W9-CDL-402

The Simon and Schuster Encyclopedia of WORLD

EDITED BY

CHIEF CONSULTANT EDITOR

WAR II

Thomas Parrish

S. L. A. Marshall

A Cord Communications Book

SIMON AND SCHUSTER

NEW YORK

Published by Simon and Schuster
A Division of Gulf & Western Corporation
Simon & Schuster Building
1230 Avenue of the Americas
New York, New York 10020

Designed by Irving Perkins
Manufactured in the United States of America
Printed and bound by The Murray Printing Co.
1 2 3 4 5 6 7 8 9 10

Library of Congress Cataloging in Publication Data

Main entry under title:

The Simon and Schuster encyclopedia of World War II.

"A Cord Communications book."
Bibliography: p.
Includes index.
1. World War, 1939–1945—Dictionaries. I. Parrish, Thomas D. II. Marshall, Samuel Lyman Atwood, 1900–1977
D740.S57 940.53'03 78-9590

ISBN 0–671–24277–6

Contents

Acknowledgments

A work of the size and scope of this encyclopedia cannot be produced without the help of a great many people. The editor is dependent not only on the services of consultants and contributors whose help is formally recognized, but on the advice and suggestions of numerous other specialists to whom he must frequently turn. One of the most pleasant discoveries one makes in editing such a book is the remarkable willingness to be of assistance with which his requests for help are met, willingness that has no thought of self but seems grounded in a genuine wish to see the book realize as much excellence as possible.

First, certainly, I must pay tribute to the consultant editors, not simply because of their profound knowledge of their special subjects but because of the thoroughness of their commitment to the book. They have given what seems unlimited time, answered what may have seemed to them unlimited questions, and in general performed tasks far beyond any expectations I might have had at the outset of the project. I also wish to thank here four contributing writers who performed various consultant services in their special areas—Joseph A. Laker, Bernard C. Nalty, John C. Reilly, Jr., and Warner Stark.

I would like to thank the following persons for assistance relating to specific questions and needs: Capt. Geoffrey Bennett, Royal Navy; Brigadier R. G. S. Bidwell, Royal United Services Institute for Defence Studies, London; Professor Wilford Bladen, University of Kentucky; Professor Charles Brockwell, University of Louisville; Sir James Butler, Trinity College, Cambridge University; Professor Arthur L. Funk, University of Florida, president of the American Committee on the History of the Second World War; Professor Louis Morton, Dartmouth College; Dr. Thomas O. Paine, president, the Northrop Corporation, former director of the National Aeronautics and Space Administration; Capt. Roger Pineau, director, U.S. Navy Memorial Museum; Professor Gordon Prange, University of Maryland; Capt. S. W. Roskill, Churchill College, Cambridge University; Henry I. Shaw, Jr., Historical Division, Headquarters, U.S. Marine Corps; Comdr. Masaji Takayama, Maritime Staff Office, Japanese Self-Defense Force, and Dr. Lawrence Thompson, former director of libraries, University of Kentucky. It is perhaps necessary to state that none of these persons has any responsibility for facts and judgments as they appear in the book; that responsibility rests with the editors, and ultimately it is mine. Thanks are due also to Dwayne Cox and Leda Roitman for their assistance in research, to Roberta Hays and Ann Pollard for secretarial services, to Eileen Caughlin for dedicated copyediting labors and to Robert Palmer for compiling the index. Other persons who helped—including numerous patient librarians—are not overlooked intentionally, and my gratitude goes to them as well.

I wish to make particular acknowledgment of the invaluable assistance of Mel Bookstein, president of Cord Communications Corporation at the time this book was conceived and through the delivery of its manuscript to Simon and Schuster. His judgments in editorial and business matters, his coordination of numerous aspects of the assembly of the project and his problem-solving abilities smoothed the path to completion. We, in turn, thank Michael Korda, Sophie Sorkin, Harriet Ripinsky and Dianne Pinkowitz, all of Simon and Schuster, for their contributions and encouragement.

As the typesetting of this book was being completed, word came of the death of Slam Marshall. I deeply regret that he will not be able to read this note of special acknowledgment for what was, first and foremost, his genuine and thorough helpfulness as Chief Consultant Editor. Anyone who ever worked with him surely knows that with General Marshall a commitment made was a commitment profoundly honored. His comments and suggestions were informative, insightful and invariably candid and direct. Slam was, it is generally agreed, one of the most important military historians and most vivid military writers of the twentieth century; he was a creative and pioneering figure in the evolution of military history as a discipline and an art. A particular, highly characteristic side of him shone through much of his work for the *Encyclopedia of World War II*—his feeling that however complex an affair war may be, it is carried on by individual human beings; it is not an encounter of bloodless abstractions, of statistics colliding on maps. Specifically, he always objected when a writer identified a force with its commander: to him it was never Patton or Manstein, for example, who attacked and advanced, but their troops, the individual men who made up the fighting force. He knew that war is not a game.

Finally, for various kindnesses of a more personal nature, I wish to thank Mr. and Mrs. Fritz F. Heimann, Westport, Conn.; Robert L. Gale, Washington, D.C.; Robert W. Pollard, Berea, Ky.; and Mr. and Mrs. Alfred H. Perrin, Berea, Ky.

THOMAS PARRISH

Photography Credits

Army Air Forces/National Archives: page 99; CBS Television Network: 420; Central Press/Pictorial Parade: 125; Defense Department (Marine Corps): 250, 437, 546, 622; Keystone Press Agency: 1, 335 left, 335 right; National Archives: 202, 252, 572, 601, 697; Navy Department/National Archives: 2, 34, 138, 148, 179, 184, 193, 258, 286, 358, 367, 411, 446, 466, 473, 475, 485, 486, 552, 582, 613, 694; Novosti from Sovfoto: 124, 586; Pictorial Parade: 236, 598; Sovfoto: 294, 615, 655, 701; United Press International: 447; U.S. Air Force: 25, 36, 41, 42, 43 top, 43 bottom, 44, 197, 257, 289, 290, 325 left, 325 right, 355, 401 left, 401 right, 402, 417, 468, 469 left, 469 right, 470, 499, 556, 595, 636, 672; U.S. Army: 20, 23, 33, 46, 64, 87, 88, 98, 110, 116, 140, 149, 152, 164, 231, 245, 264, 298, 308, 309, 310, 313, 330, 334, 378, 379, 386, 388, 392, 397, 430, 433, 445, 456, 474, 476, 480, 483, 491, 519, 522, 531, 541, 545, 617 top left, 617 top right, 617 bottom, 618 top left, 618 top right, 618 bottom, 619 top left, 619 top right, 619 bottom, 620, 661, 662, 673, 674, 677, 681, 685; U.S. Coast Guard/National Archives: 77, 461; U.S Information Agency/National Archives: 5, 421, 596, 616; U.S. Marine Corps: 338; U.S. Navy: 425, 467, 696, 698; U.S. Office of War Information/National Archives: 393; Wide World: 459, 460, 534, 574, 623.

Consultant Editors

S. L. A. Marshall, Brig. Gen. USAR (Ret.), Chief Consultant Editorn Co-founder, U.S. War Department Historical Division. Chief Combat Historian, Central Pacific Area. Chief Historian, European Theater. Author of *Armies on Wheels; Night Drop; Bastogne; Battle at Best; Pork Chop Hill,* etc.

Henry H. Adams, Capt. USNR, Naval Consultant. Former Professor of Naval History, U.S. Naval Academy. Author of *Years of Deadly Peril; 1942: The Year That Doomed the Axis; Years of Expectation,* etc.

Masataka Chihaya, Consultant Editor—Japan. Former commander, Imperial Japanese Navy, and Member, G-2 Historical Section, General Headquarters, U.S. Far East Command. Author of *Pictorial History of the Japanese Navy* (Japanese)

Brian S. Gunderson, Brig. Gen. USAF (Ret.), Air Consultant. Former Chief of the Office of Air Force History

Charles B. MacDonald, Col. USAR, Army Consultant. Former Chief, European Section, and Deputy Chief Historian for Southeast Asia, U.S. Army Center of Military History. Author of *The Mighty Endeavor; Airborne; The Siegfried Line Campaign; The Last Offensive,* etc.

Hasso von Manteuffel, General der Panzertruppen, Consultant Editor—Germany

Vladimir Petrov, Soviet Consultant. Professor of International Affairs, Institute for Sino-Soviet Studies, George Washington University. Author of *Soviet Historians and the German Invasion; A Study in Diplomacy,* etc.

Barrie Pitt, Consultant Editor—Great Britain. Editor, *History of the Second World War.* Editor in Chief, *Illustrated History of the Violent Century.* Author of *The Edge of Battle; Coronel and Falkland,* etc.

Special Consultant

Toshikazu Ohmae. Former captain, Imperial Japanese Navy; former Chief Research Officer, Military History Section, Japanese Demobilization Bureau

Maps by Richard Natkiel, Chief Cartographer, *The Economist* (London)

Contributing Writers

Senior Contributing Writers

William L. Allen Lieutenant Colonel, U.S. Army. B.A., University of Arizona; M.Ed., Northern Illinois University. Historian, U.S. Army Center of Military History

Alfred M. Beck A.B., St. Francis College; M.A., Ph.D., Georgetown University. Historian, U.S. Army Center of Military History

Eric Bergerud A.B., University of Minnesota; Fellow, U.S. Army Center of Military History

Martin Blumenson A.B., A.M., Bucknell University; A.M., Harvard University. Former Senior Historian, Office of the Chief of Military History, U.S. Department of the Army. Author of *Masters of the Art of Command; The Patton Papers* (ed.); *Eisenhower; Salerno to Cassino* (U.S. Army in World War II Series), etc.

Robert Burnett A.B., Wofford College; M.A., Ph.D., University of North Carolina. Professor of History, University of Louisville. Author of articles on modern French and European diplomatic history

Martha H. Byrd A.B., University of North Carolina; M.S., University of Tennessee. Author of *A World in Flames: A History of World War II*

Jeffrey J. Clarke A.B., Gettysburg College; M.A., Ph.D., Duke University. Historian, U.S. Army Center of Military History

Anthony Clayton M.A., Ph.D., St. Andrews University (Scotland). Senior Lecturer in Modern History, Royal Military Academy, Sandhurst (England)

Jerry W. Cooney A.B., M.A., Washington State University; Ph.D., University of New Mexico. Assistant Professor of History, University of Louisville. Author of articles on Latin-American history

Dwayne Cox B.A., Kentucky Wesleyan College; M.A., University of Louisville. Archivist, University of Louisville

Detmar Finke Schloss Bischofstein in Thüringen (Germany). Chief, General Reference Branch, U.S. Army Center of Military History

Heinrich Fraenkel Graduate of German universities. Author of *The German People Versus Hitler; Farewell to Germany;* (with Roger Manvell): *Dr. Goebbels; Hermann Göring; Heinrich Himmler,* etc.

Benis M. Frank A.B., University of Connecticut. Head of the Oral History Unit, History and Museums Division, Headquarters, U.S. Marine Corps. Author of *Okinawa: Touchstone to Victory; Halsey; Victory and Occupation* (History of U.S. Marine Corps Operations in World War II Series)

William Gleason Ph.D., Indiana University. Assistant Professor of History, University of Louisville. Author of articles on Russian and East Asian history

Jeffery A. Gunsburg B.A., University of Wisconsin; A.M., Ph.D., Duke University. Assistant Professor of History, Virginia Military Institute

E. B. Haslam B.A., Cambridge University; Diploma of Education, Unversity of London. Group Captain, Royal Air Force. Former Director of Studies (Humanities), RAF College, Cranwell (England). Head of Air Historical Branch, Royal Air Force

S. William Hines B.A., Carleton University; M.A., Ph.D., Duke University. Former Research Assistant, Department of History, Royal Military College of Canada

John E. Jessup, Jr. B.S., University of Maryland; M.A., Ph.D., Georgetown University. Former Chief, Histories Division, U.S. Army Center of Military History. President, U.S. Commission on Military History. Author of articles on Soviet foreign policy and military history

Robert B. Kebric A.B., University of Southern California; M.A., Ph.D., State University of New York. Assistant Professor of History, University of Louisville

Peter Kemp Former member, Intelligence Division, Royal Navy. Former Head, Naval Historical Branch, British Admiralty. Editor of the First Sea Lord papers of Admiral of the Fleet Lord Fisher. Author of *Victory at Sea 1939–1945; The Oxford Companion to Ships and the Sea* (ed.), etc.

Joseph Laker A.B., Marian College; M.A., Ph.D., Indiana University. Former instructor, YBU English School, Kyoto, Japan. Associate Professor of History, Wheeling College

John M. Lindley B.A., Amherst College; M.A., University of Pennsylvania; Ph.D., Duke University. Former Instructor in History, U.S. Naval Academy, and Lecturer in History, Duke University

Charles B. MacDonald Consultant Editor, the *Encyclopedia of World War II* (*see* page ix).

Roger Manvell Ph.D., D. Litt. Visiting Fellow, University of Sussex (England). Contributor to *History of the Second World War* and the *Encyclopaedia Britannica.* Coauthor (with Heinrich Fraenkel) of *The July Plot; The Canaris Conspiracy; The Hundred Days to Hitler,* etc.

Bernard C. Nalty A.B., Creighton University; M.A., Catholic University of America. Former staff member, Historical Division, U.S. Joint Chiefs of Staff. Historian, Office of Air Force History, U.S. Air Force

Walter M. Odum B.A., M.A., Florida State University. Assistant Professor of History, Eastern Kentucky University

Thomas Parrish Editor, the *Encyclopedia of World War II.* A.B., University of Chicago. Author of *Victory at Sea: The Submarine; Great Battles of History: The Bulge,* etc.

Vladimir Petrov Consultant Editor, the *Encyclopedia of World War II* (*see* page ix).

John C. Reilly, Jr. B.S., Mount Saint Mary's College; M.S.L.S., Catholic University of America. Special Projects Historian, Naval History Division, U.S. Navy Department. Contributor to McGraw-Hill *Encyclopedia of Science and Technology; Encyclopaedia Britannica; Dictionary of American Naval Fighting Ships*

Carl G. Ryant B.A., Western Reserve University; M.A., Ph.D., University of Wisconsin. Associate Professor of History and Director of the Oral History Center, University of Louisville

Robert F. Sexton B.A., Yale University; Ph.D., University of Washington. Executive Director, Office for Experiential Education, University of Kentucky

Robert Ross Smith B.A., M.A., Duke University. Chief, General History Branch, Histories Division, U.S. Army Center of Military History. Author of *The Approach to the Philippines* and *Triumph in the Philippines* (U.S. Army in World War II Series)

Warner Stark B.A., M.A., San Jose State College. Historian, Historical Office, U.S. Army Forces Command

Thomas R. Stone Lieutenant Colonel, U.S. Army. B.S., United States Military Academy; M.A., Ph.D., Rice University. Assistant Professor of History, U.S. Military Academy

Kenneth P. Werrell B.S., United States Air Force Academy; M.A., Ph.D., Duke University. Former Contract Historian, U.S. Air Force. Associate Professor of History, Radford College

Associate Contributing Writers

Marion F. Deshmukh B.A., University of California, Los Angeles; M.A., Ph.D., Columbia University. Assistant Professor of History, George Mason University

William Hammond B.A., Claretville College; S.T.B., M.A., Ph.D., Catholic University of America. Historian, U.S. Army Center of Military History

Richard A. Hunt B.A., Rutgers University; M.A., Ph.D., University of Pennsylvania. Historian, U.S. Army Center of Military History

Ronald J. Jensen B.A., Coe College; Ph.D., Indiana University. Associate Professor of History, George Mason University

Stephen A. Kamer B.A., College of the Holy Cross; M.A., University of Louisville

Bettie J. Morden Colonel, U.S. Army. B.A., M.A., Columbia University. WAC Historian, U.S. Army Center of Military History

Robert W. Pringle, Jr. A.B., M.A., Ph.D., University of Virginia. Former Historian, U.S. Army Center of Military History. Foreign Service Officer, U.S. Department of State

David A. Rosenberg B.A., American University; M.A., Ph.D., University of Chicago

Ronald Spector A.B., Johns Hopkins University; M.A., Ph.D., Yale University. Historian, U.S. Army Center of Military History

Mary K. Bonsteel Tachau A.B., Oberlin College; M.A., University of Louisville; Ph.D., University of Kentucky. Associate Professor and Chairperson of the Department of History, University of Louisville

George M. Watson, Jr. A.B., University of Maine; M.A., Niagara University; Ph.D., Catholic University of America. Historian, Office of Air Force History, U.S. Air Force

Hannah M. Zeidlik B.A., American University. Historian and Archivist, U.S. Army Center of Military History

List of Maps

Introduction

The standard for works of history that claim to transcend parochialism was well expressed by Lord Acton. Speaking of the *Cambridge Modern History,* he said, "Our Waterloo must satisfy French and English, Germans and Dutch alike." The same standard has guided those who have worked on this *Encyclopedia of World War II.* Everywhere people spoke of the need for such a book and wished its creators well, and it would not be fair to disappoint them by pretending that the point of view of one nation or another, or one actor in the drama or another, was the only one that gave a correct perspective. This is not a book of "we" and "the enemy," nor even one that attempts to favor either of the two great Western Allies, the United States and Great Britain. A look at the lists of consultant editors and contributing writers will show that a great deal of effort has been spent in an attempt to produce accuracy and balance.

The book is designed for easy use, the aim being to make the material as readily accessible as possible. For this reason, the entries are arranged in standard alphabetical order—under what seems to us the most logical heading—rather than being arranged, as is the case in some specialized encyclopedic works, by themes and topics of the editors' devising. As an editor of the *Encyclopaedia Britannica* observed many years ago, "The convenience of an arrangement of material based on a single alphabetization of subject works and proper names has established itself in the common sense of mankind."

It has also been our aim to give the reader enough information in most of the shorter entries that he will not have to spend his time chasing after cross-references unless he wishes to do so. Accordingly, a certain degree of repetition has been allowed. There are, of course, numerous cross-references for the guidance of those who wish to pursue them. A cross-reference is indicated by small capitals; thus, in the entry on President Franklin D. Roosevelt the reader is referred to the entry on Prime Minister Winston CHURCHILL. If in our judgment a cross-reference will not actually add to the reader's understanding of an entry, no cross-reference appears, even if there is an entry on that subject. Some general cross-references appear at the ends of some articles.

The fact that a given subject does not appear as the title of an entry does not mean that it is not treated in the book. The myriad possible subjects relating to the war have been reduced to a few thousand entry names; every place, every person, every entity could not of course appear in the alphabetical listing. The reader should consult the Index to see where an unlisted subject is discussed. Cross-references as separate entries have been purposely kept to a minimum (e.g., **BRITISH AIR FORCE.** *See* ROYAL AIR FORCE). Such headings could readily become almost limitless in number, and one of the prime purposes of the Index is to give the appropriate information; indeed, the Index knits together the entire book and is a vital part of it.

The lengths of the individual entries do not necessarily suggest the relative importance of the subjects, although there is in general a correlation. But sometimes, for instance, anecdotal material is included in an otherwise minor entry because of its intrinsic interest or colorfulness. This is designed to be a book for enjoyment, one that rewards the browsing reader, as well as a work of reference (and, of course, there is no reason to assume that a reference book must be austere). Here we have attempted not to follow melancholy precedent. This same thinking has guided our decision to use abbreviations only to a very limited degree. It is difficult and unpleasant, especially for one who is not a specialist in the particular subject matter, to push one's way through blocks of type bristling with strange and truncated word forms. Instead of this, we sought to invite the diplomatic historian, say, or the student, to browse among the ships and aircraft by presenting them in readable prose.

It may be useful here to mention some practical points. The editors recognize that one of the commonest uses of the *Encyclopedia* will be as a companion to reading about World War II. Partly for this reason, we define a number of specific entities (army divisions, for example) that are often referred to in the literature of the war, even though we make no attempt to define all members of the given class (all divisions in all armies).

Well-known personages (Joseph Stalin, Dwight D. Eisenhower) appear frequently with full names, where the context seems to call for them, but sometimes, in shorter entries, preeminent personages are referred to more briefly.

Since the entire book is about World War II, the term "the war" is frequently used instead of a longer form.

As a general rule, foreign titles and other usages are translated into English in headings—thus Count, not Graf, von der Schulenburg. Foreign code names appear in English when readily translatable, except in cases where they have established a strong identity in the original language (such as Operation Nordwind).

Hungarian and Japanese personal names are given in conventional Western order rather than with surname first.

Russian names appear in their standard English spelling, if they have acquired one (e.g., Kiev); in general, Webster is the authority for the spelling of Russian as of other proper names. As Edward Crankshaw has observed, "It seems to be impossible to devise an entirely consistent system of transliteration from the Cyrillic to the Roman alphabet without introducing tiresome awkwardnesses and pedantries." This we have sought to avoid, clarity being our aim. Russian first names have been anglicized where it was readily possible to do so.

As for the styles employed by the contributing writers, we have found harmony in diversity. The writers, happily, come from different backgrounds, and we have made no attempt to impose a standard prose style on them. Entries of particular length and complexity are signed with the writers' initials.

Obviously, some of the major entries, such as histories of campaigns, though long could never be long enough to be exhaustive. Such accounts necessarily cannot reflect all the complexities of titanic series of events on the order of the Soviet-German war or the fighting on the Western Front from the Normandy invasion to V-E Day. In outlining such subjects, however, we have sought for fairness and accuracy.

It should also be said that it simply was not practicable in a book of this size to list bibliographical references with the individual entries. Instead, we have provided a Bibliography of works that the editors and writers have found of greatest use. This, we believe, will be more useful to one seeking sources than would their dispersion throughout the book.

Just about a century ago the humorist Josh Billings remarked: "The trouble with people is not that they don't know but that they know so much that ain't so." Our experiences in compiling this encyclopedia suggest that things haven't changed much in the last hundred years: the closer one looked at many a locale or date, the fuzzier it seemed to become, the harder it was to fix in place. Names, times, locations—often the simplest of these varied from source to source or from memory to memory. Sometimes this elusiveness appeared to be nothing more than the result of simple error, but often it seemed the result of an event's having been given a kind of undefined precision. When did the fortress surrender? When the white flag appeared on the parapet, when the envoy entered the gates, when the document was signed, when the last man marched out of the citadel, when the public relations people released the news? All of these, perhaps. In many cases of the kind, the story varied according to the writer. What we have tried to do here is to see precisely what the tellers of the story were seeing, and to present this picture clearly. We have also tried to keep from repeating legends—tales that "ain't so"—that have come to be regarded as truths through the fact of having been repeated from author to author in the past.

Have we succeeded in these aims? Not as well as we would have wished, no doubt. We have to acknowledge that the gremlins of error are always ready not only to go on propagating but to assume new forms. So we know that in spite of our best efforts there are inadequacies and mistakes in the following pages. Unfortunately, we do not at this point know what they are, and we invite you to tell us. We genuinely hope that interested readers will help us identify the errors that have eluded our vigilance. We hope there will not be many.

THOMAS PARRISH

A

A5M. Japanese Navy Mitsubishi fighter plane (Allied code name, Claude), a series begun in 1935. The A5M1 was the Navy's first monoplane fighter to see service. The culmination of the line was the A5M4, which ceased production in 1940 but remained in full use until well after Pearl Harbor. It was powered by a 710-horsepower radial engine and had a top speed of 273 miles per hour. It carried two 7.7-mm. machine guns. About 1,000 Claudes were accepted by the Navy.

A6M. The Japanese Navy Mitsubishi *Reisen* (Zero fighter), a low-wing monoplane fighter designed primarily for agility rather than protection or endurance. Its designer was Horikoshi Jiro. Though it had been used in China as early as mid-1940, Allied knowledge of Japanese aviation was so poor that the Zero's performance still came as a surprise when the Pacific war began in December 1941. Various *Reisen* models served in first-line functions from carriers and shore bases through most of the war, though as Japan's carrier strength waned, land operation had perforce to increase in importance. Although supplanted to some extent by newer fighters during 1944–45, the Zero still made up a good part of the Japanese fighter inventory at the end of the war.

The first production Zero was the A6M2, a carrier plane with folding wing tips. This version received the Allied code name Zeke, generally applied to most later models, although the name Zero was also widely used. The 1941 A6M3 had a slightly shorter, square-tipped wing and was code-named Hap until Gen. "Hap" ARNOLD objected; the name then became Hamp. A floatplane-fighter version of the *Reisen* was designated A6M2-N and code-named Rufe. This model was extensively used from forward anchorages in the South Pacific and the Aleutians. During 1943–44 the mass-production A6M5 incorporated numerous modifications. *Reisen* production continued into 1945; during the war's last months some were modified to carry bombs while others were assigned to KAMIKAZE duty.

The Zero was perhaps the best-known Japanese aircraft of the Pacific war. A number of unsuccessful postwar attempts have been made to prove the Zero a copy rather than an indigenous Japanese design. It was so superior a dogfighting plane to existing early-war Allied aircraft that "never dogfight a Zero" became a serious maxim for Allied pilots. Zero versions varied widely in specifications. The standard A6M2 had a top speed of 317 miles per hour and was armed with two 7.7-mm. machine guns and two 20-mm. cannon. Overall production of the A6M, in all versions, was 10,938.

A6M—the Mitsubishi Zero

A7M. The Japanese Navy *Reppu* (Violent Wind) (Allied code name, Sam), designed in 1942 by Horikoshi Jiro, designer of the A6M Zero (*see* A6M), as a faster, better-armed and better-protected replacement for the Zero. The A7M1 was underpowered and unsatisfactory, but the A7M2 demonstrated superior combat performance. A further improvement, the more powerful A7M3 with four 30-mm. cannon, was selected for production late in 1944 but an earthquake, combined with bombing raids, so delayed production that it was never even tested.

A-20. Douglas Aircraft was building an export version of this twin-engine, shoulder-wing monoplane when the U.S. Army decided to place an order of its own. The American version was nicknamed the Havoc, while the British called their model the Boston. American crews flying borrowed Bostons made the first U.S. air strike against targets in occupied Europe, bombing airfields in Holland on July 4, 1942. Although the A-20C had a transparent nose, most Havocs were fitted with a solid nose that housed either four 20-mm. cannon and two .50-caliber machine guns or six .50-caliber machine guns. The most numerous model, the A-20G, of which 2,850 were built, was powered by two 1,600-horsepower Pratt and Whitney radial engines, had a top speed of 339 miles per hour at 15,600 feet and could carry 2,600 pounds of bombs. The A-20G had wing racks that could accommodate an additional 1,400 pounds.

A-24. Army version of the U.S. Navy's successful Douglas Dauntless (*see* SBD), the A-24 saw action against the Japanese in the Netherlands East Indies and in New Guinea. A convoy carrying 52 A-24s, en route to the Philippines when the Japanese struck in December 1941, was diverted to Australia, but the dive-bomber's combat debut was delayed when the switches for the machine guns were accidentally destroyed by the men assembling the planes. Lacking adequate fighter escort, the A-24 proved vulnerable to the Zero fighter (*see* A6M), and the Army soon gave up on the Dauntless, relegating it to noncombat duty.

A-26. Although the prototype of this three-place Douglas attack bomber, called the Invader, did not take to the air until July 1942, the twin-engine, shoulder-wing monoplane entered combat with the U.S. NINTH AIR

FORCE in Europe in November 1944. Two models saw wartime service, the A-26B with a solid nose fitted to carry six .50-caliber machine guns and the A-26C with a transparent "bombardier nose." Both were powered by 2,000-horsepower Pratt and Whitney radials, had top speeds in excess of 350 miles per hour and could carry two tons of bombs.

A-36. Dive-bomber version of the North American Mustang (*see* P-51), the A-36 marked the last attempt on the part of U.S. Army Air Forces to develop an aircraft especially for this purpose. The plane saw action in Sicily and Italy, but despite its diving brakes (which seldom were used) it offered no advantages over a standard fighter fitted with bomb racks.

AACHEN (Aix-la-Chapelle). The first German city (pop. 166,000) to fall to Allied troops. As men of the U.S. First Army crossed the frontier on September 11, 1944, Adolf Hitler ordered staunch defense, but the local commander deemed the cause lost and abandoned the city. Troops of the VII Corps nevertheless pursued their primary objective of penetrating two bands of the fortified WEST WALL encompassing the city. By the time that was accomplished, German forces had moved into Aachen in strength. Although encircled, the German commander refused to surrender. After heavy aerial and artillery bombardment, the 1st Division with subsequent help from the 3d Armored Division began on October 13 to clear the city. The German commander finally surrendered on October 21. Despite widespread destruction in the city, the Aachen Munster (cathedral), housing the Emperor Charlemagne's coronation chair, escaped major damage.

AARHUS. On October 31, 1944, 24 MOSQUITO fighter-bombers of the RAF Second Tactical Air Force made a low-level attack on the Jutland (Denmark) headquarters of the GESTAPO in the Aarhus University buildings. Covered by a Polish squadron of 12 Mustangs, the British fliers went in at "zero feet" through heavy flak. They destroyed both Gestapo buildings, killed 125 Germans and wounded another 40. The raid had to be carried out with great precision to avoid damaging the several hospitals adjacent to the Nazi headquarters.

AARON WARD, U.S.S. WICKES-class destroyer, commissioned 1919. Transferred to Britain in 1940, she served in the Atlantic as H.M.S. *Castleton.*

A second *Aaron Ward* was a U.S. GLEAVES-class destroyer, commissioned 1942. Her first combat was the night naval battle of GUADALCANAL, in November 1942, when she received nine shell hits. After repairs, she returned to the Solomons. On April 7, 1943, *Aaron Ward* was attacked by six Japanese planes off Guadalcanal. One bomb hit, with four near misses, sank her.

The third *Aaron Ward* was laid down as a GEARING-class destroyer but completed (1944) as a fast minelayer. She did picket duty off Okinawa and on May 3, 1945, was battered but not sunk by kamikazes.

ABADAN. Island in the Shatt-al-Arab delta (Iran), site of an oil refinery captured by a British infantry brigade on August 25, 1941. This action was part of the Anglo-Soviet occupation of Iran.

ABAIANG. A small atoll just north of TARAWA in the Gilbert Island group. Following the Tarawa operation, on November 30, 1943, scouts from the U.S. 2d Marine Division reconnoitered Abaiang and found only five Japanese soldiers, whom they took prisoner.

U.S.S. *Aaron Ward* after kamikaze attacks off Okinawa

ABBEVILLE. On May 20, 1940, German panzer units under the command of Gen. Heinz GUDERIAN captured Abbeville (France) on the Somme River, 28 miles northwest of Amiens. By taking Abbeville, Guderian was able not only to take a key port with access to the English Channel but also to cut off the BRITISH EXPEDITIONARY FORCE from its base port at Cherbourg.

ABC-1. An agreement reached between American and British planners, in 14 sessions in Washington between January and March 1941, on the strategy to be followed in the event the United States entered the war. It called for the defeat of Germany first, the maintenance of Allied positions in the Mediterranean and the strategic defensive in the Pacific theater until Germany and Italy were beaten.

ABDA COMMAND. On December 28, 1941, British and American leaders agreed to create a unified command for Allied forces in the Far East. After formal assent of the other governments involved, Gen. Sir Archibald P. WAVELL, Commander in Chief for India, became head of ABDACOM (American, British, Dutch and Australian Command). His responsibilities included command of all forces in Burma, Malaya, the Dutch East Indies and the Philippines, but his orders effectively prevented him from exercising that authority. He could not relieve subordinate commanders (each of whom represented a different national interest) and he could not interfere with the organization of national forces under his command. Rather than supreme commander in the western Pacific, Wavell functioned as a kind of supercoordinator. In that role he was expected to defend Malaya, Burma and Australia, and prepare "an all-out offensive against Japan." Neither Wavell's authority nor the resources available to ABDACOM were capable of denying Japan control of the air and sea, and the Japanese march south continued. The command was dissolved on February 25, 1942.

ABDUL. Allied code name for the Japanese Nakajima Ki 27 Army fighter (*see* KI 27). It was also called Nate, and the name Abdul was dropped in 1943.

ABE, Hiroaki (1890–1949). A career naval officer, one of Japan's most active commanders during the first year of the war. He generally commanded forward attack forces made up of battleships, cruisers and destroyers. He led the task force which attacked WAKE ISLAND and took part in the Battle of MIDWAY and numerous engagements in the struggle over GUADALCANAL. He was relieved of his command on December 20, 1942, after failing to destroy HENDERSON FIELD.

ABETZ, Otto (1903–1958). As a Nazi Party ideologue and a RIBBENTROP protégé, Abetz became the German Foreign Office representative with the German military (occupation) government at Paris in August 1940. For his prewar propaganda activity in France and for his role as a principal intermediary in Pierre LAVAL's collaboration with Nazi Germany, Abetz received a 20-year prison term from a French military court in 1949.

AB GRILLE. German code name for a type of WÜRZBURG airborne radar.

ABRAMS, Creighton W. (1914–1974). Commander of the 37th Tank Battalion, the U.S. armored column which broke through the German siege at BASTOGNE, December 26, 1944. Then a lieutenant colonel, Abrams later rose to the rank of general and at the time of his death was U.S. Army Chief of Staff.

ABRIAL, Jean (1879–1962). In the fall of 1939 Admiral Abrial took command of French naval forces operating in the North Sea. He directed the defense of the DUNKIRK perimeter during the famous evacuation of 1940. Appointed Secretary of State for the Navy at Vichy in November 1942, Abrial was tried and condemned after the liberation of France.

ABUCAY LINE. Gen. Douglas MACARTHUR's first line of defense on the BATAAN peninsula. It ran across the peninsula from Abucay, a settlement on Manila Bay, through Mount Natib to Mauban. Action began when the Japanese attacked the combined American-Philippine force on January 9, 1942.

ABUKUMA. Japanese NAGARA-class light cruiser. Veteran of nearly three years of the Pacific war, she was lost in the battle for LEYTE GULF, October 26, 1944.

ABWEHR. The intelligence office of the German armed forces. The Abwehr (the full name was Amt Auslands Abwehr) was a branch of the OKW. *See also* OKW; CANARIS, WILHELM.

ACCOLADE. Code name for planned Allied capture of Rhodes and other islands in the Aegean Sea. Although consistently urged by Prime Minister CHURCHILL in the months following the conquest of Sicily (1943), Accolade was not carried out. The plan was controversial, and a notable opponent was General MARSHALL, U.S. Chief of Staff.

ACE. Generally considered to be a fighter pilot who downs five or more enemy aircraft. The French Air Force gave one credit to each pilot involved in destroying an enemy plane. Russia and Italy kept separate count of shared kills. American units split victories into halves, quarters, thirds, etc., to apportion credit fairly. The Luftwaffe kept account of the number of engines an enemy plane had, not for the awarding of credit but for decoration purposes. However, while the Luftwaffe gave one credit per plane on shared kills, the participating pilots had to decide among themselves which one got the credit since no shared credits were allowed; generally the junior pilots were given the shared credits to build up morale and scores. Japan gave no special credit to the pilots; usually the pilot's air regiment got the credits.

The war's leading ace was the Luftwaffe's Maj. Erich HARTMANN with 352 confirmed kills (345 Soviet, 7 U.S.). The RAF's leading ace was Wing Comdr. J. E. JOHNSON with 38 kills (some authorities hold that Squadron Leader M. T. St. J. PATTLE, with over 40, was the top ace but Pattle's records were lost, so some cannot be confirmed). French aces were led by Capt. Pierre CLOSTERMANN with 33 kills. Maj. Ivan KOZHEDUB was the Soviet Union's highest ace with 62 kills. For U.S. air forces the USAAF's leading ace was Maj. Richard BONG with 40 kills, the Navy was led by Capt. David McCampbell with 34 kills, and the Marines were led by Lt. Col. Gregory Boyington with 28, six of which were with the Flying Tigers. Japan's ace was Chief Warrant Officer Hiroyashi Nishizawa with 104. Finland's ace of aces was Capt. Hans H. Wind with 75 kills.

ACHESON, Dean Gooderham (1893–1971). A well-known attorney prior to his entry into government, Acheson was active in Maryland politics and in 1933 was appointed Under Secretary of the Treasury by Franklin Roosevelt. He broke with the President in 1933 over the gold-purchase plan and monetary policies and resigned his position. He continued to support the President, however, and was active in the Committee to Defend America by Aiding the Allies after the outbreak of the war. He argued extensively for American assistance to Great Britain. He also supported in 1940 a strong statement in support of the destroyers-bases deal with Britain. Acheson returned to government service in 1941 when the President appointed him Assistant Secretary of State. He served in this position until August 1945, having general supervision over State Department divisions operating in the economic field. He played an active role in winning passage by Congress of the Lend-Lease Act of 1941. In 1943 he was permanent chairman of the Atlantic City meeting at which the United Nations Relief and Rehabilitation Administration (*see* UNRRA) was organized, and for two years served as chairman of its council. In 1944 he was delegate to the United Nations Monetary and Financial Conference in Bretton Woods, where it was decided to establish the International Bank for Reconstruction and Development and the International Monetary Fund. In 1945 Acheson became Under Secretary of State, serving under James F. Byrnes and George C. Marshall. In 1949 he succeeded General Marshall as Secretary of State.

ACHILLES, H.M.N.Z.S. New Zealand light cruiser. On December 13, 1939, the *Achilles,* along with H.M.S. Exeter and H.M.S. Ajax, caught the German pocket battleship Admiral Graf Spee off the River Plate. Though severely damaged, the *Achilles* shadowed the German ship into Montevideo, where it was later scuttled. The *Achilles* carried eight 6-inch guns and had a top speed of 31.25 knots.

ACK-ACK. British slang term for antiaircraft (AA) fire. It came from the British phonetic alphabet used in World War I, in which the letter *A* was represented by the word "Ack."

ACROBAT. Code name used by British staff in 1941 for planned advance from Cyrenaica to Tripoli. *See also* North Africa.

ACROMA. Situated not far from the Libyan port of Tobruk, Acroma afforded access from the Libyan plain up the escarpment. It was used as a British assembly base and was fortified as part of the Gazala Line in 1942.

ACTAEON NET. An antitorpedo device developed during the late stages of World War I and revived in World War II. Of relatively light mesh, it was used while the ship was in motion. *See also* antisubmarine.

ACTION GROUPS (Einsatzgruppen). Special squads operated by the German SS for the liquidation of Jews, Communists and suspected partisans (*see* SS). They were under the control of the Security Service (*see* SD) and the Security Police (Sipo), under the ultimate command of Heinrich Himmler.

ACT OF HAVANA. *See* Havana Conference.

ADACHI, Hatazo (1890–1947). A graduate of the Japanese Military Academy (1910) and the War College (1922), Lieutenant General Adachi was appointed commander of the 18th Army in November 1942, when it was formed. He commanded it during the fighting in eastern New Guinea from that time until the end of the war. In September 1947 he committed suicide, taking all responsibility for war crimes charged to his subordinates at the Rabaul prison camp.

ADAK. This island in the Aleutians was the site of an advance U.S. airfield just 250 miles from enemy-held Kiska. On August 30, 1942, amphibious forces landed unopposed at Adak, and engineers came ashore on the following day. After a hurried survey, the engineers dammed a creek, installed a drainage system and used the gravel creek bed as a temporary airstrip. On September 10 the first American plane, an old B-18, landed there. Steel mats were placed over the gravel, and combat operations commenced on the 14th when a dozen B-24s and 28 fighters took off to attack Kiska.

ADDIS ABABA. The capital and chief trade and communications center of Ethiopia. It surrendered to Italian conquest May 5, 1936, and was reclaimed by the British on April 6, 1941—thereby becoming the first national capital liberated from Axis rule.

ADDU ATOLL. A secret British naval base at the southern end of the Maldive Islands, about 600 miles southwest of Ceylon. It was designed as an alternative to Colombo, being remote from the mainland yet within covering distance. However, the threat of air attack made it an unsafe anchorage for the battleships of Adm. James Somerville's Indian Ocean fleet, which were withdrawn to Bombay and East Africa. Addu was called by the code names Base T and Port T.

ADIGE RIVER. Northern Italian river, running through Verona, which formed one of the last of a series of defense lines established by retreating German forces. When American troops of the 85th Division crossed it in April 1945, they found the line largely unmanned.

ADLER. German code name for a radio set designed for submarine-to-aircraft communication.

ADMIRAL GRAF SPEE. One of three German pocket battleships (*see* Panzerschiff), small, powerful warships designed to be superior to a cruiser and fast enough to escape from a battleship. At the outbreak of the war, the *Admiral Graf Spee* was at sea. For two months she

Smoke pours from the scuttled *Graf Spee*

raided Allied commerce in the South Atlantic and Indian Oceans. Then, on December 13, off the coast of Uruguay, she made contact with a British squadron under Commodore Sir Henry HARWOOD consisting of the heavy cruiser EXETER and the light cruisers AJAX and ACHILLES. In the ensuing Battle of the RIVER PLATE, the *Graf Spee* broke off the action and headed for Montevideo, where she was blockaded by the *Ajax* and *Achilles*. Believing that superior naval forces were waiting for him outside Montevideo, Captain LANGSDORFF, with the permission of the German high command, had the *Graf Spee* blown up on the evening of December 17, 1939.

ADMIRAL HIPPER. German heavy cruiser of 10,000 tons carrying eight 8-inch guns and heavy antiaircraft protection. She was launched in 1937. The ship suffered hull damage during the German invasion of NORWAY but after repairs remained active against the MURMANSK RUN convoy routes, though her balky turbine engines and high fuel consumption limited her use as a raider. She operated with TIRPITZ against Convoy PQ-17 in July 1942 (*see* PQ-17). *Hipper*'s equivocal performance in a dramatic battle with the escorting ships of a convoy on New Year's Eve, 1942, reinforced Hitler's resolve to lay up heavy German fleet units. *Hipper* was scuttled May 3, 1945.

ADMIRAL Q. Code name used by President Franklin D. ROOSEVELT in connection with the CASABLANCA CONFERENCE, 1943. Prime Minister Winston CHURCHILL called it "an impenetrable disguise."

ADMIRAL SCHEER. German pocket battleship (*see* PANZERSCHIFF) of 12,100 tons, carrying six 11-inch rifles. The *Scheer* represented a slight modification of the original *Deutschland* (*see* LÜTZOW) design when she was launched in 1933. Under Kapitän zur See Theodor KRANCKE, *Scheer* made a brilliantly successful 161-day commerce-raiding cruise. Breaking through the Denmark Strait in November 1940, the ship engaged a convoy, sinking a gallantly handled British armed merchant cruiser (H.M.S. JERVIS BAY) and five cargo vessels. Krancke continued his victories in the Indian Ocean, where the British Navy assembled seven cruisers and a carrier, only to have *Scheer* slip through the trap. The ship eluded other British units to return to Germany in early April 1941, and Krancke received the Knight's Cross for his exploit. *Scheer* operated against North Russian convoys in 1942. Bombed in drydock at Kiel in April 1945, *Scheer* capsized and was later buried when the dock was filled in.

ADMIRALTY ISLANDS. Manus, Los Negros and the smaller islands in the Admiralty group make up the northwest perimeter of the Bismarck Sea.

Operation Brewer, the invasion of the Admiralties, was conducted by Task Force Brewer, formed from the U.S. Army 1st Cavalry Divison. It began with a landing on Los Negros on February 29, 1944. Heavy Japanese resistance prevented capture of Los Negros until March 8, when supply vessels began entering SEEADLER HARBOR, one of the best anchorages in the Pacific. Preparatory to the landing on Manus, U.S. Army elements landed on Butjo Luo and also on Hauwei, slightly north of the new objective. The landing on Manus began on March 15; organized fighting ended on the 25th, only small pockets of resistance remaining to be eliminated. As mopping up continued, operations began against the outlying islands, with landings on Pityilu (March

30), Koruniat and Ndrilo (April 1), Rambutyo (April 3) and Pak (April 9). A U.S. naval base and an air station were established on Manus on May 18, since the capture of two airfields and an excellent large harbor in the Admiralties had the effect of hastening the tempo of operations in the Southwest Pacific area and tightening the ring of Allied bases that neutralized RABAUL.

ADMIRALTY NET DEFENCE (AND). British term for a system of heavy steel wire netting suspended from booms mounted along each side of a merchant ship, intended to catch torpedoes before they could strike the ship's hull. First mounted on ships during the late summer of 1941, by the end of the Atlantic war the nets had been fitted to some 700 merchantmen. *See also* ANTISUBMARINE.

ADOLF HITLER LINE. Name sometimes applied to two German defense lines in Italy—the GUSTAV LINE and the Führer-Senger Line. The latter was between the Gustav Line and Rome (Pico-Pontecorvo-Piedmonte) and fell in May 1944.

AERO A-100 and A-101/Ab-101. Czechoslovakian Army Air Force planes. The first two were two-seat tactical reconnaissance single-engine biplanes; the Ab-101 was the light-bomber counterpart. Most were turned over to the Slovak Air Force by the Germans.

AERO A-304. A Czechoslovakian three-place, twin-engine light reconnaissance bomber. About 15 were built; some were used by the Luftwaffe and some by the Bulgarian Air Force.

AFRIKA KORPS. The Deutsches Afrika Korps (DAK), formed to assist the Italians in Africa, was first commanded by Generalleutnant (lieutenant general—U.S. major general) Erwin ROMMEL and consisted of the 5th Light and 15th Panzer Divisions, which arrived in Africa early in 1941. In August 1941 Rommel's command was raised to the status of a panzer group, and Lt. Gen. Ludwig CRUEWELL succeeded to command of the Afrika Korps itself. The 5th Light was renamed the 21st Panzer Division, but with no change in strength or composition. Since the two panzer divisions were central to Rommel's African operations, the term Afrika Korps was popularly used to denote all Axis forces in Africa; technically it meant only the two German armored divisions. In addition, Rommel had the German 90th Light Division (four infantry battalions with strong supporting firepower) and six Italian divisions—Ariete, Trieste, Pavia, Bologna, Brescia and Savona.

The DAK had a succession of commanders. General Cruewell was shot down on a flight in May 1942, and Maj. Gen. Walther NEHRING replaced him. After being wounded at ALAM HALFA, Nehring was succeeded by Lt. Gen. Ritter von THOMA, who was taken prisoner at Alamein. Field Marshal Albert KESSELRING and Col. Fritz BAYERLEIN both served as acting commanders on occasion, and in Tunisia Gen. Gustav Fehn, Gen. Hans Cramer and Lt. Gen. Heinz Ziegler commanded. In Tunisia part of the DAK often joined other forces to form a DAK Assault Group, but Rommel was reluctant to let General von ARNIM have the complete DAK. During 1944 Rommel, as his son Manfred has written, took comfort from the fact that his beloved DAK were prisoners of the Western Allies and not in a position to be sacrificed by Hitler.

AGANO. Class of Japanese light cruisers, developed during the late 1930s and completed during the Pacific war. The Aganos, 571 feet long and displacing over 6,600 tons, had a top speed of 35 knots. Six 6-inch guns (3×2), 3-inch and 25-mm. antiaircraft guns and eight 24-inch torpedo tubes (2×4) were mounted. This class was considered undergunned and lightly protected for its size. *Agano* was sunk by a submarine off Truk in early 1944. NOSHIRO was lost at LEYTE GULF, while YAHAGI sortied from Japan with the battleship YAMATO and was lost with her. *Sakawa*, last ship of her class, survived the war and sank at Bikini as an atomic-test target ship.

AGC. U.S. Navy ship-type designation for Amphibious Force Flagship. These floating command posts were developed to provide suitable headquarters and communications facilities for the naval officer commanding an amphibious operation; the Army or Marine commander of the landing force also made his headquarters here until he could go ashore. Existence of these ships, extensively equipped with radio, radar and plotting facilities for coordination of information, was kept secret until the end of the Pacific war.

AGEDABIA. Key to defense of CYRENAICA from the west, because it gave access both to the coast road and to the tracks leading east across the desert. It lies due south of Benghazi and 250 miles from Tobruk. General ROMMEL, the Axis commander, fell back to Agedabia in December 1941 and from there launched a surprise attack the following month which threw the British back to GAZALA.

AGHEILA, EL. A small port on the Gulf of Sirte marking the western frontier of CYRENAICA. The site of an airfield and a small fort, this "bottleneck" was the far point of the British Army's first desert offensive, February 1941. It was also the starting point in ROMMEL's first desert campaign, which followed.

A GO. Japanese code name for their plan for a counterattack against an American attempt to seize the MARIANAS IN 1944. It called for land-based planes from airfields in the Marianas to attack the invasion force. They would be joined by planes from Japanese carriers, which would move into position to launch air strikes at maximum range. This was the basic plan which led to the Battle of the PHILIPPINE SEA.

AGRA. North-central Indian city that became (1942) headquarters of the Central Command of Gen. Sir Archibald WAVELL's India Command. There were three regional commands—the Northwestern, the Southern and the Eastern (the last-named being the command in confrontation with the Japanese).

AGRIGENTO. When Maj. Gen. George S. PATTON, Jr., seized this Sicilian town by a reconnaissance in force on July 15, 1943, he secured a port for the U.S. SEVENTH ARMY's supply and a bargaining point for his request to be given a more important role in the Sicilian campaign.

AINSWORTH, Walden Lee (1886–1960). U.S. Navy officer, a graduate of the Naval Academy in 1910. A gunnery officer in World War I, Ainsworth was a destroyer squadron and cruiser task group leader in the Pacific until assigned to Admiral HALSEY's staff in 1942. In 1943, as a rear admiral, he commanded the light cruiser task force that engaged in the Battles of KULA GULF and KOLOMBANGARA. He subsequently saw action in the MARIANAS, at GUAM and at LEYTE GULF.

AIRBORNE OPERATIONS. Although the Soviet Union during the 1930s was the first major power to experiment seriously with the delivery of men to the battlefield by air, the Russians during the war made little use of airborne troops. The first to do so on a large scale were the Germans, employing all three forms of air delivery: parachutes, gliders and "air landing," the latter involving bringing troops to a previously secured landing field in transport aircraft. They used air landing in 1938 in the unopposed move into Austria; small numbers of parachutists and air-landed troops against Denmark and NORWAY; gliders to take a formidable Belgian fortress, Fort EBEN EMAEL; and parachutists and air-landed troops against the Netherlands.

The greatest—and most disastrous—German airborne operation was against the Aegean island of CRETE. More than 15,000 airborne troops were involved, arriving by all three methods, while other forces arrived by sea. Although the Germans seized the island, they lost 4,000 men killed—one out of every four of the paratroopers. Crete was, said the German airborne commander, Col. Gen. Kurt STUDENT, "the grave of the German paratroopers." Having lost faith in airborne operations, Adolf HITLER sent the elite airborne divisions to fight and bleed as regular ground troops in Russia.

The first Allied airborne attack of more than battalion size was in the invasion of SICILY, when both American and British airborne forces in approximate division strength landed behind invasion beaches. So scattered were the drops, so heavy the casualties—including many shot down by Allied antiaircraft gunners mistaking the planes for enemy—that Allied commanders for a time also questioned the feasibility of airborne attack; but the very dispersion turned out to contribute to the success of the invasion, and airborne troops were from that time integral parts of Allied armies.

For the invasion of Normandy the Allies used the British 6TH AIRBORNE DIVISION behind British beaches near Caen and the U.S. 82D and 101ST AIRBORNE DIVISIONS behind Utah Beach, a total of 17,000 men arriving by parachute and glider within 24 hours. In the invasion of southern France, a provisional American-British airborne force of not quite 10,000 men participated.

In September 1944, in hope of seizing bridges over three major rivers in the Netherlands and establishing a corridor 65 miles deep through which British ground forces might advance to outflank the WEST WALL, the Allies mounted Operation Market, history's largest airborne operation (*see* MARKET-GARDEN). On the first day 20,000 airborne troops landed by parachute or glider and over a week, 36,000; but swift German reaction denied a crossing of the last river, resulting in only partial success. Casualties were high, including many incurred after link-up with ground troops when growing German strength forced Allied commanders—contrary to doctrine—to keep the elite airborne troops in the line. Participating were the British 1ST AIRBORNE DIVISION, the U.S. 82d and 101st Airborne Divisions, and the 1st Polish Parachute Brigade. During the subsequent Battle of the BULGE, those two American divisions were the only strategic reserve available, so again they had to be committed as ground troops.

For the crossing of the Rhine by the British 21ST ARMY GROUP, the British 6th Airborne Division and the U.S. 17th landed beyond the river near Wesel in Operation VARSITY. Having more transport aircraft and gliders than at the time of Operation Market, almost the entire force (22,000 men) landed on the first day. In contrast to two American divisions that crossed the river by amphibious assault, casualties were high: 41 killed in the amphibious assault, 506 in the airborne assault.

Although numbers of other airborne operations were planned in Europe, so rapid was the advance of the ground armies that by the time the detailed planning required for airborne assault could be completed, ground troops had overrun the objective. The only American division in Europe to see no action was an airborne division, the 13th.

Because the emphasis in the war in the Pacific was on amphibious assault and few transport aircraft were available, few major airborne operations were conducted. In July 1944 two American airborne battalions landed to secure an airstrip on NOEMFOOR Island off the coast of New Guinea, and in January 1945 a regiment parachuted in support of an amphibious assault on the main Philippine island of Luzon. Another American airborne regiment parachuted to recapture the island fortress of Corregidor in February 1945, at a cost of over a thousand casualties. Although the U.S. 11th Airborne Division was available for commitment, so few were the opportunities for airborne employment that the division fought primarily as a ground force. The largest airborne operation of the Pacific war was one of the first, Operation Thursday, launched in March 1944, aimed at driving the Japanese from BURMA and opening a road to the town of Myitkyina. It was mainly a glider and air-landing operation, which in the first week brought in more than 9,000 men (mainly Indian troops), 1,300 pack animals and 500,000 pounds of supplies. Japanese airborne troops were few and conducted only small-scale operations.

The basic German transport plane was the JUNKERS 52, an adaptation of a civilian aircraft; that of the Americans and British was an adaptation of the civilian DC-3 known to the Americans as the C-47 Skytrain and to the British as the Dakota (*see* C-47). Not until later stages of the war (Operation Varsity) did the C-46, specifically designed for airborne troops, appear (see C-46). Basic Allied gliders were the WACO, HORSA and HAMILCAR; the German, the DFS 230.

The types of airborne operations were varied, but the objective of most was to seize, hold or otherwise exploit important tactical objectives to assist the advance of ground or seaborne forces. Others were designed to halt enemy movement or trap enemy forces, or to take airfields or other specific objectives, such as a German heavy-water plant in Norway. Still others—usually on a small scale—assisted resistance units in occupied countries by bringing in men, supplies and equipment. In almost every case the size of the operation was limited by the availability of transport aircraft.

The airborne operations of World War II were unquestionably more costly in casualties than conventional ground operations. Virtually defenseless while dropping to earth, airborne troops were uniquely vulnerable to ground fire, and unless link-up with ground troops was swift, the relatively light arms and equipment that could be transported by air to support them left them at a disadvantage. **C.B.M.**

AIR DEFENCE OF GREAT BRITAIN (ADGB). The name given originally to an organization of the RAF bomber and fighter arms, 1925–36. It was revived between November 15, 1943, and October 15, 1944, during the preparation and carrying-out of the Normandy landings, when the name FIGHTER COMMAND was temporarily dropped.

AIR DEFENCE RESEARCH COMMITTEE. Set up in 1935 as a subcommittee of the British Committee of Imperial Defence. Its purpose, under the chairmanship of Lord Swinton, was to coordinate all Air Defence development at an interservice and interdepartment level. To this committee Sir Henry TIZARD reported the advances in radio detection made under the Air Ministry committee called the Committee for the Scientific Survey of Air Defence.

AIR MEDAL. This U.S. decoration was given in recognition of meritorious achievement while participating in aerial flight operations. Usually the award was given for the successful completion of five combat missions.

AIRPORT DEVELOPMENT PROGRAM. By a secret contract with the U.S. War Department, Pan-American Airways in 1940–42 constructed a chain of 55 airfields and bases throughout the Caribbean, Central America and northern South America, all converging on Natal in northeast Brazil. The U.S. Army would have recourse to these bases in case of war—should the respective host governments approve such use—and their strategic location could deny any invasion from Africa across the South Atlantic to the Brazilian Northeast. By late 1942 these bases were being used for training and antisubmarine patrols, and they became the "trampoline to victory" as U.S. planes carried cargo to the British in North Africa and used this route as preliminary staging across the South Atlantic, through Africa, and even to the China-Burma region.

AIR RAID PRECAUTIONS (ARP). The name given in Britain to the preparation and application of first-line passive defenses against air attack. It was essentially civil, being under the direction of the Home Office. The ARP Committee, set up in 1924, dealt with such questions as warning, prevention of damage, maintenance of vital services and movement of the seat of government.

AIR-SEA RESCUE. In 1940 both the British and the Germans began using aircraft and motor vessels to rescue airmen shot down offshore. The LUFTWAFFE used some elderly float planes for rescue work, and after each engagement in the Battle of BRITAIN the ROYAL AIR FORCE FIGHTER COMMAND sent Westland LYSANDER liaison planes, with fighter escort, to drop rubber rafts to airmen whose life jackets were keeping them afloat in the Channel. The majority of rescues were made by power boats.

Early in 1941 representatives of the Royal Air Force and the ROYAL NAVY agreed to form the joint Air-Sea Rescue Service. Because no aircraft were available at the time for its exclusive use, the new organization concentrated upon coordinating the efforts of naval units and the operational air commands, which used aircraft such as the HUDSON and the WARWICK. The service was also responsible for developing rescue equipment and was not above copying successful German innovations, such as a one-man dinghy for fighter pilots, a yellow dye marker to help search planes spot the rafts, and seaworthy floats that resembled houseboats and had bunks for four men, food, water, blankets and signal equipment. Perhaps the most valuable piece of rescue gear used by the Allies was the GIBSON GIRL, a portable radio transmitter.

When U.S. aircraft began operating from bases in the United Kingdom, the Americans at first relied on the existing rescue organization. Then, in June 1943, they set up the first elements of their own British-trained rescue service. U.S. Army fliers used P-47s to spot life rafts, report their location and protect the aircraft or motor launches making the rescue (*see* P-47). Converted B-17s could drop lifeboats, or OA-10s, Army versions of the Navy's Consolidated Catalina amphibian (*see* PBY), could touch down and make the pickup.

The air-sea rescue organization in the Mediterranean differed from that in the European theater. American units in the United Kingdom profited from British training and advice, but in the Mediterranean the American units were integrated into the British organization.

American air-sea rescue forces functioned worldwide, but despite the scope of the undertaking and the interest shown by the Joint Chiefs of Staff, there was no single rescue organization responsible for these operations. Coordination between Army and Navy was worked out within the various geographic theaters.

Effective coordination of the services took place in the Pacific, where the Army and Navy worked together to establish so-called rescue lines, positioning ships and aircraft along the paths flown by strike formations. Army rescue planes, both lifeboat-carrying B-17s and OA-10 amphibians, and Navy PBYs searched at prescribed intervals or were on alert at forward bases. Near the target was a submerged lifeguard submarine, which stood ready to move in close to Japanese-held islands. If shore batteries prevented the submarine from surfacing to take on board the downed crewmen, it could rise to periscope depth so that the men on the raft could attach a line and be towed beyond artillery range.

Throughout the Pacific war, the Navy carrier task forces continued the prewar practice of designating plane-guard destroyers to retrieve pilots who crashed on takeoff or were unable to land on board.

AIR TRANSPORT AUXILIARY SERVICE. Initially an all-male group organized in 1938, the "Air Ferry" delivered planes within Great Britain. Women pilots, known as "Ata-girls," were admitted in 1940. Approximately 900 British women served in this military corps as ferry pilots for all types of aircraft from four-engine bombers to light aircraft. They also were assigned as flight engineers, operation and control officers, ground engineers, and so on. Comdr. Pauline Gower was Director of Women's Activities. The ATA was disbanded after the war.

AIR TRANSPORT COMMAND. This wartime airline operated by U.S. Army Air Forces had its origin in a 1931 attempt to distribute supplies by air within the United States. The following year the Air Corps established a provisional air transport group with one squadron located at each of four major supply depots. This arrangement became permanent in 1937 and was undergoing tremendous expansion as America's entry into World War II approached.

Prewar plans called for the modernization and expansion of Army air transport. Orders were placed for the Douglas C-47 and the Curtiss C-46, and the military later acquired two other Douglas aircraft, the C-53 and C-54, and, though in limited numbers, the Lockheed C-69. Army Air Forces also made use of transport and tanker versions of the B-24. (See individual articles for planes.)

The volume of cargo that had to be moved by air brought a rapid growth of the Army air arm, but further impetus toward the establishment of the Air Transport Command came from an unexpected quarter. The need to deliver American-built airplanes into the hands of the British led to creation of the Air Corps Ferrying Command on May 29, 1941, and this organization expanded to form the nucleus of a worldwide transport network.

In June 1942 the Ferrying Command was redesignated Air Transport Command. Brig. Gen. Harold L. George took charge of the organization, with Cyrus R. Smith, president of American Airlines, assuming the rank of colonel to become his chief of staff. At its inception Air Transport Command was a global airline serving the War Department. Theater commanders had their own troop carrier units for local airlift, but late in the war the command extended its operations to include local service on the continent of Europe.

The air transport industry, which provided administrators such as Cyrus Smith, was a potential source of pilots, but this manpower reservoir of more than 2,500 skilled aviators could not be exploited because the airlines already were rendering considerable support to the war effort. During 1942, for instance, commercial airlines under contract to the government performed 88 percent of the War Department's air transport activity. Unable to call upon the airlines or to compete with the combat and training commands for veteran Air Corps pilots, Air Transport Command, like its predecessor the Ferrying Command, recruited whatever civilians were available—private pilots, crop dusters, even barnstormers. Aviators recruited in this fashion underwent additional training. Early in the war the newly recruited civilians were hired as temporary employees, who might receive commissions after a probationary period or might be retained in civilian status. By the end of the war, however, the command was staffed exclusively by military pilots.

The airlines aided in the training of crews for the Air Transport Command. Army Air Forces schools furnished quotas of pilots, navigators, flight engineers and radio operators. These specialists then received their final indoctrination from airline instructors.

From June 1942 until Japan's surrender, the number of officers and enlisted men assigned to Air Transport Command rose from 11,000 to almost 200,000, and its aircraft increased almost fourfold to 3,700. As the command gained in numbers, experience and proficiency, the amount of flying done under contract by commercial airlines declined steadily, dropping to 68 percent in 1943, 33 percent the following year and 19 percent by the time the war ended.

From March 1942 until September 1946, Harold George was in charge of the greatest air transportation system ever devised, and rose through successive promotions to three-star rank.

AIR WAR PLANS DIVISION/1 (AWPD/1). An estimate of "over-all production requirements required to defeat our potential enemies" requested by President Roosevelt on July 9, 1941, and submitted to him on September 11. Instead of functioning as part of the War Plans Division of the Army General Staff, the Air War Plans Division undertook the task as an agency of the Air Staff, responsible to Gen. Henry H. Arnold.

The plan that was produced adhered to the U.S. strategy outlined in the Rainbow 5 war plan, which assumed a two-front war with a strategic defensive against Japan until Germany had been defeated. To defeat Germany, the plan advocated selecting "objectives vital to the German war effort, and to the means of livelihood of the German people, and tenaciously concentrating all bombing toward the destruction of those objectives." The types of targets included the electrical power grid, the transportation network, the petroleum industry and finally the population centers. To accomplish their destruction, the American air arm would have to gain control of the air, neutralizing the German fighter force and destroying the aircraft factories that sustained it. This was a scenario for the "application of air power for the breakdown of the industrial and economic structure of Germany."

Far more detailed than the logistical summary that President Roosevelt had requested, the plan was actually a blueprint for the defeat of Germany through air power.

AITAPE. Site on north coast of New Guinea of Allied amphibious landing, April 22, 1944, made as part of General MacArthur's drive to Hollandia. The Aitape landing was made to capture airfields; the Japanese, much outnumbered, did not offer effective resistance. In July the Japanese attempted to counterattack, but the reinforced Americans repulsed them with heavy losses.

AJAX, H.M.S. Royal Navy cruiser of 6,985 tons, completed in 1934 by Vickers Armstrong. *Ajax* was armed with eight 6-inch and four (later eight) 4-inch guns, smaller weapons, eight 21-inch torpedo tubes and one aircraft. *Ajax* was one of three British cruisers that forced the German pocket battleship ADMIRAL GRAF SPEE into Montevideo, on the RIVER PLATE, on December 13, 1939. After repairs *Ajax* served throughout the war (refits excepted) in the Mediterranean, participating in numerous engagements, including the Battle of CAPE MATAPAN and the evacuation of CRETE.

AKA. U.S. Navy ship-type symbol for Cargo Ship, Attack. The AKAs were modifications of Maritime Commission cargo-ship designs which carried and launched their own complement of small landing craft. They were designed to stand off an invasion beach and, using the small craft, put supplies and equipment ashore for the use of a landing force. They were generally over 400 feet long, had displacements ranging from about 4,100 to 7,100 tons and averaged about 17 knots. Most were named after American counties.

AKAGI. Japanese aircraft carrier, originally laid down after World War I as an Amagi-class battle cruiser. Under the terms of the Washington Naval Treaty, *Amagi* and *Akagi* were to be converted to aircraft carriers as the United States was to do with LEXINGTON and SARATOGA. The severe earthquake of 1923 so damaged *Amagi* that she was scrapped on the ways and replaced by KAGA. Modernized in the late 1930s, *Akagi* took part in the PEARL HARBOR attack and was later sunk by American dive-bombers during the battle of MIDWAY. She displaced 38,200 tons and had a speed of 28 knots. She was classed with *Kaga,* although not a sister, and had a port-side island to improve landing operations when she operated with *Kaga,* which had the conventional starboard-side island.

AKERS, Sir Wallace (1888–1954). A chemist educated at Christ Church, Oxford, who spent most of his professional career with Imperial Chemical Industries. In 1941 he was assigned to the special section of the Department of Scientific and Industrial Research as director of British atomic research. He managed the negotiations with the United States and Canada on the project to develop atomic energy.

AKIZUKI. Class of Japanese destroyers. Larger and heavier than standard Japanese ships of this type, they represented a departure from the Imperial Navy's pattern of destroyer development. The Akizukis were armed with eight 3.9-inch dual-purpose (antiaircraft and surface) guns (4×2), and designed primarily to provide antiaircraft protection to carrier task groups. Before completion, torpedo tubes and depth charges were added to their armament to allow them to be used as general-purpose destroyers. Twelve Akizukis were completed, six of which were war losses. The Akizukis were referred to in wartime publications as the Terutsuki class.

AKYAB. Port on the west coast of BURMA in the ARAKAN, captured by the Japanese on March 31, 1942, during their advance through Burma. It was retaken almost three years later, in an amphibious assault (Operation Lightning) that went in shortly after dawn on January 3, 1945. There was no opposition and the port and its neighboring airfields were quickly occupied.

ALABAMA, U.S.S. SOUTH DAKOTA–class battleship, commissioned 1942. During 1943 she operated in British waters, protecting convoys bound for England and Russia. In the fall of that year she joined the U.S. Pacific Fleet. As a unit of the FAST CARRIER TASK FORCE, *Alabama* took part in operations involved with the capture of the GILBERTS, MARSHALLS, MARIANAS, Palaus, PHILIPPINES and OKINAWA. During 1944 she took part in various Pacific raids and in the Battle of the PHILIPPINE SEA. During July–August 1945 she bombarded industrial targets in Japan. *Alabama* decommissioned in 1947, and was later turned over to her name state. She is preserved as a war memorial at Mobile.

ALAGIR. A town in the Caucasus, USSR, captured by German Field Marshal von KLEIST in his advance to ORDZHONIKIDZE at the end of October 1942.

ALAMEIN, EL. A way station 50 miles west of Alexandria, Egypt. At Alamein, unlike any other place in the Western Desert, the southern flank of a potential battle line was closed. The Qattara Depression was only 40 miles inland, thus delineating a coastal passageway. Two critical battles were fought at Alamein in 1942. The first, in July, was a desperate effort of the retreating British under Sir Claude AUCHINLECK to stop a victorious Erwin ROMMEL from driving to Cairo. Rommel, his army tired from the preceding five-week campaign, overextended and experiencing crippling supply shortages, hoped to capitalize on British disorganization and broken morale and reach Cairo. Auchinleck turned to challenge him at Alamein, where the building of fortifications had begun in 1941. The sea and the Qattara Depression constricted the battlefield.

Rommel attacked the Alamein Line on July 1; by the end of the day the Axis forces were weakening and running out of supplies. On July 2 Auchinleck counterattacked and threw his enemy off balance. Equally exhausted, the two forces slugged it out for the rest of the month, with Rommel not allowed to advance east of Alamein and the British unable to drive him back to the west. However, the British success in stopping Rommel's drive contributed greatly to the second battle of Alamein, for it won time for British resupply, reinforcement and reorganization.

During the summer of 1942 both sides built up strength and defenses at Alamein. Important changes in the nature of the North African struggle took place. Generals ALEXANDER and MONTGOMERY took over for the British, while the battle for supplies swung sharply in favor of the Allies. Rommel, realizing he would be short on many requirements, for the first time began thinking defensively and laid a massive minefield. With material superiority assured, Montgomery prepared for a set-piece battle on his own terms. Rommel's attempt to force the issue by attacking at the end of August was defeated by his own shortages plus the British fortification of the ALAM HALFA ridge.

On October 23, at 9:40 P.M., the second battle of Alamein opened with a four-hour artillery barrage reminiscent of World War I. The British had overwhelming superiority in men and equipment, and they were aided by knowledge of the enemy's aims gained through ULTRA intelligence, but the Axis had built an elaborate

THE BATTLE OF EL ALAMEIN: The British, greatly superior in men and machines, broke through the Axis defenses

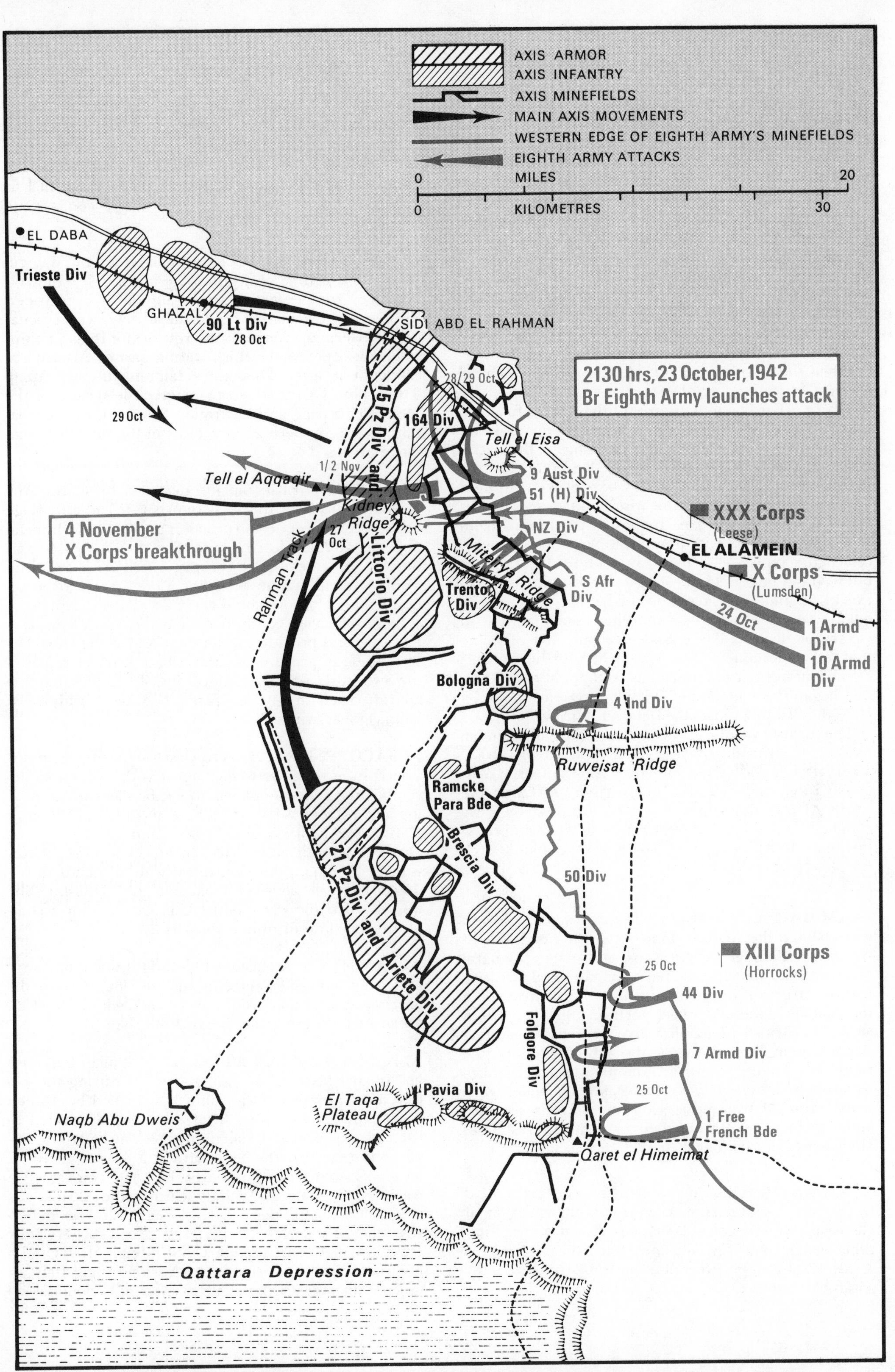

AXIS ARMOR
AXIS INFANTRY
AXIS MINEFIELDS
MAIN AXIS MOVEMENTS
WESTERN EDGE OF EIGHTH ARMY'S MINEFIELDS
EIGHTH ARMY ATTACKS
0
MILES
20
0
KILOMETRES
30
EL DABA
Trieste Div
GHAZAL
90 Lt Div
28 Oct
SIDI ABD EL RAHMAN
2130 hrs, 23 October, 1942
Br Eighth Army launches attack
28/29 Oct
29 Oct
15 Pz Div and Littorio Div
164 Div
Tell el Eisa
1/2 Nov
Tell el Aqqaqir
9 Aust Div
51 (H) Div
Kidney Ridge
XXX Corps
(Leese)
4 November
X Corps' breakthrough
27 Oct
NZ Div
EL ALAMEIN
Miteirya Ridge
X Corps
(Lumsden)
Rahman Track
Trento Div
1 S Afr Div
24 Oct
1 Armd Div
10 Armd Div
Bologna Div
4 Ind Div
Ruweisat Ridge
Ramcke Para Bde
Brescia Div
21 Pz Div and Ariete Div
50 Div
XIII Corps
(Horrocks)
25 Oct
44 Div
Folgore Div
7 Armd Div
25 Oct
Pavia Div
El Taqa Plateau
Naqb Abu Dweis
1 Free French Bde
Qaret el Himeimat
Qattara Depression

defense to a depth of five miles, utilizing large numbers of mines and well-sited antitank guns. Montgomery's plan, Lightfoot, was for the infantry to fight ahead of the tanks and clear two corridors through the minefield for the tanks to follow. After two days of extreme effort, the hoped-for gains had not been made, and Montgomery switched the main effort to the extreme north of the line, where the Australian divisions had made progress in chopping out a salient. On November 2 Operation Supercharge, essentially a repetition of Lightfoot on a concentrated sector, began just south of the Australian positions. By November 4 the Axis defenses had been penetrated, but it had been two weeks of grueling battle and heavy attrition. Alamein cost the Axis approximately 50,000 men (30,000 of them prisoners), while British losses were 13,560.

When the second battle of Alamein began, Rommel was in Germany on sick leave. HITLER urged him back to Africa, where he took control of the Axis defense on October 25 (General STUMME, commanding in Rommel's absence, had died on the morning of the 24th). There was little Rommel could do. Realizing that the British would persevere until they broke through, Rommel began planning the wisest course to save his army. On November 2 he requested permission from Hitler for a limited withdrawal; on November 3 he received the reply: "... there can be no other thought but to stand fast, yield not a yard of ground and throw every gun and every man into the battle ... As to your troops, you can show them no other road than that to victory or death." The episode was the first of many that led to Rommel's disillusionment with his Führer. Denied authority to command as he thought best, Rommel began the frustrating and bitter retreat by forced steps that led to TUNISIA the following spring.

The British victory at the second battle of Alamein marked the turning point of the struggle in Africa. Thereafter it was Allied initiative, Axis defense. Winston CHURCHILL described the significance with the words, "Up to Alamein we survived. After Alamein we conquered." Less than a week after the Alamein breakthrough the Allies invaded Africa in Operation Torch (*see* NORTHWEST AFRICA).

ALAM HALFA. The Alam Halfa ridge was roughly 15 miles behind the Alamein Line. After the first battle of ALAMEIN, General AUCHINLECK and then General MONTGOMERY anticipated that when General ROMMEL had the strength, he would attack the southern end of the Alamein Line and wheel north in the Alam Halfa area. The British prepared a heavy defense, including tanks dug in, hull down, at the western end of the ridge. On August 31, 1942, Rommel's expected attack was repulsed by strong defensive fire. Rommel withdrew, crippled by shortages of fuel and air support, and convinced that from then on material resources alone would decide the outcome.

ALAM NAYIL. This ridge (northwestern Egypt), held by the New Zealanders, marked the southern corner of General AUCHINLECK'S L-shaped ALAMEIN fortifications. From Alam Nayil the line stretched east along the ALAM HALFA ridge, with only mobile brigades to the south.

ALAMOGORDO. The birthplace of the atomic age. The memorandum from Gen. Leslie R. GROVES to Secretary of War Henry L. STIMSON opened with these sentences: "At 0530, 16 July 1945, in a remote section of the Alamogordo Air Base, New Mexico, the first full-scale test was made of the implosion type atomic fission bomb. For the first time in history there was a nuclear explosion. And what an explosion!" *See also* ATOMIC BOMB.

ALARIC (Alarich). A German plan issued on May 22, 1943, for a course of action to be taken if Fascism collapsed or Italy defected. Essentially the plan provided for German occupation of northern Italy, with evacuation by German troops of the rest of the Italian peninsula. Two operations which were a part of Alaric were carried out after Mussolini's fall on July 25, 1943. These were Operation Copenhagen, the seizure of the Mont Cenis pass, and Operation Siegfried, the occupation of the southern French coast in the Fourth Italian Army area.

ALBACORE. British biplane designed by Fairey Aircraft as a successor to the SWORDFISH. It had a fuselage of metal monocoque construction and wings with metal skeleton and fabric covering. The crew of three was housed in an enclosed cockpit. Fitted with a Bristol Taurus radial engine of either 1,065 or 1,130 horsepower, the Albacore could carry an 18-inch torpedo or a slightly heavier bomb load than the Swordfish, fly a bit faster and provide greater comfort for the crew. Despite these improvements, the Albacore never replaced the Swordfish, which remained one of Britain's first-line aircraft after the newer plane had been withdrawn from combat in 1943.

ALBACORE, U.S.S. A GATO-class submarine, commissioned June 1942. Between August of that year and December 1944 she completed 10 Pacific war patrols, sinking eight Japanese ships. These included the carrier TAIHO, the light cruiser TENRYU and two destroyers. On her eleventh patrol, *Albacore* struck a mine on November 7, 1944, and went down with all hands in the Tsugaru Strait between Hokkaido and Honshu. She was awarded the Presidential Unit Citation for accomplishments on four of her war patrols.

ALBAN HILLS. A cluster of elevations north of ANZIO and lying alongside and athwart the routes from the beachhead to Rome. They were pierced by the U.S. FIFTH ARMY at the beginning of June 1943.

ALBANIA, ITALIAN ATTACK ON. Italian influence on Albania became increasingly strong during the period after 1925 when the country was ruled by Ahmed Zogu (after 1928, called King Zog). Zog attempted to balance Yugoslav and Italian interests, although he apparently regarded the Yugoslavs as a greater threat, a judgment that cost him dearly. In 1926 Zog signed a treaty of friendship with Italy which made Albania virtually an Italian dependency. In 1927 a 20-year defensive alliance was signed, the terms of which gave Italy direction of Albanian military and foreign affairs and a favored economic position. On April 7, 1939, Italy attacked Albania; Zog was able to offer only nominal resistance to the invaders. The country was quickly joined in a personal union with Italy under the King of Italy, Victor Emmanuel III, and a puppet government was installed.

In 1943, after the surrender of Italy, the Germans restored Albanian independence and a non-Communist government was established. The Albanian Communist movement under the partisan leader, Enver Hoxha, however, was able to extend its control over most of the country even before the war ended.

ALBEMARLE. British twin-engine, twin-tailed, mid-wing monoplane, which began life as a reconnaissance bomber but, thoroughly outperformed by the Mosquito, performed mostly as a glider tug. Bristol Aircraft launched the project, but Armstrong Whitworth completed the design of this plywood-covered airplane, some 600 of which were built. Two Bristol Hercules radials gave the plane a top speed of 265 miles per hour at 10,500 feet. Service ceiling was just 18,000 feet. Albemarles took part in airborne operations in Sicily, Normandy and Holland.

ALENÇON. Important French crossroads town between Le Mans and Falaise, taken undefended on August 12, 1944, by French armored troops of the U.S. XV Corps.

ALEUTIAN ISLANDS. *See* Amchitka; Attu; Kiska.

ALEXANDER, Albert Victor (1st Earl of Hillsborough) (1885–1965). British Labour Party politician, First Lord of the Admiralty throughout the war in Winston Churchill's cabinet and that of Clement Attlee. He was subsequently Minister of Defence.

ALEXANDER OF TUNIS, 1st Earl (Sir Harold Alexander) (1891–1969). One of the most likable and respected high commanders in British history, "Alex" was known for his equable nature, charming manner, capacity for making decisions and unruffled calm under stress. He exhibited a constant optimism, founded in self-confidence and an impressive record of success.

Alexander—given the names Harold Rupert Leofric George—was the third son of the fourth earl of Caledon, and he inherited a tradition of public service and of a good life marked by dignity, orderliness and discipline. His father died when he was six; his mother was noted for her strict discipline and lack of demonstrativeness. As a child growing up on the huge estate in Ulster, Alexander developed self-reliance, courage, loyalty, and an enthusiasm for living. At Harrow he was known as well-balanced and level-headed, a boy good at games who made friends easily. He was seriously interested in painting, but after graduating from Sandhurst in 1911 he entered the Irish Guards and was soon captivated by military life.

World War I gave Alexander the opportunity to develop his capacity for leadership and discover his own feelings about war. He found "something terribly fascinating about it all," and considered it a "terrific adventure." He entered the war a lieutenant and came out a lieutenant colonel. He was in action throughout, twice wounded, three times decorated. "I have had a good weathering in this war," he wrote in 1918, and during the next 20 years he moved steadily upward. Each tour of duty brought him increased respect for his good judgment, and in 1937 he was appointed to command the 1st Division.

When war came, Alexander had his doubts about the Allied strategy as the 1st Division first took its place southeast of Lille, then moved forward to the Dyle in 1940, then joined the general retreat that ended at Dunkirk. But he held his counsel, believing always in the chain of command, and somehow he maintained morale among his men. "It does not matter in which direction you move, forwards or backwards," he said, "provided that you march on a route of your own choosing and at a time of your choice."

When the Dunkirk evacuation got under way, Lord Gort, the British Commander in Chief, was ordered home and Alexander took command of 1st Corps. Although the French later said they felt deserted by the British at Dunkirk, Alexander followed his orders—to defend Dunkirk as long as reasonable, evacuate as much of his force as he could and share evacuation facilities with the French. Alexander made every effort to help the French but he saw his main duty as being to his own corps. The British Expeditionary Force was saved—and a number of Frenchmen too—and Alexander emerged from the disastrous French campaign with increased stature. For the remainder of the year he commanded 1st Corps in northern England, then in December 1940 was appointed to the Southern Command. He soon won Winston Churchill's complete confidence, and when the Japanese invaded Burma, Churchill sent Alexander, writing later: "If we could not send an army we could at any rate send a man." Alexander's orders were to save Burma if he could, but if not, to save the army.

An unperturbed Alexander flew to Burma in March 1942 in time to make a last-gasp effort to hold Rangoon before beginning the bitter withdrawal into India. Again Alexander lost a battle but saved an army, and again his stature rose. He was slated for Operation Torch, the invasion of Northwest Africa, but in August 1942 Churchill reshaped the Middle East Command and Alexander replaced General Auchinleck as GOC Middle East. It was a formidable task, to which Alexander applied himself with his usual competence. To Gen. B. L. Montgomery, his principal subordinate, he gave freedom to plan and reorganize. Their relationship has been compared to that of the producer and director of a drama, Alexander the producer making sure his director had the time, the equipment and the support he deemed necessary. Perhaps inevitably, Montgomery seemed to overshadow Alexander, but there is no evidence that Alexander resented having his subordinate in the limelight.

In February 1943, with Alexander's force moving steadily closer to Gen. Dwight Eisenhower's Allied armies in Tunisia, Alexander was named deputy to Eisenhower, freeing Eisenhower to concentrate on political and inter-Allied problems while Alexander took operational command of the armies. Tunisia was soon cleared; the invasions of Sicily and Italy followed. Alexander proved more than equal to the challenges of an Allied command. Of him, Gen. Omar Bradley wrote: "He was easily able to comport the nationally-minded and jealous Allied personalities of his command . . . [he] brought to his command the reasonableness, patience and modesty of a great soldier."

When Eisenhower went to London to command Operation Overlord, the Normandy INVASION, he requested that Alexander go with him. Churchill was reluctant to strip the Mediterranean of both its top commanders, and loath to lose Alexander's talents in the conduct of armies. Sir Henry Maitland WILSON replaced Eisenhower, and Alexander remained as head of 15th Army Group. In this capacity he saw the Allies through the capture of Rome. On December 12, 1944, he became Allied Supreme Commander in the Mediterranean; his appointment as field marshal dated from the capture of Rome in June. The following April he had the satisfaction of seeing the German armies in Italy surrender.

After the war Alexander enjoyed a short rest. Then he went to Canada as Governor General. In 1952 he joined Churchill's second government as Minister of Defence. He stayed for two and a half years, but he did not enjoy being part of the government. His record as a minister, while not damaging his reputation, did nothing to enhance it. He retired from public life in October 1954. During the following years he painted, gardened, enjoyed his family, and served as director of various companies. He died in June 1969.

Alexander was made a viscount in 1946 and 1st Earl Alexander of Tunis in 1952. He was not a writer by inclination; both his *Despatches* and his *Memoirs* were written by others under his supervision, and are disappointing to read. We know Alexander by his actions and the way in which he affected others.

ALEXANDRIA. Although hard to defend from both land and sea, Alexandria, Egypt, served as operational and main base for the British Mediterranean Fleet and as a major supply port for the British Army in North Africa. Other Egyptian ports were too small to handle the traffic and tonnage.

ALF. Allied code name for the Japanese E7K reconnaissance floatplane (*see* E7K).

ALFIERI, Dino (1886–1966). Italian diplomat, a Fascist of long standing who first served Benito MUSSOLINI as Under Secretary of Press and Propaganda in 1935 and then as Minister of Popular Culture from 1936 to 1939. He was appointed ambassador to the Holy See in 1940 and ambassador to Berlin in 1941. After Alfieri voted against Mussolini at the Fascist Grand Council in July 1943, he fled to Switzerland. The Nazis tried him in absentia and condemned him to death. Alfieri returned to Italy in 1945 and was cleared of all charges the following year.

ALGIERS. Algiers was the easternmost point of invasion in Operation Torch, the landings in NORTHWEST AFRICA. To preserve the officially American nature of the invasion, the initial assault force was commanded by Maj. Gen. Charles W. RYDER (U.S.), with Lt. Gen. Kenneth A. N. ANDERSON (Br.) in command of the First Army units that followed. Opposition at Algiers ended on the first day of Torch; it was thereafter the scene of many political meetings, and on November 23, 1942, General EISENHOWER moved his headquarters there.

ALIAKMON LINE. Defense line on the Aliakmon River in northern Greece, held by Greek, British and Polish units in April 1941. The force of the German blitzkrieg in the Balkans made it untenable, though it was stoutly defended on April 10–12. *See also* BALKANS.

ALLAN, Robert Alexander (1914–). One of the most successful Allied commanders of coastal forces in the Mediterranean. Commander Allan, a British officer, is mainly remembered for a raid he led in Italian waters on the night of April 24–25, 1943. With a mixed squadron of British LCGs and motor gunboats and British and American motor torpedo boats, which he had trained to a high degree of excellence, he destroyed a German convoy south of Leghorn. Three armed barges which came to the aid of the convoy were then attacked. Two were sunk and the third was damaged and driven ashore. A patrol boat, escorting another convoy, was sunk by torpedo and three Italian torpedo boats engaged in mine laying were attacked, one of them being driven onto its own mines and sunk. Allan's force returned to harbor without loss or damage to either vessels or crews.

ALLEN, Terry de la Mesa (1888–1969). U.S. Army officer, a brigadier general at the time of the Pearl Harbor attack, promoted to major general in 1942. He took command of the 1st Division, which participated in the Tunisian and Sicilian campaigns. Relieved of that position by Gen. Dwight D. EISENHOWER, then ordered back to the United States in September 1943, he was placed in command of the 104th Division. Returning to Europe, Allen led the 104th (Timber Wolves) in fighting in the Netherlands in support of the right wing of the Canadian First Army attacking Antwerp. Outstandingly successful as a young division, the 104th had moved into Germany by the end of the war. A soldier with great dash and appeal to troops, Allen died shortly after his son and namesake was killed while leading a battalion in Vietnam.

ALLEN M. SUMNER, U.S.S. Destroyer and class (3,315 full-load tons; six 5-inch guns; ten 21-inch torpedo tubes; 34 knots). These destroyers followed the FLETCHER class; their hull and machinery were generally similar, but gun armament was arranged in three twin gunhouses for better forward firepower, backed by 40-mm. guns in twin and quadruple mounts. They were the first American destroyers designed to accommodate radar. Their steaming endurance proved inadequate for fleet work in the Pacific, and the design was redrawn to lengthen the hull by 14 feet. Ships built to this new design, with additional fuel tankage, became the GEARING class. Ships of the Allen M. Sumner class, with a standard (not full-load) displacement of 2,200 tons, were widely referred to as "2,200-tonners."

ALLFREY, Sir Charles Walter (1895–1964). British Army officer (lieutenant general), commander of the 5th Corps in North Africa and Italy, 1942–44. He was commander of British troops in Egypt, 1944–48.

ALLIED CONTROL COUNCIL. An organization agreed upon by Prime Minister CHURCHILL, President ROOSEVELT and Marshal STALIN, to be established in

Berlin with the responsibility of administering occupied Germany. Acting under the general guidance of the council, each of the four Allies would administer a zone. Representatives were EISENHOWER, United States; MONTGOMERY, Britain; ZHUKOV, USSR; and DE LATTRE DE TASSIGNY, France. The first formal meeting took place on June 5, 1945, when proclamations putting the council in being and detailing its responsibility were signed. More than a month later, on July 10, the first business meeting was held.

ALLIED EXPEDITIONARY FORCE. *See* SUPREME HEADQUARTERS, ALLIED EXPEDITIONARY FORCE.

ALLIED MILITARY GOVERNMENT. The necessity for military government arose when the legitimate government of an occupied nation either no longer existed, as in the case of the Third Republic in France, or was unable to exercise its functions, as in Italy in 1943–44. According to international law, military government is authoritarian, but it is not supposed to be despotic or lawless. Its purpose is to reestablish government according to law as the necessary basis for governing institutions. The Allies sought to achieve this objective in the military governments which they set up during the war and to assist in the transition to legitimate national governments led by civilians.

Throughout the war the Allies planned for military government in advance of tactical operations. Thus U.S. forces included civil affairs detachments which served as part of the staff of the military commander. Organizationally, civil affairs was a section of the General Staff (G-5). Planning and policies for military government were worked out in the civil affairs division of the War Department, which was established on March 1, 1943. In joint military operations the civil affairs division worked with the Navy and civilian agencies. In combined operations with Great Britain, the U.S. Army civil affairs division worked through the Combined Civil Affairs Committee of the Combined Chiefs of Staff.

Civil affairs officers involved in running military governments were usually experts in the fields of public safety, public health, supply, agriculture and the like. Public safety officers, for example, worked with local police forces to provide security for the Army, its equipment and personnel. They also tried to protect local resources and to preserve public order. The supply officials, health officers and other experts made sure that emergency civilian relief supplies, food, medicine, soap and coal were available. In one year in Italy the Allies distributed more than 1 million tons of relief supplies.

Public health was a serious problem for civil affairs officers. Undernourishment, lack of soap and water, broken sewers, dead animals, overcrowding and the presence of refugees were all possible causes of disease or epidemics. Thus health officers had to exterminate rodents and vermin, suppress diseases like typhus and malaria, restore water and sewage systems, and care for refugees.

Other civil affairs officers assisted local nationals in the repair or construction of war-damaged highways, bridges, railroads, public utilities, port facilities and inland waterways. They also assisted in whatever ways possible in the resumption of essential industries such as coal mining and fishing.

Allied military government took care of another population besides the civilian nationals. Military commanders were usually responsible for substantial numbers of prisoners of war; for example, after V-E Day U.S. forces held 130,000 Italian and 3 million German POWs plus another 3 million German troops disarmed following the unconditional surrender of the Third Reich. Some 420,000 German and Italian POWs had to be returned to Europe from prison camps in the United States and Hawaii. In addition to these military persons, the military governors had to supervise and coordinate the repatriation of some 5.5 million displaced persons in the liberated countries of Europe.

A final humanitarian service performed by Anglo-American military governments in Europe was the employment of experts who gave technical advice on the preservation or restoration of art objects and archives saved from destruction in the final days of the war or discovered after liberation in caches where they had been hidden away by the Nazis.

ALLIGATOR. Amphibian tractor built by Donald ROEBLING. It appeared in 1935. It was 24 feet long, weighed 14,350 pounds and was powered by a 92-horsepower Chrysler engine. This was the prototype of the LVT (landing vehicle, tracked) of World War II fame.

ALLIGATOR CREEK. A sluggish, semi-tidal stream about two miles west of Red Beach on GUADALCANAL.

ALPINE REDOUBT. *See* NATIONAL REDOUBT.

ALPINE VIOLET (Alpen Veilchen). German code name for an operation planned in early 1940. A German force of over two divisions was to help the Italians break out from Albania into Greece. Alpine Violet was canceled at the request of the Italians on January 19, 1940.

ALSOS MISSION. A cooperative project of the U.S. Army and Navy and the OFFICE OF SCIENTIFIC RESEARCH AND DEVELOPMENT, set up for purposes of nuclear intelligence. It collected information about the progress of German nuclear developments and, after the invasion in 1944, it sent teams of agents onto the Continent to capture scientists and take control of research facilities. These activities led to a number of others, popularly thought of as the roundup of German scientists. The chief scientific member of Alsos was Samuel Goudsmit, a physicist, and the principal military officer was Col. Boris Pash.

ALTMARK INCIDENT. Supply ship for the German pocket battleship ADMIRAL GRAF SPEE, the *Altmark* was pursued into Jösing Fjord in violation of neutral Norwegian waters on the night of February 16–17, 1940, by the British destroyer COSSACK. The *Cossack*'s boarding party rescued 299 British seamen taken prisoner by *Graf Spee* in her raiding career.

ALTONA. Code word used by the Germans in connection with Operation BARBAROSSA, the invasion of the

Soviet Union in 1941. "Altona" was the signal to be sent in case the offensive had to be canceled. The deadline for its use was 1300 hours on June 21.

AMAGIRI. Japanese Ayanami-class destroyer, sunk by a mine in Makassar Strait on April 23, 1944. Many wartime Allied publications refer to the Ayanami class as the Amagiri class. On August 2, 1943, the *Amagiri* collided with and sank the American PT 109, commanded by John F. KENNEDY.

AMBA ALAGI. Fortified position in northern Ethiopia, occupied by the Italians under the Duke of AOSTA after their defeat by the British in Eritrea (April 1941). British forces under Lt. Gen. Sir William PLATT and Lt. Gen. Sir Alan CUNNINGHAM converged on Amba Alagi, which fell on May 17 after two weeks of fighting. This all but ended the war in EAST AFRICA.

AMBERJACK, U.S.S. Two World War II submarines bore this name. The first was a GATO-class boat commissioned in June 1942. On her first war patrol she delivered fuel, ammunition and replacement pilots to GUADALCANAL during the early stages of the battle for that island. She also sank two small Japanese merchant ships and damaged two others. She failed to return from her third patrol, and is believed to have been sunk by two Japanese antisubmarine ships on February 16, 1943. The second *Amberjack* was a Corsair-class submarine commissioned in March 1946 after launching in December 1944. Completed after V-J Day, she saw postwar service.

AMBON (Amboina). Second largest naval base in the Netherlands East Indies, taken by Japanese forces on February 4, 1942.

AMBROSIO, Vittorio (1879–1958). Following a controversial tour of service commanding the Italian Second Army in Yugoslavia in 1941, General Ambrosio was appointed Chief of the Army General Staff in 1942. As Italy's situation worsened, he joined Marshal BADOGLIO and others working to get Italy out of the war. In February 1943 Ambrosio became head of Comando Supremo and urged MUSSOLINI to break free of German dominance. After Mussolini was replaced by Badoglio, Ambrosio worked closely with VICTOR EMMANUEL III, and after the armistice he fled with the King to Brindisi. Shortly thereafter he resigned as head of Comando Supremo and was assigned to inspection duties.

AMCHITKA. Island in the Aleutian chain, 90 miles east of KISKA. Uninhabited, it was occupied by a small U.S. Army force landed from transports on January 12, 1943. With the earlier occupation of ADAK (August 1942), seizure of Amchitka was a step toward recapture of ATTU and Kiska. An airstrip was quickly built on Amchitka and used for air strikes in support of the assault on Kiska.

AMERICA FIRST COMMITTEE. From September 1940 to December 7, 1941, this group stood at the forefront of a largely anti-British popular movement devoted to keeping the United States out of the European war. Within a few months of its founding, it had 60,000 members—in the Middle West, among veterans, pacifists, isolationists, and Republican and Democratic politicians alike. The head of the committee was Gen. Robert E. Wood, chairman of Sears, Roebuck, and its most prominent speaker was Charles A. LINDBERGH. America First acquired a tarnished image as various native American fascist groups flocked to its standard before the Japanese attack on Pearl Harbor undercut its position entirely.

AMERICAL DIVISION. The only U.S. division in World War II to bear a name rather than a number. It was formed for the defense of New Caledonia. Forty-five percent of its personnel came from Massachusetts troops of the 26th Infantry Division, the rest mostly from Illinois and North Dakota. This force, under Brig. Gen. Alexander M. PATCH, was designated Task Force 6814 and departed from New York on January 23, 1942, arriving in New Caledonia on March 12. The task force was constituted and organized as the Americal Division on May 27, 1942. A divisional element, the 164th Infantry Regiment, participated in the GUADALCANAL campaign, being one of the first U.S. Army units to conduct offensive operations in any theater. The division moved to the Fiji Islands, then served on BOUGAINVILLE and went on to the PHILIPPINES. It took part in the occupation of Japan and was inactivated December 12, 1945, at Fort Lawton, Wash. It is officially credited with the following campaigns: Guadalcanal, northern Solomons, Southern Philippines (with arrowhead) and LEYTE.

AMERICAN VOLUNTEER GROUP. Retired from the U.S. Army because of deafness, Claire L. CHENNAULT went to China in 1937 to organize and train an air force to fight the Japanese invaders. But lack of facilities, equipment and suitable trainees prevented him from accomplishing his purpose, and he was forced to try a different approach. In the spring of 1941 he returned to the United States, recruited some 90 pilots and 150 mechanics and administrators, and obtained a hundred Curtiss P-40B Tomahawk fighters, destined originally for Sweden (*see* P-40).

This force was called the American Volunteer Group; it was to be China's only effective air arm. The first contingent, some of the members carrying passports that identified them as missionaries, sailed from San Francisco in July 1941. Salaries ranged from $150 to $350 a month for ground crewmen, $600 minimum for flight crews and up to $750 for squadron commanders, with pilots eligible for a bonus of $500 for every confirmed kill in aerial combat. The volunteers painted shark teeth on the noses of their planes and styled themselves the Flying Tigers.

Training got under way at an RAF base at Toungoo, Burma, in September, but the Flying Tigers did not enter combat until December 20, 1941, when they intercepted a formation of 10 twin-engine Sally bombers and shot down six of the raiders at the cost of one P-40, whose pilot crash-landed in the jungle and returned to duty the next day with only minor injuries.

The Flying Tigers soon encountered the Japanese Zero fighter (*see* A6M). Chennault had carefully prepared them to use the ruggedness and diving ability of the P-40 to overpower this swifter, more maneuverable craft. He trained the pilots to fight in pairs, diving on the Zero, opening fire upon a plane that lacked armor and self-sealing fuel tanks, then continuing the dive at speeds the more fragile Zero could not match. Chennault also insisted that some P-40s provide overhead cover during these hit-and-run attacks.

Chennault committed a third of his force in defense of the BURMA ROAD, which carried supplies from Lashio in Burma to Kunming, China. Although the American Volunteer Group exacted a grim toll among Japanese squadrons, the Tigers were engaged in a war of attrition that they could not win. Maintenance was primitive, spare parts unobtainable and Japanese pressure unrelenting. By the end of February 1942 the Burma Road was closed, and the remnants of the squadron that had defended it were falling back across the Chinese border.

U.S. Army Air Forces sought to assume control of the Flying Tigers and dispatched some new P-40Es to China, but many of Chennault's pilots were marines or Navy men who wanted to return to their own services. Others preferred to serve with China National Air Transport or were unable to pass the Army physical examination. Enough were available to form the nucleus of the 23d Pursuit Group, organized on July 4, 1942, when the contracts signed by the original Flying Tigers had expired. This group became a component of the China Air Task Force, commanded by Chennault, who now wore the stars of an Army Air Forces brigadier general.

AMERY, Leopold (1873–1955). Statesman and journalist, Amery was born in India, the son of the head of the Indian Forest Department. As an international correspondent for the *Times* (London) he became a passionate advocate of British imperialism, remaining so through the debates of the 1930s. He opposed the MUNICH AGREEMENT, strongly criticizing the government. In 1940 he attacked Prime Minister Neville CHAMBERLAIN by quoting Cromwell: "You have sat too long here for any good you have been doing. Depart, I say, and let us have done with you. In the name of God, go." When CHURCHILL became Prime Minister, Amery accepted assignment to the India Office. He worked to bring India into free and equal partnership within the Commonwealth in the face of Indian pacifism.

AMIOT 143. A French twin-engine night bomber and reconnaissance aircraft. This plane entered service in 1935 but was obsolete by 1939. After May 1940 it was used as a transport by the VICHY air force. It flew at a maximum speed of 193 miles per hour and cruised at 155 miles per hour. It carried a five-man crew, four 7.5-mm. machine guns and a 2,866-pound bomb load, and had a range of 746 miles.

AMIOT 350. French four-place, twin-engine, medium-bomber series. The first plane in the series was the sleek Amiot 341 mail plane; the first bomber was the 340-01. These were followed by the 351-01, then the production 350 series. Few were built and used operationally. The 350 had a maximum speed of 310 miles per hour at 13,000 feet.

AMPHIBIOUS VEHICLES. Wheeled and tracked vehicles capable of navigating in water as well as on land saw considerable use during World War II. With their cross-country mobility, they were valuable in amphibious assault landings, crossing a landing beach and carrying troops and weapons directly inland without the necessity for disembarking them at the water's edge. Such vehicles also proved useful for transporting supplies and ammunition from offshore transport and cargo ships to beachhead dumps.

American amphibians included the 2½-ton DUKW, or "Duck" (*see* DUKW), widely used by British and American forces in all theaters as an amphibious cargo carrier. A number of troop-carrying, full-tracked landing vehicles, called ALLIGATORS and Buffaloes, were used by the U.S. Army and Marine Corps. Beginning with the GILBERTS invasion, LVTs were a standard feature of Pacific landing operations; some were also used by the British. The U.S. Army developed the smaller M29C Weasel amphibious cargo carrier, a web-footed version of its M29 tracked carrier. The British tested a number of designs for amphibious vehicles, wheeled and tracked; the eight-wheeled Terrapin was the only one actually produced. American vehicles saw much British service. Germany used large numbers of light 4×4 amphibian cars for reconnaissance, command and utility work. A small number of these were built by Porsche. Volkswagen produced more than 14,000 Schwimmwagen during 1942–44; a small stern propeller provided waterborne motion.

AMPHIBIOUS WARFARE. The primary American offensive tactic in the Pacific war, and the means by which the Allies took the offensive in Africa and Europe. Simply defined, an amphibious assault is an operation involving the coordinated employment of military and naval forces dispatched by sea for a landing on a hostile shore. In his final report of World War II to the Secretary of the Navy, Adm. Ernest J. KING, Commander in Chief of the U.S. Fleet, stated: "The outstanding development of this war, in the field of joint undertakings, was the perfection of amphibious operations, the most difficult of all operations in modern warfare." *See also* INVASION—NORMANDY; ITALY; NORTHWEST AFRICA; SICILY; SOUTHERN FRANCE.

AMTRAC. U.S. amphibian tractor, or amtrac, is officially designated "landing vehicle, tracked (LVT)." It was a military adaptation of Donald ROEBLING's swamp buggy, the ALLIGATOR, developed in the early 1930s for rescuing downed aviators and hurricane victims in the Florida Everglades. Its third modification appeared in the October 4, 1937, issue of *Life* magazine, arousing the interest of the Marine Corps, which was looking for an amphibian vehicle that could carry troops over coral reefs and ashore from naval vessels in an assault of a hostile beach. Nearly 16,000 amtracs of various types were built during the war. Some were armed only with .30- and .50-caliber machine guns, others mounted 37-mm. guns and 75-mm. howitzers, and still others were modified to take flamethrower kits. Some amtracs were heavily armored, while the lighter, unencumbered models were used as cargo carriers or employed in evacuating wounded to hospital ships from the beaches. Among the specialized modifications was the outfitting of individual amtracs with air conditioning and considerable radio equipment and using them as command posts.

ANAKIM. Code name for a proposed British amphibious assault on Rangoon at some time in late 1943 or early 1944. It was to be tied in with offensives in northern BURMA and the capture of important coastal points. Since it was evident by the spring of 1943 that the necessary conditions and resources would not exist, the plan was abandoned.

ANAMI, Korechika (1887–1945). A graduate of the Military Academy (1905) and the War College, Anami held many important posts in the Japanese Army. He served as aide-de-camp to Emperor HIROHITO, as director of the Tokyo Military Preparatory School and eventually as Vice-Minister of War. During much of World War II he commanded forces in China, Indonesia and New Guinea. Appointed Minister of War in Kantaro SUZUKI's cabinet (April–August 1945), Anami sought unsuccessfully to delay surrender. He committed suicide by hara-kiri at his official residence on August 15, 1945, shortly before the broadcast of Hirohito's acceptance of the Allied peace terms.

ANCON, U.S.S. A passenger and cargo vessel which the U.S. Navy converted into an amphibious command ship and equipped with elaborate radio and radar gear in 1943. It served as a flagship for amphibious landings in NORTHWEST AFRICA, at SALERNO, in Normandy (Task Force O at OMAHA BEACH) and on OKINAWA.

ÅNDALSNES. A small Norwegian port dominated by four large mountains and situated at the mouth of the Romsdal River at the head of a long fjord, site of an Allied landing in April 1940 and evacuation in May during which the town was virtually destroyed by the German attackers. Departing from Åndalsnes, a military force could approach TRONDHEIM from the south.

ANDAMAN ISLANDS. A group of islands in the Bay of Bengal, captured by the Japanese in March 1942. Plans for their recapture, under the code name BUCCANEER, were made in March 1944 but had to be shelved because of the recall of landing craft in the Indian Ocean required for Mediterranean operations. In the event, the Andaman Islands were evacuated by the Japanese at the end of 1944 and reoccupied by British forces in January 1945.

ANDERS, Wladyslaw (1892–1970). After the German attack in 1941, the Soviet Union released Polish prisoners of war held since 1939. Following his release from captivity, General Anders went with his fellow prisoners to Iran and Palestine, where they were organized into a Polish army. In Italy, Anders served as the commander of the 2d Polish Corps.

In 1945 the government-in-exile appointed General Anders commander in chief of the Polish Army. But as a staunch ally of Stanislaw MIKOLAJCZYK he was forbidden by the postwar Polish government to return to his native land. Anders died in exile in 1970. *See also* POLISH GOVERNMENT-IN-EXILE.

ANDERSON, SIR JOHN (VISCOUNT WAVERLY) (1882–1958). Educated as a mathematician at the University of Edinburgh, Anderson served in the Colonial Office, the Ministry of Shipping and the Ministry of Health, and in India as Governor of Bengal. He was elected to the House of Commons in 1938, holding his seat until 1950.

In 1938 he accepted office under Neville CHAMBERLAIN as Lord Privy Seal with special responsibilities for manpower and civil defense, and was instrumental in developing a bomb shelter which later became known as the ANDERSON SHELTER. In 1939 he became Home Secretary and Minister of Home Security, and was responsible for education plans, internment of aliens and the general transition to war, including civil defense.

Anderson became Lord President of the Council in 1940 with overall responsibility for civilian economic mobilization. He also had full responsibility for atomic research, which continued to occupy him after the war as well. In 1943 he became Chancellor of the Exchequer, a post he held until 1945 when Winston CHURCHILL left office. Never well known for his wartime services, Anderson was recognized as one of the mainstays of the British war effort by the cabinet and Churchill.

ANDERSON, Kenneth A. N. (1891–1959). British Army officer who had many qualities of the great soldier—sense of duty, courage, professional competence—but was reserved and reticent. In 1940 he commanded the British 3d Division in France during the last days of DUNKIRK. He served with the Home Forces until 1943, when, as a lieutenant general, he was given command of the FIRST ARMY in North Africa. After TUNISIA he commanded the SECOND ARMY in preparation for Normandy, but was replaced by Lt. Gen. Miles DEMPSEY before the invasion. His last military appointment was to the East African Command in 1945. From 1947 to 1952 he was much respected as the progressive Governor of Gibraltar. He was promoted to general in 1949.

ANDERSON SHELTER. When Sir John ANDERSON became Lord Privy Seal in 1938, he assumed special responsibility for manpower and civil defense. It was his belief that family air-raid shelters might well be required for the survival of the British population. He invited an old friend, the Scottish engineer Sir William Paterson, to design a shelter. This design with some modifications became known as the Anderson shelter. Made of concrete, corrugated iron and earth, this simple air-raid shelter was supplied to families in likely target areas and erected in back gardens or any other available space.

ANDREWS, Adolphus (1879–1948). A Texan, "Dolly" Andrews graduated from the U.S. Naval Academy in 1901. By 1938 he had risen to the rank of vice-admiral, and he commanded the Eastern Sea Frontier from 1941 until the end of 1943. In this command, which stretched from the Canadian border to Jacksonville, Fla., Andrews had the responsibility for carrying on the antisubmarine war against Germany and providing convoy protection. Early in the submarine war the Eastern Sea Frontier was underequipped, but during the 10 months following July 1942 no ships went down inside its barriers. Andrews developed the BUCKET BRIGADE, in which local craft escorted shipping from port to port up and down the Atlantic coast. He also coped well with the civilian pressures accompanying the proximity of the war to population centers. In 1943 Andrews retired on special duty, and in 1945 he retired from active duty. *See also* SEA FRONTIER.

ANDREWS, Frank Maxwell (1884–1943). Having graduated from the U.S. Military Academy in 1906, Andrews entered the Air Service in 1917 and by the end of World War I had risen to the rank of lieutenant colonel. When the Air Corps was permitted to establish an essentially autonomous force—the General Headquarters Air Force—in 1935, Andrews was promoted to major general and given the command, which he held until 1939. In 1941, promoted to lieutenant general, he became the first American airman to command a theater (the Caribbean); he set up a functional organization which became the model for the air arm. In February 1943 Andrews became the commander of U.S. forces in Europe, succeeding Gen. Dwight EISENHOWER. In May 1943 Andrews was killed in an aircraft accident.

ANGAUR. Southernmost island of the Palau Island group of the western Carolines. The U.S. 81st Infantry Division (less one RCT) began landing on Angaur on September 17, 1944, the 1st Marine Division having gone ashore on PELELIU, a few miles to the north, on the 15th. In three days the 81st Division cleared the southern and eastern portions of Angaur, where a large bomber base was to be constructed to support further advances toward the Philippines. A Japanese pocket held out in northwestern Angaur and was not completely eliminated until October 21. The 81st Division (and attachments) lost approximately 265 men killed and 1,335 wounded; Japanese casualties were over 1,300 killed and 45 captured.

ANGERS. French city 48 miles northeast of Nantes and three miles north of the Loire River, taken by the U.S. 5th Division on August 11, 1944.

ANGLER, U.S.S. A GATO-class submarine, commissioned October 1943. During 1944–45 she completed seven Pacific war patrols, sinking two Japanese merchantmen and a small fishing craft. She evacuated refugees from the Philippines in March 1944 and trailed Admiral KURITA's Center Force during its approach to the Philippines before the battle for LEYTE GULF. During mid-1945 she made surface gun attacks on points on the Japanese coast. Decommissioned in 1947, *Angler* was recommissioned in 1951 and served until her disposal in 1971.

ANGLO-GERMAN NAVAL TREATY (June 18, 1935). This agreement established a "permanent relationship" between the German and British navies. The treaty set the total tonnage of the German fleet at no more than 35 percent of the aggregate tonnage of the naval forces of the British Commonwealth but permitted Germany to build a submarine fleet equal to the total submarine tonnage of the Commonwealth. The agreement unilaterally modified the naval terms of the Versailles treaty and particularly disturbed France, which was less convinced than Britain that Adolf HITLER would honor his commitments. Hitler denounced the treaty on April 28, 1939.

ANGLO-ITALIAN MEDITERRANEAN AGREEMENT (April 16, 1938). This was intended to reconcile British and Italian differences particularly in regard to Ethiopia and Spain. Prime Minister Neville CHAMBERLAIN promoted the agreement in the hope that it would encourage collective security and weaken Italy's alliance with Germany.

ANGLO-POLISH ALLIANCE (August 25, 1939). This treaty formalized British assurances of military assistance to Poland in case of aggression from a European power. Britain's support of Poland was motivated in part by the accusation that Britain had encouraged the Central Powers in 1914 by failing to make clear the circumstances under which she would go to war. When Germany invaded Poland on September 1, 1939, this alliance provided the basis for Britain's declaration of war against Germany on September 3.

ANHWEI INCIDENT. In early 1938 the Anhwei province of China, lying just north of the Yangtze delta, became one of the earliest war zones of World War II. When the Japanese invaded, they destroyed the dikes of the Yellow River, flooding northern Anhwei to the Hwai River. Although the Japanese were able to maintain control of the railways leading to the more industrialized cities, the countryside remained under guerrilla control. In January 1941 Nationalist Chinese troops south of the Yangtze attacked and wiped out a 10,000-man force of the Communist New Fourth Army. This "Anhwei Incident" greatly exacerbated the hostility between the Nationalists and the Communists.

ANKLET. Allied code name for LOFOTEN ISLANDS RAID, December 26, 1941.

ANN. Allied code name for the Japanese Ki 30 light bomber (*see* KI 30).

ANNEXE, THE. Stone building (much more substantial than the Downing Street buildings) used by Winston CHURCHILL for offices and living quarters during the major part of the war.

ANSCHLUSS. The German invasion and annexation of Austria in March 1938. Adolf HITLER carefully laid the groundwork before moving against the Austrians. After carrying out a reorganization of the command of the German armed forces in order to be certain of their loyalty, he accused the Austrian Chancellor, Kurt von SCHUSCHNIGG, of violating the provisions of the Austro-German pact of July 1936, which required Germany to respect Austria's independence. Hitler summoned Schuschnigg to BERCHTESGADEN in February 1938 and threatened to invade Austria unless Schuschnigg admitted the leader of the Austrian Nazi Party, Arthur SEYSS-INQUART, into his government as Minister of the Interior, legalized the Nazi Party in Austria, and filled other cabinet posts with pro-Nazi ministers.

In an attempt to check Hitler's moves, Schuschnigg on March 9 called for a plebiscite within four days on Austria's independence. An infuriated Hitler demanded immediate cancellation of the plebiscite and the resignation of Schuschnigg. Taking their cue from Hitler, the Austrian Nazis provoked riots and unrest. Hitler again threatened an immediate invasion. In the face of Hitler's threats and the spreading disorder, Schuschnigg capitulated and handed the office of Chancellor to Seyss-Inquart. On March 12, even before the new Chancellor asked for German aid to restore public order, German troops moved into Austria. The next day Hitler declared Austria a province of Germany. For a time it was called the "Ostmark," but it soon ceased to have any special regional identity.

Hitler annexed Austria without opposition from other European powers, although German control of the country gave him strategic control of the road, rail and river communications of the middle Danube valley and frontiers with Italy, Hungary and Yugoslavia, and enabled him to strategically surround CZECHOSLOVAKIA. Despite the weakening of Italo-Austrian economic ties as a result of the Anschluss and the disquieting presence of German troops on Italy's borders, Benito MUSSOLINI could only acquiesce in Hitler's *fait accompli*. Even if he had been prepared for Hitler's startlingly swift invasion, Mussolini, no longer a guarantor of Austrian independence, had little choice but to support the actions of his Axis partner.

France and Britain also proved incapable of thwarting Hitler in Austria. France was in the midst of another cabinet shuffle, and the CHAMBERLAIN government in England, accepting Hitler's rationale for the Anschluss, was disinclined to stop him from adding to the Reich those Germans who, Hitler claimed, wanted to join it.

In a bloodless victory, Hitler added 7 million Austrians to the Reich, absorbed Austria's mines and metallurgical works, took over the Austrian National Bank and incorporated the Austrian Army into the Wehrmacht. Just as important as the gains in men and matériel was the psychological effect of the Anschluss. Reflecting on the relative ease with which he had accomplished it, Hitler was emboldened to seek more territory for the Reich. The Anschluss was a long step toward World War II.

ANSON. This Avro twin-engine monoplane, nicknamed Faithful Annie, remained in production for 17 years, with more than 10,000 planes rolling from assembly lines in the United Kingdom (A. V. Roe) and Canada (Federal Aircraft). The Anson found particular favor with the RAF because it was built principally of plywood and fabric; therefore, production required a minimum of strategic material and less skilled labor than did most World War II aircraft. A military adaptation of a six-passenger civil transport, the Anson was a standard land-based reconnaissance craft for RAF COASTAL COMMAND when the war broke out. Although in production since 1935 and approaching obsolescence, the Anson made the first aerial attack of the war on a German submarine. After Coastal Command had shelved the plane in favor of HUDSONS and WHITLEYS, it continued to serve as a transport, an ambulance plane and a gunnery, communication, navigation or bombardier trainer.

The Coastal Command Ansons featured a metal skeleton, a fabric-covered fuselage and wooden wings. Two 350-horsepower Armstrong Siddeley Cheetah radials gave Anson I a top speed of 188 miles per hour; maximum range was 660 miles at 158 miles per hour. The crew numbered three, and the standard armament consisted of one forward-firing .303-caliber machine gun and another of the same type mounted in a manually operated dorsal turret.

ANTELAT. Point in the Cyrenaican desert at the base of the Benghazi bulge, southeast of BENGHAZI. The British 7th Armored Division pursued the Italians through Antelat in January 1941. A year later (January 22,1942) Axis forces under Gen. Erwin ROMMEL took Antelat on the drive that ultimately gained Tobruk. In November 1942 Gen. Sir B. L. MONTGOMERY's British Eighth Army retook Antelat in the final offensive of the desert war. *See also* NORTH AFRICA.

ANTHONY, H.M.S. Destroyer that played a prominent part in the British assault on MADAGASCAR in May 1942. Carrying 50 Royal Marines from the battleship *Ramillies,* the *Anthony* ran the entrance to ANTSIRENE harbor on the evening of May 6 and succeeded in landing the party, which captured the naval arsenal. *Anthony* herself escaped.

ANTIAIRCRAFT DEFENSE. When the war began, antiaircraft guns for ship and land use ranged from machine guns of .30 to .50 caliber to rapid-firing shell guns of 37 to 88 mm. for land use and heavier guns of about 3 to 5.25 inches for ships. Detection was visual or by use of sound detectors, although a few early aircraft-warning radars were in various stages of development; in Britain the CH network (*see* CHAIN HOME) of radar stations had lately been completed. Heavier AA guns, usually 3-inch and up, were frequently controlled by

Antiaircraft version of the German 88-mm. gun

electromechanical directors associated with optical height finders—special AA range finders with which a plane's altitude could be determined. Machine guns and light cannon were controlled by "iron sights" or by special types of telescopic sights. Light-caliber ammunition included solid slugs, incendiaries and tracers, and impact-fuzed explosive projectiles for shell guns. These guns, intended for close-in defense against dive-bombers and strafers, had to score direct hits to have any effect. Three-inch and larger guns fired shells with mechanical time fuzes, their explosion calculated to produce a lethal pattern of blast and fragmentation. Since the fire control of the day could not keep up with an airplane on a continuous-aim basis, reliance had to be placed on barrage fire against distant planes or higher-flying horizontal bombers. The altitude, course and speed of approaching planes were determined, and the results fed into a director. This predicted the advance position of the attackers, and a barrage was fired through which the planes would have to pass to reach their target. As they passed through, fire would be adjusted to shift the barrage again to the front of the enemy formation, and the process was repeated. Large searchlights were used to assist AA gunners at night; barrage balloons were extensively used by the Allies to provide a physical obstacle.

Wartime experience brought with it the inevitable improvements. Heavy AA guns became heavier and evolved into "heavy" and "medium" families. The biggest guns were generally used in static positions, for defense of bases and rear areas; these ran from about 90 mm. to 128 mm. in caliber. Germany produced a number of twin 128-mm. automatic mounts which were used for home defense; these approximated the twin 5-inch mounts used in some contemporary destroyers. Medium AA guns, usually on towed or self-propelled mounts, averaged 20 mm. to 88 mm. World War I had seen some limited use of vehicle-mounted AA guns, but during this war they were produced in large quantities. Most such mounts were installed on tracked or half-tracked chassis for adequate mobility. Light guns were still .30 to .50 caliber in general size, although as airplane performance increased guns in the smaller caliber range came to be considered obsolete. The U.S. Army made particularly extensive use of .50-caliber weapons on single mounts atop tank turrets and truck cabs as well as on pedestal mounts in jeeps; the British did not especially care for this type of mount, and the Germans seem to have made little, if any, use of such AA weapons. Russian vehicles also lacked individual AA guns.

Naval antiaircraft weaponry tended to increase in size and number, although this varied from one navy or one theater to another. In the Pacific, ship AA batteries were enlarged as rapidly as possible, as many guns as a ship's design would permit being installed as soon as they could be produced. Wartime designs tended to be influenced by air-defense considerations, superstructures being clustered together and tophamper being reduced to allow more gun positions and better fields of fire. By comparison with their Japanese and American contemporaries, ships of the Russian, British, German, French and Italian navies often seem quite undergunned in this respect. The availability of land-based air power seems to have made it much less necessary for naval task forces to take heavy antiaircraft umbrellas to sea with them.

RADAR and the PROXIMITY FUZE considerably improved the capability of the AA gun. Radar could give gunners better and more up-to-the-minute range data than even the best optical range finders. By 1942 the U.S. Navy was equipping the directors that controlled its 5-inch shipboard AA guns with their own fire-control radars. Information from these was incorporated into the director-control solution, permitting more accurate and responsive control of heavy guns. Provision of radar range and bearing input permitted blind firing at targets obscured by darkness or cloud. When the proximity fuze was introduced in 1943, heavy AA fire further improved. It was no longer necessary for gunners to score a direct hit—a virtual impossibility—or hope that the target would walk into their barrage fire. Now, if a projectile passed within lethal range of an airplane, it would detonate itself. Proximity fuzes saw heavy service against Japanese aircraft in the Pacific, particularly against kamikaze attackers, and were used against German V-1 flying bombs over Britain (*see* V-WEAPONS).

The 20-mm. Oerlikon and 40-mm. Bofors automatic shell guns were used by the thousands, particularly by the British and American navies; they were also employed ashore. These reliable weapons became mainstays of the Allied antiair defense, throwing explosive projectiles at a high rate. Lead-computing sights were developed for the 20-mm. gun; the same sights were used as bases for simple directors for 40-mm. mounts. Director control of power-operated 40-mm. twin and quadruple mounts gave warships the ability to put up a heavy close-in antiaircraft fire; this also received great emphasis during the final months of the Pacific war for defense against kamikazes. During this period the 20-mm. was downgraded in the fleet as too light to knock a suicider from the air; where possible, many were removed from ships to make room for 40-mm. guns. By V-J Day development of blind-firing arrangements for 40-mm. batteries was well along; radar control had been introduced for fleet heavy automatic-weapon batteries during the war's final months and had seen some use.

By the end of the war, antiaircraft guns in heavier calibers and in much greater numbers than envisioned a few years before were in universal use. Control had been improved by development of higher-performance directors and lead-computing sights, with radar for greater accuracy and all-weather control. Fighter direction, guided by long-range air-search and height-finding radars and centralized in plotting rooms, coordinated defense by fighter planes; sophisticated procedures for fighter control saw considerable wartime development. There was still no total answer against air attack, though skillful coordination of defensive air cover with radar-controlled AA guns firing proximity-fuzed ammunition made antiair defense a much more formidable proposition than it had been. On the other hand, of course, the airplane itself was much faster and harder-hitting in 1945 than it had been in 1939. Late-war experimentation had included various forms of rockets and guided missiles for AA use, but these did not become operational in time for war service and could do no more than foreshadow things to come.

J.C.R.

ANTI-COMINTERN PACT. A five-year German-Japanese pact signed in November 1936. It was a reaction to the "popular front" policy adopted at the seventh and last congress of the Communist International (July–August 1935). The Anti-Comintern Pact named Communism as the chief enemy of peace in the world; a secret protocol provided for the coordination of policies directed against the Soviet Union. Italy joined the pact in 1937, Hungary and Spain in 1939. The pact was extended for a further five years in November 1941.

ANTISUBMARINE DEVICES AND TACTICS. The principal antisubmarine weapon at the beginning of World War II was the "ash-can" type depth charge, originally developed during World War I. This was dropped from stern tracks by destroyers or smaller antisubmarine ships, or was fired to one side by a depth-charge thrower. The charge was detonated by water pressure at a preset depth. Hydrophones were used to listen for the sound of a submerged submarine; early models of SONAR equipment could, within certain limits, enable a ship to determine a submarine's position and motion beneath the surface. An antisubmarine ship first had to locate its target, then predict its movement accurately enough to be able to pass directly over it to drop depth charges.

The diesel-electric submarine of this time was essentially a surface ship, capable of submerging for, by today's standards, relatively short periods. Its submerged speed was no more than a few knots. If a submarine could not surface within a certain time after submerging, its propulsive batteries exhausted their power and its crew would suffocate. As the war went on, weapons and tactics were developed to attack the submarine's weaknesses. RADAR enabled ships and planes to detect submarines on the surface at a distance, even in fog or at night. Land-based planes were used to keep known submarine transit routes and operating areas under surveillance. As escort aircraft carriers (CVE) became available, they were used both to provide air-patrol cover for convoys and as an element of carrier-destroyer escort (DE) hunter-killer groups. All this made it increasingly hazardous for a submarine to move on the surface, slowing its operation and forcing it to spend an increasing amount of time submerged. The high-frequency direction finder (*see* HF/DF), a British invention, allowed antisubmarine ships to detect brief radio transmissions from submarines and home on them.

To give a submarine less of a chance to evade an attacking ship, ahead-throwing weapons such as MOUSETRAP, HEDGEHOG and SQUID were developed. With these, an attacking ship could hurl a pattern of small depth charges at a suspected submarine before actually reaching its position, following up with a pattern of stern-dropped and side-thrown charges as it passed over the sub. The old Y-gun, firing two charges in opposite directions, had to be mounted on a ship's centerline. A new single-armed thrower, dubbed the K-gun, could be mounted in multiples along a ship's sides.

The sonar range recorder, British-devised, provided a visible plot of a ship's movements and the sonar trace of a target submarine. This meant that the underwater fire-control situation could be more easily and accurately understood and evaluated. Late-war antisubmarine attack directors mechanically combined information on the movements of one's own ship with sonar data to calculate recommended fire-control solutions.

The SNORKEL enabled a submerged U-boat to avoid detection by earlier wartime radars while running on diesels and taking in air. Later, more precise radars could pick up the snorkel head, the only part of a "snorkeling" submarine visible above the surface.

Bottom-mounted listening arrays were planted off harbors and around anchorages to detect submarines approaching fleet bases. Torpedo nets, both fixed arrays around ship berthing areas and the ADMIRALTY NET DEFENCE installed on some merchant ships, were of value against submarines and their torpedoes.

ANTONESCU, Ion (1880–1946). Rumanian politician and soldier who led the pro-German government during World War II. In 1934 he became Minister of Defense, and when King CAROL II established his corporatist dictatorship in 1938 Antonescu initially retained his position. After a few weeks, however, he was dismissed by the King for his sympathy with the most obstreperous Rumanian Fascist group, the Iron Guard.

In 1940, two days before King Carol was forced to abdicate, Antonescu was named Prime Minister. He immediately established a pro-German, Fascist dictatorship. The new regime was designated a "National Legionary State," and the Iron Guard was brought into the government. The violent excesses of the Guardists, however, soon made it necessary to eject them from the government and they became a kind of right-wing opposition. Antonescu at first gained great popularity by enacting certain domestic reforms and by joining the AXIS in the war against Russia.

As Axis fortunes declined and Rumanian casualties on the Eastern Front increased enormously, Antonescu's popularity waned. In August 1944, with Russian occupation imminent, he was overthrown by a coup d'etat headed by the young King MICHAEL. In 1946 a Rumanian Communist "People's Court" sentenced him to death, and he was executed on June 1.

ANTONOV, Alexsey (1896–1962). One of Marshal Boris SHAPOSHNIKOV's protégés, General Antonov was chief of staff of the Soviet Transcaucasian front from the outbreak of hostilities until December 11, 1942, when he was appointed Deputy Chief of the General Staff and chief of the Operations Department. Less than a month later he was detached as the GHQ representative to the Voronezh, Bryansk and Central Fronts. On his return to Moscow (March 1943) he directed the General Staff during the frequent absences of Alexander VASILEVSKY, the Chief. An excellent theoretician and executive, Antonov was highly respected by his fellow officers and, apparently, by Stalin. After being Acting Chief of the General Staff from October 1944, Antonov was appointed Chief in April 1945 and held that post until the end of the war.

ANTSIRENE (Antsirane). Town in MADAGASCAR alongside the port of Diégo-Suarez, captured by a British amphibious force on May 6, 1942. The operation was given the code name Ironclad; its object was to prevent Japanese U-boats from using Madagascar as a base from which to attack British convoys to the Middle and Far East.

ANT (Ari) TRANSPORT. Japanese nickname for troop transport by motorboats at night.

ANTWERP. The British Second Army liberated this Belgian port on September 4, 1944, with wharves and docks intact; but because the Germans held the banks of the Scheldt estuary for almost three more months, the first Allied ship did not dock until November 28. The port subsequently accounted for a third of Allied supplies entering the Continent. In the latter stages of the war the Germans tried to disrupt port operations by bombardment with V-1 and V-2 rockets but had only minimal success (*see* V-WEAPONS).

ANTWERP X. Code name for Allied antiaircraft defense of the Belgian port of Antwerp against bombardment by German V-1 and V-2 rockets (*see* V-WEAPONS). The defense employed 18,000 British and American troops and more than 500 antiaircraft guns.

ANVIL-DRAGOON. Successive code names for the Allied SOUTHERN FRANCE OPERATION. Anvil was the code name during most of the planning for the operation. Suspicion of compromised security led to the selection of another code name, and an apocryphal story has it that Churchill personally selected Dragoon because he felt that he had been "dragooned" into approving the Southern France Operation, to which he had been adamantly opposed ever since it first surfaced in Allied planning councils. Basically, the Anvil-Dragoon plan envisaged landing a strong Franco-American force along the Riviera, with a subsequent exploitation northward toward Vichy and Lyon. Once firm contact was gained with Gen. Dwight D. EISENHOWER'S SHAEF forces, the Anvil-Dragoon operations would pass from control of the Supreme Allied Commander, Mediterranean (SACMED) to Eisenhower.

ANZIO. A small port on the west coast of Italy where Anglo-American troops came ashore on January 22, 1944, and constituted a threat to German-held Rome, about 20 miles away. One of the war's major Allied operations, the landing failed to achieve its original objec-

Fifth Army troops wade ashore near Anzio

tive of forcing withdrawal of the German armies holding up Allied advance farther south against the Gustav Line around Monte Cassino. The Germans effectively hemmed in the beachhead for four months.

The rationale for the Anzio landing came from the nature of the terrain in southern Italy. Highly favorable to the defense, it restricted the Allies to a few obvious avenues of advance, which the Germans could block with relative ease. Thus the Allies after landing at Salerno on September 9, 1943, fought at great cost to inch their way northward and eventually came to a halt before the Gustav Line, anchored on the Garigliano and Rapido Rivers. It was a strong position amid towering mountain peaks with mines, barbed wire and concrete pillboxes in profusion.

Even before the advance reached the Gustav Line, the Allied Commander in Chief, Gen. Dwight D. Eisenhower, saw an end run, an amphibious operation along the west coast, as the way to end the slow, costly fighting through the forbidding terrain. On November 8 he instructed Gen. Sir Harold Alexander, the Allied ground commander, to launch such a seaborne descent in the German rear. Alexander on the same day gave the mission to Lt. Gen. Mark W. Clark, who commanded the U.S. Fifth Army. He was to put troops ashore at Anzio on beaches that were suitable for amphibious landings and yet close enough to Allied airfields for tactical air cover.

As planning proceeded, it became apparent that troops put ashore at Anzio would be so far removed from the forces on the main front as virtually to preclude an early link-up. Because of a relative paucity of Allied troops in Italy and a shortage of landing ships and other craft, only a small force could be landed at Anzio, so an early link-up would have to be achieved or the Germans would be able to wipe out the beachhead. Facing that reality, Eisenhower canceled the operation.

The Fifth Army was still fighting laboriously toward the Gustav Line when, toward the end of December, British Prime Minister Winston Churchill fell ill on the way back from the Teheran Conference. Convalescing in North Africa, Churchill insisted that the Anzio operation be executed—he "passionately" wanted Rome. After conferences on January 7 and 8, 1944, the decision was reached to launch the end run in conjunction with a major attack to batter through the Gustav Line and enter the Liri valley, which constitutes the main avenue of advance to Rome.

When British troops on January 17 and American troops three days later attacked to try to cross the Garigliano and Rapido Rivers, that prompted the German commander in Italy, Field Marshal Albert Kesselring, to move his reserve of two divisions from the vicinity of Rome to bolster the Gustav Line and prevent an Allied breakthrough. As a result, the U.S. VI Corps under Maj. Gen. John Lucas, with American and British divisions, came ashore at Anzio and nearby Nettuno on January 22 against practically no opposition.

The immediate objective was the Alban Hills, about 20 miles inland, the last natural barriér before Rome. With that high ground in hand, Lucas would be astride and could block Routes 6 and 7, the main highways leading to the capital. Yet Lucas decided that he had to get reserve troops, equipment and supplies ashore and organized before moving on the Alban Hills, and by that time the Germans had rushed units from northern and central Italy to contain him.

With additional forces arriving from southern France, Germany and Yugoslavia, the Germans on February 1 began an attack aimed at driving the forces in the beachhead into the sea. The attacks continued through much of the month and flared up again in March, but the Allied troops dug in and fought a mag-

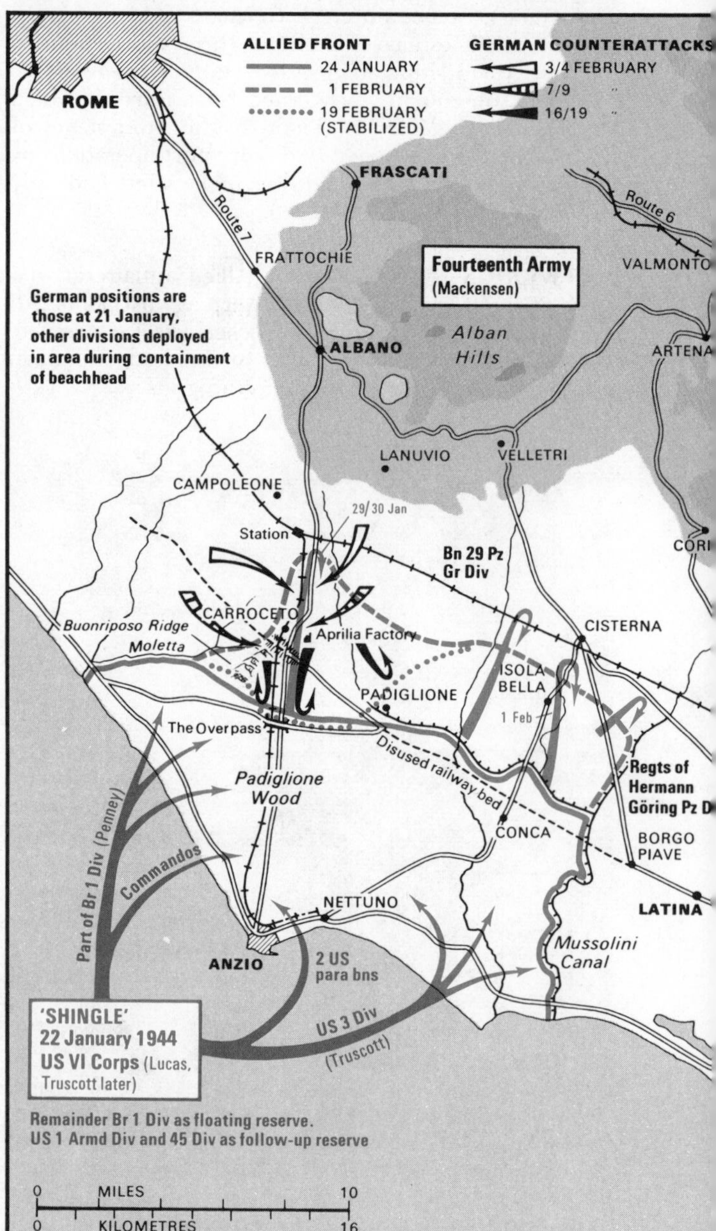

Anzio—the controversial landing

nificent defensive battle on a beachhead that had a depth of only eight miles. During the course of the fighting, General Lucas was replaced by Maj. Gen. Lucian K. Truscott, Jr. Meanwhile, the Allied forces on the main front tried desperately to gain entrance into the Liri valley, including heavy aerial and artillery bombardment of Monte Cassino on February 15 and the town of Cassino on March 15, but to no avail. The Allies also instituted a regular shuttle service of ships and craft from Naples to Anzio, a run of about 100 miles, to bring supplies, as well as an increasing number of troops, to the beachhead.

By April 1 the situation at both Anzio and the Gustav Line had reached a stalemate. While the Allied forces in the south prepared a new spring offensive in another effort to crack the Gustav Line, those at Anzio fought to hold their own while also readying an offensive to break out of the beachhead. When the offensive against the Gustav Line began on May 11, a brilliant stroke by French forces moving through almost trackless mountains penetrated the line and opened the way for American troops to advance along a corridor close to the coast. The attempt to break out of the beachhead began 12 days later on May 23, and contact between the two Allied forces was achieved within two days.

General Alexander, who had replaced General Eisenhower in overall command in Italy, directed that the forces in the beachhead cut Highways 6 and 7, escape routes for the Germans withdrawing from the Gustav Line. General Clark, on the other hand, was intent less on trapping the German armies than on capturing Rome. As a consequence, he directed his main effort toward the Italian capital, which he entered on June 4, while the bulk of the German forces escaped to fight again. **M.B./C.B.M.**

ANZIO ANNIE. Name given by American troops to one of two German 280-mm. railroad guns that shelled the ANZIO beachhead with their 562-pound projectiles. Named Leopold and Robert by their German crews, they were renamed Anzio Annie and Anzio Express by the Americans. The guns were lodged in a railroad tunnel and rolled out to fire. Although both were damaged, Anzio Annie was salvaged and is on display at the U.S. Army Ordnance Museum, Aberdeen, Md.

American GIs take a close look at Anzio Annie

AOBA. Class of Japanese heavy cruisers. *Aoba* and *Kinugasa,* built during the mid-1920s, were generally similar to the earlier FURUTAKA class but differed in many details. As built, they displaced about 9,000 tons. Over 602 feet in length, they had six 8-inch guns (3×2), antiaircraft guns and eight 24-inch torpedo tubes (2×4). *Kinugasa* was lost off GUADALCANAL in November 1942; *Aoba* continued in service until the final weeks of the war, when she was sunk in shallow Inland Sea waters by American carrier planes.

AOSTA, Amadeo, Duke of (1898–1942). Cousin of the King of Italy, the duke was Governor General of Italian East Africa and Viceroy of Ethiopia when the war began. Appointed commander in chief of Italian forces in that area, in 1940 he led troops invading British Somaliland and forced the British to evacuate. His fortunes began to decline when the British returned in 1941. In April the capital, Addis Ababa, was captured. On May 17, at AMBA ALAGI, the duke surrendered his forces. He died in 1942 while a prisoner of war in Nairobi, Kenya. *See also* EAST AFRICA.

APA. U.S. Navy ship-type symbol for Transport, Attack. The attack transport was designed to put assault troops ashore on an invasion beach, using its own complement of smaller landing craft. Early APAs were converted passenger ships, many of them formerly designated AP. Most APAs, however, were wholesale modifications of Maritime Commission cargo designs. The most numerous APA class was the 116-ship Haskell (APA-117) class, a Navy version of the VICTORY SHIP. Generally, an APA could carry an infantry regiment and its headquarters.

APAMAMA (Abemama). As part of the TARAWA operation, U.S. V Amphibious Corps Reconnaissance Company marines landed from the submarine NAUTILUS on this atoll at dawn on November 21, 1943. After a brief fire fight, assisted by gunfire from *Nautilus* and a submarine which arrived in late afternoon, the marines secured the island.

APARRI. Small city and port on the north coast of Luzon. The Japanese landed unopposed at and near Aparri on December 10, 1941, and immediately moved inland to seize and improve airfields needed to support subsequent operations on Luzon. The Japanese maintained a garrison at Aparri and operated nearby airfields throughout most of the war.

APD. U.S. Navy ship-type symbol for High Speed Transport. Earlier APDs were conversions of old FLUSH-DECK four-piper destroyers, redesignated in 1940–44. A large number of later ones were modifications of destroyer escorts, no longer so urgently needed for antisubmarine work, with troop berthing provided and large landing-craft davits mounted amidships. They were usually armed with four 3-inch guns and four 20-mm. or 40-mm. cannon.

APHRODITE. Code name of an American bombing (AZON) project. After seeing German radio-controlled, powered bombs in action in the Mediterranean, the American inventor H. J. Rand devised a version fitted with a television camera that would enable the bomb's controller to maneuver the missile precisely onto the target. The first operational mission took place on August 4, 1944, when remotely controlled B-17s each loaded with 20,000 pounds of TNT or with napalm were sent against Mimogecques, Siracourt, Watten and Wizernes, in France. A second attack against a rocket site at Watten was made on August 6, 1944. In the latter mission the crew of one drone successfully transferred control to a nearby mother ship and parachuted to safety. Despite a malfunction that prevented him from diving the drone onto the target, the controller got the B-17 to Watten, where it was shot down. One crewman from a second Aphrodite B-17 managed to parachute, but the pilot died when the lumbering plane stalled, crashed near the English coast and exploded on impact. After a controller momentarily lost contact with his drone near the English coastal city of Ipswich, General DOOLITTLE, Eighth Air Force commander, canceled further Aphrodite missions.

APHRODITE. German radar decoy used by submarines, consisting of a small balloon moored to a float. Strips of metal foil were hung from the balloon to produce a deceptive radar image; it was apparently effective.

APOGON, U.S.S. BALAO-class submarine, commissioned 1943. After eight Western Pacific war patrols, *Apogon* served as a target ship in the 1946 Bikini atomic tests. The second of two blasts sent her to the bottom of Bikini lagoon.

APOSTLE I, APOSTLE II. Code names for Allied plans to return to Norway after German surrender and cessation of all resistance in Europe (Apostle I) or German surrender in Norway while resistance continued elsewhere (Apostle II). Apostle I was initiated May 10, 1945.

APPEASEMENT POLICY. A policy allowing Germany limited gains while avoiding war. Germany's repudiation of the disarmament provisions of the Treaty of Versailles in 1935 was the first open statement of her imperialistic intentions. Beyond a few protests, the only concrete outcome was the ANGLO-GERMAN NAVAL TREATY, under which Great Britain condoned a German naval force of not more than 35 percent that of Great Britain. The reoccupation of the Rhineland by Germany in 1936 and the annexation of Austria and the Czechoslovakian SUDETENLAND in 1938 brought limited protests, which in the latter case turned at MUNICH to acquiescence. It was only in March 1939, with the German annexation of all CZECHOSLOVAKIA and the announcement of territorial demands on Poland, that the rest of Europe was convinced that Germany had indeed embarked on an imperialistic expansion. Even at this point there were still elements in all major countries wishing to avoid a second great war almost at any cost.

In essence, appeasement was an effort to satiate Hitler's Germany by peaceful concessions. The horrible slaughters of the First World War were still vividly alive in the minds of the French and British people, and air power now posed a new kind of threat. The leading spokesman and the symbol of the appeasement policy was British Prime Minister Neville CHAMBERLAIN. It is interesting to reflect that prior to the collapse of this well-intentioned but disastrous policy the word "appeasement" carried no bad connotation. Nowadays no statesman would voluntarily describe himself as an appeaser.

APPLETON, Sir Edward (1892–1965). One of the foremost physicists of his time, Appleton gained renown for his ionospheric research begun in the 1920s which led to the development of RADAR as a means of locating distant aircraft. As secretary of the British Department of Scientific and Industrial Research in World War II, he played an important role in the furtherance of radar development and in the creation of the ATOMIC BOMB. In 1947 he was awarded the Nobel Prize for Physics.

APRA HARBOR. Port on the west coast of GUAM, taken by U.S. forces in July 1944.

ARADO AR 95. A German two-place (later three) general-purpose torpedo bomber and reconnaissance twin-float biplane. It was not adopted by the LUFTWAFFE, but planes ordered by Turkey were sequestered when the war broke out and used for training. Six were sent to Spain in 1938 and nine went to Chile.

ARADO AR 196. A model introduced in 1939 as the replacement for the He 60 catapult plane. The first models went to the principal German warships. It was also used for coastal patrol duties. A total of 593 (not counting prototypes) were built. A low-wing, twin-float seaplane, with a single 970-horsepower engine, it flew 193 miles per hour maximum speed. It had two 20-mm. cannon and a 7.9-mm. machine gun forward and two flexible 7.9-mm. machine guns aft.

ARADO AR 231. A German single-place observation floatplane designed to fit in a 6.56-foot-diameter tube on a submarine. It was not a successful design, being extremely difficult to handle both on the water and in the air, and only six prototypes were built. The Focke-Achgelis Fa 330, a rotary-wing observation kite, was found to provide the same capability with none of the problems.

ARADO AR 234. This German plane, called the Blitz (Lightning), was the first jet bomber put into service by any country (the Ar 234B-2). A reconnaissance version, the 234B-1, saw action in the west in 1944, the bomber in early 1945. A single-seater, the aircraft had two turbojet engines (a third version, the 234C, had four jets mounted in pairs). Top speed of the 234B-1 was 461 miles per hour; of the 234C, 546 miles per hour. The 234B-1 was armed with two 20-mm. cannon and carried a bomb load of 2,200 pounds.

ARADO AR 240. A series of German two-place, twin-engine fighter-interceptors begun in 1935 as fighter–dive-bombers. The Ar 240 was the first plane to be fitted with remote-control dorsal and ventral barbettes mounting machine guns. Owing to its poor handling characteristics, the Ar 240 was dropped in 1943 and the similar Ar 440 was adopted for production; it too was dropped, in late 1943. The Ar 240C-0 had two 1,750-horsepower V-12 engines and flew at a maximum speed of 419 miles per hour. It carried four forward-firing

20-mm. cannon and four barbette-mounted rearward-firing 13-mm. machine guns (two to a mount).

ARAKAN. Coastal area of BURMA, on the Bay of Bengal.

ARANHA, Oswaldo (1894–1960). As Brazilian Foreign Minister from 1938 to 1944, this able diplomat and close friend of Getulio VARGAS, President of Brazil, pursued a policy of inter-Americanism and close relations with the United States. Owing largely to his urging, Brazil declared war on the Axis in early 1942, contributed to the Allies economically and in 1944 sent an expedition to fight in Italy. Aranha felt that such a military contribution would solidify the special relationship between Brazil and the United States and give to his nation a greater voice in postwar affairs. By 1944, however, internal arguments about the liberalization of the Vargas regime led to his resignation. *See also* BRAZILIAN EXPEDITIONARY FORCE.

ARAWE. The name of an island, harbor and peninsula at the southwest end of New Britain Island. It was seized by U.S. forces on December 15, 1943, as part of the larger CARTWHEEL operation for the reduction of the major Japanese base at RABAUL, in northeastern New Britain. The 112th Cavalry RCT made the landings and was later reinforced by elements of the 158th RCT and a tank company of the 1st Marine Division.

ARCADIA CONFERENCE. Held at Washington from December 22, 1941, to January 14, 1942, the conference was proposed by British Prime Minister Winston S. CHURCHILL to discuss long-range war issues after the Japanese attack on Pearl Harbor. Churchill was accompanied by the British Chiefs of Staff, his Minister of Supply (Lord BEAVERBROOK) and other top-level advisers. He lived in the White House during the conference and thus increased his ties of friendship with President Franklin D. ROOSEVELT. The British came thoroughly prepared because they had been in the war for more than two years (and therefore were more organized than the Americans) and because the outcome of the conference meant so much to them. They feared that the United States might choose to make the battle against Japan her first priority, despite FDR's oft-repeated statement that Germany was the principal enemy. Churchill hoped to ensure priority for the war against Germany as well as the promise of continued American aid to Britain.

The JOINT DECLARATION, drafted by the U.S. State Department and discussed in the cabinet before Churchill's arrival, was the primary political product of the conference. Although only the United States and Great Britain (in consultation with Russia) had really discussed this document, 26 nations had signed it by January 2, 1942. These nations pledged themselves to employ their full resources against the Axis until it was defeated, to coordinate their efforts and to continue the war together without making any separate peace. The United States was the principal force behind the declaration, for she had the freedom to say when and how she would fight while the other nations, being already committed, had no such discretion but instead were dependent upon America for support.

The term "the Big Four"—the United States, the United Kingdom, Russia and China—was first coined in connection with this declaration, since these were the initial signatories, followed by 22 other nations. France was not included because of problems involving the status of the FREE FRENCH. The United States and Britain undoubtedly took this document more seriously as an article of future international relations than did the other signatories. The British secured American confirmation on a first priority for the war against Germany—which was in fact already the U.S. plan—and the promise of continued American aid. In addition, the United States agreed to study the British proposal for a landing in French North Africa, given the code name Gymnast.

Gen. George C. MARSHALL, U.S. Chief of Staff, argued that there should be one supreme commander in charge of each area of operations, and this concept prevailed, as did the creation of a COMBINED CHIEFS OF STAFF committee. A number of combined boards were also to emerge, and two munitions boards, one in Washington and one in London, were created, each to supervise munitions made in the nation of its location. In effect, this meant that America, with by far the greater war production, had effective overall control of munitions allocation and, thus, of war policy, although she never excercised this power unilaterally.

One of the greatest impacts of the Arcadia Conference was its effect on American public opinion. Churchill's long stay in the United States helped promote pro-British attitudes there. Thus Arcadia was important to the future of American wartime relations with Britain, because it gave them a good start. In addition, it contributed to the overhaul of the American domestic war organization based on information gained from the system already developed in Britain.

The Soviet Union's absence from the meeting established a pattern of Soviet independence in part based on the fact that she was not then at war with Japan. Since U.S. Secretary of State Cordell HULL did not get along well personally with Churchill during the conference, the overall effect was to diminish the influence of Hull and his department on the future conduct of the war. *See also* COLOR PLANS.

ARCHANGEL (Arkhangelsk). Russian supply port on the White Sea to which some of the convoys carrying British and American supplies were directed. It was also the base from which a flotilla of British minesweepers operated on the approach of every convoy, sweeping it in through enemy-laid minefields. When Archangel froze up during the winter, the convoys were run to Murmansk. *See also* MURMANSK RUN; PQ-17; PQ-18.

ARCHERFISH, U.S.S. BALAO-class submarine. Commissioned in 1943, she made seven Pacific war patrols. On one of these she sank the giant Japanese aircraft carrier SHINANO in the Inland Sea (November 29, 1944).

ARCISZEWSKI, Tomasz (1877–1955). Polish Socialist Party leader and Prime Minister of the Polish (London) Government, 1944–45. Arciszewski was a socialist revolutionary from the days of the Russian Empire and the

First World War, but he also held very strong anti-Communist views. After the German occupation of Poland in 1939 Arciszewski became a leader of the underground resistance, hunted by the Germans and, until 1941, also by the Soviet NKVD (*see* NKVD). In July 1944 he was brought to London by the RAF (bringing with him important intelligence concerning German V-WEAPONS captured by the Polish underground). However, he received dwindling British and U.S. support in face of the realities of the situation, with the Soviets in control in Poland. Arciszewski, protesting in vain, found his worst apprehensions confirmed.

ARDENNES. High plateau in Belgium and Luxembourg, an extension of the same geological formation as the contiguous Eifel region of Germany, so deeply etched by serpentine streams that it has a mountainous appearance even though the highest elevation is less than 2,500 feet. Climate in winter is harsh, with frequent fog, wind and snow. A heavy patchwork of deciduous and coniferous forest and a limited roadnet add to an appearance forbidding from the military point of view. Yet when the French denied the Lorraine gateway into their country with fortifications, the Germans in both 1914 and 1940 turned to the Ardennes as a way to get at their neighbor. Adolf Hitler seized upon it in late 1944, when American forces were holding it with minimum troops in order to concentrate for offensives elsewhere, as a setting for his surprise counteroffensive to drive northwest to Antwerp and cut off Allied troops in northern Belgium and the Netherlands. Launched on December 16, 1944, it became known as the Battle of the BULGE. The official name, however, is the Battle of the Ardennes.

ARGENTA GAP. A corridor southwest of Lake Commachio (northeast Italy) near Ferrara, occupied by the British EIGHTH ARMY in April 1945.

ARGENTAN-FALAISE GAP. Term describing the distance that separated American and Canadian forces attempting to close the Falaise pocket (France) in August 1944. When the gap was finally closed, after perhaps 35,000 German troops had withdrawn, leaving most of their equipment behind, about 50,000 POWs were taken. Failure to close the gap sooner caused much controversy among Allied officers. What went wrong has never been pinpointed by historians.

ARGENTIA. Village in southeast Newfoundland on Placentia Bay. The Roosevelt-Churchill Atlantic conference (*see* ATLANTIC CHARTER) was held off Argentia.

ARGONAUT. Code name for the MALTA and YALTA CONFERENCES, January–February 1945. The Malta phase was code-named Cricket, the Yalta phase Magneto.

ARGUMENT. Code name for a series of coordinated air attacks against German factories engaged in the manufacture of airframes and the assembly of aircraft for the LUFTWAFFE. The U.S. EIGHTH and FIFTEENTH AIR FORCES were to make daylight attacks against the plants, while the Royal Air Force BOMBER COMMAND by night bombed the industrial cities where the aircraft workers lived. Despite bad weather, Argument was carried out during February 1944. The operation included a series of raids begun on the 20th of that month and known as the BIG WEEK. Following the Big Week, American bombers, escorted by fighters including the new P-51s, delivered their first blow against Berlin, bombing the capital on March 4. Other attacks against Berlin occurred in the weeks that followed, but beginning in April the B-17s and B-24s became involved in preparations for the Normandy invasion.

ARGUS, H.M.S. Royal Navy aircraft carrier of 14,000 tons, converted from the hull of an incomplete Italian passenger liner and completed in 1918. Old and slow, *Argus* had been employed only on training duties prior to 1939, and in the war she served chiefly as an aircraft transport and in training duties. Her only appearances as a fully operational aircraft carrier were the escorting of a convoy to MALTA in June 1942 and the covering of the Operation Torch landings in NORTHWEST AFRICA in November of the same year, in which operation she was damaged by a bomb. Some of her transport duties involved forays into the eastern Mediterranean to fly off fighter aircraft for Malta; she also made one voyage to Russia. Experience gained on *Argus* proved very valuable in the development of the escort carrier.

ARIMA, Masafumi (1895–1944). On October 15, 1944, Rear Admiral Arima, commanding officer of the Japanese 26th Naval Air Flotilla, led a force of 13 land-based bombers and 86 fighters against the U.S. carrier task force engaged in the preinvasion bombing of LEYTE. The force dive-bombed but did not sink the carrier FRANKLIN. Arima and 19 other fliers were lost in the attack. Before taking off, Arima had declared his intention not to return alive by ripping off his insignia of rank. He therefore came to be regarded as the first KAMIKAZE pilot of the Japanese Navy.

ARIZONA, U.S.S. Battleship commissioned in 1916, sister ship of U.S.S. PENNSYLVANIA. *Arizona* was sunk during the Japanese air raid on Pearl Harbor on December 7, 1941, with a loss of 1,103 lives. She is maintained as a memorial but contrary to common belief is not considered a commissioned Navy ship.

ARKANSAS, U.S.S. Battleship of 26,100 tons, with twelve 12-inch guns, commissioned in 1912 and somewhat modernized in 1925–27. She was slated for disposal when things began to worsen in the Atlantic during 1941, and the emergency extended her service life. During 1942–44 she served on training and Atlantic troop convoy duty. After providing heavy gunfire support to the Normandy INVASION and the siege of Cherbourg in mid-1944, she went to the Mediterranean to support the August 1944 landings in SOUTHERN FRANCE. *Arkansas* then went to the Pacific, where in 1945 she took part in the capture of Iwo JIMA and OKINAWA. The 1946 Bikini atomic tests sent her to the bottom of Bikini lagoon, where she rests today.

ARK ROYAL, H.M.S. Aircraft carrier of 22,000 tons, completed in 1938 at Birkenhead, the Royal Navy's only modern aircraft carrier at the outbreak of war. *Ark Royal* was armed with sixteen 4.5-inch guns and numerous smaller weapons, and had a maximum capacity of 72 aircraft. *Ark Royal*'s life was eventful, the ship becoming early a subject of intense German propaganda as well as physical attack. She participated in the Norwegian operations and was then sent to the Mediterranean, taking part in the attacks on the French Navy at MERS-EL-KÉBIR and later at Dakar. A member of the famous FORCE H based on GIBRALTAR, she was active in numerous operations against both the Italians and the Germans, the most noteworthy being the bombardment of Genoa and the sinking of the BISMARCK—a torpedo hit from one of *Ark Royal*'s aircraft destroying the *Bismarck*'s steering gear, a vital step in the operations leading to her destruction. On November 14, 1941, *Ark Royal* was torpedoed and sunk by the German submarine *U-81* with the loss of one man only.

ARLON. During the Battle of the BULGE, Arlon, a road center on the south edge of the ARDENNES, and the location of U.S. III Corps headquarters, was on a route which reinforcements took to relieve BASTOGNE.

ARMAVIR. City in the CAUCASUS, USSR (railroad and oil pipeline), occupied by the Germans under General von KLEIST in August 1942. In January 1943 Kleist's forces passed through Armavir on their retreat from the Caucasus.

ARMED MERCHANT CRUISER. A passenger liner, capable of reasonably fast speed, taken over by the Royal Navy and armed for combat. Some 60 ships were used as armed merchant cruisers; they were employed in patrol operations (as the RAWALPINDI). At least 15 were lost. These ships were given armaments, as available, up to 6-inch guns. Essentially, they were a stopgap measure during the earlier years of the war; beginning in 1941, they were phased out.

ARMEEABTEILUNG. A provisional German headquarters intermediate between an army and a corps—very often a reinforced corps headquarters.

ARMORED CAR. Wheeled armored vehicles, used primarily for reconnaissance and support tasks, were built and tested in the early years of motor transportation. During World War II Germany and Great Britain were the principal users of armored cars. The British at first used improvised types designed around already existing chassis, but quickly began work on specialized designs. A wide variety of types, most of them four-wheeled, were produced by such manufacturers as Daimler, Morris, Humber, Leyland, Alvis-Straussler and Bedford. Some were turretless, others had revolving turrets; armaments ranged from light machine guns to shell guns as heavy as 75 mm. Beginning in the early 1930s, Germany also produced many types. These were four-, six- and eight-wheeled, and were widely used by armored reconnaissance units and as command and communications vehicles. A light 4×4 and a heavy 8×8 were the principal wartime models. Versions of the latter were armed with a 20-mm. gun or a 75-mm. howitzer and were especially useful in such areas as Russia and North Africa. The USSR used some miscellaneous prewar armored cars during the early part of the war. The war-developed light 4×4 BA-64 was a rugged, mass-producible vehicle, similar in appearance to comparable German types. Relatively few scout cars were used by the United States, although 4×4s and half-tracks were built for this purpose; 6×6 cars were built by Ford and Chevrolet; the M6, M8 and M38 all mounted a 37-mm. gun in a turret. Most M6 production went to Britain under the name Staghound; the M8 saw some use during the latter phases of the European war. M2, M3 and M5 half-tracks were used as personnel carriers, mortar carriers and antiaircraft machine gun carriers; these were protected with light plating.

ARMY OF THE NILE. In the early months of the war the British forces in the Middle East went by the terms Army of the Delta and, later, Army of the Nile. Winston CHURCHILL frequently used "Army of the Nile" to denote the Western Desert Force.

ARNHEM. City on the Neder Rijn (Lower Rhine) river in the Netherlands whose highway bridge was the objective of the British 1st Airborne Division in September 1944 in Operation MARKET-GARDEN. The Germans annihilated a small force that gained the north end of the bridge. Arnhem was finally liberated by the Canadian FIRST ARMY on April 4, 1945.

ARNIM, Jürgen von (1891–1971). A stubborn man of iron will and surly manner, with a Prussian military background, Arnim commanded a German tank division, and later a corps, in Russia during 1941–42. He was rushed to Tunis in November 1942 to take command of the Fifth Panzer Army, and after March 8, 1943, he commanded Army Group Africa—a position General ROMMEL described as "far from enviable." On May 12, 1943, after sending a final report to the OKW, Colonel General von Arnim surrendered the remaining forces in Africa (*see* OKW). He was interned first in Britain, later in the United States.

ARNOLD, Henry Harley (1886–1950). Taught to fly by the Wright brothers in 1911, Arnold was a U.S. staff officer during World War I. Afterward, he became an advocate of an independent air arm and encouraged the development of heavily armed four-engine bombers. In 1938 he became Chief of the Air Corps as a major general. The rapid growth of the wartime air service—from fewer than 25,000 officers and men and some 4,000 planes to 2.5 million officers and men and 75,000 aircraft—was reflected in Arnold's title and rank. He became Chief of the UNITED STATES ARMY AIR FORCES in June 1941, reached lieutenant general in December and was appointed Commanding General of the Army Air Forces in March 1942. He received a fourth star in March 1943 and a fifth late in 1944. Throughout the war he sat with the JOINT CHIEFS OF STAFF and the COMBINED CHIEFS OF STAFF.

Arnold, whose nickname was "Hap," was intimately involved in even the smallest details of the functioning of U.S. Army Air Forces. In 1942, for example, he personally saw to it that parts were shipped to Australia to replace items that had previously gone astray. He undertook a 35,000-mile inspection trip, participated in the periodic conferences among Allied political leaders and championed the development of the B-29 (*see* B-29).

ARNOLD, William Richard (1881–1965). Roman Catholic priest who became a U.S. Army chaplain in 1913. In 1937 he became Chief of the Chaplain Corps, and he was promoted to major general in 1944. Known for his gentle and sympathetic manner, Arnold was raised to bishop in 1945. He collaborated with Christopher Cross in the writing of the story of the Chaplain Corps, *Soldiers of God* (1946).

ARNO LINE. German defense line in northern Italy, on the Arno River and eastward. It was in front of the GOTHIC LINE, the chief defense line in the region. The Germans withdrew from the Arno Line into the Gothic defenses at the end of August 1944.

ARNSTEIN, Daniel (1890–1960). In 1941 Arnstein, president of the New York Terminal Transportation System, was asked by President ROOSEVELT to break the BURMA ROAD bottleneck. The road was the only open supply route into China but was hopelessly bogged by bureaucratic inefficiency, corruption and inexperience. When Arnstein undertook the job in June 1941, only 4,000 tons of supplies were being moved over the 726-mile road each month, and this paucity was starving the Chinese war effort. By September, owing largely to Arnstein's efforts, shipments had doubled, and a few months later they were averaging 16,000 tons a month. The system Arnstein set up operated efficiently until the end of the war.

AROLSEN, INTERNATIONAL RED CROSS TRACING CENTER AT. Arolsen, former capital of the principality of Waldeck, is a quiet town not far from Kassel in the heart of Germany. It was to Arolsen, virtually untouched by wartime bombing, that the surviving archives of the concentration camps were brought, so that the vast task of tracing the dead, the missing, the displaced and the renamed might be undertaken with maximum efficiency. In 1955 this work was finally placed in the hands of the International Red Cross, though the organization continued to be financed by the West German Government. A staff of some 200 experts (linguists, calligraphers, archivists) was maintained, capable of dealing with between 10,000 and 20,000 inquiries a month during the 1960s. Initially Arolsen was concerned with uniting broken families and locating children purloined by the Nazis, as well as tracing facts relating to the millions of dead in the concentration camps for their kinfolk. Inquiries now tend to be of a legal nature, concerning heritage and property. Requests in a recent year amounted to about 220,000 and the master card index now totals some 38.5 million.

ARRAS. Important road center in northern France. On May 21, 1940, the British launched an attack on the flank of the German armored advance near Arras, but it lacked the strength (the only armor was two tank battalions) to be effective.

ARROMANCHES. Beach in the British sector of the Normandy INVASION front, off which was located the MULBERRY (artificial harbor) that served the Allied forces as a port.

ARSENAL-DELANNE 10. French two-seat experimental general-purpose fighter. The first prototype, the Delanne 20, was destroyed in its first flight on August 10, 1938. The second Delanne 20 flew successfully in March 1939. The military version was built by the Arsenal de l'Aéronautique at Villacoublay, where it was captured by the Germans. Tests were continued by German order, and the plane flew in October 1941. The Germans then took it to a Luftwaffe station for further tests. Powered by an 860-horsepower V-12 engine, it had a maximum speed of 342 miles per hour. It was to have had one 20-mm. cannon firing forward and two 7.5-mm. machine guns for the gunner in the rear. Its span was 33 feet 2 inches; length, 24 feet ½ inch; height, 9 feet 10 inches.

ARSENAL OF DEMOCRACY. In a fireside chat on December 29, 1940, President ROOSEVELT firmly committed the United States to continue supplying munitions to Great Britain. "We must be the great arsenal of democracy," he told the nation, thus uttering the phrase that symbolized American policy for the next year.

ARSENAL VG-30 SERIES. This French aircraft series grew out of a specification for an MS-406 replacement issued in 1937. One of four (the D-520, CAO-200 and MS-450 were the other three) designed to do this, the VG-30 series was derived from the VG-30, a lightweight fighter originally designed to replace the Caudron C-713. Only a very few of the prototypes had flown before the Germans occupied France, although 160 of the VG-33s were in various stages of assembly. The VG-33 had an 860-horsepower Hispano-Suiza V-12 engine which drove it to a maximum speed of 347 miles per hour. It carried one 20-mm. cannon with 60 rounds for four 7.5-mm. machine guns. Normal loaded weight was 5,856 pounds. It had a wingspan of 35 feet 5¼ inches, was 28 feet 4⅛ inches long, with a tail-up height of 10 feet 10⅓ inches.

ARTIFICIAL MOONLIGHT. Illumination of a battlefield by means of searchlight beams reflected off clouds. This tactic was used by the British in Normandy and the Germans at the outset of the Battle of the BULGE.

ARZEW, GULF OF. Landing Beach Z, in the Gulf of Arzew some 20 miles east of ORAN, was the major invasion area of the Center Task Force of Operation Torch (*see* NORTHWEST AFRICA). Some tanks of the U.S. 1st Armored Division were landed directly on the beaches from converted tankers, forerunners of the LST; other tanks unloaded from transports in Arzew harbor.

ASASHIO. Class of Japanese destroyers, 10 of which were completed in 1937–39. An improvement on the SHIRATSUYU class, they mounted six 5-inch guns in three twin mounts, one forward and two in a superfiring arrangement aft. Eight 24-inch torpedo tubes (2×4) were mounted amidships. Faults were found in the Asashios' machinery and hull form during early service, but these were alleviated during prewar refits. Generally speaking, this was a very successful class of ships; their basic configuration was continued in the later KAGERO, YUGUMO and SHIMAKAZE classes. Antiaircraft batteries were augmented during the war, one 5-inch mount being removed to make room; antisubmarine armaments were increased. All 10 Asashios were war losses.

ASDEVLANT. Antisubmarine Warfare Development Detachment, U.S. Atlantic Fleet. Stationed at Quonset Point, R.I., this unit developed tactics and equipment for antisubmarine warfare and trained air squadrons and crews of antisubmarine ships in the latest weapons and techniques.

ASHCAN. Code name for Allied detention center for German political prisoners of the status exemplified by Franz von PAPEN.

ASHEVILLE, U.S.S. Frigate and class. Two Canadian-built versions of the British River-class frigates (in the British definition, antisubmarine ships comparable to the U.S. destroyer escorts) were acquired by the U.S. Navy in 1942, when antisubmarine craft were in urgent demand. Armed with an American battery and British radar, they were originally classed as gunboats. When the similar TACOMA class was ordered from U.S. builders, a new type designation, Frigate (PF), was created to categorize the type. *Asheville* and her sister *Natchez* then became PF-1 and -2. Powered by reciprocating engines with twin screws, they were commissioned in the Navy but operated by Coast Guard crews.

ASPIDISTRA. Code name for a powerful radio transmitter in England, used by the British to interfere with German military transmissions.

ASSAM. State in northeastern India, the only part of India to be invaded by the Japanese during the war. Battles were fought at IMPHAL and KOHIMA in 1944. *See also* BURMA.

ASSAULT GUN. An artillery piece designed to accompany assault troops and provide immediate close-support artillery fire. These were almost always direct-fire weapons, up to 75-mm., and were used in the antitank role and the reduction of fortifications. Truly lightweight, mobile weapons were not realized until the advent of the recoilless rifle.

ASSAULT GUN, SELF-PROPELLED. This began as a lightly armored tracked vehicle mounting a relatively heavy gun and intended to be used as close-support artillery for attacking infantry and armor. For the Germans and the Russians these were cheap and easily manufactured substitutes for the tank. As the war went on, both Germany and Russia fielded heavier models. These weapons were usually mounted on a tank's hull in the front. There was no turret. Traverse and elevation were extremely limited. The Americans and British had a few models, which were mostly self-propelled artillery, of which only the self-propelled antitank guns were used up close.

ASSOCIATED POWERS. A diplomatic term meaning cooperation, not alliance, among nations for a limited objective. In World War I the United States did not formally join the "Allied Powers" and remained throughout the conflict an "Associated Power." After the Pearl Harbor attack, the powers in conflict with the AXIS were spoken of as the Associated Powers until, at the suggestion of President Roosevelt, the term UNITED NATIONS was adopted.

ASTIER DE LA VIGERIE, François d' (1886–1956). A World War I French fighter ace, d'Astier rose to command the vital Northern Zone of Air Operations in France before DUNKIRK in 1940, then retreated to North Africa with most of the French Air Force before the armistice. He later served in various capacities with the Free French.

ASTORIA, U.S.S. Two wartime American cruisers. The first *Astoria* was a NEW ORLEANS-class heavy cruiser commissioned in 1934. She took part in the Battles of the CORAL SEA and MIDWAY, escorting aircraft carriers. Supporting the landings on GUADALCANAL, *Astoria* was on patrol off that island on the night of August 8–9, 1942. With sister cruisers *Quincy* and *Vincennes* and Australian cruiser CANBERRA, she was sunk by Japanese surface forces in the Battle of SAVO ISLAND. The second *Astoria* was a CLEVELAND-class light cruiser commissioned in 1944. From December 1944 until V-J Day she operated with the FAST CARRIER TASK FORCE in the Pacific.

ASWORG. Acronym for Anti-Submarine Warfare Operations Research Group, a specialized body associated with the U.S. National Defense Research Committee. It was established April 1, 1942, with Prof. Philip M. Morse of the Massachusetts Institute of Technology as director. ASWORG was highly practical in nature, being concerned with such questions as the most effective speed and altitude for search planes, the most efficient way to deploy destroyers in search missions and the best way to use devices and inventions produced by scientists. Credit for the idea of setting up ASWORG is given to Capt. Wilder D. Baker, who was in charge of antisubmarine efforts under Adm. Ernest J. KING.

AT-6. The North American Texan, the standard U.S. Army Air Forces advanced trainer during World War II, was also used by the U.S. Navy and by America's allies. The instructor and student pilot were seated in tandem within an enclosed cockpit. A 600-horsepower Pratt and Whitney radial gave the AT-6 a top speed of slightly more than 200 miles per hour. The plane could carry one fixed, forward-firing machine gun and another on a flexible mount at the rear of the canopy. The landing gear was retractable.

AT-7. Based on the twin-engine, twin-tail Beech C-45 transport, the AT-7 Navigator was the first advanced trainer purchased by the U.S. Army Air Forces specially for navigation training. Powered by two 450-horsepower Pratt and Whitney radial engines, the plane could accommodate three students. The AT-11 Kansan was an AT-7 with the navigational equipment removed, a bomb bay and bombardier's station installed and two gun positions added. It was used to train bombardiers and aerial gunners.

Fairchild also furnished a twin-engine aircraft for the training of bomber crews. The company proposed one aircraft to train gunners, bombardiers and navigators, but the AT-21, the model that went into quantity production, was fitted out exclusively for gunnery instruction.

Also used for gunnery training was the Lockheed AT-18, which was based on the HUDSON bomber. When the power-operated dorsal turret was removed, the plane was redesignated AT-18A and used for navigation training.

AT-8. Cessna's five-seat T-50 light transport served as inspiration for a transitional aircraft used by American and Allied pilots who were moving from the AT-6 to a multiengine plane. The T-50 was a twin-engine, low-wing monoplane with retractable landing gear. When powered by 295-horsepower Lycoming radials, the trainer version bore the Army designation AT-8 and was called the Bobcat; with 245-horsepower Jacobs engines, it was the AT-17. An Army transport based on the T-50 was called the UC-78.

Because the Cessna handled so easily, Army Air Forces acquired the twin-engine, pug-nosed Curtiss AT-9, which more closely duplicated the characteristics of the modern light bomber.

ATABRINE. Trade name for quinacrine, a bitter-tasting antimalarial drug often causing temporary yellowing of the skin which was administered daily to troops in the Pacific from the end of 1942. It was originally developed in the 1920s by I. G. Farben Industries in Germany, but the research was recapitulated in the United States after Japan captured most of the world supply of quinine.

ATAGO. Japanese heavy cruiser of the TAKAO class (often called the Atago class in wartime publications). *Atago* was a workhorse throughout the Pacific war, seeing action at MIDWAY, GUADALCANAL, the BISMARCK SEA, the PHILIPPINE SEA and LEYTE GULF. She was the flagship first of Vice-Adm. Nobutake KONDO and then of Vice-Adm. Takeo KURITA. In the early morning hours of October 23, 1944, in the first phase of the battle for Leyte Gulf, *Atago* was torpedoed by the U.S. submarine *Darter* (Comdr. David McClintock). She stayed afloat long enough to enable Admiral Kurita and his staff to transfer to the battleship YAMATO, which then became the flagship of the Center Force.

ATHENIA. British passenger liner sunk by German submarine *U-30* with a loss of 128 lives on September 4, 1939. The sinking was in violation of the London Naval Agreement, which provided that passengers must be moved to a place of safety before a vessel was attacked and that merchant ships could not be armed. Germany claimed that the British had themselves destroyed the *Athenia* to provide an excuse for arming vessels in violation of the treaty.

ATIK, U.S.S. American "Q-ship," a former small cargo ship acquired at the beginning of the war and torpedoed and sunk on her shakedown cruise, March 27, 1942. American experience with Q-ships was largely negative, and little use was made of them.

ATLANTA, U.S.S. Light cruiser and class; 541 feet long, of 6,000 tons standard displacement, these were the smallest American cruisers of the war years. Designed as antiaircraft ships, similar in concept to the British Dido class, they were armed with a 5-INCH, 38-CALIBER dual-purpose main battery. *Atlanta,* JUNEAU, *San Diego* and *San Juan* were completed between December 1941 and February 1942; they had eight twin 5-inch mounts and eight 21-inch torpedo tubes (2×4). Six gun mounts were on the centerline; the remaining two were mounted in wing positions, one on either side of the after superstructure. Four later ships, similar in appearance and characteristics, had only the six centerline 5-inch mounts. *Oakland, Reno, Flint* and *Tucson,* commissioned in 1943–45, are usually known as the separate Oakland class. A final three ships, completed in 1946, made up the Juneau class. *Atlanta* and the first *Juneau* were lost in the SOLOMONS in late 1942. After the loss of *Atlanta,* the remaining ships were redesignated San Diego class.

A second *Atlanta,* a CLEVELAND-class light cruiser, commissioned in 1944. During the spring and summer of 1945, with the FAST CARRIER TASK FORCE, she took part in the final carrier strikes of the Pacific war.

ATLANTIC, BATTLE OF THE. Though to some extent it involved operations against surface raiders, the contest in the Atlantic was primarily a war between German submarines, striving to sink the ships on which the United Kingdom depended, and Allied surface and air antisubmarine forces.

As in the Pacific war, the beginning of the war in Europe saw the opening of an unlimited submarine campaign. The U-boats available to the Germans at the time operated mainly in the ocean approaches to England, making daylight attacks from periscope depth. Early results were good, and aggressive submarines exposed themselves to counterattack by British warships equipped with asdic (*see* SONAR). Antisubmarine counter-measures proved more effective than the Germans had anticipated, and submarines shifted their attention to lone ships.

The fall of France in 1940 gave Germany advance bases on the French Atlantic coast, allowing U-boats to patrol farther into that ocean and thus greatly expanding the area open to attack. British ships and planes had to be diverted from antisubmarine duty to the protection of their own coasts. As a counter to British antisubmarine tactics, the U-boat force changed their own doctrine and began surface night attacks on convoys. Again, these were successful and huge tonnages of shipping were sunk. U-boats, including some "high scorers," were lost, but the balance was profitable and the initiative was firmly in the submariners' hands.

During the early months of the war, a few German warships such as the ADMIRAL GRAF SPEE and "merchant cruisers" such as the ATLANTIS accounted for some merchant tonnage. Operating at long range in the face of overwhelming British naval strength, surface raiders never had more than a minor influence on the course of the Atlantic war. As the war went on, the "fleet in being" tactics employed with such ships as TIRPITZ, SCHARNHORST and GNEISENAU carried their share of weight in the minds of Allied admirals. The destruction of Convoy PQ-17 (*see* PQ-17) on the North Atlantic

U-boats in Bremen harbor yards

MURMANSK RUN was due, in largest part, to apprehension over the chance of a surface sortie from Norwegian bases.

British defensive measures against the new night attacks included centralized convoy routing, wide dispersal routing and strengthening of escorts. This made it more difficult for U-boats to find and attack convoys. On the other hand, expanded German submarine construction programs now began to produce results. Beginning in 1941, about 20 new U-boats a month entered service, bolstering the relatively small force with which the Kriegsmarine had entered the war. As the undersea arm expanded, however, there was some loss in crew training and experience.

During the summer of 1941 individual surface night attacks on convoys gave way to the "wolfpack" attack. Submarines patrolled areas where convoys could be expected. On making a contact, U-boats did not attack but shadowed the convoy, signaling other submarines to join in the attack. Multiple night attack meant the chance of higher kills at less risk to the submarines. Land-based long-range FOCKE-WULF FW 200 patrol planes also participated in these operations.

As U-boats extended their operating areas farther across the Atlantic, it became necessary to escort convoys through the entire transoceanic passage instead of only in the WESTERN APPROACHES to England. Since President ROOSEVELT involved the U.S. Navy to an increasing degree in the Atlantic war, however, pressure on the Royal Navy was somewhat eased. After PEARL HARBOR the U.S. Navy was officially in the submarine war, but lack of experience made it less than fully effective at first.

U-boat operations in the Caribbean and in American coastal waters were highly productive during the spring and summer of 1942. American antisubmarine measures were largely improvised and ineffective at first; it was not until the fall of that year that interlocking coastal convoys and air patrols made U-boats tend to return to the open ocean.

Two technical developments, RADAR and airborne depth bombs, were by now contributing to the antisubmarine war. Patrol planes, equipped with underwater bombs and search radar as well as high-intensity searchlights for night attack, made the U-boat transit area in the Bay of Biscay increasingly dangerous. Ship and aircraft radar could detect surfaced submarines at a distance, even at night or in foul weather. Convoy escorts' radar and HF/DF gave them effective means of defense against surfaced wolfpacks (*see* HF/DF). Large-scale shipbuilding programs were well under way in the United States and the United Kingdom. These were intended not only to produce cargo hulls faster than they could be sunk but to provide antisubmarine patrol and escort ships in more adequate numbers. Large numbers of what the British called frigates and the United States called destroyer escorts (DE), as well as escort aircraft carriers (CVE), were aimed directly at the submarine threat. Ahead-throwing antisubmarine weapons, such as HEDGEHOG and SQUID, increased ships' capabilities.

The main action shifted back into the North Atlantic late in 1942. This area was still too distant for the long-range land-based patrol planes from the United Kingdom or North America, and some extremely large wolfpacks were frequently assembled to overwhelm a convoy's escort force. Shipping losses were heavy during the winter of 1942–43.

In 1943 the balance shifted. New escort ships and CVEs were emerging in quantity. The addition of carrier antisubmarine planes to cover the mid-Atlantic area had a telling effect. The increase in numbers of available antisubmarine ships enabled hunter-killer groups, one CVE with a number of DEs, to patrol submarine operating areas. Higher frequency search radars proved valuable. U-boat wolfpacks continued to operate into the spring of 1943, but in May a pack was decisively defeated in an attack on Convoy ONS-5 (*see* ONS-5). Not only did ship sinkings drop, but submarine losses rose. During May 37 U-boats were lost; 34 went down in July. Many of these were sunk by airplanes, and a sizable proportion were sent to the bottom in the Bay of Biscay, departing on patrol or returning from it.

The U-boat force tried various expedients to right the balance. Dispersing at first into the South Atlantic to avoid an attack, they moved north again in the fall to try acoustic bombing torpedoes against escorted convoys. In October one escort ship and three merchant ships were sunk—at a cost of 22 U-boats.

Many U-boats had their antiaircraft batteries considerably augmented, receiving 37-mm. guns and twin or quadruple 20-mm. mounts. The tactic was now to remain on the surface and "shoot it out" with an attacking airplane. Results were not worthwhile, and submarine losses continued heavy.

U-boat warfare was primarily defensive through the winter of 1943–44. Relatively few boats went to sea, and the toll they took was meager. Attempts were made to attack the enormous concentration of shipping taking part in the INVASION of France (June 1944), but massive antisubmarine screening made the efforts useless.

During the latter part of 1944 the Germans introduced SNORKEL, allowing their submarines to operate without surfacing. The snorkel could not be detected by current search radars, and by using this new device and resorting to "bottoming" tactics the submarines were able to gain some protection from radar and sonar. As French bases were lost, submarines shifted to ports in Norway and Germany. Some successes were achieved during the winter of 1944–45, but by the spring of 1945

Crewmen of an Allied convoy escort ship keep a sharp lookout

new techniques and more sensitive radars had again tipped the scale. A new high-performance U-boat, the hydrogen-peroxide–fueled Type XXI, was an excellent design with unprecedented underwater performance, but it was completed too late for war service.

Throughout the war, convoy operations proved the most effective measures both in protecting convoys and in sinking U-boats. Patrol measures were far less efficient. During 1939–45 a total of 2,753 Allied ships, of 14,557,000 gross tons, were sunk at a cost of 733 German and 79 Italian submarines. **J.C.R.**

See also DÖNITZ, KARL.

ATLANTIC CHARTER. A joint declaration of President Franklin D. ROOSEVELT and Prime Minister Winston S. CHURCHILL, drawn up at their meeting at sea (PLACENTIA BAY, Newfoundland) in August 1941. The declaration was an edited blend of British and American drafts; working closely with the President and the Prime Minister were Under Secretary of State Sumner WELLES and the Permanent Under Secretary of State for Foreign Affairs, Sir Alexander CADOGAN. The declaration, which bears the date August 12, appears to have first been called the Atlantic Charter by the *Daily Herald* (London), which used the name in an editorial on August 14. The final text of the declaration was as follows.

> Joint Declaration by the President and the Prime Minister
>
> August 12, 1941
>
> The President of the United States of America and the Prime Minister, Mr. Churchill, representing His Majesty's Government in the United Kingdom, being met together, deem it right to make known certain common principles in the national policies of their respective countries on which they base their hopes for a better future for the world.
>
> First, their countries seek no aggrandizement, territorial or other.
>
> Second, they desire to see no territorial changes that do not accord with the freely expressed wishes of the peoples concerned.
>
> Third, they respect the right of all peoples to choose the form of government under which they will live; and they wish to see sovereign rights and self-government restored to those who have been forcibly deprived of them.
>
> Fourth, they will endeavor, with due respect for their existing obligations, to further the enjoyment by all states, great or small, victor or vanquished, of access, on equal terms, to the trade and to the raw materials of the world which are needed for their economic prosperity.
>
> Fifth, they desire to bring about the fullest collaboration between all nations in the economic field, with the object of securing for all improved labor standards, economic advancement, and social security.
>
> Sixth, after the final destruction of the Nazi tyranny, they hope to see established a peace which will afford to all nations the means of dwelling in safety within their own boundaries, and which will afford assurance that all the men in all the lands may live out their lives in freedom from fear and want.
>
> Seventh, such a peace should enable all men to traverse the high seas and oceans without hindrance.
>
> Eighth, they believe that all the nations of the world, for realistic as well as spiritual reasons, must come to the abandonment of the use of force. Since no future peace can be maintained if land, sea, or air armaments continue to be employed by nations which threaten, or may threaten, aggression outside of their frontiers, they believe, pending the establishment of a wider and permanent system of general security, that the disarmament of such nations is essential. They will likewise aid and encourage all other practicable measures which will lighten for peace-loving peoples the crushing burden of armaments.

ATLANTIC PATROL. Beginning in April 1941 the United States gradually increased the scope and aggressiveness of its convoy protection for British merchant ships against German U-boats. By October 31, when a U-boat sank the U.S. destroyer REUBEN JAMES, American convoy protection stretched from U.S. coastal waters to within 400 miles of Iceland (about 25° W. longitude).

ATLANTIC WALL. Fortification line built by the German occupation forces in France. The purpose was to strengthen the natural obstacles provided by the Atlantic Ocean and the beaches over which Allied invading forces would have to advance. The fortifications consisted primarily of reinforced concrete pillboxes containing machine guns, antitank weapons and light artillery pieces, supplemented by minefields and underwater and beach obstacles along the coastline. The Atlantic Wall was similar to but less elaborate than the WEST WALL and the MAGINOT LINE.

ATLANTIS. German merchant ship converted into an auxiliary cruiser and armed with six 5.9-inch guns and four torpedo tubes. She also carried two aircraft and 93 mines. She sailed from Germany on a raiding cruise on March 31, 1940, operating in the Atlantic, Pacific and Indian Oceans. During her career as a raider she sank or captured 22 Allied merchant ships totaling 145,697 tons. She was finally sunk in the South Atlantic by H.M.S. *Devonshire* on November 22, 1941.

ATOMIC BOMB. By 1939 atomic physicists in America had become convinced that uranium might be used to create a new source of energy, and they feared that the German Government might capitalize on research of the past generation to develop an instrument of unparalleled destruction. These concerns were communicated to President Franklin D. ROOSEVELT in a letter from Albert EINSTEIN, who by his international reputation gained the attention of the President. Eventually a two-pronged strategy evolved: to try to prevent Germany from producing such a weapon and to recruit teams of scientists who might be able to develop an atomic weapon before Germany could do so. To accomplish the former, British commando troops destroyed the heavy-water factory at Rjukan, Norway, and British

The atomic bombing of Nagasaki—August 9, 1945

planes bombed Trondheim, Norway, where atomic research was believed in progress. To accomplish the latter, Roosevelt and Prime Minister Winston CHURCHILL agreed that scientists in Great Britain and America (many of whom had fled Germany) should cooperate in concentrated research. In August 1942 the program was established under the code name Manhattan Engineer District (*see* MANHATTAN DISTRICT) under the administration of Brig. Gen. Leslie R. GROVES. The practical application of earlier research was demonstrated at the UNIVERSITY OF CHICAGO in December, when the first self-perpetuating nuclear chain reaction was achieved. Plutonium, a man-made fissionable material, was produced at HANFORD, Wash.; uranium 235 was separated at OAK RIDGE, Tenn.; atomic bombs were designed and constructed at LOS ALAMOS under the direction of J. Robert OPPENHEIMER. After consulting with a committee of civilian, military and scientific advisers, President Harry S. TRUMAN decided that the bomb should be used to end the war with Japan. The first of three completed bombs was tested at ALAMOGORDO on July 16, 1945. After Japan refused an ultimatum issued at the Allied POTSDAM CONFERENCE, the second bomb, with a destructive force equaling that of 20,000 tons of TNT, was dropped at HIROSHIMA on August 6 from the American bomber *Enola Gay*. The third was dropped at NAGASAKI on August 9. The vast destruction prompted Japanese surrender on August 14.

ATSUGI. A town in central Honshu, Japan, with a large airfield. The first Allied occupation forces to land in Japan did so at Atsugi on August 28, 1945, when a B-24 bomber and 47 transport planes brought 150 Fifth Air Force technicians, with advance communications and airfield equipment. These prepared the landing area to receive the 11th Airborne Division. Though this was the first landing of occupation forces, it was not the first Allied landing. A Navy PB4Y patrol bomber had encountered mechanical problems on the previous day and had landed at Atsugi to make emergency repairs before returning to its base on Iwo Jima. A fighter pilot from the carrier *Yorktown* had made an unauthorized landing on the 27th and had directed the Japanese airfield crew to paint a sign reading: "Welcome to the U.S. Army from Third Fleet."

ATTILA. Code name for the German occupation of unoccupied France. It was described in a Führer directive of December 10, 1940, as being necessary "in case those parts of the French colonial empire now controlled by General WEYGAND should show signs of revolt." By 1942 offensive action by the Western Allies began to seem the likelier possibility; a more elaborate variant called Anton, involving significant cooperation of Italian forces, was envisioned. The Attila plan, with some Italian participation, was carried out in the early hours of November 11, 1942, following the Allied invasion of NORTHWEST AFRICA.

ATTLEE, Clement Richard, 1st Earl Attlee (1883–1967). Attlee joined the Labour Party in 1907 as a result of social work in London's poverty-ridden East End. In 1913 he became a lecturer at the London School of Economics and during World War I attained the rank of major in the British Army while serving in the Middle East and in France. In 1922 he was elected Member of Parliament for Limehouse. He served in the cabinet as Chancellor of the Duchy of Lancaster (1930–31) and Postmaster General (1931), and was elected leader of the Labour Party in 1935. Prime Minister Winston CHURCHILL appointed Attlee Lord Privy Seal and Deputy Leader of the House of Commons in the wartime coalition cabinet (May 10, 1940). Attlee was a member of the British delegation to the SAN FRANCISCO CONFERENCE in 1945 that established the UNITED NATIONS.

Although seemingly diffident, Attlee could be forceful when required to exert control over conflicting personalities. This characteristic served him well when he became the first Labour leader to command an absolute majority in the House of Commons after the caretaker Conservative government suffered a staggering defeat in July 1945. The results of the election were announced in the middle of the POTSDAM CONFERENCE, requiring Attlee to take Churchill's place at the conference. He strongly supported the Big Three demand of unconditional surrender by Japan, the occupation of Germany and the plan to try Nazi leaders as war criminals.

Attlee's government lasted from July 1945 until February 1950. He remained party leader until his resignation in December 1955. His memoirs, *As It Happened,* were published in 1954.

ATTOLICO, Bernardo (1880–1942). Italian diplomat, ambassador to Germany in 1935–40 and to the Vatican in 1940–42.

ATTU. Small island at the western extremity of the American Aleutian chain, seized by the Japanese on June 7, 1942, as part of a plan to expand their initial perimeter of conquests. In late August and early September 1942 Japanese Army forces on Attu were evacuated to KISKA, but about 1,000 troops returned to Attu on October 29. By the time the U.S. 7th Infantry Division began landing on Attu on May 11, 1943, the Japanese garrison numbered about 2,400, holed up in excellent defensive terrain. The battle, except for some mopping up, was over on May 29. American losses were roughly 550 killed and 1,150 wounded; the Japanese lost their entire force (and only about 30 prisoners were taken). *See also* JAPANESE CONQUESTS, 1941–42.

AUCHINLECK, Sir Claude John Eyre (1884–). Perhaps the least known or appreciated of the major British commanders of the war, Auchinleck devoted most of his long years of military service to India and the Indian Army. In World War I he served as a captain in the Middle East against the Turks and was made a brevet lieutenant colonel. By 1926 he was recognized as the outstanding Indian Army officer of his generation. He attended the Imperial Staff College in England, where he became firm friends with John DILL, and then returned to regimental duty in India. By 1933 Auchinleck was the commander of the choice Peshawar Brigade; in 1936 he was named a major general; in 1937 he became Deputy Chief of Staff at Army headquarters at Simla. Three years later, as India's most outstanding officer, he was called to England to command 4th Corps.

The high command in England found Auchinleck likable but were often baffled by him, for beneath a surface conformity he was solitary and idiosyncratic. In late April 1940 Auchinleck was ordered to NARVIK "to secure and maintain a base in northern Norway." He arrived on May 7, just before the battle for the Low Countries began. A month later he was back in England, impressed with the importance of air support and of equipment and training suiting the terrain. He did not feel that British troops compared favorably with French or German troops, and of Norway he commented, "It is not an easy war to wage but it is interesting enough."

In June 1940 Auchinleck was given the 5th Corps in the Southern Command, and later the Southern Command itself. His businesslike manner soon made enemies, especially when he was outspoken ("We shall not win this war so long as we cling to worn-out shibboleths and snobberies") or coldly realistic in his approach. While most people liked "the Auk" and some appreciated his high critical faculty, others were nonplused or angry. Gen. B. L. MONTGOMERY, who commanded 5th Corps under Auchinleck, later wrote, "I cannot recall that we ever agreed on anything."

When Auchinleck was promoted to general and named Commander in Chief India in November 1940, he was "sorry in a way as I was *beginning* to become part and parcel of the *British,* as opposed to the *Indian,* Army." However, when Prime Minister CHURCHILL lost confidence in Gen. Sir Archibald WAVELL, Auchinleck was summoned to replace him as Commander in Chief Middle East. When he went to that theater in June 1941, Auchinleck did not take his wife because the soldiers were not allowed to have their families with them. His marriage was damaged by the separation and later ended in divorce.

From his assumption of the MIDDLE EAST COMMAND, Auchinleck was under pressure from Churchill, who wanted an immediate offensive against General ROMMEL. Auchinleck felt that he needed time for training and preparation. Within three weeks the two were at odds, but with firm confidence Auchinleck held his ground. Churchill summoned him to London, where, Auchinleck wrote his wife, "I have never had a more hectic time." Churchill reluctantly agreed to a delay in Operation CRUSADER; and later, when that offensive bogged down and Auchinleck personally intervened to ensure its continuance (November 23, 1941), he won Churchill's grudging admiration.

Churchill also supported Auchinleck staunchly during the January 1942 setback, but once the situation was stabilized the eager Prime Minister again urged an offensive and again Auchinleck insisted on having time to prepare it. Relations became more and more strained. Auchinleck stood firm and when Churchill again urged him to come to London, he refused on the ground that he could not afford to be away from his command. From then until July, when Auchinleck was relieved of his post, there was tension between him and the high command in London. Much of the problem was not so much Auchinleck's own shortcoming as the lack of a strong commander for the EIGHTH ARMY. During the confusion of the May–June 1942 battles, Auchinleck was not fully informed of the Eighth Army's losses. TOBRUK fell on June 21, and two days later Auchinleck wrote the CIGS that "the unfavorable course of the recent battle . . . impels me to ask you seriously to consider the advisability of retaining me in my command." But he was not removed from command until he had turned the defeat and rout into a victory, stabilized the front at ALAMEIN and laid the groundwork for the future success of the Eighth Army. During that time he exercised personal command of the Eighth Army, and won from Rommel the terse tribute that he "showed considerable enterprise and audacity."

Nevertheless Churchill wanted a change, and in July named Gen. Sir Harold ALEXANDER to command in the Middle East. Auchinleck was offered a new command—Iraq and Persia—which he refused to take, partly because he felt it should not be a separate command, partly because to accept it would put him in an awkward position. He went home to India. In June 1943 he was again named C-in-C India. With the creation of the Southeast Asia Command (Lord Louis MOUNTBATTEN) in November, India became the primary base and training area for Mountbatten's operations. What could have been an unpleasant or untenable arrangement worked well because Mountbatten and Auchinleck worked in close harmony. In 1946 Auchinleck was promoted to field marshal.

AUDACITY, H.M.S. In February 1940 British naval forces captured the German merchant ship *Hannover* in the Caribbean. It was refitted as an escort carrier, supplied with six U.S.-built Martlet aircraft and assigned to convoy duty in the Atlantic as H.M.S. *Audacity*. On December 21, 1941, a German U-boat sank the *Audacity* after a four-day battle between a British convoy group and a submarine wolfpack.

AUDET, Richard J. (1922–1945). A member of the Royal Canadian Air Force, Flight Lieutenant Audet downed five German planes in about two minutes during his first aerial combat. This was on December 29, 1944, when Audet's patrol attacked 12 enemy fighters. The guns of his Spitfire claimed an Me 109, then an FW 190, another Me 109 and two FW 190s in succession. While he was over Germany attacking a train on March 3, 1945, his Spitfire was struck by antiaircraft fire. Audet was killed in the crash. His victories totaled 10½.

AUGSBURG. German code word (contained in order of November 20, 1939) to be sent in case planned offensive in the west had to be delayed. It could take effect even if it reached the field commands as late as 2300 on D-1. Although Hitler pushed hard for an autumn offensive, the attack in the west did not in fact take place, of course, until May 1940. The earlier code equivalent of Augsburg was Elbe.

AUGUSTA. Sicilian port taken by the British EIGHTH ARMY on July 12, 1943.

AUGUSTA, U.S.S. NORTHAMPTON-class heavy cruiser, commissioned 1931. In 1941 she took President ROOSEVELT to Placentia Bay, Newfoundland, for his Atlantic conference with Winston CHURCHILL. *Augusta* supported the landings in North Africa in 1942, took part in Atlantic carrier task force operations and went to SCAPA FLOW in 1943 after two transatlantic convoy-escort voyages. From August to November 1943, *Augusta* covered MURMANSK RUN convoys from Scapa Flow. In 1944 she supported the landings in Normandy and southern France; in 1945 she carried President TRUMAN to Antwerp, en route to the Potsdam Conference.

AUNG SAN (1914?–1947). The Burmese insurgent leader Bogyoke (Great General) Aung San began a highly successful political career in the 1930s. An active member of the so-called Thakin group of nationalists, Aung San escaped arrest by leaving Burma in 1941. After contacting the Japanese, he organized other Thakins into a group called the Thirty Comrades, all of whom received guerrilla training by the Japanese. The Aung San–led Thirty Comrades and Burma Independence Army accompanied the Japanese in their assault on Burma and the subsequent rout of the British colonialists. Since Aung San and his followers had viewed collaboration with the Japanese not as treason but simply as a means to independence, and since he saw little real evidence of independence, he began organizing the clandestine Anti-Fascist Organization while outwardly supporting the Japanese. After contacting the British in December 1944 with a request for Allied assistance, and then surprising the Japanese by transferring his army to the Allies, Aung San and his newly named Patriotic Burmese Forces assisted in the ultimate reoccupation of Burma.

AURORA, H.M.S. Royal Navy light cruiser of 5,270 tons, completed in 1938 at Portsmouth, with an armament of six 6-inch and eight 4-inch guns, smaller weapons and six 21-inch torpedo tubes. *Aurora* served in the Home Fleet, including the operations in NORWAY, until 1941 and was then transferred to the Mediterranean, where she was the leader of FORCE K, the light forces based on MALTA, then under heavy siege. She remained in this theater, participating with distinction in numerous engagements, until 1945. After the war she was sold to the Chinese Nationalists and sunk by the CHINESE COMMUNISTS.

AUSCHWITZ. Situated 33 miles west of Cracow, Poland, Auschwitz (Pol. Oświęcim) was from summer 1941 the principal Nazi center for extermination of unwanted Jews, Poles and Slavs. A former military barracks acted as the initial headquarters, but by 1943 the camp had been extended to house 30,000 slave-labor prisoners confined in rows of barrack huts. With the additional extension known as Birkenau, accommodation was planned to rise to some 200,000; Rudolf HOESS, the commandant, claimed at NUREMBERG that he had held some 140,000 prisoners. Special war plants to exploit this labor force were set up nearby by I. G. Farben and other armaments industries. The main rail line between Cracow and Vienna ran straight through the camp complex, which came to occupy territory of several square miles. Trains bringing in new arrivals drove into a special siding serving the camp; those chosen for slave labor were housed in the huts, those destined for extermination were dispatched to the gas chambers and crematoria. It is estimated that some two million people were destroyed at Auschwitz-Birkenau between 1942 and the autumn of 1944, when the exterminations finished. When the camp was liberated by the Russians late in 1944, it had been evacuated and the gas chambers and crematoria largely destroyed. The buildings that remain have been established by the Poles as a memorial to the dead and a museum. *See also* EXTERMINATION CAMPS.

AUSTEN GUN. An Australian war-developed 9-mm. submachine gun that combined good features of the STEN GUN with others adopted from the German Schmeisser MP 38 and MP 40. It further incorporated such refinements as easy barrel changing. Its general characteristics were similar to those of the Sten, and it fired the same 9-mm. Parabellum (Luger) cartridge. Although a more sophisticated design than the Sten, it shared its practicality and ruggedness.

AUSTER. Built by British Taylorcraft, this high-wing monoplane was fabric-covered and powered by a 130-

horsepower Lycoming engine. A light plane similar to the American Cub, the Auster served as a liaison craft and artillery spotting plane.

AUSTRALIA, H.M.A.S. Heavy cruiser (eight 8-inch guns, eight 4-inch guns), sister ship of H.M.A.S. CANBERRA. *Australia* was a component of MACARTHUR'S NAVY, later the SEVENTH FLEET. She served through the Pacific war, being damaged by KAMIKAZE at LINGAYEN GULF (January 1945).

AUSTRALIAN FORCES. Australian (and New Zealand) troops were much identified with the fighting in the Middle East. "Aussies" were dispatched to Egypt in the early months of the war and in 1940–41 they fought Axis forces in the desert and in GREECE and CRETE. In 1941 Australian troops, principally the 9th Division under Gen. Sir Leslie MORSHEAD, held TOBRUK for eight months (the 9th received help from the 18th Brigade of the 7th Division). In early 1942 the bulk of the Australian forces were recalled from their service with the British Eighth Army to confront the Japanese menace; casualties in the Middle East, Malaya and the East Indies had totaled about 30,000, leaving the country short of trained soldiers. Henceforth the Australians took a prominent part in the fighting in NEW GUINEA and in subsequent Allied action in the Southwest Pacific.

AUTOCAT. U.S. Navy carrier plane with automatic mechanical VHF radio-relay equipment. Autocats were used, in small numbers, by the FAST CARRIER TASK FORCE in operations off Japan during July–August 1945. They enabled the task groups using them to receive VHF transmissions from air strikes at greater ranges than usual.

AUXILIARY TERRITORIAL SERVICE (ATS). A corps of British women whose members served as volunteers with the Army from September 9, 1938, to July 1, 1941, when they were given full military status. Women of the ATS served in over 100 military specialties (primarily at antiaircraft sites) at home and in the overseas theaters during the war. The ATS reached peak strength of 213,000 in August 1943. In 1949 the corps was renamed the Women's Royal Army Corps and admitted as an integral component of the British Regular Army.

AVALANCHE. Code name for Allied landing at SALERNO (Italy), September 9, 1943.

AVENGER. U.S. Navy name for the Grumman TBF torpedo bomber (*see* TBF).

AVIA AV-135. Czech single-seat interceptor, ordered in 1938. Its final development occurred under the Germans. Twelve were sold to Bulgaria and production ceased. This aircraft, armed with one 20-mm. cannon and two 7.9-mm. machine guns, had an 890-horsepower engine and a maximum speed of 332 miles per hour.

AVIA B-534. Single-engine biplane, Czechoslovakia's standard fighter at the time of the country's disruption, with 445 in service. Germany outfitted three squadrons of the Slovak Air Force with these, and they were used near Kiev in July 1941; many of the pilots defected to the Russians. It had a single 860-horsepower engine giving a maximum speed of 245 miles per hour and was armed with four 7.7-mm. machine guns.

AVRANCHES. Town in southwest Normandy, at the base of the Cotentin Peninsula, on the Gulf of Saint-Malo. Lying between two rivers, with north-south roads funneling through it, Avranches was a strategic prize in July 1944. It was taken by men of the U.S. 4th Armored Divison on July 30, after securing bridges over the See River. On August 1, 1944—the day U.S. 12TH ARMY GROUP (and, likewise, Lt. Gen. George Patton's THIRD ARMY) became operational—elements of the Third Army, led by the 4th and 6th Armored Divisions, poured through the Avranches corridor in the course of the Allied breakout from Normandy. *See also* WESTERN FRONT.

AXIS, THE. Originally an Italo-German statement of common interests (October 21, 1936), which was expanded into a formal military alliance (the "Pact of Steel") on May 22, 1939. It was often known as the Rome-Berlin Axis or the Berlin-Rome Axis. The term "axis" came from Benito MUSSOLINI's proclamation of the 1936 agreement as the axis around which states with common interests might collaborate. The Axis became enlarged when Japan, which had previously signed the ANTI-COMINTERN PACT, adhered to an agreement for a 10-year military alliance with Germany and Italy (September 27, 1940). Smaller countries (Hungary, Rumania, Slovakia, Bulgaria and Croatia) subsequently joined the Axis. Because she fought the Soviet Union, Finland was a participant in the war on the Axis side, and Spain, although a nonbelligerent, supplied some troops (the BLUE DIVISION) for the Eastern Front. *See also* HITLER, ADOLF.

AXIS (Achse). A German plan formulated in late July 1943 to seize control of Italy. Axis, like ALARIC, was based on the premise of Italian defection. On September 8, 1943, the Germans were informed that Italy had surrendered to the Allies, and Field Marshal KESSELRING, the Commander in Chief South, Axis, issued the code word Axis, occupied Rome and dispersed the strong Italian forces in the area. The half-million Italian troops in northern Italy and occupied France seemingly vanished into thin air. In southern Italy nine divisions were disarmed and permitted to go home. In the Balkans, Greece and the Aegean, the Italian ground forces, numbering more than 160,000 men, were with but a few exceptions completely dissolved by September 15. The Italians had offered little aid to the Allies on the Italian mainland and even less resistance to the Germans.

AXIS SALLY. *See* GILLARS, MILDRED.

AXMANN, Arthur (1913–). A product of the HITLER YOUTH, Axmann in 1940 succeeded Baldur von SCHIRACH as Reich Youth Leader. He was in the Führerbunker until after Hitler's suicide, took part in the flight the next day and is one of those who saw Martin BORMANN dead.

AYANAMI. Japanese destroyer and class. These ships, completed 1929–32, were called the "intermediate" group of "special type" destroyers, a type begun with the FUBUKI class. The 10 ships of the Ayanami class were similar to the Fubukis but had three 5-inch dual-purpose gun mounts (for antiaircraft as well as surface fire). Of 1,980 tons' displacement, they had a maximum speed of 38 knots. Nine Ayanamis were war losses.

AZON. The VB-1 ("Vertical Bomb"), developed by the U.S. Army Air Forces. It was a 1,000-pound general-purpose (high-explosive) bomb, to which a special tail incorporating a pair of radio-controlled rudders was attached. The fall of the bomb was followed by a bombardier in the dropping aircraft, with the help of a guide flare in the bomb's tail. Radio signals controlled the Azon, in azimuth only, permitting it to be guided as far as 3,000 feet to one side of what would have been the normal point of impact for an unguided bomb. It was followed by the RAZON.

AZORES. U.S. and British forces negotiated with Portugal unsuccessfully from May 1941 to October 1943 for the right to occupy the islands; finally, in October, Great Britain was granted exclusive use of Lagens Field in Terceira. However, the 6,000-foot airstrip was not sufficient, and the Americans were invited to join the British in extending it. In January 1944 the United States Naval Forces Azores was established to administer U.S. affairs on the island for antisubmarine purposes.

B

B5M9. Mitsubishi carrier torpedo bomber, same concept as B5N but with fixed gear (*see* B5N). It was produced in limited number for the Japanese Navy.

B5N. Japanese Navy Nakajima Type 97 carrier torpedo bomber (Allied code name, Kate), a folding-wing plane adopted in 1937 and used over China as a bomber. It was Japan's first-line torpedo bomber when the Pacific war began, being used as a horizontal bomber and torpedo plane at PEARL HARBOR and through the first years of the war. It was powered by a 1,000-horsepower radial engine and had a top speed of 235 miles per hour.

B6N1. Nakajima *Tenzan* (Heavenly Mountain) (Allied code name, Jill), developed as replacement for the B5N (*see* B5N). Fast and with better endurance than the earlier bomber, it saw combat in 1943–45. An improved model was designated B6N2. This plane was powered by a Mitsubishi radial engine of 1,850 horsepower and could attain a speed close to 300 miles per hour. It could carry one 1,764-pound torpedo or six bombs.

B7A1. Aichi *Ryusei* (Shooting Star) (Allied code name, Grace), a streamlined, high-performance torpedo bomber. Engine difficulties and earthquake damage to the Aichi plant limited both production and service use.

B-17. Boeing Aircraft began work on this low-wing, four-engine monoplane in 1934, intending it as a coastal defense weapons system. When the U.S. Army Air Corps issued a call for a multiengine bomber, Boeing responded with its B-17 prototype, which attained a speed of 252 miles per hour during tests in 1935. Although the plane was publicized as the Flying Fortress, export versions proved underarmed and vulnerable when used by the British in 1940 and 1941.

B-17 Flying Fortress

As the war progressed, however, the B-17 grew in weight—thanks to such refinements as armor and self-sealing gas tanks—armament and horsepower. The B-17D, in service when the Japanese attacked Pearl Harbor, had self-sealing fuel tanks but lacked power-driven gun turrets. A manually operated machine gun in a bathtub mount beneath the fuselage provided some protection against attack from the rear, but the D model had no tail gunner. The B-17E incorporated a number of changes, among them an enlarged dorsal fin that gave greater lateral stability at high altitude, but its most important improvement was in defensive armament. The plane boasted twin manually operated .50-caliber machine guns in the tail and power-operated dorsal and ventral turrets. A chin turret located beneath the bombardier's station made its appearance in the B-17G. Armament thus increased from five .30-caliber machine guns in the YB-17 to thirteen .50-caliber guns in the G model. The E model was the first Fortress to be sent to England for use by the EIGHTH AIR FORCE. A total of 512 Es were produced, to be followed by 3,400 F's.

The B-17G, of which 8,680 were built, entered service with the Eighth Air Force in 1943, made the first American raid on Berlin in March 1944 and spearheaded the daylight bombing offensive. Four supercharged Wright radial engines of 1,200 horsepower each gave the B-17G a top speed of just over 287 miles per hour at 25,000 feet and a service ceiling slightly in excess of 35,000 feet. The plane cruised at 187 miles per hour and could carry three tons of bombs a distance of 2,000 miles; it was armed with thirteen .50-caliber machine guns.

B-18. The U.S. Army Air Corps placed its first order for the Douglas Bolo in January 1936, and the type was still in service when the Japanese attacked Pearl Harbor. The plane used the wing and tail surfaces of the DC-2 commercial transport but had a deep-bellied fuselage that could accommodate 6,500 pounds of bombs. Armament was only three .30-caliber machine guns, one of them in a retractable dorsal turret. The first B-18s had a blunt nose and two 850-horsepower Wright radial engines; the B-18A and B had a sharklike nose and 1,000-horsepower engines. None of the variants could fly much faster than 200 miles per hour. B-18s fitted with primitive search radar flew patrol missions in quest of German submarines.

B-23. Douglas Aircraft proposed its B-23 Dragon in 1938 as a more powerful and aerodynamically cleaner replacement for the B-18. Based on the very successful DC-3 commercial transport, the B-23 had two 1,600-horsepower Wright engines, three. 30-caliber machine guns in nose, ventral and dorsal positions and a .50-caliber tail gun, this last an innovation for a U.S. Army Air

B-24 Liberators over Genoa, Italy

Corps bomber. First flown in 1939, the Dragon reverted early in the war to training and utility duties.

B-24. Consolidated Aircraft began designing the B-24 Liberator in 1939. The plane was intended as an improvement over the B-17 and had a greater range and bomb load than the Flying Fortress (*see* B-17). The Liberator was a slab-sided, shoulder-wing monoplane with four engines and a tricycle landing gear. Except for a few single-fin B-24Ns built in 1945, U.S. Army Air Forces Liberators had twin stabilizers. Although the B-24 saw combat in the European and Mediterranean theaters, it was especially valuable in the Pacific, where long range was essential.

Consolidated also produced three special-purpose variants of the Liberator bomber. The C-87 was a long-range transport. The C-109 was a flying tanker designed to carry aviation gasoline across the Himalayas to B-29 bases in China. The Liberator tanker was fitted with a system that pumped an inert gas into the fuel tanks as they were emptied, thus reducing the likelihood of an explosion. The third special type was the F-7 photo plane.

A wing designed by David Davis combined a high aspect ratio with a newly developed airfoil and gave the plane remarkable range and load-carrying capacity at high altitude. Yet the Liberator is best remembered for the low-level attack against the PLOESTI, Rumania, oil refineries in the summer of 1943. The B-24D used for this raid had twin-gun power turrets in the tail, belly and back. Two manually operated .50-caliber guns were located in the nose and two in the waist, bringing the total to 10. This model had four supercharged 1,200-horsepower Wright radial engines and could attain a speed of 303 miles per hour at 25,000 feet. Service ceiling was 32,000 feet. The B-24D could cruise at 200 miles per hour, had a maximum range of 2,850 miles and could carry 8,800 pounds of bombs.

B-25. The prototype of the North American Mitchell (named after Brig. Gen. Billy Mitchell) first flew in 1940. The plane was a conventional twin-engine, twin-tail medium bomber with a tricycle landing gear. In December 1941 the Mitchell drew its first blood when a B-25A sank a Japanese submarine off the Pacific coast of the United States, and in April of the following year

B-25 Mitchell

B-25Bs made the first attack of the war against targets in Japan—the famous Doolittle Raid (*see* FIRST SPECIAL AVIATION PROJECT). During 1942 a Mitchell was fitted with a solid nose that accommodated a hand-loaded 75-mm. cannon. The experiment was judged successful, despite the weapon's slow rate of fire, and some 400 B-25s were fitted with the M-4 cannon.

These B-25Gs prepared the way for the most heavily armed of all Mitchells, the H model, which carried a new and lighter 75-mm. cannon, four nose-mounted .50-caliber machine guns and four other forward-firing .50-caliber weapons in blisters alongside the fuselage. Two .50-caliber guns were in a dorsal turret, two in a tail turret and two others in waist hatches on either side of the aircraft.

In 1944 production of cannon-carrying Mitchells came to an end, and North American began turning out the B-25J with a bombardier's nose made of Plexiglas. Some J models, however, sported a solid nose that contained eight .50-caliber machine guns. Regardless of the nose, this variant mounted Pratt and Whitney radial engines rated at 1,700 horsepower and could carry 3,000 pounds of bombs. Launchers for eight 5-inch rockets could be fitted to both the B-25H and the J. Increases in gross weight—from 27,100 pounds for the B-25A to 36,047 for the B-25H and 35,000 for the J—reduced the maximum speed from 315 miles per hour to about 275.

B-26. Peyton Magruder designed the torpedo-like Martin Marauder to be powered by two of the 2,200-horsepower Pratt and Whitney R-3350 engines that were being developed for the Martin Mars flying boat. Unfortunately, work on these engines did not proceed as hoped, and he had to settle for the same manufacturer's R-2800, rated initially at 1,850 horsepower but modified by the end of the war to produce 2,000 horsepower. He also fitted the new plane with stubby wings that increased its top speed but, together with the small flaps, gave the B-26 a landing speed in the neighborhood of 100 miles per hour. Pilots used to some docile plane like the B-18 found the Marauder a "widow maker," but the number of accidents declined as a result of a revised training program that included demonstrations by men like Bob Hoover, who climaxed his aerobatic display with a dead-stick landing.

B-26 Marauder

As was true of most combat aircraft, the weight of the B-26 soared as armor and new equipment were added. Because of this growth, a larger wing was designed for later models of the Marauder, and this made for easier handling. A B-26B of 1944 had a wingspan of 71 feet—six feet more than the A model—mounted a dozen machine guns, had a crew of seven and carried some 5,000 pounds of bombs. Selection of an R-2800 engine without a turbosupercharger prevented the B-26 from becoming a 400-miles-per-hour bomber as Magruder had planned, but the Marauder did reach a top speed of 317 miles per hour. Thanks to its rugged construction, the bomber could survive speeds approaching 400 miles per hour, which it sometimes attained in a shallow dive.

B-29. The most advanced bomber of World War II, the Boeing Superfortress could carry up to 10 tons of bombs. The plane mounted eight .50-caliber machine guns in remotely controlled turrets and a 20-mm. cannon in a manned tail turret. Four 2,200-horsepower Wright twin-row radial engines drove the Superfortress at a top speed of 365 miles per hour at 25,000 feet. It cruised at 220 miles per hour and boasted a maximum range of 5,830 miles. A pressurized cabin gave the ship a distinctive cylindrical shape and enabled the crew to function at altitudes in excess of 30,000 feet.

To Gen. Henry H. ARNOLD, the B-29 represented a multimillion-dollar gamble, since the Army had approved a production contract for 250 planes before Boeing had completed so much as a wooden mock-up of the new craft. Data normally obtained through prototype testing had to come from wind tunnel and slide rule. Boeing engineers, for example, selected a high aspect ratio wing with a new airfoil, built it at quarter scale and fitted it on a Fairchild PT-19 trainer for preliminary tests.

The weight of the B-29, over 100,000 pounds fully loaded, coupled with a wing area not much larger than that of a B-17, threatened to give the new bomber the landing characteristics of a brick. Boeing engineers met this challenge by installing huge Fowler flaps that, when fully deployed, increased the lifting surface by some 20 percent.

Rushed into production before testing was under way, the Superfortress encountered a number of problems, the worst of which was a tendency of the engines to overheat and catch fire during flight. Changes in design were made so that the heat would dissipate from around the second bank of cylinders, thus giving the engines the necessary reliability.

General Arnold's gamble paid off. The biggest combat aircraft to see action during the war—wingspan 141 feet, length 99 feet—delivered its first blow on June 5,

B-29 Superfortress

1944, a shakedown mission from Chengtu, China, against Bangkok, Thailand. Just nine days later the B-29 bombed its first target in Japan, the steel-production center of Yawata. Less than four years had elapsed since the September day when Boeing had received approval for production.

The B-29 was a decisive factor in the Pacific war. In all, B-29s flew 34,790 sorties during the war and dropped just under 170,000 tons of bombs on enemy targets—and the atomic bombs on Hiroshima and Nagasaki. While 414 B-29s were lost—147 of these attributed to enemy fighters or flak—B-29 gunners were credited with destroying 1,128 Japanese aircraft.

B-32. U.S. Army Air Forces sponsored the B-32 Dominator as a possible alternative to the Boeing B-29 (*see* B-29). Despite contrary data from wind-tunnel tests, Consolidated Aircraft persisted in using twin stabilizers on the B-32 prototype, only to encounter stability problems that forced a switch to a towering single tail. As a result, the Dominator was slow in going into production, and only 15 of the four-engine, shoulder-wing bombers got to the Pacific in time to see action against the Japanese.

BA-65. Breda supplied the Italian Regia Aeronautica with this single-engine, low-wing monoplane fighter-bomber, which came in single-seat and two-place versions. The plane made its debut in 1935 in Ethiopia and was basically a ground-attack plane. Performance varied according to the power plant, either a 900-horsepower or 1,000-horsepower radial. The basic single-seat model had a top speed of 267 miles per hour and was armed with two forward-firing machine guns. The two-seater was some 30 miles per hour slower but had a third gun operated by the observer. Maximum bomb load was 2,000 pounds.

BA-88. This twin-engine, midwing attack plane designed by Breda and nicknamed *Lince* (Lynx) established a speed record in 1937. Although Mussolini retained his enthusiasm for the plane, Italian airmen found it slow (despite the installation of 1,000-horsepower Piaggio radials) and hard to handle (despite the use of a twin tail assembly in place of the original single vertical stabilizer). A few of the planes saw combat between 1940 and 1943. An attempt to convert the Lynx to a dive-bomber failed, for the choice of 840-horsepower engines reduced the top speed from 304 to 239 miles per hour.

BAB EL QATTARA. Roughly halfway between EL ALAMEIN and the Qattara Depression (northwest Egypt), Bab el Qattara was first planned as a British fortified post, or "box," in the Alamein Line. During the fighting of July 1942 General AUCHINLECK shifted his line eastward, and thereafter Bab el Qattara marked the northern edge of the Axis minefield.

BABELTHUAP. The largest island in the Palaus. Following the seizure of PELELIU and ANGAUR in September 1944, Babelthuap's Japanese garrison was isolated and neutralized, and was subjected to heavy air attacks until the end of the war.

BABI YAR. A large gully near Kiev, in the Ukraine. At Babi Yar more than 33,000 Ukrainian Jews, Soviet prisoners of war and partisans were executed and buried in two days in September 1941. These murders were part of the organized massacre program carried out by SS ACTION GROUPS.

BABS. Allied code name for the Japanese Ki 15 reconnaissance plane (*see* KI 15).

BABY BLITZ. Between January and March 1944 the Germans renewed their bombing attacks on Great Britain. Because of the small numbers of LUFTWAFFE aircraft available (550), the tough British defense and the poor quality of the German crews, these attacks were not as effective as the ongoing Allied bombing raids or the earlier German ones. Hence this campaign was called the Baby Blitz, distinguishing it from the 1940 attacks, which were called the BLITZ. During the 1944 campaign the Germans copied British night bombing tactics, using a well-trained elite of pathfinders followed by a concentrated main assault (*see* PATHFINDER BOMBING). The Germans achieved some success but suffered heavy losses.

BACHEM BA 349A. A German single-place, wooden-structured, semiexpendable rocket-propelled interceptor, also called the Natter (Viper). It had its first piloted flight in February 1944. Armed with twenty-four 55-mm. rockets in the nose, it was to be guided by radio and radar against enemy bombers. After the attack the pilot and engine descended by parachute. Thirty-six were built; none were used operationally. Powered by a 3,750-pound-thrust Walter HWK 109–509A rocket and four jettisonable 1,110-pound-thrust rockets, it flew 560 miles per hour and had a climb rate of 35,800 feet per minute for two minutes of endurance. It was 21 feet 3 inches long and had a wingspan of 13 feet 1¼ inches. An improved version, the Ba 349, flew 620 miles per hour.

BACHER, Robert Fox (1905–). American physicist, instrumental in the development of the ATOMIC BOMB as head of the bomb physics division of the Los ALAMOS laboratory. In 1940 he went to work on secret defense projects at the Massachusetts Institute of Technology Radiation Laboratory, where in 1942 he was placed in charge of the division of radar-receiver and indicator components and radar beacons. In 1943 he joined the staff of the MANHATTAN DISTRICT. At the Los Alamos laboratory Bacher became head of the experimental nuclear physics division under the direction of J. Robert OPPENHEIMER. In 1944 he became head of the bomb physics division and a member of the coordinating council for the entire Manhattan project.

BACH-ZELEWSKI, Erich von dem (1898?–1972). German SS officer (Obergruppenführer—lieutenant general), a specialist in antipartisan operations who commanded the SS forces that put down the WARSAW uprising in August 1944 (*see* SS). He was particularly admired by Adolf HITLER, who said of him: "Von dem Bach is so clever he can do anything, get around anything." In spite of his own complicity in war crimes, von dem Bach served as a prosecution witness at NUREMBERG and was not brought to trial himself until 1951, when a German court in Munich gave him a 10-year suspended sentence.

BACKBONE. Code name for possible Allied operation against Spanish Morocco in connection with the invasion of North Africa in 1942.

BADOGLIO, Pietro (1871–1956). At the end of World War I, Badoglio was Chief of the Italian General Staff. He was at first cold to the Fascist regime of Benito MUSSOLINI, but eventually he accepted it and in 1925, three years after the march on Rome, Badoglio was once again appointed Chief of Staff. In 1926 he was made a field marshal. He was Governor of Libya from 1928 to 1934. In 1935 he led Italian forces in the war against Ethiopia and ruled that country as viceroy for a short time after its conquest in 1936.

Marshal Badoglio opposed Italian entry into World War II on the grounds that Italy was unprepared, and he resigned as Chief of Staff in December 1940 after Italy's invasion of Greece turned into a disaster. He strongly dissociated himself from the Greek adventure and Mussolini's conduct of Italian affairs generally. In July 1943, when the Fascist Grand Council deposed Mussolini, Badoglio headed the government that succeeded him. On September 3, 1943, Badoglio signed an armistice with the Allies at Cassibile, which provided for the unconditional surrender of all Italian forces and for the establishment of Allied administration of the country. The position of Badoglio's government was quite ambiguous until October 13, 1943, when it declared war on Germany. With this stroke Badoglio achieved "co-belligerent" status and eased Italy's postwar situation. His second political stroke was achieved when the Soviet Union recognized his government in March 1944 and the Italian Communist Party, under Palmiro Togliatti, reversed itself and supported him.

In June 1944, following the capture of Rome, Badoglio resigned to allow the formation of a new government and retired to his family estate in Grazzano Badoglio.

BAEDEKER RAIDS. Nickname for German air raids carried out pursuant to instructions from Adolf HITLER on April 14, 1942. This order appears to have been a response to the RAF raid on Lübeck on March 28–29, 1942, in which much of this old Baltic port was destroyed. Baedeker raids (after the famous guidebooks) were attacks on cities that were not primary industrial targets but were known for their architecture and other attractions, such as Exeter, Bath, Norwich and Canterbury. The old Guildhall in York was destroyed in one of these raids. The raids were carried out during April, May and June 1942.

BAGRAMYAN, I. K. (1897–). A veteran of the Russian Imperial Army who joined the Red Army in 1921, Bagramyan was chief of staff of the Southwest Front in 1941–42 and commanded the Sixteenth Army at KURSK and BRYANSK. In 1943–45 he was in command of the First Baltic Front. During the war he rose from colonel to general and later became Marshal of the Soviet Union.

BAILEY, U.S.S. CLEMSON-class destroyer, commissioned 1919. She was transferred to Britain as part of the "destroyers for bases" agreement in 1940, and served in the Atlantic as H.M.S. *Reading.*

A second *Bailey,* a BENSON-class destroyer, was commissioned in 1942 and served in the Pacific. She earned a NAVY UNIT COMMENDATION for her part in the Battle of the KOMANDORSKI ISLANDS, where she took three 8-inch shell hits. She later supported landings in the GILBERTS, MARSHALLS, MARIANAS and Palaus. In 1945 she took part in landings on Mindanao and Borneo.

BAILEY BRIDGE. Sir Donald Coleman Bailey designed this collapsible steel bridge for the British early in the war. It could be assembled in panels; thus a destroyed bridge could be replaced in a few hours. Since the Bailey bridge was lighter than comparable American bridges, easily transported and adaptable to loads up to many tons, the U.S. Army used it extensively. The bridge proved especially valuable in Italy, where German tactics relied on bridge demolition to impede the Allied advance.

BAILLIE-GROHMAN, Harold (1888–). British naval officer who as a rear admiral attached to the staff of the Middle East Command directed the evacuation of British forces from GREECE in April 1941. He subsequently was associated with COMBINED OPERATIONS, and it was he who hoisted the White Ensign over the German naval headquarters at Kiel on May 8, 1945.

BAKA. Allied code name for the Japanese MXY7 OHKA (Cherry Blossom) suicide-attack plane. It was informally referred to in the U.S. fleet as the Gizmo before the name Baka was selected. The latter name, the Japanese word for "fool," was chosen, for possible morale purposes, as an opinion on the one-way nature of the plane's role.

BAKER ISLAND. A U.S. possession in the Central Pacific about 480 miles east of the GILBERT ISLANDS. In September 1943 it was developed as an air base for support of the American offensive against the Gilberts and

Bailey bridge

MARSHALLS; an operational airstrip was built within a week.

BAKU. Capital of the Azerbaijan Soviet Socialist Republic, on the western side of the Caspian Sea. The Bay of Baku is the best anchorage in the Caspian Sea. Baku is the center of a major oil-producing region of the Soviet Union. In the spring of 1940, the British and French Middle East commanders considered bombing the Baku region to prevent the Soviet Union from supplying Germany with oil and oil products. In 1942 seizing Baku was the objective of the First Panzer Army, which it failed to achieve.

BALANGA. Capital of Bataan province, P.I., halfway up the Bataan peninsula. It was a stop on the BATAAN death march in April 1942. Here some of the prisoners were loaded into trucks, but most had to continue on foot.

BALAO, U.S.S. Submarine and class. The second war-production class of American FLEET-TYPE SUBMARINES, 132 Balaos commissioned in 1943–45. Eighteen more were canceled. Ten were war losses; 12 earned unit citations. The Balao class closely resembled the earlier GATO class in appearance and characteristics. Like them, the Balaos had 10 torpedo tubes and a varying gun armament. Their conning towers were built to the lower silhouette of the later Gatos. The principal difference between Gato and Balao lay in the heavier hull construction of the later class.

BALBO, Italo (1896–1940). Governor General and commander in chief of Italian forces in Libya, Marshal Balbo was accidentally killed over TOBRUK in 1940 by his own antiaircraft fire. A Fascist who had led Mussolini's march on Rome in 1922, he contributed greatly to the development of the Italian Air Force between the wars. Balbo was a respected airman, and at his death Air Marshal Sir Arthur LONGMORE sent a note of respectful regret. Balbo was replaced by Marshal GRAZIANI.

BALBO. Nickname for RAF wings of four to six squadrons. The name comes from Italo BALBO, the Italian who was an early leader in mass flight. The soundness of the "big wing" concept was a matter of disagreement during the Battle of BRITAIN between Air Vice-Marshal Sir Keith PARK and the proponent of the big-wing idea, Air Vice-Marshal Sir Trafford LEIGH-MALLORY.

BALCHEN, Bernt (1899–1973). Famous as the first man to pilot an airplane over the South Pole, Balchen served with the British following the German conquest of his native Norway until September 1941, then entered U.S. Army Air Forces. For a time he commanded an airfield in Greenland and engaged in polar rescue operations, but his most important work was in connection with the Norwegian underground. He helped set up an escape route between the United Kingdom and Sweden that enabled some 5,000 Norwegians and other people to flee Nazi tyranny. He also was responsible for supplying the underground forces in Scandinavia. From November 1944 to August 1945, Colonel Balchen commanded air operations that chased the Germans from northern Norway and Finland.

BALCK, Hermann (1893–1950?). German Army officer (General der Panzertruppen, 1943), commander of Army Group G, which held in Alsace and Lorraine at the time of the Battle of the BULGE.

BALDWIN, Hanson Weightman (1903–). A graduate of the U.S. Naval Academy, Baldwin became the *New York Times* military editor and critic in 1937. Throughout World War II he was regarded as the nation's foremost military journalist, and he did several tours as a war correspondent overseas. He is the author of numerous works on military subjects.

BALI. Island in the Netherlands East Indies, separated from the eastern end of JAVA by the narrow Bali Strait. It was attacked by the Japanese on February 19, 1942, during their sweep southward through the islands. A combined force of American, British and Dutch cruisers and destroyers, commanded by Adm. Karel DOORMAN, sailed from TJILATJAP on February 18 to attack the Japanese assault force, but arrived to find that the Japanese had already landed. In scattered engagements the Dutch cruiser *Tromp* was severely damaged and a Dutch destroyer sunk. Two Japanese destroyers were damaged.

BALIKPAPAN. Oil center on the east coast of Borneo (Strait of Makassar), taken by Japanese forces on January 23, 1942. It was retaken by the Australian 7th Division on July 1–2, 1945.

BALKANS, GERMAN INVASION OF. This action was the result of a number of political, military and psychological considerations. The Italian invasion of Greece in 1940 had been ignominiously defeated by the Greeks, and the Italians were being slowly driven out of Albania. In the process Greece had become a British ally, and British forces were operating on Greek soil. The unexpected strength of the Greeks, their support by the British and the British victories against the Italians in Libya and the eastern Mediterranean had encouraged the Yugoslavs to resist German demands for cooperation. The pro-German regent, Prince PAUL, had been overthrown and replaced by a pro-Allied government under the young King PETER II. German plans for the invasion of Russia were now far advanced, and the sudden appearance of a British-supported Greek-Yugoslav bloc that could threaten the rear of the German Army was a matter of concern to Adolf HITLER. Further, the Führer was infuriated by the defiance of the Yugoslavs. He decreed that Yugoslavia was to be smashed "with merciless brutality . . . in a lightning operation."

The attack was launched on April 6, 1941, by approximately 550,000 German troops and associated Hungarian, Rumanian and Bulgarian contingents. It aimed at detaching Croatia and Slovenia in the north, driving from Bulgaria to Italian-held Albania, and thus isolating the purely Serb element, where anti-German sentiment was strongest. All this was quickly accomplished. Croatia had been seduced by German promises of independence, and there was little opposition in that quarter. Ljubljana, Zagreb and BELGRADE were captured in a few days (Belgrade on April 12), and a separate Croat state was proclaimed. The Royal Yugoslav Army was only barely mobilized and was poorly disposed for the war, and a German attack in the Vardar region in the south, though strongly resisted, was successful. Skoplje was captured, and the Germans proceeded south and west to the Monastir Gap, a strategic point at the juncture of the Albanian, Yugoslav and Greek borders.

German and Bulgarian forces captured Salonika and cut off eastern Thrace from the rest of Greece. The German and Italian forces effected a junction at Struga in Macedonia on April 12. The Germans moved to attack the Monastir Gap from the north and southeast. The ineffectiveness of Yugoslav resistance caused the Greek and British positions to be repeatedly flanked, and by April 14 the Monastir Gap position had been abandoned and a new one set up on a line running west from Mount Olympus.

Thousands of Greek troops were cut off in Albania by this move. Farther north, in what remained of Yugoslavia, the areas of Croatia, Slovenia and Bosnia had been pacified by the Germans, most of the Dalmatian coast was in Italian hands and Macedonia was almost completely occupied by Bulgarians. The Yugoslav Government and King Peter were barely able to escape to England, where they set up a government-in-exile. Only in the mountainous center of Serbia was there much resistance left.

The Greek-British Mount Olympus line was outflanked by the Germans, and the British withdrew to a line based on the pass of THERMOPYLAE. On April 21 the remaining Greek forces in the west capitulated, and the full force of the Germans fell on the British. A gallant stand at Thermopylae by Australian and New Zealand forces gave the British time to begin evacuation. On the night of April 24–25 the Germans overran Thermopylae, but the British were able to continue their evacuation until the 27th. This virtually ended the campaign on the mainland, except for minor skirmishing in Serbia and Albania. King George of Greece was able to flee on a British destroyer.

Of approximately 60,000 British troops engaged in this campaign, about 45,000 were evacuated. Of the remainder the Germans claimed 9,000 as captured, with the remaining 6,000 killed or missing. They also claimed to have taken 300,000 Serbian and 200,000 Greek prisoners. The Germans had accomplished their main objectives in a remarkably short time, although the campaign cannot properly be said to have ended until the island of CRETE was captured in late May 1941.

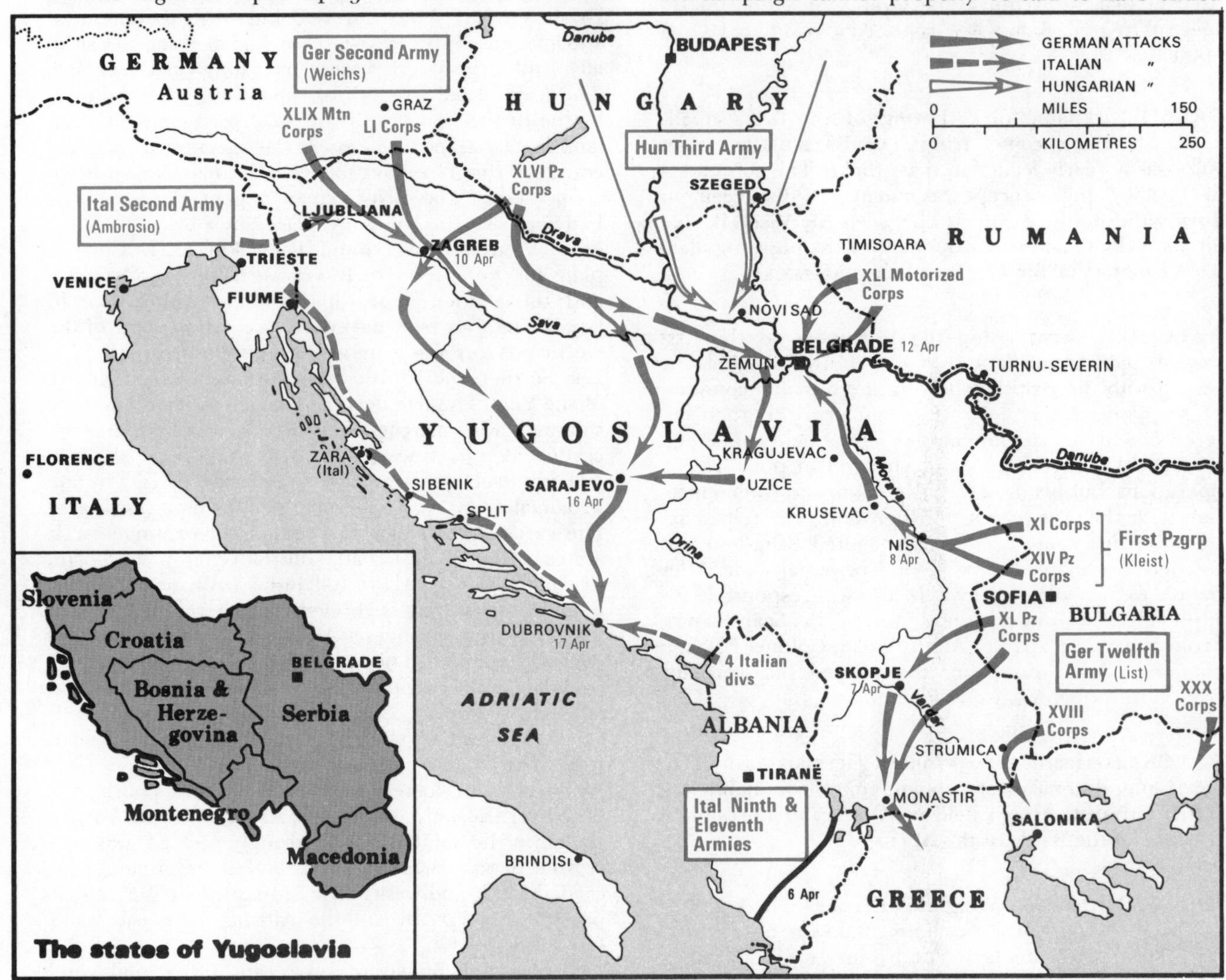

THE AXIS INVASION OF YUGOSLAVIA—from beginning to capitulation in a week and a half

BALLOON BOMB. A Japanese weapon intended to strike directly at the United States. Balloons with antipersonnel or incendiary bombs attached were launched over the Pacific. They dropped on the western parts of the North American continent. The first bomb-bearing balloon was launched on November 3, 1944; it is believed that about 1,000 reached North America. Six picnickers near Bly, Ore., were killed by the explosion of a balloon bomb in early May 1945, but little other damage was caused.

BALLOON COMMAND. The RAF Balloon Command was formed on November 1, 1938; 1,450 balloons were deployed by 47 auxiliary squadrons, including WAAF personnel, at the outbreak of war. Balloon units under the operational control of FIGHTER COMMAND protected major towns, industrial and dock areas and vulnerable points such as aircraft factories against low-flying attacks. Additional squadrons formed during the war provided barrages in the Mediterranean, the Middle and Far East, during the Normandy landings and against flying-bomb attacks.

The Balloon Command was disbanded in 1945, following V-E Day.

BALTIMORE. A twin-engine, midwing light bomber designed by the Glenn L. Martin Co. to British specifications as an improved MARYLAND. The choice of 1,660-horsepower Wright radials increased the top speed almost 25 miles per hour without affecting the 2,000-pound bomb load. The early Baltimores had four wing-mounted machine guns, two others in a manually operated ventral position and a single hand-operated dorsal gun. Later models had either a Boulton-Paul or Martin two-gun power turret atop the fuselage. The plane saw extensive service in North Africa, the Mediterranean and Italy.

BALTIMORE, U.S.S. Heavy cruiser and class. Completed in 1943–45, the class included 14 ships. Displacement was 13,600 tons; speed, 33 knots. Armament was nine 8-inch and twelve 5-inch guns, and four aircraft. A veteran of numerous actions in the Pacific, the *Baltimore* carried President ROOSEVELT to his meeting with Admiral NIMITZ and General MACARTHUR at Pearl Harbor in July 1944.

BA MAW (1893–1977). The first Premier of newly independent BURMA (1937), Ba Maw opposed Burma's participation in the war and was interned by the British in 1940.

He escaped from prison in 1942 and headed the puppet Burma regime under Japanese occupation (1943–45). His efforts resulted in a token alliance with Japan (August 1, 1943), designed to protect the population from reprisals. When the British returned, Ba Maw fled to Japan, but was allowed to return in 1946.

BANDAR SHAHPUR. An Iranian village on an island in the Khar Musa, an inlet at the head of the Persian Gulf. Bandar Shahpur was the sea terminus of the Iranian State Railway and therefore became an important port for handling Allied aid to the Soviet Union. The British took over Bandar Shahpur and began developing its facilities under the Anglo-Soviet occupation of Iran in August and September 1941. In 1942 the Allies agreed that the United States should operate the railroad and the ports of Khorramshahr (January 7, 1943) and Bandar Shahpur, control of the latter being assumed February 18, 1943, though the British aided in operations until April 1.

BANDERA, Stepan (1909–1959). Ukrainian nationalist and guerrilla leader. After one of his subordinates declared the Ukraine independent in June 1941, Bandera was arrested by the Germans. His guerrilla followers battled Germans and Soviets alike. Bandera was released by the Germans in September 1944 and encouraged fighting in the Ukraine, which lasted even after his flight to Germany in 1947. His death by poisoning was officially termed a suicide, but was considered by his followers and friends as the work of the Soviets. The Soviets used his name to describe German supporters in World War II ("Bandera gangs") and in references to the Ukrainian underground ("Banderovtsy").

BANDIT. Allied voice-radio term for an identified enemy aircraft.

BANMAUK. Burmese town northwest of Indaw, taken by Indian troops of the British 4th Corps on December 16, 1944, as Allies rolled back the Japanese in BURMA. The British made contact here with advance troops of U.S. Gen. Joseph STILWELL's Northern Combat Area Command.

BANTEN BAY. The anchorage on the north coast of Java, almost in the Sunda Strait, which was the scene of the landing of the Japanese western invasion force on the night of February 28, 1942. H.M.A.S. PERTH and U.S.S. HOUSTON, on their way from Batavia to Tjilatjap, encountered the Japanese invasion fleet but were unable to prevent the assault landing.

BANZAI CHARGE. The Japanese word *banzai* is generally translated as "May the Emperor live for 10,000 years" or "Long live the Emperor." Banzai attacks, which occurred frequently during the Pacific campaign, were frantic, usually disorganized charges, born of despair, mounted by Japanese troops shouting "Banzai!" as they rushed forward toward the enemy lines.

BÄR, Heinz (1913–1957). As a youngster, Bär enrolled in a glider club. He learned to fly powered airplanes in 1930 and joined the then-secret German Luftwaffe. In 1940 he scored the first of his 220 aerial victories, downing a French Curtiss Hawk 75. While serving with an elite Me 262 unit, Colonel Bär downed 16 Allied planes, becoming history's first jet ace.

BARBAROSSA. Code name of the German invasion of the Soviet Union, the aims of which were outlined in Hitler's Directive No. 21, issued on December 18, 1940. The "Russian Army," as the directive called it, was to be "destroyed by daring operations led by deeply penetrating armored spearheads," and the enemy was to be prevented "from withdrawing into the depths of Russia." Following the smashing of the Red Army, the Germans were to reach a line deep enough in the Soviet Union to make air attack on Germany impossible. The final objective was "to erect a barrier against Asiatic Russia on the general line Volga–Archangel."

Hitler set May 15, 1941, as the target date for the beginning of what was expected to be no more than a four- or five-month campaign. At the time the directive was issued, however, the Germans did not know that they would be involved in extensive operations in the Balkans in the spring of 1941. This involvement made it necessary to postpone the launching of Barbarossa until June 22, 1941. *See also* SOVIET-GERMAN OPERATIONS.

BARBER, Rex T. (1917–). U.S. Army flier who took part in the mission of April 18, 1943, that resulted in the death of the Japanese Adm. Isoroku YAMAMOTO, Commander in Chief of the COMBINED FLEET. Along with Capt. Thomas G. LANPHIER, Barber, a first lieutenant, claimed to have destroyed the bomber that carried the enemy naval leader. The P-38s flown by the two officers were the only aircraft of a four-plane killer group, protected by other Lightning fighters, actually in position to attack the Japanese formation—two bombers, one of them carrying Yamamoto, and their escort. Barber, who received credit for destroying one bomber, insisted that he overshot Yamamoto's plane, turned sharply and shot it down while Lanphier, also credited with downing a bomber, was climbing to engage the Japanese fighters. Which of the two actually killed Japan's leading naval strategist can never be determined.

A native of Oregon, Barber enlisted in the Army in September 1940 and during basic training proved himself a skilled rifleman. Accepted for flight training, he became an air cadet in March 1941, graduating in October of that year. During the war he shot down five Japanese aircraft. He transferred to the postwar U.S. Air Force, attaining the rank of colonel.

BARBEY, Daniel Edward (1889–1969). U.S. naval officer, a graduate of the U.S. Naval Academy in 1912, who became one of the leading amphibious-operations specialists of the war. In 1942 he went from duty in the war plans division of the Bureau of Navigation to assume command of the Service Force and then of the Amphibious Force of the Atlantic Fleet. Next he established the Navy's amphibious warfare section in Washington, and he went from there to the Southwest Pacific, establishing the new VII Amphibious Force in early 1943. As commander of the VII 'Phib, "Uncle Dan" commanded all amphibious operations in the Southwest Pacific Area and was in charge of the mop-up landings in the Philippines and Borneo. He participated in the Japanese surrender in Korea in 1945 and directed the repatriation of Japanese from Korea and China. Barbey's highest wartime rank was vice-admiral, to which he was promoted in 1944.

BARDIA. A small Cyrenaican port with Italian-built fortifications. With Sollum and Halfaya, Bardia formed a key position for the defense of TOBRUK. It was captured by the British from the Italians in January 1941; taken by the Germans in April 1941; recaptured by the British in December 1941; taken by the Germans in June 1942; and finally relieved by the British the following November.

BARHAM, H.M.S. A British battleship of 31,000 tons, completed in 1915. The *Barham* spent most of her World War II career as part of the Mediterranean Fleet under Adm. Sir Andrew CUNNINGHAM. In September 1940 she took part in the ill-fated British operations at DAKAR and six months later participated in the Battle of CAPE MATAPAN, in which she helped to sink the Italian cruiser *Zara.* She was torpedoed and sunk by a German submarine off CRETE on November 25, 1941. The *Barham,* which was modernized in the 1930s, was armed with eight 15-inch guns, twelve 6-inch guns and eight 4-inch guns and carried four aircraft. Her top speed was about 25 knots.

BARI. An important port on the Adriatic, about 60 miles up the heel of Italy from Brindisi, occupied by the British 1st Airborne Division on September 14, 1943, as a part of the Allied move from Sicily to the Italian mainland. In this operation the division was employed as infantry, coming over from Tunisia by ship rather than being airborne. On the night of December 2–3, 1943, about 30 Luftwaffe planes attacked the crowded port, blowing up two ammunition ships and thereby causing the loss of 17 other ships. The damage severely reduced the capacity of the port for three weeks.

BARKER, Ray W. (1889–). U.S. Army officer, a planner who went to Britain in 1942 to work with the British on plans for the cross-Channel operation and also on the invasion of NORTHWEST AFRICA. He held various staff posts with the U.S. Army's ETO command, and in the spring of 1943 he became deputy to Gen. Frederick E. MORGAN on the COSSAC staff. In 1944 he became deputy chief of staff of SHAEF. He was promoted to the rank of major general in 1943.

BARKLEY, Alben William (1877–1956). U.S. Senator from Kentucky, Barkley was first elected to the Senate in 1926 and held that seat until becoming Vice President under Harry TRUMAN. A strong supporter of President ROOSEVELT, Barkley was instrumental in winning support in the Senate for the SELECTIVE SERVICE and LEND-LEASE bills and also sponsored amendments to the Neutrality Act which passed the Senate in 1941. He broke with Roosevelt in 1944 over the President's tax bill veto message, claiming that it was an assault on the integrity of Congress; he resigned as majority leader of the Senate. After both houses of Congress overrode the President's veto, Barkley was unanimously reelected to Senate leadership by the Senate Democratic caucus. As chairman of the 1946 Congressional committee inquiring into Pearl Harbor, Barkley agreed with the majority report that Roosevelt and his three principal cabinet members at the time—Cordell HULL, Henry STIMSON and Frank KNOX—did not incite Japan into attacking Pearl Harbor.

BARNES, Stanley (1906–). Commander of the U.S. Navy's PT Squadron 15, which participated in the assault on SICILY as part of the screening group and in the SALERNO operation as part of the picket group. Commander Barnes and his British counterpart, Comdr. R. A. ALLAN, were known as "the Corsican Brothers."

BARNEY. Code name for U.S. submarine penetration of minefields in the Tsushima Strait and operations in the Sea of Japan, May 27–June 30, 1945. This invasion by wolfpacks completed the isolation of Japan. In 11 days on patrol the first wolfpack—HYDEMAN'S HELLCATS—sank 27 merchant ships. *See also* SUBMARINES.

BARRACUDA. Intended by Britain's Fairey Aircraft as a replacement for its ALBACORE and SWORDFISH biplane torpedo bombers, this aircraft flew for the first time in 1940 but did not enter production until 1942 because the older planes were performing satisfactorily. The single-engine, three-place Barracuda was a midwing monoplane with an externally braced tail plane mounted high on the vertical stabilizer. Fitted with Rolls-Royce Merlin liquid-cooled engines of 1,260 to 1,640 horsepower, Barracudas were capable of speeds as fast as 239 miles per hour and could carry up to 1,800 pounds of ordnance; the range was 686 miles. Besides serving as a carrier-based torpedo plane and dive-bomber, the plane performed antisubmarine reconnaissance, laid mines, dropped lifeboats on rescue missions and even flew secret agents into Nazi-occupied Europe. The Barracuda's most celebrated battle honor was the Fleet Air Arm strike against the German battleship TIRPITZ.

BARRAGE BALLOON. An unmanned captive balloon of a type first used in World War I, resembling a miniature BLIMP in appearance. Filled with hydrogen—with no crew, the safety factor provided by helium was unnecessary—and moored by heavy steel cables, barrage balloons were first used by the British and later by the Americans to protect bases and other strategic areas against low-flying air attack. They were also used by landing ships, to deter attacks on amphibious beachhead areas, and by convoys steaming in areas threatened by enemy aircraft.

BARRATT, Sir Arthur Sheridan (1891–). As an air vice-marshal (RAF), Barratt was in command of British air forces in France during the German invasion in 1940. It was a frustrating campaign for airmen as well as for ground soldiers; in particular, Barratt encountered strong French opposition to attempts to bomb Italian cities from bases in France, the French fearing enemy reprisals. After the Battle of France, Barratt was promoted to air marshal.

BARRÉ, Georges (1886–1970). French Army officer (major general) commanding in Tunisia at the time of the Allied landings in NORTHWEST AFRICA in November 1942. General Barré favored the Allied side and was the first VICHY French commander to commit his forces to battle against the Axis.

BARRIKADY GUN FACTORY. A large artillery works in the industrial area of Stalingrad. It lay between the RED OCTOBER PLANT and the Dzerzhinsky Tractor Works, and its grounds stretched down to the banks of the Volga. The Barrikady was fiercely defended by Russian troops, who held the land behind it after the Germans had occupied the buildings.

BARTON, Raymond O. (1889–). "Tubby" Barton was a U.S. Army officer who was promoted to major general in 1942 and appointed commanding general of the 4th Motorized (later Infantry) Division. He led the unit through the European campaign until, a victim of battle stress, he left to become commanding general of infantry training at Fort McClellan, Ala., in March 1945.

BARUCH, Bernard Mannes (1870–1965). Famous as the "adviser to Presidents," Baruch held high positions under President Woodrow Wilson in World War I but, though a friend of President ROOSEVELT, did not hold office in World War II. A man of great influence and capability, Baruch was one of the first members of Franklin Roosevelt's "brain trust," even though he disapproved of some of the New Deal programs. He was in agreement with Roosevelt in his apprehension of Nazi Germany and corresponded with his close friend Winston CHURCHILL about the British view of the European situation. Declining the opportunity to become war mobilization director, he became a special adviser to James F. BYRNES when the latter was Director of Economic Stabilization and later Director of War Mobilization. After the war Baruch, as U.S. delegate to the United Nations Atomic Energy Commission, presented the "Baruch plan" for the international control of atomic energy. It was vetoed by the Soviet Union.

BASE T. Code name for the British naval base at Addu Atoll in the Indian Ocean, used as an alternative to Colombo. It was also known as Port T.

BASTICO, Ettore (1876–1972). Italian Army officer who fought in the Italo-Turkish War of 1911–12, World War I, the Italo-Ethiopian War and the Spanish Civil War, when he was promoted to general. In 1940 he became Governor of the Dodecanese, and in July 1941 he was appointed Governor and commander in chief in LIBYA. General ROMMEL fought under his command, and the two often disagreed on the conduct of the African war. Mussolini named Bastico a marshal after Hitler made Rommel a field marshal, but when Rommel was put under Marshal CAVALLERO at Comando Supremo in 1942, Bastico was cut out of the chain of command. He returned to Italy in 1943 and retired in 1947. He wrote a three-volume work, *Evolution of the Art of War.*

BASTOGNE. An important road center in the ARDENNES region of Belgium, the town was the scene of an epic stand during the Battle of the BULGE by the 101ST AIRBORNE DIVISION, a combat command of the 10th Armored Division and stragglers from other American units. Securing Bastogne's roadnet became critical for the Germans when other American forces denied important roads farther north. The Fifth Panzer Army encircled the town on December 20, 1944, and two days later sent emissaries demanding surrender, to which the acting commander of the airborne division, Brig. Gen. Anthony C. MCAULIFFE, replied in American slang: "Nuts!" Clearing weather on the 23d enabled C-47 transport aircraft to parachute supplies into the perimeter. The Germans opened an all-out attack on Christmas Day, but late on the 26th tanks of the 4th Armored Division broke through to end the encirclement. Hard fighting nevertheless continued for two weeks before the Germans finally eased off. Just outside the town of Bastogne the Belgian people have erected an impressive memorial on Mardasson Hill to the American victory in the Ardennes.

BATAAN. Gen. Douglas MACARTHUR designated this peninsula west of Manila Bay as the center of American-Filipino resistance to the Japanese invasion of the PHILIPPINES. On Christmas Eve 1941 MacArthur ordered his forces to withdraw to Bataan, where supplies would be stockpiled for a last stand. Jungle, swamp and mountains made the peninsula difficult to penetrate but also hard to supply, and shortages of food and medicine plagued the Bataan Defense Force throughout the siege.

Fierce Japanese assaults, directed by Gen. Masaharu HOMMA, began on January 9 and gradually forced American and Filipino troops deeper into the pocket, but at great cost in Japanese lives. When the War Department ordered General MacArthur to leave the Philippines in March, his armies appeared to be holding the line. However, short rations weakened the 100,000 defenders who remained. Although the area was cut off from reinforcements and its new commander, Gen. Jonathan WAINWRIGHT, predicted starvation, MacArthur insisted that Bataan could hold out until May. It could not.

General Homma renewed his attack with reinforcements on April 3, 1942, and within the week Bataan surrendered. The starved survivors were then forced on a 60-mile "death march" to prison camp. Wainwright's headquarters on Corregidor Island capitulated on May 6. The sacrifice of Wainwright's command denied Japan the use of Manila Bay for a few months and provided Americans with an example of valor. But in the spring of 1942 the United States did not need another symbol to inspire it to vengeance. The Pearl Harbor attack had already aroused the nation.

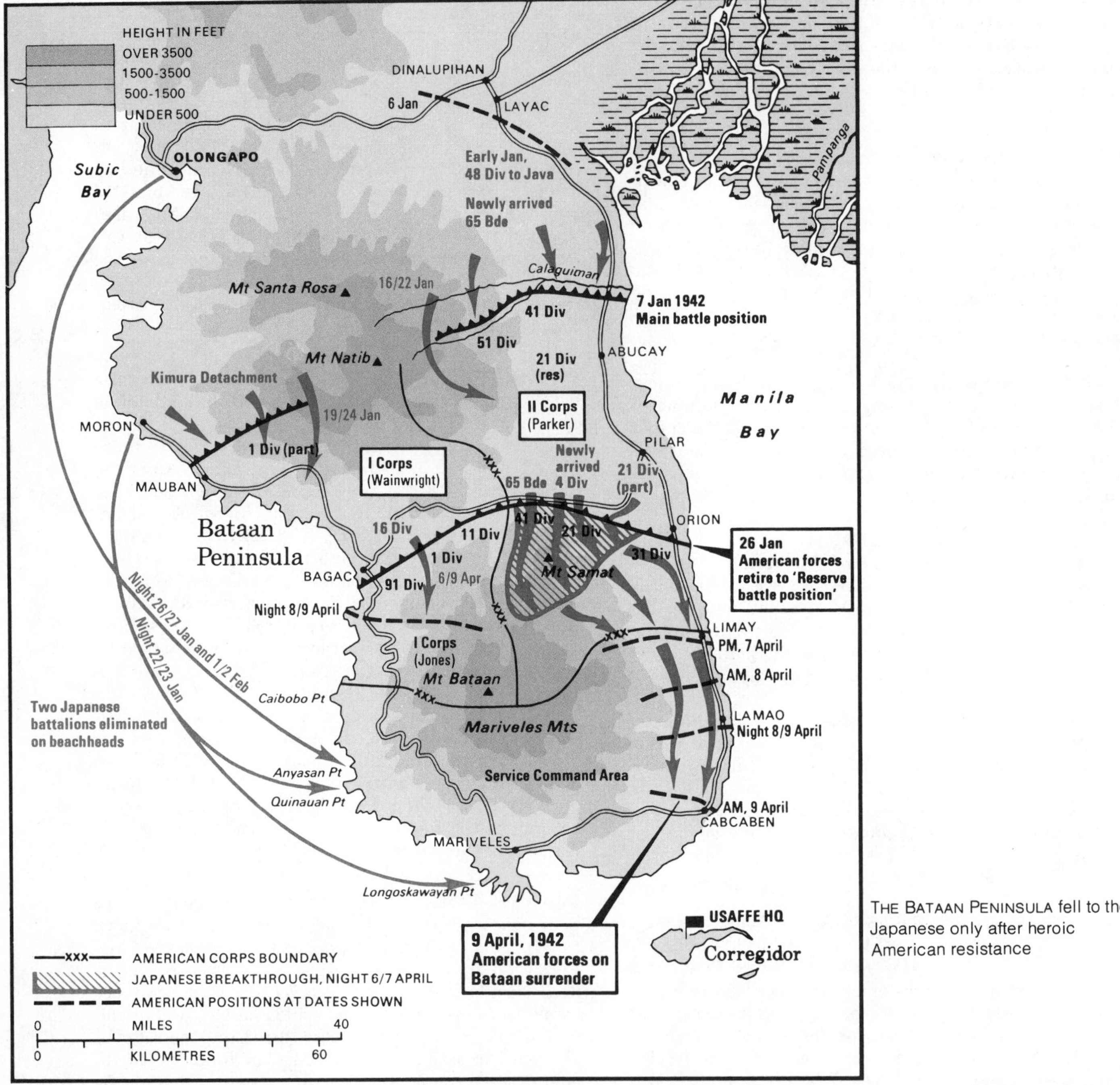

THE BATAAN PENINSULA fell to the Japanese only after heroic American resistance

BATAN. Island (in so-named group) between Formosa and Luzon, taken by the Japanese on December 8, 1941, and used by them as a fighter aircraft base for attacks on Luzon.

BATAVIA. This city (now Djakarta) on the north coast of JAVA was headquarters for the short-lived ABDA COMMAND, under the British general Sir Archibald WAVELL, from January 15 to February 25, 1942, when ABDA was dissolved in the face of the Japanese advance. The Dutch evacuated Batavia by March 5.

BATFISH, U.S.S. BALAO-class submarine. *Batfish* commissioned in 1943; she completed six war patrols. She was credited with sinking nine Japanese merchant ships, along with the destroyer *Samidare* and submarines *Ro-55*, *Ro-112* and *Ro-113*. The three submarines were sunk during a single four-day period (February 10–13, 1945).

BATOV, Pavel (1897–). After planning the defense of the Crimea, General Batov took command of the Soviet Sixty-fifth Army during the Battle of STALINGRAD. During the next two years his command was engaged in some of the heaviest fighting on the Eastern Front.

BATTIPAGLIA. A rail and road center southeast of SALERNO (Italy), one of the early objectives of the Allied forces in the landing. It was not occupied, however (except temporarily), until the tenth day of the invasion—September 18, 1943—when the Germans had withdrawn. The town was completely destroyed by Allied naval gunfire and air bombing.

BATTLE. Though superior to the biplane light bombers it replaced, this British airplane proved too slow and lightly armed to function successfully in wartime. Fairey Aviation designed the Battle, which first flew in 1936. When the war broke out, doctrine called for Battle bombers to attack during daylight without fighter escort. On September 20, 1939, the rear-seat gunner of a Battle claimed the destruction of the first German fighter downed in the war. Just 10 days later, however, unescorted daylight missions came to an abrupt end after Me 109s shot down four out of five planes in one Battle formation (*see* ME 109). Despite this disaster, the plane remained in combat. During the German thrust into France in May 1940, 71 Battles attacked enemy pontoon bridges near Sedan. Forty of the attacking bombers were shot down.

The Battle was a handsome low-wing monoplane with a transparent canopy enclosing the crew of three. Armament was one machine gun firing forward and another on a flexible mount at the rear of the crew compartment. The single 1,030-horsepower, liquid-cooled Rolls-Royce Merlin enabled the plane to carry 1,000 pounds of bombs but gave it a top speed of only 241 miles per hour.

BATTLEAXE. Code name for unsuccessful British offensive, June 1941, which was intended to destroy General ROMMEL's armor and recapture TOBRUK.

BATTLE OF THE PIPS. A surface action, fought south of the Aleutians in the dark early hours of July 26, 1943, by a U.S. naval force of two battleships, four heavy cruisers, one light cruiser and eight destroyer types against—a radar "ghost" image that convinced the American commanders that a Japanese surface force, attempting to carry reinforcements and supplies to KISKA, was within gun range. Some—not all—of the American ships' radars showed a group of "pips" that looked and acted like a formation of enemy ships. The battleships and heavy cruisers fired for a half hour at long range before the images disappeared. Reconnaissance revealed that no Japanese ships were anywhere in the area. The cause of the mirage has never been determined. It may have been a freakish long-distance reflection of radar impulses from Aleutian or Alaskan mountain peaks. This incident is a conspicuous example of the way in which the capabilities and limitations of the then-new radar often had to be discovered the hard way.

BATTLESHIP ROW. Name applied to a series of masonry mooring quays located along the southeast side of Ford Island at the U.S. PEARL HARBOR naval base. At the time of the Japanese attack in 1941 this deep-water berthing area was used for mooring battleships (hence the name), carriers and other deep-draft ships, singly or in "nests" of two ships abreast. On the morning of the attack the battleships CALIFORNIA, MARYLAND, OKLAHOMA, TENNESSEE, WEST VIRGINIA, ARIZONA and NEVADA, with the repair ship VESTAL and oiler NEOSHO, were berthed there. The sunken hull of the *Arizona* still rests where she sank that day, at Berth F-7.

BATUM (Batumi). Capital of the Adzhar Autonomous Republic, Georgian Soviet Socialist Republic, on a gulf of the Black Sea. Batum was an important oil port and the objective in 1942 of the German Seventeenth Army, which never reached it.

BAUDOUIN, Paul (1895–1964). Under Secretary of Foreign Affairs at the time of the fall of France, Baudouin served as Foreign Minister under Marshal PÉTAIN from June to October 1940 and was appointed Minister of State in 1941. A supporter of the armistice with Germany, he was strongly opposed to General DE GAULLE. He was an influential member of the VICHY government; his diary *Neuf Mois au Gouvernement* was published after the war.

BAUER, Harold W. (1908–1942). U.S. Marine fighter pilot (lieutenant colonel) who scored 11 victories. On two separate occasions in October 1942 he shot down four Japanese aircraft in action off GUADALCANAL, the second time rescuing a U.S. seaplane tender from dive-bomber attack. For this feat he was awarded the Medal of Honor. He died in action in the Solomons on November 14, 1942.

BAYERLEIN, Fritz (1899–1970). Bayerlein, who served Germany on four major fronts, was an outstanding staff officer and commander. In France in 1940, he was operations officer of General GUDERIAN's panzer corps; in Russia in 1941, the same for Guderian's Panzer Group 2. In September 1941 he went to Africa as chief of staff, first to the AFRIKA KORPS, later to General ROMMEL's Panzer Army, and finally to General MESSE. He and Rommel held each other in mutual respect; Rommel records in *The Rommel Papers* that when he left Africa, he was relieved that General Bayerlein would still be with the army.

Bayerlein was evacuated to Italy before the May 1943 surrender because he was ill, and subsequently he commanded the PANZER LEHR Division and LIII Corps. His division met the full force of Operation COBRA in France in July 1944 and was at BASTOGNE. Bayerlein fought at the Rhine and the Ruhr as a corps commander and was taken prisoner in April 1945. His highest rank was Generalleutnant. After the war he was brutally frank in analyzing his own and Germany's rôle in the conflict, and his accounts and recollections are a study of the war.

BAZOOKA. The name by which the U.S. 2.36-inch recoilless rocket launcher was generally known. The bazooka fired a hollow-charge, 3½-pound projectile up to 400 yards; it was introduced to give the infantry a powerful, easily transported weapon for use against tanks and fortifications. Other nations introduced copies, such as the British PIAT and Germany's Panzerschreck and Panzerfaust. The name "bazooka" came from a crude musical instrument used by radio comedian Bob Burns.

BCRA (Bureau Central de Renseignement et d'Action). The Free French intelligence service. Organized by "Colonel Passy" (André de Wavrin), the Central Bureau of Intelligence and Action cooperated with the British and American intelligence services in organizing the resistance to Nazi occupation.

BEACHMASTER. *See* BEACH PARTY.

BEACH PARTY. A group specifically organized to reduce confusion on landing beaches during an amphibious assault. Beach parties generally went ashore with the assault waves to place channel buoys, mark beaches for subsequent landing waves, set up beach aid and triage stations, blow up beach obstacles, establish ship-to-shore communications and generally direct invasion traffic on the beach. The individual in charge of these operations was called the beachmaster. Temporarily, he was organizer and manager of supply for the combat forces ashore, and his main task was to establish order out of confusion.

BEAR ISLAND. Lying in northern waters between the North Cape and Spitzbergen, this island was at the peak of the arc described by Allied convoys from Britain to the Soviet Union. In summer convoys were able to pass north of Bear Island, but as winter approached and the Arctic ice advanced, the convoys switched to a route to the south of the island. *See also* MURMANSK RUN; PQ-17; PQ-18.

BEAUFIGHTER. British airplane that was successful in several roles, serving as a night fighter, torpedo bomber and long-range attack plane. The Beaufighter represented an attempt to ease the burden on Britain's air industry by avoiding the necessity for extensive retooling. L. G. Frise and the Bristol Aircraft design department bobbed the nose of the low-wing BEAUFORT torpedo plane, installed two more powerful Hercules II radial engines and came up with a new fighter that utilized many Beaufort structural components. The prototype, which took to the air in July 1939, weighed eight tons but boasted a top speed comparable to that of the single-seat HURRICANE—335 miles per hour at 16,800 feet.

Even heavier and more powerful, the Beaufighter IF mounted a radar for night interception, four 20-mm. cannon and six machine guns. The IF entered RAF service in July 1940. One of these craft scored the first Beaufighter victory of the war in November, when its crew destroyed a Ju 88.

Early in the war Beaufighters began making forays against enemy shipping. Wearing Coastal Command markings, and with a navigator replacing the night fighter's radar operator, the planes operated over the Bay of Biscay. When the still more powerful Beaufighter VI appeared in 1942, some models were modified to carry torpedoes and rockets. A torpedo-carrying version was called the Torbeau.

Coastal Command made excellent use of Beaufighter X, which had a thimble nose housing an airborne intercept radar that proved equally effective in detecting ships. The Mark X, nicknamed Whispering Death by the Japanese, mounted two 1,770-horsepower Bristol Hercules radials that gave it a top speed of 303 miles per hour at 1,500 feet. Armament consisted of four 20-mm. cannon in the fuselage, six .303-caliber machine guns in the wings, a dorsal gun and one torpedo plus two 250-pound bombs or eight rockets.

BEAUFORT. The standard British Coastal Command torpedo bomber from 1940 through 1943. Bristol Aircraft designed the twin-engine, midwing monoplane, which was replaced by another Bristol product, the torpedo-carrying BEAUFIGHTER. Most Beauforts were powered by two Bristol Taurus, 1,130-horsepower radial engines. Top speed was 265 miles per hour and the normal range slightly more than a thousand miles. The plane could carry either 1,500 pounds of bombs or (externally) one 1,600-pound, 18-inch torpedo. Almost 1,400 Beauforts were built, the total evenly divided between factories in the United Kingdom and Australia.

BEAVERBROOK, William Maxwell Aitken, 1st Baron (1879–1964). British newspaper publisher and politician, nicknamed "The Beaver," a native of Canada. He was elected a Conservative (Unionist) member of Parliament in 1910 and received his title in 1917. An enormously wealthy man when he arrived in England to stay, he was interested in various ventures; for instance, he acquired, almost in passing, the controlling interest in Rolls-Royce, which he sold after failing to persuade the board to convert to mass production. In 1917 he bought control of the *Daily Express,* and he later created the *Sunday Express* and purchased the *Evening Standard.* He built the *Daily Express* into the largest newspaper in the world.

A longtime friend of Winston CHURCHILL, Beaverbrook entered Churchill's cabinet in 1940 as Minister of Aircraft Production, a specially created position. At the time, aircraft production lagged far behind schedule, and the needs imposed by the Battle of BRITAIN were urgent. Beaverbrook's biographer, A. J. P. Taylor, writes: "There can be no doubt that the production of aircraft greatly increased under his direction. Between January and April 1940 the production branch of the air ministry produced 2,729 aircraft of which 638 were fighters. Between May and August MAP [Beaverbrook's ministry] produced 4,576 aircraft, including 1,875 fighters, and repaired 1,872." In 1941 Beaverbrook was appointed Minister of State; in 1941–42 he was Minister of Supply; from 1943 to 1945, Lord Privy Seal. In 1942 he also served as a British lend-lease administrator in the United States. Earlier, in 1941, he had been head of the Anglo-American mission to Moscow, which made the agreement to supply large-scale aid to Russia, a strategy that Beaverbrook heartily favored. He also was a leading public advocate of an Allied second front in Europe. Beaverbrook was a mercurial, perhaps unpredictable figure, but a man of drive, determination and undoubted ability.

BEAVERBUGS (Beavereels, Beaverettes). Nicknames for armored cars assigned to the defense of some 250 British aircraft factories in 1940 (after Lord BEAVERBROOK, then Minister of Aircraft Production).

BECHER, Kurt (1909–). Nazi SS leader in Budapest (*see* SS) who represented Heinrich HIMMLER in making lucrative deals with Hungarian Jews able to pay for being allowed to escape the gas chamber.

BECK, Józef (1894–1944). Foreign Minister of Poland from 1932 until the outbreak of the war with Germany, Colonel Beck pursued a many-sided policy that gave him the reputation of being a devious and ambivalent power politician: a nonaggression policy with Germany after 1934, an opportunistic seizure of Czech territory during the crisis of 1938 and a continuing opposition to the Soviet Union. His frequent perceptiveness could not overcome the underlying weakness of Poland's position between two resurgent great powers or compensate for the necessity of relying for Polish safety on an increasingly irresolute French policy. Often quoted is Beck's remark that he decided to accept the British guarantee in 1939 between "two flicks of the ash" off his cigarette.

BECK, Ludwig (1880–1944). The last peacetime Chief of the German General Staff, Beck was the leader of the conspirators against Adolf HITLER and would have been the provisional regent if Hitler had been overthrown. A laconic man of iron character, but politically naïve, Beck pressed his Army superior and the Minister of War with written and oral argument against Hitler's foreign policy from 1935 to 1938. His attempts to galvanize senior German officers to resistance during the patently fraudulent von FRITSCH scandal met little success and were soon overridden by the international tension over Czechoslovakia. Respected by his peers as a man of balanced judgment, he resigned his office on August 27, 1938, in the hope of moving his brother officers and the country at large to a moral awareness, but his departure was kept secret for two months and its impact was lost in Hitler's peaceful conquest of the Czechs.

Usually associated in the conspiracy with the former mayor of Leipzig, Carl GOERDELER, Beck undertook to influence German military commanders during the war, writing finely argued and prophetic memoranda on the outcome of the conflict. Less active after a stomach cancer operation in 1943, and more given to intellectualizing than to action in any case, Beck nevertheless appeared at the BENDLERSTRASSE (Army headquarters) late in the afternoon of July 20, 1944, to issue determined orders and assurances to confused callers in the midst of the ill-fated coup against the Nazi regime. As the plot collapsed, General Friedrich FROMM, head of the German Replacement Army, regained control of the Bendlerstrasse offices and, in his hasty arrests of the military plotters in order to conceal his own dalliance with them, permitted Beck to keep his pistol. On his second attempt, Beck succeeded in ending his life; his reputation as the last true heir of the Scharnhorst tradition persists in German literature. *See also* OPPOSITION TO HITLER.

BEDA FOMM. Between Benghazi and Agedabia (Cyrenaica), Beda Fomm was the site of the decisive defeat of the Italian Tenth Army by the British, February 5–7, 1941.

BEDJA. This road center 60 miles west of Tunis figured prominently in the ebb-and-flow battles in TUNISIA in the winter of 1942–43. Elements of the British First Army occupied it in November 1942 in the Allied race for Tunis and were joined by elements of the U.S. 1st Armored Division. These forces advanced toward Tunis but the attack was forestalled, and some of the attackers withdrew to the Bedja area for refit (December 10–11). In February the British 5th Corps beat off German attacks toward Bedja, which were part of the offensive undertaken by General von ARNIM.

BEEHIVE. American name for a shaped demolition charge.

BELFAST, H.M.S. Royal Navy cruiser of 10,000 tons, completed in 1939 by Harland and Wolff. *Belfast* was armed with twelve 6-inch and twelve 4-inch guns, six 21-inch torpedo tubes and three aircraft. Badly damaged by a mine almost at the outbreak of the war, *Belfast* reentered active service late in 1942, serving in the Home Fleet on northern (Arctic) blockade patrols and convoys to Russia. On December 26, 1943, she participated in the Battle of NORTH CAPE, in which by the skillful use of radar the German battleship SCHARNHORST was caught by a superior force and destroyed. In 1944 she was included in the bombardment force covering the Normandy landings, and in 1945 she was sent to the Far East, arriving too late for any active service. *Belfast* participated in the Korean War, and is now preserved as a museum in the Pool of London.

BELFORT GAP. This historic débouché, the ancient Gate of Burgundy near the French-Swiss frontier, is a narrow passage about 15 miles wide between the Vosges Mountains to the north and the Jura Alps. Troops of the French First Army penetrated the gap in November 1944 but bogged down on the Alsatian plain before what became known as the COLMAR POCKET.

BELGIAN ARMY. At the time of the German attack on May 10, 1940, the Belgian Army consisted of about 600,000 men (although it was not fully mobilized), organized in 22 divisions. The Commander in Chief was King LEOPOLD III. *See also* FRANCE, BATTLE OF.

BELGIAN GATE. Underwater obstacle used by the Germans on the Normandy beaches. It was a steel barricade with supporters to resist impact and had three beams protruding upward with a mine fixed to each and barbed wire between. It was set in fairly deep water and was designed to be just below the surface at high tide, so that it could rip the bottoms of landing craft. *See also* ATLANTIC WALL; INVASION—NORMANDY.

BELGOROD. This city in southwest Russia, between KURSK and KHARKOV, was just inside the German lines at the end of the campaign of 1941. On February 9, 1943, it fell to Soviet forces, but it was retaken in a German counteroffensive on March 19. It was now on the flank of a Russian salient around Kursk. After the Germans lost the Battle of Kursk, Belgorod fell to advancing Russian troops on August 5, 1943.

BELGRADE. In March 1941 the Yugoslav Government under the Regent, Prince PAUL, agreed under German pressure to associate itself with the Axis, though it would not be required to participate in active war. But on March 27 a group of Army officers led by General SIMOVÍC staged a coup d'etat and after taking power repudiated the agreement with Germany. Hitler, who had counted on unresisted passage of his forces through Yugoslavia, was enraged at this defiance; with remarkable speed the Germans altered their plans for the invasion of Greece and on April 6 attacked Yugoslavia. The country was overrun in a week. Most striking, Belgrade was subjected to waves of bombing (Operation Punishment) that devastated the city, destroying government offices and killing 17,000 people.

On October 20, 1944, the occupying Germans were driven from Belgrade by the Soviet Third Ukrainian Front and Marshal TITO's Yugoslav Army.

BELL, George Kennedy Allen (1883–1958). British Anglican churchman, bishop of Chichester, who during the war years consistently refused to identify all German people with the National Socialist Party and condemned the indiscriminate Allied bombing of German churches. This criticism no doubt contributed to his failure to be selected as Archbishop of Canterbury in 1944. In 1942 Bishop Bell was used as a contact by German anti-Hitler conspirators who wished to get messages to the British Government. He was instrumental in reestablishing fellowship between the German church and other churches after the war and in the success of the first World Council of Churches meeting in 1948.

BELLINGER, Patrick (1885–1962). Rear Admiral Bellinger was U.S. Fleet Air Wing Commander at PEARL HARBOR on December 7, 1941. It was he who broadcast the message "Air raid, Pearl Harbor—This is no drill." He rose to be commander of the Air Atlantic Fleet (March 1943), in which post he successfully pursued antisubmarine warfare.

BELLOWS FIELD. One of three major U.S. Army Air Corps installations on the island of Oahu, Territory of Hawaii. The others were HICKAM and WHEELER Fields. Bellows was the least damaged of the three during the PEARL HARBOR attack. Three P-40s tried to take off from this base while the Japanese attack was in progress. One was destroyed before it could leave the ground, and the others were shot down.

BELLS. Code name for serially numbered broadcasts to U.S. Navy ships from Canberra. The coded transmissions carried information for all ships; each ship deciphered the message that applied to it. Broadcasts from Pearl Harbor, Washington and San Francisco were called "Fox."

BELOV, Pavel A. (1897–1962). Soviet officer who served in the Spanish Civil War, the occupation of Poland and the SOVIET-FINNISH WAR. When the Germans invaded Russia, Belov commanded the I Guards Cavalry Corps, which he led behind German lines for five months following the counteroffensive of December 1941. In June 1942 he took command of the Sixty-first Army, holding the post for the remainder of the war through such battles as KURSK and BERLIN. In 1944 he was promoted to colonel general. He was awarded the decoration HERO OF THE SOVIET UNION.

BELOW, Nikolaus von (1908–). For eight years HITLER's personal Luftwaffe adjutant, Colonel von Below was the last to leave the Führer's bunker as Berlin fell. He was present at Hitler's marriage to Eva Braun, witnessed Hitler's personal will and carried out of the bunker on April 29, 1945, a message to Field Marshal KEITEL in which Hitler praised his army, damned his generals and said the German aim must still be to get land in the east.

BELSEN. One of the CONCENTRATION CAMPS established by the Nazis after the war had begun, Belsen (also called Bergen-Belsen), on Lüneberg Heath, was intended to house some 8,000 prisoners, but following the hasty evacuation of the camps in Poland toward the end of the war, it was inundated with prisoners supposedly in transit. By March 1944 the number of inmates reached 42,000. A typhus epidemic was raging at the time the camp was liberated by the British in April 1945, when there were some 60,000 surviving prisoners there; some 500 were dying each day. The commandant, Josef KRAMER (the "Beast of Belsen"), had taken over only at the close of 1944, and was both unable and unwilling to do anything to relieve the situation. Trial of the Belsen staff by the British took place in a military court in Lüneberg in October 1945, and the camp is now preserved as a memorial by the Germans.

BENDLERSTRASSE. The term applied to the headquarters of the German War Ministry (Kriegsministerium), which stood on the Berlin street of the same name. As an administrative headquarters during World War II, the building housed various offices of the Army high command (*see* OKH).

BENEŠ, Eduard (1884–1948). President of CZECHOSLOVAKIA at the time of the MUNICH AGREEMENT, Beneš was one of the fathers of Czech independence. A disciple of Tomáš Masaryk, the first President of the Republic, Beneš was Foreign Minister from 1918 and President following Masaryk's death in 1935. In the latter year Beneš negotiated an alliance with the Soviet Union, and he became a prime target of the German Nazi press in its campaign against Czechoslovakia. After the disastrous proceedings at Munich, in which neither he nor any other Czech was allowed to participate, Beneš resigned as President. In 1939, however, he founded the Czech National Committee in France; in 1940, following the French collapse, the committee moved to London, where in 1941 it was recognized as the provisional government of Czechoslovakia. During the years in exile Beneš, as head of the government, was involved, in association with the British, in the direction of underground activities inside Czechoslovakia—the most famous instance being the assassination of Reinhard HEYDRICH, the Reich Protector. On May 16, 1945, Beneš returned to liberated Prague. He served as President until 1948, when he resigned following the taking of power by the Communists.

BENEVENTO. Italian city northeast of Naples, taken by the U.S. 34th Division on October 3, 1943. These troops then established a bridgehead across the Calore River.

BENGHAZI. The main port in the Jebel Akhdar region of CYRENAICA and an important center of Italian colonization. It had 65,000 inhabitants in 1941. British efforts to use its port facilities after its capture in February 1941 were thwarted by the LUFTWAFFE. On April 3, 1941, the British were driven out of Benghazi in General ROMMEL's first desert offensive. It remained in Axis hands until December 1941, when after the British advance a detachment of the Eighth Army entered it on the 24th. A month later, in the face of a new Axis offensive, the British withdrew again (January 28, 1942). It was held by the Axis until it was taken by the 10th Corps, British Eighth Army, on November 20, 1942, after the victory at ALAMEIN.

BENHAM, U.S.S. Destroyer and class (1,725 tons; four 5-inch guns; eight or sixteen 21-inch torpedo tubes; 38 to 40 knots). These single-stack ships, generally similar to the earlier GRIDLEY and later SIMS classes in appearance, carried their original torpedo battery in four quadruple mounts, two each to port and starboard. This was later modified to one mount apiece to either beam or to two centerline mounts. Topside structures were cut down during the war to allow automatic antiaircraft guns to be installed. Two of these 12 ships were war losses. Contemporary sources sometimes refer to this as the McCall class.

BENNETT, Donald Clifford Tyndall (1910–). RAF officer, an Australian, who initiated the idea of and commanded the Pathfinder Force. His highest rank was air vice-marshal. *See also* PATHFINDER BOMBING.

BENNETT, Henry Gordon (1887–1962). Australian Army officer, leader of the Australian forces (the 8th Division) in the disastrous Malayan campaign. In 1942 he led an escape of several British Imperial officers from SINGAPORE and reached Batavia. His conduct in that escape (he had violated orders) and in the Malaya battles was investigated by both military and civilian authorities. In 1946 he was charged with relinquishing his responsibilities as commanding officer in the escape. Although the military inquiry found his actions "not justified," a civilian review board concluded that he had acted in a spirit of patriotism and the belief that he was acting in the best interests of his country. The consensus is that the latter decision was a political one.

BENNETT (Bigej). Island in the south KWAJALEIN Atoll, invaded and secured by U.S. troops (7th Reconnaissance Troop, 3d Battalion, 184th Infantry) on February 5, 1944.

BENSON, U.S.S. Destroyer and class (2,030 tons; four 5-inch guns; five or ten 21-inch torpedo tubes; 36 knots), a development of the SIMS class, with a twin-stack silhouette. The first Bensons were built with five 5-inch guns; one of the after guns was soon removed to improve stability and make room for additional light antiaircraft guns. Two quintuple torpedo tube mounts were carried on the centerline. One tube mount was removed from many Bensons later in the war as antiaircraft armaments increased; some lost all their tubes in 1945. As a general rule, these ships were stationed in the Atlantic and the Mediterranean; early Bensons were involved in the Battle of the ATLANTIC before Pearl Harbor. Three ships of this class were war losses. Some sources refer to this as the Mayo class.

BERCHTESGADEN. A town in the Alps of southern Bavaria. It was the site of the fortified mountain chalet of Adolf HITLER and, for some time, of the headquarters of OKW and OKH (*see* OKW; OKH).

BERDICHEV. Ukrainian (USSR) city and rail junction, southwest of KIEV and south of ZHITOMIR, from which the Germans under General MANTEUFFEL launched a successful armored counterattack against advancing Soviet forces in November 1943. This attack recaptured Zhitomir on November 19 and helped prevent a possible German collapse on the entire southern front. On January 5, 1944, however, Berdichev was taken in the Soviet winter offensive led by General VATUTIN.

BERESFORD-PEIRSE, Sir Noel (1888–1953). General Beresford-Peirse commanded the 4th Indian Division in the first British desert offensive and the East African campaign, after which he served during Operation BATTLEAXE as the commander of the Western Desert Force. In October 1941 he went to the Sudan as GOC, and in 1942 he became GOC in Southern India.

BEREZINA RIVER. Belorussian (USSR) river in forested, swampy ground on the eastern side of the PRIPET MARSHES. This and other river systems in the area were of considerable strategic importance to both Germans and Russians, and the Soviet Navy's Dnieper Flotilla operated on the Berezina during the German advance of June 1944, denying bridges to the Germans and ferrying troops and equipment.

BEREZNIAK-ISAEV BI-1. One of three planes developed as part of the Soviet rocket target protector–interceptor program in 1941–42. All were powered by a single 1,100-pound-thrust Dushkin bifuel rocket motor designed to give a maximum flight time of 15 minutes. The BI-1 flew several times, the first powered flight being on May 15, 1942. It carried two 20-mm. cannon.

BERGEN. Important seaport, the second largest city in NORWAY, taken by the Germans on April 9, 1940.

BERGEN-BELSEN (concentration camp). *See* BELSEN.

BERGER, Gottlob (1896–1975). An early member of the German Nazi Party, chief of the SS head office (Führungsamt; *see* SS) from 1940 to the end of the war. Berger was also Heinrich HIMMLER's representative to Alfred ROSENBERG's East Ministry (in charge of occupied territories in the east), and in January 1944 he became head of the Prisoner of War Administration. He held the rank of Obergruppenführer and general in the WAFFEN SS; it was he who persuaded Himmler in 1940 that "properly Aryan" SS divisions should be recruited in the Netherlands, Norway and other occupied Western countries. Berger was named military commander in Slovakia in 1944. He paid a visit to Hitler's bunker in April 1945, when the Führer was making his decision to remain in Berlin, and has left a firsthand account of the occasion.

BERGHOF. Adolf HITLER's private mountain house (literally, "mountain court") on the OBERSALZBERG in southeastern Bavaria just south of Salzburg, Austria. Originally a small country house, called Haus Wachenfeld, it was enlarged by Hitler—and to his own design—in 1935, at which time it received the name Berghof. Because the old house was preserved within the new one and the two living rooms were connected, the ground plan, says Albert Speer, was "most impractical for the reception of official visitors." The most famous feature of the house was the enormous picture window, which looked out over the village of BERCHTESGADEN and Salzburg to the surrounding mountains.

BERGONZOLI, Annibale (1884–1973). Italian Army officer, known as "Electric Whiskers" (*Barba elettrica*), who was commander in Cyrenaica, NORTH AFRICA, when the British Desert Army won its "desert victory"—February 7, 1941. Bergonzoli became a prisoner of the British.

BERIA, Lavrenti Pavlovich (1899–1953). A Communist Party member from 1917, Beria rose through various party offices to become head of all Soviet security police forces. He began his police career in his native Georgia, transferring to Moscow in 1938 and becoming chief of the NKVD in the same year (*see* NKVD). After the outbreak of the war, Beria was appointed to the Soviet STATE DEFENSE COMMITTEE. He received marshal's rank in 1945. He retained ultimate control of all Soviet secret police work during and after the war and was the first police commissar to achieve full membership in the Politburo. The enemy of many, Beria did not long outlive Stalin; he was apparently murdered in still unclear circumstances in 1953.

BERIEV KOR-1 and KOR-2. The only floatplanes, aside from some standard land planes fitted with floats, to be used by the Soviet Navy in World War II. Built in limited numbers, the KOR-1 and KOR-2 were meant for shipboard service and use at coastal bases. The KOR-1 was introduced in 1935. The KOR-2, slightly larger overall and a little more powerful than the KOR-1, was introduced in 1940.

BERIEV MBR-2. Soviet flying boat introduced in 1932. The MBR-2*bis* model came later. Over 1,500 MBR-2s were built until production was stopped in 1941. The Soviets used them as reconnaissance planes, convoy escorts, bombers and transports. The aircraft had one 860-horsepower engine and flew at a maximum speed of 155 miles per hour. It was armed with two 7.62-mm. machine guns and could carry 661 pounds of bombs.

BERKEY, Russell Stanley (1893–). "Count" Berkey graduated from the U.S. Naval Academy in 1916 and by 1943 had risen to the rank of rear admiral. With experience in gunnery dating back to the 1920s, Berkey commanded a U.S. Navy support group of cruisers and destroyers during landing operations in the NEW GUINEA and MARIANAS campaigns, the battle for LEYTE GULF and subsequent PHILIPPINES action. His ships also provided offshore cover for minesweepers and contributed to the sinking of the Japanese battleship YAMASHIRO. In 1950 he retired with the rank of vice-admiral.

BERLIN, AIR BATTLE FOR. Berlin as the capital of Germany, the national metropolis (population 4,332,000 in 1939) and a major industrial city was a primary Allied bombing target. While cities had been bombed in the First World War (especially London), in the interwar years (Guernica, Spain, and NANKING, China) and in tactical operations in the opening phases of the Second World War (WARSAW and ROTTERDAM), both the British and the Germans were reluctant to begin strategic bombing against each other. Even the decisive Battle of BRITAIN began in 1940 without the bombing of cities. But when 10 German aircraft bombed London by accident on the night of August 24, 1940, the British retaliated with an 80-bomber raid on Berlin the next evening. Only 29 were able to drop their bombs because of cloud cover down to 2,000 feet. Five aircraft were lost on the raid; three of them ditched at sea and their crews were rescued. Further British attacks provoked German raids on London beginning on September 6, 1940.

After sporadic attacks against the German capital, the RAF launched a major bombing campaign against Berlin between November 1943 and March 1944. Berlin was a difficult target as it was a very large city, deep within Germany, necessitating a 1,150-mile round trip, and strongly defended. During the 16 major attacks in this period British BOMBER COMMAND suffered a jarring defeat with over 5 percent losses—1,077 bombers lost and 1,682 damaged on 20,224 sorties. On March 4, 1944, the first American attack on Berlin was delivered by 29 bombers of the EIGHTH AIR FORCE. The next U.S. assault on Berlin, two days later, was the costliest U.S. bomber mission of the European war, with the loss of 69 bombers of the 658 that attacked. In April the Americans again suffered heavy losses in two attacks on the city (April 11 and 29), each costing 64 bombers.

Berlin continued to be a major target. In one of the most destructive aerial attacks of the war, 1,000 virtually unopposed American bombers hit Berlin on February 3, 1945, and killed about 25,000 civilians. When the last bomb fell on Berlin on April 21, 1945, about 50,000 German civilians had been killed by bombing in the city, compared with a total of 52,000 British civilians killed by bombing. British Bomber Command alone dropped almost 51,000 tons of bombs on Berlin in 363 attacks, or about 11 percent of the tonnage dropped on industrial towns. Even before the ground war rolled across the German capital, bombing had destroyed 6,340 acres.

BERLIN, BATTLE FOR. The battle for Berlin was the closing act of the war in Europe, in truth the last battle. The Soviets planned a continuous and rapid advance on the German capital over a period of 45 days. Stalin decided to give Marshal Georgi K. ZHUKOV the honor of taking the city, and in November 1944 shifted him to the First Belorussian Front to replace Marshal K. K. ROKOSSOVSKY.

In January 1945 the Russians held a line along the border of East Prussia, down the Narew River, to Warsaw and then roughly along the Vistula River. By this time they had clear military superiority, with (according to the *Soviet Encyclopaedia*) 6 million Soviet troops and over 91,000 tanks against 3.1 million Germans and 28,500 tanks. In addition, the Russians had an overall advantage in quality of equipment and fitness of officers and men, as the Germans were increasingly relying on the VOLKSSTURM, the militia of old men and young boys.

The Soviet offensive began with a tremendous bombardment on January 12, 1945, one week ahead of schedule in response to the urgings of the Western Allies stunned by the surprise German thrust in the ARDENNES of December 1944 (although the issue in the Battle of the BULGE had by then been settled). Within four days the Russians ripped a hole 180 miles wide and 25 to 80 miles deep in the German front and sent their tanks almost unopposed behind the Germans. It appeared that nothing could stop the Soviets from dashing across Poland into Germany, and nothing in fact did. On January 26 the Russians crossed the 1939 German-Polish border and on February 1 Zhukov's men established a bridgehead at Küstrin, 40 miles from Berlin. Early in February the Red Army stood on the east bank of the Oder, with bridgeheads at Küstrin and Frankfurt. At this point the attack stalled along the line of the Oder and Neisse Rivers, because of stiffening German resistance aided by the contraction of Germany and the shifting of troops to the Eastern Front, a February thaw and Russian supply problems.

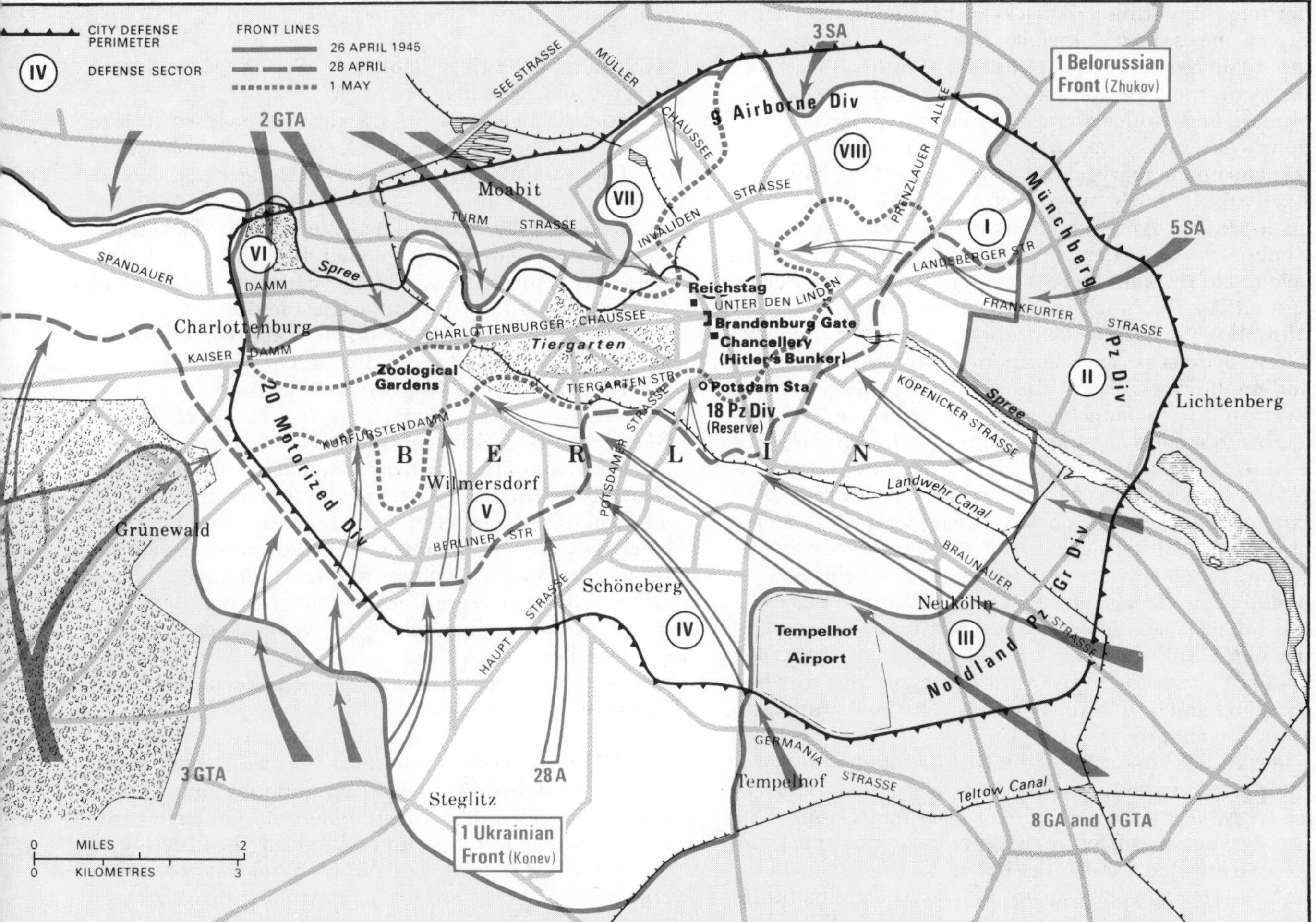

BERLIN: The battle for the German capital was a grim and destructive struggle

In the meantime U.S. troops reached the Elbe River, 60 miles from Berlin, where they stopped. Already they were 90 miles inside the zone assigned to the Soviets for postwar occupation. At this point Stalin, possibly fearing that the Western Allies would beat him to Berlin, changed the rules of the game, giving Marshal I. S. KONEV a chance to take the grand prize. It was clear that the Thousand Year Reich was in its last days. Adolf HITLER continued to live in his dream world in his underground bunker, issuing orders to phantom armies, hoping for a split among the Allies and for miracles from German SECRET WEAPONS.

The Russians consider the battle for Berlin to have begun on April 16, when they renewed their offensive after a two-and-a-half-month lull. The Soviets massed 2.5 million men (as well as 41,600 guns and mortars, 6,250 tanks and 7,500 aircraft) in three massive army groups: the First Belorussian Front under Zhukov, the First Ukrainian Front under Konev and the Second Belorussian Front under Rokossovsky. Against these formidable forces the Germans could muster only 1 million men, 10,400 guns and mortars, 1,530 tanks and a little over 3,300 aircraft (statistics from the *Soviet Encyclopaedia*).

The Soviet plan called for Zhukov's First Belorussian Front to attack out of the Küstrin bridgehead directly at Berlin, with additional attacks north and south of the city. Konev's First Ukrainian Front was to attack in three directions—toward Berlin, toward American forces on the Elbe and into Czechoslovakia. Essentially, Zhukov and Konev were to conduct a pincers operation; Rokossovsky was to operate in the north. A great bombardment marked the start of the first battle on April 16. Zhukov's troops met with stiff resistance and made slow progress, in contrast to the easier going of Konev's troops. After bitter fighting the Russians were able to cut through the German lines, bypassing Berlin, and on April 24 the First Belorussian Front linked up with the First Ukrainian Front, cutting off the city. These actions isolated 200,000 troops within the city and another 200,000 in a pocket west of Berlin. While German forces launched futile counterattacks in attempts to restore communications with Berlin, on April 25 U.S. and Soviet troops (elements of the 69th U.S. Infantry Division and the 58th Soviet Guards Rifle Division) met at TORGAU on the Elbe. By April 21 fierce house-to-house fighting in the suburbs of Berlin had begun, as Zhukov's and Konev's men fought for the honor of capturing the city. On April 30 the Reichstag was stormed by soldiers of the 171st Rifle Division and the 150th Rifle Division; it was the day that Hitler took his life. The battle raged until 3 P.M. on May 2, when the commander of Berlin defenses, Gen. Helmuth WEIDLING, surrendered.

Berlin was captured by the Russians and with it (for the period April 16 to May 8, according to the *Soviet Encyclopaedia*) a total of 480,000 German troops. The Russians admit suffering 304,000 casualties and claim to have inflicted 1 million casualties on the Germans.

A number of controversies persist over the battle for Berlin. Zhukov's broad-push strategy against Berlin has been challenged by Marshal Vassili I. CHUIKOV, who favored a concentrated attack on the capital. Another much-criticized decision was that of the Western Allies to halt at the Elbe. But U.S. Gen. Omar BRADLEY told General EISENHOWER at the time that to take Berlin might cost 100,000 casualties. "A pretty stiff price to pay for a prestige objective," Bradley said, "especially when we've got to fall back and let the other fellow take over."

BERNADOTTE, Count Folke (1895–1948). During the war Count Bernadotte served as vice-chairman of the Swedish Red Cross. He aided in the exchange of disabled German and British prisoners of war in 1943. Two years later he persuaded the Germans to transfer Danish and Norwegian political prisoners from several German camps to one camp under Swedish YMCA supervision. This work brought Bernadotte into contact with the Nazi Gestapo chief, Heinrich HIMMLER, who in April 1945 tried to arrange for the Germans to surrender to Great Britain and the United States while continuing to fight the Russians in the east. Bernadotte carried Himmler's message to Churchill and Roosevelt. These two leaders jointly turned down Himmler's proposal and called instead for an unconditional German surrender, which Himmler subsequently rejected. Bernadotte recounted his experiences in these negotiations in *The Curtain Falls* (1945). In 1948 Bernadotte served as United Nations mediator on Palestine and was assassinated by a Jewish extremist group on September 17 of that year.

BERNEY-FICKLIN, Horatio Pettus Mackintosh (1892–1961). Commander of the British 15th Infantry Brigade, Brigadier Berney-Ficklin was ordered to lead his unit in Operation Hammer, the 1940 British assault on TRONDHEIM. Maj. Gen. F. E. Hotblack, the commander of the expedition, was briefed on April 17 but suffered a stroke the same day, and Berney-Ficklin was promoted to acting major general and put in charge. While en route to SCAPA FLOW, Berney-Ficklin's plane crashed. He suffered a broken jaw and other injuries. Maj. Gen. Bernard PAGET was next appointed as commander, but before he could land, Operation Hammer was canceled. *See also* NORWAY.

BERNHARD, Prince of the Netherlands (1911–). The German-born Bernhard had been married to Princess Juliana for three years at the time of the German invasion of the Netherlands in 1940. Bernhard and Juliana escaped to London, where Bernhard earned his wings in the RAF. As a rear admiral in the Dutch Navy and a lieutenant general in the Dutch Army, Bernhard served as the commander of the Netherlands Forces of the Interior, and in 1944 he worked to fuse Dutch resistance groups into a unified force prior to the Allied liberation of his homeland.

BERNHARD. Code name for a German operation designed to disrupt the British economy by putting into circulation more than £100 million in counterfeit currency. The counterfeit notes survived the scrutiny of the Bank of England, but the plan did not achieve its objective.

BERNHARD LINE. German line of defense positions in ITALY, stretching across the peninsula from the mouth of the Garigliano River to the Adriatic. It was part of what the Allies generally called the Winter Line, the winter being that of 1943–44. In front of the Bernhard Line was the Barbara Line, which was an improvised line running from the Tyrrhenian coast to the Apennines. There were some 45,000 mines forward of the Bernhard Line and another 30,000 on its immediate approaches. The Bernhard itself was a formidable chain of defenses in depth, running from the coast up to the Sangro River, and behind it was the GUSTAV LINE, a still stronger belt of defensive positions.

BERN INCIDENT. The phrase "Bern incident" appears in a message which President ROOSEVELT sent to

Marshal Stalin concerning Operation Sunrise, the negotiations for German surrender in Italy. The British and Americans had informed the Soviets about Sunrise (also called Crossword by Winston Churchill) in mid-March. Stalin had reacted by claiming that the United States and Britain were trying to negotiate a separate peace with the Germans. In response, Roosevelt reported to Stalin on April 12, 1945, that the negotiations had apparently failed to accomplish anything. At the time Roosevelt sent this message, he was correct in his assessment of the situation; yet the talks continued throughout the month of April and they ultimately succeeded.

The first peace feeler in the Italian theater came to Allen W. Dulles, the head of the Office of Strategic Services mission in Bern, Switzerland, from a high-ranking German Catholic dignitary in November 1944. This discussion of surrender proved fruitless, but the next peace feeler, on February 25, 1945, was not. On that date a Swiss professor, Max Husmann, and an Italian businessman, Luigi Parilli, approached Capt. Max Waibel, a friend of Dulles's and a Swiss Army intelligence officer, about acting as an intermediary with the Allies in arranging German surrender in Italy in order to save northern Italy from the proposed scorched-earth policy of the retreating Germans. Waibel, in turn, introduced the negotiators to Gero Gaevernitz, a German-born, naturalized American citizen who worked with Dulles.

Encouraged by these initial talks, the intermediaries met again in Lugano, Switzerland, on March 3. In addition to Parilli, Husmann and Waibel, two SS officers and Paul Blum from Dulles's office were present. Blum was impressed by the negotiators' concern for protecting northern Italy, but he told the SS officers that some evidence of German earnestness concerning surrender was needed. He suggested that they release two Italian partisan leaders, Ferruccio Parri and Antonio Usmiani, whom the SS had caught, as a sign of their seriousness about ending the war. Less than five days later Parri and Usmiani were freed in Switzerland.

The release of the two partisans signaled the involvement of a senior SS general, Karl Wolff, in the secret negotiations. The day that Parri and Usmiani were released (March 8), Wolff, who was Heinrich Himmler's personal representative in Italy and commander of all SS forces there, and his aides and the mediators traveled to Zurich, where they met with Dulles for the first time. At this meeting Wolff assured Dulles that he was serious about saving lives and preventing the needless destruction of Italy.

Dulles had initially been skeptical that an SS general would voluntarily seek to arrange a surrender. He also knew that Wolff would have to persuade the Wehrmacht generals in Italy to cooperate, which would not be an easy task. Yet Dulles feared that if he did not manage to work out a surrender, there would be stubborn Nazi resistance in northern Italy, especially if the Germans fell back to a proposed National Redoubt for a last stand against the Allies.

Convinced of Wolff's sincerity, Dulles notified Allied headquarters of the negotiations. Field Marshal Sir Harold Alexander then sent Maj. Gen. Lyman L. Lemnitzer and British Maj. Gen. Terence S. Airey to Switzerland for a meeting with Wolff, at which they told the SS general that the Allies offered him only unconditional surrender. Wolff then returned to Italy to persuade the German commander, Field Marshal Albert Kesselring, to go along. Wolff succeeded in getting Kesselring's acquiescence, but Adolf Hitler suddenly transferred Kesselring to the Western Front and sent Gen. Heinrich von Vietinghoff to replace him in Italy. Vietinghoff was less inclined to surrender unconditionally.

In the meantime Berlin had learned that Wolff might be negotiating with the Allies. On April 2 Himmler warned Wolff against doing so, and he twice called Wolff to Berlin to explain himself. Wolff's uncertain position and the suspicions aroused in Berlin unsettled the Allies; thus headquarters ordered Dulles on April 20 to break off the talks.

In spite of Berlin's orders, Wolff and Vietinghoff decided on April 23 to continue their negotiations, and two days later Wolff informed Dulles he was ready to surrender. On April 27 the Combined Chiefs of Staff told Dulles to arrange for a German surrender at Allied headquarters in Caserta, Italy. The following day two Nazi envoys, Major Wenner, Wolff's personal adjutant, and Lt. Col. von Schweinitz, representing Vietinghoff, flew to Caserta from Switzerland. After considerable discussion of the unconditional surrender terms, the two envoys signed the surrender document with Lt. Gen. W. D. Morgan, chief of staff to Alexander, at 2 P.M. on April 29. Allowing three days for surrender orders to be passed down the German chain of command, the unconditional surrender took place at 2 P.M. local time on May 2, 1945.

BERZARIN, Nikolai E. (1904–1945). Red Army officer who commanded the Twenty-seventh Army in 1941, the Thirty-fourth Army in 1941–42, the Twentieth Army in 1943, the Thirty-ninth Army in 1943–44 and the Fifth Shock Army for the remainder of the war. He saw action in the defense of Leningrad and the battle for Berlin. Berzarin was a general and holder of the highest Russian decoration, Hero of the Soviet Union. He was killed shortly after he became the first Soviet commandant of Berlin; according to Russian sources, the cause of death was an automobile accident.

BESS. Allied code name for what was believed to be a Japanese-built version of the German Heinkel He 111 medium bomber. (*see* HE 111). During the early months of the Pacific war, it was believed that Japan was manufacturing or importing many types of German warplanes since the Japanese were said to be incapable of designing battleworthy airplanes of their own. This odd opinion was widely held at the time.

BESSON, Antoine (1876–1969). In the spring of 1940 General Besson's French Third Army Group formed a front on the Somme River following the German invasion. Despite heroic efforts, Besson was unable to reach Allied forces trapped in the Dunkirk pocket or to repel the overwhelming German forces.

BESSON MB-411. French two-place, low-wing, single-engine, submarine-borne observation floatplane. Designed and built specifically for the submarine Surcouf, the plane was housed in a cylinder aft of the conning tower. Assembly time was four minutes from the time the plane was removed from the hangar. It was raised and lowered by crane. Two MB-411s were built.

BETHE, Hans Albrecht (1906–). As chief of the theoretical physics division at Los ALAMOS from 1943 to 1946, Bethe was a key scientist in the MANHATTAN DISTRICT. He left Germany in 1933 because his mother was Jewish. He went first to England and then, in 1935, to the United States, where he continued his research in astrophysics. In 1939 he demonstrated the role of carbon in the process by which the sun turns hydrogen atoms into sunshine, and in 1940 he confirmed the theory that the forces that hold the nucleus of the atom together are transmitted by an elementary particle called the meson. Bethe became a U.S. citizen in 1941 and joined the Massachusetts Institute of Technology Radiation Laboratory in 1942. At Los Alamos, Bethe's division worked out the critical size of the fissionable mass of the ATOMIC BOMB.

BÉTHOUART, Emile (1889–). French general, a graduate of Saint-Cyr in 1909 with Alphonse JUIN and Charles DE GAULLE. Béthouart headed the French Expeditionary Corps to Norway in 1940 and directed Allied operations around NAMSOS and NARVIK. After the defeat of France, he remained in the Army and served as a divisional commander in Morocco. In November 1942, Béthouart, favoring the Allies, unsuccessfully opposed French resistance to the Allied landings in NORTHWEST AFRICA. Later he became de Gaulle's Chief of Staff for National Defense. Following the INVASION of Normandy, he took command of the French First Army Corps in northern Europe and, under the direction of DE LATTRE DE TASSIGNY, pushed his forces through the BELFORT-MULHOUSE-Rhineland area, reaching the Danube River on May 6, 1945. Shortly thereafter Béthouart became commander in chief of the French occupation forces in Austria.

BETIO. Island at the southwest tip of TARAWA Atoll in the GILBERT ISLANDS, invaded by a landing force of the U.S. 2d Marine Division on November 21, 1943, as the beginning of the Tarawa operation. Organized Japanese resistance ended on Betio on November 23.

BETTY. Allied code name for the Japanese Navy Mitsubishi G4M land-based medium bomber (*see* G4M).

BEURLING, George (1922–). A Canadian pilot in the RAF who was much decorated for his exploits in MALTA (1942), when within 14 days he shot down 27 German and Italian planes and damaged eight more planes. He was dubbed "Screwball" and became quite a celebrity among the Spitfire pilots as a result of his excellent marksmanship. In October 1942, Beurling was shot down but bailed out safely into the Mediterranean with only a heel wound.

BEVERIDGE, William Henry, 1st Baron (1879–1963). British economist who served as chairman of the London School of Economics and Political Science from 1919 to 1937. In 1940 he was named adviser on manpower to the Ministry of Labour, and in 1941 he was appointed chairman of the Interdepartmental Committee on Social Insurance and Allied Services with the goal of suggesting reforms. In 1942 the committee produced the famous "Beveridge Report," a document outlining a new social security system. It included recommendations for unemployment insurance, free medical and hospital treatment, child benefits, old age pensions and marriage and death grants. It was a blueprint for the welfare state. The plan was seen as too radical by Conservative members of Parliament but applauded by Labourites. In 1944 Beveridge was elected to the House of Commons as a Liberal, but he was defeated when he ran again in the national elections in the summer of 1945.

BEVIN, Ernest (1881–1951). A British Labour politician, Minister of Labour and National Service in Winston CHURCHILL'S wartime coalition government, Bevin was responsible for the mobilization of British manpower. He presented the extended Emergency Powers Bill to Parliament nine days after taking office in 1940. The bill gave the government absolute power over all industry and labor, and put 33 million men and women directly under Bevin's authority. In 1941 he introduced conscription for women. By a series of "essential work orders" that affected key industries, he made it illegal for workers to leave their jobs and for employers to dismiss workers without the agreement of specially appointed National Service officers. In this way he eventually reduced the time lost by industrial stoppages to something less than one hour per worker per year. Surprisingly, he rarely needed to use these emergency powers to compel obedience, but managed to secure voluntary cooperation from both trade unions and employers. He drew up the plan of postwar demobilization that was followed in 1945. In that year, after the Labour victory in the election, Bevin was appointed Foreign Secretary by the new Prime Minister, Clement ATTLEE. He then replaced Anthony EDEN at the Big Three Conference at POTSDAM.

As Minister of Labour and National Service, Bevin sought to establish a new framework of cooperation in industry and permanently raise the status of industrial and agricultural workers. It was a natural part for him to play. He had been born the son of a landless farm laborer and at 18 had become a drayman. Between the world wars he had built up, out of a number of smaller unions, his gigantic Transport and General Workers' Union, thus becoming the most powerful labor leader in the country. His presence in the wartime government was of vital importance, and he made of his office a ministerial post of the highest rank, though it had not previously been a major ministry.

BIAK. One of the Schouten Islands, lying across the entrance to Geelvink Bay in northwestern Dutch New Guinea (now West Irian). The Japanese occupied Biak in April 1942 but paid little attention to the island until late 1943. Then they decided to convert Biak into a major air base, which would be within fighter aircraft range of many of their other bases in western New Guinea. Apparently, the island was also to have become a major ground stronghold as well, and in December 1943 the Japanese sent to the island the veteran (of China) 222d Infantry of the 36th Division. However, in early May 1944 the Japanese moved their strategic main line of resistance westward, leaving Biak Island as part of a strategic outpost line of resistance that was to be held as long as possible.

Total Japanese strength on Biak, when American forces landed on May 27, 1944, was about 11,400, mainly concentrated in excellent defensive terrain dominating the area in south-central Biak where the Japanese had expended their main airfield construction effort. The combat nucleus of the garrison was the reinforced 222d Infantry, with about 3,400 troops.

Allied landings were made by the 41st Infantry Division, less the 163d RCT, most of which arrived on May 31. Opposition proved stronger than expected and progress slower than suited Lt. Gen. Walter KRUEGER, commanding the U.S. Sixth Army. Krueger thereupon sent Lt. Gen. Robert L. EICHELBERGER, the commander of the U.S. I Corps, to Biak to take over command of the Hurricane Task Force, the main part of which was Maj. Gen. Horace H. Fuller's 41st Division. Fuller was relieved as task force and division commander, and Brig. Gen. Jens A. Doe took over the division command.

The changes in command did little to speed operations on Biak. For one thing, the Japanese had organized a reinforcement program for Biak—the so-called KON OPERATION. The effort brought about 1,200 more Japanese infantrymen to Biak, not enough to affect the ultimate outcome, but sufficient to fill in defensive holes. General Eichelberger had to call for reinforcements himself, and the 34th RCT of the 24th Infantry Division arrived on June 18. Even so, it was July 22, 1944, before the last significant organized resistance on Biak had ended, and General Krueger did not "formally" end the operation until August 20. By this time FIFTH AIR FORCE planes had been using Biak fields for nearly two months, and construction for a major logistical base was well along. The operation cost the Hurricane Task Force about 400 men killed and 2,000 wounded; estimated Japanese casualties were 6,125 dead and 460 captured.

BIALYSTOK SALIENT. Area around the Soviet city of Bialystok, in which by early July 1941 the Red Army had lost some 300,000 men and 2,500 tanks.

BIBER. German one-man midget submarine, resembling a full-size submarine in appearance and carrying two torpedoes in external racks, one on either side of the lower hull. Over 300 were built.

BIDAULT, Georges (1899–1975). A graduate in history from the Sorbonne, Bidault emerged in the 1930s as a leader of the French Catholic Left. In 1940 he was captured and imprisoned by the Germans. On his release in 1941 he worked with the National Council of Resistance, of which he became head in 1943. In 1944 he founded the Mouvement Républicain Populaire, a left-wing Christian democratic party, and in that same year narrowly escaped capture by the Gestapo.

He became General DE GAULLE's Foreign Minister and in December 1944 signed the Franco-Soviet Alliance. After the war he served as Premier and in other cabinet posts. He was strongly internationalist in his views and worked for cooperation with Russia and for the success of the United Nations. He urged Communist participation in the Marshall Plan. The Communist takeover of Czechoslovakia in 1948 disillusioned him, however, and thereafter he advocated strong Western defensive policies and played an important role in the establishment of NATO.

BIDDLE, Anthony J. Drexel (1874–1948). Descendant of two of the oldest Philadelphia families, Biddle, a U.S. Marine colonel, was an internationally renowned swordsman for over 50 years and was recognized as a master of jujitsu, bayonet and knife fighting as well as of savate and defendu (a form of hand-to-hand fighting developed by the Shanghai Municipal Police in the 1920s and 1930s). He served with the Marine Corps in both world wars and as a reserve officer was often assigned to active duty in the interwar period to teach marines the forms of fighting in which he was expert. Following the attack on Pearl Harbor he was recalled to active duty at his own request at the age of 67. He taught bayonet and other forms of hand-to-hand fighting to officer trainees and other marines.

BIERUT, Boleslaw (1892–1957). Polish Communist leader who became president of the National Council of Poland in 1943 and president of the Soviet-sponsored LUBLIN COMMITTEE (the basis of the provisional government) in December 1944.

BIG APPLE. Nickname given by American soldiers to the Yaeju-dake, a formidable escarpment on OKINAWA on which the Japanese resisted attack for a week (June 1945).

BIG FOUR. The United States, the United Kingdom, the Soviet Union and China, viewed as the four great powers (as in the establishment of the UNITED NATIONS ORGANIZATION).

BIGOT. Security classification accorded the most secret planning papers for the Allied Normandy invasion, including those revealing the target area and the planned date of the assault. Distribution was limited to a small group of officers and men, who were said to be "bigoted." *See also* INVASION—NORMANDY.

BIG THREE. President Franklin D. ROOSEVELT, Prime Minister Winston S. CHURCHILL and Marshal Joseph STALIN.

BIG WEEK. A series of raids by U.S. EIGHTH and FIFTEENTH AIR FORCE B-17s and B-24s against the German aircraft industry. It began on February 20, 1944, with Eighth Air Force strikes from England against airframe manufacturing and assembly plants at Leipzig, Bernburg and Brunswick. Other targets hit through February 25 included Gotha, Regensburg, Schweinfurt, Rostock, Halberstadt, Augsburg, Stuttgart and Steyr.

In just six days Eighth Air Force bombers made some 3,300 sorties and the Italian-based Fifteenth more than 500. Almost 10,000 tons of bombs fell on the selected targets, and American intelligence believed that this weight of high explosives had seriously disrupted fighter production. The estimates proved overly optimistic, however. At Regensburg, for example, the Messerschmitt factories were bombed on the 22d and 25th

The Big Three—from left, Stalin, Roosevelt, Churchill—at the Teheran Conference, 1943

by planes from both Italy and Britain. Although production dropped from 435 planes in January 1944 to 135 in March, recovery was surprisingly rapid. Within four months the complex was operating at capacity, and this resiliency was typical of Germany's aircraft industry.

Lost during the Big Week were some 6 percent of the bombers that took part, a lesser rate than American planners had anticipated. The difference was the result of effective fighter escort, which inflicted severe losses on the Luftwaffe squadrons dispatched to intercept the bomber formations. Indeed, these aerial battles may have done more than the bombing itself to weaken the German fighter arm.

The RAF BOMBER COMMAND contributed to the success of the Big Week with night attacks against Leipzig, Stuttgart, Schweinfurt, Steyr and Augsburg. Some 2,350 planes dropped more than 9,000 tons of bombs, suffering losses of 6.6 percent.

BIKINI. An atoll with about 20 islets lying about 190 miles east of ENIWETOK and 170 miles northwest of KWAJALEIN. It was defended by five Japanese soldiers, who committed suicide on March 28, 1944, when U.S. Marines landed in one phase of Operation Flintlock Jr. *See also* MARSHALL ISLANDS.

BILLOTTE, Gaston (1875–1940). French general, who served almost continuously in the French colonies from 1894 to 1933, when he became Inspector General of Colonial Troops and a member of the Army Council (CONSEIL SUPERIEUR DE LA GUERRE). He had made his mark as a divisional commander in World War I and upon the outbreak of war in 1939 took command of the First Army Group, holding the area north of the MAGINOT LINE. By May 10, 1940, Billotte's forces included the French First, Second, Seventh and Ninth Armies and the British Expeditionary Corps. In accordance with predetermined plans, these units marched into Belgium to meet the German attack. But, as his northernmost armies wheeled into Belgium, his southern army, the Ninth, received the brunt of the German thrust through the ARDENNES and quickly collapsed. In the ensuing days General Billotte slowly moved his forces back toward the French coast, but was unable to counter the German breakthrough on his right flank. His untimely death in an automobile accident on May 23 brought further confusion to the Allied command.

BILLOTTE, Pierre (1906–). Son of Gen. Gaston BILLOTTE, the younger officer served with the French 3d Armored Division in 1940 and was taken prisoner during the Battle of FRANCE. Later he escaped and became

General DE GAULLE's chief of staff in London and Algiers.

BIRCH, John (1918–1945). As a young Baptist missionary in China, John Birch helped lead Lt. Col. James H. DOOLITTLE and his crew to safety after they parachuted following the 1942 raid on Tokyo. Birch next encountered Brig. Gen. Claire CHENNAULT, who decided to make use of the younger man's fluency in several Chinese dialects. Commissioned a second lieutenant, Birch served as an interpreter and intelligence officer but sometimes doubled as an air-to-ground liaison officer, calling down air strikes in close support of Chinese troops. He also set up a network of Chinese operatives, who had guided some 50 downed American fliers to safety by the time hostilities ended.

In May 1945, Birch, now a captain, was transferred to the OFFICE OF STRATEGIC SERVICES and began establishing an intelligence apparatus in northern China. After the Japanese had agreed to surrender, Birch headed a small detachment that was attempting to arrange for the passage of Japanese occupation troops to the coast. During this mission the detachment was stopped by Chinese Communists, who shot Birch to death on August 25, 1945.

In 1954 a retired American candy manufacturer, Robert H. W. Welch, Jr., published a biographical sketch of John Birch, whose name was used for the archconservative, anti-Communist society that Welch had founded.

BIR HACHEIM. The southernmost fortified "box" in the GAZALA LINE (Cyrenaica), defended by the FREE FRENCH under Gen. Marie Pierre KOENIG. Half his brigade was lost, in one of the most gallant actions fought by the French in World War II, before evacuation on June 10, 1942.

BIRSE, Arthur Herbert (1889–). Born in Russia of a British family, Major Birse was the chief British interpreter for all major Anglo-Soviet conferences during World War II. He had served as a linguist in World War I and volunteered his services again in 1940. As an interpreter, he worked closely with Churchill and Stalin at the Moscow, TEHERAN, YALTA, and POTSDAM Conferences. In 1967 he published an account of his experiences, *Memoirs of an Interpreter.*

BIRYUZOV, S. S. (1904–1964). Soviet Army officer who in 1942 commanded the Forty-eighth Army and then served as chief of staff of the Second Guards Army at the Battle of STALINGRAD. In 1944 Biryuzov, as a colonel general, led the Thirty-seventh Army into Rumania, Bulgaria and Yugoslavia. After Joseph STALIN's death he rose rapidly to become Chief of the General Staff of the Soviet Army.

BISCAY CROSS. German submariners' nickname for the first crude antenna, usually homemade, for the METOX radar detector. Its name came from its crosslike appearance and its use in the Bay of Biscay, heavily patrolled by Allied planes.

BISLEY. The Bristol Bisley, named for the British competitive shooting range at which trophy matches are annually conducted, was a two-seat, twin-engine ground-support airplane developed for the Royal Air Force as the manufacturer's Type 160 (AD 657). A variant of the BLENHEIM V medium bomber, it had twin radial engines that powered it at 260 miles per hour. Forty-four feet long, with a 56-foot 4-inch wingspan, the Bisley had four fixed forward-firing .303-caliber machine guns in its nose, with two more in a dorsal turret. The name Bisley was eventually dropped, and the aircraft were simply referred to as Blenheims. Blenheim V models were produced during 1942–43, but their performance was considered poor and many were lost in action.

BISMARCK. German battleship completed in 1941, one of the largest and fastest capital ships in the war. Protected by heavy armor, having a main battery of eight 15-inch guns and powered by diesel engines, the 42,000-ton *Bismarck* had a top speed of 30 knots. On May 18, 1941, she sailed from Gdynia with the heavy cruiser PRINZ EUGEN, under the command of Vice-Adm. Günther LÜTJENS, to raid British shipping in the Atlantic. On May 21 British reconnaissance located the two German warships in Bergen Fjord on the west coast of Norway. At this time 11 British convoys, including a troop convoy, were at sea. The British Home Fleet, under Adm. Sir John TOVEY, consisting of the new battleships PRINCE OF WALES and KING GEORGE V and the battle cruiser HOOD, was reinforced by other battleships and aircraft carriers from the Atlantic and the Mediterranean.

On May 22 a reconnaissance plane reported that Bergen Fjord was empty. Admiral Tovey anticipated that the Germans would come through the Denmark Strait and positioned his warships accordingly. The admiral's surmise proved correct and, in the late afternoon of the 23d, the Germans were sighted by the heavy cruisers NORFOLK and SUFFOLK. Early the next morning *Bismarck* and *Prinz Eugen* were engaged by *Hood* and *Prince of Wales* under Vice-Adm. Lancelot HOLLAND. Although the British force was nominally superior, with two capital ships and two cruisers to only one capital ship and one cruiser for the Germans, this superiority was more apparent than real. The British cruisers, which had been shadowing the *Bismarck,* were not at first in a position to engage, and *Hood* and *Prince of Wales* approached *Bismarck* at an angle which masked their main batteries. *Prince of Wales* was brand-new, one of her big guns was defective and she was yet not at full fighting efficiency, while *Hood* was 20 years old with very poor armor protection.

The defects in *Hood*'s protection became apparent soon after the battle opened. At 25,000 yards *Bismarck* scored a hit on *Hood* which started a fire in one of her ammunition lockers, and a few minutes later the huge battle cruiser blew up in a fiery explosion. Only three of her crew of some 1,400 officers and men survived. *Prince of Wales* now found herself engaged by both German warships. The British battleship scored two hits on *Bismarck,* one of which pierced an oil tank, causing an underwater leak, but at the same time she received more than half a dozen hits from the big guns of *Bismarck* and *Prinz Eugen.* Under these circumstances *Prince of Wales* broke off the action and retired. *Bismarck,* her speed reduced by the battle damage, turned south for German-occupied France, shadowed by *Norfolk* and *Suffolk.*

Toward evening *Bismarck* briefly turned and opened fire on her pursuers in order to cover the escape of *Prinz Eugen* into the South Atlantic. Admiral Tovey's forces had meanwhile been reinforced by the aircraft carrier VICTORIOUS and, late on the same evening, nine torpedo bombers from the carrier found *Bismarck* and scored a hit—which, however, failed to slow her down. This failure was doubly unfortunate, for early the next morning *Norfolk* and *Suffolk* suddenly lost radar contact with *Bismarck.* Her location remained unknown until Sunday evening (the 25th), when she was sighted in the Bay of Biscay by the U.S. Coast Guard cutter *Modoc,* which was ostensibly on weather-reporting duties. In response to *Modoc*'s signal, a long-range PBY Catalina, lent to the Royal Navy by the U.S. Navy and piloted by Ens. Leonard Smith, USN, flew to the area and, at 8:30 Monday morning, sighted *Bismarck* and radioed her position, after which the patrol plane escaped under fire. The part played by the Americans was not made public for more than 30 years. Later on the 26th the carrier ARK ROYAL, a part of FORCE H which had been ordered north from Gibraltar and was now squarely in *Bismarck*'s path, launched her torpedo planes against the German battleship. *Ark Royal*'s pilots scored two hits, one of which wrecked *Bismarck*'s steering gear and jammed her rudders. She was now unmaneuverable and steaming in the wrong direction.

At 8 A.M. the next day Admiral Tovey with *King George V* and the battleship RODNEY engaged *Bismarck,* which fought back stubbornly against the overwhelming odds. By 10:15 she was a flaming wreck with all her guns out of action. At 10:30 three torpedoes from the cruiser DORSETSHIRE, which had accompanied Admiral Tovey, finally sent the German ship to the bottom.

BISMARCK ARCHIPELAGO. Islands northeast of Papua (New Guinea), the largest being New Britain with the important base of RABAUL. Taken by the Japanese in early 1942, the Bismarcks lay astride an important axis of Allied advance and were often referred to as the "Bismarcks barrier." *See also* JAPANESE CONQUESTS; PACIFIC WAR.

BISMARCK SEA, BATTLE OF THE. This sea north of New Guinea was the site in March 1943 of repeated Allied air attacks against a 16-ship Japanese convoy bound from RABAUL, New Britain, to LAE on New Guinea's northeast coast. The ships set sail in the early morning darkness of March 1, but B-24 patrol planes spotted them later in the day. On the morning of March 2, B-17 Flying Fortresses attacked the convoy from low altitude, sinking one transport and damaging two others. A pair of destroyers rescued some 850 soldiers from the transport that went down, carried them to Lae and steamed back to rejoin the surviving vessels off the Huon Peninsula. The two arrived in time for a devastating succession of attacks by Allied planes.

Australian Beauforts struck first, delivering an unsuccessful torpedo attack. Australian Beaufighters then joined American B-17s and B-25s in bombing and strafing the convoy, and as the morning ended, A-20s and additional B-25s arrived on the scene. Damaged by bombs, the destroyer *Arashio* went out of control, rammed and sank the special service vessel *Nojima,* which had also taken hits, then went under itself. Two other destroyers and six transports received mortal damage.

The attacking planes returned that afternoon and sank another destroyer, the fourth to perish in the battle. The five surviving destroyers, aided by cruising submarines, rescued as many as they could of the troops and crewmen who had survived the day's sinkings. In all, perhaps 6,000 men lived through the battle, but fewer than a thousand reached Lae. The others were returned to Rabaul or landed at KAVIENG, New Ireland. Killed in this engagement were some 3,000 Japanese; the Allied dead numbered fewer than 20.

Several factors contributed to the victory. Allied fighters controlled the skies over the Bismarck Sea, and intelligence was able to predict the composition and time of departure of the convoy. Also, the Allies employed novel tactics. On the advice of Maj. Paul GUNN and Jack Fox of North American Aviation, they crammed the noses of their A-20s and B-25s with machine guns, then used the planes to bomb and strafe from altitudes as low as 150 feet. These aircraft might skip their bombs into the sides of the enemy vessels, as a child would skip a flat rock off the surface of a pond, or they might drop the delayed-action bombs directly onto the decks. Even the heavy bombers came in low, attacking from 6,500 feet or even lower. Most important, the Allies took advantage of sound intelligence to rehearse their tactics, employing Australian and American planes of different types in simultaneous attacks from various altitudes against beached hulks.

BISSELL, Clayton Lawrence (1896–1972). U.S. officer who graduated from Valparaiso University in 1917, joined the Air Service and downed five German aircraft. He began World War II as Gen. Joseph STILWELL's aviation officer in China. In 1942 he became commander of the TENTH AIR FORCE in the China-Burma-India Theater. A major general, Bissell returned to the United States in 1943 to become chief of air intelligence and in 1945 was appointed head of Army intelligence. After the war Bissell served as air attaché in London (1946–48), before retiring in 1950.

BIZERTE. Port, railhead and seaplane station, with primary airfield nearby, used by the Axis as a major supply center during the Tunisian campaign. Bizerte was taken by the U.S. II Corps and some French troops on May 7, 1943.

BLACK DAY (Wewak). The Japanese gave this name to August 17, 1943, when U.S. aircraft operating from PORT MORESBY bombed and strafed Japanese airfields around WEWAK (New Guinea), destroying the bulk of Japanese air power in the area.

BLACKETT, P(atrick) M. S. (1897–1974). British physicist who in 1935 was appointed to a special committee on air defense (the TIZARD Committee). He pushed the concept of operations research and was personally active in antiaircraft, naval and antisubmarine affairs. Blackett's 1941 memo, "Scientists at the Operational Level," had considerable impact and served to encourage operations research in the United States. In 1948

Blackett was awarded the Nobel Prize for Physics for his work on cosmic radiation. That same year his book, *Fear, War and the Bomb* (the American title), appeared and caused a stir because it criticized American atomic policy.

BLACK ORCHESTRA (Schwarze Kapelle). Name given in intelligence circles to the German anti-Hitler plotters. *See also* OPPOSITION TO HITLER.

BLACKOUT. The total darkening of a city or other area by extinguishing all outdoor lights and using blackout curtains on windows and other openings in buildings. Some buildings, where blackout traffic was heavy, had "light locks"—double-door arrangements allowing persons to enter and leave without letting inside light show. Blackouts were a regular way of life in theaters of war; practice blackouts were held in the United States and air-raid alarms installed. In the first years of the war, blackouts were effective against night bombers, unless a target was located near a recognizable body of water or other navigational feature that could be used as a reference point. Such techniques as the use of PATHFINDER planes, with special navigational and radar equipment, helped bombers counter blackouts. In the final months of the war, radars enabled planes to navigate their way to blacked-out targets with a high degree of accuracy.

BLACK SHIRTS. The armed, uniformed FASCIST followers of Italian dictator Benito MUSSOLINI. He used these paramilitary forces to battle with Communists and workers in his fight to win political power in Italy. Once in power, Mussolini granted the Black Shirts official status as the Militia of Volunteers.

BLACK THURSDAY. Name sometimes given to the day of the costly U.S. Eighth Air Force raid on SCHWEINFURT, Germany—October 14, 1943.

BLAKESLEE, Donald (1918–). An American, Blakeslee joined the Royal Canadian Air Force shortly after the outbreak of war. In May 1941 he went to England, being assigned to the 401st (Ram) Squadron, where he was outstanding in a number of aerial fights. He then joined the 133d EAGLE SQUADRON in Kent, a squadron of American volunteers, which together with other outfits went into American service as the 4th Fighter Group; Blakeslee later became its commander. He was one of the most famous of World War II aces, and in his work with the 4th Fighter Group he was personally credited with shooting down 15 enemy aircraft.

BLAMEY, Sir Thomas Albert (1884–1951). Australian Army officer, assigned to command the Australian army corps raised for service in the Middle East. He commanded the corps during the latter part of the first Libyan campaign and the Anzac Corps during the brief campaign in Greece in 1941. He was then appointed Deputy Commander in Chief Middle East, a post with more title than substance, but retained his command of the Australian troops in that theater. After Japan entered the war in December 1941, Blamey was recalled to Australia and appointed Commander in Chief of the Australian Army. The Australian war effort had been concentrated on supporting operations overseas, and the forces in Australia were ill equipped, ill trained and badly organized. Blamey was faced with the task of expanding the Army and bringing it to a state of readiness. With the rank of lieutenant general, he was also commander of the Allied land forces under Gen. Douglas MACARTHUR in the Southwest Pacific, and under orders from MacArthur, Blamey took personal command of the Allied land force in NEW GUINEA in September 1942. After the recapture of BUNA in 1943 he returned to his Australian Army headquarters on the mainland. From 1943 onward he played a less prominent part in the war against Japan, as the fighting shifted northward and the number of Australian troops was gradually reduced. He was contentious by nature and always a controversial figure.

BLANCHARD, Georges (1877–1954). Commander in chief of the French First Army, operating in northeastern France and central Belgium during the Battle of FRANCE in 1940. On May 25 he replaced Gen. Gaston BILLOTTE as First Army Group commander and supervised the withdrawal of his former command, the BELGIAN ARMY and the BRITISH EXPEDITIONARY FORCE toward Dunkirk. Blanchard had no more success than his predecessor in countering the German armored breakthrough to the south, and on June 1 he embarked for England.

BLANDY, William Henry Purnell (1890–1954). Rear Adm. "Spike" Blandy led his class at the U.S. Naval Academy in 1913. Between wars he acquired valuable experience in gunnery. As head of the U.S. Navy's Bureau of Ordnance early in World War II he contributed to important developments in antiaircraft weapons. In the amphibious warfare in the Pacific, he served in NEW GUINEA and the MARIANAS, at LEYTE GULF and during the battles for Iwo JIMA and OKINAWA. Following the war he became an atomic expert, heading the joint Army-Navy task force responsible for conducting the first peacetime atomic bomb tests on Bikini Atoll in the Marshall Islands.

BLASKOWITZ, Johannes von (1883–1948). A German Army infantry officer in World War I, Blaskowitz participated in the occupation of Czechoslovakia in 1939 and served as military governor of Bohemia until civil government was established. He commanded the Eighth Army in the Polish campaign and on October 1, 1939, was promoted to the rank of colonel general (Generaloberst). In late October he became Commander in Chief East (Oberbefehlshaber Ost), remaining in the position for seven months. He commanded the Ninth Army for a short period during the invasion of France and later, for an equally short period, served as military governor of northern France. From October 1940 to May 1944 he commanded the First Army in France. He was the commanding general of Army Group G from May to September 1944, when he was replaced by a younger officer. While in the command, Blaskowitz skillfully directed the withdrawal of German forces pushed back by Allied troops invading SOUTHERN FRANCE. Blaskowitz was recalled to Army Group G on December 24, 1944. He worked on the German defense in the south for a month and then was transferred to

Army Group H in the Netherlands; in April the command was redesignated and he became Commander in Chief Netherlands. After the surrender Blaskowitz told his troops to destroy their minefields. He was taken prisoner on May 8. He committed suicide in the Nuremberg prison.

BLENHEIM. Military version of Britain's Bristol 142 high-speed transport; it flew for the first time in June 1936. When it reached operational units the following year, it was the fastest medium-range bomber in the RAF, with a maximum speed of 260 miles per hour, and could outrun the Gloster GLADIATOR biplane fighter. The Blenheim was an all-metal twin-engine monoplane with one fixed forward-firing .303-caliber machine gun and a second of these weapons in a dorsal turret. The crew numbered three, and the engines were 840-horsepower Bristol Mercury radials.

Airborne radar was installed in the Blenheim IF night fighter, which saw combat over Britain in 1940 and 1941. Four additional .303-caliber guns were mounted in a tub beneath the fuselage. The bobbed-nose Blenheim I began giving way in 1939 to Blenheim IV, with an extended bombardier's nose beneath which the designers had installed a compact, rearward-firing, single-gun turret. A second gun was added to the dorsal turret.

Blenheims took part in the first two British missions of the war. In September 1939 they flew a photo-reconnaissance mission over Kiel and the following day dropped bombs on the German fleet. They were used as fighters and bombers in France and Norway and for close support missions in North Africa and the Middle East.

BLIMP. Nonrigid lighter-than-air craft used by the U.S. Navy for antisubmarine patrol, where its endurance and ability to "loiter" at slow speeds or hover at a standstill made it valuable. The principal patrol blimp was the K-14 type (K-14 through K-135); these were 251-plus feet long, with a diameter of 62 feet and an overall height of 79 feet. A "K-ship" had a gas volume of 425,000 cubic feet of helium, with a useful lifting capacity of 11,000 pounds. A K-ship carried a crew of nine or more; it was armed with a single flexible-mount .50-caliber machine gun and up to 1,200 pounds of depth charges. Two Pratt & Whitney Wasp radial engines gave it a top speed of 75 miles per hour and a patrol range of 2,000 miles. Other airships were used for training duty. Twenty-two of a new M-1 type blimp were ordered, but only four were delivered since the antisubmarine situation had improved to the extent that production capabilities could be shifted elsewhere. U.S. Navy blimp activity expanded greatly after Pearl Harbor; operating from bases in the United States and overseas, blimps patrolled coastal waters and convoy lanes and had a share in making U-boat activity increasingly difficult. One blimp—K-74—was shot down by a submarine's antiaircraft guns.

BLIND BOMBING. The technique of bombing through clouds, fog or darkness guided by airborne radar. Earlier methods of night bombing had depended on some kind of visual guidance using moonlight or artificial light.

BLITZ, THE. The terror and devastation that characterized the German blitzkrieg (blitz for short) made the name appropriate for the night air raids carried out by the LUFTWAFFE against British cities from September 1940 to May 1941. The Blitz developed after the Luftwaffe had failed in its daylight attacks to destroy the RAF fighter force.

On four nights in late August 1940 Luftflotte 3 delivered heavy attacks with only 1 percent losses against LIVERPOOL and Birkenhead. The opening of the air offensive against LONDON on September 7, 1940, marked a change in policy for the Luftwaffe. The bulk of its effort went into night raids. About 5,300 tons of high explosives were dropped on London and its suburbs on 24 nights in September. A lavish array of beacons, beam transmitters and other aids to target finding made night flying possible in weather which greatly hampered the defenses. When it became apparent that Britain could not be bludgeoned into swift surrender, the Luftwaffe decided to extend air attacks at night to the chief industrial centers throughout the country and to the main ports. The memorable raid on COVENTRY on November 14, 1940, opened a new phase of the Blitz. Some 500 German bombers dropped 500 tons of heavy explosives and nearly 900 incendiary canisters in 10 hours of attack. Great hardship and injury to life and property resulted from this, and from most attacks on industrial areas, but no irreparable damage was done to the war effort. The main offensive of the Luftwaffe ended in May 1941, as German bombers were moved to the Russian front. *See also* BABY BLITZ.

BLITZKRIEG (Lightning War). Originally a theory of military operations advanced by Gen. Hans von Seeckt when he commanded the small German Reichswehr in the 1920s. Its basic premise was that armored force operating afield pretty much on its own could ensure victory in war swiftly and cheaply. Seeckt did not himself completely believe this, because he foresaw that ascendancy of armor would inevitably bring about mass armies. When the armies of Hitler's Germany swiftly overran Poland, France and the Low Countries, these operations were popularly known as "blitzkriegs." But the term was a misnomer.

BLOCH, Claude Charles (1878–1967). An 1899 graduate of the U.S. Naval Academy and veteran of the Spanish-American War, Admiral Bloch, who had served as commander of the U.S. Fleet, was in early 1941 commandant of the Fourteenth Naval District, responsible for the naval defense of PEARL HARBOR. Before the U.S. entry into World War II, Bloch gained a reputation as a preparedness advocate, although in March 1941 he advised against the installation of baffles at Pearl Harbor to guard against aerial torpedoes recently proven capable of operation in shoal water. In late 1942 he officially retired from active duty, but he served in the United States throughout the war.

BLOCH 131. A French twin-engine, four-place, medium bomber/reconnaissance aircraft. Although production began in 1938, the plane was obsolescent by 1940 and had largely been withdrawn as a first-line aircraft. Powered by two 800-horsepower air-cooled engines, it had a maximum speed of 248 miles per hour at 13,000 feet.

BLOCH 162. A five-place, four-engine, low-winged, long-range heavy bomber similar in profile to the U.S. Flying Fortress (*see* B-17). Though it was France's most modern bomber, only one prototype was built. It fell into German hands and was used by the Luftwaffe.

BLOCH 174. A handsome three-place French light bomber/reconnaissance aircraft, of which fewer than 70 found operational use. A high-performance (329 miles per hour) and maneuverable aircraft, it was of great value in combat.

BLOCH 175. Bomber version of the 174; few were built.

BLOCH 210. France's first low-wing medium bomber with retractable landing gear. In operation since 1934, it was obsolete when the war began. Six squadrons used them briefly for night raids before the planes were relegated to a training role.

BLOCH MB-152. French single-seat interceptor-fighter developed from the mediocre MB-151 fighter and first flown on August 18, 1938. This plane went into production in early 1939. Fewer than 150 saw action; the performance was barely adequate. After the fall of France, many of the MB-152s went into VICHY service. A secret attempt at fitting them with internal auxiliary fuel tanks to increase their range was foiled by the Germans. The pilots hoped to fly the planes to North Africa if the Germans occupied Vichy. Further developments of the type, the MB-155 and MB-157, took place too late to reach normal production before the armistice. Powered by a Gnome radial 14-cylinder air-cooled engine of either 1,080 or 1,100 horsepower, this plane flew at a maximum speed of 320 miles per hour and had a range of 373 miles. It carried four 7.7-mm. machine guns. Wingspan was 13 feet 7 inches; length, 29 feet 10¼ inches; height, 12 feet 11⅞ inches. Fully loaded it weighed 5,908 pounds.

BLOCH MB-700. Single-seat fighter of all-wood, stressed-skin construction. It was developed to lessen France's dependence on critical metals in case of war. Only one was built. It was first flown on April 19, 1940. It had only 12 hours in the air when captured and burned by advancing German troops. Its 700-horsepower radial engine drove it at 342 miles per hour maximum speed. With four machine guns it weighed 3,858 pounds, and with two machine guns and two cannon it weighed 4,078 pounds.

BLOCKBUSTER. Nickname given various demolition bombs, among them the U.S. Army Air Forces' largest general-purpose bomb. Made with a light metal casing, it weighed 4,000 pounds, of which 3,986 were high explosives. The first bombs considered blockbusters were dropped by the RAF in 1941. Some blockbusters weighed as much as 11 tons.

BLOHM UND VOSS BV 40. A German single-seat glider-interceptor. This craft was made of nonstrategic materials by relatively unskilled labor. It was towed to attack height by a fighter and then released for a head-on gliding attack against bombers, falling to earth after the attack. Seven were built before the program was abandoned in late 1944 in favor of jet- and rocket-powered aircraft and missiles. It was armed with two 30-mm. cannon.

BLOHM UND VOSS BV 138. A German trimotor, long-range maritime reconnaissance flying boat. It had an abbreviated central hull with twin booms supporting the tail assembly. First flown on July 15, 1937, the BV 138 became operational in 1940; it was a very successful aircraft. A total of 279 were built. All versions could carry two 1,100-pound thrust rockets; 70 were modified for catapult operations. The BV 138C-1 had three 880-horsepower, 12-cylinder, vertically opposed diesel engines and flew at a maximum speed of 177 miles per hour. It carried two 20-mm. cannon and a 13-mm. machine gun in an open bay aft of the central engine and another on the starboard side. It also carried three 110-pound bombs or four depth charges.

BLOHM UND VOSS BV 155. A German single-seat, high-altitude interceptor powered by one 1,610-horsepower V-12 engine. Its top speed was 429 miles per hour at 52,480 feet. Only a few prototypes were built; they did not enter production.

BLOHM UND VOSS BV 222. A flying boat designed for Lufthansa's North and South Atlantic routes. Also known as the Wiking (Viking), it was the largest seaplane produced during the war. It was capable of carrying 92 troops or 72 litter cases. The BV 222C had six 1,000-horsepower diesel engines and carried five machine guns and one cannon. It flew at a maximum speed of 242 miles per hour and had a 3,790-mile range at 152 miles per hour. Its normal loaded weight was 67,572 pounds; maximum loaded weight was 108,030 pounds. It carried a 10- or 12-man crew and was 121 feet 4⅔ inches long and had a wingspan of 150 feet 11 inches.

BLOHM UND VOSS BV 238. A large, long-range patrol bomber, reconnaissance and transport flying boat projected as a replacement for the BV 138. It was the largest aircraft ever built in Germany. Only one prototype was completed and tested (1943); it was later destroyed by strafing. A land-based variant, the BV 250, was never completed. The BV 238V-1 had six Daimler-Benz 1,750-horsepower engines and flew 264 miles per hour with a weight of 154,234 pounds at 19,000 feet. It had a crew of 10; its range loaded was 2,395 miles.

BLOHM UND VOSS HA 139. A twin-engine, long-range, four-seat transport twin floatplane. Three were built for Lufthansa in 1937. At the beginning of the war the Luftwaffe commandeered the three 139s and modified them for reconnaissance and minesweeping. In the Norwegian campaign two of them were used for transporting troops and freight. No other examples were ordered.

BLONDI. Adolf HITLER's dog, an Alsatian (German shepherd) bitch. The dog, says Albert SPEER, "meant more to his master than the Führer's closest associates."

BLOODY RIDGE (Edson's Ridge), BATTLE OF. Just about 1,000 yards south of HENDERSON FIELD on GUADALCANAL, and about 100 yards north of the U.S. 1st Marine Division command post's location on September 12–14, 1942, is a ridge that has been called both Bloody Ridge—because of the ferocity of the fighting during that period—and Edson's Ridge, in honor of Col. Merritt A. EDSON, who commanded the composite group of marine raiders and paramarines who defended it.

This position was attacked initially by 3,450 Japanese assault troops belonging to the Kawaguchi Brigade, commanded by Maj. Gen. Kiyotake KAWAGUCHI, whose objective in an all-out drive on the 1st Marine Division perimeter was Henderson Field. Kawaguchi first attacked on the night of September 12 without success and was driven back. At dawn on the 13th the marines counterattacked but were unable to budge the Japanese. Despite four major bombing attacks on the ridge during the day by enemy planes, Edson's men strengthened and resupplied their positions, waiting for attacks which began, as expected, after dark. Two more came after the first, at 2130 and 2200. As the marines pulled back, preplanned artillery concentrations rained down on the attackers, disrupting their charges. All through the night Kawaguchi attacked, and while some Japanese got into the marine foxholes, each attack was thrown back. By dawn of the 14th the major Japanese effort was spent, but considerable sniping continued until the pockets were cleaned out by the marines. In all, the Japanese lost 600 men in the attacks, and another 1,500 were killed or died of wounds as they retreated back into the jungle.

BLÜCHER. Code name for the attack by the German Army Group South from the Crimea across the Kerch Straits toward the Caucasus, in the 1942 summer offensive.

BLÜCHER. German Navy cruiser, claimed to be 10,000 tons but in actual fact over 13,000, completed at Kiel late in 1939, with an armament of eight 8-inch and twelve 4.1-inch guns, smaller weapons, twelve 21-inch torpedo tubes and three aircraft. *Blücher,* potentially a very valuable unit, was sunk on her first operation, in the Dröbak Narrows of Oslofjord in April 1940.

BLUE (Blau). Code name for the German offensive in the Soviet Union in 1942. The main effort was to be made in southern Russia. In the north, Leningrad was to be taken to establish connection with the Finns. This code name was also used for the planned withdrawal of Army Group North to the Panther position in the fall and winter of 1943–44.

BLUE DIVISION. Unit of Spanish volunteers which served in the German Army on the Eastern Front from late 1941 to April 1944. The division was officially constituted on June 28, 1941, and during most of its existence maintained a fighting strength of about 20,000 men. Five air squadrons were also attached to it. Although the division officially ceased to exist on April 25, 1944, as a result of Allied pressure on the Spanish Government, a clandestine "Blue Legion" continued to serve until January 1945. During the full term of the Blue Division's existence, a total of 47,000 men served in it. It suffered 12,726 casualties, 4,260 of them killed and 8,466 wounded.

BLUIE WEST 1. Code name for an American airfield at Narsarssuak, Greenland, at the head of Tunugdliarfik Fjord, an essential link in the wartime North Atlantic air route. Work started at Bluie West 1 in September 1941. The field was located on the southern shore of Greenland (for which the United States had assumed responsibility from the government of Denmark) and lay midway between Goose Bay, Labrador, and Reykjavik, Iceland, another Danish possession under American protection. The main runway at Bluie West 1, 5,000 feet of steel matting, entered service in June 1942. The United States built two other airfields in Greenland: Bluie West 8, begun late in September 1941 on the west coast above the Arctic Circle, and Bluie East 2, finished in September 1942 at Angmagssalik on the east coast. To handle the tremendous increase in air traffic that occurred after Pearl Harbor, the United States built Patterson and Meeks Fields in Iceland near Keflavik to supplement the British-built airports at Reykjavik and Kaldadarnes.

Weather data for the North Atlantic air route came from a network of weather stations ashore and at sea. Land stations were located at Gander Lake, in Labrador, in the Baffin Bay area and at the Greenland and Iceland airfields.

BLUM, Léon (1872–1950). Blum, a Jewish Socialist, led the leftist Popular Front Government in France in 1936–37. His prolabor policies were blamed unjustly for reducing French arms production and thus leading to defeat in 1940. He was arrested by the VICHY government, then turned over to the Germans in 1943, finally being liberated in 1945. In 1946 he served as President of the Provisional Government.

BLUMENTRITT, Günther (1893–1967). German Army staff officer, operations chief for Field Marshal von RUNDSTEDT in the Polish and French campaigns and chief of staff of the Fourth Army under Field Marshal von KLUGE in Russia. Next he was chief of the operations department of the General Staff, serving in this post until September 1942, when he was posted as Rundstedt's chief of staff in OB West (*see* OB). Blumentritt assumed command of the XII SS Corps with the rank of general of infantry in September 1944 and moved to command of the Twenty-fifth Army in January 1945. In March he took command of the First Parachute Army. In the waning days of the war he was to command Army Blumentritt, a headquarters designed to control troops on the Weser line from Hameln to the Baltic coast, but by the time the headquarters was established the line had been penetrated. Blumentritt's highest rank was General der Infanterie.

BOCK, Fedor von (1880–1945). A third-generation Prussian officer, Bock served on the General Staff in World War I, then commanded a regiment of infantry with distinction. At the end of the war, as a personal friend of Wilhelm II, he tried to persuade the Kaiser to return to Berlin but was overruled by Hindenburg and Ludendorff.

Bock became a full general in 1935, and in 1938 he commanded the German marches into Austria and Czechoslovakia. Described by a contemporary as a "gaunt, bony, hard-bitten man," he was called "der Sterber" (the one who preaches death) because of his well-known lectures on a soldier's death. Adolf HITLER once said, "Nobody in the world but von Bock can teach soldiers to die."

Bock led Army Group North in the Polish campaign and Army Group B in France in 1940. He was promoted to field marshal in 1940 and in 1941 was sent to Russia to command Army Group Center. When the German advance began to slow down, Bock favored a push for Moscow rather than the broad-front strategy. At the end of November he still thought Moscow was attainable, but after the December 1 attack failed he reported he could no longer operate with his weakened troops. His own health failed, and on December 18, suffering from severe stomach pains, he was relieved of command.

It was at Bock's headquarters during 1941 that the Army conspiracy against Hitler took shape. Because of his monarchist tendencies and his friendship with Wilhelm II's son, some thought Bock could be brought into the opposition group. Although professing to loathe Nazism, Bock nevertheless refused to allow Hitler to be criticized. His critics assert that he was anxious not to jeopardize his role as conqueror of Moscow. In any event, the conspirators did not succeed in winning Bock's cooperation.

In early 1942, after Field Marshal von RUNDSTEDT was dismissed and Field Marshal von REICHENAU died, Bock was given command of Army Group South, which was to capture STALINGRAD and the Caucasus. He held command until July 13, when Hitler removed him. The circumstances are not completely clear, but apparently Bock wanted to wipe out the Russian forces at VORONEZH before continuing his advance, while Hitler wanted a direct push on Stalingrad.

BOCK'S CAR. Named for its usual pilot, Capt. Frederick C. Bock, this B-29 was flown by Maj. Charles W. Sweeney to drop an atomic bomb on NAGASAKI, Japan, August 9, 1945.

BODENSCHATZ, Karl (1890–). A Bavarian, Bodenschatz served in the German Flying Corps in World War I; he was adjutant to the famous Manfred von Richthofen and later to Hermann GÖRING. This connection with Göring resulted in Bodenschatz's becoming personal assistant and adjutant to Göring in 1933 at the Reich Air Ministry; in 1937 Bodenschatz became chief of staff of the ministry. In this capacity he played a highly important role in dealings with air attachés and other Western officers. He appears to have been at pains to convince them of Adolf HITLER's grand design and also of the might of the Luftwaffe. During the war General Bodenschatz acted as Göring's liaison officer at Hitler's headquarters, and he was injured in the July 20, 1944, assassination attempt on Hitler, being hospitalized almost until the end of the war.

BODO LINE. In the Red Army, a direct telephone line between the Kremlin and field headquarters.

BODYGUARD. Overall code name for Allied deception plans to mislead the Germans on the timing and location of D-Day (INVASION of the Continent), drawn from a remark by Winston CHURCHILL to Joseph STALIN at TEHERAN: "In war-time, truth is so precious that she should always be attended by a bodyguard of lies." The code name earlier had been Jael, after the treacherous woman of that name in the Song of Deborah in the Old Testament.

Within Jael–Bodyguard were seven major deception operations, all with the basic goal of impelling the Germans to disperse their forces thinly around the entire periphery of Europe. The first, Overthrow, and the second, Cockade, were designed to convince the Germans the Allies would invade France in 1942 and in 1943, respectively. The other five were intimately associated with the actual invasion: two pointed to an invasion of southern France; one to the Bay of Biscay; one (Zeppelin) to the Balkans (so realistic was Zeppelin that Stalin at the time and many a Western historian afterward thought Churchill genuinely wanted to invade the Balkans rather than France); and a fifth both to Norway and to the Pas de Calais.

Known as Fortitude, the last was the operation on which the success or failure of the invasion essentially rested, particularly that element of it pointing to the Pas de Calais. To convince the Germans the invasion would come there instead of in Normandy, the Allies used dummy installations, weapons, equipment and shipping; false wireless traffic; false information leaked in foreign capitals; turned German agents; and indications that the commander of the invasion would be the prominent American commander George S. PATTON, Jr. Since Patton was not to participate in early stages of the real invasion, the Germans were expected to believe that even after landings began in Normandy, the main invasion was still to come in the Pas de Calais.

When D-Day came, most German commanders did believe in the myth of an invasion in the Pas de Calais. That and bad weather helped the Allies to achieve surprise, but within a few hours the Germans captured American field orders that, from the size of the forces involved, indicated that Normandy was the main invasion. With that information Adolf HITLER released major reserves from the Pas de Calais to counterattack in Normandy. When wireless intercepts obtained through ULTRA informed the Allies of that decision, they passed word through a turned German agent whom Hitler trusted that the captured field orders constituted a deception designed to pull German reserves from the Pas de Calais and the forthcoming main invasion. Hitler promptly rescinded his order, and the Allies were able to build up forces in Normandy sufficient to deal with the German reserves before Hitler finally realized that no second invasion was coming.

BOFORS GUN. A Swedish 40-mm. air-cooled antiaircraft gun with a cyclic rate of fire of 140 rounds per minute and a 4.3-mile range, used by the United States and Britain. The U.S. Army adopted the Bofors as the 40-mm. automatic antiaircraft gun M-1 in April 1941 with the statement that it was to replace the 37-mm.

antiaircraft gun as soon as quantity manufacture was attained; that moment was not reached until October 1943. All ammunition was fixed round, either armor-piercing with tracer or high-explosive shell. Point-detonating fuzes were used rather than percussion fuzes, since the former are easier to manufacture. "Cartwheel" sights were added; the diameter of the forward ring was increased to cover targets moving 400 miles per hour at 1,000 yards. The U.S. Navy also used the gun, but in a water-cooled version, while the British used both models.

BOGAN, Gerald Francis (1894–). Rear Adm. "Jerry" Bogan served as a U.S. Navy task group commander in the Pacific and distinguished himself in carrier support operations. His name is associated with American victories in NEW GUINEA, the MARIANAS and the PHILIPPINES and the final victories over Japan. Bogan served under Adm. William F. HALSEY and as a task group commander in Vice-Adm. Marc A. MITSCHER's famous fast carrier force. He retired in 1950 with the rank of vice-admiral.

BOGDANOV, Semyon I. (1894–1960). Soviet general, commander of a tank division, then of a tank and mechanized corps, before receiving command of the Second Tank Army in September 1943 during the KURSK offensive. His command was prominent in the forcing of the Bug River in June 1944. It was honored by being redesignated the Second Guards Tank Army in January 1945 and took part in the battle for BERLIN. Bogdanov was promoted to the rank of Marshal of the Armored Forces in 1945.

BOGEY. Allied voice-radio term for an unidentified aircraft.

BOGUE, U.S.S. Escort aircraft carrier and class. Converted from merchant hulls, 10 of these ships commissioned in 1942–43; 492 feet long, with a standard displacement of 7,800 tons, they could handle 21 or more planes and had light antiaircraft armament. Eleven more of this type went to the Royal Navy. Operating a composite squadron antisubmarine patrol of fighters and torpedo planes, these carriers had a large share in the Atlantic antisubmarine war and were instrumental in defeating Germany's U-boat effort. They operated as convoy escorts or as nuclei for "hunter-killer" task groups of one CVE and a number of destroyer escorts; they also served as aircraft transports. *Bogue* and *Card* earned a PRESIDENTIAL UNIT CITATION for their service; *Block Island* fell victim to a U-boat.

BOHEMIA AND MORAVIA, PROTECTORATE OF. The form under which the Germans ruled the western two-thirds of the Czechoslovak republic, which they seized on March 15, 1939. The protectorate was largely the creation of Wilhelm Suckert, a Nazi legal expert. Bohemia and Moravia were declared to be together an autonomous part of the Reich. Germans living in the area became German citizens, while the Czech inhabitants were declared protectorate nationals. Germany controlled foreign affairs and defense, but natives administered internal matters. Emil HACHA, Czech President at the time of the occupation, was granted formal recognition as a head of state ("State President"), but he was responsible to the Reich Protector appointed by the Germans, at first Konstantin von NEURATH, later the viciously efficient Reinhard HEYDRICH, and others. The Czech bureaucracy and state operation simply transferred their allegiance to the new government. The military services were abolished, but Army officers were granted generous pensions. This system permitted the Czechs a greater role in conducting their internal affairs than was given to any other people in an occupied country, but it enabled the Germans to control the country at little cost to themselves and to exploit Czech resources effectively and ruthlessly.

BOHLEN, Charles Eustis (1904–1974). An American career diplomat fluent in Russian, "Chip" Bohlen went to the embassy in Moscow when the United States established diplomatic relations with the Soviet Union in 1933. After a two-year period back in Washington with the Division of Eastern European Affairs, he returned to Moscow, remaining there until 1940, when he was appointed second secretary of the American embassy in Tokyo. He served in Japan until the attack on Pearl Harbor in 1941, when along with the rest of the American embassy staff he was placed in internment for six months. In 1943 he returned to Moscow as first secretary of the embassy. He served as President Franklin Roosevelt's interpreter at the Big Three conference in TEHERAN. In the summer of 1944 he was asked to come to Washington to advise the U.S. delegation to the DUMBARTON OAKS meeting on international organization. In 1953 President Dwight Eisenhower appointed him ambassador to the Soviet Union. Later, he was ambassador to France.

BOHR, Niels (1885–1962). Danish physicist who went to England to study at Cambridge under Sir Ernest Rutherford. On his return to Copenhagen he developed a theory of nuclear physics that enabled him to calculate closely the frequencies of the entire system of atomic hydrogen. His achievement was recognized internationally, and he was awarded a Nobel Prize in 1942. During World War II he was rescued from occupied Denmark by the British. He then moved to Los ALAMOS, working with the Allied nuclear team. At the end of the war he returned to Copenhagen to head the nuclear physics team at the University of Copenhagen. *See also* ATOMIC BOMB.

BOLDIN, Ivan V. (1892–1965). Soviet general who, after serving in the SOVIET-FINNISH WAR, was caught in the Russian debacle of 1941, escaping three times from encirclement, once after spending 51 days behind German lines. His firm stand with the Fifteenth Army in the Vyazma area gained valuable time for the Russians. Boldin led the Fiftieth Army in the winter counteroffensive of 1941–42 near TULA, in the 1943 Battle of KURSK and the 1945 campaign into Germany. In 1944 he was promoted to colonel general. He became deputy commander of the Third Ukrainian Front in April 1945.

BOLERO. Code name of the buildup of American troops and supplies in the United Kingdom (begun in

1942) in preparation for the eventual Normandy INVASION.

BOMB. There were four types of aerial bombs: incendiary, fragmentation, armor-piercing and general purpose. General purpose bombs achieved their effect primarily from the violence of the detonation; early versions had thick casings for increased fragmentation effect, but when experience revealed greater damage from blast than from fragmentation, thinner casings came into use. Most general purpose bombs ranged in size from 100 pounds to the 4,000-pound "blockbuster," although the British, whose bombers had greater capacity than American bombers, developed a 20,000-pound Grand Slam. The bombs could be fitted with instantaneous, delayed-action, time or proximity fuzes, the last two types to achieve explosion in the air. Armor-piercing bombs were designed to penetrate the deck armor of battleships, heavy concrete structures and other hard targets and always employed delayed-action fuzes. Fragmentation or antipersonnel bombs were relatively small, ranging from 4 to 100 pounds, were usually dropped in clusters and sometimes had small parachute attachments to slow descent. Deadly against troops in the field, fragmentation bombs were also effective against vehicles, aircraft and thin-skinned installations. Incendiary bombs ranged in size from 2 to 1,000 pounds and were filled with a variety of highly combustible chemicals. Smaller types were usually dropped in clusters. In an incendiary attack, such as those on TOKYO in 1945, general purpose bombs were dropped first for blast effect, followed by incendiaries to start fires, then by more general purpose bombs to spread the fires by blast.

BOMB ALLEY. The colloquial term "bomb alley" was sometimes applied to narrow stretches of water, e.g., the English Channel or the Sicilian Narrows, where shipping was exposed to aerial attack. But the term was later applied to those areas in southeast England along the course of V-1 flying bombs, which often failed to reach their predicted target in the London area after launching from France (*see* V-WEAPONS).

BOMBARDON. A section of a breakwater used as part of an artificial harbor (*see* MULBERRY) in the Normandy INVASION. A bombardon was an air-filled float of canvas and reinforced concrete 200 feet long.

BOMBAY. British transport plane, manufactured by Bristol, used to carry troops or cargo and as a flying ambulance. Developed from an earlier Bristol commercial design, the Bombay was a rather blocky-looking high-wing, twin-engine monoplane with fixed landing gear and a twin tail. Its top speed was 192 miles per hour, and at cruising speed it had a range of 2,000 miles. Defensive .303-caliber flexible machine guns were mounted in the nose and tail. The Bombay was very similar in appearance to the Handley Page HARROW, developed, like the Bombay, during the 1930s.

BOMB DISPOSAL SQUAD. The aerial attacks on British cities produced a large number of unexploded bombs which had to be found and made safe. Companies of volunteers were formed to disarm them. One of the most notable squads—described by Churchill as the "Holy Trinity"—was composed of the Earl of Suffolk, his female secretary and his rather aged chauffeur. The War Office finally accepted responsibility for bomb disposal except for parachute mines, which were considered a job for the Royal Navy. Squads of Royal Engineers trained in bomb disposal worked in close cooperation with civilian air raid wardens and police.

BOMBER "B" PROJECT. A German program to build a long-range (2,237-mile) bomber intended not only to replace the JUNKERS JU 88 and the HEINKEL HE 111, but to carry medium-bomber design well past the level of 1939. It was to have a maximum speed of 373 miles per hour and carry an 8,820-pound bomb load to any part of the British Isles from French or Norwegian bases. Specifications were released to Arado, Dornier, Focke-Wulf and Junkers in July 1939. The contenders were the Ar 340, Do 317, FW 191 and Ju 288. The program was dropped in 1943.

BOMBER COMMAND. The Royal Air Force Bomber Command was formed in 1936, when the organization of the RAF changed from a geographical to a functional basis by role of the aircraft concerned. Its headquarters were at High Wycombe, Bucks. Bomber Command remained in existence until 1968, when it merged with Fighter Command to become RAF Strike Command.

Bomber Command was organized into groups which controlled stations and units predominantly in eastern England. At the outbreak of war in 1939 there were 33 squadrons or 480 aircraft in the command. Ten squadrons were sent to France, armed with the obsolescent BATTLE aircraft, as the Advanced Air Striking Force. No. 2 Group was armed with twin-engine BLENHEIMS, No. 3 Group operated with WELLINGTONS, No. 4 Group had WHITLEYS and No. 5 Group had HAMPDEN aircraft. The Air Officer Commanding in Chief, Air Chief Marshal Sir Edgar LUDLOW-HEWITT, recognized the deficiencies of his force in numbers, armament and load-carrying capacity. Daylight raids on German naval targets near Heligoland and Wilhelmshaven soon convinced him that to survive as a weapon of war the bomber force had to convert to night bombing. Lacking effective navigational or radio and radar aids, the night bombing attacks on targets in Germany for the first two and a half years of the war could not be described as very effective. The advent of night photographic equipment and postoperational sorties of high-flying photo-reconnaissance squadrons produced a more detailed analysis of bombing effectiveness. The Bomber Command operational research section was established in September 1941 to investigate a wide variety of problems associated with bomber operations over enemy territory.

Bomber Command's greatest wartime commander was Sir Arthur HARRIS, who was AOC-in-C from February 1942 until the end of the war. The rearming of the command with the four-engine heavy bombers designed in the mid-1930s took place from 1942 onward. The Short STIRLING, the Handley Page HALIFAX and above all the Avro LANCASTER provided means of carrying the war into the heart of occupied Europe. The development of navigational and radio/radar aids such as

Gee, Oboe and H2S improved bombing accuracy. A significant organizational change was the introduction in August 1942 of the Pathfinder Force (later No. 8 Group) with select crews whose main function was target identification and marking for the main force following up.

Among the spectacular feats of Bomber Command were the first 1,000-bomber raid on COLOGNE on May 31, 1942, the breaching of the MÖHNE and EDER dams, the fire raids on HAMBURG and the sustained offensive against the RUHR and Berlin in 1943–44. During the weeks before the Normandy landings, Bomber Command returned to precision bombing attacks by day to isolate the Normandy beachhead by cutting railway and road communications. For most of the war, however, Air Marshal Harris held to the belief in area bombing attacks on industrial targets by night.

One notable feature of the work of the command was its laying of sea mines. Over 30 percent of enemy shipping losses in European waters during the war were due to mines laid by Bomber Command. Mention must be made also of the wooden wonder, the MOSQUITO, which became a valuable aircraft for PATHFINDER, intruder, deception and bombing attacks in the last two years of the war.

By early 1945 Bomber Command had increased to 95 squadrons, with No. 6 Group consisting entirely of RCAF squadrons. The command always had a high proportion of Dominion personnel, sometimes forming their own squadron, sometimes integrated with British crew members. Allied squadrons were provided by French, Dutch and Polish air forces. Twenty-three VICTORIA CROSSES were won by pilots of bomber aircraft. Of the total of 70,253 officers, NCOs and airmen of the RAF killed or missing on operations between September 3, 1939, and August 14, 1945, 47,293 lost their lives or disappeared in operations carried out by Bomber Command. A total of 955,044 tons of bombs of all types were dropped by Bomber Command between September 1939 and V-E Day in 1945; 6,440 aircraft were missing from 199,091 dispatched on day and night raids over Germany. *See also* STRATEGIC BOMBING.

BÔNE. This Algerian port, highly valued by the Allies because it could dock 22 ships, had good rail connections and was close to a primary airfield. Bône was taken by airborne landings on November 12, 1943. It was subsequently an important transshipment point for supplies for the Tunisian front. The city is now called Annaba.

BONG, Richard I. (1920–1945). The leading American fighter ace of World War II, Bong downed 40 Japanese planes while flying P-38s in the Southwest Pacific. Much of the time his wingman was Capt. Thomas J. LYNCH, a formidable pilot in his own right, who scored 20 aerial victories. On one occasion Bong lost sight of his wingman and discovered a Zero on his tail. In shaking off this pursuer, he climbed through a cloud layer and found himself in the midst of a formation of nine Zero fighters. He immediately attacked the leader head-on, blew the Zero to pieces and then downed a second one. As the formation began to scatter, he damaged a third Japanese fighter. Bong scored eight victories during October and November 1944 while serving as a gunnery instructor. For "voluntarily and at his own request" engaging in these "repeated combat missions" he was awarded the MEDAL OF HONOR. He lost his life in August 1945 while testing a new plane at Muroc, Calif.

BONHOEFFER, Dietrich (1907–1945). A noted German Protestant theologian active in the European ecumenical movement of the 1930s who joined the protest of Martin NIEMÖLLER against Nazi control of the German Confessional Church through picked and servile prelates. During a hasty visit to Stockholm in June 1942 Bonhoeffer confided to the British bishop of Chichester the extent of the conspiracy against Hitler and solicited Allied willingness to negotiate a peace once the Nazi government had been overthrown. Arrested April 5, 1943, shortly after his friend, Abwehr agent Hans von DOHNANYI, was taken into custody, Bonhoeffer was murdered in the Flossenbürg concentration camp on April 8, 1945. His collected letters and writings from prison are among the most moving records of personal courage in adversity and of the Christian ethical motivation behind much of the German resistance to Hitler. *See also* BELL, GEORGE; OPPOSITION TO HITLER.

BONIN ISLANDS. Island group in the Pacific Ocean north of the Volcano Islands (Iwo JIMA), including Chichi Jima and Haha Jima.

BONN. Small German city on the west bank of the Rhine south of Cologne, birthplace of the composer Beethoven, captured on March 9, 1945, by the U.S. 1st Infantry Division. The city subsequently became the capital of the Federal Republic of Germany.

BONNET, Georges (1889–1973). A French Radical Socialist politician, remembered as one of the archappeasers of Hitler. Bonnet participated in the establishment of the League of Nations and served in a variety of important diplomatic and governmental positions. In 1938, he was appointed Foreign Minister. Bonnet was one of the principal figures behind the push for the MUNICH AGREEMENT, strongly pressing Czechoslovakia to agree to Anglo-French proposals for cession of the SUDETENLAND. When the Germans annexed Bohemia and Moravia in 1939 in violation of the Munich pact, Bonnet contended that the move was a *fait accompli* about which France could do nothing. Ten days after the start of the war he was transferred from the Foreign Ministry to the Justice Department. After the fall of France in 1940 he dropped into obscurity until 1944, when the French Radical Socialist meeting in Algiers announced his expulsion from the party; it was said that Bonnet had been arrested on charges of handing over Air France planes to the Germans.

BONNIER DE LA CHAPELLE, Fernand (1922–1942). An obscure young man in Algiers who played a significant part in history by assassinating Adm. Jean-François DARLAN on Christmas Eve 1942. Bonnier was a member of a group of five young anti-Nazi Frenchmen who plotted the murder. He apparently saw himself as a national hero but was condemned to death by a court-martial ordered by Gen. Henri GIRAUD and executed forthwith on the morning of December 26.

BONOMI, Ivanoe (1873–1951). The son of working-class parents, Ivanoe Bonomi was a conservative Socialist who became the Italian Premier in 1921; his coalition government fell when Benito MUSSOLINI broke with the Socialists. Bonomi retired to oblivion and political disfavor until the Allies liberated Rome in June 1944. As the leader of Rome's Committee of National Liberation, Bonomi then formed a cabinet of men from various liberation groups who did not have Fascist records.

BOOBY TRAPS. Hidden mines or charges whose firing mechanisms are so placed that the mine or charge is detonated when an apparently harmless object is disturbed by an unsuspecting person. They were employed in minefields, trees, buildings, abandoned equipment and other places likely to attract the curious. Booby traps were set off by action on a concealed explosive device; i.e., by one's lifting or disturbing an object that might be thought to be an attractive souvenir, thus releasing pressure, or by causing a pull on a concealed trip wire, or by breaking or cutting a taut cord or trip wire. Some were electrically detonated. Mines, either antipersonnel or antitank, were frequently booby-trapped; the mine had one or more secondary fuzes set to fire if it was disturbed. The Japanese frequently wired hand grenades to souvenirs, and the Germans were adept at booby-trapping houses. In addition to mines, grenades and various block explosives, artillery shells and mortar bombs were also used. Booby traps were not manufactured for use but were improvised from materials at hand.

BOOTY, OPERATION (Trophäenaktion). The Soviet dismantling of German factories and the removal of their machinery to the Soviet Union. This was started immediately after the Russian occupation.

BORGHESE, Prince Junio Valerio (1906–1974). Italian naval officer, called the Black Prince, who commanded assault craft forces in the Mediterranean. His mine-carrying two-man "human torpedoes" did severe damage to the British fleet. Overall, his operations put 73,000 tons of British shipping out of action, his force suffering only six casualties. His most effective operation was the penetration of Alexandria harbor on the night of December 18–19, 1941, which resulted in the mining of the British battleships QUEEN ELIZABETH and VALIANT, which were put out of action for several months. This was an especially severe blow to the British, since it followed by only a week the loss of the PRINCE OF WALES and the REPULSE off Malaya.

In the last phases of the war, Borghese commanded special-forces antipartisan units for Benito MUSSOLINI's rump government, the so-called Salo Republic. After the war he dabbled in neo-Fascist politics.

BORIS III, Czar of Bulgaria (1894–1943). Boris III became King of Bulgaria on October 3, 1918, when his father abdicated after the defeat of the Central Powers in World War I. Boris's ambition was to restore Bulgaria to its former size and influence; consequently, he approved of a Fascist coup d'etat in 1934 and was friendly to Hitler. Until 1941 Boris's pro-Axis policy successfully added new territory without endangering Bulgarian neutrality and autonomy, but Hitler's continued pressure on Boris to provide troops to fight Russia, a traditional Bulgarian ally, led to Boris's death on August 28, 1943, when he was shot by an anti-Nazi, pro-Russian assassin.

BOR-KOMOROVSKI, Tadeusz (1895–1966). In 1943 Gen. Tadeusz Komorovski took command of the underground Armia Krajowa (Home Army) in Poland. Though suspicious of Russian aims, he conducted guerrilla warfare against the Germans, thereby aiding the Soviet advance into Poland. He was known to his countrymen by the pseudonym "General Bor," hence his subsequent designation as "Bor-Komorovski." In August 1944, Bor-Komorovski launched an uprising in WARSAW. In a heroic and savage battle the Home Army was destroyed by the SS; the Soviet failure to help the insurgents has remained one of the most debated aspects of the war. Because of his opposition to Soviet policy, Bor-Komorovski went into exile after the war.

BORMANN, Martin (1900–1945). Bormann joined the Nazi Party in 1927 and rapidly became one of Adolf HITLER's most trusted administrators. He increased his influence in 1929 by marrying Gerda Buch, daughter of the chairman of the Nazi Party Court, responsible for maintaining party discipline. He was appointed Rudolf HESS's deputy in 1933, and the two worked diligently together as Hitler's back-room aides, supervising the many laws and decrees which the regime promulgated. An obsessive power seeker behind the scenes, Bormann brought himself directly to Hitler's attention by overseeing the construction of the BERGHOF and acting as manager for other projects of the Führer. He was honest where money was concerned, and administered the royalties Hitler received from the mass sale of MEIN KAMPF after 1933. Hess, who became surprisingly dilatory once the war had begun, increasingly left all detailed business to his deputy, which made Bormann appear indispensable. He drew ever closer to Hitler, becoming a constant member of the Führer's private entourage. When Hess flew to Scotland in 1941, Hitler placed Bormann at the head of party affairs with the rank of minister, and at the same time made him his personal aide and confidant, through whom everyone wishing to make contact with the Führer had to pass. Bormann's influence over Hitler was deeply resented by the other leaders.

Bormann was brusque and harsh with his subordinates, and his voice had an unpleasant rasp. Such loyalty as he felt to Hess evaporated immediately after his superior left Germany, and he was personally responsible for arresting all members of Hess's staff who could have been a party to his flight and for carrying out Hitler's orders that Hess's name was to be eliminated from Nazi history. Hess's wife had to seek Heinrich HIMMLER's help against Bormann's petty persecution. His loyalty to Hitler, however, was undoubted. His "protection" of the Führer often took the form of preventing him from seeing essential memoranda for the conduct of the war, because the facts might upset him; Bormann was therefore in no small measure responsible for Hitler's refusal to face the realities of the war situation. It was Bormann who caused Hitler's so-called table talk to be recorded in shorthand by Heinrich Heim.

In April 1945 Bormann stayed with Hitler in the bunker until the end. With Joseph GOEBBELS he witnessed Hitler's marriage, signing the certificate, as well as Hitler's will, in which Bormann was named executor and appointed party chancellor. Together with Goebbels, Bormann sought a truce with Marshal ZHUKOV, who continued to demand unconditional surrender. After Goebbels's suicide, Bormann was among those who sought to escape from the bunker around nine o'clock on the night of May 1. It was during this escape attempt that he was killed. Since at the time there was no absolute proof of his death, he was tried *in absentia* at NUREMBERG in 1946 and sentenced to death as a war criminal.

For many years it was rumored that Bormann had survived, and the international press has (very irresponsibly) spread frequent stories that he has been discovered in various parts of the world. In 1973 the West German Government officially pronounced him dead, his skull having been found and identified. In 1954 surviving letters to his wife were published in English under the title *The Bormann Letters.* **R.M.**

BOSE, Subhas Chandra (1897–1945). Indian nationalist political leader who led an army against the Allied forces in World War II. Before the war, Bose had broken with the independence movement led by Mohandas GANDHI. He was jailed numerous times by the British, the last time being in 1940. Shortly after his release he fled to Germany, where he organized a small body of Indian volunteers to fight against the Western powers. On Japan's entry into the war, he returned to the East and recruited a sizable INDIAN NATIONAL ARMY from among Indian Army troops captured in the Malayan campaign. One division of the INA actually took part in the Japanese invasion of India launched from Burma in 1944. After the defeat of the Japanese, his force disintegrated. He died in 1945 in a plane crash in Formosa.

BOTHA. This British airplane, built by Blackburn, joined COASTAL COMMAND just after the war broke out and soon convinced airmen that its two 880-horsepower Bristol Perseus radials did not generate power enough for a first-line torpedo bomber. The plane for a time flew reconnaissance missions, then reverted to training duty. The high-wing Botha was an ugly airplane; only the starboard half of the nose was glassed in, giving the craft a cockeyed look.

BOTTOMLEY, Sir Norman (1891–1970). After early service as a British infantry officer, Bottomley transferred to the Royal Flying Corps and the RAF. He was closely associated with the bombing offensive, being successively senior air staff officer, Bomber Command (1938–40), and commander of No. 5 Group (1940–41). He was Deputy Chief of Air Staff in the critical years 1943–45 and succeeded to command of Bomber Command when Sir Arthur HARRIS retired in 1945. He retired as an air chief marshal.

BOUGAINVILLE. Island, the largest in the SOLOMONS, which was one of the objectives in the U.S. advance toward RABAUL in 1943 because of its desirable harbors and airfield sites. By virtue of its location it served the Japanese as an advance supply and refueling base for most of the sea and air operations against the Allies at GUADALCANAL and in the central Solomons. Order-of-battle estimates placed Japanese strength at 35,000–44,000, with the bulk located in the southern part of the island. Fewer than 300 troops were estimated to be in the Cape Torokina area of Empress Augusta Bay. The landing of III Amphibious Force troops (I Marine Amphibious Corps) at Cape Torokina was given the code name Dipper. Assigned to conduct the assault was the 3d Marine Division, which would land three assault units of four landing teams each over the 12 beaches selected at Cape Torokina. The 37th Infantry Division would follow the marines ashore no later than D plus 7. Equally vital to the success of the operation was the speed with which at least three bomber and two fighter fields could be built and got into action against Rabaul.

The landing went off on schedule on November 1, 1943. A Japanese naval attempt to counteract the landings was decisively beaten off at night, and on the 7th and 8th a counterattack by Japanese troops who landed north of the beachhead was similarly repulsed. By November 26 the 3d Division had moved to the Piva River, having defeated the enemy in the Battle of Piva Forks. By January 16, 1944, the marines had been replaced by the Army AMERICAL Division. On March 8 the Japanese began an attack against the 37th Infantry Division, which culminated in a last major effort on the 24th. Three days later the enemy began a retreat from the Empress Augusta Bay area. Eventually, the Cape Torokina area was occupied by Australian forces, which by the end of the war were closing inland on Numa Numa and the last remnants of the Bougainville defenders.

BOUGIE. This Algerian port, needed by the Allies for its railroad connections and unloading facilities, was taken on November 11, 1943, by part of the British 78th Division, shipping from Algiers. The airfield of Djidjelli was occupied, and the Eastern Air Command took over November 12.

BOUNCING BETTY. Nickname given to a German antipersonnel mine detonated by trip wires. It exploded several feet above the ground, showering about 300 steel balls over a radius of several hundred feet.

BOWHILL, Sir Frederick W. (1880–1960). Formerly a British naval officer, Bowhill rose to the rank of air chief marshal after a variety of appointments—air member for personnel (1933–37), Air Officer Commanding in Chief COASTAL COMMAND (1937–41), AOC-in-C FERRYING COMMAND, Canada, and commander of the newly formed Transport Command in Britain in 1943.

BOYINGTON, Gregory (1912–). A U.S. Marine Corps ace credited with the destruction of 28 Japanese planes, Colonel Boyington commanded Marine Fighter Squadron 214 (The Black Sheep) in the central SOLOMONS area from September 12, 1943, to January 3, 1944, the day he was shot down during a fighter sweep over RABAUL—but not before he had downed his 26th, 27th and 28th enemy aircraft. He is reputed to have been one of the finest natural fighter pilots in the Marine Corps and was certainly one of its most colorful characters. He also achieved a reputation as an outstanding squadron commander in combat, based on the

U.S. marines hit the beach at Empress Augusta Bay on Bougainville

fact that he was able to transfer his skill as a fighter pilot to a group of replacements, remnants of various other squadrons and green pilots, making them into the deadly Black Sheep, a squadron of F4U Corsair pilots (*See* F4U).

A veteran of the AMERICAN VOLUNTEER GROUP (Flying Tigers), at age 31 he was the oldest pilot in Squadron 214 as well as its skipper and was, naturally enough, nicknamed "Pappy." After being shot down, he spent 20 months as a prisoner, and upon his release was ordered to Washington to receive the MEDAL OF HONOR. At the same time he was presented the nation's second highest award, the Navy Cross. He retired in 1947, at which time he was advanced to the rank of colonel.

BR-20. Designed by Fiat in 1935, the BR-20 *Cicogna* (Stork) was an Italian fast light bomber based upon lessons learned by Italian airmen in Ethiopia. The first model, which saw action in the Spanish Civil War, was a low-wing, twin-tail monoplane with four 7.7-mm. machine guns, powered by a pair of 1,000-horsepower Fiat radials and capable of carrying 3,500 pounds of bombs.

A second version, BR-20M, appeared in 1939. One of the original machine guns was replaced by a heavier 12.7-mm. weapon, and the nose was redesigned to improve visibility. This series, which had a maximum speed of 273 miles per hour, took part in daylight raids on Britain but had to be shifted to night operations because the Regia Aeronautica lacked a fighter capable of escort duty. The Italian squadrons left Western Europe early in 1941 to support the invasion of Greece. Despite their lack of defensive firepower, the planes saw extensive action from the Mediterranean to Russia before being assigned to reconnaissance and transport duty. The improved BR-20*bis* was entering service when Italy surrendered.

BRABAZON OF TARA, John Theodore Cuthbert Moore-Brabazon,1st Baron (1884–1964). British politician, Minister of Transport, 1940–41, and Minister of Aircraft Production, 1941–42. He was Britain's first licensed pilot, holding certificate No. 1 granted by the Royal Aero Club.

BRACKEN, Brendan Randall (1901–1958). British politician and publisher, intimate friend of Winston CHURCHILL. He held controlling interest in the *Economist*, the *Investors Chronicle* and the *Practitioner* (a medical journal), but his most prosperous enterprise was the *Financial Times*. In the 1930s he was one of Churchill's strongest supporters. With the declaration of war, he went to the Admiralty with Churchill as personal secretary. When Churchill formed his own wartime coalition in 1940, Bracken went with him to 10 Downing Street as parliamentary private secretary. He was one of the two or three men closest to Churchill during the war years and lived at 10 Downing Street or its annex. It is difficult to determine the amount of influence he actually exerted, but it seems certain that he prompted many of Churchill's appointments and influenced the disposition of patronage. As a publisher he was on close terms with many British and American journalists, thus paving the way for his appointment as Minister of Information in 1941. At the end of the war, Bracken was made First Lord of the Admiralty in Churchill's caretaker government. He lost his seat in the general election in 1945 but soon won another.

A colorful personality of varied background, Bracken was a self-made man with many resemblances to Churchill himself. They met when Bracken was still quite young, and the two became so close that a rumor sprang up that Bracken was Churchill's natural son. The story appears to have persisted at least in part because both were pleased by it and neither made much of an attempt to deny it.

BRADLEY, Omar Nelson (1893–). The American general who in Europe commanded over a million and a quarter men, the largest number of troops ever commanded by an American field commander. Born in Clark, Mo., Bradley as a small boy often went hunting with his father and soon became an expert shot. He maintained this skill throughout his military career. When his father died in 1908, Bradley moved with his mother to Moberly, Mo., where he went to high school. After graduation he worked in the local railroad shops, and the following year he entered West Point as a member of the class of 1915. While a cadet he continued to shoot and also played left field on the baseball team. He graduated 44 of 164 and was commissioned in the infantry. During World War I he was involved in the training of troops in the States. Disappointed that he had not seen overseas service, Bradley once told Ernie PYLE that he had spent the entire interwar period apologizing for his lack of combat experience.

Beginning in 1934, he taught tactics at West Point and later became the academy plans and training officer. From this position he moved in June 1938 to Washington to serve on the General Staff, becoming its assistant secretary as a lieutenant colonel in July 1939. He was promoted to brigadier general in February 1941 and moved to Fort Benning, Ga., to become commandant of the infantry school. While at Fort Benning he established the Officer Candidate Program, which was to commission over 45,000 officers during World War II. In February 1942, as a newly promoted major general, he took command of the 82d Infantry Division and later went to the 28th Division; both of these units were in training in the United States.

After the Battle of KASSERINE PASS he went to North Africa, where he became Gen. Dwight EISENHOWER's personal representative in the field and later was appointed as deputy to General PATTON, commander of II Corps. When Patton moved to SEVENTH ARMY, Bradley was promoted to command II Corps and led it through the remainder of the fighting in North Africa. In May 1943 his troops took BIZERTE with over 40,000 prisoners. When the enemy resistance collapsed, Bradley was shifted to Algiers, where he worked on the planning for the invasion of SICILY; in July, recently promoted to lieutenant general, he led his corps in the invasion.

Bradley was selected to command the U.S. assault army for the return to France, and in September he left II Corps for his new command. He returned to the United States to select his staff and be briefed and then traveled to England, where on October 20, 1943, he opened his FIRST ARMY headquarters in Bristol. As an additional duty he commanded the U.S. 1st Army Group, a headquarters that was part of a plan to deceive the Germans about the timing and location of the Normandy INVASION.

On June 6, under the overall command of Gen. B. L. MONTGOMERY, Bradley sent elements of his First Army ashore at Omaha and Utah Beaches. First Army forces cleared the COTENTIN PENINSULA, captured CHERBOURG and fought their way through the hedgerow country to the jump-off line for a breakout attempt—Operation COBRA, based on a plan that Bradley had personally devised. On August 1 he yielded the First Army to Lt. Gen. Courtney H. HODGES and took command of the 12TH ARMY GROUP, the position he held for the remainder of the war in Europe. When Eisenhower assumed ground command on September 1, Bradley and Montgomery had equal status as commanders of army groups.

Bradley's forces fought across France and into Germany. During the Battle of the BULGE two of the armies under 12th Army Group command, the First and NINTH, were shifted to Montgomery. But the First soon was returned, and Bradley pressed the attack. His men took the REMAGEN bridge and moved to seal the RUHR pocket, which yielded some 335,000 prisoners. Once that was accomplished, the Ninth Army again came under Bradley's command, so that he commanded four armies: First, Third, Ninth and Fifteenth. He was promoted to full general on March 12, 1945.

Though Bradley was praised by many high-ranking officials and received many decorations, his highest accolade came from the troops he led and whom he greatly respected. Many called him the "GI's general." After the war he became Administrator of Veterans' Affairs, Chief of Staff of the Army and subsequently the first Chairman of the Joint Chiefs of Staff. On September 22, 1950, he was promoted to the five-star rank of General of the Army.

BRANDENBERGER, Erich (1894–1970). German Army officer (General der Panzertruppen), who commanded the Seventh Army during the Battle of the BULGE. His army had the mission of protecting the German south and southwest flanks against attacks from the U.S. THIRD ARMY. Later Brandenberger was relieved by Hitler for defeatism, but near the end of the war he once again commanded an army, this time the Nineteenth. On May 5, 1945, at Innsbruck, Brandenberger surrendered the areas of Austria that were under his jurisdiction.

BRASILLACH, Robert (1909–1945). A French right-wing intellectual writer and journalist, Brasillach was generally favorable to collaboration with the Germans following the French defeat of 1940. He was arrested for this after the liberation, refused clemency by General DE GAULLE and executed in 1945.

BRASSARD. Code name for Allied amphibious operation launched from Corsica to capture the island of Elba, June 17, 1944. The invasion was carried out by a French colonial division with Allied naval and air support.

BRATTON, Rufus S. (1893–1958). A graduate of both the U.S. Military Academy and the Imperial Japanese Army Staff College, Colonel Bratton was uniquely qualified as head of Far Eastern military intelligence in the U.S. War Department at the beginning of World War II. He helped break the Japanese code. His intellect and ability were highly regarded by the General Staff and he seemed assured of high position. Then on December 7, 1941, his future became blighted when he delayed in getting the news of the PEARL HARBOR attack to the Army Chief of Staff, Gen. George C. MARSHALL. He served out the war as a headquarters officer of the Third Army.

BRAUCHITSCH, Walther von (1881–1948). Son of a Prussian cavalry general, this future Commander in Chief of the German Army was commissioned a lieutenant in 1900. During World War I he served as a General Staff officer. After interwar duty training the new Reichswehr and serving as inspector of artillery, in 1933 he was named commander of the East Prussian military district; when the headquarters was subsequently converted to a corps, he retained command. In April 1937 he took over the newly formed 4th Army Group at Leipzig. After the purge of the Army, Brauchitsch, on February 4, 1938, became Commander in Chief, succeeding Gen. Werner von FRITSCH. In this position he proved to be a compliant follower of Adolf HITLER. As commander he guided the Army through the fighting in POLAND, FRANCE, the BALKANS and CRETE. On July 19, 1940, he was promoted to the rank of field marshal. Brauchitsch planned the invasion of Russia and executed the initial phases of the campaign, but when in December 1941 he stated that Moscow could not then be captured and recommended to Hitler that the German forces be withdrawn to a defensive line, he was relieved, Hitler himself assuming command of the Army. The commanders of two army groups and four armies were also sacked. Though he remained on the active list, Brauchitsch saw no more active service during the war. He died in Hamburg before the start of his war crimes trial.

BRAUN, Eva (1912–1945). After the suicide in 1931 of Adolf HITLER's niece Geli Raubal, to whom he was devoted, Eva Braun, an assistant in Heinrich HOFFMANN's photographic establishment, became Hitler's mistress. She lived in his flat in Munich and later transferred to BERCHTESGADEN. Except when he was in the company of his closer associates, Hitler kept her very much in the background. It would seem that she was responsible initially for pressing her affections on Hitler, but she accepted what limited companionship he had to offer with comparatively little complaint, though it is evident from Albert SPEER's account that she suffered from neglect. She was frivolous and empty-headed and loved sports and dancing, but she was completely faithful to the Führer and, entirely of her own volition, joined him in the bunker in Berlin during his last days. He married her on April 29, 1945, shortly before their joint suicide. She was cremated beside him in the garden of the Chancellery, and the Russians were to claim later that they had exhumed her charred remains.

BRAUN, Wernher von (1912–1977). The German rocket engineer who developed the V-2 rocket, one of Hitler's secret weapons (*see* V-WEAPONS). At the age of 25, von Braun became the technical director of the German Army's rocket research center at PEENEMÜNDE, near Stettin. His orders were to produce a weapon capable of carrying a large warhead over a range much beyond that of the artillery. By 1938 von Braun had already developed the prototype of the V-2, the A-4 rocket, a self-propelled and self-steering apparatus with a maximum range of 11 miles.

But from 1940 onward his research was hindered when Hitler shifted priorities away from missile research. In 1941 von Braun pleaded with Hitler for improved research facilities, but the project did not finally get support until 1943 when Hitler demanded mass production of the V-2. Von Braun fell into disfavor and was imprisoned in 1944 when Heinrich HIMMLER attempted to gain control of the project. He was accused of planning to fly to Britain with secret documents. However, Hitler himself ordered von Braun's release, and the first V-2 was launched against Britain in September 1944. Following that a total of about 3,600 were fired against British cities until The Hague, from which most of the rockets were launched, was captured by Allied forces seven months later.

In early 1945 the scientists left Peenemünde when Russian forces came within 100 miles of it. Along with others, von Braun hid from the SS until he was able to give himself up to Allied troops. He was sent to London for interrogation and later released and sent to the United States, where he became a mainstay in the American missile program.

BRAZILIAN EXPEDITIONARY FORCE (FEB). In World War II Brazil furnished the Allies with the only ground force from a Latin-American ally. Brazil declared war against Germany and Italy in 1942, and its ships and ports played an important part in the naval war in the Atlantic. Late in 1944 an expeditionary force of 25,000 men was sent to the Italian front. One combat division was maintained at the front until the end of the war. The Brazilian force took part in some fierce fighting and suffered casualties numbering 451 killed and 2,000 wounded. During the closing days of the war an entire German division surrendered to the Brazilians. After the war the officers who had served in the FEB formed a closely knit group within the Brazilian officer corps with strong ties to the United States.

BREAKNECK RIDGE. A mass of hills and spurs in the area between Carrigara Bay and the Leyte River on the island of LEYTE, defended by the Japanese 1st Division and taken after more than two weeks of fierce fighting (November 4–22, 1944) by troops of the U.S. 24th and 32d Divisions.

BREGUET 521 (Bizerte). A huge biplane French Navy reconnaissance flying boat introduced in 1935. A three-engine design, it was based on British Short's Calcutta. The 521 equipped five naval squadrons in 1939 and was extensively used in patrolling the French seaways. After the fall of France in 1940, the plane was used by the LUFTWAFFE for air-sea rescue and other emergency missions. It cruised at 124 miles per hour with a crew of eight, was armed with five 7.5-mm. machine guns and had a range of 1,864 miles. It could carry 660 pounds of bombs.

BREGUET 690. French two-place, twin-engine multipurpose aircraft—light bomber, dive-bomber, reconnaissance and fighter plane. The series included the 690, 691, 693, 694, 695 (some of which did not enter production) and some experimental types.

BREN GUN. Light Machine Gun Marks I through IV, caliber .303, sometimes referred to as a light machine rifle. Developed at Brno, Czechoslovakia, during the 1920s, the first version of this gun was adopted by the Czech Army as the 7.92-mm. Model ZB26. The later ZB30 was also produced for Army and export use, and was also manufactured in China. Under the German occupation the Brno plant manufactured the ZB30 for the German Army. After competitive tests the Brno design had been adopted by the British in the early 1930s. It was manufactured at the Royal Small Arms Arsenal at Enfield Lock, and its English name was a combination of BRno and ENfield. The Bren was also made in Canada.

A gas-operated, air-cooled shoulder weapon capable of automatic and semiautomatic fire, the Bren had an automatic cyclic rate varying from 480 (Mark III) to 540 (Mark II) rounds per minute. A detachable box magazine, mounted on top of the gun, held 30 rounds of standard British .303-caliber rifle ammunition. The Brens Mark I and II could also take a special 100-round drum for antiaircraft work. Approximately the same length as the Lee-Enfield infantry rifle, the Bren had a butt stock and bipod and was usually fired from a prone position or, while moving, from the hip. Two special mounts were produced for the Bren. Mounted on a tripod, it could be used in the medium machine gun role; on a high free-swinging pedestal mount, it became an antiaircraft weapon. Bren guns were mounted on vehicles; the tracked Universal Carrier came to be popularly referred to as the Bren Gun Carrier. Barrel changing was quick and easy, an important feature in a light automatic gun.

Accurate, reliable and well made, the Bren was the principal wartime light machine gun of British and Commonwealth forces and served for some years after the war.

BREN GUN CARRIER. A popular term incorrectly applied to the British Universal Carrier, a small full-tracked, open-top, cross-country vehicle designed, as its name implied, for a variety of combat and utility roles. Many variants were produced in Britain, Canada and Australia. Some were produced in the United States for the United Kingdom. Various configurations were used as ambulances, personnel carriers and HQ vehicles. Others were fitted with BREN GUNS (hence the name), light antitank guns and mortars.

BRERETON, Lewis Hyde (1890–). When Japan attacked in the Pacific, Brereton was commander of U.S. Far East Air Forces in the Philippines. What has been described as a breakdown of communications with General MACARTHUR's headquarters enabled the enemy to catch Brereton's Luzon-based B-17s on the ground and destroy the bulk of his striking force. After serving in the defense of the Philippines, Brereton assumed command of Middle East Air Forces, which later became the NINTH AIR FORCE. Achieving the rank of lieutenant general in April 1944, he commanded the Ninth Air Force when it raided PLOESTI (Rumania) and remained with it until August 1944, at which time he took over the FIRST ALLIED AIRBORNE ARMY. *See also* CLARK FIELD.

BREST. For hundreds of years an important French naval base. During Allied INVASION planning, Brest's fine harbor was considered vital to support the fight for France. Core of the stout German defense of Brest was the 2d Paratroop Division under ardent Nazi Generalleutnant (Major General) Hermann RAMCKE. Hitler had ordered Ramcke to hold, and hold he did. When Brest finally fell to the U.S. VIII Corps on September 18, 1944, port facilities had been destroyed. Fighting by then was far to the east. Brest was not used as a port by the Allies.

BREST LITOVSK. After the German-Soviet partition of Poland in 1939, this city was occupied by the Soviets. Located on the new border, it was attacked at the outset of the German invasion on June 22, 1941, but Soviet infantry and NKVD troops held out for a week (*see* NKVD). Troops of the First White Russian Front retook the city on July 28, 1944.

BRETAGNE. French battleship of 22,000 tons, completed in 1915 at Brest, armed (in 1939) with ten 13.4-inch, fourteen 5.5-inch and eight 3-inch guns, and smaller weapons. *Bretagne* was part of Admiral GENSOUL's squadron attacked by the ROYAL NAVY at MERS-EL-KÉBIR on July 3, 1940; she was hit severely and shortly afterward a magazine exploded, destroying the ship and killing 977 officers and men.

BRETT, George H. (1886–1963). In 1941, while a major general and Chief of the U.S. Army Air Corps, Brett visited the United Kingdom to study the problem of providing maintenance for American-built planes being flown by the RAF. Shortly after the outbreak of war with Japan, he embarked on an inspection tour of the Middle East, India and China, but instead of returning to Washington he was sent to Australia, arriving there on December 31, 1941, to establish American air bases and direct operations from them. Promoted to lieutenant general early in January, he took command of the ragtag Allied air forces defending the Netherlands East Indies. However, organizational problems and personality clashes with General MACARTHUR's staff led to his dismissal in August 1942 as MacArthur's air commander. He was succeeded by Gen. George C. KENNEY. Later in the war General Brett headed the CA-

RIBBEAN DEFENSE COMMAND. *See also* JAPANESE CONQUESTS 1941–42.

BRETTON WOODS. Village in New Hampshire, site of the United Nations Monetary and Financial Conference in July 1944. At the conference, representatives reached an agreement to establish both the INTERNATIONAL MONETARY FUND and the INTERNATIONAL BANK FOR RECONSTRUCTION AND DEVELOPMENT. The main purposes of the International Monetary Fund were to promote international monetary cooperation, facilitate international trade, promote stability of foreign-exchange rates and make international sources of currency available to all members. It was hoped that the agreements accompanying the creation of the fund would contribute to the stabilization of foreign exchanges following the war. However, in the stresses of the aftermath of the war and the rearmament period leading up to the Korean War, many of the nations failed to maintain control over their domestic price and credit systems. Nevertheless, the fund proved to be a powerful agent for stability in the postwar era.

BREVITY. Code name of the British attack in the SOLLUM area (NORTH AFRICA), May 1941.

BREZHNEV, Leonid I. (1906–). Soviet political officer during the war, first as deputy chief political administrator of the Southern Front, then as chief of the political department of the Eighteenth Army and finally as chief political administrator of the Fourth Ukrainian Front. He saw operations in the Caucasus, the Black Sea area and the Ukraine. In 1944 he was promoted to the rank of major general. Brezhnev became first secretary of the Soviet Communist Party in 1964 and Chairman of the Presidium of the Supreme Soviet in 1977.

BRIDGES, Sir Edward, 1st Baron (1892–1969). Secretary to the British cabinet and then to the War Cabinet from 1938 until the end of the war. He was subsequently permanent secretary to H.M. Treasury and official head of the Civil Service, 1945–56. To him Winston CHURCHILL ascribed the wartime harmony which existed between civil and military staffs.

BRINDISI. On the night of September 8, 1943, after announcing that Italy had surrendered to the Allies, Marshal Pietro BADOGLIO, the head of the Italian Government in succession to MUSSOLINI, fled Rome for the south. With him were King VICTOR EMMANUEL, other members of the royal family and members of the government. They went by car to Pescara, on the Adriatic coast, and then by boat to Brindisi, on the heel of Italy. Brindisi was proclaimed "the first capital of the new Italy." The city was occupied by the British 1st Airborne Division on September 11, 1943.

BRISTOL CLASS. Term used in some contemporary and later sources to describe later-production destroyers of the U.S. BENSON and GLEAVES classes. This distinction was based on gun armament, applying to ships built with four 5-inch guns rather than with the five guns that armed the first Bensons and Gleaveses. It quickly became meaningless when the batteries of all ships of both classes were standardized at four guns.

BRITAIN, BATTLE OF. The massive air battle fought in 1940 to determine aerial supremacy over the island of Britain, and one of the fateful battles of history. After the fall of France, Adolf HITLER was faced with a problem: the British obstinately refused to admit that they as well as their ally were defeated, so it might therefore become necessary for the Germans to invade England. There is considerable disagreement about the degree to which Hitler believed in the possibility or even the desirability of mounting a successful invasion; perhaps air power by itself could effectively blockade the island or wreak sufficient damage to subdue the enemy. But in either case—and certainly if invasion were in view—the Germans believed that they had to establish control of the air over England; the German Navy was too weak to engage the British Home Fleet with any chance of success. The LUFTWAFFE must defeat the ROYAL AIR FORCE and then neutralize the Royal Navy. Then, if necessary, invasion could proceed.

The Luftwaffe began with attacks on coastal towns and shipping during July 1940, while the German Army regrouped for possible embarkation and the Navy set about gathering vessels that could serve as landing craft. The battle, called Eagle Attack (*Adlerangriff*) by the Germans, began in earnest in August. Reichsmarschall GÖRING, Commander in Chief of the Luftwaffe, gathered 2,800 aircraft in three air fleets: Field Marshal Albert KESSELRING's Air Fleet 2, operating from fields in northern France and the Low Countries; Field Marshal Hugo SPERRLE's Air Fleet 3, operating from northwestern France; and Gen. Hans-Jürgen STUMPFF's Air Fleet 5, based in Norway and Denmark. British Air Marshal Sir Hugh DOWDING's FIGHTER COMMAND had 650 operational fighters (HURRICANES and SPITFIRES) in 52 squadrons. As laid down in the Führer's directive for the battle, the Luftwaffe's first-priority targets were the RAF planes and their ground support; German strategy was to lure the British fighters into combat against supposedly superior force that would then destroy them. However, in the immediate prewar years the British had built a chain of RADAR warning stations, largely at Dowding's urging; and this radar, although unsophisticated by later standards, enabled him to concentrate superior numbers at vital spots to counter the Luftwaffe attacks. Information from the ULTRA intelligence operation was also important.

August 10 was set as the opening day of the all-out offensive, but bad weather forced postponement of this EAGLE DAY (*Adlertag*) until August 13. On this day the Luftwaffe flew 1,485 sorties, but at the end of it the Germans had lost 45 attacking planes, the British only 13 fighters (and, the truly vital statistic, only seven pilots). As they continued to meet fierce resistance, the Germans switched to heavy attacks on the main RAF bases (August 24–September 5). Large bomber formations, each escorted by 100 fighters, forced their way through the defenses and caused severe damage to airfields, communications and control centers. In this phase the Luftwaffe almost broke Fighter Command. More than 450 British fighters were destroyed, 103 pilots killed and 128 wounded. Since neither pilots nor planes could be replaced fast enough to fill the needs, and some of the airfields were out of action for varying periods, the RAF was brought to a crisis.

But Hitler and Göring saved the day. During the battle to this point, their strategy had wandered here and there as they sought to find the target whose destruction would achieve their ends. Now, in response to British air raids on Berlin—undertaken in reprisal for a German bombing of London that was carried out by mistake—the Führer and the Reichsmarschall turned to reprisals of their own. At the very moment British air defense was at its weakest, with German victory in sight, the Luftwaffe was ordered to attack London. The ensuing period of incessant aerial bombardment is known as the BLITZ. Since there was only one target, the RAF was able to concentrate its slender resources in defense, and the shattered airfields had time to recover.

The Battle of Britain was the period immortalized by CHURCHILL's "finest hour" speech, given just after the collapse of France, and London's response to the bombing was one of its finest parts. Luftwaffe losses were so great that the daylight bombing was halted. The Germans had proved unable to win daylight air supremacy. The tide had turned. On September 14–15, BOMBER COMMAND, together with light naval vessels, destroyed almost 200 barges across the Channel, about 10 percent of the total reckoned necessary for invasion (Operation SEA LION), which was declared suspended by Hitler on September 17. German daylight attacks fell off slowly, the last one occurring on September 30. The Battle of Britain had been won by the British. Now came the Blitz.

It was a battle of many resonances. Its immortals are the pilots of Fighter Command, of whom Churchill said, "Never in the field of human conflict was so much owed by so many to so few." Another part of its legend is the Spitfire, of which there were only 200 operational at the outset. And a side of it that is strangely neglected is the victorious commanding general, "Stuffy" Dowding, whose cool professionalism stood in total contrast to the wishful amateurism of Göring.

BRITISH AIR FORCE. *See* ROYAL AIR FORCE.

BRITISH ARMY. When the war began in 1939, in addition to various colonial garrisons the British Empire could field two brigades in Malaya, a division and a brigade in India, the equivalent of six infantry divisions and one armored division in the MIDDLE EAST and four divisions in FRANCE. The British Army itself, which at the end of September 1939 numbered 897,000, grew to 1,361,000 by the end of March 1940.

A force of more than 10 British divisions participated in the 1940 campaign in France. By the end of June 1940, with the evacuation of both France and NORWAY completed, British Army strength was 1,650,000.

British troops were positioned in Egypt to guard oil sources in the Middle East as well as the Suez Canal, and since the fall of France brought an end to the Western Front, the center of land operations shifted to NORTH AFRICA. If the Italians could be defeated in Libya, the southern Mediterranean coast could be opened to French Tunisia. Such a victory would open the possibility of an invasion of Europe through ITALY, Sardinia or Corsica. Thus in December 1940 the British, with two divisions, struck Italian positions in Egypt.

British attacks were successful and the Italians were driven back. German troops, however, were introduced into the theater, and under Gen. Erwin ROMMEL they attacked in March 1941. Fighting continued in the desert for more than two years. Meanwhile, in June 1941, after the British had evacuated Greece and CRETE, their fortunes improved in the south, for the Italian army in Ethiopia surrendered. By the end of the month, total strength of the British Army had risen to 2,221,000.

Malaya, Borneo and Hong Kong, all British colonies, were attacked by the Japanese in December 1941, causing Empire forces to be needed in the Far East as well as in the Middle East and in England. By the end of 1941 the British Army numbered some 2,340,000 with an infantry division in Malaya, another in India, four armored and two infantry divisions in the Middle East and six armored and 22 infantry divisions in the United Kingdom.

Combat continued on several fronts. In 1943 the campaign in North Africa was successfully concluded and both SICILY and Italy were invaded.

After a long period of planning and preparation, British and American troops invaded France on June 6, 1944. At the end of the month British Army strength was at 2,720,000, or some 40,000 higher than it had been in March. Army strength slowly increased, so that by the end of March 1945 a total of 2,802,000 were counted. By June 1945 the figure was 2,920,000.

Elements of Field Marshal MONTGOMERY's 21st Army Group comprised the contribution of the British Army to the European campaign. On May 5, 1945, Montgomery accepted the surrender of German forces in the Netherlands, Denmark and northwestern Germany.

In the Far East, British and Indian armies retook BURMA. An amphibious attack was planned to recapture Malaya, but the Japanese surrendered before it could be launched.

Total Army losses during the war were 144,079 killed, 239,575 wounded and 152,076 taken prisoner. Though these losses were severe, they were significantly lower than those suffered in World War I, when 702,410 were killed.

BRITISH BROADCASTING CORPORATION (BBC). With the outbreak of World War II, the extensive broadcasting system of the BBC became the primary, and in many cases the only, means of communication between Britain and other countries. The people of occupied countries were kept abreast of Allied progress by BBC broadcasts, and resistance movements were given encouragement (as in the V FOR VICTORY campaign). General DE GAULLE spoke over the BBC to occupied France, and his broadcasts served as the model for later projects such as "Free Yugoslavia," a Soviet-based radio system supported by the BBC.

In addition to coded messages to post commanders, the BBC sent cues for special actions on its regular programs. For example, the broadcast of the Italian surrender by Marshal BADOGLIO was to occur the evening before the Allied landing in southern Italy. In order to prevent exposure of the date, the message to surrender was cued that morning by two broadcast talks about Nazi propaganda in Argentina. On hearing these talks, the Italian Government announced the armistice.

Although it was a valuable instrument of propaganda and a source of generally sound information, the BBC occasionally allowed a touch of chauvinism or exaggeration to influence its reporting and so create problems among the Allies. According to BBC accounts, the U.S. FIFTH ARMY barely held against the German counterattack in southern ITALY until rescued by the British EIGHTH ARMY, when in reality SALERNO had been resolved before the arrival of the Eighth Army. BBC exaggeration of the resistance movements in Greece (*see* EAM; ELAS) brought extensive bombing by the Germans and protests from the Greek government-in-exile. But in spite of such misunderstandings, the BBC was indispensable to the Allied war effort.

BRITISH EXPEDITIONARY FORCE. First elements of the British Expeditionary Force (BEF) reached the Continent in September 1939. By the time of the German attack in May 1940, the force was composed of five regular and five territorial divisions. One of these units was under French command on the Saar front, while the others were under the command of Lord GORT. After an initial move forward into Belgium in May 1940 the Allies withdrew, and on May 20 the British air headquarters which supported Gort's troops displaced back to England. By the time of the surrender of Belgium, on May 27, Gort, on War Office orders which specified that his primary concern should be the safety of the BEF, was planning his own evacuation. Operation Dynamo, as the evacuation was named, was successful. By the evening of June 2, more than 338,000 Allied troops had been evacuated. Their heavy equipment, however, remained behind. *See also* FRANCE, BATTLE OF.

BRITISH NAVY. *See* ROYAL NAVY.

BRITISH SECURITY COORDINATION. Cover name for the British intelligence operation in the United States directed by Sir William STEPHENSON.

BRITTANY CAMPAIGN. After the Allied Normandy breakout—Operation COBRA, in July 1944—Maj. Gen. Troy H. MIDDLETON moved his U.S. VIII Corps through the penetration and launched his two armored divisions toward AVRANCHES on the threshold of the Brittany peninsula. On August 1, now under Lt. Gen. George S. PATTON's newly operational THIRD ARMY, Middleton sent his 6th Armored Division on a rapid dash to the west toward the port city of BREST. Meanwhile the 4th Armored moved southwest, neatly severing the peninsula from the mainland. Speed was essential, as facilities at Quiberon Bay, destination of the 4th Armored, and possibly also those at Brest were needed to land supplies for the ever growing invasion force. Patton had been told by Lt. Gen. Omar N. BRADLEY, now commander of the 12TH ARMY GROUP, to move as rapidly as possible and force the Germans back into their fortress positions before they could destroy the bridges and railroads that would be needed for the U.S. logistical effort. With the help of about 31,000 members of the FFI (Forces Françaises de l'Intérieur), who had much territory already under their control and who established roadblocks and helped to push the enemy back, the Germans were soon bottled up in SAINT-MALO, Brest and the Quiberon Bay area (including LORIENT and SAINT-NAZAIRE). So eager had Patton been to seize the peninsula and its ports that he disregarded Bradley's order to post a major force on the neck of the peninsula to guard against counterattacks. Bradley remedied the situation by changing the position of the 79th Infantry Division. The ports were stoutly defended.

Patton's attention was drawn more and more to the east, where his forces were driving toward the Seine. As the attack through France developed, it became evident that no major pause would take place on the Seine, and the Brittany ports, each day more distant from the battlefront, lost their luster. Orders were given to contain Lorient and Saint-Nazaire but to continue the siege of Brest. Bradley later said that Brest had to be taken because its garrison, including troops of the tough 2d Parachute Division, was under the command of the aggressive Generalleutnant (Major General) Hermann B. RAMCKE. Bradley felt that Ramcke, if not taken, could at any time sally forth in an attempt to disrupt Allied supply lines. He also agreed with Patton that once the American army started an operation such as this siege, it should see it through. Ramcke called up all available forces, including the local army postal unit led by the 69-year-old postmaster, as well as the paratrooper finance section and band. He stiffened his defense by spreading his best troops through all organizations with orders to keep the others fighting. Later, when a prisoner was asked why he had not surrendered after days of incessant pounding by both artillery and air strikes, his reply was, "Your propaganda leaflets may have accomplished a great deal, but the machine pistol of Oberleutnant Storz is more powerful." By early September, Patton's other forces had moved so far away that Bradley put VIII Corps and the Brittany operation under Lt. Gen. William H. SIMPSON'S NINTH ARMY, which was made operational for that mission. Brest fell on September 18. Though Lorient and Saint-Nazaire would continue to be contained until the war was over, the Brittany campaign had ended.

BROAD-FRONT STRATEGY. The concept adopted by the Western Allies for the advance into Germany after the June 6, 1944, INVASION. The strategy was planned prior to D-Day and was adhered to even though it became the subject of considerable debate and dissension as the Germans retreated in France. Essentially, it called for one advance north of the ARDENNES to the RUHR region and another south of the Ardennes. At different times, various Allied generals (MONTGOMERY, BRADLEY, PATTON) favored a single narrow thrust.

BROADHURST, Sir Harry (1905–). Royal Air Force officer, senior air staff officer to the air commander in the Western Desert, 1942, and air officer commanding the Allied Air Forces in the Western Desert, 1943. In Western Europe (1944–45), Broadhurst, an air vice-marshal, commanded 83 Group of the Allied Expeditionary Air Force.

BROKE, H.M.S. Royal Navy flotilla leader of 1,480 tons, completed in 1921 by Thornycroft. *Broke* was converted to a short-range destroyer escort in 1940, her postconversion armament being four 4.7-inch guns and one 3-inch gun, six 21-inch torpedo tubes and smaller weapons. *Broke* served chiefly in home waters, including the evacuation of Allied troops from Brest in 1940, but was lost on November 9, 1942, while on detachment in the Mediterranean. She was used in the attack on ALGIERS harbor, the object being to prevent scuttling of ships and demolitions, but came under heavy fire. At her fourth attempt she rammed and broke the harbor boom and landed her detachment of American troops, but she sustained so much damage in the operation that she sank on the following day.

BROOKE, Alan Francis (1st Viscount Alanbrooke) (1883–1963). Britain's chief professional soldier during most of the war (as Chief of the Imperial General Staff, 1941–46), Brooke was a member of one of the Northern Irish families that have traditionally supplied officers to the British Army. Brought up in France, he saw service on the Western Front in the First World War. In subsequent years he was an instructor at the Staff College and the Imperial Defence College, where he displayed particular interest in technical innovations. He held various appointments in different arms of the service, including command of the first mobile division, the ancestor of the armored divisions. Shortly before the war he was made commander of the newly established Antiaircraft Division.

On the declaration of war, Brooke, then a lieutenant general, went to France in command of the 2d Corps, British Expeditionary Force, which consisted of four raw divisions. A capable trainer, Brooke managed during the winter to develop the corps into a fighting force which played a vital part in the deliverance of the BEF in the days leading to DUNKIRK. Brooke's corps covered the flank left open by the surrender of the Belgian Army, and Brooke himself took effective charge of all British troops pressing toward the coast. Speaking of Brooke, Sir James Grigg, later Secretary of State for War, said that "by almost universal testimony, it was due largely to his skill and resolution that, not only his own corps, but the whole BEF escaped destruction on the retreat." After the Dunkirk evacuation he was sent back to France to lead the remaining British forces, but the cause by this time was hopeless. He was then appointed Commander in Chief Home Forces. As commander of Home Forces, Brooke had to build up defenses against possible German invasion, a challenging task in view of the fact that the BEF had been forced to leave all of its equipment on the Continent. When he succeeded Sir John DILL as CIGS in the black December of 1941, a regret was expressed in some professional circles that so able a British general should be removed from the field at such a critical time in Britain's fortunes. As the war progressed, however, the value of Brooke's appointment became apparent. He was able to give the British Chiefs of Staff Committee a direction and cohesiveness it had previously lacked.

Brooke was known for his self-discipline, rationality and coolness under pressure. Not the least of his achievements was his ability to counteract the impatience and impetuosity of Prime Minister Winston CHURCHILL without destroying the superb working relationship that existed between him and the Prime Minister—and this despite his severe personal disappointment when Churchill failed to arrange for his appointment as Supreme Allied Commander for the invasion of Europe. Unfortunately, however, at U.S.–British conferences and within the COMBINED CHIEFS OF STAFF, Brooke was almost invariably at swords' points with Gen. George C. MARSHALL; their mutual antipathy was a strain on Allied relationships until the end of the war.

BROOKE-POPHAM, Sir Robert (1878–1953). "Brookham," as he was affectionately called, was one of the founding members of the Royal Air Force (1912) and was the first commandant of the RAF Staff College. He later commanded in Iraq and was commandant of the Imperial Defence College. In 1933–35 he was Air Officer Commanding in Chief, Air Defence of Great Britain. After retirement as an air chief marshal in 1937 he became Governor of Kenya, but was recalled to RAF service in 1939 and in October 1940 was appointed Commander in Chief Far East. He was replaced by Lt. Gen. Sir Henry POWNALL during the fighting in MALAYA in late December 1941.

BROOKLYN, U.S.S. Light cruiser and class; the first 6-inch-gun cruisers built for the U.S. Navy since the early 1920s, seven of these ships commissioned in 1937–38. They were 608-foot flush-deck ships, displacing slightly under 10,000 tons standard, and their design emphasized the surface-combatant role with fifteen 6-inch guns in five triple turrets; forward and after superstructures were widely spaced. Eight 5-inch guns were carried in open mounts amidships. During the war two of this class, *Savannah* and *Honolulu,* had their bridge structures cut down for better antiaircraft fire; their antiaircraft guns were replaced by twin 5-inch mounts, backed up by 40-mm. guns. The other five also had their antiaircraft batteries augmented, but their basic arrangement of 5-inch guns was not altered. The later ST. LOUIS class represented an improvement on this design. *Savannah* and *Honolulu* were sold for scrap in 1959 and 1960. *Brooklyn* and NASHVILLE were sold to Chile in 1951; they served for years afterward as *O'Higgins* and *Capitan Prat.* PHILADELPHIA similarly became the Brazilian *Barroso. Phoenix* and *Boise* became the Argentine *Diecisiete de Octubre* (later *General Belgrano*) and *Nueve de Julio.*

BROWNING, Sir Frederick (1896–1965). One of the creators of the British airborne forces in World War II, including the Glider Pilot Regiment and parachute battalions and brigades. He himself commanded the 1st Airborne Division, 1941–44, and the 1st Airborne Corps, 1944, and served as deputy commander of the First Allied Airborne Army, 1944–45. He held the rank of lieutenant general. In 1945 he succeeded POWNALL as chief of staff to MOUNTBATTEN in the SOUTHEAST ASIA COMMAND.

BROWNING, Miles (1898–1954). Chief of staff to U.S. Admirals HALSEY and SPRUANCE in the Pacific. Browning was graduated from the U.S. Naval Academy in 1917 and went into naval aviation in 1923. Characterized by Samuel Eliot Morison as having a "slide-rule brain," Admiral Browning (then a captain) made important contributions to the timing of U.S. attacks in the Battle of MIDWAY.

BROWNING AUTOMATIC RIFLE (BAR). Developed by John Browning for the U.S. Army during World

War I, the BAR (M1918 and M1918A2, caliber .30) was used in large numbers by the Army, Marine Corps and Navy during World War II. The U.S. equivalent of the BREN GUN, the BAR was fed from 20-round box magazines and could fire at either of two automatic cyclic rates, 350 and 550 rounds per minute. Some wartime BARs were modified, by the Marines, to fire automatic or semiautomatic as the original production BAR had done. Gas operated, the BAR was basically similar in principle to the Bren and other comparable foreign weapons.

The original 1918 model BAR was simply a shoulder weapon. The later M1918A2 had a folding bipod, with a small monopod beneath the butt stock. This permitted more accurate automatic firing, though the BAR could be fired with reasonable accuracy in short, rapid bursts from the shoulder (its weight was 21 pounds empty, including bipod).

The BAR was accurate and reliable. Each U.S. Army rifle squad included one of these guns. The Marine Corps organized their 13-man squad around three "fire teams," each of which included a BAR. Recognizable by the characteristic sound of its relatively slow automatic fire (particularly when contrasted with the extremely rapid rate of the German MG34 and MG42 light machine guns), the BAR figured prominently in both European and Pacific theaters and continued in service through the Korean War.

BRUNEVAL. In 1942 the Germans built a radar station at Bruneval, France, on cliffs northeast of Le Havre. British Combined Operations Headquarters mounted an airborne raid on the station on the night of February 27, 1942. A force of 200 men captured the station, seizing equipment (including a WÜRZBURG device) to bring back for examination by British scientists.

BRUNSWICK (Braunschweig). Code name for the attack on the Caucasus by the German Army Group South in the 1942 summer offensive. The first phase of this offensive was known by the code name BLÜCHER.

BRUTUS. Code name for one of the two German agents (the other was GARBO) in England upon whom the Germans relied most for intelligence, though the British early turned both men. By feeding the agents occasional true information, the British maintained their veracity. Brutus proved most useful shortly after D-Day in Normandy when the Germans found copies of American field orders indicating that the Normandy landings constituted the principal invasion. Adolf HITLER had already directed his reserves to Normandy when a message from Brutus insisting that the main invasion was still to come in the Pas de Calais prompted him to cancel the order.

BRYANSK. This Soviet city 200 miles southwest of Moscow was taken by the Germans in October 1941 during the general advance on the capital. The town remained under occupation for almost two years. During that period it was the scene of heavy PARTISAN attacks on the Germans, who responded by terrorizing the civilian population. Some of the worst German atrocities of the war were committed against people living in and around Bryansk.

BRYANT, Ben (1905–). Lieutenant Commander Bryant commanded the British submarine *Sealion* during the German invasion of NORWAY in April 1940. On one occasion, while on patrol in the Skagerrak, he was hunted by German antisubmarine vessels and kept down for 45 hours, a tremendous feat of endurance on the part of the crew. During this patrol the *Sealion* was rammed by a German escort vessel and both her periscopes put out of action. Later Bryant, in command of the submarine *Safari* in the Mediterranean, attacked a convoy off the Tunisian coast, sinking an armed merchant cruiser and a tanker and driving another ship ashore. The following night, in spite of heavy antisubmarine attacks, he took the *Safari* back and hit the vessel which had been driven ashore with a torpedo, destroying her.

BT2D. Douglas Dauntless II, single-seat dive/torpedo bomber placed in production shortly before the end of the Pacific war to replace the SB2C and TBF (*see* SB2C; TBF). Manufacture was cut back after V-J Day; had the war not ended, the BT2D would have been used in the planned invasion of Japan. At V-J Day, however, it had 24 years of service ahead of it. Redesignated AD-1 in 1946 and named Skyraider, it performed with distinction in Korea and Vietnam and did not disappear from U.S. service until 1969.

BT-13. This single-engine, two-place, low-wing monoplane trainer, designed by Consolidated-Vultee, was known as the Valiant, but those who flew the craft called it the Vibrator because of the distinctive sound made by its propeller. Student and instructor sat in tandem beneath a Plexiglas canopy. The landing gear was fixed. If powered by a 450-horsepower Pratt and Whitney radial, the plane was a BT-13; if the engine was built by Wright, it was a BT-15. In its two guises, the Valiant was the standard U.S. Army Air Forces basic trainer throughout the war. More than 9,000 were built, 850 of them for the U.S. Navy.

BTM. U.S. aircraft, the Martin Mauler, competitor of the BT2D in 1945 (*see* BT2D). A single-place, multipurpose attack plane, it reflected the same design philosophy and resembled the BT2D in general appearance. It saw limited postwar service as the AM-1.

BUCCANEER. Code name for a projected Allied operation against the Andaman Islands, 1943.

BUCCANEER. U.S. Navy name for the SB2A scout bomber (*see* SB2A).

BUCHENWALD. Nazi CONCENTRATION CAMP north of Weimar, established in 1933 primarily for political prisoners. Many of the 56,000 persons who died there were Jews, but anti-Nazi Germans and non-Jews from German-occupied countries were also imprisoned at the camp. These prisoners died from starvation, general brutality and, in particular, medical experimentation. The Allies liberated Buchenwald in April 1945.

BUCKET BRIGADE. Nickname given to a temporary antisubmarine defense system employed by the United States on the East Coast in the spring of 1942. A series of anchorages, protected by nets, were set up at certain points where there were no harbors, so as to enable small coastal craft to escort merchant ships from one safe place to another. It was superseded by the interlocking convoy system. *See also* SEA FRONTIER.

BUCKINGHAM. This airplane, planned by Britain's Bristol Aircraft as a replacement for the BLENHEIM, could not compete with the immensely successful MOSQUITO and was produced in limited numbers as a fast transport. The Buckingham inspired the Buckmaster, used after the war to train light-bomber pilots and radar navigators. Both were midwing, twin-tail monoplanes powered by two 2,520-horsepower Bristol Centaurus radials and were capable of speeds in excess of 300 miles per hour.

BUCKLEY, U.S.S. Destroyer escort and class, commissioned in 1943–44 (1,400 tons standard displacement). *See also* CHARLES LAWRENCE, U.S.S.

BUCKNER, Simon Bolivar, Jr. (1886–1945). A native of Kentucky and a 1908 graduate of West Point, Buckner was commandant of cadets at that institution from 1932 to 1936. In July 1940 he was made commander of the Alaska Defense Force. He played a prominent role later in the recapture of the Aleutians from the Japanese in 1942 and 1943. He was raised to the rank of lieutenant general in 1943. After the Aleutian campaign he reported to the Central Pacific Command and was named commander of the new U.S. TENTH ARMY. In one of the last campaigns of the war, on April 1, 1945, the Tenth Army invaded OKINAWA. General Buckner was fatally wounded by an artillery shell in this campaign on June 18, 1945.

BUDANOVA, Ekaterina. Soviet woman flier, the second-ranking woman ace, with 11 victories.

BUDAPEST, BATTLE FOR. The climax of the Soviet Union's operations in the Balkans came in the three-month struggle for Budapest. Following the successful operations in Poland during the summer of 1944, the Red Army shifted its attention to the Balkans. The rapid Soviet advance and the capitulation of Bulgaria, Rumania and Hungary created a military and political vacuum in southeast Europe.

Realizing the danger to Germany's southern flank, Gen. Johannes FRIESSNER, the German commander in Hungary, sought to shorten his defensive lines. Adolf HITLER, however, forced Friessner's Army Group South to fight for every foot of the Hungarian plain. By the beginning of November the Germans were faced with an impossible military and political situation; the Magyar government had surrendered, and neither the Hungarian Army nor the people desired to fight a last-ditch battle against two Soviet army groups.

Friessner repelled the initial Soviet thrust against the Hungarian capital in late October 1944. During November, however, Gen. F. I. TOLBUKHIN's Third Ukrainian Front (army group) began the final encirclement of Budapest. In early December, Gen. Rodion MALINOVSKY's Second Ukrainian Front outflanked the city to the north. Though Hitler's attention was centered on the forthcoming ARDENNES offensive, he demanded that Friessner hold the Budapest salient to the last soldier. In December and January, Nazi offensives put off the complete destruction of the garrison, but their effort merely prolonged the agony of the defenders.

By the beginning of February 1945 there was a ration of only 75 grams of bread a day for the defenders. The fight for the city continued in the rubble and sewers until the 10th of the month. On the night of February 11, 16,000 soldiers began a desperate retreat toward their lines. Only a few hundred reached safety. Within the city, the final 33,000 defenders surrendered on February 12.

Hitler's insistence on defending the Hungarian plain and the city of Budapest compromised the defense of both flanks of the Reich by squandering the few remaining reserves of the Wehrmacht. One of the results of the fighting around Budapest was the rapid fall of Vienna and Berlin in April 1945.

BUDËNNY, Semën M. (1883–1973). Veteran Soviet military commander and founder of the Red cavalry in the Russian Civil War following the Revolution. After the German invasion in 1941, Budënny was appointed to command the Southwest Theater, in the Ukraine. In September 1941, after much of his army was encircled by the rapidly advancing German forces, he was replaced by General TIMOSHENKO. Budënny subsequently was in command of a reserve front before Moscow, and in 1942 he commanded a front in the North Caucasus. A colorful figure famous for his huge cavalryman's mustache, Budënny—like other officers who owed their prominence primarily to their friendship with Joseph STALIN—faded from the scene as the war progressed.

BUFFALO. *See* F2A.

BUGLE. Code name for widespread Allied air attacks on communications in central Germany in February 1945. Clarion was a companion operation.

BUIN. A major Japanese base at the southern end of BOUGAINVILLE, from which troops were fed down the Solomons to reinforce garrisons on the various islands. Buin held the largest concentration of Japanese forces on Bougainville, approximately 15,000 men of General HYAKUTAKE's 17th Army.

BULGANIN, Nikolai A. (1895–1975). A longtime Soviet Communist, Bulganin served in the Cheka (secret police), 1918–22, and achieved full membership in the Central Committee of the Communist Party in 1939. He served on military councils during the war and in 1944 was appointed Deputy Commissar of Defense. Subsequently, in the 1950s, he was Premier of the Soviet Union.

BULGE, BATTLE OF THE. German counteroffensive in the semimountainous ARDENNES region of Belgium and Luxembourg in December 1944, so called because of the bulge the attack created in the American lines. Its correct title is actually the Battle of the Ardennes. Involving 600,000 American troops—more than three times the number that fought on both sides at Gettys-

A Belgian woman salvages grain after the battle has passed by

burg—it was the largest pitched battle ever fought by American arms.

Even as German armies in late summer of 1944 were streaming back toward Germany following defeat in France, Adolf HITLER began contemplating a major counteroffensive against the armies of the Western Allies. He saw the possibility that a major setback to Allied arms would exacerbate tensions within the alliance and prepare the way for a separate peace on the Western Front, thereby enabling him to turn full German strength against the Soviet Union.

Hitler himself chose the Ardennes as the location of the counteroffensive. It was a region where the Supreme Allied Commander, Gen. Dwight D. EISENHOWER, was taking what he subsequently called a "calculated risk," thinning the defensive line in order to release troops for offensives under way over terrain more inviting for military operations north and south of the Ardennes. Yet as German armies had demonstrated in 1940, the Ardennes is less forbidding to military movement than it appears at first glance. Although much of the region is forested and cut by deeply incised streams, the road network is fairly extensive. Across the German frontier the contiguous EIFEL region provided dense forests where German forces might assemble in secrecy.

A quick thrust to ANTWERP, Hitler reasoned, would isolate the entire troop commitment of one of the Allies, the British 21ST ARMY GROUP, plus the U.S. NINTH ARMY and the bulk of the U.S. FIRST ARMY, which comprised roughly two-thirds of the 12TH ARMY GROUP. Even if the counteroffensive failed to lead to a separate peace in the west, it would at least erase the immediate threat to the Ruhr industrial area, just east of the Rhine River, upon which the Germans depended for coal and steel. Although the commanders who would have to execute the plan—the Commander in Chief in the West, Field Marshal Gerd von RUNDSTEDT, and the commander of Army Group B, Field Marshal Walther MODEL—considered it far too ambitious for available resources and argued against it, Hitler refused to modify the undertaking.

Hitler changed the original code name, Christrose, to conform with the cover plan he devised to conceal preparations, and called it Wacht am Rhein (Watch on the Rhine). While the main buildup occurred in the forested Eifel, the panzer concentration was north of the Eifel, ostensibly aimed at checking an American offensive toward the Rhine and the Ruhr industrial area. Only at the last minute did the panzer divisions join the buildup in the Eifel.

So basic to the plan was secrecy that Hitler forbade any radio or telephone transmissions concerning it. All orders going out over radio or telephone dealt with that apparent approaching battle. Not until a week before the target date were corps and division commanders told their assignments, and not until the night before the attack were the troops informed what they were to do. All troop movements were by night, and bad weather for several days preceding the attack was integral to the plan, a fact that necessitated several postponements of the target date, which was finally set for December 16. The shift of the panzer divisions and a final movement to assault positions began three nights earlier.

On a 60-mile front destined for assault—from the German border town of MONSCHAU in the north to ECHTERNACH in Luxembourg—only six American divisions were in the line. They were getting their first combat experience in the relatively quiet sector or were resting after hard fighting elsewhere. Only in the north near Monschau was there any appreciable concentration of troops. There, under V Corps, one infantry division was making a local attack through the lines of another division. The rest of the front was the responsibility of the VIII Corps under Maj. Gen. Troy H. MIDDLETON. A thin screen of light armored cavalry served as the link between the V and VIII Corps. Just to the south of the cavalry along a dominant ridgeline, the Schnee Eifel, in front of the road center of SAINT-VITH, was the 106th Infantry Division, newly arrived at the front, then farther south the 28th and 4th Infantry Divisions, both of which had incurred heavy losses in recent actions. A relatively inexperienced armored division, the 9th, comprised the corps reserve.

The German deception was markedly effective. General Eisenhower's intelligence officer warned that the Germans possibly might use their concentration to attack in the Ardennes, and the First Army's intelligence officer noted some indications of German buildup in the Eifel. His operations staff, however, assured the Supreme Commander there would be no attack. Although American outposts reported noise of German movement at night, that was discounted as nothing but routine relief of units. Four prisoners captured on December 15 spoke of a big offensive before Christmas, but only one impressed his interrogators as truthful.

The Germans attacked through deep snow before dawn on December 16, in some cases using artificial moonlight created by bouncing searchlight beams off low clouds. Achieving total surprise, approximately 200,000 German troops forming three armies were in the opening assault against some 83,000 Americans. The Sixth Panzer Army under Generaloberst der Waf-

U.S. Third Army vehicles move toward besieged Bastogne

fen-SS Josef ("Sepp") DIETRICH on the north wing made the main effort, seeking to capture bridges over the Meuse River within 48 hours and then strike for Antwerp. The Fifth Panzer Army under General der Panzertruppen Hasso-Eccard von MANTEUFFEL lent support on the left, aiming at the road center of Saint-Vith and pushing on alongside the Sixth Panzer Army to and over the Meuse. The Seventh Army under General der Panzertruppen Erich BRANDENBERGER provided flank protection on the south.

To speed the advance of the Sixth Panzer Army by capturing bridges with raiding parties and spreading rumors and confusion in American ranks through men disguised in American uniforms (Operation GREIF), the Germans had formed a special brigade of about 2,000 men (Panzer Brigade 156), commanded by Col. Otto SKORZENY. Under the original plan, all were to have been capable of speaking "American dialect" but in the end only 150 were so qualified and equipped. One small group in a jeep got near the Meuse and there died in the explosion of a mine. A handful of others got behind American lines but accomplished little except to prompt American sentries to use extra caution with passwords. A battalion of paratroopers was also to assist by dropping during the night of December 15 astride a major highway to block American reinforcements from the north. It was delayed for two nights because somebody forgot to provide gasoline for trucks to take the men to their planes.

The Sixth Panzer Army had the bad fortune to hit the one concentrated American force in the Ardennes. A few miles southeast of Monschau the veteran 2d Infantry Division was conducting a local attack through lines of the 99th Infantry Division. Men of the 99th held through the first day, but by nightfall the situation was so serious that the V Corps commander, Maj. Gen. Leonard T. GEROW, sent the 2d Division's uncommitted reserve regiment to back up the line. The next day, acting on his own when First Army refused to make a decision, Gerow halted his attack and committed his forces to the defensive. The orders were to hold in front of a prominent terrain feature, the Elsenborn ridge, until other units could come up. For two days and nights the 2d Division and elements of the 99th held, then on the night of December 19 withdrew to the ridge, there to be joined by the reinforcing divisions. Thus the Sixth Panzer Army attack along the northern shoulder ground to a halt.

The Sixth Panzer Army's only success to that point was achieved by a 2,000-man task force of the 1st SS Panzer Division under Lt. Col. Joachim PEIPER that penetrated the thin U.S. cavalry positions linking the 99th and 106th Divisions. After rifling gasoline stocks behind the 2d and 99th Divisions, Peiper's SS troops executed 19 unarmed American prisoners and the next day, December 17, shot up a passing convoy of an American artillery observation battalion at a crossroads near MALMÉDY. More than a hundred Americans were captured, marched into a field and mowed down with machine gun fire. A few escaped by feigning death, but 86 died in what became known as the Malmédy Massacre, the worst atrocity involving American troops during the war in Europe.

In Army Group B's center, the Fifth Panzer Army struck the 106th Division in front of Saint-Vith and thin positions of two regiments of the 28th Division in the northern reaches of Luxembourg along a stretch of high ground that American troops called the Skyline Drive. Two regiments of the green 106th Division on the Schnee Eifel ridge were quickly surrounded. Given a combat command of armor from the corps reserve, the 106th Division commander used it to reinforce the seam between his division and the 28th to the south. He figured the 7th Armored Division would come up by December 17 and could break through to the encircled regiments. The forecast of that unit's progress was undone by slick roads and 60 miles of blackout driving. By the time the lead command of the 7th Armored arrived, the Germans had drawn the noose tight. On December 19 the regiments surrendered—approximately 8,000 men—the most serious reverse incurred by American arms in the war against Germany.

A few miles farther south there should have been no contest; men of the 28th Infantry Division were so thinly spread along the Skyline Drive that the Germans could readily infiltrate between positions. Yet all day the American infantrymen held firm, aided by cooks and clerks who joined the fight. Only after the Germans during the night put in bridges across the little Our River and moved tanks across did collapse come about. Even then stragglers from one regiment rallied around the regimental command post at a crossing of the Clerf River on a main highway leading to BASTOGNE and held into the night of December 17, while the 28th Division's northernmost regiment peeled back relatively intact. At Saint-Vith the 7th Armored, a combat command of the 9th Armored, and a surviving regiment of the 106th Division formed a horseshoe-shaped defense about the town. Like the Elsenborn ridge, Saint-Vith stood as a main obstacle in the path of the Germans. Although the OKW plan called for the taking of Saint-Vith by the second day, General von Manteuffel finally got it on December 21, and even then the Americans held nearby for another day until a providential freeze provided firm footing for vehicles. Then they were authorized to withdraw.

On the south wing of the counteroffensive, General Brandenberger's Seventh Army lacked the strength in armor of the other two German armies. Yet the American defenders there—the 4th Division and a third regiment of the 28th—were as thinly spread in platoon and company outposts as were their neighbors, and the Germans could easily slip between them. Taking the outposts was another matter. In a cluster of farm buildings, one group of 21 men held for four days. Here and there small units held fast and resisted resolutely.

Within the American high command, full realization of what was happening in the Ardennes came slowly. Because the opening artillery barrages knocked out communications, reports reaching the First Army commander, Lt. Gen. Courtney H. HODGES, were at first meager. He and his superior, the 12th Army Group commander, Lt. Gen. Omar N. BRADLEY, reckoned through midafternoon of the first day that the offensive was simply a spoiling attack in reaction to the local American thrust near Monschau. The fog was no less thick at SHAEF. Yet even if the attack was local, General Eisenhower decided, the VIII Corps would need help to meet it. That was what started the 7th Armored Division moving southward toward Saint-Vith while the 10th Armored Division moved northward from the Third Army. Hodges started shifting infantry divisions to the Elsenborn ridge and farther west to extend the northern shoulder of the bulge.

By the second day more indications of the awesome power of the German thrust became unmistakable. General Hodges appealed to General Eisenhower for use of the Allied reserve, consisting of two airborne divisions. An order to move reached the two divisions that evening. By midnight of December 17, the second day, some 60,000 men and 11,000 vehicles were on the way to reinforce the defenders of the Ardennes. In the next eight days, three times those numbers would be on the move.

SHAEF's plan was to hold the northern and southern shoulders while preventing the Germans from crossing the Meuse; meanwhile the Third Army would prepare to attack from the south. Other than holding the shoulders, the staff saw three tasks as critical: deny the roads passing through Saint-Vith as long as possible; contain and then eliminate what had become a deep penetration by Task Force Peiper; and hold the road center of Bastogne. Troops were already on hand to defend Saint-Vith. To move against Peiper, the chief of staff, Gen. W. B. SMITH, sent the 82d Airborne Division. To Bastogne, in front of which stragglers of the 28th Division and a combat command each of the 9th and 10th Armored Divisions were fighting delaying actions, he committed the 101st Airborne Division.

As the scope and depth of the German penetration became apparent, General Eisenhower saw that the Germans in effect had split the 12th Army Group, making communications between forces to the north and south of the bulge nigh impossible. For that reason he transferred the U.S. First and Ninth Armies north of the bulge to command of Field Marshal Sir Bernard L. MONTGOMERY's 21st Army Group. Although General Bradley resented the decision then and lastingly, thus straining U.S. command relations at the highest level, he had no choice but to yield.

Even as the defenders of Saint-Vith held until December 21, the 82d Airborne Division blunted Task Force Peiper's penetration near the town of WERBOMONT; then, with the help of American infantry coming down from the north, the 82d by Christmas Eve eliminated the German armored task force. At Bastogne the 101st Airborne Division won the race for the town by about seven hours. The XLVII Panzer Corps encircled the town on December 20, and two days later the commanding officer sent emissaries demanding its surrender. To that the acting commander of the airborne division, Brig. Gen. Anthony C. MCAULIFFE, replied in American slang: "Nuts!"

The Germans on Christmas Day mounted a heavy armored attack to take Bastogne. But help for the defenders was on the way. With remarkable speed the commander of the Third Army, Lt. Gen. George S. PATTON, Jr., had turned his forces in a 90-degree shift to the north. On December 22 the counterattack against the southern shoulder of the bulge got moving. The 4th Armored Division broke into Bastogne the day after Christmas.

Despite the relief, still heavier fighting continued at Bastogne, since the Germans saw the city as the prize that, denied them, would make failure final. The salient was too narrow to mount a successful counterattack. Yet General Patton continued to waste troops trying for a breakthrough.

The panzer divisions of the Fifth and Sixth German Armies had by December 19 slipped past Saint-Vith to the north and south and in a corridor 20 miles wide between Bastogne and Werbomont they were struggling toward the Meuse. There were no major American reserves to stop them at first, but they did not ad-

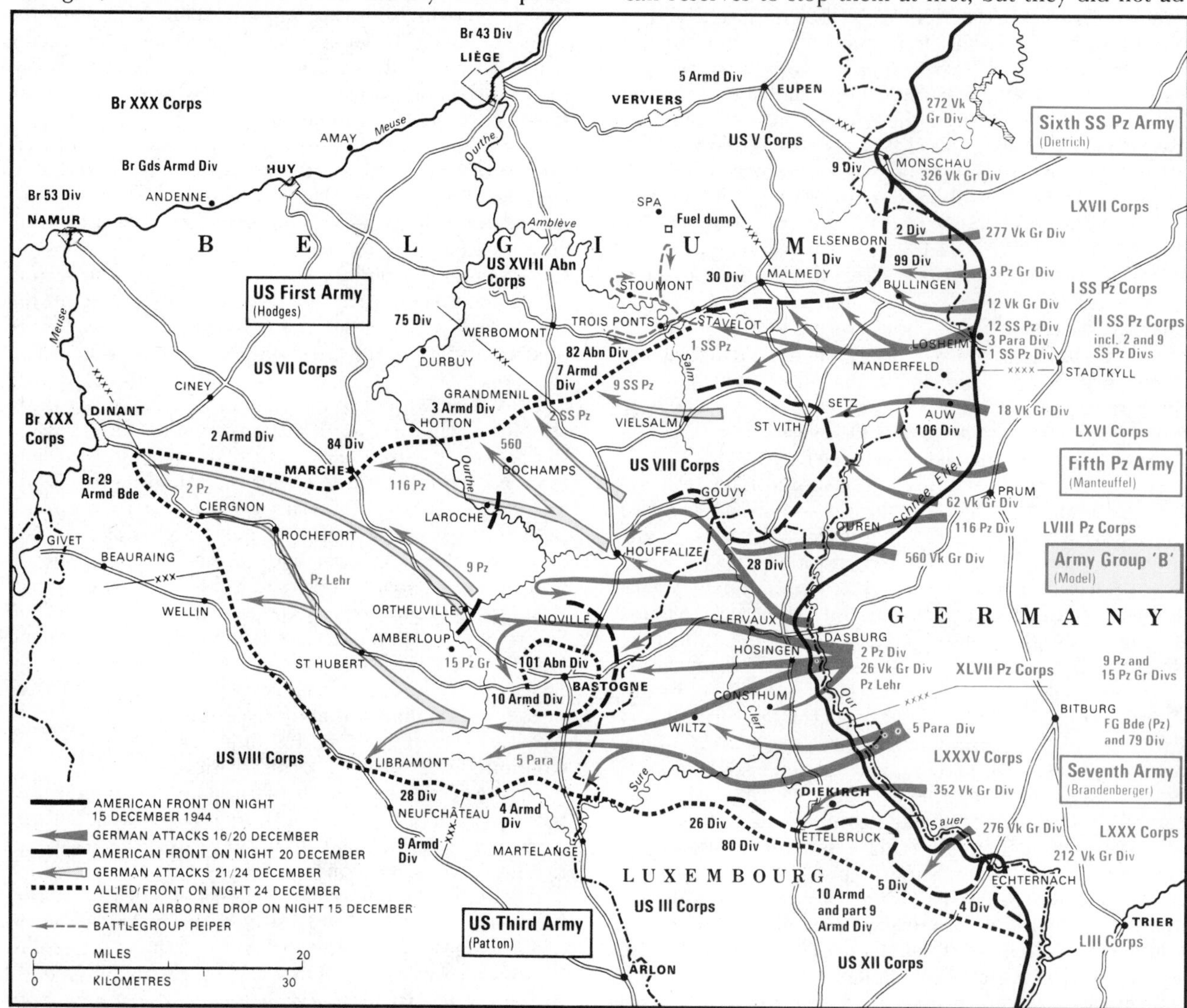

THE BATTLE OF THE BULGE: The German attacks

vance unresisted. Here and there combat fragments made up of headquarters, supply and service people helped by combat stragglers holed up in a village, at the edge of a woods, in a farmhouse at a crossroads, and opened fire. The Germans were slowed too by difficulties in bringing supplies forward over icy roads, and gasoline was soon running short. Near the town of STAVELOT an American major poured can after can of gasoline into a deep road cut and set it afire to deny German tank divisions access to a big gasoline depot. Near First Army headquarters the German spearpoint stranded for lack of fuel within one-half mile of the Army's largest POL dump (*see* POL).

A little river with two branches, the Ourthe, stood between the panzer divisions and the Meuse. Although American engineers tried to demolish the bridges, one charge northwest of Bastogne failed, enabling tanks of one of the panzer divisions to cross during the night of December 20, only 23 miles short of the Meuse. Yet there, to the amazement of American observers, they stopped. Only later was it learned that the German tank divisions were out of gas. Refueled by the 22d, three panzer divisions began a final drive intended for the Meuse. That was the night the hard freeze set in that provided firm footing for American troops to fall back from Saint-Vith; the next day the skies over the Ardennes, for the first time since the counteroffensive began, were clear enough for American fighter-bombers to operate. On December 23 the planes were out in force, attacking German columns at every opportunity. By that time General Hodges had moved additional divisions into the line behind the Ourthe.

Only one German division got through, the 2d Panzer Division, but that penetration posed a minor crisis in the Allied command. Having assembled VII Corps under Maj. Gen. J. Lawton COLLINS near the Meuse, General Hodges was withholding it on Field Marshal Montgomery's order until the German drive had run its course. Thereon Montgomery intended to counterattack. During midafternoon of Christmas Eve, the commander of the 2d Armored Division, General HARMON, reported the presence of the 2d Panzer Division a few miles short of the Meuse and asked permission to attack. Anxious to get on with undoing the damage the Germans had inflicted, General Hodges was torn by Montgomery's order to withhold VII Corps. He solved his dilemma by authorizing but not directing the armored division to withdraw and including no specific proviso against attack. That was all the commander of the American 2d Armored Division needed. He attacked successfully soon after dawn on Christmas Day.

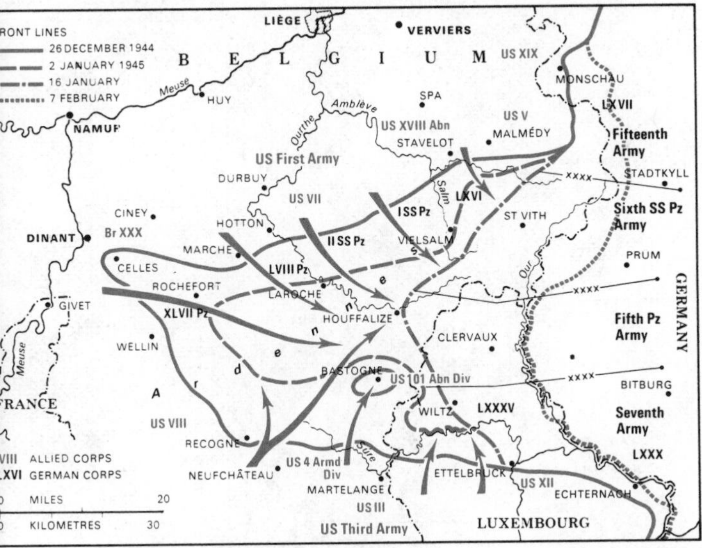

THE BULGE: Allied counterattacks

German higher commanders had become aware by Christmas Eve that the plan was defeated. On January 3, 1945, the First Army began counterattacking from the north to link early on January 16 with a 17th Airborne Division task force from the Third Army at the town of HOUFFALIZE, north of Bastogne. On January 8 Hitler authorized withdrawal from the tip of the bulge and assembly of the SS panzer divisions near the base of the bulge as a first step in quitting the Ardennes to counter a new Russian offensive on the Eastern Front. The final order to pull out came on January 22. By that time American troops had eliminated the bulge from the German offensive. It was all over by January 28.

Not only had the Germans failed to reach their main objective of Antwerp, but they had also fallen short of the interim objective of the Meuse River line. Hitler had accomplished only swift victory for the new Russian offensive, the delay for about six weeks of an Allied offensive and the deaths of tens of thousands.

Including wounded, the Germans incurred about 100,000 casualties. American casualties totaled 81,000, of which 19,000 were killed and 15,000 captured. Among small British units that fought briefly in the tip of the bulge, there were 1,400 casualties. Both sides lost heavily in weapons and equipment, probably as many as 800 tanks each, and the Germans lost a thousand planes. Yet the Americans could replace their losses in little more than a fortnight, while the Germans could not. **C.B.M./S.L.A.M.**

BULKELEY, John Duncan (1911–). A U.S. Naval Academy graduate in 1933, Lieutenant Bulkeley fought in the Philippine rearguard action of late 1941 through mid-1942. As a motor torpedo boat commander (*see* PT), he evacuated Gen. Douglas MACARTHUR and family from Luzon on March 11, 1942. The experience impressed MacArthur with the capabilities of the motor torpedo boat. Bulkeley continued to demonstrate the PT's value both in the Pacific and later in Europe, where, as a lieutenant commander, he participated in the liberation of CHERBOURG in June and July 1944. Following the war Bulkeley rose through the grades to flag rank.

BULL, Harold R. (1893–1976). U.S. Army officer who served as Assistant Chief of Staff, G-3 (operations), in 1942. In 1942–43 he was the commanding general of the Replacement School Command, Army Ground Forces. In 1943 he briefly served as commander of III Corps, but in September of that year he went to London to become deputy G-3 of COSSAC, the planning staff for the INVASION of northern France. In February 1944 he was appointed G-3 of SHAEF. He was promoted to major general in 1942. "Pinky" Bull shared his duties as SHAEF G-3 with the British general Sir John WHITELEY, but in addition he occasionally sat in as acting chief of staff to the Supreme Commander. Following the war, as a lieutenant general, he was commandant of the National War College.

BULLITT, William Christian (1891–1967). U.S. diplomat who advised President Wilson at Versailles and served as the first U.S. ambassador to the Soviet Union. His next position was as envoy to France, where he served between 1936 and 1940. Strongly pro-French, Bullitt pushed for American aid to the Allies and favored the establishment of American relations with the VICHY government.

BUNA. A group of synthetic rubbers originally developed in Germany about 1925 by I. G. Farben and sold in the United States beginning in 1937 under the name Perbunan. The trademark name Buna comes from the two chemicals from which the synthetic rubber was made, *bu*tadiene and *na*trium. After 1941 synthetic rubber became indispensable in the manufacture of rubber articles because the world's production of crude rubber was insufficient to meet the growing demand and Indonesia, the source of more than 90 percent of the world's rubber, had been captured by Japan. The Allied butadiene-based synthetic was called GR-S. One variety of Buna (Buna-N) made possible the self-sealing gasoline tank.

BUNA. The eastern terminus of the KOKODA TRAIL over the OWEN STANLEY MOUNTAINS, New Guinea. Japanese Navy forces occupied Buna on July 22, 1942. At the beginning of January 1943 it was taken by the Allies after heavy fighting.

BUNDLES FOR BRITAIN. A volunteer, humanitarian organization established on December 30, 1939, by Mrs. Natalie Wales Latham, a New York society matron. The organization gathered and shipped "bundles" of blankets, woolen garments and other warm clothing to the British people during the period of Hitler's threatened invasion and the London BLITZ. Mrs. Winston S. (Clementine) CHURCHILL became honorary sponsor of the organization, which also delivered medical supplies, surgical equipment, mobile canteens and substantial cash donations to the British. By the end of 1940 Bundles for Britain reportedly had almost 500 local branches in 46 states.

BUNGO SUIDO. A channel 20 to 25 miles wide separating the Japanese Home Islands of Kyushu and Shikoku. U.S. submarines, separately and in packs, lay in wait off the strait for profitable targets coming out into the Pacific or turning south toward the South China Sea. It was from Bungo Suido that the 69,100-ton YAMATO, one of the two largest and most heavily armored battleships in the world, steamed to her doom on April 6, 1945.

BUQ BUQ. An important supply and water center for the Italians in the fall of 1940, on the Egyptian coast near the Libyan border. It was captured by the British in December 1940, when Churchill was amused by a young officer's message, "Have arrived at the second B in Buq Buq."

BURG-EL-ARAB. Headquarters of Gen. B. L. MONTGOMERY'S British EIGHTH ARMY in 1942, at the time of the Battle of ALAMEIN.

BURKE, Arleigh Albert (1901–). A 1923 U.S. Naval Academy graduate, Burke was a surface officer with considerable experience in ordnance during the interwar period. Stationed at the Washington Navy Yard when Pearl Harbor was attacked, he was sent to the SOLOMON ISLANDS in January 1943 to command successively Destroyer Divisions 43 and 44 and Destroyer Squadron 12. During this time he developed a distinctive plan for the independent operation of destroyers in night tactical actions. He also acquired the nickname "31-knot Burke," given him for fast sailing on one particular mission. From October 1943 to March 1944 he commanded Destroyer Squadron 23 in the BOUGAINVILLE and NEW GUINEA campaigns and put his plan into effect in the Battles of EMPRESS AUGUSTA BAY, November 1, 1943, and CAPE ST. GEORGE, on November 25. In March 1944 Captain Burke became chief of staff to Vice-Adm. Marc A. MITSCHER, commander of Fast Carrier Task Force 58, and served as Mitscher's chief aide in the MARSHALLS, MARIANAS, LEYTE, IWO JIMA and OKINAWA campaigns. After the war he saw considerable important duty in Washington, the Mediterranean and Korea, and was appointed Chief of Naval Operations in 1955, serving until 1961.

BURKE-WADSWORTH ACT. The Congressional act authorizing the SELECTIVE SERVICE SYSTEM (August 27, 1940). The sponsors were Sen. Edward R. Burke of Nebraska and Rep. James W. Wadsworth of New York.

BURMA—OPERATIONS. Not regarded as a likely scene of operations by the Allies when the war began, Burma became a battleground with the fall of Malaya and SINGAPORE. Defense of Burma was, however, only one of the many responsibilities of Gen. Sir Archibald WAVELL, commander of all the Allied forces in Southeast Asia. Japanese victories shrank Wavell's command and eventually, on February 22, 1942, operational control of Burmese forces was transferred to Delhi, India.

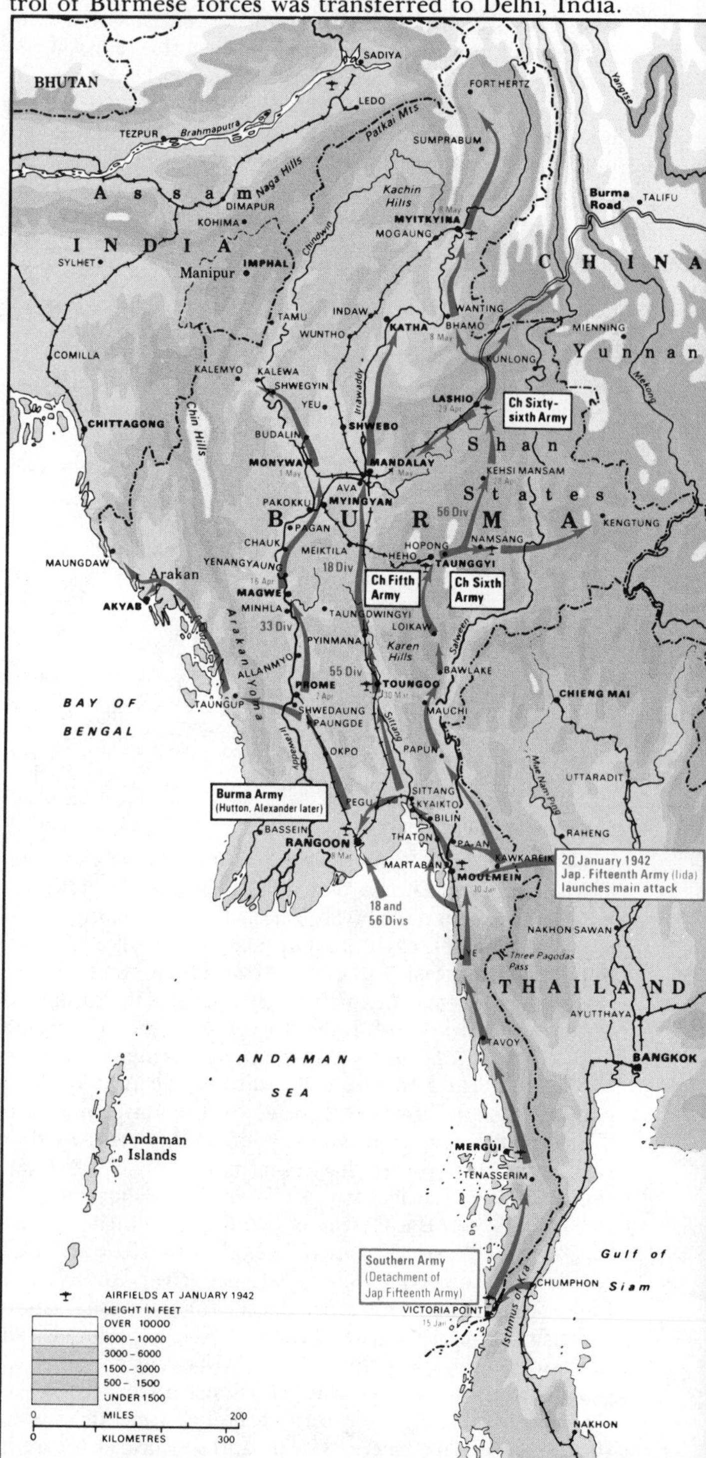

THE FALL OF BURMA came in four months

Earlier, on December 27, 1941, Wavell had put the Burma forces under the command of Lt. Gen. Thomas J. Hutton, who had been chief of staff for India.

British forces in Burma consisted primarily of the 17th Indian Division, a few British units and a locally recruited small Burma Defence Force. The British began the Burmese campaign with an unsuccessful foray into Thailand to cut bridges on the Bangkok-Malaya railway. They were forced to retire without finding the bridges.

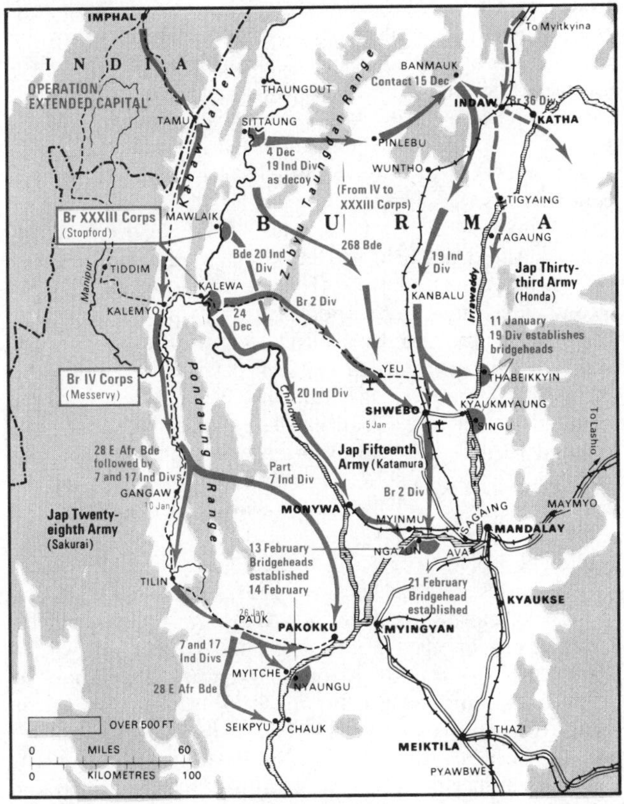

ALLIED ADVANCE IN BURMA, 1944–45—Imphal to Mandalay

The Japanese assigned the invasion of Burma to their 15th Army, under Lt. Gen. Shojiro IIDA. This army was originally made up of the 55th and the 33d Divisions, with a combined strength of 35,000 men. After Japanese victories in Malaya and the Philippines, two more divisions, the 18th and 56th, along with tank, antiaircraft and artillery units, were assigned to Burma. Air support was furnished by Gen. Hideyoshi Obata's Fifth Air Division, along with the 4th and 10th Air Brigades.

As early as December 11, 1941, Japanese forces crossed into Burma. On December 16, Victoria Point, in the southernmost part of the Burmese "tail," was occupied and the advance northward began. British preparations were quite inadequate, for it was felt that the difficult terrain would preclude any serious overland Japanese attack. The fall of MOULMEIN showed the inaccuracy of this assumption.

The British forces invariably stuck to the roads and the cleared, cultivated areas and were just as invariably outflanked and defeated by the Japanese. A major disaster occurred on February 23, 1942, when a force of 12 battalions was destroyed between the SITTANG and Bilin Rivers east of PEGU. Even before this defeat, General Wavell had decided to make a change in field commanders. General Hutton was replaced on February 22 by Gen. Sir Harold ALEXANDER, with Maj. Gen. T. J. W. Winterton as chief of staff and Lt. Gen. William J. SLIM as a corps commander.

The city of Pegu now became the point at which the British hoped to stop the Japanese and prevent them from cutting off RANGOON. The newly arrived 63d Indian Brigade engaged in savage fighting in the first week of March 1942 but was forced out of the city. On the 6th Rangoon was abandoned, leaving large stores to fall to the Japanese. As the British retreated north, sticking to the roads and usually being outflanked by the Japanese, help was received from China. A Chinese army entered Burma in mid-March, a halfhearted response to a halfhearted request for aid from General Wavell. The Chinese force was nominally under the command of Lt. Gen. Joseph W. STILWELL. Stilwell's force undertook to defend the Sittang valley east of the Pegu River and also the southern Shan States. The intelligence operation and staff work of the British were particularly inadequate. The Chinese fought well at first, although the coordination of the two forces did not proceed smoothly. The Allied effort was seriously handicapped by the presence of hordes of refugees, 400,000 of them Indians. By April 30, LASHIO, terminus of the BURMA ROAD, had fallen and all central Burma was in Japanese hands.

The retreat of the British became a disorganized rout, but the Chinese fought steadfastly until the enemy broke through to the Shan plateau. With their retreat nearly cut off, the Chinese army broke and virtually disintegrated as it fled north.

By the end of May 1942 the rainy season had begun and the Japanese had won an overwhelming victory. The three and a half months' fighting had cost the British Indian troops 3,670 killed or wounded and 6,366 missing. Burmese units had lost 363 killed or wounded and 3,064 missing. The Japanese casualties were 4,597 killed or wounded. The Allies lost 116 aircraft, the Japanese 117.

A lull occurred in the fighting at this time. The Japanese needed time to consolidate their victory, and the jungle terrain of Burma's frontier served temporarily to contain them. By late 1942 Wavell was confident that he had sufficient strength to commence small-scale offensive operations against the Japanese. He decided to seize the port of AKYAB on the ARAKAN coast. Unfortunately, this decision coincided with other events which greatly limited its chances of success. German victories made it necessary to send an infantry division and the 7th Armored Brigade to the Middle East. In India, the civil disobedience campaign of the Congress Party greatly inconvenienced the Army. Almost foredoomed, the Arakan campaign began.

Two brigades of British and Indian troops made a direct seaborne attack on Akyab. The Japanese were well dug in, and again the British grossly underestimated the Japanese ability to operate in jungle terrain. The British were thrown back, and a counterattack by Lt. Gen. Takishi Koga's 55th Division destroyed the two brigades. After suffering 2,500 casualties, the survivors were returned to India.

Fortunately, attention was diverted from this wretched affair by the activity of Brig. Orde Charles WINGATE'S CHINDIT raiders in northern Burma in mid-

February of 1943. Some 3,000 men, divided into two groups and supplied by air, operated in the rear of the Japanese lines from February to March 24, when they retreated overland to India.

The military success of the Chindits was questionable. A few bridges were blown and the enemy discomfited somewhat. The effort required a considerable deployment of supply and air support forces. Moreover, only 1,500 of the force of 3,000 survived. On the psychological side, the Chindits were a success, giving the British and Indians a much needed morale boost, and the Japanese were forced to alter their plans because of the raids.

During the remainder of 1943 Burma was relatively quiet. In the Chin Hills in the north and the Arakan area in the south there was occasional small-scale but bitter fighting, in which the Japanese invariably triumphed.

Allied plans for Burma in 1943–44 were the subject of constant conflicts between political and national interests, branches of the military and individual personalities. Gen. Claire CHENNAULT wished to air-supply his air forces in China and to make them the principal weapon against the Japanese. General Stilwell wished to campaign with a new Chinese army of 30 divisions under his command. British headquarters and Wavell wanted an overland reconquest of Burma. Wingate wanted long-range penetration brigades to play an important part, and so on. All during 1943 in the various Allied conferences first one view would prevail and then another. On the command level progress was made, however. General Wavell was made Viceroy of India, and Adm. Lord Louis MOUNTBATTEN replaced him as Supreme Commander, SOUTHEAST ASIA COMMAND (SEAC). General Stilwell became Deputy Supreme Commander, but also retained his other positions—commander in chief of U.S. air and ground forces in Southeast Asia, commander in chief of the Chinese Army in Burma and chief of staff to CHIANG KAI-SHEK. The British Eastern Army became the Fourteenth Army and was placed under the command of General Slim.

The Japanese, meanwhile, reinforced their Burmese forces, built the 250-mile BURMA RAILWAY to improve their communications and reorganized their command, placing all Burma under Burma Area Headquarters and Lt. Gen. Masakazu KAWABE. The central front was manned by the 15th Army of Lt. Gen. Renya Mutaguchi. The Arakan (southern) front was held by the 28th Army (15th, 31st and 33d Divisions and 1st INDIAN NATIONAL ARMY Division of Subhas Chandra BOSE) under Lt. Gen. Seizo Sakurai. In the north, the 33d Army (18th and 56th Divisions) faced Stilwell's Chinese forces.

At this point, both sides were planning to begin offensives as soon as possible. On January 15 Mountbatten issued a directive ordering Stilwell to attack from the north, the 4th Corps under Lt. Gen. G. A. P. SCOONES to attack on the central front, in cooperation with Wingate's Chindits, and the 15th Corps under Lt. Gen. A. F. P. Christison to attack on the Arakan front. It was hoped that the Chinese forces in YUNNAN province would join in the attack.

The Japanese beat the Allies to the punch, launching a strong attack on the Arakan front in the south on the night of February 3. General Sakurai's forces moved with the usual skill and dash, but this time the extensive retraining of the British and Indian forces paid off. Bypassed units, supplied by air, continued fighting and attacked the supply lines of the infiltrating Japanese forces. The Japanese had counted on capturing British supply dumps, but these were fiercely defended and did not fall. After some initial success, the Japanese wore themselves out, and on February 23 Sakurai ordered a general withdrawal. As he did so, the British mounted a steady attack against him.

In the north, Stilwell took direct command of his Chinese troops. With an American unit trained in the Chindit fashion (MERRILL'S MARAUDERS) operating behind Japanese lines, he launched a general attack. Characteristically, he conducted his campaign with great secrecy and without much consideration for the other fronts.

On the central front, Wingate's hold on the imagination of Allied political leaders dictated that he be given the chance to open the offensive first. On February 5 extensive long-range penetration operations were begun. By air and by infiltration, thousands of men were put behind Japanese lines. At the height of this operation, Wingate was killed in an air accident. His death deprived the Chindits of the forceful personality needed to make the whole idea work, and his political influence was lost. The Chindits soon came under the command of Stilwell, and they waned in importance as a factor in Burma.

Stilwell's offensive was a success, capturing the northern Japanese stronghold of MYITKYINA, but political factors would be his downfall. While he was waging his campaign, General Chennault's U.S. Air Force in China had launched an air offensive against the Japanese. This in turn incited the Japanese to mount an attack in China to capture his forward bases, and this offensive led to Chinese-American political difficulties, for the Chinese felt that they had unnecessarily weakened themselves to give Stilwell more troops. The result was the removal, at Chiang's insistence, of Stilwell on October 27, 1944, and his replacement by Lt. Gen. Albert C. WEDEMEYER. The field command in north Burma was taken over by Lt. Gen. Daniel I. SULTAN.

On the Yunnan front, the Chinese attacked on May 10. Though they proceeded at a leisurely pace, they tied down considerable Japanese forces.

The major battle for Burma was yet to be fought, however. On March 8, 1944, the Japanese began their long-awaited attempt to invade India, on the central front on a line from KOHIMA to IMPHAL. Three Japanese divisions (the 33d, 15th and 31st) made the attack, which caught the British by surprise. Nevertheless, the new tactics that had been devised by General Slim and used earlier with great success on the Arakan front were successful again. The Japanese were fought to a standstill at Kohima and Imphal by April 21. The British launched a counterattack, and the Japanese 15th Army began to disintegrate. By early October the British had bridgeheads across the CHINDWIN RIVER and half the Japanese 15th Army was dead—30,500 men out of an original 60,000.

In December the Allies mounted a general offensive. On the Arakan front, Akyab was captured on January 3, 1945. Ramree Island was secured by February 9 after heavy resistance. There was much heavy amphibious fighting in the many canals of this region (the so-called CHAUNG WAR). On the central front, the British Fourteenth Army advanced on a 140-mile front and captured Meiktila on March 4. In the north, General Sultan's forces advanced and by January 20, 1945, he had reopened land communications with China. On March 7 Lashio was recaptured. The Japanese tried to recapture Meiktila, but were heavily repulsed and so weakened that they had to give up Mandalay.

On May 3 an amphibious Allied landing combined with a parachute drop recaptured Rangoon, and the war in Burma was virtually over. General Slim's advancing forces destroyed all but about 4,000 or 5,000 Japanese, who managed to cross the Sittang River and escape to the east.

From the time the final offensive began, the British and Indian forces suffered losses of 4,115 killed and 13,764 wounded. The American ground force, Merrill's Marauders, had heavy going and suffered several hundred casualties. There are no accurate figures for the Chinese losses. More than 100,000 Japanese were killed in the final operations. **W.O.**

BURMA RAILWAY. The Burma Railway was a principal means of communication for the country during the war, second only to Burma's numerous rivers. Until the fall of Burma, the railway, with its spur to Lashio, was important in the delivery of supplies to the China-bound BURMA ROAD, which began at this northern Burma city. When the British reoccupied Burma in 1944 and 1945, the British Fourteenth Army used the railway and parallel roads to advance upon Rangoon.

BURMA ROAD. This famous highway was started from KUNMING (China) during 1920. The Yunnan section follows along the general route of Genghis Khan's messengers and the old spice and tea caravan trail toward Burma. It was opened during late 1939 to Wanting, a Yunnan province border village, to which the government of Burma had by then built roads to connect with their Irrawaddy River ports of Bhamo and RANGOON and with the railhead town of LASHIO. The Burma Road was opened as mostly a one-track light-surface road. The road distance from Kunming to Lashio is 717 miles.

As a result of the Japanese advance in 1942, the southern ports of China were closed and the invaders gained control of the Burma termini of the road. The defending Chinese, in an effort to stop the advancing enemy, blew up the vital Salween River bridge and destroyed 25 miles of the road along a section of the Salween River canyon.

Although an air route over the Himalaya Mountains (the HUMP) between India and China was opened, the need for a land route still existed. Opening the route meant reconstructing the Burma Road by rebuilding the sections that had been destroyed and widening or improving the rest of it. Col. Leo Dawson, a U.S. Army engineer, was placed in charge of the project as an adviser. The Chinese furnished engineers and up to 30,000 laborers at a time, as well as supplies and material. Assembling the scattered equipment (eight pieces) and making such repairs as were possible took six months. But during September 1943 reconstruction of the road was begun. The Chinese, with their hands, mattocklike shovels and bamboo baskets, and the U.S. Army's Burma Road engineers with slightly more equipment literally scratched and filled every kilometer of the road. Completed by mid-August 1944, it connected with the newly built LEDO ROAD in territory held by the Chinese.

BURP GUN. Americans gave this name to a widely used German machine pistol, the blowback-operated 9-mm. Schmeisser MP 40, which had many features in common with the U.S. Thompson submachine gun. *See also* SMALL ARMS.

BURROUGH, Sir Harold Martin (1888–). British naval officer, for the first two years of the war Assistant Chief of Naval Staff at the Admiralty. In 1942 he commanded the Allied naval forces assaulting Algiers during Operation TORCH, the NORTHWEST AFRICA landings, and followed this appointment as Flag Officer Commanding Gibraltar and Mediterranean Approaches. After the death of Adm. Sir Bertram RAMSAY in an aircraft accident in 1945, Admiral Burrough succeeded as naval commander in chief of the Allied Expeditionary Force, and was thus responsible for the final naval operations of the war in European waters. He was naval commander in chief in Germany immediately after the war.

BURROWS, Montagu Brocas (1894–1967). British Army officer who served as British military attaché to Italy, 1939–40; head of the British Military Mission to Russia, 1944; and as General Officer Commanding in Chief West Africa, 1945–46. He held the rank of lieutenant general.

BURTON ISLAND. In KWAJALEIN Atoll, invaded by troops of U.S. 7th Division (17th Infantry) on February 3, 1944, and secured the next day, despite strong resistance.

BUSCH, Ernst (1885–1945). German Army officer (field marshal, 1945) who was a corps commander in the Polish campaign in 1939 and commanded the Sixteenth Army in the invasion of the Soviet Union. In November 1943 he became commander of Army Group Center, holding the post until August 1944. In March 1945 he was appointed to a new position, one conceived out of desperation, as commander in chief in the Northwest (OB Nordwest), with authority over naval and Luftwaffe units as well as Army forces. He died in British captivity.

BUSH, Vannevar (1890–1974). A scientist and electrical engineer from Massachusetts, Bush joined the faculty of the Massachusetts Institute of Technology in 1919 and served as dean of its school of engineering, 1932–38. In 1939 he was appointed president of the Carnegie Institution of Washington, an outstanding scientific research institution. In 1940 he was appointed by President ROOSEVELT as chairman of the National Defense Research Committee, an agency designed to supplement the work of the Army and Navy in developing war materials. A year later he was assigned as director of the OFFICE OF SCIENTIFIC RESEARCH AND DE-

VELOPMENT, which was charged with general mobilization of the scientific resources of the nation, developing cooperation with the Army and Navy on broad programs of research and advising the President as to the status of scientific research and development. Bush was thus the nation's chief scientific coordinator in World War II.

BUSHIDO. Originally a code of conduct for the samurai (warrior) class in Japan—from *bushi* (warrior) and *do* (doctrine)—which evolved during the Kamakura period (1192–1333). The term itself was not used until the 16th century. The specifics of the code varied as different cultural forces made their impact on Japan from 1200 to the mid-19th century. The two major influences were Zen Buddhism and Confucianism. From the former came emphasis on the mystique of military exercises, particularly archery and swordsmanship, and indifference to danger. From Confucianism came emphasis on frugality and filial piety, although the obligation to one's feudal lord took precedence over duty to one's parents. This was in strong contrast to the Confucian tradition. Absolute obedience was stressed. The system is often compared to the Western chivalric code. In Bushido, however, there is little of the cult of romantic love, or the high status of women or the sense of *noblesse oblige* toward one's social inferiors that characterize the Western code.

Bushido was deliberately revived and adapted to modern conditions during the Meiji period in the latter 19th century. It became the official philosophy of education for Japanese of all classes until the post-World War II period, when it was dropped even in the Japanese armed forces. It is generally felt that the influence of Bushido, or at least its modern form, in the Japanese educational system made it easy for the Army to take power before the war.

BUSHY PARK. Site of SUPREME HEADQUARTERS, ALLIED EXPEDITIONARY FORCE (SHAEF) near Kingston-on-Thames, in suburban London. This headquarters, code-named Widewing, was occupied in March 1944. The U.S. Eighth Air Force also had headquarters in this part of Bushy Park. General EISENHOWER preferred the suburban location because he wanted an intermingling of officers in messes and closer contact in living quarters to accelerate the welding of an Allied command.

BUTARITARI. The main island in the MAKIN Atoll, hit in August 1942 by the U.S. Marine 2d Raider Battalion (Carlson's Raiders; *see* CARLSON, EVANS FORDYCE) and invaded on November 20, 1943, by the 27th Division Task Force under Maj. Gen. Ralph C. SMITH, of which the 165th Infantry Regimental Combat Team was the major fighting element.

BUTCHER, Harry C. (1902–). American naval officer who graduated from Iowa State College in 1924 and went into journalism, joining the Columbia Broadcasting System in 1929. After being commissioned as a lieutenant commander in the Naval Reserve, Butcher, a family friend of Gen. Dwight D. EISENHOWER, became the general's naval aide—a unique, specially created position. His diary of his experiences was published as *My Three Years with Eisenhower* (1946).

BUTT REPORT. A 1941 study of the effectiveness of British STRATEGIC BOMBING. The report said that bombing was highly inaccurate: only one-third of the bombers in most raids were coming even as close as five miles to their targets, while over the Ruhr the proportion was as low as one-tenth. One of the results of this was the adoption of the so-called area bombing strategy, which lasted until fighter-bomber escorts and better NAVIGATION AIDS became available.

BUTTRESS. Code name for projected British operation against the toe of Italy, planned as part of the Allied invasion after the conquest of Sicily.

BUZZARD. Allied code name for the Japanese Ku 7 glider (*see* KU 7), similar to the German Gotha Go 242 25-man glider in appearance and originally believed to be simply a Japanese copy. It was later learned that the Ku 7 was a Japanese design. As with the Go 242, a powered version of the Ku 7 was later produced under the designation Ki 105, and also received the code name Buzzard.

BUZZARD PATROL. Name given by Americans to an exceptionally bloody series of attacks by Navy and Marine pilots on a Japanese troop convoy to GUADALCANAL, November 13–14, 1942.

BUZZ BOMB. Nickname given by the British to the German pilotless aircraft, the V-1 (*see* V-WEAPONS).

BYERS, Clovis E. (1899–). U.S. Army officer, a major general, who served as chief of staff of the 77th Division in 1942, chief of staff of I Corps in 1942–43 and then chief of staff of the EIGHTH ARMY.

BYRNES, James Francis (1879–1972). A native of South Carolina, a close friend of Franklin ROOSEVELT and, as a U.S. Senator, one of the leading spokesmen for the Roosevelt Administration. As a member of the Senate Foreign Relations Committee, Byrnes (1939) fought for the CASH AND CARRY arms act, and he helped to steer through the SELECTIVE SERVICE and LEND-LEASE Acts. In 1941 Roosevelt appointed him to the Supreme Court to succeed Justice James McReynolds. But in October 1942, with the United States fully engaged in the war, he was asked to leave the bench by the President to serve as director of the newly created OFFICE OF ECONOMIC STABILIZATION and as chairman of the Economic Stabilization Board, which had authority to develop and administer a comprehensive national economic policy designed to hold down the cost of living and bring about the most economical use of the nation's manpower.

From this position Byrnes became chief planner and director of the American wartime economy. He became known as "Assistant President" in this period, because his authority seemed to be exceeded only by that of the President himself. In 1943 Byrnes's formal title was changed to director of the OFFICE OF WAR MOBILIZATION. In this position he made several unpopular decisions, including the suppression of horse racing, cutting down on lighting and the curtailment of civilian railroad travel. Byrnes also became one of Roosevelt's principal political and diplomatic advisers. He accompanied the President on his trip to YALTA in 1945, but shortly before Roosevelt's death, when he could see the end of the war in sight, he resigned his government position and prepared to return to the practice of law. However, President Harry TRUMAN, immediately on assuming office, asked Byrnes, whom he admired very much, to serve as adviser on foreign affairs; in July 1945 Truman appointed him Secretary of State to succeed Edward STETTINIUS. His first task was to accompany Truman to Berlin for the POTSDAM CONFERENCE. He held office until January 1947, when he resigned; he was succeeded by Gen. George C. MARSHALL.

BZURA RIVER, BATTLE ON THE. Fought between the Germans and the Poles during the second week of September 1939, this was the largest battle of the brief German-Polish war. *See also* GERMAN-POLISH OPERATIONS.

C

C-2. German ground-to-air rocket, designed for antiaircraft defense. It was designed to carry about 660 pounds of high explosives to a height of 50,000 feet. Although it was developed (under the code name Waterfall) as early as 1942, it was not put into large-scale production, the Germans concentrating instead on the long-range offensive rockets. *See also* V-WEAPONS.

C5M. Japanese Navy designation for its version of the Army Ki 15 reconnaissance plane (*see* KI 15).

C6N. Nokai *Saiun* (Painted Cloud) (Allied code name, Myrt), developed as a fast, long-range carrier reconnaissance plane by the Japanese Navy, though loss of carriers diverted it to land-based operation. Some Myrts were configured as night fighters, with a flexible 20-mm. gun in rear position.

C-46. One of Gen. Henry H. ARNOLD's gambles, like the B-29 (*see* B-29), the Curtiss C-46 Commando went into production before the prototype, intended to supplant the DC-3 on U.S. domestic commercial routes, had been fully tested. Early production models had a dolphinlike nose, but introduction of a stepped windshield improved visibility from the cockpit. Powered by two 2,000-horsepower Pratt and Whitney radial engines, the Commando could carry 45,000 pounds of cargo within its spacious fuselage, which had a unique figure-eight cross section. The C-46 had a top speed of 269 miles per hour and could cruise a distance of 1,200 miles.

Enthusiasts hailed the use of the fewest engines of the greatest possible horsepower, but cynics dubbed the C-46 the world's only two-engine four-engine plane. There were grounds for cynicism, for the rush to production left numerous flaws in the design, among them rubber hose connections that could disintegrate in an extremely dry, cold climate and allow fuel to leak onto the hot engines. Once its failings were corrected, the Commando proved its worth flying cargo from India across the Himalayas (the HUMP) to China.

C-47. Powered by two 1,200-horsepower Pratt and Whitney radial engines, the C-47 Skytrain was the military version of the Douglas DC-3 commercial transport. Fitted with bucket seats and a large loading door, the plane could carry 27 people or five tons of cargo. When used as a flying ambulance, it could accommodate 18 to

C-47 on transport duty in Egypt

24 litter patients. Its maximum speed was 230 miles per hour and its maximum range 1,600 miles. The C-47 dropped parachute troops in the European, Mediterranean, Pacific and China-Burma-India theaters, towed gliders and delivered cargo throughout the world. The Skytrain pioneered the aerial supply route across the Atlantic and hauled war matériel over the Himalayas. The C-47B had engines fitted with high-altitude blowers and could carry extra fuel for the dangerous India-China run.

The many DC-3s impressed into wartime military service carried a variety of designations. The most numerous were the C-53 Skytroopers, which had been built by Douglas for long-distance airline operations.

C-54. U.S. Army Air Forces acquired this four-engine, low-wing transport by commandeering, early in 1942, the 34 planes already on the Douglas production line. Although the DC-4A, its commercial designation, was intended as a transcontinental passenger plane, Army Air Forces used the C-54 Skymaster to carry both cargo and men over ocean as well as land. Almost a thousand Skymasters were built during the war. Four 1,200-horsepower Pratt and Whitney radial engines enabled the C-54A to carry 50 persons a distance of 3,900 miles. During the war Skymasters operated over the Himalayas, crossed the Atlantic and Indian Oceans, and established aerial routes from the west coast of the United States to Australia and the Philippines.

C-69. Destined to become one of the most successful postwar transports, Lockheed's L-49 Constellation was on the production line when the United States entered World War II. U.S. Army Air Forces took over the nine planes under construction and ordered 180 others. This beautiful, triple-fin aircraft first flew in January 1943. Its four 2,200-horsepower Wright radial engines made it the fastest transport yet acquired by the Army, with a top speed of 329 miles per hour. The plane weighed 82,000 pounds, also a record for an Army transport, and its pressurized cabin could accommodate as many as 64 passengers. Only 22 of these C-69s were built for Army Air Forces during the war.

C-200. The Macchi *Saetta* (Arrow). This Italian aircraft was the handiwork of Mario Catoldi. His plane, like R. J. Mitchell's SPITFIRE, descended from a line of Schneider Cup seaplane racers. First flown in 1937, the prototype reportedly exceeded 500 miles per hour during a dive. Early production models, however, were subject to high-speed stalls, and the airfoil had to be modified. The redesigned Arrow was now slower, but it soon earned the reputation of being one of the most maneuverable fighters of World War II. No contemporary Allied fighter could turn inside the Italian plane, and only the Spitfire could outclimb it.

The Macchi Arrow was a low-wing monoplane with a beautifully streamlined, cigar-shaped fuselage that terminated in the large cowling encircling an 870-horsepower Fiat radial engine. Maximum speed was only 312 miles per hour, and the armament consisted of two 12.7-mm. machine guns. Despite these limitations, a thousand C-200s saw service with the Regia Aeronautica. An attempt to improve performance by installing a 1,000-horsepower Fiat radial was abandoned after a version powered by a liquid-cooled engine had demonstrated its superiority.

C-202. The Macchi *Folgore* (Lightning). The C-202 evolved from the Italian firm's C-200 Arrow. The most important change was the replacement of the Arrow's Fiat radial engine with a liquid-cooled Alfa Romeo, actually a Daimler-Benz built under license, that developed 1,175 horsepower. Top speed of this single-place monoplane fighter was 370 miles per hour at 18,370 feet. The Lightning saw action in North Africa, where it proved superior to the HURRICANE and KITTYHAWK, and also in Russia. The initial armament of two 12.7-mm. machine guns was increased by the addition of two 7.7-mm. weapons or, in some versions, two 20-mm. cannon. The Italian aircraft industry produced about 1,500 of these planes.

A refinement of the Lightning was the C-205V *Veltro* (Greyhound), which retained the clean lines of its predecessor but mounted a 1,475-horsepower liquid-cooled engine that boosted the top speed to 399 miles per hour. The Greyhound was comparable in performance with the North American P-51D, (*see* P-51), but only 262 were built. Several of these fell into Allied hands when Italy surrendered; the remainder fought beside German aircraft in defense of northern Italy.

Macchi C-202 Folgore

CA-12. This plane, the Boomerang, was built by Commonwealth Aircraft Corporation (CA). Australia, facing the Japanese advance and having few modern fighters, designed and built the CA-12 prototype in four weeks. It was a fair stopgap; the 250 built were used largely in ground support and pathfinder duties. The CA-12 had a 1,200-horsepower radial engine and a top speed of 295 miles per hour, and was armed with two 20-mm. cannon, four .303-caliber machine guns and one 500-pound bomb.

CA-111. A single-engine version of the Italian Caproni Ca-101 trimotor. Retained were the boxlike fuselage, high wing and fixed landing gear. Besides flying reconnaissance missions, the plane was used to bomb and strafe partisan troops in Yugoslavia.

CA-133. A handsome Italian trimotor, high-wing monoplane with a fixed landing gear, built by Caproni. Slow but easy to handle, it saw combat with Italian forces in East Africa, Libya, Albania and Russia. Besides serving as a bomber, it was a successful trainer, troop transport and flying ambulance. The plane, powered by 450-horsepower Piaggio radials, took part in the invasion of Ethiopia and remained in service until Italy surrendered in 1943.

CA-313. This Italian aircraft and its Caproni-built lookalike, the Ca-314, saw action with the Regia Aeronautica and the Italian naval air arm. Both were low-wing, twin-engine monoplanes with glassed-in noses. Typical missions were reconnaissance, torpedo bombing and convoy escort. Standard armament was five machine guns, but two additional weapons were installed under the wings of those planes intended for the close support of ground troops.

CABANATUAN. Located approximately 75 miles north of Manila, Cabanatuan was the site of a large Japanese prisoner of war camp established for American and Filipino soldiers captured at BATAAN and CORREGIDOR. The camp was liberated by U.S. forces on January 30, 1945.

CACTUS. U.S. code name assigned to the GUADALCANAL-TULAGI area in the Solomon Islands.

CACTUS AIR FORCE. In the early days of the GUADALCANAL operation in 1942 the urgent American necessity to get everyone and everything that could fly to HENDERSON FIELD led to the frequent disregard of the niceties of squadron and group organization. The Marine air command echelon, the 1st Marine Aircraft Wing, constituted all aircraft on the island that were sent from the rear area and included naval aircraft flown in to operate from Guadalcanal when their carriers were sunk. In turn, these planes and pilots were employed according to their individual functions. This composite organization was called Cactus Air Force, because Cactus was the code name of Guadalcanal. Although predominantly Marine Corps in origin, Cactus Air Force contained Army Air Corps and Navy air units.

CACTUS EXPRESS. American nickname for the Japanese surface shuttle of supplies and reinforcements into GUADALCANAL during the campaign for that island (August 1942–February 1943). The term is derived from the code name used for Guadalcanal. The term "Tokyo Express" has been widely used in journalists' accounts and in many postwar historical works, at first for reasons of security and later because "Cactus" would have had no immediate meaning to stateside readers.

CADILLAC. U.S. Navy code name for 1945 experiments with airborne long-range search radars designed to give a fleet an extended early-warning capability. Cadillac I tested a high-powered S-band RADAR in a modified BTM fitted with a bulbous ventral radome and designated BTM-3W (*see* BTM). The plane also carried radar and communications relay equipment which fed information to receivers in a surface ship, where this information was coordinated with that received from the task force's own radars. The later Cadillac II used a modified Navy version of the B-17 bomber, designated PB1W (*see* B-17).

CADOGAN, Sir Alexander George Montagu (1884–1968). British Foreign Office official, appointed Permanent Under-Secretary of State for Foreign Affairs in 1938, replacing Sir Robert VANSITTART. As one of Winston CHURCHILL's principal foreign policy advisers, Cadogan gained renown for his cool, commonsensical, almost dispassionate approach to wartime problems. He served until 1946 and was afterward Britain's permanent representative to the United Nations, 1952–57.

CAEN. City in Normandy, scene of violent fighting in the summer of 1944 between the attacking British Second Army and German forces attempting to contain the Allied beachhead established in June. The city fell on July 9 and served as a gateway for British forces debouching onto rolling plains leading toward Paris.

CAESAR LINE. German defenses south of ROME (Arce–Ceprano), which were pierced by the U.S. 36th Division on May 30, 1944.

CAFFERY, Jefferson (1886–). American diplomat whose career spanned the years 1911 to 1955. He was American representative to the FRENCH COMMITTEE OF NATIONAL LIBERATION in 1944 and subsequently (1944–49) ambassador to France.

CAIRO. Location of the headquarters of the British MIDDLE EAST COMMAND and the site of several important meetings. In addition to the Allied CAIRO CONFERENCE, Cairo was the scene of negotiations with Rumania and Bulgaria. In time, Cairo became the general Allied headquarters in the Middle East, and it was also host to the Yugoslav and Greek governments-in-exile.

CAIRO CONFERENCE. Allied coalition conference held before and after the TEHERAN CONFERENCE in November and December 1943. The code name was Sextant. The chief participants were President ROOSEVELT, Prime Minister CHURCHILL and Generalissimo CHIANG KAI-SHEK.

During the summer of 1943 such a conference became necessary. The progress of the war had been encouraging for the Allies, and a critical point had been reached in planning for future efforts: in the balance hung the whole strategy of global warfare. Unification had to be achieved on the "beat Germany first" concept, and the roles of the United States, the USSR, Great Britain and China had to be established. Decisions also had to be made on basic strategy in Europe and against Japan.

Even the administrative aspects of Sextant—where, when and how to meet—were difficult to solve. Only after a great deal of coordination and compromise was it agreed to divide the meeting into three phases and meet at both Cairo and Teheran. The first phase, November 22–26, consisted of variously attended meetings between Roosevelt, Churchill and Chiang Kai-shek and their contingents to discuss the role of China and to set the stage for a unified meeting with Stalin. The second phase, the Eureka part of the conference at Teheran, November 28 to December 1, included a series of meetings among the triumvirate and was the focus for the more profound of the discussions. A final phase, back to Cairo from December 3 to 7, was required for Great

Britain and America to firm up plans for the invasion of France (OVERLORD and ANVIL).

Although China's status as a world power was certified in the form of the December 1 Cairo Declaration, which set forth earlier Anglo-American-Chinese agreements, it was short-lived. Among other things, President Roosevelt had promised Chiang Kai-shek that Buccaneer (an assault on the Andaman Islands) would be carried out. After returning to Cairo, Roosevelt, under pressure from Great Britain because of Overlord and Anvil priorities, especially as regarded lack of landing craft, agreed to the cancellation of Buccaneer. Stalin's promise to become an ally in the Far East, in effect decreasing the need for Anglo-American dependence on China, also influenced this decision. With this, China's role in world affairs was lessened: it was the turning point for China and its importance to the Allies in the war.

CAIRO THREE. Allied code name for Teheran, used in the planning of the TEHERAN CONFERENCE in 1943.

CALAIS. The determined defense of this Channel port by British and French forces in May 1940 gave valuable time to the defenders of DUNKIRK and thus was a vital contribution to the successful evacuation. Calais surrendered to the attacking Germans on May 27.

CALCUTTA, H.M.S. British light cruiser, launched July 9, 1918, and converted into an antiaircraft cruiser in 1939. The *Calcutta* displaced 4,200 tons and carried a main armament of eight 4-inch antiaircraft guns. Helping out during the evacuation of CRETE by British forces on May 30, 1941, the *Calcutta* was sunk by enemy aircraft early the following morning.

CALHOUN, William Lowndes (1885–1963). This great-grandson of John C. Calhoun graduated from the U.S. Naval Academy in 1906; he was decorated for heroism following the PEARL HARBOR attack. A vice-admiral, "Uncle Bill" Calhoun commanded the Service Force, Pacific Fleet, from 1939 to 1945. He performed well in this complex operation, being one of the developers of the at-sea logistics system, and in his own words handled "everything under the shining sun for the Navy and Marines which is not actually connected with fighting the ships." Calhoun retired in 1946.

CALIFORNIA, U.S.S. TENNESSEE-class battleship. Struck by Japanese bombs and torpedoes at Pearl Harbor, *California* sank in shallow water. By late March 1942 she had been refloated, and she was then sufficiently repaired so that in October of that year she was able to proceed to the United States. Here she was extensively modernized, coming out of overhaul late in 1943 a completely rebuilt ship. She returned to action during the invasion of SAIPAN in June 1944 and thereafter participated in the LEYTE and Luzon operations and the capture of OKINAWA.

CALLAGHAN, Daniel Judson (1890–1942). U.S. Navy officer, a graduate of the Naval Academy in 1911. Known affectionately to his men as "Uncle Dan," Callaghan, a rear admiral, commanded a cruiser force escorting transports to GUADALCANAL in November 1942. He was killed by Japanese gunfire in the naval battle of Guadalcanal on November 13, 1942.

CAMPBELL, Sir Ronald Hugh (1883–1953). British ambassador to France, 1939–40, and to Portugal, 1940–45. During the German offensive in May and June 1940, he was prominent in British efforts to convince France to establish an overseas government and to transport her Navy to Allied waters. Shortly before the collapse of France, he conveyed to the French cabinet at Bordeaux the British offer to unite the two countries.

CAMPBELL, U.S.C.G. The success of this U.S. Coast Guard cutter as a convoy escort in 1941 led to the general use of cutters for this purpose. The *Campbell* went on to have a busy wartime careeer in the North Atlantic.

CAMPINCHI, César (1882–1941). A decorated veteran of World War I who served several times as French Minister of the Navy. During the German invasion of France in 1940, Campinchi, a Corsican, stood stoutly with Paul REYNAUD against the proposal to seek an armistice, leaving the government when this effort failed.

CAMP O'DONNELL. Located near Tarlac on the island of Luzon, this U.S. Army camp was established during the early 1900s. It was turned over to the Philippine Government for use as an assembly and training area for the Philippine Army prior to World War II. It housed between 10,000 and 15,000 troops. Early in the war the Japanese seized the installation and turned it into a prisoner of war camp, where they concentrated about 105,000 U.S. and Philippine Army troops, Philippine Scouts and other Allied personnel. The camp was the terminal point of the infamous BATAAN death march in 1942. The death rate at the camp, because of inadequate sanitary conditions, contaminated water and lack of food and medical aid, was extraordinarily high.

CANADIAN COASTAL ZONE. The Canadian Coastal Zones, Atlantic and Pacific, were coast-defense commands comparable to the U.S. Navy's SEA FRONTIERS.

CANADIAN ESCORT FORCE. The antisubmarine force based at Halifax, Nova Scotia, which played a large and important part in the Battle of the ATLANTIC. It had the responsibility of providing the antisubmarine escort for the important HX (Halifax homeward) and SC (Sydney, Cape Breton, homeward) convoys from the Canadian coast to the MID-OCEAN MEETING POINT (MOMP), returning to Canada escorting ONF and ONS convoys (Liverpool outward, fast and slow). As the war progressed, the Canadian Escort Force grew in size and importance until at the end it played almost as large a part in the Battle of the Atlantic as the British escort forces.

CANAL DEFENSE LIGHT (CDL). Cover name for an American infrared detection device, used with notable success at REMAGEN to protect the newly captured bridge from assault by German swimmers under the command of Otto SKORZENY.

CANARIS, Wilhelm (1887–1945). Head of the ABWEHR (armed forces intelligence) from January 1935, Admiral Canaris became a prominent, if enigmatic, member of the German OPPOSITION TO HITLER, especially during the formative years of the movement. He was born in Westphalia and brought up in a wealthy, right-wing but liberal Protestant family. He entered the Navy as a cadet in 1905. He served in naval intelligence during the First World War, and he took part on the *Dresden* in the celebrated action off the Falkland Islands. When his ship was scuttled, he escaped internment and made his way back to Germany. After the war he remained in the Navy and was involved peripherally in right-wing politics.

In 1935 his restlessness, facility with languages and calculating brain led him back to intelligence work and charge of the Abwehr, a small but important department which grew in size and significance once the war began. He held the rank of admiral. At the Abwehr he became involved, along with his second-in-command, Col. Hans OSTER, in countermeasures against Adolf HITLER, whom he had distrusted from the first. Canaris provided Oster with the cover of his authority, and together they were responsible for the recruitment of many remarkable men who collectively formed the most active anti-Hitler group in the Resistance until the period in 1943 when the initiative passed to OLBRICHT and STAUFFENBERG. Early in the war, discreet but definite warnings of impending invasion by Germany were passed to Denmark, Norway, Belgium and the Netherlands, and cover was provided for such agents of the Resistance as BONHOEFFER, DOHNANYI and Josef MÜLLER, all staff members of the Abwehr. Meanwhile Canaris followed his restless path, moving around Europe, including Spain, where he used his not inconsiderable influence to keep General FRANCO neutral. On the other hand, the Abwehr as a whole functioned normally, though not very efficiently, as a wartime intelligence service; Canaris was as assiduous as Heinrich HIMMLER in exposing the Communist Rote Kapelle (*see* RED ORCHESTRA). But one by one his principal subordinates in the Resistance were arrested—Müller, Dohnanyi and Bonhoeffer among them. The Abwehr was finally dissolved and (as Himmler had always wanted) taken over by SS Intelligence; Canaris, for long entirely unsuspected, was finally himself arrested on July 23, 1944, after the abortive attempt on Hitler's life. Incarcerated in GESTAPO headquarters in the Prinz Albrechtstrasse, Canaris was interrogated by Walther Huppenkothen, one of the chief Gestapo investigators. Even in prison he managed to act as a prime source of information to his friends among the prisoners. Like Dr. Carl GOERDELER, he survived for a while by gradually leaking harmless but important-seeming information. He was executed on April 9, 1945, at Flossenbürg concentration camp.

Canaris, small of stature, volatile, was by nature devious, but he walked a tightrope of his own devising with courage and skill. It was the discovery of his diary, which he had thought destroyed, that betrayed him. No copy of this has yet come to light; two known typescripts were destroyed, one by the Gestapo and the other by Col. Werner Schrader, acting for the Resistance, but a third may still exist, possibly in the hands of the British authorities.

CANBERRA, H.M.A.S. Kent-class Australian heavy cruiser of 10,000 tons standard displacement, launched in 1928, armed with six 8-inch guns, eight 4-inch guns, twenty 40-mm. guns and sixteen 2-pounders. She had a speed of 31.5 knots. In the Battle of SAVO ISLAND, *Canberra* was set afire by Japanese torpedoes and shellfire and was ultimately scuttled.

CANNED GOODS. During the evening of August 31, 1939, Nazi SS men disguised in Polish uniforms, led by Maj. Alfred Naujocks, staged an attack on the German radio station at Gleiwitz (*see* SS). The purpose was to give seeming substance to Adolf HITLER's charges of Polish provocative acts. As part of the operation, corpses of drugged concentration camp inmates were left behind as "casualties." These persons were referred to by the code name Canned Goods.

CANNON, John K. (1892–1955). A pursuit pilot early in his career, Cannon headed the I Interceptor Command, Mitchel Field, N.Y., when the United States became involved in the war. His first combat assignment, as a brigadier general, was Commanding General, XII Air Support Command, during the Moroccan invasion, November 1942. He next assumed command of the XII Bomber Command, set up an air training organization for the Mediterranean theater and then served as Deputy Commanding General, Allied Tactical Air Force, during the conquest of Sicily and the subsequent invasion of Italy. Promoted to major general in June 1943, he soon became Commanding General, TWELFTH AIR FORCE, and while commanding the Mediterranean Allied Tactical Air Command, he was responsible for the aerial forces that took part in the August 1944 invasion of southern Europe. In March 1945, as a lieutenant general, he became commander in chief of Allied Air Forces in the Mediterranean theater. *See also* NORTHWEST AFRICA; SOUTHERN FRANCE OPERATION.

CANTON ISLAND. As part of the U.S. Central Pacific operations, SEVENTH AIR FORCE bombers operated from this atoll to strike targets in the GILBERTS.

CANT Z-501. Cantieri Riuniti dell'Adriatico (Cant) built the *Gabbiano* (Seagull), designed by Filippo Zappata, which flew for the first time in 1934 and remained in Italy's air service until 1950. This flying boat was a parasol-wing monoplane and was powered by a single 900-horsepower Isotta-Fraschini liquid-cooled engine mounted on the wing directly above the hull. A light bomber and reconnaissance craft, the Seagull mounted two or three machine guns, had a maximum range of 1,490 miles and could carry up to 1,400 pounds of bombs. The crew was two or three.

CANT Z-506B. The *Airone* (Heron), another of Filippo Zappata's designs manufactured by Cantieri Riuniti dell'Adriatico, was a trimotor, twin-float seaplane. Of mainly wooden construction, the midwing monoplane served as a reconnaissance craft and torpedo bomber. An elongated bathtub beneath the fuselage housed the bombardier and rearward-firing gunner. The Heron saw action with Italian units in the Spanish Civil War and later served with both the Italian Navy and the

Regia Aeronautica, bombing French and Greek targets and the British Mediterranean fleet. Retired as a bomber after the Axis conquest of Greece, the plane continued to fly reconnaissance, antisubmarine, convoy escort and rescue missions. As late as 1959 transport and rescue versions were active in Italian air units. The Heron had a top speed of 217 miles per hour and carried up to 3,300 pounds of bombs. At one time, this type held 16 international records for speed, distance and weight carried.

CANT Z-1007bis. Designed by Filippo Zappata and nicknamed the *Alcione* (Kingfisher), this trimotor, midwing monoplane was a refinement of a 1939 version which had proved somewhat underpowered and poorly armed. The selection of 1,000-horsepower Piaggio radials solved the first problem, but the substitution of two 12.7-mm. machine guns for two of the plane's four 7.7-mm. weapons provided only marginal defensive improvement. This second model was larger than the first, could carry either two torpedoes or 4,000 pounds of bombs and had a top speed of 280 miles per hour. Of mainly wooden construction, the rugged Kingfisher saw action with Italian squadrons in North Africa, the Mediterranean area and Russia.

CANT Z-1018. The *Leone* (Lion) was Filippo Zappata's all-metal, twin-engine successor to the Kingfisher. Powered by either 1,320-horsepower or 1,350-horsepower radials, which gave a top speed in excess of 320 miles per hour, the Lion entered service early in 1943. Work was begun on a night-fighter version, but the project never came to fruition, nor did many of the bomber models see action before Italy surrendered.

CAP BON. Immediately after the Allied breakthrough at TUNIS and BIZERTE (May 1943), the British commander, Gen. Kenneth A. N. ANDERSON, sent troops to seal off the Cap Bon peninsula to prevent any resistance on the BATAAN model by the Axis and to forestall evacuation. On May 11, with Axis units surrendering to the south, the British made a circuit of the peninsula and cleared the area.

CAPE ESPERANCE, BATTLE OF. Two months after the initial American landing on GUADALCANAL in early August 1942, the 164th Infantry Regiment was to be transported from Noumea to Guadalcanal. Distant protection was furnished by two naval forces, one organized around carrier HORNET and the other around battleship WASHINGTON. Close cover was to be provided by Rear Adm. Norman SCOTT's Task Force 64 (TF 64). In the meantime the Japanese had been making frequent CACTUS EXPRESS runs at night to reinforce their own troops. Decoded radio intercepts informed the American command that an especially important run would be made on the night of October 11. It was considered so important that it was to be preceded by a heavy day air attack from RABAUL, followed up by a night bombardment of HENDERSON FIELD by a surface strike force of three heavy cruisers under Rear Adm. Aritomo GOTO.

The Japanese reinforcement force was spotted from the air on the afternoon of the 11th and tracked until after 2200. Scott brought his force into the waters north of Guadalcanal—Ironbottom Sound—and awaited the enemy in a single column with his destroyers divided between van and rear. Radar contact with both Japanese forces was made. Scott's flagship, the heavy cruiser SAN FRANCISCO, lacked the newest radar and, for some minutes, he was not aware of the sighting. At 2330 Scott ordered a countermarch, an "in succession" turn, the order of the column being preserved. While this was happening, and after a fair amount of radar and communications confusion, the American force found itself "crossing the T" of Goto's bombardment force—heavy cruisers AOBA, KINUGASA and FURUTAKA, with two destroyers. An intense gunnery duel, aided by radar on the American side, followed. At this point Scott, confused as to the identity of the ships he saw and still hampered by inadequate radar intelligence, ordered his ships to cease firing. At the same time Goto, equally confused and believing that he was being shot at by the other Japanese force, ordered his column to turn to the right. His flagship, *Aoba,* was heavily damaged, and he was fatally wounded. In spite of Scott's order some U.S. ships continued to fire, and *Furutaka* was also damaged. After a four-minute pause, Scott ordered shooting resumed. The duel continued. The American destroyers *Duncan* and *Farenholt* were damaged; on the other side, destroyer FUBUKI was illuminated by searchlight and sent to the bottom.

Scott, by now aware of the actual situation, turned his column onto a course parallel to the retiring Japanese. The burning *Aoba* and *Furutaka* were hit again. The third Japanese cruiser, *Kinugasa*, knocked out *Boise*'s two forward turrets and put her out of action when the American cruiser snapped on a searchlight and gave the Japanese gunners an aiming point. SALT LAKE CITY swung between the two ships to give *Boise* the chance to pull out of *Kinugasa*'s fire. *Furutaka* succumbed to her injuries and went down while withdrawing. The final fatality was *Duncan.* Slowly spreading flooding and flames finally caused her loss around midday on October 12.

While this action was going on, the Japanese ships landed their cargo of 150-mm. artillery pieces, with troops and supplies, on Guadalcanal. They, too, retired during the early morning hours.

Cape Esperance was a tactical victory and morale booster for the Americans. The Japanese reinforcement convoy, however, was able to carry out its task unmolested. In that sense, then, the operation was a Japanese success. Scott, pleased with the effect he had achieved with his forces deployed in a single column, used the same rather cumbersome and inflexible formation in the later naval battle of Guadalcanal (November 1942) with unhappy results.

CAPE GLOUCESTER. On the tip of western NEW BRITAIN, site of the main U.S. landing (1st Marine Division) in the invasion of the island on December 26, 1943 (Operation Dexterity). On the 30th the Marines captured and secured Cape Gloucester airfield. Operation Dexterity was declared completed on February 10, 1944.

CAPE MATAPAN, BATTLE OF. In March 1941 Germany, planning to come to the assistance of Italy in her campaign against Greece, asked the Italians to attack British supply lines from Alexandria (Egypt) to Greece. Along with other actions, the Italian naval command ordered a surface-ship strike. This was considered risky, but feasible if surprise could be attained and if the sweep could be coordinated with effective aerial reconnaissance and air cover; the area of operations was dominated by the Royal Air Force, and air support was vital. The Italian plan called for a cruiser raid (of three divisions—the First, Third and Eighth) supported by the battleship VITTORIO VENETO. Components of the surface force sailed from various ports, and on March 27 made rendezvous east of Sicily. *Vittorio Veneto,* in which Adm. Angelo IACHINO (also spelled Jachino) flew his flag, was escorted by four destroyers. Iachino steamed eastward until the late evening of the 27th, then divided. *Vittorio Veneto* and the Third Division were to proceed to the area south of Crete to look for British forces before turning back. The other two divisions were to make a sweep into the Aegean before retiring to rendezvous with the rest of the force southwest of Greece during the afternoon of the next day. This part of the task was considered particularly hazardous, the Aegean being within range of British airfields in Greece and Crete.

Iachino's force steamed on, but the promised air support did not materialize. About midday a British flying boat spotted one cruiser division. Nothing further happened until evening, when the Italian force split as planned. At 2200 Italian naval headquarters, aware that surprise had been lost with the air sighting, ordered the Aegean force to cut its sweep short and rejoin the rest of the force in the morning, rather than the afternoon, of the 28th. Early the next morning a scout floatplane from *Vittorio Veneto* sighted four British light cruisers (*Gloucester,* PERTH, ORION and AJAX) and four destroyers, commanded by Adm. H. D. PRIDHAM-WIPPELL, about 50 miles from the Italian battleship. Iachino ordered the Third Division toward the enemy, and took *Vittorio Veneto* in support. About an hour and a half later the Italian cruisers opened fire at long range. Pridham-Wippell was outgunned; his cruisers were armed with 6-inch guns against the Italians' 8-inch, and he turned away at high speed to the southwest. The Italians chased for an hour, but neither force did any damage at the gun ranges involved. The duel did not appear productive, and the Italian division was drawing closer to British air bases. Friendly air cover still had not appeared, and Iachino ordered the cruisers and *Vittorio Veneto* to turn away to the northwest and start back toward their base at Taranto. As they withdrew, the British cruisers turned and followed out of 8-inch range. No British aircraft had been seen, and Iachino decided to try a pincers movement, in hope of catching Pridham-Wippell between the Italian battleship and the Third Division. The pincers closed, but not effectively. With the help of smokescreens and evasive maneuvering at high speed, the British ships escaped with damage to one cruiser. As *Vittorio Veneto* attacked, she was herself assailed by six carrier torpedo bombers sent by Adm. Sir Andrew CUNNINGHAM in response to Pridham-Wippell's signals. The battleship maneuvered to avoid the torpedoes; while she did so, the British cruisers drew out of range of her 15-inch guns. British scout planes were now in the area, and no axis planes were to be seen; Iachino continued on course for Taranto.

A series of British air attacks were made during the afternoon, but did no damage to the Italian cruisers. *Vittorio Veneto*, however, had her two port propellers knocked out, but using only the two starboard screws, she was able to proceed at more than 20 knots. The returning British pilots reported scoring bomb hits as well as a torpedo hit and told Cunningham that *Vittorio Veneto* was dead in the water.

Although Iachino was unaware of it, he was now being followed by Cunningham with a powerful force: the carrier FORMIDABLE, the battleships BARHAM, WARSPITE and VALIANT and nine destroyers were steaming to the rear of Pridham-Wippell's cruiser force. Cunningham had taken his force to sea in full awareness of the Italian operational plan, which had been revealed to him by a deciphered radio message provided by the highly secret British ULTRA process. On the assumption that the crippled *Vittorio Veneto* was still where his pilots had reported her, Cunningham moved ahead to finish her off after dark. Shortly after sunset British torpedo planes launched one final attack. The Italians put up heavy antiaircraft fire, helped by smoke and violent evasive action, but the heavy cruiser *Pola* was hit and brought to a standstill. The Italian command informed Iachino that intercepted radio bearings indicated British ships were about 75 miles behind him. Iachino believed that these were nothing more than patrolling destroyers, and he ordered the First Division to assist the immobilized *Pola.*

The First Division turned back in darkness. At the same time Cunningham, under the impression that a crippled *Vittorio Veneto* was lying ahead, was approaching from the opposite direction. His destroyers were in the van, followed by Pridham-Wippell's light cruisers; the three battleships sailed behind. First detecting *Pola,* then *Zara* and *Fiume,* by radar (the Italians lacked this), the British battleships and cruisers opened fire at short range. The Italian division was taken completely by surprise, having just sighted the British ships in the darkness and mistaken them for one of the other elements of their own force. A melee followed, British and Italian destroyers attacking with torpedoes through the gunfire. *Fiume* and *Zara,* with two destroyers, were sunk; a third destroyer was damaged, but she and the fourth destroyer escaped. *Pola,* her engines knocked out and without electric power, could neither steam nor shoot and had to look on. A British destroyer came alongside in the early morning hours of the 29th and took off those survivors still remaining on board before sinking the cruiser's hulk with torpedoes. The rest of the Italian force, by now miles away, could see the reflection of flames and gun flashes on the horizon. Without information on what was happening and with a damaged battleship to take care of, Iachino did not choose to go charging—literally and figuratively—into the dark. His ships proceeded to Taranto, arriving later on the 29th.

Contributing to the outcome of this operation off Cape Matapan, at the tip of Greece, were the nonappearance of promised air support and the lack of adequate intelligence concerning British movements on the part of Iachino and the Italian naval headquarters alike. Aggressive action by Cunningham and the presence of radar in his force paid off in results. The determination of the British carrier pilots who damaged *Vittorio Veneto* and *Pola* was also significant. **J.C.R.**

CAPE ST. GEORGE, BATTLE OF. On the afternoon of November 24, 1943, Capt. Arleigh BURKE's five-ship U.S. Navy Destroyer Squadron 23 was ordered to intercept a Japanese seaborne attempt at reinforcing their troops on Buka in the northwest SOLOMON ISLANDS. About 0100 on the 25th, Burke made radar contact off Cape St. George, New Ireland, with the two escorting destroyers of the five-ship Japanese force. Leaving two of his ships to attack by gunfire, Burke turned toward the Japanese flank, launched 15 torpedoes and turned away. The two unsuspecting Japanese ships blew up at the point calculated, and Burke turned his destroyers to attack the three troop-laden destroyer transports. In a running battle, the American ships sank one Japanese destroyer by gunfire and pursued the remaining two to within 60 miles of the Japanese stronghold of RABAUL on NEW BRITAIN before turning back to get under friendly air cover by dawn. A superb example of surface naval combat, the battle was later evaluated as the "almost perfect naval action" by Adm. Edward C. Kalbfus, president of the Naval War College.

CAPE VERDE ISLANDS. *See* SHRAPNEL.

CAPITAL. Code name for Allied attack across the CHINDWIN RIVER to clear northern Burma and open up a supply route to China. It was launched October 15, 1944.

CARBONI, Giacomo (1889–1973). In 1939 Benito MUSSOLINI appointed General Carboni head of the Italian intelligence service, but removed him in 1941 because of Carboni's opposition to Italian cooperation with the Nazis. Carboni then commanded the Friuli Assault Division and the Eighth Army Corps on Corsica in 1942 before being recalled to Rome in March 1943. As the commander of the motorized corps responsible for the defense of Rome, Carboni, a major general, actively plotted the removal of Mussolini.

CARENTAN. Normandy town about five miles inland between OMAHA BEACH and UTAH BEACH; one of the first objectives of the INVASION plan. It was taken on June 12, 1944, by the U.S. 101st Airborne Division after a fierce five-day fight along an exposed causeway.

CARIBBEAN SEA FRONTIER. U.S. Navy designation for the SEA FRONTIER command responsible for defense of the Caribbean from Cuba to French Guiana.

CARL, Marion E. (1915–). U.S. Marine Corps aviator and an innovator both in peacetime and in combat. During the Battle of MIDWAY in June 1942, Carl was a section leader in Marine Fighter Squadron 221 and was one of only three pilots from the squadron to survive the battle. For his outstanding performance he received his first Navy Cross. He then was transferred to VMF-223, which was one of the first Marine squadrons to operate from HENDERSON FIELD on GUADALCANAL, arriving there on August 20, 1942, at the height of the battle. Four days later he shot down two enemy bombers and a Zero. On the 26th he downed two more Japanese planes and thus became the first Marine Corps ace of the war, an exploit for which he received his second Navy Cross. Shortly thereafter he was shot down off the coast of Guadalcanal but was rescued by friendly natives, who returned him to his base. In the air battle over Guadalcanal, Carl shot down a total of 10 enemy planes, and by the end of the war he had 18 Japanese planes to his credit.

Following the war, Carl made some of the first carrier landings and takeoffs in an F-80 (Shooting Star) jet plane, became one of the Marine Corps's first helicopter pilots and earned a fourth Distinguished Flying Cross for setting a world speed record in the Douglas Skystreak in 1947. He retired from active duty in 1973 with the rank of major general.

CARLSON, Evans Fordyce (1896–1947). As a junior officer in the U.S. Marine Corps, Carlson served two tours of duty in China in the 1920s and 1930s, and he studied the Chinese language on his own time. In 1936 he returned to the United States; among his assignments was duty in the Marine guard at the Little White House at Warm Springs, Ga., where he met President Franklin D. ROOSEVELT, who took an interest in him. Carlson was ordered back to China in 1937 as a Chinese-language student in Peking and as a military observer. At the President's request, he sent back to FDR personally a number of reports dealing with politics, politicians, diplomats, military figures, American business policy and the role of the British and French in China. He made a long trek into the interior of China, to Yenan in Shensi province, to observe Chinese Communist guerrilla operations against the Japanese. He was quite impressed with Communist tactics and methods, and later, when he formed his Marine Raider battalion, he adopted the Chinese Communist motto, *Gung-ho* (Work Together).

In 1941 his recommendations concerning the formation of commando-type units in the Marine Corps were accepted, though some senior officers viewed with a jaundiced eye the organization of elite units within the corps, which they regarded as elite in itself. Carlson was given the command of the 2d Raider Battalion (first designated the 2d Separate Battalion), to be known as Carlson's Raiders. His executive officer was Maj. James ROOSEVELT, the President's son. The battalion began training in Hawaii in rubber-boat operations and working from submarines, and on August 8, 1942, it left Pearl Harbor by submarine for MAKIN Atoll in the Gilberts, where it conducted a reconnaissance in force on the 17th. On November 4 the 2d Raider Battalion landed on GUADALCANAL and for 30 days conducted a 150-mile combat and reconnaissance patrol through some of the most difficult terrain on the island. In the course of this forced march, Carlson's marines fought more than a dozen engagements with the Japanese and killed over 500 of the enemy, with minimal casualties to themselves.

In the spring of 1943 he was returned to the States for medical treatment, but returned to the Pacific in time to participate as an observer in the TARAWA assault in November. He also participated in the SAIPAN operation, being wounded while attempting to rescue a wounded marine from a front-line observation post. He retired on a physical disability and was promoted to the rank of brigadier general on July 1, 1946.

Carlson was a complex, intense person, whose integrity and bravery were above reproach. This intensity, however, coupled with his apparent approval and romantic view of the Chinese Communists, made him suspect in the eyes of some of his fellow Marine officers. Further, he was not above approaching President Roosevelt personally for hard-to-get items for his Raiders if the regular channels were clogged, and this did not endear him to his superiors. Finally, his raid on Makin had the unfortunate consequence of leading the Japanese to strengthen their outposts in the Gilberts. This led to the bloody battle on BETIO in Tarawa Atoll. It is of interest that after Carlson left his battalion following the Guadalcanal operation he was not again given a command in the war, and in 1944 the existing Raider battalions were disbanded and their officers and men used as cadres in newly formed units.

CARNEY, Robert Bostwick, Jr. (1895–). A 1916 graduate of the U.S. Naval Academy, "Mick" Carney served on the staff of Rear Adm. Arthur LeR. Bristol, Jr.'s Support Force of the Atlantic Fleet early in World War II. Later he became chief of staff to Bristol. Promoted to rear admiral in July 1943, Carney became chief of staff to Adm. William F. HALSEY. He served in this position until June 1945. Following the war, Carney rose to full admiral and served as Chief of Naval Operations.

CARNIMEO, Nicolangelo (1887–1965). Italian Army officer (general of division), a veteran of the Italo-Turkish War of 1911–12, who led the Italian defense of KEREN in EAST AFRICA in 1941.

CAROL II, King of Rumania (1893–1953). Despite training in a Prussian regiment and service in the Rumanian Army in World War I, Carol II was better known as the "playboy monarch." Carol did not become King when his father died in 1927 because he had renounced his right to the throne, and instead his son Michael (Mihai) reigned under a regency. But when Carol secretly returned to Budapest in June 1930, the regency was abolished and Carol became King. His dictatorial reign during the 1930s was unpopular, as he tried to deal with Rumania's many problems; consequently, on September 6, 1940, he abdicated in favor of his son and fled the country with his longtime mistress, Magda Lupescu. Exiled to Spain at Hitler's request, the former King agitated unsuccessfully to regain the throne. He died in Lisbon.

CAROLINE ISLANDS. This large archipelago north and northeast of NEW GUINEA includes TRUK, the site of a major Japanese base.

CARPENDER, Arthur Schuyler (1884–1960). Early in the war Vice-Admiral Carpender served as head of U.S. Naval Forces in the Southwest Pacific under Gen. Douglas MACARTHUR. MACARTHUR'S NAVY was contending with serious shortages late in 1942, and MacArthur, impressed with his evacuation from the Philippines aboard the motor torpedo boat of Lt. Comdr. JOHN D. BULKELEY, endorsed the use of PT boats by Carpender's force (*see* PT). Under Carpender "MacArthur's Navy" participated in the Battle of the BISMARCK SEA on March 25, 1943, but by then it had a new official designation, the Seventh Fleet. Later Carpender commanded the Ninth Naval District. He retired in 1946.

CARPET. An Allied airborne radar-jamming device.

CARPET BOMBING. A form of air support used to batter German forces in preparation for the Allied breakout from the Normandy beachhead (Operation COBRA). The massive bombardment was originally scheduled for the Saint-Lô area on July 24, 1944, but bad weather intervened. Not all the EIGHTH AIR FORCE planes en route to the battlefield received word that the raid had been canceled, and those that attempted to drop their bombs near friendly lines achieved results that varied from ineffectual to tragic. One fighter-bomber, for example, attacked an Allied ammunition dump, and B-17s accidentally hit American infantry. Alerted by this abortive attack, the Germans began pulling back their artillery from the area they expected to be bombed. American troops also fell back and marked their lines with colored panels in order to create a 1,500-yard safety zone between the forward positions and the nearest target box to be pounded by NINTH AIR FORCE fighter-bombers.

The rescheduled bombardment got under way on the morning of July 25. Eighth Air Force fighters flew cover as 550 Ninth Air Force fighter-bombers launched the operation with more than 200 tons of high explosives and napalm. Afterward some 1,500 B-17s and B-24s and nearly 400 medium bombers dropped about 3,500 tons of bombs on enemy positions around Saint-Lô. The dust raised by the exploding bombs obscured target markers and geographic features, so that some planes accidentally attacked friendly troops, killing more than 100 members of the 30th Infantry Division. Also killed was Lt. Gen. Lesley J. MCNAIR, chief of Army Ground Forces, who was observing operations. Despite these casualties, and bomb craters that hampered the American advance, carpet bombing did contribute to the Saint-Lô breakthrough by disrupting communications and demoralizing the German defenders.

CARRIER AIR GROUP. U.S. Navy designation (abbreviated CAG) for the complement of aircraft squadrons assigned to an aircraft carrier. At the beginning of the war, the normal air group consisted of one fighter squadron (VF); one scouting squadron (VS), flying dive-bombers but with the primary mission of fleet aerial reconnaissance; one bombing squadron (VB), also flying dive-bombers; and one torpedo squadron (VT). As the war progressed, the proportion of fighters to bombers increased, owing both to the growing need for defense against Japanese air attack and to the development of improved fighters capable of carrying bombs. By late 1943 scouting squadrons had been dropped from air groups and fighting squadrons had been enlarged. By early 1945 bombing-fighting squadrons (VBF) of fighter-bombers had been added; the nominal strength of an ESSEX-class carrier's VF and VBF squadrons was 36 planes apiece, making over two-thirds of the air group's airplane strength fighter planes. Light aircraft carriers (CVL) had smaller air groups of fighters and torpedo bombers. Escort aircraft carriers (CVE) did not have air groups but had composite squadrons (VC) of fighters and torpedo bombers, fewer in number than those carried by the CVLs.

CARRIER TRANSPORT SQUADRON. A force of CVEs and AKVs assigned to the U.S. Pacific Fleet during the last year of the war in that area and used to ferry replacement airplanes to the carrier task forces. Escort carriers assigned to this duty were sometimes referred to in documents as CVE(T).

CARTER, Worral Reed (1885–1975). "Nick" Carter distinguished himself as a U.S. Navy logistics specialist in the Pacific during World War II. He began the war as a captain but soon rose to commodore and then rear admiral. Best known for his use of the mobile supply unit, Carter devised the "floating tank farm" during the LEYTE GULF campaign, making use of obsolete tankers. He also worked with logistics during the OKINAWA campaign. Following the war he published *Beans, Bullets and Black Oil* (1953), an account of the war from the logistical point of view.

CARTON DE WIART, Sir Adrian (1880–1963). A British Army general of aristocratic Belgian parentage, Carton de Wiart had a career as a fighting soldier unique in the British Army. Leaving Oxford while he was still an undergraduate, he saw his first action as a cavalry trooper in the Boer War and was wounded. In July 1914, while serving in Somaliland suppressing a revolt, he was again wounded, losing an eye. Serving continuously on the Western Front, he was wounded four times in the First World War (a room in a fashionable London nursing home was kept reserved for him). One of his wounds resulted in the loss of an arm, which with his missing eye gave him a Nelsonic appearance. For his bravery in the field he was awarded the Victoria Cross, Britain's highest award. In 1919–21 Carton de Wiart saw further fighting as head of the British military mission in Poland at the time of the great Red Army offensive; in 1924 he retired to live on a small island on a Polish nobleman's remote estate.

In 1939 he was recalled to be head of the British mission in the brief September campaign in Poland. In April 1940 he commanded the British and French troops at NAMSOS, in the NORWAY campaign, but the German air superiority prevented the Allied forces from achieving any success. In April 1941 he was assigned to head a British mission in Yugoslavia, but en route his aircraft's engine failed and the plane crashed into the sea off Libya. The 60-year-old general swam a mile to the shore, only to be made a prisoner by the Italians. With other senior officers he was involved in several escape plots, on one occasion in Italy escaping successfully for eight days before recapture. In August 1943 he was released by the Italians in the hope that he might be a useful intermediary in impending armistice negotiations. His last appointment, for the remainder of the war, was as personal representative of Winston CHURCHILL with CHIANG KAI-SHEK in Chungking, where he once more saw action.

CARTWHEEL. Code name of Allied operations in 1943 for the seizure of the SOLOMON ISLANDS–NEW GUINEA–NEW BRITAIN–New Ireland area, with RABAUL as the ultimate objective. Cartwheel called for an advance through the Solomons to BOUGAINVILLE by Adm. William F. HALSEY's forces, accompanied by a drive up the New Guinea coast and a landing on western New Britain by Gen. Douglas MACARTHUR. Cartwheel proved to be a carefully phased series of operations, each one securing air bases for the next move. Halsey's drive opened in late June 1943 with landings on the NEW GEORGIA group. After the seizure of the important MUNDA airfield, VELLA LAVELLA was assaulted in August; landings on the Treasury and CHOISEUL Islands followed in October. The capture in November of EMPRESS AUGUSTA BAY on Bougainville completed the Solomons portion of Cartwheel. MacArthur began operations in June against SALAMAUA, New Guinea. In September the HUON PENINSULA was cleared. On December 26 beachheads were established at CAPE GLOUCESTER in New Britain. Operation Cartwheel was judged so successful by the U.S. Joint Chiefs of Staff that it was decided to bypass Rabaul completely and move toward the Philippines.

CASABLANCA. Three landing areas near this famous Moroccan city were the targets of the Western Task Force, commanded by Maj. Gen. George S. PATTON, Jr., in Operation TORCH, November 8, 1942. The French resisted vigorously; opposition was not ended until November 11.

CASABLANCA CONFERENCE. Held January 14–23, 1943, this was the first summit meeting after the Western Allies had seized the initiative in the war. After the NORTHWEST AFRICA operation (Torch), November 1942, it was essential that plans for future action be agreed upon. President ROOSEVELT wanted a three-party conference with Marshal STALIN included. "I very strongly feel that we have got to sit down at the table with the Russians," he wrote Winston CHURCHILL. Stalin, however, refused all invitations, indicating that the importance of the STALINGRAD operations would keep him home. Churchill and Roosevelt proceeded without him. Plans were made with a certain amount of zest, Roosevelt adopting the code name "Admiral Q" and Churchill jokingly suggesting that he should therefore be "Mr. P." The 40-bedroom Anfa Hotel and its surrounding villas, near Casablanca, Morocco, were requisitioned as the site. General EISENHOWER, responsible for security, considered the location risky but understood the desire to meet on liberated territory. Secrecy was in fact maintained, and the conference proceeded without incident.

The usual procedure at meetings of the leaders was for both British and American staffs to prepare and exchange papers beforehand. The staffs then arrived at the conference before Churchill and Roosevelt came, and during the meeting they were in steady consultation, working out details and reaching mutually acceptable decisions. Roosevelt and Churchill, while not present at the staff meetings, were kept constantly informed; when agreement could not be reached by the staffs, the two leaders were called in. At Casablanca, the

COMBINED CHIEFS OF STAFF met in formal session 15 times, and three times with Churchill and Roosevelt present.

The staff talks at Casablanca were lively, often forceful and sometimes heated, testifying to the growing acceptance of the coalition. Differences could be aired and resolved. Three pressures, from three directions, affected the decisions. Soviet pressure for a second front in Europe was unrelenting and understandable; for 19 months the Russians had been sustaining the major burden of fighting. Secondly, the British staff, Churchill, and to some extent Roosevelt were eager to expand operations in the Mediterranean to capitalize on the success of Torch. Thirdly, the U.S. JOINT CHIEFS OF STAFF were concerned about the Pacific and favored using all resources in the Pacific rather than supporting Mediterranean operations, if the cross-Channel invasion were not to be conducted in 1943. Admiral KING spoke strongly for naval priorities, and especially the Pacific. General MARSHALL argued for the cross-Channel invasion, his British counterpart General BROOKE for the Mediterranean. The Americans, more than the British, wanted action to help China.

Both sides made concessions. The British acknowledged the needs in the Pacific, and the Americans accepted that a cross-Channel invasion in 1943 would not be feasible. The Mediterranean offered the most positive place to employ available forces and work toward the long-term objectives of supporting Russia, weakening Germany and knocking Italy out of the war. Instrumental in negotiating the often delicate agreements was a British trio—PORTAL, SLESSOR and DILL. General Marshall recognized Dill's contribution to the final agreement in a letter stating that Dill's presence was of "vital importance," and noting that "a great deal was done by Dill to translate the American point of view into terms understandable to the British."

The major military decisions of Casablanca were:

1. The war against the U-boats in the Atlantic would have top priority until the security of the seas was achieved.

2. The effort to keep Russia supplied was to be continued.

3. The COMBINED BOMBER OFFENSIVE was to be intensified with the purpose of reducing German ability to withstand an invasion. The Americans would have the opportunity to employ their daylight bombing tactics.

4. The buildup of the U.S. strength in the United Kingdom would continue. A planning organization (*see* COSSAC) was to be set up in London to work on the cross-Channel invasion. An invasion would be attempted in 1943 only if Germany appeared near collapse, or as a token invasion to seize a bridgehead for later exploitation.

5. The U.S. Joint Chiefs of Staff were free to decide on future Pacific operations, but with the limitation that such operations should not prevent the Allies from exploiting any opportunity to defeat Germany in 1943. Plans were tentatively approved for an operation to recapture Burma in 1943, but these were never conducted as planned. To encourage China to stay in the war, the American combat air force in China was to be strengthened and the HUMP supply route expanded.

6. The North African campaign was to be concluded and Sicily was to be taken as soon as possible. July was to be the target month.

While their staffs applied themselves to reaching consensus on plans, Churchill and Roosevelt discussed a variety of matters, including the progress made in nuclear research and the growing problem of the political future of France. The conference seemed a good time to effect a reconciliation among French leaders and establish a stable temporary government. Generals GIRAUD and DE GAULLE were invited to attend to discuss these matters, but although Girard came, de Gaulle at first refused. He resented having been excluded from plans for Torch, and even after Churchill pressured him into putting in an appearance he flatly refused the Allied suggestion of a temporary government. He intended to—and did—establish one of his own. His most notable concession was probably his widely publicized if stiff handshake with Giraud.

The other decisions at Casablanca were overshadowed by a major policy decision. At the concluding press conference on Sunday, January 24, Roosevelt made the following statement: ". . . peace can come to the world only by the total elimination of German and Japanese war power. . . . The elimination of German, Japanese, and Italian war power means the unconditional surrender by Germany, Italy or [*sic*] Japan. That means a reasonable assurance of future world peace. It does not mean the destruction of the population of Germany, Italy, and Japan, but it does mean the destruction of the philosophies in those countries which are based on conquest and the subjugation of other people."

Churchill promptly supported Roosevelt and elaborated on UNCONDITIONAL SURRENDER, but he afterward claimed surprise at the announcement. The impact of the words "unconditional surrender" was possibly not appreciated beforehand. Neither the American Secretary of State nor the British Foreign Secretary had been included in the Casablanca deliberations. It is possible the words were intended more as encouragement to the Allies than as official policy toward the enemy. Most of the participants in formulating the policy afterward remembered their role incorrectly if at all. Roosevelt had included the words in the notes from which he spoke, yet he indicated that the comment was on the spur of the moment. Churchill had been in correspondence with his government about it, yet claimed to have heard of it first at the press conference.

Roosevelt and Churchill were severely criticized for the unconditional surrender policy by those who felt it prolonged Axis resistance. In defense, Churchill pointed out that the specific requirements the Allies then held for surrender were immeasurably more frightening than the vague phrase, and it should be noted that mitigating explanations and assurances were frequently given.

The conference having come to a successful conclusion, Churchill proposed to Roosevelt that they prolong their holiday by a visit to Marrakesh. The jaunt was successful, and on January 25 Roosevelt took off for home. His trip to Casablanca marked the first time that a U.S. President had flown and the first time a President had left the country in time of war. Churchill stayed in Marrakesh for a short rest, during which he painted his only wartime picture. **M.H.B.**

CASABLANCA, U.S.S. Escort aircraft carrier and class. Unlike earlier escort carriers, these ships were designed and built as carriers rather than being conversions of merchant hulls. Eighty were laid down by KAISER at Vancouver, Wash., between November 1942 and March 1944; they went into commission between July 1943 and July 1944. For speed and ease of production, hulls were built to mercantile rather than naval standards. In the Atlantic these CVEs were used principally as part of hunter-killer task forces for antisubmarine work; in the Pacific they provided, in addition, support for amphibious operations. During the last months of the war some were used as aircraft ferries to keep the FAST CARRIER TASK FORCE supplied with new planes. The ships of this class had standard displacement of 6,730 tons and were 499 feet long. They were lightly armed, carrying a single 5-inch gun plus antiaircraft batteries.

CASE GREEN (Fall Grün). Code name for the proposed German attack on CZECHOSLOVAKIA in 1938.

CASE RED (Fall Rot). German staff code name (1937) for the strategic concentration required to fight a war in the west with a subsidiary front in the southeast.

CASE WHITE (Fall Weiss). Code name for the German attack on Poland, 1939. The general plan was drawn up in the spring of 1939, and the actual order was issued to the Wehrmacht on August 31. It opened with this memorable sentence by the Führer: "Since the situation on Germany's Eastern frontier has become intolerable and all political possibilities of peaceful settlement have been exhausted, I have decided upon a *solution by force.*" The attack was ordered for 0445 on September 1, 1939.

CASEY, Richard Gardiner, Baron (1890–1976). Australian politician and diplomat, minister to the United States, 1940–42. In March 1942 he was appointed by Prime Minister Winston CHURCHILL to succeed Oliver LYTTELTON as British Minister of State Resident in the Middle East and member of the British War Cabinet. In this position he was the political and diplomatic adviser to the Commander in Chief. He was Governor of Bengal, 1944–46. Subsequently he served as Australian Minister for External Affairs (1951–60) and Governor General of Australia (1965–69).

CASE YELLOW (Fall Gelb). Code name for the German attack on the Low Countries and France. The general aims were stated in a directive of October 9, 1939. The term *Fall Gelb* referred to the invasion, not to specific operational plans, and continued to apply even though the plans were changed prior to the launching of the attack on May 10, 1940. The plan employed was called Sichelschnitt (Cut of the Sickle).

CASH AND CARRY. The Third NEUTRALITY ACT, passed by Congress on April 30, 1937, contained the first stipulation that foreign belligerent powers could purchase American supplies if they paid cash and transported them in ships of other than U.S. registry. A reflection of the isolationist mood and of the conviction that international arms credits had been a contributory cause of American entry into World War I, the cash-and-carry principle appeared also in the revised Neutrality Law of 1939, though various widespread measures to circumvent the act, such as registering American ships under foreign flags, demonstrated the division of American purpose. Most important, the 1939 law repealed the earlier embargo on actual armaments.

CASSIBILE, ARMISTICE OF. The armistice between Italy and the Allies, signed on September 3, 1943, at Cassibile, town in Sicily. With this agreement the government headed by Marshal Pietro BADOGLIO was able to extricate Italy from World War II. Italian armed forces surrendered unconditionally, and Allied military administration of Italy was accepted. Badoglio's royal government (*see* VICTOR EMMANUEL III) was allowed an existence behind Allied lines.

CASSINO. Town 87 miles southeast of Rome and close to the RAPIDO RIVER, the scene in the early months of 1944 of some of the bitterest fighting in ITALY. The town was a major position of the German winter defense, the GUSTAV LINE. The flooding of the Rapido River in the spring of 1944 made it almost impossible to use tanks and motorized equipment. The Allied breakthrough was made by infantry attacking unsupported by tanks and was extremely costly in casualties. British, Polish, French and American troops were engaged in the campaign, which reached a climax during the period May 11–20.

While the fighting was going on, the Benedictine abbey situated atop Monte Cassino, a hill which dominates the surrounding ground, became the subject of disagreement in the Allied command and heated debate in Allied newspapers. The abbey, a treasure of ancient Christendom, was said to be sheltering German defenders, and the demand was made that it be destroyed. It was suggested that the Germans could just as readily defend from the ruins of the abbey, but the proponents of destruction won the debate. A massive air raid on February 15 leveled the ancient building, but no lessening of German resistance was apparent. Although no conclusive evidence developed that the Germans had been using the abbey prior to the raid, they turned the rubble into an effective strongpoint, which was finally captured by Polish troops on May 18, 1944.

CASTELLANO, Giuseppe (1893–1977). As an aide to the Italian Chief of Staff, Gen. Vittorio AMBROSIO, Castellano represented the principal army group which opposed MUSSOLINI and successfully negotiated an armistice with the Allies in 1943. Castellano first began his negotiations with Maj. Gen. Walter Bedell SMITH of the United States and Brig. K. W. D. STRONG of Great Britain in Lisbon in August 1943. Agreement between the Italians and the Allies was not reached, however, until September 3, 1943, at CASSIBILE, Sicily, where Castellano signed the famous "Short Armistice" which ended Italian hostilities against the Allies.

CASU. Carrier Aircraft Service Unit. A self-contained U.S. Navy mobile unit designed to operate from advance island bases and at certain continental U.S. fields to provide full support services to CARRIER AIR GROUPS while these groups were separated from their carriers.

Cassino: the town, the castle atop the nearer hill, and in the distance Monte Cassino with the famous abbey

A CASU had a nominal strength of 533 officers and men, although this varied widely with individual circumstances. PATSUs—Patrol Aircraft Service Units—provided similar services to land-based patrol bombers. A SOSU (Scout-Observation Service Unit) supported units of battleship- and cruiser-based floatplanes. CASUs located in the continental United States had the additional task of training personnel for overseas CASU assignment.

CATALINA. *See* PBY.

CATANIA. The Axis drew a strong defensive line in the Sicilian plain south and west of Catania, and General MONTGOMERY'S British Eighth Army fought bitterly before taking the city on August 7, 1943.

CATAPULT. Code name for the British seizure or disabling of French warships on July 3,1940. *See* MERS-EL-KÉBIR.

CATAPULT-ARMED MERCHANT SHIP (CAM). One of a number of British merchantmen fitted with a fixed bow catapult carrying a single HURRICANE fighter. A special RAF unit, the Merchant Service Fighter Unit (MSFU), was organized in May 1941 to provide planes and trained pilots; training included special drills in bailing out and survival in the water. CAM ships were intended to provide fighter protection against German land-based bombers operating over waters outside the radius of British bases. By 1943 enough ESCORT CARRIERS and MERCHANT AIRCRAFT CARRIERS were in service for this stopgap measure to be dispensed with. For the two preceding years, the MSFU had provided the only open-ocean air cover available to Allied merchant convoys.

CATCHPOLE. Code name for the capture and occupation of ENIWETOK Atoll by the U.S. Marine V Amphibious Corps.

CATHERINE. Code name of a British plan for forcing a passage into the Baltic. It was advocated by Winston CHURCHILL in the early months of the war.

CATROUX, Georges (1877–1969). General Catroux served with distinction in Indochina and Africa and in World War I before retiring from the French Army early in 1939. Recalled after World War II began, Catroux was named Governor General of French Indochina, but was replaced in 1940 when he refused to accept the armistice between France and Germany. He then joined General DE GAULLE'S Free French movement (*see* FREE FRANCE), becoming high commissioner in Syria in late 1941. In 1943 Catroux acted as liaison between de Gaulle and General GIRAUD, serving as Governor General of Algeria and a member of the FRENCH COMMITTEE OF NATIONAL LIBERATION. In 1944 he became minister for North Africa.

CAUDRON C-714. French single-seat interceptor-fighter with a design derived from a racing plane. The C-714 was one of the few lightweight aircraft produced during the war. It first flew during tests in September and October 1938. It was mostly of wood construction and thus simply and quickly built. One hundred were ordered, but delivery was stopped at 90 in February 1940. The C-714s saw brief operational service with the all-Polish unit formed in Finland in 1940. Powered by a 450-horsepower Renault V-12 engine, the C-714 flew at a maximum speed of 302.5 miles per hour. It was armed with four 7.5-mm. machine guns and weighed 3,858 pounds fully loaded.

CAUDRON-RENAULT CR-760. French single-seat, lightweight interceptor-fighter, a progressive development of the Caudron C-714. The three prototypes showed an outstanding performance for the power available, in addition to being very maneuverable and simple to maintain. Two models were destroyed to prevent German capture. The third was completed as the CR-770–01; it too was destroyed after a few flights in order to prevent capture by the Germans. Powered by a 730-horsepower V-12 engine, the CR-760 flew at a maximum speed of 354 miles per hour. It was armed with six 7.5-mm. machine guns. The normal loaded weight was 4,092 pounds.

CAULDRON, THE. A pocket inside the GAZALA LINE (Libya) constituting a defensive position of General ROMMEL'S AFRIKA KORPS (May 30, 1942). It was completely exposed to British air attacks (hence "Cauldron"), but nevertheless—to the surprise of the British—the Afrika Korps held out and went on to take TOBRUK. *See also* NORTH AFRICA.

CAVALLA, U.S.S. GATO-class submarine. Commissioned in 1944, *Cavalla* earned a PRESIDENTIAL UNIT CITATION on her first war patrol. She effectively tracked and reported movements of Japanese naval forces leading to the Battle of the PHILIPPINE SEA, and she then torpedoed and sank the Japanese carrier SHOKAKU. By the end of the Pacific war *Cavalla* had been credited with sinking over 34,000 tons of Japanese shipping.

CAVALLERO, Ugo (1880–1943). Marshal Cavallero was named Chief of Staff of the Italian Armed Forces to replace Marshal BADOGLIO in November 1940, when the Greek campaign was at its most dismal ebb. He had a reputation for organizational ability, and under his firm hand the Italian military organization received a major revamping. Prior to 1941 the Armed Forces General Staff had exercised no command and served primarily as an advisory body, but Cavallero added intelligence and operations sections, put the service chiefs of staff directly under the Armed Forces Chief of Staff and turned Comando Supremo into a command organization comparable to Germany's OKW.

A good administrator with industrial experience, Cavallero brought to the Italian military an efficiency and order it had not previously known. He forced the Navy to exert itself to get supplies to Libya; he pressed for production of necessary military supplies. He maintained good working contact with OKW, and as head of Comando Supremo he personified the Italian policy of close alliance with Germany. When Field Marshal KESSELRING came to Italy as Germany's Commander in Chief South, he and Cavallero worked well together.

Nevertheless, Cavallero was foremost an Italian, and he was unable to avoid conflicts with the Germans. In Africa he had several stormy interviews with General ROMMEL in which Rommel seemed to get his way, but after ALAMEIN, when Cavallero felt Rommel had given unfair treatment to his Italian units, he urged Rommel's recall. Cavallero also resented Germany's accusations that Axis failure at STALINGRAD was the fault of the Italian troops there, and he objected to German demands that Germans command Italian units should the Allies invade the Balkans. Simultaneous with his change of heart over close cooperation with the Germans, there were rumors that Cavallero was planning to oust Benito MUSSOLINI and succeed him, and in February 1943 Cavallero was replaced by General AMBROSIO. Rommel's comment on Cavallero's dismissal was "Welcome news," but Ambrosio's first advice to Mussolini was to break free of the Germans.

In August 1943 Cavallero was arrested for an alleged plot, and although he was soon released, he committed suicide shortly thereafter. In January 1944, during the course of the trials held by Mussolini's rump government—the so-called Salo Republic—a document written by Cavallero shortly before his death was made public. From late 1942, when Mussolini's health failed and Italian military fortunes became hopeless, Cavallero had conspired with other military personnel to oust Mussolini and put military command in the hands of King VICTOR EMMANUEL III. He had killed himself knowing his role would soon be public knowledge.

CAVIGLIA, Enrico (1862–1945). Italian Army officer who in World War I defeated the Austrians, thereby bringing about an armistice in that theater of operations. In World War II Caviglia, who had been promoted to field marshal in 1926 but was strongly opposed to Fascism, aided Marshal Pietro BADOGLIO in ousting Benito MUSSOLINI. When the Germans occupied Rome in 1943 following the removal of Il Duce, Caviglia, against some opposition, surrendered the city to them. He later led several former Italian Army units which fought as guerrillas against the Germans.

CAVITE. U.S. navy yard on Manila Bay (Philippines), attacked and devastated by 50 to 60 Japanese bombers of the 11th Air Fleet on December 10, 1941. The bombers were able to cruise at will beyond the range of antiaircraft fire. Among the most significant losses was the Asiatic Fleet's entire stock of torpedoes for submarines.

CELESTES. Allied code name for Generalissimo CHIANG KAI-SHEK. It was used for the CAIRO CONFERENCE, November 1943.

CELLES. Belgian town four miles east of the Meuse River, the closest the Germans came in the Battle of the BULGE to their first main objective, crossing the Meuse. There on Christmas Day 1944 the U.S. 2d Armored Division with help from contingents of British armor and American planes demolished the spearhead of the 2d Panzer Division, whose tanks had run out of gasoline. The deepest German penetration was not quite 60 miles from the start line along the German frontier.

CENTRAL PACIFIC AREA. When the U.S. Joint Chiefs of Staff reorganized the command structure in the Pacific on March 30, 1942, one of the commands was designated Pacific Ocean Areas (POA) and given to Adm. Chester W. Nimitz, Commander in Chief Pacific Fleet. POA in turn was divided into three areas, one of which was the Central Pacific, which encompassed the area from latitude 42° N. to the equator and included the Hawaiian Islands, Gilberts, Marshalls, Carolines and Marianas. Lt. Gen. Robert C. Richardson was Army commander of the area.

CENTRE NC-470. French six-place crew-trainer, twin-engine, twin-float seaplane. Production began in 1938, and 24 were built. They were used for coastal reconnaissance early in the war.

CERBERUS. Code name for the dash up the English Channel of the German ships Scharnhorst, Gneisenau and Prinz Eugen, February 11–13, 1942.

CG-4. Waco Aircraft manufactured this high-wing, boxlike, 15-passenger glider. Built of wood and metal, with much of its exterior covered by fabric, the CG-4 featured a hinged nose that swung upward to discharge troops or cargo. The glider could carry a jeep with six men or a 75-mm. howitzer and five-man crew. Tested in 1942, the CG-4 Hadrian made its combat debut the following year during the invasion of Sicily, and was used in Burma as well as on the continent of Europe. An improved version, the CG-15, saw limited service near the end of the war.

CHAFF. American term for Window—radar-jamming tinfoil dropped from aircraft.

CHAIN HOME. The name given to a system of 20 early British radar stations installed during 1937–39 and named from the expression "British home chain of early-warning stations." This system covered the coast from Scapa Flow to Portsmouth; in 1941 it was extended along the southern coast, west of Portsmouth. Each station comprised four sets of antennas mounted on four 100-meter towers. It was commonly called CH.

CHAMBERLAIN, (Arthur) Neville (1869–1940). Prime Minister of Great Britain in 1937–40, identified with the policy of appeasement of the dictators Adolf Hitler and Benito Mussolini. One of his first acts was to recognize Mussolini's conquest of Ethiopia. It was his belief that a conciliatory policy toward the dictators, one aimed at meeting reasonable demands, would produce a new period of harmony in Europe. He was, he said, "a man of peace to the depths of my soul" but he did not understand the ruthless and utterly unscrupulous mentality of Hitler; he was, of course, not the first person to display limited understanding of that extraordinary personage. In the Munich Agreement of September 1938, Chamberlain accepted Hitler's demands for "self-determination" for the Sudetenland Czech minority in the belief that such appeasement would assure peace. He persuaded a willing Premier Edouard Daladier of France to agree to these demands, in spite of France's treaty obligations to Czechoslovakia. On his return to England, Chamberlain received an ecstatic welcome from the people, who wanted to believe that he had brought, in his famous phrase, "peace in our time." A movement arose to create a "National Fund of Thanksgiving" in the Prime Minister's honor, though he declined it.

After September 3, 1939, the man of peace found himself leader of a nation at war. In April 1940, following months of phony war, Chamberlain, in a speech arguing that Britain's position in relation to Germany had improved since the beginning of the war, made another celebrated utterance: Hitler, he said, had "missed the bus." Within a few days the Germans had landed in Norway, and the "phony war" was over. After the Soviet defeat of the Finns, for whom the Allies had done little, and the Allied reverses in Norway, Chamberlain resigned; the date was May 10, 1940, the day the Germans launched their attack in the west.

Although political cartoonists made Chamberlain with his furled umbrella a symbol of softness in the face of aggression, he was in fact a courageous—if stubborn and opinionated—man who attempted to live by his principles. But he never seemed to comprehend the forces with which he was compelled to deal.

CHANEY, James E. (1885–1967). American air general, a West Point graduate of 1908. In 1934 he was promoted to brigadier general and appointed to the post of Assistant Chief of the Air Corps, which he held until 1938. Promoted to major general in 1940, Chaney observed the Battle of Britain during October and November 1940; in 1941 he commanded the Special Army Observation Group in England. In 1942 he became commanding general, U.S. Army Air Forces in the British Isles, and then for a brief time in June 1942 commander of U.S. forces in the ETO. After a number of training assignments, Chaney commanded the air elements in the planning and execution of the invasion of Iwo Jima and ended the war as the island commander.

CHANNEL ISLANDS. The only British territory occupied by the Germans during World War II. Located 40 miles west of Cherbourg and 80 miles south of England, the group consists of nine islands, the largest of which is the island of Jersey. The Germans occupied the islands on June 30, 1940. The occupation ended on May 9, 1945, when the German garrison surrendered.

CHAPLAINS, THE FOUR. Four U.S. Army chaplains—two Protestant, one Catholic and one Jewish—who gave their life jackets to others when the Army transport ship Dorchester was torpedoed and sunk in the North Atlantic in February 1943. Without life jackets their chance of survival, already slim, became nonexistent. A U.S. postage stamp was later issued in their honor. The four were George L. Fox and Clark V. Poling, Protestants; John P. Washington, Roman Catholic; and Alexander D. Goode, Jew.

CHAPULTEPEC CONFERENCE. In March 1945, just prior to the San Francisco meeting of the United Nations, the Inter-American Conference on Problems of War and Peace met in Mexico City. It resulted in the Act of Chapultepec, which dealt with such matters as the joint war effort of the American nations, joint economic activities and support for the infant United Nations. The act also called for an inter-American treaty declaring that an attack on one American nation was an attack on all and requiring concerted action against such aggressor nations. This principle of mutual defense, established in the Charter of the United Nations later that year, would later be invoked as the justification for such regional alliances as NATO. As its final act, this conference established conditions by which Argentina (whose neutrality generally favored the Axis throughout the war) could rejoin the community of Western Hemisphere nations. Argentina was to declare war on the Axis, join the Allied war effort, democratize its government and adhere fully to the pledges of the Chapultepec Conference. Quickly, if reluctantly, Argentina agreed to these conditions so as to attend the San Francisco meeting of the United Nations.

CHARAN KANOA. Town on SAIPAN, center of the four-mile front on which the U.S. 2d and 4th Marine Divisions landed on June 15, 1944. It was taken that day.

CHARLEMAGNE DIVISION. When the Nazis formed the Charlemagne, or 33d Waffen-Grenadier, Division in November 1944, they amalgamated the French Waffen SS and the LVF (Légion des Volontaires Françaises Contre le Bolchévisme). Consisting of some 7,340 Frenchmen, not all of whom served voluntarily, the division wore German uniforms while fighting the Soviets in Pomerania and in Berlin in the war's last months.

CHARLES LAWRENCE, U.S.S. High-speed transport and class. Forty former BUCKLEY-class destroyer escorts received a conversion similar to that given to the CROSLEY class. Their 3-inch-gun battery was, in many ships, replaced by a single forward 5-INCH 38-CALIBER gun.

CHARLES-ROUX, François (1879–1961). French diplomat who served as ambassador to the Vatican (1932–40) and was appointed secretary general of the Ministry of Foreign Affairs in 1940. In 1949 he published his memoir *Cinq Mois Tragiques aux Affaires Étrangères (21 Mai–1 Novembre, 1940).* Although not a cabinet minister, he offered some resistance to the French Government's rush to armistice in 1940.

CHASTITY. Code name of Allied plan for constructing an artificial harbor at Quiberon Bay, Brittany, in 1944. The plan was never executed.

CHAUNG WAR. A unique campaign fought by British forces in the ARAKAN west coastal area of BURMA from December 1944 to May 1945. This part of the Burmese coast consists of low-lying mangrove swamps and islands intersected by hundreds of narrow waterways. Bad as the terrain was, it served as a major line of communication and supply for forces moving to or from India; hence, it was vital that the British control it once they had launched their campaign to reconquer Burma in 1944. Both the British and the Japanese used scores of small, shallow-draft motor launches and motor torpedo boats. In addition, any other available vessels which could be used were put to work. Armed landing craft, sampans and barges cruised the chaungs, or waterways. The fighting was characterized by sudden, violent encounters at very close range. The Japanese, after heavy losses, were forced to relinquish their hold on the area. The fighting prefigured in many ways the campaign that would be waged by the U.S. Navy in the Delta region of South Vietnam in the 1960s.

CHAUTEMPS, Camille (1885–1963). French politician and Radical Socialist Party champion of keeping France out of war. Chautemps supported the VICHY regime and served as its Vice-Premier in Algiers. He spent most of the war in Washington as a spokesman for Vichy but broke with the regime as the war turned. His conviction for treason *in absentia* was later rescinded.

CHEMICAL MORTAR. Models M1A1 and M2 were 4.2-inch rifled mortars developed by the U.S. Army's Chemical Warfare Service (CWS) from the British World War I smooth-bore Stokes 4-inch mortar. The 4.2-inch bore came from rifling the Stokes, which added two-tenths of an inch. The 4.2 was first used in Sicily, and it was soon demanded on all fronts; the heaviest use later was in the Pacific. The weapon was originally designed to lob chemical shells into enemy lines; early in the war the Army decided that a heavy-explosive capability would be useful. The M1A1's explosive range of 2,400 yards was inadequate. After experimentation a 3,200-yard range was achieved, but a new barrel, the M2, had to be adopted to accommodate the increased propellant charge. The M2's range was increased to 4,400 yards by use of removable propellant discs which the crew could manipulate to obtain the maximum range or the minimum range of 340 yards. Even more range was demanded, and several attempts to improve the M2, including a jet accelerator mounted on the shell, were tried and dropped. The CWS saw that the M2 had reached the end and began development of the E37 mortar, which was completed too late to be used in the war.

CHENGTU. This city, the capital of China's Szechwan province, was chosen as the principal mainland base for B-29 operations against the Japanese home islands (*see* B-29). The city lay in the densely populated and intensely cultivated Min River valley, some 200 miles northwest of Chungking, then the national capital, and 400 miles from Kunming, the Chinese terminus of the air route across the HUMP. Perhaps a half-million persons labored on four bomber bases and their satellite fighter airfields at Chengtu; almost all the work was done by hand. The task, worthy of Hercules, played havoc with the region's agriculture. Maj. Gen. Claire L. CHENNAULT, in command of the China-based Fourteenth Air Force, had proposed basing the B-29s at Kweilin, which was closer to Japan, but his superior, Gen. Joseph W. STILWELL, quickly pointed out that an estimated 50 Chinese divisions, all of them supplied by air over the Hump, would be required to protect that site. Allied planners settled for the more distant Chengtu, because it seemed more secure. Unfortunately, Chinese Nationalist military strength had so diminished by the end of January 1945 that the airfields had to be abandoned. By this time, the main B-29 effort against Japan was originating in the MARIANAS. Some Superfortresses continued to use fields elsewhere in China, usually to attack targets in Japanese-held portions of the Asian mainland. *See also* CHINA.

CHENNAULT, Claire L. (1890–1958). A pilot since 1919, Chennault was a specialist in fighter tactics. After serving in the interwar years as chief of U.S. Army Air Corps fighter training, he expressed his views in the book *The Role of Defensive Pursuit* (1935), in which he dissented from the official doctrine that bombers needed no protection. Retired from U.S. service in 1937 because of bad hearing, Colonel Chennault accepted an offer to train fighter pilots for the Chinese Government. Because China lacked the human and material resources with which to organize an effective air arm, he returned to the United States early in 1941 to recruit pilots trained by the American armed forces. These men formed the AMERICAN VOLUNTEER GROUP—the famous Flying Tigers—which he commanded until April 1942, when he was recalled to active duty by the U.S. Army and promoted to brigadier general, the rank he had held in the Chinese armed services. He then assumed command of the Army Air Forces units in China, which evolved into the Fourteenth Air Force. As a major general commanding this organization, he advocated the buildup of China-based air power at the expense of increasing the effectiveness of the Chinese ground armies.

This view put him in direct opposition to Gen. Joseph W. STILWELL, the American chief of staff to CHIANG KAI-SHEK; the Generalissimo favored Chennault. However, logistical problems and the ineffectuality of the Chinese Army were factors that militated against any larger air offensive from Chinese bases. The Chinese phase of the war was one in which frustation and bitterness were common emotions, and the clash between Chennault and Stilwell was a prime example of this. Chennault resigned his command on July 6, 1945; Stilwell had already gone.

CHERBOURG. Scene of much fighting since the 13th century, Cherbourg is a seaport on the northern edge of the COTENTIN PENINSULA. Early capture of the port was a prime task of the U.S. FIRST ARMY in Operation Overlord (the Normandy INVASION). The city fell on June 27, 1944, and within three weeks supply ships began using the harbor. Although the front soon passed far to the east, Cherbourg remained a major port for the entry of American supplies through much of the war. In November 1944, for example, 433,000 tons passed through the port.

CHERNYAKHOVSKY, I. D. (1906–1945). Soviet general, commander of a tank division when the Germans invaded Russia in 1941. He did well in the 1941 retreat, serving with the XVIII Tank Corps south of Leningrad until the summer of 1942. Between July 1942 and April 1944, Chernyakhovsky commanded the Sixtieth Army, which fought in the KURSK offensive of 1943. Promoted to general of army in 1944, he commanded the Western front, which became the Third Belorussian Front. He was one of the youngest Soviet generals and was considered a brilliant officer. His troops took Minsk, Vilna and Kaunas and penetrated into East Prussia. In February 1945 he was killed by German fire outside Königsberg.

CHERRY. Allied code name for the Japanese H5Y1 utility flying boat (*see* H5Y1).

CHERWELL, Lord (Frederick A. Lindemann) (1886–1957). British physicist and scientific adviser to Winston CHURCHILL, educated at the University of Berlin and the Sorbonne (doctorate in physics, 1910). In 1915 Lindemann went to work at the Royal Aircraft Factory at Farnborough, the chief aeronautical experimental institution in Britain. His theoretical and practical work, including personal flight tests, resulted in the first scientific explanation of an aircraft spin. Later, at Oxford, he raised the Clarendon Laboratory to the level of a first-rate research establishment.

Lindemann met Churchill in 1921 and the two established a friendship that endured. Churchill nicknamed him "the Prof." In the 1930s Churchill, recognizing the threat of Hitler, pressed for the establishment of a scientific committee. Lindemann joined the resulting TIZARD Committee in 1935, but because of friction soon left. When Churchill became Prime Minister in 1940, Lindemann was there as adviser, close friend and loyal associate, and was a strong influence. During the war he held the post of Paymaster General (1942–45) and was the only scientist in the British cabinet. He wrote 2,000 memos to Churchill, backing original research and pushing such projects as the bending of German navigational beams, hollow charges, proximity fuzes and microwave radar. Lindemann was not always wise or correct. He overestimated the effect of the bombing of German cities, asserting that it could break German morale, an idea that carried force with Churchill and was put into action with questionable results. Another dubious action was his delay of an effective antiradar device (*see* WINDOW) for over a year. When Churchill returned to political power in the early 1950s Lindemann was made the chief of the British nuclear program (1951–53).

Decidedly brilliant, Lindemann wielded great power under Churchill and participated in and influenced numerous important wartime decisions. Yet his aloof manner and acid personality made him a difficult associate for many and detracted from his positive contributions.

CHESHIRE, Leonard (1917–). A distinguished RAF bomber pilot and commander of No. 617 Squadron, the precision bombers. He was awarded the Victoria Cross for bravery in air operations from June 1940 to July 1944. He left the RAF in 1946 and worked in the establishing of the Cheshire Homes for physically handicapped persons.

CHETNIKS. The guerrilla forces of the royalist Serbian Yugoslav leader, Gen. Draža MIHAJLOVIĆ. During the German attack on the BALKANS in April 1941 the Royal Yugoslavian Army had performed very unevenly, reflecting the powerful internal tensions of the South Slav state. Croat units had mutined, and many had welcomed the Germans. After the regular phase of the war had ended and the King and his government had fled, resistance based on Serbian nationalism began, headed by then Colonel Mihajlović. In late 1941 these fighters, called Chetniks, received considerable acclaim in the West. But later in the war they were displaced in the esteem of the Allies by the PARTISANS, led by Marshal TITO.

CHIANG KAI-SHEK (1887–1975). Also known as Chiang Chung-cheng, Chiang was President of China from 1943 and Allied Supreme Commander of the China Theater of Operations, and, as commander of Chinese armies, was usually called the Generalissimo.

He studied for a military career, taking both Chinese and Japanese training and serving in the Japanese Army in 1909–11. After returning to China he joined the revolutionists opposing the imperial Manchu government, and in 1918 he became associated with Sun Yat-sen, leader of the KUOMINTANG, the revolutionary coalition of forces. In 1925, the year of Sun's death, Chiang became commander in chief of the revolutionary army. Two years later, in a bloody coup, he broke with the Communists, who were also participants in the Kuomintang, and in 1928 he established a Nationalist Chinese government in NANKING.

China was at war with Japan essentially after 1931, completely after 1937, and after the devastation of Shanghai and Nanking, Chiang retreated with his government to CHUNGKING, a city selected for its remote location in the heart of the country. The Japanese attack on Pearl Harbor made Chiang an American ally engaged in battle with the enemy; the U.S. Government was therefore eager to extend him military and economic aid, and looked to China as a fourth great power in the UNITED NATIONS alliance. In 1943 Chiang attended the CAIRO CONFERENCE with President Roosevelt and Prime Minister Churchill. His relations with his Western allies were marked by continuing tensions; a notable example was the protracted feud between the Generalissimo and the American general Joseph W. STILWELL. The British, for their part, did not share the sanguine official American view of China's potential contribution to the Allied war effort, nor did a number of leading figures in the U.S. armed forces.

Among the many problems faced by Americans working to aid the Chiang Kai-shek government was the long-standing hostility between the Nationalists and the CHINESE COMMUNISTS, each group appearing to many observers to view its own survival as a war aim more important than unified effort to defeat the Japanese invader. Amid all the intrigues that swirled about him, Chiang remained a skillful politician, adept at dealing with dissension and factionalism. To this trait he owed his lengthy survival in power. *See also* CHINA.

CHIANG KAI-SHEK, Mme. (1898–). The wife of Generalissimo CHIANG KAI-SHEK, Mme. Chiang (nee Mei-ling [or Mayling] Soong) was educated in the United States at Wellesley College. She returned to China and in 1927 married Chiang. A strong and vivid personality and a controversial figure, Mme. Chiang was active in the Chinese resistance to Japan. In 1942 she traveled to the United States, where she was a guest at the White House and addressed Congress, the first private citizen to do so. She appealed for more help in the Pacific war and pointed out that Japan controlled more resources than Germany. A member of the distinguished Soong family of Shanghai, she was the sister of T. V. SOONG, Mme. Sun Yat-sen and Mme. H. H. Kung.

CHICAGO, U.S.S. NORTHAMPTON-class heavy cruiser, commissioned 1931. She was part of the CORAL SEA operation and supported the landing on GUADALCANAL; she was damaged by a torpedo in the Battle of SAVO ISLAND. Returning after repairs, she arrived once more in the South Pacific just in time to be torpedoed and sunk in the Battle of RENNELL ISLAND.

CHICHIBU, Prince (1902–1953). Born in Tokyo, the second son of Emperor Taisho, Chichibu remained throughout his life the principal rival of his older brother, Emperor HIROHITO. Self-assured and polished, Chichibu several times traveled to Europe and the United States. He was generally pro-Western, and though he was a critic of Army intervention in political affairs, his closest friends were those connected with the dissident Kodoha (Imperial Way) faction of the Army, which engaged in several attempted coups d'état and assassinations during the 1930s.

CHIEFS OF STAFF COMMITTEE. Originally a subcommittee—composed of the First Sea Lord, the Chief of the Imperial General Staff and the Chief of the Air Staff—of the British Committee of Imperial Defence. Following the major reorganization of the high command in 1937–38, the Chiefs of Staff, under the chairmanship of the Minister for Coordination of Defence, later to be known as Minister of Defence, had the duty of advising the government on all matters relating to defense. With the outbreak of war in 1939, such matters of operational priority and the like as the committee was unable to resolve among its members were referred to the War Cabinet. The Chiefs of Staff Committee was served by subcommittees on planning and intelligence, composed of the directors of plans and intelligence of the three services. After the entry of the United States into the war, a close relationship with the American JOINT CHIEFS OF STAFF was developed, and the two bodies met from time to time as the COMBINED CHIEFS OF STAFF.

CHIFLEY, Joseph Benedict (1885–1951). This former railroad worker rose to prominence during the war years, becoming Australian Prime Minister in 1945. In October 1941, when the Labour Party under John CURTIN came to power, Chifley took office as Treasurer. He also served as production executive and was given responsibilities for postwar planning. He was impressed with the plan put forward by Sir William BEVERIDGE in Britain, basing many of his own proposals on this model. He became acting Prime Minister on April 30, 1945, succeeding to the office on July 12, when Curtin died.

CHI-HA. The Japanese Type 97 medium TANK, developed in 1936–37. It became the standard Japanese battle tank of World War II, and a number of improved versions were produced to incorporate the results of experience. The Chi-He was a modification having a different gun and more powerful engine. Some of its armor was thicker.

CHIKUMA. Japanese TONE-class heavy cruiser. Completed in 1939, she operated with fast carrier and other striking forces before being lost to American air attack at the battle for LEYTE GULF.

CHINA-BURMA-INDIA THEATER. The China-Burma-India Theater (CBI) came into being when the United States fulfilled a pledge to assist the Supreme Commander of the Chinese Theater, Generalissimo CHIANG KAI-SHEK, in carrying out China's wartime mission on the Asian mainland. Chiang had asked for an American general to serve as his chief of staff. Named to this position was an officer with an extensive background in Chinese affairs, the energetic but truculent Lt. Gen. Joseph W. STILWELL, who was also designated as commanding general of the CBI.

Prior to departing for China, the CBI staff received only very broad guidance. The orders assigning Stilwell to China, besides naming him chief of Chiang's staff, appointed him as commanding general of the "United States Army Forces in the Chinese Theater of Operations, Burma, and India," with instructions to "increase the effectiveness of the United States assistance to the Chinese Government for the prosecution of the war and to assist in improving the combat efficiency of the Chinese Army."

On February 24, 1942, the CBI staff began to arrive in Karachi, India. Stilwell assumed command of the U.S. Army Forces, which included all former American Military Mission to China (AMMISCA) personnel, on March 4, the day he arrived in Chungking to set up headquarters and meet with the Generalissimo. Chiang promptly placed him in command of the Chinese Expeditionary Force (CEF) in BURMA. At this time the Japanese were beginning a drive to capture all of Burma. RANGOON had fallen to their advance on March 6, and they immediately began to press northward against Allied forces consisting of the CEF and a British corps. The CEF was composed of the Chinese 5th Army, which was disposed along Burma's upper Sittang River and the BURMA ROAD; the 6th Army, which was deployed in the Shan States protecting Burma's east flank; and the 66th Army, in reserve in China but eventually to be committed against the Japanese. The British corps was generally located in west Burma along the Irrawaddy River. During April and May 1942 the four divisions of the Japanese 15th Army involved in the conquest of Burma drove the Allied defenders back to India and China, completing the blockade of China.

The CBI, in accomplishing its tasks relating to supply, transportation and training the Chinese during the nearly two-year period the Japanese occupied Burma and threatened India and China, was faced with numerous difficulties, many of which resulted from differences between General Stilwell and Chiang Kai-shek. Its organization and subheadquarters varied over the months to meet different situations, including the ever present problem of a complex command relationship with the other Allies. This was particularly true concerning the Southeast Asia Command (SEAC), an organizational entity suggested by Prime Minister CHURCHILL and agreed to by the United States as an improved command and control establishment in the area. SEAC was formally established on November 15, 1943, with Stilwell serving as the Deputy Supreme Commander under Adm. Lord Louis MOUNTBATTEN. At the time SEAC was formed, the commander of the U.S. Army forces (Stilwell), in addition to being deputy SEAC commander, was commanding general of the Northern Combat Area Command, chief of staff to the Generalissimo and commander of the Chinese Army in India. Other hindrances to operations were internal or-

U.S. Army instructor trains Chinese soldiers in the use of the .30-caliber machine gun

ganizational and personality problems, a prime example being the CBI relationship with the subordinate U.S. Fourteenth Air Force and its commander, Maj. Gen. Claire L. CHENNAULT.

Problems notwithstanding, the CBI succeeded in training Chinese forces sufficient in number to render important assistance in the recapture of Burma. Training bases were located in Ramgarh, India, where emphasis was on the training of entire units, and in Yunnan, China, where the technique was to train individuals who would return to their units and in turn train them with the assistance of American liaison groups detailed from the Yunnan training centers.

Logistics efforts in the CBI were guided for Stilwell by Brig. Gen. Raymond A. WHEELER and managed by a headquarters in New Delhi and various base and advance depots. This primary CBI mission was fraught with complexities of time, distance and scheduling. Supply deliveries to China improved continuously, however, as a result of the airlift over the HUMP and, beginning in 1944, the completion of the LEDO ROAD and a pipeline to Yunnan.

After numerous delays—the underlying reason being the low priority accorded China, Burma and India in the overall Allied scheme of operations for the war—CBI forces began to retake Burma in the fall of 1943. The first effort was in the form of a Chinese screen for the advance of the Ledo Road. Before that time only LONG-RANGE PENETRATION GROUPS had operated in Burma, and as a result of the CAIRO CONFERENCE of November and December 1943 it was evident that operations in Burma would be considerably reduced from those envisioned during the previous months of planning. By December 1943 the road had been pushed to Shingbwiyang as Stilwell's India-trained 38th Chinese Division entered the Hukawng valley in northwest Burma. Thus the Burma campaign was under way even though the detailed plan had not been approved by the Combined Chiefs of Staff.

During January 1944, since the Chinese were advancing only slowly down the valley, Stilwell took personal command in the field to urge faster movement. Myitkyina was the ultimate objective. In early February the Japanese attacked on the ARAKAN front, an effort that was decisively defeated by Lt. Gen. William SLIM's British Fourteenth Army. During March, in another effort, this one lasting several months, the Japanese attacked the IMPHAL front. This operation was also thwarted by the British, but not without difficulty and not before a three-month blockade of the city had been broken. Meanwhile, the Chinese forces under Stilwell were gradually pushing the Japanese south through the Hukawng along the proposed Ledo route, but enemy resistance stiffened appreciably and fighting became severe. The Chinese were assisted in their efforts by the maneuvers of the 5307 Provisional Unit (*see* MERRILL'S MARAUDERS), which operated deep in northern Burma behind Japanese lines. By July 1 the Japanese were definitely showing signs of weakening, a process that was accelerated by the long-awaited and strongly urged opening of the Salween campaign by the Chinese Yunnan-trained (Y-Force) divisions. Pressure was now being applied to the Japanese in northern Burma from two flanks. On August 3, 1944, after a lengthy siege, Myitkyina fell to the Stilwell-led Chinese.

During the rest of the year, advances by the Chinese slowed greatly and achievements on both fronts were disappointing. It was during this period that the schism between Stilwell and Chiang became extreme. President ROOSEVELT was forced to recall the general to appease the Generalissimo, who had refused to accept the further services of Stilwell in operations against the Japanese in eastern China. Stilwell was ordered to return to the United States on October 18, and the CBI was split into two entities. Maj. Gen. Albert C. WEDEMEYER took over Stilwell's duties in China, while Lt. Gen. Daniel I. SULTAN assumed those in the India-Burma theater. General Wheeler (now a lieutenant general) became Deputy Supreme Commander in SEAC, and for the first time Mountbatten had an assistant who would have undivided allegiance and would not be engaged in other duties of command. By the middle of 1945 all of Burma had been reoccupied by the Allied forces under the direction of SEAC. **W.L.A.**

CHINA INCIDENT. Japanese euphemism for operations in CHINA.

CHINA—OPERATIONS. For China, World War II began long before Germany's invasion of Poland or Japan's sudden attack at Pearl Harbor. War in China started officially on July 7, 1937, when the Japanese occupied an area near Peiping in what was called the "Lukouchiao Incident." This date—"triple seven"—did not mark the first instance of aggression, but was simply the time that China's collective will was aroused to defeat Japan. The bases of the conflict were established years earlier: the Nationalist government, its predominant political party (the KUOMINTANG), the Nationalist leader CHIANG KAI-SHEK, the Chinese Army and the CHINESE COMMUNISTS all had varied but important roles.

Provocations by Japan before 1937 had been numerous. As early as 1914 the Japanese had violated Chinese neutrality. After 1922 Japan's first goal in China became MANCHURIA, with its potential wealth and its strategic location as a buffer between Japan and Russia. On September 18, 1931, using a minor incident as provocation, the Japanese captured Mukden, and in spite of a Chinese appeal to the League of Nations, occupied all of Manchuria by January 1932. The League offered no help, and China had to accept an armistice in which the invaders were to return north of the Great Wall. Shortly thereafter, Japan proceeded to recognize the previously established (by the Japanese) independent state of Manchukuo. On January 28, 1932, again with minimal provocation, Shanghai was attacked; this incident was finally settled in April with a declaration of truce. After a brief interlude Japan returned to active aggression in 1935. Confrontations and negotiations continued through late 1936, as the Japanese attempted to detach five more northern provinces from Chinese jurisdiction. At this point a Japanese-Manchukuoan attack on Suiyuan province caused a temporary halt in what had been continuing negotiations.

But also in this period it became clear to all concerned, although not specifically agreed upon until after July 7, 1937, that it would be to the Communist advantage to join the Nationalist effort in the resistance against the common enemy. The first half of 1937 saw moderation of Japanese policies toward China, but this trend was brought to a halt on July 7. The incident at Lukouchiao consisted of an exchange of shots between Japanese troops on maneuvers and the Chinese garrison at Wanping, a Peiping suburb located at the eastern end of the Lukouchiao (Marco Polo) Bridge. The Japanese used the incident as an excuse for sending in reinforcements, and within three weeks Peiping was encircled.

Chiang was now determined to resist to the end, but until Pearl Harbor China suffered mostly defeats, trading territory for time. On August 13, 1937, after an incident near Shanghai, Chinese soldiers and Japanese reinforcements engaged in fierce fighting, and war had now spread to eastern China. Chinese troops poured into the Shanghai area in the first of several major battles during this initial phase of the war. Shanghai, strategically important to the security of the Nationalist capital at NANKING, was the scene of the bloodiest of these battles. Before the November 12 Japanese victory at Shanghai, some 300,000 Chinese had become casualties, while Japan's losses were estimated at 40,000. Chinese forces then retreated to Nanking, which fell on December 13. (Before its fall, however, the government was removed temporarily to Hankow. It later moved to CHUNGKING, where it remained for the duration.) It was during the battle for Nanking that Japanese bombers sank the American gunboat *Panay*; the United States demanded and received an apology and an indemnity from Japan.

Although the Chinese Army suffered reversal after reversal in 1938, one bright spot was the firm defeat of Japanese forces at Taierchwang, a rural town northwest of Hsuchow, and the checking of attempts to encircle the defending Chinese. Because of this six-month defense in the Hsuchow area, China's government at Hankow was given a short but needed respite. Another success was the Chinese Red Army ambush and defeat of a Japanese column in Shansi province. Following these setbacks, however, the Japanese succeeded in capturing Hsuchow on May 20, 1938. With strongly reinforced armies, they advanced upon Hankow from the north, reduced it to rubble and occupied it on October 25. The Chinese cities of Wuchang and Hanyang, to the south, were evacuated by the Chinese on the same day. In the meantime, the Japanese had also captured Kaifeng, capital of Honan province (June 6); Anking, capital of Anhwei province (June 12); and Canton (October 21).

With the fall of Hankow, the first phase of China's war came to an end. The Japanese now controlled the Peiping area, the Canton area in the south, Hankow and portions of central China and the Shanghai-Nanking area in the east. The Yellow, West and Yangtze Rivers, the coast and its major cities were also controlled by the invaders.

Japan began to consolidate its gains in the so-called second phase of the war. What battles were fought were, for the most part, won by the Japanese. But the Chinese, under such generals as Li Tsung-jen (the Battle of Tsaoyang), HSUEH YUEH (at Changsha) and Pai Chung-hsi (at Kunlungkwan), had some successes, in spite of an overall defensive strategy to "yield in front, close in on the flanks and rear, and attack thinly manned defense points and lines of communication." The capture of Nanning in late 1939 marked the maximum extent of Japanese operations against China until a drive on Chekiang in 1942. But Nanning's capture put Japan in a position to threaten French Indochina, which the Japanese Army in fact occupied in 1940. The result was that China's last eastern line of communication—the Yunnan-Indochina railroad—was no longer available.

At this point all of China's great industrial centers were in Japanese hands; the lack of production facilities for war material was one reason for Chiang's defensive strategy. Another reason was that the government had learned that the Communists in the north (*see* YENAN) were actually conserving their strength for the inevitable clash with the Nationalists. In order to counter MAO TSE-TUNG's policy of "cooperation with the Kuomintang and struggle against it at the same time," the government had to employ troops in a blockade of the Communist forces, a diversion of effort from the main goal of defeating the Japanese. An additional factor dictating defense was Japan's firm possession of air superiority, this in spite of efforts by the AMERICAN VOLUNTEER GROUP (AVG) flying in China. In late 1941 air support by Col. Claire CHENNAULT's group was about the only useful American effort in China. Such was Chennault's continuous success that he was revered by Chinese soldier and civilian alike, and he was always well regarded by Chiang Kai-shek. (The AVG was ultimately inducted into the U.S. Army Air Forces. At first it was called the China Air Task Force, but later it was reconstituted as the FOURTEENTH AIR FORCE.) As the decade of the 1930s drew to a close, Soviet aid to Chiang also decreased; with the signing of a Japanese-Soviet neutrality pact in April 1941, Russian assistance ceased altogether. The United States, however, was beginning to emerge as a strong and sympathetic ally, and would remain so for years after the war.

The generally accepted date for the beginning of the third phase of the war in the China theater is December 7, 1941. Concurrently with the attack on Pearl Harbor the Japanese began to close the ring around China, hoping to strangle the country into eventual submission. In rapid succession the Japanese conquered Malaya and the British island fortress of SINGAPORE; the Netherlands East Indies; and finally, in May 1942, BURMA. After securing Burma, Japanese forces actually occupied portions of YUNNAN province in China. The Japanese occupation of Burma and the loss to the Allies of the last overland route to China—RANGOON to KUNMING (the BURMA ROAD)—was a disastrous blow to the Chinese war effort. An already difficult resupply situation was made even more difficult.

On December 9, 1941, after years of fighting, China joined the Allies with a formal declaration of war; on January 3, 1942, President ROOSEVELT announced that "General Chiang Kai-shek," as he termed the Chinese leader, had accepted supreme command over all forces of all nations in the Chinese theater. On March 4, Lt. Gen. Joseph W. STILWELL, in response to a request by the Generalissimo for an American chief of staff, arrived in Chungking. In addition to his duties as chief of staff, Stilwell, as commanding general of the CHINA-BURMA-INDIA THEATER (CBI), assumed responsibility for all former American Military Mission to China (AMMISCA) personnel, the current American advisory

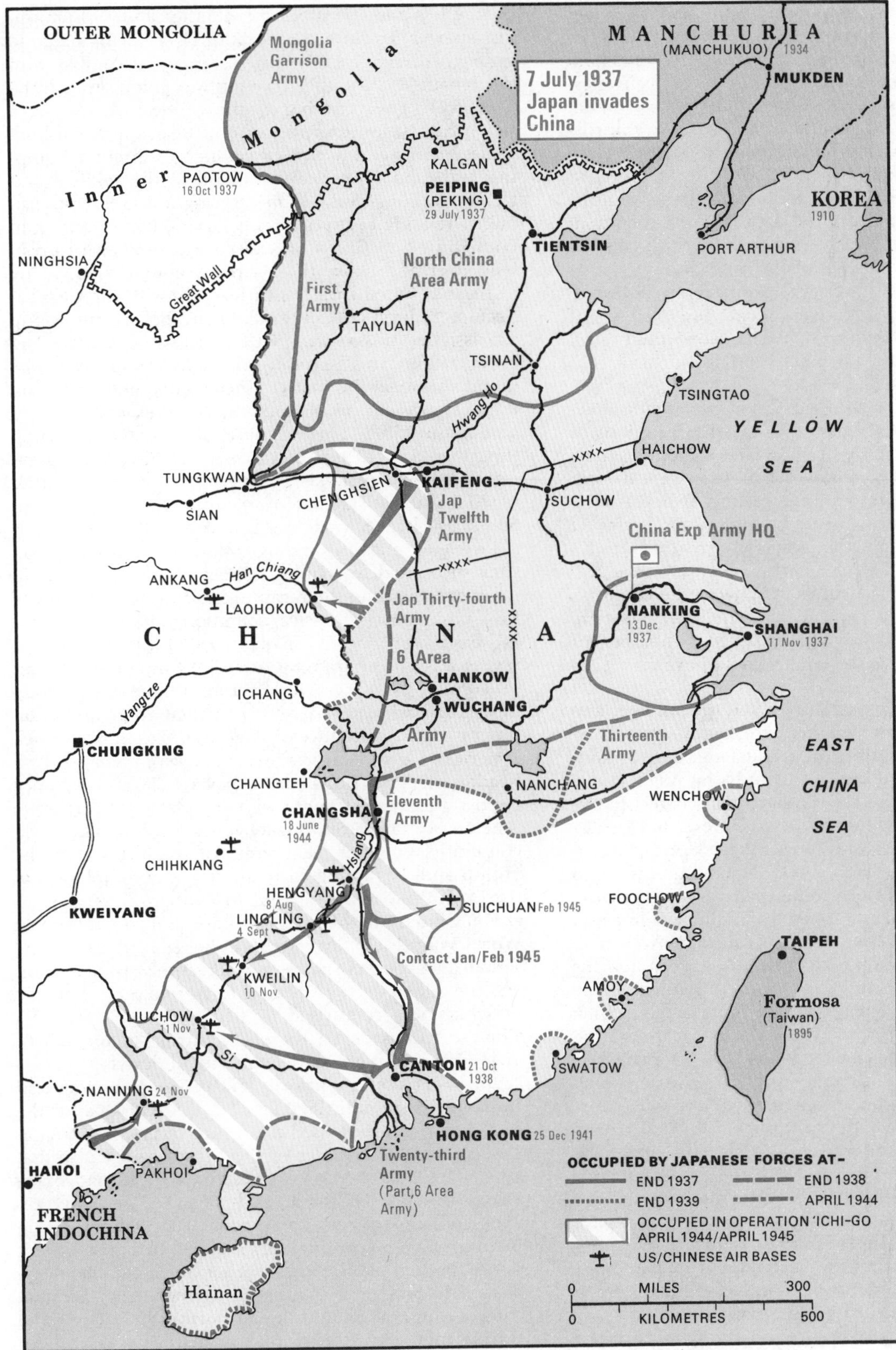

CHINA—the areas held by Japanese forces. For the Chinese the war began in 1937

effort. An extremely complicated command situation, made even more complex as time went on, greatly affected the efficiency of the U.S. effort in China until late 1944. With a mission to "increase the effectiveness of United States assistance to the Chinese Government for the prosecution of the war and to assist in improving the combat efficiency of the Chinese Army," General Stilwell soon found that he had one of the most difficult jobs of the war. The Generalissimo promptly placed Stilwell in command of the Chinese Expeditionary Force in Burma, which, along with British colonial forces, was being driven out of the country by the Japanese. Even though they were thoroughly defeated, these troops would eventually form the nucleus of American-trained Chinese divisions that would meet with success on the field of battle, both in Burma and in China.

In late 1941 and early 1942 China's economic situation was bleak at best, in spite of massive injections of American money. There was, however, something to be said for the military situation. While American, British, Dutch and Chinese forces were reeling in defeat elsewhere, Chinese forces were holding their own. At Changsha, for example, the Japanese were driven to retreat after a battle lasting nearly a month. What was happening, in effect, was that in spite of the country's greatly weakened economic and military position, Chinese forces were keeping occupied a number of Japanese divisions that the enemy could have used elsewhere.

As a result of the loss of Burma and the last overland supply route, Chinese fighting efficiency began to be impaired, notwithstanding a gradual increase in tonnage flown over the HUMP from India by Allied transports. Stilwell proposed a two-part plan to rectify the extremely critical situation of the Chinese: the re-formation of the Chinese Army and an attack on Burma to restore the vital overland lines of communication to Kunming. Stilwell's efforts to get plans accepted by the Allies were greatly handicapped by an initial withdrawal of U.S. aircraft to the Middle East, a move which caused the Generalissimo to issue three demands for the maintenance of China in the war: U.S. divisions for the recapture of Burma, increased aircraft in China and increased aerial transportation of supplies over the Hump. After complex negotiations and compromises, the Chinese agreed to a modified form of the demands; the agreement provided a basis for U.S. assistance during the war. In essence, the requirement for U.S. troops was eliminated and the amount of airlifted tonnage reduced. During the period in which the three demands were being settled, Stilwell began efforts to organize the CBI, pressed for a training program to prepare Chinese divisions in India for their return to Burma—the nucleus being the Chinese troops who had been driven from northwest Burma—and made plans for a new 30-division force (to be increased in a later proposal). Chiang Kai-shek did not initially agree with the 30-division plan, often reminding Stilwell that U.S. promises of assistance were not being fulfilled. This was true, the underlying reasons being transportation difficulties and the low priority accorded China by the Allies.

In 1942 Japanese strength in continental China was on the increase, and the Chinese Government was receiving less and less support from the Chinese Communist quarter. In China preparations were being made to train 30 divisions (Y-Force) for eventual combat with the Japanese, and other training was going on in India (X-Force). The readying of the Chinese Army was a slow process, however, because of delays in furnishing replacements and in the distribution of essential equipment, the poor physical condition of the soldiers and lack of training. Stilwell, in carrying out U.S. responsibilities relating to supply, transportation and training in both India and China, was faced with numerous problems over and above those already enumerated; many of these resulted from his differences with the Generalissimo. Stilwell's main instrument for accomplishing the assigned mission, the CBI structure, had a varying organization and several subheadquarters over the months to meet the many difficult situations, including the ever present problem of the complex relationships among the Allies. This was particularly true concerning the Allied SOUTHEAST ASIA COMMAND (SEAC), an organizational entity established in November 1943 because of Allied dissatisfaction over progress of the war in Southeast Asia; Stilwell was also its deputy commander.

Problems notwithstanding, Stilwell and Chiang Kai-shek succeeded in training Chinese forces sufficient in number to assist in the recapture of Burma and provide for—ultimately—offensive operations in China. Training bases were located in Ramgarh, India, where emphasis was on the training of entire Chinese units, and in Yunnan province, where the technique was to train individuals who would return to their units and train them with the assistance of American liaison personnel. American logistics efforts for China were managed by a headquarters in India and various base and advance depots; they were fraught with complexities of priority, time and distance. Supply deliveries to China improved constantly, however, as a result of the airlift over the Hump and, beginning early in 1945, the completion of the LEDO ROAD and a pipeline to Yunnan.

For China, one of the most important operations of World War II was not fought on her soil. It was of vital significance because it reopened supply routes. This was the Allied drive to recapture Burma, no small part of which was comprised of Chinese forces. Stilwell's Chinese troops began to retake Burma in the fall of 1943 after numerous delays, the underlying reason again being the low priority given China, Burma and India in the overall Allied scheme of operations for the war. The first effort used the troops trained in India as a screen for the advance of the Ledo Road. Up to that time only LONG-RANGE PENETRATION GROUPS had operated in Burma, and as a result of the CAIRO CONFERENCE in late 1943 it was evident that operations in Burma would be considerably reduced from those envisioned earlier. By December 1943 the road had been pushed to Shingbwiyang, as the Chinese 38th Division entered the Hukawng valley in northwest Burma. The Burma campaign, therefore, was in reality well under way even though the plans had not yet been approved. While British forces were fighting off and defeating the Japanese to the south, the Chinese pushed slowly toward their first objective, Myitkyina, which fell to them on August 3, 1944. In the meantime—May 11, 1944—the Chinese had attacked across the SALWEEN RIVER with Yunnan-trained divisions. This operation had been delayed considerably, owing to political differences between Chiang Kai-shek and the Allies, but when it finally began, pressure was being brought to bear on the Japanese, and for the first time from two different flanks. Although Burma was not completely reoccupied by the Allies until May 1945 (the Chinese did not participate in the final thrust against Rangoon), the campaign enabled the first convoy of supplies to arrive in Kunming in January by way of the Ledo Road.

It was during this general period (October 1944) that the long-standing differences of opinion between Chiang Kai-shek and Stilwell reached their peak. President Roosevelt was forced to recall Stilwell to appease the Generalissimo, who had refused to accept Stilwell's further services in operations against the Japanese in eastern China. The CBI was split into two theaters of operation, with Maj. Gen. Albert C. WEDEMEYER taking on Stilwell's duties in China in what was now known as the China Theater (CT).

While Chinese divisions were conducting successful campaigns in Burma, the situation in China was somewhat different. Morale in the country was low because of inflation and poor governmental administration. The Japanese, aware of the poor state of the economy and still occupying eastern China, chose this time to launch a major offensive effort. The objectives of Operation ICHI-GO, as it was called, were to forestall U.S. bombing of Japan from bases at Kweilin and Liuchow, to secure the Kweilin-Liuchow area for possible future offensives, to restore operation of the north-south transcontinental railway and to destroy "the backbone of the Chinese Army and force increased deterioration" of the Chungking government. On April 18, 1944, the Japanese began with efforts to seize control of the Peiping-Hankow railway. Despite stiff Chinese resistance and effective U.S. and Chinese air support, the Japanese secured the railway in mid-June, killing a number of high-ranking Chinese officers and capturing Loyang, the ancient capital of Honan, in the process.

Fresh from these successes, the Japanese planned and very capably carried out a large-scale pincers movement in Hunan province, capturing Changsha on June 18, 1944, and moved on to Hengyang, an important railway center. Assisted by Chennault's Fourteenth Air Force, 16,275 Chinese defenders held off six Japanese divisions for 46 days. In spite of the Chinese effort, however, the Japanese took Hengyang on August 8, and in early 1945 they controlled the Hankow-Canton railway. With fresh reinforcements, the Japanese continued their westerly advance, beginning with an effort to take Kweilin and Liuchow with a force that eventually totaled some 400,000 troops. Kweilin fell on November 10, 1944, Liuchow on the 11th, and by early December both Tuyan and Kweiyang in Kweichow province were in Japanese hands. The situation in Kunming and Chungking was tense, as a very real Japanese threat loomed.

When General Wedemeyer arrived in Chungking after assuming command on October 31, 1944, two situations required his immediate attention. The first was the defense of the Kweilin airfield, and the second, absolutely vital, was the defense of Kunming. Wedemeyer was not unfamiliar with the situation in China, having served previously as deputy chief of staff to SEAC's Supreme Commander, Adm. Lord Louis MOUNTBATTEN. Wedemeyer's official mission was to advise and assist the Chinese in their conduct of military operations and, regarding U.S. forces, to carry out air operations from China. The Generalissimo welcomed his new adviser, and Wedemeyer's disarming personality and ability to exercise diplomacy and tact made his advice palatable to the Chinese during this very difficult time.

With the cooperation of the Generalissimo, Wedemeyer set to work to help the Chinese stem the Japanese advance in Kweichow province by airlifting in some 23,000 fresh troops and by ordering Gen. Fu Tso-yi to engage the Japanese in northern China to prevent their reinforcing the Kweiyang area. To ease the situation in Kunming, Wedemeyer directed the planning of a well-organized defense (Operation Alpha). He set up machinery to facilitate closer understanding between the two Allies. On a somewhat longer term the CT, under Wedemeyer's close direction, made substantial progress in improving the lot of the Chinese soldier; planned for and began the execution of a large-scale effort to reopen continental China's eastern seaports (Operation Beta, ultimately Carborando); and by war's end had 39 Chinese divisions undergoing training.

By the spring of 1945 the situation had begun to look somewhat brighter. The increased cooperation between the United States and China—although not without its setbacks, an example being difficulties in getting the defense of Kunming under way—resulted in tangible improvement, as in the Chinese defeat of Japan's China Expeditionary Army in two separate instances. The first was the reversal of a Japanese offensive in the Hunan-Hupeh area (March–August), during which the Chinese inflicted heavy casualties and regained air bases captured in the initial Japanese assault. The second was the suppressing of the Japanese Chihchiang campaign (western Hunan) in April–June. With the intention of neutralizing a Chinese-American air base at Chihchiang, the Japanese began an assault with some 80,000 men and made considerable gains, but were then driven back beyond their original lines. The Chinese, for the first time in the war, now possessed the initiative, though helped by the fact that the Japanese were beginning to withdraw their forces toward the homeland. When V-J Day came, the Chinese were preparing for the offensive in the Canton–Hong Kong–Fukien area with the express purpose of reopening China's east coast.

Even before the cessation of hostilities it was apparent that peace would not come easily in China. The enmity between the Nationalists and the Communists was deep and would end, in 1949, with a Communist victory. But it was nevertheless true that out of all the complexities, frustrations and intrigues of wartime China had come victory over the invader. **W.L.A.**

CHINDIT. A soldier of a British LONG-RANGE PENETRATION GROUP. In the summer of 1942, Brig. Orde WINGATE formed the 77th Indian Infantry Brigade from British, Gurkha and Burmese battalions. Known as Chindits after a mythical Hindu figure, these troops were trained to act as raiders and guerrillas. In February 1943, Wingate took 3,000 men of this mixed force across the CHINDWIN RIVER into north Burma. After six weeks of operations against Japanese lines of communications, Wingate's force exfiltrated into India and China. Though the Chindits lost over one-third of their number to disease and the enemy, Wingate believed that future long-range penetration groups could paralyze the enemy's rear. At the QUEBEC CONFERENCE in the fall of 1943, he convinced both Churchill and Roosevelt that light infantry brigades supported and supplied by air could survive in the enemy's rear.

The second Chindit operation began in March 1944. On March 16, 9,000 troops and 1,000 mules were landed by glider behind Japanese lines, and by March 20 three Chindit brigades were operating. Only 18 days later, Major General Wingate, as he had become, was killed in an aircraft accident; his tactics were, however, to be successfully practiced by his successors. Under General LENTAIGNE the Chindit force disrupted Japanese supply lines and forced an abortive end to the Japanese offensive at IMPHAL. The success of the Chindits was achieved at a high price. By July 1944 the bulk of the men were dead, wounded, sick or exhausted.

The Chindits were as controversial as their tactics. Many staff officers regarded them as eccentric and undependable. But despite their detractors' claims, they played an important role in the recapture of Burma.

CHINDWIN RIVER. Situated in BURMA and paralleling the Indian border, this primary tributary of the Irrawaddy River was a major obstacle for both Allied and Japanese forces during World War II. The Chindwin was crossed with difficulty by the Allies at several locations as they were driven from Burma in 1942. Planning in 1944 (code-named CAPITAL) called for a recrossing of the river by elements of the British Fourteenth Army. This was accomplished in force on November 19 at Sittaung and December 3 at KALEWA against elements of the Japanese 15th Army. The last occupied port on the Chindwin—Monywa—was recaptured on January 22, 1945.

CHINESE ARMY. In 1937, when the Japanese commenced full-scale hostilities against China after the Marco Polo Bridge incident, the army of CHIANG KAI-SHEK, the leader of the Nationalist government, numbered about 2 million troops, who were inadequately organized, trained and equipped. The other Chinese force was the army of the CHINESE COMMUNISTS, consisting of about 150,000 troops. These two armies were officially allies. *See also* CHINA.

CHINESE COMMUNISTS. On the eve of the full-scale war between China and Japan in 1937, the Chinese Communists under MAO TSE-TUNG were stationed in Yenan in northern Shensi province, behind Japanese lines and beyond the reach of CHIANG KAI-SHEK and the Nationalist Chinese in Nanking. During the 1930s the Nationalists and the Communists had fought each other, but in September 1937, following the Japanese attack on Shanghai, they agreed to refrain from civil war and form a united front. Under the agreement the Communists toned down their economic program and renamed the Red Army the Eighth Route Army, and the Nationalists pledged to work for the establishment of democratic freedoms for the Chinese people.

After the Japanese conquest of Nanking the Nationalists moved up the Yangtze River to CHUNGKING, the Communists remaining virtually alone as an effective political and military force. Militarily the Communists expanded their power both by direct recruitment and by encouraging and eventually incorporating into their own ranks a variety of self-defense and anti-Japanese guerrilla units that had formed spontaneously in the wake of the invasion and the abusive treatment of the population by the Japanese. The guerrilla tactics recommended by Mao for the war were identical with those he had employed in the struggle against the Nationalists. They consisted in "avoiding strength and striking at weakness," concentrating one's forces to annihilate the enemy units one by one and emphasizing the killing of enemy soldiers rather than the conquest of territory or strongpoints.

Politically the Communists applied the three-thirds system, under which local government in the guerrilla areas was composed of one-third Communists, one-third from other organizations and one-third nonparty people. The appeal to all classes in the name of unity against the enemy was strengthened by moderate economic policies involving a limitation of rent but no confiscation of land.

By 1940 the Eighth Route Army counted some 400,000 regular troops and full-time guerrillas. In June, Chiang and Mao reached a new arrangement which permitted the Communists a free hand north of the Yellow River. However, when a portion of the Communist forces operating in central China had not crossed the Yellow River by the end of the year the Nationalists attacked and annihilated it in January 1941. This incident marked the end of any real collaboration between the two groups. For the rest of the war the Communists ceased to make even a pretense of obeying Nationalist directives and continuously increased their prestige as the staunchest defenders of China's national integrity.

The summer of 1944 saw the first important contact between Mao and representatives of the U.S. Government. In August a U.S. military mission accompanied by diplomat John Service was established in Yenan. At the same time President Roosevelt attempted to improve relations between the Nationalists and Communists by placing Gen. Joseph W. STILWELL in direct command of all Chinese troops. As a natural corollary of the plan for a unified command of all armies, Roosevelt shortly proposed a coalition government for China with Communist participation. The ideas were formally endorsed by Mao but Chiang Kai-shek refused to go along, and Stilwell soon was recalled. Subsequent efforts to bring Mao and Chiang together failed, and by the end of the war the Communists and Nationalists prepared to resume internal hostilities for control of China.

CHI-NI. The Japanese Type 98 light TANK, developed in 1938 but not placed in production until the Pacific war had begun.

CHI-NU. A Japanese medium TANK, using the Chi-He chassis but armed with a 75-mm. field gun (*see* CHI-HA). It was produced in limited numbers.

CHI-RO. The Japanese Type 89 medium TANK, designed for use with infantry and tested in 1929. It was a first-line tank during the earlier years of the Sino-Japanese War and during the campaign in the PHILIPPINES.

CHI-TO. The Japanese Type 4 medium TANK, a wartime development with a 75-mm. antiaircraft-type gun. Comparable to the American M4 Sherman in weight and gun caliber, it was produced too late for overseas service. It would have been used to oppose the projected Allied invasion of Japan.

CHITOSE. Second ship of the Japanese CHIYODA class, built as seaplane carriers but later converted to aircraft carriers. A veteran of the Battle of the PHILIPPINE SEA, she was lost in the battle for LEYTE GULF.

CHIYODA. Class of Japanese seaplane carriers built to carry, launch and recover reconnaissance seaplanes; 631 feet 6 inches long and displacing over 11,000 tons, *Chiyoda* and her sister CHITOSE could handle 24 floatplanes. In early 1941 *Chitose* was modified to handle 12 midget submarines, to be launched through stern doors. *Chiyoda* was then similarly converted. During the winter of 1942–43 both ships were again converted, this time to conventional aircraft carriers with a capacity of 30 planes. Completed during the following winter, both ships took part in the Battle of the PHILIPPINE SEA and were later lost as part of Adm. Jisaburo OZAWA's decoy force in the battle for LEYTE GULF.

CHOCOLATE DROP HILL. Hill 130 northeast of Ishimmi on OKINAWA, called Chocolate Drop because of its resemblance to that form of candy, became the objective of the U.S. 77th Infantry Division on May 11, 1945. Against deeply entrenched and determined Japanese defenders, the U.S. troops fought for nine days before this position was captured.

CHOISEUL. A densely forested island in the northern SOLOMONS, asssaulted on the night of October 27–28, 1943, by the U.S. 2d Marine Parachute Battalion in a raid intended to deceive the Japanese concerning U.S. intentions at BOUGAINVILLE. The battalion was withdrawn on November 4 after engaging in a number of punishing firefights with Japanese defenders.

CHOKAI. Japanese TAKAO-class heavy cruiser, completed in 1932. She saw wide service with the COMBINED FLEET, frequently as a flagship—she flew Vice-Adm. Gunichi MIKAWA's flag at the Battle of SAVO ISLAND—and enjoyed the reputation of being an elite ship. *Chokai* was lost in October 1944, during the battle for LEYTE GULF.

CHOLTITZ, Dietrich von (1894–1966). Born into a Prussian military family, Choltitz was schooled in the Saxon cadet corps. During the war he served as a regimental commander at the siege of SEVASTOPOL. Later he saw combat in Army Group Center. On June 18, 1944, Choltitz, now a Generalleutnant, assumed command of LXXXIV Corps on the COTENTIN PENINSULA. The American Operation COBRA went through his sector on July 25, and he was replaced on the 28th. Adolf HITLER, on August 7, appointed him commanding general and military commander of Greater Paris. As the Allies approached, Choltitz, though ordered by Hitler to burn the city, decided to defend outside of Paris, and thus the city was saved. He was captured by the Allies on August 25, 1944.

CHOU EN-LAI (1898–1976). Chinese Communist leader who was active in the Communist revolution in China in 1919–20 and joined Sun Yat-sen in the KUOMINTANG. When CHIANG KAI-SHEK ordered the arrest of Communists, Chou escaped and joined in the organization of the Chinese Red Army. Despite the civil war fought with the Nationalists throughout the 1930s, Chou continued to urge compromise in a united effort against the Japanese. As a result, when Chiang was kidnapped by a dissident Kuomintang general in 1936, Chou and the Communists were largely responsible for his release. When the united front between the Communists and Nationalist forces was effected, Chou was made military adviser to Chiang and in 1938 became vice-director of the political department of the military council of the Communist Eighth Route Army. But the rupture reopened in 1941 when Chiang refused Communist demands and attacked a Communist force.

By the end of the war Chou was second only to MAO TSE-TUNG in the Communist Party. He played a leading part in negotiations leading to temporary truce between the Kuomintang and the Communists in 1946. After the Communist victory, Chou served as Premier of the People's Republic.

CHRISTIAN X, King of Denmark (1870–1947). King Christian refused to flee to England when Denmark was occupied by the Germans in 1940 and carried out a policy of limited collaboration in order to protect the Danes from full-scale German repression. The Germans had little success in their attempt to establish the "new order" in Denmark. Martial law was declared in 1943 because of increasing opposition and actual revolt. King Christian became something of a folk hero by protecting Danish Jews. He was said to have worn the Star of David and attended synagogue, and to have asserted that "there are no Jews in Denmark, only my people."

CHRISTIE, Ralph Waldo (1893–). U.S. Navy officer, a graduate of the Naval Academy in 1915. One of the first graduates of the submarine school, Christie was a specialist in torpedoes and a leading commander of submarine forces. He served as a captain in the Eastern Australia Submarine Group in the Southwest Pacific, later becoming commander of Task Force 42 (August 1942) at Brisbane. He was appointed Commander of Submarines South Pacific at Perth and Fremantle in early 1943; he had shortly before been promoted to rear admiral. He served in this post until December 1944, when at Adm. Thomas KINKAID's request, but for no stated reason, he was relieved. He then took command of the Bremerton (Wash.) navy yard.

CHRISTROSE. Early German code name for a counteroffensive in the ARDENNES region of Belgium and Luxembourg in December 1944, later changed to Watch on the Rhine (Wacht am Rhein). *See also* BULGE, BATTLE OF THE

General Chuikov (second from left) in his command bunker at Stalingrad

CHUIKOV, Vassili (1900–). Prior to the Soviet-German war, Chuikov, as a Soviet general, took part in both the occupation of eastern Poland and the Soviet-Finnish War. In 1941 he served as an adviser to Chiang Kai-shek, but returned from Chungking in May 1942 to take command of the Sixty-second Army. After a series of setbacks at the hands of Gen. Friedrich Paulus's Sixth Army, the Sixty-second Army was given responsibility for the defense of Stalingrad. Though in the first days of the battle the German Army was able to reach the Volga, Chuikov controlled the critical sectors of the city. From September to November 1942 the Sixty-second Army fought house by house for the city. By the end of the siege the German force was exhausted, and the way was clear for the great Soviet counteroffensive of November 19. Following the capitulation of the Sixth Army, Chuikov's command won a number of victories. April 1945 found Chuikov and his Eighth Guards Army fighting in Berlin.

During Nikita Khrushchev's ascendancy, Chuikov's star rose to new heights. In 1960–65 he served as chief of Soviet forces in Germany. During the same year he managed to write two studies of the war, glorifying his and Khrushchev's role in the defeat of the Nazi invader. Subsequently, Chuikov was attacked by Soviet historians for falsifying the history of the Second World War. Later accounts of the Stalingrad and Berlin campaigns downplayed Chuikov's role and emphasized that of Marshal Zhukov. But however harsh the verdict of Soviet historians, Marshal Chuikov's defense of Stalingrad remains one of the Red Army's great achievements.

CHUNGKING. Located in Szechwan province, on the north bank of the Yangtze River, Chungking was, beginning in 1938, the wartime capital of the Chinese Nationalist government, under the leadership of Chiang Kai-shek.

CHURCHILL, Clementine (1885–1977). Wife of Sir Winston Churchill. The daughter of Sir Henry and Lady Blanche Hozier, she was, her son Randolph wrote, "a striking beauty and one of the most admired girls of her generation." She and the future Prime Minister were married in 1908 and, Churchill observed many years later, "lived happily ever after." During the war she often accompanied her husband to various conferences and meetings. She was an effective ambassador and took the lead in such projects as the British Aid to Russia fund.

CHURCHILL, Randolph (1911–1968). The only son of Sir Winston Churchill, Randolph Churchill achieved success as a popular journalist in the 1930s and was Conservative Member of Parliament for Preston, 1940–45. During World War II he served in the Middle East and Yugoslavia as an intelligence officer. At the time of his death he had completed two volumes of what was to be the definitive biography of his father. The work was continued by Martin Gilbert.

CHURCHILL, Sir Winston (Leonard) Spencer (1874–1965). "No statesman save Alfred has done England such service as Churchill," wrote the British historian Sir Arthur Bryant. This is a remarkable tribute, encompassing as it does the whole sweep of English history, but there is little disagreement that in the summer of 1940 the island was in the gravest danger that had threatened her since 1066—when in fact she succumbed—and that, as Bryant said, Churchill's "courage made her the hope of the world."

Together with this courage were imaginative brilliance, resourcefulness and a mastery of phrase and image that contributed to Churchill's subsequent winning of the Nobel Prize for Literature. As numerous observers (including many who worked with him) have pointed out, there was also impatience and even impetuosity, which were to a considerable extent the natural corollaries of his virtues.

Like other dominant historical figures—the Lincolns, the Napoleons—Churchill inevitably acquired a cluster of myths as well as a verifiable history. And, like any political figure, he had his detractors. But his associates and subordinates, although often challenging his plans and disagreeing with his decisions, appear generally to have shared the view of Churchill's chief wartime military adviser, Field Marshal Alan BROOKE. Brooke, himself a man of strong opinions, speaks of the insignificance of the "defects that arose out of [Churchill's] very greatness," and in the diary he kept during the war he wrote of the Prime Minister: "He is quite the most wonderful man I have ever met . . . occasionally such human beings make their appearance on this earth—human beings who stand out head and shoulders above all the others."

Britain's wartime leader was born at Blenheim Palace, the seat of the Dukes of Marlborough, on November 30, 1874. His father was the eccentric Lord Randolph Churchill, who had a dazzling but brief career in British politics, and his mother was the former Jennie Jerome, daughter of the colorful Leonard Jerome of New York. It was this aspect of his parentage that gave rise to the later observation that "Churchill is half American and all English." The story of Churchill's youth and beginnings in politics is told in many of his own writings—notably *My Early Life*—and in various biographical works, including the multivolume biography begun by his son Randolph and carried on by the historian Martin Gilbert. It has also been dramatized in a film.

Churchill's experience in the First World War is of profound importance in understanding some of his later attitudes and, equally, in understanding attitudes toward him. As First Lord of the Admiralty,

Prime Minister Churchill visits an antiaircraft unit in London, October 1941

Churchill—eager, imaginative, impetuous—looked for ways to break the deadlock gripping the great armies in France. Horrified at the bloodiness of the struggle, in 1915 he supported the use of British sea power in an expedition to the Dardanelles that would "raise the Balkans in the rear of Germany" and open a supply and communications route to Russia through the Black Sea. The operation, poorly conducted, ended disastrously, and as the man identified with it, Churchill was banished from the cabinet. He then saw service on the Western Front as a lieutenant colonel, commanding the 6th Battalion of the Royal Scots Fusiliers. In July 1917 Churchill returned to the cabinet, this time under Lloyd George, as Minister of Munitions.

During the first postwar decade Churchill was a prominent member of different cabinets, but his strenuous opposition to the government's willingness to discuss concessions with Mohandas K. GANDHI in India led to his resignation from the Conservative Party's ruling group and to his subsequent exclusion from office in the 1930s. Thus he was not in a position of political power but "in the wilderness" during the rise of Adolf HITLER's Third Reich, though he was an influential political figure and a widely read writer. Throughout the decade he called for the building up of British strength and the curbing of German power. At the time of the MUNICH AGREEMENT in 1938 he denounced the pact with the dictators reached by the APPEASEMENT-minded Prime Minister, Neville CHAMBERLAIN, and despite his unwavering hostility to Communism, urged the British Government to work toward an understanding with the Soviet Union about opposing Hitler in Eastern Europe.

At six o'clock on the evening of September 3, 1939, the day Britain declared war on Germany, the Admiralty radioed the fleet: "Winston is back." He was First Lord again, the post he had held a quarter of a century earlier when war had come. In April 1940 the Allies were outwitted and outmaneuvered by the Germans in NORWAY, but even though the Royal Navy did not appear to advantage, the hostility of the House of Commons and the public was directed at Chamberlain rather than Churchill, and just as the German Army struck in the West on May 10, the Prime Minister resigned. Churchill's hour had come. No longer would he be forced to operate from a subordinate position. As he later wrote with remarkable self-assurance: "I was conscious of a profound sense of relief. At last I had authority to give direction over the whole scene."

On May 13 the new Prime Minister told the House: "I have nothing to offer but blood, toil, tears and sweat." It was the first of a series of memorable utterances which, as the crisis intensified, made him the eloquent symbol not only of British defiance of Hitler but of freedom itself. At the time of the capitulation of France he spoke the famous words: "Let us therefore brace ourselves to our duties, and so bear ourselves that, if the British Empire and its Commonwealth last for a thousand years, men will still say, 'This was their finest hour.'" His portly, pugnacious figure, his cigar, his V sign, all combined to make him seem the embodiment of the British people, John Bull himself.

Churchill's basic war policy was simple and direct: nothing was to distract Britain from the task of defeating Hitler; any ally, even Communist, was welcome in this effort; the friendship and assistance of the United States was of paramount importance. Churchill's cultivation of the last-named, his close relationship with President ROOSEVELT, must rank among the highest of his services to his country. Another deeply rooted belief was that Britain must avoid the static bloodletting that had characterized the Western Front in World War I.

Through correspondence (in which he signed himself "Former Naval Person") and intermediaries Churchill built up a friendship with the President. The first yields of this was the DESTROYERS-BASES DEAL in 1940, and in 1941 came LEND-LEASE. In August 1941 President and Prime Minister met off Newfoundland in a conference that became famous as the ATLANTIC CHARTER meeting. The Japanese attack on PEARL HARBOR in December 1941, with its consequent involvement of the United States in the war, immediately meant to Churchill that, whatever difficulties might lie ahead, the war was won and Britain was saved. Led by Churchill and Roosevelt, the United States and Britain created what was, for all its stresses, the closest alliance in modern history. Military operations were planned and carried out by the COMBINED CHIEFS OF STAFF, unified commands established in theaters of operations and joint organizations set up for the allocation of resources.

A source of controversy during the war, and a matter of debate since, was Churchill's true view of the plan to win the war in Europe by a cross-Channel INVASION and subsequent advance into Germany. Many observers, particularly Americans, felt that he wanted only a peripheral strategy—that the Battle of the Somme was in his bones and that he would never favor major land operations, even mobile operations. Certainly he favored Mediterranean operations, but whatever his feelings, once the die was cast for Operation OVERLORD he gave it firm support; in fact, he became creatively involved in the details of it, encouraging the development of technical innovations (such as MULBERRY harbors) that played an important part in the success of the landings.

He also constantly looked to postwar Europe, when there would be no Central European power facing the Soviet Union, and sought to restore and build up France in order to have some counterweight to Russian might on the Continent. This was of particular concern because there was at the time little reason to suppose that the United States would maintain forces in Europe for any considerable time after the end of the war.

In May 1945, after victory over Germany, Churchill's wartime coalition government was broken up. An election was held in July and, to the surprise of much of the world, the Labour Party dealt a sweeping defeat to the Conservatives and their illustrious leader. At the time, Churchill was representing Britain at the POTSDAM CONFERENCE, though he had flown home for the election; his successor, Clement ATTLEE, returned to Germany. That day Mrs. Churchill said to her husband, "It may well be a blessing in disguise." "At the moment," he replied, "it seems quite effectively disguised."

Churchill returned to office in 1951 and retired in 1955. In his long career he wrote some 20 books, not including collections of speeches and papers. Especially notable were his biography of his father; *The World Crisis*, his account of the First World War; his study of his ancestor, the first Duke of Marlborough; and his *Second World War.*

At Churchill's death on January 24, 1965, Queen Elizabeth sent this message to Lady Churchill: "The whole world is the poorer by the loss of his many-sided genius, while the survival of this country and the sister nations of the Commonwealth, in the face of the greatest danger that has ever threatened them, will be a perpetual memorial to his leadership, his vision, and his indomitable courage."

Churchill will always be known in history as the great war leader, the man who defied Hitler during Britain's darkest hour. But he was a man of many moods—mischievous as well as brave, boyish as well as statesmanlike. Dean ACHESON wrote of him: "What can one say of a man of whom everything has been said, of whom every hyperbole is an understatement?" It is perhaps instructive to remember that in the 1930s, when he was in his sixties, he was thought by many students of politics to be a failure, a dilettante, washed up. **T. P.**

CHURCHILL TANK. *See* TANK.

CHU TEH (1886–1976). Strategist of the Chinese People's Liberation Army. After service with the Imperial Chinese Army and several warlords, Chu Teh joined the Chinese Communist Party in the 1920s. Along with MAO TSE-TUNG, he developed a military strategy to supplement the party's political struggle in the rural areas. Chu's forces did not contest Japanese control; rather, they sought to broaden Communist influence behind Japanese lines, with the aim of establishing control over the rural population of north China.

CIANO, Galeazzo (1903–1944). Count Ciano took part in the Fascist march on Rome in 1922 and subsequently held a number of posts in the Italian diplomatic corps and wrote for various Fascist newspapers. In 1930 he married Edda Mussolini, the daughter of the dictator, and his career was guaranteed. He was successively chief of the press bureau (1933), Under Secretary of State for press and propaganda (1934) and member of the Fascist Grand Council. He was regarded by many as Mussolini's likely successor.

After taking time off to command a bomber squadron in the war with Ethiopia, he became Minister of Foreign Affairs in 1936. As Foreign Minister, Count Ciano exhibited a capricious instability. He advocated an alliance with Germany during 1936–39, although he had strong reservations about Germany's influence in Spain during that country's civil war. After the signing of the Rome-Berlin AXIS agreement, Ciano sought and received assurance that the Germans would not begin hostilities without first consulting Italy. This assurance was violated when the Germans attacked Poland in September 1939. Disturbed and angered, Ciano urged a policy of discreet disentanglement from Germany, but the sudden collapse of France made this policy impossible and Italy entered the war as an ally of the Reich.

After the failure of the German Army in Russia and the entry of the United States in the war, Ciano urged a separate peace for Italy. Mussolini became suspicious of him and had him demoted to ambassador to the Vatican in February 1943. Ciano and his fellow conspirators had sufficient power, however, to depose Mussolini, in a dramatic meeting of the Grand Council on July 24–25, 1943.

Mussolini shortly afterward was rescued by the Germans and established a Fascist republic in northern Italy. The new government in Rome turned against Ciano and brought charges of dishonesty and corruption against him. Ciano had nowhere to go. He fled to the north, where he was seized by Mussolini sympathizers, acting under some German pressure, and was tried and shot on January 11, 1944.

CICERO. German code name for Elias Basna, an Albanian who sold British secrets to members of the German embassy in Ankara, Turkey. Cicero had access to these plans, which he photographed, as the valet of the British ambassador, Sir Hughe KNATCHBULL-HUGESSEN. After the war it was found that the money the Germans had paid was counterfeit.

CIGARETTE CAMPS. These were established in France in 1944 as assembly areas for U.S. supplies, equipment and troops arriving on the Continent for forward areas. The camps were named after American cigarette brands, such as Lucky Strike, Philip Morris, Twenty Grand and Old Gold. At the end of the European war they were used to house and process troops and equipment for redeployment to the Pacific or transfer home.

CILIAX, Otto (1891–1964). German Navy officer who, in February 1942, as a vice-admiral, was flag officer commanding the ships SCHARNHORST, GNEISENAU and PRINZ EUGEN at Brest. On February 11–13 he led this force in its "Channel dash" past British defenders to home waters, a feat that caused the *Times* (London) to remark that "nothing more mortifying to the pride of British seapower has happened in home waters since the seventeenth century." However, the transfer of these heavy ships to the North Sea removed an immediate threat to Allied shipping in the Atlantic. In 1943 Ciliax was promoted to full admiral and placed in command of German naval forces based in Norway. An officer with a reputation as a martinet, Admiral Ciliax was called by the men under him the Black Czar.

CIRCUS OPERATIONS. The defeat of the LUFTWAFFE in the Battle of BRITAIN and the withdrawal of German aircraft to the Russian and Mediterranean fronts provided opportunities for RAF fighter and bomber aircraft to put pressure on the Luftwaffe in Western Europe. Daylight offensive raids using fighter-escorted bombers to entice German fighters to battle were known as circus operations.

CITADEL (Zitadelle). German code word for the attack on the KURSK salient (USSR) in July 1943. Originally planned for the spring, Citadel was put off until July by Hitler to enable the German armored forces to be supplied with new tanks.

CIVIL AIR PATROL. Established on December 1, 1941, this U.S. organization was made up of civilian aviators, mechanics, radio operators and other volunteers whose skills and equipment might contribute to the national defense. Both men and women were eligible for membership. The new organization was responsible to the OFFICE OF CIVILIAN DEFENSE, headed by Fiorello H. LAGUARDIA, World War I airman and mayor of New York, but provision was made for close coordination with the War and Navy Departments. The first national commander of the Civil Air Patrol was Maj. Gen. John F. Curry, who served until his transfer in March 1942. His successor was Earle L. Johnson, director of aeronautics for the state of Ohio, who took a commission as captain in the U.S. Army Air Forces and rose to the grade of colonel.

After Pearl Harbor the Army found a variety of uses for the Civil Air Patrol. These included courier flights, the delivery of medicines and supplies, searching for downed planes and helping to train ground observers, searchlight crews and other elements of the nation's air defenses. The patrol, however, did its most important work in searching for marauding German submarines. In April 1943 the Office of Civilian Defense relinquished control over the Civil Air Patrol, which became an auxiliary of the Army Air Forces. U-boat captains, unaware that Civil Air Patrol planes carried no weapons, dived when caught on the surface. On one occasion off the New Jersey coast, a submarine dived into the muddy bottom and became stuck fast. The unarmed Civil Air Patrol plane circled overhead, radioing for help, but none came; the submarine worked itself free and escaped. This incident, and similar escapes, persuaded the War Department to allow the civilian airmen to carry depth charges or light bombs.

The coastal patrol flourished for about 18 months, being completely phased out by the end of 1943. Because naval aircraft were becoming available, the light planes were no longer needed. During the antisubmarine operations the Civil Air Patrol had flown almost a quarter-million hours and had received credit for spotting 173 submarines and sinking or damaging two. In addition, the organization had reported 91 friendly vessels in distress and contributed to the rescue of 363 persons.

CIVIL DEFENSE. Civil defense in World War II consisted of all nonmilitary actions which combatant nations took to reduce the loss of life and property from enemy attack. Civil defense work involved the construction or designation of bomb shelters, the enforcing of blackouts or dimouts, and the supplying of gas masks to civilians, as was done in Britain. Although the normal agencies of local government handled civil defense operations, they were assisted by volunteers. Civilians in Britain and the United States served voluntarily in the Royal Observer Corps and the Ground Observer Corps, respectively, reporting aircraft movements. American civilians also manned the CIVIL AIR PATROL (established December 1, 1941), which hunted enemy submarines, towed practice targets, helped in search and rescue missions and trained pilots for the air forces.

CLAPPER, Raymond (1892–1944). Clapper was probably the most widely read correspondent and columnist in the United States during the war years. He served in the Washington bureau of United Press (as it then was) and then with the Scripps-Howard syndicate as a columnist. In February 1944, while on an assignment in the Pacific, he died in an airplane crash.

CLARION. Attacks by Allied air forces in February 1945 designed to disrupt transportation systems throughout Germany.

CLARK, Joseph James (1893–1971). "Jocko" Clark, from Oklahoma and part Cherokee Indian, graduated from the U.S. Naval Academy in 1918. In Operation Torch, the invasion of NORTHWEST AFRICA (1942), he commanded the carrier SUWANNEE. Given command of the new carrier YORKTOWN, Captain Clark went to the Pacific, where his aircraft destroyed three-quarters of the Japanese installations on MARCUS ISLAND on August 31, 1943. Known for his unorthodox dress and colorful language, Clark became a rear admiral on January 31, 1944. He soon distinguished himself as a carrier task force commander in the Pacific, and his determined strikes against the "Jimas" in June 1944 convinced his aviators to dub him president of the "Jocko Jima Development Corporation." The striking power of Admiral Clark's carriers proved a major factor in the PHILIPPINE SEA, the capture of OKINAWA and attacks on the Japanese home islands. Following the war Clark served as Assistant Chief of Naval Operations for air.

CLARK, Mark Wayne (1896–). Tall, gangling and energetic, combining sound ability with personal charm, Mark Clark (called Wayne by his friends) fought in three major wars but is best remembered as commander of the U.S. FIFTH ARMY in ITALY in 1943–44.

Clark graduated from West Point in 1917, saw action and was wounded in World War I, and began World War II as a staff officer with Gen. Lesley MCNAIR and the Army Ground Forces. In rapid succession he was chief of staff of AGF (May 1942), commander of II Corps (June 1942), commander of American ground forces in Europe (July 1942) and deputy commander in chief under General EISENHOWER for the invasion of French NORTHWEST AFRICA. In the last capacity he went to Algiers to confer secretly with the French prior to the Operation Torch landings. His account of that cloak-and-dagger mission, complete with the comic relief of lost trousers and refuge in an empty wine cellar, made one of the war's most captivating adventure stories. After the Torch invasion was under way, Clark handled the delicate negotiations leading up the the securing of French cooperation. He afterward defended the DARLAN deal as proper under the complex and difficult circumstances.

Clark was eager to have a command of his own, and in January 1943 he was given the Fifth Army. It was then a training organization, but in July it was assigned to the invasion of Italy. Clark tackled the planning for Italy with enthusiasm. He was already known in Army circles as hardworking and aggressive—"not afraid to take rather desperate chances," in the view of one observer. Eisenhower called him the "best organizer, planner and trainer of troops that I have met," while others pointed out that people "couldn't help but like him." Clark had to draw on all these talents, as well as his sense of humor and a deft touch for questions of morale and public relations, during the following months. The Italian campaign, which he saw through to its conclusion in May 1945, was difficult. The Axis defended favorable terrain, the Allied forces were heterogeneous, political problems were ticklish and the theater did not receive top priority in men or supplies. But having begun the campaign, Clark elected to stay with it. In January 1944 he was named commander of the planned invasion of southern France (Operation Anvil), but at his request he was relieved of the Anvil command at the end of February.

Clark suffered through a commander's "helpless feeling" during the SALERNO landings of September 1943, and when the critical nature of the landings became evident he moved his headquarters ashore. By September 15 he could assure his men that the "beachhead is secure . . . we are here to stay."

Operation Shingle, an amphibious landing at ANZIO to help the advance, became an issue once the hard drive up the Italian peninsula began. Clark was in favor, even enthusiastic, "provided that necessary means are made available." In retrospect he thought it would have been better to keep his forces together, but he exerted every effort to make the Anzio operation a success. The concurrent attacks at CASSINO were pushed relentlessly; they included crossing the RAPIDO RIVER with the U.S. 36th Division. The crossing failed, and two years later a group of former officers of the division asked the Senate Military Affairs Committee not to approve Clark's promotion to the permanent rank of major general because of his "blunder" at the Rapido. The War Department concluded that Clark had exercised "sound judgment" and his promotion was confirmed.

Another controversy arose in February 1944, as the Fifth Army struggled to conquer Cassino and move on to Rome. General FREYBERG, leading troops against the Cassino defenses, requested that the Monte Cassino abbey be destroyed by bombing. Clark opposed the bombing for military, religious and sentimental reasons. He made his position clear, but he bowed to the wishes of his superior, General ALEXANDER, and Freyberg because of the joint nature of the effort. The destruction of the abbey precipitated a storm of protest, and, as Clark had feared, did not end the struggle for Cassino. Not until June 4, 1944, did the Fifth Army enter ROME.

After Rome was in Allied hands, strength in Italy was reduced so that Anvil could be launched. In private Clark opposed Anvil, later calling it "one of the outstanding political mistakes of the war." He argued for a continued strong drive through Italy, but this was not the decision and General MARSHALL later noted that Clark said nothing publicly at the time: "He was a very good soldier and very loyal."

Clark was named commander of the 15th Army Group in November 1944, replacing Alexander, who became Supreme Commander in the Mediterranean. When he accepted the unconditional surrender of the Axis in Italy in May 1945, Clark felt "agonized relief." The 20-month campaign had been arduous, but its basic purpose—to prevent the Axis from employing their full strength in France and Russia—had been achieved.

In July 1945, Clark, a full general since March, went to Austria to head the U.S. occupation forces There his charm, wit and flair for public relations eased tensions as he applied himself to helping the Austrians without antagonizing the Russians, but he gradually became disillusioned over the prospects for a lasting peace.

In the spring of 1947 the "American Eagle," as Winston Churchill dubbed him, returned to the United States to take over command of the Sixth Army. He became commander of the United Nations forces in Korea in May 1952, and in July 1953 he signed the truce ending the Korean conflict. Later he acknowledged a feeling of frustration that it might be "unfinished business."

Clark retired from military service in October 1953, marking the end of a career that had brought him two heterogeneous commands (17 countries in Korea and representatives of 26 nationalities in Italy) and a series of controversial events. He freely expressed his views on the latter in two books, *Calculated Risk* (1950) and *From the Danube to the Yalu* (1954). Following his retirement, he became president of The Citadel (1954–66), a military college in Charleston, S.C. **M.H.B.**

CLARKE, Bruce Cooper (1901–). A 1925 graduate of West Point, Clarke served with the Engineers until 1942. After a period as chief of staff of the U.S. 4th Armored Division, in November 1943 Colonel Clarke took over Combat Command A. In November 1944 he became commander of Combat Command B, 7th Armored Division, and was soon promoted to brigadier general. During the BULGE the 7th Armored was shifted to the south. Clarke took charge at SAINT-VITH and coordinated a delaying action which helped to upset the German advance and allowed an American defense to be established behind him.

CLARK FIELD. At this base north of Manila, Japanese bombers destroyed two squadrons of B-17s on the afternoon of December 8, 1941. The American planes were preparing to attack Japanese installations on Formosa as soon as weather over the island improved enough to permit adequate reconnaissance. Maj. Gen. Lewis H. BRERETON, who commanded Far East Air Forces, was under the impression that General MACARTHUR had approved massing the bombers at Clark Field prior to attacking Formosa, but MacArthur later insisted that he knew nothing of the Brereton proposal and was under the impression that the B-17s had been flown to Del Monte airfield on Mindanao Island, well beyond the range of Japanese bombers. Brereton, however, had kept the two squadrons at Clark because the primitive conditions at Del Monte, and the additional distance involved, would prevent the Flying Fortresses from going promptly into action in the event of war. Unfortunately, lack of an adequate air raid warning net enabled the enemy to take advantage of this confusion and launch the surprise attack. Clark Field was taken almost intact from the U.S. forces and served the Japanese as their largest base outside the homeland. It was recaptured by General MacArthur's forces in January 1945.

CLAUDE. Allied code name for the Mitsubishi A5M Japanese Navy fighter (*see* A5M).

CLAY, Lucius Du Bignon (1897–1978). A 1918 graduate of the U.S. Military Academy, Clay served in a variety of capacities with the Army Engineers until the outbreak of the war. In 1942 he was promoted to brigadier general and assigned to Washington as Deputy Chief of

Staff for requirements and resources. From July 1942 to October 1944 he was Assistant Chief of Staff for matériel. In 1944 he was sent to France to command the Normandy base section. He was then assigned to the Office of War Mobilization and Reconversion. In 1945, promoted to lieutenant general, he became, under Gen. Dwight D. EISENHOWER, deputy military governor of the U.S. Zone of Germany, responsible for establishing military government in the zone and for representing the United States in governing Germany as a whole. He subsequently became one of the outstanding figures in the development of German self-government.

CLEMSON, U.S.S. Destroyer and class (1,308 tons full load; antiaircraft: four 4-inch/50, one 3-inch/23; twelve 21-inch torpedo tubes; 35 knots). Destroyers Nos. 186–347, the second of two classes of FLUSH-DECKERS laid down during World War I, were nicknamed "long-leggers," since their 375-ton oil capacity gave them better steaming endurance than the similar WICKES class. Built during a period when machinery and skilled workmen were scarce, the Clemsons were frequently overweight and sometimes slightly inferior in performance to the Wickes class. Most of the surviving Clemsons were altered to at least some extent during World War II.

CLERF. Town in Luxembourg on the Clerf River approximately four miles from the German frontier. There stragglers from the U.S. 28th Infantry Division, rudely handled in early fighting in the Battle of the BULGE, rallied around a regimental headquarters and held up the German advance for more than a day, helping to enable American reserves to form for defense of the critical crossroads town of Bastogne.

CLEVELAND. British name for the U.S. Navy SBC scout bomber (*see* SBC).

CLEVELAND, U.S.S. Light cruiser and class, of 14,400 tons, with twelve 6-inch guns and a speed of 31.6 knots. It was the most numerous cruiser class projected by any navy; a total of 50 ships were laid down or ordered. Twenty-seven were completed to the original design. Nine more were finished as INDEPENDENCE-class light aircraft carriers. One ship was canceled at the end of the war; two more, *Fargo* and *Huntington,* were completed to a modified single-stack design. Eleven more ships would have been completed as Fargos, but were canceled in 1945; some of these had not yet been laid down.

The Cleveland class was a development of the BROOKLYN and ST. LOUIS classes, having the same length and 55 inches more beam, with improved compartmentation for better underwater protection. They were designed with more effective antiaircraft defense in mind; superstructures were grouped amidships, and four 6-inch triple turrets (as against five in the Brooklyns and St. Louises) were mounted, to make room for a secondary battery of six 5-INCH 38-CALIBER twin mounts, plus an automatic-weapon battery (which was steadily increased through the Pacific war). After the first nine Clevelands were built, the remainder were completed with a new bridge structure designed for all-around command and control of the ship and her battery.

The first two Clevelands were commissioned in June 1942; in August of that year, *Cleveland* conducted the final pre-combat tests of the new PROXIMITY FUZE for 5-inch antiaircraft ammunition in Chesapeake Bay. Ten ships of this class were in commission by the end of 1943, 20 by the end of 1944. They formed a part of the FAST CARRIER TASK FORCE in the Pacific, where their speed and antiaircraft armament made them useful partners for the fleet carriers. Clevelands also took part in some of the surface actions of the latter stages of the SOLOMON ISLANDS campaign and in the amphibious operations of 1943–45.

CLIPPER. Code name of the Allied operation to reduce the GEILENKIRCHEN salient in the Roer River area, November 1944.

CLOSTERMANN, Pierre (1922–). The only Frenchman to command a Royal Air Force squadron, Clostermann downed 33 German aircraft. He scored 24 of these victories between December 1944 and March 1945 while flying a Hawker TEMPEST. He achieved the rank of wing commander.

COASTAL COMMAND. When the Royal Air Force established functional commands in 1936, Coastal Command was formed. At the outbreak of war in 1939 the command was a modest force of 19 flying boat and land-based squadrons. Its bombs were 100-pound or 250-pound antisubmarine and soon proved to be unsuitable. A special 250-pound depth charge had to be developed quickly. The three operational roles of the command were anti-U-boat activity, antishipping strikes and reconnaissance. The two main areas of operation were the North Sea and the ATLANTIC. Protection of shipping in coastal convoys was the main North Sea task, along with assistance to the ROYAL NAVY in its blockade of German ports. In the Atlantic the main tasks were protection of shipping and providing air cover for convoys.

When the Germans overran France, Norway and the Low Countries, the tasks of Coastal Command and the Royal Navy were made immeasurably more difficult. However, they succeeded in driving the U-boats into the Atlantic Ocean. A squadron of SUNDERLAND flying boats was operating from Iceland as early as September 1940. Closing the mid-Atlantic air-cover gap became a paramount necessity in the anti-U-boat warfare. By the middle of 1943 very-long-range B-24 Liberators from Iceland and the United States along with Canadian aircraft had provided air cover for the North Atlantic route and as far south as Lagos on the West African coast. Cooperation with surface escort groups improved, especially under Sir John SLESSOR as Air Officer Commanding in Chief. The use of the LEIGH LIGHT and centimetric ASV RADAR helped to track and destroy the U-boats. Coastal Command also assisted in providing air cover for the Russian convoys in 1942. The command's strike wings operated BEAUFIGHTER and MOSQUITO aircraft against shipping off the coasts of occupied Europe. In its reconnaissance role Coastal Command made an important contribution to the early development of photographic reconnaissance with specially equipped SPITFIRES having a range of 1,450 miles.

During the war Coastal Command aircraft sank 184 U-boats and destroyed more than 478,000 tons of shipping. Four Victoria Crosses, three posthumously, were awarded to air crews of Coastal Command for operations in the Mediterranean and the South Atlantic. Among its less spectacular tasks Coastal Command included some 30 meteorological sorties daily toward the end of the war in the European theater alone. From April 1941 Coastal Command came under the operational control of the Admiralty, but the method of operating and the independence of the command were always safeguarded through its commander.

COASTAL PICKET PATROL. An Atlantic antisubmarine effort organized by the U.S. Coast Guard in May 1942. It was made up of civilian yachts and motorboats, mostly with civilian crews, armed with small guns and depth charges. Although there were at one point 550 of these boats (they were nicknamed the "Hooligan Navy"), they lacked the speed and the armament to make kills. After the winter of 1942–43 they were superseded by Coast Guard vessels.

COASTWATCHERS. Australians and New Zealanders who operated, singly or in small groups, on islands of the SOLOMON and BISMARCK groups with the help of local natives. After the Japanese advanced into the South Pacific, these prewar government administrators and island planters concealed themselves in accordance with a plan devised by the Australian Navy. During the long campaigns to recapture the Solomons and neutralize RABAUL, coastwatchers using radio transmitters provided Allied commands with a steady flow of information on threatening movements of Japanese ships and planes. Air raids heading southeast along the Solomons from Rabaul were spotted by coastwatchers, who reported them in time to allow GUADALCANAL-based fighters to meet the attackers. Their role in the South Pacific war was carried out without fanfare or applause, and it required a special kind of solitary courage.

COBRA. Code name for the Allied Normandy breakout. After a carpet of bombs was dropped ahead of the U.S. VII Corps, Cobra called for infantry divisions to break through the enemy lines and hold the shoulders of the penetration; then armored and motorized infantry units would pour through the gap. After several delays Cobra was launched on July 25, 1944. Gen. Omar N. BRADLEY later called Cobra "the most decisive battle of our war in western Europe."

COCHRAN, Jacqueline (1910?–). Already a famous racing pilot when war broke out in 1939, Jacqueline Cochran organized a group of American women to serve in Britain's Air Transport Auxiliary, performing such duties as ferrying aircraft from factory to operational unit. She had suggested a similar organization to assist the U.S. Army Air Corps, and after the United States entered the conflict she took charge of the WOMEN'S AIR FORCE SERVICE PILOTS (WASP), who did similar noncombat jobs within the United States. Her association with WASP continued until December 1944, when the organization disbanded.

COCHRAN, Philip C. (1910–). During the Allied offensive in BURMA, launched in March 1944, Cochran, a U.S. officer, commanded the 5318th Air Unit, which supported British Brig. Orde WINGATE's Special Force. Cochran's "Air Commando" group had 25 C-47s and C-46s, plus 225 gliders to carry troops, a hundred light planes and 6 helicopters for liaison work, and 30 P-51 fighter-bombers along with a dozen B-25Hs. The aerial supply effort proved beyond the capacity of Cochran's few transports, and Brig. Gen. William Old's troop carrier command relieved the air commandos of all but glider deliveries.

Cochran had commanded a fighter squadron in the North African campaign, and by the end of the war he had attained the rank of brigadier general. He served as inspiration for Col. Flip Corkin, a character in Milton Caniff's comic strip *Terry and the Pirates*.

COCHRANE, Sir Ralph (1895–). RAF officer who first served in the Royal Navy. As Air Officer Commanding No. 5 Group he was responsible for the development of night precision bombing. The DAM BUSTERS raid, the sinking of the battleship TIRPITZ and attacks on V-WEAPON sites were carried out under his direction. An air chief marshal, he retired in 1952, his last appointment being Vice-Chief of Air Staff.

COCKADE. Code name for one of the opening moves in a worldwide Allied deception plan known as JAEL, Cockade was designed to convince the Germans that the Allies would invade the Continent in 1943. There were three subplans: Starkey—to simulate a British invasion of the Pas de Calais with sufficient realism to draw the LUFTWAFFE into a costly engagement; Tindall—to indicate an Anglo-Russian invasion of northern Norway; and Wadham—to suggest an American invasion of Brittany. To provide realism, the FRENCH RESISTANCE had to be convinced of imminent invasion and prompted to step up guerrilla attacks, a dangerous procedure since the Resistance might surface and the Germans wreak wholesale vengeance. Because the Germans failed to make any major response to Cockade, the deception had to be termed a failure. Although the French Resistance displayed considerable discipline in failing to surface, the increased activity prompted the Germans to launch a concentrated effort to uncover Resistance leaders, resulting in a temporary paralysis of the movement.

COCKCROFT, Sir John (1897–1967). A pioneer in nuclear research in Britain, Cockcroft was a prominent figure in the installation of Britain's first RADAR chain. During the war he served as chief superintendent, Air Defence Research and Development Establishment (1941–44). In 1944 he went to Canada to take charge of atomic matters for the National Research Council. In 1951 he was awarded the Nobel Prize for Physics.

COCKEREL. Code name, used in Allied voice radio, for IFF (*see* IFF).

COLDITZ. A medieval fortress in central Germany used as an "escape-proof" prison for Allied fliers who had attempted to escape from other camps. It was floodlighted, patrolled by dogs, enclosed by barbed wire and surrounded by walls and moats. It held about 600 prisoners of various nationalities and ranks, some of whom managed to escape.

COLLINS, Joseph Lawton (1896–). Known as "Lightning Joe" from the code name of a division he commanded on GUADALCANAL, Collins subsequently led the U.S. VII Corps ashore at UTAH BEACH on D-Day and through the remainder of the campaign in Europe. The British commander, Field Marshal Sir B. L. MONTGOMERY, deemed him one of the most aggressive American corps commanders and specifically asked for him for a counterattack role during the Battle of the BULGE, and Gen. Omar N. BRADLEY called him "one of the most outstanding field commanders in Europe."

Born in New Orleans, Collins graduated from West Point in 1917. Following the attack on Pearl Harbor, he was sent to Hawaii to work on the defenses of the islands, and in May 1942 became commanding general of the 25th Infantry Division on Guadalcanal. After further fighting on NEW GEORGIA, Collins was sent to Europe, where in February 1944 he assumed command of VII Corps. Collins's corps led the American breakout from the Normandy beachhead, helped close the ARGENTAN-FALAISE GAP and captured AACHEN, the first major German city to fall to the Allies. After stopping the Germans in the tip of the Bulge, Collins and VII Corps moved back to the vicinity of Aachen, attacked to the Rhine, captured Cologne and helped exploit the REMAGEN bridgehead. After helping seal the RUHR pocket, the corps continued eastward to the Elbe River. On April 16, 1945, Collins was promoted to lieutenant general.

When Japan surrendered, Collins and his staff were in California preparing to go to the Pacific. Following the war, he served a term as U.S. Army Chief of Staff.

COLMAR POCKET. A holdout position of the German Nineteenth Army on the west bank of the Rhine River around the Alsatian city of Colmar. Stopping a drive by an undermanned French First Army through the Belfort Gap in November 1944, the Germans held the pocket in what amounted to a stalemate for more than two months, in the process posing a threat to Allied troops to the north and south. In a counteroffensive begun in the last hours of 1944 (Operation Nordwind), forces from the pocket drove northward to threaten the city of Strasbourg but were stopped short of the objective. In the face of a renewed French drive that began in mid-January 1945 and included help from the U.S. XXI Corps, the last German resistance in the pocket ended on February 9.

COLOGNE—THE THOUSAND BOMBER RAID. The British Air Staff had always believed that the true function of the heavy bomber was to concentrate strategic attacks against the sources of enemy strength—in his industrial areas. In 1939–41 it became clear that bomber losses in daylight raids would be insupportable in the face of antiaircraft and enemy fighters. Night bombing in these years proved to be inaccurate owing to navigational errors, weather, enemy defenses and a lack of scientific aids to target identification. There was a certain falling off of enthusiasm and belief in the effectiveness of strategic bombing. Air Marshal A. T. HARRIS, who became Air Officer Commanding in Chief Bomber Command in February 1942, decided that the way to silence objections of political opponents to area bombing and the demands of the Royal Navy and the Army for diversions of his bombers would be to carry out a massive raid, concentrated in time and space, of 1,000 bombers (Operation Millennium). The target chosen was Cologne, on the Rhine River. The raid was to be led by WELLINGTONS and STIRLINGS, equipped with the Gee NAVIGATION AID, to set the target alight in a time span of 15 minutes. The entire remaining force was to bomb in the next hour except for the new four-engine bombers, the LANCASTERS and HALIFAXES, which were just appearing in the command. These were to bomb in the last 15 minutes. The whole raid was to be accomplished in one and a half hours.

To amass a force of 1,000, Harris had to call on all the serviceable bombers from his own command plus some from Flying Training Command and from the bomber Operational Training Units. At the last moment the Admiralty refused to allow the use of 250 aircraft from Coastal Command. Nevertheless, he enlisted 1,046 bombers, of which, on the night of May 30, 1942, over 900 were known to have attacked the target. Casualties were not high, and photographic reconnaissance showed that about a third of the total area of Cologne had been heavily damaged. The first 1,000-bomber raid was a demonstration of what strategic bombing could do given the aircraft, bombs and navigation aids to accurate target marking.

COLONEL BRITTON. Name used by Douglas Ritchie (b. 1905) of the BRITISH BROADCASTING CORPORATION, whose broadcasts to occupied Europe encouraged resistance to the Germans, most notably through the "V campaign." *See also* V FOR VICTORY.

COLONEL WARDEN. Code name used by Prime Minister Winston CHURCHILL in connection with travel to various wartime conferences.

COLORADO. Code name used by British for CRETE in 1941 operations.

COLORADO, U.S.S. Battleship and class, of 32,600 tons, with eight 16-inch guns (4×2), commissioned in 1921–23. *Colorado, Maryland* and *West Virginia* were identical to the TENNESSEE class in dimensions and appearance except for their twin 16-inch turrets in place of the Tennessees' 14-inch triples. *Maryland* was damaged at PEARL HARBOR; *West Virginia,* hard hit, sank in shallow water. During 1942 *Colorado* and *Maryland* were slightly modified for better antiaircraft defense. *West Virginia* was salvaged and steamed back to the United States; in 1943–44 she was thoroughly modernized in the same manner as the Tennessee class. *Colorado* and *Maryland,* as bombardment and gunfire-support ships, took part in the Pacific amphibious offensive beginning with the seizure of the GILBERTS in November 1943. *West Virginia* returned to duty in time for the LEYTE operation. With *Maryland,* she stood in the battle line at Surigao Strait during the battle for LEYTE GULF. All three ships served through V-J Day.

COLOR PLANS. Code name for U.S. strategic plans drawn up in the 1920s and 1930s by the Joint Planning Committee, an arm of the Joint Army and Navy Board. They were so called because foreign countries that were possible adversaries were designated by colors, Japan—the most likely enemy—being orange. The color plans were superseded by the RAINBOW plans.

COLUMBIA, U.S.S. Light cruiser, second ship of the CLEVELAND class. Commissioned in July 1942, *Columbia* took part in the SOLOMONS campaign, including the Battle of RENNELL ISLAND. During the battle for BOUGAINVILLE she fought in the surface action at EMPRESS AUGUSTA BAY, and continued her support work in the Solomons area through the end of 1943. In 1944 she took part in the capture of the Green Islands and of Emirau Island before providing gunnery support for the landing on PELELIU. During October and November of that year she supported the invasion of LEYTE and took part in the battle for LEYTE GULF. In December she covered landings on MINDORO. She was severely damaged by two KAMIKAZE planes in Lingayen Gulf in January 1945. She returned from shipyard repairs in time to back up landings on Borneo and to support late-war sweeps against Japanese shipping in the East China Sea.

COMBAT AIR PATROL (CAP). U.S. Navy term for a defensive umbrella of fighter planes deployed over a naval force or operating area. Its principal mission was destruction of enemy aircraft. A CAP was responsible for intercepting approaching enemy planes as far as possible from the area being defended, breaking up attacks and shooting down "snooper" scout planes before they could obtain information. A CAP might be stationed at various altitudes, or at various positions with relation to its own forces, depending on the kind of attack expected. Effective use of the CAP was greatly increased by development of radar detection and radio fighter-direction technique.

COMBAT INFANTRY BADGE. Commonly known as the CIB, the Combat Infantry Badge was first authorized by the U.S. War Department on October 27, 1943 (War Department Circular 269-1) for issue to individuals recommended by a regimental commander or higher authority who had performed in infantry units in combat. The same circular authorized the establishment of the Expert Infantry Badge. If 65 percent or more of a unit's personnel had the CIB, the unit could be awarded a Combat Infantry Streamer for its guidon. Award of the CIB was made retroactive to service on or after December 7, 1941. Subsequent changes in regulations limited issuance to officers, warrant officers and enlisted men serving in the infantry, specifically excluding Medical Corps personnel and chaplains. In July 1944 Congress authorized an additional payment of $5 a month to enlisted men holding the CIB unless the award was withdrawn because of transfer to the Medical Corps or Army Air Corps. Payment of the special money was made retroactive to December 7, 1941.

COMBINED BOMBER OFFENSIVE. The loosely coordinated Anglo-American air offensive against Germany's military, industrial and economic system. The so-called Casablanca Directive, issued on January 21, 1943, called for the kind of strategic air offensive outlined in AWPD/1 and reflected American optimism concerning the ability of unescorted B-17s and B-24s to fight their way deep inside Germany during daylight to deliver precision attacks on industrial targets (*see* AIR WAR PLANS DIVISION/1). General EAKER, who commanded the U.S. bombing force in Britain, maintained that with 300 bombers he could carry out such an air offensive without incurring losses in excess of 4 percent.

One bombardment specialist, Britain's Air Chief Marshal Sir Arthur HARRIS, felt that American confidence in daylight precision bombing was disastrously misplaced. He advocated using the cloak of darkness to bomb area targets, leveling the houses where German workers lived rather than the factories where they worked. Harris, however, was not present at the CASABLANCA CONFERENCE to argue these views.

The senior British airman at the conference, Air Chief Marshal Sir Charles PORTAL, shared Harris's doubts, but two considerations kept him from opposing the preparation of a directive that reflected American views. The first of these was his desire to promote Anglo-American harmony, a particularly compelling motive since he seemed destined for an important post in the Allied hierarchy of command. Second, he apparently felt obliged to acknowledge the growing American contribution, in troops and ships as well as aircraft, to the joint war effort.

The directive itself was scarcely deserving of the name, for it did not ensure coordination, save to state that the Americans would bomb by day and the British by night. It did, however, establish general objectives: German submarine construction yards, the aircraft industry, transportation, the oil industry and other industrial facilities. Both Harris and Eaker remained free to use their bombers as they desired, establishing any target priority that they wished.

COMBINED CHIEFS OF STAFF. The Anglo-American command committee set up at the Washington ARCADIA CONFERENCE following American entry into the war. The operating body sat in Washington and was made up of the U.S. service chiefs and representatives of the British service chiefs. All the chiefs also met frequently at major conferences during the war.

COMBINED FLEET. When the war began, the third most powerful navy belonged to the Japanese, whose primary naval force was embodied in the Combined Fleet. This naval force was somewhat analogous to the United States Fleet, with its Atlantic and Pacific Fleets, except that the Combined Fleet had only one geographic area of concern, the Pacific Ocean. The order of battle of the Combined Fleet was not fixed but was different at various times. At the time of its massive defeat in the battle for LEYTE GULF in October 1944, it consisted of the Advance Force (submarines), the Mobile Force, the 1st Striking Force, the 2d Striking Force and the Land-based Air Force, except for such stationary forces as the Southeast Area, Southwest Area, North Area and China Area Forces. With its virtual destruction in this battle, the Japanese Navy could no longer influence the course of the war. The term

"Combined Fleet" is often used to refer to the command headquarters in Japan rather than the fleet *qua* fleet.

COMBINED OPERATIONS. The British term for amphibious and airborne raiding operations launched against Axis positions in occupied Europe and North Africa. This type of operation began in June 1940 with the fall of France. Initially they were small raids against outlying positions of little military significance, gradually increasing in size and scope through the DIEPPE raid of August 19, 1942, and culminating in the amphibious/airborne assaults on Europe in 1944. The Combined Operations Development Centre had been established in Britain in 1936 to develop suitable craft for landing operations. In 1940 highly trained units called COMMANDOS were organized for irregular hit-and-run operations against the Continent under the direction of the Combined Operations Command.

COMET. Code name for a proposed Allied airborne operation in the Arnhem-Nijmegen (Netherlands) area in September 1944. It was succeeded by MARKET-GARDEN.

COMMANDO. *See* C-46.

COMMANDO. On June 5, 1940, Lt. Col. Dudley Clarke, military assistant to the Chief of the British Imperial General Staff, Sir John DILL, recommended to his chief that the War Office establish a special unit trained to carry out guerrilla operations against the Germans. This unit, Clarke contended, could apply irregular tactics to regular warfare. Their raids would be particularly useful since the British had been pushed off the Continent and the regular forces were in no position to mount a large-scale attack across the Channel. Small operations would boost British morale and be a painful reminder to the Germans of the extensive coastline, stretching from the Arctic Circle to Spain, which they had to guard.

Clarke's idea quickly won the approval of his seniors, and on June 8, 1940, Section MO9 was established in the War Office to implement it. The only condition which Prime Minister CHURCHILL had set was that no unit should be diverted from the principal mission of the defense of Britain. The name Commando came from the mobile Boer units which kept the British off balance during the Boer War (1899–1902).

Since Commando units would be specially organized and trained, the War Office decided to rely upon volunteers rather than convert an already existing unit into a Commando team. By calling for volunteers the Commandos were able to get officers who were more youthful than those already in charge of existing units. In addition, volunteers would presumably be more willing to undertake the risky operations that Commando units would perform and better able to learn the techniques of guerrilla warfare. Still another advantage of a volunteer force was that no one would be committed to the conventional organization of an infantry battalion. Thus organizational structure could be modified or changed as necessary for particular operations.

Initially, a Commando organization consisted of a headquarters and 10 troops, each with three officers and 47 men. After the first few raids had shown some problems with this structure, Brig. J. C. Haydon, commander of the Special Service Brigade (the Commandos) reorganized the Commando into a headquarters and six troops instead of 10. This reorganization eliminated 12 officers in each unit—a convenient way of weeding out those found unsuitable; also each troop was now to include 62 enlisted men, a more effective number tactically. In each case the commanding officer of each troop was a volunteer who had then selected his own officers. These three officers had, in turn, recruited volunteers from already existing units to fill up the Commando ranks. Those who volunteered, whether officer or enlisted, had to be good soldiers, young, physically fit, able to drive motor vehicles and unlikely to get seasick. The result of the initial recruiting was a volunteer unit composed of a cross section of British military units, national geography and regulars and reservists.

Commando training was first held at Inveraray, but in December 1942 the training site was shifted to Achnacarry Castle in Scotland. At Achnacarry the combination of physical isolation and rugged terrain and coastline proved to be ideal for teaching guerrilla tactics. Lt. Col. Charles Vaughan, a 28-year regular, put potential commandos through a physically demanding training course which included realistic exercises in which live ammunition was used. By the end of the war some 25,000 soldiers, including U.S. RANGERS, Belgians, Norwegians, Frenchmen, Dutchmen and Poles, had completed the Commando training course.

Despite limited training, the first Commando raid took place very soon after Churchill had approved the plan for the new unit. On June 23–24, 1940, an inconclusive raid was made on the Boulogne–Le Touquet area of France. Following another minor raid, against the German garrison on the island of Guernsey on July 14–15, Section MO9 came under the supervision of Admiral of the Fleet Sir Roger KEYES, who had become director of the COMBINED OPERATIONS Command. Keyes held that post until October 27, 1941, when he was succeeded by Lord Louis MOUNTBATTEN.

From the coast of France the Commandos turned their attention to the Norwegian coastline. Twice Commando forces made successful raids on the LOFOTEN ISLANDS off Norway; the first was in February, the second in December 1941. In addition, the Commandos took part in a Combined Operations raid on Spitzbergen, under the command of Brig. A. E. Potts, on September 3, 1941. In this raid the British forces set fire to 450,000 tons of coal and 275,000 gallons of petroleum products.

In February 1941 another Commando unit, known as Layforce, under the command of Lt. Col. (later major general) Robert E. LAYCOCK, departed for the Middle East as a Special Service Force. It carried out a raid at BARDIA, in Libya, in April and fought a rearguard action at Sphakia, CRETE, during the British withdrawal on May 26–31. Layforce suffered some 600 casualties on Crete. On June 7–8 a Layforce unit outflanked a VICHY French force at Kafr Bada, Syria, taking a strong redoubt in the path of advancing Allied units. The most spectacular operation of Layforce came on November 17–18, 1941, when Lt. Col. Geoffrey KEYES led a raid on what was thought to be Gen. Erwin ROMMEL's headquarters at Beda Littoria, North Africa. The objective was to kill or capture the Desert Fox prior to General AUCHINLECK's attack on TOBRUK. Although the raiders succeeded in getting into a building, they failed to find the general. Only two members of this raiding party returned to Allied lines.

Layforce had no monopoly on daring operations in 1941. A raid on the German garrison at VAAGSØ, Norway, on December 27 involved 51 officers and 525 men in some fierce fighting.

SAINT-NAZAIRE, France, was the next major Commando target. The objective in Operation Chariot was the destruction of the drydock and other facilities. The largest Commando raid took place nearly six months after Saint-Nazaire, at DIEPPE on August 18–19, 1942. In this operation two Commando units covered the north and south flanks of a 6,000-man largely Canadian force. The southern Commando unit destroyed the coastal battery at Varengeville, but the northern unit had trouble landing when it encountered a German force offshore. Once the unit landed, it met heavy resistance and withdrew without doing much damage. The entire raid was a costly one; the Canadian and British forces lost 3,670 men killed, wounded or captured.

Throughout 1942 the Commandos staged a number of small raids, such as the two-man raid on Boulogne harbor which sank a German tanker with a limpet mine, but after the Allied invasion of NORTHWEST AFRICA in November 1942 the Commandos were used more and more to spearhead large-scale amphibious operations by conventional forces. In the last two and a half years of the war Commando units operated in North Africa, Italy, Sicily, Burma, Madagascar and Normandy. One mark of the special valor demonstrated by Commandos during the war was their winning of 479 individual decorations, including eight Victoria Crosses.

COMMISSAR ORDER. A Führer order of June 6, 1941—just prior to the German attack on the Soviet Union—decreeing that the political commissars of the Red Army "when captured in battle or in resistance are on principle to be disposed of by gunshot immediately"; i.e., they were to be completely denied the treatment normally given to prisoners of war. The executions were to be carried out by SD detachments (*see* SD).

COMMITTEE TO DEFEND AMERICA BY AIDING THE ALLIES. Following the outbreak of war in 1939, American internationalists, led by the Kansas newspaperman William Allen WHITE, formed the Non-Partisan Committee for Peace through Revision of the Neutrality Law. Although the committee was a decisive factor in swinging public opinion behind repeal of the American arms embargo, it fell into inactivity during the PHONY WAR. Following the renewal of fighting in the spring of 1940, the committee was reorganized on May 17 as the Committee to Defend America by Aiding the Allies. It soon had more than 600 local branches, which undertook a national campaign to muster public support for American aid to the Allies short of war.

COMMUNICATIONS ZONE (Com Z). The headquarters controlling administrative and logistical functions (i.e., Services of Supply) behind American armies in western Europe, commanded by Lt. Gen. John C. H. LEE. Troops performed such diverse functions as operating ports, transporting supplies by truck and rail, rebuilding railroads, defending rear installations, processing and housing reinforcements, operating hospitals and burying the dead.

COMPASS. Code name for British attack on Italian Army in NORTH AFRICA, December 7, 1940.

COMPIEGNE. At Rethondes, in the Forest of Compiègne north of Paris, the Franco-German armistice was signed on June 22, 1940. The area was overrun by the U.S. 4th Infantry Division at the beginning of September 1944.

COMPOSITION C. The U.S. designation for a British-developed plastic explosive used in demolition charges. It was a mixture of RDX with a nonexplosive plasticizer (*see* RDX), and was widely used by the Army in mop-up operations.

COMPTON, Arthur Holly (1892–1962). A distinguished American physicist, Compton was dean of the division of physical sciences and chairman of the department of physics at the UNIVERSITY OF CHICAGO in 1940. Because of his knowledge of nuclear physics he was brought into the MANHATTAN DISTRICT early in its development. In 1941 he was made chairman of the National Academy of Sciences committee which was evaluating the military importance of uranium, and later in 1941 he became one of the program chiefs of the ATOMIC BOMB project itself. He was director of the metallurgical project centered at the University of Chicago; here he was in charge of studies relating to the chain reaction. In 1943 this work was transferred to LOS ALAMOS. Under Compton's direction at Chicago and also at OAK RIDGE methods were developed for producing the plutonium used in the atomic bombs. The first atomic chain reaction was produced at Chicago on December 2, 1942. Compton, a Nobel Prize winner for physics in 1927, was installed as president of Washington University in St. Louis in 1945.

COMPTON, Karl Taylor (1887–1954). American physicist, president of the Massachusetts Institute of Technology, 1930–48, and an important scientific adviser to the U.S. Government during the war. He established the radiation laboratory at MIT, the leading American center for RADAR research. He was the older brother of Arthur Holly COMPTON.

COM Z. *See* COMMUNICATIONS ZONE.

CONANT, James Bryant (1893–1978). American chemist, professor of organic chemistry at Harvard and, 1933–53, president of the university. During World War II he administered Harvard with particular attention to the requirements of the Army and the Navy and planned for postwar reconversion to meet the special needs of returning servicemen. In 1941 he was sent to England as head of a three-man commission to confer with British scientists on new scientific developments, including knowledge gained in atomic research. That same year he was made chairman of the National Defense Research Committee and in that capacity advised the government on top-secret matters related to the development of the ATOMIC BOMB.

CONCENTRATION CAMPS. On Adolf HITLER's appointment as Chancellor of Germany in January 1933, Hermann GÖRING was named minister of the interior for the state of Prussia, by far the largest state in the German federal system. This gave Göring charge of security and of the police, whom he immediately restaffed with Nazi sympathizers in key posts, at the same time establishing the GESTAPO as secret security police. Many people alleged to have been actively opposed to Hitler were taken into "protective custody," and concentration camps—hastily established by the SA and the SS—were set up to receive them (*see* SA; SS). (The idea, said Göring cynically, came from the British practice during the Boer War.) Heinrich HIMMLER, as police president in Bavaria, Germany's second largest state, founded his own "model" concentration camp at DACHAU, near Munich, in March 1933. By Christmas some 27,000 prisoners were said to be held in these camps, many of which were "unauthorized" establishments set up by local SA strong-arm groups out to avenge themselves on their political enemies. Göring, who in 1934 was to hand over the nation's camps to Himmler as head of the SS, did not favor such unauthorized camps and sought to have them closed. Many short-term detainees were released after it was deemed they had learned their lesson.

The "authorized" camps flourished during the 1930s as centers of correction for political dissidents, with growing ill-treatment, floggings and torture being used as methods of coercion. Dachau, under Theodor Eicke, became the training center for SS men specializing as camp guards and administrators; the alumni included Rudolf HOESS and Adolf EICHMANN. Further camps were established, among the more notorious being Sachsenhausen (near Berlin-Oranienburg) in 1936, BUCHENWALD (near Weimar) in 1937, Flossenbürg (in the Upper Palatinate) and Mauthausen (near Linz) in 1938, and Ravensbrück (in Mecklenburg) in 1939. Ravensbrück was to specialize in training women guards. The number of concentration camps increased with the need to enforce the innumerable decrees by means of which Hitler transformed Germany into a police state. Prisoners were used as forced labor in quarries and armaments factories, and in the building of new camps even before the war started and changed the whole nature and pattern of the concentration camp system.

The Jews of Germany and Austria had been persecuted and driven into exile in large numbers during the prewar period; by 1939 some two-thirds had gone. With the invasion of Poland in 1939, western Europe in 1940 and Russia in 1941, the Nazis were faced with millions of unwanted Jews, many in the east being impoverished. There were 3.3 million in Poland, 2.1 million in western Russia, and 1.5 million in Czechoslovakia, Hungary and Rumania. They were herded mercilessly into ghettos and camps, which by 1941 were established for extermination as well as for slave labor. Concentration camps were established on a greatly enlarged scale in the occupied territories and were used indiscriminately to house political prisoners, criminals, Russian prisoners of war, Jews, Gypsies and unwanted Slavs. Many camps in Polish territory shared the roles of extermination centers and labor camps, and a new list of sinister names such as AUSCHWITZ and TREBLINKA in Poland, Natzweiler in the Vosges area and BELSEN in Germany came into being. There were in all 30 principal camps operating during the war, with hundreds of subsidiaries, usually set up as bases for slave labor used in the war plants. It has been claimed that at any one time during the war the camps collectively held at least a million prisoners, with newcomers rapidly replacing those who died either through extermination or from the privations of camp life combined with slave labor. The camps also became organized centers of pillage, of which the section known as "Canada" in Auschwitz was the most noted for its thorough organization. The belongings of the victims were sorted and packed by squads of prisoners and returned to Germany in the trains that had brought the newest arrivals.

A further horrifying practice in the camps was the use of prisoners for so-called medical experiments. These were conducted in a highly unscientific, actually murderous, manner by incompetent and sadistic doctors from the 350 medical practitioners who had joined the SS. Among the worst of the projects were Dr. Sigmund RASCHER's experiments at Dachau with low-pressure chambers and with freezing, the inflicting of gas-gangrenous wounds on girls at Ravensbrück, the hideous attempts at sterilization in Auschwitz and Ravensbrück, and the inducing of epidemic hepatitis at Sachsenhausen and typhus at Buchenwald. Over 100 prisoners were gassed at the Oranienburg camp in order to provide a collection of skeletons for the Institute for Practical Research in Military Science, founded by Himmler in 1942.

When Germany's empire began to collapse and the Russian armies moved into Poland, the camps were closed down as necessary and the prisoners were marched west, many dying by the wayside. The Russians entered Auschwitz in January 1945. By then the central camps and their numerous satellites numbered around 100 inside Germany, holding some 500,000 "Aryans" and 200,000 Jews. By 1944 approaches had been made to Himmler, KALTENBRUNNER, MÜLLER, Hoess, Eichmann and others to release Jewish prisoners and to permit Red Cross personnel from Switzerland and Sweden to bring what relief they could to the vastly overcrowded camps. Red Cross parcels for non-Jewish prisoners had been permitted entry since 1943 (though their contents were often rifled by the guards); 751,000 parcels were sent between November 1943 and May 1945. A Red Cross official penetrated Auschwitz in September 1944, but later attempts to visit the camps met only with frustration. It was not until April 1945 that officials saw Theresienstadt, the so-called model camp for Jews, and relief was brought in trucks to prisoners on a forced march from Oranienburg. By March a typhus epidemic had broken out at Belsen, where some 60,000 prisoners were crammed into a facility intended for 8,000. This camp was handed over to the British on April 15. The world then knew at last what a Nazi concentration camp was like.

After the war all surviving concentration camp records were assembled by the Red Cross in their International Tracing Center at AROLSEN. **R.M.**

CONCRETE SHIPS. Ships built of steel-reinforced concrete had been used at the time of World War I, to a limited extent, along with smaller lighters and barges. During World War II the same expedient was tried, both to save critical steel and to enable shipbuilders not set up to use steel to take part in the wartime ship program. World War II concrete ships were non-self-propelled barges at first; later orders called for powered ships as well. A number of different designs were produced and used to carry oil and other bulk cargoes.

CONDOR. *See* FOCKE-WULF FW 200.

CONINGHAM, Sir Arthur (1895–1948). British air marshal, a pioneer in Army-Air cooperation and the original architect of the tactical air force concept. As commander of the Desert Air Force portion of Sir Arthur TEDDER's Middle East Air Force, 1941–43, he was responsible for RAF operations at El ALAMEIN and Tripoli, and as commander of the 1st Allied (North African) Tactical Air Force, 1943–44, he controlled tactical air elements during the conquest of TUNISIA, PANTELLERIA and SICILY, and during the subsequent Allied campaign in southern ITALY. In 1944–45 he commanded the 2d Tactical Air Force.

CONNALLY, Tom (Thomas Terry) (1877–1963). U.S. Senator from Texas, originally elected in 1928 and reelected in 1934 and 1940. As a member of the Senate Foreign Relations Committee and later as chairman of the committee, he was an outspoken advocate of President Roosevelt's foreign policy and led the fight for enactment of the SELECTIVE SERVICE bill in 1940.

CONOLLY, Richard Lansing (1892–1962). A 1914 graduate of the U.S. Naval Academy, Conolly began World War II as a captain and rose to the rank of vice-admiral, seeing duty in both Europe and the Pacific and distinguishing himself in amphibious warfare. He commanded a major amphibious task force in the invasion of SICILY in 1943, and his Pacific operations included action in the MARSHALLS, at LEYTE GULF and in the liberation of the PHILIPPINES. Conolly and his wife died in a plane crash.

CONSEIL SUPERIEUR DE LA GUERRE. Highest body within the peacetime French Army. It consisted of the Minister of War as president, the Inspector General of the Army (designated as wartime Commander in Chief) as vice-president, any living marshals of France and those ranking generals designated to high command posts during time of war. From 1936 to 1939 the council functioned as an advisory body under the leadership of Army chief Gen. Maurice GAMELIN and War Minister Edouard DALADIER, although the latter normally deferred to the military members on matters of doctrine and organization. Key meetings took place in 1936, 1937 and 1938, when the council discussed the merits of establishing various types of armored formations, but the members decided to create only a small number of heavy tank brigades when the proper equipment became available. The council had no wartime function. In English it is called the Army Council, the Army War Council or the Supreme War Council.

CONSPICUOUS GALLANTRY MEDAL. Prior to 1943 only enlisted men of the Royal Navy or Royal Marines or men of the merchant navy who had displayed conspicuous gallantry in action with the enemy could receive the CGM. The Royal Air Force instituted its own CGM to recognize gallantry in air operations against the enemy by its NCOs, glider pilots and observers.

CONTE DI CAVOUR. Generally known as *Cavour*, this Italian battleship of 23,600 tons was completed at La Spezia in 1915 and completely rebuilt and modernized in the 1930s. *Cavour*'s armament in June 1940 was ten 12.6-inch, twelve 4.7-inch and eight 3.9-inch guns, smaller weapons and two aircraft. On November 11, 1940, *Cavour* was so badly damaged by the British naval aviation's attack on TARANTO (21 aircraft from the aircraft carriers ILLUSTRIOUS and EAGLE, though only the former vessel actually participated in the operation) that she foundered. With great difficulty she was refloated and taken to Trieste for repairs, but these were never completed. She was captured by German forces in September 1943 but further heavily damaged by air attacks in 1945.

CONVOY COLLEGE. Ocean area around Formosa, given the nickname because of the rich prizes offered to U.S. submarines. In 1944 the "campus" was occupied by various wolfpacks. *See also* SUBMARINE.

COOKE, Charles Maynard, Jr. (1886–1970). Following his graduation from the University of Arkansas, "Savvy" Cooke entered the U.S. Naval Academy and graduated second in the class of 1910. Commanding officer of the U.S.S. *Pennsylvania* at Pearl Harbor, Cooke soon became chief of staff to Admiral Ernest J. KING, where his "clarity of vision and power of analysis" won him, as King's top planner, a Distinguished Service Medal. After the war Cooke earned a reputation as a student of world affairs. He remained vocal following retirement.

COOPER, Alfred Duff (1890–1954). An influential British politician, an opponent of APPEASEMENT in the 1930s. Duff Cooper was at the War Office under Stanley Baldwin (1935–37), and in 1937 when Neville CHAMBERLAIN became Prime Minister, Cooper was offered the post of First Lord of the Admiralty. Believing that war was inevitable, he worked to prepare the Navy for the conflict, but Chamberlain did not support his efforts. Cooper continued to feel (after an initial period in which he had trusted in the League of Nations) that Great Britain must oppose any power seeking to dominate the Continent and that it was a mistake to have more than one major enemy at a time. When the Czechoslovak crisis developed in the autumn of 1938, he had difficulty obtaining approval for mobilizing the fleet. When Chamberlain returned from MUNICH, Cooper denounced the agreement in the House of Commons as unworkable and meaningless and resigned from the cabinet. He accepted an offer from Lord BEAVERBROOK to write a weekly article for the *Evening Standard* and in 1939–40 embarked on an extended lecture tour of the United States. When Winston CHURCHILL succeeded Chamberlain, Cooper was given the position of Minister of Information (1940). In 1941 he left the ministry after a frustrating period, accepting the sinecure post of chancellor of the duchy of Lancaster. In August he left for the Far East on behalf of the War Cabinet, with orders to examine the arrangements for consultation and coordination among the various British authorities. After PEARL HARBOR he was appointed resident cabinet minister at SINGAPORE and told to establish a war council. But the appointment of a supreme commander for the theater made his efforts in the Far East meaningless—and he returned to England to find that some imputed to him a share of the responsibility for the loss of Singapore.

An admirer of General DE GAULLE, he served as British representative with the FRENCH COMMITTEE OF NATIONAL LIBERATION established in North Africa under the general. In September 1944 he was moved to Paris, and in November he was appointed British ambassador to France. During three years' residence in France he did much to heal the wounds left by the war.

CORAL SEA, BATTLE OF THE. After the fall of the Netherlands East Indies in early 1942, the Japanese planned Operation Mo, involving the seizure of PORT MORESBY, at the southeastern tip of NEW GUINEA, with landings in the Solomons on GUADALCANAL and TULAGI. This would serve as a step toward the capture of Nauru and Ocean Islands, as well as providing air bases from which Australia could be attacked and driven out of the war. Three landing forces were organized. Two were aimed at Port Moresby and Tulagi; the third was to set up a seaplane reconnaissance base in the Louisiade Islands, southeast of New Guinea. An American counterattack was expected; as the U.S. fleet moved into the Coral Sea, east of Australia and south of the Solomons, it was to be caught between two pincers and destroyed. One of the jaws of this stroke was commanded by Rear Adm. Aritomo GOTO, commanding the light carrier SHOHO, four heavy cruisers and one destroyer. The other was Vice-Adm. Takeo TAKAGI's force, with the new fleet carriers SHOKAKU and ZUIKAKU, two heavy cruisers and six destroyers. The Mo plan directed the seizure of Tulagi on May 3; the striking forces would then screen the Port Moresby invasion force, which would go ashore on the 10th.

By mid-April, thanks to radio code intercepts, Admiral NIMITZ, the U.S. Pacific commander, knew enough about the Japanese plan to evaluate the projected thrust. Rear Adm. Frank Jack FLETCHER was already in the South Pacific with Task Force 17, built around carrier YORKTOWN. Rear Adm. Aubrey FITCH sailed from Hawaii with Task Force 11 (carrier LEXINGTON and escorting ships). On May 1 the two forces met south of the New Hebrides, and on the 4th they launched an air strike at the newly landed Japanese forces at Tulagi. Later that day British Rear Adm. J. G. CRACE joined with Task Force 44, two Australian heavy cruisers and one American heavy cruiser. On the 6th the three forces were combined into a single Task Force 17, under Fletcher. Besides *Yorktown* and *Lexington*, Fletcher now had eight heavy cruisers and 11 destroyers. A fueling group, two oilers with two destroyers, operated separately.

Fletcher planned to attack the Japanese forces as soon as he knew their location. Early on May 7 he sent Crace, with a task group of three cruisers and two destroyers, to the Louisiades to intercept any thrust at Port Moresby. Later that morning the American oiler *Neosho* and destroyer *Sims* were sighted and attacked by

U.S.S. *Lexington* was a casualty of the Coral Sea battle

Japanese carrier planes. *Sims* was sunk; *Neosho* was left a drifting hulk. While the Japanese concentrated on these two targets, under the impression that *Neosho* was an aircraft carrier (as search planes had incorrectly reported), American carrier planes hit Goto's force and sank *Shoho*. During the afternoon *Shokaku* and *Zuikaku* launched an attack force. They did not find the American carriers, but met fighters from *Yorktown* and *Lexington*; some of the Japanese planes were downed.

The main carrier duel of the Battle of the Coral Sea, the first naval action in history in which two fleets engaged without coming within sight of each other, began on the morning of May 8. An American search plane sighted *Shokaku* and *Zuikaku*; Fletcher immediately launched a strike. *Shokaku* was hit; gasoline fires were started and her flight deck was damaged. Meanwhile, Takagi had learned the position of the American carriers and sent out his own attack. At nearly the same time the American air groups were attacking, the Japanese aircraft struck. In spite of the efforts of covering fighters and the ships' antiaircraft gunners, Japanese torpedo bombers were able to get into position to launch their weapons in a crisscross pattern from both sides of *Lexington*'s bow. The carrier took two hits on her port side, followed by three hits by Japanese divebombers. She suffered some flooding in her engineering spaces; fires were started and her elevators were knocked out. *Yorktown*, somewhat more maneuverable than the longer *Lexington*, dodged eight torpedoes and took only one bomb hit on her flight deck; she could still land and launch planes.

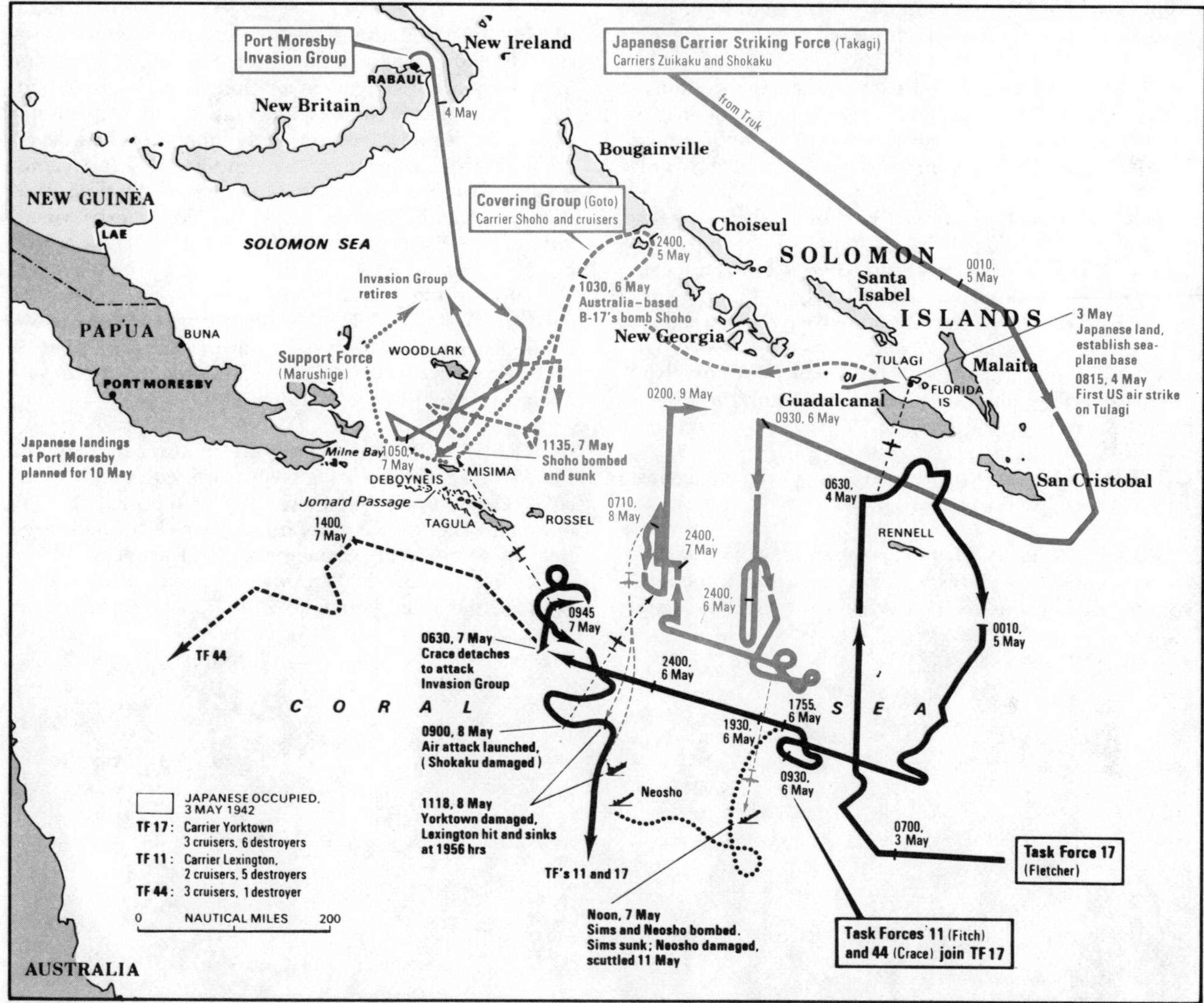

THE BATTLE OF THE CORAL SEA, which halted the Japanese drive to Port Moresby, was a key American strategic victory

About an hour after the air battle ended, *Lexington*'s crew had cured a slight list; most of her fires had been put out, and she was able to recover planes. But gasoline vapor was accumulating below decks from leaking fuel lines, and at midday these were detonated by an unshielded electric motor. A heavy explosion was followed by intense fires. These spread and began to set off ammunition. After more than four hours' effort, the crew was ordered to abandon ship. Nearby destroyers and cruisers picked up survivors as the ship burned more furiously. A destroyer fired two torpedoes into *Lexington*; after one last explosion she sank.

Coral Sea was a tactical victory for the Japanese. The loss of one of the few big U.S. carriers outweighed the sinking of *Shoho* and the damaging of *Shokaku*. The strategic result, however, was different. The drive for Port Moresby had failed; the Japanese transports turned back when their covering force was unable to destroy Fletcher's task force as planned. Damage to

Shokaku and heavy losses to *Zuikaku*'s air group kept both ships out of the Battle of MIDWAY in June; the presence of these two modern carriers might have contributed to a Japanese victory. **J.C.R.**

CORAP, André (1878–1953). General Corap served with distinction in the French colonial forces. In 1940 he commanded the ill-fated French Ninth Army, which took the full shock of the German drive through the ARDENNES. He has been unjustly blamed for the collapse of his badly outmatched forces.

CORBIN, Charles (1881–). French career diplomat, ambassador to Britain and a strong supporter of Anglo-French cooperation. Corbin was one of the sponsors of the DECLARATION OF UNION in 1940.

CORK AND ORRERY, 12th Earl of (William Henry Dudley Boyle) (1873–1967). Admiral of the Fleet the Earl of Cork and Orrery had been Commander in Chief of the British Home Fleet in 1933–35. On April 10, 1940, Lord Cork was appointed naval commander of the force designated to take NARVIK, Norway. His command was expanded and he led all forces involved in the Narvik operation from April 21 until he evacuated the area in early June.

CORKSCREW. Code name of Allied operations against PANTELLERIA, June 1943.

CORLETT, Charles H. (1889–1971). Cowboy Pete, as he was known to the U.S. Army, as a major general commanded troops in the invasion of ATTU in 1943. Then in early 1944 he commanded the 7th Infantry Division at KWAJALEIN. One of the few Pacific generals transferred to Europe at the time of the Normandy INVASION, he took over U.S. XIX Corps and led it until after the battle for AACHEN and the HÜRTGEN FOREST, when he was relieved primarily because of continuing friction with the commander of U.S. First Army, Gen. C. H. HODGES. An intensely serious soldier, enigmatic of mien, Corlett was an able tactician.

CORONET. Code name assigned to the planned invasion of the Japanese island of Honshu scheduled for March 1946 but overtaken by the surrender of Japan. The war ended while Coronet was still in its planning stages, but a broad outline of the operation was developed. Two U.S. armies, the Eighth and Tenth, comprised of nine infantry and two armored divisions, plus three Marine divisions of III Amphibious Corps, would land on the Pacific beaches of the Kanto Plain, covered by the Third and Fifth Fleets, with the primary objective of crushing Japanese resistance on the plain. The occupation of the Tokyo-Yokohama area would follow. Immediately behind the assault armies ashore would be the First Army, redeployed from Europe, with an airborne and 10 infantry divisions.

CORREGIDOR. Dominating the entrance to Manila Bay, Corregidor was a heavily fortified island which surrendered to the Japanese on May 6, 1942, after an epic four-month defense during which it had been heavily bombarded by enemy air and artillery. In the effort to recapture it, U.S. planes began a pre-invasion bombardment on January 22, 1945. On February 16,

American soldiers in Malinta Tunnel on Corregidor in April 1942

after a heavy air and naval gunfire preparation, landings began at 8:30 A.M. with a drop by the Army 503d Parachute Regimental Combat Team and a landing across the beaches by the reinforced 3d Battalion, 34th Infantry. The beachhead was established as the two assault units linked up without difficulty; the enemy had been shaken by the heavy bombardment and apparently taken by surprise. On the 26th, after 10 days of heavy fighting, operations on Corregidor were ended except for mopping up. Gen. Douglas MACARTHUR returned to Corregidor on March 2, 1945, after having left it nearly three years earlier, to raise the American flag over the island once more.

CORSAIR. *See* F4U.

CORSAIR, U.S.S. Submarine and class; the third class of wartime FLEET-TYPE SUBMARINES, these were like the earlier BALAO class except that their internal arrangements were specifically designed to accommodate RADAR and newer SONARS and their associated equipment. Twenty-seven Corsair-class submarines commissioned in 1945–46; 93 more were canceled. Slightly heavier than the GATO and Balao classes, these submarines were known as "1,570-tonners."

CORSAIR FLEET. Officially assigned name for the U.S. force more customarily referred to as the HOOLIGAN NAVY.

CORVETTE. British designation for small, mass-produced Flower-class seagoing antisubmarine escort ships. Designed to meet the urgent early-war need for quantities of antisubmarine ships, the Flowers were patterned on ocean whale-catching ships. Armed with one 4-inch gun, antiaircraft weapons and depth charges, along with asdic (*see* SONAR) and, later, RADAR, corvettes were seaworthy under terrible North Atlantic conditions but were anything but comfortable for their crews. Like many other weapons, the Flower class filled an essential role when they were desperately needed. Some were used by the U.S. Navy as the Temptress class, and were officially classified as corvettes in that service also.

COSSAC. Acronym for "Chief of Staff to the Supreme Allied Commander" (of the Allied Expeditionary Force in Europe). Actually, the title was used for both the headquarters and the officer himself. The COSSAC staff came into being to conduct preliminary planning for the cross-Channel INVASION; its head was the British Lt. Gen. F. E. MORGAN.

COSSACK, H.M.S. British destroyer involved in the rescue of British prisoners from the German ship *Altmark* (*see* ALTMARK INCIDENT).

COTA, Norman D. (1893–1971). U.S. Army officer, known as "Dutch," who after service in North Africa in 1942 was transferred to England to become the U.S. adviser on the staff of Adm. Lord Louis MOUNTBATTEN, Chief of Combined Operations. As assistant division commander of the 29th Infantry Division, he was later placed in charge of its units committed to the Normandy assault. In this capacity he became the first American general officer to land on D-Day. His heroism that day was such that he was awarded the DSC. On August 13, 1944, Cota, as a major general, took command of the 28th Infantry Division in the midst of combat. He led the division across France, to include a march down the Champs Elysées to pacify Paris, through the action at HÜRTGEN FOREST and the Battle of the BULGE. Overwhelmed by enemy strength in the opening fighting in the Bulge, the division nevertheless broke into small delaying groups that bought critical time, enabling other units to assemble for defense of the road center of BASTOGNE. Cota commanded the 28th Division until the end of the war. To his peers, he was a gallant figure.

COTENTIN PENINSULA. The tongue of land projecting from Normandy, at the end of which is CHERBOURG. The U.S. First Army (VII Corps) was charged with cutting the Cotentin and taking Cherbourg, which fell on June 27,1944.

COURAGEOUS, H.M.S. Royal Navy aircraft carrier of 22,500 tons, completed in 1917 by Armstrong as a battle cruiser and converted to an aircraft carrier in 1924–29, with an armament (in 1939) of sixteen 4.7-inch guns, smaller weapons and 48 aircraft. *Courageous* was the Royal Navy's first major loss, being torpedoed and sunk by the German submarine *U-29* in the WESTERN APPROACHES on September 17, 1939. Her captain, W. T. Makeig-Jones, went down with his ship, remaining alone on the bridge and saluting the flag in accordance with a theory of duty held by a number of Royal Navy officers; shortly afterward the Admiralty officially discouraged this waste of life—and often waste of important intelligence. Over 500 officers and men were lost.

COVENTRY. English manufacturing center for armaments, munitions and aircraft components (as well as a historic city), subjected to a very heavy German air raid the night of November 14, 1940. Operation Moonlight Sonata, as the Germans called it, was carried out in retaliation for the British bombing of Munich on November 8, the 17th anniversary of Adolf HITLER's Beer Hall Putsch of 1923. The LUFTWAFFE sent 449 bombers, which dropped 503 tons of high explosives and 881 incendiary canisters during the 10 hours of the raid. The medieval center of the city was hard hit, many businesses and other civilian targets, including St. Michael's Cathedral, being destroyed. At least 554 persons were killed and 865 wounded, and essential services and industrial production were disrupted for some time. The raid marked the Luftwaffe's switch from bombing London to striking at strategic targets and saw the first use of the radio-beam navigation system X GERÄT. In recent years it has been asserted that the British knew of the German plan for the raid from ULTRA intelligence but did not take protective action through fear of revealing the fact that they were reading enemy transmissions. But the point remains disputed.

CR-25. Fiat designed this Italian twin-engine, three-place, low-wing monoplane as a high-speed, long-range, heavily armed fighter-bomber. First flown in 1939, the plane was deficient in firepower, with either four 7.7-mm. or two 12.7-mm. forward-firing machine guns plus, a dorsal turret with a single 12.7-mm. weapon. The few that were built served Italy's air arm as transports.

CR-32. This Fiat biplane fighter, designed by Celestino Rosatelli and first flown in 1933, continued in production until the autumn of 1939. By the time Italy entered the war in 1940, the Regia Aeronautica had some 400 of the planes on hand, most of them with second-line units. The single-seat craft had an open cockpit and a fixed landing gear with streamlined wheel covers. Armament of the final production model was two 12.7-mm. machine guns firing through the propeller arc. In addition, it could carry a dozen small fragmentation bombs. A 600-horsepower Fiat liquid-cooled engine gave the plane a top speed of 221 miles per hour at 9,840 feet.

CR-42. The Fiat *Falco* (Falcon) was the last biplane fighter manufactured by any of the World War II combatants. Production ceased in 1942 after the Italian air service had accepted almost 1,800 of the planes. Designed by Celestino Rosatelli, the single-seat, open-cockpit Falcon had a welded steel frame with metal covering forward and fabric aft. The wings also were fabric-covered, and the landing gear was not retractable. The usual power plant was an 840-horsepower Fiat radial, and the armament consisted of a pair of 12.7-mm. machine guns. Top speed was 266 miles per hour at 13,120 feet. The installation of a 1,010-horsepower Daimler-Benz liquid-cooled engine gave an experimental version the incredible top speed of 323 miles per hour, but the Regia Aeronautica realized that even so the Falcon was inferior to the monoplane fighters of 1941.

Before the war, Sweden, Hungary and Belgium purchased this Italian fighter. Of the 25 serving the Belgian air arm, 13 were destroyed during the first German air attacks in May 1940. Wearing Italian colors, the Falcon saw combat against the French, played a minor part in the Battle of Britain and saw extensive action in the Mediterranean and North Africa theaters.

CRACE, Sir John Gregory (1887–1968). Crace joined the Royal Navy in 1902 and served throughout World War I. During World War II he commanded the Australian squadron which took part in the various actions in the CORAL SEA in 1942. In that year he retired as a vice-admiral but continued to serve as admiral superintendent of Chatham Dockyard until 1946. He was promoted admiral on the retired list in 1945.

CRAFT, Clarence B. (1922?– ?). A U.S. Army private first class, Craft became a hero in the fighting in the Shuri area of OKINAWA by killing 58 Japanese defenders, mostly with hand grenades, in about 15 minutes. A 23-year-old, he was new to combat.

C RATION. U.S. Army field ration, developed shortly before World War II to provide troops with a nutritious meal having a modest amount of variety and easily prepared by the individual soldier without recourse to a field kitchen. Each meal was contained in two cans. The first held one of three "main courses"—stew, hash or meat and beans. The second can included large crackers called C-Ration biscuits, with such additional items as candy, sugar and powdered fruit juice or coffee.

CREAGH, Sir Michael O'Moore (1891–1970). British Army officer, commander of the 7th Armored Division (the "Desert Rats"), Middle East, 1939–41; commander, 3d Armored Group, 1941–42. He held the rank of major general.

CREASY, Sir George Elvey (1895–1972). Commander of the Royal Navy's 1st Destroyer Flotilla from the outbreak of the war until 1940, when he was brought to the Admiralty as director of the Anti-Submarine Division. After commanding the battleship DUKE OF YORK in 1942–43, he became chief of staff to Adm. Sir Bertram RAMSAY during the planning for Operation NEPTUNE, the naval side of the INVASION of northwest Europe (Normandy). On promotion to rear admiral during that appointment, he became Admiral Commanding Submarines, a post he held until 1946. He served in various postwar appointments of importance.

CRERAR, Henry Duncan Graham (1888–1965). One of the most distinguished military leaders in Canada's history and the first Canadian general to command Canadian forces in the field. After serving as Chief of General Staff, 1940–41, Crerar became commander of the 2d Canadian Division Overseas. In 1942–44 he was General Officer Commanding, 1st Canadian Corps, United Kingdom and Italy. In 1944 he took command of the Canadian FIRST ARMY. In the Canadian offensive against the lower Rhine, commencing in February 1945, eight British divisions and most of the 21ST ARMY GROUP were assigned to Crerar until he eventually commanded more than 500,000 men. He retired in 1946.

CRETE. In April 1941, as the Allied front in Macedonia crumbled beneath the German assault, the island of Crete took on a new importance for the British military planners. Initially perceived as a refueling and support station for the campaign in Greece, it had to ready itself to defend against a likely German invasion and to serve as a refuge for the troops defeated in Greece. For the Germans the possession of Crete would have several advantages. It would provide air and sea bases that would ensure domination of the eastern Mediterranean. With the acquisition of Crete the Axis could launch air attacks against points in Egypt and North Africa, and the sea route from the Danube through the Dardanelles and the Corinth Canal, which was essential to Italy, especially for oil transportation, would be made secure.

Axis success in Greece gave Gen. Kurt STUDENT, who commanded the airborne corps, Fliegerkorps XI, a long-awaited opportunity to attempt a series of island-hopping assaults. He envisioned Crete as the first of several such attacks eventually leading to the Suez Canal. Although Adolf HITLER on April 21, 1941, approved Student's scheme regarding Crete, his strategic view was more limited; the Crete plan itself was hastily conceived within the course of a month.

On the morning of May 20 the largest German airborne attack ever attempted, Operation Mercury (Merkur), got under way under the command of Gen. Alexander LÖHR. The Germans were well prepared for the operation. Löhr had some 13,000 men of the 7th Air Division and Assault Regiment and about 9,000 mountain troops. His air force was also formidable: some 700 transports, 80 gliders, 430 bombers and 180 fighters were available for the operation. To meet this force the British, under the command of the New Zealand general Bernard FREYBERG, had in mid-May only 24 serviceable fighter aircraft on the island. British land forces consisted of some 28,000 troops, the majority—21,000—being tired men recently evacuated from Greece.

The German invasion plan consisted of dropping airborne troops at the three main airfields, which were all located on the north coast of Crete. These fields were MÁLEME, Canea-Suda-Rétimo and HERÁKLION. The Germans planned to take over the airfields and the local beaches and then fan out to establish a line that would seal off the area until reinforcements could be sent in.

After several hours of sustained bombing on the morning of May 20, the assault commenced. The plan broke down at Heráklion and Rétimo, where the paratroops were either wiped out or beaten back by the British defenders. But the Battle of Crete was lost and won at Máleme. The Germans succeeded in catching the defenders, still shaken from the bombing, with their heads down. By nightfall Máleme airfield belonged to the attackers. Resupply of equipment and troops enabled them to retain their position in the face of valiant British counterattacks.

On the British side resupply was becoming an increasingly hazardous undertaking. Several ships were lost to German air attacks. On May 24 the British commanders, in a reply to a request from London for assessment of the situation in Crete, stated that the scale of air attacks made it no longer feasible for the Navy to operate by day. The Navy concluded that it could not guarantee to prevent German seaborne landings without suffering severe losses which, it was argued, would compromise the British command of the eastern Mediterranean.

By May 27 the Germans, who had dropped between 20,000 and 30,000 troops on the island, were extending their positions. At the same time the British, after concluding that reinforcement was impossible since it would have grave effects on other commitments in the Middle East, ordered the island evacuated. It was the Royal Navy's task to rescue the defenders. The Navy performed admirably, rescuing nearly 18,000 men, but not without sustaining substantial losses. In casualties the Navy suffered 1,828 men killed and 183 wounded. One aircraft carrier was sunk, three battleships damaged, three cruisers and six destroyers sunk, and six cruisers and seven destroyers damaged. The Royal Air Force lost seven Wellingtons, 16 medium bombers and 23 fighters. British ground troops killed in Crete numbered nearly 1,800, while an additional 1,800 were wounded and 12,000 taken prisoner.

Yet the German losses were no less severe. Two hundred and twenty planes were destroyed and nearly 150 damaged. The statistics on German manpower were nearly 2,000 killed, over 2,000 wounded and another 2,000 missing. These figures may well have prompted the Germans to reconsider the effectiveness of airborne attack, since they never again attempted one on such a large scale.

CRICKET. Code name for the preliminary British-American phase of the YALTA CONFERENCE, at MALTA on January 30–February 2, 1945. The code name of the entire Malta-Yalta meeting was Argonaut.

CRIMEA, THE. This peninsula, because of its strategic location by the Black Sea as well as its proximity to the oil-rich Caucasus, was important to Germans and Russians alike. In addition, Adolf HITLER had special plans for the Crimea, hoping to convert the area into a purely German colony from which all foreigners would be excluded. By the end of 1941 the entire Crimea was in German hands, with the exception of SEVASTOPOL, which held out until July 1942. The tenacious Soviet defense of Sevastopol helped to slow the German offensive, which would otherwise have moved on into the Caucasus across the Kerch Strait. German occupation of the Crimea lasted until 1944. In the end Hitler's infatuation with the area led to a disastrous defeat at Sevastopol, where the Germans, ordered to hold out indefinitely by the Führer, lost nearly 100,000 men.

CRIPPS, Sir (Richard) Stafford (1889–1952). British Labour politician, ambassador to the Soviet Union 1940–42 and Minister of Aircraft Production in 1942–45. He headed the Cripps Mission to India in 1942, which almost succeeded in obtaining Indian political support for the Allied war effort in return for the promise of full autonomy for India after the war. In 1945 Cripps took office in the ATTLEE government.

CROCKER, Sir John Tredinnick (1896–1963). British Army officer, the first officer of the Royal Tank Corps and Royal Tank Regiment to command an army corps in the field, to become a commander in chief overseas and to sit in the Army Council. He was commander, 6th Armored Division, 1940–41; commander, 2d Armored Group, Eastern Command, 1941–42; commander, 9th Corps, 1943; commander, 1st Corps, 1944–45, during the invasion of France and Germany.

CROMWELL. British code word meaning "invasion imminent." It was issued by the headquarters of Home Forces on September 7, 1940—not because an actual invasion was about to take place but because the commanders, on putting together the evidence they had, deemed invasion likely at this time. On learning that Cromwell had been issued, some local commanders ordered church bells rung, an action that was supposed to warn of parachute-troop landings. Cromwell was kept in force for 12 days. There was a widespread and long-persistent rumor, complete with details, that the Germans had in fact mounted an invasion but had been repulsed by flaming oil and other measures, but this was not so.

CROMWELL TANK. *See* TANK.

CROSLEY, U.S.S. High-speed transport and class. Former destroyer escorts of the RUDDEROW class, these 54 ships were built up amidships to provide troop accommodations. BUCKLEY-class DEs, similarly converted, became the CHARLES LAWRENCE class. APDs (*see* APD) were used to transport and land raiding parties and pre-invasion underwater demolition teams.

CROSSBOW. Code name for Allied operations against the German vengeance weapons—V-1 flying bombs and V-2 rockets. As early as November 1939 the British got their first inkling that Germany was developing long-range weapons of a revolutionary type, and by the spring of 1943 enough intelligence had been gathered to cause the launching of a photo-reconnaissance effort that resulted in the taking of over a million aerial pictures. One of these, taken over the Baltic isle of PEENEMÜNDE in May 1943, fell into the hands of Flight Officer Constance Babington-Smith, a photo interpreter, who detected an elevated launching ramp and a small airplane with no cockpit. Her identification of the V-1 resulted in a night attack against Peenemünde on August 17, 1943, a raid that caused the enemy to accelerate plans for the dispersal of rocket development and manufacturing facilities.

Aerial photography also disclosed a burgeoning number of concrete structures, located near the Channel coast, that were correctly identified as launch sites or rocket-support installations. American B-17s joined the attack on these sites on August 27, bombing what proved to be a rocket-fuel plant at Watten, in the Pas de Calais area. The earliest Crossbow targets in France consisted of heavy concrete structures such as the one at Watten, but photo interpreters soon discovered rapidly proliferating ski sites, so named because they resembled 300-foot skis placed on edge. Additional reconnaissance sorties ferreted out new sites, fighter-bombers went into action against them and heavy bombers joined the attack. By mid-June 1944 American and British planes had dropped some 36,000 tons of bombs, apparently knocking out the French launch sites, at a cost of 771 lives and 154 aircraft.

Then, on the night of June 12, an undetected launcher in the Pas de Calais region sent a V-1 sputtering toward London, and within 24 hours some 300 flying bombs had been dispatched against the United Kingdom. To meet this threat the British employed fighter patrols, radar-controlled antiaircraft guns and barrage balloons. Crossbow now entered a new phase.

The Allies refused to launch a sustained aerial offensive against the V-1 installations, but they did divert some heavy bombers from strikes against German industry and employ tactical aircraft that might otherwise have been supporting the advance inland from the Normandy beaches. Most of the attacks were directed against permanent launch facilities, but the Germans were now using improvised sites that were extremely hard to pinpoint. Air strikes on firing batteries and manufacturing centers failed to end the V-1 menace, and the "buzz bombs" continued to take off from French soil until early September, when Allied troops overran the launch sites.

V-1 operations continued from Holland, though on a lesser scale, as the Germans used obsolete aircraft like the He 111 to carry the V-1s piggyback to launch points over the North Sea. Allied night fighters, together with the difficulty of flying the overloaded aerial launchers, caused heavy casualties among the German airmen. Meanwhile, construction began on launching ramps in Holland, which commenced operation on March 5 and dispatched their last flying bomb on March 29.

The deadliest defensive weapons, though by a small margin, were the land-based antiaircraft guns, which accounted for 1,866 buzz bombs, while fighters claimed 1,847. Twelve V-1s fell victim to shipboard antiaircraft weapons, and 232 collided with balloon cables. This first of Hitler's vengeance weapons killed 2,855 and seriously injured 6,268.

On September 8, 1944, the second vengeance weapon made its combat debut, as the first of 1,115 V-2 rockets exploded in a London suburb. Until March 27, 1945, when the last rocket fell, London was the principal target, though the port of Antwerp, Belgium, came under heavy attack. The speed and trajectory of the V-2 made aerial interception impossible, but Allied planes could bomb the probable launch complexes and support installations in Holland, where misdirected attacks near The Hague caused casualties among Dutch civilians. Although the V-2 did not disrupt the advance of Allied arms, it did kill 6,139 persons in the London area and seriously injure an additional 17,239. *See also* V-WEAPONS.

CROSSWORD. Code name given by Winston CHURCHILL to the operation that brought about the surrender of German forces in Italy in May 1945. This secret operation was called Sunrise by the negotiators on the spot. *See also* DULLES, Allen W.

CROWLEY, Leo Thomas (1890–). Previously chairman of the Federal Deposit Insurance Corp. in Washington, Crowley in March 1942 was appointed U.S. Alien Property Custodian. Then, upon the creation of a new super-agency, the Office of Economic Warfare, Crowley was appointed administrator. In September 1943 this office, the Office of Lend-Lease Administration and the Office of Foreign Relief and Rehabilitation Operations were consolidated into the Foreign Economic Administration, with Crowley as director.

CRUEWELL, Ludwig (1892–1958). German Army officer, a World War I veteran who became an outstanding panzer commander in World War II. Achieving the rank of major general in 1939, he commanded a tank division in Yugoslavia in 1941 and in September of that year went to Africa to serve under General ROMMEL, succeeding to command of AFRIKA KORPS when Rommel became commander of the armies in Africa. In May 1942 Cruewell was captured by the British.

CRUSADER. Code name for major British North African operation directed by General AUCHINLECK, November 1941, which relieved the siege of TOBRUK and recaptured CYRENAICA.

CRUSADER TANK. *See* TANK.

CRUTCHLEY, Sir Victor Alexander Charles (1893–). British naval officer, awarded the Victoria Cross during World War I. At the start of World War II he was captain of H.M.S. WARSPITE, and he became commodore of the Royal Navy Barracks at Devonport in 1940. In 1942 he relieved Rear Admiral CRACE in command of the Australian naval squadron which operated with the

U.S. Pacific Fleet in the war against Japan. In 1945 he was appointed Flag Officer Gibraltar.

C-STOFF. A German rocket-fuel mixture of hydrazine hydrate and methyl alcohol.

CUB. U.S. Navy term for a self-contained mobile unit capable of setting up and operating a medium-size advance supply base to support forces afloat. A Cub, smaller than a LION, provided fuel, supplies and ammunition.

CULTIVATOR NUMBER 6. An earth-cutting machine devised in 1939–40 on the impulse of Winston CHURCHILL, its purpose being to make a large groove through which infantry and tanks could readily reach enemy front lines. It was of course created with the trench-warfare conditions of the First World War in mind and did not find application in the Second. Churchill observed, however, "I am responsible but impenitent."

CULVERIN. Code name of a plan much discussed in 1943 for an Allied attack on the Japanese-held Netherlands East Indies, particularly the northern tip of Sumatra. Culverin was not carried out.

CUMMINGS, William (1902–1945). American Roman Catholic priest who is credited with having said "There are no atheists in foxholes." A civilian in Manila when the war began, he was captured at BATAAN and died of starvation on a Japanese prison ship.

CUNNINGHAM, Sir Alan (1887–). In 1940–41 Lt. Gen. Sir Alan Cunningham, GOC Kenya, commanded the offensive that captured Kismayu and then covered the thousand miles to Addis Ababa swiftly and with little loss of life. In August 1941 he left Kenya to command the EIGHTH ARMY in the Western Desert, but during the CRUSADER offensive General AUCHINLECK, who felt that Cunningham was thinking too defensively, replaced him with Lt. Gen. Neil RITCHIE. After leaving Eighth Army, Cunningham served as commandant of the Staff College, Camberley; GOC Northern Ireland; and GOC Eastern Command.

CUNNINGHAM, Sir Andrew Browne (1883–1963). Admiral Cunningham, later Viscount Cunningham of Hyndhope, was, by general agreement, one of the truly outstanding naval leaders of the war. He was especially admired by General EISENHOWER, who after working with him in North Africa used him as a standard; So-and-so, Eisenhower would say by way of praise, was almost as good as Cunningham.

Cunningham made his name as a destroyer captain during the First World War, and between the two world wars his career followed the normal naval pattern. He reached flag rank in 1932. He disliked all staff work and, in his own words, an appointment to the Admiralty "filled him with horror." When the First Sea Lord, Sir Roger Backhouse, fell seriously ill in March 1939, Cunningham assumed his duties, representing the Navy at the meetings of the Committee of Imperial Defence, but with the international situation degenerating rapidly into war and with no sign of Backhouse's health improving (in fact he died in July 1939), it was decided to bring Sir Alfred Dudley POUND, Commander in Chief Mediterranean, home as First Sea Lord, replacing him with Cunningham, with the rank of acting admiral.

So it was that Cunningham at the outbreak of the war was commanding in the Mediterranean. It proved an admirable appointment, for Cunningham had the invaluable quality of inspiring supreme confidence in all who served with him. He was the very picture of a fighting admiral, with a genial countenance and piercing blue eyes and a memory that never forgot the face of anyone who had served with him. Although the Italian Navy far outnumbered the British Mediterranean Fleet, in skill and expertise it was vastly inferior.

When Italy declared war in 1940, Cunningham was almost at once deprived of his main fleet base at MALTA, but he recognized that the small island was the key to the whole Mediterranean and African campaign. It was his task to keep Malta supplied with weapons, ammunition, oil and food, but to a bold commander this also presented opportunities of hitting at the Italians. And Cunningham was nothing if not bold. The FLEET AIR ARM attack on TARANTO in 1940 put three Italian battleships out of action, and the night battle of CAPE MATAPAN in 1941 sent three 10,000-ton Italian cruisers and two destroyers to the bottom without loss to Cunningham's fleet. With these two strokes he achieved a moral ascendancy over the enemy that was virtually absolute.

When the Italian lack of success in North Africa and Greece brought German army and air forces to their aid, the tide in the Mediterranean turned dangerously. German dive-bombers made the running of supplies to Malta extremely hazardous, and the successive evacuations of British forces from Greece and then from Crete were immensely costly in ships, particularly destroyers. Yet Cunningham was as indomitable in defeat as he had been in victory. Somehow the essential tasks were performed; Malta was kept supplied—though at increasing cost in ships and crews—and the fortress of TOBRUK, cut off by Axis armies, was regularly replenished by the battered ships of Cunningham's command.

In June 1942 Cunningham arrived in Washington as the First Sea Lord's representative on the COMBINED CHIEFS OF STAFF Committee, but after three months he returned to action as naval commander in chief for the landings in NORTHWEST AFRICA. The victory in Africa in May 1943 removed all the threats against Malta, and it was from this central base in the Mediterranean that Cunningham was able to plan and execute the great amphibious assaults which turned the Mediterranean Sea into a vast Allied lake and knocked Italy out of the war. The crowning vindication of his whole strategic concept of the Mediterranean campaign came when the surrendered Italian fleet anchored under the guns of Malta, led there by H.M.S. WARSPITE, his flagship at the start of the war.

Cunningham had by now reached the rank of Admiral of the Fleet, and in a matter of weeks he was to be appointed to the highest position in the naval hierarchy, that of First Sea Lord, following the death of Sir Dudley Pound. In June 1946 he retired to his home at Bishop's Waltham, close enough to Portsmouth to keep in contact with the Navy which he had served so well.

CUNNINGHAM, Sir John (1885–1962). Vice-admiral commanding the First Cruiser Squadron at the outbreak of the war, Cunningham was in command of the naval force supporting General DE GAULLE's abortive attempt to occupy DAKAR in 1940. After two years in the Admiralty as Fourth Sea Lord he went to the Mediterranean as Commander in Chief Levant at the time of the Allied invasion of North Africa, and succeeded Adm. Sir Andrew CUNNINGHAM (no relation) as Commander in Chief Mediterranean when the latter was recalled to London to become First Sea Lord. After the end of the war he again succeeded Sir Andrew Cunningham, serving as First Sea Lord from 1946 to 1948, when he retired.

CURLY. Allied code name given to a German 21-inch submarine torpedo incorporating a mechanism causing it to pursue a looping course in search of a target.

CURTIN, John (1885–1945). Australian political leader, elected in 1935 to head the Labour Party. In 1939 he pledged that the party would give full support to the war against Germany but, because of party rules, he refused to join in a coalition government. In 1941 Sir Arthur William FADDEN's ministry was defeated in a vote of censure; Curtin thus became Prime Minister a few weeks before Japan entered the war.

Because Australia's field forces were serving in the Middle East, the entry of Japan seemed to present an immediately critical situation, and Curtin directly asked the United States for aid. Australia, to add to the impact of this request, made a separate declaration of war against Japan in 1941 instead of entering (as she had in 1939 against Germany) by virtue of the British declaration. But Curtin said he had been misunderstood: he believed fully in the British Commonwealth but he also knew that it alone could not save Australia as the Japanese forces moved southward.

Despite his previous attitudes, he did not hesitate to introduce conscription in Australia. He was, however, confronted with parliamentary difficulties between 1941 and 1943. His cabinet was inexperienced and the Labour Party was not in the majority in the Senate and was sometimes in difficulty in the House, where the Prime Minister was dependent upon the votes of the independent members and where in June 1943 his ministry escaped a censure motion by only one vote. In the general election of 1943, however, he won a huge victory, and for the first time since 1914 the Labour Party had a majority in both houses. Curtin visited London in 1944 and while returning home he became seriously ill; although he was able to resume his duties, the illness led to serious congestion of the lungs. He died in June 1945.

CUSHING, James (1910?–1963). U.S. Army officer (lieutenant colonel) who after the fall of the PHILIPPINES acted as commander of guerrilla forces on the island of Cebu. In April 1944 he was demoted to private in a radiogram from General MACARTHUR because he released a high-ranking Japanese prisoner (Admiral FUKUDOME) in order to stop reprisals on civilians. He was later reinstated.

CUTLER, Elliot Carr (1888–1947). In the early years of the war, Dr. Cutler headed the medical aid division of the Massachusetts Committee on Public Safety, organizing a system of emergency preparedness which served as a national model. A lieutenant colonel in the Army Medical Corps Reserve, he was called to active service in 1942 as chief consultant in surgery and later chief of professional services, Office of the Chief Surgeon, European Theater of Operations. As a result of his work, he was promoted ultimately to brigadier general and awarded numerous U.S. and foreign decorations.

Cutler performed the first successful surgery on the valves of the human heart in 1923. His book *Atlas of Surgery* was a medical classic of its time.

CVETKOVIĆ, Dragiša (1893–1969). Prime Minister of Yugoslavia from 1939 to 1941. Though he made efforts to reconcile the Serbs, Croats and Slovenes in his country to bolster national unity and a foreign policy of neutrality, Cvetković eventually yielded to Adolf HITLER's pressure and formally joined the TRIPARTITE PACT on March 25, 1941. Three days later a bloodless coup deposed Cvetković and the regency of Prince PAUL in favor of leaders who were not pro-Axis.

CYPRESS. Allied code name for a Japanese primary trainer used by the Army as the Ki 86 and by the Navy as the K9W1 (*see* KI 86; K9W1).

CYRENAICA. The eastern province of Libya, scene of most of the fighting in North Africa during 1940–42. Cyrenaica is part of the Western Desert, but the Jebel Akhdar (Green Mountains) region around BENGHAZI, sometimes called the Cyrenaican Bulge, has fresh water and can support limited settlement and cultivation.

CZECHOSLOVAKIA. One of the longest steps toward World War II was taken in MUNICH in 1938, when the SUDETENLAND in Czechoslovakia was handed over to the Germans. During the depressed 1930s there had in fact been considerable discontent in that area, occupied by ethnic Germans, partly because the people were German, but also because unemployment was particularly high there and because the presence of border fortifications caused the Czech authorities to institute some security measures that were regarded as repressive. The Sudeten Nazis were able to magnify all these grievances and were duly rewarded at Munich, when the territory was transferred to Germany—and with it the strategic areas and fortifications. With German connivance, Slovakia became autonomous, resulting in a truly hyphenated Czecho-Slovakia. On March 15, 1939, this rump republic disappeared when the Germans occupied BOHEMIA AND MORAVIA.

The Czech National Committee, first in France and then, after the defeat of France, in England, assumed the leadership of anti-Nazi Czechs and allied itself with the resistance at home. In May 1942, at its direction, Reinhard HEYDRICH, the Reich Protector, was murdered, a deed that expressed the authority of the government-in-exile and may have had some value for morale purposes but that led to a wave of savage repression, the most famous instance of which was the destruction of the village of LIDICE. In early 1944 the Red Army appeared in the eastern tip of Czechoslovakia, but its progress was slow and a Slovak rebellion that began in August was put down by the Germans. On May 4, 1945, Prague rose against the occupying Germans; after four days of fighting the Germans acknowledged defeat and departed. The Red Army moved in on May 11, and on May 16 Eduard BENEŠ, the head of the government-in-exile, returned to take the lead in re-creating the republic.

D

D1A2-K. A Japanese Navy Aichi trainer (Allied code name, Susie) used to a limited extent.

D3A. Aichi Type 99 carrier dive-bomber (Allied code name, Val), the Japanese Navy's most important such aircraft during the first years of the Pacific war. The D3A1 was characterized by its radial engine, elliptical wings and stabilizers, underwing dive brakes and fixed landing gear. The later D3A2 had a more powerful engine (1,300 horsepower—up from 1,075) and a more streamlined "greenhouse." It carried about 820 pounds of bombs.

Aichi D3A2 goes into action

D4Y. Japanese Navy–designed *Suisei* (Comet) (Allied code name, Judy) carrier dive-bomber. Four versions, designated D4Y1 through D4Y4, were produced, varying in power plant and performance. The *Suisei* was used for reconnaissance as well as dive-bombing and KAMIKAZE attacks. Some were fitted for night interception in 1945, with a 20-mm. gun mounted in a SCHRÄGE MUSIK–type installation.

DACHAU. The so-called model CONCENTRATION CAMP founded by Heinrich HIMMLER in March 1933 with SS Col. Theodor Eicke as its first commandant. Many SS personnel who were later to be prominent in concentration camp administration were trained at Dachau, including Rudolf HOESS, who was in charge at AUSCHWITZ. Dachau became one of the centers for the hideous experiments with human victims conducted by SS Dr. Sigmund RASCHER, who studied the possibilities of human survival in low-pressure chambers and when subjected to intense freezing. The camp, located near Munich, was liberated by the Allied armies on April 29, 1945, and later became the site for a memorial to the great numbers who died there.

DAI ICHI BUILDING. Office building in downtown Tokyo, across from the moat around the imperial palace. It became the headquarters of Gen. Douglas MACARTHUR for the occupation of Japan.

DAISY CUTTER. A U.S. general-purpose BOMB equipped with an extension, approximately 36 inches long, on its nose fuze to ensure its detonation above the ground, making it particularly effective against personnel.

DAKAR. On September 23, 1940, a combined British and Free French force attempted a landing at Dakar, on the West African coast. Their object was to occupy the city as a starting point to rally the French African colonies to General DE GAULLE. The mission—Operation Menace—lost its secrecy, floundered in fog and met resistance. Faced with failure, the force withdrew. After the Allied invasion of French North Africa in 1942, Governor General Pierre Boisson negotiated with the Americans and arranged for the full cooperation of French West Africa.

DAKOTA. *See* C-47.

DALADIER, Edouard (1884–1970). French Radical Socialist politician and protégé of Radical leader Edouard HERRIOT, Daladier entered politics in 1919. Three times Premier, in 1933, 1934 and, his longest tenure, 1938–40, the misnamed "Bull of Vaucluse" was also Minister of War between 1936 and 1940 and thus bore the greatest political responsibility for France's defense preparations. In 1936 Daladier sponsored a large rearmament program and a limited program to nationalize selected war industries. He also became closely associated with the Army Commander in Chief, Maurice GAMELIN, to whom he deferred on most military matters, devoting his own efforts to attempts to create coalition governments capable of handling France's complex economic, social and diplomatic problems.

Although a staunch republican, Daladier—who had survived Verdun—had a keen appreciation of the effects of the nation's World War I experience, and his restrained policies doubtless reflected the feelings of many Frenchmen. Suspicious of conservative Army leaders, he felt comfortable with the moderate Gamelin and his cautious strategy based on economic mobilization and a draftee army. For France, the next war would have to be one of economic rather than manpower attrition. Daladier thus led his party in opposing a more offensive military policy of the type advocated by Paul REYNAUD and Charles DE GAULLE, and tended to believe that the Army's main task would be to guard the country's frontiers rather than actively assist her East European allies.

Once Germany's attack on Poland forced a French declaration of war, Daladier was content to let Gamelin's lengthy mobilization process slowly proceed.

Dachau: GIs hold SS guards at gunpoint

The defection of the French Communist Party, and the hope of the Right that France's war effort could somehow be directed against Bolshevik Russia, narrowed the Premier's base of support and limited his scope of action. Characterized as sluggish, plodding but tireless, he was never able to unite either Parliament or the people behind the war effort. After an autumn and winter of what was called the PHONY WAR, his government came under increasing criticism for the Army's inactivity. However, it was the SOVIET-FINNISH WAR, which began in December 1939, that led to Daladier's downfall.

In January 1940 France and Britain began making plans to assist Finland with troops and supplies, to be sent through neutral Norway and Sweden. Their real purpose appears to have been to gain a foothold in Scandinavia and cut Germany off from her principal source of iron ore. But the end of Finnish resistance on March 12 brought the project to a halt, and Daladier was blamed for both the Russian victory and the Allied failure to interdict German trade. Proponents of war with Germany wanted a stronger leader at the helm, and opponents hoped for a weaker successor. As a result, on March 20, 1940, Daladier resigned the premiership; he was succeeded the next day by his Finance Minister and political rival, Paul Reynaud.

Still a powerful leader in the key Radical Party, Daladier was able to retain his portfolio as Minister of War, and he continued to defend Gamelin and his conduct of the war. Thus, although militarily strong, France was still politically weak on the eve of the German attack in May. The French debacle at SEDAN finally led to the ouster of both Daladier and Gamelin, although the former stayed in the government as Minister of Foreign Affairs until June 5.

Arrested by the VICHY government in September 1940, Daladier was tried at RIOM early in 1942 for his part in the French defeat, but defended himself vigorously and with honor. Handed over to the Germans the following year, he was liberated in 1945 and successfully reentered politics after the end of the war.

DALTON, Hugh (1887–1962). A Labour member of the British Parliament after World War I, Dalton served as parliamentary undersecretary at the Foreign Office between 1929 and 1931 under Prime Minister Ramsay MacDonald. In Winston CHURCHILL's wartime coalition cabinet he became Minister of Economic Warfare (1940) and President of the Board of Trade (1942). In 1945 he was named Chancellor of the Exchequer by Clement ATTLEE, but he later was forced to resign as the result of a budget leakage.

DAMASKINOS, Archbishop (1891–1949). When the peasant-born Damaskinos was elected archbishop of Athens and all Greece in 1938, the pro-Nazi Premier Joannes METAXAS annulled the election and exiled Damaskinos to a monastery. After the Germans occupied Greece, Damaskinos returned to Athens in 1941 as archbishop and fought the Germans with all the power of his office, even offering himself as a hostage to the Nazis. Throughout the war he aided the Greek resistance movement and war internees. After the Allies liberated Greece, Damaskinos served as Regent, from December 31, 1944, to September 28, 1946 (part of this time as Premier), when he stepped down in favor of King GEORGE II.

DAM BUSTERS. On the night of May 16, 1943, No. 617 Squadron, RAF, under Wing Comdr. Guy GIBSON, carried out a precision bombing raid which breached the Möhne and Eder dams in Germany. The squadron was specially trained in low-level flying and SKIP BOMBING techniques and used a new rotating bomb designed by Barnes WALLIS. The aim of the operation was to release the water vital to Ruhr industry from the Möhne, Eder, Sorpe, Lister and Schwelme dams. The results of the raid, though devastating, were not as great as the breaching of the Sorpe dam would have caused. The story of the Dam Busters is told in Guy Gibson's book *Enemy Coast Ahead* (1946) and in Paul Brickhill's *Dam Busters* (1951).

DANZIG. This Baltic port on the Vistula River, with a 96 percent German population, became a free city under a League of Nations high commissioner in 1920 to provide a seaport for newly independent Poland. With a German internal administration but a foreign policy and a customs office controlled by Poland, and a vocal Polish minority, Danzig was the source of German-Polish friction even before the local elections of May 1933 handed the city to the indigenous Nazi Party under Gauleiter Albert Forster. Though there was some intermittent improvement in affairs after the German-Polish nonaggression pact of 1934, the city became the focus of international tension after October 1938, when Adolf HITLER demanded the political, if not the economic, reunification of Danzig with the Reich and concessions for an extraterritorial railroad and motor road across the Polish Corridor, separating Danzig from Germany proper.

Through the summer of 1939 Hitler alternated cajolery with threats. In July the French newspaper *L'Œuvre* published an editorial with a title that became a symbol of shortsighted appeasement: "Why Die for Danzig?" Having decided on war by early August 1939 despite the British guarantee to Poland, Hitler kept up a diplomatic pretense. But the League high commissioner was sent packing, and Danzig was forcibly returned to Germany, as the war began on September 1, 1939, with the old battleship SCHLESWIG-HOLSTEIN firing from Danzig harbor in support of German troops operating in the Polish Corridor.

DANZIG. German code word (contained in order of November 20, 1939) to proceed with planned offensive in the west. The armies were supposed to be ready to deliver the offensive "at a moment's notice" in order to "take immediate advantage of favorable weather." Although Hitler pushed hard for an autumn offensive, the attack in the west did not in fact take place until May 1940. The earlier code equivalent of Danzig was Rhein (Rhine).

D'AQUINO, Iva. *See* TOKYO ROSE.

DAR 10F. This airplane (DAR stands for Darjavna Aeroplanna Rabotilnitza—State Airplane Factory) was a Bulgarian-designed and -built two-place, single-engine light bomber and dive-bomber. It was the only Bulgarian combat aircraft of indigenous design to be manufactured; it was not used in operations. Powered by a 950-horsepower radial engine, it had a maximum speed of 295 miles per hour and carried one 550-pound or four 110-pound bombs.

DARBY, William Orlando (1911–1945). U.S. Army officer, then a major, assigned by General EISENHOWER to interview and select officers for a specialized force that came to be known as the RANGERS. Colonel Darby was killed in action in Italy shortly before the end of the war while leading a combat team of the 10th Mountain Division.

DARLAN, Jean François (1881–1942). In June 1940 Admiral Darlan, Commander in Chief of the French Navy, assured Winston CHURCHILL that the French fleet would never fall into German hands. France surrendered, but Darlan did not order the French fleet to sail to British or neutral ports. A few days later he gave his allegiance to Marshal Philippe PÉTAIN and accepted a position as Minister of Marine in the VICHY regime. After February 1941, as Vice-Premier of Vichy, Darlan pursued a policy of limited cooperation with the Axis, but during this same period he confided to the U.S. ambassador, William D. LEAHY, that he would dissociate himself from collaboration if supported with adequate strength. Neither the Germans nor the Allies knew whether or not Darlan could be trusted.

Early in 1942 Darlan gave up his ministerial posts but was made head of all French forces, and in November 1942 he was in Algiers at the time of the Allied invasion. His authority was accepted by the French in North Africa, and General EISENHOWER designated him political head of French North Africa. The move was severely criticized. Darlan was assassinated on Christmas Eve by a French fanatic.

Much attacked in the press, distrusted by both countrymen and foreigners, Darlan left his best defense in the form of a letter to Churchill dated December 4, 1942, in which he stated simply: "I was obliged from January 1941 to April 1942 to adopt a policy which would prevent France and its Empire from being occupied and crushed by the Axis Powers." Although he bitterly opposed Darlan's handling of the fleet, Churchill paid careful tribute to Darlan and noted that, as he had promised, the French fleet never fell into German hands.

DARNAND, Joseph (1897–1945). A leading French collaborator with the Germans, head of an SS-style police force (*see* SS) called the Milice (militia) which fought the underground. After the war he was executed for treason.

DAUNTLESS. *See* SBD.

DAUNTLESS DOTTY. The U.S. B-29, piloted by Brig. Gen. Emmett ("Rosie") O'DONNELL, that led the first Superfortress attack upon Tokyo, launched on November 24, 1944, from the Marianas. *See also* B-29.

DAUTRY, Raoul (1880–1951). Noted French civil engineer and railroad expert who on September 13, 1939, was appointed Minister of Armaments. This summons to office, coming right after the start of the war and only eight months before the German invasion, allowed him little time to try to remedy the deficiencies resulting from years of neglect.

DAVE. Allied code name for the Nakajima E8N Japanese Navy reconnaissance floatplane (*see* E8N).

DAVIDSON, Lyal Ament (1886–1950). A 1910 graduate of the U.S. Naval Academy with an M.S. from Columbia in 1917, Davidson served as teacher as well as sailor prior to World War II. In November 1941 he became a rear admiral. He saw action as an attack group commander in several major western operations: TORCH, HUSKY, AVALANCHE and ANVIL-DRAGOON. In the invasion of SOUTHERN FRANCE he had overall command of naval gunfire. Davidson was decorated for his part in the operations off the north Sicilian coast. He retired in 1946.

DAVIES, Joseph Edward (1876–1958). American lawyer and politician who served as ambassador to the Soviet Union, 1936–38, and to Belgium, 1938–40. His best-selling memoirs *Mission to Moscow* (1941) showed the Soviet Union in a highly favorable light. During the war Davies worked as a special assistant to the Secretary of State in connection with various international conferences and performed special assignments for Presidents ROOSEVELT AND TRUMAN.

DAVIS, Elmer Holmes (1890–1958). From 1915 to 1924 Davis served as a reporter and editorial writer for the *New York Times*. Subsequently he wrote fiction, plays and essays. In 1939 he entered radio broadcasting as a news analyst for the Columbia Broadcasting System; this led to his appointment as director of the OFFICE OF WAR INFORMATION (OWI) in 1942. He held the position through World War II, being in effect the chief information officer for the entire American war effort. When the war ended, the OWI was dissolved and Davis, with his familiar Middle Western voice, returned to broadcasting as a regular commentator for the American Broadcasting Company.

DAVISON, Ralph Eugene (1895–1972). Rear Admiral Davison commanded a task group of fast carriers in the U.S. THIRD FLEET under Adm. William F. HALSEY during the LEYTE GULF campaign. His carrier attacks proved especially important during the Formosa air battle and the Battle of Cape Engaño (Leyte Gulf) in October 1944. Later he commanded another task force under Adm. Raymond A. SPRUANCE and the FIFTH FLEET. His carriers contributed air strikes against IWO JIMA in February and March 1945 and at OKINAWA immediately afterward. His task group was dissolved on April 17, 1945.

DAWLEY, Ernest Joseph (1886–). U.S. Army officer, member of the class of 1910 at West Point. On September 9, 1943, Dawley, a major general, was in command of the VI Corps in the invasion of ITALY at SALERNO. During the fighting on the beachhead his superiors lost confidence in him, and on September 20 he was relieved by Maj. Gen. John P. LUCAS, who was in turn to suffer a similar fate at ANZIO. Dawley reverted to the rank of colonel but was subsequently promoted to brigadier general and assigned to training and replacement commands.

DBX (Depth Bomb Explosive). A mixture of RDX, aluminum nitrate, TNT and powdered aluminum, American-developed to replace TORPEX. It used half the amount of then-critical RDX as Torpex and was half again as powerful as TNT when detonated underwater. When the RDX supply became adequate for wartime demands, DBX was shelved. *See also* RDX.

DD TANK. U.S. M4 medium tanks were equipped with detachable canvas "bloomers"—pleated screens that could be raised to float the tanks. The tanks had a duplex drive (hence "DD"), twin propellers for swimming as well as the normal tank drive for land. *See also* TANK.

DEANE, John R. (1896–). U.S. Army officer (major general) who participated in the Moscow CONFERENCE of foreign ministers in 1943 and remained in the Soviet Union as head of the U.S. Military Mission, serving in this post until the end of the war. He had previously been U.S. secretary of the COMBINED CHIEFS OF STAFF.

DEATH VALLEY. Valley in SAIPAN about 1,000 yards wide running north and south to the east of Mount Tapotchau—so called because Japanese artillery commanded it from the heights on either side. The slow advance of American infantrymen (27th Division) resulted in the dismissal of the division commander, Maj. Gen. Ralph C. SMITH, by Marine Lt. Gen. Holland M. SMITH.

DECLARATION OF LIMA. *See* LIMA CONFERENCE.

DECLARATION OF PANAMA. *See* PANAMA CONFERENCE.

DECLARATION OF UNION. A proposal for permanent union of the British and French empires and governments originated by Jean MONNET and Charles CORBIN and designed to bolster French morale and to keep France in the war. On June 16, 1940, Winston CHURCHILL and Charles DE GAULLE discussed this scheme, which was endorsed by the British cabinet but was not voted upon by the French cabinet.

DECORATIONS. *See specific decoration.*

DEFENSE COMMITTEE OF THE USSR. *See* State Defense Committee.

DEFENSIVELY EQUIPPED MERCHANT SHIPS (DEMS). The DEMS Organisation was established by the Royal Navy, in collaboration with the British merchant navy, to provide a measure of defensive armament to merchant shipping. Planning for this began in mid-1939. Guns were collected and distributed and ships made ready to receive them. Reservists and merchant sailors were trained in their use. Even with this preparation, the number of weapons and trained gunners proved quite inadequate for a world war. The nuclei of DEMS units were prewar reservists, but during the war thousands of recruits had to be procured and trained. Even then, the number of seagoing personnel available was still inadequate, and help had to be requested from the Army. Army guns and gunners were provided, to the extent possible, for shipboard use. A Maritime Regiment of Royal Artillery was created; this regiment numbered 14,000 men by 1944.

The guns available during the early war years were usually old ones, often surplus weapons removed from scrapped warships and stored years before. They varied extensively in type and caliber; anything that would work was used. Antiaircraft guns were in particularly short supply for a long while even for Navy ships, let alone for merchantmen. The 20-mm. Oerlikon and 40-mm. Bofors guns were especially coveted for use in European and Mediterranean waters, where Axis air attack was a constant threat. A worldwide system of redistribution of guns and crews was put into effect, whereby ships would have guns added or removed as they entered or departed areas of particular danger. By the end of the European war, Britain and the Commonwealth had armed some 9,500 ships, most of them oceangoing; like their counterparts in the U.S. Navy Armed Guard crews, men of the DEMS Organisation had done a deadly, difficult and largely unrecognized job with distinction. Many of them, especially in the Battle of the Atlantic, performed heroically against U-boats or Luftwaffe raiders.

DEFIANT. In 1935 the British Air Ministry called for the construction of a fighter in which all the armament was concentrated in a single power-driven turret. Boulton-Paul responded with the low-wing Defiant, powered by a 1,030-horsepower Merlin liquid-cooled engine and not much larger than a Hawker Hurricane. This resemblance to the Hurricane, which carried eight forward-firing machine guns, resulted in an impressive string of victories at Dunkirk, when German pilots mistook two-place Defiants for Hurricanes and attacked from the rear, diving into the murderous fire of four .303-caliber weapons. Luftwaffe airmen quickly realized the error, commenced attacking from the front and forced Fighter Command to shift the Defiant to night operations. During 1941, 13 squadrons of radar-equipped Defiants saw service in the nighttime defense of Great Britain. Defiant II, with a slightly more powerful engine, appeared in 1941; production ceased in February 1943.

DE GAULLE, Charles (1890–1970). One of France's foremost patriots and statesmen of the 20th century, de Gaulle emerged from relative obscurity during World War II to command the continuing French war effort after 1940. His character and many of his wartime policies were the result of a long period of development as an officer in the French Army. Prior to World War I, de Gaulle worked under the then Colonel Philippe Pétain and supported the future marshal's stress on firepower and his unsuccessful challenge to existing French offensive doctrines. During World War I, de Gaulle served with distinction as a company-grade infantry officer until his capture at Verdun in 1916. His unusual height (6 feet 4 inches) thwarted his attempts to escape, and the 32 months of confinement that followed seemed only to deepen his intense self-reliance, aloofness and penchant for thought and study. During this time he wrote the first draft of *Discord Among the Enemy,* published in 1924.

Following the 1918 armistice, de Gaulle joined the French volunteers fighting in Russia under Pilsudski and later, after renewing his friendship with Marshal Pétain, devoted himself to the study of history and military strategy. As a lecturer at the French War College and later as secretary general of the Council of National Defense, he began to question many of the military doctrines that were becoming rooted in the French Army as a result of its wartime experience. The Army's growing emphasis on firepower, detailed planning and defensive warfare to the detriment of other factors was

General de Gaulle leads a victory parade through the streets of Paris. With him are General Leclerc (center) and General Koenig

challenged by de Gaulle, and his stand gradually brought him into conflict with most of his superiors and finally with the marshal himself.

De Gaulle's first major work, *The Edge of the Sword,* published in 1932, stressed the importance of character and the mark of the individual, rather than the organization, on history. His second major book, *Vers l'Armée de Métier* (published in English as *The Army of the Future*), was more openly revolutionary. Here de Gaulle recommended that the Army return to an offensive strategy by creating a new, powerful striking force based on armored divisions and other modern equipment. Excessively praised, the work hardly reflected genius. After 1934 the controversial author allied himself with a leading French politician, Paul REYNAUD, to further his ideas, and in 1935 Reynaud officially asked the French cabinet to adopt a force similar to the one proposed by de Gaulle. But the idea was rejected by parliamentary and military leaders alike, and during the next five years de Gaulle lost most of his authority as a military spokesman.

De Gaulle's situation at first changed little with the outbreak of war in 1939. The outspoken officer had commanded tank units since 1937 and was now appointed commander of tanks in the French Fifth Army, a position with little command authority since most of the attached tank battalions were parceled out to corps and divisions for operational employment. However, de Gaulle continued to push his ideas and, following Germany's successful campaign in Poland, sent a letter to a number of leading French generals and politicians pointing out the danger of a similar attack against France and again urging the creation of a cohesive armored force. Ignored yet another time, de Gaulle hoped for a change when Reynaud succeeded Edouard DALADIER as Premier, but was again frustrated when the latter managed to retain his portfolio as Minister of War. The French Commander in Chief, Maurice GAMELIN, did relent enough to promise de Gaulle eventual command of the 4th Armored Division, which was to be organized in May, but nothing was done about the dispersion of French armor among existing infantry and cavalry units.

The Battle of FRANCE yielded only further disappointments for de Gaulle, who at 49 was the youngest general in the French Army. Assuming command of the 4th Armored in early May, he was ordered to take what was then a loose collection of newly organized battalions to the southern edge of the German breakthrough and cover several infantry formations moving up to protect Paris. On May 18 de Gaulle's unit began one of the few offensive actions undertaken by the French Army, pushing north from the Aisne River near Laon. However, his partial advance was not followed up and instead the division was transferred west to Abbeville, where it exhausted itself trying to eliminate German bridgeheads over the Somme.

On June 6, 1940, de Gaulle left the front for Paris to become Under Secretary of State to the Minister of National Defense (and War), Reynaud having finally taken the latter position away from Daladier. Henceforth de Gaulle's efforts were devoted to shoring up the sagging determination of the cabinet to continue the war effort. In this task he was opposed not only by the new French Army commander, Gen. Maxime WEYGAND, but also by his old commander and former mentor, Marshal Pétain. On June 9 de Gaulle met with Winston CHURCHILL in London to coordinate the war effort.

Returning to France, de Gaulle found the military situation worse and the government fleeing Paris. He immediately urged Reynaud to replace the pessimistic Weygand and argued for a final stand in Brittany or for provisions at least to be made to continue the war from North Africa. In this, de Gaulle was frustrated as much by Reynaud's weakening will as by the efforts of Pétain and other "defeatists." When he returned from his second meeting with Churchill on June 16, Reynaud had resigned; Pétain quickly formed a new government. At that point de Gaulle was virtually kidnapped from France by Maj. Gen. Sir Edward L. SPEARS and flown to London (some say to the extreme displeasure of Churchill, whom Spears represented in Paris). On the announcement of Pétain's request for an armistice on June 18, he began his personal campaign to keep France in the struggle. He was not to return to France until June 14, 1944.

During the next week, with the support of the British Government, de Gaulle began a series of radio broadcasts from London denouncing the armistice and later the Pétain government and appealing to all Frenchmen for support. Special appeals were made to French forces still in Britain and to the individual colonies, but the results were disappointing. Only two colonial generals declared for de Gaulle, and the Pétain regime quickly condemned the general as a traitor. Undaunted, de Gaulle went about his self-appointed task of preserving the honor and greatness of France. He looked the part—a commanding presence, with erect bearing and distinctive features (including an elephantine nose that was the delight of cartoonists). His confidence, his boldness and even his hauteur and arrogance he believed essential to his task. "Je suis la France," he proclaimed. His creation of what was to be called the Free French (later, the Fighting French) military forces proved to be an agonizing task, as is made plain in the entry FREE FRANCE.

By May 1944 de Gaulle's movement had created a provisional government of France. Prior to the Normandy INVASION in June, de Gaulle had a major contest with his reluctant allies. The U.S. Government wished to move into France with no political commitments, whereas de Gaulle demanded that his provisional government have full political authority over any liberated French territory. The situation was saved when the Allied Supreme Commander, Gen. Dwight EISENHOWER, privately agreed to recognize no French political power other than de Gaulle. In any case, once the invasion proved successful and the Allies began their drive through France, most Frenchmen rallied to de Gaulle and the question of American or British approval became moot. Then, on August 26, 1944, the long-exiled leader entered newly liberated Paris and the welcome was tumultuous. In a meeting with the National Council for the Resistance he reiterated his thesis that it was unnecessary to reestablish the republic since the VICHY regime had always been illegal and the Third Republic, in concept, had never ceased to exist. As promised, the provisional government arrived in France the following month and in November created a provisional consultative assembly with representatives of all Free French and Resistance organizations as well as a number of former deputies of the Third Republic.

De Gaulle's triumphs were short-lived. He visited Moscow in December 1944 to sign a Franco-Soviet pact, but was not invited to the YALTA CONFERENCE. At home, his troubles were more pressing. Although he managed to dissolve or nationalize most of the paramilitary Resistance organizations and ward off French Communist demands for local autonomy, he was unable to cope with the country's great economic problems. Despite the nationalization of many key industries in an effort to restore order, inflation became rampant and the black market flourished. De Gaulle's efforts to establish a strong central government also met with failure. The French supported by a wide margin his referendum seeking to create a new constitution, but the October 1945 elections for a constitutional assembly were dominated by older political leaders who distrusted the general's desire for a strong executive. De Gaulle himself remained committed to a democratic form of government, which he associated with France's history and her "grandeur," and had no intention of becoming a dictator. But in the hope that his absence would make the new delegates more amenable to creating a stronger government, he finally resigned as provisional president on January 20, 1946. He would not return actively to politics until 1958, when, as Premier, he was again faced with the task of creating a new constitution. He became President of France in 1959.

De Gaulle served as President until April 1969, when he resigned after an unsatisfactory vote in a referendum on a minor detail of France's new regional structure. He retired to his home in Colombey-les-Deux-Eglises, where he died suddenly on November 10, 1970, just short of his 80th birthday. He was survived by his wife, Yvonne Vendroux de Gaulle, whom he had married in 1921, and two children. He was also survived by France, and in announcing his death President Pompidou declared, "France is a widow." **J.C./M.H.B.**

DEGAUSSING. The process by which a ship was rendered nonmagnetic (by means of electrical coils bearing a current that neutralized the magnetic field of the ship) and as a result of which it would not detonate magnetic MINES. It was developed by the British in 1939–40.

DE GUINGAND, Sir Francis (1900–). A graduate of the Royal Military College at Sandhurst, de Guingand served in 1939–40 as military assistant to the British Secretary of State for War. After a tour in intelligence he became in 1942 the director of military intelligence for the Middle East. In July of that year he was named chief of staff of the British EIGHTH ARMY. Gen. Sir Bernard L. MONTGOMERY arrived in August, and de Guingand got along so well with his new commander that in April 1943 he was promoted to major general and given the responsibility of planning for the invasion of SICILY. This division of effort permitted Montgomery to devote his full attention to military operations in northern TUNISIA. De Guingand moved with Montgomery to England in 1944 and remained in the position of chief of staff of the 21st ARMY GROUP to the end of the war. Well liked by General EISENHOWER, the diplomatic de Guingand was often able to resolve misunderstandings between Montgomery and the Supreme Commander.

DEIR EL SHEIN. A "box" in the Alamein Line in Egypt, taken by Gen. Erwin ROMMEL's forces in the First Battle of ALAMEIN, July 1, 1942. This was the Germans' deepest penetration into Egypt.

DELESTRAINT, Charles (1879–1945). Captured in the opening battles of World War I, Delestraint returned to serve in the French armored forces, commanding a unit in which Charles de Gaulle saw service. General Delestraint retired in 1939 but was called back to duty as a senior staff officer and commander in the French armored forces. He continued active opposition to the Germans after the armistice, taking command of the Gaullist SECRET ARMY in 1943. He was arrested by the Germans that summer and ultimately shot by them at Dachau.

DEMON. Code name for the evacuation of British forces from Greece, April 24–May 1, 1941. Demon was also the name given to the British occupation of ABADAN, Persia, August 25, 1941. In American usage, DEMON was the code name for the U.S. Navy.

DEMPSEY, Sir Miles (1896–1969). British Army officer, a veteran of World War I, who in 1940 commanded the 13th Infantry Brigade in France and fought in the rear guard which covered the DUNKIRK evacuation. Back in England he served with the Canadians; then, after ALAMEIN, he took over the 13th Corps, which he led in SICILY and in the invasion of ITALY. Dempsey assumed command of the British SECOND ARMY in January 1944. He was knighted for his work in Normandy. A lieutenant general, Dempsey retained his command until the German surrender, at which time elements of the Second Army were east of the Elbe River.

DENTZ, Fernand (1871–1945). As military governor of Paris in 1940, General Dentz surrendered the city to the Germans. Named high commissioner in SYRIA, he directed the defense of that territory against a British–Free French invasion in 1941, for which he was convicted in 1945. He died in prison. *See also* FREE FRANCE.

DER GROSSE SCHLAG (The Great Blow). Code name for the part in the Battle of the BULGE played by the LUFTWAFFE. The Great Blow was delivered on New Year's Day 1945, by which time the land battle had gone against the Germans.

DE RUYTER. Netherlands cruiser of 6,450 tons completed at Schiedam in 1935. *De Ruyter* was armed with seven 5.9-inch guns and smaller antiaircraft weapons and carried two aircraft. She was the flagship of Adm. Karel DOORMAN in February 1942. Doorman's squadron, which consisted of two 8-inch- and three 6-inch-gun cruisers—British, Netherlands, American and Australian—and a number of destroyers, was ordered to repel a Japanese invasion fleet heading for JAVA. The squadron, however, had only weak air cover, its ships had not trained together and most of the crews were exhausted. In consequence, on meeting the Japanese escorting force, including 8-inch-gun cruisers, Doorman's cruiser squadron was destroyed despite tenacious fighting. *De Ruyter* herself blew up following a torpedo hit from the Japanese cruiser HAGURO. The destruction of the squadron revealed to the Allies for the first time that certain Japanese cruisers had been rearmed with 8-inch guns and that the Japanese LONG LANCE 24-inch torpedo was an exceptionally powerful weapon.

DESERT ARMY. The British Army that fought in North Africa in 1940–43 started as the Western Desert Force (June 1940), expanded into the 13th Corps (January 1941) and finally grew into the EIGHTH ARMY (September 1941).

DESERT RATS. Affectionate nickname for the men of the British 7th Armored Division in North Africa, who took as their emblem the Libyan jerboa. This desert rat is quick and has a reputation for survival.

DESTROYER ESCORT. A type of seagoing antisubmarine patrol and escort ship, mass-produced in the United States by prefabrication. Between late 1941 and mid-1943, 1,005 DEs were ordered. Seventy-eight of these went to England; six were transferred to France. Six more, originally commissioned in the U.S. Navy, were transferred to Brazil in 1944 for duty in the South Atlantic. In the fall of 1943, 305 ships were canceled, and 135 more during 1944, as the Allies gained control of the Atlantic and shipbuilding priorities shifted from antisubmarine ships to the landing craft needed for amphibious offensives in the Atlantic and Pacific. DEs were built to six different designs, identified not only by the conventional lead-ship designation but by a letter code denoting the combination of machinery plant and gun armament carried:

Evarts (DE-5) class, type GMT (diesel-electric, 3-inch guns, short hull)
Buckley (DE-51) class, type TE (turboelectric, 3-inch guns, long hull)
Cannon (DE-99) class, type DET (diesel-electric, 3-inch guns, long hull)
Edsall (DE-129) class, type FMR (Fairbanks-Morse geared diesels, 3-inch guns, long hull)
Rudderow (DE-224) class, type TEV (turboelectric, 5-inch guns, long hull)
John C. Butler (DE-339) class, type WGT (Westinghouse geared turbines, 5-inch guns, long hull)

The earliest design was the Evarts class, drawn up by Gibbs & Cox to British specifications. These ships, 289 feet 5 inches long, were referred to as "short hull" escorts; the other classes, measuring 306 feet, were known as "long hull" types. DEs were armed with two 5-INCH 38-caliber or three 3-inch 50-caliber dual-purpose guns and 40-mm. and 20-mm. antiaircraft guns. Some earlier DEs mounted 1.1-inch guns in lieu of 40-mm. weapons. Many had a triple 21-inch torpedo tube mount, removed earlier from old FLUSH-DECKERS (destroyers). All carried depth-charge tracks and side-throwing depth-charge projectors; these were later supplemented, in many ships, by ahead-throwing antisubmarine projectors.

Though slower than contemporary fleet destroyers (trial speeds, depending upon the class involved, ran from 20.9 to 24.3 knots), DEs proved better antisubmarine ships because of their superior maneuverability. The most remarkable accomplishment of a wartime DE was that of *England*, credited with sinking five Japanese submarines and assisting in the sinking of a sixth, May 19–31, 1944; this earned her a PRESIDENTIAL UNIT CITATION. Ninety-four ships of the Buckley and Rudderow classes were converted to high-speed transports (APD), capable of carrying and landing a company of troops; they were used to transport raiding parties and underwater demolition teams.

DESTROYERS–BASES DEAL. In May 1940, shortly after becoming Prime Minister, Winston CHURCHILL asked President ROOSEVELT for "the loan of forty or fifty of your older destroyers to bridge the gap between what we have now and the large new construction we put in hand at the beginning of the war." After the fall of France in June, the need was widely seen in Washington as urgent, but the President was forbidden by law to dispose of any military matériel unless it was certified by the appropriate service chief as useless for American defense. Finally Roosevelt decided to link the transfer of the destroyers to the acquisition by the United States of leases for naval and air bases in British possessions in the western Atlantic; the total exchange, or deal, was clearly a strengthening of American defense, as the law required. As finally announced on September 3, 1940, the United States transferred 50 destroyers of World War I vintage to Britain and received the rights to 99-year leases on bases in Newfoundland, Bermuda, the Bahamas, Jamaica, Antigua, St. Lucia, Trinidad and British Guiana. A vital if intangible aspect of the exchange was the fact that for the United States it was a long step forward in the undeclared war.

DEUTSCHLAND (ship). *See* LÜTZOW.

DEVASTATOR. *See* TBD.

DEVEREUX, James P. S. (1903–). U.S. Marine officer, commissioned from the ranks in 1925, who commanded the Marine detachment (from the 1st Defense Battalion) on WAKE ISLAND in December 1941. He and the other survivors of the Japanese attack spent the war years in prison camps. He was on active duty until 1948, retiring as a brigadier general.

DEVERS, Jacob Loucks (1887–). Commander of the U.S. 6th Army Group during the campaign in Europe. Devers graduated from West Point in 1909. He did not serve overseas during World War I, but carried out various assignments in France and Germany from May to August 1919, when he reverted to his permanent rank of captain. He graduated from the Command and General Staff College in 1926 and the Army War College in 1933. In October 1940, as a temporary major general, he became commanding general of the 9th Infantry Division. Gen. George C. MARSHALL in August 1941 personally selected Devers to head the Army's growing armored force at Fort Knox, Ky., and later sent him to North Africa as a personal observer. Devers was promoted to lieutenant general in September 1942.

Moving on to England, Devers in May 1943 became Commanding General, EUROPEAN THEATER OF OPERATIONS, U.S. ARMY (ETOUSA), more or less as a caretaker for Gen. Dwight EISENHOWER. When Eisenhower took over the Supreme Command (and ETOUSA) in England, Devers, effective December 31, 1943, replaced Eisenhower as Commanding General, NORTH AFRICAN THEATER OF OPERATIONS, U.S. ARMY (NATOUSA); Devers also became the Deputy Supreme Allied Commander, Mediterranean (Deputy SACMED). In September 1944 he became commander of the 6th Army Group, which consisted of the U.S. SEVENTH ARMY and the French First Army. This army group, for which Eisenhower envisaged a relatively minor role compared with those of Gen. Omar BRADLEY's 12th Army Group and Gen. Sir B. L. MONTGOMERY's 21st Army Group, played a significant role in the defeat of Germany, a contribution that could well have been of much greater importance had Eisenhower employed Devers's command to its full potential.

Of charming mien and winning smile, Devers possessed boyish features, noticeable ears and slightly bowed legs. He was popular with troops, but Eisenhower doubted his judgment. Devers ran his army group quite differently from the fashion of his American opposite, Bradley of 12th Army Group. Devers commanded in a rather easy manner, leaving detailed planning to his two principal subordinates—PATCH of Seventh Army and de LATTRE DE TASSIGNY of French First Army. For the most part Bradley dealt only with his army commanders, whereas Devers was a familiar figure at the headquarters of his armies, corps and divisions.

Following the war Devers (who was made four-star general in March 1945) became Commanding General, Army Ground Forces. He retired in November 1949.

DEWEY, Thomas Edmund (1902–1971). A lawyer, Dewey was a special prosecutor and then district attorney in New York City. In 1938, as a result of his increasing popularity, he was selected by the Republican Party as its nominee to challenge Herbert Lehman, the Democratic governor of New York; Dewey lost by a small margin. As a result of his showing in the gubernatorial election, he was a strong contender for the Republican nomination for President in 1940, but Wendell L. WILLKIE won the nomination on the sixth ballot. After a brief period back in private law practice, Dewey again ran for governor in 1942 and this time was successful. He was reelected for a second term in 1946 and for a third term in 1950. Meanwhile, in 1944 he had won the Republican presidential nomination, but in November was defeated by Franklin ROOSEVELT. Four years later, in 1948, Dewey again ran for the presidency, but was again defeated, this time by Harry TRUMAN.

The United States was the only one of the belligerents to hold an election during the fighting, and in his 1944 campaign Dewey had the difficult problem of attacking the President while supporting the war and the American commanders.

DE WITT, John Lesesne (1880–1962). Commissioned a second lieutenant in the U.S. Army in October 1898, De Witt served with the 42d (Rainbow) Division in World War I. He was promoted to lieutenant general in 1939. Between March 1941 and September 1943 he commanded the Western Defense Area (the West Coast). He then became commandant of the Army and Navy Staff College, a position he held until November 1945. *See also* EVACUATION OF JAPANESE-AMERICANS.

DEWOITINE D-520. French single-engine, single-seat, low-wing fighter carrying one 20-mm. cannon and four 7.5-mm. machine guns. It was designed by a team led by Emile Dewoitine at the Société Nationale de Constructions Aéronautiques du Midi in 1937. Trials were completed in March 1939, and production began shortly thereafter. By the time of the Franco-German armistice, 411 had been built. Undoubtedly France's best and most successful fighter, the D-520 accounted for 114 enemy shot down and 39 probables. Adopted by the VICHY air force as the standard fighter, it was kept in limited production throughout the war. After Germany took over unoccupied France in November 1942, the D-520s were commandeered and used as fighter-trainers for the LUFTWAFFE or given to the Italian Regia Aeronautica for a similar purpose. Some were employed operationally by the air forces of Bulgaria and Rumania. As the Germans began retreating from southern France, former French pilots took over surviving models, formed a squadron and fought Axis forces. The plane flew at a maximum speed of 329 miles per hour and had a normal range of 620 miles. Loaded weight, 6,129 pounds maximum; wingspan, 33 feet 5½ inches; length, 28 feet 8½ inches.

DEYO, Morton Leyndholm (1887–1973). A 1911 graduate of the U.S. Naval Academy, Deyo began the war as a captain and rose to the rank of rear admiral (1943), seeing action in both the Atlantic and the Pacific. At first he commanded destroyer escorts in the Atlantic, but D-Day found him in command of the bombardment group for UTAH BEACH. Deyo's firepower served not only to take the beachhead but to support it, and eventually all gunfire support came under his command. On June 25, 1944, Deyo's offshore bombardment contributed to the Army's capture and clearing of CHERBOURG. Deyo went to the Pacific in 1945 to command a bombardment group of battleships and cruisers. His task force for gunfire cover at OKINAWA, the largest assembled for a Pacific operation, proved of crucial importance, the Okinawa invasion being especially dependent upon naval gunfire. Deyo retired in 1949 as a vice-admiral.

DIADEM. Code name for the 1944 Allied spring offensive in ITALY, begun May 11.

DICK. In 1937 20 Seversky Model 2PA two-place fighter-bombers, an export model similar to the U.S. Army's P-35 fighter, were sold to Japan. During the war, Allied intelligence incorrectly believed that the 2PA had been placed in production in Japan, and assigned this code name to it.

DIEPPE. Small French port on the English Channel. In order to test the German defenses along the ATLANTIC WALL, as well as their own tactics, the Allies staged an amphibious assault on the town of Dieppe on the morning of August 19, 1942. The attacking force was composed of 5,100 Canadians and 1,000 British COMMANDOS and American RANGERS. Supported by 252 ships, none larger than a destroyer, and 69 squadrons of aircraft, this miniature force was doomed from the beginning. Tactical intelligence was totally insufficient, and prior planning for both the assault and the eventual evacuation was woefully inadequate.

The invasion force was compromised before it reached Dieppe, as one naval squadron was engaged by a German coastal convoy. Though the Commandos had some success once ashore, the seven Canadian battalions fought from impossible positions. With no heavy gunfire from the sea and only intermittent close air support, the Canadians suffered terrible losses. Three-quarters of them were killed, wounded or taken prisoner within six hours, as all seven battalion commanders became casualties. Communications between the beach and the task force commander, Maj. Gen. J. H. Roberts of the 2d Canadian Division, broke down as the situation in Dieppe deteriorated.

Though the debacle made good propaganda for the Nazis, it had its value for the Allies. What was learned led to the improvements in intelligence, communications, air support, naval gunfire and tactical operations that were made before the landing at Normandy 22 months later. As the official Canadian historian wrote: "The casualties sustained in the raid at Dieppe were part of the price for the knowledge that enabled the great operation of 1944 to be carried out at a cost in blood smaller than even the most optimistic had ventured to hope."

The foregoing discussion represents the orthodox view of the Dieppe raid. A different picture is presented in the book *A Man Called Intrepid,* which describes the intelligence activities during the war of Sir William STEPHENSON. This operation (Jubilee), according to the Stephenson papers, served complex strategic and intelligence purposes. It "deceived the enemy into thinking the slaves of Nazidom were about to be freed. When it seemed to fail, Jubilee deceived the enemy about how the Second Front would be created." In other words, the outcome was entirely expected.

DIETL, Eduard (1890–1944). German Army officer, leader of ski and mountain troops, who commanded land forces at the NARVIK landing in NORWAY in 1940. He later (1942–44) commanded mountain troops in Finland, attaining the rank of colonel general. He was killed in an airplane crash.

DIETRICH, Josef (1892–1966). The illegitimate son of a German peasant servant girl, "Sepp" Dietrich received little education and as a youth worked variously as a farm laborer and a bellboy until 1911, when he entered the German Army. During World War I he was promoted to the rank of sergeant and was decorated for bravery. In 1919 he joined the Bavarian provincial police, but he was soon fired. Later he joined the newly formed Nazi Brown Shirts (*see* SA) of Ernst RÖHM. In 1928 he became a member of the NSDAP, the Nazi Party.

He worked for a time in the party's publishing headquarters. Thereafter he assisted in the formation of the Black Shirts (*see* SS) in Bavaria. In 1933 he was made Gruppenführer and assigned the task of selecting Adolf HITLER's bodyguard SS unit, which would become the Leibstandarte SS Adolf Hitler. He took a leading part in the slaughter of Hitler's SA opponents in the 1934 party purge. In 1938 the Leibstandarte unit became a motorized infantry unit, and an independent part of the Army. Later it became a panzer division; it remained under Dietrich's command until 1944. During that period Dietrich was a successful field commander in Russia.

At the time of the anti-Hitler plot, Dietrich favored vigorous measures against the conspirators. He was awarded promotions, first to Oberstgruppenführer and then to Generaloberst (colonel general). For the ARDENNES offensive (the Battle of the BULGE), he was given command of the Sixth Panzer Army, the main German striking force—probably because Hitler considered him a highly loyal Nazi. Troops under his general command perpetrated the notorious MALMÉDY outrage, in which 120 captured American prisoners were massacred.

In 1946 he was arrested and tried for his responsibility in this affair. He was convicted and sentenced to life imprisonment. In 1955 he was pardoned and released from Landsberg Prison as a parolee. For a time he worked as a clerk. In 1957 he was again arrested and tried by a Munich court for his part in the 1934 execution of the leaders of the SA. He was again convicted and sentenced to 18 months in prison.

DIETRICH, Otto (1892–1954). A native of Essen, Dietrich had established himself as a journalist when he joined Adolf HITLER's inner circle in 1931. In 1933 he was appointed Reich press chief and from 1937 was head of the press section in the Ministry of Propaganda. He remained in direct personal touch with Hitler while at the same time occupying the uneasy position of being technically subordinate to Joseph GOEBBELS. Interned after the war by the British in Fallingbostal, he wrote a study of Hitler in 1946, which was published posthumously (1955) and appeared in English as *The Hitler I Knew* (1957). This is one of the more reliable accounts to come from a former Nazi source. Dietrich was finally released from prison in 1952. *See also* NATIONAL SOCIALIST GERMAN WORKERS' PARTY.

DILL, Sir John Greer (1881–1944). Dill was one of the very few senior British Army officers to occupy high command posts in both world wars. At the end of World War I he was chief of the Operations Branch at GHQ with the temporary rank of brigadier. At the onset of World War II he was appointed commander, 1st Corps, British Expeditionary Force (1939–40), but a month before the start of the German offensive in 1940 he was recalled to England to take up the post of Vice-Chief of the Imperial General Staff. In May he became CIGS.

It was Dill's misfortune to assume the latter post at the nadir of Britain's military fortunes in the war. Concerned about the potential misuse of British force, patient and thorough in thought and action, he came increasingly to be regarded as overcautious, obstructive and unimaginative by Winston CHURCHILL, always eager for offensive action. Ultimately, Dill's position as

CIGS became intolerable and, exhausted physically and mentally, he could no longer withstand the pressures on him. At the end of 1941 he was replaced by Sir Alan BROOKE and was appointed to head the British Joint Staff Mission to the United States.

As senior British representative at the meetings of the Anglo-American COMBINED CHIEFS OF STAFF, Dill came to acquire enormous prestige with American strategic planners, notably Ernest KING, MARSHALL and ROOSEVELT. Upon his death in 1944, Roosevelt termed him "the most important figure in the remarkable accord which has been developed in the combined operations of our two countries." During his time in Washington, no man did more than Dill to promote Anglo-American harmony at senior strategic levels. He was buried in Arlington National Cemetery, the only foreigner to be so honored.

DIMOUT. American term for the reduced illumination adopted in coastal cities to diminish the bright glare against which ships were being torpedoed and sunk by patrolling U-boats. It was tried in other areas during the earlier stages of the war, when the possibility of Axis air attack was believed real. It did not require total darkening.

DINAH. Allied code name for the Japanese Army Ki 46 reconnaissance plane (*see* KI 46).

DINANT. Belgian town at the western tip of the ARDENNES region where in 1940 the German 7th Panzer Division under a commander destined for fame in North Africa, Erwin ROMMEL, secured the first bridgehead across the Meuse River. In the Allied drive to the German frontier in late 1944, the American 9th Infantry Division took the town against little resistance. During the Battle of the BULGE a German patrol driving a captured jeep and wearing American uniforms almost reached the Meuse bridge at Dinant, but the jeep hit a mine and all were killed.

DISTINGUISHED FLYING CROSS. A U.S. decoration established in 1926 for active-duty or reserve airmen of the Army, Navy and Coast Guard who distinguished themselves by "heroism or extraordinary achievement while participating in an aerial flight." Among the earliest recipients was Charles A. LINDBERGH, who held a commission in the Air Corps Reserve at the time of his New York–to-Paris flight. Congress later approved Distinguished Flying Crosses for other transatlantic pioneers, including Amelia Earhart and Italo BALBO, the Italian airman.

During World War II the basis for this award varied according to combat theater. In general, the recipient had to complete a specific number or type of missions or fly a certain number of hours in combat. Sometimes, however, the Distinguished Flying Cross was awarded for some heroic exploit, such as shooting down one or more enemy aircraft or bringing back a crippled bomber to a safe landing.

The Royal Air Force and other Allied air forces also had such decorations.

DISTINGUISHED FLYING MEDAL. British decoration instituted in 1918 for bestowal on warrant and noncommissioned officers and men of the Royal Air Force (and Fleet Air Arm from April 9, 1941) for acts of gallantry when flying in active operations against the enemy.

DISTINGUISHED SERVICE CROSS. An American award, the DSC was first authorized in 1918 and is awarded to any person who, while serving in any capacity in the Army, distinguishes himself by extraordinary heroism against an armed enemy of the United States. A number of foreigners have won the DSC for heroism while attached to the Army. Ranking immediately after the MEDAL OF HONOR in order of precedence, the bronze cross-shaped medal is suspended from a dark blue ribbon with red and white edges.

DISTINGUISHED SERVICE MEDAL. U.S. Army and Navy decoration, originally established in 1919, for "exceptionally meritorious service to the government in a duty of great responsibility." It was not a combat decoration but was given for distinguished service in administrative, technical and other support fields.

DISTINGUISHED SERVICE ORDER. Established in 1886, the DSO is awarded to officers of the British armed forces for individual instances of meritorious or distinguished service in war. In 1942 members of the merchant navy became eligible to receive the DSO for bravery while serving in close contact with the Royal Navy in action against the enemy.

DISTINGUISHED UNIT CITATION. Award established in 1942 for units of the U.S. armed forces and those of cobelligerents that demonstrated extraordinary heroism in action against an armed enemy on or after December 7, 1941. The requirements for the type of heroic act necessary for the award were the same as those established for a DISTINGUISHED SERVICE CROSS to an individual. The award, worn over the left breast pocket, is a dark blue ribbon framed in a decorative gold-colored frame.

DIVINE WIND. *See* KAMIKAZE.

DIVING TANKS. In preparation for the invasion of England, a number of German Mark III and Mark IV tanks were sealed against water and rubber caps were supplied for the gun muzzles. Though these tanks found no employment in the English Channel, they were used by the Germans at the crossing of the Bug River on June 22, 1941, which began the invasion of the Soviet Union. *See also* TANK.

DIXON, Robert. A U.S. Navy lieutenant commander who led a scout bomber squadron from the carrier LEXINGTON at the Battle of the CORAL SEA on May 7, 1942, Dixon reported the sinking of the Japanese light carrier SHOHO in these memorable words: "Scratch one flattop! Dixon to carrier. Scratch one flattop!" The *Shoho* was the first large Japanese ship sunk by the Americans in the war.

DMS or DSM. The U.S. Navy converted old World War I four-stacker destroyers and, later in the war, newer destroyers to high-speed destroyer minesweepers

(DMS). The newer ones reached the Pacific in time for OKINAWA in early 1945 and carried fire control radar and three dual-purpose 5-INCH 38-caliber guns. They could sweep a 150-yard width of water while steaming at 15 knots.

DNIEPER RIVER. This 1,400-mile north-south river was an important factor in the German-Soviet war. The original aim of the Germans was to encircle and annihilate the main Russian forces west of the Dnieper, which is 300 miles inside the Soviet Union. But, though victories were achieved, this great encirclement eluded them. In early July the Germans crossed the Dnieper on a side front. In September 1943 the Russians pushed them back to the Dnieper at numerous points and crossed the river near KIEV, Kremenchug and Dnepropetrovsk during the first week of October.

DOBBIE, Sir William (1879–1964). A British Army Royal Engineers general in retirement at the outbreak of the war, Dobbie was appointed Governor of MALTA in the spring of 1940, and held the post for the first two years of the war in the Mediterranean. For most of this time Malta was under continuous Italian and later German air attack, which killed numbers of civilians, destroyed Maltese buildings and property and imposed virtual blockade conditions. It fell to Dobbie to mobilize Malta's resources for the siege, to arrest a small number of leading (and a larger number of less prominent) Maltese for pro-Italian activities, to disperse and shelter the population in face of the air attacks and to keep as much of the normal civilian government running as was possible. His most important achievement was, however, in maintaining morale. A strictly religious man in the Protestant Cromwellian tradition, he communicated his own courage and piety to the Maltese in broadcasts several times each week, giving the island's equally devout Roman Catholic inhabitants pride and courage to endure their ordeals. In 1942, exhausted, General Dobbie was replaced by Lord GORT.

DOC. Allied code name assigned to the MESSERSCHMITT ME 110, incorrectly thought in the early months of the Pacific war to have been in use by the Japanese.

DOHNANYI, Hans von (1902–1945). A prominent member of the German OPPOSITION TO HITLER, Dohnanyi was the son of the celebrated composer. In 1925 he married Christine Bonhoeffer, sister of Klaus and Dietrich BONHOEFFER. A doctor of law, he was attached to the Reich Ministry of Justice and in 1938 became a judge in the Supreme Court at Leipzig. A close associate of Admiral CANARIS and Hans OSTER, he was responsible for compiling secret legal evidence against the Nazis. At the beginning of the war he joined Canaris and Oster in the ABWEHR, where he became the "back room" organizer for the resistance and a prime keeper of its documentation. His arrest came in April 1943. Subject to constant interrogation, Dohnanyi developed his own form of resistance by deliberately infecting himself with diphtheria, the means being smuggled into the prison by his wife. This enabled him to spend much time in the hospital, free from interrogation, but naturally it permanently affected his health. With the discovery of his collection of anti-Nazi documentation in September 1944, the case against him was complete. He was indicted and finally executed in April 1945.

Dohnanyi was a man of the greatest courage and the highest character; his letters to his wife are among the most moving writings to have come out of the horrors of imprisonment by the Gestapo. His brother-in-law Dietrich Bonhoeffer, who had been arrested at the same time as he was, was with him in prison.

DOLLMAN, Friedrich (1876–1944). German Army officer who was appointed commander of the Seventh Army in September 1939 and led it in victorious fighting against the French in 1940. The army was subsequently on occupation duty in Normandy and Brittany and was the force opposing the Allied INVASION on June 6, 1944. Within a month Dollman, a colonel general, was dead of a heart attack.

DONETS BASIN (Donbas). A major industrial region of the USSR, located in the eastern Ukraine just north of the Black Sea. When the Germans overran the Donbas in 1941, Russia lost over 60 percent of her coal output. During the occupation the Germans tried to extract coal, iron and other industrial products from the region, but the attempt had little success, owing to the passive resistance of the native population. The Donbas was liberated by the Red Army in the late summer of 1943.

DÖNITZ, Karl (1891–). Successively the commander of the GERMAN NAVY's U-boat arm and Commander in Chief of the German Navy during the war, Admiral Dönitz became the head of the German Government after Adolf HITLER's suicide in late April 1945. Born September 16, 1891, in the Berlin suburb of Grunau, Dönitz came from a Prussian family of civil servants and landowners. He served aboard the cruiser *Breslau* in Turkish and Russian waters in World War I, participating in a spectacular raid against the Russian Black Sea port of Novorossisk in 1916. In that year he returned home to begin training in submarines, later appearing in the Mediterranean in command of *U-68*. While single-handedly stalking an English convoy off Sicily on October 4, 1918, his boat's longitudinal stability control failed, and Dönitz, forced to surface in the middle of the British force, spent a number of months in captivity, mulling, between attempts at escape, the futility of independent, single-ship U-boat operations.

He spent the 15 years following the war slowly advancing through the ranks, but associated with surface units. In November 1934, as a captain, he commanded the cruiser *Emden* on an extended cruise to the Indian Ocean lasting until July 1935. On his return he was assigned to command of the U-boat arm of the resurgent German Navy, which was permitted 45 percent of the submarine strength of the British Navy under the ANGLO-GERMAN NAVAL TREATY of June 1935. From the outset Dönitz established firm control of the technical and, equally important, the tactical innovations of the German submarine fleet. He concentrated on the dependable 517-ton Type VII U-boat, with later variants, as the mainstay of the service while endorsing refinements in range and speed in the Types IX, IXD2, XB (minelaying submarine) and XIV supply submarine. He relentlessly drilled his crews in the techniques of massed U-boat operations, the wolfpack tactics that were to be his contribution to naval warfare and the scourge of British-American and Russian sea supply lines in the first half of the war.

The coming of the war caught Dönitz's command with a total of 57 boats available, only 39 of them ready for sea, and the first two years revealed serious irregularities in German torpedoes, yet the training and skill of his commanders brought some spectacular results, as in Günther PRIEN's daring penetration of the British base at SCAPA FLOW. Dönitz, promoted to rear admiral in October 1939, was a strong believer in the human touch, and had the confidence of his crews through the worst adversity; he catered to them and continued to send off and meet the war patrols personally on the docks.

With the French Biscay coast in German hands after June 1940, Dönitz eventually established his headquarters near Lorient and continued the campaign that had destroyed nearly a thousand warships and merchantmen by the end of 1941 alone. He argued against the dissipation of German undersea forces in theaters other than the North Atlantic. PEARL HARBOR was as much a surprise to the German high command as it was to the United States, and it took Dönitz until mid-January 1942 to deploy U-boats—usually Type IX, of longer range than Type VII—to American shores, in what was termed Operation Drumbeat (Paukenschlag). They had excellent hunting against merchant shipping still running under peacetime routine and against inexperienced American naval crews; not until April 1942 did an American destroyer sink a U-boat in American waters.

On January 30, 1943, Dönitz was appointed Commander in Chief of the Navy, succeeding Erich RAEDER, whose increasingly stormy relations with Hitler over the value of heavy surface units had led to his resignation earlier in the month. Dönitz's elevation to the command and the rank of Grossadmiral (grand admiral) stemmed from Hitler's appreciation of his technical qualifications and his calm demeanor rather than from his political loyalty. Dönitz succeeded in getting additional steel allocations for a 1943 building program heavily concentrating on smaller ships, including E-boats and U-boats, to the exclusion of the heavy units so discredited with Hitler, and he hastened work on the advanced Types XXI and XXIII boats and improvements such as the acoustic and magnetic torpedoes.

Predisposed by his strict traditional upbringing and by his naval career to acceptance of what he perceived as the accomplishments of National Socialism and its sense of purpose amid the confusion of Weimar democracy, Dönitz went to war in 1939 with no illusions about the difficulties of winning, but his political attitude was uncomplicated by moral nuance; he maintained throughout the war and at the NUREMBERG TRIALS afterward that his profession made him an instrument of state policy and permitted no hesitation once war was declared. He regarded the perpetrators of the attempt on Hitler's life on July 20, 1944, as traitors in this light, though later professing to understand their moral revulsion at Nazi atrocities unknown to him as a naval officer who, in fact, knew little of political conditions or of mass murder and who had protected Jewish officers or Navy men with Jewish wives.

In the last gasp of the war, following a contingency plan for dividing control of the Reich split into a northern and a southern enclave, Dönitz went to Ploen in Holstein to establish civil authority in the north (April 22, 1945), where in the midst of general collapse on the 30th he received Martin BORMANN's radioed advice that Hitler was dead and that he, Dönitz, was the new head of state. His regime moved to the old naval cadet school near Flensburg on May 2, 1945, its leader rejecting the pleas of HIMMLER and RIBBENTROP for roles in the new government. With a civilian rump cabinet presided over by the career civil servant and former Finance Minister Count Lutz SCHWERIN VON KROSIGK, Dönitz claimed to represent the German state, still in existence despite the defeat of German arms, a fiction persisting until his arrest with his entire entourage on May 23, 1945.

Tried at Nuremberg by the International Military Tribunal for his part in the German war effort and convicted of crimes against the peace and war crimes, Dönitz was sentenced to 10 years' imprisonment at SPANDAU. He was released in October 1956. **A.M.B.**

See also ATLANTIC, BATTLE OF THE.

DONOVAN, William J. (1883–1959). A New York lawyer and World War I hero, Donovan was appointed by President ROOSEVELT in 1941 to head the Office of Coordinator of Information, shortly afterward renamed the OFFICE OF STRATEGIC SERVICES (OSS). As director of OSS, "Wild Bill" Donovan presided over an oddly assorted group that included Wall Street bankers, acrobats, college professors, movie stars and scientists. Charged with responsibility for espionage, sabotage, intelligence and propaganda, the OSS operated throughout Europe and the Far East. An unorthodox yet effective administrator and a skilled bureaucratic infighter, Donovan, who was made a major general, incurred the wrath of many old-line military men and civil servants but won the loyalty and respect of his OSS colleagues.

DOOLITTLE, James H. (1896–). A record-breaking racing pilot, a pioneer in instrument flying and an oil-company executive, Jimmy Doolittle was called to active U.S. air duty from the reserve in 1940. After conferring with leaders of the auto industry concerning the possible conversion of their plants to aircraft production, he undertook a fact-finding mission to Great Britain. His best-remembered wartime exploit was the Doolittle Raid of April 18, 1942, when he led 16 B-25s from the carrier HORNET to bomb targets in Tokyo, Yokohama, Yokosuka, Kobe and Nagoya. This daring undertaking earned him the MEDAL OF HONOR.

A lieutenant colonel when he took off from the *Hornet,* Doolittle was advanced to brigadier general the day after the attack on Tokyo. In 1943, as a lieutenant general, he commanded the FIFTEENTH AIR FORCE, and from January 1944 through the end of the war, the EIGHTH AIR FORCE.

Doolittle was a many-sided airman: a flamboyant flier, an effective commander, a scientific student of aviation. *See also* FIRST SPECIAL AVIATION PROJECT.

DOORMAN, Karel (1889–1942). Admiral in the Royal Netherlands Navy, commander of the combined force of Dutch, British, American and Australian cruisers and destroyers which was formed on February 14,

1942, to combat the Japanese advance through the Netherlands East Indies. The force operated under severe handicaps since it had never worked together at sea as an integrated force, had had no opportunity to develop any tactical doctrine and had no common communications system. Its first major operation was the Battle of the JAVA SEA on February 27, 1942. Outranged and without air support, Doorman's force suffered a severe defeat. Among the losses was the Dutch cruiser DE RUYTER, flying Admiral Doorman's flag, and he was lost with his ship.

DORA. German gun, the largest to see action in the war. Dora had a 31½-inch bore and fired up to 7-ton projectiles a distance of 24 miles. *See also* GUSTAV.

DORA LINE (Hitler Line). Located between CASSINO and the ALBAN HILLS (Italy), one of the major positions by which the Germans hoped to check the Allied advance on ROME. With the capture of Cassino on May 18, 1944, the Germans fell back to the next prepared position, the so-called Hitler Line. When Field Marshal KESSELRING realized that the line could not be held long, he renamed it the Dora Line.

DORCHESTER. U.S. Army transport, formerly a commercial passenger ship. Taken over for Army use in January 1942, she was used to carry troops and supplies to Newfoundland and Greenland. She was torpedoed by a U-boat in February 1943 and sank with heavy loss of life; in this sinking the Four CHAPLAINS earned fame by sacrificing their life jackets to give others a chance to save their lives.

DORNBERGER, Walter (1895–). Dornberger was responsible for development of the V-2 rocket (called A-4 by the German scientists who devised it) which battered London from September 1944 through March of the following year. An artilleryman during World War I, Dornberger joined the postwar Reichswehr, studied mechanical engineering at Army expense and in 1930 took charge of military rocket development. He established a test center near Berlin and assembled a gifted staff that included a young student named Wernher von BRAUN.

Dornberger's early experiments so impressed the Army leadership that in 1934, the year after Adolf HITLER came to power, he and his organization were transferred to PEENEMÜNDE, an island in the Baltic, where he supervised development of the A-4. The rockets were manufactured in an underground plant near Nordhausen in central Germany.

In May 1945 both Dornberger and von Braun surrendered to American troops. Later the two men came to the United States, where von Braun was instrumental in developing rockets for the exploration of space. Dornberger, despite his fascination with space travel, did not join forces with his former colleague but worked for a time as a missile consultant to the Air Force and eventually became prominent in the aerospace industry. *See also* V-WEAPONS.

DORNIER DO 17. German medium bomber whose lean lines caused it to be widely known as the Flying Pencil. The basic Do 17 was designed in 1934 in response to Deutsche Lufthansa's desire for a mail-passenger plane for service between European cities, but the airline rejected the prototypes because it deemed the passenger accommodations inadequate. However, officials of the LUFTWAFFE saw in the Do 17 a fast, short-range bomber. With various modifications, including a twin-rudder assembly in place of the original single fin (this change being made to eliminate some tendency to yaw, and thus to provide a steadier bombing platform) and 770-horsepower 12-cylinder Hispano-Suiza engines, one of the prototypes in 1935 turned in a test performance of 243 miles per hour. In 1937 another version of the Do 17 with 1,000-horsepower Daimler-Benz engines created a sensation in an international meet at Zurich by flying faster than any foreign fighter (let alone bomber).

Production began with the Do 17E-1, which had two 750-horsepower BMW VI-7.3 engines, giving it a top speed of 220 miles per hour. Many of these planes were sent to Spain for duty with the German forces aiding General FRANCO. In 1939 the last line of Do 17s, the Z series, entered production; these had Bramo 323P 1,000-horsepower radial engines which could drive them at a maximum speed of 263 miles per hour. The Do 17Z-2, the standard version, had a range of 745 miles with a bomb load of 2,200 pounds. An export version was called the Do 215A, and it retained this designation when taken over by the Luftwaffe instead of being sold to foreign customers; some planes with modifications received 215B designations.

The Do 17 saw service throughout the war, with various engines and other alterations. It was particularly successful in operations in Poland but much less so in the Battle of BRITAIN.

DORNIER DO 18. A German monoplane originally produced as a transatlantic mail plane and used throughout the war as a reconnaissance and air-sea rescue flying boat. It was powered by two 880-horsepower diesel engines mounted in a single nacelle above the wing, one driving a normal propeller, the other a pusher prop. It carried one 13-mm. machine gun, one 20-mm. cannon and four 110-pound bombs. Its maximum speed was 165 miles per hour, and its range was 2,175 miles. A Do 18D was the first German plane downed by a British fighter in World War II, attacked on September 25, 1939, by a Blackburn SKUA from the carrier ARK ROYAL.

DORNIER DO 24. A trimotor reconnaissance and transport flying boat. Originally ordered by the Dutch Government for work in the East Indies, many ended up in Luftwaffe service. The DO 24T had three 1,000-horsepower radial engines and flew 211 miles per hour maximum speed. The maximum range was 2,950 miles. Some were pressed into service for the invasion of NORWAY in April 1940, and later models were used for air-sea rescue work.

DORNIER DO 26. A long-range transport flying boat, delivered to Lufthansa in 1939 for nonstop Atlantic mail flights. It was powered by four 700-horsepower diesel engines mounted in tandem pairs at the end of the wing center section. The rear engines drove pusher props which swung up on takeoff to clear the spray.

Only six were built. It flew at a maximum speed of 208 miles per hour and had a maximum range of 5,592 miles.

DORNIER DO 217. Basically a twin-engine, four-place heavy bomber, this series ran from the Do 217A to the Do 217P (the letters H and I were not assigned, and the R model was a modified Do 317). An entirely new aircraft begun in 1937, it externally resembled the old Do 17 series. Production ceased in 1943, with a total of 1,366 bombers, 364 night fighters and some early prototypes being built. Some of the bombers were modified to carry standoff missiles. The Do 217 was a successful plane, but it suffered from weak defensive armament. From the K through M series, the forward fuselage nose was entirely glazed paneling and the stepped pilot's compartment was eliminated; the Do 217N-2 was a night fighter with a nose similar to the J. The Do 217M-1 had two 1,750-horsepower engines and flew at a maximum speed of 348 miles per hour. Armed with six machine guns, it had a range with internal fuel of 1,335 miles at 248 miles per hour.

DORNIER DO 335. Germany's most unconventional piston-engine fighter, also known as *Pfeil* (Arrow). It had two 1,900-horsepower engines, one mounted in front driving a tractor propeller, one mounted midship driving a pusher propeller behind the tail. Both a single-place fighter-bomber and a two-place night-fighter version were built; none were operational by V-E Day. It flew 474 miles per hour maximum speed (the 335A-1) with a 1,280-mile range. It was 45 feet 5¼ inches long with a 45-foot, 3½-inch wingspan. Armed with one 30-mm. cannon and two 15-mm. machine guns, it also carried 1,100 pounds of bombs.

DORSETSHIRE, H.M.S. Royal Navy cruiser of 9,975 tons, completed at Portsmouth in 1931, armed (in 1939) with eight 8-inch and eight 4-inch guns, smaller weapons, eight 21-inch torpedo tubes and one aircraft. *Dorsetshire* served in the East Indies to 1940 and was then moved to the Atlantic, taking part in the abortive attack on the French battleship RICHELIEU at DAKAR in July 1940 and firing the final torpedoes into the BISMARCK in May 1941. Moved to the Far East, *Dorsetshire*, in company with a similar cruiser, *Cornwall*, was destroyed by Japanese carrier-borne aircraft off Ceylon on April 5, 1942.

DOSS, Desmond T. U.S. Army medic in the 307th Regiment, 77th Infantry Division. During the battle for OKINAWA, Pfc. Doss saved many lives, frequently exposing himself to Japanese fire, and was wounded twice. For these actions between April 29 and May 21, 1945, he was awarded the MEDAL OF HONOR. Doss was a conscientious objector.

DOUGLAS OF KIRTLESIDE, 1st Baron (Sir William Sholto Douglas) (1893–1969). Douglas served in the Royal Flying Corps and became a career RAF officer after a brief spell in civil aviation. In World War II he was chief of FIGHTER COMMAND, succeeding Air Marshal Hugh DOWDING (November 1940). Afterward he was successively commander in chief of the RAF in the Middle East and then of COASTAL COMMAND. After the war he was British member of the ALLIED CONTROL COUNCIL for Germany. As such, he had to confirm the death sentences on Nazi war criminals. Sholto Douglas was an aggressive fighter pilot and a shrewd judge of men. This combination made him a great commander in war and a noted aviation executive in peace. He achieved the rank of Marshal of the Royal Air Force and received a peerage.

DOUMENC, Joseph (1880–1948). A French general, graduate of the Ecole Polytechnique, Doumenc made his mark in the FRENCH ARMY as a logistical expert. In August 1939 he was chief French representative in the barren Anglo-French-Soviet talks in Moscow (*see* SOVIET-GERMAN NONAGGRESSION PACT), and the following January became Major General (i.e., Chief of Staff) of the French Army. In this position Doumenc headed an administrative and logistical headquarters at Montry, midway between the command post of the Army Commander in Chief, Gen. Maurice GAMELIN, at VINCENNES and that of the Northeastern Front commander, Gen. Alphonse GEORGES, at La Ferté-sous-Jouarre. Doumenc's staff provided support for all French land forces until the armistice in June 1940. During the VICHY period Doumenc headed Army efforts to support refugees and civilian reconstruction.

DOWDING, 1st Baron (Sir Hugh) (1882–1970). This name will be associated in history with the epic summer of 1940. Lord Dowding's memorial in Westminster Abbey bears the words "He Led the Few in the Battle of Britain." Educated at Winchester, Dowding sought a career in the Royal Artillery. Then he joined the Royal Flying Corps and served in France, where he had what was probably an ominous difference of opinion with "Boom" Trenchard, founder of the RAF, on a technical problem. He was nicknamed "Stuffy," probably because of a certain austerity of manner which concealed his innate charm and lack of side. He was air commander in Transjordan and Palestine in 1929. From 1930 to 1936 he was Air Council Member for supply and research. The expansion of the RAF had begun, and Dowding was responsible for many of the major decisions in the development of monoplane fighters armed with eight machine guns and of the chain of RADAR stations along the coasts. From 1936 to late 1940 he was Air Officer Commanding in Chief, FIGHTER COMMAND. Thus in peace and war he was uniquely responsible for the defense of the British Isles against the numerically superior LUFTWAFFE.

When the Germans attacked in France on May 10, 1940, Dowding came under continual heavy pressure from Prime Minster CHURCHILL and the French Government to send more and more fighters to the Continent. He resolutely stuck to his demand that the defense of Britain should not be put in peril. Despite this, his fighter force gave a good account of itself in covering the withdrawal of British and French ground forces across the beaches at DUNKIRK. Assisted principally by Air Vice-Marshal Keith PARK, who commanded No. 11 Group, Dowding fought the Battle of BRITAIN from his headquarters at Bentley Priory. His personal devotion to duty compelled him to spend not only his days in the Operations Room but his nights visiting the units developing the night-fighter techniques urgently needed to counter the night-bomber threat.

After the Germans canceled the preparations for the invasion of England, Dowding was somewhat abruptly replaced by Sholto DOUGLAS at Fighter Command. Though he had been the winning strategist in one of history's most fateful battles, his laurels were comparatively meager. He seems to have been on the losing side in a doctrinal battle within the RAF. He visited the United States and Canada in 1941, wrote his dispatch on the Battle of Britain and, as an air chief marshal, retired from active service in 1942. In September 1969 he sat in a wheelchair among his former pilots at the premiere of the film *Battle of Britain.*

DOWNFALL. Code name for planned Allied invasion of Japan. *See also* CORONET; OLYMPIC.

DP. This abbreviation for "displaced person" became a familiar term during the war. Uncounted millions of people were displaced from their homes by military operations, bombing, deportation as forced laborers, etc., in Europe and Asia. In the last phases of the war there was a mass movement of Germans westward to escape the Red Army. It was estimated that the total number of DPs, German and Allied, in Germany might have been as high as 30 million. In China there were more than 20 million; no accurate figure could be determined. In Japan there were perhaps 12 million.

DP. Abbreviation for "deep penetration," a British term for BOMBS designed for ballistic penetration of a target as well as for explosive effect. It was applied to armor-piercing and semi-armor-piercing bombs, as well as to the extra-heavy GRAND SLAM and Tall Boy bombs, which were designated general-purpose bombs but depended for their effect on penetration by sheer weight into the earth before detonating to produce heavy shock waves. DP is also an abbreviation for "dual purpose" or "double purpose," referring to guns designed for use against both surface and air targets.

DRACULA. Code word for an Allied air-seaborne attack on the RANGOON area. Because of Allied successes in late 1944 and early 1945 in their overland advance south into BURMA, Adm. Lord MOUNTBATTEN, the Supreme Commander, decided on February 23, 1945, to seize Rangoon from that direction. But because this advance became slowed, a modified Dracula was carried out which culminated in the reoccupation of Rangoon on May 3, 1945.

DRAGOON. *See* ANVIL-DRAGOON.

D RATION. An emergency field ration developed by the U.S. Army. It consisted of a bar of specially developed chocolate, processed to stay hard in hot climates and vitamin-fortified, intended to furnish the eater with the nutritional equivalent of a meal when other food was not available. The chocolate had a very hard texture, and for the sake of his teeth, the user had to approach it with a certain amount of caution.

DRESDEN. The bombing of this German city in 1945 is frequently cited as an example of aerial overkill and it came to be one of the most controversial actions of the entire war. In January 1945 a renewal of the Russian offensive from the east caused Anglo-American planners to look for ways to employ the combined bomber force to assist the Soviet effort. In their files was a plan called Thunderclap, drafted in the summer of 1944, which aimed at shattering German civilian morale. Although the recent Ardennes battle had demonstrated Germany's residual strength and determination, Air Chief Marshal Sir Arthur HARRIS, chief of BOMBER COMMAND, and some of his British colleagues proposed Thunderclap raids against Berlin and other large cities, among them Dresden, to create new hordes of refugees that would disrupt the movement of troops and supplies. Prime Minister CHURCHILL, eager to find some means of "harrying the German retreat from Breslau," seized upon this suggestion.

Next, the Allied leaders met at YALTA, where on February 4 the Soviet delegation requested air attacks to "paralyze" Berlin and Leipzig; however, they showed no further interest in Anglo-American strategic bombing. In the absence of any more specific request, Harris, Air Chief Marshal Charles PORTAL of the RAF and U.S. Gen. Carl SPAATZ saw no need to alter the modified Thunderclap plan for the devastation of the surviving eastern German cities. This offensive had begun on February 3 with a U.S. EIGHTH AIR FORCE daylight raid on Berlin. Anglo-American attacks followed against such places as Munich, Leipzig and Dresden, with the Americans bombing by RADAR and achieving results not unlike those obtained by the British in their nighttime "city busting."

Dresden had come under American air attack in October 1944 and again in January 1945, but these raids were feeble in comparison with the destruction wrought by Bomber Command and the Eighth Air Force on February 13–15; there also were follow-up attacks on March 2 and April 15. No one knows the extent of the casualties; an estimated 35,000 (some say many more) of the million or so townspeople and refugees perished in the February bombings alone.

These attacks, along with Thunderclap poundings of Berlin, Chemnitz and Cottbus, inspired press reports of "deliberate terror bombing" as a "ruthless expedient" to hasten victory. Actually Harris was merely continuing his policy of area bombing, which had originated as an attempt to reduce production by attacking German workers in their homes rather than bombing their factories. In the United States, Gen. George C. MARSHALL tried to reconcile the conflict between newspaper reports of terror bombing and official statements calling it precision bombardment. Rather than admit a change of policy, he merely declared that Dresden had been obliterated at the request of the Russians, an apparent misreading of the memorandum presented at Yalta.

Meanwhile, Churchill had been having second thoughts about the revival of Thunderclap and its application in eastern Germany. "The destruction of Dresden," he told his military advisers on March 28, 1945, "remains a serious query against the conduct of Allied bombing." He warned of the folly of any "bombing of German cities simply for the sake of increasing the terror" and as a result coming into possession "of an utterly ruined land." He quickly withdrew this memorandum, however, and issued a substitute that contained no specific reference either to terrorism or to Dresden. He nevertheless urged that "we . . . see to it that our attacks do not do more harm to ourselves in the long run than . . . to the enemy's war effort."

DSM. *See* DMS.

DUBOSE, Laurance Toombs (1893–1967). U.S. naval officer who distinguished himself as a task force commander in the Pacific in charge of gunfire and bombardment for amphibious operations. As commanding officer of the U.S.S. PORTLAND, he was torpedoed at GUADALCANAL. Promoted to rear admiral, he commanded a task force at BOUGAINVILLE, where he was in charge of the light cruisers and destroyers providing gunfire cover for the invasion. Samuel Eliot MORISON said of DuBose's efforts there that "seldom has there been such effective coverage of an invasion." DuBose continued with his task force of cruisers and destroyers through the campaigns in the GILBERT and MARSHALL ISLANDS and at LEYTE GULF.

DUCE, IL (The Leader). The title used by Benito MUSSOLINI, dictator of Italy. It symbolized Mussolini's belief that he was the successor to the Caesars of Rome, the man who would restore Italy to its former power and prestige.

DUCK. U.S. Navy name for the J2F; U.S. Army nickname for the DUKW (*see* J2F; DUKW).

DUGOUT SUNDAY. Name given to October 25, 1942, on GUADALCANAL because heavy rains had turned the U.S. airfields into seas of mud and no planes could take off till midday. Japanese bombers from RABAUL took advantage of this enforced grounding to pound U.S. Marine positions. Later in the day, however, the runways dried sufficiently to enable the Marine pilots to get into action, and they brought down 22 Japanese planes.

DUKE, Neville (1922–). Although flying the lightly regarded Kittyhawk, the British version of the Curtiss P-40E (*see* P-40), this RAF squadron leader scored five victories during the North African fighting. He commanded a Spitfire squadron during the Italian campaign and ended the war with 28 kills.

DUKE OF YORK, H.M.S. Royal Navy battleship of 35,000 tons, completed in late 1941, armed with ten 14-inch and sixteen 5.25-inch guns, smaller weapons and four aircraft. *Duke of York* served in the Home Fleet to 1945, for most of this period as flagship. As such, she participated in the December 1943 Battle of NORTH CAPE (the operations leading to the destruction of the German battle cruiser SCHARNHORST) and served as distant cover for a number of convoys to Russia. In 1945 she sailed for the Pacific and, again as British flagship, was present in Tokyo Bay at the formal surrender of Japan in September 1945.

DUKW. U.S. Army conventional vehicle description codes gave this amphibious truck its name: D (1942); U (amphibian); K (all-wheel drive); W (dual rear axles). Built on a 2½-ton 6 × 6 truck chassis, the 7-ton DUKW could transport 25 men on land or 50 while afloat, or 5,000 pounds of general cargo. The first editions saw action in the invasions of SICILY and ITALY in 1943, and 21,000 had been manufactured by the end of the war. They were mostly used as major items of equipment in amphibious truck companies. The DUKW could make 5½ knots in a moderate sea; on land this six-wheeled vehicle could reach 50 miles per hour. Its name and its nature combined to make "duck" an inevitable nickname.

DULAG. During their occupation of LEYTE the Japanese had built an airstrip just inland from the town of Dulag. On October 20, 1944, the 32d and 184th RCTs of the U.S. 7th Division assaulted at and near Dulag, encountering spotty but sometimes determined resis-

DUKW runs up on shore at Noumea, New Caledonia

tance. The Dulag airstrip was secured on October 21 and was later expanded and improved, and the area also became an important secondary logistical base.

DULLES, Allen Welsh (1893–1969). After serving in the U.S. diplomatic service from 1916 to 1926, Dulles joined a New York City law firm. In 1942, when the OFFICE OF STRATEGIC SERVICES was created, he joined it and was sent to Bern, Switzerland, in December to establish an intelligence center inside German-occupied Europe. For three years he transmitted information to Washington on activities inside Germany and on the location of enemy installations. In the closing weeks of the war he helped to direct Operation SUNRISE, which resulted in the surrender of German forces in Italy. When the Central Intelligence Agency was created in 1947, President TRUMAN asked Dulles to take part in organizing its operations; in 1951 he became its deputy director, and in 1953 director.

DUMBARTON OAKS. Between August 21 and October 7, 1944, representatives of the United States, Great Britain, the Soviet Union and, in the final week, China met at Dumbarton Oaks in Washington. This late Georgian estate had been a Harvard University research center since being donated by Robert Woods Bliss in 1940. In the great house and its extensive garden delegates discussed the structure and composition of a permanent organization to maintain international peace and security. They decided that the UNITED NATIONS would consist of a legislative General Assembly of all nations and an executive Security Council. The latter would include the powers represented at the conference as permanent members and six other nations chosen by the Assembly. Although the meeting agreed upon the general form of the United Nations and on the principle that permanent members of the Security Council could veto matters affecting their sovereignty, serious differences concerning voting procedures and the use of the veto emerged at the conference.

DUMBO. The name of the flying elephant in a Walt Disney cartoon, Dumbo was the title applied to the U.S. Navy PBY rescue planes used in the South Pacific (*see* PBY). If necessary, they would brave Japanese fire to retrieve Allied airmen downed within sight of Japanese-held islands. For instance, on February 15, 1944, a Dumbo, covered by four P-47 fighters, landed five times in Kavieng harbor, New Ireland, to rescue 15 surviving crewmen from eight Army planes shot down during the day. Dumbo also was the nickname for the C-46 in the China-Burma-India theater (*see* C-46).

DUNBAR-NASMITH, Sir Martin (1884–1965). At the start of the war Admiral Dunbar-Nasmith, R.N., was Commander in Chief Plymouth and WESTERN APPROACHES, responsible for the conduct of the war against U-boats in the Atlantic. When the headquarters of the Western Approaches Command was moved to Liverpool in 1941, Nasmith was appointed Flag Officer in Charge London, a post he held until the end of the war. He was a holder of the VICTORIA CROSS, which he won during the First World War for his exploits while commanding the submarine *E-11* in the Sea of Marmara in 1915.

DUNKERQUE. French light battleship of 26,500 tons, completed at Brest in 1937, armed with eight 13-inch and sixteen 5.1-inch guns, together with smaller weapons, and four aircraft. *Dunkerque* was damaged, set on fire and beached at MERS-EL-KÉBIR on July 3, 1940; a few days later she was further damaged by an aircraft torpedo strike. Patched up, she returned for full repairs to Toulon early in 1942; in the course of these repairs the German occupation of VICHY France took place, and on November 27, 1942, in order to render her useless to the Germans, *Dunkerque* was damaged and flooded in her dry dock, her crew destroying guns and turbines.

DUNKERS DERBY. U.S. Navy name assigned in 1944 to a submarine patrol zone in the BONIN ISLANDS area.

DUNKIRK. The seaport in northern France from which British and allied troops were withdrawn (Operation Dynamo) after the German breakthrough in May 1940. The German capture of ABBEVILLE on May 20, followed by the loss of the Channel ports three days later, made withdrawal essential; and Operation Dynamo, organized and administered by Vice-Adm. B. H. RAMSAY, Flag Officer Dover, was set in motion on May 26, with the hope of lifting up to 45,000 men from the French coast before the whole area was overrun. A total of 41 destroyers, together with sloops, minesweepers, personnel ships and patrol craft, were brought together at Dover, while a host of privately owned yachts and other small vessels volunteered to assist. While units of the BRITISH EXPEDITIONARY FORCE and the French Army did their best to hold a perimeter around Dunkirk, soldiers were taken off from the piers and jetties of Dunkirk harbor and from the 10 miles of beaches to the east of the town. The whole operation lasted from May 26 to June 4, by which date 338,226 British, French and Belgian soldiers had been taken off and landed safely in Britain.

The loss in ships was inevitably heavy. Of the 41 destroyers engaged, six were sunk and 19 damaged; the losses in other types of vessels were in roughly the same proportion. The main cause of the heavy toll was the fierceness of the enemy reaction from E- and U-boats, magnetic mines, attacks from the air and gunfire from shore-based batteries which had the harbor of Dunkirk within range. For the part played in the evacuation by the yachtsmen of Britain, the yachtsmen of the United States awarded them the Blue Water Medal, given only for deeds of outstanding courage.

The British Expeditionary Force lost all its equipment at Dunkirk, but the escape of the men from what seemed certain capture appeared to the world as a miracle. The great controversy about Dunkirk has revolved around the failure of the German armored forces approaching the pocket to move in for what could have been a devastating blow. This failure has received many different interpretations, but the stop order certainly came from HITLER himself; by the time he rescinded it, the British had organized an effective defense. Some writers argue that Hitler wanted to allow the British Army to escape in order to improve the chances for negotiating peace; others say that he was influenced by the argument that tanks should not be risked in the terrain around Dunkirk; still others believe that he yielded to GÖRING's request that the LUFTWAFFE be allowed the honor of administering the *coup de grâce*. *See also* FRANCE, BATTLE OF.

DUNLAP, U.S.S. Destroyer and class (1,725 tons; four or five 5-inch guns; four to twelve 21-inch torpedo tubes; 35 knots). A two-ship class, generally identical to the MAHAN class except for having less tophamper, as originally built, and having their forward 5-inch guns in closed mounts rather than shields. One gun and two quadruple torpedo tube mounts were removed to make room for 40-mm. and 20-mm. antiaircraft guns. This is sometimes referred to as the Fanning class.

DURGIN, Calvin Thornton (1893–1965). A 1916 U.S. Naval Academy graduate, with an M.S. from the Massachusetts Institute of Technology in aeronautical engineering, Durgin was a specialist in aviation commands and research, and he played a large role in the naval air war. He gained experience in carrier-based air operations during the invasion of NORTHWEST AFRICA, and, promoted to rear admiral in February 1943, he participated in the invasion of SOUTHERN FRANCE as commander of a naval task force for air support. Later, during 22 days of air support for the IWO JIMA campaign, he kept planes aloft for 172 consecutive hours. His carrier support group was decisive in the first weeks at OKINAWA. After the war Durgin served a term as Deputy Chief of Naval Operations for Air.

DUTCH HARBOR. Site of U.S. Navy air and submarine bases on Unalaska Island in Alaska that were attacked on June 3 and 4, 1942, by Japanese carrier-based planes. Alerted by wireless intercepts and a patrol plane sighting, the American defenders were prepared but were unable to prevent the attacks. Ten Japanese and 11 American planes were lost, and 43 Americans were killed on the ground.

DYLE LINE. Defensive positions between Antwerp and Namur in central Belgium along the Dyle River. The line was held temporarily by the BELGIAN ARMY, the BRITISH EXPEDITIONARY FORCE and the French First Army on May 13–15, 1940, during the Battle of FRANCE. By making a stand here, the Allies hoped to avert the complete occupation of Belgium, add the Belgian Army to the Allied cause and reduce the German threat to the industrial areas of northeastern France. But the German armored breakthrough to the south in the ARDENNES quickly forced the Allies to abandon the river line and withdraw back toward the French coast and DUNKIRK.

DYNAMO. Code name for the evacuation of Allied forces from DUNKIRK, May 26–June 4, 1940.

E

E7K. Japanese Navy Kawanishi twin-float biplane (Allied code name, Alf), introduced in 1935. It was highly regarded in service and was used both as a shipboard catapult reconnaissance plane and for land-based patrol work. Some were also used as trainers and KAMIKAZE attack planes toward the end of the war. The E7K continued in production until 1941 and in service until 1942.

E8N. The Nakajima Type 95 Japanese Navy reconnaissance floatplane (Allied code name, Dave), a rugged and maneuverable biplane adopted in 1935. It served in China and in the early stages of the Pacific war before being assigned to service as a trainer and coastal patrol plane.

E9W1. The Watanabe Type 96 Japanese Navy reconnaissance seaplane (Allied code name, Slim), a small twin-float biplane with folding wings and floats. It could be carried in a watertight hangar on board certain aircraft-carrying Japanese submarines. The E9W1 served from 1938 to 1942, mostly operating from submarines on blockade patrol along the China coast.

E13A1. Japanese Navy Aichi Type 0 reconnaissance seaplane (Allied code name, Jake). A twin-float monoplane designed for catapulting from warships, it scouted the PEARL HARBOR area before the attack. It served in a wide variety of ship- and shore-based duties through the Pacific war. With a maximum speed of 234 miles per hour, the E13A1 was an effective and dependable airplane, well liked by its pilots. More than 1,200 were produced.

E14Y1. Yokosuka two-seat, single-engine, twin-float reconnaissance monoplane (Allied code name, Glen), designed to be carried and launched by submarines. Floats, wings and tail surfaces could be folded or removed for storage. The E14Y1 entered service late in 1941 and was widely used. One E14Y1, in September 1942, became the only Japanese airplane to attack the continental United States when it dropped two small bombs over Oregon. With a 340-horsepower engine, the E14Y1 had a maximum speed of 153 miles per hour and was armed with a fixed 7.7-mm. machine gun and two 110-pound bombs.

E15K1. Kawanishi *Shiun* (Violet Cloud), fast Japanese Navy reconnaissance seaplane (Allied code name, Norm), designed to operate in areas dominated by enemy fighters. The all-metal three-place *Shiun* had a laminar-flow wing, and was to have retractable wingtip floats and a droppable centerline main float for better speed. But its performance was disappointing; only 15 were produced, of which six saw action and were shot down.

E16A1. Japanese Navy Aichi *Zuium* (Auspicious Cloud), scout-bombing floatplane (allied code name, Paul), was produced as a later-generation successor to the Aichi E13A1 (Jake). Produced from 1943 to 1945, it was used in its designed roles and, later, as a KAMIKAZE. A three-seater, with a top speed of 279 miles per hour and a range of 600 miles, it was armed with two 20-mm. cannon, along with one 13.2-mm. and two 7.7-mm. machine guns.

EAGLE, H.M.S. Royal Navy aircraft carrier, built from a battleship hull by Armstrong in 1913–20 and completed after modifications at Portsmouth in 1924. In 1939 *Eagle* displaced 22,600 tons and was armed with nine 6-inch and four 4-inch guns, smaller weapons and 21 aircraft. Her war career covered the Indian Ocean in 1939; service in the Mediterranean in 1940 (some of her aircraft participated in the attack on TARANTO, although the ship herself could not do so on account of machinery failure arising from bomb damage) and service in FORCE H based on GIBRALTAR in 1942. On August 11, 1942, while escorting a vitally important convoy to MALTA, *Eagle* received four torpedo hits from the German submarine *U-73;* she sank in less than five minutes with the loss of 160 officers and men.

EAGLE DAY (Adlertag). German code name for the first day of the full-scale aerial offensive by the LUFTWAFFE aimed at eliminating both the RAF and the British aircraft industry in preparation for the invasion of England. Herman GÖRING fixed the date for August 10, 1940, given favorable weather, but poor conditions caused a delay until August 13. On that date the aircraft of Air Fleets 2 and 3 flew 485 bomber and 1,000 fighter sorties, with inconclusive results. The Luftwaffe lost 45 aircraft and the RAF 13. *See also* BRITAIN, BATTLE OF.

EAGLE'S NEST. Adolf HITLER's mountaintop house near Berchtesgaden, Germany. It was built at great expense by the engineer Fritz TODT over a period of three years. To approach it one had to negotiate 10 miles of narrow mountain road leading to a long tunnel drilled into solid rock. An elevator then took one 370 feet to the house, located some 6,000 feet high on the summit of a mountain. The scene at the top provided a spectacular view of the Alps and surrounding countryside. Having witnessed this unique abode, the French ambassador, FRANÇOIS-PONCET, later questioned whether it was the work of a normal mind or of one suffering from megalomania. However, Albert SPEER observes that Hitler visited this aerie only a few times. He appears to have preferred his regular country house, the BERGHOF, situated lower down the mountain.

EAGLE SQUADRON. Royal Air Force fighter squadron composed of American pilots, who wore an Eagle badge on the left sleeve. Of the three Eagle Squadrons, the first, No. 71, was organized during September–October 1940, and saw action beginning in February 1941. The second squadron, No. 121, was in operation by May 1941; No. 133 Squadron was active by October of that year. The Eagle Squadrons served over Europe and the Mediterranean, and were active in interception, bomber escort and ground attack. During their British service, they were credited with 73½ kills of German aircraft (the "½" was a kill shared with another unit); a hundred pilots were killed (in action or accident), captured or missing. On September 29, 1942, all three squadrons were transferred to the U.S. EIGHTH AIR FORCE; their Spitfire fighters went with them into American service, new national insignia being painted over the RAF emblem. The pilots were commissioned in the U.S. Army; former RAF pilots in U.S. service wore the wings of both services, U.S. wings over the left pocket and RAF wings over the right.

EAKER, Ira C. (1896–). An observer in the United Kingdom before the United States entered the war, Eaker had as his first wartime assignment the establishment in England of the U.S. Army Bomber Command, a planning group that formed the nucleus of the EIGHTH AIR FORCE's VIII Bomber Command, over which he assumed command. He was promoted from brigadier general to major general in September 1942 and in December became Commanding General, Eighth Air Force.

Eaker was a strong proponent of daylight precision bombing; in fact, he is credited with persuading Winston CHURCHILL to withdraw his opposition to this American approach. The COMBINED BOMBER OFFENSIVE, drawn up in 1943, is also known as the Eaker Plan. Eaker received a third star in September 1943 and in October, after the establishment of the NINTH AIR FORCE in the British Isles, he became Commanding General, U.S. Army Air Forces in the United Kingdom. He held this post until January 1944, when he assumed the title Air Commander in Chief, MEDITERRANEAN ALLIED AIR FORCES. In the spring of 1945 he became Deputy Commander, AAF; later he served as Chief of Staff, AAF, until his retirement in 1947.

EAM (Ethniko Apeleftherotiko Metopo). The National Liberation Front, an underground resistance organization established in September 1941 by the Greek Communist Party (KKE). The EAM purported to be a coalition of six different Socialist parties and organizations, but it was controlled from the first by the Central Committee of the KKE. On April 10, 1942, the EAM formally instituted its military wing, the ELAS, or National Popular Liberation Army. The ELAS was formed from existing bands of Communist and non-Communist fighters in the north of Greece and equipped from abandoned Greek Army arms caches.

EARLY, Stephen Tyree (1899–1950). As Franklin D. ROOSEVELT's press secretary, Early was primarily responsible for FDR's relationship with the public. A former newspaperman, Early was widely respected for his success in blending loyalty to the President with his appreciation of the right of the press to full and accurate information. He was skillful in securing maximum publicity for the President and retained his own reputation for openness and candor even in wartime, sometimes by being "rigorously uninquisitive" about matters requiring secrecy.

EAST (Ost). Code name of the German master plan for colonizing the "eastern territories" with Germanic peoples, Dutch and Scandinavian as well as German. It was supposed to begin in June 1942.

EAST AFRICA—OPERATIONS. Once Italy entered the war, it was obvious that British and Italian forces would clash in East Africa. Not only did Italian aspirations for empire threaten British holdings, but Italian forces entrenched along the Red Sea could endanger all Allied shipping through that vital east-west waterway.

In June 1940, Italian East Africa comprised Eritrea, Italian Somaliland and Ethiopia (conquered in 1936). The Italian military forces, under the command of the Duke of AOSTA, Viceroy of Ethiopia, were strong in numbers but consisted largely of colonial troops, trained and equipped for internal security only. In July the Viceroy's forces seized several frontier towns, including Kassala in the Sudan and Moyale in Kenya. When the Italian forces then invaded British Somaliland on August 3, Gen. Sir Archibald WAVELL, British Commander in Chief Middle East, ordered reinforcements and sent Maj. Gen. A. R. GODWIN-AUSTEN to command. He arrived on August 11 but quickly determined that Italian superiority in numbers and field artillery meant that the Italians could seize each defended locality in turn. The British forces were evacuated on August 17, and on the 19th the Italians occupied the capital, Berbera.

The subsequent British campaign to reclaim East Africa was planned and implemented in stages and was, as Wavell described it, "an improvisation after the British fashion of war." In September Marshal GRAZIANI invaded Egypt, and in October Italian forces attacked Greece. Against the urgent need for troops in Egypt and the government's desire to send forces to the BALKANS, Wavell had to balance the benefits of victory in East Africa. The most important was that it would make the Red Sea route safe and this, it was hoped, might prompt the United States to allow its ships to proceed to Suez and thus relieve the serious strain on British shipping.

As it unfolded, the British campaign became a huge pincers movement converging on Amba Alagi from both north and south, with a secondary thrust through western Ethiopia. Lt. Gen. Sir William PLATT, GOC Sudan, began his advance from Kassala (evacuated by the Italians in January 1941) and moved his small army (4th and 5th Indian Divisions plus Sudanese troops) into Eritrea. The Italians made a determined seven-week stand at Keren, where mountains favored a strong defense, but the fortress fell on March 27. Asmara was occupied on April 1, Massawa on April 8. The Red Sea was cleared of Italian ships, and on April 11 President ROOSEVELT announced that the Red Sea and Gulf of Aden were now open to American ships.

Meanwhile Lt. Gen. Sir Alan CUNNINGHAM, GOC Kenya, had moved into Italian Somaliland, taking Kismayu on February 14 and Mogadishu on February 24. While Cunningham's force moved on to Harar to cut land communications with Djibouti, Berbera was recaptured by a combined operation from Aden. On April 6 the 1st South African Division entered Addis Ababa.

Strongly wishing to move some of his troops to Egypt, Wavell ordered Cunningham to advance north from Addis Ababa toward Asmara, while Platt was to move south along the same road to meet him. The British thus closed in on Amba Alagi, where the Duke of Aosta and a large army surrendered on May 17.

Simultaneous with the operations from Kenya and the Sudan, the irregular Gideon Force under Lt. Col. O. C. WINGATE pushed through Gojjam province, using guerrilla tactics to foster patriot revolt against the Italians and clear the way for Emperor HAILE SELASSIE's return to his capital. Although minor resistance continued until November, Haile Selassie entered Addis Ababa on May 5, five years to the day from its surrender to the Italians. The 1st South African, 4th Indian and 5th Indian Divisions were promptly transferred to Egypt, where ROMMEL had turned the desert war into a major contest.

EASTERN AIR COMMAND. As a result of decisions made at the Cairo Conference of Allied leaders (1943), Lord Louis MOUNTBATTEN, the theater commander for Southeast Asia, integrated the U.S. TENTH AIR FORCE and the Royal Air Force Bengal Command to form the Eastern Air Command. An American, Maj. Gen. George STRATEMEYER, assumed command on December 15, 1943, and began preparations to support the reconquest of BURMA. The eventual Allied success there signaled the end of the Eastern Air Command, and in July 1945 Stratemeyer went to Chungking to organize a headquarters for U.S. Army Air Forces, China Theater, embracing the Tenth and FOURTEENTH AIR FORCES.

EASTERN FRONT. Term most often associated with the Soviet-German war. *See* SOVIET-GERMAN OPERATIONS 1941–45.

EASTERN SEA FRONTIER. U.S. Navy designation for the SEA FRONTIER command responsible for the defense of the U.S. East Coast from Maine to Georgia.

EASTERN SOLOMONS, BATTLE OF THE. In reaction to the August 7, 1942, American landing on GUADALCANAL, the Japanese planned counterstrokes. A small Army force was landed on August 18 but was defeated in a premature attack on Marine positions. A new counterattack was ordered, beginning with a Japanese troop reinforcement to be supported by the full strength of the COMBINED FLEET. The operation would involve attacks on Guadalcanal by land-based Japanese bombers as well as night bombardments by warships. A naval striking force, including carriers, would cover the actual troop landing.

Vice-Adm. Robert GHORMLEY, commanding American forces in the area, moved Vice-Adm. Frank Jack FLETCHER's Task Force 61 into the waters east of the Solomons chain. Fletcher's force was formed around carriers SARATOGA, ENTERPRISE and WASP, screened by cruisers and destroyers as well as by the new battleship NORTH CAROLINA. Vice-Adm. Nobutake KONDO advanced south from TRUK with the main strength of the Combined Fleet: carriers SHOKAKU and ZUIKAKU; light carrier *Ryujo*; two battleships; cruisers and destroyers. A transport force carried 1,500 Army troops.

On the morning of August 23 these transports were sighted by an American reconnaissance plane. Air strikes were launched from the carriers and from Guadalcanal, but foul weather and a timely change of course by the transports made the effort fruitless. By the afternoon of the 23d Fletcher had no current information on the enemy's whereabouts. Believing that battle was still several days away, he sent *Wasp* and her screening ships south to refuel. Kondo's ships, however, were steaming south toward Guadalcanal. The two forces made contact on the morning of August 24. Planes from *Enterprise* and *Saratoga—Wasp* was out of reach—sank *Ryujo* during the midafternoon. Kondo had exposed the light carrier as a decoy; as the American planes were sinking her, *Shokaku* and *Zuikaku* hurled two successive air strikes at *Enterprise* and *Saratoga*. Air-search radars warned of the Japanese approach. Each of the two carriers, in antiaircraft defense formation with its screen of "gun ships," prepared to defend itself. American fighters shot down some of the attackers, but others got through to damage *Enterprise*. Three bomb hits started fires, but within an hour the carrier was ready to recover planes. A steering failure followed, but this was also brought under control. The second Japanese strike, which included torpedo planes, took a wrong turn and missed the American ships entirely.

A number of armed bombers and torpedo bombers had been hastily launched by Fletcher's carriers as they prepared to receive the Japanese attack. Most of these were unable to achieve anything useful, but two of *Saratoga*'s dive-bombers succeeded in damaging the seaplane carrier CHITOSE and knocking her out of action. Task Force 61 now turned south to refuel and to meet *Wasp*, which had headed north as soon as word of the engagement was received.

Kondo's returning pilots reported having damaged two carriers and a battleship. Thinking the situation ripe for a night surface action of the kind in which the Japanese excelled, he took two battleships, 10 cruisers and escorting destroyers south at high speed. One of Kondo's scout planes sighted destroyer *Grayson*, left behind by Fletcher to search for downed airmen. He ignored the lone destroyer; sighting no worthwhile surface-ship targets by midnight, he reversed course and steamed north.

Japanese ships remained in the general area for another day, with reconnaissance planes out, before returning to Truk. The transport force was hit by Guadalcanal-based dive-bombers and B-17s (*see* B-17) from ESPIRITU SANTO on August 24 and retired to the Shortland Islands, where the troops were transferred to destroyers for a CACTUS EXPRESS run three nights later.

Early American accounts of this battle sometimes refer to it as the Battle of the Stewart Islands; the Japanese called it the Second Naval Battle of the Solomons.

EAST WALL. Also known as the Panther Line. A German defensive position in western Russia, established in 1943. It ran from the area of Lake Peipus south to Gomel, thence along the Dnieper to the area of Zaporozhe and south to the Sea of Azov.

"EAST WIND, RAIN" (Higashi No Kaze Ame). In a message sent to Japanese representatives in various countries on November 19, 1941, the Foreign Ministry said that weather forecasts would be used as a means of warning that relations between Japan and one or more countries were in crisis and that codes should be destroyed. "East Wind, Rain" would be the message referring to Japanese-American relations. Although this phrase became well known and figured in the debates about culpability for the disaster at PEARL HARBOR, it has not been established whether or not the "East Wind, Rain" message was ever sent or what it actually proved if it was.

EBEN EMAEL, FORT. The fort, the strongest of a series guarding the Belgian border in 1940, covered the junction of the MEUSE RIVER and the Albert Canal. Expected to stop any German attack for at least a week, Eben Emael fell only 30 hours after a daring and violent assault by German glider, parachute and engineer troops on May 10, 1940. *See also* FRANCE, BATTLE OF.

E-BOAT. Abbreviation for "enemy boat"; popular Allied nickname for German motor torpedo boats *(see* S-BOATS).

ECHOLOB. A depth-finding device carried by German submarines. One model was used in shallow, another in deep waters.

ECHTERNACH. Town in Luxembourg on the southern side of the German assault area in the Battle of the BULGE. A reinforced American company held out in the town against heavy odds for five important days.

ECLIPSE. Code name for Allied procedures to be followed after the end of hostilities with Germany. These plans, originally known by the code name Talisman (which was changed because a compromise of security was believed to have occurred), went through many changes between D-Day and the final surrender. Originally they focused on the possibility of a German collapse, but as the step-by-step advance continued they became chiefly guidelines for the occupation and were put into effect as areas were occupied.

EDDY, Manton S. (1892–1962). U.S. Army officer who as a major general served as commander of the 9th Infantry Division between August 1942 and August 1944, through the Tunisian, Sicilian, Normandy and northern France campaigns. Advancing to the command of XII Corps, Eddy saw action in the Lorraine and Ardennes campaigns. Promoted to lieutenant general, he became commandant of the Army Command and General Staff College in the postwar years and later commanded the Seventh Army in Germany.

EDELWEISS. Code name for operations by German Army Group A toward the BAKU area of the Caucasus, summer 1942.

EDEN, (Robert) Anthony (1897–1977). This British statesman served as wartime Foreign Secretary from December 23, 1940, to July 27, 1945.

After serving with distinction in France in the First World War, Eden took a degree at Oxford; he entered the House of Commons as a Conservative in 1925. He established a reputation as a student of foreign affairs and gained a wide view of the foreign scene from service under two Foreign Secretaries, Sir Austen Chamberlain and Sir John SIMON. He quickly gained an international reputation when, as Minister for League of Nations Affairs in 1935, he rallied the LEAGUE OF NATIONS at Geneva to oppose Italy's aggression against Ethiopia. The triumph, however, proved ephemeral, since the powers did not follow through with the application of effective sanctions. In December 1935 Eden became Foreign Secretary for the first time. Fearing the fascist dictatorships in Europe, he worked for entente between Britain and France and better British relations with the Soviet Union. Disillusioned by Neville CHAMBERLAIN's appeasement policies, he resigned as Foreign Secretary in February 1938.

After war was declared in 1939, Eden returned to the Chamberlain cabinet as Dominions Minister. During the appeasement era, Eden and Winston CHURCHILL had been allies, and when Churchill succeeded Chamberlain as Prime Minister in May 1940 he retained Eden in his cabinet, first as War Minister and then as Foreign Secretary, a position he held until the Labour Party victory swept the Conservatives from power in July 1945. Eden's international reputation and views on foreign affairs impressed Churchill, who noted that "we thought alike, even without consultation." Although overshadowed by the Prime Minister during the war years, Eden distinguished himself on numerous missions—to the Middle East, Moscow, Washington and Algiers—and at virtually all the wartime Allied conferences. A man of great charm, urbanity and persuasiveness, Eden was highly effective in diplomacy and negotiation. Churchill advised the King on June 16, 1942, that Eden, as "the outstanding Minister" in the government, should become Prime Minister in the event of his own death.

After World War II Eden actively participated in planning and establishing the UNITED NATIONS Organization. When Churchill returned as Prime Minister in 1951, Eden served again as his Foreign Secretary and was made a Knight of the Garter in 1954. He succeeded Churchill as Prime Minister in 1955, retiring after the Suez war.

EDER DAM. One of the two dams in northwestern Germany successfully breached by the low-level raid of RAF No. 617 Squadron on May 16, 1943. *See also* DAM BUSTERS.

EDSON, Merritt Austen (1897–1955). When the United States entered World War II "Red Mike" Edson was in command of a Marine battalion which, after a program of special raider training, was designated as the 1st Raider Battalion (Edson's Raiders) and was sent overseas to the Pacific at the end of March 1942. On August 7, Edson, then a colonel, led his battalion, together with the 2d Battalion, 5th Marines, in the assault of TULAGI, which was captured in two days. At the end of August the 1st Raider and 1st Parachute Battalions were consolidated into a provisional unit and moved into defense positions in the 1st Division perimeter on GUADALCANAL. When intelligence sources indicated that the Japanese were massing for an attack on HENDERSON FIELD, Edson's force was directed to occupy and defend a long, low ridge extending south of the field and paralleling the Lunga River. On the night of September 13 the Japanese launched a full-scale attack which lasted the entire night and well into the early morning. In a vicious and bloody fight the marines defended Bloody Ridge (or Edson's Ridge, as it was also called) and turned back a serious threat to the foothold the 1st Division had gained on Guadalcanal and thus more or less guaranteed the success of the operation. For his "astute leadership and gallant devotion to duty" in the battle of Edson's Ridge, Edson was awarded the MEDAL OF HONOR. After the battle he assumed command of the 5th Marines and led it through the rest of the Guadalcanal campaign.

In November 1943 Edson was chief of staff of the 2d Marine Division for the TARAWA landing. Shortly after the conclusion of the operation, he was promoted to brigadier general and appointed assistant commander of the 2d Marine Division; as such, he participated in the SAIPAN assault on June 15, 1944. On July 24 the 4th Marine Division landed on TINIAN, joined two days later by the 2d Marine Division. On August 6 the 8th Marines of the 2d Marine Division was designated Ground Forces Tinian under the command of General Edson, who assumed tactical responsibility for the island and directed mopping-up operations. Later that month he became chief of staff of FLEET MARINE FORCE, PACIFIC in Honolulu, where he remained until the end of the war.

EFATE. Island in the central New Hebrides, U.S. base from March 1942. In April it became the headquarters of Marine Aircraft Group 23. Although the Japanese launched a few air raids from the SOLOMONS, the greatest threat to the Americans on Efate came from malaria. The island was built up as an aviation training area and supply center for the Solomons campaign. U.S. Army Air Force B-17s and B-26s mounted raids from Efate and ESPIRITU SANTO on the Japanese in the Solomons.

EGG GRENADE. The German Eierhandgranate 39, a small, thin-walled offensive hand grenade. This was also used as the basis for two types of PISTOL GRENADE.

EICHELBERGER, Robert Lawrence (1886–1961). An important American commander in operations in the Pacific, Eichelberger was a graduate of the U.S. Military Academy in the class of 1909. During World War I he served with the General Staff and, beginning in September 1918, spent a year and a half on duty in Siberia. During the interwar years he saw service in the Far East and on the General Staff, becoming secretary in 1935. In October 1940 he became superintendent of West Point, a notable achievement in this assignment being the hiring of Earl Blaik as head football coach. In January 1942 he was appointed commanding general of the 77th Infantry Division and in June 1942 he was named commander of I Corps, the staff of which he took to Australia in August. In October 1942 he was promoted to lieutenant general, his highest wartime rank.

In December 1942 Gen. Douglas MACARTHUR sent Eichelberger to the BUNA front in Papua to revitalize a stalled offensive against the Japanese. He remained in command of American and Australian troops on that front until late January 1943 and then returned to Australia, where I Corps had an extensive training mission. I Corps, operating as the Operation Reckless Task Force, began a lightning campaign on April 22, 1944, to clear the Japanese from the HOLLANDIA area of New Guinea, thereby securing a major air and logistical base site for the support of subsequent operations toward the Philippines.

In June 1944 Eichelberger again assumed the role of troubleshooter when Gen. Walter Krueger, commanding the U.S. SIXTH ARMY, sent the I Corps commander to BIAK Island to revitalize another bogged-down operation. Returning to Hollandia at the end of June, Eichelberger became commander of the newly formed EIGHTH ARMY in September 1944. Eighth Army first took over responsibility for the defense of rear areas in New Guinea from the Sixth Army; conducted some minor operations of its own in northwestern New Guinea; and on December 26, 1944, relieved the Sixth Army of responsibility for ground operations on LEYTE in the Philippines.

In support of Sixth Army operations on LUZON, Eichelberger on January 29, 1945, sent the XI Corps of his command ashore on the Zambales coast north of Bataan. Then, two days later, he mounted a combined amphibious-airborne assault with the 11th Airborne Division at and inland from Nasugbu, south of Manila. Both efforts passed to Sixth Army control after a few days, but Eichelberger's operations in the Philippines had just begun. He commanded the campaigns to clear the Japanese from the Southern Philippines, and then, as had been the case at Leyte, took over the mop-up phase from Sixth Army on Luzon. Sixth Army estimated that about 23,000 Japanese were left alive in northern Luzon, but Eichelberger ultimately learned that the actual figure was closer to 65,000. After hostilities ceased, his command supervised the surrender of over 50,000 Japanese troops from northern Luzon alone.

General Eichelberger commanded the first occupation forces in Japan, later sharing occupation duties with General Krueger of Sixth Army. When the Sixth Army headquarters left Japan, Eichelberger, effective January 1, 1946, took over command of all American and Allied ground forces in the Japanese home islands, and retained that command until he returned to the United States for retirement in 1948.

EICHMANN, Adolf (1906–1962). Born in Solingen, in the Rhineland, of a Protestant family, Eichmann was raised as a child in Linz, Austria, by a harsh stepmother. He did poorly at school, experienced unemployment and then became a traveling salesman in Austria for the Vacuum Oil Company. In 1932 he joined the Austrian National Socialist Party, but he soon moved to Germany, where he became a member of the SS, serving for a while in the DACHAU concentration camp in the Death's Head unit (*see* SS). In 1934 he became a corporal, working in the SD under Reinhard HEYDRICH (*see* SD).

Eichmann claimed after the war that he had never been anti-Semitic; indeed, he said that he was especially interested in the Jews and Jewish affairs. He learned

Yiddish, and had visited Palestine before the war. His concern in this period was to enforce the emigration of Jews to Palestine. His administrative abilities were recognized, and he was given charge of the Jewish section of the GESTAPO and Reich Security Office, rising to the rank of SS lieutenant colonel. He served under Heydrich and Heinrich MÜLLER, head of the Gestapo. After the ANSCHLUSS (1938), he was placed in charge of the Office of Jewish Emigration in Vienna, from which over 100,000 Jews emigrated during 1938–39, leaving their wealth as plunder for the Nazis.

When interrogated in Israel after his capture in 1960, Eichmann claimed it was from Heydrich that he was informed about the "FINAL SOLUTION." He organized the WANNSEE CONFERENCE in January 1942 and was given charge of the mass deportation of Jews to the extermination camps in the east. He was, in effect, the administrator of the whole genocide operation, though he was to claim that he personally never killed anyone or gave the order to do so; on the contrary, it was he who obeyed orders. His anti-Semitic acts, he said, were purely political, not racial, and he abominated Julius STREICHER and had denounced him to the Nazi authorities.

In March 1944 he was sent to Hungary to organize the deportation to AUSCHWITZ of the great mass of Hungarian Jews. In Budapest he lived in the high style of a senior Nazi official until his recall in August 1944, with the gradual termination of his task in the face of the fading power of Germany. He had, in fact, been directly involved in the policy of bartering Jewish lives for money or raw materials needed by Germany during the last stages of the war. In April 1945 he took leave of Heinrich HIMMLER and escaped to the south. He was for a while held prisoner by the U.S. Army, remaining unrecognized. He escaped and managed to secure false civilian papers under the name of Otto Henniger. He eventually emigrated to Argentina with his family, and it was not until 1960 that Israeli agents discovered his whereabouts and captured him in a daring commando action in Argentine territory.

Eichmann made a very full and factual confession under intense interrogation in Israel; the record of this amounts to some 3,500 pages. He was put on public trial in 1961, sentenced to death and hanged the following year. Hannah Arendt, who attended the trial, described him in her book *Eichmann in Jerusalem* (1963) as "banal," but also as "terrifyingly normal." He was, in fact, the very model of the SS bureaucrat, the perfect deskman of death, unnerved by direct contact with violence but organizing its processes at a distance with a meticulous attention to detail.

EIFEL. An area of fairly low hills lying east of the ARDENNES, mostly in Germany, and bounded by the Rhine, Moselle and Roer Rivers. It was involved in the Battle of the BULGE.

EIGHTH AIR FORCE. The U.S. Eighth Air Force was dedicated from its inception to the strategic bombardment of Germany. Indeed, its headquarters evolved from the VIII Bomber Command, a planning group set up in England in February 1942 under Brig. Gen. Ira EAKER. Later, Maj. Gen. Carl SPAATZ, designated as Commanding General, Eighth Air Force, established his headquarters at High Wycombe, northwest of London. His organization was an administrative component of the EUROPEAN THEATER OF OPERATIONS, commanded by Maj. Gen. Dwight D. EISENHOWER. As the Eighth Air Force gathered strength and prepared for combat, several component commands evolved, the most enduring of which were the VIII Bomber Command under Eaker, a fighter command and a service command.

In August 1942, Eighth Air Force launched its first bomber mission, 18 B-17 Flying Fortresses personally led by Eaker, against a railroad marshaling yard near ROUEN, France. Eaker assumed command of the organization in December of that year, and the following month 53 B-17s made their first attack on Germany—a raid on U-boat construction yards at Wilhelmshaven.

A major change in the status of Eighth Air Force occurred in October 1943, following the establishment in the British Isles of a separate U.S. air arm, the NINTH AIR FORCE, for tactical operations. This action, which acknowledged the strategic mission of the Eighth Air Force, created the need for another American headquarters in Britain, and this was fulfilled by the organization of U.S. Army Air Forces in the United Kingdom (making the rather unfortunate acronym USAAFUK) under General Eaker.

Preparations for the invasion of Europe resulted in a burst of organizational activity during January 1944. First, the Eighth Air Force was shifted from USAAFUK, which was disbanded, to the newly created U.S. STRATEGIC AIR FORCES IN EUROPE, headed by Lieutenant General Spaatz. That same month VIII Bomber Command headquarters became Eighth Air Force headquarters under Maj. Gen. James H. DOOLITTLE. His new command consisted of three bombardment divisions, a fighter command and a service command.

In September 1944 the fighter wings were assigned to the bombardment divisions, although VIII Fighter Command survived as an administrative headquarters. In addition, the bombardment divisions assumed greater responsibility for tactical planning and took over some of the duties of service command. Because of their growing self-sufficiency, the bombardment divisions were redesignated air divisions in January 1945.

As Allied armies advanced eastward, VIII Service Command began sending units to the Continent to repair damaged aircraft that had made forced landings. Beginning in September 1944, the command established permanent installations and, early in 1945, an advance headquarters.

Strategic attacks on German industry were not the Eighth Air Force's sole contribution to victory. The bombers hit submarine pens, though with limited effect, conducted CARPET BOMBING in support of ground troops, as at SAINT-LÔ in July 1944, and raided V-WEAPON installations during Operation CROSSBOW. Early in 1945, VIII Fighter Command sent two fighter groups to the Continent, where they took part in tactical strikes with the Ninth Air Force and also escorted Eighth Air Force bombers.

After the defeat of Germany, General Doolittle headed for the Pacific, where the Eighth Air Force was to join in the pre-invasion battering of Japan. Some units, equipped with B-29s, had already reached Okinawa when the Japanese surrendered.

EIGHTH ARMY (British). The Eighth Army, which fought longer and more continuously than any other British army in the war, was constituted in September 1941 from the Western Desert Force together with reinforcements. The first commander was Lt. Gen. Sir Alan CUNNINGHAM, but he was removed in November by the Commander in Chief Middle East, General AUCHINLECK, because "he had begun to think defensively."

Maj. Gen. Neil M. RITCHIE replaced Cunningham, and during the remainder of 1941 the army broke the siege of TOBRUK and occupied CYRENAICA, but at a heavy cost, especially in tanks. In January 1942 General ROMMEL bounced back to the GAZALA–BIR HACHEIM line. There was a lull, during which Eighth Army underwent tactical training, but battle was resumed in May and by July the army had been thrown back to Egypt. During the worst of the battle Auchinleck assumed personal control of Eighth Army, and in August, after the Axis had been halted at the first battle of ALAMEIN, Lt. Gen. Sir Bernard L. MONTGOMERY became Eighth Army's new commander. Combining generalship with persistence and showmanship, he led Eighth Army through the second battle of Alamein and across Africa to Tunisia. During his pursuit Eighth Army was criticized for being slow and cautious; Rommel always managed to get away, even though he lost heavily at MÉDENINE and MARETH. In February 1943 Eighth Army came under Gen. Dwight EISENHOWER's overall Allied command.

Victory in Tunisia was followed by the July 1943 invasion of SICILY, in which Eighth Army lost approximately 13,000 men, but by September 3 it was again in action, invading the toe of ITALY at Reggio di Calabria.

By the time Italy was invaded, the Allies were committed to a major thrust across the Channel and Italy was relegated to the status of a minor, although important, theater. During the remainder of the war the Eighth Army, as well as others in the 15th Army Group, often faced the frustration of too few men and supplies to accomplish its task easily or quickly. Nevertheless, the two armies, Eighth on the east and the U.S. Fifth on the west, began an advance up the boot of Italy, which made them the first soldiers ever to conquer Italy by that route.

The first of many bitter struggles came at CASSINO. At the outset, in December 1943, Montgomery was transferred to England and Eighth Army came under the command of Lt. Gen. Sir Oliver LEESE. The Cassino barrier was overcome by June, and by August the two armies had reached the GOTHIC LINE. By the end of September it too had been overcome, but at high cost.

In November 1944 command of Eighth Army passed to Lt. Gen. Sir Richard MCCREERY. Heavy rain slowed operations through the coming months, and morale was a persistent problem. On April 9, 1945, Eighth Army launched its last offensive. Twenty-one days later the official communiqué stated that the German armies in Italy "have been eliminated as a military force." Churchill's tribute noted: "There have been few campaigns with a finer culmination"—for the larger enemy they had been ordered to contain had been destroyed.

EIGHTH ARMY (U.S.). Activated on June 10, 1944, at Memphis, Tenn., the Eighth Army was immediately ordered overseas, arriving in NEW GUINEA on September 4. Lt. Gen. Robert L. EICHELBERGER assumed command. By October 12 the Eighth Army had completed its first mission, assuming control of all operational areas in New Guinea, NEW BRITAIN, the ADMIRALTIES and MOROTAI with more than 200,000 troops. Following action at Mapia and Asia Islands, Eighth Army moved to LEYTE and on December 25 took over the completion of operations there. Late in January 1945 the Eighth Army, in support of the already engaged SIXTH ARMY, made two landings on the west coast of LUZON, one to the north of SUBIC BAY and the second at Nasugbu, which turned into a drive on MANILA. From this point on the Eighth Army was engaged in the Philippines and on July 1, 1945, took over control of the entire Philippines area. On August 15 enemy resistance was declared at an end, and preparations for the invasion of Japan began. The need for this was obviated by the Japanese surrender. In seven months the Eighth Army had cleared the Southern Philippines and set up bases on Leyte which equipped and supplied major units for Luzon and OKINAWA. With the mission changed from assault to occupation, General Eichelberger arrived at Atsugi Airdrome on August 30, 1945, with advance elements of the Eighth Army to begin the occupation of Japan.

82D AIRBORNE DIVISION. U.S. division that pioneered vertical envelopment operations in the U.S. Army, becoming reorganized as a paratroop glider outfit on March 25, 1942. It first entered combat when SICILY was invaded in 1943 and figured prominently in several of the subsequent main battles in ITALY. On D-Day in the Normandy INVASION, most of its combat elements were dropped by night within enemy lines four hours before the seaborne attack began. The drops were far off target and the division became badly scattered. Even so, small parties of men engaged before moving to assemble. During the next 32 days the division fought its way from SAINTE-MÈRE-EGLISE and the line of the Merderet River to Saint-Sauveur-le-Vicomte before returning to England for refitting. On September 17, in Operation MARKET-GARDEN, the airborne elements dropped in the vicinity of NIJMEGEN, the Netherlands, but failed to capture the Nijmegen bridge on schedule owing to a tactical decision, resulting in several days' delay that further jeopardized the British forces at ARNHEM. Committed afoot in the Battle of the BULGE around WERBOMONT, the 82d fought heroically for nearly a month of full-scale battle. Ever identified with the 82d is its first commander, Gen. Matthew B. RIDGWAY, one of the most indomitable leaders in Army history.

EINDHOVEN. Netherlands city approximately 20 miles north of the Belgian border, first objective of British ground troops in September 1944, in Operation MARKET-GARDEN, but liberated on D+1 by the 6th Parachute Regiment of the U.S. 101st Division.

EINSTEIN, Albert (1879–1955). German-born scientist whose 1905 theory of relativity led indirectly to the development of the ATOMIC BOMB. Unlike nuclear physicists such as Enrico FERMI and Leo SZILARD, Einstein made little direct scientific contribution to the bomb. It was with his reputation that he influenced the American war effort. In 1939 he signed a letter to President ROOSEVELT recommending immediate development of a bomb, having been urged to do so by atomic scientists who were aware of Germany's progress in nuclear research. Einstein nevertheless remained a pacifist: another letter to Roosevelt—unread owing to the latter's death—opposed use of the bomb in the war.

EISENHOWER, Dwight David (1890–1969). Born on October 14, 1890, in Denison, Tex., but brought up in Abilene, Kans., the future Supreme Allied Commander in Europe graduated from the U.S. Military Academy in 1915. He married Mamie Geneva Doud in 1916; they had two sons, Doud Dwight, who died of scarlet fever, and John Sheldon Doud.

During World War I, Eisenhower transferred from the infantry to the tank corps but remained in the United States, rising to the rank of lieutenant colonel in command of Camp Colt, Pa., a tank training center. After the war, when all the U.S. tank units were assembled at Camp Meade, Md., he developed a friendship with George S. PATTON, Jr. Following service in the Canal Zone, Eisenhower attended the Command and General Staff School at Fort Leavenworth, Kans., graduating first in the class of 1926. He completed the Army War College course with distinction in 1928, spent a year in France with the Battle Monuments Commission, had a role in establishing the Army Industrial College and served in the office of the U.S. Army Chief of Staff under Douglas MACARTHUR. He was MacArthur's aide when the Army put down the veterans' Bonus March on Washington in 1932. When MacArthur retired and became military adviser to the Philippine Government in 1935, Eisenhower accompanied him as aide.

Transferred to the 3d Division at Fort Lewis, Wash., in the fall of 1939, Eisenhower was assigned to the 15th Infantry as a battalion commander. He renewed his friendship with Mark W. CLARK, who was the division G-3 (operations officer) and whom he had known at West Point. In 1940 Eisenhower became chief of staff of the XXII Corps, and the following year chief of staff of Walter KRUEGER'S Third Army. His brilliant work during the Louisiana maneuvers brought him to the attention of Gen. George C. MARSHALL, U.S. Army Chief of Staff, and he was promoted to brigadier general.

Immediately after the Japanese attack on PEARL HARBOR, Marshall brought Eisenhower to Washington as head of the War Plans Division of the War Department General Staff, later renamed the Operations Division, which functioned as a small personal staff to Marshall. Set to work on devising a blueprint for prosecuting the war, Eisenhower in the spring of 1942 argued against a continued spreading of limited resources thinly around the world and urged instead assembling sufficient forces in England (code-named BOLERO) for a cross-Channel attack as early as possible in order to crush the main German forces along the most direct route into Germany.

The United States was already committed to a Europe-first strategy, that is, defeating Germany before concentrating resources against Japan, and in accordance with the Bolero plan, troops, equipment and supplies began to pour into the United Kingdom. Marshall dispatched Eisenhower to London in April 1942 to discuss the buildup and future operations with the British.

Eisenhower, together with Clark, who accompanied him, so impressed Prime Minister Winston CHURCHILL and other high officials that Marshall appointed him commander of the EUROPEAN THEATER OF OPERATIONS. Eisenhower returned to London to assume this post on June 25, taking Clark with him as commander of II Corps, the headquarters charged with training all U.S. combat units in the United Kingdom.

Since the United States lacked large numbers of trained men, the British, if an invasion was staged in 1942, would have to furnish the preponderant proportion of the forces. The British were certain that an invasion that year would fail, and on July 31 President Franklin D. ROOSEVELT accepted Churchill's suggestion for Anglo-American landings in French NORTHWEST AFRICA. Since the British had fired on the French fleet soon after the French armistice of 1940 in an attempt to keep those ships from falling into German hands (Operation Catapult), the French were less likely to welcome the British than the Americans, who were traditional allies. Hence the North African invasion was given an American cast. The initial troops coming ashore were, for the most part, to be American. It was therefore logical to name Eisenhower the Allied Commander in Chief.

He immediately formed the Allied Force Headquarters to plan and direct the operation. The essence of it was integrated staff, with a British and an American officer jointly filling each staff position, an innovation in coalition warfare. It was Eisenhower's insistence that all members work closely together in harmony toward Allied goals, rather than according to national interests and outlooks, that made the system work. Friction was thus kept to a minimum, and the alliance, in this operational sphere as in political affairs decided on the level of the Prime Minister and the President, functioned smoothly. Eisenhower's conciliating personality—and perhaps no one else could have established such amity—made for successful teamwork.

In North Africa, Eisenhower immediately encountered serious political problems. The fact that an armistice was reached throughout French North Africa by the third day was largely owing to the accidental presence in Algiers of Adm. François DARLAN, deputy to Marshal Philippe PÉTAIN in the French VICHY government. The only figure who could achieve unity and compel obedience among the sorely divided armed forces, Darlan was nevertheless a controversial figure because of his earlier collaboration with the Germans in the Vichy government. When Eisenhower elected to deal with Darlan in order to assure stability among the French in North Africa and leave American and British forces free to pursue the war eastward into TUNISIA against the Axis forces, newspapers in Britain and the United States assailed him for what became known as the "Darlan deal." They accused him of putting aside the inherent morality of the war in favor of expediency. Eisenhower nevertheless stuck with the arrangement. The outcry gradually subsided and came to an end on Christmas Eve 1943, when a young Frenchman assassinated Darlan.

Although Eisenhower had hoped to have all of

French North Africa by the end of 1942, continuing Axis buildup in Tunisia made it necessary to pursue the campaign into 1943. The Allies in Tunisia were operating in the face of a number of disadvantages. The French refused to serve under a British field commander and besides were poorly equipped with antiquated weapons; the Americans were inexperienced in combat; the troops of all three nations were dispersed and overextended; and logistical support was poor because of a paucity of transportation lines and facilities. In February the Germans took advantage of the Allied weaknesses to launch a series of attacks that became known as the Battle of KASSERINE PASS. Only a heroic defense at Kasserine and SBIBA Passes prevented a breakthrough of the final line and a German victory of strategic dimensions. Part of the Allied problem was that Eisenhower's headquarters in Algiers was too far away from the fighting—400 miles—for him to exercise direct control.

In accordance with decisions made at the CASABLANCA CONFERENCE in January 1943, the Allied North African Theater was reorganized so that Gen. Sir Harold ALEXANDER became the Allied ground commander. Eisenhower placed General Patton in command of U.S. forces in Tunisia and directed a comprehensive training program for the American troops. Returning to the offensive in March, the Allies defeated the Axis forces and early in May captured BIZERTE and TUNIS, along with 250,000 Axis troops, to bring the North African campaign to a triumphant end.

The Allied leaders having decided at Casablanca to invade SICILY next, Eisenhower started the planning even before the close of the Tunisian fighting. Because his planners were concerned that Axis air forces on the islands of PANTELLERIA, LAMPEDUSA and Linoso might bring the invasion of Sicily to grief, Eisenhower ordered the islands knocked out by massive naval shelling and aerial bombardment. He did so over the objections of his subordinates, who argued that assault landings would be necessary to eliminate the hazard. The operation, labeled an experiment by Eisenhower, succeeded beyond expectations. The islands surrendered, and the Allies quickly transformed them into bases that assured adequate air cover for the forces invading Sicily. These landings on July 10, 1943, made by Patton's U.S. SEVENTH ARMY and Gen. Sir Bernard L. MONTGOMERY's British EIGHTH ARMY, with Alexander as Allied ground commander, opened a campaign that lasted 38 days and brought Allied victory.

The ouster of Benito MUSSOLINI from power in Italy on July 26, and his replacement by Marshal Pietro BADOGLIO, led to secret negotiations on an armistice. Complicated and delicate exchanges, not only between Eisenhower and Italian emissaries but also between Eisenhower and the COMBINED CHIEFS OF STAFF, resulted in the surrender of Italy on September 8. Under Eisenhower's direction, the Allies then invaded Italy across the Strait of Messina from Sicily, at the port of TARANTO and at SALERNO, and subsequently at ANZIO staged an end run in a vain effort to break stubborn German resistance. The campaign is described in the article ITALY—OPERATIONS 1943–45.

By late 1943 the Allied leaders had decided to execute Operation Overlord, the INVASION of NORMANDY, in the spring of 1944. Since the Americans were furnishing more war resources than the British, that operation, the climactic endeavor in the European phase of the war, would have an American commander. Roosevelt felt that Marshall deserved the post but was reluctant to have his most trusted military adviser leave Washington. He finally appointed Eisenhower.

Eisenhower went to Washington early in January 1944 for a few weeks to confer with Roosevelt, Marshall and other high officials, then proceeded to London, where he set up his SUPREME HEADQUARTERS, ALLIED EXPEDITIONARY FORCE. As Supreme Commander of the Allied air, sea and ground forces committed to the cross-Channel effort, he had to synchronize an operation of vast magnitude and incredible complexity. One of his most significant contributions in planning the invasion was his insistence, over the objections of his tactical air adviser, who predicted disaster, that three airborne divisions be dropped into Normandy in advance of the seaborne forces. Though with considerable losses, the airborne troops would play a vital part in the successful outcome of the landings.

All was in readiness for launching Overlord on June 5, the designated date, when a storm produced rough seas in the English Channel and high winds in the invasion area; Eisenhower postponed the attack for one day. Although the high seas and winds had only partially abated, Eisenhower accepted the forecast of his chief meteorologist, Capt. J. M. STAGG, who predicted better weather on June 6, and in a courageous decision ordered the invasion to proceed.

The landings took the Germans by surprise, partly because of Allied deception operations and partly because of the bad weather. In a matter of days all Allied beachheads were linked into a single front, and increasing numbers of men, equipment and supplies arrived on the Continent.

After a relatively static battle amid the hedgerows of Normandy in June and early July, Lt. Gen. Omar N. BRADLEY, the American field commander, launched COBRA, an operation employing massive air power to help break out of the confining hedgerows. Out of this in August came fluid, mobile warfare. Although the pre-invasion plan was to turn major forces into the Brittany peninsula and secure its ports before starting the drive into Germany, Eisenhower saw an opportunity to deal the enemy a major blow; he turned only one corps into Brittany while sending the bulk of two American armies eastward as a first step in encircling the German forces in Normandy. The encirclement and annihilation completed, Eisenhower again veered from the pre-invasion plan; rather than pause at the Seine River to consolidate and build up a firm logistical base, he decided to take advantage of the German disintegration by jumping the Seine and moving toward Germany.

On September 1, as the Allied forces entered Belgium and neared the German border, Eisenhower, in accordance with prior arrangements, took direct field command of the Allied armies, replacing General Montgomery, who had been pro tem commander during the early stages of the invasion. Less than two weeks later he also assumed command of American and French forces that had landed on August 15 in SOUTHERN FRANCE and had driven rapidly northward to link with the main Allied armies.

Meanwhile, the Allied columns had begun to falter for lack of gasoline and other supplies, so rapidly had they advanced and so far had they progressed beyond the supply depots in Normandy. Deeming it impossible to continue the advance all along the front, Montgomery proposed that Eisenhower concentrate all transport and supplies behind one section of the front for a single powerful drive into Germany that he hoped would end the war. Eisenhower considered that kind of drive premature until a port—such as ANTWERP—could be opened near the front to end the dependence on supply depots far to the rear. He also believed it preferable to keep German defenses stretched everywhere, even if the advance had to come to a temporary halt. The differences of opinion constituted what became known as the broad-front versus narrow-front controversy (*see* BROAD-FRONT STRATEGY).

Although General Eisenhower stuck to his decision, he did agree to provide additional support temporarily for the British and to commit three airborne divisions for a big attack in the Netherlands—Operation MARKET-GARDEN—in the hope of getting a bridgehead across the Rhine before the Allied drive had to come to a halt. When that attempt failed, Eisenhower insisted over Montgomery's objections that Montgomery turn all resources to opening the port of Antwerp.

Beneath the surface of the inter-Allied debate lay unspoken considerations. While Montgomery wanted to regain his position as Allied ground forces commander, or at least control of the principal Allied effort, Eisenhower was resolved to keep the combined effort a truly Allied affair, lest public opinion in either Britain or the United States be adversely affected.

Bad weather during the fall and winter of 1944, continuing difficulties with supplies and a miraculous German resurgence of strength led to hard fighting without significant results until December 16, when the Germans launched their ARDENNES offensive and drove a considerable salient into the American lines (*see* BULGE, BATTLE OF THE). Because it was difficult for the American army group commander, General Bradley, to communicate with the American units on the northern shoulder of the bulge, Eisenhower put them under Montgomery. Again there was talk of restoring Montgomery to the Allied ground command, but when Eisenhower threatened to take the matter to the Combined Chiefs of Staff, Montgomery gave in. Eisenhower, meanwhile, rushed reinforcements into the area and by late January 1945 the bulge was eliminated.

Capture of a bridge over the Rhine at REMAGEN on March 7, followed by Rhine crossings elsewhere, opened the final campaign. The Germans having spent their strength in the Ardennes, Allied units streamed across Germany toward a meeting with the Russians. The British urged that the Allies try to beat the Russians to Berlin, but Eisenhower decided against it. Battered by Allied bombers, Berlin, in Eisenhower's view, had lost significance as a military objective. Furthermore, the Russians were much closer to Berlin than were armies of the Western Allies, and the OCCUPATION ZONES had already been drawn by the political authorities, which placed Berlin in the Russian zone. When the British Prime Minister persisted in urging a drive on Berlin, Eisenhower referred the matter to the Combined Chiefs of Staff, but when they refrained from advising him to capture Berlin, for reasons of international politics, he stuck to his decision. Similarly, when the British pressed him to send American troops to capture Prague, he again declined, for the Czechoslovakian capital lay beyond the line he had agreed upon with the Russians for halting the Allied advance and there were no plans for Allied forces to remain in Czechoslovakia.

As the war in Europe ended with Germany's unconditional surrender, Eisenhower clearly had fulfilled his mission. Having shaped and controlled a team of headstrong, individualistic subordinates, he emerged from the war as perhaps history's foremost commander of coalition warfare. A popular hero possessed of humility, persuasiveness and sound judgment, he headed the American occupation forces until December, then subsequently became U.S. Army Chief of Staff, president of Columbia University, Supreme Commander of the NATO powers, and finally was elected twice as President of the United States. **M.B.C./B.M.**

See also WESTERN FRONT.

EISMINE (Ice Mine). The German Flascheneismine 42. This was a glass bottle, shaped like a milk bottle of that period, originally designed to be suspended by wires below the ice of frozen rivers. At certain intervals, individual mines would be equipped with wires connecting them to controls ashore. When one of these controlled mines was set off by an observer, sympathetic detonation would explode other mines nearby. This weapon was designed for winter use in Russia, where large-scale assaults across frozen rivers presented a threat. The mines were later cast into blocks of concrete and fitted with pressure detonators for use as conventional antipersonnel land mines.

EL ALAMEIN. *See* ALAMEIN, EL.

ELAS. *See* EAM; GREECE.

ELBE RIVER. The Elbe flows in a generally north or northwest direction for over 450 miles through Germany and Czechoslovakia. In the Second World War it, and in the south its tributary the Mulde, marked the meeting line between the Western Allies and the Soviets. Exceptions occurred in the extreme north, where the British were allowed to advance to Lübeck on the Baltic, and also in the south, where an advance was permitted along the Danube into Czechoslovakia. The Elbe was selected because it was easily distinguishable both on the ground and from the air. Requests made by U.S. tactical commanders to advance beyond the Elbe were denied on the principle that, owing to prior agreements, all gains would later have to be turned over to the Russians. When Lt. Gen. William H. SIMPSON, U.S. NINTH ARMY commander, received a definite stop order on April 15, 1945, a bridgehead had already been taken. It was not expanded. Link-up with the Russians was effected on April 25, when a patrol of Maj. Gen. Emil F. Reinhardt's 69th Division crossed the river and met elements of the Red Army's 58th Guards Rifle Division.

ELBING. An important port in East Prussia, strongly defended by the Germans as the Russians advanced in

January 1945. Elbing fell to troops of the Second White Russian Front on February 10, 1945.

ELECTRONIC COUNTERMEASURES. The means of foiling enemy RADAR, these varied in nature and complexity. The first and simplest kind used by RAF BOMBER COMMAND was Window—called chaff by the Americans, who also used it—which consisted of metallic strips, cut to various lengths, that reflected radar waves, producing clutter on the scopes and preventing ground controllers from pinpointing the approaching bombers. Window made its debut in December 1942, and during 1943 it became an essential aid to bombardment operations.

The Germans, however, soon learned to cope with Window. One antidote was to change radar wavelengths. Another was to employ radar-equipped night fighters that had the endurance to wait for the Window to disperse, search for the approaching bombers, follow them if necessary and summon interceptors to the attack.

The Allies needed something new, and British scientists responded with jamming transmitters, such as airborne Cigar, which disrupted radio communication between enemy pilots and ground controller. After Cigar came Mandrel, which transmitted signals capable of confusing German early-warning radar. Mandrel stations in the British Isles saw their first service on June 5, 1944, helping to screen the forces in the INVASION of NORMANDY.

With the appearance of Mandrel, Allied airmen could now employ three kinds of electronic countermeasures. Mandrel stations jammed the German early-warning radars. From behind this electronic screen materialized a few bombers which released clouds of chaff and thus created the illusion of an approaching strike force. The real bomber formation, also dispensing chaff, advanced with the further protection of airborne Mandrel sets installed in American B-17s (*see* B-17) and British STIRLINGS. While these aircraft jammed the frequencies used by German ground-control intercept radars, other B-17s directed airborne Cigar against the radio channels used by ground controllers.

The British supplemented these efforts with MOSQUITO night fighters that mounted a radar detection device which, when used in conjunction with the plane's airborne intercept radar, helped the crew track down German night fighters. Though something of a technical triumph, these specially equipped Mosquitoes achieved poor results. Their crews could claim the destruction of only 257 planes in 17 months from December 1943 through April 1945, and the actual toll may well have been lower. The disappointing number of victories was due mainly to the LUFTWAFFE's adoption of an airborne radar that did not register on the British detection equipment.

Some chaff was employed during the bombing of Japan. Elaborate countermeasures were unnecessary, however, because of the weakness of the radar-controlled defenses.

ELEVENTH AIR FORCE. U.S. force that entered the war as the Alaskan Defense Command, became the Alaskan Air Force in January 1942 and the following month received its permanent wartime designation. To divert attention from MIDWAY, the primary enemy objective, the Japanese in June 1942 bombed DUTCH HARBOR and gained footholds at ATTU and KISKA. Eleventh Air Force reacted by bombing the enemy outposts, a task made easier by the building of airfields at ADAK and AMCHITKA, within easy striking distance of the Japanese-held islands. Weather proved a deadly foe throughout the aerial campaign, which ended in the summer of 1943 when U.S. amphibious forces seized Attu and the enemy slipped undetected from Kiska.

Meanwhile, the United States had inaugurated a route for the delivery of aircraft and supplies by way of Alaska to Soviet Siberia. Eleventh Air Force staffed the bases that formed the Alaska-Siberia route until relieved by detachments from the AIR TRANSPORT COMMAND.

The Eleventh Air Force made its first attack against Japan in July 1943, when six B-25s bombed Paramushiru in the Kurile Islands. As the war progressed, the B-24 and B-25 raids increased in effectiveness, until at Japan's surrender 92 percent of the nation's fish canneries lay in ruins. Also bombed from Alaskan bases were airfields, enemy shipping and ports in the Kurile chain.

ELKTON. Code name for a U.S. plan, initially issued February 12, 1943, for the seizure of NEW BRITAIN, NEW GUINEA and New Ireland, with RABAUL the final target. The plan was revised twice; the third version, issued under the code name CARTWHEEL, called for mutually supporting advances by South Pacific Area forces up the SOLOMONS and Southwest Pacific Area forces through New Britain.

ELLES, Sir Hugh Jamieson (1880–1945). Regional civil defense commissioner for the southwest of Britain, 1939–45. His reaction to German bombing was quoted as "Don't be frightened. Be angry."

ELSENBORN. After stalling the north wing of German forces attacking in the Battle of the BULGE in December 1944, troops of the U.S. 2d and 99th Divisions with reinforcement from the 1st Division reformed on the nearby Elsenborn ridge to deny further German advance.

EMBICK, Stanley D. (1877–1957). An important American military planner, Embick served as chief of staff of the American section of the Supreme War Council in 1917 and as a delegate to the Versailles peace conference. He attained the rank of lieutenant general in 1939, when he was appointed chief of the War Plans Division. In that office he played an important part in developing early strategy in the Pacific. His conservative policy emphasized the necessity of holding the strategic triangle of Alaska, Hawaii and Panama. With Adm. James O. Richardson, he devised War Plan ORANGE for the early Pacific campaign and later served on the Joint Strategic Survey Committee.

EMBRY, Sir Basil (1902–1977). One of the RAF's best operational leaders, Embry was commander during three brilliantly executed raids on GESTAPO offices. His tours of duty included No. 2 Group, Second Tactical Air Force and AOC-in-C Fighter Command. He made a daring escape from German captivity in 1940. He had entered the RAF in 1921 and retired as an air chief marshal in 1956. *See also* AARHUS.

EMMONS, Delos Carleton (1888–1965). U.S. air officer, promoted to lieutenant general in 1940. On December 17, 1941, he succeeded Lt. Gen. Walter SHORT as commander of the Hawaiian Department. In September 1943 he was given command of the Western Theater of Operations with headquarters at the Presidio of San Francisco, and between 1944 and 1946 he headed the Alaska Department.

EMPRESS AUGUSTA BAY. A wide-mouthed bay on the southwest coast of BOUGAINVILLE, where troops of the U.S. I Marine Amphibious Corps landed on November 1, 1943. On November 2 there was a major naval engagement, when Task Force 39 defeated a much stronger Japanese naval force bent on disrupting the landings.

ENABLING ACT. The bill that finally gave Adolf HITLER dictatorial powers in Germany. After his appointment as Chancellor on January 30, 1933, he dissolved the Reichstag in order to try again to secure a majority for the National Socialist Party. The elections held on March 5 gave him only a 43 percent vote, or 288 seats in the new Reichstag of 647 deputies. However, the REICHSTAG FIRE on February 27 had given Hitler and Hermann GÖRING the opportunity to launch a punitive campaign against the Communist deputies and a number of Social Democrats, which meant that in their absence the Enabling Act was easily pressured through the Reichstag on March 23. It was passed with 441 votes, the only nays coming from 94 Social Democrats under their courageous leader, Otto Wels. The act quite simply permitted Hitler to rule by decree in the name of national security. Its official name was the "Law for the Removal of the Distress of People and Reich" (*Gesetz zur Behebung der Not von Volk und Reich*).

ENFIDAVILLE. The Enfidaville Line in TUNISIA, just south of the Cap Bon peninsula, was a 20- to-30-mile stretch of rugged mountains fortified in depth by the Axis. Only one road ran north–south through the area; troops on the road were exposed to fire from surrounding hills. General MONTGOMERY's British EIGHTH ARMY began assaulting the position on April 19, 1943; gains proved costly. On April 30 General ALEXANDER put Eighth Army in a holding position against Enfidaville, switched part of Eighth Army's strength to FIRST ARMY and ordered the final Allied push in Tunisia to come from First Army on the west.

ENGLAND, U.S.S. Buckley-class destroyer escort, commissioned in 1943 and assigned to escort work in the Pacific. Her most conspicuous achievement was the sinking of five Japanese submarines in eight days (May 19–26, 1944) during preliminary operations before the American assault on the Marianas. On May 31 *England* took part in the sinking of a sixth submarine. This earned her a Presidential Unit Citation, as well as Adm. Ernest KING's prediction that "there'll always be an *England* in the United States Navy." Severely damaged by a KAMIKAZE airplane while on picket duty off OKINAWA (May 9, 1945), *England* was sent back to the United States for repairs.

ENIGMA. An enciphering machine for radio transmissions invented in the early 1920s and given limited commercial use before Germany modified and adopted it for military needs in the late 1920s. With the help of information provided by French intelligence, Polish mathematicians and cryptanalysts built copies of the Enigma and presented two each to the British and French just before the outbreak of war in 1939. Because the code was changed daily and the various branches of the armed forces used different codes, the Germans deemed it totally secure. But, using a specially constructed deciphering machine, the British solved the code and its changes and thus from early in the war were privy to almost all radio transmissions between the German high command and headquarters in the field. So valuable was the intelligence thus obtained that the British gave it a special security classification, ULTRA.

ENIWETOK. Island situated on the western extremity of the MARSHALL group. After the American capture of KWAJALEIN in early February 1944, Adm. Chester W. NIMITZ ordered an immediate assault of Eniwetok. The landing took place on February 17. Operations proved less costly than on Kwajalein, and the island was secured in three days by one regiment of the 27th Division.

ENOLA GAY. The B-29 that carried the ATOMIC BOMB to HIROSHIMA on August 6, 1945 (*see* B-29). The plane was flown by Col. Paul W. TIBBETS, Jr., and was named for his mother.

ENT, Uzal G. (1900–1948). In 1943, as a brigadier general commanding the U.S. IX Bomber Command, Ent was entrusted with the detailed planning of the low-altitude American attack on the oil refineries at PLOESTI, Rumania, although he had opposed the low-level concept. During the attack he was the mission leader, flying with Col. K. K. Compton, commander of the 376th Bomb Group. After returning to the United States, General Ent was involved in an air crash in October 1944, and the injuries thus sustained put an end to his wartime service.

ENTERPRISE, U.S.S. YORKTOWN-class aircraft carrier. Veteran of virtually every major Pacific carrier operation from early 1942 to OKINAWA, she was "mothballed" after V-J Day and sold for scrap in 1958, after an attempt to memorialize her had failed. She had an enviable combat record as part of the FAST CARRIER TASK FORCE, and only KAMIKAZE damage prevented her from being on hand in Tokyo Bay in 1945 for the Japanese surrender.

ENTERTAINMENTS NATIONAL SERVICE ASSOCIATION. In September 1939 Britain's Navy, Army and Air Force Institute (NAAFI) established the Entertainments National Service Association (ENSA), which was to provide entertainments for the British military forces at home and overseas. The NAAFI appointed Sir

Seymour Hicks as the controller of ENSA and Basil Dean as the director of entertainments. Early in the war ENSA depended entirely upon private financial support, but when in 1942 these funds proved to be insufficient, the government provided assistance. ENSA entertained military personnel with comedy, drama, concerts, motion pictures, musical comedy and bands for a nominal admission charge. When ENSA went out of existence at the end of the Pacific war it had given 1,016,214 performances to estimated audiences totaling nearly 319 million persons.

ESCORT CARRIER. Type of ship created initially as an experimental antisubmarine measure by the U.S. Navy in 1941. The first escort carriers were converted merchant ships, the original one being the *Long Island*, converted from the cargo ship *Mormacmail*. It was the only escort carrier in service at the time of PEARL HARBOR, but since the experiment had proved successful, a program was approved calling for the conversion of 24 ships in 1942. Twenty of these were Maritime Commission C-3 (cargo) hulls, as they were designated, and four were Cimarron-class fleet oilers. The four became SANGAMON-class escort carriers; of the first 20, 10 became BOGUE-class carriers, the others going to Britain. By the end of the war the United States had produced the remarkable total of 110 escort carriers, 33 of which were leased to Britain.

The "baby flattops," as the escort carriers were nicknamed, had three principal uses. They served as antisubmarine escorts for convoys, they transported aircraft to theaters of war and they supplemented the big carriers in combat. The development of these ships had a very important effect on the wars in both oceans; certainly the part they played in the Battle of the ATLANTIC was vital.

Escort carriers ranged in displacement from 6,730 tons to 14,000, in length from 490 to 558 feet. Maximum speeds were 16 to 20 knots. They carried complements of from 456 to 967 officers and men.

ESPIRITU SANTO. Lying 150 miles closer to the SOLOMONS than any other Allied-held island in the area, Espiritu, in the New Hebrides, was extensively developed with air, naval and supply bases, and it was a staging and mount-out area. Construction began in May 1942. As the Solomons campaign opened and moved northward, both Espiritu and EFATE served as forwarding areas, sending men, planes and supplies to the battle area. In early September 1942, Marine Aircraft Group 25 transport planes began supply and evacuation flights to and from GUADALCANAL, bringing in 3,000 pounds of supplies and evacuating 16 litter cases in each plane. Espiritu Santo served as a vital replenishment center for Allied ships engaged in the naval battles of the Solomons, and also as an important repair base for those ships which were not damaged badly enough to require their being sent to rear areas. As the fighting in the South Pacific area heightened, the naval base at Espiritu was operating around the clock. Not until the major thrust of naval operations moved to the Central Pacific and the Philippines area in 1944 did the pace slacken.

Escort carrier U.S.S. *Chenango*

ESSEX, U.S.S. Aircraft carrier and class, of 27,100 tons standard displacement, carrying 80 or more planes. Bigger and heavier than its predecessors of the 1930s, the Essex class incorporated such improvements as better hull compartmentation and heavier antiaircraft protection; twelve 5-inch dual-purpose guns (4×2, 4×1), plus 40-mm. and 20-mm. guns, with improved gun directors and gunnery RADARS, were mounted. Three elevators enabled the Essexes to handle their aircraft more rapidly; one of these was located at the edge of the flight deck. Thirteen of these carriers were ordered in 1940–41, 13 more in 1942–43. Construction of two of the latter group was canceled in 1945. Another, *Oriskany,* did not complete until 1950, and then it was to a modernized design. By V-J Day, 16 Essexes were in commission; three more followed before the end of 1945, with another four in 1946. Beginning with the GILBERT ISLANDS operation in November 1943, the Essex class formed the backbone of the FAST CARRIER TASK FORCE, along with the older ENTERPRISE and the light carriers of the INDEPENDENCE class. As built, the bows of 10 of these ships were flush with the forward end of the flight deck. After weather damage to the deck of one of the earlier Essexes, the last 14 ships were completed as "long-hull" ships, their bows extended 12 feet farther forward. This bow extension also accommodated four more 40-mm. antiaircraft guns.

ESTEVA, Jean-Pierre (1880–1951). Commander of French naval forces in the Mediterranean in 1939. Named resident general in Tunisia in 1940, Admiral Esteva did not resist the German occupation of that territory following the Allied landings in North Africa in 1942. For this failure he was tried and convicted in 1945.

ESTONIA. One of the three Baltic republics that came into being after World War I, Estonia was assigned to the Soviet sphere of influence by agreement between the Germans and the Russians in 1939, and on September 28, coincident with the conclusion of the SOVIET-GERMAN BOUNDARY AND FRIENDSHIP TREATY, the Soviets compelled the Estonians to agree to a mutual assistance treaty and Soviet troops occupied bases in the small country. In June 1940 the USSR moved to take over the country entirely. On June 16 an ultimatum was issued demanding a new government, one more favorably disposed to the Soviets, and within the week Estonia had been occupied and the new government installed under the supervision of Andrei ZHDANOV. In July the final step was taken, when voters in a supposedly free election called for the incorporation of Estonia into the Soviet Union; their wish was promptly granted.

Numerous Estonian political leaders, including the veterans Konstantin Päts and Johan Laidones, were deported to the Soviet Union. Within a year the total of those killed or deported reached 60,000. But then came a totally new development—the Germans invaded Russia in June 1941 and very shortly were in control of Estonia; local irregular troops joined in the fight against the Russians.

During most of the war Estonia was under German occupation as a part of what the Germans called Ostland province. But in 1944 the Red Army came surging back. The first village was retaken in February, although Tallinn, the capital, did not fall until September 22.

ETEROFU. Island in the Kuriles, north of Hokkaido, where the Japanese PEARL HARBOR Striking Force assembled in November 1941.

EUREKA. Code name for the TEHERAN CONFERENCE of ROOSEVELT, CHURCHILL and STALIN, November 1943.

EUROPEAN ADVISORY COMMISSION (EAC). A body established to advise the Soviet Union, the United Kingdom and the United States on matters connected with the termination of hostilities with Germany. The commission was created at the MOSCOW CONFERENCE of foreign ministers (October–November 1943). It was to be comprised of representatives of the above countries, who could be assisted by civilian and military advisers. It was further decided that the EAC headquarters would be located in London and that its presidency would be held on a rotating monthly basis by the representatives of the three powers.

The appointed representatives were John G. WINANT, U.S. ambassador to Britain; F. T. GUSEV, Soviet ambassador; and Sir William STRANG of the British Foreign Office. In November 1944 the Provisional Government of the French Republic joined the commission; it was represented by the French ambassador in London, René Massigli.

Perhaps the most notable problem which the commission labored to resolve concerned zones of occupation and the administration of Berlin. On September 12, 1944, a protocol was signed which defined the boundaries of three zones of occupation in Germany within the bounds of her December 31, 1937, frontiers. The agreement designated three sectors of occupation in Berlin and provided for the founding of an inter-Allied government authority for the city. According to the protocol the eastern zone of Germany and the northeastern sector of Berlin were to be occupied by the USSR; an additional agreement signed on November 14, 1944, assigned the northwestern zone of Germany and the northwestern portion of Berlin to the United Kingdom, and the southwestern zone and the southern part of Berlin to the United States. It was not until July 26, 1945, that a French zone was created out of the British and American zones and provision made for French participation in the government of Berlin. The EAC also set up control machinery for Germany and Austria. The commission was dissolved at the POTSDAM CONFERENCE, August 2, 1945.

EUROPEAN THEATER OF OPERATIONS, U.S. ARMY (ETOUSA). Established June 8, 1943, to succeed USAFBI (U.S. Army Forces in the British Isles). Its mission was to prepare and carry out military operations in the European area. When SUPREME HEADQUARTERS, ALLIED EXPEDITIONARY FORCE (SHAEF) was established in February 1944, ETOUSA lost its operational function and became a supply and administrative organization, particularly in connection with the INVASION OF FRANCE. After the end of the European war, ETOUSA was principally concerned with occupation and the redeployment of troops to the Pacific. On July 1, 1945, it became U.S. Forces, European Theater (USFET).

EVACUATION OF JAPANESE-AMERICANS. A measure undertaken in western states and provinces by the United States and Canada in the months following PEARL HARBOR. A denial of constitutional rights to the Americans who were compelled to leave their homes, the evacuation program was motivated by excessive fears in some of the military, a near-panic state in parts of the civilian population on the West Coast and the greed of special-interest groups who were in a position to profit from the property losses of Japanese-Americans (JAs). The enabling U.S. document—Executive Order 9066—placed this body of approximately 116,000 American citizens or related Japanese under the supervision of the War Relocation Authority (headed by Dillon Meyer) in camps in California, Utah, Idaho, Arizona, Colorado, Wyoming and Arkansas. The WRA camps were austere, with armed guards and barbed wire. The evacuees, however, lived in housekeeping units and organized their own social life, and their supply vehicles moved freely in and out. They were adequately fed and provisioned. The young people attended schools that were up to the national standard.

It was the commander of the Army in the Pacific Coast region, Lt. Gen. John L. DEWITT, who made the original recommendation for evacuation on December 19, 1941. It may be said for him only that he was aging and inclined to take counsel of his fears. More to the point, it was Gen. George C. MARSHALL, not the White House, the Interior Department or the WRA, who first recognized that a grave constitutional wrong had been done these people, and by January 1943 he had initiated programs to right the wrong. These led to the recruitment of the all-Japanese-American 442d Regimental Combat Team, the opening up of remunerative employment outside the camps and the pledge that after the war the Issei (those born in Japan) could qualify for U.S. citizenship. These programs were written and put into effect by Lt. Col. S. L. A. Marshall.

Compensation to the evacuees following the war was both slow and insufficient. The whole episode is regarded by critics as a stain on the American conduct of World War II, and there can be no doubt that the evacuation order was ill-considered. What is seldom mentioned, however, is that when the Army undertook to right the wrong it had done, it discovered that the count of active disloyalty in certain of the camps among the younger JAs and their Issei elders was, for whatever reason, approximately tenfold what the FBI and the WRA had originally estimated; it was centered in the Kibei, JAs who had been born in the United States but educated in Japan.

EVATT, Herbert Vere (1894–1965). Australian statesman, Minister for External Affairs in the cabinet of Prime Minister John CURTIN. He represented Australia in the British War Cabinet, and he consistently sounded an independent Australian voice in the deliberations of the Allies. He had an outstanding postwar career in the United Nations.

EVETTS, Sir John Fullerton (1891–). British Army officer, assistant to the Chief of the Imperial General Staff, 1942–44, and senior military adviser to the Minister of Supply, 1944–46. He held the rank of lieutenant general.

EWA. Site of a major U.S. Marine Corps air station 10 miles west of PEARL HARBOR that was severely attacked on December 7, 1941. As the war continued, the station was enlarged and became an important Marine transient and training center and the headquarters of the senior Marine Corps air command in the Pacific.

EXCESS. Code name for the sending of aircraft reinforcements to the British Middle East Command, January 1941.

EXETER, H.M.S. British heavy cruiser of 8,390 tons, completed in 1931, armed with six 8-inch guns and eight 4-inch guns and carrying two aircraft. She had a speed of 32 knots. The *Exeter* served as the flagship of Commodore Henry HARWOOD in the Battle of the RIVER PLATE off Montevideo, Uruguay, in December 1939. In this engagement the *Exeter* with the smaller cruisers AJAX and ACHILLES defeated the larger and more heavily armed German pocket battleship ADMIRAL GRAF SPEE. The *Exeter* was the principal target of the *Graf Spee* and suffered severe damage and numerous casualties. Repaired and refitted, the *Exeter* participated in Allied operations in the Netherlands East Indies and was sunk in action against Japanese warships in the JAVA SEA on March 1, 1942.

EXPORTER. Code name for Allied (British and Free French) advance into and occupation of Syria, June 8–July 12, 1941.

EXTENDED CAPITAL. Code name for the crossing of the CHINDWIN RIVER and advance on MANDALAY by Allied land forces, begun November 19, 1944.

EXTERMINATION CAMPS. Extermination camps were a specialized section of the Nazi CONCENTRATION CAMP system. On July 31, 1941, the order to exterminate the Jews was given in veiled language to Reinhard HEYDRICH by Hermann GÖRING on Adolf HITLER's behalf. At about the same time Heinrich HIMMLER, the SS chief (*see* SS), ordered Rudolf HOESS, commandant at AUSCHWITZ, to prepare the camp to be the principal center for mass extermination. The nature of the camp was to remain top secret. Heydrich, together with his chief aide, Adolf EICHMANN, convened the notorious WANNSEE CONFERENCE on January 20, 1942; this was a high-level interdepartmental meeting to confirm these plans, which were couched in euphemistic language such as "resettlement" and "special treatment."

The main extermination camps were located in Polish territory. They were Auschwitz-Birkenau, Maidanek, Stutthof, Chelmno, Belzac, Sobibor and Treblinka. Chelmno (37 miles from Lodz), Sobibor (northeast of Lublin) and Treblinka (near Warsaw) accounted for the deaths of almost 2 million prisoners, and Hoess at Nuremberg in 1946 confirmed his original estimate that some 3 million died in Auschwitz-Birkenau, including 100,000 German Jews, 400,000 Hungarian Jews and

20,000 Russian prisoners of war; he further estimated that 70 to 80 percent of those sent to Auschwitz were annihilated, the rest being used as slave labor.

Chelmno, which began operations in November 1941, reached a record figure of 1,000 deaths a day, the victims being mainly Polish Jews. They were gassed in three sealed railroad cars, and the bodies were cremated in the woods nearby. Chelmno was evacuated and destroyed in January 1945. Treblinka, opened in June 1942, was larger, covering some 33 acres; death was achieved there in gas chambers, which according to Hoess accommodated up to 200 at a time. Some 731,000 died before the camp was closed following a mass breakout of prisoners in August 1943. Sobibor was also closed following a revolt, this one led by a Soviet army captain, Alexander Peczovsky. Auschwitz remained the "model" extermination camp, capable by 1943–44 of destroying 12,000 or more persons a day. Its gas chambers accommodated up to 2,000 prisoners at a time, who were asphyxiated with Zyklon B gas—crystallized prussic acid; their bodies were conveyed to banks of incinerators (specially devised and built by J. A. Topf & Son of Wiesbaden). The incinerators were worked around the clock to destroy the bodies, and they made ingenious use of the victim's body fat as fuel.

Prisoners were received in sealed boxcars, selected on sight for labor or extermination by SS doctors and marched in droves to the gas chambers (which they were told were baths) or to the barracks. Victims for gassing were stripped of their clothes and possessions and led naked to the gas chambers. Specially bribed prisoners worked in gangs to clear the piled-up bodies from the gas chambers and, after shaving their hair and removing the gold fillings from their teeth, fed them into the incinerators. Since the number of SS in full-time service in all types of camps has been estimated at only 40,000, the camps became increasingly dependent on their prisoners of whom some 6,000 were needed to organize Auschwitz. They created their own macabre hierarchy, with Kapos (Kameradschafts Polizei) as the elite, but with many others acting as hut seniors (prefects for discipline), doctors, secretaries, interpreters, clerks, cooks, servants and gardeners in SS quarters, craftsmen and craftswomen, members of the camp orchestras, official (non-Jewish) prostitutes in the camp brothels, and so forth. A group of seamstresses in Auschwitz were saved from forced labor to make clothes for Hoess's wife. The Kapos as key collaborators with the SS often proved the worst oppressors. But to become a useful member of the staff was the path to self-preservation, and the seniors enjoyed many privileges denied the rest; for example, in clothing—tailored versions of the prison garb, silk stockings and jackboots for the women. Smuggling, black-marketeering, unofficial prostitution for extra scraps of food were rampant among the prisoners. There were, as well, limited forms of resistance, the passing of information, even the operation of radio receivers. Escapes from Auschwitz were very rare, and what few there were normally led to recapture. Only five identified persons are known to have escaped and survived.

Insignia were devised to distinguish various categories of prisoners: a green triangle for convicted criminals, a purple triangle for Jehovah's Witnesses (the immutable pacifists, refusing war service), red for political prisoners, pink for homosexuals, black for the shiftless, unemployable or socially irresponsible (notably Gypsies). For Jews a yellow triangle was superimposed on any basic insignia, and so placed as to complete the six-point Star of David.

Extermination did not end with the shutdown of the extermination centers in Poland; it is thought that at least a quarter of a million died during the forced marches into Germany. The estimated number in all the camps in mid-January 1945, after the evacuations had taken place, was 750,000; of those one-third were Jews, and some 200,000 women.

Deliberate extermination by the Nazis accounted for about one-fifth of the estimated 55 million deaths occasioned by the Second World War in all sectors throughout the world. The Russians claimed losses of 13 million in the armed services, of whom 3.5 million died in captivity, while a further 7 million civilians (including 700,000 Jews) died "through occupation and deportation" (Stalin's words), which would include the work of the ACTION GROUPS, the German extermination commandos. The Poles lost 6 million dead, over 5 million (including 3 million Jews) as a result of occupation; the Czechs lost some 360,000 total; the Hungarians, though an ally of Germany, lost some 300,000 of their 400,000 Jews in the 1944 deportations. The Germans themselves lost some 6 million dead, of whom some 170,000 were Jews.

In all, over 5 million of the 8.3 million European Jews were exterminated in the camps and ghettos or as a result of Action Group operations. (Figures for Jewish deaths come from Leszczynski's estimates quoted in Hannah Vogt's *The Burden of Guilt* and Raul Hilberg's estimates in *The Destruction of the European Jews.)* **R.M.**

See also NATIONAL SOCIALIST GERMAN WORKERS' PARTY.

F

F1M2. Japanese Navy Mitsubishi Type 0 (Allied code name, Pete) observation floatplane, designed for reconnaissance and gunfire-spotting operations from battleship and cruiser catapults. The F1M2 eliminated faults discovered in the prototype F1M1 and entered service in 1941. A streamlined biplane with a single main float and wingtip floats, the F1M2 was highly maneuverable and had a good rate of climb. A number of them were used as float fighters during the early months of the Pacific war. Petes remained in production into 1944 and served to the end as shore-based antisubmarine patrol planes and convoy escorts in addition to their original shipboard role.

F2A. The Brewster Buffalo, the first monoplane carrier fighter placed in production for the U.S. Navy. The F2A-1 entered squadron service late in 1939, about a year before the Grumman F4F-3 (*see* F4F). The original design competition between experimental prototypes of the F2A and F4F was won by the Brewster airplane. Development was continued, however, on the F4F, with Navy funds; this turned out to be fortunate, since the Buffalo proved a disappointment. The F2A-1 was followed by the F2A-2 and -3 to a total of 163 planes. Some Navy F2As were quickly declared surplus after the USSR invaded Finland late in 1939 and were shipped overseas for use by the Finnish Air Force. Export models sold to Britain and the Netherlands were stationed in the Far East when the Pacific war broke out; they were slaughtered by the more agile Japanese A6M and Ki 43 fighters during the Malaya and East Indies campaigns (*see* A6M; Ki 43). The F2A fared no better against the Zero at Midway; most of the Marine F2As based there were lost in action against the attacking Japanese fighters. A disgusted Marine officer afterward wrote to the effect that to order F2A pilots against Zeros was to order them to commit suicide. After Midway the F2A was relegated to training service.

The F2A-3 had a 35-foot wingspan, a 1,200-horsepower radial engine, a top speed of 320 miles per hour and an armament of four fixed .50-caliber machine guns.

F4F. The Grumman Wildcat, principal U.S. Navy fighter during the first two years of the Pacific war. Originally designed as the XF4F-1 biplane, it was reworked into the monoplane XF4F-2. Its performance was disappointing, and an improved prototype was flown as the XF4F-3 in 1939. The first production model was the F4F-3, delivered late in 1940. A barrel-like, radial-engine midwing fighter with squared wing and tail surfaces, the F4F-3 had a 1,200-horsepower engine which gave it a maximum speed of 328 miles per hour. It had fixed (nonfolding) wings and four wing-mounted .50-caliber machine guns. The F4F-3 continued in production for Navy and Marine use into 1941, when it was followed by the F4F-4. This version had folding wings and six .50-caliber wing guns, plus some pilot armor. From Pearl Harbor until late in 1943 the F4F, supplemented to some extent by the F2A and F4U (*see* F2A; F4U), was the sea services' first-line fighter. Combat with Japanese fighters, particularly the A6M2 Zero (*see* A6M), revealed deficiencies which had to be compensated for. Compared with the A6M2, the F4F was slow; the Zero could climb faster and turn inside the Wildcat. The F4F, on the other hand, was sturdier; its greater weight made it faster in a dive, and many pilots survived in badly damaged F4Fs. In combat it was vital for F4Fs to gain superior altitude and make a diving attack wherever possible; Japanese planes at higher altitudes could pretty much engage or avoid action at will. F4F pilots quickly discovered that, all else being equal, dogfighting a Zero was simply another form of suicide. Navy pilots also criticized the use of six .50-calibers in the F4F-4 after the battles of the Coral Sea and Midway. Four guns, they felt, were enough to do fatal damage to any plane they could hit; replacement of four guns by six had cut down on rounds-per-gun ammunition capacity, giving a pilot in a prolonged aerial combat less actual firing time. Grumman production of Wildcats ended in May 1943, to allow the plant to concentrate on production of the new F6F fighter (*see* F6F). However, a General Motors organization, its Eastern Aircraft Division, was set up to produce Wildcats as well as a version of the Grumman TBF torpedo bomber (*see* TBF). This plant began production late in 1942; its first Wildcat was designated FM-1. This was essentially an F4F-4 with the user-recommended four wing guns and increased ammunition. In the fall of 1943 production was shifted to an improved Wildcat, designated FM-2. This was a production version of the Grumman-developed XF4F-8, with four wing guns and a higher vertical tail which distinguished it from other Wildcat models. Lighter than the earlier planes and with a more powerful engine, it had a better rate of climb. Production of the FM-2 continued into late 1945; more of these were produced than of all other Wildcat models combined. Export models of the Wildcat, differing in details from their American counterparts, were delivered to the Royal Navy. The Martlets I through III were fixed-wing F4F-3 variants; the Martlet IV corresponded to the F4F-4. "Stock" FM-1s went to England as the Martlet V; by the time the FM-2 was available for British use, in 1944, its Royal Navy name had been standardized with that of its American cousin and it went into service as the Wildcat VI. A total of 7,905 Wildcats were manufactured, 1,978 by Grumman and 5,927 by General Motors; 1,082 of these went to Britain.

F4U. The Vought Corsair U.S. Navy single-engine fighter. Design work began on this plane in 1938, and in 1940 the XF4U-1 appeared. It was a large, radial-engine, low-wing monoplane; to enable its large propeller to clear the ground, its wings were given the in-

F4U Corsair

verted-gull form which was to become its principal identification. Its performance was good, but a number of major changes were made in the prototype to reflect early European-war experience. The first U.S. Navy production contract for 584 F4U-1s came in 1941, and the first production F4U-1 was delivered in mid-1942. Corsairs went to the Navy and Marines; beginning in February 1943, the Marines flew combat missions in the SOLOMONS with land-based F4U-1s.

One of the changes that had been made to the prototype XF4U-1 had involved addition of more fuel capacity in the fuselage; this required the cockpit to be moved three feet aft to make room for the new fuel tank, placing the pilot over the trailing edge of the large wing. This, with other problems, led the Navy to pronounce the F4U-1 unsuitable for carrier duty after trials in late 1942 and early 1943. This first Corsair had a conventional sliding "razorback" cockpit canopy; the F4U-1A, introduced in 1943, had a slightly raised cockpit with a "bulged" canopy for better pilot vision. Other modifications were intended to improve landing behavior, still another Navy complaint. Both F4U-1 and -1A were armed with six .50-caliber wing guns. The F4U-1C, on the other hand, had four 20-mm. guns. In 1944 the F4U-1D followed. This had a more powerful engine, providing a speed of 425 miles per hour, and six .50-calibers. Twin pylons under the wing roots could each handle a 1,000-pound bomb or a droppable fuel tank. As an alternate load, eight 5-inch rockets could be carried on wing launchers. A night-fighter design, the XF4U-2, was studied at the time the United States entered the Pacific war, but never produced; 12 standard F4U-1s were modified to carry four wing guns and wingtip-mounted RADAR equipment, and were redesignated F4U-2. All 12 operated in the Pacific, some from carriers and others from an island base. Further development led to the introduction in late 1944 of the F4U-4. This faster Corsair had a redesigned cockpit with pilot armor, as well as other improvements including a large four-blade propeller. By the Okinawa campaign, the F4U-4 was in service in quantity. The improvements incorporated into the F4U-1A and -1D had finally led to the Corsair's acceptance for carrier work in mid-1944. By the end of that year, two squadrons of them were flying with the FAST CARRIER TASK FORCE, based on U.S.S. ESSEX. F4Us were operating from six of the Carrier Force's 17 carriers, assigned as fighter-bombers to Bombing-Fighting (VBF) Squadrons.

Other production versions of the Corsair included the photo-reconnaissance F4U-1P and -4P; the cannon-armed F4U-4C, with four 20-mm. guns; and in 1945, the F4U-4E and -4N, night fighters with four 20-mm. guns and improved wingtip radars. The F4U-4B was originally intended for Britain but was diverted to U.S. use. An excellent aircraft with a long and distinguished record, called "the finest shipboard fighter of World War II," the F4U did not replace the F6F in war service, though supplementing it to a considerable extent in the Pacific war's final months (*see* F6F).

Corsairs were manufactured by Brewster, which produced equivalents to the F4U-1, -1A and -1D as the F3A-1, -1A and -1D; Brewster's production ended in mid-1944. Goodyear also built parallel models as the FG-1, -1A and -1D. Unlike the other folding-wing Corsair models, the FG-1 had a fixed wing and was furnished to Marine squadrons. The later F2G, built by Goodyear, was a bubble-canopy model, designed for high performance at low altitudes in reaction to the KAMIKAZE menace; it was developed too late for service. Only 10 out of a contract for 418 F2G-1s and 10 F2G-2s were built. Over a thousand Corsairs were transferred to the Royal Navy, beginning in mid-1943. The British, in fact, had the F4U in carrier service some months before the U.S. Navy did so. About 16 inches was shaved from each wing to allow them to fold under the lower decks of British carriers. The Corsairs I, II, III and IV were the Royal Navy versions of the F4U-1, F4U-1A, F3A-1D and FG-1D, respectively.

F-5. Like many other Italian fighters, this aircraft was both underpowered and inadequately armed. A Caproni-Vizzola product, it mounted an 840-horsepower radial engine and carried a pair of 12.7-mm. machine guns located in the wing roots. Fourteen of the clean-looking, wood-and-metal, low-wing monoplanes saw action as night fighters in defense of Rome.

F6F. The Grumman Hellcat, U.S. Navy carrier fighter. Air actions of the early months of the Pacific war made it glaringly apparent that the then standard F4F and F2A Navy and Marine fighters were inadequate (*see* F2A; F4F). An existing design, the XF6F-1, had been worked on since mid-1941 by Grumman as an eventual replacement for the F4F; to get the most up-to-date input, designers traveled to Pearl Harbor to interview carrier pilots and obtain their opinions. One of the prototypes was modified in the light of what had been learned in Hawaii, and designated XF6F-3; it had a Pratt and Whitney R-2800-10 engine and was flown on June 26, 1942. Production was given high priority; the first production F6F-3 was accepted in September 1942 and 10 were delivered before the end of that year. Production of Grumman's other designs, the F4F and TBF (*see* TBF), had been shifted to General Motors' Eastern Division plant to free Grumman to concentrate on their new fighter. By early 1943 Hellcats were flying from carriers. On August 31, 1943, in an attack on MARCUS ISLAND, the F6F-3 saw its first combat. By mid-1944 the F6F had become the Navy's principal carrier fighter, supplanting the F4F in fleet carrier service, though the F4F and its derivative, the FM, remained in escort carrier (CVE) use. During 1944 the F6F-5, differing but little externally from the F6F-3 but incorporating numerous refinements, entered service. Other production variants included the radar-equipped F6F-3E, -3N and -5N night fighters. By the time production ceased in November 1945, more than 12,000 Hellcats had been turned out. More than 1,200 of them were supplied to the British FLEET AIR ARM, which flew the F6F-3 as the Hellcat I and the F6F-5 as the Hellcat II. They also received F6F-5Ns, which were designated Hellcat N.F. II.

Both the F6F-3 and -5 were armed with six wing-mounted .50-caliber machine guns. The F6F-5 could, in addition, carry two 1,000-pound bombs or six 5-inch rockets for surface attack. During the last months of the Pacific war, when the fighter complements of fleet carriers were steadily increased for defense against KAMIKAZE attack, this fighter-bomber capability made the Hellcat particularly useful.

The F6F-3 had a span of 42 feet 10 inches, a 2,250-horsepower radial engine, a top speed of 375 miles per hour at 17,500 feet and a maximum range (with external fuel tank) of 1,590 miles at 160 miles per hour. Slight additional streamlining increased the maximum speed of the F6F-5 to 386 miles per hour.

The Hellcat did not receive the kind of publicity accorded the F4U Corsair (*see* F4U), either during or after the war, nor did it serve in Korea as did the F4U. It is, to some extent, one of the forgotten aircraft of World War II. Its place in the history of the Pacific war, however, is real. It is no exaggeration to say that its share in winning air superiority in the Pacific was of critical importance. Even in the 1945 operations of the FAST CARRIER TASK FORCE, the bulk of the American and British shipboard fighters were Hellcats. Some late-war Japanese fighters, notably the N1K1-J *Shiden* and the Ki 84 *Hayate,* equaled or surpassed it in performance (*see* N1K1-J; KI 84). This was not enough, however, to overcome the Allied advantage of numbers and superior pilot training and experience. Approximately 75 percent of the air-to-air kills scored by American carrier pilots in the Pacific were made in F6Fs.

F7F. The Grumman Tigercat, U.S. Navy twin-engine monoplane fighter. Designed for use from shore bases and with the large new Midway-class carriers in mind, the F7F developed from the experimental F5F Skyrocket twin-engine fighter tested before Pearl Harbor. As the F7F went into production, it was earmarked for anti-KAMIKAZE service, for which its high rate of climb (over 4,500 feet per minute) and good armament (four wing 20-mm. guns and four nose .50-caliber machine guns) made it desirable. Intended for assignment to Marine land-based squadrons in the Pacific, the Tigercat was too late for combat, and production was cut back after V-J Day.

F-51. *See* P-51.

FADDEN, Sir Arthur William (1895–). Australian political leader who was acting Prime Minister when Sir Robert MENZIES was in London for lengthy discussions in 1941. Australians were not pleased with the use made of their forces by the British Government in the Middle East and Greece, and on August 28, 1941, Fadden replaced Menzies as Prime Minister, Menzies retaining an important post in the cabinet. The change was not enough to still the criticism, and on October 3, 1941, the Fadden cabinet gave way to the Labour government of John CURTIN.

FAÏD. A pass in the eastern Dorsal (Tunisian mountain chain) leading west from Sfax, Faïd was important to the Axis for flank protection. General von ARNIM seized Faïd at the end of January 1943, and on February 14 the KASSERINE offensive opened through the pass.

FAIRCHILD, Muir S. (1894–1950). Postwar commandant of the Air University and later Vice-Chief of Staff of the Air Force, Fairchild achieved a reputation as a U.S. Air Force intellectual. During the war he rose from lieutenant colonel to major general, serving as the first secretary of the Air Staff at headquarters in Washington in 1941. Later he became Assistant Chief of the Air Corps and director of military requirements on the Air Staff. He was a member of the Joint Strategic Survey Committee of the JOINT CHIEFS OF STAFF.

FAIREY FOX. A two-place reconnaissance, observation and light-bombing single-engine biplane that constituted the most numerous aircraft in Belgium's Aeronautique Militaire. Built in Belgium from a 1925 design and slightly updated, it was obsolescent when the war began.

FALAISE. *See* ARGENTAN-FALAISE.

FALKENHAUSEN, Alexander von (1878–1966). German Army officer (General der Infanterie, 1940), commander in Belgium and northern France from 1940 to 1944. He sympathized to some degree with the OPPOSITION TO HITLER and had discussions with various plotters. He was arrested and imprisoned after the July 20, 1944, attempt on Hitler's life. He was subsequently in a prison camp with Léon BLUM, the former French Premier, who later deleted his name from the French list of German war criminals. But, although there were many witnesses in his favor, a Belgian court in Liège found him guilty of conspiracy in the shooting of 240 hostages. He had already spent four years in prison awaiting trial and was released shortly after being convicted.

FALKENHORST, Nicholas von (1885–1968). German Army officer (original family name, Jastrzembski) who served in World War I and in the peacetime Army, rising to command of the XXI Corps, which he led in the Polish campaign in 1939. For this service he was promoted to General der Infanterie. He was advanced as the leader of the Norwegian operation when it was determined that the use of a corps commander and his staff would accelerate planning. Falkenhorst's main qualification for the task was his experience as a staff officer during the 1918 German intervention in Finland. He had worked with the Navy in 1918 and now would do so again. The Norwegian operation was a success. Promoted to Generaloberst (colonel general) in July 1940, Falkenhorst stayed in Norway as armed forces commander until ordered to return to Germany late in the war.

FALSE TARGET SHELL, FALSE TARGET CAN. U.S. Navy adaptations of the concept used in the German PILLENWERFER. The False Target Shell Mark 1 was similar in dimensions to a signal flare used by submerged American submarines as a distress signal, and was designed to be fired from the same launcher. After firing, the shell broke up and released six small cups of lithium hydride. On contact with water, the chemical reacted to produce hydrogen bubbles which returned a SONAR signal like that of a submerged submarine. The later False Target Can Mark 2 was a sealed tube containing nine small chemical cups.

FANFARE. Overall code name for Allied operations in the Mediterranean area.

FARMAN F-222. French four-engine heavy bomber. Obsolescent in 1939, it was used for reconnaissance and the dropping of propaganda leaflets. After the 1940 armistice it was used as a transport by the VICHY government.

FAROUK (1920–1965). As King of Egypt, Farouk supported the British—albeit reluctantly—but retained AXIS sympathizers in his government. When the Axis threat to Cairo was severe in 1942, the British forced Farouk to dismiss a pro-German Prime Minister and name a Wafd Party member in his place. But this political party had little influence, and tension continued. After the war Farouk complained bitterly of 40 years of British misrule in Egypt.

FARRAGUT, U.S.S. Destroyer and class (1,700 tons; four or five 5-inch guns; eight 21-inch torpedo tubes; 36 knots). Eight of these ships commissioned in 1934–35, the first new American destroyer design since World War I and the first U.S. destroyer to mount all guns and tubes on the centerline. Raised-forecastle ships with two stacks, the Farraguts introduced the 5-INCH 38-caliber rapid-fire dual-purpose gun to the fleet. Their relative cost and sophistication, compared with the earlier FLUSH-DECKERS, earned them the nickname "Goldplaters."

FASCIST PARTY. The ruling political party in Italy from 1922 to 1943, founded by Benito MUSSOLINI. Fascism was highly totalitarian and in theory required strict regimentation in all aspects of national life. The movement became the philosophical underpinning for similar parties in Germany (National Socialism) and elsewhere. The word "fascism" is derived from the Latin *fasces,* the bundle of rods with an ax which were carried as a symbol of authority before ancient Roman magistrates. In the turmoil following World War I, Mussolini founded the Fasci di Combattimento. The Fasci, like the Nazis in Germany, had a loose and contradictory program, but in 1921 became allied with the landowners and industrialists, offering a bulwark against socialist radicalism and disorder.

In 1922 Mussolini staged the "march on Rome," with his Fascists, and the King—unnecessarily, it appears—asked him to form a new government. Mussolini established a totalitarian regime in which the state was completely identified with the Fascist Party, which in turn was identified with its leader (Il Duce). The Fascist regime was overthrown in July 1943 and was saved only for a brief period by the Germans. That rump government ended in the spring of 1945.

Fascism as a principle had been widely accepted in many countries by the mid-1930s. It influenced the governments of Germany, Austria, Hungary, Poland, Spain, Rumania, Bulgaria, Greece, Japan and later VICHY France. *See also* NATIONAL SOCIALIST GERMAN WORKERS' PARTY.

FAST CARRIER TASK FORCE. The aircraft-carrier striking force of the U.S. Pacific Fleet. This was constituted as the fleet's major TASK FORCE. It was divided into task groups, usually four, each normally including three to five carriers (CV and CVL) with an escort of fast battleships, cruisers and destroyers. A supporting task group of fuel and supply ships kept the carrier task groups provided with logistic support, although it was not under command of the carrier task force commander. Task groups operated at a distance from each other to avoid presenting too large a target to enemy attack, working together or independently as the situation required. The Fast Carrier Task Force came into being in 1943 as new ESSEX- and INDEPENDENCE-class carriers began to join the fleet. From the beginning of the Central Pacific drive, opened late in that year with the capture of the GILBERT ISLANDS, this force ran interference for the Allied amphibious offensives by launching far-ranging air strikes and gun bombardments at selected landing objectives as well as on air and naval bases from which the landings might be contested. During and after a landing, carrier planes supported troops on the ground. Later this task was assumed by escort carrier groups, freeing the fast carriers for distant support jobs. If the Japanese posed a counterstroke, the carrier force was charged with meeting it.

During the Gilberts operation (November–December 1943) it was designated the Carrier Force (Task Force 50) and commanded by Rear Adm. Charles POWNALL. In January 1944 it was designated the Fast Carrier Force (Task Force 58) under Rear Adm. Marc MITSCHER. Under this name it took part in operations in the MARSHALLS, NEW GUINEA and the MARIANAS. It was redesignated Task Force 38 for the capture of the PHILIPPINES. The carrier force alternated numbers again for Iwo JIMA and the first part of the OKINAWA campaign, being Task Force 58 until May 1945, when Vice-Adm. John MCCAIN relieved Admiral Mitscher. As Task Force 38 the fast carriers finished the battle for Okinawa and spearheaded the final sea and air offensive against the Japanese home islands (July–August 1945). During its final year of operations, the Fast Carrier Force was joined by the British Pacific Fleet, a carrier force identified as Task Force 37 or 57.

FAT MAN. So called because it was heavier and bulkier than the bomb that leveled Hiroshima, this ATOMIC BOMB destroyed Nagasaki on August 9, 1945. Fat Man weighed 10,000 pounds and measured 10 feet 8 inches in length by 5 feet in diameter.

FAULHABER, Michael (1869–1952). A fearless preacher against the Nazis, Cardinal Faulhaber had been archbishop of Munich from 1917, and was 64 when Hitler became Chancellor. Once chaplain general of the Bavarian Army, he was the first Roman Catholic bishop to be decorated with the IRON CROSS for courage in war. He later became a pacifist, and a supporter of the Jewish cause when the Jews came under attack. His sermons were printed and openly circulated in the Catholic community in spite of stringent prohibitions, and he was the stoutest champion of the Catholic Church against various forms of persecution, such as the closing of church schools. In 1938 his house was attacked by Nazi mobs, but this did not stop him from attacking Hitler's euthanasia of the insane in 1940. Owing to his powerful position in the Catholic community, the Nazi authorities felt it wiser to take no direct action against him, but they ignored all his protests.

FAUSTPATRONE. A German hand-launched antitank weapon consisting of a shaped-charge projectile with a tubular tail and four small tail fins. It was fired from a projector which was a simple metal tube containing a propellant charge and firing mechanism. Its rated effective range was 33 yards. This weapon is commonly referred to as the Panzerfaust (tank fist).

FECHTELER, William Morrow (1896–1967). A U.S. Naval Academy graduate in 1916, Fechteler became a rear admiral in January 1944 and gained a reputation as an attack group commander in the Pacific. During April and May 1944 in the HOLLANDIA operation of the NEW GUINEA campaign, he commanded the Central Attack Group. Skilled in amphibious warfare, Fechteler led attack groups in the LEYTE GULF campaign and the subsequent liberation of the PHILIPPINES. In 1946 he became a vice-admiral, in 1950 a full admiral and in 1951 Chief of Naval Operations.

FEGEN, Edward Fogarty (1895–1940). Captain of the British armed merchant cruiser JERVIS BAY, who won a posthumous VICTORIA CROSS for his conduct of the encounter with the ADMIRAL SCHEER.

FELIX. Code name for a planned German operation in Spain in early November 1940. It was to take Gibraltar and deny the British any foothold on the Iberian Peninsula or in the Atlantic islands. Felix was based on the supposition that Spain would enter the war on the side of the Axis powers. When this did not happen, Felix was canceled.

FELLGIEBEL, Erich (1888–1944). The German Army's chief signal officer during World War II, General (der Signaltruppen) Fellgiebel took an active part in the conspiracy to eliminate Hitler and was executed on September 4, 1944 (*see* OPPOSITION TO HITLER).

FELSENNEST. Headquarters used by Adolf HITLER during the campaign in the west in 1940. Felsennest (Aerie) was located near Münstereifel, 25 miles southwest of Bonn.

FEREBEE, Thomas W. (1918–). The bombardier on board the B-29 *Enola Gay,* which dropped the ATOMIC BOMB "Little Boy" on HIROSHIMA, August 6, 1945.

FERMI, Enrico (1901–1954). Italian-born winner of the Nobel Prize for Physics (1938), Enrico Fermi emigrated to the United States in early 1939. In the ensuing years he contributed immeasurably to the creation of the first ATOMIC BOMB. In March 1939 Fermi, who in 1934 was probably the first man to split the uranium atom (and thus unwittingly struck the initial sparks of a chain reaction), tried without success to interest the Navy Department in the possibilities of an atomic bomb. Several of Fermi's associates then prevailed upon Albert EINSTEIN to send a letter to President ROOSEVELT, which resulted, finally, in action on the part of the U.S. Government. The first sustained and controlled release of nuclear energy occurred at the UNIVERSITY OF CHICAGO in December 1942 when, under Fermi's direction, an atomic pile was set into operation. Transferred to Los ALAMOS in 1943 as chief consultant for all nuclear physics experiments, Fermi saw the realization of his efforts and those of other scientists when the first fission bomb was detonated at Trinity Site on July 16, 1945.

FERRYING COMMAND. The evolutionary link between the U.S. Army's prewar air transport organization and the wartime Air Transport Command. In 1940 the British agreed to fly newly acquired American-built airplanes from the factories across the Atlantic to the United Kingdom, but they could not find enough pilots for so ambitious an undertaking. Gen. Henry H. ARNOLD responded by volunteering the services of Army Air Corps aviators to fly the planes to a point of embarkation, where British pilots would take over the transatlantic flight. Existing legislation required that belligerent nations adhere to a CASH AND CARRY policy and prevented American airmen from delivering the planes directly to the British Isles.

The Air Corps Ferrying Command came into being in May 1941. Under the command of Col. Robert Olds, the new organization soon established a transatlantic passenger service, using converted B-24s to fly American military officers and civilians on fact-finding missions to Great Britain, the Middle East and the Soviet Union. Further expansion occurred after Pearl Harbor, when Ferrying Command began delivering aircraft and flying passengers to all the combat theaters.

FESTUNG EUROPA. Literally, "Fortress Europe," a phrase said to have been used by the Germans for German-occupied Europe, though there is no evidence that it actually was employed by Adolf HITLER or other German leaders.

FFI. Acronym for Forces Françaises de l'Intérieur (French Forces of the Interior). *See* FRENCH RESISTANCE.

FIDO. U.S. homing torpedo carried by naval patrol aircraft (TBF-1 Avengers; *see* TBF) for use against submarines.

FIEBIG, Martin (1891–1947). German Luftwaffe officer (General der Flieger) who commanded the VIII Air Corps, which attempted vainly to supply the SIXTH ARMY at Stalingrad.

FIELD ARTILLERY. During World War II the various armies utilized different and often confusing systems to designate their weapons. In addition, artillery pieces were continually being modified and each modification was usually given a new model number. To avoid entanglement in these numbers, the light and medium artillery pieces of the various combatants which are discussed here will be designated by caliber. For example, the workhorse weapon of the U.S. field artillery inventory was the 105-mm. howitzer. This piece, which featured a split trail and two-wheel carriage, weighed about 2¼ tons and could fire a 32-pound projectile some 12,200 yards. A short-barreled version of the 105 was used by airborne artillerymen. The weapon also came in a self-propelled model. At first a half-track was used; then the piece was mounted on a tank chassis. Great Britain fielded the 25-Pounder, an 87.6-mm. howitzer which weighed about two tons. As a budgetary measure, early 25-Pounders were mounted on 18-Pounder carriages which were already in the inventory. This weapon, called the 18/25, could achieve a range of 12,800 yards. With a 25-Pounder carriage, the range was extended to 13,400 yards. Variations of the 25-Pounder included the "Baby 25-Pounder," a lighter weapon featuring a shorter barrel, used for jungle operations. The 25-Pounder was also produced in self-propelled versions.

German field artillery was of many types. A piece which saw much use was the 10.5-cm. (105-mm.) howitzer. This split-trailed, two-wheeled weapon weighed about 1.9 tons and with a 33-pound shell had a maximum range of 10,300 yards. The Germans also employed self-propelled weapons. In the east the Germans fought an army well equipped with field artillery. A variety of Soviet pieces were seen, a real mainstay being the 76-mm. (or 76.2-mm.) field gun which, with a 14-pound shell, ranged to 15,260 yards. This weapon featured a long barrel and split trails. As the war progressed, 85-mm. and 100-mm. weapons appeared. The 100-mm. gun attained a range of 23,000 yards. Self-propelled artillery also had an important place in the Soviet inventory. Like the Russians and Germans, the Japanese fielded a number of weapons. A primary factor in most Japanese designs was mobility of the piece; thus weight was a major consideration. Two 75-mm. weapons which saw much action were the mountain gun, featuring a long split trail, and the regimental gun, of an old design, which had a box trail. These weapons had a 7,000-yard range and weighed only 1,200 pounds. The Japanese also had a 105-mm. split-trailed howitzer. The design of this weapon, which usually was pulled by six horses, was not up to modern standards.

All nations had medium-sized field artillery weapons. A general idea of what could be seen in combat can be gained from the following brief account. Both guns and howitzers, towed and self-propelled, of 155 mm. were fielded by the Americans. The British Army was supported by 4.5-inch (104-mm.) and 5.5-inch (140-mm.) guns. On the other side of the hill, the Germans used a 15-cm. howitzer with a 14-foot barrel—an extremely long barrel for a howitzer. When the weapon was prepared for movement, the barrel had to be retracted. Russian armies were supported by 122-mm. and 152-mm. weapons, both of which came in gun and howitzer configurations and both of which were seen in towed and self-propelled versions. The Japanese fielded two types of 15-cm. howitzers. While one was of a fairly recent—1936—vintage, the other model went back to 1915. These weapons, light and medium, combined to give the infantrymen and tankers highly mobile weapons systems which were capable, when properly served, of delivering a large volume of timely and highly effective fire.

FIESELER FI 167. A German biplane torpedo bomber and reconnaissance plane, originally meant for the proposed aircraft carrier *Graf Zeppelin*. Two prototypes and 12 Fi 167A-Os were built and used in experiments until 1943.

FIFE, James (1897–). A 1918 graduate of the U.S. Naval Academy, Fife became a submariner early in his career. During the war, as a commander, he served as chief of staff to Capt. John WILKES, commander of submarines in the Asiatic Fleet. A rear admiral by 1944, Fife took command of U.S. Navy submarines for the entire Southwest Pacific. He remained in this position until the end of 1945. He retired in 1955.

FIFTEENTH AIR FORCE. Elements of the Bomber Command, North African Air Forces, formed the nucleus of the U.S. Fifteenth Air Force, which was organized on November 1, 1943, during the Italian campaign. The new air force was to use recently captured airfields in southern Italy to bomb strategic targets in the industrial north, in Austria, in southern France and in Germany. Maj. Gen. James H. DOOLITTLE took command of the Fifteenth at its inception, but he soon received orders to take over the EIGHTH AIR FORCE in England. He was replaced at the Fifteenth by Maj. Gen. Nathan F. TWINING on January 1, 1944.

In complementing the efforts of Doolittle's Eighth Air Force, Twining's airmen inaugurated a series of shuttle missions in which American planes bombed enemy targets en route to bases in the Soviet Union. But the destruction of an Eighth Air Force contingent on the ground at POLTAVA in the Ukraine and the generally poor cooperation from Russian leaders cooled American enthusiasm for the project, especially since it soon became apparent that the Fifteenth Air Force, flying from Italian bases, could hit all the worthwhile strategic targets that lay beyond the range of squadrons based in England.

Among the targets hammered by Fifteenth Air Force bombers were synthetic-oil plants in Czechoslovakia and Poland and the oil refineries at PLOESTI, Rumania. In addition, they supported Allied ground armies by attacking rail yards, supply and communication lines and depots as part of Operation Strangle, the aerial effort to isolate German armies in northern Italy. Fighter units flying P-38s and P-51s attacked truck convoys, trains, bridges and airfields, in addition to escorting the bombers and engaging in aerial combat with German fighters.

FIFTEENTH ARMY (U.S.). Force that became operational in Europe in January 1945, its primary mission being to relieve the other armies of the 12th ARMY GROUP of mop-up and occupation duties as they advanced into Germany. Its strength was six divisions. Its commander was Maj. Gen. Leonard T. GEROW.

FIFTH AIR FORCE. When the surviving elements of the Philippine-based U.S. Far East Air Forces reached Australia early in 1942, they were reorganized to form the nucleus of the Fifth Air Force. Planes from this organization flew reconnaissance missions as Allied forces checked the Japanese at the Battle of the CORAL SEA and prepared to take the offensive in the SOLOMON ISLANDS. In August 1942 Maj. Gen. George C. KENNEY took command and employed the Fifth Air Force to support the Allied advance in NEW GUINEA.

Besides bombing Japanese strongpoints and airstrips, Fifth Air Force planes flew troops and supplies from Australia to Port Moresby, New Guinea, then across the Owen Stanley Mountains to the battle area, and attacked enemy convoys attempting to reinforce the New Guinea garrison. During the Battle of the BISMARCK SEA, March 2–4, 1943, Fifth Air Force P-38s, A-20s, B-17s and B-25s joined Australian Beaufighters in low-altitude attacks that sank every vessel in a 22-ship convoy.

As the New Guinea campaign neared a successful conclusion, Fifth Air Force intensified its bombardment of RABAUL, the Japanese bastion on New Britain. While preparing for the return to the Philippines, Fifth Air Force was turned over to Maj. Gen. Ennis C. WHITEHEAD and incorporated, together with the Thirteenth Air Force, in General Kenney's new Far East Air Forces in June 1944. Beginning in November 1944, Whitehead's fliers supported operations to reconquer the Philippines. From bases in the Philippines, Fifth Air Force bombers hit targets in the Netherlands East Indies and on Formosa. As the war ended, Okinawa-based units were bombing Japan.

V AMPHIBIOUS FORCE. A U.S. naval command activated on August 15, 1943, as a component of the Fifth Fleet to plan amphibious operations and to coordinate training of all subordinate surface and ground units to be committed in these operations. Under the command of Adm. Richmond Kelly TURNER, who led it from its inception until the end of the war, when he also was Commander, Amphibious Forces, Pacific Fleet, VPhibFor directed the following operations: Galvanic (GILBERT ISLANDS, MAKIN), November 1943; Flintlock (MARSHALLS) and Catchpole (Kusaie, ENIWETOK, WAKE ISLAND), January–February 1944; FORAGER (MARIANAS), June 1944; Detachment (IWO JIMA), February–March 1945; ICEBERG (OKINAWA), April 1945; and the occupation of southern Honshu at the end of the war.

FIFTH ARMY (U.S.). An American field army that fought in ITALY; the headquarters was the first to be activated outside the United States during the war. It came into being in Algiers on January 5, 1943, and was placed under the command of Lt. Gen. Mark W. CLARK, Lt. Gen. Dwight D. EISENHOWER's deputy commander in chief of the Allied forces—the Anglo-American land, sea and air forces that had in November 1942 invaded NORTHWEST AFRICA and were then campaigning in TUNISIA. Clark's chief of staff and indispensable principal assistant was Maj. Gen. Alfred GRUENTHER.

The Fifth Army was created to form an equivalent organization to the British First Army under Lt. Gen. Sir Kenneth A. N. ANDERSON, who directed British, American and French units. After some discussion, Fifth Army headquarters was established at Oujda, near the border between Algeria and French Morocco. As the highest American field command in North Africa, the headquarters assumed administrative control over Maj. Gen. Lloyd R. FREDENDALL's II Corps in Tunisia and somewhat closer control over Maj. Gen. George S. PATTON, Jr.'s I Armored Corps in French Morocco. The missions of the Fifth Army headquarters were diverse. First, it had to ensure that the population of the enormous area outside the North African combat zone remained calm and peaceful. Second, it had to be prepared to counter hostile action in Spanish Morocco. Third, and most important, the Fifth Army headquarters became an immense training organization; it operated a host of installations to teach officers and soldiers, British, French and American, the basics and the specialties of warfare.

Shortly before the invasion of SICILY, the Fifth Army was assigned another mission: operations in the Mediterranean beyond Sicily, should such operations be directed. As a consequence, the Fifth Army headquarters drew plans for invasions of SARDINIA, Corsica and the southern mainland of Italy. In August 1943 the COMBINED CHIEFS OF STAFF approved a descent on ITALY, specifically landings to be executed by the Fifth Army in the Naples region. Fifth Army's plan, code-named Avalanche, projected operations at SALERNO with the British 10th Corps of two divisions and the U.S. VI Corps of one division coming ashore on September 9.

Even though Italy had surrendered, the German opposition at Salerno almost brought about an American disaster. German troops threatened to split the Allied beachhead at the Sele River, which separated the 10th Corps and VI Corps. Intensified naval shelling and air support, dogged tenacity on the ground, the drop of part of an airborne division into the beachhead and the arrival of additional divisions gave the Fifth Army a clear-cut victory by September 20.

After a 10-day battle to pierce the passes through the Sorrento mountain mass, the Fifth Army took Naples. While engineers began to rehabilitate the port destroyed by the Germans, the combat troops pushed north to the VOLTURNO RIVER. They crossed the Volturno in October in a well-synchronized attack and pushed into the mountainous terrain south of the RAPIDO and Garigliano Rivers. The Germans had fortified this ground in order to anchor a stubborn defensive effort. Grim fighting followed in what the Allies called the German Winter Line.

The arrival in Italy of the U.S. II Corps headquarters gave the Fifth Army more flexibility, and the coming of the French Expeditionary Corps with two divisions gave it more strength. Thus it was that in the beginning of 1944 the Fifth Army launched an amphibious operation at ANZIO (code-named Shingle) designed to make an end run around the German defenses and thereby come into quick possession of Rome.

A coordinated attack by the British 10th and the French corps culminated in an effort by the U.S. II Corps on January 20 to cross the Rapido River and gain entrance into the Liri River valley for a subsequent drive to make contact with the U.S. VI Corps coming ashore at Anzio. The British crossed the Garigliano, but the Americans failed to cross the Rapido. The large-scale offensive had, however, drawn German reserve formations away from the Rome area, and consequently the VI Corps landings at Anzio on January 22 were virtually unopposed.

The Fifth Army now had two fronts—the Anzio beachhead and the main line at the Garigliano, the Rapido and CASSINO—separated by 75 miles of German-held territory. While the forces at Anzio held against a massive German attempt in February to dislodge them, the troops at the main line battled vainly to move up the Liri valley to reach the besieged beachhead. A stalemate settled over both fronts while the Germans tried to recover from their exhaustion.

On May 11, after most of the British Eighth Army had been brought across the Apennines into the western coastal sector and the French corps and the U.S. II Corps had been augmented by two new divisions each, the battle for ROME opened on the main front. This time, on May 25, the Fifth Army succeeded in making contact with the beachhead forces, which launched their own attack. This pressure compelled the Germans to withdraw and abandon Rome, which fell to the Fifth Army on June 4.

Detaching the VI Corps and three divisions for the invasion of SOUTHERN FRANCE, the Fifth Army pursued the Germans 150 miles up the Italian peninsula to the Arno River, but there on July 23 the advance ran out of energy. Attacks in September and October made a small breach in the GOTHIC LINE, which the Germans had erected to protect the Po River valley. But except for minor action, the campaign in the northern Apennines became dormant during the severe weather of the winter months.

In November, when Gen. Sir Harold ALEXANDER was elevated to the position of Supreme Allied Commander in the Mediterranean, Clark replaced him in command of the 15th Army Group. Lt. Gen. Lucian TRUSCOTT, Jr., moved up from command of the VI Corps, then in France, to command of the Fifth Army. He led the army, now augmented by the IV Corps and several additional divisions, in the final drive across the Po valley that started on April 5, 1945, and ended with the surrender of the German forces in Italy on May 2.

FIFTH COLUMN. Term used to describe any widespread subversion of a nation's defenses during wartime. To achieve its greatest effect, such subversion should penetrate every part of society and the military. The term was invented during the Spanish Civil War by the colorful Nationalist general Queipo de Llano in one of his famous radio broadcasts striking at the Republican cause. Queipo claimed that Madrid was under attack from four Nationalist columns and from a "fifth column" within the city—secret Nationalist supporters.

FIFTH FLEET (U.S.). Established in August 1943 as the U.S. Navy's Central Pacific Force under Adm. Raymond SPRUANCE, this became the Fifth Fleet on April 26, 1944. (Until the latter date, the term "Fifth Fleet" was used for the *ships* of the Central Pacific Force, which also included amphibious forces and land-based aircraft.) As the Navy's mobile striking force, the Fifth Fleet took part in the capture of the GILBERTS (as the Central Pacific Force) and MARSHALLS, supported the spring 1944 landings in NEW GUINEA and participated in the seizure of the MARIANAS and the Battle of the PHILIPPINE SEA. In September 1944 this force became the THIRD FLEET for the duration of the PHILIPPINES campaign, under a system by which Admirals William F. HALSEY and Spruance were to alternate command. As the Fifth Fleet, once again under Spruance, the force took part in the Iwo JIMA operation and the early stages of the battle for OKINAWA. In May 1945 it again became the Third Fleet, which it remained until V-J Day. The Third Fleet and Fifth Fleet were then simultaneously established to participate in the occupation of Japan.

FIGHTER COMMAND. When the Royal Air Force was reorganized into a system of functional commands, the defense of Great Britain against aerial attack was made the responsibility of Fighter Command. This was formed on July 14, 1936, at Bentley Priory, Stanmore, Middlesex, and its first AOC-in-C was Air Marshal Sir Hugh DOWDING, later Lord Dowding. In 1939 the command was given the additional task of protecting coastal shipping to within 40 miles of the coast. The defense against air attack was deployed through fighter groups, which in the spring of 1940 were numbered 9 through 14; of these, No. 11 and No. 12 Group bore the brunt of the aerial fighting in the Battle of BRITAIN. In addition, the AOC-in-C took under his control the chain of RADAR stations erected to give early warning of air raids, the OBSERVER Corps, BALLOON COMMAND and units of the Army's Anti-Aircraft Command for operations and combined training.

The Battle of Britain, which officially lasted from July 10 to October 31, 1940, was the proving time for the operational effectiveness and resilience of Fighter Command, which had suffered fighter losses in the squadrons dispatched to NORWAY and FRANCE. On July 10, 1940, Fighter Command had 52 squadrons, mostly HURRICANES and SPITFIRES, to oppose the LUFTWAFFE's attacking force of some 2,750 bombers and fighters. The Luftwaffe's failure to establish a favorable air situation over the Channel and southeast England led to the postponement of Operation SEA LION (German invasion) in October 1940. Fighter Command was then faced with a longer and tougher challenge—the night bomber—with the BLITZ on British industry and residential areas. The development of airborne radar (AI) and the introduction to service of BEAUFIGHTER and MOSQUITO aircraft eventually led to success against the Luftwaffe intruders. Fighter Command, after mid-1941 in particular, contributed to the offensive sweeps against the Luftwaffe in France and the Low Countries and also dispatched a mission of two Hurricane squadrons to northern Russia in August 1941. The air support provided by Fighter Command to the mainly Canadian-forces raid on DIEPPE in August 1942 was a rehearsal for the air cover needed eventually for Operation OVERLORD in June 1944.

With the formation of the Allied Expeditionary Air Force on November 15, 1943, Fighter Command assumed a primarily defensive role and reverted to the title AIR DEFENCE OF GREAT BRITAIN (ADGB). However, when the Allied armies had penetrated deep into France, ADGB regained its preferred title of Fighter Command in 1944. One of the most sinister opponents of Fighter Command then appeared, in the shape of the doodlebug, or V-1 flying bombs (*see* V-WEAPONS). By the middle of August 1944, 15 day-fighter and 10 night-fighter squadrons were being employed against the flying bombs; 1,847 were claimed destroyed by aircraft of Fighter Command out of 5,000 which flew over British territory.

With the end of hostilities, Fighter Command suffered the contraction common to other forces in peacetime, and eventually, on April 30, 1968, the name Fighter Command disappeared when a new formation, Strike Command, was created, uniting the former Bomber and Fighter Commands.

FIGHTING FRANCE (France Combattante). The French resistance movement organized by Charles DE GAULLE in London in June 1940, after the fall of France, and originally called FREE FRANCE. The name "Fighting France" was adopted in July 1942.

FIGHTING LADY. A popular nickname given to the U.S. aircraft carrier YORKTOWN, stemming from a wartime motion picture made under that title about her exploits.

FINAL SOLUTION (Endlösung). The term used by Nazi officials to veil the extermination of the Jews. It appeared notably at the conclusion of Hermann GÖRING's written instruction sent to Reinhard HEYDRICH on July 31, 1941, following the invasion of Russia: ". . . I instruct you further to submit to me as soon as possible a general plan showing the measures for organization and for action necessary to carry out the desired final solution [*Endlösung*] of the Jewish question." The notorious WANNSEE CONFERENCE, convened by Heydrich and Adolf EICHMANN on January 20, 1942, was an official interdepartmental meeting to discuss, in veiled language, the organization of the "final solution." The minutes survive, and they form one of the regime's most damaging documents.

FINSCHHAFEN. Small port on the HUON PENINSULA in northeast NEW GUINEA. Fearing that Japanese troops retreating from LAE would reach Finschhafen, General MACARTHUR ordered Australian troops to land there on September 22, 1943, just six days after they had captured Lae. Fierce Japanese resistance delayed capture of the port until October 3.

FINUCANE, Brendan (1920–1942). Wing Commander "Paddy" Finucane, born in Dublin in 1920, joined No. 65 Squadron, RAF, in July 1940. During the Battle of BRITAIN and later, he proved to be one of the RAF's best fighter pilots. He was credited with 32 enemy aircraft destroyed, and was awarded the DISTINGUISHED SERVICE ORDER and the DISTINGUISHED FLYING CROSS with two bars. He was killed in action in July 1942.

FIRE BOMB. An aerial bomb containing an incendiary agent such as magnesium, white phosphorus or jellied petroleum. Magnesium types were used by the Germans during the London BLITZ. Jellied petroleum became a household word: napalm. Some incendiary bombs were known by nicknames, such as the MOLOTOV BREADBASKET of the Soviet-Finnish War and the KENNEY COCKTAIL in the Southwest Pacific. Fire bombs were also called incendiary bombs.

FIREBRAND. This British aircraft, built by Blackburn, began life as a low-wing, single-seat, carrier-based fighter powered by a 2,305-horsepower Sabre III liquid-cooled engine and mounting four 20-mm. cannon. Even as it was being readied for deck landing tests, the British Admiralty realized that it was superior to the existing SEAFIRE in only one respect—the ability to carry weight. As a result, Firebrand II emerged as a single-seat "torpedo-strike fighter," able to carry an aerial torpedo. Only a dozen Firebrand IIs were built.

Meanwhile, the Royal Air Force was exercising its priority over the Sabre engine, which it wanted for the Hawker TYPHOON. Hence another power plant had to be used in the Firebrand. Two Firebrand II airframes were therefore modified to accommodate a Centaurus air-cooled radial engine developing 2,520 horsepower. The radial-powered Firebrand III suffered somewhat from directional instability, so a larger fin was installed on Firebrand IV, which flew for the first time in May 1945, too late for wartime service.

FIREBRAND. Code name for the Allied occupation of Corsica, September–October 1943. The invasion was carried out on the order of General EISENHOWER, Supreme Allied Commander in the Mediterranean, and was led by the French Gen. Alphonse JUIN. It began on September 11 with the sailing of a French submarine from Algiers to Corsica with a small French force. The final German withdrawal came on October 4. Participating in the expulsion of the Germans were local patriots, the Battalion du Choc, GOUMS of the 4th Moroccan Mountain Division and a small U.S. OSS group (*see* OFFICE OF STRATEGIC SERVICES).

FIREFLY. A design team headed by H. E. Chaplin produced the Fairey Firefly as its response to a 1939 request by the British Admiralty for two new carrier fighters, one with foward-firing armament and the other with all its firepower in a multigun turret. Chaplin's group chose to respond to the former requirement, designing a conventional-looking two-place, low-wing airplane mounting four 20-mm. cannon and powered by a 1,730-horsepower Rolls-Royce Griffon liquid-cooled engine. Some wartime Fireflies boasted a 1,765-horsepower Griffon, but all of them had the characteristic chin radiator and elliptical wing. The plane entered combat against the Germans in July 1944, attacking the TIRPITZ at anchor in a Norwegian fjord. The Firefly also saw action against the Japanese; in fact, most of its service with the FLEET AIR ARM was in the Pacific theater. Although classed as a "shipboard reconnaissance fighter," it could carry eight rockets or two 1,000-pound bombs. Maximum speed was 316 miles per hour at 14,000 feet. A RADAR-equipped version served as a night fighter.

1st AIRBORNE DIVISION (British). This division's first major action came at Syracuse in SICILY on July 9, 1943. The unit captured its objective, a vital road bridge, despite having 47 of its 134 gliders blown into the sea. The 1st Airborne subsequently landed west of ARNHEM, the Netherlands, on September 17, 1944, as part of Operation MARKET (air drop)-GARDEN (ground thrust). It took the Arnhem bridgehead after fierce combat, but it was cut off from General MONTGOMERY's other forces when infantry relief failed to link up with it. Finally, on the 25th, the division was withdrawn from Arnhem, having lost some 7,000 men killed, wounded or missing.

FIRST ALLIED AIRBORNE ARMY. Headquarters established August 2, 1944, under U.S. Lt. Gen. Lewis H. BRERETON to afford centralized control over training and operational planning for all Allied airborne troops and units flying troop carrier aircraft in the European theater. Located near the famous British racecourse at Ascot, the headquarters functioned directly under the Supreme Allied Commander. Essentially a planning and coordinating headquarters, it had no supply function and no facilities for operating in the field. Once ground troops established contact with the airborne troops during an operation, the airborne units came under ground command. The army had no assigned corps but could employ when required the British Airborne Corps (Lt. Gen. F. A. M. BROWNING) and the American XVIII Airborne Corps (Maj. Gen. Matthew B. RIDGWAY). Major units were the British 1st and 6th AIRBORNE DIVISIONS and 38 and 46 Groups, Royal Air Force, and the U.S. 13th, 17th, 82d and 101st Airborne Divisions (see separate articles for the 82d and 101st) and IX Troop Carrier Command. The army also controlled the Combined Air Transport Operations Room, an agency for coordinating the hauling of freight and personnel by air, including aerial supply for the ground armies.

FIRST ARMY (British). Force created as the British contribution to Operation Torch (the invasion of NORTHWEST AFRICA). It landed at Algiers on November 8, 1942, as the Eastern Task Force and immediately became the British First Army, under the command of Lt. Gen. Sir Kenneth A. N. ANDERSON. It fought through the Tunisian operations in 1943 and was then disbanded.

FIRST ARMY (Canadian). The First Canadian Army, comprising the 1st and 2d Corps, was formed in England on April 6, 1942. Its combatant forces, some of which had been in England since December 1939, were not employed in significant offensive action until August 1942, when some 5,000 Canadians took part in the bloody raid on DIEPPE. Almost 2,000 became prisoners of war.

In July 1943 the 1st Canadian Division and the 1st Canadian Armored Tank Brigade took part in the invasion of SICILY—the first occasion in the war when Canadian troops were employed in large numbers in a major campaign; 485 Canadians were killed in action during the offensive. In the following month the same units cooperated in the Allied assault on the mainland of ITALY, and in the ensuing months, they advanced through Potenza, Campobasso, Vinchiatura, across the SANGRO and the Moro and into Ortona by the end of the year. In 1944 the 1st Canadian Corps took part in the Liri valley offensive (May–June) and advanced across the Metauro and Foglia, through the GOTHIC LINE and across the Savio and Lamone to the Senio (December). In February 1945 the corps was withdrawn from Italy to rejoin the 2d Canadian Corps in the NIJMEGEN area and the Reichswald perimeter in northwestern Europe. A total of 91,579 officers and men had served in the Italian theater, of whom 5,800 had been killed.

While the 1st Corps campaigned in Italy, the 3d Division of the 2d Corps had landed on the Normandy beaches on D-Day. Joined by the remainder of the 2d Corps, the Canadians assisted in the taking of CAEN (July 1944), captured Vetrières (July), operated in the Falaise area (August) and entered ROUEN (August). In the ensuing Allied pursuit of the Germans through France and Belgium, the Canadians reached Dieppe and Ostend in September 1944, and entered Calais and Boulogne in the same month. Throughout the Battle of the SCHELDT and the winter on the Meuse which followed (September 1944–February 1945), the Canadians took SOUTH BEVELAND and WALCHEREN and maintained a holding action in the Nijmegen salient.

The 2d Canadian Corps took part in the final push into Germany beginning in February 1945, launching an offensive through the Reichswald, a large forest just across the Dutch-German border. In March the two Canadian Army corps were united and advanced together across the Rhine. In the remainder of the war, Canadians operated extensively in Germany and northern Holland. By the time the European war ended, the First Canadian Army's formations (including foreign army units) had captured 192,000 Germans. Some 470,000 Canadians had operated in the Northwest European theater, of whom more than 12,000 had been killed. *See also* INVASION—NORMANDY; WESTERN FRONT.

FIRST ARMY (U.S.). The oldest numerically designated U.S. field army, created in France in 1918 with Gen. John J. Pershing as commander. The headquarters was reactivated early in World War II at Governors Island, N.Y., and went to England in October 1943 to begin planning for the American role in the invasion of northwestern Europe. At a boys' school, Clifton College in Bristol, a newly designated commander joined the staff: Lt. Gen. Omar N. BRADLEY, who brought with him several members of his former staff of the II Corps that had fought in North Africa and Sicily. It was foreordained that when sufficient American forces had arrived on the Continent to constitute an army group, Bradley was to move up to that command while Lt. Gen. Courtney H. HODGES, who reached England in the spring of 1944, took over the First Army.

From the pre-invasion stage in England through V-E Day, two corps headquarters were always with the First Army—the V and VII Corps. As was the custom, others came and went as the tactical situation dictated, but the two others that saw most service with the First Army were the VIII and XIX Corps. Divisions too came and went, but several of the U.S. Army's oldest formations were almost always under the First Army's command: the 1st, 2d, 4th and 9th Infantry Divisions and the 2d and 3d Armored Divisions. The armored divisions were "old style," possessing a hundred more medium tanks than did divisions organized later, so that, contrary to press reports that the Third Army was "top-heavy" with armor, the First Army almost always had more tanks than any other American army. Throughout the war the army had "an indissoluble operational partnership" with the IX Tactical Air Command, oldest tactical support component of the Ninth Air Force, commanded by Maj. Gen. Elwood R. QUESADA.

In operations the First Army achieved a remarkable series of "firsts": first (with British and Canadians) ashore in Normandy, first to break out of the beachhead, first into Paris, first across the Seine River, first across the German frontier, first across the Rhine River and first to contact the Russians in central Germany. The only serious reversal the army incurred was in the Battle of the BULGE in December 1944 when the surprise German counteroffensive struck in the Ardennes region of Belgium and Luxembourg, where Hodges had thinned the line in order to concentrate for an offensive in more open terrain to the north.

The headquarters and many of its units were the first to be deployed from Europe after the war ended, for the First Army was scheduled to spearhead the planned invasion of Japan. *See also* WESTERN FRONT.

FIRST POLISH PARACHUTE BRIGADE. Assigned to the British 1st Airborne Division for the ARNHEM operation (*see* MARKET-GARDEN), September 1944, the brigade was to seize critical terrain on the left bank of the Rhine. Like the other elements of the 1st Airborne Division, the First Polish Parachute Brigade encountered stiff resistance.

FIRST SPECIAL AVIATION PROJECT. The cover name for the first U.S. bombing of Japan, an undertaking that originated early in 1942 with two naval officers, Captains Francis S. Low and Donald W. Duncan, who proposed that Army B-25s be launched from an aircraft carrier. Adm. Ernest J. KING, Commander in Chief, U.S. Fleet, referred them to Lt. Gen. Henry H. ARNOLD, Commanding General of the Army Air Forces, who was enthusiastic about the scheme. Arnold then called upon Lt. Col. James H. DOOLITTLE to take charge of modifying the aircraft and training crews for the operation.

To prepare the B-25s for this secret mission, additional fuel tanks were installed, the radios were removed and only twin .50-caliber machine guns in the upper turret and a single .30-caliber in the nose were retained as defensive armament. The volunteer crews trained at Eglin Field, Fla., where they practiced low-altitude bombing using the specially built MARK TWAIN bombsight, a device made from about 20 cents' worth of metal. The pilots learned from U.S. Navy Lt. Henry L. Miller how to take off in the 500 feet that would be available to them on a carrier deck.

On April 2, 1942, U.S.S. HORNET steamed from San Francisco carrying Doolittle's men and their 16 B-25s. The carrier made rendezvous with another task group, formed around the carrier ENTERPRISE, and laid a course for the Western Pacific. A Japanese patrol boat spotted the American ships and managed to radio a warning before it was sunk. As a result, Vice-Adm. William F. HALSEY, the task force commander, decided that he had no choice but to launch the bombers.

Doolittle and his men caught the Japanese unpre-

Bound for Japan, a B-25 takes off from the flight deck of the U.S.S. *Hornet*

pared and successfully attacked military targets at Tokyo, Yokohama, Yokosuka, Kobe and Nagoya. Though they did not cause major damage, they gave American morale a great boost. The raid actually caused more material destruction to Japan than the plan had anticipated, and the moral shock to the Japanese people was tremendous. The principal strategic result of the raid was that it influenced Japanese planners to attempt to secure their homeland by advancing on MIDWAY, an operation that ended in disaster for Japan. It also caused the recall of several Zero fighter squadrons from the outer perimeter; none had been left to defend Japan.

The raiders had planned to land at airfields in China, but the necessary preparations had not been made to receive them. In addition, weather over the mainland was bad, and without radio beacons to guide them the airmen became lost and ran low on fuel. One B-25 turned northward and landed safely at an airfield about 40 miles north of Vladivostok in the USSR, where the crew was interned for a year until an escape to Iran could be arranged. Of the other 15 planes, four crash-landed and the crews of 11 (including Doolittle's) took to their parachutes. One man was killed parachuting, and two drowned when their plane ditched off the coast. Japanese patrols captured eight of the raiders. Three were executed as war criminals, one died in prison and four survived 40 months of solitary confinement in prison and were freed after hostilities had ended. For his role in the daring venture, Doolittle received the MEDAL OF HONOR and an immediate promotion to brigadier general.

At the time, President ROOSEVELT declared that the planes had taken off from Shangri-La, a Tibetan paradise described in the James Hilton novel *Lost Horizon*. A year passed before the public learned that the bombers had been launched from the *Hornet*, which by that time had fallen victim to the Japanese.

FISH, Hamilton (1888–1972). U.S. Representative from New York, Fish was a vocal isolationist until the Japanese attack on Pearl Harbor in 1941. In the spring of 1939 he had established the National Committee to Keep America Out of Foreign Wars, in which he was active until 1941 as an opponent of the Roosevelt Administration's policies and as an advocate of better relations with Japan and Germany. But with American involvement in the war, Fish changed his position and announced that the American people "should present a united front in support of the President of the United States."

FITCH, Aubrey Wray (1883–1978). "Jake" Fitch, a U.S. Naval Academy graduate of 1907, began the war commanding a task force in Adm. Chester NIMITZ's Pacific Fleet. In this capacity he fought in the Battle of the CORAL SEA. By late 1942, now a vice-admiral, he had taken overall command of aircraft in the South Pacific, coordinating U.S. Navy, Army, Marine and New Zealand units. Fitch kept a low profile, attracting little attention for the air war in the SOLOMONS, though he there developed a strategy of bombardment, invasion and use of the newly captured base to launch further air operations. In 1944 Fitch returned to Washington to become Deputy Chief of Naval Operations for Air. When he became superintendent of the Naval Academy in 1945, he instituted a new emphasis on aeronautics.

5-INCH 38. Term used in referring to the U.S. Navy 5-inch 38-caliber dual-purpose gun; in documents and official correspondence it is expressed as 5"/38. A widely used and long-lived naval gun, the 5"/38 was developed in the early 1930s to give destroyers a reasonably heavy gun suitable for use against surface or air targets. During World War II it was the principal heavy antiaircraft gun of the U.S. fleet. In closed twin mounts and in closed or open single mounts, it saw service in every type of surface warship as well as in many fleet auxiliaries and in DEFENSIVELY EQUIPPED MERCHANT SHIPS. It fired semifixed ammunition, with a 54-pound projectile; these could be explosive shells, star shells or white-phosphorus rounds. The 5"/38 was capable of a high rate of sustained fire, limited only by the strength and endurance of its crew; it had a horizontal range of 18,000 yards and an antiaircraft range of 37,300 feet. Thousands of 5-inch 38s were in service by V-J Day, and the gun is still in use by the U.S. and other navies 40 years after its introduction to service.

FLAIL TANK. A TANK with a minesweeping device attached; the device was basically two arms extending from the vehicle's sides or hull which held a revolving drum that had lengths of heavy chain attached. The chains struck the earth, detonating any mines and clearing a path. There were two main types. The most numerous was the Sherman M4-A4 "Crab" flail, which could clear a lane 10 feet wide while moving 1½ miles an hour. It was first used in Normandy and was employed throughout the European campaign by the British and U.S. armies. The "Scorpion" minesweeper was built on the hull of a turretless Matilda and moved at 2 miles an hour; it was used in the desert campaigns.

FLAK. Abbreviation of *Fl*ieger*a*bwehr*k*anone, German for "antiaircraft gun." Allied pilots, especially American, used the term to denote antiaircraft fire.

FLAK WAGON. U.S. service slang term for self-propelled antiaircraft gun mounts—light antiaircraft guns mounted on tank or half-track chassis.

FLAMETHROWER. Essentially an offensive weapon that fires a stream of burning liquid or semiliquid from a nozzle. Generally it has four major components: a fuel storage system, a compressed gas storage system, a flame gun and an igniter. The gun has two triggers, one to release the fuel, the other to ignite it as it passes through the nozzle. The most widely used were the portable, one-man flamethrowers. Flamethrowers were also mounted on tanks and armored cars; the British had some emplaced in stationary fortifications in case of German invasion attempts. The Americans developed an aerial flamethrower, the aeroflame, and tested it successfully. It was not adopted, since NAPALM did a better job.

FLANDIN, Pierre Etienne (1889–1958). French political figure, a minister in various cabinets beginning in 1924, who served as Premier (1934–35) and Foreign Minister (1936) and was a participant in the VICHY regime. Marshal PÉTAIN appointed Flandin Foreign Minister in December 1940, but he held the post only until the following February. During this time he was in effect the chief minister of the Vichy government, a role in which he replaced Pierre LAVAL. Tried after the war by a French tribunal, Flandin was sentenced to five years' "national indignity." His defense was bolstered by a letter from Winston CHURCHILL, who recalled Flandin's prewar attempts to oppose Adolf HITLER.

FLASHER, U.S.S. GATO-class submarine, completed in 1943, which is credited with sinking the greatest total enemy tonnage. On her six war patrols she destroyed 100,231 tons of shipping. The commanders of *Flasher* were Reuben T. Whitaker and George W. Grider. Ranking second in tonnage sunk was *Rasher* (99,901 tons); third was *Barb* (96,628).

FLASH RED. U.S. Pacific Fleet radio signal, standardized early in 1944, meaning that enemy planes were near and an air attack was imminent. Flash Blue indicated that unidentified planes were in the vicinity and an attack was possible. Flash White meant that enemy aircraft had left the area, or that unidentified planes had been identified as friendly; this was a verbal all-clear signal.

FLAX. Code name for operation by Allied air forces (with P-40s and Spitfires) to disrupt the flow of Axis air transport from Italy and Sicily to Tunisia, beginning April 5, 1943. This operation, designed to sever General ROMMEL's supply line into TUNIS, was of great help to final Allied ground operations in Tunisia (Operation Vulcan), though it had been planned before Vulcan was conceived.

FLEET AIR ARM. The aviation force of the Royal Navy. During World War I its predecessor had been the Royal Naval Air Service, but in 1918 this was taken into the Royal Air Force. In 1924 a Fleet Air Arm was created within the RAF, most of whose personnel were Navy and whose aircraft were designed and built by the Air Force to Navy requirements; this last feature has been criticized as a reason for the relative obsolescence of British naval aircraft when war came. The Fleet Air Arm came under the operational control of the Navy, but its shore establishment was controlled by the RAF. Finally, in 1938, total control of the FAA was transferred to the Navy. Since support had been provided by the RAF, the Navy had no maintenance or repair personnel; through the war years it was necessary for the Navy to rely on borrowed Air Force people as it gradually trained its own men to replace them both ashore and afloat. During the war FAA pilots flew the same general types of missions as their American counterparts, operating from ships and from shore airfields. British carriers joined forces with the U.S. Pacific Fleet to take part in the final offensive against Japan.

FAA aircraft were a combination of prewar Air Ministry designs for naval use, such as the WALRUS, SWORDFISH and SKUA; modifications of RAF land-based planes, such as the Sea Hurricane (*see* HURRICANE) and SEAFIRE; wartime Admiralty designs, such as the BARRACUDA; and lend-lease American types such as the MARTLET (later Wildcat), Hellcat (*see* F6F), Corsair (*see* F4U) and Avenger (*see* TBF).

FLEET MARINE FORCE, PACIFIC. The origins of the senior U.S. Marine Corps command in the Pacific can be found in the 2d Joint Training Force, a joint Marine-Army amphibious training organization which, after several redesignations, moved to Pearl Harbor in September 1943, becoming V Amphibious Corps (VAC). In addition to its training duties, VAC became responsible for planning and conducting amphibious assaults. In March 1944 Lt. Gen. Holland M. SMITH, commander of VAC, was given as an additional duty complete administrative control and logistical responsibility for all Fleet Marine Force units in the Central Pacific. With the onset of operations in the MARIANAS in 1944, two task forces were established—one to conduct the SAIPAN and TINIAN landings and a second to direct the GUAM operation. VAC conducted the former; III Amphibious Corps (IIIAC)—so redesignated from I Marine Amphibious Corps, which had directed operations up the SOLOMONS ladder—had control of the latter. In order for General Smith to exercise tactical command of both IIIAC and VAC, a higher headquarters, Fleet Marine Force, Pacific, was organized on September 17, 1944. By the time of the surrender of Japan in September 1945, FMFPac consisted of the Service Command, FMFPac; the III and V Amphibious Corps, comprised of six Marine divisions; and Aircraft, Fleet Marine Force, Pacific, with four Marine aircraft wings and Marine Fleet Air, West Coast.

FLEETS, U.S. NAVY. At the time of PEARL HARBOR the U.S. Navy's forces afloat were organized into an Atlantic and a Pacific Fleet. Both were under the overall direction of the Commander in Chief, U.S. Fleet. A small Asiatic Fleet was based in the Philippines, but after the fall of the "Malay Barrier" it ceased to exist. Various forces were established to work in specific geographic areas. On March 15, 1943, Adm. Ernest J. KING directed that these forces be designated as numbered fleets, those in the Atlantic being given even numbers and those in the Pacific odd numbers. This basic system is followed today. These numbered fleets existed during World War II:

- THIRD FLEET, established March 15, 1943. Formerly South Pacific Force.
- Fourth Fleet, established March 15, 1943, disestablished April 15, 1945. Formerly South Atlantic Force.
- FIFTH FLEET, established April 26, 1944. Formerly Central Pacific Force.
- Seventh Fleet, established February 19, 1943. Formerly Southwest Pacific Force.
- Eighth Fleet, established March 15, 1943, disestablished April 15, 1945. Formerly Naval Forces, Northwest African Waters.
- TENTH FLEET, established May 20, 1943, disestablished June 12, 1945.
- Twelfth Fleet, established March 15, 1943. Formerly Naval Forces, Europe.

The Tenth Fleet was a shore-based command, set up to direct American antisubmarine operations in the Atlantic. The Seventh Fleet was primarily concerned with the amphibious campaign in the Southwest Pacific. During the last part of the Pacific war, the Pacific Fleet's principal striking force was alternately designated the

Third Fleet, under command of Adm. William F. Halsey, and the Fifth Fleet, commanded by Adm. Raymond A. Spruance. This dual arrangement permitted each fleet commander to concentrate on planning the next operation while his alternate was conducting the current one.

FLEET-TYPE SUBMARINES. General U.S. Navy term for the three operationally similar Gato, Balao and Corsair classes, the principal wartime American submarine types.

FLEISCHER, Carl (1883–1942). Norwegian Army officer, commander of the 6th District in the far north at the time of the German invasion in 1940. Fleischer soon took over the province of North Norway, which had been cut off from the main government. His division operated until the Allied withdrawal. Fleischer accompanied the Norwegian Government to England. In 1942 he was named military attaché in Ottawa, as well as commander of the Norwegian forces then located in Canada. *See also* Norway—Operations.

FLETCHER, Frank Jack (1885–1973). Born into a Navy family and a 1906 graduate of the U.S. Naval Academy, Fletcher won a Medal of Honor at Vera Cruz in 1914 and saw service in World War I. As a vice-admiral in World War II, Fletcher worked with carrier-based aircraft in the Pacific.

He was in command of the cruiser *Minneapolis* when the Japanese attacked Pearl Harbor, his ship being one of the few at sea during that disaster. Following the attack, Adm. Husband E. Kimmel chose Fletcher to lead the operation to relieve Wake Island; however, Fletcher experienced refueling delays, leading Adm. W. S. Pye, Kimmel's temporary successor, to abandon the attempt.

Fletcher's most distinguished action came in the decisive battles of the Coral Sea and Midway. The Coral Sea was a tactical victory for the Allies in that it preserved communications with Australia, and although he lost the carrier Lexington there, Fletcher played no small part in the victory. His task force intercepted the Japanese fleet headed for Port Moresby and fought a four-day air battle, May 4–8, 1942. Midway was, of course, the turning point of the Pacific war. Japan lost four carriers and much of her air power, but Fletcher lost another carrier, the Yorktown. After the *Yorktown* (Fletcher's flagship) was hit, Vice-Adm. Raymond A. Spruance directed the battle.

Fletcher saw further action in the Pacific, his task force participating in the Guadalcanal campaign. In this fighting his ship, the Saratoga, was hit and Fletcher wounded. He returned to Washington for temporary duty. Although Fletcher had participated successfully in several major battles, they had all gone badly for him in some way. The crucial victories of the Coral Sea and Midway remained his brightest moments. He retired in 1947.

FLETCHER. Class of U.S. destroyers. These flush-deck 2,050-ton ships, popularly called "2,100-tonners," followed the Benson and Gleaves classes in design sequence and began to go into commission during the summer of 1942. Their designed armament consisted of five closed-mount dual-purpose 5-inch guns and two quintuple banks of 21-inch torpedo tubes. The original design called for one 1.1-inch quadruple antiaircraft gun mount, and some of the early Fletchers were completed with this. It was soon replaced by a twin 40-mm. mount. As the war went on, further additions were made to the antiaircraft battery, many ships losing their second set of torpedo tubes to make way for AA guns. Serving primarily in the Pacific, Fletcher-class destroyers became the "classic" American destroyer of that war. They took part in every major campaign from the Solomons to the final carrier strikes of 1945, and were considered good and useful ships. One hundred and nineteen Fletchers were built under orders placed in 1940; after Pearl Harbor, additional orders to yards already building them produced 56 more "Repeat Fletchers." Nineteen Fletchers were war losses; nine received unit citations.

F-LIGHTER. German beaching craft (163 feet) resembling the LST (*see* LST). During the fighting in Italy the Germans employed F-lighters in the supply of their forces from ports in northern Italy and on the French Riviera.

FLINTLOCK. Code name of the U.S. invasion of the Marshall Islands, the attacks on Kwajalein and Majuro Atolls and on Roi, Namur and Kwajalein Islands by Army, Marine and Navy forces, January 31–February 7, 1944.

FLOATING CHRYSANTHEMUMS (Kikusui). The Japanese name for their large-scale aerial kamikaze offensive against American forces off Okinawa. Beginning on April 6, 1945, 10 heavy assaults were mounted through June 22. Both Army and Navy planes were involved, the number totaling 1,465 aircraft. Numbers of planes taking part in individual *kikusui* attacks ranged from 355 in the first raid to 45 in the last. Approximately 450 individual suicide sorties, not part of the large-scale Floating Chrysanthemums operation, were also hurled at U.S. naval forces at Okinawa.

FLUSH-DECKERS. U.S. Navy nickname for three classes of World War I–era destroyers—the Caldwell, Wickes and Clemson classes—which earned it for their flush-decked hulls, a novelty in comparison with earlier American destroyers with their prominent raised forecastles. The six Caldwells were prototypes, with two machinery arrangements; three had triple stacks, the others having the four-funnel silhouette that would characterize the 273 ships of the Wickes and Clemson classes. Four single-purpose 4-inch guns were the normal battery, with one 3-inch antiaircraft gun. All 279 flush-deckers went into commission between October 1917 and August 1922. Even after new ships began to join the fleet in the mid-1930s, flush-deckers continued to form a large part of the destroyer force. Many were still active when the U.S. Navy began to take part in the Battle of the Atlantic before Pearl Harbor. The flush-decker Reuben James, sunk on October 31, 1941, while escorting a British convoy, was the first U.S. warship lost to hostile action during World War II. Flush-deckers served in the Atlantic and Pacific throughout the war as fleet destroyers and in auxiliary roles as fast transports (APD), small seaplane tenders (AVD), minelayers (DM) and minesweepers (DMS); some became experimental auxiliaries (AG) or training ships. Fifty of these ships were transferred to the Royal Navy by President ROOSEVELT (*see* DESTROYERS–BASES DEAL).

During the war years British and American flushdeckers received varying modifications. Some had their 4-inch guns replaced by 3-inch dual-purpose weapons. Torpedo batteries were reduced, rearranged or removed. Light antiaircraft guns and new antisubmarine armament were added; stacks were lowered, and many ships lost one. New electronics, including RADAR and SONAR, were added.

FLYING BARN DOOR. Nickname for the British WHITLEY bomber.

FLYING BOMB. Allied name for the German FZG 76 (Fern Ziel Gerät—Long Range Target Apparatus). This weapon was best known as the V-1 (Vergeltungswaffe 1—Reprisal Weapon No. 1) and to the British as the "doodlebug." While the name "flying bomb" fits a number of other weapons, it generally denotes the V-1. *See also* V-WEAPONS.

FLYING BOXCAR. Official name for the U.S. C-119 but used as a nickname by soldiers for both the C-82 and the C-87.

FLYING ELEPHANT. Code name for the Japanese operation involving the launching of balloons carrying incendiary bombs against the continental United States in 1944–45. *See also* BALLOON BOMB.

FLYING FORTRESS. *See* B-17.

FLYING PENCIL. A British-originated nickname for the German DORNIER Do 17 medium bomber, from its slim appearance.

FLYING PORCUPINE. Nickname given by the Germans to the British SUNDERLAND flying boat, because of its heavy (eight-gun) armament.

FLYING TIGERS. Nickname of the AMERICAN VOLUNTEER GROUP and of the FOURTEENTH AIR FORCE.

FM-1. Designation of two aircraft: the Bell Airacuda, a U.S. Army experimental "bomber destroyer" that was never put into production; and a version of the Grumman F4F-4 Wildcat (*see* F4F), with four fixed .50-caliber machine guns in lieu of the F4F-4's six, produced by General Motors' Eastern Division beginning in 1942. The FM-2 was a lighter and more powerful version of the General Motors–built Wildcat. It was the final production model of the F4F.

Manufacture of the F4F was transferred by the Navy from Grumman to General Motors in order to free the Grumman plant to concentrate on the F6F Hellcat. GM undertook to adapt mass-production techniques to airplane manufacturing.

FOCKE-WULF FW 187A. A twin-engine German fighter aircraft also known as Falke (Falcon), designed in 1936; nine were built. The last three were used in Norway in 1940.

FOCKE-WULF FW 189. A very successful twin-engine, three-place tactical reconnaissance and liaison monoplane known as the Uhu (Owl). About 800 were built. It was a twin-boom plane which carried its crew in a glazed housing mounted in the center of the wing. Powered by two 465-horsepower V-12 engines, it flew at 217 miles per hour maximum speed. It was armed with six machine guns and carried four 110-pound bombs. It could fight off fighters and absorb great amounts of punishment, though in the latter part of the war it could not survive in combat because of its low speed.

FOCKE-WULF FW 190. A series first flown on June 1, 1939. About 100 were tested operationally in mid-1941, and by the end of the war 13,367 FW 190 fighters and 6,634 FW 190 fighter-bombers had been built, a majority of the fighters A-series aircraft. It was the outstanding fighter of the war, possessing the best all-around flying capabilities in terms of speed and maneuverabil-

Focke-Wulf FW 190

ity at low and high altitudes; it was also an excellent gun and bomb platform. Although other fighters may have had an edge in one or two areas, none combined the FW 190's overall capabilities. The FW 190A-8 had a 1,700-horsepower (2,100-horsepower with supplementary fuel injection), 14-cylinder radial engine which drove it to a maximum speed of 402 miles per hour. It was armed with two MG 131 13-mm. cowl machine guns and four MG 151 20-mm. wing cannon. It weighed 9,750 pounds fully loaded and was 29 feet long and had a wingspan of 34 feet 5½ inches.

The FW 190B was an adaptation of the A series for fighting at high altitudes. Dubbed the "Kanguruh" because of a belly-mounted supercharger, it was supplanted in 1944 by the D series—essentially an A model with an in-line engine, a longer nose and a lengthened tail frame. Although it was a spectacular performer, reaching 426 miles per hour and considered by many fighter pilots to be the finest piston-engine fighter to enter LUFTWAFFE service, relatively few were built. The FW 190F and 190G were single-seat, close-support fighters, armored and modified for carrying bombs, rockets and even torpedoes. The FW 190F-3 could do 394 miles per hour; it carried a 1,100-pound bomb load.

FOCKE-WULF FW 200. An improvised maritime reconnaissance bomber, also known as Kondor (Condor). It was designed in 1936 as a Lufthansa transatlantic transport, but its success as a commerce raider, eyes for the U-boats, a reconnaissance plane and a transport is attested to by the huge number of ships it sank and the tremendous Allied effort to eliminate it. Although very durable, it lacked armor and the fuel lines were vulnerable to attack. It was also plagued with structural failures throughout its career, primarily failure of the rear spar which resulted in the aircraft breaking its back on landing. The FW 200-3/U4 was a seven-place plane with four 9-cylinder, 1,000-horsepower radials (1,200-horsepower at takeoff and 940-horsepower at 13,120 feet). Its most economical speed was 152 miles per hour with a 2,210-mile range. Its defense armament was one 7.9-mm. machine gun in a dorsal turret, a flexible 13-mm. machine gun mounted dorsally aft, a 20-mm. cannon on each side, a ventrally mounted 7.9-mm. machine gun forward and a 9.9-mm. machine gun aft. It carried a 4,626-pound bomb load.

FOCKE-WULF 1000×1000×1000 B Project. German project to develop a bomber capable of carrying a 1,000-kilogram bomb load at 1,000 kilometers per hour for a distance of 1,000 kilometers.

FOCKE-WULF TA 152. A refinement of the FW 190D. At first there were few differences between that plane and the Ta 152. The Ta 152 used a 1,200-horsepower radial engine. Several models were planned, but few of the type were ever built. The Ta 152C flew 463 miles per hour maximum speed and carried one 30-mm. and four 20-mm. cannon. The prefix Ta denoted Prof. Kurt Tank, chief of Focke-Wulf aircraft projects.

FOGGIA. This Italian city across the Apennines from Naples was seemingly important to the Allies because of airfields in the vicinity, and was occupied by troops of the British Eighth Army (13th Corps) on October 1, 1943. There has been considerable debate about the value of the air facilities that existed at the time the Allies took Foggia.

FOKKER D-XXI. Dutch single-radial-engine, low-wing fighter, designed in 1936. It was used by Republican Spain, Finland and Denmark, but only 29 were serviceable when Germany invaded the Netherlands. Although limited by low speed (286 miles per hour), the sturdy D-XXIs gave a good account of themselves against the LUFTWAFFE until, after three days, the surviving aircraft had to be grounded for lack of ammunition.

FOKKER G-IA. Heavily armed Dutch twin-engine, twin-boom heavy fighter and close-support fighter; 33 were in service when Germany attacked. Those not destroyed on the ground fought until all were lost. The G-IA had two 830-horsepower radials, giving 295 miles per hour maximum speed, and was armed with eight forward-firing 7.9-mm. machine guns and one rear 7.9-mm. machine gun or two 23-mm. cannon and two 7.9-mm. machine guns forward and one 7.9-mm. in the rear.

FONDOUK GAP. Pass in northern Tunisia leading to the Kairouan plain. Allied forces attempted to seize the gap on March 27, 1943, but ran into stiff opposition from Axis forces. This was the first divisional action of the U.S. 34th Division, and it fell back and established defensive positions.

FOOCHOW (Minhow). A seaport city in Fukien province in southeast China that was fought over in 1944–45 by Japanese and Chinese armies. Foochow was finally liberated on May 18, 1945.

FORAGER. Code name for U.S. invasion of the MARIANA ISLANDS. Pre-invasion attacks began June 11, 1944; the first landing, at SAIPAN by U.S. Marines, was on June 15.

FORBES, Sir Charles Morton (1880–1960). Flag commander to Admiral Jellicoe during the First World War, Forbes held several important commands between the two wars and in 1938 became commander in chief of the British Home Fleet, an appointment he still held when war was declared. He was in chief command at sea during the Norwegian campaign of 1940, and although the Germans eventually succeeded in occupying the whole of NORWAY, their losses at sea were considerably greater than those of the Home Fleet. In December 1940 Forbes was appointed Commander in Chief Plymouth. As well as conducting extensive warfare on U-boats—in conjunction with COASTAL COMMAND of the RAF—he carried out many actions against enemy destroyers and convoys passing along the north coast of France and organized raids on enemy posts ashore, of which the most successful and spectacular was the combined operations assault on SAINT-NAZAIRE in March 1942.

FORCE H. British naval squadron assembled at Gibraltar in June 1940. It was created to fill the vacuum left in the western Mediterranean when France quit the war. Commanded by Vice-Adm. Sir James SOMERVILLE, Force H consisted of the carrier ARK ROYAL, the battle cruiser HOOD, the battleships VALIANT and RESOLUTION, two cruisers and 11 destroyers. Its first assignment was the disabling of the French fleet at MERS-EL-KÉBIR. It participated in many other missions, notably the pursuit of the BISMARCK and the landings in NORTHWEST AFRICA, in SICILY and at SALERNO, as well as providing escorts for MALTA-bound convoys.

FORCE K. British striking force of cruisers and destroyers based at MALTA in October 1941. In December it suffered severe losses when, en route to intercept an Italian convoy, several of its ships were sunk or damaged.

FORCE 141. Allied headquarters set up by General EISENHOWER to plan the invasion of SICILY, so called from the number of the room in the St. George's Hotel, Algiers, where the members of the group first met. It was established in January 1943 and became an independent operational headquarters on May 15, at the end of the Tunisian campaign.

FORCE Z. Code name of the British fleet consisting of the battleship PRINCE OF WALES, the battle cruiser REPULSE and escorting destroyers, which was sent to the Far East in late 1941. The two capital ships were sunk by Japanese air attack on December 10, 1941.

FORD ISLAND. A large island in the middle of PEARL HARBOR, the site of a U.S. naval air station. It was heavily bombed on December 7, 1941. Ship moorings, including BATTLESHIP Row, were located along its shores.

FORMER NAVAL PERSON. A code name used by Winston CHURCHILL to refer to himself in communications with President ROOSEVELT. When the personal correspondence between the two began in 1939, Churchill, as First Lord of the Admiralty, signed himself "Naval Person." "Former" was added in the letter of May 15, 1940, Churchill's first after leaving the Admiralty and becoming Prime Minister.

FORMIDABLE, H.M.S. ILLUSTRIOUS-class fleet aircraft carrier of 23,000 tons standard displacement, armed with sixteen 4.5-inch dual-purpose guns and numerous 40-mm. and 20-mm. antiaircraft guns. She was completed in 1940. *Formidable* played an important part in the Mediterranean, notably in the Battle of CAPE MATAPAN in March 1941. In early 1942 she went to the Indian Ocean, and finished the war as part of Task Force 57, the British force attached to the U.S. fleet in the Pacific. She was damaged by a KAMIKAZE attack in the Ryukyus in May 1945.

FORMOSA. Allied planners envisioned that this large island (now Taiwan) in the China Sea would serve as the final stepping-stone in the invasion of Japan. Among the Allied plans considered during the CAIRO CONFERENCE of November 1943 was one in which Admiral NIMITZ's forces would push through the Central Pacific in a series of operations culminating in an assault on Formosa before the final drive on Japan. As the Pacific campaign developed, many different options arose for Allied planners, and in mid-1944 they were confronted with having to make a choice of either Luzon or Formosa as a major objective. In October 1944 the decision was made to mount operations against Luzon, Iwo JIMA and OKINAWA in turn, and Formosa at a later date if conditions in the Pacific and Europe warranted and troops and shipping became available. Despite the fact that it was not a primary objective for an amphibious assault, Formosa was subjected to many heavy air raids emanating from U.S. Navy carrier forces once they began operating in the China Sea in late 1944.

FORRESTAL, James Vincent (1892–1949). Like many prominent New Yorkers in the ROOSEVELT Administration, James Forrestal came to Washington after a successful business career. A graduate of Princeton University and a Navy veteran of World War I, he left the presidency of the Wall Street firm Dillon, Read and Co., to become administrative assistant to President Roosevelt in 1940. In August of that year he was sworn in as Under Secretary of the Navy; he served in that post four years. His able administration of the procurement office and strong advocacy of naval supremacy won him appointment as Secretary of the Navy on May 10, 1944. Forrestal was the only cabinet member to continue in office in the TRUMAN Administration. He supported President Truman's effort to unify the direction of the various military services, and became the first Secretary of Defense in 1947.

FORTITUDE. Code name of the cover plan designed to mislead the Germans as to the site of the 1944 invasion of the Continent. Fortitude North was designed to focus German attention on a possible invasion of Norway, Fortitude South on the Pas de Calais region of the French coast.

FORT SHAFTER. The oldest U.S. Army post in Hawaii, headquarters for U.S. Army forces staging into the Central Pacific area during the war.

FOSS, Joseph Jacob (1915–). A native of South Dakota, Foss was a captain and executive officer of his U.S. Marine squadron (VMF-121) when it arrived on GUADALCANAL on October 9, 1942, to begin operations from HENDERSON FIELD. Flying his Grumman F4F-4 Wildcat (*see* F4F) almost daily from October 9 to November 19 to engage Japanese air and naval forces attempting to dislodge the 1st Marine Division from the island and U.S. and Allied naval forces from the surrounding waters, Foss shot down 23 enemy planes and damaged a number of others so severely that they presumably did not survive. During this period he also led a number of escort missions covering bombing, reconnaissance and photo missions. After being relieved for rest, the squadron returned to Guadalcanal in January 1943 and remained there until the end of the month. This brief period enabled Foss to break World War I "Ace of Aces" Eddie RICKENBACKER's record score of 25 enemy planes downed; on January 15 Foss shot down three planes to raise his total to 26. His skill as a pilot and his inspiring leadership together with his record of kills led to his being awarded the MEDAL OF HONOR in May 1943.

FOULKES, Charles (1903–). Canadian Army officer who was chief of staff, First Canadian Army, 1943–44. He commanded the 2d Canadian Division, 1944, and the 1st Corps, 1944–45, on the WESTERN FRONT. His highest wartime rank was lieutenant general. He was afterward Canada's Chief of General Staff (1945–51) and Chairman of the Chiefs of Staff (1951–60).

FOUR FREEDOMS. In his annual message to the U.S. Congress of January 6, 1941, President Franklin D. ROOSEVELT formulated what became the classic statement of the principles for which America would fight: freedom of speech and expression, freedom to worship God, freedom from want and freedom from fear, for all the world's peoples.

442D REGIMENTAL COMBAT TEAM. Comprised of Japanese-Americans except for the top command, this unique battle group was authorized on February 1, 1943, as an instrument of high national policy. The object was to ensure the well-being of the Japanese-American community in the postwar world; the policy originated in the office of the Army Chief of Staff. The units were the 442d Infantry Regiment, the 552d Field Artillery Battalion and the 232d Engineer Battalion. They were filled with volunteers from among the Nisei of the mainland and Hawaii and via the draft, the islanders comprising a disproportionate percentage of the volunteers as the command cadre. One such Nisei unit, the 100th Battalion of the Hawaiian National Guard, was already in being and shipped early for combat duty in Africa, where it joined the 34th Infantry Division. The 442d formed and trained at Fort Shelby, Miss., where it became an object of more rapt attention by high-ranking officers than any other unit in the Army. The RCT arrived in Italy in May 1944, where it served in battle until September of that year. It then moved to France, where it fought two campaigns before again displacing to Italy to finish the war. The 442d earned four DISTINGUISHED UNIT CITATIONS, having incurred 9,486 casualties, or three times its table-of-organization strength; and more than 18,000 individual decorations were awarded. As one consequence of its participation, the Japanese-born Issei in the United States became eligible for citizenship.

FOUR-NATION DECLARATION. At the October 1943 MOSCOW CONFERENCE, the United States, the United Kingdom, the Soviet Union and China pledged joint action in both war and peace. There were promises of postwar arms regulation and the avoidance of armed conflict except to maintain the peace. And they agreed to establish, as soon as possible, "a general international organization, based on the principle of the sovereign equality of all peace-loving states, and open to membership by all such states, large and small, for the maintenance of international peace and security." Thus the postwar UNITED NATIONS was suggested and the concept of a "Big Four," which included China, was advanced.

FOURTEENTH AIR FORCE. The successor of the AMERICAN VOLUNTEER GROUP, recruited by retired U.S. Air Corps officer Claire L. CHENNAULT, which had gone into action against the Japanese in 1941. Once U.S. Army Air Forces had decided to establish an American air command in China, these Flying Tigers formed a nucleus for the China Air Task Force, also commanded by Chennault, now restored to active duty as a brigadier general in the U.S. Army. The task force, set up in July 1942, consisted at first of 34 P-40s and seven B-25s (*see* P-40; B-25). By March of the following year, however, Chennault's organization had become powerful enough to function independently of the TENTH AIR FORCE, and it emerged as the Fourteenth.

Newly arrived B-24s (*see* B-24) began attacking enemy shipping off the China coast as Chennault attempted to sever the supply lines upon which the Japanese forces in China depended, thus forcing the enemy to relax their grip on the country. Unfortunately, the Fourteenth Air Force was operating at the end of a 16,000-mile supply line that had as its last segment a harrowing flight over the Himalayas. The Japanese could sustain their China expeditionary force far more easily than the Americans could keep Fourteenth Air Force planes in the air. Stung by the bombing, the enemy attacked the poorly trained Chinese ground armies and overran many of Chennault's air bases.

Defeated elsewhere, the Japanese in May 1945 ordered their forces in China to retreat toward the coast. Chennault's airmen harassed the enemy as they fell back. During this final phase of the air war in China, the Fourteenth Air Force destroyed more than 600 locomotives, 900 railroad cars and 2,000 sampans and barges. Chennault's units also assisted Chinese ground forces and hit ports and coastal airfields. *See also* CHINA—OPERATIONS; HUMP, THE.

FOURTEENTH ARMY (British). Along with other organizational changes in India, the British Fourteenth Army was formed on October 15, 1943, in preparation for the establishment on November 15 of the Allied Southeast Asia Command (SEAC). Under the command of Lt. Gen. Sir William J. SLIM, the Fourteenth took over the operational tasks of the abolished Eastern Army and responsibility for security of Assam and Bengal east of the Meghna River. Eventually to be subordinate to SEAC through the 11th Army Group, the Fourteenth Army and its subordinate units wasted no time in getting into action.

Initially, the Fourteenth Army consisted of two corps, the 15th on the Arakan front and the 4th on the central front. Another unit, 33d Corps, at first temporarily under the Indian Command, arrived as a reinforcement on April 2, 1944. The 15th Corps was detached from the Fourteenth Army on November 15, 1944, when Arakan front operations became the responsibility of Allied Land Forces Southeast Asia (ALFSEA).

Facing the British during the Fourteenth Army's share of the Allied campaign to recapture BURMA were elements of Japan's Burma Area Army. Early in 1944 the Japanese attacked strongly in two locations—on the Arakan front and in the area of IMPHAL and KOHIMA. But the first threat was rapidly eliminated, and by June 22 the Fourteenth Army had reopened the road between Imphal and Kohima, signaling the end, after bitter fighting, of the last major Japanese offensive in the India-Burma area.

From December 1944 to early May 1945 the 4th and

33d Corps fought methodically southward in a series of complex maneuvers, and by May 3 only bits and pieces remained of the once strong Japanese forces. At the end of May, Fourteenth Army headquarters moved to India to begin planning for Operation Zipper, the invasion of Malaya; its duties in Burma were passed on to the newly formed Twelfth Army. Although the invasion of Malaya was not necessary, the Fourteenth did perform occupation duties there until it was deactivated on November 1, 1945.

FOURTH ARMY (U.S.). Activated in August 1932 as one of the four new field armies created by the War Department, the Fourth Army just before World War II was assigned the mission of constituting the Western Defense Command, which had to defend the Pacific coast and Alaska. After the war began, the Western Defense Command became active, using Fourth Army personnel, and was known as the Western Defense Command and Fourth Army. The Fourth Air Force was added, along with additional ground forces to defend KISKA and ATTU Islands. The Fourth Army separated from the Western Defense Command on September 18, 1943, and reorganized at San Jose, Calif. In April 1944 the bulk of the Fourth Army staff was ordered overseas to establish the NINTH ARMY, and in August the newly reorganized staff was alerted for overseas duty to organize the FIFTEENTH ARMY. The Fourth Army had furnished the staffs for two additional field armies and had trained and equipped at least half of the combat units shipped overseas. By September 1944 the Fourth Army had absorbed all of the Second Army's duties west of the Mississippi. It remained in the United States throughout the war.

FOURTH OF JULY RAID. On July 4, 1942, the 15th Bombardment Squadron (Light) became the first American unit to attack a target in occupied Europe. Six of the squadron's crews, flying American-built Douglas Bostons (*see* A-20) supplied them by the Royal Air Force, joined six British crews of No. 226 Squadron in attacking four airfields in Holland. Owing to heavy antiaircraft fire, only two of the American crews actually bombed their assigned targets; two of the American-manned planes were shot down and a third was badly damaged.

FOX. Code name for serially numbered broadcasts to U.S. Navy ships from Pearl Harbor. The coded transmissions carried information for all ships; each ship deciphered the message that applied to it. Broadcasts from Canberra were called "Bells."

FOXHOLE. A protection pit for one or two men, usually dug by the occupants. A foxhole was generally cut hastily but might be made more secure as time and materials permitted.

FRANCE, BATTLE OF. The German campaign in western Europe during the spring of 1940, usually called the Battle of France, passed through three general stages. The opening phase from May 10 to 16 included the invasion of Holland and Belgium, the fall of EBEN EMAEL and other Belgian frontier defenses and the Allied counteradvance to the MEUSE and Dyle Rivers (*see* DYLE LINE) in order to meet and contain the German invaders in concert with the BELGIAN ARMY. The second stage encompassed the main German thrust through the ARDENNES Forest in southern Belgium and across the Meuse near SEDAN with the bulk of their armored divisions on May 15. Once the French lines were pierced, the mobile German forces quickly drove west to the sea, splitting the Allied forces in two and forcing the northern Allied armies, including the BRITISH EXPEDITIONARY FORCE (BEF), out of Belgium and back to the English Channel. The Belgians surrendered on May 27, the French First Army capitulated on June 1 and the last naval vessel left DUNKIRK on June 3. The final stage began two days later when the GERMAN ARMY attacked the remaining French forces, which had established a thin defensive line north of PARIS. The French front was quickly breached, leading to a general withdrawal south. Paris fell on June 14, the MAGINOT LINE was surrounded four days later and shortly after midnight on June 25 an armistice went into effect, ending the struggle with about two-thirds of France in German control. (Actually, a Franco-German armistice was signed on June 22 at COMPIÈGNE; hostilities officially ceased six hours after the signing of a Franco-Italian armistice on June 24.)

On the eve of the battle the opposing forces were approximately equal. Germany had marshaled 118 infantry divisions, 10 armored (PANZER) and 8 motorized infantry divisions, and 1 cavalry and 1 parachute division on the Western Front. These forces were controlled by 3 army group, 10 army and 38 corps headquarters. In the north, Army Group B (General von BOCK), opposite Holland and northern Belgium, included 3 panzer divisions, an airborne division and 27 infantry divisions. In the center, opposite southern Belgium and the Ardennes, was Army Group A (von RUNDSTEDT), Germany's strongest force, with 7 panzer and 36 infantry divisions. To the south, opposite the Maginot Line, was the relatively weak Army Group C (von LEEB) with 19 infantry divisions. About 40 more infantry divisions were in general reserve.

The key units were the 10 panzer divisions. In Army Group B the 9th Panzer Division operated independently, while the 3d and 4th Panzers belonged to the XVI Panzer Corps (HOEPPNER). Of the seven in Army Group A, the 5th and 7th (ROMMEL) Panzer Divisions belonged to the XV Corps (HOTH), while the special von KLEIST Armored Group controlled the 1st, 2d and 10th Panzers of the XIX Corps (GUDERIAN) and the 6th and 8th Panzers of the XLI Corps (REINHARDT), as well as four motorized infantry divisions. Each of the panzer divisions had about 325 mixed armored vehicles with motorized infantry, artillery and support units.

Against Germany's 138 divisions, France put about 100 on her northeastern frontier, including 68 foot, 7 motorized and the equivalent of 14 fortress infantry divisions, 5 cavalry divisions and 4 cavalry brigades, 3 armored cavalry divisions and 3 brigade-size heavy armored divisions. A fourth armored division (DE GAULLE), along with many ad hoc infantry and cavalry formations, was slapped together during the ensuing battle, and several units were transferred north from other fronts. To this must be added the 11 British divisions (including 1 armored division which arrived during the battle), 22 Belgian and 10 Dutch divisions, for a grand total of 144 Allied divisions.

German armor advances in France

The Anglo-French forces were disposed in three army groups. Groups Two and Three, with about 50 divisions, stood behind the Maginot Line, while the best Allied units belonged to Army Group One (BILLOTTE), covering the exposed Belgian frontier. In the extreme north was the French Seventh Army (GIRAUD) with 7 divisions, including 1 armored cavalry and 1 motorized infantry division. Next came the BEF (Lord GORT) with 9 infantry divisions and 1 tank brigade. On the British southern flank was the French First Army (BLANCHARD) with 8 first-rate infantry divisions and the Cavalry Corps (Prioux) of 2 armored cavalry divisions. Farther south, behind the Ardennes and along the Meuse, were the Ninth (CORAP) and Second (HUNTZIGER) Armies with 16 divisions, including 4 cavalry divisions, 4 second-class infantry divisions (Series B) of older reservists and several fortress detachments. The southern edge of the Second Army rested on the northern tip of the Maginot Line.

It should be noted that the French armor was divided among 3 armored cavalry divisions, 3 heavy armored divisions (in reserve) and over 40 independent tank battalions providing direct support to infantry units. In addition, the 5 cavalry and 7 motorized infantry divisions had separate armored components. But with the exception of Gen. René Prioux's Cavalry Corps, none of the French armored or motorized formations operated in concert.

The major antagonists were well endowed with modern equipment and weapons. SMALL ARMS, including automatic weapons, were excellent on both sides. French heavy, field and antitank artillery was superior in quality and more plentiful than that of their opponents, though much of this equipment was still horse-drawn in both armies. In antiaircraft artillery the Germans took a strong lead, and their heavier 88-mm. pieces proved to be deadly dual-purpose weapons. The two sides employed about the same number of armored vehicles—slightly over 4,000—but the French machines tended to be slower and more heavily armed and armored, while the German vehicles were spacious and fast, built for maneuver. British armor was a hodgepodge of heavily armored "infantry" TANKS and thin-skinned "cruiser" and reconnaissance machines. But the most important fact was the concentration of German armor and vehicles in the panzer divisions and panzer corps.

In aircraft, Germany had a decided numerical superiority as well as a slight qualitative edge. Against about 1,000 Allied fighters and 400 bombers in the northeast, the LUFTWAFFE employed some 1,100 fighters, approximately the same number of horizontal bombers and about 325 special dive-bombers (STUKAS). France and Britain had no aircraft comparable with the Stuka, and most of France's 750 first-line fighters were slower than their counterparts. More significant, the German Air Force was organized to support the Army's tactical operations, whereas the tactical role of Allied air power was limited to reconnaissance and air defense. Moreover, both Britain and France retained large numbers of aircraft in their interiors for strategic air defense. (Paradoxically, both Allied air forces were numerically

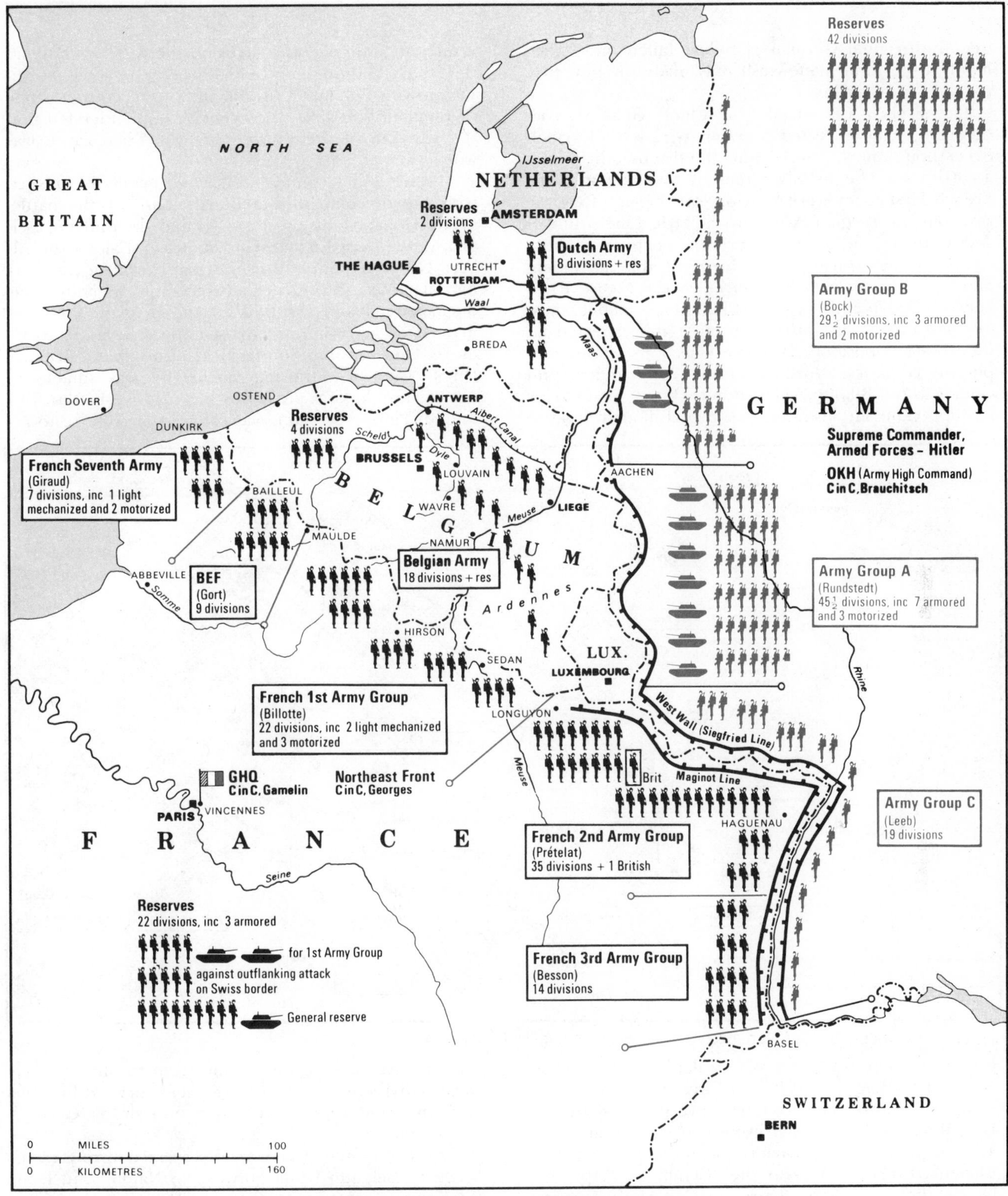

THE OPPOSING FORCES IN THE WEST on the eve of the German invasion—May 1940

stronger at the close of the battle than at the beginning.) As in the case of armor, the Allies were not organized to use what they had most effectively.

At first, the German high command planned to launch an attack through northern Belgium similar to the World War I modified Schlieffen plan. Most of their mobile forces were thus allotted to Army Group B, which was expected only to secure Holland, Belgium and small sections of northeastern France along the Channel. Unlike 1914, the thrust was not to extend south to and past Paris, and hence was not expected to be decisive. The commander of Army Group A, Gen. Gerd von Rundstedt, and his chief of staff, Gen. Erich von MANSTEIN, objected to the plan, and over the initial opposition of Army chief Gen. Walther von BRAUCHITSCH, convinced Adolf HITLER that the main German thrust should be directed through southern Belgium at Sedan and from there to the Channel coast. The northern Allied armies would thus be caught between Army Groups A and B, and destroyed. The fact that the original German plan had fallen into Allied hands after an airplane crash only made the new proposal more appealing.

The French Commander in Chief, Gen. Maurice GAMELIN, also expected another 1914-style German drive though northern Belgium and disposed his forces accordingly. The mobile forces of the BEF and the French First Army were to swing east through Belgium and join the Belgian Army on the Dyle Line south of ANTWERP. To the south, the French Second and Ninth Armies would constitute the hinge of this movement and were to entrench themselves on the Meuse River between Sedan and NAMUR. Although less mobile, most of these forces were already in place and expected no immediate opposition. Over the objections of Gen. Alphonse GEORGES, Northeast Front commander, and Gen. Gaston Billotte, commander of the First Army Group, Gamelin also insisted that Billotte's reserve army, the Seventh, race across northern Belgium to aid the Dutch. Although there had been no military coordination with Belgium and Holland, owing to their hope of remaining neutral, the French commander felt that the addition of their armies to the Allied cause was worth the risk.

The opposing commanders were generally satisfied with the outcome of the initial phase of the battle. While Holland quickly collapsed and the outlying Belgian defenses at LIÈGE, MAASTRICHT and along the Albert Canal fell rapidly to German airborne and armored units, the Allied advance into Belgium was unchallenged and the bulk of the Belgian Army remained intact. Gen. Henri Giraud's Seventh Army moved quickly into southern Holland, but since the Dutch were withdrawing north, he was unable to achieve any linkup and, after inconclusive battles with the 9th Panzer Division, was ordered on May 12 to re-

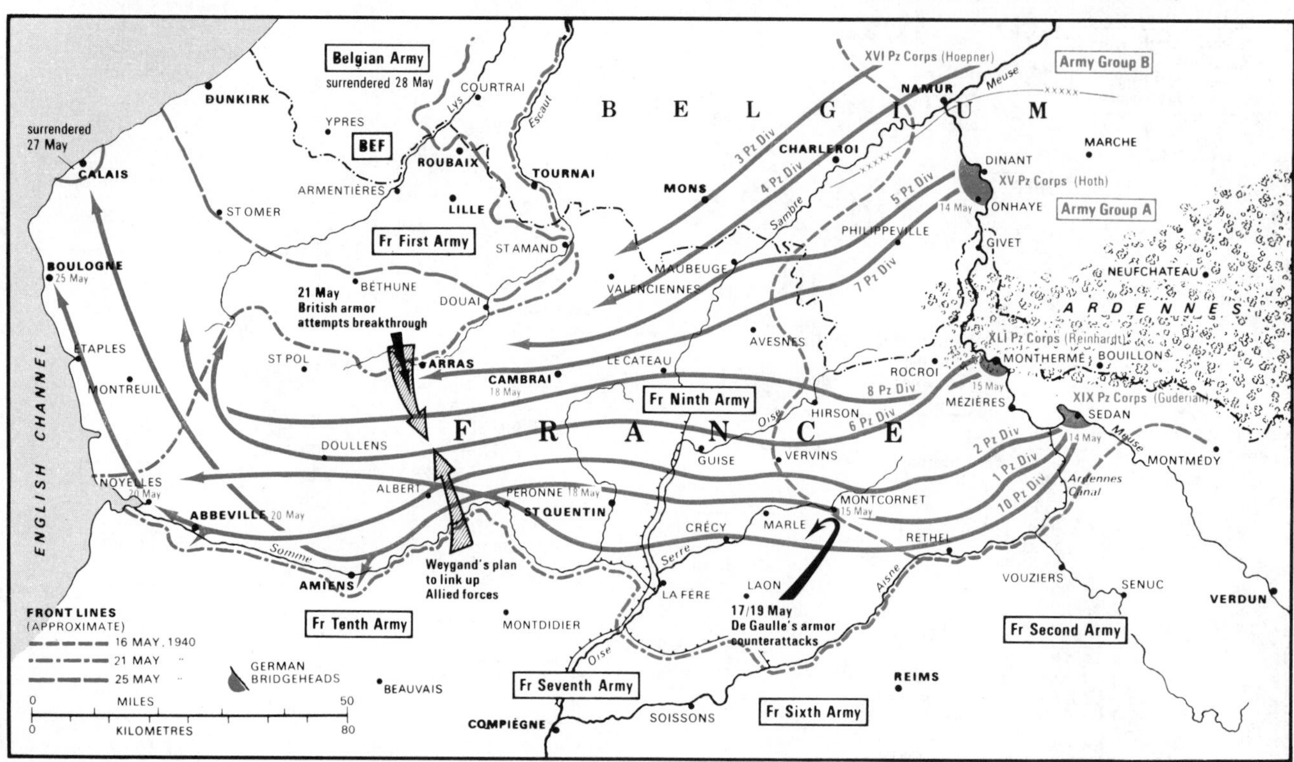

THE GERMAN SWEEP: By May 20, panzers had thrust to the English Channel

group his forces on the northern flank of the Belgian Army. The Belgian and British forces were busy occupying a defensive line around Antwerp and along the Dyle River, with little interference. More critical to the French plan was the establishment of Gen. Georges Blanchard's First Army in the "Gembloux Gap," between the Dyle and Meuse Rivers. Here General Prioux's Cavalry Corps fought a fierce delaying action with Gen. Erich Hoeppner's XVI Panzer Corps on May 11–14. Losses were heavy, but Prioux won enough time to allow Blanchard's infantry to arrive in place. Then, in expectation of further German attacks around Gembloux, the armored cavalry forces were split up among the infantry divisions and Georges committed two of his three reserve armored divisions to Blanchard. South of Namur, Gen. André Corap's Ninth Army moved into place, and the remaining French forces continued to work on their defensive positions along the Meuse. The only discordant note here came from the five French cavalry divisions which had been sent forward into the Ardennes and reported running into strong German opposition.

On May 15 the Allied armies seemed firmly established in Belgium from Antwerp to Namur but, from the German point of view, they had entered Manstein's trap and it was only necessary to slam the door shut. So as not to force the Allies back too early, the XVI Panzer Corps was withdrawn from the Gembloux area on May 16 and sent south to the Ardennes, where the bulk of the German panzers were located. It was here that the main German attack took place.

The French Ninth Army was to hold the Meuse River from Namur south to Sedan, about 75 miles, with five divisions on line—the 5th Motorized, the 18th, 22d and 61st Infantry and the 102d Fortress Division. The first three had to move up to the Meuse from the French border, while the 61st, a Series B division of older reservists, and the static 102d already were in prepared positions. Two more divisions stood in reserve. South of the 102d, the Second Army defended the Sedan area, a sector of about 25 miles, with the 3d North African and two Series B divisions, the 55th and 71st. The defenders occupied a network of half-completed field fortifications which in no way could be considered an extension of the Maginot Line.

On May 10 the seven panzer divisions pushed across the frontiers of Belgium and Luxembourg and through the narrow Ardennes roads. The XV and XLI Panzer Corps headed for the Ninth Army's positions on the Meuse, while Gen. Heinz Guderian's XIX Corps, followed by the XIV Motorized Corps, aimed straight for Sedan. On May 11 and 12 these units pushed the French cavalry back and arrived quickly at the Meuse. In the center, Gen. G.-H. Reinhardt's XLI Corps attacked but made no impression against the well-dug-in 61st and 102d Divisions. The German thrusts to the north and south, however, were more successful. In the north, the French 18th and 22d Divisions took their time moving up to the Meuse and allowed an advance party of German infantry to gain a foothold on the western bank near Dinant on the evening of May 12. French counterattacks the following day were sluggish and uncoordinated, and failed to eject the weak German force. German reinforcements enlarged the bridgehead on May 13, and by the following day tanks of the 5th and 7th Panzers were crossing the river, forcing Corap to move his entire army back.

To the south, before Sedan, Guderian's forces arrived on May 12 and attacked the following morning across the Meuse with assault infantry supported by direct-fire weapons and tactical aircraft. Again the French failed to launch effective counterattacks and allowed the Germans to expand their initial penetrations. By the morning of May 14 the 55th and 71st Divisions had been overrun and German armor was crossing the Meuse and pushing west.

The breakthroughs at Dinant and Sedan spelled the end of the Ninth Army. By May 15 the 102d and 61st Divisions were caught between the advancing Germans and, together with several confused reserve divisions, quickly destroyed. Only the long-retreating cavalry units managed to extricate themselves. The fate of the three French heavy armored divisions was even more tragic. One moved from the rear of the French First Army south toward Dinant on May 14 but was unable to link up with any friendly forces and was overrun while refueling the following morning. A second followed the first but was scattered by the rapid German advance before it had a chance to deploy. Finally, the third arrived south of Sedan on May 13 but, instead of attacking, was broken up and used to cover the flank of the rest of the Second Army. In fact, from May 15 to 20, as the German armor continued to drive west toward the coast, the French high command continued to pile its reserve units on the flanks of the German breakthrough in a vain effort to reestablish a continuous front. Each day they supposed that the German attack would exhaust itself and they would be able to launch a series of slow, methodical counterattacks. But the only serious ripostes during this period were made by Gen. Charles de Gaulle's 4th Armord Division on May 17 and 19 from Laon and by British armor attacking south from Arras on May 21. Neither thrust was reinforced, and both were easily beaten back. The German panzers had been followed closely by motorized and foot infantry columns, which secured the flanks of the advance and organized bridgeheads for further attacks. Gamelin's dismissal and replacement on May 19 by Gen. Maxime WEYGAND failed to alter the situation.

The French high command had had its eyes fixed on the Gembloux Gap and had failed to discern the German thrust through the Ardennes until about May 15, long after the Ninth Army had collapsed. From May 12 to 14, Allied air power was concentrated in northern Belgium to protect the Allied forward movement and was switched to the Ardennes sector only after the Germans had crossed the Meuse. None of the Allied generals had thought the enemy capable of pushing through the Ardennes Forest and then mounting sustained attacks over a major river against prepared defensive positions in the span of three or four days. It was the tempo of the German attack that prevented the French from reacting effectively. The paralysis that seemed to take place during the ensuing period was perhaps only the result of their initial psychological shock coupled with their inability to predict German intentions. As long as the German armor kept moving, the French were unable to put together a current picture of the battlefield and deploy their reserve forces accordingly. Many Frenchmen felt that the main German objective was Paris rather than the Channel coast. And, of course, the commitment of most of the Allied mobile forces to northern Belgium early in the campaign limited their options during the second stage of the battle.

The Allied forces above Namur began withdrawing west on May 16 and, using their armored cavalry and reserve units to cover their rear, slowly backed up to the Franco-Belgian coast. Only Hitler's decision on May 24 to halt the panzer advance to Dunkirk prevented a greater disaster. As it was, the surrender of the Belgian Army on May 27 opened up more gaps in the Allied line and spurred the British-led evacuation which had begun at Dunkirk. Then, while the bulk of the French First Army was trapped at Lille, the remaining Allied forces of Army Group One headed for the coast. Despite determined intervention by the Luftwaffe, between May 26 and June 4 about 338,000 troops, including 110,000 French soldiers, were ferried safely to Britain. Nevertheless, the net loss of over 60 Allied divisions signified the end of France.

During the final phase of the campaign, some 60 weak French divisions faced over twice as many German formations. Most critical was the northern front above Paris, where some 40 French divisions defended 225 miles along the SOMME and Aisne Rivers. Here Weygand ordered his troops to establish a series of small strongpoints, or HEDGEHOGS, which would continue to resist even when bypassed by German armor. All French mobile forces were to be concentrated in three mobile reserves which would counterattack any German breakthrough. However, from about May 24 to June 5, while the German panzers rested, the remaining French armored units had been hurled against German bridgeheads at Péronne and ABBEVILLE in a mistaken effort to strengthen the French defensive line.

As a result, when the Germans launched their final assaults there was almost no French armored reserve to meet them.

German armor was now reorganized into five panzer corps of two armored divisions and one motorized infantry division each. On June 5 three panzer corps attacked across the Somme, and on June 9 the remaining two pushed over the Aisne. This time French infantry resisted bitterly, but after several days of fierce fighting the panzers again pushed through the French line, Weygand's strongpoints were overrun and the French were forced to withdraw south. On June 14 the Germans entered Paris, and they began to outflank the forces on the Maginot Line. The decision to evacuate the line was made too late, and by June 17 the four armies on the frontier were cut off, resulting in the surrender of 400,000 troops five days later. The Italian declaration of war on June 10 was only a footnote.

As the remaining French forces fell back to the LOIRE RIVER and the interior of France, the determination of the French high command to continue the struggle dissolved. Weygand strongly advised French Premier Paul REYNAUD against continuing the war from North Africa, and neither he nor the French Navy made any preparations to that end. Instead, Weygand and Marshal Philippe PÉTAIN, who had been brought into the government because of his immense military prestige, insisted that France request an armistice. Reynaud demurred at first, but as the remaining French military forces began to dissolve and the German advance throughout France continued, he finally resigned on June 16. Pétain took office the same day and immediately asked for terms. A cease-fire was declared on June 20; then came the armistices of June 22 and June 24 (the latter effective June 25), formally ending the struggle. German dead totaled 40,000, to 100,000 for France—nothing like the 3 million on both sides for the same stakes in World War I. At least for France, the war of attrition would not be repeated. But the debacle had stunned the world.

On the German side, great credit was due not only to Manstein, the chief designer of the strategic plan, but to Heinz Guderian, who put his long-held theories about armor into practice in leading the German advance to the sea. In the words of B. H. LIDDELL HART, the British military historian and prophet of armored warfare, "The Battle of France is one of history's most striking examples of the decisive effect of a new idea, carried out by a dynamic executant." **J.C.**

FRANCK, James (1882–1964). A German physicist, corecipient of the Nobel Prize for Physics in 1925. Franck emigrated to the United States in 1935, where he conducted research in photochemistry and atomic physics. He worked on the ATOMIC BOMB project but opposed the dropping of the bomb, favoring instead a demonstration of its power.

FRANCO, Francisco (1892–1975). Leader of the Nationalists during the Spanish Civil War, who defeated the opposing Republican forces and became head of the Spanish state. In spite of the military aid and personnel that Benito MUSSOLINI and Adolf HITLER provided to Franco's forces during the Civil War, Franco refused to enter World War II in alliance with the Axis powers. Hitler was thus unable to establish a fascist bloc in southern Europe and seal off the Mediterranean, and this failure left French North Africa vulnerable to the moves of his enemies.

On October 23, 1940, during the period when Hitler was all-conquering, he found in Franco a worthy and wily dialectical opponent. During a nine-hour meeting at the town of Hendaye, on the Franco-Spanish border, the Spanish Caudillo argued so tiresomely and evaded commitments so deftly that the Führer was later moved to remark to Mussolini: "Rather than go through that again, I would prefer to have three or four teeth pulled out."

FRANÇOIS-PONCET, André (1887–1978). French ambassador to Berlin (1931–38) and to Rome (1938–40) and a member of the Académie Française. During World War II François-Poncet was coordinator of the Paris and VICHY press before going into exile in 1943. He published several volumes about these troubled years in French history, including *Souvenir d'une Ambassade à Berlin* (1946), *De Versailles à Potsdam* (1947) and *Au Palais Farnèse, Souvenirs d'une Ambassade à Rome* (1961).

FRANGIBLE GRENADE. U.S. Army term for a MOLOTOV COCKTAIL. It consisted of a glass bottle filled with thickened gasoline; gasoline and alcohol; hydrocyanic acid; or a smoke-producing compound. The incendiary versions had an igniter taped or clamped to the bottle to set off the contents when the bottle was shattered.

FRANK, Anne (1929–1945). Born in Germany, Anne Frank emigrated to Amsterdam with her parents in 1933. During the German occupation the family, which was Jewish, and four friends hid for two years in rooms behind a warehouse. Dutch friends sustained them until the GESTAPO discovered their refuge in 1944 and sent them to a concentration camp. Anne died in BERGEN-BELSEN; only her father survived. Anne's *Diary of a Young Girl,* composed while in hiding, is a sensitive portrait of adolescence and a poignant testament to human courage.

FRANK, Hans (1900–1946). Born at Karlsruhe in Baden, Frank completed his legal training in 1926 and, after a period of service in the SA (*see* SA), became legal adviser to Adolf HITLER. He was an intelligent man, though of somewhat unstable character, and his background and seeming administrative ability led to his rapid promotion by Hitler, first as head of the party's legal department in 1929, and then as state minister of justice for Bavaria (1933), Reich Commissioner of Justice and Minister without Portfolio, as well as president of the Law Academy, which he founded. In 1939 he was appointed governor general of the central Polish territory not annexed by Germany or Russia, known as the Government General. With headquarters at Wavel Castle, Krakow, his punitive rule aimed at the enslavement of the Poles and the extermination of the Jews. When the Germans were faced with defeat, his morale collapsed. His rule in Poland ended in August 1944, and after the war he faced trial in NUREMBERG as a major war criminal. In emotional terms, he admitted his guilt, and while in captivity he compiled a lengthy autobiographical diary. He was sentenced to death and hanged in October 1946.

FRANK, Karl Hermann (1898–1946). With Konrad HENLEIN, Frank was one of the leaders of the Sudeten German Party. After HITLER's takeover of the whole of CZECHOSLOVAKIA in 1939, he was made secretary of state for the Protectorate of BOHEMIA AND MORAVIA. He was sentenced to death by a postwar Czech court and publicly hanged near Prague on May 22, 1946. *See also* LIDICE.

FRANKLIN, U.S.S. ESSEX-class aircraft carrier. Commissioned in January 1944, *Franklin* began her wartime career by taking part in the capture of the MARIANAS during June–August 1944. Diversionary strikes on the Bonins were followed by support of the capture of PELELIU in September. While supporting the capture of LEYTE in October, she was slightly damaged by a KAMIKAZE plane. Two days later an aerial bomb damaged one of her aircraft elevators, but she continued to send off air strike and support missions through the battle for LEYTE GULF. Off SAMAR on October 30 a kamikaze crashed through her flight deck, killing and wounding nearly 120 men. The carrier underwent repairs in the United States and in March 1945 rejoined the FAST CARRIER TASK FORCE for strikes against Japan in support of the approaching landing on OKINAWA. On the morning of March 19 a single Japanese bomber dove out of overhanging clouds without being detected by radar. It dropped two bombs; one struck near the center of *Franklin*'s flight deck, the other toward the stern. Both tore through the deck and exploded belowdecks; aviation gasoline burst into flames, while ammunition, bombs and torpedo and rocket warheads detonated. Not quite 50 miles from Japan, the carrier went dead in the water as intense fires raged. Through the efforts of her crew, the fires were brought under control and *Franklin* was saved. Power was eventually restored, and the ship steamed to Pearl Harbor and thence to New York for repair.

FRASER, Peter (1884–1950). New Zealand Labour Party leader, a native of England. In World War I he strongly opposed conscription of men without the conscription of wealth, and found himself in jail. When Labour came to power in 1935 he served as Minister of Education and was active in preparing the groundwork for the National Health Service and the Social Security Act of 1938. When war broke out, Prime Minister Michael Savage was a dying man and Fraser was Acting Prime Minister. In April 1940, upon Savage's death, he succeeded to the office. At that point he began to exert an influence far beyond the limits of New Zealand. Flying frequently to London and attending prime ministers' conferences, he built up a reputation for sound judgment and statesmanship. He was an influential participant in the SAN FRANCISCO CONFERENCE of 1945, which founded the UNITED NATIONS.

FRASER OF NORTH CAPE, Bruce Austin, 1st Baron (1888–). British admiral, known during the war as Sir Bruce Fraser, who as commander in chief of the Home Fleet directed the action off NORTH CAPE against the German battle cruiser SCHARNHORST on December 26, 1943, which resulted in the sinking of this menace to the northern convoys. Admiral Fraser had been Third Sea Lord (1939–42) and second-in-command of the Home Fleet (1942) prior to his appointment as commander, a post he held in 1943–44. In the summer of 1943 he declined Prime Minister CHURCHILL's offer of the position of First Sea Lord in succession to Adm. Sir Alfred Dudley POUND; he appears to have shared the general view that the man for the job was Adm. Sir Andrew CUNNINGHAM, who did in fact receive the appointment. In August 1944 Fraser became commander of the Eastern Fleet in the Indian Ocean, and in November he assumed command of the new Pacific Fleet, which joined the U.S. Navy in operations against the Japanese. After the war (1948–51) Fraser served as First Sea Lord and Chief of the Naval Staff.

FREDENDALL, Lloyd R. (1884–). General Fredendall, experienced in army training, was selected by U.S. Chief of Staff Gen. George C. MARSHALL to command the U.S. II Corps and the Center Task Force of Torch, the 1942 NORTHWEST AFRICA operation. After the successful operations at ORAN, II Corps was stationed at the southern end of the Tunisian battle line. There Fredendall kept his headquarters well to the rear, with an emphasis on security that made a poor impression on his chief, Gen. Dwight D. EISENHOWER. Fredendall did not work well with the British or the French, had little patience with the political problems of the war and tended to speak in a casual slang that often was unclear and sometimes gave offense. After the Battle of KASSERINE he was replaced by Gen. George S. PATTON and assigned to training soldiers in the United States, a job well suited to his talents. He rose to the rank of lieutenant general with the Second Army and commanded the Central Defense Command until its consolidation with the Eastern Defense Command in January 1944.

FREE CORPS (Freikorps). Units of German World War I veterans which, with the support of the Army, gave armed aid to various right-wing causes in the years following the war. Freikorps volunteers made up some of the early membership of the Nazi Party. *See also* NATIONAL SOCIALIST GERMAN WORKERS' PARTY.

FREE FRANCE. The French resistance movement organized by Charles DE GAULLE in London in 1940.

Only six weeks after Hitler's armies smashed into France in May 1940, the French Government decided to accept the inevitability of a German victory and signed an armistice (June 22). General de Gaulle had fled to London on June 17. In a dramatic broadcast on June 18 over the BBC, which Prime Minister Winston CHURCHILL had put at his disposal, the general announced that only a battle had been lost, and not the war. At this uncertain moment he expressed confidence in Britain's determination to continue the fight and in the inevitability of America's providing economic assistance to the anti-Axis cause. Boldly he challenged Frenchmen not to despair and urged volunteers to join him in London in a Free France movment that would continue the fight to save France from totalitarianism. "Whatever happens, the flame of French resistance must not and shall not die," he concluded. Thus was initiated the first French resistance movement in World War II.

Few Frenchmen heard de Gaulle's prophetic and revolutionary appeal, and for those who did, his hopes and aspirations appeared at the least premature in 1940. The French Government responded by ordering the general to return to France immediately, and when he refused, a military tribunal sentenced him to death *in absentia.* Now branded a traitor, de Gaulle failed in his efforts to persuade prominent Frenchmen to join and lead Free France, and by the end of July 1940 the number of Free French volunteers totaled only 7,000.

Undaunted by these disappointments, the rebel general persisted in his mission, encouraged on June 28 by Churchill's recognition of him as the leader of Free France. British cooperation was important to the Free France movement in these early months of existence, for it permitted the Free French to recruit troops from the French exiles in England and allowed Free France to continue its patriotic broadcasts over the BBC.

As the only French resistance movement in the early months of the war, Free France was important to Britain, but de Gaulle's ambitious, egotistical and aloof manner rankled the British from the beginning, and the relationship remained a troubled one throughout the war. Indeed, on July 3, 1940, the British dealt Free France a severe setback by attacking MERS-EL-KÉBIR, the French naval base near ORAN, Algeria, sinking and damaging several French ships. This incident hardened anti-British and anti–Free French sentiments in metropolitan France and enhanced Marshal PÉTAIN's position as the French leader most likely to save France from more destruction.

The British attack on Mers-el-Kébir also intensified the loyalty of France's North African territories to the VICHY regime, thus dashing the Free French hope of winning the allegiance of these important colonies—and of moving their headquarters from England to a base on French soil. But territorial aspirations were revived on August 26 when the Governor General of Chad, Félix Éboué, proclaimed Chad's allegiance to Free France. Within three months French Equatorial Africa, the Congo, Oubangui-Chari, the Cameroons and Gabon were consolidated with Chad into a Free French African state.

As Free French attention focused on black Africa as a base of operations against the Axis, de Gaulle proposed to the British the capture of DAKAR, the important French naval base in French West Africa. The resulting operation was a fiasco. In London the Battle of Britain was raging; and the British unilaterally terminated the venture on September 26. Churchill publicly reaffirmed his continued confidence in and support of Free France, but the Anglo-American press made de Gaulle the scapegoat of the Dakar debacle.

After the failure to capture Dakar, de Gaulle made a tour of French Equatorial Africa. He began on October 8 and before his departure on November 17 had established the Defense Council of the Empire to administer Free French territories. By the end of 1940 French possessions in India, New Caledonia and the New Hebrides had joined the African territories in acknowledging the authority of Free France. Also in 1940 the Governor General of Indochina, Georges CATROUX, went to London to join Free France, and Gen. Paul LEGENTILHOMME, the commander in French Somaliland, abandoned his troops, who remained loyal to Vichy, to give his allegiance to de Gaulle.

From the African territories Free France initiated its first military expeditions against the Axis under Jacques de Hautecloque, better known as General LECLERC, one of Free France's most successful commanders. In 1940–41 Free French troops captured Kufra in southern Libya, distinguished themselves in the battle of SIDI BARRANI in Egypt, participated in expeditions in Eritrea and Ethiopia and attempted but failed in a land blockade of Djibouti, French Somaliland.

In June and July 1941, 6,000 Free French soldiers joined a British army in the invasion and defeat of the Vichy forces in SYRIA. When the British, without consulting Free France, offered the defeated Vichy troops repatriation in return for control of the Levant territories, de Gaulle furiously ordered his troops to ignore the proposed settlement. After heated Anglo–Free French discussions, the British conceded to Free France the mandatory rights in Syria and Lebanon, an agreement formalized in November 1942. De Gaulle also won permission to recruit volunteers for Free France from the Vichy army of 25,000 men, but only 127 officers and 6,000 troops chose to join Free France. The aftermath of the Syrian campaign embittered Free French relations with Britain; and though Syria had been freed from Vichy control, the campaign had added little to Free French military prestige.

Although praised for their valiant fight in delaying the advance of Field Marshal ROMMEL's army at BIR HACHEIM in Libya in June 1942, where one-fifth of Gen. Marie Pierre KOENIG's Free French troops were lost in battle, and for their part in the Battle of ALAMEIN, the Free French army remained largely ignored by the Allies. Indeed, after two years of war the military impact of the Free French had been noble but minor and the number of volunteers joining Free France had been disappointing. The Free French army in 1942 numbered no more than 100,000 troops, and these were scattered throughout French territories and were dependent on the Allies for weapons and support. A Free French navy of 50 ships and 3,600 sailors and a merchant fleet of 170 ships and 5,000 sailors had played an important role in the battle for control of the ATLANTIC, during which it lost a quarter of its men, but nevertheless remained an auxiliary force to the British fleet. A small Free French air corps also existed and proudly claimed by 1943 that its pilots had downed 300 enemy aircraft.

Despite its military forces, Free France had developed primarily as a political movement with its headquarters in London at No. 4 Carlton Gardens. Here de Gaulle established a competent personal staff consisting of Hettier de Boislambert, Pierre Tissier, Geoffroy de Courcel, his *chef de cabinet,* and Capt. André de Wavrin, better known by his alias, Passy, who became an important figure in the Free French intelligence operations. Other influential advisers to de Gaulle included Hervé Alphand, René Cassin, Maurice Dejean, Gaston Palewski, René Pleven, Maurice Schumann and Jacques Soustelle. The failure of any prominent French politician to join the movement had made Free France overwhelmingly Gaullist in character by 1942. To strengthen the political image of Free France, de Gaulle established the French National Committee, an administrative cabinet, on September 24, 1941. It took on the appearance of a government-in-exile and was in due course recognized by Britain and the Soviet Union, but not by the United States.

In 1942 a resistance movement developed in metropolitan France, and the French National Committee began to seek its support by sending Free French agents to the mainland. Throughout 1942 Free French prestige increased as Allied military strength mounted, Vichy collaboration with Germany increased and belief in ultimate Axis victory diminished. But intrigues and quarrels continued to plague the movement, and an anti-Gaullist whispering campaign mounted by non–Free French exiles in London persisted. Dissension within the Gaullist ranks was reflected most notably in the case of Admiral MUSELIER, who had accepted de Gaulle's leadership of the Free French although his military rank was higher than that of the general. Friction between the two developed as Muselier disputed de Gaulle's policies. The climax came in the spring of 1942 when, after various disputes, the admiral boldly challenged de Gaulle's leadership of Free France, but his move failed for lack of support.

The German invasion of the Soviet Union in June 1941 was a turning point in the war for the Free French. Now Germany faced a two-front war, but equally significant for the Free French was the opportunity to escape absolute dependence on British support by turning to the Soviet Union. The USSR responded to Free French overtures for an alliance by its recognition of the French National Committee as the official French regime (September 1941). As the Communist role in the French home resistance became significant, maintaining good Soviet–Free French relations increased in importance. De Gaulle threw Free French support behind the Soviet Union's demands for establishing a military second front in France. The USSR reciprocated by encouraging the French Communists to support de Gaulle's leadership of a united FRENCH RESISTANCE.

To broaden the appeal of Free France to other resistance groups, de Gaulle changed the name of the organization to France Combattante (Fighting France) in July 1942. The Soviets acknowledged this change and proclaimed Fighting France the only legitimate authority to organize the French war effort at home and abroad.

This recognition served as a catalyst unifying all resistance movements under the London regime. In early 1942 de Gaulle had sent Jean Moulin as his special emissary to France, and by May 1943 Moulin had organized the Conseil National de la Résistance (CNR). The CNR comprised representatives from all resistance movements, labor unions and antifascist political parties, and its demand for the formation and recognition of a French provisional government under de Gaulle strengthened the general's position in the struggle for power with Gen. Henri GIRAUD in Algiers in 1943, after the Allied occupation of NORTHWEST AFRICA. Giraud had been supported most strongly by the Americans. American–Free French relations, in fact, had been dismal since the fall of France, because the United States had (and usefully for the Allied cause) recognized Vichy as the official French regime. Political and diplomatic considerations aside, de Gaulle's demeanor offended many Americans, including President ROOSEVELT and Secretary of State Cordell HULL, both of whom did little to hide their personal dislike for him.

Although de Gaulle was photographed shaking hands—rather frigidly—with Giraud at the CASABLANCA CONFERENCE, the general's meeting with Giraud, Roosevelt and Churchill was less than cordial and utterly failed in its purpose of reconciling the Gaullists and Giraudists. Indeed de Gaulle adamantly maintained his conviction that Vichy supporters were French traitors and that only Fighting France had the right to continue the struggle against the Axis. The Algerian political situation developed into one of the most complex of the war, and de Gaulle entered the combat with the odds against him. But his strategy worked, thanks to Giraud's political incompetence and the failure of Anglo-American leaders to understand de Gaulle's character and strength. Still hoping for a rapprochement between the Gaullist and Giraudist factions, the Allies persuaded Giraud to invite de Gaulle to Algiers to share the leadership of a common French authority. With the blessing of the Allies, the FRENCH COMMITTEE OF NATIONAL LIBERATION was created on June 3, with de Gaulle and Giraud as co-leaders. De Gaulle quickly asserted his leadership in the committee, which declared itself to be the administrative authority of France and set as its goal the restoration of French freedoms and republican ideals; within two months Giraud was eliminated as a serious rival for the leadership.

In November 1943 the Consultative Assembly was established in Algiers as a legislative arm of the Committee of National Liberation. Acting as a constitutional assembly, the Consultative Assembly, with encouragement from de Gaulle, rejected the restoration of the Third Republic in postwar France, but postponed formulating a new governmental structure until France was liberated. The Anglo-American efforts to counter this action by reestablishing the Third Republic as a provisional government for France misfired, and on July 3, 1944, de Gaulle's Committee of National Liberation formally proclaimed itself the Provisional Government of the French Republic.

As the Axis retreated on all battlefronts, resistance forces at home and in Algiers recognized de Gaulle's leadership of a united French resistance. Fighting France, though not losing its identity, was integrated with the larger resistance movement. Free French forces were united with other resistance units, and in 1944 French resistance armies totaled 400,000 troops, but, as had been the case with Free French soldiers earlier in the war, they remained scattered and poorly equipped, thus limiting their effectiveness. The largest concentration of French troops—230,000 mostly former Vichy soldiers now supporting de Gaulle—was based in Algiers, but half of them were committed to battle in the Italian campaign.

A week after the Normandy INVASION of June 6, 1944, de Gaulle returned to France for the first time since 1940. Arriving near Bayeux, he toured the area briefly and returned to London, but not before appointing a Gaullist governor in liberated Normandy. While the Battle of France continued in Europe, de Gaulle visited Algiers, Italy and the United States and returned to Normandy on August 20. At that time a

French uprising in Paris was quickly brought under control by the German garrison, and the French 2d Armored Division under General Leclerc was ordered there by U.S. Gen. Omar N. BRADLEY to crush resistance. The city became liberated on August 25.

Though shots were still heard in Paris, de Gaulle's triumphal entry on August 26 was the climax of the long and frustrating struggle begun as the lone voice of Free France in London. Beginning with the Free French movement, the French Resistance had restored French pride and the will to fight after the humiliation of defeat in 1940. **R.B.**

FREEMAN, Sir Wilfrid (1888–1953). A Sandhurst-trained officer and a senior member of the Royal Flying Corps in World War I, Freeman joined the Royal Air Force in 1919. In the course of a distinguished peacetime career he was RAF commander in Palestine and Transjordan in 1930 and commandant of the RAF Staff College. As Air Member for Research and Development he was one of the driving forces in the RAF rearmament programs before World War II. In 1938 he became Air Member for Development and Production, and he was attached to the Ministry of Aircraft Production in 1940. That November he became Vice-Chief of the Air Staff; the Chief, Sir Charles PORTAL, was his close friend and confidant. He retired from the RAF as an air chief marshal in 1942 and served for the duration of the war as chief executive to the Ministry of Aircraft Production.

FREETOWN ESCORT FORCE. A British force originally of seven armed merchant cruisers, based on Freetown (Africa), which was employed to provide the ocean escort for SL (Sierra Leone homeward) convoys until they were taken over by WESTERN APPROACHES escorts. In addition to the armed merchant cruisers, a number of small antisubmarine trawlers formed part of the force for local defense duties. Because of the large number of SL convoys, some had to sail unescorted, and the large concentration of undefended merchant traffic caused by this shortage of escort attracted U-boats to the area. At the end of 1940 the first two of six corvettes arrived at Freetown to augment the escort force, the other four following in 1941. Additional reinforcements came from the United States, first after the passage of the LEND-LEASE ACT, when 10 Coast Guard cutters were allocated to the Freetown Escort Force (June 1941), and again when the involvement of the U.S. Navy in Atlantic convoy duties in September 1941 made three Western Approaches escort groups available for redistribution to Gibraltar and Freetown.

FREISLER, Roland (1893–1945). Described by Adolf HITLER as "our Vishinsky," Freisler was a prisoner of war in Russia during the First World War and on his release became a Communist, acting as chairman of the Workers' and Soldiers' Council that took brief control of Kassel in 1918. Joining the Nazi Party in 1925, he became undersecretary in the Prussian Ministry of Justice. He rose to president of the Nazi People's Court in Berlin in 1942. He was a merciless cross-examiner; among his notable targets were the Scholls in 1943 (*see* WHITE ROSE) and the men tried for the attempt on Hitler's life in 1944. Freisler was killed on February 3, 1945, during an air raid that occurred as he was about to hear the case of the prominent resistance conspirator Fabian von SCHLABRENDORFF. *See also* OPPOSITION TO HITLER.

FRENCH AIR FORCE. In May 1940, at the time of the German attack, the French Air Force (l'Armée de l'Air) and Naval Air Force had some 600 to 700 modern fighters but only about 60 medium bombers, plus 90 low-level and dive-bombers, ready for action. A further 400 British aircraft were also in France, of which some 70 were modern fighters. The French forces were divided into two Zones of Air Operations facing Germany, the more important being the Northern Zone, under Gen. François d'ASTIER DE LA VIGERIE, which was to control virtually the whole of French air strength in the vital air space over Belgium and northern France. Above d'Astier a central headquarters under Gen. Marcel TÊTU controlled all French aviation working with the ground forces (with a British staff coordinating British air action in France), while strategic air war remained Gen. Joseph VUILLEMIN's responsibility.

On May 10, 1940, the LUFTWAFFE opened HITLER's invasion of the west by attacking with 3,500 modern aircraft, including 1,050 superior fighters, 1,100 medium bombers and 325 STUKAS. Outnumbered because the British refused to commit the bulk of their air strength (including initially all their SPITFIRES) over the Continent, the French Air Force was unable to stop the Luftwaffe from achieving decisive air superiority over the German breakthrough front. Allied bomber attacks did inflict some delay on the invaders, the tardy Spitfires helped rescue Allied troops from DUNKIRK and French air reserves and burgeoning aircraft production managed to keep pace with the attrition of the battle. Nonetheless, the numerically superior Luftwaffe proved a critical element in the rapid French defeat. By the end of the air war the French had lost 700 aircraft, while claiming 1,000 enemy planes shot down.

Following the defeat a number of French airmen joined Gen. Charles DE GAULLE and the RAF, one group serving (the only Western Allied force to do so) on the Russian front—the famous NORMANDIE SQUADRON.

FRENCH ARMY. In peacetime, the French Army was supervised by the Minister of War, a key cabinet member. Within the War Ministry were the branch and functional directorates, inspectorates and various administrative offices. The Army General Staff operated semi-independently and was charged with the development of doctrine, the formulation of plans, research and development, and supervision of the military school system. France, including Algeria, was divided into 21 mobilization districts which oversaw the training of two-year draftees and prepared detailed mobilization plans in support of the national program. The Army's highest coordinating body was the Army Council (*see* CONSEIL SUPERIEUR DE LA GUERRE), presided over by the War Minister and the Inspector General of the Army. The Inspector General, or "Generalissimo," was designated Commander in Chief in wartime and since 1935 had also been Chief of the General Staff. The Ministry of National Defense had been established in 1938, and although technically superior to the other defense agencies, it had only a small staff and served as a loose coordinating body.

Upon mobilization, the standing army of 900,000 men was slowly augmented by some 5 million reservists. While the regular force guarded the frontiers, these reservists traveled to predesignated mobilization centers to form the bulk of the wartime army. By May 10, 1940, the French Army consisted of about 119 divisions, of which 100 were stationed opposite the northeastern frontier. Of the 75 infantry divisions there, 16 were overseas units, 18 were Series A divisions of younger reservists, and 16 were Series B divisions of older classes. In addition, there were 5 half-mechanized cavalry divisions and the equivalent of 6 armored and 14 fortress divisions. Control of these forces was vested in 3 army group, 8 army and approximately 30 corps headquarters, with the Commander in Chief depending directly on an augmented General Staff for support. Other units garrisoned the Spanish and Italian frontiers, defended the colonies and were engaged in NORWAY.

French military doctrine and strategy rested heavily on the experience of the First World War. Emphasis was placed on total mobilization of the nation's resources and on the need to reduce battlefield casualties. French military leaders were convinced that the war would be long and that economic and social organization together with technological superiority would be the decisive factors. Time would be required to bring all the Allied resources into play, while a blockaded Germany grew weaker. Because of the concentration of French industry in the northeast, any German attack would have to be stopped at the frontier; hence the emphasis on fortifications and defensive tactics. For these same reasons, the Army put a premium on offensive and defensive firepower rather than on maneuver, and stressed the importance of maintaining a "continuous front." French armored units were divided among infantry and cavalry units to help these formations perform their traditional missions. One exception was the late establishment of several small tank brigades composed of heavily armored machines designed to punch through the opposing defenses. Enemy armored attacks would be repelled by obstacles, artillery, special antitank cannon and units of the General Reserve. The FRENCH AIR FORCE was expected to provide reconnaissance and air security for the Army, but there was little thought of direct tactical cooperation between the two services.

Immediately following the 1940 defeat, many military observers blamed the poor French showing on faulty equipment and shortages of matériel. Nothing could be further from the truth. French matériel was generally excellent and, despite some gaps, was available in sufficient quantity. Specific shortages included assault rifles, antiaircraft artillery and antitank mines. However, French antitank, field and heavy artillery was superior. Although, as was the case in most European armies, most French transport was horse-drawn, the quantity of motorized transport was in no way inferior to that of the GERMAN ARMY. French armored vehicles were slower, but more heavily armed and armored, than their German counterparts, and the two armies employed approximately the same number in 1940—about 3,500. However, the bulk of the French machines were not organized into divisions and larger formations. French military technology was used to bolster existing formations rather than serving as the basis for a concentrated striking force similar to the massed German PANZER divisions.

The armistice army imposed by the German victors was officially established on November 25, 1940, and consisted of about 100,000 men in eight small divisions and two corps-like headquarters. With the exception of those units in NORTHWEST AFRICA, little modern equipment—tanks and powerful artillery in particular—was allowed. Although augmented by a number of secret organizations and hidden equipment depots, the new army had little offensive value and could offer only a show of resistance to any challenger. The ground forces of Gen. Charles DE GAULLE's FREE FRANCE were not much better and until 1943 numbered only several battalions of volunteers and colonial troops outfitted by the British. Most notable were Jacques LECLERC's two brigades of about 13,000 men serving in North Africa under British command from 1941 to 1943.

The entry of the United States into the war and the ensuing invasion of North Africa gave the Free French military leaders a chance to rebuild and expand their army. With American matériel, a new force was created consisting of two corps headquarters and eight divisions, including three fully equipped armored divisions, and, during the liberation of France, four more infantry divisions were ultimately raised. Based on this expansion, the French leaders were able to place an expeditionary corps in Italy of four divisions numbering 105,000 men, and in 1944 sent the First Army under Gen. Jean de LATTRE DE TASSIGNY into France with two corps—12 divisions numbering over 200,000 men. The FRENCH RESISTANCE movement in metropolitan France consisted of about 300,000 members, but lacked any central organization. Upon liberation, most of these units were either disbanded on orders from de Gaulle or incorporated into the regular army. **J.C.**

FRENCH COMMITTEE OF NATIONAL LIBERATION. Also called the Algiers Committee, the French Committee of National Liberation met for the first time in Algiers on June 3, 1943. Its purpose was to provide a genuine coalition or nonpartisan trusteeship for France until liberation. Generals Charles DE GAULLE and Henri GIRAUD were co-chairmen, but de Gaulle quickly obtained control. On May 15, 1944, he proclaimed the committee to be the provisional government of France, and on October 23, 1944, it was recognized by the U.S. and British Governments.

FRENCH NAVY. France began the war with a powerful naval force of 7 battleships, 19 cruisers, 71 destroyers, 76 submarines and a host of auxiliaries. Of the battleships, two, the STRASBOURG and the DUNKERQUE, were new, and three of the five older capital ships had been extensively modernized. All of the remaining fleet units had been built during the preceding 13 years. In addition, two new "super battleships," the RICHELIEU and the JEAN BART, were nearing completion. Unlike the French Army, the naval service was composed almost entirely of regular personnel and constituted an extremely close-knit group. Major bases included Brest on the North Atlantic; Toulon, Mers-el-Kébir and Bizerte in the Mediterranean; and Casablanca and Dakar on the west coast of Africa. France's colonial empire also provided many minor stations from the Caribbean to the Far East.

At the top of the naval hierarchy was Admiral of the Fleet François DARLAN. During the interwar period the small National Defense Ministry was too weak to coordinate the activities of the three services and as a result the Navy was virtually independent. The objective of prewar French naval planners had been to maintain a fleet stronger than the combined navies of Germany and Italy. Such a force would make France less dependent on the Royal Navy and give the nation a greater degree of political flexibility. However, the cost of the needed ships was perhaps greater than was warranted by the contribution of the resulting fleet to the security of France.

Specific problems within the Navy included inadequate shipboard antiaircraft defense, the absence of RADAR and the primitive state of French SONAR equipment. Another serious shortcoming was the weakness of French naval aviation. This large fleet had only a single aging aircraft carrier.

Under the terms of the armistice with the Axis powers that went into effect on June 25, 1940, the Navy was required to assemble at designated ports and be disarmed under German or Italian supervision. Only those vessels needed to defend the colonies were to remain operational. In practice, however, the Germans did little to enforce these provisions and were content simply to have the French ships withdraw from the Allied war effort. The British were not so trusting and, fearing that Darlan's ships would fall into Axis hands, took harsh measures to neutralize the French fleet. At MERS-EL-KÉBIR (the naval base at ORAN) a powerful British naval force caught Adm. Marcel GENSOUL's battle fleet at anchor and, upon Gensoul's refusal to sail to a British port, opened fire on the immobilized French, sinking the battleship BRETAGNE and damaging several other units. Other French warships were seized by force in Great Britain, while in Alexandria Vice-Adm. René GODFROY's task force was interned by a "gentlemen's agreement" and without bloodshed. Other major pieces of the fleet gradually collected at Toulon, Casablanca, DAKAR and Fort-de-France (Martinique). Dakar sheltered the *Richelieu* and, bolstered by shore batteries and cruiser reinforcements from Toulon, stood off a joint Free French–Royal Navy assault in September 1940. French naval units were less successful defending Syria in 1941 and Indochina in 1945, but a local encounter with the Thai Navy earlier had been decided decisively in favor of France.

The naval component of Charles DE GAULLE's FREE FRANCE movement began on June 28, 1940, under retired Vice-Adm. Emile MUSELIER. Almost immediately, however, the growing hostility between France and Britain undercut the admiral's efforts. The bulk of French naval personnel interned by the British refused to rally to de Gaulle, and French naval commanders at colonial ports were even less enthusiastic, especially after Mers-el-Kébir. Thus the Free French Navy did not become an important force; it never consisted of more than a few escorts, submarines and auxiliaries. The nomination of Admiral Darlan as Marshal PÉTAIN's Minister of Marine solidified the Navy's loyalty to the VICHY regime and was a major factor in France's active opposition to the Allied invasion of NORTHWEST AFRICA on November 8, 1942.

German troops occupied Vichy France on November 11 but carefully avoided the area around Toulon, hoping the French ships would remain immobilized in the base. Only on November 27 did the Germans finally occupy the port, leading the French commander, Adm. Jean de LABORDE, still under the orders of Pétain, to scuttle more than 70 fleet units, including 3 battleships, 7 cruisers, 32 destroyers, 16 submarines, 18 sloops and 1 seaplane tender.

The new French Navy that emerged from this wreckage was built around 4 battleships, 9 cruisers and 11 destroyers, and reinforced by many smaller units built in American and British yards. U.S. shipyards also modernized several major French units with advanced radar and antiaircraft equipment.

FRENCH RESISTANCE. Opposition to the Germans began in France with the German conquest in June 1940 (much of the story is told in the entry FREE FRANCE). Recruitment of regular officers for Gen. Charles DE GAULLE's Free French forces soon declined, however, as the VICHY regime became established in succession to the Third Republic. But as the German occupation showed itself to be not simply a military occupation but, through the activities of the SS (*see* SS) and the GESTAPO, a means of nazification of the country (and of looting it for the benefit of the Germans), the French Resistance developed, culminating in the rising and liberation of 1944.

The Resistance was made up of persons and groups of all types, with widely disparate political views, united by their opposition to the occupiers. A highly complex organization grew up to direct and coordinate its activities, which involved forces outside France as well. At its head in France was the Conseil National de la Résistance (CNR), headed by Georges BIDAULT, and coordinate with this was the de Gaulle government in Algiers after June 1943—the FRENCH COMMITTEE OF NATIONAL LIBERATION. The CNR had recognized the leadership of de Gaulle in May 1943, so that out of all the Resistance movements a single provisional government was able to emerge in 1944.

The military arm of the Resistance in France was the French Forces of the Interior (FFI), established February 1, 1944. In principle the FFI unified all the various armed Resistance groups—the SECRET ARMY of the Gaullists, the Francs-Tireurs et Partisans Français (FTPF) of the Communists and the Army Resistance Organization (ORA), which looked to Gen. Henri GIRAUD. In fact, however, the Communists kept the FTPF separate. Nevertheless, the French Resistance was a highly organized force by the time of the Allied INVASION in June 1944, and its armed agents played an important part in the operations.

FRÈRE, Aubert (1881–1944). Prior to the Battle of FRANCE, General Frère commanded the French 4th Corps along the MAGINOT LINE, but on May 17, 1940, was ordered to form a new Seventh Army to protect PARIS. Although he was successful in establishing his forces north of the capital along the SOMME RIVER on the southern edge of the German advance, he was unable to take the offensive and assist Gen. Georges

BLANCHARD's trapped Army Group One to the north. In the ensuing battles of June his Seventh Army was repeatedly pushed south and gradually fell apart. Following the armistice Frère served in the Army of VICHY until September 1942, and he later became involved with the FRENCH RESISTANCE. He was arrested in 1943 and died in a German prison camp the following year.

FRETTER-PICO, Maximilian (1892–). German Army officer, a corps commander on the Eastern Front and, from July 1944, commander of the SIXTH ARMY (successor to the Sixth Army lost at STALINGRAD). This force was all but wiped out in Rumania in August; General Fretter-Pico commanded the remnants in subsequent Rumanian and Hungarian operations.

FREYBERG, Bernard (1889–1963). General Freyberg, who led his New Zealand troops through NORTH AFRICA, GREECE, CRETE, SICILY and ITALY, was called by Winston CHURCHILL a "salamander," who throve in the fire and was "literally shot to pieces without being affected physically or in spirit." Twelve times wounded and often facing goals that seemed unattainable, Freyberg retained his own equilibrium plus the respect and affection of his men. He first retired from British service in 1937, after a full and colorful military career that had made him a popular hero. He was famed for feats of valor, and received the first of four DSOs for a one-man diversionary operation at Gallipoli. At 27 he became the youngest brigadier in the British Army, and on December 16, 1917, he was awarded the VICTORIA CROSS.

In 1939 Major General Freyberg, matured and mellowed, still physically powerful, became commander of the New Zealand Division, readying for service in Africa. He had been raised in New Zealand, and his ties with the New Zealanders proved firm and lasting. (After the war, from 1946 to 1952, he served them as Governor General.) The New Zealand Division became one of the elite units of the EIGHTH ARMY, and in 1942 General ROMMEL wrote that he would "have been very much happier if it had been safely tucked away in our prison camps instead of still facing us."

Freyberg and the New Zealanders faced the Axis from 1940 until 1945. In 1941 Freyberg took command of the British resistance on Crete, and the defeat that ensued marked his last independent command. Three years later, at CASSINO, Freyberg came in for unfavorable comment because the destruction of the Monte Cassino abbey by bombing, an action he had strongly advocated, proved of doubtful value. But taken as a whole, his military career was remarkable.

FRICK, Wilhelm (1877–1946). An early Nazi Party member who was arrested with Adolf HITLER after the attempted putsch in Munich in 1923. He was Reich Minister of the Interior from 1933 to 1943 and then (1943–45) Reich Protector of BOHEMIA AND MORAVIA. He was tried at NUREMBERG and hanged on October 16, 1946.

FRIEDEBURG, Hans Georg von (1895–1945). German naval officer who served on U-boats in the First World War and in the Second was commanding admiral of submarines after Adm. Karl DÖNITZ. In May 1945 Friedeburg, who held the rank of Generaladmiral and was the last Commander in Chief of the Navy, was cosigner of the German capitulations at Reims and Berlin. He committed suicide shortly thereafter.

FRIEDMAN, William Frederick (1891–1969). An American cryptologist who headed the Army team that broke the Japanese codes in 1940. Besides inventing various coding devices, Colonel Friedman won prizes for his work showing that Shakespeare was indeed the author of the literature credited to his name. *See also* MAGIC.

FRIENDLY. Allied voice-radio term for an identified friendly aircraft. It was also applied to Allied persons, material and objects generally.

FRIESSNER, Johannes (1892–1971). German Army officer, in 1942 a major general commanding a division on the Eastern Front, in 1943 a lieutenant general commanding the XXIII Corps. In July 1944 Friessner was appointed to the command of Army Group North, in the Baltic area, but was then transferred to command of Army Group South, in the Ukraine, his rank being General der Infanterie. His final rank was Generaloberst.

FRITSCH, Werner, Baron von (1880–1939). German Army officer, Commander in Chief of the Army in 1938, dismissed by Adolf HITLER in bizarre circumstances. Colonel General Baron von Fritsch, no admirer of the Nazis, had incurred the hostility of high-ranking members of the party (notably Heinrich HIMMLER), and Hitler himself was displeased with Fritsch's opposition to his expansionist aims. In the wake of the dismissal in January 1938 of the War Minister, Field Marshal von Blomberg, Himmler charged that Fritsch had engaged in illegal homosexual conduct. In Hitler's presence, Fritsch was confronted with the procurer who claimed to have witnessed the act; Fritsch appears to have been too shocked to make an effective defense. Later investigation by the Army showed that the accuser, one Schmidt, had for years been blackmailing a retired Major *Frisch*. Nevertheless, Fritsch was removed from command, and the Army's attempts to defend him were swallowed up in the preparations for the move into Austria. In September 1939, while serving by his own desire in his old regiment, he was killed in the German attack on Warsaw.

FROMM, Friedrich (1888–1945). Chief of the German Replacement Army, responsible for training military manpower, Colonel General Fromm remained on the fringes of the conspiracy against Hitler. When it was clear that the bomb plot of July 20, 1944, had failed, Fromm sought to exculpate himself by executing the active conspirators in the BENDLERSTRASSE. Despite his efforts to avoid complicity, Fromm was arrested on July 21, 1944, and executed in January 1945. *See also* OPPOSITION TO HITLER.

FRONT. Soviet term equivalent to "army group."

FUBUKI. Class of Japanese destroyers, completed 1928–29. These "Special Type" (*Toku Gata*) ships set the general pattern for future Japanese destroyer construction in World War II. Raised-forecastle ships with three enclosed 5-inch twin gun mounts and nine 24-inch torpedo tubes (3×3), the Fubuki class had a modern twin-stack silhouette and represented a major advance in destroyer design. The 10 ships of this class were followed by 10 more of the similar Ayanami class (completed in 1929–32) and four of the Akatsuki class (completed in 1932–33), the latter having a slightly different silhouette. All three classes were referred to by the Japanese as Special Type destroyers; the Ayanamis and Akatsukis are frequently described as subgroups within the Fubuki class. Many Allied wartime sources also refer to this entire group of ships as the Fubuki class, applying the terms "Shinonome group," "Amagiri group" and "Hibiki group" to the Fubuki, Ayanami and Akatsuki classes, respectively. The three classes, like other Japanese destroyers, were extensively rearmed during the war to provide better antiaircraft and antisubmarine capability. All 10 Fubukis were war losses.

FUCHIDA, Mitsuo (1902–1976). One of Japan's most skilled fliers and a veteran of the war with China, Commander Fuchida was picked to command the air attack against PEARL HARBOR in 1941. Although he created some confusion among his pilots by signaling twice, the attack was a great success. The Japanese lost only 29 planes (out of 363). Fuchida himself was the last to leave the battle area and return to the Japanese carriers. He unsuccessfully tried to persuade Admirals NAGUMO and KUSAKA to launch a second attack against Pearl Harbor. Fuchida also helped to plan the MIDWAY attack. Ill with appendicitis, he climbed to the flight deck of the flagship AKAGI to see the attack get under way. He was injured when *Akagi* was hit. In 1943 and 1944 Fuchida served as one of the senior staff officers of Adm. Mineichi KOGA, commander of the COMBINED FLEET.

After the war Fuchida became a rice farmer in his home district near Osaka. He converted to Christianity and became a nondenominational preacher. During the 1950s he frequently traveled to the United States and Canada to minister to Japanese immigrants in those two countries. In December 1966 he took out papers to become a United States citizen. Both his children are American citizens living in the United States.

FÜHRER (Leader). The title officially assumed by Adolf HITLER immediately after the death of President von Hindenburg on August 2, 1934. Hitler wrote much about the leadership principle (FÜHRERPRINZIP) in MEIN KAMPF, and when he took the title of Führer and Reich Chancellor (Reichskanzler) he was also following the example of MUSSOLINI, who assumed the title Il Duce (leader). At one stroke he combined in himself the offices of President, Chancellor, Commander in Chief of the Armed Forces and head of the ruling Nazi Party. Prior to this, it had been customary to refer to him inside the party as the Chief (Chef). From 1934 the obligatory title of address was "Mein Führer."

FUJITA, Nobuo (1911–). Japanese flying officer, the only Axis pilot to bomb the mainland United States during the war. His two incendiary raids on an Oregon forest took place on September 9 and 29, 1942. The submarine *I-25* served as mother ship for his small seaplane.

FUKUDOME, Shigeru (1891–1971). A graduate of the Naval Academy (1913) and the Naval Staff College (1926), Fukudome served as chief of staff of the Japanese COMBINED FLEET under both Isoroku YAMAMOTO and Mineichi KOGA. Following Koga's death off Mindanao in March 1944, Fukudome, a vice-admiral, became commander in chief of the Sixth Air Base and the Second Air Fleet, based on FORMOSA, and later of the Tenth Air Fleet at Singapore. He was convicted of war crimes by the tribunal in Singapore. Following his release from prison he became a member of the 12-man commission advising the Japanese Government on the reorganization of its defense program.

FUKUOKA. City on Kyushu (Japan) where 24 American B-29 crewmen were victims of a Japanese atrocity (beheading) in the last days of the war, 1945.

FULLER, John Frederick Charles (1878–1966). A British soldier, military critic and historian, Fuller served in the Boer War and World War I. A companionable man with a puckish humor, he was known to his intimates as Boney and rated by his peers the most brilliant military thinker of the 20th century. He first drew attention when as a junior officer he codified the principles of war. His writings on strategy, tactics and leadership are classics. In World War I, as chief of staff of the British Tank Corps, he planned the first successful tank assault, at Cambrai on November 20, 1916. In his Plan 1919 he advocated the employment of armor en masse to end the war, which project was aborted by the 1918 armistice. He gained star rank as the war terminated. In 1923 he became chief instructor at Camberley Staff College, and was subsequently named assistant to the Chief of the Imperial General Staff, where he offended higher authority by his unremitting advocacy of mechanization and motorization. His ultimate break with the Army occurred in 1933, when as a major general he responded to a posting as governor of the Bombay District, India, a move that virtually shelved him, by publishing *Generalship, Its Diseases and Their Cure,* which he intended as an affront to the high command.

As is the common fate of prophets, Fuller was discounted and viewed as an extremist in his own country. He further lost prestige and credit because of his association with the British extreme right wing.

Widely studied abroad and taken with the utmost seriousness, particularly in Germany and Russia, his writings led to the rebuilding of modern armies beginning in the 1920s. In France, Charles DE GAULLE as a military theorist drew heavily from Fuller's ideas. Fuller's most famous work on armored warfare, *Field Service Regulations III,* a compilation of his lectures published in 1933, is the cornerstone of his worldwide reputation as the father of modern war, a title that he never relished.

Fuller's work and influence are sometimes compared with those of his British contemporary B. H. LIDDELL HART. Both were outstanding military theoreticians and historians, but Fuller had also been in his time a preeminent practitioner. The two were close personal friends rather than rivals, and Liddell Hart was ever ready to acknowledge his great debt to Fuller, his preceptor, backer and idol. **S.L.A.M.**

FULMAR. A Fairey Aviation design team headed by Marcelle Lobelle offered the Fulmar in response to a 1937 request by the British Air Ministry for a two-place shipboard fighter that, like the HURRICANE and the SPITFIRE, would mount eight forward-firing guns. The second crewman would be a navigator, who could find the way back to the aircraft carrier after long overwater missions. Lobelle and his colleagues designed a low-wing monoplane that was rugged and maneuverable, but too slow. The improved Fulmar II had a 1,300-horsepower liquid-cooled Merlin that produced a top speed of only 272 miles per hour at 7,250 feet. The plane nevertheless enjoyed success against Italian fighters in the Mediterranean area, and during the winter of 1944–45 some Fulmars helped protect North Atlantic convoys bound for the Soviet Union.

FUNAFUTI. This atoll, located in the Ellice Islands, between the Samoan group and the GILBERTS, was an important outpost in the line of communication between the United States and Australia. It was first occupied on October 5, 1942, by the U.S. Marine 5th Defense Battalion. In April 1943 heavy bombers of the SEVENTH AIR FORCE began operating from a strip on the atoll to hit targets in the Gilberts.

FUNK, Walther (1890–1960). A German journalist, editor during the 1920s of a Berlin financial newspaper (*Die Börsenzeitung*), who joined the Nazi Party in 1931 and became an important link between party leaders and businessmen. In 1933 Funk was appointed chief of the press section in the Ministry of Propaganda, and in February 1938 he succeeded Dr. Hjalmar SCHACHT, who had resigned, as Minister of Economics. In 1939 Funk became president of the Reichsbank as well. For his part in Nazi crimes he was sentenced at NUREMBERG to life imprisonment; he was released in 1958.

FURIOUS, H.M.S. Royal Navy aircraft carrier, 22,450 tons, completed in 1917 by Armstrong as a battle cruiser and converted to an aircraft carrier in a series of reconstructions, with (in 1939) twelve 4-inch guns and smaller weapons, and 33 aircraft. *Furious* served in the Home Fleet until 1944, her service including the August 1942 conveying of SPITFIRES within flying range of MALTA, covering the North African landings and providing the aircraft for the April 1944 attack on the TIRPITZ. At the end of 1944 *Furious* was reduced to reserve, her 1917 hull and exceptionally reliable engines being finally worn out. She was the only Royal Navy 1939 aircraft carrier to remain afloat throughout the entire war.

FURUTAKA. Class of Japanese heavy cruisers, completed in 1926. *Furutaka* and *Kako* were the first modern Japanese heavy cruisers; their design was supervised by Vice-Adm. Yuzuru Hiraga, who had been responsible for YUBARI. As built, they had six 7.9-inch (200-mm.) guns in single mounts, plus 12 fixed 24-inch torpedo tubes, on a loaded displacement of 8,100 tons. During 1937–39 they were modernized, being fitted with six new 8-inch (203-mm.) guns (3×2) and eight 24-inch torpedo tubes in two trainable quadruple mounts. Both ships were active through the early months of the war and were lost in the SOLOMONS area in August (*Kako*) and October (*Furutaka*) 1942.

FUSO. Class of Japanese battleships, of about 34,000 tons, with twelve 14-inch guns. Built during World War I, *Fuso* and YAMASHIRO went through two modernizations between the wars, which gave them elaborate tower foremasts, *Fuso*'s being the most exaggerated. Their relatively low speed kept them out of major action until 1944, when both were lost in the battle for LEYTE GULF.

G

G3M. Mitsubishi Type 96 two-engine, land-based medium bomber (Allied code name, Nell). It was widely used in China in the early years of the Pacific war, though by then considered obsolescent. Nells took part, along with G4M1 torpedo bombers (*see* G4M), in the sinking of PRINCE OF WALES and REPULSE off Malaya in December 1941.

G4M. Mitsubishi Type 1 two-engine, land-based torpedo bomber (Allied code name, Betty), first used in China in 1941. It served through the Pacific war and became one of the best-known Japanese aircraft. Self-sealing fuel tanks were omitted from the design for maximum endurance; this, however, made the G4M1 and the longer-range G4M2 highly vulnerable to enemy gunfire. The G4M3 had self-sealing tanks at some sacrifice in range, but only a small number of these were built. Some G4Ms were later used as transports and cargo planes. In 1945 a number were modified to carry the Model 11 OHKA "human bomb." A small number of escort-fighter versions of the Type 1 design were built by the Navy early in the war under the designation G6M1.

G6M1. Japanese Navy escort fighter version of the G4M (above).

G8N1. Nakajima *Renzan* (Mountain Range) (Allied code name, Rita), a fast, four-engine, land-based bomber designed for the Japanese Navy and flown late in 1944. Four prototypes were built, but it never entered production.

G-50. The Fiat *Freccia* (Arrow) flew for the first time in 1937. Designed by Giuseppe Gabrielli, this single-seat, low-wing monoplane was the first all-metal fighter manufactured in Italy. Only the control surfaces were fabric-covered. It incorporated two characteristic features of Italian fighter design: it was higly maneuverable but lightly armed (two 12.7-mm. machine guns). Although modern in appearance, with enclosed cockpit and retractable landing gear, this clean-looking airplane was relatively slow: the 840-horsepower Fiat radial engine gave it a top speed that did not reach 300 miles per hour. Despite the lack of firepower and speed, the Regia Aeronautica used the Arrow over the British Isles, Greece and North Africa.

G-55. The Fiat *Centauro* (Centaur) evolved from the G-50 Arrow (above) and had both an adequate engine, a 1,475-horsepower, liquid-cooled Fiat, and sufficient firepower, three 20-mm. cannon and two 12.7-mm. machine guns. Capable of 385 miles per hour and boasting a service ceiling in excess of 42,000 feet, this single-seat, low-wing monoplane was intended for service with the Regia Aeronautica but did not appear until after Italy had surrendered. However, the German-sponsored government in the north ordered 1,000 of the G-55s. Difficulties in producing engines limited production to 105 units, and only one operational group, based at Turin, was actually equipped with Centaurs. The improved G-56 was undergoing testing when the war ended and did not go into production.

GABÈS. A city on the Tunisian coast midway between Tunis and Tripoli. Twelve miles inland a chain of lakes and marshes (the Chotts) and a range of ridges made the coastal plain between Gabès and the Wadi Akarit, 15 miles north, a bottleneck capable of strong defense. After the Battle of the MARETH LINE, Field Marshal ROMMEL's panzer army withdrew behind the Wadi Akarit, where the British EIGHTH ARMY dislodged it on April 6, 1943.

GABRESKI, Francis S. (1919–). Although stationed at WHEELER FIELD, Hawaii, when the Japanese attacked in December 1941, Colonel Gabreski scored all his 31 aerial victories against the Germans. He arrived in the United Kingdom in November 1942, served for a time as American liaison officer to the RAF No. 315 Squadron (Polish), then joined the 56th Fighter Group, U.S. Army Air Forces, and became one of the war's deadliest P-47 pilots (*see* P-47). His combat career was cut short in July 1944 when he was shot down over enemy territory. He was a prisoner of war until Germany surrendered in May 1945.

GAEVERNITZ, Gero von Schulze (1901–1970). An American businessman of German parentage (his father was one of the authors of the Weimar constitution) who had important contacts with the German OPPOSITION TO HITLER. He was resident in Switzerland at the beginning of the war and subsequently worked with Allen DULLES and the OFFICE OF STRATEGIC SERVICES in efforts to overthrow Hitler and end the war. *See also* BERN INCIDENT.

GAFFEY, Hugh Jerome (1895–1946). U.S. Army officer, chief of staff of the II Corps in Africa in 1943. He was promoted to major general that year and commanded the 2d Armored Division in Africa and SICILY and the 4th Armored Division in western Europe. He also served for a period as General PATTON's chief of staff when he commanded the THIRD ARMY.

GAFSA. A small oasis on the road between Tébessa and GABÈS (Tunisia), Gafsa was strategic because Allied troops based there could attack to separate Field Marshal ROMMEL's and General von ARNIM's forces, as well as stop an Axis drive toward Tébessa from the south. The nearby Thélepte airfield added to the town's importance. Gafsa was occupied by the U.S. II Corps in January 1943, evacuated February 14–15 during the KASSERINE attack and retaken by the Allies on March

16–17 to draw Axis forces away from the British EIGHTH ARMY at the MARETH LINE.

GALAHAD. Code name given an American LONG-RANGE PENETRATION unit in BURMA. Commanded initially by Brig. Gen. Frank D. MERRILL and also known as MERRILL'S MARAUDERS or the 5307th Composite Unit (Provisional), Galahad saw heavy action in Burma from March to August 1944. Particularly noteworthy were the Marauders' efforts at Walawbum, Inkangahtawng, Nhpum Ga and MYITKYINA, where they materially assisted Lt. Gen. Joseph W. STILWELL in his drive to recapture northern Burma.

GALE, Sir Humfrey Myddelton (1890–1971). British Army officer, a specialist in administration. In July 1941 he became chief administrative officer to Gen. Sir Alan BROOKE, Commander in Chief, Home Forces. In August 1942 he was appointed to the same post at Gen. Dwight EISENHOWER'S Allied Force Headquarters in the Mediterranean, serving there until February 1944, when he came to Eisenhower's new SHAEF headquarters (*see* SUPREME HEADQUARTERS, ALLIED EXPEDITIONARY FORCE) as a deputy chief of staff and chief administrative officer. He held the rank of lieutenant general.

GALEN, Clemens August, Count von (1878–1946). German Roman Catholic clergyman, appointed bishop of Münster in 1933. Throughout the period of the Third Reich he courageously spoke out against Nazi racial theories (particularly anti-Semitism) and against the persecution of the churches, both Catholic and Protestant. Even after the war he continued his protests, objecting to what he considered unjust acts of the occupation authorities.

GALLAND, Adolf (1912–). German fighter pilot and key LUFTWAFFE commander. Galland began his career with gliders in Germany and received pilot's training secretly in Italy in 1933. In 1937 he volunteered for the Condor Legion, a German air unit serving with Nationalist forces in the Spanish Civil War. After his service there, Galland was recalled to serve in Germany as a director of ground support operations.

When the war began, he was serving with a ground support unit. Later he was assigned to a fighter squadron in the west, and after shooting down a number of Allied planes was promoted to wing commander. For a time he was Germany's leading ace. In mid-1941 he was promoted to General of the Fighter Arm, becoming at 29 the youngest general in the German services. Before being grounded, he had downed 103 aircraft.

Galland commanded the German fighter forces in the west until the end of the war and was responsible for many technical innovations in aerial combat. He consistently advocated greater emphasis on the fighter arm, but was just as consistently overruled by Hermann GÖRING, the chief of the Luftwaffe, and by Adolf HITLER, who favored bombers. At the end of the war Galland held the rank of lieutenant general. After the war he served for a number of years as a technical adviser to the Argentine Air Force, and on his return to Germany became a consultant to the German aerospace industry.

GALLERY, Daniel Vincent (1901–1977). U.S. Navy officer who, as commander of the *Guadalcanal* escort carrier group off the Cape Verde Islands in June 1944, assisted in the capture of the German submarine *U-505*, whose code books enabled naval experts to decipher the German naval code. Captain Gallery had the submarine towed to Bermuda, and after the war it became a permanent exhibit of the Museum of Science and Industry in Chicago.

GALVANIC. Code name for the U.S. capture and occupation of and development of bases in the GILBERT ISLANDS and, initially, Nauru. As revised, Galvanic assigned to forces under Adm. Richmond Kelly TURNER and Maj. Gen. Holland M. SMITH the mission of capturing, defending and developing bases at MAKIN, TARAWA and APAMAMA. Successful landings on Tarawa and Makin took place on November, 20, 1943, and on Apamama on the 21st.

GAMELIN, Maurice (1872–1958). Graduating from Saint-Cyr in 1891, the future World War II French Commander in Chief served on the staff of Marshal Joseph Joffre and was credited with having some influence on his chief's successful maneuvers during the Battle of the Marne in 1914. Thereafter Gamelin served in a number of key staff positions and in 1917 became one of the Army's youngest division commanders. In the 1920s the rapidly rising officer headed the French military mission to Brazil and commanded French forces in the Near East, and in 1930 he was named Deputy Chief of the General Staff. Because of his staunch republican reputation, French politicians regarded Gamelin as a counter to his conservative superior, Gen. Maxime WEYGAND, and when the latter became Army chief in 1931 Gamelin succeeded him as Chief of the General Staff. Finally, upon the retirement of Weygand in 1935, Gamelin was chosen over Gen. Alphonse GEORGES to head the Army, a position he held until his dismissal in 1940.

Gamelin has often been characterized as an ivory-tower intellectual whose talents were more cerebral than physical, but who was nevertheless limited by the lessons of World War I. But his cautious strategy and emphasis on the defensive were in tune with France's interwar mood as the country slowly recovered from the deep wounds of World War I. The days of mass offensives by infantry were over, and Gamelin hoped to employ French military technology and organization to avoid the frightful manpower losses of the past. The survival of France depended on extensive planning for a rapid mobilization of partially trained reservists, with little margin for error. To this end, Gamelin relied on centralized planning and the formalization of doctrine, strategy and tactics. Unlike Weygand, Gamelin retained command of the General Staff and commissioned Georges to review and codify all French military doctrine. Gamelin was convinced that machine weapons and new military theories could be satisfactorily reconciled with the lessons of World War I and incorporated into one basic framework. The result was the institution of a rigid tactical doctrine that emphasized firepower and the proper techniques of defensive and offensive combat. To Gamelin, the operation of semi-independent armored formations on some broad battlefield made no sense for France. As a result, those armored formations established in the Army under Gamelin tended to be much smaller and more specialized than their German counterparts.

Gamelin's actions as wartime commander followed in this pattern. He personally supervised all plans and indirectly all operations. In his role of Chief of Staff for National Defense, he also devoted time to coordinating the larger French war effort and, in January 1940, delegated operational responsibility for the Northeast Front (against Germany) to Georges. Gamelin was content to wait behind the MAGINOT LINE while France mobilized her manpower and industrial resources; he did not plan to take the offensive until 1941. If Germany attacked first, Gamelin expected another sweep through the Belgian plains and consequently prepared to move north and meet the Germans head-on with French and British mobile forces. Such a maneuver would enable the Belgian Army to join the Allied forces, preserve the greater part of Belgium from German occupation and keep the battle away from France. Georges was to be merely the executor of his commander's plans.

Gamelin was severely criticized for his conduct during the May 1940 attack. In January he had withdrawn from the Northeast Command Center back to VINCENNES with a portion of the Army's staff not concerned with day-to-day operations. Already past the age of mandatory peacetime retirement, he may well have felt that his replacement was imminent, a feeling that would have been reinforced by the fall of his principal political sponsor, Premier Edouard DALADIER, in March. Criticism was also mounting over the Army's inactivity and Gamelin's failure to assist Poland or push the Norwegian campaign more vigorously. Perhaps because of these reasons, he failed to intervene in the conduct of the May battles, even after it became apparent that Georges had lost control, and his strange attitude of calm detachment remained until his dismissal on May 19.

In September 1940 Gamelin was arrested by the VICHY government and interned, and in 1942 he was put on trial at RIOM for his role in the French defeat. The taciturn general refused to participate or defend himself and was jailed until 1943 and then deported to Germany. A prisoner at Buchenwald and later at Itter, Gamelin was finally freed in May 1945 by advancing American troops.

GANDHI, Mohandas Karamchand (1869–1948). The principal Indian leader of the 20th century, called the Mahatma (great soul). By the time of the outbreak of war in 1939, Gandhi had spent over 20 years working for Indian independence and was the recognized leader of the movement. The Indian Congress Party (Gandhi's) was quick to demand independence from Great Britain as a condition of Indian cooperation, and when they failed to receive satisfaction, the provincial ministries resigned.

In 1941 Gandhi maintained that the Japanese were unlikely to attack a free India, but if they did, he contended, the attack must be met with the kind of civil disobedience that had been used on the British, even though this might result in the loss of a large number of Indian lives. In 1942, after Congress adopted the "Quit India" policy (which essentially meant civil disobedience), Gandhi and other Congress leaders were arrested. For a time he undertook one of his famous prison fasts, and, though the British continued to stand firm against independence, he was released from jail in May 1944 because of his physical frailty.

Continuing to work as he had throughout his career for solution to the Hindu-Moslem disagreements, Gandhi felt he had failed when in 1947 the country was partitioned between the two groups and tragedy resulted. His pleas for cooperation angered the militant Hindus, and one of these assassinated him in Delhi as he was leading people in prayer.

GARBO. Code name for one of the two German agents (the other was BRUTUS) in England upon whom the Germans most relied for intelligence. The British early turned both men; by feeding the agents occasional true information, the British maintained their veracity, thus enabling them to plant false information as desired.

GARDEN. *See* MARKET-GARDEN.

GARRETT 60-mm. SHOULDER MORTAR, MARK 1. Developed by the U.S. Navy and Marines, this was a standard 60-mm. mortar barrel machined down to reduce weight. It was fitted with a butt stock containing a recoil spring, plus a small folding bipod and a sight. Designed to provide accurate short-range, flat-trajectory explosive fire against enemy vehicles and positions, it could be set up and fired in conventional high-trajectory fashion if desired. A small number of these weapons were produced in 1944. Some were sent into the field, but the Garrett mortar never attained wide use.

GATO, U.S.S. Submarine and class; the first of three war-production classes of FLEET-TYPE submarines, 73 Gatos commissioned in 1942–43. Three hundred eleven feet long, with a surfaced displacement of 1,525 tons, the Gato class had a surfaced speed of 20 knots and a typical crew of 85. Six 21-inch torpedo tubes were mounted in the bow, four more in the stern. Gun armaments varied; early Gatos had a single 3-inch gun, later ones were built with a 4-inch. Antiaircraft guns and RADAR were later added; 5-inch guns replaced lighter deck guns in some submarines as the war went on. Nineteen Gatos were war losses; 16 of them earned the PRESIDENTIAL UNIT CITATION or NAVY UNIT COMMENDATION. Early Gatos had a high-sided conning tower; this was soon cut down to present a smaller silhouette and to allow room for antiaircraft guns.

GAVIN, James M. (1907–). As the assistant commander of the U.S. 82D AIRBORNE DIVISION, General Gavin led the unit's parachute invasion in Normandy on D-Day. After August 1944 he was the commanding general of the division and directed its airborne assault at NIJMEGEN and its ground operations in the Battle of the BULGE. He was called Slim Jim.

GAY, Hobart R. (1894–). A U.S. cavalry officer and one of the Army's outstanding athletes, Hap Gay was a close friend of Gen. George S. PATTON, Jr. That friendship ripened on the polo field. In World War II, Gay was first chief of staff of I Armored Corps in North

Africa. In 1943 he was made chief of staff of Patton's SEVENTH ARMY before the invasion of Sicily. In 1944 he became chief of staff of the THIRD ARMY, Patton's new command. Patton once described Gay as "the bravest man I ever knew." Gay's rank on retirement was lieutenant general. His nickname was not a play on his family name but was given him because under stress he wore a nigh perpetual smile.

GAZALA. A pass from the Libyan coastal plain up the escarpment. It was held by the British 50th Division and 1st South African Division as the northernmost point of the GAZALA LINE, and on May 26, 1942, it caught the opening blow of Erwin ROMMEL's summer offensive. The British held Gazala until a breakthrough to the south threatened encirclement on June 13.

GAZALA LINE. A series of fortified positions in CYRENAICA stretching from Gazala, on the coast, 40 miles south to BIR HACHEIM. Built by the British between February and May 1942, it was the first fortified defense line employed in the desert war. Field Marshal ROMMEL described it as having been planned with "great skill" and being a "very tough nut" to crack. Rommel's attack on the Gazala Line opened May 26, and by June 15 Bir Hacheim had fallen and the Germans were advancing toward TOBRUK. *See also* NORTH AFRICA.

GEARING, U.S.S. Destroyer and class, a wartime development of the ALLEN M. SUMNER class. Gearings had 14 feet added amidships to provide additional fuel tankage and to remedy what was considered the inadequate Pacific steaming endurance of the earlier ships. They were otherwise alike in appearance and armament. Some Gearings were converted to RADAR picket ships during 1945 as a result of lessons learned at OKINAWA; a high tripod mast, with a height-finding radar antenna, was added amidships in place of one torpedo tube mount.

GEE. *See* NAVIGATION AIDS.

GEHLEN, Reinhard (1902–). German intelligence officer. From late 1942 until the conclusion of the war, General Gehlen directed Foreign Armies East, the intelligence branch of the OKH that dealt with the Red Army (*see* OKH). Gehlen was an exacting commander, who provided Adolf HITLER with accurate and important information about Soviet formations. Though his analysis was accepted by many staff officers, it was disregarded by Hitler with fatal effects for Germany. After the war (till 1972) Gehlen directed the intelligence service of the German Federal Republic.

GEIGER, Roy Stanley (1885–1947). A native of Florida and a graduate of Stetson University, Geiger enlisted in the U.S. Marine Corps in 1907 and was commissioned in 1909. One of the first fliers in the Marine Corps, he commanded a squadron of the First Marine Aviation Force in France during World War I. During the interwar period he was engaged in the development of close air-support tactics in alliance with ground Marine officers working on the development of amphibious-warfare assault techniques.

By the time the United States entered World War II, Geiger was not only one of the most experienced Marine aviation commanders, he was one of the best educated, having attended most of the high-level U.S. service schools. He was commanding general of the 1st Marine Aircraft Wing on GUADALCANAL from September 3 to November 4, 1942. His command shot down 268 Japanese planes, damaged as many more, and sank a number of ships. For his outstanding demonstration of leadership, Geiger was awarded a gold star in lieu of a second NAVY CROSS. He returned to the United States in May 1943 to become director of Marine Corps aviation, but in November went back to the Pacific to take over command of I Marine Amphibious Corps, relieving Lt. Gen. Alexander A. VANDEGRIFT on the 9th, just eight days after Vandegrift had led the successful landing on BOUGAINVILLE at EMPRESS AUGUSTA BAY.

Following this operation, Geiger returned with his command headquarters (which was redesignated III Amphibious Corps in April 1944) to Guadalcanal, where it began plans for the recapture of GUAM in July 1944 and of PELELIU the following September. In April 1945, Geiger led his corps of two divisions, as part of the TENTH ARMY, in the invasion of OKINAWA. When Lt. Gen. Simon Bolivar BUCKNER, Jr., was killed in June, Geiger, now a lieutenant general, briefly served as commander of the Tenth Army. This was the first time that a Marine Corps general had commanded a unit of this size. He was awarded the DISTINGUISHED SERVICE MEDAL for his conduct of the Bougainville operation and two gold stars in lieu of second and third awards of the same medal for his direction of the Guam and Peleliu operations. In July 1945 he assumed command of FLEET MARINE FORCE, PACIFIC.

GEILENKIRCHEN. German town on the Little Wurm River north of Aachen, on the fringes of the frontier fortifications of the WEST WALL. Advance of the U.S. NINTH ARMY east and northeast of the town in early November 1944 left the Germans in possession of West Wall positions that became known as the Geilenkirchen salient. Troops of the U.S. 84th Division took the town on November 19, and the entire salient was eliminated by the 23d.

GELA. General PATTON's Seventh Army landed in the Gulf of Gela (*see* SICILY) on July 10, 1943, in Operation Husky. For two days the Axis opposition at Gela was intense, at one time threatening the landing beaches.

GENDA, Minoru (1904–). After graduating from the Japanese Naval Academy, Genda joined the Navy's air force, becoming one of Adm. Isoroku YAMAMOTO's most capable and trusted subordinates. As Adm. Chuichi NAGUMO's chief operations officer, Commander Genda played a major part in perfecting the shallow-running-torpedo attack used at PEARL HARBOR. He was also in charge of operations at MIDWAY, where the Japanese Navy suffered a disastrous defeat. After the war Genda joined the Kawaminami Shipbuilding Co. In 1954 he entered the Japanese Air Self-Defense Force, rising to general in 1956 and serving as Commander in Chief in 1959–62.

GENERAL H. H. ARNOLD SPECIAL. During a visit in January 1944 to a Boeing plant at Wichita, Kans.,

Gen. H. H. ARNOLD asked how many B-29s would be completed that month. Upon learning the number, he walked down the production line, selected a skeletal fuselage "just a little beyond that goal" and announced, "This is the plane I want this month." The factory met the challenge, and this bomber, called the *General H. H. Arnold Special,* saw combat in the Pacific. In November 1944, after bombing Omura, Japan, the plane ran low on fuel and headed for Vladivostok, USSR, where it landed safely. The Russians eventually repatriated the crew by way of Iran, but they kept the plane, one of several that landed in the Soviet Union and became prototypes for its postwar bomber fleet.

GENERAL-PURPOSE BOMB. U.S. Army and Navy term for a thin-walled, high-explosive bomb designed for maximum blast effect. GP bombs were used in sizes ranging from 100 to 2,000 pounds.

GENEVA CONVENTION. Actually there were, beginning in 1864, a number of Geneva conventions or treaties attempting to regulate the circumstances under which war was waged and the treatment of participants. Public attention during World War II was particularly directed to the 1929 Convention Relating to the Treatment of Prisoners of War, which called for humane treatment, for making information about prisoners available and for permitting visits to prison camps by representatives of neutral states. These principles were at least formally adhered to in the European war in the west; they did not apply on the Eastern Front or in Asia.

GENOCIDE. Created out of a combination of the Greek *genos* (race or kind) and the Latin *-cide* (killer), "genocide" was coined by the American-Polish jurist Raphael Lemkin in *Axis Rule in Occupied Europe* (1944). But, as Sartre has said, "Genocide is as old as history." In December 1948 the United Nations proclaimed genocide as a new crime to be recognized under international law and called for an international court to deal with instances of it. So far no court of this kind has been set up. The crime of genocide—the mass slaughter of communities on the grounds of race, religion or occupation of land coveted by others—has occurred frequently in history; for example, the massacres by Genghis Khan (much admired by HIMMLER) in the 13th century, Pizarro's extermination of the Incas and the French slaughter of the Huguenots in the 16th century, the European-American slave trade extending from the 16th to the 19th centuries (with aggregate deaths amounting to an estimated 30 million), and finally the systematic Nazi extermination of the Jews, soberly estimated at 5.1 million by Raul Hilberg in *The Destruction of the European Jews* (1961).

GENSOUL, Marcel (1880–1974). A competent if unimaginative officer, Admiral Gensoul commanded the main striking force of the French Navy lying docked at ORAN following the Franco-German armistice. On July 3, 1940, a British fleet attacked, putting most of the French ships out of action, after Gensoul refused a British ultimatum contrary to the terms of the armistice.

GENTILE, Don S. (1920–1951). Despite having some 300 civilian flying hours, Don Gentile was rejected when he sought to enlist in the prewar U.S. Army Air Corps. The Royal Air Force accepted him in 1940, however, and he scored his first two victories while flying a SPITFIRE with the EAGLE SQUADRON. After transferring to the U.S. Army Air Forces, he teamed with John T. GODFREY, flying P-51s (*see* P-51). Gentile received credit for an additional 19.84 aerial victories, mostly against Me 109s and FW 190s, and Godfrey was credited with 16.33. Over half of Gentile's victories came during one month—March 1944. Winston CHURCHILL was reported to have referred to the pair as the Damon and Pythias of the 20th century, and according to legend, Hermann GÖRING offered to sacrifice two squadrons for the capture of "the Italian Gentile and the Englishman Godfrey."

GEORGE II, King of the Hellenes (1890–1947). Succeeding to the Greek throne in 1922, the King was deposed in 1923 after a series of uprisings. He spent 11 years in exile but was recalled by the Greek Assembly in 1935. His popularity grew when the Greek Army pushed the invading Italians back into ALBANIA in October 1940, but he was forced to flee to Crete after the Germans invaded Greece and approached Athens in April 1941. He reached London in September 1941 and formed a government-in-exile. In radio broadcasts he continued to ask Greeks to defend themselves against the Germans and pledged to restore democratic rule after the war. But opposition to the monarchy was growing in Greece, and the King was encouraged not to return until a plebiscite could be held. Factional fighting broke out. In 1944 King George, responding to Winston CHURCHILL's request, appointed a temporary regent and agreed not to return to Greece unless asked to do so by a national plebiscite. In the vote held in 1946, the Greek people voted for the monarchy and King George went home. *See also* BALKANS; GREECE.

GEORGE VI (1895–1952), "of the United Kingdom of Great Britain and Northern Ireland and the British Dominions beyond the seas, King, Defender of the Faith, Emperor of India," in the words of his title. Called to the throne following the abdication of his older brother Edward VIII in 1936, George VI died in 1952 more beloved in Britain than any monarch for 300 years. A shy, diffident man with a strong sense of duty and love of his family, George VI provided the British people with a type of leadership different from that of Churchill but complementary to it. The royal standard flew over Buckingham Palace throughout the air raids in London; ordinary people saw there a head of state sharing their concerns and facing the same dangers with a firm Christian faith. Perhaps his greatest strength was his wife, Queen Elizabeth (referred to after George VI's death as the Queen Mother); the monarchy was a true husband-and-wife partnership.

George VI saw his duties in war much as they were in peace, at the political level: to advise, encourage and warn his ministers and to further national unity; to assist in international negotiations, particularly those with other monarchs or the President of the United States He also sought to lead his people, if not as of old on the battlefield, at least by example in his capital under heavy attack, and by encouragement, tramping over the rubble of bomb-damaged cities and making innumerable visits to military, naval and air force units in Britain. Plans were made for his departure to other areas of Britain or, if necessary, to Canada, and for the evacuation of his daughters, in the event of a German landing. But the King insisted that this was not necessary, even proposing to lead a last sortie himself if a German invasion were proving successful. The King's enormous political importance and the risks involved prevented his making journeys outside Britain until the tide of the war had turned in the Allies' favor. Then in June 1943 he visited British and Commonwealth forces in North Africa and Malta. In June 1944 he visited the Normandy beachhead and in October 1944 the recently liberated Low Countries.

GEORGES, Alphonse (1875–1951). Georges served as Marshal Ferdinand Foch's operations chief in 1918 and as Marshal Philippe PÉTAIN's chief of staff during the Riff wars, and in 1932 was appointed to the CONSEIL SUPÉRIEUR DE LA GUERRE. Two years later he was badly wounded when King Alexander of Yugoslavia was assassinated at Marseilles, and he apparently never completely recovered. In 1935 Georges was a leading candidate to succeed Gen. Maxime WEYGAND as head of the French Army, but Gen. Maurice GAMELIN was chosen for the post, and for the next five years Georges served as Gamelin's deputy. During this period he headed an important Army commission that was charged with reviewing and codifying all tactical doctrine.

Upon the outbreak of World War II, General Georges became deputy commander (under Gamelin) for the Northeast Front (opposite Germany), but had little real power. In the reorganization of the French high command in January 1940, Gamelin gave Georges direct command of the Northeast Front and made him responsible for liaison with all Allied forces there. Georges, however, later complained with some justice that Gamelin had retained control of all planning and had left Georges with only operational responsibilities.

When the German Army attacked on May 10, Georges delegated responsibility for liaison with the British forces to Gen. Gaston BILLOTTE, heading the French Army Group One, while he supervised the integration of the BELGIAN ARMY into his defensive forces. When several days later Georges finally perceived that the main German thrust was being directed through the ARDENNES, he was unable to organize an effective counterattack and instead tried hopelessly to "contain" the armored breakthrough. Psychologically exhausted, he was relieved of operational responsibility on May 19 but continued to assist Gamelin's successor, General Weygand, until the armistice.

Georges played little part in the VICHY regime, and in 1943 he joined General DE GAULLE and General GIRAUD in North Africa as a member of the FRENCH COMMITTEE OF NATIONAL LIBERATION.

GÉRAUD, André. *See* PERTINAX.

GERMAN AIR FORCE. *See* LUFTWAFFE.

GERMAN-AMERICAN BUND. The chief Nazi organ in the United States after 1936 was the Deutschamerikanische Volksbund, or German-American People's League. Led by the German-born Fritz KUHN, the Bund, as it was generally known, spread Nazi propaganda and anti-Semitism. At its peak in 1939, this quasi-military organization had a membership of about 8,300 in more than 80 active cells throughout the country.

GERMAN ARMY. In early December 1940 the Organization Branch of the German Army High Command (*see* OKH) prepared a chart showing the numerical development of the Army. This chart, drawn up at the request of the National Defense Branch of the German Armed Forces High Command (OKW/L), was to be used for planning; it contained the figures for the dates September 1, 1939, May 1, 1940, and December 1, 1940. Similar compilations on a monthly basis were issued during the war at least until January 1, 1945. The major categories covered were the number of higher headquarters—army corps and above—and the number of division-type units. Although most of the categories in the charts (*see* pp. 222–23) are self-explanatory, some will need clarification. Under the listing of Higher Headquarters, the Military Commanders were mostly the occupation headquarters in the western and southern areas. The Commanders of the Army Rear Area were located in the rear area of the army groups operating in Russia. The Commanders in the Security, later Operational, Areas were located as occupation headquarters mostly in Italy and the Balkans. Under the listing of Division-Type Units, the Corps Groups and Division Groups consisted of the remaining elements of divisions annihilated on the Eastern Front which were gathered to be used as the cadres for new divisions organized in Germany.

For its first operation of the war, the invasion of Poland, the German Army had available about 60 divisions, including 6 panzer divisions and 8 mechanized divisions; the number of men involved was 1.25–1.5 million. In May 1940 the Army had mobilized a total of about 5 million men, of whom some 2.5 million were deployed in the west, in about 135 divisions, including 10 armored divisions and motorized or mechanized divisions variously estimated from 6 to 9. The panzer forces included about 2,500 tanks. For the invasion of Russia in 1941 the German Army assembled about 3 million men (including satellite forces numbering about 200,000), organized in approximately 160 divisions, of which 19 were the reorganized (half the original tank strength) panzer divisions and 14 were motorized. Tank strength available was somewhat more than 3,000, perhaps as many as 4,000. To counter the expected Allied invasion, in June 1944, the Germans had deployed 58 divisions in the west, of which 10 were panzer divisions and some 33 were second-line—either coast defense or training.

During the war the Wehrmacht (all arms) mobilized about 12.5 million men; about 3 million (some estimates run as high as 3.5 million) were killed and more than 7 million wounded.

GERMAN ARMY GENERAL STAFF. The origins of the German Army General Staff (Generalstab des

GERMAN HIGHER HEADQUARTERS, GERMAN FIELD ARMY

September 1, 1939–January 1, 1945

	1939 Sep 1	1940 May 1	1941 Jun 1	1942 Jul 1	1943 Jul 1	1944 Jul 1	1945 Jan 1
Army Group HQ	3	4	4	5	7	10	11
Army HQ	8	8	13	19	17	20	21
Military Commanders	—	—	4	5	5	9	4
Panzer Groups	—	—	4	—	—	1	—
Group XXI (Norway)	—	1	—	—	—	—	—
Corps HQ	18	26	31	39	46	49	48
Mountain Corps HQ	1	1	3	4	4	8	8
Panzer Corps HQ (formerly Motorized Corps HQ)	4	7	12	12	13	14	18
Cavalry Corps HQ	—	—	—	—	—	—	1
Corps HQ for Special Employment	—	8	12	3	—	—	—
Commanders of the Army Rear Area	—	—	3	3	5	1	—
Commanders in the Operational Areas (formerly Security Areas)	—	—	3	3	5	4	2
Reserve Corps HQ (from the Replacement Army)	—	—	—	—	5	3	—
SS Headquarters							
SS Corps HQ	—	—	—	—	—	1	4
SS Mountain Corps HQ	—	—	—	—	—	1	2
SS Panzer Corps HQ	—	—	—	—	1	3	4
SS Cavalry Corps HQ	—	—	—	—	—	—	1

Heeres–GenStdH) go back to the early days of Brandenburg-Prussia, when the forerunner of the staff system was created by Frederick William, the Great Elector of Brandenburg (ruled 1640–88). Although the term General Staff was used during that period, it did not refer to a particular group or corps of specially trained staff officers as it did later. There was no permanent field army staff. Such a staff had to be reassembled at each time of war. It consisted of several senior aides to transmit orders; a quartermaster general who was an engineer officer, responsible for selecting campsites, reconnoitering routes of march and constructing field and permanent fortifications; a captain of guides who had to know the terrain and to provide local guides; a wagonmaster general who controlled the army transport; a field chaplain, a surgeon, and an apothecary; a provost marshal-general charged with the observance of discipline and the care of prisoners; and a commissary general responsible for the supply, quartering and financial affairs of the Army.

The structure of the Prussian Army staff remained basically the same until the reforms introduced after the Napoleonic defeats of 1806. These reforms were brought about primarily by Lt. Col. Gerhard von Scharnhorst and his disciples. From a small group of carefully selected officers, trained by Scharnhorst, there developed during and after the wars of liberation against Napoleon a precisely constructed, permanent general staff system and the expert advisers to serve it. The general staff system with a central authority known as the Great General Staff (Grosser Generalstab) exercised its control through the troop general staffs at the corps and division headquarters. The German Army General Staff Corps was developed in the 19th century as a separate branch of the service to provide the expert advisers on planned or actual operations. Down to the division level any staff position whose holder had the responsibility of advising on operations was to be filled by a member of the General Staff Corps.

Both the General Staff and the General Staff Corps were prohibited by the Treaty of Versailles. But both institutions were continued under different designations until 1935, when they resumed their original names. The Chief of the General Staff was also the chief of the General Staff Corps. Personnel matters pertaining to the General Staff Corps were handled separately from those of other officers by the Central Division (Zentral Abteilung) of the General Staff. In addition to the Central Division, the General Staff consisted of five senior officers called Oberquartiermeister who controlled 12 branches. The Oberquartiermeister I had Branch 1 (operations), Branch 6 (rear echelons), Branch 9 (topography) and Branch 10 (maneuvers); Oberquartiermeister II had Branch 4 (field training) and Branch 11 (military schools and officer training); Oberquartiermeister III had Branch 2 (organization) and Branch 8 (technical services); Oberquartiermeister IV had Branch 3 (Foreign Armies East) and Branch 12 (Foreign Armies West); Oberquartiermeister V had Branch 7 (military science) and the historical branch.

GERMAN ARMY GROUPS
I. Poland, 1939

Army Group South (Poland) was organized to control the German armies advancing against western Galicia and Warsaw. Upon completion of the Polish campaign Army Group South (Poland) was redesignated Com-

GERMAN FIELD ARMY, DIVISION-TYPE UNITS

September 1, 1939–January 1, 1945

	1939 Sep 1	1940 May 1	1941 Jun 1	1942 Jul 1	1943 Jul 1	1944 Jul 1	1945 Jan 1
Infantry Divisions	56	137	142	145	145	139	168
Corps Groups	—	—	—	—	—	5	—
Division Groups	—	—	—	—	—	25	—
Air Force Field Divs.	—	—	—	—	—	11	4
Inf. Divs. w/Ger. Cadres	—	—	—	3	4	4	4
Static Inf. Divisions	—	—	—	—	7	29	5
Fortress Div. 133 (Crete)	—	—	—	1	1	1	1
Jäger Divisions	4	—	1	7	10	11	11
Ski-Jäger Divisions	—	—	—	—	—	1	1
Mountain Divisions	3	3	6	7	7	7	8
Panzer Gren. Divisions	4	4	4	11	10	10	10
Panzer Divisions	9	10	16	25	20	24	25
Panzer Div. Norway	—	—	—	—	1	—	—
Artillery Division	—	—	—	—	—	—	—
Cavalry Div. w/ Ger. Cad.	1	1	—	—	—	—	—
Cavalry Brigade	—	—	—	—	—	2	2
Storm Div. Rhodes	—	—	—	—	1	1	—
Brandenburg Division	—	—	—	—	1	1	—
Security Divisions	—	—	9	11	11	12	5
Occupation Divisions	—	—	15	5	14	—	—
Field Training Divisions	—	—	—	—	4	2	4
Div. HQ for Spec. Empl.	—	—	—	7	3	3	12
HQ Fortress Div. 41	—	—	—	—	—	1	—
Waffen SS							
SS Infantry Divs.	—	—	—	—	1	2	5
SS Brig. (horse-drawn)	—	—	—	1	1	—	—
SS Mountain Divisions	—	—	—	—	2	3	3
SS Panzer-Gren. Divs.	1	2	3	3	4	3	5
SS Panzer Divisions	—	—	—	—	—	7	7
SS Brig. (motorized)	—	—	—	—	2	3	1
SS Cavalry Division	—	—	—	1	1	1	3
From Replacement Troops							
Replacement and Res. Divs.	15	26	31	33	50	41	31
Army Troops							
Panzer Gren. Brigs.	—	—	—	—	—	—	1
Panzer Brigs.	—	—	—	—	—	1	3
Führer Gren. Brig.	—	—	—	—	—	—	1
Führer Escort Brig.	—	—	—	—	—	1	1
Misc. Div.-Type Units							
Mountain Div. w/Ger. Cadre	—	—	—	—	—	—	1
SS Mountain Brigade	—	—	—	—	—	—	—
Replacement							
Replacement Brigades	—	—	—	—	—	—	2
Gren. Training Brig.	—	—	—	—	—	1	—
For Inf. Divs. w/ Ger. Cadre	—	—	—	—	—	—	—
Bicycle Jäger Brig.	—	—	—	—	—	—	—

D.F.

COMPARATIVE FIREPOWER OF THE U.S. AND GERMAN 1944-TYPE INFANTRY DIVISIONS

	U.S.	German 1944
Strength (officers and enlisted men)	*14,037*	*12,769*
Rifles; carbines	11,507	9,069
Pistols	1,228	1,981
Submachine guns	295	1,503
Light machine guns and automatic rifles	539	566
Heavy machine guns	90	90
60-mm. mortars	90	—
81-mm mortars	54	48
120-mm. mortars	—	28
Bazookas	558*	108†
Flame throwers	—	20
U.S. .50-caliber machine guns; German 20-mm. antiaircraft guns	237	12
37-mm. antitank guns	13	—
57-mm. antitank guns	57	—
75-mm. antitank guns	—	35
75-mm. infantry howitzers	—	18
105-mm. howitzers	54‡	36
U.S. 155-mm. howitzers; German 150-mm. howitzers	12	18§

*Also had 2,131 rifle grenade launchers.
†Either bazookas or antitank rifles.
‡Eighteen were found in the cannon companies of the infantry regiments.
§Six were infantry howitzers, two in an infantry howitzer company assigned to each infantry regiment. Each howitzer company had, in addition, six 75-mm. howitzers.
SOURCE: U.S. Army Center of Military History.

mander in Chief East (Oberost) and took command of the entire Eastern Front in early October 1939. The need for a third army group headquarters in the planned campaign against France became evident in mid-October. Army Group South (Poland) was named to fill this spot, and the command of the Eastern Front was transferred to Frontier Army Command Center at Lodz. The Army Group South (Poland) headquarters was transferred to the Western Front on October 18, 1939. (*See* Army Group A [France], *below.*)

Army Group North (Poland) was organized to control the German armies breaking through the Polish Corridor to and from East Prussia. Upon completion of the Polish campaign Army Group North (Poland) headquarters was transferred to the Western Front (early October 1939). (*See* Army Group B [France #1], *below.*)

II. Western Front

Army Group C (France) was organized to control the German armies from the North Sea to Lake Constance. Command of the north and central sectors of the Western Front was transferred from Army Group C (France) to Army Group B (France #1) on October 10, 1939. After the French campaign in 1940 Army Group C (France) was relieved of its French occupation sector by Army Group D and transferred to Dresden in October 1940. (*See* Army Group North [Russia #1], *below.*)

Army Group B (France #1) was organized by redesignation of Army Group North (Poland) headquarters in early October 1939. Command of the southern sector of Army Group B (France #1) was transferred to Army Group A (France) in late October 1939. Army Group B (France #1) headquarters was transferred to the Eastern Front in September 1940. (*See* Army Group Center [Russia #1], *below.*)

Army Group A (France) was organized by redesignation of the headquarters Army Group South (Poland) in late October 1939. The commanding general of Army Group A (France) was appointed Commander in Chief West as an additional duty as of October 30, 1940. Army Group A (France) was relieved of its occupation duties by Army Group D and transferred to the east in April 1941. (*See* Army Group South [Russia #1], *below.*)

Army Group D was organized in October 1940 to take command of the Army Group C (France) area. Army Group D also relieved Army Group A (France) of its area command, and of the overall command as Commander in Chief West, on April 14, 1941. This combined army group and theater headquarters continued until the spring of 1944, when elements of Army Group D were used to organize Army Group G headquarters. The Army Group D designation was finally dropped in early November 1944.

Army Group G was organized in April–May 1944 with the Army Group D elements of the OB West headquarters (*see* OB). The mission of Army Group G was to prepare the defense of the French Atlantic coast south of the Loire, of the Franco-Spanish border and of the French Mediterranean coast against a possible Allied invasion. Until September 9, 1944, Army Group G headquarters did not have full army group status, being designated as an Armee-Gruppe, a lower-echelon headquarters. This treatment was attributed to Adolf HITLER's dislike of Gen. Johannes von BLASKOWITZ, the army group commander. In late January 1945 Army Group G took command of the front sector of Army Group Oberrhein. Army Group G surrendered to the Allies on May 6, 1945.

Army Group Oberrhein was organized in late No-

GERMAN CHAIN OF COMMAND IN THE WEST, MAY 1944

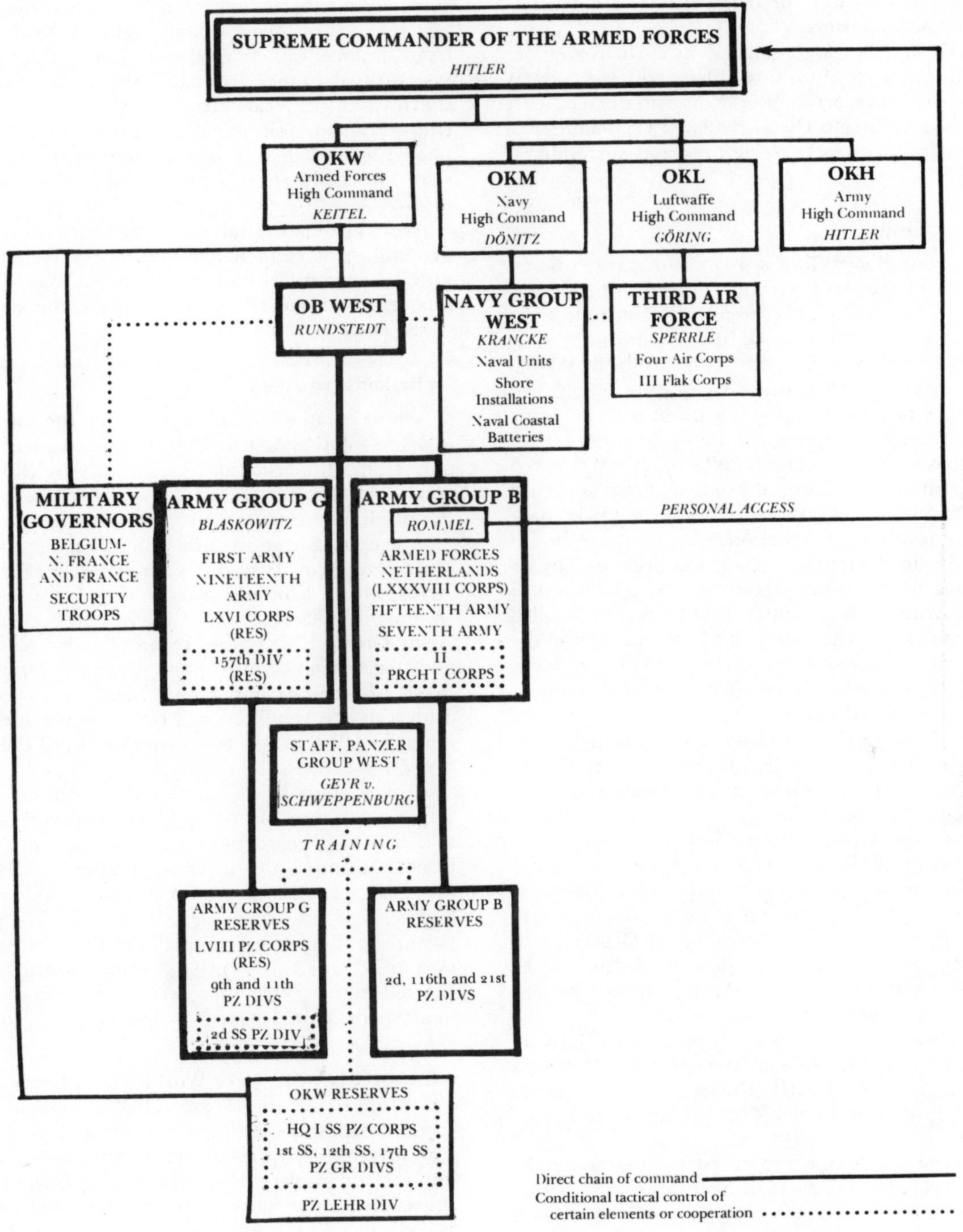

SOURCE: U.S. Army Center of Military History.

vember 1944 under the command of Reichsführer SS Heinrich HIMMLER to secure and defend the line of the upper Rhine River from Binwald to the Swiss border. Army Group G took over the sector of Army Group Oberrhein in late January 1945. Elements of Army Group Oberrhein were sent to Army Group Weichsel, and other elements were used to organize a new Eleventh Army headquarters.

Army Group H was organized in early November 1944 from elements of various disbanded headquarters to defend the Dutch area under command of Gen. Kurt STUDENT. Army Group H was renamed Commander in Chief Northwest in early April 1945 and surrendered on May 4.

III. Eastern Front

Army Group South (Russia #1) was organized by redesignation of the Army Group A (France) headquarters. Army Group South (Russia #1) controlled the German armies advancing toward KIEV and ROSTOV in June 1941. It was redesignated Army Group B (Russia) at the start of the German offensive in June 1942, when the southern part of its sector was taken over by Army Group A (Russia #1), to control the German armies advancing toward KURSK and STALINGRAD. It was relieved of command on the Eastern Front in February 1943 and sent to Vinnitsa at disposal of OKW (*see* OKW). (*See* Army Group B [Italy–France], *below.*)

Army Group Center (Russia #1) was organized by redesignation of the headquarters of Army Group B (France). Army Group Center (Russia #1) controlled the German armies charged with a breakthrough in the direction of SMOLENSK in June 1941. It was redesignated as Army Group North (Russia #2) in January 1945 and deactivated in April 1945.

Army Group North (Russia #1) was organized by redesignation of Army Group C (France). Army Group North (Russia #1) controlled the German armies advancing into the Baltic states in June 1941. It was redesignated Army Group Kurland in January 1945.

Army Group A (Russia #1) was organized to control the German armies advancing into the North Caucasus in June 1942. It was redesignated Army Group South Ukraine in April 1944, and then as Army Group South (Russia #3) in September 1944. Army Group South (Russia #3) was redesignated Army Group Ostmark during the last days of the war.

Army Group Weichsel was organized in January 1945 to close the gap between Army Group A (Russia #2) and Army Group Center (Russia #1) in an effort to keep East Prussia from being cut off from the rest of the Reich.

Army Group Don was organized by upgrading the Eleventh Army headquarters in November 1942. Army Group Don was redesignated as Army Group South (Russia #2) in February 1943, and then as Army Group North Ukraine in April 1944. Army Group North Ukraine was redesignated as Army Group A (Russia #2) in September 1944, and finally as Army Group Center (Russia #2) in January 1945.

IV. Africa–Italy–France

Army Group Africa was organized on February 23, 1942, to control the Fifth Panzer Army and the First Italian Army in Tunisia. Army Group Africa surrendered to the Allies on May 12, 1943.

Army Group B (Italy–France) was organized from elements of former Army Group B (Russia) under command of Field Marshal ROMMEL in early July 1943. Army Group B (Italy–France) controlled all German forces in northern Italy until November 1943, when it was relieved by Army Group C (Italy). Army Group B (Italy–France) was charged with preparations against an INVASION of France from England in late 1943. After the invasion of France by the Allies, Army Group B (Italy–France) took part in the German operations and played a leading role in the ARDENNES counteroffensive. The army group surrendered in the Ruhr Pocket in early April 1945.

Army Group C (Italy) was organized to control the ground force elements under Field Marshal KESSELRING's command in Italy in November 1943. This headquarters and the troops under its command surrendered in early May 1945.

V. Balkans, 1943–45

Army Group E was organized from the former headquarters of the Armed Forces Commander Southeast and from the headquarters of the Twelfth German Army in January 1943. The commander of Army Group E was concurrently the Commander in Chief Southeast (OB Südost) and controlled Serbia, Croatia and Crete. Army Group E was relieved as OB Südost by Army Group F in late August 1943, as well as of the command in Serbia and Croatia. At the same time, Army Group E was made responsible for all of Greece and the Aegean Islands. Army Group G assumed command of Army Group F's area and again became OB Südost in late March 1945. Army Group E was subordinated to OB Südwest from April 22 until the capitulation on May 8, 1945.

Army Group F was organized on August 28, 1943, under the command of Field Marshal von WEICHS to take control of the entire southeastern theater of operations as Commander in Chief Southeast (OB Südost). Hungary was dropped from the command of the OB Südost as of late April 1944. In late March 1945 Army Group F relinquished command as OB Südost to Army Group E. On April 1, 1945, Army Group F was disbanded and its elements were to reinforce the headquarters of Army Group Weichsel. **D.F.**

GERMAN NAVY. After World War I, Germany's navy was reduced by the Treaty of Versailles to six antiquated battleships, six light cruisers and 12 destroyers. The future, too, appeared bleak, since restrictions were imposed on replacement vessels. The first of the new ships, *Emden* (launched January 1925), soon to be followed by *Karlsruhe* and *Köln,* adhered to the guidelines—6,000 tons and 6-inch guns—set down for cruiser replacements, but with *Deutschland* and, later, ADMIRAL SCHEER and ADMIRAL GRAF SPEE, a revolutionary warship was introduced which partially skirted the treaty's limitations—the "pocket battleship," (or PANZERSCHIFF). Designed as long-range raiders, these novel warships combined the size of a heavy cruiser with the firepower of a battleship, thus being virtually invulnerable to all but the most powerful units of enemy fleets and giving Germany a much greater naval capacity than would seem indicated by the terms of Versailles.

With HITLER's denunciation of the treaty in 1935 and the signing of the ANGLO-GERMAN NAVAL TREATY, Germany began to rebuild her navy in earnest and reactivated her U-boat arm. On the premise that war with Britain was inevitable, Grand Admiral Erich RAEDER was assigned the task of making the German Navy competitive with the ROYAL NAVY by 1945, and in 1939 the famous Z-PLAN was proposed. However, Hitler began the war soon afterward, and, as a further disappointment, Raeder found that his own political aloofness had cost the Navy a leading role in Hitler's war plans. Nonetheless, German naval strength at the beginning of World War II was formidable. In addition to units already mentioned, Germany had ready or soon to be completed two battle cruisers, SCHARNHORST and GNEISENAU; two battleships, BISMARCK and TIRPITZ; three heavy cruisers, ADMIRAL HIPPER, BLÜCHER and PRINZ EUGEN; three light cruisers, LEIPZIG, NÜRNBERG and *Königsberg;* and numerous destroyers, torpedo boats and U-boats.

Even before the formal declaration of war, the German surface raiders were at sea, *Graf Spee* patrolling south of the equator, *Deutschland* the North Atlantic. Once hostilities began, the raiders were to attack commerce and, by disguise and rapid movement, confuse the Royal Navy as to their strength and number. The cruise of the *Graf Spee* shaped up to be the most dramatic of the early war at sea. After sinking nine ships in the South Atlantic and Indian Ocean, *Graf Spee* was engaged by the three cruisers of Commo. Henry HARWOOD's South America Division in the Battle of the RIVER PLATE (December 13, 1939). The first serious naval confrontation of the war ended in a resounding victory for the British.

The destruction of *Graf Spee,* and, almost coincidentally, the torpedoing and crippling of *Leipzig* and *Nürnberg* in home waters, provided an inauspicious preface to the fleet's participation in the occupation of NORWAY and Denmark in the spring of 1940. Desiring to establish bases for both surface units and U-boats, especially in Norway, Raeder persistently urged German control over that country's sea lanes, which, among other things, brought precious iron ore to Germany from NARVIK in the north. The boarding of *Altmark, Graf Spee*'s supply ship, by the British in neutral Norwegian waters (*see* ALTMARK INCIDENT), and the obvious fact that the Allies could supply Finland in her pressing war against the Russians only through Narvik, pointed out the necessity of controlling Scandinavia. On April 9, 1940 (by which time Finland had already fallen), Operation WESER EXERCISE (Weserübung) was launched. The conquest of Denmark and Norway was swift. The fleet, however, was badly damaged. Besides 10 destroyers lost at Narvik, peripheral actions resulted in the sinking of *Blücher, Königsberg, Karlsruhe* and four U-boats; and *Scharnhorst, Gneisenau,* LÜTZOW (the renamed *Deutschland*) and *Hipper* were all in need of repairs.

The fall of Norway and the defeat of France in 1940 greatly enhanced the effectiveness of German sea power. Now the Atlantic was much more accessible. Joining the conventional surface raiders, repaired and freed for Atlantic duty after the cancellation of the invasion of Britain, was a fleet of converted merchantmen that packed the firepower of cruisers. Appearing harmless, the disguised hybrids could approach their victims without arousing suspicion. By the time they were discovered, it was usually too late for the victim to escape. Between 1940 and 1942 these ships plied the oceans of the world, racking up staggering amounts of tonnage. Among the most successful were ATLANTIS, PINGUIN, which preyed upon the whaling fleets of the Antarctic, and *Thor.* Their successes were complemented by *Admiral Scheer,* which demonstrated the true capacity of the pocket battleship by completing the most productive sortie ever made by a lone German warship (October 1940–April 1941); *Scharnhorst* and *Gneisenau,* which, before docking at Brest, had had a brilliant cruise (January–March 1941) under Adm. Günther LÜTJENS; and *Hipper,* which, after a slow start, managed to sink seven enemy vessels. In early 1941 the prospects for German sea power had never looked better.

By May 1941 the first of Germany's new battleships, *Bismarck,* was ready for sea. Accompanied by the heavy cruiser *Prinz Eugen,* the *Bismarck* presented the most formidable challenge the Royal Navy had faced thus far in the war. Originally planned as a part of Operation Rhine Exercise (Rheinübung), by which Admiral Raeder hoped to win control of the North Atlantic and, thereby, ensure Hitler's continued interest in the fleet (once the Russian front had opened), *Bismarck*'s first sortie was to be coordinated with *Scharnhorst* and *Gneisenau* at Brest in a double-fisted action against British shipping. But the Brest squadron was not operational by the designated time and Rheinübung began without them, *Bismarck* and *Prinz Eugen* departing for the Atlantic on May 18. The sortie on the 27th ended with the sinking of the *Bismarck.* After its loss the German Navy continued to be plagued with troubles. *Scharnhorst, Gneisenau* and *Prinz Eugen* at Brest had all been incapacitated by the RAF as of July 1941, and any chance of another Rheinübung, this time including *Bismarck*'s newly completed sister, *Tirpitz,* was eliminated. The vulnerability of the ships at Brest, and Hitler's conviction of the necessity of protecting Norway, led to one of the most daring operations of the German Navy in World War II—the "Channel Dash." Accompanied by LUFTWAFFE and destroyer escort (one of the few German combined air–sea operations of the war), the Brest squadron, seaworthy again, steamed toward home on the night of February 11, 1942. The Channel Dash was a complete triumph for the Germans, who, sailing under the very noses of the British, demonstrated that they could still strike wherever and whenever they pleased. For the *Gneisenau,* however, the voyage was to be her last. She was hit by bombs at Kiel, her repairs were never completed and eventually she was decommissioned, her guns removed to be used as coastal emplacements—a humiliating end for the once proud warship. Concentrated in the north, the German Navy would now begin to raid the Arctic sea lanes serving Russia.

The German fleet, though impressive, proved relatively ineffective in its raiding of the Russian convoys, while dangerously exposing itself to destruction by heavy Allied escort vessels: the *Tirpitz,* on her very first sortie, almost suffered the same fate as her sister *Bismarck.* Even Raeder's ambitious Operation Rösselsprung, which included *Tirpitz, Scheer, Hipper* and their destroyers (*Lützow* had temporarily run aground)—one of the most powerful battle fleets ever assembled by the Germans—came to naught. Before the ships could even get close to their target—the ill-fated Convoy PQ-17—it had been destroyed by the Luftwaffe and U-boats (*see* PQ-17), which exhibited far greater efficiency in dealing with the northern convoys. Nonetheless, the mere presence of the fleet was a powerful deterrent, and the Allies always had to consider it in their convoy planning. Allied pressure in the Mediterranean, however, soon caused the Luftwaffe to move southward, and better defense against U-boats began to limit their capabilities. The charge of interdicting the northern convoy routes now fell mainly upon the fleet, which, late in 1942, had been restricted in its activities by a cautious Hitler and was running low on fuel. The Battle of North Cape (Barents Sea) demonstrated just how ineffective the fleet had become when, on December 31, 1942, two British cruisers and five destroyers beat off an attack by *Lützow, Hipper* and their destroyers. Hitler, convinced of the fleet's uselessness, ordered it scrapped, prompting the resignation of Raeder on January 30, 1943. He was replaced by Adm. Karl DÖNITZ, head of the U-boat arm. Dönitz, a better politician than Raeder and the man who would eventually head Germany for a brief period after Hitler's death, won a reprieve for the fleet, convincing Hitler that without it the Allies could concentrate everything they had on the U-boats, the most successful branch of the German Navy.

Beginning with the unauthorized sinking of the liner ATHENIA on September 3, 1939, the U-boats proceeded to pile up incredible records in the early years of the war. In the first four months, they sank more than 100 ships, including the aircraft carrier COURAGEOUS, and Günther PRIEN accomplished what seemed an impossible task by torpedoing and sinking the battleship ROYAL OAK in SCAPA FLOW, anchorage of the British Home Fleet. The fall of Norway and France in 1940 provided U-boats, as well as the surface raiders, with easy access to the Atlantic, and they increased their monthly tonnage totals significantly. The top U-boat ace of the war, Otto KRETSCHMER, had already accounted for about 350,000 tons before his capture by British destroyers in March 1941. With the advent of the "WOLFPACKS"—U-boats attacking in groups—the tonnage continued to mount; 1942 was the greatest year for U-boats, which sank 1,160 ships totaling 6,266,215 tons. The most impressive single action of the war came in mid-March 1943, when U-boats sank over 20 ships of combined Allied convoys SC-122 and HX-229, losing only one of their own. However, improved Allied tactics, utilizing long-range aircraft, aircraft carriers and escorts with RADAR, soon began to pay off in the Battle of the ATLANTIC and also in the Mediterranean. Tonnage sunk by U-boats steadily declined as their losses rose dramatically. Over 50 were destroyed in April–May 1943, and heavy casualties continued into 1944. German attempts to remedy the situation by equipping U-boats with SNORKELS, so that they could evade detection by not having to surface, and by designing new models with greater speed and performance came too late to challenge Allied control of the sea lanes. The war they were fighting was eventually lost, but not before they had sunk more than 14 million tons of Allied shipping. Of the 1,162 U-boats built during the war, 785 were destroyed, 156 surrendered and the rest were scuttled.

With increasing Allied dominance over air and sea, the remainder of the German surface fleet, like the U-boats, was doomed. The loss of *Scharnhorst* off the North Cape on December 26, 1943, signaled the beginning of the end. *Scharnhorst* had always been the mainstay of the fleet, having been involved in one way or another in practically all important German naval actions, and, with *Gneisenau,* had chalked up one of the more impressive kills of the war, the British aircraft carrier GLORIOUS, during the Norway campaign of 1940. While attacking an Allied convoy to Russia, *Scharnhorst* was challenged by the battleship DUKE OF YORK and her cruisers and was sunk. Of the heavy units of the German fleet still functional, only *Tirpitz, Lützow, Scheer* and *Prinz Eugen* remained, and *Tirpitz*'s luck would soon run out. The career of *Tirpitz* could hardly be called an eventful one. The only time her guns were fired in combat was to neutralize gun emplacements at Spitsbergen. But the threat she posed made her a primary target for the British. During her short existence *Tirpitz* never wandered far from Norwegian waters, and it is appropriate that there would be her grave (November 12, 1944).

With the end of *Tirpitz,* German naval strength was limited to the Baltic, where fuel shortages hampered the fleet's already declining activities. Troubles were compounded when *Prinz Eugen* accidentally rammed *Leipzig,* taking her out of the war. The last service the fleet provided was the evacuation of troops and refugees from the east in face of the advancing Red Army. These operations, which took place between January and May 1945, were directed by Dönitz and proved remarkably successful. The final days of the war were disastrous for the fleet. *Scheer,* already inactive, was bombed at KIEL on April 9, and *Lützow, Köln* and *Emden* suffered similar fates. *Hipper* and the unfinished heavy cruiser *Seydlitz* were scuttled, while the never completed aircraft carrier *Graf Zeppelin* (which Raeder had wanted badly in the early stages of the war) was wrecked. The only significant units of the German Navy still afloat were *Prinz Eugen, Nürnberg* and the crippled *Leipzig.* They were turned over to the Allies. **R.K.**

GERMAN-POLISH OPERATIONS—1939. On August 25, 1939, Great Britain proclaimed a formal alliance with Poland, confirming the earlier guarantee given by the British Government. On the same day Adolf HITLER's Fascist ally, Benito MUSSOLINI, indicated that Italy was not ready to participate in a war. Although these were both significant setbacks for Hitler, they did not deflect him from his aim of attacking Poland, He did, however, postpone the assault, which was scheduled for the morning of August 26.

On August 31, after several days of diplomatic efforts to isolate Poland, the Führer signed his "Directive No. 1 for the Conduct of the War." During the night SS units (*see* SS) staged "incidents" along the Polish-German border and conducted a faked "Polish" raid on a German radio station at Gleiwitz, in Silesia; these maneuvers were intended to make the Poles appear to be the aggressors and seem to have had some temporary success. At 4:17 on the morning of September 1 the war began as the Germans began firing on Polish posts in DANZIG, and at 4:45 German armies crossed the frontier. The ensuing campaign has been described by the British military critic B. H. Liddell Hart as "the first demonstration, and proof, in war of the theory of mobile warfare by armoured and air forces in combination."

The German plan called for a short war. The Poles were to be knocked out before the British and French could give them any effective aid, and there was the further thought that a quick defeat of Poland might convince the Western Allies that there was no reason to continue the war. Two groups of armies were to invade Poland: Army Group North, commanded by Col. Gen. Fedor von Bock, was to attack eastward into the Polish Corridor and southward from East Prussia. Army Group South, under Col. Gen. Gerd von Rundstedt, was to strike northeast from Silesia and Slovakia. The strength of these army groups, as given by the Chief of the German Army General Staff, Col. Gen. Franz Halder, was 630,000 and 886,000 troops, respectively. Of the approximately 60 divisions involved, six were armored—a small component, but the vital one. The northern armies were supported by 500 bombers, 180 dive-bombers and 120 fighters. The southern group had comparable air support.

The Poles deployed their seven armies and some smaller groupings (about 1 million men) along all the country's frontiers, rather than falling back to the river lines (Narew-Vistula-San) and awaiting French and British support; to do the latter would have meant sacrificing the country's industrial base. Actually, neither alternative offered much prospect of success, although some of the Polish leaders expected Allied attacks in the west to draw off some German strength.

In the first days of the war the Luftwaffe attacked the Polish airfields, destroying runways, hangars and fuel stores, though not, as is often said, annihilating the Air Force itself. The German fliers then systematically disrupted railroads and communication lines. Even by the end of the first day, Polish troop movements had been thrown into chaos. The initial phase of the campaign, the breakthrough on the German-Polish borders, ended before the week was over. By September 5 the two armies of Bock's Army Group North had cut across the Polish Corridor and commenced moving to the southeast. By September 7 the Tenth Army had advanced northeastward to within 36 miles of Warsaw; the Polish Government had fled the capital on the 6th.

In the second phase of the campaign, the Germans completely destroyed the Polish armed forces. The German plan called for a double double envelopment, the first part being a giant encirclement of Polish forces west of the Vistula River. When intelligence reports revealed that large numbers of Polish troops had fled across the Vistula, the high command ordered the second encirclement, penetrating deeper and reaching eastward to the Bug River. The Germans might have progressed even faster than they did had they themselves not entertained some doubts about the ability of mobile forces to take care of themselves when far ahead of the infantry.

The only major crisis the Germans faced during the campaign developed when the Polish forces around Kutno, bypassed during the first week of fighting, counterattacked toward Warsaw. The German Eighth and Tenth Armies deployed some of their divisions to meet the attack, and by September 19 this German pincers movement had overwhelmed the Kutno force, which surrendered with 100,000 men. This engagement, called the Battle on the Bzura River, was the largest of the campaign, and it was the last major Polish act of resistance.

A spectacular aspect of the war was the advance of General der Panzertruppen Heinz Guderian's XIX Panzer Corps, which swept southward from East Prussia past Brest-Litovsk and made contact with the spearhead of the Tenth Army at Wlodawa, 30 miles south of Brest-Litovsk, during the third week of September.

By September 19 the war had unofficially ended, although Warsaw held out until September 27. The last organized resistance ended on October 5, when 17,000 Polish troops surrendered at Kock, southeast of Warsaw. During the entire campaign the Germans took some 694,000 Polish prisoners; the Poles also lost about 66,000 killed and 200,000 wounded. German losses were estimated at 14,000 killed and missing and 30,000 wounded.

On September 17, in conformity with the Soviet-German Nonaggression Pact, two Soviet army groups marched into Poland. There was little the Poles could do to resist. A secret protocol to the pact delineated the German and Russian spheres in eastern Europe. But on September 29 a new agreement (the Soviet-German Boundary and Friendship Treaty) was signed, altering the terms of the original treaty. Germany received the provinces of Lublin and Warsaw eastward to the Bug, while the Soviet Union in exchange was allowed to incorporate Lithuania into its sphere. This Ribbentrop-Molotov revision placed much of the Soviet border on the Curzon Line, drawn by the Western Allies after World War I (and never accepted by Poland), and that is essentially where it has remained.

GEROW, Leonard Townsend (1888–1972). A U.S. Army officer, Gerow moved from his post as chief of the War Plans Division to command of the 29th Division in 1942. The next year he became commander of U.S. field forces in Europe. He was the commanding general of the V Corps at Omaha Beach during the D-Day invasion and in 1945 was given command of the Fifteenth Army and promoted to lieutenant general. Known by the nickname "Gee," he was universally respected for an unfaltering integrity.

GERSTENBERG, Alfred (1893–1959). Luftwaffe officer (lieutenant general), air attaché in Bucharest and in 1944 commander of all Luftwaffe forces (air and ground) in Rumania. He was taken by surprise by Rumania's change of sides in August and was subsequently imprisoned by the Soviets.

GESTAPO (*Ge*heime *Sta*ats*po*lizei—Secret State Police). The Nazi-instituted German secret police organization, which, together with the SA and the SS (*see* SA; SS), formed the basic apparatus of repression in the Third Reich. Unlike the SA and the SS, the Gestapo was not created until the Nazis had come to power. Originally operating in the state of Prussia, it received its name in April 1933, after Hermann Göring (as minister of the interior of Prussia) had purged the state police, putting Nazi supporters in all key posts, and had also taken over the Berlin Police Bureau 1A (the already existing state political police).

On April 26, 1933, Gestapo headquarters was established at 8 Prinz-Albrechtstrasse in Berlin, a building that soon became notorious as the Gestapo's chief interrogation center and prison. Similar political police forces were set up in other German states by Heinrich HIMMLER during the period from April 1933 to April 1934, first of all in Bavaria, where Himmler had been appointed president of police, and later in Hamburg, Mecklenburg, Lübeck, Württemberg, Baden, Hesse, Thuringia and Anhalt. This extension of Himmler's powers was in response to HITLER's demand for centralization of functions in place of the old state autonomy. In 1934 Göring's ambitions extended into wider (and more popular) fields, and he ceded his Prussian Gestapo to Himmler on April 20, along with the state CONCENTRATION CAMPS he had established. The camps were placed in the hands of the SS, which Himmler also controlled. Himmler moved his headquarters from Munich to Berlin, taking full control of the uniformed national SS movement and the national Gestapo forces.

From now on the SS, the SD (Sicherheitsdienst, the SS intelligence service) and the Gestapo were to march in close step together, and were often indistinguishable except from the inside, where differentiation was jealously maintained. Together they made up the police state. After the RÖHM purge of June 30, 1934 (*see* NIGHT OF THE LONG KNIVES), the power of the SA diminished sharply, and the SS took precedence as the national force sustaining the Nazi regime. The Gestapo received official recognition as an independent national police force in February 1936, when it was placed in the charge of Heinrich MÜLLER, a career police officer, an efficient and rather mild-mannered man who disappeared completely after the war.

In 1939 the Gestapo became a division of the Reichssicherheitshauptamt (RSHA, the Reich Main Security Office), under Himmler's subordinate, Reinhard HEYDRICH. Thus, in effect, it became merged with the SS, while nevertheless retaining its individual identity.

The Gestapo extended its control to the occupied countries. Its agents frequently operated in plain clothes, arresting men and women without warning or spying on their movements until they judged the moment right to seize them. The notorious Nacht und Nebel Erlass (*see* NIGHT AND FOG DECREE) of December 1941—directed primarily against occupied countries in the west—enabled the Gestapo to arrest individuals and make them "disappear," wiping out all record of them so that relatives who sought to know their fate would be told there was no record of their existence, inside or outside Germany.

Confinement of persons without trial in prison or concentration camp, which had become normal practice, was greatly intensified in war conditions. Interrogation under torture was also normal practice; prisoners were stripped, humiliated and subjected to the cruelest forms of torture, some of medieval origin (thumbscrew and rack), some more modern (electric shocks applied to the most sensitive parts of the body). A prominent member of the German Resistance, Dr. Fabian von SCHLABRENDORFF, who survived the regime, has described in his book *The Secret War Against Hitler* how he was tortured in order to induce him to reveal the names of his fellow conspirators, and how the torture stopped immediately when he broke his silence and gave information (which was in effect quite harmless to anyone still alive). Jacques Delarue in his book *Gestapo* describes the operation of the secret political police in France. With headquarters in Paris, there were Gestapo branches in 17 regional centers, including Bordeaux, Nancy, Rouen, Lyons, Marseilles, Montpellier and Vichy. The Gestapo used agents and collaborators to spy and gather information, especially against resistance workers.

In the NUREMBERG TRIALS the Gestapo was indicted as a criminal organization, and its close interrelations with the SD and the Criminal Police (Kripo) revealed. The Gestapo was shown to have been involved in every aspect of terrorization practiced by the Nazis—the persecution and extermination of the Jews, brutalities and murder in the concentration camps, excesses in the administration of occupied territories, the operation of the slave labor programs and the maltreatment of prisoners of war—and its agents were thus collectively condemned as war criminals.

GEYR VON SCHWEPPENBURG, Leo, Baron (1886–1974). German Army officer (General der Panzertruppen), a tank expert who in 1944 was the commander of Panzer Group West, the staff set up to take charge of armored forces in the counterattack against the expected Allied INVASION. Unlike Field Marshal ROMMEL, he favored a mobile counterattacking force rather than a defense based on defeating the invasion on the beaches.

GHORMLEY, Robert Lee (1883–1958). A 1906 graduate of the U.S. Naval Academy, Ghormley became known as a planner. In 1940 he was an observer in London; described as a "mystery man" by the newspapers, Ghormley kept his "eyes open and mouth shut." His mission was unprecedented, since the U.S. Navy had never employed such a high-ranking observer while still at peace. In March 1942 Ghormley left his diplomatic post for a more active one in the South Pacific, his duty being to organize the U.S. Navy there. A vice-admiral, Ghormley kept a low profile as he organized the assault on the SOLOMON ISLANDS to save communications with Australia and New Zealand. The task was difficult, involving a landing on hostile shores in dangerous waters, against an enemy with land-based aircraft. Ghormley's planning, and the results it led to, not only preserved communications with Australia and New Zealand but provided bases in the Solomons for further attacks in the Southwest Pacific. In October 1942, however, Adm. William F. HALSEY replaced him; Ghormley had been deemed insufficiently aggressive during the desperate fighting at GUADALCANAL. He returned to Washington to work with the headquarters of Adm. Ernest J. KING, Commander in Chief of the U.S. Fleet. Later in the war he commanded the HAWAIIAN SEA FRONTIER, and after V-E Day he directed the disarmament and demobilization of the German Navy.

GI. This famous term became an all-purpose noun, adjective, verb and adverb during the war, and has remained so. As a noun, it referred to the individual American soldier. As an adjective, it was used to describe something that was issued by the Army or that conformed to Army regulations (as a GI haircut); a person who was a stickler for Army usage was said to be "strictly GI." The verb GI was used for cleaning and scrubbing, as of a barracks floor. The adverb described behavior and actions that were in accord with military rules.

The letters GI are widely taken to be an abbreviation for "government issue" or "general issue," but in fact were originally used as an abbreviation for "galvanized iron" (as for garbage cans) by supply clerks.

GI BILL OF RIGHTS. Perhaps one of the most significant pieces of American wartime legislation, although its effects were largely socioeconomic and occurred in the postwar era, the GI Bill, or Servicemen's Readjustment Act of 1944 (Public Law 346, 78th Congress), was signed into law by President ROOSEVELT on June 22, 1944.

On October 27, 1943, the President had presented to Congress an outline of proposed veterans' educational benefits. Within a month, on November 23, this message was followed by a second, which detailed the remainder of his legislative package. Basically, he requested at least one calendar year of supported education (and a selective allocation of up to three additional years) for all veterans honorably discharged with six or more months of service after September 16, 1940 (the date of the Selective Service and Training Act). Beyond this there was a reaffirmation of existing benefits in terms of government life insurance, government guarantees on commercial life insurance premiums, hospitalization and medical care, rehabilitation benefits for the disabled, pension rights, suspension of some civilian-incurred obligations (Soldiers' and Sailors' Civil Relief Act of 1940) and reemployment rights. To these were added mustering-out pay, provision of uniform federal unemployment benefits and Social Security credit for time spent in the service.

Roosevelt's basic rationale, apart from a feeling of obligation to aid returning veterans, was that this further education would benefit both them and the nation as a whole and would also serve as a cushion against unemployment. Early reaction to the program was basically favorable, with disagreement involving such matters as whether there should be any restrictions on educational benefits beyond the first year and whether the U.S. Office of Education or the Veterans Administration

GIs in Normandy grab some sleep in their foxhole

should control the program. But on January 10, 1944, the American Legion presented to Congress its plan, publicized two days earlier as "a bill of rights for G.I. Joe and G.I. Jane"—the so-called omnibus bill, soon named the GI Bill of Rights. This unified all proposed benefits in one legislative package. The basic philosophy of the proposal was that World War II veterans should secure benefits at least equal to those provided World War I returnees. Furthermore, such benefits should be centralized in one administrative unit—the Veterans Administration. The result should be that veterans could resume civilian life at the point where they had left it to enter the service.

Basically the Legion measure merely repeated FDR's program with two differing features: the provision of a centralized administration and the plan to provide federally guaranteed loans for homes and farms. Philosophically, the bills differed in that Roosevelt had tied veterans' benefits to overall domestic reconversion plans, whereas the Legion was interested only in programs specifically for veterans. This latter stance was undoubtedly a combined product of the Legion's genuine concern for returning service personnel and a desire to appeal to a large number of potential new members.

Once the omnibus bill was introduced, Roosevelt allowed the Legion to carry the battle, and their bill, in revised form, passed the Senate unanimously in March 1944. The House required more debate, but a substitute measure, largely the work of Congressman John Rankin, a Mississippi Democrat, passed that chamber in May. A final measure, after going through conference committee, secured joint passage and presidential signature in June 1944. This measure provided loans for homes and businesses up to a maximum of $2,000 at 4 percent interest, subsistence and tuition for higher education or other approved training for a period equal to the time spent in service plus 12 months and unemployment benefits up to $20 a week for a maximum of 52 weeks (the so-called 52–20 Club).

Changes were subsequently made in the act, but by 1955 4.3 million home loans, worth about $33 billion, had been granted, accounting for 20 percent of all new homes built in the first postwar decade. By that time 3,782,000 people had used the home-loan-guarantee benefits and 5,322,000 had used the readjustment allowance. About 7 million veterans, approximately 50.5 percent of all World War II veterans in civilian life, had taken education or training, representing a federal investment of $14.5 billion. Included in this group were 250,000 blacks who took advantage of the opportunity to go to college.

Socially the ramifications were great. Apart from establishing a new basis for federal participation in housing and education programs, the GI Bill meant that a large segment of the population whose traditional socioeconomic circumstances, intensified by the Great Depression, might have denied them home or business ownership and further education (with the resultant entrance into the professions) had now achieved those goals and moved forward into the American middle class.

GIBRALTAR. British naval base that commands the western entrance to the Mediterranean Sea. It was the headquarters of the Mediterranean Command, and after the entry of Italy into the war in June 1940 was also the base of an independent squadron known as FORCE H, comprised initially of two battleships, one aircraft carrier, one cruiser and four destroyers. It was from Gibraltar that the escort forces for the supply convoys to MALTA were organized. In November 1942 Gibraltar became the command headquarters for Operation Torch, the Allied landings in NORTHWEST AFRICA which, in conjunction with the advance of the EIGHTH ARMY from Egypt, cleared all Axis forces from Africa and opened the Mediterranean to Allied seaborne traffic throughout its length.

GIBSON, Guy (1918–1944). Leader of the RAF Lancaster force from No. 617 Squadron (the DAM BUSTERS), which carried out the famous bombing raids on the MÖHNE and EDER dams in May 1943. Gibson, a wing commander, was killed when his plane crashed near Steenbergen, Holland, returning from a raid on Rheydt on September 19, 1944. He received the VICTORIA CROSS for his conduct as leader of the Möhne dam raid.

GIBSON GIRL. A portable radio transmitter used in Allied air–sea rescue operations. The downed flier could, by turning a crank, broadcast an SOS on the international distress frequency. At first a kite served to raise the antenna, but a balloon filled from a gas cylinder proved more satisfactory.

GIFFARD, Sir George (1886–1964). British Army officer who in the first two years of the war occupied the positions of military secretary to the Secretary of State for War (1939) and General Officer Commanding Palestine and Transjordan (1940). He then served as first commander in chief, West Africa (1940–42), during which period he was the only senior British officer then in service with experience of jungle fighting (acquired in Africa in World War I). As General Officer Commanding Eastern Army, India (1942–43), Giffard supplied administrative expertise that paved the way for the Allied conquest of BURMA. Subsequently, he served under Lord Louis MOUNTBATTEN as commander in chief, 11th Army Group, SOUTHEAST ASIA COMMAND, until removed by the latter in 1944 for reasons of incompatibility.

GIFFEN, Robert Carlisle (1886–1962). Early in the war, Rear Admiral Giffen, a graduate of the U.S. Naval Academy in 1907, participated in the Battle of the ATLANTIC. After serving in supply convoys to Russia, he took part in Operation Torch, the invasion of NORTHWEST AFRICA. His covering group encountered French destroyers off Casablanca and engaged them in a battle. After Torch, Giffen brought part of his force halfway around the world to the battle for RENNELL ISLAND. His cover and fire support groups also took part in the Aleutian and MARSHALL ISLANDS compaigns. In May 1944 "Ike" Giffen took command of the CARIBBEAN SEA FRONTIER as a vice-admiral.

GI JOE DINERS. Rest stops for truck drivers in pursuit operations east of the Rhine River behind the U.S. SEV-

ENTH ARMY. To speed deliveries along an express truck route, drivers could exchange cold rations for hot food.

GILBERT ISLANDS. Group southeast of the MARSHALLS, occupied by the Japanese in December 1941. The most strategically important islands were TARAWA (also the largest), ABAIANG and APAMAMA. Although the capture of the Marshalls was initially considered desirable by the Americans as the first step on the march westward to Tokyo, so little intelligence was available on these islands that Allied planners decided to move first into the Gilberts, since they could provide bases from which reconnaissance planes could investigate the nearby Marshalls. Besides, the defenses of the Gilberts appeared weaker than those of the Marshalls, and the Gilberts were near enough to permit South Pacific naval forces to support operations mounted against them. Finally, control of the Gilberts would reduce the Japanese threat to American bases in the Ellice Islands and Samoa as well as protect the line of communications to Australia and New Zealand. Therefore, on July 20, 1943, the Joint Chiefs of Staff directed Adm. Chester W. NIMITZ to begin planning for the capture of bases on Tarawa and Apamama in the Gilberts, and Nauru Island, although, in the end, the last objective was canceled and MAKIN Atoll substituted instead. The code name assigned to the operation was GALVANIC. Successful landings were made on Tarawa and Makin by the 2d Marine Division and the 27th Infantry Division respectively on November 20, 1943, and on Apamama by Marine scouts of V Amphibious Corps Reconnaissance Company on the 21st (secured the same day). Resistance on Tarawa and Makin ended on the 23d.

GILLARS, Mildred Elizabeth (1900–). Known to the world as Axis Sally, Miss Gillars, an American, was a onetime aspiring actress who was teaching English in Berlin at the outbreak of the war. She soon began broadcasting on the German radio, and when American troops arrived in the Mediterranean her programs of music and talk attempted to undermine the morale of the GIs by raising doubts about the war and by describing, in salty language, how the men back home were seducing the women the soldiers had left behind. She was, however, more popular with the GIs than was the official Army radio, and it was her playing of the record of the song "Lili Marlene" that led to its great popularity among Allied soldiers. At her trial in 1949, Miss Gillars said that she had done it all for the love of Max Otto Koischwitz, a staff member of the Foreign Ministry. Convicted of treason, she was paroled in 1961.

GILLEM, Alvan C., Jr. (1888–1973). Commissioned from the ranks in 1911, Gillem while stationed in the United States during World War II commanded in sequence the Third Armored Division, II Armored Corps, Desert Training Center and the Armored Force. In December 1943 he assumed command of the XIII Corps, which he trained until he went overseas in July 1944, as a major general. Under the NINTH ARMY, XIII Corps went operational in November, and Gillem commanded it until the end of the war in Europe. According to the Ninth Army commander, General SIMPSON, he "handled his corps in a masterful fashion."

GIRAUD, Henri (1879–1949). In 1939 General Giraud commanded the French Seventh Army and in May 1940 had the mission of advancing across northern Belgium to aid the embattled Dutch. When this effort was frustrated in southern Holland, he moved his forces back to Belgium to link up with the rest of the Allied forces. On May 15 Giraud replaced Gen. André CORAP, whose Ninth Army, opposite the Ardennes, was in a state of imminent collapse. But the appointment came too late: Giraud's headquarters was overrun and the new commander captured before he had had an opportunity to act.

Held prisoner at Königstein, Giraud escaped in April 1942 and made his way to VICHY France, but there abstained from all public political and military activity. In secret, however, he supervised planning for France's reentry into the war against Germany and argued for an Allied landing in southern France. When notified of the impending Allied invasion of NORTHWEST AFRICA in November 1942, Giraud was surprised at the news but agreed to take charge of all French forces there and assist the Allied armies however possible. President Franklin D. ROOSEVELT felt that Giraud would prove more acceptable than the leader of FREE FRANCE, Charles DE GAULLE, to French officers there and would be able to rally enough support to halt any opposition to the landings. But the defending French forces remained loyal to Marshal Philippe PÉTAIN. The Marshal's chief assistant, Adm. François DARLAN, happened to be visiting Algeria at the time and ordered the Army to resist.

With the assassination of Darlan on December 24, the United States once again swung its support to Giraud, and he became High Commissioner for French Africa as well as Army Commander in Chief. This set the stage for his duel with de Gaulle, who had never supported Giraud's original appointment and who now refused to recognize the new command arrangement. In January 1943 the Allies managed to arrange a meeting between the two men at Casablanca, but neither would agree to accept subordination to the other. If the older Giraud spoke for the officers of the French North African army, de Gaulle represented the Free French forces, which were already engaged in combat. Finally, in May, the two agreed to head a central FRENCH COMMITTEE OF NATIONAL LIBERATION on an equal basis, and this served as a beginning for the integration of the two forces.

During the next 12 months the Allies gradually recognized the committee as the de facto government of France, but Giraud slowly lost his American support. A conservative professional soldier, he was no match for the more Machiavellian supporters of de Gaulle. Also, he was personally difficult, arrogant and ill-tempered. De Gaulle's early stand against Germany and Giraud's apolitical stance made the former more popular with both Winston CHURCHILL and the FRENCH RESISTANCE. As a result, in August 1943, Giraud was forced to step down from his political position and, as Army Commander in Chief, devoted himself to reorganizing and reequipping the French military forces.

A final showdown between Giraud and de Gaulle came in April 1944, when the latter established a defense-level staff which threatened to bypass Giraud's authority. Giraud objected but at first refused to resign.

De Gaulle then offered Giraud the post of Inspector General of the Army and, when he declined the new position, persuaded the committee to relieve him of all command responsibilities. But by this time, Giraud's task of rebuilding the Army was largely complete.

GISEVIUS, Hans Bernd (1903–1974). A career German civil servant, Gisevius briefly found himself a GESTAPO official after the Nazi seizure of power, but managed to extricate himself and joined the resistance movement. Later he was taken by Hans OSTER into the ABWEHR, and finally posted to the German consul general's office in Zurich, where he maintained a liaison with Allen DULLES of the OFFICE OF STRATEGIC SERVICES on behalf of the German resistance. Gisevius, who was later to write a highly colorful account of the resistance, *To the Bitter End* (1948), acted as go-between, knowing everyone of importance in the resistance and frequently returning to Germany to renew his contacts and pass on information. He gave sensational evidence against Hermann GÖRING during the NUREMBERG TRIALS. *See also* OPPOSITION TO HITLER.

GIULIO CESARE. Italian battleship, sister ship of the CONTE DI CAVOUR. She was damaged in action off Calabria on July 9, 1940, being hit by fire from H.M.S. WARSPITE, but survived unscathed the British torpedo attack on TARANTO on November 11, 1940, which put three other battleships out of action. With other elements of the Italian fleet, *Giulio Cesare* was surrendered to the Allies in September 1943. (The Italian Navy actually baptized this ship with the full name of the person it honored—*Caio Giulio Cesare*—but it is customarily given without the praenomen.)

GLADIATOR. This Gloster product, designed by a team headed by H. P. Folland, was the last biplane fighter to see service with Britain's ROYAL AIR FORCE and FLEET AIR ARM. Flown for the first time in 1934, the single-seat Gladiator remained in production from July 1936 until April 1940. Some 500 planes rolled from the assembly line, about 200 of them destined for export to Latvia, Lithuania, Sweden, China, Belgium, Eire, Norway, Iraq, Portugal and Greece. British versions mounted four machine guns, two in the lower wing and two in the cowling. An 840-horsepower Bristol Mercury radial engine gave the plane a top speed of 253 miles per hour at 14,500 feet, a range of 410 miles and a service ceiling of 33,000 feet.

The installation of an arrester hook, hard points for catapult operation and a compartment for an inflatable life raft slightly reduced the performance of Fleet Air Arm Gladiators. These Sea Gladiators saw action over the North Sea and Mediterranean. In 1940 the defense of MALTA depended for a time on four of the biplanes. One served as reserve for the other three, which bore the nicknames Faith, Hope and Charity. During 1940 modern American-built Grumman MARTLETS replaced most of the Sea Gladiators.

GLASMINE 43(f). German antipersonnel land mine with a glass body, intended to be undetectable by electronic mine detectors.

GLEAVES, U.S.S. Destroyer and class (2,060 tons; four 5-inch guns; five or ten 21-inch torpedo tubes; 37 knots). Externally almost identical to the BENSON class, *Gleaves* and 65 sisters were built to a modification of the original design prepared by Gibbs & Cox. This incorporated higher-pressure, higher-temperature machinery which was highly controversial at the time of construction but proved satisfactory in wartime service. In armament and service the Gleaves class followed the general pattern of the Bensons; 24 of them became high-speed minesweepers, with minesweeping gear replacing the aftermost 5-inch gun. The first Gleaves-class destroyers went into commission, like the first Bensons, in 1940–41. As the state of emergency deepened, further orders were placed for follow-on ships; the bulk of this class commissioned in 1942–43. They saw extensive service, primarily in the Atlantic and Mediterranean, before being decommissioned after V-J Day. Contemporary official and unofficial publications often refer to these ships as the Livermore or Bristol class, sometimes with a slightly different breakdown of ships between this and the Benson class.

GLIDER. The glider became a weapon of war on May 10, 1940, when German troops landed in such craft to seize bridges across the Albert Canal in Belgium and to capture Fort EBEN EMAEL, a reputedly impregnable border strongpoint. The metal-and-plywood DFS 230 gliders landed atop the fort and disgorged specially trained men who disabled the gun turrets and observation cupolas using hollow-charge explosives designed to focus their destructive force. This descent upon Eben Emael was the culmination of a "sport" flying program begun in Germany after the Treaty of Versailles had placed limitations on heavier-than-air craft.

In April 1941, when Germany intervened against the British expeditionary units in Greece, glider-borne engineers helped seize a bridge across the Corinth Canal. Following their successes along the Albert and Corinth Canals, the Germans employed similar 10-man gliders to land some 750 assault troops on the island of CRETE. The glider units landed successfully, but the parachute forces that were the backbone of the operation suffered grievously when they landed amid the main defensive positions. Crete fell to the Germans, but the cost of victory convinced HITLER that further airborne operations would be folly. Gliders were used, however, in September 1943 to rescue the deposed dictator Benito MUSSOLINI from his Italian captors, and in July of the following year in an attack against a Resistance stronghold in France.

Ironically, the airborne descent upon Crete encouraged the Allies even as it dismayed Hitler. Gliders were especially important in airborne warfare because they could carry the light artillery, jeeps and antitank weapons that were essential if the airborne units were to survive until friendly armor and infantry could link up with them. The Americans relied on the boxlike Waco glider (*see* CG-4); the British employed the more graceful Airspeed HORSA.

Allied glider troops first saw action in SICILY. High winds on the night of July 9, 1943, scattered the gliders in the first airborne assault wave, and several came down at sea. Some 250 British troops drowned. Subsequent glider assaults in Sicily suffered casualties from friendly as well as hostile fire, demonstrating forcibly the need for careful coordination.

Despite the Sicilian experience, the Allies persisted in airborne operations involving both American and British gliders. More than 850 gliders participated in the INVASION of France in June 1944. Some 450 descended upon SOUTHERN FRANCE in August of that year, and about the same number saw action during the September 1944 invasion of Holland. The final airborne operation of the European war was the crossing of the Rhine in March 1945, which required a large number of gliders—more than 1,300.

A smaller number of Waco gliders—fewer than 100—also saw action in BURMA with Col. Philip COCHRAN's air commando force. The aircraft descended behind Japanese lines to deliver supplies and equipment to long-range penetration groups.

GLIDER BOMB. A type of bomb, generally in the form of a miniature aircraft and equipped with radio-controllable control surfaces. Glider bombs were designed to be towed or carried within striking range of their targets. On release, they were guided by the mother plane in their final gliding approach. The German HENSCHEL Hs 293 severely damaged the U.S. light cruiser *Savannah* off SALERNO in September 1943 and later destroyed the Italian battleship *Roma*. The U.S. Navy tested a number of these devices, to which it gave the contracted name "glomb." Troop-carrying gliders were tested as gliding bombs but proved unsatisfactory, and three new designs, like miniature airplanes in appearance, were prepared.

GLOIRE. French cruiser and class, completed in 1937. These ships were of 7,600 tons standard displacement and carried nine 6-inch and eight 3.5-inch guns and numerous antiaircraft guns. Along with other French vessels, three Gloires were scuttled in TOULON harbor on November 27, 1942, so that they would not fall into German hands.

GLORIOUS, H.M.S. Royal Navy aircraft carrier, 22,500 tons, completed in 1917 by Harland and Wolff as a battle cruiser and converted to an aircraft carrier in 1925–30 with (in 1939) sixteen 4.7-inch guns and smaller weapons, and 48 aircraft. On June 8, 1940, returning from Norway, *Glorious* was sunk by the German battle cruisers SCHARNHORST and GNEISENAU. For reasons never ascertained, the carrier had not maintained an air reconnaissance, although her only escort was two destroyers, both also sunk. Almost all her crew were lost.

GLOWWORM, H.M.S. Royal Navy destroyer, 1,345 tons, completed in 1936 by Thorneycroft and armed with four 4.7-inch guns, smaller weapons and eight 21-inch torpedo tubes. On April 8, 1940, *Glowworm,* which had been escorting the battle cruiser RENOWN off Norway, became detached and encountered the German 8-inch-gun heavy cruiser ADMIRAL HIPPER. Overwhelmed by *Hipper*'s vastly superior armament, *Glowworm* turned on her enemy and rammed her before sinking. Only one officer and 30 members of her crew were rescued, but the sacrifice of the others was not in vain; the damage caused to the *Hipper* necessitated her return to Germany. More important, the gallantry of *Glowworm*'s crew made a great impression on the seamen of the German Navy, many of whom had been raised to believe in British decadence. The captain of the *Glowworm,* Lt. Comdr. Gerard ROOPE, was awarded a posthumous VICTORIA CROSS.

GNAT. Geman acoustic torpedo.

GNEISENAU. German battle cruiser launched in 1936, sister ship of SCHARNHORST. She displaced 26,000 tons and carried a main armament of nine 11-inch guns. She participated with *Scharnhorst* in the invasion of NORWAY in 1940. After a commerce-raiding cruise in the North Atlantic with *Scharnhorst,* she returned to Brest. On February 11, 1942, in the company of *Scharnhorst* and PRINZ EUGEN, *Gneisenau* made a spectacular dash up the English Channel in daylight to Wilhelmshaven. Damaged in RAF raids on Kiel in February 1942, the ship was decommissioned in July and was scuttled at Gdynia at the end of the war.

GNEISENAU LINE. When Soviet troops attacked the German positions in the CRIMEA on April 8, 1944, they found the German Seventeenth Army making a stand along the Gneisenau Line south of the Perekop isthmus. This defensive position, which flanked Simferopol, failed to hold the Russians, who pushed on to liberate SEVASTOPOL on May 9.

GODFREY, John Henry (1888–1971). Royal Navy officer (vice-admiral), director of naval intelligence 1939–42 (his personal assistant was Lt. Comdr. Ian Fleming, the author of the James Bond novels). Admiral Godfrey had previously served as captain of the battle cruiser REPULSE.

GODFREY, John T. (1922–1958). Godfrey, an American, joined the Royal Canadian Air Force in mid-1941, received his wings the following year and in April 1943 transferred to U.S. Army Air Forces. Flying with the 4th Fighter Group, he teamed with Don GENTILE and became an ace before his 21st birthday. During two combat tours in Europe he shot down 18 German planes and destroyed an equal number on the ground. In August 1944 he was downed by enemy flak and taken prisoner. He escaped as the war in Europe was ending and reached the safety of Allied lines.

GODFROY, René (1885–). In 1940 Admiral Godfroy commanded a division of French cruisers working in the eastern Mediterranean. At the Franco-German armistice his force lay in Alexandria harbor, where it was demobilized by agreement with the British. This force rejoined the Allies in 1943, at which time Godfroy retired.

GODWIN-AUSTEN, Sir Alfred (1889–1963). General Godwin-Austen was sent to British Somaliland in 1940 to prevent Italian conquest if possible, and otherwise to arrange a British withdrawal. Evacuation became necessary, and afterward he commanded the 12th African Division in Kenya. He went to North Africa as commander of the 13th Corps of the EIGHTH ARMY in the fall of 1941, but early in February 1942, after ROMMEL had pushed Eighth Army back to the GAZALA LINE, Godwin-Austen asked to be relieved of command because he sensed a lack of confidence in his leadership. After North Africa he served as vice-quartermaster general at the War Office and principal administrative officer at Army headquarters in India.

GOEBBELS, (Paul) Joseph (1897–1945). Goebbels, as chief of Nazi Party propaganda from 1929 and German Minister for Propaganda and Public Enlightenment from March 1933 to the end of the war, was a master in his field—the outstanding exponent in this century of political propaganda. He learned the basic principles of propaganda from Adolf HITLER, but brought his own malevolent personal flair to the work. For Goebbels the aim of propaganda was to implant in the public a desired point of view, to manipulate the minds of a sufficient number of people to achieve a given political objective, namely, the seizure of power by the party through so-called legitimate means (i.e., within the German republican constitution).

Once this objective had been achieved and Hitler had obtained the right (through the ENABLING ACT of March 1933) to rule by decree, Goebbels's propaganda moved into another gear. All the media of public expression became subject to uniform control in their presentation and interpretation of news and public affairs to the exclusion of all criticism or counterargument. With the coming of war, all news was "processed" or suppressed to secure the maximum response of the nation or its subjects in occupied territories to Hitler's immediate objectives.

Throughout this prolonged period Goebbels's ingenuity never ceased to operate; if on occasion he miscalculated (as in the case of the burning of the books in 1933) or was nonplused (as on the occasion of Rudolf HESS's flight to Britain in 1941), he seldom failed to bring an astute judgment to bear on the interpretation of events in such a way as to command (admittedly with the backing of the police state) some kind of positive response from the majority of the German people, even during the last two years of a war which had turned from triumph to catastrophe. As a performer, he was a master orator and broadcaster; as a writer and diarist, he was a caustic, egocentric commentator and manipulator of historical interpretation. Vain, malicious, fertile of ideas, greedy for power and influence and admiration, he often claimed he could have made a far greater fortune out of advanced advertising techniques than he made out of politics. In a sense, Hitler was his product, an image (or succession of images) he had devised to sell to the German people and to the world.

Dr. Goebbels with Adolf Hitler

Born on October 29, 1897, of petit bourgeois stock, Goebbels was brought up in Rheydt, a town in the industrial Ruhr. He was partially crippled in childhood by infantile paralysis, but compensated for this early weakness by developing a sharp, precocious intellect. Intended by his family for the Catholic priesthood, he lost his faith during adolescence and became a cynic, scraping together the money (in one instance from a Catholic charitable society) that enabled him to enter the University of Heidelberg in 1917. Surviving letters covering the period of his university studies and after (he achieved his doctorate in 1921 with a thesis on the Romantic drama) reveal an extraordinary narcissism, which is also to be found in a romantic autobiographical novel, *Michael,* written in diary form around 1922 but only published in 1929 (with significant additions introducing the character of a Hitler-like messiah). He wrote poetic dramas, articles and other works without success, and kept a diary (parts of which survive) recording his love affairs in detail and revealing the troubled nature (bordering on sadomasochism) of his relationship with a young schoolteacher called Else. After a period of economic hardship he got work in 1923 as a caller in the Cologne stock exchange. Failing to break into the theater, he turned in desperation to politics, in which he had become interested during 1923. He joined the staff of the northern wing of the Nazi Party in 1925, when he was 28, and made rapid headway as an itinerant agitator and assistant editor of party literature.

This was the period when divergence was developing between this faction (dominated by the brothers Gregor and Otto Strasser) and Hitler, who was reorganizing the party in the south following his release from LANDSBERG. Goebbels meanwhile was discovering his outstanding gifts as a speaker, which fed his starved vanity and fulfilled his frustrated histrionic ambitions. The section of his diary (written in the same self-laudatory style as *Michael*) which survives covers the significant period August 1925 to October 1926. (See *The Early Goebbels Diaries,* edited by Helmut Heiben [1962].) This was a crucial time in Goebbels's career, revealing his opportunistic switching to Hitler's viewpoint after initial hostility to him, his selection by Hitler as a speaker and his appointment in 1926 as party gauleiter (district leader) in "red" Berlin, one of the principal centers of Communist activity.

Hitler obviously intended the work in Berlin to be this brilliant young man's baptism of fire. Breaking off his enervating love affair with Else, he fought the party's battle in Berlin with a will from 1926 to 1928, when Hitler invited him to be one of the party's 12 deputies in the Reichstag. In 1929 Hitler made him head of the party's propaganda operations. Goebbels proved himself in Berlin first of all on the platform, where he spoke with tireless energy, caustic humor and an unscrupulous capacity to smear his opponents, notably the Jewish chief of police, Bernhard Weiss. He used provocative, highly entertaining posters; he engineered acts of violence to attract attention—street incidents between the Nazis and the Communists; he made his meetings "occasions" where anything might happen to please the strong-arm members of the movement, building up mass rallies that filled the Berlin Sportpalast. He brought wounded party members onto the platform, and dressed up others to be put on display as stretcher cases. He was insolent to the police if they intervened, in order to disconcert them. Like Hitler he turned court appearances into occasions for intimidating the authorities, and defied the ban on party meetings by holding them in some disguised form. He founded a weekly propaganda journal, *Der Angriff (Attack).* He learned how to be constantly adaptable in order to exploit the changing mood of the public he was attempting to manipulate. The whole story as he viewed it is told in his book *Kampf um Berlin* (1934).

One of the factors which led to Hitler's choosing Goebbels as a Reichstag deputy was that a deputy could not be prevented from public speaking, a ban which was constantly being imposed on Goebbels in Berlin. He knew how to incite his followers—how to make them march and demonstrate in the streets, smash the windows of Jewish-owned shops, beat up Communists. When on occasion a follower was killed, Goebbels would deliver an emotional political oration by the graveside. He knew this was a crucial period for the Nazis, especially during the economic depression which began in 1929 with its consequent mass unemployment, which helped to bring the Nazis a vast increase in votes in the 1930 Reichstag election.

In December 1931, at the age of 34, Goebbels married Magda Quandt, an elegant and wealthy divorcée who had a deep devotion to Hitler. Now Goebbels achieved social position—life in a luxurious Berlin apartment (where Hitler spent much time resting, talking and listening to music), the prestige of being a Reichstag deputy with free first-class travel on the railways, outstanding success as Hitler's principal propagandist and, in the great struggle for power during the next two years, his chief campaign manager. The year 1932 was to be one of ceaseless fighting for votes, but it was also one of exciting ups and downs which kept Goebbels constantly at the helm of the campaign—a position he loved, working alongside his leader. Hitler's personal magnetism was exploited to the utmost in campaigns conducted for the first time by means of air hops across the country. Though Goebbels's strategy was a triumph of organization, the seizure of power eluded their grasp. By the fall, time was not on their side. Hitler resorted to backroom intrigue, mostly with Franz von PAPEN, to achieve the Chancellorship in January 1933. Goebbels conducted during January a brilliant campaign in the Lilliputian state of Lippe, winning it to acclaim in the Nazi press as a great national comeback.

In the campaigns of 1932 which finally led to victory, every available medium had been used—the party press, the newly available loudspeaker equipment making it possible to address mass rallies, loudspeaker vans in the streets, mass-produced gramophone recordings, strident cartoonlike posters, propaganda films. Rallies, marching, banners, music had swelled the Storm Troopers (*see* SA) from some 400,000 in 1930 to 3 million by 1933; there were Nazi children's organizations, youth organizations, women's organizations. Meanwhile, street fighting, intimidation of the property-owning bourgeoisie, violent disruption of opposition meetings all brought to public attention that it was dangerous to oppose the Nazis. In Prussia alone 461 political riots took place in June and July 1932, with 82 people killed. "The party must always be kept with the steam up," said Goebbels. "We must make up our minds to live dangerously. We are always strongest on the offensive. We must never allow ourselves to fall back on mere defense." With Hermann GÖRING working on the industrialists ("Stem Communism!"), Goebbels worked on the masses ("Stem Jewish exploitation! Vote for the man who will solve unemployment!"). Goebbels's lust for power was intimately linked with his love for self-display. The actor and the propagandist were one. He rehearsed his speeches and gestures with the aid of mirrors, and his techniques were studied by all the Nazi speakers.

Hitler was made Chancellor on January 30, 1933. Immediately another election was announced; another campaign had to be fought and won. The REICHSTAG FIRE intervened, and Goebbels used it against the Communists in another propaganda drive. The Nazis increased their vote sufficiently to force passage of the Enabling Act (in the absence of Communist and some other opposition deputies, many of them under arrest following the fire). On March 14 Goebbels was made Minister of Propaganda and Public Enlightenment, responsible—as Hitler put it—for the "spiritual direction of the nation." Jews were now totally banned from participation in any medium of public expression. (Goebbels's vicious anti-Semitism was to reach its climax in the notorious, nationwide pogrom of November 7, 1938, which he personally instigated.) But in February 1933 both press and radio had to be muzzled as a first action in the big new campaign of Gleichschaltung (political coordination—penetration of Nazi ideology into all areas of national life). The Führerkult was on.

By 1932 there were 121 Nazi newspapers and periodicals with a total circulation of a million, led by the early party organ *Völkischer Beobachter,* with a circulation of 127,000. After the Reichstag fire in February 1933, the Communist and Social Democratic press began to be banned, and Germany's 4,700 journals started to disappear or to change their character; the end of 1933 saw 1,500 publishing houses put out of business. By 1934 the Nazi press was represented by 436 journals, and the rest of the "independent" press was under Nazi control—a long-term operation skillfully achieved so that the non-Nazi readership would be broken in gradually. Every newspaper man was "always and foremost a propagandist." On October 4, 1933, a decree was issued which made every editor an "official," forbidden to publish anything deemed injurious to the state or to act or write independently; the editor became a censor, and all journalists had to hold a license to practice their profession. Conferences were constantly called to give editors "guidance." By 1939, Max Amann (secretary of Goebbels's press office) employed 600 editors in chief; by 1944, 82 percent of the German press had come directly under Amann's control.

In comparison, taking control of broadcasting was easy, since it was already run by the state. Cheap, officially sponsored radio sets (incapable of receiving foreign broadcasts) were put on the market, so that by 1939 70 percent of German households had receivers (the highest percentage in the world at that time), while loudspeakers were installed in streets and factories and elsewhere to transmit important announcements and speeches. Broadcasts to foreign countries began (for example, to Austria, the Saar, Poland; and by short wave to the United States, Central and South America and, by the end of 1933, Africa, Asia and Australia—in the appropriate languages). Taking control of the film industry (an important segment of it already centralized within Alfred Hugenberg's business empire) was not difficult; the state gradually acquired financial interests in film companies, wholly acquiring Hugenberg's company in 1937, and also exercised control, through granting or withholding subsidy, though Goebbels was wise enough to keep the mainstream of production on a purely entertainment level. Propaganda came largely through newsreels, documentaries and occasional prestige feature productions. The work of the ministry was channeled through seven specialized sections.

In September 1933 the Reich Chamber of Culture was established to work closely with Goebbels's ministry. The chamber had specialist sections for broadcasting, press, literature, fine arts, theater, music and film. Each art was censored. In literature, a decree of April 1934 required all new work to receive a permit before publication, and in April 1935 a list of forbidden books was sent to publishers to prevent their reissue. In May 1935 a decree forbade "antisocial" jokes in cabarets. In November 1936 Goebbels prohibited all criticism of the arts in the press, and in 1937 he purged the public galleries of "degenerate" art. Conferences were constantly held to advise writers, artists, performers and publishers concerning their duties to the state. As for foreign journalists, Goebbels attempted to muzzle them but had little success, though over 50 correspondents were forced to leave Germany as *personae non gratae* during the 1930s.

An elaborate organization was built up to disseminate the Nazi viewpoint abroad. In 1934, 260 million marks (about $50 million) was spent on propaganda outside Germany; 300 German-language newspapers appeared abroad, and the Germans acquired some financial hold over about 350 foreign newspapers as well as sponsoring news agencies that put out free copy and photographs. German embassies had propaganda attachés, while indoctrinated German journalists were posted abroad. This area of Goebbles's activities drew near to that of Hess, the person who was responsible for bringing German nationals abroad under Hitler's influence. In 1937 it was estimated that German-sponsored organizations abroad had a subsidy of some $50 million.

Goebbels constantly wrote articles and gave broadcasts, demanding high fees for the services he himself imposed on the broadcasting system and the publishers. He had lavish properties—an island estate in Wannsee and a lakeside estate on the Bogensee, both within easy reach of Berlin—but the family lived relatively simply and ate frugally. Goebbels's personal indulgences extended to his clothes, which were expensive and varied. Though his marriage resulted in the birth of five daughters and one son between 1932 and 1940, he was consistently unfaithful to Magda, using his charm to seduce innumerable women, many of them actresses. His affair with the youthful Czech actress Lida Baarova nearly led to divorce in 1938, but Hitler disapproved and the foreign mistress was banished, her career ruined.

In the early years of the war, the period of success for Hitler's armies, there was little difficulty for Goebbels's propaganda. He simply saw to it that the right version of the news was directed to the right people at the right time. He followed the sudden volte-face of the SOVIET-GERMAN NONAGGRESSION PACT by himself performing a volte-face in his newspapers, jettisoning past recriminations overnight and extolling the new relationship. Publishing became increasingly centralized in Max Amann's Eher Verlag, the old party publishing house which dated back to the 1920s but which had grown during the 1930s into a vast empire; the wartime press circulation of 24.6 million copies represented largely party-owned publications. With the conquest of new territories, Goebbels's control extended to broadcasting, publishing and film-making activities abroad. He either acquired or built new radio transmitters and, in the case of Prague, greatly enlarged film-making facilities.

Germans were allowed to listen to broadcasts from all the occupied countries (except Denmark, which was still nominally independent), but only those ministers and officials with special monitoring permits were supposed to listen to enemy radio. Home broadcasting was divided between instruction (news, political talks, war reports, propaganda) and cultural entertainment (predominantly music). Hans Fritzsche (later to be tried and acquitted in the NUREMBERG TRIALS) was the star commentator. Wardens throughout the nation ensured that the people in their districts listened to all important broadcasts. Goebbels established a broadcasting channel for the armed forces, which also had their own journals and libraries of approved books, as well as propaganda and training films. Propaganda films for the public were shown not only in the cinemas but also by means of mobile vans, as in Britain.

"News policy is a cardinal political affair," Goebbels said. "During a war, news should be given out for instruction rather than for information." The foreign-language broadcasts became of great importance, as did the German-language service to German listeners abroad. Broadcasting never ceased throughout the whole 24 hours, including the shortwave services to distant parts. The service directed to England consisted largely of news and music, together with news commentaries; during the early years of the war Goebbels exploited the commentaries broadcast by William JOYCE, Lord Haw Haw. At home, morale was sustained by presenting culture alongside propaganda in the form of good music, by the continued existence of the state theaters (355 were said to be operating in 1941) and by keeping the production of films going right up to the end of the war. Feature films remained largely entertainment, but many reflected nationalistic, as distinct from specifically Nazi, themes, such as the series about Frederick the Great. Newsreels grew in length, extending sometimes to 45 minutes, and they used the magnificent footage of German service cameramen, whose casualty rate was higher than that of the normal serviceman. Special prestige war films, such as *Baptism of Fire* (the graphic Luftwaffe film about the Polish campaign) and *Victory in the West* (about the fall of Western Europe), were released from time to time. Virulent propaganda films, such as *Der Ewige Jude,* smeared the Jewish people; others attacked the character of Germany's enemies.

Goebbels by the midwar years craved a further extension of his powers; he wanted control of the whole of civilian life in Germany. Propaganda, important though it was, no longer satisfied him. He had seen the power of Göring, Heinrich HIMMLER and Martin BORMANN increasing, while his own remained the same. He kept a voluminous diary, dictated at all hours, sections of which (1942–43) survived the destruction of Berlin and form an interesting commentary on his day-to-day life. (They appeared in translation as *The Goebbels Diaries* [1948], edited by Louis P. Lochner.) The diary reveals his approval of the extermination of the Jews and his total admiration for Hitler, tempered with momentary criticism and worry about the Führer's health. When after the surrender of Stalingrad (January 31, 1943) the war began to turn against Germany, Goebbels's propaganda policy hardened into advocacy of "total war," which he proclaimed in a histrionic speech in the Sportpalast in February 1943. As Hitler and the other Nazi leaders withdrew increasingly from the public eye, Goebbels fearlessly went out among the people at the height of the bombings. His assiduity was finally rewarded when Hitler made him Reich Trustee for the Total War on July 26, 1944, a week after the abortive attempt on the Führer's life (*see* OPPOSITION TO HITLER). Goebbels, who had been in Berlin on July 20, had acted with great presence of mind in the crisis.

During the last months of the war Goebbels stayed close to Hitler, encouraging him to continue his resistance in an increasingly impossible situation. Goebbels's propaganda line was that Germany should go down with Hitler in a final Götterdämmerung. He delivered his last, melancholy broadcast on April 19, 1945, the eve of Hitler's birthday. He and Hitler felt that their death wish should be adopted by the 80 million German people, who were expected to destroy the nation's resources and die resisting the invaders. Goebbels, his wife and children shared, along with Bormann, Hitler's living tomb beneath the ground; Goebbels and Bormann were witnesses to Hitler's marriage on April 29 to Eva BRAUN and to his will. After Hitler's suicide on April 30 Goebbels became, by the terms of Hitler's will, Chancellor of Germany.

Goebbels and his wife had themselves decided on a family suicide. Unsuccessful attempts were made to negotiate with the Russians. Then, on the evening of April 30, Goebbels and his wife poisoned their sleeping children and took their own lives. Their partially cremated bodies were found by the Russians. **R.M.**

GOERDELER, Carl Friedrich (1884–1945). In their investigation of the July 20, 1944, attempt on Adolf HITLER's life, GESTAPO agents searched Army headquarters in the BENDLERSTRASSE. In a safe they found various incriminating documents, including a list of ministers who were supposed to make up the new provisional government. At the head of the government was to be Dr. Carl Goerdeler, former mayor of Leipzig. The fact that such a list actually existed in so prominent a place—where it was readily found—is evidence of the anti-Hitler group's inexperience as conspirators.

Son of a district judge who in 1899 became a member of the Prussian parliament, Goerdeler was born in Schneidemühl and brought up in a well-to-do Prussian home where right-wing politics were a matter of course. Trained in law, banking and commerce at Tübingen University, he became after war service a municipal administrator, serving as deputy mayor of Königsberg in 1920–30 and then mayor of Leipzig. He was an inflexible nationalist with an authoritarian slant to his nature; he disliked the Weimar government and was not averse initially to Nazism. His distinction as an administrator led him to become economic adviser to Adolf Hitler and Reich Price Commissioner in 1934–35. But he soon realized that Nazi intransigence ran counter to his strict moral principles. His disaffection found drastic expression in 1937, when he resigned as mayor of Leipzig because Nazi authorities, against his express orders, had removed the memorial to the city's famous composer, Felix Mendelssohn, a Jew.

Goerdeler became a confirmed opponent of Nazism from this period and joined Ludwig BECK, who had resigned as Chief of the General Staff in protest of Hitler's prowar policies, to form the initial spearhead of right-wing opposition to Hitler, the two representing the military and civilian wings of the movement. If Goerdeler sometimes displayed a rash courage and outspokenness, he also brought a tireless energy to recruiting for the German resistance. As the circle widened, Goerdeler's staunch individualism and lack of discretion in what he said became something of an embarrassment to the movement. Meanwhile, feeling that the West should be warned of Hitler's real intentions in Europe and apprised of the extent of the opposition in Germany itself, he visited Britain and the United States, and in 1939 he met Winston CHURCHILL. After war broke out, he constantly tried to encourage peace feelers through his contacts in Sweden and Switzerland.

When it became plain that no action other than the assassination of Hitler would have any effect on those elements in the Army who might join in a coup d'état once it was achieved for them by others, or would move the British Government to agree on peace terms with an interim government, Goerdeler (though opposed to actually killing Hitler) lined up with those planning a shadow cabinet to take over, being cast in the role of future Chancellor. He continued to make contacts with senior military men, such as Field Marshal von KLUGE, who had shown diffident interest. Using bogus papers supplied by the ABWEHR, he even traveled to Smolensk to see Kluge, commanding on the Eastern Front. By 1943, however, a younger wing, to be led by Count von STAUFFENBERG, was entering the German resistance, and Goerdeler was too old and too set in his outlook to agree with their more liberal views.

The Gestapo were not without interest in Goerdeler, though preferring to watch him rather than arrest him, and he was warned to go into hiding before the July 20 attempt. He was arrested on August 12, 1944, and held by the Gestapo, who subjected him to continuous interrogation. He developed his own clever technique of self-preservation without betrayal of his colleagues—endless talk laced with tantalizing revelations requiring much research and further questioning by his persecutors. He was condemned to death on September 8 but was kept in confinement so that he could write memoranda on political and economic matters which the Gestapo and the SS hoped would be useful to the state.

Although the conspirators associated with Goerdeler had complained at times of his indiscretion and overoptimism, he had given the activities of the plotters a shaping moral integrity. Along with the other leaders of the plot, he also gave his life. He was hanged on February 2, 1945. *See also* OPPOSITION TO HITLER.

GOLD BEACH. The westernmost (Asnelles) of the three British beaches in the INVASION of NORMANDY. It was assaulted by the British 30th Corps.

GOLD STAR MEDAL. This Soviet award, often referred to as the Order of the Gold Star, was presented to individuals, both military and civilian, who accomplished outstanding feats contributing to the Soviet Union's honor and material development during the war. It is awarded, along with the Order of Lenin, to a person named HERO OF THE SOVIET UNION.

GOLIATH. Code name for a German Navy radio station that could transmit to submarines beneath the surface.

GOLIATH. A remote-controlled miniature tank filled with explosives, used by the Germans at ANZIO (Italy) in the attack on the bridgehead in February 1944. The Goliaths were supposed to confuse the Allied defenders as to the location of German attacks but were not effective.

GOLIKOV, Filip I. (1900–). A Soviet general who served in the invasion of Poland and the SOVIET-FINNISH WAR and in 1941 headed a LEND-LEASE mission to London and Washington. In the 1941 campaign he commanded the Tenth Army, and in the winter offensive of 1941–42 his forces cracked the German lines at TULA. In 1942 he commanded the Bryansk Front, then the Voronezh Front. Golikov led part of the assault against the Italians and Hungarians at STALINGRAD and was deputy commander of the Stalingrad army groups in 1942–43. In early 1943 his forces retook KURSK, KHARKOV and ROSTOV. He was appointed Deputy Minister of Defense and chief of personnel of the Red Army later that year, a post he held until 1950.

GOLOVANOV, Alexander Y. (1903–). Golovanov was a colonel in 1941, commanding the 81st Long Range Division in support of the Soviet defense of the Moscow area. In March 1942 he was promoted to general and given command of the Air Force for Long Range Operations (AFLRO), more commonly called the Long Range Bomber Command, which was directly subordinate to the General Headquarters of the SOVIET HIGH COMMAND. Although it appears that Golovanov continued in command, the relatively few references to his wartime activities tend to place him as Marshal ZHUKOV's aviation adviser, especially at STALINGRAD. The end of the war found him in command of the Eighteenth Air Army, which was formerly a part of AFLRO but was given separate status in June 1944. His highest rank was aviation chief marshal.

GOLOVKO, Arseniy G. (1906–1962). Soviet admiral, commander of the Northern Fleet between 1940 and 1945. His forces helped get Allied supply convoys to Russia and took part in the 1944 Petsamo-Kirkenes operation which liberated Russian territory north of the Arctic Circle and northern Norway. He was promoted to vice-admiral in 1942 and to admiral in 1944. Between 1945 and 1954 Golovko served as Chief of the Navy General Staff.

GOLUBINKA. Headquarters of the German SIXTH ARMY on the west side of the Don River near STALINGRAD.

GOMORRAH. Code name for RAF bombing of HAMBURG, July–August 1943, during which the use of the new countermeasure WINDOW enabled the bombers to conduct repeated attacks with relative impunity.

GONA. A native mission about seven miles north of BUNA Mission on the northern coast of Papua, NEW GUINEA, this was the place from which the Japanese mounted an unsuccessful attack on PORT MORESBY. An Australian counterattack in October 1942 forced the Japanese to contract their positions into a perimeter defense of Buna and Gona. Gona fell to Australian troops on December 9, 1942, after some hard fighting.

GOODWOOD. Code name of British Second Army offensive southeast of CAEN (Normandy), July 18, 1944. The strategic purpose of this attack has been the subject of considerable controversy. *See also* WESTERN FRONT.

GOOSEBERRY. Code name for a blockship used as part of a breakwater in a MULBERRY harbor (the name for the artificial harbor developed for the INVASION of NORMANDY.)

GORDOV, Vassili N. (1896–1951). This Soviet general is first listed as chief of staff of the Twenty-first Army in the vicinity of the Sula River in September 1941. By July 7, 1942, as a lieutenant general, he was commanding general of the Sixty-fourth Army. Five days later, on July 12, the STALINGRAD front was formed and the Sixty-fourth Army passed to Marshal TIMOSHENKO's new command with orders to hold the left bank of the Don River. On July 23 Gordov succeeded Timoshenko as the front commander. When the high command divided the overly large formation into two fronts, General YEREMENKO was given command of the other front. After August 13 Gordov was Yeremenko's deputy for a new, enlarged Stalingrad Front, but at the end of September he was replaced by General ROKOSSOVSKY.

GÖRING, Hermann (1893–1946). Göring's position as second only to Adolf HITLER in the establishment and maintenance of the Nazi regime is unassailable, although his influence waned after 1942. His close and jealous rivals were Joseph GOEBBELS and, in the later years of the war, Heinrich HIMMLER and Martin BORMANN. But none received, as Göring did in 1939, Hitler's public acknowledgment as his "successor." Rudolf HESS, commonly called Hitler's deputy, was never more than his deputy at the head of the party, as distinct from the state.

At the NUREMBERG TRIALS after the war, Göring was inevitably the principal defendant, the self-appointed spokesman for the regime. A man of great ability and guileful intelligence, he sought to be considered a political *condottiere,* even a gangster, whose only interest was the successful accretion of power by strong-arm methods. His overweening ambition, his vanity and self-display (enlarged by his drug addiction), reached absurd proportions, but he did not mind exciting laughter, which he accepted as a sign of admiration. His gravest weakness was his inability to retain interest in anything that could not be achieved quickly; his wartime neglect of the LUFTWAFFE once it became strained beyond its resources (and so, in his view, failed him) led to his virtual retirement, under the excuse of ill health, during the last years of the war. He preferred to concentrate on his country estate, his hunting forays and his (largely purloined) art collection rather than on the day-to-day conduct of the war.

Göring was born on January 12, 1893, in a sanatorium in Bavaria to which his mother had been sent from Haiti, where her husband, Heinrich Ernst Göring, was German consul general. Franziska was his second wife, a woman of modest Bavarian stock, and Hermann was her fourth child. Heinrich Göring was near retirement, and the family settled for a while in Berlin in 1896, living in straitened circumstances. Franziska submitted readily to the protestations of a partly Jewish lover, the wealthy Ritter von Epenstein, family doctor and a friend of long standing, who offered the Görings residence in one of his two castles in Bavaria, Veldenstein, near Nuremberg, where Franziska lived discreetly as Epenstein's mistress. The castle with its ornate furnishings provided Hermann in his youth with a consciousness of class; he was a domineering boy, difficult at school and spoiled. He loved rough games and mountaineering, and he was brought up to regard his godfather, Epenstein, as a foster parent—while his father succumbed to alcohol and old age. At the age of 16, Göring was sent to the military training college at Lichterfelde (Kadetten-Anstalt), near Berlin; responding well to this form of education, he earned in 1912, at age 19, a commission in the Infantry Regiment Prinz Wilhelm No. 112 at Mulhausen. At this time the family's circumstances changed; Epenstein decided to marry, and the Görings went to live in Munich, where Heinrich died in 1913. (It is noteworthy that the connection with the Epensteins was not entirely broken. In 1939 Epenstein's widow died, and in her will the castle of Mauterndorf was bequeathed to the Göring family.)

Göring's World War I service was distinguished. Encouraged by a friend, Bruno LOERZER, he transferred to the embryonic Army Air Force. In 1915 he qualified as a pilot, flying fighters and becoming a well-known air ace. By 1917 he was commanding a squadron of fighters, and he won the coveted decoration Pour le Mérite. In July 1918, at the age of 25, he succeeded the legendary Manfred von Richthofen as commander of the Richthofen squadron. The following November, after the war was over, Göring was disgusted by the conditions of the armistice; he felt the Army had been dishonored. He was demobilized with the rank of captain and left Germany for Denmark and eventually Sweden, taking up a career as a civilian pilot and acting as sales agent for the Heiniken parachute. In Sweden he fell in love with the Baroness Carin von Kantzow, whose mother was English and who divorced her husband in order to be free to marry Göring; meanwhile, he returned to Germany to try to consolidate his business career. They married in Munich in February 1923, a few months after Göring had met Hitler and joined the Nazi Party.

Göring had fallen completely under the spell of Hitler's nationalism, while the former air ace was exactly the kind of man Hitler felt he needed to take charge of the Storm Troopers (*see* SA). "I gave him a disheveled rabble," said Hitler. "In a very short time he had organized a division of 11,000 men." At the age of 30, Göring stood second to Ernst RÖHM, Hitler's "chief of staff," aged 36, who had belonged to the party since its founding. Röhm and Göring became Hitler's principal lieutenants in the unsuccessful Munich putsch of November 1923, in the course of which Göring was badly wounded in the groin. His arrest was ordered by the Munich authorities, and he was spirited across the border into Austria by his wife and sympathizers, including—significantly—some of the police. Göring's neglected wound having turned gangrenous, he was given morphine, to which he was to become a near lifelong addict. He was kept in a hospital in Innsbruck until Christmas. The Görings, now dependent largely on financial help from sympathizers, moved to Italy when his notoriety as a Nazi made him *persona non grata* in Austria.

They were to remain in exile until 1927. In Italy, Göring studied art, and on one occasion met Benito MUSSOLINI. In May 1925 he and his wife went to Sweden to be near Carin's family; both by now were in poor health. Carin was a near invalid with a weak heart. Göring, hypochondriac, fat and flabby, was certified a dangerous drug addict and confined in Langbro mental institution on September 1, 1925; he was not declared cured until 1926. He returned to Germany alone when President von Hindenburg proclaimed a political amnesty in autumn 1927. Göring returned not only to rejoin Hitler but to reestablish himself in the business world, especially in the field of aviation. His wife joined him later.

Hitler was in no hurry to reemploy his former aide, though he foresaw his potential use as a contact man, especially among industrialists. Göring and his wife represented in his eyes social "class." Hitler eventually accepted him as one of the party's candidates for the Reichstag, in which he became a deputy in May 1928, representing Bavaria, along with another of Hitler's protégés, Joseph Goebbels, now party gauleiter of Berlin. Their brief from Hitler was to disrupt, embarrassing the Social Democrats and the government as much as possible. Göring, enjoying his new status, became the "salon Nazi," establishing confidence among the right-wing nationalists and upper-class industrialists and bankers, such as Fritz Thyssen and Hjalmar SCHACHT, while Goebbels and the Nazi "radicals" gathered support among the working class (and, after the onset of the Great Depression, the growing numbers of the unemployed).

Determined to seize power by overtly legal means, Hitler made the Reichstag his ultimate arena, and Göring his principal representative. It was Göring who accompanied Hitler when, from 1931, he had to meet formally with President von Hindenburg. After the election of July 1932, the second landslide in favor of the Nazis, who gained 230 seats, Göring was elected president of the Reichstag. Now he could boast a palace in his own right. Carin, however, was not there to share his glory; worn out by the troubles of her married life and her illnesses, she had died in Stockholm the previous October.

Göring as president of the Reichstag had little respect for protocol; he attempted to oust the Chancellor, von PAPEN, from office by deliberately framing a vote of censure. Although the Nazis lost seats in the next election (November 1932), Göring was reelected president. After Hitler finally became Chancellor, Göring received a seat in his cabinet and was made commissioner for aviation and minister of the interior in Prussia, by far the largest and most powerful of the German states (with its administration in Berlin alongside the federal administration). He immediately set about restaffing the Prussian police force by placing Nazi supporters in key positions and creating auxiliary police forces manned by SA and SS men (*see* SS). He remodeled the already existing political police, renaming them the Geheime Staatspolizei (the GESTAPO), and established CONCENTRATION CAMPS to deal with political dissidents. On February 27, 1933, the REICHSTAG FIRE occurred; whether or not it was deliberately instigated by Göring, he took immediate advantage of it to arrest prominent Communists and even Social Democrats, including many Reichstag deputies. The fire came only a few days before the next Reichstag election on March 5, in which the Nazis polled their final vote in what still passed as a free choice—17,270,000 votes, 43 percent of those cast. Even with arrests of their key opponents and intimidation of the rest, the Nazis could still not command an absolute majority in the Reichstag. Nevertheless, with so many empty seats and with Göring as a scarcely impartial president, Hitler secured passage of the ENABLING ACT, which gave him power to rule Germany by decree.

Although at this stage Göring was a dedicated worker, devoting time and energy to his many offices of state, he was not slow to feather his own nest. He had two official palaces—as president of the Reichstag and as the minister of the interior for Prussia—as well as a luxurious apartment in the Kaiserdamm. His grandiose nature found full expression at the public expense, most of all in the great country house Carinhall (dedicated to his late wife, whose remains were reinterred there in 1934). As Master of the German Hunt, he developed this mansion from an old hunting lodge on a vast 100,000-acre estate in the forests north of Berlin; his game laws were models of their kind.

Göring had no conscience where money or property was concerned; now that he was in a position of supreme power, graft on a giant scale operated in his favor through his industrial contacts. He thought of himself as a Renaissance prince, and his weight rose eventually to 280 pounds. His clothes became notorious for their gaudiness and extravagance; uniforms, hunting costumes and the like all expressed his vanity, as did his splendid flashing rings. Jewels were an obsession with him. His bumptious good humor and occasional self-mockery excused much, and his bonhomie in contrast to the dourness of many Nazi headmen made him relatively welcome in the social life of the diplomatic corps in Berlin. His birthday became the occasion for an opera ball and lavish gifts from all over the nation. He organized hunting parties on his estate, attended by ambassadors and diplomats from abroad. (When in 1940 he became Reichsmarschall, he had a coat of arms created—a mailed fist holding a bludgeon. He liked to be called "Der Eiserne," the iron man.) Nonetheless, he liked also to be thought a man of feeling, and he became the self-appointed patron of the fine arts and of the theater and the opera. Although always sentimentally loyal to the memory of his late wife, from 1932 he associated closely with a well-known actress, Emmy Sonnemann, a divorcée whom he married in an elaborate ceremony on April 10, 1935. They were to be a devoted couple, and a daughter, Edda, their only child, was born in 1938.

Göring was to occupy during the 1930s a succession of offices in addition to those he already held. One, however, he relinquished—control of the Prussian Gestapo and the concentration camps, which he (no doubt gladly) ceded to Himmler in 1934, the year in which he played the leading part, along with Himmler, in the downfall of Röhm and the bloody purge called the NIGHT OF THE LONG KNIVES. His air commission became a ministry, covering the secret development of an air force, later to be called the Luftwaffe; the German air arm was established in March 1935, and tours of service in the Spanish War gave Göring's pilots important battle training.

Göring's ambition, however, went beyond this; he wanted to take possession of the whole economy of Germany insofar as it was directed toward a future war of expansion, and in September 1936 Hitler responded by making him National Commissioner for the Four-Year Plan for the German economy; feeling supplanted by this move, Dr. Schacht, Hitler's Economics Minister and Plenipotentiary for War Economy, resigned in November 1937. Göring also aimed at becoming Hitler's roving ambassador abroad; indeed, he became a constant visitor to Mussolini in Italy, and played host at home to such visiting dignitaries as the Duke of Windsor, Lord HALIFAX, Charles LINDBERGH and Sumner WELLES. In 1939 Hitler finally declared Göring his "successor," thus making him second man in Germany. There seemed no limit to Göring's ambition, and his ebullience was by now conditioned by his resort to paracodeine, a mild derivative of morphine. He became a secret patient of Prof. Hubert Kahle, who had a sanatorium near Cologne and had devised a quick, but temporary, means for withdrawal from certain drugs. Göring was forced to resort to this temporary cure at intervals during the rest of his life, but his addiction was common gossip in Germany, and was said to account for the extravagances in his behavior. (He was finally to be taken off drugs by the Americans when in captivity in 1945.)

With Röhm gone, Göring had ambitions to become (as Röhm had hoped to become before him) Minister of War, and willingly joined in the devious plots of 1938 surrounding the downfall of Field Marshal von Blomberg, War Minister and Commander in Chief of the Armed Forces, and of his possible successor, General von FRITSCH, Commander in Chief of the Army, who was falsely charged with homosexuality by the Gestapo. Göring failed in this particular ambition, since Hitler took over both the ministry and the command of the Wehrmacht. Göring presided over the court of honor which the Army insisted should examine the Gestapo's case against Fritsch, but since the final session coincided with the move into Austria in 1938, Göring washed his hands of the business, knowing that Fritsch was already ruined. Göring himself conducted by telephone the final blackmail of Kurt von SCHUSCHNIGG, the Austrian Chancellor, and President Wilhelm Miklas on the night of March 11, 1938, which led to the downfall of Austria. German troops had been stationed along the border ready to march the moment the signal was given.

Göring also figured in the persecution of the Jews, presiding over the notorious high-level conference following the pogrom of November 10, 1938. He regarded the destruction of property with disfavor: "I wish you had killed 200 Jews and not destroyed such properties," he grumbled. Göring in fact was worried about the precipitate way in which Hitler was directing Germany's destiny in the direction of war without adequate preparation. He considered 1942 the first year in which Germany would be ready to wage a major war. It was for this reason only that he became an advocate during 1939 for the maintenance of peace. So long as Hitler acquired his territories, such as Austria, the SUDETENLAND or CZECHOSLOVAKIA as a whole, by hard-fisted negotiation or sheer blackmail, Göring was happy, and the thought of disrupting his luxurious life to enter upon the rigors of war went against his nature. When Poland appeared to be the territory upon which Britain and France would be prepared to make a stand, Göring came to be regarded as the moderate in the Nazi hierarchy, not only by the diplomatic corps in Berlin but by such interventionists as the Swedish businessman Birger Dahlerus, who used his acquaintance with Göring to introduce him to an unofficial delegation of British businessmen for a peace-promoting conference in August 1939. Dahlerus, who has left an account of his desperate, last-minute efforts to avert war in his book *The Last Attempt,* draws remarkable portraits of both Hitler and Göring. He was convinced of Göring's sincerity in these discussions, which lasted until after the start of hostilities.

"Leave it to my Luftwaffe," declared Göring as soon as the invasion of Poland was due to begin. Using the technique called blitzkrieg, Göring's dive-bombers attacked Polish airfields, destroying hangars and fuel dumps. The Luftwaffe battered central Warsaw, leaving its buildings empty shells. The Luftwaffe feature film *Baptism of Fire,* introduced by Göring himself, boasted about the feat after the short-lived campaign was over. Later, in 1940, the same merciless treatment was given to ROTTERDAM, where 800 people were killed. "Leave it to my Luftwaffe" was to be Göring's continual gloat.

In 1940 Göring had the largest air force in the world, 3,500 operational aircraft; he was never again to be so powerful as now, when in July Hitler made him Reichsmarschall des Grossdeutschen Reiches. But after the fall of France, Göring met his first reversal in the failure of the Luftwaffe to give the ROYAL AIR FORCE the *coup de grâce;* both sides sustained heavy losses, but the SPITFIRES, working around the clock, proved far too damaging during the key period of the Battle of BRITAIN, from mid-August 1940 on. Göring supervised operations personally (when not hunting or resting at Carinhall) from his luxurious train, on which he was accompanied by his manservant, Robert Kropp, his doctor and his nurse.

Hitler, averse to conducting a sea operation with his depleted navy, abandoned the attempt to subdue Britain from the air and turned his attention to preparations for his principal campaign—Operation BARBAROSSA against Russia. The Luftwaffe in 1940–41 began to find its firepower inadequate. Hitler's intuitive strategy had always laid emphasis on bombers and fighter-bombers in his war of aggression rather than on fighters needed for defense, and Göring found himself required to maintain the defense of Germany with an insufficient number of fighters. Göring had boasted that no enemy bomber would ever penetrate the Fatherland. "If they do, you can call me Meier," he had joked. But by the start of the Russian campaign the Luftwaffe would be spread out along a 2,000-mile series of fronts. It failed even to subdue the RAF in its defense of MALTA. The RAF began to raid the German industrial centers during 1941, and the first of the massive 1,000-bomber raids came in May 1942.

Turning, as ever, to new interests which promised dividends, Göring took energetic charge of plans for the spoliation of Russia. The Ukraine was to become the granary of Germany. "Many millions of people will be starved to death, if we take out of the country the things we need," wrote Göring in a directive of May 2, 1941. It was Göring who sent Reinhard HEYDRICH on July 31, 1941, the secret order, couched in veiled terms, concerning the "FINAL SOLUTION" of the "Jewish problem." (At Nuremberg these documents were to be the most damning that Göring had to seek to explain away under cross-examination.) Sumner WELLES, visiting Germany in March 1940, had found Göring "monstrous" in girth, flushed and wearing an emerald ring an inch square; Count CIANO, observing him in November 1941 in Italy, thought him "bloated and overbearing" and still obsessed by his jewels. He was utterly callous about the suffering of civilians in occupied territories.

The problems the Luftwaffe faced as a result of trying to live up to Hitler's and Göring's demands took a heavy toll; such well-known senior officers as UDET and JESCHONNEK (the chief of staff) committed suicide; MÖLDERS was killed in a plane crash. GALLAND, commander of the Fighter Arm and unafraid of Göring, tried to force him to stand up to Hitler about the supply of fighters, but Göring only quailed before the Führer's opposition. In 1942 Albert SPEER was appointed Minister for Armaments, bringing real capacity for organization into the sphere of war production, where Göring still held the now empty rank of Economic Plenipotentiary. By the spring of 1944 Speer was delivering some 3,000 aircraft a month, but it was too late to affect the outcome of the war, and fuel was becoming scarce. Göring's last boast on behalf of the Luftwaffe was that he would keep General PAULUS supplied by air in the STALINGRAD salient during the desperate days of January 1943. But while German soldiers were dying from freezing and starvation before the final capitulation, Göring was holding his usual elaborate birthday celebrations in Berlin.

With the United States in the war, the bombing of Germany was redoubled after 1942, and Göring found it expedient to withdraw himself as far as Hitler would permit. His place in Hitler's esteem was taken by Goebbels, Himmler and Bormann.

Under cover of ill health Göring avoided every duty he could, gave way further to his drug addiction (he was swallowing up to 100 paracodeine pills a day) and concentrated on his vast art collection (valued after the war at $150 million), made up of gifts from industry and municipalities, purchases using state funds and depredations from Jewish art collections. The collection was kept principally at Carinhall, but also in his palaces in Berlin and in his southern castle of Mauterndorf. Late in 1944 Göring and his staff were preoccupied with organizing the removal of the principal collection from Carinhall to the south. Trainloads of treasures and furniture were evacuated in the weeks prior to the end of the war, while Göring himself traveled south accompanied by a fleet of cars, after saying good-bye to an indifferent Hitler on April 20, 1945.

Göring's egocentric but well-meant attempts to persuade Hitler to allow him to take over leadership in the Reich, radio-communicated to the bunker on April 23, cost him instant dismissal and house arrest by embarrassed SS men that night. Still regarding himself as Germany's plenipotentiary, however, Göring endeavored to surrender in style to the Americans on May 8, and after some feting (for which the U.S. Army commanders concerned were reprimanded by General EISENHOWER), he was flown on May 21 to the prison center reserved for important detainees in Mondorf, near Luxembourg. It was called Ashcan. Göring's attempts to ingratiate himself with his captors and to treat with Eisenhower "man to man" completely failed. He accepted normal prison conditions with good grace and consented to be taken off drugs, which caused him some temporary suffering but cleared his mind for the ordeal of the Nuremberg trial that began the following October.

Göring was inevitably the principal defendant. He regarded himself as spokesman for the regime and conducted at great length as brilliant a defense as was conceivably possible. But he was unable in the end to survive severe cross-examination, and he knew all along that a death sentence was inevitable. When refused execution by shooting instead of hanging, he took his own life on the night of October 15, 1946, using cyanide capsules he had successfully concealed throughout his captivity. He left a suicide letter for the American prison commandant, Colonel Andrus, which was only released for publication in September 1967. **R.M.**

GORSHKOV, Sergey G. (1910–). A talented Soviet admiral, commander of ships and formations in the Black Sea Squadron between 1931 and 1944. As commander of the Azov Military Flotilla, Gorshkov participated in the defense of the CRIMEA and the Caucasus and in the Battle of STALINGRAD. In 1944 he commanded the Danube Military Flotilla. Gorshkov ended the war as chief of the operations department, Black Sea Fleet. His strategic concepts were appreciated by STALIN's successors, and in 1956 he was appointed Commander in Chief of the Soviet Navy.

GORT, 6th Viscount (John Standish Surtees Prendergast Vereker) (1886–1946). A British Army officer with an outstanding reputation for gallantry in battle derived from his service in World War I—for which he won the VICTORIA CROSS, the DSO and two bars and the MILITARY CROSS—Gort was selected in 1937 as Chief of the Imperial General Staff over the heads of several senior officers, including Sir John DILL. As commander in chief of the BRITISH EXPEDITIONARY FORCE in France in 1939–40 he was unable to prevent the German victories in May, but his order that two divisions fill the gap between the British and Belgian armies in the face of the German offensive probably saved the BEF from annihilation. Relieved by Dill that same month, Gort then served as Inspector General to the Forces, 1940–41, as Commander in Chief GIBRALTAR, 1941–42, and as Commander in Chief MALTA, 1942–44, where his leadership was instrumental in saving the island from the Germans. Gort was promoted to field marshal in 1943. In 1944–45 he served as high commissioner and Commander in Chief Palestine and high commissioner for Transjordan.

GOTHA GO 229. One of many advanced fighters built by Germany at the end of the war. It was an all-wing turbojet-driven plane that never reached production. A prototype flew in 1944 but burned up; the Go 229A-0 flew 640 miles per hour.

GOTHA GO 242. German glider that could carry more than 2½ tons of cargo or 25 troops. Towed by JUNKERS JU 52s, they carried reinforcements and supplies to the forces in Africa.

GOTHIC LINE. The final German defense line in Italy, running across the peninsula above Florence, from south of La Spezia to Pesaro on the Adriatic. In front of it was a delaying line along the Arno River. It began receiving Allied pressure in August 1943 (British EIGHTH ARMY) and was successfully penetrated by British and American (FIFTH ARMY) forces.

GOTO, Aritomo (1888–1942). A Japanese rear admiral, Goto commanded the task force which captured GUAM on December 10, 1941. He later participated in the seizure of WAKE ISLAND, the Battle of the CORAL SEA and the attempted invasion of PORT MORESBY. He died during the Battle of CAPE ESPERANCE on October 12, 1942.

GOTT, William Henry Ewart (1897–1942). In the first years of the war, Gott—known as "Strafer"—was the most outstanding of the British desert commanders. As commander of the 7th Armored Division, EIGHTH

Army, he was prominent in British action against the Italian armies in Libya in 1941, and as commander of 13th Corps, Eighth Army, he was involved in the British defeat at Gazala. In August 1942, a lieutenant general, Gott was selected by Winston Churchill to be commander of the Eighth Army, but was killed en route to his command when his transport aircraft was shot down. He was replaced by Lt. Gen. Sir Bernard L. Montgomery, and the entire conduct of the desert war was thereby affected.

GOUMS. French colonial light infantry raised in Morocco. Established in 1908, Goums were originally native territorial troops or police used primarily to supplement regular French units in North Africa. Only after the outbreak of World War II were they slowly incorporated into the regular army. Each Goum consisted of 175 to 200 "goumiers" led by 10 or 12 French cadre. Four or five Goums were grouped into a *tabor,* and three tabors were joined to form a tabor group. At all levels mule teams provided most of the transportation, and the heaviest weapons carried were mortars and light antitank cannon. Four Moroccan tabor groups participated in World War II, taking part in the Italian and French campaigns of 1943–45.

Goumiers were known for their skill with the knife

GOURDOU-LESEURRE GL-810 and GL-812. These French light three-place observation and scout twin-float seaplanes, designed for use on warships or from coastal bases, entered service in 1931 and, despite their obsolescence, were still operational in some numbers with shore-based units during the war.

GOURDOU-LESEURRE GL-832 HY. French two-place catapult observation and scout twin-float seaplane. Along with the Potez 452 and GL-810 (above), it was the standard catapult plane for French cruisers in the mid-1930s. About 30 were built, of which eight were first-line equipment in the early stages of World War II.

GOVOROV, Leonid A. (1896–1955). Soviet general who served as a private in the Czar's army and then in the Red Army. An artilleryman, he was removed for a time during the purges of the 1930s but was restored and went on to fight in the Soviet-Finnish War. In the 1941 Battle of Moscow, Govorov, a lieutenant general, was deputy commander of the Moscow Reserve. He was given command of the Fifth Army after a few days as chief of the artillery on the Western Front. In 1942 Govorov was promoted to colonel general and commanded the Leningrad Front, breaking the encirclement of the city in January 1943. In June 1944 he took command of the successful offensive against Finland. Govorov was promoted to field marshal in 1944 and participated in operations in the Baltic area.

GRAHAM-BOWER, Ursula (1915–). British anthropologist who put her friendship with the Naga Hills people of northeast India to good use when Japanese forces surged across the border from Burma in 1944. She set up a system of watching and guarding trails which helped Allied prisoners escape from Burma. She also organized Naga ambushes of Japanese search parties. Her mother, in England, was quoted as saying of her: "an extraordinary girl."

GRAND ALLIANCE. Winston Churchill often used this term in referring to the coalition of the United States, the United Kingdom and the Soviet Union, although—at the suggestion of President Roosevelt—the alliance of all the powers fighting the Axis was officially called the United Nations. "Grand Alliance" had a special meaning for Churchill, since this term was applied to England and her allies in the War of the Spanish Succession (1701–14), in which Churchill's ancestor the Duke of Marlborough won fame.

GRAND MUFTI OF JERUSALEM. *See* Husseini.

GRAND QUARTIER GENERALE (GQG). One of the three headquarters maintained by the French high command in 1940; it was at Montry, east of Paris. Although its name—Grand General Headquarters—implies supremacy, the impression is misleading. Its Generalissimo, General Gamelin, maintained a separate "command post" at Vincennes, and the commander of the Northeast Front (i.e., the front against the Germans), General Georges, had his own headquarters at La Ferté-sous-Jouarre. GQG was under the direction of General Doumenc. Various sections of the staff were divided between Montry and La Ferté. No one has subsequently defended this arrangement as having any merit whatever. It was utterly inefficient, and communication among the three points was poor. This three-headed command seems to have resulted from domestic political factors and personal animosities, which took precedence over the needs of the time.

GRAND SLAM. A 22,000-pound bomb produced in experimental quantities, but too late for war use. It was first manufactured by the British, and then taken up in modified form by the United States. The British referred to it as a DP (deep penetration) bomb, while its American designation was T14.

GRANITE. Code name for U.S. overall plan for operations to be conducted in the Central Pacific. Granite was to begin with a carrier raid on TRUK on March 24, 1944, in support of an invasion of the ADMIRALTY ISLANDS and KAVIENG on New Ireland; capture of ENIWETOK and Ujelong Atolls in the MARSHALLS (Catchpole), May 1; capture of Mortlock and TRUK in the Carolines, August 1; invasion of the MARIANAS (Forager), November 1. If, however, Truk could be bypassed, it was proposed that the Palaus be invaded instead on August 1. Granite also alerted the U.S. Army 27th Division to be prepared to seize Eniwetok. Under Granite II, a revised plan, Truk and Kavieng were to be bypassed, the Forager date reset for June 15 (with SAIPAN and TINIAN included), to be followed by landings in the Palaus. The latter were rescheduled for September 15 with landings on PELELIU and ANGAUR. The final Central Pacific operation, with a tentative date of February 15, 1945, was to be either southern FORMOSA (Causeway) and Amoy or the island of Luzon. In October 1944 the Joint Chiefs of Staff canceled the Formosa-Amoy operation in favor of Luzon and OKINAWA.

GRANT TANK. British designation for a modified U.S. M3 TANK.

GRAVE. Dutch town, site of a 1,500-foot bridge across the Maas River that was one of the prime initial objectives of the U.S. 82D AIRBORNE DIVISION in the ARNHEM operation (September 17, 1944).

GRAY, Augustine Heard (1888–). "Gus" Gray, the U.S. Navy's "Oil King of the Pacific," served as a captain in Adm. Monroe KELLY's Northern Attack Group during the invasion of NORTHWEST AFRICA, in which he had charge of transports. His real distinction came in the Pacific, however, where, as a commodore, he commanded a service squadron under Vice-Adm. William L. CALHOUN. His work in logistics went a long way toward the goal of integrating tactics and logistics. His efficiency as a supplier of oil to the fighting ships is suggested by his nickname. Gray retired in 1947 as a rear admiral.

GRAZIANI, Rodolfo (1882–1955). Graziani entered the Italian Army in 1908 and saw hard fighting during World War I. He made a reputation for severity and cruelty, as well as for outstanding administrative ability, during succeeding service in Libya, as Governor of Libya (1930–34) and as Viceroy and Commander in Chief in Ethiopia in 1936–37, when he was made a marshal. He became Chief of Army Staff in 1939 and in 1940 was named Commander in Chief of the Armed Forces in Libya.

In advancing against Egypt, he moved slowly. When MUSSOLINI ordered him to get going, he did so feeling, according to Count CIANO, that he was moving into a struggle between "a flea and an elephant." After the defeat at BEDA FOMM he left North Africa and resigned his post.

Graziani became the Minister of War in Mussolini's Fascist puppet government in 1943. He was captured by Italian partisans in April 1945 and indicted for high treason. In May 1950 a military court sentenced him to prison, but he was freed by amnesty in August and thereafter became a leader of the Italian Social Movement Party.

GREAT ARTISTE, THE. Maj. Charles W. Sweeney's B-29, which served as an observation plane during the HIROSHIMA mission, August 6, and the NAGASAKI mission, August 9, 1945.

GREATER EAST ASIA CO-PROSPERITY SPHERE. Term the Japanese used to designate a "new order" in Asia, including areas they had determined to seize during their early war efforts. The sphere was also intended to include territories under Japanese domination as a result of World War I agreements and strategic areas they had already seized before December 1941, i.e., industrial regions (Korea, Manchuria, China) and sources of raw materials (French Indochina, Malaya, Burma, the Philippines and the Netherlands East Indies). It was around the Co-Prosperity Sphere that the Japanese prepared their defensive perimeter. They felt that the quick occupation and development of this region would lead to a negotiated peace, leaving Japan in possession of the territory.

GREAT MARIANAS TURKEY SHOOT. U.S. Navy nickname given to the aerial portion of the Battle of the PHILIPPINE SEA, in which over 200 Japanese aircraft were downed while attacking the American FAST CARRIER TASK FORCE (June 19, 1944).

GREAT PATRIOTIC WAR (Velíkaya Otéchestvennaya Voina). The official Soviet name for the 1941–45 war with Germany and the brief 1945 Soviet campaign in the Far East.

GREAT SATURN. *See* SATURN.

GRECHKO, Andrei A. (1903–1976). Beginning his long career during the Russian Civil War, Grechko rose through the Red Army ranks as a cavalryman and officer. One of Gen. Boris SHAPOSHNIKOV's protégés, he graduated from the Frunze Military Academy in 1936 and the General Staff Academy in 1941. That same year he commanded first a cavalry division and later a cavalry corps. In April 1942 Grechko was promoted to the command of the Twelfth Army. In the next year and a half he commanded the Forty-seventh, Eighteenth and Fifty-sixth Armies and, in October 1943, became deputy commander of the First Ukrainian Front. Two months later, General of the Army Grechko was given command of the First Guards Army, a post he retained until the end of the war.

GREECE—CIVIL WAR. The underground political life of Greece during the German occupation was complicated in the extreme, but as time passed the Communist-led National Liberation Front (*see* EAM), by dint of its long experience in working underground and its savage internal discipline, became the dominant power. Its chief rival was the liberal-republican EDES (National Democratic Army) of Col. Napoleon ZERVAS. The royalist government-in-exile could count on the support of only the small organization of unemployed Army officers (the EOA), which operated in a limited area of the northern Peloponnesus. Nowhere in Greece could any of these organizations count on the support of the rural masses, whose political attitude was indifference. Their support was gained by judicious use of terrorism. Recruits were gotten the same way. British irritation at what they considered to be the internal squabbling of the resistance groups resulted in the signing of a "National Bands Agreement" by the EAM/ELAS (ELAS was the National Popular Liberation Army, the military arm of EAM), the EDES and the Socialist Party in July 1943.

Most of the effective acts of sabotage against the Germans and Italians during the occupation were carried out by special teams of British agents with the reluctant support of the EAM/ELAS. On its own, it did only enough to ensure British support and supplies. By October 12, 1943, the EAM/ELAS felt secure enough to launch a broad attack against all other guerrilla forces in Greece, particularly the EDES. The Greek civil war can be said to have begun then. The EAM/ELAS moved with an openness that caused some to allege that it had entered a secret truce with the Germans, although it is more likely that the Germans simply stood aside to let the rival Greeks go at each other.

In February 1944 British pressure once again brought about an armistice, the so-called Plaka agreement, which was signed on February 29. The KKE (Communist Party) now moved from military to political action. On March 26 a rival government to the exiled royalist one in London was set up in the mountains as the Political Committee of National Liberation (PEEA). The Soviet Union immediately recognized it as the official Greek government. British pressure was once again brought to bear, and the PEEA agreed to abridge temporarily its independent status and accept a number of cabinet positions in the royalist government-in-exile.

The EAM/ELAS used 1944 to consolidate its position, recruiting personnel and establishing training centers. It even initiated a naval program and at one time had 100 small armed vessels operating. The British had by now become somewhat wary of the goals of their putative allies, and as British support waned, Russian support took its place. Greece now became part of a larger international picture. Allied agreements had assigned the Balkans to the Soviet Union, but Winston CHURCHILL had insisted at a meeting in Moscow in October 1944 that Greece be excepted. At a conference at Caserta, Italy, in September 1944 pledges had been exacted from Gen. Stephanos SARAPHIS of ELAS and Colonel Zervas of EDES to cooperate with the British Army when it arrived. Both organizations were assigned "spheres of influence." In fact, the Germans left more or less of their own accord when the advance of the Red Army made their position untenable.

Sensing the end, EAM/ELAS began aggressively extending its area of control. In October 1944 a hastily put together British force occupied strategic positions throughout Greece and an "Operation Rat Week," a program of harassing the retreating Germans, was put into effect. The royalist George PAPANDREOU was installed in Athens, but King GEORGE agreed not to return until a plebiscite on the question of the monarchy was held. The more significant actions occurred in the northern Balkans. There by November, Communist regimes were in power in Albania, Yugoslavia and Bulgaria—all across Greece's rugged frontier.

EAM/ELAS quietly but forcefully began pushing out rival EDES forces throughout Greece. The weakness of the British forces in Athens and Salonika was duly noted. A powerful international press campaign was launched portraying EAM/ELAS as rural reformers and dedicated killers of Germans. British GHQ in Athens was reluctant to do anything to impede their takeover of the country. In the countryside outside Athens thousands of people were arrested and shot, wholesale massacres occurring in some places as EAM moved to exterminate all its enemies. When noted at all, these events were presented in the press as execution of collaborators or "Fascist elements." The Papandreou government became increasingly helpless as its representatives were not allowed into the hinterland. EAM now began to infiltrate Athens with thousands of agents, and a number of its combat units were pulled around the city.

Gen. Sir Ronald SCOBIE, heading the British GHQ, began nervously urging negotiation on General Saraphis. Saraphis stalled, then agreed to merge ELAS with a new national army and relinquish his police functions to the government in return for concessions. In fact, he was furiously preparing an armed takeover of the country.

On December 2, 1944, he struck. A demonstration was held in Athens which soon became a riot. A general strike was called. ELAS uniformed troops moved into the Athens suburbs, and EDES forces all over Greece were attacked. By the 4th, British troops were engaged with Saraphis's forces in both Athens and Salonika, and it appeared that they would be overcome. Thus, while the war in Europe had months more to go, the world was treated to the spectacle of the hot beginning of the Cold War. Field Marshal ALEXANDER (who became Supreme Allied Commander, Mediterranean, on the 19th) flew into Athens and observed how desperate the situation was.

On December 12, EAM/ELAS asked what would be the British cease-fire terms. General Scobie said that ELAS must desist and evacuate Attica. Fighting continued. At this time the British were receiving extremely harsh criticism in the international press, particularly in America. Even nominally conservative papers portrayed the British as the aggressors. In spite of this, British forces were reinforced and were able gradually to secure the Athens and Salonika regions. On Christmas Eve 1944, Winston Churchill came to Greece and presided over a conference held at Athens. All parties were represented, and little was accomplished other than to name Archbishop DAMASKINOS as regent. The American press criticism had now become intense.

On the fighting front EAM/ELAS was giving way to the British, but in the hinterland it virtually destroyed the EDES and other rival guerrilla forces. The combination of enormous quantities of German supplies and a vigorous terrorist campaign gave EAM/ELAS the upper hand everywhere. On January 15, 1945, a cease-fire went into effect. Out of 75,000 British troops engaged, there were 2,100 casualties, including 237 killed. ELAS casualties were no doubt higher, and no one knows how many anti-Communist Greeks were killed. One result of ELAS savagery in the countryside was the enormous increase in the numbers and power of the most extreme right-wing of all Greek underground forces, the theretofore insignificant X organization led by the fanatical royalist Gen. George Grivas. It quickly replaced the now virtually destroyed liberal EDES as EAM/ELAS's most dangerous foe. In terrorist activity, X was willing to match EAM/ELAS atrocity for atrocity.

As World War II ended, the nervous truce between the rival Greek forces continued. On February 12, 1946, the civil war broke out again, and this time it would not end until the United States had become deeply enmeshed in this violent chapter in the Cold War. **W.O.**

GREENOCK. This Scottish port was one of the three operational bases of the WESTERN APPROACHES Command.

GREENWOOD, Arthur (1880–1954). British politician who in the 1930s was a prominent spokesman for the Labour Party in foreign affairs, criticizing strongly the government's policy in Manchuria, Abyssinia and Spain. As deputy party leader to Clement ATTLEE after 1935, he argued consistently for Britain to resist outside aggression. In 1940, as a leading Labourite, he entered the War Cabinet as minister without portfolio, acquiring responsibility for postwar reconstruction; he was responsible for the appointment of the famous BEVERIDGE committee. In February 1942, however, he was removed from the government.

GREER, U.S.S. WICKES-class destroyer, commissioned in 1918. In reserve when the European war broke out in 1939, *Greer* was recommissioned for service in the Atlantic and Caribbean. As the United States edged closer to war in the Atlantic, *Greer* found herself en route to Iceland on September 4, 1941, with passengers and mail for the American garrison stationed there. At 0840 a patrolling British airplane signaled to her that a U-boat had crash-dived about 10 miles ahead to escape attack by the bomber. *Greer* increased speed and began to zigzag as she headed for the submarine's reported position; she went to battle stations and began a SONAR search. At 0920 she made sound contact with the submerged submarine; she maneuvered to retain contact and began to broadcast plain-language position reports as current operating instructions required. Forty minutes later the British aircraft asked whether *Greer* intended to attack. Receiving a negative reply, the British pilot dropped four depth bombs and departed at 1100. *Greer* continued to track the U-boat; at 1240 the submarine turned and fired a single torpedo, which passed astern of the ship. *Greer* then attacked, dropping a pattern of depth charges; the submarine replied with a second torpedo, which missed. The destroyer had now lost sound contact and began to search for the U-boat. At 1415 a British destroyer arrived on the scene and proposed a coordinated search. *Greer* declined, and the British ship left. About an hour later *Greer*, believing that she had regained contact with the U-boat, dropped another depth-charge pattern, without result. Contact was again lost; *Greer* searched until 1840 before breaking off her effort and resuming her voyage.

This incident was first announced by the Navy without comment, but on September 11 President ROOSEVELT declared in a radio speech that the U-boat had made a "deliberate" and unprovoked attack on *Greer*, whose identity was "unmistakable." Roosevelt called this an act of "piracy," and made public orders that had already been placed in effect. These were the "shoot on sight" orders. The first of these had been given late in July 1941, when Admiral Ernest J. KING ordered Atlantic Fleet convoy escort ships and aircraft to attack Axis submarines or surface raiders on sight; the second came on September 1, when this order was extended to patrolling ships and planes not operating with convoys.

Greer remained on Atlantic convoy and patrol duty into early 1944, when she was relegated to training and utility work. She decommissioned in July 1945 and was sold for scrap.

GREIF. Code name for a special German brigade under Lt. Col. Otto SKORZENY, scheduled to seize bridges over the Meuse River and spread confusion in American rear positions during the Battle of the BULGE. Skorzeny tried to recruit German soldiers who spoke the American idiom, but only 150 of a force of 2,000 so qualified. Nor were enough captured American uniforms, vehicles and equipment available to outfit the entire force as planned. Only a few of Skorzeny's men made it through American lines and none reached the Meuse bridges, but as word of the operation spread, sentries double-checked all who passed and military police bolstered the guards of senior commanders.

GREIM, Robert Ritter von (1892–1945). A much-decorated veteran of World War I, Ritter von Greim was one of the abler LUFTWAFFE high officers in World War II. He commanded an air corps and an air fleet on the Eastern Front. On April 24, 1945, he was summoned from Munich to Berlin by Adolf HITLER; he was flown by Hanna REITSCH, the famous woman test pilot. On the last leg of the trip (the evening of the 26th) the plane was hit over the Tiergarten in Berlin by enemy fire, von Greim suffering an injury to his foot. When he arrived at the Führerbunker, he was informed that he was now Commander in Chief of the Luftwaffe, in succession to Hermann GÖRING, and a field marshal. On April 29 the Führer gave him another mission—to arrest Heinrich HIMMLER, regarded by Hitler as a traitor for attempting to deal with the Western powers. None of these promotions and orders could have substantive significance at this point; when von Greim was captured soon afterward by American troops, he observed that "I am head of the Luftwaffe but I have no Luftwaffe." He committed suicide on May 24, 1945.

GRENADE. Code name for the U.S. NINTH ARMY's portion of Field Marshal MONTGOMERY's post-BULGE double envelopment which was designed to result in a link-up on the Rhine River with Operation VERITABLE being executed by the CANADIAN FIRST ARMY. Owing to high water in the Roer River (the enemy opened dams), the operation, planned for February 10, 1945, was not launched until the 23d. It was extremely successful.

GRETTON, Sir Peter W. (1912–). Royal Navy admiral who made a considerable reputation for himself as a brilliant commander of convoy escort groups during the war. Ill health after the war cut short a promising naval career, Gretton having to resign as a vice-admiral holding the post of Deputy Chief of the Naval Staff.

GREW, Joseph Clark (1880–1965). U.S. foreign service official who began his career with diplomatic posts in Cairo, Mexico City, St. Petersburg (Leningrad) and Berlin. After World War I he was envoy to Denmark and then Switzerland. In 1927 he was made ambassador to Turkey, a post he held until 1932, when he was appointed ambassador to Japan. Generally conciliatory in his relations with the Japanese, Grew relayed the distress of the United States over Japanese encroachment in China in 1939. As early as January 1941 he passed on to the State Department the rumor he had picked up that Japan had plans for a "surprise mass attack at Pearl Harbor in case of 'trouble' with the United States." After the attack on PEARL HARBOR, Grew and his staff were confined in Tokyo and not returned to the United States until the summer of 1942. In 1944, despite controversy over his opinion that the Emperor of Japan should be retained on the throne, he was appointed Under Secretary of State. He retired in 1945.

GRIDLEY, U.S.S. Destroyer and class (1,725 tons; four 5-inch guns; eight to sixteen 21-inch torpedo tubes; 38 to 40 knots). Ten ships of this class commissioned in 1937. Torpedo tubes were arranged in four quadruple mounts, two each to either beam. Detail plans for eight ships were drawn by the Navy; these eight ships are sometimes referred to in contemporary publications as the Bagley class. The first two ships, *Gridley* and *Craven*, were built to details drawn up by Bethlehem Steel, and differ in details from their sisters. Light antiaircraft guns were added during the war years, with much topside detail being removed to make room. Most of these ships kept their original 16 tubes, unlike the later BENHAM class. Three were war losses. Some contemporary publications refer to the Gridley class as the Craven class.

GRIFFITH, Samuel Blair, II (1906–). U.S. Marine officer. Before the United States entered the war, Griffith and a fellow Marine officer made an inspection tour of British commando training facilities. The experience stood him in good stead as executive and later commanding officer of the 1st Raider Battalion (EDSON's Raiders) in operations on GUADALCANAL and NEW GEORGIA. He received the NAVY CROSS for heroic action during the battle of the Matanikau on Guadalcanal, September 27, 1942, when he refused to relinquish command of the troops despite his severe wounds, because he was the only surviving field-grade officer in the unit. For his conduct in command of the battalion during the New Georgia campaign in the period July 7–10, 1943, he was awarded the Army DISTINGUISHED SERVICE CROSS.

Griffith returned to Quantico, Va., to command the Officer Candidate School in 1944, and before the war ended in the Pacific he went back to command the 21st Marines, 3d Marine Division, on Guam. He retired in 1956 as a brigadier general and entered Oxford University, where he was awarded a doctorate in Chinese military history.

GROMYKO, Andrei A. (1909–). Longtime Soviet Foreign Minister, an agricultural economist by education, Gromyko entered the foreign service in 1939 as head of the Department of American Countries. After serving in the embassy in Washington as counselor, in 1943 he was appointed to succeed Maxim LITVINOV as ambassador to the United States and Cuba. He was a representative of the USSR at various international meetings, including DUMBARTON OAKS, the founding meeting of the UNITED NATIONS at SAN FRANCISCO, and at YALTA and POTSDAM.

GROVES, Leslie Richard (1896–1970). U.S. Army engineer officer, who graduated from West Point in 1918 after a year at the University of Washington and two years at the Massachusetts Institute of Technology. In 1941 he was deputy chief of Army construction. In September 1942 he was promoted to brigadier general and given command of the super-secret MANHATTAN DISTRICT, the cover for the Allied ATOMIC BOMB project. Groves was the man-who-gets-things-done type, a driving force who kept the operation organized, controlled and moving. Under his charge installations such as those at LOS ALAMOS, OAK RIDGE and HANFORD were built. In 1944 he was promoted to major general.

Certainly a primary factor in the success of the atomic program was the forceful leadership provided by Groves. He supervised the expenditure of more than $2 billion and the work of more than 125,000 people.

GRUENTHER, Alfred Maximilian (1899–). U.S. Army officer, a graduate of West Point in the class of 1917 (although he was not commissioned until 1918 because of a surplus of second lieutenants). Despite this delayed beginning, Gruenther went on to become renowned for the brilliance of his staff work, during World War II becoming known in many quarters as the "brain of the Army." In 1941–42 he was chief of staff of the Third Army. He then was named deputy chief of staff of Allied Force Headquarters (General EISENHOWER's headquarters for planning the NORTHWEST AFRICA operation). In 1943 Gruenther became chief of staff of the FIFTH ARMY and the Army's youngest major general; he was the principal planner of the U.S. landings on SICILY and at SALERNO and ANZIO. In 1944 he moved as chief of staff with the Fifth Army commander, Gen. Mark CLARK, when Clark was appointed to command of the 15th Army Group in Italy. Between 1953 and his retirement in 1956, Gruenther was Supreme Allied Commander in Europe (NATO). Even as a junior officer Gruenther became internationally known as an expert bridge player, referee and writer on the subject.

GRUPPENHORCHGERÄT (GHG). A German multi-unit hydrophone consisting of numerous receivers fitted in pattern on either side of the hull of a submarine or light surface ship. It was also fitted to the hull of the heavy cruiser PRINZ EUGEN, which used it during the

BISMARCK-VS.-HOOD engagement in 1941; it was not known until after the war that the German Navy had used this type of passive SONAR in so large a ship. U-boats used GHG as an accurate directional hydrophone with an effective range up to 10 miles under good conditions.

GUADALCANAL. On August 7, 1942, in the first American offensive of the war, Maj. Gen. Alexander A. VANDEGRIFT's 1st Marine Division made successful landings in the SOLOMON ISLANDS on Guadalcanal, Gavutu and TULAGI. Fortunately, there was no enemy opposition to the assault, with the exception of two Japanese air raids in the afternoon, for the debarkation of men and supplies, which had begun smoothly in the morning, turned into chaos. While wheeled and tracked vehicles and artillery moved inland, supplies began piling up on the beaches in disorder, and marines in later waves wandered around looking for someone to tell them where to go. The move inland lagged, and as night fell, defensive lines were set. Despite the absence of any Japanese, the darkness was punctured by the fire of nervous and trigger-happy marines who began seeing things in the night. Nonetheless, discipline and order were soon restored.

Late on the afternoon of the 8th, the 5th Marines moved straight ahead to gain the airfield, while the 1st Marines circled around and entered it from the inland or southern side. The landings had apparently taken the Japanese by surprise, and they had fled into the jungle in disarray. But during the night of August 8, a Japanese cruiser force came down the SLOT into Sealark Channel and shattered Australian Rear Adm. V. A. C. CRUTCHLEY's screening force in the Battle of SAVO ISLAND. With this force gone, what remained of the invasion fleet sailed away in face of the strong Japanese naval threat, with some marines and most of the supplies still on board. Fortunately, in their haste to go, the Japanese had abandoned heavy construction equipment, which the marines used to good advantage to complete the airfield the Japanese had been building. Vandegrift was left with 11,145 men on Guadalcanal and 6,805 others who had landed on Gavutu and Tulagi and were still on those islands.

In Tokyo on August 8, Imperial General Headquarters ordered Lt. Gen. Harukichi HYAKUTAKE to drive the Americans off Guadalcanal; to accomplish this mission, he was given 50,000 men and command of the 17th Army, based on RABAUL. He quickly began a series of day and night bombings of Guadalcanal. Meanwhile, the waters around the island were controlled by the Japanese Navy—until August 20 when American fighters and dive-bombers arrived. The field they landed on was named HENDERSON FIELD in honor of Maj. Lofton R. Henderson, a Marine pilot who had been killed in the Battle of MIDWAY in June.

In his eagerness to rid Guadalcanal of the Americans, General Hyakutake sent in Col. Kiyono ICHIKI's force to attack the eastern perimeter of the 1st Division. On the night of August 20 the Ichiki force threw itself against Marine positions on the western bank of the Ilu River (mistakenly identified in the early stages of the battle as the TENARU). Twice Ichiki attacked, only to be thwarted both times. Because the continued existence of a Japanese force here was too great a threat to his meager force, Vandegrift ordered a reserve battalion to cross upstream of the river and swing north and around in an envelopment of the enemy. In the late afternoon of the 21st, after being completely encircled by the marines and subjected to bombing and strafing

Japanese dead after Tenaru River battle on Guadalcanal

from the planes which had landed the day before, the Ichiki force was no longer effective as a military unit. Only a handful of the soldiers, led by Colonel Ichiki himself, escaped into the jungle and headed east for Taivu, farther up the coast. Here Ichiki burned his regimental colors and committed hara-kiri.

This was the first in a number of attempts to throw the Americans off the island. Shortly thereafter, Edson's Raiders, who had made the Tulagi landing, were brought to Guadalcanal and on September 7–8 raided the Japanese base at Taivu, acquiring considerable intelligence information. They learned, for instance, that Maj. Gen. Kiyotake KAWAGUCHI's reinforced 35th Brigade had already landed on Guadalcanal and was preparing for an attack on Henderson Field. The Raiders and the remnants of the 1st Parachute Battalion, which had faced a determined enemy on Gavutu and Tanambogo, were formed into a composite battalion under Col. Merritt A. EDSON and on September 12 moved to a low grassy ridge a mile south of the airfield. That afternoon the ridge, rather than the airfield as had been customary in the previous days, was subjected to heavy bombing, heralding a ground attack. Shortly after nightfall a Japanese cruiser and three destroyers began shelling the ridge while Kawaguchi's troops probed Edson's positions without success. He tried again on the night of the 13th, but was driven back once more, losing 1,200 men in the two attempts. This fighting was to go down in history as the Battle of BLOODY RIDGE, and for his outstanding leadership and heroism Colonel Edson was awarded the MEDAL OF HONOR.

Undaunted by their heavy losses, the Japanese continued to pour men onto Guadalcanal, landing them at night from barges and transports at CAPE ESPERANCE, on the coast about 25 miles west of Henderson Field. In September and October, Hyakutake was able to bring in about 20,000 men in this manner. At the same time, Vandegrift also was receiving reinforcements. The 7th Marines, third infantry regiment of the 1st Division, was brought in from Samoa, and later the Army 164th Infantry of the AMERICAL DIVISION, a total of 6,000 men, was landed and put into the line, now giving the Marine general more than 23,000 Americans on the island. Not all were effectives, however, for malaria, which is endemic to Guadalcanal, was taking its toll together with battle casualties.

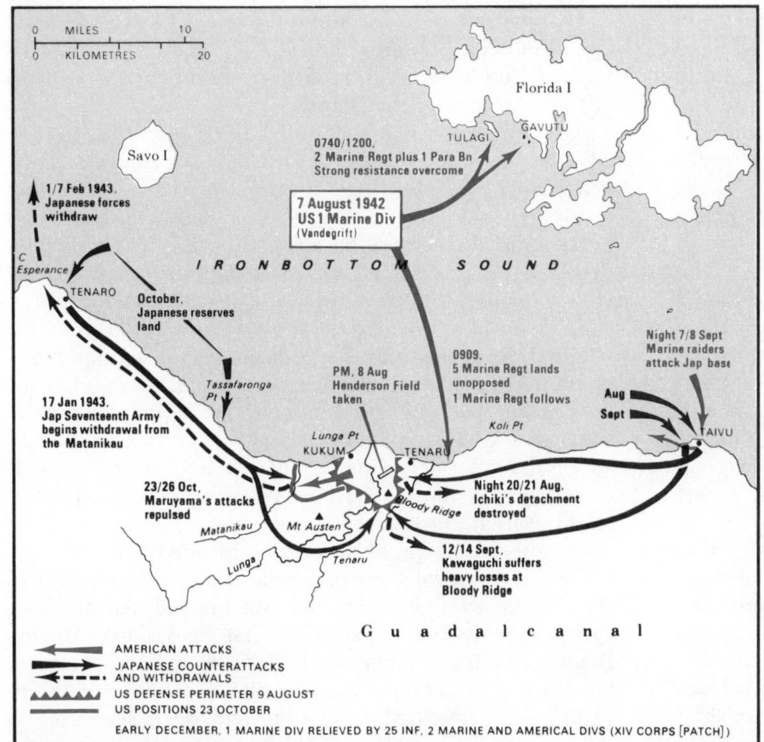

GUADALCANAL—the campaign that saw the United States take the offensive in the Pacific

On October 23 Hyakutake attacked with 5,600 men of his 2d (Sendai) Division across the Matanikau River; he was forced back in the face of heavy artillery fire. He attacked the next night, with the same results, and was forced to withdraw on the 25th, leaving behind some 3,500 dead. It was time now for the Americans to go on the offensive. On November 4, Vandegrift was reinforced by the 8th Marines of the 2d Marine Division and began widening his perimeter. Also on the 4th, the 2d Raider Battalion (CARLSON's Raiders) landed at Aola Bay some 40 miles east of the LUNGA River—near the site of the initial landings on August 7—to begin an epic 150-mile month-long trek through the jungle. In the course of it, the Raiders fought more than a dozen actions, killing 500 of the enemy and driving the rest into the interior.

In a two-day battle beginning late on the 19th, two Marine battalions ran head-on into Hyakutake, who once more was heading for the airfield. The Japanese were forced to do an about-face and leave the area, but not without heavy losses.

The third regiment of the Americal Division, the 132d Infantry, arrived on December 8, at which time the command of the island was passed from Vandegrift to Maj. Gen. Alexander M. PATCH. That same day, the

5th Marines sailed for Australia, followed soon after by the remainder of the division and other Marine support units. A few days later the Americal Division was joined by the Army 25th Infantry Division. The XIV Corps, as Patch's command was now designated, began a drive to the west, closing in on Cape Esperance on February 9, 1943. However, Hyakutake had successfully evacuated 13,000 men, despite continuous heavy pounding by American air and naval forces. In the six-month campaign, the Japanese lost approximately 25,000 dead, 600 planes and 24 ships. Marine losses were 1,044 dead, 2,894 wounded and 55 missing. U.S. Army casualties were 446 dead, 1,910 wounded. In the naval battles off the island, Allied losses were the same as the Japanese, 24 ships, but Japanese loss in tonnage was greater.

On February 9, 1943, organized resistance on Guadalcanal ended. **B.M.F.**

An important aspect of the Guadalcanal operation was the naval actions, which included the Battle of Savo Island, the Battle of the EASTERN SOLOMONS, the Battle of Cape Esperance, the Battle of SANTA CRUZ and the climactic engagement that determined the outcome of the campaign, the naval battle of Guadalcanal, fought November 12–15, 1942.

It began on the afternoon of November 12 with a Japanese bomber attack on American transports in Lunga Roads. The attack was easily beaten off by the Americans, with numbers of the Bettys being downed by antiaircraft fire. That night, however, the air attack was followed by the arrival of a strong Japanese surface force—a TOKYO EXPRESS, under the command of Vice-Adm. Hiroake ABE, including two battleships, a light cruiser and destroyers. This was actually a bombardment group sent to dispose of the U.S. Marine force at Henderson Field. It encountered the transport escort groups, commanded by Rear Adm. Daniel J. CALLAGHAN and Rear Adm. Norman SCOTT, Callaghan being the officer in tactical command. A wild melee resulted in the small hours of the 13th. The Japanese battleship HIEI was severely crippled and two destroyers were sunk; on the American side, two cruisers, the ATLANTA and the JUNEAU, were sunk, as well as four destroyers. Next morning American carrier fliers finished off the damaged *Hiei*. Both American admirals were killed in the action, but they had managed to thwart the Japanese bombardment mission.

That night the Japanese returned with two heavy cruisers, which battered Henderson Field for more than half an hour. On the following day (November 14) a force of 11 Japanese transports commanded by Rear Adm. Raizo TANAKA was pounced on by Navy and Marine Corps fliers from Henderson Field and from the carrier ENTERPRISE. Six of the Japanese transports went down. Tanaka, however, landed his surviving troops on Guadalcanal.

Meanwhile Vice-Adm. Nobutake KONDO's bombardment group—consisting of the battleship KIRISHIMA, two cruisers and 14 destroyers—was en route to Guadalcanal, his mission being to cover Tanaka's transports. However, powerful American forces were likewise on the move about 100 miles south of Guadalcanal—the battleships WASHINGTON and SOUTH DAKOTA, with destroyers, under the command of Rear Adm. Willis LEE. The two fleets met in IRONBOTTOM SOUND, the clash beginning about three-quarters of an hour before midnight on the 14th. The American destroyers were put out of action early in the fight, two of them being sunk; Lee was thus deprived of any destroyer screen, and a further disaster occurred when the *South Dakota* suffered a power failure. This left the *Washington* to carry the fight to the enemy, which she did with great effectiveness. The *Kirishima* was battered by 16-inch and smaller shells and put out of action within a few minutes; she was scuttled early the next morning. Two Japanese cruisers took heavy fire and were put out of action for a number of months. Five American destroyers were damaged, one of them being sunk by American gunfire after the battle. The *South Dakota* took 42 hits from Japanese big guns but survived.

The battle was over in less than two hours. Kondo began withdrawing at 0025; the *Washington* pursued the retreating Japanese for some minutes. Thus ended the last large-scale Japanese attempt to reinforce the garrison on Guadalcanal. The Americans now took control of the seas around the island.

GUAM. At 1115 on December 8, 1941 (December 7, Pearl Harbor time), three hours after the military governor of Guam received word that PEARL HARBOR had been attacked, SAIPAN-based Japanese bombers began the first in a series of raids on Guam. At that time Guam's only protection was a 153-man Marine garrison, an 80-man Insular Guard Force, an ill-armed and -trained volunteer naval militia and 271 regular Navy personnel. The heaviest weapons on the island were .30-caliber machine guns. Faced with a Japanese invasion force of nearly 6,000 troops, Guam was forced to surrender on December 10, after a defense of sorts. It would be two and a half years before the Americans could even attempt to win it back.

On July 21, 1944, after 13 days of one of the heaviest pre-invasion naval gunfire preparations of any target in the Pacific to that date, the Marine III Amphibious Corps (3d Marine Division and 1st Provisional Marine Brigade, with the Army 77th Division in corps reserve) landed on Guam. By nightfall the two beachheads invaded by the two Marine units had been secured. By August 10, Ritidian Point at the north of the island was reached and the island declared secure. However, mopping up continued well into 1945.

GUBBINS, Sir Colin McVean (1896–1976). British Army officer, a specialist in guerrilla tactics, sabotage and other forms of irregular warfare. A native of the Hebrides, he saw varied service in the interwar years and at the outbreak of World War II was chief of the British military mission to Poland; he was responsible for saving much of the Polish knowledge of the German cipher machine ENIGMA. In 1940 he served with the COMMANDOS and helped found the SPECIAL OPERATIONS EXECUTIVE. In 1943 he succeeded to the title of "D"—chief of the SOE. His highest wartime rank was major general.

GUDERIAN, Heinz (1888–1954). Germany Army officer, a pioneer of tank warfare and one of its outstanding practitioners in World War II; he has been called, with good reason, the architect of the panzer forces. The son of an officer, he was born at Kulm on the Vistula. After service as a staff officer in World War I, he became an advocate of mechanized and armored warfare. His theories attracted the attention of Adolf HITLER in 1935 and he received rapid promotion, becoming Chief of Mobile Troops, with the rank of General der Panzertruppen, in 1938. In Poland in September 1939, as commander of the XIX Corps, he proved the soundness of his *Blitzkrieg* theories. He supported the idea of attacking in the west in 1940 through the ARDENNES, and in May his panzer corps made the fateful crossing of the Meuse at SEDAN and thrust with astonishing speed across northern France, thus giving dramatic proof that armored forces were capable of fast, independent action—and thereby cutting off the Allied armies in Belgium. The impetuosity of his drive seems to have surprised some of his own superiors as well as the British and French commanders. In July 1940 he was promoted to colonel general.

In October 1941 Guderian was appointed to command of the Second Panzer Army in Russia, but after quarreling with Hitler and with his superior, Field Marshal von KLUGE, he fell out of favor and was removed from his post. In March 1943, however, after the defeat at STALINGRAD, Hitler turned to him, appointing him Inspector General of Armored Troops. In July 1944, immediately after the attempt to assassinate Hitler, the Führer appointed Guderian acting Chief of the General Staff in succession to Gen. Kurt ZEITZLER. In this position he had occasion to differ openly with Hitler as Germany's fortunes declined, and on March 28, 1945, he was sent on leave.

Guderian was a pivotal figure in the war. If he had not been in command at the Sedan breakthrough, the entire Battle of FRANCE might well have gone differently, with incalculable consequences.

General Guderian

GUILLAUME, Augustin (1895–). French general who served in North Africa before and during World War II. In 1943–44 he commanded Algerian troops fighting with the Allies and in 1944–45 led his forces into Alsace and then Germany. He rose to become Chief of Staff of French forces after the war. He is also a distinguished military writer.

GUISAN, Henri (1874–1960). An agronomist and then a full-time citizen-soldier in the Swiss tradition, General Guisan commanded Switzerland's armed forces during World War II. His discreetly pro-Allied stance favored Allied intelligence operations in this vital neutral base inside occupied Europe.

GULF SEA FRONTIER. U.S. Navy designation for the SEA FRONTIER command responsible for the defense of the U.S. East Coast from the Georgia-Florida line to Mexico.

GULLION, Allen Wyatt (1880–1946). U.S. Army officer who organized and became the first head of the Provost Marshal-General's Department, a post he held between 1941 and 1944. He then joined Gen. Dwight D. EISENHOWER'S staff in France and was later chief of the displaced persons branch of Allied headquarters.

GUMRAK. Village west of STALINGRAD, site of headquarters of General PAULUS. The Gumrak airfield was the last one remaining in German hands.

GUN FIRE CONTROL SYSTEM. A term developed late in the war by the U.S. Navy to refer to an entire complex of devices used, in combination, to control the shooting of naval guns. It was generally given to integrated combinations of equipment designed for use with medium- and smaller-caliber dual-purpose antiaircraft guns, and was not normally retroactively applied. It was also called fire control.

GUNN, Paul I. (1900–1957). A veteran of 21 years with the U.S. Navy and the Marine Corps, "Pappy" Gunn was living in the Philippines at the outbreak of the Pacific war. He was employed as a pilot and operations manager by the Philippine Air Lines. After December 7, 1941—using the firm's five twin-engine Beechcrafts, and later shifting to Army transports—Gunn and his pilots shuttled men and supplies throughout the embattled islands and then helped with the evacuation to Australia. There he helped organize an air transport service for the SOUTHWEST PACIFIC theater. He also experimented with the installation of batteries of forward-firing guns in the noses of A-20s and B-25s, improvisations that paid off handsomely in the destruction of enemy shipping (*see* A-20; B-25).

GURKHA. The family name of the ruling house of Nepal, used to denote Nepalese troops serving as mercenaries in the British Army. During World War II Gurkhas fought with great distinction in East Africa, North Africa, Italy and Burma and elsewhere in Southeast Asia. They have served Britain with enormous loyalty in every theater of war since their incorporation after the Indian Mutiny and are now the only non-British troops to have the honor of mounting guard at the royal palaces.

GUSEV, Fedor T. (1905–). Soviet diplomat who entered the foreign service in 1937 and during the war was ambassador to Canada (1942–43) and to Great Britain (1943–46). In the latter post he also served as Soviet representative on the EUROPEAN ADVISORY COMMISSION, and he was an adviser at the Allied conferences at TEHERAN, YALTA and POTSDAM.

GUSTAV. Name the Germans gave to one of two 80-cm. Kanone E (Eisenbahnlafette—railroad gun) L40-6s. Gustav was the war's largest gun and the largest ever built. Krupp began the design in 1937 and completed production in 1943. The only record of operational use was at the siege of SEVASTOPOL. The weapon traveled in sections to the site and was then assembled; the mounting straddled two sets of standard-gauge tracks with 80 wheels holding the 1,350-ton weight. A 250-man crew was required for assembly and firing, and a special detachment of 4,120 men commanded by a major general was needed to man, maintain and protect it; a colonel and 500 men were needed for day-to-day operation. A 1¾-ton propelling charge threw a 7½-ton concrete-piercing shell 23 miles or a 5-ton high-explosive shell 29 miles. The rate of fire was two rounds per hour. The other gun, Dora, never left the proving ground.

GUSTAV LINE. One of a series of German defensive lines in Italy south of Rome. It was based on the Garigliano and RAPIDO RIVERS and the formidable Monte CASSINO and, sitting behind the Barbara and BERNHARD Lines, was designed not merely to delay the Allied advance but to be held if possible. It included gun pits blasted out of rock, concrete bunkers, turreted machine gun emplacements, barbed wire and minefields—dominated by the heights of Monte Cassino. The main assault by the Allies was begun on May 11, 1944, and they had smashed through by May 17 and reached Rome by June 4.

GUZZONI, Alfredo (1887–1965). General Guzzoni's career in the Italian Army spanned both world wars. In 1939 he commanded an army corps in Albania. Subsequently he went to General Headquarters in Rome, where he served as Under Secretary of State for War. In 1943 he came out of retirement to take command of the Sixth Army in SICILY at the time of the Allied landings there. The Germans arrested Guzzoni in October 1943 but subsequently freed him.

GYMNAST. Code name of early (1941) plans for British occupation of NORTHWEST AFRICA. It was succeeded by SUPER-GYMNAST and, ultimately, by TORCH.

GYPSY MOTH. This classic sports biplane, built by de Havilland, was an elementary trainer for the ROYAL AIR FORCE from 1932 until 1947. It was a two-place aircraft of wood-and-metal construction covered with fabric. The wings were swept back slightly, with the upper wing staggered forward of the lower and placed ahead of the open cockpits to facilitate escape by parachute. Overseas production took place in Canada, Australia and New Zealand. A radio-controlled version, the Queen Bee, functioned as a target drone.

H

H_2S. A British 10-cm. blind-bombing RADAR, using a PPI (plan position indicator) scope and mounted in a ventral position in British and, later, in American heavy bombers. Its PPI presentation, which gave a panoramic "picture," made it suitable for use as a "bombsight" radar, though its relatively low frequency made it less than ideally accurate. H_2S was used for PATHFINDER BOMBING, radar-equipped lead planes guiding bomber formations to their targets. Later models incorporated detail improvements. The H_2X was an American 3-cm. version, developed by the Radiation Laboratory of the Massachusetts Institute of Technology. Its higher frequency gave a sharper PPI image, making the H_2X—nicknamed Mickey—a more accurate horizontal-bombing radar. *See also* NAVIGATION AIDS.

H6K. Japanese Navy Kawanishi patrol flying boat (Allied code name, Mavis), introduced prewar as the H6K2, with the H6K4 and H6K5 being improved wartime versions. The H6K4 had a wingspan of 131 feet 2¼ inches, a maximum weight of nearly 17½ tons, a maximum speed of 208 miles per hour and a maximum range of over 3,000 miles. Defensive armament consisted of a 20-mm. gun and four 7.7-mm. machine guns. Up to 3,500 pounds of bombs or torpedoes could be carried. The H6K's fuselage had a lean, upward-curving appearance and a twin tail. Four radial engines were mounted on the single wing, which was carried on struts above the fuselage. Wingtip floats were fixed. The H6K was a reliable flying boat but was replaced in production by the faster, better-protected and more heavily armed H8K (below). A transport version was produced as the H6K2-L.

H8K. The Japanese Navy Kawanishi H8K1 patrol flying boat (Allied code name, Emily) entered operation in March 1942, when two were used in a bombing attack on Oahu. A fast, long-range, heavily armed aircraft, the H8K1 was developed as an improved replacement for the H6K (above). It had a maximum weight of over 24 tons and a wingspan of 124 feet 8½ inches; four radial engines gave it a top speed of 234 miles per hour. It was armed with five 20-mm. and three 7.7-mm. automatic guns and up to 3,528 pounds of bombs, torpedoes or depth bombs on underwing racks. The H8K1 and the later H8K2, incorporating more powerful engines and detail refinements, were highly effective in service. A deep-hulled, high-wing monoplane with a single tail, the H8K superficially resembled the British Short SUNDERLAND. A transport version was produced as the H8K2-L *Seiku* (Clear Sky).

HAAKON VII (1872–1957). King of Norway from 1905, when he was elected after the dissolution of union between Norway and Sweden. Haakon refused to recognize the Nazi government of Vidkun QUISLING or to abdicate when the Germans invaded his nation in 1940. On the other hand, he rallied no resistance. Instead he established a government-in-exile in London. Haakon's return to Norway in June 1945 following the German defeat was an occasion for national rejoicing.

HABBAKUK. Code name for a self-propelled floating airfield to be made of ice with an admixture of wood pulp. The aim of this British proposal was to give fighter support to troops on invasion beachheads in Normandy, but for a number of reasons Habbakuk was never put into operation.

HABBANIYA. The British maintained an air training base at this desert city on the Euphrates (Iraq). On May 2, 1941, the garrison (augmented by a British battalion from India) was attacked by Iraqi troops at the command of the pro-German Prime Minister, RASHID ALI. The defense, led by the commander of the flying school, Air Vice-Marshal Harry Smart, was highly effective. With air support the defenders raided enemy lines. On May 5 the besiegers withdrew. They were followed, prisoners were taken and a column of reinforcements was destroyed by aircraft.

HACHA, Emil (1872–1945). Born in Bohemia, Dr. Hacha entered the Austrian state service after his education at Prague University. By 1925 he had advanced to the position of president of the Czechoslovak High Court of Administration and member of the Hague International Court. When Czech President Eduard BENEŠ resigned under German pressure in late 1938, Hacha, an undisguised reactionary, was elected to take his place despite his never having been in politics. As President, Hacha gradually saw his powers undermined as the Nazis took control of the country. As a German puppet ruler, Hacha survived the war but died while awaiting trial on charges of traitorous collaboration.

HAGEN LINE. German defense line before BRYANSK (USSR). The Germans were forced back to it after the failure of their attack on the KURSK salient in July 1943.

HAGURO. Japanese NACHI-class first-class (heavy) cruiser of 10,000 tons, completed in 1929. She carried ten 8-inch guns. She fought throughout the war, participating in the Battle of the JAVA SEA, the fighting at BOUGAINVILLE in November 1943 and as part of Admiral KURITA's battle line off SAMAR (the battle for LEYTE GULF) in October 1944. She was torpedoed in May 1945.

HAHN, Otto (1879–1968). German chemist who in 1938 produced radioactive isotopes by bombarding uranium with neutrons. He developed the theory of fission, concluding that molecules must have split and thereby created great energy. The discovery caused a scientific sensation, in that it presented the possibility of a chain reaction of neutron production and thus the creation of atomic energy. The 1944 Nobel Prize for Chemistry was awarded to Hahn for his discovery. For various reasons, however, the German Government gave only limited support to nuclear research and development.

HAILE SELASSIE (1892–1975). When driven out of Ethiopia by the Italians in 1936, Emperor Haile Selassie went to Geneva to plead for Ethiopia, then into exile in Britain. At the beginning of Britain's EAST AFRICA campaign he moved to Khartoum to encourage the British to utilize patriot revolt in the campaign. Led by Gen. Orde WINGATE's Gideon Force, the indomitable little man of great dignity and courage marched through the wilds of western Ethiopia to rally his people and regain his capital. He continued to fight for Ethiopia, insisting on becoming a charter member of the United Nations and on signing the peace treaty as a cobelligerent. After the war he worked to reform and modernize his country. He was deposed by a group of Army officers in September 1974.

HAISLIP, Wade Hampton (1889–1971). U.S. Army officer who organized the 85th Infantry Division and commanded it in 1942–43. He advanced to command of the XV Corps and served with it through the Normandy, French and Rhineland campaigns.

As a first lieutenant at Fort Sam Houston, Haislip introduced 2d Lt. Dwight D. EISENHOWER to a young lady named Mamie Doud, who would become Mrs. Eisenhower.

HAKKO ICHIU. Japanese expression, also transliterated *Hakko-ichi-u,* meaning "under Heaven a single household" or "the bringing of the eight corners of the world under one roof." In the Japan of Meiji and of HIROHITO, this ancient phrase was used by some nationalist elements in the sense of a Japanese dominance of the Far East, with major-power strength and self-sufficiency; during the 1930s it became an element of government policy. Admiral YAMAMOTO used the expression in the operation order under which the Japanese Navy opened the Pacific war, referring to the "vast and far-reaching fundamental principle, the goal of our nation—*Hakko ichiu.*"

HALDER, Franz (1884–1972). Gen. Ludwig BECK's successor as Chief of the GERMAN ARMY GENERAL STAFF (1938), Halder remained in this post through the early and spectacular German military successes of the war, being dismissed by Adolf HITLER in 1942. A member of the military circle discussing the overthrow of Hitler before the war and in its first stages, Halder underwent an agony of indecision over the conflict between his principles and his loyalty to duty in Hitler's service. He spent the last months of the war in a concentration camp.

Born in Würzburg of a long line of soldiers on June 30, 1884, Halder received a classical education in Munich. Beginning his military career as an officer aspirant with the 3d Royal Bavarian Field Artillery Regiment in the Bavarian capital, he advanced later through General Staff study at the Bavarian War College from 1911 to 1914, and remained in some form of staff work with only two exceptions throughout his entire service, the latter being as commander of the 7th Infantry Division in 1937. Called to Berlin from that assignment, Halder put to use his mastery of military training techniques in directing the Army maneuvers of that year, the largest held since the reintroduction of conscription in the German Army in 1935. Assigned to the General Staff thereafter, Halder became Oberquartiermeister I (Deputy Chief of Staff) under Beck in April 1938, as the crisis over CZECHOSLOVAKIA reached its climax.

Frequently described as a phlegmatic, professorial personality, Halder was in fact deeply sensitive, often moved to tears, and a strongly religious Protestant. Said by many sources to have been ready to begin a coup against Hitler upon receipt of any orders to invade Czechoslovakia, Halder desisted with the bloodless German diplomatic victory, which immeasurably increased Hitler's prestige, making it impossible in Halder's view to displace him in the wake of such a clear triumph. Halder all but withdrew from the anti-Hitler conspiracy, though he remained accessible to its members. His behavior after the MUNICH AGREEMENT prompted members of the conspiracy to comment on his loss of will and shattered nerves.

Halder became at the same time the chief spokesman for Army concern over Hitler's military dilettantism, though he carried on the staff work that planned German offensives. He reached frequent impasses with Hitler on plans for a western offensive in Europe in late 1939, Hitler in his pathological suspicion of the General Staff even banishing from his presence the notebooks Halder habitually carried to his staff conferences and which later became the basis for his famous war diary. Seeking only a defensive posture after Poland's collapse, Halder led a number of senior officers in professional and technical opposition to the offensive until November 5, 1939, when he suffered a collapse of nerve following a meeting in which Hitler rebuked von BRAUCHITSCH, the Army Commander in Chief, for defeatism when the latter presented the Army's arguments to the dictator; the Chief of Staff, also present and deeply shaken, hastily ordered the destruction of all anti-Hitler resistance documents within his control at the ZOSSEN General Staff headquarters. After a similar tirade from Hitler on November 23, repeated entreaties from his opposition colleagues could not move Halder to his former commitment, and his acceptance of Hitler's plans grew with the development of German military strength in the west in early 1940. The stunning successes of the Scandinavian and western European operations confirmed Hitler's faith in his own intuition and his contempt for the generals, though they also vindicated Halder's training methods and demonstrated the quality of German doctrine.

Halder's traditional staff conceptions collided again with Hitler's analysis and his politically tinged military orders in the BALKANS campaign, the differences growing in intensity during the planning and execution of the invasion of Russia. Hitler formulated a divergent strategy aiming at LENINGRAD and the Don Basin at once, while the General Staff regarded Moscow, the center of the Russian transport net, as the main objective. The course of the campaign, influenced by Hitler's interference even in tactical maneuvers, led Halder to the conclusion in August 1941 that Russian manpower reserves had been grossly underestimated and that German technical superiority could not surmount that disadvantage. On December 19, 1941, after the failure to take Moscow, Hitler accepted the weak and ill von Brauchitsch's resignation, becoming Commander in Chief himself; Halder remained out of a sense of duty, living on borrowed time for the next nine months.

With the German advance into the Caucasus in May 1942, Halder identified new Russian divisions and confronted Hitler continually with hard facts. Hitler, having already pronounced the Russians finished and requiring only one last blow to collapse utterly, furiously rejected this information. After Halder's reiteration of his view of the general situation in late summer 1942 and his prediction of disaster on the flanks of the German thrust toward STALINGRAD, Hitler dismissed the Chief of Staff in a rage on September 24, shrieking that he would find a staff chief less given to the traditional spirit and more imbued with revolutionary National Socialism. Halder retired to the obscurity of family life at Oberstdorf in Bavaria for nearly two years.

Though not directly involved in the attempt on Hitler's life on July 20, 1944, Halder was arrested with his wife and daughter on the following day for his continued contacts with General Beck and Carl GOERDELER, who figured prominently in the conspiracy. Kept for months in blacked-out solitary confinement in the Flossenbürg concentration camp, Halder escaped execution when, on April 29, 1945, German troops released him from captivity, and with a company of ranking prisoners including Fabian von SCHLABRENDORFF, Kurt SCHUSCHNIGG of Austria and Leon BLUM of France, the entire party surrendered to American troops at Niederdorf in the Austrian Tyrol on May 4.

As the last Chief of the General Staff, Halder after the war was a symbol to his former subordinates of a proud and long-lived military and intellectual tradition. Working with U.S. Army historians, he joined in a search program that, enlisting the help of German officer prisoners, eventually produced some 2,400 monographs on German military policy and operations in the 25 years prior to 1945. *See also* FRANCE, BATTLE OF; SOVIET-GERMAN OPERATIONS. **A.M.B.**

HALFAYA PASS. Sixty-five miles east of TOBRUK, this was a strategic point in the desert war because it was one of the few places where vehicles could negotiate the 500-foot escarpment from the coastal plain to the desert plateau. It was renamed "Hellfire Pass" after bitter fighting during Operation BATTLEAXE, June 1941.

HALF-TRACK VEHICLES. A compromise between the wheeled and full-track vehicle, the half-track had the disadvantages of both without the full advantages of either. The German and American models were the best of type, the former because the track bogies extended to about 75 percent of the vehicle's length, the latter because of front-wheel drive. The United States, Germany and France, in that order, built the most half-tracks.

HALIFAX, Edward Frederick Lindley Wood, 1st Earl (1881–1959). British Secretary of State for Foreign Affairs, 1938–40, and ambassador to Washington, 1941–46. For a time in May 1940 it looked as though this leading British political figure might become Prime Minister. Neville CHAMBERLAIN was retiring and the choice was between Halifax and Winston CHURCHILL. Although Halifax had had a long career in high offices, including a term as Viceroy of India (as Lord Irwin), it seems remarkable that at this time of crisis he was considered at all, since he had been one of Britain's most influential proponents of the policy of APPEASEMENT in the late 1930s. In those years he had been convinced that understanding in international diplomacy could be achieved through rational negotiation and that, through discussion, recourse to violent means might be avoided. Instead, the foreign policy of appeasement to which Halifax subscribed came to be viewed as weakness by Italy and Germany.

Slow to realize the course of events in Europe, quick to shut his eyes to the unpleasant realities of international European diplomacy in the late 1930s, Halifax was not, as his biographer Lord Birkenhead admits, fit to preside over the Foreign Office at such a moment in history. As ambassador to the United States, however, he was extremely successful, establishing warm relationships with members of the Roosevelt Administration and acquiring considerable popularity with the public through tours to different parts of the country.

HALIFAX. Nova Scotia port, the terminus for convoys from Britain to North America (the OB—later ON—convoys). The slower convoys (ONS) usually called at Sydney, Cape Breton Island.

HALIFAX. The first British four-engine bomber to attack a target in Germany. It made more than 75,000 wartime sorties, dropping 227,610 tons of bombs. Like the Avro LANCASTER, this Handley Page aircraft evolved from a twin-engine design. A shortage of Rolls-Royce Vulture engines, two of which were to power the plane, forced its designers to substitute four of the more readily available Rolls-Royce Merlins. First flown in 1939, the slab-sided, midwing, twin-tail monoplane participated in daylight raids, including the July 1941 attack on the SCHARNHORST at La Pallice, France, before concentrating on night bombardment. The Halifax also ferried gliders and towed them into combat, served as an airborne radio-jamming station, flew overwater re-

Halifax

connaissance and parachuted arms and agents into Nazi-occupied Europe.

The rugged bomber carried a crew of seven and could carry up to 13,000 pounds of bombs. Early models had a top speed of 265 miles per hour and a range of 1,860 miles. Replacement of the liquid-cooled 1,280-horsepower Merlins with 1,390-horsepower versions, installation of new engine cowlings and enlargement of the tail fins increased speed and stability. The early versions had power-operated gun turrets in the nose and tail; the nose turret proved superfluous and was replaced with a manually operated machine gun. The weight thus saved was invested in a two-gun dorsal turret. Halifax VI, intended for service against the Japanese, had four 1,800-horsepower Bristol Hercules radials that boosted the top speed beyond 300 miles per hour.

As new models were produced, the earlier ones were turned over to Coastal Command for submarine patrol and minelaying.

HALL, John Lesslie, Jr. (1891–1978). A 1913 graduate of the U.S. Naval Academy, Hall served as commanding officer of the U.S.S. ARKANSAS in 1940–41 and held various staff jobs into 1942. A rear admiral, he then saw action in the Mediterranean, and in November 1943 took command of an attack force stationed in England; he commanded that force at the OMAHA BEACH landing. Transferred to the Pacific late in the war, he led another attack force at OKINAWA. "Jimmy" Hall retired in 1953.

HALPRO. Code name for the Halverson project, a plan whereby a U.S. B-24 detachment (*see* B-24) led by Col. Harry A. Halverson would ferry 23 of the bombers to China, by way of the Middle East and India, in order to bomb Japan from Chinese airfields. Since their intended base in China had been overrun by the Japanese and war had been officially declared against Rumania on June 5, 1942, the men and planes were detained in North Africa for a special mission against the oil refineries at PLOESTI, Rumania. On June 11 Halverson led 12 of the Liberators (a 13th turned back) across the Mediterranean, over neutral Turkish territory, and hit the target. Damage to the refineries was minor, and the raid served mainly to alert the defenders to the possibility of future attack. None of the B-24 crewmen were killed or wounded, though one bomber crash-landed and four others ran low on fuel and had to put down in Turkey. Because Field Marshal ROMMEL at the time was threatening Egypt, the detachment was kept in North Africa and Halpro was abandoned.

HALSEY, William Frederick, Jr. (1882–1959). Son of a U.S. Navy officer, Halsey was a member of the Naval Academy class of 1904 and as a destroyer officer in World War I won the NAVY CROSS for distinguished service. He experienced a combination of sea duty and shore assignments, and in 1935 won his wings as a pilot, which enabled him to take over aviation command billets. His first such assignment was command of SARATOGA, a carrier.

At the time of the PEARL HARBOR attack, Vice-Admiral Halsey was at sea in command of Task Force 2 with his flag in the carrier ENTERPRISE. The command was split, and Halsey's section, redesignated Task Force 8, continued on to reinforce WAKE ISLAND. At this point he issued his famous Battle Order No. 1, which put *Enterprise* on a war footing, meaning that all planes were armed and other steps taken for immediate combat in expectation that war was imminent. It was an early demonstration of the aggressive attitude that was to be Halsey's hallmark throughout the PACIFIC WAR. His physical appearance itself gave an impression of aggressiveness, dash, dynamism and toughness. His speech was salty, his manner brusque, while his beetle-browed, bulldog-like visage added to the effect. He was revered by his subordinates, for he was always approachable, always solicitous of his men.

It was fortunate for the United States that Halsey and his task force were at sea when the Japanese struck Pearl Harbor, since the *Enterprise* and other carriers were spared the fate that befell the battleships of the Pacific Fleet at anchor at Oahu. Soon after the attack, in one of the first U.S. naval offensives of the war (February 1942), Halsey successfully raided the Gilberts and Wotje, Maloelap, Roi-Namur and Kwajalein in the Marshall Islands with little Japanese response. After returning to Pearl for a short time, Halsey, with his command redesignated Task Force 16, set out to harass the Japanese on Wake, and on the way home hit Marcus Island. On April 13 he rendezvoused with the carrier HORNET, which carried 16 B-25 bombers commanded by Lt. Col. James H. DOOLITTLE, and set a course which would en-

Admiral Halsey

able these Army Air Corps planes to be launched for the famous raid on Tokyo (*see* FIRST SPECIAL AVIATION PROJECT). In addition to his command of TF 16, Halsey had been designated Commander, Carriers, Pacific Fleet, and also Commander, Carrier Division 2.

Because of illness, Halsey was unable to lead his TF 16 in the Battle of MIDWAY in May 1942. After treatment on the mainland he returned in September and on October 18, 1942, was appointed Commander of South Pacific Forces and Area, replacing Vice-Adm. Robert L. GHORMLEY. In this post he supervised the GUADALCANAL operations.

As news of Halsey's appointment spread through the fleet in the South Pacific (SoPac) and among the troops on Guadalcanal, it acted like some sort of miracle tonic. Because of his flamboyance, his record of early victories in the war and the publicity his every action received, Halsey had become a symbol of aggressive and forthright action. To many, the issue with the Japanese in SoPac now was no longer in doubt. Early on during his new command, Halsey coined a slogan, "Kill Japs, Kill Japs, Kill More Japs," which became the operative motto in SoPac. Although Halsey's appearance in SoPac raised morale, it did not result in an immediate turnaround of the military situation or in dramatic American victories. By February 1943, with the invasion of the RUSSELL ISLANDS, the U.S. offensive up the SOLOMONS chain began, and in slightly more than a year's time Halsey had succeeded in climbing the Solomons ladder, pushing the Japanese back and firmly putting the Allies on the offensive.

Halsey commanded the THIRD FLEET and at the same time wore a second hat as ComSoPac. He was relieved of the latter on June 15, 1944, and ordered to take the fleet to sea, which was much to his liking. On the 17th he reported to Admiral NIMITZ at Pearl Harbor and began planning for operations in the Central Pacific. With Halsey's arrival, Nimitz now had two teams—the other being the FIFTH FLEET (Admiral SPRUANCE). The same ships continued in action but the commanders changed. While Fifth Fleet staff planned and trained, Third Fleet was out conducting operations. Third Fleet's first assignment in the Central Pacific was the assault and occupation of the western CAROLINE ISLANDS. At the beginning of October it steamed from Ulithi to begin preliminary operations in support of General MACARTHUR's landing at LEYTE on October 20. This involvement with the Leyte operation led to Halsey's controversial role in the battle for LEYTE GULF, October 23–25, described in that entry.

Halsey and the Third Fleet remained in Philippine waters supporting the Seventh Fleet until MacArthur's land-based planes could take over. When released by the SWPA command, Halsey's carrier planes hit LUZON and Iwo Jima, and then in late November he withdrew to Ulithi to replenish and reorganize. On December 11 the Third Fleet steamed forth again, this time to support MacArthur's MINDORO landing by hitting LUZON on a number of consecutive days. At this point, on December 17, a great typhoon hit the fleet, causing a large loss in lives, the loss of three destroyers and considerable damage to ships. Halsey was brought before a court of inquiry for his handling of the fleet under these circumstances. Despite his being held culpable in the matter, it was felt that the importance of his continuing in command of the fleet outweighed any need to mete out punishment. In June 1945, in Okinawan waters, Third Fleet was again surprised by a typhoon and suffered considerable damage, though not as much as in the previous December. Nonetheless, Halsey and his subordinate commanders were called before a court of inquiry, which criticized them for failing to take appropriate measures.

The final phase of the war for Halsey began on July 1, when the fleet began operations against the home islands of Japan. Tokyo was first hit on July 10, and other targets on succeeding days, with minimal Japanese opposition. From the first appearance of the Third Fleet, there was no part of Japan that was safe from Halsey's planes or guns. Third Fleet continued almost daily operations against Japan proper until August 9, when Halsey had to suspend all action while the second atomic bomb was dropped on the enemy. The fleet was ready to begin action again on August 12, but Nimitz ordered Halsey to cancel all strikes and proceed with caution to the Tokyo area. All offensive operations against Japan were canceled on the 15th, following word that Japan had capitulated.

Halsey was present during the surrender ceremony on board U.S.S. *Missouri* on September 2, backing up Admiral Nimitz, who signed the surrender document for the United States. Spruance relieved Halsey on September 20 when Third Fleet became Fifth Fleet again. However, Third Fleet was reconstituted at Pearl Harbor with different ships and sailed home to the West Coast to participate in Navy Day celebrations there on October 27. Halsey had a hero's welcome. On November 22 he hauled down his flag as Third Fleet commander for the last time and headed for Washington for a special assignment in the office of the Chief of Naval Operations. In December he was promoted to fleet admiral. He remained on active duty until April 1947.

B.M.F.

HAMBRO, Carl (1885–1964). Norwegian statesman, president of the Storting and president of the 1939 League of Nations Assembly that expelled the Soviet Union from membership for aggression against Finland. After the German invasion of NORWAY in April 1940, he fled the country and went to the United States. In 1945 he was chairman of the Norwegian delegation to the San Francisco UNITED NATIONS conference.

HAMBURG RAID. RAF BOMBER COMMAND carried out attacks on Hamburg on no fewer than 187 occasions in the years 1940–45. But the heaviest concentration of bombing and the greatest destruction wrought were in the raids of late July and early August 1943. This period has been called the Battle of Hamburg.

By mid-1943 Sir Arthur HARRIS had in his hands a force of four-engine bombers whose navigational and target-marker capabilities had been enhanced by the introduction of Oboe (*see* NAVIGATION AIDS), a PATHFINDER force and H2S (*see* H2S). Finally he was given permission by the War Cabinet to use WINDOW, a jamming device which would blind German RADAR. Hamburg was chosen as the target because of its importance to both German war industry and morale and because, as a seaport, it was within Oboe range and would show up well on H2S.

On the night of July 24, 1943, a force of LANCASTERS, HALIFAXES, STIRLINGS and WELLINGTONS was sent against Hamburg; 728 aircraft claimed to have attacked the target. The bomber loss rate was low, mainly because the first use of Window produced a paralyzing effect on the German radar-controlled air defenses. Destruction was widespread, though not greater than other towns had suffered previously. But the battle was continued when by day on July 25 and 26 Gen. Ira C. EAKER'S U.S. Eighth Bomber Command kept up the bombing. MOSQUITO aircraft continued the harassment by night. On July 27 the second major night area bombing raid was carried out; 722 aircraft claimed to have attacked. When Mosquitoes attacked on the night of July 28, fires were still burning. The third major raid was on the night of July 29, when 699 aircraft claimed to have attacked. By this time the Germans had resorted to a running voice commentary on the attack to assist their night fighters and to counter the confusion caused by the use of Window. The final action came on the night of August 2.

From postwar records, especially the reports of the police president at Hamburg, it is known that the bombing raids were devastating. A million people were said to have fled from the city and the terror of the fire storm which swept through the bombed areas. According to the official historian, two-thirds as many people—at least 31,000 and probably closer to 50,000—were killed by bombing in one week as were killed in the whole war by bombing in the United Kingdom.

Albert SPEER and the Nazi hierarchy were apprehensive of the effect that such raids on other major cities might produce. Speer told Adolf HITLER that if such attacks were made on six other German cities devoted to war production, it would bring "a rapid end to the war." In the event, Hamburg was allowed to recover and was given special treatment by the Nazi authorities to aid its housing problems.

Bomber Command made 3,095 sorties in the four major attacks of the Battle of Hamburg. Nearly 9,000 tons of bombs, about half of them incendiaries, were dropped, and the casualty rate was 2.8 percent lost and 5.6 percent aircraft damaged.

HAMILCAR. Glider designed by General Aircraft to meet a British Air Ministry requirement for a glider capable of carrying a 7-ton tank. Weighing 37,000 pounds when fully loaded, it was the heaviest glider used by the Allies. Almost 400 of these high-wing monoplanes were built, and 70 of them saw action in the Normandy INVASION.

HAMMELBURG. After American forces crossed the Main River (Germany) at Aschaffenburg, General PATTON decided that an effort to liberate POWs held near Hammelburg, north of Würzburg, would be made. He gave the mission to XII Corps and remained adamant even when the commanders of both the corps and the 4th Armored Division tried to dissuade him. A small armored task force was sent out on March 26, 1945. Though the liberators reached the camp, the task force was destroyed on the return trip. Of the 307 men who started, 15 infiltrated back along with a few prisoners, 9 were killed, 16 were missing, 32 were wounded and the rest captured. The Hammelburg camp was liberated on April 6, but all POWs except those seriously wounded had been evacuated. Among the wounded was Patton's son-in-law. Though Patton later claimed he did not know of the presence of his relative in the camp when he ordered the raid, indications are that from intelligence reports he was able to deduce the chances were good that Col. John Waters was there.

HAMMER. Code name for the Allied operation designed to recapture TRONDHEIM, Norway, in April 1940. A direct attack by a large seaborne force was to be supported by naval gunfire and air attacks. As the plan would require that most of the British Home Fleet be concentrated within range of German aircraft, Hammer was abandoned.

HAMMOND, N. G. L. (1907–). British lieutenant colonel who served in Greece, Crete and Syria. As a member of the British Military Mission to Greece (1943–44), with the assignment of coordinating and developing the activities, both military and political, of the various Greek resistance groups, Hammond displayed remarkable resourcefulness. After the war he resumed academic life and in 1962 became a professor of Greek at the University of Bristol.

HAMP. Allied code name for the "clipped wing" A6M3 model of the Mitsubishi A6M Zero Japanese fighter (*see* A6M). It was also called "Hap," before its identity was established as a Zero variant (Zeke 32).

HAMPDEN. The last of Britain's prewar medium bombers, this aircraft acquired the nickname Flying Panhandle because the crew, bombs and armament were concentrated in the forward section, from which a single, tubular boom extended rearward, supporting the tail plane and twin rudders. Of all-metal, stressed-skin construction, the Hampden was a midwing monoplane powered by two 1,000-horsepower Bristol Pegasus radials. A variant powered by Napier Dagger in-line engines, called the Hereford, served mainly as a trainer.

Despite a top speed of 254 miles per hour, a bomb load of 4,000 pounds and a range in excess of 1,000 miles, the Hampden proved unsatisfactory for daylight bombardment. In particular, the armament of five machine guns proved inadequate. The planes were more successful as night bombers, however, remaining with BOMBER COMMAND until September 1942 and with COASTAL COMMAND, where they flew antisubmarine patrols, until December of the following year.

HANDS UP. Code name of a planned Allied air-sea operation to establish a port in Quiberon Bay, France.

HANDY, Thomas (1892–). U.S. Army officer who graduated from Virginia Military Institute in 1914 and saw action in World War I. Between 1936 and 1940 he served in the War Plans Division, a post to which he returned in 1941. Promoted to major general in 1942, Handy became assistant chief of staff, Operations Division. After rising to the rank of lieutenant general and the post of deputy chief of staff in 1944, he added a fourth star in 1945. He was appointed Commander in Chief U.S. Army European Command in 1949.

Throughout World War II Handy was rated as one of the two or three top brains of the Army General Staff. He was in fact the top director of operations.

HANFORD. Common designation for Hanford Engineer Works, established in southeastern Washington State as part of the ATOMIC BOMB project. Its purpose was to produce plutonium from U-238. It was located in a very isolated area because of the fear of accidental explosion. Plutonium produced at this plant was used in "Fat Man," the bomb dropped on NAGASAKI.

HANFSTAENGL, Ernst (1887–1975). Member of a wealthy Munich family who owned an art publishing house, "Putzi" Hanfstaengl had an American mother, was a graduate of Harvard (class of 1909) and spent the years of the First World War in New York. Returning to Germany, he formed an early friendship with Adolf HITLER, and in 1922 offered him cheerful and cultivated companionship as well as money (in dollars—of the utmost value during the period of inflation). After the failure of the Munich putsch, Hitler took refuge in the Hanfstaengl house, and it was there he was arrested on November 11, 1923. After Hitler's confinement in LANDSBERG, Hanfstaengl continued to be one of his patrons, always present on the fringe of the movement, an amused and amusing spectator but a person seldom taken seriously by the Nazi leaders. Hitler appointed him chief of his foreign-press department in 1933.

Later Hanfstaengl became alienated as a result of a bizarre practical joke played on him by Nazis who considered him to be "soft." They hustled him into an airplane (this was during the Spanish Civil War) and told him he was going to be flown to Spain and put out there. In fact, the plane merely circled round and round inside Germany, landing where it had taken off. Hanfstaengl took this as a warning and fled the country, spending part of the war years in nominal internment in Washington as White House adviser on German affairs. He published two entertaining and revealing books on the period, *Hitler, the Missing Years* (1957) and *Zwischen Weissem und Braunem Haus* (1970).

HANGÖ. Finnish port at the mouth of the Gulf of Finland. The Finnish refusal to lease or sell it to the Soviet Union was one of the immediate causes of the Soviet attack in 1939. Hangö was taken over by the Russians after the 1940 armistice and retaken by the Finns in 1941. After the 1944 armistice between Finland and the Allies the Soviet Government relinquished its claim to Hangö.

HANSON, Robert M. (1920–1944). The third-highest-scoring U.S. Marine fighter pilot of the war, with 25 kills. He won the MEDAL OF HONOR for missions in November 1943 and January 1944. In 17 days in January 1944 he downed 20 Japanese aircraft. Hanson was killed while strafing Cape St. George in February 1944.

HARA-KIRI GULCH. Nickname for a canyon on SAIPAN constituting a strong Japanese defensive position, cleared by the U.S. 165th Infantry on July 7, 1944.

HARDER, U.S.S. GATO-class submarine, commissioned 1942. Beginning her war activity in the Pacific in mid-1943, *Harder* successfully carried out five combat patrols. During her sixth patrol, on August 24, 1944, she was sunk by depth charges. Between June 1943 and August 1944 she had sunk nine Japanese cargo ships and one tanker, in addition to destroyers *Ikazuchi, Minatsuki, Hayanami* and *Tanikaze* and escort ships *Matsuwa* and *Hiburi*. Her first and only commanding officer, Comdr. Samuel D. Dealey, was posthumously awarded the MEDAL OF HONOR; *Harder* received a PRESIDENTIAL UNIT CITATION for her aggressive and highly productive actions.

HARDY, H.M.S. Royal Navy destroyer (flotilla leader) of 1,500 tons, completed in 1937 by Cammell Laird. *Hardy*'s armament included five 4.7-inch guns, smaller weapons and eight 21-inch torpedo tubes. *Hardy* led four H-class destroyers of the 2d Flotilla into the NARVIK (Norway) fjords early on the morning of April 10, 1940, to attack German ships engaged in landing operations. The flotilla was unaware of the superiority of the German forces but had the advantage of surprise. Two German destroyers and an important ammunition ship were sunk and three destroyers damaged; the British losses were *Hardy* and one destroyer, with another damaged but escorted to safety. The flotilla captain, B. A. W. Warburton-Lee, was killed; he was awarded a posthumous VICTORIA CROSS.

HARMON, Ernest Nason (1894–). U.S. Army officer who began the war as chief of staff of Headquarters, Armored Force. In 1942–43 he commanded the 2d Armored Division in the NORTHWEST AFRICA campaign. In 1943–44 he commanded the 1st Armored Division in ITALY. A major general, Harmon returned to the 2d Armored Division in 1944, and ended the war as commanding general of the XXII Corps. As an armored commander he was the ideal type, admired by his peers and men as a hard-charging leader.

HARMON, Millard Fillmore (1888–1945). U.S. Army air officer who commanded the Second Air Force in 1941–42 as a major general. After serving as Chief of Air Staff HQ AAF, he became the commander of all U.S. Army air forces on GUADALCANAL and the South Pacific islands in 1943 as a lieutenant general and then, in 1944, commander of all Army Air Force units in the Pacific area. Harmon was lost on a routine flight to Hawaii in February 1945.

HARPOON. Code name for British convoy from Gibraltar to Malta, June 1942. Only two of six ships made port.

HARRIMAN, (William) Averell (1891–). American businessman who became an important diplomatic figure during the war. In 1941 he took charge of LEND-LEASE arrangements in London, where he had built up a close relationship with Prime Minister Winston CHURCHILL. In the summer of 1941 Harriman and Lord BEAVERBROOK led a mission to Moscow to establish working relationships with the Russians after the German invasion; Harriman was among those who believed that the Soviet Union could withstand the assault. Although he favored cooperation with the Russians, he also favored firmness in dealing with them. In October

1943 he was appointed ambassador to Moscow, serving until February 1946. He was an important participant in wartime meetings of the Allied leaders, and while ambassador he met regularly with Joseph STALIN. After the war he served in a variety of offices and as an unofficial foreign policy adviser to Presidents.

HARRIS, Sir Arthur Travers (1892–). A colorful and controversial figure who from February 1942 until September 1945 was Air Officer Commanding in Chief BOMBER COMMAND. English by birth, Harris spent some of his adolescent years in Rhodesia. He became a soldier and transferred via the Royal Flying Corps to the ROYAL AIR FORCE in 1919. In a distinguished career he commanded bomber-transport squadrons at home and in the Middle East. He attended the Army Staff College course in 1928 and qualified on flying boats. Tours of duty in intelligence and plans at the Air Ministry in the 1930s allowed him to exercise a direct influence on the evaluations made of the war that threatened and on the specifications for the new four-engine bombers. He was AOC Palestine and Transjordan in 1938 and in 1939 commanded No. 5 Bomber Group in Britain. He began to develop his special technique for aerial mining.

He became AOC-in-C Bomber Command at a propitious moment, when new equipment was beginning to appear. Under his direct personal inspiration and leadership Bomber Command grew in size and capability. The development of PATHFINDER techniques and of saturation and precision attacks reflected his professional drive and competence. He saw the bomber offensive not only as a means of striking directly at the source of military might in Germany but as a means of obviating the vast slaughter of men in stalemated ground battles of the World War I Passchendaele and Somme type. Despite the frequent weakening of his force and the diversions to other targets, particularly those demanded by the Royal Navy, Harris had the support of the Prime Minister and the War Cabinet. Though not an extrovert among his officers and men and not often seen around his operational stations, Harris also won the confidence and loyalty of his crews, in the air and on the ground. He was "Bert" or "Bomber" Harris to them. He picked his headquarters team carefully and kept it with him; his group commanders were chosen men. His relations with the Air Ministry were not always easy because he resented interference with his interpretation of directives once they were given to him.

Harris's knowledge of the complicated operational, technical and meteorological factors affecting bomber operations by night was unequaled. Under him, scientific aids and operational research helped to fashion a fearsome weapon of war—the STRATEGIC BOMBING force. His favorable assessment of the capability of his force made him a believer in area bombing by night, and the force showed itself capable, when the air situation was suitable, of precision bombing by day in Normandy before and after the D-Day landings. He cooperated wholly with the U.S. Army Air Forces and shared headquarters accommodations with them in the early days. His relations with Generals SPAATZ, EAKER and ARNOLD were warm.

When peace came, bombing became an unpopular subject, particularly among politicians. There are many who think that Harris and his Bomber Command did not receive the accolades they merited. Whatever the ultimate historical assessment, Harris was surely one of the most dominant command figures of World War II. **E.B.H.**

HARROW. This airplane was designed by Britain's Handley Page corporation as a transport, then converted for use as a bomber. On the eve of war, however, RAF BOMBER COMMAND acquired Vickers WELLINGTONS to replace the Harrows, which received streamlined noses, had their armament removed and became transports. The Harrow was a twin-engine, high-wing monoplane with twin tails and fixed landing gear. The skeleton was metal, but wings, fuselage and tail surfaces were fabric-covered.

HARSTAD. Norwegian port on the island of Hinnöy on the approach route to NARVIK. At the start of the Norwegian campaign in April 1940 it was the site of the headquarters of Maj. Gen. Carl FLEISCHER's 6th Command District. Later it was used by Maj. Gen. P. J. MACKESY as a base to support his attack on Narvik. British troops started landing on April 15 and were evacuated in early June.

HART, Thomas Charles (1877–1971). An 1897 graduate of the U.S. Naval Academy, Admiral Hart commanded the U.S. Asiatic Fleet from 1939 until early 1942. His conferences with British officers in the Far East prior to the U.S. entry into the war built up useful relationships. After December 7, 1941, Hart led the U.S. Asiatic Fleet from its position near Manila to safer waters in the Netherlands East Indies. He resigned his command in February 1942, however, following a controversy with the Dutch Vice-Adm. Conrad HELFRICH. From his Connecticut farm, Hart wrote articles for the *Saturday Evening Post* during 1942 criticizing U.S. preparations at Pearl Harbor prior to the Japanese attack.

HARTMANN, Erich (1922–). An Me 109 pilot, this LUFTWAFFE ace saw action on both the Eastern and Western Fronts, flew 1,425 missions, participated in some 800 dogfights and downed 352 planes. On a single day in 1944 he downed six Russian planes, refueled and returned to shoot down five more. Sixteen times he had to parachute to safety or crash-land a badly damaged Me 109. Once the Russians captured him after a forced landing, but he escaped that same day and returned to action. He was a prominent figure in the building of West German military air power.

HARUNA. Japanese fast battleship completed (as a battle cruiser) at Kobe in 1916; she was fully modernized in the 1930s, which increased her displacement to 31,700 tons. *Haruna*'s World War II armament comprised eight 14-inch, fourteen 6-inch and eight 5-inch guns together with smaller weapons; by the end of the war her antiaircraft armament had been increased to twelve 5-inch and approximately a hundred smaller AA guns. *Haruna* served in the Southern Force of the Japanese Navy in 1941. In 1942–43 her service included the Indian Ocean foray, MIDWAY and the GUADALCANAL operations. The ship also participated in the battle for LEYTE GULF and was finally sunk at Kure following attacks by U.S. Navy carrier-borne aircraft on July 28, 1945.

HARWOOD, Sir Henry (1880–1950). Commodore in command of the South America Division of the Royal Navy's America and West Indies Station at the outbreak of the war. On December 13, 1939, with the cruisers AJAX, ACHILLES and EXETER, he intercepted the German pocket battleship ADMIRAL GRAF SPEE, which had heavier guns and thicker armor than any of his three ships, and brought her to action—the Battle of the RIVER PLATE. Harwood was promoted to rear admiral and knighted for the considerable success of this engagement.

In 1940 he was appointed an assistant chief of staff at the Admiralty and in 1942 was selected by the Prime Minister to relieve Adm. Sir Andrew CUNNINGHAM as Commander in Chief Mediterranean, with the acting rank of admiral. Growing ill health made him unequal to the task, and in early 1943 he relinquished the command, returning to Britain to occupy for a few months the less demanding post of Admiral Commanding the Orkneys and Shetland. He was finally invalided from the Navy in 1945.

HASSELL, Ulrich von (1881–1944). Career diplomat and German ambassador in Italy from 1932 to 1938, Hassell was retired from office because of his acknowledged dislike of Nazism. He belonged to an aristocratic Hanover family and was the son-in-law of Admiral von Tirpitz. A staunch conservative who favored restoration of the monarchy, Hassell became a prominent member of the German OPPOSITION TO HITLER and a friend of its leaders among the older generation, seeking to bring as many together in harmony as possible, including the KREISAU CIRCLE. From 1938 to 1944 he maintained a secret diary that is a primary source for the history of the period. Using various contacts with the British, he did what he could during the early months of the war to initiate peace negotiations with the British, with the proviso that Hitler first be deposed. After the unsuccessful attempt on Hitler's life in July 1944, Hassell, a longtime suspect of the GESTAPO, was arrested, tried by the People's Court and hanged as a traitor in September 1944.

HATANAKA, Kenji (1912–1945). A career Japanese Army officer, Major Hatanaka was the principal leader of the abortive coup d'état of August 14–15, 1945, which attempted to prevent Japan's surrender to the Allies. Hatanaka murdered his superior officer, Gen. Takeshi Mori, when Mori refused to sanction the Army seizure of power. Led by Hatanaka, some of the troops of the Imperial Guards Division seized the palace grounds and instituted a search for the phonograph record containing the Emperor's surrender address to the nation. Hatanaka shot himself in the palace compound when the mutiny failed.

HATS. Code name for an operation designed to reinforce the British Mediterranean Fleet in September 1940 by the passage from west to east of the battleship VALIANT, the new carrier ILLUSTRIOUS and the antiaircraft cruisers CALCUTTA and COVENTRY. The opportunity was also taken to reinforce the land and air defenses of MALTA. The ships left Gibraltar on August 30, and the whole passage was completed without any serious opposition.

HATSUHARU. Class of Japanese destroyers of the mid-1930s. Planned under the 1,500-ton destroyer displacement limitation imposed by the London Naval Treaty of 1930, this class was designed with a raised forecastle, one twin 5-inch gun mount forward with a second one aft and a single 5-inch mount above the forward twin. After the first two ships of the class, *Hatsuharu* and *Nenohi*, had been completed they were discovered to lack stability. The single 5-inch mount was moved aft and located in a back-to-back position with the after gun mount. The bridge structure was cut down, and the battery of nine 24-inch torpedo tubes (3×3) was reduced to six (2×3). The four remaining ships of this class were completed to this new configuration; wartime changes removed the single 5-inch gun mount and added antiaircraft guns and additional depth charges. All of this class were war losses. The subsequent SHIRATSUYU class resembled the Hatsuharus.

HAUSSER, Paul (1880–1972). German Army officer, retired in 1932, who like many others found a continuation of his career in the Verfügungstruppe (the Armed SS—later called the WAFFEN SS) after 1933. In 1936 he became inspector of the Verfügungstruppe and was subsequently an SS divisional and corps commander. He served in the USSR and, as a colonel general, commanded the Seventh Army in Normandy, being wounded in the fighting at Falaise, and later was in command of Army Group G.

HAVANA CONFERENCE. This second conference of foreign ministers of American states met in Havana in July 1940 with Secretary of State Cordell HULL leading the U.S. delegation. From this conference, held shortly after the fall of France, came the Act of Havana, which provided that North and South American territories belonging to European powers, if in danger of falling into hostile hands, could be taken over and jointly administered by the American republics pending the restoration of independence in their conquered mother countries. If an emergency arose, individual nations of the Americas could assume temporary control of these orphaned possessions, subject to a review by the American states. This later proviso justified the American administration of Danish Greenland throughout World War II.

The Havana declaration and a later treaty ratified by two-thirds of the American states effectively multilateralized the Monroe Doctrine. Although Germany threatened Latin America during the conference with postwar economic retaliation, the act revealed the extent of continental solidarity in the face of the 1940 German victories.

HAVOC. *See* A-20.

HAWAIIAN SEA FRONTIER. U.S. Navy designation for the SEA FRONTIER command responsible for the defense of the waters around the Hawaiian Islands.

HAYATE. Japanese KAMIKAZE-class destroyer sunk off WAKE ISLAND by coastal guns on December 11, 1941, thus becoming the first Japanese ship sunk in the war.

HBX. A war-developed American explosive designed as a substitute for TORPEX in underwater explosive work and loaded in aircraft depth bombs. It was a mixture of RDX (*see* RDX), TNT, powdered aluminum and a "desensitizer" intended to make it more resistant to shock and rough handling.

HEATH, Sir Lewis Macclesfield (1885–1954). British officer who entered the Indian Army in 1906 and in 1941 had advanced to the rank of lieutenant general. He served in Eritrea (EAST AFRICA) and in December 1941 was responsible for the defense of northern Malaya as commander of the 3d Indian Corps. His force retreated to SINGAPORE Island, where, together with other British units, it surrendered to the Japanese on February 15. General Heath was taken prisoner.

HECHT. Name given to the German Type XXVIIA midget submarine.

HEDGEHOG. Antitank obstacle made of three crossed angle irons. In Normandy the Germans moved a large number of hedgehogs to the beaches and set them up as underwater obstacles.

HEDGEHOG (Igelstellung). Nickname for one of the fortified defensive perimeters set up by the German Army in Russia after the Soviet counterattacks in the winter of 1941–42. The Germans held these hedgehogs instead of attempting to maintain a continuous line.

HEDGEHOG. U.S. Navy name for an ahead-throwing antisubmarine weapon for surface ships. Twenty-four 7.2-inch depth charges were fired in a pattern ahead of the attacking ship. These charges did not explode automatically but went off only if one of them actually hit the target submarine and exploded; this set off the remaining charges by sympathetic detonation. This meant that the surface ship's SONAR would not be deafened by useless explosions if the charges fell wide of their target, allowing the attacker a better chance to hold sound contact and deliver an accurate pattern of side-thrown and stern-dropped charges.

HEDGEROW. A dense row of bushes or trees growing in a wall-like mound of earth and forming a fencelike boundary. In Normandy and Brittany hedgerows greatly impeded the advance of Allied forces, offering protection to the defending Germans and obstacles to armored and infantry units. They were trench-strengthened and connected with tunnels.

HEDGEROW CUTTER. U.S. Army Sgt. Curtis G. Culin, Jr., devised this steel-toothed earth-moving attachment for tanks in the summer of 1944. Welded to the front, it enabled tanks to plow through the ubiquitous hedgerows in Normandy rather than climb them, and thereby maintain guns in firing position and prevent exposure of the vulnerable tank bottom. Gen. Omar N. BRADLEY, commander of the First Army, ordered it mass-produced. The original device was made from antitank obstacles taken from the invasion beaches.

Hedgerow cutter affixed to a light tank

HEERMANN, U.S.S. FLETCHER-class destroyer. Commissioned in 1943, she took part in amphibious and convoy operations in the Pacific. With Rear Adm. Thomas SPRAGUE's Escort Carrier Group, *Heermann* had a distinguished share in the Samar surface action which formed part of the battle for LEYTE GULF. After repairs she returned to join the FAST CARRIER TASK FORCE in operations through V-J Day.

HEINKEL, Ernest (1888–1958). Dr. Heinkel was the builder of the HEINKEL HE 111s and others which formed the backbone of the LUFTWAFFE from 1939 to 1945. When these planes first appeared, they were rated as the top fighter aircraft. Yet Heinkel fell into disfavor with Nazi authorities because of his blunt criticism of Luftwaffe leadership. After the war he was arrested and his holdings confiscated; in 1948 he was tried by an Allied court on charges of contributing to Nazi armament strength. Evidence was introduced that he had been associated with an anti-HITLER resistance group, and the following year he was freed and authorized to return to his profession. Heinkel remains one of the most famous names in German aviation.

HEINKEL HE 46. A German two-place, single-engine, short-range tactical reconnaissance and army liaison plane. Designed as a biplane in 1931, the He 46 was produced as a high-wing monoplane. Standard until 1936, it was being phased out when the war began. It was kept in limited service until 1943, after which it was used only in night harassment duties against the Russians with small bombs. It had a 650-horsepower engine and a maximum range of 620 miles. It was armed with one 7.9-mm. machine gun and the bombs.

HEINKEL HE 59. A twin-engine, twin-float biplane originally built in 1930 as a torpedo-bomber and reconnaissance plane for the clandestine LUFTWAFFE. It made its operational debut in the Spanish Civil War and continued in use to 1943, when it was phased out.

HEINKEL HE 60. A two-place, single-engine shipboard reconnaissance twin-float seaplane. First flown in 1933, it continued in limited service to 1943, when it was supplanted by the ARADO AR 196.

HEINKEL HE 100D. German mystery fighter, for a time given the designation He 113. Much publicized as the 113, the plane never did in fact carry that title. It got the 100 designation in the design stage and, though it was generally believed that it entered service, it was never accepted for operational use. Only 12 were built, not counting the six prototypes. In a successful attempt to mislead Allied intelligence, the 12 He 100Ds were repainted with varying insignia and many photos were distributed leading to the belief that a great number were in use. One prototype, the He 100V-8, raised the world speed record to 746.606 kilometers (463.92 miles) per hour in 1939. Despite the He 100D's superior performance over the standard MESSERSCHMITT ME 109E, it did not find favor with the command. A plan to build them in Japan failed. The 12 production planes were used to protect the main Heinkel factory.

HEINKEL HE 111. This plane was first revealed to the public as a civil transport, although observers noted the limited seating arrangements. Actually, the first prototype flown prior to public exhibition was a bomber; the He 111 was really a bomber that could double as a commercial transport. Its first operational use was in Spain. Beginning in 1938 with the P series, a shorter, more oval, glazed-nose model was produced, eliminating the more normal broken upper fuselage contour marking the pilot's position. In 1939 the He 111 was the LUFTWAFFE's standard level bomber. It continued in production until 1944, more than 7,300 being built. Of the series the most widely used version was the He 111H-6, which not only served as a bomber but also performed a variety of other duties, including that of flying platform for launching missiles at Britain. The He 111H-6 was a five-place, twin-engine medium bomber capable of flying 1,212 miles at 205 miles per hour with a full bomb load. It was armed with one nose-mounted 20-mm. cannon, five MG 15 machine guns and one MG 17 machine gun fixed in the tail, and it could carry a bomb load of over 5,500 pounds.

HEINKEL HE 112B. A low-wing monoplane designed to compete with the MESSERSCHMITT ME 109 fighter. Thirty were delivered before the war and used briefly by the LUFTWAFFE. Seventeen went to Spain and 12 to Japan (the A7 *Hei*) in 1938. An average machine, it flew 317 miles per hour carrying two cannon, two machine guns and six 22-pound bombs.

HEINKEL HE 114. A two-seat, single-engine reconnaissance sesquiplane with twin floats. It was obsolescent when the war began but still saw considerable service, though only a few had been built.

HEINKEL HE 115. One of the best floatplanes used during the war. It performed well in or out of the water, and was the LUFTWAFFE's most important torpedo bomber and reconnaissance floatplane serving in the Atlantic and the Baltic, Mediterranean and North Seas. The three-place, midwing, twin-engine, twin-float plane flew at a maximum speed of 203 miles per hour and carried two flexible 7.9-mm. machine guns plus a 1,750-pound torpedo and two 550-pound bombs or five 550-pound bombs.

HEINKEL HE 116B. A plane originally designed for Lufthansa's planned mail route to the Far East via Afghanistan and also for service across the South Atlantic. First flown in 1937, the four-engine plane never entered quantity production (only 14 were built) and served only over Germany or German-held territory as a photoreconnaissance plane.

HEINKEL HE 162A. A single-place, jet-powered German fighter, the last combat aircraft to enter production in Germany. The Salamander (after the mythical creature that had the ability to live through fire) or Volksjäger (People's Fighter), as it was also known, went from drawing board to flight in 69 days and was first flown on December 6, 1944. It was built of nonstrategic materials (wood, duralumin, some steel); its construction was simple enough for semiskilled labor. Only 116 were built, though many were in advanced assembly stages when the war ended. None, apparently, were used in combat. Powered by a 1,760-pound static-thrust turbojet engine, it flew at a maximum speed of 522 miles per hour and was armed with two 20-mm. cannon (later, two MG 151/20 machine guns).

HEINKEL HE 170. A three-place, single-engine, short-to-medium-range reconnaissance plane. Designed in the early 1930s, this plane, also known as Blitz (Lightning), may have been more responsible for reestablishing Germany as a leading aircraft producer than any other type. The 1932 prototype civil plane could outrun any extant fighter. The first plane to display the elliptical wing form that was considered almost a Heinkel trademark, it was an outstanding aerodynamic achievement for its time. By World War II it was confined to courier duties, but some saw combat with the Hungarian Air Force.

HEINKEL HE 177. One of Germany's few strategic bombers, also known as Greif (Griffin). It was championed by Lt. Gen. Walther Wever, first Chief of Staff of the LUFTWAFFE, who died before he could ensure Germany's strategic capability. After his death the program was stopped; it began again in 1938, but owing to wrangling among officials and a series of operating problems, the plane never reached full potential and was disliked by its crews. It had four engines linked into pairs, so that it was effectively twin-engined. Capable of a maximum speed of 303 miles per hour, it carried six machine guns and two cannon plus a 6,500-pound bomb load.

HEINKEL HE 219. A specialized high-altitude, twin-engine fighter, also known as Uhu (Owl), first flown in 1942. Fast, maneuverable and with devastating firepower, the He 219 was the only piston-engine German night fighter capable of meeting the RAF MOSQUITO on equal terms. Only 274 were built, including several prototypes. Although popular with air and ground crews alike, it was abandoned in favor of the JUNKERS JU 88. The He 219A-7R1 had two 1,900-horsepower V-12 engines and flew at a top speed of 416 miles per hour. Maximum ceiling was 41,660 feet.

HEINKEL HE 277. Developed unofficially by Heinkel, this plane was a four-separate-engine version of the He 177. Official sanction came too late in the war for the plane to achieve operational status, and only eight were completed before all heavy-bomber development was canceled on July 3, 1944, in favor of the emergency fighter program.

HEINKEL HE 280. The world's first turbojet-powered fighter plane. First flown on April 2, 1941, it was technically advanced, having the first powered ejection seat ever used. Despite its proven superiority over piston-driven planes, the German Government refused to sanction production, favoring instead the MESSERSCHMITT ME 262, which had one-third more range capability. Existing only in the prototype stage, it flew at a speed of 578 miles per hour and carried three 20-mm. cannon.

HEINRICI, Gotthard (1886–1971). German Army officer, member of a family that had been soldiers since the 12th century. Heinrici was prominent in the fighting on the Eastern Front, being appointed to command of the Fourth Army in January 1942, after the failure of the German drive on Moscow, and to command of the First Panzer Army in August 1944. A highly professional military man with the reputation of being a master of defensive tactics, Heinrici succeeded Heinrich HIMMLER on March 20, 1945, as commander of Army Group Vistula. On April 17 he was made responsible for the defense of Berlin but was relieved of his command on April 28 after ordering a withdrawal despite Adolf HITLER's wish to the contrary. His highest rank was colonel general.

HEISENBERG, Werner Karl (1901–1976). A German physicist, discoverer of the "uncertainty principle," Heisenberg was awarded the 1932 Nobel Prize for his work in quantum mechanics. He was associated with Niels BOHR in Copenhagen and in 1927–41 was a professor at Leipzig. He had proposed the creation of a nuclear reactor in 1939, and when the Germans occupied Norway they developed a plant capable of producing heavy water in industrial quantities; they also controlled Europe's largest stock of uranium compounds, in Belgium. But progress on the project was slow and by 1943 it had become essentially moribund—members of Adolf HITLER's staff were dubious about the real prospects of developing a bomb, as was Heisenberg himself. He is said to have discouraged the project because of his disapproval of the Hitler regime.

HELENA, U.S.S. ST. LOUIS–class light cruiser, commissioned 1939. Damaged at PEARL HARBOR, *Helena* returned to action in the Solomons as the battle for GUADALCANAL began in August 1942. She was in the screen escorting carrier WASP when that ship was torpedoed and sunk; in October she took part in the Battle of CAPE ESPERANCE. She was part of the critical naval battle of Guadalcanal in November; during January 1943 she bombarded Japanese positions on NEW GEORGIA. During the Battle of KULA GULF, *Helena* was struck by several Japanese surface-ship torpedoes and went to the bottom. For her work at Guadalcanal, Cape Esperance and Kula Gulf she became the first ship to earn the NAVY UNIT COMMENDATION.

HELFRICH, Conrad Emile Lambert (1886–1962). The Dutch naval commander in chief in the East Indies at the outbreak of the war with Japan; Rear Admiral DOORMAN was his second-in-command. After the disastrous Battle of the JAVA SEA on February 27, 1942—in which Doorman was lost—and the subsequent annihilation of Allied ships in SUNDA STRAITS, Helfrich resigned his command on March 1, since by then he had virtually no Allied ships left to command.

HELLCAT. *See* F6F.

HELLDIVER. *See* SB2C.

HENDERSON, Leon (1895–). American economist active at various levels of administration in the New Deal. In 1940 President ROOSEVELT appointed him to the Advisory Commission of the Council on National Defense to head work on prices. In 1941 the Office of Price Administration and Civilian Supply was created, consolidating the price and consumer divisions of the National Defense Advisory Commission; Henderson was named chief administrator. Later that year the office was reorganized as the OFFICE OF PRICE ADMINISTRATION. By 1942 the OPA was given authority to establish a rationing system governing retail sales. Henderson was also empowered to prohibit unnecessary increases in rents and to prevent hoarding, profiteering, speculation and other practices which contributed to inflation. The rationing program was designed to provide equitable distribution of scarce goods and to protect the interest of consumers. It was carried out by several thousand local rationing boards. Price schedules were also provided, establishing controls on more than 50 percent of all goods sold wholesale.

HENDERSON, Sir Nevile Meyrick (1882–1942). British diplomat, ambassador to Germany in the crucial prewar years 1937–39. He had previously served in various stations, reaching ambassadorial rank in 1935, when he was posted to Argentina. He was closely identified with Prime Minister Neville CHAMBERLAIN's policy of APPEASEMENT, so much so as to draw considerable criticism in the British press (for example, he was called "our Nazi British ambassador at Berlin"). In justification of his approach he subsequently (1940) wrote: "Many may regard my persistence as convicting me of the lack of any intellectual understanding of Nazi or even German mentality . . . but even today I do not regret having tried to believe in Germany's honor and good sense. Whatever happens, I shall always persist in thinking that it was right to make the attempt, that nothing was lost by making it, but that, on the contrary, we should never have entered upon this war as a united Empire and nation . . . if the attempt had not been made." His book has been described as "a masterpiece of self-pleading."

HENDERSON FIELD. The Japanese began this airfield on GUADALCANAL in 1942, and it was one of the primary reasons that Guadalcanal was selected for capture by U.S. planners. Completed by the Marines and ready for air operations in less than a week after the initial landings, the field was named for Maj. Lofton R. Henderson, who led Marine dive-bombers and was killed in the Battle of MIDWAY.

HENLEIN, Konrad (1898–1945). As the leader of the German minority in Czechoslovakia (the Sudetendeutsch), Henlein organized and led a Nazi fifth column that precipitated the MUNICH crisis. The growth of a virulent nationalist movement within the Czech republic helped persuade the British Government to grant concessions to Adolf HITLER during the Munich negotiations. Henlein served the Nazi Party during the war as a gauleiter (district leader). He committed suicide after his arrest by Czech resistance forces in 1945.

HENLEY. This British aircraft, intended by Hawker as a monoplane light bomber, flew for the first time in 1937. The Air Ministry decided, however, that the single-engine, single-seat Henley was inadequate to the demands of modern war and shifted the plane to towing targets, at which it replaced a collection of lumbering biplanes that were too slow for realistic gunnery practice. Beginning in 1942, the Henley gave way to the Miles MARTINET and Boulton-Paul DEFIANT.

HENSCHEL HS 123. Germany's first single-phase, close-support, dive-bomber biplane. Adopted in the summer of 1936, it made its operational debut in the Spanish Civil War as a close-support plane. About 37 were operational in 1939, and these performed the first close-support missions of the war. Operational models went out of service in mid-1944. It carried two 7.9-mm. cowl machine guns, two 20-mm. cannon in the wing joints above the wheels, a 550-pound bomb under the fuselage and four 110-pound bombs under the wings.

HENSCHEL HS 126. A two-place, high-wing, single-engine tactical reconnaissance and army liaison plane. This plane equipped most of the LUFTWAFFE's reconnaissance squadrons at the beginning of the war. Although a good plane for its job, it was phased out to nonoperational roles by the end of 1942 in favor of the FOCKE-WULF FW 189. However, some fought on in night harassment and antipartisan duties in the Balkans, Estonia and Latvia.

HENSCHEL HS 293. German glider bomb that was controlled by radio from the aircraft that launched it. When airborne, it received an initial thrust from a rocket engine. The Hs 293 carried a warhead of 1,100 pounds.

HERÁKLION (Candia). The main airfield on CRETE (the others were MÁLEME and Rétimo), against which the Germans launched paratroops in May 1941. Use of the airstrip soon became impossible, but a heroic stand caused heavy German losses before the British were forced to evacuate the island by sea.

HERALD. U.S. Navy code name for systems of fixed SONAR equipment used to detect and track submarines entering a harbor or anchorage area. The original QBC-1 equipment was developed when the Herald program was initiated in 1941. The later QBD, QCP and QCW-through-QCZ systems were lighter and more compact, better adapted to overseas use.

HERCULES (Herkules). Code name for planned Axis attack on Malta in 1942. Because of General ROMMEL's successes in North Africa, Hercules was postponed by Adolf HITLER until the conquest of Egypt was completed. Hercules therefore went into the category of operations that were never mounted.

HERING, Pierre (1874–1963). A technical and artillery officer, General Hering rose to prominence in the French Army before the war as an advocate of armor. Recalled from retirement during the German invasion, he commanded the Army of Paris in the long retreat of June 1940, until the Franco-German armistice.

HERMANN. Nickname for LUFTWAFFE operations in the Battle of the BULGE; properly called "Der Grosse Schlag" (Great Blow).

HERMES, H.M.S. Royal Navy aircraft carrier, 10,850 tons, completed in 1922 at Devonport. *Hermes* was an experimental small design, with an armament of six 5.5-inch and three 4-inch guns, together with smaller weapons, but carrying only 15 aircraft. Considered too slow and weak for the European theater, she was employed in the South Atlantic (including the abortive DAKAR attack) and in the Indian Ocean, where she was sunk off Ceylon by Japanese carrier-borne dive-bombers on April 9, 1942. She was the last major unit of the Royal Navy to be lost in the war.

HERON (Fischreiher). Code name for the attack by the German Army Group B on STALINGRAD in the 1942 summer offensive.

HERO OF THE SOVIET UNION. Since 1939, the title of highest distinction in the USSR. It is symbolized by a single gold star and is awarded to both military personnel and civilians, Soviet and foreign. The title identifies individuals or organizations that have performed heroic deeds or outstanding feats. The recipient also receives automatic membership in the ORDER OF LENIN (1930).

HERRENVOLK. "Master race"—the term adopted by the Nazis to describe the Germanic people, the so-called Aryans. The concept was one of the principal points of attack in Allied anti-HITLER propaganda. The completely unscientific notion of an Aryan race stemmed from the equally unscientific theories of Social Darwinism, originated late in the 19th century by such advocates of selective breeding as Joseph Gobineau and Houston Stewart Chamberlain.

HERRING, Sir Edmund Francis (1892–). Australian Army officer prominently involved in the fighting in NEW GUINEA from 1942. He was commander, 6th Division, Australian Infantry Forces, 1941–42; General Officer Commanding Northern Territory Force, 1942; GOC II Australian Corps, 1942; GOC New Guinea

Force, 1942–43; GOC I Australian Corps, 1942–44. He held the rank of lieutenant general.

HERRIOT, Edouard (1872–1957). Three-time Premier of France, Herriot in 1936 became president of the Chamber of Deputies. He remained in France after the German occupation in June 1940 and, though he had strongly opposed the Nazis, appeared to accommodate himself to VICHY. But in 1942, when Marshal PÉTAIN dissolved the permanent bureaus of the Senate and the Chamber of Deputies, Herriot was one of the authors of a letter of protest. He was arrested and imprisoned in Germany. In April 1945 he was liberated by Russian troops.

HERRMANN, Hajo (1914?–). German LUFTWAFFE officer, a bomber pilot who in 1943 developed Wild Boar (Wildesau) tactics for the night air defense of German cities. Utilizing a flak-free zone, the Wild Boars attacked the British bombers, which were illuminated by massed searchlights and by the flames resulting from bombing. Herrmann's tactics produced considerable success at Cologne, HAMBURG and BERLIN, and he was promoted from major to colonel. He later was captured by the Russians and imprisoned until 1955.

HERSHEY, Lewis B. (1893–1977). After serving from 1936 as secretary and executive officer of the Joint Army and Navy Selective Service Committee (which planned the organization created following passage of the U.S. Selective Training and Service Act of 1940), General Hershey quickly rose to deputy director (December 1940) and to director (July 1941) of the SELECTIVE SERVICE SYSTEM. In that capacity Hershey, who became a major general on April 16, 1942, was responsible for the efficient registration of 40 million men, of whom about 10.1 million were inducted during the more than six and a half years the 1940 act was in force.

HESS, Rudolf (1894–). Son of a German businessman, Hess was born in Alexandria, Egypt, but from the age of 14 was educated in Germany. He served in the same regiment as Adolf HITLER during World War I, and he completed training as an officer pilot in October 1918. His markedly right-wing views led him to take part in the street fighting against the postwar Communist state government in Bavaria, and he served in the FREE CORPS. In 1920 he became an adult student at Munich University; in April of the same year he joined the embryonic Nazi Party, this being the period in which Hitler was taking control. He was drawn to Hitler from the start, and became his close aide and confidant from 1921. He played a prominent part in the Munich putsch of November 8, 1923. Following its failure, he voluntarily submitted himself for trial, in order to share Hitler's confinement in LANDSBERG castle during 1924. There he assisted Hitler in the composition of MEIN KAMPF in an advisory, but not (as commonly alleged) secretarial, capacity. His influential teacher, Prof. Karl Haushofer—the expounder of geopolitics—was among Hess's regular visitors, and Hitler undoubtedly consolidated his own geopolitical views in conversation with Haushofer and Hess.

During 1925–32 Hess acted as Hitler's confidential aide, using his administrative ability to further the conspiracy for power. He was inseparable from Hitler, believing completely in his leader's destiny. He was cold and somewhat withdrawn, essentially a back-room man, though he could take his place effectively on a platform. His face was stern and handsome, his eyes fierce and penetrating. He was a vegetarian and a nonsmoker, with his own unorthodox ideas about health. He was also a firm believer in astrology. In 1927 he married Ilse Pröhl, another of Hitler's dedicated supporters; his son, Wolf Rüdiger, was not born until 1937. He acted as Hitler's contact man with the upper-class stratum in German society, dealing, for example, with the banker Fritz Thyssen, who became one of the party's wealthy supporters. In December 1932 Hess was placed in charge of the central party commission to control the political activities of the party, and in April 1933, after the seizure of power, he became Hitler's deputy (*Stellvertreter*) as party leader (not, as commonly thought, his deputy head of state), and in December Reich Minister Without Portfolio. Later, in 1938–39, he was to become a member of the Secret Cabinet Council and the Council of Ministers for the Defense of the Reich. He was also a member of the Reichstag from 1933.

The affairs of the party and the state became increasingly integrated. Hess's administrative duties involved supervision of all laws and decrees of the Reich, and he was also in charge of political relations between the Reich and ethnic Germans living abroad—the purpose being to foster pan-German feeling and loyalty. His headquarters were the Brown House in Munich, and from 1933 his chief aide was Martin BORMANN. Hess was signatory to much punitive legislation, including decrees which led to persecution of Jews and later of Poles.

During his career, Hess had maintained his interest in flying and, although forbidden to fly by Hitler once war was declared, he secretly trained himself (with the help of Willy Messerschmitt) to pilot the new Messerschmitt Me 110. With the Russian campaign in secret preparation, Hess (who shared Hitler's view that Anglo-Saxon England ought to be party to the attack on Russia) flew to Scotland in the Messerschmitt on a mission, entirely of his own devising, to bring about peace with Britain. He landed by parachute in Scotland on Saturday, May 10, 1941, around 11 o'clock at night.

All sober evidence points to the fact that Hitler knew nothing of this harebrained adventure until receiving a letter Hess left in which he explained the mission and made the suggestion that, if it failed, the Führer should announce that he had lost his reason. Hitler, consumed by rage and anxiety at what he held to be Hess's betrayal of faith, dismissed him from all his offices and purged his name from Nazi records, announcing in the press that Hess had indeed lost his reason. Bormann, ever power-seeking, took Hess's place as Hitler's confidant.

Churchill played the affair coolly. Hess was kept in custody and interviewed by various persons, including the Duke of Hamilton (whom he wrongly claimed to have met during the Olympic Games in Berlin in 1936), Ivone Kirkpatrick (a former senior staff member at the British embassy in Berlin) and Lord BEAVERBROOK. When it was clear to him that his mission was of no avail, Hess adopted the tactic of pretending amnesia in an effort to be repatriated. He accused his captors of trying to poison him, and twice attempted suicide while in British hands. By the time he was put on trial at NUREMBERG in 1945, he had become the most celebrated psychiatric case in medical history, examined by teams of British, American and Russian psychiatrists. While sending perfectly rational and affectionate letters to his family, he adopted in public the distracted air of the amnesiac, though he caused instant sensation in Nuremberg when on November 30 he declared his loss of memory to have been simulated. He later relapsed into his normal state of indifference to the trial, however, only reviving to make a crazy, rambling statement which the president of the court was forced to interrupt. It would appear this was a further subterfuge to gain clemency. Hess was found guilty only of conspiracy and crimes against peace, and not of war crimes. Against the wishes of the Soviet representatives, who urged his execution, he was sentenced to life imprisonment.

Hess was to remain confined in SPANDAU prison in the British sector of Berlin after all those sentenced to various terms of imprisonment had served their time and been released. Renewed pleas for remission of his sentence on account of his age only met with Russian obduracy. **R.M.**

HEUSINGER, Adolf Ernest (1897–). German Army officer (Generalleutnant), head of the operations section of the high command (*see* OKH) from September 1942 to July 20, 1944, in which capacity he was also Deputy Chief of the General Staff. Heusinger joined the General Staff in 1937 and succeeded Gen. Günther BLUMENTRITT in the operations post. On July 20, 1944, when the bomb planted by Colonel von STAUFFENBERG exploded in Adolf HITLER's headquarters, Heusinger was standing on the Führer's immediate right and was speaking at the time of the explosion. Although he had some connection with the conspirators, he had not been warned of this particular attempt on Hitler's life, and he suffered injuries. Along with many other officers he was quickly arrested, but he survived incarceration to play an important part in West German military affairs in the postwar years, serving as military adviser to the government and later as Chairman of the German Joint Chiefs of Staff (1957–61) and as Chairman of the NATO Military Committee (1961–64).

HEWITT, (Henry) Kent (1887–1972). Hewitt graduated from the U.S. Naval Academy in 1906 and served in battleships, destroyers and patrol craft and in staff positions. As a rear admiral, he commanded task groups in the NEUTRALITY PATROL during 1941. In April 1942 he was given command of the Amphibious Force, Atlantic Fleet, where he directed training of landing-craft crews and Army landing forces. He commanded U.S. naval forces in the invasions of NORTHWEST AFRICA and SICILY, and served as Allied naval force commander during the landings at SALERNO, ANZIO and SOUTHERN FRANCE. From February 1943 he was Commander, United States Naval Forces Northwest African Waters (designated the Eighth Fleet in March of that year). In April 1945 he returned to the United States for duty in connection with the Pearl Harbor investigation. Hewitt ended the war with the rank of admiral.

HEXOGEN. The German name for the explosive RDX (*see* RDX).

HEYDRICH, Reinhard (1904–1942). The principal Nazi agent in the GENOCIDE campaign against the Jews, Heydrich, an able SS officer (*see* SS), was distinguished only by being in the forefront of the worst crimes against humanity practiced by the Nazis. He came of a musical family; his father was a composer and head of the Halle Conservatory, his mother a professional teacher of voice and piano. Heydrich at first seemed destined for a musical career; he was an accomplished violinist, as well as an able all-around student and sportsman. As a youth he saw service in the FREE CORPS movement, where his taste for violence and thuggery found initial expression. In 1922, at the age of 18, he met Wilhelm CANARIS through the latter's wife, another amateur musician; as a result he became a naval cadet on Canaris's ship, the *Berlin.* By 1930 he was chief signals officer, but his career in the Navy was ruined when an affair with the daughter of a steel magnate who had influence with Admiral RAEDER led to demands that he be cashiered if he failed to marry the girl. Since he was by now engaged to Lina von Ostau, he turned the alternative down. He married Lina in December 1931, some nine months after his dismissal from the service.

Through his wife, who was involved with the Nazi movement, Heydrich secured an interview with Heinrich HIMMLER, who had become head of the SS in 1929. Himmler, impressed by Heydrich's icy, unscrupulous intelligence and his blond "Aryan" good looks, offered him the chance to form an intelligence and security service for the SS, the Sicherheitsdienst (*see* SD). Himmler, a desk man, needed a man of action on whom he could depend, and saw this in Heydrich. He also knew that Heydrich had a weak point—his maternal grandmother was alleged to have been Jewish. Heydrich used his powers in the SS to cover this up; indeed, his supposed touch of Jewish blood made him all the more virulently anti-Semitic.

The files of the SS were now in Heydrich's hands, and they grew into a carefully indexed dossier on everyone of importance in the party and the state, secret information from which power through blackmail, "protective custody" and punitive interrogation sprang. The SD was soon allied closely with the GESTAPO, which could act on information supplied by Heydrich. Heydrich built up the evidence which led to the assassinations during the NIGHT OF THE LONG KNIVES in 1934. He came to despise Himmler as an indecisive weakling given to racial theorizing when action was needed. He rose rapidly to become Himmler's deputy at the head of the SS and Gestapo, and his abilities attracted the attention of Adolf HITLER himself. In 1938 he was placed in charge of police activities in Austria after the ANSCHLUSS. In 1939 Heydrich was entrusted with the task of creating the bogus border incident at Gleiwitz which Hitler used to cover his attack on Poland; later he took charge of the brutal "housecleaning" operation in Poland, with its forcible expropriation and mass movement of victims in the depth of winter. He was also in charge of the ACTION GROUPS (Einsatzgruppen) responsible for the mass murder of Jews and political officials undertaken in the wake of the German advance into Russia, and of the organization of the whole genocide operation. His close lieutenants included Adolf EICHMANN and Odilo Globocnik. He was called "the Hangman."

It was from Hermann GÖRING, not Himmler, that Heydrich received on July 31, 1941, his written instruction to undertake the FINAL SOLUTION of the Jewish "problem." In the organization of the extermination centers (with AUSCHWITZ at their head) and the roundups and transport of Jews from all over German-occupied Europe, Eichmann acted as his able second-in-command. Heydrich's ambition was to outclass all Hitler's deputies, including Himmler, and become second only to Hitler himself. He seemed to be on the way to achieving this when in September 1941 Hitler appointed him Reich Protector of BOHEMIA AND MORAVIA, with the rank of Minister of the Third Reich, while at the same time requiring him to maintain supervision of the genocide operation. It was in Prague on June 4, 1942, that he died of wounds sustained in an attack on May 29 by Czech resistance men sent in from Britain. His death was avenged by the SS in their notorious extermination of the Czech village of LIDICE, and he was accorded a state funeral by Hitler. **R.M.**

HEYDTE, Friedrich August, Baron von der (1907–). Colonel von der Heydte, who before the war had been a professor of international law, was in early December 1944 the commandant of the German Parachute Army Combat School. This veteran of the Crete campaign, a cousin of Count Klaus von STAUFFENBERG and an early member of the July 20 conspiracy against Adolf HITLER, was on December 8 ordered to form a unit for a special mission in connection with the ARDENNES offensive (the BULGE). He was to drop at night into the rough area north of Malmédy, open roads in the vicinity for the leading German units and block enemy attempts to reinforce. His operation would be called Hohes Venn. It was to be a difficult one, and the available forces were inexperienced. It did not in fact accomplish many of its purposes, and von der Heydte was taken prisoner on December 23. Even so, Hohes Venn had contributed to the confusion that initially was widespread behind the Allied lines.

HF/DF (Huff-Duff). A British-designed radio direction finder that could pick up transmissions from U-boats and allow convoy escorts or hunter-killer (antisubmarine) ships to determine their position. Extensively used from the autumn of 1941 on, it could rapidly obtain bearing, even on signals too brief to be detected by conventional RDFs. HF/DF played perhaps an even greater role in the Atlantic antisubmarine war than RADAR. The German Navy never realized that such a device was being used against it.

HICKAM FIELD. The most important U.S. Air Corps installation in the Hawaiian Islands, Hickam Field was badly damaged during the Japanese attack on PEARL HARBOR. Hangars, shops, administrative offices and maintenance equipment were destroyed. When the last bomb had fallen, only 79 of 231 Hawaii-based Army planes remained available for action, and some 200 airmen were dead or missing. Most of the losses occurred at Hickam Field.

Two flights totaling 12 B-17s, which were bound from Hamilton Field, Calif., for the Philippines by way of Hickam Field, arrived over Oahu during the attack. The pilots found themselves dodging enemy fighters and simultaneously trying to avoid American antiaircraft fire. One B-17 was destroyed and two more were badly damaged, but the others landed safely at Hickam or elsewhere on the island.

HIEI. Japanese KONGO-class battleship, severely damaged during action with an American cruiser force off GUADALCANAL during the night of November 12, 1942. She was further pounded by daylight air attack on the 13th before finally being scuttled.

HIGASHIKUNI, Prince Naruhiko (1887–). Second cousin of the Japanese Emperor Meiji and uncle of Emperor HIROHITO by marriage. After eight years of study in France (1920–27), Higashikuni held a number of important Army commands, rising to the rank of general in 1937. In 1935 he became a member of the Supreme Military Council. He served as Prime Minister between August and October 1945, but resigned when he became dissatisfied with a number of the occupation's reform directives.

HIGGINS BOAT. The leading U.S. industrial pioneer in the design and manufacture of landing craft in World War II was Andrew J. Higgins, who before the war had developed a "Eureka" boat which was designed for operations in shallow waters and could beach and retract easily. Its chief characteristics were its shallow draft and protected propeller, its capability of beaching by its bow and its small turning circle, which enabled it to leave a beach quickly and turn out to open water without danger of broaching in a heavy surf. The addition of a ramp bow, together with its reliable engine, made it the most versatile and ubiquitous landing craft developed for the war. Officially designated "landing craft, vehicle, personnel" (LCVP), it had a length of 36 feet overall and a beam of 10 feet 5¼ inches, and could carry 36 fully equipped troops or a 6,000-pound vehicle or 8,100 pounds of general cargo. It had a speed of 9 knots in reasonably calm water. The draft was only 3 feet aft and 2 feet 2 inches forward. The boat was armed with two .30-caliber machine guns.

HILL, Harry Wilbur (1890–1971). A graduate of the U.S. Naval Academy in 1911, Hill served with the U.S. battleship fleet attached to the Royal Navy in World War I. In 1942 he commanded the cruiser *Wichita*, engaged in North Atlantic convoy duty. Promoted to rear admiral in September 1942, Hill was given command of Battleship Division 4, supporting the battle for GUADALCANAL. In September 1943 he became commander of Amphibious Group 2. He participated in the battles for TARAWA and ENIWETOK, was second-in-command of the SAIPAN operation and directed the assault of TINIAN. In 1945 he served as deputy commander of the Iwo JIMA force and commanded the 5th Amphibious Force at OKINAWA, being promoted to the rank of vice-admiral. Following the war Hill became the first commandant of the Army and Navy Staff College (later renamed the National War College) and in 1950–52 was superintendent of the Naval Academy.

HILLDRING, John Henry (1895–). U.S. Army officer, Assistant Chief of Staff in the War Department between December 1941 and June 1942. He then became the commander of the 84th Infantry Division during the division's training period in the United States. In April 1943 he returned to the War Department and became the first director of the Civil Affairs Division and a member of the Combined Chiefs of Staffs' Civil Affairs Committee. Hilldring was promoted to major general in 1942.

HILLMAN, Sidney (1887–1946). A native of Lithuania, Hillman moved to Chicago, became involved in labor activities in the clothing industry and in 1914 was elected first president of the new Amalgamated Clothing Workers of America. His continued work in labor, including his role as a founder of the Congress of Industrial Organizations in the 1930s, led to his becoming a national spokesman for labor. In 1940 President ROOSEVELT appointed him to the Advisory Commission of the Council on National Defense as head of the labor division. Hillman's duties were to see that there was an adequate labor supply for defense industries and that work stoppages were held to a minimum. He was also responsible for the training and retraining of workers for new jobs in defense industries.

When the OFFICE OF PRODUCTION MANAGEMENT was created in 1941, Hillman was appointed associate director general; he was also a member of the Supply Priorities and Allocation Board. In 1942, when the OPM was replaced by the WAR PRODUCTION BOARD, Hillman became director of the labor division of the new agency. In 1943 he became chairman of the CIO's Political Action Committee. At the time of the 1944 Democratic convention, President Roosevelt was said to have told his aides apropos of the choice of a Vice-Presidential candidate: "Clear it with Sidney." The phrase was used by Republican campaign speakers, the implication seeming to be that the Democrats were controlled by left-leaning labor leaders.

HIMMELBETT. A German night air-defense concept. A target area with its approaches was blocked off into "boxes," in which ground-controlled night fighters were vectored toward approaching bomber formations until they could pick them up with their own airborne RADARS and go in to the attack.

HIMMLER, Heinrich (1900–1945). Son of a schoolmaster, Prof. Gebhard Himmler, former tutor to the Bavarian royal household, Himmler was born in Munich, received a conventional Catholic upbringing and entered German military service in 1917, becoming an officer cadet. After the war, still having a taste for militarism, he served in the local FREE CORPS. In 1919 he became a student of agriculture at the University of Munich, qualifying in 1922. He grew up prudish, chaste and studious, his right-wing views and anti-Semitism revealed early in his unpublished diary. His early link with Nazism came through contact with Ernst RÖHM, and he played a minor part in the abortive putsch of November 1923, having joined the party the previous August. In 1925, being in search of a job, he entered full-time politics, joining both the staff of Otto and Gregor Strasser and the local SS (*see* SS). His assiduity caught the attention of Adolf HITLER, who made him deputy head of party propaganda in 1926, and in 1929 chief of the small SS force, then some 280 strong; he received the pompous title "Reichsführer SS." In 1930 he became a party deputy in the Reichstag.

In 1928 Himmler had married Marga Concerzowo, a nurse of Polish origin; she was seven years older than he and shared his thrifty nature and his unorthodox views about health and medicine. With her modest capital they bought a farm in Waltrudering, near Munich. The minor profits from this enterprise, run largely by Marga, supplemented Himmler's small stipend. In 1929, they had a daughter, Gudrun. Himmler was later, 1942 and 1944, to have two children, a boy and a girl, by his recognized mistress of this period, a secretary called Hedwig.

Unlike the other Nazi leaders, Himmler began his climb to power behind the scenes. He was an idealist, concerned to see the vindication of his racial beliefs rather than foster his private fortunes. He never sought the public eye. He tried to live within his relatively modest means and was as meticulous in keeping his personal accounts as he was in checking the racial purity of his SS men and their brides, following the establishment of an SS marriage code in 1932. He was determined that his black-uniformed forces should become the knights of Nazism, the elite. Imbued with the principles of racial "Aryanism" implanted in him by Walter Darré, author of *Blood and Soil* (and derived from late 19th-century neo-Darwinism, as expounded in Günther's book, *Racial Science*), Himmler firmly believed the future lay with the blond, Nordic peoples reared in pagan simplicity and dedicated to the twin duties of tilling the good earth and fighting the good fight for German supremacy over all inferior races, whose sole function would be to work for the master race.

In 1931 Darré was placed in charge of the SS department founded to research the ethnic qualities of the various European peoples and check the racial credentials of those who sought to join the SS. Every SS man had to carry a Sippenbuch (a genealogical stud book) and prove the purity of his stock as far back as 1750. In addition, he had to meet standards of health and athletic prowess which Himmler himself, owing to the weakness of his constitution, could not attain. Without his knowledge, the records were faked in his favor, as they were to be for many of the SS.

In 1931, Reinhard HEYDRICH (aged 27) was introduced to Himmler (aged 31), who at once recognized in this tall, blond, athletic prodigy the cold-blooded man he needed to carry out the disciplines he was so skilled at devising on paper. Heydrich was placed in charge of the Sicherheitsdienst, the Security Service (*see* SD), which meant at this stage building up dossiers on everyone of importance to the Nazis, whether inside or outside the party. Heydrich was the opposite of Himmler, ruthlessly energetic in action while Himmler was essentially a desk man, weak, apt to be indecisive when in difficulties, pedantic but always calculating. Heydrich became, in effect, Himmler's second-in-command and took off his shoulders the burden which the SS inherited once power was won.

Himmler's rise was tortuous. First, the SS rapidly grew in strength during 1932, reaching 30,000; it stood in uneasy relationship to Röhm's massive army of the Storm Troopers (*see* SA). Himmler raised the status of the SS by offering members of the aristocracy honorary rank; even archbishops accepted membership. During the period of the seizure of power in 1933, however, Himmler received only the minor office of Bavarian president of police, while Hermann GÖRING, as minister of the interior in the great state of Prussia, built up a new pro-Nazi police system and founded the GESTAPO as his secret political police. During 1933–34 Himmler took action to consolidate what power he could. In March 1933 he founded DACHAU as a "model" CONCENTRATION CAMP for political dissidents in Bavaria and staffed it with SS men, some of whom were later to become infamous. Himmler's carefully worded disciplinary regulations were models of back-room brutality. Then, from October 1933 to March 1934, he began to widen the range of his influence by taking command of the political police in other states, as part of Hitler's new policy of centralization. He achieved his ambition at this stage when, in April 1934, Göring formally handed over to him control of the Gestapo, and the concentration camp system. Himmler's authority in this field now being complete on a national scale, he took up residence in Berlin, leaving his wife and family in a small lakeside property on the Tegernsee in Bavaria. Though he always loved his daughter Gudrun, he gradually became estranged from his wife and kept her very much in the background.

The next consolidation of Himmler's power came through an alliance with Göring in bringing about the downfall of Röhm. Hitler was always slow to take action against old and familiar supporters, but Röhm's manifest ambition was to take control of the Army, 100,000 strong, and merge it with the SA rabble of street fighters, which had risen during the years of mass unemployment to some 3 million unpaid volunteers. Göring, Himmler and Heydrich dredged up all the evidence they could find to smear Röhm not only concerning his conduct and that of his immediate circle of SA commanders as noted homosexuals, but also concerning his alleged readiness to stage a coup d'état (of which, in fact, there was little evidence). Hitler was finally moved to take violent action on June 30, 1934, and there followed the NIGHT OF THE LONG KNIVES—the purge of the SA leadership, as well as of others considered inimical to the Nazi state—in which hundreds were put to death under the supervision of Göring, Himmler and Heydrich. When all was over, the SA fell into abeyance as an organization, while the SS, allied to the Gestapo, became an independent force representing the formidable teeth of the regime, with sanctions of arrest, interrogation under torture and imprisonment in the concentration camps. The SS was itself purged of its less desirable recruits and reduced to a workable national force of some 200,000 men. They were armed and conducted their own paramilitary training, swearing, like the Army after the death of President von Hindenburg, an oath of personal loyalty to Hitler as head of the state. Eventually, in fulfillment of Hitler's orders, the SS supplied the equivalent of a division of battle-trained men, the genesis of the wartime Waffen SS.

Himmler's obsession with historical, even mythological, ceremonial led him to found the SS Order of Teutonic Knights, with its ultimate headquarters in a castle built in medieval style at Wewelsburg in the forests near Paderborn, Westphalia. This castle was run, or was supposed to be run, like a monastery, an SS "retreat," with Himmler as superior general of the order. Heydrich, needless to say, ridiculed these fantasies of his boss.

In June 1936 Himmler was made chief of police of the Reich in the Ministry of the Interior, and in the same year the Gestapo received official recognition as a special nationwide police force with absolute powers which could not be questioned. Himmler was, in effect, given his own powers of action independent of the Minister of the Interior, Wilhelm FRICK. He was so inspired by his new position that he conducted a special ceremony associating himself with Emperor Heinrich I (Henry the Fowler), the 1,000th anniversary of whose death occurred that year. In 1938 Himmler even took issue with the Army by preparing the wholly fabricated case against Gen. Werner von FRITSCH, Commander in Chief of the Army, who was accused of homosexuality. The high command insisted on contesting the case but was foiled, largely because the Austrian ANSCHLUSS came about at exactly the same time. Both Himmler and Heydrich were by then preoccupied with the details of extending their police state to the new territory incorporated into the Reich. The Austrian police were put in the charge of Ernst KALTENBRUNNER, while the purge of Jews was conducted by Adolf EICHMANN, with orders to expedite their emigration.

In 1939 Himmler's health began to give way under the strain of his earnest endeavors to live up to the high responsibilities he had been given. Although still a comparatively young man, he suffered from acute nervous headaches and stomach cramps, and his fastidious attitude to health made him all the more tense and fearful. His resort to nature cures yielded little, but in 1939 he was introduced to Felix KERSTEN, a Finnish masseur with a lucrative international practice. Kersten's "miraculous hands" always brought him complete, if temporary, relief, and during the war years he was to fall under Kersten's sway. He retained Kersten permanently, for a time virtually impounding him in Berlin.

Himmler had already pledged his concentration camp prisoners to war work before the war began, and his name was given to the horrifying hoax Hitler played to initiate the invasion of Poland. Operation Himmler (also called CANNED GOODS) involved the use of political prisoners, specially killed for the purpose, to represent the bodies of Polish invaders who had supposedly crossed the border into Germany. With Poland conquered, the SS became responsible for the appalling atrocities that followed. Himmler in effect delegated actions against the 3 million Jews in Poland to Heydrich. He ordered the movement of ethnic Germans into territory incorporated into the Reich, regardless of the hardships to those evicted or, for that matter, to those favored by being moved in from their homes farther east. In all, over half a million people of German stock were shifted, and a million and a half Poles and Jews expelled to make room for them. And it was Himmler who in the summer of 1941 personally conveyed to Rudolf HOESS, commandant of the Auschwitz concentration camp, the order that his camp should become the greatest single center for the extermination of the Jews and Slavs. The ACTION GROUPS, responsible for the murder of a million or more people in Russia behind the German advance in 1941, were also Himmler's ultimate responsibility. So was the destruction of the WARSAW ghetto in 1943. Ridding Europe of the Jews became his obsession.

Heydrich used the genocide campaign initiated in 1941 as the stepping-stone to power independent of Himmler, a position he achieved when, in September 1941, Hitler appointed him Reich Protector in Czechoslovakia (where he was to be assassinated the following year). By this time Himmler had other aides whose services were kept fully stretched, but (unlike Heydrich) they were kept firmly in their separate places—Hoess in charge of genocide in Auschwitz, Eichmann in charge of the general administration of the FINAL SOLUTION for the Jews of Europe, Heinrich MÜLLER in charge of the Gestapo, Walter SCHELLENBERG in charge of SS intelligence (the SD) and (after Heydrich's assassination in 1942) Kaltenbrunner as Heydrich's successor in charge of SS security and the concentration camps.

Himmler was free now to think of a further extension of his powers in fields he felt would be most helpful to Hitler in his dedicated pursuit of war. He moved about in his special armored train, "Heinrich," supervising the work of the SS in the occupied territories; he gave speeches to the SS leadership and the Army on the need for ruthlessness in matters of racial purity, urged the use of slave labor and explained, in highly select company, the need for extermination.

Himmler had already been prepared for the crime of genocide through the SS campaign for "mercy killing" ordered by Hitler in 1939 and lasting until 1941. Viktor Brack, son of the doctor who had delivered Marga Himmler of her daughter in 1929, was given charge of this "euthanasia" program, which resulted in the killing of some 60,000 people suffering from the severe forms of mental illness; secret extermination centers were set up under the control of selected SS doctors and nurses. The program was finally exposed, and Hitler himself countermanded it when public protest, particularly by the churches, became embarrassing. Himmler was also to take some personal interest in the barbarous medical experiments which SS doctors carried out in various concentration camps, including sterilization of the "racially undesirable" and "research" involving death for some prisoners. These experiments were conducted for Himmler's special Institute for Practical Research in Military Science to further his Ahnenerbe (Ancestral Heritage Community).

Himmler also warmly supported the establishment of homes for unmarried mothers, the so-called Lebensborn institutions, to which SS men had to contribute from their pay. For him, SS men were the fount of life, and suitable girls should be proud to bear racially pure children conceived by them, whether legitimate or illegitimate. The one thing Himmler would not tolerate was homosexuality; this practice was the equivalent of racial sabotage. So were sexual relations between German women and men of inferior race, such as Polish slave workers on the farms; when such cases came to light, they were severely punished. On the other hand, Himmler recommended the expropriation of foreign, non-German children whose appearance seemed to guarantee them to be of good racial stock; many were taken from their homes and reared by German foster parents. Their presence speeded the consolidation of the Aryan master race in the heartland of Germany.

Himmler was by now in a unique position of power; although never an intimate member of Hitler's domestic circle, in the way Joseph GOEBBELS, Göring and Albert SPEER were or had been, Himmler held himself to be coequal with them in the eyes of the Führer, and he was a frequent visitor to Hitler's headquarters. He normally set up his own field headquarters alongside Hitler's, so as to be available for Hitler's regular war conferences. He was responsible for security behind the German Army lines, and during 1941–43 was frequently in Zhitomir in the Ukraine, near Hitler's headquarters at Vinnitsa on the Eastern Front, and later established himself near Rastenburg in East Prussia, Hitler's principal headquarters during the latter period of the war. In 1943 he became Minister of the Interior.

He was deeply concerned over Hitler's state of health, physical and mental, as he revealed to Kersten in December 1942 when he showed him a secret medical report on the Führer; this paper purported to show that Hitler was suffering from progressive paralysis originating from syphilis incurred in youth and left untreated. (This is now proven to have been untrue.) In the hierarchy surrounding the Führer, Himmler trusted only himself as the regime's eventual successor should Hitler collapse. Himmler's lifelong military ambitions began to be roused: he already controlled the SS (and, loosely, its military wing, the Waffen SS), but he had no place in the Army high command. It was because of his suspicion that Himmler might have interests which went beyond the present autocracy of the Führer that Carl Langbehn, a lawyer who was sympathetic to the resistance but who also acted on occasion as an informant for Himmler, arranged that Johannes von POPITZ meet with Himmler on behalf of the resistance to sound him out concerning the position Germany would be in if the Führer were for any reason, no longer in control. Meetings took place in 1943 but did nothing except to excite Himmler's curiosity. The initial, tentative inquiries concerning the prospects for negotiating peace, in which Himmler had shown a distant but continual interest as early as 1942, were put at first in the hands of Langbehn, and later of Schellenberg himself, as head of the SD. Himmler's self-protective sense of caution was naturally foremost in this area, but he revealed his interest to Kersten, on whom he became increasingly dependent both physically and psychologically as the war turned against Germany.

Himmler's ambitions are revealed in his attempt to secure control over the secret V-2 rocket, in his successful move to acquire armed forces intelligence (the ABWEHR) in February 1944, but above all in his appointment by Hitler, on a sudden impulse, as commander in chief of the home-based Replacement Army in place of Col. Gen. Friedrich FROMM. This was on July 20, 1944, the day of the abortive attempt on Hitler's life. Himmler arrived in Berlin that night to take full charge of proceedings against the network of conspirators, who were interrogated by Kaltenbrunner and his men and tried by Roland FREISLER. At the same time, as commander in chief of the Replacement Army he finally secured control of the V-2 rocket. But what proved to be disastrous was his appointment on December 10 as commander of Army Group Oberrhein, possibly to utilize the Replacement Army as part of Hitler's attempt to push back the victorious Allied advance. His failure in military command was total. When things went wrong he blamed the service generals. Hitler transferred him to the Vistula front to stem the Russians—an amateur sent to relieve the professionals in a hopeless situation—where he helped only to make matters worse. Eventually, General GUDERIAN persuaded him to resign from active command in March 1945, though he still retained nominal command of the Replacement Army and the Waffen SS. He now retired to his favorite sanatorium, Hohenlychen, about 70 miles north of Berlin.

It was in Hohenlychen that Himmler intensified his association with those determined to bring about peace and, in particular, relieve the prisoners in the concentration camps (whom Hitler wanted totally destroyed along with the camp buildings). Himmler's visitors included Count BERNADOTTE of Sweden and Kersten, who lived now in Stockholm and was also concerned to save the prisoners. On March 12 Himmler was induced to sign an agreement that the camps should be handed over intact with their prisoners still alive, and on March 14 a further agreement that Dutch cities and the Zuyder Zee dam should be spared attack by V-2 rockets. On April 20 Himmler was back in Berlin for Hitler's birthday celebrations, but the next day he met with Norbert Masur, director of the Swedish section of the World Jewish Congress of New York, who had traveled to Germany incognito. The meeting, organized by Kersten and Schellenberg, led to the release of Jewish women prisoners from Ravensbrück for evacuation to Sweden.

Himmler's main concern by now was to make contact with General EISENHOWER and, as commander of the Replacement Army, initiate peace negotiations, using Bernadotte as intermediary. Late in April he moved from the danger zone of Hohenlychen to Schwerin, which was near Admiral DÖNITZ's headquarters in the north. Then, on April 28, news of his attempted peace negotiations was leaked to the Allied press. Hitler learned of Himmler's betrayal through a monitored radio report and in a convulsive rage dismissed him from all his offices and ordered his arrest, orders which, in the chaotic circumstances of the time, never reached Dönitz.

With the collapse of the Reich following Hitler's suicide, Himmler attempted to maintain his position in the new government at Flensburg, but Dönitz refused to deal with him. Finally dismissed by Dönitz, the new Führer, Himmler left Flensburg on May 10 and, traveling incognito, was finally captured on May 23 by the British, to whom he revealed his identity. He managed to commit suicide shortly afterward, using a phial of cyanide concealed in his teeth. His body was buried in an unmarked grave near Lüneburg. **R.M.**

HIRANUMA, Kiichiro (1867–1952). Vice-president of the Japanese Emperor's Privy Council from 1926 to 1936 and president from 1936 to 1939 and again in 1945. Hiranuma served as Prime Minister between January and August 1938 and then as Vice–Prime Minister, Home Minister and Minister Without Portfolio in the second KONOYE cabinet. He negotiated with WANG CHING-WEI in 1942 to give China's pro-Japanese Nanking regime greater independence from Japan. Several times Hiranuma was attacked and nearly assassinated by ultranationalists who disagreed with his politics. Convicted and sentenced to life imprisonment as a war criminal in 1948, Hiranuma died in 1952.

HIROHITO (1901–). Emperor of Japan since 1926. The role of the Japanese Emperor until the end of World War II is difficult to understand. On the one hand, he was, according to tradition, a direct descendant of the ancient sun goddess; he was, therefore, to remain above politics and to transcend party feuds, since he represented the entire nation. The Emperor presided over the Imperial Conference, a group of top-ranking civilian and military leaders, and said nothing, his mere presence making any decision legal. On the other hand, the Emperor wielded considerable influence, since he was in the unique position of being able to present his views on governmental matters without being held responsible. More significantly, his subjects regarded him as a god and every man and woman was pledged to serve him unto death. Finally, under the 1889 constitution he was Commander in Chief of the Armed Forces.

During World War II, Hirohito, himself a modest and studious man, broke tradition and expressed his opinion at the Imperial Conference on a number of occasions. Thus in 1941 he cautioned the Japanese supreme command about the dangers of war and recommended negotiations with the United States. Though he approved the decision to attack PEARL HARBOR, as early as February 1942 Hirohito urged his Prime Minister, TOJO, to end the war. Three years later, in the midst of the American bombing of Japan, Hirohito played an active role in the search for peace by urging acceptance of the Allied surrender demand. At the surrender of Japan, Hirohito was forced by the Allies to renounce his divinity, though he was permitted to retain the title Emperor and to function as the symbolic head of state.

HIROSHIMA. A port on the southwest coast of Japan, Hiroshima will forever remain in history as the first community to be destroyed by a nuclear bomb. This city was the primary target for the USAAF's 509th Composite Group, which had trained to drop the bomb. The alternate targets were KOKURA and NAGASAKI.

On August 6, 1945, B-29 weather planes reconnoitered the three cities, and another Superfortress, the *Enola Gay,* took off from Tinian carrying a 9,000-pound bomb called "Little Boy." At the controls of the aircraft was Col. Paul W. TIBBETS, Jr., the group commander. Once the plane was in the air, two naval officers, Capt. William S. PARSONS and Lt. Morris R. Jeppson, completed assembling the bomb, and near Iwo Jima word came that the weather was good over Hiroshima. Tibbets headed for the city in the company of two observation planes, also B-29s, Maj. Charles W. Sweeney's THE GREAT ARTISTE and Capt. George W. Marquardt's NO. 91.

At 0815 Hiroshima time, Maj. Thomas W. FEREBEE released the bomb from 31,600 feet. It detonated 47 seconds later at a height of 660 yards (600 meters) over central Hiroshima, generating for 1/10,000 of a second a heat of 300,000° C. The plane, with engines at maximum power, was by then six miles from the holocaust. Following the blinding heat flash, the blast radiating from the bomb devastated the city, immediately flattening virtually every building within a 2,000-yard radius of the hypocenter of the explosion, and destroying those to a radius of 4,000 yards. A few highly resistant concrete shells (including the now-famous skeletonized dome and its supporting base, retained as a permanent memorial) were left; the rest was rubble, dust, dead bodies and horribly mutilated people. The mushroom cloud that rose from the bomb's fireball ascended to 50,000 feet. Three days later, on August 9, a second atom bomb of a different type, nicknamed "Fat Man," was dropped on Nagasaki. At midday on August 15, the Emperor broadcast to the nation and to the world the message of Japan's surrender.

The human toll at Hiroshima and Nagasaki is estimated by Japanese sources as 240,000 dead—many expiring in lingering agony from burns and radiation aftereffects—37,425 injured and 13,983 finally accounted missing. These figures include all who eventually died from aftereffects. American figures for the dead are substantially less: 66,000 to 78,000 dead in Hiroshima and 39,000 in Nagasaki. John Hersey's figure for the dead in Hiroshima is around 100,000. The number subjected to radiation has been estimated by the Japanese to be 300,000. The aftereffect of the bomb in Hiroshima was the generation of spontaneous fires, reaching their climax between 10 in the morning and 2 in the afternoon of August 6, but lasting up to three days in an area with a radius of some 2,000 meters from the hypocenter. Black rain fell torrentially over the western sector of the city up to 4,000 meters from the center.

Hiroshima was a well-chosen target; its normal population of 240,000 civilians was doubled by the presence of a large number of military and naval personnel. No one in Japan realized for some time what actually had caused the devastation. People outside Hiroshima could only offer help to the streams of dazed and mutilated people pouring out of the city. The first detailed account to reach the world was that of John Hersey, filling an entire issue of *The New Yorker* in August 1946 and based on intensive interviews revealing the experiences of six survivors. In 1955, 10 years after the holocaust, there appeared the most remarkable record of the event so far to have been published in English translation—Dr. Michihito Hachiya's *Hiroshima Diary,* a detailed account from both the human and medical points of view of his experiences between August 6 and September 30, 1945. He was himself badly injured but managed to assist in organizing a medical center amid the ruins of central Hiroshima.

An official Japanese film unit was sent during August into both Hiroshima and Nagasaki to record the devastation and the aftereffects on those exposed to radiation. The footage, finished under American supervision, was confiscated by the Americans; some few scenes were eventually released for use in newsreels and documentaries. A print of the total material shot was officially returned to Japan in 1968, and both the Japanese and the Americans have since then released documentaries incorporating considerable footage.

The site in Hiroshima beneath the hypocenter of the bomb is now occupied by a memorial museum set in grounds called Peace Park. The museum contains models, photographs and relics, both horrifying and pathetic, of August 6, 1945.

HIROTA, Koki (1878–1948). A very capable diplomat, Hirota served Japan as ambassador to the Soviet Union (1930–32), Foreign Minister (1933–36 and 1937–38) and Prime Minister (March 1936–June 1937). As Prime Minister, Hirota tied Japan to Germany and Italy in the ANTI-COMINTERN PACT and coordinated Japanese plans for expansion into China. Hirota was created a peer in 1937, following the dissolution of his cabinet. A close ally of Mitsuru Toyama, leader of the ultranationalist and pro-expansion Black Dragon Society, Hirota was judged guilty of war crimes and was hanged on December 23, 1948.

HIRYU. Second ship of the SORYU class of Japanese aircraft carriers. The most striking difference between *Hiryu* and her sister *Soryu* was the position of *Hiryu*'s island structure, on the port side of the flight deck. After taking part in the PEARL HARBOR attack, *Hiryu* was lost at MIDWAY in June 1942.

HISS, Alger (1904–). A graduate of the Harvard Law School, Hiss was a member of the staffs of various Washington departments from 1933 and during the war participated as a State Department employee in international conferences. He served as secretary general for the founding meeting of the UNITED NATIONS at SAN FRANCISCO in 1945. His fame came in the late 1940s as the result of allegations that he had earlier been involved in espionage on behalf of the Communists. He was convicted of perjury in 1950 and sentenced to five years in prison; he was released in 1954.

HITLER, Adolf (1889–1945). Hitler was born an Austrian, at Braunau-on-Inn on the Austrian-German border. His father, Alois Hitler, who was nearing retirement at the time of Adolf's birth, was a customs official of authoritarian character, a man of little education. His mother, Klara, 23 years younger than her husband, had been Alois's mistress before their marriage, which was his third. Alois's family name had been Schicklgruber, but had been legally changed to Hitler in 1876, possibly to secure an inheritance.

As soon as Adolf was old enough to enter into conflict with his father—around the age of 11 or 12—he did so over the desire to begin study to become an artist. Alois refused categorically; he wanted his son to become a civil servant. As a result, Adolf began deliberately to do badly at school. Alois died in January 1903, when Adolf was 14, and his mother, who took him to Linz to live, was prepared to indulge his dreams of becoming an artist or, failing that, an architect. In MEIN KAMPF, written a quarter of a century later, Hitler was to romanticize his youth and rationalize the reasons for his failure at school and his inability subsequently to win a place in the Academy of Fine Arts, for which he applied in 1907 and again in 1908.

In 1907 his mother died. This proved a deep blow, for in spite of the egocentric self-indulgence which was already characteristic of him, he had loved his mother. He had both venerated and exploited her, an attitude to women he was to retain in his maturity. He transferred his semidependence to his hunchback spinster aunt, Johanna Pölzl, cadging money from her when his orphan's allowance of about $5 a month and his modest inheritance from his mother's estate proved insufficient for his austere needs. Posing as a student while living in Vienna, Hitler rejected family pressures to work at some settled occupation, and the somewhat idealized portrait of him drawn by his student friend of the period, August Kubizek, is of a dreamer living self-indulgently but in near-poverty—reading, drawing, walking, talking endlessly about art and politics, going to the opera when he could get hold of the tickets. He was, it seems, shy of girls, and was at once an ascetic and an idler, although already entertaining thoughts of some messianic mission.

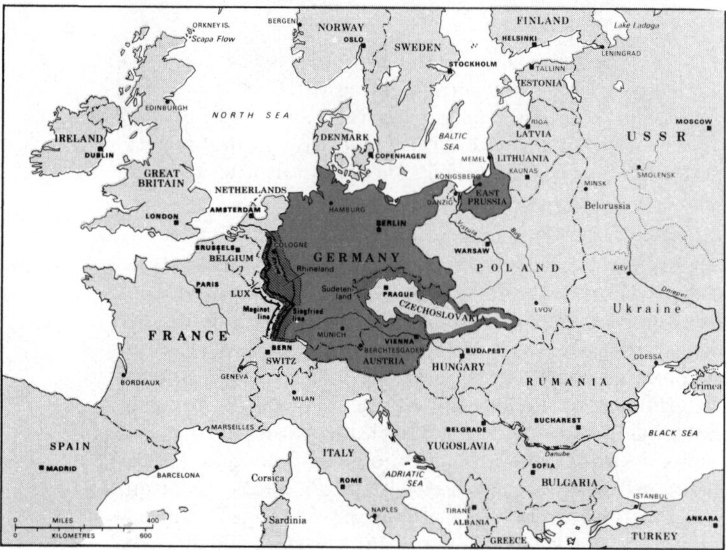

THE EXPANSION OF GERMANY under Hitler, 1936–39

For a short while, in 1909, Hitler lived like a hobo. Then he moved to the comparative comfort of a state men's hostel. From December 1909 until 1913 he eked out his minute pension and the frequent gifts from his aunt with money earned from drawing and painting, which in fact was not inconsiderable. He finally left Vienna for Munich in May 1913, at the age of 24; he appears to have been driven to seek refuge abroad from military service in the army of a state he openly despised for its betrayal of its Germanic heritage. (Robert Payne in his biography of Hitler [1973] cites an unpublished manuscript [preserved in the New York Public Library] written by Hitler's sister-in-law Bridget, wife of his elder half-brother, Alois, stating Hitler became an unwanted guest while they were living in Liverpool, England, staying from November 1912 until the spring of 1913. She claimed that he used the birth certificate of his younger brother, Edmund, who had died in 1900, to help him avoid military service.) By now he was a ceaseless expounder of his nationalistic and racial theories. Once in Munich, however, he was forced by the authorities to return to Linz in January 1914, but was found to be medically "unfit for combatant duties." Immediately after he was free of his legal obligations in Austria, he returned to Munich and when the war started, volunteered for service in the German Army. In spite of his supposed unfitness, he was accepted. He served with some distinction in the Bavarian List regiment; though he did not advance beyond the rank of lance corporal, he won the Iron Cross (First Class). He was severely gassed and temporarily blinded in October 1918, when the war was near an end. He was profoundly shocked by the terms of the armistice. The betrayal (as he saw it) of the German Army became mixed in his mind with the prejudices of his youth (his hatred of the Jews and other "contaminating" people who sapped the German character; his hatred of Marxism, which had threatened Germany briefly after the war and taken its toll of Russia; his hatred of the Social Democrats, who were the primary supporters of the constitution of the new Weimar Republic, a form of parliamentary government Hitler despised). By now, the concept of the leadership principle which would be expounded in *Mein Kampf* was growing in his mind and, while still in uniform, he turned increasingly to politics.

Back in Munich, he was sent by the Army authorities to investigate Anton Drexler's German Workers' Party, a small nationalistic organization which he decided to join with a view to taking it over. He renamed it the NATIONAL SOCIALIST GERMAN WORKERS' PARTY (or "Nazi" Party), and adopted a platform of self-determination for all ethnic Germans, abolition of the Versailles treaty, confiscation of Jewish capital and removal of the Jews from a German state with a centralized, authoritarian government. At the same time, early in 1920, he left the Army to devote himself to his political career.

The year 1920 began to see the formation of the leadership corps who were to be prominent in the Nazi movement. Ernst RÖHM, the Army captain and FREE CORPS commander, and Rudolf HESS, the ascetic student of geopolitics, both joined the party in 1920; Julius STREICHER and Hermann GÖRING joined in 1922, while Heinrich HIMMLER became one of Röhm's recruits in 1923. Meanwhile, the movement had taken over a journal, the *Völkischer Beobachter,* in 1920. As the single outstanding personality in the party, Hitler became its acknowledged leader in July 1921. In November of that same year he founded the Storm Troopers (*see* SA), which would be headed by Göring. They were followed in March 1923 by the first, rudimentary form of the SS, his personal bodyguard (*see* SS). In 1922 Hitler served a month's imprisonment, part of a three-month sentence for creating a disturbance. By November 1923, with the SA now some 20,000 strong, Hitler felt the movement he had established along with Gen. Erich Ludendorff and other right-wing supporters in September to be powerful enough to launch, during a state of emergency in Bavaria, the abortive putsch of November 8.

The failure of the putsch led to Hitler's arrest and his subsequent trial in February 1924. He made this hearing the occasion for an eloquent exposition of his political beliefs. He was given a five-year sentence, of which he served only one year—and that in the comfortable place of honorable detention for political prisoners, LANDSBERG castle, where he could receive visitors and live on lavish gifts of food that poured in from supporters. Here he composed the first part of his semiautobiographical political testament, *Mein Kampf*. Meanwhile, the Nazi Party had been disbanded, Hitler having resigned from his leadership post during the period of his confinement. After the remission of his sentence on December 20, 1924, he refounded the party, but in March 1925 he was forbidden to speak in Bavaria, Prussia and other states. He had to depend on others to speak in public for him until 1927–28, when he regained the right to public platforms in the principal states. He had determined now to fight for power constitutionally through the regional and federal elections.

This intense activity, both before and after the Munich putsch, had brought Hitler into touch with a widening range of people who favored the nationalistic and racist views he put forward with the burning zeal of a prophet. Not only his roughneck followers were attracted; society men like Ernst HANFSTAENGL and Kurt Lüdecke (both of whom were to write books about him) sought his company, and women belonging to the distinguished Wagner and Bechstein families were among those magnetized into becoming his patrons. Between them they taught him the rudiments of polite social behavior. In his early, insolvent days they picked up his bills, gave him food and encouraged him to look for support among the moneyed classes, the aristocracy and the industrialists.

In 1925 Hitler renounced his Austrian citizenship. (He was to remain stateless until February 1932, when he finally acquired German citizenship so that he could run for the German presidency.) At the same time he reformed his leadership corps: Hess remained, but Röhm had resigned and was eventually to go to Latin America, while Göring was in exile fighting his drug addiction. Among Hitler's principal aides between 1925 and 1928, apart from Hess, were Gregor Strasser (later to become to some small degree a rival for the party leadership) and Joseph GOEBBELS, a rising young agitator who took over party organization for Berlin in 1926. Göring returned to favor in 1928, while Himmler was given charge of the small SS force in 1929. Meanwhile, Hitler had organized a great party rally in Nuremberg in 1927; party membership rose from 27,000 in 1925 to 108,000 in 1928, when the party polled 810,000 votes and gained 12 seats in the Reichstag.

The years 1929 and 1930 were to prove very successful for both Hitler and the party. With the economic recession, the rise in unemployment (to 3 million in 1930) and the increasing threat represented by the swelling ranks of the Communists, Hitler and his party seemed the only firm nationalist bulwark in face of the weakness and dissension within the governing classes. Money came from the industrialists. Though it was by no means on the lavish scale so often claimed, it was in sufficient quantity to raise Hitler's standard of living substantially and enable him to acquire the luxurious party headquarters, the Brown House in Munich (formally opened early in 1931). In the Reichstag elections of 1930 the Nazis polled nearly 6.5 million votes and gained 107 seats, becoming second only to the Social Democrats, the Communists by comparison winning only 77 seats. The movement was also spreading abroad, with National Socialist representation in the assemblies of both Austria and Danzig.

Hitler's much-debated relationship with women was a prominent factor in his life about this time. All the available evidence (as painstakingly assembled by his German biographer Werner Maser) points to the fact that he was quite normal sexually, though probably retarded somewhat in early manhood because of his ascetic habits. His response to women during the 1920s appears to have been to seek out those who would mother him, acting as patrons of his movement while at the same time providing him with domestic and other comforts to ease his spartan existence. Mostly these were older women, or if nearer his own age, were socially far better placed than he was. But as his star rose, mothering by women gave way to awe and admiration in those whom he attracted. At the same time, his tastes seem to have changed when he was around 40. He became increasingly attracted to girls much younger than himself, pretty and without marked character.

Kubizek reveals Hitler's remarkable adolescent infatuation with a girl called Stephanie, whom as a youth he had loved only from a distance, never disillusioning himself by actually meeting her. Although in maturity he treated women with an almost old-fashioned gallantry, he never hid his view in private that he regarded them as very subsidiary as a sex to men. He had the good sense to realize that his Führer image, his charisma, required that he should not marry. However prudish during his youth, he must have forfeited his virginity at some time, whether in Vienna, in Munich, during the war or during the 1920s. His name was coupled with those of many girls, culminating in his relationship with his niece Geli Raubal, 19 years younger than he. After Geli's suicide in his apartment (1931), Hitler himself appears to have contemplated suicide. Maser claims she had been his mistress and remained in memory his one real love; he also points out that their devotion to him drove several other women to attempted suicide—Eva BRAUN (two attempts), Maria Reiter, Unity Mitford, Inge Ley and others. The actual reason for Geli's suicide became the cause for speculation from the moment it occurred. Was it because Hitler tyrannized her, made her subject to unnatural sexual practices, tried to prevent her from enjoying other love affairs or drove her mad with jealousy because of his association with Eva Braun, whom he had first met in 1929?

Of those who knew him intimately, Hanfstaengl always claimed (with his wife) that Hitler was impotent and that he had seen Hitler's lewd drawings of Geli, while Albert SPEER has claimed that by the mid-1930s Eva was increasingly lonely and that Hitler's lovemaking either had become infrequent or had been abandoned altogether. She was jealous, too, of the attentions he paid to other women when away from BERCHTESGADEN, where she was mostly required to live.

The period 1931–32 represents the next stage of the advance to power. It was a testing time for Hitler's strength of character, the period of temptation to accept a secondary position as Vice-Chancellor to Franz von PAPEN. Hitler, supported primarily by Göring and Goebbels, insisted to everyone, from President von Hindenburg (who received him for the first time in October 1931) and the successive Chancellors Brüning, von Papen and Schleicher down to the rank and file of the party, that it was to be the chancellorship or nothing. In 1931 Röhm returned from Bolivia to take charge of the SA on Hitler's invitation; the SA increased to 300,000 during the year. And Göring became president of the Reichstag after the election of July 1932, when the Nazis polled 13.7 million votes and achieved 230 seats in the Reichstag.

Meanwhile Hitler had fought (and, as anticipated, lost) the 1932 election for the presidency, achieving in the second round of voting 13.4 million votes. The successive campaigns of 1932 (for the presidency, the Reichstag elections, the state elections) were conducted with increasing violence in the streets and at political meetings and rallies, largely in fighting between the SA and the Communists. During the campaigns Hitler and Goebbels never ceased to speak at rallies throughout the country, traveling by air and working around the clock.

In the November Reichstag elections the Nazis lost some 2 million votes; as the economic situation was showing the first signs of improvement, support for the party was beginning to wane. Goebbels as campaign manager was in despair, but Hitler resorted to intense negotiation behind the scenes to recoup his position. He met with Papen on January 4, 1933, at the house in Cologne of Kurt von Schröder, the banker. This meeting was crucial in bringing about the downfall of Chancellor Schleicher and the appointment on January 30 of Hitler as Chancellor. Hindenburg had been under pressure from several sources to give the office to Hitler; Papen and Hjalmar SCHACHT, the latter representing an important group of industrialists, had been particularly active.

Hitler's cabinet contained only two Nazi members, Göring and Wilhelm FRICK. The remaining eight ministers were right-wingers led by Papen, the new Vice-Chancellor, who believed he and his colleagues could keep Hitler under control once he had got what he wanted. The next election (in which the Nazis hoped to achieve a majority in the Reichstag) was called for March 5, and during the intervening weeks everything was done to secure the foothold that had been gained. Contrary to Papen's woefully misguided expectations, the Communists and Social Democrats were subject to continual harassment, culminating in wholesale arrests following the REICHSTAG FIRE on February 27. Göring worked day and night as minister of the interior of Prussia to nazify the command in the Prussian police, and he supplemented the police with a massive force of SA and SS auxiliaries. But the election still failed to give Hitler the absolute majority he sought, though in this last nominally free election the party secured some 43 percent of the vote, which gave him 288 deputies in a house made up of 647 members. The Reichstag was opened with traditional ceremony in Potsdam, attended by Hindenburg and the old military establishment dressed in style. When on March 23 Hitler presented the ENABLING ACT, giving him the power to rule by decree, it was passed because so many deputies belonging to the opposition were absent or under arrest; only the Social Democrats voted against the bill. The third and final phase in the seizure of power was complete, and rule by decree, with total disregard of the Reichstag as a lawmaking body, followed.

The policy now was as speedy a national nazification, or coordination (Gleichschaltung), as possible. During the six years before the outbreak of war in 1939, Hitler was occupied first in restructuring the state and secondly in conducting foreign policy and the expansion of Germany to the east. The state diets were dissolved to bring the nation into a single administrative system controlled by a unified police force—including the secret political police, the GESTAPO, and Hitler's disciplined national force, the SS (all under Himmler's control). The SS replaced the SA as the primary coercive force after the purge of Röhm and his associates in the summer of 1934. In this bloody action many old opponents were killed, including Schleicher and Gregor Strasser. All means of communication came under state control through Goebbels's Ministry of Propaganda. Jews were removed from public life, persecuted, dispossessed and driven into exile, 235,000 leaving during the period 1935–38. No political parties other than the National Socialists were permitted after July 1933, while the state and the party became increasingly coordinated. Labor and industry alike came under exacting control, administered at first by Schacht and later by Göring; the economy was put on a war footing.

On the death of Hindenburg (August 2, 1934), Hitler combined the offices of President and Chancellor, calling himself FÜHRER and Reich Chancellor, to whom all officers and men in the armed forces (the only independent entities left in the state) had to swear an oath of personal allegiance. In a plebiscite conducted by the Nazis with every degree of nationwide coercion, Hitler obtained a vote of confidence from 90 percent of the German people out of a 95.7 percent poll. (Four and a quarter million voted against him.) Conscription for the Army was introduced in March 1935, and in September the notorious "Law for the Protection of German Blood and German Honor" (the Nuremberg Laws) prohibiting intermarriage between Jews and Germans. In 1938, after the fall of Field Marshal von Blomberg (War Minister since 1933) and General von FRITSCH (Commander in Chief of the Army), Hitler made himself Minister for War and put a close follower, Joachim von RIBBENTROP, at the head of the Foreign Ministry.

Turning to foreign policy, Hitler attempted to consolidate the powerful Catholic opinion in Germany in his favor by concluding a concordat with the Holy See in July 1933. In October he withdrew Germany from the League of Nations. In 1935 he gained the Saar for the Reich, following a plebiscite that polled 91 percent in favor of return to Germany. In 1936 he took a grave risk in occupying the demilitarized Rhineland and repudiating the LOCARNO treaties; the supine reaction of France and Britain encouraged him to go further in his challenges to the Western powers. Having first met MUSSOLINI in Venice in 1934, he established the Rome-Berlin AXIS in 1936, the year in which he also signed the ANTI-COMINTERN PACT with Japan.

In 1938, using diplomatic blackmail, he occupied Austria, making it part of the German Reich, and shortly afterward he inveigled the Western powers into forcing CZECHOSLOVAKIA to yield the SUDETENLAND—his so-called final demand in Europe—at MUNICH. In March 1939 German troops entered the whole of Czechoslovakia, after Hitler had forced the aged Czech President, Emil HACHA, to accept German "protection." In the same month he took over MEMEL. In August 1939 he brought off the wholly unexpected SOVIET-GERMAN NONAGGRESSION PACT, thus obtaining the temporary security of his borders in the east. Secret clauses in this agreement predetermined what parts of eastern Poland STALIN could occupy once Hitler had invaded that country—the next on his list of conquests in the territories east of Germany. Thus, before the Polish campaign, in a series of brilliant and wholly unscrupulous diplomatic strokes, Hitler had increased by over half the size of the German Reich in less than five years.

During this period of expansion, successful largely because of the unexpected effrontery with which Hitler disregarded all established codes of international conduct, he did not change his petit bourgeois style of living, though he acquired the capacity to deal effectively with diplomats and heads of state. Visiting delegates were impressed by his grasp of affairs and phenomenal memory for detail, though his apparent courtesy often gave way to his habit of subjecting visitors, however eminent, to long speeches on his policy of the moment.

The one great monument to Hitler's architectural ambitions for the Berlin of the future was the massive chancellery that SPEER completed for him in January 1939. For his private relaxation Hitler constructed the BERGHOF in his mountain estate above Berchtesgaden in the OBERSALZBERG (Bavaria). Here he gathered his small group of intimates; he had no friends, only followers, in his domestic circle. They existed to sustain his ego, listening patiently if wearily to the incessant talk that lasted far into the night and thus lessened the hours of his insomnia. Hitler tended to turn day into night, to retire in the small hours and rise late in the morning, to work intermittently and, when he felt like it, to idle away his time, even in periods of crisis.

It was during the 1930s that Hitler began to develop hypochondria. Contrary to a great deal of rumor, his basic health record was virtually normal. Since 1923 he had, however, had a tremor in his left arm (possibly of psychosomatic origin) which tended to recur when he became deeply worried. He took pep pills made up of kola, caffeine and sugar before delivering any major speech or undertaking exhausting engagements. In 1931 he became a vegetarian and also gave up drinking beer. He did not smoke and did not permit others to smoke in his presence. But during the 1930s he suffered recurrent gastric pains, and he feared as his voice grew hoarser that he had cancer of the throat. He was relieved to find that the hoarseness was due to benign polyps of the vocal cords, which were removed. He complained of cardiac pains. From 1936 he placed himself almost entirely in the hands of the society physician Theodor MORELL. Dr. Morell prescribed a variety of pills, including stimulants that excited his patient, increasing his aggressive tendencies.

More important was the development in Hitler of an obsessive desire to fulfill his political destiny (as he visualized it) as rapidly as possible, before he suffered an incapacitating heart attack. From 1941 his health was to deteriorate markedly under the strain of war, increasing his fits of temper at what he held to be the dilatory nature of the high command. Stomach pains, debility, headaches and nausea were among his symptoms; he also suffered from frequent colds and influenza. From 1943 he aged visibly. The tremor in his left arm was more pronounced, and it appeared also in the left leg; he dragged his left foot when walking. His spine developed a curvature, which caused him to stoop. His sight also deteriorated, but was never chronically affected; he had had to wear spectacles for normal reading for some time. Like Hindenburg, he was able to read his speeches without the aid of spectacles by having them printed by a machine with giant type. The assassination attempt of July 1944 did not seem to affect him as much as might have been expected; his survival in fact encouraged him to feel that he was the chosen one of Providence. But he suffered a slight heart attack in mid-September 1944, which confined him to bed until October. He twice underwent complete medical examinations, in 1940 and 1944, by Dr. Erwin Giesing, whose diagnoses survive and are fully quoted and discussed by the biographer Werner Maser. His memory lost little of its phenomenal quality, but his mental capacity to conduct total war was gravely impaired. At 56 Hitler was a prematurely aged, sick and neurotic man, his mind no longer flexible, his features masklike, his eyes quite protuberant.

It is necessary to understand Hitler's obsession with his health in order to understand his attitude to the conduct of the war. His personal anxieties always influenced his judgment, hastening the timing of campaigns and making him insist on rigorous aggression. Also, political considerations commonly took precedence over considerations of military strategy. Hitler was in a hurry to determine the pattern of events so that his successor, whoever he might be, would find himself fully committed. He wanted to start his war before his fiftieth birthday. The Second World War was thus the culmination of the policy forecast in *Mein Kampf;* Hitler was nothing if not consistent when it came to the broader objectives behind his actions. However, his failing health tended to make him an indecisive commander in the field.

Hitler's strategy depended on the BLITZKRIEG, calculated to achieve quick results at minimal cost in men and equipment. In 1939 the German armaments industry was not in a position to supply the needs of a long war. Hitler's success as a conqueror depended on immediate, startling victories, and this was precisely what happened in Poland, NORWAY and FRANCE, though with significant losses in German sea power. Only in the case of BRITAIN did Hitler face a strategic deadlock, with severe losses of planes and crews. Typically, he turned his back on a campaign that obviously was not going to produce quick results, while entertaining delusions that Britain would eventually come to her senses and sue for peace. Deflected by Mussolini's inability to complete his campaign in the BALKANS without German aid, Hitler unleashed a ruthless blitzkrieg. It succeeded, but the price was a late start to the assault on Russia, though this appeared at first to be astonishingly successful. Hitler's second failure was his inability to bring about a full-scale, decisive defeat of the Soviet Union before the fatal winter of 1941–42.

Thereafter, Hitler chose a strategy governed by political and economic considerations, advancing in the Ukraine and the south as far east as STALINGRAD. His forces became gravely overextended, being in operation from the environs of LENINGRAD and MOSCOW out to the extreme southeastern front in the Caucasus, in the Mediterranean and North Africa, and along the seaboard of the Atlantic from the Arctic Circle to the south of France. In the end, Germany itself became insufficiently protected—first from ceaseless Allied bombing and finally from attack by land simultaneously from the east and the west.

Hitler's genius in both politics and war depended on lack of scruple or humanity, intuitive skill in outfacing his opponents, and charismatic success that stifled criticism. There was little latitude for him in decline; surrounded largely by yes-men in the high command, he directed the late, unsuccessful phases of the war with increasing loss of self-confidence. At the same time, he refused to consider the views of the few men of common sense left in the high command, who opposed his cruel waste of people and massive sacrifice of equipment and would have spared Germany the catastrophic losses to which his intransigence submitted her. In the end his was, as Maser puts it, an ersatz strategy: Hitler was no military genius in defeat and ill health. His final, self-deluding conduct of the war from the confines of the bunker in Berlin could only lead to his complete humiliation. He preferred suicide to capture or death by the enemy, and it was his final desire that Germany and the German people should be destroyed along with the Führer they had "betrayed." The most sensible act of the final months was his lucid, if overrationalized, analysis of his errors in strategy published posthumously as *The Testament of Adolf Hitler,* transcribed under Martin BORMANN's supervision in February 1945.

On April 29, 1945, Hitler married Eva Braun, who of her own volition had joined him in the bunker. Then he dictated his last will and testament. Bormann and Goebbels, last of the Nazi hierarchy to stay with the Führer, witnessed both his marriage certificate and the typescript of the legal documents. On April 30 Hitler and his new wife died by suicide. Their bodies were burned. Maser denies that the remains exhumed by the Russians and described in such detail by Lev Bezymenski in his book *The Death of Adolf Hitler* (1968) were actually those of Hitler, since they do not sufficiently correspond to the known details of his physiology.

With the passage of time, historians, biographers and psychologists will no doubt combine to arrive at some unprejudiced evaluation of Hitler. The magnitude of the suffering caused by Hitler and Nazi Germany in Europe remains so dark and bitter a memory that objective judgment of him may well have to wait another century. The map of Central Europe has been substantially redrawn as a result of the conflicts occasioned by Hitler's short-lived Reich, which he dreamed would last a thousand years. The fascination that Hitler holds for so many people is due less to the personality of the man—which apart from recordings of his voice and his image on film must now depend largely on contemporary descriptions—than to a kind of awe inspired by the unparalleled degree of power he achieved in so short a time and his capacity to take complete psychological possession of a great modern nation.

To all outward appearance he remains commonplace and unattractive, speaking a heavily accented German in a harsh and brutal way. What has to be taken into account is that within this man of petit bourgeois background existed a ruthless, uncompromising mind of exceptional strength and a will to power which from the age of 30 made him hypnotically irresistible to those susceptible to his nationalistic fervor. His unique qualities included his capacity to command men from all walks of life, to intimidate the weak and uncertain and to follow without deviation the destiny he had prescribed for himself and the German people. It is notable that Mussolini, until Hitler's rise the leading exponent of fascist dictatorship, was incapable of sustaining other than second place to him. Although always critical of Hitler, he was nevertheless overawed and fascinated by him. Comparison with Napoleon inevitably comes to mind. Hitler conquered a greater empire in a shorter time—and lost it faster. Hitler's gravest weakness, his lack of humanity, enabled him to sacrifice his soldiers on a scale Napoleon could never have entertained. Hitler had little or no feeling for anyone, and genocide was to him no more than a necessary fulfillment of his ethnic prejudice and the need to clear the ground for territorial possession.

The pattern of Hitler's thought is revealed in his *Table Talk,* the ruminations that Bormann recorded during the early war years, before the Führer's deterioration set in. It is a strange, alarming combination of prejudice and insight, rabid rationalization and occasional acute observation, the fruits of wide reading and considerable thought, all bent to sustain his own idiosyncratic understanding of history, human nature, the arts and sciences. *Table Talk* also reveals his marked sense of humor, little shown in public except for scathing sarcasm; even his private humor was largely at the expense of others. His belief in himself extended to a semireligious belief in "Providence," which had made him, he claimed, the greatest German of the century. He spoke of himself in mystical terms, fulfilling his destiny with the "assurance of a sleepwalker." However, according to Percy Ernst Schramm in his book, Hitler was not (as is commonly thought) superstitious. Without *Table Talk* Hitler cannot be rightfully understood, but although it raises his stature well above the commonplace, it does nothing to lighten the burden of inhumanity he must carry in history. As Trevor-Roper has put it, it is only too easy to underestimate the capacity of Hitler's mind because it is repellent.

He undoubtedly possessed genius which, combined with his ruthless willpower, brought him rapidly to the top and made his leadership of the German people at this difficult time in their national history seem inevitable. His genius lay in speechmaking, in propaganda, in his intuitive skill in handling opponents weaker or more deluded than himself, and in directing his carefully calculated moves toward ever increasing power, both military and diplomatic. He took comparatively few risks in the key moments in his career, except at the beginning, when he was inexperienced (the 1923 November putsch), and at the end, when his judgment was clouded and his self-confidence eroded. All the other ventures were shrewdly timed. Yet Hitler's personality may well remain at bottom an enigma, for, in spite of his evident genius and even his sensitivity, his nature remained warped, restricted, vulgar, egocentric, prejudiced and fundamentally inhumane. He was, says Trevor-Roper, "the coarsest, cruellest, least magnanimous conqueror the world has ever known." **R.M.**

HITLER YOUTH. Nazi youth organization, an important element in National Socialism's program of establishing complete control over every segment of life within the German state. The most prominent Nazi involved with the Hitler Youth movement was Baldur von

SCHIRACH, who became Youth Leader of the German Reich in June 1933. He literally took over other German youth movements, seizing millions of dollars' worth of property. To extend their control over German youth, the Nazis outlawed all other youth organizations (1936) and conscripted children into the Hitler Youth (1939). Under the system children were organized by ages into various cadres and were sent to special schools. From this program of political education the Nazis hoped to produce their future leaders. It was to this group that Hitler turned for the final defense of Berlin. *See also* NATIONAL SOCIALIST GERMAN WORKERS' PARTY.

HIT PARADE. U.S. Navy name, assigned in 1944 to a submarine operating area off the eastern coast of Japan.

HIWI. A Soviet volunteer, generally a prisoner of war, who worked for the German Army in Russia in such capacities as laborer, truck driver and groom. The name comes from the German *Hilfswilliger* (volunteer auxiliaries). In practice, many of the *Hiwis* participated in the fighting.

HIYO. Class of Japanese aircraft carriers. Originally begun as passenger ships, they were converted to carriers and completed in 1942. *Hiyo* and her sister JUNYO saw considerable war service. *Hiyo* was lost to American air attack in the battle of the PHILIPPINE SEA; *Junyo* survived the war in battered condition and was later scrapped. Displacing about 27,500 tons, the Hiyos were nearly 720 feet long, with a speed of 25-plus knots and a capacity of more than 50 planes.

HNS. U.S. Navy designation for the R-4 helicopter (*see* R-4).

HOARE, Sir Samuel (1880–1959). British statesman and diplomat. He was Secretary of State for Air (1922–29), for Foreign Affairs (1935) and for Home Affairs (1937–39), First Lord of the Admiralty (1936–37) and ambassador to Spain (1940–44). He is remembered as the co-creator of the quickly discredited Hoare-Laval Pact (1935), an attempt to appease MUSSOLINI by recognizing some of his claims in Ethiopia while at the same time preserving some independence for the country. The plan was blown away by popular indignation, and Hoare was replaced as Foreign Secretary by Anthony EDEN.

HOBART, H.M.A.S. This 7,105-ton cruiser of the Royal Australian Navy operated throughout the war in the Pacific. During the Japanese drive through the Netherlands East Indies in the early months of 1942, she formed part of Rear Admiral DOORMAN's force of Dutch, American, British and Australian cruisers and destroyers, based at Batavia, which suffered heavily in many actions in and around the JAVA SEA. Later that year she operated with American task forces in the Battle of the CORAL SEA and in the GUADALCANAL campaign. In 1945 she took part, as support ship, in the Australian assaults of Tarakau and BALIKPAPAN in Borneo.

HOBBY, Oveta Culp (1905–). As a result of her work as a civilian consultant in the War Department's Bureau of Public Relations (1941–42), Mrs. Hobby was selected by U.S. Chief of Staff Gen. George C. MARSHALL in May 1942 to be director of the Women's Army Auxiliary Corps. After a bill was passed on July 1, 1943, which established the WOMEN'S ARMY CORPS as a part of the Army of the United States (the expanded wartime Army), Mrs. Hobby was sworn in as the first member of the WAC and took the oath of office as a colonel. She continued in the job of director until July 12, 1945, when she resigned owing to ill health. Credited with having performed an extremely difficult job with great success, Colonel Hobby was awarded the DISTINGUISHED SERVICE MEDAL upon leaving the WAC. In later years Mrs. Hobby continued to be active in business, politics and national and community affairs. She served as the first Secretary of the Department of Health, Education and Welfare (1953–55).

HOBGOBLIN. Allied code name for the island of PANTELLERIA, in the Mediterranean.

HO CHI MINH (1890–1969). Born Nguyen Van Thanh, Ho Chi Minh (He Who Enlightens) took his better-known name when he began his wartime effort to organize a Communist and non-Communist coalition in Vietnam, the Viet Minh. Emerging as its leader at the end of the war, Ho was the coalition's driving force. The Viet Minh was the only anti-Japanese movement of consequence in Vietnam; it was responsible for occasional forays against the Japanese and for gathering intelligence. Ho Chi Minh subsequently became the leader of the Democratic Republic of Vietnam.

HODGE, John R. (1893–1963). U.S. Army officer who saw World War I service in France and was stationed in Luxembourg after the armistice. His World War II career was in the Pacific. He was assistant division commander of the 25th Infantry Division on GUADALCANAL, and in June 1943 he assumed command of the AMERICAL DIVISION. When the 43d Division was involved in a tough fight on NEW GEORGIA, Hodge was temporarily put in command. In August 1943, after the fall of New Georgia, he returned to the Americal for the BOUGAINVILLE operation. Hodge became commanding general of XXIV Corps in April 1944, leading the corps on LEYTE and OKINAWA. On June 6, 1945, he was promoted to lieutenant general.

HODGES, Courtney Hicks (1887–1966). So taciturn was Courtney Hodges, so averse to personal publicity and lacking in attention-provoking personal eccentricity, that the Supreme Allied Commander, Gen. Dwight D. EISENHOWER, at one point asked his public relations staff to focus on Hodges in order to obtain recognition for his command, the U.S. FIRST ARMY. General Eisenhower was so concerned that Hodges and his superior, Gen. Omar N. BRADLEY, were lacking due recognition of their abilities and accomplishments that this factor entered into his decision in the spring of 1945, during the drive across Germany, to shift the Allied main effort from the British 21ST ARMY GROUP to Bradley's 12TH ARMY GROUP, which included Hodges's First Army.

Georgia-born, Hodges at 18 failed geometry at the U.S. Military Academy, but enlisted as a private and after three years won a competition that brought him an officer's commission only a year later than his former classmates. After serving in the Philippines and chasing Pancho Villa in Mexico, he commanded a battalion in the Meuse-Argonne campaign of World War I, in the course of which he was awarded the Distinguished Service Cross for valor.

During interwar service at the infantry school at Fort Benning, Ga., Hodges impressed the man who would be the World War II Chief of Staff, Gen. George C. MARSHALL, and on another tour in the Philippines he served with Eisenhower, then a lieutenant colonel. When World War II began, General Marshall brought Hodges to Washington as Chief of Infantry. In the spring of 1944 Hodges went to England to be deputy to Omar Bradley, who was commanding the First Army and was to move up to army group command, with Hodges taking over the First Army. Assuming command on August 1, he made few changes, for his methods and those of Bradley were markedly similar.

Of medium height with graying hair and mustache, Hodges looked more businessman than soldier. He seldom found it necessary to raise his voice, yet he was firm and demanding with subordinates. He was also cold and colorless and had little appeal to the ranks. He insisted on detailed planning from his staff. General Bradley once remarked that he had "implicit faith in his judgment, skill and restraint." Perhaps the only time Hodges's calm mien appeared ruffled was during the Battle of the BULGE when the severe blow the Germans had dealt his forces hit home. In the first days of the battle many of his headquarters people were in a near-panic state.

Retiring soon after the war with four stars, General Hodges indulged his long-standing interests in duck hunting and fine guns and wines.

HOEPNER, Erich (1886–1944). Colonel General Hoepner was a bold and aggressive German tank commander who led a panzer corps in the west and a panzer group in the invasion of the Soviet Union. He was humiliated by Adolf HITLER and retired from the Army during the Führer's recriminatory wholesale dismissals of officers following the failure of the Moscow offensive in December 1941. An outspoken man and a convinced opponent of the Nazi regime even before the war, Hoepner was to have been Commander in Chief of the German Army had Hitler been eliminated on July 20, 1944. Arrested in the BENDLERSTRASSE when the officers' revolt failed, he was executed on August 8, 1944. *See also* OPPOSITION TO HITLER.

HOESS, Rudolf (1900–1947). Brought up in a devout German Catholic family and intended for the priesthood, Hoess ran away to join the Army, became a member of the postwar FREE CORPS and joined the Nazi Party in 1922. In 1923 he was involved in a brutal political murder, for which he was sentenced to 10 years' imprisonment, but served only five. He joined the SS in 1933 (*see* SS), and in 1934 became a member of staff at DACHAU concentration camp. In 1938 he became adjutant to the commandant at the Sachsenhausen camp. His insensitive acceptance of the principle that "orders are orders" commended him to Heinrich HIMMLER, and he rose steadily in the CONCENTRATION CAMP administration to become one of Himmler's most trusted officers. He was given charge from 1940 to 1943 of the key extermination camp at AUSCHWITZ. His imperturbability while testifying at NUREMBERG to his skill in exterminating 2 million prisoners horrified his listeners, and the near-pious attitude he adopted in the memoirs he wrote while in captivity reveals to the fullest extent what Nazi indoctrination could mean. He appeared to experience no sense of guilt; he had merely fulfilled meticulously an unpleasant duty. He was finally sentenced to death by a Polish people's court, taken to Auschwitz and hanged on the site where he had once administered mass extermination.

HOFACKER, Cäsar von (1896–1944). Lieutenant Colonel Hofacker was a cousin of the anti-HITLER conspirator Count von STAUFFENBERG, and one of his close aides during the period preceding the attempt on Hitler's life in July 1944. One of Field Marshal von KLUGE's staff officers in France, Hofacker acted as liaison between Berlin and General von STÜLPNAGEL in France, and it was intended that he should be Germany's ambassador to France if the attempt succeeded and an interim military government was established in Germany. On July 20, 1944, he acted in close association with Stülpnagel, accompanying him as principal advocate on the abortive final mission to Kluge's headquarters at La Roche–Guyon to involve the field marshal directly in the conspiracy. Subsequently, Hofacker was arrested in Paris by the Gestapo and taken to Berlin for interrogation. He was tried along with Stülpnagel on August 29 and condemned to death. He was not executed, however, until December 20, 1944.

HOFFMANN, Heinrich (1885–1957). Official photographer to Adolf HITLER (and the only person allowed officially to photograph him), Hoffmann claimed to have taken 2.5 million photographs of Hitler between 1922 and 1945. He and his family became close personal friends of the Führer. Born in Fürth, Hoffmann was apprenticed to his father, who was court photographer to the Bavarian royal house. Later he worked with E. O. Hoppe in London, and he returned to Germany to found his own studio in Munich in 1909, specializing in political news photographs. A considerable collection of his unique studies of Hitler is preserved in an archive administered by his son. It was through Hoffmann that Hitler met Eva BRAUN, who was Hoffmann's receptionist in 1929, and also Dr. Theodor MORELL, who in 1936 cured Hoffmann of what appeared to be a fatal illness, and so became Hitler's trusted medical adviser. Hoffmann's daughter Henrietta married Baldur von SCHIRACH, the HITLER YOUTH leader (she was granted a divorce in 1946).

HOGE, William Morris (1894–). U.S. Army officer who commanded Combat Command B, 9th Armored Division, when men of that unit seized the REMAGEN bridge across the Rhine River on March 7, 1945. An engineer officer and a veteran of World War I, he had in 1942 commanded engineer units building the Alaskan Highway. He was commander of the Provisional Engineer Special Brigade Group in support of the

V Corps at OMAHA BEACH in the Normandy INVASION. After commanding the unit which operated the Brittany ports and later Le Havre, the 16th Major Port, he assumed command of the unit that took the Remagen bridge to establish the first Allied bridgehead over the Rhine. In March 1945 he assumed command of the 4th Armored Division and led it throughout the remainder of the war. He was promoted to major general on May 2, 1945.

HOLCOMB, Thomas (1879–1965). In 1936, as a U.S. Marine brigadier general, Holcomb was jumped over more senior general officers by President ROOSEVELT, who appointed him the 17th Commandant of the Marine Corps, an organization whose size at that time—at 16,000 men—was smaller than the New York City police department. In 1940, when Holcomb was reappointed for a second four-year tour, the corps was expanding. In July 1941 its size reached 53,886; a year later, after Pearl Harbor, it had increased to 143,388.

Holcomb's position as Commandant was somewhat incongruous, for while he was head of the Marine Corps, he had no operational control of the troops in the field. The Commandant's role is best explained by noting that under the provisions of Navy General Order 241, the charter for the Fleet Marine Force (FMF) issued in 1933, the Commandant of the Marine Corps (CMC) was to maintain the Marine expeditionary force in readiness for operations with the fleet, since the force was to be part of the fleet for "tactical employment." Under this charter, CMC was also to designate the units comprising the FMF; they were to be under his command except when they were embarked with the fleet or engaged in fleet exercises. At the onset of the war, CMC did control the FMF, or parts of it. The declaration of war changed this command relationship for all practical purposes, primarily because most of the FMF operated under the tactical control of fleet commanders. Thereafter, the Commandant was responsible only for administration of the Marine Corps and for internal planning. But the manner in which Holcomb provided the Fleet Marine Force with fully trained and equipped marines and the most modern tools of war available is generally considered to have been exemplary. He kept fully abreast of all developments concerning his marines through numerous field inspections, visits to the commands overseas and continuous correspondence with his commanders in the Pacific. On January 20, 1942, he was promoted to lieutenant general, becoming the highest-ranking officer ever to head the Marine Corps.

During his tenure, the Corps fielded four divisions and four aircraft wings and burgeoned to a strength of over 300,000 men and women. Holcomb requested retirement at the age of 64, suggesting that someone younger should replace him in order to meet the increasing demands of the war. He was retired with a fourth star on December 31, 1943, and three months later, in March 1944, he was confirmed by the Senate as U.S. Minister to the Union of South Africa—a position he filled for four years.

HOLLAND, Lancelot Ernest (1887–1941). Royal Navy officer, Assistant Chief of the Naval Staff 1937–38, appointed commander of the 2d Battle Squadron, 1939. In May 1941 Holland, now a vice-admiral, was in command of the battle cruiser HOOD, the battleship PRINCE OF WALES and their escorting destroyers when they engaged the German battleship BISMARCK in the Denmark Strait. Holland lost his life when his flagship, *Hood*, blew up and sank after being hit by plunging fire from *Bismarck*.

HOLLANDIA. Prewar seat of local government in Dutch NEW GUINEA, occupied by the Japanese in April 1942. In September 1943 they began a belated effort to turn the area into a major air and logistical base, but Allied air strikes virtually destroyed Japanese air power at Hollandia during March and April 1944. On April 22 the Operation Reckless Task Force (actually, the U.S. I Corps) began landings at Humboldt and Tanamerah Bays with the 41st and 24th Divisions, respectively. The 11,000-man Japanese garrison of air and service troops could put up little resistance, and the inland airfield area was secured by April 26. Hollandia became a major air and logistical base for General MACARTHUR's forces and ultimately also the site of the major headquarters of the Southwest Pacific Area, which moved up to Hollandia from Australia.

HOLLIDT, Karl (1891–). German Army officer (colonel general), commander of a corps and an ad hoc group at STALINGRAD and subsequently commander of a new Sixth Army in the Ukraine (successor to the SIXTH ARMY lost at Stalingrad). He was removed from this post in April 1944.

HOLLIS, Sir Leslie Chasemore (1897–1963). British general, senior military assistant secretary to the WAR CABINET, 1939–45.

HOLY MOSES. Nickname for the U.S. Navy–developed 5-inch HVAR (*see* HVAR).

HOLZMINE 42. A German wooden-box antivehicle land mine, its wooden casing intended to be undetectable by electronic mine detectors.

HOME GUARD. Confronted with Hitler's threatened invasion of England, the British Secretary of State for War, Anthony EDEN, proposed on May 14, 1940, that an organization to be called the Local Defence Volunteers (later renamed the Home Guard) assist in defending the country against the Germans. Any male Briton between the ages of 17 and 65 was eligible to join the Home Guard. Volunteers turned out enthusiastically in response to Eden's call; consequently enrollment in the Guard peaked at about 500,000 men. With the aid of weapons made in the United States, the force was well equipped by July 1940. Once the danger of German invasion had subsided, the Home Guard served as an integral part of the general framework of British defenses by manning antiaircraft and coastal defenses. In the spring of 1944 the Guard was particularly helpful during the preparations for the Allied invasion of France, when it carried out many routine and security-related duties, thereby freeing regular forces for tasks related to the invasion.

HOMMA, Masaharu (1887–1946). Homma served as a Japanese Army observer with British forces in France during World War I. During the 1920s he was first Japan's resident army officer in India and then military attaché in London. As chief of the press section of the War Ministry, he had the task of defending the Japanese Army's seizure of Manchuria in 1931–32. In the late 1930s he commanded Japanese forces in northern China. In December 1941 Homma, a lieutenant general, was appointed the Supreme Commander of Japanese Army Forces in the Philippines. Although ultimately victorious, he was relieved of his command and placed on the reserve list in June 1942 for failure to achieve a speedier, less costly victory. Held responsible for the BATAAN death march, Homma was convicted of war crimes in Manila and executed by firing squad in 1946.

HONEY. British nickname for the American M3 series light TANK.

HONG KONG. Even before the outbreak of war with Japan, the British realized that from a military standpoint Hong Kong was a liability rather than an asset. The emergence of Japan as a strong naval and air power and the development by the Japanese of FORMOSA rendered Hong Kong indefensible as an independent strategic point. Prior to the war Hong Kong was the headquarters of the Royal Navy's China Squadron. The garrison was small, consisting normally of four British and Indian regiments with contingents of artillery, engineers and other supporting units. There was also a volunteer Defense Force. The garrison commander in December 1941 was Maj. Gen. C. M. MALTBY. In effect, Hong Kong was a "hostage of fortune," and it fell before the Japanese onslaught on Christmas Day 1941. It remained in Japanese hands until September 16, 1945, when during a quiet ceremony a Japanese general signed a surrender agreement and the Union Jack was rehoisted on the grounds of Government House, where the surrender had taken place.

HOOD, H.M.S. Royal Navy battle cruiser, 42,100 tons, completed in 1920 by John Brown, with an armament (at the time of her loss in 1941) of eight 15-inch guns, fourteen 4-inch guns, a number of smaller weapons and four 21-inch torpedo tubes. Prior to her dramatic loss, *Hood* had served in the Atlantic and home waters; in July 1940 she had been the flagship of FORCE H, which bombarded the French fleet at MERS-EL-KÉBIR. In May 1941 she flew the flag of the second-in-command, Home Fleet, and in company with the battleship PRINCE OF WALES (so new that neither was her work-up complete nor were all her builders' craftsmen returned home) she sailed to encounter the new German battleship BISMARCK, which had come out in company with the PRINZ EUGEN, a heavy cruiser. In the course of a brief action—in which *Hood* had scored hits on her adversary—the *Bismarck*'s fifth salvo exploded *Hood*'s aft 15-inch magazine, a blow which led to the destruction of the ship in a matter of seconds, 1,418 officers and men being killed and only three surviving. The disaster was due primarily to *Hood*'s age, in particular to the absence of deck armor sufficient to protect her against the plunging fire available in 1941. In addition to the material loss of so valuable a ship and so many men, the loss of the *Hood* was a great symbolic blow. A British naval-fiction writer, D. Reeman, wrote later of her: "But the *Hood* had been different. She had been more than just a ship. Huge, beautiful and arrogant, she had cruised the world between the wars, showed the flag in dozens of foreign ports, lain at anchor at reviews ablaze in coloured lights and bedecked with bunting to the delight of old and young alike. To the public at large she *was* the Royal Navy."

HOOLIGAN NAVY. U.S. Navy slang term for the Coast Guard. Coast Guardsmen, operating during wartime under Navy command, turned their particular type of seamanship to good account, especially in such areas as antisubmarine patrol and amphibious landing operations. Besides their own cutters, "Hooligans" manned many PFs and DEs as well as landing ships and craft. The expression "Hooligan Navy" was also applied to the wartime COASTAL PICKET PATROL, or Corsair Fleet. *See also* UNITED STATES COAST GUARD.

HOOVER, J(ohn) Edgar (1895–1972). Born and educated in Washington, D.C., Hoover entered the U.S. Department of Justice in 1917; in 1919 he was appointed special assistant to the Attorney General, and in 1924 he became director of the Bureau of Investigation, the position he held for the remainder of his life. As director of what was renamed the Federal Bureau of Investigation, he established training programs that revolutionized law enforcement and led to the development of professional standards in the field. The power and size of the bureau grew immensely between 1924 and the war years, partly because of increased responsibilities resulting from Congressional enactments, including the federal bank robbery acts, kidnapping acts, stolen property acts and antiracketeering acts. In 1939 a Presidential order gave the FBI chief responsibility for handling espionage, sabotage and related cases and for conducting intelligence and counterespionage functions. By 1941 almost 70,000 security cases had been dealt with by the FBI. In addition to investigating spy rings and supervising internment of enemy aliens after the outbreak of the war, agents of the FBI inspected approximately 3,300 key industrial facilities which furnished war materials, in order to improve protection against espionage and sabotage.

HOOVER, John Howard (1887–1970). Hoover began the war as a rear admiral in charge of the U.S. Navy's CARIBBEAN SEA FRONTIER. The decentralized nature of the command made Hoover's job a difficult one, and along with his general responsibility he had to watch the French islands of Guadeloupe and Martinique. Subsequently he commanded all land-based air operations for the invasions of the GILBERTS, MARSHALLS and MARIANAS in the Pacific. He then took command of Forward Areas of the Pacific, a post important in the LEYTE GULF campaign and the final actions against Japan. He had been a vice-admiral since 1942.

HOPKINS, Harry Lloyd (1890–1946). President ROOSEVELT's closest and most trusted adviser during most of the war, Hopkins was a native of Iowa and had a distinguished career in social work prior to entering the government. His first association with Roosevelt came about when the then governor of New York appointed him executive director of the state relief administration in 1931. In 1933 Hopkins was appointed head of the Federal Emergency Relief Administration. In this capacity he administered the largest public relief program ever undertaken, dealing with 14 million unemployed people. In 1935 he organized the Works Progress Administration, the famous WPA.

During the war years Hopkins's close relationship with Roosevelt enabled him to serve as a special personal envoy to leaders of other countries as well as, for a time, to administer the LEND-LEASE program. He met with Winston CHURCHILL in January 1941 to bring the message from the President that the United States would stand by Britain and that the two countries would make every effort to win the war together. As the President's personal representative, and also as lend-lease administrator, Hopkins visited Moscow in July 1941 to confer with STALIN on Soviet needs after the German invasion. When the United States entered the war he worked as a personal link between the President and the Chiefs of Staff and was involved in the development of strategy. Actually, his services are not readily summed up by titles and positions. His relationship with Churchill was perhaps the area of his greatest usefulness—"that extraordinary man," said Churchill, "who played, and was to play, a sometimes decisive part in the whole movement of the war. His was a soul that flamed out of a frail and failing body." And, Churchill added, "Everyone who came in contact with Harry Hopkins in the long struggle will confirm what I have set down about his remarkable personality." Because of Hopkins's impatience with equivocation and irrelevant detail, Churchill dubbed him "Lord Root of the Matter."

Hopkins's services were contributed in spite of chronic ill health. Shortly after the death of President Roosevelt he undertook a mission to Moscow for President TRUMAN, where he met with Stalin on a number of issues in contention, including Soviet actions in Poland and the impasse that had developed at the UNITED NATIONS conference in San Francisco concerning the veto. Hopkins had some success with respect to Poland and succeeded in breaking the deadlock over the veto and, in addition, reached an agreement with Stalin for a Big Three meeting (the POTSDAM CONFERENCE). In early July 1945 Hopkins resigned as an adviser to Truman, and he died the following January.

HORE-BELISHA, (Isaac) Leslie, Baron (1893–1957). In the immediate prewar years Hore-Belisha was primarily responsible, as British Secretary of State for War, for improving the condition of the Army through substantial reforms in personnel, equipment and organization. But his own strong personality and methods of action aroused such resentment and criticism in War Office circles that he was forced to resign in 1940.

HORII, Tomitaro (1890–1942). A graduate of the Japanese Military Academy in 1911, Major General Horii became the commander of the 55th Infantry Corps in August 1940. Shortly before the outbreak of the Pacific war, he was assigned to the command of the newly formed South Sea Detachment (with the 55th Corps as its nucleus). The force's first mission was to take GUAM; in late January 1942 it was ordered to take RABAUL. In August 1942 it was given the mission of taking PORT MORESBY, New Guinea, overland through BUNA and KOKODA. But Horii's advance was halted at Kokoda and he was turned back to the coast. Horii was killed in action on November 23, 1942; he was posthumously promoted to lieutenant general.

HORNET, U.S.S. Aircraft carrier, a somewhat improved version of the earlier YORKTOWN class but virtually identical in appearance and general characteristics, differing in detail and in her bridge structure. Commissioned in 1941, *Hornet* arrived in the Pacific after PEARL HARBOR. Her first major operation involved launching Lt. Col. James DOOLITTLE's 16 B-25 medium bombers for their April 1942 raid on Japan (*see* FIRST SPECIAL AVIATION PROJECT). With *Yorktown* and ENTERPRISE, she took part in the Battle of MIDWAY. *Hornet* was lost in October 1942 in the SOLOMONS Battle of SANTA CRUZ.

A second *Hornet,* an ESSEX-class aircraft carrier, commissioned in November 1943 and served with the FAST CARRIER TASK FORCE through V-J Day.

HORRIFIED. Allied code name for SICILY.

HORROCKS, Sir Brian (1895–). Horrocks, a lieutenant general in the British Army, was known as an enthusiastic, highly strung man, capable of great charm or biting anger, and a forceful commander. He spent practically all of World War I as a POW. General MONTGOMERY thought highly of Horrocks and requested him for leadership of the 13th Corps of EIGHTH ARMY in August 1942. In 1944 Horrocks commanded 30th Corps, under Montgomery's 21ST ARMY GROUP, in its drive across northern Europe. His corps was outstanding in the rapid drive across Belgium and the Netherlands in 1944, but suffered a setback in the ARNHEM battle of September 1944, during which Horrocks experienced "the blackest moment of my life." His memoirs, *A Full Life,* were published in 1960.

HORSA. British high-wing monoplane glider of wooden construction, with tricycle-type landing gear, manufactured by Airspeed Ltd. Capable of carrying as many as 24 soldiers and a crew of two, the Horsa made its combat debut in November 1942 during a raid to destroy a German-operated heavy-water plant in Norway. The RAF acquired some 3,600 of these craft, which participated in every major British airborne operation of the war, including those in SICILY in July 1943 and during the Normandy INVASION. The Horsa II had a hinged nose to permit the loading of light vehicles. Even so, in U.S. operations the Horsa proved to be a crash-prone carrier and extremely dangerous to personnel.

HORSE ISLAND. Code name for BUTARITARI Island of MAKIN Atoll in the GILBERT ISLANDS.

HORTHY, Miklós (1868–1957). Admiral in the Austro-Hungarian Navy during World War I, who became leader of the White (anti-Communist) regime in Hungary following the war and was Regent from 1920 to 1944. During the 1930s the Horthy regime, befriended and supported by Nazi Germany, acquired territory at

U.S.S. *Hornet* undergoes dive-bomber and torpedo attacks in the Santa Cruz battle

the expense of its European neighbors. After Germany's invasion of the Soviet Union in 1941, the Horthy regime allied itself with the Reich in the war in the east. Adolf HITLER in turn supported the Horthy regime as long as it supported his interests. As the war began to go badly for Germany, relations between the two became strained. In the summer of 1944 Admiral Horthy attempted to prevent the Nazi deportation of Hungarian Jews. In October 1944 he entered into negotiations for an armistice with the Soviet Union and issued an order for surrender. As a consequence the Germans forced Horthy to retract his order and to abdicate as Regent on October 16, 1944. They then deported him to Austria. He was liberated in May 1945 by the Americans.

HORTON, Sir Max (1883–1951). One of the Royal Navy's outstanding commanders of the war, but one who only very rarely flew his flag at sea. Horton had had an outstanding record as a submarine commander in the First World War; in 1937 he was appointed to command the Royal Navy's Reserve Fleet and was largely responsible for the war readiness of so many of Britain's older ships and reserve crews in 1939. From September to December 1939 Horton commanded the Northern Patrol, an ad hoc force of old cruisers and ARMED MERCHANT CRUISERS tightening the maritime blockade of Germany. From 1940 to 1942 he was Flag Officer Submarines, entirely responsible for all training and administration and in part for operations; under his command British submarines achieved a number of successes. He was promoted to admiral in 1941.

After refusing command of the Home Fleet, Horton was appointed Commander in Chief WESTERN APPROACHES at the height of the Battle of the ATLANTIC in November 1942. As poacher turned gamekeeper, Horton made a decisive contribution to victory in the Atlantic, bringing to the scene additions to tactical doctrine, improved training, the results of scientific research and his own experience both in command and in the most effective use of older ships and the newer ones becoming available. Perhaps his most noteworthy contribution was the formation of "support groups" of special hunter forces not specifically concerned with day-to-day escort commitments. Horton remained in this appointment until the end of the war.

As a man Admiral Horton was very devout, but ruthless and of most uncertain temper; he nevertheless commanded the affection and respect of all who served under him.

HOSOGAYA, Hoshiro (1888–1964). After serving as commander in chief of the Japanese Fleet in Central China Waters (December 1940–July 1941), Vice-Admiral Hosogaya was appointed commander in chief of the Japanese Fifth Fleet, which was responsible for Japanese defenses in the North Pacific. He was in overall command of the invasion of the Aleutians in March 1942 and the seizure of ATTU and KISKA. Following the Battle of the KOMANDORSKI ISLANDS in the North Pacific in March 1943, Hosogaya lost his command and was placed on the reserve list.

HOSPITAL SHIP. In the U.S. Navy, designated by the symbol AH. Under the terms of international law these ships were forbidden to take any part in military operations or to carry troops or war matériel. They were painted white with conspicuous Red Cross identification and were brightly lighted at night. The U.S. Army also operated hospital ships, as did Britain and Japan.

HOSSBACH, Friedrich (1894–). Adjutant to Adolf HITLER in 1934–38, Colonel (later General der Infanterie) Hossbach is remembered because he took minutes of one of Hitler's most important prewar secret conferences, at which the Führer disclosed his plans for future aggression to an inner circle of ministers. This was on November 5, 1937, and those present were Blomberg (War Minister), FRITSCH (Army commander), RAEDER (Navy), GÖRING (Luftwaffe) and NEURATH (Foreign Minister). Hitler spoke of the need for German territorial expansion (Lebensraum) and the need to overcome Britain and France before German armed supremacy was overtaken by the rearmament of the Western powers. He also forecast German seizure of Austria and Czechoslovakia. The notes of this meeting are known as the Hossbach minutes or Hossbach memorandum. An interesting, unorthodox view of this conference appears in *The Origins of the Second World War* by A. J. P. Taylor. Hossbach was dismissed from command of the Fourth Army in January 1945.

HOTH, Hermann (1885–1971). Following service in the German Army in World War I, Hoth held a position in the training department of the Ministry of War. By 1936 he was a divisional commander. In 1941 Adolf HITLER rewarded Hoth with promotion to colonel general for his service as a tank commander (XV Panzer Corps) in the invasion of Poland and the overrunning of the Low Countries and FRANCE.

In the invasion of Russia, Hoth had command of Panzer Group 3 in Field Marshal von BOCK's Army Group Center, whose initial objective was Moscow. In January 1942 Hitler placed Hoth in command of the Fourth Panzer Army, and in mid-July he was ordered to assist PAULUS's SIXTH ARMY in the attack on STALINGRAD. By early September Hoth's army had reached the suburbs of Stalingrad, but shortly thereafter the whole German advance on the city stalled as winter and stubborn Russian resistance prevented the Germans from capturing the city. When a Soviet counteroffensive in late December encircled the Sixth Army, Hoth was ordered to break through and relieve Paulus. The Soviet defense proved too stubborn, and Hoth's tanks were unable to reach the Sixth Army, which eventually surrendered to the Soviets.

After the defeat at Stalingrad, the Fourth Panzer Army took part in the summer offensive of 1943. In the Battle of KURSK (July), Hoth's armor made considerable progress against the Russians, but it was to no avail because Hitler called off the offensive owing to weaknesses elsewhere in the German line. In the battle for KIEV (November 1943) the Fourth Panzer Army was unable to stop the Soviet offensive and had to retreat to the west. Hitler was so angered by the loss of Kiev that he dismissed Hoth on December 10, even though he had been continuously in action since June 1941 and was one of Germany's most experienced tank generals. Militarily, Hitler had objected to Hoth's mobility on the defensive, which the Führer felt represented a defeatist attitude.

Hoth was tried and convicted at NUREMBERG in 1948 of war crimes and crimes against humanity. He received a sentence of 15 years' imprisonment, but was released on amnesty after serving six years.

HOTROCKS. Code name for Mount SURIBACHI, Iwo Jima, site of the famous flag-raising by men of the U.S. 28th Marines.

HOTSPUR. Designed by Britain's General Aircraft, this was the standard RAF training glider. It was a midwing monoplane with dual controls, arranged in tandem, for instructor and student pilot.

HOUFFALIZE. Belgian crossroads town in the center of the ARDENNES region, taken by the 116th Panzer Division on December 19, 1944, during the Battle of the BULGE. As the Germans withdrew from the Ardennes in January 1945 under pressure from the U.S. First and Third Armies from north and south, task forces of the two armies met early on January 16 at Houffalize, thus sealing off the battleground known as the Bulge.

HOUSTON, U.S.S. NORTHAMPTON-class heavy cruiser, commissioned in 1930. When the Pacific war broke out, she was flagship of Adm. Thomas HART's U.S. Asiatic Fleet. During the early weeks of 1942 she took part in some of the engagements leading up to the Battle of the JAVA SEA, in which she and the Australian light cruiser PERTH were the only surviving Allied ships. In the evening of February 28 the two cruisers attacked Japanese invasion shipping at BANTEN BAY, Java; in the action that followed, both were sent to the bottom. *Houston*'s service earned her a PRESIDENTIAL UNIT CITATION.

The second wartime *Houston*, a CLEVELAND-class light cruiser, commissioned late in 1943. Joining the FAST CARRIER TASK FORCE in mid-1944, she took part in the capture of the MARIANAS and the Battle of the PHILIPPINE SEA. In the fall she supported the invasion of the Palaus. During carrier-force attacks on Formosa in preparation for the LEYTE landing, *Houston* took an aerial torpedo in her engine room. Her power gone, she had to be taken under tow. While she was being towed two days later, another Japanese torpedo bomber placed a hit in her stern. After repairs at Ulithi, she was able to sail for New York for permanent repair, which extended through V-J Day.

HSUEH YUEH (1896–). With experience gained from several prewar revolutionary army commands, Hsueh Yueh—the "Tiger of Hunan"—became one of the key Chinese generals of the war. His primary contribution was as commander in chief of the 9th War Area in eastern China, where he faced various Japanese offensives with great skill. Hsueh, praised by Gen. Claire CHENNAULT as a superb tactician, went on to hold various executive positions in the postwar Nationalist Chinese government.

HSÜ YUNG-CH'ANG (1889–1959). As a career officer in China's prewar revolutionary army, Gen. Hsü Yung-ch'ang served in various capacities, such as provincial governor and army commander. With the reorganization of the Chinese Military Affairs Commission in 1938, Hsü became the Minister of the Military Operations Board, which functioned during the war as the general staff of the Nationalist military establishment. From World War II until shortly before his death he held various high offices in the Nationalist Chinese government.

HUBE, Hans Valentin (1890–1944). German Army officer (General der Panzertruppen, 1942; colonel general, 1944), who directed withdrawal from SICILY in 1943, commanded a corps in ITALY and was an army commander on the Eastern Front.

HUDSON. Military variant of the American-built Lockheed Model 14 transport, used by the British. It was reaching RAF COASTAL COMMAND when the war broke out. Although purchased by the British for navigation training, these twin-engine, all-metal monoplanes replaced the Avro ANSON on antisubmarine patrol and overwater reconnaissance missions, especially during the Battle of the ATLANTIC. Some Hudsons carried lifeboats for rescue work; others reverted to their transport role after they had become obsolete as combat aircraft. Hudsons tracked the German prison ship *Altmark* to neutral Norwegian waters, where it was boarded and the captured seamen released (*see* ALTMARK INCIDENT). In August 1941 a Hudson attacked a German submarine and forced it to surrender. Easily recognized by its twin tails, its onionlike dorsal turret and the rails for its Fowler flaps, the Hudson was powered in its earlier versions by 1,100-horsepower Wright Cyclone radials and carried a crew of four. Later models boasted 1,200-horsepower Pratt and Whitney radials that increased the top speed from 246 to 284 miles per hour, and the plane could carry up to four 500-pound depth charges. Late-model Hudsons served U.S. Army Air Forces as A-28s and AT-18s; the U.S. Navy designation was PBO-1.

HUEBNER, Clarence Ralph (1888–1972). An up-from-the-ranks U.S. soldier who ultimately rose to four stars, Huebner was in charge of training on the General Staff early in the war. He later commanded the 1st Infantry Division in battle and went on to other high posts. Gruff in manner, dogmatic as a decision-maker, a stern disciplinarian, he fashioned a celebrated career out of study and an iron will.

HULL, Cordell (1871–1955). Hull was elected to the U.S. House of Representatives from Tennessee in 1906 and served until 1921; after two years in private life he returned between 1923 and 1931. He was elected to the Senate in 1930. A deeply committed supporter of Woodrow Wilson, Hull had favored the League of Nations and deplored the U.S. failure to participate.

He was appointed by President ROOSEVELT as Secretary of State in 1933. He did much in the 1930s to develop solid relationships with Latin America (the Good Neighbor Policy) and to bring about the reciprocal lowering of tariffs. Hull conducted the fateful negotiations with Japan in the fall of 1941. He displayed considerable patience, but there was actually little chance that the American and Japanese positions with respect to China could be reconciled, though some critics have argued that U.S. intransigence was to some extent responsible for the ascendancy of the war group in Japan.

Hull was valuable to Roosevelt because of his great prestige on Capitol Hill, particularly among conservatives, and he was a dedicated if sometimes stubborn worker for his aims. Throughout the war he was especially vigorous in supporting the development of the UNITED NATIONS and was later called by Roosevelt the father of the United Nations. Hull resigned in 1944; his term of service was the longest of any Secretary of State.

HULL, John E. (1895–1974). U.S. Army officer, chief of the European Theater section of the General Staff and a distinguished strategist. No West Pointer but a graduate of Miami (Ohio) University, Hull became an Army careerist in World War I. In World War II, as a brigadier, he shared with Gen. Thomas HANDY the direction of the Operations Division (OPD), which virtually ran Army affairs. Later, as a four-star general, Hull was Supreme Commander, Far East. Extremely modest, "Ed" Hull was highly popular with his fellow soldiers.

HUMP, THE. When the Japanese captured RANGOON in March 1942, a new route had to be found to reach the BURMA ROAD, China's lifeline. A hastily drawn plan called for supplies to move by rail from Calcutta to Sadiya in the Brahmaputra Valley of easternmost India. There aircraft would take on the cargo and fly it some 200 miles across the Naga Hills to Myitkyina, Burma, for shipment by barge down the Irrawaddy River to Bhamo, where river and road intersected. At Bhamo, trucks would take over for the final leg to KUNMING, China. Before the key airfield at Myitkyina could be improved and the complicated operation begun, the Japanese overran the region. The only remaining supply route was by air over the Hump—from airfields in the Brahmaputra Valley, across the towering Himalayas to Kunming in Yunnan province, a distance of some 550 miles. This route led over the 10,000-foot Patkai Range and the Chindwin River valley, bounded on the east by the 14,000-foot Kumon Mountains, and crossed a series of 14,000- to 16,000-foot ridges separated by the West

The Hump

Irrawaddy, East Irrawaddy, Salween and Mekong River valleys (the Hump itself was the 15,000-foot Satsung Range between the Salween and Mekong Rivers).

The route, also called the Aluminum Trail because of the crashed planes that served as guideposts, was inaugurated in April 1942 by a gasoline-laden transport, and by midsummer of that year deliveries had reached 700 tons in a single month. The handful of C-47s that pioneered the operation gave way to larger and more numerous types—C-87s and C-109 tankers, C-46s and C-54s—so that in its final year the route over the Hump averaged some 45,000 tons per month. The total carried in 1942–45 was 650,000 tons.

HUNTZIGER, Charles (1880–1941). General Huntziger served in the French Army during World War I. In May 1940 his Second Army defended the southern ARDENNES front. Reservist troops of his command broke under air bombardment and let the Germans under Gen. Heinz GUDERIAN through at Sedan, but subsequently the Second Army fought well. General Huntziger ended the campaign in command of an army group, was a reluctant signer of the Franco-German armistice, then became Minister of War under VICHY, dying in an air crash on his way to North Africa for an inspection.

HUON PENINSULA. After defeat at GUADALCANAL and Papua, the Japanese hoped to anchor their position in NEW GUINEA with bases at LAE and FINSCHHAFEN on this peninsula on the Huon Gulf. However, a series of skillfully executed amphibious operations from June to December 1943 by General MACARTHUR's forces cleared the peninsula.

HURLEY, Patrick Jay (1883–1963). U.S. Secretary of War in the Hoover Administration (1929–33), Hurley was called to active military duty in the fall of 1941, and after the Japanese attack on PEARL HARBOR was promoted to brigadier general. He was ordered to the Southwest Pacific to direct efforts at running the Japanese blockade of the Philippines with supplies for Gen. Douglas MACARTHUR. After being wounded in 1942 he was assigned as minister to New Zealand and also sent to Moscow to consult with STALIN. In November 1943 he went to China as President ROOSEVELT's representative to make arrangements for CHIANG KAI-SHEK's meeting with the President and Winston CHURCHILL at the CAIRO CONFERENCE. In August 1944 he returned to China with the assignment of keeping the Chinese Nationalist army in the war and harmonizing relationships between the Chinese and American military establishments. Later he was appointed U.S. ambassador to

China, and he initiated conferences with Chinese leaders designed to end the civil war in that country. He remained in China until November 1945, when he resigned his position in protest against what he saw as maneuvers by the Department of State to sabotage his efforts to reconcile the Nationalists and the CHINESE COMMUNISTS. His public blast at the department was an early feature of the great American postwar debate over China. *See also* CHINA; STILWELL, JOSEPH WARREN.

HURRICANE. In 1934 Sydney Camm was designing a monoplane based on Hawker's successful Fury biplane fighter. Upon learning that Rolls-Royce was developing a new liquid-cooled engine, later named the Merlin, he altered his plans to accommodate this power plant. When the British Air Ministry insisted upon eight .303-caliber machine guns, twice the armament he had planned, Camm mounted four in each wing to fire outside the propeller arc. From his drawing board came a metal-cowled, fabric-covered, low-wing monoplane with an enclosed cockpit and exceptionally clean lines. The 990-horsepower Merlin C turned a two-bladed wooden propeller and enabled the Hurricane to reach 315 miles per hour at 16,200 feet, thus making it the first Royal Air Force fighter to exceed 300 miles per hour in level flight.

By the time of the Battle of BRITAIN, Hurricane I formed the backbone of FIGHTER COMMAND and was credited with destroying more German aircraft than all other planes combined. A 1,030-horsepower Merlin had been installed, along with a new metal propeller and metal wings; these changes increased the top speed to 324 miles per hour. Camm's airplane proved to be rugged, hard-hitting, easily repaired and more maneuverable than the MESSERSCHMITT ME 109E under 20,000 feet. Some Hurricane I's were fitted with four 20-mm. cannon, but only a handful of these saw action during the BLITZ.

A formation of Hurricanes. These aircraft are Hurricane IIs, a more heavily armed version of the famous Battle of Britain fighters

Hurricane I also served the FLEET AIR ARM both as a carrier fighter and as a "Hurricat" (or "Sea Hurricane"), which was catapulted from merchant vessels to intercept marauding bombers. The more powerful Hurricane II remained with Royal Navy carrier squadrons into 1943. It had folding wings for carrier operations.

The RAF Hurricane underwent several changes that converted it from an interceptor to a fighter-bomber. The more common ground-support versions, Hurricane IIB and C, mounted a 1,460-horsepower Merlin XX, had a top speed of 342 miles per hour at 22,000 feet and could carry up to 1,000 pounds of bombs. The usual armament was four 20-mm. cannon, though some carried twelve .303-caliber machine guns and the IIE series boasted two 40-mm. cannon slung under the wings for use against tanks.

Before the war, Hurricane I's had been exported to Finland, Yugoslavia, Belgium, Rumania and Turkey. One plane reached Poland prior to the outbreak of war, and another went to Iran. The plane was built under license in Yugoslavia and Belgium. Wartime production took place in Canada as well as in the United Kingdom. After the German invasion, the Soviet Union received almost 3,000 late-model Hurricanes, some of them Canadian-built. Other wartime recipients included Egypt, India and Turkey. Production ended in September 1944 after the manufacture of more than 14,000 Hurricanes.

HÜRTGEN FOREST. Lying southeast of the German border city of Aachen, the forest is some 20 miles long and 10 miles wide, primarily coniferous woodland with occasional villages perched on high, bald ridges. Much of it is trackless except for firebreaks that cut the forest into grids. Although the forest mass includes the Wenau and Rötgen Forests, both Americans and Germans who fought there during the fall and winter of 1944–45 in some of the most severe fighting of the war knew it all as the Hürtgen Forest. It has been called the Argonne of World War II, and Ernest Hemingway said it was "Passchendaele with tree bursts."

As troops of the U.S. FIRST ARMY crossed the German border in early September, the commander, Lt. Gen. Courtney H. HODGES, directed the 9th Infantry Division to sweep the forest against expected minor resistance, securing right-flank protection for a main effort in more open terrain around Aachen to penetrate German border fortifications, the WEST WALL. Although the German Seventh Army was at first ill-prepared to defend, it benefited from the hardships faced by the American units, which, fatigued and overextended, had to surmount the convoluted terrain, dense trees, the pillboxes of the West Wall and a dearth of roads. In attacks through September and into October, the 9th Division gained less than two miles at a cost of 4,500 casualties.

The entire American drive having stalled, General Hodges directed as a preliminary to a new offensive in November that the 28th Infantry Division push through the forest and seize high ground at Schmidt.

But when rain and fog delayed the main offensive, German reserves were free to move against the lone division. So intense was the fight—6,000 casualties, one of the most costly American divisional actions of the war—that the division acquired a nickname derived from the experience: the "Bloody Bucket," after its red keystone-shaped shoulder patch.

Five other divisions tried in succession to clear the forest: the 1st, 4th, 8th and 83d Infantry Divisions and the 5th Armored Division. Everywhere the fighting was plodding and costly. Antipersonnel mines, shells bursting in treetops to bathe the floor of the forest with deadly fragments, patrols and ambushes behind opposing lines, quilts of broken branches, trees transformed by artillery fire to look like giant jagged toothpicks, constant effort to maintain direction amid dense growth that looked disconcertingly like all the rest, persistent rain and mud, and then sleet and snow: it was a miserable existence for men of both sides.

The stalwart German defense was attributable in part to the forest itself; in part to German plans for a major counteroffensive to be launched farther south in December (the Battle of the BULGE), which would have been jeopardized had the Americans crossed the Roer River in the Hürtgen Forest; and in part to presence of the Roer dams, which the Germans could use to flood the Roer and isolate any American force that had crossed. American difficulties also were attributable to unimaginative frontal attacks made usually by one division at a time.

Not until mid-December was most of the forest taken, and of approximately 120,000 Americans who fought there, 33,000 became casualties. German losses were about the same, but the Germans did succeed in maintaining the prerequisite for a counteroffensive. Once that was over, the Americans still had to capture the Roer dams. The 9th and 78th Divisions did that in February 1945, but not before the Germans released floodwaters that delayed a crossing of the Roer for two weeks. **C.B.M.**

HU SHIH (1891–1962). Western educated, including a Ph.D. from Columbia and numerous honorary degrees from the United States and Europe, Dr. Hu Shih was a leading intellectual in revolutionary China. Best known for his prewar advocacy of the use of the spoken language in literary writing, the influential philosopher and educator served as ambassador to the United States from 1939 to 1945, where one of his missions was to seek funds for China's war effort.

HUSKY. Code name for the invasion of SICILY by Allied forces, July 10, 1943.

HUSSEINI, Amin el (1893–1974). Muslim leader who, as Grand Mufti of Jerusalem, organized Arab support for the Axis. In 1941 he was instrumental in the plot that overthrew Iraqi Prime Minister Nuri es-Said and replaced him with RASHID ALI. Later Husseini and Rashid Ali vied for leadership of the Arab movement; HITLER favored the Grand Mufti, possibly because his red hair and blue eyes seemed evidence of Aryan descent.

HVALFJORDUR. U.S. naval base in Iceland, established to support convoy activities. It was known, unflatteringly, as Valley Forge.

HVAR (High-Velocity Aircraft Rocket). A faster version of the earlier U.S. Navy 5-inch AR (Aircraft Rocket), introduced in combat in August 1944. It used a modified 5-inch-gun projectile for a warhead and had a more powerful motor than the earlier rocket. It was referred to either by its designation, pronounced "havar," or by the nickname Holy Moses. A highly effective and popular weapon, the HVAR was in great demand in European and Pacific theaters alike, and had to be rationed to spread the available supply around fairly.

HYAKUTAKE, Harukichi (1888–1947). The younger brother of two famous Japanese admirals, Harukichi Hyakutake entered the Army. After studying at the Military Academy and Military Staff College, he held a number of staff positions before being appointed director of the Hiroshima Military Preparatory School. During the war Hyakutake commanded the 17th Army stationed at RABAUL. In August 1942 he took personal command of Japanese efforts to retain control of GUADALCANAL and the other SOLOMON ISLANDS. After the Japanese defeat there, Hyakutake, a lieutenant general, and his remaining troops were withdrawn to fight again later in BOUGAINVILLE and surrounding islands.

HYDEMAN'S HELLCATS. Nickname of a U.S. submarine wolfpack, under Comdr. E. T. Hydeman in *Sea Dog,* which led the penetration of the Sea of Japan in Operation BARNEY. The Hellcats (nine submarines) sank 57,000 tons of shipping in 11 days.

HYUGA. Japanese battleship, second ship of the ISE class. Like *Ise,* she survived until late July 1945 before being sunk by carrier aircraft.

I

I-BOAT. U.S. Navy term for large Japanese oceangoing submarines, designated "I-Class Submarines" by the Japanese Navy. These submarines were identified by numbers prefixed by the letter *I*, the first character in one of the Japanese alphabet systems. Medium, or so-called coastal, submarines (many of these were used for ocean operations) were identified by the prefix *Ro*, the second character. Small attack and transport submarines (excluding midget submarines and KAITEN types) were identified by the third symbol, *Ha*.

IACHINO (JACHINO), Angelo (1889–1976). Italian admiral (ammiraglio d'armata), commander of the naval forces 1940–43. Admiral Iachino commanded the Italian fleet in the Battle of CAPE MATAPAN. After the war he wrote a number of books treating the war at sea.

IAR 80. Rumanian (Industria Aeronautica Romana) single-radial-engine, low-wing, open-cockpit fighter, introduced in 1941. About 120 IAR 80s were built, and besides being employed on home defense duties, some served alongside units of the LUFTWAFFE in the German invasion of Russia. A respectable but not excellent fighter, the IAR 80 had a 940-horsepower engine, 343 miles per hour maximum speed and armament of two 20-mm. cannon and four 7.7-mm. machine guns.

IBN-SAUD, Abdul-Aziz (1880–1953). King of Saudi Arabia (1932–53), ibn-Saud was the great modernizer of his country. During the war he maintained his policy of friendship toward Britain and, as events progressed, welcomed American technical advisers. Saudi Arabia thus survived the war without becoming an area of conflict, unlike its neighbors. In February 1945, after the Yalta Conference, ibn-Saud met separately with President ROOSEVELT and Prime Minister CHURCHILL as they returned home. "He still lived the existence of a patriarchal king of the Arabian desert," Churchill said later, "with his forty living sons and the seventy ladies of his harem, and three of the four official wives, as prescribed by the Prophet, one vacancy being kept."

ICEBERG. Code name of the U.S. operation in which one or more positions in the Nansei Shoto (Ryukyu Islands) were to be seized in three phases. Phase I called for capture of the southern part of OKINAWA and small adjacent islands and initial development of base facilities, as Okinawa was to be used as a staging and mount-out base in the final operations against the Japanese home islands. In Phase II, IE SHIMA and the remainder of Okinawa were to be seized and base development continued in the newly captured areas. Then in Phase III, further positions in the Ryukyus, including the Sakishima Gunto, were to be taken and developed with forces available. In late April 1945, Phase III plans for the operations against Miyako and Kikai Jima in the Sakishimas were canceled and all base development efforts and troops slated for employment on these and other islands of the Ryukyus were assigned to Okinawa.

ICELAND. On July 8, 1941, after a somewhat reluctant invitation from the government of Iceland, U.S. marines relieved the British garrison in Iceland. The U.S. Navy then began escorting merchant ships, including those of "any nationality which may join," between Iceland and the United States—an important step for a still-neutral nation to take. The Navy developed a base at Hvalfjordur to support these tasks. As the war progressed, Iceland served as a vital base for air coverage of convoys. *See also* ATLANTIC, BATTLE OF THE.

ICHIGAYA HEIGHTS. Location in Tokyo of the Japanese War Ministry and the General Staff.

ICHI GO (Operation One). Japanese operation to consolidate holdings in eastern China and to capture U.S. air bases established there. It was mounted on April 18, 1944, and continued successfully throughout the rest of the year and into the first months of 1945, forcing the abandonment of the American airfields.

ICHIKI, Kiyono (1892–1942). A career Japanese Army officer, Ichiki landed on GUADALCANAL on August 18, 1942, with half of the 2d Battalion of Japan's 28th Infantry. The following day a U.S. Marine patrol discovered one of Ichiki's patrols and destroyed it, capturing maps, charts and diaries. Realizing that his forces had been discovered, Ichiki decided to attack as quickly as possible, without waiting for the arrival of the second half of his battalion. Early in the morning of August 21 he launched his assault on HENDERSON FIELD with only 790 men. They were decisively defeated at the TENARU RIVER. Following his defeat Ichiki committed hara-kiri. Only 130 Japanese survived the attack, while the Americans suffered losses of 35 dead and 75 wounded.

ICHIMARU, Toshinosuke (1891–1945). A graduate of the Japanese Naval Academy, Ichimaru was a career officer who during much of the war served as commander of a number of naval land-based air forces. In August 1944 he was made commander of the 27th Air Flotilla (land-based air force) at Iwo JIMA and given overall command of Japanese naval forces on the island. He appears to have died in late March 1945 during the last stages of the battle for the island, but his body was never recovered. His rank was rear admiral.

ICKES, Harold LeClaire (1874–1952). American lawyer and reporter, a Republican who was Secretary of the Interior throughout the ROOSEVELT Administration and into 1946 and was an important energy figure during the war as solid-fuels administrator (from 1941), petroleum administrator (from 1942) and coal-mines administrator (from 1943). Known as the "Old Curmudgeon," which he called himself in his autobiography, Ickes was a colorful, outspoken man and a strong conservationist.

IDA, Masataka (1912–). A career Japanese Army officer and protégé of Gen. Korechika ANAMI, then War Minister, Ida was one of the leaders of the attempted coup d'état of August 14–15, 1945. The rebels seized the palace compound and unsuccessfully attempted to prevent Japan's surrender. Ida, a lieutenant colonel, was a member of the Imperial Guards Division. He fell into disgrace following the failure of the attempted coup when he decided not to commit suicide as expected. Following the end of the war he divorced his wife and changed his family name to Iwata.

IE SHIMA. A small island approximately three and a half miles northwest of Motobu Peninsula in the center of OKINAWA. Elements of the U.S. 77th Infantry Division landed on April 16, 1945, and the island was declared secure on the 21st after fighting in which a heavy price was exacted from both attackers and defenders. The famous war correspondent Ernie PYLE was killed on Ie Shima.

IFF (Identification, Friend or Foe). A type of Allied-developed electronic device which enabled friendly ships and planes to identify themselves electronically. A RADAR pip wears no national insignia. Without visual confirmation, there was no way to tell whether a particular radar contact was friendly or hostile. IFF was designed to solve this problem. Used as an auxiliary to search and fire-control radars, early IFF systems involved an interrogator-responsor in ships or shore positions. This device sent out challenging radar pulses. These were picked up by a challenged airplane and triggered a transponder; this automatically (if it was switched on) sent back a coded signal which appeared as a characteristic pip on the challenging radar's screen. Later airborne IFF, used in radar-equipped planes, had its own interrogator-responsor so that the plane could challenge a target it picked up. Certain modified late-model aircraft IFF gear could also transmit "rooster" beacon signals to allow other IFF-equipped planes to home in on them. An emergency IFF setting caused a plane's transponder to send out a special distress signal which produced a telltale pip on a receiving screen. Early IFF antennas were separate units; by the later war years IFF antennas were incorporated into search or fire-control radar antennas.

IGNATOV, Peter and Elena. In peacetime Peter Ignatov was a Soviet mechanic and his wife Elena looked after their home. But the onslaught of the German Army and the consequent development of partisan warfare turned Peter into the leader of a guerrilla "army" and Elena into a proficient killer in that army. As the Germans retreated in 1943, partisan armies retreated with them—harassing, cutting communications, killing. The Ignatovs were honored in a *Pravda* editorial and two Ignatov sons were named HERO OF THE SOVIET UNION after they reportedly died blowing up a German ammunition train.

I GO. Japanese operational code name. In early 1943, with GUADALCANAL lost and U.S. air operations moving increasingly farther north in the SOLOMONS, Japanese Army leaders decided to build up their air strength to confront American air power and to attack Allied shipping in what they called the Southeast area, around Australia. When not enough Army planes could be obtained to support this effort, Adm. Isoroku YAMAMOTO, commander of the COMBINED FLEET at TRUK, decided to assist the operation, entitled I Go. He sent carrier aircraft from Truk to join other naval planes based at fields on Rabaul, Ballale, Kavieng, Buka and Buin. He also moved his headquarters to Rabaul to direct the operation, which was to involve more than 300 Japanese planes.

The first phase of I Go began on April 1, 1943, with a fighter and bomber strike on the RUSSELLS, which had been taken by the Americans on February 21. Air-to-air combat continued for three hours before the Japanese were driven off with severe losses. The next phase of the operation took place on April 7, when I Go attackers headed for a large concentration of American shipping in the waters around Guadalcanal. COASTWATCHERS on New Georgia flashed the warning to Adm. William F. HALSEY, who then dispersed his ships, including a bombardment group steaming north to shell MUNDA and Vila. To combat the 117 Japanese fighters and 71 bombers, the U.S. air command in the Solomons sent up 76 fighters.

Since neither U.S. nor Japanese air loss claims in World War II are noted for their accuracy, it has always been difficult to determine actual loss figures. But, in this case, it is safe to say that the Japanese lost considerably more planes and pilots than did the Americans. Satisfied nonetheless that his fliers had accomplished their mission, Yamamoto turned his attention to the Allies in New Guinea, and on April 11 he dispatched a raid against shipping in Oro Bay, and, the next day, against PORT MORESBY. On the 15th Japanese bombers hit MILNE BAY. Calling I Go a success following this last raid, Yamamoto ended it and returned his command to Truk. However, he had been fooled by his pilots' over-optimistic reports, for Allied losses in the Solomons and New Guinea totaled only 1 destroyer, 1 tanker, 1 corvette, 2 merchant ships and 25 planes.

IIDA, Shojiro (1888–). The "Conqueror of Burma," General Iida commanded the Japanese 15th Army's invasion of BURMA from Malaya in 1942. After the Japanese victory, Iida and his staff quickly helped to establish a Provisional Administrative Committee of Burmans under BA MAW to set up a civilian government and a new Burmese Army under Gen. AUNG SAN. Favorably impressed by Iida, Ba Maw called him an ideal samurai who, though devoted to the Japanese Emperor, warrior code and nation, still empathized with Burmans. Iida attempted unsuccessfully to prevent abuse of the Burmese by Japanese occupation troops.

ILLUSTRIOUS, H.M.S. Royal Navy aircraft carrier of 23,000 tons, completed in May 1940 by Vickers-Armstrong and armed with sixteen 4.5-inch guns and smaller weapons. *Illustrious* could carry 40 to 50 aircraft, depending on their size; an important feature of her design was an armored flight deck. On completion she was sent to the Mediterranean, taking part in various operations in 1940, the most noteworthy being the attack on TARANTO in November. In January 1941, while escorting a convoy to MALTA, *Illustrious* was badly damaged by Stuka (Ju 87) dive-bombers, which secured seven hits, setting the ship on fire; the armored flight deck saved her from destruction. Repairs in the United States followed, after which *Illustrious*'s further service included covering the Allied landings on MADAGASCAR in 1942, Home Fleet work and cover for the SALERNO landings in 1943 and British Pacific Fleet work in 1944 and 1945. Among these latter operations were strikes on Sumatra, JAVA, islands in the Sakishima Gunto and FORMOSA.

ILYUSHIN IL-2. Sergei Ilyushin, the Soviet designer, won a 200,000-ruble prize for designing this attack bomber, the renowned Stormovik. Sheathed in heavy armor, it worked closely with ground forces to destroy tanks and other vehicles and to strafe enemy troops. It was appropriately armed for such missions, carrying two 20-mm. cannon, one 12.7-mm. machine gun and two 7.62-mm. machine guns. It also carried about 800 pounds of bombs or eight rockets. Top speed was 257 miles per hour, which was produced by a 1,600-horsepower in-line engine.

As a single-seater, the Stormovik was just entering service at the time of the German attack in 1941. In 1942 a two-seater version was produced; this one featured the 12.7-mm. machine gun, which was operated by the second crew member, facing rearward. The Stormovik is said to have had the lowest percentage of loss of any aircraft on the Eastern Front.

Ilyushin Il-2 Stormovik

ILYUSHIN IL-4. The basic design of this type aircraft (the DB-3, alias ZKB-26) was first used in 1936; it was the mainstay of the Soviet medium-bomber forces. It was also used by the Soviet Navy as a torpedo bomber. Naval Il-4s bombed Berlin on August 8, 1941, in a morale-building raid. The first versions were powered by two 1,110-horsepower engines and flew at a maximum speed of 277 miles per hour. The plane carried a three- or four-man crew, three 7.62-mm. machine guns and 4,398 pounds of bombs (or one 18-inch torpedo). Dimensions: wingspan, 70.4 feet; length, 48.7 feet; height, 13.9 feet.

IMAMURA, Hitoshi (1886–1968). One of Japan's most successful and versatile generals, Imamura served during the 1920s and '30s in a variety of staff and command positions. In 1936–37 he was vice-chief of staff of the KWANTUNG ARMY. Imamura took command of Japan's 16th Army in 1941 and led the victorious invasion of JAVA. Once in control of Java, Imamura fostered liberal occupation policies and released political prisoners in an effort to win Indonesian support for Japan's expansionist policies. Made a full general in 1943, he was given command of the 17th and 18th Armies and ordered to retake the SOLOMON ISLANDS. He established his headquarters at RABAUL, but in spite of major efforts to resupply and reinforce his troops on GUADALCANAL, he was ultimately forced to order their withdrawal in 1943. Convicted of war crimes at the end of the war, Imamura was sent to Sugamo prison. He was paroled in 1954.

IMPERATOR. Code name for a proposed Allied tip-and-run raid on the French coast in 1942. It would have been a small-scale SLEDGEHAMMER.

IMPERIAL GENERAL HEADQUARTERS. The senior joint Japanese command for prosecution of the war. IGHQ was a term rather than a real organization. It was used to denote the co-equal status of the Tokyo-based headquarters of the Army and Navy General Staffs and their subordinate general and special staff sections. This duality of command typified the Japanese military system in the war not only at the highest level but also in the lower echelons. The joint Army-Navy concept prevailed in the field, but sometimes interservice rivalries prevented the development of a smooth working relationship.

IMPHAL. Scene of the major battle of the Japanese invasion of India in the spring of 1944, Imphal was the chief town of Manipur province. Through it ran the only all-weather highway on the Burma-India frontier. The invasion of India was to coincide with a political effort by the Japanese to subvert British control of that country. The invading force, under the command of Lt. Gen. Renya Mutaguchi, totaled some 100,000 men, including the 15th, 31st and 33d Divisions as well as one division of the INDIAN NATIONAL ARMY under Subhas Chandra BOSE, an Indian nationalist politician who had fled to the Japanese in 1941. The British mustered a force of Indian Army troops which was roughly equivalent in number at the beginning of the offensive but was constantly reinforced as the campaign progressed. The 17th, 20th and 23d Indian Army Divisions, the 2d British Division and the 11th East African Division were the principal Allied units engaged. The overall commander was Lt. Gen. Sir William J. SLIM.

In the fighting around Imphal the British suffered 13,000 casualties, the Japanese 50,000. The campaign was a complete disaster for the Japanese, owing mainly to their inadequate supply system and weak air support. Following the failure of their invasion attempt, they were subsequently driven out of most of BURMA before the war's end.

INDEPENDENCE. Code name for the Allied blockade of Bay of Biscay ports occupied by Germans (March

1945). Independence was also the early name for the operation later called VENERABLE.

INDEPENDENCE, U.S.S. Aircraft carrier and class of nine ships, originally laid down as CLEVELAND-class light cruisers; during 1942 the decision was made to complete them as aircraft carriers to meet the urgent need for such ships. They commissioned between January and December 1943. They had a standard displacement of 11,000 tons and a nominal capacity of 45 planes; at 610 feet, they were 245 feet shorter than the full-size fleet carriers of the ESSEX class and had slightly over half their aircraft capacity. Their speed, however, was slightly higher, and the Independences were assigned to operate with the Essexes in the FAST CARRIER TASK FORCE. To distinguish them from their larger consorts, the Independence class were redesignated Small Aircraft Carriers (CVL) in mid-1943, and were referred to as "light carriers." The first combat operation for one of this class came in September 1943, when *Independence*, with Essex-class carriers *Yorktown* and *Essex*, attacked MARCUS ISLAND. As the rest of this class came into service, they took part in task force air strikes from the invasion of the GILBERT ISLANDS to the final attacks on the Japanese home islands, and participated in the battles of LEYTE GULF and the PHILIPPINE SEA. *Independence* served as an atomic target ship at Bikini in 1946, surviving the two blasts in battered condition.

INDIANA, U.S.S. Battleship and class (including MASSACHUSETTS and ALABAMA). *Indiana* was of 35,000 tons standard displacement and had nine 16-inch guns and twenty 5-inch guns (four more than the nearly identical SOUTH DAKOTA; these ships are often referred to as being of the same class). The Indiana also carried fifty-six 40-mm. and forty 20-mm. antiaircraft guns. They were commissioned in 1942. *Indiana* was sent from the Atlantic to the Pacific in 1942 and saw a great deal of action as part of a task group and as a component of Adm. Willis LEE's battle line.

INDIANAPOLIS, U.S.S. PORTLAND-class heavy cruiser. Commissioned in 1932, *Indianapolis* was in the Pacific Fleet at the time of PEARL HARBOR. After screening carriers LEXINGTON and YORKTOWN in early raids against Japanese island bases, she operated in the Aleutians until the recapture of KISKA (August 1943). In the fall of that year she became Vice-Adm. Raymond SPRUANCE's Fifth Fleet flagship. In this role she took part in the capture of the GILBERTS and MARSHALLS and in carrier task force attacks on the western CAROLINES. In mid-1944 she participated in the seizure of the MARIANAS and in the Battle of the PHILIPPINE SEA. In September she supported the capture of PELELIU.

After an overhaul *Indianapolis* joined the FAST CARRIER TASK FORCE in February 1945 and took part in the first carrier attack on Japan since General DOOLITTLE's single strike of April 1942. During February and March she operated in support of the capture of Iwo JIMA and in pre-invasion attacks on OKINAWA. Severely damaged by a KAMIKAZE plane on March 31, the eve of the Okinawa landing, *Indianapolis* was able to return to the United States under her own power after emergency repairs.

Ready for sea, *Indianapolis* sailed from San Francisco on July 16, 1945, carrying elements of the ATOMIC BOMBS that were soon to be dropped on Hiroshima and Nagasaki. After delivering this top-secret cargo at Tinian, she paused at Guam before sailing from that island on July 28. Steaming to Leyte Gulf without escort—Japanese submarines had not been the kind of threat that U-boats had been in the Atlantic; it was also felt that her speed would protect her—she was spotted by the Japanese submarine *I-58* during the night of July 29. At 15 minutes past midnight two torpedoes smashed into *Indianapolis*'s hull, forward on the starboard side. Twelve minutes later the cruiser rolled over and sank. From survivors' later estimates, about 300 to 350 of her crew of 1,199 men went down with their ship. Some 850 to 900 men were left in the water.

The worst part of the tragedy was just beginning. Because of radio difficulties, no one else realized that the cruiser had been lost. Electrical power had been knocked out when *Indianapolis* was torpedoed, and no SOS could be sent during the minutes before the ship went down. When she had departed Guam, the cruiser had sent a standard radio message ahead to Leyte to report that she was on her way. Atmospheric interference scrambled the signal, and Leyte received an unintelligible garble. *Indianapolis* should have arrived on July 31, but no overdue report was filed; Leyte had no idea that the ship should be expected.

Survivors were sighted by a patrolling plane at midmorning on August 2, 82 hours after the ship had gone down. All ships and planes within reach were directed to the area; the search for survivors continued until August 8. Only 316 of the original crew of 1,199 were rescued.

INDIAN NATIONAL ARMY. Organization founded by the anti-British revolutionary leader Subhas Chandra BOSE, who advocated a Free India movement aligned with the AXIS. He organized the Indian National Army in 1943 from Indian POWs in Japanese hands. About 40,000 declared their adherence to Free India; of these, some 7,000 fought with the Japanese 15th Army in the IMPHAL and KOHIMA battles.

INDISPENSABLE STRAIT. The channel between southeast GUADALCANAL and Malaita.

INDOCHINA. With the collapse of France in June 1940, French-controlled Indochina became an object of contention—the United States and Britain versus Japan. Prior to 1940, the Yunnan railway linking the port city of Haiphong in northern Indochina with KUNMING in southern China had been one of the principal supply routes into Chiang Kai-shek's China.

The Japanese promptly took advantage of the French surrender in Europe to demand that the new VICHY government of Marshal PÉTAIN halt the flow of supplies to China and allow Japanese troops to be stationed in northern Indochina. In addition, the Japanese wished to use the French airfields in the north and utilize Indochinese railroads for troop movements. After vainly appealing to the United States for military aid, the French Government yielded in September 1940.

The following summer the Japanese returned with new demands. On July 21, 1941, the French were forced to agree to allow the Japanese to use airfields in southern as well as northern Indochina and to station an unlimited number of troops in the colony. Saigon and Camranh Bay were to be used by the Japanese as naval bases. Although still nominally under French rule, Indochina was from this point on effectively occupied by the Japanese. The United States responded to the Japanese moves by freezing all Japanese assets and placing an embargo on the export of petroleum products to Japan. PEARL HARBOR followed five months later.

Indochina saw no significant military operations during the remainder of the war. French efforts to organize an anti-Japanese underground were halfhearted and largely unsuccessful. In northern Indochina, nationalist Vietnamese guerrillas led by HO CHI MINH had more success. Ho's "Viet Minh" fighters aided the Allies in China by supplying intelligence and information on Allied POWs. In March 1945 the Japanese military command deposed the French administration of Governor General Jean Decoux and assumed direct control of Indochina. The French could offer little resistance, and Indochina remained under Japanese control until the end of the war.

INDOMITABLE, H.M.S. Royal Navy aircraft carrier of 23,000 tons, completed late in 1941 by Vickers-Armstrong and armed with sixteen 4.5-inch guns and smaller weapons. *Indomitable* had a capacity of 40 to 50 aircraft, depending on their size, and an armored flight deck. On completion she served first in the Indian Ocean in 1942, participating in the occupation of MADAGASCAR; she was then ordered home for use in the August 1942 PEDESTAL convoy to Malta, in which she was damaged. *Indomitable* was next used in the SICILY operations in 1943, being again damaged, after which she was transferred to the Pacific Fleet, where she served until the end of the war, taking part in strikes on targets in Sumatra and the Sakishima Gunto. She was struck by a Japanese KAMIKAZE but suffered little damage: the kamikaze bounced off the armor into the sea.

INFATUATE. Code name of Allied operation to capture WALCHEREN ISLAND and free the SCHELDT River approaches to ANTWERP, November 1, 1944.

INFLUX. Code name for a proposed British occupation of Sicily, studied as a possible operation early in the war (1941).

INGERSOLL, Royal Eason (1883–1976). Graduated from the U.S. Naval Academy in 1905, Ingersoll rose to rear admiral in 1938, vice-admiral in January 1942 and admiral in July 1942. Soon after U.S. entry into the war, he became commander of the Atlantic Fleet, responsible for transportation, communication, troop transport, supply lines and the defense of the Western Hemisphere. Until May 1943, when the TENTH FLEET was established, Ingersoll was in charge of antisubmarine warfare as well. He also helped direct the invasion of French Morocco in November 1942. In November 1944 Ingersoll took command of the WESTERN SEA FRONTIER. He retired in 1946.

INGRAM, Jonas Howard (1886–1952). A graduate of the Naval Academy (where he was a famous football player and coach) in 1907, Ingram became a rear admiral in 1941 and was promoted to vice-admiral the following year. As commander of the South Atlantic Force (later the Fourth Fleet), Ingram cleared Brazilian waters of German submarines and led naval operations in the South Atlantic. In November 1944 he was appointed Commander in Chief of the Atlantic Fleet, where he countered the Germans' last-ditch submarine efforts.

INÖNÜ, Ismet (1884–1973). President of Turkey in 1938–50, Inönü was courted during the war by both Axis and Allies. But, though Turkey had signed a treaty in 1939 pledging to give assistance to Britain and France in case of war, she remained neutral through most of the war, opposed to Germany but fearful that she would win. After the German victories in the Balkans in 1941, Turkey was strategically isolated from the Western powers. In 1943, following the TEHERAN CONFERENCE, Inönü met with CHURCHILL and ROOSEVELT at Cairo; Churchill, in particular, had consistently pushed for Turkish entry into the war. But Inönü wanted military aid that the Allies were unable to supply. Inönü seemed so concerned over the necessity, as he saw it, to refuse the Anglo-American urging that Roosevelt admitted that, if he were a Turk, he too would need more guarantees than were being offered. In the summer of 1944 Turkey severed diplomatic relations with Germany, thus closing down a major Nazi espionage center, and in February 1945 Inönü's government declared war.

One of the pioneer statesmen of modern Turkey, Inönü later (1961–65) served his country as Premier.

INOUYE, Shigeyoshi (1889–). A career naval officer, Vice-Admiral Inouye commanded Japan's Fourth Fleet, stationed at TRUK at the outbreak of the war. He was in overall command of the forces that invaded and conquered GUAM and WAKE ISLAND, though actual operations were conducted by Adm. Aritomo GOTO. Inouye also helped to plan and mount the unsuccessful PORT MORESBY invasion. Relieved of command in October 1942, Inouye became superintendent of the Naval Academy. In August 1944 he was appointed Vice-Minister of the Navy. A peace advocate from 1943 on, Inouye became a member of Japan's Supreme War Council in May 1945, being promoted to admiral.

INTERNATIONAL BANK FOR RECONSTRUCTION AND DEVELOPMENT. Three principal organs of world economic policy were established in 1945: the International Bank for Reconstruction and Development, the INTERNATIONAL MONETARY FUND and the International Trade Organization. These organizations were the result of sentiment felt throughout the war that international monetary cooperation and management were necessary for creating the kind of world envisioned at the end of the war. The final plans for the bank were decided at the International Monetary and Financial Conference at BRETTON WOODS, N.H., in 1944, and it became operational on December 27, 1945. The purpose of the bank—usually called the World Bank—was to provide funds for postwar reconstruction and development throughout the world.

INTERNATIONAL MILITARY TRIBUNAL. The name given to two judicial bodies, those conducting the Nuremberg and Tokyo trials of accused war criminals. The tribunal for Nuremberg was established under the London Charter of August, 8, 1945, and the trials opened on November 20, 1945. This set a precedent followed in the establishment of the International Military Tribunal for the Far East, which began sitting in May 1946.

INTERNATIONAL MILITARY TRIBUNAL FOR THE FAR EAST. The principal trials were held at Tokyo; 25 Japanese leaders were found guilty of war crimes, seven being sentenced to death and the rest to life imprisonment. Other trials were held in Hong Kong, Singapore and some smaller cities. More than 900 persons were sentenced to death, mostly for crimes committed against civilians in occupied areas.

INTERNATIONAL MONETARY FUND. This fund, along with the International Bank for Reconstruction and Development, was agreed upon at the International Monetary and Financial Conference held at Bretton Woods, N.H., in July 1944. The fund and the bank formally came into existence in December 1945 when all the final agreements and arrangements were made. Both institutions were designed to promote the balanced growth of world trade and the maintenance of high levels of employment. The fund's primary purpose was to maintain orderly currency practices; by establishing a suitable pattern of exchange rates among member currencies, the fund would ensure reasonable stability in exchange rates while providing for orderly changes when necessary. Secondly, the fund was charged with eliminating harmful restrictions on international payments and discriminatory currency arrangements. Its resources of currency and gold could be made available to member nations to meet deficits in their international payments.

INTREPID, U.S.S. Essex-class aircraft carrier, commissioned in 1943. She took part in operations against the Marshall Islands and in the February 1944 raid on Truk; during that operation she was struck by an aerial torpedo. After supporting the invasions of the Palaus and the Philippines and taking part in the battle for Leyte Gulf, she was again damaged, this time by two kamikaze planes. *Intrepid* later participated in attacks on Japan and Okinawa before being put out of action a third time, this time by a suicide plane that crashed through her flight deck. She returned to the Pacific only weeks before the end of the war.

INVASION—NORMANDY. When on D-Day—June 6, 1944—Allied armies landed in Normandy on the northwestern coast of France, possibly the one most critical event of World War II unfolded; for upon the outcome of the invasion hung the fate of Europe. If the invasion failed, the United States might turn its full attention to the enemy in the Pacific—Japan—leaving Great Britain alone, most of its resources spent in mounting the invasion. That would enable Nazi Germany to muster all its strength against the Soviet Union. By the time American forces returned to Europe—if, indeed, they ever returned—Germany might be master of the entire Continent.

Although fewer Allied ground troops went ashore on D-Day than on the first day of the earlier invasion of Sicily, the invasion of Normandy was in the aggregate history's greatest amphibious operation, involving on the first day 5,000 ships, the largest armada ever assembled; 11,000 sorties by Allied aircraft following months of preliminary bombardment; and approximately 154,000 American, British and Canadian soldiers (70,500 American, 83,115 British and Canadian), including 23,000 arriving by parachute and glider. It involved, too, a long-range deception plan on a scale the world had never before known and the clandestine operations of tens of thousands of resistance fighters in the Nazi-occupied countries of western Europe.

Preparation for the invasion had begun more than two and a half years earlier, in September 1941, when the Joint Planning Staff of the British military services drew up a first plan, known as Roundup, for a return to the Continent in the event the German armies, for whatever reason, had to fall back on their homeland. Yet Roundup was a plan prepared in recognition of the dearth of British resources in the wake of the evacuation from Dunkirk and was based on the understanding that no invasion would be attempted until German strength was sharply depleted.

The United States had been in the war less than three months when, early in 1942, an obscure major general in the Operations Division of the War Department, one destined to play a principal role in the eventual invasion, Dwight D. Eisenhower, introduced a radical concept that foreshadowed a long-lasting conflict between the British and the Americans over the proper strategy to be employed in defeating Germany. Deploring an apparent perilous spreading of limited American resources around the globe, Eisenhower convinced the U.S. Army's Chief of Staff, Gen. George C. Marshall, that the time had come not only to reaffirm a previously agreed-upon strategy of defeating Germany before concentrating on Japan but also to make a specific commitment to include a time and place for invading Europe.

Marshall in turn presented a plan to President Franklin D. Roosevelt based on an early American buildup in Britain (code-named Bolero) to support an invasion of France (given the British code name, Roundup) within a year, around the first of April 1943; but should the Soviet Union show signs of collapse, an emergency invasion (code-named Sledgehammer) might have to be mounted before the end of 1942. When Roosevelt endorsed the proposal, Marshall headed a delegation to go to London to sell it to the British.

Sharply conscious of the forbidding losses incurred by British ground armies on the Continent in World War I, the British Prime Minister, Winston Churchill, and his military advisers were adamantly opposed to what they saw as an impetuous American adventure. The way to defeat Germany in their view was to pound the enemy with air and sea power while nibbling away with small ground attacks on the periphery of Nazi conquests. Only when the Germans were near collapse, their far-reaching tentacles cut off, should the Allies confront them directly on the ground.

Particularly concerned lest the Americans insist on an emergency invasion (Sledgehammer), Churchill came to the United States in June 1942 with the specific goal of convincing Roosevelt that such an invasion in 1942 would only sacrifice Allied troops on French beaches. Aware that Roosevelt was anxious to begin some direct confrontation with the German armies to provide the American public with a sense of getting on toward victory, Churchill proposed instead an invasion of French NORTHWEST AFRICA, which was controlled by the collaborationist VICHY government. Although General Marshall argued eloquently that invading Northwest Africa would do little to help the Russians and would slow buildup for the eventual invasion of Europe, Roosevelt sided with Churchill. There would be no invasion of Europe in 1942. Nor, as Marshall predicted while speaking against the Northwest Africa operation, would one be possible in 1943.

Meanwhile, although buildup of American forces in Britain was slow, primarily because of a shortage of shipping, enough troops were on hand to justify creating an American command, the EUROPEAN THEATER OF OPERATIONS, United States Army (ETOUSA). He who early had argued for a quick move against the Continent, General Eisenhower, was appointed as the commander. When it came to selecting a commander for the Northwest Africa invasion—who, all agreed, should be an American because of the strong antipathy between the Vichy French and the British—Eisenhower was conveniently at hand.

As the campaign in Northwest Africa proceeded long beyond the invasion in November 1942, Roosevelt, Churchill and the COMBINED CHIEFS OF STAFF met in January 1943 at CASABLANCA to consider the future conduct of the war. A relative paucity of Allied resources, including shipping, obviously precluded an invasion of Europe across the English Channel until 1944. That forced the Americans to accept a continuation of what they termed the British peripheral strategy and led to the invasion of SICILY and eventually of ITALY. But the Allied leaders did agree to continue American buildup in Britain for an eventual cross-Channel invasion. Although nobody wanted to name a supreme Allied commander for the invasion until it became apparent which nation would provide the preponderance of troops, all recognized that planning for the operation had to get under way. That led in March 1943 to designation of a chief of staff to a nonexistent supreme commander; the assignment went to a British general, Sir Frederick MORGAN, who established a combined American-British headquarters known as COSSAC, for Chief of Staff to the Supreme Allied Commander (*see* COSSAC).

Setting up in Norfolk House on St. James's Square in

The Allied invasion commanders (from left): General Bradley, U.S. ground commander; Admiral Ramsay, Allied naval commander; Air Chief Marshal Tedder, Deputy Supreme Commander; General Eisenhower, Supreme Allied Commander; General Montgomery, British (and, initially, Allied) ground commander; Air Chief Marshal Leigh-Mallory, Allied air commander; General Smith, chief of staff

London, General Morgan saw COSSAC not only as a planning staff but also as a coordinating staff for all activities contributing to the invasion. That inevitably involved deception to mislead the Germans as to the time and place of the invasion. For this the British already had a broad plan known as JAEL, which involved whispering campaigns in diplomatic posts around the world and various feints to keep German eyes focused anywhere but on the coast of northwestern France. Basic to the deception was ULTRA, code name for intelligence obtained from intercepts of German radio traffic (made possible by the British early in the war having broken the code of the standard German radio enciphering machine, the ENIGMA). Through Ultra the Allied high command knew what the Germans expected the Allies to do and thus could plant information either to reinforce an existing wrong view or to create another. One of the most effective methods was to feed information through compromised German agents, most of it false but enough of it true—and thus sometimes involving sacrifice of Allied troops, agents or resistance forces in occupied countries—to maintain the credibility of the German agents.

One of the first plans prepared by COSSAC was a ruse, COCKADE, designed to keep German troops in western Europe and off the hard-pressed Russian front by fostering the expectation of Allied invasion in 1943. Later in the year the Russians were brought in on the deception to help point to Allied invasion of the Balkans and Norway, and subsequently to mislead the Germans to believe that a Russian offensive designed to coincide with the invasion would come off several months later than it actually was planned. Once the Russians were involved, Jael was rechristened BODYGUARD, after a remark by Churchill to the Russian leader, Marshal Joseph STALIN, that truth in war is so important that it must be protected by a bodyguard of lies.

Other COSSAC plans were RANKIN, a blueprint for occupying the Continent should the Germans suddenly collapse, and OVERLORD, a full-scale invasion of France across the Channel. The bulk of the planning centered on Overlord. As directed by the Combined Chiefs of Staff, the target date was May 1944. The assault was to take place along 25 miles of coastline in Normandy extending westward from the mouth of the Orne River near Caen, plus a simultaneous supporting invasion of SOUTHERN FRANCE.

Who was to command the invasion remained to be decided. At a time when an early invasion appeared in prospect, in which case the British would have to furnish most of the troops, Churchill promised the job to the Chief of the Imperial General Staff, Field Marshal Sir Alan BROOKE. But when it became clear that the invasion would not be made until 1944, the promise proved short-lived. Aware that the United States would provide most of the troops and resources once the campaign on the Continent was under way, the U.S. Chiefs of Staff wanted an American commander. Deeming the British still lukewarm to a cross-Channel attack until the Germans were thoroughly beaten down, they also saw an American commander as a guarantee that the assault would be launched within a reasonable time. That led inevitably to consideration of General Marshall for the post, with the prospect that General Eisenhower would succeed him as Chief of Staff.

There the matter stood until November 1943, when Allied leaders met with Marshal Stalin in TEHERAN. Concerned that the invasion proceed on schedule, Stalin pressed Roosevelt to name a supreme commander. Since the target date was less than six months away, a decision was essential in any case. In deliberating, Roosevelt deemed Marshall better prepared than Eisenhower to handle relations with American commanders in the Pacific and with Congress. When Marshall himself decorously declined to express a preference, the President said, in effect, "I could not sleep at night with you out of the country." A few days later he informed Eisenhower that he was to be the Supreme Allied Commander.

Arriving in London early in 1944, Eisenhower changed COSSAC into SUPREME HEADQUARTERS, ALLIED EXPEDITIONARY FORCE (SHAEF). While appreciative of the job General Morgan had done, he wanted to bring his former chief of staff, Lt. Gen. Walter Bedell SMITH, into the headquarters. Morgan graciously agreed to accept a position as deputy chief of staff. As Eisenhower determined, COSSAC's plan for Overlord was sound. Studying the results of a hit-and-run raid against the French coast in 1942 at DIEPPE, in which the raiders incurred heavy losses, the early planners had concluded that the strength of German defenses required not a number of separate assaults by relatively small units but an immense concentration of power in a single main landing. The invasion site would have to be close to at least one major port, would have to provide a good road network leading inland and would have to lie within easy range of fighter aircraft based in Britain. The latter consideration fairly well limited the choice to the coast from the Belgian-French border to Cherbourg, including the Pas de Calais across the Strait of Dover, the region already tested around Dieppe and that part of Normandy along the base of the Cotentin Peninsula between Caen and Cherbourg. The first two choices presented totally unsheltered beaches which, because of proximity to Britain, probably would be most heavily fortified. That left only the beaches of the Cotentin.

While agreeing in principle with COSSAC's plan, Eisenhower believed it had to be strengthened and broadened. Instead of a 25-mile front, he wanted 40 miles; instead of three divisions, five. Yet how to obtain enough landing craft to accommodate such a force? To provide them, he recommended postponing the simultaneous subsidiary invasion of Southern France, thereby making landing craft from the Mediterranean area available for the main invasion. A question of postponing Overlord for a month also arose. Although a month's delay would reduce the amount of good campaigning weather on the Continent before winter set in, would give the Germans that much more time to strengthen beach defenses and might afford the enemy time to bring to bear a new weapon that British intelligence had detected—a pilotless aircraft or bomb subsequently known as the V-1 (*see* V-WEAPONS)—it had the virtue of gaining an additional month of good flying weather for Allied aircraft. It was vital to afford Allied airmen more time to cripple French railroads and knock out highway bridges so that German reserves could not move quickly against the invasion. It was vital also for what was deemed the *sine qua non* for success of the invasion—the crippling of the German air arm, the LUFTWAFFE. Given those reasons, the Combined Chiefs sanctioned the delay.

In the meantime, the cast of forces and commanders and the specific roles for the invasion were emerging. The overall ground command was to be vested in a British general, Sir Bernard L. MONTGOMERY, and his headquarters, the British 21st ARMY GROUP. The British SECOND ARMY under Lt. Gen. Sir Miles C. DEMPSEY was to go ashore on the east on three beaches labeled SWORD, JUNO and GOLD, extending westward from the mouth of the Orne River. The American FIRST ARMY under Lt. Gen. Omar N. BRADLEY was to land farther west on beaches called OMAHA and UTAH, on either side of the mouth of the Vire River. A British airborne division was to assist British landings by seizing high ground and enemy batteries east of the Orne, while two American airborne divisions were to land behind UTAH Beach to secure routes of egress through marshes backing the beach.

The follow-up force consisted of the Canadian FIRST ARMY under Lt. Gen. H. D. G. CRERAR and, somewhat later, the American THIRD ARMY under Lt. Gen. George S. PATTON, Jr. Once Patton's army was ashore,

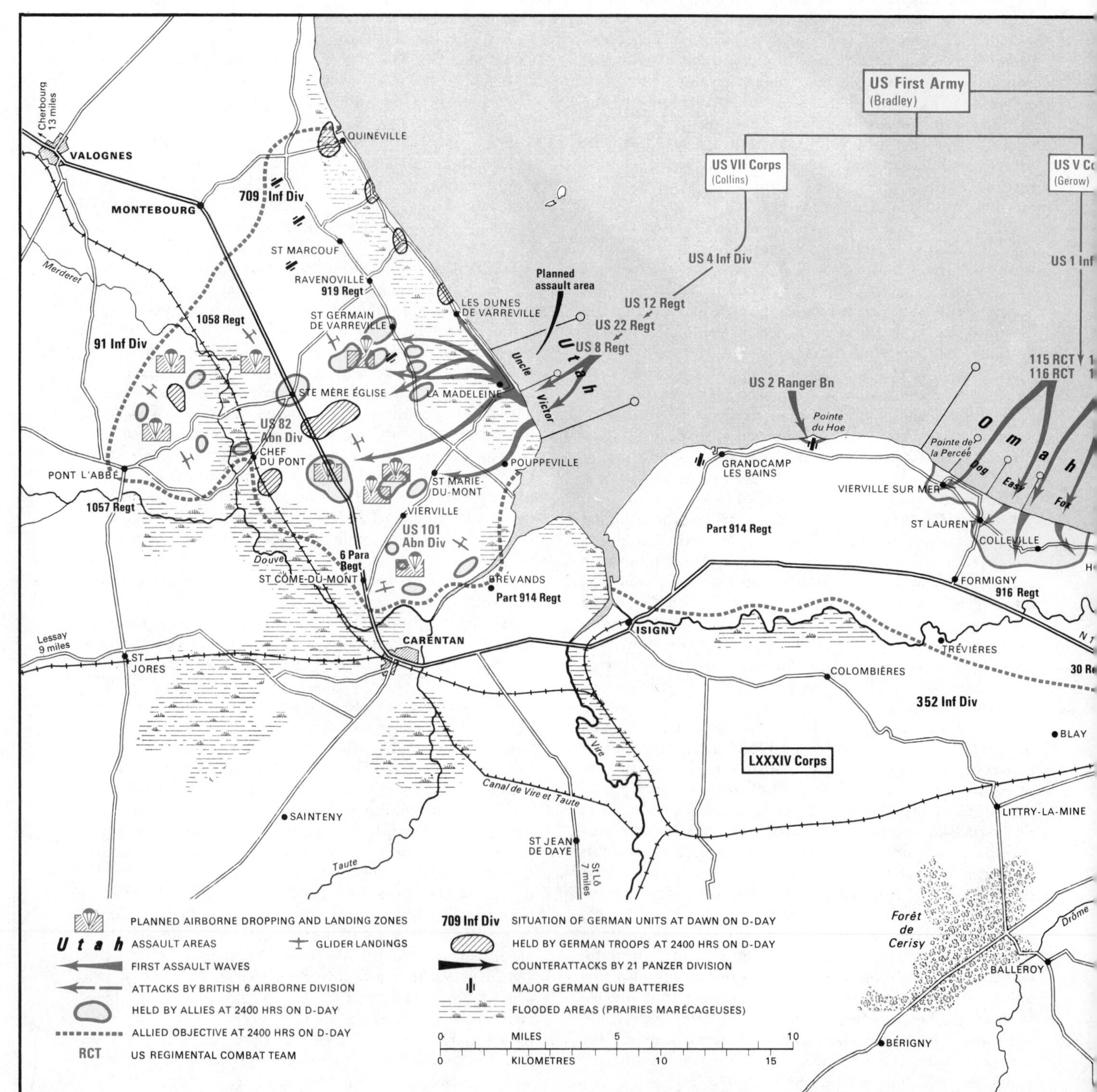

D-DAY—the Allied dispositions and the opposing German forces as the supreme amphibious operation was launched

the Americans were to create the 12TH ARMY GROUP under General Bradley, although Montgomery was to remain as the overall ground commander until Eisenhower brought his own headquarters to the Continent. Only after strong Allied forces had been concentrated in a lodgment area extending from the Seine River in the north to the Loire River in the south, which would include the major ports of Cherbourg and Brest, was a final drive into Germany to begin.

Eisenhower's deputy commander, Air Chief Marshal Sir Arthur W. TEDDER, acted as coordinator of the air forces, consisting of the tactical air forces under Air Chief Marshal Sir Trafford LEIGH-MALLORY and the strategic air forces, the latter composed of the Royal Air Force BOMBER COMMAND under Air Chief Marshal Sir Arthur T. HARRIS and the U.S. Strategic Air Forces under Lt. Gen. Carl SPAATZ. Adm. Sir Bertram H. RAMSAY commanded the naval forces.

Although the taking of major ports figured prominently in the planning, the Allied armies were to be supplied at first over the beaches by landing craft and amphibious trucks. Two artificial prefabricated ports, known by the code name MULBERRY, were later to be towed into place, and great coils of rubber hose were to

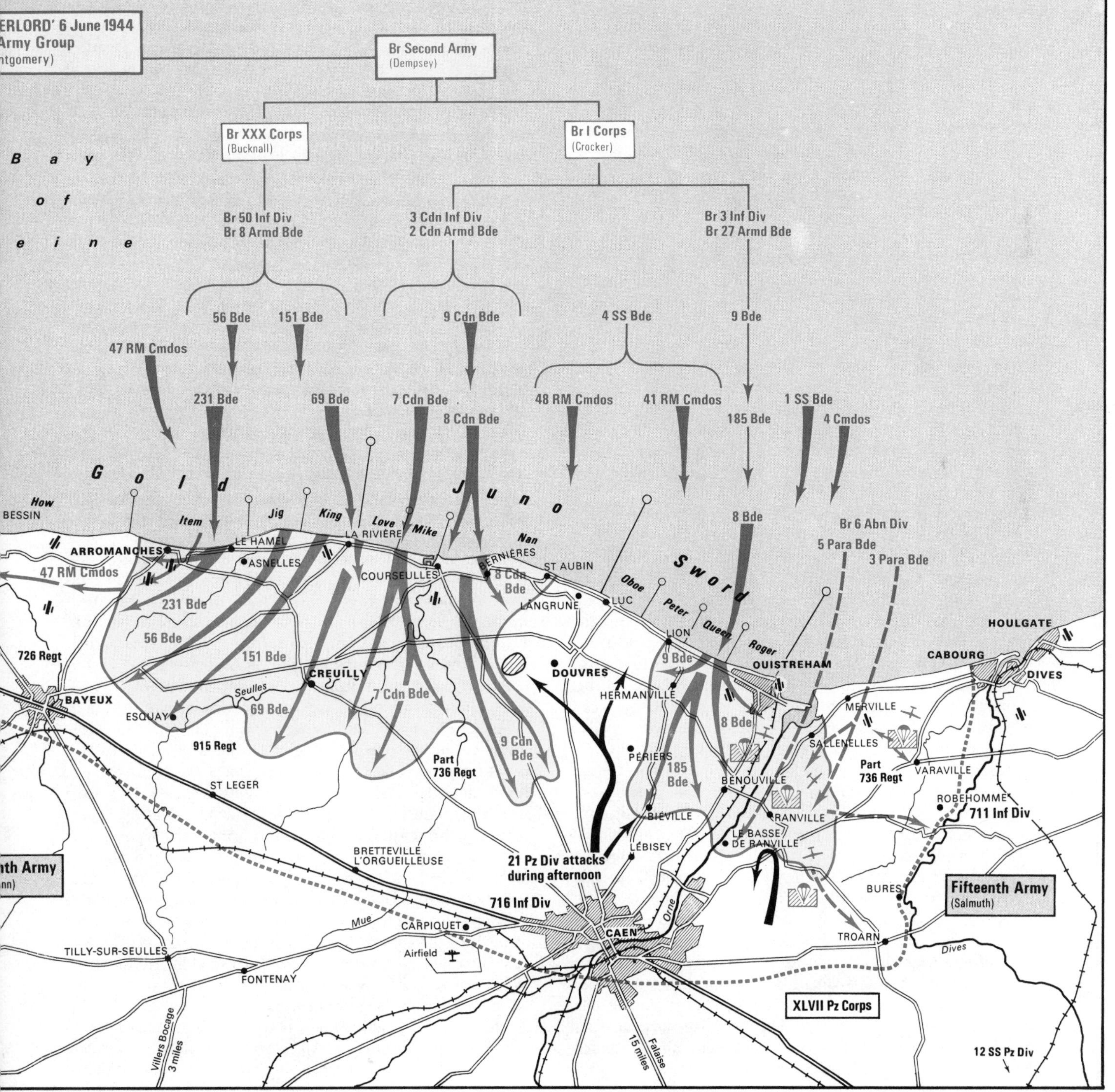

be laid on the floor of the Channel for piping fuel to the Continent—called PLUTO for Pipe Line Under the Ocean. Some tanks were equipped with canvas "bloomers" so that they could swim ashore. Steel mesh mats were to provide footing on sand. In case the Germans employed gas warfare, the troops were to carry gas masks and wear uniforms impregnated with a malodorous antigas chemical.

So vast was the paraphernalia accumulated in Britain for support of the invasion that pundits quipped that if it hadn't been for the barrage balloons protecting British cities against low-flying enemy aircraft, the island would have sunk. Artillery, antiaircraft guns, ambulances, trucks, tanks, bulldozers, observation planes, laundries, hospitals, field kitchens, locomotives, railroad rolling stock, even dental fillings—the south of England was a bulging warehouse. The 5,000-ship armada included landing craft, troop transports, cargo ships, coasters, minesweepers, almost 900 warships ranging from torpedo boats to battleships, even midget submarines to guide assault craft through early morning darkness to the beaches. American aircraft alone totaled almost 13,000 planes, including more than 4,500 big bombers.

Eisenhower set the specific target date for June 5. Six days before that, troops who for weeks had been cordoned off from the English countryside in barbed-wire enclosures and watched by some 2,000 counterintelligence agents began to climb gangways to landing craft and transports in harbors all along the southern and southwestern coasts of England. Troops that were to go by air assembled at predesignated airfields. Coded messages broadcast by the BRITISH BROADCASTING CORPORATION alerted the FRENCH RESISTANCE to prepare to sabotage German communications. All was ready for one of history's most dramatic and momentous events, but two big questions remained: What did the Germans know? And what about the weather?

Although the Allied commanders could not know it until their troops were ashore, their deception had been remarkably successful. As time for the invasion neared, the focus of the deception had shifted from such regions as the Balkans and Norway to the Pas de Calais, for so immense was the Allied concentration in Britain that an invasion of France obviously was in the offing. The object was to pin the strongest German force, the Fifteenth Army, in the Pas de Calais, along with the German PANZER reserve, leaving the defense of Normandy to the weaker Seventh Army, which was overextended through also bearing responsibility for Brittany. Bombing attacks, sabotage by the French Resistance, false messages from compromised German agents—all concentrated on the Pas de Calais with only minimal attention to Normandy. So too the intelligence specialists fostered the impression that the Allies had some 90 divisions for the invasion (they had in fact 39), so that even after the Normandy invasion the fiction could be preserved that Normandy was but a preliminary and the main invasion in the Pas de Calais was still to come.

Under Operation Fortitude, a fictitious American force—the 1st Army Group under General Patton—ostensibly assembled just across the Channel from the Pas de Calais. Dummy troop installations, false radio traffic, dummy landing craft in the estuary of the Thames River, huge but unoccupied tent encampments, dummy tanks—all contributed to the deception. After the Normandy landings and Patton's move to the Continent, the chief of U.S. Army Ground Forces, Lt. Gen. Lesley J. MCNAIR, arrived to continue the fiction, and when he was killed while observing the fighting in Normandy, another senior American commander took his place in the ruse. As the date for the invasion neared, none of the German high command in France doubted that the invasion would strike the Pas de Calais, including the commander in chief in the west, Field Marshal Gerd von RUNDSTEDT, and his top field commander, Field Marshal Erwin ROMMEL, commander of Army Group B. The Führer himself, Adolf HITLER, had an intuition that the invasion would come in Normandy, but he lacked sufficient conviction to impel his commanders to make other than nominal reinforcement there.

On the eve of D-Day, General Eisenhower's weather adviser, Group Capt. J. M. STAGG, was optimistic at first; but on the night of June 3, with the troops already embarked, all optimism faded. The designated day of June 5, Stagg reported, would be overcast with high winds and a cloud base too low for flying, and conditions were so unsettled that he could venture no forecast more than 24 hours ahead. The first step was to call back convoys already at sea, then to face the terrible dilemma that Stagg's revelation posed. As Eisenhower pondered the alternatives, wind and rain swirled around his command trailer. They could still go on June 6, but if not then, the convoys would have to be recalled and refueled, and the next time tidal conditions would be right would be on June 19. That and the first possible date in July would mean disembarking troops, with the morale and security problems that disembarkation entailed.

In a dramatic meeting the night of June 4, General Eisenhower heard from Stagg encouraging if not good news: a new weather front should move up the Channel the next day, meaning that on June 6 the rains would stop, the winds decrease to a degree and the cloud cover rise just enough for bombers to operate. After polling principal subordinates, Eisenhower made the momentous decision to proceed with the invasion on June 6 and confirmed it at a final briefing after midnight. Airborne troops were to begin coming to earth in France in the first minutes of June 6, followed by seaborne American troops landing at 6:30 A.M., and within the next hour, depending upon tidal conditions, British and Canadian troops. The decision was irrevocable.

As Eisenhower made his fateful decision, the Germans remained ignorant of the time and place of the invasion. They had learned the code name Overlord, but that did them little good, partly because Overlord was the name for the broad overall invasion plan, whereas the actual landing operations went by another code name, NEPTUNE. They had also learned that to alert the French Resistance that invasion was imminent, the BBC would broadcast the first line of a poem by the French poet Paul Verlaine, to be followed by the second line when the invasion was to come within 48 hours. Yet few German commanders had faith in that intelligence. Why would the Allies announce over the radio in advance when they were coming?

One who did believe it was the intelligence officer of the Fifteenth Army in the Pas de Calais. When he heard the broadcast of the second line on the night of

June 5 he informed his commander, who put the Fifteenth Army on the alert. Nobody notified the Seventh Army in Normandy, and neither the overall German commander, Rundstedt, nor the commander of Army Group B, Rommel, put much store by the information, particularly since almost gale-force winds were churning the Channel. Rommel in any case was on his way back to Germany to visit his wife.

D-Day was 15 minutes old when the first Allied soldiers came to Normandy—pathfinders and special assault teams of three airborne divisions: the British SIXTH DIVISION and the American 82D and 101ST DIVISIONS. As men and women of the French Resistance moved to assigned tasks, the main bodies of the divisions followed, but thick clouds and heavy German antiaircraft fire interfered. The men came to earth badly scattered, particularly the Americans, some dropping as far as 35 miles from their objectives. Yet the dispersion when combined with the dropping of dummy parachutists, fused with firecrackers, far from the invasion site helped mislead German commanders. Most of them saw the airborne assault as nothing more than a raid or at most a diversionary attack.

As the airborne landings continued, Field Marshal von Rundstedt nevertheless decided that even if the assault was a diversionary attack, it had to be defeated. Around 4 A.M. he ordered two panzer divisions to prepare for counterattack, but when he reported what he had done to the high command in Germany, word came back to halt the divisions pending approval from Hitler. That would be a long time coming, for Hitler's staff was reluctant to disturb the Führer's sleep.

A little before 5 A.M. the chief of staff of the Seventh Army defending Normandy and Brittany reported to Rommel's headquarters that Allied ships were converging on the coast between the mouths of the Orne and Vire Rivers. In the absence of Rommel, his chief of staff, Lt. Gen. Hans SPEIDEL, ordered a panzer division to head for Caen to counterattack, but it was after daylight before the division could move, and Allied aircraft made a shambles of the attempt. The burden of defeating the invasion thus fell primarily on those German soldiers already in position in the fortifications of the ATLANTIC WALL or in close reserve in coastal villages and towns.

It was still dark when Allied tactical bombers began to range the entire northwestern coast of France; then at 5:50 A.M. a heavy Allied naval bombardment opened. At 6:30 A.M., H-hour for landings at Omaha and Utah Beaches, American troops began to touch down, many of them depressingly seasick from the pitching of the landing craft in the heavy surf. At Utah the 4th Infantry Division under the VII Corps had little difficulty getting ashore, for gently sloping sands there proved to be one of the weak points in the Atlantic Wall. In less than three hours the 4th Division was in full control of the landing sites and men were pushing over causeways toward higher ground where paratroopers and glider troops of the American airborne divisions awaited their arrival. Some 23,000 men came ashore during the day with remarkably light losses—210 dead and wounded.

Some 10 miles up the coast at Omaha the story was strikingly different. There steep bluffs more than 150 feet high added to the effectiveness of the fortifications, and a forest of antilanding obstacles denied the sloping beach to the troops. Manning the defenses was one of the best German divisions in Normandy, one that Allied intelligence had failed to detect until only a few days before the invasion. German artillery took the landing craft under heavy fire, and as those that survived lowered their ramps, machine gun fire poured in on the troops. Hundreds died, but somehow little knots of men made it across the exposed beach to temporary refuge behind a sea wall and a line of dunes.

Few of the amphibious tanks made it ashore to provide close-in fire support, but an intrepid few among those men bunched behind the precarious cover nevertheless began to work their way up the bluffs. Local German commanders reported to their superiors at various times during the day that the invasion at Omaha had failed, and offshore General Bradley followed the proceedings aboard his command ship, U.S.S. *Augusta,* with deep concern; but by noon small disorganized parties of men had climbed the bluffs to cut a highway that ran along them. By nightfall men of the 1st Infantry Division and an attached regiment of the 29th Infantry Division, both operating under the V Corps, held a precarious foothold nowhere more than a mile and a half deep, but they were ashore nevertheless. At a nearby promontory called POINTE DU HOE, two Ranger battalions had in the meantime scaled cliffs with rope ladders to take out big guns of a German coastal battery. At Omaha some 2,500 men fell, but 34,000 others made it ashore.

No such crisis arose up the coast to the east at British and Canadian beaches. There because of differing tidal conditions the Canadian 3d Division and the British 3d and 50th Divisions stormed ashore from half an hour to an hour later than the American troops. They benefited from additional naval bombardment that the delays made possible and from the absence of towering bluffs and a top-ranked German division as at Omaha. Before the day was out British and Canadian troops were several miles inland with contact established with the airborne division beyond the Orne River. In late afternoon, as the German panzer division that had been ordered to counterattack at last arrived, British warships took the panzers and panzer grenadiers under such a devastating fire that further German advance was impossible. In the day's assault the Canadians lost 1,074 men; the British, approximately 3,000.

It was 4 P.M. on D-Day before Hitler at last approved Rundstedt's employing two other divisions from the panzer reserve, which, in view of Allied aerial superiority, could move only after nightfall. Because Allied deception had been remarkably effective and because Hitler had been sleeping and then had vacillated, German power that could have spelled defeat for the invasion had been withheld. The rest of the armored reserve in France—five divisions—and the 19 divisions of the Fifteenth Army in the Pas de Calais stood impotently by.

The next day, after word reached Hitler that German troops had found copies of U.S. operational orders indicating that the landings in Normandy constituted the main invasion, he ordered the panzer reserve into action, but Allied intelligence was ready for just such an emergency. Through Ultra the Allied command learned of Hitler's order, and through a compromised German agent known as BRUTUS it sent word that the American corps orders were a plant. The main invasion, Brutus reported, was still to come in the Pas de Calais. Hitler retracted his order.

Allied armies were ashore in Normandy, but their hold was still tenuous. Forces in the two American beachheads had to link up and to establish contact with the American airborne divisions, and a gap still existed between the American beachheads and those of the British and Canadians. The beach at Omaha was a shambles, still raked by German shelling and small arms fire. Allied losses totaled something over 9,000 men, probably a third of them killed. Some 2,500 of the losses were in airborne troops, although there were grounds for encouragement in that some planners (and Air Marshal Tedder) had predicted losses among airborne troops of 80 percent, and actual losses were 15 percent.

Had Allied commanders known of the near-bankruptcy on the German side, they would have had more cause for encouragement. The Seventh Army had thrown into the battle every major unit that stood in the Cotentin, and committing units from Brittany and elsewhere would take time. Every movement was in any case subject to attack from Allied planes, and like Hitler himself, the commander of the Seventh Army was reluctant to commit himself completely lest the Allies stage a second landing, perhaps in Brittany. Meanwhile, Rundstedt, Rommel and Hitler—their eyes blurred by Allied deception—continued to believe that a bigger landing was still to come in the Pas de Calais. D-Day was a tremendous achievement for Allied arms and American, British and Canadian fighting men, but it also owed an immeasurable debt to Ultra and to the deception that Ultra made possible. **C.B.M.**

IOWA, U.S.S. U.S. battleship and class. They were of 45,000 tons standard displacement and had nine 16-inch guns. Six ships of this class were laid down *(Iowa,* NEW JERSEY, MISSOURI, *Wisconsin, Illinois* and *Kentucky);* only the first four were completed, going into commission in 1943–44. The last two were suspended before completion. These, the last American battleships built, were over 887 feet long and had 212,000 horsepower to give them a designed speed of over 32 knots. Their 16-inch guns were longer and slightly more powerful than those that armed the earlier NORTH CAROLINA and SOUTH DAKOTA classes. *Iowa,* the first of the class to commission (February 1943), carried President ROOSEVELT to the TEHERAN CONFERENCE and back. Thereafter she and her sisters went to the Pacific, where they joined the earlier fast battleships in screening the carrier task force during operations off the MARSHALLS, MARIANAS, Palaus, PHILIPPINES, IWO JIMA and OKINAWA. *Missouri,* because she bore the name of the home state of the new President Truman, was designated as the site of the signing of the documents that ended the Pacific war on September 3, 1945. All four ships are now in the Navy's Inactive Fleet, *Iowa* and *Wisconsin* at Philadelphia and *New Jersey* and *Missouri* at Bremerton, Wash.

IRAN. The entry of the Soviet Union into the war (June 22, 1941) and the consequent desire of Britain to send her munitions and other supplies gave Iran a position of strategic importance. The British and Soviet Governments therefore demanded that the Iranian Government expel German agents and other nationals. On Iran's refusal, British and Soviet forces entered the country (August 25, 1941). Within three days Iranian resistance, which was only mild, collapsed entirely. On September 16 the Shah abdicated in favor of his son, and the next day British and Soviet forces occupied Teheran. Only limited detachments were required to maintain the Allied occupation. On January 29, 1942, Britain and the USSR signed a treaty with Iran whereby Iran agreed to remain neutral and the Allies agreed to withdraw six months after the end of hostilities. The Persian Corridor became the principal route for Western supplies to Russia. *See also* ABADAN.

IRAQ. The Anglo-Iraqi treaty of 1930 gave Britain the right to maintain air bases—Basra and HABBANIYA—in Iraq and to have access to the necessary transit for men and supplies, but in March 1941 the pro-German RASHID ALI became Prime Minister and appealed to Germany for aid, which, fortunately for the Allies, was limited and late. On May 2 Rashid Ali's forces attacked the British at Habbaniya but were defeated. Rashid Ali retreated to Baghdad; British troops pursued the Iraqis, and on May 30 Rashid Ali fled to Iran. The pro-British Regent, who had been expelled, returned to power. On January 16, 1943, Iraq declared war on the three chief AXIS powers.

IRONBOTTOM SOUND. The waters between GUADALCANAL and Florida Islands in the SOLOMONS, given that name as a series of bitterly fought naval actions sent an increasing number of ships to its bottom.

IRONCLAD. Code name for British occupation of Diégo Suarez, MADAGASCAR, May 8, 1942.

IRON CROSS. Established as a Prussian order for bravery by King Frederick William III in 1813, the Iron Cross was awarded in eight classes in World War II. The decoration was a cross pattée in black iron with a silver edge. It had a swastika in the center and the date 1939 on the lower limb of the cross.

IRONSIDE, Sir William Edmund (1880–1959). Chief of the British Imperial General Staff, 1939–40. Despite a long and distinguished military career in the decades before World War II, General Ironside had never served in the War Office before he became CIGS. Overburdened by work and associated with Britain's poor military performance early in the war, Ironside proved unequal to the demands made upon his position—as did his successor as CIGS, Sir John DILL—and lost his command in 1940. He was promoted to field marshal.

IRRAWADDY RIVER. Along with its tributaries, the Irrawaddy River constituted the principal means of internal communication for BURMA, and thus was strategically important during the war. During March, April and early May 1942 the Irrawaddy valley was used as a main northward avenue of advance by two persistent divisions of the Japanese 15th Army, the 18th Division (against MANDALAY) and the 33d Division (against Yenangaung).

Two years later, as the tide began to turn against the

Japanese, the Irrawaddy, which had been an obstacle tc Allied withdrawal in 1942, was used as an Allied avenue of approach. During operations in October–December 1944 in northern Burma, the river was crossed by British forces at several locations near Bhamo as they advanced against elements of the Japanese 18th and 56th Divisions. Early in the British FOURTEENTH ARMY offensive of December 12, 1944, to May 3, 1945, which culminated in the reoccupation of Burma, the Irrawaddy was crossed at various points bordering central Burma. This was followed by an Allied advance down the valley to Prome, the town being entered concurrently with the recapture of RANGOON.

IRWIN, Noel Mackintosh Stuart (1892–1972). British Army officer who commanded a brigade in the BRITISH EXPEDITIONARY FORCE in 1939–40 and was the army commander of the abortive Anglo-French DAKAR expedition in September 1940. In 1942–43 Irwin, a lieutenant general, commanded the Eastern Army on the BURMA front until relieved temporarily by Sir George GIFFARD and ultimately by Sir William SLIM.

IRWIN, Stafford Leroy (1893–1955). "Red" Irwin was a U.S. Army officer given command of the 9th Division's artillery in 1942. In this capacity he led the artillery on a forced march from Oran to Tunisia in February 1943 to intervene decisively in the Battle of the KASSERINE PASS. He was promoted to major general in 1943 and named commander of the 5th Infantry Division, a post he held through the fighting in northern France, Belgium and Germany. In April 1945 Irwin received command of the XII Corps.

ISABELLA. Code name for proposed German operations to occupy the Atlantic coast of the Iberian Peninsula, 1941. The proposed operation was later called Ilona, but it was never mounted.

ISE. Class of two Japanese battleships, of 36,000 tons, with twelve 14-inch guns. As modernized before the war, *Ise* and her sister ship, HYUGA, had the characteristic Japanese battleship "pagoda" foremasts, a large single stack and six twin turrets. In reaction to heavy carrier losses at Midway and in the Solomons, both ships were refitted in 1943. The two after turrets were replaced by an aircraft deck covering a hangar for 22 dive-bombers. In action, planes were to be launched by two catapults. Antiaircraft guns were increased; in 1944 a battery of antiaircraft rocket launchers was installed in each ship. For lack of trained pilots, neither of these ships was ever used as a carrier. They took part in the battle for LEYTE GULF, without planes, as part of a decoy force. Late in July 1945 both were sunk in shallow water by carrier planes.

ISIGNY. Town at the base of the COTENTIN PENINSULA (France), taken by U.S. 29th Division on the night of June 8–9, 1944.

ISLEY FIELD. Name given to Aslito airfield, SAIPAN, by U.S. forces (it had previously been renamed Conroy Field, after Col. Gardiner J. Conroy, 165th Infantry, killed at MAKIN Atoll). The name honored Comdr. Robert H. Isely, a U.S. Navy flier lost over Saipan. The spelling "Isley" is one of those errors that, through the force of repetition, become immutable.

ISMAY, Sir Hastings Lionel (1887–1965). When war broke out in 1939, "Pug" Ismay had enjoyed a long and eminent career in the British Committee of Imperial Defence as assistant secretary (1925–30), deputy secretary (1936–38) and, finally, secretary in succession to the renowned Lord Hankey (1938–39). In 1939–40 he served the War Cabinet as deputy military secretary. Then when Winston CHURCHILL became Prime Minister, Ismay became chief of staff to the War Cabinet (1940–45). In this capacity he was outstandingly successful in establishing a close and effective working relationship between Churchill and the Chiefs of Staff, his tact and diplomacy being admired by all who came in contact with him. Throughout the war, all of Churchill's military correspondence passed through his hands, and it was perhaps he more than any other who ran the British war machine. Subsequently (1952–57) Ismay was the first Secretary General of NATO.

ISOLATIONISM. A vocal segment of American public and political opinion in the interwar era opposed involvement in international affairs. This attitude emerged from the disillusionment that followed the First World War and gained adherents as the threat of war reappeared in the 1930s. It has become identified with a number of U.S. Senators, including Henry Cabot Lodge, leader of the fight against participation in the League of Nations; William E. Borah, who opposed cooperation with an international court; and Gerald P. Nye, whose investigations into the armaments industry helped precipitate the NEUTRALITY ACTS of 1935–37. Other public figures, such as William Randolph Hearst and Charles A. LINDBERGH, helped make isolationism a political movement by 1940. In that year the AMERICA FIRST COMMITTEE, dedicated to keeping the United States out of the war, organized to rally public opinion.

IS-WAS. U.S. Navy slang term for the Torpedo Angle Solver, Mark 7, so called because it compares the past and present positions of a ship. This hand-held circular slide rule, similar in appearance and concept to hand-operated computers used by aviators for navigation, was used in submarines, destroyers and destroyer escorts to solve the torpedo fire-control problem. It did not replace the various electromechanical torpedo directors in use, but assisted a ship's conning officer in determining his firing approach and getting into proper position to use his torpedoes.

ITALIAN AIR FORCE (Regia Aeronautica). Considering that its foundations were laid by Giulio Douhet, MUSSOLINI's first Under Secretary for Air and the leading thinker between the wars in the field of the strategic use of air power, the Italian Air Force fell far short of what might have been expected. Before the war it was thought of as one of Europe's best. In 1920, 1921 and 1926 Italian planes won the Schneider trophy; in 1927–28 a Macchi seaplane powered by a Fiat engine set world speed records. At the opening of the war the Italians had about 2,500 planes in operating squadrons; however, only 11,000 more were produced during the war.

The Regia Aeronautica had its greatest period of development under Marshal Italo BALBO, who was succeeded by Gen. Giuseppe Valle, known as a brilliant technician, and later (1941) by Gen. Francesco Pricolo, the author of several books on tactics. After 1935, however, the Regia Aeronautica declined; despite the operations of a large research center, Guidonia, the development of planes failed to keep up with that in other countries. The reason lay in part with Italy's industrial and technical weakness.

The Italian planes were obsolescent at the outbreak of war. The standard fighter was the Fiat CR-42, a very maneuverable aircraft, having a top speed of 272 miles per hour as compared with 335 for the British Hurricane. The Savoia-Marchetti SM-79 bomber (*see* SM-79), veteran of the Spanish Civil War, was an efficient weight-carrying bomber but was soon outclassed. Italy's new planes were not a match for either their German or British counterparts, and the air force founded by Douhet was unprepared for strategic bombing.

The Italian failure to knock MALTA out of the war early in 1940–41 greatly increased the British ability to fight in NORTH AFRICA, where the Italian Air Force was soon dissipated. In Libya in December 1940 Italy had 140 bombers and 191 fighters when the RAF attacked the Italian airfields. Most of the planes were lost. Short on spares, fuel and service, the Italian air strength quickly declined. In EAST AFRICA also, most of the 325 aircraft with which the Italians opened the campaign were destroyed.

After the initial Cyrenaican campaign in North Africa, the Italian Air Force was no longer a serious threat to the Allies. German aircraft took over in the theater, and the Italians concentrated on reconnaissance and supply, as well as assisting in the bombing of Malta.

ITALIAN ARMY. The Italian Army, whose officers and men were bound by oath to the King, played almost no role in Benito MUSSOLINI's Fascist revolution. The militia (BLACK SHIRTS) was later created by Mussolini, and the members swore allegiance to him personally. Militia officers held rank equal in status to regular Army officers, even though Black Shirt divisions numbered only 8,000 men to a regular division's 13,000. Black Shirt divisions played important roles in Ethiopia and Spain in the 1930s.

The Army fought against the gradual erosion of its position, but in 1933 Mussolini permanently took over the War Ministry. Old regimental distinctions were abolished, the goose step and Fascist salute were introduced and joining the FASCIST PARTY became the surest means of advancement. Favoritism and corruption allowed the wrong kind of officer to reach the higher ranks, with resulting loss of morale and confidence for the entire service.

The lack of sound central direction soon became evident when Mussolini plunged Italy into war in 1940. The Army was unprepared. According to Count CIANO, the Foreign Minister, only 10 divisions were ready to fight in January 1940. Artillery was weak and mostly of 1918 vintage. The Army's early moves were poorly conceived and led to defeats from which it never recovered, in either strength or morale. Mussolini's plans for NORTH AFRICA were not militarily sound. When he decided to invade Greece, Mussolini halved the estimates of enemy strength given him by his intelligence and allowed his staffs only three weeks to get ready for the invasion. Military disaster soon followed.

After the Battle of BEDA FOMM (February 1941), the Italians had lost 130,000 men in North Africa; during the summer of 1941 they lost another 289,000 in EAST AFRICA. Six Italian divisions served with the German Gen. Erwin ROMMEL, and after ALAMEIN (November 1942) Rommel wrote that the defeats they suffered were not the fault of the Italian soldier, who was "willing, unselfish and a good comrade." Poor equipment contributed to the Italian soldier's lack of enthusiasm, which was seldom equated with lack of bravery but rather with the absence of military morale or a passionately held cause for which to fight.

Despite Italy's continuing defeats, Mussolini still wanted to play a big part in the war. In 1942 approximately 1.2 million Italian soldiers were on foreign soil. Hitler was at first reluctant to accept Italian help; later he begged for it. In Russia, the Italian Eighth Army of 217,000 men was the force the Russians broke through at STALINGRAD. As Italy's situation continued to worsen, some Army leaders wanted to oust Mussolini and bring an end to the war, but the primary impetus for Mussolini's dismissal came from civilian efforts.

By September 1943, with the Allied invasion of Italy threatening, only 12 divisions were available for Italy's defense. The Italian surrender negotiations were complex and painful. To a great degree the Italians had become dependent on German strength; now, wanting to get out, they were too weak and entangled to escape without German reprisal.

Marshal BADOGLIO's announcement of surrender on September 8, 1943, found the Army without instructions. When the Germans moved swiftly to seize Rome, the Italians fought briefly but soon ceased resistance. Many soldiers simply threw down their weapons and disappeared into the countryside, and the Germans soon effected Italian surrender throughout the rest of the country. Some Italian units joined the Germans to continue fighting; some were sent to Germany as workers; many simply went home. Allied efforts to encourage the Italians to fight the Germans were largely ineffective. Some units of the regular Army joined with the Allies, but the primary contribution of Italian combatants toward the liberation of Italy was partisan activity behind the lines in northern Italy.

ITALIAN NAVY. The Italian Navy went through World War II with some crippling disadvantages, yet more than any other branch of the service, it managed to maintain morale and cohesion. Since there was a minimum of FASCIST PARTY influence in the Navy, long-established traditions were not lost.

The Italian Navy knew of RADAR but had not developed it, nor did it have a naval air arm, for Benito MUSSOLINI had deemed Italy to be one big aircraft carrier and fleet air unnecessary. With the exception of a few antiquated reconnaissance planes, the Navy was dependent on the Air Force for reconnaissance or protection, and coordination was seldom as good as needed. Although Adm. Sir Andrew CUNNINGHAM, commander of the British Mediterranean fleet, considered Italian reconnaissance very good, the Italians blamed it for many of their failures. A third problem, and by far the greatest, was shortage of fuel oil. Partly for this reason, the Navy opposed plans for invading Greece, but Mussolini disregarded the advice.

As of June 10, 1940, the Italian Navy had 4 battleships in service and 4 others fitting out, 8 heavy cruisers, 14 light cruisers, 128 destroyer types and 115 submarines.

The fall of France (June 1940) gave the Italian Navy a fighting chance in the Mediterranean, but the November 1940 British attack on TARANTO (which Italians blamed on their poor reconnaissance and slowness to install nets) hurt them badly. Adm. Arturo RICCARDI became Chief of Staff in December 1940, and when the German AFRIKA KORPS went to NORTH AFRICA in the spring of 1941, he took charge of the Italian Navy's new responsibility to keep it supplied. The bulk of the Italian naval effort from that point on was devoted to convoying men and materials to Africa. Its success was directly proportional to conditions at MALTA, and in June 1941 a high of 125,076 tons of material was taken to Libya. But the shortage of fuel oil had begun to cripple the Italian effort. This, together with Mussolini's reluctance to use the fleet (he did not want to risk losing it), meant exercising a restraint that earned the Italians a wartime reputation, perhaps not deserved, of being reluctant to fight. By April 1942 the fuel reserve was depleted and operations were totally dependent on monthly deliveries from Germany. The situation continued, even after the loss of Libya and the start of the enormous commitment by the Germans in TUNISIA. For Tunisia also, the Italian Navy handled troop and supply movements, utilizing the 10 remaining operational destroyers for transporting troops across the "Death Route."

By the time of the invasion of SICILY (July 1943) the Italian fleet could only serve as a fleet in being, but its existence was still a threat to the Allies. Admiral Raffaele De Courten became Navy Minister in July 1943. He knew nothing of the Italian armistice agreements until they were a reality, but he took the lead in obeying the orders of his government to take the fleet to Malta. The Italian Navy did not look upon this as a surrender; morale and unity remained relatively high. Perhaps for that reason it was relatively easy for the Navy to cooperate with the Allies. The Navy's fine record of Mediterranean assistance after September 1943 (especially in the use of their naval yards, well stocked before the war) contributed significantly to enabling Italy to emerge from the war relatively intact.

During the war the Italian Navy also operated submarines in the Atlantic to a limited extent, the main point of interest being frequent undersea crossing of the Straits of Gibraltar without loss. The Navy had also conducted experiments with midget submarines, explosive motorboats and guided two-man torpedoes, and with such unorthodox craft had disabled the British battleships VALIANT and QUEEN ELIZABETH in Alexandria harbor. Admiral Cunningham paid tribute to their "cold-blooded bravery and enterprise." The expertise of this special section, the 10th MAS Flotilla, was made available to the Allies after September 1943 and subsequently used against Germany.

The historical office of the Italian Navy records 339 ships of all types (excluding merchant marine) lost between June 10, 1940, and September 7, 1943 (314,298 total tons), plus 565 ships of the merchant marine (2,018,616 gross tons). Navy men lost numbered 24,660 before the armistice; 4,177 afterward.

ITALY—OPERATIONS 1943–45. The series of battles on the mainland of Italy started on September 3, 1943, with the Anglo-American invasion and ended on May 2, 1945, with the German surrender. The impetus for the British and Americans to commit their forces in Italy developed chiefly out of circumstances. The conquest of SICILY in August 1943 placed Allied troops a scant two miles across the Straits of Messina from the toe of Italy. The ousting of Benito MUSSOLINI from power the month before, his replacement by Marshal Pietro BADOGLIO and the secret attempts of that new government to come to terms with the Allies indicated a distinct possibility of eliminating Italy from the war. Suspicious that Italy might terminate the alliance with Germany and make peace with the Allies, Adolf HITLER had virtually occupied the mainland with troops ostensibly sent to help the Italians repel an Allied invasion. To enable the Italians to capitulate, the Allies were thus required to engage the Germans on the Italian homeland.

This resolved an impasse in Anglo-American strategic planning over the issue of whether to continue major offensive operations in the Mediterranean, as the British wished, or to shift resources from North Africa to the United Kingdom, as the Americans desired, in order to make possible an earlier cross-Channel attack. At the CASABLANCA CONFERENCE in January 1943 the Allies, unable to agree on the fundamental strategic question, had decided merely to go from North Africa to seize Sicily. In May at the Washington Conference (*see* TRIDENT), while they agreed definitely to launch a cross-Channel invasion in the future as the main endeavor of the war, they confirmed their decision for Sicily. Whether they would continue the offensive momentum in the Mediterranean beyond Sicily would depend on how the situation developed.

To prepare for the contingency of maintaining the offensive in the Mediterranean area, Gen. Mark W. CLARK'S U.S. FIFTH ARMY, located in French Morocco and Algeria, began in June to draw plans for a variety of operations. There were two major targets: (1) Sardinia and Corsica, and (2) the mainland of southern Italy—the shinbone, the toe, the instep and the heel. Toward the end of August, when Badoglio was ready to surrender and Allied intelligence information indicated that Hitler would withdraw his troops to strong defensive positions in the Apennines of northern Italy in the event of Allied landings, the COMBINED CHIEFS OF STAFF, with the approval of President Franklin D. ROOSEVELT and Prime Minister Winston S. CHURCHILL, instructed Gen. Dwight D. EISENHOWER, the theater commander, to invade southern Italy for the following purposes: to capture the port of Naples and the important airfield complex around Foggia, which would make further operations possible; and to bring to battle and tie down as many German forces as possible in order to draw German troops from other areas, mainly the Eastern Front.

Thus, after several weeks of heavy bombardment on the Italian mainland, with Gen. Sir Harold ALEXANDER'S 15th Army Group in command of the Allied ground forces, Gen. Sir Bernard MONTGOMERY'S British

EIGHTH ARMY crossed the Straits of Messina on September 3, landing against slight opposition, on the toe near Reggio. Two German divisions began to withdraw slowly, leaving obstructions in their wake. On the same day, against no resistance, warships put a British division ashore at Taranto in the heel. Six days later, on September 9, following the announcement of the Italian capitulation, a British and an American corps of Clark's Fifth Army landed on the beaches of SALERNO. The Salerno invaders met immediate resistance, for the Germans fought to keep open the routes of escape for those troops retiring from the toe. The battle was fierce. Salerno was at the maximum range of Allied planes supporting the invasion forces. Shortages in shipping prevented rapid reinforcement of the Allied beachhead. The critical day was September 13, when a German attack came close to reaching the shoreline and destroying the Allied forces. Stubborn ground defense, the drop of an American parachute regiment into the beachhead, the diversion of strategic bombers to furnish close support at the battlefield and the rushing of warships to increase naval bombardment of German shore positions were the principal factors that won the engagement for the Allies. On September 20, with all the German forces in the toe having extricated themselves, the Germans at Salerno began to give way and move to the north. Eleven days later, on October 1, the U.S. Fifth Army entered into the destroyed port of Naples, and the British Eighth Army, having crossed the peninsula to the east coast, took the Foggia airfields.

With the first objectives in hand, Eisenhower directed Alexander to fulfill the second: tie down the Germans. Thus the two field armies, separated by the Apennines, started to advance slowly to the north against Gen. Heinrich von VIETINGHOFF's Tenth Army, which, in accordance with Hitler's policy, gave way grudgingly. While a huge force of naval experts and Army engineers worked to rehabilitate Naples, the Fifth Army reached and, after a heavy attack, crossed the Volturno River in mid-October. A vast fleet of strategic bombers flew into Foggia to establish an important base for air operations, and the Eighth Army, after fierce fighting, reduced Ortona and Orsogna.

By this time Rome had emerged as the only immediate Allied objective of meaning. Rome was a major psychological symbol. Its capture would mark the falling of the first Axis capital, while, conversely, its retention by the Germans would signal success in maintaining a German presence in Italy. By seizing Rome the Allies could reinstall King VICTOR EMMANUEL and the Badoglio government, located temporarily in Bari, in their national capital. Furthermore, by taking Rome the Allies would come into possession of airfields closer to Germany. And the Germans would be compelled to pull back 100 miles to defensive positions in the northern Apennines.

Hitler had come to recognize this also. Gen. Albert KESSELRING, his commander in chief in Italy, had pointed out the advantages of denying Rome to the Allies. Furthermore, he persuaded the Führer that he could stop the Allied northward march below Rome because the mountainous terrain offered decisive advantages to troops fighting a defensive campaign. Hitler consequently changed his mind about giving up southern Italy. He instructed Kesselring to hold fast, dispatched Gen. Erwin ROMMEL (to whom he had thought of giving command in Italy) to France to prepare the coastal defenses against an expected cross-Channel invasion and ordered the movement of reinforcements from northern Italy to bolster Kesselring's troops.

Apprised by intelligence of Hitler's intention to fight it out below Rome, Eisenhower on November 8 ordered Alexander to open the battle for Rome. On the same day Alexander issued his instructions for the capture of Rome. He wished the Eighth Army to take Pescara, then swing westward to threaten the capital. The Fifth Army was to drive to the entrance of the Liri valley, make an amphibious end run to outflank the German defenses, then drive to the city.

But Kesselring had constructed a massive defensive

U.S. infantrymen eat their 1943 Christmas dinner on a haystack in Italy

British soldiers search a house in an Italian mountain village

system across the Italian peninsula that the Allies called the Winter Line. In reality it consisted of three major obstacles. A heavy outpost named the Barbara Line barred the approaches to two strongly fortified main lines of defense, the BERNHARD LINE and the even more formidable positions called the GUSTAV LINE. In a winter of unusual severity, the troops fighting from these prepared defenses blocked the Allied advance toward Rome. The Battle of San Pietro symbolized the difficulties of this part of the campaign.

Because of the weather and the exhaustion of his men, Clark brought his offensive to a halt far short of the Liri valley entrance. He had been unable to mount an amphibious venture to outflank the German defenses because of a shortage of shipping and troops. Nor had Montgomery been able to do more than get his effort toward Rome started. He reached and secured the Sangro River, and there he ceased major operations. At the end of 1943 the two Allied armies rested, sought to keep warm and awaited developments. They soon arrived in the form of decisions concerning the Allied prosecution of the war in Europe. Returning from conferences with CHIANG KAI-SHEK in Cairo and with STALIN in TEHERAN, Roosevelt and Churchill were pledged to execute the cross-Channel attack in the spring of 1944. Eisenhower was appointed the Supreme Allied Commander of the effort, and Montgomery was designated as the commander of the British ground forces. Replacing Eisenhower, Gen. Henry Maitland WILSON became Supreme Commander in the Mediterranean, and Gen. Oliver LEESE succeeded Montgomery.

Even more significant for the course of the Italian campaign was the illness of Churchill and his subsequent convalescence in Morocco. Passionately desiring Rome, Churchill, through personal communication with Roosevelt during the early days of January 1944, succeeded in assembling sufficient landing ships and craft to make an amphibious operation possible. In order to guarantee a sufficiency of resources, Leese's army would remain quiet while Clark's army made the push against Rome. But first Clark would have to batter through the Bernhard Line, reach the line of the Garigliano and RAPIDO Rivers, cross this water and enter into the Liri valley. Paradoxically, he had to attract additional German defenders to the Gustav Line in order to ensure success in the amphibious landings, while at the same time he had to crack the already difficult defenses in order to rush up the Liri valley and make contact with the beachhead.

Consequently, in preliminary operations that merged imperceptibly into the opening of the battle for Rome, the Fifth Army fought hard through early January. Managing to reach the Garigliano and Rapido Rivers, the army was now in direct contact with the Gustav Line. The Rome operation could be said to have started with the crossing of the lower Garigliano near the coast by Gen. Richard MCCREERY's British 10th Corps on January 17. As Gen. Alphonse Juin's French Expeditionary Corps jockeyed in difficult mountains to threaten Cassino, Maj. Gen. Geoffrey Keyes's U.S. II Corps attacked across the Rapido on January 20. The U.S. 36th Division took heavy casualties and failed to cross the river that day or the next. Later the operation would become highly controversial, the division commander charging Clark with recklessness and bad judgment, Clark defending his order on the ground of necessity. The truth probably lay in between, with both at fault.

Yet the pressure on the Gustav Line, particularly the breach made by the British near the coast, prompted Kesselring to send his reserves from the Rome area to bolster the defenses. As a consequence, on January 22, Gen. John LUCAS's U.S. VI Corps, with British and American units, came ashore against virtually no opposition at ANZIO and Nettuno, 20 miles below Rome, and thereby threatened the rear of the Gustav Line, 75 miles to the south. In order to make good the threat, Lucas had to strike inland about 15 miles and seize the Alban Hills, high ground that constituted the last barrier before Rome and controlled the two main highways into the city, Routes 6 and 7. But Hitler's reaction to the Anzio landings was instantaneous. He immediately ordered units from France, Germany, northern Italy and Yugoslavia to converge on Anzio and remove at once what he termed an "abscess" on the German positions. Learning through the ULTRA intelligence reports of Hitler's intention, Clark advised Lucas not to head for the Alban Hills but to dig in and prepare to meet the inevitable German counterattack. Massed German forces of Col. Gen. Eberhard von MACKENSEN's Fourteenth Army sought to eradicate the beachhead early in February, but the Allied troops took the attacks without breaking and maintained a precarious hold over their territory, even though they were under constant fire by the Germans on the Alban Hills. Continual reinforcements of combat troops, a shuttle service of landing ships from Naples bringing ammunition and other supplies, naval shelling, air bombardment and heroic steadfastness on the ground enabled the beachhead to resist being engulfed.

Now there were two fronts in Italy, the main front at

the Gustav Line and the subsidiary front at the beleaguered beachhead. In order to compensate Clark for the reinforcements he was sending to Anzio and also to provide him increased strength to break the Gustav Line, Alexander moved a British and a New Zealand division across the Apennines from the Eighth Army to the Fifth Army zone and formed them into a provisional corps under Gen. Bernard FREYBERG. Clark then scheduled an attack against Monte CASSINO, the dominating hill overlooking not only the Garigliano-Rapido but also the Liri. If Freyberg could take that high ground, he would break the Gustav Line and permit the entrance of troops into the Liri valley for a plunge to Anzio.

The more Freyberg studied his problem, the more he became convinced that the Benedictine abbey on top of Monte Cassino, theretofore untouched by Allied artillery and bombers, was the key to the German defense. Believing that German troops occupied the monastery and therefore had unexcelled observation over the Allied positions, he asked Clark for a bombardment of the structure. Clark refused. He was virtually certain that the building housed no Germans. He was also conscious of Allied policy that proscribed destruction of religious and historical monuments. Freyberg insisted, and finally Clark passed the request to his superior, Alexander, who approved the bombing. Meanwhile, Freyberg's modest request of 36 bombers had swollen into an enormous effort. The air forces had decided that Monte Cassino would provide a perfect example of the effectiveness of air power. As a result, a thousand planes bombed the abbey on February 15 and obliterated it. Yet the removal of this structure had no effect on Freyberg's subsequent attack. The Allies were able to gain neither the heights of Monte Cassino nor entrance into the Liri valley. Now that the Allies had destroyed the sanctity of the abbey, the Germans moved into the ruins and erected strong defensive positions.

Another Allied effort had similar results in March. On the 15th, bombers devastated the town of Cassino. Yet the ground attack of Freyberg's corps failed to permit the entrance of Allied forces into the Liri valley for an advance to the Anzio beachhead. At that point the Italian campaign fell quiet. Both sides rested, built up their strengths and awaited the arrival of spring for the inevitable resumption of major operations.

Still obsessed by the necessity to get into the Liri valley and to link up with the Anzio beachhead, Alexander brought most of the Eighth Army across the Apennines. In his Operation DIADEM, launched on May 11,

Italian partisan runs for cover as his comrades watch for a German sniper

Alexander threw an immense amount of resources against the Germans. What broke the Gustav Line was the extraordinary advance of Juin's French Corps across mountains deemed altogether impassable. Forging ahead, the French troops loosened up the defenses. A few days later, by virtue of the French advance, General ANDERS's Polish Corps stormed across Monte Cassino and captured the monastery, thereby opening up the Liri valley. Americans in the coastal zone sped forward and on May 24 made contact with the Anzio beachhead forces.

Now, with the German forces disintegrating, two courses of action were possible for the Allies. They could drive into Rome, or they could try to trap and

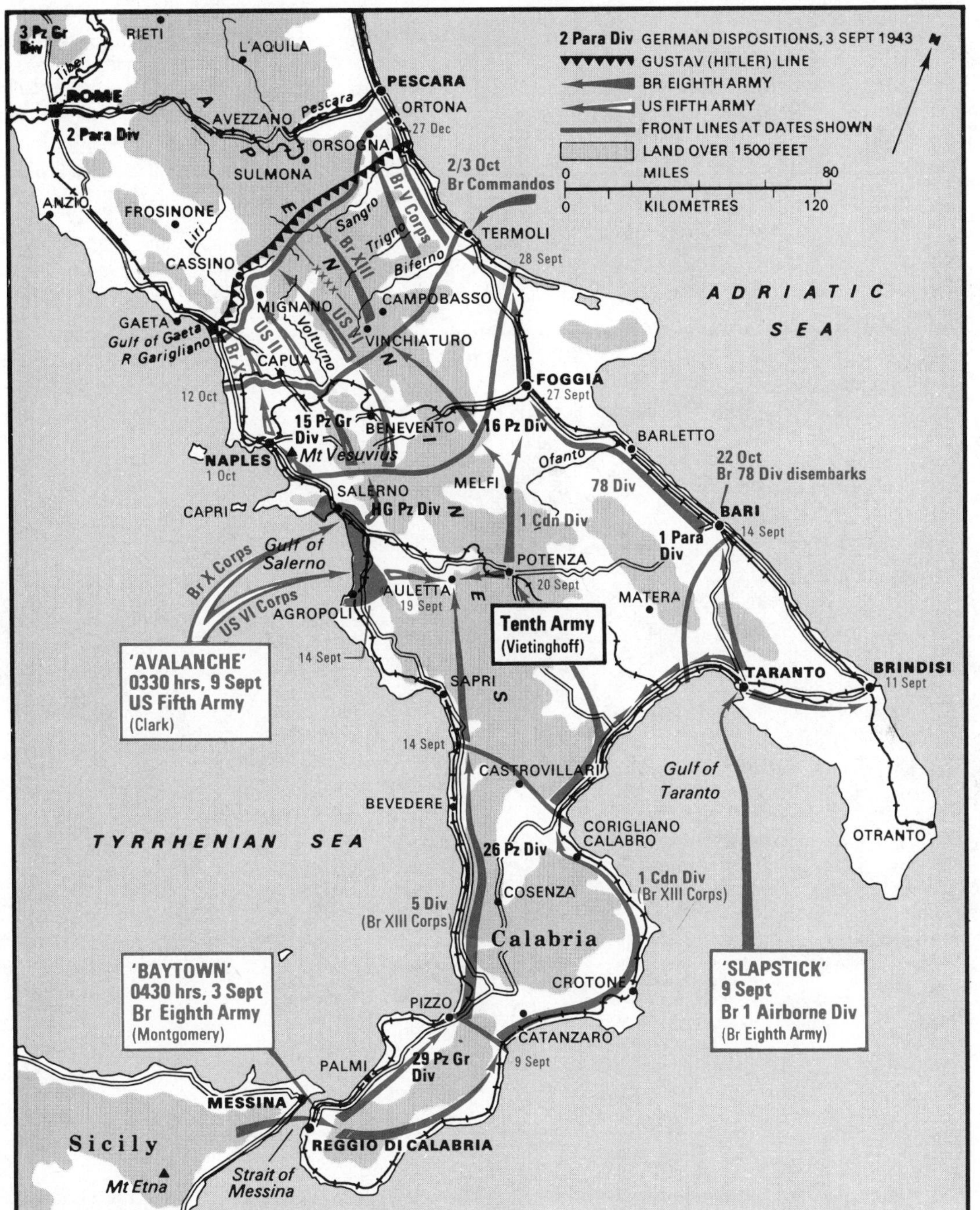

ITALY: The end of 1943 saw the Allies at the Gustav Line

destroy the Tenth Army withdrawing up the Liri valley from Cassino. To Alexander, the latter seemed more beneficial, and he therefore ordered Clark to drive eastward from Anzio to Valmontone to cut the two main highways leading to Rome and block the German retreat. But Clark doubted that he could reach Valmontone in time to block the German escape, for he estimated there were enough secondary roads through the mountains to guarantee the German movements. And he was enticed by the prize of entering Rome, an objective that Roosevelt and U.S. Army Chief of Staff George C. MARSHALL had urged upon him in December. He therefore tried to fulfill both missions. He sent a reduced force eastward toward Valmontone while directing the bulk of his units north toward Rome.

Fighting desperately and skillfully, the Germans

managed to evade entrapment while denying the Allies entrance into Rome. At last, having extricated their troops from the Liri valley and having lost Monte Artemisio, the key to Rome, they left the city to the Allies, who entered it on June 5 and captured the newspaper headlines of the world. The fame and the glory were brief, for the invasion of Normandy took place on the following day, totally eclipsing interest in the Italian campaign, which became a subsidiary front in the European war. The Allies pursued the Germans north of Rome, taking Leghorn, Pisa and Venice in the process. Even Bologna seemed within reach, but the arrival of winter weather and the shelter of the GOTHIC LINE defenses in the northern Apennines brought Allied offensive operations to a temporary halt.

By now, although Clark had had to make available an American corps and a substantial number of French units for the invasion of Southern France in August, his Fifth Army was composed of more national troop contingents than any other field army. In addition to American and British units, he commanded a BRAZILIAN EXPEDITIONARY FORCE, Italian units (which were granted the status of cobelligerents), French, New Zealanders and Indians. In November, when Wilson went to Washington to replace the deceased Sir John DILL as British representative to the Combined Chiefs of Staff

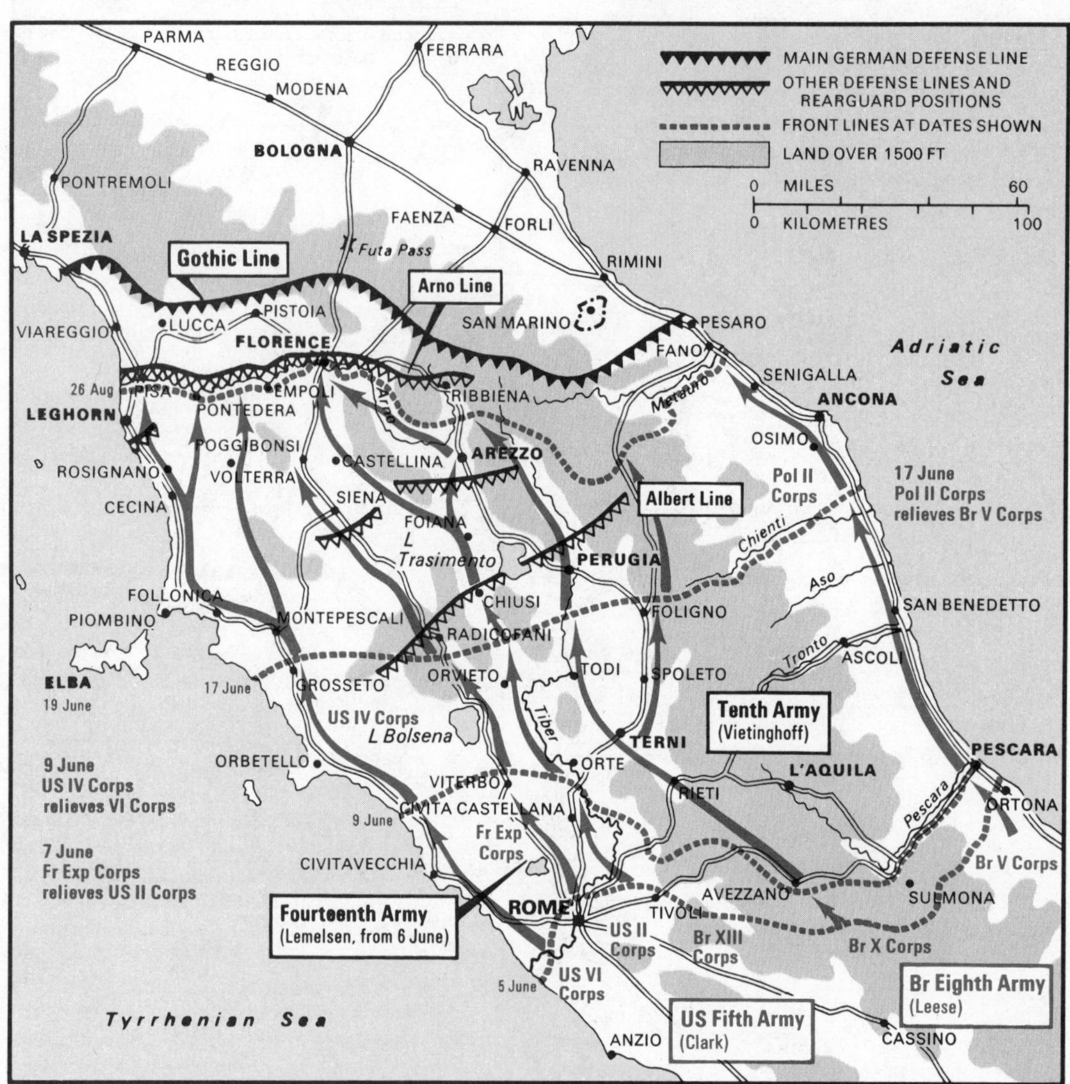

ITALY: the Allied push to the Germans' Gothic Line in the north

and Alexander replaced him in command of the theater, Clark moved up to head the 15th Army Group, which controlled the Fifth and Eighth Armies. At that point Clark additionally had under him Poles, South Africans, Canadians, even a Jewish Brigade from Palestine. No field force in World War II was more an international mixture.

Fighting in northern Italy during the winter of 1944–45 was impossible. But in the spring of 1945 Clark opened an offensive. The Fifth Army, now under Gen. Lucian TRUSCOTT, and the Eighth Army, now under McCreery, surged forward, broke the Gothic Line, took Bologna and moved toward Aosta, the Brenner Pass and Trieste. With the Allied armies moving wherever they wished, with Italian partisans ever more active and with German forces in a state of utter disintegration and rout, Vietinghoff, who had succeeded Kesselring as theater commander, and Karl WOLFF, representing the SS forces, jointly surrendered their troops to Clark on May 2, several days before the total capitulation of Germany at Reims and Berlin.

The Italian campaign featured bitter mountain warfare devoid of the reckless, slashing movements seen in France and Germany. The shortness of the front, restricted to the width of the peninsula, and the limited avenues of advance, dictated by the terrain, made the Italian fighting a campaign of painful progress. The Allies, using the bulk of their resources in western Europe and drawing upon their slender resources in Italy for the invasion of southern France, never had enough troop units to establish a clear-cut superiority over the Germans. At the same time, the Germans demonstrated an unexcelled skill in waging defensive warfare by imaginatively utilizing ground exceptionally suited for delay and obstruction.

The question has often been raised whether the Italian campaign, forced pretty much by the British, was necessary for the Allied victory. Without Allied presence in Italy, the bombardment of Germany and of southeastern Europe would have been less effective; the support of Tito's forces in Yugoslavia would have been less efficient; and the German strength on the Western and Eastern Fronts would have been far more formidable. The Allied Italian campaign was a necessary component of the giant ring that squeezed the life out of the Nazi state. **M.B.**

I (Infantry) TANK. British category of TANKS designed for cooperation with infantry. I-tanks included the Matilda I and II and the Valentine, the latter being produced in very large numbers.

ITO, Seiichi (1890–1945). A career Japanese naval officer who served in important staff positions both before and during the war. As Vice-Chief of the Naval General Staff in late 1941, Ito strongly urged that Japan delay sending its final note to the United States until just before the PEARL HARBOR attack. Late in the war he favored the use of KAMIKAZE attacks on American naval vessels. A vice-admiral, Ito led Japan's final naval sortie against the Allies as fleet commander in April 1945. He stayed aboard the sinking YAMATO during this attack, perishing with his fleet.

IVANOV. A code name used by Joseph STALIN in Soviet military transmissions.

IWABUCHI, Sanji (1893–1945). A Japanese naval officer, a graduate of the Naval Academy in 1915. Iwabuchi was made commanding officer of the battleship KIRISHIMA in April 1942; he commanded her in the Battle of MIDWAY and a number of engagements off GUADALCANAL until she was sunk off SAVO ISLAND in November 1942. In May 1943 he was promoted to rear admiral. He was named commander of the 31st Naval Base Force in MANILA in November 1944. In this capacity he made a determined defense of the city, which turned it into rubble. Iwabuchi himself was killed in the battle in February 1945. He was posthumously promoted to vice-admiral.

IWO JIMA. The U.S. assault on Iwo Jima, in the Bonin Islands, took place on February 19, 1945, when Maj. Gen. Harry SCHMIDT's V Amphibious Corps (4th and 5th Marine Divisions, with the 3d Marine Division in reserve) began landing at two minutes after the scheduled H-hour of 0900. The Americans wanted Iwo Jima as a base for fighter planes that would escort B-29s attacking Japan from fields on TINIAN and as a haven for bombers in trouble on the 2,800-mile round trip. Beginning in December, the island was subjected to the most intensive preparation given to any target in the Pacific war up to that time. Although the Marines asked the Navy for a 10-day preinvasion bombardment, the Navy supplied only three days' worth, setting off a debate that has gone on ever since.

The landings met with little initial opposition; it appeared that the preinvasion air and naval gunfire had been effective and that the two divisions would be able to gain their respective objectives—the 5th Division driving across the lower part of the pork-chop-shaped island and taking the 550-foot landmark Mount Suribachi, an extinct volcano; and the 4th capturing one of the two airstrips, Motoyama No. 1. But neither objective was gained, for as soon as the gunfire lifted from the beaches and the air support moved inland and the marines began to advance, the defenders brought all of their firepower to bear on the beachhead—mortars, artillery, machine guns and other automatic weapons. From late morning until early afternoon, few landing craft could make the beach, and not until late afternoon were the reserves able to come ashore. When the advance was halted for the night, Marine lines stretched across the base of Suribachi, moved northeast along the coast, swerved around the edge of Motoyama No. 1 and ended near the East Boat Basin, far short of the day's objectives.

The first night ashore was marked by small enemy probes into the line and attempts at infiltration with minor attacks, but no massive counterattack as was expected. The American attack resumed the next day with the 5th Division heading in two directions, the right flank toward the north while the 28th Marines on the left began the assault of Mount Suribachi. It took three days for the height to be captured. On the 23d,

Japanese emerge from their hiding place to surrender

when the crest was taken, there were two flag-raisings. In the first, an American flag carried to the top by one of the combat platoons was raised, but it was too small to be seen from the beaches; a second, larger flag was obtained from an LST and fastened to a long pole, which was erected by five marines and a Navy hospital corpsman. It was this flag-raising that was immortalized in the photograph taken by Associated Press photographer Joe ROSENTHAL. While the 28th Marines had been taking Mount Suribachi, the drive to the north had begun on the 20th by the two divisions, but it ended almost as soon as it had begun, in the face of determined Japanese resistance.

An all-out attack was mounted on the 24th behind a tremendous naval gunfire, artillery (most Marine artillery had been landed early and set in place behind the beachhead), carrier air and tank artillery preparation. Fifteen Marine tanks were able to negotiate to and across a second airstrip, Motoyama No. 2. Aiding in this attack was the 3d Division, now ashore (less its 3d Marines, which was still on shipboard as corps reserve) and in the middle of the line. By February 28 the second airfield had been taken and attacks directed on the fortified hills beyond it. The 5th Division was balked in its progress by enemy positions on Hill 362A—one of three key terrain features in the Hill 362 complex—while on the right the 4th Division was being held up by strongly defended positions on and around Hill 382. These points were the strongest links in Gen. Tadamichi KURIBAYASHI's defensive chain across the island. By March 1 both had been taken, but ahead lay 362B and C. The first was taken after a period of fierce fighting on the 3d, and the second after a predawn surprise attack mounted without benefit of artillery by the 3d Division; it was in American hands by midafternoon. Bypassed, however, were two strongly contested positions, the Amphitheater and Turkey Knob. The former was a natural bowl, the second a massive rock formation. During the bloody fighting, ending March 10, to take these two positions in the main Japanese defense line, the entire region was dubbed the Meat Grinder. Prior to this date, on the evening of March 8, the Japanese had mounted an unsuccessful counterattack, which was finally put down by noon of the following day, at which time it became possible for Marine patrols to proceed all the way to the coast.

This marked the final phase of the battle for Iwo Jima. The remainder of the fighting consisted of mopping up bypassed pockets, including a remnant under General Kuribayashi's personal command at Kitano Point at the extreme north of the island. With the assistance of the 3d Division, this point was taken on March 25 and the island declared secure. The fighting was not over, however, for in the early morning of the 26th a last-ditch BANZAI attack was launched against the bivouac area of support troops near Airfield No. 2.

The conquest of Iwo Jima was costly—5,931 marines killed, 17,372 wounded. Their sacrifice made possible a safe haven for 2,251 heavy bombers carrying 24,761 Americans in the course of raids over Japan. The Japanese troops on Iwo Jima, nearly 23,000, were annihilated almost to the last man. As Admiral NIMITZ put it, "On Iwo Jima, uncommon valor was a common virtue."

B.M.F.

J

J1N1. The Naka *Gekko* (Moonlight) (Allied code name, Irving), a two-engine land-based reconnaissance plane and night fighter. Developed by Japan as a long-range fighter, it was originally used as a reconnaissance plane owing to problems in producing the rather complicated remote-controlled rearward-firing armament installation designed for it. In 1943 an adaptation of the SCHRÄGE MUSIK installation was fitted and tested against night bombers over RABAUL. It proved successful, and *Gekkos* were thus adopted as night fighters. Some carried RADAR; others had a 20-mm. gun in a dorsal turret. They were used against B-29s over Japan, and also for suicide attacks.

J2F. The Grumman Duck, a U.S. Navy amphibian utility biplane. Evolved from the Grumman JF series, the first J2F flew in 1935. Various versions were built for the Navy and Marines under the designations J2F-1 through -5. In 1942 production was transferred to the Columbia Aircraft Corp. to enable Grumman to focus on the new F6F fighter (*see* F6F). Columbia manufactured Ducks under the designation J2F-6 (an exception to the Navy rule that aircraft designed by one manufacturer but produced by another would bear a separate designation) into 1945. The J2F proved rugged and dependable in service, and was used for antisubmarine patrol and aerial photography as well as for target towing. Like the earlier JF, the J2F had its single main float faired into the fuselage (rather than suspended by struts), as had been done with the series of Loening Army and Navy floatplanes of the 1920s and 1930s.

J2M. The Mitsubishi J2M Thunderbolt, code-named Jack by Allied airmen, was designed as a land-based fighter for the Japanese Navy. It was heavy by Japanese standards, weighing more than three tons, and the production model mounted four cannon. Jack also had a supercharger which enabled it to climb high enough to challenge American B-29s. Although a prototype flew in March 1942, two years passed before the plane was being manufactured in appreciable numbers. The delay resulted from difficulties in perfecting an adequate engine. The Kasei 13, with a complicated and balky propeller extension shaft, was replaced by the more powerful Kasei 23. The new power plant gave the J2M a top speed of about 370 miles per hour at 19,000 feet, but engine failure continued to plague the aircraft. Because of its speed and climbing ability, the Jack—with two 20-mm. cannon and two 7.1-mm. machine guns—was an excellent interceptor, and some 500 served in the defense of the home islands.

J8M1. The Mitsubishi *Shusui* (Rigorous Sword) (no Allied code name), a Japanese rocket-powered adaptation of the design of the German MESSERSCHMITT ME 163 interceptor. Developed in 1944–45, it flew only once—and that unsuccessfully—before V-J Day.

JABO. German abbreviation, also used as a slang term, for Jagdbomber (fighter-bomber).

JACK, U.S.S. American FLEET-TYPE submarine, commissioned in 1943; she made nine Pacific war patrols. *Jack* was credited with sinking 16 Japanese ships of various sizes. During her last patrols, in 1945, she performed offshore "lifeguard" duty as carrier planes and land-based bombers struck the Japanese home islands.

JACKSON, Robert Houghwout (1892–1954). A native of Pennsylvania and a lawyer in New York State, Jackson went to Washington in 1934 as general counsel to the Bureau of Internal Revenue. His most impressive case was that against Andrew Mellon, former Secretary of the Treasury, for income tax evasion. In 1936 he went to the Department of Justice and in 1940 he became Attorney General of the United States.

A great deal of Jackson's work as Attorney General dealt with questions related to the war. He was responsible for building the legal basis for the exchange with Britain in 1940 of 50 destroyers for naval and air bases in British possessions (the DESTROYERS–BASES DEAL).

In June 1941 he was appointed an associate justice of the Supreme Court. In May 1945 President TRUMAN chose him as chief counsel for the United States in preparing the prosecution's charges in the war crimes trials against Axis leaders. In this capacity he helped to organize the INTERNATIONAL MILITARY TRIBUNAL. His work was aimed at establishing the principle that starting a war of aggression is a crime against mankind and one for which the perpetrators must be apprehended and punished. Jackson played a leading role in drawing up the indictments against 24 German war criminals and six Nazi organizations, charging them with complicity in the conspiracy to wage an aggressive war and perpetrating crimes against mankind. Later Jackson was asked to give the opening statement for the prosecution when the trials got under way in NUREMBERG on November 20, 1945. He was active throughout the trials and developed a reputation for clear and thoughtful statement of the difficult legal issues involved in the prosecution. He also at times became quite emotionally involved in the proceedings.

JACOB, Sir Edward Ian Claud (1899–). British Army officer (lieutenant general) who was junior military assistant secretary to the WAR CABINET in 1939–46. Winston CHURCHILL remarked that the debt to Jacob, HOLLIS and ISMAY for their wartime service was immeasurable *(Their Finest Hour)*; all his military correspondence was handled by this team.

JACOB JONES, U.S.S. Destroyer of the WICKES class, first commissioned in 1919. After prewar NEUTRALITY PATROL service, *Jacob Jones* spent the period from December 1941 through February 1942 on Atlantic convoy duty. On the morning of February 28, 1942, she was torpedoed by *U-578* and went down. Only 12 survivors were rescued from the icy waters. An older destroyer of the same name had been torpedoed and sunk by a U-boat during World War I. A new *Jacob Jones*, an Edsall-class destroyer escort, was commissioned in 1943 and saw escort and antisubmarine patrol duty in the Atlantic and Mediterranean.

JAEL. Code name for a worldwide deception plan to mislead the Germans about Allied tactics and strategy, with particular attention to the INVASION of Normandy. Devised primarily by the British but with American participation, it was named for the Biblical prophetess in the Book of Judges who did away with an enemy of the Canaanites by driving a tent peg into his temple while he slept as a guest in her tent. The code name was later changed to BODYGUARD.

JAGUAR. Code name for British air reinforcements to MALTA, 1941.

JAMES, Clifton (1897–). British actor who was the central figure in one of the Allied deception plans prior to the INVASION of France in June 1944. He bore a considerable resemblance to Gen. Sir B. L. MONTGOMERY, commander of the assaulting Allied ground forces, and posed as the general in Gibraltar just before the launching of the invasion. The Germans were supposed to conclude that if the enemy general was in Gibraltar he could not be leading an assault on the coast of Normandy.

JAPANESE AIRCRAFT—ALLIED CODE NAMES. Identification of Japanese aircraft by the Allies during the early months of the Pacific war was characterized by confusion and error. Little was known about operational Japanese planes, and the systems of nomenclature used by the Japanese Army and Navy were themselves complex. To provide a tool for use in the field, work was begun during the middle of 1942 by the Air Technical Intelligence Unit of the Allied Air Forces, Southwest Pacific Area. Code names were assigned to identified types of Japanese planes; their use spread, and within a few months these names had been standardized for Anglo-American use. With a few exceptions, fighters and floatplanes were given male first names (Zeke, Tony); bombers and flying boats received female names (Mavis, Val); transports also got women's names, but beginning with the letter T (Thora); trainers were named for trees (Cypress); and gliders received the names of birds (Buzzard). This system generally worked well, although, as noted under some individual code names, the inevitable errors cropped up. Code names were given to some nonexistent types, as well as to a few old planes thought to be still in use. The object of this arrangement, however, was not to provide a precise cataloging scheme for researchers but to give the people who needed it a reasonably reliable method of identifying and describing the planes they saw in combat. In this, it succeeded. A descendant of this scheme is today used to identify Soviet-bloc aircraft.

JAPANESE ARMY. Between World War I and the expansion of aggression in China in 1937, the Japanese Army reached a peak strength of about 300,000 officers and men. They were organized into 17 divisions and a number of special units such as cavalry and artillery brigades and air and antiaircraft regiments. In 1937 the Army began a rapid growth. Existing units were brought up to full strength and additional units were organized, resulting in an Army of 51 active divisions, with a total strength of about 1.7 million men. During 1941–45 the Army grew to a peak strength of approximately 5 million men, organized into 140 divisions and numerous special-purpose units.

The Army was commanded from a headquarters in Tokyo, which was under the Chief of Staff. His principal assistants were the Inspector General of Military Training and the Inspector General of Aviation. Defense areas were established as needed, wherever Japanese forces were engaged in military operations in the Pacific and on the Asian continent. These areas were under the control of the various Japanese armies; each had its commander in chief.

At the outset of the Pacific war (December 8, 1941, in Japan) the bulk of the Japanese Army (38 divisions) was deployed in China and Manchuria. The forces available for the attack were given the following assignments: 23d Army—Hong Kong; 14th Army—Philippines; 15th Army—Thailand and Burma; 16th Army—Netherlands East Indies; 25th Army—Malaya (also northern Sumatra and North Borneo). *See also* JAPANESE CONQUESTS 1941–42; PACIFIC WAR 1942–45.

JAPANESE ARMY AIRCRAFT DESIGNATIONS. Like the JAPANESE NAVY, the Army used a number of different systems through the years to designate its aircraft. Two principal schemes were in use during the Pacific war. Ki *(Kitai)* numbers were assigned to individual designs, with various suffixes being added to indicate modifications and variants on the basic design. Type numbers, similar to those used by the Navy and based on the Japanese-calendar year of adoption, were also applied to airplanes. Thus the Army Type 97 heavy bomber was accepted for production in the year 2597, or 1937; it also bore the designation Ki 21. In this volume, Japanese Army aircraft are identified under their Ki numbers. As will be noted under individual entries, some Army planes were also referred to by names. This never became a universal practice.

Japanese Army Name	*Kitai Designation*
Hayabusa	Ki 43 fighter
Shoki	Ki 44 fighter
Toryu	Ki 45 fighter
Shinshitei	Ki 46 reconnaissance plane
Donryu	Ki 49 bomber
Guntei	Ki 51 scout-bomber
Hien	Ki 61 fighter
Hiryu	Ki 67 bomber
Hayate	Ki 84 fighter

JAPANESE CONQUESTS 1941–42. The Japanese entered the war with but limited objectives and with no

BUILDUP TO THE PACIFIC WAR: The expansion of the Japanese Empire, 1933–4

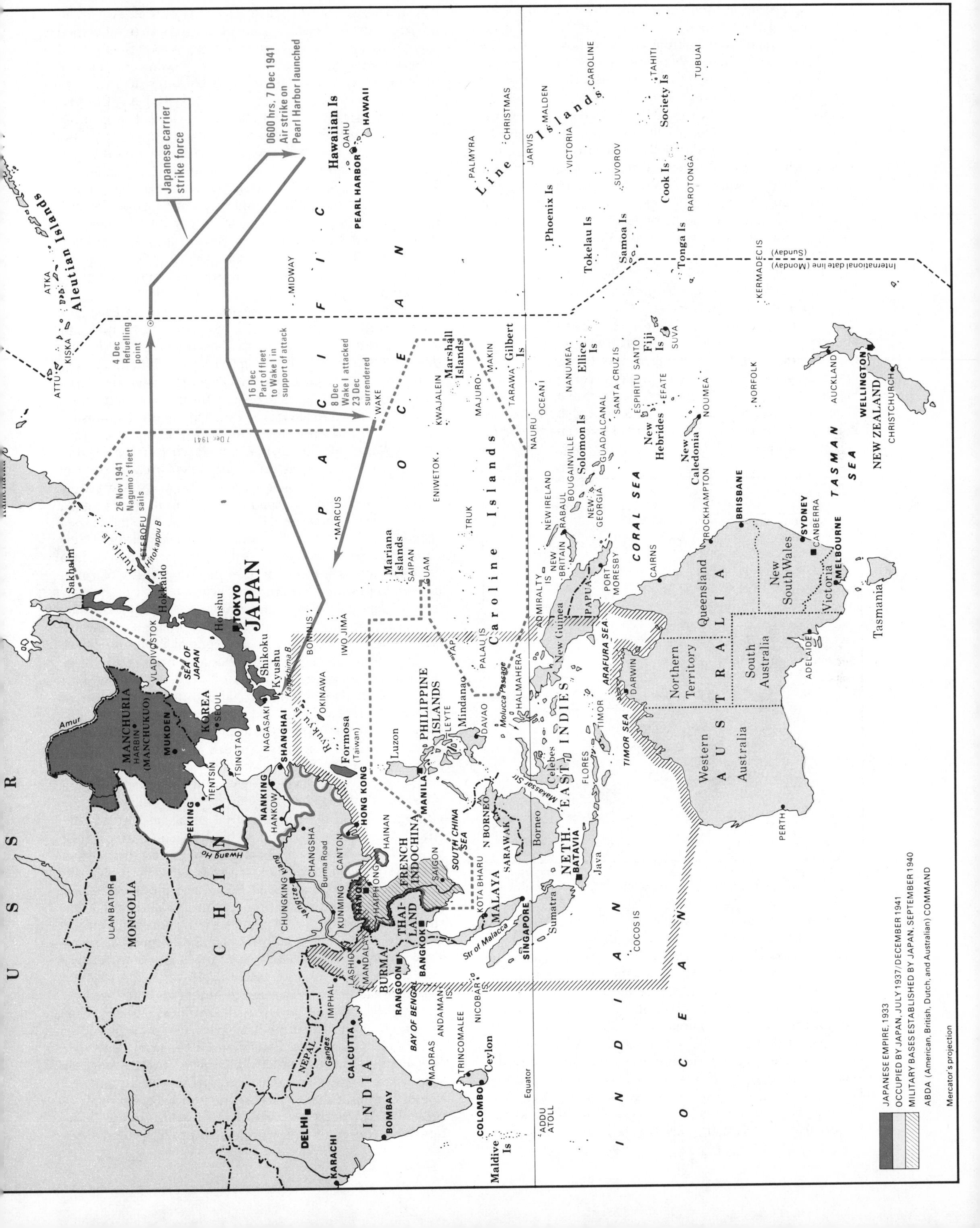

JAPANESE EMPIRE, 1933
OCCUPIED BY JAPAN, JULY 1937/DECEMBER 1941
MILITARY BASES ESTABLISHED BY JAPAN, SEPTEMBER 1940
ABDA (American, British, Dutch, and Australian) COMMAND
Mercator's projection
Japanese carrier strike force
0600 hrs, 7 Dec 1941 Air strike on Pearl Harbor launched
4 Dec Refuelling point
26 Nov 1941 Nagumo's fleet sails
16 Dec Part of fleet to Wake I in support of attack
8 Dec Wake I attacked 23 Dec surrendered
7 Dec 1941
International date line (Monday) (Sunday)
Equator
U S S R
C H I N A
MANCHURIA
(MANCHUKUO)
KOREA
JAPAN
TOKYO
MONGOLIA
INDIA
BURMA
THAI-LAND
FRENCH INDOCHINA
MALAYA
PHILIPPINE ISLANDS
NETH. EAST INDIES
AUSTRALIA
NEW ZEALAND
P A C I F I C O C E A N
I N D I A N O C E A N
CORAL SEA
TASMAN SEA
SOUTH CHINA SEA
BAY OF BENGAL
SEA OF JAPAN
ARAFURA SEA
TIMOR SEA
Aleutian Islands
Hawaiian Is
PEARL HARBOR
Marshall Islands
Caroline Islands
Mariana Islands
Gilbert Is
Ellice Is
Solomon Is
New Hebrides
New Caledonia
Fiji Is
Samoa Is
Tonga Is
Phoenix Is
Tokelau Is
Line Islands
Cook Is
Society Is
WAKE
MIDWAY
GUAM
SAIPAN
MARCUS
IWO JIMA
OKINAWA
Formosa (Taiwan)
HONG KONG
SHANGHAI
MANILA
SINGAPORE
BATAVIA
RANGOON
BANGKOK
HANOI
SAIGON
CALCUTTA
DELHI
BOMBAY
KARACHI
COLOMBO
Ceylon
PEKING
NANKING
CHUNGKING
Burma Road
DARWIN
BRISBANE
SYDNEY
CANBERRA
MELBOURNE
WELLINGTON
Borneo
Sumatra
Java
Celebes
New Guinea
PORT MORESBY
RABAUL
GUADALCANAL
Northern Territory
Queensland
Western Australia
South Australia
New South Wales
Victoria
Tasmania

plan to press home their offensives to destroy the military forces of the nations opposing them. Instead, as of December 1941, they intended only to knock out the U.S. Asiatic and Pacific Fleets, to destroy British naval power in Southeast Asia, to destroy Allied air power in the Western Pacific and Southeast Asia, to seize the NETHERLANDS EAST INDIES and Malaya (including the British defensive bastion of SINGAPORE), to occupy the PHILIPPINE ISLANDS and, finally, to secure firm control over a defensive perimeter stretching south from the KURILE ISLANDS through WAKE ISLAND, the MARIANA ISLANDS, the CAROLINES, the GILBERTS and the MARSHALLS, back southwest to RABAUL on the island of NEW BRITAIN and thence west along the north coast of NEW GUINEA. In Southeast Asia the perimeter was to include not only the Netherlands East Indies but also French INDOCHINA—into which the Japanese had moved in 1940—THAILAND and BURMA. The Japanese also intended to bring their stuttering operations in CHINA to a successful conclusion by overrunning southeastern China. Following attainment of the foregoing objectives, they fully expected to obtain from the United States and Britain a negotiated peace that would leave Japan in firm possession of a GREATER EAST ASIA CO-PROSPERITY SPHERE which, behind the defensive perimeter, would be open to Japanese exploitation.

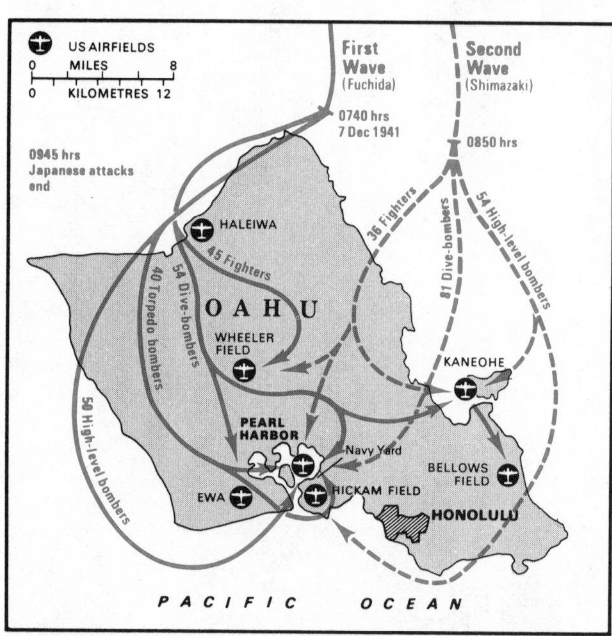

DECEMBER 7, 1941—The Japanese attack on Oahu

Quickly, in late 1941 and early 1942, the Japanese moved out to their planned perimeter. The attack on PEARL HARBOR came on December 7, 1941. The same day (December 8 in the Far East) the Japanese invaded Malaya and Thailand and made their first landing on Philippine soil, at BATAAN Island north of Luzon. On the 9th they occupied Bangkok, Thailand, and invaded the Gilbert Islands. The small American garrison on GUAM surrendered on December 10, the same day the Japanese landed near APARRI and VIGAN in northern Luzon. The Japanese started into Burma on December 11, and the next day landed at LEGASPI, in southeastern Luzon. By the 13th, the day the Japanese made their first landings on Borneo in the East Indies, American air strength in the Philippines had been virtually wiped out or withdrawn. On the 20th the Japanese invaded the southern Philippines at Davao, MINDANAO, and two days later undertook their main landings at LINGAYEN GULF, Luzon. By January 7 the bulk of Gen. Douglas MACARTHUR's forces on Luzon had withdrawn into the BATAAN Peninsula. Meanwhile, on December 23, Wake Island fell to the Japanese, and the next day they invaded Jolo Island of the Sulu Archipelago in the southwestern Philippines. HONG KONG surrendered on December 25, and in mid-January the Japanese undertook additional landings in the East Indies. On January 23 they secured Rabaul on New Britain and KAVIENG on New Ireland, and undertook to secure their southeastern flank with the seizure of Kieta, on BOUGAINVILLE of the SOLOMON ISLANDS.

On February 8 the Japanese expanded to Gasmata, on the south-central coast of New Britain. The 14th saw them landing on Sumatra in the Indies, and the next day the British-Australian garrison at Singapore surrendered. During the period February 18–20 the Japanese extended their hold on the Indies to include BALI and TIMOR, and on March 1 came the main landings on JAVA, the most important island in the East Indies. Java fell on March 9. Meanwhile on March 8–10, the Japanese seized LAE, SALAMAUA and FINSCHHAFEN on the northeast shore of New Guinea. Early in April they began a series of landings along the north coast of Dutch New Guinea and on the 6th of that month secured the ADMIRALTY ISLANDS, north of eastern New Guinea. These advances, coupled with the moves into New Britain, secured for the Japanese their planned defensive perimeter on the southeast.

On April 9 Filipino-American forces on Bataan surrendered. During the next week the Japanese moved to Cebu and PANAY Islands in the central Philippines and on the 29th undertook additional landings on Mindanao in the south. The 6th of May saw the end of resistance in the Philippines, and on the 18th, for all practical purposes, the Japanese completed the conquest of Burma. Japan was in possession of the Greater East Asia Co-Prosperity Sphere except for coveted areas on mainland China.

But the successes had not brought the ends the Japanese had hoped. No negotiated peace talks with the United States and Britain had taken place. Instead, the Allies gave strong indications that they could and would strike back long before the Japanese expected such action. As early as February 1, 1942, for example, the U.S. Pacific Fleet had launched a carrier-based air raid against Japanese installations on the Gilbert and Marshall Islands, and on April 18 had come the famed Doolittle B-25 raid on Tokyo (*see* FIRST SPECIAL AVIATION PROJECT). And, further, the Japanese offensive operations had not gone entirely to schedule. Before the outbreak of war Japanese planners had allocated 50 days to the conquest of the Philippines; instead, that campaign had consumed nearly six months. The Burma operations had also taken longer than expected. Worse still, from the Japanese point of view, American forces had begun to establish and protect an air and sea line of communications across the South Pacific to Australia. By April 1942 it had become obvious to the Japanese that the Allies were, unless stopped, going to develop Australia as a major base for future offensive operations.

The Japanese answer was to attempt to expand the perimeter they had already secured, and for this purpose they returned to plans considered but not approved before December 7, 1941. Discarding as beyond their means a plan to invade Australia, the Japanese decided to cut the developing line of communications from the United States to Australia by seizing NEW CALEDONIA, the Fiji Islands and Samoa. Flank protection for the new perimeter on the south was to be obtained by seizing PORT MORESBY, on the southern coast of eastern New Guinea; on the north, by seizing bases in the American Aleutian Islands; in the center, by the occupation of MIDWAY Island.

On the south the Japanese reinforced their holdings on Bougainville, moved into the SHORTLAND ISLANDS and on May 3, 1942, reached TULAGI in the southeastern Solomon chain off GUADALCANAL. The next step was to be the capture of Port Moresby, but this was frustrated by the naval battle of the CORAL SEA on May 7 and 8. The Battle of Midway, also mainly naval in nature, took place on June 3–5 and saved the island for the United States. The Japanese secured ATTU and KISKA in the Aleutians on June 7 and on July 21–22 landed in the BUNA–Gona area on the north shore of New Guinea and immediately began an overland advance toward Port Moresby, an advance not halted until September 16. Meanwhile, on August 7, the 1st Marine Division, landing on Tulagi and Guadalcanal, halted further Japanese expansion toward New Caledonia and Fiji. The Japanese made one more offensive effort in New Guinea, landing on August 26 at MILNE BAY on the island's southeast tip. This, too, came to naught, and the Allies had the situation at Milne Bay cleaned up by September 5. Finally, on May 12, 1943, U.S. forces began the reconquest of Attu and on July 29 of the same year the Japanese withdrew from Kiska. By this time it had become amply clear that the Japanese had long since overreached themselves. *See also* PACIFIC WAR. **R.R.S.**

JAPANESE MANDATED ISLANDS. For having participated in World War I on the Allied side by seizing German holdings on the Shantung Peninsula in China, Japan was ceded a mandate by the League of Nations of former German-owned islands in the North Pacific—the MARSHALL, the CAROLINE and the MARIANA groups. Countries given a mandate over former enemy-held territories were to improve the condition of life of the people inhabiting those mandates and prepare them for self-government. Because the League of Nations exercised no real supervision over the conduct of the mandates, and in fact had no real power, Japan was able to build up and fortify bases in the islands without interference from league members.

JAPANESE NAVY. Like the U.S. NAVY, the Imperial Japanese Navy at the beginning of the Pacific war was oriented in the direction of conventional surface warfare. It was organized around a battle line of 12 battleships, ranging in age and power from the brand-new YAMATO and MUSASHI (over 71,000 tons fully loaded, nine 18.1-inch guns) to the four British-designed ships of the KONGO class, completed early in World War I (nearly 32,000 tons, eight 14-inch guns). The older Japanese battleships had been extensively modernized between the wars, in much the same manner as contemporary capital ships of foreign navies.

Japan had built the first from-the-keel-up aircraft carrier, *Hosho*, in 1922 and had shown a keen interest in naval aviation. By late 1941 the Imperial Navy had 10 carriers of various types and sizes. Shipboard and land-based naval aviation had seen extensive service during the China campaign, which gave Navy fliers a priceless background of experience. Cruiser (18 heavy, 18 light) and destroyer (113) forces, like those of other navies, were a mixture of early post–World War I construction and newer types built during the 1930s. With the possibility of a naval war with the United States in mind, Japan realized that since resources and treaty limitations prevented competition in quantity, the quality of its naval forces must be as high as possible. Ship designers stressed seakeeping and hitting power; during the years before PEARL HARBOR, cruisers and newer destroyers were armed with the powerful 24-inch oxygen-fueled LONG LANCE torpedo. Training was severely realistic and thorough.

Japanese submarines were good in quality, and the crews highly trained. Submarines were intended for use with the fleet rather than for independent raiding of the kind conducted by the German and U.S. Navies. This principle proved deficient in practice, with results being not at all in proportion to the numbers (113 in December 1941).

Japanese antisubmarine warfare was generally ineffective. Few antisubmarine ships existed, and there were no construction programs until late in the war; by that time, most of the damage had already been done. RADAR and SONAR lagged behind developments in Britain and the United States, although the Japanese did employ countermeasures against widely used Allied radars.

Though the Japanese surface-fleet menace declined as the war went on, and submarines never proved a real danger to the Allies, aviation was continually effective. Air attack was always considered the real threat in the Pacific; ships' radar and antiaircraft batteries were steadily increased to meet it. The quality of shipboard aviation declined as the war progressed, however; the Japanese did not rotate experienced squadrons so that they could pass their experience along to new pilots, but instead kept them in front-line service. Heavy losses at the CORAL SEA, MIDWAY and GUADALCANAL (1942–43) meant that by 1944, though Japanese carrier aviation had planes, it had few experienced pilots. While the remaining veterans were probably superior to the average Allied pilots, being much more experienced, the overall quality of Allied fliers was by now better than the average of the Japanese Naval Air Force, leavened as it was with relatively inexperienced men. Heavy losses in the GREAT MARIANAS TURKEY SHOOT (June 1944) underscored this. By October 1944, when Admiral OZAWA's carrier force sortied from Japan for the LEYTE GULF action, it was a paper tiger—new carriers with few planes and few pilots. Two battleships (ISE and HYUGA) had been converted to hermaphrodite "battleship-carriers" with catapults and plane-handling decks replacing their after turrets, but there were no planes for them.

The KAMIKAZE suicide weapon was the new feature of

the final year of the war. It really pitted the "warrior spirit" against Western machinery. By the end of the Philippines campaign in early 1945, kamikazes had been used in some numbers, and there was a large-scale kamikaze offensive during the Okinawa campaign. The kamikaze attack was the first operational guided-missile warfare, having, however, a human pilot rather than guidance machinery. Kaiten suicide torpedoes were also developed and deployed in numbers. *See also* Combined Fleet.

JAPANESE NAVY AIRCRAFT DESIGNATIONS. Operational aircraft were designated according to two principal systems, a letter-number system somewhat similar in concept to that followed by the U.S. Navy and a war-adopted arrangement of aircraft names. Beginning in the late 1920s, letter-number designations came into use. These consisted of a capital letter indicating the type of aircraft (e.g., A—carrier fighter; D—carrier bomber; F—observation floatplane; H—flying boat; J—land-based fighter; S—night fighter); a number indicating its place in the sequence of designs of that particular type produced for the Navy; another capital letter, indicating the firm responsible for the design; and a numeral denoting the individual model within that basic design. A minor modification within a model was indicated by a lower-case letter. Thus, the A6M5c would be a carrier fighter (A), the sixth design of its type since adoption of this designation system (6), designed by Mitsubishi (M), the fifth version of the basic A6M design (5) and a slight modification of the model A6M5 (c), not sufficient to warrant a new model number. When a plane of one type was modified for a different mission, it received the type letter of the new mission as a suffix. Thus, a trainer (K) version of the A6M2 fighter was designated A6M2-K. These model designations are the entries under which Japanese naval aircraft are identified in this volume.

In 1943 names were also assigned to new naval airplanes in addition to the designations just described. These were given in accordance with certain name categories; for instance, training planes were named after flowers, trees or plants; bombers were named for heavenly bodies; patrol planes were named for seas. In addition to these systems, airplanes designed from 1931 on were given project numbers, or *Shi* numbers, based on the year of the reign of the Emperor Hirohito in which the project was begun; 1932, for example, was the seventh year of this reign, and projects begun during that year were identified as 7-*Shi*. To distinguish among different types of planes developed during the same year, the aircraft type was also specified. A full title might read, for example, Navy Experimental 11-*Shi* Reconnaissance Seaplane. Type numbers were also used; a number based on the year of adoption, according to the Japanese calendar, was combined with a system of model numbers indicating the specific version of that design. The A6M3 fighter, for instance, was also known as the Type 0 (Zero) Fighter Model 32. This system was discarded late in 1942.

Japanese Navy Name	*Letter–Number Designation*
Kyofu	N1K1 fighter
Shiden	N1K1-J fighter
Reppu	A7M fighter
Keiun	R2Y1 reconnaissance plane
Shusui	J8M1 fighter
Ginga	P1Y1 bomber (*see also* Kyokko)
Ryusei	B7A1 torpedo bomber
Suisei	D4Y dive-bomber
Saiun	C6N reconnaissance plane
Gekko	J1N1 reconnaissance plane and night fighter
Tenzan	B6N bomber
Reisen	A6M Zero fighter
Kyokko	P1Y1 night fighter
Shiun	E15K1 reconnaissance plane
Zuiun	E16A1 floatplane bomber
Renzan	G8N1 bomber
Momiji	K9W1 trainer
Seiran	M6A1 attack floatplane

JAVA. A strategically important link in the Japanese defensive perimeter as well as the most populous island in the Netherlands East Indies, Java was invaded by elements of the Japanese 16th Army on February 28, 1942. The island was firmly under Japanese control by March 9, their success having been hastened by the Allied defeat in the Battle of the Java Sea, frequent preinvasion aerial bombardments of principal ports and airfields and the increasingly exhausted state of the Allied defenders. With the conquest of Java the Japanese had complete control of the Netherlands East Indies, and Australia was now in much greater danger. The island was reoccupied only with difficulty after the termination of hostilities, owing to opposition to the reestablishment of Dutch rule.

JAVA. Netherlands light cruiser (6,670 standard tons; ten 5.9-inch guns, eight 40-mm. guns, 12 mines; 31 knots), completed in 1925. She served with the ABDA Command force in its attempt to defend the Netherlands East Indies, and was finally sunk by Japanese cruiser torpedoes in the Battle of the Java Sea, February 27, 1942. A sister ship, *Sumatra*, served in the European theater and was used as part of the artificial harbor off the Normandy beachhead in 1944 (*see also* Mulberry).

JAVA SEA, BATTLE OF THE. In early 1942 the naval portion of the Japanese southward drive into the Netherlands East Indies (now Indonesia), under the overall command of Vice-Adm. Nobutake Kondo, was divided into two main prongs. The Eastern Force was commanded by Vice-Adm. Ibo Takahashi, the Western Force by Vice-Adm. Jisaburo Ozawa. To meet this, a joint Allied organization called the ABDA (American-British-Dutch-Australian) Command was established on January 15, 1942. Its naval element was first commanded by Adm. Thomas Hart, commander in chief of the U.S. Asiatic Fleet. To this new command was given the task of holding what was optimistically called the Malay Barrier.

During January, Japanese landings were made on Sumatra, Borneo and Celebes. In February, Japanese forces moved into Timor and Bali. Protests by the Netherlands government-in-exile, which had not been consulted when ABDA was established, led to Hart's replacement on February 16 by Vice-Adm. C. E. L. Hel-

FRICH of the Royal Netherlands Navy. Helfrich assumed command of an organization which, like the rest of ABDA, was willing enough but was plagued by differences in material, language, signals and tactical doctrines, as well as lack of adequate command and coordination.

Attempts during late January and into February to resist the Japanese advance were unproductive of any real result. For the final defense of Java, ABDA had a force of 2 heavy cruisers (British EXETER and American HOUSTON); 3 light cruisers (Dutch DE RUYTER and JAVA; Australian PERTH); and 5 American, 3 British and 3 Dutch destroyers. These ships were under the tactical command of Rear Adm. Karel W. F. M. DOORMAN, who flew his flag on *Java*.

Kondo, on the other hand, had an array of task groups numbering 7 carriers; 1 seaplane carrier; 1 battleship; 13 heavy and 6 light cruisers; and 57 destroyers, plus a seaplane tender and smaller mine and patrol craft. Ninety-seven ships carried troops and cargo in two large transport groups. The various transport and support forces deployed from Indochina and the Philippines to await the scheduled assault on Java, set for February 28. Among these forces were Rear Adm. Takeo TAKAGI's 3 cruisers (2 heavy, 1 light) and 7 destroyers, which steamed out of Makassar Strait to run interference for one of the transport convoys.

At this point the ABDA Command, as an overall unit, was dissolved. The Dutch, with the few other Allied ships still available, were determined to fight. Aerial sightings of Japanese forces made it apparent that an attack on Java was imminent. From February 25 to the 27th, Doorman searched for the Japanese. On the 27th he took his worn ships and tired crews into Surabaya, but new contact reports brought orders from Helfrich for an attack. Doorman, without pausing, turned out to sea in such haste that there was not even time to work out a plan of operations. His five cruisers sailed northwest from Surabaya into the Java Sea, screened by 10 destroyers. He was soon spotted by floatplanes from Takagi's cruiser force. Shortly after 1600, Japanese warships were sighted ahead; this was Takagi's group, which had by now been reinforced by Rear Adm. Shoji Nishimura with a light cruiser and six destroyers. Takagi's heavy cruisers NACHI and HAGURO opened fire at long range with their 8-inch guns. His screen commander, Rear Adm. Raizo TANAKA, took his flagship (the light cruiser JINTSU) and his seven destroyers to closer range and began firing on the Allied destroyer screen with *Jintsu*'s 5.5-inch guns.

A few minutes later Doorman turned his column to the left to keep Takagi from crossing his T, closing the range as he did so to let his 6-inch-gun light cruisers open fire. The shooting continued; Doorman turned to close the range further, and Takagi ordered a torpedo attack. Tanaka's and Nishimura's squadrons fired salvos, joined by *Haguro*, but at this long range no hits resulted. Takagi had observation floatplanes spotting his gunfire, while Doorman did not. The Japanese destroyers compounded this Allied disadvantage by laying a smoke screen, which prevented spotting from Doorman's ships.

By now the Japanese transport convoy was in sight. Tanaka decided to force a decision before the troop ships could be harmed; his ships having reloaded torpedoes, he attacked the approaching Allied cruiser column with torpedoes and gunfire. An 8-inch projectile from *Haguro* seriously damaged *Exeter*, slowing her down. This threw Doorman's column into confusion as ships turned in different directions, some captains under the mistaken impression that the formation was changing course. One of Tanaka's torpedoes sank the Dutch destroyer *Kortenaer*, and the disordered Allied ships turned south, away from the Japanese. Takagi now fired torpedoes from his heavy cruisers and from Nishimura's destroyer squadron. This increased the confusion as Allied ships took evasive action. The British destroyer *Electra* was badly hit in the gunnery duel that followed. Tanaka took *Jintsu* and two destroyers after the wounded *Exeter*, but a counterattack by three Allied destroyers foiled this attempt; turning back, Tanaka joined in finishing off *Electra*.

By 1730 Doorman had reformed his force; he headed southeast as he kept up an intermittent gun engagement with Takagi's cruisers. *Houston* took two 8-inch duds that damaged her hull and started an oil leak even though they did not explode. Takagi's ships began to close, but another Japanese torpedo attack missed its mark. At sunset Doorman ordered his four American destroyers to cover his withdrawal. The destroyers fired their torpedoes but did so at a long-enough range to give the Japanese ample time to maneuver, and no hits were scored.

Lacking knowledge of Doorman's intentions, Takagi put each of his destroyer squadrons in position to block one of the possible approaches to the troop convoy, which was now some 20 miles to the northwest. Doorman turned in that direction, searching for the invasion force. A little over an hour after sunset the opposing cruiser forces again sighted each other. In a running gun duel, Doorman now headed west along the northern coast of Java. The American destroyers, their torpedoes expended, turned east toward Surabaya to refuel as Doorman had earlier instructed them. A Dutch mine sank the British destroyer *Jupiter*, and Doorman now swung his ships to the north, detaching his last remaining destroyer to rescue survivors from the sunken *Kortenaer*. The Allied cruisers exchanged further shots with *Nachi* and *Haguro*; another Japanese torpedo spread hit *Java* and *De Ruyter*. Both ships were set afire and sank not long afterward. Doorman went down with his flagship.

At the last, he had ordered his two remaining ships, *Houston* and *Perth*, to head for Batavia (now Djakarta), on the north coast of Java near SUNDA STRAITS. On this same day, the American seaplane tender LANGLEY sank under Japanese air attack while attempting to carry Army P-40 fighters and pilots in to Java (*see* P-40). In the final battle of Sunda Straits, during the night of February 28–March 1, *Perth* and *Houston* were lost. *Exeter*, attempting to reach safety, was sent to the bottom during the morning of March 1. Three American destroyers and the oiler *Pecos* were sunk. The "Malay Barrier" was gone; only a few Allied destroyers and smaller ships remained afloat, and these were ordered to make their way to Australia. On March 1 the ABDA naval command officially ceased to exist. By the 9th the Japanese were in control of Java. **J.R.**

JD. U.S. Navy designation for the Army A-20 (*see* A-20).

JEAN BART. French battleship of 35,000 tons, with a 15-inch main battery. Incomplete at the time of her flight from France in June 1940 to avoid falling into German hands, the ship remained under VICHY French control at Casablanca. Immobile in the harbor, *Jean Bart* engaged U.S.S. MASSACHUSETTS during the Allied invasion of North Africa on November 8, 1942, and was *hors de combat* after a 14-inch shell jammed both her forward turrets.

JEANNE D'ARC. French cruiser, launched in 1930, of 6,496 tons standard displacement, armed with eight 6.1-inch and numerous antiaircraft guns. She participated in the occupation of Corsica in September 1943.

JEANNENEY, Jules (1864–1957). President of the French Senate, 1932–42. In 1940 Jeanneney presided over the Senate's deliberations and vote (229–1) that terminated the Third Republic and created a new constitution giving Marshal PÉTAIN full executive powers in VICHY France.

JEDBURGH. Three-man American-British-French teams were parachuted in uniform into German-occupied France to train and assist French Resistance forces. Each team was called a Jedburgh. The code name, often said to have come from the place in Scotland where the teams were trained, was actually, according to British intelligence sources, picked at random from a schoolbook.

JEEP. U.S. Army truck, ¼-ton, 4×4, Command Reconnaissance. A small, four-wheel personnel and utility car with what has come to be a universally recognized appearance, it had an 80-inch wheelbase, an overall length of 131 inches and a gross weight of 3,240 pounds. The jeep could carry five passengers or 800 pounds of payload, and could tow a 37-mm. antitank gun or a light trailer. Its 54-horsepower, four-cylinder gasoline engine had a rated fuel consumption, with the vehicle loaded, of 20 miles per gallon. Ground clearance was 8¾ inches. Jeeps were used as command, light reconnaissance and general utility vehicles. Some were adapted to carry stretchers; many were equipped with a pedestal-mounted .50-caliber machine gun.

Produced by the thousands, jeeps were used by all U.S. services; many were provided to Allied powers. This rugged, no-frills car served in every theater, and military and civilian descendants are in production today. The name came from its designation, *G*eneral *P*urpose, and was probably influenced by the popularity of Eugene the Jeep, a wonder-working character in the comic strip *Thimble Theatre* (Popeye). The jeep was first military-tested in December 1940, having been designed and built by a Toledo motor manufacturer, Willys.

JEFFERIS, Sir Millis Rowland (1899–1963). British Army officer (major general), employed 1940–45 by the Ministry of Defence in the development of special war weapons, notably aerial antitank missiles and an infantry antitank gun. For his war performance, Jefferis was described by Churchill as brilliant. Afterward he was chief superintendent of the Military Engineering Experimental Establishment, 1950–53.

JEHEEMY. An elevated framework, on four rubber-tire wheels, used for removing stranded small landing craft from a beach. It was pushed into place over a landing craft by a bulldozer or other suitable vehicle. The craft was secured to the frame by chain tackle, and the Jeheemy was then rolled out into water deep enough for the landing craft to float.

JERRICAN (jerry can). A British-originated nickname for the standard fuel or water can developed by the German Army for use with vehicles. Easily handled, these cans were carried in brackets or other external stowage. The jerrican was sturdier and easier to handle than the thinner-walled commercial-type tins used for this purpose by the British. The U.S. Army adopted the idea after encountering them in North Africa, producing a version differing in details from the original. German water cans were distinguished from fuel cans by a prominent white cross painted on each side.

JERVIS BAY, H.M.S. Royal Navy armed merchant cruiser of 14,000 tons, completed as a passenger liner for the Aberdeen and Commonwealth Line by Vickers-Armstrong in 1922 and armed in 1939 with eight single hand-operated 6-inch guns and two 3-inch antiaircraft weapons. In November 1940 (at the height of the British convoy escort vessel shortage) *Jervis Bay* formed the sole escorting ship for a westbound Atlantic convoy. On November 5 *Jervis Bay* sighted the German pocket battleship ADMIRAL SCHEER at dusk. It was no match, of course, but she engaged the *Scheer* as best she could, ordering her convoy to scatter. Although *Jervis Bay* was disposed of with little difficulty, the time—22 minutes—it took enabled the convoy's 37 ships to scatter in a smoke screen and the darkness of evening so widely that the *Scheer* could only find and sink five of them.

The *Jervis Bay*'s captain, E. S. Fogarty FEGEN, was badly injured early in the action but continued to direct the fight until a further explosion killed him. He was awarded a posthumous VICTORIA CROSS on the initiative of King GEORGE VI himself. A number of survivors from the *Jervis Bay* were rescued by the Swedish ship *Stureholm*, whose captain, Sven Olander, after consultation with his crew decided that although neutral they could not leave a scene of such gallantry without an attempt at rescue, whatever the risks involved for themselves.

JESCHONNEK, Hans (1899–1943). A German Army lieutenant by the age of 15, Jeschonnek became a pilot in 1917, serving in Jagdstaffel 40 with Erhard MILCH. After World War I Jeschonnek was involved with the development in Russia of the secret German air force. In September 1933 he became staff officer to the Secretary of State for Air (Milch). In 1937 he was appointed head of operations of the LUFTWAFFE General Staff, and on February 1, 1939, he was made Chief of Staff. For various reasons, his earlier close relationship with Milch had by this time turned into a feud, a state of affairs not untypical of the Luftwaffe high command. As the war progressed, Hermann GÖRING, Commander in Chief of the Luftwaffe, tended to bypass Jeschonnek and his staff, and Milch took over more and more responsibilities as Göring himself neglected his duties. In addition, Jeschonnek received increasing blame for the

Allied bombing of Germany, Hitler preferring to accuse him rather than his favorite, Göring. The pressure overwhelmed Jeschonnek and he committed suicide in August 1943. His highest rank was colonel general.

JINTSU. Japanese SENDAI-class light cruiser, lost in the night battle of KOLOMBANGARA, July 1943.

JM. U.S. Navy designation for the Army A-26 (*see* A-26).

JODL, Alfred (1890–1946). German Army officer, a veteran of service in World War I as an artillery officer with Bavarian units. Between the wars he served in staff and intelligence posts. In 1939 he was artillery commander in Vienna; he was promoted to major general during this service. At the beginning of the war he was assigned to the OKW operations office (*see* OKW), of which he quickly became the chief. He held this position throughout the war, working directly with Field Marshal Wilhelm KEITEL, the chief of OKW, and with Adolf HITLER. Being an abler and more independent person than Keitel, Jodl was perhaps the most important German planner after the Führer himself (although, because of the curious schism that grew up in the German higher echelons, OKW did not direct the campaign on the Eastern Front). In his diary Jodl presents instances of his opposing Hitler on questions of strategy; his method seems to have been one of indirection and subtlety, and was perhaps not always as effective as he appeared to think. Jodl was promoted to General der Artillerie in 1940 and to colonel general in 1944. He was among those injured in the July 20, 1944, attempt on Hitler's life. Jodl signed the instrument of surrender at Allied headquarters (SHAEF) in Reims on May 7, 1945. In 1946 he was convicted of war crimes, it having been demonstrated that he had signed orders for the execution of prisoners of war. He was hanged on October 16, 1946.

JOHN C. BUTLER, U.S.S. Destroyer escort and class. In appearance these ships were like the RUDDEROW class, with low bridges and two closed 5-INCH 38-caliber gun mounts, but had Westinghouse geared turbines. Seventy-four completed; 211 more were canceled.

JOHNSON, James Edgar (1915–). RAF ACE who led the Western Allies in victories against the Luftwaffe with 38 kills, all fighters—most of them coming in 1943–44. Johnson, who was known as Johnnie, participated in the DIEPPE raid as leader of No. 610 Squadron, and later as a wing commander he escorted more than 50 American bombing missions over Germany. He remained in the RAF after the war, retiring as an air vice-marshal, and became a leading writer on aerial warfare.

JOHNSON, Leon W. (1904–). Commander of the U.S. 44th Bomb Group, nicknamed the Eight Balls, during the August 1943 PLOESTI raid. Colonel Johnson won the MEDAL OF HONOR for electing to "carry out his planned low-level attack despite the thoroughly alerted defenses, the destructive antiaircraft fire, enemy fighter airplanes, the imminent danger of exploding delayed action bombs from the previous element, of oil fires and explosions, and of intense smoke obscuring the target." He later commanded the 14th Bomb Wing and was promoted to brigadier general.

JOHNSON, Robert S. (1920–). Johnson entered U.S. Army Air Forces in November 1941, completed his pilot training the following July and in January 1943 went to the United Kingdom. He flew his first P-47 mission in April 1943 and his last in May 1944 (*see* P-47). During fewer than 13 months of combat Lieutenant Colonel Johnson scored 28 aerial victories, to rank second to Col. Francis GABRESKI among the American aces in the European Theater of Operations. He then commanded an operational training unit and after the war joined Republic Aviation, manufacturer of the P-47 Thunderbolt which he had flown so skillfully.

JOINT CHIEFS OF STAFF. At the beginning of 1942 President ROOSEVELT created a committee of American military staff commanders to coordinate operational strategy for the armed services. JCS consisted of Gen. George C. MARSHALL, Army Chief of Staff; Adm. Ernest J. KING, Commander in Chief of the U.S. Fleet and Chief of Naval Operations; and Gen. Henry H. ARNOLD, Commanding General, Army Air Forces. Adm. William D. LEAHY, chief of staff to the President, presided over the committee after July 1942. It was established as the American component of the COMBINED CHIEFS OF STAFF of Great Britain and the United States, which was charged with preparing and implementing general Allied strategy. Although an Army-Navy Joint Board had existed before 1942, American staff chiefs had not met regularly and had no secretariat or planning agency. Service chiefs traditionally had dealt individually with the President and conducted military operations without formal coordination. Although JCS did not end service rivalries, it did unify strategic planning for American forces. The committee also ensured a high degree of interservice cooperation by appointing a single commander for each military operation.

JOINT DECLARATION. Statement signed at the White House on January 1, 1942, by representatives of 26 nations, declaring the creation of the alliance against the AXIS powers. It was a blend of drafts by President ROOSEVELT and Prime Minister CHURCHILL. The text reads as follows:

> *A Joint Declaration by the United States of America, the United Kingdom of Great Britain and Northern Ireland, the Union of Soviet Socialist Republics, China, Australia, Belgium, Canada, Costa Rica, Cuba, Czechoslovakia, the Dominican Republic, El Salvador, Greece, Guatemala, Haiti, Honduras, India, Luxembourg, the Netherlands, New Zealand, Nicaragua, Norway, Panama, Poland, South Africa, and Yugoslavia.* The Governments signatory hereto,
>
> Having subscribed to a common program of purposes and principles embodied in the Joint Declaration of the President of the United States of America and the Prime Minister of the United Kingdom of Great Britain and Northern Ireland, dated August 14, 1941, known as the ATLANTIC CHARTER.
>
> Being convinced that complete victory over their

enemies is essential to defend life, liberty, independence, and religious freedom, and to preserve human rights and justice in their own lands as well as in other lands, and that they are now engaged in a common struggle against savage and brutal forces seeking to subjugate the world, DECLARE:

(1) Each Government pledges itself to employ its full resources, military or economic, against those members of the Tri-Partite Pact and its adherents with which such Government is at war.

(2) Each Government pledges itself to cooperate with the Governments signatory hereto, and not to make a separate armistice or peace with the enemies.

The foregoing declaration may be adhered to by other Nations which are, or may be, rendering material assistance and contributions to the struggle for victory over Hitlerism.

JOINT PLANNING STAFF. Policy and strategic planning group composed of four members—representing the Army, Navy, Army Air and Navy Air—serving the U.S. JOINT CHIEFS OF STAFF. The four had their own staff of assistants, the most important part of which was the Joint War Plans Committee that drafted studies and strategic plans for all major joint or combined operations. The Joint Planning Staff with a comparable British group comprised the Combined Planning Staff serving the COMBINED CHIEFS OF STAFF.

JONES, Albert Monmouth (1890–1967). U.S. Army officer who was sent to the Philippines in 1940, where he commanded the 31st Infantry Regiment. In 1941–42 he was commanding general of the 51st Filipino Division and then of the 1st Filipino Corps. Promoted to major general, Jones was captured at BATAAN, endured the death march and survived 40 months of Japanese captivity.

JONES, Jesse Holman (1874–1956). Texas (Tennessee-born) banker and construction magnate of wide business interests who became chairman of the Reconstruction Finance Corporation in 1933 and retained the position while serving as Secretary of Commerce in 1940–45. The RFC supplied the financing for the construction of war plants.

JOUBERT DE LA FERTÉ, Sir Philip (1887–1965). RAF officer who joined the Royal Flying Corps in 1913 and served in France in World War I. Between 1930 and 1934 he was commandant of the RAF Staff College. He headed COASTAL COMMAND in 1936–37 and again in 1941–43. He was promoted to air chief marshal in 1941, and in 1942 he pushed the concept of "planned flying and maintenance" that rationalized both operations and maintenance and increased efficiency (operational hours to maintenance man-hours) 30 to 40 percent. In addition, he advocated heavier antisubmarine bombs, low-altitude bombsights, improved depth charge fuzes, operations research, airborne search RADAR, a unified North Atlantic command and tests of aircraft camouflage. In the fall of 1943 he became deputy chief of staff for information and civil affairs on Lord Louis MOUNTBATTEN's Southeast Asia Command staff.

JOYCE, William (1906–1946). Known to the British as "Lord Haw Haw" when he broadcast to Britain for Joseph GOEBBELS, the German Propaganda Minister, during the earlier years of the war, Joyce had belonged to the fascist movement in England before leaving for Germany in 1939. The supercilious, sinister irony of his voice appealed to the British sense of humor, and he built up a largely bogus reputation for "accuracy" in his exposure of alleged weaknesses in the British war effort. Born in New York City of an English mother and an Irish-American father, he went to England in 1921 and graduated with first-class honors at London University. Arrested at Flensburg after the war, he was tried for high treason at the Old Bailey in London and sentenced to death. He declared that he was an American citizen, but nevertheless at the time of his broadcasts he was in possession of a British passport. He was finally executed following the failure of appeals made to the Court of Appeal and to the House of Lords.

JUBILANT. Code name for planned Allied airborne operations to protect and supply Allied prisoners in POW camps in the event of a German collapse following the Normandy invasion.

JUBILEE. Code name for the Allied raid on DIEPPE (France), August 19, 1942.

JUIN, Alphonse (1888–1967). In 1940 General Juin led the French 15th Motorized Infantry Division in Belgium and northern France, compiling a brilliant combat record before his trapped division was forced to surrender at Lille. Released at VICHY's behest, he became commander in chief of French forces in North Africa and brought them back into the war following Allied landings there in late 1942. In 1944 he commanded the French corps in ITALY, and by the end of the war was Chief of Staff of the French National Defense. Marshal Juin later held a high command under NATO. He died in 1967 and was buried in the Invalides.

JUNEAU, U.S.S. ATLANTA-class light cruiser, commissioned in 1942. She served briefly on Caribbean patrol before going to the South Pacific. She was escorting the carrier WASP when that ship was sunk by a Japanese submarine (September 15, 1942). She then operated with the carrier task group involved in the Battle of SANTA CRUZ. On November 12, 1942, off GUADALCANAL, *Juneau* helped to repel Japanese air attacks against transports landing reinforcement troops on the island. During the night of November 12–13 she took part in the cruiser night action that formed the first portion of the naval battle of Guadalcanal and was severely damaged by a torpedo. While retiring from the area shortly after 1100 on the 13th, she was hit by another torpedo, this time from a Japanese submarine. Her magazines exploded, and she quickly went to the bottom with all but 10 of her crew. Lost with *Juneau* were the five SULLIVAN BROTHERS. It was a famous incident.

JUNKERS JU 52/3M. German trimotor freighter developed in the early 1930s (the LUFTWAFFE employed it in the Spanish Civil War as a bomber). It was also used for towing gliders. This famous airplane helped make history in the invasion of NORWAY, this being the first time transport aircraft had played a major part in military operations. Twelve groups were used; they delivered almost 30,000 men, as well as supplies. The plane, nicknamed "Iron Annie," carried 18 men besides the crew. It had a top speed of about 165 miles per hour and a range of 800 miles, and was armed with one 13-mm. and two 7.9-mm. machine guns.

JUNKERS JU 86. Twin-engine bomber, transport and reconnaissance aircraft, some versions of which had a ceiling of about 41,000 feet. The Ju 86P had a top speed of about 240 miles per hour.

JUNKERS JU 87. This angular, ugly dive-bomber gained early wartime fame as the "Stuka"—although this term, an abbreviation of Sturzkampfflugzeug, is actually generic for dive-bombers. The Ju 87 was the first bomber employed in the war, being used in the initial German attacks in Poland. There and in the 1940 fighting in the Low Countries and France, it had tremendous success as a ground-support weapon, capitalizing as much on the terror evoked by its screeching engines when the plane was in its headlong plunge as on the actual effect of its bombs. In the Battle of BRITAIN, however, a situation where the LUFTWAFFE did not have control of the air, the Ju 87's inadequacies became apparent. It was slow, not very maneuverable and, hence, ready prey for the RAF's HURRICANES and SPITFIRES; losses were heavy. The Ju 87B was the standard version in 1938–40; it had an 1,100-horsepower Jumo 211D engine. In 1940 it was supplanted by the more streamlined Ju 87D, with an improved 1,400-horsepower Jumo 211J engine. This series had a top speed of 255 miles per hour and was armed with two 7.9-mm. MG 81 and two 7.9-mm. MG 17 machine guns. Its standard bomb load was about 2,000 pounds, but for a short range it could carry up to 3,960 pounds. In the years 1937–44, 5,709 Ju 87s were produced.

Junkers Ju 87

JUNKERS JU 88. The most widely produced and most versatile German aircraft of the war—bomber, day and night fighter (*see* JU 88C) and ground-support and reconnaissance plane. Design work began in January 1936, and the first Ju 88V-1 (D-AQEN) flew on December 21, 1936; the Ju 88 entered production in 1938. After combat experience, modifications were made to produce the Ju 88A-4, which had a top speed of 293 miles per hour at 17,380 feet and a range of about 1,500 miles; it was powered by two 1,400-horsepower Jumo 211J engines. A B series was developed but did not go into full production. The later Ju 88S bombers had twin 1,730-horsepower BMW radial engines. The Ju 88A-4 could carry about 5,000 pounds of bombs (with rocket-assisted takeoff, up to 7,940 pounds of bombs could be lifted). About 9,000 Ju 88 bombers were built; production of Ju 88s of all types totaled about 15,000.

Junkers Ju 88

JUNKERS JU 88C. An adaptation of the Ju 88 bomber for night fighting; originally designed as a heavy fighter (Zerstörer), with some being built for this purpose, it was used as an interim night fighter. Soon fully developed in this role, it became one of the most widely used night fighters, with at least 2,500 being delivered. The Ju 88C-6c had two 1,410-horsepower V-12 Jumo in-line engines and a top speed of 311 miles per hour. It carried three forward-firing 20-mm. and three 7.9-mm. machine guns and one rearward-firing 13-mm. machine gun. Some versions carried two 20-mm. SCHRÄGE MUSIK cannon. Airborne RADAR was also carried.

JUNKERS JU 88G. A four-seat, twin-engine night-fighter version of the Ju 88 bomber. Widely used, it carried RADAR, had two 1,725-horsepower V-12 engines and had a top speed of 389 miles per hour. It was armed with four forward-firing 20-mm. cannon, one rear-mounted 13-mm. machine gun and two machine guns in a SCHRÄGE MUSIK mounting. In 1940–45, 3,964 Ju 88 fighter versions were delivered to the LUFTWAFFE. Of 28 Luftwaffe night-fighter Gruppen in January 1945, 16 were entirely or partially equipped with Ju 88Gs.

JUNKERS JU 188. A stretched version of the Ju 88, this aircraft entered service (Ju 188E-1) in 1942. Different versions of the Ju 188 varied considerably in characteristics. The E-1 could carry 6,600 pounds of bombs; it had two 1,700-horsepower BMW radial engines. The Ju 188A, produced later, had two 1,776-horsepower Jumo 213A engines, which drove it at a maximum speed of about 325 miles per hour. One version, the Ju 188S, reached almost 430 miles per hour. Popular with air crews, Ju 188s were produced in reconnaissance (the D and F) as well as bomber versions; the totals were 466 bombers and 570 reconnaissance versions.

JUNKERS JU 252. Transport plane designed to be the successor to the Ju 52/3M, which it did not in fact supplant. Only 15 Ju 252s were produced, since it drew heavily on metal in limited supply.

JUNKERS JU 290. A four-engine patrol bomber and transport employed by the LUFTWAFFE primarily in the Atlantic and the Mediterranean; it mainly performed reconnaissance duties. The Ju 290 could carry 40 men, had a top speed of 280 miles per hour and was armed with 20-mm. cannon and machine guns.

JUNKERS JU 352. Aircraft (called the Hercules) similar to the Ju 252 but needing less metal. About 50 were produced. *See also* JUNKERS JU 252.

JUNKERS JU 388J (Störtebeker). One of the last variants of the Ju 88 series to be built. A four-place, high-altitude night fighter, it was built in an attempt to knock out the RAF's night-flying MOSQUITO. Only three were produced, however, since the HEINKEL HE 219 was considered a better night fighter. The Störtebeker carried two 20-mm. and two 30-mm. cannon, was equipped with RADAR and flew at 362 miles per hour maximum.

JUNKERS JU 390. A six-engine bomber designed to reach New York from German bases in Europe. It was developed in 1943, but only two prototypes were built. The Ju 390V-1 was flown at Dessau in August 1943 as an unarmed cargo plane carrying 22,000 pounds for 4,970 miles. One of the giant planes, delivered in January 1944, used its 32-hour endurance for a transatlantic patrol said to have turned back only 12½ miles short of the American coast north of New York.

JUNO BEACH. Code name of the center British assault area (the Courseulles-sur-Mer beach) in the Normandy INVASION, June 6, 1944.

JUNYO. Japanese aircraft carrier, second ship of the HIYO class. Active through most of the Pacific war, she ended it bomb-damaged and out of action for lack of carrier air crews. She was later scrapped.

JUPITER. Code name for a proposed Allied operation to liberate northern Norway. It was much favored by Winston CHURCHILL in 1942 as a means of beginning the Allied return to the Continent, but the idea received little support from the military staffs.

K

K3M. Japanese Navy Mitsubishi trainer, which appeared in two important versions, the K3M2, built by Mitsubishi, and the K3M3, built by Watanabe.

K-9 CORPS. In 1942 the U.S. Army Quartermaster Corps began to train dogs for sentry, roving patrol, messenger and mine-detection duty. Of the 10,425 dogs which the QMC trained for the Army, Navy and Coast Guard, some 9,300 served as sentries. Both the Marines and the Army also trained dogs for scouting operations in the jungles of Pacific islands. The name of the corps may be noted as an instance of official humor.

K9W-1. The Tachikawa *Momiji* (Maple) (Allied code name, Cypress), a Japanese Navy version of the Army's Ki 86 primary trainer (*see* KI 86).

KADENA AIRFIELD. Base located just inland from the Hagushi beaches, site of U.S. landings on OKINAWA on April 1, 1945. Despite Japanese plans to render Kadena and other airfields on the island unusable, it was captured by 10 A.M. the day of the assault.

KAGA. Japanese aircraft carrier, originally laid down after World War I as one of two battleships of the Tosa class. Under the Washington Naval Treaty, both ships were to have been disposed of before completion. The 1923 Japanese earthquake, however, severely damaged the incomplete battle cruiser *Amagi,* which had been selected for conversion to an aircraft carrier along with her sister AKAGI. In *Amagi*'s place, *Kaga* was completed as one of Japan's first two large fleet carriers. Part of the carrier task force that opened the Pacific war by attacking PEARL HARBOR, *Kaga* was sunk in June 1942 by American dive-bombers in the Battle of MIDWAY. *Kaga* and *Akagi* were not sister ships of the same class, differing in dimensions and characteristics.

KAGERO. A class of Japanese destroyers. Eighteen Kageros were built just before Japan entered the war. A development of the ASASHIO class, they had the same armament and general appearance but embodied improvements in stability and hull form. Fast, long-range ships, the Kageros, with the Asashios and the first ships of the YUGUMO class, formed the backbone of Japan's first-line destroyer force during the early years of the Pacific war. This successful class had their antiaircraft and antisubmarine armament increased during the war years. One of this class, *Hamakaze,* was the first Japanese destroyer to be fitted with RADAR.

KA GO (Operation Ka). Japanese code name for their August 1942 operation to reinforce GUADALCANAL, which resulted in the Battle of the EASTERN SOLOMONS.

KAIN, Edgar (1918–1940). RAF pilot from New Zealand, one of the war's first aces, with 17 kills from November 1939 to May 1940. During the Battle of FRANCE, in May alone he shot down 12 German planes, three of them in one day. The next month "Cobber," as he was known, was killed, not in combat but in a flying accident.

KAIRYU (Sea Dragon). A Japanese two-man submarine developed from earlier models. Produced in 1945, it was powered by a combination automotive engine and electric motor. Some kairyus had two 18-inch torpedoes slung beneath the hull; others had an explosive warhead for suicide attack. Their slow speed (7.5 to 10 knots at most) and limited range suited them to coast defense only. Some kairyus were built as trainers, with two periscopes in an enlarged conning tower. None became operational.

KAISER, Henry John (1882–1967). American industrialist famous for his monumental feats of ship production in World War II. The sterotypical self-made man, he dropped out of school at 13, advanced rapidly in business and in 1912 entered the construction field. His company worked on such projects as the Boulder, Bonneville and Grand Coulee Dams and the piers of the San Francisco–Oakland Bay Bridge. In World War II he pioneered the use of assembly-line methods, prefabrication and new welding techniques in the production of ships. The shipyards operated by his firm built almost one-third of the merchant ships constructed in America during the war, as well as 50 escort carriers—a total of 1,460 vessels. In 1942 one of his yards (Richmond, Calif.) set a record by launching a 10,500-ton ship four and a half days after her keel was laid and delivering her three days after that. At the Navy's request Kaiser became chairman of Brewster Aircraft Co. in 1943, holding the position for a little over a year. For a time he was associated with Howard Hughes on a flying-boat contract, but when the order was reduced to one aircraft Kaiser withdrew. Following the war Kaiser was for several years in the automobile business with Joseph W. Frazer. When he died, his enterprises had assets of $2.5 billion and employed 90,000 workers.

KAITEN. Japanese one-man "human torpedo." Modified from the 24-inch LONG LANCE oxygen-propelled torpedo, the kaiten was wider and longer than the Long Lance but had many components in common with it. It was controlled by a pilot, seated in a small cockpit with a compass and periscope. Developed during 1942–43, it became operational in small numbers late in 1944. Many surviving Japanese submarines, as well as some surface ships, were converted to carry kaitens and launch them when within range of an enemy target. Submarines of the larger I-BOAT type could carry six kaitens; before launching, the pilot entered his weapon through a lock from inside the submarine. The overall effect of the kaiten is less than certain. Although contemporary Japanese sources claimed good results, American sources point to no more than a small number of ships hit by kaitens.

The principal kaiten was the Type 1, over 48 feet long and armed with a 3,400-pound warhead. Speeds and ranges varied from 85,300 yards at 12 knots to 25,100 yards at 30 knots. These were produced and used in large numbers. The Type 2 had the same warhead, but was slightly longer and had a hydrogen-peroxide power plant with a top speed of 40 knots. The experimental Type 3 was faster, but never entered production. The Type 4 kaiten succeeded the Type 2, returning to the Long Lance propulsion system in the interest of quick production. Like the Type 2, it could make 40 knots, but it had a 4,000-pound warhead. Many Type 2 and 4 hulls had been built by V-J Day, but production problems were insurmountable and no more than a few were completed.

KALACH. At this Russian town west of STALINGRAD, the Soviet Don and Stalingrad Fronts (army groups) met on November 22, 1942, completing the encirclement of the German SIXTH ARMY. Earlier Kalach had been the scene of several main engagements.

KALEMYO. This small town on the eastern edge of central BURMA was left to the Japanese on May 12, 1942, as elements of the British Burma Army withdrew from the KALEWA vicinity, en route to India. On November 15, 1944, it was reoccupied without opposition—having been found deserted and in ruins—by elements of the British 33d Corps as the Allies began their reconquest of Burma.

KALEWA. Town in BURMA, 130 miles south of IMPHAL, taken by British 33d Corps on December 4, 1944.

KALININ. City northwest of Moscow taken by the Germans in their 1941 advance but retaken by Soviet troops in their counteroffensive (December 16, 1941). The Kalinin front then advanced as far as Rzhev before the offensive halted.

KALININ BAY, U.S.S. Escort aircraft carrier of 6,730 tons displacement (commissioned November 27, 1943), which sustained heavy damage in the battle for LEYTE GULF, though still remaining afloat and in formation. She took 13 hits from the 8-inch guns of Japanese cruisers and also was hit by fire from a battleship. After the controls were knocked out, the crew steered her by hand.

KALLIO, Kyosti (1873–1940). Kyosti Kallio spent a lifetime in Finnish politics. Elected President in 1937, he valiantly attempted to preserve Finnish democracy and constitutional rule against the military force of the Soviets in the war of 1939–40. Kallio resigned his office on November 28, 1940, owing to ill health, and died shortly thereafter.

KALTENBRUNNER, Ernst (1903–1946). SS general and from 1943 head of the Reich Main Security Office (RSHA), in succession to the murdered Reinhard HEYDRICH, though at first with reduced power. Kaltenbrunner was born in Ried, Austria; he qualified as a doctor of law and political economy in 1926. At one stage he earned his living as a coal miner. He joined the Austrian Nazi Party in 1932, acting as its legal adviser, and he was twice arrested and kept for a short time in custody. Allying himself with Arthur SEYSS-INQUART, he rose to the rank of SS lieutenant general. Following the ANSCHLUSS (1938), he became chief of police for Austria, specializing in intelligence. In 1943, Heinrich HIMMLER named him chief of RSHA, which included the Security Police, the Criminal Police and the Security Service (*see* SD), although aware of the strong antagonism that had grown up between Kaltenbrunner and Heydrich. Kaltenbrunner assumed control of the GESTAPO, with Heinrich ("Gestapo") MÜLLER as his technical subordinate.

In 1944, with the collapse of Admiral CANARIS's authority, the duties of military intelligence (the ABWEHR) were added to Kaltenbrunner's department, and he grew in power to such an extent that he enjoyed a confidential relationship with Adolf HITLER and, like Heydrich before him, was often able to evade the authority of Himmler. He therefore became directly responsible for atrocities on a mass scale, along with Adolf EICHMANN, who was officially another of his subordinates. He was determined until the end to exterminate the Jews held in captivity. As was shown during the NUREMBERG TRIALS, his signature was attached to innumerable incriminating documents, including orders to massacre prisoners of war.

Kaltenbrunner took personal charge of many inquiries, and his name became notorious. He cross-examined Canaris, who remarked on his cold eyes and "murderer's paws." Kaltenbrunner was indeed a huge, coarse man, given to drinking and having an expressionless face. He was in active charge of investigations following the attempt on Hitler's life. Toward the end of the war, he decided to negotiate with the Red Cross concerning relief for the concentration camps, in order to cover himself as far as possible; compromised as he was, it would appear that by March 1945 he was prepared to hand over the camps intact to the liberating forces, and he even allowed Red Cross officials access to certain camps to bring in relief. After the war he was finally captured in the house of his mistress, following a gun battle.

On the witness stand at Nuremberg, Kaltenbrunner, faced with document after document bearing his signature, firmly denied complicity in the exterminations; he attempted to hide behind the complex interlacing of authority among Himmler, Müller and himself. He alleged that when he finally heard of the existence of the camps in 1944 he remonstrated with both Hitler and Himmler. His attempt at self-defense was, however, torn apart under cross-examination, and he was sentenced to death and executed.

KAMIKAZE. Americans first experienced the Japanese kamikaze (divine wind) phenomenon—that is, the suicide pilots of the Special Attack Corps—in the PHILIPPINES in 1944. Japanese naval aviators attempted to deprive American invasion shipping at LEYTE of its air cover by crashing the flattops of the accompanying carrier forces. At first, these suicide missions were a temporary expedient only, but initial successes led the Japanese to continue the attacks both in the Philippines and elsewhere. In particular, a combined force of about 1,815 planes carried out well-organized suicide raids at OKINAWA.

During the first few days of April 1945 the toll of damaged and sunk American shipping grew at an alarming rate while naval casualties mounted in proportion. By April 6 Admiral TOYODA, commander of the COMBINED FLEET, completed plans to launch from Kyushu the first of 10 general air attacks, entitled KIKUSUI, which would continue until June 22. Before these attacks (*see* TEN GO) ended, a total of 1,465 kamikaze planes from Kyushu sank 26 American ships and damaged 164 others. Overall, Japanese sources say, 7,852 aircraft (2,393 of them kamikazes) were used, from all bases, in this campaign. In the end the kamikaze concept proved unsuccessful. Nevertheless, in the final plans for defense of the Japanese home islands the role of the kamikazes was to be paramount. Fortunately for both sides, the war ended before they were employed.

KAMIKAZE. Japanese destroyer and class (nine ships) built during the 1920s, a fact that made them of the same vintage as the American FLUSH-DECKERS. They were 1,270-ton ships, 336 feet in length, and were armed with four 4.7-inch guns and six 21-inch torpedo tubes; during the war they were extensively rearmed, the antiaircraft and antisubmarine capacity being increased. Top speed, as they were originally built, was about 37 knots. Ships of this class were characterized by an unusual broken forecastle forward of the bridge. *See also* HAYATE; YUNAGI.

KAMMHUBER LINE. A system of German night-fighter operating areas designed to cover the likely bomber routes from England, first set up in 1942. Approaching bomber formations were picked up by ground RADAR, and fighters were then vectored in on them. Its name came from Gen. Josef Kammhuber (b. 1896), general in command of night fighters.

KANE, John R. (1907–). Nicknamed "Killer," Colonel Kane received the MEDAL OF HONOR for leading the U.S. 98th Bomb Group against PLOESTI, Rumania, in August 1943: "By his gallant courage, brilliant leadership, and superior flying skill, he and the formation under his command successfully attacked this vast refinery . . ." After returning to the United States, he served as commander of various air bases.

KANGAROO. Name for a British armored personnel carrier.

KARELIAN ISTHMUS. An area between the Gulf of Finland and Lake LADOGA. In 1939, before the SOVIET-FINNISH WAR, it belonged to Finland, including the ancient city of VIIPURI. By the terms of the Soviet-Finnish peace treaty, the Karelian Isthmus was ceded to the Soviet Union. Later, after the German blockade of LENINGRAD in 1941, the isthmus was retaken by the Finns. It was finally retaken by the Red Army in 1944 and today forms part of the Soviet Union.

KARL MORTAR (Karl Mörser). Generic name for the German self-propelled field howitzers, which were the heaviest field equipment to see service in the war. Built in two calibers, 540-mm. and 600-mm., they were mounted on the same tracked carriage. Special equipment enabled long-distance moves over rails or roads. Three of each caliber were built: the 600-mm. weighed 132 tons and was 35 feet 6 inches long. Powered by a 500-horsepower diesel engine, it traveled at a speed of three miles per hour over good ground. It fired a 4,850-pound shell able to penetrate 98½ inches of concrete or 17¾ inches of armor plate.

KASSEL. An industrial city on the Fulda River in modern West Germany, important during the war as a manufacturing center for tanks and aircraft. It was almost completely destroyed by Allied bombing and ground fighting. It was captured by troops of the U.S. 80th Division (THIRD ARMY) on April 4, 1945.

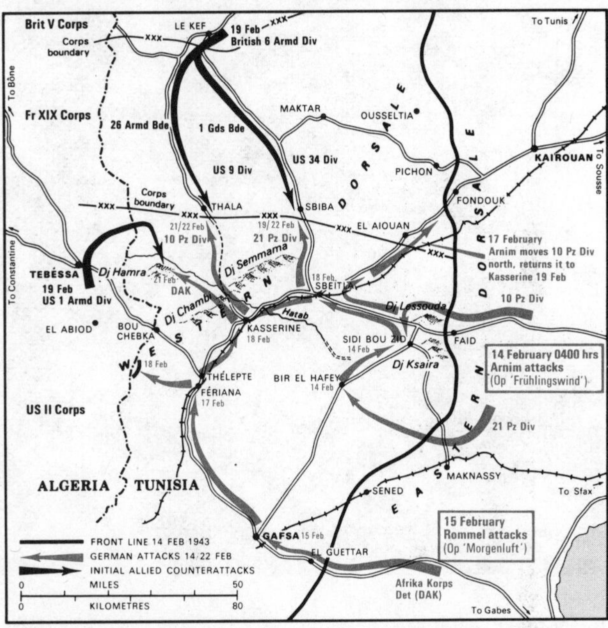

THE KASSERINE PASS was for the Allies a series of crises

KASSERINE PASS. A gap in the Tunisian mountain chain called the Western Dorsal, this pass gave its name to the Axis offensive that opened February 14, 1943, through FAÏD PASS. After pushing the Allies out of SIDI BOU ZID and SBEÏTLA, the Axis attacked Kasserine on February 19 and broke through the next day. Field Marshal Erwin ROMMEL then attacked north toward THALA, but the Allies, after fumbling under the initial offensive, had rallied a strong defense. Unable to penetrate at Thala, Rommel's forces retreated back through Kasserine on February 23. The Allies did not pursue aggressively enough to destroy his force. German casualties numbered 989; 535 Italians were captured. The U.S. II Corps figured its casualties at more than 6,000 (approximately 300 dead, 3,000 wounded, 3,000 missing). *See also* NORTHWEST AFRICA.

KATYN. A forest near Smolensk, USSR, where mass graves containing the corpses of some 4,000 Polish officers and troops were discovered in the spring of 1943. Along with 11,000 others never accounted for, they had surrendered to the Soviets in the fall of 1939 as the remnants of the Polish Army fled from the advancing Germans. Medical examination established that the executions in the Katyn Forest took place in the spring of

Kasserine Pass area

1940, a fact immediately publicized by the German propaganda machine.

The Polish government-in-exile, then headed by General SIKORSKI, asked the Soviet Government to investigate the case and determine the circumstances under which the executions took place. The Soviet response was to break diplomatic relations with Sikorski's government, accusing it of advancing the Nazi cause by helping to spread GOEBBELS's propaganda. Moscow also asserted that the crime was committed by the Germans after they had invaded Russia in the summer of 1941.

The breaking of Soviet-Polish relations was of considerable embarrassment to the governments of the United States and Great Britain, which refused to lend support to Sikorski's request; they felt that the need to maintain good relations with the Soviet Union, then carrying the main burden of war against the common enemy, was of far greater importance. The Katyn massacre initially was among the charges brought up against the principal Nazi war criminals at Nuremberg, but the charge was quietly dropped toward the end of the trials.

KATYUSHA. A Soviet rocket mortar, generally 82-mm. in caliber. The launcher rails for the solid-fuel, fin-stabilized rocket were mounted on tanks, trucks, carts and river vessels as well as on ground mounts. Being area (not precision) weapons, Katyushas were most often constructed in large launcher assemblies of 32 to 48. The range was 6,500 yards. They were first used at SMOLENSK in March 1941. They were called Stalin Organs by the Germans.

KAVIENG. Town on the island of New Ireland in the BISMARCK ARCHIPELAGO, site of an important Japanese air base. Although Kavieng was bombed from the air and bombarded from the sea, it was bypassed by Allied forces and left in isolation until the end of the war.

KAWABE, Masakazu (1886–1965). Older brother of Torashiro KAWABE, Masakazu graduated from the Japanese Military Academy (1907) and the Military War College (1915). In early 1942 Kawabe became chief of staff of the Japanese army in China. In 1943 he assumed command of the army in BURMA. Following a costly and unsuccessful invasion of India, Kawabe was relieved of his command in Burma and appointed commander of Japan's Central Area until he was made commander of Army Air Forces in 1945. General Kawabe commanded the First Army until the demobilization of Japan's military establishment later the same year. Masakazu Kawabe is frequently referred to as Shozo Kawabe in histories of World War II, "Shozo" being another reading of his given name.

KAWABE, Torashiro (1890–1960). Younger brother of Gen. Masakazu KAWABE, Torashiro attended both the Military Academy and the Military War College. He served as a staff officer of the Japanese KWANTUNG ARMY in Manchuria and of the Imperial General Staff in Tokyo. He was chief of staff of the Home Defense Forces from September 1941 until he became Army Vice-Chief of Staff in April 1945. In this capacity Lieutenant General Kawabe headed the 16-man delegation to Manila in August 1945 to discuss details of Japan's surrender and to receive instructions on the demobilization of Japanese military forces from the United States command. After the end of the war Kawabe served as a member of the 12-man commission advising the Japanese Government on armaments.

KAWAGUCHI, Kiyotake (1892–1961). When the U.S. hold on GUADALCANAL appeared to be assured, in late August 1942, Lt. Gen. Harukichi HYAKUTAKE, commander of the Japanese 17th Army at RABAUL, committed Major General Kawaguchi and 3,500 men to help throw the Marines off the island. After running a gauntlet of fire from U.S. ships and planes while in transit to Guadalcanal, he finally landed with a reduced force and was given the primary mission of capturing HENDERSON FIELD, in which he was unsuccessful. After this futile effort Kawaguchi returned to Japan, where he was placed on the reserve list in April 1943.

KEARBY, Neel E. (1911–1944). U.S. Army pilot, a colonel who commanded the 348th Fighter Group, FIFTH AIR FORCE. On October 11, 1943, he led a flight of four fighters to Wewak, New Guinea, and attacked 12 Japanese bombers escorted by 36 fighters. Colonel Kearby shot down six, for which he received the MEDAL OF HONOR. He scored a total of 22 kills before he was killed in action on March 5, 1944.

KEARNY, U.S.S. GLEAVES-class destroyer, commissioned in 1940. While escorting a convoy in the North Atlantic on October 17, 1941 (about a month after President ROOSEVELT issued his order to shoot on sight), and depth-charging the suspected location of a U-boat, *Kearny* was damaged by a torpedo but survived. She later took part in Atlantic convoy duty and in the NORTHWEST AFRICA landings. After further Atlantic convoy operations, she participated in gunfire support operations at ANZIO and in the landing in SOUTHERN FRANCE. *See also* GREER, U.S.S.

KEELHAUL. Code name for one of the operations involving forced repatriation of Russian nationals and émigrés to the USSR at the end of the war. This name, applied to one specific instance, has been popularly used in referring to the entire forced-repatriation program.

KEENAN, Joseph Berry (1888–1954). American lawyer who served in the Justice Department between 1933 and 1939 and gained fame for prosecuting "Machine Gun" Kelly and helping frame the Lindbergh kidnap laws. He was the chief prosecutor in the Tokyo war crimes trials, which in 1946 tried 28 top Japanese, including former Premier Hideki TOJO (*see* INTERNATIONAL MILITARY TRIBUNAL FOR THE FAR EAST).

KEITEL, Wilhelm (1882–1946). German Army officer who from February 1938 until May 1945 was Chief of the High Command of the Armed Forces (*see* OKW). As chief of staff to Adolf HITLER, Keitel seems to have kept his position by frequent use of the words "Jawohl, mein Führer"; he is frequently referred to as a "lackey." One of the generals described him as "Hitler's head clerk." His rank was field marshal.

Keitel came from a middle-class Hanoverian family of officers with an anti-Prussian tradition. He entered the artillery in 1901 and served on the staff of the War Ministry in World War I and afterward. Albert SPEER, who often observed the Keitel-Hitler relationship, thought Keitel hated his own weakness but no longer tried to form his own opinions on strategy and operations, knowing that he would be replaced if he did. There is no evidence that, as one of those closest to Hitler, he ever questioned a decision of the Führer's or encouraged discussion of an issue. Instead, he forbade any criticism or defeatism to be expressed in Hitler's presence, leading Speer to observe that Keitel and others like him were partly to blame for Hitler's belief in his own superhuman qualities. For instance, Speer and General ZEITZLER, Chief of the General Staff, recorded that after the SIXTH ARMY was encircled at STALINGRAD, Zeitzler asked Keitel to support him in urging the Führer to evacuate the pocket. Keitel agreed, but when Zeitzler made the plea Keitel interrupted, "My Führer! Do not leave the Volga!"

Keitel was at Hitler's side for seven years. He took part in the Austrian ANSCHLUSS, the MUNICH Conference, the plans for war, the shaping of the NEW ORDER. He read out the armistice terms to the French in June 1940; he signed the surrender of Germany in Berlin on May 8, 1945. He was imprisoned and tried at NUREMBERG, where in his closing statement he said that he would choose death rather than be entangled again in such horrors. He was found guilty of war crimes and hanged on October 16, 1946.

KELLY, Charles E. (1921–). U.S. Army sergeant (143d Infantry Regiment, 36th Division) who in September 1943 distinguished himself in action around Altavilla, Italy, killing 40 Germans. For his bravery "Commando" Kelly was awarded the MEDAL OF HONOR. Kelly's story, *One Man's War*, appeared in the *Saturday Evening Post* and as a book.

KELLY, Colin P. (1915–1941). Two days after the attack on PEARL HARBOR, Captain Kelly took off from CLARK FIELD, Luzon, to bomb Japanese shipping. He scored a direct hit on a transport—believed at the time to be the battleship HARUNA—but his Air Force B-17 was set ablaze by gunfire from a Zero apparently flown by Saburo SAKAI, who went on to score 64 wartime victories. One member of the B-17 crew was killed, and Kelly ordered the other six to bail out. They survived, but he perished when the plane exploded. Kelly's act of sacrifice was judged worthy of the DISTINGUISHED SER-

VICE CROSS, and he was acclaimed as one of the first American war heroes.

KELLY, Monroe (1886–1956). A 1909 graduate of the U.S. Naval Academy, Kelly earned a reputation as a naval diplomat. In November 1941 he became a rear admiral, serving after Pearl Harbor as chief of staff to the Commander in Chief, U.S. Fleet. Kelly received a DISTINGUISHED SERVICE MEDAL for his work in the occupation of French Morocco. In 1943 he became commander of the New York Naval Shipyard and in 1944 commander of the Third Naval District, with headquarters in New York City. He retired as a vice-admiral.

KEMPEITAI. The Japanese military police organization. The soldiers comprising it were *kempei*.

KEMPF, Werner (1886–1964). German officer who played a prominent part in the motorization of the Army. He commanded a tank brigade and later a tank division in the campaign in Poland in 1939 and subsequently, as a General der Panzertruppen, commanded the Eighth Army.

KEMPKA, Erich (1910–1975). Adolf HITLER's longtime personal chauffeur, an Obersturmbannführer in the SS (*see* SS), who also served as the Führer's transportation officer.

KENNAN, George Frost (1904–). An American diplomat and specialist in Soviet affairs, Kennan entered the foreign service in 1926. In 1929 he was posted to Berlin with the assignment of studying Russia, since officials of the State Department presumed that in the near future the United States would establish diplomatic relations with the Soviets, and in 1933 he accompanied the newly appointed ambassador, William C. BULLITT, to Moscow as his Soviet specialist. He subsequently served in Prague and Berlin (being interned for five months after the United States entered the war) and returned to Moscow in 1944, where he was adviser to Ambassador Averell HARRIMAN. Kennan came to wide public notice after the war for his writings advocating "containment" of Communist power and later as a scholarly writer on Russian affairs and diplomacy generally. He served as ambassador to the Soviet Union for a time in the 1950s.

KENNEDY, Edward (1905–1963). Correspondent for the Associated Press who released the story of the German surrender at REIMS (May 7, 1945) 24 hours before the official time set for the disclosure. Kennedy, a veteran reporter, was "disaccredited" by SHAEF and ordered home.

KENNEDY, John Fitzgerald (1917–1963). Kennedy, a native of Brookline, Mass., was unsuccessful in his attempts to enlist in the U.S. Army in 1941 because of a back injury. He later joined the Navy and was assigned to a motor torpedo boat squadron. He was sent to the South Pacific in 1943 in command of a PT boat (*see* PT). While participating in operations in the SOLOMON ISLANDS on August 2, 1943, the boat was rammed by a Japanese destroyer. Kennedy and the other survivors of the crash were forced to swim for approximately five hours to a small island. Through a series of daring efforts to alert other PT boats in the area by swimming into the straits around the island, and eventually swimming to another island and relaying a message on a coconut to New Zealand forces in the area, Kennedy managed to save his men. Because of injuries sustained in the operation, he was sent to a hospital in the United States in 1943 and did not again see active duty. In 1946 he embarked on a political career which culminated in his election in 1960 as President of the United States. He was assassinated on November 22, 1963.

KENNEDY, Joseph Patrick (1888–1969). American businessman who served as ambassador to Britain from 1937 to early 1941. Although he admired the way the British fought on after the fall of France, he was skeptical of their chances against Germany. On returning to the United States in 1941, he testified against the LEND-LEASE bill but, though strongly opposed to American involvement in the war, did argue, somewhat paradoxically, for aid to Britain. Kennedy's support of the isolationist position militated against his being offered any significant post during the war. He was the father of President John F. KENNEDY.

KENNEY, George C. (1889–1977). When the Japanese attacked Pearl Harbor, Kenney was in charge of the Air Materiel Division of the U.S. Army Air Forces at Wright Field, Dayton, Ohio. As he had told the commanding general of the AAF, Gen. Henry H. ARNOLD, sometime earlier, he would be unwilling to "stand around counting airplanes coming out of factories" in the event of war, so Arnold now appointed him commanding general of the Fourth Air Force, with headquarters at San Francisco, which was responsible for air defense, reconnaissance and training along the Pacific coast.

Kenney next went to Australia, where in August 1942 he replaced Gen. George H. BRETT as Gen. Douglas MACARTHUR's chief air officer. He then set up the FIFTH AIR FORCE and later incorporated this organization and the THIRTEENTH AIR FORCE into the Far East Air Forces, which he headed for the remainder of the war. His first wartime combat operation was the neutralization of the Japanese base at RABAUL, New Britain; his last was the bombing of targets on Kyushu with B-24s based on Okinawa.

He was one of the great innovators of the Pacific war. For example, he employed parachute fragmentation bombs, which he had helped develop during the 1930s, against Japanese airfields, and he encouraged Paul "Pappy" GUNN in his modifying of aircraft and devising of tactics for low-altitude attacks on Japanese shipping.

An outstandingly successful commander, Kenney combined an aggressive, often cocky manner with a down-to-earth, pragmatic approach to problems. Not the least of his accomplishments was his ability to assert his independence while at the same time maintaining a harmonious relationship with General MacArthur. And he became legendary for his devotion to his "boys."

KENNEY COCKTAIL. A FIRE BOMB used by Lt. Gen. George C. KENNEY's Allied airmen in the Southwest Pacific. These "cocktails" were adaptations of incendiary and GP (general-purpose) bombs made by filling an

M-47 100-pound bomb with white phosphorus. Detonation on a hard surface resulted in a burst with a radius of 150 feet.

KENT, DUKE OF (Prince George) (1902–1942). At the beginning of the war the duke gave up the post of Governor General of Australia, to which he had just been appointed, in favor of active war work. As chief welfare officer of the RAF Home Command, he visited RAF installations, and it was on a flight to bases in Iceland that he was killed when his plane crashed (August 25, 1942). While in North America during the previous year, he had developed a strong friendship with President ROOSEVELT, who became godfather of his youngest child.

KERAMA RETTO. Group of eight large and some smaller islands to the west of OKINAWA which were seized by the U.S. 77th Infantry Division on March 26–27, 1945, as a prelude to the major landing on Okinawa on April 1. They proved to be invaluable as an advance logistics base as the Okinawa operation wore on.

KERCH PENINSULA. This easternmost appendage of the CRIMEA was a major arena of Soviet counterattack. As the German operations around SEVASTOPOL continued to mount, the Red Army landed in strength first in the vicinity of the city of Kerch (December 26, 1941) and two days later at Feodosia. By January 18, 1942, the German Eleventh Army, supported by two Rumanian mountain brigades, had cleared Feodosia and established a defensive line across the neck of the peninsula at Parpach. For five months the front remained relatively static. On May 8 the Germans began Operation Bustard to clear the peninsula. Ten days later the task was completed with the capture of 170,000 Red Army soldiers.

KEREN. Situated on the edge of the Asmara plateau in Eritrea, Keren is separated from the valley by a formidable wall of hills to a height of 5,800 feet. Access is through the Dongolaas gorge, by road and light railway. In 1941 the Italians under General Frusci held the town for almost eight weeks against British attacks, but in doing so they suffered 3,000 casualties and thereafter their resistance in Eritrea was dispirited.

KERR, Sir Archibald Clark (1st Baron Inverchapel) (1882–1951). British diplomat, ambassador to China (1937–42) and then to the Soviet Union. He had an extremely good relationship with CHIANG KAI-SHEK and developed a similar one with STALIN. It has been suggested that his efforts helped maintain Anglo-Soviet relations despite Stalin's mistrust of the British, and that his understanding of Stalin made it possible for him to convey many of Stalin's attitudes to the Allies. His advice was an important factor in the meeting of the Big Three at TEHERAN in 1943. After the war he was appointed ambassador to the United States.

KERSTEN, Felix (1898–1960). A masseur who brought relief to Heinrich HIMMLER's stomach cramps and who attained a considerable degree of psychological influence over the Reichsführer SS during the war years. Two years older than Himmler, Kersten had (according to his own account) led a very varied life. Born in Estonia, he had at first trained for agriculture before serving in the Finnish Army during the war against Russia in 1919, after which he had taken Finnish citizenship. Discovering his gift for massage while in an army hospital, he had trained under the celebrated Chinese masseur, Dr. Ko, in Berlin, and taken over his lucrative practice in 1925. His patients were mostly distinguished persons, and he established treatment centers in Holland as well as in Germany. In 1937 he married a young German girl. His first treatment of Himmler took place in March 1939, and he was so successful in bringing immediate, though temporary, relief where all others had failed that the Reichsführer confined him to Germany (by controlling his visa) and virtually commandeered his services.

By his own account, Kersten set out to influence Himmler, especially in relation to the Jews, obtaining whatever individual releases he could, and eventually allying himself with Walter SCHELLENBERG in order to press Himmler to undertake secret peace negotiations. In September 1943 Kersten was able to move his family to Sweden, though he continued to spend much time in Germany. In 1953 Kersten became a Swedish citizen. His memoirs, in diary form, first published in German in 1953 and in English in 1956, are a primary source of information about Himmler, though they should be read guardedly.

KESSEL, DER (The Caldron). Germans' name for the STALINGRAD pocket in which they were trapped after November 23, 1942. The term was also used generically for such pockets.

KESSELRING, Albert (1885–1960). The German commander identified with the skillful and tenacious defense of ITALY, Kesselring began his Army career as an artillery officer and in World War I served on divisional and corps staffs. After routine assignments in the postwar years—a period in which he acquired a reputation as an administrative expert—he went to the still-illicit air force in 1933, serving as head of administration for Erhard MILCH, the state secretary of the Air Ministry. In 1936, following the death of Gen. Walther Wever, Kesselring was appointed to succeed him as Chief of Staff of the LUFTWAFFE. In this command position, Kesselring's relationship with Milch was strained, and in 1937 he was transferred to an operational command. In September 1939 he commanded Air Fleet I in the Polish operations, and it was his planes that bombed Warsaw. In January 1940 he took over Air Fleet 2, which he commanded in the Low Countries and France; this was the force that attacked ROTTERDAM and bombed the Allied armies at DUNKIRK. On June 30, 1940, after the German victory over FRANCE, Kesselring was raised to the rank of field marshal. Air Fleet 2 was then in the thick of the Battle of BRITAIN, in which it lost almost a thousand planes.

In June–December 1941 Kesselring's air fleet participated in the campaign in the Soviet Union on the central front. When the air fleet was transferred to the Mediterranean area in December 1941, Kesselring acquired the additional duties of Commander in Chief South (OB Süd). Here the side of his personality that had earned him the nickname "Smiling Albert" proved valuable; his charm enabled him to develop close rela-

Field Marshal Kesselring (left) with U.S. Maj. Gen. Maxwell D. Taylor

tionships with Italian leaders, including Benito Mussolini himself. In October 1942, shortly before the Allied landings in Northwest Africa, Adolf Hitler gave Kesselring command of all German armed forces in the Mediterranean, except for the army in North Africa (Panzerarmee Afrika), and this force came under his purview when the fighting moved into Tunisia.

After the Allied invasion of Italy, Kesselring showed extraordinary resourcefulness in conducting the long, slow retreat up the peninsula that kept the Allies from quick victory. The terrain was highly favorable to the defense, to be sure, but the field marshal showed ingenuity and tenacity in making use of it. In October 1944 he was injured and was out of action for several months, and in March 1945 he was appointed Commander in Chief West in succession to Field Marshal Gerd von Rundstedt. He surrendered the southern portion of the divided German forces on May 7, 1945.

Kesselring was sentenced to death in 1947 as a war criminal for involvement in the shooting of 320 Italian prisoners (the so-called Ardeatine Caves massacre), but the sentence was commuted to life imprisonment and he was released in October 1952. He was subsequently president of the Stahlhelm, a veterans' organization.

KEYES, Geoffrey C. T. (1917–1941). Son of Admiral of the Fleet Sir Roger Keyes, Geoffrey Keyes was the British Commando officer who led a raid on the German Afrika Korps headquarters at Beda Littoria, near the Cyrenaican coast, at midnight on November 17, 1941, with the object of killing Gen. Erwin Rommel. The party, cut to a handful after a difficult landing from two submarines, assaulted a two-story house that was not actually Rommel's quarters but was used by the supply staff. Four men entered the structure and killed 30 German officers in classic Commando style before being beaten off with heavy losses, Keyes taking a fatal machine pistol burst. Though Keyes, a lieutenant colonel at 24, won a posthumous Victoria Cross for his daring, the raid would have been a failure in any case, owing to faulty intelligence work in Cairo; at the time Rommel was not even in the area but was in Athens on a return trip to Africa from Rome.

KEYES, Roger John Brownlow, Baron (1872–1945). Britain's first director of the Combined Operations Command, 1940–41—a role for which he was particularly suited by virtue of his familiarity with the technicalities of amphibious warfare, derived from his experiences at the Dardanelles, Ostend and Zeebrugge in World War I. His patriotism and personal courage were an inspiration to all who knew him, but critics have held that his enthusiasm sometimes blinded him to grim practicalities.

KHARKOV. Located in the eastern Ukraine, and the fourth largest city in the Soviet Union at the outbreak of World War II, Kharkov was captured by the Germans in May 1942. Nine months later, following the German defeat at Stalingrad, the Russians retook the city. After the war the Battle of Kharkov occasioned some bitter denunciations of Joseph Stalin by Nikita Khrushchev, then the leader of the Soviet Government. In his secret report to the Twentieth Party Congress in 1956, Khrushchev blamed Stalin for the Kharkov defeat, claiming that Stalin's "no retreat" orders led to the needless encirclement and capture of thousands of Russian soldiers.

KHOZEDUB, Ivan N. (1920–). Soviet air officer (major), the leading Red Air Force ace of the war, with 62 kills.

KHRULEV, Andrei V. (1892–1962). Khrulev, whose highest rank was General of the Army, was chief of supply when Stalin in August 1941 appointed him the first chief of rear services of the Red Army. He was also appointed Minister of Railways and held both posts until the end of the war.

KHRUSHCHEV, Nikita S. (1894–1971). The man who would one day rule the Soviet Union was made a full member of the Politburo in March 1939. During the war years he helped supervise the annexation of eastern Poland to the USSR and was responsible for the evacuation of industrial resources from the path of the German advance. He served on the military councils of both the Western and Southwest Fronts. At the time of the Kharkov disaster (May 12, 1942) he was Marshal Timoshenko's political adviser. He would later—during his denunciation of Stalin (February 1956)—try to absolve himself of any responsibility for the debacle. Khrushchev was appointed lieutenant general in 1943, and following the liberation of Kiev in November of that year he resumed the duties of first secretary of the Central Committee of the Ukrainian Communist Party.

He is credited with the suppression of the Ukrainian nationalist guerrillas and the return of the region to firm Soviet control.

KI (Kitai). An abbreviation (*Kitai* means "aircraft") used as a prefix to aircraft model numbers by the Japanese Army, beginning with the Type 93 heavy bomber. Army aircraft were identified by their Ki number (with suffixes to indicate modifications of the basic design), by a type number based on the year of adoption according to the Japanese calendar (e.g., Type 97=year 2597=A.D. 1937) and, in many cases, by a name. For the sake of simplicity, the Allies assigned code names to most known Japanese aircraft types. The entries that follow are not a comprehensive list of all Ki numbers, but include aircraft that seem significant or that saw extensive war service. Manufacturer, type number, name and Allied code name are given where they apply.

KI 21. Mitsubishi Type 97 twin-engine bomber (Allied code name, Sally). It served from early in the China war until mid-1944 in a major combat role, although its inadequate defensive armament made it vulnerable to strong fighter attack. The Ki 21 Model 2 was armed with one 12.7-mm. and five 7.7-mm. machine guns, and could carry 2,000 pounds of bombs.

KI 27. Nakajima Type 97 (Allied code names, Abdul, Nate), Japan's first monoplane fighter with a low wing and the first to have an enclosed cockpit. A maneuverable single-seat aircraft, it was a contemporary of the A5M Navy fighter (*see* A5M), which it resembled in general terms. The Ki 27 fighter-bomber was used against Soviet fighters in prewar border fighting and took part in early Pacific operations, being finally replaced by the KI 43. Capable of a maximum speed of 286 miles per hour, Nate was armed with two 7.7-mm. machine guns.

Nakajima Ki 27

KI 30. Mitsubishi Type 97 single-engine bomber (Allied code name, Ann), a large airplane with an internal bomb bay. It was used principally in China and the Philippines in the initial Southwest Pacific operations of 1941–42; 700 were built by Mitsubishi and Tachikawa. The Ki 30 carried a 660-pound bomb load and was armed with two 7.7-mm. machine guns.

KI 32. Kawasaki Type 98 single-engine bomber (Allied code name, Mary), produced in 1938–40 and used, for the most part, in China. About 800 were built, but they were withdrawn from service shortly after the outbreak of the war. It was armed with three 7.7-mm. machine guns and carried 660 pounds of bombs.

KI 36. Kawasaki Type 98 (Allied code name, Ida) short-range reconnaissance plane, a single-engine monoplane with fixed landing gear. It served, for the most part, in China. Some were later adapted to the KAMIKAZE role. A dual-control trainer version of this design was designated Ki 55, and identified by the same Allied code name. It had two 7.7-mm. machine guns and a bomb load of 330 pounds.

KI 43. Nakajima *Hayabusa* (Falcon) (Allied code name, Oscar), a fighter similar to the A6M Zero in general appearance and frequently confused with it by Allied observers (*see* A6M). It served throughout the Pacific war and was the most widely produced Japanese Army fighter of the war; 5,878 were produced in various versions. The Ki 43 was armed with two 12.7-mm. machine guns. Its 1,130-horsepower radial engine gave it a top speed of 320 miles per hour.

KI 44. Nakajima *Shoki* (Demon) (Allied code name, Tojo), a powerful radial-engine fighter whose design stressed speed and rate of climb rather than maneuverability. This high-performance aircraft was mostly used for defense against B-29s (*see* B-29). It carried four 12.7-mm. machine guns. Powered by a 1,520-horsepower radial engine, it had a very good maximum speed of 376 miles per hour.

KI 45. Kawasaki *Toryu* (Dragon Slayer) (Allied code name, Nick), a twin-engine fighter first produced in 1941 and continued throughout the Pacific war. Originally designed as a long-range escort and night fighter, it was used as a bomber interceptor and strike fighter. Beginning in 1944, some Ki 45s had two .50-caliber machine guns mounted in an upward-firing, remote-controlled SCHRÄGE MUSIK installation, and were used as night fighters in defense of Japan. The Ki 45 Model 1 was armed with a 20-mm. shell gun and two 12.7-mm. machine guns; it could also carry 1,100 pounds of bombs.

KI 46. Mitsubishi Type 100 *Shinshitei* (headquarters reconnaissance plane) (Allied code name, Dinah). Aerodynamically, the Ki 46 was one of the finest machines produced by any of the combatants in World War II.

Mitsubishi Ki 46

Designed as a fast, long-range scout plane, it acquired modifications that improved its speed and range still further; it depended on its speed (up to 375 miles per hour) for protection. Some were converted to heavy fighters to attack B-17s and B-29s (*see* B-17; B-29). The Dinah saw general service throughout the Pacific war; 1,738 were produced.

KI 48. Kawasaki Type 99 twin-engine bomber (Allied code name, Lily). Produced from 1940 to 1944, it saw general service in the Pacific but was considered only mediocre. The Ki 48 Model 1 was armed with four 7.7-mm. machine guns and 660 pounds of bombs.

KI 49. Nakajima Type 100 *Donryu* (Dragon Swallower) (Allied code name, Helen), a twin-engine bomber developed to replace the KI 21, with improved speed and armament. It was operational principally from 1942 through 1944, and was used primarily for transport and antisubmarine duties, especially after the superior Mitsubishi KI 67 *Hiryu* (Peggy) entered the operational inventory. The Ki 49 was armed with one 20-mm. shell gun and five 7.7-mm. machine guns, and carried a 1,600-pound bomb load.

KI 51. Mitsubishi Type 99 *Guntei* (Army reconnaissance) (Allied code name, Sonia) reconnaissance aircraft and dive-bomber. This maneuverable aircraft, designed for ground attack, was used in China and the Pacific, and remained in production into 1945. The Ki 51 had a single flexible 7.7-mm. machine gun and two 12.7-mm. or 7.7-mm. fixed forward-firing guns, along with a 450-pound bomb capacity.

KI 54. Tachikawa Type 1 advanced trainer (Allied code name, Hickory). As was the case with comparable twin-engine U.S. trainers, a number of versions were produced for various types of specialized training. Some Ki 54s were used for KAMIKAZE attacks, and toward the end of the war some were modified as 5-to-9-seat transports. Approximately 1,200 were produced.

KI 55. A trainer version (Allied code name, Ida) of the KI 36.

KI 56. Tachikawa Type 1 transport and cargo plane (Allied code name, Thalia), a Japanese modification of the Lockheed Super Electra twin-engine passenger-plane design. The Ki 56 was used, along with an earlier unmodified Super Electra copy produced as the Type *Ro*, as a troop transport and heavy-cargo carrier.

KI 57. Mitsubishi Type 100 twin-engine transport (Allied code name, Topsy), a design derivative of the KI 21 bomber. The standard crew was four men, and the plane could carry up to 11 passengers. It had a maximum speed of 292 miles per hour.

KI 61. Kawasaki *Hien* (Flying Swallow) (Allied code name, Tony). With a liquid-cooled engine and "razorback" cockpit canopy, this plane superficially resembled the MESSERSCHMITT ME 109F or 109G, and was thought at first to be a Japanese version of it. It appeared in combat during the spring of 1944, and operated in the Southwest Pacific and over the Japanese home islands. A radial-engine version of this design was designated the KI 100. The Ki 61 had two 20-mm. guns and two 12.7-mm. machine guns, and could carry a 450-pound bomb load.

KI 67. Mitsubishi Type 4 *Hiryu* (Flying Dragon) twin-engine bomber (Allied code name, Peggy). A streamlined, maneuverable plane, it was used during 1944–45 as a bomber and torpedo aircraft. Although only in full operational service for the last 10 months of the war, it was by far the best Japanese bomber. Forty-four copies of a heavy-fighter version were produced to attack B-29s over Japan (*see* B-29), but its lack of supercharging prevented it from reaching the bombers at high altitudes. Powered by two 2,000-horsepower radial engines, it had a maximum speed of 334 miles per hour. With a crew varying from six to eight, it could carry up to 1,760 pounds of bombs or one 1,760-pound torpedo.

KI 76. Nihon Kokusai Type 3 liaison plane (Allied code name, Stella), a single-engine, high-wing light plane used for command and utility work. A few were fitted with tail hooks and depth-charge racks and operated from the Army ship *Akitsu Maru* for convoy escort. The standard Stella had one defensive 7.7-mm. machine gun.

KI 84. Nakajima Type 4 *Hayate* (Gale) (Allied code name, Frank), a highly effective fighter introduced in 1944. It was sometimes employed as a dive-bomber, in which role it was capable of carrying two under-wing bombs of up to 550 pounds each. The *Hayate* had twin 20-mm. guns and two 12.7-mm. machine guns. It operated to good effect in the PHILIPPINES and off OKINAWA, and was especially well regarded by its opponents. The *Hayate* later served as a bomber-interceptor over Japan. A modification with some back armor for the pilot was designated Ki 113, while another version with wooden framing was designated KI 106.

KI 86. Tachikawa Type 4 (Allied code name, Cypress) primary trainer, a small, highly maneuverable Japanese version of the German Bucker Bu 131 Jungmann. It was widely used through the Pacific war. A variant was produced for the Navy as the K9W-1 (*see* K9W-1).

KI 100. A radial-engine version (no Allied code name) of the Kawasaki KI 61. Because of problems in the production of the Ki 61's liquid-cooled engine, a radial power plant was installed in the Ki 61 airframe. The resulting fighter was highly satisfactory and was used in defense of Japan during 1944–45. Earlier Ki 100s had the "razorback" cockpit canopy of the Ki 61, while later models had a more typical raised canopy for all-around vision. Like the Ki 61, the Ki 100 was armed with two 20-mm. shell guns and two 12.7-mm. machine guns.

KI 102. Kawasaki heavy attack fighter (Allied code name, Randy), developed late in the war. The standard production model was the Ki 102b, but only a few of these were made. The plane was heavily armed, carrying one 57-mm. cannon, two 20-mm. cannon and a 12.7-mm. machine gun; it could also accommodate a bomb load of 1,100 pounds. A twin-engine aircraft, the Ki 102 had a top speed of 360 miles per hour.

KI 105. Japanese Army designation for a twin-engine modification of the Kokusai Ku 7 transport glider. Like the Ku 7, it received the Allied code name Buzzard.

KI 106. A production variant of the Ki 84 fighter (no Allied code name), armed with two 20-mm. shell guns and two 12.7-mm. machine guns.

KIDD, Isaac Campbell (1884–1941). A 1906 graduate of the U.S. Naval Academy, Kidd became a rear admiral in 1940. On December 7, 1941, he had command of Battleship Division Number One of the Pacific Fleet. In the PEARL HARBOR attack, Kidd took his position on the bridge of the U.S.S. ARIZONA and remained there until killed in an explosion. He was the first American naval officer of flag rank to die in combat. He received the MEDAL OF HONOR posthumously for "conspicuous devotion to duty, extraordinary courage and complete disregard for his own life."

KIDO, Koichi (1889–1977). Japanese Emperor HIROHITO's Lord Keeper of the Privy Seal from June 1940. In the latter part of the war Kido was prominent among those urging acceptance of Allied peace terms. In December 1945 he was arrested by the occupation authorities. Sentenced to life imprisonment for war crimes, Kido was paroled in 1956.

KIEL. German Baltic port, the site of a state-owned shipyard which built diesel engines, submarines and, late in the war, bow sections for long-range submarines. A nearby satellite plant fabricated sections of submarines and built air-driven torpedoes. The latter facility emerged undamaged from the war. The main shipyard, however, underwent 36 attacks by British and American bombers. According to the U.S. Strategic Bombing Survey, RAF BOMBER COMMAND inflicted the heaviest damage in two April 1945 raids. On the night of April 9–10, 59.5 tons of bombs fell on Kiel, scoring 49 hits on factory buildings and sinking several ships, including the pocket battleship ADMIRAL SCHEER. The April 13–14 attack totaled 119.5 tons of bombs and resulted in 124 hits, five of them on the power plant, which had been put temporarily out of action by the earlier bombing. Until the power plant was demolished, Allied bombs had not interfered with scheduled production, the wartime managers claimed, although some workers had remained at home to repair damage caused by bombs that fell in residential areas.

KIEV. Capital of the Ukraine and scene of one of the most spectacular Soviet defeats of the war. In September 1941, in the face of German encirclement, Joseph STALIN rejected the advice of his generals to withdraw from Kiev and ordered instead a defense of the city. Subsequent authorization by Stalin to abandon Kiev did not prevent the death or capture of several hundred thousand Russian soldiers. However, the significance of the Battle of Kiev extended beyond the magnitude of Germany's success in the Ukraine. Historians agree that the time spent on the Kiev operation was a contributing factor in the failure of the Germans to reach the gates of Moscow before the winter set in.

KIKUSUI. Japanese cover name for the general air attack against OKINAWA, heavily dependent upon KAMIKAZE tactics. *Kikusui* literally means "floating chrysanthemum." The characters making up this word were part of the crest of a 15th-century hero who supported the Emperor in a civil war against heavy odds.

KILINDINI. Deepwater port which served the city of Mombasa in the Kenya protectorate on the east coast of Africa. Both the British Royal Navy and the Royal Air Force had bases there, which helped provide logistic support for the British EAST AFRICA campaign against the Italians in 1941.

KILROY. A name popularized by American soldiers who scribbled "Kilroy was here" on walls and objects wherever they traveled. Accounts of the term's origin conflict. One has it that a member of the Air Transport Command first used the name in 1943 on a notice posted for his friend Sgt. Francis J. Kilroy and that other men in the ATC imitated the sign as a joke. Another story says that Kilroy was a shipyard inspector who signed his work for the benefit of his supervisor.

KIMMEL, Husband Edward (1882–1968). U.S. Navy officer, a graduate of the Naval Academy in 1904. Kimmel was executive officer of the battleship *New York* in World War I, became a rear admiral in 1937 and was appointed Commander of Cruisers, Battle Force, U.S. Fleet, in 1939. As an admiral, he became Commander in Chief of the United States Fleet (renamed the Pacific Fleet), based at PEARL HARBOR, on February 1, 1941, and was thus in command at the time of the Japanese attack on December 7, 1941. As an inevitable result of the success of the attack, Kimmel, who had enjoyed a reputation as a highly capable officer, received much of the blame for the unreadiness and poor response of the U.S. naval forces there.

After the initial attacks on Pearl Harbor, WAKE ISLAND and GUAM, Kimmel moved to strengthen the bombed bases. In late December he dispatched a relieving force to Wake, which had been captured by the Japanese, but the force was recalled by Adm. W. S. PYE, who temporarily replaced Kimmel in command. On December 31 Adm. Chester W. NIMITZ was appointed Commander in Chief of the Pacific Fleet. Kimmel, accused of dereliction of duty by a board of inquiry, retired in 1942; he was, however, cleared of the charge in 1946 by a Congressional inquiry, which found many causes for the tragedy at Pearl Harbor. Kimmel published his account of the events leading up to Pearl Harbor in his book *Admiral Kimmel's Story* in 1955.

KING, Edward Postell, Jr. (1884–1958). U.S. Army major general forced to surrender at BATAAN in 1942. He survived captivity as Gen. Jonathan WAINWRIGHT's cellmate.

KING, Ernest Joseph (1878–1956). The chief American naval figure of the war, Admiral King played a decisive strategic role. Following PEARL HARBOR, he was appointed Commander in Chief of the United States Fleet, and in March 1942 he was given the additional post of Chief of Naval Operations. In December 1944 he was promoted to the new five-star rank, fleet admi-

Admiral King (in front seat) tours Saipan with Marine Lt. Gen. Holland M. Smith (standing) and Adm. Chester W. Nimitz

ral. By the time of Japan's surrender, King commanded the largest fleet ever assembled, surpassing the combined naval strength of all other nations in the world. His armada numbered more than 92,000 ships of all types—including 8 battleships, 48 cruisers, 27 aircraft carriers, 110 escort carriers, 352 destroyers and 203 submarines; 23,880 operating aircraft; 335,471 naval officers and 2,926,252 sailors; and 37,664 Marine officers commanding 443,647 enlisted personnel.

A 1901 graduate of the U.S. Naval Academy, King was awarded a Distinguished Service Medal and later a gold star for his submarine salvage operations during the 1920s. In 1927 he qualified as a naval aviator, and after several aviation commands became assistant chief of the Bureau of Aeronautics in 1928. He commanded the naval air station at Hampton Roads, Va., and the carrier *Lexington*, and after a Naval War College course became chief of the Bureau of Aeronautics in 1933. Subsequently he commanded an aircraft base force, an aircraft scouting force and an aircraft battle force. In February 1941 he became commander of the Atlantic Fleet.

King's heavy responsibility in the dual administrative roles of Commander in Chief of the U.S. Fleet and Chief of Naval Operations in World War II demanded a smoothly functioning chain of command. His philosophy was never to assume tasks or decisions he could delegate elsewhere; the supreme commander should remain free to make decisions for which he alone had responsibility. Underequipped, King faced a two-front war. This forced him to expedite the rebuilding of the fleet and meanwhile to adopt a defensive posture in both oceans, at least initially. In the Atlantic, King's primary responsibilities were to keep communications with Great Britain open and to guarantee the security of the Western Hemisphere. In the Pacific, the strategy was to hold key positions, prevent further offensives by the Japanese and take the offensive as soon as possible. King had responsibility, furthermore, for coordinating joint U.S. force operations and joint operations with the Allies. World War II, like no other conflict, demanded cooperative strategic planning between services and allies, and as a member of the Combined Chiefs of Staff, King made no small contribution in this field.

In November 1942, with Operation Torch in Northwest Africa, the Americans took the offensive sooner than expected. During the next year the Atlantic submarine war turned in the Allies' favor. The Navy provided fire support and transportation for major amphibious landings in Sicily, Italy and Southern France, and for the invasion of Normandy. By this time the Navy's role in Europe had become a supportive one, the bulk of the war having shifted to land and air. The Pacific war, however, was primarily the Navy's. Originally submarines comprised the only American offensive force in the Pacific, but with American victories in the Coral Sea and at Midway the winds changed. As the U.S. fleet grew in the Pacific and Americans began to stack up amphibious victories, King's emphasis upon carriers as opposed to battleships paid dividends. The Americans took the offensive and eventually carried the war to the home islands of Japan.

King was sometimes criticized as being battleship oriented. Far from a traditionalist, however, King presided over great innovations in naval warfare. His prewar experience prepared him well for the new kind of sea war, with its emphasis on air power and the aircraft carrier. Naval air provided not only a new striking force but also air cover for another operation perfected during King's command, the amphibious invasion. And the complex nature of amphibious warfare forced a new emphasis on logistics.

Besides his naval contribution to the war, King also made a diplomatic one—although his personal style, stern and abrupt, was not in the traditional diplomatic mode. Since he directed naval strategy, King attended the great wartime conferences of leaders as an adviser to President ROOSEVELT. He was present at the drafting of the ATLANTIC CHARTER in August 1941 and at the CASABLANCA, CAIRO, TEHERAN, YALTA and POTSDAM CONFERENCES. During these strategic meetings King consistently urged delegates to hasten the war against Germany so that he could move adequate forces to the Pacific, where he thought the United States had a special responsibility.

King received many decorations and much praise for his performance in World War II. He relished the pomp and regalia of his position, and enjoyed his reputation as an exacting taskmaster. He told of a boatswain's mate who, when asked how he got along with his captain, replied: "The Captain, he's a good man to a good man. Him and me, we gets along fine." King retired in 1945. **D.C.**

KING, William Lyon Mackenzie (1874–1950). Canadian Liberal Party leader who served as Prime Minister not only during the war but for some years before and after (1921–30, except for temporary periods, and 1935–48). In the early days of the war King and President Franklin D. ROOSEVELT worked for cooperation between their two countries on defense questions (*see* OGDENSBURG AGREEMENT, 1940). King was also the official host for the two QUEBEC CONFERENCES of 1943 and 1944. In his prosecution of the war he encountered perhaps his most severe problem in connection with conscription. French Canadians in particular were opposed to it, though a draft act for home service was passed in 1942. The Prime Minister managed to delay the issue until 1944, when losses in the European fighting demanded an increasing number of replacements and enabling legislation was enacted.

KINGFISHER. Name applied to the U.S. Navy OS2U floatplane (*see* OS2U). The Royal Navy called it the Kingfisher I.

KING GEORGE V, H.M.S. Royal Navy battleship of 35,000 tons, completed late in 1940 by Vickers Armstrong and armed with ten 14-inch and sixteen 5.25-inch guns, smaller weapons and three aircraft. *King George V* joined the Home Fleet, becoming flagship; she served in various North Sea and Atlantic operations, including those leading to the destruction of the BISMARCK. In May 1943 she was transferred to the Mediterranean for the invasion of SICILY and subsequent operations. In 1944 *King George V* was moved to the Pacific, serving for a while as British Pacific Fleet flagship. She participated as cover for the British aircraft carrier strikes on Palembang and the Sakishima Gunto, and in July 1945 served in U.S. Adm. William F. HALSEY's bombardment force against the Japanese mainland—the last occasion a Royal Navy battleship was to fire its main armament in action.

KINGPIN. Code name used to designate the French general Henri GIRAUD when he was transported from France to Gibraltar and North Africa in 1942.

KING'S AFRICAN RIFLES. The regimental name for African battalions raised in the British colonies of Kenya, Uganda, Tanganyika, British Somaliland and Nyasaland. The number of these battalions (five at the outbreak of war) was quickly increased in 1939 and 1940. The battalions were formed from men of many tribes but all from the same territory; each had British officers and some British NCOs. No Africans were commissioned. KAR battalions participated in the destruction of Italy's African empire in 1940–41 and in the forcible occupation of MADAGASCAR in 1942, where African soldiers from British Africa fought French colonial African troops. In 1943 the 11th East African Division was formed for service in BURMA. In all, one battalion went from British Somaliland, two battalions from Kenya, three from Tanganyika and four each from Uganda and Nyasaland, together with African soldiers of the Northern Rhodesian Regiment (two battalions) and the Rhodesian African Rifles (one battalion); all participated in the Burma campaign from 1943 to 1945.

Mention should also be made of numerous African labor units recruited in every British African possession; these men, in the thousands, served the Allied war effort in a variety of ways, chiefly in the Middle East. Those who served outside their own territories were volunteers, but conscription was often applied for local military needs within home territories.

KING'S CROSS. A key road junction in the TOBRUK perimeter (Libya), about five miles south of the town itself. It was taken by Gen. Erwin ROMMEL's forces (Rommel himself was on the scene) on June 20, 1942.

KING TIGER TANK. *See* TANK.

KINKAID, Thomas Cassin (1888–1972). U.S. Navy officer, a graduate of the Naval Academy in 1908. Kinkaid served in World War I and was the technical adviser to the American delegation at the Geneva Disarmament Conference in 1932. As a rear admiral, he figured in several Pacific naval engagements in 1942, including the CORAL SEA, MIDWAY, SANTA CRUZ and GUADALCANAL. In January 1943 Kinkaid took over the Aleutian campaign as Commander North Pacific Fleet, and in November of that year became commander of the SEVENTH FLEET under Gen. Douglas MACARTHUR. As a vice-admiral, he participated in the American victory at LEYTE GULF and covered General MacArthur's campaigns on LEYTE and Luzon. After the war Kinkaid became Commander Eastern Sea Frontier (1946), retiring in 1950. No American naval commander in World War II was more highly respected in his own service.

KINZEL, Eberhard (1897–1945). German Army General Staff officer who served in intelligence as chief of the Foreign Armies East section, which dealt principally with military intelligence concerning the RED ARMY. In April 1942 he was replaced by Reinhard GEHLEN and subsequently served as an army group chief of staff.

KIPPENBERGER, Sir Howard Karl (1897–1957). New Zealand officer who saw action in NORTH AFRICA, Greece and CRETE as a battalion and brigade commander. In 1944 he was given command of the 2d New Zealand Division in Italy. Later in that year he was severely wounded, losing both legs. Afterward he was official war historian to the New Zealand forces.

KIRISHIMA. Japanese KONGO-class battleship, sunk in a gunnery duel with U.S.S. WASHINGTON in the night battle of GUADALCANAL, November 14–15, 1942. This was the only instance in the Pacific war of a battleship's being sunk by another battleship in a gunnery duel.

KIRK, Alan Goodrich (1888–1963). A 1909 graduate of the U.S. Naval Academy, Kirk saw service as naval attaché in London in 1939–41. In March 1941 he became director of the Office of Naval Intelligence, and in October he was given command of a division of ships and soon became a rear admiral. After PEARL HARBOR some critics tried, on the whole unsuccessfully, to blame Kirk's Office of Naval Intelligence for the Navy's lack of preparedness. Kirk returned to London as naval attaché in March 1942, but in 1943 was given command of the Atlantic Fleet's Amphibious Force. His amphibious task force unloaded men and supplies during the invasion of SICILY with only 90 casualties, and Kirk received the LEGION OF MERIT for his conduct of the operation. Later that year he acquired command of another task force, this one training for the INVASION of Normandy. At Normandy his ships came so close to the shore that they sometimes fired by visual aim, and captains in his command almost grounded their vessels. In October 1944 Kirk took command of the U.S. naval forces in France. He was promoted to vice-admiral in September 1944, and he retired with the rank of admiral. In 1949–52 he was U.S. ambassador to the Soviet Union.

KIRK, Norman T. (1888–1960). U.S. Army orthopedic surgeon credited with treating at least one-third of the American major amputees in World War I. His book *Amputation: Operative Techniques* (1924) became a standard textbook in the field. Promoted to major general in 1943, Kirk served as the Surgeon General between 1943 and 1947.

KIRKENES. Port city of northern NORWAY, near the Russian frontier. Not long after the German invasion, Allied leaders considered placing a battalion in Kirkenes to assist the Norwegians in their effort to hold border territory.

KISHINEV. In the area of this city, the capital of Bessarabia, the Soviet Second and Third Ukrainian Fronts trapped the bulk of the German Sixth Army (a successor to the SIXTH ARMY lost at Stalingrad), together with Rumanian and other German elements, in an offensive begun on August 20, 1944.

KISKA. Island in the western Aleutians occupied by the Japanese on June 7, 1942, the same day the Japanese took ATTU. After the loss of Attu in May 1943, the Japanese decided that Kiska, to the east of Attu, could no longer be held. Japanese submarines began evacuating sick, wounded and civilians early in June, and on July 29 the last of the garrison, some 5,000 troops, was evacuated by surface vessels. Allied (American and Canadian) forces landed on Kiska on August 15, 1943, finding the island deserted.

KITA, Nagao (1895–). Appointed Japanese consul general in Honolulu in 1940 after holding a number of diplomatic posts, Kita was responsible for setting up intelligence networks in Hawaii and funneling reports, especially those of Takeo YOSHIKAWA concerning PEARL HARBOR, on to Tokyo. These reports aided the Japanese Navy considerably in planning the raid on Pearl Harbor. Kita was arrested on December 7, 1941, along with other members of the Japanese consulate, but was repatriated to Japan in 1942 in the general exchange of diplomats.

KLEIST, Paul Ludwig Ewald von (1881–1954). Member of one of the oldest landowning familes in Prussia, Kleist in World War I was an officer of the German General Staff, serving with the VII Corps. Adolf HITLER dismissed Kleist along with six other Army generals and six air generals in his 1938 purge of senior military leaders; Kleist's dismissal was partly due to his quarrel with Hitler over the dismissal of General von FRITSCH, but he was reinstated at the outbreak of World War II.

Serving under General von RUNDSTEDT on the Western Front, Kleist played a key role in the invasion of FRANCE. With an army of tanks and motorized troops under his command (Panzer Group Kleist), he broke through the Allied lines, crossed the Meuse River and rolled across northern France (though much of the credit for this thrusting advance must be given to one of Kleist's corps commanders, Gen. Heinz GUDERIAN).

Having demonstrated his skill as a panzer commander on the Western Front, Kleist later assumed command of the German First Panzer Group in Yugoslavia; operating in conjunction with the LUFTWAFFE, Kleist's tanks captured Belgrade on April 12, 1941. That summer, in the invasion of the Soviet Union, he crossed the Dnieper River on a 75-mile-wide front, assisting in the pincers movement ordered by Rundstedt which captured KIEV in September. He was subsequently at the siege of SEVASTOPOL and, despite heavy losses, his army captured ROSTOV on the Don on November 22, 1941. At Rostov, Marshal Semën TIMOSHENKO was able to halt the German advance. Forced to abandon Rostov, Kleist's troops fell back along the Sea of Azov, finally reestablishing their lines at TAGANROG.

The following summer Kleist's Army Group A recaptured Rostov, took MAIKOP to the south and encroached upon the Grozny oil fields. But the Soviet stand at STALINGRAD in the winter of 1942–43 halted the German offensive for good. When the Soviet armies took the offensive after Stalingrad, Kleist had to retreat once more. The subsequent German reverses in the Ukraine infuriated Hitler, who relieved Kleist and MANSTEIN, his commanders in the south, replacing them with MODEL and SCHÖRNER on March 30, 1944.

After the German armies had fallen back toward Berlin, the British Army eventually captured Kleist in 1945. He was subsequently extradited to Yugoslavia, where in 1948 he was sentenced to 15 years in prison. The following year the Yugoslavs turned him over to the Russians, who sent him to prison for war crimes against the Soviet people. He died in a Soviet prison on November 5, 1954.

KLOPPER, Hendrik Balzazer (1902–). South African Army officer, commander of the 3d South African Infantry Brigade, 1942; commander, 2d South African Division, 1942 (May–June). He surrendered the forces under his command at Tobruk in June 1942 to Gen. Erwin Rommel's soldiers—the climax of Rommel's career. Some 33,000 Allied combatants were taken prisoner, including almost a third of all South Africa's forces in the field. The suddenness of the collapse at Tobruk was a particular shock to Britain; Winston Churchill felt that it was one of the heaviest blows of the war. In October 1943 Klopper escaped from his German captors and made his way back to South Africa, where he subsequently held domestic commands. His highest wartime rank was major general. In the years after the war he rose to the rank of general and served as Commandant-General of Union Defence Forces.

KLUGE, Hans Günther von (1882–1944). Born in Posen of an old German military family, Kluge was commissioned in the artillery in 1901. He served in various staff and command positions during the First World War, and in the interwar years rose rapidly through the ranks of the service. In 1939 and 1940 he led the Fourth Army with extraordinary success in Poland and France. He was appointed to command Army Group Center, facing Moscow, during the Russian campaign in December 1941. After fighting some severe defensive battles, Kluge replaced Field Marshal Gerd von Rundstedt as Commander in Chief West, headquartered in Paris, in July 1944. Facing the rapidly growing power of the Allied armies in Normandy and realizing that the destruction of the German forces was inevitable when Adolf Hitler refused to send reinforcements or to order a retreat, Kluge became increasingly pessimistic about the outcome of the war. He was relieved of his command on August 17, 1944, after Hitler suspected him of involvement in the July 1944 plot against the Führer's life.

Kluge had shared the motives of the conspirators and had been involved in earlier discussions with Army officers to overthrow Hitler, but he had disapproved of assassination and had no prior knowledge of the July attempt to murder Hitler. Despondent over the failure of his forces to counter the Allied onslaught and knowing that Hitler suspected him of complicity in the July conspiracy, Kluge committed suicide en route to Berlin in or around Metz, in northeastern France, on August 19, 1944. He held the rank of field marshal.

KLUNKER. A sarcastic U.S. Army Air Forces nickname for the P-400 fighter on Guadalcanal in 1942–43 (*see* P-400).

KNATCHBULL-HUGESSEN, Sir Hughe (1886–1971). British ambassador in Ankara from 1939 to 1944, Sir Hughe became involved in the notorious Cicero spy episode. In 1943 the ambassador's Albanian valet offered to sell the Germans (represented by the secret service agent C. L. Moyzisch, an attaché at the German embassy) photographs of top-secret documents in the ambassador's safe; his price was £20,000 (about $100,000). Ankara was a key diplomatic post owing to the crucial position of neutral Turkey and therefore received many classified documents, both political and military. The documents photographed revealed not only the progress of Anglo-Turkish relations during the period when Turkey was under pressure to enter the war on the Allied side, but also the contents of the discussion at Cairo in November 1943 among Roosevelt, Churchill and Chiang Kai-shek, and those at the Teheran Conference. The Germans were highly suspicious of this wealth of information, feeling the whole matter too good to be true and the documents a plant. When Moyzisch's secretary deserted to the Allies in 1944, Cicero's activities ceased. He had received in all some £300,000 ($1.5 million), most of which, however, was paid in forged notes. Knatchbull-Hugessen served subsequently as ambassador in Brussels until his retirement in 1947.

KNEE MORTAR. Japanese Model 10 (1921) 50-mm. grenade launcher. This mortar was 20 inches long, weighed 5½ pounds and had a range of 65 to 175 yards, depending on the projectile being used. Designed for platoon use, its main utilization was firing flares. It was called the knee mortar by Americans in the mistaken belief that the curved baseplate was meant to rest on the knee, rather than the ground, for firing.

KNICKEBEIN. Code word used by the Luftwaffe for navigational apparatus employed in 1940 in bombing England. It produced a split radio beam along which the pilot flew until he intersected another beam; this intersection marked the target. Knickebein was put into use in late August 1940, but British intelligence anticipated it and in a few days countermeasures were at work jamming the beams. *See also* NAVIGATION AIDS.

KNIGHTSBRIDGE. One of the fortified positions, or "boxes," comprising the Gazala Line (Cyrenaica). It was held by the British Guards until Gen. Erwin Rommel's tank victory of June 13, 1942.

KNOBELSDORFF, Otto von (1886–1966). German Army officer, a General der Panzertruppen from 1942, who commanded panzer corps in 1942 and 1943 and in 1944 was commander of the First Army in the west.

KNOX, (William) Franklin (1874–1944). Col. Frank Knox, as he was known, was publisher of the Chicago *Daily News;* the "colonel" came from his World War I service in France in the field artillery. In 1936 he was the Republican candidate for Vice-President, running with Alf Landon. In 1940 President Roosevelt, attempting to broaden his administration in the dark days following the fall of France, appointed Knox as Secretary of the Navy; at the same time Henry L. Stimson, another prominent Republican, was named Secretary of War. Knox was attacked by some of his fellow Republicans, but he said that he was "an American first and a Republican afterward." Knox was a considerable success as Secretary of the Navy, and after the United States entered the war he presided over the growth of the fleet into the largest the world had ever seen. Samuel Eliot Morison says of him that he "quickly acquired a grasp of naval business and became one of the best secretaries the Navy ever had."

KNUDSEN, William Signius (1879–1948). Christened Signius Wilhelm Poul Knudsen, William S. Knudsen was born in Denmark. After coming to America, he rose steadily through the ranks of the automobile industry, first with Ford and then with Chevrolet. In 1937 he became president of General Motors, and in 1940 President ROOSEVELT put him in charge of production for the National Defense Advisory Commission. On January 7, 1941, FDR created by executive order the OFFICE OF PRODUCTION MANAGEMENT and appointed Knudsen its director general for production. His co-director was Sidney HILLMAN, president of the Amalgamated Clothing Workers, who was in charge of labor.

When the WAR PRODUCTION BOARD was established in 1942, with a single head—Donald M. Nelson—Knudsen was thus superseded; however, he was then drafted by the War Department as its director of production with the rank of lieutenant general. In that capacity he traveled throughout the country settling labor disputes and speeding production, particularly in the aircraft industry. For his successful efforts he received the DISTINGUISHED SERVICE MEDAL on May 25, 1944, from Secretary of War Henry L. STIMSON, who called him "the master troubleshooter on the biggest job the world has ever seen." On Knudsen's retirement from this post on May 29, 1945, he received the Oak Leaf Cluster.

KOCH, Erich (1896– ?). An old Nazi adherent who was gauleiter (district leader) for East Prussia in 1930–45, Koch was in 1941 made also Reich Commissioner for the Ukraine. He remained a trusted member of Adolf HITLER's hierarchy of officials and voiced faithfully the party line about Russia. In a speech in Kiev in March 1943 he said: "We are a master race, which must remember that the lowliest German worker is racially and biologically a thousand times more valuable than the population here." He was extradited to Poland in 1950, and has not been heard of since. *See also* EAST (plan).

KOCH, Ilse (1906–1967). Wife of SS Col. Karl Koch, commandant of the BUCHENWALD concentration camp from its founding in 1937, the year the two were married. Daughter of a foreman in Dresden, Ilse had been a secretary in Berlin prior to becoming Koch's mistress. Both she and Koch were notorious for their sadistic tendencies, which found expression in the torture of prisoners, and for criminality. By 1943 the SS themselves had to intervene, conducting investigations lasting two years, not into mass murder at the camp, but into bad discipline and theft at the Nazi Party's expense. Koch was sentenced to death and executed, but Ilse (known as the Red Witch of Buchenwald) was acquitted. However, she was indicted by the Americans in 1947, and her trial, widely reported in the press, produced sensational evidence, including allegations that she had ordered lampshades to be made from the skin of male prisoners with interesting tattoos. She admitted promiscuous behavior with SS officers and even with prisoners. Since she was pregnant, she received a life sentence and was spared execution; the sentence was subsequently commuted to four years. In 1950 she was brought before a German court, charged with 45 murders and 135 attempted murders and given a life sentence once more. She committed suicide while in jail.

KÖCHLING, Friedrich (1893–1970). German Army officer, commander of the LXXXI Corps on the Western Front in the latter stages of the war.

KOELTZ, Louis (1884–1970). A French Army specialist in intelligence during World War I and after. In 1939 he was chief of staff of the French Eighth Army but soon after became Deputy Chief of Staff for Operations at French General Headquarters, where he served during the 1940 campaign. After the armistice he became Director of Armistice Services, then commander of the Algiers Military District (1941). Following the Allied landings in late 1942, General Koeltz led French troops against the Germans in TUNISIA. He later served as a senior liaison officer to the Allies.

KOENIG, Marie-Pierre (1898–1970). Koenig volunteered for the French Army in 1917, then following the end of World War I entered the Foreign Legion and fought in North Africa. He was with the legion in NORWAY in the spring of 1940. After the Franco-German armistice he joined General DE GAULLE. In 1942 his Free French brigade's stubborn defense of BIR HACHEIM (North Africa) against General ROMMEL put FREE FRANCE into battle prominence for the first time. Subsequently he commanded the French Forces of the Interior (*see* FRENCH RESISTANCE) inside occupied France. General Koenig served briefly in the mid-1950s as Minister of National Defense.

KOGA, Hidemasa (1919–1945). A career Japanese Army officer and member of the Imperial Guards Division, Major Koga participated in the attempted coup d'état of August 14–15, 1945. Rebel soldiers seized the imperial palace and attempted to prevent the surrender of Japan. Koga was Hideki TOJO's son-in-law. Following the failure of the coup, Koga killed himself in the office of his superior, Gen. Takeshi Mori, who had been slain during the mutiny.

KOGA, Mineichi (1885–1944). A graduate of the Japanese Naval Academy, Koga rose to command of Japan's COMBINED FLEET in April 1943 following the death of Adm. Isoroku YAMAMOTO. Before achieving this command, Koga had served as Vice-Chief of the Naval General Staff and commander of the Yokosuka Naval Station. He also participated in the Japanese assault on HONG KONG. During his command of the Combined Fleet for 11 months (late April 1943–March 31, 1944) Koga continually hoped to lure the Americans into one big knockout battle that would turn the war in Japan's favor, through his Plan Z. The Americans, who had captured a copy of Plan Z on Hollandia, waged a war of attrition against Japanese air power in the Pacific islands and so whittled away Koga's air strength that he was forced to withdraw his forces to the Philippines. He died during the withdrawal when his plane was lost in a fog at sea while headed for Davao, Japan's principal settlement in the southern Philippines. Soemu TOYODA succeeded him as commander of the Combined Fleet. Koga's highest rank was vice-admiral.

KOHIMA. A town in the Indian province of Manipur, close to the Burmese border, the scene of a notable siege during the Japanese invasion of India in the spring of 1944. Kohima lies at an elevation of 5,000 feet astride the only all-weather road on the Burma-India frontier. The town was defended by 500 men of the 4th Battalion of the Royal West Kent Regiment and some

Indian Army troops. The attackers were virtually the whole Japanese 31st Division. The siege began on April 5 and was lifted on the 20th, after the defenders had suffered nearly 300 casualties. *See also* BURMA.

KOISO, Kuniaki (1880–1950). A graduate of the Japanese Military Academy and of the War College, Koiso held numerous important Army posts in Manchuria, China and Korea. He was involved in General Staff work and served as both Vice-Minister and Minister of War in the 1930s. Following his retirement from military service, Koiso served as Governor General of Korea from 1942 to 1944. Joining with Adm. Mitsumasa YONAI and others in 1944 to oust Hideki TOJO from the government, Koiso became Tojo's successor as Prime Minister (October 1944). He resigned in April 1945 as the war in Europe was coming to an end. He was convicted by the INTERNATIONAL MILITARY TRIBUNAL FOR THE FAR EAST of crimes against peace and sentenced to life imprisonment. He died in prison.

KOKODA TRAIL. Route over the OWEN STANLEY MOUNTAINS (New Guinea), rising as high as 8,500 feet. It connected PORT MORESBY with BUNA, on the north coast, by way of Kokoda. Kokoda itself was taken from the Japanese by the Australian 25th Brigade on November 2, 1942.

KOKURA. This city on the northern coast of Kyushu (now part of Kitakyushu), Japan, was the scene of unquestionably the greatest deliverance in history. On August 9, 1945, it was the primary target for the dropping of the second ATOMIC BOMB, but smoke and haze obscured the city and after three runs the crew of the bomb-carrying B-29 Superfortress turned away and headed for NAGASAKI. *See also* HIROSHIMA.

KOLBERG. Near this port on the Pomeranian coast, the Soviet First Belorussian Front broke through to the Baltic on March 4, 1945. The town, ordered by Adolf HITLER to be made into a fortress, held out until March 18—the last German pocket on the Baltic coast between the Polish Corridor and Stettin Bay.

KOLLER, Karl (1898–1951). German air officer, the last Chief of Staff of the LUFTWAFFE, 1944–45. An able officer, Koller was on the staff of Air Fleet 3 (General SPERRLE) during the Battle of BRITAIN and later was the fleet's chief of operations. In 1942 he became chief of staff of Air Fleet 2, being promoted to the rank of General der Flieger. Prior to being appointed Luftwaffe Chief of Staff, he served as director of operations. He became disgusted with his chief, Reichsmarschall Hermann GÖRING, because of Göring's increasing neglect of his duties as the war developed more and more unfavorably for Germany, but he agreed to accept the post of Chief of Staff in succession to Gen. Werner KREIPE. In the last days of the war he flew from Berlin to BERCHTESGADEN to inform Göring of Hitler's decision to die in the capital.

KOLOMBANGARA, BATTLE OF. A week after the Battle of KULA GULF, July 1943, U.S. Rear Adm. Walden AINSWORTH was ordered to the area to meet an expected Japanese destroyer reinforcement run. In the evening of the 12th Ainsworth departed Tulagi with Task Force 18: light cruisers HONOLULU and ST. LOUIS, New Zealand light cruiser *Leander* and 10 destroyers organized into two destroyer squadrons. Shortly after midnight Ainsworth's force was north of Kula Gulf. A patrolling plane reported the approach of a Japanese force. Ainsworth formed his ships in column and increased speed to meet the enemy. At 0100 RADAR contact was made.

The Japanese force consisted of light cruiser JINTSU and five destroyers, under Rear Adm. Shunji Izaki, running interference for four other destroyers loaded with troops to be landed at Vila, on NEW GEORGIA, near the southern end of Kula Gulf.

Ainsworth turned his cruisers to unmask their 6-inch guns, and at 0109 he ordered his destroyers to launch a torpedo attack. He expected his radar-guided attack to surprise the Japanese. Izaki, however, had a new radar-wave detector which had long since warned him of the Americans' presence, and had planned a surprise of his own.

At 0108 the Japanese ships began firing torpedoes. Within minutes a general action exploded. *Jintsu* was shattered by heavy radar-controlled cruiser gunfire, plus two destroyer torpedoes. Izaki and most of the Japanese cruiser's crew were lost. A Japanese torpedo damaged *Leander,* and matters became generally confused as four of the Japanese destroyers retired northward to reload torpedoes. The fifth destroyer remained in the area where *Jintsu* had been stricken.

Ainsworth moved north as well, with his two undamaged cruisers and five destroyers. His other five destroyers—Squadron 21—were unable to find any enemy ships on their radars, and failed to receive Ainsworth's radio order to search to the north. Assuming that the rest of the American force had retired back down the SLOT toward Tulagi, they set their course in that direction.

Ainsworth was unaware of this. He headed north, expecting further oppostion. At 0156 his radar detected ships over 11 miles ahead. Not knowing that the five destroyers of Squadron 21 had left the area, he was unsure whether this contact was friendly or enemy. Holding fire, he tried to take a count of his force by radio. Minutes passed; at 0203 Ainsworth ordered star shells fired to light up the unknown ships. The contacts were seen on the radar screens to be turning away. Deciding that they were Japanese, Ainsworth ordered his ships to turn to the right and bring their broadsides to bear. The Japanese destroyer commander, who had been watching the Americans approach, salvoed his four ships' torpedoes just as Task Force 18 began its turn.

The Japanese destroyers, their torpedoes in the water, quickly withdrew. Just as the American ships were ready to fire, *St. Louis* was hit by a torpedo. *Honolulu* dodged several others, but was hit in the bow and then—by a dud—in the stern. Destroyer *Gwin* was mortally hit and set ablaze by another LONG LANCE torpedo.

St. Louis and *Honolulu* limped home, following already damaged *Leander. Gwin* lingered until daylight before being scuttled as beyond salvage. Ainsworth's retiring ships were attacked at daybreak by land-based Japanese planes, but by this time American fighters were overhead and the raid was driven off.

The Japanese destroyer transports in the meantime

had turned and headed for the far side of Kolombangara, where they quickly landed their troops. As in the Kula Gulf action of the preceding week, the Japanese had succeeded in their reinforcement mission. They had also put three Allied cruisers out of action and sunk one destroyer, at a cost of one old light cruiser.

KOLOMBANGARA ISLAND. Japanese forces landed on this island in the central SOLOMONS despite a costly naval battle on July 12–13, 1943 (also called the second battle of KULA GULF). They were bypassed but not isolated after Allied forces landed on VELLA LAVELLA to the northwest, and were evacuated during the 10 days ending October 3. Subsequently the 11th Defense Battalion, U.S. Marine Corps, was stationed on Kolombangara to protect the harbor at Kula Gulf, from which troops on NEW GEORGIA were supplied.

KOLTSO. Soviet attack on the Germans at STALINGRAD. *See also* RING.

KOMANDORSKI ISLANDS, BATTLE OF THE. In late March 1943 a small U.S. task group under Rear Adm. Charles H. MCMORRIS, consisting of heavy cruiser SALT LAKE CITY, light cruiser *Richmond* and four destroyers, had been operating west of ATTU, in the Aleutians, and south of the Komandorskis to forestall expected Japanese efforts to reinforce their garrison on Attu. Before sunrise on March 26, McMorris's force made RADAR contact with a number of ships, at first believed to be Japanese cargo ships or transports with a light escort. As the contacts became visible to the eye, they proved to be two heavy cruisers, two light cruisers, four destroyers and two converted merchant cruisers under the command of Vice-Adm. Boshiro HOSOGAYA. At 0840 a gunnery duel began at long range, with most of the Japanese attention going to *Salt Lake City.* McMorris, outgunned by the heavier batteries of the Japanese force, turned away at 25 knots while the opposing cruisers exchanged salvos.

In a seesaw long-range running duel, both the Japanese heavy cruiser *Nachi* and *Salt Lake City* were damaged. Japanese torpedoes were fired without effect; American destroyers laid smoke screens, which helped. *Salt Lake City* received a final 8-inch hit at 1103. Her after engine room flooded; then her after boilers lost power. Sea water contaminated her fuel lines and doused the remaining oil burners. The cruiser went dead in the water. Though her after turrets were still firing, most of her ammunition was gone.

McMorris ordered three of his destroyers to attack with torpedoes. At this point Hosogaya, low on fuel and unaware of *Salt Lake City*'s predicament, mistook some long-range shell splashes for bomb hits. Thinking his force under American air attack, he turned and began to withdraw. The Japanese cargo ships—the two auxiliary cruisers referred to—retired, unable to deliver their loads. Hosogaya's supply mission had failed in its purpose, and the admiral was soon relieved for his failure to press home the attack.

KOMURA, Keizo (1896–). A graduate of the Japanese Naval Academy in 1917 and of the Naval War College in 1929, Rear Admiral Komura participated in many of the notable naval engagements of the Pacific war. As commanding officer of the cruiser CHIKUMA he took part in the PEARL HARBOR attack, the carrier task force's subsequent operation in the Indian Ocean, the Battle of MIDWAY and the Battle of SANTA CRUZ, in the last of which his ship was damaged. From December 1942 to June 1943 he was commanding officer of the battleship FUSO and from June to December of that year of the battleship MUSASHI. He was promoted to rear admiral in November 1943 and subsequently became chief of staff of the First Task Force, in which capacity he was involved in the Battle of the PHILIPPINE SEA in June 1944. In October 1944 he took command of the 1st Carrier Division, heading it in the battle for LEYTE GULF. In January 1945 he was transferred to command of the 2d Destroyer Squadron, taking part in the last sortie of the giant battleship YAMATO. In May 1945 he became chief of staff of Yokosuka naval base on Tokyo Bay.

KONDO, Nobutake (1886–1953). A career Japanese naval officer, Kondo was Vice-Chief of the Naval General Staff before the war. As commander of Japan's Second Fleet during the first two years of the war, Admiral Kondo had overall command of many operations against the Allied powers. Forces under his command carried out the invasions of the PHILIPPINES, Malaya and JAVA. He provided the main support forces for the attempted invasion of MIDWAY. Later, Kondo was active in the SOLOMONS, taking part in the Battles of SANTA CRUZ and GUADALCANAL. He was appointed a member of the Supreme War Council in May 1945.

KONEV, Ivan S. (1897–1973). After service with the Czarist Army in World War I, Konev joined the Red Army and the Communist Party in 1918. During the Russian Civil War he served as a political commissar. In the interwar years he completed his military education and rose to command of a division.

At the time of the German invasion, Konev was the acting commander of the Transcaucasian Military District. He was recalled to Moscow in the fall of 1941 and given command of an army. During the Soviet offensive around Moscow in December 1941, Konev commanded the Kalinin Front (army group) in the decisive struggle for the northern flank. By the beginning of 1942 his command had forced the invaders back over 100 miles.

Konev came to prominence during the great Soviet offensives of 1943–45, holding the command of the Second and First Ukrainian Fronts. As a Marshal of the Soviet Union, Konev led the million men of the First Ukrainian Front in the climactic battle for BERLIN.

Konev's reputation as a conductor of Soviet offensive operations is challenged only by Marshal ZHUKOV's. At Moscow and KURSK, in Poland, and in East Prussia and Berlin, he demonstrated great capability in handling masses of infantry in the attack. Following the war Konev held a number of key political and military posts, including commander of the Warsaw Pact forces and commander of the Soviet forces in Germany.

KONGO. Class of Japanese battleships, displacing over 31,000 tons, with eight 14-inch guns. Built to a British design shortly before World War I as battle cruisers, these four ships (*Kongo,* HARUNA, HIEI, KIRISHIMA) were extensively modernized during the 1930s. Their machinery revamped and protection increased, they were reclassified as fast battleships, with a speed slightly over 30 knots. All four ships saw extensive war service. *Kirishima* and *Hiei* were lost in the SOLOMONS in November 1942, *Kongo* was sunk in November 1944 off Formosa by a submarine and *Haruna* succumbed to carrier-plane attack in the Inland Sea late in July 1945. Before their loss *Kongo* and *Haruna* had had their antiaircraft armament extensively increased and had been equipped with RADAR.

KÖNIGSBERG. In January 1945 German forces in East Prussia fell back into Königsberg (now Kaliningrad, USSR), where they were invested by the Third Belorussian Front. The city held out until April 9, when Gen. Otto LASCH, the commander, surrendered. When the Red Army entered the city, it became, in the words of the British historian Albert Seaton, "the scene of the most fearful barbarity and atrocity."

KON OPERATION. On May 9, 1944, the Japanese withdrew their southeastern strategic main line of resistance to the western tip of NEW GUINEA, leaving BIAK Island, in Geelvink Bay, as a position on a strategic outpost line of resistance. As such, Biak could expect no significant reinforcements. Meanwhile, the Japanese Navy was speeding preparations for the A Operation (*see* A Go), envisaged as a final showdown with the U.S. Pacific Fleet. A Go, for which the Japanese had issued an alert order to the COMBINED FLEET on May 3, was expected to take place in the general vicinity of the Palau Islands, although the Japanese did not discount the possibility that the naval battle might occur off the Mariana Islands or in the region of Geelvink Bay. To provide land-based air support to the Combined Fleet during A Go, the Japanese Naval Air Service began sending planes to western New Guinea (including Biak), the Marianas, the Carolines and the Palaus. On May 20, just a week before the Allied landing on Biak, the striking force of the Combined Fleet, based at Tawitawi in the Sulu Archipelago in the Philippines, was alerted to sally forth for A Go at a moment's notice. By this time the Japanese had concluded that the next major Allied advance in the Pacific would be directed against the Mariana Islands, and they were quite surprised when the Biak Island landing took place first.

The Japanese Navy thereupon decided that the fleet would be at a marked disadvantage if, during A Go, it had to deal with Allied aircraft from Biak fields. Accordingly, the Japanese moved at least half the fleet's land-based air strength in the Central Pacific to bases in western New Guinea, the western Carolines and the Halmaheras. Next, the Navy prevailed upon the Japanese Army to cooperate in an effort to send major reinforcements to Biak, starting with the shipment of the 2d Amphibious Brigade. For this purpose the Japanese Navy broke up the A Go fleet concentration at Tawitawi. The first effort to reinforce Biak began on May 30, but the Japanese called off the attempt on June 3 because the transports and combat vessels had been sighted and shadowed by Allied aircraft and submarines. A second Kon Operation began on June 7, this time involving the transfer of two battalions of the 219th Infantry, 35th Division, from Sorong in western New Guinea to Biak. Allied aircraft struck the Japanese convoy, which turned back after cutting loose some towed troop barges. The upshot was that perhaps 100 Japanese troops reached Biak.

Despite learning that the main carrier striking force of the U.S. Pacific Fleet had begun moving westward from the Marshall Islands—thus presaging the A Go Operation—the Japanese Navy initiated a third Kon Operation on June 10, this one including a naval force that could have overwhelmed American naval strength in the Biak region. On June 13, before the third Kon had actually developed, the Japanese Navy called off the attempt and assembled all available naval strength in the western Pacific for A Go. What followed was the great naval engagement known on the Allied side as the Battle of the PHILIPPINE SEA.

The Japanese Navy had counted heavily on land-based air support for A Go, but as a result of Kon movements only 20 percent of the Navy's land-based air strength in the Central Pacific was available for fleet support during A Go. Furthermore, preoccupation with Kon undoubtedly delayed the deployment of the Japanese Navy for A Go and put an additional strain on men and ships. The effects of the Kon maneuvering on A Go are difficult to measure, but it cannot be doubted that for the Japanese the effects were adverse.

A footnote to the maneuvering of major Japanese naval units—both air and surface—during Kon is the fact that from about May 30 to June 25, 1944, the Japanese also undertook to reinforce Biak by troop barges. Making short hops from western New Guinea and NOEMFOOR Island, the barges, traveling under cover of darkness, did manage to land approximately 1,200 troops on Biak. **R.R.S.**

KONOYE, Fumimaro, Prince (1891–1945). Born into the prestigious Japanese Fujiwara clan, Konoye was educated at the Peers' School and the First Higher School. He entered Tokyo Imperial University but soon transferred to Kyoto Imperial University, which had a freer intellectual atmosphere. At Kyoto he came under the influence of Dr. Hajime Kawakami, then one of Japan's leading socialists. In 1914 he translated Oscar Wilde's *The Soul of Man Under Socialism,* publishing it in the student magazine *Shinshisho* (New Current of Thought), which resulted in the banning of the periodical. Konoye graduated from the Kyoto University Law School in 1917 and was given a job in the Home Ministry in spite of his leftist leanings. He had already become a member of the House of Peers in 1916. He worked for passage of a universal male suffrage law and served as secretary to Kimmochi Saionji during the Paris peace conference in 1919. He became president of the House of Peers in 1933, a position his father had held many years previously.

Konoye was seen as the ideal Prime Minister in the late 1930s, as a man who could bring about the cooperation of the various factions of society (political, military and bureaucratic) whose mutual hostility so divided Japan. Between 1937 and 1941 Konoye served three times as Prime Minister and once as Vice-Prime Minister in the Hiranuma cabinet. But he was unable to control the military or reach an agreement with the United States which would prevent war. He remained politically inactive throughout much of the war. In 1945 he began to promote efforts to achieve peace. When he learned that he might be placed on trial for "war crimes" in late 1945, Konoye committed suicide by taking poison.

KONSTANTINOV. Code name used in Soviet military transmissions for Marshal Georgi ZHUKOV.

KORIZIS, Alexander (1885–1941). When Korizis became Premier of Greece on January 29, 1941, he assumed the leadership of a country involved in a war with both Italy and Germany. Korizis was neither a politician nor a soldier like his predecessor, Joannes METAXAS, who had died in office, and was unable to halt the bloodshed. Depressed over the suffering which war had brought to Greece, Korizis committed suicide on April 18, 1941.

KORSUN. A provincial town in the southwestern Ukraine, where elements of six German divisions were encircled in January 1944. The decision to effect a breakout was made after a long and costly debate at OKW (*see* OKW). Though 30,000 German soldiers escaped from the Cherkassy Pocket, as it became known, the German Army in the southern Ukraine suffered a significant tactical defeat.

KORTEN, Günther (1898–1944). German air officer, Chief of Staff of the LUFTWAFFE from August 25, 1943, to his death on July 22, 1944. A former staff officer under Erhard MILCH, state secretary of the Air Ministry, he was commander of Air Fleet 1 at the time of his appointment to succeed Gen. Hans JESCHONNEK, who had committed suicide. Korten had increasing difficulties with Hermann GÖRING, the Commander in Chief of the Luftwaffe, and declared his intention of resigning as Chief of Staff. However, he was fatally wounded in the July 20, 1944, attempt on Adolf HITLER's life.

KOS. Aegean island occupied by British forces on September 13, 1943, after the Italian surrender, and used as an air base—the only Allied air base in the Aegean. On October 3 the Germans invaded Kos, completing the seizure the following day.

KOSCIUSKO DIVISION. A Russian-trained division of Polish forces, drawn from those Polish citizens in the Soviet Union who did not leave for Iran and the Middle East with Wladyslaw ANDERS. The Kosciusko Division first appeared in the summer of 1943, and in its first engagement fought bravely and with heavy casualties. In 1944 it accompanied the Red Army into Poland.

KOSYGIN, Aleksei Nikolaevich (1904–). Trained as an engineer, Kosygin joined the Communist Party in 1927. His rapid advance began in 1938 during the great purge under Joseph STALIN, when he was named Commissar of Textile Industries. In 1940 he became vice-chairman of the Council of People's Commissars, with special responsibility for all consumer goods industries. A year later he was named Premier of the Russian Federated Soviet Socialist Republic and remained in that post throughout the war. He subsequently became Premier of the USSR.

KOTA BHARU. Located on the east coast of Malaya just south of the Malayan–Thai border, Kota Bharu and its British-occupied airfield was one of four locations chosen as targets for the first Japanese attacks of World War II on the Western powers. About 1 A.M. Malayan time, December 8, 1941, an amphibious force belonging to the 18th Division, Japanese 25th Army, under command of Lt. Gen. Tomoyuki YAMASHITA, the "Lion of Manchuria," began its assault on the British. This strike, against defenses established by the 8th Indian Infantry Brigade, 9th Indian Division, III Indian Corps, commanded by Brig. B. W. Key, was a success in spite of British artillery fire and attacks by Australian HUDSON aircraft against the Japanese transports and landing craft. After an ineffectual counterattack by Key, a rumor that the Kota Bharu airfield was under attack led to its abandonment, and the Japanese thrust south to SINGAPORE had begun in earnest.

KOTELNIKOVO. From this town about 90 miles southwest of STALINGRAD, General von MANSTEIN launched his unsuccessful attempt to relieve the German SIXTH ARMY in the Stalingrad pocket, December 12, 1942. Kotelnikovo itself was retaken by Red Army forces on December 29.

KOVPAK, Sidor A. (1887–1967). Soviet PARTISAN commander operating in the Ukraine. In 1943 he led a long-range raid into Galicia and in 1944 another into Poland, the western Ukraine and western Belorussia. In 1943 he was promoted to the rank of major general.

KOZHEDUB, I. N. (1920–). The leading Soviet fighter ace, with 62 victories. The list that he headed contained the names of two women—Lt. Lily Litvak (killed in action, 1943), who downed seven planes, and Lt. Katya Budanova, who destroyed six enemy planes in aerial combat.

KRA ISTHMUS. The neck of land in the south of Thailand, on which two Japanese divisions landed on December 8, 1941, beginning the drive to SINGAPORE.

KRAMER, Alwyn D. (1903–). U.S. naval officer (a lieutenant commander in 1941) with the Office of Naval Intelligence. Kramer was in charge of translating and disseminating the Japanese code intercepts (*see* MAGIC), including the final message delivered on the morning of the PEARL HARBOR attack. A Japanese-language expert, he was a precise and meticulous person, well suited for his specialty.

KRAMER, Josef (1906–1945). After joining the SS in 1932 (*see* SS), Kramer entered the CONCENTRATION CAMP service in 1934, rising in 1940 to become Rudolf HOESS's deputy at AUSCHWITZ, where in 1944 he supervised the extermination of some 300,000 Jews from Hungary. He was also for a short while commandant of the Natzweiler camp. He became commandant of BELSEN in December 1944, and the worst period of that camp's history began when it became the uncontrolled dumping ground for tens of thousands of dying prisoners evacuated from camps overrun by the Russian advance. Kramer, the so-called Beast of Belsen, was, like Hoess, a heartless bureaucrat rather than a sadist;

he was concerned only to do his duty by Nazi standards and remained completely untouched by the suffering around him. The British took charge of the camp in April 1945. Kramer was tried for war crimes and executed in November 1945.

KRANCKE, Theodor (1893–1973). German naval officer (admiral, 1943). In October 1940 he was given command of the pocket battleship ADMIRAL SCHEER, which he took to sea in what was the most successful voyage of a lone German warship. In 1942–43 Krancke was naval liaison officer at OKW (*see* OKW). He then became naval commander in chief in the west, the position he held at the time of the Allied INVASION of Normandy.

KRASNODAR. Railroad junction and regional center on the Kuban River in the northern Caucasus (USSR), seized by the Germans in their advance in the summer of 1942. Part of the bridgehead that the Germans tried to hold after their defeat at STALINGRAD, Krasnodar was retaken by Soviet troops on February 12, 1943.

K RATION. U.S. Army field ration, originally developed for airborne troops. It consisted of three small cardboard boxes, a day's ration, containing a breakfast, dinner and supper unit. Each unit had a small can of a protein food, plus biscuits, a candy or fruit bar, instant coffee or powdered fruit-juice concentrate, sugar, chewing gum and cigarettes. The flavors were much criticized. With the C RATION and the 10-IN-1 RATION, the K Ration was a major item in the diet of troops in the field, particularly in the Pacific, early in the war.

KREBS, Hans (1898–1945?). German Army officer, the last Chief of the General Staff. Prior to his appointment to this post on April 1, 1945, Krebs had served in a variety of staff officer jobs. He began his Army career as an infantry officer in World War I, but in 1939 he moved to the intelligence division of the General Staff. From December 1939 to March 1941 he served as chief of staff to the VII Corps. He was then appointed a deputy to Gen. Ernst Köstring, German military attaché in Moscow. He acted for Köstring in the latter's illness during the months prior to the German attack on Russia (June 22, 1941).

Krebs then held a succession of staff positions on the Eastern Front. From January 1942 to September 1944 he was chief of staff of the Ninth Army. He next served under Generals Ernst BUSCH and Walther MODEL as chief of staff to Army Group Center and Army Group B, respectively.

Hitler brought Krebs to Berlin in early 1945 when he and the Chief of the General Staff, Gen. Heinz GUDERIAN, were planning the operations of Army Group Vistula. Guderian had persuaded Hitler to appoint Gen. Walter WENCK, Guderian's protégé, to the staff of Army Group Vistula to ensure that he (Guderian) would have some control over the operations. When Wenck was injured, Hitler replaced him with Krebs, whom one historian has described as a "Nazi general," that is, a Nazi Party man, who was "known for his unquenchable optimism and his chameleonlike ability to adapt to the views of his superiors."

Following a violent argument between Hitler and Guderian on March 27, 1945, Krebs was appointed Acting Chief of Staff; Guderian had been ordered to take six weeks' sick leave, an order tantamount to dismissal. With Krebs in Guderian's place, Hitler would not have to deal with an argumentative Chief of Staff in working out a defense of Berlin in the final weeks of the war.

After Hitler's suicide on April 30, Krebs acted as liaison between the Führer's de facto successors, GOEBBELS and BORMANN, and the Russians. At one o'clock on the morning of May 1, Krebs crossed the German-Soviet lines to inform the Soviets that Hitler was dead and to negotiate an armistice that would allow the government of Adm. Karl DÖNITZ to function in Berlin. The Soviet response was to agree to let Dönitz come to Berlin but also to demand an unconditional surrender by the Third Reich. Krebs returned to Hitler's bunker, reported the Soviet terms and declared that he would commit suicide. He probably took his own life later on May 1 or on the following day when the Red Army captured the bunker.

KREIPE, Werner (1905–). German LUFTWAFFE officer, in 1940 chief of operations of Air Fleet 3, which fought in the Battle of BRITAIN. On August 1, 1944, Kreipe, a lieutenant general, was appointed Chief of the General Staff of the Luftwaffe in succession to Gen. Günther KORTEN, who was killed in the July 20, 1944, attempt on Adolf HITLER's life. Kreipe is said to have been preferred by Reichsmarschall Hermann GÖRING, the Commander in Chief of the Luftwaffe, over such men as Ritter von GREIM and Karl KOLLER because he was more likely to follow Göring's lead. However, Kreipe did not win favor with Hitler, the Führer regarding him as merely "a typical staff-officer type," and he was replaced by Koller on November 2, 1944. After the war Kreipe worked for the West German Government.

KREISAU CIRCLE. A group of German intellectuals opposing Adolf HITLER, who met—mostly on weekends—at the estate of Count Helmuth von MOLTKE in Kreisau, Silesia. The members of the circle were strongly believing Christians, both Protestants and Catholics. They were for the most part opposed to any form of violence against Hitler, but debated constantly how best to bring about the salvation and regeneration of Germany by means other than assassination. However, they suffered guilt by association as a result of their close contact with the more active opposition movement, to which some of them belonged, and many leading members of the circle were tried and executed after the July 1944 attempt on Hitler's life, including Count von Moltke, Adam von TROTT ZU SOLZ, Peter YORCK, Father Alfred Delp and Count Fritz von der SCHULENBURG (not to be confused with the former ambassador to the Soviet Union). *See also* OPPOSITION TO HITLER.

KRETSCHMER, Otto (1912–). The German U-boat ace of World War II, who sank approximately 267,000 tons of Allied shipping before being captured by the British destroyers H.M.S. *Walker* and H.M.S. *Vanoc* on March 27, 1941. Kretschmer was the first U-boat commander to surpass the quarter-million-ton mark, and on one voyage his *U-99* accounted for seven ships, the most tonnage ever sunk during a single patrol He lived out the war as a prisoner in Britain and Canada but remained active by secretly passing useful information back to Germany. He was a recipient of the Knight's Cross with Oak Leaves and Swords.

KRISTIANSAND. Located on the north side of the entrance to the Skagerrak, Kristiansand was the site of the headquarters of the Norwegian 3d Command District. A small airfield was also located there. After being initially turned back by the coastal defenders, a German seaborne force was able to enter the harbor on April 9, 1940, when, owing to poor visibility, the Norwegians thought they saw French ensigns. By the time they realized their mistake, it was too late. Kristiansand was later used as a German air base.

KRONSTADT. A large Soviet naval base located in the Gulf of Finland just outside LENINGRAD. Kronstadt remained in Russian hands throughout the German siege of Leningrad. Both Kronstadt and Leningrad were bases of the Baltic Red Banner Fleet, which rarely stirred from harbor but did use its guns to aid Soviet forces in the land fighting.

KRUEGER, Walter (1881–1967). Born in Flatow, West Prussia (now a part of East Germany), Krueger came to the United States when he was eight years old and was educated in public schools in the Midwest. A veteran of the Spanish-American War in the U.S. Volunteers, he reenlisted as a private in the Regular Army in June 1899, beginning a career that continued until 1946. In 1901 he was commissioned a second lieutenant. He served in the Philippines and on the Mexican border and in World War I saw duty in France, becoming chief of the Tank Corps of the AEF.

In March 1939 (having been promoted to major general on February 1 of that year) Krueger became the commanding general of the 2d Infantry Division. From October 1940 to May 1941 he commanded the VIII Corps, and as a lieutenant general (May 16, 1941) he was appointed to the command of the Third Army. The deputy chief of staff and then chief of staff of the Third Army was Col. Dwight D. EISENHOWER. In January 1943 Krueger and the forward staff echelon of the new SIXTH ARMY were ordered to Australia. Krueger's initial missions in Australia were training troops and planning for future operations. His command launched its first operations in June 1943, but not as Sixth Army. Rather, Sixth Army, under the code name Alamo Force, operated as a special task force directly under Gen. Douglas MACARTHUR's command—which was largely a device to avoid placing substantial American forces under the operational control of Australian generals. It was not until the invasion of LEYTE in October 1944 that General Krueger conducted an operation as Commanding General, Sixth Army.

Beginning in June 1943, Krueger commanded almost all Southwest Pacific Area offensive ground operations in NEW GUINEA, the BISMARCK ARCHIPELAGO and the PHILIPPINES. As Alamo Force/Sixth Army moved forward, the U.S. EIGHTH ARMY or Australian forces took over in rear areas; the highlights for Sixth Army were the invasion of Leyte and the reconquest of Luzon. The only major operations Krueger did not command from June 1943 to the end of the war were the Eighth Army's campaigns in the Southern Philippines and the Australian invasion of Borneo.

On becoming 64, Krueger retired as a major general on January 31, 1945, but was recalled to active duty the next day as a lieutenant general. He turned over final operations on Luzon to Eighth Army on July 1, 1945, and began planning for the invasion of Japan, the first step of which was to be under his command. The war ended before invasion became necessary, and Krueger's Sixth Army moved to Japan on September 20 to share occupation duties with Gen. Robert EICHELBERGER's Eighth Army. On December 31 Krueger was relieved of further occupation duties, and HQ Sixth Army was inactivated on January 26, 1946.

A pragmatist rather than a theoretician, Krueger was a believer in rather basic strategy and thorough preparation. Tactically, his inclinations were somewhat akin to those of the British Gen. Sir B. L. MONTGOMERY, for he was reluctant to move until he was sure he had the strength deployed to carry an attack through to a successful conclusion. A strict disciplinarian, he sought the best equipment and supply for his men. He possessed a sometimes volatile temper, which showed itself when carelessness on the part of a subordinate offended. He was called a soldier's soldier.

KRUPP VON BOHLEN UND HALBACH, Alfried (1907–1967). From 1943 president and chief owner of the Krupp armaments firm. He was arrested in 1945 by the Allies and tried in lieu of his ailing father (Gustav); in 1948 he was sentenced to 12 years and confiscation of his fortune, but the verdict was canceled by U.S. High Commissioner John J. MCCLOY. Though Krupp was ordered to dispose of his coal and steel properties, this was not done.

KRUPP WORKS. Founded by Alfred Krupp and greatly extended by his son Friedrich, the Krupp iron and steel works at Essen, Germany, became one of the most powerful industrial combines in the world and the largest manufacturer of arms in the First World War. In the mid-1930s the factory was the center of German rearmament. Bombing had destroyed 70 percent of the works by 1945, and the Allies confiscated the remainder, but the courts restored the company to the family in 1951.

KRYLOV, Nikolai I. (1903–1972). A RED ARMY officer, Krylov was General CHUIKOV's chief of staff in the Sixty-second Army at STALINGRAD (September 1942). In 1944–45 Krylov commanded the Fifth Army, first in the Third Belorussian Front, participating in the capture of KÖNIGSBERG, and later as the spearhead of General MERETSKOV's First Far Eastern Front in the attack on the Japanese KWANTUNG ARMY.

KÜBELWAGEN. Nickname (meaning "roadster") for a German four-wheeled light car.

KÜCHLER, Georg von (1881–1968). A Junker who joined the German Army in 1901, Küchler saw service in World War I as a General Staff officer whose specialty was artillery. By 1936 he had risen to the rank of lieutenant general, and in the following year he took command of the I Corps at Königsberg. In 1939 he commanded the German force that occupied MEMEL when it was taken from Lithuania.

In the invasion of Poland in September 1939, Küchler commanded the Third Army in General von BOCK's Army Group North. The following spring, in the invasion of the Low Countries and France, Küchler again served under Bock, as the commander of the Eighteenth Army, which broke the Dutch defenses at Yssel and the Grebbe line, took Moerbeke and then headed for DUNKIRK, which it occupied on June 4 1940, following the Allied evacuation from that city.

In the invasion of Russia the next year, Küchler's Eighteenth Army, which totaled 11 divisions, was part of General von LEEB's Army Group North. When Leeb was unable to take LENINGRAD in the winter of 1941–42, Adolf HITLER replaced him with Küchler, who was ordered to accomplish what his predecessor had failed to do. But Küchler, too, was unable to capture the city; instead of taking Leningrad, his armies were forced to retreat under pressure from a Russian offensive. Küchler held command of Army Group North for two years, until the Führer's disapproval of a retreat caused his replacement by Gen. Walther MODEL on January 31, 1944. Küchler had risen to the rank of field marshal.

KUHN, Fritz (1896–1951). The self-appointed Führer of the GERMAN-AMERICAN BUND, widely overrated as a FIFTH COLUMN organization in the United States. Convicted of embezzlement and forgery, Kuhn went to prison in November 1940.

KUIBYSHEV. A city on the Volga, the relocation site during World War II of a number of agencies of the Soviet Government, the military and the offices of the Central Committee of the Communist Party. Most of the state treasure and the entire diplomatic corps were also moved to Kuibyshev when German forces threatened Moscow in October 1941. Some agencies returned in 1943, some at the end of the war.

KULA GULF, BATTLE OF. Kula Gulf is a body of water bounded on the west by the Solomons island of KOLOMBANGARA, on the east by NEW GEORGIA and on the north by the SLOT. At its southern end is the small island of Arundel. At Vila, on the Kolombangara coast near the southern end of Kula Gulf, the Japanese had an airstrip. At the time of this action (July 6, 1943), American troops had just landed on the southern coast of New Georgia and on the adjacent islands of RENDOVA and Vangunu. Intelligence reports indicated that a force of Japanese destroyers would make a run on the night of July 5–6 to reinforce their garrison on Kolombangara. To counter this, Rear Adm. Walden AINSWORTH with Task Group 36.1 (light cruisers *Honolulu*, ST. LOUIS and HELENA and four destroyers) moved north through the Slot; shortly after midnight on the 6th they were off the northern entrance to Kula Gulf.

The total Japanese transport force consisted of 10 destroyers under Rear Adm. Teruo Akiyama. Two transport units were made up of three and four destroyers, respectively; these carried troops and supplies. The remaining three destroyers formed the support unit, with Akiyama in flagship *Niizuki*. Akiyama took his force into Kula Gulf from the northwest; his three-ship transport unit arrived at Vila and began to unload. He countermarched the rest of his force at the southern end of the gulf before turning north and ordering the second, four-ship transport group also to head for Vila. With his three-ship support unit, he continued to steam toward the head of Kula Gulf.

At 0140 American RADARS picked up the Japanese support group and second transport group. Ainsworth deployed his ships for radar-controlled gun action. At 0147 the Japanese sighted the American force; Akiyama prepared for torpedo action and ordered his second transport group (then heading for Vila) to turn northward and join him. Ten minutes later, Ainsworth's ships opened up, pouring rapid 6-inch fire in the direction of Akiyama's force. *Niizuki* was hit and put out of action before she could fire, but the two remaining support group destroyers quickly fired salvos of 24-inch LONG LANCE torpedoes. Three torpedoes smashed into *Helena*, blowing her bow off and leaving her sinking. The two remaining Japanese ships then cleared the area; Ainsworth's ships now opened fire on the approaching second transport group. Two of the four Japanese destroyers were damaged; all four turned back toward Vila. With no further contacts visible, Ainsworth departed the Kula Gulf area at 0330.

The two Japanese transport groups landed their cargoes at Vila. On the return trip north, destroyer *Nagatsuki* grounded and could not be freed. Air attack on the following day wrecked her. Another ship of this force, AMAGIRI, attempted to rescue survivors from sunken *Niizuki* but was taken under fire by the destroyers *Nicholas* and *Radford*. After a fruitless exchange of torpedoes and minor damage to *Amagiri*, the latter turned away from the area. *Nicholas* and *Radford* later exchanged fire with destroyer *Mochizuki*, also homeward bound. This action was over by about 0615. Kula Gulf had resulted in the loss of an American cruiser against two Japanese destroyers, with damage to several more Japanese ships. The intended reinforcement operation was accomplished, although Akiyama lost his life when *Niizuki* went down.

KUMA. Class of Japanese light cruisers. Built after World War I to follow the TENRYU class, they displaced 5,500 tons and mounted seven 5.5-inch guns and eight 21-inch torpedo tubes. *Kuma, Tama, Oi* and *Kiso* were war losses; *Kitakami* was scrapped after V-J Day. *Tama* and *Kiso* operated in the North Pacific. *Oi* and *Kitakami* had three guns removed and their decks sponsoned out to each side to accommodate forty 24-inch torpedo tubes (10×4). Later, both ships were converted to MIDGET SUBMARINE carriers.

KUNG, H. H. (K'ung Hsiang-hsi) (1881–1967). Chinese financier, brother-in-law of CHIANG KAI-SHEK. A graduate of Oberlin College in Ohio, Kung was an important member of the Chiang Kai-shek entourage. He was Vice-President of the Executive Yuan, and thus head of the government, and Finance Minister.

KUNMING. Capital of Yunnan province, the city of Kunming was important to the wartime survival of China. Various major headquarters and training facilities were located in or around the city, and both the

BURMA ROAD and the China airlift (the HUMP flights) terminated in Kunming. When threatened by the Japanese in late 1944, Kunming was the focus of an extensive plan of defense called Alpha.

KUOMINTANG. The Kuomintang (literally, National People's Party) controlled most of China from 1928 until 1949, when it was defeated by the Communist forces under MAO TSE-TUNG and driven to the offshore island of Taiwan. The party was formed from a number of small revolutionary groups in 1912 by Sun Yat-sen. Its ideology in principle bore superfical resemblances to western parties of the center. Dr. Sun's Three People's Principles—nationalism, democracy and people's livelihood—were its basic tenets. As time wore on, however, the constant military involvement of the Kuomintang, first in civil wars and then in conflict with Japan, caused the party to assume a more nationalistic and authoritarian mold. In addition, Chinese traditional culture was strongly emphasized, in contrast to the Communist Party, which considered most of the traditional Chinese culture as the worthless product of an evil social system.

In its early years the Kuomintang, with Soviet aid, was able to extend its control over most of the country and to suppress the provincial warlords. Sun Yat-sen died in 1925, and his role was gradually filled by CHIANG KAI-SHEK. The Communist Party had been an integral but independent part of the Kuomintang under Dr. Sun, but in 1927–28 Chiang determined to force the Communists into line or destroy them. Thousands of Communists were killed, the survivors making their escape by the famous "Long March" of the Eighth Route Army to YENAN, in the remote northwest.

During the long war with Japan (1937–45), the Kuomintang became a strongly militaristic, nationalistic party under the authoritarian rule of Chiang Kai-shek.

KURIBAYASHI, Tadamichi (1891–1945). In May 1944 Lieutenant General Kuribayashi, commander of the Japanese 109th Division, was chosen to defend IWO JIMA to the last. He arrived at his new command in early June and set his 17,500 men, including the naval force there, to digging in. But American power in the form of the Marine amphibious assault was overwhelming, and the Iwo garrison bravely fought to just about the last man. Kuribayashi's command was in radio contact with the Chichi Jima garrison until March 23, 1945, after which nothing further was heard from Iwo Jima. Although his body was never found, it is believed that General Kuribayashi died on March 22. He was posthumously promoted to general.

KURILE ISLANDS. An island chain between Hokkaido and Kamchatka, awarded to the Soviet Union for its entry into the war against Japan. It was from Tankan Bay in the Kuriles that Admiral NAGUMO's fleet sailed for the attack on PEARL HARBOR.

KURITA, Takeo (1889–1977). Born into a family of scholars, Kurita chose to be a career Japanese naval officer. He had considerable experience before the war skippering destroyers and commanding destroyer squadrons and a cruiser division. He commanded a cruiser division and then a battleship division providing cover for the invasions of JAVA, MIDWAY and GUADALCANAL. A vice-admiral, he commanded the most important remnants of the Japanese Navy in 1943–44. His fleet was severely defeated at the battle for LEYTE GULF in October 1944.

KUROCHKIN, Pavel A. (1900–). Soviet general, commander of an army in the SOVIET-FINNISH WAR. In 1941 he took over the Transbaikal Military District and, later, the Western Military District. After breaking out of the SMOLENSK pocket, he led the Northwest Front (Eleventh and Thirty-fourth Armies) during the Soviet offensive in the winter of 1941–42. In 1944 he left that command for the Second Belorussian Front, then the Sixtieth Soviet Army and finally the First and Fourth Ukrainian Fronts. Kurochkin was awarded the distinction HERO OF THE SOVIET UNION.

KURSK, BATTLE OF. Though the statistics are not dependable, Kursk is often termed the largest armored battle in history. Determined to offset the defeat at STALINGRAD in the spring of 1943, the German high command chose the Kursk sector for a major offensive operation. Jutting westward, the Kursk bulge seemed to present favorable conditions for the encirclement and subsequent destruction of the Soviet Central Front and VORONEZH FRONT forces defending the area. The operation was named CITADEL. The successful completion of Citadel was to trigger Operations Panther and Habicht, wherein other German forces would strike southeastward behind the Soviet Southwest Front, seeking to destroy the south wing of Russia's defensive positions.

Fifty German divisions, including 16 panzer and motorized divisions, were concentrated for the operation. In the operations order, surprise and maximum concentration on a narrow sector were emphasized as the touchstones of success. By the end of June 1943 the Germans facing Kursk numbered about 900,000 troops, supported by 2,700 tanks and assault guns, 10,000 pieces of artillery and 2,000 aircraft. On July 1 Adolf HITLER, at his East Prussian headquarters, ordered that the offensive begin on July 5. Effective Soviet intelligence pointed to the Kursk salient as the scene of the next threat. Marshal ZHUKOV's plan (Operation KUTUZOV) was to allow the German attack to get under way and then counterattack.

The Germans launched Citadel with a heavy air preparation followed by a southward attack by the Ninth Army on a 35-mile front along an OREL–Kursk axis. By the end of the day the Soviet lines in General ROKOSSOVSKY's Central Front had been breached. To the south of the Kursk salient the Fourth Panzer Army attacked northward along a 30-mile front westward of BELGOROD. In two hours General VATUTIN's Voronezh Front lines had been penetrated. But, although the initial assaults were successful, heavy Soviet artillery concentrations, a sudden violent thunderstorm and extensive minefields stopped the Germans there. Another German assault east of Belgorod made only minimal advances after crossing the DONETS. By July 8 the German offensive was practically stopped by the reaction of the Soviet forces. Unlike their performance at Moscow and Stalingrad, the Russians had prepared their operations in advance, and were further helped by the German delay in launching the offensive.

THE BATTLE OF KURSK: The Soviet forces on the offensive

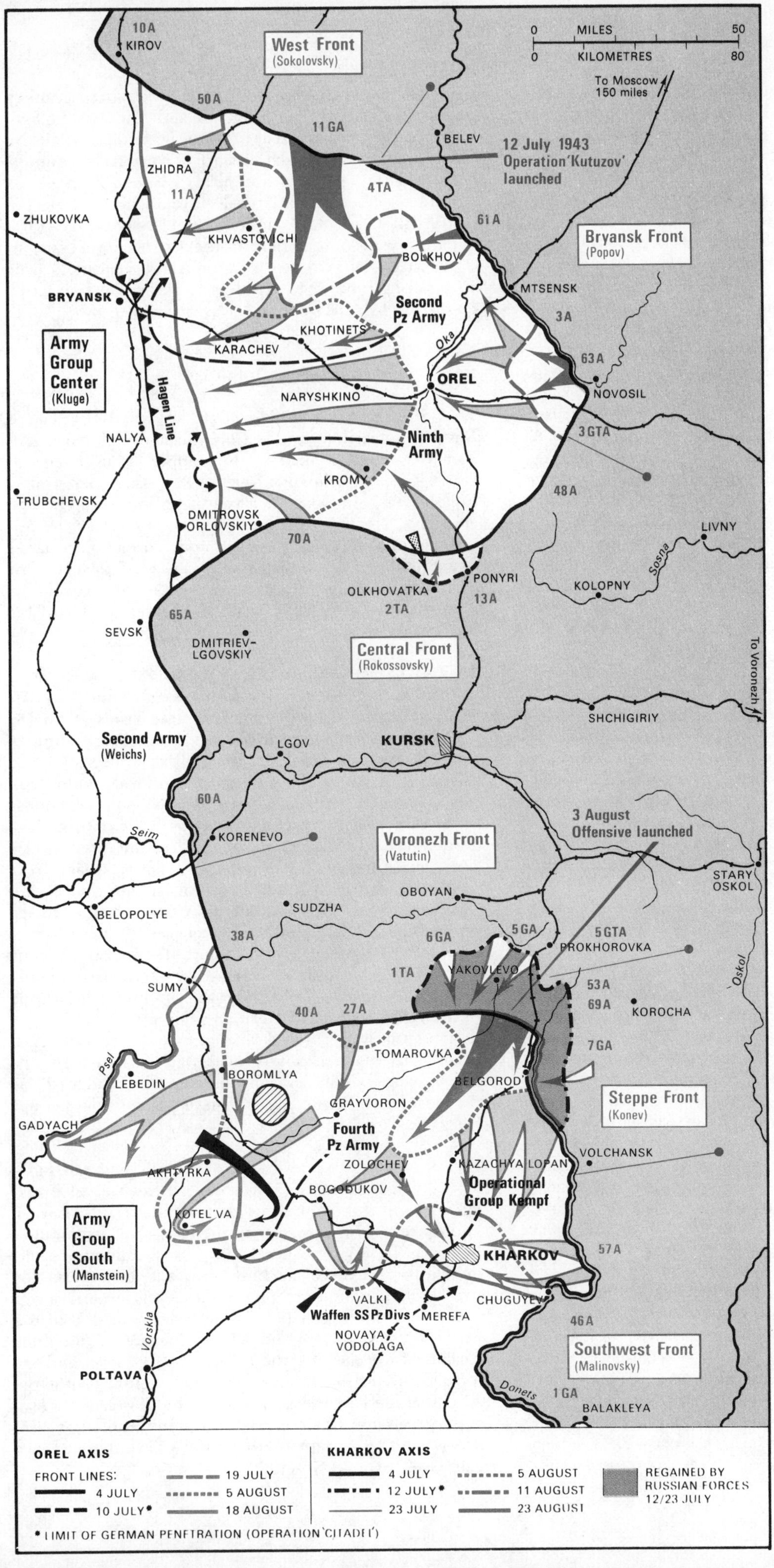
West Front
(Sokolovsky)
Bryansk Front
(Popov)
Central Front
(Rokossovsky)
Voronezh Front
(Vatutin)
Steppe Front
(Konev)
Southwest Front
(Malinovsky)
Army Group Center
(Kluge)
Second Army
(Weichs)
Army Group South
(Manstein)
Second Pz Army
Ninth Army
Fourth Pz Army
Operational Group Kempf
Waffen SS Pz Divs
Hagen Line
12 July 1943 Operation 'Kutuzov' launched
3 August Offensive launched
To Moscow 150 miles
To Voronezh
MILES 0 50
KILOMETRES 0 80
KIROV
ZHIDRA
ZHUKOVKA
KHVASTOVICHI
BELEV
BOLKHOV
MTSENSK
BRYANSK
KARACHEV
KHOTINETS
OREL
NOVOSIL
NARYSHKINO
NALYA
KROMY
TRUBCHEVSK
DMITROVSK ORLOVSKIY
LIVNY
PONYRI
OLKHOVATKA
KOLPNY
SEVSK
DMITRIEV-LGOVSKIY
SHCHIGIRIY
KURSK
LGOV
KORENEVO
STARY OSKOL
OBOYAN
SUDZHA
BELOPOL'YE
PROKHOROVKA
YAKOVLEVO
SUMY
KOROCHA
TOMAROVKA
BOROMLYA
LEBEDIN
BELGOROD
GRAYVORON
GADYACH
VOLCHANSK
AKHTYRKA
ZOLOCHEV
KAZACHYA LOPAN
BOGODUKOV
KOTEL'VA
KHARKOV
VALKI
MEREFA
CHUGUYEV
NOVAYA VODOLAGA
POLTAVA
BALAKLEYA
Oka
Sosna
Seim
Psel
Vorskla
Oskol
Donets
10A
50A
11GA
11A
4TA
61A
3A
63A
3GTA
48A
70A
13A
2TA
65A
60A
38A
6GA
5GA
5GTA
1TA
53A
69A
40A
27A
7GA
57A
46A
1GA
ORFL AXIS
FRONT LINES:
4 JULY
10 JULY*
19 JULY
5 AUGUST
18 AUGUST
KHARKOV AXIS
4 JULY
12 JULY*
23 JULY
5 AUGUST
11 AUGUST
23 AUGUST
REGAINED BY RUSSIAN FORCES 12/23 JULY
* LIMIT OF GERMAN PENETRATION (OPERATION 'CITADEL')

On July 12 the Soviets opened their counteroffensive. Now convinced that the bulk of German power was committed against Kursk, the Russians launched an attack against the Orel salient to the north of the Kursk bulge. Composed of elements of the BRYANSK (General POPOV) and Western (General SOKOLOVSKY) Fronts, this counteroffensive was so successful that German Army Group Center (General von KLUGE) was required to withdraw four committed and reserve divisions from the Ninth Army.

To the south of Kursk, the German advance was moving again. Vatutin's reserves were committed, and still the Germans made progress. By nightfall on July 13 a sizable Soviet force had been trapped between two panzer corps.

The complex tactical situation became more confused when on July 13 Hitler directed the termination of Citadel. Although Army Group South (General von MANSTEIN) was allowed to continue against Vatutin with the aim of dealing a partial defeat to the Russians, even this slender hope vanished on July 17. Coincidentally Hitler ordered the II SS Panzer Corps out of the line to prepare for movement to Italy, and the Soviet Southwest and South Fronts opened an attack against Manstein's right flank.

Following an initial Russian success, the action in the south took on a seesaw quality, with neither side being able to make meaningful progress. Still the battle continued until August 6. As a precaution the Germans began preparation of a defensive position, the HAGEN LINE, across the base of the Orel salient on July 16. On August 14 General MODEL, now in command of German forces in the Orel salient, began withdrawing to the Hagen Line. By August 17 the withdrawal was complete; the end of the Battle of Kursk is generally associated with this date. To the south, however, Soviet troops were on the move driving westward. Thus Kursk, often described as one of the greatest land battles in history (more than 2 million men were engaged), became the signal for the general weakening of German power on the Eastern Front. **J.E.J.**

KURUSU, Saburo (1888–1954). While Japanese consul in Chicago (1913–19), Kurusu married Alice Little, an American. Thereafter he held posts of increasing importance in the Philippines, Chile, Italy, Germany and Peru. As Japan's ambassador to Germany he helped negotiate the TRIPARTITE PACT of 1940. Considered an expert on the United States, Kurusu was sent to Washington in November 1941 to assist Ambassador Kichisaburo NOMURA in his abortive negotiations with Secretary of State Cordell HULL. After being repatriated following the PEARL HARBOR attack, Kurusu toured Japan giving speeches to encourage the Japanese war effort and then retired from the foreign service.

KUSAKA, Ryunosuke (1893–1971). The son of a Japanese business executive, Kusaka chose the Navy as a career, graduating from the Naval Academy in 1913 and the Naval War College in 1926. He specialized in naval aviation, captaining the aircraft carriers *Hosho* and AKAGI and commanding Japan's 24th Air Flotilla. In April 1941 Kusaka was appointed chief of staff under Adm. Chuichi NAGUMO of Japan's 1st Air Fleet, which was to carry out the attack on PEARL HARBOR. Kusaka played a major role in formulating Japanese strategy and tactics at both Pearl Harbor and MIDWAY. Following Japan's serious defeat at Midway, he dissuaded the fleet commander and chief staff officers from committing suicide. A rear admiral, Kusaka served as Nagumo's chief of staff until November 1942. He became chief of staff under Adm. Soemu TOYODA, Japan's new commander of the COMBINED FLEET, in April 1944. Kusaka was a cautious and realistic officer who strongly opposed fruitless sorties against superior enemy forces. His final rank was vice-admiral.

KUTUZOV. Code name for the Soviet counteroffensive in the KURSK salient, July 1943.

KUUSINEN, Otto (1881–1964). An Old Bolshevik of Finnish extraction, and a Comintern functionary, Kuusinen was made head of the puppet "Finnish Democratic Republic" shortly after the RED ARMY penetrated Finland early in December 1939, and immediately concluded a "treaty" with the Soviet Union. After the Soviet assault had come to a halt and Moscow negotiated peace with Helsinki, Kuusinen's so-called government was quietly dissolved and he was relegated to relative obscurity in the Soviet Union for the remainder of his life. *See also* SOVIET-FINNISH WAR.

KUZNETSOV, Nikolai G. (1902–1974). Soviet naval officer, appointed People's Commissar of the Navy in 1939, when he was only 37. His rapid rise was due to Joseph STALIN's liking for him and to the opportunities opened up as a result of the political purges of the 1930s. In 1940 Kuznetsov, a full admiral, added the post of Commander in Chief of the Navy to his ministerial duties. Known as a strong disciplinarian, he discarded the Navy's egalitarian postrevolutionary practices, insisting instead that the officers wear dress uniforms with gold braid. Admiral Kuznetsov was the prime mover in the building up of the Soviet cruiser and submarine fleet and was widely called the father of the modern Soviet Navy. Although the fleet is not considered to have pursued an aggressive course against the German Navy, it did claim the sinking of hundreds of thousands of tons of German shipping.

After the war Admiral Kuznetsov's career and reputation, like those of other Soviet figures, had their ups and downs, but in 1965 he became "rehabilitated" as the result of being praised in a speech by Leonid BREZHNEV.

KV. Soviet TANK series based on the T-100/SMK tank. The KV (for Klimenti Voroshilov) series was of excellent design and went through several variants. Larger and more heavily armed than the heaviest German tank of 1940, the KV-1 weighed 46.35 tons, carried one 76-mm. gun and three machine guns and had a crew of five. It had a 550-horsepower diesel engine and a top speed of 22 miles per hour. The series consisted of the KV-1, KV-1A, KV-1B and KV-1C, the KV-1S (a lighter variant of the KV-1C), the KV-85 (larger turret and 85-mm. gun) and the KV-2-1, an experimental prototype. Also included in the series were the KV-2A, a close-support version which carried a 152-mm. howitzer, and the KV-2B, a variant of the KV-2A. From this series came the IS, or JS (Joseph STALIN) series.

KWAJALEIN. American victories at TARAWA and MAKIN in November 1943 encouraged Adm. Chester W. NIMITZ, U.S. commander in the Pacific, to bypass the eastern MARSHALLS and seize Kwajalein Atoll in the western portion instead. The twin islands of ROI and NAMUR in the northern portion of the atoll were assigned to the 4th Marine Division, while the more heavily defended Kwajalein Island in the south of the atoll was given to the Army 7th Infantry Division as an objective. After capturing small nearby islands beforehand, Army troops landed on Kwajalein on February 1, 1944. Following five days of determined enemy resistance, Kwajalein fell on February 6, and the entire atoll was declared secured. The assault was marked by the most intense artillery bombardment of World War II.

KWANTUNG ARMY. A quasi-independent Japanese force in Manchuria, originally established in 1905 (by international agreement) to guard the South Manchurian Railway and protect other Japanese interests. In 1931 officers of the Kwantung Army, acting on their own, led the takeover of Manchuria, which was renamed MANCHUKUO. In 1938–39 the army fought a series of battles with Soviet forces (the SOVIET-JAPANESE BORDER CONFLICT), and in the final stages of the war in August 1945, when it numbered about 700,000 men, it was engaged by invading Soviet troops.

KYOKKO (Aurora). Japanese name for a night-fighter version of the P1Y1 (*see* P1Y1).

L

L-2, L-3, L-4, L-5. In 1941 the U.S. Army Air Corps called on three manufacturers of light planes—Aeronca, Piper and Taylorcraft—to provide samples of their standard aircraft for evaluation as artillery spotters. The tests proved successful, and a variety of light planes saw wartime service adjusting artillery fire, performing liaison and observation missions and even serving as aerial ambulances. All were high-wing monoplanes powered by 65-horsepower Continental engines that gave them top speeds under 100 miles per hour. Taylorcraft built the L-2, Aeronca the L-3 and Piper the L-4—all nicknamed the Grasshopper. Stinson entered the field somewhat later than the others, producing the L-5 Sentinel, which was based on its three-place Voyager sport plane. More powerful than the others, the L-5 boasted a 185-horsepower Lycoming engine. The Navy version of the Sentinel was designated the OY-1 ("Y," the designation for Consolidated, because Stinson had been absorbed by Consolidated before the Navy began acquiring the plane).

LABORDE, Jean de (1878–). In 1939 Admiral de Laborde was in command of French naval forces in the Atlantic theater. After the 1940 armistice he commanded the French fleet at TOULON, which was scuttled at his order in late 1942 when the Germans attempted to seize it. He was convicted following the war for failing to bring the fleet over to the Allies.

LACEY, James Harry (1917–). RAF officer (squadron leader) who was the top ACE of the Battle of BRITAIN. His total number of kills in all actions was 28. He was known by the nickname Ginger.

LA CHAMBRE, Guy (1898–1957). A World War I veteran and moderate liberal politician, La Chambre was French Air Minister from early 1938 to March 1940. He worked to bring up French air strength, in part by purchasing American planes. Following the 1940 defeat he was imprisoned by the VICHY government.

LADOGA, LAKE. A strategically important lake in the northwestern part of the Soviet Union. It became the linchpin in the defense of LENINGRAD against the Germans. Many of the supplies that meant the city's survival were convoyed across the lake's frozen surface during the winter of 1941–42.

LAE. Town, port and airstrip site near the mouth of the Markham River at the western bight of the Huon Peninsula in northeast NEW GUINEA. The Japanese, virtually unopposed, secured the Lae area on March 8, 1942, but made little effort to develop it until after January 1943. Constant Allied air attacks made it impossible for the Japanese to attain their development objectives. As part of the CARTWHEEL campaign, the Australian 9th Division began landing west of Lae on September 4, 1943, and shortly thereafter the Australian 25th Infantry Brigade Group began driving southeast toward Lae from NADZAB in the Markham River valley. The Australians had firm control over the area by September 16. The Allies rapidly developed the Lae region as a base for the support of future operations northwest toward the PHILIPPINES.

LAFAYETTE. The French transatlantic liner *Normandie* was acquired by the U.S. Navy in December 1941 for conversion to a troop transport and renamed *Lafayette*. Early in 1942 work on her conversion began. On February 9 a fire broke out on board; water pumped in to fight the blaze caused her to capsize, and she sank in the early hours of the 10th. The 18-month salvage job that followed, one of the most massive and difficult on record, righted *Lafayette* in August 1943. She was drydocked, but the condition of her hull and machinery was judged too badly deteriorated to make further work practicable.

LA GUARDIA, Fiorello Henry (1882–1947). American politician, most famous as mayor of New York (1934–45), who served in various war-related posts. He was chairman of the U.S. section of the Canada–U.S. Joint Defense Board (August 1940), and in 1941–42 he served as the first director of the OFFICE OF CIVILIAN DEFENSE. After the war (March–December 1946) he was director general of the United Nations Relief and Rehabilitation Administration (*see* UNRRA).

LA HAYE-DU-PUITS. Crossroads village in Normandy located west of CARENTAN on an east–west road that crosses the base of the COTENTIN PENINSULA. It was taken by the VIII Corps, U.S. First Army, on July 8, 1944, after several days of stiff fighting.

LAMMERDING, Heinz (1905–1971). German SS general, commander of the SS panzer division Das Reich. Troops of that division participated in one of the war's worst atrocities, the massacre of French civilians at the village of ORADOUR-SUR-GLANE.

LAMMERS, Hans Heinrich (1879–1962). German civil servant, chief of the Reich Chancellery from 1933 to 1945, first as Secretary of State and, after 1937, as Reich Minister. He was sentenced to 20 years' imprisonment at Nuremberg but was released in 1952.

LAMON BAY. Bay on the east coast of LUZON, site of a Japanese landing on December 24, 1941.

LAMPEDUSA. Allied airplanes began an assault on this Mediterranean island on June 11, 1943, the day that nearby PANTELLERIA surrendered. Lampedusa, reduced from the air, surrendered unconditionally on June 12.

LAMPSON, Sir Miles (1st Baron Killearn) (1880–1964). As British ambassador to Egypt and high commissioner for the Sudan, 1936–46, Lampson was blamed for alienating patriotic Egyptians when in February 1942 he almost forced the abdication of King FAROUK over the latter's refusal to accept as Prime Minister a British nominee for the post.

LANCASTER. The most successful of Britain's heavy bombers, this aircraft started its distinguished career as an Avro Manchester airframe modified to accommodate four Rolls-Royce Merlin liquid-cooled engines instead of two Vultures. The Avro company called the prototype Manchester III before settling on the name Lancaster. The improved bomber was a midwing, twin-tail monoplane with two .303-caliber machine guns in nose, ventral and dorsal turrets and a four-gun turret in the tail. The seldom-used ventral turret was eventually removed. The Lancaster could carry seven tons of bombs or, with the H_2S RADAR and dorsal turret removed, a single 22,000-pound bomb. With four 1,460-horsepower Merlins, the plane could cruise some 1,600 miles at 210 miles per hour carrying 14,000 pounds of munitions.

The Lancaster made its combat debut in March 1942 and by the end of the war had flown 156,000 sorties and dropped more than 600,000 tons of bombs. Among the targets hit by Lancasters were the MÖHNE and EDER DAMS and the rocket development center at PEENEMÜNDE. Although best known for its contribution to the night attacks on German industrial cities, the Lancaster also participated in some of BOMBER COMMAND's rare daylight precision strikes, hitting a diesel factory at Augsburg in April 1942 and sinking the battleship TIRPITZ in November 1944.

LAND, Emory S. (1879–1971). U.S. rear admiral who retired in 1937 and in 1938 was appointed chairman of the U.S. Maritime Commission; in 1942 he became administrator of the War Shipping Administration.

LANDING CRAFT. A general term applied to smaller boats and craft used to land troops, vehicles, weapons and supplies on a hostile beach. The U.S. Navy generally applied this term to non-seagoing craft less than 200 feet long, distinguishing them from LANDING SHIPS. At the outbreak of the war Japan was possibly ahead of Britain and the United States, owing to the demands of operations in China. War in Europe spurred British development, and the Americans followed suit before and after Pearl Harbor. Serious efforts, their urgency varying with the relative priority given to amphibious operations as the war progressed, were devoted to evolving extensive families of landing craft. Germany developed some craft for its projected invasion of England, and later for other uses. By 1944 a large and specialized variety of Anglo-American landing craft had been devised. Besides landing various combinations of troops and hardware, the craft provided support services ranging from casualty evacuation and hot meals for boat crews to close-in gunfire support, emergency repairs and fighter direction. (See separate LC entries.)

Lancaster

LANDING SHIPS. Oceangoing ships built or converted to carry and land troops and their equipment on an invasion beach. The U.S. Navy defined a landing ship, as distinguished from a LANDING CRAFT, as a seagoing ship 200 feet or more in length. As with landing craft, a wide variety of ships were devoted to this purpose by Japan, Britain and the United States. Some landing ships, such as the American AKA and APA or the British LSI, remained off a beach and sent their troops and cargoes ashore in landing craft. Others, such as the LST and LCI, were designed to land directly on a beach. (See separate LS entries.)

LANDSBERG. The fortress prison in beautiful surroundings at Landsberg am Lech, Bavaria, in which Adolf HITLER was incarcerated from November 11, 1923, to December 20, 1924, following his conviction for his part in the Munich putsch in November 1923. Landsberg was known in Germany not as a prison but as a *Festung,* which signifies a place of "honorable" detainment suitable, for example, for a duelist committed for homicide. Built in 1909 in medieval style, it housed many political prisoners.

LANGLEY, U.S.S. Aircraft carrier, the U.S. Navy's first (1922). Converted into a seaplane tender in 1937, she was sunk by Japanese bombers off TJILATJAP on February 27, 1942. The second U.S.S. *Langley,* also an aircraft carrier, INDEPENDENCE class, was commissioned in August 1943. She was a veteran of the PHILIPPINE SEA and LEYTE GULF battles.

LANGSDORFF, Hans (1890–1939). The commanding officer of the German pocket battleship ADMIRAL GRAF SPEE, which commenced commerce-raiding operations against British shipping in the South Atlantic in the autumn of 1939. Captain Langsdorff commanded the ship in the Battle of the RIVER PLATE on December 13, 1939, when he encountered the British South American Division and subsequently was forced to seek refuge in the neutral harbor of Montevideo. Under extreme pressure and beset by indecision and rumors, Langsdorff felt compelled to blow up his ship in the estuary of the Rio de la Plata, having received permission from his superiors for this action. Then, interned with his crew in Argentina, he committed suicide during the night of December 19–20, 1939.

LANPHIER, Thomas G. (1915–). U.S. pilot who took part in the destruction of the plane carrying Japanese Adm. Isoroku YAMAMOTO from Rabaul to Kahili airfield on Bougainville. A message containing the admiral's itinerary was intercepted and decoded. U.S. Secretary of the Navy Frank KNOX was notified, and he immediately issued orders to "destroy" Yamamoto. The task of intercepting the admiral's plane and its escort went to Maj. John W. Mitchell of the 339th Fighter Squadron, a unit that flew P-38s, the only available planes with range enough for the flight from Guadalcanal to Kahili and back—a mission of nearly a thousand miles. On April 18, 1943, the mission got under way. Sixteen P-38s arrived over Bougainville. Mitchell led the 12-plane escort, and Captain Lanphier the four aircraft in the execution squad. Yamamoto flying in one of two Mitsubishi Betty bombers, arrived on schedule, and within minutes he was dead. Either Lanphier or Lt. Rex T. BARBER had shot down the bomber that was carrying the admiral; Lanphier is generally considered to have done so. One member of the cover unit, Lt. Raymond K. Hine, was killed.

LA PALLICE. Port on the west coast of France, near La Rochelle, used by the Germans as a submarine base.

LA ROCHE-GUYON. Town on the Seine below Paris, headquarters of German Army Group B at the time of the INVASION of NORMANDY, and an Allied tactical objective in the sweep through France.

LARSEN, Leif (1906–). Norwegian resistance leader, prominent in the operation of the "Shetland bus"—an organized boat service between the Shetland Islands and Norway. It carried men trained to conduct underground activities and ferried supplies (by the end of 1944, 400 tons of arms and 60 radio sets had been transported to Norway). The Norwegians also participated in operations such as the LOFOTEN ISLANDS and VAAGSØ raids.

LARSON, Westside T. (1892–1977). U.S. Army Air Forces officer who commanded the Antisubmarine Command in 1942–43. Promoted to major general in 1943, he was given command of the Third Air Force. In August 1945 he became commanding general of the Eighth Fighter Command in the Pacific.

LASCH, Otto (1893–1971). German Army officer (General der Infanterie, 1944) who was in command of the garrison at KÖNIGSBERG, which held out against enormous odds through February and March 1945 but capitulated to Soviet forces on April 9. For this surrender Lasch was condemned to death in absentia by Adolf HITLER, and his wife and two daughters were arrested. Lasch himself was taken prisoner by the Russians and was not released until 1955.

LASHIO. The northern Burmese city of Lashio, historically important because of its location at the end of the BURMA RAILWAY and the beginning of the BURMA ROAD, became even more valuable to the Allies as the sole overland supply link to China after the Japanese occupation of northern Indochina and the resultant closing of the Yunnan–Indochina Railway. But in 1942, as one part of a three-pronged advance aimed at the capture of all BURMA, the Japanese drive to Lashio was a complete success. LEND-LEASE supplies totaling some 44,000 tons, awaiting shipment to China via the Burma Road, were lost to the Japanese when Lashio fell on April 29, 1942, after a five-hour battle. Recapture of Lashio occurred on March 6–7, 1945, the city being entered by the Chinese 38th Division after the northeast corner of Burma had been taken from the Japanese.

LATÉCOÈRE 290. French single-engine, three-place, twin-float torpedo bomber, first produced in 1932. About 35 were built. Some were used operationally during the early stages of the war.

LATÉCOÈRE 298. French single-engine, low-wing torpedo bomber and reconnaissance seaplane, introduced in 1936. Two hundred were built, equipping five naval air squadrons. The 298 was widely used, especially in the Mediterranean against the Italians. It had a maximum speed of 186 miles per hour and a cruising speed of 167 miles per hour. Its range was 497 to 1,367 miles, depending on load and mission; it carried a two- or three-man crew (the three-man crew was for reconnaissance duty). It carried three 7.5-mm. machine guns and a 1,477-pound bomb load or one torpedo.

LATTRE DE TASSIGNY, Jean-Marie de (1889–1952). A French cavalry officer in World War I, in which he fought brilliantly, suffering four wounds. Following the war de Lattre switched to the infantry and fought in Morocco until 1926, then attended the French Staff College. In the early 1930s he served as the favored aide of Gen. Maxime WEYGAND, then Commander in Chief–designate of the French Army. Following Weygand's retirement in 1935, de Lattre joined the staff of Gen. Alphonse GEORGES, chief assistant to Weygand's successor, Gen. Maurice GAMELIN. During the early months of quiet on the Western Front, de Lattre sought a command, getting first a brigade and then the crack 14th Infantry Division. His unit, one of the first reserves thrown into the breach following the German breakthrough at SEDAN in May 1940, fought bitterly and successfully to contain the southward thrust of General GUDERIAN's armor. For the rest of the six-weeks' campaign, General de Lattre's unit held off repeated enemy attacks and maintained its cohesion through the long retreat which ended in the south of France.

Following the armistice de Lattre got a high command in the small army left to VICHY France, working to rebuild morale and planning for the day of revenge against the invader. In late 1942 he attempted to resist the German move into Unoccupied France and was arrested, but escaped and reached Algiers in the fall of 1943. There he took command of the French First Army, which, formed from former Vichy forces and Free French units, landed in SOUTHERN FRANCE in August 1944 and pushed north toward Alsace and the German frontier. Here he resisted a fierce German counterattack during the winter, then drove on in the spring of 1945 over the Rhine River in a surprise operation into southern Germany.

After the war de Lattre held high French and NATO commands, then served with some success as French high commissioner and Commander in Chief in Indochina from 1950 to 1952. He died in 1952 and was posthumously named marshal of France.

LATVIA. The pre–World War II independent Latvian state was created as a result of the collapse of Russia in 1917 and Germany in 1918. But in 1939 its fate was sealed by a secret protocol of the SOVIET-GERMAN NON-AGGRESSION PACT, which relegated Latvia to the Soviet sphere of influence. In October 1939 Latvia was forced to sign a dictated treaty of mutual assistance by which the Soviet Union was granted military bases on Latvian territory. On June 16, 1940, Latvia was invaded by the RED ARMY and a puppet government under the Latvian Communist August Kirchensteins was set up. Mass deportations and executions, which stripped the country of its intelligentsia, followed and, after a Soviet-sponsored referendum in August, Latvia became a constituent republic of the USSR. Latvia was occupied by German forces from July 1941 to October 1944. The Germans suppressed Latvian national aspirations, but the deportations and executions did not stop. Latvia during this time was part of "Reichskomissariat Ostland," which included the other Baltic states and part of Belorussia.

When the Germans retreated in late 1944, some 65,000 Latvians fled with them or escaped to Sweden. Upon the return of the Soviets, the deportations began again, 105,000 people being removed in 1945 and 1946 alone, and Latvia again became the Latvian Soviet Socialist Republic.

LAUREL, José Pacaino (1891–1959). In October 1943 the leaders of the Japanese occupation forces picked Laurel, an associate justice of the Philippine Supreme Court, to be President of the Philippines. When the Allies liberated the Philippines in 1945, the Japanese moved Laurel and his government to Tokyo. At the end of the war Laurel was imprisoned, returned to the Philippines and tried on 143 counts of treason. The trial was never completed, and in 1948 an amnesty proclamation set him free.

LAVAL, Pierre (1883–1945). The French political figure most identified with the policy of collaboration with the Germans, Laval held high cabinet offices (including the Premiership) at various times in the 1930s and was head of the government under the VICHY regime after the fall of France in 1940. A Socialist in his early days, he moved to the right as his career progressed. He served in the Chamber of Deputies during the First World War and again in the 1920s and became a senator in 1927. During the period he served in various cabinet offices, becoming known as a skillful harmonizer of differing interests—something of a fixer, actually. He also became a rich man through his legal practice and various business enterprises.

In 1931 Laval became Premier, in 1934 Foreign Minister and in 1935 Premier again (he retained the Foreign Ministry as well). He worked for rapprochement with Italy, one of his efforts being the Hoare-Laval agreement to give Benito MUSSOLINI a free hand in Ethiopia; outraged British public opinion caused the agreement to be abandoned. After 1936 Laval was out of the government until the summer of 1940, when, after playing a leading part in the dissolution of the Third Republic and the installation of Marshal Philippe PÉTAIN as Head of State of the new Vichy regime, he became head of the government (his title was Vice-President of the Council of Ministers). He was the leading spokesman for cooperation with the victorious Germans, being convinced that France must ally herself with Hitler's "wave of the future."

In December 1940 Pétain dismissed Laval as Premier, but he was recalled in 1942. He now took one of the steps that made him hated by Frenchmen: he agreed to provide French workers for factories in Germany. There is evidence that Laval believed himself to be working in the best interests of France in his dealings with Adolf HITLER, and he in fact argued with the Führer in efforts to drive a good bargain for his country. But to most Frenchmen he became the symbol of collaboration with the Nazis. In 1945 he was taken to Germany and then to Austria, and at the end of the war he fled to Spain. He agreed to return to France and stand trial for treason; the ensuing proceeding was, by any account, extremely unfair and irregular. Nevertheless, it ended in Laval's conviction, and he was executed by a firing squad on October 15, 1945.

LAVOCHKIN LA-5. Late in 1941 the Soviet Union's S. Lavochkin adapted an LaGG-3 (below) airframe to take a two-row 14-cylinder radial engine; the plane was first flown at the end of 1941. The trials showed it to be 25 miles per hour faster than the German MESSERSCHMITT ME 109F at low altitudes as well as being highly maneuverable. It was rarely flown above 16,000 feet, since it was at its best close to the ground. Many German pilots stalled and crashed trying to follow it in a tight turn. The plane immediately supplanted the LaGG-3. It appeared first in the autumn battles around STALINGRAD, and earned the title "Wooden Saver of Stalingrad." In 1943 an improved version, the La-5FN (FN—Forsirovannii Nyeposredstvenny, or Boosted Engine—equipped with direct fuel injection), became operational. Of mixed wood and metal construction, it was lighter and faster than the La-5. The La-5FN was powered by one 1,650-horsepower 14-cylinder radial engine and had a top speed of 401 miles per hour at sea level. It was armed with two 20-mm. cannon and could carry 330 pounds of bombs or other ordnance. It weighed 7,406 pounds fully loaded. Dimensions: wingspan, 32 feet 1¾ inches; length, 27 feet 10¾ inches; height, 9 feet 3 inches.

LAVOCHKIN LA-7. An aerodynamically refined, more powerful and more heavily armed version of the La-5FN (above) with a basic structure identical to the latter. The La-7 equipped a large part of the Soviet air forces at the close of the war. Two variants were built; one had a rocket-assist motor on the interceptor version to boost combat speed, and the other, the La-7UTI, was a two-seat reconnaissance and liaison version. Powered by a 14-cylinder 1,775-horsepower engine, the plane flew at a maximum speed of 420 miles per hour. It was armed with three 20-mm. cannon plus six rockets or two 110- or 220-pound bombs. Dimensions: wingspan, 32 feet 1¾ inches; length, 27 feet 10¾ inches; height, 9 feet 2 inches.

LAVOCHKIN LA-9. The final development of the Soviet single-seat fighters. Developed by S. Lavochkin, this plane was radically different in structure from the others in the series but bore a close external resemblance to them. It was of stressed-skin, all-metal construction. Since deliveries began just before the war ended, it probably saw no more than limited action. It was powered by an 1,870-horsepower 14-cylinder engine and flew 428 miles per hour maximum speed. It was armed with four 20-mm. cannon.

LAVOCHKIN LAGG-3. Russian single-seat interceptor and fighter-bomber designed by Lavochkin, with the assistance of engineers Gorbunov and Gudkov. The project began in 1938 to develop a new fighter, which eventually came to be the best Soviet plane of the war. It entered production in 1940 as the LaGG-1, but after structural and control modifications it was designated the LaGG-3. Although made of wood and canvas, it was very sturdy. It became operational during the early part of 1941, and though numerically the most important Soviet fighter in the early and middle war years, it was replaced in the summer of that year by the La-5 (above). Powered by a 1,210-horsepower V-12 engine, it flew at a maximum speed of 348 miles per hour and cruised at 280 miles per hour; its maximum range with internal fuel was 404 miles. It carried a variety of armament, the most common being one 20-mm. cannon, one 12.7-mm. and two 7.62-mm. machine guns, plus six RS082 rockets or 484 pounds of bombs. Normal loaded weight was 7,032 pounds—very low compared with other planes of the same type. Dimensions: wingspan, 32 feet 1¾ inches; length, 29 feet 1¼ inches; height, 8 feet 10 inches.

Lavochkin LaGG-3

LAWRENCE, Ernest Orlando (1901–1958). American physicist, chief inventor of the cyclotron. He and his associates were the first persons to carry out the artificial disintegration of matter. In the course of their experiments numerous new isotopes were formed, many of which were found to be radioactive and therefore of great biological and medical value for the study of cancer and other malignant tumors. With the establishment of the ATOMIC BOMB project, the Lawrence cyclotron was used in the electromagnetic separation of uranium 235. Lawrence was a major figure in the development of the bomb. He was on the faculty of the University of California from 1928.

LAWRENCE, Geoffrey (Baron Trevethin and Baron Oaksey) (1880–1971). British jurist, president of the INTERNATIONAL MILITARY TRIBUNAL at Nuremberg, 1945–46.

LAWSON, Ted W. (1917–). The pilot of the B-25 *Ruptured Duck,* which participated in the Doolittle raid of April 18, 1942, the first Allied air attack on Japan (*see* FIRST SPECIAL AVIATION PROJECT). Lawson's plane successfully bombed targets in Tokyo, but over China it ran low on fuel in bad weather. Lawson had to crash-land in shallow water along the coast. He and his crewmen got ashore, where they met friendly Chinese who led them to safety. During the overland journey, 1st Lt. Thomas White, an Army doctor who had served as a volunteer gunner on one of the bombers, had to amputate Lawson's left leg, which had been mangled in the crash. Back in the United States, Captain Lawson told his story, with the help of journalist Bob Considine, in the book *Thirty Seconds Over Tokyo,* which became a motion picture.

LAYCOCK, Sir Robert (1907–1968). British Army officer, one of the first COMMANDO leaders. In November 1941 he took part in a raid behind German lines in North Africa which included an attack on General ROMMEL's supposed headquarters. Laycock, then a colonel, and Sgt. J. Terry were the only ones to get back, all the others being killed or taken prisoner; they wandered in the desert for almost six weeks before reaching British lines. As commander of the Special Services Brigade in 1942–43, Laycock was responsible for the training and organization of all Special Services troops in Britain. In 1943 Laycock was promoted to major general, and in 1943–47 he was Chief of COMBINED OPERATIONS in succession to Lord Louis MOUNTBATTEN and adviser to the Chiefs of Staff on amphibious warfare. *See also* KEYES, GEOFFREY C. T.

LC(FF). U.S. Navy ship-type symbol for Landing Craft (Flotilla Flagship), a modification of the basic LCI(L) hull to serve as a flagship for groups of LCI types (below). Instead of troop accommodations, it had spaces for communications equipment and for a unit commander and his staff.

LCI(G). U.S. Navy ship-type symbol for Landing Craft, Infantry (Gunboat). Six different modifications of the basic LCI(L) hull (below) were produced, armed with combinations of 3-inch, 40-mm. or 20-mm. guns; .50-caliber machine guns; and rocket launchers. They were used for close support of amphibious landings and, in the South Pacific, against Japanese small-craft traffic.

LCI(L). U.S. Navy ship-type designation for Landing Craft, Infantry (Large). A seagoing troop-landing craft, the LCI(L) was 160 feet long and displaced 387 tons loaded, with a top speed slightly over 15 knots. Armed with 20-mm. antiaircraft guns, it carried nearly 200 troops and was widely used in both major theaters.

LCI(M). U.S. Navy ship-type symbol for Landing Craft, Infantry (Mortar), similar to the LCI(G) (above) but armed with three 4.2-inch mortars and designed to lay down high-angle barrage fire before an assault landing. An LCI(M) also had one 40-mm. and four 20-mm. guns.

LCI(R). U.S. Navy ship-type symbol for Landing Craft, Infantry (Rocket). Besides one 40-mm. and four 20-mm. guns, it was armed with six 5-inch bombardment-rocket launchers. Its basic function was like that of the LCI(M) (above), and it was used in Pacific landings in 1944–45.

LCM. U.S. Navy ship-type symbol for Landing Craft, Mechanized, an amphibious craft that could take personnel and tanks onto beaches for unloading.

LCS(L) (3). U.S. Navy ship-type symbol for Landing Craft, Support (Large) (Mark 3), a built-for-the-purpose modification of the LCI(L) hull, entirely rearranged internally and armed with 40-mm. and 20-mm. guns and bombardment-rocket launchers. Some had a single 3-inch gun. A development of the LCI(G) (above), it had the same basic functions.

LCS(S). U.S. Navy ship-type symbol for Landing Craft, Support (Small). Two versions of this 36-foot 8-inch small craft were built to deliver close-support automatic-weapon and rocket fire to amphibious assault waves. The Mark 1 (LCS [S] [1]) carried two or three .50-caliber and/or .30-caliber machine guns and smoke pots; some had one or more guns removed to make room for rocket launchers. The Mark 2 had a standard armament of one twin .50-caliber mount, two single .30-caliber guns, two 12-rail bombardment-rocket projectors and smoke pots. Both types of craft could be carried by landing ships and launched by booms or davits.

LCT. U.S. Navy ship-type symbol for Landing Craft, Tank. Different types of this craft were produced and used by Britain and the United States; all were generally open, bargelike types with a bow ramp. They differed in configuration and dimensions but had the same general function and capabilities. The short-range LCT, depending on the specific model, could carry from four to eight medium tanks or an equivalent weight of vehicles or cargo. An LCT could be transported empty on the upper deck of an LST and slid off sideways into the water to be loaded for landing. The LSD was also designed to carry loaded LCTs in its floodable well deck. *See also* LST; LSD.

LEAFLET RAIDS. American and British bombers dropped nearly 6 billion pieces of propaganda and information over Europe between September 1939 and the end of the war. A variety of civilian and military agencies produced the leaflets, but most came out of the Psychological Warfare Division of SHAEF. The leaflets had diverse purposes. Some were intended to boost the morale of civilians under German occupation; others aimed at undermining German will or, after D-Day, informed people of the campaign and gave instructions to members of the resistance.

The single, briefly worded sheets were simply tossed from bomb bays until the U.S. Army Air Force developed a leaflet bomb in 1944. Each bomber carried 12 bombs, with 80,000 leaflets in each bomb. This enabled as many as seven or eight sites to be targeted during each sortie. Modified B-17 bombers of the Special Leaflet Squadron (422d BS, 305th Bomb Group), organized in September 1943, conducted 537 sorties from its British base (Chelveston) in an eight-month period without losing a plane. Later the squadron converted to B-24s. Leaflet raids multiplied after D-Day and included one sortie on the morning of June 6 to warn French coastal settlements of the INVASION. From then on leaflet drops, aimed primarily at Germans, increased steadily for the duration of the war. During 319 night operations, 1.5 billion leaflets were dropped over Germany, Norway, Denmark, France, Belgium and the Netherlands.

LEAGUE OF NATIONS. Founded by the victorious powers of World War I, the league was in operation from 1920 to 1946. Throughout the 1930s, it was confronted by one crisis after another. After the Japanese invasion of Manchuria, the league's report, which maintained that Manchuria should be returned to China, was rejected by Japan, and Japan withdrew from the league. The result made it clear that the league was unable to protect China against aggression. But a more promising development was the new "collective security" attitude of the Soviet Union. In 1935 the league reacted promptly when Benito MUSSOLINI invaded Ethiopia, employing economic sanctions against the aggressor. But oil was not included, and Britain and France did not really support stringent measures.

The failure of the league to deal effectively with the invasion of Ethiopia moved it into its final period of decay. From July 1936, when Italy and Germany joined in the Rome–Berlin AXIS, the important diplomatic activity was conducted directly between the nations involved. The league played no part in such crucial events as the Spanish Civil War, the Japanese invasion of China, the German annexation of Austria and Czechoslovakia and the Italian conquest of Albania. The impulse for creation of an effective international organization appeared to be strengthened during the Second World War, however, and the result was the establishment of the UNITED NATIONS.

LEAHY, William Daniel (1875–1959). After a U.S. Navy career that began during the Philippine insurrection and culminated in a term as Chief of Naval Operations (1937–39), Admiral Leahy came out of retirement in 1940 to become ambassador to VICHY France. The next year President ROOSEVELT made Leahy his personal chief of staff, and for the duration of the war he presided over the JOINT CHIEFS OF STAFF. Leahy chaired the meetings and signed JCS recommendations, but he never usurped the President's role as Commander in Chief. He conveyed the advice of the service heads to the President and loyally implemented his decisions. Although an outspoken man, Leahy did not provide commanding leadership in deciding issues of military strategy, but he was Roosevelt's foremost source of information on such questions and his constant companion at wartime conferences. He, along with Harry HOPKINS, was authorized to originate messages to Winston CHURCHILL and other British leaders through the White House Map Room. Only these two and the President had this authority. In December 1944 Roosevelt honored Leahy with the new rank of five-star fleet admiral.

Leahy remained chief of staff under President TRUMAN until 1949 and in addition served briefly, in 1946, as director of the Central Intelligence Group, an agency that unsuccessfully attempted to plan and coordinate all foreign intelligence work.

LEATHERS, Frederick, Viscount (1883–1965). As British Minister of War Transport in 1941–45, Leathers, a shipping executive, was the man primarily responsible for the preservation of Britain's external and internal communications at a time when the country's survival depended on them.

LEBRUN, Albert (1871–1950). President of France, originally elected in 1932 and reelected in 1939. Although under the Third Republic the President did not wield executive power, his personality and convictions could prove important, since he chose the Premier (the president of the Council of Ministers) and the state of French politics was such that the life of cabinets was short and the choice of a Premier had frequently to be made—and among the leaders of numerous competing parties, there often being no obvious person for the post. Lebrun, a former senator, was not known as a man of strong views. He played an essentially passive role in the French crisis of 1940 and on July 13 left office, the Third Republic having been abolished. He was later arrested by the Germans. *See also* FRANCE, BATTLE OF.

LECKWITZ. Village in Saxony, about two miles from the Elbe River, where American and Russian soldiers first sighted each other in 1945. The American party, led by 1st Lt. Albert Kotzebue (Company G, 273d Infantry), proceeded on to the Elbe and near the town of Strehla made contact with Lt. Col. Alexander T. Gardiev, commander of the Soviet 175th Rifle Regiment. Because Lieutenant Kotzebue reported his location incorrectly, his superiors were unable to confirm the contact, and the first meeting is therefore generally said to have taken place at TORGAU.

LECLERC, Jacques Philippe (1902–). A modern d'Artagnan, Leclerc was captured by the Germans in France in 1940, escaped, rejoined the French Army, was recaptured, escaped a second time and joined Gen. Charles DE GAULLE in London. He then went to Chad as military governor and commanding general of French Equatorial Africa. In January 1943 he and his Free French force joined the British EIGHTH ARMY at Tripoli, having marched 1,500 miles across the Sahara, destroying Italian posts as they went (*see* FREE FRANCE).

General Leclerc was commander of the French 2d Armored Division, which participated in the Normandy INVASION. He fought with distinction at ARGENTAN, and was chosen to accept the German surrender in PARIS. Described by Sir Alan BROOKE as "hard-bitten, capable, and of great charm" and by Gen. Omar BRADLEY as "a magnificent tank commander," Leclerc made an important contribution to the dignity of France as well as to the Allied military effort. His real name was de Hauteclocque; "Leclerc" was adopted in an effort to spare his family from persecution by the Germans.

LEDO ROAD. Route from Ledo, Assam, to Bhamo, Burma, part of the land supply route from India to China. The Japanese capture of the Burmese section of the BURMA ROAD in June 1942 severed the land route to China and forced the Allies to airlift ammunition and matériel over the section of the Himalayas known as "the HUMP." In the fall of 1942 American engineers began building a road between Ledo and the old Burma Road. When the new link was finished it soon carried more tonnage to north Burma than the air route. In early 1945 it was officially named the Stilwell Road by CHIANG KAI-SHEK in honor of Gen. Joseph W. STILWELL.

LEE, John Clifford Hodges (1887–1958). U.S. Army officer, commander of the 2d Infantry Division in 1941–42, who served for most of the war as Commanding General, Services of Supply, or COM Z, in ETO, in which role he directed the largest logistical operation in history. Known as an excellent administrator, he was promoted to lieutenant general in 1944 and made deputy commander of U.S. forces in the theater. A devout churchman, somewhat pompous in manner—his initials gave him the nicknames "Courthouse" and "Jesus Christ Himself"—he was conspicuously loyal to his staff and subordinates as well as higher authority, though he would sometimes oppose the Supreme Commander on principle. While in command in Italy in the postwar period, he was the subject of attacks by the newspaper correspondent Robert Ruark, who accused him of living in an excessively lavish style.

LEE, Willis Augustus, Jr. (1888–1945). "Ching" Lee, a Kentuckian by birth, entered the U.S. Navy in 1904; he became a rear admiral in 1942. Best remembered for his decisive action at GUADALCANAL (1942), Lee turned the tide there with his group of battleships and cruisers. At a crucial moment, when victory hung in the balance, Lee radioed the message: "Stand aside. I'm coming through. This is Ching Lee." In the spring of 1944 Lee and Vice-Adm. Marc A. MITSCHER directed attacks on TRUK Island and Japanese strongholds in the CAROLINES. At FORMOSA and the RYUKYUS in the fall of 1944, Lee was second in command to Adm. William F. HALSEY. He died near the end of the war while conducting research to counter Japanese KAMIKAZE attacks.

LEEB, Wilhelm Ritter von (1876–1956). Born and educated in Bavaria, Leeb entered the Bavarian Army in 1895, serving in a variety of assignments, including participation in the German Expeditionary Corps mission to China (1901–02) and duty with the Prussian General Staff (1909–11). He saw service in World War I, and in the interwar period held several commands; notably, he took part in crushing Adolf HITLER's Munich putsch of 1923 as commander of the Bavarian artillery.

Despite this antagonistic encounter with Hitler, Leeb was recalled to active duty by the Führer in 1938 after having been retired earlier in the year. The aristocratic and austere general was placed in command of part of the German Army that moved into the SUDETENLAND after the MUNICH AGREEMENT. Two years later Leeb commanded Army Group C on the Western Front. In recognition of his victory over the French in Alsace-Lorraine, Hitler in July 1940 awarded Leeb the Knight's Cross of the IRON CROSS and promoted him to field marshal in a ceremony in which 12 field marshal's batons were awarded.

Leeb next commanded Army Group North in the invasion of Russia. His armies attacked from East Prussia through the Baltic states toward LENINGRAD. But when the conservative Leeb was unable to cope with Hitler's maneuvering of his armies, he asked to be relieved. Hitler accepted this offer of resignation in January 1942 and put General von KÜCHLER in command of Army Group North.

Leeb's reward for failing to take Leningrad was retirement. Captured by the U.S. SEVENTH ARMY in early May 1945, he spent three years in prison prior to trial at NUREMBERG, where he was found guilty of one charge of war crimes. He was sentenced to three years' imprisonment, but since he had already served that length of time he was released.

LEEPER, Sir Reginald W. Allen (1888–1968). Head of the British Political Warfare Executive, 1939–43, and Ambassador to GREECE, 1943–48.

LEESE, Sir Oliver William Hargreaves (1894–1978). British Army officer, a veteran of World War I, in which he was wounded three times. In 1940 he was deputy chief of staff of the BRITISH EXPEDITIONARY FORCE in France, escaping from DUNKIRK in a small boat. In 1942, as a lieutenant general, he became a corps commander in the EIGHTH ARMY in the Middle East, and he led the corps in SICILY and ITALY in 1943. At the end of 1943 he was appointed commander of the Eighth Army, in succession to Gen. Bernard MONTGOMERY. He next served as Commander in Chief, Allied Land Force Southeast Asia, in 1944–45, and General Officer Commanding in Chief, Eastern Command, in 1945–46.

LEE TANK. British designation for U.S. M3 TANK.

LEGASPI. This city in southeast Luzon, on the Bicol Peninsula, was the site of port and air facilities. It was seized by the Japanese in an unopposed landing on December 12, 1941. It was returned to American hands as the result of a landing (also unopposed) on April 1, 1945. The airstrip became operational on April 7.

LEGENTILHOMME, Paul (1884–1975). Commander of French troops in Somaliland in 1940. He was the first French general to join DE GAULLE following the Franco-German armistice, and commanded the forces of FREE FRANCE in East Africa and Syria, later holding administrative positions.

LÉGER, Alexis Saint-Léger (1887–1975). From 1933 to March 1940 Léger was secretary general of the French Foreign Ministry. He took a hard line against Adolf HITLER, urging an active stand with Britain and the Soviet Union against German encroachments. Following the French defeat in 1940, Léger came to the United States. He was also a noted poet, writing under the name St.-John Perse.

LEGHORN. This important northern Italian port fell to the U.S. 34th Division on July 19, 1944, thereby shortening the Allied supply lines.

LEGION OF MERIT. Established by the U.S. Congress on July 20, 1942, the LOM is the first U.S. decoration instituted for award to foreigners as well as the first U.S. medal that can be awarded in one of four possible degrees. It is awarded to U.S. military personnel (without degree) or military personnel of friendly armed forces who since September 8, 1939, have distinguished themselves by exceptionally meritorious conduct in the performance of outstanding services.

LEIGH LIGHT. An extremely high intensity airborne searchlight, British-designed, for use in night attacks on surfaced U-boats by patrol bombers. It was not used for scanning but was switched on to assist the bomber in its attack run on the target.

LEIGH-MALLORY, Sir Trafford (1892–1944). A career RAF officer who commanded No. 12 Group, FIGHTER COMMAND, during the Battle of BRITAIN in 1940. Afterward he took command of No. 11 Group, and in November 1942 became commander in chief of Fighter Command. At the close of 1943 he was appointed to command of the Allied Expeditionary Air Force under Gen. Dwight EISENHOWER; in this post he was in charge of the tactical air forces supporting the INVASION of Normandy and subsequent operations. In the autumn of 1944 Leigh-Mallory, an air chief marshal (from December 1943), was given a new appointment as air commander in chief, Southeast Asia Command, but in November he was killed in an aircraft crash in France en route to take up the appointment. An ambitious and aggressive officer, he was the center of some instances of intraservice rivalry. His quarrel with Air Marshal Keith PARK in 1940 over the employment of fighters in "big wings" became notorious.

LEIPZIG. Attacked by nearly 800 RAF bombers on the night of February 19, 1944, the aircraft-production complex at this city was the first target of Allied aircraft during the intensified assault that acquired the name BIG WEEK. Seventy-eight bombers, almost 10 percent of the attacking force, never returned to England. On February 20 more than 1,000 bombers (941 of them B-17s and B-24s) attacked Leipzig again. Production of the Ju 88 plant was stopped for a month and 40 Me 109s were destroyed, along with the factory, at the city's Erla plant. Leipzig fell to the U.S. First Army's 2d and 69th Divisions on April 19, 1945, following diehard German resistance.

LEIPZIG. German light cruiser, launched in October 1929. The *Leipzig* displaced 6,650 tons and had a top speed of 32 knots. She was armed with nine 5.9-inch and six 3.5-inch guns and twelve 21-inch torpedo tubes, and carried two aircraft. The *Leipzig* was the only significant German warship besides the PRINZ EUGEN and the NÜRNBERG to survive the war. She was scuttled in the North Sea with a load of poison gas in July 1946.

LE KEF. Important road center in northern Tunisia, Field Marshal ROMMEL's original objective at the time of the KASSERINE PASS battle (February 1943). Rommel gave up the attempt to reach Le Kef on February 22.

LEMAY, Curtis E. (1906–). Originally a pursuit pilot, LeMay was transferred to bombardment, where he earned a reputation as one of the most skillful navigators in the prewar U.S. Army Air Corps. In 1942, while a colonel, he trained the 305th Bomb Group, which he later led against the Germans. A keen student of tactics, later commander of the 3d Air Division, he continued to be a mission leader in such important strikes as the REGENSBURG raid. He concluded that evasive maneuvering during the bomb run afforded no additional protection to air crews but merely scattered bombs all over the landscape. The success attained by his group demonstrated the importance of maintaining the defensive formation and flying a straight-in bomb run.

As a major general commanding the XXI Bomber Command with headquarters on GUAM, he revolutionized the bombing of Japan. Because the B-29 had not achieved the expected destruction in high-altitude precision strikes, LeMay ordered the plane stripped of much of its defensive armament and used for low-level night attacks with incendiary bombs (*see* B-29). As LeMay had anticipated, enemy defenses could not cope with these attacks, which exploited the vulnerability of Japanese cities to fire.

LEMELSEN, Joachim (1888–1954). German Army officer (General der Panzertruppen), a corps commander on the Russian front and an army commander in Italy. His final command was the Fourteenth Army.

LEMNITZER, Lyman L. (1899–). U.S. Army officer who served on the General Staff before becoming commanding general of the 34th Antiaircraft Brigade in 1942. As assistant chief of staff at Allied Force Headquarters, he accompanied Gen. Mark CLARK on his secret mission to North Africa in October 1942. Their attempt to persuade the French to welcome U.S. and British troops failed. In 1943 Lemnitzer served as deputy chief of staff of the FIFTH ARMY, before returning to command the 34th Brigade. He then became deputy chief of staff of the 15th Army Group in SICILY and ITALY. In 1944 he was promoted to major general, becoming deputy chief of staff, Supreme Allied Command Mediterranean, where he finished the war. In 1960–62 Lemnitzer, as a full general, was chairman of the Joint Chiefs of Staff, and between 1962 and his retirement in 1969 he served as the Supreme Allied Commander in Europe (NATO). Greatly respected as a strategist, one of the most durable soldiers of his time, his powers in no degree diminished even in advanced age, Lemnitzer was a highly popular commander at all levels in the U.S. armed services.

LEND-LEASE. The Lend-Lease Act (passed March 11, 1941) was originally conceived by President ROOSEVELT as a means of helping Great Britain win the war without direct United States intervention. The program was gradually expanded to include other Allied nations. The act provided that the President could "sell, transfer title to, exchange, lease, lend or otherwise dispose of" defense articles to the government of any country whose defense he thought vital to the defense of the United States. In return the United States was to receive "payment or repayment in kind or property, or any other direct or indirect benefit" which the President deemed satisfactory. In other words, the President was given the authority to determine what defense items or materials could be used best by the Allies or by the military forces of the United States. Immediately after signing the Lend-Lease Act, Roosevelt declared that the defense of Great Britain was vital to the defense of the United States and asked the Secretary of the Navy to turn over 28 motor torpedo boats and submarine chasers to the British along with matériel for arming merchant ships. He made a similar declaration about Greece, and transferred guns, shells and infantry equipment to the Greek Army.

In March 1941 the first lend-lease funds, $7 billion, were appropriated by Congress; a further $21 billion was later appropriated. In addition, almost $26 billion was authorized for lend-lease from the budgets of the War and Navy Departments. Edward R. STETTINIUS, Jr., was named administrator when the Office of Lend-Lease Administration was established (October 28, 1941). Of lend-lease assistance, almost $47 billion out of $50 billion was given to the British, the Russians, the French and the Chinese but aid was granted to 38 countries, including 19 American republics. Reverse lend-lease came back in the amount of approximately $8 billion, and returns in kind totaled approximately $2 billion. After the war a lend-lease settlement was arranged between the United States and Great Britain. It was agreed that the "net sum due from the United Kingdom to the United States for the settlement of lend-lease and reciprocal aid, for the acquisition of surplus property and the United States' interest in installations located in the United Kingdom, and for the settlement of claims shall be $650 million." The British had actually been given over $31 billion of aid.

The principle of lend-lease actually was put into effect when the United States transferred to Britain surplus stocks of munitions valued at $43 million, after the evacuation from DUNKIRK, where the British lost large quantities of military supplies. But the NEUTRALITY ACT of 1935 (amended and revised in 1937) called for an embargo of shipments from the United States to countries involved in war and prohibited the purchases of securities issued by warring countries. In 1939, when war seemed imminent, the Secretary of State, Cordell HULL, submitted proposals for modification of the neutrality legislation, pointing out that "no matter how much we may wish or may try to dissociate ourselves from world events, we cannot achieve this dissociation." Under the Neutrality Act of 1939, the embargo provision of the earlier legislation was repealed. The new act insisted on CASH AND CARRY, i.e., exports to belligerents were not to involve the extending of credit or the use of United States vessels. Under the cash-and-carry rule,

Britain was compelled to finance its increasing purchases from the United States from its dollar resources, which rapidly declined. Hence the need for such a mechanism as lend-lease, described to Parliament by Winston CHURCHILL as "the most unsordid act in the history of any nation."

After September 25, 1943, lend-lease was administered by the Foreign Economic Administration, directed by Leo T. CROWLEY.

LENINGRAD, BATTLE OF. By mid-August 1941 German troops, though weakened by steady fighting, had managed to advance to the environs of Leningrad, the second city of the Soviet Union. Soviet artillery at Gatchina (Krasnogvardeysk), one of the six major fortified areas around Leningrad, opened fire on August 19, signaling the beginning of the battle for the city. On August 25 German forces broke into the area of Kolpino and reached Schlüsselburg. Three days later, on August 28, the October Railway Line to Moscow was cut, and by September 6 German forces in some strength had closed on the southern approaches to the city.

As the defenses were being prepared against the Germans approaching from the south, the Soviets had also to keep watch in the north, where by August 20 pressure applied by the Finnish Southeastern Army had forced the evacuation of VIIPURI (Vyborg) at the north end of the KARELIAN ISTHMUS. While the Finns and Germans drove forward on land, Leningrad was subjected to incessant aerial bombardment. Although ill-equipped, Soviet air units gave what they could to the defense. By September 15, according to Soviet sources, 500 German planes had been destroyed. At the same time what was left of the Red Baltic Fleet was anchored within the perimeter, and the ships added their guns to the city's defenses. Many of the ships' crews were put ashore, where they fought as infantry. By mid-September it appeared that the Germans would inundate the defenses.

On September 12 General ZHUKOV was ordered to take command at Leningrad. Within a week of his arrival, Zhukov had shocked the RED ARMY into finding itself and the tide of the German attack was broken, though not without fearful Soviet casualties. On September 26 the Soviet command discovered that the Germans were digging in along their line south of the Neva. To the north, the Finns, having recovered the territory lost in 1940, discontinued their offense.

Although the front had stabilized, it would have been precipitate to conclude that the attacks on the city had ceased. Yet this is what Zhukov reported to Joseph STALIN on October 6; at the same time he reported sightings of heavy German armor movements south toward Moscow. This assessment most likely convinced Stalin to order Zhukov to Moscow for consultation on the increasing threat to the capital and, subsequently, to give him command of the Western Front.

In Leningrad, the extreme difficulties caused by the incessant bombing and shelling were compounded by the shortage of food; no more than a trickle of supplies managed to get through. Strict rationing was enforced, and violators were shot or sent to the front to work in labor units. The supplies that did come in were most often ferried across Lake Ladoga by naval units of the lake flotilla; food, raw materials and fuel went into Leningrad, and evacuees and industrial equipment and products came out. Supporting the waterborne operation was an airlift using Aeroflot aircraft. About 45 tons of supplies a day each way were carried in and out of the city, including guns and ammunition produced for use on other fronts.

This resupply effort had not gone unnoticed by the Germans, and Field Marshal von LEEB concluded that he should attempt to extend his lines along the southern littoral of Lake Ladoga so as to interdict the supply route. But Hitler ordered instead a drive on TIKHVIN, thence north to the Svir River to link up with the Finns. In effect, the two moves would accomplish the same result, but HITLER was also interested in seizing the bauxite facilities near Tikhvin. Initially, the German attack went well, and for Leningrad the result of this advance was near-starvation. Inbound supplies were held up awaiting the outcome of the battle, and with the lake beginning to ice over, plans were made to use an ice road to replace the convoy. On November 22 the first trucks made the passage and Leningrad was at least momentarily saved. The road remained open throughout the winter, moving supplies to Leningrad and bringing out material and evacuees. More than 500,000 people were removed from the city by this means, but several hundred thousand starved to death. In December the Germans withdrew from Tikhvin, removing that threat to the supply lines.

The Soviet winter offensive (1941–42) against the German center was supported by a major operation in the Leningrad area. On January 7 MERETSKOV's Volkhov Front attacked to the rear of the northward-oriented German Eighteenth Army. But the Soviets failed to appreciate the stamina and resilience of the German and allied forces, and as the battle wore on large Soviet forces, including VLASOV's Second Shock Army, were surrounded and eventually lost. The Leningrad siege continued, the theater being relegated to secondary status by the Germans until they could muster sufficient strength to complete the encirclement and subsequent reduction of the city. Following the capture of SEVASTOPOL (July 1, 1942), Hitler ordered MANSTEIN and the Eleventh Army to move north from the Crimea and take Leningrad. Instead of the army moving *in toto*, however, bits and pieces were broken off and attached to other commands to such an extent that the army ceased to be an effective unit. Even so, Manstein went to Leningrad and took command of Army Group North. Before he could act, however, Meretskov's forces again took the offensive (August). Hitler ordered Manstein to concentrate on the Volkhov Front, and once again Leningrad received a respite. This time, actually, it was permanent relief. The Germans were not able to contain the Soviet attack until November; Manstein, in the interim, had been moved to the Don front.

Before the Germans could regroup and attack Leningrad in force, the Soviets executed their plan to open a land corridor into Leningrad. Called Operation Spark (Iskra), the plan called for Leningrad and Volkhov Front forces to breach the German lines in the Schlüsselburg–Sinyavino area, the 10-mile wedge that separated the two fronts on the southern shore of Lake Ladoga. On January 12, 1943, the attack began. Six days later, on January 18, after extremely hard fighting and great losses on both sides, the link-up was made. As a result the whole southern shore of the lake was cleared of German troops to a depth of seven miles. Much bitter fighting followed, and it was not until the end of 1943 that the breach could be widened to any appreciable depth. By January 20, 1944, the German Northern Wall, propagandized as impregnable, had been breached and Novgorod liberated. On January 24 Pushkin and Pavlovsk were retaken, and two days later Gatchina fell. By the 27th the Germans had been driven more than 50 miles from Leningrad. The siege was over. J.E.J.

LENTAIGNE, Walter David Alexander (1899–1955). British Army officer who succeeded Gen. Orde WINGATE as commander of the CHINDITS in BURMA when the latter was killed. The Chindits were responsible for considerable disruption of Japanese communications in Burma while under Wingate's command, and the task facing Lentaigne was chiefly to extricate them. His highest wartime rank was lieutenant general.

LEOPOLD III, King of the Belgians (1901–). The son of King Albert I, who resisted German aggression in World War I, Leopold (ruled 1934–51) led his country into a policy of "independence"—neutrality in the German-Allied dispute—to which he adhered, despite increasing proof of aggressive German intentions, until Adolf HITLER invaded Belgium in 1940. Trapped with his army by the German breakthrough, Leopold chose to capitulate separately from his British and French allies, provoking violent discord with the refugee Belgian Government and leading eventually to his own abdication in 1951.

LERWICK. British twin-engine seaplane, Saunders-Roe's replacement for its highly successful London twin-engine, biplane flying boat which served RAF COASTAL COMMAND from 1936 to 1941. The Lerwick monoplane, though thoroughly modern in appearance, lasted about one year before being shelved because of instability in flight and inability to recover from stalls.

LES GUEUX. Dutch underground organization that harassed German occupation forces. The name, meaning "the beggars," was a revival of that of a 16th-century group that opposed the Spanish conquerors.

LETOV S-328. Czech single-radial-engine biplane used as a reconnaissance plane and light bomber, designed in 1933. It was confiscated by the LUFTWAFFE and assigned to pilot schools, though a few were used in the Slovak and Bulgarian Air Forces. Three were captured in 1944 by partisans and used against the Germans. The S-328 had a 560-horsepower engine, 176 miles per hour top speed and armament of four 7.7-mm. machine guns.

LEUTZE, U.S.S. FLETCHER-class destroyer. Commissioned in 1944, she arrived in the Pacific war zone in time to provide gunfire support for the landing on PELELIU. Support of the LEYTE landing was quickly followed by the Surigao Strait night action, part of the battle for LEYTE GULF. In January 1945 *Leutze* took part in the invasion of Luzon, and the next month in the assault on IWO JIMA. Late in March she took part in the pre-landing bombardment of OKINAWA. On April 6, off Okinawa, *Leutze* was severely damaged by a KAMIKAZE plane. After voyage repairs, she returned to the United States.

LEVASSEUR PL-15. French two- or four-place, single-engine, twin-float biplane torpedo bomber. It was introduced in 1932, and was one of the oldest floatplanes in use in 1939.

LEXINGTON, U.S.S. Aircraft carrier and class (with SARATOGA), completed in 1927. These were ships of 33,000 tons standard displacement, with a maximum speed of 33 knots; they carried 90 aircraft. They were laid down as battle cruisers and converted to carriers while under construction. "Lady Lex" took torpedo and bomb hits in the Battle of the CORAL SEA and finally, after suffering two internal explosions, was abandoned. She was then sunk by an American destroyer. A successor *Lexington* (ESSEX class) joined the new FIFTH FLEET in 1943. She served as flagship for Vice-Adm. Marc MITSCHER, commander of the FAST CARRIER TASK FORCE.

LEY, Robert (1890–1945). One of Adolf HITLER's early followers, who became head of the German Labor Front (Deutsche Arbeitsfront) in May 1933 and remained in this position until the end of the Third Reich in 1945. An air force veteran of World War I, Dr. Ley was a chemist by profession and worked for I. G. Farben. He joined the Nazi Party in 1925, became a gauleiter (district leader) in the Rhineland and in 1930 was elected to the Reichstag. As director of the Labor Front, Ley organized the elaborate "Strength through Joy" program of sports, outings and vacation trips for workers. His activities were endlessly varied, since the Labor Front was the largest enterprise of the kind ever known in Western history. Ley, who has been termed "pathologically uncouth," was afflicted with a drinking problem, and his private life has been described as unsavory. At NUREMBERG he committed suicide on October 25, 1945.

LEYTE. One of the eastern Visayan Islands lying midway between Luzon and Mindanao, Leyte was the first part of the PHILIPPINES retaken by American forces. After a two-day naval bombardment the SIXTH ARMY (Lt. Gen. Walter KRUEGER) landed on October 22, 1944, accompanied by Gen. Douglas MACARTHUR and Philippine President Sergio OSMEÑA.

With Maj. Gen. Franklin C. SIBERT's X Corps on the north and Maj. Gen. John R. HODGE's XXIV Corps to the south, the Sixth Army secured the broad north-central valley by November 2, forcing Lt. Gen. Sosaku Suzuki's Japanese 35th Army into the island's north-south mountain backbone. During the mopping-up phase Krueger was able to secure the south coast of Samar Island, just north of Leyte, but his two-corps drive on the western, Japanese-held port of ORMOC was halted by bitter fighting in Leyte's mountains and jungle valleys. Temporarily frustrated, Krueger launched an amphibious assault against Leyte's western shore on December 7, secured Ormoc three days later and by December 20 had taken the last Japanese port. After the failure of a daring airborne attack on American airfields on December 6, Suzuki was finally forced to disperse the remaining troops that could not escape by sea.

On December 15 control of the Leyte campaign passed from the U.S. Sixth to the U.S. EIGHTH ARMY, and the remnants of the Japanese forces were cleared during January and February of the following year. The hard-fought campaign cost the Americans some 3,500 dead and 12,000 casualties; Japanese losses totaled 55,000 to 60,000 dead but only 389 prisoners. From their foothold at Leyte, American forces would now move north and south against the larger islands.

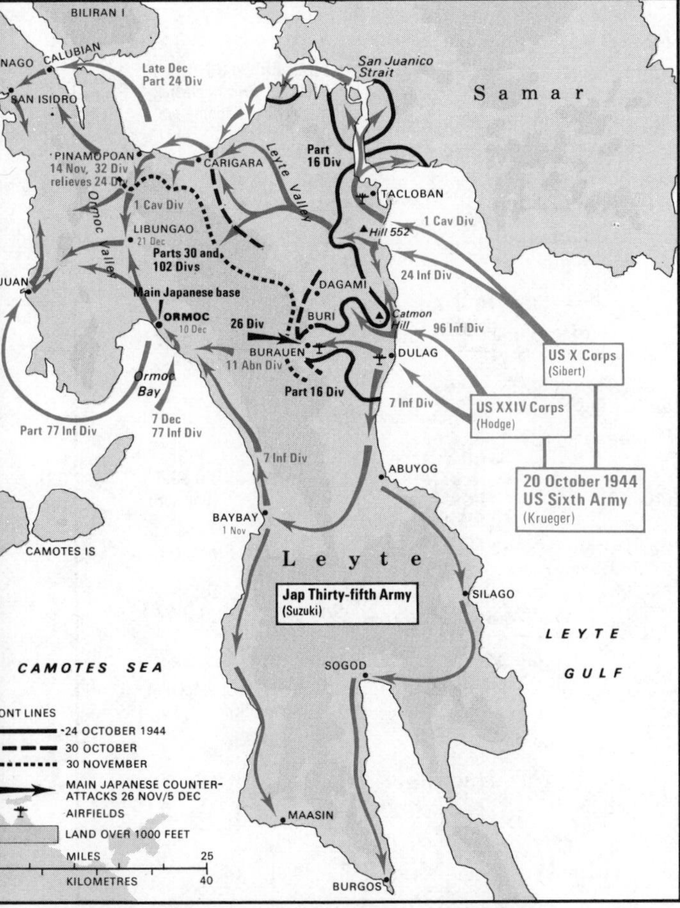

LEYTE: The Americans returned to the Philippines

LEYTE GULF, BATTLE FOR. Triggered by Gen. Douglas MACARTHUR's invasion of LEYTE on October 20, 1944, the battle for Leyte Gulf took place October 23–26. To counter the American assault landing in the PHILIPPINES, the Japanese Imperial General Headquarters ordered Operation Sho I (*see* SHO GO) executed. The concept underlying Sho I was relatively simple. A comparatively weak force consisting of 1 heavy and 3 light carriers, carrying a greatly reduced complement—a mere 116 planes—plus 2 battleships, 3 cruisers and 9 destroyers was to steam south toward Luzon from bases in the Inland Sea, then turn about, luring Adm. William F. HALSEY and his THIRD FLEET away from the scene of amphibious operations at Leyte. This action would then permit two other Japanese surface forces—one to come through San Bernardino Strait and the other through Surigao Strait—to make simultaneous attacks at dawn on October 25 on all American amphibious shipping in Leyte Gulf. At the same time Japanese land-based planes would attack Third Fleet carriers. Finally, KAMIKAZES would begin their suicide attacks on shipping in Leyte Gulf.

A great daring gamble, Sho I committed to action virtually all the remnants of the once powerful Japanese Navy in one rash attack. Considerable credit must be given to Japanese planners, who correctly assessed what Halsey's reaction would be to the decoy force. They based the working of Sho I on the fact that San Bernardino Strait would be left open once Halsey took off north after the carriers. Further, the use of carriers for decoy purposes was extremely clever, because all during the pre-invasion strikes against Formosa and the Ryukyus, Third Fleet had encountered neither the carriers nor carrier air.

The engagements encompassed in the battle for Leyte Gulf were four in number: the action in the Sibuyan Sea, October 24; the action in the Surigao Strait, October 24–25; the battle off Samar Island, October 25; and the battle off Cape Engaño, October 25–26. These, taken together, make Leyte Gulf the greatest naval battle ever fought.

The battle opened on the 23d as U.S. submarines off Palawan Island sighted the Center Force of the three groups approaching Leyte from different directions, and sank three cruisers. Task Force 38 aircraft located and heavily attacked both this force south of Mindoro in the Sibuyan Sea, sinking the giant battleship MUSASHI, and the Southern Force steaming through the Sulu Sea. Meanwhile, Third Fleet ships came under increasingly stringent and damaging air attacks, in which the carrier PRINCETON was mortally wounded and a light cruiser and five destroyers were damaged. During the night of October 24–25 Third Fleet fast carriers moved north from San Bernardino Strait to be in position for dawn attacks against the Northern Force decoy carriers. San Bernardino Strait was now open in accordance with Japanese expectations, and the Center Force, including four battleships and five cruisers, steamed through and turned south toward Leyte Gulf.

During this same night the Southern Force entered Surigao Strait, where it was virtually destroyed by Rear Adm. Jesse B. OLDENDORF's force of battleships, cruisers, destroyers and PT boats. The Center Force, having passed relatively unmolested into the Philippine Sea during the night, attacked the SEVENTH FLEET's 16 escort carriers and 21 screening vessels under Rear Adm. Thomas L. SPRAGUE, protecting the Leyte Gulf beachhead area. The brunt of the attack fell on the northernmost unit, under Rear Adm. C. A. F. SPRAGUE, which bravely staved off the Japanese at a cost of two of the escort carriers and three ships of the screen, together with a number of other vessels damaged to varying degrees, and the loss of a number of lives. After mounting this attack, the Japanese Center Force retired without taking advantage of its favorable situation.

At the same time, Halsey's carrier aircraft had located and mounted attacks on the Northern Force in the vicinity of Cape Engaño on the morning of October 25. All this time Halsey was unaware of what was going on at Leyte Gulf until, while the Japanese ships were being polished off in Surigao Strait, Vice-Adm. Thomas C. KINKAID, Seventh Fleet commander, radioed Halsey for help in saving the beachhead. Halsey changed Third Fleet's course 180 degrees and headed south at full

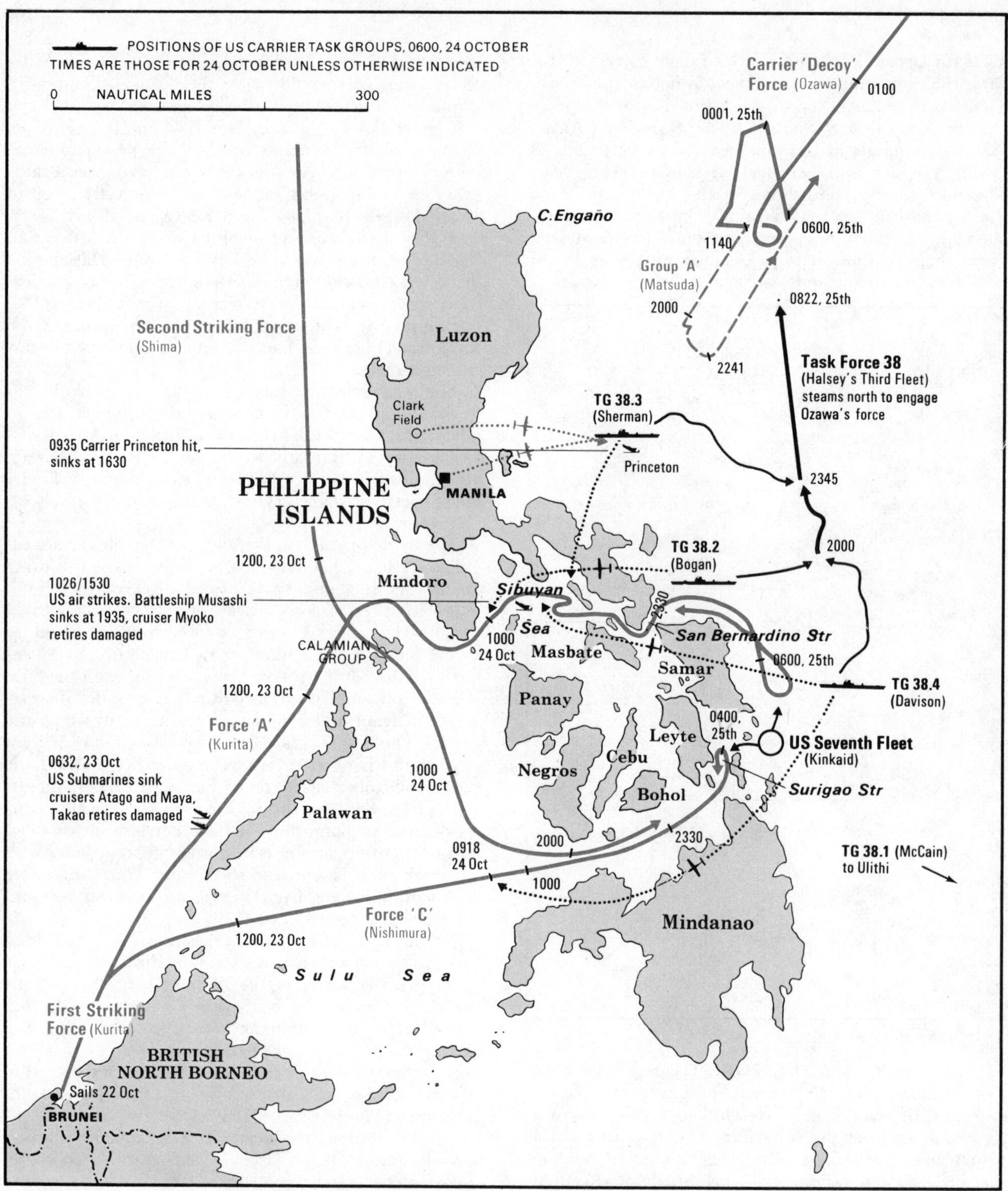

THE BATTLE FOR LEYTE GULF: The Japanese plan to destroy U.S. land and naval forces

speed. At this point he was only 42 miles from the pitiful remnants of the Japanese Northern Force and closing fast. It took him 23 hours to get back to Leyte Gulf, by which time the danger was dissipated and the Japanese were on the run. On the 26th the battle for Leyte Gulf ended as U.S. land- and carrier-based aircraft found and attacked the retreating Japanese cripples which had survived the battle.

In the entire battle the Japanese lost 4 carriers, 3 battleships, including *Musashi,* 6 cruisers and 14 destroyers. The rest of the Sho I force fought its way back to Brunei Bay on the northwest coast of Borneo, reaching it on October 28. Besides ships, the Japanese lost hundreds of their trained pilots and 7,500 to 10,000 sailors. **B.F.**

LIAISON PLANES. These craft performed a variety of wartime tasks, such as reconnaissance, artillery spotting, evacuation of wounded and light transport. Perhaps the most famous of the type was Germany's Fieseler STORCH, a high-wing monoplane with an elaborate array of wing slots and flaps to reduce landing and

Night action in Surigao Strait, as seen from U.S.S. *Pennsylvania*

takeoff distance. In April 1945 Hanna REITSCH relied on the single-engine Storch to make the last flight to Adolf HITLER's headquarters in Berlin. She used a rubble-strewn street for a runway.

The Allies had similar planes. The British, for example, made extensive use of the Westland LYSANDER single-engine monoplane to infiltrate agents into occupied Europe. On the eve of America's entry into the war, the Army Air Corps acquired the Ryan Dragonfly, which embodied the same concepts as the Storch. The Army, however, abandoned the Dragonfly and bought large numbers of light planes such as the Piper Cub and the Stinson Voyager. *See also* L-2, L-3, L-4, L-5.

LIBERATOR. *See* B-24.

LIBERTY SHIP. A mass-produced merchant cargo ship designed by the U.S. Maritime Commission in the hope of producing a type that could be built more rapidly than U-boats could sink them. The Liberty design emphasized simplicity of construction, and used reciprocating engines to permit builders of turbines, diesels and electric motors to concentrate on production for naval use. The basic Liberty cargo-ship design was identified by the Maritime Commission designation EC2-S-C1. Other variants were specially designed to carry tanks, crated airplanes or liquid fuel. Between 1939 and 1945 the Maritime Commission built 5,777 cargo ships; 2,770 of these were Liberties. A few Liberty ships were used by the U.S. Navy, but the great majority were operated by civilian shipping firms.

LICATA. Licata, Sicily, was needed as a supply port by General PATTON's SEVENTH ARMY. It was seized and opened to shipping July 10, 1943, the first day of the invasion.

LICHTENSTEIN. Code name of German interception RADAR, used in night-fighter models of the JUNKERS JU 88 and MESSERSCHMITT ME 110. The Lichtenstein BC (FuG 202) was introduced early in 1942. Later versions were the Lichtenstein SN-2 (FuG 220), C-1 (FuG 212) and SN-3 (FuG 228).

LIDDELL HART, Sir Basil Henry (1895–1970). British military commentator, theoretician and historian, one of the most creative and influential strategists of the 20th century. In World War I he served in the British infantry at Ypres and the Somme. He retired as a captain in 1927. When he redrafted the *Infantry Training Manual* in 1920 he expounded the "expanded torrent" method of attack based on wartime infiltration tactics. He advocated surprise, mobility, mechanization, armor and air power. He made these points continually, especially as the military correspondent of the *Daily Telegraph* (1925–35) and of *The Times* (1935–39).

Some of his ideas were adopted by the Germans in evolving the BLITZKRIEG tactic. As personal adviser to the War Minister, Leslie HORE-BELISHA, in 1937–38, Liddell Hart constantly pressed his ideas and the need for reform within the British Army. Relations with senior generals became so strained that he resigned the post, though he served as an adviser during the war. He wrote more than 30 books, including *History of the Second World War.*

LIDICE. A Czech village that became a symbol of Nazi barbarity. After the death of Reinhard HEYDRICH following the bombing of his car (May 29, 1942), his successor in BOHEMIA-MORAVIA, Karl Hermann FRANK, decided on "a special repressive action to give the Czechs a lesson in propriety." Because two men from Lidice had left Czechoslovakia in 1939 and were serving in the RAF, Frank picked Lidice as the place for the "lesson." On June 9, 1942, a convoy of Germans arrived and sealed off the village; all the inhabitants were ordered to assemble in the square. A child and a woman who attempted to escape were shot. The male population of the village was locked up in the buildings of a farm. All the 195 women (except seven who were shot) were sent to Ravensbrück concentration camp, where about 50 of them died. The children were also taken to a concentration camp. The men (numbering 172, including boys over 16) were taken from the farm buildings in batches of 10 and shot. After everyone was disposed of, the German Security Police burned and dynamited the houses of the village and leveled the ruins. A camera crew recorded the entire proceedings. The name of Lidice, said the Germans in the newspaper *Der Neue Tag,* "has been erased from the records." But the eradication was short-lived. A town in Illinois and another in Mexico each took the name Lidice. And Edna St. Vincent Millay wrote a poem, "The Murder of Lidice," which enshrined Lidice as a symbol of resistance to tyranny. The village has not been rebuilt.

LIÈGE. Belgian industrial city on the Meuse River at the northern edge of the ARDENNES. Blocking a major invasion route from Germany, the city was heavily fortified in both world wars. In both cases defenders of its great forts made epic stands, in 1940 the last fort surrendering 17 days after the city itself fell on May 12, but with little influence on the overall campaign. After the U.S. 3d Armored Division captured Liège on September 7, 1944, it became an American logistical and hospital center and target of some 2,000 German V-1 and V-2 rockets.

LIFEBOAT RATION. An emergency ration, packed for the use of the crews of shipwrecked or torpedoed naval and merchant ships. This varied according to the country of origin. The U.S. lifeboat ration, packed in a large rectangular can, included small cans of a fruit-and-nut mixture called pemmican, C RATION biscuits, D RATION chocolate and malted-milk tablets. It was intended to provide an extremely compact, nonperishable ration which could furnish stranded sailors enough vitamins and calories to keep them alive.

LIGHTFOOT. Code name for General MONTGOMERY's plan for the second Battle of ALAMEIN, October 23, 1942. Lightfoot called for the infantry, with massive artillery support, to break enemy lines, after which the armor would pass through the breach and hold the area.

LIGHTNING. *See* P-38.

LILLEHAMMER. Town located a little less than 120 miles north of OSLO, on one of the two main routes to TRONDHEIM. In the NORWAY campaign in 1940, Allied forces positioned near Lillehammer failed to stem the German attempt to break out from Oslo to link with other German troops in Trondheim.

LILO. Code name for a planned breakwater device using floating air bags, designed to be used off the Normandy beaches in connection with artificial harbors. Although the Lilo did not work out, it was a partial parent of the BOMBARDON.

LIMA CONFERENCE (1938). This, the Eighth International Conference of American States, was mainly concerned with joint action by American republics against possible aggression or subversion by non-American powers. The Declaration of Lima, approved December 24, 1938, both supported joint action by American states to meet a common threat and stated that foreign ministers of all the republics should meet upon the call of any single one of them. This conference witnessed the first strong evidence of the doctrine of continental solidarity, even though Argentina would not accept that doctrine in all its implications, then or later.

LINCOLN. British bomber, built by Avro, a stretched version of the LANCASTER. It came into service only in 1945, not in time to see operational duty.

LINDBERGH, Charles Augustus (1902–1974). Before the war Lindbergh had toured German aircraft factories, with the cooperation of Hermann GÖRING, and had been greatly impressed by the power of the LUFTWAFFE and the industry that supported it. He reported his observations to U.S. authorities. After the European war began, he became a prominent opponent of American entry, looking upon the war as a purely foreign quarrel. After PEARL HARBOR he toured the Pacific as a technical representative of the United Aircraft Corp., parent of the firms that built the Vought Corsair and its Pratt and Whitney engine. Besides working with the Marines who flew the Corsair, he helped the P-38 units serving in Lt. Gen. George KENNEY's FIFTH AIR FORCE. Lindbergh drew upon his vast experience—including his pioneering solo flight from New York to Paris—to instruct the younger pilots in extending the range of their fighters by careful attention to throttle setting and fuel mixture. He also flew several combat missions. While flying a P-38 on a mission to observe fighter coverage of a bomber raid on the island of Guam, he shot down a Japanese plane. Since he was a civilian and not supposed to engage in combat, his kill was not revealed to the public.

LINDEMANN, F. A. *See* CHERWELL.

LINDEMANN, Georg (1884–1963). German Army officer (colonel general, 1942) who served in France and on the Eastern Front. It was his division that in June 1942 captured the Soviet general Andrei VLASOV. In March 1944 Lindemann was appointed to command of Army Group North in Russia; he was replaced in July by Gen. Johannes FRIESSNER.

LINGAYEN GULF. Gulf on the west coast of Luzon, about 120 miles north of MANILA, which was the site of the main Japanese invasion landings, December 22, 1941 (14th Army). This same gulf was also the site, a little more than three years later, of the landing of the U.S. SIXTH ARMY (Gen. Walter KRUEGER) when the Americans returned to Luzon (January 9, 1945).

LINGGA ROADS. An anchorage in the Lingga Archipelago, a group of small islands at the eastern end of the Strait of Malacca, just south of Singapore. The main surface force of the Japanese COMBINED FLEET was based here in the summer of 1944, after the Battle of the PHILIPPINE SEA, to prepare for the anticipated SHO Go operation. Lingga Roads was chosen as convenient to the oil supplies of the Netherlands East Indies and outside the reach of Allied air attack. The Lingga area was the site of intensive training operations up to the time the Japanese fleet sailed for LEYTE GULF.

LINLITHGOW, Victor Alexander John Hope, 2d Marquess (1887–1952). As Viceroy of India in 1936–43, Linlithgow faced domestic political strife and Congress Party hostility to India's participation in the British war effort. Prominent in his mobilization of India for war was his creation of an Indian department of supply and, in October 1941, of the National Defence Council, which in its first two years recruited more than 2 million men for the Allied cause.

LINTON, John W. L. (1905–1943). Captain of the British submarine *Turbulent,* which in 1942 and 1943 was engaged in operations against enemy sea communications to Tripoli. Linton, a lieutenant commander, was a remarkably successful submarine captain, frequently taking his boat in to point-blank range before attacking. In one raid he wiped out a convoy of four supply ships and a destroyer, and in a similar later attack sank two ships and a destroyer during a night operation. H.M.S. *Turbulent,* with Linton still commanding her, was mined in March 1943. Linton was awarded a posthumous VICTORIA CROSS for his gallantry in these operations.

LION. U.S. Navy term for a self-contained mobile unit incorporating the men and equipment necessary to set up a large advance naval base. This "packaged" organization, when set up on an island in a forward area, could provide service and repairs, except for serious cases, to a large naval force. It was larger and more extensive than a CUB, providing such things as supply and medical service, communications, fuel and ordnance repairs.

LIORÉ NIEUPORT LN–40. French light bomber used by the Navy for antisubmarine work and, after the German invasion in 1940, for ground support.

LIORÉ-ET-OLIVIER H43. French three-place, single-engine, observation-scout twin-float seaplane. This craft was first flown in 1934, but extensive modifications delayed production until 1939. A total of 20 were built.

LIORÉ-ET-OLIVIER H257bis and H258. French six-place, twin-engine, twin-float biplane torpedo bomber. The H257 and H258 were almost identical except for the H258's larger engines. They were used operationally during the war, and one was still in service in June 1944. About 50 were built.

LIORÉ-ET-OLIVIER LEO 45. French medium bomber produced by Lioré-et-Olivier, operated from December 1936 as a nationalized division of the Société Nationale de Constructions Aéronautiques de Sud-Est under a law providing for government acquisition of defense industries. A fast, streamlined, twin-engine, low-wing monoplane, the LeO 45 had an unusual twin tail whose vertical surfaces extended downward from the tail plane, giving its tail a unique "inverted" appearance. It had a crew of four, and carried its bomb load in an internal bay. Produced in some quantity, the LeO 45 served in French North Africa after the fall of France in 1940. It had a top speed of 310 miles per hour, a range of about 750 miles and a bomb load of 3,000 or more pounds.

LIORÉ-ET-OLIVIER LEO 451. France's only modern medium bomber. Introduced in 1939, it was widely used by l'Armée de l'Air to good effect. Its maximum speed was 307 miles per hour; it cruised at 227 miles per hour. It carried a two- or three-man crew and was armed with one 20-mm. cannon and four 7.5-mm. machine guns. It carried 880 pounds of bombs and had a range of 1,367 miles.

LIPSKI, Josef (1894–1958). Polish ambassador in Berlin from October 1933 to the outbreak of the war on September 1, 1939.

LISCOME BAY, U.S.S. A KAISER-built CASABLANCA-class escort aircraft carrier, commissioned in 1943, which supported the capture of the GILBERT ISLANDS. Early in the morning of November 24, 1943, she was torpedoed by the Japanese submarine *I-175* while steaming with a task group near the Gilberts. After a heavy magazine explosion, followed by fire, the carrier rolled over and sank about six minutes after the two torpedoes struck. Six hundred and forty-six of her crew went down with her. Survivors were picked up by the U.S.S. *Leonard Wood.*

LIST, Siegmund Wilhelm (1880–1971). German Army officer, named a field marshal in 1940 following his successful leadership of the Fourteenth Army in Poland and the Twelfth Army in FRANCE. Early in 1941 List reached an agreement with the Bulgarian General Staff permitting the passage of German troops through Bulgaria, and he subsequently commanded the Twelfth Army of 15 divisions, four of them armored, in its campaign in the BALKANS. He was then tapped for command of Army Group A, ordered to seize the Caucasus in the summer of 1942. By August List and his army had reached their maximum advance, and when List told Adolf Hitler that Germany did not have the resources to win the war, he was called to Hitler's forward headquarters at Vinnitsa, where he gave a calm appraisal of the situation. Hitler listened cordially, restated his objectives, said nothing of reinforcements and removed List from command.

LITHUANIA. Lithuanian independence was gained after a period of extremely complex military and diplomatic maneuvering in the period 1917–20 involving Russia, Germany and Poland; the country was admitted to the League of Nations in 1920. But her fate was sealed by the Soviet-German Nonaggression Pact signed in August 1939. A secret protocol to this treaty made the northern boundary of Lithuania "the boundary of the sphere of influence of Germany and the USSR" and apparently allowed for her continued independence. This arrangement was revised in the Soviet-German Boundary and Friendship Treaty in September 1939, in which Lithuania was secretly assigned to the Soviet Union. On October 10, 1939, the Lithuanians were forced to sign a mutual assistance treaty with the Soviets, permitting Soviet garrisons in Lithuania.

After the fall of France on June 15, 1940, Moscow issued an ultimatum demanding that Lithuania immediately form a government "friendly to the Soviet Union." While the Lithuanians were considering this document, on the same day the Red Army invaded and occupied the country. An obscure Communist journalist, Justas Paleckis, was made Premier of the puppet Communist government. After a rigged referendum on August 3, Lithuania was declared a constituent republic of the USSR. During this first period of Russian occupation, from June 1940 to June 1941, 5,000 Lithuanians were reportedly executed and another 40,000 were deported to Siberia, including virtually all the politicians, journalists, government officials, teachers and professional people in the country.

The Germans, who occupied Lithuania from June 1941 to July 1944, were firmly opposed to restoration of Lithuanian national identity. Whatever few members of the intelligentsia that the Russians had overlooked, they seized. A policy of Germanization was effected, and German colonists were brought in. Except for the Jewish population, which was exterminated, the Germans did not persecute the Lithuanians.

When the Red Army reoccupied Lithuania, large-scale destruction and dispersal of the people took place. Between 1944 and 1949 an estimated 350,000 Lithuanians were exiled to Siberia, not to return until after Stalin's death.

LITTLE, Sir Charles James Colebrooke (1882–1973). Royal Navy officer (admiral), Lord Commissioner of the Admiralty and Chief of Naval Personnel in 1938–41. He was head of the British Joint Staff Mission in Washington in 1941–42, and commander in chief, Portsmouth, in 1942–45.

LITTLE, U.S.S. With Comdr. Madison Hall in command, the destroyer *Little* was one of 150 such vessels assigned to support the Allied invasion of Okinawa, which began on April 1, 1945. During the evening of May 3 the *Little* was struck by four of an estimated 21 fiercely attacking kamikazes. She sank 12 minutes after the first hit; casualties were 6 dead, 79 wounded and 24 missing.

LITTLE BLITZ WEEK. Name given to the week of July 24, 1943, when the U.S. Eighth Air Force bombed 16 important enemy targets in Norway and Germany. One of the targets was Hamburg, the Americans here joining the RAF Bomber Command in attacks of unprecedented destructiveness.

LITTLE BOY. Code name, replacing Thin Man, for the atomic bomb that destroyed Hiroshima on August 6, 1945. The weapon was 10 feet long and 28 inches in diameter, and weighed 9,000 pounds. It was slimmer and lighter than Fat Man, the bomb that razed Nagasaki. Its explosive yield was equal to about 20,000 tons of conventional high explosives.

LITTLE DAVID. A 914-mm. mortar, the T-1. Weighing 172,000 pounds, it was the only American super-heavy weapon. It broke into two assemblies for transport. A 218-pound propelling charge threw a 3,650-pound projectile about 9,000 yards. Although development began in March 1944 with the aim of obtaining weapons capable of destroying fortifications expected to be found in Europe, development problems prevented use of the mortar in Europe, and plans for Pacific employment terminated when Japan surrendered.

LITTLE MAGINOT LINE. French defense line along the border with Italy.

LITTLE SATURN. Code name for offensive by the Soviet Southwest Front and other forces against the German effort to relieve the Sixth Army at Stalingrad, launched December 16, 1942. *See also* Saturn.

LITTORIO. Allied wartime name for what the Italian Navy called the Vittorio Veneto class of battleships. Four modern ships, of 38,000 tons and armed with nine 15-inch guns (3×3), were projected. Vittorio Veneto and *Littorio* were laid down in 1934 and completed in 1940. *Roma* and *Impero* were laid down in 1938. *Roma* was completed in 1942; *Impero* was never finished. *Vittorio Veneto* operated in the Mediterranean during 1940–42; after Italy's surrender in 1943 she was interned in Egypt. *Littorio* took part in operations after Italy's entry into the European war in 1940. Seriously damaged by aerial torpedoes at Taranto on November 12 of that year, she was repaired and returned to service in the fall of 1941. In June 1943 she was renamed *Italia.* Damaged by German air attack while en route to Malta after the Italian surrender, she spent the rest of the war interned with *Vittorio Veneto.* Both ships decommissioned in 1948 and were scrapped. *Roma* never saw combat. Like *Vittorio Veneto* and *Italia,* she sailed for Malta in September 1943. During this voyage she was sent to the bottom, with heavy casualties, by a German glider bomb. The fourth ship, *Impero,* remained an incomplete hulk until she was sunk early in 1945 by American bombers. After the war she was raised and scrapped.

These ships had an unusual Italian-designed hull-protection system intended to provide an effective defense against torpedoes. It was "retrofitted" into the CONTE DI CAVOUR, GIULIO CESARE and two other older ships when they were extensively modernized in the 1930s. While ingenious, it was not perfect, as damage to *Littorio* at Taranto indicated.

LITVINOV, Maxim M. (1876–1951). Litvinov, born Meir Walach, was a native of Russian Poland. An Old Bolshevik, he served as Commissar of Foreign Affairs from 1930 until May 1939, when he was replaced by V. M. MOLOTOV in the realignment of Soviet foreign policy that preceded the SOVIET-GERMAN NONAGGRESSION PACT (August 1939). His removal was undoubtedly prompted by his identification with the earlier Soviet policy opposing Germany and by his Jewish parentage. Litvinov remained in obscurity until the German attack on the USSR brought about a rapprochement with the United States. This led to his being appointed ambassador to the United States on November 6, 1941; he remained at that post until August 21, 1943, when he was replaced by Andrei A. GROMYKO. He was the Soviet signer of the United Nations Declaration of January 1, 1942. On returning to Moscow he was appointed Deputy Commissar of Foreign Affairs, a post he held until his retirement in August 1946.

LIVADIA PALACE. The building in which the YALTA CONFERENCE (1945) was held.

LIVERPOOL. This English port was an important factor in the Battle of the ATLANTIC as one of the three bases of the WESTERN APPROACHES Command.

LLEWELLIN, John Jestyn (1893–1957). Colonel (later Lord) Llewellin was an important figure in supply in the war. A member of the British cabinet as President of the Board of Trade and then Minister of Aircraft Production in 1942, he became Minister Resident for Supply in Washington later in 1942, handling coordination of Anglo-American war supplies. He served as Minister of Food in Britain from 1943 to 1945.

LLOYD, Sir Hugh (1894–1972). Royal Air Force commander at MALTA in 1941 when the bombing raids were at their peak. After serving on Air Marshal Sir Arthur TEDDER's staff in the Middle East, he commanded the Northwest Africa Coastal Air Force. An air chief marshal, he was to command a British bombing force had the Japanese not surrendered.

LOBNITZ. A 200-foot-long semifloating pierhead, with four steel legs, part of the seaward element of a MULBERRY harbor. Because the legs were called spuds, that name was also applied to the pierheads themselves.

LOCAL DEFENCE VOLUNTEERS. The original name of the British HOME GUARD.

LOCARNO PACTS. A series of related treaties negotiated primarily by Gustav Stresemann (Germany), Aristide Briand (France) and Sir Austen Chamberlain (Britain) at Locarno, Switzerland, in October 1925 and formally signed in London on December 1, 1925. The treaties aimed to promote European collective security and to prevent the scourge of war. The pacts included (1) the Rhineland Pact, by which Britain, France, Germany, Italy and Belgium mutually guaranteed Germany's existing borders with France and Belgium; (2) identical arbitration and nonaggression conventions between Germany and France and Germany and Belgium; (3) identical arbitration conventions between Germany and Poland and Germany and Czechoslovakia; and (4) identical guarantee treaties between France and Poland and France and Czechoslovakia. The expression "the spirit of Locarno" was in general use until the mid-1930s, the implication being that a stabilized peace was indeed at hand.

LOCKWOOD, Charles Andrews, Jr. (1890–1967). A graduate of the U.S. Naval Academy in 1912, Lockwood became a division commander of submarines in 1935, and in 1942, with headquarters at PEARL HARBOR and the rank of rear admiral, took charge of the Pacific submarine force (as Commander Submarines Pacific Fleet—Comsubpac). His ships sank more than 1,000 Japanese vessels. These included a battleship, seven carriers and five cruisers, but the heaviest toll was taken of Japanese troop and supply transports. The submarines also served in rescue missions for B-29 bomber crews (*see* B-29) downed between Iwo JIMA and Japan. For his service in the submarine war, Admiral Lockwood received two gold stars and the LEGION OF MERIT. Following the war he collaborated on books on submarine warfare. His final rank was vice-admiral.

LOERZER, Bruno (1892–1960). German flier, a prominent World War I ace and friend of Hermann GÖRING. In 1933 he was made head of the Air Sports League, which was in reality a device for training pilots. After 1935 he openly served as an officer in the new LUFTWAFFE. In 1940, a General der Flieger, he commanded II Air Corps, one of the units assigned to establish German air superiority over the English Channel following the fall of France. He was subsequently in charge of the Luftwaffe personnel department. In general, he appears to have owed his positions more to Göring's patronage than to his own ability.

LOFOTEN ISLANDS RAID. In 1941 British COMMANDO units carried out two raids on the Lofoten Islands, off the northwest coast of German-occupied Norway. The first raid, on March 4, under the overall command of Brig. J. C. Haydon, had four objectives: (1) to destroy fish-oil factories which produced glycerine, used in the manufacture of explosives; (2) to sink enemy shipping; (3) to enlist volunteers for Norwegian forces in Great Britain; and (4) to capture Norwegian collaborators. Both this raid and a similar one December 26–28 were very successful in causing economic damage and military harassment to the Germans.

LÖHR, Alexander (1885–1947). German LUFTWAFFE officer who began his military career in 1906 as a lieutenant in a Hungarian infantry regiment, served as a staff officer in the Austro-Hungarian Army in World War I and after the war became an air officer in the army of the Austrian republic. In 1936 he became commander of the Austrian Air Force. After Germany absorbed Austria in the 1938 ANSCHLUSS, Löhr became a general in the Luftwaffe. In 1939, as a General der

Flieger, he took command of Air Fleet 4, which he commanded in Poland in 1939, in the BALKANS in 1941 and in the campaign in Russia. He was promoted to colonel general in May 1941. After 1942 he held army commands in the Balkans. In 1947 he was convicted of war crimes by a Yugoslav court. He was hanged on March 16, 1947.

LONDONDERRY. One of the three operational bases of the WESTERN APPROACHES Command.

LONG LANCE. Japanese oxygen-powered, Type 93, 24-inch TORPEDO, furnished to cruisers and all but the oldest destroyers during the years just before the outbreak of the Pacific war. The product of long experimentation, this unusually powerful and effective weapon weighed over 6,000 pounds and carried an explosive warhead of over 1,000 pounds. It had three speed settings; at 49 knots it could travel nearly 11 miles. Thorough Japanese security measures kept the very existence of the Long Lance a secret until well into the war; in mid-1943 rumors of an unusually fast, hard-hitting, long-range enemy torpedo were circulating among the Americans in the Pacific, but it was even later than this that any definite information was picked up.

LONGMORE, Sir Arthur (1885–1970). One of the earliest British officers to learn to fly, Longmore had a distinguished career in the Royal Naval Air Service and the RAF. He was knighted in 1935 and was named Air Officer Commanding in Chief Middle East in May 1940. He prepared the air support for General WAVELL's advance through Libya in December 1940. He retired in 1942 with the rank of air chief marshal.

LONG RANGE DESERT GROUP. A special British unit in North Africa, created in 1940 for intelligence and sabotage. Its volunteers headquartered at Siwa Oasis and Kufra and sent out reconnaissance patrols, sometimes staying in "road watch" for three months at a time. After 1941 the LRDG often guided patrols of SPECIAL AIR SERVICE troops or COMMANDOS to special targets, picking them up again after the raids had been completed.

LONG-RANGE PENETRATION GROUP. A type of Allied guerrilla unit formed in BURMA for operations in Japanese-held territory. Its aim was to seize strongpoints that would serve as bases for operations to cut communications, acquire information useful for planning air attacks and otherwise harass the enemy. The originator of the idea was Brig. Orde WINGATE. *See also* CHINDITS; GALAHAD.

LONGSTOP HILL. A bitterly contested hill in TUNISIA, tactically important for control of the Medjerda valley, Longstop (actually Hill 290) was first assaulted by the Allies on December 22–24, 1942, but left in Axis control. In April 1943 the "Christmas Hill" was taken by the British after another costly battle.

LONG TOM. Nickname for the 155-mm. gun also called M1A1. The M1A1 was adopted and standardized in 1938 by the U.S. Army Ordnance Department. It was put into quantity production when the war began and served in almost every theater. The gun fired two types of semifixed shells, the M101 High Explosive (94.71 pounds) or the M112 B1 Armor Piercing (99 pounds), over a maximum distance of 25,715 yards. It could fire one round per minute.

LOOMIS, Alfred Lee (1887–1975). This remarkably versatile man, a lawyer and financier as well as a physicist, was head of the RADAR research division of the U.S. Office of Scientific Research and Development and was one of the principal developers of LORAN, the navigation aid. He was also associated with the nuclear research of Ernest O. LAWRENCE.

LOPATIN, A. I. As a major general who commanded a corps in the Twenty-sixth Army, this Soviet officer was able to break out of a German encirclement in the Ukraine in September 1941. In November 1941 he was in command of the Thirty-seventh Army, which took part in the recapture of ROSTOV (November 29), the first important Soviet victory. In February 1942 Lopatin, already a lieutenant general, was still in command of the Thirty-seventh Army, now a part of MALINOVSKY's Southern Front. The Battle of STALINGRAD found him in command of the Sixty-second Army, which was later credited with the heroic defense of the city. Praised by ZHUKOV as the man who preserved his army to save Stalingrad, he was at the same time roundly criticized by CHUIKOV, who saw him as a "plump and fair" individual, "outwardly very calm" but lacking self-confidence and unable to stand up to harsh conditions. *See also* SOVIET-GERMAN OPERATIONS 1941–45.

LORAN. *Lo*ng *ra*nge *n*avigation, a form of radio navigation in use by the U.S. Navy by 1944. Short-pulse radio signals are broadcast from pairs of shore-based stations and received by a ship using a receiver which measures the difference in time of arrival of the two signals. This measured time difference is entered onto prepared tables or loran charts to determine a line of position on the earth's surface. The intersection of two of these lines gives a loran fix. Loran lines of position can also be used in combination with celestial lines to plot a position. Improved loran systems are in use today.

LORD HAW HAW. *See* JOYCE, WILLIAM.

LORENZ BEAM. The LUFTWAFFE developed in the late 1930s a bombing beam to direct their bombers onto a correct course to targets in England. This KNICKEBEIN beam was received in the bomber aircraft on the normal blind-landing radio equipment and worked on the blind-landing (Lorenz) principle.

LORIENT. French port made into a submarine base and headquarters by the German Navy. Even after Lorient lost its usefulness to the Germans following the Allied advances in France, the garrison held out, not surrendering until the end of the war.

LORRAINE. French battleship of 22,189 tons, launched in 1913 and rebuilt in 1934–35. She carried eight 13.4-inch guns (one turret had been removed to make room for an airplane and catapult), fourteen 5.5-inch guns and numerous smaller ones. She was the heaviest ship of the French Force X attached to Adm. Sir Andrew CUNNINGHAM's force at Alexandria at the time of the fall of France in 1940, and was peaceably neutralized.

LOS ALAMOS. In 1942 the MANHATTAN DISTRICT (the ATOMIC BOMB project) established its secret laboratory in this area of north-central New Mexico, and the town of Los Alamos ("The Poplars") developed as a result.

LOSHEIM GAP. In the Eifel region of Germany along the upper reaches of the Kyll River near the Belgian frontier, the gap constitutes a militarily strategic débouché between the SCHNEE EIFEL ridge to the south and the Weisserstein watershed to the north. German forces invading Belgium used the gap to advantage in 1914, 1940 and 1944.

LOTHIAN, Philip Henry Kerr, 11th Marquess (1882–1940). British ambassador to the United States in 1939–40, whose speeches to the American people were instrumental in gaining sympathy and support for the British war effort, especially during Britain's darkest days. Earlier, Lothian had been identified with the APPEASEMENT-minded group in England.

LOUIE THE LOUSE. American nickname for Japanese floatplanes, principally based at Rekata Bay, Santa Isabel Island, and flown over Marine positions on GUADALCANAL as a form of night harassment. One or two of these airplanes orbited over the HENDERSON FIELD area each night, beginning in October 1942, dropping small bombs essentially at random and also dropping parachute flares if Japanese surface ships were in the vicinity, to mark the general target area for their gunfire. From the *put-put* sound of their engines, these planes were also dubbed "Washing-Machine Charlie."

LOUISVILLE, U.S.S. NORTHAMPTON-class heavy cruiser, commissioned 1931. With the Pacific Fleet when the war broke out, she took part in early raids before going to the Aleutians in mid-1942. There she served on escort and bombardment duty. In January 1944 she was sent to the South Pacific, where she supported operations against the MARSHALLS and raids against Japanese-held islands. *Louisville* was involved in the capture of the Palaus and LEYTE, including the Surigao Strait night action. Damaged by two KAMIKAZES off Luzon early in January 1945, she joined the OKINAWA operation after repairs. Hit by another kamikaze early in June, she returned from a refit in time to take part in Pacific occupation duty.

LOW, Francis Stuart (1894–1964). A graduate of the U.S. Naval Academy in 1915, Low worked under Adm. Ernest J. KING in the antisubmarine war in the Atlantic. In 1943–45 he served as chief of staff for the newly organized TENTH FLEET, the force that, working with the British, broke the German submarine menace with surface and air craft. Low also commanded a cruiser division in the OKINAWA campaign. He was promoted to rear admiral in 1942. Following the war Low commanded the Western Sea Frontier. He was promoted to vice-admiral in 1947.

LSD. U.S. Navy ship-type symbol for Landing Ship, Dock. The largest landing ship of World War II, this was a seagoing ship with a large drydock built into the after part of its hull. Designed to carry loaded landing craft or vehicles into a beachhead area, the LSD had large ballast tanks which, when filled, trimmed the ship down by the stern so that the well deck could be flooded. The landing craft or amphibious vehicles then proceeded out a stern gate under their own power. These 458-foot ships could carry two or three loaded LCTs or 14 loaded LCMs or 40-plus LVTs or DUKWs (see individual entries for these craft). LSDs also served as mobile drydocks for emergency beachhead repairs to landing craft.

LSM. U.S. Navy ship-type symbol for Landing Ship, Medium. Smaller than the LST (below), the LSM had a vehicle-carrying capacity comparable to that of the LCT. Unlike the LCT, however, the LSM was an ocean-going ship with long range and good sea-keeping ability, designed to operate in conjunction with the LCI(L). (*See* LCT; LCI[L].) It could land tanks, artillery or cargo directly on an invasion beach by means of a bow ramp. In appearance the LSM somewhat resembled a small aircraft carrier, with a cylindrical bridge–wheelhouse structure offset to starboard to make room for a vehicle well deck extending the length of the hull.

LSM(R). U.S. Navy ship-type designation for Landing Ship, Medium (Rocket). Modified from the basic LSM hull, several versions of this type differed in configuration and details. All had one 5-inch gun with combinations of 40-mm. and 20-mm. guns. Their principal armament consisted of different types of barrage-rocket launchers for blanketing landing areas. Like the LCI(R), the LSM(R) was used in the later Pacific invasions (*see* LCI[R]).

LST. U.S. Navy ship-type symbol for Landing Ship, Tank. The LST was a big, flat-bottomed ship designed to transport tanks and vehicles of comparable size across large ocean distances and land them directly on a beach. It was used for many other tasks as well. LSTs hauled troops and cargo, and at Normandy and later they were used for emergency casualty evacuation. Tanks and heavy vehicles were carried in a hold, or "tank deck." When the ship beached, two bow doors were opened and a ramp lowered to allow the vehicles to drive ashore. Cargo, as well as lighter vehicles, could be carried on an LST's upper deck. As an alternative, an unloaded LCT might be carried there (*see* LCT). The LST, produced in the United States and Britain in several versions, was one of the most useful designs of World War II. Many LSTs were modified to serve as repair ships or hospital ships and to do a myriad of other jobs. Its large size and limited speed led many sailors to insist that the letters LST actually stood for Large, Slow Target.

LSV. U.S. Navy ship-type symbol for Landing Ship, Vehicle, a seagoing ship designed to transport 44–52 amphibious vehicles to a landing area, unloading them into the water across a stern ramp while still in deep water. Two classes of LSVs were generally similar in characteristics and configuration, the twin-stack Catskill (LSV-1) class and the single-stack Osage (LSV-3) class. A total of six of these ships (LSV-1 through -6) commissioned in 1944–45 and saw service in some late-war amphibious operations.

LÜBECK. The British Air Staff became convinced in the autumn of 1941 that saturation incendiary tactics were likely to prove more destructive in air raids on Germany than conventional high-explosive attacks. Lübeck was chosen as the first target to test this theory. The medieval construction in the Altstadt (Old City) made the buildings inflammable, it was on the coast and recognizable—though beyond the range of Gee (*see* NAVIGATION AIDS)—and it was known to be lightly defended. Two hundred thirty-four aircraft of BOMBER COMMAND were ordered to attack Lübeck in full moon and good weather on the night of March 28, 1942. Subsequent photographic reconnaissance showed that 45 to 50 percent of the city had suffered heavy damage. Postwar surveys confirmed this and also the panic it produced in high quarters in Berlin.

LUBLIN COMMITTEE. After the Soviet Government broke relations with the Polish government-in-exile over the KATYN massacre issue in April 1943, Moscow began to transform the Union of Polish Patriots into a pro-Soviet governmental body for postwar Poland. Having won CHURCHILL and ROOSEVELT (at the TEHERAN CONFERENCE) to his views regarding Poland, STALIN felt free to proceed with the formation in Warsaw of the Communist-dominated National Council, officially announced as existing on January 1, 1944, by the Soviet radio. In spite of the protests of the London-based Polish Government, Great Britain and the United States attempted to work out a compromise solution with the Soviets. These attempts failed, as Stalin responded by creating, in July 1944, the Polish Committee of National Liberation (commonly called the Lublin Committee), with temporary headquarters in Lublin. It was given limited administrative powers over the Polish territory liberated from the Germans. On December 31, 1944, it was reconstituted as the provisional government of Poland and promptly recognized as such by the Soviet Government. At the YALTA CONFERENCE the Allies agreed that the Lublin Committee should serve as a base for the Polish Government, but it was to be joined by several Poles from London. This government was finally formed in June 1945 and was quickly recognized by the United States and Great Britain.

LUCAS, John Porter (1890–1949). U.S. Army officer who served as Gen. Dwight D. EISENHOWER's personal deputy in 1943. A major general, he later commanded II Corps in SICILY and VI Corps in Italy. Despondent prior to the ANZIO landing, convinced he was headed for disaster, he employed his troops timidly, though they were little opposed, and was shortly relieved of his command.

LUCHT, Walther (1882–1949). German Army officer (General der Artillerie), commander of the LXVI Corps (infantry) of the Fifth Panzer Army in the Battle of the BULGE. In April 1945 he became commander of the Eleventh Army in Germany.

LUCKY. Code name for the U.S. THIRD ARMY under Lt. Gen. George S. PATTON, Jr. Patton's advance headquarters was known as Lucky Forward.

LUCKY STRIKE. Code name for a plan considered by the Allies that would have called for capture of the Seine ports rather than Brittany following the INVASION of Normandy.

LUCY. Code name of a spy ring operating through Switzerland in 1939–43 and also of its head, Rudolf Roessler, a German Communist. Though the details of the functioning of the Lucy ring remain matters of debate, it appears that a group of anti-Nazi German officers in Berlin relayed information about German operational plans to Roessler and his associates in Lucerne. This information was then radioed to the Allies. The plans were of particular value to the Russians, who, once convinced of the authenticity of the information, made direct use of it in planning their own strategy. Roessler is often spoken of as one of the greatest spies of all time.

LUDENDORFF BRIDGE. Railroad bridge across the Rhine River at REMAGEN, named for the German general of World War I. As American troops approached, demolitions damaged the bridge, but armored infantrymen of Combat Command B, 9th Armored Division, rushed across (March 7, 1945). The bridge collapsed on March 17, but not before an American bridgehead was secure.

LUDLOW-HEWITT, Sir Edgar (1886–1973). Inspector General of the ROYAL AIR FORCE for most of the war. An Army officer, he transferred to the air in World War I. He was commandant of the RAF Staff College in 1926–30 and AOC-in-C BOMBER COMMAND in 1937–40. His incisive analytical thinking did much to remedy the worst deficiencies of RAF navigation and bombing training. He rose to the rank of air chief marshal.

LUFTWAFFE. The German Air Force (Luftwaffe, in German) was officially unveiled by Adolf HITLER and Hermann GÖRING in March 1935, but in fact it had been developing constantly since 1920. By 1936 the Germans were testing the MESSERSCHMITT ME 109 and ME 110 fighters, the JUNKERS JU 88, DORNIER DO 17 and HEINKEL HE 111 bombers and the JUNKERS JU 87 and HENSCHEL HS 123 dive-bombers.

In August 1936 the Germans entered the Spanish Civil War; in November the Condor Legion was sent to support General Franco's forces. It established air superiority only after the introduction of the Me 109 fighter and He 111 and Do 17 bombers in the summer of 1937; later Ju 87 and Hs 123 dive-bombers appeared. Here the Luftwaffe developed their ground-support (tactical) techniques, but strategic bombing theory and practice were neglected.

By August 1, 1938, at the start of the MUNICH crisis, the Luftwaffe had 1,669 serviceable aircraft, among which were 453 fighters, 582 bombers and 159 dive-bombers. By the eve of World War II in 1939 the

Luftwaffe had profited from the year Munich had given it. There were now 3,750 aircraft, including 1,170 bombers, 335 dive-bombers, 1,125 single-engine fighters (mostly Me 109s) and 195 twin-engine fighters (mostly Me 110s). The aircraft were superior to those of any other European power at the time. None of the bombers could be classed as strategic; the Luftwaffe neglected this type after the death of Gen. Walther Wever, the first Chief of Staff, in 1936.

The basic flying unit in the Luftwaffe was the *Gruppe* of about 30 planes. It held three *Staffeln* (equivalent to a squadron), of 9 or 10 aircraft apiece. Bomber and fighter units were organized into *Geschwader* (equivalent to an RAF group) of three Gruppen, or about 90 aircraft. While the sizes of Staffeln, Gruppen and Geschwader were fairly constant, the strength of the largest formation, the *Luftflotte* (air fleet), with a *Luftgau* (air district) for administration and a *Fliegerdivision* for operations, was not fixed. The strength of an air fleet varied during the war between 200 and 1,250 aircraft.

The attack in Poland tested Luftwaffe theories of close support of Army operations. The test was passed brilliantly. About 1,600 aircraft swamped the Poles' largely obsolescent force of about 500 planes (although the Luftwaffe lost 734 of their military personnel and 285 aircraft). After rest and refit the Luftwaffe supported the attack on NORWAY in 1940 with about 1,000 aircraft divided evenly between operational and transport types, led by Fliegerkorps X, which crushed Norwegian resistance.

In the Battle of FRANCE the Luftwaffe used about 3,530 planes, from a first-line strength of about 4,500, along with 475 transports and 45 gliders for operations in Holland. Air operations were commanded by Luftflotte 2 under Gen. Albert KESSELRING and Luftflotte 3 under Gen. Hugo SPERRLE. Once again the Army–Air Force close cooperation swept opposition ahead of it.

After the Battle of France the Luftwaffe regrouped for the final stage of the western campaign. Luftflotte 2 with I, II and IX Fliegerkorps and Luftflotte 3 with V, VI and VIII Fliegerkorps moved to the assault of BRITAIN; the strength was about 2,600 aircraft, including about 850 bombers, 280 Ju 87s and 980 fighters of both types. There were 190 planes in Fliegerkorps X in Norway for diversion. The Battle of Britain began in August 1940 and ended in October with German defeat in the air, their first of the war. The Luftwaffe turned now to bombing England by night in the BLITZ from October 1940 to May 1941.

In June 1941 the Luftwaffe deployed Luftflotten 1, 2 and 4 against the Russians, with a total of 2,770 aircraft out of a first-line strength of 4,300; included were 775 bombers, 310 Ju 87s and 920 twin- and single-engine fighters. Initially brilliantly successful, almost forcing the Russians from the air, the Luftwaffe felt the constant pressure of fighting over vast distances, as well as the strain of the war on other fronts, and had to change its tactics. By the end of 1943 it was dividing its strength roughly equally between the offensive and the defensive forces.

The year 1943 marked the turn from an offensive to an overall defensive German air strategy. Operational strength fell to 4,000 aircraft, and reserves were nonexistent. Both aircraft production and air-crew training struggled to keep up with demand. Through the rest of the war German air strength in the east hovered between 1,600 and 1,800 aircraft. The all-out Allied bomber assault on Germany so strained the Luftwaffe structure that it was reduced to an almost completely defensive role by the end of 1943. Despite the development of jet-powered fighters—which the Luftwaffe was unable to exploit fully—the Allies' aerial superiority in numbers, quality of aircraft and crews doomed the Luftwaffe by late 1944; by early 1945 it was a small force of largely semiobsolescent planes. The last of the Luftwaffe, some 1,500 planes of all types, surrendered on May 8, 1945. **W.S.**

LUGER. A reworked version of an 1893 design by an American, Connecticut gunsmith and inventor Hugo Borchardt, the original Luger took its name in 1900 from Georg Luger, a designer at the Ludwig Löwe small-arms factory in Berlin, which employed Borchardt after he had brought his models there in search of a market. The 8-shot, grip-magazine-fed, semiautomatic, recoil-operated pistol with a toggle-joint breech action first appeared as a 7.65-mm. piece, being later rechambered for a 9-mm. (Parabellum) round. Adopted by the German Navy as an officer's sidearm in 1904, the Luger found acceptance in the German Army in 1908. Designated *Pistole 08,* the Luger remained in service in World War II as one of two standard officer's sidearms. The more common 4¼-inch-barrel pistol also underwent modification that resulted in a model with a 9-inch barrel, equipped with a rifle stock and a graduated leaf rear sight. A specially adapted drum magazine increased either model's capacity to 32 rounds. Inevitably compared with the American Colt M-1911 or M-1911 A1 .45-caliber semiautomatic, the Luger, a particularly prized war souvenir, is conceded to be better balanced and slightly more accurate but has far less shock effect than the U.S. weapon. *See also* SMALL ARMS.

LULEA. Swedish port through which Germany received much of her iron ore. The important strategic fact was that Lulea was icebound during the winter, which meant that the Swedish ore had to be sent by rail to NARVIK, in Norway, and thence by ship to Germany. This situation was one of the factors directing the attention of the British and German staffs to Norway.

LUMBERJACK. Code name for the advance to the Rhine in the Cologne area by the U.S. FIRST ARMY and farther south by the THIRD ARMY, February 1945.

LUMSDEN, Herbert (1897–1945). British Army officer who saw service in Belgium and in North Africa, where he commanded, successively, the 30th and the 10th Corps, EIGHTH ARMY, in 1942–43. He was not in favor with General MONTGOMERY, the Eighth Army commander, and in 1943 went to the Pacific as Winston CHURCHILL's special representative with General MACARTHUR. He was killed in January 1945 when a Japanese plane crashed the bridge of the U.S.S. NEW MEXICO, on which he was standing. His highest rank was lieutenant general.

LÜNEBURG HEATH. Located about 25 miles southwest of Hamburg, Lüneburg Heath was the site of Field Marshal MONTGOMERY's tactical headquarters in early

May 1945. It was at this headquarters, on May 4, that German officers signed an instrument of surrender (effective 8 A.M. on May 5) for forces in Holland, Denmark, northwest Germany, the German islands and Schleswig-Holstein.

LUNGA POINT. Place on GUADALCANAL near which the initial landings took place on August 7, 1942, by elements of the U.S. 1st Marine Division.

LUSTRE. Code name for the movement of British troops from Egypt to Greece in March 1941, one of the more debatable operations of the war. *See also* BALKANS.

LUTES, Leroy (1890–). U.S. Army officer who in 1942, as a major general, became director of operations, Headquarters Services of Supply (which later became Plans and Operations, Army Service Forces). He held this position for the entire war (serving as acting chief of staff, Headquarters SOS, September through November 1943). He was promoted to lieutenant general in 1945.

LÜTJENS, Günther (1889–1941). German naval squadron commander. After seeing successful action during the Norwegian campaign of April 1940, Admiral Lütjens went down with the battleship BISMARCK on May 27, 1941.

LÜTTWITZ, Heinrich, Baron von (1895–1970). German Army officer (General der Panzertruppen, 1944) who commanded the XLVII Panzer Corps in the Battle of the BULGE.

LÜTZOW. German armored ship of 11,700 tons and carrying six 11-inch guns, launched in 1931 as the *Deutschland.* The so-called pocket battleship (*see* PANZERSCHIFF) was a circumvention of the intent of the Treaty of Versailles to limit German naval power by allowing Germany warships no larger than 10,000 tons. Sacrificing armor protection for speed and employing welded fittings throughout, *Deutschland* had an advertised ability to outrun any ship she could not outgun. Operating as a raider in the early months of the war, she included among her successes the capture of an American freighter (the *City of Flint*), but returned to Germany to be rechristened *Lützow* in 1940 because of Adolf HITLER's concern for the propaganda effect if a ship bearing the name *Deutschland* should be lost. She was redesignated a heavy cruiser at the same time. She saw action off NORWAY in 1940 and later in a dramatic New Year's Eve 1942 battle with convoy escorts, and she was heavily damaged in air raids. She was scuttled in May 1945.

LUZON. The largest and northernmost island in the Philippine archipelago, the scene of two of the largest campaigns of the Pacific war. *See also* PHILIPPINES.

LVT. U.S. Navy type symbol for Landing Vehicle, Tracked. Somewhat resembling a tank in appearance, the LVT could "swim" at 4 to 5.4 knots; unlike other amphibious vehicles, it did not use a propeller in the water but was driven by paddle-like cleats on its tracks. On dry land it could move at 15 to 25 miles per hour. It was first used at GUADALCANAL. An extensive family of LVTs was produced.

LYNCH, Thomas J. (1916–1944). U.S. Army Air Force officer (major) who engaged in rivalry with Maj. Richard BONG in the Pacific, ending up with 20 kills. On March 9, 1944, while on a two-man patrol with Bong, he was shot down off the coast of New Guinea.

LYSANDER. A two-place, single-engine plane used by the RAF for working with the Army in reconnaissance, artillery spotting and liaison. During the DUNKIRK evacuation, Lysanders dropped supplies to British troops, and attacked enemy positions with fragmentation bombs carried on racks extending outward from the streamlined wheel covers. Lysanders fitted with large external fuel tanks and ladders for ease of exit from the enclosed cockpit landed Allied agents in enemy-held territory. This Westland-built product was a high-wing monoplane with a glassed-in cabin and a fixed landing gear. The 890-horsepower Bristol Mercury radial gave it a top speed of 219 miles per hour. Armament was three .303-caliber machine guns, two firing forward and one in the rear cockpit.

LYTTELTON, Oliver, 1st Viscount Chandos (1893–1972). British businessman and politician, President of the Board of Trade and member of the Privy Council, 1940–41. In June 1941 he was appointed to the new position of Minister of State in the Middle East, which carried a seat in the War Cabinet; in this post he acted as political counselor to the Commander in Chief in the Middle East. In 1942 he was given another new position, Minister of Production (and member of the War Cabinet), which he held until 1945.

M

M-1 RIFLE. Also called the Garand, this weapon was originally designed for the U.S. experimental caliber .276 as part of a program, begun in 1921, to find a suitable semiautomatic rifle. In 1931 the .276 cartridge program was discontinued by Gen. Douglas MacArthur, then Chief of Staff, who ordered that all small arms of the rifle and machine-gun category were to use the .30-caliber ammunition. In the rifle competitions of 1929 only the Garand was considered superior and chosen for further development. The name came from its designer, John C. Garand, a civilian employee of the Ordnance Department at the Springfield Armory. The rifle was officially adopted by the Army in 1936, and production began the same year. In 1940, as the result of tests and field use, the rifle's gas port system and muzzle construction were modified, and it became the standard U.S. Army rifle. During the war manufacture was contracted out to such diverse companies as Winchester Repeating Arms, the Singer and White sewing machine companies and IBM. The weapon is semiautomatic, operated by a blowback system, weighs 9½ pounds, is 43 inches long (59 inches with bayonet) and carries eight rounds in an open block clip. The ammunition most used was the U.S. .30 M1906 round with an extreme range at maximum elevation of 3,300 yards and an effective combat range of 400–700 yards.

M-1, M-2 CARBINE. Introduction of the U.S. carbine was influenced by the submachine gun and by the average soldier's inefficiency with the pistol; it was also a concession to the needs of specialist units such as engineer, signal, armor and others requiring a weapon for use in emergencies. The M-1 carbine was meant mainly to replace the Model 1911 Colt .45-caliber pistol. It was initiated by the Army's Ordnance Department technical staff under the direction of Col. René R. Studler, Small Arms Development Branch. The early models and cartridges were made for the Army by the Winchester Repeating Arms Company, who modified their .32 sporting cartridge. The carbine is a gas-actuated, blowback weapon almost identical to the M-1 rifle. It utilizes a magazine holding 15 rounds and has an effective range of about 300 yards. M-1 refers both to the carbine itself and to the cartridge (caliber .30), a smaller cartridge than the M-1 rifle cartridge. One modification of the weapon was the paratrooper M1A1, Cal. .30, which had a folding wire stock; another, the M-2 carbine, had a fully automatic capability, firing up to 775 rounds per minute.

M-I OPERATION. More fully Mike-I, the code name for the main U.S. invasion of Luzon at Lingayen Gulf on January 9, 1945. Mike-I was one of a series of operations contained in Gen. Douglas MacArthur's strategic plan—Musketeer III, September 26, 1944—for the reconquest of the Philippines, and other Mike operations followed Mike-I. Mike-I was not a detailed campaign plan; rather, the concept assumed that after a successful landing on the southern shore of Lingayen Gulf the U.S. Sixth Army would drive south through the central plains of Luzon as rapidly as possible to seize Manila and secure Manila Bay. More detailed operational plans would be developed as the campaign progressed.

M3. A light tank series, also called the General Stuart, after the Confederate cavalry general J. E. B. Stuart. Adopted on July 5, 1940, the first type, the M3, was of all-riveted construction. The second, the M3A1, was the same except for a cast turret, and the third, the M3A3, had a cast turret and semi-welded hull. All were armed with a 37-mm. gun and .30-caliber machine gun in the turret, an antiaircraft .30-caliber machine gun on the turret and a ball-mounted .30-caliber machine gun in the hull. On the M3 only were two sponson-mounted .30-caliber machine guns. All were powered by radial air-cooled engines except for a few diesel-powered ones built for the British. The tank saw action in virtually every theater of the war, including the Eastern Front in Russia. The British tank forces, with whom it found great favor, nicknamed it "Honey."

M-3, M-3A1 SUBMACHINE GUN. Nicknamed the "Grease Gun" owing to resemblance to one, this U.S. weapon was adopted in 1943 and issued the same year. Partial inspiration for the M-3 came from the Finnish Suomi submachine gun, as the M-3's breechblock is also in one piece with a fixed stud in the countersunk face of the bolt for firing when the round is chambered. The weapon was of simple design and easily mass-produced, using stampings and readily fabricated metal parts; it was extremely reliable. It was fully automatic only, blowback actuated, using the .45-caliber pistol ammunition. It weighed 10.3 pounds, carried a 30-round magazine and had a cyclic rate of fire of 450 rounds per minute. It was issued to troops not normally assigned to infantry duty.

M6A1. Japanese Navy Aichi *Seiran* (Mountain Haze) (no Allied code name), a streamlined twin-float plane designed to be carried in pairs on aircraft-carrying submarines. It was intended for use in an attack on the Panama Canal, which was rehearsed but never carried out. Only 28 were built.

MAASTRICHT. An important communications center and the capital of the Dutch province of Limburg. On May 11, 1940, the second day of the German invasion, the city came under attack. Maastricht was retaken by the Americans in September 1944.

McAFEE, Mildred (1900–). Director of the WAVES (*W*omen *A*ccepted for *V*olunteer *E*mergency *S*ervice; later [1944] renamed Women's Reserve of the United

States Navy) from August 1942 to January 1946. Appointed as a lieutenant commander in the Naval Reserve, Miss McAfee was promoted to captain in 1943. She was president of Wellesley College in Massachusetts from 1936 to 1949, taking a leave of absence for her work with the Navy. In August 1945 she married Douglas Horton, a clergyman. In January 1946 Captain Horton left the Navy and returned to her position at Wellesley.

MacARTHUR, Douglas (1880–1964). One of America's most brilliant and controversial generals, MacArthur was the third son of Arthur MacArthur, a Civil War Medal of Honor winner and later the senior officer in the U.S. Army. Douglas MacArthur graduated first in his class at West Point in 1903 with the highest academic record achieved in a quarter of a century. Entering the engineers, he became an aide to his father in 1905 and then served as aide to President Theodore Roosevelt in 1906–07. In World War I, as chief of staff and later commander of the 42d (Rainbow) Division, MacArthur was nicknamed "the Dude" because he cut a dashing figure in his unorthodox attire—heavy muffler, bright turtleneck sweater, floppy hat, loose field jacket and riding crop. Wounded several times and frequently cited for bravery, he was promoted in June 1918 to brigadier general, becoming the youngest American division commander. He attracted considerable attention; Secretary of War Newton Baker, for example, called him America's best front-line general in World War I.

Between June 1919 and June 1922, MacArthur served as superintendent of West Point. He pushed needed reforms, broadening and modernizing the curriculum, stiffening entrance examinations, updating military training, introducing intramurals and relaxing discipline. Many of his reforms were only temporary, but MacArthur's dedication to the work could not be questioned. In 1925 MacArthur became America's youngest major general; he served as a judge in the court-martial of "Billy" Mitchell, the air-power advocate whose fight against the military and naval traditionalists was the talk of the country. In October 1930 MacArthur was appointed Chief of Staff of the Army.

During the desperate years of the Depression, MacArthur did his best to preserve the Army and especially to protect the officer corps, and he favored air power and armor. The most dramatic incident during MacArthur's tenure as Chief of Staff, an incident that would besmirch his reputation, was his personal direction of the suppression of the Bonus Army in Washington in July 1932; in this effort he was aided by Majors Dwight Eisenhower and George Patton. MacArthur never changed his view that only a small portion of the men were veterans, that a significant number had criminal records and that, in his words, "careful needling by the Communists turned them into a sullen mob." None

General MacArthur (second from left) with U.S. and Philippine officers wades ashore at Leyte, October 20, 1944

of these assertions was correct, and he was severely criticized by the press for his conduct. MacArthur, a political conservative, frequently made no distinction among Communists, liberals and pacifists. Although MacArthur was hostile to Roosevelt and his New Deal, the new President extended the Chief of Staff's term by one year.

In 1935 MacArthur stepped down as Chief of Staff and went to the Philippines as military adviser to the Commonwealth government. He accepted its rank of field marshal in 1936, even though his aide Eisenhower advised against it, regarding it as "pompous and rather ridiculous to be the field marshal of a virtually nonexisting army." MacArthur not only proposed the title, but also designed a sharkskin uniform for it. He retired from the U.S. Army in 1937. He proposed a 10-year plan to make the Philippines into the "Switzerland of Asia," with universal military training, a large citizen army, PT boats and a small air force. His optimism infected Washington planners and moved them to change their original idea that the Philippines could not be held in case of war. In July 1941 MacArthur was recalled to service, being appointed Commanding General, United States Army Forces in the Far East.

The initial Japanese invasion of the Philippines came on December 10, 1941, with the main assault following on December 22; by January 7, 1942, American and Filipino units had withdrawn into the Bataan Peninsula. MacArthur was ordered out of Luzon in February and left for Australia by PT boat on March 11. MacArthur's words on his arrival, "I came through and I shall return," will be long remembered. The phrase, it has been observed, also illustrates the general's ego, for he insisted that the "I" remain despite urgings that it be replaced by a collective "we." For his role in the defense of the Philippines, MacArthur received the Medal of Honor. He was never reconciled to the "Germany first" strategy, which he felt deprived the Philippines of deserved support.

In April 1942 he became Supreme Commander of the newly activated Southwest Pacific Area (Australia, most of the Indies, the Philippines), while Adm. Chester Nimitz was given command of the Pacific Ocean Areas. New Guinea was held despite fierce attacks and the weakness of Allied forces there. The Japanese were thwarted by the American naval victories at the Coral Sea and Midway, the Marine landings on Guadalcanal and the stalling of the Japanese drive in New Guinea in September 1942. The pattern of the fighting under MacArthur was the bold use of air and sea power, leapfrogging Japanese positions. The enemy was hit at New Britain, New Georgia, Bougainville and the Admiralty Islands. In 1944 MacArthur and Nimitz differed on strategy. The general stressed that America could not skip the Philippines and attack Formosa, as the Navy desired, without breaking a solemn moral commitment to the Filipinos. MacArthur won the day; Leyte was invaded in October 1944, Luzon in January 1945.

In December 1944 MacArthur was promoted to General of the Army (five stars), and in April 1945 he was given command of all U.S. Army units in the Pacific. He arrived in Japan on August 30, 1945, and presided over the surrender ceremonies on the deck of the U.S. battleship Missouri in Tokyo Bay on September 2. MacArthur was made Supreme Commander of the Allied Powers in Japan (SCAP); in this post he supervised the restoration of the Japanese economy and the building of a new state.

When the United States entered the Korean War in the summer of 1950, MacArthur was made commander of U.S. and United Nations forces. After defeating the North Koreans and moving up to the Yalu River in late 1950, Allied forces were surprised and badly beaten by Chinese Communist forces in the winter of 1950–51. Because MacArthur violated an order from the White House and the Defense Secretary, he was recalled in early 1951. He had not come home after World War II, and he was now greeted as a conquering hero. His speech to a joint session of Congress (with the phrase "Old soldiers never die, they just fade away") was the finale to a long and remarkable career. **K.P.W.**

MacARTHUR'S NAVY. American nickname given to the Navy landing ships and craft and Seventh Fleet support ships that operated under the command of Gen. Douglas MacArthur in the Southwest Pacific Area.

McAULIFFE, Anthony C. (1898–1975). U.S. Army officer who became legendary for his one-word reply to a German demand for surrender at Bastogne in the Battle of the Bulge: "Nuts!" McAuliffe, a 1919 graduate of West Point, was in 1944 a brigadier general and artillery commander of the 101st Airborne Division, which was rushed into the Bulge fighting as ground troops. McAuliffe was acting division commander, owing to the absence on leave of Maj. Gen. Maxwell

General McAuliffe

TAYLOR. On December 22 a German party under a white flag brought an "honorable surrender" ultimatum into the encircled town; the alternative, said "the German commander," was "annihilation." McAuliffe, who was in command of all the American forces in Bastogne, at first did not take the demand seriously but finally was induced to put on paper his spontaneous oral response. His note read:

To the German Commander:
Nuts!
—The American Commander

The rumor later grew that the general had used somewhat stronger language which was toned down for the public, but this does not seem to have been the case. The German commander whose name did not appear on the demand was Gen. Heinrich von LÜTTWITZ.

McAuliffe, whose handling of the defense of Bastogne was widely praised, was promoted to major general. Subsequently he served in high commands, including in the mid-1950s the post of Commander in Chief, U.S. Army in Europe.

McCAIN, John Sidney (1884–1945). A 1906 graduate of the U.S. Naval Academy, McCain later became a pilot and early in World War II served as chief of the Bureau of Naval Aeronautics and Deputy Chief of Naval Operations for Air. Promoted to vice-admiral in August 1943, McCain commanded the carrier task force of the THIRD FLEET, planes under his direction taking part in action over PELELIU, LEYTE GULF, the PHILIPPINE SEA, MINDORO, LUZON, FORMOSA, the RYUKYUS and the Japanese homeland. His planes once sank 49 Japanese ships in a single day. Between July 10 and August 14, 1945, McCain's aviators located and destroyed 3,000 grounded enemy planes. The admiral received decorations from Great Britain as well as the United States for his role in the naval air war. He died soon after taking part in the formal Japanese surrender on the MISSOURI.

McCAMPBELL, David (1910–). U.S. Navy aviator who won the MEDAL OF HONOR for action in the two battles of the PHILIPPINE SEA, June 19, 1944, in which he claimed seven victories, and October 24, 1944, in which he had nine. He commanded Air Group 15 attached to the U.S.S. ESSEX. Captain McCampbell ran his score up to 34 kills to become the leading American naval ace of the war.

McCLOY, John Jay (1895–). A New York lawyer who joined the U.S. War Department in 1940 as a special consultant to Secretary Henry L. STIMSON and became Assistant Secretary of War in April 1941, a position he held until he resigned in November 1945. In this capacity he was chairman of the combined civil affairs committee of the COMBINED CHIEFS OF STAFF and War Department member of the State, War and Navy Department coordinating committee. As a general assistant to Stimson he was primarily concerned with the organization and maintenance of the Army during the war period. Toward the end of the war he was engaged in the political aspects of dealing with the liberated territories, in the preparation of armistice and surrender terms and in the administration of occupied territories. He also helped plan the war crimes trials, and was later U.S. military governor in Germany.

McCLUSKY, Clarence Wade, Jr. (1902–1976). U.S. Navy flier, a lieutenant commander, who commanded the air group of SBD dive-bombers (*see* SBD) from the carrier ENTERPRISE during the Battle of MIDWAY. He made the key decision to turn north when the Japanese fleet was not where it was reported to be and led the victorious attack on the Japanese carriers.

McCREERY, Sir Richard (1898–1967). British Army officer who was, in General ALEXANDER's words, "one of those rare soldiers who are both exceptionally fine staff officers and fine commanding officers in the field." In 1940 he was with the BRITISH EXPEDITIONARY FORCE, and after DUNKIRK with the Home Forces. In North Africa he was for a brief time tank adviser to General AUCHINLECK, and in August 1942 he became chief of staff to Alexander, Commander in Chief in the Middle East. In September 1943 he commanded the British 10th Corps in the SALERNO landings and led it through the fighting at CASSINO. General McCreery became commander of the EIGHTH ARMY in November 1944 and was with it at the Axis surrender in May 1945. He commanded the British occupation forces in Austria until 1946. In 1959 McCreery precipitated a storm by writing critically of MONTGOMERY's conduct of the ALAMEIN battle and pursuit.

McGUIRE, Thomas B. (1920–1945). America's second-ranking (after Maj. Richard I. BONG) World War II ace, McGuire shot down 38 Japanese planes in some 20 months of combat. On a Christmas Day 1944 escort mission over Luzon, his squadron of 15 P-38s was attacked by 20 Japanese fighters. He shot down three of these planes and on the next day downed four others. McGuire, an Air Force major, met his death on January 7, 1945, when his P-38 stalled and crashed as he attempted a tight turn in order to come to the aid of a squadron member who had been jumped by an enemy fighter. His exploits earned him the MEDAL OF HONOR.

MACHINE GUN. *See* SMALL ARMS.

MACKELVIE, Jay Ward (1890–). U.S. Army officer (brigadier general, 1942) who took command of XII Corps artillery in 1943 and in 1944 became commander of the 90th Division, leading it in Normandy. On June 13, 1944, after the division had made a poor showing in its first combat experience, MacKelvie was relieved without prejudice. After serving briefly in the headquarters of ETO, in September 1944 he became artillery commander of the 80th Division.

MACKENSEN, Eberhard von (1889–1969). German Army officer, son of the famous Field Marshal von Mackensen of World War I. Eberhard von Mackensen began his Army career in his father's old hussar regiment. In World War II Mackensen commanded a tank corps and later the First PANZER ARMY on the Eastern Front. He was replaced in 1943 by Gen. H. V. HUBE and was subsequently transferred to Italy, where, a colonel general, he took over the Fourteenth Army, defending against Allied landings at ANZIO. Mackensen was given the task of eliminating the Allied beachhead, but in spite of his efforts through February 1944 the struggle ended in a stalemate. After the war Mackensen was indicted for being involved in the shooting of hostages. A British court in Rome sentenced him to life imprisonment, but he was released in 1952.

McKEOGH, Michael. A U.S. Army sergeant, "Mickey" McKeogh served as Gen. Dwight D. EISENHOWER's orderly. He was remembered by Ike for his loyalty and devotion. In December 1944 he married WAC Cpl. Pearlie Hargrove, Ike's staff driver.

MACKESY, Pierse Joseph (1883–1956). British Army officer, commander of an infantry brigade in Palestine just before the war and at the time of the Norwegian campaign the commander of the British 49th Division. A major general, he used his divisional headquarters when he led the army contingent for operations in the NARVIK area from April to mid-May 1940, when he turned over command to Lt. Gen. Sir Claude AUCHINLECK.

McLAIN, Raymond S. (1890–1954). A National Guardsman, this Oklahoma banker served as a machine-gun-company commander in World War I and as commanding general of the 90th Infantry Division in World War II. His two predecessors in the 90th had been relieved, but in a short time McLain so transformed the division that three months later, when he was promoted to the command of XIX Corps, he left a unit later described by Gen. Omar N. BRADLEY as "one of the finest divisions in combat on the Allied front." When ordered to stop his advance into Germany, McLain had a bridgehead across the Elbe. In June 1945 he was promoted to lieutenant general.

MACLEAN, Fitzroy (1911–). A former British diplomat and a Member of Parliament in 1943, Brigadier Maclean had an adventurous time in Yugoslavia as Winston CHURCHILL's liaison officer to Marshal TITO and his PARTISANS. He played a prominent part in influencing the Allies to assist Tito in his struggle against the Axis and to grant him preferment over his domestic opponents.

MacLEISH, Archibald (1892–). A leading American poet who in 1939 was chosen by President ROOSEVELT to serve as Librarian of Congress. In 1941 he was appointed director of the Office of Facts and Figures, an agency established for the purpose of facilitating the dissemination of information to the public on the defense policies and activities of the government. When the office was merged into the OFFICE OF WAR INFORMATION (1942), MacLeish became assistant director of the new agency. In 1944–45 he was Assistant Secretary of State for public and cultural relations. After the war he played a prominent part in the development of UNESCO.

MACMILLAN, Harold (1894–). British Conservative political figure, an opponent of the prewar APPEASEMENT policy, who rendered important wartime service as British political adviser at General EISENHOWER's Allied Force Headquarters in NORTHWEST AFRICA. His American counterpart was Ambassador Robert MURPHY. Macmillan played a part in the Italian armistice negotiations and in November 1943 was appointed British high commissioner for Italy. Ultimately he participated in political discussions and settlements throughout the Mediterranean area. Macmillan served as Prime Minister in 1957–63.

McMORRIS, Charles Horatio (1890–1954). U.S. naval officer who graduated fifth in his class (1912) at the Naval Academy, where his intelligence gained him the nickname "Soc" (for Socrates). McMorris saw Atlantic service in World War I and after a mixture of sea and shore duty in the interwar period graduated from the Naval War College in 1938. In 1939–41 he was operations officer of the Hawaiian detachment of the U.S. Fleet; he then became war plans officer of the Pacific Fleet, serving until April 1942. After a period of sea duty as commander of the cruiser SAN FRANCISCO and of a cruiser-destroyer task force at the Battle of the KOMANDORSKI ISLANDS, he became chief of staff of the Pacific Fleet (June 1943), serving for the balance of the war. His highest wartime rank was rear admiral.

McNAIR, Lesley J. (1883–1944). During his World War I service in France, where he was on the staff of the U.S. 1st Division and later in GHQ, AEF, McNair was promoted to brigadier general (October 1, 1918), just 14 years after he graduated from West Point, but following the war he reverted to the rank of major. By 1937 he had regained his star, and two years later he became commandant of the Command and General Staff School. McNair is known as the man who trained the World War II American army, for he established a new rigorous system under which units in training experienced conditions close to actual combat. As head of the Army Ground Forces, McNair was responsible for the entire cycle: activation, training and evaluation of new divisions. In June 1941 he was promoted to lieutenant general. Since his name was well known to the Germans, for a short time in 1944 he served as commander of the phantom 1st Army Group, which was supposed to be stationed in England. This fictitious army group appeared to threaten the Pas de Calais area during the early stages of operations on the Continent. Such a threat, it was hoped, would fix the German forces located in the Pas de Calais. On July 25, while observing the CARPET BOMBING which was the first stage in Gen. Omar BRADLEY's breakthrough attempt, Operation COBRA, McNair was killed by a bomb that fell short of its target.

McNARNEY, Joseph T. (1893–1972). U.S. Army officer who became an aviator on the eve of World War I, served in that conflict and held a variety of peacetime command and staff assignments. When the Japanese attacked PEARL HARBOR, McNarney was a brigadier general acting as chief of staff for a group of American military observers in London. Upon returning to the United States, he joined the Roberts Commission, headed by Supreme Court Justice Owen J. ROBERTS, which investigated the Japanese attack on Pearl Harbor. He received a promotion to major general in January 1942 and became chairman of a War Department committee charged with reorganizing the Army. Appointed

Deputy Chief of Staff in March, he was promoted to lieutenant general in June; in his position he was, in fact, Vice-Chief to General MARSHALL. He arrived in the MEDITERRANEAN THEATER in October 1944 and served first as deputy theater commander and then as commanding general of U.S. Army forces in the theater. He received a fourth star in March 1945, and shortly after V-E Day succeeded General EISENHOWER as Commander of ETO.

McNAUGHTON, Andrew George (1887–). Canada's Chief of General Staff in 1929–35, McNaughton during the war served as commander, 1st Canadian Division, 1939–40; commander, 7th Corps, 1940; commander, Canadian Corps Overseas, 1940–42; and General Officer Commanding in Chief, CANADIAN FIRST ARMY Overseas, 1942–44. A lieutenant general, he retired in November 1944 to become Minister of National Defence, resigning in August 1945. Afterward he was president of the Atomic Energy Control Board of Canada, 1946–48.

McNUTT, Paul Vories (1891–1955). A native of Indiana, governor of the state from 1933 to 1937. After serving as U.S. high commissioner to the Philippines, McNutt was appointed (1939) Federal Security Administrator, with administrative control over the Civilian Conservation Corps, the National Youth Administration, the Office of Education, the Public Health Service, the Social Security Board and the U.S. Employment Service. In 1940 he was appointed coordinator of all health, medical, welfare, nutrition, recreation and related activities affecting national defense. When the Office of Defense, Health and Welfare Services was established in 1941, he was named director. In 1942–45 he was chairman of the WAR MANPOWER COMMISSION, designed to ensure the availability of manpower for war production. After the war he returned to the Philippines as high commissioner and then ambassador.

MACON, Robert C. (1890–). U.S. Army officer who commanded the 7th Infantry Regiment in the 1942 invasion of NORTHWEST AFRICA. In 1943 he became the assistant commander of the 83d Infantry Division. He was promoted to major general in 1944 and named commanding general of the 83d Division, engaged in the ETO. A lanky individual, casual in manner, Macon was a strong, fighting leader. His division had a bridgehead across the Elbe and was bound for Berlin when by order the advance was halted on April 12, 1945.

MADAGASCAR. Large island off the east coast of Africa, now the independent Malagasy Republic, the scene of operations that involved British and VICHY French forces in May and September 1942. After the successes of the Japanese fleet against the Royal Navy in the Indian Ocean in the early months of 1942, there was fear that the Japanese might follow up their advantage and seek a base in the western part of the Indian Ocean. Madagascar seemed a likely target, since the well-equipped French bases on the island could easily accommodate Japanese forces. In April a large British naval force was assembled at Durban to transport and land on Madagascar two brigades of Royal Marines. The target of the action was the large French naval base at Diego Suarez on the northern part of the island. In heavy fighting on May 5, 6 and 7 the French bases were occupied or neutralized. The civil administration of the island was left in the hands of the Vichy French authorities, who signed a treaty of capitulation. In September the British Government came to the conclusion that the Vichy French authorities, particularly the governor, were collaborating with the enemy. Once again, heavy British forces were moved to the island and were landed in concert with attacks by British forces already present. There was little fight left in the French, however, and the capital, Antananarivo (Tananarive), fell on September 23 after only a few days of light skirmishing.

MADANG. Town on the northeast shore of NEW GUINEA, with a fair harbor and good sites for airfields. The Japanese secured the area on December 19, 1942, the same time that they occupied the WEWAK area to the northwest. During the early months of 1943 the Japanese developed Madang into an important air and logistical base, and it was one of the major objectives of the Allied CARTWHEEL campaign. A major Allied operation to seize Madang never came off, for other bases in eastern New Guinea proved adequate substitutes. The Japanese themselves ultimately abandoned Madang, pulling their forces west to Wewak, and Australian troops, moving overland, occupied the town and base area on April 24, 1944.

MADDOX, U.S.S. The name of three ships, the first one a WICKES-class destroyer, commissioned in 1919. Transferred to Britain in 1940, she was renamed H.M.S. *Georgetown* and served in the Atlantic before being transferred to the USSR and renamed *Doblestnyi*.

The second *Maddox* was a GLEAVES-class destroyer, commissioned in 1942. After convoy work in the Atlantic, *Maddox* supported the invasion of SICILY. Here, on July 10, 1943, she was hit by a bomb from a German dive-bomber. Her after magazine exploded, and she quickly sank with most of her crew.

The third *Maddox* was an ALLEN M. SUMNER–class destroyer. Commissioned in 1944, she joined the FAST CARRIER TASK FORCE and supported the invasions of MINDORO and LUZON. Damaged by a KAMIKAZE off Formosa in January 1945, *Maddox* rejoined the fleet for carrier strikes in support of the battle for OKINAWA. After final strikes against Japan in July–August 1945, she took part in the occupation of Japan and Korea.

MADURAI BOMB. Alternate Japanese name for the OHKA rocket kamikaze bomb.

MAEDA ESCARPMENT. Retaining this position in the southern third of OKINAWA was a vital part of the Japanese 32d Army defense plans because, if captured, Maeda would afford the Americans a commanding view of all the Japanese positions as far south as the Shuri foothills, while possession of it guaranteed the Japanese observation to the north, east and west into American lines. The region surrounding Maeda was the scene of furious fighting from April 26 to May 3, 1945, when elements of the 307th Infantry, 77th Infantry Division, reached the top of the escarpment and held it despite heavy enemy fire from reverse slope positions and adjacent Japanese positions, as well as desperate counterattacks.

MAE WEST. Orange or yellow life jacket worn around the chest, inflatable by means of carbon dioxide cartridges, blown up manually if the cartridges fail or are lost.

MAGDEBURG. City in central Germany on the Elbe River, entered briefly by reconnaissance troops of the U.S. 2d Armored Division on April 11, 1945, and captured on April 18 after a two-day assault by parts of that unit and the 30th Infantry Division.

MAGIC. In 1939–40 the U.S. Army and Navy were intensively engaged in an effort to "read" the coded messages which the Japanese Government was sending to its agents around the world. Rear Adm. Walter S. Anderson, director of the Office of Naval Intelligence (ONI) employed the term "magic" to refer to any decrypted Japanese code message. Operation MAGIC was the name assigned to the overall program devoted to breaking the Japanese codes.

In 1929 Secretary of State Henry L. STIMSON had ordered the existing, moderate operations in cryptology curtailed because he believed that "gentlemen do not read each other's mail." Thus when the Japanese built a cipher machine, subsequently known as the Red machine, for the transmission of their diplomatic messages by automated ciphers, the machine withstood American efforts to discover its manner of operation until 1935, when the ONI reconstructed the machine by means of analysis and intrigue.

By 1937 the Japanese had reason to believe that American intelligence experts might have compromised or broken some of their code systems. Capt. Jinsaburo Ito of the Imperial Japanese Navy invented a new cipher machine which consisted of a battery of standard, six-level, 25-point relays (electrically controlled switches). This machine, which American cryptologists subsequently labeled the Purple machine, worked on the principle of a telephone switchboard. Once it was put into operation, the Purple machine defied all efforts by U.S. cryptologists to crack its messages.

The Purple code system remained secure until Col. William FRIEDMAN, a U.S. Army intelligence officer, and his team finally cracked it on September 25, 1940, when the first fully intelligible, ungarbled text was recovered with the code machine they had designed. The triumph was even more remarkable than it seemed at the time because neither Friedman nor any of his associates had ever seen the Japanese machine, nor were they aware of its principles of operation or its components. Unfortunately, Colonel Friedman suffered a nervous breakdown as a consequence of his 19-month effort to crack the Purple code; thus he was not available for work on the Japanese codes in the months preceding PEARL HARBOR.

By the time the Purple code, which was then the highest-priority Japanese diplomatic code, fell to Friedman's analysis, Operation Magic was well under way. Both the Army and the Navy had special intelligence sections that decoded Japanese messages. The Navy called its section the Communications Security Unit (OP-20-G). It had a staff in 1941 of about 300 persons, under the supervision of Comdr. Laurence F. SAFFORD. After Safford's unit had decrypted a message, it sent the message to a special section of ONI headed by Lt. Comdr. A. D, KRAMER, a skilled Japanese-language linguist, whose staff of only six translators rendered the message into English. ONI then determined which Purple messages should be routed to civilian and military leaders for their information.

With surprisingly little duplication of effort and interservice rivalry, the Army Signal Intelligence Section (SIS) of the Signal Corps also intercepted, decrypted and translated Japanese coded messages. By December 1941 SIS had a staff of 224 in Washington and 150 persons working in the field on Operation Magic. The Army's head of Far Eastern intelligence selected the persons to whom decrypted Purple messages were distributed.

Procedures in the operation were slow and cumbersome. Since the Japanese used a variety of codes, some of which the cryptologists had never broken, there was always a backlog of undecoded and untranslated messages. Purple messages always got first priority from both services in decoding, translation and distribution. Yet the value of Purple messages was limited, since Purple was a top-secret diplomatic code. No intercepts of military significance found in Purple transmissions were sent to the State Department. Thus American diplomatic analysts had only half the picture of Japanese intentions. The Navy encountered more difficulty when the Japanese changed their top-secret Flag Officers' code in November 1940. Navy intelligence had first broken this code in 1926, but OP-20-G was unable to crack it again before Pearl Harbor. Consequently both the Navy and the Army, which had never broken the Japanese Army code, had little specific insight as to Japanese military plans in 1941.

Working under great pressure, inadequately staffed and lacking any one person or office that could get an overview of Japanese intentions from the accumulated magics, American intelligence experts had many pieces to a gigantic puzzle but little idea of the overall design of that puzzle in the fall of 1941. They had, nevertheless, drawn three primary conclusions from the magics they had read. They concluded that Japan would not attack Russia in support of Germany; that Japan would strike to the south; and that war would be likely to break out on the weekend of November 29, 1941. They lacked, however, the part of the puzzle which identified the place of attack, and all they had available to solve that question were ambiguous clues. When November 29 came and went without any Japanese attack, no one knew what the Japanese intended.

The subsequent attack on Pearl Harbor soon resolved the intelligence ambiguities, but Operation Magic did not cease with the outbreak of war with Japan. Cryptanalysis of the Japanese codes continued throughout the war, with the biggest payoff coming at the Battle of MIDWAY. Through reading the Japanese naval code prior to that battle, U.S. commanders knew the Japanese objectives, the approximate direction of approach, and the approximate date of attack. Consequently, numerically inferior U.S. forces were able to overcome the Japanese superiority.

MAGINOT LINE. A French Minister of War, André Maginot, gave his name to this line of concrete and steel fortifications that stretched from Luxembourg to Switzerland along the French border with Germany. The barrier, with its heavy artillery enclosed in bombproof casements, was conceived as an impregnable defense against a German threat. The French Government, when it constructed the line between 1930 and 1935, assumed that it would hold any surprise attack until the Army could mobilize to meet it. Thus the Maginot Line tended to justify a small peacetime Army and reflected the defensive mentality of French policymakers. The German Army circumvented this defense by advancing through Belgium in 1940. Though such a move was no surprise to the Allies, the cost and the objections by the Belgians that it would consign them to Germany in the event of war had prevented the extension of the line along the Franco-Belgian border.

MAGISTER. Introduced in 1937, this was the first monoplane trainer acquired by Britain's Royal Air Force. The craft was built of wood and plywood, the landing gear was fixed, and pupil and instructor sat in open tandem cockpits. A 130-horsepower de Havilland Gypsy Major engine gave this low-wing product of Miles Aircraft a top speed of 132 miles per hour. Split flaps reduced the landing speed to a mere 42 miles per hour.

MAGNET. Code name for U.S. forces in Northern Ireland; also applied to the movement of the forces to this destination (early 1942).

MAHAN, U.S.S. Destroyer and class (1,726 tons; four or five 5-inch guns; four to twelve 21-inch torpedo tubes; 39 knots). Sixteen of these ships completed in 1936–37; they were two-stackers with advanced engineering plants for their time. Their torpedo battery was arranged in three quadruple mounts, one on the centerline and one to either side. Like other destroyers, they began to go through a series of modifications beginning in 1941. One gun was removed, light antiaircraft guns were progressively added and some ships finished the war with one torpedo tube mount. Six ships were war losses. Two others, *Cassin* and *Downes*, were sunk at PEARL HARBOR. Their machinery was salvaged and shipped back to the United States, where new ships were built around the old machinery, with the same names and numbers.

MAHURIN, Walker M. (1918–). While serving in the U.S. EIGHTH AIR FORCE, Mahurin shot down 21 German planes, probably downed a 22d and damaged three others. Shot down over occupied Europe in March 1944, he avoided capture and returned to England, thanks to the efforts of the French underground. Later he commanded the 3d Fighter Group in the Pacific, where he shot down one Japanese plane; attaining the grade of lieutenant colonel, he took over the 3d Air Command Wing.

MAIKOP. The third most important oil center in the Caucasus (USSR) after BAKU and Grozny. The Germans captured Maikop in August 1942, during their lightninglike sweep down through the Caucasus. Prior to their evacuation the Russians blew up the oil installations, thus preventing enemy exploitation of this valuable resource.

MAINZ. This Rhineland city was taken by the U.S. 90th Division (THIRD ARMY) on March 22, 1945. It then served as a springboard for a crossing of the river, at the direction of General PATTON, by the U.S. 80th Division.

MAISKY, Ivan (1884–1975). Soviet diplomat, originally a Menshevik, who switched his position to the winning Bolshevik side. He became ambassador to Britain in 1932, holding that post until 1942. Maisky did well in the position, especially in the difficult years of the SOVIET-GERMAN NONAGGRESSION PACT (1939–41). Prior to the German invasion in June 1941, Maisky sent messages to the Kremlin warning of the coming attack. In July 1941 he concluded a treaty with the Polish government-in-exile in London, which established relations between the two parties, called for the forming of a Polish army in the Soviet Union and declared the Soviet-German Pact of 1939 null and void but left the question of the future Soviet-Polish frontier open. That same month he also reached an agreement with the Czech government-in-exile. Maisky helped to arrange for FREE FRANCE to establish the NORMANDIE SQUADRON to fight on the Eastern Front. He participated in Anthony EDEN's talks with STALIN and MOLOTOV in Moscow (1941), Winston CHURCHILL's and Eden's meeting with Molotov in London (1942) and the YALTA and POTSDAM CONFERENCES of 1945. In 1943 he was appointed Deputy People's Commissar for Foreign Affairs, and he served as chairman of the Allied Commission on Repartitions in 1945.

MAJESTIC. Code name for the projected Allied invasion of the island of Kyushu, Japan.

MAJOR MARTIN. "Maj. William Martin, Royal Marines" was the identity given a corpse by the British Naval Intelligence Division in a ruse carried out to convince the Germans that an invasion of the Balkans was the next operation scheduled after the Allied victory in North Africa in 1943. The body, equipped with a courier's briefcase containing appropriately deceptive documentation, was floated ashore off the coast of Spain on April 30, 1943. Many Axis leaders, including Adolf HITLER himself, accepted the major's news as confirmation of their belief that such was the Allied plan. The story is told in Ewen Montagu, *The Man Who Never Was* (1954). The operational code name was Mincemeat.

MAJURO. The target of a U.S. V Amphibious Corps Reconnaissance Company landing on the night of January 30, 1944. The atoll, in the MARSHALL ISLANDS, was secured without opposition on the 31st and became a principal operating base for Central Pacific forces until after the MARIANAS were secured. On May 4 the U.S. Naval Base and Naval Air Facility, Majuro Atoll, was established.

MAKASSAR STRAIT, BATTLE OF. The first sizable American naval engagement of the war, fought off BALIKPAPAN, Borneo. On January 24, 1942, four U.S.

destroyers attacked Japanese shipping, causing serious losses.

MAKIN. The northernmost projection of the GILBERT ISLANDS, this atoll was the secondary target when in November 1943 counteroffensive operations against Japan were begun in the Central Pacific theater, the primary target being TARAWA Island, 105 miles to the south. As planning was being completed for Operation GALVANIC, Makin, which was needed for an airstrip, was suddenly substituted for Nauru, because of the latter's formidable heights and greater distance from the MARSHALL ISLANDS. Weakly garrisoned by the Japanese, though heavily fortified, Makin Atoll was overrun and occupied by U.S. Army troops in four days of battle (November 20–23). A reinforced Korean labor battalion stationed there had taken up arms to assist the defense. The end was distinguished by the shortest victory message of the war, "Makin Taken."

MAKINO, Shiro (1893–1945). A graduate of the Japanese Military Academy (1914) and the War College (1922), Lieutenant General Makino became commander of the 16th Division in March 1944. In that capacity he was in command of the Japanese garrison force on LEYTE when the Allies landed in October 1944. He was reported killed in action.

MAKNASSY. A gap in the Eastern Dorsal (TUNISIA), leading west from SFAX. In March 1943 General PATTON and U.S. II Corps seized Maknassy while the British EIGHTH ARMY defeated the Axis at MARETH and the Chotts, but efforts to advance east of Maknassy to cut the Italian Tenth Army's line of communication or retreat failed.

MALAN, Adolph Gysbert (1910–1963). Born in South Africa, "Sailor" Malan joined the RAF in 1936. He was a brilliant fighter pilot, credited with destroying 32 enemy aircraft in World War II. He received the DISTINGUISHED SERVICE ORDER and bar and the DISTINGUISHED FLYING CROSS and bar. He commanded No. 74 Squadron in the Battle of BRITAIN.

MALAYA, H.M.S. Royal Navy battleship, completed in 1915 by Armstrong and only partially modernized in 1935–36. She displaced 31,000 tons and in 1939 was armed with eight 15-inch, twelve 6-inch and eight 4-inch guns, smaller weapons and four aircraft. *Malaya* served in Indian Ocean and Atlantic convoy escort forces in 1939–40, in FORCE H based on GIBRALTAR in 1941 (including the bombardment of Genoa) and from the end of 1941 to 1943 in the Home Fleet. In 1943 she was reduced to training and reserve.

MÁLEME. Key airfield on the north coast of CRETE, assaulted by German paratroopers on May 20, 1941, and taken (with very heavy losses) from the New Zealand 5th Brigade on May 21. Additional German troops were then flown in.

MALENKOV, Georgi M. (1902–). An intimate associate of Joseph STALIN, Malenkov secured his future through his role in the elimination of the opposition to Stalin in the purges of 1937–38. In February 1941 he became a candidate member of the Politburo and a close collaborator of Stalin in the party's General Secretariat. After the German attack in June 1941 he became a member of the STATE DEFENSE COMMITTEE, where he was responsible for aircraft production.

MALINOVSKY, Rodion (1898–1967). During the critical battle for STALINGRAD, General Malinovsky commanded the Second Guards Army. Following the Red Army's victory on the Volga, he commanded the Southwest Front and the Third and Second Ukrainian Fronts (army groups). Finally, as commanding officer of the Transbaikal Front, he helped defeat the Japanese KWANTUNG ARMY in Siberia. Malinovsky, who achieved the rank of Marshal of the Soviet Union, served as Minister of Defense from 1957 until his death in 1967.

MALINTA TUNNEL. The main reinforced-concrete subterranean tunnel on CORREGIDOR Island. It was used as shelter and living space by Corregidor's defenders during the 1942 siege by the Japanese. Japanese defenders retreated to it during the 1945 recapture of the island, and its entrances were sealed off. Malinta Tunnel consisted of a main passageway with a number of wings, or "laterals," opening out to either side.

MALMÉDY. Picturesque Belgian town near which on December 17, 1944, during the Battle of the BULGE, a task force commanded by Lt. Col. Joachim PEIPER from the German 1st SS Panzer Division came upon a convoy of Battery B, U.S. 285th Field Artillery Observation Battalion. Herding approximately a hundred captured Americans into a field, German troops opened fire with pistols and machine guns. A few feigned death and escaped, but 86 were murdered, the worst atrocity of the war in Europe involving American troops. After the war 73 Germans including Peiper were convicted of responsibility in the massacre, but none was executed and none served full sentence, primarily because the U.S. Senate Armed Forces Committee questioned procedures under which the trials were conducted. The Belgians have erected a monument on the site bearing names of the victims.

MALTA. The Maltese Islands, lying in the central Mediterranean only 60 miles from Sicily and 140 miles from the mainland of Europe, provided a vital naval and air base for British control of the Mediterranean. From Malta, British planes and ships could strike Axis supply routes from Italy to Africa, and from the time Italy entered the war until late 1942 Malta was under steady Axis attack. The British, under attack at home, reinforced Malta with as many planes and antiaircraft guns as they could spare, and in August 1941, 35 percent of General ROMMEL's supply ships were sunk. In October the figure increased to 63 percent, and Italian Foreign Minister CIANO wrote that the Italians had given up trying to get convoys through because the British had "slaughtered us." The Germans then decided to neutralize Malta by a bombing blitz from Sicily, directed by Field Marshal Albert KESSELRING, Commander in Chief South.

As LUFTWAFFE bombing of Malta intensified, British losses mounted and Axis supplies increasingly got through, and in January 1942 Rommel bounced back from El Agheila to retake the western half of Cyrenaica, including the airfields within striking distance of Malta.

In April 1942 Rommel was preparing for what proved to be his final campaign in Africa. He flew to Germany to persuade Adolf Hitler to capture Malta and thus ensure his supplies. Admiral Raeder also urged the capture of Malta, and Operation Hercules was tentatively set for July. Two parachute divisions—one German, one Italian—were to seize a bridgehead which would be reinforced by six to eight divisions of seaborne Italian troops. Hitler was not enthusiastic, and plans called for Malta to be completely neutralized before the assault.

The air attacks on Malta steadily intensified, reaching a peak in April. Luftwaffe's planes pounded the island night and day, and in addition preyed on the surrounding sea lanes to prevent convoys of supplies from reaching the island. When only two out of 17 British convoy ships got through, the British reluctantly stopped their efforts to reinforce Malta by sea. The Maltese were dependent on outside supply for food as well as war materials, but morale remained high throughout their long ordeal. They tunneled into the soft limestone of their island for protection, and in April King George VI awarded them the George Cross "to bear witness to a heroism and devotion that will long be famous in history." It was the first time a medal had been conferred on a people of the Commonwealth.

The crucial British need was to get fighter planes to Malta. So long as Rommel held the western half of Cyrenaica, the Spitfires could not reach Malta from a land base. The Malta crisis prompted an unusual action in early May, when Winston Churchill ordered General Auchinleck, against the latter's judgment, to launch an offensive no later than June. Rommel opened his own offensive on May 26, but by then the crisis was easing. Spitfires, flown from the decks of carriers H.M.S. Eagle and U.S.S. Wasp, reached the island, and slowly but surely Malta regained its fighting strength.

Operation Hercules was never conducted, and after the war General Student, who was to have commanded the German paratroopers in the capture of Malta, told the British military historian B. H. Liddell Hart that in June he was summoned to Hitler's headquarters for a conference. Hitler had just talked with General Cruewell from Africa, who had given him an unfavorable account of Italian morale and especially of the Italian Navy. Deciding that if the Royal Navy contested the capture of Malta the Italian Navy would

Bodies of American soldiers lie in the snow after the Malmédy massacre

abandon its mission, Hitler postponed the assault. It was never reinstated.

The result was Axis defeat. As Rommel drove toward Egypt, planes from Malta again reduced his supplies to a trickle. In the *Rommel Papers*, Rommel cites the failure to take Malta as the main reason for his problems at ALAMEIN. Churchill, writing in *The Hinge of Fate*, says that Malta's heroic defense formed the keystone of the struggle for the Middle East.

By June 1943 Malta's civilian casualties numbered 1,436 killed, 3,415 wounded. **M.H.B.**

MALTBY, Christopher Michael (1891–). British Army officer who commanded British troops in China in 1941, and was military commander of HONG KONG in the fighting against the Japanese in December 1941. His rank was major general.

MALYSHEV, Vyacheslav A. (1902–1957). Beginning his career as a railroad mechanic and then a locomotive engineer, Malyshev rose to important Soviet economic administrative posts during World War II, heading tank production and serving as deputy chairman of the Council of Ministers. For his work in the war he was given the rank of lieutenant general. After the war he directed Soviet naval development and, in the 1950s, nuclear programs.

MANCHESTER. This British aircraft, a twin-engine bomber built by Avro, proved a failure. Designed expressly for the Rolls-Royce Vulture, a 1,760-horsepower liquid-cooled engine, the Manchester carried a crew of seven and had a range of 1,630 miles with 10,350 pounds of bombs. Armament consisted of eight .303-caliber machine guns in power-operated turrets. Two of the weapons were in the nose, two atop the fuselage and four in the tail. The plane went into action in February 1941 against Brest, France, but was withdrawn from combat in June 1942 because of recurring trouble with the Vulture engines, which were underpowered and unreliable. *See also* LANCASTER.

MANCHUKUO. In 1931 the Japanese Army seized Manchuria, and a year later recognized this old Chinese region as the nation of Manchukuo under a puppet, Pu-yi, who had abdicated the Manchu throne of China as an infant in 1912. A League of Nations commission of inquiry condemned the seizure; Japan responded by withdrawing from the league. Manchuria was used by the Japanese Army in 1933 and 1934 to spark a series of smaller incidents that established its control over parts of Inner Mongolia and the areas of northern China around Peking. These incidents served as the background for the full-scale war between Japan and China that erupted in 1937. *See also* CHINA.

MANDALAY. The second largest city in BURMA, in May 1942 defended against the Japanese by Chinese troops under the command of Lt. Gen. Joseph W. STILWELL. In spite of the resoluteness of the defense, the Japanese prevailed and the Chinese garrison was forced to flee to China and India. In March 1945 Mandalay was recaptured during the British offensive by British and Chinese troops under the overall command of Lt. Gen. Sir William J. SLIM.

MANDEL, Georges (1885–1944). Conservative French politician (born Jeroboam Rothschild) during the late Third Republic, once a protégé of Georges Clemenceau. Prior to World War II, Mandel served in several governments as Colonial Minister and consistently opposed the interwar German resurgence. On May 19, 1940, in the midst of the Battle of FRANCE, Prime Minister Paul REYNAUD strengthened his cabinet by moving Mandel from the Colonial office to the Ministry of the Interior, a key wartime post. During the following weeks Mandel staunchly opposed the proponents of an armistice, but finally resigned on July 16 after Reynaud was replaced by Marshal Philippe PÉTAIN. Several days later Mandel, a Jew, was arrested by French officials; he was imprisoned, then handed over to the Germans and, after two years in Nazi concentration camps, turned back to officials of VICHY France and murdered by Pétain's militia on July 7, 1944.

MANDIBLES. Code name for proposed British plan, originated in 1941, for the capture of Rhodes.

MANHATTAN DISTRICT. Short for Manhattan Engineer District, the district of the U.S. Army Corps of Engineers established in June 1942 for construction of the production plants required in the development of the ATOMIC BOMB; it was at first called the DSM Project (for Development of Substitute Materials). The Manhattan District, under the direction of Brig. Gen. Leslie R. GROVES, took over administrative control of all aspects of the development of the atomic bomb, scientific as well as engineering and construction, and its name became synonymous with the overall project. It is often termed Manhattan Project.

MANILA. Long known as the "Pearl of the Orient," Manila was not only the economic, political and communications center of the Philippines but also, before World War II, the focus of American military and naval planning in the Far East. Prewar plans led to the construction of the defenses of the magnificent harbor of Manila Bay. War plan ORANGE was based on the assumption that in the event of war with Japan, American-Philippine forces would retain control over Manila Bay while the U.S. Pacific Fleet fought its way there from the fleet base at Pearl Harbor in Hawaii. And even if the city itself could not be held, at least the American-led forces could deny the Japanese access to Manila Bay for the six months the Orange Plan required.

During the months before the Japanese attacked the Philippines, Manila became the entrepôt and transshipment point for military supplies and troops concentrating in the islands under Gen. Douglas MACARTHUR, while after the outbreak of war all efforts were devoted to moving matériel out of the city. As early as December 22, 1941, MacArthur, who obviously wanted to avoid the destruction of Manila, informed the War Department that he intended to declare it an open city and withdraw all supplies and personnel to BATAAN and CORREGIDOR. Headquarters—both Army and Navy—began moving out of the city during the night of December 24, and on the 26th MacArthur declared Manila an open city.

To that date only a few misdirected Japanese planes

had attacked the city proper, causing little damage, but on the 27th Japanese Navy aircraft, later joined by Japanese Army planes, began a series of strong attacks against the port area and other obvious military targets. The Japanese, however, had some justification for ignoring the "open city" declaration, for American rear-echelon troops continued to move supplies out of Manila until New Year's Eve. On January 2, 1942, the Japanese entered Manila unopposed.

Under the Japanese, Manila continued to be the commercial, political and military center of the Philippines. It also became the main military supply depot for Japanese forces in the New Guinea area, the Netherlands East Indies, Indochina and Malaya. Manila was likewise the central supply point for the Japanese 14th Area Army, which, under Gen. Tomoyuki Yamashita, was responsible for the defense of the Philippines. But Yamashita had no centralized control over logistical installations in Manila—not even over all Japanese Army logistical operations—until after January 1, 1945, hardly a week before the U.S. Sixth Army invaded Luzon. He never gained any real control over Japanese Navy logistical activities in the Manila Bay area. Yamashita had no intention of defending Manila or, except for token delaying forces, of attempting to hold Manila Bay. He considered the city indefensible, given his means, and like MacArthur he had no desire to preside over its destruction. But the Japanese Navy, with its Manila Naval Defense Force, thought otherwise.

General MacArthur's plans for the reconquest of Luzon forcused on the early recapture of Manila and the equally early opening of Manila Bay. To this end the Sixth Army began landing at Lingayen Gulf, with little difficulty, on January 9, 1945, and by the 11th it had secured a firm beachhead. Then, while I Corps moved to protect Sixth Army's left flank, Gen. Walter Krueger, the army commander, started XIV Corps south through the Central Plains toward Manila. MacArthur was none too happy with the pace of XIV Corps, and by January 17 he had begun pressing Krueger for faster progress. Again on January 30 MacArthur urged Krueger on, and the next day XIV Corps, having deployed sufficient troops for a concerted drive on Manila, began its final push to the city. Late on February 3 the leading units of the 1st Cavalry Division, on the left of XIV Corps, entered the eastern part of Manila, and next day the 37th Infantry Division came streaming in on the west. On the same day, February 4, the 11th Airborne Division, which had mounted a combined amphibious-airborne assault—under Eighth Army control—well to the south of Manila, reached the southern outskirts of the city.

Almost to the end MacArthur hoped that Manila would fall without much fighting or damage, and his headquarters had even evolved plans for a great victory parade through the city. By February 6, however, it had become obvious that strong Japanese forces were going to fight for Manila, and the parade plans were quietly laid aside.

By evening on February 7, XIV Corps had cleared most of Manila north of the bisecting Pasig River. The Japanese made no concerted effort to hold northern Manila, and the fighting there stemmed largely from XIV Corps's attempts to prevent Japanese units north of the Pasig from escaping to the mountains east of the city. During the period February 8–12 elements of the 1st Cavalry Division encircled the city on the east and south, making contact with the 11th Airborne Division at the southern outskirts. Meanwhile, on February 7, the 37th Infantry Division had begun an assault cross-

Street fighting was heavy in the great Manila battle

ing of the Pasig near the center of the city. For this effort earlier restrictions on artillery and other ground-support fire had to be lifted. All pretense at saving the buildings in the southern part of Manila had to be abandoned, for American casualties had begun mounting at an alarming rate in assaults against the Japanese defenses.

The final defensive area, defined by February 12, covered a piece of ground extending some three miles north to south and about a mile inland from the shore of Manila Bay. This area contained the most modern, reinforced-concrete buildings as well as the stone, Spanish-built old city of Intramuros (within the walls of which were also located some modern buildings erected during the American presence). To defend this final area the Manila Naval Defense Force had left about 6,000 troops of all categories. These Japanese were trapped like rats and they knew it; they would also fight like cornered rats.

What followed was a costly war of attrition as the 1st Cavalry and 37th Infantry Divisions assaulted each fortified, Japanese-held building behind the unrestricted support fire of artillery, tanks, tank destroyers and mortars—fire that usually ground the Japanese strongpoints into near rubble. By February 23 most of the remaining Japanese had been pushed back into Intramuros and into three Philippine Commonwealth government buildings off the southeast corner of the walled city.

Tactical commanders responsible for reducing the final defenses wanted to employ air bombardment to raze the last strongpoints and also proposed the use of aerial napalm bombardment to burn the Japanese out. General MacArthur, who felt aerial bombardment would be too inaccurate, forbade such action. He did not, however, place any restrictions on ground-based bombardment, an awesome amount of which preceded the 37th Division's assault against Intramuros on February 23. The support fire virtually razed the walled city as effectively as aerial bombardment would have, and the issue at Intramuros was decided by dusk on February 24. The same fate—destruction—befell the three government buildings during the period February 26–March 3, and at the end of the latter day organized resistance within the city had collapsed.

American casualties in the Manila metropolitan area from February 3 through March 3 numbered approximately 1,000 troops killed and 5,500 wounded. The Manila Naval Defense Force (including its attached Japanese Army units) lost at least 12,500 men killed, while perhaps 4,500 troops escaped to the hills and mountains east of Manila.

But the cost to Manila and the Philippines cannot be measured in terms of military casualties alone. For one thing, some 100,000 Filipino civilians lost their lives during the battle, many of them during an unbridled series of atrocities in the southern part of the city. Large sectors of the city—including the governmental center—had been destroyed or damaged beyond repair; public transportation no longer existed; the water and sewerage systems required extensive repair, and the water that did run was unpotable; electric power was nonexistent; 39 bridges had been destroyed, including the six major spans over the Pasig River. So great were the problems of port repair and the clearing of obstacles from Manila Bay that it was mid-April before American forces could make profitable use of the port facilities. For a city left in Manila's condition there could be no return to normal. Instead, Manila's economic, political and social life had to begin over from scratch. **R.R.S.**

MANNA. Code name of British expedition to GREECE, October 1943.

MANNERHEIM, Carol Gustaf Emil, Baron (1867–1951). A descendant of Swedish nobility who had settled in Finland, Mannerheim became a second lieutenant in the Imperial Russian Army in 1889. When Finland declared independence in October 1917, Mannerheim, who had risen to the rank of lieutenant general, returned home, where he organized the White Guards. With these troops and German aid he defeated the Bolshevik-supported Red Guards in the brief civil war of 1918. He then became Regent, holding the post until defeated in the presidential election of July 1919. From then to 1931 he lived in semiretirement, directing the Mannerheim Child Welfare League and the Finnish Red Cross. In 1931 he became head of the National Defense Council, and in 1933 he was made field marshal. He reorganized the Army and built a 65-mile defense line, later called the MANNERHEIM LINE, across Finland's southeastern frontier.

He led Finland's armed forces in their heroic but ultimately unsuccessful resistance to Soviet aggression in the Winter War (1939–40) and again in the Continuation War (1941–44), when Finland, hoping to regain its lost territory, became Germany's cobelligerent in attacking Russia. Mannerheim was appointed president to negotiate a separate peace when the Germans began retreating. Finland withdrew from the war on September 4, 1944. Mannerheim opened the new legislature in April 1945 but resigned the presidency on March 4, 1946, because of ill health. His last years were spent in retirement, mostly in Switzerland and Sweden. *See also* SOVIET-FINNISH WAR.

MANNERHEIM LINE. A 65-mile series of trenches, obstacles and 119 reinforced bunkers along a series of lakes and rivers in the KARELIAN ISTHMUS, Finland's southeastern frontier. It was named for the Finnish Commander in Chief, Marshal MANNERHEIM.

MANNHEIM. Rhineland city, the object of the first RAF night area raid on Germany, December 16–17, 1940. Little damage was done to the target.

MANSTEIN, Fritz Erich von (1887–1973). German Army officer who acquired the reputation among many commentators of being the outstanding German strategist of the war. The son of an artillery officer, Eduard von Lewinski, Manstein took the surname of his uncle General von Manstein, by whom he was adopted. He entered the Army in 1906 in the Third Regiment of Foot Guards.

During World War I, Manstein served mainly in staff positions, seeing duty on the Eastern and Western Fronts and in the Balkans. He was severely wounded in November 1914. Following the war he held various staff and regimental appointments in the Reichswehr, in 1935 becoming chief of the operations branch of the General Staff of the Army. In 1936, as a Generalmajor (equivalent to brigadier general), he was appointed Oberquartiermeister I, which made him deputy to Gen. Ludwig BECK, Chief of the General Staff. In the purge of the Army following the dismissal of the Commander in Chief, General von FRITSCH, in February 1938, Manstein was relieved of his staff appointment and given command of the 18th Infantry Division. In the autumn of 1938, however, he participated in the occupation of the SUDETENLAND as chief of staff to General von LEEB.

During the campaign in Poland in 1939, Manstein served as chief of staff to General von RUNDSTEDT, commander of Army Group South. In October he accompanied Rundstedt to the Western Front as chief of staff of Army Group A, which at that stage had only a secondary role in the German plan of attack. Manstein, however, believed that the contemplated replay of the old Schlieffen plan of World War I was unlikely to produce decisive results; he favored instead a surprise drive through the supposedly impenetrable ARDENNES. This Manstein plan became the key to the astonishing German victory of May 1940. It was adopted by Adolf HITLER against the opposition of Field Marshal von BRAUCHITSCH, the Commander in Chief of the Army, and General HALDER, the Chief of Staff, and only after documents containing the original plan had fallen into Belgian hands. Manstein was thus the architect of the German triumph in the Battle of FRANCE, in which he held a field command—the XXXVIII Corps.

In March 1941 he was appointed to command of the LVI Panzer Corps, which he led in the advance on LENINGRAD in June and July. In September he was promoted to command of the Eleventh Army, on the southern wing of the German advance into the Soviet Union. His forces defeated the Russians in the CRIMEA, and after a siege took SEVASTOPOL at the beginning of July 1942. Manstein was rewarded with promotion to field marshal. In August the Führer, upset at the lack of progress in the Leningrad area, gave Manstein the assignment of taking this fortress, but the general's main effort had to be devoted to countering a Russian offensive south of Lake LADOGA.

In November the Eleventh Army, augmented by other units, was designated Army Group Don and thrown into the STALINGRAD campaign; General PAULUS's SIXTH ARMY came under the formal though not effective command of Manstein (this because Hitler issued direct orders by radio to Paulus). In December Manstein launched a vain attempt to rescue Sixth Army (Operation Winter Storm). Although this operation was not successful, Manstein's skillful direction helped save the German southern wing in extremely heavy fighting against Soviet attacks. In February 1943 Manstein's command was redesignated Army Group South, and the field marshal led it in a counteroffensive against the Russians in the KHARKOV area, winning a significant victory and stabilizing the front for a time. Manstein's army group participated in the last German offensive in Russia, Operation Citadel, the attempt to eliminate the Soviet KURSK salient, in July 1943. After the failure and cancellation of this offensive, Manstein led his forces through a series of difficult defensive battles, culminating in withdrawal behind the Dnieper River.

On March 30, 1944, Hitler's personal airplane landed at Manstein's headquarters at Lvov. It had come to take the field marshal, along with Field Marshal von KLEIST, to Hitler's house at the Obersalzberg, where the two men were dismissed from their commands. Manstein, once Hitler's man of the hour and the brain behind Germany's greatest triumph of the war, had fallen into disfavor. He did not hold another command during the war.

In 1949 Manstein was convicted by a British military court of war crimes committed in Russia. He was sentenced to 18 years' imprisonment; the sentence was later reduced to 12 years, and he was released after serving four.

MANTES-GASSICOURT. Thirty miles from Paris, site of the first Allied crossing of the Seine River after the breakout from the Normandy beachhead. The crossing was made on the night of August 19, 1944, by troops of the U.S. 79th Division. The first men across (313th Infantry) walked on a narrow footpath on top of a dam.

MANTEUFFEL, Hasso-Eccard von (1897–). German Army officer who became known as a dynamic and resourceful commander. He began his career as a cavalry officer and remained on the active list during the Weimar Republic, but in 1934 he changed to the armored forces, seeing prewar service on the staff of the Inspectorate of Panzer Troops. By 1943 he had risen to command of a division in TUNISIA. Evacuated from Africa in May 1943, he later commanded the 7th Panzer Division in the Soviet Union. In February 1944 Manteuffel was transferred to the Grossdeutschland Panzer Division, which he commanded in Rumania and East Prussia. Later in the year, as a General der Panzertruppen, Manteuffel was given command of the Fifth PANZER ARMY, which he led during the Ardennes counteroffensive (Battle of the BULGE). In March 1945 he was transferred to the Eastern Front, where he assumed command of the Third Panzer Army. On May 3, along with thousands of his troops, Manteuffel surrendered to soldiers of the U.S. 8th Infantry Division.

MANUS. One of the two major islands of the Admiralties group (Los Negros is the other). The two islands are separated only by a narrow channel. On February 29, 1944, an Allied 1,000-man reconnaissance in force landed on Los Negros, accompanied by Gen. Douglas MACARTHUR. Although American troops were heavily outnumbered at the outset, MacArthur ordered them to hold as reinforcements were rushed in. After withstanding counterattacks, American units moved onto Manus on March 15. The two islands, with the fine SEEADLER Harbor, were secure on April 3.

MAO TSE-TUNG (1893–1976). Educated at Changsha Normal College, Mao joined the Communist Party upon its formation in China at Shanghai in 1921. Thereafter he dedicated his life to the party—teaching Communism, editing newspapers and organizing peasant unions. In 1934 he led his followers on the Long March to Yenan province in an effort to establish a power base from which he could fight CHIANG KAI-SHEK's Nationalist party, the KUOMINTANG. When war broke out with the Japanese in 1937, Mao promoted an anti-Japanese United Front involving both the Kuomintang and the Communists. During the war with Japan, Mao lived in Yenan, where he worked out his political and military ideas, especially his theories of guerrilla warfare. In 1942–44 he instituted a broad "rectification" program designed to tighten party discipline and to purge the party of undesirables. When the Seventh Party Congress met in April 1945, Mao was elected chairman of the Central Committee and of the Revolutionary Council. Following the end of hostilities with Japan in August 1945, the Communists made some effort to effect a reconciliation with the Kuomintang, but when this failed, civil war resumed in mid-1946. Within three years Mao's Communists had driven the Nationalists from mainland China to the island of Taiwan (Formosa). *See also* CHINA; CHINESE COMMUNISTS.

MAQUIS. A unit of guerrilla fighters or PARTISANS, especially in France—though the French use the term generically. It is also used for a member of a maquis. The Allies often used "maquis" to mean French Forces of the Interior as a whole, using "maqui" as the singular form. *See also* FRENCH RESISTANCE.

MARACAIBO. A British landing ship fitted with a large bow ramp for tanks. Maracaibos were converted oil tankers (named after the oil port) and were the prototypes of the LST (*see* LST).

MARBLEHEAD, U.S.S. OMAHA-class light cruiser. Commissioned in 1924, *Marblehead* was part of the U.S. Asiatic Fleet when the Pacific war began. Severely damaged during the East Indies campaign early in 1942, she returned to the United States under her own power. After extensive repairs she then operated in the South Atlantic and Mediterranean, supporting the 1944 landings in SOUTHERN FRANCE.

MARCUS ISLAND. Japanese-held island east of Iwo JIMA, bombarded at various times by U.S. planes and ships, including an attack by the THIRD FLEET task group on October 9, 1944, on the eve of the American assault on LEYTE. Various dispersed targets were attacked at this time in order to confuse the Japanese as to American intentions.

MARDER. German one-man midget submarine carrying a single torpedo; about 300 were produced.

MARETH LINE. The Mareth Line (North Africa) ran 22 miles from the sea to the Matmata Hills. Part of the defenses were underground, and the WADI Zigzaou in front gave added protection. In March 1943 the positions were manned by a weakened but still formidable German-Italian force under General MESSE; Field Marshal ROMMEL had left for Germany. General MONTGOMERY's British EIGHTH ARMY attacked the Mareth Line on March 20. The main weight was behind the 30th Corps on the right; General FREYBERG with a provisional New Zealand corps (27,000 men) led a wide flanking movement through the Matmata Hills. After two days, when 30th Corps did not make the expected breakthrough, Montgomery switched the weight of attack to Freyberg (SUPERCHARGE II). Breakthrough was achieved on March 27. Although the Axis lost 7,000 prisoners, they avoided annihilation and withdrew to the Chott position behind the Wadi Akarit.

MARGARET (MARGARETEN) LINE. German defense line southwest of BUDAPEST, built in late 1944.

MARIANA ISLANDS. The strategic value of the Marianas had as its major factor the need for bases from which B-29s could bomb Japan (*see* B-29). The most important islands in the group were the five in the southern Marianas—GUAM, Rota, Aguijan, TINIAN and SAIPAN. The first of these scheduled for assault was Saipan, since it was, in both the military and geographic sense, the center of the group. It could serve as the base from which Tinian could be attacked, and both Guam and Rota could be isolated and subjected to air raids.

Thus Saipan was the target for attack on June 15, 1944, mounted by the Northern Troops and Landing Force, commanded by Lt. Gen. Holland M. SMITH. After one of the most difficult battles in the Central Pacific campaign, Saipan was declared secure on July 9 and planning began for Tinian. The 4th Marine Division landed on Tinian on July 24, followed two days later by the 2d Marine Division. Organized resistance ended on August 1. While Saipan and Tinian were in the planning stages, Southern Troops and Landing Force were planning for the Guam operation, to be conducted under the command of Maj. Gen. Roy S. GEIGER. The Guam landing was set to take place on June 18, three days after Saipan, but for various reasons it was postponed until July 21.

Beginning July 8, Guam was subjected to a continuous 13-day naval and air bombardment. Despite both the best naval gunfire preparation of the Pacific war to date and the early securing of the beachheads, the invading Marine forces came under intense mortar, artillery and small arms fire from the cliffs above the beaches, suffering heavy casualties. By July 31 the beachheads had been linked up, and the pursuit of the Japanese to the north of the island began. All organized resistance ended on Guam with the Marines cleaning up the northern tip of the island on August 10, although many Japanese bypassed positions had yet to be reduced.

MARIE. Code name of proposed British operation against Djibouti, French Somaliland, 1941.

MARIN, Louis (1871–1960). Lawyer, anthropologist and fiercely patriotic right-wing politician who served in the Chamber of Deputies from 1905 representing a constituency in his native northeastern France. He held cabinet posts and was a principal right-wing leader following World War I, and as a member of Paul REYNAUD's cabinet stoutly resisted signing the armistice with Germany in 1940. Marin fled to London in 1944 and served in the new French Parliament thereafter.

MARITA. Code name of the German attack on Greece, 1941. *See* BALKANS.

MARKET-GARDEN. Code words for the two phases of an airborne and armored operation in September 1944. The ground phase, called Garden and launched by

Allied trucks cross the Nijmegen bridge under heavy German shellfire—Operation Market-Garden

Field Marshal Sir Bernard MONTGOMERY on September 17, called for the British SECOND ARMY to outflank the German WEST WALL in an armored thrust aimed at ARNHEM. In Operation Market Allied airborne troops were to seize key waterways and railheads in advance of Montgomery's tank column. Although paratroopers captured several bridges and even took and held the Arnhem bridge for some time, the joint operation failed, as the tanks did not reach that bridge before the German counterattack. *See also* WESTERN FRONT.

MARK TWAIN. The name given to a low-altitude bombsight devised by Capt. Charles Ross Greening, one of the B-25 pilots, for use in the Doolittle raid against Japan (*see* FIRST SPECIAL AVIATION PROJECT). The sight, made from about 20 cents' worth of materials, consisted of a movable sighting bar attached to a vertical plane upon which settings between 20 and 80 degrees had been inscribed. Approaching the target, the bombardier set the bar at the mark prescribed for his plane's speed and altitude. He then sighted down the bar and released his bombs when the target disappeared from view. Not only was Greening's Mark Twain more accurate at a very low level than the NORDEN BOMBSIGHT, but its use avoided the possibility of the secret Norden falling into Japanese hands.

MARS. Code name of the 5332d Brigade (Provisional), a U.S. task force operating in the CHINA-BURMA-INDIA THEATER.

MARSEILLE, Hans-Joachim (1919–1942). German flier who, though only No. 29 on the list of German World War II ACES, had the most kills (158) in the west (including the Mediterranean). Known as the "Star of Africa," Marseille was an unmilitary, rather undisciplined figure whose good looks made him as popular as a movie idol among German women. He was killed September 30, 1942, when his Messerschmitt Me 109 caught fire and, after staying with it for a time, he was unable to open his parachute.

MARSEILLES. Southern French port taken by troops of the 2d Corps, French Army "B" (subsequently French First Army), on August 28, 1944. Its use as a supply port providing an alternate line of communications into France was a basic objective of the Allied invasion of SOUTHERN FRANCE.

MARSHALL, George Catlett (1880–1959). A remarkable man by any standards, Marshall was the top-ranking U.S. Army officer of the war, and probably the most influential Allied strategist. He was not a product

General Marshall

of West Point; instead, this Pennsylvanian was a 1901 graduate of the Virginia Military Institute, where he was first captain. He subsequently finished first in his class at the Fort Leavenworth infantry and cavalry school, and his performance with National Guard units in New England and on maneuvers in the Philippines enhanced his reputation. In a pre–World War I training post, Marshall received one of the most unusual efficiency reports in Army history. To the form question whether he would like this man under his command, Lt. Col. Johnson Hagood commented, "Yes, but I would prefer to serve under his command." Hagood also wrote that Marshall was "a military genius" and merited a promotion to "brigadier general in the regular Army, and every day this is postponed is a loss to the Army and the nation."

During World War I, Marshall served as a staff officer. He went to France with the 1st Division in 1917 as training and operations officer. In July 1918 he was attached to General Headquarters, where he helped plan the Saint-Mihiel offensive; in October he became chief of operations of the First Army. Though Marshall built a solid record as a staff officer and organizer and advanced to colonel in World War I, he did not acquire command experience and he was outdistanced in rank by some of his peers, including Hugh A. Drum and Douglas MacArthur.

Between 1919 and 1924 Marshall served as aide to Gen. John J. Pershing, the top American soldier in World War I, who became Chief of Staff in 1921. The two developed a deep friendship, and Pershing remained for the rest of his life a supporter of Marshall.

A tour in China followed this duty. In 1927 Marshall became an instructor at the Army War College, and between 1927 and 1932 he served as assistant commandant of the infantry school at Fort Benning, Ga. He was in charge of the academic department, which he strongly influenced, especially pushing flexibility and improvisation; as he wrote, he aimed at "an almost complete revamping of the instruction and technique." The position gave Marshall a close look at many of the officers who would hold senior positions in the coming war. The generation trained at Benning under him came to be known as "Marshall men."

Throughout the period between the wars, General Pershing, as a chief adviser to the White House, was the main influence in determining the Army Chief of Staff succession. A prime concern in 1939 was the selection of the next chief, who would almost inevitably be responsible for building up a force capable of engagement in the conflict already flaming in Asia and looming ahead in Europe. Although Marshall ranked in seniority behind 21 major generals and 11 brigadier generals, regulations required that the Chief of Staff be able to serve his full four-year term before retirement at age 64, which ruled out all but four of the others. His two real rivals were, like Marshall, non–West Pointers and former members of the First Army in World War I, Hugh Drum and John L. DeWitt. Marshall had won President Roosevelt's respect, and in the course of working with Harry Hopkins had made a highly favorable impression on this influential figure. Marshall was appointed Acting Chief of Staff on July 1, 1939, and then on the day Germany invaded Poland (September 1, 1939) Chief of Staff and full general.

Marshall played a key role in the Allied victory in World War II, Winston Churchill calling him the "Organizer of Victory" and the "American Carnot," but some of his most important contributions came in the years 1939–41, before American entry into the war. He supervised the buildup of the U.S. Army from 174,000 men and 1,064 aircraft in 1939 to 8.3 million men and 64,000 airplanes in 1945. He pushed preparedness in the pre–Pearl Harbor years, and the respect with which he was regarded by Congress was in good measure responsible for the enactment of the peacetime draft. In those years he also worked closely with the British in developing strategic plans for the coalition he knew to be inevitable. Marshall realized the airmen's thirst for independence and gave them considerable autonomy and support while keeping them within the Army. Under Marshall, the Army was reorganized in 1942 into three branches, Army Ground Forces, Army Air Forces and Services of Supply (later, Army Service Forces).

Marshall became the main architect of the basic American strategy in World War II: beat Germany first, as quickly and cheaply as possible, then set about finishing the war in the Pacific. Not only was it his design; he was the main instrument in maintaining that course. Priority for the Pacific theater was championed by Douglas MacArthur, the Chinese, the U.S. Navy and a portion of the public and Congress. A political strategy calling for major action in the Mediterranean theater was pushed by the British and especially by Churchill. Against all this pressure Marshall stood firm in his support of the Germany-first strategy and the invasion of France.

Another key decision in which Marshall played a critical role was the question of command of the cross-Channel INVASION. The Americans and British had agreed that the country that supplied the bulk of the troops would also supply the commander. By 1944 this was clearly the United States, and most war leaders as well as the U.S. Army expected that man to be Marshall. But Roosevelt, who had promised the prime post to Marshall, had second thoughts. He told Marshall, as the general recalled later, "I didn't feel I could sleep at ease if you were out of Washington." He gave Marshall the chance to express his desire for the job, but the general refused to do so, saying he would serve wherever the President desired. He thus chose duty, remaining in Washington; his protégé, Dwight D. EISENHOWER, received the invasion command. Incredible as it seems in retrospect, politicians hostile to Roosevelt accused him of seeking to send General Marshall overseas for political reasons.

Marshall stood firmly behind his men in the field, an outstanding example being his unwavering support of General Eisenhower. The Chief of Staff backed Eisenhower when he needed backing most—over the DARLAN deal in 1942, the retention of Gen. George S. PATTON after he had slapped a hospitalized soldier, the control of air power in the invasion and the BROAD-FRONT STRATEGY, and in his relations with the ever difficult Field Marshal Sir Bernard MONTGOMERY. But the two were not on a first-name basis; practically no one called Marshall "George." Eisenhower later recalled that Marshall once slipped and called him Ike but made up for it by calling him Eisenhower five times in the next sentence.

Marshall also kept the President at arm's length. Roosevelt's style was to call people by their first name, but he rarely called Marshall "George." The Chief of Staff was careful to meet Roosevelt only formally, since he knew how polite assent in private could be construed by Roosevelt as solemn agreement. Thus Marshall declined to meet the President at Hyde Park or Warm Springs.

In December 1944 Marshall received his fifth star. There was discussion over what a five-star general would be called, Marshall opposing "field marshal" (hardly wanting to be "Marshal Marshall"). In deference to his old boss Pershing, the title created was General of the Army, to differentiate it from Pershing's rank of General of the Armies.

General Marshall's postwar career was one of profound service. In November 1945, shortly after he stepped down from his post as Chief of Staff, President TRUMAN appointed him to head a mission to China. Though he was able to get a truce between the Communists and the Nationalists within three weeks, it did not last. Marshall ended his China mission in January 1947. The next month he became Secretary of State, the first and only career Army officer to hold that post. Marshall's speech at Harvard University in June 1947 was the genesis of the crucially important, massive and successful American aid to western Europe known as the Marshall Plan. For his part in the economic recovery of Europe, Marshall received the Nobel Peace Prize in 1953. Marshall ended his public career as Secretary of Defense between September 1950 and September 1951

Marshall was very much concerned with the morale of his troops and especially with casualties. He was receptive to new ideas and encouraged flexibility and improvisation. Awesome in his bearing, Marshall commanded by assent, being able to get his subordinates to want to obey. His superlative talent was his ability to present his case in a winning manner to soldiers, the public and especially to Congress. He was an excellent judge of men and made remarkably few mistakes in his choices of top Army leaders. As might be expected, he had his negative points, but few of them. He was not only demanding of himself but of his subordinates, yet by habit he was gently spoken.

The general's self-discipline, integrity and hard work won him respect from world leaders. "There was no military glamour about him and nothing of the martinet," wrote Dean ACHESON. "Yet to all of us he was always 'General Marshall.' The title fitted him as though he had been baptized with it."

MARSHALL ISLANDS. This group consists of two island chains, Ratak (Sunrise) in the east and Ralik (Sunset) in the west. KWAJALEIN, the largest atoll in the world, lies near the center of the Marshalls, 955 miles from TRUK. The atolls in the group that held the greatest military importance by late 1943 were Mille, Maloelap and Wotje in the Ratak chain, and Jaluit, Kwajalein and ENIWETOK in the Ralik group. With the exception of Jaluit, which was a seaplane base, all the rest of the Ratak atolls were sites of enemy airfields, and those in the Ralik chain were most suitable for naval anchorages. The objectives selected for the invasion of the Marshalls (Operation Flintlock) were MAJURO and Kwajalein Atolls.

Majuro is located 220 nautical miles southeast of Kwajalein. Because of the size of the Kwajalein group, two landing forces were organized. The Northern Landing Force (U.S. 4th Marine Division) was to seize the twin islands of ROI and NAMUR, joined by a narrow causeway and a sand spit. Some 44 miles below in the southeastern portion of the atoll, Kwajalein Island was the objective of the Southern Landing Force (7th Infantry Division). The first phase of Flintlock began on January 31, 1944, as the 25th Marines seized small islands on the northeast rim of Kwajalein Atoll from which emplaced U.S. artillery could support the Roi–Namur landing. On the same day, Majuro was secured without resistance. On February 1 both Northern and Southern Landing Forces assaulted their targets, with Roi and Namur being secured on the 2d and Kwajalein on the 4th.

MARSTON MAT. Prefabricated aluminum strips or "planks," longitudinally ribbed for strength and perforated with rows of holes for lightness, used to construct advance airstrips by the U.S. Army and Navy. Extensive use of Marston mat, combined with rapid leveling and smoothing of the ground where it was to be laid, allowed advance landing fields to be put in operation virtually overnight. This material got its name during 1941 Army maneuvers, when it was first used near the town of Marston, N.C.

MARTEL, Sir Giffard Le Quesne (1889–1958). In the interwar period this British Army officer was closely associated with the development of both the light tank and the machine-gun carrier. As commander of the Royal Armored Corps in 1940–42, he preserved a personal association with the Tank Corps which dated from its beginnings in World War I. In 1943 he became head of the British military mission in Moscow. He held the rank of lieutenant general.

MARTINET. British airplane, designed by Miles Aircraft as a target tug. The Martinet made its first flight in 1942. The plane was based on the firm's MASTER, retaining the same wing but acquiring a longer nose and enlarged canopy. The engine was an 870-horsepower Bristol Mercury radial. Miles also produced a radio-controlled version called the Queen Martinet.

MARTLET. Royal Navy designation for the U.S. F4F (*see* F4F).

MARU. A Japanese word used as the second portion of the names of merchant ships, as *Teiyo Maru, Hikawa Maru.* It was not applied to warships. It became an American wartime slang term; a Japanese ship was frequently referred to as "a Maru."

MARU MORGUE. U.S. Navy name assigned in 1944 to a submarine operating area in the waters around the Nansei Shoto chain, southwest of Japan.

MARYLAND. Designed by the Glenn L. Martin Co. to meet a U.S. Army requirement for a twin-engine attack plane, the Maryland failed to impress American officials but was ordered by the French Government. After the fall of France the balance of the order went to the British, who used Marylands as light bombers and reconnaissance craft in North Africa and the Mediterranean area. A Maryland based at Malta conducted the reconnaissance that preceded the carrier attack on the Italian fleet at TARANTO in November 1940. Powered by two 1,200-horsepower Pratt and Whitney radials, the all-metal monoplane could carry 2,000 pounds of bombs and reach a top speed of 278 miles per hour. Armament was only six machine guns, four in the wings and one each in the dorsal and ventral positions.

MARYLAND, U.S.S. COLORADO-class battleship, commissioned in 1921. Slightly damaged at PEARL HARBOR, she was for some time used for patrol and escort work. Beginning with the capture of the GILBERT ISLANDS at the end of 1943, *Maryland* served as a heavy bombardment and gunfire support ship. She took part in the invasions of the MARSHALLS, MARIANAS, Palaus, PHILIPPINES and OKINAWA. Off SAIPAN in June 1944 she was damaged by a Japanese aerial torpedo. At Okinawa in April 1945 a KAMIKAZE inflicted casualties and some damage. In Surigao Strait during the battle for LEYTE GULF, *Maryland* took part in the last gunnery engagement of a naval battle line. Her 1945 kamikaze damage repaired, she returned troops to the United States.

MASARYK, Jan Garrigue (1886–1948). The foremost Czech diplomat in World War II, one of the leaders of the Czech government-in-exile in London. Through Masaryk's good offices, the British Government recognized the "shadow government" of Eduard BENEŠ on July 19, 1941. Throughout the war Masaryk spent much of his time speaking before the Allied nations on behalf of the occupied countries of Europe. In 1943 he represented Czechoslovakia at the founding conference of the United Nations Relief and Rehabilitation Administration (*see* UNRRA) in Washington. He died mysteriously on March 10, 1948. The official cause of death was suicide or an accidental fall from a high window, but many people believed that Masaryk had been murdered because he was an anti-Communist in a newly Communist nation.

MAS BOAT. Italian designation (*M*otoscafi *A*nti-*S*iluranti) for motor torpedo boats, well thought of in the Italian Navy. Their crews used a favorite motto of Gabriele d'Annunzio: *Memento audere semper* ("Remember always to dare"), the initials of which matched the designation of the boats.

MASLENNIKOV, Ivan I. (1901–). Soviet general, commander of the Twenty-ninth Army and then of the Thirty-ninth Army in 1941 and 1942. He fought on the North Caucasus front through 1943. In 1944 he was promoted to colonel general and appointed to command of the Forty-second Army and then of the Third Baltic Front in operations in the Baltic area.

MASON-MACFARLANE, Sir Frank Noel (1889–1953). British Army officer who served successively as Director of Military Intelligence (1939–40); Deputy Governor of GIBRALTAR (1940–41); head of the British Military Mission to Moscow (1941) and Governor and Commander in Chief of Gibraltar (1942–43). His most notable position was as head of the Allied Control Commission (1944), in which capacity he was responsible for the creation of Italian democratic government after the fall of Rome. He was a lieutenant general.

MASSACHUSETTS, U.S.S. INDIANA-class battleship, commissioned in 1942. She supported the American landings at CASABLANCA in November 1942 and later saw service in the Pacific, where she was part of Adm. Willis LEE's battle line.

MASSAWA. A small Italian fleet stationed at Massawa, Eritrea, posed a threat to British shipping in the Red Sea. During the EAST AFRICA campaign the ships were attacked by air power, and before Massawa fell to the British on April 8, 1941, the last of the Italian destroyers had been sunk—some of them scuttled by their crews.

MASSILIA. French passenger liner which sailed from Bordeaux for North Africa on June 21, 1940, carrying members of the French Government (29 deputies and one senator), including some of the leading opponents of armistice with Germany (César CAMPINCHI, Edouard DALADIER, Yvon Delbos, Georges MANDEL, Tony Revillon). This move was supposed to have been part of a transfer of government to North Africa, but the plan collapsed amid the vacillations and intrigues of those last days of the Third Republic. The *Massilia* arrived at Casablanca on June 24.

MASSY, Hugh Royds Stokes (1884–1965). British Army officer, Deputy Chief of the Imperial General

Staff, who on April 22, 1940, was appointed commander of all British and French forces in NORWAY except those in the NARVIK area. He was told to work with the Norwegians to establish Allied control in central Norway. Owing to the termination of the Norwegian campaign, however, neither Massy nor his headquarters ever left London.

MAST, Charles-Emmanuel (1889–). French Army officer, commander of a North African division in France in 1940. He commanded the Algerian division in late 1942 in VICHY North Africa, and plotted with the Americans to assist Allied landings there. The plot failed, but following the landings General Mast served FREE FRANCE as an administrator.

MASTER. A British two-place, wood-and-plywood advanced trainer, designed by G. G. Miles, powered by a 715-horsepower Rolls-Royce liquid-cooled Kestrel, an 870-horsepower Bristol Mercury radial or an 825-horsepower Pratt and Whitney Wasp Junior radial engine. More than 3,000 of these planes were built for the RAF before Miles Aircraft ceased production in 1942.

MATEUR. A Tunisian road and railway hub southwest of BIZERTE, Mateur was essential if Bizerte was to be taken by the Allies from the interior. In the U.S. II Corps offensive that opened April 23, 1943, Gen. Omar N. BRADLEY planned for the infantry to clear the hills approaching Mateur, after which the 1st Armored Division was to seize the city. The Axis withdrew from one side of Mateur as the 1st Armored Division entered the other on May 3. A few prisoners were taken.

MATHEWS, Vera Laughton (1888–1959). The director of Britain's WOMEN'S ROYAL NAVAL SERVICE (the "Wrens") from 1939 to 1946.

MATSU. Class of Japanese destroyers. Designed for mass production to replace war losses, these ships were somewhat comparable to American DESTROYER ESCORTS in size. Unlike the DE, however, the Matsus were intended for a more conventional destroyer role and were armed with 5-inch guns and torpedo tubes. Their 28-knot speed made them faster than the DE but slower than the usual fleet destroyer. A second group of Matsus, modified and further simplified, was built. Thirty-two ships of both groups were constructed; nine more were never finished, while another 90 were planned but never begun. Ten of the Matsu class were lost; one more was written off as a total loss after aerial bombing.

MATSUOKA, Yosuke (1880–1946). Born in Yamaguchi prefecture, Japan, Matsuoka went to Portland, Ore., at the age of 13 with a cousin. Following his graduation from the University of Oregon in 1900 with a law degree, he returned to Japan and joined the foreign service. For 20 years he held a variety of diplomatic posts in China, the United States and Europe. After his retirement from the foreign service in 1921, Matsuoka became director (1921–26), vice-president (1927–29) and president (1935–39) of the South Manchuria Railway Co., which was responsible for the overall economic development of Manchuria. A strong defender of Japanese interests in Manchuria and China, Matsuoka served as a member of the House of Representatives (1930–34). As Japan's chief delegate to the League of Nations in 1933, he formally withdrew Japan from the league after it accepted the Lytton Report, which was critical of Japanese expansion into Manchuria and its creation of MANCHUKUO. Matsuoka was appointed Foreign Minister in Prince KONOYE's second cabinet (July 1940–July 1941). He strongly favored the TRIPARTITE PACT among Germany, Italy and Japan and the SOVIET-JAPANESE NEUTRALITY PACT of 1941. Designated a war criminal by the Allied powers, Matsuoka died shortly after the Tokyo war crimes trials began and his name was dropped from the list of defendants.

MATTERHORN. Code name of a U.S. plan calling for long-range strategic air attacks by XX Bomber Command from India and the CHENGTU area of China against Japan in 1944–45. The operation was not significantly successful, and was superseded by raids from bases in the Pacific.

MAULDIN, William Henry (1921–). The preeminent U.S. Army artist-cartoonist of World War II, Bill Mauldin is often called the Bruce Bairnsfather of that conflict (Bairnsfather played a comparable role for the British in World War I). To troops, he was a heroic figure. A Southwesterner, he entered military service through the Arizona National Guard, and by 1943 he was doing duty in Sicily. His cartoons in the STARS AND STRIPES reflected the grim humor of the front. The originals of his famous characters, Willie and Joe, are prized exhibits in the Smithsonian Institution, and he has written numerous best-sellers recounting his military service.

MAURICE. Code name of the Allied operation in the 1940 Norwegian campaign designed to attack TRONDHEIM via NAMSOS. Commander of the Maurice force was Major General CARTON DE WIART.

MAYA. Japanese heavy cruiser of the TAKAO class (often called in wartime publications the Atago class). *Maya* saw extensive action in the Pacific war, from GUADALCANAL to the KOMANDORSKI ISLANDS to LEYTE GULF. She was sunk in the opening hours of the Leyte Gulf battle by the U.S. submarine *Dace* (Comdr. B. D. M. Claggett).

MEACON. British radio device employed to counter German radio navigational beams used by bombers in the Battle of BRITAIN. A Meacon station rebroadcast the German signal, thus interfering with its use for directional purposes.

MECHILI. A central point in the network of tracks traversing the WESTERN DESERT. An ancient caravan center, called the "heart" of Cyrenaica, Mechili is 50 miles inland. British forces cut through Mechili in February 1941, but in April General ROMMEL's forces did likewise, heading east, and after defeating the British at Mechili drove on toward TOBRUK.

MEDAL OF HONOR. The highest U.S. military decoration, awarded by the President in the name of the Congress to a member of the armed forces who distinguishes himself by conspicuous gallantry and intrepidity above and beyond the call of duty. During World War II the Army and Navy issued slightly different versions of the medal. Originally approved by Congress during the Civil War, the Medal of Honor is the oldest U.S. decoration in continuous use. It was awarded by special legislation to the Unknown Soldier of World War II. The medal is worn around the neck on a ribbon of light blue silk and is suspended from a folded ribbon embroidered with 13 white stars.

MÉDENINE. On March 6, 1943, Field Marshal Erwin ROMMEL fought his last battle in Africa at Médenine in Tunisia. His plan was to strike the British EIGHTH ARMY on its southwest flank, cut through and divide the forces and then destroy the bulk of them. Preliminary moves were spotted by the British. The Axis lost the advantage of surprise and encountered a strong defense, with antitank guns sited in depth and field artillery under centralized control for massed fire on prearranged squares. The battle opened in early morning and by evening the Axis was defeated with heavy losses. Rommel left Africa three days later.

MEDICINE. The treatment of the wounded was, in general, considerably more effective in World War II than in World War I (American deaths per 100 wounded were 4.5 in the second war, 8.1 in the first). There were several reasons for this improvement. The first involved the greater speed with which the wounded were brought to medical attention, through the extensive use of surgical field hospitals close to the fighting areas and the much greater use of air evacuation. And the advances in medicine itself—the improvements in technique, the use of blood banks and plasma and the development of new drugs—saved many lives. The most remarkable feature here was probably the use of miracle drugs—sulfonamides and penicillin.

MEDITERRANEAN AIR COMMAND. Allied command that became operational on February 18, 1943, under Air Chief Marshal Sir Arthur TEDDER. It brought under one command the U.S. TWELFTH and NINTH AIR FORCES, the RAF Eastern Air Command and three RAF area commands—Middle East, Malta and Gibraltar. Under the new organization there were three areas: Middle East Air Command (Air Chief Marshal Sir Sholto DOUGLAS), Malta Air Command (Air Vice-Marshal Sir Keith PARK) and Northwest African Air Forces (Maj. Gen. Carl SPAATZ).

MEDITERRANEAN ALLIED AIR FORCES. A consolidation of MEDITERRANEAN AIR COMMAND with the NORTHWEST AFRICAN AIR FORCES, the MAAF was created at the CAIRO CONFERENCE in November 1943 and formed in early December. Air Chief Marshal Sir Arthur TEDDER commanded until his appointment to Operation OVERLORD; Maj. Gen. Ira C. EAKER took command on January 1, 1944. MAAF included both strategical and tactical air forces in the Mediterranean theater.

MEDITERRANEAN THEATER. The Mediterranean theater was one of the first to become active, and it remained so until the end of the war. What started as a small conflict between the British and Italians in 1940 became in late 1942 a major campaign pitting the combined Axis against the combined Western Allies. There were numerous changes in organization and command as the situation changed and different portions of the vast theater were involved.

In the summer of 1939 the British reorganized their peacetime Mediterranean commands. Lt. Gen. Sir Archibald WAVELL was named General Officer Commanding in Chief, to command army units in Egypt, the Sudan, Palestine, Transjordan and Cyprus and to prepare plans for any troops in Iraq, Aden, British Somali-

U.S. medics treat an infantryman wounded in the Hürtgen Forest fighting

land and the Persian Gulf area. The Royal Air Force Middle East Command, under Air Marshal Sir William Mitchell, covered essentially the same territory, with the addition of Malta. Adm. Sir Andrew CUNNINGHAM, Commander in Chief Mediterranean, had responsibility for the Mediterranean Sea only, while the East Indies Command retained control of the Red Sea and the Gulf of Aden. Mitchell, Wavell and Cunningham jointly formed the Mediterranean High Command.

In May 1940, in the first of many command changes for the theater, Air Chief Marshal Sir Arthur LONGMORE replaced Mitchell. In May 1941 Air Chief Marshal Sir Arthur TEDDER replaced Longmore; in July Gen. Sir Claude AUCHINLECK replaced Wavell. The far-flung command, posing extreme difficulties for its commanders, was reorganized in September to put the East African countries in a separate command and free Auchinleck for North Africa. In a further effort to ease the command burden, Persia (Iran) and Iraq were detached and put in a separate command in August 1942.

The Mediterranean assumed new importance when U.S.-British forces landed in NORTHWEST AFRICA in November 1942. The operation had an Allied command under Gen. Dwight D. EISENHOWER, but Gen. Sir Harold ALEXANDER, who had replaced Auchinleck in August 1942, continued as commander of the British MIDDLE EAST COMMAND until early 1943. At that time a major reorganization of British-American forces in the Mediterranean brought the British EIGHTH ARMY under Eisenhower's command as Allied Commander in Chief, North Africa; Alexander became Deputy Commander in Chief. All Allied air forces operating in the Mediterranean came under Air Chief Marshal Tedder.

As the Allied forces in the Mediterranean concluded the Tunisian campaign, conquered SICILY and began the long advance up the boot of ITALY, further command changes took place. At the end of 1943 the Royal Navy abolished its Levant Command and put the entire Mediterranean under Adm. Sir John CUNNINGHAM. On January 8, 1944, Gen. Sir Henry Maitland WILSON replaced Eisenhower, and the title was changed to Allied Commander in Chief, Mediterranean Theater. On March 9, 1944, the title was changed to Supreme Allied Commander, Mediterranean Theater. In December 1944 Field Marshal Sir Harold Alexander was named to the post, and he held it until the end of the war.

The Mediterranean was the subject of lively debate over strategy. Some Axis leaders, led by Admiral RAEDER and Field Marshal ROMMEL, favored a pincers movement through the oil-rich Middle East, with Rommel's forces from the west moving to join forces from Russia. Some Allied strategists, led by Winston CHURCHILL, argued for an Allied push from the Mediterranean through the Balkans to Germany. Neither strategy was adopted.

For the Germans, the Mediterranean theater served only to tie up numerous forces and provide a distraction from the Russian front. No major strategic goal was at stake. The Mediterranean Sea remained an open link from Britain to the Far East, and later in the war the Allies used it as a major supply route to send aid to Russia through the Persian Gulf. Many American troops received their first combat experience in North Africa, where the Allies also tested and proved the soundness of a combined command.

MEDITERRANEAN THEATER OF OPERATIONS. The Mediterranean Theater of Operations, U.S. Army, became operational in a reorganization on November 1, 1944. Prior to that date the operations in French North Africa were within the boundaries of, first, the EUROPEAN THEATER OF OPERATIONS, then the separate NORTH AFRICAN THEATER OF OPERATIONS.

MEDJERDA RIVER. The Medjerda, flowing northeast through MEDJEZ EL BAB to the coast roughly halfway between Tunis and Bizerte, bisected the Allied front in TUNISIA. The Medjerda valley, particularly such defensible points as LONGSTOP HILL, was the scene of heavy fighting between November 1942 and May 1943, when the British 5th Corps cleared the valley.

MEDJEZ EL BAB. A key road junction on the Medjerda River, in TUNISIA, Medjez el Bab was seized by the Germans on November 20, 1942, and then by the British 78th Division on November 25. On December 11 an Axis assault at Medjez el Bab halted the drive for Tunis until spring.

MEIKTILA. Important town and rail center in BURMA taken from the Japanese by the British 17th Indian Division on March 3, 1945. The Japanese counterattacked, besieging the British force in the town, but they began withdrawing on March 28–29 as they found it necessary to fall back in the general area.

MEIN KAMPF (My Struggle). Adolf HITLER's autobiography and political-ideological testament, the first volume of which (subtitled *A Reckoning*) was composed in LANDSBERG fortress in 1924 and published in July 1925, seven months after his release. A second part, entitled *The National Socialist Movement,* was added in 1926, and from 1930 the standard edition of *Mein Kampf* included both parts.

Hitler had been considering committing his thoughts to paper since 1922, and a proposal from Max Amann, the Nazi Party's publisher, that he should write his autobiography while he had the leisure to do so in Landsberg led to this outpouring of his wild surmises about the history and destiny of the German people. Such autobiography as appears in its pages is a mixture of fact and fancy, linking his youthful development to the myth of "Aryan" supremacy to which he had devoted his career. The style of the book is turgid, even illiterate, reflecting the fact that it was dictated in phases with little editorial preparation or planning, though Rudolf HESS, who was better educated than Hitler, assisted by acting as adviser. The book is oratorical rather than literary, and subject to long-winded, tangential asides, such as Hitler's attacks on academic studies, which he likens to a costly, empty envelope.

The first volume, *A Reckoning,* traces Hitler's upbringing in Austria, which he calls a "sham" state whose German elements were subject to inferior racial influences, notably the Jews, and a Social Democratic government so weak that it became the mere tool of the Marxists. He claimed he acquired his anti-Semitism in Vienna, and also learned there to despise the system of government through parliamentary debate, favoring in its place outright leadership from the top. Only through purposive, God-given leadership can the German people rehabilitate their lost racial identity and reassert their supremacy in Europe. Once their ethnic supremacy is reestablished, he says, the Germans must acquire much needed territory to the east. But such a reawakening requires urgent propaganda, a new art in politics of which he had made himself a master. In his celebrated chapter on the subject, Hitler claims that propaganda's appeal must be to emotion, not to reason, and that its aim is to swing the stupid and unthinking masses, who are "feminine by nature and attitude."

After giving some account of his own experiences, he inveighs against what he deems the Jewish influence in Germany which led to her betrayal and defeat in 1918. The Jews he calls the source of all degeneracy, with their own special link to Marxism. Hitler stands for purification of the German race, the purging of alien elements from its bloodstream, the expropriation and banishment of the Jews as the parasites and seducers of honest German working people. It is to achieve this, he claims, that he took over the German Workers' Party.

In the second volume, *The National Socialist Movement,* Hitler reiterates and enlarges upon the arguments of the first, examining the nature of leadership and its dependence on brilliant oratory. The party he has developed must successfully oppose the Communists, meeting violence with violence and bypassing the timid, democratic bourgeois. He emphasizes the importance of the Storm Trooper movement (*see* SA), which inherits the spirit of the FREE CORPS. Revolution depends on alliance between "a great, creative, renewing idea" and a strong-arm force. The Weimar Republic he sees as doomed, a bourgeois "intermezzo" in Germany's postwar development which will soon respond to the leader and his trained supporters.

Sales of *Mein Kampf* were small prior to 1930: 23,000 of Volume I and 13,000 of Volume II. An inexpensive "People's Edition" appeared in 1930, and by 1932 its sales totaled 194,000. By the end of 1933, the first year of Hitler's Chancellorship, 1.5 million copies had been sold, and it has been estimated that sales amounted to 8 or 9 million during Hitler's lifetime. Presentation copies were frequently ordered—for example, for every bridal couple. Several versions of *Mein Kampf* appeared in English in the United States and Britain, and it was translated into the principal European languages as well as Arabic, Tamil and Japanese. *See also* NATIONAL SOCIALIST GERMAN WORKERS' PARTY.

MEITNER, Lise (1878–1968). A physicist and mathematician who first calculated the energy that would result from the splitting of the atom and thus helped lay the theoretical groundwork for the development of the ATOMIC BOMB. Because she was Jewish she was forced to flee Germany, and continued her work in Sweden.

MEMEL. East Prussian port (given to Lithuania after World War I and reabsorbed by Germany in 1939), invested by the Soviet First Baltic Front in early October 1944. The pocket held out until January 28, 1945.

MENACE. Code name of the Anglo–Free French expedition to DAKAR, September 1940.

MENGELE, Fritz (1911–). One of the worst of criminal Nazi doctors, SS Captain Mengele took part in Adolf HITLER's euthanasia program in 1940, which led to the deaths of 60,000 persons held to be incurably insane. At AUSCHWITZ he was second to Dr. Hans Klein, whom he succeeded as chief medical officer when Klein was posted to BELSEN. His horribly arrogant way of classifying new prisoners was notorious; he would stand looking them over, indicating with a flick of the thumb or a movement of his cane those who were to die and those who were to become slave laborers. He also conducted bogus experiments in pathology concerning the origins of dwarfs, cripples and twins, and research into methods of promoting multiple births. He was cynical, licentious, vain; one of his prisoner-assistants spoke of his "detached, haughty air, his continual whistling, his absurd orders, his frigid cruelty." After the war he escaped and made his way to Latin America, possibly to Paraguay. There were naturally many rumors about him, including one that he had been shot by a Christian Jew called Erich Erdstein. *See also* FINAL SOLUTION.

MENZIES, Sir Robert Gordon (1894–1978). An Australian cabinet minister during the 1930s who in 1939 was elected leader of the United Australia Party and two days later became Prime Minister. A declaration of war came from the Menzies cabinet immediately upon the outbreak of World War II on September 3, 1939, and he introduced compulsory military training the following month. After a five-month absence in Britain, Eire and elsewhere, Menzies returned in May 1941 to find growing opposition in Parliament, resulting from defeats in which Australian troops had taken part and from the Labour Party's insistence that the Prime Minister remain in Australia and not return to London. He consequently resigned in August 1941 but was again elected leader of the United Australia Party in 1943. He returned as Prime Minister in 1949 and held the post continuously until 1966.

MENZIES, Sir Stewart Graham (1890–1968). British Army officer, a member of Sir Douglas Haig's staff in World War I, who was head of Britain's Secret Intelligence Service (MI6) from 1939 to 1951. Menzies, a major general, presided over the unfolding of the ULTRA secret (the decrypting of German radio transmissions) and was the directing brain among Britain's cover planners. His position carried the title "C."

MERCHANT AIRCRAFT CARRIER (MAC). British merchant ship fitted with a flight deck and a small "island" superstructure which made it resemble an ESCORT CARRIER. Like the earlier CATAPULT-ARMED MERCHANT SHIP (CAM) the MAC was designed as a stopgap measure to provide some fighter protection against German long-range land-based bombers in areas of the North Atlantic outside the range of British land-based planes. Unlike the CAM ships, though, these ships could recover their aircraft after an action. Converted from oil tankers and grain carriers, with cargo spaces left intact, they continued to carry cargoes while planes operated from their flight decks. Nineteen ships in all were modified into MAC ships. Widespread introduction of mass-produced escort carriers made further conversions unnecessary. The average MAC was armed with a 4-inch gun and a few 20-mm. antiaircraft guns, based a unit of four fighters and had a merchant-service crew; pilots and air unit support personnel came from the Royal Navy.

MERCHANT MARINE. The U.S. War Shipping Administration took control of merchant marine operations in February 1942. It absorbed 131 operators of U.S. flag ships, recruited and trained merchant seamen and dealt with the 22 maritime unions which represented many of the men who served aboard the famous LIBERTY and VICTORY SHIPS. These ships took the brunt of the Axis submarine attacks on U.S. merchant shipping, especially in 1942–43. In addition to supplying Allied forces in Europe and the Pacific, the merchant marine also carried troops to North Africa, Normandy and the Pacific islands. Of the 250,000 men who voluntarily served in the U.S. merchant marine in World War II, 5,638 died as the result of enemy action.

MERCURY (Merkur). Code name for the German occupation of CRETE, May 1941.

MERETSKOV, Kiril A. (1897–). Red Army officer, a veteran of the Bolshevik Revolution and the Civil War. In 1940 he commanded the Seventh Separate Army in the Finnish campaign. By the end of the year he was Chief of the Soviet General Staff, but in January 1941 he was replaced by Georgi ZHUKOV. At various times he was the Soviet GHQ representative to the Northwest Front and commander of the Volkhov and Karelian Fronts; finally, he commanded the First Far Eastern Front during the offensive against the Japanese KWANTUNG ARMY. A Marshal of the Soviet Union, he was one of the few recipients of the ORDER OF VICTORY.

MERKERS. On April 4, 1945, in a salt mine at this German village near Eisenach, the U.S. 358th Infantry (THIRD ARMY) found the Nazi "treasure"—the bulk of the German gold reserve, vast stores of German and foreign currency and hundreds of works of art looted from the conquered countries of Europe.

MERRILL, Aaron Stanton (1890–1961). A 1912 graduate of the U.S. Naval Academy, "Tip" Merrill taught naval science at Tulane University in 1941–42. Sent to the Pacific as captain of the U.S.S. INDIANA, Merrill was promoted to rear admiral in January 1943 and was named commander of a cruiser and destroyer task force. His first battle experience, at GUADALCANAL, proved important later during the BOUGAINVILLE campaign at EMPRESS AUGUSTA BAY. There Merrill distinguished himself in night action against a Japanese surface force, thereby preserving the beachhead. He was the first admiral to use RADAR in action, this occurring in Kula Gulf in the SOLOMONS in March 1943.

MERRILL, Frank D. (1903–1955). A West Point graduate born in Massachusetts, General Merrill was commander of the 5307th Composite Unit (Provisional), better known as MERRILL'S MARAUDERS, the original U.S. experiment in LONG-RANGE PENETRATION tactics. He assumed command of the unit on January 6, 1944, as a brigadier general, after it had been formed in India of volunteers from other U.S. Army units. Trained in the doctrine of British Brig. Orde C. WINGATE and referred to as GALAHAD, the unit became Lt. Gen. Joseph STILWELL'S most dependable combat element during the drive to recapture northern BURMA. On March 31, 1944, Merrill was evacuated over his protest owing to serious illness, but not before Galahad had distinguished itself at Walawbum and Inkangahtawng and had begun an assault on Nhpum Ga. He later served as chief of staff of the Tenth and Sixth Armies, and retired from the service in 1947. His highest rank was major general.

MERRILL'S MARAUDERS. Nickname given to the U.S. 5307th Provisional Unit in honor of their first commander, Maj. Gen. Frank D. MERRILL. They were also known as Merrill's Raiders.

MERSA MATRÛH. A small Egyptian port between TOBRUK and ALEXANDRIA, developed and fortified by the British as an advance supply base for their Desert Army. During the Axis advance of June 1942, the British attempted to hold at Mersa Matrûh, but the Axis succeeded in capturing the fortress with its sizable quantities of stores.

MERS-EL-KÉBIR. After the Franco-German armistice of June 1940, the British War Cabinet decided it could not risk having the French fleet fall into Axis hands, and the attitude of the French Navy high command was doubtful. Vice-Adm. Sir James SOMERVILLE and FORCE H confronted French Adm. Marcel GENSOUL at Mers-el-Kébir, the naval base near Oran, with the request that the French either sail with the British, turn their ships over to the British, take their ships to the West Indies for the duration of the war or sink them. If none of these options was taken, Somerville warned, he would use force "to prevent your ships from falling into German or Italian hands." Gensoul refused; the British fired on his ships. One battle cruiser escaped, but the remainder were either destroyed or damaged so severely the British knew they could not be used against them. To Winston CHURCHILL, though he thought the action necessary, it was "a hateful decision, the most unnatural and painful in which I have ever been concerned."

MESSE, Giovanni (1883–1968). Italian Army officer who went to Russia in 1941 as head of the Italian Expeditionary Corps. In early 1943, when Field Marshal Erwin ROMMEL'S army in Africa was reorganized, Messe became commander of the First Italian Army in TUNISIA. When he was taken prisoner at Tunis, Benito MUSSOLINI promptly made him a marshal, but Messe was nevertheless one of the first Italian generals in captivity to switch sides. He became Chief of Staff of the Italian Army under Pietro BADOGLIO'S government, but his role in Russia had alienated many and in 1945 he was replaced.

MESSERSCHMITT, Willy (1898–). German aircraft designer and manufacturer (see note on terminology in MESSERSCHMITT ME 109 entry).

Messerschmitt Me 109

MESSERSCHMITT ME 109. German fighter designed by Prof. Willy MESSERSCHMITT. It was manufactured in larger quantities than any other warplane in World War II. Total production of the Me 109 amounted to 30,124 aircraft from 1940 to 1945, and early production (1937–39) was more than 2,300. This may well be the highest production of any combat plane in history.

In 1939 the Me 109E was superior to any other existing fighter, with the possible exception of the SPITFIRE; its only handicap was its short range. It was the fourth basic service model of a fighter built to meet a 1934 specification. Earlier models served in the Spanish Civil War and a specially equipped Me 109V-13 established a new world speed record of 379.38 miles per hour on November 11, 1937. The first production E-series plane reached units in the spring of 1939. Direct fuel injection was standard equipment by September 1939. Several variants were built, among them a fighter-bomber and a fighter for the carrier *Graf Zeppelin.* The Me 109E-1 was powered by an 1,100-horsepower inverted V-12 engine and flew 354 miles per hour maximum speed. Armed with two 20-mm. cannon and two 7.9-mm. machine guns, it weighed 5,523 pounds fully loaded. It was 28 feet 4 inches long and had a 32-foot 4½-inch wingspan.

A note on Messerschmitt terminology: Professor Messerschmitt originally was designer for the Bayerische Flugzeugwerke A.G., the predecessor company to his own Messerschmitt A.G. The Me 109 and other Messerschmitt aircraft are therefore often referred to by the designation "Bf" instead of "Me." However, all the Messerschmitt aircraft described here were manufactured by Messerschmitt A.G., long after the Bayerische Flugzeugwerke had been dissolved. "Me" seems, accordingly, the more suitable designation.

MESSERSCHMITT ME 109F. The result of an extensive program of aerodynamic refinement of the basic ME 109, begun in 1940. The first units of the Me 109F-1 became operational in January 1941. Some problems with tail spar failure were quickly solved, and the plane proved an excellent fighter, outclassing the SPITFIRE V at altitude. A tropical version was built for North African service; several other variants were also produced. The Me 109F-3 had a fuel-injected 1,300-horsepower inverted V-12 engine and flew 390 miles per hour top speed at 20,000 feet. It carried one 15-mm. engine-mounted cannon and two 7.9-mm. machine guns. Fully loaded it weighed 6,054 pounds; 29 feet ½ inch long, it had a 32-foot 6½ inch wingspan.

MESSERSCHMITT ME 109G. This model, also known as Gustav, was basically an F-series airframe with a new Daimler-Benz DB 605 A engine; it supplanted all other Me 109 models by the end of 1942. The 109G suffered from constant operational demands for increased firepower and additional equipment, which resulted in heavier weight and drag and no power or lift increases. As a result of this, flying performance suffered. The G was widely used, existing in several versions, variously armed. Powered by a Daimler-Benz engine giving up to 1,800 horsepower, the G-10/R-2 reached a speed of 425 miles per hour. The Me 109K was the last production type of the Me 109. It differed only in a few structural details from the G-10 model. It went into operation in January 1945. The letter *I* was not assigned to any Me 109s, and *J* was given to a Spanish-built series.

MESSERSCHMITT ME 109H. A specialized high-altitude version of the basic ME 109. A small number of prototypes were built but were found unsatisfactory in testing because of wing vibration, and the design was dropped in favor of the FOCKE-WULF TA 152.

MESSERSCHMITT ME 110C through H. A series developed in the first serious attempt to produce a strategic fighter capable of escorting bombers deep into enemy territory and fighting off hostile fighters. First flown in 1936, it was only a little slower than the HURRICANE. Equipping GÖRING's elite Zerstörer (Destroyer) squadrons, the plane did well in Poland and France against largely obsolescent enemy types. Because of its lack of maneuverability and speed against RAF SPITFIRES and Hurricanes, it was a complete disaster in the Battle of BRITAIN and had to be withdrawn. When ME 210 production was halted in April 1942, a serious gap was opened in Germany's twin-engine fighter program; Me 110 production, which had been tapering off, therefore picked up with the G and H models. The latter series had its greatest success as a night fighter. The Me 110C-4, a three-place, long-range day and escort fighter, was powered by two 1,100-horsepower inverted V-12 engines and flew 349 miles per hour maximum speed. It was armed with four forward-firing 7.9-mm. machine guns and two 20-mm. cannon, along with one

Messerschmitt Me 110

free-mounted 7.9-mm. machine gun. The last 40 models were delivered in January 1945.

MESSERSCHMITT ME 163. The only interceptor-fighter powered solely by a rocket motor to be used operationally. Dr. Alexander Lippisch headed the development team. Known also as Komet, it first flew in the spring of 1941. Its first operational use was in July 1944, against B-17s, although without success (*see* B-17). A single-place, target-defense interceptor powered by a 3,750-pound thrust rocket engine, it flew 596 miles per hour maximum speed. It climbed at a rate of 16,000 feet per minute—time to 30,000 feet was 2.6 minutes. The plane carried two 30-mm. cannon and 24 underwing rockets, or four rockets in each wing mounted to fire upward.

MESSERSCHMITT ME 209A-2. A model developed to provide a successor to the Me 109 and a competitor to the Focke-Wulf FW 190 and Ta 152. The Me 209A-2 was a modernized and more powerful development of the earlier series; 65 percent of the new plane was composed of components of the older series. The prototype flew in November 1943, but the fighter never entered production.

MESSERSCHMITT ME 210. A two-place, twin-engine, medium-range fighter, first projected in 1937 as a successor to the Me 110. It was planned as more versatile and powerful, but a pre-production order for 1,000 was a costly error. Once it was operational numerous accidents occurred with the units using it, primarily because of serious instability, and despite great numbers of modifications, it suffered an appalling accident rate. Production ceased in April 1942, with a loss of 600 aircraft to the German war effort and 30 million Reichsmarks to the Messerschmitt A.G.—and a diminution of Professor Messerschmitt's power and prestige. A total of 352 were built. Armed with two cannon and two machine guns firing forward and two remote-controlled, barbette-mounted, rear-firing machine guns, it flew at a maximum speed of 385 miles per hour.

MESSERSCHMITT ME 262. The first turbojet fighter to become operational in the war. Its first flight was in July 1942 but, owing to official indifference, production was not begun until the end of 1943. The first jet fighter unit was formed in November 1944, but Adolf Hitler did not give the Me 262 priority until 1945. Of the 1,433 built, fewer than 15 percent were used operationally. The plane was meant to be a fighter, but many were wasted in the role of attack bomber. The Me 262A-1A was powered by two 1,980-pound static-thrust turbojets and flew at a maximum speed of 540 miles per hour at 23,000 feet. It was armed with four 30-mm. cannon plus twenty-four 5-cm. rockets.

Messerschmitt Me 262B-2 (night-fighter version of the Me 262)

MESSERSCHMITT ME 263A. An improved version of the Me 163 (above), a prototype was finished in August 1944 as the Ju 248V-1. It never entered production.

MESSERSCHMITT ME 321 and ME 323. In the earlier phases of the war—notably, in Belgium and Crete—the Germans used gliders as weapons of invasion. Later, larger gliders were used to carry troops and supplies to forces in North Africa. The giant of German gliders was the Messerschmitt Me 321, a monster with a wingspan of 181 feet and a lift capacity of 40,000 pounds. So large was it, in fact, that it quickly acquired six engines and became the Me 323, a transport ferrying men, gasoline and supplies to North Africa and returning with wounded. The slow Me 323s were easy targets for Allied airmen. *See also* glider.

MESSERSCHMITT ME 410. A greatly improved model of the Me 210, which was used chiefly as a heavy fighter, interceptor and night fighter. A total of 1,013 of the Hornisse (Hornet) model were built, not counting 108 built in Hungary. Powered by two 1,750-horsepower inverted V-12 engines, it flew 388 miles per hour maximum speed. The Me 410A-1-U2 carried four forward-firing 20-mm. cannon and two 7.9-mm. machine guns plus two rear-firing 13-mm. machine guns in remote-controlled barbettes.

MESSERVY, Sir Frank Walter (1893–1974). As commander of the British 9th Infantry Brigade during General Platt's advance to Ethiopia, Messervy distinguished himself at the Battle of Keren in 1941. As commander of the 4th Indian Division in the Western Desert he won fame during the fighting around Sidi Omar, when the forces under his command checked General Rommel's offensive into Egypt (November 1941). During Sir Claude Auchinleck's retreat from Benghazi, Messervy commanded the 1st British Armored Division until its destruction, following which he succeeded Gen. J. C. "Jock" Campbell as commander of the 7th Armored Division (Desert Rats). Relieved of his command by General Ritchie, the Eighth Army commander, he served subsequently in a number of positions before assuming command in 1943 of the 7th Indian Division at Arakan. In 1944–45 he commanded the 4th Corps during the Burma campaign.

In his reputation for bravery and for inspiring leadership, General Messervy was one of the war's outstanding generals, constantly in the midst of heavy fighting. On a number of occasions his forces were cut off and his own headquarters overrun; in the Western Desert, he was once a prisoner for 18 hours before escaping. To many, his name became virtually a legend and a synonym for gallantry.

MESSINA. A port city in the northeast corner of Sicily, the key to the Sicilian campaign. Allied forces entered the city on August 17, 1943, but most of the Axis troops had been evacuated across the Strait of Messina to Italy, thus denying the Allies a complete victory.

METAXAS, Joannes (1871–1941). Greek military leader and politician, dictator from 1936 to 1941. In 1936 he was the head of a small ultraroyalist party, and for his loyalty King GEORGE II appointed him Prime Minister, an office which he quickly transformed to dictator. Metaxas's regime resembled other right-wing governments of the times, although some economic and social reforms were made. He was successful in uniting the country behind him to oppose the Italian invasion of 1940.

METAXAS LINE. Greek defense line in Macedonia (1941). Having no flank protection because of the quick German defeat of Yugoslav forces, it was abandoned by the Greek defense forces. *See also* BALKANS.

METEOR. Originally called the Thunderbolt, this British plane was the only Allied jet fighter to see wartime operational service. Gloster designers, headed by W. G. Carter, commenced work early in 1940. Engines were a problem from the outset. Since none of the turbojets likely to be available for the new plane was powerful enough for a first-line fighter, Carter and his colleagues had to plan on using two power plants. Even so, the pair of Rover W.2B turbojets installed in the prototype did not develop thrust enough for takeoff. After ground tests, more powerful engines were substituted.

A dizzying succession of engines were tried in the Meteor I before the Rolls-Royce Welland became standard. One of these planes went to the United States for study, in exchange for a sample of the Bell Airacomet. Meteor I scored Britain's first confirmed jet victory on August 4, 1944, when a Royal Air Force pilot found that his guns had jammed and used a wing tip to nudge a German V-1 into a crash dive.

Meteor III also saw combat in Europe. Powered by two Rolls-Royce Derwent engines, this version went into action in April 1945 and attacked ground targets during the final weeks of the war. (Meteor II existed only in prototype.)

The Meteor was a low-wing, single-seat monoplane with a tricycle landing gear. The cockpit was atop the fuselage just forward of the wing, and the horizontal stabilizer was located high on the fin where it was not affected by the jet exhaust. The two engines were mounted in nacelles well out on the wing. Except for power plants, differences between Meteor I and III were minor. The later version, however, was capable of 493 miles per hour at 30,000 feet, 83 miles faster than Meteor I, and had a service ceiling of 44,000 feet, 4,000 feet higher than the Welland-powered version. Both mounted four 20-mm. cannon.

The change of names from Thunderbolt to Meteor was a concession to U.S. Army Air Forces, which was acquiring the Republic P-47 Thunderbolt (*see* P-47) at the time the British jet was having preliminary tests.

METOX. A German submarine-mounted RADAR search receiver (FuMB 1), whose original homemade antenna earned the nickname BISCAY CROSS. Later models incorporated improvements. It was incapable of detecting newer Allied higher-frequency radars.

METZ. One of the first targets of the Allied late-autumn offensive in 1944. Metz—the old capital of Lorraine—was surrounded by U.S. XX Corps (THIRD ARMY) on November 19 and capture was completed on the 23d. The greatest difficulty was in reducing old forts on the outskirts dating from the late 19th century.

MEUSE RIVER. The line of the Meuse was an important element in the defense of Belgium and France in 1940, but it was easily crossed by the German Army Group B in the north and by Army Group A, which came through the ARDENNES.

MEXICAN AIR UNIT. Mexico entered the war against the AXIS on May 30, 1942. Her contribution to the war was mainly economic until February 1945, when Squadron 201 of the Mexican Air Force was dispatched to the Pacific. It was equipped with the P-47 Thunderbolt fighter aircraft (*see* P-47) and saw service in the PHILIPPINES and in attacks on Japanese-held FORMOSA. Eight men were lost in action. By sending the squadron into action, Mexico became one of the two Latin American belligerents in World War II to have actual fighting forces involved, the other being Brazil.

MEYER, John Charles (1919–1975). Piloting a North American P-51D Mustang (*see* P-51), this U.S. ace shot down 24 German planes and destroyed 13 others on the ground. On one occasion he made a single-handed attack on a formation of 20 or more FW 190s, downing four of them. His last two victories, also over FW 190s, came within 90 seconds of takeoff. German fighters began strafing the airfield at Chievres, Belgium, as Lieutenant Colonel Meyer's patrol roared along the runway. He shot down the first plane as his own Mustang was becoming airborne, then climbed to 3,000 feet and downed the second. Later a general, Meyer commanded the U.S. Strategic Air Command in the early 1970s.

MICHAEL I (1921–). The last King of Rumania, Michael (Mihai) came to the throne on September 6, 1940, as a result of a coup which overthrew his father, CAROL II. Until August 1944 Michael was forced to accept governments more or less imposed on him by Germany and her supporters within the country, notably Gen. Ion ANTONESCU and the Rumanian Fascist Party, the Iron Guard. As German defeat became more certain and Russian armies approached Rumania's eastern frontier, the Germans appeared to be on the verge of an outright seizure of the country. On the night of August 23, Michael, with the aid of loyal generals, staged a coup d'état, arresting Antonescu and his cabinet. The new government then accepted unconditional surrender to the forces of the United Nations, and the King ordered his military forces to fight with the Russians. An official armistice was signed on September 12 in Moscow, and Rumania formally came over to the Allied side.

In the postwar period, despite Western protests, the Soviet occupation forces assisted the local Communists in their progressive taking of power. By 1947 the participation of non-Communists in the government was virtually impossible, and on December 30 the government announced the abdication of King Michael and the establishment of a "People's Republic." Michael left Rumania on January 3, 1948.

MICHELIER, Felix (1887–1966). Admiral Michelier served as the French naval representative on the Franco-German armistice commission, then commanded French naval forces at CASABLANCA, where he directed resistance to the Allied landings in late 1942. He was commander of French naval forces under Admiral DARLAN until Darlan's assassination in December 1942.

MICHIELS, Oscar (1881–1946). General Michiels, a staff officer and division commander, became Chief of Staff of the Belgian Army in February 1940 and held his post until the Belgian armistice with Germany on May 28, 1940. In this role he carried out the orders of the King and served as his military adviser.

MICKEY. Nickname for H_2X RADAR bombing device—an American adaptation of the British H_2S (*see* H_2S; NAVIGATION AIDS).

MICKEY FINNS. A U.S. Navy submarine wolfpack, commanded by Capt. W. V. O'Regan, that operated off Formosa and China (*see* CONVOY COLLEGE) in 1944. The submarines were *Guardfish, Piranha, Thresher* and APOGON.

MIDDLE EAST COMMAND. The British Middle East Command was a vast one, stretching from Persia (Iran) to the Sudan; it was the headquarters under whose control the desert war in NORTH AFRICA was fought. The wartime commanders were Gen. Sir Archibald WAVELL (till June 1941) and Gen. Sir Claude AUCHINLECK. In August 1942 Prime Minister CHURCHILL divided the Middle East Command into the Persia and Iraq Command under Gen. Sir Henry Maitland WILSON and the new Middle East Command (Egypt, Palestine and Syria) under Gen. Sir. Harold ALEXANDER. Wilson's task was to protect the reserves of Near Eastern oil and the supply lines with Russia. Alexander's mission was to destroy the German-Italian army in North Africa.

MIDDLETON, Troy (1889–1976). A U.S. colonel of infantry in World War I, this Mississippian retired in 1937 after a 29-year military career to become dean of administration at Louisiana State University. Middleton returned to the Army in World War II and commanded the 45th Infantry Division in SICILY. He was hospitalized because of a knee injury, and when Gen. Dwight EISENHOWER, who wanted him for a European command, heard of it, he said, "I would rather have Troy Middleton commanding VIII Corps from a stretcher than anyone else I know in perfect health." Middleton commanded the VIII Corps throughout the European fighting. His corps participated in Operation COBRA, took BREST and held positions in the ARDENNES when the Germans launched the BULGE attack. Middleton's staff virtually collapsed, but he was steady as a rock. Gen. Omar BRADLEY later praised Middleton for his ability to rally and delay the enemy advance. Following the Bulge, Middleton led his corps across Germany. Rugged, tough-minded and a hard cusser, he retired as a lieutenant general.

MIDGET SUBMARINE. Miniature submarines of various types were used by Italy and Britain, and to a somewhat lesser extent by Germany and Japan. The first use of midgets in World War II was made by Italy; in September 1941 they sank three cargo ships at Gibraltar. The weapon used was essentially a two-man controllable torpedo, battery-powered, with a 500-pound detachable warhead. Its crew, wearing protective suits and oxygen gear, rode it astraddle. Although it was something less than ideal, the Italians used it with courage in numerous efforts against enemy warships and merchantmen in the Mediterranean before the Italian-Allied armistice in 1943.

A British two-man human torpedo, the Chariot, patterned after the Italian weapon, was developed in 1942. Armed with a 600-pound detachable warhead, it was used in the Atlantic, Mediterranean and Pacific. Another development, the X-Craft, was a true midget submarine, 45 feet long and carrying a crew of four. Diesel electric propulsion enabled it to operate at sea for some days; it had two periscopes, bunks and primitive cooking arrangements. It did not have torpedo-launching gear; a diver left the craft through an air lock to plant limpet mines or bottom charges. A Motorized Submersible Canoe, or MSC, nicknamed Sleeping Beauty, was a small powered surface craft designed for launching from submarines or torpedo boats; it could submerge to make its approach and attack, and was used for various types of clandestine operations. In 1942 Chariots were tried against the German battleship TIRPITZ, moored in a Norwegian fjord, but failed. In the following year X-Craft were sent against her; two of them succeeded in planting bottom charges, which crippled the big ship. Two X-Craft were used as navigational markers for one of the Normandy landings; taking up their stations off the beach, they flashed colored lights to guide approaching invasion craft. British midgets took part in the Italian campaign; in February 1944 they sank the Italian heavy cruiser *Bolzano* at La Spezia. Improved Chariots and X-Craft went to the Far East in 1944–45; X-Craft crippled the Japanese heavy cruiser TAKAO at Singapore in July 1945.

Japan used both midget submarines, in the conventional sense of the term, and human suicide torpedoes. The first Japanese midgets encountered were the Type A, used at PEARL HARBOR and, later, at Sydney, Australia. One of these damaged the British battleship *Ramillies* at Diégo-Suarez, MADAGASCAR. The Type A was 78½ feet long, was powered by an electric motor and had a crew of two. Armed with two 18-inch bow torpedo tubes, it was fast but had a short range since it could not recharge its batteries. Intended for coastal use or for launching from a submarine or seaplane carrier, the Type A was later replaced by newer midgets and relegated to training duty. The experimental Type B midget, completed in 1943, had a diesel engine for surface propulsion and battery recharging. It led to the Type C, generally similar to the Type A but with a three-man crew and a greater radius of action. The Type D midget was named Koryu (Dragon Larva). More seaworthy than the Type C, it had a more powerful diesel. After successful trials of the prototype, prefabricated mass production was begun. The bombing of factories delayed production, and Koryus entered service more slowly than had been hoped. With a streamlined hull and conning tower, the Koryu had a five-man crew and two torpedo tubes. If no torpedoes were available, an explosive warhead could be fitted for suicide use. Some Koryus were used in the defense of the PHILIPPINES and OKINAWA.

During 1943–44 the Kairyu (Sea Dragon) was developed from the Type A. This smaller craft was the victim of production problems; many boats varied in dimensions and other details. It was produced into 1945 along with the Koryu. Like the other craft, many Kairyus were armed with warheads rather than torpedoes and were sent on KAMIKAZE missions. Designed for rapid mass production, the Kairyu was 55½ feet long, had a gasoline/electric power plant and carried its two 18-inch torpedoes slung under its hull. Five models of KAITEN suicide torpedoes were developed or produced.

After the British attack on *Tirpitz*, a special German force called the Kleinkampfmittelverband, or "K-Force," was organized late in 1943 for small-scale underwater operations using midget submarines, small surface craft and frogmen. Experiments were carried out with salvaged British Chariots. Early in 1944 the battery-powered Hecht (Pike), based on the British vehicle, was tried. It had only a small punch—one limpet mine—and was soon assigned to training work. Mobile, self-contained units called Marineeinsatzkommandos (MEK) were now equipped with the one-man Neger (Negro), a controllable vehicle with a small cockpit. This actually was not a submersible but relied on its size to make it less noticeable. Some Negers, armed with a live torpedo slung underneath, were used off ANZIO in 1944. This operation led the Germans to conclude that the Neger, if improved, was workable. Others were used against the Normandy INVASION force, but with small success. A one-man submarine, Biber (Beaver), was developed in 1944. This carried two torpedoes, one slung externally underneath each side of its hull. Its propulsion was gasoline/electric; the pilot had to wear oxygen equipment owing to the Biber's small air capacity when closed up. During late 1944 and early 1945 some Bibers operated off France and Holland. The two-man Seehund (Seal) went into production late in 1944 and was used from Dutch bases during early 1945. The diesel electric Seehund had a better performance than earlier German midgets; strongly built, it could resist depth charges. Like Biber, it carried two torpedoes. Employed to good effect against Allied supply convoys supporting the land offensive on the WESTERN FRONT, it was later used to carry supply cylinders to besieged German coastal garrisons. *See also* MOLCH.

MID-OCEAN MEETING POINTS (MOMPS). At the meeting of Prime Minister Winston CHURCHILL and President Franklin D. ROOSEVELT at ARGENTIA on August 10, 1941, it was agreed to implement the American "Western Hemisphere Defense Plan No. 4," under which, *inter alia*, the U.S. Navy was allowed to escort convoys comprising ships not of American registry as far as a Mid-Ocean Meeting Point, initially fixed at 22° W. and north of latitude 58° N., from which point a British escort force took over the convoy. The actual position of the MOMP could be changed as required to suit individual conditions of endurance and weather.

MIDWAY, BATTLE OF. In May 1942 the strategic initiative in the Pacific remained with Japan. In little more than five months the U.S. Pacific battleship force had been hard hit at PEARL HARBOR and the PHILIPPINES, Malaya and the East Indies had been overrun. An offensive aimed at the capture of PORT MORESBY as a step toward the ultimate neutralization of Australia had been stopped at the Battle of the CORAL SEA, early in May, but the general pattern of success could hardly help pleasing the Japanese planners.

Under the direction of Adm. Isoroku YAMAMOTO, a new plan was prepared. The COMBINED FLEET was to move in strength eastward to seize Midway Atoll, toward the west end of the Hawaiian chain and about a thousand miles west of Pearl Harbor. A diversionary thrust to the north was to capture the Aleutian islands of ATTU and KISKA. Capture of Midway would give Japan an advance base that could serve as an early-

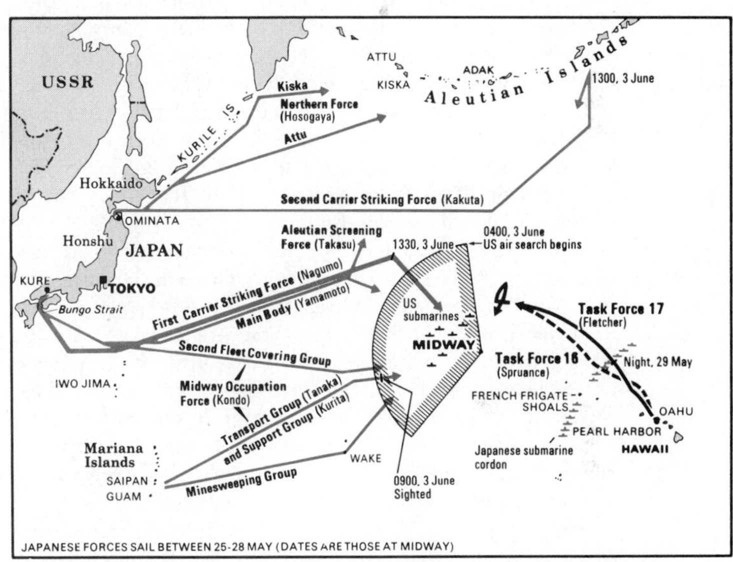

MIDWAY: The Japanese plan (top) was elaborate, but the battle developed into one of the major Allied victories of the war

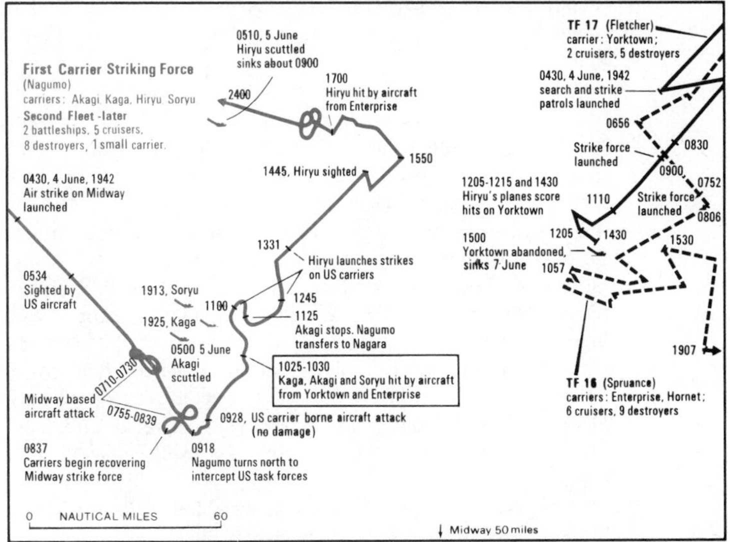

warning outpost and a possible threat to Pearl Harbor, the only major American fleet base west of California.

More important, in Yamamoto's mind, was the challenge such an assault would pose to Adm. Chester NIMITZ's Pacific Fleet. Threatening Midway, he felt, would force the Americans to face him in a decisive sea battle that Japan should win. Yamamoto had long insisted that Japan could not hope for victory in a protracted war with the United States; something conclusive had to be done before American resources could be fully mobilized. If the Pacific Fleet could be badly beaten, this might be discouraging enough to create a mood in the United States favorable to a negotiated peace. The Japanese strategic plan was complex, requiring excellent timing and coordination among widely separated elements. The principal thrust was to come from Vice-Adm. Chuichi NAGUMO's Carrier Striking Force (carriers AKAGI, KAGA, HIRYU and SORYU and escorting ships). This force was followed by a transport group carrying landing troops. After carrier strikes, beginning on June 4, had knocked out Midway's defenses, the transports would put their troops ashore on the 6th. Further support would come from Vice-Adm. Nobutake KONDO's Main Support Force—two battleships, four heavy cruisers, and destroyers. While the Midway phase of the operation was proceeding, Rear Adm. Kakuji Kakuta was to send an air strike against the Alaskan air base at DUTCH HARBOR from two light carriers. Kakuta would be followed by a small transport force, which would stage landings on Attu and Kiska. A Guard Force (four battleships, two cruisers, and destroyers) was to take its position between Hawaii and the Aleutians in case Nimitz should send part of his fleet north to counter the Japanese northern stroke. Finally, Admiral Yamamoto himself would be northwest of Midway with three battleships—including his flagship, YAMATO—the old small carrier *Hosho* and screening destroyers. From here he could move to support either the Midway or the Aleutian attack forces as the operation unfolded.

Thus by June 3 Midway faced Nagumo's carrier force to the northwest, the invasion force of transports was approaching from the west and Yamamoto's battleships were between the other two elements and farther to the rear. Japanese submarines had formed a patrol line between Midway and Pearl Harbor to warn of the approach of the U.S. fleet, believed to be still at Pearl Harbor.

Admiral Nimitz, commanding the Pacific Fleet from his Hawaiian headquarters, had one vital advantage: American intelligence had broken the Japanese naval code and could read intercepted message traffic. This put Nimitz in the priceless position of knowing Yamamoto's intentions. By the time the Japanese reconnaissance submarines took up their stations, they were too late; the American carrier force was at sea, behind them. Rear Adm. Frank Jack FLETCHER, with Task Force 17 (carrier YORKTOWN, two cruisers, six destroyers) made rendezvous with Rear Adm. Raymond SPRUANCE's Task Force 16 (carriers ENTERPRISE and HORNET, six cruisers, nine destroyers) several hundred miles north of Midway. Fletcher assumed overall command.

Early on June 3 messages warned Midway that Dutch Harbor was under air attack. Patrol planes later spotted the Japanese transport group, and reported it as the main striking force. B-17s (*see* B-17) attacked the transports from high altitude and claimed hits, though none were actually scored. After midnight, in the early hours of June 4, four PBY flying boats (*see* PBY) from Midway attacked with torpedoes; one oiler was hit and damaged.

During the night of June 3–4, Nagumo's carriers approached Midway from the northwest. Fletcher's task forces, unknown to the Japanese, were steaming to take position north of Midway within scouting range of Nagumo's anticipated morning position. At 0430 on June 4 Nagumo launched search planes to scout for possible American ships and sent off 108 carrier planes for the first strike at Midway. Marine fighters intercepted this force, but the outnumbered defenders were badly shot up and the Japanese attack did extensive damage. After observing the results, the Japanese strike commander reported that a second attack would be required.

Nagumo had held back a force of planes, including B5N Kate torpedo bombers (*see* B5N), for use against any American naval force that might be sighted. The Kates were armed with torpedoes. On receiving the message from his Midway strike leader, Nagumo ordered the torpedo bombers rearmed with bombs, intending to send them against Midway. This was a time-consuming operation, which involved lowering each plane to the hangar deck. To speed things up, torpedoes were left on the hangar decks of the carriers instead of being properly struck below to the magazines.

Beginning at 0710 Nagumo's carriers came under a series of uncoordinated attacks by planes from Midway. Four Army B-26 Marauder medium bombers (*see* B-26) and six Navy TBF Avenger torpedo bombers (*see* TBF) made torpedo attacks; two B-26s and five TBFs were shot down. The next attack came from 16 Marine SB2U Vindicator dive-bombers (*see* SB2U); these were followed by 15 Army B-17s, which dropped their bombs from 20,000 feet. Eleven more Marine SB2Us followed the Fortresses. Antiaircraft fire and Zero fighters fended off these attacks, and no hits were scored on the Japanese ships.

While this was happening, scout planes from Nagumo's force were searching the area for American ships. At 0728 one of these planes reported sighting a force of 10 ships 200 miles from the Japanese carriers. The pilot did not identify the ships by type. Without knowing whether American carriers were present, Nagumo could not be sure whether he should continue with the second Midway attack or divert these planes to a strike against the ships. He decided that the American ships were the more important target and ordered the rearming of his torpedo bombers stopped. He would go ahead and attack this new contact with whatever his planes had on their racks. At 0758 the scout plane reported the U.S. force as five cruisers and 25 destroyers; not until 0820 did the pilot finally inform Nagumo that one of the enemy ships "appears to be a carrier." This news made a timely attack vital. But 10 minutes later the Midway attack planes began to return. Nagumo decided to recover these planes immediately instead of launching his strike at the American contact. The "ready" planes were struck below, and the Midway planes landed. Rearming and refueling began immediately.

About the time the Japanese carriers began to fight off the Midway-based air attacks, planes were taking off from Spruance's *Enterprise* and *Hornet*; 116 planes—fighters, torpedo planes and dive-bombers—set course for the reported Japanese carriers. The three types of planes, flying at different speeds and altitudes, became separated. On arriving at the predicted enemy position, the American planes found nothing. Nagumo, instead of continuing toward Midway, had turned toward the American carrier force while he readied his air strike. *Hornet*'s dive-bombers and fighters never managed to find the Japanese carriers. Her torpedo squadron—Torpedo Eight—sighted smoke on the horizon and followed it to find Nagumo's ships.

The Japanese force was ready for them. Heavy fighter attack and antiaircraft fire knocked down all 15 of Torpedo Eight's TBD Devastators (*see* TBD); one pilot survived. *Enterprise*'s Torpedo Six made a similar run against the same opposition; 10 of 14 planes went down. Fletcher's *Yorktown* had launched her squadrons after Spruance's strike had departed. As with the other air groups, *Yorktown*'s torpedo squadron was the first into action. Torpedo Five attacked, losing 11 planes; two survived. The three torpedo squadrons had sacrificed themselves apparently to no avail. But from 0925 until after 1000 they had kept Nagumo's ships maneuvering to avoid torpedoes and thus unable to launch their own air strike. The carriers' fighter cover had been drawn down toward the surface to attack the torpedo planes.

At this moment the dive-bomber squadrons from *Yorktown* and *Enterprise* arrived overhead from separate directions. As the last of the torpedo bombers went down, Nagumo ordered his carriers to turn into the wind and launch aircraft. Preparations for takeoff were abruptly shattered as dive-bombers came down on *Akagi, Soryu* and *Kaga*. Hits on all three set off massive fires and explosions from the armed and fueled planes on their decks and from torpedoes still sitting on the hangar decks. Within minutes all three ships were ablaze and out of action. *Hiryu*, some miles away, was not hit.

Rear Adm. Tamon YAMAGUCHI, in *Hiryu*, ordered out what he had available—18 D3A1 Val dive-bombers (*see* D3A1) and six fighters. These were followed by 10 B5N torpedo bombers with six fighters. The first attack got through to *Yorktown*, scoring three bomb hits and leaving the carrier dead in the water. Damage was temporarily repaired, and in a little over an hour *Yorktown* was steaming and operating planes. Then came *Hiryu*'s second attack, and two torpedoes tore into *Yorktown*'s side. The carrier lost power and listed; her captain, believing she would capsize, ordered the crew to abandon ship. Spruance then assumed U.S. tactical command.

At this same time, scout planes from *Yorktown* were reporting *Hiryu*'s position. Dive-bombers from *Enterprise* found her and made four hits, crippling her and starting fatal fires.

Yamamoto, receiving word of the fate of his carriers, moved his heavy surface force forward, contemplating a night battle with what he believed to be a badly damaged American fleet. But as he received messages giving him a clearer picture of the situation, he decided on a general retirement and turned back in the dark early hours of June 5.

The burning Japanese carriers went down; *Kaga* and *Soryu* sank during the evening of the 4th, while *Hiryu* and *Akagi* were finished by torpedoes from their own destroyers early the next morning. Nagumo shifted his flag to an escorting cruiser. Yamaguchi, considered an aggressive and able officer, went down with *Hiryu*. *Yorktown* was still afloat on the morning of the 5th, and a salvage party was put aboard. The carrier was taken under tow and proceeded slowly toward Hawaii with a destroyer screen. The destroyer *Hammann* came alongside to provide power needed for electric pumps. In the early afternoon of June 6 the Japanese submarine *I-168* got inside the destroyer screen. Two torpedoes hit *Yorktown*; a third blew *Hammann* in two and quickly sank her. *Yorktown* hung on some hours longer, but early in the morning of the 7th she rolled over and went down.

Other contacts were made during the 6th. The heavy cruisers MOGAMI and MIKUMA had collided during the night of June 4–5. The two ships were attacked by Marine dive-bombers from Midway on the morning of the 5th, with damage to *Mikuma*. Carrier bombers located the cruisers on the 6th. *Mogami* was damaged and believed sunk; *Mikuma* was accounted for as sunk.

The consequences of Midway were profound. Not only had the Japanese lost four of their six first-line fleet carriers, but their losses in trained, experienced airmen were to prove serious. After Pearl Harbor and the Coral Sea, Midway had provided emphatic confirmation of the power of the aircraft carrier striking force. The slaughter of the American torpedo squadrons, attacking alone against heavy oppostion, pointed out the need for coordination of the efforts of fighters, dive-bombers and torpedo planes. Air groups had to fight as air groups, not as isolated squadrons. With Midway, the initiative in the Pacific passed to the Americans. The next big move was to be the August 1942 American landing on GUADALCANAL—the first step in the three-year offensive that would decide the Pacific war. **J.C.R.**

MIG-1. A Soviet open-cockpit, single-seat fighter, the first plane designed by the team of Artem I. Mikoyan and Mikhail I. Gurevich. Begun in 1939 as the I-61, it made its first flight in April 1940. The plane's hurried production was apparent in its poor flying characteristics. Although 2,000 were built and it was used operationally, it was soon supplanted, in 1941, by the MiG-3 (below). The MiG-1 was powered by a 1,200-horsepower V-12 engine and flew at a maximum speed of 365 miles per hour. It carried two 7.62-mm. machine guns and one 12.7-mm. machine gun, along with some bombs or rockets.

MIG-3. A further development of the MiG-1 (above). Begun in 1940, it was completed in 1941 and became operational in June of that year. While it was fast, its overall performance was not up to that of the LUFTWAFFE fighters. Better fighters, such as the YAKOLEV YAK-3, were available, and although produced in considerable numbers, by the end of 1943 the MiG-3 was no longer used by front-line interceptor units, and it was relegated to reconnaissance duties. Powered by a 1,350-horsepower V-12 engine, it had a maximum speed of 407 miles per hour. It was armed with two

7.62-mm. machine guns and one 12.7-mm. machine gun and could carry rockets and bombs.

MIG-5. The MiG-5's airframe was essentially the same as that of the MiG-3 (above) except for the engine, a 1,600-horsepower 14-cylinder radial. Its estimated top speed was 370 miles per hour. It carried four 7.62-mm. machine guns and rockets or bombs if needed. A few of these planes saw service in 1943. It was replaced by the LAVOCHKIN LA-5.

MIHAJLOVIĆ, Draža (1893–1946). Following the rapid German conquest of Yugoslavia, General Mihajlović organized a resistance to the Axis invaders in Serbia. His troops were known as CHETNIKS, and he was appointed Minister of Defense by the Yugoslav government-in-exile in London. Shortly after the beginning of resistance against the occupiers, Mihajlović found himself at war with Josip Broz (*see* TITO) and his Communist PARTISANS. Mihajlović sought to minimize casualties, and he made periodic truces with the Germans. His reputation as a nationalist leader waned through the war both at home and abroad. In Yugoslavia, he operated only in Serbia. At TEHERAN, the Allies decided to support the more active and ruthless Tito.

After the liberation of Yugoslavia, Mihajlović went into hiding. He was captured on March 13, 1946, accused of collaboration with the Germans and executed four months later at Belgrade.

MIKASA, Takahito, Prince (1915–). The fourth son of Japanese Emperor Taisho and the younger brother of Emperor HIROHITO, Prince Mikasa graduated from the Peers' School (1932), the Military Academy (1936) and the Army Staff College (1941). Attached to the 15th Cavalry Regiment, Mikasa served as a staff officer at Nanking in 1943. He resigned from the Army with the rank of major in 1945. In the final phases of the war, he supported those who wished to make peace.

MIKAWA, Gunichi (1888–). One of Japan's most active naval commanders, Mikawa took part in both the PEARL HARBOR and MIDWAY operations before going to RABAUL in mid-1942. As commander in chief of Japan's Eighth Fleet (Outer South Seas Force) at Rabaul, Mikawa had the task of reinforcing Japanese forces on GUADALCANAL and preventing American buildup on the island. Although Mikawa and his commanders defeated U.S. naval forces a number of times, notably in the Battle of SAVO ISLAND on August 8–9, 1942, he failed to achieve his main objectives. After his defeat at the Battle of the BISMARCK SEA in March 1943, Mikawa returned to Tokyo. Later he became commander of Japan's Southwest Area Forces and of Japanese air forces in the PHILIPPINES. His highest rank was vice-admiral.

MIKOLAJCZYK, Stanislaw (1901–1966). A member of the Peasant Party, Mikolajczyk served as Prime Minister of the Polish government-in-exile from July 1943 to November 1944. Though not as famous as his predecessor, General SIKORSKI, he was a skillful and ardent defender of Polish interests. Mikolajczyk quarreled with the British and the Americans over the issues of the postwar boundaries of the Polish state, the KATYN massacre and the WARSAW uprising, but received no support because ROOSEVELT and CHURCHILL were reluctant to clash with STALIN over Polish interests. In 1945 Mikolajczyk returned to Poland as Deputy Prime Minister, but two years later had to go into exile.

MIKUMA. Japanese MOGAMI-class cruiser. During the night of February 28–March 1, 1942, she and other Japanese ships sank the Allied cruisers H.M.A.S. PERTH and U.S.S. HOUSTON in BANTEN BAY, off Java. *Mikuma* was herself sunk on June 6, 1942, just after the Battle of MIDWAY, by U.S. carrier-based aircraft.

MILCH, Erhard (1892–1972). The real architect of the German LUFTWAFFE, as deputy to Herman GÖRING and state secretary of the Air Ministry, Milch had been an outstanding executive in commercial aviation. A German Army veteran of World War I, he entered the aviation industry as an administrator in the early 1920s and in 1925 was appointed one of the directors of the new national airline, Deutsche Lufthansa, becoming chief executive of the line in 1929. He proved extremely capable in both the technical and financial spheres. He developed a friendship with Göring, which in 1933 led to his becoming deputy to this leading Nazi in his capacity of "Reich Commissioner of Aviation," the euphemistic name for the office of the still-secret air force. Since Göring was heavily involved in the politics of the Third Reich, Milch with his drive and competence became the effective operating head of the shadow Air Ministry; he also became a strong supporter of Adolf HITLER, a view which he maintained throughout the war. In March 1935 the existence of the Luftwaffe was announced to the world, and in this same month Milch was given the rank of lieutenant general. In 1938 he was promoted to colonel general, and after the victory in the west in 1940 he was made a field marshal.

As the war developed, Reichsmarschall Göring, the Commander in Chief of the Luftwaffe, did less and less detailed work, spending much of his time at his estate, Carinhall. Hence Milch became for most purposes the real chief executive of the air force. As the situation worsened on the Eastern Front, Milch organized an extremely efficient large-scale operation for repairing damaged aircraft. He also took the brunt of Hitler's wrath when trying—in vain—to convince the Führer that the MESSERSCHMITT ME 262 (the first operational jet plane) should be employed as the fighter it was designed to be rather than recast as a bomber.

In a U.S. military trial at NUREMBERG in 1947, Milch was sentenced to life imprisonment; the sentence was later reduced to 15 years, and he was released in 1955. There has been much speculation about Milch's parentage, having to do with the allegation (a fatal one for a government official in the Third Reich) that his father was Jewish. In order to acquire full "Aryan" status, it is said, Milch concocted documentary evidence that his mother conceived him out of wedlock. Other sources—notably Milch's biographer David Irving—dispute this story, saying both that Milch's legal father was not Jewish and that in fact he was fathered by his mother's lover, who was "unquestionably Aryan" and who, Irving says, "wanted to marry her—a union which would have been disallowed by the Church but not illegal in those days." But, he observes, "so awful were the implications that Erhard Milch knew that this one fact about his parentage could never be revealed." The implications concern incest, since this lover is said to have been the uncle of Milch's mother.

MILCHKUH (Milk Cow). German term for special cargo U-boats fitted to refuel and resupply other submarines at sea. With surface supply ships driven from the seas, these boats assumed considerable importance in the attempt to keep patrolling U-boats on station for as long as possible. Results were disappointing; the Milchkühe were slow to submerge, which made them vulnerable to attacking aircraft, and all were eventually lost.

MILES, Sherman (1882–1966). U.S. Army officer, chief of Army intelligence at the time of the PEARL HARBOR attack in 1941. He became a major general in 1942.

MILITARY COUNCIL. A RED ARMY command device at the front and army levels. Operational orders were not valid unless signed by the council (soviet), which consisted of the commander of the front or army, his chief of staff and the political member. The political member was a Communist Party official appointed by headquarters in Moscow. From October 1942 these officials held military ranks.

MILITARY CROSS. Instituted in 1914, the Military Cross is awarded for bravery to British Army officers below the rank of major. Officers in the Royal Air Force are eligible for the award for gallant service on the ground.

MILK RUN. Slang term used by U.S. Army Air Force flying crews for an uneventful mission, or a mission that was expected to be easy.

MILLENNIUM. Code name of the British 1,000-plane (*see* THOUSAND PLAN) air raid on COLOGNE, Germany, May 30–31, 1942.

MILNE BAY. The Japanese, as part of their operations directed at the seizure of PORT MORESBY, decided to wipe out the Allied air base at Milne Bay, NEW GUINEA. Vastly underestimating the strength of the Allied garrison (which included six Australian infantry battalions), they landed about 1,500 troops at Milne Bay during the night of August 25–26, 1942. The Japanese began withdrawing under counterattack on August 31, and during the night of September 5–6 virtually the last of them boarded ship to be evacuated. The Japanese lost some 600 troops killed; Australian losses were about 125 killed and 200 wounded; U.S. Army forces lost 1 killed and 2 wounded. Work continued at Milne Bay, which was developed into a major base for the support of subsequent operations, especially those of CARTWHEEL.

MINCEMEAT. Code name for the famous Allied deception plan "The Man Who Never Was." *See also* MAJOR MARTIN.

MINDANAO. The southernmost and second largest island in the PHILIPPINES archipelago. Desiring to use Mindanao as a stage for operations against Borneo, the Japanese landed at Davao on the east coast on December 20, 1941, and at Cotabato on the west coast on April 29, 1942. Filipino forces under Brig. Gen. William SHARP were helpless against the Japanese and withdrew to mountain retreats. Although preparing for guerrilla operations, Sharp was ordered to surrender by Lt. Gen. Jonathan WAINWRIGHT on May 6.

Four years later the task of reconquering Mindanao was given to Lt. Gen. Robert EICHELBERGER's newly formed U.S. EIGHTH ARMY. A series of landings, beginning April 17, 1945, took place on the north, south and east coasts. Although the 102,000 starving Japanese troops resisted to the best of their ability, American forces and Filipino guerrillas had forced them into isolated pockets in the mountains by mid-July. Sporadic resistance continued until the end of the war.

MINDORO. Island, largely undeveloped, in the Visayan Islands of the central PHILIPPINES. The Japanese landed unopposed on the northern shore of the island on February 27, 1942, but undertook no significant military construction on the island during the war, and in December 1944 their garrison numbered less than 1,500 troops. The U.S. Western Visayan Task Force made an unopposed amphibious landing in southwestern Mindoro on December 15, 1944, to secure airfield sites to support the invasion of LUZON, as well as subsequent operations to the south and west. The first of three major airfields on Mindoro was operational on December 20. Japanese casualties were about 170 killed and 15 taken prisoner; total Allied casualties numbered over 475 men killed and 385 wounded, most of them stemming from KAMIKAZE attacks against Allied shipping, together with one Japanese naval raid.

MINE, LAND. Defensive weapons designed to delay and restrict enemy movements. The quickest means of setting up defensive positions, mines can be used as standing patrols to guard an area or to channel attacks into zones covered by prepared fields of fire, and can make up for a lack of manpower, as used by the Germans in the WESTERN DESERT and by the Japanese at OKINAWA. In World War II there were two general kinds, antipersonnel and antitank mines. The former consisted of a small amount of high explosive, usually less than a pound, fitted with a detonator actuated by pressure or by cutting a trip wire. Generally, they were laid beneath the ground. They were of two types—the bounding, as the German S-mine, and the blast type, as the British Shrapnel Mine, Mark II, a trip-wire model with a 30-yard casualty effect.

Antitank mines were used to immobilize or destroy enemy tanks or other vehicles. They could be laid on top of or beneath the ground and carried between 3 and 22 pounds of high explosive in a casing fitted with a primary fuze, with provision for one or more secondary detonators. They usually required 300–400 pounds' pressure to set them off, though some could be set off by a running man. One of the lightest was the French Light Antitank Mine, which had 5½ pounds of explosive and required 300–500 pounds' pressure to be actuated. The German Teller Mine 42, one of the largest, carried 12 pounds of explosive and needed 240–400 pounds to be set off; the American M1A1 antitank mine was essentially a copy of it. All these mines were pressure actuated.

There were some general-purpose mines used, as the British No. 75 Hawkins Grenade Mine, Mark I, which, although it was light, could disable a vehicle or cause personnel casualties. It was copied by the Americans and improved, as the M-7 mine, but was developed too late for general use. Some mines were improvised from available materials, such as artillery or mortar shells, grenades or blocks of explosive, when standard materials were in short supply; some fuzes were specially developed for these uses.

MINE, NAVAL. World War II mines were of the contact (exploded by coming into direct contact with a ship's hull) or influence (exploded by passage of a ship within a certain distance) type. Contact mines were usually moored; they floated at a preset distance below the surface at the end of a cable attached to an anchor. Influence mines were acoustic (detonated by sound waves from a ship's engines and propellers) or magnetic (detonated by the pull of a ship's magnetic field). These were bottom mines, i.e., planted on the bottom of a channel or other area. A type of pressure mine, activated by the fluctuation in water pressure caused by the passing of a ship, was used by the Germans during the late stages of the war, but not in sufficient numbers to prove significant.

Controllable mines were planted as a defensive measure in strategic bodies of water. Unlike other types of mines, these did not explode until they were deliberately set off from a control station ashore. Thus one's own ships could traverse such a mined area at will.

MINGALADON. A key airfield north of RANGOON (Burma). From this field British and American fighter pilots in early 1942 fought a desperate delaying battle against the invading Japanese forces. It was retaken by the RAF on May 2, 1944.

MINNIE MOUSE. Subcaliber practice rocket used with the U.S. Navy MOUSETRAP antisubmarine rocket launcher for training. A considerable amount of training was required to make crews adept with this weapon. Minnie Mouse economized on propellant, then in critical supply as rockets of all kinds came into worldwide use in great numbers, while at the same time allowing realistic training.

MINOL. A British combination of TNT, ammonium nitrate and powdered aluminum. Introduced early in 1943 to increase the power of depth charges, it had a higher shock and blast effect than TNT, making it suitable for this type of work.

MINSK. A Belorussian city midway between Warsaw and Moscow, captured (July 1941) in the second week of the German attack on the Soviet Union by Field Marshal von BOCK's Army Group Center. The city remained in German hands until recaptured by General ROKOSSOVSKY's Second Belorussian Front on July 3, 1944, in a lightning stroke that brought wholesale capture of German troops.

MIRGOROD. One of three cities in the Ukraine, USSR, used in 1944 as bases by U.S. FIFTEENTH and EIGHTH AIR FORCES on SHUTTLE BOMBING raids. *See also* POLTAVA.

MISSISSIPPI, U.S.S. NEW MEXICO–class battleship. When the Pacific war began, *Mississippi* was on Atlantic patrol duty. With her sister ships *New Mexico* and *Idaho*, she was shifted to the Pacific to help replace the battleships knocked out of action at Pearl Harbor. Through 1942 and early 1943 she served on patrol, convoy and training duty. In mid-1943 she supported operations in the Aleutians, then went to the GILBERT ISLANDS. While she was bombarding MAKIN Atoll in November 1943 an accidental turret explosion killed 43 of her crew. In January 1944, *Mississippi* shelled KWAJALEIN as part of the campaign to seize the MARSHALL ISLANDS. Two months later she bombarded the Japanese base at KAVIENG, New Ireland. After overhaul she supported landings in the Palaus and on LEYTE. On the night of October 24–25, 1944, she formed part of the battle line at the Surigao Strait action, a phase of the battle for LEYTE GULF. During bombardment operations off LUZON early in 1945 she was struck by a KAMIKAZE plane, but she continued on the gun line into February. After repairs she went on to take part in the capture of OKINAWA. *Mississippi* was present in Tokyo Bay during the Japanese surrender. She then returned home for conversion to an experimental gunnery ship.

MISSOURI, U.S.S. IOWA-class battleship. Commissioned in June 1944, *Missouri* was the last American battleship to go into service. She took part in the operations of the FAST CARRIER TASK FORCE during the final months of the Pacific war and provided gunfire support for the capture of IWO JIMA and OKINAWA. Since she was named in honor of President TRUMAN's home state, she was designated as the scene of the surrender ceremony in Tokyo Bay on September 2, 1945. Now a unit of the Inactive Fleet at Bremerton, Wash., she is visited by thousands of people every year.

MITSCHER, Marc Andrew (1887–1947). A 1910 U.S. Naval Academy graduate, Mitscher was a pioneer naval aviator whose early service included duty as pilot of the NC-1 seaplane during the 1919 transatlantic flight of the NC-4. Captain of the U.S.S. HORNET when Pearl Harbor was attacked, Mitscher commanded that aircraft carrier on the Doolittle raid against Tokyo on April 18, 1942 (*see* FIRST SPECIAL AVIATION PROJECT), and in the Battle of MIDWAY, June 3–7, 1942. In 1943 he was Commander, Fleet Air, SOLOMON ISLANDS, and was the overall tactical commander of the operation that shot down Japanese Adm. Isoruku YAMAMOTO on April 18, 1943. In January 1944 he became commander of Carrier Division Three, which later became FAST CARRIER TASK FORCE 58. He stayed in that post, as a vice-admiral, through the rest of the war. He welded the fast carriers into a fighting team that fought the Battles of the PHILIPPINE SEA, June 19–20, 1944, and LEYTE GULF, October 24–25, 1944, and bested the Japanese KAMIKAZES in the OKINAWA campaign in the spring of 1945. Offered the post of Chief of Naval Operations by Secretary of the Navy James V. FORRESTAL after the war, Mitscher turned it down to become com-

Admiral Mitscher

mander of the Eighth Fleet and then Commander in Chief Atlantic Fleet, where he served until his death in February 1947.

MODEL, Walther (1891–1945). A German infantry officer in World War I and a staff officer in the training branch of the War Ministry at the beginning of World War II, Model cast his lot with Adolf HITLER rather than the tradition-ridden hierarchy of the Wehrmacht. His manner was rough, but his energy and aggressiveness as a soldier earned him a special relationship with Hitler, which enabled Model to speak to the Führer with unusual frankness, ignore impossible orders or act first and seek permission later. His loyalty was unquestioned; after the July 20, 1944, attempt on Hitler's life, he was the first commander on the Eastern Front to send a telegram reaffirming his allegiance.

Model served as a staff officer with the IV Corps in Poland and the Sixteenth Army in France. In 1941 in Russia he commanded the 3d Panzer Division, leading the German drive to the DNIEPER, and earned the respect of Gen. Heinz GUDERIAN, who described him as a "bold, inexhaustible soldier" who won the confidence of his men by habitual disregard for his personal safety and by his intolerance of lazy or incompetent subordinates.

Model continued to serve on the Eastern Front, where he earned the nicknames "Lion of Defense" and "the Führer's Fireman" because Hitler switched him to North, South, and Center Fronts in turn, attempting to stem the Russian tide. When in August 1944 the WESTERN FRONT also was threatening to collapse, Hitler sent Model to replace Field Marshal von KLUGE as concurrently Commander in Chief West and commander of Army Group B. One of Model's first actions was to send Hitler a blunt message describing the situation in the west as untenable. In September Field Marshal von RUNDSTEDT, Kluge's predecessor, was reinstated as CinC West, Model retaining command of Army Group B, which was surrounded in the RUHR pocket in April 1945. To avoid surrender, Model dissolved the army group on April 17, freeing its members to make their way home individually, join another front or surrender. He is reported to have shot himself on April 21, after asking, "Have we done everything to justify our actions in the light of history? What is there left to a commander in defeat?"

MOGADISHU. Capital of Italian Somaliland (1941) and an important port on the Indian Ocean. It was occupied by Lt. Gen. Sir Alan CUNNINGHAM's British African forces on February 25, 1941, and yielded important stores of motor fuel.

MOGAMI. Japanese heavy cruiser and class, of more than 11,000 tons loaded, with ten 8-inch guns (5×2) and twelve 24-inch torpedo tubes (4×3). *Mogami*, MIKUMA, *Kumano* and *Suzuya* were orginally completed in 1935–37 as light cruisers armed with fifteen 6.1-inch (155-mm.) guns in five triple turrets. By the end of 1939 all four ships had been rearmed as heavy cruisers with 8-inch guns. Eight 5-inch antiaircraft guns were later backed up by 25-mm. antiaircraft automatic shell guns and 12.7-mm. machine guns. All four Mogamis saw extensive combat service. *Mikuma*, lost at MIDWAY, was the first Japanese heavy cruiser sunk during the war. *Mogami* was damaged in the same action. She was then refitted, an airplane-handling deck replacing her two after turrets. Eleven scout floatplanes could be carried by *Mogami* in her new rig. *Mogami* and *Suzuya* were lost at LEYTE GULF; *Kumano* went down under air attack a month later. Their design incorporating lessons learned in the design and construction of earlier Japanese heavy cruisers, the Mogamis were powerful and effective warships.

MOGILEV. One of the German strongpoints on the upper Dnieper River, taken by the Second White Russian Front in the 1944 Soviet summer offensive (June 28).

MÖHNE DAM. The most familiar of the names of the targets of RAF No. 617 Squadron on the dam-busting raid of May 16, 1943. The Möhne dam, in northwestern Germany, was breached after the fifth aircraft had attacked with a new type of bomb. *See also* DAM BUSTERS.

MOLCH. German one-man MIDGET SUBMARINE with its internal cockpit near the stern. It carried two torpedoes in external racks, one to each side of the lower hull. Nearly 400 were built.

MÖLDERS, Werner (1913–1941). Outstanding German flier and air commander, an ace in both the Spanish Civil War (14 kills) and World War II (101). He was the first person in the war to down 100 enemy planes. At the age of 28, as a colonel, he was made General of the Fighter Arm and, though forbidden to fly, continued to do so occasionally in Russia. He was summoned to Berlin in November 1941 for the funeral of Ernst UDET, the Luftwaffe technical chief; he was killed on the way when his plane, not piloted by him, crashed in severe weather.

MOLINIÉ, Jean-Baptiste (1880–1971). Commander of the French 25th division, General Molinié advanced into Holland to meet the German invasion of 1940, repelling an armored attack. Trapped by the German breakthrough, Molinié succeeded by seniority to command of the remains of the French First Army, which fought at Lille at the end of May, diverting German strength from DUNKIRK.

MOLOTOV, Vyacheslav M. (1890–). Veteran member of the Soviet Politburo and one of Joseph STALIN's closest associates before World War II. In 1939 Molotov (whose original surname was Skriabin) was appointed Commissar for Foreign Affairs and figured prominently in the negotiations with Germany which led to the conclusion of the SOVIET-GERMAN NONAGGRESSION PACT.

During the war Molotov's position in the Soviet Government was second only to Stalin's. In June 1941 Molotov announced the German invasion of the country and concluded his broadcast with a dramatic appeal to the Russian people: "Our cause is just. The enemy will be beaten. Victory will be ours."

Molotov became a member of the STATE DEFENSE COMMITTEE, which was a combined civilian and military policy-making body, and served on it throughout the war. He traveled to London and Washington in 1942 for talks designed to coordinate Allied military strategy against HITLER. At that time Stalin wanted Britain and the United States to open up a SECOND FRONT somewhere in western Europe in order to relieve German pressure on Russia. Molotov obtained the promise of a second front in principle but not, as it turned out, in fact. Historians agree that the failure in 1942 to reach real accord over the questions of an Allied invasion of Europe and of war aims soured Soviet attitudes toward the Western Allies for the duration of the war.

In 1943 (at TEHERAN) and 1945 (at YALTA and POTSDAM), Molotov, along with Stalin, represented the Soviet Union at the great conferences that were held to decide the fate of Europe after the war. Molotov also headed the Soviet delegation to the founding conference of the UNITED NATIONS in San Francisco in 1945.

MOLOTOV BREADBASKET. Nickname, of British origin, given to a type of cluster bomb which broke up in flight to scatter a large number of small incendiary bombs or pellets.

MOLOTOV COCKTAIL. Frangible incendiary grenade, made from a glass bottle filled with gasoline with a cloth wick in the neck. The user poured gas on the wick, ignited it and threw the bottle; the bottle burst and the gasoline went up in flames. Despite their crudeness, Molotov cocktails could put tanks and mechanized vehicles out of action, and they could be produced quickly and easily. First used in the Spanish Civil War, they got their nickname from the extensive use made of them in the SOVIET-FINNISH WAR of 1939–40.

MOLTKE, Helmuth, Count von (1907–1945). A legal expert on the ABWEHR staff, Moltke was, with Count Peter YORCK VON WARTENBURG, the founder of the KREISAU CIRCLE of native German opponents to Adolf HITLER, a loose assembly named after Moltke's Silesian estate. Consisting of members of both political wings, clerics, professional scholars, administrators, economists and diplomats, the group formulated and discussed the nature of a principled postwar German society and its place in an internationally federated European union, the latter conception gaining increasing weight among other, more traditional-minded resistance circles. Moltke contributed notably to the socialist character of the Kreisau group before his arrest in January 1944; he was executed at the Ploetzensee prison on January 23, 1945. *See also* OPPOSITION TO HITLER.

MONCKTON, Walter Turner, Viscount (1891–1965). Head of the British propaganda and information services in Cairo, 1941–45.

MONDORF. Village in Luxembourg; its Palace Hotel was the temporary place of confinement for high-ranking German officers and Nazi officials shortly after the German surrender.

MONNET, Jean (1888–). French expert on international finance and organization. A leader in seeking airplanes and munitions from the United States, Monnet chaired the Anglo-French Economic Coordinating Committee after war was declared in 1939. He was one of the creators of the Anglo-French DECLARATION OF UNION. After the fall of France in 1940, he was asked by Winston CHURCHILL to serve on the British Supply Council in Washington, and in 1943 he represented the American and BRITISH MUNITIONS ASSIGNMENTS BOARD in Algiers. He assisted in merging the French Giraudist and Gaullist factions and became the commissioner of arms and supplies for the FRENCH COMMITTEE OF NATIONAL LIBERATION.

Monnet had served on the Allied Supreme Economic Council during World War I and afterward was Deputy Secretary-General of the League of Nations. His contributions to the European unity movement after World War II earned him the nickname "Mr. Europe."

MONROVIA, U.S.S. Attack transport, begun as a cargo ship, acquired by the Navy as a transport, commissioned in December 1942 and redesignated an amphibious transport in February 1943. She took part in the invasion of SICILY before going to the Pacific to participate in the capture of TARAWA, KWAJALEIN, SAIPAN, LEYTE, LUZON and OKINAWA.

MONSABERT, Joseph de Goislard de (1887–). French Army officer, commander of a division in Algeria in 1940. Following Allied landings there in 1942, General Monsabert led French troops against the Germans in TUNISIA, commanded a division in ITALY and finally the 2d Corps of the French First Army in Alsace and southern Germany.

MONSCHAU. Picturesque German border town with timbered houses southeast of Aachen, a prewar haven for German honeymooners. Troops of the U.S. 9th Infantry Division captured it in mid-September 1944. Although the town was an early German objective in the Battle of the BULGE in December, men of the U.S. 78th Infantry Division successfully defended it.

MONTCALM. French GLOIRE-class light cruiser, launched in 1935, of 7,600 tons. She carried nine 6-inch guns. *Montcalm* was part of the squadron dispatched to DAKAR in September 1940 just prior to the attempted British–Free French landing. She later, in Fighting French hands, participated in the occupation of Corsica.

MONTÉLIMAR. Small city in southern France on the east bank of the Rhône River about 90 miles north of the Mediterranean coast and a like distance south of Lyon. Just north of Montélimar the main railroad and highway leading to Lyon passed through a defile, where during the period August 21–31, 1944, the reinforced 36th Infantry Division of the VI Corps, U.S. SEVENTH ARMY, made an unsuccessful attempt to cut off the German LXXXV Corps of Nineteenth Army. German matériel losses during this battle were heavy but not decisive; for example, the 11th Panzer Division managed to bring over 30 of its 40-odd medium tanks through the defile. German personnel losses were about 600 men killed, 1,500 wounded and 5,800 taken prisoner. The losses of the reinforced 36th Division were approximately 150 men killed, 885 wounded and 290 missing (most of the latter taken prisoner). *See also* SOUTHERN FRANCE OPERATION.

MONTEREY, U.S.S. INDEPENDENCE-class light aircraft carrier, commissioned in June 1943. Begun as the CLEVELAND-class light cruiser *Dayton,* she completed as the carrier *Monterey* and went to the Pacific to join the FAST CARRIER TASK FORCE for the GILBERTS and MARSHALLS operations, followed by 1944 Pacific raids and support of the LEYTE landings. Damaged by a typhoon in December of that year, she returned from shipyard repairs to take part in air strikes in support of the capture of OKINAWA. *Monterey* participated in final carrier task force strikes against Japan, and after the end of the war brought home troops from the Pacific and Europe. President Gerald Ford saw wartime Pacific sea duty on *Monterey* as a young man.

MONTGOMERY, U.S.S. WICKES-class destroyer, commissioned in 1918. Decommissioned in 1937, she went back into service in 1939 and was in the Pacific when PEARL HARBOR was attacked. *Montgomery* served on patrol, convoy and minelaying duty (she had been converted to a light minelayer in 1931) until August 1943, when she was damaged in a collision while laying a minefield in the SOLOMONS. After repairs, she continued her work. In September 1944 she supported the capture of PELELIU and ANGAUR in the Carolines. Anchored off the island of Ngulu on October 17, 1944, she was struck by a drifting mine, which caused severe flooding. After repairs she returned to San Francisco.

MONTGOMERY OF ALAMEIN, Bernard Law Montgomery, 1st Viscount (1887–1976). British general, one of the outstanding Allied military leaders and one of the most controversial. Modesty was not among his virtues. He considered it vital to effective leadership for a commander to be visible, distinctive and well known; he achieved this by a variety of means, some natural and some contrived. His tendency to be outspoken, insensitive and domineering made him difficult to work with, and a reviewer called his *Memoirs* "a testimonial to the magnificent forbearance of General EISENHOWER."

Montgomery was one of nine children. Their father was a bishop; the family income was modest. He described his childhood as "unhappy," with many fierce clashes of will between himself and his mother. In school at St. Paul's and later at Sandhurst he hurled himself into sports, but sometimes had scholastic troubles. He soon developed the personal philosophy that life is a "stern struggle" and hard work and integrity are essential for success. Later he added a third requisite—moral courage. Montgomery entered the Army in 1908, serving first in India. He developed habits of asceticism that stayed with him—no alcohol, no tobacco, early hours.

Montgomery found much to question about the conduct of operations in World War I, when he served in France, and after the war he decided to dedicate himself to his profession and master its details. He went to the Staff College at Camberley and later was asked to rewrite the manual for infantry training. In 1927 he married Betty Carver, a widow, and a son, David, was born in 1928. The marriage was very happy, but Betty Montgomery died in 1937. After her death Montgomery devoted himself exclusively to military life, and in 1939, as a major general, he was given command of the 3d Division.

As part of the BRITISH EXPEDITIONARY FORCE, the 3d Division was evacuated from DUNKIRK in May 1940, and for the next two years Montgomery served in England, where he concentrated on training. His emphasis was on achieving physical and mental fitness in his men, weeding out incompetent officers and instilling a sense of urgency and discipline. He later called those two years of preparing for war the basis of all his future success. He had a role in planning the controversial DIEPPE raid, but left England before it was conducted.

In August 1942 Lieutenant General Montgomery was tapped for the FIRST ARMY in Operation Torch, the invasion of NORTHWEST AFRICA, but he was ordered to the EIGHTH ARMY in Egypt when Gen. "Strafer" GOTT was killed. He was pleased at the appointment, and immediately (sometimes tactlessly) began establishing his tone of command. Gen. Sir Harold ALEXANDER, whom Montgomery admired and liked, was his superior officer, but tended to let Montgomery have his head. Monty, as he was known, has been criticized for taking over the plans of others as if they were his own and taking too much credit for ending the Eighth Army's series of defeats, but beginning with ALAMEIN, Montgomery commanded a series of victories until he accepted the German surrender on LÜNEBURG HEATH on May 4, 1945.

Alamein was a set-piece battle; victory was slow in coming, and Montgomery had a chance to test his philosophy of "decision in action and calmness in the crisis." After Alamein, Montgomery pursued Gen. Erwin ROMMEL's broken army across North Africa to TUNISIA; Montgomery's critics point out that Rommel always managed to escape annihilation at Montgomery's hands. Characteristics that Montgomery continued to show throughout the war were evident in Africa—precision, punctuality and caution. With the exception of the MARKET-GARDEN operation at ARNHEM in 1944, his battle plans were based on force, close control and frontal assault rather than maneuver or daring. Persistence was his key to success.

In North Africa the Axis armies were finally cornered between Montgomery and the Torch forces in Tunisia. Montgomery was next scheduled for SICILY. He imposed his own plan on the Sicily operation, at least the British part of it, and it has been criticized for being too cautious. After Sicily was taken, Montgomery and the Eighth Army invaded the tip of ITALY on September 3, 1943. He stayed with the Eighth Army in the Italian campaign until the end of December, when he left to command the 21st Army Group, then preparing in England for the INVASION of NORMANDY. Until Gen. DWIGHT D. EISENHOWER, the Supreme Commander, could move his headquarters to France, Montgomery was to be his deputy in command of all ground forces.

Before the Normandy invasion, Montgomery visited all the men of his army group, giving everyone a chance to see and hear him. He was ashore in Normandy by June 8. While Montgomery fought bitterly in the CAEN sector, Gen. Omar BRADLEY's U.S. forces gradually occupied the rest of Normandy. On August 1 Bradley's 12TH ARMY GROUP became operational, and Gen. George S. PATTON's THIRD ARMY broke out of Normandy and turned the war into one of movement. On September 1 Eisenhower took over from Montgomery as commander of all ground forces, and Montgomery was promoted to field marshal. A conflict between Montgomery and the Americans soon developed, as Montgomery wanted Eisenhower to let him make a single northern thrust into Germany. Supply and support for Montgomery's plan would have immobilized Patton and placed the numerically superior Americans in a subordinate position. Besides, Montgomery had not displayed an aptitude for daring, thrusting action, and Eisenhower, firmly supported by Bradley, held out for the planned BROAD-FRONT STRATEGY.

Because supply shortages often cramped Allied plans, the issue of Montgomery's single thrust versus the broad front cropped up repeatedly. A concurrent British argument that Montgomery should serve as commander of ground forces because Eisenhower had too many responsibilities became bitter after the ARDENNES offensive (the Battle of the BULGE), during which Montgomery was given temporary command of those American forces north of the German salient. Montgomery added fuel to the flames by a tactless news conference in which he presented himself as the rescuer of the Americans, and at one point Bradley was ready to resign if Montgomery were given command. Montgomery pressed his views vigorously, but when it became apparent he had lost his arguments, he served loyally under Eisenhower. His contributions to the battle of Europe were immense, and his plan for Operation Market-Garden, even though it failed, was one of the most imaginative of the European campaign.

After the German surrender Montgomery became commander in chief of the British forces of occupation and British member of the ALLIED CONTROL COUNCIL in Germany. In June 1946 he was named Chief of the Imperial General Staff, a post he held for two and a half years. From 1951 to 1958 he was Deputy Supreme Allied Commander in Europe (NATO). His accounts of the war years may be found in *El Alamein to the River Sangro; Normandy to the Baltic;* and his controversial *Memoirs.* **M.H.B.**

MOORE, Bryant Edward (1894–1951). U.S. Army officer who commanded the 164th Infantry Regiment on GUADALCANAL. In 1943 he was promoted to brigadier general and assigned to the 104th Infantry Division in the ETO. In 1945 he was raised to major general and given command of the 8th Infantry Division. He was killed while on a flying mission early in the Korean War.

MOORE, James E. (1902–). During the war Moore, a 1924 graduate of West Point, served on the U.S. War Department General Staff and as chief of staff of the 35th Division, the 30th Division, the XII Corps, the FOURTH ARMY and the NINTH ARMY. He ended the war with the rank of major general.

MORAN, Charles McMoran Wilson, Baron (1882–1977). Personal physician to Winston CHURCHILL, 1940–65. Lord Moran's book *The Struggle for Survival* is a controversial close-up presentation of Churchill's performance in the war and after.

MORANE-SAULNIER MS-406. A single-seat fighter, the MS-406 was numerically the most important fighter available to the French Armée de l'Air at the outset of the war. It equipped four pursuit squadrons, each of three groups of 25 planes. Though a reliable plane with good flying characteristics, it was outclassed by its opponents, being somewhat slow and underpowered. The standard MS-406 was powered by an 860-horsepower Hispano-Suiza 12-cylinder liquid-cooled in-line engine. It flew at a top speed of 302 miles per hour with a normal range of 497 miles (932 miles with two 32-imperial-gallon external tanks). It was armed with a 20-mm. cannon that fired through the hub and two 7.5-mm. machine guns. Wingspan, 34 feet 9¾ inches; length, 26 feet 9¼ inches; height, 9 feet 3¾ inches; loaded weight, 5,000 to 5,997 pounds.

MORANE-SALUNIER MS-450. French single-seat interceptor-fighter designed to replace the MS-406 (above). Three prototypes were built; the first one flew on April 1, 1939. Another plane, the D-520, was chosen to replace the MS-406, but the company continued development of the MS-450 on its own. The MS-450 was accepted by the Swiss Government and built under license as the D-3802.

MORELL, Theodor (1887–1948). Adolf HITLER's personal physician, Professor Morell was of Huguenot extraction, the son of a schoolmaster. He claimed to have studied under the bacteriologist Ilya Mechnikov, professor at the Pasteur Institute, who had died in 1916. For a time he was a ship's doctor on passenger liners, but later he set up a fashionable and lucrative practice in Berlin, specializing in skin and venereal diseases. Introduced to Hitler by the photographer Heinrich HOFFMANN, whom he had cured of a serious illness, Morell took charge of Hitler medically from 1936, and used his body like a laboratory for his unseemly concoctions—notably Multiflor (capsules of bacteria from the testicles and intestines of animals), phosphorus, dextrose and hormone tablets. By the latter part of the war, according to Sir Hugh Trevor-Roper, Morell was daily using some 28 different drugs on Hitler, largely by injection, together with Dr. Köster's Antigas Pills, a prepared blend of strychnine and belladonna. Morell made a fortune from patenting medicines that Hitler's patronage had enabled him to develop. It was alleged that his annual salary was 60,000 marks, plus 24,000 marks for expenses (the total equal to perhaps $30,000 at the time), and that he amassed further wealth out of a truly unique enterprise—a delousing monopoly made compulsory for the Wehrmacht and the Labor Front. He last saw Hitler on April 22, 1945, eight days before the Führer's suicide.

MORGAN, Sir Frederick (1894–1967). British Army officer who had extensive experience as an Allied planner. Early in the war General Morgan had a field command (an armored group) in France. In October 1942 he was assigned to Gen. Dwight EISENHOWER to plan a possible subsidiary landing as part of the invasion of NORTHWEST AFRICA (Operation Torch) or as a counter to a German move through Spain. Then he was directed to plan an invasion of Sardinia, which did not materialize, and he worked on plans for assaulting SICILY—a planning assignment that was later given to the armies that carried out the invasion. In March 1943 Morgan was appointed chief of staff to the Supreme Allied Commander (Designate) (COSSAC), with instructions to prepare a plan for the cross-Channel INVASION (Operation Overlord). To this end, Morgan assembled a staff from all three services, British and American both, but soon found himself handicapped by lack of funds and lack of a Supreme Allied Commander. His original plan was revised after Eisenhower was appointed to the latter position: landing craft were added to the assault, the assault front widened with two divisions added and the date for invasion set back from May to June. This strengthening was at Eisenhower's insistence. Concurrent with Overlord, Morgan was also responsible for preparing a feint to prevent the Germans from concentrating against the Russian or Italian front.

Until the end of the war Morgan was the deputy chief of staff in Eisenhower's headquarters, and as such, became a thorn in the side of General MONTGOMERY, who accused him of supporting Eisenhower's ideas at the expense of his own. *See also* SUPREME HEADQUARTERS, ALLIED EXPEDITIONARY FORCE.

MORGAN, Sir William Duthie (1891–1977). British Army officer who was, successively, chief of the general staff, Home Forces, 1942–43; General Officer Commanding in Chief Southern Command, 1944; chief of staff to the Supreme Allied Commander Mediterranean, 1945; Supreme Allied Commander Mediterranean, 1945–47.

MORGENTHAU, Henry, Jr. (1891–1967). Close friend and adviser to President Franklin D. ROOSEVELT, Morgenthau was Secretary of the Treasury from 1934 until 1945 and in that capacity was responsible for the development of a system of finance for the war effort relying on the sale of war bonds and on taxation to dry up inflationary excess profits. He also took an active interest in foreign relations and made a series of recommendations (usually unpopular) in that area including the so-called MORGENTHAU PLAN for postwar Germany, rejected by Roosevelt and so disliked by Harry S. TRUMAN that upon becoming President he asked Morgenthau to retire.

MORGENTHAU PLAN. In September 1944 the U.S. Treasury Department, under Secretary Henry MORGENTHAU, prepared a proposal for the economic disposition of Germany after the war. The plan envisioned the creation of an "agricultural and pastoral" Germany in order to prevent its rearmament. The industrial regions of the Saar and Ruhr were to be stripped of their factories, either through destruction or through removal as reparations. Morgenthau presented the plan to ROOSEVELT and CHURCHILL at the QUEBEC CONFERENCE, and they initialed their agreement to a statement of the idea. Within a matter of weeks advisers to the two leaders, particularly STIMSON, HULL, HOPKINS and EDEN persuaded them that the plan was dangerous and impracticable, and it died a natural death.

MORISON, Samuel Eliot (1887–1976). A Harvard history professor and author of a number of important works on American history, Morison was commissioned in the United States Naval Reserve in 1942 with the task of preparing a comprehensive history of American naval operations during World War II. Together with a small staff of assistants, Morison participated in many of the most important naval campaigns and battles in both the Atlantic and Pacific. His *History of United States Naval Operations in World War II* appeared in 15 volumes between 1950 and 1962.

MOROTAI. Northernmost island of the Halmahera group, between NEW GUINEA and the PHILIPPINES, and an airfield stepping-stone on the Allied way to the Philippines. The U.S. 31st Infantry Division began landing on Morotai on September 15, 1944, against little opposition.

MORRISON, Herbert Stanley (1888–1965). In 1915 Morrison became secretary of the London Labour Party, and in due course he rose to prominence in the national party. Returned to Parliament as a Labour member in 1935, after having been out for four years, Morrison became one of the three Labour members of the CHURCHILL coalition government in May 1940 as Minister of Supply. In October 1940 he became Home Secretary and Minister of Home Security. In 1941 he became a member of the War Cabinet. With the breakup of the coalition government in May 1945 and the victory of the Labour Party in the general election of July, Morrison became leader of the House of Commons and Lord President of the Council.

As Minister of Home Security under Churchill, Morrison inaugurated the National Fire Service and organized a nightly guard on industrial and public buildings as a precaution against air attacks using incendiary bombs. As Home Secretary he had responsibilities relating to censorship and control over the release of persons whose actions were considered prejudicial to the war effort.

MORRISON SHELTER. Named for British Home Secretary Herbert MORRISON, this bomb shelter was designed for use by a family and could be set up indoors. It was 2 feet 9 inches high, and the top was a steel plate that could serve as a table. The sides were of wire mesh. The Morrison shelter was developed too late to be of much use in the BLITZ of 1940–41, but more than half a million had been distributed by November 1941 and were thus available in later attacks.

MORSHEAD, Leslie (1889–1959). A schoolteacher turned soldier, Morshead made an outstanding record in World War I, returned to civilian life and in 1939 again joined the Army in his native Australia. In Africa he commanded the newly formed 9th Australian Division, which caught the brunt of General ROMMEL's first African offensive. Displaying resolute leadership, Morshead led his men through the TOBRUK siege, winning from them the sobriquet "Ming the Merciless," later affectionately softened to "Ming." Promoted to lieutenant general and given command of the Australian Imperial Forces in the Middle East, Morshead led the 9th Division through ALAMEIN and then went to the Southwest Pacific. For a short time he commanded NEW GUINEA Force, and as GOC I Australian Corps he directed the operation to take Borneo. After the war he returned to civilian life in Australia.

MORTAIN. Town in Brittany a few miles inland from AVRANCHES. On August 7, 1944, the Germans made a strong armored counterattack against the U.S. FIRST ARMY in an effort to drive through to the sea at Avranches and cut off American armored spearheads that had passed well beyond the town. The Germans took Mortain, holding it until August 12, but never came close to gaining Avranches. The German thrust became known as the "Mortain counterattack."

MOSCICKI, Ignacy (1867–1946). When the Germans began to agitate for the occupation of DANZIG in 1939, Dr. Moscicki, an internationally famous chemist who had been President of Poland since 1926, stated (in June) that he was determined to defend Danzig against Nazi aggression at any cost. But the subsequent German attack on Poland forced Moscicki to flee to Paris, where he resigned as President.

MOSCOW, BATTLE OF. One of the major battles of the war. The German attack on Moscow, capital of the Soviet Union and hub of all Russian railways, was directed by Field Marshal Fedor von BOCK, ably assisted by his tank commander, Gen. Heinz GUDERIAN. Within one month of the German invasion of Russia in June 1941, Bock's forces reached SMOLENSK, several hundred miles west of Moscow. Here Adolf HITLER ordered a halt in the advance while Guderian turned south to assist Army Group South near KIEV in the Ukraine. This resulted in a lengthy delay in the assault on Moscow, which did not resume until October. Nevertheless, by the middle of October the Germans were just 60 miles west of the capital, and in the fighting that followed several units reached the suburbs of the city itself. The final German drive, aiming to encircle Moscow and to cut it off from supplies, reached Klin in the north and TULA in the south. By December, as the winter set in, the Germans were bogged down in the snow and the roads were impassable for wheeled vehicles. On December 8, 1941, Hitler announced a halt in the German offensive. The battle ended with Moscow still in Russian hands. *See also* SOVIET-GERMAN OPERATIONS 1941–45.

MOSCOW CONFERENCE. This meeting of the Big Three foreign ministers—Cordell HULL (U.S.), Anthony EDEN (U.K.) and V. M. MOLOTOV (USSR)—was held in Moscow, October 19–30, 1943. It reflected Soviet mistrust of the Western Allies caused by their failure to open a SECOND FRONT against Germany, by their exclusion of the Soviet Union from administering occupied Italy and by their attempts to advance plans for a postwar organization of eastern Europe which the Soviets considered contrary to their interests. The Soviets agreed in principle to facilitate air transport between the United States and Russia, to allow weather stations in Siberia and to permit setting up airfields for SHUTTLE BOMBING of Germany by American planes. But implementation of these agreements later encountered roadblocks placed by Soviet authorities. The principal document of the conference was the Joint Four-Power Declaration (signed also by China's ambassador to the Soviet Union), stating the Allies' determination to continue the war against the Axis until the latter surrendered unconditionally, laying the foundation for postwar peace by creating the UNITED NATIONS ORGANIZATION and pledging consultation and cooperation in establishing a peaceful and secure world.

MOSES, Raymond G. (1891–1974). U.S. Army officer who served as assistant chief of staff (G-4—Supply) in the War Department, with the rank of brigadier general.

MOSLEY, Sir Oswald Ernald (1896–). British political figure, a man of early promise and frequently spoken of as a future Prime Minister, who in 1932 founded the British Union of Fascists. A Conservative when first elected to Parliament in 1918, he moved through the ranks of the independents to become (1924) a member of the Labour Party, and in 1929–30 he served in the cabinet. His response to the agonies of the Depression was to found his Fascist party and, a figure of charismatic appeal, he had by 1934 acquired perhaps 30,000 adherents. In May 1940 he was imprisoned and his Union of Fascists broken up. His release in 1943 on the grounds of ill health was met with outcries from much of the public, but the Churchill government stuck to its decision.

MOSQUITO. For most of the war the fastest airplane in Britain's ROYAL AIR FORCE, the Mosquito was dreamed up in 1938 by de Havilland as a private venture. Not until the outbreak of war did the government show any enthusiasm for an unarmed bomber built of wood. Then, in December 1939, the firm received an official invitation to submit the Mosquito design as a possible high-speed light bomber. For a time after the DUNKIRK evacuation, the initial order for 50 of the planes seemed destined for termination, but the project survived and a Mosquito prototype took to the air in November 1940 with Geoffrey de Havilland, elder son of Sir Geoffrey, at the controls. Instead of 50 bombers, the company was to turn out 20 bombers and 30 fighter variants, an indication of the plane's versatility. During the war the Mosquito served as bomber, fighter and reconnaissance plane.

Powered by two Rolls-Royce Merlin liquid-cooled engines, varying in output from 1,230 to 1,710 horsepower, some models were capable of maximum speeds as great as 425 miles per hour at over 25,000 feet. In appearance the Mosquito was a compact, shoulder-wing monoplane with a blister canopy that enclosed the two-man crew.

The first Mosquito to fly was the bomber prototype, which attained 400 miles per hour. In May 1942 the plane took part in its first strike of the war, a high-speed daylight attack on COLOGNE, following a 1,000-plane raid on the previous night. Among its more remarkable achievements was the September 1942 rooftop attack that destroyed GESTAPO headquarters at Oslo, Norway. Fitted with OBOE and other NAVIGATION AIDS and carrying incendiaries, the Mosquito served as a pathfinder, marking nighttime targets for British heavy bombers. The plane also proved effective in attacking V-1 sites during Operation CROSSBOW. Designed originally to carry a thousand pounds of bombs, Mosquitos with enlarged bomb bays were by the end of the war carrying 4,000-pound weapons against targets as far distant as Berlin.

The second prototype, the Mosquito fighter, had a strengthened main wing spar to permit more violent maneuvers than were executed by a bomber. Standard armament of the fighter models was four 20-mm. cannon and four .303-caliber machine guns. Fitted with RADAR, this plane roamed the skies of Europe in search of German night fighters. Mosquito fighters based in the United Kingdom received credit for destroying 60 V-1 buzz bombs and 10 times as many German planes. In addition, the Mosquito flew intruder missions, attacked trains and bridges and destroyed shipping in the European, Mediterranean and Far Eastern areas. In strikes against ships, the fighters sometimes mounted a 57-mm. gun or carried as many as eight 60-pound rockets. Since it could carry a pair of 500-pound bombs, the Mosquito fighter could serve as pathfinder or conduct precision strikes such as the February 18, 1944, attack on the Amiens jail, which breached the wall and made possible the escape of 258 FRENCH RESISTANCE fighters imprisoned there. (Unfortunately, many were recaptured and others died in the raid.)

Mosquito

The third Mosquito prototype to take to the air was the reconnaissance version, which flew for the first time in June 1941, not quite a month after the fighter. The Mosquito was so successful as a photographic plane that several bombers were converted for this purpose. Indeed, a Mosquito took the photos of PEENEMÜNDE that confirmed the existence of the V-1 flying bomb. In August 1945 a Mosquito based on the Coco Islands in the Indian Ocean flew a nine-hour, 2,600-mile mission, photographing Penang, off the Malay peninsula, and portions of the China mainland.

The only British-built fully operational aircraft to have been designed and produced between the declaration of war in 1939 and the cease-fire in 1945, the Mosquito earned renown as by far the most versatile military aircraft of the war, possibly of all time.

MOTOR GUNBOAT (MGB). British term for a small high-speed craft, similar to a PT in general characteristics but armed with automatic guns rather than torpedoes (*see* PT).

MOULD, Peter W. O. (1917–1941). RAF Flight Lieutenant Mould shot down a DORNIER Do 17 on October 30, 1939, when serving with No. 1 Squadron in France; it was the first British kill of the war. He survived the Battle of FRANCE and claimed at least seven aircraft destroyed. He was an instructor during the Battle of BRITAIN before being posted to command No. 185 Squadron in MALTA. He was presumed killed on October 1, 1941.

MOULMEIN. Important Burmese port located at the mouth of the Salween River, captured on January 31, 1942, by elements of the Japanese 15th Army in its drive to occupy BURMA, but only after fierce hand-to-hand fighting with the British defenders. The city was reoccupied peacefully by the British shortly after the formal surrender of Japan.

MOUNTBATTEN OF BURMA, Earl (Lord Louis Mountbatten) (1900–). A distinguished signal specialist, Mountbatten was at the outbreak of the Second World War captain of the 5th Destroyer Flotilla in H.M.S. *Kelly*. In 1941 he was selected to relieve Admiral of the Fleet Sir Roger KEYES in charge of combined operations, a post which in 1942 was renamed Chief of COMBINED OPERATIONS, with membership in the CHIEFS OF STAFF COMMITTEE. He was intimately concerned in the initial planning for Operation Overlord, the INVASION of northwest Europe. In 1943 he was selected, at a meeting in Quebec of Prime Minister CHURCHILL, President ROOSEVELT and the COMBINED CHIEFS OF STAFF, to become Supreme Allied Commander SOUTHEAST ASIA, and it was under his overall command that the war in this area was brought to a successful conclusion with the complete defeat of the Japanese and the recapture of SINGAPORE.

After the war Mountbatten—now Earl Mountbatten of Burma—left the naval service for a short period from March 1947 to June 1948 to become Viceroy of India and, after the grant of independence, Governor General. Subsequently he returned to the Royal Navy, rising to the post of First Sea Lord, which he relinquished in 1959 to become chairman of the Chiefs of Staff Committee.

MOUSETRAP. The U.S. Navy ahead-throwing Rocket Launcher Mark 20, developed in 1942 as a lightweight counterpart to HEDGEHOG. It was a simple fixed framework, supporting four side-by-side launching rails. Its projectile was a Hedgehog bomb with a solid-fuel rocket motor installed in its tail. Rocket propulsion eliminated the recoil of Hedgehog, which used a powder charge to launch each of its bombs. In 1943 the enlarged Mark 22 Mousetrap launcher, similar to the Mark 20 but with a double-deck arrangement of eight rocket rails, was introduced.

MOYNE, Walter Edward Guinness, Baron (1880–1944). British statesman and diplomat, Secretary of State for the Colonies, 1940–42; deputy minister of state in Cairo, 1942–44; and minister resident in the Middle East, 1944, when he was assassinated by Jewish Stern Gang terrorists. Zionist organizations later denounced the killing.

MOZHAISK. Central point of a Soviet defense line before Moscow in 1941.

MUIRHEAD-GOULD, Gerald (1887–1945). Captain in Charge, Royal Navy, at Sydney, Australia, in 1940, Muirhead-Gould remained in that post as Flag Officer in Command after his promotion to rear admiral in 1941. He had been naval attaché in Berlin between the world wars and spoke German fluently, and in 1944, when the Allied invasion of northwest Europe was going well, was recalled from Australia to be appointed Flag Officer in Charge, Western Germany. He received the surrender of Heligoland in 1945. He died of a heart attack shortly afterward.

MUKDEN INCIDENT. The affair that led to the Japanese seizure of Manchuria and thus to increased pressures for Japanese expansion in China in the 1930s. On September 18, 1931, the Japanese Army secretly dynamited a section of the Southern Manchurian Railway. The explosion was the excuse to "bring order" by sending troops to occupy the nearby town of Mukden. Although Tokyo shortly ordered the military to limit its hostilities, the Japanese Army ignored the civilian authorities and swept over the entire northern province.

MULBERRY. Code name for a type of artificial harbor designed for use in the Allied INVASION of Normandy. The intended invasion area lacked deepwater ports for unloading the vast quantities of supplies, weapons and vehicles required to support the landing forces. Two artificial harbors, called Mulberries, were planned, one each in the British and American landing areas. Old ships were sunk to form a breakwater, beginning on D-Day; these were to create areas of sheltered water where cargo ships could unload and small patrol and landing craft could take shelter from storms. Another feature of the Mulberry was its use of concrete caissons, called PHOENIXES, towed into place and sunk. Pontoon piers and causeways were also used for mooring and for landing of vehicles. A smaller artificial harbor in the American beachhead area, called a Gooseberry, was planned for small craft. The British Mulberry, off Arromanches, gave satisfactory results. The American Mulberry, off OMAHA BEACH, was less successful. It was severely damaged by a heavy storm (June 19–21, 1944) before it could be completed, and construction was abandoned. Logistic support for the American landing was provided by conventional over-the-beach means.

MULHOUSE. Alsatian city near the German frontier, taken in the Allied autumn 1944 offensive (November 22) by the French 1st Army (General LATTRE DE TASSIGNY).

MÜLLER, Heinrich (1896– ?). A former police officer in Munich who became an SS officer (*see* SS) and was put in charge of the GESTAPO in 1936. Known as "Gestapo Müller," he was notorious for his admiration of the Soviet police, and his efficient administration made the Gestapo feared throughout Germany and the German-occupied territories. Essentially the bureaucrat, he was mild-mannered and even pleasant in company. After the war he totally disappeared and was never brought to trial. Müller was directly involved in the Gleiwitz border incident, which gave HITLER his excuse for invading Poland in 1939; he provided the dozen or so condemned prisoners who were killed and then disguised as Polish corpses. Müller was last seen in the bunker with Hitler during the final days of the war; he was long thought to be dead, but a grave alleged to be his was opened by order of the authorities in 1964 and found to contain two corpses neither of which could be his. If he did survive the war, he may have fled to Latin America or the Soviet Union.

MÜLLER, Josef (1898–). Lawyer and influential member of the Catholic community in Munich, Müller was a close friend of the anti-Nazi Cardinal Michael von FAULHABER, archbishop of Munich. At the outbreak of the war, Hans OSTER enlisted his services for the ABWEHR, posting him to Rome. There he was able, through his contacts in the Vatican—notably Fr. Robert Leiber and Msgr. Ludwig Kaas—to communicate with the British in order to win the Pope's cooperation in initiating peace negotiations. These efforts were aimed at influencing the German high command to unseat Adolf HITLER. Müller composed the celebrated "X" report, which incorporated the kind of conditions to which, it was hoped, the Western Allies might agree. Müller was finally arrested in April 1943 along with other prominent dissidents in the Abwehr, notably Dietrich BONHOEFFER and Hans von DOHNANYI. Confined until the end of the war and constantly interrogated, Müller narrowly escaped execution, but survived to become one of the principal exponents of the role of the Abwehr in the German resistance. Famous for his courage and good humor, he has always been known by the nickname of his schooldays, Ochsensepp (Joe the Ox).

MUNDA. Munda, or Munda Point, is in the southwest part of NEW GEORGIA. Relatively flat and well protected from both the landward and seaward sides, it was an excellent site for an airfield. When Australian COASTWATCHERS discovered Japanese airfield construction beginning at Munda in 1942 and relayed this information to Admiral HALSEY'S SoPac headquarters, the immediate response was a series of bombing raids, which continued into 1943. Allied capture of the airfield would provide a base close to RABAUL, a major Allied objective. Accordingly, such plans were made, with D-day set for June 30, 1943. The New Georgia operation actually began on June 2, but the Munda airfield did not fall until August 5.

MUNICH AGREEMENT. The result of a four-power conference in Munich on September 29–30, 1938, at which Germany was represented by Adolf HITLER, Britain by Prime Minister Neville CHAMBERLAIN, France by Premier Edouard DALADIER and Italy by Benito MUSSOLINI. The agreement permitted Germany to annex the Sudeten area of CZECHOSLOVAKIA, which contained approximately 3 million ethnic Germans. Czechoslovakia was not represented in the deliberations.

The crisis that precipitated this agreement focused on the principle of nationality and the right of minorities to self-determination. Hitler's demand that the Sudeten Germans be included in the German Reich threatened the existence of Czechoslovakia, which had been awarded the SUDETENLAND at Versailles in 1919 for the purpose of giving her a sound strategic frontier with Germany; previously, the Sudeten territories had been a part, not of the Kaiser's Germany, but of the Austro-Hungarian Empire. Since 1934 Konrad HENLEIN'S Sudeten Nazi Party had increasingly inflamed Czecho-German relations, though the Czechs had made efforts to satisfy Sudeten German grievances.

After the German ANSCHLUSS with Austria in March 1938, the threat of a Czechoslovak-German clash over the Sudetenland intensified. With Hitler stridently demanding self-determination for the Sudeten Germans, Prime Minister Chamberlain vigorously attempted through diplomacy to defuse the crisis, which seemed likely to lead to a general war. In September Chamberlain met with Hitler at BERCHTESGADEN and at Godesberg, and he persuaded French Premier Daladier to join with Britain in pressing Czechoslovakia to cede the Sudeten region to Germany. On September 28 Hitler threatened to march into Czechoslovakia. Mobilization in Germany, Czechoslovakia and France began. Hitler's ally Mussolini suddenly became alarmed by the threat of war and spoke for a negotiated settlement. Consequently the four powers agreed to meet at Munich on September 29 to discuss the crisis. Within a little more than 12 hours Hitler, Mussolini, Chamberlain and Daladier accepted the "Mussolini" proposals, which had in fact originated in Berlin, and war was avoided.

The agreement permitted Germany to occupy the Sudetenland in four phases by October 10, 1938. The four powers agreed to establish an international commission to determine the new Czechoslovak-German border and to use plebiscites in the districts with ethnically mixed population. In a separate agreement Britain and France guaranteed the new frontier of Czechoslovakia with Germany, which Hitler and Mussolini agreed to accept, but only after disputes with Polish and Hungarian minorities in Czechoslovakia were resolved. An Anglo-German pact, which promised frequent consultation between the two powers aimed at keeping the peace in Europe, was also signed by Hitler and Chamberlain.

Under duress from her friends Britain and France, Czechoslovakia reluctantly accepted the Munich agreement, but the remainder of Europe—and the United States—breathed a sigh of relief that war had been averted.

In March 1939, as the Slovak separatists declared independence from Prague, German troops occupied the Czech lands which became the Protectorate of BOHEMIA–MORAVIA, ruled directly from Berlin. By a German-Italian "arbitrage," southern Slovak regions, populated by ethnic Magyars, were awarded to Hungary, while Poland seized the district of Teschen. Hungary also occupied Ruthenia, the easternmost province of Czechoslovakia. Encouraged by Western acquiescence in the dismemberment of Czechoslovakia, Hitler ordered, on April 1, preparations for attack on Poland.

Munich has become a symbol of weakness: democracies confronted with an aggressive totalitarian power surrendered their high principles and defaulted on their international obligations in order to appease the aggressor, and still failed to buy peace. At the time, Munich was denounced by such Western statesmen as Winston CHURCHILL and Paul REYNAUD, and it prompted Joseph STALIN, who saw in Munich the threat of an all-European alliance against the Soviet Union, to begin secret negotiations with Berlin.

MUNITIONS ASSIGNMENTS BOARD. Combined U.S.–British agency established in January 1942, with staffs in both Washington and London. It maintained a continuous inventory of American and British munitions resources and had the responsibility of allocating war material to the various Allies. Harry L. HOPKINS was the chairman.

MURMANSK RUN. The most direct route between Great Britain and the Soviet Union was by convoy around the northern tip of Norway to Murmansk. However, the weather and the danger from German U-boats, surface raiders and aircraft limited the quantity of goods that could be sent by this route. During the period June 1941 to September 1943, over one-fifth of all supplies moved by convoy to Murmansk were lost. In one convoy, PQ-17, 21 of 33 ships were lost (*see* PQ-17). It was not until late 1943 that the Royal Navy was able to stifle the German threat to the convoys. *See also* LEND-LEASE.

MURPHY, Audie (1924–1971). A native of Texas, one of the most decorated American soldiers of World War II. Murphy received the Medal of Honor for his heroism during an encounter with the Germans in eastern France in January 1945. In addition, he received 27 other decorations, including the DISTINGUISHED SERvice Cross, the Legion of Merit, the Silver Star (with Oak Leaf Cluster) and the Croix de Guerre (with palm). After the war Murphy wrote his autobiography, *To Hell and Back,* and began an acting career in which he first played himself in the film version of the book and went on to appear in some 40 movies in the 1950s and 1960s.

MURPHY, Robert D. (1894–1978). A career diplomat who worked directly with the Allied military establishments throughout most of the war, Murphy is best known for his efforts in North Africa from late 1940 until early 1943. As the senior U.S. State Department official in this complex situation, Murphy worked to win the support of the French in Africa and to further preparations for the Allied landings. This involved coordinating subversive activities, propaganda and political warfare with the military efforts. The judgment Murphy brought to these tasks is a matter of some debate. Certainly he (in step with official Washington, to be sure) was strongly opposed to General de Gaulle's Free France, and perhaps in consequence he overestimated the appeal of Gen. Henri Giraud, who proved to have no authority over the French North African forces. Stephen Ambrose, a leading Eisenhower scholar, says that Murphy "made promises he could not keep and predictions that were hopelessly mistaken."

President Roosevelt appointed Murphy as his personal representative with the rank of minister to French North Africa, and Murphy also served as the chief civil affairs officer on the staff of the Supreme Commander, Allied Force Headquarters (AFHQ). For his work in Africa he was awarded the Distinguished Service Medal in December 1942.

Murphy and his British counterpart, Harold Macmillan, were active in political-military affairs and particularly in the negotiations for the Italian armistice. In September 1943 Murphy became a member of the Mediterranean Advisory Commission with the rank of ambassador; the following month he was appointed political adviser to AFHQ, and after September 1944 he served as U.S. political adviser for Germany. His wartime experiences are recounted with thoroughness and humor in his book *Diplomat Among Warriors* (1964). After the war Murphy served as director of the Office of German and Austrian Affairs, was ambassador to Belgium and Japan and held other State Department posts.

MURRAY, George Dominic (1890–1956). Murray qualified as a naval aviator in 1915, and was in command of the carrier U.S.S. Enterprise at the time of Pearl Harbor. His planes were the only American carrier-based air involved in that battle. A rear admiral, Murray commanded a carrier task force at Santa Cruz Island in October 1942. He later worked in naval air training. He formally accepted the Japanese surrender on Truk Atoll in September 1945.

MURROW, Edward Roscoe (1908–1965). American radio broadcaster, famous for his vivid and convincing reports from London during the Blitz. "This is London," his solemn voice intoned at the beginning of each broadcast, and this introduction, which became a sort of trademark, was the call for silence in many an American household. Murrow began working for the Columbia Broadcasting System in 1935 and in 1937 became CBS director of programs in London. When Adolf Hitler took over Austria in 1938, Murrow flew to Vienna and made personal broadcasts from the city, these being among the first news broadcasts from abroad over CBS. He built a staff of radio news correspondents in Europe that became famous. When the war ended in Europe he returned to the United States to become vice-president and director of public affairs for CBS, but soon resumed active broadcasting.

Ed Murrow in London

MUSASHI. Japanese battleship, second ship of the Yamato class. She was lost in the Sibuyan Sea phase of the battle for LEYTE GULF (October 1944), after absorbing multiple torpedo and heavy-bomb hits.

MUSELIER, Émile (1882–1965). A French vice-admiral in 1939, Muselier joined General DE GAULLE following the Franco-German armistice of 1940, becoming the naval commissioner of FREE FRANCE. But he proved insubordinate to de Gaulle (whom he outranked) and separated himself from the Gaullists in 1941, losing all influence.

MUSSOLINI, Benito (1883–1945). The man who ruled Italy as Duce (Leader) for 21 years was a strange mixture of strength and weakness, confidence and uncertainty, practicality and romanticism, expediency and dogmatism. The greatest accomplishment of his public career was to restore Italy's confidence in itself after the devastating experience of World War I. His greatest mistake was to lead Italy into World War II, for which the people, the economy and the military establishment were not adequately prepared.

Mussolini was born in the province of Forli in 1883. His father was a blacksmith, antireligious and politically discontented; his mother, a strong person, was a schoolteacher. In school he showed an intelligence as lively as his temper, and by age 18 he had qualified and found work as a teacher. Restless and ambitious, he began to drift. For several years he associated with various revolutionary groups, and at 25 he joined the staff of a socialist newspaper in Trento. Two years later, when he became a secretary for the Socialist Party in Forli, he had already become strongly nationalistic and fully convinced that violence was fundamental to social change.

From that time on he lived up to the name Benito, which had been given him in honor of the Mexican revolutionary Benito Juárez. As editor of a small Socialist paper he advocated the doctrine that socialism was war and that there was no room in war for softness. His leadership in the party grew, and in 1912 he became editor of *Avanti*, the Socialist Party's official organ. He was a strong and effective journalist. Years later, when as Premier he was thanked for having received a journalist, he replied that he was a journalist by trade, and should he lose his present job it would be through journalism that he would earn his bread and butter.

At the beginning of World War I Mussolini first advocated complete neutrality, then began to call for intervention on the Allied side. He argued that war would promote social revolution in Italy, but the Socialists disagreed and he was obliged to leave *Avanti*. He promptly began publishing his own daily paper, *Il Popolo d'Italia*, advocating his interventionist beliefs. Mus-

In a daring operation on September 12, 1943, German commandos take Mussolini from Italian custody

solini insisted that a victory of Prussian reactionary principles would reduce the level of human civilization. He served in the war as a private, but was wounded and returned to his paper.

Capitalizing on postwar fears of a Bolshevist revolution and general discontent with the peace terms, Mussolini organized the Fasci di Combattimento in 1919. It was a new political movement, deriving its name from the fasces, or bundles of reeds, used by the Romans as a symbol of authority. The new Fascists were strongly nationalistic and called for a constituent assembly, the abolition of the Senate and control of the factories by the workers. When strikes threatened the country, the Fascists organized armed bands, the Black Shirts, which rapidly took over the state's function of maintaining order. As the FASCIST PARTY grew, more Fascists won seats in elections, and when a Fascist convention in Naples (October 24, 1922) offered the opportunity for a concerted march on the capital to demand power, the King asked Mussolini to form a government.

From the beginning of his leadership, Mussolini's government showed the weaknesses that eventually caused its downfall, but often they were hidden from all but the most keenly observant by a façade of progress greatly exaggerated by propaganda. Gradually Mussolini drew more and more power into his hands. The role of the cabinet decreased; a party Grand Council, with appointed members, became the most powerful body in the government. The armed squads were legitimated and became a personal army; legislative and judicial powers were shifted to the Duce; opposing political parties were outlawed. An economic reorganization, a Fascist alternative to communism or capitalism called the corporative state, put control of the government and the economy together in an ever expanding bureaucracy.

As his power increased, Mussolini became more intolerant of criticism. The greater in scope his decisions had to be, the less he was able to accept advice or help. Those around him became yes-men, strengthening his conviction that he was always right and effectively hiding from him and the public view the lack of soundness in administration and the shallowness of policy making. Although foreign statesmen were often conscious of his inconsistencies and unpredictability, Mussolini gained the admiration of both foreigners and Italians. There was little Italian protest as freedoms gave way to the repressions of a totalitarian state, and to Mussolini this was proof that the people wanted not to rule but "to be ruled and to be left in peace." "The crowd is like a woman," he once told an interviewer. "The crowd loves strong men."

Mussolini possibly could have overcome financial, administrative and economic weaknesses and turned his Fascist-corporative state into a long-term success had he not adopted an aggressive posture in foreign affairs. Until the Fascists came to power in 1922, Fascism was a movement with its goal being the attainment of power. Once power was attained, it became necessary to give Fascism some dimensions, and after borrowing bits of doctrine and philosophy from various sources, Mussolini tied them all together with bellicose nationalism. He began to extend Italy's influence in the Balkans and Austria, and by 1936 was ready for his first foreign aggression—the conquest of Ethiopia (Abyssinia). It was designed not only to erase the memory of defeat by the Abyssinians in 1896, but to launch a new Roman Empire that would recapture the grandeur that was Rome.

Between October 1935 and May 1936 the Ethiopians were systematically defeated by superior Italian arms and equipment, while the other powers watched and talked. The war was popular among Italians, and during the year after its conclusion Mussolini reached his high point in power and prestige. But having successfully defied the League of Nations over Ethiopia gave the Duce an illusion of power that increasingly marred his judgment. He intervened in the Spanish Civil War, expecting quick additional prestige; but the war was long, and Italy gained little prestige and lost appreciably in men and material. Not only did the two foreign adventures cost Italy much and profit it little, but they strained relations with France and Britain and pushed Italy closer to alliance with Germany—an alliance half feared, half desired.

Unfortunately for Italy, Mussolini was superficial in his approach to foreign relations as well as to domestic matters. Lacking broad background knowledge, he based policy on fear, prejudice and jealousy. In 1935 an ambassador described him as "the victim, not the master, of his destiny." Diametrically opposed to Germany on anti-Semitism and Pan-Germanism, thinking Adolf HITLER's racial theories ridiculous, and fundamentally disliking the Germans as aggressive and domineering, Mussolini nevertheless led Italy into the AXIS alliance in 1936.

Similarities existed between Mussolini's Italy and Hitler's Germany, but Mussolini, although senior in age and time in power, could see that after 1933 the German dictatorship was more powerful and efficient. Mussolini reacted with admiration, envy and fear, attracted to Hitler, wrote his son-in-law Count CIANO, by something "deeply rooted in his make-up." Hitler seems genuinely to have admired the Duce, acknowledging him as his only equal and granting him unswerving loyalty. By 1937, when Hitler touched Mussolini's vanity by entertaining him with an elaborate state visit, the pattern of their relationship was established. Hitler did the talking, made the decisions and told the Duce only what he chose. Mussolini listened and agreed, only to fume later, "The Germans are unbearable." Yet in Hitler's presence Mussolini was quiet and deferential. Throughout the war, whenever relations between the two dictators became strained, Hitler could restore harmony and renew his influence by a personal meeting.

Not until 1939 did the Axis alliance become a military alliance. Although his generals thought Italy's military power negligible, Hitler wanted Mussolini as an ally badly enough to woo him with patience and subtlety and, having won him, to offer him assistance in building up his war machine. Italy was in no economic or military condition to wage war, but it is difficult to determine how clearly Mussolini understood this. Ciano described him as nervous and disturbed. "Until now he had lived under the illusion that a real war would not be waged. The prospect of an imminent clash in which he might remain an outsider disturbs him and, to use his words, humiliates him."

The fear of being left out of the glory seemed the primary motivation when Mussolini declared war on

France in June 1940. He did not consult his ministers or military advisers, who had warned him that Italy was unready for war and that little of substance had been done to prepare. For even though the romantic adventurer in Mussolini could lead him to dreams of conquest, he appears to have had little practical conception of the means whereby such dreams are made reality. He believed morale to be the only thing that mattered, and he failed to see that morale would be determined in the long run by a soldier's confidence in his equipment and the chances for victory.

Italy floundered in the war. The initial attack on an already defeated France made slight gains; advances in Africa soon turned into humiliating reverses. The British crippled the Italian Mediterranean fleet. Debacle in Greece made it necessary to request German help. As early as 1942 the King, military leaders and statesmen of Italy were seeking ways to get Italy out of the war.

Mussolini himself seemed powerless. By the end of 1940 he had lost hope of bringing Italy's involvement to an honorable end. He endured the war, hating his sycophantic dependency on Germany, yet sustained and even at times buoyed by Hitler's influence and optimism. He was eager to participate when Germany invaded Russia; he cheerfully declared war on the United States. At times he lost himself in a fog of unrealities, apparently blind and deaf to the rising sentiment against him. In June 1942 he flew to Africa, where he intended to ride a white horse in a victory parade through the streets of Cairo. By the time he reached Libya, the Axis had been stopped at ALAMEIN. Mussolini considered the episode a turning point. His health collapsed; severe depression was compounded by physical suffering. He began to isolate himself, bitter and broken, to await the end.

When the Allies invaded SICILY in July 1943, the Italian leaders had the leverage they needed to act. The Fascist Grand Council met on July 24 and voted 19 to 7 for a no-confidence motion. When Mussolini reported to the King, he was put under protective arrest. The King asked Marshal BADOGLIO to form a government.

Mussolini accepted his new position quietly, without protest. He seemed resigned. But on September 12 he was "liberated" from Italian custody by Hitler's commando Otto SKORZENY and taken to Germany. There he was reunited with his wife Rachele, who had given him her loyalty, borne him six children and quietly allowed him freedom to pursue numerous romantic alliances. Mussolini seemed content, but Hitler had plans to give Fascism a rebirth, and a revivified Duce was to be the figurehead.

For the next 19 months Mussolini played the role Hitler expected of him, but not as vigorously as Hitler would have liked. The headquarters of the reborn Fascist state, the Salò Republic, was at Gargagno on Lake Garda. Like much of Mussolini's life, Salò was a sham. The most noteworthy incident was a trial in which five of the members of the Grand Council who voted against Mussolini in July 1943 were sentenced to death. His son-in-law Ciano was one of them, and of the episode Mussolini wrote, "In the many agitations of my life, what happened at Verona [the trial and execution] has been the most dramatic chapter. Sentiment and *raison d'état* have sharply collided in my spirit."

In April 1945 the Third Reich was collapsing, and Allied forces in Italy moved closer to Lake Garda. Mussolini and his government moved, but there was no place to go. On April 27 Mussolini and his mistress, Clara PETACCI, were captured by Italian partisans; on the 28th they were shot. On April 29 their bodies were hung, head down, from the girder of a filling station. That evening the bodies were removed by order of the Allied authorities, and Mussolini was secretly buried in Milan. Twelve years later the body was reburied beside his son Bruno at Predappio. The tombstone bears the emblem of the fasces. **M.H.B.**

MUTSU. Japanese battleship, second ship of the NAGATO class. She served with *Nagato* during the first year and a half of the Pacific war. In June 1943 she sank in the Inland Sea after a severe explosion, the cause of which was never determined.

MXY7. Japanese Navy designation for the OHKA suicide-attack plane.

MYOKO. Class of four Japanese heavy cruisers. These were referred to by the Allies as the NACHI class.

MYITKYINA. A town in northern BURMA, occupied by the Japanese on May 8, 1942, as they drove British and Chinese defenders from the country. Needed by the Allies in the reestablishment of a land route to China (the LEDO ROAD), Myitkyina was the object of a major Allied offensive. After a two-month siege, the town fell on August 3, 1944, but not before 972 Chinese and 272 Americans had lost their lives.

MYSHKOVA RIVER. The line reached by the German 6th Panzer Division on December 19, 1942, in the attempt to relieve the SIXTH ARMY in STALINGRAD. This line was about 30 miles from the city, and was the closest Field Marshal von MANSTEIN's relief effort was able to come.

N

N1K1. Japanese Navy Kawanishi *Kyofu* (Mighty Wind) (Allied code name, Rex), floatplane fighter that came into service in 1942. A single-engine plane with a top speed of about 300 miles per hour, the N1K1 was the basis for the land-based N1K1-J (below).

N1K1-J. Japanese Navy Kawanishi *Shiden* (Violet Lightning) (Allied code name, George) land-based fighter developed in 1943 from the N1K1 floatplane. An improved version was the N1K2-J *Shiden-Kai*, simplified for ease in production and redesigned to eliminate flaws discovered in the original *Shiden.* These fighters served in the PHILIPPINES and OKINAWA campaigns, where they gave a good account of themselves. Armed with four 20-mm. wing guns, the N1K1-J was considered one of the best Japanese fighters of the war.

NACHI. American designation for what the Japanese Navy referred to as the Myoko-class heavy cruisers *Myoko, Nachi,* HAGURO and *Ashigara*, completed in the late 1920s. Designed to combine maximum speed and hitting power within the displacement limits imposed in 1922 by international agreement (the Washington Treaty), they were better protected than the earlier AOBA class. Modified during the 1930s, they entered the Pacific war with ten 8-inch guns (5×2), eight 5-inch antiaircraft guns (4×2) and sixteen 24-inch torpedo tubes. During the war, torpedo armaments were reduced and RADAR and additional antiaircraft guns were added. *Nachi, Haguro* and *Ashigara* were war losses. *Myoko*, damaged, was surrendered at the end of the war.

NADZAB. A small settlement with an airfield northwest of LAE on the HUON PENINSULA of NEW GUINEA. It was the scene of the first Allied airborne operation in the Pacific, on September 5, 1943, when the U.S. 503d Parachute Regiment was dropped on the airfield. Later in the day the 7th Australian Division was flown in and helped to capture Lae.

NAFUTAN POINT. On the extreme southeast corner of SAIPAN, the area was wrongly believed by the Americans to be heavily defended by Japanese troops. But as the attacking U.S. forces pushed inland, the defenders employed a holding action and then withdrew to previously prepared positions on Nafutan, where they put up a fanatic resistance to the attacking 27th Division, June 18–27, 1944.

NAGA HILLS. A spur of the Himalayas whose peaks form part of the border between India (Assam) and BURMA, the Naga Hills barrier was one reason why communications between the two countries were exceedingly difficult. The LEDO ROAD—conceived by Lt. Gen. Joseph W. STILWELL and the key to the resupply of China beginning in January 1945—crossed this formidable range of mountains.

NAGANO, Osami (1880–1947). Japanese naval officer who during the 1920s and 1930s held increasingly important positions and became involved in diplomacy and naval planning and development. He opposed alliance with Germany and Italy and favored coming to terms with the United States, but when diplomacy failed he urged forceful expansion into the Pacific and Southeast Asia. He supported Admiral YAMAMOTO's plans to attack PEARL HARBOR. Accused by the Allied powers of being a war criminal, Admiral Nagano died while on trial in Tokyo in 1947. He had held almost every post of consequence in the Japanese Navy, including director of the Naval Academy, Navy Minister in the Hirota cabinet in 1936, Commander in Chief of the COMBINED FLEET in 1937, and Chief of the Naval General Staff from April 9, 1941, to February 21, 1944.

NAGARA. Class of Japanese light cruisers, similar to the earlier TENRYU and KUMA classes in general appearance (over 5,500 tons, seven 5.5-inch guns) but armed with eight 24-inch torpedo tubes. Like other light cruisers of their age, they were used in cruiser forces and as destroyer squadron flagships. *Yura*, of this class, was lost in October 1942. *Nagara*, with sister ships *Abukuma, Isuzu, Kinu* and *Natori*, had her torpedo battery increased to 24 tubes (6×4) and her antiaircraft defense strengthened. All the rest but *Isuzu* were lost during 1944; *Isuzu* followed in April 1945.

NAGASAKI. When the HIROSHIMA bomb (August 6, 1945) failed to bring about an immediate Japanese surrender, the United States launched a second atomic attack. The primary target was Kokura, site of an Army arsenal, with the industrial city of Nagasaki as alternate. Selected to deliver the 10,000-pound FAT MAN, the only atomic weapon then available, was Maj. Charles W. Sweeney, who traded B-29s with Capt. Frederick C. Bock and flew *Bock's Car* instead of his usual plane, *The Great Artiste*.

The weather over Kokura on August 9 was unsuitable for bombing, so Sweeney flew to cloud-blanketed Nagasaki, where his bombardier, Capt. Kermit Beahan, found a hole in the overcast and, at 1058 Nagasaki time, released the bomb. Since they did not have fuel enough for the return flight to Tinian, Sweeney and Bock, who flew the observation plane, diverted to Okinawa and landed safely.

Because broken terrain checked the blast effect, structural damage at the more modern city of Nagasaki was less than at Hiroshima. Nevertheless, known dead numbered 23,753 and the injured 23,345. Estimates of total casualties vary widely.

NAGATO. Class of Japanese battleships, of about 37,000 tons, with eight 16-inch guns. The first Japanese 16-inch-gun battleships, *Nagato* and *Mutsu* were completed after World War I. They were modernized before World War II and made up a battleship division of the COMBINED FLEET; before the commissioning of *Yamato, Nagato* was the fleet's flagship. *Matsu* was destroyed by an explosion. *Nagato* survived the war in damaged condition and was sunk at Bikini during the 1946 atomic tests.

NAGOYA. One of the three targets of the American 1942 Doolittle raid (*see* FIRST SPECIAL AVIATION PROJECT), this Japanese industrial city was devastated by incendiary bombing during the night of March 10–11, 1945. *See also* STRATEGIC BOMBING.

NAGUMO, Chuichi (1887–1944). As commander of Japan's 1st Air Fleet, Nagumo, a vice-admiral, was in direct charge of the attacks on PEARL HARBOR, Northwest Australia, the Netherlands East Indies, India and Ceylon between December 1941 and May 1942. A strong advocate of combining air and sea power, Nagumo commanded Japanese forces in their greatest victories. Following his loss of four carriers at the Battle of MIDWAY, Nagumo appears to have lost his aggressiveness and effectiveness. Relieved of the command of Japan's carrier force in 1943, Nagumo was placed in charge of a small naval flotilla in the Marianas. He committed suicide with a pistol on July 1, 1944, on Saipan, just before the American invasion.

Admiral Nagumo

NAHA. The largest city on OKINAWA as well as in the Ryukyu Islands, Naha boasted a fine harbor and airfield, both tactical objectives of the U.S. TENTH ARMY. Units of the 6th Marine Division captured Naha on May 27, 1945.

NAMBU. Term applied to the Japanese 8-mm. service semiautomatic pistol, from the name of its designer, Col. Kijiro Nambu. It was also widely applied to the 6.5-mm. Model 11 light machine gun, commonly called Nambu Keiki (a contraction of Nambu Keikikanju, or Nambu machine gun) by the Japanese.

NAMHKAM. Situated in northern BURMA on the border with China (Yunnan province), Namhkam was occupied by the Japanese in May 1942 as they completed their invasion of Burma. Its recapture was planned for mid-December 1944 as part of the NORTHERN COMBAT AREA COMMAND's portion of Operation CAPITAL. Actual Allied reoccupation occurred on January 15, 1945, when the Chinese 30th Division took the town with ease.

NAMSOS. Norwegian timber port, northeast of TRONDHEIM and about 20 miles from the mouth of the Namsenfjord. Namsos, which is near good anchorage and is on a railroad, was selected as the site of Allied landings for Operation MAURICE in the 1940 NORWAY campaign.

NAMUR. At the northernmost part of KWAJALEIN Atoll, Namur Island is joined to ROI by a narrow causeway and a strip of beach. The Japanese had constructed numerous concrete buildings on the island, which was also covered with palms, breadfruit trees and brush. It was assaulted by the U.S. 24th Marines on February 1, 1944, and secured the next day.

NAN. Technical code name applied to infrared signaling equipment developed and used by the U.S. Navy. It included signal searchlights, yardarm beacons and portable beach markers for use in landing operations. NAN equipment was familiarly nicknamed Nancy, a term applied to infrared signaling in general.

NANCY. The historic metropolis of the portion of eastern France known as Lorraine, Nancy was a primary objective in General PATTON's U.S. THIRD ARMY drive through France to Germany. An important highway and railroad center, Nancy itself was occupied without opposition by a Third Army task force on September 15, 1944. It had been evacuated by the German First Army under Gen. der Panzertruppen Otto von KNOBELSDORFF in favor of more important defensive positions.

NANKING. City on the Yangtze River, capital of China from 1928 until the Nationalist government withdrew to Hankow in 1937. In December 1937 Nanking fell to the Japanese, a capitulation accompanied by atrocities on a huge scale (about 42,000 civilians were massacred by Japanese soldiers). On December 12 Japanese planes sank the U.S. gunboat *Panay* near Nanking; two British ships were also attacked. In 1940 the Japanese made Nanking the seat of the puppet government they established under WANG CHING-WEI.

NAPALM. A powdered gasoline thickener, a metallic salt derived from naphtha, used in American fire bombs and flamethrower fuel. Early in the war, combat units used oil, sometimes in combination with lime and rosin, to help the gasoline used in these weapons stick to the surfaces upon which it fell and to make it burn more intensely. Gradually napalm came to refer to the thickened gasoline as well as to the thickener itself.

The earliest of the so-called napalm bombs were auxiliary fuel tanks filled with the liquid and ignited by a bomb fuze or white phosphorus grenade. Sometimes barrels of napalm were dropped on a target and ignited by machine-gun fire. At the end of the war, however, two standard types of bombs were in use. One consisted of an M-47 casing for a 100-pound gasoline bomb (the key bomb used by U.S. B-29 pathfinders [*see* B-29] to mark the center of Tokyo with a rough, blazing X in the great fire raid on March 10, 1945) filled with 69 pounds of the thicker napalm. The other was the 500-pound M-76, which contained an explosive charge that scattered gobs of burning napalm over a radius of 100 feet.

NAPLES. The King's Dragoon Guards (British) of the U.S. Fifth Army entered Naples on October 1, 1943. Allied salvage specialists, under the command of Commo. William A. Sullivan, efficiently restored the port to usable condition, and it was thereafter of prime importance to the Anglo-American armies.

NAQB EL DWEIS. Southernmost "box" in the Alamein defense line, Egypt.

NARA, Akira (1888–1964). A graduate of the Japanese Military Academy (1911) and the War College (1920), Lieutenant General Nara took command of the 65th Brigade in November 1941. He commanded this force in the 1942 fighting on the Bataan Peninsula. He retired from active duty in late 1942.

NAREW RIVER. German defense line in Poland, north of Warsaw, 1944–45.

NARVIK. Located on a peninsula in the Ofotfjord at the inner end of the Arctic Vestfjord, Narvik was the Norwegian terminus of the single-track Lapland Railroad. It was over this line that Swedish iron ore traveled to the ore-crushing plants located in Narvik. Anchorage was available for 30 ships. Since Narvik was the only ice-free port through which Swedish iron ore could pass to Germany, in late 1939 the British Ministry of Economic Warfare determined that loss of the use of the Narvik port would have a serious effect on German industry. Early in 1940 plans were made to land the main portion of an Allied relief expedition to Finland at Narvik; but the Finns surrendered to the USSR before the plan could be executed. Narvik fell to the Germans on April 9 after a struggle that cost almost 300 Norwegian lives. The city was retaken by the Allies on May 28, but within a few days they evacuated it because of the collapse on the Western Front. German troops reentered the town on June 6. *See also* Norway.

NARWHAL, U.S.S. Submarine, commissioned in 1930, one of two large submarines built as long-range "cruiser subs." *Narwhal* and her sister Nautilus were 371 feet long, displaced 2,730 tons (surfaced) and had ten 21-inch torpedo tubes and the heavy surface armament of two 6-inch guns. During 1942 and the first part of 1943 *Narwhal* made six war patrols in the Pacific. Among her accomplishments was the landing of Army scouts on Attu Island in the Aleutians for a preliminary reconnaissance before the actual assault on the island. Her last nine war patrols (October 1943–October 1944) were clandestine supply and evacuation missions in support of the Filipino resistance movement.

NASHVILLE, U.S.S. Brooklyn-class light cruiser, commissioned in 1938. After Neutrality Patrol service in the Atlantic during 1941, *Nashville* spent the first three months after Pearl Harbor on convoy escort duty. She then escorted carrier Hornet during the April 1942 Doolittle raid on Japan (*see* First Special Aviation Project). *Nashville* operated in the Aleutians during the summer and fall of 1942; in December she began operations in the Solomons area. During a night bombardment in May 1943 a powder explosion killed or wounded 35 men in one of her forward turrets. After repairs and overhaul she joined the Fast Carrier Task Force in air strikes against Marcus and Wake Islands. From late 1943 into 1944, *Nashville* provided gunfire support to operations in New Guinea and the central Solomons; she was Gen. Douglas MacArthur's flagship during the landings at Hollandia, Tanahmerah Bay and Aitape in April 1944. She again flew MacArthur's flag during landings on Morotai (September 1944) and during the Leyte landings (October).

While steaming toward Mindoro as flagship of the Visayan Attack Force on December 13, 1944, *Nashville* was hit by a kamikaze, which crashed into the open upper deck amidships, where much of her antiaircraft battery was sited in open positions. Explosions and a raging gasoline fire killed or injured 323 of her crew. A period of major repairs followed, and *Nashville* returned to the Pacific in time to cover landings on Borneo and take part in occupation duty at Shanghai. She made two transpacific voyages with troops returning to the United States; during her second she took a crippled transport in tow and brought her safely to San Francisco. Decommissioned in 1946, she was sold to Chile in 1951, serving afterward as *Capitán Prat*.

NASU, Yumio (1892–1942). A graduate of the Japanese Military Academy (1913) and the War College (1923), Major General Nasu became commander of the 2d Infantry Corps in November 1940. In that capacity he participated in the Guadalcanal campaign. He was killed in action in October 1942 and was promoted to lieutenant general posthumously.

NATIONAL COMMITTEE FOR FREE GERMANY. Organized in Moscow in July 1943 from prominent anti-Nazi officers captured by the Red Army (including such personalities as Field Marshal Paulus), the Free Germany Committee, as it was commonly called, became an important part of the Soviet propaganda effort directed against Adolf Hitler's regime. The committee's appeals to German soldiers to defect met only limited success because the well-founded fear of Soviet captivity was widespread in the Wehrmacht. With the exception of a few members who joined the ranks of German Communists, the committee had no role in the postwar organization of the Soviet zone of occupation of Germany.

NATIONAL GUARD. A reserve component of the United States Army. It is under state control in peacetime and an Army component only when called up to active federal service. The National Guard was ordered into active military service for one year (later extended to the duration of the war) by a joint resolution of Congress, approved August 27, 1940. Induction began on September 16, 1940, and continued through a number of months. A total of 300,034 men were brought into federal service in formed and trained units, comprising 18 combat divisions and 143 nondivisional units. The divisions were the 26th through the 38th, the 40th and 41st, and the 43d through the 45th. Since the Army was reducing the number of organic divisional infantry regiments from four to three when the Guard was called in, a number of the Guard regiments were surplus. These were used as cadres to form other divisions. National Guard units participated in 34 separate campaigns and seven assault landings, winning 148 DISTINGUISHED UNIT CITATIONS, and 14 Guardsmen won the MEDAL OF HONOR.

NATIONAL REDOUBT (Alpine Redoubt). Over a period of time Allied intelligence received a number of reports which indicated that a sizable German force, said to be largely composed of the best men from SS and Gestapo units, would attempt to prolong the war indefinitely. These troops would move to the mountainous area of southern Bavaria, western Austria and northern Italy, and prepare to withstand a siege. As the industrial and agricultural resources of the region were scant, most intelligence officers discounted any threat of long duration. Since the terrain was excellent for any type of resistance, however, the area was cleared. It was later determined that though some devout Nazis had pushed for a full-fledged Alpine redoubt, no formal plan for such a scheme ever existed.

NATIONAL SERVICE ACT. The (British) National Service Act of September 3, 1939, made all men between the ages of 19 and 41 eligible for military service and based deferment on occupation. This law proved inadequate and was changed in December 1941 to provide more manpower. The upper age limit was raised to 61, and women between the ages of 20 and 30 were to be compelled to serve in the auxiliary services, civil defense or industrial jobs.

NATIONAL SOCIALIST GERMAN WORKERS' PARTY (Nationalsozialistische Deutsche Arbeiterpartei). On March 7, 1918, Anton Drexler, a Munich locksmith, established a Committee of Independent Workers in order to develop a nationalist viewpoint among working-class Germans. This led to the founding in January 1919 of the German Workers' Party, which Drexler set up along with a journalist, Karl Harrer. Activity was confined to beer-hall discussions and membership was sparse when Adolf HITLER, then an instructor in the political department of the Army's Munich District Command, was sent to observe one of the party's meetings. During the meeting (September 12, 1919) he became enraged by a suggestion that Bavaria should separate from the Reich, and spoke so vehemently that he was invited to meet the organizing committee, made up of six men. Hitler became the committee's seventh member and a speaker for the group, taking charge of the party's propaganda in 1920. Trying out his capacity as an orator and agitator, he held some 2,000 people spellbound at a meeting on February 24. In effect, Hitler was to take over the organization of this obscure and ill-defined political group; he ousted his associates and renamed the party the National Socialist German Workers' Party, or Nazi Party, at the same time resigning from the Army and devoting himself to full-time political activity. He issued an initial 25-point program along strongly nationalist lines. A parallel movement had also developed in Vienna and in the Sudetenland, the Viennese being the first to use the swastika (Hakenkreuz), in 1918. The movements did not amalgamate at this stage, but kept in touch.

Meanwhile in Munich the party developed in some strength, aided by the presence of an Army officer with FREE CORPS connections, Capt. Ernst RÖHM. Former Free Corps men joined the party in some numbers, forming strong-arm groups—the Sturmabteilung; (*see* SA)—to protect their political meetings. The party acquired its own newspaper, the *Völkischer Beobachter* (the name means "People's Observer," "people's" having some connotation of racial orientation), with secret financial aid from the Army and from Dietrich Eckart, a nationalist writer who became editor. In July 1921 Hitler became the elected president of the party. The socialist element in the party program was spurious, a sop to win support from the working class, though Hitler wanted support from all sections of society.

Other early recruits to party membership were the former Army officers Rudolf HESS and Hermann GÖRING, and the party began to attract financial support from certain wealthy right-wing families, into whose homes Hitler was invited as a rising star in politics. He also formed an association with the violently nationalist General Ludendorff. This connection encouraged him to stage the abortive Munich putsch of November 1923. This coup aimed at supplanting the Bavarian state government, with a view to overthrowing in turn the republican government in Berlin. Both the party and the *Völkischer Beobachter* were in consequence banned, and Hitler was arrested. He resigned from the party leadership for the duration of his confinement in LANDSBERG castle, though he used his trial to enhance his personal position as a national political figure. His year's incarceration during 1924 in Landsberg led to the party's temporary disintegration, though in any case it was illegal. It had to be totally reorganized by Hitler in 1925, following his release: "I shall need five years before the movement is on top again," he said.

Hitler also assumed leadership of the Austrian Nazi Party at this stage (1926). In Germany a system of party gauleiters (district leaders) was set up throughout the country to organize meetings and rallies and conduct propaganda. Joseph GOEBBELS was made gauleiter of Berlin in 1926. Party headquarters were established in the Brown House in Munich, and a succession of rallies were held in Weimar (1926) and in Nuremberg (1927, 1929, 1933), growing in strength and becoming annual during the mid-1930s. Other annual events included the rally of party veterans in November at the Bürgerbräukeller in Munich to commemorate the 1923 putsch.

The years 1925 to 1931 were the years of Hitler's success in the often difficult and frustrating task of rebuilding the party. His policy now was to achieve power through "legal" means, that is, by manipulation of the Constitution. His platform was based mainly on hostility to the Weimar government, to the Versailles treaty and to the Marxists, whom Hitler chose to identify with the Jews. He managed to increase the party's share of the national vote out of all recognition between 1928 and July 1932. Party membership rose between 1925 and 1929 from 27,000 to 178,000, and the Nazis hotly contested elections on the federal, state and municipal levels, with gradually increasing success from 1930. But their success in the Reichstag elections was phenomenal, going from 810,000 votes in 1928 to almost 13.75 million in July 1932. In the subsequent election (November 1932), however, the Nazis lost ground, their vote dropping by some 2 million and the number of their deputies correspondingly reduced from 230 to 196. Their success had in fact been closely related to the rise of unemployment; in November the economic recession was ending. Hitler, as party leader, also contested the presidency against Hindenburg in 1932, losing the election but nonetheless achieving 13.4 million votes (more than 36 percent of those cast). With hectic maneuvering behind the scenes, playing off the successive Chancellors, PAPEN and Schleicher, against each other, Hitler won the Chancellorship and pushed the party vote up to 17.3 million in the Reichstag election of March 5, 1933. Following the REICHSTAG FIRE of February 27, most of the Communist deputies and his key opponents among the Social Democrats had been ousted, and the ENABLING ACT, making him a dictator who could rule by decree, was passed on March 24, 1933. In the last free vote cast by the German electorate, therefore, Hitler achieved 6 million additional votes, representing support by 44 percent of the electorate. By a decree of July 14, 1933, the Nazi Party was constituted the only political party in Germany.

Thereafter, the organization of the party and the state gradually merged, with Hitler ruling by decree. Hess became deputy head of the party (and in effect its controller on Hitler's behalf, with Martin BORMANN as his principal aide). On the death of President von Hindenburg, Hitler made himself Führer, Chancellor and Commander in Chief of the Army, as well as leader of the party in a one-party system. The party, however, kept its identity throughout the regime, with all those occupying key positions, however minor (such as civil servants and teachers), required to be party members. The gauleiters, as district party representatives, were powerful figures until the end of the war. Hitler in his will bequeathed the party leadership to Bormann, who held this office nominally during the last hours of the Nazi Reich. **R.M.**

NATIONAL WAR LABOR BOARD. U.S. agency established on January 12, 1942, succeeding the National Defense Mediation Board. In addition to its mediating function in labor disputes, it acquired the power of regulating wage increases and decreases. Membership included four representatives each from industry, labor and the public. William H. Davis was the chairman.

NAUTILUS, U.S.S. Submarine commissioned in 1930. The sister ship of NARWHAL, *Nautilus* took part in the MIDWAY campaign. With submarine *Argonaut*, she transported marines to MAKIN in August 1942 for a raid on that atoll. In September 1943 she conducted a photoreconnaissance of the GILBERTS in preparation for the coming capture of that island group. In November, just before the first Gilbert landings, *Nautilus* put a landing force ashore on APAMAMA. Like *Narwhal, Nautilus* now began a series of supply missions in support of the Filipino underground, making six such trips altogether.

NAVAL DISTRICT. A U.S. Navy shore-based command responsible for military control of naval activities within a specific area of United States territory. The district commandant's duties involved local defense; transportation and logistic support for district and other naval forces; communications; and local administrative services. Such activities as shipbuilding and ship maintenance at navy yards came under the military command of district commandants.

The naval district system was inaugurated in 1903; by 1940 there were 16 numbered districts, whose areas of responsibility ranged from upper New England (1st Naval District, headquartered at Boston) to the Philippines (16th Naval District, with headquarters at Cavite). On December 8, 1941, naval activities in the Washington and Annapolis areas were formally constituted as the Severn River Naval Command (SRNC) and Potomac River Naval Command (PRNC), both separate entities amounting to miniature naval districts. Some changes took place in district boundaries during the war years. The 16th Naval District became a dead letter when the Japanese occupied the Philippines, and was not reestablished when the islands were recaptured in 1944–45. On April 15, 1944, Alaska and the Aleutians, originally part of the 13th District, became a new 17th District. By agreement with the governments involved, the waters off Venezuela and the Guianas, as well as Bermuda and Newfoundland, were included in naval districts for defensive and shipping-control purposes on a temporary basis after Pearl Harbor.

When the SEA FRONTIERS were established in 1941 and assumed overall responsibility for offshore defense, naval district commandants became task group commanders under the overall control of the sea frontier commanders in charge of their areas.

NAVICERT. A system begun by the British at the beginning of the European war of inspecting cargoes of merchant ships flying neutral flags. This was done either at the loading port or at designated contraband-control points. Ships receiving a clean bill of health from the contraband standpoint were given an inspection certificate, called a Navicert for short. This was intended to reduce, if not eliminate, the need for at-sea searches of neutral shipping.

NAVIGATION AIDS. In summer 1940 the Germans introduced a navigation aid, accurate to within one square mile, for the night bombardment of urban areas. Called Knickebein (crooked leg), the system featured two intersecting radio beams. The bomber followed the first beam—a continuous tone delineated by a series of Morse code dashes on one edge and dots on the other—until it encountered the second, which had a distinctly different tone. Generally the beams crossed a short distance from the target, and the raider flew a prescribed course for a given time before releasing its bombs.

Alert to the possible existence of such a device, the British in June presumed that it existed, and they promptly began developing countermeasures. At first, they resorted to improvised jamming devices—medical diathermy sets installed in automobiles and at police stations within likely target areas—in an attempt to blot out the radio beams. More successful were the attempts to distort the German signal instead of drowning it out. Radio transmitters in the United Kingdom broadcast the German signal, broadening the beam until it was too wide to provide the necessary accuracy. This practice was called bending the beam. Another countermeasure was to introduce a false cross beam, so that the enemy would drop his bombs some distance from the intended target. The leader in these efforts was the young scientist R. V. Jones (b. 1911).

The Germans also used a series of direction-finding stations on the Continent, each with its own signal, to enable bomber crews to obtain periodic radio fixes and accurately determine the position of their aircraft. The British reacted by broadcasting stronger signals that masked the German signals and caused navigators to miscalculate their position.

The LUFTWAFFE countered with a new system that was more difficult to jam. Within a wide masking beam the Germans transmitted, on a different frequency, a narrow guidance beam that was intersected by three other beams. The first two provided warning; then, upon receipt of the third signal, the bombardier set a device that automatically released the bombs after the plane had flown a prescribed time.

When British countermeasure transmitters proved able to confuse this latest method of navigating, the Germans eliminated the cross beams, employing instead ranging signals that enabled the crew to check the distance flown along the main beam. By this time, however, the bombing offensive against Britain was ending.

In the meantime, the RAF BOMBER COMMAND had discovered that normal methods of aerial navigation were pitifully inaccurate for night bombardment missions over Germany and occupied Europe. One solution was Gee, a navigation aid tested in the summer of 1941 and put into general use in March of the following year. This system employed paired master and slave stations in the United Kingdom and an airborne receiver that converted the radio signals into pulses visible on a cathode-ray tube. The navigator plotted on a special chart the time interval between signals from the paired stations in order to calculate his position relative to them. Until the Germans began jamming it, Gee was a valuable short-range navigation aid, but it was not accurate enough for blind bombing.

Next came Oboe, based on the latest German method, which entered service in December 1942 and proved more accurate than Gee. A control station in the United Kingdom broadcast a directional beam for the Oboe-equipped bomber and tracked the plane on radar. The controller was able to guide the bomber directly to its target. Because the radar wave did not conform to the curvature of the earth, Oboe was limited in range. Also, a control station could handle only one aircraft at a time.

MOSQUITO bombers used a variant of Oboe, called G-H. With this set, distance measuring and computation of the plane's position was done by the crew rather than at the ground station.

January 1943 saw the introduction of H_2S, which had no range limitation since it was an airborne RADAR installed in the bomber. This navigation aid stemmed from a search radar used by COASTAL COMMAND aircraft to detect vessels on the surface of the sea. A rotating H_2S transmitter scanned the ground and a receiver picked up the radar return, displaying it on a cathode tube. Land, urban areas and water gave distinctive images, which the navigator used, in conjunction with maps, to establish the position of his aircraft. Seldom was the H_2S picture clear enough or in sufficient detail to permit precision bombing, and navigational accuracy varied according to the skill of the operator in interpreting the radar image.

As early as September 1943 American bombers of the EIGHTH AIR FORCE had used H_2S, but the British, barely able to meet their own needs, could not furnish sets to their American ally. Fortunately, the Radiation Laboratory of the Massachusetts Institute of Technology developed an improved version, H_2X. Manufactured in the United States, H_2X was tested in November 1943 by Pathfinder B-17s (*see* B-17) in an attack on Wilhelmshaven. Pathfinders carrying H_2X—or sometimes Oboe, G-H or H_2S—helped the Eighth Air Force sustain its share of the COMBINED BOMBER OFFENSIVE regardless of cloud cover.

A further refinement in navigation aids was Micro-H, a combination of G-H and H_2X introduced by Eighth Air Force Liberators in November 1944. The bombers followed G-H beams emanating from stations in France until roughly 35 miles from the target. At this point, the navigator switched to H_2X.

In the Pacific, B-24s (*see* B-24) carrying H_2X saw action over Formosa. The B-29s (*see* B-29) that attacked Japan also carried radar, the AN/APQ-13, which was suitable for area bombing even though it lacked the clear definition of a genuine radar bombsight. LORAN, long-range air navigation, was particularly helpful during night attacks, when cloud cover over Japan tended to dissipate, thus reducing atmospheric interference with the signal. Developed by the U.S. Navy, loran utilized ground stations at known locations, special plotting charts and an airborne receiver with a cathode tube. The system was similar in operation to the British Gee. **B.C.N.**

NAVY ARMED GUARD. U.S. Navy gun crews, placed on board merchant ships to give them some measure of self-defense capability. They were the American counterparts to the British DEFENSIVELY EQUIPPED MERCHANT SHIP organization. Depending on their size and expected area of operation, as well as on the availability of appropriate ordnance, ships were armed with various .30- and .50-caliber machine guns, as well as 20- and 40-mm. automatic guns and 3-, 4- and 5-inch naval guns. As in England, automatic antiaircraft guns were in short supply until production could match the urgent demands of the combatant fleets.

NAVY CROSS. U.S. Navy decoration, established in 1919, for "extraordinary heroism in connection with military operations against an armed enemy." Ranked between the MEDAL OF HONOR and the DISTINGUISHED SERVICE MEDAL, it was thus the Navy's second-highest award.

NAVY UNIT COMMENDATION. A U.S. Navy and Marine Corps citation, authorized by the Secretary of the Navy on December 18, 1944. Ranking second to the PRESIDENTIAL UNIT CITATION, it was to be awarded to any ship, aircraft or other unit which, after December 7, 1941, distinguished itself by "outstanding heroism in action against the enemy, but not sufficiently to justify the Presidential Unit Citation." A unit could also earn it for outstanding work not involving actual combat, but "in support of military operations." It was considered the equivalent of the award of a SILVER STAR or LEGION OF MERIT to an individual.

NAZI PARTY. *See* NATIONAL SOCIALIST GERMAN WORKERS' PARTY.

NAZI-SOVIET PACT. *See* SOVIET-GERMAN NON-AGGRESSION PACT.

NEALE, Robert H. American fighter pilot who flew with the AMERICAN VOLUNTEER GROUP (the Flying Tigers) and was the unit's highest scorer, downing 16 Japanese aircraft.

NEAME, Sir Philip (1888–1978). General Neame was put in command of the stripped-down British Desert Force in CYRENAICA at the end of February 1941. The Commander in Chief Middle East, General WAVELL, cognizant of the force's weakness, ordered Neame to fight a delaying action and retreat, conserving forces, should an enemy attack be made. General ROMMEL's first offensive began March 31. Wavell sent General O'CONNOR to the front to assist Neame, but both were taken prisoner by the Axis on April 6. Although Neame lacked prior experience with mechanized desert warfare, his peers have judged that he handled the retreat as well as could be done with existing forces.

NEBE, Artur (1894–1945). German police official who was chief of the Berlin criminal police before the Nazis came to power. In 1933 he became chief of the criminal police of the Reich. A nominal member of the Nazi Party, as a General der Polizei he held corresponding rank in the SS (*see* SS), and in 1941–42 he was in charge of some of the notorious ACTION GROUPS in Minsk and Smolensk (though he is said to have led these murder squads as "humanely" as possible). He had some involvement with the OPPOSITION TO HITLER, saving some leaders through timely warnings. He was found out, sentenced to death by a Nazi court and executed.

NEBELWERFER. Although this German term literally means "smoke thrower" and the first Nebelwerfers were chemical mortars, the name came to be applied to rocket launchers—particularly the 150-mm. Nebelwerfer 41 and its 210-mm. successor. The rockets launched by the six-barrel weapon produced a screeching sound, hence the nickname by Allied troops, "screaming meemies." The 41 was fired at a rate of six rounds every 90 seconds and had a range up to about 7,700 yards.

NEGER. German one-man midget surface torpedo boat. *See also* MIDGET SUBMARINE.

NEGROS. After the Japanese conquest of the PHILIPPINES in 1942, a large number of Filipino troops on this island in the Visayan group did not surrender but instead came to form the nucleus of a guerrilla force under Lt. Col. Salvador Abcede (Philippine Army). In March 1945 the Japanese garrison on the island numbered nearly 15,000, including an infantry brigade, while Colonel Abcede had about 14,000 guerrillas under his command, over half of them armed one way or another. The U.S. 40th Division began landing on Negros on March 29. A vicious battle ensued in the mountains of northwestern Negros, but by June 2 the Americans had overcome most of the organized opposition.

NEHRING, Walther (1892–). German panzer commander and staff officer (General der Panzertruppen, 1942) who was commanding officer of the AFRIKA KORPS under Field Marshal Erwin ROMMEL, the commander in chief of German forces in NORTH AFRICA. Nehring was wounded in the Battle of ALAM HALFA on August 31, 1942. In November 1943 he was placed in temporary command of Axis forces in TUNISIA, successfully parrying Allied attacks. On December 9, 1943, he was succeeded as Axis commander by Gen. Jürgen von ARNIM. Nehring subsequently commanded the XXIV Panzer Corps on the Eastern Front.

NEHRU, Jawaharlal (1889–1964). After a legal education in England, Nehru returned to his native India to participate in the movement for Indian independence. He was president of the Indian Congress party twice and was the most important national leader next to Mohandas GANDHI. Nehru sought complete independence for India rather than dominion status, which had been Gandhi's aim, and was much more radical in demanding a socialist, nationalist and strong anti-British program. After the Congress party adopted a civil disobe-

British soldier demonstrates the operation of a Nebelwerfer

dience campaign in 1942, Nehru and other leaders were arrested and sent to prison; he was not released until June 1945. In 1946 he was named president of the Congress party. In 1947 he bacame the first Prime Minister of independent India.

NEISSE RIVER. Two rivers of this name flow into the Oder River, one to the east of Breslau (now Wroclaw, Poland), the other considerably to the west. They figured in sometimes ambiguous discussions between the Western Allies and the Soviet Union concerning the fixing of the western boundary of postwar Poland. In spite of Anglo-American protests, the line Oder–Western Neisse became the boundary.

NELSON, Donald Marr (1888–1959). A native of Missouri and an executive of Sears, Roebuck and Co. who in 1940 served as U.S. Coordinator of Defense Purchases, where his knowledge virtually revolutionized practices in the defense program. When the WAR PRODUCTION BOARD was created in January 1942, Nelson was appointed chairman, with full authority over the armament program. The difficult and controversial position made him virtual dictator of American industry, with responsibility for the production of planes, tanks, guns, merchant ships and all other munitions and equipment. The monetary commitments under his authority were approximately $150 billion and involved what were considered drastic moves, such as his curtailment or restriction of the production of automobiles, refrigerators, typewriters, radios and other articles for civilian use in order to increase the production of war materials.

In the summer of 1944 a dispute erupted between the WPB and the Army and Navy concerning the WPB's plans to allow limited reconversion to peacetime production. Nelson had long felt that the services desired too great a degree of domination over production; their opposition to his announced plans seemed a fresh instance of this. But he failed to receive the support of the President, and was dispatched on a special mission to China, being succeeded as chairman of the WPB by Julius A. Krug.

NELSON, H.M.S. Royal Navy battleship of 34,000 tons, completed by Armstrong in 1927, armed with nine 16-inch (all forward), twelve 6-inch and six 4.7-inch guns, numerous smaller weapons, two 24.5-inch torpedo tubes and one aircraft. From 1939 to 1942 *Nelson* served in the Home Fleet. She participated in the August 1942 convoy to MALTA (*see* PEDESTAL) and was transferred to the Mediterranean FORCE H in 1943, assisting in the Sicilian and the various Italian landings; she then returned to home waters for bombardment support for the Normandy landings. After refit in the United States, *Nelson* was sent to the Far East; her slow speed, however, limited her employment to subsidiary operations off Sumatra and Malaya.

NEPTUNE. Code name for the naval side of Operation Overlord, the Allied INVASION of northwest Europe in 1944. The naval Allied commander in chief was Adm. Sir Bertram RAMSAY, who had planned and directed the North African and Sicilian assaults. His main task was to organize the naval aspect of the assault—putting five divisions ashore simultaneously on the coast of Normandy, supporting their landing with heavy naval gunfire, sweeping lanes through the German minefields through which the assault craft and supporting ships could steam in safety, removing the underwater obstacles with which the Germans had obstructed the beaches—and to direct the vast business of landing the follow-up divisions and supplies. All this had to be coordinated with the army and air plans for the invasion. The naval plan involved some 7,000 ships of all types and sizes, of which over 1,200 were warships ranging from battleships to MIDGET SUBMARINES; more than 4,100 were landing ships and craft to put the armies ashore, and 846 were merchant ships to supply them.

Another part of Operation Neptune was the protection of this great armada of ships from attack by German U-boats from the west and E-BOATS and other attack craft from the east. Ten escort groups of destroyers, frigates and sloops, together with aircraft from COASTAL COMMAND, patrolled the western end of the English Channel as an anti-U-boat screen, while day and night patrols of destroyers and motor torpedo boats guarded the eastern approach to the invasion area.

NEST EGG. Code name of the Allied plan for occupation of the Channel Islands after German evacuation or surrender. It was initiated May 9, 1945.

NETHERLANDS INTERIOR FORCES. The Dutch underground, one of the most effective resistance organizations in Europe. It provided intelligence on the Germans and was especially notable for the help it gave to Allied parachutists and glidermen. Many of its leaders were clergymen.

NETTUNO. Airstrip at the ANZIO beachhead, Italy.

NEURATH, Konstantin, Baron von (1873–1956). German career diplomat, descendant of three generations of cabinet ministers in Württemberg, who entered the consular service in 1903, rose to be ambassador to Italy and in 1932, during the government of Franz von PAPEN, was appointed Foreign Minister. He continued in this position during the first five years of the Nazi regime, but in February 1938, at the time the leaders of the Army (Blomberg and FRITSCH) were being dismissed, was replaced by the Nazi Joachim von RIBBENTROP. After the fall of Czechoslovakia (March 1939), Neurath was appointed Reich Protector of BOHEMIA–MORAVIA; he was apparently chosen for the post because he was not identified with the Nazis and would thus appear to be a moderate. He said later that the appointment took him by "complete surprise." In 1941 he was sent on sick leave, being replaced as Protector by the formidable Reinhard HEYDRICH. At NUREMBERG, Neurath was sentenced to 15 years' imprisonment, but he was released for reasons of health in 1954.

NEUTRALITY ACTS. A series of laws enacted by the U.S. Congress in the 1930s with the aim of keeping the United States out of war. In 1935 legislation prohibited trading with belligerents, in 1936 loans to belligerent governments were banned and in 1937 a new law required military items to be paid for by foreign governments before they could leave the country. On November 4, 1939, after the outbreak of the war in Europe, Congress passed a new neutrality law, which permitted belligerents (in fact, Britain and France) to obtain arms on a CASH AND CARRY basis. On November 13, 1941, Congress repealed the requirement that prohibited the arming of American merchant ships and their entry into combat zones.

NEUTRALITY PATROL. The maintenance by the American republics of a zone in the western Atlantic in which belligerent powers were prohibited from conducting operations. *See also* PANAMA CONFERENCE.

NEVADA, U.S.S. Battleship and class, of 29,000 tons, with ten 14-inch guns. The two ships of this class, *Nevada* and OKLAHOMA, commissioned in 1916 and were modernized in 1927–29, receiving two prominent tripod masts like those of the PENNSYLVANIA class. Both were at PEARL HARBOR. *Oklahoma,* hit by bombs and torpedoes, capsized and sank with heavy loss of life. *Nevada*, the only battleship to get under way that morning, was seriously damaged as she headed for the open sea and had to be beached. She was refloated, repaired and partially modernized. Returning to service in 1943, she took part in the capture of ATTU and then went to the Atlantic. Here she escorted troop convoys to Europe before participating in the INVASION of Normandy and of SOUTHERN FRANCE. Back in the Pacific, she supported the landings on IWO JIMA and OKINAWA. After taking part in the occupation of Japan, she served as an atomic-test target ship at Bikini.

NEWALL, Lord (Sir Cyril Newall) (1886–1963). RAF officer, Chief of the Air Staff in the critical period 1937–40 when the ROYAL AIR FORCE was reequipping and having to face the first shocks of war against an aggressive and better-armed enemy air force. Formerly an Army officer, Newall transferred to air in World War I, and his distinguished career culminated in elevation to the post of CAS. A Marshal of the Royal Air Force (and later Lord Newall), he became Governor General of New Zealand on retirement from the RAF.

NEW BRITAIN. The largest island in the BISMARCK ARCHIPELAGO. Midway along its coasts, Talasea in the north and Gasmata in the south offered good airfield sites from which missions could be flown against RABAUL, the ultimate target in this area of the war. On December 26, 1943, the U.S. 1st Marine Division landed at Cape Gloucester on the northwest point of New Britain. *See also* PACIFIC WAR 1942–45.

NEW CALEDONIA. This major island was an important stage in the air ferry route from the United States to Australia. It had a dual strategic value; first, it lies at the end of a string of islands stretching across the Pacific, and flanks the northeast approaches to Australia from NEW GUINEA and the SOLOMONS; further, it holds valuable nickel and chrome deposits, both tempting prizes to the Japanese. On March 12, 1942, elements of the AMERICAL DIVISION arrived in Noumea, the major city, to garrison the island. When South Pacific Forces and Area, a naval command, was formed, its headquarters was set up in Noumea.

NEWFOUNDLAND ESCORT FORCE. A force of convoy escorts, principally sloops and corvettes, based on St. John's, Newfoundland, and used mainly for the escort westward of slow Allied convoys. After turning over the convoys to British escorts at the MID-OCEAN MEETING POINT, the Newfoundland escorts brought back convoys bound for Canada and the United States.

NEW GEORGIA. The largest of the cluster of islands in the New Georgia group in the central SOLOMONS. A tortuous, misshapen mass with a spiny ridge of peaks, it is 45 miles long and 20 miles wide with rugged approaches. The Japanese arrived in the New Georgia group in mid-November 1942 and began construction of an airfield, which threatened American positions in the lower Solomons, especially on GUADALCANAL. On June 21, 1943, elements of the Marine 4th Raider Battalion landed at Segi Point to begin operations in eastern New Georgia. The island was finally secured on August 25 as Army units seized Bairoko harbor.

NEW GUINEA. New Guinea, one of the world's largest islands, was divided into Netherlands New Guinea, comprising the western half of the island; Northeast New Guinea; and Papua, the latter two parts administered by Australia. The Japanese began operations against New Guinea on March 8, 1942, with landings in the Huon Gulf of Northeast New Guinea at LAE and SALAMAUA. Bases were established to protect RABAUL, the great southern defensive bastion of the newly conquered empire. However, the Japanese high command soon decided that further operations in the Southwest Pacific should be undertaken to isolate Australia. PORT MORESBY, a major port on the southern shore of the Papuan peninsula, was the key objective. Undoubtedly, a quick operation against Port Moresby in March would have been successful, as the Australian garrison was very small. Before the Japanese had completed their preparations, however, Australian defenses were strengthened, owing in large part to the return of Australian troops from the Middle East. In addition, American land and naval forces began a rapid buildup in Australia. As of April 1942, Australian and American forces in the SOUTHWEST PACIFIC AREA were under the command of Gen. Douglas MACARTHUR; the Australian Gen. Sir Thomas BLAMEY was appointed commander of Allied Land Forces.

The first Japanese attempt to seize Port Moresby was thwarted by the U.S. Navy in the Battle of the CORAL SEA on May 4–8. Although an American carrier was sunk, the Japanese fleet, including troop ships bound for Port Moresby, was forced to withdraw. After the victory at MIDWAY, American planners decided that Allied forces were strong enough to begin the seizure of the New Guinea–NEW BRITAIN area and the reduction of Rabaul. On July 2 General MacArthur was instructed that among his tasks for the offensive was to be the capture of Lae, Salamaua and the northwest coast of New Guinea. However, Allied operations were forestalled on July 22 when a Japanese reinforced regiment landed at GONA, situated on the northern coast of the Papuan peninsula, captured neighboring BUNA and moved inland. By July 29 the Japanese, much to MacArthur's surprise, had succeeded in capturing KOKODA, the key to the best pass through the OWEN STANLEY MOUN-

TAINS. The advance continued through wild terrain, bringing the Japanese within 30 miles of Port Moresby. But the Australian defenses stiffened, and Allied aircraft harried communications; the Japanese were halted, and were gradually pushed back. Meanwhile, their situation on GUADALCANAL was worsening. To add to their problems, an amphibious assault, intended to aid the drive from Kokoda, was repulsed in MILNE BAY at the tip of the Papuan peninsula (August 25–September 5).

After stopping the Japanese, Australian and American troops went over to the offensive at once. Initial operations were aimed at Buna, where Japanese survivors of the Port Moresby offensive had constructed formidable defenses. Fighting at Buna began November 19 and dragged on until January 22, 1943. While the Allies prepared for further operations, the Japanese suffered a sharp blow in March when a major supply convoy bound for Lae was decimated by Allied aircraft in the BISMARCK SEA. Concentrated Japanese air attacks in April intended to regain air superiority were also costly failures. In March the JOINT CHIEFS OF STAFF decided that not enough troops could be deployed in the Pacific to allow for the capture of Rabaul in 1943. Hence MacArthur was ordered to proceed toward western New Britain while Adm. William F. HALSEY cleared the SOLOMONS and took BOUGAINVILLE (Operation CARTWHEEL).

In line with these instructions, MacArthur began the next phase of Allied operations, which lasted from June to September. In a series of complicated converging airborne-amphibious-ground attacks, MacArthur managed to feign a move on Salamaua, and then seized Lae from behind. The Allies capitalized on this success by immediately landing at FINSCHHAFEN (September 22), the main port on the strategic HUON PENINSULA. On September 23 General Blamey arrived in Port Moresby to take direct command of the forces in New Guinea.

U.S. infantry reinforcements come ashore on New Georgia

Meanwhile, in August, the Joint Chiefs of Staff had decided that Rabaul had been so weakened that it could be bypassed. To assure the isolation of Rabaul, MacArthur's troops seized Cape Gloucester on western New Britain in December. No longer having to worry about Rabaul, MacArthur was now anxious to move up the northern coast of New Guinea in preparation for landings in the Philippines. The first Allied move in 1944 was a landing at Saidor on January 2, which nearly succeeded in cutting off the Japanese force retreating from Lae. When Australian troops marching from Finschhafen reached Saidor a week later, American amphibious troops were freed for the daring seizure of the Admiralty Islands in February.

MacArthur next surprised the Japanese 18th Army at Wewak by landing behind it at Aitape and Hollandia in April, even though the troop ships were beyond the range of land-based air cover. The continuing Australian advance up the coast completed the entrapment of the 18th Army. Isolated and starving, the Japanese were left for the Australians to mop up. Further landings at Sarmi on May 17, and at Sansapor, at the western tip of Netherlands New Guinea, were made in preparation for the Leyte campaign. In November the Australians assumed responsibility for eastern New Guinea and began operations against bypassed Japanese, whose resistance continued until the end of the war. **E.B.**

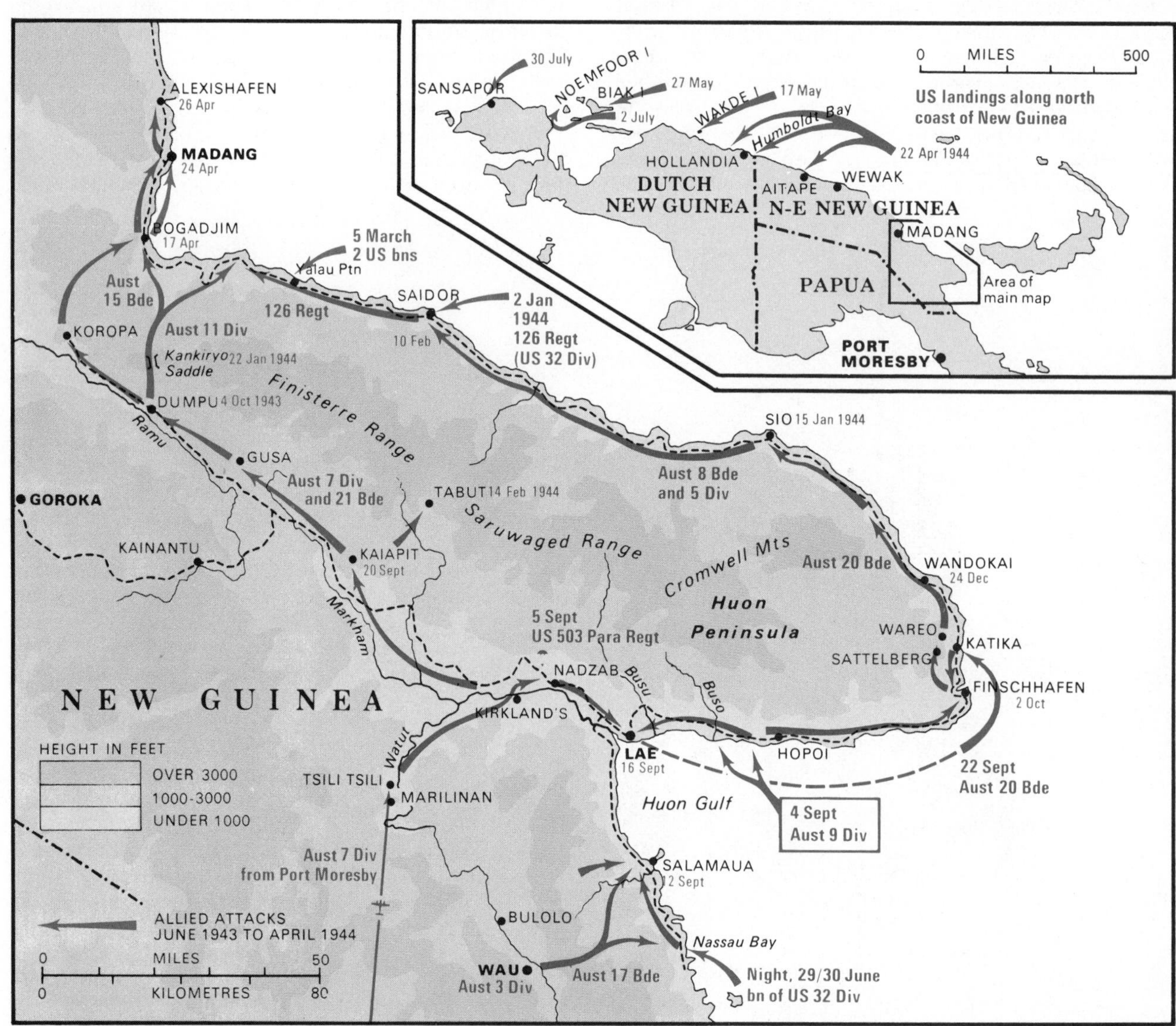

New Guinea: 1943 saw a succession of Allied operations against the Japanese

NEW HEBRIDES. The most important of these islands in the war were Espiritu Santo and Efate. The strategic value of this group lies in the fact that it guarded the vital line of communication from the United States to the Southwest Pacific area and Australia and also provided airfields and staging and training bases for operations in this theater of the war.

NEW JERSEY, U.S.S. Iowa-class battleship. Commissioned in 1943, she operated with the Fast Carrier Task Force from the capture of the Marshall Islands (January 1944 to the assault on Okinawa (April 1945). From February to April 1944 she flew the flag of Adm. Raymond Spruance, commanding the Fifth Fleet; the following August she became the flagship of the Third Fleet commander, Adm. William Halsey. In January 1945 Halsey hauled down his flag and *New Jersey* became flagship of a battleship division. For a short while she served as flagship of various commanders of naval occupation forces after V-J Day, and she returned to the United States in February 1946 with troops traveling home for discharge. Subsequently decommissioned, *New Jersey* was recommissioned for service in Korea and went back into commission (April 1968–December 1969) for Vietnam service, the last American battleship to see active duty. She is now berthed in the Navy's inactive fleet at Bremerton, Wash.

NEW MEXICO, U.S.S. Battleship and class (33,400 tons; twelve 14-inch guns). The class included *New Mexico*, MISSISSIPPI and *Idaho*. Commissioned in 1917–19, they were extensively modernized in 1930–34. Rebuilt with massive foretowers instead of their original cage masts, they were the most modern battleships in the U.S. fleet until completion of the NORTH CAROLINA class in 1941. They served on the NEUTRALITY PATROL through 1941. Sent to the Pacific early in 1942 to redress the post–Pearl Harbor capital-ship balance, they operated in that theater for the rest of the war. Like other older battleships, they were actively employed as shore bombardment and naval-gunfire support ships.

NEW OPERATIONAL POLICY. A revised estimate of Japanese war aims, drawn up in September 1943 by IMPERIAL GENERAL HEADQUARTERS. It described an "absolute national defense sphere"—the minimum area that must remain under Japanese control. The line ran Burma–Malaya–western New Guinea–Carolines–Marianas–Kuriles.

NEW ORDER (German). The term used for Adolf HITLER's policy aiming at a German-dominated Europe. In the European new order the so-called Aryan blond peoples were to be the key racial stock to be developed as the HERRENVOLK (master race). All others, notably the Poles and other Slavs, would become slave laborers, while the Jews would be exterminated. "Aryan" was, of course, an entirely mythical racial concept, stemming from 19th-century neo-Darwinistic theory.

NEW ORDER (Japanese). The TRIPARTITE PACT of 1940 formally recognized the leadership of Japan in the establishment of a "New Order" in Greater East Asia. This statement of Japanese hegemony, particularly in Korea, Manchuria and China, in the Tripartite Pact meant that Germany and Italy acknowledged that Japan would use whatever means were necessary to achieve effective political influence and economic control in Asia.

NEW ORLEANS, U.S.S. Heavy cruiser and class including seven ships, commissioned in 1934–37. They were 588 feet long; displacements varied but were slightly under the 10,000-ton treaty limitation under which the ships were built. Armed with the same battery as the NORTHAMPTON class (nine 8-inch guns [3×3]), they had prominent tower bridges and after superstructures but omitted the high tripod masts characteristic of earlier American heavy cruisers. Slightly shorter than the Northampton and PORTLAND classes, they had heavier armor protection, and their fire control installation was more advanced. Three of this class—ASTORIA, QUINCY and VINCENNES—were lost together in the Solomons night battle of SAVO (August 1942). SAN FRANCISCO distinguished herself in the naval battle of GUADALCANAL. *New Orleans* and *San Francisco*, with *Minneapolis* and TUSCALOOSA, were given radar and additional antiaircraft guns during the war years.

NEWTON, John Henry (1881–1948). U.S. naval officer, a member of the Naval Academy class of 1905. At the time of PEARL HARBOR, Newton, then a rear admiral, was at sea with a task force, including the carrier LEXINGTON, bound for Midway to deliver a force of scout bombers; thus the "Lady Lex" was not at home when the Japanese attack came and was saved for her role in the CORAL SEA battle. Newton served as deputy to Adm. Chester W. NIMITZ, Commander in Chief of the Pacific Fleet, and in a command rearrangement at the beginning of 1944 went to the South Pacific Area as deputy to Adm. William F. HALSEY, whom he succeeded as ComSoPac in June 1944.

NEW YORK, U.S.S. Battleship and class, of 27,000 tons, with ten 14-inch guns (5×2). The first American ships armed with 14-inch weapons, *New York* and TEXAS commissioned in 1914 and were modernized in 1925–27. Both were on Atlantic duty when the Pacific war began. *New York* escorted Atlantic troop convoys through mid-1943, interrupted only by the November 1942 NORTHWEST AFRICA landings. Then she was assigned to gunnery-training duty in Chesapeake Bay; this continued through the summer of 1944, along with midshipman training. In 1945 she provided gunnery support to landings on Iwo JIMA and OKINAWA.

NEW YORK (AMERIKA) BOMBER. *See* JUNKERS JU 390.

NEW ZEALAND FORCES. At the beginning of the war New Zealand dispatched troops to Egypt, the plan being that they would train in installations there before going to Europe to participate in the fighting. However, the contemplated positional war in Europe did not materialize, and the New Zealanders found themselves involved against the Axis in NORTH AFRICA. In 1941 New Zealand contingents were among the British forces in Greece and CRETE, and in later phases of the war they were represented in the armies that returned to the Continent.

NGESEBUS. A small island off the northern tip of PELELIU. It held gun positions which fired on U.S. Marine units on Peleliu. Ngesebus was taken on September 28, 1944, by the 3d Battalion, 5th Marines, in a two-day operation only 13 days after the initial landings on Peleliu.

NICHOLS FIELD. Air base on the outskirts of MANILA that figured prominently in prewar American plans for the defense of the PHILIPPINES. Based there when the Japanese attacked were a squadron of P-40Es, the most modern pursuit planes in the islands (*see* P-40), along with P-40Bs and P-35s (*see* P-35). On December 8, 1941, pursuit planes took off from Nichols to intercept Japanese bombers headed for CLARK FIELD but failed to locate the attacking formation, which all but wiped out the total B-17 contingent available for the defense of the Philippines (*see* B-17).

Nichols itself came under attack on the early morning of December 9, and as a result the antiaircraft defenses were strengthened. Nevertheless, the additional guns could not stop the Japanese, who returned on the 10th in overwhelming strength to bomb and strafe both the airfield and the naval base at CAVITE. Nichols Field and the other permanent installations around Manila soon fell to the Japanese, as the Americans and their Filipino allies retreated to the BATAAN peninsula.

NICOBAR ISLANDS. The Nicobars, northerly island extensions of Sumatra and important to the Japanese Indian Ocean Front, were completely occupied by the Japanese by May 1942. Used as bases for two mixed infantry brigades, as airfields and as radar stations, and falling under various Japanese command and control authorities, the islands were the subject of Allied air and sea attacks toward the end of the war. They were never invaded, though assault was feared by the Japanese, and were still under Japanese control at the end of the war. The Allies received formal surrender on October 9, 1945, and evacuation of all Japanese troops was completed in December.

NIELSON FIELD. U.S. air base at MANILA, heavily bombed by the Japanese on December 10, 1941.

NIEMÖLLER, Martin (1892–). A legendary figure for much of his life, Niemöller was a German submarine commander in World War I, winning the highest award for bravery, POUR LE MÉRITE. Afterward he studied theology and in 1931 became vicar (Confessional Church) of Dahlem, a well-to-do suburb of Berlin. Following the advent of Adolf HITLER, Niemöller's sermons against racism, concentration camps and other Nazi beliefs and practices achieved world fame. On June 27, 1937, he said to a congregation including, conspicuously, observers from the SS (*see* SS): "We have no more thought of using our own powers to escape the arm of the authorities than had the apostles of old. No more are we ready to keep silent at man's behest when God commands us to speak." Three days later he was arrested. He was subsequently confined in Sachsenhausen and later DACHAU concentration camp, being liberated in 1945. After the war he resumed his very active church career.

NIGHT AND FOG DECREE (Nacht und Nebel Erlass). This order, issued by Adolf HITLER on December 7, 1941, directed German occupation authorities in western Europe to dispose of certain persons "endangering German security" in a novel way—not by execution but by making them disappear into "night and fog" in Germany. As explained by General KEITEL in a subsequent directive, intimidation could be achieved "either by capital punishment or by measures by which the relatives of the criminal and the population do not know his fate." The number of persons transported under this decree has not been established, but there were few known survivors.

NIGHT OF THE LONG KNIVES. The supreme act of recrimination perpetrated by HITLER, GÖRING and HIMMLER on June 30, 1934, primarily against Ernst RÖHM and the SA leadership (*see* SA), but also taking in many of those who had in one way or another opposed the Führer's ambitions during the period 1932–34—notably the former Chancellor, Gen. Kurt von Schleicher, and Hitler's prime critic in the Nazi Party, Gregor Strasser. Röhm, who had been overly ambitious to be Minister of War and thus combine his vast SA following with the standing German Army under his single control, was, along with other SA leaders, arrested by Hitler in person and imprisoned in Munich, while in Berlin Göring and Himmler supervised the arrest and formal executions of a further list of suspects and opponents. "The Night of the Long Knives" (the name was given it by the Nazis themselves) spanned June 30–July 1. Hitler admitted subsequently that 77 persons had been executed, with Röhm at the head of the list; but taking the nation as a whole, it is likely the final toll of victims was nearer 200. Old scores were settled in many parts of Germany on all levels before the purge was brought to a halt.

NIJMEGEN. City on the Waal River, the Netherlands, a pivotal objective of the U.S. 82D AIRBORNE DIVISION in Operation MARKET-GARDEN, September 17, 1944. The great bridge at Nijmegen remained under German fire for months after the city's capture by Allied forces.

NIKITIN-SEVCHENKO IS-1. Development began in the USSR in 1939 to combine the maneuverability and short-landing-and-takeoff characteristics of a biplane with the high speeds of a monoplane. The IS-1 was an I-153 fuselage fitted with a gull-type upper wing and a hydraulically retractable lower wing which the pilot could change at will. The prototype flew fairly well, proving the design concept. The IS-2, a slightly improved version, came shortly after the IS-1. Despite its success the design was dropped, as performance improvement was marginal and the hydraulic system was hard to maintain during field operations. Its top speed as a monoplane was 285 miles per hour (estimated), while it could cruise at 180 miles per hour (estimated) as a biplane.

NIMITZ, Chester William (1885–1966). When Admiral Nimitz took over the U.S. Pacific Fleet on December 31, 1941, many of his battleships were incapacitated in PEARL HARBOR. But a new kind of sea war, the war of the carriers, was just beginning. By the end of the war Nimitz commanded 6,256 ships, 14,847 combat aircraft and 2 million personnel, including six Marine divisions.

The grandson of a sea captain, Nimitz grew up on his grandfather's sea stories. Despite this he first applied to West Point, but eventually entered the Naval Academy at age 15, where he was on the rowing crew, and graduated seventh in the class of 1905. Nimitz became seasick on his first voyage, but soon became an expert in submarines and earned a reputation for mastery of his business as a naval officer. In 1940 two names were under consideration as commander of the Pacific Fleet. One was Nimitz, the other Adm. Husband E. KIMMEL.

Following Pearl Harbor and Kimmel's dismissal, Nimitz took command of the Pacific Fleet—but with reluctance; he would have preferred sea duty. To the surprise of many, he did not "clean house" after succeeding Kimmel, but proceeded with deliberation to rebuild the fleet. According to Samuel Eliot MORISON, morale in the fleet "rose several hundred percent." An excellent judge of character and an astute handler of men, Nimitz gathered a capable cadre of subordinates to cover the 65 million square miles under his command. His officers included Admirals William F. HALSEY, Raymond A. SPRUANCE, Marc A. MITSCHER, Richmond Kelly TURNER and Thomas C. KINKAID.

Although major operations were not immediately possible, Nimitz began to launch carrier air strikes against Japanese bases in the GILBERT and MARSHALL ISLANDS, on WAKE ISLAND and in NEW GUINEA. The necessity of protecting communications with Australia brought American forces into contact with the Japanese in the area of New Guinea, NEW BRITAIN and the SOLOMONS. As a result, American and Japanese forces met in the CORAL SEA. This battle was a strategic victory for the Americans, denying the Coral Sea to the Japanese and preserving communications with Australia.

Even before the Coral Sea, American intelligence had wind of a Japanese plan to reenter the Central Pacific. Nimitz mobilized all units, including the carriers ENTERPRISE, HORNET and YORKTOWN, 8 cruisers, 14 destroyers and 20 submarines. He then divided the command, and on June 3, 1942, the three-day Battle of MIDWAY began. Navy carrier, Marine and Army aircraft sank four Japanese carriers, a cruiser and a destroyer; gave the Japanese Navy its first taste of defeat; and ended the enemy threat to Hawaii, the Panama Canal and the West Coast of the United States. Japanese operations thereafter were largely confined to the South Pacific.

Admiral Nimitz (center) takes a look at Tarawa, November 1943. His companions are Generals Robert Richardson (left) and Julian Smith

The development of a Japanese air base on GUADALCANAL threatened the American base on NEW CALEDONIA, and Nimitz decided to move before the enemy fortified Guadalcanal further. On August 7, 1942, the 1st Marine Division (General VANDEGRIFT) landed, commencing the first amphibious operation against the enemy. The Japanese reaction was fierce, and the outcome in doubt; Guadalcanal witnessed possibly the most desperate fighting of the war. The Americans suffered heavy losses on August 9 at SAVO ISLAND, but repulsed Japanese efforts at reinforcement and by December controlled sea and air in the southern Solomons.

Fortified with more ships and planes, Nimitz was able in 1943 to begin a general offensive in the Central Pacific. A Central Pacific force under Spruance, the hero of Midway, began to capture Japanese strongholds and bases needed for later operations. Beginning with an amphibious operation against the Gilbert Islands, the Americans forced the Japanese back with victories in the MARIANAS and the PHILIPPINE SEA, at IWO JIMA and OKINAWA. Submarines made a decided contribution to Nimitz's war, accounting for two-thirds of Japan's losses in merchant shipping and one-third of her combat tonnage losses. As the U.S. fleet approached Tokyo Bay, planes began to strike against the Japanese homeland. At the time of Japan's surrender, the Nimitz command had sunk more than two-thirds of Japan's major combat vessels and had been responsible for 85 percent of her losses in merchant tonnage. Nimitz was promoted to Fleet Admiral on December 19, 1944.

Following the Japanese surrender, Nimitz returned to the United States, succeeding Adm. Ernest J. KING as Chief of Naval Operations. For his activities during World War II, he received decorations from the United States and 11 foreign countries, plus honorary degrees from 15 universities. He had proved himself an outstanding organizer, a thoughtful strategist and a decisive commander. In an oversimplification that is nevertheless suggestive, Edwin P. Hoyt said of the Pacific admirals that "Halsey was the man to win a battle for you, Spruance was the man to win a campaign, but Nimitz was the man to win a war." He was tremendously popular with the enlisted people of both Army and Navy. **D.C.**

NINE-POWER TREATY. Perhaps the most significant of several agreements to emerge from the Washington Naval Conference (November 1921–February 1922), the Nine-Power Treaty of February 6, 1922 was an agreement that seemed at the time to give international sanction to the classic American Open Door Policy by binding the United States, Britain and Japan in particular (the other signatories were Belgium, China, France, Italy, the Netherlands and Portugal) "to respect the sovereignty, the independence, and the territorial and administrative integrity of China." Japan soon violated the treaty through her assertion of power in the Far

East during the 1930s, a prelude to the approaching world war.

NINTH AIR FORCE. This U.S. force had its beginnings in the Halverson Detachment (*see* HALPRO), which bombed PLOESTI, Rumania, in the summer of 1942. That handful of B-24s was absorbed into Maj. Gen. Lewis H. BRERETON's Middle East Air Forces, which consisted mainly of heavy bombers that were employed against General ROMMEL's bases at TOBRUK and BENGHAZI in Libya and against harbors in Greece and on CRETE. Medium bombers and fighters arrived later in the year and helped support the British offensive that began at El ALAMEIN in October. On November 12, 1942, the Middle East Air Force became the Ninth Air Force.

After its redesignation, Brereton's force continued to support the advance in North Africa and also bombed targets in Italy and on the Mediterranean isles; Rome was first hit in July 1943. Planes from the Ninth and TWELFTH AIR FORCES waged an aerial campaign that ended in June 1943 with the surrender of the Italian troops that garrisoned the island of PANTELLERIA. This operation was followed by air strikes and an airborne attack on SICILY. During the Sicilian fighting, Brereton launched his North African–based B-24s on Operation Tidal Wave against the Ploesti oil refineries.

In September 1943 Army air organization in Europe was adjusted to support the approaching cross-Channel INVASION. The Ninth Air Force became a tactical striking force and joined the EIGHTH AIR FORCE in the newly created U.S. Army Air Forces in the United Kingdom. From bases in the British Isles, Ninth Air Force fighter-bombers, attack planes and medium bombers severed rail lines, shot up airfields and flak towers, and destroyed bridges in preparation for the June 6, 1944, invasion of Normandy. They also attacked launch sites that the Germans were preparing for the V-WEAPONS attack against Britain. On D-Day Brereton's airmen flew the transports that dropped parachutists and towed gliders during the airborne portion of the assault. Afterward, Brereton and his successor, Maj. Gen. Hoyt S. VANDENBERG, used the Ninth to support the advance across France, employing C-47s to deliver fuel to General PATTON's armored column. The Ninth Air Force helped to check the Ardennes counterattack (the BULGE), provided gliders and transports for the crossing of the Rhine and joined in the final conquest of Germany.

NINTH ARMY (U.S.). Activated at Fort Sam Houston, Tex., on April 14, 1944, as the Eighth Army but redesignated the Ninth on May 22, 1944, to avoid confusion with the British Eighth Army. Commanded by Lt. Gen. William H. SIMPSON throughout its operational life, the Ninth established headquarters at Bristol, England, on June 29, 1944, in preparation for operations on the Continent. It became operational on September 5, 1944, under command of 12TH ARMY GROUP, and took over the tasks of reducing BREST, holding German forces in LORIENT and SAINT-NAZAIRE and protecting the army group's southern flank along the Loire River to Orléans. Brest fell on September 20 and in October the Ninth Army moved east to the ARDENNES between FIRST and THIRD ARMIES. A few weeks later it moved to the northern flank of the U.S. armies. Because of these sudden and distant moves, portions of Ninth Army were operating simultaneously in five countries—France, Belgium, Luxembourg, the Netherlands and Germany. It maintained this position, with the First Army on the right and the British on the left, until the end of the war. During the Battle of the BULGE, the Rhine crossing and the envelopment of the RUHR, Ninth Army was in fact attached to Field Marshal MONTGOMERY's 21ST ARMY GROUP. Otherwise it served under General BRADLEY's 12th Army Group.

Ninth Army's November offensive drove through a gap in the SIEGFRIED LINE north of Aachen and ended at the Roer River in December 1944. Resuming the attack in February 1945, the Ninth advanced from the Roer to the Rhine and made an assault crossing on March 24, 1945, in cooperation with the British SECOND ARMY. Sealing off the northern Ruhr, it advanced eastward to join the U.S. First Army at Lippstadt on April 1, completing the greatest double envelopment of the war. Ninth Army participated in the continuing advance into Germany, moving 230 miles in 19 days, and was the first Allied army to reach and cross the Elbe River. On April 12, when ordered to halt its advance, its forward elements held a firm bridgehead and were preparing to move the last 53 miles to Berlin.

After the fighting ended on May 8, Ninth Army carried out occupation and military-government duties. As of May 21, 1945, it comprised five corps (VII, VIII, XIII, XVI and XIX)—17 infantry and five armored divisions—with a peak strength of over 650,000. The European mission was completed on June 15, 1945, and the Ninth returned to the United States to prepare to embark for the Pacific theater; however, these plans were canceled when Japan surrendered, and the Ninth Army was inactivated on October 10, 1945, at Fort Bragg, N.C.

NISHIZAWA, Hiroyoshi (1920–1944). Called "Devil" by his comrades, this Japanese ace scored 104 aerial victories, at least 90 of them against American forces. He flew a Zero (*see* A6M) and wrung the maximum performance from that agile fighter. Nishizawa met his death on October 26, 1944, at Clark Field, LUZON, when Navy Hellcats shot down the transport he was piloting.

NKVD (Narodnyi Kommissariat Vnutrennykh Del). The Soviet People's Commissariat of Internal Affairs came into being in July 1934, with the renaming of the OGPU (Unified State Political Administration). It was successively headed by Henrik Yagoda (executed in 1937), Nikolai Yezhov (executed apparently in 1939) and Lavrenti BERIA (executed in 1953). In addition to performing its political police and counterintelligence functions, the NKVD controlled regular police (militia), the concentration camp system, fire departments throughout the country, geological exploration and geodetic surveys. It maintained a vast intelligence network abroad, conducted subversive operations and controlled the operational links of the Comintern Executive Committee with foreign Communist parties.

With the outbreak of the war, NKVD activities expanded. It conducted massive purges in eastern Poland, annexed in 1939, and in the Baltic states and Bessarabia, annexed in 1940. Purges were accompanied by wholesale deportations to Siberia and executions of the elements of the population considered hostile to the Soviet state; the latter included up to 15,000 Polish officers who surrendered to the Soviets in September 1939. After the German invasion had begun, NKVD squads carried out mass executions of political prisoners, particularly those in the cities and towns about to be abandoned to the advancing Germans.

While the NKVD's main role during the war was guarding rear areas and carrying out counterintelligence operations, it was also involved in searching for draft dodgers and conducting political surveillance in military units. Special NKVD squads were often placed behind fighting Army units, with orders to open fire against those retreating without authorization and to capture deserters, who were then "tried" by special NKVD tribunals for "treason." Another major NKVD role in the war was the enforcement of discipline among PARTISAN units operating in German-controlled territory. As the tide of the war turned and the Red Army began to liberate territories formerly occupied by the Germans, the NKVD's functions were extended to locating and punishing war criminals, collaborators and others who were deemed to have aided and abetted the occupiers.

NOBALL. Name given to German rocket-launching sites by Allied air forces attacking them. Unofficially, it was also given to the operation to eliminate them.

NOBLE, Sir Percy (1880–1955). Admiral Noble was the Royal Navy's Commander in Chief China at the outbreak of the war, and in 1941, when the headquarters of the WESTERN APPROACHES Command was transferred from Plymouth to Liverpool, he became its commander in chief with responsibility for conducting the war against U-boats in the Atlantic. By the time he left the command the British antisubmarine forces had reached a degree of training and organization that gave his successor, Adm. Sir Max HORTON, a lasting foundation on which to mount his victory over the U-boats. Noble followed his 18 months at Liverpool with service in Washington as head of the British Admiralty delegation. The tact, firmness and common sense that he brought to the various deliberations of the COMBINED CHIEFS OF STAFF did much to ensure the smooth agreement in operational planning that existed between the British and American Navies. He retired in January 1945, and his services in Washington were acknowledged by the awards of the British GBE and the American LEGION OF MERIT in the degree of commander.

Noble has one other small claim to fame. When he was a sub-lieutenant he was detailed for duty with the naval guard of honor at the funeral of Queen Victoria. The horses drawing the gun carriage bearing the coffin became restive and started to kick, and Noble suggested that they be unhitched and the gun carriage drawn by the naval guard. The result was so impressive that the precedent set then has been followed in every subsequent royal funeral. *See also* ATLANTIC, BATTLE OF THE.

NOEMFOOR. Small island in Geelvink Bay of western NEW GUINEA, occupied by the Japanese in late 1943. In the spring of 1944 the Japanese began developing Noemfoor into an air base, and by the time the Allies landed on nearby BIAK Island on May 27, 1944, they had completed two airstrips and started a third. They also used Noemfoor as a way station for troop-laden barges attempting to reinforce Biak during the KON OPERATION. The U.S. 158th RCT (Separate) landed on Noemfoor on July 2, 1944. Next day a battalion of the 503d Parachute Infantry (Separate) dropped on one of the Japanese airstrips and was followed on the 4th by a second battalion. Casualties were high because of the rough condition of the drop zone, and the rest of the 503d came in by water.

At the time of the landing there were about 2,250 Japanese on Noemfoor, the defensive garrison being built around a reinforced battalion of the 219th Infantry, 35th Division. There were also some 600 Formosan labor troops and 400 Javanese slave laborers, whose condition was nearly unbelievable. (The Javanese were the survivors of an initial shipment of some 3,000.) No hard fighting took place on Noemfoor, which for the 158th and 503d Infantry Regiments was more or less a mopping-up operation. By the end of August 1944 almost 2,000 Japanese troops had been killed or found dead, and about 250 had been captured. Formosan POWs numbered about 600.

NOGUÈS, Auguste (1876–1971). After holding political and military positions in both France and Morocco, General Noguès was named by Léon BLUM's French Popular Front government as Resident General of Morocco in 1936. When war broke out he was made commander in chief of all French forces in North Africa and cracked down on German sympathizers; after France fell he hounded partisans of FREE FRANCE and enforced German racial laws. His adaptability won him the nickname "General No-Yes." In November 1942 he ordered resistance to the Allied landings but requested an armistice on November 10 after receiving orders from Adm. François DARLAN to stop the fighting. The Allies thereafter supported him as Resident General of Morocco because he could maintain order. Distinguished-looking, with a close-clipped mustache and handsome uniforms, Noguès was an impressive figure but not overly trusted by anyone. After Darlan's assassination in December 1942, Noguès was deputy high commissioner for French North Africa, and in June 1943 he resigned and went to Portugal. He was tried in absentia in 1947 and sentenced to 20 years' hard labor, and when he returned to France in 1956 he was arrested but shortly released.

NOMURA, Kichisaburo (1887–1964). One of Japan's most capable naval career officers, Nomura fought in the Russo-Japanese War, served as naval attaché in Russia and the United States and held a number of important bureaucratic posts in the Navy. He was a delegate to Versailles and to the Washington Naval Conference. After resigning from the Navy in 1937, Admiral Nomura became a member of the Supreme War Council and president of the Peers' School. In 1939 he accepted the post of Foreign Minister in Nobuyuki Abe's cabinet and was appointed ambassador to the United States in the following year. It was he who was involved in the difficult and abortive negotiations preceding the PEARL HARBOR attack. He retired from the diplomatic service after being repatriated to Japan in 1942.

NONFRATERNIZATION POLICY. Embodied in a directive from the Allied COMBINED CHIEFS OF STAFF (who proclaimed the policy in September 1944), this prohibited all "mingling with the Germans upon terms of friendliness, familiarity, or intimacy, individually or in groups in official or unofficial dealings." F. S. V. Donnison, a British official historian, described it as an attempt "to send the whole German people to Coventry largely in order to express disgust for the bestialities of Nazism." Strict enforcement of the rule proved impracticable in both official and personal spheres, but it officially remained in force until several months after the German surrender.

NORDEN BOMBSIGHT. A precision optical device that incorporated a gyrostabilized automatic pilot to keep the bomber straight and level during the bomb run. Invented by Carl L. Norden, a civilian consultant employed by the U.S. Navy (with Capt. Frederick L. Entwistle, assistant research chief of the Navy Bureau of Ordnance), the bombsight favorably impressed U.S. Army observers during 1931 tests against an obsolete warship. As a result, the Army Air Corps ordered its own Norden bombsights the following year.

Improvements in the sight and refinements in tactics during the 1930s enabled tight formations to be flown, and compact bomb patterns with excellent results on the target range were obtained. Clear weather and undisturbed bomb runs with the Norden bombsight gave rise to the legend of "dropping a bomb in a pickle barrel." Peacetime achievements could not, however, be duplicated in wartime when attacking through cloud cover, amid bursting antiaircraft shells and swarms of enemy interceptors. *See also* SPERRY BOMBSIGHT.

NORDHAUSEN. Town on the southern side of the Harz Mountains in central Germany, site of a Nazi complex—a concentration camp, a slave-labor camp with a capacity of 30,000 and underground factories, one of them for manufacturing V-2 rockets (*see* V-WEAPONS). When the laborers became incapable of working, they were left to die and their remains were cremated in camp ovens. Nordhausen was occupied by the U.S. 3d Armored Division on April 11, 1945.

NORDLING, Raoul (1882–1962). The Swedish consul general in Paris, who interceded with the German commandant, Gen. Dietrich von CHOLTITZ, on behalf of French political prisoners and helped arrange a truce, August 1944. *See also* PARIS, LIBERATION OF.

NORDWIND (North Wind). Code name for a German counteroffensive in northern Alsace beginning just before midnight on December 31, 1944; it was designed to take pressure off German forces attacking in the Battle of the BULGE. The U.S. SEVENTH ARMY having extended its lines to free troops of the U.S. THIRD ARMY to counterattack in the Bulge, thinly held Seventh Army positions in a salient in the extreme northeastern corner of France were vulnerable. Attacking southward from the Saar region in the vicinity of the town of Bitche, the German First Army hoped to gain the Saverne Gap through the Vosges Mountains, there to meet a northward thrust by the Nineteenth Army from the COLMAR POCKET and trap seven American divisions along the Rhine River.

Forewarned by intelligence gleaned from prisoners, the Supreme Allied Commander, Gen. Dwight D. EISENHOWER, contemplated withdrawing to the Vosges. Since that would mean relinquishing the historic city of STRASBOURG, the French protested so vehemently that Eisenhower reconsidered. He authorized withdrawing only about 20 miles from the extreme northeastern corner of the salient and adjusted the boundary between the U.S. Seventh and First French Armies to give the French responsibility for defending Strasbourg.

In the main thrust by the First Army, the Germans advanced half the distance to the Saverne Gap, but swift American counterattack had by the fourth day driven them back. Divining that the Americans might withdraw from the northeastern tip of the salient, Adolf HITLER directed a shift in German effort eastward to the Wissembourg Gap; but despite the enemy pressure, the planned American withdrawal proceeded in an orderly manner.

Meanwhile, the Nineteenth Army forged a small bridgehead across the Rhine north of Strasbourg, and in company with the advance northward from the Colmar Pocket threatened the city. The thrust from the north got within seven miles of Strasbourg before hastily committed American reserves stopped it. The move from the south got within 13 miles before French troops halted it at the last bridge short of the city.

NORFOLK, H.M.S. Royal Navy heavy cruiser of 9,925 tons, completed by Fairfield in 1930, armed (in wartime) with eight 8-inch and eight 4-inch guns, smaller weapons, eight 21-inch torpedo tubes and one aircraft. *Norfolk* served throughout the war in the Home Fleet. She played an important part in shadowing the BISMARCK after the destruction of the HOOD, and she was included in the covering force of a number of convoys to Russia, participating in the operations leading to the destruction of the SCHARNHORST in December 1943. In June 1945 *Norfolk* transported King HAAKON of Norway back to Oslo amid scenes of tremendous jubilation.

NORFOLK HOUSE. At St. James's Square, London, Norfolk House was occupied by Allied Force Headquarters from August 4, 1942, during the planning of the invasion of NORTHWEST AFRICA.

NORMANDIE SQUADRON. A squadron of French fighter pilots serving in Russia. Formed in 1942, it entered action in 1943. The squadron grew to a full air regiment under the name Normandie-Nieman.

NORMANDY INVASION. *See* INVASION—NORMANDY.

NORRIE, Charles Willoughby Noke, Baron (1893–). British Army officer, General Officer Commanding 1st Armored Division, 1940–41; GOC 30th Corps, EIGHTH ARMY, in the Middle East, 1941–42; commander, Royal Armored Corps, 1943.

NORSTAD, Lauris (1907–). A U.S. Army cavalry officer before becoming an aviator, Norstad was a major when the United States entered the war. By February 1942 he was a lieutenant colonel and a member of Gen.

Henry H. ARNOLD's principal planning agency. He went overseas as a colonel to become assistant chief of staff for operations, TWELFTH AIR FORCE, and later held the same staff position in NORTHWEST AFRICAN AIR FORCES. Promoted to brigadier general in March 1943, he became director of operations, MEDITERRANEAN ALLIED AIR FORCES, in December of that year. In August 1944 he returned to Washington to become chief of staff, TWENTIETH AIR FORCE, with additional duty as Deputy Chief of the Air Staff. He received a second star in June 1945, while serving as director of plans and operations for the War Department.

In his subsequent career General Norstad served as Supreme Allied Commander Europe, responsible for NATO military planning and operations.

NORTH AFRICA—OPERATIONS. Benito MUSSOLINI, with ambitions for a new Mediterranean empire, carried the war to North Africa in 1940. The Italian Tenth Army, under Marshal Rodolfo GRAZIANI, built up its strength in CYRENAICA and crossed the Egyptian border in September. The British, under treaty rights granted by Egypt in 1936 for protection of the SUEZ CANAL, had prepared for Graziani's move. The MIDDLE EAST COMMAND, under Gen. Sir Archibald WAVELL, with headquarters in Cairo, had approximately 82,000 men scattered from the Sudan to Palestine. In Egypt, facing Graziani, was Lt. Gen. Sir Richard O'CONNOR with two divisions. O'Connor harassed the advancing Italians, who halted just over the Egyptian border at SIDI BARRANI.

During October attention focused on the Italian invasion of Greece, but in December O'Connor seized the initiative in Egypt. In a series of bold and imaginative moves, the small British Western Desert Force struck the Italians at their weakest and most isolated posts. With astounding speed, the British captured Sidi Barrani and BARDIA. TOBRUK was taken January 21,1941. Graziani's Tenth Army seeming disorganized (90,000 men had surrendered) and the leadership unaggressive, O'Connor and Wavell decided to press on for a major victory.

While the 6th Australian Division pursued Graziani's army along the coast road toward BENGHAZI, the 7th Armored Division cut across the desert through MECHILI to intercept it. The maneuver caught the retreating Italians between the two British divisions, and in the Battle at BEDA FOMM on February 5–7 Wavell's forces won a victory of total annihilation against great odds. Over 113,000 prisoners, more than the total attacking force, were taken. Not only did the British have a moral boost from winning their first land victory in the war, but pressure was lifted from the Suez Canal, and in April the successful conclusion of the war in Ethiopia (*see* EAST AFRICA) opened the Red Sea to both British and U.S. ships. (This 1940–41 North African campaign was the subject of the official film *Desert Victory*.)

Contrary to appearances, the war in North Africa had only begun. Mussolini had bogged down in Greece, and Adolf HITLER determined he must come to his ally's assistance. Major German forces swept through Yugoslavia, Greece and Crete between April 6 and May 27, while to Libya Hitler sent two armored divisions, the AFRIKA KORPS, and their commanding general, Erwin ROMMEL. Hitler's plan for Africa was to keep the Italians bolstered enough to stay in the war. Rommel was subordinated to the Italian high command; his orders were for defensive action.

While Hitler turned his attention toward the June invasion of Russia, General Rommel surveyed opportunities in Africa. The Western Desert, in many ways like an ocean, was conducive to the fluid, mobile warfare he favored; the strategic objectives of an African campaign were unlimited. On the map, many a worried British observer traced the course that Rommel himself saw—a pincers move through the Middle East to link up with forces in the Russian Caucasus. Rommel perceived that the British facing him were weak, for Wavell had sent forces to East Africa, Greece and CRETE. Why give Wavell time to strengthen his forces? Not even waiting for all his troops to arrive, Rommel opened his first desert campaign on March 31, 1941, at El AGHEILA. The British forces began to fall back, and Rommel exploited every move. The tempo accelerated. A series of skirmishes destroyed the British armor, and General O'Connor, a resourceful commander, was captured. Rommel sent a force across the desert through Mechili that threatened to capture the 9th Australian Division, retreating along the coast road. A stand had to be made to stop the rout, and the best available place for it was Tobruk. Wavell consulted with his other Mediterranean commanders, Air Chief Marshal Sir Arthur LONGMORE and Adm. Sir Andrew CUNNINGHAM. Cunningham felt the Navy could keep a garrison at Tobruk supplied by sea; Longmore could provide air cover for the convoys.

The 9th Australian Division got within the Tobruk perimeter the first week in April, and under the vigorous leadership of Gen. Leslie MORSHEAD the troops hurriedly repaired the old Italian defenses and settled in for a siege. Fighting was severe around the perimeter in April, but Rommel could not break into Tobruk. Neither could he advance far beyond Tobruk, leaving its garrison to constitute a threat to his rear. Both the British and the Axis spent the summer months consolidating their strength and preparing for another major battle, which did not open until November.

By November 1941 the situation had changed. General Wavell, insufficiently aggressive in CHURCHILL's eyes, had been sent to India, and Gen. Sir Claude AUCHINLECK had replaced him as the British commander in the Middle East. He had an enlarged force of two corps, called the EIGHTH ARMY, and frantic attempts were being made to supply and train them for the new type of mobile, armored conflict that Rommel was imposing in the desert. After Operation Battleaxe failed to relieve the siege of Tobruk in June 1941, Auchinleck devoted more time to preparation. On November 17, with control of the Mediterranean–Suez route to Asia at stake, Auchinleck opened his major campaign, Operation Crusader.

For a month the battle was heated and at times desperate. Huge armored clashes brought heavy losses to both sides. But the Germans had a better antitank gun, the dual-purpose 88 mm., and better tanks, and the British tended to divide their forces and commit their units piecemeal, compounding their losses. At one time Rommel was so sure of victory that he sent his Afrika Korps on a dramatic drive around the British army toward Egypt. Auchinleck forbade a British withdrawal, the battle continued and the Axis force backtracked.

Gradually seizing the initiative, the British relieved the siege of Tobruk on December 7 and pursued Rommel across Cyrenaica to El Agheila, his starting point in February.

Simultaneous with the lifting of the siege of Tobruk, Japan entered the war. Two Australian divisions in Africa were immediately sent to Asia. Exploiting his enemy's new weakness, Rommel sprang back and recaptured that portion of Cyrenaica containing airfields within striking distance of MALTA.

Both British and Axis forces in Africa were totally dependent on supplies brought from elsewhere, and the Mediterranean supply routes were vital. The British had bases at GIBRALTAR, ALEXANDRIA and Malta. Because of the great distances, only from Malta could effective, steady harassment of the Axis supply routes be maintained. At Rommel's urging, in January 1942 Hitler sent LUFTWAFFE bombers under Field Marshal Albert KESSELRING to Sicily, with the mission of eliminating Malta. There were tentative plans to seize the island later. While the Luftwaffe blitzed Malta, Rommel's supplies got through, and in May he renewed his offensive.

The British had prepared the GAZALA LINE defenses, utilizing a number of fortified strongpoints with mobile units to connect them, but the mobile units proved unable to halt Rommel's armor, which swept around the southernmost box, BIR HACHEIM, and headed for Tobruk. The British armor, reinforced with U.S. Grant tanks, succeeded in stopping Rommel and forcing the Afrika Korps into a defensive bridgehead in the middle of the British line. From this CAULDRON the Afrika Korps countered the British attacks and gradually reduced the British tank strength. Without armored support, Bir Hacheim could not hold. By June 13 the Gazala Line was crumbling and Rommel was in full tilt across the desert, headed for Cairo. A feeble effort to stop him at Tobruk brought only embarrassment. Tobruk fell in a day, and the Afrika Korps streamed east. Hitler made Rommel a field marshal; Mussolini planned to hold a victory parade in Cairo.

The new field marshal, already suffering from supply shortages and needing replacements, considered halting to consolidate. Malta had not yet been eliminated, and Allied air power was striking back at both the Luftwaffe and Axis shipping. But Rommel decided to press on, capitalizing on the British confusion and broken morale. During the last two days of June the two armies raced across the desert, the British seeking to take up positions at the ALAMEIN bottleneck and halt the advance. Both sides were exhausted by July 1, when the first battle of Alamein began. Neither could prevail, and after a month of grim slugging, the armies settled in to rest, refit and prepare for a major battle.

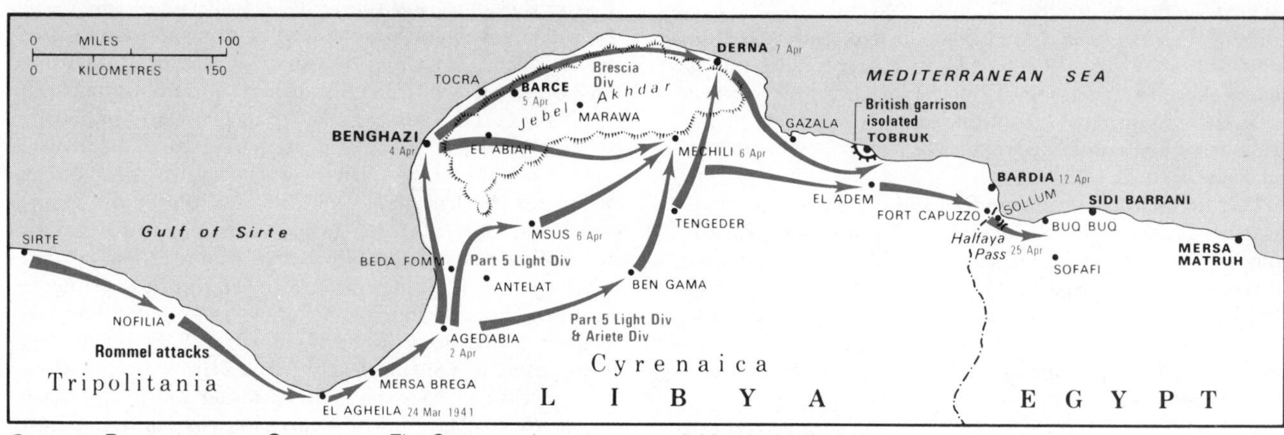

GENERAL ROMMEL ON THE OFFENSIVE—The German advance eastward, March–April 1941

Early in August Gen. Sir Harold ALEXANDER replaced Auchinleck, and Gen. Sir Bernard MONTGOMERY, a match for Rommel in self-confidence and determination, assumed field command of Eighth Army. Preparations were made to deflect the obvious Axis offensive at ALAM HALFA, and after defeating Rommel's bid there in September, Montgomery took the time to accumulate an overwhelming superiority in equipment and to train his men thoroughly. Hitler had not seized Malta, and the island was built up and once more serving as a base for attacks on Axis supply routes. Knowing he would not have fuel, Rommel prepared for defensive warfare behind a massive minefield.

The second battle of Alamein began October 23, 1942. By November 4, after cruel but decisive attrition, the British had broken the Axis defense. The Afrika Korps began a dismal retreat toward Tunis. They were hampered by lack of fuel and transport, as well as by Hitler's refusal to countenance retreat as a policy. Rommel, who had not been in Africa at the opening of the battle, managed to keep the Afrika Korps intact, but at the sacrifice of his less mobile units (primarily Italians), and with the realization that the strategic possibilities were gone. On November 8 Allied forces invaded NORTHWEST AFRICA in Operation Torch. The Axis armies in Africa were trapped between superior forces. Late 1942, marked not only by Alamein and Torch but by Russian control at STALINGRAD and American victory at GUADALCANAL, was a turning point in the war.

M.H.B.

NORTH AFRICAN THEATER OF OPERATIONS, U.S. ARMY. Abbreviated NATOUSA, this U.S. command was established at Algiers under Gen. Dwight D. EISENHOWER on February 4, 1943. In addition to North Africa it included Spain, Italy and several islands in the Mediterranean, these all being transferred from the EUROPEAN THEATER OF OPERATIONS. Gen. Jacob L. DEVERS succeeded General Eisenhower in command of NATOUSA on January 8, 1944; Gen. Joseph T. McNARNEY replaced Devers on October 23, 1944. On November 1, 1944, the theater was redesignated the MEDITERRANEAN THEATER OF OPERATIONS (MTOUSA). On

March 1, 1945, Northwest Africa was taken over by the new Africa–Middle East Theater (AMET).

NORTHAMPTON, U.S.S. Heavy cruiser and class (of six), commissioned in 1930–31. Fifteen feet longer and slightly heavier than the PENSACOLA class, the Northamptons had a raised forecastle and mounted a nine-gun 8-inch battery in three triple turrets. Their protection was comparable to *Pensacola*'s. HOUSTON was lost shortly after the JAVA SEA action in early 1942; *Northampton* and CHICAGO were lost during the SOLOMONS campaign. *Chester*, LOUISVILLE and AUGUSTA were extensively refitted; their high tripod foremasts were lowered, and lower main tripods were replaced by lighter masts. RADAR and additional automatic antiaircraft guns were added.

NORTH CAROLINA, U.S.S. Battleship and class, commissioned in 1941. These 27-knot-plus ships, 729 feet long and 35,000 tons, with nine 16-inch guns (3×3), were the first American capital ships built since the Washington Treaty of 1922 limiting size. With massive tower masts supporting their gun directors, *North Carolina* and WASHINGTON set the general pattern of overall appearance for later American battleships of the SOUTH DAKOTA and IOWA classes. The secondary battery consisted of twenty 5-INCH 38-caliber dual-purpose guns (10×2) arranged amidships, five twin mounts to each side. Light antiaircraft batteries were considerably augmented during the war, and electronics installations were expanded into full "suits" of search and gunnery RADARS. In the Atlantic when the Pacific war began, both ships went to the Pacific Fleet in the spring of 1942. From the GILBERTS operation, in late 1943, through to V-J Day, the North Carolinas served with the FAST CARRIER TASK FORCE.

NORTHERN COMBAT AREA COMMAND. Established at Ledo, India, on February 1, 1944, to direct growing Allied forces in northern BURMA, the Northern Combat Area Command (NCAC) was originally an American command which was responsible for American, British and Indian service and combat troops. Its personnel were also the American staff of a Chinese-American headquarters, Chih Hui Pu, which commanded Chinese forces. NCAC ultimately (and informally) superseded the Chinese-American organization, serving as the senior Allied headquarters in northern Burma.

NORTHERN LIGHT (Nordlicht). Code name for German operations designed to capture LENINGRAD, summer 1942. These operations were at first given the code name Fire Magic (Feuerzauber).

NORTHERN SHIP LANE PATROL. An American submarine-spotting effort, in which converted yachts patrolled convoy routes in offshore North Atlantic waters. *See also* ATLANTIC, BATTLE OF THE.

NORTHWEST AFRICAN AIR FORCES. Under Air Chief Marshal Sir Arthur TEDDER's MEDITERRANEAN AIR COMMAND, Maj. Gen. Carl SPAATZ organized the Northwest African Air Forces into functional organizations. Administrative headquarters was maintained at Algiers; operational headquarters was at Constantine with British and American officers. Maj. Gen. James H. DOOLITTLE commanded the Northwest African Strategic Air Forces (bombers and their fighter escorts), and Air Marshal Sir Arthur CONINGHAM the Northwest African Tactical Air Forces.

NORTHWEST AFRICA—OPERATIONS. The Allied decision to conduct Operation Torch (the invasion of Northwest Africa) was not made until July 1942. There were compelling reasons why Allied soldiers needed to open another front against the AXIS, but it was no easy matter to decide where and how. The Americans favored an operation called Roundup—an invasion of the Continent across the English Channel. Although the British agreed that such an operation would eventually be necessary, they felt the Allies did not yet have sufficient strength to conduct it. American planners gradually assented—many with reluctance—but political and military reasons still necessitated action. The Russians were fighting for their lives for the second summer, and only in Libya were the Western Allies meeting the European Axis.

President ROOSEVELT strongly advocated action in North Africa, which would be possible with existing resources and would also serve to open the Mediterranean, make it easier to get supplies to the Russians through the Persian Gulf and draw Axis strength away from both the British EIGHTH ARMY in Libya and the hard-pressed Russians. An earlier plan, named GYMNAST, was revived. After the staffs had engaged in heated discussions, Roosevelt directed his military advisers to reach an agreement with the British on an operation that could be undertaken in 1942. The decision was for Torch. Three landings were planned—at CASABLANCA, ORAN and ALGIERS. From Algiers the British FIRST ARMY would drive immediately toward TUNISIA, hoping to seize all of French North Africa before the Axis could send sufficient reinforcements to turn it into a major battleground.

The command arrangements for Torch introduced some American figures who were to play key roles in the war. Maj. Gen. Dwight D. EISENHOWER was commander in chief; his deputy was Maj. Gen. Mark CLARK. The Western Task Force, coming from the United States and composed of U.S. troops, was commanded by Maj. Gen. George S. PATTON, Jr. For political reasons, it was deemed necessary to give the invasion an American character: French North Africa supported the VICHY regime, which had broken relations with the British but maintained relations with the United States. Considerable efforts were made before the invasion to determine the degree of support that could be expected from the French and to pave the way for cooperation.

All three landings of Torch, on November 8, 1942, were successful. There were losses caused by the inexperience of the troops, and much was learned about the requirements of an amphibious assault. At all three invasion sites the French offered opposition, but it varied in intensity and duration. At Algiers, the Eastern Task Force met light resistance and on shore all was calm by evening. At Oran, the landings were largely unopposed, but heavy opposition was met ashore and the fighting there lasted until noon of November 10. The heaviest fighting was at Casablanca, where ships as well as shore-based guns and ground forces opposed the invasion. The fighting at Casablanca ended November 11, brought about in large measure by a political move.

Torch posed unusual political-diplomatic problems, for the French, whose territory was being invaded, were not the enemy. Not since the invasion of Canada in 1775 had the Americans faced a comparable situation. Not only did the British and Americans not want to destroy French lives or property, but they wanted the French as active allies in the war against the Axis. They looked upon Torch as liberation, not conquest. But liberation was no simple matter, for the French themselves were divided in allegiance between Gen. Charles de Gaulle and the Vichy regime of Marshal Philippe Pétain.

Hoping to find a French leader around whom all Frenchmen could rally, the Allies slipped Gen. Henri Giraud into Africa, only to find that the French North African leaders would not accept his authority. The authority they would accept was that of Admiral of the Fleet Jean François Darlan, who was powerful in the Vichy regime and yet had at times hinted he would cooperate with the Allies. Darlan was in Algeria on personal business. He agreed to cooperate, and issued orders for the French to cease opposition. By the terms of the Darlan agreement, the French would help the Allies and provide sanction for military operations, while the Allies would stay out of French internal affairs. Darlan was authorized to handle French affairs until the military campaign in Africa was concluded; General Giraud was put in command of French military forces in Northwest Africa. This agreement—the so-called Darlan deal—provoked strong controversy in Britain and the United States. But to the generals it was simply a practical measure to avoid fighting the French and to expedite the main task—fighting the Germans.

While the political negotiations with the French were still in process, Lt. Gen. Kenneth Anderson led the British First Army eastward from Algeria toward Tunisia. Haste was everything, for a major battle could be avoided if the Allies could beat the Axis to the Tunisian ports. Not lacking in determination, but short of tangible elements like supplies and motor transport, Anderson had to fight a poor railroad and highway system plus early winter rains that turned roads and airfields into seas of mud. Air superiority was lost when the only hard-surfaced airfields, near Tunis and Bizerte, were taken over by the Axis. The French troops in Tunisia stalled for time before making a commitment, and before they had arrayed themselves with Anderson, Hitler had begun pouring reinforcements into Tunisia by both sea and air. Generaloberst Jürgen von Arnim was sent to command; his forces in northern Tunisia were separated from Field Marshal Erwin Rommel's Afrika Korps in Libya by some 1,200 miles.

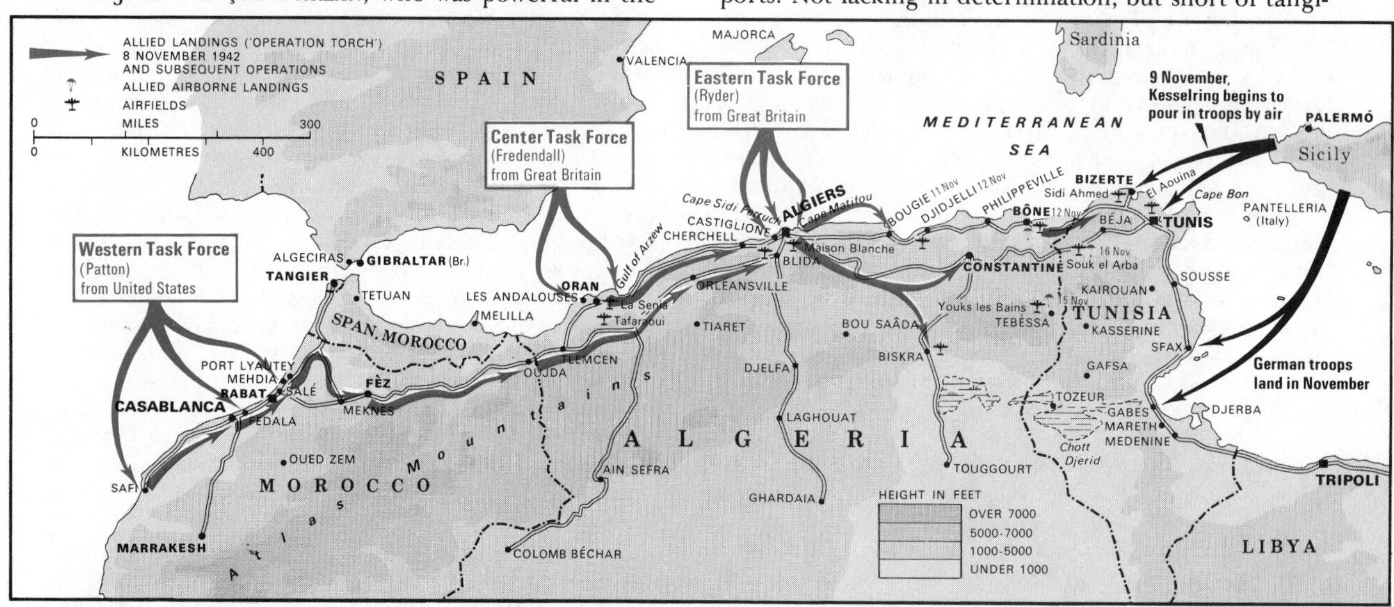

Operation Torch, the landings in Northwest Africa, put the Anglo-American allies into joint action against the Axis

Within days it was obvious to General Anderson that the supply situation was running against the Allies. Air landings were made at Bône and Bougie to seize forward supply ports, but the African transport network could not meet the heavy demands being made on it. The Axis supply lines from Italy were relatively short, and once troops and supplies were in Tunisia, the Axis fought from favored positions because the coastal areas were ringed by hills that could be effectively defended. On November 17 the British and Germans met in the first of many Tunisian battles, but neither side could dislodge the other. Realizing that Anderson would need more strength to take Tunisia, Eisenhower began committing American units to the front, but there was a limit to the number that could be kept supplied. In late November Anderson pushed an offensive as far as Tébourba, but the Allies could go no farther and early in December Axis counterattacks pushed them back.

Reluctant to abandon hopes of ending the Tunisian battle before winter, Eisenhower and Anderson made one more effort, late in December. One of the first steps was to be the capture of Longstop Hill, but when pouring rain, mud and inadequate supplies combined with stiff Axis opposition to bring Allied defeat at Longstop, the Allied generals had to admit that they had lost the race for Tunisia. It would be necessary to stop, consolidate strength, build a supply base and prepare for a battle when the winter rains ended.

Neither side stayed idle during the months of preparation for the final confrontation. There was appreciable sparring for limited tactical objectives, and in mid-February an Axis offensive turned into a serious threat to the Allied position. By that time Rommel's forces had been pushed westward across Africa to the borders of Tunisia; Tripoli was occupied by Eighth Army on January 23. As Rommel and Arnim came physically closer, their differences and rivalries intensified. Rommel, as he wrote, resented the huge amounts of men and supplies sent to Arnim, when he had been denied similar supply backing for his own North African campaign.

In February Arnim decided to push against the passes in the Eastern Dorsal to increase the flank strength of his Tunisian position. Rommel, whose forces would participate in the same operation, saw in it the opportunity to turn Axis defeat into victory by striking from the GABÈS–GAFSA area northwest to cut the Allied forces off from their bases of supply. There was friction between Rommel and Arnim over goals and the allocation of troops. Had the Axis forces been under one command, the February offensive might have been a much more serious threat. Even so, it gave the Allies a sobering setback. Arnim's troops struck through FAÏD PASS and moved across Sbeïtla plain to KASSERINE. Rommel's forces moved up through Gafsa and struck at Kasserine Pass, breaking through on February 20 and then threatening THALA and TÉBESSA—key areas giving access to positions in the Allied rear.

The Axis Kasserine offensive fell against part of the U.S. II Corps, commanded by Maj. Gen. Lloyd FREDENDALL, which held the very end of the Allied line. The Americans were not only thinly extended, but understrength and inexperienced. These conditions had been realized and accepted as one of the hazards of the campaign. Unable to counter the Axis thrusts, the Americans retreated through Kasserine but held firmly behind the pass, particularly at Thala. Rommel decided the large strategic aim could not be achieved and favored retreating to MARETH to meet Gen. Sir Bernard MONTGOMERY, who was pushing from the south. The Axis withdrew, and the Americans reoccupied Kasserine.

This experience was turned to good use in improving American command and training. Kasserine emphasized to the Allies the need for tight command, and after the battle Gen. Sir Harold ALEXANDER, Eisenhower's deputy, took command of the diverse Allied ground forces. All the Axis forces came under the command of Rommel, who wanted to pull his southern forces back and consolidate strength in a smaller area of Tunisia. He was denied permission to do so.

Early in March, Rommel struck Montgomery's Eighth Army at MÉDENINE, hoping to divide, envelop and dispose of his old adversary. It was a task beyond the capabilities of the weakened Afrika Korps. Montgomery, whose move across Africa from ALAMEIN was carefully paced and constantly assured of overwhelming material supply, met Rommel at Médenine with confidence. Anticipating the attack, he planned the defense with particular attention to antitank guns. On March 6 Rommel's forces attacked the Médenine positions four times. They were repulsed each time. Disheartened, realizing that only defeat faced the Axis in Africa, Rommel left for Germany to confer with Adolf Hitler. He never came back to Africa.

Two weeks later Eighth Army attacked the Axis position at MARETH. It was the strongest obstacle since Alamein, occupying a gap between the sea and the rugged Matmata Hills some 20 miles inland. When the main assault, by 30th Corps on the right, did not make the expected gains, Montgomery shifted the weight of the assault to Gen. Bernard FREYBERG and a provisional New Zealand Corps, which was meeting success with a wide flanking maneuver. The Germans retreated to the Chott position behind the WADI Akarit; there Eighth Army attacked on April 6. Soon in full retreat, Rom-

French troops in North Africa receive instructions in the use of American equipment

mel's famous desert army moved up the coast toward ENFIDAVILLE. It was time for the showdown.

For the final Allied drive against the Axis (now under Arnim), General Eisenhower requested that the U.S. II Corps, which had been squeezed out of the line when the Axis retreated north to Enfidaville, be moved to the north of the front and be given an active role. Alexander agreed, and II Corps, now under Maj. Gen. Omar N. BRADLEY, moved into position between BÉDJA and the sea.

The last week of April and the first week of May 1943 were days of hard fighting in Tunisia. The Axis troops were under orders to defend to the death, and their positions were adaptable to strong defense. At Enfidaville, on the south, the Axis stronghold was so formidable that Alexander put Eighth Army into a holding position and moved part of its strength to First Army's front on the west. The final push came from the west, well supported by both air power and artillery. Slowly but inexorably the Allies drove across the hills toward Mateur and up the Medjerda valley toward Tunis. Bizerte fell to II Corps and Tunis to First Army on May 7, and thereafter concluding operations went quickly. The CAP BON peninsula was sealed off to prevent any possibility of a prolonged resistance. On May 12 the last of the Axis in Africa surrendered.

As General von Arnim and 240,000 Axis soldiers marched into captivity, the 32-month struggle for North Africa came to an end. The total effort, since 1940, had cost the Axis a total of 950,000 men; 2.4 million gross tons of shipping; 8,000 aircraft; 6,200 guns; 2,500 tanks; 70,000 trucks. Although Allied losses in matériel were also heavy, in men Allied losses were substantially less. Now, with North Africa secure, the Allies were in a favorable position to control the Mediterranean and move against Italy or the Balkans. Perhaps more important, an Allied command had been tested and proved workable; American troops had gained valuable battle experience; and the requirements of amphibious assault had been tested. **M.H.B.**

NORTHWESTERN APPROACHES. The area of sea north of Ireland and west of Scotland, and including the northern half of the Irish Sea. At the start of the war it was part of the ROSYTH Command, but on February 7, 1941, when the headquarters of the WESTERN APPROACHES Command was moved from Plymouth to Liverpool, it became part of that command.

NORTHWESTERN EXPEDITIONARY FORCE. Anglo-French force in NORWAY, 1940. Lt. Gen. Sir Claude AUCHINLECK was appointed Commander in Chief–Designate of Anglo-French Military Forces and of the British Air Component in Norway. He was given a directive from the Vice-Chief of the Imperial General Staff to take command, under Adm. Lord CORK AND

The French battleship *Jean Bart* was battered in the fighting at Casablanca

Allied leaders meet in Tunis. Front (from left): Gen. Dwight D. Eisenhower, Air Chief Marshal Sir Arthur Tedder, Gen. Sir Harold Alexander, Adm. Sir Andrew Cunningham. Back (from left): Harold Macmillan, Maj. Gen. Walter Bedell Smith, Commo. R. M. Dick (chief of staff to Admiral Cunningham), Air Vice Marshal Sir Philip Wigglesworth

ORRERY, if "you consider that local conditions necessitate." Upon arrival, Auchinleck saw that Lord Cork and the Army commander, Gen. P. J. MACKESY, were in serious disagreement. On May 13, 1940, Auchinleck decided to take over from Mackesy. The land and air forces which Auchinleck then commanded were given the title Northwestern Expeditionary Force.

NORTHWESTERN SEA FRONTIER. U.S. Navy designation for the SEA FRONTIER command responsible for the defense of the U.S. West Coast from Oregon through Alaska. Its area of responsibility was divided in two by the CANADIAN COASTAL ZONE, which protected Canada's Pacific coast. In 1944 this Sea Frontier was abolished, and its area was added to the WESTERN SEA FRONTIER.

NORWAY—OPERATIONS. Though Adolf HITLER told his subordinates early in the war that he would prefer a neutral Norway, in fact a neutral Scandinavia, he stated that if the Allies planned to enlarge the scope of hostilities, he would beat them to the punch. Norway with its long coastline and numerous ports had great attractions for Germany, a power which had suffered under a blockade in the First World War. Not only would the Allies, particularly the British, be denied control of the trade routes which ran from and near Norway, but they would not be able to occupy bases from which they could threaten the German control of the Baltic. Conversely, Germany would gain such bases and thus weaken any British attempts at blockade. Conquest of Norway would also secure the sea passage, through the NORWEGIAN LEADS, that was used by ships carrying Swedish iron ore loaded at the Norwegian port of NARVIK.

Discussion in Britain (some of which was printed in the newspapers) of the possibility of violating Norwegian neutrality, along with other perceived threats, caused Hitler, who had not definitely decided to attack, to direct that invasion plans be prepared. On February 21, 1940, Hitler summoned the commander of the XXI Corps, General der Infanterie Nicholas von FALKENHORST, put him in charge of the operation with a staff composed of officers from all three services and told him that German troops were to be in Norway prior to those of the Allies.

On April 1, after Falkenhorst had had over a month to prepare, Hitler decided to attack. German troops were to land in Norway and Denmark on April 9. German ships began to move on the 7th, the very day that, after much indecision, British ships were en route to mine the Norwegian Leads.

There were naval contacts on April 8. On the next day German ships landed small units at the widely separated key cities of OSLO, KRISTIANSAND, BERGEN, TRONDHEIM and Narvik. Though none of the detachments numbered over 2,000 men, the Germans were generally able to achieve superiority in both soldiers and material. Paratroopers aided in the securing of airfields. Since Denmark fell on April 9, German air support could operate from Danish airstrips, located much closer than those in Germany.

Contrary to the situation in Denmark, Norway did not capitulate in a single day. The naval expedition ordered to take Oslo was held off long enough for the Norwegian royal family, the cabinet and most of the Parliament to leave the city. When the Germans demanded that King HAAKON VII accept a government led by the head of the Norwegian Nazis, Vidkun QUISLING, the King declared that he would rather abdicate. His ministers supported the King's stand, and a decision to resist was made.

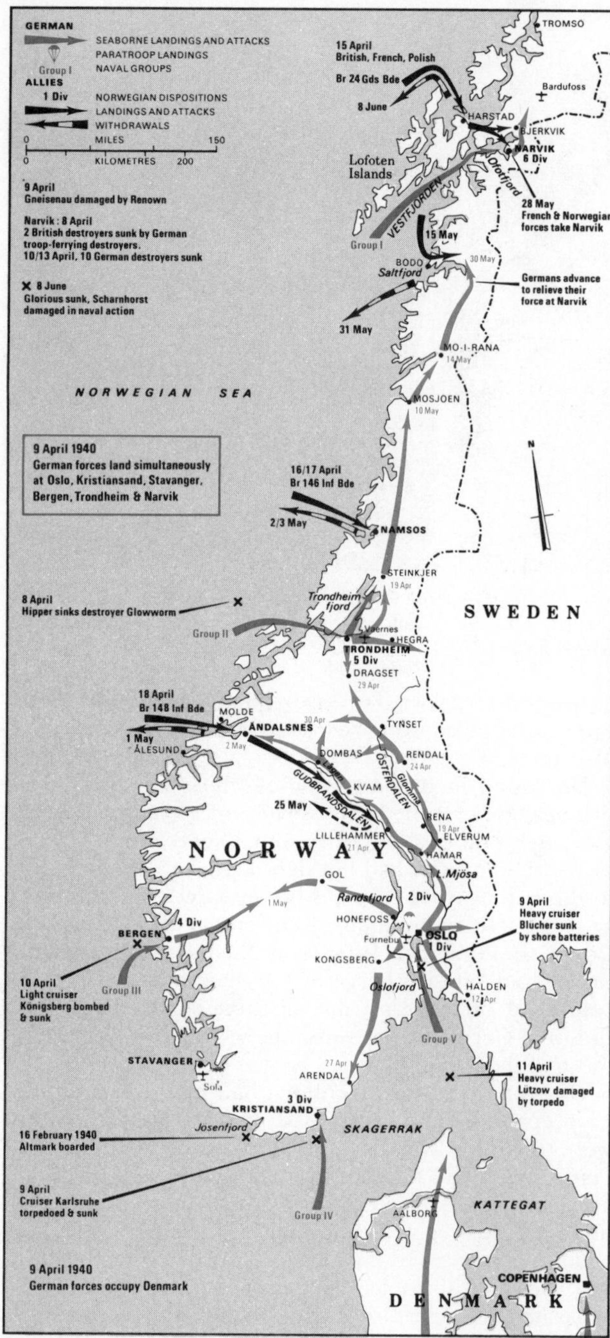

THE NORWAY CAMPAIGN—German speed, Allied frustration

By April 11 the energetic Col. Otto RUGE had been promoted to major general and installed as the Commander in Chief of the Norwegian armed forces. Meanwhile coastal cities had fallen and German fuel and supply ships were arriving with weapons and equipment. To both the Norwegians and the rest of the world, the attackers proclaimed that they had come to protect Norway from an imminent Allied invasion. Allied help was soon to arrive, but its effectiveness was severely hampered by German aircraft. Land-based airplanes, many flying out of Danish airfields, inflicted casualties and caused the British to abandon any plan to use surface ships to cut the German sea line of communication through the Skagerrak, the body of water which separates Norway and Denmark.

By April 16 virtually all of southern Norway had fallen under German control. After several changes in plans, Allied troops with the mission of taking Trondheim had landed at ÅNDALSNES and NAMSOS. This try was unsuccessful, and by May 3 the Allies had been pushed out of central Norway.

More fighting took place in the Narvik area to the north, and the town was taken by the Allies. In early June, however, because of the critical situation in France, the Allied forces were evacuated. The King and his government accompanied the withdrawing forces to England, where a government-in-exile was established. General Ruge decided to stay in Norway with his men. Ruge negotiated an armistice, and the campaign ended.

German confidence soared as a result both of the end of the Norwegian campaign and the events at DUNKIRK that had taken place shortly before. Success in Norway demonstrated to friend and foe alike what German interservice cooperation could achieve. Other benefits included the safeguarding of critical supply lines along the Norwegian coast and the acquisition of air and submarine bases. Victory in Norway was won at a cost, as a number of German cruisers and destroyers were lost or damaged. These losses later hampered the effectiveness of the GERMAN NAVY.

Ships were lost by the Allies also, many to land-based aircraft. One of the most important lessons learned in this campaign was the vulnerability of ships without air cover to such attacks. **T.R.S.**

NORWEGIAN LEADS. Deep sheltered-water passage between the Norwegian mainland and offshore island groups. The Norwegian Leads stretch almost the entire distance from Stavanger to the North Cape. The Leads were Norwegian territorial waters; thus as long as NORWAY remained neutral, German ships could enter the Leads far north of the Arctic Circle or at the iron ore port of NARVIK and safely travel south until they came under the protection of friendly planes and submarines. Operation WILFRED, the long-debated British mining of the Leads, began on April 8, 1940, but some elements of the operation were canceled when it was learned that the German fleet was out. Between the nights of April 13 and April 25 magnetic mines were air-dropped along the coast. German losses to mines were 12 ships, while a number of ships of neutral nations were also sunk. The British cost was 11 planes. Once the Norwegian campaign ended, the German victors carefully guarded their route through the Leads.

NOSHIRO. Japanese AGANO-class light cruiser which saw action at RABAUL, the GILBERT ISLANDS and the MARIANAS, and as part of Admiral KURITA's Center Force in the battle off Samar (*see* LEYTE GULF). U.S. carrier aircraft sank the *Noshiro* northwest of Panay, during the withdrawal of Kurita's force from Leyte.

NO TRANSFER RESOLUTION. In June 1940 the U.S. Congress, concerned about the status of the colonies of Denmark, Holland and France in the New World after the fall of their mother countries to Germany, reaffirmed in a joint resolution the famous "no transfer" clause of the Monroe Doctrine. This 1940 resolution stated firmly that the United States would oppose the transfer of territory in the New World from one non-American power to another. Although the resolution was ill received by Germany, the United States thereby served notice that it would tolerate no German territorial acquisitions in the Western Hemisphere. *See also* HAVANA CONFERENCE.

NOUMEA. The capital of NEW CALEDONIA, whose magnificent harbor provided the primary staging area for Allied landings in the SOLOMONS and NEW GUINEA.

NOVGOROD. Ancient Russian city located at the northern end of Lake Ilmen. By August 20, 1941, Soviet forces had been pushed back to Novgorod by the German drive on LENINGRAD about 70 miles farther north. Novgorod fell the next day. In the ensuing months of subjugation, the Nazis systematically ravaged the city's monuments, some of which dated from the ninth century. Novgorod was liberated by General MERETSKOV's Volkhov Front on January 17, 1944.

NOVIKOV, Alexander A. (1900–1976). Leading Soviet air commander. Chief of Staff of the Air Force during the SOVIET-FINNISH WAR, in 1941–42 Novikov commanded air operations on the LENINGRAD front, becoming a lieutenant general in 1941. Between 1942 and 1946 he was the Commander in Chief of the RED AIR FORCE, helping restore it after the German onslaught in 1941. Novikov personally directed air operations in the Battle of STALINGRAD and was promoted to colonel general in 1943. In 1944 he became the USSR's first marshal of the Air Force. Novikov fell out of STALIN's favor in 1946 and dropped out of sight until the dictator's death in 1953.

NOVOGRAD-VOLYNSKY. Ukrainian town northwest of KIEV and just south of the PRIPET MARSHES. It figured prominently in the defense before Kiev in June–July 1941, being first defended by ROKOSSOVSKY's IX Mechanized Corps. The city was taken by the Germans in July 1941 and was not liberated until January 1944.

NOVOROSSISK. Soviet Black Sea naval base, taken by the Germans on September 6, 1942, and retaken by the Red Army on September 16, 1943.

NOWOTNY, Walter (1920–1944). LUFTWAFFE ace, with 255 kills on the Eastern Front and three more in the west. He was removed from Russia first to serve as commander of a training wing and then as head of what became known as Kommando Nowotny, for testing the jet MESSERSCHMITT ME 262. While in a Me 262 he was killed in action with U.S. Mustangs (*see* P-51).

NSZ (Narodowe Sily Zbrojne). National Armed Forces, a political party and armed underground group of the extreme right, formed in German-occupied Poland. The NSZ conducted operations against the Germans and Russians during the war and also attacked Polish Jews who were able to escape the Nazis. After the war the NSZ continued to oppose the Russians and the new Polish Communist state. For a time it was led by Boleslaw Piasecki, who would later achieve prominence in the Communist regime. By 1947 it had been completely suppressed by the Polish Government.

NO. 91. This B-29, commanded by Capt. George W. Marquardt, carried scientific gear and military and civilian observers during the August 6, 1945, atomic attack on HIROSHIMA. Its nickname was an abbreviation of its number: 44–27291.

NUREMBERG. On the night of March 30–31, 1944, RAF BOMBER COMMAND dispatched 795 bombers to Nuremberg. The losses were appallingly heavy, 94 planes being shot down and 71 damaged. As a result, heavy night penetration of German air space was suspended, although it is also true that at this time Allied bombing efforts were scheduled to be switched to France to help prepare the way for the Normandy INVASION. Peculiarly, the target of the raid was strictly the Old City, one of the architectural treasures of Europe.

NUREMBERG TRIALS. When the occupation of Germany was completed by the Allied forces, there began the formidable task of bringing to some form of justice the vast number of war criminals. It was a task that would last until 1948, when the German courts were authorized to take over this responsible act of retribution. There were many legal and moral problems involved, for it was only too easy to turn retribution into revenge or to apply a retroactive form of law, that is, a legal code that did not exist at the time the crimes were committed. Many of the worst culprits (notably Adolf HITLER and Heinrich HIMMLER) were dead; many had escaped the country (Adolf EICHMANN, for instance) or gone into hiding (for example, Rudolf HOESS, who was not arrested until March 1946). Others, such as the defendants at the initial trial held at Nuremberg under joint Allied control—the INTERNATIONAL MILITARY TRIBUNAL—were already under arrest. Other notable trials followed in the four zones under the control of the particular Allied nation in authority.

The International Military Tribunal at Nuremberg was unique in judicial history. Its legal basis was established at a conference in London of jurists from the four victorious nations convened on June 26, 1945. Agreement on a statute for the court was finally reached and signed on August 8, and this was subsequently subscribed to by 23 nations. The trials were, however, open to criticism not only because they applied a code of law retroactively, but because they adopted an Anglo-American form of procedure unfamiliar to the German people and because the accusers were also the judges. However, Dr. Robert Woetzel in *The Nuremberg Trials and International Law* claims the tribunal was properly grounded in international law and has created a precedent for the future. Certainly it led to an almost immediate and relatively systematic exposure before the eyes of the world of the appalling culpability of the Nazi regime, in the form of massive documentary evidence and reiterated personal testimony.

The defendants were:

Hermann Göring	**Karl Dönitz**
Rudolf Hess	**Erich Raeder**
Joachim von Ribbentrop	**Baldur von Schirach**
Alfred Rosenberg	**Fritz Sauckel**
Wilhelm Keitel	**Alfred Jodl**
Ernst Kaltenbrunner	**Franz von Papen**
Hans Frank	**Arthur Seyss-Inquart**
Wilhelm Frick	**Albert Speer**
Julius Streicher	**Constantin von Neurath**
Hjalmar Schacht	**Hans Fritzsche**
Walter Funk	**Martin Bormann** (*in absentia*)

Robert Ley would also have stood trial, but he committed suicide in his cell on October 25, 1945. The defendants had, in fact, been flown to Nuremberg on August 12 and confined in cells within the virtually undamaged Palace of Justice, where the trials were held. Not only were the prisoners kept under heavy guard by the Americans, they were also placed under psychiatric observation, the psychiatrists' reports being published subsequently: *Twenty-two Cells in Nuremberg* (1947) by Douglas M. Kelley and *Nuremberg Diary* (1947) by G. M. Gilbert.

The charges were grouped under four main headings:

(1) The Common Plan or Conspiracy, relating to the seizure of power in Germany and its utilization to achieve foreign aggression.

(2) Crimes against Peace—the planning, preparation, initiating and waging of wars of aggression, in violation of international treaties.

(3) War Crimes in countries and territories occupied by German Armed Forces and on the high seas—murder and ill-treatment of civilian populations, deportations for slave labor, killing of prisoners of war and hostages, wanton destruction of cities, towns and villages, plunder of public and private property, conscription of civilian labor and Germanization of occupied territories.

(4) Crimes against Humanity—murder, extermination, enslavement, deportation, persecution on political, racial and religious grounds.

The defendants were presented on October 18, 1945, with a copy of the indictment, some 25,000 words long, and they were permitted to choose their German defense lawyers from a list prepared by the Allied authorities. The main costs of the trials, conducted in German and interpreted by simultaneous translation into English, French and Russian, were borne by the United States. The proceedings were fully recorded, and key moments were covered on sound film. The world press was represented on the opening day by 250 journalists, of whom only five were German.

The court proceedings were to become interminable, lasting in all 218 days, occupied as follows:

1945	November 20. The indictment read
1945–46	November to March. Case for the prosecution
1946	March to July. Case for the defendants
	July. Final speeches for defense and prosecution
	July–August. Trial of indicted organizations
	August 31. Final statements by defendants
	September 30. Judgments read
	October 1. Conclusion of trial
	October 15 (night). Executions

The parallel trials in Tokyo lasted 417 days.

The tribunal consisted of Lord Justice Lawrence of Britain, who acted as president, with Mr. Justice Birkett as his alternate; Francis Biddle and Judge John J. Parker (U.S.); Prof. Donnedieu de Vabres and M. le Conseiller Falco (France); and Maj. Gen. I. T. Nikitchenko and Lt. Col. A. F. Volchkov (USSR). The teams of prosecutors for each country were led by Justice Robert H. Jackson (U.S.), H.M. Attorney-General Sir Hartley Shawcross (U.K.), François de Menthon and later Auguste Champetier de Ribes (France) and Gen. R. A. Rudenko (USSR). The American commission was responsible for the immense task of collating, condensing and translating the vast body of documentary evidence fed into the trials—including selections from some 350,000 affidavits, as well as innumerable interrogations and evidence derived from captured Nazi archives; the tribunal heard the testimony of well over a hundred witnesses.

During the first day of the trial—November 20, 1945—the lengthy indictment was read out. Two defendants, Hess and Kaltenbrunner, were absent because of illness. On the second day each prisoner, including Hess but still excluding Kaltenbrunner (who had had a heart attack), declared himself "not guilty." The massive case for the prosecution then began, and became in effect a history of the Third Reich presented in terms of the four counts named above and as reflected in the respective careers of each defendant. This was followed by the cases against the indicted organizations (and, through them, the key individuals responsible for their activities): the Reich cabinet, the leadership corps of the Nazi Party, the SS, the SD (SS intelligence), the Gestapo, the SA and the high command of the German armed forces (OKW). (See separate entries for these organizations.)

The record of the trials as published in Nuremberg in English fills 23 volumes, amounting to some 6 million words, while the documentary evidence fills a further 19 volumes. Behind it all lay the malignant personality of the dead Führer, whom only Göring went out of his way to defend, though Keitel asserted Hitler's genius as a military strategist, betrayed (he said) by the evil influence of Himmler, Goebbels and Bormann. The defendants were largely divided between those who were penitent (Frank, a newly converted Catholic; Schirach;

Funk; Speer, who was always reasonable and factual), those who were enraged at being there at all (notably Schacht, who considered himself a member of the German resistance), those who kept as aloof and uninvolved as possible (Papen and Neurath), the service chiefs who considered the trial inapplicable to their case, since they had been in uniform and required to obey orders (Raeder, Dönitz, Keitel and Jodl), and those determined to brazen it out (such as Kaltenbrunner and Streicher). The two exceptions were Göring, who in private conversation was contrite but in the courtroom was often spokesman for the leadership principle as promulgated in MEIN KAMPF, was at times impatient or ironic at the lack of detailed knowledge in his accusers and was devious under severe cross-examination (as, for example, when questioned concerning his knowledge of the EXTERMINATION CAMPS, which he continued to deny); and Hess, who feigned amnesia except for the electrifying moment on November 30, 1945, when he suddenly got up and asserted that his loss of memory was simulated and that he accepted full responsibility for what he had done. After this outburst, however, he relapsed once again into his obliviousness.

Many witnesses gave startling evidence; for example, Erwin Lahousen's testimony about the existence of the OPPOSITION TO HITLER within the ABWEHR and about the parts played by several defendants in the exterminations in Poland, Hans GISEVIUS's bitter statements about Göring's participation in various Nazi scandals, HOESS's cold-bloodedly factual declaration about extermination in Auschwitz and Otto OHLENDORF's testimony about the crimes of the ACTION GROUPS in Russia.

Of the cross-examiners, the most penetrating and persistent was the British Sir David Maxwell-Fyfe, and the most emotional and deeply moved was the American Robert H. Jackson. For the first time the great wealth of documentary evidence against the Nazis was exposed to public scrutiny. Speer shocked some of his fellow defendants (notably Göring) by declaring that he had come to regard Hitler as "a selfish, destructive force that had no consideration for the German people." But undoubtedly the hearing of Göring's case was the highlight of the trial, since he was inevitably the foremost defendant. "I am determined to go down in German history as a great man," he declared to the psychiatrist, Dr. Kelley. No less than 13 days was spent in his defense, and Göring behaved throughout like an actor performing the greatest role of his life. He was often lucid in his exposition, often humorous and entertaining, always determined to dominate the proceedings as a triton among the minnows, anxious to show off the fullness of his knowledge and memory for detail. His often impertinent assertions, interruptions and evasions eventually made Jackson lose his temper, and the trial had to be recessed. Maxwell-Fyfe hammered at him over the extermination camps, and was equally severe in his treatment of Papen and Neurath when they attempted to evade any responsibility for what had happened.

So the trials dragged on, month after month. Finally, the defense attorneys took two more weeks winding up their cases; the prosecutors, in their final statements, used up a further four days. Another month was spent exploring the evils of the accused organizations. On September 30, after the lapse of a month while the judges considered their verdicts, came the judgment:

Condemned to death: Göring, Streicher, Frick, Ribbentrop, Kaltenbrunner, Sauckel, Keitel, Jodl, Frank, Rosenberg, Seyss-Inquart.

Condemned to imprisonment: Hess (life), Funk (life), Raeder (life), Speer (20 years), Schirach (20 years), Neurath (15 years), Dönitz (10 years).

Acquitted: Schacht, Papen, Fritzsche.

Papen and Fritzsche, as distinct from Schacht, could not believe their good fortune. They were, however, subject to retrial at the hands of the Germans. Göring alone refused to face the hangman along with the others awaiting death; when his request to be shot like a soldier was refused, he took his own life on the night he was due to hang, October 14, swallowing a capsule of cyanide which he had kept concealed. Col. Burton C. Andrus, U.S. Army governor of Nuremberg prison, revealed in 1967 the text of a suicide letter Göring had left for him explaining that he had managed to conceal two capsules throughout his captivity.

The International Military Tribunal war crimes trials were the first of a network of trials conducted by the Allies of those accused of Nazi crimes. Twelve additional trials took place in Nuremberg, starting in October 1946 and spanning some 1,200 days in court. The transcripts occupy 330,000 pages. These cases included that against the SS Action Group participants, the specialist killers who caused the death of 1 million people in German-occupied Russia; the outstanding defendant was Otto Ohlendorf, who was in charge of Action Group D in 1941–42. Another of these trials, lasting eight months between December 1946 and July 1947, was that of the SS doctors, who had conducted the so-called scientific experiments on the prisoners in the concentration camps. **R.M.**

NÜRNBERG. German light cruiser, launched in December 1934. The *Nürnberg* was the only significant German warship besides the PRINZ EUGEN and the LEIPZIG to survive the war. She served as the *Admiral Makarov* in the Soviet Navy until 1959. She displaced 6,710 tons and had a top speed of 32 knots. She was armed with nine 5.9-inch and eight 3.5-inch guns and twelve 21-inch torpedo tubes, and carried two aircraft.

NYE, Sir Archibald (1895–1967). British Army officer who served as Vice-Chief of the Imperial General Staff, 1941–46. Nye, a lieutenant general, represented Field Marshal Sir Alan BROOKE, the chief (CIGS), at various conferences and meetings and gained the respect of Prime Minister CHURCHILL and Brooke for his intelligence and the care with which he executed policy.

NYE, Gerald (1892–1971). U.S. Senator from North Dakota, whose Senate committee investigated the role played by U.S. munitions and weapons industries in World War I. His charge that the munitions industry's desire for profits had helped drag the United States into the war stirred up isolationist sentiment and led to the passage of NEUTRALITY ACTS from 1935 to 1937.

O

OA-10A. U.S. Army designation for its version of the PBY flying boat (*see* PBY). Ordered from Canadian-Vickers for the Navy as the PBV-1, 230 of these airplanes were produced and delivered to the Army as the OA-10A. They were principally used for air–sea search and rescue in the Pacific.

OAK (Eiche). Code name of the German rescue of Benito MUSSOLINI from the custody of Marshal BADOGLIO's government on September 13, 1943; the exploit was carried out under the direction of Otto SKORZENY. Mussolini had been moved to a hotel on the Gran Sasso d'Italia in the Abruzzi Apennine Mountains. Skorzeny landed with a small SS force, overawed the *carabinieri* guarding Mussolini and whisked the prisoner away in a small Fieseler-STORCH airplane.

OAK RIDGE. An important center involved in the production of the ATOMIC BOMB was the Clinton Engineer Works, located at what became the city of Oak Ridge, Tenn. In 1943 the Du Pont Co. constructed several plants on a 70-acre site on the Clinch River near Clinton to obtain U-235 and plutonium.

OB. Abbreviation for the German Oberbefehlshaber (commander in chief). It was used to signify the headquarters of German theater commanders: OB Nordwest (Northwest—northwest Germany, Denmark and the Netherlands); OB Süd (South—southern Germany and several army groups on the Eastern Front); OB Südost (Southeast—the Balkans); OB Südwest (Southwest—Italy); OB West (West—France, Belgium and the Netherlands). OB West, for example, is translated "Headquarters, Commander in Chief West."

O'BANNON, U.S.S. FLETCHER-class destroyer, commissioned in 1942. She joined the Pacific Fleet in the fall of that year and served with distinction in the naval battle of GUADALCANAL (November 1942) and the Battles of KULA GULF (July 1943) and VELLA LAVELLA (October 1943). During 1944 *O'Bannon* supported landing operations in New Guinea and screened the transport area off the Leyte landing beaches during the battle for LEYTE GULF. Through mid-1945 she continued to support assaults on Japanese-held islands in the PHILIPPINES and to cover landings on Borneo. During June–August 1945 she screened escort carrier strikes on OKINAWA and FAST CARRIER TASK FORCE attacks on Japan.

OBERSALZBERG. Mountain (6,400 feet) in southern Germany, near the town of Berchtesgaden and the Austrian border; site of Adolf HITLER's country house, the BERGHOF.

OBOE. British code name for a 222–228 megacycle RADAR blind-bombing system, first used successfully when the Battle of the RUHR opened on the night of March 5, 1943, with an attack by RAF LANCASTER bombers on the KRUPP armament works at Essen, Germany.

OBSERVER CORPS. When the AIR DEFENCE OF GREAT BRITAIN was set up in 1925, recruiting began for a new Observer Corps to report the movement of aircraft across those parts of Great Britain which lay open to attack. The corps was a civilian body, raised and paid through the chief constables of their area. In 1936 the Observer Corps came under FIGHTER COMMAND. By 1939 the corps was ready for war, but wide tracts in the north and west of the country lacked coverage. The observers were particularly useful in reporting low-flying intruders operating below RADAR cover so that the sector controllers could build up a picture of attacks and feint attacks. In 1941 the title Royal Observer Corps was granted in recognition of the corps's valuable services.

OCCUPATION ZONES. Substantial discussion among the Allies during the war was devoted to the problem of postwar policy toward a defeated Germany, especially the question whether the Reich should be allowed to remain unified or should be divided into several states. Progress toward an agreed policy was achieved at the MOSCOW CONFERENCE of foreign ministers (October 1943). This meeting formulated the initial occupation zones for the Big Three powers and stipulated that control machinery for the occupation would be set up. The foreign ministers also agreed to establish the EUROPEAN ADVISORY COMMISSION (EAC) to help formulate policy for a defeated Germany. The EAC began operation on January 14, 1944, and worked out the lines of division between the Soviet zone and the British and American zones and for the joint administration of Berlin. The Russian zone would extend to 200 miles west of Berlin. The British would occupy the north-

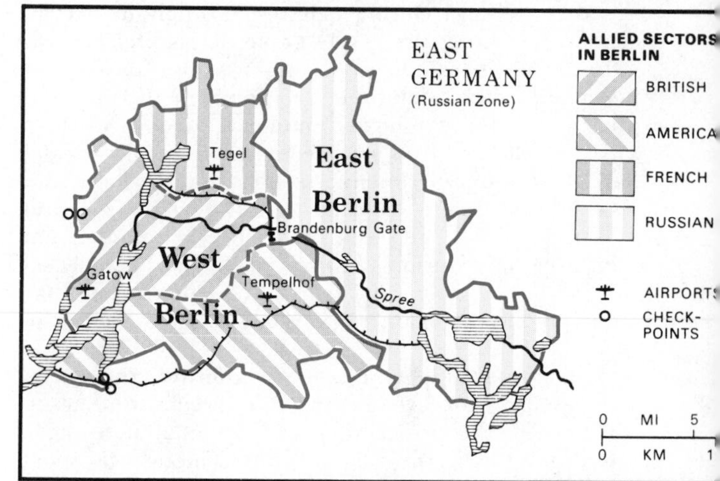

BERLIN—the Allied sectors

western part of Germany; the Americans would control the area south of the Saar and the Lower Palatinate. By the time Germany surrendered in May 1945, France had joined the Big Three as an occupying power. The French zone, which included the Rhineland and the Saar, was carved out of the British and American zones. France was also given a zone of occupation in Berlin.

The formal period of occupation began on June 5, 1945, when General EISENHOWER, Field Marshal MONTGOMERY, Marshal ZHUKOV and General de LATTRE DE TASSIGNY met in Berlin and signed a declaration by which the four powers assumed supreme authority in Germany. They also set up the ALLIED CONTROL COUNCIL to coordinate occupation policy in accordance with protocols drafted by the EAC. The occupation of Berlin was analogous to that of the German state. The Soviet sector comprised 156 square miles on the eastern side of the city; the Western powers controlled 186 square miles in the west. Three air corridors over the Soviet zone which were set up on November 30, 1945, provided lines of transit for air traffic to the three western zones of the city.

The Allies set up four occupation zones in Austria following V-E Day; Vienna was also divided into four zones. As was the case in Germany, the four military commanders decided policy for the Austrian state. The Soviet zone in Austria included Lower Austria, in which Vienna is situated, and Burgenland. The British zone covered Steiermark, Carinthia and the eastern Tyrol. The French zone included Voralberg and the western Tyrol. The American zone included Upper Austria and backed up on its German occupation zone. In October 1945 the Allies recognized Premier Karl Renner's government as the all-Austrian government, but the occupation of the country lasted until May 15, 1955.

The division of Korea into occupation zones came about in a much different way from that followed in the European cases. The communiqué issued by Roosevelt, Churchill and Chiang Kai-shek at the first CAIRO CONFERENCE (November 1943) stated that these three leaders were "determined that in due course Korea shall become free and independent." The Allies reaffirmed this goal at the POTSDAM CONFERENCE.

OCCUPATION ZONES of the Allies in Germany and Austria

Following the Soviet declaration of war on Japan and the subsequent Japanese surrender, the Russians agreed with the other Allies to accept the surrender of Japanese forces north of the 38th parallel, which roughly bisected Korea. The Americans would do the same south of the 38th parallel. This decision to disarm the Japanese north and south of a temporary military line was more the result of accident than of design. Yet contrary at least to American expectations, this convenient division of Korea became two rigid zones of occupation.

O'CONNOR, Sir Richard (1889–). General WAVELL, British Commander in Chief in the Middle East, requested his old friend General O'Connor as commander of the Western Desert Force in 1940. True to his motto, "Offensive action wherever possible," O'Connor led the Desert Force in the well-planned and successful action against the Italians between December 8, 1940, and February 5, 1941. He was captured at the front in April 1941 and held in captivity in Italy until December 1943, when he escaped. June 1944 found O'Connor in command of the 8th Corps in Normandy. He was highly respected as a fighting leader who showed a good balance between aggressiveness and caution, and his period of captivity was a considerable Allied loss.

OCTAGON. Code name for the second American-British QUEBEC CONFERENCE, September 12–16, 1944.

O'DANIEL, John Wilson (1894–1975). "Iron Mike" O'Daniel was a U.S. Army officer who saw action in North Africa and SICILY and at SALERNO and ANZIO. In February 1944 he became commanding general of the 3d Infantry Division at Anzio; he led the division in the operation and across Germany to BERCHTESGADEN. He earned his nickname in World War I when a bullet passed through his face while he was serving as lieutenant in the company commanded by Mark W. CLARK. In the postwar years he served in Korea and South Vietnam, his highest rank being lieutenant general. He was one of the modern Army's characters, loved by his associates and men for his sunny disposition and wry humor.

ODEND'HAL, Jean (1884–1957). French admiral, chief of the French naval mission to London in 1939–40, which coordinated French naval operations with the British. Expelled from the British Admiralty when the British took action against French naval forces following the Franco-German armistice, Odend'hal was repatriated to France.

ODER–NEISSE LINE. The much-disputed line of these rivers became the western boundary of Poland at the end of the war. *See also* NEISSE RIVER.

ODESSA. Located on the Black Sea, Odessa was prior to World War II the main Soviet naval base for the western section of the Black Sea. Odessa as well as that portion of the southern Ukraine stretching from Bessarabia to the Bug River was Rumania's reward for participation in the war against the Soviet Union. The territory was incorporated into Rumania under the name Transnistria (Land Beyond the Dniester). The Red Army reclaimed Odessa as well as "Transnistria" and Bessarabia in April 1944.

O'DONNELL, Emmett (1905–1971). "Rosie" O'Donnell was an athlete and later a coach at the U.S. Military Academy. He transferred from infantry to aviation and won his wings in 1930. After a variety of assignments, in September 1941 he led a squadron of B-17s from Hawaii to the PHILIPPINES, the first mass flight across the western Pacific (*see* B-17). After the outbreak of war, he fought the Japanese in the Philippines and in the Netherlands East Indies. He was promoted from major to lieutenant colonel in January 1942, then became a colonel in March when he went to India to serve as assistant chief of staff for operations at TENTH AIR FORCE headquarters.

O'Donnell returned to the United States in March 1943 and became chief of an advisory committee established by Gen. Henry H. ARNOLD. In February 1944 he received a promotion to brigadier general and joined the B-29 program (*see* B-29). He trained a Superfortress bombardment wing, then went to the Pacific, where he led the first B-29 strike against Tokyo in November 1944. He was with the Marianas-based bomber units for the remainder of the war.

OFFICE FOR EMERGENCY MANAGEMENT. During the war the U.S. Government, under authority of the Reorganization Act of 1939, created units to carry on wartime functions, rather than assigning new emergency tasks to already existing agencies. Following this centralization, an administrative order in 1940 established the Office for Emergency Management within the Executive Office of the President for the purpose of coordinating and directing all emergency agencies.

OFFICE OF CIVILIAN DEFENSE. U.S. agency established in May 1941 "to provide for necessary cooperation with state and local governments in respect of measures for adequate protection of the civilian population in emergency periods." The first director was Mayor Fiorello H. LA GUARDIA of New York; Eleanor ROOSEVELT became assistant director. This team had various difficulties with conservative members of Congress; in fact, the OCD, which had little in the way of line authority but was a coordinating group, was surprisingly controversial. At the time of Pearl Harbor there were about 3.5 million volunteers and 7,000 defense committees in operation. Two years later there were more than 11 million volunteers and 11,400 local defense councils. Shortly after the United States entered the war, La Guardia retired from the OCD (as did Mrs. Roosevelt), being succeeded by James M. Landis.

OFFICE OF DEFENSE TRANSPORTATION. U.S. agency created in December 1941 to coordinate the work of transportation agencies and organizations. Joseph B. Eastman was appointed director on January 2, 1942.

OFFICE OF ECONOMIC STABILIZATION. U.S. agency created within the OFFICE FOR EMERGENCY MANAGEMENT in October 1942 for the purpose of formulating policy in the area of wage stabilization and the control of living costs. The first director was former Supreme Court Justice James F. BYRNES. In May 1943 Byrnes resigned to become director of the OFFICE OF WAR MOBILIZATION. He was succeeded by Fred M. VINSON, a federal judge.

OFFICE OF PRICE ADMINISTRATION. This U.S. agency was originally established as the Office of Price Administration and Civilian Supply within the OFFICE FOR EMERGENCY MANAGEMENT in April 1941. The office assumed the responsibilities and incorporated the staff of the adviser on price stabilization of the National Defense Advisory Commission. Its name was changed to the Office of Price Administration in August 1941, and its responsibilities for civilian supply were transferred to the WAR PRODUCTION BOARD. The OPA was then established as an independent agency in January 1942, with its principal functions being price control, rent control and rationing.

The most pressing economic problem faced by the OPA resulted from the expansion of government outlays which rapidly increased national income at the same time as there was a slowdown in the volume of civilian goods produced. The gap between purchasing power and supply presented the possibility of disastrous inflation. Directors of the OPA were, successively, Leon HENDERSON, Prentiss M. Brown and Chester Bowles.

OFFICE OF PRODUCTION MANAGEMENT. U.S. agency established within the OFFICE FOR EMERGENCY MANAGEMENT in January 1941. Under its jurisdiction were placed the coordination of national defense purchases; small-business activities; research and statistics; and advisers on industrial materials and industrial production. Broad powers over the supply of materials required for national defense and over the means of production were granted to the office. The director general of OPM was William S. KNUDSEN; the associate director general was Sidney HILLMAN. The functions of OPM were transferred to the WAR PRODUCTION BOARD in January 1942.

OFFICE OF SCIENTIFIC RESEARCH AND DEVELOPMENT. U.S. agency established in the OFFICE FOR EMERGENCY MANAGEMENT on June 28, 1941, with Dr. Vannevar BUSH as director. It included the National Defense Research Committee and the Committee on Medical Research. The OSRD had the mission of developing new equipment and helping to see that it came into use. During the war OSRD let about $500 million in contracts for the development of new weapons, notable examples being the PROXIMITY FUZE and the ATOMIC BOMB.

OFFICE OF STRATEGIC SERVICES. U.S. entry into World War II found the nation with an ineffective intelligence system. The Office of the Coordinator of Information (COI), formed in July 1941, was unequal to the problems caused by the unclear areas of jurisdiction and the bureaucratic rivalries in the intelligence community. Since early 1941 American agents, including Col. William J. "Wild Bill" DONOVAN, friend and confidant of President ROOSEVELT, had been in London studying the British SPECIAL OPERATIONS EXECUTIVE (SOE). When on July 13, 1942, Roosevelt created the OSS to replace COI and named Donovan as its director, the SOE served as the model. Many of the COI functions, such as those dealing with domestic information services, were turned over to the newly formed OFFICE OF WAR INFORMATION. Thereafter OSS was charged with the collection and analysis of foreign information and with carrying out special operations under the control of the JOINT CHIEFS OF STAFF.

Although the OSS was capable of operating worldwide, it was prohibited from involvement in Latin America, because of an agreement with the FBI, and in the Southwest Pacific, because General MACARTHUR refused to allow it to operate there. MacArthur was not alone in his dislike of the clandestine nature of the OSS. This view was shared at the time by a number of the U.S. leaders—especially in the Army, Navy and FBI—who distrusted the unorthodox, individualist makeup of the group. Even so, OSS began to operate; it drew on all walks of life, including the military, to fill its ranks. Eventually, as many as 12,000 people would be on duty either in the headquarters or in subordinate activities in the United States and overseas. Although the organization of OSS was constantly changing, its major operations fell into three categories: propaganda to boost or break morale, as the case might be; research and analysis of information concerning all areas where U.S. forces might operate; secret intelligence pertaining to sabotage, spying, demolitions, clandestine radio communications and paramilitary operations. Although the first two elements performed tasks vital to the war effort, it was the special intelligence operations that acquired most of the glamour and drama associated with OSS.

As early as September 1942 OSS had integrated its operations with those of the SOE. Much of the initial training of American personnel was given by the British. In October 1943 a small OSS team aided in the capture of Corsica. In BURMA, OSS-led guerrillas were credited with killing or wounding over 15,000 Japanese troops. Beginning in late 1943, hundreds of OSS, British and other Allied three-man teams were sent into France and the Low Countries to organize and equip local resistance groups for participation in the forthcoming invasion of Europe. Similar activities took place in other theaters, with many acts of personal heroism; in all, some 830 members of OSS were decorated during the war. In neutral Bern, Switzerland, OSS mission chief Allen DULLES, who was later to serve as first director of the Central Intelligence Agency, operated one of the most successful espionage rings of the war. Dulles's agents penetrated the German Foreign Office and the GESTAPO, and the American master spy was able to negotiate the secret surrender of all German troops in northern Italy a week before V-E Day.

Although Donovan remained the director until the end of the war, he was unable to convince President TRUMAN that OSS had a place in peacetime. On October 1, 1945, OSS ceased to exist, and its functions, records and personnel were divided between the State and War Departments.

OFFICE OF THE COORDINATOR OF INTER-AMERICAN AFFAIRS. U.S. wartime agency, established in 1940, whose field of operation was Latin America. Under its first coordinator, Nelson A. ROCKEFELLER, its functions included curtailment of Axis influence in the Latin American press and economy, American propaganda to Latin America, news services and implementation of American aid to Latin America in such diverse areas as health and sanitation, transportation and economic programs.

OFFICE OF WAR INFORMATION. Authorized by President ROOSEVELT on June 13, 1942, the OWI had the mission of giving direction to war propaganda and official information flow. It was headed by Elmer DAVIS, probably the most popular newscaster of his day, and its activities were supervised by three celebrated deputies, Robert E. Sherwood, Leo Rosten and Milton S. Eisenhower. Initially the OWI was charged with providing all information to forces overseas, but that purview was yielded to the Army following negotiations between Davis and Lt. Col. S. L. A. Marshall, then chief of Army Orientation. With the support and facilities of the Army Signal Corps, Marshall then organized the Army News Service, which in postwar years became the Armed Services Information Service. Both at home and abroad, the operations of OWI were regarded as efficient and markedly successful. The office was abolished shortly after the end of the war.

OFFICE OF WAR MOBILIZATION. President ROOSEVELT created this U.S. agency early in 1943 at the suggestion of James F. BYRNES. The office, of which Byrnes became director, had broad authority over the allocation of civilian manpower and resources during the war. Although designed as a superagency to coordinate and plan war production, it functioned as a White House mediator between conflicting production agencies. "Assistant President" Byrnes chaired a council that included the Secretaries of the Army and the Navy and the heads of the WAR PRODUCTION BOARD, War Food

Administration and OFFICE OF ECONOMIC STABILIZATION. As referee, Byrnes's office attempted to soothe rivalries and dampen disputes before they became disruptive or embarrassed the Administration. Legislation sponsored by Harry TRUMAN's Senate investigating committee transformed OWM into the Office of War Mobilization and Reconversion in 1944 and gave it authority over matters related to the transition to peacetime production.

OGDENSBURG AGREEMENT. In mid-August 1940 President Franklin D. ROOSEVELT and Canadian Prime Minister W. L. Mackenzie KING met in Ogdensburg, N.Y., during U.S. Army maneuvers. There the two leaders agreed to establish the Permanent Joint Board on Defense to analyze common defense problems. Although Canada was a belligerent and the United States a neutral, it was understood by this action that the United States would tolerate no Axis takeover, penetration or influence in Canada, regardless of the outcome of events in Europe.

O'HARE, Edward Henry (1914–1943). President ROOSEVELT called the U.S. Navy Hellcat pilot "Butch" O'Hare one of the greatest combat fliers of all time. O'Hare shot down five Japanese planes single-handedly in an air battle at BOUGAINVILLE in February 1942, a feat that won him the MEDAL OF HONOR and promotion to lieutenant commander. He was killed in action in November 1943 while operating off the carrier ENTERPRISE during the GILBERT ISLANDS campaign. O'Hare Field on APAMAMA Atoll was named in his honor as was the Chicago international airport.

OHKA (Cherry Blossom). Designed principally as a coast-defense weapon against Allied invasion, this Japanese Navy "human bomb" (Allied code name, Baka ["Fool"]) carried a 1,760-pound explosive warhead (1,320 pounds in the Model 22) and was powered by a rocket (Model 11) or a jet engine (Model 22). Model 11, designed to be carried to the target area by a modified G4M bomber (*see* G4M), was hampered by its short range. The Model 22 was produced too late for combat. Three later versions were intended to be launched by the G8N1 bomber (*see* G8N1), by a tow plane and from a land-based catapult, respectively. A further turbojet variant, Model 43, was planned. One- and two-seat versions of this piloted suicide bomb were produced.

Ohka bomb

OHLENDORF, Otto (1907–1951). A student of economics, philosophy and sociology, holder of a doctor's degree in jurisprudence, Professor Ohlendorf was born in Hohen Egelsen, Hanover. He was typical of the German intellectuals attracted into the SS, which he joined in 1926 (*see* SS). He entered Reinhard HEYDRICH's SD, the SS intelligence service, in 1936 and took charge of its cultural, economic and legal affairs (*see* SD). In 1941 he was, to use his own term, "conscripted" to lead one of the SS ACTION GROUPS charged with pursuing and killing Russian Jews, Communist officials and PARTISANS behind the German lines of advance. After the war he gave evidence before the INTERNATIONAL MILITARY TRIBUNAL (NUREMBERG TRIALS) and later was principal defendant in the Action Group trial, speaking of his duties with remarkable frankness. He was sentenced to death and hanged at Landsberg prison in 1951.

OHRDRUF. Town in central Germany near Gotha, site of the first CONCENTRATION CAMP encountered by American troops (4th Armored Division, Third Army). After being forced by the Americans to tour the camp, the burgomaster of Ohrdruf and his wife went home and hanged themselves.

OIKAWA, Koshiro (1883–1958). A graduate of the Japanese Naval Academy (1903), Oikawa served as a naval aide-de-camp to the Crown Prince between 1915 and 1922. After captaining several warships and serving in the Naval General Staff office, he became president of the Naval Academy in 1933. He later served as commander in chief of the China Fleet and commander in chief of the Yokosuka Naval Station. Promoted to full admiral in 1939, Oikawa was Navy Minister from July 1940 to October 1941 in the second and third KONOYE cabinets. Politically a moderate, Oikawa favored negotiating with the United States as long as possible, and he strongly opposed Yosuke MATSUOKA's proposals to join with Germany in attacking the Soviet Union in the summer of 1941. Oikawa became Chief of the Naval General Staff in 1944 with the fall of Hideki TOJO and Shigetaro SHIMADA. He held this post until May 1945.

OKAMURA, Yasuji (1884–1966). Japanese Army officer, a graduate of the Military Academy (1904) and the Military War College (1913). Okamura once went to China to serve as military adviser to the Chinese war lord Sun Chuang-fang. After returning to Japan he served for some years in the Army General Staff office in Tokyo. As vice-chief of staff of the KWANTUNG ARMY in the 1930s he helped bring about the Manchurian invasion of 1931–32 and the invasion of northern China in 1937. Promoted to full general in 1941, Okamura became a member of the Supreme War Council and commander in chief of the Japanese Army in northern China. He replaced Gen. Shunroku Hata as commander in chief of the Japanese Army in the whole of China on November 22, 1944. Less than a year later he surrendered these forces to Gen. Ho Ying-chin of the Nationalist Chinese army. Briefly thrown into a Shanghai prison as a war criminal, Okamura was released to become an adviser to CHIANG KAI-SHEK in his fight against the Chinese Communists. After returning to Japan in 1949, he assisted in the creation of the Japanese Self-Defense Force and became the head of the Japanese Veterans Association.

O'KANE, Richard Hetherington (1911–). U.S. Navy officer (Naval Academy class of 1934), commander of the submarine *Tang*, which sank 24 Japanese ships on five patrols, making O'Kane the leading American submarine commander in number of enemy ships sunk. On the night of October 24–25, 1944, *Tang* was sunk by one of its own torpedoes; Commander O'Kane and the seven other survivors spent the rest of the war as Japanese prisoners.

OKH (Oberkommando des Heeres). The German Army High Command. The OKH was composed of the Commander in Chief of the Army (Oberbefehlshaber des Heeres—ObdH), the Army General Staff, the Army Personnel Office and the Commander in Chief of the Replacement Army. The Commander in Chief of the Army was the highest command and administrative echelon of the German Army in time of war (Kriegsheer), which consisted of the Field Army (Feldheer) and the Replacement Army (Ersatzheer). He conducted the operations of the Field Army and was responsible for the organization, training, replacement and armament of the entire Army. Directly subordinated to the ObdH were:

(1) The Chief of the Army General Staff (Chef des Generalstabes des Heeres), the senior adviser to the ObdH in all questions concerning the conduct of military operations, and his permanent deputy;

(2) The chief of the Army Personnel Office (Chef des Heeres-Personalamtes), the adviser to the ObdH on officer personnel matters relating to the Army in time of war (after 1942 General Staff officer personnel matters were also handled by this office);

(3) The highest command echelons of the Field Army (Oberste Kommandostellen des Feldheeres), i.e., army groups, etc.;

(4) The commander of the Replacement Army (Befehlshaber des Ersatzheeres), responsible to the ObdH for the training, replacement and arming of the Army, including the development, procurement and acceptance of all arms, ammunition and equipment for the Army and for all areas of Army administration.

OKINAWA. Operation Iceberg, the invasion of the Ryukyu Islands, with the main landing on the western beaches of Okinawa, took place on April 1, 1945—Easter Sunday, or L Day, as it was designated. Mounting the invasion was the U.S. TENTH ARMY, commanded by Lt. Gen. Simon Bolivar BUCKNER, Jr. In the Tenth Army order of battle was the III Marine Amphibious Corps (1st and 6th Marine Divisions in assault and the 2d Marine Division [a demonstration force]) and the Army XXIV Corps (7th, 77th and 96th Divisions, with the 27th Division in Army reserve).

Okinawa is approximately 60 miles long and 2 to 18 miles wide, extremely rugged and mountainous in the north, and in the south, below the narrow Ishikawa Isthmus, more level and cultivated, but still having rolling ridges and steep escarpments, which become more pronounced in the southernmost portion of the island. According to the invasion plan, after cutting the island in half III Amphibious Corps marines would swing north and directly across the island, and the Army XXIV Corps would head south. In an amphibious operation conducted in now-familiar fashion, the Tenth Army put more than 16,000 combat troops ashore in the first hour of Operation Iceberg against little or no enemy gunfire and no mines or other obstacles on the beach. Immediately the question arose, Where are the Japanese? The answer was that Lt. Gen. Mitsuru USHIJIMA, commanding general of the 32d Army, had decided not to defend at the beaches, and instead had developed three concentric defense rings around his headquarters deep in the bowels of SHURI CASTLE.

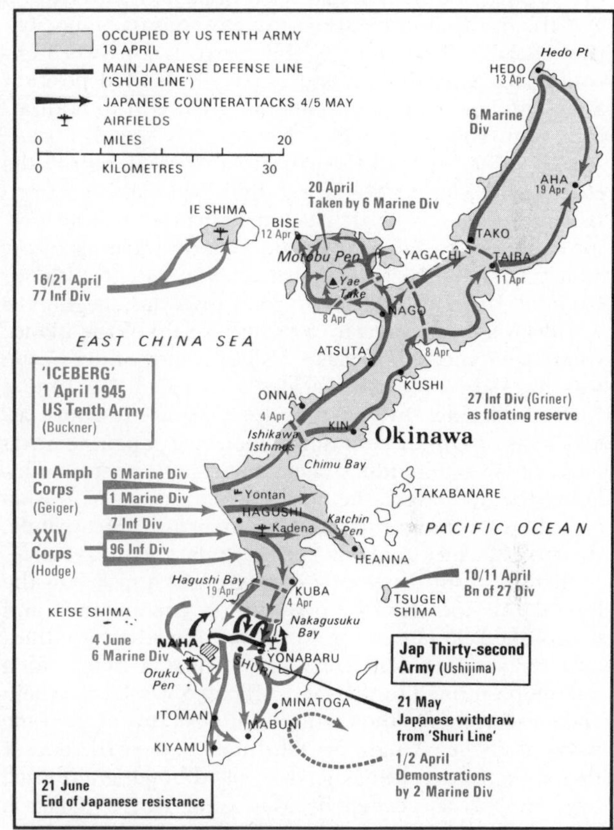

OKINAWA—the last island battle

By April 4 the 1st Marine Division had cut the island in two, reaching Katchin Peninsula on the east coast, while the 6th Marine Division had secured Yontan airfield and headed north to attack Motobu Peninsula, where some 2,000 Japanese had set up a solid and well-organized defense system built around 1,200-foot-high Yae Take, the most prominent feature of Motobu. The attack on Motobu began April 12 and the peninsula was cleared in a week, while the 22d Marines, one of the 6th Division's three infantry regiments, swept the entire rugged north of the island against little or no opposition. During this time the 1st Marine Division fought against guerrilla-type units in the mountains of the Ishikawa Isthmus.

On April 4 the XXIV Corps line wheeled to the right and headed south after having crossed the island in its zone. The toughness of the Japanese outer Shuri defense rings caused advances to be marked in yards, as the Americans met both forward and reverse slope positions which were heavily fortified, honeycombed with caves and tunnels and mutually supporting. On April 22 the 1st Marine Division entered on the right of the XXIV Corps line in the drive south, and on May 1 the III Amphibious Corps took over responsibility for that zone of action, joined several days later by the 6th Division. The Tenth Army line now consisted, from left to right, of the 7th and 77th Infantry Divisions and the 1st and 6th Marine Divisions.

On May 4 General Ushijima mounted a massive counterattack, which had some initial success but was quickly subdued. Opposite the 6th Division was SUGAR LOAF HILL, part of the Shuri defense system, and opposite the 1st Marine Division was Shuri Castle itself. By the 18th the Shuri line had been breached, and on the 23d the 6th Division entered the environs of NAHA. On the left side of the line, XXIV Corps troops were encountering one difficult and fiercely defended position after another, and taking them at great cost to both attacker and defender.

Meanwhile, the more than 1,000 U.S. ships off the coast of the island were facing their own baptism of fire from a number of KAMIKAZE attacks, whose main targets were the destroyers that provided early warning of air attacks and the big carriers at anchor. On the island, General Ushijima, faced by four divisions, began his withdrawal from Shuri to the southern tip of the island, where he expected to make his last stand. Shuri Castle was entered by the 5th Marines on May 29. On June 4 the 6th Marine Division mounted a shore-to-shore attack against Oroku Peninsula, where the Japanese naval garrison was defending. Ten days later, after annihilating the defenders, the marines secured the peninsula and then joined in the attack in the south. Meanwhile, the 7th Marines took the precipitous and heavily defended Kunishi Ridge in a daring night attack. On the left of the line, XXIV Corps troops encountered and demolished Japanese strongpoints one after another, and by June 17 had come up against a determined enemy positioned in the very difficult Yuza Dake–Yaeju Dake escarpment; they took these positions after some particularly heavy fighting. On June 18, near the end of the battle, General Buckner was killed by Japanese shell fire. He was succeeded by Maj. Gen. Roy S. GEIGER, commander of III Amphibious Corps, who directed the campaign to its completion.

All during the battle for Okinawa, ground forces were supported by Marine and Navy air, with planes flying both from carriers and from captured enemy airfields, which were made operable within a few days of the initial landings.

By June 21 the southern end of the island had been reached and, except for small bypassed pockets of enemy resistance, the fighting was over. General Geiger declared Okinawa secured, and the next day the American flag was raised. In the early morning hours of the previous day, as American patrols neared his cave hideout, General Ushijima and his chief of staff, General Cho, had committed hara-kiri.

Overall American losses in the land battle were 7,374 killed, 31,807 wounded and 239 missing. At sea and in the air, the Navy reported 36 ships sunk, 368 damaged, 763 aircraft lost, 4,907 seamen killed or missing, and another 4,874 wounded. This was the highest total of American casualties experienced in any campaign against the Japanese (the figures reported by the different services vary slightly). Japanese losses were even higher and more grievous—a total of 107,539 dead, with 27,764 sealed in caves, and 10,755 taken prisoner. Many of this number were Okinawan civilians caught up in the fighting.

While Okinawa was being developed as a springboard for the attack on the Japanese home islands, the two ATOMIC BOMBS were dropped and the war ended. Okinawa was truly the last battle. **B.M.F.**

OKLAHOMA, U.S.S. The second battleship of the NEVADA class. At PEARL HARBOR she was struck by Japanese bombs and aerial torpedoes, capsized and went down with heavy casualties. In a massive wartime salvage operation, she was righted and refloated. Her hulk beyond practical repair, she rested at pierside until being sold for scrap in 1946. While being towed to the West Coast of the United States in 1947, she parted her towline and plunged to the bottom of the Pacific.

OKTYABRJSKY, Filip S. (1899–1969). Soviet naval officer who changed his name from Ivanov to Oktyabrjsky in honor of the October Revolution (1917). He commanded the Black Sea Fleet during the war and was promoted to admiral in 1944.

OKULICKI, Leopold Bronislaw (1898–1946). The last commander of the Polish resistance forces, one of 16 Polish leaders who went to Moscow in June 1945 to negotiate about the future of their country. Instead of negotiating, the Soviets arrested Okulicki and the others and tried them for alleged crimes against the Soviet Union and for collaboration with the Germans. Okulicki pleaded guilty to all charges, was convicted and sentenced to 10 years' imprisonment. He died in a Soviet prison.

OKW (Oberkommando der Wehrmacht). For some time prior to his resignation in January 1938, Field Marshal Werner von Blomberg, the Reich Defense Minister and Commander in Chief of the German Armed Forces, had been attempting to create an armed forces high command. In this effort he had the full backing of Adolf HITLER and of his own subordinates in the Defense Ministry, Brig. Gen. Wilhelm KEITEL, chief of the armed forces office (Wehrmachtamt), and Col. Alfred JODL, chief of the national defense division (Abteilung Landesverteidigung). Blomberg was strenuously opposed in his endeavors by both the Army and Navy high commands. The Minister for Aviation and Commander in Chief of the Luftwaffe, Gen. Hermann GÖRING, generally gave Blomberg's attempts more or less sincere support.

Upon Blomberg's departure, Hitler carried through the creation of an armed forces high command soon after he personally assumed command of the German armed forces in February 1938. He abolished the Defense Ministry and redesignated the armed forces office of that ministry as the Armed Forces High Command (Oberkommando der Wehrmacht—OKW). The OKW was to function as Hitler's military staff under his direct command, and General Keitel was appointed its chief.

According to the mobilization plan that went into effect in late August 1939, the OKW was organized as follows:

The office of the chief, which consisted of Keitel and a few officers and clerks.

The central administrative division, which carried out the internal administration of the OKW.

The armed forces operations office (Wehrmachtführungsamt) under Jodl, which consisted of three divisions—national defense, armed forces communications and armed forces propaganda. The mission of the national defense division was to handle all questions concerning military operations. It kept the chief of OKW and Hitler informed of the military situation and coordinated and prepared the sections of Hitler's directives concerning military operations. The communications and propaganda divisions were concerned with the matters indicated by their titles.

The armed forces intelligence office (Amt Auslands Abwehr), the largest office in the OKW, under Adm. Wilhelm CANARIS. It controlled the collection and dissemination to the armed services of all clandestine military intelligence and conducted military sabotage and counterintelligence matters.

The armed forces administrative office (Allgemeines Wehrmachtamt), which coordinated miscellaneous areas—including scientific research, prisoner-of-war matters and casualty statistics—common to the three services.

The armed forces war production office (Wehrwirtschaftsamt), which had as its mission the procurement and allocation of all raw materials and production facilities needed for the war effort.

Various small units, such as military justice, legal and fiscal divisions, made up the rest of the OKW.

During the time of quasi peace between February 1938 and the outbreak of war in September 1939, the OKW's primary mission was the preparation of an overall national defense plan. It issued several amendments to the then current plan of June 1937 and prepared the comprehensive national defense plan issued in April 1939. The OKW during this time also participated in the planning for the occupation of Austria (the ANSCHLUSS), CZECHOSLOVAKIA and MEMEL.

From the outbreak of the war until the summer of 1941 the OKW continued to function as Hitler's personal military staff, working in close cooperation with the high commands of the three services. From that time on, the OKW also began to develop into a supreme ground force headquarters. This development had started with the creation of the first armed forces commanders (Wehrmachtsbefehlshaber) in the Netherlands and in Norway. Both of these commanders received their orders directly from the chief of OKW according to Hitler's direction.

By the end of May 1942 the following headquarters were tactically subordinated to the OKW: Commander in Chief West (France and Belgium); commander of German troops in Denmark; the armed forces commanders in the Netherlands, Norway and the Southeast (Balkans); the armed forces commanders Ostland (Central Russia) and the Ukraine, who controlled the occupied areas in the rear of the German armies in Russia; and the Army of Lapland (Northern Finland). The Commander in Chief South (Italy and North Africa) was added to OKW's theaters in October 1942. The ostensible purpose of these assignments was to relieve the Army high command of some of its burdens so as to enable it to concentrate on the main ground combat theater in Russia.

Following the Allied invasion of NORTHWEST AFRICA, more and more of the OKW theaters were drawn into combat operations. Now the OKW on a greatly increasing scale assumed the functions of a ground force headquarters. At the same time the earlier function of

As Supreme Commander of the Armed Forces, Adolf Hitler (right) received minutely detailed reports from the chief of the OKW staff, Field Marshal Wilhelm Keitel (second from left), and from the service chiefs, including Reichsmarschall Hermann Göring (left), commander of the Luftwaffe. Also listening to the Führer's observations in this 1941 meeting is Heinrich Himmler, head of the SS

Grand Admiral Erich Raeder, head of the German Navy from 1928 until 1943, opposed the creation of OKW.

the OKW as an overall advisory and coordinating staff for the Commander in Chief of the Armed Forces became more and more tenuous.

OLBRICHT, Friedrich (1888–1944). Born in Leisnig in Saxony, Colonel General Olbricht was a career German Army officer, serving both in action and on the Army General Staff. From 1938 to 1940 he was commander of the 24th Infantry Division, and he took part in the Polish campaign. In March 1940 he became second-in-command to Gen. Friedrich FROMM, commander of the Replacement Army (Ersatzheer). A devout Christian, close friend of BECK, OSTER, GOERDELER, HOEPNER and others involved in the German resistance, he was profoundly opposed to Adolf HITLER and worked closely with Count von STAUFFENBERG. He became the principal executive of the abortive coup d'état of July 20, 1944, and initiated Operation VALKYRIE, designed to achieve the military takeover of the Berlin administrative center following the death of Hitler. After the failure of the attempt, he was executed along with Stauffenberg by order of Fromm, following a summary court-martial that same night. *See also* OPPOSITION TO HITLER.

OLDENBURG. Name given to a German plan for the exploitation of territory occupied in the Soviet Union. The planning staff observed that "there is no doubt that millions of people will starve to death in Russia if we take out of the country the things necessary for us." The sentence has been read either as a statement of gruesome fact or as a caution against excess.

OLDENDORF, Jesse Barrett (1887–). U.S. Navy officer, a graduate of the Naval Academy in 1909. He served as commandant of the Aruba-Curaçao area and at Trinidad (1942–43), where he organized rescue operations. He saw Pacific service in the MARSHALLS, the CAROLINES and the MARIANAS, and at LEYTE GULF, where he commanded the bombardment and fire support group of the Seventh Fleet. As commander of this group (his rank was rear admiral), Oldendorf destroyed the Japanese force in Surigao Strait and helped ensure an American victory. After this battle Oldendorf led the battle squadron at LINGAYEN GULF. He was later injured in an accident off OKINAWA (March 1945).

OLEANDER. Code name of AKYAB, on the coast of Burma.

OLIVE. Code name for Allied attack on the GOTHIC LINE (Italy), August 1944.

OLIVER, Lunsford Everett (1889–). U.S. Army officer who commanded an armored combat command in the North African landings (Oran) in 1942 and as a major general led the 5th Armored Division in the 1944 and 1945 campaigns in northern France and Germany.

OLYMPIC. Code name for the Allied invasion of Kyushu scheduled for November 1, 1945. It was to be the first phase of Operation Downfall, the overall assault on the Japanese home islands, and was to be followed by CORONET, the invasion of Honshu. Gen. Walter KRUEGER's U.S. SIXTH ARMY was assigned to Olympic.

OMAHA, U.S.S. Light cruiser and class. Four-stack ships resembling the World War I FLUSH-DECKERS (destroyers) in appearance, these 10 cruisers, with twelve 6-inch guns, commissioned in 1923–28. Already obsolete before Pearl Harbor, the entire class remained active through V-J Day. *Milwaukee*, lent to the USSR in 1944, was renamed *Murmansk*. Wartime modifications removed two 6-inch guns and added RADAR and some antiaircraft guns, but did not alter the ships' general appearance.

OMAHA BEACH. One of the two Normandy beaches (Colleville-Vierville) assigned to American forces for D-Day landings, June 6, 1944. Units of the U.S. V Corps, FIRST ARMY, there met the fiercest resistance of any Allied force on D-Day. German 88 batteries and a high tide caused most of the casualties. More critical, however, was the virtual paralysis of the great body of the survivors owing to the impact of seasickness and panic. On D-Day the landing forces barely avoided total defeat under the steep bluffs at Omaha. Had this happened, the whole INVASION would likely have failed.

101ST AIRBORNE DIVISION. U.S. division, always known as the Screaming Eagles, which came into being

U.S. infantrymen go ashore at Omaha Beach

on August 15, 1942. Its battle record in World War II is without blemish: its people captured every assigned objective and in defense never yielded. Dropped behind UTAH BEACH by night four hours before the first seaborne landings of the Normandy INVASION, its combat elements, though much scattered, still cleared all of the approaches to the sector where the 4th Infantry Division would make shore. Next, two of its regiments overwhelmed the stoutly defended German fortifications at CARENTAN.

Operating airborne from bases in England during the invasion of the Netherlands on September 17, 1944 (Operation MARKET-GARDEN), the Eagles wholly cleared their part of the route over which the British 30th Corps was to advance, capturing EINDHOVEN and St. Oedenrode and fighting great battles at Best and around Heeswick. The division's most notable feat came later at BASTOGNE, Belgium, during the Battle of the Ardennes (the BULGE), which opened December 16, 1944: there it was under full siege for almost a month, during one week of which it was totally enveloped by four enemy divisions. For its stand it was awarded the Presidential Unit Citation. As with the 82d and other sky soldier outfits, most of the personnel were two-time volunteers—at enlistment time and when the call came for airborne service. **S.L.A.M.**

ONISHI, Takijiro (1891–1945). A Japanese career naval officer, Onishi was a strong advocate of naval air power. As chief of staff of the 11th Air Fleet, Onishi and Comdr. Minoru GENDA, staff officer of the 1st Air Fleet, conducted research on the feasibility of Adm. Isoruku YAMAMOTO's plan to attack PEARL HARBOR. Onishi also ordered the attacks on the PHILIPPINES on December 8, 1941, in spite of the bad weather. In late 1944 Onishi was appointed commander of the 1st Air Fleet in the Philippines and created a special task force of pilots to crash-dive their bomb-laden planes into American ships in order to turn the ever worsening tide of the war once and for all. These KAMIKAZE suicide squads made American attacks on Japanese forces more costly, but failed to bring victory to Japan. A vice-admiral, Onishi was appointed Vice-Chief of the Naval General Staff in May 1945 and in this position strongly supported the Army generals who wished to continue the war. He committed suicide by slitting his abdomen and stabbing himself in the chest and throat shortly after the Emperor's broadcast of surrender.

ONS-5. The spring of 1943 had seen large numbers of Allied ship sinkings at a relatively small cost in U-boats. In April the available German submarines were deployed in three North ATLANTIC barrier lines in an effort to cover every possible route that might be taken by a convoy. By late April, 47 submarines were on station.

The slow westbound Convoy ONS-5 (43 merchantmen escorted by 2 destroyers, 1 frigate, 4 Flower-class corvettes and 2 former fishing trawlers converted to armed rescue ships) was sighted by one of the patrolling U-boats early on April 28. Fifteen boats were vectored in on the convoy, but their radio transmissions were detected by HF/DF gear in two convoy escort ships and their positions were plotted (*see* HF/DF). The escorts, knowing the general positions of the approaching submarines, made offensive sweeps to throw them off balance and compel them to submerge. On the night of April 28–29, a series of poorly coordinated attacks were made on the convoy. No ships were lost.

The first kill was scored in the early morning of the 29th, when a freighter was sunk. Late in the day a U-boat was damaged by a patrolling flying boat. The next several days were stormy. The convoy was scattered, but continuous air cover by land-based bombers kept submarines at a distance. The storm let up on May 2, long enough to reassemble most of the convoy; stragglers were quickly herded into groups of their own. At this time a support group of antisubmarine ships came out from Newfoundland to reinforce the convoy.

By May 4 some escort ships had had to be detached to refuel. Fifty-one U-boats were being redeployed between Greenland and Newfoundland to attack the convoy. As long as light lasted, land-based planes continued to keep the submarines at bay. One Canadian PBY, (*see* PBY) sank a U-boat as it stalked a convoy straggler. With nightfall, patrol planes withdrew. Thirty submarines closed in on ONS-5 through calming seas. During the night of May 4–5, seven merchantmen were lost. The battle continued through the following day; five more cargo ships went down, along with one U-boat. Admiral DÖNITZ, chief of the German submarine force, ordered an all-out attack for the night of May 5. Thick fog disrupted the submariners' attempts, and aggressive work by the convoy escort ships sank four U-boats and damaged two more. By the morning of May 6, ONS-5 was within range of Newfoundland-based air cover. Realizing that further effort would be futile, Dönitz called off his submarines, and the convoy went on its way without further attack.

During this voyage 13 merchant ships had been lost. Five U-boats, however, had been sunk by escort ships; a patrolling airplane sank a sixth. Land-based air support in foul weather, along with good convoy discipline and an aggressive defense by escort ships, had succeeded against heavy odds in holding down ship and crew losses. RADAR and HF/DF had had their share in the convoy's defense. This was the last occasion on which a convoy would be attacked in such massive force; ONS-5 was something of an Atlantic turning point and represented a real victory for this convoy and her escorts.

OPPENHEIM. German town at which troops of the U.S. THIRD ARMY first crossed the Rhine River, March 22, 1945.

OPPENHEIMER, J. Robert (1904–1967). American physicist, a native of New York City, who studied at Cambridge and Göttingen and served as a professor of physics at both the California Institute of Technology (from 1928) and the University of California at Berkeley (from 1929). In his prewar career he received international attention for his work on the quantum theory, which laid the basis for the application of quantum mechanics to the study of molecules. At the University of California he worked with Dr. Ernest O. LAWRENCE in investigating the structure of the atom and in developing the cyclotron.

Early in the war, when it was decided to try to develop atomic energy for military purposes, Oppenheimer was asked to help in the project. He played a leading role in organizing and conducting experiments which led to the creation of the ATOMIC BOMB. In 1943 he became director at Los ALAMOS, where the bomb was actually built. By July 1945 an experimental bomb had been developed and a successful test conducted at ALAMOGORDO. After the war Oppenheimer became director of the Institute for Advanced Study at Princeton, N.J., and he served as chairman of the General Advisory Committee of the U.S. Atomic Energy Commission (1947–52).

In 1954 his career took a tragic personal turn, when the commission permanently removed his security clearance following a hearing, the step being prompted partly by his left-wing associations of earlier days and partly by his opposition to pushing ahead with development of the hydrogen bomb. In 1963, however, the commission presented him its Fermi Prize.

OPPOSITION TO HITLER. It is important to remember that there was considerable resistance to Adolf HITLER in Germany throughout the duration of the regime, in spite of the overwhelming support he received from a great part of the German people. Once he had assumed full dictatorial powers through the ENABLING ACT of March 1933, and in effect identified loyalty to the state with loyalty to himself—reinforced in the case of members of the armed forces by the oath of personal loyalty imposed in 1934—opposition to Hitler amounted to high treason. This put active members of the German resistance in the position of traitors, as distinct from the position of resistance workers in the occupied countries after 1939, who were patriots.

Active resistance took two main forms: individual and in organized groups, on both the political left and the right. Individual opposition occurred either clandestinely or openly, according to the choice and circumstances of the persons involved, and originated in every class and political persuasion. Most open opponents died for their beliefs, either inside or outside the prisons and concentration camps. Celebrated examples include the youthful brother and sister Hans and Sophie Scholl, who attempted to establish a student revolt against Hitler and founded the so-called WHITE ROSE movement in Munich. They were utterly unprotected from the forces which soon bore down upon them; they were arrested, tried by the notorious judge Roland FREISLER in the Nazi People's Court, condemned to death and executed in February 1942. However, a very few in high places who openly opposed Hitler on certain matters remained immune, even from the GESTAPO; such were Bishop Count von GALEN and Cardinal Michael von FAULHABER of Bavaria, who preached against Nazism and anti-Semitism during the 1930s, when the churches were still relatively strong. The official policy in the case of such people was to ostracize and ridicule them, isolating them rather than arresting them, which would have caused too great an outcry at the time. But the inmates of the prisons and concentration camps included a leavening of German individualists who had in one way or another made their disapproval felt, though most Germans opposed to Hitler lay low and said and did as little as possible. Some, however, showed compassion in small ways to Jews, to concentration camp prisoners serving in work gangs outside the camps, to slave laborers on the farms and the like, to whom they surreptitiously gave food.

The German resistance movement in the fullest sense worked clandestinely in groups and eventually evolved an organized faction of individuals determined, if necessary at the cost of their lives, to remove the head of state by a coup d'état. However, opinions differed sharply among these people as to means. The celebrated KREISAU CIRCLE of aristocrats and intellectuals, which was founded in 1939 by Count Helmuth von MOLTKE and included among its members such ardent Anglophiles as Count Peter YORCK VON WARTENBURG and the former Rhodes scholar Adam von TROTT ZU SOLZ, did not favor taking any drastic action against Hitler, though the opinion of certain members hardened considerably as Hitler led Germany deeper and deeper into catastrophe. Most members, including Moltke himself, eventually met death at the hands of the Nazi executioners. But the essential nature of their opposition lay in the values they hoped to keep alive until better times returned to Germany.

The history of active opposition, though involving many courageous civilians, lies almost entirely within the German Army. It grew initially out of the sheer resentment felt by certain highly placed officers at the crude militarism Hitler advocated during the 1930s and the unscrupulous methods he used to displace those who opposed him. The actual center of gravity for organized opposition within the Army tended to shift during the course of the years, but it began during the mid-1930s inside the ABWEHR, the department of military intelligence, where Adm. Wilhelm CANARIS, head of intelligence from 1935, and his chief of staff, Maj. Gen. Hans OSTER, had become disaffected following the NIGHT OF THE LONG KNIVES in 1934 and the sudden, wholly unexpected imposition of the oath of allegiance to Hitler on all members of the armed forces. At the same time, Gen. Ludwig BECK, Chief of the General Staff and an officer of the old school, was determinedly opposed to the aggression inherent in Hitler's European policy, which, in his particular position, he was among the first to recognize. Meanwhile, on the civilian side Hans von DOHNANYI, a member of the staff of the Ministry of Justice, had begun the systematic collection of evidence against the regime, while in 1937 the mayor of Leipzig, Carl GOERDELER, at first a supporter of Hitler and an economic adviser to the new regime, turned violently against Nazism and became one of its most outspoken critics. Often talking openly to the point of indiscretion, he ceaselessly organized opposition in every field, civilian and military, that was open to him.

The middle years of the decade were years of apparent success for Hitler. Germany was rapidly assuming a position in the forefront of the European powers. Its economy was irrevocably set in the direction of rearmament; the Rome-Berlin AXIS proclaimed the brotherhood of fascism. But Hitler alienated conservative elements in the Wehrmacht high command through the unseemly way in which he managed to disgrace Field Marshal Werner von Blomberg, Commander in Chief of the Armed Forces and Minister of War, whose bride was revealed as a former prostitute, and Gen. Werner von FRITSCH, Commander in Chief of the Army, who was charged with homosexuality and, though proved innocent, left with his career in ruins. Beck, unable to stay the acceleration of Hitler's plans for aggressive war, resigned in August 1938 and became the titular head of the resistance movement, which was strengthened by the addition of many important adherents on all levels, including Ulrich von HASSELL, who was dismissed the same year from his position as ambassador to Italy.

A conspiracy within the high command to arrest Hitler is said to have existed but to have collapsed as soon as it was learned that British Prime Minister Neville CHAMBERLAIN was prepared to fly to Germany to act as mediator when Hitler was threatening invasion of CZECHOSLOVAKIA. Hitler's amazing diplomatic coup at MUNICH in September 1938 took what little wind was left out of the sails of the Army conspirators. Meanwhile, energetic representatives of the German resistance, in particular Goerdeler, Maj. Ewald von Kleist-Schmenzin (a friend of Canaris) and Fabian von SCHLABRENDORFF, were sent to Britain to urge any kind of support possible to stop the development of German militarism to the point of war. They met, among others, Lord Lloyd, Lord HALIFAX and Winston CHURCHILL. The British reaction was largely negative; in their estimation, overt action by the resistance against Hitler would have spoken far louder than words. But no action was taken.

On the declaration of war, Hassell momentarily moved into the forefront; during the early months of hostilities, 1939–40, he held two clandestine meetings with a wholly unofficial, self-appointed go-between, J. Lonsdale Bryans, who had a somewhat tenuous link with Lord Halifax. The object was to test the British reaction to tentative peace terms to be put forward by an interim authority that would be established by the resistance after the downfall of Hitler. The terms, right-wing in tone, were of the kind approved by Beck, Goerdeler, Canaris and Oster, who were by now more or less firmly aligned with Hassell. Meanwhile, parallel with Hassell's efforts, a Catholic agent in close touch with Canaris and a member of the wartime Abwehr, Josef MÜLLER, through diplomatic contacts in the Vatican, was bringing pressure to bear on the Pope to come forward as peacemaker between Britain and France and Germany, again without success. The so-called peace terms were redrafted in a form which came to be known as the "X Report" ; it was drawn up by Dohnanyi, who had joined Canaris on the staff of the Abwehr, as had the influential Protestant pastor Dietrich BONHOEFFER, who in 1942 was to have a secret meeting with the English bishop George BELL in Sweden. Appeals for public recognition by the British of the resistance movement were to be firmly turned down by Anthony EDEN. Churchill insisted that action must come first; by that time UNCONDITIONAL SURRENDER had become the Allied war aim.

Much of this clandestine effort, however, had taken place during the quiet PHONY WAR period. But recruiting worthwhile support among the Army high command was proving ever more difficult to achieve and became virtually impossible once Hitler had swept triumphantly into western Europe. Oster, backed by Canaris, had played the dangerous game of trying to forewarn Denmark, Norway, Holland and Belgium of the plans for invasion, only to be met by blank disbelief. In the face of the fall of France and what appeared to be the imminent fall of Britain, the resistance, weak, irresolute and very small in numbers, could do little but discuss their problems endlessly among themselves. However, a brave man of the younger generation, Gen. Henning von TRESCKOW, stationed on the Eastern Front after the invasion of Russia, began to plan the capture or assassination of Hitler; he endeavored to ensure the support of Field Marshal von KLUGE, who held a command in the east and offered wavering encouragement to the conspirators, to which they clung desperately. In March 1943 Tresckow and his aide, Schlabrendorff, placed a bomb on Hitler's aircraft before it took off to return to the Führer's headquarters in East Prussia after a visit to Kluge, but the bomb failed to function.

Initiative passed to the younger generation of officers during 1943 in the person of Col. Count Claus von STAUFFENBERG, following the arrest of members of the Canaris circle, including Dohnanyi, Müller and Bonhoeffer. Oster and Canaris were to remain free for the time being, though powerless to exercise further influence. While on leave in Berlin, Tresckow began work on VALKYRIE, the cover plan to bring the Replacement Army into action following Hitler's assassination. He was followed as chief planner of the coup in October by Stauffenberg, whose severe war injuries led to his acceptance of a staff appointment in the Replacement Army under Gen. Friedrich FROMM.

Following Tresckow's abortive attempt in 1943, two young officers had volunteered to make suicide attempts on Hitler's life; they were Axel von dem Bussche and Ewald von Kleist. Neither was successful; Hitler eluded them, but at least their lives were spared along with his. However, in 1944 the GESTAPO began to close in; Moltke was arrested in January. The Abwehr was disbanded; Canaris, though forced into retirement, was still unsuspected. Julius Leber, the contact for the resistance with the clandestine Socialist movement, was arrested in July, a month after the Allied invasion of France. Goerdeler was in hiding. The resistance, spearheaded now by Stauffenberg and Gen. Friedrich OLBRICHT, Fromm's chief of staff, working under Beck's nominal guidance, finally set up a last, elaborate plan to kill Hitler, if at all possible along with Hermann GÖRING and Heinrich HIMMLER. This was to take place at one or the other of the Führer's distant headquarters, such as the Wolf's Lair at Rastenburg in East Prussia. Stauffenberg, who now had access to Hitler's war conferences (and who as a disabled war hero was quite unsuspected of disaffection and never searched), volunteered to carry and place the bomb.

The date finally chosen was July 20, 1944, and Stauffenberg, accompanied by his cousin Col. Cäsar von HOFACKER, flew from Berlin to Rastenburg with the time bomb in his briefcase. Though the bomb exploded, the briefcase in which it was concealed had been moved after Stauffenberg left the conference; this chance event probably saved Hitler's life. The principal conspirators in Berlin (including Stauffenberg, who had flown back immediately from Rastenburg) met with a tragic end when the plot finally collapsed. Beck committed suicide, as did Tresckow on the Eastern Front. In France the steps of the coup had been carried out according to plan under the supervision of Gen. Karl Heinrich von STÜLPNAGEL, though to no effect once the conspiracy in Berlin had failed. Hitler and the Gestapo took a terrible toll of everone suspected of disaffection, and the trials which followed in August and September 1944 under Freisler led to the execution, sooner or later, of numerous famous men of the resistance, including Moltke, Hassell, Yorck, Stülpnagel, Goerdeler, Leber, Oster, Canaris and Bonhoeffer. **R.M.**

ORADOUR-SUR-GLÂNE. Village in southwestern France (Haute-Vienne), scene of one of the worst atrocities of the war. Frustrated by hit-and-run attacks by French guerrillas delaying movement of the 2d SS "Das Reich" Panzer Division to Normandy in July 1944, the Germans summarily shot all the males, burned women and children alive in the church and razed the village. A thousand perished. The French maintain the village in its razed form as a memorial to the victims.

ORAN. A vital port for the logistical support of the Allied armies in Africa, Oran (Algeria) was the target for the Center Task Force of Operation TORCH. Maj. Gen. Lloyd R. FREDENDALL commanded the U.S. 1st Division and parts of the 1st Armored Division in the assault (November 8, 1942). Although Oran was well protected with coastal guns and lay in a defensible basin ringed by hills, opposition was overcome within two days of the landings.

ORANGE. U.S. code name for Japan and for the strategic plan drawn up in event of war with Japan. "Orange" was also code for a U.S. general officer. *See also* COLOR PLANS.

ORDER OF LENIN (Orden Lenina). This Soviet decoration, first authorized in 1930, was awarded to individuals and groups, both civilian and military, who during World War II distinguished themselves by notable achievement in any sphere of national activity. There is some question as to the relative order of precedence of this award during the war years, but it was certainly among the highest decorations to be awarded; the recipient of a HERO OF THE SOVIET UNION or Hero of Socialist Labor was automatically given the Order of Lenin along with the GOLD STAR Medal. The medal is a portrait of Lenin surrounded by a gold wreath and red banner emblazoned with Lenin's name.

ORDER OF SUVOROV. A Soviet military award presented to high-ranking commanders and their deputies for operations in which the enemy is defeated.

ORDER OF THE RED BANNER. A Soviet award presented to both civilian and military individuals, units and associations for outstanding merit.

ORDER OF VICTORY (Orden Pobedy). This Soviet decoration, established November 8, 1943, is the most expensive and lavish award originating in World War II. Designed to be worn over the right breast, the Order of Victory is a five-pointed star, two inches in diameter, made of platinum overlaid with blue and red enamel and encrusted with 135 diamonds. The center of the star is flat and depicts the Spassky Gate in the Kremlin Wall. Only the most senior commanders were authorized to receive this award. Several were awarded to foreign officers, such as Gen. Dwight EISENHOWER and Field Marshal Sir Bernard MONTGOMERY.

ORDZHONIKIDZE. A town, once known as Vladikovkoz and Dzaudzhikau, strategically situated in the Caucasus at the northern end of the Georgian Military Road. In September–October 1942, Ordzhonikidze became the pivotal point in the Nalchik defensive operations against the attempt of German Army Group A to divide the Soviet forces protecting the approaches to Grozny, Tbilisi and BAKU. The failure of the German drive at Ordzhonikidze and the concurrent action at STALINGRAD changed the nature and strategy of the Caucasus campaign.

OREL. Central Russian city, approximately 250 miles south of Moscow, captured by the Germans in October 1941 during the assault on Moscow. The German occupation of Orel lasted for almost two years and was a constant concern to the Soviet leaders because of its salient threat to the capital. During this period the Germans inflicted numerous atrocities on the civilian population, which shrank from 114,000 inhabitants at the start of the war to 30,000 by 1943. Orel was also the scene of considerable PARTISAN warfare conducted by hastily organized civilian detachments, who succeeded in tying down large numbers of German troops.

ORGANIZATION TODT. German construction organization, a paramilitary arm of the Nazi Party. The name came from the founder, Dr. Fritz TODT.

ORIENT. Code name of a German plan, drawn up in July 1941, for invasion of the Middle East. It was predicated on a successful outcome of the war in Russia in 1941; the requisite conditions therefore never existed.

ORION, H.M.S. Royal Navy cruiser of 7,151 tons, completed at Devonport in 1933, armed with eight 6-inch and eight 4-inch guns, smaller weapons, eight 21-inch torpedo tubes and one aircraft. *Orion* served in the Mediterranean from 1940 to 1945; her service included a number of engagements, notably the Battle of CAPE MATAPAN, and she was for a while a member of FORCE K based on MALTA. She was badly damaged in the withdrawal from CRETE in 1941, sustaining heavy casualties among her own crew and the troops she was carrying. She participated in the landings on the mainland of ITALY in 1943 and the Normandy INVASION in 1944, after which she returned to the Mediterranean for further bombardment work at the SOUTHERN FRANCE landings and in support of the Allied armies in Italy.

ORION–BAGAC LINE. Gen. Douglas MACARTHUR's primary position for the defense of the BATAAN peninsula; it ran directly east–west. The Japanese first struck the line on January 26, 1942. American and Philippine forces held, despite meager supplies. Following a four-week lull the Japanese offensive was renewed on April 3, after a savage bombardment. Breakout was almost immediate and was soon followed by the capitulation of American and Philippine forces on Bataan on April 8.

ORMOC. On October 23, 1944, just three days after the U.S. SIXTH ARMY landed on LEYTE, the Japanese began sending in reinforcements through the port of Ormoc until, by December 10, they had shipped in more than 45,000 troops and 10,000 tons of supplies. The U.S. 77th Division had begun landing, unopposed, about three miles south of Ormoc on December 7, and secured Ormoc—which was utterly destroyed by air and artillery bombardment—by evening on December 10. The 77th Division's casualties were approximately 125 men killed, 330 wounded and 15 missing; an estimated 1,500 Japanese had been killed.

ORNE RIVER. The bridges across this river in Normandy were important objectives of the British 6TH AIRBORNE DIVISION in the predawn assault on D-Day, June 6, 1944.

ORO BAY. Oro Bay lies on the northern coast of Papua, NEW GUINEA, about 20 miles southeast of Buna. It was used as a supply point and training area by the U.S. 1st Marine Division prior to and during the CAPE GLOUCESTER operation. In the early part of 1943 it was often subjected to heavy Japanese air attacks.

ORSCHOLZ SWITCH (Orscholz Sehnenstellung). A spur of the German WEST WALL south of Trier. It was attacked by the U.S. 94th Division during late January and February 1945, and the pocket of German defenders it protected was finally cleaned out on February 22.

ORSHA. A German bastion town on the upper Dnieper River, USSR, on the Moscow–Minsk highway. The Germans fought a remarkable defensive battle in this sector against Soviet forces in the autumn of 1943. Adolf HITLER ordered Orsha to be held at all costs, but it fell in the 1944 Soviet summer offensive in June.

OS2U. The Vought-Sikorsky Kingfisher, a U.S. Navy two-seat observation floatplane introduced to the fleet in 1940 and widely used from battleships and cruisers.

OS2U Kingfisher does spotting duty at the landing on Angaur, September 17, 1944

It carried two .30-caliber machine guns. Built, like other American naval floatplanes, to take interchangeable wheels or floats, OS2Us flew antisubmarine patrols from land bases and flew gunfire-spotting, rescue and antisubmarine patrol missions from ships. Produced by the Naval Aircraft Factory as the OS2N, these planes were also provided to the Royal Navy, which designated them Kingfisher I. Models produced: OS2U-1, OS2U-2, OS2U-3 (OS2N-1). Though relatively low-powered, the OS2U proved itself a rugged and dependable aircraft of its type. It was replaced, in part, by the SC (*see* SC), but many OS2Us were still in fleet service by V-J Day.

OSAKA. Japanese city devastated by U.S. fire-bombing raid in March 1945. Also, it was a designated but missed target in the Doolittle raid against Japan (*see* FIRST SPECIAL AVIATION PROJECT). *See also* STRATEGIC BOMBING.

OSE. U.S. Edo Aircraft experimental single-seat observation floatplane with a Ranger in-line liquid-cooled engine, designed for catapult operation. Twelve OSE-1s were built, but the type was too late for war service and was never placed in production.

OSHIMA, Hiroshi (1886–1975). Japanese Army officer who had strong ties with Germany, having served in Berlin as assistant military attaché in the 1920s and as military attaché in the 1930s. He favored and helped negotiate both the ANTI-COMINTERN PACT (1936) and the TRIPARTITE PACT (1937), which allied Japan with Germany and Italy. He was created a lieutenant general in 1940 shortly before his appointment as ambassador to Germany, a position he held throughout the war. Convicted of war crimes in Tokyo, Oshima was sentenced to life imprisonment, but was paroled in 1955.

OSLO. The capital of NORWAY, Oslo was surrendered to the Germans on April 9, 1940. A challenge issued by a Norwegian patrol boat to a convoy of German ships at the mouth of the Oslofjord alerted the Norwegian Government to the impending danger. The German cruiser BLÜCHER, carrying staff personnel and GESTAPO agents, was sunk on the way in, with a loss of 1,000 lives. Though the other ships turned and landed their troops a distance from the city, Oslo was declared open when six companies of airborne troops marched into the capital. The royal family, cabinet and most of the members of Parliament escaped on a special train which headed for Hamar, some 70 miles to the northwest.

OSMEÑA, Sergio (1898–1961). Philippine politician and statesman, and close friend of Manuel QUEZON, the first President of the PHILIPPINES. Osmeña's long and successful career in law and politics culminated in his election as Vice-President twice, in 1935 and in 1941, with Quezon as President. When the Japanese invaded the country, Osmeña fled with Quezon to Washington and there served in the government-in-exile. In 1944, on President Quezon's death, he became President, and in October of the same year he returned to his homeland with the American forces. In the first postwar election (April 1946) he was defeated for the presidency by Manuel ROXAS.

OSTER, Hans (1888–1945). Chief of staff to Admiral CANARIS at Army Military Intelligence (the ABWEHR) and a principal organizer of German Army OPPOSITION TO HITLER, Major General Oster was a career officer who at one stage (1932) had been temporarily dismissed from the service owing to a "scandalous" love affair. He had turned against Hitler early on, primarily because his former chief of the Abwehr, Maj. Gen. Kurt von Bredow, had been among those killed in the RÖHM purge of 1934, and his opposition was confirmed by the Blomberg and FRITSCH scandals of 1938 (when these two officers holding the highest posts in the Army were dismissed by Hitler in a particularly shabby way, which included the use of false evidence about personal conduct), especially as Oster himself was chosen to deliver to Blomberg the news of his dismissal.

Handsome, elegant, dashing but incautious, Oster was the opposite in character to Canaris, but they became close and trusting colleagues in their dedication to resistance, organizing the secret collection of documents incriminating the Nazi regime. Oster was responsible for drafting the so-called Oster Study (an initial outline for an Army coup d'état), and worked closely with DOHNANYI, BONHOEFFER and Josef MÜLLER following their recruitment to the wartime Abwehr. It was Oster who in 1940 took grave risks in giving clandestine warnings of imminent invasion, notably to Holland and Belgium—Oster's so-called treason. He narrowly escaped full exposure at the time of Dohnanyi's arrest in April 1943, being suspended pending investigation. He was finally arrested after the attempt on Hitler's life in July 1944 and was subjected to intensive interrogation. He was executed on April 9, 1945.

OSTTRUPPEN. The name, meaning "Eastern troops," which the Germans gave to Red Army deserters who volunteered to serve in the Wehrmacht. Many of these Russian volunteers were motivated to join the Nazi forces by a hatred of Communism. They wore their own distinctive uniforms, and their estimated size in 1942 was at least 500,000 men.

OTT, Eugen (1890–1966). German Army officer who in 1933 was appointed military attaché in Tokyo, and from 1938 to 1942 served as German ambassador to Japan. General Ott resigned after his friend Richard SORGE was discovered to be a top Soviet spy.

OTTO. The original—and temporary—designation for Operation BARBAROSSA, the German invasion of the Soviet Union.

OUMANSKY, Constantine A. (1902–1945). Soviet diplomat who began as a newspaperman, joining the overseas service of Tass in 1924. In 1936 he became counselor to the Soviet embassy in Washington, in June 1938 the chargé d'affaires and in May 1939 ambassador to the United States, one of the youngest men to serve as such. Oumansky held that post during 1939–40, difficult times for Soviet-American relations because of the conclusion of the SOVIET-GERMAN NONAGGRESSION PACT in August 1939, and his personal traits did not endear him to Washington officials. In November 1941 he accompanied an American mission to Moscow for talks on LEND-LEASE. In 1943 he became the Soviet ambassador to Mexico. He played a role in the establishment of relations between a number of Latin American countries and the Soviet Union. In January 1945 he was killed in an aircraft crash at Mexico City.

OVERCAST. Code name for U.S. military project designed to bring German scientists and engineers to the United States, originally on a temporary basis. It was established in July 1945, the purpose being to "assist in shortening the Japanese war and to aid our postwar military research." In the first group of seven to come to the United States was Wernher von BRAUN. Competition for the services of the scientists was brisk, not only between the Western Allies and the Soviet Union but among the Western Allies themselves; in fact, at this time the U.S. efforts do not appear to have had any basis in "Cold War" thinking.

OVERLORD. The code name of the Allied cross-Channel INVASION in the spring of 1944. The naval part of the operation was called NEPTUNE.

OVERSTRAETEN, Raoul van (1885–). Belgian career soldier, aide to King Albert I and then military adviser to King LEOPOLD III. As such, General van Overstraeten played a crucial role in Belgian military policy. During the German invasion of May 1940, he ran the Belgian Army under Leopold's direction; however, he opposed the King's negotiation of a separate Belgian armistice with the Germans.

OWEN STANLEY MOUNTAINS. Mountain range in eastern NEW GUINEA that figured prominently in the fighting in 1942. *See also* KOKODA TRAIL.

OXFORD. Called the Ox-box by those who flew it, Britain's Airspeed Oxford was a twin-engine, low-wing trainer and utility transport. When it was used to train aerial gunners, a dorsal turret was installed. The two 370-horsepower Armstrong Siddeley Cheetah radial engines were replaced in later models by 475-horsepower Pratt and Whitney Wasp Juniors, and the added power increased the maximum speed from 188 to 202 miles per hour.

OYODO. Japanese light cruiser–command ship completed in 1944, displacing 8,100 tons. *Oyodo* was designed to be a fast flagship for striking groups of submarines and aircraft. She was given an armament of six 6.1-inch and eight 3.9-inch guns and numerous smaller weapons. It was intended that she should carry six fast-strike aircraft in a quarterdeck hangar. The aircraft for this purpose, however, were never built, and *Oyodo* received only the usual two scouting aircraft. The ship often served as a command flagship, with only limited participation in operations, though she was present at LEYTE GULF. She was eventually destroyed in Kure harbor by U.S. Navy carrier-borne aircraft on July 28, 1945.

OZAWA, Jisaburo (1886–1966). A graduate of the Japanese Naval Academy in 1909, Ozawa rose gradually in the Navy, attaining the rank of rear admiral in 1936. In February of the following year he became Chief of Staff of the COMBINED FLEET. Promoted to vice-admiral in 1940, Ozawa was soon appointed president of the Naval Academy. In October 1941 he received an active fleet command and participated in Japan's seizure of Indonesia, Malaya and the PHILIPPINES. In November 1942 Ozawa relieved Adm. Chuichi NAGUMO of his command of the Third Fleet, which contained most of Japan's carriers; his force played an important part in the Battle of the PHILIPPINE SEA and the battle for LEYTE GULF. Ozawa remained in this key post until November 1944, when he was appointed Vice-Chief of the Naval General Staff and president of the Naval War College. He was appointed commander of the Combined Fleet in late May 1945 following the failure of Adm. Soemu TOYODA to prevent the American seizure of OKINAWA.

Admiral Ozawa

P

P1Y1. Japanese Navy–designed *Ginga* (Milky Way) (Allied code name, Frances), a land-based two-engine dive-bomber. It entered service in 1944 and later was used in KAMIKAZE attacks. Some P1Y1s were built by Kawasaki as the RADAR-equipped *Kyokko* (Aurora) night fighter, but these were still in the test stage when the war ended.

P-26. The Boeing Peashooter, the first low-wing fighter used by the U.S. Army Air Corps, saw combat against the Japanese soon after PEARL HARBOR, some 10 years after it emerged from the drawing board. A single 570-horsepower Pratt and Whitney radial gave the plane a top speed of just 234 miles per hour, and the armament was only two .30-caliber machine guns. In December 1941 Filipino pilots climbed into the open cockpits of their obsolete P-26s to oppose modern Japanese aircraft, and Capt. Jesús Villamor actually shot down an enemy bomber in the few days before the Philippine air arm was wiped out.

P-35. Small U.S. single-seat fighter, built by Seversky (later reorganized as Republic Aviation). The P-35 was obsolete by 1941, but 48 of the planes were in the hands of Filipino pilots, who used them against the invading Japanese. After two days of combat, only two of these aircraft survived. The P-35 mounted only two machine guns and had a top speed of 310 miles per hour.

P-36. Design of this U.S. single-engine, single-seat fighter was begun by Curtiss-Wright in 1934, about the time that the concepts that became the Hawker HURRICANE, Supermarine SPITFIRE and MESSERSCHMITT ME 109 were taking shape. Unfortunately, the P-36 proved inferior to these planes. It was undergunned, with at most three .30-caliber and one .50-caliber weapon, and its radial engine gave it a top speed not much in excess of 300 miles per hour. A few U.S. Army Air Corps P-36s saw action early in the war against Japan, and a number of Hawk 75s, the export version, fought in the French air arm during 1939 and 1940.

P-38. U.S. twin-engine, twin-boom, single-seat fighter that made a spectacular debut in 1939, establishing a transcontinental speed record on its first long-distance flight. Unfortunately, the venture ended with a crash landing on a Long Island golf course. Nicknamed the Lightning, this Lockheed product was designed under the supervision of Clarence "Kelly" Johnson. In Europe it acquired another nickname: the Germans called it *der Gabelschwanz Teufel* (Fork-tailed Devil).

Early P-38s, through the G models, had sharklike nacelles housing liquid-cooled, supercharged Allison engines that developed a maximum of 1,325 horsepower. Models H through M had Allisons of either 1,425 or 1,475 horsepower with "beard" radiators that marred the plane's sleek lines. Armament was one 20-mm. cannon and four .50-caliber machine guns mounted in the pod that housed the cockpit. An unarmed photoreconnaissance version, the F-5, also saw wartime service. Although the maximum speed attributed to the P-38 was 414 miles per hour at 25,000 feet, even the early models could approach the speed of sound in a shallow dive.

P-38 Lightnings

P-39. Bell Aircraft produced an unusual U.S. aircraft in the P-39 Airacobra, a low-wing, single-place fighter. The liquid-cooled Allison engine was located behind the pilot, and the drive shaft passed beneath the cockpit. This arrangement permitted easy stowage of the tricycle landing gear, and left room for a 37-mm. cannon that fired through a hollow propeller hub. Horsepower, originally 1,150, was boosted by 15 percent, but weight also increased, so that the maximum speed advanced only some 5 percent, to 376 miles per hour at 15,000 feet.

A disappointment as an interceptor, the plane proved rugged and deadly in close support of ground troops. The Soviet Union received roughly half of the P-39s that were built, and Russian pilots reportedly were pleased with the craft's performance.

P-40. This Curtiss product was intended as a liquid-cooled replacement for the same company's radial-engine P-36 (above). The XP-40 was a production model P-36 modified to accommodate the new Allison engine. The experimental model so impressed the U.S. Army Air Corps that in 1939 Curtiss received a contract for 524 aircraft. The P-40 remained in production until December 1944, with a total of 12,302 planes being accepted for service. This fighter saw action with the U.S. Army (as the Warhawk), with the British (as the Tomahawk and the Kittyhawk), with the French and with the AMERICAN VOLUNTEER GROUP in China. Canada, Australia, South Africa and the Soviet Union also used the P-40.

Despite the extended production run and its wide usage, the P-40 was not a popular airplane. Although durable and easy to fly, it performed poorly at high altitude and was far more successful in bombing attacks or strafing runs than in aerial combat. The P-40B was powered by an 1,150-horsepower Allison, which gave it a service ceiling of 32,400 feet and a maximum speed of 352 miles per hour at 15,000 feet. Both speed and ceiling declined in the P-40C because of the installation of additional equipment, such as self-sealing fuel tanks. The lightweight P-40N-CU-1 Warhawk, of which only 400 were built, was the fastest of the breed, reaching 378 miles per hour at 10,500 feet. Later P-40Ns, however, were built with standard equipment and armament, so that their top speed declined by some 14 miles per hour.

P-40 is concealed by bamboo trees at a base in India

P-47. Republic Aviation's chief designer, Alexander Kartveli, was reputed to have used the back of an envelope to make the preliminary sketch of the highly successful P-47 Thunderbolt. If so, the basic idea behind this drawing had evolved through a series of Kartveli designs—the P-35, the P-43 (which saw wartime service with the Chinese air arm) and the unsuccessful P-44. The Thunderbolt, however, was far more powerful than any of its U.S. Army Air Forces ancestors.

The barrel-chested P-47, with its graceful elliptical wing, had a Pratt and Whitney Double Wasp engine, a twin-row radial developing 2,000 horsepower. When the prototype XP-47B took to the skies in May 1941 it was the heaviest fighter in the world, but despite its weight the plane attained a speed of 412 miles per hour.

Production models of the P-47 fought both the Germans and the Japanese. In Europe, Thunderbolts served for a time as bomber escorts, but they surrendered this mission to the longer-range P-51 Mustangs (below) and concentrated on ground attacks on airfields and lines of communication. When the V-1 buzz bomb appeared, Republic countered with the P-47M, which had an enlarged turbosupercharger and a water-injection system that in emergencies could boost horsepower to 2,800. This model, and the N which followed, could exceed 450 miles per hour at 30,000 feet.

Thunderbolt pilots downed 3,752 German planes and destroyed 3,315 on the ground. Squadrons using the P-47 also reported the destruction of 86,000 railroad cars, 9,000 locomotives, 68,000 trucks and 6,000 armored vehicles.

P-47 Thunderbolt

P-51. North American Aviation first proposed this plane as a substitute for the Curtiss P-40 (above), which a British purchasing mission was planning to buy for the Royal Air Force. A design team headed by Raymond Rice and Edgar Schmued pioneered in fitting the new laminar-flow wing to a fighter plane. Their product, Mustang I, saw action with the RAF and proved to be the best American-built fighter that the British had thus far acquired. The plane's sole major defect was its Allison engine, which performed poorly at high altitude.

Despite this limitation, U.S. Army Air Forces commenced ordering fighter (P-51), photoreconnaissance (F-6) and dive-bomber (A-36) versions of the Mustang. Whatever its use, the plane could be recognized by its squared wings and the air intake beneath the fuselage. Beginning with the P-51D, a bubble canopy was installed.

As the U.S. Army was acquiring its first Mustangs, the RAF tried installing a 1,600-horsepower Rolls-Royce Merlin instead of the 1,200-horsepower Allison.

P-51 Mustangs

The different liquid-cooled engine gave Mustang II a top speed of 427 miles per hour, an increase of 37 miles per hour over the speed of Mustang I, and raised the service ceiling from 31,350 to 42,000 feet. The fastest Mustang was the P-51H, whose Packard-built Merlin gave it a top speed of 487 miles per hour at 25,000 feet.

Fitted with a Packard version of the Merlin engine, the single-seat P-51 became an outstanding fighter. Auxiliary fuel tanks enabled it to escort American bombers all the way to Berlin. In the European theater, P-51s flew more than 200,000 sorties, shot down 4,950 enemy planes and destroyed 4,131 on the ground. The plane also saw service in the Pacific, where it escorted Marianas-based B-29s on missions against Japan.

P-59. The Bell Airacomet, the first turbojet aircraft built in the United States, took to the air in October 1942. Even after refinements in design had been made, this twin-jet, midwing fighter had a maximum speed of only 409 miles per hour at 35,000 feet and was therefore slower than many propeller-driven fighters. As a result the P-59 never saw combat, but a number were built and used for experiments and training.

P-61. Northrop Aviation began designing this twin-engine, twin-boom U.S. night fighter in 1940; a prototype took to the skies in 1942. Dubbed the Black Widow, the P-61 weighed some 16 tons fully loaded and had a crew of two (three in the B model) housed in a large nacelle that also contained the RADAR, a remotely controlled dorsal turret and four fixed guns mounted in the belly to fire forward. Despite the P-61's size, its two 2,800-horsepower supercharged engines gave it a top speed in excess of 400 miles per hour and a service ceiling above 40,000 feet. Unfortunately, the most powerful model, the P-61C, appeared too late for the war, and the P-61As and Bs that saw combat were unable to reach enemy bombers flying much above 31,000 feet.

P-63. The Bell Kingcobra resembled a slightly enlarged version of the Airacobra (*see* P-39), even to the location of the engine and the cannon firing through the propeller hub, but the newer plane was actually an entirely different design. The first Kingcobras mounted a 1,325-horsepower Allison engine such as was used on the most advanced of the P-39s. The P-63, however, had a service ceiling of 38,000 feet and a maximum speed of 410 miles per hour at 25,000 feet, compared with 35,000 feet and 376 miles per hour at 15,000 feet for the P-39Q.

Most of the Kingcobras served with the Soviet air arm. Some of those used by U.S. Army Air Forces were fitted with 1,400 pounds of armor and used as targets for gunnery students firing frangible plastic bullets.

P-70. A night-fighter version of the Douglas A-20 (*see* A-20); RADAR-equipped it figured in two wartime experiments while wearing Royal Air Force markings. The British fitted the craft, which they called the Havoc, with the Long Aerial Mine, an explosive charge attached to a 2,000-foot cable that was trailed across the path of German night-bomber formations. The device was a failure.

Other Havocs mounted the Turbinlite, a 2.7-billion-candlepower searchlight used to illuminate targets for accompanying fighters that lacked radar.

U.S. Army Air Forces employed some P-70s as trainers, and also used a few as night fighters in the Pacific theater, where they soon gave way to the P-61 Black Widow (above).

P-80. In June 1943 a Lockheed Aircraft design team, headed by Clarence "Kelly" Johnson, began work on a fighter built around the de Havilland H-1 turbojet engine, which was to be manufactured in the United States by Allis-Chalmers. Just 143 days after work started, a prototype XP-80 made two successful test flights at Muroc Army Airfield in California. When the American version of the H-1 fell far behind schedule, Lockheed substituted the General Electric J-33, developed by Allison and rated at 4,000 pounds' thrust.

The P-80 Shooting Star featured a laminar-flow wing modified with a sharp leading edge. Air intakes for the turbojet engine were on either side of the fuselage just forward of the wing root. Armament was increased from five to six .50-caliber machine guns grouped in the nose. U.S. Army Air Forces accepted 13 YP-80As for service test, beginning in October 1944. Two of these planes reached Italy shortly before the war in Europe ended, but did not see combat.

P-108B. This four-engine, low-wing Piaggio monoplane, which served as a heavy bomber and transport, was among the most heavily armed of Italian aircraft, carrying eight 12.7-mm. machine guns. The first Italian heavy bomber, it entered service in 1942. Single weapons were located in the nose and belly and on both sides of the fuselage at the waist position. Atop each of the outboard engine nacelles was a two-gun powered turret manipulated by remote control. The plane could carry more than 7,000 pounds of bombs or three 18-inch torpedoes, and the four 1,500-horsepower radial engines gave it a top speed of 267 miles per hour.

P-400. Designation applied to Bell Airacobra fighters built for the RAF and taken over after Pearl Harbor for U.S. Army use. The most conspicuous difference between the P-400 and the Army's P-39 (*see* P-39) was the use of a 20-mm. gun through the propeller hub in place of the 37-mm. gun used in planes built for U.S. service. P-400s were sent to the South Pacific, operating out of GUADALCANAL. Squadrons using them coined the nickname "Klunker" to express their opinion of the P-400 as an opponent for more agile Japanese fighters.

PAASIKIVI, Juho K. (1870–1956). Finnish statesman, leader of the opposition Coalition Party and minister to Sweden at the time of the outbreak of the SOVIET-FINNISH WAR. Paasikivi played the key role in negotiating the armistice and the treaty which concluded that war. He joined the government as Minister Without Portfolio in December 1939, and after signing the peace treaty became ambassador to Moscow. After the resumption of Soviet-Finnish hostilities in June 1941, he became the chief advocate of a separate peace with the Soviet Union. As Prime Minister after November 1944, he negotiated the new peace treaty, and from March 1946 until his death was President of Finland.

PACIFIC OCEAN AREAS. One of two major Allied theaters of operations into which the Pacific was divided in April 1942; the other was the SOUTHWEST PACIFIC AREA, under the command of Gen. Douglas MACARTHUR. The Pacific Ocean Areas (abbreviated POA) were placed under the command of Adm. Chester NIMITZ, who was already Commander in Chief, U.S. Pacific Fleet (CINCPAC); Nimitz's title now became Commander in Chief, U.S. Pacific Fleet and Pacific Ocean Areas (CINCPAC/CINCPOA). Nimitz's area command consisted of the North Pacific Area, the Central Pacific Area and the South Pacific Area. Individual area commanders in these three zones operated under Nimitz's orders. MacArthur's Southwest Pacific Area included the waters around Australia, New Guinea, the Bismarck and Solomon groups, the Netherlands East Indies and the Philippines. Just before the August 1942 landing on Guadalcanal, the boundary of the Southwest Pacific Area was moved slightly to the west to bring the southern Solomons inside the South Pacific Area. A Southeast Pacific Area had been established in December 1941. This was a defensive zone, taking in the waters off the west coasts of Central and South America.

PACIFIC WAR—1942–45. Despite their stunning victories in December 1941 and the first months of 1942 (*see* JAPANESE CONQUESTS) and the skillful tactics that made them possible, the Japanese had lost the war, practically speaking, at the outset. Before the fighting began, the Americans had broken the Japanese code, enabling them to anticipate Japanese moves. Hitler's drive into Russia stalled, leaving the Axis opposed by a strong land foe in Euroasia. PEARL HARBOR itself was a hollow Japanese victory: the very success of the raid had shown dramatically that the aircraft carrier, not the battleship, was the heart of a modern navy, and the American fleet had lost no carriers at Pearl Harbor. By April 1942 six American and three British carriers were operating in the Pacific and Indian Oceans, compared with the Japanese 10. Most important, the Japanese command had wrongly forecast the reaction of the American people to Pearl Harbor. The United States immediately began building a military machine fully capable of waging a two-front war.

Before the Japanese attack, the planners had decided that in case of a two-front war the struggle against Germany would receive priority. Nevertheless, American Far Eastern and Australian ground forces were heavily reinforced during Japan's run of victories. As long as communications between Hawaii and Australia remained secure, the Allied buildup could continue. Eventually the Japanese defensive perimeter could be threatened from several different directions.

Perceiving the danger, the Japanese in the spring of 1942 pursued a number of operations intended to isolate Australia and bring the American fleet to battle. The first of these efforts failed when a task force intended for PORT MORESBY, NEW GUINEA, was turned back by the American fleet at the Battle of the CORAL SEA in May. Then disaster struck the Imperial Fleet when Adm. Isoruku YAMAMOTO, seeking a decisive naval victory, led a huge force against MIDWAY Island. On the afternoon of June 4 American carrier-based planes caught the Japanese by surprise and succeeded in sinking all four of the Japanese carriers, while losing only one. Despite the defeat at Midway, the Japanese proceeded with a series of successful landings in the SOLOMONS. Since they had lost naval superiority, however, these last Japanese victories proved short-lived.

After Midway the JOINT CHIEFS OF STAFF decided to go over to a limited three-phase offensive aimed at securing communications with Australia and reducing the important Japanese base at RABAUL. Phase One sought the seizure of bases in the southern Solomons. Phase Two envisioned an advance through the Solomons and a drive up New Guinea to the HUON PENINSULA. In Phase Three the two drives would converge on Rabaul. The offensive began on August 7 with a landing on GUADALCANAL. The Japanese, favorably situated at Rabaul and TRUK, reacted vigorously. Their small garrison on Guadalcanal was reinforced. They contested control of the sea in the South Pacific in a series of sharp surface engagements. The battle became far greater than had been expected by the Americans. Despite some bad moments, however, American superiority in men and material began to show. By November four reinforced U.S. divisions were on Guadalcanal. Japanese troops counterattacked fiercely, but in February 1943 were forced to evacuate, after heavy losses in men, ships and planes.

While fighting raged in the Solomons, the Japanese attempted an overland drive on Port Moresby, only to be thwarted by Australian defenders some 20 miles from their objective. Gen. Douglas MACARTHUR's American and Australian troops pursued the Japanese, who finally took up strongly entrenched positions around BUNA and GONA on Papua's northeastern coast. The Allies assaulted the Buna-Gona area in November, but the Japanese were not dislodged until January 1943, after weeks of hard fighting.

The Japanese tried vainly to restore the situation in the Southwest Pacific by sending heavy reinforcements

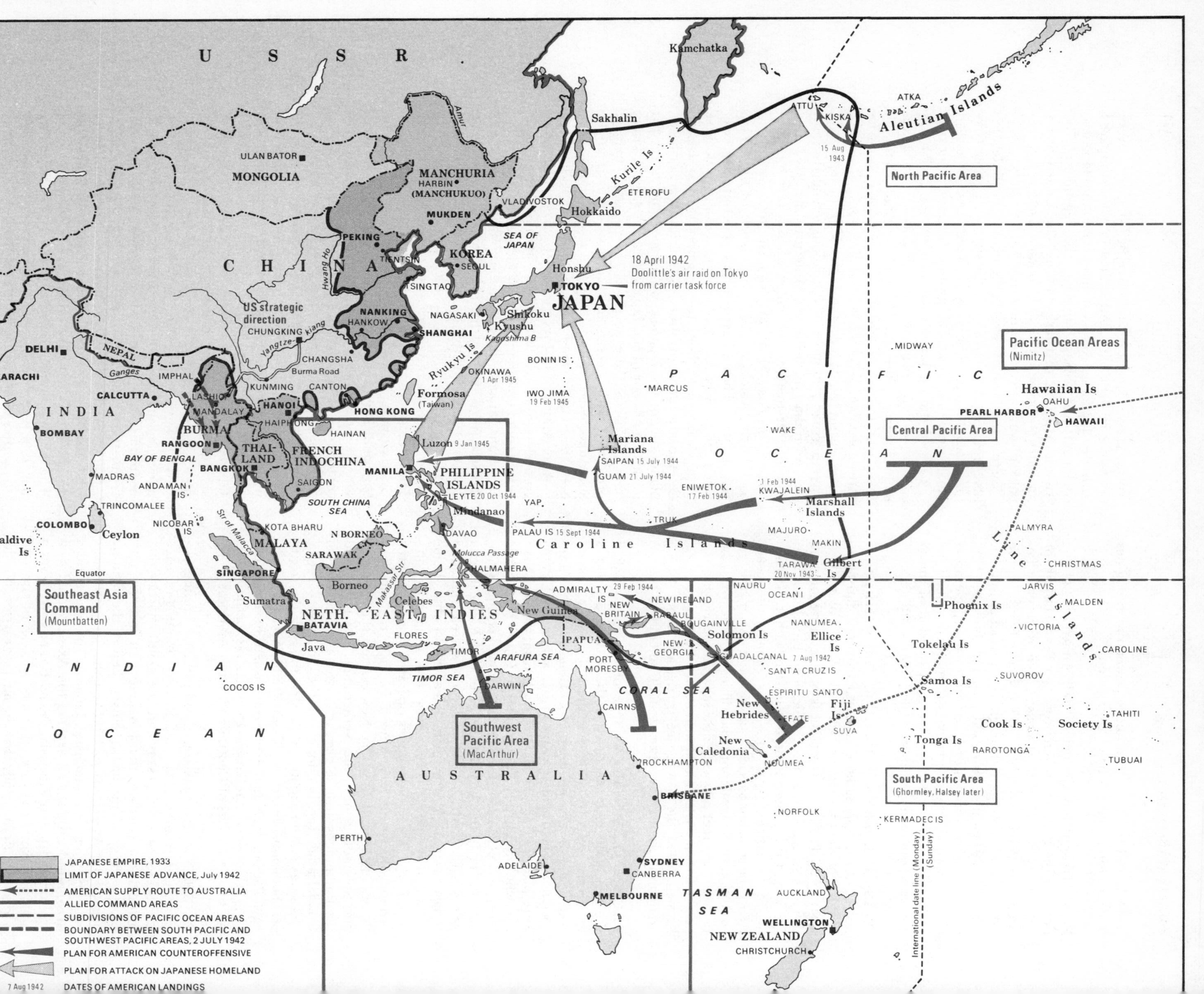

THE PACIFIC WAR—the Allies on the offensive, 1942–45

to New Guinea and the Solomons. In March 1943 a large Japanese convoy bound for LAE was shattered in the Battle of the BISMARCK SEA by U.S. Army land-based planes. In April a concentrated Japanese air offensive from Rabaul that was aimed at regaining air superiority in the Southwest Pacific ended in dismal failure. This defeat was indicative of a serious turn of events for Japan. New types of American planes, with expertly trained pilots, had ended Japan's initial qualitative superiority in the air. The new American ESSEX-class carriers, which began appearing in 1943, were superior to anything the Japanese could put forward. In short, as 1943 progressed the Japanese increasingly found themselves outclassed.

In March 1943 the Joint Chiefs determined that without reinforcements U.S. forces could not take Rabaul that year, as originally planned. Since Europe had first call on resources, a less ambitious aim was substituted. Operation CARTWHEEL called for an advance in 1943 to BOUGAINVILLE by Adm. William F. HALSEY'S South Pacific forces and to western NEW BRITAIN by MacArthur. The drive up the Solomons began in July. In operations typical of the South Pacific, Halsey executed a series of landings designed to secure air bases and bypass Japanese strongpoints. In November a successful assault was made on EMPRESS AUGUSTA BAY on Bougainville, thus completing Halsey's portion of the offensive. MacArthur's advance in New Guinea kept pace; intricate land, airborne and amphibious operations succeeded in clearing the Huon Peninsula in September. On December 26 beachheads were established at CAPE GLOUCESTER on western New Britain. During the Allied advance, continuous air battles so weakened Rabaul's defenses that Japanese air and naval forces were withdrawn to Truk. Consequently, the U.S. command concluded that Rabaul could be bypassed altogether.

Meanwhile, long-range planning for the final defeat of Japan was well under way. Originally, the Joint Chiefs believed that FORMOSA eventually must be captured and air bases established in China to cut communications between Japan and the East Indies, to initiate

U.S. battleships provided intensive preinvasion bombardment of Japanese-held islands. Here the *Tennessee* pounds Iwo Jima

a bomber offensive against Japanese industry and to prepare for an invasion of Japan. Despite hopes to the contrary, the British were unable to spare sufficient resources for a major drive through BURMA and Southeast Asia. The defeat of Japan was therefore regarded as essentially an American project. Initially the Joint Chiefs—Adm. Ernest J. KING in particular—thought it could best be accomplished by a drive through the Central Pacific, with a secondary advance up New Guinea. King and Adm. Chester NIMITZ, the Commander in Chief of Pacific Ocean Areas, argued that the Central Pacific route would be easier to support logistically, would allow full advantage to be taken of the fleet's mobility, would strike at Japan's vulnerable east flank and would permit the earliest possible employment of the Army's new B-29 bomber (*see* B-29) from bases in the Marianas. MacArthur argued vehemently that the main drive should be made up New Guinea and into the PHILIPPINES. He claimed that the Southwest Pacific route was shorter, would avoid costly island assaults and would allow better utilization of land-based air power.

The argument went back and forth for some months. As the American buildup in the Pacific continued, however, it became possible to begin both drives. In 1944 the dispute shifted emphasis. Admiral King and some others at JCS asserted that the Philippines could be bypassed and Formosa assaulted directly. MacArthur, along with many commanders on the spot, favored the seizure of the entire Philippine archipelago, claiming that the United States had a moral obligation to reconquer the Philippines and that Luzon could be made into the "England of the Pacific" in preparation for an invasion of Japan. Even Nimitz, although uncertain about an invasion of Luzon, believed that bases in the Philippines were requisite for a drive on Formosa. So the Allies conducted a two-pronged drive which was to converge on the Philippines. Ultimately, logistical considerations settled the Formosa-versus-Luzon debate in favor of the Luzon plan.

The Central Pacific offensive began on November 20, 1943, when Nimitz sent Army and Marine troops to the GILBERT ISLANDS to seize air bases for subsequent landings in the MARSHALLS. Troops and supplies embarked from Hawaii on specially designed assault shipping and sailed 2,000 miles to be landed by newly developed LANDING CRAFT and AMPHIBIOUS VEHICLES. Air support was delivered by Seventh Fleet's carrier strike force. MAKIN Atoll, the Army objective, fell after a sharp fight. Marines landing on TARAWA had a much more difficult time. Since American amphibious doctrine had not yet been refined by experience, coordination of naval gunfire and air attacks was faulty, and a ferocious struggle took place before the Japanese garrison was exterminated. In January 1944 the drive continued into the central Marshalls, with the easy capture of MAJURO and KWAJALEIN. Surprised by this weak resistance, Nimitz advanced the schedule of his drive 10 weeks by landing on ENIWETOK Atoll in the western Marshalls on February 17. At the same time the carrier strike force conducted a raid on Truk, considered Japan's primary bastion in the Central Pacific. This raid revealed that Truk had virtually been abandoned, and Nimitz therefore decided it could be bypassed, further accelerating the tempo of the Central Pacific advance.

General MacArthur was likewise able to advance his own timetable. A landing at Saidor in January 1944 nearly succeeded in trapping Japanese troops retreating from the Huon Peninsula. In February a daring operation led to the capture of the ADMIRALTY ISLANDS.

Hat-wearing New Zealand troops relieve Americans on Vella Lavella Island, September 1943

U.S. Third Fleet steams off the coast of Japan at the end of the war

MacArthur then persuaded Nimitz to lend carrier support for landings at HOLLANDIA and AITAPE behind Japanese forces at WEWAK. Although the Japanese counterattacked, they were trapped between the Americans at Aitape and the Australians marching up the coast. After seizing Hollandia, American units jumped 125 miles northwest on May 17 to capture an air base site at WAKDE Island. Ten days later a leap of 180 miles led to the capture of BIAK Island.

From Biak, Army planes could harry the Japanese fleet that was assembling in Philippine waters for a showdown with Nimitz's forces. To counter this threat, the Japanese deployed half of their land-based air strength from the Central Pacific against MacArthur. They also prepared a sizable naval strike force to expel the Americans from Biak. In June, however, they learned that the American fleet was off the Marianas. The Biak operation was canceled, and a hastily prepared sortie was made against Nimitz. Lacking land-based air, the Japanese were unable to surprise the American fleet, and they suffered another crushing defeat at the Battle of the PHILIPPINE SEA. Although Nimitz did not realize the extent of the damage to the Japanese fleet, the American carrier strike force had once again proved to be the decisive weapon in the Pacific war.

On June 15 Marine and Army divisions landed on SAIPAN in the Marianas. The three-week struggle for Saipan was one of the fiercest engaged in by Nimitz's troops. Nevertheless, the outcome was not really in doubt, and in July Nimitz was able to proceed on GUAM and TINIAN. By November, B-29s based in the Marianas would begin to fly missions against Japan.

After the capture of the Marianas, the two Allied drives quickly converged. At the end of July, MacArthur's troops took SANSAPOR on the northwestern tip of New Guinea. On September 15 they landed on MOROTAI Island between New Guinea and the Philippines. At the same time Nimitz seized PELELIU and ANGAUR in the Palau Islands and secured a forward anchorage for the fleet at ULITHI in the Carolines. In the seven months since the capture of the Admiralties, MacArthur's forces had advanced 1,500 miles. In the 10 months of the Central Pacific drive Nimitz had advanced 4,500 miles, from Hawaii to the Palaus. By mid-September 1944 preparations were under way for reentering the Philippines.

Originally it had been planned to invade MINDANAO in November and LUZON in February 1945. However, Halsey's carriers supporting the MOROTAI operation had met unexpectedly light opposition from the Japanese in the central and southern Philippines. MacArthur and Nimitz therefore proposed to JCS that Mindanao be bypassed in favor of a landing on LEYTE in October. This was a welcome possibility for MacArthur, since Admiral King was still advocating an advance on Formosa rather than on Luzon. With operations speeded up, MacArthur proposed to invade Luzon in mid-December. As Formosa could not be assaulted until February, King gave way; MacArthur would be allowed to invade Luzon, although once the Japanese fleet was neutralized, Central Pacific forces would move against Iwo Jima in the Bonins and then against Okinawa.

The main assault on Leyte occurred on October 20. Because the establishment of American air bases on Leyte would ensure the conquest of Luzon and the severing of communications with the Indies, the Japanese determined to fight the decisive battle on Leyte. Ground and air reinforcements were sent to the island, and the Navy prepared a desperate gambit to destroy MacArthur's troopships and block the Philippines: while a Japanese carrier strike force (carrying few planes) lured Halsey away from Leyte, a battleship attack force would move from the south and smash the American invasion. The resulting battle for Leyte Gulf was the largest naval engagement in history. Halsey in fact took the bait, but he succeeded in sinking all four Japanese carriers. The battleships got perilously close to Leyte Gulf but were turned away by old American battleships and escort carriers. In all, the Japanese lost four carriers, three battleships and 10 cruisers. After Leyte Gulf, the Imperial Fleet ceased to be a factor in the war.

Having won uncontested control of the sea, MacArthur's troops proceeded with the destruction of the Japanese garrison on Leyte. Despite miserable weather and difficult terrain, most of the important areas on the island were secure by late December. The remaining Japanese retreated to the mountains in a state of semi-starvation. Sporadic resistance continued until the end of the war.

The Luzon campaign began on December 15 with the quick seizure of an air base on Mindoro 150 miles south of Manila. Just as the Japanese had in 1941, MacArthur chose Lingayen Gulf for the site of the main blow. On January 9, 1945, four divisions landed there, with two more soon to follow. Gen. Tomoyuki Yamashita, victor at Singapore and now Japanese commander in the Philippines, believed that the battle for Luzon had already been lost at Leyte. Realizing that his troops could not be reinforced, he decided not to make a concentrated defense of the Central Plains–Manila Bay region. Rather, he determined to make a fighting withdrawal toward mountain strongholds in north-central Luzon, pinning down as many American troops as possible to prevent their deployment against Japan itself. Thus the Americans were able to progress steadily from Lingayen Gulf toward Manila. They were aided by the landing near Subic Bay of another corps, which quickly sealed off the Bataan peninsula. On February 3 American troops reached Manila. However, Japanese naval troops, in spite of Yamashita's orders, were determined to defend the city. A month of harsh house-to-house fighting was required before Manila could be secured.

By mid-March Manila Bay was open to Allied shipping, but a sizable salvage and repair job was required before it could be fully used. MacArthur continued to reinforce Luzon, and the fight became the largest land battle of the Pacific war. Steady pressure was maintained on Yamashita, and his forces were slowly isolated

American and Australian troops cross the Francisco River near Salamaua, New Guinea, September 1943

in pockets. As happened often in the later stages of the war, Japanese troops had to face starvation as well as superior opposition. Nevertheless, resistance of a sort continued on Luzon until Japan's surrender.

Beginning in late February, American forces had begun the reconquest of the southern Philippines. By May landings had been made on Palawan, Mindanao, Panay, Cebu and Negros. Despite some hard fighting, the Japanese were in every case either destroyed or forced to withdraw to the mountains. In these operations, as well as on Luzon, Filipino guerrilla units were a significant aid. In May the Australians began the last offensive in the Southwest Pacific Area with the first of a series of landings on Borneo.

While MacArthur was turning Luzon into the England of the Pacific, Central Pacific forces, again operating independently, determined to bring the war to Japan's doorstep. Iwo Jima was sought as an air base for fighters and medium bombers operating against Japan; it could also serve as an emergency base for B-29s unable to return to the Marianas. On February 19 three Marine divisions landed on the eight-square-mile island and encountered the most elaborate defensive network faced in the Pacific war. Fanatically defended by 21,000 Japanese troops, Iwo Jima cost the marines a month of bloody combat, and nearly 7,000 men killed.

On April 1 two Army and two Marine divisions landed on Okinawa in the Ryukyus and were soon reinforced by two more Army divisions. The 117,000 Japanese defenders retreated to prepared cave and tunnel defenses in the inland hills. As American troops began one of the harshest land battles of the war, Nimitz's naval forces faced a concentrated assault by Japanese KAMIKAZE planes which succeeded in sinking some 25 ships and damaging 165 more. By the time Okinawa was declared secure on June 21, 12,520 Americans had lost their lives, including the Tenth Army commander, Lt. Gen. Simon B. BUCKNER. Some 110,000 Japanese troops were also killed in an extraordinary display of fanatic, fatalistic courage.

The possession of air bases on Okinawa put American fighters and bombers within easy range of the Japanese mainland. Operating from forward anchorages in the Ryukyus, the fleet kept in almost continuous action against Japan. Advanced planning was under way for Operation Olympic, the invasion of Kyushu, scheduled for November 1, 1945. To prepare for this invasion, a concentrated air offensive was launched against the home islands. U.S. Army Air Force planes from the Philippines, the Marianas, Iwo Jima and Okinawa bombed mainland targets continually. In July, Halsey boldly took his THIRD FLEET into Japanese waters, launching 1,000-plane carrier attacks and even bombarding shore installations from battleships. A British carrier strike force joined in the assault. The B-29s, employing new low-level saturation tactics, by Japanese estimate killed 260,000 people and left 9.2 million homeless. American submarines continued their largely unheralded operations, which, along with air power, virtually destroyed the Japanese merchant fleet.

After Okinawa most Japanese leaders realized that the situation was hopeless. As early as May approaches were made through the Soviet Union for a conditional surrender. Since the Allies, as highlighted by the famous POTSDAM Declaration in July 1945, insisted on unconditional surrender, nothing was accomplished. Some fanatics in the Japanese Army resisted any moves for peace, preferring to fight to the end on the home islands. President TRUMAN, supported by most of his military and civilian advisers, decided that dropping the newly developed ATOMIC BOMB on Japan might force capitulation and make unnecessary an invasion, which, it was feared, might cost 1 million Allied casualties. On August 6 the first atomic bomb was dropped on HIROSHIMA. On August 9, as previously agreed, the Soviet Union entered the war. The same day a second bomb was delivered on NAGASAKI. The next day the Japanese offered to surrender if the Emperor could be retained. To this point President Truman agreed. The Emperor announced surrender on August 15. On September 2 the surrender agreement was signed on the deck of the U.S.S. MISSOURI in Tokyo Bay. **E.B.**

PACT OF STEEL. The signing of a formal military alliance between Germany and Italy had been among HITLER's objectives since his visit to Rome in May 1938, although both MUSSOLINI and his Foreign Minister, Count CIANO, managed to avoid hard commitments on paper until the so-called Pact of Steel was finally agreed upon a year later, and signed in Berlin on May 22, 1939. The pact declared that Germany and Italy were "determined to act side by side and with united forces" for their own security and for the maintenance of peace, and that each would come to the aid of the other should hostilities ever break out.

PADDOCK. Underground headquarters near Hampstead, London, for the British War Cabinet and military staffs, to be used if German bombing rendered government offices unusable. It was used only once, in a rehearsal in September 1940.

PAGET, Sir Bernard Charles Tolver (1888–1961). British Army officer who performed outstanding service in the NORWAY campaign in 1940 and was Commander in Chief Home Forces in 1942–43. Paget gained recognition for his excellent system of training troops—notably through the use of live ammunition in exercises to simulate actual battle conditions—and for the high morale which he inspired in the soldiers under his command. He trained the British armies that participated in the INVASION of Normandy. Subsequently, he commanded British forces in the Middle East. His highest wartime rank was general.

PAKFRONT. Abbreviated form of Panzerabwehrkanonenfront, meaning "antitank gun front." The Germans developed the Pakfront tactic in 1943 to counter Soviet attacks employing a great number of tanks. They scattered groups of up to 10 antitank guns over a defended area, with each group commanded by one man whose job was to concentrate fire on a single Russian tank.

PALDASKI. Naval base in Estonia, at the entrace to the Gulf of Finland, taken over by the Soviets in 1939 following the conclusion of the SOVIET-GERMAN NONAGGRESSION PACT.

PALERMO. Palermo, SICILY, was occupied by General PATTON's U.S. SEVENTH ARMY on July 22, 1943, after a sweep from the southern coast of the island. Opposition was not severe, but it was the first dramatic American drive of the war and a tremendous morale booster.

PALLET LOADING. World War II technique in which cargo was assembled into large cubes strapped to wooden platforms called pallets. The pallet stood clear of the floor on crossbeams; the blades of a forklift could be inserted under the pallet and the entire cube could be handled as a single item.

PALM SUNDAY MASSACRE. The destruction on April 18, 1943, of a large group of German JUNKERS JU 52 transports that were attempting to fly supplies across the Mediterranean to German forces in North Africa. In an engagement of about 10 minutes, Allied fighters (58 U.S. P-40 Warhawks [*see* P-40] and 12 RAF SPITFIRES) shot down at least 51 of the lumbering trimotor transports and 16 of the escorting fighters. Allied losses were six P-40s and one Spitfire.

PANAMA CONFERENCE. In accordance with the Declaration of Lima of 1938, American foreign ministers (with Under Secretary of State Sumner WELLES as the chief United States delegate) met in Panama in September 1939, shortly after the outbreak of war in Europe. Very rapidly this conference adopted the Declaration of Panama, which declared the neutrality of the American states, forbade the entry of belligerent submarines into the harbors of American nations, called for the curtailment of subversion by belligerents and proclaimed a safety zone around the Americas (but excluded belligerent Canada). At this conference various agencies of economic aid and cooperation were created to help Latin-American nations.

PANAMA SEA FRONTIER. U.S. Navy designation for the SEA FRONTIER command responsible for the defense of the eastern and western approaches to the Panama Canal Zone.

PANAY. Large, well-settled island in the Visayan group of the central PHILIPPINES. The Japanese first landed on Panay on April 16, 1942. U.S. forces on the island, under Col. Albert F. Christie, were well prepared to undertake protracted guerrilla warfare, but he perforce joined in the general surrender in May. During the course of the Japanese occupation Col. Marcario L. Peralta (Philippine Army) organized on Panay one of the most effective guerrilla units in the Philippines. By March 1945 Peralta had under his command 22,500 men, half of them armed, and controlled much of Panay against a Japanese garrison of some 2,750. The reinforced 186th RCT of the U.S. 41st Division encountered no opposition when it landed on Panay on March 18, 1945.

PANTALOON. Allied code name for NAPLES, Italy.

PANTELLERIA. A small, rocky island about 150 miles northwest of MALTA, developed by the Italians as a base for E-BOATS. Plans for its capture were put forward by the COMBINED OPERATIONS Command in October 1940 but were abandoned as impracticable. In June 1943, following the successful Allied campaign in NORTH AFRICA, Pantelleria surrendered to a British naval force after a short air bombardment, the one time in history that such has happened.

PANTHER TANK. German medium-heavy TANK.

PANZER. The German word for "armor." It was popularly used on both sides to refer to tanks or as an adjective (as panzer attack, panzer breakthrough, etc.). In German use it might refer to any tank; used by the Allies, it usually referred specifically to German armor.

PANZER ARMIES (German). *First–Fourth Panzer Armies*: During the Polish campaign the German armored forces were controlled by four corps headquarters. These corps headquarters had been upgraded to four numbered panzer groups, 1 to 4, by the beginning of the Russian campaign. Panzer Groups 1 and 2 were renamed the First and Second Panzer Armies respectively in October 1941, and Panzer Groups 3 and 4 the Third and Fourth Panzer Armies in January 1942. All four panzer armies were in action on the Eastern Front for the remainder of the war and were disbanded in May 1945.

Fifth Panzer Army (Africa): The German headquarters in TUNISIA, the XC Corps, was renamed the Fifth Panzer Army in early December 1942. The Fifth Panzer Army served in North Africa and surrendered to the Allies on May 9, 1943.

Fifth Panzer Army (France): Panzer Group West, organized in France in December 1943 to control German armor in case of an Allied invasion, was redesignated the Fifth Panzer Army in August 1944. It fought in Normandy and in the Battle of the BULGE, and was disbanded in mid-April 1945.

Sixth Panzer Army: Organized under the command of SS Gen. Sepp DIETRICH in September 1944 to rehabilitate armored divisions withdrawn from the WESTERN FRONT. The Sixth Panzer Army took part in the Battle of the Bulge, was transferred to the Eastern Front and surrendered in May 1945.

Panzer Army Africa/German-Italian Panzer Army: Panzer Group Africa, organized as Gen. Erwin ROMMEL's headquarters in Africa in August 1941, was renamed Panzer Army Africa in January 1942. It was renamed again as the German-Italian Panzer Army in October 1942. It was deactivated on February 20, 1943.

PANZERBUCHSE. German term for an antitank rifle, a shoulder-fired weapon designed for use against armor. Early bolt-operated arms of this type had appeared in World War I. World War II types were also manually operated, but weapons developed later in the war in Germany and Russia were semiautomatic. The Solothurn 20-mm. rifle was of this latter type, with a box magazine and a telescopic sight which could be illuminated for night firing.

PANZERFAUST. Popular name for the German antitank FAUSTPATRONE.

PANZERGRENADIER. The German term for mechanized infantry, i.e., troops equipped with HALF-TRACK personnel carriers and attached to PANZER (armored) divisions. The term was applied to the troops themselves and also to their units (e.g., a panzergrenadier battalion). Motorized (motorisierte) organizations, as differentiated from panzergrenadier units, were equipped with motor transport but were not part of a panzer organization (division, corps, etc.).

PANZERHANDMINE. A German antitank explosive charge, its paper-composition body shaped like a bottle and containing a shaped charge arranged to deliver its force toward the bottom of the "bottle." Magnets were fastened around the bottom to enable the user to stick the panzerhandmine to a vehicle or other metal surface before triggering a delay igniter.

PANZER LEHR. Formerly a German armored demonstration unit, the Panzer Lehr division was committed in Normandy in the battle for the HEDGEROWS, where it quickly lost a third of its tanks. During the preliminary bombing for Operation COBRA, the division sustained severe casualties. In the Battle of the BULGE, Panzer Lehr was one of three divisions encircling BASTOGNE. A later attempt to relieve elements of the 2d Panzer in the CELLES pocket failed. Subsequently Panzer Lehr opposed the Canadians during Operation VERITABLE and was later caught in the RUHR pocket. Remnants surrendered on April 15. Its most celebrated commander was Lt. Gen. Fritz BAYERLEIN, who had been General ROMMEL's chief of staff.

PANZERSCHIFF. The German Navy's designation for the "supercruisers" *Deutschland* (later LÜTZOW), ADMIRAL SCHEER and ADMIRAL GRAF SPEE. These ships, similar to conventional German and foreign 8-inch- and 6-inch-gun cruisers in size and protection but armed with six 11-inch turret guns (and capable of doing 26 knots or more), presented something of a classification problem, since nothing like them existed elsewhere. The Germans resolved this situation, which originated in the Versailles Treaty's provision limiting their "capital ship" size to 10,000 tons' displacement, by adopting the term *Panzerschiff*. They were popularly known as "pocket battleships," a term liked by the Germans since it magnified their strength in the public mind and, later, by the British since it magnified the impact of their victory in the Battle of the RIVER PLATE (1939). But the panzerschiffe were not true battleships, lacking the size, hitting power and protection of contemporary battleships; the term "pocket battleship" has no technical significance. During the war the two surviving panzerschiffe, *Lützow* and *Admiral Scheer*, were redesignated heavy cruisers (schwere Kreuzer) by the German Navy.

PANZERSCHNELLMINE. Either of two models of a German wooden-box antitank mine, similar in concept to the SCHUHMINE but heavier.

PANZERWURFMINE. A German shaped-charge antitank grenade designed to be thrown at a target. It had a wooden handle, to which were attached four spring-ribbed canvas fins. When the grenade was thrown, these fins sprang open to steady it in flight.

PAPAGOS, Alexander (1883–1955). When the Italians invaded Greece on October 28, 1940, General Papagos led the Greek forces which repelled the aggressors. The following spring the Germans came to the aid of their Axis ally and overran Greece. The Germans arrested Papagos, who was interned as a hostage at DACHAU and other concentration camps. Freed in 1945, Papagos put down Greek Communist rebels in 1949.

PAPANDREOU, George (1888–1968). Greek politician (Radical Socialist) who was brought out of occupied GREECE in 1944 to Cairo to become Premier of the Greek government-in-exile (April 26). Representatives of the Communist-led EAM joined his cabinet but quit it when the Premier ordered the dissolution of resistance groups (*see* EAM). Civil strife followed, with order being imposed by British forces. Papandreou was succeeded in 1945 by Nicolas Plastiras.

PAPEN, Franz von (1879–1969). Born in Werl, Westphalia, member of a well-to-do landowning German family, Papen served during World War I as military attaché in the German embassy in Washington (where he was declared *persona non grata* and ordered home in 1915). After war service he entered politics and became active in the Catholic Center Party; a convinced right-wing monarchist, he rose to prominence through his social aptitude and charm. He possessed guile rather than intelligence. A soft-spoken authoritarian, he found sufficient favor with the aged President von Hindenburg to become Chancellor on June 1, 1932, during the troubled period immediately preceding Adolf HITLER's coming to power. He at least achieved the distinction of being a Chancellor who never had an opportunity to address the Reichstag, and in November 1932 he was forced to resign in favor of Gen. Kurt von Schleicher, a devious manipulator who had been responsible in the first place for maneuvering him into temporary power. Papen negotiated throughout the period with Hitler, hoping to render him tractable by making him Vice-Chancellor, and he was finally instrumental in Hitler's becoming Chancellor in Schleicher's place. This followed an agreement he reached with Hitler at the house of the Cologne banker Kurt von Schröder on January 4, 1933.

When Hitler became Chancellor on January 30, 1933, Papen was his Vice-Chancellor. Following the passage of the ENABLING ACT of March 1933, which assured his dictatorship, Hitler completely outwitted Papen's futile attempts to control him. When Papen realized the impossibility of his position, he made his single gesture of protest in a celebrated speech at the University of Marburg in which he urged moderation. Through Hermann GÖRING's intervention he was spared assassination during the 1934 purge, in which Schleicher lost his life. Dismissed from office, Papen continued to serve the Führer as ambassador to Austria, paving the way for the ANSCHLUSS of 1938, and finally as ambassador to Turkey, where he watched over Turkish neutrality until the final severance of German-Turkish relations in August 1944.

Arrested in April 1945, Papen was tried before the INTERNATIONAL MILITARY TRIBUNAL (NUREMBERG TRIALS); he was found not guilty of conspiracy and released. A subsequent denazification trial was instituted by the German authorities in 1947, and he was sentenced to eight years' imprisonment as a prominent Nazi, but eventually was released on appeal. In 1952 he published his interesting but devious *Memoirs*. In 1968, the year before his death, he published another book, *Vom Scheitern einer Demokratie*.

PAPPMINE. A German antitank mine with a body made of paperboard (Pappe). Its nonmetallic construction was designed to foil electronic mine detectors.

PAPUA. *See* NEW GUINEA.

PARIS, LIBERATION OF. Captured intact by the Germans in 1940, the city of Paris with its architectural splendors was one of Adolf HITLER's most cherished prizes. It was also, despite the rigors of the German occupation, still by far the largest and most highly industrialized city in France—and possession of it remained the sign of authority for most Frenchmen.

When the Western Allies landed in Normandy on June 6, then broke the German front at AVRANCHES and raced into the clear in early August 1944, Paris was up for grabs. Engaging in a multicornered tug of war, four major parties wrestled for control of the prize. First was the German occupier: early in August Hitler, still shaken by the abortive officers' coup of July 20, called Gen. Dietrich von CHOLTITZ from the Russian front to defend Paris at all costs or, failing that, to leave it in ruins. The second party was the Western Allied commander, Gen. Dwight EISENHOWER: preoccupied with pushing his pursuit of the Germans to the limit and facing steadily increasing logistics constraints, Ike was determined that Paris should be bypassed and left for a later day. The third player in the game was the Communist resistance movement in Paris, led by Col. Henri ("Rol") Tanguy: the Communists were the strongest element of the FRENCH RESISTANCE and were determined to seize Paris on their own hook as a step toward increasing their political position, even at the cost of ruining the city. The last party to the dispute was FREE FRANCE and the movement's leader, Gen. Charles DE GAULLE: cooling his heels impatiently in Algiers, de Gaulle sought to restrain the Resistance inside Paris while pushing the Allies to take Paris from the outside, all the while intriguing to get himself into the city as soon as possible.

The denouement of this struggle began on August 19, when the Resistance, forced to action by Tanguy, threw up barricades and turned hidden weapons on the German garrison. Choltitz had not yet received the heavy reinforcements promised by Hitler, nor did he wish to bring the magnificent city down in ruins. He temporized and finally agreed to a makeshift truce with the Gaullist Resistance arranged by the Swedish consul general, Raoul NORDLING. This arrangement soon broke down, however, and Choltitz reluctantly sent tanks against the insurgents, who appealed urgently for Allied help. Meanwhile, de Gaulle arrived in France and hurriedly prepared to send the sole French force available to him, General LECLERC's 2d Armored Division, to the scene. His sustained pressure, plus intelligence from inside the city that Paris could be seized cheaply before German reinforcements arrived, finally persuaded Eisenhower to change his mind and order the taking of the city on August 23. Leclerc's force with

French Resistance fighters roll down a Paris street in their truck, nicknamed "Le Terrible"

the American 4th Infantry Division broke into Paris on August 25, with de Gaulle one day behind. Despite the most pressing demands from Hitler, Choltitz surrendered the city intact, thus preserving his honor; de Gaulle won his prize and forestalled the Communists.

PARK, Sir Keith (1892–1975). Park shares with Lord DOWDING the distinction of leading the ROYAL AIR FORCE fighter force to victory in the Battle of BRITAIN. He commanded No. 11 Group, with responsibility for air defense of the area from Southampton to Norwich (southeast England). A vivid account of Park in action is given by Winston CHURCHILL (in *Their Finest Hour*), who visited the headquarters of No. 11 Group on September 15, 1940 (which, as the culminating day of the battle, became the date for Battle of Britain Day). Yet, despite the fact that the British fighters were victorious, Park, like Dowding, was removed from active command as soon as the battle had been won. He appears to have been a loser in one of the intraservice doctrinal squabbles familiar in every country: he had won his battle, certainly, but not in the right way—the right way being the "big wing" formation advocated and practiced by Air Vice-Marshal LEIGH-MALLORY. Park later wrote: "To my dying day I shall feel bitter at the base intrigue which was used to remove Dowding and myself as soon as we had won the Battle of Britain."

In December 1940 he was transferred to a training group. Later he got back into action as Air Officer Commanding at MALTA, where his fighter experience was invaluable. In 1944 he took command of RAF forces in the Middle East and then became Allied air commander in Southeast Asia. In 1946, as an air chief marshal, he retired to his native New Zealand.

PARKER, George M. (1889–1968). U.S. Army officer assigned to the PHILIPPINES in 1941, the same year he was promoted to brigadier general and then to major general. Parker commanded the II Philippine Corps and was captured at BATAAN. He survived the death march and Japanese captivity.

PARKS, Floyd Lavinius (1896–1959). U.S. Army officer who served as deputy chief of staff of Army Ground Forces. He was advanced to chief of staff of AGF before being assigned to the 69th Infantry Division as assistant division commander. After serving in that position in 1943–44 he became chief of staff of the FIRST ALLIED AIRBORNE ARMY in 1944 and commanding general in 1945, the same year he was promoted to major general. A former National Guardsman, an intimate of Gen. George C. MARSHALL and one of his prime advisers on public and political relations, Parks at the time of retirement was a lieutenant general commanding the First Army.

PARRY ISLAND. In ENIWETOK Atoll, invaded and secured by U.S. 22d Marines on February 22, 1944.

PARSONS, William Sterling (1901–1953). A 1922 graduate of the U.S. Naval Academy, Captain Parsons assembled in flight the trigger of the ATOMIC BOMB dropped on HIROSHIMA. "If anything happens, then we lose only the plane, the crew and the bomb," he explained. Following the war Parsons worked in ordnance and with atomic and other special weapons, taking part in the atomic bomb test on Bikini Atoll in the Marshall Islands. Parsons won a DISTINGUISHED SERVICE MEDAL and an Army SILVER STAR for his assembly of the Hiroshima bomb trigger, and was a rear admiral at the time of his death.

PARTISANS. During the war nearly every German-occupied country had bands of partisans that operated behind the lines disrupting communications and carrying out sabotage, espionage and acts of terrorism. On occasion these bands helped downed Allied pilots escape capture by the Germans.

After the fall of France in June 1940, the FRENCH RESISTANCE started spontaneously. Initially Resistance groups worked to assist Englishmen, Frenchmen who were escaped POWs, Jews or other anti-Nazis to get out of France. These activities received formal recognition in December when a two-page news sheet called *Résistance* appeared. Soon other tracts, pamphlets and papers began to circulate, calling on the French people to abandon defeatism. After the German invasion of Russia, French Communists formed a National Liberation Front with a military wing known as the Francs-Tireurs et Partisans Français.

Although a gulf grew up between these groups and Charles DE GAULLE's FREE FRANCE, based in England, the partisans in France recognized de Gaulle as their leader. On January 1, 1942, de Gaulle sent Jean Moulin to France to form the Resistance into a unified command. Moulin was eventually betrayed to the Nazis, but before he died by torture he had welded the *maquisards*, as the partisans were called, into the Conseil National de la Résistance (CNR). The *maquis* groups grew in strength and organization: in one eight-day period in May 1944 they were able to stop all German rail traffic in Brittany so that Allied intelligence could see how the Nazis would react. After the Normandy INVASION, the Resistance played a strong role in Operation DRAGOON and in the liberation of France.

Partisan bands in the BALKANS were as dedicated and daring as those in France, but owing to the political situation in Yugoslavia and GREECE, no unified underground was possible in either of those countries. In Yugoslavia the Serbo-Croat feud and the tendency of the Communists to use partisan groups self-servingly complicated resistance to the Nazis. In April 1941 Draža MIHAJLOVIĆ began to organize Serbian nationalists (*see* CHETNIKS) to fight the Germans and the supporters of the Croat collaborator Ante Pavelić. Although Mihajlović received British aid, he depended on the support of various Serbian groups which fought under Italian command against Communist partisans. Thus he was charged with collaboration by a rival group headed by a Croat named Josip Broz (*see* TITO), who was a Moscow-trained Communist. Tito had begun fighting the Germans in June 1941; he claimed to be a Yugoslav nationalist rather than a Serbian patriot. He met with Mihajlović in October 1941, but the two could not cooperate. Consequently the Chetniks and Tito's Partisans sometimes fought the Germans and sometimes fought each other. The British began supporting Tito and his Partisans in September 1943, and in May 1944 they withdrew their support from Mihajlović. With the arrival of the Soviet armies that fall, the Partisans helped the Soviets to liberate Yugoslavia.

In Greece there were at least three rival anti-Axis partisan groups. The Greek National Liberation Front (*see* EAM) with its military arm known as the ELAS (Popular Liberation Army) was led by Stephanos SARAPHIS and was Communist-dominated. Col. Napoleon ZERVAS led the conservative Greek National Democratic Army (EDES). A third group, the National and Social Liberation group (EKKA), was led by Gen. Dimitrios Psaros. The EKKA was not as strong as the other two bands, especially after Psaros, a non-Communist, was murdered.

Beginning in September 1942, a British military mission to Greece supported the Greek partisans with money, arms and ammunition, and tried to get them to cooperate in fighting the Germans. In the two years the British mission was in Greece, it was never fully successful in achieving this goal because the partisan groups were continually struggling for predominance in Greek affairs.

Partisan warfare in the Soviet Union began immediately after the German invasion in 1941. At first Russian guerrilla bands were small, ineffectual and usually isolated. Communist Party and NKVD efforts (*see* NKVD) to organize the partisan bands were not fruitful until after the Soviet winter offensive of 1941–42. The offensive rekindled Russian confidence in the government, which, when it was combined with growing resentment of the German occupation, gave rise to vigorous partisan activity. The Soviets systematically organized, trained and equipped partisan bands. By the summer of 1942 some of them numbered over 1,000 men and women each. The total number of partisans was estimated to be between 150,000 and 200,000.

The Soviet high command eventually brought these bands under their direct control by radio communication and by the establishment of army control staffs. The great majority of the partisan units operated in the rear areas of German Army Groups North and Center, especially in the Bryansk Forest.

Führer Directive No. 46, which Adolf HITLER issued on August 18, 1942, defined the Nazi policies of anti-partisan warfare and served as an indication of how seriously partisan raids had hampered Wehrmacht operations. The Germans tried to control partisan warfare by winning over the local populations and by recruiting OSTTRUPPEN to fight the guerrillas. The latter tactic was more successful.

The partisans in ITALY caused serious problems for the German armies there. Open partisan warfare in Italy began following the flight of King VICTOR EMMANUEL and Marshal Pietro BADOGLIO from Rome on September 9, 1943. For the next 20 months the partisans in northern Italy harassed the Germans and the Italian Fascists.

The roots of Italian partisan activity went back to MUSSOLINI'S takeover in the 1920s, but this opposition to Fascism became militant when the Anti-Fascist Committee led by Ivanoe BONOMI became the Committee of National Liberation (CLN). The partisan army, known as the Resistenza Armata (RA), represented the CLN or CLNAI (CLN for Northern Italy) in united action against their enemies. In 1944 the various bands in the CLNAI achieved greater coordination among themselves and with Allied intelligence agencies. Thus they were even able to call a successful general strike on March 1, 1944.

PAT, ORGANIZATION. An escape organization operating in France after DUNKIRK. Originally it helped Allied soldiers to reach Spain; later it chiefly handled the crews of planes that were shot down. The name came from Lt. Comdr. Patrick O'Leary, *nom de guerre* of Albert Guérisse (b. 1911), a Belgian doctor who directed the organization in 1941–43, being arrested in the latter year.

PATCH, Alexander McCarrell, Jr. (1889–1945). U.S. Army officer who as a major general organized various units into the AMERICAL (*Ameri*can–New *Cal*edonian) DIVISION in 1942. In December 1942 Patch took over command of American forces on GUADALCANAL, concluding the battle there in February 1943. He next served as commander of the Desert Training Center. He was promoted to lieutenant general in 1944 and given command of the SEVENTH ARMY, which invaded SOUTHERN FRANCE in August 1944. His forces fought into Germany and Austria. General EISENHOWER regarded him as his ablest army commander in the ETO.

PATHFINDER BOMBING. A British-developed technique of night strategic bombing in which "pathfinder" planes would navigate their way to the blacked-out objective in advance of the main formations and mark the target area with flares and incendiaries. Its accuracy was not spectacular but was adequate for the sort of CARPET BOMBING practiced by the night-attacking RAF BOMBER COMMAND. Something similar was tried by bomb-carrying U.S. Army P-38 fighters (*see* P-38) in the Pacific. A modified P-38 with a glassed-in "bomber nose" carrying a bombardier and a NORDEN BOMBSIGHT would act as guide for a formation of other fighter-bombers in a horizontal bombing run; on signal from the bombardier in the lead plane, the formation would salvo its bombs. Late in the war, pathfinder planes in both the European and Pacific theaters used the H_2S blind-bombing RADAR to guide themselves to their targets (*see* H_2S).

PATRIA. Passenger ship that served Grand Admiral Karl DÖNITZ as a residence while he was at Flensburg, on the Danish border, as German head of state in succession to Adolf HITLER. The Dönitz government was dissolved by the Allies on May 23, 1945.

PATTERSON, Robert Porter (1891–1952). For the five years following his appointment as U.S. Assistant Secretary of War in July 1940, Patterson directed the Army's procurement program. As one of the most energetic and persistent administrators in wartime Washington, the former lawyer and judge earned the nickname "Old Thorough." When Secretary of War Henry L. STIMSON retired in 1945, President TRUMAN appointed Patterson, like Stimson a New York Republican, in his place. He retired in 1947, later to die in an air crash.

PATTLE, Marmaduke T. St. John (1914–1941). South African RAF pilot considered the leading British and possibly the leading Western Allied fighter ace of the war, with more than 40 kills. "Pat" Pattle scored his early victories in a Gloster GLADIATOR against the Italians in the Middle East in 1940. In November 1940 his squadron was sent to Greece, where Pattle, who became a squadron leader, was the top ace of the campaign, flying first a Gladiator and then a HURRICANE. On April 20, 1941, after having shot down three German fighters, he himself fell to two Germans. His precise victory score is unknown, because the records of his squadron were destroyed in the British evacuation from Greece.

PATTON, George Smith, Jr. (1885–1945). From Casablanca to Czechoslovakia, George Patton led American troops with a boldness that roused fear in the Axis and awe (and sometimes consternation) in the Allies. A cavalryman converted to armor, Patton believed that speed of movement decreased casualties, and his operations were characterized by mobility and dramatic thrusts.

From his earliest childhood in California, Patton wanted to be a soldier. He believed his destiny was to be a great warrior, and he pursued it with single-minded dedication. He came from a well-to-do family with a strong military tradition, and after a year at the Virginia Military Institute he went to West Point. "The only thing I am good at is military," he wrote his father, and after graduation in 1909 he chose the cavalry. He worked hard, was aggressive and efficient, studied military history and philosophy as well as tactics and weaponry, and by 1916 was known as an officer of special promise. He displayed initiative with Pershing in Mexico in 1916, later went to France as part of Pershing's staff and in November 1917 became one of the first American officers assigned to tanks. Undaunted by the challenge of having no precedents—and initially no tanks—Patton threw himself into the tasks of organization and training. Under his command the 304th Brigade, Tank Corps, fought at Saint-Mihiel and in the Meuse-Argonne offensive. Patton demonstrated both the potential of tanks and his own dynamic leadership, but he was badly wounded, and before he could get back in combat the war was over.

General Patton

Between the wars the tanks were assigned to the infantry and Patton went back to the horse cavalry, but he retained his interest in armor, followed the progress of the German armed forces and studied FULLER and LIDDELL HART on the use of tanks. He had a penchant for getting into trouble, however, and in the late 1930s his career seemed to be on the wane.

Patton's tendency toward trouble stemmed from his outspokenness, a touch of the dramatic and his conception of what a good soldier must be—hard, tough and disciplined. "War is very simple, direct and ruthless. It takes a simple, direct and ruthless man to wage war," he wrote. By looks and actions he portrayed the ruthless soldier—swashbuckling, profane, insensitive. His biographers and family confirm that much of this was an act—an image carefully cultivated for the dual purpose of overcoming his own fears and doubts and of helping his men overcome their instinct of self-preservation so that they could function in combat. He believed that morale and élan could make the difference between defeat and victory, and he insisted always on discipline and attention to detail. He was hated or worshiped, and he himself was full of contradictions. He practiced his "war face" before a mirror, but the suffering of his men often moved him to tears. He was an egotist with driving ambition, but he was tortured by self-doubt. He believed sweat could save blood, and he drove his men without mercy. He wrote poetry, unabashedly prayed on his knees, believed in *déjà vu* and was devoted to his wife, the former Beatrice Ayer. Patton's public behavior served to mask a sensitivity he felt was inconsistent with soldiering.

In July 1940 Patton was assigned a brigade in the newly formed 2d Armored Division; in December he became a major general and the division commander. He shaped the armored units around dash, speed and boldness, epitomized in his phrase, "Catch the enemy by the nose and then kick him in the pants." The Patton legend began to emerge as he sought ways to maintain personal leadership despite the growing size of his command. Highly spiced language and lively pep talks intrigued his men and made good newspaper copy.

In July 1942 General MARSHALL named Patton commander of the Western Task Force of Torch, the NORTHWEST AFRICA operation. Patton threw himself into the preparations, and when congestion on the beach threatened the success of the operation he spent 18 hours on the scene giving physical assistance as well as setting an example of determination. The initial phase of Torch over, Patton faced the delicate and often misunderstood task of supporting the French authorities and laying the foundation for Allied-French cooperation. Martin Blumenson, editor of *The Patton*

Papers, concludes that as a diplomat he displayed strength mixed with charm and a shrewd understanding. By February 1943 Patton was busy organizing the SEVENTH ARMY and preparing for the invasion of SICILY—a process interrupted from March 6 to April 14, when he took command of the disorganized II Corps to bring it to a state of battle-worthiness.

The Sicilian campaign established Patton as a popular hero—a ground gainer who could deliver morale-building victories—but it almost ended Patton's career. As Axis opposition intensified and the drive for MESSINA slowed to a crawl, Patton suffered from tension and impatience. While visiting a hospital on August 3 he met a young man who said he "couldn't take it." Patton gave the soldier a tongue-lashing and slapped him with his gloves. A similar incident occurred on August 10. Convinced that Patton's emotional intenseness contributed to his value as a leader, General EISENHOWER, the Allied commander, tried to handle the matter privately. A chastened Patton apologized personally to all concerned, but the story hit the press and the public became irate. Patton's usefulness was temporarily ended, and for the next 11 months he cooled his heels, chafed at his inactivity and pleaded to be allowed back in the fight. In January 1944 he was given command of the THIRD ARMY, but his role was not announced and his army did not become operational until August 1, 1944.

When the Third Army burst through AVRANCHES to sweep Brittany and entrap the Germans at Falaise (*see* ARGENTAN-FALAISE GAP), Patton was in his element, viewing his whole life as preparation for this campaign. He was now subordinate to Gen. Omar BRADLEY, who had served under him in Sicily, but he accepted the reversal in role without a murmur, and Marshall's winning team—Eisenhower, Bradley, Patton—worked with harmony and effectiveness. There was less harmony between Patton and British Field Marshal MONTGOMERY, who was systematic and methodical where Patton favored rapid exploitation. As the campaign across France took shape, Patton and Montgomery frequently urged different approaches. Rivalry between the two intensified, and as logistics tightened they became competitors for supplies. When the Third Army was halted in its drive, a frustrated Patton began fighting for the right to continue his advance.

Patton made one of his most dramatic contributions in December 1944, when he disengaged three divisions, turned them 90 degrees and moved them across icy roads to the relief of besieged BASTOGNE in three days. In the final days of April and May he led Third Army southeastward across Germany to meet the Russians. Denied authority to advance as far as Prague, he ended the war with Third Army over the borders of Czechoslovakia and Austria.

Patton hoped to be transferred to the Pacific, but he was retained in Bavaria as military governor. Ever outspoken, he was soon in trouble, first for privately advocating fighting the Russians to ensure freedom for the people of eastern Europe, and then for advocating using capable ex-Nazis in the tasks of reconstruction. In October 1945 he was removed from command of Third Army. Two months later he was fatally injured in an automobile accident near Mannheim. He was buried near Hamm, Luxembourg. Patton's highest rank was general, to which he was promoted in 1945.

In battle Patton lived by the creed "Attack, always attack." Under his leadership, Third Army covered more ground and captured more prisoners than any army before it in American history. His personal philosophy, his ebullient personality and his military thinking can be followed in *War As I Knew It* and the more complete *Patton Papers*. **M.H.B.**

PAUL, Prince, of Yugoslavia (1893–1976). The Oxford-educated Prince Paul was a scholar and aesthete who became Regent of Yugoslavia when his cousin, King Alexander, was assassinated in 1934. He served as Regent until March 26, 1941, when an anti-Nazi coup forced him to resign; he had maintained a pro-Nazi orientation designed to preserve Yugoslav neutrality. Following the coup PETER II became King, and Paul fled first to Greece and then in 1943 to South Africa.

PAUL JONES, U.S.S. CLEMSON-class destroyer, commissioned in 1921. As a unit of the U.S. Asiatic Fleet, she took part in the defense of the Malay Barrier after Pearl Harbor. After the Battle of the JAVA SEA sealed the fate of the East Indies, *Paul Jones* returned to the United States and began nine months of Eastern Pacific convoy duty. In May 1943 she began a tour of similar duty in the Atlantic, followed by service as a training ship and as part of a convoy-refueling group in the Eastern Atlantic.

PAULUS, Friedrich (1890–1957). A German Army career staff officer until 1942, Paulus succeeded to command of the SIXTH ARMY in January 1942, on the death of Field Marshal von REICHENAU, and he is the German general identified with the Battle of STALINGRAD. After three months of bitter fighting the Sixth Army took most of the city by November 1942, only to be sealed off in the rubble they had just captured by an encircling Soviet army. As the Russian siege tightened, Paulus found himself between the conflicting dictates of Adolf HITLER, in whom he had great faith and who ordered him to hold Stalin's namesake city at all costs, and his desire to salvage his army by breaking out. In the end, he did neither. Supplies provided by the LUFTWAFFE and a promotion to field marshal did not prevent German defeat, but they may have contributed to Paulus's indecision. With his army reduced to a starving, defenseless remnant, Paulus disobeyed Hitler and surrendered on January 31, 1943. He was then denounced by the Führer. Later in the war Paulus broadcast for the Russian NATIONAL COMMITTEE FOR FREE GERMANY. At Nuremberg he testified for the Soviet prosecution, and in 1953 he took up residence in East Germany.

Paulus's wife Elena Constance, a member of a Rumanian royal family, was a significant figure in her own right. She disliked Hitler as much as her husband admired him, and she was opposed both to the war and specifically to the invasion of the Soviet Union.

PB2B. A version of the U.S. Navy PBY-6A flying boat (*see* PBY), manufactured by Boeing at its Vancouver (Canada) plant. Unlike the PBY-6A, and like the PBN-1 (*see* PBN), it was not an amphibian.

PB2Y. The Consolidated Coronado, a U.S. Navy patrol bomber that came into service in 1941 (as the PB2Y-2;

subsequent versions ranged up to the PB2Y-5). A four-engine flying boat, the Coronado was powered by Pratt & Whitney 1,200-horsepower radials, had a range of about 1,400 miles and carried a crew of 10. Its top speed was about 220 miles per hour. The Coronado was armed with eight .50-caliber machine guns and could carry up to 8,000 pounds of bombs internally and four bombs or depth charges (or two torpedoes) outside. The PB2Y-3R was a transport and cargo version that could lift 44 people (in addition to five crewmen) or 16,000 pounds of cargo.

PB4Y. U.S. Navy designation for its version of the U.S. Army B-24 bomber (*see* B-24), built by Consolidated. The PB4-Y1, also called the Liberator, resembled the B24D and was widely used from 1942 for long-range antisubmarine patrol. It was armed with surface-search radar and depth charges, and its long endurance was considered particularly desirable for this type of ocean operation. The PB4Y-2 Privateer, a derivation used only by the Navy, had a lengthened forward fuselage, modified engine nacelles and a high single tail in place of the twin tail characteristic of the PB4Y-1 and Army B-24. Its engines were not supercharged, on the assumption that ocean patrol work would be done at lower altitudes where supercharging would be unnecessary. Like the B-24, the Privateer carried bombs or depth charges in an internal bomb bay. A few PB4Y-2s were modified, toward the end of the war, to carry a Bat antiship GLIDER BOMB beneath each wing. Twelve .50-caliber machine guns were carried by the PB4Y-2 in power-operated twin mounts. Although the PB4Y-2 did not see any considerable amount of wartime use, it continued in service with the Navy, Coast Guard and French Navy for some years afterward.

PBJ. U.S. Navy designation for its versions of the B-25 Army medium bomber (*see* B-25). With other types, a number of B-25s were furnished to the Navy under a July 1942 agreement allowing the Navy to share in production of land-based bombers suitable for use as ocean patrol airplanes. All Navy B-25s were designated PBJ-1, with a suffix letter corresponding to the equivalent Army model. Thus, the PBJ-1C corresponded to the B-25C. The PBJ-1D, -1G, -1H and -1J were later deliveries. Some differences in armament and electronics existed between Army and Navy equivalents; for example, some PBJs carried search RADARS in nose or wing-tip positions for ocean search work. Most of the Navy-acquired PBJs were used by Marine squadrons in the Pacific. Marine pilots generally liked the PBJ, considering it a rugged and pleasant airplane to fly, without conspicuous vices.

PBM. The Martin Mariner, a U.S. Navy patrol flying boat introduced in 1939. It was produced until 1947, in versions PBM-1 through -5. The Mariner had a crew of seven or eight and could carry as much as 8,000 pounds of bombs; one transport version could accommodate 20 passengers. A larger and heavier plane than the famous PBY Catalina (*see* PBY), the Mariner was powered by twin radial engines (up to 1,900 horsepower) and attained a speed of about 210 miles per hour.

PBN. A version of the U.S. Navy PBY-6A flying boat (*see* PBY), produced by the Naval Aircraft Factory, Philadelphia, as the PBN-1. Unlike the PBY-6A, the PBN-1 was not an amphibian.

PBV. U.S. Navy designation for a version of the PBY flying boat (below) ordered from Canadian-Vickers. These planes were reassigned to the Army, to which they were delivered under the designation OA-10A (*see* OA-10A).

PBY. The Consolidated Catalina, U.S. Navy patrol flying boat. It was designed and tested in 1933–35 as the XP3Y-1; production aircraft were ordered in 1935 as the PBY-1. This first model entered service in 1936. Its appearance was unique, and was to characterize this and all later models of the airplane. A fairly conventional-looking flying-boat hull with a single tail having its horizontal plane set midway to the top was surmounted by a single, nearly rectangular wing on which the plane's twin radial engines were mounted. Wing-tip floats were hinged down when the aircraft was waterborne, retracted for flight. The PBY's configuration was so distinctive that during World War II the saying was that the only thing in the world that resembled a PBY was another PBY.

The PBY-1 was soon followed by the PBY-2, -3, -4 and -5. By Pearl Harbor the last three models were in service, along with the amphibian PBY-5A. The PBY-4 introduced the large side blisters for beam-firing machine guns that were to become a recognition characteristic for wartime Catalinas. Late-production PBY-5As had a wingspan of 104 feet and a gross weight of nearly 18 tons. Two 1,200-horsepower engines gave them a top speed of 175 miles per hour and a range of 2,350 miles. Two .30-caliber machine guns were mounted in the nose, with a third in a ventral hatch; single .50-caliber guns were carried in side blisters abaft the wing. Four thousand pounds of bombs could be carried. Later in the war a final amphibian model, the PBY-6A, was produced. Canadian-Vickers manufactured amphibian Catalinas under the designation PBV-1A; these were delivered to the Army Air Forces as the OA-10A. Later production went to Canada under the name Canso. Boeing of Canada built these planes as the PB2B-1 and -2. The Naval Aircraft Factory, at the Philadelphia navy yard, turned them out as the improved

PBY Catalina

PBN-1 Nomad. Some PBY-6As went to the Army as the OA-10B. Catalina production ended in the spring of 1945. Nearly 3,300 had been built; a version of the PBY is said to have been manufactured in the USSR under the designation GST. During its service the PBY earned a well-deserved reputation as a rugged and reliable airplane. It lacked the performance and armament of many other American and foreign seaplanes, such as the PBM Mariner (*see* PBM), which was replacing it by the end of the war; it was, however, available in some quantity when it was needed, and it performed capably in a wide variety of roles ranging from search-and-rescue to ocean reconnaissance in the Atlantic and Pacific theaters alike. Catalinas were used by British Commonwealth powers as well as by the USSR. While most of them were disposed of shortly after the war, some continued in American service as rescue planes and in Naval Reserve training duty for a number of years afterward.

PEARKES, George Randolph (1888–). Canadian Army officer (major general) who commanded the 1st Canadian Division, 1940–42, and was General Officer Commanding in Chief, Pacific Command, Canada, 1942–45. He was subsequently (1957–60) Minister of National Defence of Canada.

PEARL HARBOR. Pearl Harbor, a fine natural harbor on the island of Oahu, in the Hawaiian Islands, became a U.S. naval base early in the 20th century, but not until U.S.–Japanese relations became seriously strained in the late 1930s did it assume unusual importance. In April 1940 the U.S. Fleet was sent to Pearl to serve as a deterrent to Japanese aggression. Adm. J. O. Richardson, the Commander in Chief, protested the decision to base at Pearl, but there the fleet stayed. In February 1941 Richardson was replaced by Adm. Husband E. KIMMEL, and the U.S. Fleet was renamed the U.S. Pacific Fleet.

In January 1941 Adm. Isoruku YAMAMOTO, Commander in Chief of Japan's COMBINED FLEET, ordered his staffs to develop plans for a carrier-borne air strike on Pearl Harbor as one of the opening blows of the war. The operation would depart from the generally accepted doctrine of carriers as a protective force for battleships and utilize them as an offensive air weapon. Late in August 1941 Yamamoto disclosed the Pearl Harbor plan to the Naval General Staff, but the reaction was negative. Yamamoto insisted; if the Japanese Government were determined to go to war with the United States, he strongly believed Japan's only chance of success lay in a quick war in which the U.S. Pacific Fleet was defeated before American production got fully mobilized.

The Pearl Harbor plan was adopted, and the Striking Force, containing six carriers under the command of Vice-Adm. Chuichi NAGUMO, sailed from the Kurile Islands on November 26 and set a course toward Hawaii north of the usual shipping lanes. Despite rough seas, refueling was accomplished without trouble. The force was undetected en route. On December 2 Nagumo received confirming orders to proceed with the attack,

Battleship Row after the Japanese strike. Left to right: *West Virginia, Tennessee, Arizona*

and at 6 A.M. on December 7 (Hawaiian time) planes began taking off for Pearl, 275 miles to the south of the carriers' position.

The first Japanese assault hit Pearl Harbor at 7:55 A.M., just as the base was coming to life for a quiet Sunday morning. Seven U.S. battleships, moored in a neat row along Ford Island, in the middle of the harbor, were the primary target. The Japanese torpedo planes came in close—there was little or no opposition during the initial moments of the attack—and dropped torpedoes that had been fitted with special fins to make them run true in shallow water. The torpedoes were followed by specially adapted armor-piercing shells dropped as bombs. Not a single battleship escaped damage. Within 30 minutes the power of the U.S. Pacific Fleet was gone—except for the fleet's three aircraft carriers (ENTERPRISE, LEXINGTON and SARATOGA), which were at sea. This exception proved vital for the future conduct of the war.

The Japanese attack consisted of 363 planes in two waves, the second about 45 minutes after the first. By

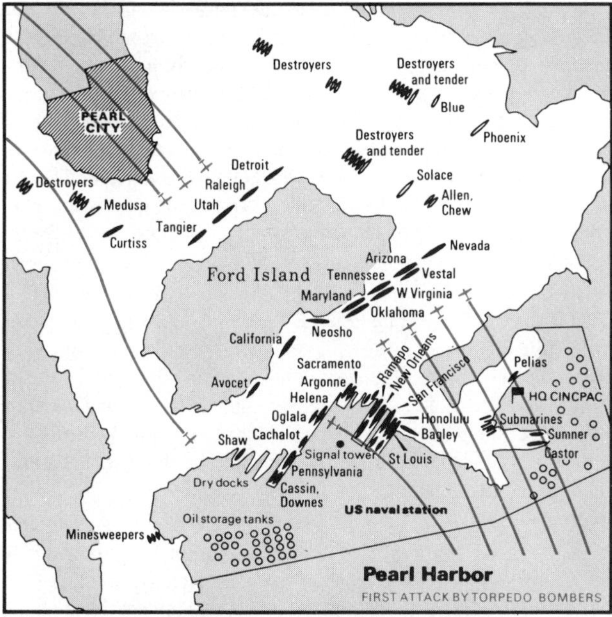

PEARL HARBOR—the Japanese attack on Battleship Row

10 A.M. they had done their damage and departed. Of the eight U.S. battleships (including PENNSYLVANIA in dry dock), all but two would eventually be repaired and rejoin the fleet, but ARIZONA and OKLAHOMA were lost, and for the moment not one was fit to fight. Two destroyers and a target ship were lost; three cruisers and a destroyer were damaged. Oahu's air strength was almost wiped out. On the airfields the Army planes were lined up wing tip to wing tip to be guarded against sabotage. Very few got into the air to meet the enemy, and the remainder were perfect targets. More than 2,400 Americans were killed. Japanese losses were slight—29 planes, approximately 100 lives and 5 MIDGET SUBMARINES, which played a minor role in the events of December 7.

The details of the Pearl Harbor attack have attracted less attention than the reasons why the Americans were caught so woefully unprepared. Official investigations were begun at once, and Admiral Kimmel and Maj. Gen. Walter C. SHORT, in charge of Army operations at Oahu, were soon relieved of command. Yet both men had labored under the handicap of not knowing everything that was going on behind the scenes, and even those in Washington who knew the most did not suspect an attack on Pearl Harbor. Short and Kimmel also had to weigh the demands of training against the importance of a state of full alert. On November 24 they had received a message warning that the "chances of favorable outcome of negotiations with Japan [are] very doubtful . . . a surprise aggressive movement in any direction including attack on Philippines or Guam is a possibility." On November 26 Secretary of State Cordell HULL rejected the "final proposals" of the Japanese diplomats, and on November 27 Kimmel received a stronger warning from Washington: "This dispatch is to be considered a war warning. Negotiations with Japan looking toward stabilization of conditions in the Pacific have ceased. An aggressive move by Japan is expected within the next few days. The number and equipment of Japanese troops and the organization of naval task forces indicates an amphibious expedition against either the Philippines, Thai or Kra Peninsula or possibly Borneo. Execute appropriate defensive deployment . . ."

General Short, alerted through the office of the Chief of Staff, General MARSHALL, followed plans formulated to protect against sabotage, which was considered a likely threat. When Washington found out that the Japanese diplomats had requested a 1 P.M. appointment (dawn in Hawaii) for Sunday, December 7, General Marshall sent General Short a message advising accordingly. This dispatch was handled by the transmitting officers with remarkable negligence, together with an admixture of Army-Navy rivalry incredible to a layman. In the end it went by Western Union and did not reach Short until after the attack, but it is doubtful in any case that it would have served to alert the base. Other warning signs, less vague than Washington's conjectures, were ignored. A private who was manning the island's new RADAR post saw the incoming Japanese planes on his screen and reported them, only to have his observation dismissed as "nothing to worry about." The destroyer WARD located and sank a Japanese midget submarine inside the harbor, but the reports produced no alert. The atmosphere was one of peace, not war, and the Americans made the mistake of acting on what they expected the enemy to do, which was strike in the Far East. It must also be remembered that carrier strikes were a new form of warfare and their chances of achieving surprise were high.

The next day President ROOSEVELT asked Congress to declare war on Japan, calling December 7 "a date which will live in infamy."

Because the Pearl Harbor attack served to unite the American people and bring them into the war with the determination to win, it has been called a strategic mistake on the part of the Japanese. It has also been called a tactical mistake, for in their eagerness to sink the battleships the Japanese did not strike the repair facilities or the oil storage depots—key elements in Pearl's rapid recovery. And the aircraft carriers, which were soon to be involved in a new kind of sea war, were not at home. *See also* MAGIC.

PEDESTAL. Code name of a major British convoy to MALTA in August 1942. It consisted of 14 merchant ships escorted by a very large naval force, including the battleships NELSON and RODNEY. Air attack was heavy, and only five of the merchant ships got through, but the supplies they carried were of vital importance to Malta.

PEEL MARSHES (De Peel). A 60-square-mile lowland in the Netherlands east of EINDHOVEN where a thinly spread U.S. 7th Armored Division attacked in October 1944 to broaden the base of a salient created by Operation MARKET-GARDEN. Two German divisions counterattacked on October 27 but achieved only minor gains. Ostensibly for failure to clear the marshes, the division commander, Maj. Gen. L. McDonald Silvester, was relieved, but it eventually required two British corps to do the job, which was not finally accomplished until December 3.

PEENEMÜNDE. Town on the Pomeranian coast of Germany, site (from 1937) of the German rocket development complex where the V-WEAPONS were created. Gen. Walter DORNBERGER was the director of the project and Wernher von BRAUN was the technical director. On August 7, 1943, the RAF delivered a 597-bomber attack on the installations, but the damage was not as heavy as had been hoped. Scientists continued working at Peenemünde until the advance of the Red Army in 1945.

PEGU. A southern BURMA town situated between the Sittang and Irrawaddy Rivers, railway-oriented Pegu was initially bypassed by the Japanese as they marched west on RANGOON in March 1942. Over two years later the British 17th Indian Division recaptured Pegu on April 30–May 1, 1945, in its drive south toward Rangoon.

PEIPER, Joachim (Jochen) (1915–1976). Only 29 at the time of the Battle of the BULGE and young for his grade—Obersturmbannführer (lieutenant colonel), WAFFEN SS—Peiper, formerly an adjutant to Heinrich HIMMLER, had already won laurels on the Eastern Front. As the commander of a task force of the 1st SS Panzer Division, he led the spearhead of the Sixth PANZER ARMY. His troops were charged with the MALMÉDY massacre as well as with the killing of other American POWs and unarmed Belgian civilians. Though he crossed the Salm River, his command was eventually trapped and only 800 of the 2,000 men he started with returned to German lines.

PEIRSE, Sir Richard (1892–1970). Peirse joined the RAF from the Royal Naval Air Service. After a distinguished career he served as commander in chief of BOMBER COMMAND in 1940–42, when the command was rearming with four-engine aircraft. In 1943 he became Allied air commander, SOUTHEAST ASIA COMMAND, under Lord Louis MOUNTBATTEN. His highest rank was air chief marshal.

PELELIU. The Palau Islands were an important part of Japan's main defense line, which flanked the American thrust into the Philippines. Assigned to conduct the invasion of the Palaus, Operation Stalemate, with landings on Peleliu and ANGAUR to the south, was III Marine Amphibious Corps, with its 1st Marine Division directed to take Peleliu.

Peleliu is dominated by a long, precipitous ridge called Umurbrogol, honeycombed with caves and masked by dense jungle growth. A coral reef, backed by mangrove swamps, ringed the entire island. The Japanese very effectively employed these features in developing an almost impregnable defense. Peleliu was assaulted on September 15, 1944, with all three 1st Marine Division infantry regiments landing abreast. The most difficult fighting was experienced by the 1st Marines, which ran into underwater obstacles on the beach, mutually defended and heavily fortified concrete pillboxes and determined enemy resistance. By the end of the first day ashore, over 200 Marines had been killed and 900 wounded, an indication of what the rest of the fighting was to be like.

It took nine weeks to reduce Japanese resistance in the Umurbrogol pocket. The 1st Marine Division was relieved by the 81st Infantry Division on October 16. Finally, on November 7, the soldiers overcame the last enemy resistance on the island. Nonetheless, for years afterward a number of Japanese soldiers who had been hiding in the caves and swamps of Peleliu continued to hold out, not believing the war was over. This little-heralded battle cost 1,794 American dead and 8,000 wounded. Almost the entire Japanese garrison was wiped out; only 302 enemy were captured or surrendered.

PELTZ, Dietrich (1914–). German LUFTWAFFE officer (lieutenant colonel), appointed by Hermann GÖRING as assault leader against England (Angriffsführer England) following devastating Allied raids on German cities in early 1943. The German retaliatory attacks, made early in 1944, became known as the BABY BLITZ.

PENANG. Because of its strategic location just off the west coast of Malaya, the island of Penang—and the city of George Town—was vital to the British defense of Malaya. In Japanese hands, it could provide a base from which to launch amphibious attacks all along the west coast, outflanking the defenders. Early in December 1941 the Japanese had begun advancing southward through the Unfederated Malay State of Kedah, and this advance was not stopped by the British. Acting on an earlier decision by the Far East War Council that he could order an evacuation if necessary, Lt. Gen. Sir Lewis HEATH, commander of III Indian Corps, made the decision to evacuate the European population of Penang during the night of December 16–17, 1941. The evacuation was poorly planned: many items of importance were left intact to be used by the Japanese, including 3,000 tons of tin ingots, a radio station and boats in the harbor. Because most of the Malay and Chinese community were left behind to face the Japanese occupation, the evacuation was viewed with distaste by the Asian population of SINGAPORE, who feared the same treatment.

PENITENT. Code name for Allied operations on the Dalmatian coast (Yugoslavia) proposed during the latter years of the war.

PENNSYLVANIA, U.S.S. Battleship and class, commissioned in 1916. They were of 33,100 tons standard displacement and had twelve 14-inch guns. *Pennsylvania* and her sister ARIZONA were extensively modernized in 1929–31, when they were fitted with two tripod masts. Both were at PEARL HARBOR; *Pennsylvania* suffered minor damage, but *Arizona* was demolished by a bomb which set off her forward magazines. Photos of the stricken *Arizona*, her forward tripod canted at an angle, were widely used for morale purposes. *Pennsylvania* received a partial wartime modernization late in 1942, losing her mainmast and receiving dual-purpose 5-inch twin secondary gun mounts and smaller antiaircraft guns. Through the rest of the Pacific war she served in the Aleutians and as a bombardment and gunfire-support ship during the island offensives from MAKIN to LINGAYEN GULF. Again overhauled in 1945 in expectation of the final landings in Japan, she was hit by a Japanese aerial torpedo at OKINAWA in the final days of the war. Seriously damaged, she was sufficiently repaired to enable her to serve as a target ship in the Bikini atomic bomb tests in 1946, and was finally sunk as a gunnery target in 1948.

PENSACOLA, U.S.S. Heavy cruiser and class, commissioned in 1929–30. *Pensacola* and SALT LAKE CITY, rakish flush-deck 10,000-ton ships built under the size limitation of the Washington Treaty of 1922, were identifiable by their unique 10-gun battery arranged in four turrets, triples over twins. Wartime improvements included addition of RADAR and light antiaircraft guns; low tripod mainmasts were replaced by low towers supporting gun directors. *Pensacola*, battle-damaged, had her high tripod foremast lowered, giving her a rather peculiar appearance. Both ships served through the Pacific war, and were ultimately expended as ordnance targets after serving as Bikini atomic-test ships in 1946.

PENTATHLON PATROL. U.S. Navy name for a coordinated submarine patrol which operated off the southern MARIANAS until their capture in 1944.

PENTOLITE. A 50–50 mix of PETN (*see* PETN) and TNT, used in grenades because of its high sensitivity and shattering power.

PERCIVAL, Arthur Ernest (1887–1966). Beginning his career as a private in the British Army, Percival rose to the rank of lieutenant general and was appointed to the Malaya Command in April 1941. In this capacity on February 15, 1942, he surrendered the city of SINGAPORE and some 64,000 defenders to the Japanese after they had concluded a successful advance down the Malay Peninsula. Percival was widely criticized for his conduct of the defense of both Malaya and Singapore, but some of the blame could be apportioned to British prewar military thinking, which had conceived of attack only from the sea.

PEREKOP ISTHMUS. The northern gateway to the CRIMEA (USSR), five miles wide. It was the scene of bitter, very heavy fighting in October 1941, the Germans finally breaking through the Russian defenses on October 28. By April 1944 the tide of war had reversed, and it was the Germans who were locked behind Perekop defenses, which were both stormed and outflanked by Soviet forces in an attack launched on April 8.

PERKHUSHKOVO. Headquarters of the Soviet Western Front set up in October 1941 for the defense of Moscow.

PERÓN, Juan Domingo (1895–1974). Argentine Army officer with experience of, and admiration for, Benito MUSSOLINI'S Italy prior to the war. Colonel Perón was a leading member of a cabal of fascist-minded officers, and after the military coup of 1943 solidified his political influence by nationalistic and reformist appeals to the urban working class. In his drive toward political power he was aided by his mistress and later wife, Eva Duarte. Though he was criticized within and outside Argentina for his fascist sympathies, his political power increased so much that shortly after the war he was elected President of Argentina. It was the existence of such sympathies that made Argentina a place of refuge for many Germans after the collapse of the Reich.

PERTH, H.M.A.S. Modified Leander-class light cruiser, launched as H.M.S. *Amphion* July 27, 1934, but later transferred to the Royal Australian Navy. The *Perth* displaced 6,980 tons and carried a main battery of eight 6-inch guns. After seeing considerable action in the Mediterranean in the early stages of the war, the *Perth* became part of the combined Dutch, British and American fleet guarding the Netherlands East Indies. In those waters, on March 1, 1942, during action in BANTEN BAY, the *Perth* was sunk by the Japanese.

PERTINAX (pseudonym of André Géraud) (1882–1974). French journalist who served as foreign politics expert for *Echo de Paris* (1917–38) and as editor of *L'Europe Nouvelle* (1938–40). Soon after World War I Pertinax warned that a revival of German power would produce a new crisis and argued for a strong Anglo-French alliance as a balance to Germany. After the Franco-German armistice in 1940, he was one of the first journalists to flee France. Pertinax spent most of the war years in the United States, where he wrote *Les Fossoyeurs, Défaite Militaire de la France, Armistice, Contre-révolution* (1943), which was translated into English as *The Gravediggers of France* (1944). He renewed his journalistic career in 1944 as diplomatic correspondent for *France Soir*.

PETACCI, Clara (Claretta) (1912–1945). The mistress of the Italian Fascist dictator Benito MUSSOLINI from 1936 until their death together in 1945. In spite of Mussolini's notorious appetite for women, Petacci became virtual consort shortly after meeting the Duce. Although Mussolini treated her badly and on occasion tried to break off the affair, she had considerable influence over him, and her family gained from the relationship. On Mussolini's fall from power in 1943 and his subsequent rescue by the Germans, Petacci joined him in the north of Italy. As the end neared, her affection for him apparently never wavered. After capture in April 1945, Mussolini inadvertently betrayed the disguise of his mistress by asking that a message be taken to her. Once she was captured, Petacci requested to be killed with Mussolini, and they both were shot by the partisan leader Walter Audisio at Mezzegra on April 28, 1945. The next day their bodies, along with those of sixteen other Fascist notables, including Claretta's brother Marcello, were hung by their heels from the girders of a gasoline station in a public square of Milan.

PÉTAIN, Henri Philippe (1856–1951). Rarely has a military career embraced such extremes of triumph and execration as that of Marshal Pétain, who saved the French Army in the First World War and in the Second led the nation in its capitulation to the Germans. A graduate of Saint-Cyr, the French military academy, Pétain taught at the War College, where he evolved a theory of warfare favoring the defensive. Such thinking ran contrary to the prevailing French doctrine of the offensive and "toujours l'audace," of which Marshal Ferdinand Foch was a leading spokesman, and Pétain accordingly advanced slowly through the ranks, not becoming a general until 1914, after war had come. In 1916 he was celebrated as the hero of Verdun, but his most important contribution to the Allied cause was his restoring of order following the French Army mutinies in 1917; his adroit mixture of firmness and conciliation kept the troops in the line and preserved the Army for the operations of 1918. His Allied contemporaries, however, rated him an ingrained pessimist.

In the interwar period Pétain, who became a marshal in 1918, was one of the guiding figures of the military establishment, serving as vice-president of the Supreme War Council and Inspector General of the Army. He gave his own color to the Army. His political convictions were unexceptional for a high-ranking Army officer: although he associated with no particular party or group, he was vaguely anti-Masonic, anti-British, anti-Semitic and anti-German. He deplored the "decadence" of France and, above all, he thought that the country must have order.

On May 18, 1940, as the German armor was sweeping across northern France, Premier Paul REYNAUD appointed Pétain Vice-Premier, and a month later the 84-year-old marshal was called to form a new cabinet. He did so, and immediately asked the victorious Germans for an armistice. The French Government withdrew to VICHY after the conclusion of the armistice, and in the third of France not occupied by the Germans, Pétain set out to form a new state based on "Work, Family and Fatherland."

In 1942, after the Germans forced him to reappoint Pierre LAVAL as Premier, the marshal withdrew from active participation in the work of the government. The Allied landings in North Africa in November 1942 led to the German occupation of all of France after November 11, but Pétain continued as the titular head of an essentially powerless government until the summer of 1944. He was removed by the Germans to the castle of Sigmaringen in Germany. After the war he was returned to France, tried by a French court and condemned to death. The sentence was immediately commuted to life imprisonment, which was served on the Ile d'Yeu off the Atlantic coast.

PETER II, King of Yugoslavia (1923–1970). Peter II came to power on March 27, 1941, when a coup d'état organized by leaders of the armed forces overthrew the pro-Axis government of his uncle the Regent, Prince PAUL, who fled the country. Germany and Italy would not tolerate an unfriendly government in the dominant Balkan state, however, and on April 6 the Axis powers invaded the country; by the 16th the Yugoslav Army had virtually disintegrated. The boy king and his cabinet fled the country and set up a government-in-exile in London. From London the King attempted to direct and coordinate the guerrilla operations of the royalist CHETNIK movement of Gen. Draža MIHAJLOVIĆ, but eventually the Allies deemed the rival guerrilla movement of the Croatian Communist Josip Broz (*see* TITO) more worthy of support, and the defeat of the monarchists then became inevitable.

PETLYAKOV PE-2. Twin-engine, high-altitude Soviet fighter designed in 1938 by V. M. Petlyakov. The design was soon changed to a light-bomber, ground-support, reconnaissance and night-bomber type. It was one of the most versatile Soviet aircraft of the war, operational from 1941 on. The later versions held a slight edge over the speed of enemy fighters. The Pe-2 had two 1,100-horsepower engines and flew at a speed of 336 miles per hour, carrying a crew of two. It was armed with one 12.7-mm. machine gun and four 7.62-mm. machine guns and could carry 2,200 pounds of bombs. Dimensions: wingspan, 56.4 feet; length, 41.6 feet; weight, 16,976 pounds.

PETLYAKOV PE-8. The Soviet Union's only heavy strategic bomber. A limited number were built 1940–44. It was used in raids on Germany, including a few on Berlin. Powered by four 1,450-horsepower engines, it had a top speed of 276 miles per hour. It carried a crew of 11 and was armed with two 20-mm. guns, two 12.7-mm. machine guns and two 7.62-mm. machine guns and carried 8,796 pounds of bombs. Dimensions: wingspan, 131 feet; length, 73.9 feet; height, 20 feet.

PETN (pentaerythritol tetranitrate). An explosive widely employed by Allies and Axis alike. Developed in 1901, it was not used to any extent until after World War I. PETN was employed in detonators and booster charges; combined with TNT, it was used to fill grenades and smaller-caliber projectiles. Approximately equal to RDX (*see* RDX) and nitroglycerin in explosive power but more sensitive than RDX, PETN was one of the most potent of World War II explosives.

PETREL (Q-6). The Petrel, manufactured by Percival Aircraft, first appeared in 1937 on England's internal air routes as a civilian aircraft. A light twin-engine, low-wing cabin monoplane carrying six passengers, it was the fastest of airline aircraft, with a cruising speed of 181 miles per hour. In 1938 seven Mark V versions were completed for the Royal Air Force; they were given the military designation Petrel and served alongside their civilian counterparts as communications aircraft.

PETROV, Ivan E. (1896–). Soviet general, commander of the Special Maritime Army, which conducted a tenacious defense of the Black Sea port of ODESSA in 1941. In 1942–43 Petrov led the Black Sea Group, which operated in the Caucasus along the Black Sea between Sochi and Novorossisk. In 1944 he commanded the Fourth Ukrainian Front, which advanced into the Carpathians against the Germans. During the war he rose in rank from major general to general.

PHILADELPHIA, U.S.S. BROOKLYN-class light cruiser, launched November 17, 1936, at the Philadelphia navy yard. The *Philadelphia* displaced 9,700 tons and carried a main armament of fifteen 6-inch guns. She saw service mainly in the Atlantic and was the flagship of Rear Adm. L. A. DAVIDSON of the Southern Attack Group of Task Force 34, which covered the Allied landings in French Morocco in November 1942.

PHILIP, Prince of Hesse (1896–). A member of German royal houses, nephew of Kaiser Wilhelm II, Prince Philip was an Obergruppenführer (equivalent to lieutenant general) in the Nazi SS (*see* SS). Because he was married to Princess Mafalda, second daughter of King VICTOR EMMANUEL III, he was sometimes used by Adolf HITLER for diplomatic assignments in Italy. He acted as go-between for Hitler with Benito MUSSOLINI at the time of the Austrian ANSCHLUSS in 1938, assuring the Führer of Mussolini's acquiescence in the German takeover. It was then that Hitler swore unwavering loyalty to Mussolini, a pledge redeemed in 1943 when a German commando operation under Otto SKORZENY rescued the Duce from detention after his overthrow. Prince Philip and his wife were both accused of having been aware of the conspiracy against Mussolini and were arrested and imprisoned in Germany.

PHILIPPINES, THE. The Philippine archipelago was the scene of two major campaigns in the PACIFIC WAR: the JAPANESE CONQUEST, lasting from December 8, 1941, to May 7, 1942, and the American reconquest, initiated October 17, 1944, and incomplete at the end of the war. The archipelago is divided into three sections. LUZON, the largest and northernmost island, lies some 550 miles from the China coast; MANILA, the Philippine capital and a great port, is situated on Luzon's west coast. MINDANAO, the second major island, is some 500 miles south of Manila. Between Luzon and Mindanao are some 7,000 islands collectively known as the Visayans; Panay, MINDORO, Samar, Negros and LEYTE are the major islands.

On the eve of the war, six reserve Philippine divisions, one Philippine regular division, the Philippine Scouts and the U.S. Philippine Division (reinforced by the U.S. 26th Cavalry) were allocated to the defense of LUZON. Elements of three Philippine divisions were deployed for the defense of Mindanao and the Visayans. In all, Gen. Douglas MACARTHUR, commander of the U.S. Army Forces Far East (USAFFE), disposed of some 135,000 men. Of Japan's 51 divisions and 59 brigades, 10 divisions and 4 brigades were allocated to the overall offensive. The 14th Army (Lt. Gen. Masaharu HOMMA), comprised of two reinforced divisions (16th and 48th), was assigned to the Philippines.

Japanese success at the very outset was total. Although the Philippine garrison had gone on full war alert on November 27 and American forces had received word of the PEARL HARBOR attack some hours before local attacks, Japanese air strikes from Formosa destroyed half of MacArthur's air force on the ground in attacks commencing at noon on December 8 (local time). The striking force of the small U.S. Asiatic Fleet fled south the same day, to be followed on December 11 by the remnants of the American bomber force; the bombers had not launched a single strike.

Philippine guerrillas on Luzon make use of captured Japanese equipment, including the 7.7-mm. heavy machine gun

Japanese forces followed up the air strikes with landings at three points in northernmost Luzon on December 10. The purpose of these assaults was to obtain air bases for further operations and, as MacArthur surmised, they did not constitute the main landing. However, the soon-launched main blow shattered MacArthur's plan to contest control of the Philippines. On December 22, 43,000 Japanese, including the 48th Division, landed at LINGAYEN GULF, north of Manila on the west coast. On December 24 elements of the 16th Division landed at LAMON BAY to the south of Manila on the east coast. The Filipino units were put to flight. MacArthur decided on a phased withdrawal to BATAAN, much in accordance with prewar planning. This decision was reinforced by Japanese advances from the Lamon Bay front. North Luzon Force, commanded by Maj. Gen. Jonathan M. WAINWRIGHT, was ordered to hold on a series of five defensive lines, while the two-division South Luzon Force was to withdraw toward Bataan. Manila was declared an open city on December 26.

By January 7 all American troops on Luzon had withdrawn to a partially prepared battle line running from Mauban to ABUCAY on Bataan. Once they were deployed and he was able to utilize his strong artillery, MacArthur's position was formidable. But the supply situation was ominous. At the outbreak of the war a supply convoy had been steaming toward Manila. Shocked by the defeat at Pearl Harbor, naval planners conceded the ultimate loss of the Philippines and diverted the convoy to Australia, despite MacArthur's objections. USAFFE was totally isolated.

On January 9, despite the withdrawal of the 48th Division for operations against Java, General Homma ini-

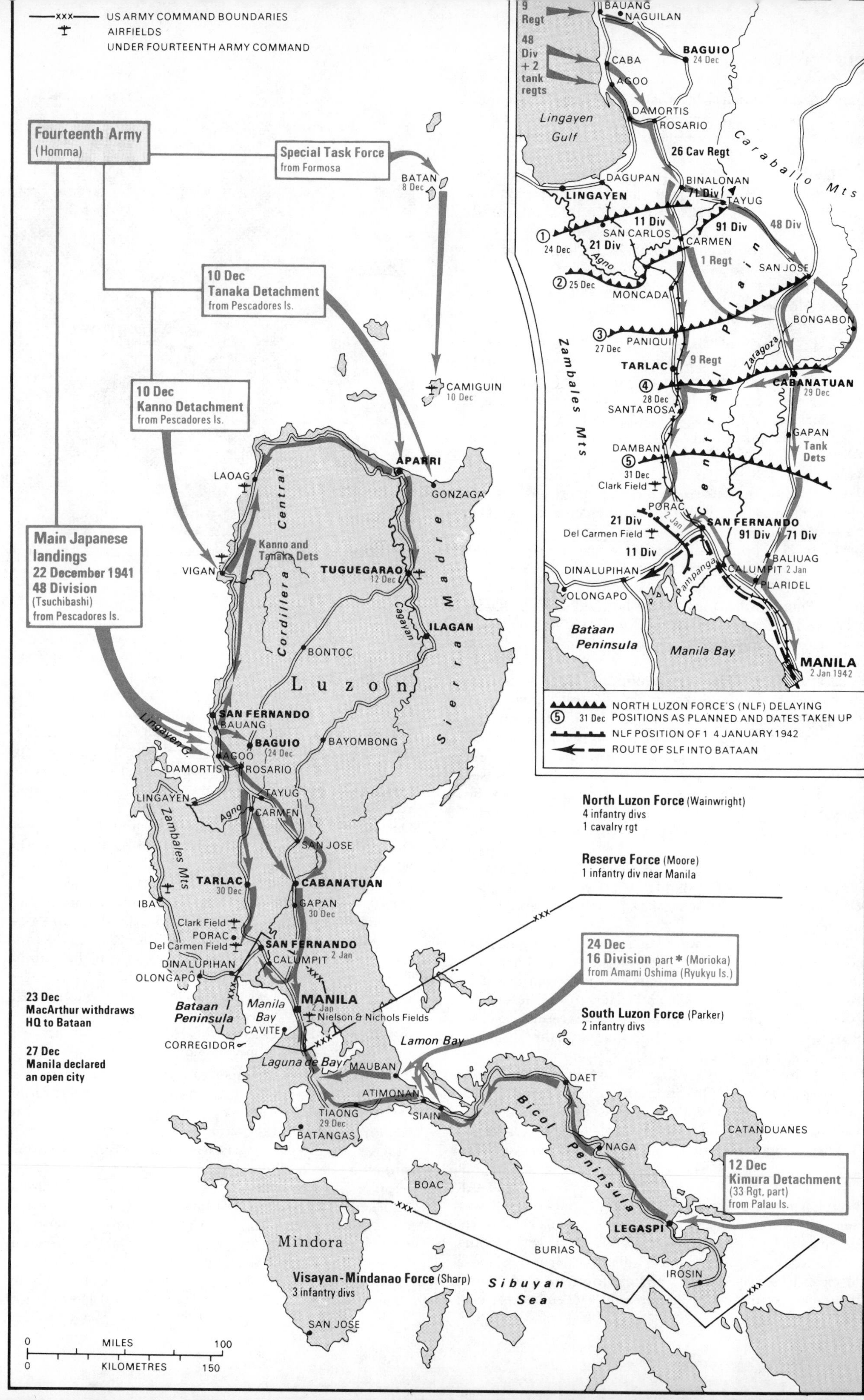

US ARMY COMMAND BOUNDARIES
AIRFIELDS
UNDER FOURTEENTH ARMY COMMAND
Fourteenth Army (Homma)
Special Task Force from Formosa
10 Dec Tanaka Detachment from Pescadores Is.
10 Dec Kanno Detachment from Pescadores Is.
Main Japanese landings 22 December 1941 48 Division (Tsuchibashi) from Pescadores Is.
24 Dec 16 Division part * (Morioka) from Amami Oshima (Ryukyu Is.)
12 Dec Kimura Detachment (33 Rgt, part) from Palau Is.
North Luzon Force (Wainwright) 4 infantry divs 1 cavalry rgt
Reserve Force (Moore) 1 infantry div near Manila
South Luzon Force (Parker) 2 infantry divs
Visayan-Mindanao Force (Sharp) 3 infantry divs
23 Dec MacArthur withdraws HQ to Bataan
27 Dec Manila declared an open city
NORTH LUZON FORCE'S (NLF) DELAYING POSITIONS AS PLANNED AND DATES TAKEN UP
NLF POSITION OF 1 4 JANUARY 1942
ROUTE OF SLF INTO BATAAN
Luzon
Mindora
Sibuyan Sea
Lingayen Gulf
Manila Bay
Bataan Peninsula
Bicol Peninsula
Cordillera Central
Sierra Madre
Zambales Mts
Caraballo Mts
Central Plain
MILES 0 100
KILOMETRES 0 150

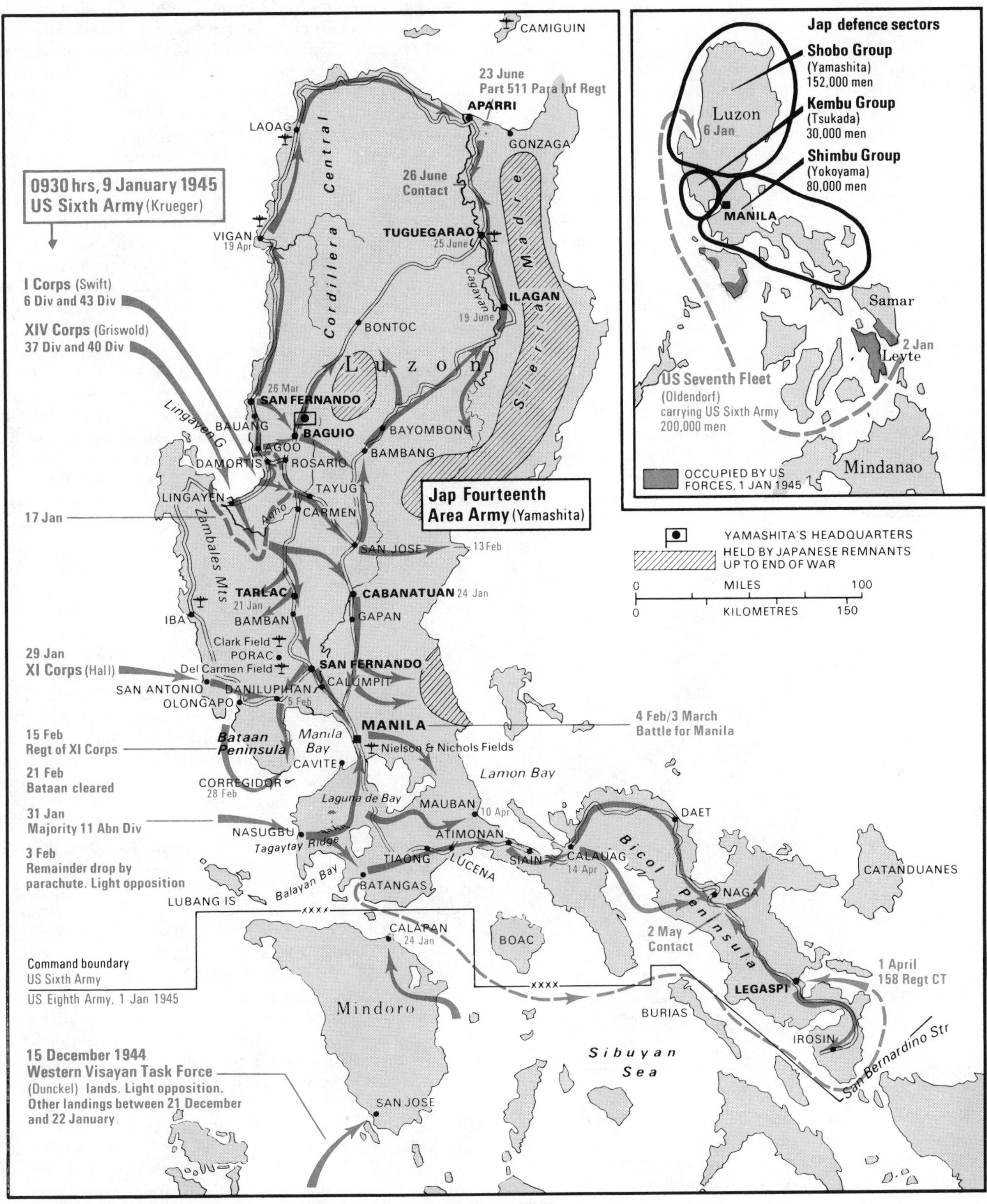

RETURN TO LUZON: American forces took the island, January–March 1945

LUZON, the largest of the Philippine Islands, was quickly taken by the Japanese—except for Bataan and Corregidor

tiated an offensive against the Mauban–Abucay line. After 10 days of continuous fighting, the Japanese pentrated it near Mauban. MacArthur was forced to withdraw again, this time to the shorter ORION–BAGAC LINE. Two Japanese attempts to land regiments by barge behind the new USAFFE lines ended in failure. On January 27 the Japanese assaulted the main battle line. Although a penetration was achieved on the USAFFE left flank, General Wainwright was able to counterattack and reduce the pocket. On February 8 General Homma suspended the offensive, realizing that he was not yet strong enough to force MacArthur's position. However, the fighting had seriously depleted USAFFE's supplies, especially vital artillery shell stockpiles. On January 6 the food ration had been cut in half, only to be halved again on April 1. The outcome was not in doubt; the United States could only buy time.

Realizing that the Philippines were doomed, President ROOSEVELT ordered MacArthur to leave his post and assume command of Allied forces in the Southwest Pacific. On March 12 the general left CORREGIDOR on a PT boat en route to Australia. Wainwright assumed command of the Philippines, and Maj. Gen. Edward P. KING was given operational command on Bataan.

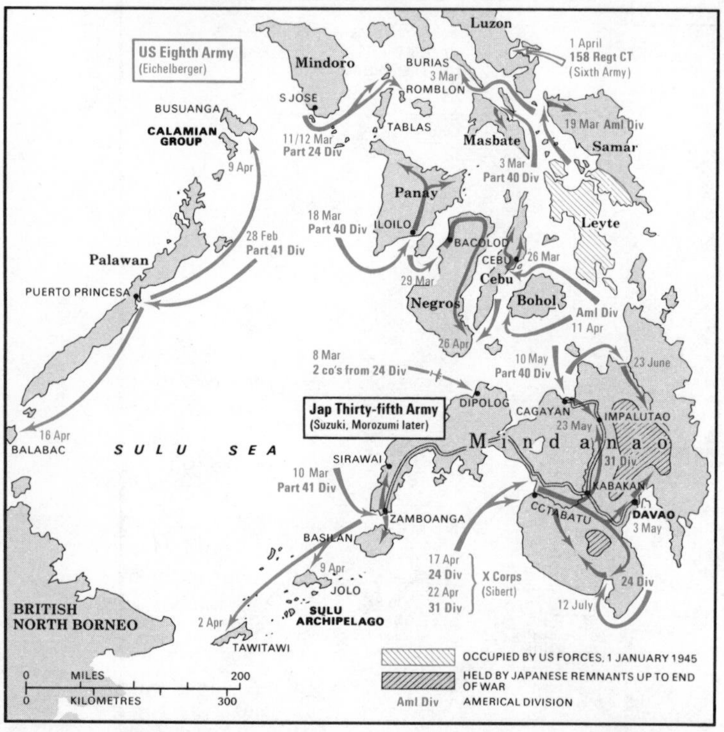

THE PHILIPPINES: U.S. Eighth Army took the smaller islands

By mid-March Homma had received enough reinforcements to enable him to increase air and artillery bombardment. On April 3 a furious Japanese assault shattered the right flank of the Orion–Bagac line. The Japanese, brushing aside counterattacks, began a headlong advance down the shores of Manila Bay toward the southern tip of Bataan. On April 9, realizing that the situation was hopeless, General King, although under orders to attack, surrendered the Luzon Force. Filipino and American prisoners then began the infamous Bataan death march into captivity.

Homma was angered that King's surrender order only affected troops on Bataan. Wainwright's 11,000-man garrison continued to hold out on the fortified island of Corregidor in the entrance to Manila Bay. In addition, Brig. Gen. William F. SHARP still commanded elements of three Philippine divisions on Mindanao which had retreated to mountain bases after being scattered by two Japanese brigades in March. To end resistance, the Japanese bombarded Corregidor for several weeks; on May 5 they landed a battalion. His defending troops dazed, Wainwright sought to initiate surrender negotiations. Homma insisted on the simultaneous surrender of Sharp's forces. After some confusion Wainwright acquiesced, and official resistance ended in the Philippines on May 6. However, Homma could not force the surrender of every individual Filipino, and the Japanese were plagued by a partisan campaign throughout the war. Nor did Homma receive personal satisfaction for his victory. Because it had required five months rather than the scheduled two, he was recalled to Tokyo.

Despite the time gained by USAFFE's stand, the fall of the Philippines was the worst defeat suffered by American arms at the hands of foreign ground forces since the War of 1812. Yet within a year planning was under way for the final defeat of Japan. The precise role of operations aimed at reconquest of the Philippines, however, was in doubt well into 1944. By the spring of 1943 the JOINT CHIEFS OF STAFF had decided that an invasion of the Japanese mainland would be necessary for victory, and they believed that before the invasion it would be necessary to subject Japan to heavy air bombardment and to sever communications between the Japanese mainland and forces in Southeast Asia. To achieve these goals, the Joint Chiefs thought the United States would have to establish air bases in China, which required the control for logistical purposes of a Chinese port and control of the entrance to the South China Sea. It was agreed that establishment of air bases on Mindanao or in the Visayans would have to precede a move into China.

However, the Joint Chiefs began to have doubts about the need for Philippine bases as increasing American strength and the success of "island hopping" opened the possibility of more daring and extended operations. Adm. Ernest J. KING, Chief of Naval Operations, began to argue strongly that American forces should bypass the Philippines altogether and assault Formosa. Formosa, he said, was more strategically placed, would enable B-29s to carry heavier bomb loads than possible from the Philippines and was better situated in relationship to China. But Adm. Chester NIMITZ, the U.S. commander in the Pacific, asserted that any move on Formosa required air bases in the Philippines to neutralize Japanese air power on Luzon. General MacArthur, having made his much publicized promise to return, never wavered. He argued that conquest of the entire archipelago was vital.

With some reluctance, the Joint Chiefs yielded to the commanders on the spot. But Nimitz viewed an offensive in the central Philippines as a necessary step toward the conquest of Formosa. MacArthur believed initial operations in the Philippines must be followed by an invasion of Luzon. The dispute raged for some weeks before MacArthur prevailed. He continually stressed that American prestige in Asia required a total reconquest of the Philippines. This argument won a powerful ally in Adm. William D. LEAHY, the President's Chief of Staff. The Japanese offensive in China had succeeded in overruning American air bases, thus eliminating an important argument for operations against Formosa. More important, logistical requirements of the Formosa operation meant that it could not be mounted before February 1945, whereas MacArthur could, it was believed, move to Luzon before the end of 1944. On October 3 the Joint Chiefs instructed MacArthur to proceed.

For operations against LEYTE the United States created the largest amphibious force yet used in the Pacific. Ground forces were under Lt. Gen. Walter KRUEGER, commander of the SIXTH ARMY. Amphibious operations and naval support were supplied by the SEVENTH FLEET, commanded by Vice-Adm. Thomas C. KINKAID. Land-based air support was the responsibility of Lt. Gen. George C. KENNEY. MacArthur had overall command of air, ground and naval forces directly allocated to the assault. However, Adm. William F. HALSEY's THIRD FLEET, containing the main naval strike force of fast carriers and fast battleships, was assigned the task of eliminating the Japanese fleet if it offered battle, and was under the ultimate control of Admiral Nimitz, not MacArthur. The division of naval forces between Kinkaid and Halsey was to result in a measure of confusion during the battle for LEYTE GULF.

The main blow commenced on October 20, when General Krueger landed four infantry divisions on the east coast of Leyte. Resistance was spotty, and American forces were able to capture the important air bases near TACLOBAN and DULAG within four days. Caught by surprise and desperately in need of a decisive victory, Japanese naval planners initiated a daring plan. Japan's remaining aircraft carriers, almost bare of aircraft in any case, were to be offered to Halsey as bait. With Halsey's strike force occupied, another naval column, spearheaded by seven battleships, was to crush Kinkaid's invasion force. The resulting series of naval and air actions on October 23–26, collectively known as the battle for LEYTE GULF, was the largest naval battle of all time; 282 vessels and hundreds of airplanes took part (the Battle of Jutland in 1916 saw the employment of 250 ships and five seaplanes). Although the Japanese succeeded in luring Halsey away from Kinkaid, stubborn resistance by Seventh Fleet escort vessels prevented—just barely—the Japanese battleships from reaching American invasion forces. The JAPANESE NAVY, once master of the Pacific, was henceforth not a major factor in the war.

To coincide with the naval sortie, Imperial GHQ ordered the immediate reinforcement of Leyte. Gen. Tomoyuki YAMASHITA, commander of Japanese forces in the Philippines, opposed an all-out struggle for Leyte, wishing to preserve his resources for the inevitable invasion of Luzon. Despite the naval defeat, Tokyo ordered Yamashita to proceed with the reinforcement of Leyte. Between October 23 and December 11 the Japanese built their garrison up from 15,000 to 60,000 men by means of a convoy to ORMOC on Leyte's west coast, suffering heavy transport losses in the process. However, by November 2 American forces had reached Carigara Bay on the north coast and Abuyog midway down the east coast, capturing all five Japanese airfields on their way. Torrential rains hampered operations severely for some weeks. Stalemate was averted on December 10, when American amphibious forces captured Ormoc. Remnants of the Japanese forces withdrew to the mountains of northwestern Leyte and continued organized resistance into the spring of 1945.

By mid-November Yamashita realized that Leyte was lost. He also realized that no chance existed to defeat MacArthur on Luzon. He therefore determined to stay on the defensive and divert as many American troops as possible, for as long as possible, from operations against the mainland. From this point of view, the defense of Leyte was not a total failure. MacArthur was forced to postpone the scheduled December 20 landing on Luzon until January 9, 1945. He planned to land at Lingayen Gulf, just as Homma had three years earlier. After air bases were established, there was to be a rapid drive of overwhelming force on Manila. Once Manila Bay was cleared for American shipping, Luzon could be made into the "England of the Pacific" in preparation for an invasion of Japan. By the beginning of 1945 American strength had reached staggering proportions. MacArthur's combined command alone numbered almost 1.5 million men. Nimitz controlled the bulk of the Navy's 61,000 vessels and 37,000 aircraft. Although all the American forces could not be gathered for a single operation, the Japanese position, as General Yamashita knew, was hopeless.

The Luzon campaign was initiated with the rapid capture of air bases on the island of Mindoro, 150 miles south of Manila. On January 9 four divisions went ashore at Lingayen Gulf. The defenders put up stiff resistance, but an American breakout to the Central Plain could not be prevented. Driving hard, American forces reached the outskirts of Manila on February 3. However, 25,000 Japanese naval personnel, not under direct command of Yamashita, attempted to hold the city. A fierce house-to-house struggle was waged for a month before Manila was declared secure; it left much of the city in ruins. Meanwhile, secondary landings were made at San Antonio and Mariveles to prevent the Japanese from withdrawing to Bataan. On February 16 a spectacular airborne and amphibious assault was launched against Corregidor, leading to its capture, after vicious fighting, on February 26. By mid-March Manila Bay was open to Allied shipping, but extensive repairs were required before full use of the harbor was restored.

Yamashita's dwindling forces made good their retreat into the mountains. However, supply shortages ruled out any local counterattacks. As the battle continued, the possibility of starvation became a danger for the Japanese. On April 27 the U.S. 37th and 33d Divisions, in conjunction with powerful Filipino guerrilla forces, captured the Philippine summer capital of Baguio. Rugged mountain fighting then commenced, slowly leading to the isolation of the three Japanese defensive groups. For all practical purposes, MacArthur had control of Luzon by June. However, Yamashita's semi-starved army continued resistance until the end of the war. In all, MacArthur had utilized 10 divisions, plus additional regiments, for the conquest of Luzon.

While the primary battle raged on Luzon, MacArthur ordered Lt. Gen. Robert L. EICHELBERGER, commander of the EIGHTH ARMY, to clear the southern Philippines. Such operations were desirable because the southern islands were better situated for isolating the East Indies, because American air bases there could support Australian landings on Borneo and because there was concern for the safety of the population in bypassed islands. Operations commenced on February 28 with a landing on Palawan Island. On March 10 amphibious forces came ashore on Mindanao's southwestern coast. In rapid succession landings occurred on Panay, Cebu, Negros and Bohol. Further landings were made in southern and northern Mindanao. Concurrently, American forces advanced southwest down the Sulu archipelago toward Borneo. Filipino guerrillas were an important element in many of these operations. Japanese resistance was often fierce. As on Luzon, Japanese troops were able to retreat to the mountains and hold out until the surrender. In most cases, however, organized resistance ended by June.

The second battle for the Philippines was the largest of the Pacific war; in fact, American efforts there exceeded those in North Africa or Italy. In all, the American conquest of the Philippines eliminated 450,000 Japanese troops, weakened Japanese air power and led to the final destruction of the Imperial fleet. American casualties were 62,143, including 13,700 killed. **E.B.**

PHILIPPINE SEA, BATTLE OF THE. On June 15, 1944, three divisions of American troops (two Marine, one Army) landed on SAIPAN, in the MARIANAS. Seizure of this island chain posed a new threat to Japanese sea routes to the East Indies and Southeast Asia, and it would also place Japan itself within easy range of Allied heavy bombers. The Japanese placed Operation A (*see* A Go) in effect, and Vice-Adm. Jisaburo OZAWA put to sea with his First Mobile Fleet. This included fleet carriers SHOKAKU, ZUIKAKU and TAIHO; medium carriers HIYO and JUNYO; and light carriers ZUIHO, RYUJO, CHITOSE and CHIYODA, escorted by battleships, cruisers and destroyers. Ozawa's goal was the relief of Saipan, with the destruction of the supporting American naval forces.

Adm. Raymond SPRUANCE, in overall command of the Marianas operation, was west of Saipan with the FAST CARRIER TASK FORCE (Task Force 58), commanded by Vice-Adm. Marc MITSCHER. This force included 15 carriers and light carriers grouped into four task groups, with their screening cruisers and destroyers. Six fast modern battleships, normally part of the carrier task groups, had been detached and formed into a fifth task group, the Battle Line. The five groups, spaced 12 to 15 miles apart, were disposed to repel either a direct Japanese drive for Saipan from the west or an end run around the American fleet. The Battle Line was held ready to meet a surface attack, should Ozawa launch one. Although Admiral Spruance was embarked in one of the ships of TF 58, he left Mitscher in tactical command, issuing general orders and leaving the actual conduct of the expected battle to his junior.

Ozawa approached from the southwest, his force in two principal elements. The Van Force, under Vice-Adm. Takeo KURITA, included three light carriers and a relatively heavy screen of surface ships. A hundred miles to the rear, Ozawa's main body was formed around the other six carriers and their screens. He was weak in carrier planes—430 against Mitscher's 891—and this disadvantage was weighted even more heavily against him by the relative inexperience of most of his air crews.

During the afternoon of June 18 Japanese scout planes spotted TF 58 about 200 miles west of Saipan. Kurita's Van Force moved ahead to a position 300 miles from the American force, outside the striking range of Mitscher's planes. The Japanese plan called for their attack to be launched while still out of the American reach, taking advantage of the better range of their carrier planes. After attacking TF 58, the Japanese planes were to continue on to the Marianas and land on GUAM to refuel and rearm before taking off for a second attack on the way back to their carriers. They were to be joined in the attack by land-based planes from Guam, flown there to take part in this operation. Neither Japanese admiral was aware that heavy carrier air strikes by TF 58 had already whittled the Guam-based Japanese strength down to a fraction.

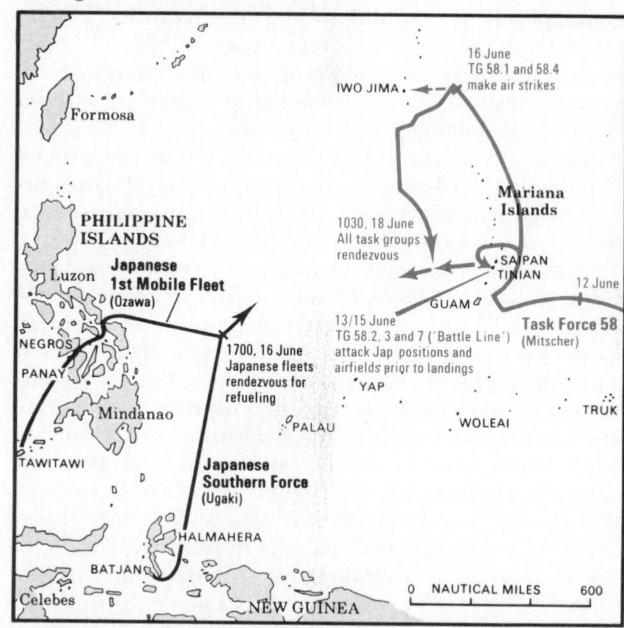

THE BATTLE OF THE PHILIPPINE SEA—the "Great Turkey Shoot"

Early on June 19 the Japanese carriers launched more than 300 planes in five groups of varying sizes. In a series of air and antiaircraft actions beginning shortly after 1030 and continuing until after 1600, 243 Japanese planes were downed, at a cost of 31 American aircraft. Four of Mitscher's ships suffered minor damage; none were sunk or put out of action. This victory, dubbed the Great Marianas Turkey Shoot by Mitscher's jubilant pilots, was the product of good RADAR fighter direction; the qualities of the F6F (*see* F6F), well established as a potent carrier fighter; and, finally, the better training of the American pilots.

While this was happening, submarine torpedoes sank the first-line Japanese carriers *Taiho* and *Shokaku*. Ozawa directed a night retirement to the northwest to refuel; he intended to attack again the next morning, after having received his pilots' early reports that TF 58 had been badly damaged. Under the impression that many of his missing planes had landed in the Marianas as planned and would soon return, he still planned to renew the battle on the 21st. Late in the afternoon of the 20th an intercepted signal from an American scout plane told Ozawa that his force had been spotted and that he could expect an attack. The Japanese force increased speed to draw out of reach of a pre-dusk attack, but too late; Mitscher had meanwhile been closing the distance between the two fleets.

If he launched an immediate attack, Mitscher realized, he could still get in a blow against Ozawa's fleet before darkness fell. This would require a night return and recovery, something new for most of the American pilots. Mitscher judged the opportunity worth the risk, and launched a 216-plane strike. Carrier *Hiyo* was mortally hit; *Zuikaku* was severely damaged and set ablaze, as was *Chiyoda*. Battleship HARUNA and heavy cruiser MAYA were damaged; 65 Japanese planes were lost, at a cost of 20 planes to the attackers. Two of the oilers that were to have refueled Ozawa's fleet were sunk. The Japanese admiral abandoned thoughts of further combat, aware now that the reports he had received had been exaggerated, and turned his force westward.

Mitscher's strike force re-formed and turned back toward their carriers. Darkness was falling and fuel was running low. Planes began to ditch from battle damage or lack of gasoline. As returning planes began to approach the task force in the dark, Mitscher defied the possibility of lurking submarines or "snooper" planes and ordered his ships to turn on their lights. Besides the flight-deck illumination customary for night carrier landings, ships' running lights were switched on. Searchlights beckoned to the incoming pilots, and 5-inch guns fired star shell. Many planes landed more or less safely, but others had to ditch near the task force for lack of a clear deck to land on. All in all, 80 planes crashed on carrier decks or went into the water during the return flight. Mitscher's ships combed the waters that night and through the next day for survivors. By the 21st Ozawa was out of striking range; that evening Task Force 58 turned back for the Marianas. The last "classic" carrier-versus-carrier battle of the Pacific war was over.

The battle for LEYTE GULF is referred to in many wartime documents and publications as the second battle of the Philippine Sea, with the June action just described being called the first battle. **J.C.R.**

PHILIPPINE SEA FRONTIER. U.S. Navy designation for the SEA FRONTIER command responsible for the defense of the PHILIPPINES. The Japanese overran this area in 1941–42, at which time the sea frontiers were little more than paper organizations. The Philippine Sea Frontier was reconstituted at the liberation, and dissolved when the Philippines became independent in 1946.

PHILLIPS, Sir Tom (1888–1941). In May 1939 Adm. Sir Dudley POUND, coming to the British Admiralty as First Sea Lord, selected Admiral Phillips to be his Deputy (later Vice-) Chief of Naval Staff. After Winston CHURCHILL became Prime Minister and Minister of Defence in 1940, the diminutive Phillips—he was known as Tom Thumb—found himself more and more out of accord with Churchill's views and overall direction of strategy, and by 1941 all contact between the two men had virtually ceased. In May 1941 he was given the "dormant" appointment of Commander in Chief Eastern Fleet, though he remained Vice-Chief of Naval Staff until October 1941. He then sailed for the Far East in the battleship PRINCE OF WALES, picking up the elderly battle cruiser REPULSE on the way. These were the only capital ships of his fleet, although it had been intended that the aircraft carrier INDOMITABLE should join him. She was, however, not available, having been damaged in an accident. Phillips with his two ships arrived at SINGAPORE on December 2, six days before the Japanese amphibious attack on the north of Malaya. The ships sailed on the evening of the attack, and on December 10 were sunk by torpedo bombers. Admiral Phillips was not among the survivors.

PHIPPS, Sir Eric (1875–1945). British ambassador to France in 1937–39, whose warnings to the British Government regarding the extent of the demoralization of the French cabinet went unheeded until the collapse of France in 1940. Phipps worked closely with French Foreign Minister Georges BONNET in efforts to appease Germany, as at the time of MUNICH.

PHOENIX. The largest features of the MULBERRY artificial harbors used by the Allies in the Normandy INVASION were the Phoenix concrete caissons. Each of these breakwaters, conservatively called "six-story office buildings lying on their sides," was between 174 and 204 feet long; the largest displaced 6,044 tons. They were towed into place, seacocks were opened and they settled on the floor of the Channel.

PHONY WAR (Twilight War, Sitzkrieg). The name given by Western journalists to the relatively calm first eight months of World War II on the Western Front. The FRENCH ARMY, owing to the enormous losses it had sustained during World War I, was committed to defense. The MAGINOT LINE was regarded as impregnable, and the fighting spirit of the Army in September 1939 was in grave question. The result was that the French awaited the expected German attack and confined their own operations to occasional strong patrols and probing and intelligence missions. On the other side of the front the Germans were inactive because they had at first only 23 divisions arrayed against more than a hundred mobilized by the French, the remainder of the GERMAN ARMY being used against the Poles. Although the Polish campaign was concluded by October, redeploying and refitting the German Army took considerably more time. The European war was livened by the German attack on Denmark and Norway in April 1940. The Norwegian campaign was rendered insignificant, however, and the "phony war" definitely ended by the German attack in the west on May 10, 1940.

PHOTO INTERPRETER. Trained specialists examined aerial photography, sometimes using stereoscopic equipment, in order to discover information of military value, such as bomb damage, fortifications or the topography of an area of operations. British photo interpreters, for example, were able to demonstrate the inaccuracy of night precision bombing without benefit of navigation aids as attempted by RAF BOMBER COMMAND in 1940–41.

In the Pacific, photo interpreters charted tidal and beach conditions, as well as enemy defensive positions. By studying the number of latrines built along the shoreline at Betio Island, TARAWA Atoll, American interpreters arrived at an accurate estimate of the size of the garrison. Not all the photographic information required for operations in the Pacific came from aerial pictures; photos taken through submarine periscopes were invaluable in determining beach gradients.

PICUDA, U.S.S. BALAO-class submarine, commissioned in 1943. During an active Pacific career, *Picuda* completed six war patrols (1944–45). All but the first and sixth were spent in WOLFPACK operations. *Picuda* accounted for 12 Japanese ships, including gunboat *Hashidate* and destroyer *Yunagi*.

PIERLOT, Hubert (1883–1963). Belgian Minister of Foreign Affairs, who fled the country when the Germans overran it in 1940. He went first to France and then, when that nation fell, moved on to Great Britain via Spain and Portugal, barely escaping the Germans each time. In London, Pierlot served as Premier of the Belgian government-in-exile from 1940 to 1944. This government fought the Axis through Belgium's colonies.

PIGSTICK. Code name of Allied advance toward AKYAB, Burma. The plan was canceled when landing craft were withdrawn to the Mediterranean.

PILE, Sir Frederick Alfred (1884–1976). British Army officer, General Officer Commanding in Chief, Antiaircraft Command, 1939–45. In rather adverse circumstances, General Pile worked to build up antiaircraft defenses before the war broke out. He attained the rank of general.

PILLBOX. A small defensive fortification, usually of reinforced concrete (in the Pacific, frequently of earth and heavy logs).

PILLENWERFER. German device which ejected chemical "pills" through tubes in a submarine's hull. Two minutes after ejection the pills began to dissolve, creating a bubbling target which reflected SONAR waves and created the impression of a submerged U-boat. It was used in attempts to deceive the sonar operators of Allied antisubmarine ships. The Italian Navy developed its own version of this device, referred to in Allied publications as a Submarine Bubble Target Ejector. Equivalent devices, called FALSE TARGET SHELLS (FTS) and FALSE TARGET CANS (FTC), were produced for use by American submarines, and tested late in 1943.

PILLSBURY, U.S.S. CLEMSON-class destroyer, commissioned in 1920. Assigned to the U.S. Asiatic Fleet when the Pacific war began, she took part in the defense of the Netherlands East Indies. After a night action in Badoeng Strait (February 19–20, 1942) *Pillsbury*, her torpedoes expended, was ordered south to Australia. Intercepted by Japanese naval forces in Bali Strait early in March, she was sunk with all hands.

A second *Pillsbury* was an Edsall-class destroyer escort, commissioned in 1943. As part of a hunter-killer task group commanded by Capt. Daniel V. Gallery, *Pillsbury* took part in the capture of the German submarine *U-505* on June 4, 1944. For this capture, considered of great intelligence value, the ships of Gallery's task group were awarded the PRESIDENTIAL UNIT CITATION. So tight was security that even the bare fact of the award was not made public until after V-E Day. Shortly before the Atlantic war ended, *Pillsbury*, operating with another antisubmarine group, sank *U-546*.

PIMPERNEL. Code name for an Allied RADAR-jamming transmitter equipped with its own monitoring receiver which automatically kept the transmitter tuned to the frequency of the enemy radar being jammed.

PINETREE. Code name of U.S. EIGHTH AIR FORCE Bomber Command at High Wycombe, England, about 30 miles from London and less than five miles from RAF BOMBER COMMAND.

PINGUIN. German merchant ship converted into an auxiliary cruiser and armed with six 5.9-inch guns and four torpedo tubes. In addition, she carried 300 mines and two aircraft. She sailed from Germany on June 22, 1940, to operate as a raider in the Atlantic, Indian and Antarctic Oceans, and sank 17 ships and 11 whalers of 136,551 total tonnage. She was finally sunk off the Seychelles Islands on May 8, 1941.

PIRYATIN. Town in the Ukraine east of Kiev, site of one of the three Soviet bases made available to U.S. Air Force bombers in 1944. *See also* POLTAVA.

PISTOL GRENADE. Any of a number of small German explosive grenades designed to be fired from the Walther signal pistol. They were intended to give this Very-pistol-like arm an offensive capability. Early pistol grenades were modifications of the standard EGG GRENADE; later ones were specifically designed for this use.

PITOMNIK. As the main airfield of the STALINGRAD garrison, Pitomnik was the major resupply and evacuation point for General PAULUS's German SIXTH ARMY. The Soviet capture of Pitomnik in January 1943 doomed Sixth Army to an early defeat.

PIUS XII (Eugenio Pacelli) (1876–1958). Supreme head of the Roman Catholic Church during World War II, Pius was Pope from March 1939 to 1958. His career in the church prior to his election as Pope was spent almost entirely in the Vatican Secretariat of State, and by 1929 he had risen to the position of secretary of state. He brought many of the diplomat's skills and weaknesses with him when he was elected Pope in 1939. His policies during the war have been the subject of considerable debate. As papal secretary of state, he had earned the dislike of the Nazi regime in Germany, which opposed his election to the papacy. Once the war began, he was under pressure from certain European Catholic circles to proclaim an anti-Communist crusade, but this influence he resisted. On the other hand, he limited his protests against the Nazi extermination of the Jews to discreet diplomatic utterances, although he did shelter thousands of Jews in the Vatican itself during the war.

To what degree his actions reflected his true opinions, and just what his true opinions were, are moot questions. There is no doubt that he was by nature a rather timid individual, and his timidity may have been increased by the diplomat's turn of mind which he acquired during his lifetime.

PLACENTIA BAY. Atlantic inlet in southeastern Newfoundland, site of the Roosevelt-Churchill conference in August 1941. *See also* ATLANTIC CHARTER.

PLAN D. One of the two alternative plans, proposed by General GAMELIN, under which the Anglo-French Allies intended to meet a German invasion of Belgium. It called for an Allied advance into Belgium to the line Antwerp-Dyle-Meuse (the *D* was for Dyle). Plan D was officially adopted by the Allied Supreme Council on November 17, 1939. It was not designed to counter what in fact happened in 1940—a heavy German attack through the ARDENNES. *See also* PLAN E.

PLAN E. One of the two alternative plans—the other being PLAN D—under which the Anglo-French Allies intended to meet a German invasion of Belgium. Under this plan the left wing of the Allied armies would make a relatively modest advance to the Scheldt River (Escaut in French, hence the *E* designation).

PLATT, Sir William (1885–). From 1939 to 1941 Platt was British commander in the Sudan. After successful completion of the campaign that conquered Eritrea and helped to liberate Ethiopia, he was promoted to lieutenant general and named head of the newly activated East African Command. In July 1942, as commander of all British troops in MADAGASCAR, he urged forceful British operations to ensure that the island would not come under Japanese control through concessions by the VICHY government. The operations ended in November 1942, and Platt handed over responsibility for administration of Madagascar to General LEGENTILHOMME of the Free French. *See also* EAST AFRICA.

PLOESTI RAID. On August 1, 1943, 177 U.S. B-24Ds (*see* B-24), each carrying more than 4,000 pounds of explosives, took off from bases in Libya to bomb the oil refineries at Ploesti, Rumania. The formation, commanded by Brig. Gen. Uzal G. ENT, flew high over the Mediterranean, roared across the mountains of Albania and Yugoslavia and crossed the Danube River in Bulgaria. At Pitesti, Rumania, the bombers dropped to 500

Waves of B-24s fly over the Concordia Vega oil refinery, Ploesti

feet, in accordance with the controversial plan for a low-level attack decided on by Maj. Gen. Lewis H. BRERETON, commander of the NINTH AIR FORCE. The 389th Bomb Group turned away to deliver a successful attack against Campina, its assigned target. Two other groups, the 376th and the 93d, became lost, however, and flew to the outskirts of Bucharest, alerting the defenses, before orienting themselves and heading for Ploesti. The 98th and 44th Bomb Groups approached Ploesti as planned, but they found that B-24s of the 376th Group, forced by intense antiaircraft fire to hit targets of opportunity, had set oil fires that cloaked the area in dense smoke. Dodging chimneys that leaped from the concealing smoke, shaken by the explosion of delayed-action bombs dropped by the 376th, the two groups bored in and bombed their targets.

Five participants in the Ploesti raid earned the MEDAL OF HONOR for heroism during the confused fighting. They were Col. John R. KANE, Col. Leon W. JOHNSON, Lt. Col. Addison Baker, Maj. John J. Jerstad and 2d Lt. Lloyd Hughes. Lost in the operation, called Tidal Wave, were 54 bombers, 41 of them shot down by Ploesti's intrepid defenders, and 532 men killed or captured. The attack caused extensive fires but, thanks to the work of well-drilled damage control teams, the refineries soon were back in production. Subsequent air raids inflicted further damage, but Ploesti was never an easy target, and it did not stop functioning until the end of August 1944. In September the Russians occupied the ruins. Overall, more than 350 bombers were lost in the continual attempts to knock out Germany's oil supply.

PLÖTZENSEE PRISON. The place of execution, near Berlin, of the persons condemned to death in the July 20, 1944, conspiracy against Adolf HITLER (*see* OPPOSITION TO HITLER).

PLUNDER. Code name for the 21ST ARMY GROUP (General MONTGOMERY) crossing of the Rhine, begun March 23, 1945.

PLUNKETT-ERNLE-ERLE-DRAX, Sir Reginald (1880–1967). Royal Navy officer who at the start of the war was Commander in Chief the Nore (eastern England) and had considerable responsibility for the protection of coastal convoys and for minesweeping along the east coast of Britain. He retired in 1941 and for two years served in the HOME GUARD before returning to sea service in 1943 as a commodore of ocean convoys. Admiral Drax was the naval member of the British military mission that, with its French counterpart, engaged in abortive negotiations with the Russians in Moscow during August 1939.

PLUTO. Acronym for "pipe line under the ocean," the designation of the underwater pipeline carrying gasoline from England to Allied forces in France.

POCKET BATTLESHIP. *See* PANZERSCHIFF.

POINTBLANK. Code name for both the COMBINED BOMBER OFFENSIVE and a revision of the Casablanca Directive that brought a degree of coordination to the operation. The Pointblank Directive, adopted on May 14, 1943, authorized a joint Anglo-American bomber offensive launched from the United Kingdom "to accomplish the progressive destruction and dislocation of the German military, industrial, and economic system, and the undermining of the morale of the German people to a point where the capacity for armed resistance is fatally weakened . . . so as to permit initiation of final combined operations on the continent."

The Quadrant Conference (QUEBEC, August 1943) specifically declared Pointblank to be the primary preinvasion effort against Germany.

POINTE DU HOE. A 100-foot cliff to the west of OMAHA BEACH (Normandy), believed on D-Day, June 6, 1944, to be the site of a battery of six 155-mm. German howitzers. U.S. RANGERS scaled the cliff and discovered that the guns had been removed from their emplacements; they were later found a few hundred yards inland, their crews having fled.

POKRYSHKIN, Alexander (1913–). One of the Soviet Union's greatest air ACES, Major Pokryshkin shot down 59 German planes and was himself reported to have been shot down three times. He was three times honored as a HERO OF THE SOVIET UNION, received the U.S. DISTINGUISHED SERVICE MEDAL and became a lieutenant general.

POL. Abbreviation for "petroleum oil lubricant." POL was Class III supply, which included all fuels and lubricants for both air and ground units.

POLAR CIRCUIT. U.S. Navy name, assigned 1944, to a submarine patrol area off the KURILE ISLANDS.

POLIKARPOV I-15. Soviet single-seat, general-purpose biplane fighter with a gull-shaped upper wing, designed by Nikolai N. Polikarpov in the early 1930s. A modified version of the I-15, an excellent plane for its time, set a world altitude record of 47,818 feet in 1935. Over 550 I-15s and I-15*bis* models served in the Spanish Civil War, where they gained the nickname Chato (Flat Nose). The I-15s were obsolescent by 1939, but some were used against Finland and others served in the ground-support role during the first few weeks of the German invasion. The I-15*bis* was an improved version with greater speed and more visibility for the pilot. Another variant was the I-153, which had a retractable landing gear. It had a larger engine (1,000 horsepower to the 750 horsepower of the I-15*bis*).

POLIKARPOV I-16. The first low-wing monoplane interceptor with retractable landing gear to enter service anywhere. Some experts claimed that the designer, Nikolai N. Polikarpov, got his inspiration from the Boeing P-26, but the I-16 was under test before the first P-26 went into service. The first of the I-16s—the I-16, Type 1—came into service in 1934. It carried two 7.62-mm. machine guns in the wings and flew at a maximum speed of 224 miles per hour. Four hundred seventy-five I-16s were used in Spain, where the Republicans called it the Mosca (Fly) and their opponents called it the Rata (Rat). Development of the I-16 type continued until 1942. Numerically it was Russia's most important fighter at the beginning of World War II, and it bore the brunt of the LUFTWAFFE's initial offensive. It continued in front-line service until early 1943. The I-16, Type 24, had a 1,000-horsepower radial engine and flew 325 miles per hour maximum speed. It carried two 20-mm. cannon and two 7.62-mm. machine guns. Dimensions: wingspan, 29 feet 6½ inches; length, 20 feet 1¾ inches; height, 8 feet 5 inches.

POLIKARPOV I-17. Soviet single-seat, single-engine, low-wing monoplane with retractable landing gear. It was first flown in 1934 but was not produced in great numbers, even though it was in first-line service in 1942. It flew at 305 miles per hour and carried one 20-mm. cannon, two 7.62-mm. machine guns and two 110-pound bombs.

POLISH ARMY. In September 1939 the Polish Army consisted of 30 active divisions, 10 reserve divisions and 12 cavalry divisions, only one of which was motorized. The potential mobilization strength of the Army was some 2.5 million men. However, it had several deficiencies. It had no armored divisions, was short of antitank and antiaircraft weapons and lacked the air power necessary to cover and support its troops. An even more serious deficiency than these material shortages was the outdated military thinking of the Polish commanders.

POLISH GOVERNMENT-IN-EXILE. Following the German invasion of their homeland in 1939, the Poles established a government-in-exile in London headed by President Wladyslaw Raczkiewicz, Premier Wladyslaw SIKORSKI and Vice-Premier Stanislaw MIKOLAJCZYK. The German attack on Russia in 1941 forced the Polish Government to follow the Anglo-American policy of friendship toward the Soviets despite traditional animosities and the fact that the Soviets had occupied eastern Poland in 1939; then the discovery of the KATYN Forest massacre of Polish officers caused a deep revulsion toward the Soviet Union among the Poles. After Mikolajczyk became Premier upon the death of his predecessor in July 1943, he repeatedly sought Anglo-American assurances of a free and independent Poland in postwar Europe. Mikolajczyk's efforts failed to persuade the Allies, who at YALTA acceded to STALIN's desire for a coalition government in Poland which would include the Communist LUBLIN Poles.

POLTAVA. At sunset on June 21, 1944, a lone German HEINKEL HE 177 reconnaissance plane photographed the airfield at Poltava in the Soviet Ukraine, where 73 B-17s (*see* B-17) had landed after bombing factories and rail yards deep within Germany. These planes were part of a SHUTTLE BOMBING force—163 EIGHTH AIR FORCE Flying Fortresses and their fighter escort—that had left the United Kingdom earlier in the day. Since a B-17 shot down on an earlier shuttle-bombing mission had carried photographs showing the American bombers on Russian airfields, the German mission over Poltava merely confirmed the presence of the Flying Fortresses.

After dark the LUFTWAFFE attacked with more than 50 JUNKERS JU 88 and HEINKEL HE 111 bombers, escorted by FOCKE-WULF FW 190 and MESSERSCHMITT ME 109 fighters. Wave after wave dropped its bombs by the light of flares, destroying 47 B-17s and damaging 19. Amid this destruction, one American was killed and another mortally wounded.

The Poltava raid caused misgivings about continued Soviet-American cooperation in the shuttle-bombing project. The Russians had promised adequate protection for the bases, but they had no RADAR-directed night fighters, their antiaircraft defenses consisted mainly of machine guns mounted on trucks and most of their fire fighters had nothing more effective than buckets and shovels. Lt. Gen. Carl SPAATZ, in overall command of American strategic bombers in Europe, decided after Poltava to postpone further participation of his B-17s until the shuttle-bombing concept could be reconsidered.

PONOMARENKO, Pantaleimon (1902–). First secretary of the Belorussian Communist Party and chief of the Central Headquarters of Partisan Activities in the Soviet Union. Under Ponomarenko's direction, hundreds of thousands of PARTISANS carried out large-scale operations, demolishing highways, railroads and bridges behind the German lines. The partisans were especially active around Moscow and in parts of the Ukraine and Belorussia. In 1943 Ponomarenko was promoted to the rank of lieutenant general.

PONTE OLIVO AIRFIELD. Key airfield near GELA, SICILY, taken by U.S. airborne and seaborne forces at the outset of operations on the island. The airfield fell to troops of the 1st Division on July 12, 1943. Elements of the 82D AIRBORNE DIVISION had previously taken the high ground near the field.

POORTEN, Hein ter (1887–). One of the first Dutch Army officers to obtain a pilot's license, General ter Poorten was a strong advocate of air power. The bulk of his career was spent in the Netherlands colonies in Asia, and in October 1941 he was made commander in chief of the Netherlands East Indies Army. On March 2, 1942, he was named to command of United Nations armies fighting the Japanese in JAVA, but eight days later the fighting was over and General ter Poorten was interned by the enemy.

POPITZ, Johannes von (1884–1945). One of the more ambiguous figures who served the resistance in Nazi Germany. A civil servant who was an early supporter of Adolf HITLER, Professor Popitz became minister of finance for the state of Prussia. He held right-wing views and belonged to the circle in which Ulrich von HASSELL moved. He was scheduled to become finance minister in the emergency government designed to take over after the assassination of Hitler. He is remarkable for having advocated an approach to Heinrich HIMMLER in 1943 to sound out the possibilities of an SS coup d'état against Hitler. On August 26, 1943, Popitz was introduced to Himmler (recently appointed Minister of the Interior) by Carl Langbehn, a member of the resistance having personal contacts with him. The results were naturally inconclusive, and Himmler (cautious as ever) had Popitz shadowed by the GESTAPO. He was finally arrested on July 21, 1944, after the attempt on Hitler's life. He was subjected to prolonged interrogation, and for this purpose and that of writing general memoranda on statecraft (like his fellow opposition figure, Dr. GOERDELER) was preserved from inevitable execution until the final days of the regime. He died on February 2, 1945. *See also* OPPOSITION TO HITLER.

POPOV, Dusko (1910–). A young Yugoslav from a well-to-do family who became an important double agent for British intelligence, working in London and for a time in the United States. His code name was Tricycle. He is said to have been the model for Ian Fleming's James Bond.

POPOV, Markian (1902–1969). A Red Army staff officer and army commander, General Popov won distinction during his service at LENINGRAD in the opening year of the war, and later as a commander during the STALINGRAD offensive.

POPSKI'S PRIVATE ARMY. British raiding force in NORTH AFRICA and ITALY, founded and led by Vladimir Peniakoff (1897–1951), who was called Popski. A cosmopolite, Popski was a Belgian of Russian parentage, and developed a thorough knowledge of the desert while a businessman in Egypt. He joined the British Army at the beginning of the war and formed his company-size reconnaissance and raiding force, which acquired the official name Popski's Private Army.

PORCUPINE. U.S. Navy nickname for an experimental 32-rail MOUSETRAP-rocket launcher designed for mounting in an LCM (*see* LCM). It was developed in 1943 to clear a path through beachhead minefields and obstacles. The Porcupine was not accepted for production, but its principle was used in designing the WOOFUS.

PORSCHE, Ferdinand (1875–1951). Professor Porsche, the eminent motor car designer and builder—he founded his own works in Stuttgart in the 1930s—during the war was in charge of Volkswagen production, the vehicles largely being used by the AFRIKA KORPS, and of the design and development of TANKS, notably the Tiger.

PORTAL, Sir Charles (Viscount Portal of Hungerford) (1893–1971). Marshal of the ROYAL AIR FORCE, Chief of Air Staff from October 25, 1940, to the end of December 1945. Throughout the war Portal was a key member of the Chiefs of Staff, who advised Winston CHURCHILL and with their American colleagues helped to plan and direct war strategy in the COMBINED CHIEFS OF STAFF.

Educated at Winchester and Christ Church, Oxford, Portal served briefly as a dispatch rider in the Royal Engineers before transferring to the Royal Flying Corps as an observer and then as a pilot. He was given a permanent commission in the RAF, attended the first course at the RAF Staff College in 1922 and soon became recognized as one marked for advancement and distinction. He was a disciple of "Boom" Trenchard, founder of the RAF, and as such believed firmly in the offensive and the strategic bombing force. During his tour of duty as Air Officer Commanding in Aden in 1934 he developed the technique of air control of dissident tribes. After serving as Air Member for Personnel he became AOC-in-C BOMBER COMMAND in April 1940. With a small force and a multiplicity of war plans and demands to meet, he nevertheless assisted the efforts of FIGHTER COMMAND by bombing German invasion barges on the Belgian and French coasts and by attacks on German-held aerodromes.

He was the youngest of the Chiefs of Staff when appointed, but probably the best educated of them, academically and scientifically. He gave himself completely to his work, so much so that he appeared to be aloof and unapproachable to his juniors. He lunched when he could in solitary and respected privacy at the Travellers Club. But in committee, and particularly when working with his American colleagues, he was held in the highest regard. His judgment and balance were generally unmatched, and the Prime Minister relied very much on his views. His close personal friendship with Sir Wilfrid FREEMAN, whom he had as his Vice-Chief from November 1940 to October 1942, was a source of strength to him. He was a loyal supporter of Sir Arthur HARRIS, chief of Bomber Command, though not without an occasional disagreement with him about the use of the bombing force. Portal held the Royal Air Force together, not a light task when it included such strong and sometimes disagreeing leaders as Harris, TEDDER, DOUGLAS, DOWDING and SLESSOR. Though convinced of the war-winning value of Bomber Command, Portal recognized the need for the combined operations which developed into the INVASION and the overrunning of occupied Europe. He established eventually a standard of cooperation with the other services that won admiration and gratitude.

That respect was symbolized nationally in May 1975, when a monument to Lord Portal was placed outside the Ministry of Defence in Whitehall, facing south across the river whence the enemy came. The statue flanking his is of Lord Trenchard.

PORT-EN-BESSIN. Village on the edge of GOLD BEACH (Normandy), taken by the British 47th Royal Marine COMMANDO (30th Corps) on June 7, 1944.

PORTER, U.S.S. Destroyer and class (2,130 tons; six to eight 5-inch single-purpose or five 5-inch dual-purpose guns; four to eight 21-inch torpedo tubes; 35 knots). Eight of these large (for their time) ships commissioned in 1936–37.

PORTES, Countess Hélène de (? –1940). The daughter of a wealthy Marseille merchant and the wife of Count Jean de Portes, Hélène de Portes was a lioness of the Paris social scene in the late 1930s. In 1938 she became the mistress of Paul REYNAUD, who, though he was twice her age, left his wife for her. During the chaotic retreat of Reynaud's government from Paris in the spring of 1940, Mme. de Portes served Reynaud as an unofficial administrative assistant, constantly intervening in government business and pushing Reynaud (unsuccessfully) to agree to an armistice with Germany. Following Reynaud's resignation and the signing of the armistice in late June 1940, the two were driving south with the distraught Reynaud at the wheel when the car hit a tree, injuring Reynaud and killing his mistress instantly.

PORTLAND, U.S.S. Heavy cruiser and class. *Portland* and INDIANAPOLIS commissioned in 1932–33. Modified NORTHAMPTONS, they had the same nine-gun 8-inch battery (3×3), but were 10 feet longer and 600 tons heavier; their protection was on a somewhat better scale, and their tophamper was lower and less prominent. Wartime refits increased their antiaircraft protection and provided search and fire-control RADARS.

PORT-LYAUTEY. One of the three landing areas for the Western Task Force of Operation Torch (the invasion of NORTHWEST AFRICA). The Port-Lyautey assault, commanded by Maj. Gen. Lucian K. TRUSCOTT, Jr., was the most complicated and difficult of the CASABLANCA landings. Heavy surf, confusion on the beaches, stiff opposition and difficult terrain made for a precarious situation the night of November 7–8, 1942. The concreted airfield was secured on November 10, and just before midnight came a request to discuss cessation of hostilities, which thereupon ended.

PORT MORESBY. Town on the south coast of the southeastern portion of NEW GUINEA, before the war the administrative center of the Australian Territory of Papua. Port Moresby had minor port and airfield facilities, and a potential for development into a major military base. The Japanese recognized this potential, and in planning their second-phase offensives to cut the lines of communication between the United States and Australia, decided that Port Moresby would have to be seized to protect their own right (south) flank as they moved east and southeast beyond New Guinea.

When the United States came into the war, the Australian garrison at Port Moresby consisted of an understrength infantry battalion. Given available resources, Australia was hard put to reinforce the area, but in January 1942 sent forward another infantry battalion and began work to improve the airfield facilities. In March 1942 the Japanese began aerial bombardment of Port Moresby, and the next month the first American troops, engineer and antiaircraft artillery, arrived. In May the Japanese made their first attempt to seize Port Moresby by an amphibious operation, but this effort came to grief as a result of the Battle of the CORAL SEA. Diverted by their invasion of the Aleutians and the Battle of MIDWAY, the Japanese turned their attention back to Port Moresby in July. That month they landed troops on the north coast of New Guinea in the BUNA–GONA area, with the intent of seizing Port Moresby by means of an overland thrust across the rugged OWEN STANLEY MOUNTAINS.

After buildup and reconnaissance, the Japanese launched their overland offensive on August 26. By September 16 they were scarcely 25 miles from Port Moresby, but largely because of supply difficulties and the demands of operations elsewhere, the offensive collapsed and the Japanese began withdrawing to what was to prove the bloody shambles of the Buna–Gona beachhead.

From November 1942 until Gen. Douglas MACARTHUR's headquarters moved to Hollandia, Dutch New Guinea, in mid-1944, Port Moresby served as an advance command post for GHQ SWPA, primarily to overcome difficulties of radio communications from Australia to the forward areas.

PORTO FARINA. About 20 miles east of Bizerte, TUNISIA. Some 9,000 Germans surrendered to Allied forces at the town on May 9, 1943, in the final phase of operations in Tunisia.

PORT OF EMBARKATION (POE). U.S. Army term for a designated port at which troops were put aboard transport ships for overseas movement. Ports of embarkation were operated by the Army Transportation Corps. Wartime ports of embarkation were located at Boston, New York, Hampton Roads, Va., Charleston, S.C., New Orleans, Los Angeles, San Francisco and Seattle. The Seattle POE operated two subports, located at Portland, Ore., and Prince Rupert, British Columbia. Temporary short-term subports were operated by the Boston POE at Montreal, Quebec; Halifax, Nova Scotia; and Providence, R.I. The New Orleans POE operated a temporary subport at Mobile, Ala. Temporary subports at Juneau and Excursion Inlet, Alaska, were managed from the Seattle POE and used solely for shipment of cargo to Alaska. Cargo ports were located at Searsport, Me., Philadelphia and Baltimore. A total of 7,293,354 troops, civilians and prisoners of war passed through these ports between Pearl Harbor and V-J Day, and the ports handled 126,787,875 tons of cargo.

PORT T. Code name for the British naval base at Addu Atoll in the Indian Ocean, used as an alternative to Colombo. It was also known as Base T.

POSKREBYSHEV, Alexander N. (1891?–1966). One of the closest associates of Joseph STALIN; in 1935 Stalin put him in charge of a unit in his personal secretariat called the Special Secret Political Section of State Security, which Poskrebyshev in fact took part in creating and which directed the purges and simultaneously supervised the secret police (*see* NKVD). Very little known outside the party–government hierarchy, Poskrebyshev was made lieutenant general after the outbreak of the war and later twice awarded the ORDER OF LENIN. He retained the confidence of Stalin until the latter's death and was greatly feared by the highest Soviet officials. He came into public view only once, in 1952, when he delivered one of the key speeches at the Nineteenth Congress of the Communist Party of the Soviet Union, and he disappeared from sight immediately after Stalin's death. He was known to be writing his memoirs in the early 1960s; he died in a Moscow hospital, apparently of natural causes.

POTENZA. Important road center in southern ITALY, 50 miles inland from SALERNO, taken by a Canadian contingent of the British EIGHTH ARMY on September 20, 1943.

POTEZ 631. French two-seat long-range escort fighter and bomber-interceptor. It was built to a 1934 specification and first flew in 1936; production models reached their squadrons in 1937. Many were purchased or built under license by foreign governments. Unable to fill the fighter-interceptor role, they were used as night fighters and ground-support aircraft. Powered by two 660-horsepower radial engines, the plane had a maximum speed of 276.5 miles per hour. It carried two

20-mm. cannon, six 7.5-mm. machine guns forward and two flexible 7.5-mm. machine guns aft. It weighed 9,921 pounds fully loaded.

POTEZ 671. French two-seat, twin-engine, long-range escort fighter and bomber-interceptor, which had not reached full production by the fall of France in 1940.

POTSDAM CONFERENCE. Sometimes called the Berlin Conference, this meeting was held between July 17 and August 2, 1945. The U.S. delegation was headed by President Harry S. TRUMAN, the Soviet by Premier Joseph STALIN and the British by Prime Minister Winston CHURCHILL, who after the Conservatives' electoral defeat was replaced on July 28 by Clement ATTLEE. The conference was necessitated by the surrender of Germany, but discussions covered a number of European political and territorial issues and the prosecution of the war in the Pacific.

There were difficulties in convening the conference. Truman, who became President upon the death of ROOSEVELT on April 12, 1945, had wanted to meet Stalin separately, but this idea was strongly opposed by Churchill. Truman delayed the conference to coincide with the test of the first ATOMIC BOMB in New Mexico (scheduled for July 16), believing that the new weapon would ensure victory in the Far East and give the United States additional prestige. The focus of the conference discussions, however, was Europe.

In a series of agreements, the Big Three resolved administrative, economic and political questions regarding the governing of occupied Germany. They created the ALLIED CONTROL COUNCIL (ACC) for coordinating their policies, but since each of them retained full sovereignty within their respective OCCUPATION ZONES, coordination became a function of their goodwill and mutual understanding. ACC decisions required unanimity; i.e., each power could veto anything it felt was contrary to its interests. There was little disagreement at the conference about general principles of denazification, democratization and demilitarization of Germany. Formal partitioning of Germany, which the Allies considered at TEHERAN and YALTA, did not take place, although theoretically it could become part of the future peace treaty with an all-German government, expected to emerge after the full democratization of the German society had been achieved.

The conference approved the principle of reparations to the Soviet Union and other countries which had been victims of the Nazi aggression. These reparations were to be paid, not out of the current German production, but by removal of property and equipment from the zones of occupation. In return for industrial equipment from the Western zones, the Soviets were obligated to send back agricultural products from their zone, an obligation which they did not fulfill, causing the Western powers to terminate deliveries of capital goods in the spring of 1946. The Potsdam agreement to treat Germany as "one economic whole" was not implemented; because of recurring conflicts in the ACC, movement of goods and persons between the Soviet and the Western zones (except in Berlin) was discontinued early in 1947.

In disposing of territorial questions, the conference followed the agreements reached at Yalta. East Prussia was partitioned between the Soviet Union and Poland, and the so-called ODER–NEISSE territory of eastern Germany was transferred to the Polish administration. Although regarded as a temporary arrangement pending the future peace treaty with Germany, the massive expulsion of the German population from these territories was in fact final. The conference also agreed that ethnic Germans from Czechoslovakia, Hungary and Poland, numbering over 6 million, would be resettled in occupied Germany.

The Big Three agreed to establish the Council of Foreign Ministers to prepare draft treaties with the defeated Axis nations. China was to participate in drafting the treaty with Japan; France later became a member of the Council of Foreign Ministers (and obtained a zone of occupation, carved out of the U.S. zone). Soviet attempts to make the Western powers recognize provisional regimes in Rumania and Bulgaria failed; only the government of Poland, reconstituted by the inclusion of representatives of the Polish government-in-exile, won recognition. Soviet demands for a trusteeship of Libya, Italy's former African colony, and for a base in the Dardanelles or the Dodecanese Islands were rebuffed.

Among other decisions of the conference were the disposal of the Germany Navy and merchant marine (to be divided among the USSR, Britain and the United States, except for the submarines, which were to be scuttled); formation of the International Military Tribunal to prosecute Nazi war criminals; and creation of the Allied Berlin Kommandatura to administer jointly the former German capital and supervise the Berlin city government to be elected.

The Potsdam Conference appeared to be a success to some contemporary observers. It set in motion a mechanism for the conclusion of peace treaties with former enemy nations and seemed to ensure temporarily Allied cooperation in governing Germany. Its decisions on territorial issues, however, implicitly recognized Soviet de facto occupation of central and eastern Europe: only Czechoslovakia escaped Soviet dominance for a while. But the Big Three political decisions proved to be unenforceable, as the East–West conflict, arising from the differences in objectives, policies and attitudes of the Soviet Union and the Western Allies, began to erode the wartime spirit of cooperation. **V.P.**

POUND, Sir (Alfred) Dudley (1877–1943). From his earliest days in the ROYAL NAVY, Pound was marked as an officer likely to go far in his career. After serving as flag captain in H.M.S. *Colossus* in the Battle of Jutland, he was called to the Admiralty as head of a new section whose duty it was to foresee and think out problems. This section developed into the Plans Division, and in 1922 he became its director. His appointments between the two world wars alternated between sea commands and naval staff posts at the Admiralty, and in 1935 he was selected as Commander in Chief Mediterranean to relieve Adm. Sir William Fisher. Shortly before he was due to take over the command, the Ethiopian crisis came to a head and it was decided, because of his knowledge of Mediterranean strategy, to retain Admiral Fisher in the Mediterranean. Pound offered to become his chief of staff, although now a full admiral, when he learned that a relief for that officer was required. His offer was accepted, and he served in that position until the crisis eased sufficiently for Fisher to return home in 1936 and for Pound to take over.

Pound was a superb trainer of a fleet. He had evolved a series of tactical drills and exercises to bring ships and squadrons to a high pitch of excellence, and he trained the captains of his ships to take immediate action when required without waiting for the order to do so. Under his hand the Mediterranean Fleet grew in skill, dash and tactical expertise. The resignation of the First Sea Lord (Sir Roger Backhouse) because of ill health early in 1939 brought Pound home to step into his shoes. He took office in June of that year, to enter into four years of arduous work. He was now 62, but faced the future with a fortitude of mind and toughness of body that was to see him through the anxious years until the final victory was in sight.

Pound's achievements as First Sea Lord form virtually the history of the war at sea. It was his broad strategical thought that fashioned the ultimate overwhelming successes in the Mediterranean, the ATLANTIC and the Arctic. That there were operational setbacks in the day-to-day course of the war was of course inevitable, but behind them lay Pound's overall strategic concept to which he held firm through thick and thin, and which inevitably increased the pressure on Germany, month by month and year by year, until the net was drawn tight.

It was not until June 1942 that a deputy First Sea Lord was appointed to take some of the strain off Pound's shoulders, and it came too late to bring the relief which his health needed. For three years he had carried the burden, almost single-handed, of the whole conduct of the war at sea, a tremendous strain on a man of his age. But he could see clearly, even then, that the worst of the naval war was over. In January 1943 he assured the COMBINED CHIEFS OF STAFF, meeting at CASABLANCA with Prime Minister CHURCHILL and President ROOSEVELT, that the balance of the sea war was swinging so decisively in favor of the Allies that the end was in sight.

In July 1943 Pound's wife died, a blow from which he found it hard to recover. But by that time he had seen his assurances at Casablanca come true, he had witnessed the final defeat of the U-boats in the Atlantic and he knew that the road was now open to inevitable victory. Yet he was to have no personal share in it when it came. Though he was worn out by the strain of four years of lofty and lonely command, his supreme strength of will took him, with the Prime Minister, to QUEBEC for another meeting with the President and the Combined Chiefs of Staff. There he collapsed. He was brought home to England, and died in a London hospital on Trafalgar Day, October 21. After a funeral service in Westminster Abbey, his ashes were scattered at sea. **P.K.K.**

POUR LE MÉRITE. Established in 1740 by Frederick the Great of Prussia, the order Pour le Mérite was limited by statute in 1810 to a purely martial award. Although there now exists a "peace class" for scientists and artists, the "Blue Max," as the award was popularly called, won fame as a German award for military merit. In World War II it was replaced by the Knight's Cross of the Iron Cross.

POWNALL, Charles Alan (1887–). U.S. naval officer, a graduate of the Naval Academy in 1910, who became a specialist in aviation, graduating from the Naval Aviation School at Pensacola in 1927. In 1938–41 he was commander of the carrier ENTERPRISE, and he went on to command carrier task forces in the Central Pacific Area. Subsequently he commanded the air forces of the Pacific Fleet. He retired as a vice-admiral in 1949.

POWNALL, Sir Henry (1887–1961). British Army officer, director of military operations and intelligence, War Office, 1938–41; Commander in Chief Far East, 1941–42; Commander in Chief Ceylon, 1942–43; Commander in Chief Persia and Iraq, 1943; chief of staff, SOUTHEAST ASIA COMMAND, 1943–44.

POZNAN (Posen). This city in western Poland was the first great objective of the First Belorussian Front in the Soviet 1945 offensive. Though surrounded, German forces in Poznan kept up resistance until February 23.

PQ-17. Convoy PQ-17, sailing from Iceland to northern Russia in July 1942, suffered heavily from air and submarine attacks by German forces in the Arctic Ocean. Losses in previous convoys, in both merchant ships and escorting naval vessels, had made it advisable to restrict convoys until the winter darkness provided some protection, but this caution was overruled by the political need to make gestures of continuing support to the Russians. Convoy PQ-17 consisted of 35 merchant ships with a close escort of 6 destroyers, 4 corvettes and 2 antiaircraft ships, a close-support force of 4 cruisers and 3 destroyers and distant cover provided by the Home Fleet, reinforced by 2 heavy ships of the U.S. Navy.

By July 4, the convoy having passed north of BEAR ISLAND, air and U-boat attacks were being made, though without causing any heavy loss. British air reconnaissance showed that German heavy ships (TIRPITZ, ADMIRAL HIPPER, ADMIRAL SCHEER, LÜTZOW) had left their Norwegian bases and were steaming north to Altenfjord, the naval anchorage at the top of the North Cape. Calculations made in the Admiralty indicated that these ships could reach the vicinity of the convoy during the night of July 4–5, and in the face of this danger the convoy was ordered to scatter and the close-support force to withdraw to the west. In fact, the German ships were still at anchor in Altenfjord, and it was not until noon on July 5 that they sailed, only to return to harbor a few hours later. There was nothing left for them to do, as the U-boats and torpedo bombers were accounting for the scattered convoy.

When the order to scatter was received, the cruiser covering force withdrew westward, as ordered. The six destroyers of the close escort went with them, expecting to meet the German ships on their way up to the convoy and engage them. Unfortunately, these destroyers remained with the covering force after it was apparent that there were no German ships present, and the merchant vessels were deprived of their support. Of the 35 ships of the convoy, only 11 reached their destination in Russia, the remaining 24 being sunk by U-boats and torpedo bombers. The Admiralty decision to withdraw the heavy covering force infuriated Adm. Ernest J. KING, the U.S. Chief of Naval Operations, and made him reluctant to have American and British ships operating together. *See also* MURMANSK RUN.

PQ-18. The convoy that followed the ill-fated PQ-17 (above) to northern Russia, sailing from Iceland in September 1942. It consisted of 39 merchant ships with a close escort of 2 destroyers, 2 antiaircraft ships, 2 submarines, 4 corvettes, 3 minesweepers and 4 trawlers, but in addition it was accompanied by an escort carrier, H.M.S. *Avenger*, with 2 destroyers, and a "fighting destroyer escort," consisting of the cruiser *Scylla* and 16 destroyers. The Germans, after their success against Convoy PQ-17, decided to leave the attack to U-boats and aircraft, and sent out 12 U-boats to concentrate against the convoy and increased the air striking force to 92 torpedo bombers and 133 long-range bombers and dive-bombers.

The most severe loss to the convoy was caused by an attack by 40 torpedo bombers on the afternoon of September 13, when eight ships were sunk. When the convoy reached Russian waters on September 18 it had lost 10 ships through air attack and three from attacks by U-boats, but the cost to the enemy was 41 aircraft shot down and three U-boats sunk. *See also* MURMANSK RUN.

PRAGUE UPRISING. In late April 1945 the British Chiefs of Staff pointed out to Gen. Dwight EISENHOWER the political advantages they believed would accrue to the Western Allies if their armies should get to Prague before the Soviets. The Supreme Allied Commander's answer was that apart from all logistic, tactical or strategical considerations, he personally "would be loath to hazard American lives for purely political purposes." Thus Eisenhower decided that the Red Army should liberate Prague since it was already in the area.

As part of this decision not to send U.S. forces to Prague, Eisenhower informed General MARSHALL, the U.S. Chief of Staff, that he would not order General PATTON's Third Army on to the Czech capital unless specifically ordered to do so by the COMBINED CHIEFS OF STAFF. On April 30 Eisenhower notified the Soviets that his forces would move as far east as the Karlsbad–Pilsen–Budweis line. Four days later he told the Soviet high command that if they wished, Patton's forces could advance as far as the west bank of the Moldau, on which Prague is situated. The Russian Chief of Staff, Gen. Alexsey ANTONOV, replied on May 5, requesting that Eisenhower hold his forces at the Pilsen line. Eisenhower complied, and thereby left Prague to the Soviets.

While Eisenhower and Antonov were exchanging messages concerning their respective forces in Czechoslovakia, the citizens of Prague tried to settle their fate themselves. On the night of May 1–2 Czech PARTISANS blew up several bridges outside Prague. On May 4 students tore off German street names. By the following day the city, which was relatively untouched by war despite the Germans' six-year occupation, was in revolt. The partisans hoped to prevent the Germans from destroying property before the Allies liberated the city and to ensure that postwar Czechoslovakia would be a democracy.

The uprising became serious on the morning of May 5 when the Prague radio station read the news in Czech only, rather than in both German and Czech. The Germans tried to take over the radio station but found the announcers barricaded inside. When they finally invaded the station on the 8th, the radio personnel fled to a church and continued to broadcast the message of liberation. In the meantime barricades had gone up all over the city.

The German forces in Prague were relatively weak. They had no tanks or artillery. But the Czechs were poorly equipped also. Since the Czech radio had informed the world of the uprising in Prague, Czech Foreign Minister Hubert Ripka in London appealed to the Western Allies for help. Gen. Stanislav Bosy of the Czech military mission appealed directly to Patton to send his Third Army on to Prague. Prime Minister CHURCHILL wrote to Eisenhower on May 7 urging him to get to Prague before the Soviets. In spite of these pleas, SHAEF complied with the Soviet request of May 5 to keep its forces on the Pilsen line. Eisenhower kept Moscow informed of the military situation in Czechoslovakia so that the Soviets would not be able to complain that the Germans had stopped fighting the Western armies but not the Red Army, especially after the formal German capitulation on May 8.

While Eisenhower kept Patton's army at Pilsen, the Reich Protector of Bohemia and Moravia, Karl Hermann FRANK, appealed to Hitler's successor, Adm. Karl DÖNITZ, for help. Two divisions were ordered to Prague. To meet this new threat, the Revolutionary Czech National Council sought help on May 6 from the nearby U.S. forces. Patton wanted to proceed to Prague, but he was told not to.

Unable to get aid from the Americans, the Czechs had in the meantime turned to Lt. Gen. Andrei VLASOV, commander of the Russian Army of Liberation (*see* ROA), Russians fighting for Germany against Soviet Communism. Vlasov and the commander of the 1st ROA division, Gen. Sergei K. Bunyachenko, agreed to bring their 20,000 men to Prague from Beroun, about 25 miles southwest of the capital. The ROA arrived in time on May 8 to fight off the German reinforcements and clear the city of Germans. Then the ROA pulled out of the city.

With the German forces defeated, Frank's commanding general, Rudolf Toussaint, met with the Revolutionary Czech National Council. He argued with the Czechs for more than four hours over permission for the German troops to march west and surrender to the Americans. The Czechs finally agreed; thus by the time Marshal Ivan KONEV's First Ukrainian Front reached Prague the following day, the city was free of Germans. The Soviet liberators then rounded up the soldiers in Vlasov's army and took charge of German soldiers handed over by the Americans.

PRAUN, Albert (1894–1975). German Army officer (General der Nachrichtentruppen, 1944) who as chief of the Signal Corps did not carry out Adolf HITLER's order to destroy all communications facilities in the last days of the war.

PRESIDENT HARRISON. American President Lines passenger ship, chartered by the U.S. Navy late in 1941 to evacuate Navy and Marine personnel from Chinese ports. She made one such voyage to Shanghai from the Philippines; on her second trip the Pacific war broke out, and she was pursued by a Japanese cruiser off the

Chinese coast. Her captain ran her onto a reef in an effort to make her useless to the enemy. Salvaged by the Japanese, she operated under the name *Kachidoki Maru* until the American submarine *Pampanito* torpedoed and sank her on September 12, 1944.

PRESIDENTIAL UNIT CITATION. A U.S. Navy and Marine Corps citation, authorized by Presidential order on February 6, 1942, for award to any ship, aircraft or Navy or Marine unit that on or after October 16, 1941, was singled out for "outstanding performance in action." Presidential Unit Citations, or "PUCs," were awarded to a number of ships, task organizations, Marine units and shore-based units of various types. The PUC was the higher-ranking of two unit awards established during the war, the lesser being the NAVY UNIT COMMENDATION. *See also* DISTINGUISHED UNIT CITATION.

PRÉTELAT, Gaston (1874–1969). Chief of staff to General Gouraud in World War I, General Prételat commanded the French Army Group Two on the MAGINOT LINE in 1940. In June his troops were trapped when his superiors failed to heed his plea for an early retreat from the line.

PRIDHAM-WIPPELL, Sir Henry (1885–1952). Commander of the light forces of the British Mediterranean Fleet at the Battle of CAPE MATAPAN on March 28, 1941. His ships were next engaged in the withdrawal of British forces from Greece a month later. After being appointed second-in-command of the Mediterranean Fleet, Admiral Pridham-Wippell was in H.M.S. BARHAM when she was torpedoed and blew up on November 25, 1941; he was picked up after swimming for 45 minutes, having given his life belt to an injured seaman. On leaving the Mediterranean in 1942 he became Flag Officer Dover, holding that appointment until the end of the war. His final appointment was as Commander in Chief Plymouth, and he retired in 1948.

PRIEN, Günther (1908–1941). Commander of the German submarine *U-47*, which penetrated the swirling passage to the main British fleet anchorage at SCAPA FLOW on the night of October 13–14, 1939. Prien fired two torpedo salvos in the confined waters, sinking the British battleship ROYAL OAK, and made a skillful escape on the surface without loss to his own command. Prien died in action on March 8, 1941, when the *U-47* was sunk by the British destroyer *Wolverine*.

PRINCE OF WALES, H.M.S. Built by Cammell Laird, this Royal Navy battleship of 35,000 tons carried ten 14-inch guns, sixteen 5.25-inch guns and an array of 2-pounder Bofors, Oerlikons and machine guns. As the fastest battleship in the Royal Navy, the *Prince of Wales* was assigned to guard the Denmark Strait against German warships. In May 1941, shortly after her commissioning and with dockyard workmen still aboard, she engaged the battleship BISMARCK and damaged her fuel tanks sufficiently to force her toward the French coast, where other British ships destroyed her. *Prince of Wales* carried Prime Minister CHURCHILL to the ATLANTIC CHARTER conference to meet President ROOSEVELT off Newfoundland in August 1941. Japanese aircraft sank *Prince of Wales* in the Gulf of Siam during the invasion of Malaya on December 10, 1941. Acting Admiral Sir Tom PHILLIPS, commander of FORCE Z, went to the bottom with the ship.

PRINCETON, U.S.S. INDEPENDENCE-class light aircraft carrier, commissioned in 1943. Sent to the Pacific, she operated with the FAST CARRIER TASK FORCE from the seizure of the GILBERTS through the Battle of the PHILIPPINE SEA to the invasion of LEYTE. On October 24, 1944, during the battle for LEYTE GULF, a Japanese dive-bomber hit *Princeton* with a single bomb. Exploding belowdecks, the bomb set off fires and explosions that eventually went out of control; blast and fragments damaged several ships that attempted to assist *Princeton*. The light cruiser *Birmingham* was badly damaged by one heavy detonation; 385 of her crew were killed or injured. After a massive final explosion, *Princeton* sank.

PRINZ EUGEN. German heavy cruiser of 10,000 tons, launched in August 1938, with eight 8-inch rifles as main armament. The ship accompanied the ill-fated BISMARCK on her attempt to break out into the Atlantic in May 1941. A participant in the Channel dash of February 1942, *Prinz Eugen* ended her career as a target in postwar American atomic bomb tests in the Pacific. *See also* GNEISENAU.

PRIPET MARSHES. A great swamp in western Russia, near the Polish border. It stretches for about 150 miles north and south and is about 300 miles across. Aside from a road or two on causeways, few paths crossed it at the time of the Second World War. Its significance was that, since it was largely impassable for vehicles, it divided the Eastern Front into northern and southern parts. *See also* SOVIET-GERMAN OPERATIONS.

PRISONERS OF WAR. In the last phases of the war, the number of prisoners held by all participants was estimated to be 4 million. The figure was based on some reasonably precise information (such as that concerning men of the Western Allies held in Germany) and on estimates to complete the picture. Allied prisoners in Germany numbered over 1.7 million (765,000 French, 550,000 Italian, 200,000 British and Imperial, 125,000 Yugoslav, 90,000 American). The Japanese held 145,000 Allied prisoners (108,000 British and Imperial, 22,000 Dutch, 15,000 American). There were no figures concerning Chinese soldiers in Japanese captivity, prisoners held by USSR or Russians taken prisoner. Axis prisoners, exclusive of those held by the Soviet Union, numbered about 630,000 Germans, 430,000 Italians and 11,600 Japanese (because of Italy's switching sides, she had men in the camps of both).

PRIVATEER. Name applied to the U.S. Navy PB4Y-2 (*see* PB4Y).

PROCTOR. Based on the Hills Vega Gull four-place sport plane, the Proctor was manufactured by Percival Aircraft as a communication trainer for the ROYAL AIR FORCE. It was a low-wing monoplane with a streamlined fixed landing gear, a wooden internal structure, a plywood-covered fuselage and fabric-covered wings and tail surfaces. The power plant was a single 210-horsepower de Havilland Gypsy Queen.

PROVENCE. French battleship of 22,189 tons, launched in 1913 and refitted in the 1930s. She carried ten 13.4-inch guns, fourteen 5.5-inch guns and numerous smaller ones. She was beached in the British attack on the French fleet at MERS-EL-KÉBIR in July 1940 and scuttled at TOULON on November 27, 1942.

PROXIMITY FUZE. A type of fuze developed in Britain and the United States and first tested in 1942. It incorporated a tiny transceiver that emitted radio waves after firing. When the projectile passed within range of an object, its waves were reflected with enough strength to trigger the fuze and explode the projectile. Referred to in the U.S. service as a variable-time (VT) fuze for security reasons, it was a major contribution to air defense. Before its development a wide margin of error was inherent in heavy antiaircraft gunnery. Fire control was not precise or rapid enough to predict the movements of attacking airplanes and calculate the exact point at which mechanical fuzes would have to go off to score fatal damage. Barrages of exploding projectiles had to be laid down in front of attacking planes, in the hope that at least some of them would fly into danger. The VT fuze raised the percentage of hits, since each projectile could now do its own sensing and explode itself if it passed close enough to a target to inflict damage. Proximity fuzes were later produced for bombardment rockets, to sense the nearness of ground and produce air bursts. German researchers were working on various types of these fuzes when the war ended.

PSKOV. German bastion town in northwest Russia, the anchor of a north–south defense line taken up after retreat from the LENINGRAD area in January 1944. Lakes Peipus and Pskov made up the main portion of the line.

PT. U.S. Navy ship-type symbol for Motor Torpedo Boat. Seventy PTs of various types were acquired by the Navy during 1939–41. Mass-produced boats ordered after these were of three types. The 78-foot PT-71 class was built by Higgins; the Electric Boat Company (Elco) produced the 80-foot PT-103 class; and the 70-foot PT-368 class was built by various boatyards to a British design by Vosper. They carried two or four torpedoes in tubes or launching racks, along with automatic weapons. During the war many modifications were made to suit the circumstances. Some PTs carried depth charges or smoke generators; many had their gun armaments enlarged in the field for use against enemy small craft. A considerable number of Elco and Vosper boats were transferred to Allied navies.

PT-16. The military version of the Ryan sport plane, this was the first low-wing primary trainer used by the U.S. Army Air Corps. The PT-16 was a two-place, open-cockpit plane with an externally braced wing and fixed landing gear. Ryan also built the PT-20, PT-21 and PT-22, basically the same airplane as the PT-16 except for different engines and changes in streamlining.

The Ryan planes were soon joined by other low-wing primary trainers built by Fairchild. Although lacking the external braces common to the Ryan series, the Fairchilds had the usual fixed landing gear. A change of engine marked the principal difference between the PT-19 and the Fairchild PT-23. Some PT-19s were fitted with canopies and redesignated PT-26.

PT-17. The Stearman Kaydet was one of a series of biplane primary trainers built for the U.S. Army and Navy by this company, which became a division of Boeing Aircraft. Some 5,000 Kaydets were manufactured for the Army alone. The PT-17 and its sister aircraft were fabric-covered and had two open cockpits and a fixed landing gear. A 220-horsepower Continental radial engine gave the plane a top speed of 135 miles per hour.

PT-109. Commissioned in New York on June 16, 1942, and placed in service July 10, 1942, *PT-109* was dispatched with the rest of Elco-built Motor Torpedo Boat Squadron 5 (PTs 103–114) to Panama, where she was assigned to Squadron 2 for service in the SOLOMONS. After seeing various action while patrolling the SLOT, the *109* came under the command of Lt. John F. KENNEDY, later to become the 35th President of the United States. At about 2:30 on the morning of August 2, 1943, in an encounter with four Japanese destroyers, the *109* was rammed and sunk by AMAGIRI in the Blackett Strait off KOLOMBANGARA Island. Kennedy and 10 other survivors swam to a nearby island. Following several attempts to secure help, they were finally rescued on August 8.

PTC. U.S. Navy ship-type symbol for Motorboat, Submarine Chaser. This was an antisubmarine version of an early 70-foot PT design by Elco (*see* PT), armed with depth charges and two twin .50-caliber machine gun mounts. PTC-1 through -12 were placed in service in March 1941 as Motor Boat Submarine Chaser Squadron 1. The type proved unsatisfactory, since no suitable SONAR equipment could be developed for their use, and by July 1941 all 12 PTCs had been transferred to Britain, where they were used as motor gunboats.

PUGILIST GALLOP. Code name of the original Allied plan for an attack by the British EIGHTH ARMY on the MARETH LINE in TUNISIA, March 1943. Lack of success caused a shift to a new plan, SUPERCHARGE II.

PULLER, Lewis Burwell (1898–1971). One of the most decorated U.S. marines in history, Puller had already won two NAVY CROSSES (for outstanding performance of duty in the Nicaragua campaign in 1931 and 1932) by the time he took his battalion overseas in 1942. He was nicknamed "Chesty" because of his bantam rooster strut. Even before the war he had attained an enviable reputation as an outstanding small-unit leader and trainer of young officers.

Puller and the 7th Marines joined the rest of the 1st Marine Division on GUADALCANAL in September 1942. Puller won his third Navy Cross for the action on the night of October 24–25 when his battalion, although stretched over a mile-long portion of the defense perimeter, provided the only defense between HENDERSON FIELD and an attacking Japanese regiment. In pouring jungle rain on a dark night, the enemy attacked Puller's lines repeatedly, only to be thrown back each time. The battalion was in the forefront of the fighting throughout the stay of the division on Guadalcanal, and after that campaign Puller was appointed executive officer of the 7th Marines for the CAPE GLOUCESTER operation, which began with the 1st Division's landing on December 26, 1943.

Puller won his fourth Navy Cross when the commanders of two of the 7th's battalions were wounded and he took over their units, moving through heavy machine gun and mortar fire to reorganize and lead them in a successful attack on a strongly fortified Japanese position. Promoted to colonel, he led the 1st Marines in the PELELIU operation, which began with the landing on September 15, 1944. In this assault the 1st Marines met perhaps the stiffest opposition of any of the 1st Division regiments, suffering 65 percent casualties.

In November 1944 Puller returned to the United States, remaining there for the rest of the war in command of a training unit. He went on to greater fame during the Korean War, where he won his fifth Navy Cross. He retired as a result of physical disability in 1955 with the rank of lieutenant general. A mark of his fighting spirit may be seen in the fact that in 1966 he requested to return to active duty, but was turned down because of his age.

PUNISHMENT. Code name for German intensive bombing of BELGRADE on April 6–8, 1941. *See* BALKANS.

PUPPCHEN. German two-wheel rocket launcher.

PURDY, U.S.S. ALLEN M. SUMNER–class destroyer. Commissioned in 1944, *Purdy* took part in the battle for OKINAWA. On RADAR picket station off that island on April 12, 1945, *Purdy* and the destroyer *Cassin Young* were severely damaged in a KAMIKAZE attack.

PURIĆ, Bodžidar (1891– ?). King PETER II chose Dr. Purić, a career diplomat, to be Premier of the Yugoslav government-in-exile on August 10, 1943, because Purić was a Serb who supported the PARTISAN resistance efforts of Gen. Draža MIHAJLOVIĆ. Once the Allied leaders decided at TEHERAN that they would back Marshal TITO rather than Mihajlović, the British pressed Peter to dismiss his pro-CHETNIK Premier. On June 1, 1944, the King did so.

PURPLE HEART. U.S. decoration awarded to Army, Navy and Coast Guard personnel killed or wounded by enemy action. The reinstitution of a medal originated by George Washington, it was also awarded, to a very limited extent, for meritorious service other than wounds until September 1942.

PV. The U.S. Navy Lockheed aircraft Ventura and Harpoon, developed from that company's HUDSON medium bomber, entered service late in 1942 as part of a program to supply the Navy with fast, well-armed patrol planes for use in ocean areas where enemy fighter opposition could be expected and flying boats were too vulnerable. The original PV-1 was essentially the same as the Army's B-34 and was named Ventura. The PV-2, named Harpoon, had a fixed forward-firing machine gun armament as well as flexible defensive guns. The PV-3, also named Ventura, came from Lockheed British-export Model 37 bomber production taken over for Navy use. After V-J Day the PV-1 and -3 passed out of service. The PV-2 continued on active duty for some years thereafter, for both Navy and Naval Reserve use.

The PV-2 was 52 feet long, with a 75-foot wingspan. Two 2,000-horsepower radial engines gave it a top speed of 280 miles per hour; its search radius, at cruising speed of 185 miles per hour, was 630 miles. Two .50-caliber machine guns were carried in a flexible ventral mount, with two more in a dorsal power turret; five fixed guns were mounted in the nose. Up to two tons of bombs could be carried in an internal bomb bay; another ton could be mounted on external wing racks. The crew, depending on the assigned mission, numbered four or five. For long-range antisubmarine patrol, depth charges and an additional bomb-bay fuel tank could be carried, as well as droppable wing fuel tanks. As the war went on, PVs were equipped with search RADAR.

PVO (Protivovzdushnaya Oborona). The Soviet antiaircraft defense. The PVO was the part of the Red Air Force system charged with protecting specific targets from aerial attack or enemy reconnaissance. During the war the PVO system was staffed primarily by women.

PY. Designation for private yachts taken over by the U.S. Navy for patrol duty.

PYE, William Satterlee (1880–1959). A 1901 graduate of the U.S. Naval Academy, Pye served in the Navy's War Plans Division before the war and in this capacity drafted the basic war plan for the Pacific. In January 1941 Pye, a vice-admiral, took a command in the Pacific, and following PEARL HARBOR he temporarily replaced Adm. Husband E. KIMMEL as commander of the Pacific Fleet. Although respected for his strategic ability, Pye was criticized for his decision to abandon WAKE ISLAND, and with it America's first chance to avenge Pearl Harbor—although other critics blame the Wake Island fiasco primarily on Adm. Frank Jack FLETCHER's insistence on engaging in a time-consuming refueling operation. Pye aided Adm. Chester NIMITZ in the latter's early days as commander of the Pacific Fleet and later served as president of the Naval War College.

PYKRETE. The substance to be used in the floating airstrip called HABBAKUK. The name came from the surname of the inventor, Pyke.

PYLE, Ernest Taylor (1900–1945). Specializing in telling the personal side of war, Ernie Pyle was the best-known American journalist of World War II, beloved both by the GI whom he wrote about and the people at home. Six columns a week printed in over 300 newspapers attested to his popularity, the Pulitzer Prize in 1943 to his professional skill. After studying journalism at Indiana University, Pyle reported for a variety of newspapers in the 1920s and in 1932 became managing editor of the Washington *Daily News.* He left that post in 1935 to work as a roving reporter, in which work he developed the folksy, down-home style that he carried over into his war reporting. As a Scripps-Howard correspondent, he told of the tribulations of the soldier, sailor and airman, all the while professing his own personal frailties and fears. He was with American troops from 1942 through 1944 in North Africa, Sicily, Italy and France, and in 1945 moved to the Pacific. There the small, shy newsman fell victim on April 18 to Japanese sniper fire on the little island of IE SHIMA near OKINAWA.

Pz.Kpfw. Abbreviation of Panzerkampfwagen, the German term for TANK, used with Roman or Arabic numerals (e.g., Pz.Kpfw. III; Pz.Kpfw. 35t) to identify tank designs. The form Pz.Kw. was also employed, both designations sometimes appearing without periods.

PZL P-11. Polish single-engine fighter, called Jedenstka (the Eleventh), with high gull-wing configuration, built by Panstvove Zaklady Lotnicze (PZL). Designed in 1930, it entered service in 1933. It made up the bulk of Poland's fighter force in 1939; 125 were formed in 12 squadrons, which lasted 17 days and accounted for 126 enemy aircraft. Seven were left when Poland surrendered. This plane had a 645-horsepower engine and a top speed of 242 miles per hour, and was armed with two 7.7-mm. machine guns.

PZL P-24. Similar to the PZL P-11 (above). It was never used by the Poles but was exported in large numbers to Turkey, Rumania, Bulgaria and Greece. The latter had four squadrons of P-24s, which fought Italian planes in 1940. The P-24F version had a 970-horsepower engine and a maximum speed of 267 miles per hour, and was armed with two 20-mm. cannon and two 7.7-mm. machine guns.

PZL P-37B. Polish four-man, twin-engine, all-metal, stressed-skin monoplane bomber of compact design. It was one of the most formidable products of the Polish air industry. Called the Loś (Elk), this plane first flew in 1936, but only 36 of the approximately 100 built were fully equipped for operational duties. The Loś did a fine job against the German armor concentrations, and later well over 40 of these aircraft were flown to Rumania, where they were taken over by the Rumanian Air Force for use against Russia throughout the war. The Loś had two 918-horsepower engines and a maximum speed of 273 miles per hour. It carried three 7.7-mm. machine guns and could deliver 5,688 pounds of bombs.

PZL P-50. Polish single-radial-engine, low-wing, all-metal fighter, designed in 1936 and first flown in 1939. Only two were built. It had a top speed of 280 miles per hour and was to carry four 7.7-mm. machine guns.

Q

Q SHIP. An American revival of a British World War I idea—the use of heavily armed ships disguised as merchantmen, the purpose being to sink unsuspecting U-boats. Q ships, also called mystery ships, were employed in the ATLANTIC in 1942 but produced no results; two of them were sunk by German submarines. The project was abandoned.

QATTARA DEPRESSION. A below-sea-level, lifeless area of salt flats in northwest Egypt. Considered impassable, and separated from the desert by precipitous cliffs, it was a significant military factor. It stretches 150 miles from the Siwa Oasis to a point 40 miles south of ALAMEIN, thus forming the southern anchor of the Alamein Line.

QUEBEC CONFERENCES. Allied diplomacy during World War II was characterized by a series of conferences, two of which met at Quebec and were code-named Quadrant (1943) and OCTAGON (1944).

The *Quadrant* conference, August 14–24, 1943, was attended by President Franklin D. ROOSEVELT, Prime Minister Winston CHURCHILL, their chief advisers and the COMBINED CHIEFS OF STAFF, and included for the first time a representative from China. Roosevelt and Churchill had originally hoped for a meeting with Premier Joseph STALIN, but he remained aloof. In the months preceding the conference Stalin had made such friendly gestures as abolishing the Comintern and establishing a rapprochement with the Orthodox Church, but he continued his insistent demands for an Allied SECOND FRONT in western Europe. On the military fronts at the time of the conference the Allies were taking the initiative against the Japanese, had swarmed over SICILY and were preparing to invade the Italian mainland.

Military considerations dominated the conference discussions, the primary issue being the British insistence on a concentrated military thrust in ITALY aimed ultimately at the Balkans as against the American demand that there be no shift in military strategy that would delay Operation Overlord, the Allied INVASION of France. The American position triumphed, and the conference reaffirmed May 1, 1944, as the execution date for the Normandy invasion. In other actions the conference ordered Gen. Dwight D. EISENHOWER to seize Sardinia and Corsica, to accept the unconditional surrender of Italy and to keep "unrelenting pressure" on the German forces in Italy. It was agreed to intensify Allied military operations in the Far East, particularly in Burma. The SOUTHEAST ASIA COMMAND was created; Adm. Lord Louis MOUNTBATTEN was appointed the Supreme Allied Commander, and Gen. Joseph STILWELL was named his deputy. The conference acknowledged the FRENCH COMMITTEE OF NATIONAL LIBERATION as the government of the French overseas territories and received the report of the Chiefs of the Naval Staffs that the Battle of the ATLANTIC had turned in favor of the Allies.

The *Octagon* conference met on September 12–16, 1944, in the wake of reports from every battle front of great Allied victories but just before the heroic failure of the Battle of ARNHEM to end the war with Germany quickly. Efforts to follow the first Churchill, Roosevelt and Stalin meeting at TEHERAN with a second Big Three conference had failed, and for the second time Churchill and Roosevelt met at Quebec with their political and military advisers, this time to review plans for final victory in Europe and in the Far East.

The principal subjects discussed at this conference were the demarcation of German OCCUPATION ZONES and the postwar treatment of Germany. The U.S. Secretary of the Treasury, Henry MORGENTHAU, Jr., proposed a "Program to Prevent Germany from Starting a World War III," which was tentatively approved by Churchill and Roosevelt. The MORGENTHAU PLAN linked German military might to her economic and industrial power and concluded that the solution to German bellicosity was the "pastoralizing" of postwar Germany. The plan was rejected within a month.

Of growing concern to Churchill and Roosevelt was the future freedom and stability of eastern Europe. To establish a basis for postwar political harmony they agreed to press for the union of rival resistance groups in Poland and in Yugoslavia.

Regarding Far East operations, Churchill promised Roosevelt that the main British fleet would participate in the major operations against Japan under the U.S. supreme command. Specific plans were also made for the capture of RANGOON, Burma.

QUEEN. Code name for the war's heaviest aerial bombardment in direct support of ground troops, mounted on November 16, 1944, to help the U.S. FIRST and NINTH ARMIES break through to the Roer River east of AACHEN. A total of 2,807 planes (2,379 heavy bombers, 80 mediums, 348 fighter-bombers) dropped 10,097 tons of bombs. Although German losses were heavy, the targets were too spread out and the bomb safety line too far ahead of the American troops to precipitate breakthrough.

QUEEN BEE. Name given to a variant of the de Havilland TIGER MOTH trainer, an obsolescent British aircraft that saw some service in the war.

QUEEN ELIZABETH. British passenger liner used as a troop transport. *See also* QUEEN MARY.

QUEEN ELIZABETH, H.M.S. Royal Navy battleship of 31,100 tons, completed at Portsmouth in 1914 and rebuilt in 1937–40. Her World War II armament comprised eight 15-inch and twenty 4.5-inch guns, smaller weapons and four aircraft. *Queen Elizabeth* served initially in the Home Fleet but was moved to the Mediterranean in time to take part in the evacuation from CRETE and other operations. In December 1941 she and VALIANT were severely damaged in an audacious attack by Italian "human torpedoes" in ALEXANDRIA harbor; the delayed-action mines caused extensive flooding, but both ships remained on even keels and the full extent of the damage was concealed. After lengthy repairs in the United States, *Queen Elizabeth* served in the Indian Ocean, initially protecting convoys and later in a bombardment role in support of land operations along the BURMA coast.

QUEENFISH, U.S.S. BALAO-class submarine, commissioned in 1944. During her first two Pacific war patrols, *Queenfish* sank seven Japanese ships to earn a PRESIDENTIAL UNIT CITATION. Her third patrol was uneventful. On April 1, 1945, during her fourth patrol, she sank the Japanese passenger-cargo ship *Awa Maru*; however, *Awa Maru*'s safe passage had been guaranteed by the United States, and this sinking has been the subject of controversy.

QUEEN MARY. This giant British ocean liner (1,019 feet, 81,235 tons) ferried approximately 570,000 Allied troops across the Atlantic during the war. The *Mary* and her sister "Queen," the *Elizabeth,* could carry 15,000 troops between New York and Britain in less than five days. She made 10 eastward voyages in 1942 and 20 more during the first half of 1943, bringing troops for the buildup prior to the Allied invasion of Europe. Earlier she served as a transport between Australia and the Middle East. The employment of large, fast luxury liners like the *Mary* was much more expedient than using ordinary troop convoys. While her speed prevented the attendance of escorts (she had broken the North Atlantic crossing record in 1938), the *Mary* nonetheless completed the war unscathed, though the Germans reported her sunk on several occasions. After the war she resumed service with Cunard Lines until 1967, when she was sold to the city of Long Beach, Calif., to be used as a floating hotel and convention center.

QUESADA, Elwood R. (1904–). Pete Quesada's first wartime assignment as a U.S. Army Air Forces officer was command, as a major, of a pursuit group. In January 1942 he became a lieutenant colonel, and by the end of the year he was a brigadier general and wing commander. He went to Africa early in 1943, where he took over the XII Fighter Command, leading that organization during the Tunisian, Sicilian and Corsican campaigns and the invasion of Italy. In October 1943 he was appointed Commanding General, IX Fighter Command. The following spring he received a promotion to major general and became Commanding General, Ninth Tactical Air Command. While he was serving in this post the Allies invaded Europe, and Quesada established an advance headquarters on the Normandy beaches, from which he began directing tactical air operations on D plus 1. He returned to the United States in April 1945 to become Deputy Chief of Staff for intelligence on the Air Staff. In 1947 he was promoted to lieutenant general.

QUEZON, Manuel (1878–1944). President of the Philippine Commonwealth from its founding in 1935 to his death. He fled with American forces after the fall of Manila following the Japanese invasion in December 1941, and in May 1942 established a provisional Philippine government-in-exile in Washington. He was a constant ally of the United States.

QUINAN, Sir Edward Pellew (1884–1960). British Army officer (general) commander of forces in Iran and Iraq, 1941–42. He commanded the Tenth Army in 1942–43 and the Northwestern Army in India in 1943, retiring in that year.

QUINCY, U.S.S. NEW ORLEANS–class heavy cruiser, commissioned in 1936. In 1941 she served in the Atlantic NEUTRALITY PATROL, and she operated in the North Atlantic in early 1942. She supported landings on GUADALCANAL and TULAGI in August 1942. On the night of August 8–9, with sister ships ASTORIA and VINCENNES, she was lost in the Battle of SAVO ISLAND.

The second U.S.S. *Quincy* was a BALTIMORE-class heavy cruiser, commissioned in 1943. In 1944 she supported the INVASION of Normandy and the SOUTHERN FRANCE landing. In January and February 1945, *Quincy* transported President ROOSEVELT to Malta on the first leg of his journey to the YALTA CONFERENCE. Roosevelt returned to *Quincy*, then in Egypt, in mid-February for the voyage back to the United States. In April *Quincy* joined the Pacific Fleet and took part in final FAST CARRIER TASK FORCE operations against Japan.

QUISLING, Vidkun (1887–1945). The man whose last name became a synonym for "fifth columnist" began a promising career as a Norwegian General Staff officer in 1911, acquiring some experience in international affairs during assignments as military attaché in Russia. By 1931, though he had dallied with socialist elements in Russia and at home, his fascist ideology had surfaced in coherent form during his brief leadership of a small group of believers in Nordic racial superiority. After holding office as Defense Minister in the conservative Agrarian Party government from 1931 to 1933, a post he handled badly and used as a platform for lashing Norwegian leftist parties, Quisling formed the Nasjonal Samling (National Union) Party, in which he exercised absolute power. His fortunes declined with the party's poor showings in national elections, and by the outbreak of World War II Quisling's failure as a politician was apparent, which prompted him to seek German support. A series of meetings introduced him to Alfred ROSENBERG, Admiral RAEDER and Adolf HITLER, laying the groundwork for his collaboration with German occupation forces.

When the Norwegian government fled Oslo on April 9, 1940, the German invaders approved Quisling's formation of his own government based on a pro-German, anti-British policy. Though the German military commanders and the appointed Reichskommissar for Norway maintained ambivalent attitudes toward him, dismissing him momentarily on April 15, 1940, Quisling remained a figurehead in the country throughout the war, becoming Minister President in 1942. He offered little as a manifestation of indigenous Norwegian fascism and was roundly unpopular in spite of the growth of the Nasjonal Samling during the occupation.

Tried for treason by the postwar Norwegian Government, Quisling was executed on October 24, 1945. A self-deluding and opportunistic but intelligent man, he went to his death insisting that, although he had relied on Hitler for his power, Hitler had been his student in the realm of fascist political ideas. *See also* NORWAY.

R

R2Y1. *Keiun* (Lucky Cloud) (no Allied code name), a short-range, high-performance land-based Yokosuka aircraft developed for high-altitude reconnaissance from bases in Japan against naval forces. Two supercharged engines were mounted behind the cockpit, connected to the six-bladed single propeller by a 12-foot shaft. Its specifications called for a speed of 488 miles per hour at over 32,000 feet. Only one R2Y1 was produced; a jet-propelled R2Y2 was in the planning stage when the war ended.

R-4. America's first successful military helicopter, the R-4 was a descendant of Igor Sikorsky's single-rotor VS-300 of 1939. The R-4 carried a crew of two, seated side by side in an enclosed cabin. A single 180-horsepower Warner radial engine, located in the fuselage aft of the cabin, drove a 38-foot horizontal rotor and a small antitorque rotor mounted on the right side of a boom extending from the rear of the fuselage. Top speed was about 75 miles per hour, and the maximum range was 130 miles.

RABAUL. On January 23, 1942, the Japanese captured this important Australian base on Gazelle Peninsula at the eastern end of NEW BRITAIN. From Rabaul—with its two harbors, Simpson Harbor and Blanche Bay—the Japanese could dominate the entire NEW GUINEA–New Britain–SOLOMONS area, threaten Australia or even mount operations against that country and sever the line of communications from the United States to her ports. Hence, Rabaul was a prize whose recovery was paramount in Allied planning. By late 1942 the Japanese had made it the powerful hub of their air base system in what they called the Southeast Area. In September 1943, on the eve of the major Allied air offensive against Rabaul, the Japanese 11th Air Fleet based there numbered about 300 planes and 10,000 men, of whom perhaps 1,500 were flying personnel. In addition, at TRUK, some 795 miles away, were two carrier air groups with about 300 planes ready to reinforce Rabaul if needed.

In the early days of the war there were so few Allied planes in the South Pacific, with only a bare number of them having the range to attack Rabaul and return home, that the basic objective of Allied planners was the capture of air bases in the Solomons and the Bismarck Archipelago area within fighter plane range of Rabaul. These drives culminated in the landing on BOUGAINVILLE at EMPRESS AUGUSTA BAY on November 1, 1943, and at CAPE GLOUCESTER on New Britain nearly two months later.

The first major strike in the air offensive that eventually neutralized Rabaul (Rabaul was considered too strongly defended for an amphibious operation to be risked) was dispatched on October 12, 1943, by 349 SOUTHWEST PACIFIC AREA (FIFTH AIR FORCE) aircraft. From that date on, day and night raids were conducted by both land- and carrier-based planes. In all, 29,354 sorties were sent against the Japanese base and 20,967 tons of bombs were dropped. These were not milk runs, for the enemy had 367 antiaircraft guns, raising a strong steel umbrella over the target. All the troops in the area—some 91,000—were surrendered on September 6, 1945.

RADAR. *Ra*dio *d*etection *a*nd *r*anging (radar) equipment was in operational use by the Allies prior to the beginning of the war, having undergone a long and often hesitant development. There is no doubt about the significance of the contribution made by the invention: its possession by the Allies not only shortened the war but made victory possible at a lower cost in both men and machines.

Radar equipment of all kinds—land-based, shipboard and airborne—saw early, significant and continued use in the war. Its first contribution was the vital defensive part it played in the Battle of BRITAIN in 1940. In this case, radar was represented by an early-warning system, installed beginning in 1937 as the CHAIN HOME radar (RDF-1). For the United States, radar made its well-known debut at PEARL HARBOR, when two Army Signal Corps privates gave unheeded warning, 57 minutes in advance, of the Japanese air attack. Subsequently, the value of Allied radar was demonstrated with ever increasing frequency. Radar was responsible for forcing German submarines to operate underwater, thus decreasing their effectiveness. It made possible effective antiaircraft and shipboard fire control, well demonstrated during the second battle of SAVO ISLAND. It brought about accurate navigation for both airplanes and fighting ships during periods of limited visibility.

The evolution of radar is one of the world's classic examples of parallel discovery. It was not the invention of any one person but was an amalgamation of many related ideas, the first being Heinrich Hertz's discovery in 1880 that metal would reflect radio waves. The development reached culmination through key discoveries made from 1922 to 1939 by scientists in the U.S. Navy Research Laboratory and the U.S. Signal Corps Laboratory and by others in Britain and Germany. The efforts of the Allies bore fruit in spite of all sorts of problems: lack of money and support; competition from other systems, such as infrared; and state-of-the-art obstacles. The Germans had good radar equipment by 1940 and made considerable use of it, but the Japanese, who had only poor equipment available at the beginning of the war, never used radar effectively.

RADAR DEPTH. U.S. Navy term for a semi-submerged condition in which a submarine's upper conning tower was above the surface. Most wartime submarine torpedo-control RADARS had their antennas mounted on the conning tower; this was the only way in which they could be used. At this depth the submarine was slow and vulnerable to attack. Adoption of the ST periscope radar in 1945 was intended to correct this, because only the periscope was above the surface (although the range of this radar was shorter).

RADAR PICKET. U.S. Navy term for a RADAR-equipped ship stationed in a distant screen around an operating area to give early warning of approaching air attack. Radar picket ships were first extensively used in the OKINAWA operation (April–June 1945) to counter the Japanese KAMIKAZE aircraft, destroyers and destroyer escorts being used for the purpose.

RADFORD, Arthur William (1896–1973). A 1916 graduate of the U.S. Naval Academy, Radford won his wings in 1920. Promoted to rear admiral in 1942, Radford spent the early war years as director of aviation training, the citation for his performance in this post congratulating him for "sound and decisive judgment" and "consistently high standards." Ordered to sea in July 1943, he led air attacks on BAKER, MAKIN and TARAWA Islands. He later served in Vice-Adm. Marc A. MITSCHER's task force, his group conducting air strikes against Tokyo, Iwo JIMA, Kyushu and OKINAWA. He rose to full admiral following the war and served as chairman of the Joint Chiefs of Staff.

RADIO AND RADAR COUNTERMEASURES. General U.S. term, abbreviated RCM, describing what today are called ELECTRONIC COUNTERMEASURES (ECM). RCM included RADAR countermeasures (RADCM) alone, and communications countermeasures (COMCM). It covered the use of electronic devices (receivers, jammers) and mechanical devices (dummy radar reflectors, WINDOW).

RAEDER, Erich (1876–1960). German naval officer who entered the Imperial Navy in 1894, was promoted to the rank of commander in 1911 and saw active service in World War I—he survived the sinking of the battleship *Lützow* at Jutland. For a time after the war he conducted research in the naval archives. In 1925 he was promoted to vice-admiral and in 1928 to admiral, receiving the latter rank when he was appointed Chief of the Naval Staff (Chef der Marineleitung). In this office he devoted himself to the development of the GERMAN NAVY and was in full accord with the violations of the Versailles Treaty that were involved; he felt that without these secret moves, Germany would be unable to have any navy at all. It was during his tenure that the famous pocket battleships were designed (*see* PANZERSCHIFF), though he at first did not believe in the idea of commerce-raiding vessels. However, he reversed himself when he became convinced of the merit of these ships.

In 1935 Adolf HITLER appointed Raeder Commander in Chief of the Navy, and he was given the rank of Generaladmiral in the following year; in 1939 he was promoted to grand admiral (Grossadmiral). The war came earlier than Raeder had hoped or expected, and he found himself in command of a navy that was still quite small. Nevertheless, it gave a good account of itself in the invasion of NORWAY, though it suffered heavy losses. It was never in any position to challenge the British fleet. On January 30, 1943, Raeder, after strong disagreement with Hitler about the scrapping of heavy ships, retired from his post. Raeder was regarded as a highly professional officer, a strong disciplinarian and a hard worker. He was given a life sentence at Nuremberg but was released in 1955.

RAINBOW. Code name for a group of U.S. war plans, developed during the period beginning in mid-1939, to meet the possibility of a combined threat from the three Axis powers. Since the early 1900s colors had been used in war planning and war gaming to identify the various powers involved. Blue, for instance, meant the United States; Red identified Britain; Black was Germany; and Orange meant Japan. Since these new plans involved combinations of opponents, they were called Rainbow. Five Rainbow plans were eventually drawn up, each based on a different strategic situation. Rainbow 1 envisioned the United States going to war with no major allies, and was principally aimed at the defense of the Western Hemisphere and Hawaii. In Rainbow 2, the United States was allied with Britain and France. Some American forces would operate in Europe and the Atlantic, and an early Pacific offensive was planned. Rainbow 3 again had the United States entering a war without allies. The Western Hemisphere would be defended and an early offensive mounted in the Pacific. In Rainbow 4, the United States likewise had no allies and would go on the defensive in South America and the Pacific while carrying out operations in the Eastern Atlantic. Rainbow 5 involved Britain, France and the United States in an early joint offensive in Europe. The Pacific would be a defensive theater until success was assured in the Atlantic area. Work on these overall plans, and on related detailed service plans for their implementation, continued as World War II broke out and developed during 1939–41. The degree of emphasis placed on this or that Rainbow plan varied as the military situation changed.

RALSTON, James Layton (1881–1948). Minister of National Defence of Canada, 1940–44. His insistence on conscription as the only feasible method of reinforcing Canadian troops in the European theater in November 1944 provoked a political crisis which ended only with his resignation from the cabinet.

RAMCKE, Hermann Bernhard (1889–1968). German airborne commander who originally served in the old Imperial Navy, later transferring to the Reichswehr. He entered the parachute service in 1940; a major general in 1942, he commanded the 2d Parachute (Fallschirm) Brigade in Africa and later the 2d Parachute Division. In 1944, now a General der Fallschirmtruppen, he was in charge of the defense of BREST, where he was made prisoner by the U.S. 29th Division some days before the siege of the city ended.

RAMILLIES, H.M.S. Royal Navy battleship of 29,150 tons, built on the Clyde and completed by Cammell Laird in 1917, with an armament (in 1939) of eight 15-inch, twelve 6-inch and eight 4-inch guns, smaller weapons and four 21-inch torpedo tubes. Of her class, by 1939 too old and slow for many types of work, *Ramillies* had the most successful wartime career. In 1940–41 she was used on a variety of duties, mostly convoy escort, in both the Mediterranean and the ATLANTIC; in 1942 she served in the Indian Ocean, participating in the MADAGASCAR operations, at the end of which she was torpedoed by Japanese MIDGET SUBMARINES. After repairs she participated in both the Normandy INVASION and the SOUTHERN FRANCE landings of June and August 1944 in a bombardment role, before reduction to reserve at the end of 1944.

RAMSAY, Sir Bertram Home (1883–1945). One of the first officers in the Royal Navy to qualify as a staff officer; after a distinguished career he was placed on the retired list in 1938. During World War I Ramsay had spent two years in the Dover Patrol as a captain. On the outbreak of World War II he was the obvious choice, although still on the retired list, to become Flag Officer Dover, an appointment that in 1940 brought him responsibility for the evacuation of the BRITISH EXPEDITIONARY FORCE from DUNKIRK (Operation Dynamo) following the German breakthrough into France. After the operation Ramsay was called to London to report direct to the King, who knighted him on the spot.

In 1942 Admiral Ramsay was selected to command the Allied navies assembled for the invasion of NORTHWEST AFRICA, but there were some objections raised at so great a naval fleet being placed under the command of an admiral still on the retired list. This problem was solved by bringing Adm. Sir Andrew CUNNINGHAM back from the United States to take over the chief naval command, with Ramsay as his deputy. The North African landings, which owed much to Ramsay's initial planning and his later work as liaison officer between British and American authorities, were completely successful, and he followed this by planning for the assault on SICILY, commanding the Eastern Task Force at the actual landings.

In 1943 Ramsay was restored to the active list. He returned to England to become naval commander in chief of the Allied Expeditionary Force for the INVASION of Normandy. All the naval planning (Operation Neptune) fell to him—the sweeping of the enemy minefields, the putting ashore of five divisions on the coast of France in the face of the enemy and the whole burden of supplying reinforcements and replenishment to follow the first landings. It was all a brilliant success, and this greatest of all combined operations was achieved at a cost in casualties far less than had been expected. As the Allied armies advanced through France, Belgium and Holland, Ramsay set up his headquarters outside Paris to be nearer the scene of operations. It was while at his headquarters, in January 1945, that he lost his life when the aircraft in which he was to travel to attend a conference at 21st Army Group headquarters crashed on takeoff.

RAM TANK. A Canadian "cruiser TANK" (a relatively fast, lightly armored type) design developed during 1940–41, incorporating many mechanical components of the American M3 tank (*see* M3) but with a Canadian-designed hull, turret and gun. The finished product had the distinctive suspension of the M3 (very similar to that of the M4 Sherman), with a hull and turret vaguely suggestive of the M4. The name Ram, inspired by the family coat of arms of the chief of the Canadian armored forces, was given the new vehicle. The Ram I had a British 2-pounder (40-mm.) gun, while the Ram II was armed with a 6-pounder (57-mm.).

RANGER, U.S.S. Aircraft carrier, commissioned in 1934. The 14,500-ton *Ranger* was a specimen of the "small carrier" advocated at that time by some officers as preferable to bigger ships. Her wartime service was in the Atlantic, where her planes supported the 1942 landings in North Africa. She carried about 80 aircraft.

RANGERS. The U.S. Army Rangers were the American counterparts of the British COMMANDOS. They were specially trained and equipped soldiers who carried out surprise raids behind enemy lines, usually involving demolition and intelligence work. As light infantry, the Rangers also received training in beach assaults. Normally they were among the first units ashore in an amphibious operation.

Heirs to the tradition of Robert Rogers and his Rangers of 1757 in the French and Indian War, the Rangers of World War II were organized in 1942 and 1943 from volunteers. Rather than redesignating existing infantry battalions, the War Department decided that units involved in special or unconventional warfare should be made up entirely of volunteers.

Six Ranger battalions were organized during the war. The 1st Ranger Battalion was activated on June 19, 1942, at Carrickfergus, Northern Ireland. As did many others who fought for the Allies in special warfare, members of this unit trained with the Commandos in Scotland. The next Ranger battalion was the 2d, activated on April 1, 1943, in Tennessee. It was followed by two provisional battalions, the 3d and 4th, organized in North Africa on May 21 and 29, 1943, respectively. The final two battalions, the 5th and 6th, were activated on July 21, 1943, and September 25, 1944. The 6th Battalion was converted and redesignated from the 98th Field Artillery.

The six Ranger battalions saw their full share of combat operations. The 1st through 5th Battalions served in the European, North African and Middle Eastern theaters. Only the 6th Battalion fought in the Pacific theater. In official Army records, the Rangers are credited with having served in the following campaigns: Algeria-Morocco; Tunisia; Sicily; Naples-Foggia; Anzio; Rome-Arno; Normandy; Northern France; Southern France; Rhineland; Ardennes-Alsace; Central Europe; Aleutian Islands; New Guinea; Leyte; and Luzon.

Two other U.S. infantry units, although not part of the Rangers, nevertheless carried out unconventional warfare operations: the 1st Special Service Force, established on July 9, 1942, and the 5307th Composite Unit (Provisional). The 1st Special Service Force was trained to operate behind enemy lines when snow covered Europe. It was made up of volunteers, such as lumberjacks, game wardens and professional skiers, who had skills applicable to this kind of work. It was an unusual unit in that about half its personnel came from Canada. The experiment in U.S.–Canadian cooperation worked well, and the unit performed very creditably in France.

The 5307th Composite Unit, better known as MERRILL'S MARAUDERS, was organized in October 1943 and operated along the LEDO ROAD in Burma under Brig. Gen. Frank D. MERRILL. All its volunteers were trained in jungle fighting. The unit was subsequently reorganized on August 10, 1944, as the 475th Infantry Regiment.

RANGOON. Rangoon, capital of BURMA and an important port, served for the Allies as the principal point of entry for critical China-bound supplies prior to the first months of 1942. The city, suffering from more than two months of Japanese aerial bombardment, fell on March 6, 1942, to elements of the Japanese 15th Army as it began its quest to capture all of Burma. Allied fortunes turned in 1944 and 1945, but not without effort; the British FOURTEENTH ARMY, commanded by Lt. Gen. Sir William SLIM, met considerable resistance in a six-month campaign to retake Rangoon. After the reoccupation of most of central Burma, General Slim sent his motorized 5th and 17th Indian Divisions and the bulk of his armor by road and rail from Mandalay to Rangoon, bypassing formidable Japanese forces. On April 27, 1945, as the 17th Indian Division neared Rangoon, several task groups of the British 26th Indian Division put to sea for air and amphibious assaults on the port city. An attack on Rangoon's seaward defenses began on May 1, and the city, whose name means "end of strife," was reoccupied by the British on May 3.

RANKIN PLANS. Allied contingency plans relating to possible return to the European continent under various conditions. Rankin A was a plan to return in case German strength should give evidence of weakening at some time before the scheduled date for the Normandy invasion. Rankin B was a plan to land if the Germans withdrew from France or Norway. Rankin C was a plan to return in case of German unconditional surrender.

RAPIDO RIVER. Italian river flowing past the foot of Monte CASSINO to a junction with the Liri River, the two combining to form the Garigliano. In January 1944 Allied plans called for multiple crossings of the swollen stream, behind which was the GUSTAV LINE, coincident with an "end run" landing at ANZIO. A diversionary attack by French divisions of the U.S. FIFTH ARMY succeeded in getting a foothold inside the Gustav Line, and downstream, forces of the British 10th Corps gained a small bridgehead over the Garigliano (another attempt failing), which drew German reserves to the sector. In the main attack (January 20) by the U.S. II Corps, the 36th Infantry Division encountered intense opposition, took heavy casualties and on January 22 abandoned the tiny bridgehead the troops had established. On January 24 and 25 a regiment of the 34th Infantry Division got across upstream from Cassino, but the offensive as a whole was deemed a failure. The Rapido downstream from Cassino was not crossed until May 11, when the British 13th Corps did so as part of a fresh and successful Allied offensive. The Rapido attack by the 36th Division generated much controversy, including an inconclusive postwar Congressional investigation.

RASCHER, Sigmund (1909–1945). One of the worst of the Nazi criminal doctors, Rascher was originally attached to the Luftwaffe but later seconded to the SS. He carried out secret experiments at DACHAU concentration camp in 1941–42, investigating the reactions of the human body in high-pressure chambers and its resistance to cold. Seventy out of the 200 men he used died following the first group of tests, and 90 following the second group. Heinrich HIMMLER, the SS chief, took a personal interest in these experiments, which were subsequently revealed to have had no scientific validity. The facts were exposed during the Doctors' Trial in Nuremberg from December 1946 to July 1947. But Rascher was not there to answer for his crimes. He and his wife had been arrested in 1944 for child abduction, and Himmler, who had acted as "godfather" to the Raschers' supposed children, found he had been deceived. Rascher was shot at Dachau and his wife hanged.

RASEINIAI. The scene of a surprise for the Wehrmacht on the northern front in Russia, when on June 24, 1941, superheavy Soviet KV-1 and KV-2 TANKS gave the advancing German panzers a hard battle. But the Germans' superior skill at that time in handling armor still won the day.

RASHID ALI (1892–1944?). Iraqi politician who resigned as Premier in January 1941 but in April led an Axis-supported coup d'état that established a "government of national defense." In May fighting broke out between Rashid Ali's forces and the British garrison at HABBANIYA air base, and after further conflict Baghdad was occupied by the British and Rashid Ali fled to Iran. The dash of the British column from Transjordan to Habbaniya was one of the most spectacular strokes in that phase of the war.

RASTENBURG. A town in East Prussia having historical links with the Teutonic Knights, Rastenburg became notable because Adolf HITLER established in the pine forests nearby his military headquarters known as the WOLF'S LAIR (Wolfsschanze). It was here on July 20, 1944, that the celebrated attempt on his life was made by Count von STAUFFENBERG acting for the German resistance movement.

RAT EXPRESS. Japanese nickname for the transfer of troops by means of destroyers trying to make a stealthy run in the dark of night. *See also* ANT TRANSPORT.

RAVENSBRÜCK. Nazi CONCENTRATION CAMP in Mecklenburg; it was established for female prisoners.

RAWALPINDI, H.M.S. Royal Navy armed merchant cruiser, formerly a Peninsular & Oriental Steamship Co. liner, of 16,697 tons. *Rawalpindi*, equipped with a weak armament of hand-loaded 6-inch guns, encountered the German battle cruisers SCHARNHORST and GNEISENAU on November 23, 1939, and was sunk with heavy loss of life after a brief action of 14 minutes. Her captain, E. C. Kennedy, went down with his ship, one of a school of British naval captains who regarded it as their duty to do so.

RAWLINGS, Sir (Henry) Bernard H. (1889–1962). Captain of the British battleship VALIANT at the outbreak of the Second World War. On promotion to flag rank in 1940, Admiral Rawlings commanded the 1st Battle Cruiser Squadron in the Home Fleet before being sent to the Mediterranean in 1941 to command the 7th Cruiser Squadron, in which he saw some of the fierce fighting around Greece and CRETE and along the North African coast. After other appointments he was selected as second-in-command of the British Pacific Fleet for the last part of the war against Japan and commanded the British task forces during all their operations in that ocean. He retired in 1946.

RAYBURN, Sam (1882–1961). A strong ally of President ROOSEVELT, Rayburn was elected Democratic leader of the U.S. House of Representatives in 1937 and in 1940 became Speaker of the House. Renowned as a master parliamentarian, he presided over the House during one of the closest and most important votes in its history—the passage, by 203 to 202, of the extension of the SELECTIVE SERVICE Act in 1941. He went on to serve as Speaker longer than anyone else in American history.

RAZON. The VB-3 guided bomb, developed by the U.S. Army Air Forces. Like the AZON, it was a 1,000-pound general-purpose bomb with a special tail section fitted. The Razon was released from a conventional bombsight at a high altitude. Two bombardiers, using special sights, controlled it, one each in range and azimuth (bearing). Control switches transmitted radio signals to a receiver in the tail of the bomb, activating the ailerons to make small corrections in its flight. A colored flare in the tail of the bomb, ignited after release, permitted the bombardiers to follow its fall.

R-BOAT. German light motor minesweeper, comparable in size to a motor torpedo boat, called Raumboot (R-boot). It was also used for light patrol and convoy work.

RDX. Also called cyclotrimethylenetrinitramine or cyclonite. A powerful explosive discovered in 1899 but not extensively used until World War II. Both Allies and Axis used it in detonators and as an ingredient for bursting charges for bombs and shells; it was too sensitive to be used alone. RDX was called T4 by the Italians and Hexogen by the Germans.

RE-2000. The Reggiane *Falco* I (Falcon) closely resembled the Seversky P-35 (*see* P-35). This low-wing, single-seat airplane, though exceptionally maneuverable, lost out to the Macchi C-200 (*see* C-200) in the Italian 1938 fighter competition. The Italian Navy, however, outfitted one squadron with the Falcon I and tested a few as catapult fighters. Another 170 were sold to the governments of Sweden and Hungary. The plane's greatest failing was its inadequate armament, a pair of 12.7-mm. machine guns.

By installing a 1,175-horsepower liquid-cooled Alfa Romeo engine in place of the 986-horsepower Piaggio radial, Reggiane increased the speed slightly at no sacrifice in maneuverability. The Re-2001 Falcon II joined the ITALIAN AIR FORCE, and after Italy's surrender participated as a night fighter in the defense of German-held northern Italy. The usual armament was two 12.7-mm. and two 7.7-mm. machine guns, but the night-fighter version carried one 20-mm. cannon under each wing.

Another offshoot of Falcon I was the radial-powered Re-2002 *Ariete* (Ram), which saw action as a fighter-bomber and reconnaissance plane. This craft could carry 1,433 pounds of bombs and the usual four machine guns.

RE-2005. The Reggiane *Sagittaria* (Archer) was among the most heavily armed of Italian fighters, mounting three 20-mm. cannon and two 12.7-mm. machine guns. A 1,475-horsepower liquid-cooled Fiat engine gave the handsome low-wing monoplane a top speed of 390 miles per hour. This single-seat fighter appeared in 1943 and served mostly with Italian units that cast their lot with the Germans. During the collapse of the European Axis, the plane fought in northern Italy, Hungary and Germany. Fewer than 300 were built.

RECKLESS. Code name of U.S. operation against HOLLANDIA, New Guinea, April 1944.

RED AIR FORCE. The Germans had close to 3,000 aircraft at their disposal in eastern Europe when the invasion of the Soviet Union was launched. Opposing this armada the Soviets had more than 7,500 planes, including 3,000 fighters. Even so, the LUFTWAFFE greatly outclassed the Red air units in experience, equipment and training. None of the numerous types of Soviet fighters were a match for the MESSERSCHMITT ME 109. All other categories of Soviet aircraft either fell short of or merely matched their German counterparts. But of prime importance was the clear fact that the German attack surprised the Russians and the preliminary strikes on Soviet air bases wreaked havoc. This factor and the generally poor showing of those Soviet fighters that did get airborne resulted in the destruction of nearly 3,000 Red aircraft in the first 10 days of fighting.

Losses continued at an extremely high rate throughout the remainder of the year. Had it not been for individual acts of extreme heroism and the dogged determination of all involved to defeat the enemy, the air war would likely have been lost. That the Luftwaffe was overcommitted soon became apparent, as German air units were constantly shifted from front to front and even between theaters. Actions such as that at VORONEZH proved that Soviet air units could function well given the right leadership (Sergei RUDENKO) and equipment. At STALINGRAD Gen. Alexander GOLOVANOV's Long Range Bomber Command aircraft transported troops and supplies to the beleaguered defenders. By now (late 1942) German air supremacy was on the wane, and concentrated Soviet attacks against German forward air bases further limited the Luftwaffe's effectiveness. Through 1943 and 1944, aided by increasing numbers of aircraft and by the U.S.–British strategic bombing in the west, Soviet air superiority grew. Close air support of ground operations became a major effort of the Soviet air force, and the ILYUSHIN IL-2 Stormovik became one of the better-known aircraft of the war, using as it did the first aircraft rockets against armor.

By the end of the war the Red Air Force had 18 air armies equipped with the newest aircraft, such as the YAKOVLEV YAK-3, a fast, low-altitude fighter. By late 1944 the Soviets were even able to go over to the offensive in the air, conducting bombing raids on Budapest and other central European targets. *See also* SOVIET-GERMAN OPERATIONS.

RED ARMY. On June 22, 1941, the date of the German invasion, the USSR had on her western front about 3 million men; another 1 million were serving in other parts of the country. Peak strength reached during the war was about 12.5 million. The Soviet armies in contact with the Germans were organized in July 1941 in three "theaters," or groups of fronts: Marshal Kliment VOROSHILOV's Northwest Front (32 divisions), Marshal Semën TIMOSHENKO's Western Front (47 divisions) and Marshal Semën BUDËNNY's Southwest Front (69 divisions). These theaters were frequently reorganized during the war as the strategic situation changed.

The Red Army was the product of the Bolshevik Revolution, and until 1935 had no saluting and, in fact, no rank system. In the following years, however, it was made much more conventional and soldiers were given increased pay and amenities.

Like most armies, the Red Army was made up principally of infantry (rifle) divisions, which in the first year and a half of the war increased from 175 to 442. Prior to the German successes in western Europe in 1940, Soviet tank strength was dispersed throughout the Army, rather than being gathered into armored divisions; some reorganization along panzer division lines had been completed when the Germans struck.

In 1941 the Russians had very large numbers of tanks and aircraft (but most of this equipment was obsolete). A unique feature of the Red Army in 1941 was the existence of 30 cavalry regiments, which proved of some value in the Russian climate and terrain. *See also* SOVIET-GERMAN OPERATIONS.

RED ARMY GENERAL STAFF (Generalnyi Shtab RKKA). On January 14, 1941, Georgi ZHUKOV, a relatively junior officer, was appointed Chief of Staff in place of Gen. Kiril MERETSKOV. In July, following the German invasion of the Soviet Union, Joseph STALIN sent Zhukov to aid Marshal Klimenti VOROSHILOV in the defense of LENINGRAD, and Gen. Boris SHAPOSHNIKOV, a previous Chief of Staff, took the position again. In June 1942 severe illness forced Shaposhnikov to retire to less strenuous duties; the chief of operations, Gen. A. M. VASILEVKSY, was appointed to succeed him. Gen. A. I. ANTONOV took Vasilevsky's place as chief of operations and subsequently was named Deputy Chief of Staff. (These positions were not simply desk jobs; Marshal S. M. SHTEMENKO has observed that Vasilevsky and Antonov were often sent to the front by Stalin to help with operations.) In October 1944 Antonov was appointed Acting Chief of the General Staff; in April 1945 he received the full appointment and held the post until the end of the war. The General Staff served as the tactical working group for the SOVIET HIGH COMMAND.

RED BALL EXPRESS. An improvised one-way truck transport system that supplied fuel and provisions for the swift Allied advance through France in the late summer of 1944. Between August 29 and September 15, 6,000 trucks carried 135,000 tons of supplies on two highways between Saint-Lô and Chartres. Truck companies competing to be first-with-the-most ignored traffic regulations, speed limits and wear and tear on their vehicles to get supplies forward and keep Allied armies moving. The system was improvised by Maj. Gen. Frank A. Ross, chief of transportation.

RED CROSS. Established in 1863 as an international humanitarian agency dedicated to the treatment of wounded combatants regardless of the side they fought on, the Red Cross served ably in World War II. It not only collected whole blood from donors to be used as

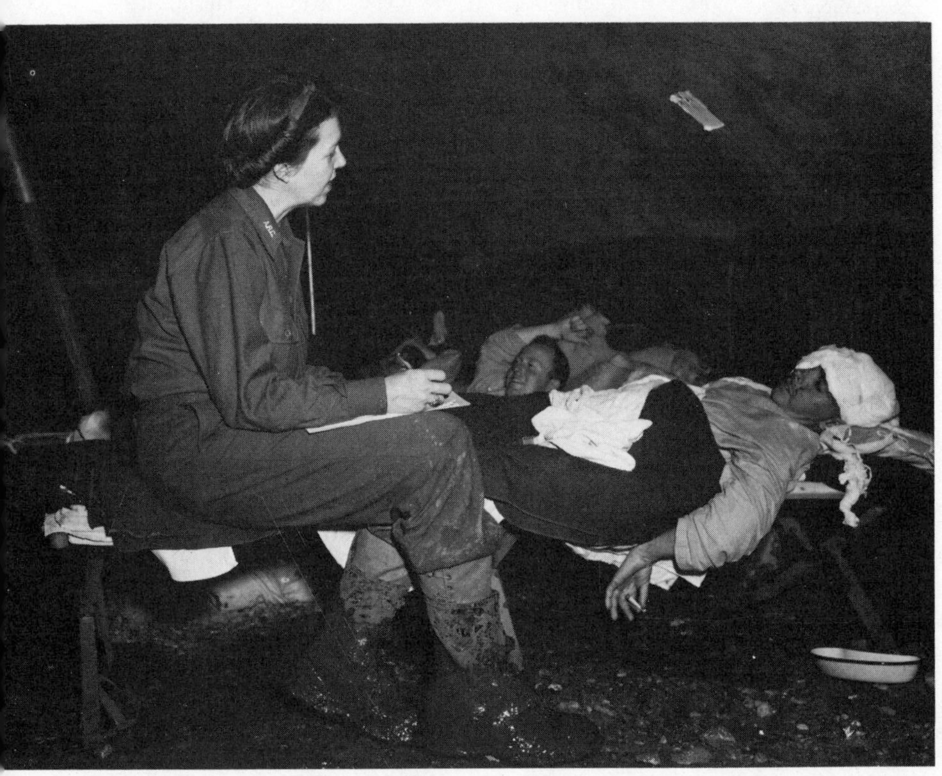

At an evacuation hospital in Italy, a Red Cross worker writes a letter home for a wounded American soldier

plasma, but also provided ambulances, hospitals and medical and nursing care to wounded soldiers and civilian victims of war. It operated canteens for troops in transit, located families and friends displaced by war, conducted major relief programs for war refugees and gave courses in first aid and nutrition to volunteers.

REDFISH, U.S.S. BALAO-class submarine, completed in 1944, that disposed of two Japanese carriers in December 1944, damaging and putting out of service the JUNYO on December 9 and sinking the new *Unryu* on December 19. The skipper of the *Redfish* was Comdr. L. D. "Sandy" McGregor.

RED HOUSE. The "Commissar's House," this brick strongpoint was the scene of fierce fighting at STALINGRAD on November 9, 1942.

REDLINE. Radio circuits set up in September 1944 for communication between the Supreme Allied Commander in Europe and the army group commanders.

RED NAVY. The German plan for the invasion of the Soviet Union in 1941 was almost exclusively for a land campaign. The only naval operation coordinated into the plan called for a few units of the GERMAN NAVY to support Army Group North in its drive on LENINGRAD. Five submarines and a small force of motor torpedo boats and minesweepers comprised the forces assigned. The Soviet Baltic Fleet, on the other hand, consisted of 2 battleships, 3 cruisers, about 40 destroyers, over 90 submarines and 20 minelayers. The Germans planned to neutralize or destroy the bulk of this fleet by combined air attack and ground operations designed to capture the several significant naval bases along the axis of advance.

When the German invasion began, the Soviet Navy was not prepared. The purges of the 1930s had affected naval leadership as well as that of the other armed forces. Adm. Nikolai G. KUZNETSOV, the Commissar of the Navy, had had only two years (from April 1939) to try to rebuild the fleet; neither the building program nor his other reforms had had time to be tested. This unpreparedness was immediately apparent. During the first six months of the war the Germans lost only one cargo ship, the 3,700-ton *Baltenland,* to torpedoes (and two to mines), while the Soviets lost about 25 submarines, mostly to German mines in the waters near KRONSTADT. Results were equally poor in the Black Sea and in the Arctic.

The German air attack along with the effort mounted by the Finnish Air Force destroyed the major part of the Red Navy's air arm in the first weeks of the war. What remained was transferred to serve with the air armies supporting the RED ARMY. By the end of 1941 most of the Soviet fleet still afloat in the Baltic was under the antiaircraft cover of Leningrad's defenses, where the ships' guns were made a part of the artillery support available to the defenders and the ships' crews went ashore to fight as infantry. Many sailors, for instance, took part in the defense of the Gangut peninsula at the mouth of the Gulf of Finland.

To the south, the German drive into the Ukraine and the CRIMEA and their absolute mastery of the air forced the Soviet Black Sea Fleet into a seaport-defense role. It was not until later in the war that Red naval units ventured to sea and participated in several important amphibious operations. In the Barents Sea, Soviet submarines operated with only moderate success against enemy convoys heading for Kirkenes and Petsamo.

According to Soviet claims, 3.6 million tons of enemy shipping were sunk by submarine attack from 1941 to 1945. Western estimates put the total at a more modest 300,000 tons. In any case, the point can be made that the Red Fleet's submarines took the lead in carrying the war to the enemy, while the general rule for surface ships was passive defense. Only the motor torpedo boats of the "mosquito fleets" achieved any creditable results, and then not until late in the war.

Since the time of the Civil War the Navy had been more or less subordinated to the Army in the chain of command, and it remained so during the war years, with naval units under the operational control of the local army front commander. As much as any other factor, this restricted seaborne operations to flank support of land actions, convoying, integration into the defense of cities and logistic resupply. Similarly, the Navy's loss of the air arm served to restrict the fleet's activities, since it gave the Germans almost uncontested air superiority over the seas and increased the vulnerability of Soviet ships to air attack. Two aspects of the Navy's contribution do deserve mention, however, as having been significant: the river flotillas and the naval infantry units. Forty-two brigades of naval infantry and a number of independent battalions served in ground combat roles, especially at Leningrad and on the Black Sea, and the flotillas supported land operations.

The Navy's losses during the war included a battleship and a cruiser, both sunk by enemy air attack, and about 36 destroyers. A number of unfinished ships on the stocks at Leningrad and Nikolayev were damaged, most of them beyond recovery. Over 50 submarines were sunk, although about the same number were built during the war years. No major surface ships were constructed in the Soviet Union during that period. Added to the Red Fleet were a British battleship, a U.S. cruiser and numerous lesser ships, all loaned to the USSR and all subsequently returned.

At the end of the war, the USSR collected its share of naval booty—a number of vessels from the Italian Navy, which had surrendered in 1943, and an undetermined quantity of intact submarines, hulls, machinery and tools from the Germans.

RED OCTOBER PLANT. A factory in the STALINGRAD industrial district, scene of intense and prolonged fighting October–December 1942.

RED ORCHESTRA. Known to the Germans as Rote Kapelle, the Red Orchestra was one of the most successful intelligence networks of the war. Under the direction of Leopold Trepper, a Polish Communist, the network controlled agents and informers throughout Nazi-occupied Europe, including an officer in the Luftwaffe high command in Berlin. Though broken by Nazi counterintelligence in 1942, the organization had channeled thousands of intelligence reports to the chief intelligence directorate of the Red Army in Moscow.

REEVES, John Walter (1888–1967). A U.S. Naval Academy graduate of 1911, Reeves earned his wings in 1936. He fitted out the carrier WASP and served as her commanding officer in 1939–42. In the latter year he became a rear admiral and took command of the Alaska sector of the NORTHWESTERN SEA FRONTIER. In 1943–44 he commanded a Pacific Fleet carrier division, and during the last months of the war held a command in the Caroline Islands. Following the war he served as chief of naval air training at Pensacola, Fla.

REGENSBURG. Target of a massive daylight attack by U.S. EIGHTH AIR FORCE B-17s on August 17, 1943. *See also* B-17; SCHWEINFURT.

REGGIO DI CALABRIA. Site of the landing of the British EIGHTH ARMY in ITALY, September 3, 1943.

REICH DEFENSE COUNCIL (Reichsverteidigungsrat). A group established by Adolf HITLER in 1933 originally to stimulate secret rearmament. It met only twice (as in 1939 to discuss mobilization for war), but various committees did considerable work. The chairman was Hermann GÖRING.

REICHENAU, Walther von (1884–1942). A strong German Army proponent of National Socialism even before Adolf HITLER came to power, Reichenau seems to have seen the Nazi movement as a vehicle for his own advancement. He supported Hitler at the time of the RÖHM purge in 1934, and he commanded ever larger army formations during the Austrian crisis of 1938, the Polish campaign in 1939 and the French campaign in 1940; in July 1940 he was one of nine generals advanced to field marshal by the Führer. In the invasion of the Soviet Union in 1941, Reichenau commanded the SIXTH ARMY. He died of a stroke in January 1942, shortly after taking over Field Marshal von RUNDSTEDT's Army Group South.

REICHSTAG FIRE. On February 27, 1933, barely a week before the decisive German elections of March 5, a student passing the Reichstag (parliament building) at 9:05 in the evening saw a half-naked man with a burning brand silhouetted against a window on the first floor of the building. By 9:27 the great session chamber was exploding in flames; meanwhile the student and other witnesses had summoned the police and firemen. The half-naked youth was found to be a Dutchman, Marinus van der Lubbe, an arsonist who boasted he alone had caused the conflagration. Adolf HITLER and Hermann GÖRING immediately seized on the fire as the work of Communist conspirators; it was, they alleged, the prelude to a coup d'état. Wholesale arrests were ordered, including those of Georgi Dimitroff and other noted Communists, who were later charged with arson along with van der Lubbe. However, it was plain that the chamber had been well prepared with inflammable chemicals, and it was universally suspected that the Nazis themselves were guilty, using van der Lubbe as a willing scapegoat. At the trial the following September, the Communists proved that they were not involved, but van der Lubbe was executed. Since the war the controversy has continued as to whether or not the Nazis were implicated. In a lengthy book on the subject, *Der Reichstagsbrand* (1962), Fritz Tobias sought to exonerate them; more recently, a team of historians led by Prof. Walther Hofer of Bern University sought, in *Der Reichstagsbrand* (1972), to reestablish Nazi complicity.

REIMS. Gen. Dwight EISENHOWER established SUPREME HEADQUARTERS, ALLIED EXPEDITIONARY FORCE (SHAEF) in this city in northern France early in 1945. The headquarters was in a red brick building of a boys' school, the Collège Moderne et Technique des Garçons, Ecole Supérieur de Commerce. On May 5–7 it was the site of negotiations for the general surrender of German forces. HITLER's successor, Grand Admiral Karl DÖNITZ, sent representatives to Reims authorized to surrender only the troops on the Western Front, in hopes of withdrawing more men from the Russian front to surrender to the West. Since Allied agreements stipulated a simultaneous capitulation on the two fronts, Eisenhower refused, and threatened to end negotiations. At 2:41 A.M. on May 7, Col. Gen. Alfred JODL signed a general surrender. Soviet authorities wanted a second surrender, which took place before Allied representatives the next day in Berlin.

REINECKE, Hermann (1888–1972). German Army officer (General der Infanterie, 1942), a supporter of the Nazis who on July 20, 1944, after the attempt on Adolf HITLER's life, took command of troops in Berlin loyal to the Führer. He was closely connected with the People's Court and its notorious judge, Roland FREISLER. Reinecke was sentenced to life imprisonment for involvement in war crimes.

REINHARDT, Georg-Hans (1887–1963). German Army officer who in the invasion of the Low Countries and FRANCE in 1940 commanded the XLI Panzer Corps in KLEIST's panzer group. Following the fall of France, the corps was shifted to the Eastern Front for the invasion of Russia as a part of Gen. Erich HOEPNER's Fourth Panzer Army in LEEB's Army Group North. With over 60 percent of Hoepner's armor under his command, Reinhardt initially attacked Kovno. After that city fell, Reinhardt's tanks sped toward LENINGRAD where they cracked the perimeter of the city on September 12, 1941. At that point they had reached what was probably the closest advance that the Germans would make to Leningrad.

In October 1941 Reinhardt took over Gen. Hermann HOTH's Third Panzer Group in the late autumn drive on Moscow. Reinhardt's forces fought almost continuously throughout 1942 and 1943 as part of Army Group Center's continuing offensive. On August 16, 1944, Reinhardt was made commander of Army Group Center, which shortly thereafter had to fall back to defend East Prussia, especially KÖNIGSBERG, against the Soviet incursion. Unable to offer effective resistance to the Russian offensive, he was relieved of command on January 26, 1945. His highest rank was colonel general.

REITSCH, Hanna (1912–). German flier, the only woman to be awarded the IRON CROSS during the war. Originally a medical student, she quit to indulge her passion for gliding and flying (she once held the world gliding record for women—five and a half hours). Her niche in history comes from the fact that it was she who flew Gen. Ritter von GREIM to Berlin on April 26, 1945, in response to HITLER'S summons to the general, who was appointed Commander in Chief of the LUFTWAFFE, in succession to Hermann GÖRING. It was a hazardous flight and the plane was hit over the Tiergarten by Russian antiaircraft fire; Ritter von Greim was wounded in the foot. Her role in the endeavor seems to have stirred Reitsch, a fervent Nazi, who wrote an account of life in the Führerbunker in those final days. Following the war she resumed her flying career in various countries, becoming the friend of such national leaders as Indira Gandhi and Kwame Nkrumah.

REMAGEN. Site of a strategic railway bridge—the Ludendorff Bridge—over the Rhine named after the World War I commander Erich Ludendorff. On March 7, 1945, members of the U.S. 9th Armored Division tried to seize the bridge just as German engineers prepared to blow it. The explosion damaged the bridge but left it still standing. Under cover of tank fire the riflemen reached the east bank to establish the first Allied bridgehead across the Rhine. The bridge collapsed 10 days later, but not before adequate tactical bridges were in place. In American annals there is no military operation more decisive in its impact on the enemy.

REMER, Otto Ernst (1912–). As a German Army major commanding the guard battalion at Döberitz, outside Berlin, Remer was one of the principal officers upon whom the anti-HITLER conspirators relied on July 20, 1944, to put a cordon round the Wilhelmstrasse in Berlin. Instead Remer, a convinced Nazi and a brave soldier who held the Knight's Cross with Oak Leaves, placed himself at the disposal of Joseph GOEBBELS, the only Nazi minister in Berlin on the day of the attempt on Hitler's life. Goebbels put Remer in direct touch with Hitler on the telephone; the major was created a colonel on the spot, and took his orders directly from Hitler and Goebbels in the action to suppress the conspirators. It was his men who supplied the execution squad that shot STAUFFENBERG and his associates. After the war Remer was leader of the neo-Nazi Socialist Reich Party in 1949–52. In 1952 he was sentenced by a court in Brunswick to four months' imprisonment for his denigration of the German resistance to Hitler. But instead of serving his sentence, he escaped, apparently fleeing to Egypt. *See also* OPPOSITION TO HITLER.

RENARD R-31. Belgian two-place, single-engine tactical reconnaissance and Army liaison plane. It was the only aircraft of Belgian design and construction to be

U.S. First Army men and equipment cross the Ludendorff Bridge, Remagen

used operationally in the 18 days of Belgian resistance in 1940.

RENDOVA. Island in the southern portion of the NEW GEORGIA group, separated from the island of New Georgia by Blanche Channel. Troops of the U.S. 43d Division landed on Rendova on June 30, 1943, and secured the island on July 2, at which time the buildup for the invasion of MUNDA began.

RENDULIC, Lothar (1887–1971). German Army officer who came from an old Austrian family of soldiers. He began his military service as a member of the Austrian General Staff and subsequently served as military attaché in London and Paris. During this period he became a fervent admirer of National Socialism. In the German Army he served on the Eastern Front from 1941, rising to corps commander. In August 1943 he was transferred to the Balkans, where he commanded the II Panzer Corps. In July 1944 Rendulic took charge of German troops in Finland (20th Mountain Army) in succession to Gen. Eduard DIETL, who was killed in a plane crash. Admired by Adolf HITLER, Rendulic in January 1945 began a series of army group commands on the Eastern Front (Army Groups North, Kurland and South). The designations underwent various changes, and Rendulic at one time or another was on every part of the narrowing front. In April he took command of Army Group South, covering VIENNA. His highest rank was colonel general.

RENNELL ISLAND, BATTLE OF. In late January 1943, unaware that the Japanese were preparing to evacuate GUADALCANAL, Adm. William F. HALSEY's intelligence staff predicted a large-scale effort to reinforce the island. U.S. Army troops were due to land on Guadalcanal at the end of the month, and to protect this movement, powerful surface forces were deployed. Close support was the responsibility of Rear Adm. Robert C. GIFFEN's Task Force 18, which advanced toward Guadalcanal from the south on the afternoon of January 29. Japanese land-based planes shadowed the American force through that afternoon; submarines also tracked Giffen and reported his movements. American fighter cover retired at dusk, and Giffen continued on without air screening. His six cruisers steamed in two parallel columns at 24 knots, his eight destroyers deployed in an arc ahead of them—a poor formation for defense against air attack. But, newly arrived in the Pacific from the Mediterranean, Giffen had had no experience of heavy Japanese aerial opposition, and he left his force with no orders concerning it.

G4M Betty twin-engine, land-based bombers (*see* G4M) delivered a torpedo attack just after dusk, without result. TF 18 continued on course, formation unchanged. Scout planes marked the movement of the American force with floating lights and flares; a second Betty attack hit heavy cruiser LOUISVILLE with a dud torpedo. Some bombers were knocked down by antiaircraft fire. Air attacks continued, and a crashing Betty splattered heavy cruiser CHICAGO with burning gasoline. More bombers aimed for this illuminated target; *Chicago* was hit by two torpedoes in succession. Flooding was followed by loss of power; the cruiser went dead in the water as her damage-control parties tried to keep her afloat. But the Japanese pilots lost track of the task force in the darkness, and soon turned away. *Chicago*'s crew got matters under control and restored some boiler power. The ship was taken under tow, and slowly made off toward Espiritu Santo.

With morning, air cover was once more provided. Two Japanese "snooper" planes appeared; the first was shot down, but the second got away. Under orders to leave *Chicago* and proceed to the New Hebrides—by this time the original plan was a dead letter—Giffen and the rest of his force parted company from her in midafternoon. *Chicago,* towed by a fleet tug and screened by six destroyers, continued at her slow pace. Shortly after 4 P.M., 12 Bettys were spotted by American carrier fighters on combat air patrol. The bombers were heading for carrier ENTERPRISE, operating some distance away, but, seeing the protecting fighters, turned on *Chicago.* Fighters shot down three Bettys, but the remaining nine dove to the attack. More bombers fell to antiaircraft guns and pursuing F4Fs (*see* F4F), but *Chicago* took three torpedoes. She went down at about 4:45.

Although *Chicago* had finally been lost, the planned American reinforcement of Guadalcanal proceeded unharmed. The Japanese bomber force had focused on Giffen's task force while the transports offloaded their soldiers without aerial opposition. Japanese night torpedo attack doctrine had been proved sound. Until new weapons and procedures could be developed to deal with it, it would continue to be a menace.

RENNES. City at the base of the Brittany peninsula (France), taken by troops of the U.S. 8th Division, THIRD ARMY, on August 4, 1944.

RENOWN, H.M.S. Royal Navy battle cruiser of 32,000 tons, completed in 1916 and modernized and reconstructed in the 1930s. Sister ship of the REPULSE, the *Renown* carried six 15-inch guns and twenty 4-inch guns and four aircraft. She served throughout World War II in the Atlantic and Mediterranean, most notably in the Norwegian campaign and as flagship of FORCE H under Vice-Adm. Sir James SOMERVILLE.

REPULSE, H.M.S. Royal Navy battle cruiser of 32,000 tons, completed in 1916 and twice modernized. *Repulse* took part in the Norwegian campaign and acted as escort for ATLANTIC convoys during 1940 and 1941. In November 1941 she was ordered to SINGAPORE in company with H.M.S. PRINCE OF WALES under Rear Adm. Sir Tom PHILLIPS. On December 10, 1941, she was sunk off the east coast of Malaya by Japanese bombers and torpedo planes. *Repulse* carried six 15-inch guns, six 4-inch and several other antiaircraft guns.

RESERVE FRONT. A feature of the Soviet defense of Moscow in 1941, a front (army group) set up in the rear of the active front, so that it would still be in place if the active front collapsed or, alternatively, could move forward to support the active front if the latter succeeded in checking the Germans.

RESOLUTION, H.M.S. Royal Navy battleship of 29,150 tons, completed by Palmers in 1917 and not modernized prior to 1939. She was armed with eight

15-inch, twelve 6-inch and eight 4-inch guns, smaller weapons and one aircraft. *Resolution* initially served on ATLANTIC convoy escort duties. In June 1940 she was moved to Gibraltar and participated in the bombardment of the French fleet at MERS-EL-KÉBIR. In September 1940 when bombarding DAKAR in support of the abortive expedition intended to replace the VICHY French administration by one headed by General DE GAULLE, *Resolution* was hit by French shore batteries and subsequently by a torpedo from the Vichy French submarine *Bévéziers*. Badly damaged, she returned with difficulty to Gibraltar. After lengthy repairs in the United States, *Resolution* served in the Indian Ocean in 1942 and 1943; in 1944 she returned to Britain for use as a training ship.

RETRIBUTION. Code name for the Allied sea and air operation to prevent any of the German and Italian forces trapped in TUNISIA from reaching Italian territory after the Allied victory in North Africa. The operation lasted from April to June 1943 and was completely successful. It was the occasion of Adm. Sir Andrew CUNNINGHAM's famous signal to his fleet: "Sink, burn and destroy."

RETROBOMB. U.S. Navy term for a type of rocket-propelled small aircraft bomb designed for use by MAD (magnetic anomaly detection)–equipped planes. It had a rocket in its tail, and was fired backward from underwing launch rails to lay a pattern of 24 bombs. The rocket motors almost instantly burned out when they had brought the bombs to a standstill in midair; the charges then fell vertically into the water, where—if the magnetic contact was authentic—a submerged U-boat would be.

REUBEN JAMES, U.S.S. A FLUSH-DECKER (CLEMSON class) destroyer, completed in 1920, that became the first American warship to be sunk during the war when she was torpedoed on October 31, 1941, by the German submarine *U-562*. The attack occurred during the period when the United States was giving Britain all aid "short of war"; with four other destroyers, *Reuben James*, a 1,193-tonner, was escorting a North Atlantic convoy about 600 miles west of Ireland. She sank in five minutes with the loss of 115 officers and men. Explosion of her depth charges increased the loss of life. The *Reuben James* incident followed by two weeks the torpedo attack on the U.S.S. KEARNY.

A successor *Reuben James*, a destroyer escort, was commissioned in 1943.

REYNAUD, Paul (1878–1966). Leading French conservative politician who served successively as Minister of Finance, Colonies and Justice during the early 1930s. A consistent foe of German resurgence, Reynaud allied himself with Charles DE GAULLE in 1934 and unsuccessfully urged the government to establish an offensive army based on armored divisions. In the ensuing years, the emerging national leader took a strong stand against appeasement, and he fully supported the war effort against Germany. In November 1938 Reynaud had become Finance Minister in the DALADIER government, and on March 21, 1940, he succeeded Edouard Daladier as Premier and Minister of Foreign Affairs.

As Premier, Reynaud hoped to unify the nation behind the war effort and immediately pushed for more positive military measures against Germany. One of his first acts was to resurrect Allied plans to eliminate Germany's source of iron ore in Scandinavia and thus tighten the existing blockade. At the same time, on March 28, Reynaud cemented the Anglo-French alliance by concluding an agreement forbidding either party from signing a separate peace or armistice. Reynaud's coalition government, however, proved exceedingly weak. Daladier, his political rival, remained Minister of War and would not tolerate criticism of his protégé, Army Commander in Chief Maurice GAMELIN. After the German conquest of Denmark and NORWAY in April and May, Reynaud appeared ready to dismiss Gamelin, but the main German attack against FRANCE on May 10 stayed his hand.

The initial defeat of the Allied forces on the northeastern frontier forced Reynaud to take stronger measures. Marshal Philippe PÉTAIN was brought into the cabinet on May 18 to strengthen the image of the government, and Reynaud himself took over the War Ministry, installed a staunch supporter, Georges MANDEL, in the Ministry of the Interior and replaced Gamelin with Gen. Maxime WEYGAND. Later, on June 5, de Gaulle became Reynaud's personal military adviser. But these measures were unable to reverse the tide of the war against France, and as the remaining French defenses began to collapse during the first weeks of June, pressure began to mount on Reynaud to ask for a separate armistice.

Despite encouragement from de Gaulle, Mandel, Winston CHURCHILL and others, Reynaud's will now began to weaken. On June 13 he raised with Churchill the question of releasing France from the March 28 agreement, and when his military chiefs insisted that it was hopeless to continue the struggle from Brittany or North Africa, his determination to continue the war weakened still further. Neither Reynaud's desperate requests for massive aid from the United States nor an unorthodox proposal for a political union of France and Britain offered relief. Finally, with most of his government leaning toward some sort of armistice, Reynaud gave way and on June 16 resigned, fully aware of the views of his successor, Marshal Pétain.

In September 1940 Reynaud was arrested and interned by the VICHY regime, and in 1942 deported to Germany. Incarcerated at Oranienburg and Itter, he was freed in 1945 and became a leading politician in postwar France.

REYNOLDS, Quentin Jones (1902–1965). American journalist. In 1941 his book *The Wounded Don't Cry*, about wartime England, was on the best-seller list. That year Reynolds was appointed press officer to Averell HARRIMAN on the latter's trip to Moscow. He covered the war on many fronts, including NORTHWEST AFRICA, SICILY, SALERNO, Palestine and the SOUTHWEST PACIFIC.

RHINE RIVER. The great natural German defense barrier and strongest water obstacle in the west, first crossed by the Allies on March 7, 1945, when men of the U.S. 9th Armored Division, FIRST ARMY, seized the Ludendorff railroad bridge at REMAGEN.

RHINO FERRY. An American-designed pontoon barge, 42 feet by 176 feet, powered by large outboard engines. It had a capacity of 30 to 40 vehicles and was designed to carry vehicles and cargo ashore from amphibious transports and large landing ships, such as LSTs (*see* LST), at landing beaches where the slope was too gradual to allow heavy beaching ships or craft to unload directly onto the beach.

RHUBARB. Air Marshal Sholto DOUGLAS determined to assume an offensive posture "leaning forward into France" when he took over FIGHTER COMMAND from Air Marshal Sir Hugh DOWDING in 1940. One way was to send fighters over enemy coastal areas. Fighter sweeps by small forces against ground-attack targets were code-named Rhubarb operations.

RIBBENTROP, Joachim von (1893–1946). The future Foreign Minister of the Third Reich was born on April 30, 1893, in Wesel, on the Rhine River. The son of Sophie (Hertwig) and Richard Ribbentrop, both of whom were commoners, he attended the Imperial Lyceum at Metz and later received further education in France, Great Britain and Switzerland. While studying in London, Ribbentrop worked for a time as a clerk in an importing company. In 1910 he traveled to the United States, visiting New York and Boston, where he worked part-time as a free-lance journalist. Ribbentrop then went to Canada, where he held a variety of jobs until war broke out in 1914. Returning to Germany, he joined the 12th Regiment of hussars and subsequently won the IRON CROSS for bravery in action. In addition to his military experiences, Ribbentrop got his first exposure to diplomatic service when he took part in Franz von PAPEN's military mission to the United States. Both officers subsequently went to Turkey in an effort to promote the German cause in that nation.

In 1919 Ribbentrop was a member of the German delegation to the Versailles Peace Conference. Despite his military and diplomatic service between 1914 and 1920, however, Ribbentrop was unable to get an official post in the Weimar Republic. Consequently he turned to private business, speculating in inflated German marks and working as a traveling wine salesman for a French firm. He then joined the German champagne firm of Henckel-Trocken and in 1920 married the daughter of one of the firm's owners.

During the 1920s Ribbentrop, though a socialist, became a very rich man as a joint owner of Henckel-Trocken. In 1926 he persuaded his rich aunt, who had helped finance his education, to adopt him so that he could add the aristocratic "von" to his name. In 1927, ironically in view of later events, he solicited the aid of a wealthy Jewish banker in organizing the Impregona Importing Co.

Motivated partly by the hope of putting his Jewish competition out of business, Ribbentrop became a convert to National Socialism in 1928. The following year he met Adolf HITLER for the first time. He cooperated with Hitler partly in the expectation that this association would aid his business ventures. At the same time, he did not break with his Jewish banking connections, just in case Hitler's help might prove insufficient for his purposes.

Acting as a mediator between Hitler and the German Government in the early 1930s, Ribbentrop arranged the important meetings in January 1933 between Hitler and Papen and Hitler and Oskar von Hindenburg, son of the President. These meetings led directly to Hitler's becoming Chancellor on January 30. As a principal agent in the formation of the Nazi government, Ribbentrop promoted both his champagne and his National Socialist ideology at home and abroad. Hitler rewarded him by appointing him Reich Commissioner for Disarmament in 1934. Simultaneously, Hitler began to rearm Germany. The following year Ribbentrop became ambassador-at-large. In this office he organized his own agency for political espionage and the promotion of Nazism abroad. He also negotiated the ANGLO-GERMAN NAVAL TREATY of June 1935.

Hitler appointed Ribbentrop his ambassador to Great Britain in the summer of 1936. In the two years in which he held this post Ribbentrop mixed with English society, made powerful friends and joined some of the more exclusive clubs in London. While serving as ambassador to the Court of St. James's, Ribbentrop gained further recognition and prominence by signing the original ANTI-COMINTERN PACT with Japan in November 1936. Although Konstantin von NEURATH was the German Foreign Minister, Hitler had Ribbentrop sign the pact in his stead. Hitler had come to consider him a diplomatic genius and was to call him, with considerable exaggeration, a "second Bismarck." In fact, though Ribbentrop did go on to achieve various diplomatic successes, he had few admirers, being considered by most people as pompous and incompetent. While he was in London in the late 1930s Ribbentrop's earlier Anglophilia gradually turned to Anglophobia. Following the abdication of Edward VIII, whom Ribbentrop had known in English society, he paid his respects to the new monarch, GEORGE VI, with a Nazi salute and a "Heil Hitler" twice repeated.

In early 1938 Hitler eased Neurath out of the Nazi government and installed Ribbentrop as Foreign Minister. In this post he built up an enormous Foreign Office and developed an association with Heinrich HIMMLER, the SS chief (*see* SS). Ribbentrop went on to negotiate the MUNICH AGREEMENT of September 1938, the December 1938 declaration of friendship with the French and the March 1939 occupation of Czechoslovakia. On August 23, 1939, Ribbentrop showed the world how skillful a diplomat he was when he signed in Moscow the SOVIET-GERMAN NONAGGRESSION PACT. During this period Ribbentrop also advised Hitler that in his judgment Great Britain would not go to war to defend Poland should the Germans attack that nation.

After the war broke out in the fall of 1939 Ribbentrop traveled extensively promoting Nazism and the Third Reich. "Iago," as Ribbentrop was called by jealous Nazi leaders, eventually prodded Benito MUSSOLINI into joining the war in 1940 when the fall of France was imminent. Ribbentrop's successes as a diplomat were not enough, however, to maintain his influence throughout the war. Dependent upon Hitler's goodwill, Ribbentrop lost much of his power when his Foreign Office was discredited by the implication of various members in the July 1944 plot on Hitler's life. Once Berlin fell, Ribbentrop disappeared until he was found by the British in Hamburg in June 1945. He subsequently stood trial before the INTERNATIONAL MILI-

TARY TRIBUNAL at Nuremberg. The court judged him "responsible for war crimes and crimes against humanity because of his activities with respect to occupied countries and Axis satellites." Condemned to death, Ribbentrop was hanged on October 16, 1946. **R.M.**

RICCARDI, Arturo (1878–1966). Italian admiral, director general of personnel in the Ministry of Marine between 1935 and 1940 and Chief of the Naval Staff and Under Secretary of State for the Navy from 1940. Between 1941 and 1943 Riccardi, who was a specialist in aerial warfare, conferred frequently with senior German naval officers on the defense of Italy.

RICHARDSON, Robert Charlwood, Jr. (1882–1954). U.S. Army officer (lieutenant general, 1943) who held high administrative posts in the Pacific. He commanded the Hawaiian Department, served as Commanding General, U.S. Army Forces in the Central Pacific, and in 1944 became Commanding General, U.S. Army Forces in the PACIFIC OCEAN AREAS. In these posts he did not exercise operational control over troops but was primarily concerned with training and logistics. He was involved in an imbroglio with Marine Lt. Gen. Holland M. "Howlin' Mad" SMITH over the controversial relief by the latter of Army Maj. Gen. Ralph SMITH, commander of the 27th Division on SAIPAN, in June 1944. Richardson visited Saipan, reviewed Army units and presented decorations without having made arrangements through Holland Smith. When the Marine commander objected, Richardson is said to have replied, "I want you to know you cannot push the Army around the way you have been doing."

RICHELIEU. French Navy battleship of 35,000 tons, completed at Brest early in 1940. Her armament after 1943 comprised eight 15-inch and fifteen 6-inch guns, numerous smaller weapons and four aircraft. *Richelieu* was undergoing trials at the time of the French collapse in 1940 and she was ordered to DAKAR, where she became the object of attacks by the Royal Navy. The first attacks, in July 1940, were mounted from H.M.S. HERMES. They included depth charges dropped near the battleship by a gallant motorboat team and an aircraft attack; the former failed, as the charges did not explode, but the latter caused serious damage. In September 1940 *Richelieu* was one of the prizes which the British and General DE GAULLE hoped to obtain with the Dakar expedition, but de Gaulle's overtures were rejected and the expedition withdrew, several British ships being damaged. In 1943, after the Allied landings in Northwest Africa, *Richelieu* was moved to the United States for repairs and rearming. She then joined first the British Home Fleet and later the British Indian Ocean Fleet, participating in strike operations against Japanese installations in the Netherlands East Indies.

RICHTHOFEN, Wolfram, Baron von (1895–1945). One of the early officers in the revived German Air Force, Richthofen flew in the First World War in the squadron of his famous cousin Manfred. He was chief of staff of the Condor Legion, the German force that fought for General FRANCO in the Spanish Civil War; in this post he acquired experience with dive-bombing and other techniques that were put to use in World War II. Richthofen was involved in activities on the Western and Eastern Fronts during the war. He directed the bombing of Warsaw in 1939, and his VIII Air Corps dive-bombers were instrumental in the German Army's advance through Belgium and FRANCE in 1940 and in the taking of CRETE in 1941. The VIII Air Corps, however, had less success in its efforts to establish air superiority over the English Channel after the fall of France; its JUNKERS Ju 87s were riddled by RAF SPITFIRES and HURRICANES. Richthofen commanded in other theaters as the war progressed, but the great days of the LUFTWAFFE were behind it. He was promoted to field marshal in 1943, and in 1944 he had a serious brain operation.

RICKENBACKER, Edward Vernon (1890–1973). "Captain Eddie" was America's leading fighter ace of World War I, with 26 victories, and a holder of the MEDAL OF HONOR. A civilian during World War II, he served as a special observer for Gen. Henry H. ARNOLD, Commanding General of U.S. Army Air Forces, and for Secretary of War Henry L. STIMSON. While he was returning from a trip to the Soviet Union in October 1942, his plane crashed in the Pacific. Rickenbacker and his surviving companions underwent a 27-day ordeal before their raft was sighted and they were rescued.

RIDGWAY, Matthew Bunker (1895–). A soldier with an exceptionally active career from the time of his graduation from the U.S. Military Academy, Ridgway worked in the War Plans Division of the War Department in 1939–42. In 1942, as a major general, he took command of the newly reorganized 82D AIRBORNE DIVISION. He made combat jumps with the 82d in SICILY and Normandy, and also led it in ITALY and through the early part of Operation OVERLORD until he became commanding general of XVII Airborne Corps just before the liberation of the Netherlands. At the end of 1950 he took command of the U.S. Eighth Army following its massive defeat in North Korea, and his turnabout of that army, his infusing of it in a short time with his own aggressive spirit, is regarded as one of the greatest achievements ever by an American general. When Gen. Douglas MACARTHUR was recalled, Ridgway, with four-star rank, took over the Supreme Command in Tokyo. Subsequently he served in Europe as Supreme Commander at SHAPE (Allied Supreme Headquarters), and in 1953 he became Chief of Staff of the Army. But he did not get along with his former chief, President EISENHOWER, because he fought too hard to maintain Army manpower levels at a time when the White House was bent on retrenchment. As a soldier, he was not unduly concerned about power and place but he was certain of his worth. He seemed to love danger, his troops sensed that he did not hold back from any risk, and that was part of his command mystique.

RIEFENSTAHL, Leni (1902–). A German screen actress starring in mountaineering films and a film director, Riefenstahl became a member of Adolf HITLER's entourage in the early 1930s. Her enthusiasm for his mission, as she understood it, led Hitler in 1934 to invite her to make a prestige feature film about himself and the movement—to which he gave the title *Triumph* *of the Will*—appointing her director without consultation with Joseph GOEBBELS, whose bitter resentment made him her enemy. The film featured the most massive party rally in the history of Nazism—the gathering held in Nuremberg in September 1934, involving some 200,000 participants, including Nazi youth, the workers of the Labor Service (Arbeitsdienst) armed with spades, the SA and SS carrying their swastika banners and regalia (*see* SA; SS). There were torchlight processions and mass displays staged for the benefit of the camera, all backed by Nazi music with its hymnlike emotionalism. Hitler's succession of speeches, amplified through loudspeakers (of which he had been an early user), summarized what he felt he had achieved and his hopes for the future. The film reflected the nation's response to the Führer after some 18 months of dictatorship and belonged to the "honeymoon" period of national enthusiasm, though the bloody RÖHM purge had taken place a bare two months previously.

The international acclaim given *Triumph of the Will* led to Riefenstahl's being invited by the Olympic Committee to film the games in Germany in 1936. This gave her a further opportunity to place Hitler center-stage in a prestige film with world distribution. Her coverage of the games remains unique, rivaled only by Kon Ichikawa's film of the 1964 games. After this triumph she fell from favor as a result of Goebbels's hostility.

RIFLE. *See* SMALL ARMS.

RIGA. Capital of Latvia, this important naval base on the Baltic was defended by the Germans behind the Sigulda Line. It fell to the Soviet Second and Third Baltic Fronts on October 13, 1944.

RING (Koltso). Code name of the Soviet operation for the reduction of STALINGRAD, January 1943.

RINTELEN, Enno von (1884–1949). German Army officer (General der Infanterie) who was military attaché in Rome and German liaison officer with Comando Supremo.

RIO CONFERENCE. Immediately following the Japanese attack on Pearl Harbor, the United States directed notes to all American republics requesting a consultative meeting of foreign ministers as quickly as possible. The notes referred to the resolution adopted at the HAVANA CONFERENCE in 1940 whereby the American states would deliberate about any hostile action upon any one of them by a non-American power. The American republics agreed to such a meeting in Rio de Janeiro during the latter half of January 1942, and in the meantime more than half the nations either declared war on the AXIS or severed diplomatic relations.

The press of international affairs made it impossible for U.S. Secretary of State Cordell HULL to attend this meeting, and in his stead was Under Secretary of State Sumner WELLES. Before the departure of the U.S. delegation it was agreed that emphasis should be placed upon getting all the republics to declare jointly a complete severance of relations with the Axis.

It was quickly apparent at Rio that the main obstacle to such a strong declaration would, as usual, be Argentina. The Argentine Government had attempted in early January to induce smaller Latin-American nations to oppose the United States plan of a complete severance of relations, and at Rio the Argentine opposition continued. Too many prominent figures in the Argentine Government believed in the inevitability of an Axis victory; the long Argentine opposition to the United States in inter-American affairs was also a contributory factor. Chile, on the other hand, was dubious about the value of such a resolution, as it feared for the safety of its long, exposed coastline and, in addition, was then only weakly governed by a caretaker government. Nevertheless, the U.S. delegation received instructions from Washington to accept no compromise with Argentina, since it was now believed (and rightly so) that the presence of Axis diplomats anywhere in the Americas would mean subversion and espionage.

Regardless of his instructions, Welles did agree to a compromise over the issue of severance of relations, and it was simply *recommended* that the American states break relations. When Hull learned of this compromise (reached under Argentine pressure), he was enraged; this event undoubtedly contributed to Welles's eventual departure from the State Department. Welles, on the other hand, stressed the need for a unanimity of republics with regard to that resolution.

While the political events at this conference were uppermost in the minds of all participants, important work was accomplished in other areas as well. Measures were taken to curb Axis subversion, to interdict commerce with the Axis, to increase production of strategic materials, to create an Inter-American Defense Board, to develop commercial relations and transportation facilities and to consider postwar problems. Although in the areas of transportation, economic aid and economic cooperation, the United States could not fulfill the desires of Latin Americans and could not commit itself to continue such activities after the war, the delegates were nevertheless able to discover grounds for agreement. As for actions against the Axis, very shortly all Latin-American nations with the exception of Argentina had either declared war on the Axis or severed relations. The Rio Conference was thus a triumph for continental solidarity and the prosecution of the war. From this conference onward, the great bulk of the Americas were solidly aligned against the Axis and the goals of the United States were almost completely accomplished.

RIOM TRIAL. Sponsored by the VICHY French regime of Marshal Philippe PÉTAIN and by Nazi Germany, the French judicial proceedings at Riom were undertaken in order to prove that leading French politicians of the Third Republic were responsible for initiating World War II and for the political corruption that supposedly lay behind France's military defeat. In defiance of existing laws, the marshal personally picked the members of the special "court," and testimony was gathered secretly during 1940 and 1941. The public trials began on February 19, 1942. Among the accused were former Premiers Léon BLUM, Edouard DALADIER and Paul REYNAUD, Air Minister Pierre Cot and the wartime Commander in Chief of the Army, Gen. Maurice GAMELIN. Allowed to speak freely, the defendants were able to refute most of the charges made by the court and to challenge the legitimacy of the entire proceedings. Embarrassed by this turn of events, Pétain suspended the trial in April, and the court was never reconvened.

RITCHIE, Sir Neil Methuen (1897–). British Army officer who was deputy chief of staff to Gen. Sir Claude AUCHINLECK, Commander in Chief in the Middle East, 1941, and took command of the EIGHTH ARMY on the removal of Lt. Gen. Sir Alan CUNNINGHAM in November 1941 after the slowing of Operation CRUSADER, a desert offensive. Ritchie, although an experienced staff officer, had had little experience of command. At first he was successful in pursuing the offensive, but by June 1942 General ROMMEL was at the gates of TOBRUK, which fell on June 21. Ritchie was replaced in command of the Eighth Army by Auchinleck himself; it had been his initial misfortune to be pitted against the legendary Desert Fox. He later returned to combat command as a corps commander in the fighting in western Europe, 1944–45.

RIVER PLATE (Rio de la Plata), BATTLE OF THE. On December 13, 1939, the German pocket battleship ADMIRAL GRAF SPEE, commanded by Kapitän zur See Hans LANGSDORFF, encountered the British South America Division (Force G) off the estuary of the Rio de la Plata. Since September the German vessel had pursued a successful course of commerce raiding in the South Atlantic, greatly alarming the British Admiralty. Commo. Henry HARWOOD, commander of the South America Division of the America and West Indies Squadron, had been weighing intelligence reports and readying his command. When the German ship was sighted, the British force consisted of H.M.S. EXETER (heavy cruiser), commanded by Capt. F. S. Bell; H.M.S. AJAX (light cruiser), commanded by Capt. Charles Woodhouse; and H.M.N.Z.S. ACHILLES (light cruiser), commanded by Capt. W. E. Parry. Commodore Harwood's flagship for the Battle of the Plate was the *Ajax*.

Inasmuch as the ships of Force G would be heavily outgunned by the German vessel, Commodore Harwood had devised the tactic of forcing the *Graf Spee* to divide its fire. The *Exeter* would attack on one flank and the *Ajax* and *Achilles*, in close company, on the other. In the early morning of December 13 the two forces met, with the *Exeter* suffering heavily from the German ship's 11-inch guns, but Harwood's tactics enabled the *Achilles* and *Ajax* to strike some telling blows with their relatively small 6-inch batteries. Perhaps confused from a blow on the head, Langsdorff ordered the damaged (although not severely so) *Graf Spee* to break off action and seek refuge in the neutral harbor of Montevideo.

There, in a cat-and-mouse game of diplomacy, intelligence operations, bluff and rumor, the British were able to cause the *Graf Spee* to be detained long enough to permit the arrival of H.M.S. *Cumberland* (heavy cruiser) from the Falkland Islands. They also managed to create the impression that other reinforcements were on hand, though none could in fact arrive until December 19. The *Exeter*, heavily battered and in no condition for further combat, repaired to the Falklands for refit.

Captain Langsdorff, in the meantime, felt he could not break out to sea in the face of the rumored superior British forces, and he did not desire to see his ship interned, as it would sooner or later have to be, in a neutral port. He therefore requested permission from his superiors to blow up the ship in the estuary of the Rio de la Plata, which was done on the evening of December 17. Most of his crew and the captain himself were then interned in Argentina, where they had been taken shortly before the destruction of their ship. Langsdorff committed suicide two days later.

Not only did this British victory raise Allied morale in the period of the "Sitzkrieg," it cleared the South Atlantic for British shipping. Commodore Harwood and his crews were generously rewarded by promotions and decorations, and rightly so, since by a combination of audacity, bluff and superior tactics, a technically inferior British force had defeated the German ship in one of the last classic surface-to-surface actions on the high seas. As for the interned German crew, many of them made their way back to Germany when the Argentine Government turned a blind eye to their movements. But the British aggressiveness had proved to both their allies and enemies that they would spare no effort to command the Atlantic, regardless of German raiders or the earlier Declaration of Panama (*see* PANAMA CONFERENCE) that had created a neutrality zone near the Americas, a zone that no belligerent respected.

RO-57. A twin-engine, single-seat monoplane fighter designed for Italy's Industrie Meccaniche e Aeronautiche Meridionali by a team headed by Giovanni Galasso. First produced in 1942, the plane featured an all-metal fuselage and wooden wing. Two large engine nacelles created the illusion of power, but the Fiat radial engines developed only 840 horsepower each. Maximum speed was 311 miles per hour at 16,400 feet, and the service ceiling was 25,590 feet. Because its performance was inadequate for an interceptor, the plane was fitted with diving brakes and employed as a dive-bomber and fighter-bomber. Two 20-mm. cannon were added to the original pair of 12.7-mm. machine guns. A successor, the two-place, twin-engine Ro-58, was based on the MESSERSCHMITT ME 110 and featured 1,175-horsepower engines and five 20-mm. cannon. Italy surrendered before this model went into production.

ROA (Russkaya Osvoboditelnaya Armiya). The Russian Liberation Army, organized in Germany by Lt. Gen. Andrei VLASOV as what he and other former Soviet soldiers and civilians hoped might become the nucleus of a free Russian army and government. The ROA movement foundered on a combination of obstacles. These included the general opposition of the Nazi regime to any such attempt as Vlasov's to create a truly autonomous Russia, as well as the inability of anti-Communists of various nationalities (Ukrainian, Great Russian, etc.) to put their national differences aside until Joseph STALIN could be removed. Ironically, the only military action in which the ROA took part as a major force was in 1945 when it joined its efforts with those of the Czech resistance to free PRAGUE from the German occupiers. Some ROA survivors surrendered to U.S. Army forces and were for the most part returned to the USSR; the others were rounded up by Soviet soldiers.

ROATTA, Mario (1887–1968). Italian Army officer who led Italian troops at Málaga in 1937 in the Spanish Civil War before becoming military attaché in Berlin in 1939. He became Chief of the General Staff in March

1941. Nearly a year later he took command of the Second Army in the Balkans; he returned to the post of Chief of Staff in June 1943. Although he kept his job after Benito MUSSOLINI was overthrown, Roatta was eventually dismissed (November 12, 1943) because of his past associations with Fascists. Put on trial by an Italian court for war crimes in 1945, Roatta escaped; he was sentenced to life imprisonment *in absentia*. An appeals court subsequently overturned the sentence in 1948, but Roatta did not return to Rome until 1965. His highest wartime rank was lieutenant general.

ROBB, Sir James (1895–1968). After service in the Royal Flying Corps in World War I, J. M. Robb became a career officer in the RAF. He was deputy commander of the NORTHWEST AFRICAN AIR FORCES in 1943 and later deputy chief of staff (Air) at SHAEF. He was knighted in 1945 and received two U.S. decorations, Officer of the Legion of Merit (1943) and the Distinguished Service Medal (1945). He retired as Air Chief Marshal.

ROBERTS, Owen Josephus (1875–1955). Associate Justice of the U.S. Supreme Court, appointed by Presidential order on December 18, 1941, to head an inquiry into the Japanese attack on PEARL HARBOR. The report of the Roberts commission was submitted on January 24, 1942. This was the first of eight executive, Congressional and service investigations of Pearl Harbor. None established any clear-cut culpability for the Japanese success in achieving surprise.

ROBIN MOOR. American-flag merchant ship, torpedoed by the German submarine *U-69* in the South Atlantic on May 21, 1941, while en route from the United States to South Africa. Her crew took to their lifeboats and spent 18 days in the water before rescue.

ROC. Blackburn, the British aircraft firm, attempted in 1937 to combine its SKUA low-wing dive-bomber with the Boulton-Paul four-gun powered turret in order to produce a shipboard fighter capable of pulling alongside an enemy bomber and downing it with a devastating broadside. Forward-firing guns were unnecessary according to this concept, which left the plane mortally vulnerable to head-on attack. Production began in 1938 and ended in 1940 after 136 Rocs had been built. The concept behind the design was faulty, and the plane a failure.

ROCCA DELLE CAMINATE. Headquarters from which Benito MUSSOLINI directed his puppet Italian Social Republic (proclaimed September 15, 1943). It was near Gargnano on Lake Garda in northern Italy.

ROCKEFELLER, Nelson A. (1908–). As war approached, President ROOSEVELT and his advisers became concerned about United States relations with Latin America, and Nelson Rockefeller was chosen in 1940 to be coordinator of the Office of Inter-American Affairs (CIAA). Prior to and during the war, Rockefeller was engaged in propaganda efforts in Latin America and in the instigation and coordination of projects concerned with health, sanitation, education and economic aid to the region. He also busied himself with certain anti-Axis activities and trade agreements with Latin-American nations. In December 1944 Rockefeller was appointed Assistant Secretary of State for Latin-American Affairs. In that position his most important contributions were the call for the CHAPULTEPEC CONFERENCE, at which the American states gave Argentina the opportunity to rejoin the hemispheric community, and his acceptance for the United States of regional world organizations. In later years Rockefeller was governor of New York and Vice-President of the United States.

ROCKET. Although known for some centuries and used in combat during the Napoleonic Wars and the War of 1812 (hence Francis Scott Key's reference to "the rocket's red glare"), rockets saw their first extensive military use during World War II. Though a rocket was bigger and heavier than a gun projectile carrying an equivalent weight of explosive, it could be fired from a launcher which was a great deal lighter and simpler than a gun. Its lack of recoil made it a good aircraft weapon for ground attack.

Rockets of various types and sizes, many of them described in this volume under their individual names, were fired from ships, planes, vehicles and wheeled artillery-type launcher mounts. Used from planes, rockets were valuable for attacking ground or water targets where explosive effect was needed and where better accuracy was required than could be attained with bombs. Land- and sea-based rockets, launched in heavy salvos, were popular with British, German, Soviet and American forces for area bombardment and neutralization of enemy defenses. Rockets were not weapons of precision, and thus could not be used for close fire support for ground troops. This made them, for the most part, unsuitable for naval combat, although some PT boats in the South Pacific employed rocket launchers against shore targets and small craft (*see* PT).

Wartime rockets were generally fired from tube- or rail-type launchers. However, it was discovered that an ignited rocket had adequate stability on its own, and airplanes began using "zero-length" launchers—small stubs beneath the wings—thus lessening the aerodynamic drag. Toward the end of the war, PROXIMITY FUZES were developed for use with American aerial rockets.

ROCKET, 4.5-inch aircraft. An American-developed weapon intended to give airplanes greater gunnery power than could be provided by conventional guns, whose recoil was a limiting factor. First tested in 1941–42, the 4.5-inch rocket was in service by 1943, though many problems were encountered. The early M8 rocket was launched from an underwing BAZOOKA-like tube. Its tail fins folded to allow it to fit the tube; when fired, they snapped out into flying position. This gave the weapon the name Folding-Fin Aircraft Rocket (FFAR). Later improvements included substitution of zero-length post launchers (small stubs under the wings) for the bulky tubes; this allowed larger fixed fins for better accuracy. These improved rockets were extensively used in Europe and the Pacific; they were also used to some extent from ground launchers for area bombardment. As used by aircraft, the M8 rocket was found insufficiently powerful and accurate. Work was begun in

1944 on a redesigned "super" 4.5-inch weapon. By the time this was ready for use, the 5-inch HVAR (*see* HVAR) had been adopted by the U.S. Army and Navy. Some requirement for the new 4.5-inch rocket developed in 1945, but the Pacific war ended before it could appear in service.

ROCKET, 4.5-inch barrage. Developed by the U.S. Navy in 1942 for support of amphibious assaults, this weapon combined the motor of the MOUSETRAP rocket with a 20-pound general-purpose bomb, and had an 1,100-yard range. The launcher was designed to be as small and light as possible to allow it to be mounted in landing craft and carried in toward a landing beach. The first simple 12-rocket launcher, the Mark 1, was used in the NORTHWEST AFRICA landings in November 1942. A simpler Mark 8 launcher resembled the Mark 1; both were nicknamed "egg-crate" launchers from their appearance. Mark 8 launchers could be controlled in multiples from a central control panel. During 1943 the automatic Mark 7 launcher was developed; this had a single launching rail, but was gravity-fed from a magazine. It rapidly replaced the earlier launchers in support craft, although Mark 8 launchers were used by PT boats in the Pacific (*see* PT). A later Mark 11 launcher was automatic in operation, but did not supplant the Mark 7. The 4.5-inch bombardment rockets were used in large numbers in the Mediterranean, Atlantic and Pacific through 1943 and 1944, arming converted LCTs and LCI(L)s. *See also* LCI(L), LCT.

RODNEY, H.M.S. Royal Navy battleship of 34,000 tons, completed by Cammell Laird in 1927, armed with nine 16-inch (all forward), twelve 6-inch and six 4.7-inch guns, numerous smaller weapons, two 24.5-inch torpedo tubes and two aircraft. *Rodney* served in the Home Fleet from 1939 to 1942, taking part in the Norwegian campaign, convoy operations and the final stages of the sinking of the BISMARCK. In 1942 *Rodney* participated in the August convoy to MALTA (Operation PEDESTAL) and covered the North African landings; in 1943 she was transferred to the Mediterranean FORCE H and assisted in the Sicilian and the various Italian landings. In 1944 she returned to home waters for bombardment support at the Normandy INVASION and the reduction of German garrisons in the CHANNEL ISLANDS.

ROEBLING, Donald (1909–1950). The grandson of Col. Washington Roebling, builder of the Brooklyn Bridge, Donald Roebling was the inventor in 1935 of an amphibious tank, called the ALLIGATOR.

ROER DAMS. The British Ministry of Economic Warfare believed the release of water from the Möhne, Sorpe, Eder, Lister and Schwelme dams would disrupt Germany's Ruhr industry. The Sorpe, with a compacted earth barrier around a concrete core, differed from the masonry walls of the other dams and was judged impossible to attack. The Möhne had the largest capacity and became the priority target. *See also* DAM BUSTERS.

ROGACHEV. German bastion town on the upper DNIEPER RIVER (USSR). It fell to the Soviet First Belorussian Front on February 24, 1944.

RÖHM, Ernst (1887–1934). One of the chief builders of the German Nazi Party, Major Röhm was a much-wounded veteran of World War I who, as a political officer, supported the infant NATIONAL SOCIALIST GERMAN WORKERS' PARTY and became one of its pioneer members. He thus helped launch the political career of Adolf HITLER and became the organizer and leader of the SA, the Nazi Storm Troopers (*see* SA). Röhm and Hitler were in chronic disagreement over the importance to be given the SA, however, and in 1925 Röhm resigned and went to South America; but in 1930 he returned at Hitler's request and reassumed command of the SA. The division between the two was nevertheless fundamental, and in 1934 Hitler ended it in violent fashion: Röhm was one of the perhaps 200 persons executed in the NIGHT OF THE LONG KNIVES.

ROI. At the northern apex of KWAJALEIN Atoll, Roi Island was attached to NAMUR by a narrow causeway and a strip of sand. Its importance was based on the large airfield the Japanese had built on it. On February 1, 1944, the U.S. 23d Marines landed and completed its mop-up of the island the same day. Within a short time U.S. aircraft were operating from this newly captured field.

ROKOSSOVSKY, Konstantin K. (1896–1968). Born in Poland, Rokossovsky began his long military career during the First World War as an NCO in the Imperial Russian Army. After the Revolution he served first in the Red Guard, then in the Red Cavalry. He spent the early 1930s as the commander of the 7th Samara Cavalry Division in Semën TIMOSHENKO's III Cavalry Corps. In 1936–37 he commanded the V Cavalry Corps. Then Rokossovsky was swept up in STALIN's purge of the Army and thrown into prison. It is believed that he was released in the spring of 1940 and restored as a major general to command a corps in the Kiev Military District under Georgi ZHUKOV. At the end of 1940 he was reassigned to command the IX Mechanized Corps, a newly activated organization in the Kiev Military District.

The German attack on the Soviet Union in 1941 found Rokossovsky with this corps, which took part in the first actions in the Lutsk-Rovno area. In July 1941 Rokossovsky was given command of a special group protecting SMOLENSK. After the retreat across the DNIEPER in August 1941, he took command of the Sixteenth Army. He remained with this formation throughout the first winter of the war, often finding his army headquarters group moved to a new region as part of a patchwork development of the defenses of Moscow. Throughout most of this period Rokossovsky was under Zhukov's command. Although in his book *A Soldier's Duty (Soldatskij dolg)* he outlines his long association and friendship with Zhukov, Rokossovsky is highly critical of Zhukov's actions and on more than one occasion blames him for failures.

From the summer of 1942 Rokossovsky commanded a succession of fronts (Bryansk, Don, Central, First Belorussian and Second Belorussian). Commanding the Don Front, Rokossovsky was responsible for the encirclement and destruction of large German forces at STALINGRAD and accepted the surrender of Field Marshal PAULUS. He later took part in the great KURSK battle.

His forces then crossed the Dnieper and after a series of battles his Second Belorussian Front joined with the First Belorussian and First Ukrainian Fronts in the drive on BERLIN. The end of the war found Rokossovsky's armies on the Baltic coast and the Elbe.

ROLIK GROUP. A "Horatius at the Bridge" operation by four Russian soldiers in STALINGRAD, who held the sides of a ravine in which troops of the Red Army 138th Division were isolated and fought off German attacks.

ROMA. Italian battleship of 35,000 tons, completed at Trieste in 1942 and armed with nine 15-inch, twelve 6-inch and twelve 3.5-inch guns, smaller weapons and three aircraft. *Roma*, serving as fleet flagship, was sunk off Corsica while leading the ITALIAN NAVY to surrender on September 9, 1943. She was hit by German radio-controlled FX 1,400-kg. bombs (not glider bombs, as is often stated) dropped from DORNIER Do 217 aircraft, and exploded shortly afterward with heavy loss of life.

ROMANENKO, Prokop L. (1897–1949). Red Army officer (lieutenant general) who commanded the Fifth Armored Army in the Battle of STALINGRAD and subsequently was commanding general of the Forty-eighth Army.

ROME. Declared an open city by German Field Marshal KESSELRING, Rome was entered by troops of the U.S. FIFTH ARMY on June 4, 1944. This was the culmination of a drive begun on May 11. *See also* ITALY.

ROMMEL, Erwin (1891–1944). This German general was not only his country's most popular war hero but was respected by his adversaries to an unusual degree. A man of mercurial temperament and tremendous energy, Rommel often displayed brilliance in the tactical handling of his forces.

Until 1940 Rommel was an obscure Wehrmacht officer. The son of a schoolmaster, he joined the Army as a young man and served capably in World War I, when he received the highest German decoration, POUR LE MÉRITE, after the Caporetto offensive of 1917. Not deemed to be of General Staff caliber, he held routine positions after the war. In 1933 he was appointed military instructor to the SA (*see* SA) and later taught at the infantry schools at Dresden and Wiener-Neustadt. He attracted Adolf HITLER's attention as dynamic and unorthodox, and when war broke out he became commander of Hitler's personal headquarters. With a keen sense of timing that often served him well, Rommel asked for a PANZER command after the Polish campaign and was given the 7th ("Ghost") Panzer Division. During the succeeding drive across FRANCE to the Channel coast, he established his command pattern and made his name as a panzer leader. He led from the front, often taking personal charge of the battle, and he was quick to exploit his opponent's mistakes or weaknesses. He strove at all times to keep his enemy off balance by mobile and flexible offensive action.

In early 1941 Hitler named Rommel to command the AFRIKA KORPS, sent to Libya to sustain the Italians. His orders were for defensive action only, but according to his own account, by the time he reached Africa he had decided to depart from instructions because unusual opportunities confronted him. With only half his allotted German troops on hand, he opened the first desert offensive on March 31 and swept the understrength British out of CYRENAICA and back into Egypt. Both his personal traits and his command and tactical approaches lent themselves well to the fluid desert war, and from mid-1941 until late 1942 Rommel dominated the North African theater.

Although Hitler consistently denied Rommel sufficient strength to turn his victories into a decisive offensive, he exploited Rommel's success and his likable personality to build him into a popular war hero. Rommel's victories offset German defeats in Russia, and Rommel could be safely exalted since he was not judged to be politically ambitious or likely to vie with Hitler for power. Hitler named his desert general a field marshal on June 22, 1942, the day after he captured TOBRUK, but Rommel wrote his wife that he would have preferred another division.

In many respects Rommel was politically naïve. Although not a Nazi, he admired Hitler even though he had little respect for some of the other German leaders. He considered himself a military man, and as such he displayed daring and skill. With a sure instinct for making the most of his resources and concentrating his strength, he baffled a succession of British commanders and came to be so highly regarded by the British EIGHTH ARMY that General AUCHINLECK, who later called Rommel "a master of improvisation," felt it expedient to try to deflate the notion that Rommel was either magician or superman. Auchinleck issued a letter to his commanders urging them "to dispel by all possible means the idea that Rommel represents something

Field Marshal Rommel (left) inspects German defenses in Normandy

more than an ordinary German general." Yet the fact remained—Rommel was hardly ordinary. When he sprang back from defeat to recapture the western half of Cyrenaica in January 1942, Winston CHURCHILL paid him a rare tribute in the House of Commons: "We have a very daring and skilful opponent against us, and, may I say across the havoc of war, a great general."

Much of Rommel's popularity stemmed from his "clean" approach to warfare. More than any other theater of the war, NORTH AFRICA was a traditional trial of skill between worthy opponents. There were no SS troops (*see* SS) in Africa, and all prisoners were treated with decency and respect. Rommel had a sound grasp of psychology and used it in the handling of his enemy as well as his own men. If he demanded much from his men, he gave no less of himself. He worked hard, fought hard, lived simply, talked easily with his troops, and was devoted to his wife and son. He was a visible leader, known to his men and enjoying the charmed life of one who seems constantly to court death but never comes to harm. His bravery, luck and ability to bounce back and turn defeat into victory became legendary.

Rommel had failings as well as strengths. He was overly impatient with the difficulties of logistics and administration. He tended to be arrogant, and he had little use for the Italian Comando Supremo under whom he fought. His temper often flared with his staff, and he found it hard to delegate authority, even though his tendency to stay at the front meant that he was often not available when needed at his headquarters. His staff found him fair, though hard to work with, and the younger men adored him because he gave energetic junior officers the opportunity to prove themselves.

By late 1942 Rommel's African heyday was ending. The British acquired dynamic and confident leadership along with overwhelming material superiority, while Rommel's supplies dwindled to nothing. During the Battle of ALAMEIN and the succeeding retreat to TUNISIA, when Hitler consistently denied him permission to make strategic withdrawals to save his men, Rommel became disillusioned and bitter. His health weakened, and after the battles at KASSERINE and MÉDENINE he was recalled from Africa. Hitler considered him for commander in Italy, but Albert KESSELRING was appointed instead. Rommel wrote his wife that he suspected Kesselring got the appointment because he had shown more optimism about holding Italy. By December 1943 Rommel's son Manfred was aware that his father was doubting Hitler's leadership. Rommel had learned of the EXTERMINATION CAMP policy, and during succeeding months he gradually transferred his loyalty to his country as opposed to his Führer.

In January 1944 Rommel was given command of Army Group B, stationed in France to meet the expected Allied invasion. He and RUNDSTEDT, overall commander in the west, differed on strategy. The latter favored a defense in depth after the Allies were ashore, but Rommel favored a defense of the beaches because he doubted Germany's ability to fight effectively in the face of Allied air superiority. The result was a compromise, but Rommel had neither time nor resources to prepare the defense he deemed necessary.

Shortly after the Normandy INVASION, Rommel and Rundstedt appealed to Hitler to withdraw to defensible lines. Hitler would not listen. Rommel's disillusionment grew. During the preceding months he had been contacted by several persons involved in the conspiracy to overthrow Hitler. Rommel was asked to be either interim head of state or Commander in Chief of the Armed Forces when Hitler was taken into custody. Although he did not condone killing the Führer, Rommel thought Hitler should be arrested by the Army and tried before a German court. He agreed to cooperate as requested.

Meanwhile the fighting in Normandy continued, and on July 15 Rommel wrote Hitler, "The unequal struggle is nearing its end." He begged the Führer "to draw the proper conclusions without delay." Two days later Rommel's skull was fractured when his staff car was strafed by a low-flying Allied aircraft. He was in the hospital when the conspirators made their July 20 attempt on Hitler's life. During succeeding weeks Hitler learned of Rommel's role and decreed his death. According to Field Marshal KEITEL's later testimony, Hitler realized that the truth would create a terrible scandal. Consequently, Rommel was given the option of standing trial or taking poison; if he chose the latter, he was assured, his family would not be molested. On October 14, 1944, Rommel swallowed the poison the SS provided. He was given a state funeral, and it was announced that he had died of his earlier wounds.

After World War I Rommel wrote a book on infantry tactics, and during World War II he kept a detailed journal, with plans to write another book. Edited into *The Rommel Papers*, his notes and his letters to his wife (whom he wrote almost daily) reveal a man of great dedication, enthusiasm and talent. **M.H.B.**

ROMMELSSPARGEL (Rommel's asparagus). Name given the great forests of stakes driven in the ground in areas suitable for aircraft landing behind the beach in Normandy. They were planned by Field Marshal ROMMEL as part of the overall defenses.

ROMULO, Carlos Peña (1901–). Philippine diplomat, author and journalist. Romulo, who received part of his education in the United States, won a Pulitzer Prize for a series of articles about the Far East in which he correctly predicted the course of Japanese policy. When the war began, he entered the service as Gen. Douglas MACARTHUR's press aide, with the rank of major. He escaped from BATAAN with the general and served for a while in Australia, rising eventually to the rank of brigadier general. He was Secretary of Information and Public Relations in President Manuel QUEZON's war cabinet in exile in 1943, Secretary of Public Instruction in the cabinet of President Sergio OSMEÑA in 1944 and resident commissioner of the Philippines to the United States from 1944 to 1946. After the war Romulo was a prominent figure in the United Nations.

ROOPE, Gerald B. (1905–1940). Commander of H.M.S. *Glowworm* in April 1940, when she was part of a force operating in Norwegian waters to cover minelaying off the Norwegian coast. On April 6 one of her crew fell overboard, and the *Glowworm* parted company to search for him. Heavy weather on April 7 prevented her from rejoining the force, and on the morning of the 8th, sighting two German destroyers, she engaged one *(Berndt von Arnim)* in a running fight. Within a few minutes she sighted the 14,000-ton German cruiser ADMIRAL HIPPER and came under very heavy fire. Continually hit, she closed her giant adversary and damaged her by ramming before she was sunk. It was not until the few survivors were released from their prisoner-of-war camp after the war that details of the action became known, and Roope was awarded a posthumous VICTORIA CROSS for his gallantry.

ROOSEVELT, (Anna) Eleanor (1884–1962). Eleanor Roosevelt married her cousin Franklin D. ROOSEVELT on March 17, 1905. Between 1907 and 1916 five children—Anna, James, Elliott, Franklin, Jr., and John—were born, and from the early years of their marriage Eleanor faced both private responsibilities to her family and broader duties as the wife of a public figure. Painfully shy and often overshadowed by Franklin's forceful mother, she met the challenges of her life with courage and good sense. She developed her interests in education, social problems and politics, and when Franklin was crippled with polio in 1921 she was instrumental in sustaining his interests and helping him resume an active life of public service.

By 1933 Eleanor had set the pattern for her life: active, energetic involvement with a warm and sincere interest in people and the problems of society. She helped her husband by traveling, observing and reporting to him, and under his tutelage she developed a perceptive eye. In addition, she had interests in a school and a furniture factory, was active in women's Democratic Party activities and social projects, edited a magazine and frequently spoke or wrote for the public. When she became First Lady, she told her friends she would "be myself, as always."

She continued to serve as her husband's observer. She went where time or circumstances prevented his going—to soup kitchens, coal mines, slums, hospitals and prisons. She reported to the President, and he respected her judgment. Although she deprecated her influence, she realized the contributions she could make, and she made certain the President was exposed to persons and points of view that might otherwise have been kept from him. Through her daily newspaper column (in over 25 years she never missed a deadline) she sometimes paved the way for her husband's programs, and she has been called the conscience of the New Deal. In her autobiography she called herself a "spur," and judged that although "the spurring was not always wanted or welcome," she was one who served her husband's purposes.

During the war years Eleanor Roosevelt made several extended trips at the President's request. In England in the fall of 1942, she inspected the war damage, observed women's war efforts and visited American servicemen in hospitals and camps. Even Winston CHURCHILL, with whom she had the courage to argue matters of difference, praised her contribution to Anglo-American solidarity.

She went to the Southwest Pacific in 1943. In a trip that included 17 islands, as well as Australia and New Zealand, she saw roughly 400,000 men in camps and hospitals, and left behind her a warmth and good will that caused Adm. William F. HALSEY to say that she "accomplished more good" than anyone else to visit the theater. She lost 30 pounds and returned exhausted, but was more than ever determined to work toward a world free from the stupidity of war. Quick to perceive that worldwide racial dignity and freedom were basic to postwar stability, she worked tirelessly to promote concepts of racial equality.

When her role as First Lady ended in April 1945, she was 61, and for the first time in her life free to develop a life of her own. She joked about wearing a lace cap and retiring to her fireside, but when President Harry S. TRUMAN asked her to serve with the UNITED NATIONS she accepted, viewing it as a way in which she could help in building the peace. She was chairman of the commission that drafted the Universal Declaration of Human Rights, adopted by the General Assembly in 1948. By 1952, when she resigned following the election of Gen. Dwight D. EISENHOWER as President, she had earned worldwide respect for her contributions to the common cause of humanity. She continued to serve with the American Association for the United Nations, and later President John F. KENNEDY reappointed her a delegate. Failing health forced her to decline reappointment after 1961.

Her 78 years are testimonial to her belief that "life was meant to be lived." As wife, mother, politician, humanitarian, columnist, teacher, lecturer, diplomat and ambassador, she worked with astounding energy. Not least among her accomplishments was the added scope she gave to the concept of womanhood and the role of the First Lady.

ROOSEVELT, Elliott (1910–). Second son of the President of the United States, Elliott Roosevelt was called to active duty from the Army Air Corps reserve in 1940. In the summer of 1941, while a captain, he took part in an aerial survey of the east coast of Greenland in quest of sites for airfields. This search failed to turn up an acceptable location, though a base eventually was built at Angmagssalik on the east coast. He served in NORTHWEST AFRICA, where he attained the rank of colonel while commanding the Northwest African Photo Reconnaissance Wing. During 1944 he served as a reconnaissance specialist on the staff of U.S. STRATEGIC AIR FORCES IN EUROPE. He became a brigadier general in February 1945.

ROOSEVELT, Franklin Delano (1882–1945). As President from March 1933 until his death in April 1945, Franklin Roosevelt led the United States through its most severe economic crisis and its most costly war. His long term of office (he is the only U.S. President to be reelected three times) was marked by innovation, determination and great faith in the world's future. He has been criticized for lack of original thinking and praised for his resourcefulness in bringing persons of outstanding ability into his administration. He has been accused of seeking to be a dictator and praised for becoming the savior of democracy. He has been denounced for expanding the power of government and lauded as the benefactor of the common man. Few modern American political figures have attracted such extremes of devotion and dislike.

Roosevelt's family had wealth and social prominence.

He graduated from Harvard, studied law at Columbia and passed the New York bar examination, but his primary interest was politics. He was influenced by his distant cousin Theodore Roosevelt, and in 1905 he married Theodore's niece Eleanor ROOSEVELT.

Roosevelt's political career began in 1910 with his election to the first of two terms in the New York state senate. These were followed by seven years as Assistant Secretary of the Navy; ships and the sea were a love that he retained throughout his life. In 1920 he ran for Vice-President with James M. Cox, but Harding and Coolidge won in a Republican sweep. A serious attack of poliomyelitis the following year kept Roosevelt out of active public life until 1928, when he was elected governor of New York. A vigorous campaign and a dynamic administration silenced those who doubted his physical stamina, but even though he had made a dramatic recovery from polio he never regained the use of his legs, and for the remainder of his life he had to rely on braces, a cane or a wheelchair. He accepted his infirmity uncomplainingly, and did not allow his crippled legs to slow his advance. His personal interest in polio therapy led him to establish the Warm Springs Foundation in Georgia for the treatment of polio victims, and for many years on his birthday gala balls were held across the country to raise money for polio research. After he became crippled, Roosevelt learned to campaign from a car, to enlist the help of his wife as his "eyes and ears" in places where he could not easily go and to make skillful use of radio for reaching the people. He had a rich, vibrant voice, could speak in a warm, intimate manner and had a jaunty, debonair appearance. In 1932, with the country floundering in the Depression, he was elected to the Presidency by a landslide—472 to 59 electoral votes.

His handling of the Depression was marked by his philosophy that the powers of government should be used for the benefit of the people. Programs were initiated to get money into the economy; drastic measures were taken to raise farm prices, stimulate business and reform certain economic and banking practices. The Social Security program came into being. New tax laws had the effect of starting a redistribution of American wealth. These measures—collectively called the New Deal—were not uniformly popular or successful, and controversy over their constitutionality became an issue. When the Supreme Court began ruling against the New Deal, Roosevelt attempted to win legislation that would enable him to appoint more justices, but there was a Congressional and public outcry and he had to back down. Although it seemed to be his most serious political defeat, it was so only in appearance, because the court quickly began to uphold the key measures of his administration.

By the time the Supreme Court issue was blowing over, war was threatening in Europe and the Far East. Having built his unusual political strength by moving across party lines to draw in all those of like philosophical mind, Roosevelt tried to lead the American people toward an early realization of the consequences to America of conflicts in Europe and Asia. He fought, unsuccessfully, for revision of the NEUTRALITY ACTS to enable the United States to help victims of aggression, and in October 1937 he spoke of "quarantining" aggressors. American isolationist sentiment was strong, there was an outcry of protest and alarm, and Roosevelt retreated to a slower-paced leadership. Not until Germany invaded Poland in 1939 did Congress revise the neutrality laws to allow CASH AND CARRY, and during the ensuing year Roosevelt requested modest increases for armaments and defense. In a decision known to only a very few, he authorized research into atomic energy and set the Manhattan Project (the ATOMIC BOMB) in motion. He strengthened his cabinet by the addition of two prominent Republicans, Henry L. STIMSON as Secretary of War and Frank KNOX as Secretary of the Navy, but in the election of 1940, when Roosevelt ran for an unprecedented third term against Wendell

President Roosevelt tours a war plant. The officer escorting the President is Gen. Brehon B. Somervell, head of the Army Service Forces

WILLKIE, both candidates pledged to keep the nation out of war.

The first important achievement of Roosevelt's third term was the LEND-LEASE Act, passed in March 1941 after a lengthy Congressional debate. The concept was Roosevelt's. Convinced that victory by Germany and Italy would be disastrous for the United States, and realizing that Britain's resources were almost depleted and she could not long continue to buy war goods on the cash-and-carry plan, Roosevelt sought a way to get rid of "the silly, foolish, old dollar sign" and put the economic resources of America at Britain's disposal. "All aid short of war" and the "arsenal of democracy" were American policy until the Pearl Harbor attack on December 7, 1941. After Germany invaded Russia, lend-lease was extended to the Russians also. The war goods were useless if German U-boats sank them before they reached their destination, and gradually the U.S. Navy began to take an active role in protecting convoys in the ATLANTIC.

During the period of the "undeclared war" in the Atlantic, Roosevelt continued to emphasize the importance to the free world of an AXIS defeat and to move steadily but cautiously forward in preparing the country for defense. Economic mobilization proceeded rapidly; a two-ocean navy was under construction. To ensure that the two nations would be ready to work together if the United States became actively involved in the war, joint British–U.S. staff talks were held in January 1941, and in August Roosevelt journeyed to Newfoundland for a meeting with Prime Minister Winston CHURCHILL. Their meeting, at which the ATLANTIC CHARTER was formulated, was the beginning of a firm friendship and paved the way for what later became the pattern of the Allied coalition—top-level conferences by the heads of state and their military staffs in which strategic decisions were hammered out and resources allotted to implement them.

As early as 1932 Roosevelt had called the Presidency "pre-eminently a place of moral leadership," and during the war years he exerted his major efforts in the fields of Allied relations, strategy and planning for the future peace. He relied heavily on his military leaders, particularly George C. MARSHALL, for military decision-making. Only once, when he insisted that American troops get into action in Europe in 1942, did he overrule his military advisers.

Much of Roosevelt's personal faith and energy went into the planning of the UNITED NATIONS. More than two decades earlier Roosevelt had campaigned vigorously for the LEAGUE OF NATIONS. Now, with the power of the Presidency behind him, he sought to convince Americans of the importance of world cooperation and simultaneously to build from the war's wreckage a world in which peaceful cooperation would be feasible. It was soon obvious that Germany and Japan would be defeated, and Roosevelt felt the future stability of the world lay largely in developing friendly relations with the Russians. Tackling Russian reserve, secrecy and occasional churlishness as hurdles to a worthwhile goal, Roosevelt sought to win Joseph STALIN's friendship and trust. At the TEHERAN CONFERENCE in November 1943, such friendship seemed attainable. Before the end of the war numerous problems arose, particularly in eastern Europe. Churchill expressed fear of Stalin's intentions, but Roosevelt, though aware of difficulties, continued to feel that the hope of future world peace lay in obtaining Soviet cooperation.

Shortly after being elected to a fourth term, Roosevelt, who had retained a physical and mental vigor that astounded his critics, began to show signs of stress and age. He was at Warm Springs, resting and looking forward to attending the United Nations SAN FRANCISCO CONFERENCE, when he died of a massive cerebral hemorrhage. The date was April 12, 1945—two weeks before the conference convened, four months before atomic power became a reality. He had played a leading role in the development of both, but as his funeral train made its way to Hyde Park thousands of Americans lined the tracks to mourn a political leader they would remember primarily as a friend. **M.H.B.**

ROOSEVELT, James (1907–). The oldest son of President Franklin D. ROOSEVELT, James Roosevelt completed various tours of active duty in the Marine Corps Reserve prior to the war. He also served as personal secretary and aide to his father during a number of international conferences and as the President's representative on inspection trips to the Middle and Far East before the United States entered the war.

As executive officer of the 2d Raider Battalion (Carlson's Raiders), he participated in the assault of MAKIN Atoll in the Gilberts in August 1942. For his exemplary courage during this action he was awarded the NAVY CROSS. He returned to the United States in October 1942 to take command of the newly formed 4th Raider Battalion and bring it back overseas. While training for the New Georgia operation, Roosevelt was hospitalized and then evacuated to the States. He returned to the Pacific in 1943 and for the rest of the war served as an intelligence officer on a number of major staffs during various operations.

Colonel Roosevelt transferred to the inactive list in October 1945 and was elected to Congress from the state of California in 1954. He retired from the Marine Corps Reserve in 1959 in the rank of brigadier general.

ROOSEVELT, Theodore, Jr. (1887–1944). U.S. Army officer (son of the 26th President), assistant commander of the 1st Division at ORAN in the NORTHWEST AFRICA operation and of the 4th Division in the Normandy INVASION. He was relieved from his post during the fighting in SICILY in a general command shuffle to improve discipline in the division. But he was returned to action in Normandy, through the help of his longtime friend Gen. George C. MARSHALL. General Roosevelt died on July 12 of a heart attack. An explorer and politician, Roosevelt had earlier served as Governor General of the Philippines.

ROOSTER. A mode of late-wartime Allied IFF operation (*see* IFF) in which certain designated equipment could transmit a beacon signal which allowed other planes to home on them.

ROSE, Maurice (1899–1945). U.S. Army officer who served as chief of staff of the 2d Armored Division in 1942–43. As a major general he became the commanding general of the 3d Armored Division, which he led until he was killed in action in Germany on March 30, 1945.

ROSENBERG, Alfred (1893–1946). Often called the "philosopher" of the Nazi Party, Rosenberg was a Baltic German, a native of Tallinn, who studied in Russia and graduated from the University of Moscow in 1917. He went to Berlin in 1918 and thence to Munich, where he began working with right-wing and Russian émigré groups, including, in 1919, the fledgling German Workers' Party, which became the Nazi Party. He became an intellectual influence on Adolf HITLER, having much to do with the phrasing of Hitler's denunciations of Judaism and Bolshevism as twin evils; Rosenberg appears to have advanced these ideas not out of expediency but out of fervent conviction. In 1923 he took over the editorship of the *Völkischer Beobachter*, the party newspaper. After the Nazis came to power in 1933, Rosenberg was given the title "Chief of the Foreign Political Office." He held many positions of a more or less ideological nature, the most spectacular of which was "Führer's Deputy for Supervision of the Entire Spiritual and Ideological Training of the Nazi Party." During the war he became a general in the SS (*see* SS).

In 1941 he was appointed Reich Minister for the Occupied Eastern Territories. His zealous application of his racial beliefs rapidly alienated the numerous Russians who had welcomed the German invaders. At Nuremberg he was charged with organizing the plunder of the occupied areas, helping to formulate the policies of forced Germanization of the areas, exploiting forced labor and exterminating Jews and members of other groups. He was hanged on October 16, 1946. *See also* NATIONAL SOCIALIST GERMAN WORKERS' PARTY.

ROSENMAN, Samuel Irving (1896–1973). President Franklin D. ROOSEVELT's personal counsel and chief speechwriter, who had served on the New York Supreme Court in 1932–43, resigning from it to accept the counsel's position. Previously, Judge Rosenman had been associated with the President in an informal way, and in 1929–32 had served as counsel to then Governor Roosevelt.

ROSENTHAL, Joseph J. (1911–). Associated Press photographer who was with the U.S. Marine forces which invaded Iwo JIMA. He was present on Mount SURIBACHI on February 23, 1945, when five marines and a Navy hospital corpsman were struggling to raise the American flag. He was awarded the Pultizer Prize in 1945 for his classic photograph, which became perhaps the most famous picture of the war, and the scene was later depicted in the largest bronze statue in the world—the Marine Corps War Memorial, Arlington, Va.

ROSTOV. "Gateway to the Caucasus" and scene of a fierce battle in November 1941 in which the Red Army successfully defended the city from German capture, the first major Soviet victory of the war. The victory was important in a double sense, for it helped reduce German pressure on Moscow and quite possibly saved the Soviet capital from enemy capture. In July 1942 the Germans again attacked, and this time took the city. In sharp contrast to their staunchness in 1941, the Russians panicked and abandoned Rostov, a development which led to numerous executions on STALIN's orders of Russian generals and officers. Finally, in February 1943, shortly after the German defeat at STALINGRAD, the Russians recaptured the city.

ROSYTH. Until April 1938 Rosyth, in the Firth of Forth, was designated as the base for the British Home Fleet in the event of war with Germany. Because Rosyth was strategically less suitable than SCAPA FLOW, the Home Fleet was moved about until March 1940, when Scapa had acquired sufficient defenses to serve as the main base.

ROTMISTROV, Pavel A. (1901–). Red Army officer, a leading authority on tank warfare, who as a lieutenant general commanded a tank corps at the Battle of STALINGRAD. In 1943 he was promoted to colonel general and to the command of the Fifth Guards Armored Army. Rotmistrov commanded this army at KURSK, his tank engagement at Prokhorovka being one of the biggest of the war. In 1944 he was promoted to the rank of marshal and Deputy Commander of the Armored Forces.

ROTTERDAM. The German bombing of Rotterdam on May 14, 1940, was one of the symbolic acts of the war. Coming while negotiations for surrender were under way, it seemed to represent Nazi wantonness and terrorism at its worst and, together with later attacks on English cities, played an important part in influencing British opinion in favor of indiscriminate attacks on German cities. Yet the bombing was the direct result of confusion and error. On May 13 German tanks were poised to enter the city, in which resistance was strong, and German paratroopers at the Willems Bridge were under heavy fire. Gen. Rudolf Schmidt, the German commander, demanded that Rotterdam surrender; the Dutch commander, Col. P. Scharoo, delayed, part of the confusion resulting from the Dutch high command's insistence that the German ultimatum have a proper signature. General Schmidt obliged, but vital time had been lost, and a mix-up in German communications caused his order to delay the planned LUFTWAFFE raid to be lost somewhere in the delivery chain. Schmidt had given Scharoo until 4:20 P.M. to surrender, but at three o'clock 100 He 111s appeared. Germans on the ground sent up red flares, waving the bombers off, but in the smoke and haze most of the fliers failed to see them, and 57 of the attackers roared over the city at 2,000 feet, dropping 97 tons of high explosive on the target area, without killing any of the Germans fighting in the area of the bridge. The raid was thoroughly effective, and only the surrender of the city averted a second one.

The Allies unintentionally strengthened German propaganda claims by extreme exaggeration of the casualties from the raid. Rather than 25,000 or 30,000 killed, as the Allies said, the dead amounted to 814. And even though a communications breakdown was directly responsible for the raid's being carried out, it is also true that some of the German commanders were glad of the opportunity to demonstrate the power of the Luftwaffe and thus overawe the people of other cities and countries.

ROTTERDAM APPARATUS. German code name for PPI (plan position indicator)–equipped centimetric search RADARS retrieved, in damaged condition, from two downed British planes early in 1943. Undamaged components were assembled into one working set, and its unexpected performance spurred a feverish race to develop countermeasures against such radars as well as similar search sets for German use. The discovery came as a shock; German authorities had hitherto considered centimetric radar impracticable.

ROUEN. Port on the Seine River below Paris, heavily damaged by bombing in 1940 and 1944 because it was a key transportation center. Following the Normandy INVASION, Lt. Gen. Sir Henry D. G. CRERAR's Canadian FIRST ARMY liberated the city on August 31, 1944.

ROUEN-SOTTEVILLE. On August 17, 1942, the U.S. EIGHTH AIR FORCE bomber command made its first strike of the war, launching 12 B-17Es, escorted by British SPITFIRES, against the Sotteville railroad marshaling yards at Rouen, France. The Flying Fortresses, with Gen. Ira C. EAKER flying as an observer in the lead plane of the second flight, dropped some 37,000 pounds of bombs from 23,000 feet, with about half of these exploding directly within the target area. Enemy antiaircraft and fighter opposition was light, and none of the bombers that took part in the daylight raid was lost. *See also* B-17.

ROUNDUP. Code name of various Allied plans for a cross-Channel attack. As commonly used, it designates the assault on northwest Europe agreed on in 1942 and having the target date April 1, 1943. It was superseded by OVERLORD.

ROVER JOE. Nickname for air controllers that accompanied Allied armies in Italy in order to effect coordination between air and ground forces.

ROXAS, Manuel (1892–1948). General Roxas, a Philippine politician who had served as Speaker of the House of Representatives in the Commonwealth government, was taken prisoner by the Japanese on Mindanao in 1942. An order from General HOMMA's headquarters calling for his secret execution turned out to have been issued in Homma's name but without his authorization, and Roxas survived to become the first President of the Philippine Republic (1946–48).

ROYAL AIR FORCE. The Royal Air Force came into being as an independent service on April 1, 1918, as a result of the union of the former Royal Flying Corps and the Royal Naval Air Service. Despite attempts by the older services, usually associated with Treasury demands for economy in defense expenditure, the RAF preserved its independent existence. With Britain facing the growing threat of a resurgent Germany under the Nazi regime after 1933 and possible enemies in the Far East and in the Mediterranean, the RAF had to undergo a rapid expansion in manpower and equipment. The creation of functional commands (e.g., FIGHTER COMMAND) in 1936 was the first step in putting the RAF on a war basis.

Overall direction of the Royal Air Force was vested in the Air Council of the Air Ministry. The Air Council consisted of the political and military leaders of the service, principals being the Secretary of State for Air and the Chief of Air Staff. When war was declared, the Royal Air Force had a total of 1,911 first-line aircraft, compared with the German total of 4,161. Bombers were mainly of the two-engine variety, but the first STIRLINGS and HALIFAXES were appearing. The best fighters were the SPITFIRE I and V and the HURRICANE I and II. Coastal aircraft were a mix of land-based ANSONS, HUDSONS and BLENHEIMS with some flying boats, the best of which was the SUNDERLAND I. The strength of the RAF at the outbreak of war was 20,033 air crew and 153,925 ground personnel, with 1,734 members of the WOMEN'S AUXILIARY AIR FORCE. The total force of men and women was 175,692. In May 1945 the air crew totals were 144,488 RAF together with 41,107 Dominion personnel. Ground personnel numbered 831,541 RAF and 33,976 Dominion. The WAAF component consisted of 157,286 WAAF and 445 Dominion. The total force of men and women in the RAF was 1,208,843, and in addition 29,763 Allied personnel were enrolled.

During the war the RAF operated continuously over Europe, the North Atlantic and the seas around the British Isles. It frustrated the LUFTWAFFE's attempts to win air superiority as a prelude to the invasion of the British Isles in 1940. It supported the Army in drawn-out campaigns in NORTH AFRICA, the Mediterranean, ITALY, the BALKANS and the Far East. It played a major role with its U.S. partners—the EIGHTH, NINTH and FIFTEENTH U.S. Army Air Forces—in the air offensive preceding and complementing the Allied INVASION of Europe, which led to the final defeat of Hitler's Germany. In the bomber offensive the Royal Air Force made its biggest effort in terms of logistics, number of aircraft, personnel and casualties. The official history records that "of a total of 70,253 officers, noncommissioned officers and airmen of the Royal Air Force killed or missing on operations between September 3, 1939, and August 14, 1945, 47,293 lost their lives or disappeared in operations carried out by BOMBER COMMAND."

The Air Council, which had to formulate the administrative plans to meet the demands on the Air Force made by the political leaders of the nation and the CHIEFS OF STAFF COMMITTEE, succeeded in retaining in position certain key figures who provided continuous leadership during the bulk of the war years. The Secretary of State for Air was Sir Archibald SINCLAIR, the Chief of Air Staff was Sir Charles PORTAL, the Air Member for Supply and Organization was Sir Christopher Courtney and the Permanent Under Secretary was Sir Arthur Street. These, assisted by staff and commanders who stayed in their posts for long tours—especially Sir Arthur HARRIS at Bomber Command—gave the solid support needed by the operational squadrons in the theaters of war.

ROYAL AUSTRALIAN AIR FORCE. At the time war broke out, the RAAF comprised about 300 officers and 3,000 men. RAAF squadrons operated in Europe, the Middle East, India-Burma and the Far East in bomber, fighter, transport and maritime roles. Over 10,000 officers and men were killed in action. Australia played a big part in the Empire Air Training Scheme (the training of fliers in the dominions), and the RAAF provided 27,387 air crew, of whom 10,882 were pilots, all trained in the Commonwealth. At the end of the war the RAAF was operating more than 50 squadrons in the Pacific theater alone. A wing of Mustang fighters went to Japan in 1945 as part of the air component of the British Commonwealth Occupation Forces, but by 1946 full-scale demobilization of the RAAF was well under way.

ROYAL CANADIAN AIR FORCE. Canadian airmen made a significant contribution to aviation in World War I as part of the Royal Flying Corps and the RAF. Distinguished names like Bishop, Barker, McLeod and Collishaw will be remembered. A nucleus of Canadian squadrons had been formed with the RAF, but the Canadian Air Force itself dates from 1920; the prefix Royal was granted in 1923. The establishment of the new force was necessarily limited by peacetime financial stringency, but in 1937 the Flying Training School at Trenton, Ont., added a program to train crews specifically for the RAF. In 1939 the Empire Air Training Scheme was adopted. No less than 360 schools and associated units were set up in Canada; 137,739 trained air crew, of whom 54,000 were pilots, emerged from the Canadian Training Scheme, and a considerable proportion of the cost was met by Canada herself as part of her contribution to the war effort. Many of those trained as air crew came from the United States. Although a number of them returned to become part of the U.S. Army Air Forces after Pearl Harbor, hundreds remained in the Canadian Air Force until the war was over.

The Transatlantic Ferry Service was inaugurated in November 1940 to speed up delivery of aircraft to Britain. Canadian pilots flew with other nationalities to ferry across the Atlantic thousands of Canadian- and American-built aircraft. Canadian airmen served with the RAF either as individuals or in complete units. No. 1 Squadron RCAF fought in the Battle of BRITAIN, and No. 6 Group in BOMBER COMMAND was composed of Canadian squadrons, mostly based in Yorkshire. At sea RCAF maritime squadrons played a vital part in the Battle of the ATLANTIC.

ROYAL MARINE. Code name for a British plan to lay floating mines in the Rhine, Moselle and Meuse Rivers early in the war. The mines were so designed that they would become harmless by the time they reached neutral portions of the river. The original plan was to lay them in March and April 1940, both by launching them from the French-held banks of the rivers and by dropping them from aircraft. The French Government asked for a delay, however, because it feared reprisals. Finally, on May 14, when the German armies were well on the move, mines were released into the Rhine, but the operation was rendered futile by the speed of the German victory in FRANCE.

ROYAL NAVY. By the start of the Second World War in 1939, the naval forces of Great Britain had taken up their traditional war stations and war organization. The main striking force at home, consisting of battleships, battle cruisers, aircraft carriers, cruisers and destroyers, was the Home Fleet, based at SCAPA FLOW, the traditional distant blockade base for a war against Germany. There was a Channel Force of battleships and cruisers based at Portsmouth, a Humber Force of cruisers and destroyers, with the Humber River on the east coast as its base, and destroyer forces at the various main naval bases available for local operations. The only fleet outside home waters was in the Mediterranean, consisting of battleships, a carrier, cruisers, destroyers and submarines, with the other foreign commands—North Atlantic, South Atlantic, America and West Indies, East Indies and China—having squadrons of cruisers and destroyers (the China Command having submarines in addition). The Royal Australian Navy disposed 5 cruisers and 3 destroyers, the Royal Canadian Navy had 6 destroyers and the Royal New Zealand Division of the Royal Navy (not an independent navy until October 1941) consisted of 2 cruisers and 2 small escort vessels.

The overall strength of the British navy, excluding ships undergoing major refits (2 battleships, 1 battle cruiser, 6 cruisers, 14 destroyers) and the Commonwealth navies, amounted to 12 battleships and battle cruisers, 8 carriers, 35 fleet cruisers, 23 convoy cruisers, 100 fleet destroyers, 101 escort destroyers, sloops and similar vessels, and 38 submarines. New ships under construction were 2 battleships, 2 carriers, 5 cruisers, 1 destroyer and 2 submarines of the 1936 program; 3 battleships, 2 carriers, 6 cruisers, 15 destroyers and 6 submarines of the 1937 program; 2 carriers, 8 cruisers, 16 destroyers and 3 submarines of the 1938 and 1939 programs. Of smaller warships, 24 escort vessels, 40 minesweepers and 4 fast minelayers were on the building stocks. Following the declaration of war, an emergency building program was superimposed on the 1939 program, designed to add 6 cruisers, 58 destroyers and escort destroyers, 60 antisubmarine corvettes, 24 submarines and 16 minesweepers to the strength of the Royal Navy. And as the war progressed, new building programs in 1940 and 1941 added yet more ships in substantial numbers, particularly escort carriers, destroyers, antisubmarine frigates, sloops and corvettes, submarines and minesweepers.

As in any war against a continental power, the first and major task of the Navy was to establish as strict a blockade as possible against all enemy seaborne trade. Within a few days of the outbreak of war, German shipping had either been swept off the oceans or immobilized in whichever foreign ports they happened to be in when war was declared. Some of them attempted to run the blockade in an attempt to reach home; few succeeded.

For the first week or two of the war there was some anxiety whether Germany's partners in the Axis, Italy and Japan, would come in on the side of Germany. When it became apparent that they were not going to do so, it became possible to reduce the Mediterranean Fleet and the China Squadron, bringing the ships home to assist in the blockade and other tasks. The squadrons stationed elsewhere abroad were left as they were, and some in fact were reinforced, to try to deal with the German raider warfare which began to build up in the oceans within a few weeks. An early success in foreign seas was the action fought off the RIVER PLATE on December 13, 1939, which resulted in the scuttling of the German pocket battleship ADMIRAL GRAF SPEE.

It was perhaps propitious for the Royal Navy that the

Donaldson liner ATHENIA was torpedoed by a U-boat and sunk on the first day of the war. There had been some ambivalence in the Navy's outlook on the need to introduce a convoy system for merchant shipping at the start of the war, some authorities holding it unnecessary until sinkings from U-boat attack had reached a level which surpassed Britain's ability to replace tonnage lost through new construction. The sinking of the *Athenia* by *U-30* changed all that, and within two or three days of war being declared, a convoy system was in operation. This requirement highlighted one of the main failures of interwar naval policy in Britain, revealing not only a chronic shortage of escort vessels but also a severe lack of speed and endurance in those which had been built. At first, escorts could only take a convoy from Britain out to 14° W., meeting an incoming convoy on that longitude and escorting it in. During the next two years the limit was pushed out to 19° W. before, by the end of 1941, end-to-end ATLANTIC escort was achieved. Convoys to other destinations were similarly limited in scope until the new long-legged escorts, under construction, became operational.

The first major test of the Home Fleet was the German invasion and occupation of NORWAY (April–May 1940). One of the main lessons learned during that campaign was the inability of ships to operate under continuous air attack without their own air cover, a painful lesson for the Royal Navy, which lost a number of ships through direct air attack. But the occupation of Norway by Germany was to pose more difficult problems for Britain. Norway's many protected deepwater anchorages were fine bases for GERMAN NAVY ships, which, simply by their presence there, automatically tied down ships of the Home Fleet, a classic example of the "fleet in being" theory of naval strategy. Other ports were quickly adapted as U-boat bases, bringing the U-boats many hundreds of miles nearer their patrol areas in the Atlantic.

The occupation of Denmark and Norway was followed within a month by the attack on the Low Countries and FRANCE. A disastrous campaign on the Allied side brought Germany a yet greater prize than the Norwegian bases through her occupation of the French naval bases on the coast of the Bay of Biscay—BREST, SAINT-NAZAIRE, LORIENT and Bordeaux. From these bases German U-boats now had a new access to the Atlantic, cutting their passage to and from their patrol areas by more than 1,000 miles and thus giving them that much more time on patrol. The Royal Navy had little part to play in this essentially land campaign beyond being called upon to lift the British Army from the beaches at DUNKIRK (and elsewhere) when they became cut off by the German advance.

With the fall of France, Italy entered the war on the side of Germany, bringing yet more naval problems. Her geographical position in the center of the Mediterranean made the British main naval base at MALTA untenable, and the fleet was forced to move into the eastern Mediterranean, with its base at ALEXANDRIA. In the original alliance at the start of the war, the security of the western Mediterranean was the province of the FRENCH NAVY; it was now to fall to Britain to fill that gap. An independent squadron of one battleship, one battle cruiser and one aircraft carrier, all that could be spared from the Home Fleet, was formed and was based at GIBRALTAR to seal up the entrance to the Mediterranean through the Strait of Gibraltar.

The basic naval strategy at this stage of the war (1940) was to hold a line out in the Atlantic from Norway to Gibraltar, with Britain as a fortress inside that wide arc of ocean. It was expected, as the war progressed and German naval forces were worn down and gradually eliminated, that the ocean line could be drawn inward until Allied command of the sea would leave the European coastline open to invasion. There was always full recognition in Britain that for the war to be won, the final confrontation would have to come on the mainland of Europe, with the decisive battle fought between the armies and air forces of the two sides, but there was equally full recognition that no such battle could ever be fought unless the seas around Europe were under complete Allied domination.

The naval strategy in the Mediterranean was basically similar to that in the Atlantic—to hold firm at both ends (Suez and Gibraltar) and exert pressure from them eventually to dominate the whole length of that inland sea. But there were complications, both in the need to deny the enemy possession of the strategic central position of Malta and in the fact that a land campaign was being waged in NORTH AFRICA. British retention of Malta was essential, since it was the one strong base from which supply lines to the enemy armies in Africa could be harried and cut by submarine and air attack; if Malta were lost, the land war in Africa would also be lost. No one realized this more forcefully than Adm. Sir Andrew CUNNINGHAM, Commander in Chief of the Mediterranean Fleet, and from the day that Italy entered the war he determined, in spite of the great disparity in numbers between the opposing fleets, to achieve his objective by establishing supremacy over the ITALIAN NAVY. Two major victories in fairly rapid succession—the FLEET AIR ARM attack on the Italian battleships at TARANTO and the night action off CAPE MATAPAN—put the Italian Navy on the defensive, and all through the desperate days to come it was never allowed to switch from defensive to offensive. Even when German military and air forces arrived in strength in the Mediterranean to bolster Italian morale, even when severe losses of British warships in the fighting around Greece, CRETE and Malta reduced Cunningham's forces to a shadow of their former strength, that determination never wavered.

The main naval battle of the first four years of the war was that fought in the Atlantic and Arctic Oceans against German U-boats. Adm. Karl DÖNITZ, who commanded the U-boat fleet, was not slow to understand that Germany's only chance of winning the war was through a successful campaign against British seaborne trade. This was, as it has always been, the Achilles' heel of an island nation dependent on a steady flow of imports to remain operational. Dönitz, himself a U-boat captain of the First World War, had trained his captains in two new tactics which gave promise of great results. The first of these was the surface attack at night, when the tiny silhouette of a submarine's conning tower is virtually invisible to the defense. The second tactic was to organize submarines at sea to operate in packs, made up of as many as 20 boats, as circumstances allowed, and to bring them all in to the target before an attack was made. To neither of these tactics had the Royal

Navy any answer during the early years of the war, and the Battle of the Atlantic was a long-drawn-out and evenly balanced campaign. Until it was won, there could be no return to Europe to engage Germany in the decisive battle that could bring final victory; and it was because of this that the Atlantic campaign became the dominating concern of the Royal Navy, assisted by the Royal Canadian Navy and, later, by the U.S. NAVY. This vital campaign was won only just in time (May 1943). With the threat of U-boat attack removed in the Atlantic, the way was now open for the concentration in Britain of the armies and their weapons and supplies with which to mount the assault on Europe.

While the Atlantic campaign was in full swing, a smaller but no less desperate naval war was being fought in the Arctic—on the sea route north of Norway to MURMANSK, USSR. But at the end of this particular small campaign, as in the Atlantic, victory was achieved and the last convoys sailed regularly without hindrance or loss.

In the Mediterranean, the year 1942 was a vital one. Malta, the linchpin of British naval strategy in that theater, was still holding firm against German and Italian attack, though at a savagely increasing cost in naval and merchant ships sunk. The supply convoys to Malta produced some of the bitterest battles of the whole naval war, but just enough merchant ships got through to keep the island 's defense alive. In the land campaign in North Africa, Field Marshal ROMMEL and his AFRIKA KORPS drove the British forces back to within striking distance of Cairo, and for a time the situation in the Middle East became desperate, with the loss of two battleships of the Mediterranean Fleet to Italian human torpedoes making the task yet more difficult. But the tide of battle in the Mediterranean theater was turned with the land victory at ALAMEIN in October 1942 and the almost simultaneous Anglo–U.S. assaults in NORTHWEST AFRICA, which brought the German and Italian forces under attack on two fronts. Although there was much bitter fighting still to be done in Europe, total victory in Africa had been achieved by May 1943; the naval contribution had been the almost complete denial of seaborne supplies to the enemy armies. The success in North Africa not only removed the threat to Malta but opened the whole Mediterranean to Allied convoys which could sustain the inevitable follow-up assaults on SICILY and ITALY.

By the end of 1943 the naval war in the European theater had been virtually won, even though there was still 18 months of very hard fighting to come. The Atlantic Ocean was wide open to a stream of convoys bringing men, munitions and supplies for the final assault on Europe. The Arctic, too, was open for supplies to Russia. The naval blockade of Germany, held far out in the oceans during the dark days of 1940, 1941 and 1942, was now closing in and becoming a stranglehold, and planning for the Normandy INVASION was progressing unhindered by anything the Germans could do. It was launched on June 6, 1944, and on the naval side involved some 7,000 ships, of which over 1,200 were warships ranging from battleships to MIDGET SUBMARINES. The majority of these warships were British, as were the two prefabricated MULBERRY harbors towed across the English Channel and assembled on the coast of France. The successful landing of the Allied armies and their supplies, and their sustenance during the weeks of fighting to establish a firm bridgehead ashore, was the last great naval operation of the war in Europe, though the clearance of ports along the coast for the more efficient supply of the advancing armies was still a naval commitment. The opening of Antwerp as a supply port, for instance, was only achieved after a bitterly fought naval action at the mouth of the Scheldt River.

British naval operations on the other side of the world, where Japan had entered the war on the side of Germany and Italy in December 1941, were always secondary in comparison with the operations of the U.S. fleet, the dominant partner in this theater of operations. The war had opened there with considerable defeats for both partners, and it took many months before the Japanese advance in the Pacific could be stopped, stabilized and finally reversed. The main British theater of operations against the Japanese was the Indian Ocean, which included the waters around Burma, where there was much fighting. It was only in the last few months, after the victory in Europe, that a British fleet was sent to the Pacific to fight alongside the U.S. Navy. By that time only the final battles remained to be fought, and even in these it was the U.S. fleet which took the preponderant share. In the Indian Ocean, which was a purely British commitment, the advance of the army through Burma and its eventual recapture of Singapore were sustained by the Royal Navy in those waters.

If one can take the naval war as a whole, the overall balance of endeavor was not uneven. If the PACIFIC WAR was overwhelmingly a United States commitment, that in European waters was equally overwhelmingly a British effort.

With the final victory over Japan, the Second World War came to an end. Of the three British services engaged, Navy, Army and Air, the cost had borne most heavily, in terms of casualties, on the Royal Navy, whose losses in personnel engaged amounted to 9.3 percent, compared with 9.0 percent for the Royal Air Force and 6.1 percent for the Army. Total losses in ships amounted to 4 battleships, 2 battle cruisers, 5 aircraft carriers, 3 escort carriers, 2 catapult ships, 33 cruisers, 154 destroyers, 90 submarines, 13 sloops, 3 cutters, 11 frigates, 38 corvettes, 39 minesweepers, 1 monitor, 10 minelayers, 6 antiaircraft ships, 15 armed merchant cruisers and 2 submarine and destroyer depot ships. Of this total, 169 ships were lost in the Mediterranean, 119 in home waters and 84 in the North Atlantic. **P.K.K.**

ROYAL OAK, H.M.S. Royal Navy battleship of 29,150 tons, completed at Devonport in 1916 and refitted but not modernized prior to 1939. *Royal Oak* was sunk on October 14, 1939, in SCAPA FLOW anchorage as a result of a daring attack by the German submarine *U-47*. Günther PRIEN, the *U-47*'s captain, also mistakenly claimed damage to other ships. Of her crew, 833 perished. It was the first such naval loss to Britain.

ROYAL SOVEREIGN, H.M.S. Royal Navy battleship of 29,150 tons, completed in 1916 at Portsmouth and not modernized. *Royal Sovereign* was armed with eight 15-inch, twelve 6-inch and eight 4-inch guns, smaller weapons and one aircraft. She served on convoy escort duties chiefly in the ATLANTIC but occasionally in the Mediterranean until 1942, when she joined the Far Eastern Fleet. In 1944 she was made over to the Red Navy on loan and served under the name *Archangelsk.* Despite her age and limited value, the Soviet authorities were reluctant to return her to Britain at the end of the war, only doing so in 1949.

ROYAL TIGER TANK. German heavy TANK (Tiger II).

ROYAL WEST AFRICAN FRONTIER FORCE. The name dates from 1897, when the force was first raised by the British, and was used later to cover troops raised in the four British West African colonies of Nigeria, Gold Coast (now Ghana), Sierra Leone and Gambia. In these units West African troops, organized into two brigades, played a notable part in the operations against the Italians in Somalia and Ethiopia in January–October 1941. After the Japanese entry into the war West African forces were expanded into two divisions, the 81st and 82d West African Divisions, and sent to the BURMA front, where they fought in various operations beteen 1943 and 1945.

RS-14. This Italian aircraft, built by Fiat and flown for the first time in 1938, was a beautifully streamlined, midwing, twin-engine, twin-float monoplane. Maximum speed of the all-metal seaplane was a creditable 242 miles per hour, but the armament was only three machine guns. Capable of carrying bombs or depth charges, the RS-14 flew reconnaissance, overwater patrol, convoy protection and air–sea rescue missions.

RUDDEROW, U.S.S. Destroyer escort and class. Turboelectric powered, these ships were similar to the JOHN C. BUTLER class in appearance, with a low bridge and two closed 5-INCH 38-caliber gun mounts. Fifty-four of the 81 ships of this class, designated type TEV, completed as fast transports (*see* APD) of the CROSLEY class; 187 more were canceled.

RUDENKO, Sergei I. (1904–). Soviet air officer who commanded the Sixteenth Air Army, which fought in the Battles of STALINGRAD, and KURSK and the invasion of Germany. Rudenko was later promoted to the rank of marshal of aviation.

RUGE, Friedrich Oskar (1894–). German admiral who as commander of Naval Forces West was associated with Field Marshal Erwin ROMMEL in the defense of Normandy at the time of the Allied INVASION in 1944. A successful writer on military affairs, in postwar years he was closely associated with U.S. military forces in West Germany.

RUGE, Otto (1882–1961). Inspector General of Infantry, Colonel Ruge became Commander in Chief of the Norwegian Army, being promoted to major general, on April 11, 1940, and served till June 8. He replaced Maj. Gen. Kristian Laake, who retired because of age. Ruge was energetic and pushed for continued resistance to the German invaders, but by the time he took over, they had already seized many divisional and regimental headquarters as well as much equipment. Ruge chose to stay with his men at the end of the campaign. He negotiated an armistice, was taken by the Germans and remained in captivity, first in Norway, then in Germany, until the end of the war. *See also* NORWAY.

RUHR. The valley of the Ruhr River, the heart of the German iron and steel industry, was a principal objective of Allied ground and air operations. In particular, the Ruhr was a favorite target of RAF BOMBER COMMAND. A notable series of raids was the "Battle of the Ruhr," 43 large attacks between March and July 1943, most of which were on Essen, Cologne, Aachen, Bochum, Duisburg, Wuppertal, Düsseldorf and Dortmund.

The Ruhr region was also the objective of the Allied armies following the breakout in Normandy in July–August 1944. In March–April 1945 Allied armies encircled the German Army Group B and two corps of Army Group H in the Ruhr (this envelopment is also known as the Battle of the Ruhr).

RUMYANTSEV. Code name of the Soviet counteroffensive at the Battle of KURSK (August 1943). It covered attacks by the Voronezh and Steppe Fronts.

RUNDSTEDT, Karl Rudolf Gerd von (1875–1953). Rundstedt was born on December 12, 1875, in Aschersleben, Prussia, of an aristocratic Brandenburg family. His father was a general in the Prussian Army, and from his early youth Rundstedt was groomed for a career in the military. After his graduation from the Mili-

Field Marshal von Rundstedt

tary Academy and the General Staff College, he commanded an infantry regiment; he was a major at the beginning of World War I. For his contributions during the campaign in Alsace, he was promoted to chief of staff of corps on both the Eastern and Western Fronts. He also served with the Turkish General Staff. Rundstedt remained on the active list during the Weimar Republic, having the rank of lieutenant colonel and commanding the Third Military Area headquarters (Wehrkreiskommando). During the 1920s he was responsible for the development of the *Einheit* system of battlefield operation. This was a system by which each German infantry command was composed of a small number of self-sufficient units.

From 1933 to 1938 Rundstedt headed the First Army Group. He retired in 1938, but was recalled to active duty in 1939 to command the group of armies which swept across Poland from the south during September. His forces took Krakow, Lodz and Przemysl, driving the Poles from two strategic rivers, the San and the Vistula, leading to the fall of Warsaw. During the western campaign of 1940, Rundstedt led Army Group A, the center group of armies which struck at FRANCE through the ARDENNES, flanked the MAGINOT LINE and pushed to the sea. After the victory over France, Rundstedt was promoted to field marshal.

In the following year he commanded Army Group South in the invasion of Russia. He drove his armies through the Ukraine, destroying Marshal Semën BUDËNNY's army group and capturing KIEV. But in 1942 Rundstedt was defeated at ROSTOV by the Russians under Marshal S. K. TIMOSHENKO; Rundstedt was removed from his Russian command and transferred to France, being put in charge of all defenses from Bayonne to Norway.

When the Allies landed on the Normandy coast in June 6, 1944, Field Marshal von Rundstedt was the German supreme commander in western Europe. After suggesting to Adolf HITLER's headquarters that the war should be ended, he was removed from his command on July 6 and replaced by Field Marshal Günther von KLUGE. Kluge, too, was unable to stem the Allied advance, and Rundstedt was reinstated in command in September. He was in nominal command in the Battle of the BULGE in December (the Allies called it at the time the "Rundstedt offensive," though the field marshal actually opposed the plan).

On March 13, 1945, when Germany's defeat was imminent, Rundstedt retired from active duty. On May 1 at Bad Tolz, 23 miles south of Munich, he was taken prisoner by troops of the 141st Regiment of the U.S. 36th Infantry Division. He was held in British custody for trial before a war crimes tribunal, but because of ill health he was never tried. On May 26, 1949, he was released from a British military hospital in Hamburg. He died in Hannover on February 24, 1953.

RUPERTUS, William Henry (1889–1945). In the U.S. 1st Marine Division GUADALCANAL operation, Brigadier General Rupertus, the assistant division commander, led the force which attacked TULAGI, later going over to Guadalcanal to assist in that operation. He was promoted to major general and assumed command of the division in July 1943 when Gen. Alexander VANDEGRIFT became commander of the I Marine Amphibious Corps. Rupertus led the 1st Marine Division in the landing at CAPE GLOUCESTER on December 26, 1943, and in the assault of PELELIU on September 15, 1944. In November he relinquished command of the division and returned home, where he was assigned as commandant of the Marine Corps schools in Quantico, Va. He died of a heart attack on March 25, 1945.

RUPTURED DUCK. Nickname for a lapel pin given U.S. servicemen upon discharge. The round button enclosed a standing eagle whose wingspan extended beyond the circle.

RUSH-BAGOT AGREEMENT. The U.S.–British Rush-Bagot Agreement of 1817, which neutralized the Great Lakes after the War of 1812, was modified in 1940 and later during the war. The revisions, made by the United States and Canada, allowed naval construction, training and testing to be carried out on the Great Lakes.

RUSSELL ISLANDS. Lying 30–35 miles northwest of Cape Esperance on GUADALCANAL are two large islands, Pavuvu and Banika, which comprise the Russells. The accident of location rather than any strategic significance made this group Adm. William F. HALSEY's first objective (1943) after Guadalcanal was secured. For this operation the U.S. 43d Infantry Division—less one of its regimental combat teams, and reinforced by the 3d Marine Raider Battalion and the antiaircraft elements of the 11th Marine Defense Battalion and assorted naval construction units—was designated. The operation went off on February 21, 1943, without opposition. Banika was built up to become a large supply base; in 1944, after conclusion of the CAPE GLOUCESTER operation, Pavuvu became the home for the 1st Marine Division, which staged from here for both the PELELIU and OKINAWA landings.

RUTTER. Code name of the original Allied plan for a raid on DIEPPE. The operation was canceled and later remounted as JUBILEE, August 19, 1942.

RUWEISAT RIDGE. A desert rise in Egypt, 10 miles from the coast, effectively dividing the ALAMEIN Line into northern and southern portions. Twice, in July 1942, it was the scene of bitter fighting as the British EIGHTH ARMY tried to dislodge the Axis and gain control of the Alamein positions.

RYDER, Charles W. (1892–1960). U.S. Army officer who served as chief of staff of the VI Army Corps in 1941–42, the year he was promoted to major general. Ryder was assigned to the 90th Infantry Division in 1942 and then was given command of the 34th Division. In the landings in NORTHWEST AFRICA he temporarily acted as commander of the assault force at Algiers, as part of the attempt to give the operation a thoroughly American flavor. He then led his division through the ensuing campaign and in ITALY. He was subsequently shifted to the Pacific as commander of the IX Corps.

RYUJO. Japanese light aircraft carrier (10,600 tons), completed in 1931. She carried 48 airplanes. *Ryujo* saw extensive service in the early part of the war, from the PHILIPPINES, where she launched the first attack on December 8, 1941, to the Aleutians in June 1942, to the EASTERN SOLOMONS, where she was sunk on August 24, 1942, by U.S. carrier-based aircraft.

RYUKAKU. Incorrect reading for the characters spelling the name of the Japanese light aircraft carrier SHOHO, sunk in the Battle of the CORAL SEA. Japanese characters may be sounded in different ways, and this ship's name was read as *Ryukaku*; she is frequently referred to by this name in wartime writing.

RYUKYU ISLANDS. Known as the Nansei Shoto in Japanese, this island chain stretches from the Japanese home islands to Formosa. Because of their location and the fact that several of the islands, including OKINAWA, were suitable for air bases, the Ryukyus appeared vital to the island-hopping advance against Japan. After extensive preparation, marines landed on Okinawa on April 1, 1945.

S

SA (Sturmabteilungen—Storm Troopers). Created and organized from ex-servicemen by Maj. Ernst RÖHM, the SA members—the Brown Shirts—were in the 1920s the strong-arm squads of the Nazi Party. They engaged in frequent street clashes with Communists and Socialists and generally sought to paralyze the functioning of government. Radical and anticapitalist, the SA was nationally organized by Röhm in 1931 into 21 districts. Now separated from the Nazi Party, it established its own training schools. By 1933 it had 2.3 million members.

With the split of the SA from the party, a dispute arose between Adolf HITLER and Röhm over the proper role of the SA. Hitler viewed it as an instrument of political intimidation and clearly subordinate to the party, while Röhm treated it as independent of the Nazi movement. Röhm's goal was to build up secretly the armed forces forbidden to Germany by the Treaty of Versailles. Hitler saw the SA only as a means to power; he was opposed to making the SA an independent army.

After Hitler took power, the dispute over the role of the SA became pronounced. The SA advocated expansion of the armed forces and political revolution. The regular army was as disturbed as Hitler at the thought of an independent armed SA. In a swift move Hitler in 1934 had Röhm killed and purged the SA (*see* NIGHT OF THE LONG KNIVES). With the destruction of the SA as a political force, Hitler sought to win the confidence of the Army, assuring its command that it was the sole armed force of the Reich. Not only did Hitler destroy a political rival by eliminating the SA, he also won the backing of the German military. *See also* NATIONAL SOCIALIST GERMAN WORKERS' PARTY.

SABUROV, A. N. (1908–). Soviet general who commanded a special battalion in the defense of KIEV in 1941. During the rest of the war he helped organize and lead PARTISANS.

SACHS, Alexander (1893–1973). Dr. Sachs, a Russian-born economist, won a place in history on October 11, 1939, when he read aloud to President ROOSEVELT a letter signed by Albert EINSTEIN in which the possibilities of "a nuclear chain reaction in a large mass of uranium" were discussed. It was, so far as is known, the first intimation the President had of the feasibility of the ATOMIC BOMB. Sachs had been chosen as spokesman by Leo SZILARD, Eugene WIGNER and other scientists who were concerned about German progress in nuclear research.

SACRED COW. Designated the C-54C, this unique plane was President ROOSEVELT's personal transport. It had an electrically operated elevator that enabled the President to board without leaving his wheelchair. The *Sacred Cow*, also used for a time by President Harry S. TRUMAN, had a conference room as well as passenger accommodations. A pane of bulletproof glass was installed in the window behind which the President sat, but there was no armor plate.

SAFFORD, Laurence Frye (1894–1973). A graduate of the U.S. Naval Academy who served as assistant director of naval communications for cryptographic research in World War II. He had been one of the pioneers in the U.S. attack on the Japanese codes, working in partnership with the Army's Col. William FRIEDMAN. Captain Safford invented 20 coding systems and devices. *See also* MAGIC.

SAINTE-MÈRE-EGLISE. Crossroads town in Normandy inland from UTAH BEACH. When it was taken by paratroopers of the U.S. 82D AIRBORNE DIVISION early on D-Day (June 6, 1944), it became the first French town liberated by American arms.

SAINT-LEU-D'ESSERENT. Site near Paris of a cavern in which the Germans stored V-1 bombs (*see* V-WEAPONS) in 1944. It held about 2,000 bombs; in July it was destroyed in an RAF raid.

SAINT-LÔ. Fortress town in northwestern France on the Vire River. At the time of the Normandy INVASION, the headquarters of the German LXXXIV Corps was located there. Because Saint-Lô was a major communications center for the area, it was an objective assigned to the invading American forces. It was captured on July 18, 1944.

ST. LOUIS, U.S.S. Light cruiser and class, commissioned in 1939. The two ships were 10,000-tonners, similar to the earlier BROOKLYN class in hull and battery, but their superstructure was more closely clustered forward and aft of their two stacks. Instead of the single open-mount 5-inch 25-caliber antiaircraft guns of the Brooklyns, they had eight 5-INCH 38-caliber guns in four twin mounts, and improved fire control equipment. *St. Louis* survived the war; HELENA was lost in the 1943 Battle of KULA GULF. Sold to Brazil in 1951, *St. Louis* was renamed *Tamandare*.

SAINT-MALO. Located on the Brittany Peninsula, Saint-Malo is a Channel seaport and was thus desired by the invading Allies. German defenders used both old fortifications and newly constructed defenses to turn the city into a fortress, not only to deny the Allies the use of the port but also to fix the attacking forces. The scheme was successful, for German troops far behind the line had caused the commitment of an American division to a siege operation. Saint-Malo fell on August 17, 1944, but the Ile de Cézembre, 4,000 yards offshore, held out for two additional weeks.

SAINT-NAZAIRE. Naval base on the Biscay coast of France on which a spectacular Allied combined operations assault was made on the night of March 27–28, 1942. When the German battleship TIRPITZ was known to be operational, the possibility of a foray by her into the Atlantic, as had happened with the BISMARCK, was anticipated by the British Admiralty, which decided to make an attempt to destroy the only dock in western France capable of taking her. This was the *Normandie* lock at Saint-Nazaire (1,148 feet by 164 feet), to which access was gained direct from the Loire River. The plan, as finally evolved, was for a destroyer, with three tons of explosive aboard, to ram the outer caisson of the lock. She was to be escorted up the river estuary by one motor gunboat, one motor torpedo boat and 16 motor launches, all carrying troops designed to land and blow up the dock and other installations.

The plan, called Chariot, involved a sea passage of 400 miles followed by a five-mile journey up a heavily guarded estuary, but the planners hoped for complete surprise. Because of the numerous sandbanks in the estuary, the operation could be mounted only at the height of the spring tides, a condition which occurred at 1:30 A.M. on March 28. The destroyer selected was H.M.S. *Campbeltown*, one of the 50 over-age American destroyers transferred to Britain in the DESTROYERS–BASES DEAL of 1940.

The force sailed from Falmouth on the afternoon of March 26, those on board being 62 naval officers and 291 men, and 44 officers and 224 other ranks of the COMMANDOS. Despite being sighted by a U-boat, they were not effectively discovered by the enemy until they were two miles short of their target, and although they were illuminated by shore-based searchlights, the force commander, Comdr. R. E. D. Ryder, gained another two or three minutes of immunity by giving false identification signals. But by that time the Germans had established the nationality of the vessels, and intense fire was opened on them from both banks. Increasing to full speed, the *Campbeltown* made direct for the lock and at 1:34 A.M. (four minutes after the scheduled time) rammed the caisson at her maximum speed, her bows being embedded in it to a depth of 36 feet. The three-ton charge she carried was timed to explode in two and a half hours. An hour later, after Commander Ryder had landed and satisfied himself that the *Campbeltown* was in position, he ordered the motor torpedo boat to fire her torpedoes, also timed to explode later, into the lock gates of the Saint-Nazaire basin.

At the same time, the Commandos were being landed from the *Campbeltown* and from as many of the motor launches as could get alongside. Once ashore they set about their task of destruction. But the enemy fire was getting so hot and the small craft suffering so much damage that withdrawal was essential. Only seven of the original 18 escorts were still capable of movement, and taking on board as many wounded and others as they could, they set off downriver but were intercepted by German torpedo boats. By the time the action was over, only three of the small craft were still on hand. One had been sunk by the torpedo boats, three others had disappeared out to sea. Destroyers took on board the crews and passengers of the three small craft and returned to Plymouth. Later that day the three motor launches which had proceeded out to sea reached Falmouth under their own power.

The total losses in killed and missing were 85 naval and 59 military personnel, though many others re-

Submarine pens at Saint-Nazaire

mained as prisoners until the end of the war. Fourteen of the small craft engaged were also lost.

It was almost noon on the next day when the *Campbeltown* finally blew up, wrecking the caisson. A large number of German senior officers were on board at the time to inspect her, and all lost their lives. An hour later the torpedoes that had been fired into the lock gates also exploded, causing more casualties. These repeated explosions caused the German troops to panic and they opened fire, killing hundreds of their own men and a large number of French dockyard workers. **P.K.K.**

SAINT-OMER. Located some 40 miles WNW of Lille (France), Saint-Omer had been often fought over in past wars. On September 5, 1944, the town was taken by the 1st Polish Armored Division.

SAINT PIERRE AND MIQUELON. French islands off Newfoundland, taken over from VICHY control by a Free French naval force under Adm. Emile MUSELIER on December 24, 1941. The action had diplomatic ramifications, since the U.S. State Department seems to have preferred that the occupation be carried out, if at all, by a Canadian force, and in fact called for a restoration of the *status quo ante*. A plebiscite, however, showed overwhelming sentiment for FREE FRANCE.

SAINT-VALERY-EN-CAUX. Located west of Dieppe on the English Channel, Saint-Valery-en-Caux was taken by the British 51st (Highland) Division, then serving as a part of the First Canadian Army, on September 2, 1944. In June 1940 much of the division had been surrounded and captured there.

SAINT-VITH. Belgian town close to the German border where in December 1944 American troops for a week denied critical roads to the German Fifth Panzer Army attacking in the Battle of the BULGE. Beginning on December 16, the attack soon isolated two regiments of the 106th Division on the nearby SCHNEE EIFEL ridge. Although the 7th Armored Division moved by forced march to assist, the division was unable to reach the trapped regiments, which surrendered on December 19. Men of the 7th Armored joined with a surviving regiment of the 106th, a regiment of the 28th Division and a combat command of the 9th Armored Division to form a horseshoe-shaped defense about the town. Although the Germans took Saint-Vith on December 21, the Americans held nearby for another day until a providential freeze provided firm ground for vehicles and they were authorized to withdraw. Of 22,000 defenders, 6,000 were killed or wounded and 8,000 were captured on the ridge, but the delay afforded time for a new line to form behind the Salm River 10 miles to the rear. The 7th Armored Division recaptured Saint-Vith on January 23, 1945.

SAIPAN. U.S. forces seized the MARIANA ISLANDS of Saipan, TINIAN and GUAM because the Navy needed advance bases for operations against the Philippines and the Air Force needed fields from which B-29s could bomb Japan.

A second objective of the Mariana operations was to

U.S. marines advance on the town of Garapan, Saipan

lure the Japanese Combined Fleet out of its anchorage at TRUK for a decisive engagement; the result was the GREAT MARIANAS TURKEY SHOOT and the first Battle of the PHILIPPINE SEA, in which the enemy suffered disastrous losses.

Saipan was the objective of the 2d and 4th Marine Divisions, with the 27th Infantry Division as floating reserve; D-day was June 15, 1944. The landing across the reefs off the beaches was beset by heavy Japanese fire, which caused 2,000 casualties the first day and required the commitment of the 27th Division.

By D plus 1 the 4th Division had attacked straight ahead and the 2d Division had penetrated to Charan Kanoa, the sugar mill town inland. At 3:30 on the morning of the 17th the Japanese mounted a heavy tank-led attack, which caused considerable damage and casualties before it was stopped. By the 18th the 4th Division had crossed Saipan to Magicienne Bay on the east coast, while two Army regiments, the 105th and 165th Infantry, began clearing out the southern end of the island.

On June 20, as the 2d Division wheeled in line to face the north, the 4th Division moved to the right side of the line and the 27th Division to the center in a coordinated drive to the northern tip of the island, jumping off on the 23d. When the attack of the Army division bogged down, Lt. Gen. Holland M. SMITH, the Marine commander of the entire operation, removed the division's commanding general, Maj. Gen. Ralph C. SMITH, an action that generated considerable interservice controversy. The Army subsequently sustained Ralph Smith.

In the narrow part of Saipan to the north, the 4th and 27th Divisions pressed the attack. Marpi Point, at the tip of the island, was reached on July 9, when the island was declared secure. Here one of the most dramatic and tragic events of the war occurred as many entire families of civilians, egged on by Japanese soldiers, leaped to their deaths from the 220-foot cliff, while marines looked on, horrified, unable to stop the suicides.

The defeat in the Battle of the Philippine Sea combined with the loss of Saipan forced Premier Hideki Tojo to submit his resignation to the Emperor, and a new Japanese government was formed.

SAITO, Yoshitsugu (1890–1944). A graduate of the Japanese Military Academy (1912) and the War College (1924), Lieutenant General Saito became commander of the 43d Division in April 1944. In this capacity he commanded the garrison force on SAIPAN, where he was killed in action in July.

SAKAI, Saburo (1916–). One of Japan's greatest air ACES, Sakai took part in more than 200 air battles during World War II and is credited with shooting down 64 Allied planes. He fought in a variety of planes but recorded his greatest successes in the Zero (*see* A6M). A Navy pilot, Sakai fought in CHINA (1938–41), the PHILIPPINES, JAVA and the PACIFIC. In August 1942 he was seriously wounded, eventually losing his right eye. For almost two years thereafter he served as a flight trainer at air bases in the Japanese home islands. He was briefly permitted to become a fighter pilot again in mid-1944 in spite of having only one good eye. He was promoted to naval ensign in late 1944.

SAKHALIN (Karafuto). Prior to World War II the southern half of this island in the Sea of Okhotsk north of Hokkaido was Japanese, having been taken as a result of the Russo-Japanese War of 1905. Between 1918 and 1924 the Japanese temporarily occupied all the island. When the Soviet Union entered the war against Japan in late 1945 Russian forces took all of the island, and after the war the entire Japanese population was expelled.

SAKONJU, Naomasa (1890–1948). A graduate of the Japanese Naval Academy in 1912, Rear Admiral Sakonju was naval attaché in Thailand when the Pacific war broke out and remained in the post until July 1943. In September 1943 he was made commander of the 16th Division, in which he played an important part in the fighting off LEYTE in the fall of 1944; his transport unit carried troops to the island with considerable success. In October 1944 Sakonju was promoted to vice-admiral, and in December he became chief of staff of the China Area Fleet. After the war he was found guilty of war crimes and executed.

SALAMAUA. Unopposed, the Japanese secured the Salamaua area, on the Huon Gulf of northeast NEW GUINEA, beginning March 8, 1942, the same day they seized LAE, 18 miles to the north. They developed an air and supply base at Salamaua. But by the end of June 1943 they had for some time been under pressure from Australian troops positioned in the inland mountains, and then a small American force—ultimately built up to the reinforced 162d RCT, 41st Infantry Division—began adding pressure from the south, along the coast. The main body of the Japanese garrison, which perhaps numbered over 7,000 troops at peak strength, began withdrawing toward Lae on September 11. The next day Australian troops secured the town of Salamaua and its nearby airstrip.

SALAZAR, Antonio de Oliveira (1889–1970). Premier, sometime President and virtual dictator of Portugal for 36 years. Although his regime is usually described as fascist, Salazar never headed a political mass movement of the type of the Nazi or Fascist Party. He generated even less charismatic appeal than Francisco FRANCO in Spain.

During the war Portugal was neutral, but her neutrality conformed to the conditions of the ancient Anglo-Portuguese alliance. Salazar permitted a large Allied base to be constructed in the AZORES, which was a major factor in controlling German submarines in the Atlantic.

Salazar suffered a crippling stroke in 1968. He was replaced as Premier, but he was never told of the change.

SALERNO. Port in southern Italy, on an inlet of the Tyrrhenian Sea, the scene of an Allied amphibious landing (Operation Avalanche) on September 9, 1943, designed to capture the port of NAPLES. The U.S. FIFTH ARMY, comprising one American and one British corps, commanded by Gen. Mark CLARK, was landed by a joint

British and American naval force under the command of U.S. Vice-Adm. H. Kent HEWITT, air cover being provided from recently captured airfields in Sicily and naval aircraft from five British carriers under Rear Adm. Sir Philip VIAN. Fierce German counterattacks held up the advance ashore for six days, and withdrawal appeared imminent until the British battleships WARSPITE and VALIANT arrived from Malta and were able with their 15-inch guns to halt, and eventually drive back, the German attacks. On September 15 contact was made with the British EIGHTH ARMY, advancing up the coast from Reggio, where it had been landed, 150 miles to the south. Operation Avalanche is notable as the first occasion on which the Germans used heavy bombs guided by radio. The American cruiser *Savannah* and the British cruiser *Uganda* were both hit and severely damaged on September 11, and on September 16 *Warspite* was heavily damaged, having to be towed back to Malta. *See also* ITALY.

SALLADA, Harold B. (1895–). U.S. naval aviator, commander of escort carrier forces in the Pacific. He was promoted to rear admiral in 1944. In June 1945 he became chief of the Bureau of Aeronautics.

SALMON TRAP (Lachsfang). Code name for the planned German capture of the Murmansk railroad in 1942, the aim being to cut off supplies from the west to the Soviet Union. This particular trap was not sprung.

SALM RIVER. Stream in the Ardennes, running southeast from the Amblève River. In the Battle of the BULGE, the Salm was an Allied defense line behind SAINT-VITH.

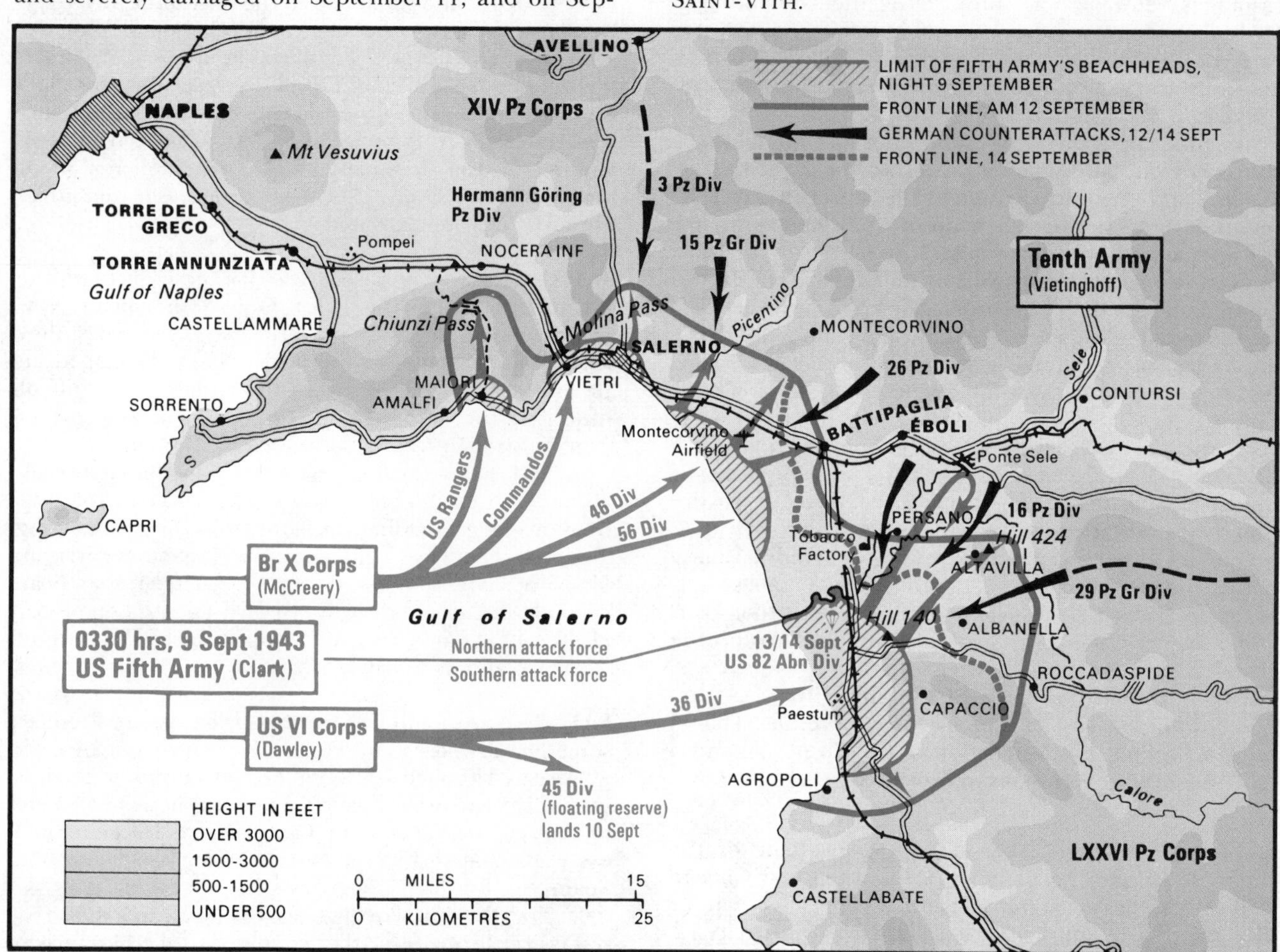

SALERNO was the main Allied landing in southern Italy. The invading U.S. Fifth Army was actually international

SALMUTH, Hans von (1888–1962). German Army officer (colonel general, 1942) who was an army commander on the Eastern Front in 1942–43 and commanded the Fifteenth Army in Normandy at the time of the Allied INVASION.

SALT LAKE CITY, U.S.S. PENSACOLA-class heavy cruiser, launched January 23, 1929, at the New York Shipbuilding Company. The *Salt Lake City* displaced 9,100 tons and carried a main battery of ten 8-inch guns. Her main wartime action was in the Battle of CAPE ESPERANCE off GUADALCANAL on October 11–12, 1942, and in the indecisive Battle of the KOMANDORSKI ISLANDS in Alaskan waters, March 26, 1943, where a small task group under Rear Adm. Charles H. McMORRIS fought a somewhat larger Japanese force. The battle was unique in that there was a complete absence of combat aircraft on either side. The *Salt Lake City* received considerable damage in the battle but suffered remarkably few casualties.

SALWEEN RIVER. Second in size in BURMA only to the Irrawaddy River, the broad southern Salween was crossed on February 21, 1942, by the 33d and 55th Divisions of the Japanese 15th Army during their January–March westward advance against RANGOON. After the capture of Rangoon the Salween valley served as one of the three northward routes of advance for the Japanese when they occupied the rest of Burma. Two years later, as the Allies began to take the offensive, the upper Salween, called the Angry River by the Chinese, was crossed in three places on May 11, 1944—the commencement date of the Salween campaign by the Chinese Army.

SAMAR. One of the eastern Visayan Islands in the PHILIPPINES, lying midway between LUZON and MINDANAO, seized by American forces in early 1945 with little Japanese opposition. *See also* LEYTE GULF, BATTLE FOR.

SAMLAND (Zemland). The East Prussian peninsula on which KÖNIGSBERG is situated, the scene of fierce fighting in February and March 1945; in fact, some German forces held out until mid-April. The Red Army used the name of the peninsula to denote operations against Königsberg.

SANANANDA. Village in NEW GUINEA that fell to Allied (U.S.–Australian) forces in the climax of the Papua campaign, January 17, 1943.

SANATESCU, Constantin (1885–1947). When King CAROL II abdicated the Rumanian throne in 1940, General Sanatescu supported Carol's son MICHAEL, acting as Regent for the young king. Following an anti-Nazi coup in August 1944, Michael selected Sanatescu as his Prime Minister. As Prime Minister, Sanatescu tried to eliminate the pro-Fascist members of the government in order to satisfy Soviet demands. Failing to meet those demands, Sanatescu resigned and subsequently retired from the Army in 1945.

SAN BERNARDINO STRAIT. Lying between the southeastern tip of Luzon and the northern end of Samar in the PHILIPPINES, the strait is approximately 27 miles long and five miles wide at its narrowest part. It provides the main entrance into the Philippines from the Pacific, and through its unguarded channel on the night of October 24–25, 1944, a Japanese naval force steamed in in an unsuccessful attempt to destroy General MACARTHUR's landing operation at LEYTE.

SAN DEMETRIO. When shellfire from a German surface raider set the cargo of the British tanker *San Demetrio* aflame on November 5, 1940, the crew escaped in open boats. They spent 24 hours on the cold sea before they climbed aboard their damaged vessel, got the fire under control and then navigated the ship 1,000 miles to a Scottish port.

SANDFORD, Daniel Arthur (1882–). British Army officer who served in Ethiopia. Brigadier Sandford was head of Mission 101, which entered Ethiopia six months before British troops to assist anti-Italian patriots in 1940. After the British victory in EAST AFRICA, he was adviser to Emperor HAILE SELASSIE.

SANDOMIERZ. Taken from the Germans by the Soviet First Ukrainian Front on August 18, 1944, this Polish town on the west bank of the Vistula served as the springboard for the front's attack, as part of the Soviet winter offensive, on January 12, 1945.

SANDYS, Duncan Edwin (1st Baron Duncan-Sandys) (1908–). Son-in-law of Winston CHURCHILL and a leading opponent of Britain's prewar APPEASEMENT POLICY, Sandys (pronounced Sands) held various government positions during the war, including Minister of Works in 1944–45. He chaired a special War Cabinet committee concerned with defense against German flying bombs and rockets (*see* V-WEAPONS).

SAN FRANCISCO, U.S.S. NEW ORLEANS–class heavy cruiser, launched March 9, 1933, at the Mare Island (Calif.) navy yard. The *San Francisco* displaced 9,950 tons and carried a main battery of nine 8-inch guns. The ship took part in almost all the battles in late 1942 off the island of GUADALCANAL, including the decisive naval battle. On November 13, in this action, the *San Francisco* suffered heavy damage and her captain, Cassin Young, and the commander of a transport escort group, Rear Adm. Daniel J. CALLAGHAN, were both killed on board. Fire from the *San Francisco* at close range was the major factor in disabling the Japanese battleship HIEI, which was finished off the next day by aircraft. The *San Francisco* was repaired and subsequently served until the end of the war.

SAN FRANCISCO CONFERENCE. The international meeting at which the UNITED NATIONS ORGANIZATION was established. (The term United Nations had previously been used to denote the nations allied in opposition to the AXIS powers.) The conference convened in San Francisco on April 25, 1945. The resulting document, the Charter of the United Nations, was signed on June 26 and went into force on October 24, 1945.

The agenda of the conference grew largely out of the DUMBARTON OAKS proposals, to which were added items resulting from the Big Three discussions at YALTA and subsequent exchanges. Forty nations besides the sponsoring powers—the United States, Britain, the USSR and China—had submitted 72 other proposals, and these, along with 24 amendments proposed by the sponsors, were incorporated into the agenda.

It is of interest that this was the first international conference in modern times that was not dominated by Europe. Only nine continental European states west of the Soviet Union were represented; on the other hand, there were 21 American republics, seven Near Eastern states, six Commonwealth nations, three Soviet republics, two republics from the Far East and two African states. All of the 26 states that had originally signed the JOINT DECLARATION of the United Nations were represented. Poland, although it did not have a government, was permitted to become an original member of the United Nations, making a total of 51.

The preliminary sessions of the conference were chaired by members of the Big Four. An international secretariat provided translators and handled administration. General strategy sessions were held by the Big Four (France was later included). In the final charter, the General Assembly was given more power than had been envisioned at Dumbarton Oaks. Political issues were central to the conference from the beginning, notably disagreements between the Western powers and the Soviet Union over the admission of the Ukraine and Argentina and recognition of the Polish Government. The question of the great powers' veto in the Security Council was generally debated.

SANGAMON, U.S.S. ESCORT CARRIER and class. *Sangamon* commissioned on August 25, 1942. Like other early escort carriers, she was converted from an oil tanker; in her previous incarnation she was the *Esso Trenton*. The Sangamon-class designation was given to a group including also the *Chenango*, the SANTEE and the SUWANNEE. As a component of the Northern Attack Group, the *Sangamon* played an important part in the American landings in Morocco in November 1942, when both she and her crew were brand-new. Subsequently she was active in the Central Pacific, at LEYTE GULF and off OKINAWA, where she was heavily damaged, but not sunk, by a KAMIKAZE attack.

SANGRO RIVER. Italian river flowing into the Adriatic, forming with the RAPIDO and Garigliano Rivers and the Apennine Mountains a natural defense line across the peninsula south of Rome. Behind this line the Germans constructed the fortified GUSTAV LINE. In late November 1943 the British EIGHTH ARMY established bridgeheads across the Sangro, but the British commander, Gen. Sir Bernard MONTGOMERY, halted the offensive after heavy losses in late December. *See also* ITALY.

SAN JOSE. Small town in southwestern MINDORO in the PHILIPPINES. American troops captured San Jose and the nearby airfield on December 15, 1944, after an unopposed amphibious landing. The prewar strip, however, could not be expanded, and American and Australian engineers quickly began work at other sites to the south and southwest of San Jose. The first of three new fields was operational on December 20.

SANSAPOR. Village and plantation on the northwest shore of the VOGELKOP Peninsula of northwestern NEW GUINEA. The 1st Infantry of the U.S. 6th Infantry Division landed unopposed near Sansapor on July 30, 1944, and took Sansapor the next day. U.S. Army engineers opened a fighter strip on the mainland on September 3. The 6th Infantry Division staged from the Sansapor base for the invasion of Luzon, in the PHILIPPINES, in January 1945.

SANTA CRUZ, BATTLE OF. As the Japanese Navy's share in a major effort to drive U.S. forces from GUADALCANAL, in October 1942 Adm. Isoroku YAMAMOTO sent his COMBINED FLEET against the American naval forces operating in the SOLOMONS area. Vice-Adm. Nobutake KONDO deployed an advance force which included carrier JUNYO, battleships KONGO and HARUNA, 4 heavy cruisers, 1 light cruiser and 14 destroyers. Under Kondo's overall command, Vice-Adm. Chuichi NAGUMO had a striking force consisting of carriers SHOKAKU and ZUIKAKU, light carrier ZUIHO, battleships HIEI and KIRISHIMA, 4 heavy cruisers, 1 light cruiser and 15 destroyers.

The American force included Rear Adm. Thomas KINKAID's Task Force 61 (carrier ENTERPRISE, battleship SOUTH DAKOTA, 1 heavy cruiser, 1 light cruiser, 8 destroyers) and Rear Adm. George MURRAY's Task Force 17 (carrier HORNET, 2 heavy cruisers, 2 light cruisers, 6 destroyers). Both sides could draw on land-based air support. An American surface combat force, Rear Adm. Willis LEE's Task Force 64 (battleship WASHINGTON, 1 heavy cruiser, 2 light cruisers, 6 destroyers), was operating in the general area but did not take part in the coming action.

Orders issued to Kinkaid and Murray called for their carrier task forces to pass north of the Santa Cruz Islands, a small island group lying east of the Solomons and north of the NEW HEBRIDES, and then turn southeastward to be in position to intercept any Japanese fleet approaching Guadalcanal. An incorrect report (later retracted) that HENDERSON FIELD had been recaptured by Japanese ground forces left Kondo and Nagumo in doubt as to the actual state of the battle on Guadalcanal; they were also in the dark as to American fleet movements. Early on October 25 *Enterprise* planes began to search for the Japanese fleet. At midday a patrolling American flying boat sighted the advance of the Japanese force northwest of the Santa Cruz Islands. Realizing they had been sighted, the Japanese changed course to the north, and the *Enterprise* planes found nothing. A number of returning planes were damaged in landing or forced to ditch for lack of fuel.

During the night of October 25–26 Nagumo's carriers steamed to the north. Reports of the Guadalcanal fighting were still confused, and the Japanese admiral wanted a clearer picture of the situation. The American task forces similarly headed northward, intending to attack as soon as the opportunity presented itself. More contact reports were received from scouting flying boats, and from Vice-Adm. William F. HALSEY, the South Pacific commander, came the brief order: "Attack. Repeat. Attack."

Early the next day, American and Japanese scout planes sighted the respective fleets. Japanese fighters drove off the scouts that spotted the carriers, but two others found light carrier *Zuiho* and scored two hits, which made her flight deck useless and started fires. Both the Japanese and the American carrier forces now launched strikes, which actually passed each other en route to their targets. Japanese fighters attacked the American planes, shooting down several fighters and several torpedo bombers at a cost of three of their own number. Shortly after 9 A.M. planes from *Shokaku* and *Zuikaku* began their attack, scoring bomb and torpedo hits on *Hornet*. About a half hour later, American planes made a number of bomb hits on *Shokaku*, seriously damaging her and putting her out of action. Cruiser CHIKUMA was also damaged.

Damage-control efforts to save *Hornet* were begun. A second wave of Japanese planes now struck the *Enterprise* task force. Covering fighters and intense antiaircraft fire did their best as this attack came in, but three bombs struck *Enterprise*. Forty minutes later a further attack wave inflicted minor damage on *Enterprise* and landed a bomb on the heavy armor of one of *South Dakota*'s forward turrets. Another bomb damaged light cruiser *San Juan*. Repair efforts in *Hornet* continued, but in midafternoon more Japanese torpedo bombers

(Kates) came in, planting a torpedo in her side. One of still more Kates scored another hit, and the order was passed to abandon ship. Two accompanying destroyers fired torpedoes into the stricken carrier, but she refused to sink.

Kondo, feeling his day's work had been successful, sent his strong surface forces forward to seek out the enemy, following in support with undamaged *Zuikaku* and *Junyo*. As the surface ships drew closer to *Hornet*, with "snooper" floatplanes flying ahead, the American destroyers attempted to sink the carrier with gunfire. Failing in this, they withdrew. Unable to take *Hornet* in tow, the Japanese finally sank her with torpedoes before turning north. While Santa Cruz was a tactical victory for Japan, the attempt to recapture Henderson Field on Guadalcanal had failed; the tide of battle on that island was not turned. **J.C.R.**

SANTEE, U.S.S. Cimarron-class fleet oiler converted in 1942 to an ESCORT CARRIER, along with SANGAMON, SUWANNEE and *Chenango*. These ships were used for antisubmarine patrol and for covering amphibious operations, seeing service in the NORTHWEST AFRICA landings. *Santee* helped catch and sink the German blockade runner *Kota Nopan* in 1943, and she participated with her sister escort carriers in the battle off SAMAR (LEYTE GULF) on October 25, 1944.

SANTO TOMAS UNIVERSITY. Campus in Manila operated by the Japanese as a prison camp for Allied combatants and civilians—men, women and children. It held about 3,700 people, under conditions of deprivation that shocked and angered rescuing GIs. The camp was liberated on February 4, 1945, by a column from the U.S. 1st Cavalry Division.

SARAPHIS, Stephanos (1890–1957). When Italy attacked Greece in 1940, Saraphis was in prison because of his participation in an abortive republican uprising; he received a grant of amnesty from the Greek Government. In 1943 he joined the Communist-inspired guerrilla band ELAS (National Liberation Front), the military arm of the EAM (National Liberation Party) (*see* EAM). Saraphis, a lieutenant general, soon became the commander of the ELAS. Although he was not a Communist, Saraphis was deported in 1946 for his association with the ELAS. After a period of time in a forced labor camp, he received his freedom in 1951. *See also* GREECE—CIVIL WAR.

SARATOGA, U.S.S. LEXINGTON-class aircraft carrier, completed on a hull originally laid down in 1920 as a battle cruiser and commissioned in 1927. At San Diego when the Pacific war began, she took Marine fighters on board and sailed to relieve WAKE ISLAND, only to be recalled before she could reach the besieged outpost. Operating off Hawaii in January 1942, she was hit by a Japanese submarine torpedo. Repairs were completed, but she returned just days too late for the Battle of MIDWAY. Sailing to the South Pacific, "Sara" participated in the early weeks of the battle for GUADALCANAL. Another submarine torpedo damaged her at the end of August. By November she was again ready for sea, and into late 1943 she provided air support for operations in the SOLOMONS and against RABAUL. During November 1943 *Saratoga* supported the capture of the GILBERTS. In early 1944 she assisted in the invasion of the MARSHALLS and then joined the British Eastern Fleet in the Indian Ocean. During April and May she operated with the British carrier ILLUSTRIOUS, striking Japanese targets in the East Indies. After an overhaul she spent the fall and winter of 1944–45 operating out of Pearl Harbor, training night-fighter squadrons. In January 1945 she joined ENTERPRISE to provide night-fighter cover for the capture of Iwo JIMA; a Japanese air raid severely damaged *Saratoga*, inflicting heavy casualties.

At Bikini in 1946, the old carrier served as an atomic bomb target ship and went down after the second test blast.

SARDINIA. Once the aim of Allied invasion plans (Operation Brimstone), which were dropped because of the success of the campaign in SICILY, Sardinia was taken on September 18, 1943, without a shot, by a force embarked in two British motor torpedo boats.

SATO, Kenryo (1895–1975). Japanese Army officer, one of Premier Hideki Tojo's most trusted and influential advisers throughout much of the war. Sato became a member of the Government Planning Board in 1937. Four years later he entered the Military Affairs Bureau of the Ministry of War. From April 1942 to December 1944 he served as chief of the bureau. Following the fall of Tojo, Sato was demoted to assistant chief of staff of the Chinese Expeditionary Forces. Promoted to lieutenant general in March 1945, he was given command of the 37th Division of the Japanese Army in Indochina. The INTERNATIONAL MILITARY TRIBUNAL FOR THE FAR EAST sentenced Sato to life imprisonment for "crimes against peace" in 1948, but he was paroled in 1956.

SATO, Naotake (1882–1971). Japanese diplomat who, after serving for a number of years in different European capitals in a variety of minor posts, became in turn minister to Poland, Belgium and France. In 1937 he was appointed Foreign Minister in Senjuro Hayashi's cabinet, but he was forced into retirement in the same year because of his opposition to the ANTI-COMINTERN PACT of 1936. When he took the post of ambassador to the Soviet Union in late February 1942, many Western newsmen believed that his mission was to lure the Soviets into complacency before a Japanese attack. He served as Japan's ambassador to the Soviet Union throughout the war.

SATURN. Code name for planned Soviet operation toward ROSTOV, December 1942. *See also* LITTLE SATURN.

SAUCKEL, Fritz (1894–1946). A member of the German Nazi Party from 1923, Sauckel was party gauleiter and after 1933 governor of Thuringia. In March 1942 he was appointed to an office with the title Generalbevollmächtigter für Arbeitseinsatz (translated as Minister of Labor with Special Powers, or Plenipotentiary General for the Allocation of Labor), which meant that he was in charge of the SLAVE LABOR program. He was hanged at Nuremberg on October 10, 1946.

SAVO ISLAND, BATTLE OF. Shortly after midnight on August 9, 1942, a Japanese force under Vice-Adm. Gunichi MIKAWA surprised and sank four unprepared Allied cruisers and damaged another in the waters around Savo Island, off GUADALCANAL. Sometimes called the Battle of the Five Sitting Ducks, the engagement lasted just over half an hour; the damage to the attacking Japanese was negligible. The Allies lost the U.S. cruisers ASTORIA, QUINCY and VINCENNES and the Australian cruiser CANBERRA, plus a destroyer; casualties in killed and wounded totaled about 2,000. The Allied commander, Rear Adm. Richmond K. TURNER, survived the fiasco to become famous as a practitioner of amphibious warfare.

Wartime documents and publications refer to as many as six "Battles of Savo," often in contradictory fashion, causing some confusion to the reader searching contemporary sources. The night action of August 9, 1942, known today as the Battle of Savo, was known then as the First Battle of Savo, or First Savo. CAPE ESPERANCE (October 11–12, 1942) was called Second Savo. SANTA CRUZ (October 26–27, 1942) was referred to as Third Savo. The two night surface actions (nights of November 12–13 and November 14–15, 1942), constituting what was later called the naval battle of GUADALCANAL, were then called Third and Fourth Savo; both actions, taken together, were sometimes referred to as the Battle of the Solomons, a term also used by the Japanese. TASSAFARONGA (night of November 30–December 1, 1942) was variously referred to as Fourth, Fifth or Sixth Savo, also as the Battle of LUNGA POINT.

SBC. U.S. Navy dive-bomber, a biplane that saw service early in the war (those used by the Royal Navy were called Clevelands). The SBC, built by Curtiss, could carry an 1,100-to-1,300-pound bomb and had a top speed of 240 miles per hour. The operational versions were the SBC-3 and -4.

SB2C. Originally manufactured for the U.S. Navy by Curtiss-Wright, the Helldiver was the most widely used dive-bomber in the war in spite of the fact that, because of production delays, it did not see action until late 1943. An all-metal, low-wing monoplane with a crew of two, it was powered by engines ranging from 1,700 to 2,100 horsepower, bore various armaments from five .50-caliber machine guns to two wing-mounted .20-mm. cannon to 5-inch rockets, and carried 1,000 pounds of bombs internally. The SB2C saw service with the U.S. Army Air Forces as the A-25A, was also manufactured by the Canadians and was eventually used by the British, French and Italians; 7,200 editions had been built by 1949, when it was withdrawn from service with the Navy.

SB2U. This Vought-manufactured U.S. aircraft was named the Vindicator in 1939 with the production of the SB2U-3. With a crew of two, this low-winged dive-bomber carried various armaments, depending on the series, and could handle up to 1,000-pound bomb loads. Production ceased in 1941, 237 having been built; of these, 167 saw service with the U.S. Navy and Marines (at MIDWAY), 20 were used by the French and 50 were purchased by the British (who called the plane the V-156 Chesapeake) for use by the FLEET AIR ARM.

SBD. U.S. airplane originally built by Northrop as the BT; Douglas Aircraft Corp. purchased the production facility and began manufacture of the craft as the SBD in 1940. A total of 5,936 were built until production ceased with the SBD-6 series. Powered by a single engine of from 700 to 1,350 horsepower, depending on the series, and carrying up to 1,000 pounds of bombs, this low-wing monoplane, called the Dauntless, was the most successful U.S. dive-bomber of World War II. Although it was employed by the Army as the A-24, most versions were used by the Navy. SBDs had their first battle experience at PEARL HARBOR, a few days later sank the first Japanese submarine and were the principal air weapon during the Battles of the CORAL SEA and MIDWAY and in the SOLOMON ISLANDS campaign.

SBEÏTLA. A small, ancient Roman town in the Sbeïtla plain (TUNISIA), a flat, semiarid stretch about 50 miles long, between the FAÏD and KASSERINE Passes. The Axis attacked Sbeïtla on the night of February 16–17, 1943; the Americans evacuated it during the 17th.

SBIBA PASS. Key pass in TUNISIA east of the KASSERINE PASS, stoutly defended during the Kasserine battle by American, British and French units.

S-BOAT. German motor torpedo boats were designated Schnellboote (abbreviated S-Boote). A number of production groups of these craft, superficially similar in appearance, were produced from the early 1930s into the war years. Ranging from 28 to 34.9 meters in length and from 35 to 42 knots in designed speed, they were all armed with two fixed forward-firing torpedo tubes and had various combinations of light automatic guns. S-boats were popularly called E-boats (Enemy boats) by British and American sources. "S-boat" was also a U.S. Navy nickname for the surviving old submarines of the post–World War I years.

SBD Dauntless over Wake Island, October 1943

SC. The Curtiss Seahawk, a high-performance U.S. Navy observation floatplane designed to replace the SOC and OS2U (*see* SOC; OS2U) on battleship and cruiser catapults. A low-wing, single-seat monoplane with one 1,350-horsepower radial engine, the SC-1 was fairly widely distributed in the fleet by the end of the Pacific war. The improved SC-2 was produced too late for war service. This was the last catapult floatplane used for scout-observation duty in the U.S. Navy, being replaced by 1949 by helicopters.

SCAEF. Supreme Commander, Allied Expeditionary Force; the designation of Gen. Dwight D. EISENHOWER during the 1944–45 campaign in northwest Europe.

SCAPA FLOW. The main base of the British Home Fleet in World War II. Located in the Orkney Islands north of mainland Scotland, it provided easy access to the ATLANTIC and command of the North Sea. In 1919 the German Navy had been interned and had scuttled itself at Scapa Flow, a humiliation which was partly avenged by a daring naval exploit at the beginning of World War II. On October 14, 1939, Oberleutnant Günther PRIEN, the commander of the German *U-47*, penetrated the defenses of Scapa Flow and sank the battleship ROYAL OAK. The shock hastened the improvement of defenses at Scapa Flow, which proved impenetrable for the remainder of the war.

SCHACHT, (Horace Greeley) Hjalmar (1877–1970). The "financial wizard" of the Third Reich, Dr. Schacht was the son of parents who were originally Danish, and his father later became an American citizen. A banker, Schacht got into politics after World War I by becoming a founder of the Democratic State Party. In 1923 he was appointed president of the Reichsbank, but resigned in 1930 because of his opposition to the Young Plan for the payment of war debts. As 1933 approached, Schacht gave his support to Adolf HITLER, although he never joined the Nazi Party, and when Hitler came to power Schacht was reappointed president of the Reichsbank. From 1934 to 1937 he was also Minister of Economics, a post which he left after feuding with Hermann GÖRING, chief of the "Four-Year Plan" for economic development; although Schacht had been instrumental in organizing the German economy to serve Hitler's purposes, he was opposed to Göring's program of autarky. Schacht increasingly disagreed with Hitler as well, and in January 1939 he resigned as president of the Reichsbank. He had a limited involvement in the OPPOSITION TO HITLER and was imprisoned after the July 20, 1944, assassination attempt. At the NUREMBERG TRIALS he was one of three defendants to be acquitted.

SCHARNHORST. Launched in 1936 as the sister ship to GNEISENAU, the battle cruiser *Scharnhorst* (26,000 tons) took part in the invasion of NORWAY in 1940, but after commerce-raiding cruises with *Gneisenau* in 1941 she remained in refuge at Brest, where RAF raids damaged her. Additional damage sustained from mines during the Channel dash from Brest to Wilhelmshaven in February 1942 immobilized her until early 1943. She later operated from northern Norway against the Allied convoy routes to Russia until December 26, 1943, when she single-handedly engaged a British force, including the battleship DUKE OF YORK, off Norway's North Cape (the engagement is called the Battle of North Cape). *Scharnhorst* went down with 1,864 men, leaving only TIRPITZ in northern waters as the last German heavy surface unit threatening the MURMANSK convoys.

SCHAUB, Julius (1898–1970). One of Adolf HITLER's earliest Nazi Party comrades, who participated in the abortive Munich putsch in 1923 and was with Hitler in LANDSBERG prison. Schaub became Hitler's constant companion and also his chauffeur.

SCHELDT ESTUARY. Mouth of the Scheldt River in Belgium, providing seaward access to Antwerp, 55 miles inland. British troops capturing Antwerp in September 1944 failed to clear the banks of the estuary or to block an isthmus leading from SOUTH BEVELAND ISLAND, which forms part of the north bank. Although trapped on the south bank, at least 65,000 men of the German Fifteenth Army escaped across the estuary and down the isthmus. Clearing the banks cost 13,000 Allied casualties, mainly Canadians, and not until late November were Allied ships able to reach Antwerp.

SCHELLENBERG, Walter (1910–1952). A student of medicine and law at the University of Bonn, Schellenberg became during the 1930s one of Heinrich HIMMLER's bright young intellectuals in the SS intelligence service, the SD (*see* SD), and he gradually drew closer to his chief, of whom he made a close psychological study. In November 1939 Schellenberg abducted two British intelligence officers, Capt. S. Payne Best and Maj. R. H. Stevens, from Venlo, a Dutch border town, so that they might be said to be implicated in the attempt on Adolf HITLER's life which had taken place in Munich on November 8. Schellenberg's highly entertaining memoirs, written after the war, show how he relished such missions, which advanced him in Himmler's favor. He became acting head of the SD foreign intelligence in June 1941, eventually holding the rank of SS lieutenant general.

In the latter phase of the war Schellenberg became one of Himmler's closest political advisers; as Germany's situation worsened, he urged Himmler to take the initiative in seeking a negotiated peace. Allying himself with Felix KERSTEN, Himmler's equally influential masseur, he did what he could to overcome Himmler's excessive diffidence and caution. Together, Schellenberg and Kersten pressured Himmler into easing the genocide operation against the Jews. Schellenberg brought Himmler into direct contact with enemy agents and neutral go-betweens; through him Himmler met the Swiss President, Jean-Marie Musi, and the meeting led to the barter of Jewish lives for Swiss francs and equipment that Germany urgently needed. Himmler also met with Norbert Masur of the World Jewish Congress of New York and the Swedish Count Folke BERNADOTTE, representing the International Red Cross, both in April 1945. Rumors of the discussions with Bernadotte reached the Allied press and led to Hitler's enraged dismissal of Himmler on April 28. After the war Schellenberg was tried and sentenced (1949) to six years' imprisonment, but was released in 1951 on grounds of ill health. After his release he wrote his memoirs.

SCHIRACH, Baldur von (1907–1974). Head of the HITLER YOUTH from 1931 and Reich Youth Leader from 1933, Schirach became a minister in 1936 and in 1940 gauleiter of Vienna and Reich Defense Commissioner. (Arthur AXMANN in effect succeeded Schirach as Minister for Youth in 1940.) Brought up in Weimar, where his father was in charge for a while of the Court (later National) Theater, Schirach drifted into National Socialism in his youth and became a party member, serving in the SA in 1925 (*see* SA). By 1929 he had become head of the Nazi student movement at the University of Munich. After 1933 he was responsible to Adolf HITLER for preparing the youth of both sexes (all of whom had to join the Hitler Youth by law) for their role in the Third Reich. By 1938, 1.2 million Hitler Youth were receiving regular training in small-bore rifle shooting, 74,000 were organized in flying units and 45,000 were receiving marine training and other forms of military instruction. At the NUREMBERG TRIALS after the war, Schirach admitted: "It is my guilt that I have trained youth for a man who became a mass murderer." They were marched and paraded, brainwashed into belief in the Nazi mythology, induced to adopt anti-Semitism. However, Schirach was finally condemned as much for his persecution and deportation of the Viennese Jews as for his influence over Germany's youth.

After the war Schirach had for a time been believed dead; he was working in disguise as an interpreter for the Americans. Finally, in June 1945, he surrendered of his own free will. He was sentenced to 20 years' imprisonment for crimes against humanity, being finally released from SPANDAU in 1966. Schirach was of a romantic, idealistic turn of mind and wrote verse in praise of Hitler; later he became something of a *bon viveur. See also* NATIONAL SOCIALIST GERMAN WORKERS' PARTY.

SCHLABRENDORFF, Fabian von (1907–). One of the survivors of Nazi vengeance after the 1944 bomb plot against Adolf HITLER failed, Schlabrendorff has provided one of the few firsthand accounts of the entire conspiracy (*Revolt Against Hitler*). A persistent participant in the prewar attempts to overthrow Hitler, he was later on the staff of General von TRESCKOW at Army Group Center in Smolensk, where he maintained liaison with General OLBRICHT and others in Berlin. On March 13, 1943, during the Führer's visit to the headquarters of Field Marshal von KLUGE, Schlabrendorff personally set the fuze on a plastic composition bomb, shaped to resemble two liquor bottles and wrapped in paper, which was carried onto Hitler's aircraft and timed to explode during the return flight to RASTENBURG, Hitler's East Prussian headquarters. When the attempt, known as Operation Flash, miscarried, Schlabrendorff hastened to Rastenburg to retrieve the bomb, only to discover that the detonator had functioned but had inexplicably failed to set off the charge. Imprisoned and tortured after July 20, 1944, Schlabrendorff was liberated by advancing American troops on May 4, 1945. *See also* OPPOSITION TO HITLER.

SCHLESIEN. German battleship launched in 1906 and converted in 1935–36 into a training ship for practice in shore bombardment. She was subsequently used to help wipe out the Polish resistance to the Nazis at the naval base at Hela in the Gulf of Danzig in September 1939.

SCHLESWIG-HOLSTEIN. German battleship completed in 1908 and reconstructed during the 1920s as a training ship and coast-defense vessel. She fired the opening guns of World War II at DANZIG on September 1, 1939, at 5:45 A.M. The *Schleswig-Holstein* served throughout the war and was sunk by Allied aircraft in the Baltic in 1945.

SCHLIEBEN, Karl Wilhelm von (1894–1964). German Army officer who commanded both panzer and infantry divisions. On June 23, 1944, Schlieben, a lieutenant general, took over command of the besieged fortress of CHERBOURG, but on the 26th he was made prisoner by the U.S. 9th Division. He nevertheless refused to order the garrison to surrender, and resistance did not cease until the next day.

SCHLÜSSELBURG. German bastion town (after September 15, 1941) in the rear of LENINGRAD, on Lake Ladoga. The Russians retook it in January 1943.

SCHMID, Joseph (1901–). German LUFTWAFFE officer (Generalmajor), in 1940 chief of intelligence (Abteilung 5). His responsibilities included estimating the strength of the ROYAL AIR FORCE during the Battle of BRITAIN. "Beppo" Schmid consistently underestimated the number of SPITFIRES and HURRICANES available to the British, and at the same time he failed to realize the extent of the damage inflicted on air installations by the German attacks.

SCHMIDT, Arthur (1895–). German Army officer (lieutenant general), chief of staff of the SIXTH ARMY, which surrendered to the Russians at STALINGRAD. An able and aggressive soldier, he favored holding out as long as possible, despite the hopelessness of the situation, and was in extreme contention with General PAULUS, the army commander.

SCHMIDT, Harry (1886–1968). Commissioned a second lieutenant in the U.S. Marines in 1909, General Schmidt was serving at Headquarters Marine Corps in Washington as assistant to the Commandant at the beginning of the war. In August 1943 he activated the 4th Marine Division and was its first commander, leading it in the assault of ROI and NAMUR in the Marshall Islands and in the SAIPAN operation. In July 1944 he assumed command of V Amphibious Corps and led the 2d and 4th Marine Divisions in the capture of TINIAN. The following February he commanded the corps in the assault and capture of IWO JIMA. At the end of the war he took his corps into the occupation of Japan. Schmidt returned to the United States in February 1946 and retired in four-star rank in July 1948.

SCHMIDT, Paul (1899–1970). German interpreter, a career staff member of the Foreign Office from the 1920s. He was chief interpreter for various foreign ministers, including Joachim von RIBBENTROP, and at times interpreted for Adolf HITLER, as at MUNICH. He had the ability to translate not sentence by sentence but by memorizing chunks of 10 minutes or so at a time.

SCHMUNDT, Rudolf (1896–1944). General Schmundt, who served as Adolf HITLER's Wehrmacht adjutant and as chief of the Wehrmacht Personnel Office, died of wounds sustained in the bomb explosion at RASTENBURG in the unsuccessful attempt to kill Hitler on July 20, 1944. *See also* OPPOSITION TO HITLER.

SCHNAUFER, Heinz-Wolfgang (1922–1947). German fighter pilot, the LUFTWAFFE's top night-fighter ace, with 121 kills. The much decorated Schnaufer found his prey among the RAF LANCASTERS and HALIFAXES that bombed Germany; the British nicknamed him the "Night Ghost of St. Trond," after the name of his base in Belgium. RAF squadrons were sent out with special instructions to get Schnaufer, but none did. He survived the war only to die in a car accident in France. His MESSERSCHMITT 110 was subsequently put on show in Hyde Park, London. The victory-marked rudder of this aircraft is on view in the Imperial War Museum.

SCHNEE EIFEL. Prominent ridgeline inside the German frontier near SAINT-VITH, Belgium. Although fortified as part of the WEST WALL, the ridge fell to the U.S. 4th Infantry Division in September 1944. When the Germans attacked in December in the Battle of the BULGE, two defending regiments of the inexperienced 106th Division were surrounded. They surrendered on December 19, the largest capitulation (8,000 men) of American troops during the war in Europe. The 4th Division took the ridge again in February 1945.

SCHNIEWIND, Otto (1887–1964). German naval officer, veteran of World War I, who was from 1937 Chief of the Naval Staff (Marinewehramt im Oberkommando der Kriegsmarine). He attained the rank of admiral in 1940 and was promoted to Generaladmiral in 1944.

SCHOFIELD BARRACKS. The home in 1941 of the principal U.S. Army unit in Hawaii, the Hawaiian Division. Schofield is situated in the center of the main plateau of Oahu, about 10 miles inland from PEARL HARBOR. It became the main training base and chief staging post for U.S. Army forces in the Central Pacific Area.

SCHÖRNER, Ferdinand (1892–1973). German Army officer, an infantry veteran of World War I who in World War II served with mountain troops (1939–43), becoming a corps commander. In March 1944 he began a series of assignments as an army group commander on the Eastern Front—Army Group A (South Ukraine), Army Group North, Army Group Center. He took up the last command in January 1945 in Silesia, where, he told Albert SPEER, his forces existed in name only. Nevertheless, his eagerness to fight made him a favorite of Adolf HITLER, and after the Führer's death he was one of the two designated recipients of the will, along with Admiral DÖNITZ. He was appointed a field marshal in the last weeks of the war.

SCHRÄGE MUSIK (Jazz Music). Fixed guns mounted to fire either forward and up or rearward and up at an oblique angle (*schräge Musik* literally means "slant music"). This equipment was mounted in the fuselage behind the crew compartment on German night fighters.

SCHUHMINE (Shoe Mine). German antipersonnel mine containing a ½-pound charge, packed in a plywood box. Two models of the Schuhmine 42, differing in their igniters and in the shape of their containers, were used.

SCHULENBURG, Friedrich Werner, Count von der (1875–1944). As German ambassador to Moscow from October 1934 until the German attack on the Soviet Union, Schulenburg was among the principals in negotiating the SOVIET-GERMAN NONAGGRESSION PACT of 1939, sincere in his traditional and prosaic belief that cooperation with Russia was to Germany's long-run advantage. Horrified at the reversal of this policy with Adolf HITLER's assault on Russia, Schulenburg approached the circle of conspirators against Nazism through Ulrich von HASSELL after the Stalingrad debacle, offering his intercession with Joseph STALIN in working for a general peace. Though widely discussed, the suggestion never came to realization, but its author was executed for his adherence to the conspiracy on November 10, 1944.

SCHUSCHNIGG, Kurt von (1897–1977). In July 1934 Schuschnigg, the Austrian Minister of Justice and Minister of Education (Christian Socialist Party) became Chancellor in succession to Engelbert Dollfuss, who was murdered by Nazis attempting a coup. As the Germans moved toward incorporating Austria into the Reich, Schuschnigg resisted as much as he was able. He was bullied by Adolf HITLER in a memorable meeting at BERCHTESGADEN on February 12, 1938, and in a last desperate effort to keep Austria independent asked for a plebiscite on the question. But the Germans forced the cancellation of the vote, and Schuschnigg resigned as Chancellor, handing over to Arthur SEYSS-INQUART. After the ANSCHLUSS, Schuschnigg was arrested by the GESTAPO; he spent the war years in concentration camps. In 1948 he went to live in the United States, where he taught and lectured.

SCHUTZENMINE. German term for two different models of a type of antipersonnel land mine. It consisted of an outer case containing an inner canister. The canister held a charge of TNT or amatol, surrounded by a large number of steel shot. At the bottom of the canister was an ejection charge of gunpowder. When the mine was tripped, the ejection charge forced the canister into the air, to a height of three to five feet. The explosion of the charge then sent the shrapnel-like steel balls spraying out in all directions, up to as much as 200 yards from the mine. This weapon combined the features of an antipersonnel mine with the air-burst capability of an artillery projectile. The Schutzenmine 35 was nicknamed the "Fruit Tin" by the British. The later Schutzenmine 44 followed the same principle but differed in detail.

SCHWEINFURT. This Bavarian city, a center for the manufacture of ball bearings, was first bombed by the

U.S. Eighth Air Force on August 17, 1943, as part of a coordinated operation in which 146 B-17s attacked the Messerschmitt factory at Regensburg and continued on to airfields in North Africa, while another 230 Flying Fortresses hit the vital ball-bearing factories and returned to England. (*see* B-17).

The Regensburg force took off on time, thanks mainly to a cram course in blind flying that its commander, Brig. Gen. Curtis E. LeMay, had insisted upon, but both the fighter escort and the Schweinfurt strike force were delayed by bad weather. German fighters appeared just eight minutes after LeMay's B-17s crossed the European coast and kept up their attack for almost two hours, until the bomber formation reached Regensburg. The defenders shot down 18 B-17s en route to North Africa. The bombing was considered accurate, however, despite the fierce opposition. Unfortunately, the North African airfields lacked facilities for the bombers and their crews, and plans for shuttle bombing between England and North Africa had to be shelved.

The Schweinfurt raiders were to have followed LeMay's force by 10 minutes, but weather delayed them three hours, and this disruption proved deadly. German fighters, having refueled and rearmed in anticipation that the Regensburg formation would return to Britain, were ready for this new incursion. Fighters swarmed over the Flying Fortresses until the bombers reached Schweinfurt, where antiaircraft gunners opened fire. The Germans downed 36 B-17s, bringing the total losses for the two missions to 60 aircraft and 600 crewmen killed or captured. The attack did have a decided effect, causing a temporary 38 percent decline in ball-bearing production, but it also convinced the Germans that they should begin dispersing their factories and importing ball bearings from neutral Sweden.

A second attack on Schweinfurt took place on October 14, 1943 ("Black Thursday"), and it was a repetition

Smoke rises from Schweinfurt during the October 1943 raid

of the first, with 60 of 291 B-17s going down over enemy territory, 5 others being abandoned when the crews parachuted over England and 17 sustaining damage that was beyond repair. Again some 600 officers and men were lost. Although the day's bombing was remarkably accurate, Germany had already begun carrying out the dispersal plans drawn up after the first raid. Schweinfurt was only half as important a target in October as it had been in August. The second Schweinfurt raid was the heaviest of 16 against the city and was the most expensive air attack of the war. It exploded the theory of the self-defending bomber formation, forcing the Americans to curtail their daylight bombing offensive until technical developments allowed the fighters to accompany them round trip.

SCHWERIN VON KROSIGK, Lutz, Count (1887–1976). German civil servant, a Rhodes scholar who entered the Ministry of Finance in 1920 and remained in the government until the end of the DÖNITZ administration in 1945. Schwerin von Krosigk was appointed Minister of Finance by Chancellor von PAPEN in 1932 and, remarkably, kept this office throughout the Nazi era and even in the short-lived Dönitz government, when he also was Foreign Minister. In 1949 he was sentenced to 10 years' imprisonment as a war criminal, but was released in 1951.

SCOBIE, Sir Ronald (1893–1969). British Army officer who was chief of staff to the Commander in Chief Middle East, 1943–44. In 1944 Scobie, a lieutenant general, commanded British troops sent to GREECE to take over control of the country from the various guerrilla organizations and to maintain order until the establishment of a constitutional administration.

SCOONES, Sir Geoffry Allen Percival (1893–1975). British Army officer who served as director of military operations and intelligence in India, 1941–42, and as commander of the 4th Corps in BURMA, 1942–44. He led this corps in the IMPHAL and KOHIMA fighting. In 1945–46 Scoones was General Officer Commanding in Chief, Central Command, India, being promoted to general in 1946.

SCORCHER. Code name for the British occupation and defense of CRETE, May–June 1941.

SCOTT, Norman (1889–1942). A 1911 graduate of the U.S. Naval Academy, Scott saw combat action in World War I, but when the United States entered World War II he was in a staff job in the office of the Chief of Naval Operations. He eagerly sought a more active role in the war effort, Adm. Raymond A. SPRUANCE recalling that Scott "made things so miserable for everyone around him in Washington that he finally got what he wanted—sea duty." A rear admiral from June 1942, Scott commanded a Pacific task force until his death in action at GUADALCANAL, when his ship, the ATLANTA, was hit on November 13, 1942.

SCOTT, Robert L., Jr. (1908–). A veteran of the Flying Tigers (the AMERICAN VOLUNTEER GROUP), Scott transferred to U.S. Army Air Forces in the spring of 1942, took command of the 23d Fighter Group and soon had scored 10 of his 13 aerial victories. This early wartime service inspired his popular book *God Is My Co-Pilot.* After a tour as an instructor in the United States, Colonel Scott returned overseas to pioneer in the use of rocket-firing fighters against Japanese shipping off OKINAWA and against enemy rail transportation in China.

SCULPIN, U.S.S. Salmon-class submarine (1,450 tons). On November 19, 1943, *Sculpin* (Comdr. Fred Connaway) was sunk off TRUK by gunfire from the Japanese destroyer YAMAGUMO.

SD (Sicherheitsdienst—Security Service). The intelligence and espionage arm of the German Nazi SS (*see* SS). Its full name was Sicherheitsdienst des Reichsführers SS, i.e., the Security Service of the Reich Leader of the SS—Heinrich HIMMLER. The SD was built up by Reinhard HEYDRICH, under whose direction it became a formidable center of information and power. In 1939 the SD, the Criminal Police and the GESTAPO were all made divisions of the Reich Security Main Office (Reichssicherheitshauptamt), with Heydrich as chief. After Heydrich's assassination these forces were directed by Ernst KALTENBRUNNER.

SEABEES. Name given to U.S. Navy Construction Battalions (abbreviated CB). These were formed to provide essential construction and maintenance services in combat areas. Established in January 1942, Construction Battalions served worldwide and established a lasting reputation for ability and ingenuity under any circumstances and in any climate. Each battalion was organized to operate as a self-sufficient unit. As the scope of Seabee work grew and the numbers of men required to handle it similarly increased, Naval Construction Regiments and Brigades were organized, but the battalion remained the basic Seabee unit. By V-J Day the Seabees included 246,000 men organized into 338 Construction Battalions and special units. Seabees tended to be somewhat older than the average sailor, since men who already had essential skills were particularly desired. Their wartime accomplishments validated their motto—"We build, we fight"—and caused Adm. William F. HALSEY to list the bulldozer as one of the four decisive weapons of the Pacific war (after the submarine, RADAR and the airplane).

SEABORG, Glenn Theodore (1912–). American chemist who became an instructor at the University of California in 1939 and in 1942 joined the metallurgical laboratory at the UNIVERSITY OF CHICAGO to work on the ATOMIC BOMB project. At Chicago his interest was in isolating element 94, plutonium—which turned out to be a crucial element in the production of the atomic bomb. His work was the basis for the creation of giant plutonium-producing nuclear reactors which furnished large quantities of plutonium for the atomic bomb stockpile. Following the war he resumed his academic career at Berkeley. In 1951 he was co-winner of the Nobel Prize for Chemistry, and he was later chairman of the Atomic Energy Commission.

SEAFIRE. The aircraft carrier version of R. J. Mitchell's Supermarine SPITFIRE. When the war began, Britain's Fleet Air Arm did not have an adequate fighter. To fill this void, the Hurricane was pressed into service, followed in 1941 by a Spitfire VB fitted with an arrester hook. The first 166 Seafires were converted Spitfire Vs with a variety of Merlin engines but a standard armament of two 20-mm. cannon and four 303-caliber machine guns. The first actual production model, Seafire IIC, saw action during the invasion of Sicily in July 1943.

Seafire III was the first model to have folding wings, a difficult innovation because of the thinness of the wing section. The solution was to fold the wings upward near the root, with the tips folding downward to reduce overall height and facilitate storage on the hangar deck. More than a thousand Seafire IIIs were built. This model saw action during the Salerno landing in September 1943 and the Normandy invasion in June 1944. It also served in the Far East, taking part in strikes against Japanese-held Sumatra early in 1945. The single-seat Seafire III had a 1,470-horsepower liquid-cooled Rolls-Royce Merlin that provided a top speed of 352 miles per hour at 12,250 feet and a service ceiling of 33,800 feet. It had a maximum range of 750 miles with a drop tank and could carry one 500-pound bomb or two 250-pound bombs.

When the war ended, Seafire XV was entering service. Powered by an 1,850-horsepower Rolls-Royce Griffon liquid-cooled engine, it had a top speed of 383 miles per hour and a service ceiling of 35,500 feet. Like the Merlin-powered versions, it mounted two 20-mm. cannon and four .303-caliber machine guns.

SEA FRONTIER. U.S. Navy term for a type of area command first established on July 1, 1941, as naval coastal frontiers. They were responsible for offshore coast defense and antisubmarine patrol. By the latter war years, sea frontier commanders directed extensive forces of inshore and seagoing patrol ships and craft, as well as large numbers of land-based patrol planes and blimps. The Atlantic and Pacific coasts of Canada were protected by equivalent commands.

SEAGRAVE, Gordon Stifler (1897–1965). Seagrave, the famous "Burma Surgeon," was the son, grandson and great-grandson of missionaries to Burma. Although he returned to the United States at the age of 12 and was educated at Johns Hopkins University, his overriding commitment was to the poor of Burma. After his graduation he returned to the country, where, starting with a small wooden house in which he cared for one patient, he eventually built a 22-unit hospital complex. During World War II Seagrave received a commission as a major in the U.S. Medical Corps. In this capacity he set up base hospitals and cared for the wounded until the Japanese invasion forced him out of Burma. In 1944 he returned and rebuilt his ruined hospital.

SEAGULL. U.S. Navy name for the SOC and SO3C scout-observation floatplanes (*see* SOC; SO3C).

SEAHORSE, U.S.S. While on patrol east of the Philippines, this submarine reported to Adm. Raymond A. Spruance, the U.S. Fifth Fleet commander, that on June 15, 1944 (the previous day), it had spotted Vice-Adm. Matome Ugaki's battleship force headed in a northerly direction. Fearing a massing of Japanese naval forces in defense of the Marianas, Spruance decided to commit reinforcements to the Saipan invasion and to postpone the assault on Guam until July 21.

SEA LION (Seelöwe). This is probably the most famous code name a nonexistent operation has ever had. It was given to the operation described in Adolf Hitler's Directive No. 16, dated July 16, 1940, dealing with "preparations for a landing operation against England." The much-quoted opening section reads as follows: "Since England, in spite of her hopeless military situation, shows no signs of being ready to come to an understanding, I have decided to prepare a landing operation against England and, if necessary, carry it out. The aim of this operation will be to eliminate the English homeland as a base for the prosecution of the war against Germany and, if necessary, to occupy it completely."

Preparations were to be complete by the middle of August. The directive recognized, however, that certain conditions had to be achieved before the operation would be possible. First, the RAF had to be made "morally and physically" incapable of attacking the German invasion force. Second, mine-free corridors had to be swept across the Channel. Third, the entrances to the Channel must be sealed off with minefields. Fourth, strong coastal artillery must be in place to cover the invasion force. Fifth, the Royal Navy should be diverted by actions in the North Sea and the Mediterranean and weakened at home by air and torpedo attacks.

Thus the general plan called for the Luftwaffe to establish air superiority, for the Navy to wall off the invasion waters with minefields and for the Army to go across. But the first condition was never met. Instead, there was the Battle of Britain.

SEALION, U.S.S. Sargo-class submarine, commissioned in 1939 and destroyed by Japanese bombs at Cavite (Philippines) on December 10, 1941. Sunk by two bomb hits, she was pronounced beyond salvage and was blown up before Manila was evacuated by retreating American forces.

The second Sealion was a Balao-class submarine, commissioned in 1944. In six Pacific war patrols she picked up downed fliers and rescued Allied prisoners of war from a sunken Japanese freighter. Off Formosa in the early morning hours of November 21, 1944, *Sealion* torpedoed and sank the Japanese battleship Kongo.

SEA OTTER. A single-engine biplane amphibian, designed by Supermarine and built by Saunders-Roe, used as a rescue craft by the Royal Air Force and Fleet Air Arm. The hull of this British airplane was metal and the wings fabric-covered. The lower wing was attached to the fuselage just behind the enclosed cockpit. The 855-horsepower Bristol Mercury radial engine was mounted on the upper wing directly above the hull. The prototype flew in 1938, but the last of 290 Sea Otters did not roll from the production line until 1946.

SECOND ARMY (British). The army activated in the summer of 1943 as the United Kingdom component of the 21st Army Group, the Allied (later exclusively

British) ground force for the INVASION of Normandy. Gen. Sir Miles DEMPSEY came from the Italian fighting to take command of the Second Army in January 1944; he led it in the invasion and throughout the remainder of the war in France, Belgium, the Netherlands and Germany.

Following the Normandy landings, the Second Army was involved in the much-debated and argued-about fighting in the CAEN sector, where, though its progress was slow, it drew onto itself the bulk of the German defense forces, thus setting up the conditions for a large-scale American advance. This was said to have been the aim of Gen. Sir Bernard MONTGOMERY, then the overall ground commander, but there were a number of misunderstandings concerning the plan between the general and Allied headquarters. During this period the Second Army consisted of 12½ divisions (including 3 armored and 1 airborne), augmented by 7 independent armored brigades and 3 independent infantry brigades—the total being equivalent to about 16 divisions.

In September the Second Army moved into Belgium, took Brussels and Antwerp and provided the ground force for the unsuccessful ARNHEM operation (*see* MARKET-GARDEN). It subsequently conducted operations in the Netherlands, moved into Germany, put units across the Rhine on March 23, 1945, and drove to the Elbe. It captured Hamburg on May 3. *See also* WESTERN FRONT.

SECOND FRONT. A contentious issue between the USSR and the Western Allies in 1942–44 was the timing for establishing a "second front" against Germany, the Eastern Front being considered the first front. Neither NORTHWEST AFRICA nor ITALY was deemed a front in this sense by critics of the Anglo-Americans, who pressed for the INVASION of France (June 6, 1944). With reference to the cry for a second front, General EISENHOWER observed in *Crusade in Europe* that "the impatience of the public clearly demonstrated a complete lack of appreciation of the problems involved, particularly of the time that must elapse before any such operation could be launched." Nevertheless, the Allied staffs did consider such operations as SLEDGEHAMMER, which proved to be unfeasible.

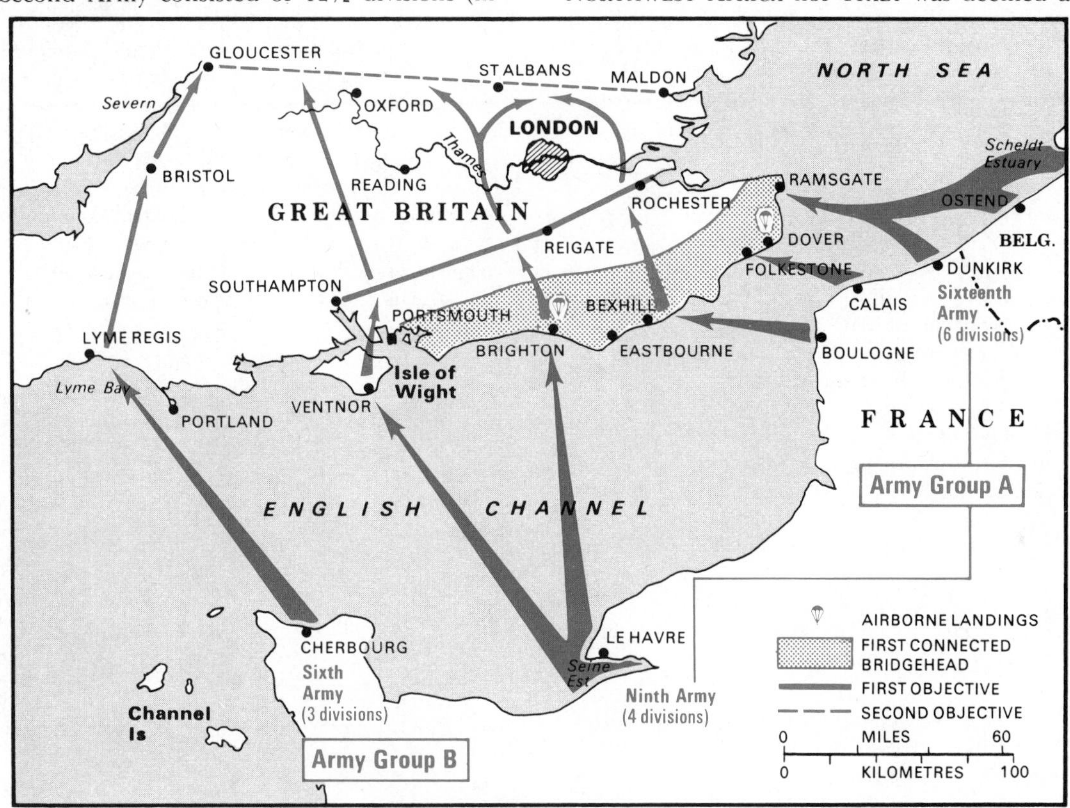

OPERATION SEA LION: German plans for the invasion of England

SECRET ARMY (l'Armée Secrète). Culmination of Gen. Charles DE GAULLE's efforts to unify FRENCH RESISTANCE groups during the war. Created by the Conseil National de la Résistance, the Secret Army was intended to be the framework for Allied-French underground cooperation. Its leadership was decimated by the GESTAPO, which was aware of its being organized, but after reorganization and decentralization the Resistance continued limited operations in most parts of France, making valuable contributions to the war effort.

SECRET WEAPONS. A theme that recurred throughout the war years was the idea that German scientists were developing "secret" or "miracle" weapons that would exercise a decisive influence on the outcome of the war. This was true in the Allied countries, where respect for German science was great; it was also true in Germany, where the government deliberately spread such stories in the later years to bolster morale in the face of defeat on all sides. The idea, of course, had substance, as was demonstrated by the V-1 pilotless aircraft, the V-2 rocket (*see* V-WEAPONS) and the MESSERSCHMITT ME 262 jet plane.

The notion of secret weapons came from a speech Adolf HITLER made in Danzig in 1939, when he spoke of an unknown weapon. A British Air Ministry study of the records made at the time revealed references to such projects as bacterial warfare, gliding bombs, pilotless aircraft, rockets, death rays and magnetic mines. Later the British learned that work on rockets was being carried out at PEENEMÜNDE, on the Baltic. The clue to the pilotless aircraft came from the discovery of the launching sites on the French coast.

A continuing Allied concern had to do with the possibility that the Germans were developing an atomic bomb; the ALSOS MISSION was set up to investigate German progress in nuclear research and development. As we now know, the Germans did not produce nuclear weapons; according to Albert SPEER, they abandoned the attempt in 1942. So strong were the rumors of secret weapons in north Germany in the last months of the war that a group of generals asked Speer on January 13, 1945, whether they could "still count on the introduction of new weapons." He replied, as he recalled it, "We will never have a secret weapon that will win the war in one blow."

SEDAN. Town in northeastern France in the ARDENNES, scene of Napoleon III's defeat in the Franco-Prussian War of 1870, near which on May 13, 1940, a German armored corps under Gen. Heinz GUDERIAN made an assault crossing of the Meuse River, leading to the German breakthrough of French positions and the rapid drive to the English Channel.

SEEADLER HARBOR. Port in the ADMIRALTY ISLANDS, taken from the Japanese in early March 1944. It was developed by the U.S. Navy as a major fleet base.

SEEHUND. Name given to the German Type XXVIIB MIDGET SUBMARINE.

SEEKUH (Sea Cow). German submariners' nickname for their large Type IX long-range U-boats.

SEELUFTSTREITKRÄFTE. The units of the German Navy's small air force, which were separate from LUFTWAFFE control.

SEIKU (Clear Sky). Japanese Navy name for the H8K2-L transport version of the H8K patrol flying boat (*see* H8K).

SELBORNE, Roundell Cecil Palmer, 3d Earl (1887–1971). British Minister of Economic Warfare, 1942–45.

SELECTIVE SERVICE SYSTEM. The U.S. Selective Service System was created by the Selective Training and Service Act of 1940. Liability for military service, with a few exceptions, was placed on all males aged 21 through 35; selection was to be by citizens from the local communities through Selective Service Boards. According to the 1940 act, the first American peacetime draft, not more than 900,000 men were to be in training at any one time and inducted men were to serve for a period of 12 months or less. In August 1941 the 12-month limitation was removed. The President was given authority to defer men from service because of age, occupation or dependency, but deferments were made on an individual basis and not on the basis of membership in an occupational group or employment in any particular plant or institution. The act also carried a reemployment provision which sought to guarantee that the soldier would be rehired in the position he left when he entered the service.

The Selective Service System was administered by a civilian agency under the direction of the President. The local boards carried out the processes of registration, classification and delivery of the draftee for induction. Selective Service was also given the responsibility for administering the reemployment provisions of the act. There were six separate registrations from October 1940 through January 1943, enrolling a total of almost 36 million males within the United States. Although under the initial act men between 21 and 36 were liable for military service, in August 1941 Congress limited the ages of induction to 21 to 27 and provided that men aged 28 should be released from duty. After PEARL HARBOR, however, men 20 through 44 were made eligible for Selective Service; in November 1942, 18- and 19-year-olds were made liable for service. Then in December 1942 the maximum age for service was dropped from 44 to 37, and this age remained the upper limit until the end of the war. The period of service was considered to be the duration of the war and six months following—"duration and six" was the popular phrase.

SELF-PROPELLED ARTILLERY. Artillery pieces mounted on tracked, half-track or wheeled vehicle chassis. A general term covering assault guns, intended to provide mobile close-in support for attacking infantry, and tank destroyers, or self-propelled antitank guns designed to knock out armored vehicles. SP artillery was nothing new—it had appeared during World War I—but during World War II a wide variety of models were used in great numbers by virtually all the warring powers. They ranged from heavy-caliber guns and howitzers to light automatic weapons, the latter usually in multiple mounts for antiaircraft use. Configurations varied. Gun mounts could be traversing (rotating) or nontraversing (fixed to fire forward, capable of elevation and sometimes a few degrees of traverse). Each type had its advantages and drawbacks. The fixed mount (e.g., German Sturmgeschütz III, Jagdpanther; Soviet SU-85, SU-100; Italian Carro Semovente M13/40; U.S. M7 Priest) had a generally lower silhouette and could be given good frontal protection. On the other hand, it could not quickly shift its gun to either side to attack a new target; to traverse the gun, it was necessary to traverse the vehicle itself. SP weapons with traversing mounts (e.g., U.S. M10, M36) were more flexible, but had higher silhouettes.

SENDAI. Class of Japanese light cruisers, last of the series of older-pattern 5.5-inch-gun cruisers of the 1920s developed from the original TENRYU-class design. *Sendai*, JINTSU and *Naka* displaced nearly 5,600 tons and had seven 5.5-inch guns and eight 24-inch torpedo tubes. *Sendai* and *Jintsu* were lost in the central Solomons in 1943; an air attack on TRUK early in 1944 sank *Naka*.

SENGER UND ETTERLIN, Fridolin Rudolf von (1891–1963). German panzer leader who was also a writer on military affairs. A Rhodes scholar, Senger was a veteran of World War I who stayed in the Reichswehr. In 1940 he was chief of the German delegation at the meeting of the Franco-Italian armistice commission. In 1942 he commanded a panzer division on the Eastern Front. In June 1943 he was put in command of German troops in SICILY; he subsequently commanded the XIV Panzer Corps, which fought at Monte CASSINO.

SERAFIMOVICH. Bridgehead across the Don River held by the Red Army as the Germans advanced to STALINGRAD. It was the springboard for an attack opening the Soviet winter offensive (November 19, 1942) and aimed at the encirclement of the Germans.

SERAPH, H.M.S. British submarine of 640 tons, based on Gibraltar in 1943. In November of that year she carried out two unusual missions in connection with the imminent Allied invasion of North Africa. The first involved the secret landing, west of Algiers, of Maj. Gen. Mark CLARK and the other U.S. Army officers for a conference with French officers, and reembarking them two days later for return to Gibraltar. The second operation, following immediately, involved sailing to the coast of France and taking on at night Gen. Henri GIRAUD, who had escaped from a German prison and was to command FREE FRANCE's forces in North Africa, and his staff. The *Seraph* was commanded by Lt. N. L. A. Jewell in both these missions, although Capt. Jerauld WRIGHT, U.S. Navy, was also on board to give the mission an American flavor and thus soothe any anti-British feelings on the part of the French.

SEROV, Ivan (1908–). A prominent officer in the Soviet secret police, Serov was responsible for the brutal sovietization of the Baltic states following the SOVIET-GERMAN NONAGGRESSION PACT of 1939. In 1940 he was in charge of the NKVD in the Ukraine (*see* NKVD), and after 1941 he was Deputy Minister of State Security; in 1943–44 he conducted mass deportations of Chechens, Ingushes, Kalmyks and Crimean Tatars. In 1945 General Serov was promoted to deputy supreme commander of Soviet forces in Germany, in charge of counterintelligence operations.

SEVASTOPOL. On October 20, 1941, German forces launched an attack across the PEREKOP ISTHMUS on the Soviet defense lines of the CRIMEA and 10 days later succeeded in penetrating the barrier. Thereafter, German and Rumanian forces poured into the peninsula, some heading for Kerch, the rest for Sevastopol, at the southwest corner of the peninsula. On December 17 General von MANSTEIN's Eleventh Army attacked the fortress city. Although the attack was repulsed, the Soviets were alarmed; the high command ordered a diversion to relieve the pressure. Soviet amphibious landings in the Kerch-Feodosia area not only relieved momentarily the pressure on Sevastopol but forced the Germans to withdraw from the KERCH PENINSULA, at the easternmost tip of the Crimea. Manstein had to turn his attention to clearing the Kerch area (Operation Bustard) before concentrating against Sevastopol. The Kerch Peninsula was finally cleared by mid-May 1942; two Soviet armies were practically wiped out in the battle, with the capture of almost 170,000 RED ARMY soldiers.

Manstein's force then turned to conquering Sevastopol. The Eleventh Army's 203,000 German and Rumanian troops were opposed by a Soviet garrison of about 110,000 soldiers and marines. Leaving the XLII Corps to guard the Kerch Peninsula, Manstein arranged the LII Corps on the right (north), the Rumanian Mountain Corps in the center and the XXX Corps on the left. The ground assault began on June 7, following five days of aerial and artillery bombardment. By June 17, when the second phase of the offensive ended, deep penetrations had been made in the north and the south. When the Soviets had to abandon their remaining airfields and ammunition began to run out, the high command had no choice but to order the withdrawal of the forces in the perimeter (June 30). The Black Sea Fleet of the RED NAVY carried out a successful evacuation, which was complete by July 3. The next day Germany officially announced the occupation of the demolished city. About 30,000 Soviet defenders were rounded up from hiding places, to swell the total to more than 90,000 captured. Adolf HITLER promoted Manstein to field marshal and ordered a special badge for the men of the Eleventh Army.

Sevastopol remained in German hands until 1944, when TOLBUKHIN's Fourth Ukrainian Front and YEREMENKO's Coastal Army entered the Crimea in April. The attack to recapture Sevastopol began on May 7. With double the number of artillery pieces that the Germans had employed in 1942, the offensive began against the German Seventeenth Army. By May 9 the city was once again in Soviet hands. Twelve German and Rumanian divisions had been annihilated.

SEVENTH AIR FORCE. In February 1942 the U.S. Hawaiian Air Force became the Seventh Air Force and began waging war against the Japanese on a battlefield that extended eventually from Oahu to OKINAWA and covered an expanse of ocean measuring 3,000 by 5,000 miles.

Seventh Air Force B-17s and B-26s (*see* B-17; B-26) took part in the Battle of MIDWAY in June 1942, but inflicted little damage on the enemy. From July through December of that year a B-17 group, commanded by Col. LaVerne Saunders, took part in the SOLOMONS campaign. Other B-17s then joined B-24s in attacking WAKE ISLAND and other Japanese outposts in support of the Central Pacific advance through the GILBERTS and MARSHALLS to the MARIANAS.

During this amphibious offensive, Seventh Air Force bombers battered the Japanese base at TRUK and helped neutralize other enemy strongpoints in the Carolines. From bases in the Marianas, the planes hit the Volcano and Bonin Islands, repeatedly hammering Iwo JIMA, where Marine amphibious forces landed in February 1945. Once Iwo Jima was secured, it became a base for fighters escorting B-29s against Japan and an emergency field for the bombers themselves (*see* B-29).

In the summer of 1945 the Seventh Air Force became a component of Gen. George C. KENNEY's Far East Air Forces. Although some fighter units remained at Iwo Jima, others accompanied the bomber squadrons to Okinawa, the principal base from which the Seventh Air Force launched strikes against Japan.

7th ARMORED DIVISION (U.S.). In August 1944, shortly after arriving on the Continent, the division participated in the THIRD ARMY drive on the Seine. When the BULGE assault hit the FIRST ARMY in December, the 7th Armored, then a part of the NINTH ARMY, was quickly shifted to the affected area. After traveling over slippery roads clogged with refugees and displacing support units, elements of the division reached SAINT-VITH and held in that area for several critical days. This delay upset the German attack timetable.

SEVENTH ARMY (U.S.). Activated while at sea (July 10, 1943) in the invasion convoy off SICILY, the Seventh was actually the first American field army to see action in the war. It was created by the redesignation of I Armored Corps (Reinforced), under the command of Lt. Gen. George S. PATTON, Jr. The units making it up were the 1st, 3d, 9th and 45th Infantry Divisions, the 82D AIRBORNE DIVISION and the 1st and 2d Armored Divisions.

In the July–August Sicilian operations, the Seventh Army fought in the western part of the island, taking Palermo on July 22, and then moved northeast, racing the British EIGHTH ARMY for Messina. A regimental combat team of the U.S. 3d Division entered Messina on the morning of August 17.

The next assignment for the Seventh was the SOUTHERN FRANCE OPERATION, initially code-named Anvil and later Dragoon. General Patton was transferred to England, and on January 1, 1944, Lt. Gen. Mark W. CLARK took command of the Seventh (while retaining command of the FIFTH ARMY in Italy) to oversee the planning of the invasion of southern France. Operations in Italy proving to be slower than anticipated, Clark handed over command of the Seventh on March 2, 1944, to Lt. Gen. Alexander M. PATCH, former U.S. commander on Guadalcanal.

On August 15, 1944, the Seventh Army assaulted the French Riviera beaches. The army now consisted of the 3d, 36th and 45th Infantry Divisions (comprising VI Corps), the 1st Airborne Task Force and five French divisions organized as French Army B. Within a month these American and French forces had liberated all of southern France and advanced to the Vosges Mountains. On September 15 the French force became an independent command (French First Army).

During the Battle of the BULGE, the Seventh Army covered much of the frontage of the U.S. THIRD ARMY (Patton), freeing the latter for counteroffensive operations. The Seventh then resumed its advance, eliminating (together with the French First Army) German resistance in the COLMAR POCKET in February and crossing the Rhine on March 26; it took Nuremberg on April 20 and Munich on April 30. On May 4 elements of the army crossed the Brenner Pass and linked up with troops of the Fifth Army.

After the end of the fighting, the Seventh Army performed occupation duty in Germany until March 31, 1946, when it was inactivated in Europe. In addition to the units mentioned, other divisions saw extensive service with the army. They included the 4th, 42d, 44th, 63d, 70th, 71st, 79th, 100th and 103d Infantry Divisions; the 10th, 12th, 13th, 14th and 20th Armored Divisions; and the 101ST AIRBORNE DIVISION. *See also* WESTERN FRONT.

SEVENTH FLEET (U.S.). One of the three numbered fleets in the Pacific, originally Naval Forces Southwest Pacific. The numbered designations were formally adopted on March 15, 1943. The first Seventh Fleet commander was Vice-Adm. Arthur S. CARPENDER; he was succeeded on November 26, 1943, by Vice-Adm. Thomas C. KINKAID. VII Amphibious Force (the "VII 'Phib") was commanded by Rear Adm. Daniel BARBEY.

SEVERSKY, Alexander de (1894–1974). Born in Tiflis, Russia, de Seversky served in the imperial air service during World War I and lost a leg as a result of injuries sustained in combat. After emigrating to the United States he became a major in the Army Air Corps Reserve, a title he used throughout his career. In 1931 he organized Seversky Aircraft Corp. to manufacture a low-wing, all-metal monoplane capable of being fitted with either wheels or floats. The product, the single-engine SEV-3, established a seaplane speed record and was the first in a series of distinguished aircraft, among them the Seversky P-35 and the Republic P-47 (*see* P-35; P-47), both designed by Alexander Kartveli, who joined the firm in 1934.

When the P-35 failed to attract foreign buyers, Seversky Aircraft had to seek new financing and was reorganized as Republic Aviation, with de Seversky stepping down from the company's presidency to become a member of the board of directors.

A skillful polemicist on behalf of air power, Major de Seversky updated the ideas of the Italian theorist Giulio Douhet in the 1920s and set them forth in the book *Victory Through Air Power*, which in 1943 became a popular motion picture. His theme, however, was not sustained by the war's developments.

SEXTANT. Code name for the U.S.–British–Chinese CAIRO CONFERENCE, held just before and after the U.S.–British–Soviet conference at TEHERAN.

SEYDLITZ. German HIPPER-class heavy cruiser, launched in 1939 but not completed. She was of 15,200 tons standard displacement. *Seydlitz* was blown up at Königsberg in April 1945.

SEYDLITZ-KURZBACH, Walter Kurt von (1888–1976). German Army officer, a major general commanding a division at the beginning of the war. At STALINGRAD, Seydlitz commanded the LI Corps and, a man of ability and independent judgment, urged General PAULUS, the commander of the SIXTH ARMY, to break out of the encirclement by attacking to the southwest. Paulus refused, but Seydlitz, on his own, began withdrawing his corps. This news came to Adolf HITLER's ears but, strangely, he blamed Paulus for the withdrawal and removed Seydlitz, whom he admired, from the control of Sixth Army headquarters. After surrender to Soviet forces, Seydlitz headed the NATIONAL COMMITTEE FOR FREE GERMANY, organized by the Russians. Later he was imprisoned by the Soviets and was not released until 1955.

SEYFFARDT, Hendrik Alexander (1872–1943). The Chief of Staff of the Dutch Army from 1929 to 1934, when he retired as a lieutenant general; the German occupation of the Netherlands brought Seyffardt out of retirement, and he formed a volunteer unit called the "Vrijkorps," which fought for the Axis in Russia. Seyffardt paid dearly for his collaboration with the Germans, being assassinated in The Hague on February 5, 1943.

SEYSS-INQUART, Arthur (1892–1946). Austrian politician who joined the Nazi Party in 1928 and quickly became one of its leaders. In 1938, Adolf HITLER, after his bullying meeting with Austrian Chancellor Kurt von SCHUSCHNIGG at BERCHTESGADEN, demanded that Seyss-Inquart be appointed Austrian Minister of the Interior; under this heavy pressure Schuschnigg made the appointment. After Schuschnigg resigned and German troops were on the way, Seyss-Inquart was appointed Chancellor. Once the Germans had occupied Austria, he was made Governor (Reichs Statthalter). From May 1939 until the end of the Hitler regime, Seyss-Inquart held the title Minister Without Portfolio in Hitler's cabinet. Most of this time (from May 1940) he served as Reich Commissioner for Occupied Holland. He was found guilty of war crimes and hanged at Nuremberg.

SFAX. A key Tunisian port, Sfax was seized by the Germans in November 1942 and held until April 10, 1943.

SFORZA, Carlo (1872?–1952). Prominent Italian anti-Fascist who spent the Mussolini era in exile, becoming widely known in the United States. After the fall of Mussolini, Count Sforza urged Italian entry into the war on the Allied side.

SHAEF. One of the most famous acronyms of the war, standing for SUPREME HEADQUARTERS, ALLIED EXPEDITIONARY FORCE—the force that fought in western Europe from the INVASION on June 6, 1944, to the German surrender.

SHANGRI-LA. The name of the mythical city in James Hilton's novel *Lost Horizon*, "Shangri-La" was the answer President ROOSEVELT gave when asked where the bombers came from that attacked Japan in the April 1942 raid (*see* FIRST SPECIAL AVIATION PROJECT). In commemoration an ESSEX-class carrier was given the name *Shangri-La*.

SHAPOSHNIKOV, Boris M. (1882–1945). An officer in the Imperial Russian Army at the time of the Bolshevik Revolution, Shaposhnikov joined the Red Army (May 1918) and served with great distinction in numerous assignments. He became one of the great Soviet military intellectuals; his writings, especially the three-volume *The Brain of the Army*, are highly regarded. Shaposhnikov is thought to have been Joseph STALIN's military mentor, and as such was one of the few high officers to have survived the purge of 1937–38. In 1937 he was appointed Chief of the General Staff, and he is credited with the authorship of the plan for Soviet occupation of eastern Poland (1939) and with developing effective operational planning after the early disasters of the Finnish campaign.

Poor health caused Shaposhnikov to resign as Chief of Staff in 1940, but in a shake-up in July 1941, following the German invasion, he was reappointed to the post by Stalin in succession to General ZHUKOV. He served until June 1942, when severe illness forced him to resign for good. He continued his career as chief of the Military Historical Administration, serving in this post until his death.

SHARP, William Frederick (1885–1947). U.S. Army officer assigned to the PHILIPPINES in 1941. A major general, he commanded U.S. forces on Mindanao, being forced to surrender in 1942. He endured Japanese captivity.

SHARPENER. Code name of General EISENHOWER's advance command post at Portsmouth, England, May 1944. When the headquarters was enlarged (July 1), it acquired the code name Shipmate. It was then a tent city capable of housing 1,400 persons.

SHAW, U.S.S. MAHAN-class destroyer, commissioned in 1936. *Shaw* was in dry dock at PEARL HARBOR on December 7, 1941; three Japanese bombs caused severe fires that exploded her forward magazines and destroyed the forepart of the ship. Temporary repairs patched her shattered hull; by mid-1942 she had been rebuilt, with a new bow, and in the fall she returned to duty in the South Pacific, where she saw extensive service.

SHAWCROSS, Hartley William, 1st Baron (1902–). British political figure who as Attorney General in the ATTLEE cabinet in 1945 became British chief prosecutor at the NUREMBERG TRIALS.

SHCHERBAKOV, Alexander S. (1901–1945). Soviet political leader, a member of the Politburo, who served as the head of the Main Political Administration of the Armed Forces during the war. In 1943 he was promoted to colonel general. His death in 1945 was later attributed (1953) by Stalin's controlled press to a plot by certain Kremlin doctors, most of them Jews, to murder Soviet leaders. The plot was alleged to have been concocted by "Jewish-American-British intelligence."

SHEFFIELD, H.M.S. Royal Navy cruiser of 9,400 tons, completed in 1937 by Vickers Armstrong, armed with twelve 6-inch and eight 4-inch guns, smaller weapons, six 21-inch torpedo tubes and three aircraft. *Sheffield* served in the Home Fleet throughout the war, except in 1940–41 when she was part of FORCE H based in GIBRALTAR. *Sheffield*'s record of service was outstanding among Royal Navy cruisers, the ship distinguishing herself in the Norwegian campaign, in her service with Force H (including the bombardment of Genoa), in her critically important shadowing of the BISMARCK, in the North African landings and the sinking of the SCHARNHORST.

SHELLBURST. Code name of a small advance headquarters established on August 7, 1944, by General EISENHOWER in a tent and trailer camp near Tournières, France, 12 miles southwest of Bayeux.

SHERMAN, Forrest Percival (1896–1951). U.S. Navy officer, a Naval Academy graduate of 1918, who was in war plans when the United States entered the war and served as a planner until assigned to Adm. Ernest J. KING as an aviation adviser. He then was commanding officer of the aircraft carrier WASP, which was torpedoed and sunk in September 1942. He was subsequently appointed deputy chief of staff to Adm. Chester W. NIMITZ, commander in chief in the Pacific; served as chief of staff of the air force of the Pacific Fleet; and from late 1943 to the end of the war was chief of Nimitz's war plans division (and thus Nimitz's top planner). His rank was rear admiral. After the war Sherman served as commander of the U.S. Sixth Fleet in the Mediterranean; he became Chief of Naval Operations in November 1949.

SHERMAN, Frederick Carl (1888–1957). U.S. Navy officer, a graduate of the Naval Academy in 1910. A submarine commander in World War I, Sherman became commanding officer of the aircraft carrier LEXINGTON in 1940 and, after her sinking in the Battle of the CORAL SEA, was appointed successively assistant chief of staff to the commander in chief of the Pacific Fleet, commander of Carrier Division 2 of the FAST CARRIER TASK FORCE, Pacific Fleet (in the SOLOMONS GILBERTS, MARSHALLS and MARIANAS, and at LEYTE GULF), and commander of Fleet Air West Coast. In July 1945 Sherman, a rear admiral, became commander of the 1st Carrier Task Force, Pacific Fleet. After the war he served as commander of the Fifth Fleet until his retirement in 1947.

SHERMAN TANK. British designation (and common U.S. name) for the U.S. M4 TANK.

SHIGEMITSU, Mamoru (1887–1957). Called "Shiggy" by American newsmen, Shigemitsu graduated with a law degree from Tokyo Imperial University. He then entered the Japanese foreign service. After serving in a variety of minor diplomatic posts in the United States and Europe, Shigemitsu was sent to China as Japan's ambassador in 1931. The following year he lost a leg when a Korean threw a bomb among the Japanese dignitaries gathered at Hong Kew park in Shanghai in celebration of Japan's seizure of that city from the Chinese. Shigemitsu thereafter wore a wooden leg. From 1933 to 1936 he was Vice-Minister of Foreign Affairs. He served as ambassador to the Soviet Union (1936–38), to Great Britain (1938–41) and to WANG CHING-WEI's Nanking (China) regime (1942–43). Shigemitsu was appointed Foreign Minister in April 1943 and remained at this post until April 1945.

Chosen Foreign Minister again in August 1945 to serve in Prince HIGASHIKUNI's first postwar cabinet, Shigemitsu, together with Gen. Yoshijiro UMEZU, signed the document of surrender aboard the MISSOURI on September 2, 1945. He was convicted of war crimes by the INTERNATIONAL MILITARY TRIBUNAL FOR THE FAR EAST and served seven years' imprisonment. Following his release from prison Shigemitsu again became Foreign Minister and helped negotiate Japan's peace treaty with the Soviet Union and her entry into the United Nations.

SHIGURE. Japanese destroyer of the SHIRATSUYU class. During the SOLOMONS fighting she acquired a reputation as a lucky ship, coming through some severe actions unharmed. She was finally lost in January 1945.

SHIMADA, Shigetaro (1883–1976). A graduate of the Japanese Naval Academy, Shimada served as naval attaché in Rome during World War I. He rose gradually to important posts in the Japanese Navy in the 1930s, including commander in chief of the Second Fleet, commander in chief of the China Fleet and commander of the Yokosuka Naval Station. Admiral Shimada was named Navy Minister in October 1941 and also Chief of the Navy General Staff on February 21, 1944. Called Premier Hideki TOJO's "briefcase carrier" by his Navy critics, Admiral Shimada worked very cooperatively with the Premier in trying to coordinate the war efforts of the Army and Navy. Replaced as Navy Minister by Mitsumasa YONAI on July 17, 1944, when the Tojo cabinet fell, Shimada was ousted as Chief of the Navy General Staff on August 2, 1944. He retired from active service in January 1945. Sentenced to life imprisonment by the INTERNATIONAL MILITARY TRIBUNAL FOR THE FAR EAST, Shimada was paroled in 1955.

SHIMAKAZE. Japanese destroyer, generally similar in appearance to the ASASHIO, KAGERO and YUGUMO classes but some 25 feet longer. Completed in 1943, she was built with a new high-pressure, high-temperature engineering plant which gave her a top speed of more than 40 knots. Armed with six 5-inch guns in three twin mounts, *Shimakaze* mounted three quintuple banks of 24-inch torpedo tubes on the centerline, giving her the most powerful torpedo broadside ever built into a destroyer. She was lost in the Philippines in November 1944; 16 more ships of her type were projected in 1942 but were never built.

SHIMOSE. A Japanese explosive, first used in the 1890s and still in use for boosters and bursting charges during World War II. Composed of nearly pure picric acid, it was somewhat more sensitive than TNT and was rated as being slightly more powerful. One or two published works have referred to Shimose as having some special "secret weapon" potency; this seems exaggerated.

SHINANO. Originally designed as a superbattleship of the YAMATO type, the Japanese warship *Shinano* was converted to an aircraft carrier after the Battle of MIDWAY had demonstrated the importance of this type of ship. As completed in 1944 she was the largest and probably the most heavily armored carrier in the world, displacing 69,100 tons. On her maiden cruise she was torpedoed off the Japanese coast by the American submarine ARCHERFISH, and sank several hours later.

SHINGLE. Code name of the Allied amphibious operation at ANZIO, Italy, January 22, 1944.

SHIRATSUYU. Class of Japanese destroyers. An improved version of the HATSUHARU class, these 10 ships were armed and configured like the earlier class except for having eight 24-inch torpedo tubes (2×4) and more compact bridges. The last four Shiratsuyus incorporated various improvements; their funnels were shaped differently, giving them a silhouette suggestive of the later ASASHIO class. All 10 Shiratsuyus were war losses. This class is referred to as the Shigure class in wartime Allied publications.

SHIRER, William Lawrence (1904–). American writer, a correspondent for the Columbia Broadcasting System in Berlin before the United States entered the war. He wrote the best-selling *Berlin Diary* in 1941. He also worked as a war reporter. Since the war he has written *The End of a Berlin Diary* (1947), *The Rise and Fall of the Third Reich* (1960) and *The Collapse of the Third Republic: An Inquiry into the Fall of France in 1940* (1969).

SHO GO (Victory Operation). A Japanese plan developed during the summer of 1944 after the loss of the MARIANAS for the defense of the inner Empire against invasion. The thrust of the next U.S. offensive was not known; all possibilities had to be provided for, and four area plans were drawn up within the overall Sho concept. Sho-Ichi-Go (Sho No. 1 Operation) provided for defense of the PHILIPPINES, which the Japanese believed the most likely Allied target; it was the general plan under which the battle for LEYTE GULF was fought. Sho-Ni-Go (Sho No. 2) covered the defense of the Ryukyus and FORMOSA; Sho-San-Go (No. 3) covered defense of the Japanese home islands. Defense of the KURILES and Hokkaido was provided for in Sho-Yon-Go (No. 4). Under the general Sho plan, the area attacked was to be designated the "theater of decisive battle." All available Japanese forces would then be concentrated there to counterattack. When it became clear that the Philippines were the next American invasion objective, Imperial General Headquarters placed Sho-Ichi-Go in effect; Leyte Gulf followed.

SHOHO. Class of Japanese light aircraft carriers. *Shoho* and ZUIHO were originally laid down as fast fleet oilers, but then named *Tsurugizaki* and *Takasaki* and ordered completed as submarine tenders. *Tsurugizaki* served for several years in this role; *Takasaki* was nearing completion when, in a second change, she was finally finished in 1940 as a light carrier and renamed *Zuiho*. In 1941 *Tsurugizaki* was similarly converted and renamed *Shoho*. *Shoho* was lost in the Battle of the CORAL SEA. *Zuiho* served capably until October 1944, when she was lost in the battle for LEYTE GULF.

SHOKAKU. Class of Japanese aircraft carriers, completed shortly before the beginning of the Pacific war. *Shokaku* and ZUIKAKU, called the most advanced carriers in service when new, took part in the attack on PEARL HARBOR and formed a strong element of Japan's fast carrier strength into 1944. *Shokaku* was lost during the Battle of the PHILIPPINE SEA; *Zuikaku* was sunk at LEYTE GULF, four months later. With a capacity of 84 planes, the Shokaku class were 844-plus feet long and displaced over 25,000 tons.

SHORE FIRE CONTROL. A U.S. term for the technique for calling and controlling naval gunfire support from an invasion beachhead, first experimented with during the prewar years. Shore Fire Control Parties (SFCP) went ashore with landing troops, working with aerial spotters and ships' fire-control personnel to direct naval gunfire onto targets as needed.

SHORT, Walter Campbell (1880–1949). U.S. Army officer who as a lieutenant general commanded the Hawaiian Department between February and December 17, 1941. Along with Adm. Husband E. KIMMEL he was held responsible for the PEARL HARBOR disaster, and he was replaced by Lt. Gen. Delos C. EMMONS. The Pearl Harbor committee headed by Justice Owen J. ROBERTS charged Short with "dereliction of duty" and errors of judgment. He retired in 1942. Short was never granted a court-martial and always maintained that his conscience was clear.

SHORTLAND ISLANDS. Group in the SOLOMONS used as bases by the Japanese for harrying American operations. Airfields in the Shortlands were neutralized by U.S. task forces at the time of the invasion of BOUGAINVILLE (November 1, 1943).

SHOULDER MORTAR. *See* GARRETT 60-mm. SHOULDER MORTAR, MARK 1.

SHOUP, David Monroe (1904–). At the outbreak of the war, Shoup was in Iceland serving as operations officer of the U.S. 1st Marine Brigade. He sailed for the Pacific in September 1942. Promoted to colonel, he was given command of the 2d Marines, which was to spearhead the assault on TARAWA on November 20, 1943. In this operation he won the MEDAL OF HONOR for assuming command of all marines on the island when the division command group was unable to land because of the heavy fighting and overwhelming Japanese fire disrupting the assault waves. In December 1943 Shoup became chief of staff of the division and as such participated in the SAIPAN and TINIAN operations, returning to the United States in October 1944 after two years overseas. In later years he was Commandant of the Marine Corps.

SHRAPNEL. Code name for a tentative British operation by which a combined operations force would seize a base in the Cape Verde Islands in the event of a German occupation of GIBRALTAR. The plans were drawn up in 1940 when it seemed possible that Spain might join forces with Germany and open the way to Gibraltar. The necessity to put Shrapnel into operation never arose.

SHTEMENKO, Sergei M. (1907–1976). Shtemenko began his long Soviet military career in 1926. He later studied at the Frunze Military Academy, graduating in August 1939, and was assigned to the General Staff. He saw service in the Polish campaign and, later, in the Finnish campaign. From that point until the end of the war Shtemenko served on the General Staff in Moscow. He was appointed deputy chief of operations in April 1943 and one month later was named chief of the department. By the end of the hostilities, as a general of army, he had become deputy chief of the General Staff.

SHUMILOV, Mikhail S. (1898–). Soviet Army officer who commanded the Sixty-fourth Army in the Battle of

STALINGRAD, where he received the surrender of German Field Marshal PAULUS. For its performance his unit was renamed the Seventh Guards Army. Shumilov led it in the Battle of KURSK and the 1944–45 thrust into Hungary and Austria. Shumilov's highest rank was colonel general.

SHURI CASTLE. Shuri (on OKINAWA) was the ancient capital of the Ryukyuan kingdom, and Shuri Castle, a solid citadel, stood on a high hill in the midst of a natural fortress area. The Japanese 32d Army chose Shuri Castle as its headquarters; it was the center of a number of concentric defense perimeters which formed the main battle positions, with the strongest installations facing north toward the Hagushi landing beaches. Located in the U.S. 1st Marine Division zone of action, Shuri Castle was the objective of an attack beginning on May 21, 1945, and ending on the 31st when the 5th Marines raised the U.S. flag over it.

SHUTTLE BOMBING. American airmen hoped to launch shuttle-bombing attacks against Japan, with Army bombers taking off from bases in the western Pacific, hitting Japanese targets, rearming and refueling at Soviet bases, then bombing Japan again on the return flight. Marshal STALIN refused, however, to participate in the scheme.

Shuttle bombing had even greater appeal in Europe, where attacks from different directions, and a choice among exit routes, would force the Germans to disperse the massed defenses through which British-based aircraft had to fight their way. An attempt to use North African airfields came to naught because these installations lacked the facilities to accommodate large numbers of bombers and their crews. The Soviet Union seemed to offer better possibilities.

As early as 1942, American planners had begun considering the use of bases in the Soviet Union, and serious negotiations with the Soviet Government got under way the following autumn. Stalin was reluctant, however, to have more than a thousand Americans stationed at the airfields the bombers would use. Not until the spring of 1944 did U.S. Strategic Air Forces in Europe (USSTAF) receive the necessary clearances to begin using three Russian bases—Mirgorod, Piryatin and POLTAVA—which had been specially prepared to receive the American bombers and their fighter escort.

On June 2, 1944, Lt. Gen. Ira C. EAKER led a formation of FIFTEENTH AIR FORCE B-17s, escorted by P-51s (*see* B-17; P-51), that bombed the Debrecen railroad marshaling yards in Hungary, en route from Italy to the Soviet Union. On June 6 the American planes bombed Galatz, Rumania, and on the 11th they hit Foscani airfield, Rumania, and continued onward to Italy.

The second shuttle mission, conducted by the EIGHTH AIR FORCE, damaged targets near Berlin but ended in disaster when German bombers attacked Poltava during the night of June 21–22, 1944, destroying 47 B-17s and damaging 19 others. The surviving Flying Fortresses took off for bases farther to the east, thus escaping additional losses on the following night when the Germans bombed Mirgorod and destroyed stockpiles of fuel and bombs. On June 26 the 71 surviving B-17s, escorted by 55 P-51s, bombed the oil refinery at Drohobyez in Poland and continued to Italy. Then, on July 5, they returned to England, bombing the rail yard at Béziers, France, on the way.

Because of the inadequate early-warning radar and ground defenses the Russians had provided for the three airfields, Lt. Gen. Carl SPAATZ, in command of USSTAF, questioned the wisdom of sending more B-17s to the Soviet Union. As a result, the next two missions were flown by bomb-laden P-38s (*see* P-38) with P-51s. July, Italian-based fighter-bombers struck the PLOESTI refineries and hit supply lines in the Balkans. During their nine days in the Soviet Union the aircraft attacked targets in Poland, and on July 26 they raided Ploesti and Bucharest, Rumania, on the way back to Italy. The second P-38 shuttle mission lasted from July 31 until August 6 and was devoted mainly to attacks on airfields.

As this last P-38 mission was concluding, 76 B-17s and 64 P-51s took off from Great Britain bound for Russia, en route bombing an airplane plant near Gdynia, Poland. While in the Soviet Union the force attacked an oil refinery in Poland, then battered the Balkan airfields on the return flight, which was made by way of Italy.

General Spaatz now proposed a combined bombing attack and supply drop in support of the uprising by Polish patriots in WARSAW. Stalin was backing a Communist faction and refused to aid the Warsaw Poles, even though Soviet troops were nearby across the Vistula. This refusal has been the subject of much debate, the Soviets claiming that the uprising was premature. Not until September 12 did the Soviet Government approve such a support mission, and bad weather delayed the effort until the 18th. By that time the portion of Warsaw held by the Poles was so small that accurate delivery of cargo was impossible.

The shuttle-bombing campaign, which had borne the appropriate code name Frantic, had as its final chapter the bombing by B-17s of a rail yard in Hungary during the flight to Italy. The eastward advance from the Normandy beaches resulted in the acquisition of fighter bases from which American planes could harry the battered LUFTWAFFE. Meanwhile, Russian forces were advancing westward and overrunning the cities that provided worthwhile targets for Russian-based B-17s. The success of Allied arms, as well as political differences between the United States and the Soviet Union, brought Frantic to an end.

SIAULIAI. Important junction on the railroad from Riga, Latvia, to East Prussia, taken by Red Army forces on July 27, 1944. The loss of Siauliai was a severe threat to German forces to the north.

SIBERT, Edwin L. (1897–). U.S. Army brigadier general who in 1944 became assistant chief of staff, G-2, 12TH ARMY GROUP. He served in this post (which meant that he was Gen. Omar BRADLEY's chief intelligence officer) for the remainder of the war. Previously he had served with the 7th Division.

SIBERT, Franklin C. (1891–). U.S. Army officer who served on Gen. Joseph STILWELL's CHINA-BURMA-INDIA staff in 1942 as a major general. A respected infantry commander, Sibert participated in Stilwell's famous "walkout" from BURMA. Between 1942 and 1944 he commanded the 6th Infantry Division in the Pacific theater. In 1944 he took command of the X Corps in the PHILIPPINES.

SICILY—OPERATIONS. The Allied invasion of Sicily, Operation Husky, was decided upon at the CASABLANCA CONFERENCE in January 1943. Its primary objective was to clear the central Mediterranean for Allied shipping; secondary objectives were to keep Axis forces drawn away from the Russian front and to knock ITALY out of the war. The overall commander was Gen. Dwight D. EISENHOWER, who had established a highly effective inter-Allied headquarters for the invasion of NORTHWEST AFRICA and the subsequent operations.

Husky, launched on July 10, 1943, involved landing eight divisions on a 100-mile front; in terms of initial assault strength alone, it was the largest amphibious assault of the entire war. Several new landing craft—LST, LCT, LCM and DUKW—were tried, with great success. Gen. B. L. MONTGOMERY's British EIGHTH ARMY landed south of Syracuse, while Gen. George S. PATTON's U.S. SEVENTH ARMY went ashore in the Gulf of Gela.

High winds caused heavy losses in paratroop landings behind the army invasion fronts, but despite rough seas the amphibious landings went well. Although the Seventh Army met vigorous opposition from the Hermann Göring Division and Italian troops, by nightfall of July 11 the beaches were secure and the drive inland could begin. There were roughly 230,000 Axis troops in Sicily, mostly Italians, and for the campaign to be completely successful those troops had to be prevented from escaping to Italy. The key, then, was Messina—the northeastern point of the island, only three miles from the toe of Italy and the obvious evacuation point. The Allies had to reach Messina before the Axis could concentrate in the point. With that goal, Montgomery's Eighth Army immediately began an advance north.

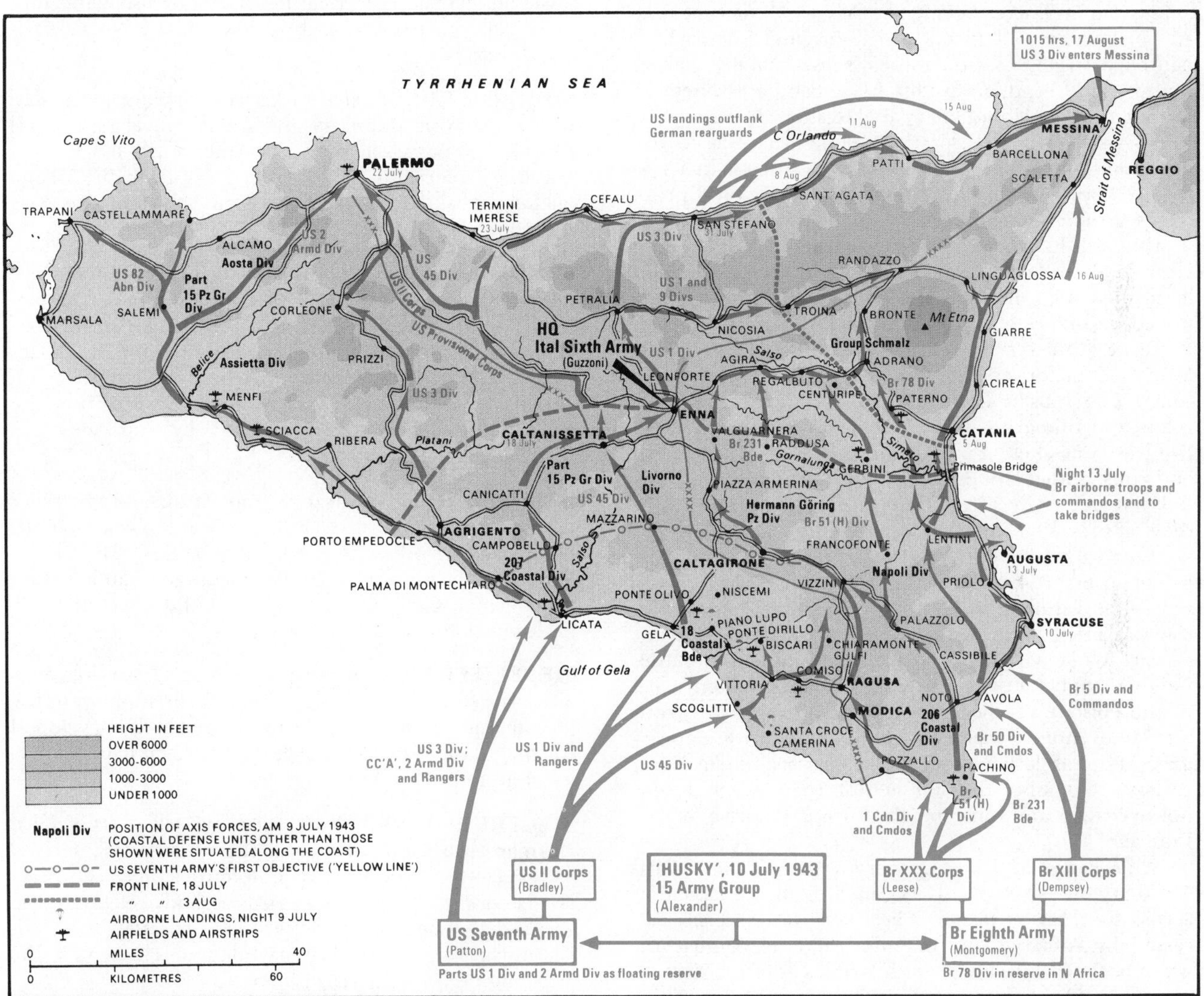

SICILY was cleared by Anglo-American forces in 38 days

Syracuse and Augusta were taken without difficulty by July 12, but in the plain south of Catania the Axis concentrated a strong defense and the Eighth Army advance slowed down. Montgomery then ordered a two-pronged attack: 13th Corps would advance directly against Catania, while 30th Corps swung left to get around Mount Etna on the west.

Montgomery's changes in the battle plan precipitated a small crisis that had far-reaching repercussions. General Patton's Seventh Army had been delegated a supporting role in Husky, but now Patton saw even that possibility taken away, since Montgomery had assigned to his own 30th Corps the roads that Seventh Army needed for its flank advance. Patton looked around for another opportunity, then sent a reconnaissance in force to Agrigento and Porto Empedocle, west of Gela. The measure was successful, and having secured a port for his army's supply, Patton appealed to Gen. Harold ALEXANDER, who as Eisenhower's deputy was in charge of ground operations, for permission to drive for Palermo. Alexander agreed, and Seventh Army began a dashing thrust west and north, taking Palermo on July 22 and then heading east toward Messina. American morale soared as American soldiers made their first dramatic drive of the war.

Messina no longer belonged solely to Montgomery as an objective, as it had under the original plan, which had been largely of Montgomery's own making. Patton was given his head, and with a fierce competitiveness he set out to beat Montgomery to Messina. The same rivalry—partly personal, partly nationalistic—was to follow Montgomery and Patton on across Europe in 1944. It kept both generals at a sharp edge, but posed problems for their commanders.

Although its advance so far had been relatively easy, after Seventh Army headed for Messina the opposition intensified. Eighth Army also continued to meet determined resistance; Catania did not fall until August 7. While Eighth Army worked around both sides of Mount Etna, Seventh Army fought along the north coast. The Axis utilized mountainous terrain, narrow roads and numerous bridges to build a nasty defense. Progress was slow. Twice, on August 8 and 11, naval end runs landed troops behind the German lines. They did not decisively affect the German withdrawal, but they impressed Winston CHURCHILL and planted the seed for ANZIO the following January.

The pressure on both troops and commanders was severe, and during the push for Messina General Patton was involved in an incident that nearly ended his career. While visiting a hospital, he slapped a battle-fatigued soldier in the face with his glove. When word of the episode reached the public, Patton was in trouble. He eventually made both public and private apologies, and was left without an active assignment from August 1943 until the summer of 1944, when Eisenhower called on him for the armored drive across France.

While Patton and Montgomery were pushing toward Messina, the Axis troops began a skillful evacuation across the Messina Strait. They were not severely harassed by Allied planes or ships, and by August 17, when both Seventh and Eighth Armies entered Messina (Seventh only slightly before Eighth), most of the Axis forces, including their vehicles and equipment, had escaped to Italy.

Husky was a short campaign (38 days) that achieved its objectives, even though it was less than a resounding Allied success. It cost nearly 20,000 Allied casualties, and although 12,000 German troops were killed or captured, more than 39,000 escaped to Italy. Italian casualties were high (147,000, primarily prisoners), but the Italians played a minor role in the campaign. The plan for Husky has been criticized as not utilizing Allied air and naval power to the full. On the positive side, the campaign gave American soldiers and sailors and their commanders vital experience; it cleared the Mediterranean for Allied use; and it provided the final impetus Italy needed to get out of the war. MUSSOLINI was asked to resign on July 25. On August 19 Marshal BADOGLIO began discussing surrender terms with the Allies. **M.H.B.**

SICKLE. Code name for the buildup of the U.S. EIGHTH AIR FORCE in Britain.

SIDI BARRANI. The far point of the Italian invasion of Egypt in September 1940. The British recaptured it on December 10, seizing control of the coast road and quickly driving the Italians out of Egypt with heavy losses. It was the first meaningful test of force and mobility between the contending sides in the North African desert.

SIDI BOU ZID. Twelve miles west of Faïd (TUNISIA), the roads from Maknassy and Gafsa converged at Sidi Bou Zid, an oasis village of 500 Arabs and a few French families. Americans were driven away from the village on February 14, 1943, in the early stages of the Axis KASSERINE offensive.

SIDI MUFTAH. Two spots in the Western Desert were identified by the name Sidi Muftah: an area on the plateau southeast of SIDI REZEGH where British armor concentrated, and the defended locality near the Trigh Capuzzo, west of KNIGHTSBRIDGE, where the British 150th Infantry Brigade held out for three days during the GAZALA battles while surrounded by superior Axis forces.

SIDI REZEGH. Sidi Rezegh and its airfield, 20 miles southeast of TOBRUK (Cyrenaica), were pivotal points, fiercely contested, in the CRUSADER battles of late 1941. Five times possession of the area changed hands before the German Gen. Erwin ROMMEL withdrew to the GAZALA position in early December.

SIEBEL FERRY. German pontoon raft, carrying antiaircraft weapons, used as a transport for supplies in the Mediterranean. Siebel ferries were originally developed for the planned invasion of England. Each had a capacity of 40 tons.

SIEGFRIED LINE. Name used by Allied troops for German frontier fortifications, the WEST WALL, derived either from a World War I defensive line, the Siegfriedstellung, or the Siegfried legend celebrated in Richard Wagner's operas, and made popular by a British music hall tune, "We're Going to Hang Out the Washing on the Siegfried Line."

SIKORSKI, Wladyslaw (1881–1943). A leader of the Polish nationalist movement before World War I, General Sikorski served as Premier, Interior Minister and War Minister of Poland during the 1920s. In 1928 he was dismissed from the Army by Marshal Josef Pilsudski, who had taken over the government. In 1939 Marshal Edward SMIGLY-RYDZ, who had succeeded Pilsudski, refused Sikorski's request for an assignment to active service against Germany. But after the collapse of Poland, Sikorski—a patriot of zeal and determination—became Premier of the Polish government-in-exile in Paris. He succeeded in building up an army of 100,000 men, and served as commander in chief of the Polish legions that fought in various theaters. After the fall of France the provisional Polish government moved to London. On June 23, 1941, Sikorski reached an agreement with Moscow that invalidated the Soviet-German division of Poland in 1939. But he ran afoul of the Russians on the question of the Polish officers massacred at KATYN. The Russians broke diplomatic relations with Sikorski's government in April 1943. On July 4, 1943, General Sikorski was killed in a plane crash at Gibraltar.

SILVER STAR. The third-highest U.S. military award for heroism. The decoration consists of a bronze star with a small silver star in the center. The Silver Star was first authorized on July 9, 1918, and was made retroactive to the Spanish-American War. Prior to 1932, when the present design was approved, the award was designated by a small silver star worn on the appropriate campaign ribbon. During World War II the Silver Star was awarded for heroism against the enemy that did not warrant presentation of the MEDAL OF HONOR, DISTINGUISHED SERVICE CROSS or NAVY CROSS.

SIMON, John Allsebrook Simon, 1st Viscount (1873–1954). Prominent British Conservative political figure in the years preceding the war, as Foreign Secretary, 1931–35; Home Secretary, 1935–37; Chancellor of the Exchequer, 1937–40. Simon was a strong supporter of the APPEASEMENT POLICY. As Lord Chancellor under Winston CHURCHILL during the war, he was not a member of the War Cabinet and had little to do with the conduct of the war.

SIMONDS, Guy Grenville (1903–1974). Canadian Army officer who served in North Africa, Sicily and Italy and on the Western Front. Simonds was chief of staff of the Canadian FIRST ARMY and then commander of the 1st Division in Sicily, 1943. He was then successively commander of the 5th Canadian Armored Division, the 2d Corps and the Canadian First Army in 1945. He was the originator of the armored infantry carrier, first used in the Allied offensive near CAEN in 1944. He was called by Field Marshal Bernard MONTGOMERY "the best product of the Allied side." His highest wartime rank was lieutenant general. After the war (1951–55) he was Canada's Chief of General Staff.

SIMOVIĆ, Dušan (1882–1962). In 1938 General Simović was appointed commanding general of the Yugoslav Air Force. On March 27, 1941, he led a coup d'état that overthrew the government of Premier Dragisha CVETKOVIĆ and the Regent, Prince PAUL, three days after it had signed an agreement to collaborate with Germany. PETER II was proclaimed King, and Simović became Premier. However, the Germans quickly crushed Yugoslavia, and a government-in-exile was set up in London. Simović resigned as Premier of this government in 1942. *See also* BALKANS.

SIMPSON, William Hood (1888–). Tall and completely bald, with a profile often compared to that of a weathered Indian chief, "Big Simp" Simpson was an impressive leader of troops. Prior to leading the U.S. NINTH ARMY into action in the Brittany peninsula in September 1944, Simpson had had a varied career. Son of a Confederate veteran, he was born and raised in the vicinity of Weatherford, Tex., west of Fort Worth. A graduate of West Point, he was an officer in the 33d Division and became division chief of staff shortly after the armistice in 1918. Simpson's interwar duties included attendance at service schools appropriate to his rank, battalion command, General Staff work and service as an instructor at the Army War College. Then followed assignments as regimental commander, assistant division commander, commander of an infantry replacement center, commander of the 35th Infantry Division, of the 30th Division and of the XII Corps. He excelled at all levels and hence was selected for more and more responsible jobs.

In September 1943 Simpson was promoted to lieutenant general; he was given command of the FOURTH ARMY and in spring 1944 of the Eighth (soon renumbered the Ninth). His smoothly operating staff, closely supervised by Ninth Army chief of staff Maj. Gen. James E. MOORE, received much praise from subordinate commanders. Ninth Army was under the command at various times of Gen. Omar N. BRADLEY and Field Marshal Bernard L. MONTGOMERY, as Simpson led it from Brittany into Belgium and across the Roer, Rhine and Elbe Rivers to final victory. Of this period General of the Army Dwight D. EISENHOWER later wrote: "If Simpson ever made a mistake as an army commander, it never came to my attention." Eisenhower personally commended Simpson for his ability to work with the British. Simpson's leadership earned the praise of King GEORGE VI as well as other honors. General Eisenhower aptly summed up Simpson when he wrote: "Alert, intelligent, and professionally capable, he was the type of leader that American soldiers deserve." Simpson was promoted to general on the retired list.

SIMS, U.S.S. Destroyer and class (1,770 tons; four 5-inch guns; eight 21-inch torpedo tubes; 38 knots). As built, these ships featured a prominent single stack and five 5-inch guns. Twelve torpedo tubes were carried in three quadruple mounts, one on the centerline and one on either beam. For better stability, one gun and one torpedo tube mount were soon removed; tophamper was cut down and topside weights removed or relocated. This process continued as light antiaircraft guns and electronics were added through the war. The Sims and earlier classes saw extensive service in the Atlantic and Pacific theaters through the first half of the war; five of the 12 ships of this class were war losses. As improved new destroyers became available in quantity, the older ships were gradually relegated to secondary duty.

SINCLAIR, Sir Archibald (1890–1970). Leader of the Liberal Party in the British House of Commons from 1935, Sinclair was Secretary of State for Air from May 1940 until the end of the wartime coalition in May 1945. His close relationship with Winston CHURCHILL was based partly on their former service in the 6th Royal Scots Fusiliers in 1916, when Sinclair was second-in-command to Colonel Churchill. Sinclair was a typically courteous and upright member of the Establishment. He became Lord Thurso, a Scottish peer.

SINGAPORE. Publicized as an impregnable British bastion in the Far East, Singapore, together with its naval base, was occupied by the Japanese on February 15, 1942, a month in advance of the time called for in their war plans.

The effort to capture Singapore began on December 8, 1941, when the Japanese 25th Army, under the command of Lt. Gen. Tomoyuki YAMASHITA, the "Lion of Manchuria," landed troops on the east coast of Malaya, at KOTA BHARU, and on the eastern shores of Thailand at Singora and Patini. Nearly concurrent with these landings, the Japanese 11th Air Fleet bombed Singapore itself, the first of many such attacks to be suffered by the island before its fall. Lt. Gen. Arthur PERCIVAL, commander of the Malaya Command, was responsible for the overall defense of colonial Malaya. Percival's 3d Indian Corps, commanded by Lt. Gen. Sir Lewis HEATH, which was initially responsible for Malayan defenses north of the state of Johore, took the brunt of an immediate and aggressive Japanese advance down the Malay Peninsula. During the ensuing weeks the British suffered defeat after defeat—the most critical being at Jitra, the Slim River and the Muar River—as Japanese troops occupied the entire peninsula, including Johore, the jump-off point for Singapore Island.

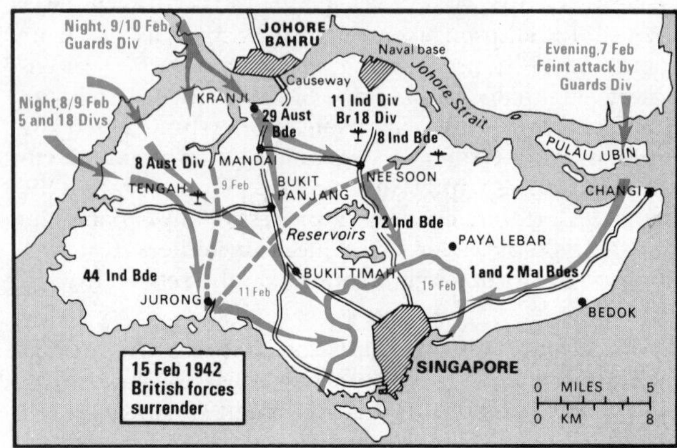

SINGAPORE ISLAND fell in a week of fighting

A British evacuation from the mainland to Singapore was completed by January 31, 1942. Air superiority had been lost—the Japanese had begun daylight air raids on Singapore early in January—and the Japanese controlled the seas east of Malaya, a contributing factor having been the December 10 sinking of H.M.S. PRINCE OF WALES and H.M.S. REPULSE by Japanese aircraft off the Malayan coast. General Percival then organized an island defense consisting of three sectors: Western Area (the Australian Imperial Force, Malaya), Northern Area (3d Indian Corps), and Southern Area (Singapore Fortress troops and others).

After a short respite, with activity being confined to artillery and air bombardments, the Japanese began landing on February 8 on the northwest corner of the island, driving a wedge into Australian defensive positions. In spite of the dispatch of reinforcements to the Western Area, Japanese invaders soon reached Tengah airfield, and on February 9 landed another force west of the causeway connecting the island and the mainland. By the 10th, Japanese troops had deepened their penetration and General Percival had promulgated an order establishing an eventual final defense on the southern portion of the island, where, aside from Singapore town, Kalang airdrome, the reservoirs and supply depots were located.

The Japanese pressed the attack, and on February 12 British beach defenses on the east and southeast coasts were pulled in to strengthen the defensive perimeter around the town. To make matters worse, ammunition and food supply rapidly ran low. On the 13th and 14th Japanese forces further compressed the British with main thrusts against the western flank of the defensive perimeter. The last British flotilla left Singapore on the 13th, but on the 14th it was devastated by a Japanese air attack. Early on February 15 General Percival decided to surrender unconditionally, effective that evening.

In losing Singapore, the western anchor of the Malay Barrier and home of the strongest British fleet in the East, and in surrendering some 130,000 local, British, Indian and Australian troops, Britain suffered what was generally acknowledged to be her most humiliating defeat in World War II. **W.H.A.**

SIRTE (Syrte). Town on the Gulf of Sidra (Sirte), Libya, where Gen. Erwin ROMMEL's German troops first clashed with British forces, February–March 1942. Sirte was taken by the British EIGHTH ARMY on December 25, 1942, in its drive to Tunisia.

SITTANG RIVER. The Sittang River, one of BURMA's largest, came into prominence early in 1942 as the Japanese, in their first Burma campaign, were beginning their mission of severing communications between RANGOON and KUNMING, China. Advancing westward out of Thailand, elements of the Japanese 15th Army, specifically the 33d and 55th Divisions, crowned previous successes with a devastating attack on two brigades of the British 17th Indian Division, which on February 22–23 were situated on the east bank of the Sittang in the vicinity of a bridge. Called the Battle of Sittang Bridge, this action marked the first of many bloody victories as the Japanese marched northward through Burma after capturing Rangoon. As the Allies reoccupied Burma during the first half of 1945, a reversal of the 1942 disaster occurred when elements of the 17th Indian Division, having set up strongpoints along escape routes of the remnants of the 28th and 33d Divisions, extracted heavy casualties as the Japanese moved eastward and crossed the Sittang River.

SITZKRIEG. A sarcastic British takeoff on the German word *Blitzkrieg,* applied to the period of static PHONY WAR on the Western Front between the fall of Poland in 1939 and the 1940 German offensive that led to the collapse of France.

6th AIRBORNE DIVISION (British). This division parachuted into the CAEN area of France in the early hours of June 6, 1944. The division's objectives were to seize and hold the Orne bridges between Caen and the sea; to deny the Germans the use of the area between the Orne and Dives Rivers; and to silence a battery which threatened the left flank of the Allied landings. The 6th captured not only the bridges over the Orne but also three bridges over the Dives. In addition they silenced a German battery at Merville. *See also* INVASION—NORMANDY.

SIXTH AIR FORCE. On February 5, 1942, the U.S. Caribbean Air Force was redesignated Sixth Air Force. For the remainder of the war, this command provided aerial defense for the Panama Canal, trained air crews for combat operations in the tropics and helped patrol the Caribbean in search of marauding German submarines.

SIXTH ARMY (German). The force famous as the army that was destroyed at STALINGRAD. Earlier in the war it had played an important role in Poland and in the campaign in the west, in the latter as part of Gen. Fedor von BOCK's Army Group B. Its commanding officer was Gen. Walther von REICHENAU. In the planned invasion of England, the Sixth Army was to sail from Cherbourg to Lyme Bay west of Portland Bill for an attack north toward the Severn estuary. After the cancellation of Operation SEA LION, the Sixth Army was transferred to the Eastern Front, where it became part of Field Marshal Gerd von RUNDSTEDT's Army Group South in the invasion of Russia in June 1941. When Reichenau was appointed to replace Rundstedt in December 1941, Reichenau's chief of staff in 1940, Gen. Friedrich PAULUS, succeeded to command of the Sixth Army. A staff officer during almost all of his career, Paulus successfully led the army in the operations at KHARKOV in May 1942, the Sixth Army and Field Marshal Paul von KLEIST's First Panzer Army together taking 214,000 prisoners, along with 1,200 tanks and 2,000 guns.

On June 28, 1942, the main German summer offensive began, the Sixth Army advancing eastward toward the Volga between the Fourth Panzer Army to the north and the First Panzer Army to the south. Initially the Sixth Army made substantial progress along the corridor between the Don and Donets Rivers. Then the advance slowed, owing to battle losses and the ever lengthening line of communications. In addition, Soviet resistance prevented a final push for Stalingrad until late August. But from this time the Sixth Army was caught up in the great battle for Stalin's namesake city, in which it perished. It lost 28,000 men between November 22 and December 23, primarily because of starvation and exhaustion. By the end of the year the Russians had taken 60,000 of its men prisoner. The Sixth Army had well over 200,000 men in Stalingrad (its strength on paper was 246,000), and of these about 200,000 died or were taken prisoner by the end of the fighting on February 2, 1943. Of the 91,000 said by the Russians to have been taken prisoner, only a few thousand ever saw Germany again.

In March 1943 a new Sixth Army was constituted from Army Group Hollidt under the command of Gen. Karl HOLLIDT. *See also* SOVIET-GERMAN OPERATIONS 1941–45.

SIXTH ARMY (U.S.). This army was activated at Fort Sam Houston, Tex., on January 25, 1943. The cadre came from Third Army headquarters. Lt. Gen. Walter KRUEGER, who had been Third Army commander when Sixth Army was activated, assumed command on February 16, 1943, and commanded the unit throughout the war. The army's size varied with the availability of forces and requirements of the missions assigned; corps composition ranged from one to three, including at various times the I, X, XIV and XXIV Corps. Operations from late April 1943 to September 25, 1944, were carried out by Task Force Alamo, the headquarters of which were the same as that of the Sixth Army; i.e., units assigned to Sixth Army comprised the Alamo force and the two were identical.

The Sixth Army was assigned to the Pacific Theater of Operations; its first combat was in July 1943. It served in the NEW GUINEA, BISMARCK ARCHIPELAGO, LEYTE and LUZON campaigns. Sixth Army headquarters landed in Japan on September 25, 1945, and carried out occupational duties until January 28, 1946, when the headquarters was inactivated. It was reactivated on March 1, 1946, at the Presidio of San Francisco, where it is still stationed.

6th ARMY GROUP. One of two American army group headquarters to operate in France and Germany, activated on August 1, 1944, at Bastia on the island of Corsica. Although the commander, Lt. Gen. Jacob L. DEVERS, had been involved as deputy commander of the Mediterranean theater in planning for the invasion of SOUTHERN FRANCE, operational command of the landings was at army level, so that the 6th Army Group became operational only on September 15, after troops from southern France had established contact with main Allied forces in northern France. The principal components of the command were the U.S. SEVENTH ARMY and the French First Army.

From the first, the Supreme Allied Commander, Gen. Dwight D. EISENHOWER, looked upon the 6th Army Group as a supporting command with the mission of assisting a main Allied advance by the U.S. 12TH ARMY GROUP and the British 21ST ARMY GROUP. Thus General Devers's command, advancing through the rugged Vosges Mountains of northeastern France and facing no objectives across the Rhine River that were vital to the German war effort, was destined throughout the war to play a secondary role.

As in the other Allied commands, its supply lines were overextended, and the armies of the 6th Army Group through the autumn of 1944 were reduced to slow, methodical advances. By late November they were nevertheless through the Vosges and at places had drawn up to the Rhine, but the Germans maintained a sizable bridgehead on southern reaches of the Alsatian plain known as the COLMAR POCKET. In response to Devers's request to shift his forces northward in hope of gaining a more active role, General Eisenhower agreed, but with the proviso that Devers quickly eliminate the pocket. That proved impossible until early February 1945; in the meantime, as Eisenhower had feared, the pocket served the Germans in mounting a counteroffensive (Operation NORDWIND). Although Devers could point to the fact that he had but two armies to the 12th Army Group's three and far fewer divisions and that the French lacked replacements and adequate logistical support, that failed to salve Eisenhower's irritation fully.

In a general Allied offensive in November 1944, the smaller 6th Army Group nevertheless gained more ground than the others, bringing the U.S. Seventh Army up to the Rhine on a broad front and prompting Devers to press for Rhine crossings. Since no other forces were in position to support such a drive, since the frontier fortifications of the West Wall and harsh terrain strengthened German defense of the Rhine and since there were no decisive objectives that far south, Eisenhower denied the request.

After eliminating the Colmar pocket and minor German gains achieved in Nordwind, the 6th Army Group shifted northwestward to face the West Wall in front of the Saar industrial region. A big attack in March cleared the Saar and again brought the two armies up against the Rhine. The Seventh Army gained the east bank on either side of Worms on March 26, while the French staged a surprise crossing near Speyer before daylight on the 31st. A rapid drive across southern Germany followed with entry into Austria in late April and linkup with Americans from Italy on May 4 at the Brenner Pass. The next day the German Army Group G surrendered to General Devers. The headquarters was deactivated on July 20.

SKATE, U.S.S. Balao-class submarine. Between 1943 and 1945 she completed seven war patrols in the Pacific. She was later used as a Bikini atomic-test target ship.

SKIP BOMBING. Tactic originated by Maj. Gen. George C. Kenney and his aide Maj. William Benn during the Southwest Pacific fighting. While en route to Australia in 1942, where Kenney was to take command of Allied air forces, the two men discussed the feasibility of attacking a ship broadside from an altitude of about 50 feet, releasing a bomb fitted with a five-second delayed-action fuze. The bomb, they believed, would skip along the water for about a hundred feet, activate the fuze upon striking the side of the ship, sink beneath the water and detonate at a depth that would damage the bottom of the vessel. Kenney's airmen discovered after hours of practice that they could blow out the bottom of a ship if they released the bomb at a distance of 300 yards while flying at 200 miles per hour 200 feet above the sea. During the Southwest Pacific campaign, planes as large as B-17s and B-24s (*see* B-17; B-24) performed skip bombing. *See also* Dam Busters; Wallis, Barnes.

SKIPJACK, U.S.S. Salmon-class submarine. Commissioned in 1938, *Skipjack* completed 10 Pacific war patrols by the end of 1944. She was reassigned to training duty in the Atlantic near the end of the war. *Skipjack* was sunk at Bikini in the 1946 atomic bomb tests.

SKODA WORKS. Czechoslovak (originally Austrian) arsenal, the third-largest producer of armaments in Europe in 1939, when it was taken over by the Germans on their annexation of Czechoslovakia. Czech tank production was of first importance to the Wehrmacht, in particular the LTM-35, redesignated by the Germans the Pz. Kw. 35(t), and the TNHP, redesignated the Pz. Kw. 38(t).

SKORZENY, Otto (1908–1975). Probably the most spectacular officer of the Nazi SS (*see* SS), Skorzeny was once known as the "most dangerous man in Europe" as the result of his exploits, the most famous of which was the daring glider raid that snatched Benito Mussolini from captivity on a mountaintop. A native of Vienna, Skorzeny was an early member of the Nazi Party and

Colonel Skorzeny

the SS; he achieved the rank of Standartenführer (colonel) in 1943. He fought with the Waffen SS in France, Yugoslavia and the USSR and in 1943 was assigned to the Security Office (RSHA—Reichssicherheitshauptamt), working under Walter Schellenberg in the organization of espionage activities. In this capacity he led the commando squad that freed Mussolini on September 12, 1943, after the dictator had been turned out of office. He also organized Operation Greif, which during the Battle of the Bulge infiltrated Germans in American uniforms behind Allied lines; although the extent of this operation was exaggerated by the Allies, it did cause great confusion. Skorzeny also set afloat rumors that General Eisenhower was the object of an assassination plot. In 1947 Skorzeny was tried by a U.S. Army court for war crimes and acquitted. He subsequently escaped internment in Germany and went to Spain, where he became a prosperous businessman.

SKUA. The first British-designed dive-bomber and the first monoplane to join the Fleet Air Arm. The Skua was an all-metal, low-wing, two-place carrier aircraft. Blackburn Aircraft produced the plane, which had four forward-firing machine guns and a fifth weapon on a flexible mount at the rear of the canopy. The graceful-looking Skua carried one 500-pound bomb internally. A 905-horsepower Bristol Perseus radial gave the plane a top speed of 194 miles per hour. This aircraft, which saw combat service between 1939 and 1941, was the first British naval aircraft to down a German warplane and the only British dive-bomber to sink a major German warship (the cruiser Königsberg).

SKUNK. U.S. Navy term for an unidentified surface RADAR contact, equivalent to the use of *bogey* when referring to aircraft.

SKYTRAIN. *See* C-47.

SLAPSTICK. Code name for the occupation of Taranto, Italy, by the British 1ST AIRBORNE DIVISION on September 9, 1943. The division was brought across the Mediterranean from Bizerte, Tunisia, in light cruisers and minelayers, and the landing was not opposed.

SLAVE LABOR. "Of the 5 million foreign workers who have come to Germany, fewer than 200,000 have come voluntarily," said Fritz SAUCKEL, Adolf HITLER's Plenipotentiary General for the Allocation of Labor, in March 1944. Large numbers of people from the occupied territories, especially in the east, were sent to Germany for every kind of labor, replacing the men serving in the fighting forces and working particularly in Albert SPEER's munitions plants. More than a million came from Poland. Prisoners of war were also coerced into war work. When men were needed, the Nazi authorities thought nothing of taking them by force from any of the occupied countries. The Netherlands, for example, reported during the NUREMBERG TRIALS: "In November 1944 the Germans began a ruthless campaign to enlist labor forces; they bypassed the labor exchanges. Without warning they singled out whole town areas, arrested people in the streets or in their homes, and deported them." Beginning in March 1942 youths and girls of 18 to 25 were deported from the Netherlands; in October 1942 Belgian men between the ages of 18 and 50 and women between 18 and 35 could be taken away. Slave labor began to be exploited soon after the occupation of Poland for men between 18 and 60. By July 1942 almost 2 million workers had been sent to Germany, and by April 1943 Sauckel reported to Hitler that a further 3.6 million workers had been introduced into industry and that 1.6 million prisoners of war were also employed. Some 40 percent of the armaments workers in Germany at the time were forced labor.

Slave labor took many forms. The most fortunate were the isolated workers assigned to German farmers, who often treated them well. The worst off were the concentration camp prisoners singled out on arrival at AUSCHWITZ for labor rather than extermination. Their lives were in any case forfeit; as they died from ill treatment, malnutrition or disease, they could be only too readily replaced. Heinrich HIMMLER's intention was to exploit the labor the more able-bodied prisoners represented and make money for the SS (*see* SS) by supplying camp labor at a price to armaments manufacturers. Firms applied to the SS Main Economic and Administration Office for an allocation of this cheap labor at daily rates ranging from 4 to 8 marks (approximately $1–$2); the turnover at BUCHENWALD alone became worth between 1 and 1.5 million marks a month to the SS. Rudolf HOESS testified at Nuremberg that the 13 major concentration camps in German-occupied Europe controlled some 900 subsidiary labor camps holding anywhere from 100 to 10,000 prisoners. Firms such as Siemens and I. G. Farben built subsidiary plants near Auschwitz to make use of the prison labor force (women as well as men) supplied them by the SS; the daily work period was from 10 to 11 hours. The SS were responsible for the supervision of prisoners while at work.

Workers who came to Germany not technically as prisoners but as "voluntary" or conscripted workers were normally housed in camps, where the conditions became almost as bad as those in the concentration camps themselves. Speer, however, insisted the workers be adequately fed, though he admits he turned a blind eye to the cruelties involved in seizing men from their homes and deporting them for forced labor. When the war came to an end, a great part of the refugee problem arose from the great army of ill-nourished and penniless workers wandering on foot back in the direction of their countries of origin or waiting helplessly to be repatriated by the Allied authorities.

Though Sauckel was condemned to death at Nuremberg and hanged for his part in this terrible enterprise, Speer was spared death and given a 20-year sentence on the grounds of his courageous opposition to Hitler during the final phase of the war. Speer made no attempt to conceal his part in the affair. When on trial at Nuremberg, he said, "The workers were brought to Germany largely against their will, and I had no objection to their being brought to Germany against their will. On the contrary, during the first period, until the autumn of 1942, I certainly used all my energy to see that as many workers as possible should be brought to Germany in this manner."

SLEDGEHAMMER. Code name for a proposed British-American landing on the coast of France in late 1942. A product of the American staff, the plan was viewed as an emergency one, to be undertaken if the Soviet armies appeared to be reaching the point of collapse. The idea was to gain and hold a beachhead as a sort of suicide SECOND FRONT, thus relieving some of the German pressure on the Russians. Sledgehammer also would have served the desired purpose of bringing U.S. troops into combat with the Germans in 1942, an aim that was actually realized with the invasion of French NORTHWEST AFRICA. Fortunately for the Allies (fortunate because, as the fiery German repulse of the DIEPPE landing demonstrated, the Wehrmacht was in full control in France in 1942), the operation remained only a suggested plan.

SLESSOR, Sir John (1897–). A Royal Air Force officer, Slessor was Director of Plans in 1937–39 and took part in the Anglo-American (ABC) staff conversations in Washington in 1941. After commanding No. 5 Bomber Group he became AOC-in-C COASTAL COMMAND and decisively increased the effectiveness of his maritime force in the Battle of the ATLANTIC. He made an equally significant contribution as commander of RAF forces in the Mediterranean and Middle East, 1944–45. When the war ended he was made Air Member for Personnel and in due course became Chief of Air Staff (1950–52). He achieved the rank of Marshal of the Royal Air Force.

SLIM, William Joseph (Viscount Slim) (1891–1970). After joining the Royal Warwickshire Regiment in 1914 as a private, the future Field Marshal Viscount Slim rose steadily up the military ladder and was a brigadier

General Slim

by the time World War II began. He saw wartime desert duty in IRAQ, SYRIA and IRAN as commander of the 10th Indian Division and then was sent to BURMA. He was disappointed at leaving his desert command; of desert fighting he said, "The desert suits the British, and so does fighting in it. You can see your man."

Arriving in Burma on March 19, 1942, as a lieutenant general, Slim was appointed by General WAVELL, Commander in Chief India, as commander of the 1st Burma Corps (Burcorps), which was just being formed from the Imperial troops. The situation on Slim's arrival was bleak: one of his units, the 17th Indian Division, had recently suffered an unnerving defeat at the hands of the Japanese in a retreat across the SITTANG RIVER, and the Japanese were beginning a strong advance into Burma's heartland. Although he attempted to regain the offensive in the face of Japanese advances, Slim was unable to do so for long. His troops were exhausted, casualties had been heavy, air superiority belonged to the Japanese and no clear strategic objective had been established for the Allied campaign in Burma. By May 14 the British forces had been driven into Assam.

After this retreat into India, Slim took command of the newly formed 15th Indian Corps, supervising intensive training to prepare it for battle in the jungles against the Japanese. In October 1943 Slim was made commander of SOUTHEAST ASIA COMMAND'S (SEAC) newly established British FOURTEENTH ARMY. Early in 1944, the army repulsed a Japanese attack against the ARAKAN front and defeated a lengthy siege at IMPHAL. After these successes Slim's army, initially with three corps, including the 15th, went on the offensive (code-named CAPITAL), crossed the CHINDWIN RIVER and helped eject the Japanese Army from Burma, inflicting some 347,000 casualties in the process.

In 1945 Slim was appointed commander in chief of Allied land forces in Southeast Asia. One of Britain's most successful field commanders, he was appointed after the war Chief of the Imperial General Staff and later served as Governor General of Australia.

SLOT, THE. American nickname for the otherwise unidentified body of water that runs the length of the SOLOMONS chain between BOUGAINVILLE and GUADALCANAL. It is approximately 280 miles long and 30 to 50 miles wide. Its orientation, along the general axis between Guadalcanal at its southeast end and the Japanese base at RABAUL, New Britain, some 300 miles beyond its northwest entrance, made it a heavily traveled waterway during the struggle for the Solomons.

SM-79. Italian aircraft built by Savoia-Marchetti, designed by Alessandro Marchetti as Italy's entry in the 1934 England-to-Australia race sponsored by Sir MacPherson Robertson, a British publisher. The first production models, though intended as bombers, emerged from the production line as compact, high-speed transports but were promptly converted to their original purpose. Nicknamed the *Sparviero* (Sparrowhawk), the bomber was a low-wing, trimotor monoplane of wood-and-metal construction. In 1938 an SM-79 established five world speed records carrying a specified weight over a measured course. Average speed was 290.81 miles per hour for 2,000 kilometers and 293.29 miles per hour for 1,000 kilometers.

The plane had a distinctive hump above the pilot's compartment. This bulge served as fairing for the dorsal gunner, who fired a 12.7-mm. machine gun, and also housed a fixed forward-firing weapon. Either one 12.7-mm. or two 7.7-mm. guns were fired through hatches in the waist. The bombardier aimed from a bathtub slung beneath the fuselage aft of the wing and also manned a rearward-firing 12.7-mm. machine gun. Three 780-horsepower Alfa Romeo radials gave the early Sparrowhawks a top speed approaching 270 miles per hour. Three 1,000-horsepower Piaggio radial engines were later installed, enabling the plane to carry two 450-mm. torpedoes or 4,400 pounds of bombs.

The Sparrowhawk was a rugged, easy-to-handle airplane. In its different versions, it proved a successful bomber and land-based torpedo plane. A few were still serving as trainers and transports as late as 1952.

SM-81. The *Pipistrello* (Bat), an Italian trimotor, low-wing monoplane with a fixed landing gear. First flown in 1933, this Savoia-Marchetti bomber and transport saw combat in Ethiopia and Spain and with the wartime Regia Aeronautica in North Africa, Greece, Albania and Russia. Of mixed wood-and-metal construction, the Bat was manned by a crew of five, had a top speed of 217 miles per hour and could carry 4,000 pounds of bombs 900 miles. The engines were 900-horsepower Piaggio radials. Armament consisted of two-gun, semi-retractable ventral and dorsal turrets. A fifth 7.7-mm. machine gun could be fired by hand from hatches on either side of the fuselage. The bombardier sighted through a window in a gondola fitted beneath the fuselage aft of the engine. Despite its size and lack of speed, the Bat served as a torpedo plane, attacking British shipping in the Mediterranean.

SM-84. A replacement for another Savoia-Marchetti trimotor, the SM-79 Sparrowhawk (above), this was a twin-tail, low-wing monoplane powered by 1,000-horsepower Piaggio radial engines. The plane lacked the older craft's humpback, which was replaced by a dorsal turret. Armament was four 12.7-mm. machine guns, and ordnance capacity was 4,410 pounds of bombs or two torpedoes. Top speed was 266 miles per hour at 11,500 feet. Less numerous than the Sparrowhawk, this type joined Italy's air arm in 1941 and remained in service until 1948.

SM-85. Flown for the first time in 1938, the SM-85 was designed by Savoia-Marchetti as a single-place, twin-engine dive-bomber for Italy's Regia Aeronautica. Built largely of wood and fitted with diving brakes, the plane could carry more than 1,000 pounds of bombs. Poor flying characteristics and the inadequacy of its 500-horsepower Piaggio radial engines doomed it to failure. Only 32 were built, and these saw very little action before giving way to JUNKERS JU 87Bs (Stukas) provided by the Germans.

SMALL ARMS. The essential small arms of World War II can be grouped as follows: rifles and semiautomatic rifles; automatic rifles and light machine guns; submachine guns, carbines and pistols. Rifles—for example, the bolt-action German Mauser Gewehr 1898 (KAR 98); the British Lee-Enfield SMLE No. 1, Mark III; and the semiautomatic U.S. M-1 (*see* M-1 RIFLE)—made up the greater number of infantry weapons during the conflict. The automatic rifle was the basic supporting weapon of the infantry platoon, although the numbers of these weapons per company in a given army at any given time varied according to circumstances and tactical requirements. Typical weapons in this group were the British BREN Light Machine Gun, Mark I and Mark II (.303 caliber); the Japanese M1936 (Model 96) or M1939 (Model 99) of 6.5 mm.; the U.S. BROWNING AUTOMATIC RIFLE M1918A2 (BAR A2); and the German Dreyse-Solothurn MG 34 and MG 42, both of 7.92 mm. Also in this group one may include the medium machine guns, such as the water-cooled Browning M1917A1 (.30 caliber), the Vickers-Maxim Mark I/w Tripod Mark IV, the air-cooled Japanese Hotchkiss M1932 (Model 92) and the U.S. Browning M1919A4.

As for submachine guns, carbines and pistols, there was a wide variety. Generally, submachine guns were used for special purposes, issued to vehicle crews or used for assault. The most famous of these were the U.S. Thompson submachine gun M1928A1; the British STEN GUN, Marks I, II and III; the German Schmeisser MP38; and the Suomi submachine gun as modified by the Russians—the PPSH-41 (BURP GUN). Carbines were used in place of light automatic weapons, and the U.S. Carbine M1, .30-caliber semiautomatic, was typical. Pistols were carried by officers, troops handling crew-served weapons, MPs and airmen. These were usually automatics (really semiautomatics) as the American .45-caliber Automatic Pistol M1911 and M1911A1, the German LUGER or WALTHER P-38 and the Russian 7.62-mm. Tokarev. The British preferred revolvers, using the British Service Pistol, Mark I and II.

SMIGLY-RYDZ, Edward (1886–1943?). In 1935 Marshal Smigly-Rydz ("Smigly" was an acquired name meaning "lightning") succeeded Jozef Pilsudski as virtual dictator of Poland, and he was thus the national leader and military chief when the Germans invaded in 1939. Various observers have criticized the disposition of the Polish forces and the Army's naïve faith in the cavalry, but the Poles had little chance in any case. After the Russians moved into eastern Poland, Smigly-Rydz escaped to Rumania, and later he returned to join the Polish underground. He is believed to have been killed by the Germans in 1943.

SMITH, Albert C. (1894–1974). U.S. Army officer, a brigadier general in 1942, who in 1944 was named commanding general of the 14th Armored Division. He was promoted to major general in 1945.

SMITH, Allan Edward (1892–). "Hoke" Smith began the war as a captain in the U.S. Navy commanding the battleship SOUTH DAKOTA during the GILBERT and MARSHALL campaigns. After promotion to rear admiral, Smith commanded groups responsible for preliminary gunfire and cover during the LEYTE, IWO JIMA, Ryukyus and OKINAWA invasions. Following the war he served as president of the Naval War College.

SMITH, Edward H. (1889–1961). U.S. Coast Guard officer—known as "Iceberg" Smith—very much involved in oceanographic studies. In 1939–40 he commanded the International Ice Patrol (which tracks icebergs). Promoted to rear admiral in 1942, Smith commanded Task Force 24 (the Coast Guard's Eastern U.S. Area) between 1943 and 1945. Coast Guard forces under his direction were active in keeping the Germans from using Greenland as a base for weather observations (which would have been of great value in planning U-boat operations).

SMITH, Holland McTyeire (1882–1967). Sometimes called the father of modern U.S. amphibious warfare, and nicknamed "Howlin' Mad," General Smith was involved both in the development of amphibious warfare doctrine and, as the senior Marine officer in the Pacific during World War II, was its foremost practitioner.

In the years prior to the war, Smith was director of operations and training at Headquarters Marine Corps in Washington and then was assistant to the Commandant until 1939, when, upon his promotion to major general, he was placed in command of the 1st Marine Brigade; in February 1941 the brigade was redesignated the 1st Marine Division. In June 1941 Smith assumed command of the organization which became the Amphibious Force, Atlantic Fleet.

In August 1942 he moved to the West Coast to take command of the Amphibious Corps, Pacific Fleet, which trained the 2d and 3d Marine Divisions and the 7th Infantry Division before they went overseas into combat. His command prepared U.S. and Canadian Army units for the KISKA and ATTU landings. Amphibious Corps, Pacific Fleet, was redesignated V Amphibious Corps and set up headquarters at Pearl Harbor in September 1943 to begin planning for the GILBERTS operation. As commander of VAC, Smith directed the successful Marine and Army landings in the MARSHALLS and on SAIPAN and TINIAN in the MARIANA ISLANDS.

It was during the Saipan operation in July 1944 that the rancorous Smith versus Smith controversy erupted, after Lt. Gen. Holland Smith relieved Army Maj. Gen. Ralph SMITH, commander of the 27th Infantry Division, for "all-round poor performance" of the division. It became the most malodorous U.S. interservice feud of the war. Ralph Smith was ultimately sustained by the Army high command.

In August 1944 Smith took over command of the newly formed FLEET MARINE FORCE, Pacific, which was the senior Marine Corps organization in the Pacific and under which III and V Amphibious Corps operated. Under the aegis of FMFPac, the two corps took GUAM, IWO JIMA and OKINAWA. As commanding general of FMFPac, Smith was Admiral NIMITZ's senior Marine adviser. But in the new arrangement his authority was purely nominal.

In July 1945, after nearly two years overseas, in which his marines played a very large role in the defeat of Japan, General Smith was transferred to the United States to assume command of the Training and Replacement Command at Camp Pendleton, Calif. He held this job until May 1946, when, at the age of 64 and after 41 years of active duty, he retired.

SMITH, John L. (1914–1972). U.S. Marine aviator, commander of Marine Fighter Squadron 223, the first on GUADALCANAL. Captain Smith, who received the MEDAL OF HONOR, recorded 19 kills.

SMITH, Julian Constable (1885–1975). One of the Marine Corps's outstanding leaders in amphibious warfare, and in fact one of its developers, Smith was promoted to brigadier general before World War II. He took command of the 2d Marine Division in the spring of 1943, leading it into the battle for TARAWA. He also was Commanding General, Expeditionary Troops, THIRD FLEET, in which capacity he was responsible for the capture of the southern Palaus and ULITHI. After a short tour with Fleet Marine Force, Pacific, he returned to the United States in December 1944, taking command of the Department of the Pacific in San Francisco. He retired in February 1946.

SMITH, Ralph C. (1893–). U.S. Army officer who was promoted to major general and given command of the 27th Division in 1942. He held that position until 1944, when, on SAIPAN, he was relieved by Marine Lt. Gen. Holland M. "Howlin' Mad" SMITH because of the 27th's alleged inefficiency and lack of aggressiveness and his own disobedience of orders. A full-scale controversy developed between the Army on one side and the Navy and Marine Corps on the other, the Army accusing Holland Smith of being prejudiced against it. The matter was looked into by an Army board, chaired by Lt. Gen. SIMON B. BUCKNER, which concluded that the relief was not "justified by the facts." The Navy—and Admiral KING himself—dismissed the findings as one-sided, and no further official action was taken.

SMITH, Walter Bedell (1895–1961). Some say "Beetle" Smith, as his contemporaries knew him, had the countenance of a bulldog; he needed at least the temperament of one in order to fill his assigned role as hatchet man for an affable Supreme Allied Commander, Gen. Dwight D. EISENHOWER. He may have acquired that—along with a brusque manner and a salty vocabulary—in his first service as a private in the Indiana National Guard. Entering the U.S. Army in 1917 as an infantry reserve officer, he served in France with the 4th Division. When George C. MARSHALL became the Army's wartime Chief of Staff, he called in Major Smith, a protégé, to be assistant to the secretary of the General Staff; he moved up to secretary in September 1941 and in February 1942 was named U.S. secretary of the COMBINED CHIEFS OF STAFF.

Just before the invasion of North Africa, Marshall sent Smith to England to be Eisenhower's chief of staff. General Smith filled that role until the German surrender, which he stage-managed for his boss. Eisenhower subsequently called him "the general manager of the war." Following the war Smith served as ambassador to the Soviet Union, director of the Central Intelligence Agency and Undersecretary of State. He died as a full general at age 65 of a heart attack.

SMOLENSK, BATTLE OF. Located on the upper Dnieper River, Smolensk is a strategically important Soviet rail and communications center. The Battle of Smolensk is generally considered to have begun with the German seizure of VITEBSK on July 9, 1941, and was not so much a battle to save the city as it was a fight by the Soviets to stem the German sweep into the heart of Russia and, especially, to win time to strengthen the defenses of Moscow. As the battle opened, the main Soviet forces in the area were of Marshal TIMOSHENKO's Western Sector (as of July 2)—the Twenty-first Army south of Smolensk generally in the Mogilev-Gomel area, the Twentieth Army between Vitebsk and Smolensk, the Sixteenth Army in the area east of the city itself and the Nineteenth Army to the west. Other Soviet forces in the area strengthened the northern and southern ends of the line.

The German plan was to send the Second and Third Panzer Groups against the center immediately instead of waiting for the Twentieth and Ninth field armies, which were still to the rear. The relatively large concentration of Soviet troops in the Smolensk region led HALDER and BRAUCHITSCH of the German high command to predict that the gateway to Moscow, Smolensk, would be the arena for engaging and destroying a large enemy force in one decisive battle. The fighting at Smolensk reached its peak between July 21 and August 7. On July 24 Timoshenko reported to the SOVIET HIGH COMMAND that the Sixteenth Army still held most of the city and that, although also caught in the German ring, the Twentieth Army had withstood a series of large-scale attacks on its positions.

By the end of July the German high command, seeing their blitzkrieg bogging down, had renewed the drive to reduce the city and cut off the Soviet forces not already surrounded. In one attempt at Yartsevo, the 17th and 20th Panzer Divisions were thrown against the newly formed Rokossovsky Group. Soviet artillery and ROKOSSOVSKY's effective defense stopped the assault, with heavy German casualties. Of equal importance was the appearance of the new T-34 TANK, which for the first time gave the Russians some parity in armor. About this same time (July 30) Marshal ZHUKOV was named to command the Reserve Front, located some distance to the rear 100 miles east of Smolensk. Instead of putting his six-army command to the task of building a static defense position before Moscow, Zhukov began to move forward, though not until the Germans had taken Smolensk (August 6).

Soviet forces recaptured the city, which had been heavily fortified by the Germans, on September 25, 1943, suffering enormous casualties in the seven armies Marshal SOKOLOVSKY was required to commit to the battle. *See also* SOVIET-GERMAN OPERATIONS 1941–45.

SMUTS, Jan Christiaan (1870–1950). South African soldier and statesman. Smuts had been one of the Boer commando leaders in the Second Boer War at the turn of the century; he then became reconciled to the British and a great admirer of them, developing a philosophy of the British Commonwealth and Empire as a voluntary union of free peoples devoted to the cause of world peace. In World War I he first suppressed a revolt at home and then commanded the Allied forces in the German East Africa campaign. He next moved to London to serve in the Imperial War Cabinet, where *inter alia* he was a strong supporter of the formation of a separate Royal Air Force and was a leading architect of the League of Nations. From 1919 to 1924 he was Prime Minister of South Africa, from 1924 to 1933 in opposition and from 1933 a minister in a coalition government. At the outbreak of war the Prime Minister, Gen. James B. M. Hertzog, favored neutrality; Smuts favored war. The issue, put to a free vote in the House of Assembly, was won by Smuts's supporters after a dramatic debate, Smuts again becoming Prime Minister.

For obvious strategic reasons South Africa's support was of enormous importance to Great Britain, Smuts himself becoming one of Winston CHURCHILL's most trusted confidants. Under Smuts's inspiration and direction volunteer units and formations of the South African Army fought in Somalia and Ethiopia, and then in NORTH AFRICA and ITALY; combatant units were all white, nonwhites being restricted to auxiliary and labor work. But the war brought out the best and the worst in Smuts. At his best he was a Commonwealth statesman of the widest vision and steadfastness on the world scene, but on the home political scene he seemed increasingly to shrink away from his own country's mounting internal problems.

SMYTH REPORT. The popular name for *Atomic Energy for Military Purposes* (1945) by Henry DeWolf Smyth, chairman of the department of physics at Princeton University. The book, sponsored by the War Department, told the story of the development of the ATOMIC BOMB.

SNORKEL (Schnorkel, Schnorchel). A hollow retractable mast, of prewar Dutch design, fitted to German U-boats during the latter part of the war. It contained tubes for fresh-air intake and for engine exhaust. By raising the head of its snorkel above the surface, a submarine could cruise submerged on its diesel engines while replenishing its air supply and recharging its storage batteries. A U-boat could thus remain submerged for extended periods, presenting less of a target at a time when airplane and surface-ship RADAR was making life extremely uncertain for submarines. When the snorkel was first introduced, existing Allied radars were not sensitive enough to pick up the exposed head when it was raised; later radars, however, were capable of doing so when capably used. The British and Americans spelled this word "snorkel," and in this form it passed into the English language.

SNOWFLAKE. A powerful rocket flare developed by the Allies to counter night surface attacks on convoys by German submarines.

SOC. The Curtiss Seagull, U.S. Navy scout-observation floatplane, a radial-engine two-place biplane with interchangeable wheels and floats. Delivery of the SOC-1 began in 1935. This was followed by the wheels-only SOC-2 and -2A, the latter equipped with a tail hook for carrier landing. The SOC-3 reverted to interchangeable landing gear, while several -3As had wheels and tail hooks. SOC-3 and -3A equivalents were also produced by the Naval Aircraft Factory at the Philadelphia navy yard as the SON-1 and -1A. Three SOC-4s were built for the Coast Guard. SOC production ended in 1938. SOCs first equipped cruiser scouting squadrons, then battleship observation squadrons. Others flew from carriers and shore bases. The SO3C (*see* SO3C), introduced in 1942, was intended to replace the SOC. The SO3C's inferior performance gave the older plane a new lease on life. Although generally replaced for battleship and some cruiser use by the OS2U (*see* OS2U), a fair number of SOCs were still in service at the end of the war.

Although it did not match some other floatplanes in performance, the SOC served for some 10 years in considerable numbers and demonstrated a ruggedness and dependability that made it valuable beyond its allotted time. The SOC-3 had a 550-horsepower engine giving it, in float configuration, a top speed of 162 miles per hour and a 900-mile range at economical speed of 97 miles per hour. It had one fixed forward-firing .30-caliber machine gun, with another on the observer's flexible mount. Wing racks could carry two 100-pound bombs or two 325-pound depth bombs.

SO3C. The U.S. Navy Curtiss Seagull, a light monoplane scout-observation catapult floatplane with interchangeable wheels/floats landing gear. It was developed as a high-performance replacement for the SOC and given the same name (*see* SOC). Design work began in 1937, but problems had to be ironed out and fleet delivery did not begin until 1942. During the next two years 800 production planes were manufactured in SO3C-1, -2 and -3 models. Performance was disappointing, and plans to replace the SOC were dropped; the newer plane saw only limited operational service from cruisers, and by 1944, when SO3C production was terminated, it had been relegated to subsidiary duties. The Royal Navy received 150 SO3C-2C models; these were designated Seamews and used as trainers. Many U.S. Navy Seagulls were converted to radio-controlled target drones; 30 of these, redesignated SO3C-1K, went

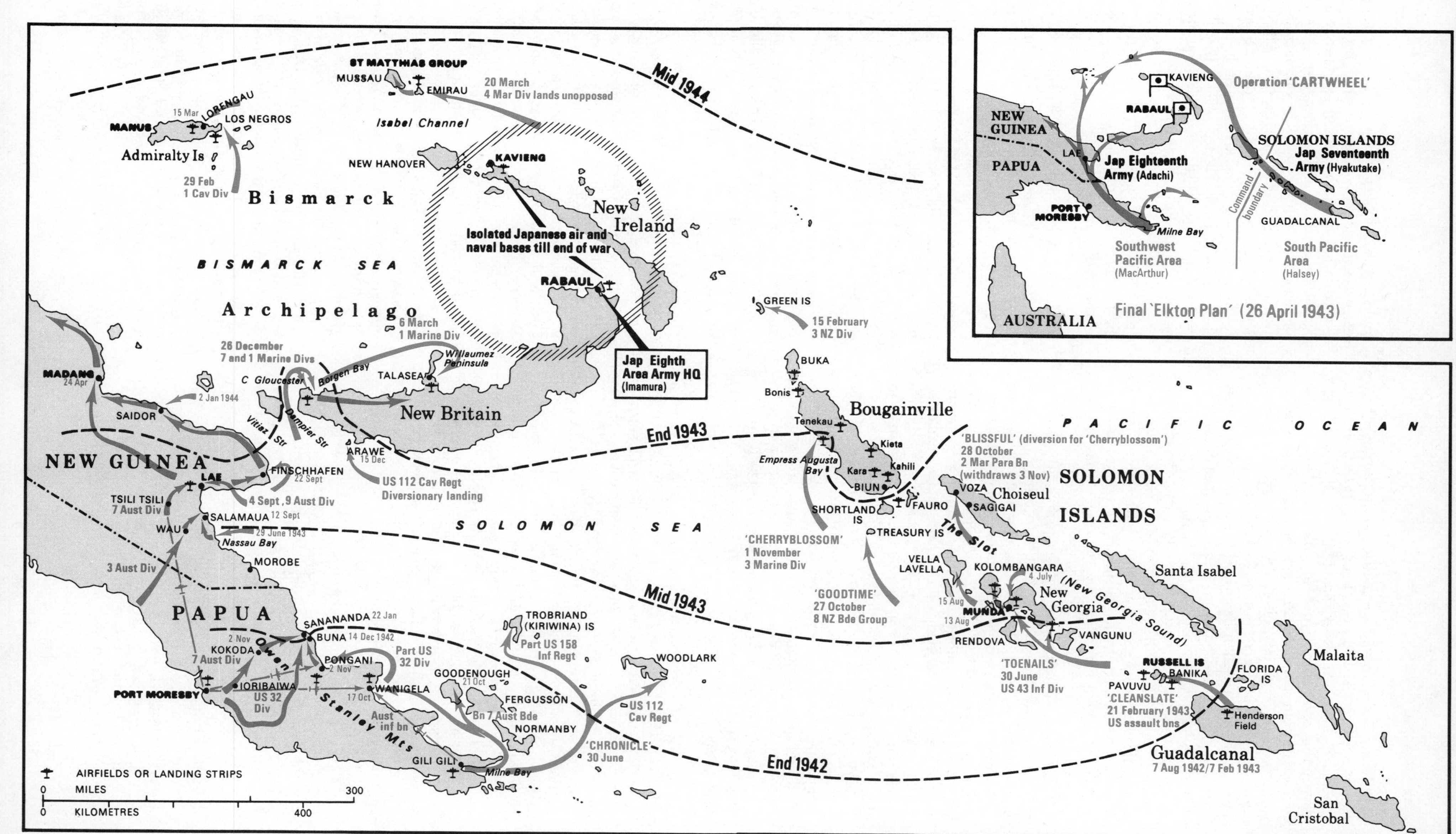

Final 'Elkton Plan' (26 April 1943)
Operation 'CARTWHEEL'
NEW GUINEA
PAPUA
LAE
PORT MORESBY
Milne Bay
KAVIENG
RABAUL
Jap Eighteenth Army (Adachi)
SOLOMON ISLANDS
Jap Seventeenth Army (Hyakutake)
Command boundary
GUADALCANAL
Southwest Pacific Area (MacArthur)
South Pacific Area (Halsey)
AUSTRALIA
ST MATTHIAS GROUP
MUSSAU
EMIRAU
20 March
4 Mar Div lands unopposed
Mid 1944
Isabel Channel
MANUS
15 Mar
LORENGAU
LOS NEGROS
Admiralty Is
29 Feb
1 Cav Div
NEW HANOVER
Bismarck
BISMARCK SEA
Archipelago
New Ireland
Isolated Japanese air and naval bases till end of war
Jap Eighth Area Army HQ (Imamura)
6 March
1 Marine Div
26 December
7 and 1 Marine Divs
Willaumez Peninsula
TALASEA
Borgen Bay
C Gloucester
New Britain
MADANG
24 Apr
2 Jan 1944
SAIDOR
Vitiaz Str
Dampier Str
ARAWE
15 Dec
US 112 Cav Regt
Diversionary landing
End 1943
NEW GUINEA
FINSCHHAFEN
22 Sept
4 Sept, 9 Aust Div
TSILI TSILI
7 Aust Div
SALAMAUA 12 Sept
29 June 1943
Nassau Bay
WAU
MOROBE
3 Aust Div
PAPUA
SOLOMON SEA
SANANANDA 22 Jan
BUNA 14 Dec 1942
2 Nov
KOKODA
7 Aust Div
Owen Stanley Mts
PONGANI
2 Nov
Part US 32 Div
PORT MORESBY
IORIBAIWA
US 32 Div
17 Oct
WANIGELA
Aust inf bn
GOODENOUGH
21 Oct
FERGUSSON
Bn 7 Aust Bde
NORMANBY
GILI GILI
Milne Bay
TROBRIAND (KIRIWINA) IS
Part US 158 Inf Regt
WOODLARK
US 112 Cav Regt
'CHRONICLE'
30 June
End 1942
Mid 1943
GREEN IS
15 February
3 NZ Div
BUKA
Bonis
Bougainville
Tenekau
Empress Augusta Bay
Kieta
Kara
Kahili
BIUN
SHORTLAND IS
FAURO
TREASURY IS
'CHERRYBLOSSOM'
1 November
3 Marine Div
'GOODTIME'
27 October
8 NZ Bde Group
PACIFIC OCEAN
'BLISSFUL' (diversion for 'Cherryblossom')
28 October
2 Mar Para Bn
(withdraws 3 Nov)
SOLOMON ISLANDS
VOZA
Choiseul
SAGIGAI
The Slot
VELLA LAVELLA
KOLOMBANGARA
4 July
15 Aug
13 Aug
MUNDA
New Georgia
(New Georgia Sound)
RENDOVA
VANGUNU
'TOENAILS'
30 June
US 43 Inf Div
Santa Isabel
Malaita
RUSSELL IS
BANIKA
PAVUVU
'CLEANSLATE'
21 February 1943
US assault bns
FLORIDA IS
Henderson Field
Guadalcanal
7 Aug 1942/7 Feb 1943
San Cristobal
AIRFIELDS OR LANDING STRIPS
MILES
0
300
KILOMETRES
0
400

to Britain, where they were called Queen Seamews. Curtiss planned an improved SO3C-4, and the Ryan Co. was to have built a slightly redesigned variant, the SOR-1; both projects were abandoned. The SO3C-2 had a 600-horsepower air-cooled engine, with a maximum speed of 190 miles per hour and a range of 830 miles at 122 miles per hour. It had one fixed and one flexible .30-caliber machine gun and could carry two 100-pound bombs or one 325-pound depth bomb.

SOKOLOVSKY, Vasili D. (1897–1968). Soviet general (later Marshal of the Soviet Union) who helped to organize the defense of MOSCOW in 1941.

SOLA. Largest Norwegian airfield, located near STAVANGER on the southwest coast. Its capture on April 9, 1940, gave the Germans a base from which they could bomb British ships.

SOLLUM. An Egyptian port of some importance, near the Libyan frontier; also the site of a pass up the escarpment. Sollum and HALFAYA, six miles south, were key positions in the British BATTLEAXE offensive (June 1941) and the struggle for TOBRUK.

SOLOMON ISLANDS. Lying in the western Pacific east of NEW GUINEA, the Solomons constitute a double mountain chain running northwest to southeast for about 700 miles between the BISMARCK ARCHIPELAGO and the NEW HEBRIDES. Though the northern islands of BOUGAINVILLE, Buka and Green are politically part of the New Guinea district, geographically they are the northernmost links of the Solomons chain. There are several offshoot islands well away from the main chain: Ontong Java Atoll (Lord Howe Island) to the northeast; RENNELL, due south of GUADALCANAL; and the SANTA CRUZ group to the southeast. All are considered part of the Solomons. The terrain in the Solomons is typical of that entire World War II strategic area—jungle and hills that are extremely difficult to move through and over, which meant that ground combat was localized along the littoral and that air and surface engagements played a large part in the fighting. The major islands of the northern chain—CHOISEUL, Santa Isabel and Malaita—held few natural military objectives, which was true also of San Cristobal, the southernmost of the island chain.

The other large islands of the Solomons—Guadalcanal, Bougainville and NEW GEORGIA—had sizable harbors and enough airfield sites to make them strategic objectives in the drive against RABAUL, the ultimate strategic objective in the South Pacific campaigns. Each of the following major objectives embraced small nearby islands, as noted: TULAGI and Florida together with Guadalcanal; VELLA LAVELLA and KOLOMBANGARA with New Georgia; and Buka and the SHORTLAND–Treasury Islands with Bougainville. One further target group, about 30 miles northwest of CAPE ESPERANCE on Guadalcanal, was the RUSSELLS, with the two islands of Banika and Pavuvu.

Following are the major Solomon Islands and their satellites and the dates they were invaded: Guadalcanal, Tulagi, Florida, Gavutu, Tanambogo—August 7, 1942; Russell Islands—February 21, 1943; Vangunu and Rendova in the New Georgia group—June 30, 1943; Vella Lavella—August 15, 1943; Treasury Islands—October 27, 1943; Choiseul (diversionary raid)—October 28, 1943; Bougainville—November 1, 1943.

SOMERS, U.S.S. Destroyer and class (2,130 tons; six to eight 5-inch single-purpose guns, or five 5-inch dual-purpose guns; eight to twelve 21-inch torpedo tubes; 39 knots). These ships mounted the same eight-gun single-purpose battery as the PORTER class, but incorporated improved high-pressure, high-temperature steam plants. Boilers were trunked into a single stack, which allowed deck space for three quadruple torpedo tube mounts on the centerline. Early in the war one tube mount and one after gun mount were removed to improve stability and to make room for antiaircraft guns. Two of the five ships of this class were completely rebuilt, with new bridges and five 5-inch dual-purpose guns. One of this class, *Warrington*, foundered in an Atlantic hurricane in 1944.

SOMERVELL, Brehon Burke (1892–1955). A U.S. Army officer in World War I, Somervell directed civilian engineering and construction projects in the 1920s and '30s and in 1936–40 was WPA administrator for New York City. In 1941 he was made Assistant Chief of Staff for supplies. In 1942, as a lieutenant general, he became commanding general of the Services of Supply (Army Service Forces). In 1945 he was promoted to full general.

SOMERVILLE, Sir James Fownes (1882–1949). Admiral Somerville was the Royal Navy's Commander in Chief East Indies in 1938, but early in 1939 he was invalided home with pulmonary tuberculosis and placed on the retired list. Although he made a complete recovery, he was not then reinstated on the active list. During the evacuation of the BRITISH EXPEDITIONARY FORCE from DUNKIRK in May–June 1940 he offered his services to Admiral RAMSAY, Flag Officer Dover, and did much to ease the burden on Ramsay's shoulders during those desperate nine days. With the entry of Italy into the war and the need to keep a powerful naval force at GIBRALTAR, Somerville was appointed in command, and it fell to him to cover and fight through many vital convoys to MALTA. During the chase of the German battleship BISMARCK in the Atlantic in May 1941, it was his FORCE H, steaming up from Gibraltar, which dealt the blow that immobilized the *Bismarck*, a torpedo attack from his carrier, ARK ROYAL, damaging the *Bismarck*'s rudder.

After the entry of Japan into the war, Somerville was selected (March 1942) to command the hurriedly organized Eastern Fleet in the Indian Ocean. He held this appointment until 1944, when he was at last reinstated on the active list and sent to Washington as head of the British Admiralty delegation. He remained there until the end of 1945, being promoted to Admiral of the Fleet while he was there.

SOMUA TANK. French medium TANK.

SONAR. The name is an acronym derived from *so*und *na*vigation *r*anging. Sonar, developed long before World War II, includes all types of underwater sound

THE SOLOMON ISLANDS were the scene of a series of American landings opposed by rain and jungle as well as by the Japanese

devices used for listening, echo ranging and locating of obstacles. Its best known wartime use was for Allied detection of German and Japanese submarines.

Prior to World War I, devices based on sonar principles were used for navigation, and in the latter half of that war purely acoustical listening apparatus was used, somewhat ineffectually, to detect German submarines. During the last few months of World War I the Anti-Submarine Devices Investigation Committee (from the initial letters the British equivalent term for sonar, asdic, was derived) was formed among the Allies to coordinate underwater-sound research efforts. It was dissolved at the end of the war, and the member nations pursued their own interests until the catalyst of World War II arrived.

Progress in the interval between the wars was relatively slow. The primary U.S. agency involved, beginning in 1923, was the Naval Research Laboratory, which contributed to a wide variety of other military research efforts. Emphasis during those years was placed on supersonic echo ranging, and depth indicators began to be produced commercially. Like RADAR, sonar reaped the benefits of related advances in the field of electronics. New knowledge of thermal characteristics of the ocean, improved training techniques and parallel efforts on the part of the British and others were also important to the evolution of sonar, and by the beginning of World War II all parties possessed operational sonar equipment. During the war, production, research and training increased at a rapid pace, as did cooperation and exchange of information among the Allies. Nevertheless, the Allies initially lost the Battle of the ATLANTIC: in the beginning, German U-boats sank Allied shipping faster than it could be replaced.

The need for action was effectively demonstrated in July 1942, when U-boats sank 143 ships in the Atlantic. The U.S. Navy Department took on the task of analyzing the total problem, an effort which resulted in great refinements in the training of sonar operators, in operational tactics and in knowledge of the sonar-affecting characteristics of the ocean. Radio SONOBUOYS were developed, as was the "console sonar," which, with all the latest refinements, could detect minefields, calculate U-boat depths using the echo sounder, indicate the presence of oncoming torpedoes and plot accurate ranges, bearings and time-to-fire of weapons. With such concentrated efforts, the Allied success ratio began to rise rapidly, aided by refinements in the use of radar. During 1943 the Allies were sinking an average of 22 enemy submarines a month, up from three a month at the beginning of the war. So effective did Allied antisubmarine tactics become that the U.S.S. ENGLAND was able to sink six Japanese submarines in 11 days, a record for the war. At the end of the war, the tally of enemy submarines sunk stood at 70 percent for the British and 30 percent for the Americans, with a substantial portion of the kills being made possible by sonar equipment of all types.

SONOBUOY. A small combination hydrophone and radio transmitter. When dropped near the suspected position of a submarine, it would radio the sounds picked up to a nearby airplane or blimp. First produced in late 1942, the sonobuoy was a significant contribution to the antisubmarine effort.

SOONG, T. V. (1894?–1971). Educated at Harvard and holder of many top governmental posts in Nationalist China, including those of Premier and Foreign Minister, T. V. Soong (born Tse-ven Sung) was for the most part a staunch supporter of Generalissimo CHIANG KAI-SHEK and the right wing of the KUOMINTANG. Soong's major contribution to the Chinese war effort was as chief negotiator in obtaining monetary support. In 1941, for example, he obtained a $100 million loan from the United States in exchange for China's keeping occupied some 1 million Japanese troops who could possibly have been elsewhere. Throughout the war he served as mediator between the Generalissimo and senior American officers such as Lt. Gen. Joseph STILWELL and his replacement, Lt. Gen. Albert WEDEMEYER.

SOP. *S*tandard *O*perating *P*rocedure. U.S. Army abbreviation for prescribed field-service procedures. The term came into popular use during the war to describe any standard or established way of doing something.

SORGE, Richard (1895–1944). As a Soviet spy on close terms with the German embassy in Tokyo, Sorge passed German and Japanese strategic secrets to his superiors in Red Army intelligence from 1933 to 1941. Born in Russia of a German father and a Russian mother, he grew up in Germany. A Communist after October 1918, he led the cosmopolitan existence of a Comintern agent in assignments in Europe and Asia, moving to Shanghai in 1930 and to Tokyo in 1933, using the cover of a journalist (correspondent for the *Frankfurter Zeitung*), a profession in which he had a justly deserved reputation. Sorge's informants in Tokyo included various Japanese, but he was also privy to German embassy files, messages and confidential discussions.

His military sources enabled Sorge, among others, to inform Joseph STALIN in May 1941 of the impending German attack on the Soviet Union, naming June 20 as the date for the invasion. From German speculation and reliable Japanese analyses of Japanese military plans, Sorge also concluded that Japan's strategic interests lay to the south in Asia and in the Pacific, not in Siberia, which view he related as well to Russian military intelligence officers in Moscow. Whether Stalin heeded any of the information coming to him from Sorge or other sources cannot be positively asserted, but there is some evidence that he felt able—though perhaps reluctantly—to pull troops out of eastern Siberia in the fall of 1941 for the defense of Moscow because of Sorge's reports. If so, this was of the highest importance.

Sorge, arrested suddenly and to the great surprise of the German embassy staff on October 16, 1941, was hanged on November 7, 1944.

SORPE DAM. One of the targets of the RAF DAM BUSTERS. A suitable bomb for breaching the Sorpe dam was not available, and this dam was given a lower priority in the attack by No. 617 Squadron on May 16, 1943. Two LANCASTERS made their runs, but the dam withstood the bombs.

SORYU. Class of Japanese aircraft carriers completed in 1937. Displacing nearly 16,000 tons (*Soryu*) and over 17,000 tons (HIRYU), the two ships of this class were

746 feet long and could handle 73 planes; they were considered very effective ships. *Hiryu* had her island superstructure on the port side (a feature unique to her and to AKAGI), while *Soryu* mounted her island in the usual starboard position. These two ships formed a carrier division of the PEARL HARBOR attack force; both were sunk by American carrier dive-bombers at MIDWAY, where, with *Akagi* and KAGA, they made up Adm. Chuichi NAGUMO's striking force. The captain of *Soryu*, a particularly well respected officer named Yanagimoto, refused all attempts at rescue and was last seen on the bridge, sword in hand, singing the Japanese national anthem.

SOSNKOWSKI, Casimir (1885–1969). Polish Army officer, second-in-command when the Germans attacked in 1939. Although the Poles were unable to withstand the German onslaught, Sosnkowski won the only Polish victory over the invaders, at Przemysl. The Germans subsequently encircled Sosnkowski's force at Lvov, which forced the general and a handful of followers to escape from the Germans and the encroaching Soviet forces by disguising themselves as peasants. Sosnkowski eventually reached London, where he served as commander of the army of the Polish government-in-exile. Sosnkowski, who was both strongly anti-Fascist and anti-Communist, left the government in late 1944.

SOUND-RANGE RECORDER. Invented by the British early in the war, this device contained a roll of chemically treated graph paper and an automatic stylus which traced the impulses received by a ship's SONAR. This created a visible "plot" which could be used to classify and identify the signals received. More important, this visible trace enabled the attacking ship to calculate the relative movement of ship and submarine, making antisubmarine operations something less of a hit-or-miss affair. Range recorders were used both by the British and the Americans.

SOUSSE. Port city in TUNISIA seized by the Germans in November 1942 and held by them until April 11, 1943, when the Axis evacuated it in their retreat toward Enfidaville.

SOUTH AFRICAN AIR FORCE. At the outbreak of the war, SAAF squadrons operated in EAST AFRICA and in the maritime role on shipping and antisubmarine reconnaissance. The WESTERN DESERT was the scene of some of the memorable operations of the SAAF, and by the end of 1943 there were 16 squadrons operating in the Middle East. The SAAF also took part in the fighting in SICILY and ITALY and in the Battle of the ATLANTIC off the coast of West Africa. At its wartime peak the SAAF comprised 35 operational squadrons with a total strength of 45,000 personnel, including 6,500 women. Capt. Edwin Swales, of No. 582 Squadron in the Pathfinder Force, won the only South African Air VICTORIA CROSS of the war. Two famous fighter pilots in the Battle of BRITAIN were South Africans—"Sailor" MALAN and E. J. Morris. SAAF casualties in the war totaled 2,112.

SOUTH BEVELAND ISLAND. With WALCHEREN ISLAND to the west, South Beveland forms the north bank of the SCHELDT ESTUARY connecting ANTWERP with the sea. The Canadian FIRST ARMY attacked on October 2, 1944, to seal an isthmus connecting the island to the mainland, then to clear the island. Confined to a narrow front, the fight took the rest of the month, despite an assist from an amphibious assault across the estuary from the south bank.

SOUTH DAKOTA, U.S.S. Battleship of 35,000 tons standard displacement, having nine 16-inch guns and sixteen 5-inch guns, four fewer than the nearly identical INDIANA class (*Indiana*, MASSACHUSETTS and ALABAMA). All four had the same basic armament and the same general displacement as the NORTH CAROLINA class, but were over 49 feet shorter to permit a better degree of hull protection. Their superstructures were more compact to allow better all-around fields of antiaircraft fire. Commissioned in the spring and summer of 1942, these ships generally served in the Pacific, with the exception of a North Atlantic tour of duty in 1943 for *South Dakota*. For the most part, they accompanied the FAST CARRIER TASK FORCE, their extensive gun batteries lending protection against air attack. All four ships ended the Pacific war with the Third Fleet off Japan. They decommissioned in 1946–47.

SOUTHEAST ASIA COMMAND. Formally brought into existence on November 15, 1943, the Allied Southeast Asia Command (SEAC) was intended to relieve the India Command of responsibility for operations against the Japanese in BURMA, THAILAND (Siam), Malaya and SINGAPORE and to defend Ceylon and the northeast frontier of India. SEAC was commanded by a British Supreme Allied Commander—for nearly all of its existence Adm. Lord Louis MOUNTBATTEN—and an American deputy, the first holder of the position being Lt. Gen. Joseph W. STILWELL. Organizational problems notwithstanding, SEAC forces were successful in expelling the Japanese from Burma, enduring great hardships in order to do so. After the formal surrender of Japan, SEAC took steps to expedite the transition to peace, including the rescue of some 96,000 Allied internees and prisoners of war, the disarmament and repatriation of all Japanese troops and the return of the countries involved to appropriate civilian control. SEAC ceased to exist on November 30, 1946.

SOUTHERN FRANCE OPERATION. When on August 15, 1944, troops of the U.S. SEVENTH ARMY landed on the coast of southern France while an American-British airborne task force of division size came to earth a few miles inland, it was the culmination of one of the lengthiest and most divisive debates to agitate Allied command circles during the war in Europe. The Supreme Allied Commander, Gen. Dwight D. EISENHOWER, wanted landings to support the main INVASION of Normandy. The British Prime Minister, Winston CHURCHILL, wanted the resources used for pursuing the campaign in ITALY and into central Europe and the Balkans. Although Eisenhower's view prevailed, a shortage of landing craft made it impossible to execute the two invasions simultaneously, so that the landings in southern France—known originally by the code name Anvil, then later by Dragoon—occurred almost six weeks after the invasion of Normandy.

By that time most of the reserves of German Army Group G under Generaloberst Johannes von BLASKOWITZ had been moved from the south to oppose the Allies in northern France, and with only 11 divisions remaining to defend not only the Riviera beaches but also the Biscay coast, Blaskowitz had no real hope of defeating the invasion. Behind a heavy air and naval bombardment, contingents of the U.S. 3d, 36th and 45th Infantry Divisions under the VI Corps of Lt. Gen. Alexander M. PATCH's Seventh Army came ashore just after dawn between St. Tropez and Cannes. The sea was calm, the weather ideal. The preliminary bombardment having silenced many German positions, casualties were strikingly light, a total of 520 in the seaborne force, with fewer than a hundred killed. The airborne troops encountered even less opposition, and by nightfall most were in contact with the seaborne troops. Some 9,000 men arrived by air, 77,000 men and 12,000 vehicles by sea.

The next day the French 1st Infantry and 3d Algerian Divisions—part of what was known at the time as French Army B under Gen. Jean de LATTRE DE TASSIGNY—came ashore over beaches already secured by the Americans and turned from assembly areas against the major ports of Toulon and Marseilles. On the third day Adolf HITLER ordered General Blaskowitz to leave forces to deny the major ports while pulling the rest of Army Group G back into the Vosges Mountains of northeastern France.

On board U.S.S. *Philadelphia,* crewmen pass ammunition to gunners firing on beaches of southern France, August 15, 1944

As the Germans retreated, fighters of the FRENCH RESISTANCE harried them. Only the fortified banks of the Gironde estuary, denying access to the port of Bordeaux, remained to the Germans, who withered there for some months. The only sharp fighting was for Toulon and Marseilles, but both ports fell on August 28, two weeks after the invasion.

Main contingents of the VI Corps meanwhile advanced up the valley of the Rhône River in hope of trapping German divisions retreating from southwestern France 75 miles inland at the road center of Montélimar, famous for the production of nougats, while a smaller column, spearheaded by a composite armored task force, proceeded up the Route Napoléon toward Grenoble. As the armor neared Grenoble, the corps commander, Maj. Gen. Lucian K. TRUSCOTT, Jr., ordered the armor and other forces to shift westward to the Rhône valley. The order came too late. German forces turned to fight at the town and held it long enough for most of the retreating troops to get away.

Aided by the FRENCH RESISTANCE and by planes of the U.S. XII Tactical Air Command, the pursuit continued up both major corridors, with French troops providing an assist west of the Rhône. Lyons, France's third city, fell on September 2 with virtually no opposition, and French armor took Dijon one week later. That night a French armored reconnaissance group operating west of Dijon met a patrol from a French armored division on the south flank of the U.S. THIRD ARMY, marking the link-up of the main Allied forces from Normandy with those from southern France. Four days later headquarters of the U.S. 6TH ARMY GROUP, under Lt. Gen. Jacob L. DEVERS, took direction of the U.S. Seventh and French First Armies and came under General Eisenhower's overall command.

As the advance proceeded into the foothills of the Vosges, German resistance stiffened, while the speed of the race from the Riviera and the long supply lines began to tell on Allied units. The invasion of southern France by any measure was nevertheless a resounding success, carrying almost 500 miles in just over a month and capturing approximately 100,000 Germans in the process. The ports of Toulon and Marseilles subsequently served as supply bases for the 6th Army Group. Given the scope of Allied victory in Normandy, the Germans probably would have withdrawn from southern France without a second invasion, but General Eisenhower and his planners could not have known that before the machinery of the subsidiary invasion was already in operation. **C.B.M.**

SOUTHERN RESOURCES REGION. In Japanese usage, the East Indies and adjacent areas.

SOUTH PACIFIC FORCES AND AREA. SoPac, as South Pacific Forces and Area was elided, was established on March 30, 1942, when the U.S. JOINT CHIEFS OF STAFF realigned command arrangements, organization and direction of the war effort in the Pacific. Adm. Chester W. NIMITZ, Commander in Chief, Pacific Fleet, was given a second hat as Commander in Chief, Pacific Ocean Areas (Cincpoa). SoPac, one of three area com-

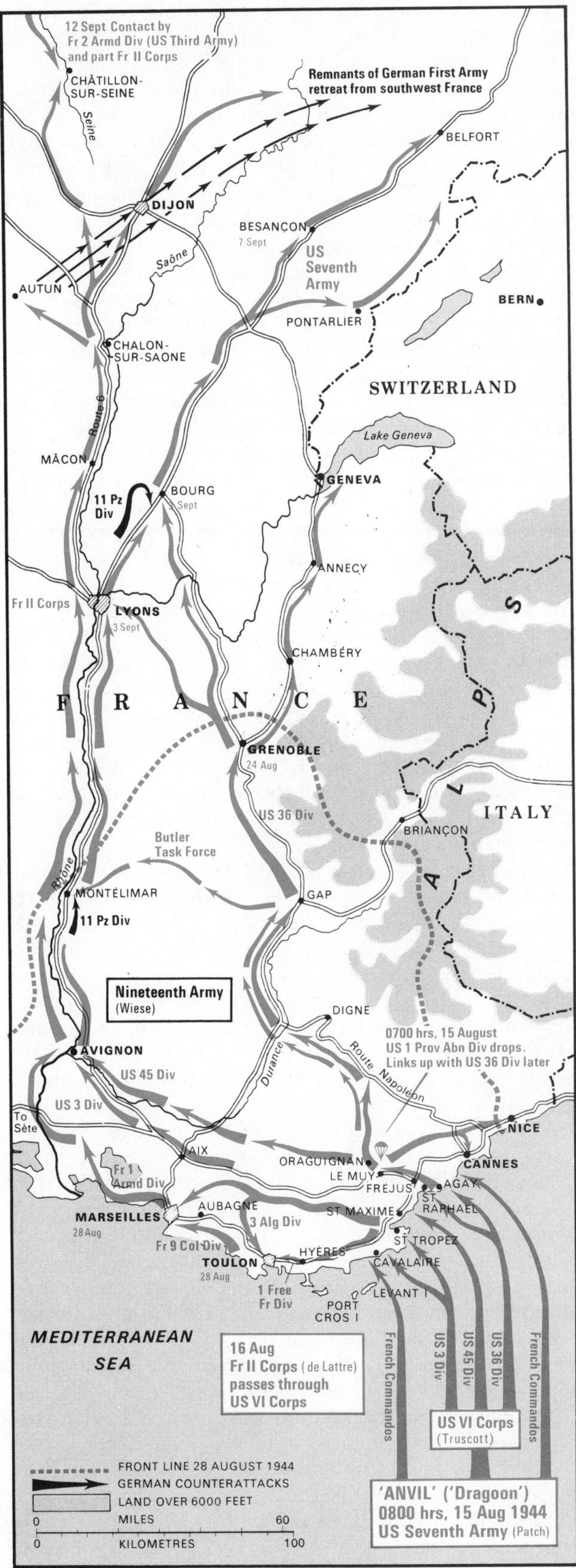

ANVIL-DRAGOON—the landings in Southern France

mands assigned to Cincpoa, encompassed the region from the equator to the South Pole, including the Ellice, Phoenix, Marquesa, Tuamotu, Samoa, Fiji and NEW HEBRIDES island groups, as well as New Zealand and NEW CALEDONIA. Although Vice-Adm. Robert L. GHORMLEY received his appointment as ComSoPac on April 13, he did not assume command for some weeks, arriving at his new headquarters in Auckland on May 21, 1942. For the SOLOMON ISLANDS campaign, SoPac headquarters was moved to Noumea, New Caledonia. The forces in Ghormley's command included all the garrisons in the area (60,000 Army troops plus some air units); an ANZAC (Australian and New Zealand) naval force; the U.S. 1st Marine Division, then en route to SoPac; and whatever other forces might be assigned.

As finally organized, SoPac consisted of South Pacific Amphibious Forces under the command of Rear Adm. Richmond Kelly TURNER; South Pacific Naval Forces, held by Ghormley himself; U.S. Army Forces South Pacific, commanded by Maj. Gen. Millard F. HARMON; and South Pacific Air Forces, commanded by Rear Adm. John S. MCCAIN. Ghormley's first task was to plan for the GUADALCANAL operation. On October 18 he was relieved as ComSoPac by Vice-Adm. William F. HALSEY, Jr., who served in the post until June 15, 1944, when he was relieved by Vice-Adm. John H. NEWTON. By that time the major fighting in the Pacific had shiftd to the CENTRAL and SOUTHWEST PACIFIC AREAS.

SOUTHWESTERN APPROACHES. The area of sea south of Ireland and west and south of England, including the southern half of the Irish Sea and the western part of the English Channel. At the start of the war it was known as the WESTERN APPROACHES Command, with headquarters at Plymouth, and remained in that command when the headquarters was moved to Liverpool on February 7, 1941.

SOUTHWEST PACIFIC AREA. SWPA, as this area was abbreviated (also SoWesPac), was given to Gen. Douglas MACARTHUR, Supreme Commander, Allied Forces, on March 30, 1942, when the U.S. JOINT CHIEFS OF STAFF divided the Pacific war zone into two theater commands. Geographically, MacArthur's command included the PHILIPPINES, Australia and all that lies between them, the whole of NEW GUINEA and all of the BISMARCK ARCHIPELAGO. The forces under General MacArthur in SWPA included Allied Naval Forces (Rear Adm. Arthur S. CARPENDER); Allied Land Forces (Gen. Sir Thomas BLAMEY, Australian Army); Allied Air Forces (Maj. Gen. George C. KENNEY); U.S. Army Services of Supply (Brig. Gen. Richard J. Marshall). In addition, two other units were assigned—U.S. Army Forces in the Philippines and U.S. Army Forces, Far East, both of which were inactive. MacArthur retained command of SWPA all through the war and also, on April 3, 1945, was designated Commander in Chief, U.S. Army Forces, Pacific, with control of all the Army units in that theater (less those in the North and Southeast Pacific). He was given this new command by the Joint Chiefs of Staff, who recognized that the March 30, 1942, directive needed revision in view of the impending operations against the Japanese homeland, which would be conducted primarily by Army troops.

SOUTHWICK HOUSE. Headquarters of Adm. Sir Bertram Ramsay, near Portsmouth, England. Here, on June 4, 1944, General Eisenhower made the decision to go ahead with the invasion of Normandy despite a weather outlook that was at best hazardous. *See also* Stagg, James Martin.

SOVIET-FINNISH WAR (1939–40). Following the German annexation of Austria, the Soviet Government initiated secret negotiations with Finland in Helsinki (April 1938), suggesting joint security measures aimed at blocking the Gulf of Finland to the naval forces of a third power. The Finns declined, citing their traditional neutrality and the requirement of territorial integrity. After the Munich Conference (September 1938), alarmed at the prospect of a European war, the Soviets renewed their demands, this time requesting a lease for 30 years of a number of islands in the gulf. After the signing of the Soviet-German Nonaggression Pact in 1939 and the establishment of Soviet military bases in Estonia, Latvia and Lithuania, the demands were expanded to include Finland's Hangö Peninsula and Karelian Isthmus as well as the Rybachi Peninsula in the north. During the negotiations in Moscow in October 1939, Stalin offered to compensate Finland for her losses by twice as many square miles of territory in Soviet Karelia. Although refused diplomatic support by any European powers, the Finns rejected the Soviet demands. The talks in Moscow were broken off and, after a brief anti-Finnish propaganda campaign, Red Army troops attacked Finland on a broad front, concentrating major effort on the Karelian Isthmus.

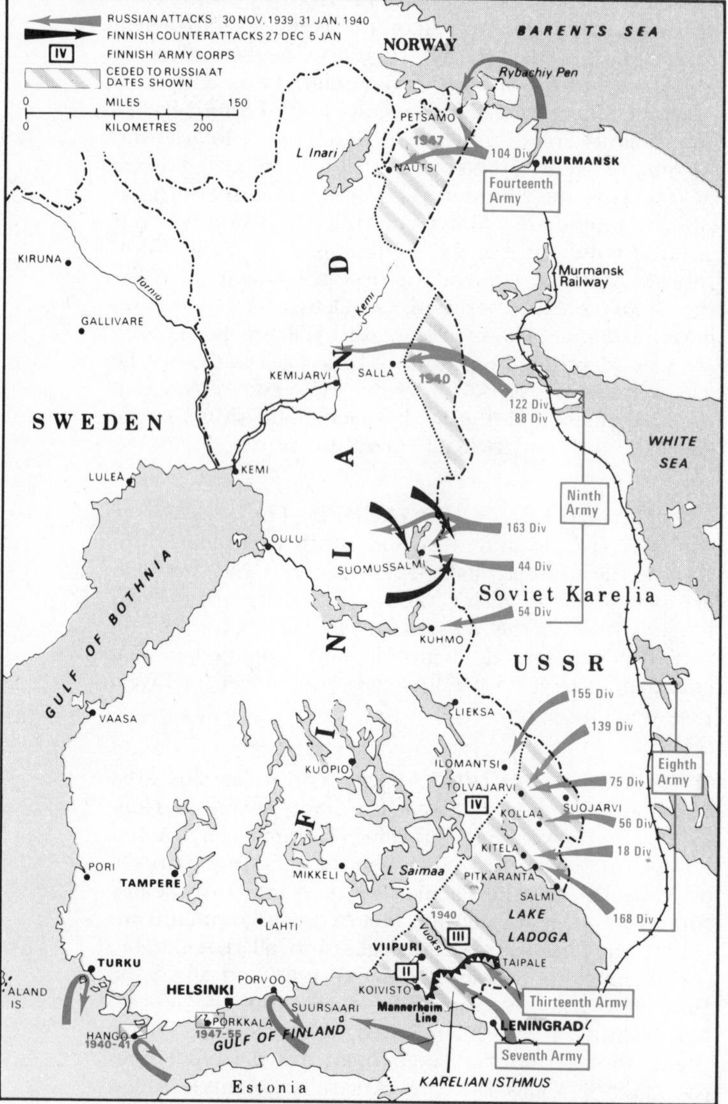

THE WINTER WAR: For two months a surprising stalemate

The war demonstrated astonishing deficiencies in the Red Army, whose losses in the attempt to break through the Mannerheim Line exceeded fivefold those of the Finns. The attack was halted after six weeks of fighting. In January 1940 the Soviet Government created the Northwest Front under the command of Marshal Timoshenko, and in mid-February, after extensive preparations, two armies (Seventh and Thirteenth) consisting of more than 35 divisions, with heavy air and naval support, resumed the offensive against 15 undermanned Finnish divisions. By March 1, having broken through the Finnish defenses with further heavy losses, the Red Army captured Viipuri.

During the war Finland received some military aid from Great Britain and France, who then regarded the Soviet Union as an ally of Germany. There were plans to send a few thousand volunteers to help the Finns, although none in fact arrived. The outburst of public indignation at the Soviet aggression against a small and neutral country led to the expulsion of the Soviet Union from the League of Nations in December 1939. President Roosevelt declared a "moral embargo" on trade with the Soviets, which remained in force for more than a year.

The Finnish Government realized early that this political and military support was insufficient to stiffen resistance for very long. Its appeals to Sweden for mediation went unheeded. Germany, bound to the Soviet Union by the 1939 pact and the subsequent treaty, refused to intercede. Great Britain and France likewise declined, wanting the Finns to fight as long as possible. Having assessed the situation, the Finns accepted the Soviet terms, extended late in February, and on March 13, 1940, the peace was signed, granting the Soviet Union the territories it had initially demanded.

In signing the peace, the Soviet Government abandoned the goal of eventually annexing Finland. The creation in Moscow of a "government of the Finnish Democratic Republic" headed by the old Comintern hand Otto Kuusinen, which, on December 2, 1939, had signed a treaty with the Soviets, conceding everything Stalin wanted, had indicated for Finland the fate which later befell Estonia, Latvia and Lithuania. Kuusinen's government was quietly dissolved, never to be mentioned in Soviet history books.

Stalin's relative moderation was dictated by the demonstrated military weakness of the Red Army, which lost close to half a million troops in the Winter War, and by Soviet fears that further efforts to subdue Finland might precipitate an all-European coalition against the Soviet Union, perhaps with the participation of Germany and backed by the United States.

The revelation of Soviet weakness was duly registered by the general staffs of France and Great Britain, as well as by the German General Staff. All parties downgraded the Red Army, and Stalin himself determined to keep the Soviet Union out of war for as long as possible, even at the high cost of appeasing HITLER and supplying Germany with strategic commodities. **V.P.**

SOVIET-GERMAN BOUNDARY AND FRIENDSHIP TREATY. Agreement signed by the Soviet and German foreign ministers, MOLOTOV and RIBBENTROP, in Moscow on September 29, 1939, after the German defeat of Poland; it amended the SOVIET-GERMAN NONAGGRESSION PACT by assigning to Germany the province of Lublin and eastern regions of the province of Warsaw in exchange for Lithuania, which, in consideration of Joseph STALIN's wishes, was consigned to the Soviet "sphere of influence." Additional secret protocols provided for migration of ethnic Germans residing in the Soviet sphere to the Reich and for the suppression of nationalist Polish agitation on both sides of the new frontier. The Soviets also undertook to facilitate the flow of goods between Germany and Rumania, Iran and Afghanistan and to supply Germany with additional quantities of oil, equal to those produced by the oil fields in former Poland. The treaty also laid the foundation for expansion of economic relations between the two countries.

SOVIET-GERMAN NONAGGRESSION PACT. This momentous agreement (often called the Nazi-Soviet Pact), which took less than 24 hours to negotiate, was signed in Moscow on August 23, 1939. It cleared the way for the German attack on Poland, thus marking the beginning of the Second World War. In Adolf HITLER's mind, Soviet benevolent neutrality was imperative for implementation of his military plan; he paid for it by recognition of a Soviet sphere of influence extending to Finland, ESTONIA and LATVIA and of the Soviet right to annex eastern Poland and Bessarabia. In addition to Soviet neutrality, Germany gained a steady supply of vital strategic minerals and foodstuffs in exchange for deliveries of industrial equipment and machinery.

Joseph STALIN's motives in signing the pact were complex. Starting with the reoccupation of the Rhineland in 1936, he had viewed with growing alarm the collapse of the Versailles security system in Europe and considered the rearmament of Germany as posing a potential threat to the Soviet Union. Painfully aware of the enormous weaknesses of the Soviet Union and of the growing threat of Japan in the Far East, where large-scale clashes were taking place along the Manchurian and Mongolian borders, Stalin embarked on a conscious policy aimed at fomenting and exploiting "internal contradictions in the imperialist camp" by facilitating a conflict between Great Britain and France on the one side and Germany on the other. On the assumption that Germany was the weaker power, Stalin began to signal to Berlin his receptiveness to the idea of a rapprochement between the two countries. His speech of March 10, 1939, at the Eighteenth Communist Party Congress condemning Anglo-French imperialism, and his replacement of Maxim LITVINOV as Commissar of Foreign Affairs by V. M. MOLOTOV in May, were duly recorded in Berlin, paving the way for mutual accommodation. Although the Nazi seizure of Prague in March had visibly split the Munich "front," showing to the British and French the futility of appeasing Hitler, Stalin did not deviate from his chosen tactic.

The Moscow conversations with low-level British and French delegations which began in April had convinced Stalin that London and Paris merely wanted to assure an anti-German posture by the Soviet Union while committing themselves as little as possible to a joint action against Germany if the latter attacked Russia. The failure of the Western powers to secure the consent of Poland and Rumania to the passage of the Red Army across their territories in case of war and to accommodate Soviet political and strategic interests in eastern Europe only strengthened Stalin's determination to effect rapprochement with Germany while keeping the Soviet Union out of the armed conflict. Aware of Hitler's impatience to conclude the deal before the attack on Poland (scheduled for September 1, 1939), Stalin played for time in order to obtain the best terms for the Soviet Union, while stringing along France and Great Britain in inconclusive talks in Moscow.

The pact, signed by Molotov and German Foreign Minister RIBBENTROP, bound the two governments to refrain from any aggressive action against each other; to lend no support to any third power at war with one of the signatories; to consult on problems affecting their common interests and settle their disputes "through friendly exchange of opinion"; and to ratify the pact "within the shortest possible time." The secret protocol (to this day not acknowledged by Soviet historians) provided for a de facto partitioning of eastern Europe.

While the secret trade agreement, signed on August 19, was seen as being mutually beneficial, the advice of the German Foreign Office to Japan, conveyed on August 22, "to bring about a period of quiet in Japanese-Russian relations," assured the Soviet Union a much-desired peace in the Far East.

The conclusion of the pact shocked most Western statesmen and Russia-watchers, who had erroneously believed that the presumably implacable ideological conflict between Communism and Nazism had automatically made the Soviet Union a quasi-partner of the Western democracies. In fact, the deep-seated mistrust the Soviets had had since the October Revolution of *all* imperialist powers, particularly France and Great Britain, was neither invalidated nor displaced by the rise of Nazi Germany. British sympathies for German expansionist aspirations, widespread among the Tories, were known in Moscow no less than British efforts to befriend Fascist Italy.

Soviet historians constantly assert that by effecting rapprochement with Germany, Russia had gained time for strengthening its military position in preparation for the future conflict. In retrospect, however, it appears certain that Stalin had miscalculated. He overestimated the power of France and her allies and underestimated the rapidity and scope of possible German successes, the achievement of which enabled Hitler to turn against Russia long before the latter could become strong enough to withstand the onslaught. The pact also had a demoralizing effect upon the Soviet people, who during the two years of partnership with Germany were conditioned by Communist propaganda to believe that the Germans had become friends, thus making the Soviet people psychologically unready for war. **V.P.**

SOVIET-GERMAN OPERATIONS 1941–45. There is no mystery about the reasons for the German attack on the Soviet Union on June 22, 1941. Adolf Hitler, the German dictator, had always looked on Communism as his worst enemy and had long coveted the resources of the Soviet Union. In Mein Kampf he wrote: "If the Urals, with its immeasurable treasure of raw materials, Siberia, with its rich forests, and the Ukraine, with its limitless grain fields, were to lie in Germany, this country under National Socialist leadership would swim in plenty." The dream of this wealth inspired Hitler to resume the old *Drang nach Osten*, the push to the east which the Kaiser had pursued before him.

Until the invasion of Russia, Nazi Germany had never engaged in a campaign longer than two months or fought on a front of more than 300 miles. In their attempt to conquer Russia, however, the Germans spread their forces along a broken front of 1,800 miles from the Arctic Ocean to the Caucasus. Instead of carrying off another blitzkrieg, they involved themselves in a grim war which sapped their strength for three long years. The invading German forces were organized in three groups: Army Group North, Army Group Center and Army Group South. Five air fleets, totaling more than 3,200 planes, and 20 armored divisions, with their 8,000 tanks, were part of 180 divisions mobilized by Hitler for the invasion of Russia.

The Red Army had 158 infantry divisions ready to meet the attack. Red air strength was estimated at 6,000 combat planes, and of tanks there were 54 brigades, each with 200 armored vehicles. Some 300 new divisions of reserves were mobilized within half a year after the invasion began. The potential power of the Red Army was seriously underestimated by the Germans.

On June 22, 1941, after nearly two years of conquest, the Axis commanded the population and resources of 15 European countries. The USSR had a population of approximately 192 million—more than Germany and all her unwilling vassals combined—and the Soviet peoples were spread over one-sixth of the earth's surface, a continental territory so vast that even Hitler must have doubted the possibility of conquering it. The German attack achieved tactical surprise. They drove forward in three parallel columns. In the north the group of armies under Field Marshal Wilhelm Ritter von Leeb directed their efforts against Leningrad through the Baltic states. In the center the main effort, an attack against Moscow via Smolensk, was led by Field Marshal Fedor von Bock. Kiev was the target city of the southern group of armies sweeping through the Ukraine with Field Marshal Gerd von Rundstedt in command. Although these key cities were apparent objectives of the listed groups of armies, it must always be borne in mind that the Wehrmacht's primary objective was the destruction of the Soviet armed forces. Tactics designed to gain this primary objective were evident in every engagement. The Germans sought to utilize their armor for piercing the Soviet lines, for cutting lines of communication and then for trapping large bodies of Soviet troops, who were quickly surrounded by a solid ring of rapidly moving German infantry. Hitler wanted to smash Soviet resistance in one hard, fast blow.

Red Army troops storm a German position

The German Invasion of the Soviet Union was the beginning of months of unprecedented victories

FINLAND
Lake Onega
LAKE LADOGA
Svir
TURKU
VIIPURI
SWEDEN
HELSINKI
Twenty-third Army
Forty-second & Fifty-second Armies
Gulf of Finland
HANGÖ (USSR)
3 Dec, 1941 Evacuated by Russia
VOLKHOV
Eighth Army
LENINGRAD
TIKHVIN
TALLINN
NARVA
Fifty-fourth Army
Fourth Army
Volkhov
Luga
BALTIC
Estonia
LUGA
Fifty-ninth Army
Second Shock Army
SEA
TARTU
NOVGOROD
L Peipus
L Ilmen
Eleventh Army
Northwest Front (Voroshilov)
STARAYA RUSSA
VENTSPILS
PSKOV
Thirty-fourth Army
Lovat
Third Shock Army
OSTROV
KHOLM
Volga
RIGA
OSTASHKOV
Twenty-seventh Army
KALININ
Latvia
Velikaya
Twenty-second Army
Dvina
REZEKNE
Twenty-ninth Army
Army Group North (Leeb)
SIAULIAI
IDRITSA
VELIKIYE LUKI
Eighth Army
DAUGAVPILS
BELYY
RZHEV
MEMEL
MOSCOW
Eighteenth Army
Lithuania
Thirtieth Army
Nineteenth Army
VELIZH
Neman
POLOTSK
Sixteenth Army
VYAZMA
Thirty-second Army
Fourth Pzgrp
KAUNUS
VITEBSK
YARTSEVO
Sixteenth Army
Twentieth Army
EAST PRUSSIA
Eleventh Army
VILNYUS
SMOLENSK
KALUGA
Ninth Army
YELNYA
Dnieper
Third Pzgrp
Twenty-fourth Army
NOVI BORISOV
Moscow Highway
ORSHA
TULA
Twenty-eighth Army
Berezina
West Front (Timoshenko)
GRODNO
MINSK
MOGILEV
ROSLAVL
Forty-third Army
Third Army
NOVO BYKHOV
KRICHEV
Army Group Center (Bock)
BIALYSTOK
GORODISHCHE
Fiftieth Army
BRYANSK
Tenth Army
Sozh
BOBRUYSK
OREL
Belorussia
Fourth Army
WARSAW
Third Army
Twenty-first Army
GOMEL
STARODUB
Fourth Army
Second Pzgrp
BREST-LITOVSK
PINSK
Pripet
RECHITSA
Second Pzgrp
Thirteenth Army
Vistula
Pripet Marshes
MOZYR
NOVGOROD SEVERSKI
KURSK
POLAND
CHERNIGOV
Desna
Southwest Front (Budënny)
KOVEL
Bug
BAKHMACH
KONOTOP
Sixth Army
KOROSTEN
Fortieth Army
First Pzgrp
Fifth Army
Fifth Army
Second Army
ROVNO
KIEV
Thirty-seventh Army
LOKHVITSA
Seventeenth Army
ZHITOMIR
KHARKOV
LVOV
Twenty-first Army
Sixth Army
BERDICHEV
KAZATIN
Psel
Donets
TERNOPOL
POLTAVA
First Pzgrp
Thirty-eighth Army
Slovakia
Dniester
CHERKASSY
KREMENCHUG
Twenty-sixth Army
Ukraine
Carpathian Mts
KAMENETS-PODOLSKY
VINNITSA
Sixth Army
Army Group South (Rundstedt)
UMAN
Twelfth Army
DNEPROPETROVSK
Twelfth Army
CHERNOVTSY
PERVOMAYSK
Rum Third Army
Eighteenth Army
ZAPOROZHYE
HUNGARY
Yuzhni Bug
KRIVOY ROG
Eighteenth Army
Prut
Seventeenth Army
Eleventh Army
Dnieper
Moldavia
Eleventh Army
KISHINEV
MELITOPOL
NIKOLAYEV
Ninth Army
Rum Fourth Army
ODESSA
16 Oct
Ninth Army
PEREKOP
Sea of Azov
Fifty-first Army
STALIN LINE
FRONT LINE, 21 JUNE 1941
" " 9 JULY
" " 1 SEPTEMBER
" " 30 SEPTEMBER
RUSSIAN COUNTERATTACKS
TRAPPED RUSSIAN POCKETS
Crimea
RUMANIA
SEVASTOPOL
BUCHAREST
0 MILES 200
CONSTANTA
Danube
0 KILOMETRES 300
BLACK SEA

The Soviet-German war can be categorized into seven major campaigns:

1. The German advance, to the Battle of Moscow (June 22–December 1941)
2. First Soviet winter counteroffensive (December 1941–May 1942)
3. Second German offensive, to the Battle of Stalingrad (June–November 1942)

SOVIET COUNTERATTACKS took territory from the invaders

4. Battle of Stalingrad and the Soviet counteroffensive, to July 1943
5. Battles of Orel and Kursk and the Soviet offensive, to spring 1944
6. Soviet summer offensive of 1944: entry into Rumania, Hungary and Poland
7. Final Soviet offensive, to the end of the war (January–May 1945)

In the first of these campaigns, Leeb progressed rapidly until he was at the gates of Leningrad. Finland entered the war on June 26 and attacked Leningrad from the north. Leningrad was heroically defended and did not fall, although it was invested by September 8, 1941.

The main effort, directed toward Moscow by Army Group Center, was most successful. A series of double envelopments put Bock east of Smolensk by August 7. He had taken more than 850,000 Red Army prisoners in this 360-mile advance, but Soviet defenses stiffened as the Wehrmacht approached Moscow, and the tardiness of the southern group of armies necessitated a slow advance so as to protect Bock's right wing. After the Kiev encirclement by Army Group South, the central group endeavored to surround Moscow. Although two salients north and south of the capital were dangerously close to meeting, the Russians took the offensive and the Germans went no farther than their December 7 line, which was 25 miles from Moscow at its closest point.

A concentration of forces, coupled with better-prepared defenses, slowed Rundstedt and Army Group South. The resistance in the Kiev area held up the German advance for two months. German success in the battles of Uman and Gomel then made possible the encirclement and capture of Kiev, which was accomplished by the end of September. In September the CRIMEA was attacked, but Soviet resistance near KERCH and SEVASTOPOL kept those areas out of German hands. ODESSA was lost, however, and by the end of the offensive ROSTOV was in German hands.

In the first winter of the war in Russia, the Germans went into defensive positions. The generals had wanted to do this before snow fell and the vain drive on Moscow extended their lines, but Hitler had refused to listen to them. His conflict with the Army came to a head when he relieved Field Marshal Walther von BRAUCHITSCH, the commander in chief (December 1941), and, declaring that henceforth he would follow his own "intuition," named himself as successor. But he proved no match for the severity of the Russian winter. German troops in summer clothing perished. Soviet PARTISANS cut their supply and communications lines. The bitter cold froze lubricating oil and cracked the cylinders of engines in tanks, planes and trucks. Supply and transport broke down over the vast distances of Russian territory which had been overrun but not conquered. Nevertheless, the Germans dug in. They began repairs on the great power plant at Dnepropetrovsk, reclaimed mines, distributed steam tractors in the Ukraine to speed production of food for the armies and altered the railroad gauge for German rolling stock. Conscript Poles and prisoners of war were put to work building lines of defense in the rear. The Germans reversed the positions of the old STALIN LINE west of the DNIEPER and finished lines along the Bug and Oder Rivers which the Soviets had started over a year before.

The Soviets launched the *first winter counteroffensive* because they thought the Wehrmacht was poorly prepared to weather the winter. They were also convinced that German reserves had been exhausted by heavy casualties. On this score the Russians were mistaken; in fact, the rest of the world, like the Germans, wondered that it was not the Soviet Union which was exhausted. This idea was equally false. This first Soviet offensive was an attempt to drive westward along the entire line. It relieved the pressure on Moscow by destroying the threatening German salients and pushing back the north–south battle line in the Moscow area. Leningrad, however, was not relieved. The greatest gains were made in the south. Rostov was quickly retaken, and the Germans were thrust back 120 miles in that area. An unsuccessful attempt to relieve Sevastopol was made, and a large Soviet offensive operation to recapture Kharkov was also a failure.

The *second German offensive*, from June to November 1942, included the end of the siege of Sevastopol, after 10 months, on July 2, 1942. All organized Soviet resistance in the Crimea ceased a few days later. Beginning their summer offensive in June, the Germans took Rostov within a month and swept into the CAUCASUS. But the objective of the main thrust of the German offensive was the city of STALINGRAD. Stalingrad was important because its capture would give German troops a way to Astrakhan, a vital southern terminus of rail and river communication; holding the VOLGA at this point would cut to a trickle the northward flow of petroleum. Second, the capture of Stalingrad would facilitate the German conquest of the Caucasus and deny the Russians a point from which the winter offensive of 1942–43 could be launched. Third, the seizure might make possible a German move north behind Moscow. Finally, the capture of the city was important in itself, since Stalingrad was one of the foremost Soviet industrial centers. An all-out effort was made to capture Stalingrad in November 1942. This was the high-water mark of the German invasion. By now the front was 2,100 miles long.

The *Soviet counteroffensive* began at Stalingrad on No-

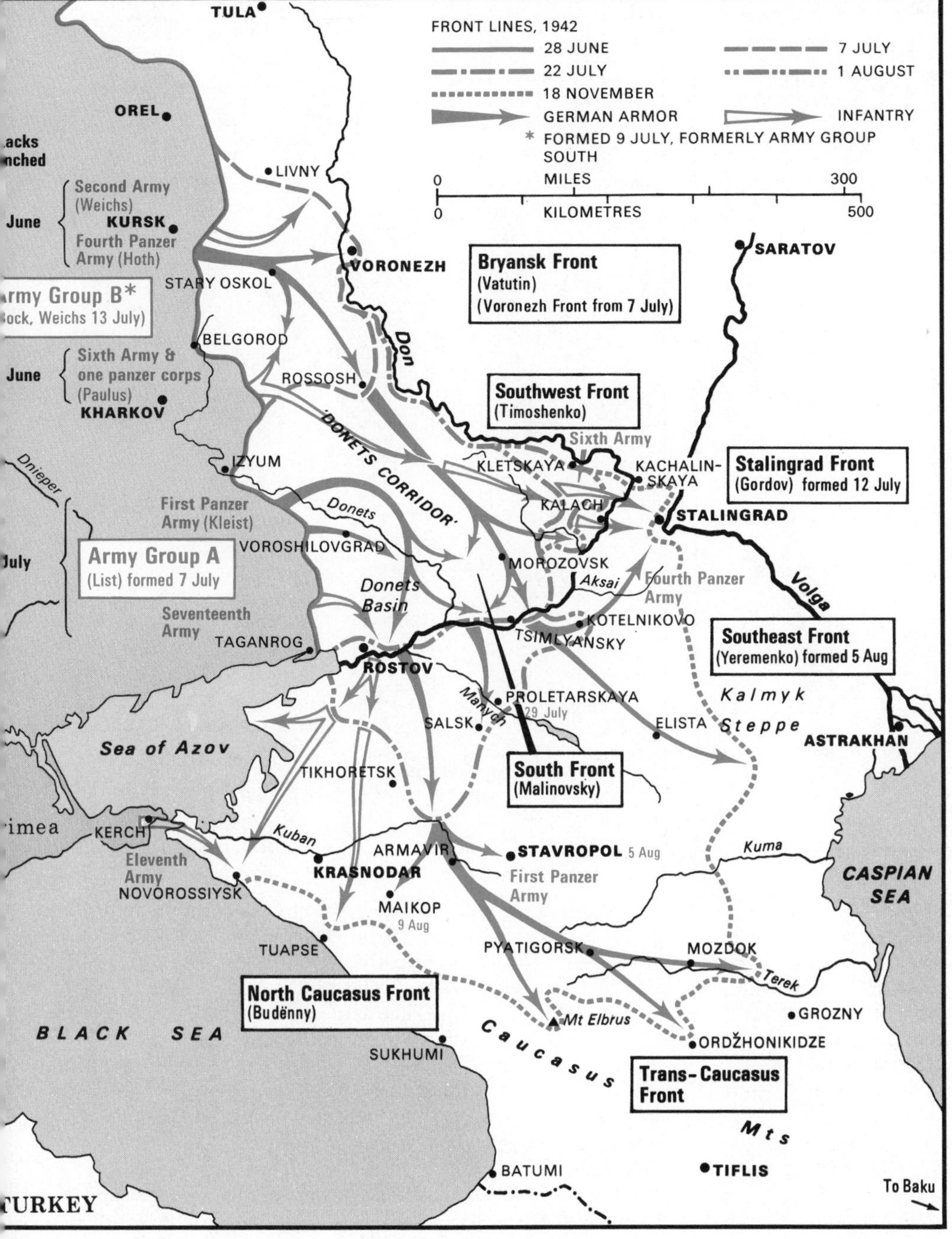

RUSSIA, 1942: The German summer offensive reached toward the Volga and the Caucasus

vember 19, 1942. The objectives of the offensive, to be pushed all along the Russo-German front, were the reduction of the VYAZMA–Rzhev salient, the Stalingrad salient, the OREL salient and the Grozny salient and the disengagement of the anchor of the German line at Leningrad. Gen. Georgi ZHUKOV directed the offensive in the Stalingrad sector. A double envelopment of Gen. Friedrich PAULUS's SIXTH ARMY was accomplished, and on February 2, 1943, the last Wehrmacht forces surrendered. The Stalingrad battle is considered the turning point in the east. Further Soviet gains were made all along the front and Rostov returned to Russian hands, but Leningrad was not relieved. The Germans were forced to evacuate the Vyazma–Rzhev, Grozny and Stalingrad salients. By July 1943 the Soviets had made gains all along the line since launching their offensive at Stalingrad the preceding November.

The Soviet 1942–43 *winter offensive* had found the German defenses around Orel strong enough that a salient was formed into the Soviet line, north of KURSK. Each side wanted to reduce its dangerous salient. The Germans needed to shorten their lines; the Soviets wanted to open the Moscow–Orel–Kursk line of communications. The Germans struck first, both north and south of Kursk. The Soviets had by now mastered the technique of stopping the Wehrmacht's envelopment tactics. When the German armor was committed, the Soviet forces struck hard at the Orel salient from the east and south. Unprecedented artillery barrages, with 250 artillery pieces per mile on the 20-mile front, preceded the attack. The Germans did not reduce the Kursk salient. Then the Soviets, in their first successful *summer offensive*, succeeded in capturing Orel and later Smolensk, Kharkov and TAGANROG. The Soviet offen-

THE SOVIET RESURGENCE, 1942–43

THE GERMAN RETREAT from Russia, 1944

sive was brilliantly successful, and the Germans' contemplated summer offensive became a retreat. Only north of VELIKYE LUKI did the line remain stabilized. The Soviet forces were rolling forward and had enough of an advantage in manpower so that they could push at one point and then, after German resources were committed, make a parallel main effort at a weak point. These tactics were to be employed by the Soviets until V-E Day.

After the capture of Gomel (November 26, 1943), the Soviets prepared their forces for the recapture of Kiev, hoping to trap many German troops there. The city was taken in one day, but there were few prisoners, as the German troops had been pulled out to occupy stronger positions in the Dnieper bend. Having taken Kiev, the Soviets sought to envelop the German left and entrap the forces strung along the lower Dnieper. In October 1943 the Kuban bridgehead had been liquidated, giving the Soviets greater control of the Sea of Azov and the Black Sea and ending the German threat to the Caucasus. In the north a major Soviet offensive was launched on January 15, 1944, to relieve Leningrad after 28 months of siege. It continued westward until early March, when it halted at the line Narva–Lake Peipus–VITEBSK. The Soviet forces went on the offensive in the Crimea in April 1944. A series of devastating whirlwind attacks cleared the Germans from the peninsula in a month. Sevastopol was retaken by the Russians within two days of the launching of their attack on the city. The offensives after July 1943 had brought back much territory to the Soviets. The Germans had lost heavily in personnel and equipment, and Hitler had had to extend his control over Axis satellite nations that were threatened by the Soviet Army.

The first major drive in the Soviet *summer offensive* of 1944 was in the Vitebsk–Zhlobin sector. Other drives, to the north and south, would commence when German

THE EASTERN FRONT in the final phases, 1944–45

reserves were committed to that sector, the gateway to a drive against East Prussia. On June 23 four Soviet fronts (army groups) launched a major offensive on a 300-mile front. By July 3 Soviet troops were on prewar Polish soil. At the end of July one army group was crossing the Vistula, knocking at WARSAW's door. On August 1 Poles in Warsaw under General BOR rose in what they believed to be a behind-the-lines attack coordinated with a Soviet attack on the city from the east. The Soviet forces, because of political reasons and possibly because of overextended lines of communication, failed to support this uprising; the underground army in Warsaw was wiped out by the Germans. The entire chapter remains one of the most bitterly controversial episodes of the war.

The Soviet offensive south of the PRIPET MARSHES began on July 14, 1944. Within two weeks Soviet troops were in Lvov. This offensive preceded the important drive into the Balkans by two fronts, directed by Marshal A. M. VASILEVSKY. The drive began on August 20. Three days later Rumania capitulated; subsequently she declared war on Germany and Hungary. The Germans fought hard to save the PLOESTI oil fields. Neutral Bulgaria, under German pressure, violated her neutrality, and the USSR declared war against her, a war that lasted 24 hours. Immediately after surrendering, Bulgaria declared war on Germany and Hungary. In early October, Gen. Rodion MALINOVSKY's front had entered Hungary. BUDAPEST was surrounded within a month, but the city did not surrender. In the meantime Gen. F. I. TOLBUKHIN's front was advancing on Belgrade. Partisan forces in Yugoslavia were aiding the Soviet advance. In the north Gen. L. A. GOVOROV opened an attack against the Finns in June 1944. The drive was successful and led to Finland's capitulation in September. This was a particularly hard blow to the German war economy.

In the *final Soviet offensive* of January–May 1945, Budapest fell in mid-February after 14 weeks of siege. Although the southern groups were now in a position to start a push toward VIENNA, all Soviet efforts were bent to support the drive on the northern front that had begun on January 12. The main objectives of this drive were East Prussia, Pomerania, BERLIN and Silesia. The Soviets hoped to achieve them by multiple penetrations of the northern front, followed by a rapid exploitation across Poland to the ODER RIVER east of Berlin; envelopment and isolation of East Prussia and Silesia and possibly of Pomerania; capture of the great industrial area of Silesia; and a threat toward Vienna that might subsequently cut behind the main front from the south.

Warsaw fell on January 17, 1945. Operations against East Prussia were not unlike the Russian offensive in that area in 1914, but this time the Russians instead of the Germans won at Tannenberg. At the end of February the Soviets swung to the north, hoping to push the Germans into the Baltic. By the end of the winter offensive, March 20, the Soviets had reached the Baltic and were strung along the Oder. The Western Allied forces were preparing to cross the Rhine at this time. As the northern armies slowed down, the Balkan armies moved forward. By April 13 Vienna was occupied. During this period the Red Army in the north regrouped forces and improved its positions preparatory to its final drive. On April 16 the Russians moved forward along 200 miles of the Oder, closely supported by artillery and air forces. Zhukov's First Belorussian Front was to drive on the city of Berlin. Within 10 days Berlin was encircled. That same day, April 25, elements of the U.S. First Army met elements of the First Ukrainian Front at TORGAU on the Elbe. Berlin fell on May 2. The final capitulation of German forces came on May 8. **J.C.J.**

SOVIET GUARDS. The Guards title was first awarded after August 1941 to military units which distinguished themselves in combat action. A number of stories exist as to the origin of the title, the most prevalent having to do with 28 men of Maj. Gen. I. V. Panfilov's 316th Rifle Division who gave their lives destroying 50 German tanks outside Moscow. Individual members of the recipient units are authorized to wear a special badge, a laurel wreath encircling a red star with a red banner bearing the word "Guards" in Russian.

SOVIET HIGH COMMAND. The General Headquarters of the High Command of the Armed Forces of the USSR (Stavka Glavnovo Komandovaniya Vooruzhennykh Sil SSSR)—the Stavka, as it was generally called—was established June 23, 1941. In its first stages the Stavka consisted of TIMOSHENKO, the People's Commissar of Defense, who served as chairman; ZHUKOV, Chief of the General Staff, which was subsumed into the Stavka; VOROSHILOV; BUDËNNY; KUZNETSOV, People's Commissar of the Navy; MOLOTOV; and STALIN. In addition, a permanent board of advisers was set up, which included SHAPOSHNIKOV, MERETSKOV, VATUTIN, VORONOV, ZHDANOV, A. I. Mikoyan and N. A. Voznesensky. Marshal Shaposhnikov was probably the architect of the Stavka, as his earlier work *The Brain of the Army (Mozq Armii)* outlines most of the organizational concepts that were employed. Even so, no movement toward such an organization, not even planning for wartime conditions, preceded the German attack. Therefore, as Admiral Kuznetsov pointed out, the organization was not "scrupulously tested and perfected in times of peace." It followed, of course, that the lack of planning for war would affect the tactical deployment of the armed forces. The subsequent debacles in the battles of the frontiers, the obvious lack of contingency plans and the destruction of the Soviet Air Force were all symptomatic of this failure.

By August, Stalin, the Supreme Commander of the Armed Forces, had emerged as the sole leader of all phases of the effort to defeat Germany (he had taken over the duties of Commissar of Defense on July 19). Inevitably this led to overcentralization of authority, creating problems of command and stultifying initiative at all levels. Yet within the limits of the situation Stalin proved himself in effective control of operations. Since the war, and especially since Stalin's death, many Soviet commanders have commented unfavorably on the workings of the Stavka; e.g., Stalin's technique of dispatching senior staff officers, such as Zhukov and A. M. VASILEVSKY, to supervise a unit's activities, thereby usurping the commander's authority and prerogatives. Marshal S. M. SHTEMENKO has criticized the policy which kept the Chief of the General Staff (Vasilevsky) in the field rather than supervising the staff.

Operating through the Commissariat of Defense, the Stavka ran the General Staff and the staffs of the various administrations and service arms. The primary tactical planning group was the RED ARMY GENERAL STAFF (Generalnyi Shtab RKKA). The General Staff, though the working body of the Stavka, was not subordinate to it, and answered directly to Stalin. In theory and in practice, the Supreme Commander's first deputy, Zhukov, had no authority regarding the General Staff. In effect, this system removed the Stavka itself from the chain of command and added to Stalin's personal power.

SOVIET-JAPANESE BORDER CONFLICT (1938–39). The Soviets had regarded Japan as a threat since the Japanese had attempted to seize the Russian Far East during the Civil War. The Japanese invasion of Manchuria in 1931 and the tensions resulting from encroachments upon the Soviet-owned Chinese Eastern Railroad prompted the Soviet Government to create the Independent Far Eastern Army. When Japan invaded northern China in 1937, the Soviets began assisting China in its resistance, regarding the Japanese army in Manchuria, 300,000 strong, as a potential menace to Russia.

Under the pretext that the boundary line was imprecise, on July 29, 1938, two Japanese regiments attacked Soviet positions near Vladivostok, in the area where the boundaries of the Soviet Union, Korea and Manchuria converge, and having penetrated two and a half miles into Soviet territory, began to build fortifications. The Soviets counterattacked with superior forces on August 6 and forced the Japanese to withdraw into Manchuria. On the 9th the latter made an attempt to regain the lost ground, but the next day were repulsed again. The armistice followed shortly thereafter.

The second round of hostilities was preceded by a series of border raids by the forces of the Japanese KWANTUNG ARMY in January–February 1939, in the vicinity of Nomon-Han. The attack on May 11 was directed against the border troops of the Mongolian republic; in an enveloping movement, the Japanese soon reached the banks of the Khalkhin Gol River. Invoking their mutual defense treaty of 1936, the Soviets sent their troops into Mongolia. By mid-August fighting was in full swing, involving several divisions and hundreds of tanks and airplanes on both sides. The joint Soviet-Mongolian forces under the command of General ZHUKOV launched a counteroffensive on August 20, encircling and then destroying the bulk of the Japanese 6th Army. Perhaps because of the signing of the SOVIET-GERMAN NONAGGRESSION PACT on August 22, the Japanese decided not to undertake further incursions into Soviet and Mongolian territories. On September 16, 1939, an armistice and the creation of the joint border commission were announced, and peace ruled the Soviet Far East until 1945.

SOVIET-JAPANESE NEUTRALITY PACT. This agreement, providing for neutrality in the case of an attack by a third country, was concluded on April 13, 1941, during Japanese Foreign Minister Yosuke MATSUOKA's brief stopover in Moscow on his way from Berlin to Tokyo. It was preceded by prolonged negotiations, which had reached an impasse because of the Soviet demands that Japan return southern SAKHALIN, surrender her concessions in northern Sakhalin and abandon her ambition to dominate China. During his talks in Berlin, however, Matsuoka had decided that in spite of the tensions in the BALKANS following the coup d'état in Belgrade and the subsequent German invasion of Yugoslavia, there would be no war between Germany and Russia. Since Japan was ready to launch a new offensive to the south, protection in the north appeared desirable. The Soviets, by then already anticipating the German attack and fearful of a two-front war, scaled down their demands, obtaining only Japanese concessions in Sakhalin. In spite of the pact, Japan continued to maintain her large KWANTUNG ARMY in Manchuria, and until victory in the Battle of KURSK in 1943 the Soviet command reckoned with the possibility of a Japanese attack. The collapse of Germany permitted the Soviets to eliminate the Japanese menace in the Far East. In April 1945 the Soviet Government denounced the pact (concluded for the term of five years) and, in accord with the wishes of its Western allies, on August 9, 1945, declared war on Japan and invaded Manchuria.

SPAAK, Paul-Henri (1899–1972). Belgian statesman and Socialist leader who served in London during World War II as Belgium's foreign minister in exile. He headed Belgium's delegation to the UNITED NATIONS organizing conference in San Francisco and was selected the first president of the U.N. General Assembly.

SPAATZ, Carl (1891–1974). After serving as an American air observer in Great Britain, "Tooey" Spaatz returned to the United States and was serving as Chief of the Air Staff when the Japanese attacked PEARL HARBOR. Promoted to major general, he went back to Britain, where in June 1942 he took command of the EIGHTH AIR FORCE and launched America's air war against Germany. His next assignment was Commanding General, TWELFTH AIR FORCE, during the North African fighting. In February 1943 he organized and took command of the NORTHWEST AFRICAN AIR FORCES. Promoted to lieutenant general in March, he became Deputy Commanding General, MEDITERRANEAN ALLIED AIR FORCES, then went to the United Kingdom in January 1944 to become Commanding General, U.S. STRATEGIC AIR FORCES IN EUROPE (including the Eighth Air Force in England and the FIFTEENTH AIR FORCE, based in Italy). He received a fourth star in March 1945, returned briefly to Army Air Forces headquarters, then went to GUAM to command U.S. STRATEGIC AIR FORCES PACIFIC (the Eighth and TWENTIETH AIR FORCES), the post he held at the end of the war.

Spaatz was thus America's preeminent air commander in both hemispheres—the highest-ranking wielder of strategic air power. In the last and most dramatic act of the war, he was the overall commander who waited at TINIAN for the ENOLA GAY to return from the HIROSHIMA mission.

SPANDAU. A prison in the West Berlin area of the same name wherein the seven Nazi leaders sentenced to imprisonment at the NUREMBERG TRIALS of 1946 were confined under four-power control. Originally a fortress dating from the 16th century, Spandau has room for as many as 600 prisoners, and in the past was used as a political prison. The seven convicted war criminals were brought to Spandau from Nuremberg on July 18, 1947. They were Rudolf HESS, Walther FUNK, Karl DÖNITZ, Erich RAEDER, Baldur von SCHIRACH, Konstantin von NEURATH and Albert SPEER. Since 1947 each controlling power has taken its monthly turns supervising the prison, each employing its own prison director and guards. Spandau prison is divided into two security sectors, an outer and an inner; steel doors secure the inner cell block. The garden used by the inmates is covered by machine gun posts. One by one the prisoners have been released—Neurath in 1954, Raeder in 1955, Dönitz in 1956, Funk in 1957, Schirach and Speer much later (1966)—leaving only Hess. All attempts by the Western Allies to have Hess released have thus far been categorically rejected by the Soviets. One probable reason is that access to Spandau gives them a foothold in West Berlin.

SPARS. Women's component of the United States Coast Guard Reserve, established November 23, 1942; the acronym stands for the Coast Guard motto *Semper Paratus*—Always Ready. The wartime director was Capt. Dorothy C. Stratton (November 1942 to January 1946). Peak wartime strength of 10,000 enlisted women and 1,000 officers was attained in November 1944. The women were assigned shore duties in the United States, Hawaii and Alaska, primarily in administrative positions. This U.S. women's corps did not continue as a permanent part of the postwar military establishment as did the Women's Army Corps and the Women Reserves of the Navy, but was completely demobilized in 1946.

SPEARS, Sir Edward Louis (1886–1974). Famous World War I British military interpreter (half French by birth) with the French who in May 1940 was sent to France by Winston CHURCHILL to act as his representative with Premier Paul REYNAUD. On his return to England during the collapse of France, Spears (the name was originally Spiers) brought with him Charles DE GAULLE and thereby initiated FREE FRANCE, a movement which was to have an important political and psychological role in the course of the war. Spears did this on his own initiative. De Gaulle was most reluctant to go, and Churchill was said to have been highly indignant that Spears had brought him. A major general, Spears was also a Member of Parliament.

SPECIAL AIR SERVICE. British unit formed originally to operate behind Axis lines in the desert. After the end of the NORTH AFRICA campaign, it was formed into three regiments, one to operate in France, one in Italy and one, renamed the Special Boat Service, in the Aegean. Later, two French battalions and a Belgian company were formed to operate with the British in their own countries. Generally, SAS troops worked independently, but on a few occasions they collaborated with resistance forces.

SPECIAL ATTACK CORPS. The KAMIKAZE fliers who first appeared at the LEYTE landing, October 1944.

SPECIAL BOAT SECTION. A British unit, part of a COMMANDO specially trained to attack shipping in enemy-held harbors. The attacks were carried out by canoes, usually carried to their destinations in submarines, trawlers or small craft; the crews of the canoes, trained as frogmen, laid limpets (small mines) and depth charges against the hulls of enemy ships. Perhaps the most spectacular Special Boat Section attack was that mounted on December 7, 1942, in the Gironde River (France), when four large ships that had run the blockade were seriously damaged and put out of action for many months. The episode was later the subject of a successful film, *The Cockleshell Heroes*.

SPECIAL OPERATIONS EXECUTIVE. British organization established in November 1940 to encourage, direct and supply resistance groups in countries occupied by Germany. It was responsible to the Minister of

Economic Warfare. SOE agents operated in the Balkans, the Baltic and central Europe and were especially employed in France, working with the FRENCH RESISTANCE. In 1943 the American OFFICE OF STRATEGIC SERVICES began operating through agents in France, and by January 1944 the Special Operations branch of the OSS had amalgamated with the SOE.

SPECIAL OPERATIONS GROUPS. U.S. teams, 11 in all, armed and trained to fight with the FRENCH RESISTANCE.

SPEER, Albert (1905–). One of the youngest of the Nazi hierarchy, Speer was also one of the most gifted men to serve Adolf HITLER. Speer's father was a prominent architect, and he himself trained for the same profession. It was as an architect, in fact, that he first caught Hitler's attention; he had refurbished party district headquarters in Berlin and the Ministry of Propaganda, and had designed the overall display in the Nuremberg stadium. He had joined the party only in 1931, having been magnetized by Hitler's personality when he heard him speak. At 28, Speer became Hitler's designer-architect in chief, producing grandiose designs for the rebuilding of Berlin, none of which were realized except Hitler's own Chancellery, completed at the beginning of 1939. In 1937 there was a $250 million design for the Nuremberg Congress stadium which won Speer the Grand Prix at the Paris World's Fair. But his outstanding administrative ability was revealed in his capacity to complete work by what appeared to be an impossible deadline.

In 1942 when Hitler's Minister of Armaments, Fritz TODT, was killed in an air crash, Speer was (to his surprise) appointed Minister for Armaments and Munitions, and in 1943 he took charge of total war production. He performed his task with exemplary skill throughout the period of reversal on the war fronts and the increasingly severe disruptions of production caused by intensive Allied bombing. He expanded the system of slave labor originated by Todt, and this became the prime reason for his sentence following the NUREMBERG TRIALS.

Speer was in a unique position to judge the point at which Germany could no longer win the war, and in 1944 his patriotism began to outbalance his desire to serve Hitler. Reason asserted itself, and his innate common sense forced him to recognize the utterly destructive nature of Hitler's megalomania. Hitler and Martin BORMANN—who increasingly stood between the Führer and those who might disturb him with evidence of Germany's impending defeat—refused to accept the moral of Speer's memoranda, which was that Germany should seek to end the war. Although Hitler realized that Speer was opposed to his total war policy, he refused to accept a proffered resignation and took no punitive action even when in April 1945 Speer countermanded Hitler's express orders that Germany was to undergo destruction by scorched earth as the price of "betraying" the Führer. There seems no doubt that Hitler held his young minister, only 40 years old at the end of the war, to be a fellow artist of whom, in his own egocentric way, he was genuinely fond.

Speer even went so far as to consider gassing Hitler in the bunker, but such an attempt proved impracticable. Speer and Gen. Heinz GUDERIAN remained the last men to try to face Hitler with the truth. Both managed to survive. Speer took his leave in April, traveling north to Admiral DÖNITZ's headquarters. He was interrogated by the Americans in mid-May, and later in the month arrested by the British at Flensburg. One of the principal defendants at the NUREMBERG TRIALS, he was judged guilty of war crimes and crimes against humanity and received a 20-year sentence. This he served at SPANDAU prison, being released on October 1, 1966.

During his imprisonment Speer drafted his memoirs, which he revised and checked after his release. The result was the most thorough and reliable account of Hitler and the regime to come from a former Nazi leader. In the book, Speer fully acknowledges his past guilt as an exploiter of slave labor. The memoirs appeared in German in 1969, and in English translation in 1970.

SPEIDEL, Hans (1897–). German Army officer who as a lieutenant general was chief of staff to Field Marshal Erwin ROMMEL in France at the time of the Allied INVASION of Normandy. Speidel was involved in the OPPOSITION TO HITLER, and it was he who persuaded Rommel to join. On July 9, 1944, Speidel was arrested on the orders of Heinrich HIMMLER; he spent eight months in the Gestapo cellar in Prinz-Albrechtstrasse but, inexplicably, was one of only a few of the conspirators who escaped execution. After the war he had a career in the West German Army.

SPERRLE, Hugo (1885–1953). German air commander, a veteran of World War I, in which he became commander of the Air Reconnaissance School of Cologne and flight commander of the Fourth Army. Sperrle was able to stay in the Army despite the severe limitations imposed by the Treaty of Versailles, and with the advent of Adolf HITLER in 1933 he was made commander of an infantry regiment. Later he was brought into Hermann GÖRING's new Air Ministry. In 1935 he became a major general and was appointed commander of the 5th Air District (Munich).

In 1936 Sperrle was given command of the Condor Legion, a German air unit organized to aid the Nationalists during the Spanish Civil War. After differences with Nazi Party leaders, he was relieved of his command in Spain in 1937 and reassigned to command of LUFTWAFFE Group 2. When World War II began he was chief of Air Fleet 3, which he commanded in the attack on England in 1940. Subsequently Sperrle was transferred to the Luftwaffe's Ordnance Department, with the rank of colonel general. He served in that capacity until 1944, when he was relieved.

Sperrle had knowledge of the plot against Hitler in 1944, but he managed to escape retribution by the Nazis. The Allied military court in Nuremberg freed him on November 22, 1948.

SPERRY BOMBSIGHT. A precision device, named for its U.S. inventor, Elmer A. Sperry, that made its U.S. Army Air Corps debut in 1933 and remained in production for a decade. Even though the Army decided in September 1943 to stop purchasing the Sperry and its associated automatic pilot, those already on hand saw service for the remainder of the war. The Flying Fortresses and Liberators sent to the United Kingdom prior to Pearl Harbor carried the Sperry bombsight. The Army hoped to protect the more sensitive NORDEN BOMBSIGHT in case some of the bombers went down over German-held Europe. Royal Air Force bombardiers used the Sperry in high-altitude attacks with disappointing results.

SPEZIA, LA. Italian naval base on the Ligurian Sea, near Genoa.

SPICHALSKY, Maryan (1906–). In 1942 Colonel Spichalsky helped to found the Communist Party in Poland. He formed Communist PARTISAN detachments to fight the Nazis and served as political chief in the People's Army. Spichalsky was also the mayor of Warsaw and a representative of the Polish Committee of National Liberation, better known as the LUBLIN COMMITTEE, which sought a pro-Soviet government for Poland at the end of the war.

SPITFIRE. This famous British airplane, designed by R. J. Mitchell, was descended from a line of Supermarine racing seaplanes that had won the Schneider Cup three times, gaining permanent possession of this trophy for the United Kingdom and exceeding 400 miles per hour in accomplishing the feat. The Spitfire was Supermarine's response to an Air Ministry requirement for an eight-gun fighter. First flown in 1936, the prototype made extensive use of stressed-metal skin, though the control surfaces were fabric-covered. A 990-horsepower Rolls-Royce Merlin liquid-cooled engine turned a two-bladed wooden propeller. On the ground the narrow track of the landing gear gave the plane a somewhat fragile look, but in the air its clean lines and graceful elliptical wing made it a thing of beauty.

Spitfire I, which became a legend in the Battle of BRITAIN, incorporated armor, a bulletproof windscreen, a raised canopy that gave the pilot better visibility and a 1,030-horsepower Merlin. Compared with its principal foe, the MESSERSCHMITT ME 109, the Spitfire was only a shade faster but had a definite edge in maneuverability. The German fighter, however, enjoyed a superiority in diving and climbing, and its armament had greater range, though a lesser concentration of fire, than the Spitfire's eight .303-caliber Browning machine guns.

A total of 21 Spitfire variants entered service with the ROYAL AIR FORCE during the war, as the plane grew in size and improved in performance. At first the changes consisted in the installation of successively more powerful Merlins and the substitution of a wing that housed two 20-mm. cannon and four .303-caliber machine guns. Spitfire V, however, did violence to the plane's original lines, as designers cropped the wing tips to increase the roll rate and installed a chin-type dust filter on models intended for combat in the desert.

Spitfire

Some Spitfires, I's as well as later models, were stripped of their armament, fitted with cameras and used for aerial reconnaissance. Well suited to this mission was Spitfire VI, intended as a high-altitude interceptor and fitted with a pressurized cabin, four-bladed propeller and elongated wing tips.

Spitfire VI blazed the trail for a second high-altitude model, Spitfire VII, which mounted a 1,710-horsepower Merlin that produced a top speed of 408 miles per hour at 25,000 feet. Spitfire VIII lacked the VII's pressurized cabin, featured the dust filter introduced on Spitfire V and fought at low and medium altitudes.

By the beginning of 1942 the new German FOCKE-WULF FW 190 and improvements to the Me 109 threatened the ascendancy of the Spitfire. Supermarine undertook an emergency program that resulted in Spitfire IX, which came in low-, medium- and high-altitude versions. The 1,470-horsepower Merlin used in Spitfire V gave way to a 1,720-horsepower type (1,710 in the high-altitude IX) that turned a four-bladed propeller and increased the top speed from 374 miles per hour at 13,000 feet to 404 miles per hour at 21,000 feet. Spitfire IX proved to be the most numerous of the breed, 5,665 of them emerging from the assembly line.

These alterations did not restore the Spitfire's supremacy, and the next change involved the replacement of the Merlin engine, last used in Spitfire XVI, with a Rolls-Royce Griffon. A series of transitional models demonstrated different versions of the liquid-cooled Griffon, and one of these planes succeeded in downing an Me 262 jet fighter in aerial combat. Spitfire XXI was the first Griffon-powered Spitfire selected for mass production, but only 122 had been built when hostilities ended. The 2,050-horsepower engine gave the plane a top speed of 454 miles per hour at 26,000 feet and a service ceiling of 43,500 feet.

The Spitfire remained in production until 1947, when the last of 20,334 planes was accepted by the RAF. The final 2,053 mounted Griffon engines, all the others Merlins.

SPOONER, Ernest (1887–1942). Captain of H.M.S. REPULSE at the outbreak of the war, Spooner in 1941 was appointed Rear Admiral Malaya and Admiral Superintendent of Singapore Dockyard. As such he was in charge of the local naval defense of SINGAPORE. When the Japanese captured Singapore in February 1942, Spooner escaped in the launch ML 310, which ran ashore on the island of Tjebia, 20 miles north of Banka, and was damaged beyond repair. After evading the Japanese for two months, Spooner suddenly collapsed and died on the island on April 15, 1942.

SPRAGUE, Clifton Albert F. (1896–1955). Described as "all Navy," this 1918 graduate of the U.S. Naval Academy was a specialist in naval aviation. At PEARL

HARBOR his seaplane tender *Tangier* fired the first shots on Japanese planes the morning of December 7, 1941. Sprague commanded the carrier WASP at the PHILIPPINE SEA, and in August 1944 became a rear admiral. His escort carrier group won special distinction in October 1944 at the battle off Samar (*see* LEYTE GULF). Later Sprague commanded escort carrier divisions at Iwo JIMA and OKINAWA. Following the war, Sprague continued his interest in naval air.

SPRAGUE, Thomas Lamison (1894–1972). A 1917 graduate of the U.S. Naval Academy, Rear Admiral Sprague fought his most distinguished action of World War II during the battle for LEYTE GULF, late in 1944. For the preliminary amphibious operations, Sprague had responsibility for providing air cover for troops, maintaining air supremacy and neutralizing Japanese planes; despite bad weather, he was successful. His task group of escort carriers took part in the Battle of Surigao Strait, and in the battle off Samar (Leyte Gulf) came under the first full-scale KAMIKAZE attack of the war. Sprague retired in 1952 as a full admiral.

SPRING. Code name of the Canadian attack in Normandy, July 1944, coinciding with Operations COBRA and GOODWOOD.

SPRUANCE, Raymond Ames (1886–1969). Adm. William L. CALHOUN once described Spruance as a "cold-blooded fighting fool," a characterization that takes account both of Spruance's prudence and of his aggressiveness. As the result of his actions at MIDWAY and his leadership of American naval forces in the Central Pacific, Spruance rose from rear admiral to full admiral. He received decorations from the United States and foreign countries, and as a four-star admiral saw action at TRUK Atoll in the MARSHALLS aboard a ship engaged in the actual combat, an unprecedented act for an officer of his rank.

Spruance graduated 25th in the 1906 class at the U.S. Naval Academy. In 1940 he was promoted to rear admiral and given command of the Tenth Naval District, the Caribbean area, with headquarters in San Juan, Puerto Rico. The next year he took command of a division of cruisers in the Pacific; he was in this position when the Japanese advanced toward Midway in June 1942. At Midway Spruance came into the limelight when he assumed tactical command after the flagship of Vice-Adm. Frank J. FLETCHER, the YORKTOWN, was severely damaged, and even before this happened he had handled his planes to great effect. In the words of Adm. Chester NIMITZ, commander of the Pacific Fleet, Spruance "did a remarkable job." Although outnumbered, Spruance deployed his strength cleverly, routing the enemy, in the process sinking at least 10 warships, including all four carriers, downing 275 planes and killing 4,800 Japanese. Midway was a great moral victory for the United States, and for his actions there Spruance received the DISTINGUISHED SERVICE MEDAL.

After Midway, Spruance became chief of staff to Admiral Nimitz, where he played a vital role in planning operations in the SOLOMONS and the Central Pacific. In 1943 Nimitz gave Spruance command of the new Central Pacific force (the FIFTH FLEET). Spruance's campaign planning in this position proved decisive in defeating the Japanese. His first objective was the GILBERT ISLANDS. The Japanese heavy fortifications on BETIO in TARAWA Atoll were attacked beginning November 21, 1943. The battle continued for over three days and cost 2,950 American casualties, but eventually gave U.S. forces possession of the Gilberts. Spruance directed this joint operation; Adm. Richmond Kelly TURNER led amphibious operations for Spruance, and Marine Maj. Gen. Holland M. "Howlin' Mad" SMITH commanded assault troops.

Within two months Spruance was attacking KWAJALEIN Atoll in the Marshall Islands. Supported by air from planes based in the Gilberts, Spruance's offensive won quick success. Shore-based air support came from Rear Adm. John H. HOOVER and carrier air support from Rear Adm. Marc A. MITSCHER. On February 10, 1944, President Franklin D. ROOSEVELT nominated Spruance for promotion to full admiral.

The Americans had Kwajalein, but the Japanese still held strongholds in the Marshalls. At Truk in mid-February his force sank at least 19 enemy ships, possibly as many as 26, and downed 200 planes, with U.S. losses amounting to only 17 aircraft. Commentators attributed Spruance's success in the Marshalls to his exhaustive planning, especially his imaginative use of Mitscher's task force.

In late March 1944 Spruance assaulted the CAROLINES. Mitscher's task force, under Spruance's command, participated in the HOLLANDIA invasion in NEW GUINEA. In mid-June 1944 preliminary bombardment

Admiral Spruance

of SAIPAN by Mitscher's planes and Spruance's naval guns began. The admirals hoped for a classic surface battle, but only carrier aircraft could reach the Japanese ships. After a Japanese aerial counterattack on the Fifth Fleet was repulsed, Mitscher caught the retreating enemy on June 19 at the Battle of the PHILIPPINE SEA, downing 402 planes and sinking six ships. British Prime Minister Winston S. CHURCHILL congratulated Spruance for his capture of Saipan. Meanwhile, units under Spruance successfully protected the MARIANAS invasion force.

In August 1944 Admiral Nimitz announced that Adm. William F. HALSEY'S THIRD FLEET and Spruance's Fifth would henceforth work as two separate planning and operating teams, alternating blows at the enemy. Spruance commanded the force invading Iwo JIMA (February 1945) and OKINAWA (April 1945). The latter included 1,200 vessels and 548,000 men. Spruance had been among the first to advocate the capture of Iwo Jima and Okinawa.

On November 5, 1945, Spruance relinquished command of the Fifth Fleet, but soon succeeded Nimitz as commander of the Pacific Fleet. He continued in this position until February 1946, when he became president of the U.S. Naval War College. Spruance's DISTINGUISHED SERVICE MEDAL had two gold stars by the end of the war. He also held the NAVY CROSS and Army Distinguished Service Medal. Great Britain made him an honorary Companion of the Order of the Bath.

Commentators agree that Spruance's personality was an ideal one for amphibious warfare. Such complex operations require a mind capable of mastering sweeping plans and small details alike; one must be able to coordinate landings, naval and air bombardment and logistics. In addition to possessing these qualities and abilities, Spruance was a leader. A biographer compared him to David Farragut as "not rash, but a go-ahead man ... Our men will fight to the death for him." Historian S. E. Morison said that "there was no one to equal Spruance." **D.C.**

SQUID. A long-range ahead-throwing depth-charge projector developed by the Royal Navy. A three-barreled mortar, controlled from the asdic SOUND-RANGE RECORDER, Squid fired a finned depth charge, its hydrostatic fuze automatically set by input from the asdic depth-prediction gear. Its effective forward range was approximately 300 yards.

SS (Schutzstaffel—Protection Detachment). The SS (the Black Shirts) was organized on Adolf HITLER'S orders in 1925 to provide protection for National Socialist Party meetings after the SA (Sturmabteilungen) (*see* SA) was made illegal. In 1926 the SA was again legalized and the SS suffered a brief setback. This changed in 1929 when Hitler appointed Heinrich HIMMLER as Reichsführer (Reich Leader) SS. Himmler immediately began to expand the SS, which then had a total strength of 280 men. Until Hitler assumed power in 1933 the SS was combating other political parties and strengthening its position within the party. But other agencies within the party, primarily the SA under Ernst RÖHM, looked with jealous eyes at Himmler's growing empire. These party rivals were soon put in their place. The SS wiped out the SA leadership, as well as many others who had aroused their displeasure, in the bloody purge of June 30, 1934 (the NIGHT OF THE LONG KNIVES). Hitler, who had believed himself threatened by the SA leaders, conferred upon the SS the status of an independent party organization in July 1934.

Himmler added the German police forces to his empire between 1933 and 1939, and with them those elements of power that made him the most feared party leader in Germany. He gained control of the police by absorbing them from one German state after another. When Himmler was appointed Minister of the Interior in June 1936 the police were under his dominance. He combined the office of Minister of the Interior with that of the Reichsführer SS and formally systematized this union with the creation of the Reich Security Main Office (Reichssicherheitshauptamt—RSHA) in 1939. The RSHA consolidated the Party Security Service (Sicherheitsdienst—SD) and those branches of the state police dealing with criminal and political offenses (*see* SD).

The SS had grown to a total of over 240,000 men by early 1939 and was broadly divided as follows: (1) the General SS (Allgemeine SS), all the voluntary part-time members; (2) the SS Verfügungstruppe, more commonly known as the WAFFEN SS; (3) the Death's-Head Formations (SS Totenkopf Verbände), who guarded the concentration camps; (4) the SD, the Party Security Service; and (5) the SS Race and Settlement Service (SS Rasse- und Siedlungsamt).

Himmler controlled the above organizations through three SS main offices (SS–Hauptämter) under the collective title Reich Command SS (Reichsführung–SS). By 1940 the Reich Command SS had to be enlarged and a number of other SS main offices created to take care of Himmler's ever expanding duties. The Reich Command SS was now composed of Himmler's personal staff, 10 SS main offices and one independent SS office.

STACHIEWICZ, Waclaw (1894–1973). Chief of Staff of the Polish Army who in 1936 began to modernize and improve the quality of the Army and its officer corps. The improvements in military effectiveness that Stachiewicz wanted came slowly, and in mid-1939 he turned to Poland's ally, Great Britain, for help. Despite these joint efforts to prepare the Polish Army, it was unable to withstand the German onslaught in September 1939.

STAGG, James Martin (1900–1975). An RAF officer, the chief meteorological adviser to the Supreme Commander, Allied Expeditionary Force, 1943–45. It was on the basis of Group Captain Stagg's interpretation of the weather charts on the eve of D-Day that General EISENHOWER took the decision to launch the INVASION of Normandy by the Allied forces. In all of recorded military history, no staff officer has played a more direct forcing hand in the making of a main decision.

STALIN, Joseph (1879–1953). Born J. V. Dzhugashvili, the future Soviet dictator began his revolutionary activity in 1898, became prominent in party and government affairs after the 1917 October Revolution and, having defeated his opponents in the leadership struggle following Lenin's death, consolidated his personal power in the bloody purges of the 1930s. In the last purge, which began in the spring of 1937, a third of the RED ARMY officers were liquidated, including 3 out of 5 marshals, all 11 Deputy Commissars of Defense and 13 of 15 generals of the Army. All commanders of military districts, all corps commanders, almost all brigade and division commanders and about half of all regiment commanders were purged—many more than were killed in action during four years of war against Germany. Deterioration of the professional competence of the Red Army and its morale was the single most important factor accounting for Soviet defeats in 1941–42.

Although the signing of the SOVIET-GERMAN NONAGGRESSION PACT in 1939 only briefly slowed down Soviet war preparations, Stalin's expectation that the war in the west would be prolonged led to grievous delays in implementing modernization of the military equipment and to reckless deployment of forces in the immediate frontier area. Fortifications along the old frontier with Poland were dismantled, large armored units were inexplicably disbanded and no plans for a defensive war were developed in the General Staff: for doctrinal reasons it was mandatory to assume that war would be fought on enemy territory.

The German attack on June 22, 1941, stunned Stalin. For two weeks he took no part in mobilizing the war effort, and even after his assumption of the title Supreme Commander in Chief his role for a while remained perfunctory; much of his attempt to stem the German offensive was reduced to terrorizing Red Army commanders, some of whom he ordered shot for unauthorized retreat.

As the war progressed, however, Stalin displayed increasing ability to select talented persons to administer the mobilization of Soviet resources and to utilize his unique dictatorial powers through the highly centralized mechanism of the STATE DEFENSE COMMITTEE. He was credited with a remarkable capacity for retaining vast stores of information, with being in constant touch with the situation in all the military and civilian sectors and with having a mastery of detail. But while choosing capable men for key appointments, Stalin jealously guarded his own authority and his prerogative to approve every plan in its smallest particulars. He was noted for constant meddling in the execution of plans and for his extreme reluctance to delegate responsibility to his subordinates.

There seems to be a consensus among those who watched him closely during the war that Stalin had an extraordinary grasp of general war objectives and long-range strategic plans. He also had a talent for adjusting the conduct of military operations to economic and political realities. In the planning of operations themselves, however, his contribution was limited, to say the least. Whenever he took part in planning campaigns

Soviet street fighters go on the attack in Stalingrad

and directing battles, he invariably made serious errors. Among the most prominent of Stalin's blunders were his delay in permitting the KIEV army group to withdraw in the summer of 1941, resulting in a loss of 700,000 troops; his insistence on the dispersal of the Soviet offensive capacity after the successful counteroffensive at Moscow in the winter of 1942; and his erroneous prediction of the nature and direction of the German summer offensive in 1942. Coupled with his excessively optimistic assessment of the strength of the Red Army, this last miscalculation resulted in his ordering of the enormously costly attempts to recapture KHARKOV.

Soviet marshals and generals whose memories of the great purges were fresh were extremely reluctant to question Stalin. They feared his wrath much more than the prospect of needless losses of thousands of troops to the enemy, and often obeyed him against their better judgment: however unrealistic Stalin's orders were, they had to be followed. Only at the early stage of the German invasion, when Stalin himself was demoralized, and during the defense of Moscow late in 1941 was the conduct of military operations entrusted to his lieutenants. Stalin also seems to have displayed self-doubt during the crisis in the summer of 1942 and in the early stages of the STALINGRAD battle.

In spite of all the deficiencies of Stalin's military leadership, historians as well as major Army and Navy commanders who wrote their memoirs tend to agree that the authority of Stalin as unchallengeable leader and a symbolic rallying point for Soviet resistance to foreign invasion was a key ingredient in the successful prosecution of the war. Although with some delay, Stalin realized the need to inspire people with the spirit of nationalism and patriotism, abandoning the discredited Communist sloganeering in favor of resurrecting the past glories of Mother Russia.

In dealing with his Western allies, Stalin skillfully exploited the great psychological advantage resulting from Russia's bearing the brunt of the struggle against the common enemy. The failure of his early efforts to have political and territorial objectives of the war defined in a binding agreement with Winston CHURCHILL and Franklin D. ROOSEVELT made him anticipate the conflict with the West once victory had been achieved. This realization was strengthened by what he saw as delays in the opening of the SECOND FRONT at a time when Russia needed it the most. Yet he extracted maximum material assistance from the United States under the LEND-LEASE agreements, and in the wartime conferences at TEHERAN, YALTA and POTSDAM secured substantial concessions on outstanding issues. In the end, however, it was the advance of the Red Army into the heart of Europe in the last stage of the war that put Stalin into a position to confront his allies with a series of *faits accomplis*, thus making sure that Soviet interests, as he interpreted them, were adequately protected. The last act of the war—the attack on Japan in August 1945—brought Soviet territorial gains in the Far East and eliminated Japanese power from the continent of Asia. Although he failed to attain such objectives as a military base in the Dardanelles, a Soviet trusteeship of Tripolitania or territorial expansion at the expense of Turkey and Iran, Stalin could feel satisfied that victory in the war resulted in universal recognition of the Soviet Union as a great world power. *See also* SOVIET-GERMAN OPERATIONS 1941–45. **V.P.**

STALINGRAD, BATTLE OF. This decisive battle had two phases: (1) the German attack and eventual occupation of Stalingrad, which lasted from August to November 1942; (2) the Soviet counteroffensive, which began in mid-November and ended with the liquidation of the German SIXTH ARMY under Gen. Friedrich PAULUS.

The Germans planned a pincers attack on Stalingrad for August 23. The Sixth Army was to attack from the the northwest, the Fourth Panzer Army from the

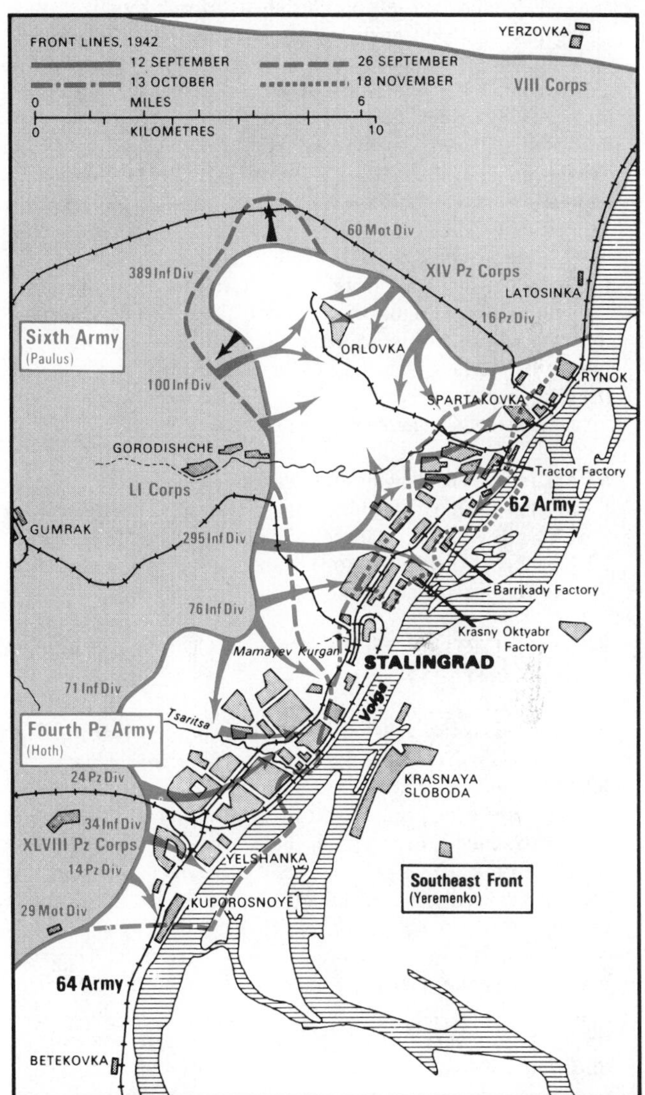

STALINGRAD, as winter arrived, 1942

southwest. Although mobile German units soon reached the Volga above Stalingrad, the Russians held the German pincers apart. Eventually the Germans completed a semicircle around the city to the west. They repeatedly pressed the Soviets with attacks in what soon became a war of attrition. Concentrated German attacks, however, met concentrated Soviet defense; thus the invaders did not reach the suburbs of Stalingrad until September.

The German move on Stalingrad consisted of a direct assault from the west. During this period Stalingrad was bombed and shelled, being completely destroyed, but the Soviet Army under Gen. Vasili CHUIKOV was ordered to defend the area at all costs and, as a result, the German capture of Stalingrad was achieved in the face of enormous losses inflicted by the besieged garrison.

On November 19 the Red Army counterattacked from points north and south of the German salient in Stalingrad and within five days succeeded in cutting off any retreat by the Sixth Army. In mid-December Field Marshal Fritz Erich von MANSTEIN's Army Group Don tried to break through the circle from the south and assist the entrapped armies. However, the Russians checked Operation Winter Storm, as the relief operation was called, some 30 miles short of its objective.

Paulus, trapped inside the devastated city, appealed to Adolf HITLER for permission to surrender, but the Führer ordered the Sixth Army to fight on. Soon the Russians mounted their own offensive against the beleaguered forces. By the end of January 1943 they had destroyed the Sixth Army. Ironically, Hitler had promoted Paulus to the rank of field marshal on January 30; thus he became the first German officer of that rank ever to be taken prisoner. Hitler's policy of defense to the last was more costly than one field marshal, however. The Germans lost more than 200,000 men at Stalingrad. The Russians had achieved their most notable and dramatic victory of the war. Stalingrad was the turning point of World War II in Europe. *See also* SOVIET-GERMAN OPERATIONS 1941–45.

STALIN LINE. Soviet defense line in 1941, running from the Gulf of Finland near Narva through Pskov and Mogilev, before Gomel, turning southwest north of Kiev, then southeast before Kamenets-Podolsk and following the line of the Dniester to the Black Sea.

STALIN ORGAN (Stalin Orgel). German nickname for the KATYUSHA.

STALIN TANK. Popular term for the IS (Joseph Stalin) TANK series derived from the KV tank series (*see* KV). It was a virtual redesign of the latter made to accommodate a heavier gun and larger turret. The series was introduced in 1942 and was kept in production until after the war. The IS-1, the first production model, carried a 122-mm. gun; the IS-2, a major production type (2,250 were built), and the IS-3, a complete redesign with sloping armor all round and a ballistically excellent turret, carried a 122-mm. gun and two machine guns. It had a crew of four, weighed 45.8 tons, was powered by a 519-horsepower diesel engine and had a maximum speed of 25 miles per hour.

STANDLEY, William Harrison (1872–1963). Admiral Standley, a veteran of the Spanish-American War, was U.S. Chief of Naval Operations in 1937–38. He retired with the rank of rear admiral but was recalled to active service in March 1941. In the fall of 1941 he went to Russia as a member of an Allied aid mission, and in February 1942 he was appointed ambassador to the Soviet Union. His resignation was announced on October 1, 1943.

STANLEY, Oliver Frederick George (1896–1950). British political figure who served in 1940 as Secretary of State for War. He also held the offices of president of the Board of Trade (1937–40) and Secretary of State for the Colonies (1942–45).

STANMORE. The name is associated with RAF FIGHTER COMMAND and the Battle of BRITAIN. RAF Stanmore Park was opened in 1938 and was the location of Balloon Command HQ as well as the administrative and domestic support station for Headquarters Fighter Command, a mile or so away at Bentley Priory.

STARAYA RUSSA. German-held bastion town in northwest Russia, south of Lake Ilmen, retaken by the Red Army on February 18, 1944.

STARFISH. Code name used by the British for decoy fires designed to simulate the effects of incendiary bombs dropped as markers. The use of these devices saved property and many lives by leading German bombers away from their allotted targets, particularly British cities.

STARK, Harold Raynsford (1880–1972). U.S. Navy officer, a graduate of the Naval Academy in 1903, Chief of Naval Operations at the time of PEARL HARBOR in 1941. "Betty" Stark became commander of the cruiser division of the U.S. Fleet in 1937 and commander of the cruisers in the Battle Force in 1938. He was named Chief of Naval Operations on August 1, 1939, with the rank of admiral. After the attack on Pearl Harbor, Stark was felt to have been less than thorough in relaying warnings of possible Japanese movements to Adm. Husband E. KIMMEL on Oahu. In March 1942 Stark was sent to London as commander of U.S. Naval Forces in Europe, being replaced as CNO by Adm. Ernest J. KING, Commander in Chief of the United States Fleet, who was already in fact the operating head of the Navy; Stark's position as CNO had become redundant. Stark filled the European command throughout the war; he served as chief liaison between American and British naval forces. One of his principal contributions was that, some months before Pearl Harbor, he teamed with Gen. George C. MARSHALL to write the main strategy for the United States in the event of world war.

STARKEY. Code name of an Allied operation in 1943 designed to lead the Germans to expect an invasion in the Pas de Calais area. It was part of Operation COCKADE.

STARS AND STRIPES. The U.S. soldier's newspaper of World War II took its name from the weekly of Pershing's World War I Expeditionary Force. The latter was a scholarly publication, in contrast to the weekly that first appeared in London in April 1942, the columns of which featured news from the home front. Seven months later the paper became a daily, partly in response to pressure from the White House, President ROOSEVELT being concerned to thwart the Chicago *Tribune*, which was preparing to publish for troops overseas. As military operations expanded, other soldier dailies by the same name began publishing in North Africa, Italy, France, the Hawaiian Islands and other areas. They were of different quality, according to the editorship and staffing. The edition published in Italy, for example, was superior. The Paris paper, on the other hand, was a source of constant irritation to higher commands. Violating regulations, it ridiculed officership and made slighting comparisons between Allied and enemy main weapons. Lt. Gen. W. B. SMITH, chief of staff to the Supreme Commander, became convinced that a Communist cell had infiltrated the paper and ordered an investigation, then called it off because the end of the war was approaching. All of the papers, however, were generally popular with the rank and file, and the *Stars and Stripes*, a model of sound journalism, remains the official news organ for American forces stationed abroad.

STARVATION. Code name of an American operation to plant mines around the Japanese home islands between March 1945 and the end of the war. More than 11,000 mines were sown by submarines and aircraft.

STATE DEFENSE COMMITTEE (Gosudarstvenny Komitet Oborony). Referred to as GOKO or GKO, the Soviet State Defense Committee was established in the days following the German invasion. It was officially responsible for all aspects of the war—military, political and economic. The first members were STALIN, chairman; MOLOTOV, TIMOSHENKO, VOROSHILOV, BUDËNNY, SHAPOSHNIKOV, ZHUKOV and KUZNETSOV. *See also* SOVIET HIGH COMMAND.

STAUFFENBERG, Claus Schenk, Count von (1907–1944). Stauffenberg won an assured place in history by his remarkable exploit in placing a time bomb under Adolf HITLER's map table in the Wolf's Lair, the Führer's headquarters at Rastenburg, on July 20, 1944. This assassination attempt was the culmination of a year of energetic leadership he brought to the ill-fated German OPPOSITION TO HITLER. In many other respects Stauffenberg was one of the outstanding younger offi-

Count von Stauffenberg (extreme left) at the Führer's headquarters. Hitler is in the center

cers in the German Army. His family held themselves to be descendants of the ancient Swabian nobility; on his mother's side he belonged to the Gneisenau family, who had established the Prussian General Staff, and the Yorck family, famous in German military history of Napoleonic times. From his mother, too, he inherited his taste for literature and the arts, which in adolescence centered in the symbolist poet Stefan George, from whose philosophy he absorbed, among many principles, the idea that the mind must control the body. Poor health never held him back from the physical exertion needed to succeed in his chosen career in the Army. From George he absorbed too his love of intellectual discussion, his dedication to his country and his idealistic impulses—impulses which the poet maintained should lead to action. Stauffenberg was brought up and remained a Catholic.

After achieving an outstanding record at the infantry school at Dresden and the cavalry school at Hanover, Stauffenberg was commissioned a second lieutenant on January 1, 1930. The following year he married Nina von Lerchenfeld, whose family belonged to the Bavarian nobility, and with whom he was to have five children. In 1936, though he was only 28, his brilliance qualified him to enter the exclusive circle of the General Staff College. In common with all members of the armed forces, he had to swear the oath of loyalty to Hitler imposed in August 1934, and there is controversy among his biographers as to the nature and degree of his initial tolerance of Hitler's role in Germany's destiny—since Hitler at first appeared, in spite of the regrettable excesses of his followers, to be expressing an idealistic view. Stauffenberg's widow, however, denied strongly that he ever held Hitler in any regard.

In 1938, Stauffenberg, now a captain, became logistics officer to Lt. Gen. Erich HOEPNER, supervising supplies for his division when it entered Sudeten territory in 1938. Later he was to serve in Poland. There is no doubt that he was openly ambitious and that his powerful personality and bent for argument hampered him when it came to promotion. But in May 1940 he was posted at the age of 32 to the organization section of the German General Staff and sent to France, where his grasp of affairs and unremitting energy brought him to the attention of his senior officers. It would seem that Stauffenberg's active opposition to Hitler took shape at this time, inspired by his observation of SS activities (*see* SS). Promoted to major in 1942, he was in a position to observe Nazi war policy both in the west and later in the east after the German invasion of Russia. He began to be openly critical of Hitler's malign influence over the high command.

In January 1943 Stauffenberg was promoted to lieutenant colonel and appointed senior staff officer (operations) to the 10th Panzer Division in North Africa. On April 7 his staff car was attacked by low-flying aircraft and he received severe injuries, losing his right hand and forearm, the third and fourth fingers of his left hand and his left eye. He refused pain-killing drugs, and after his recovery insisted on continuing to serve. He accepted the position of chief of staff to Gen. Friedrich OLBRICHT at the General Army Office in Berlin. Olbricht was a leading member of the military wing of the conspiracy to assassinate Hitler. By August 1943 Stauffenberg can be said to have become a principal in the resistance. However, his acute and ruthless mind did not endear him to some of the members of the diverse, if small, and often politically reactionary resistance circle, notably Carl GOERDELER. The problem was compounded when he advocated, purely for strategic reasons, a peace approach to Russia.

Stauffenberg volunteered to place a time bomb in Hitler's headquarters because he was the only member of the inner circle of the resistance to attend Hitler's staff conferences. Also, as a severely incapacitated war hero, he was spared the search normally experienced by anyone attending the conferences. Stauffenberg carried the bomb in his briefcase on three occasions—on July 11, 1944, to Berchtesgaden and to Rastenburg (to which Hitler moved on July 14) on July 15 and finally on July 20. On the two earlier occasions the attempt was abandoned because Heinrich HIMMLER and Hermann GÖRING were absent. On July 20, regardless of absences, he placed the bomb under Hitler's map table and left the conference to take a telephone call (as he claimed). He managed to bluff his way out of the complex before it was sealed off after the explosion and fly back to Berlin to take part in the abortive coup d'état. He was convinced Hitler was dead. When the conspiracy foundered around 10 o'clock that night, Stauffenberg was summarily court-martialed by Gen. Friedrich FROMM (whom he had earlier placed under arrest) and, along with Olbricht and others, executed. **R.M.**

STAUNING, Thorvald (1873–1942). Danish political figure who became Prime Minister for the first time in 1924. He then held other offices before becoming Prime Minister again in 1935. When the Germans occupied Denmark in 1940, Stauning tried to preserve his country's autonomy within the context of Nazi domination. He died in office on May 3, 1942.

STAVANGER. Seaport in southern NORWAY. Early on April 9, 1940, German paratroopers jumped into and occupied Sola airfield, Norway's largest, which is located eight miles southwest of Stavanger. Sola is the continental airfield that is closest to SCAPA FLOW, the chief British naval base. Unfortified, Stavanger was soon in German hands.

STAVELOT. Belgian town on the Amblève River where on December 17–18, 1944, during the Battle of the BULGE, a small American detachment under Maj. Paul J. Solis delayed the spearhead of the Sixth Panzer Army (Task Force PEIPER) for over 24 hours. Pouring gasoline into a road cut, Solis set it ablaze to deny the Germans access to critically needed fuel.

STEELHEAD, U.S.S. GATO-class submarine, commissioned in 1942. She completed five Pacific war patrols before a serious fire, during a stateside shipyard overhaul, made an extended repair necessary. She returned to service in mid-1945, performing "lifeguard" duty in the Caroline Islands and patrolling off Tokyo Bay. She performed training duty for a short while after V-J Day and went out of commission in 1946.

STEINER, Felix (1896–1966). A German Army officer who in 1935 retired from the Army and joined the Nazi SS (*see* SS), which developed its own divisions (WAFFEN

SS) paralleling those of the Army itself. Steiner commanded SS panzer units on the Eastern Front, in 1945 taking command of the Eleventh Panzer Army. He had been given the rank of Obergruppenführer (equivalent to lieutenant general) in 1944. At the finale of the war outside Berlin, Steiner had an assortment of troops (Group Steiner), to which Hitler vainly turned in the hope that it could block the advance of Marshal ZHUKOV's armies.

STEINHARDT, Laurence Adolph (1892–1950). A native of New York City, Steinhardt was appointed U.S. ambassador to the Soviet Union in 1939. He was responsible for diplomatic assessment of Russia's wartime activities and intentions. In January 1942 he became ambassador to Turkey.

STEN GUN. British 9-mm. submachine gun, produced through most of the war in Marks I through V. This simple, mass-produced blowback weapon without elaborate refinements was widely used by British and Commonwealth forces and was dropped into occupied Europe for underground use. The original Sten Mark I had a wooden hand guard and grip beneath the barrel, as well as a flash hider. The later Marks II through IV abandoned these fripperies; one of these models looked like something that had been put together in a pipefitter's basement. It was cheap and reasonably reliable and could be produced in quantity; this was all that mattered. The final model, the Mark V, had wooden handgrips and a wooden butt stock, with a permanently attached angular socket bayonet. All Stens could be fired single-shot or automatic; the Mark V was designed for more accurate single-shot firing and was issued to British airborne troops.

The Mark II Sten, typical of the "gas pipe" versions of this weapon, was 30 inches long from butt to muzzle, weighed about 8¼ pounds fully loaded and fired the 9-mm. Parabellum (Luger) cartridge to an effective range of about 200 yards at a cyclic rate of 500 to 550 rounds per minute. The Sten used box magazines holding 32 rounds apiece.

STEPHENSON, Sir William Samuel (1896–). British (Canadian-born) intelligence officer, director of British Security Coordination in America, 1940–45, with headquarters in New York. British Security Coordination was the cover name for the British intelligence network. Stephenson served as a channel of communication on intelligence and other matters between CHURCHILL and ROOSEVELT. A remarkably versatile man, he was a World War I flying ace and later a pioneer in electronics. He was known by the code name Intrepid.

STETTINIUS, Edward Reilly, Jr. (1900–1949). This American industrialist was brought to Washington by Franklin ROOSEVELT at the beginning of the war to serve as chairman of the War Resources Board; by the end of the war he was Secretary of State. At the War Resources Board, his responsibilities were to determine which raw materials would be needed if the United States were to enter the war. In May 1940 he was appointed to the National Defense Advisory Commission, with responsibility for industrial materials; he had resigned his chairmanship of the board of the United States Steel Corp. He served with the new OFFICE OF PRODUCTION MANAGEMENT, where his main functions related to the conservation of raw materials. Later in 1941 he was appointed administrator of the LEND-LEASE program, and in 1943 he published *Lend-Lease: Weapon for Victory*.

In October 1943 Stettinius became Under Secretary of State. The DUMBARTON OAKS conference in mid-1944 was also his direct responsibility; he collaborated with representatives from Britain, the USSR and China in preparing proposals for a world organization, later the UNITED NATIONS. He became Secretary of State on December 1, 1944. He accompanied Roosevelt to YALTA in 1945 and was a United States delegate to the U.N. conference in San Francisco.

STICKY BOMB. British grenade, intended for use against armored vehicles. It was most useful as a portable demolition charge, planted by hand. Weighing 2½ pounds, the grenade consisted of a flask of high explosive in a metal casing that was removed before use. The flask was covered with a sticky envelope by which the charge was to attach itself to the target. The bomb would not stick to a sloping surface that was muddy, wet or oily. This grenade saw a great deal of use in guerrilla operations.

STIEFF, Helmut (1901–1944). Born in Deutsch-Eylau, Major General Stieff was a German career officer who became head of the organization branch in the Army high command. He occupied a prominent position in the German Army resistance movement. At one stage it was intended that he should himself make the bomb attempt on Hitler's life, and he was the custodian of the time bombs which were to be used. It was he who prepared the bomb for STAUFFENBERG on July 20, 1944. After the failure of the attempt, he was arrested, tried by Roland FREISLER in August 1944 along with the other principal defendants, and executed. *See also* OPPOSITION TO HITLER.

STIELHANDGRANATE (Stick Hand Grenade). The well-known German "potato masher" grenade. Three models were used in World War II. The Stielhandgranate 24 and Stielhandgranate 39 were similar in design and size; the 24 carried 6 ounces of TNT, while the 39 had 22 ounces. Both types consisted of a thin-metal can-shaped head, screwed onto a hollow wooden handle. These grenades were essentially the same in construction and functioning as the earlier model used in World War I. The later Stielhandgranate 43 had its pull-igniter knob mounted on the grenade head, which was often fitted with a fragmentation sleeve, a segmented metal sleeve designed to add fragment effect to explosive blast.

STILWELL, Joseph Warren (1883–1946). A native of Florida, Stilwell graduated from West Point in 1904 and saw service in the Philippines. In World War I he was a U.S. staff officer in France. Between the wars came the experience that determined his future career—he had two tours of duty in China (1926–29 and, as military attaché in Peking, 1935–39; he had first visited the country in 1911). He learned the Chinese language and developed a wide knowledge of the Chinese people.

After Pearl Harbor he was promoted to lieutenant general and sent back to China as chief of staff to CHIANG KAI-SHEK and commander of U.S. forces in the theater. In 1942 he had command of the Chinese Fifth and Sixth Armies in BURMA and was driven from the country in a 140-mile "walkout" through difficult terrain; he stayed with his men. In 1943 his complex and unprecedented responsibilities were augmented by his being named deputy commander of the Allied SOUTHEAST ASIA COMMAND, under Lord Louis MOUNTBATTEN. In 1944, now a full general, he was recalled from the CHINA-BURMA-INDIA THEATER as a result of friction between himself and Chiang over the disposition of Chinese troops and numerous other chronic issues. His opinion of the Generalissimo is suggested by the name he gave Chiang in his diary: the Peanut. In 1945 Stilwell was appointed commander of the U.S. Tenth Army in OKINAWA. In this capacity he accepted the surrender of Japanese troops scattered throughout the Ryukyus.

Stilwell—"Vinegar Joe" to the press, "Uncle Joe" to his American troops (though he was strangely ill at ease with enlisted people)—was a complex person and one whom many found it difficult to work with. Those close to him, however, were devoted to him. *See also* CHINA.

STIMSON, Henry Lewis (1867–1950). This American statesman, a leading member of the New York Republican establishment, served the country in cabinet office under three Presidents. His last time in the cabinet was as Secretary of War under Franklin ROOSEVELT, from 1940 to 1945. Three decades earlier he had held the same office under President Taft (1911–13), and under President Hoover he served as Secretary of State (1929–33). A graduate of Yale University and the Harvard Law School, Stimson became associated with Elihu Root's Wall Street law firm and rapidly rose to a partnership. In 1927 President Coolidge appointed him Governor of the Philippines, the position he held immediately before becoming Secretary of State. In the latter post he advanced in 1931 the so-called Stimson Doctrine for nonrecognition of Japanese conquests in Manchuria—a position that disappointed many critics of Japanese expansionism, since it called for no action. But no one would argue that in 1931 the people of the Depression-ridden United States were in any mood for overseas adventure.

In June 1940, in the aftermath of the collapse of France, President Roosevelt appointed Stimson and another prominent Republican, Col. Frank KNOX, to the cabinet. Stimson, a strong advocate of aid to Britain, pushed American preparedness. He also was a point of attraction for numerous fellow Republicans who entered government service. Stimson's age proved to be no great handicap to him as Secretary; he displayed a great deal of energy and tenacity, and in particular became a leader in setting atomic policy, being one of the inner circle who originally favored the project. In concurrence with his panel of scientific advisers, he recommended to President TRUMAN that the bomb be employed.

STINGRAY, U.S.S. Salmon-class submarine. Commissioned in 1938, she was in the Philippines when war began in the Pacific. She completed 16 war patrols. On "lifeguard" duty off Guam in June 1944, she rescued four downed airmen, the fourth being saved under fire. Unable to surface because of Japanese shore-battery fire, *Stingray* approached the swimming pilot at periscope depth. Seizing the submarine's periscope, he was towed to safety. During the fall of 1944 *Stingray* carried out two supply missions to the Japanese-held Philippines; early in 1945 she landed reconnaissance parties at points on Celebes.

STIRLING, David (1915–). British officer in North Africa who in 1941 founded the SPECIAL AIR SERVICE, a force that worked behind enemy lines destroying aircraft and disrupting other transportation. Called by the Germans the "phantom major" (he was promoted to lieutenant colonel in 1942), he was captured in January 1943 after betrayal by local Arabs to the Germans.

STIRLING. Produced by Short Brothers, this British aircraft was intended from its inception as a four-engine heavy bomber and benefited from test flights with a manned half-scale model powered by light-plane engines. Despite the careful preproduction testing, the Stirling suffered from several handicaps. The bomb bay was divided into two compartments, which prevented the plane from carrying bombs larger than 4,000 pounds. The low aspect ratio of the wing made sense because of the loaded weight of 31 tons, but limited the service ceiling to a mere 17,000 feet. The Stirling was a shoulder-wing, all-metal monoplane with a slab-sided fuselage and single vertical stabilizer.

The first four-engine bomber to join RAF BOMBER COMMAND, the Stirling served from August 1940 until March 1944. It flew on its first raid in February 1941 against oil storage tanks in Rotterdam. It took part in the attack on the SCHARNHORST in July 1941 and the thousand-plane raids of 1942 but faded from prominence during the following year, assuming such duties as minelaying, radio and radar jamming, towing gliders and parachuting agents into German-held territory. The last of the Stirlings served as transports.

The most common bomber version, Stirling III, carried two-gun power turrets in the nose and atop the fuselage, plus a four-gun turret in the tail. Four 1,650-horsepower Bristol Hercules radials powered the plane, which had a top speed of 270 miles per hour, could cruise 2,010 miles with 3,500 pounds of bombs and could carry a maximum bomb load of 14,000 pounds.

STOPFORD, Sir Montagu George North (1892–1971). British Army officer (lieutenant general) who was an outstanding figure in the fighting in India and BURMA as commander of the 33d Indian Corps, which relieved the garrison at KOHIMA in April 1944 and participated in the pursuit of the Japanese across Burma. Stopford was commander of the 17th Infantry Brigade, BRITISH EXPEDITIONARY FORCE, in 1939–40; General Officer Commanding, 56th (London) Division, 1941–42; commandant of the Staff College, 1942–43. In 1943 he went to Burma in command of the 33d Indian Corps, the post he held until 1945.

STORCH. The Fieseler Fi 156 Storch (Stork), a high-wing, single-engine monoplane used by the German Army in large numbers for command transport, liaison, artillery spotting and general utility work. With a top speed of 109 miles per hour, the Storch had a slow landing speed and could land and take off from restricted spaces and rough fields. A rugged, dependable airplane, it was well liked by the troops who used it. Numbers of them continued to fly for private owners after the war. The most famous use of a Storch was in Otto SKORZENY's 1943 rescue of MUSSOLINI.

STOUMONT. Belgian town in the valley of the Amblève River where on December 19, 1944, during the Battle of the BULGE, a hastily committed battalion of the U.S. 30th Division delayed the spearhead of the Sixth Panzer Army (Task Force PEIPER) for several hours, forcing gasoline-short German tanks to use up critical fuel and providing time for an American tank company to be outfitted with tanks from a repair depot and block further advance to the west. As infantry reinforcements arrived, German egress from the valley was denied. The 30th Division retook the town on the 22d.

STRAIGHT FLUSH. The U.S. B-29 that flew as the weather plane for the ATOMIC BOMB attack on HIROSHIMA, August 6, 1945.

STRANG, Sir William (1893–1978). Under Secretary in the British Foreign Office from 1939 until 1943, Strang served as the United Kingdom's representative to the EUROPEAN ADVISORY COMMISSION in 1943–45. He was the author of the "exportable surpluses" theory and insisted upon Russia's obligation to provide for western Europe foodstuffs from the occupied eastern European countries. In 1939 he had participated in the abortive Anglo-French-Soviet negotiations in Moscow. Though an able official, he was a subordinate-enough figure to suggest that the British did not take the prospect of an alliance with Russia very seriously.

STRANGLE. Code name of an Allied air operation, begun in March 1944, "to reduce the enemy's flow of supplies to a level which will make it impractical for him to maintain and operate his forces in central ITALY." First priority went to rail transportation, thus forcing the Germans to turn to the highways, which then became the prime target of Allied airmen. At first the attackers sought to achieve simultaneous interdiction using swarms of fighter-bombers all along the rail lines leading south from the Po valley, but results here and lessons learned from similar efforts in France caused them to concentrate on marshaling yards, bridges, viaducts and other choke points. Medium and heavy bombers proved effective against rail yards, and the Allied Coastal Air Force sent WELLINGTONS, Mitchells (*see* B-25) and BEAUFIGHTERS against inshore shipping.

Strangle hampered the enemy supply effort, but the Germans maintained their forces by impressing Italian food and trucks for their own use and by moving at night whenever possible. The defenders had, however, been weakened by May 11, when the Allies began their drive on Rome.

STRASBOURG. Historic French city on the Rhine River, looked upon symbolically as the capital of the ancient provinces of Alsace and Lorraine, which the French were forced to surrender following the Franco-Prussian War of 1870 and again following the defeat of 1940.

The French 2d Armored Division having recaptured Strasbourg on November 23, 1944, the French were appalled when in the face of a pending German counteroffensive in Alsace (Operation NORDWIND), the Supreme Allied Commander, Gen. Dwight D. EISENHOWER, contemplated withdrawing to a sturdier defensive line in the Vosges Mountains to the west and abandoning the city. Relenting in the face of French protests, Eisenhower shifted responsibility for defending Strasbourg from American to French troops, who stopped the German thrust short of the city.

STRASBOURG. French light battleship of 26,500 tons, completed at Saint-Nazaire in 1938, armed with eight 13-inch and sixteen 5.1-inch guns, together with smaller weapons and four aircraft. By the brilliant seamanship of her captain, Collinet, *Strasbourg* managed to escape unscathed from the Royal Navy's attack on MERS-EL-KÉBIR on July 3, 1940, reaching TOULON damaged only by one aircraft torpedo hit. When the Germans moved to seize the French ships on November 27, 1942, *Strasbourg* was the flagship of the French naval commander at Toulon, Admiral de LABORDE. With German tanks rushing through the dockyard toward her, Laborde gave the order "Scuttle" to his flagship and fleet; *Strasbourg*'s crew destroyed the gun turrets and scuttled the ship.

STRATEGIC BOMBING. At the outset of the war in Europe, RAF BOMBER COMMAND attempted daylight attacks against military targets and tried to keep German civilian casualties at a minimum. Since losses among the small, unescorted formations at times reached 50 percent, the effort verged on the suicidal and was promptly abandoned. Meanwhile, leaflet-carrying aircraft were droning, almost with impunity, through the night skies of Germany. Bomber Command therefore shifted to night operations against factories and military installations. Losses declined, but even in bright moonlight the results were poor, and the smoke that hovered over the industrial RUHR valley frustrated even the best-trained bombardiers. A new course was therefore decided on—night raids designed primarily to force Germany's industrial workers to desert their jobs. The targets were to be industrial cities rather than individual factories or military installations.

In the meantime the United States had entered the war, and Army Air Forces B-17Es had been sent to Britain (*see* B-17). In the summer of 1942 these planes, usually with fighter escort, made their first daylight strikes against German-occupied Europe. The British doubted the feasibility of a sustained aerial offensive against Germany conducted by day, but the Americans—believing strongly in daylight precision bombing—resisted all attempts to absorb them into an Allied night bombing force. Coordination between the two strategic bombing campaigns was necessary, and this was provided by a directive drawn up as a result of the conference of Allied leaders held at CASABLANCA in January 1943.

This document attempted to establish priorities for a systematic Anglo-American air attack upon Germany's war-making potential. The targets, in order of importance, were submarine yards, the aircraft industry, transportation, the oil industry and other industrial targets. By summer, however, the submarine menace seemed less grave, and Allied planners had come to realize that first priority would have to go to the destruction of the German fighter force.

The emphasis on destroying segments of enemy industry did not affect the employment of Bomber Command. Air Marshal Sir Arthur HARRIS, chief of Bomber Command, resisted the idea of bombing what he termed "panacea targets" and continued his nighttime battering of German cities to "dehouse" the workers who inhabited them. During August 1943 these tactics were employed on four raids that incinerated HAMBURG, killing some 50,000 persons.

The Americans, meanwhile, were discovering that bomber formations could not penetrate deep into Germany without fighter escort. Serious losses resulted during two daylight precision strikes, in August and October 1943, against the ball-bearing factories at distant SCHWEINFURT, one of the panacea targets against which Harris inveighed. Only the arrival of the P-51 Mustang (*see* P-51) enabled the daylight offensive to continue. This fighter, when fitted with jettisonable auxiliary fuel tanks, could escort the bombers even to Berlin itself.

The destruction of Germany's fighter force proved a difficult undertaking. Precision attacks on aircraft plants were less effective than American planners had expected; indeed, production of first-line aircraft actually increased despite the raids. This statistic is misleading, however, for the number of skilled German pilots was fast declining, in part the result of the deadly escort that now accompanied the American bombers. Also, while Bomber Command completed its devastation of the Ruhr, the B-17s and B-24s (*see* B-24) in mid-1944 launched a systematic attack on the synthetic-oil industry. The LUFTWAFFE began feeling the effects of the oil offensive as early as the fall of 1944, and as the bomb tonnage directed at these plants increased, Germany's air arm literally "ran out of gas." This destruction of the synthetic-oil facilities and the Allied conquest of the Ruhr left the bombers with few worthwhile strategic targets. The air war in Europe ended with a series of attacks on German transportation.

Clearly, the strategic bomber helped defeat Germany, though not precisely in the manner predicted by its enthusiasts. Despite the battering received from Harris's squadrons, Germany's workers did not desert their machines, though absences and casualties did complicate production. Similarly, German factories, except for the synthetic-oil plants, proved far more resilient than American planners expected, and, also contrary to expectation, bomber formations could not survive sustained fighter attack without escort. Finally, the distinction between area bombing and precision attack had become blurred as the fight wore on.

Strategic bombardment became operative against Japan when the new B-29s (*see* B-29), operating from bases in China, began high-altitude precision strikes against Japanese industry in the summer of 1944. The Chinese airfields were at the end of a long and arduous supply line, which meant that no sustained offensive could be mounted from them, and, furthermore, Japanese ground forces soon made them untenable. Operations from the recently captured MARIANA ISLANDS got under way in November 1944, but small formations, attempting to hit precise targets from 30,000 feet, did not achieve the anticipated results. With the arrival of Maj. Gen. Curtis E. LEMAY, the Marianas-based B-29s scrapped precision bombing in favor of area attack with incendiary bombs.

When incendiary attack from high altitude proved disappointing, LeMay decided to exploit Japan's inadequate night defenses by bringing his bombers over Japanese cities at low altitude during darkness. The first such raid took place on the night of March 9–10, 1945, left much of TOKYO in ashes and inaugurated a series of similarly destructive attacks against Japanese cities, which, because of the extensive use of wood in their construction, were mortally vulnerable to fire.

By the time the fire raids began, Japan was critically short of planes, trained pilots and oil. Her fleet was all but destroyed. The destruction of more factories was hardly necessary. Area attacks using incendiaries, followed by the dropping of two ATOMIC BOMBS—supreme strategic bombardment—forced Japanese authorities to accept the necessity of surrender. **B.N.**

STRATEGIC BOMBING SURVEY, U.S. A combined civilian-military organization established by the Secretary of War on November 3, 1944, by direction of the President. Headed by Franklin D'Olier, the organization, which called for 300 civilians, 350 military officers and 500 enlisted men, was initially headquartered in London. Its original mission was to compile an expert, objective study of the effects of air attack on Germany, to be used as a basis for planning the final aerial assault on Japan and also for planning postwar defense policy. On August 15, 1945, with the end of the Pacific war, President TRUMAN directed the survey to make a similar study of the Pacific campaign. The results of the survey's work were published in two series of reports (European War and Pacific War), totaling 316 individual titles. They have been extensively used as sources of information on operations, as well as on the industrial resources and war efforts of Germany and Japan.

STRATEMEYER, George E. (1890–1969). A brigadier general when the United States entered the war, Stratemeyer became a major general in June 1942 and served for about a year as Chief of the Air Staff for Gen. Henry H. ARNOLD. From Washington he went to the CHINA-BURMA-INDIA THEATER, where he was both air adviser to the theater commander and commanding general of the India-Burma sector. In December 1943 he assumed command of U.S. Army Air Forces throughout the theater. Promoted to lieutenant general in May 1945, he received a new assignment in July, becoming Commanding General, U.S. Army Air Forces in China.

STREICHER, Julius (1885–1946). A former Nuremberg schoolmaster and a man of coarse and brutal habits, Streicher entered politics in 1911. He joined the

Nazi Party in 1921, amalgamating his own anti-Semitic German Socialist Party with Adolf HITLER's movement, and he took part in the abortive putsch in Munich in 1923. He was notorious for his obscene and provocative anti-Semitic journal, *Der Stürmer,* which he founded in 1922 and edited himself until 1933. It circulated at first only in Bavaria; after 1933 it achieved a national circulation of half a million, as well as being put on prominent display as a wall newspaper. It therefore received semiofficial support from the Nazi Party until it was finally discontinued in 1943.

Streicher was party gauleiter of Franconia from 1925 until 1940, after which he fell into disfavor on account of his disreputable conduct. The other Nazi leaders disliked him intensely, and it was only Hitler's curious, conservative loyalty to his original supporters that sustained him in office for so long. During the war period he lived in enforced retirement, working as a farmer. His private interests included collecting pornography. He was tried as a war criminal at Nuremberg and executed; his speeches and writings were deemed to have constituted incitement to mass murder. *See also* NATIONAL SOCIALIST GERMAN WORKERS' PARTY.

STRONG, George Veazey (1880–1946). U.S. Army officer who before American entry into the war was chief of the Army planning staff. In this capacity Strong, a major general, was one of three officers (the others were Rear Adm. Robert L. GHORMLEY and Maj. Gen. Delos C. EMMONS) who represented the United States in Anglo-American staff conferences in London in August–September 1940, at the height of the Battle of BRITAIN. Strong and his colleagues reported to their chiefs in highly favorable terms on the British resistance to the Germans, thus helping to influence American policy toward increased assistance to Britain. In 1941 General Strong took a domestic command (8th Corps Area), and in 1942 he was named head of the Military Intelligence Division. He retired in 1944 but was recalled to serve with the JOINT CHIEFS OF STAFF. He was an adviser at the DUMBARTON OAKS conference and at the Pan-American Conference of 1945.

STRONG, Kenneth William Dobson (1900–). British Army officer, head of the intelligence staff for Gen. Dwight EISENHOWER at SUPREME HEADQUARTERS, ALLIED EXPEDITIONARY FORCE. Before the war Strong had served as assistant military attaché in Berlin, and for the first year and a half of the war he was head of the German section of the War Office. In 1942–43 he was head of intelligence of the Home Forces and in 1943–44 chief of intelligence of Allied Force Headquarters in the Mediterranean. His highest wartime rank was major general. Subsequently (1964–66) General Strong was the first director general of intelligence at the Ministry of Defence.

STROOP, Jürgen (1901–1951). The German SS officer and police general who suppressed the WARSAW ghetto uprising in 1943. Brigadeführer Stroop produced a detailed report, called *The Warsaw Ghetto Is No More.* He was sentenced to death by an American court at Dachau in 1947 for the shooting of hostages in Greece and then was tried in Poland for the killing of the Jews in the Warsaw ghetto. He was hanged in Warsaw in 1951.

STRUBLE, Arthur Dewey (1894–). A 1915 graduate of the U.S. Naval Academy, Struble served in the office of the Chief of Naval Operations from 1942 to 1944, when he became chief of staff for Adm. Alan G. KIRK in Operation Overlord (the INVASION of Normandy). Rear Admiral Struble saw his greatest action in the Pacific, however, where he commanded an attack group at LEYTE GULF and other campaigns in the Philippines. In September 1945 he became commander of amphibious forces for the Pacific Fleet. He retired in 1956.

STRYDONCK DE BURKEL, Victor van (1876–1961). Belgian general who, after the fall of Belgium in May 1940, escaped to England and became commander of the Free Belgian Forces. In September 1944, as the Allied armies freed his country, he returned to lead the Belgian military mission to General EISENHOWER's headquarters.

STUART. *See* TANK.

STUDENT, Kurt (1890–1978). Germany's chief airborne commander, General Student was involved on all fronts of the war. In 1940 he commanded the parachute troops that secured bridges over the Rhine in the Netherlands. In 1941–43 he commanded XI Parachute Corps (Fliegerkorps), which in May 1941 led the spectacular and unprecedented but costly conquest of CRETE. Student was an energetic officer, respected by Adolf HITLER, and in the fall of 1944 he was put in command of a formation called the First Parachute Army against the Allies in Belgium; he was later given command of Army Group H (First Parachute and Fifteenth Armies) in the west. Hence Student, now a colonel general, was not only commander in chief of airborne forces but was an important ground commander. In April, as the defenses of BERLIN were disintegrating, Generals KEITEL and JODL, the chief German staff officers, sought to have Student assume command of the army group north of the city in succession to Gen. Gotthard HEINRICI. But the time for the defense of Berlin was past.

STUDIE ENGLAND. German plan for the invasion of England, produced in May 1940 by the Naval War Staff Operations Division, under Rear Adm. Kurt Fricke.

STUKA. *See* JUNKERS JU 87.

STÜLPNAGEL, Karl Heinrich von (1886–1944). Stülpnagel was German military governor of France, 1942–44, and the principal instigator of the coup d'état in France on behalf of the Army resistance movement in Germany. He had trained originally in the infantry school at Dresden at the same time as Erwin ROMMEL, who by 1944 also favored a coup against Adolf HITLER. Rommel had remained a friend of Stülpnagel, who relied a great deal on Rommel's popularity and influence on the day of action. When Rommel was seriously wounded on July 17, 1944, Stülpnagel was the only commanding general in France wholeheartedly dedicated to the conspiracy. Nevertheless, he and those of his junior officers involved with him were highly successful in their operation, arresting the senior officers of the SS and the Gestapo on the evening of July 20, though they failed to win over Field Marshal von KLUGE, Commander in Chief West, when the latter realized that Hitler had not in fact been killed. Placed in an impossible position, Stülpnagel attempted suicide but failed. He was arrested, tried by Roland FREISLER in the Nazi People's Court and executed in August 1944. *See also* OPPOSITION TO HITLER.

STUMME, Georg (1886–1942). German Army officer, a lieutenant general at the beginning of the war, promoted to General der Panzertruppen in 1941 just before the invasion of the Soviet Union, in which he participated as a corps commander. His career took a bizarre turn in the following June (1942) when a staff officer of one of his divisions allowed plans for an attack to fall into Soviet hands. Stumme and his chief of staff were held responsible for the lapse, and both were sentenced to imprisonment; however, Stumme's sentence was commuted and he was dispatched to NORTH AFRICA, where in September he succeeded the ailing Field Marshal ROMMEL as temporary commander of the Axis forces. Stumme was thus in command when the second battle of ALAMEIN opened in October. On October 24, the second day of the battle, he drove to the front, where his car encountered heavy fire. The general fell from the car and died of a heart attack.

STUMP, Felix Budwell (1894–1972). U.S. Navy officer, a graduate of the Naval Academy in 1917. By 1940 Stump had become commanding officer of the aircraft carrier ENTERPRISE. In 1942 he became director of the combined Allied intelligence operations in the Pacific. In 1943 he was appointed commander of the new carrier LEXINGTON for the naval operations in the MARSHALLS to be carried out in early 1944, and later in 1944, as a rear admiral, he commanded an escort carrier group at LEYTE GULF. After the war Stump became U.S. commander in chief in the Pacific (1953–58).

STUMPFF, Hans Jürgen (1889–1968). German air officer who joined the General Staff of the LUFTWAFFE in 1934, becoming Chief of Staff in 1937, a post he held until 1939. In 1940 Stumpff led the Luftwaffe in operations in NORWAY and in May became commander in chief in the area and commander of Air Fleet (Luftflotte) 5, which participated, though in a minor way, in the Battle of BRITAIN. In the latter phases of the war he commanded the home air force (Luftflotte Reich).

STUTTGART RAIDS. Although RAF BOMBER COMMAND made several raids on Stuttgart in 1940–42, the first major raid took place in March 1943. It was a failure, because the main force arrived too late behind the target markers. A raid on October 7, 1943, was more successful, with a small loss of aircraft. Successful heavy attacks were launched in February and March 1944, again with small casualties. The ball-bearing plant was one of the main objectives. In all, Bomber Command dropped 21,016 tons of bombs on Stuttgart in the period 1940–45.

SUBAŠIĆ, Ivan (1892–1955). Yugoslav politician who was *ban* (governor) of Croatia at the time of the German invasion in 1941. In 1944 he was selected by King PETER to form a government that would be acceptable to Marshal TITO, and agreements were reached that preserved a measure of harmony till the end of hostilities.

SUBIC BAY. Natural harbor in the Philippines, separated from Manila Bay, 10 miles east, by the Bataan peninsula, used as an American naval base.

SUDA BAY. The chief harbor of CRETE, occupied by the British at the end of October 1940. It fell to German airborne attackers on May 26, 1941.

SUDETENLAND. Region of CZECHOSLOVAKIA along the frontier with Germany. It held about 3.25 million ethnic Germans, who after the rise of Adolf HITLER became increasingly pro-Nazi. Although there was much talk at the time about the Sudeten Germans "returning" to Germany, they had never in fact been part of a modern German state but, as part of Bohemia, had belonged to the Holy Roman Empire and its successor, Austria. Nevertheless, Hitler used the situation of the Sudeten Germans as a minority in the Czech state to spearhead his diplomatic propaganda attack on Czechoslovakia. At MUNICH the four powers (Britain, France, Germany, Italy) agreed to the transfer of the Sudeten districts to Germany. The Czech Government was not consulted.

SUEZ CANAL. The Suez Canal was the most vulnerable point in the British artery of sea communications with the Far East, and the need to protect it prompted British resistance to Italian threats to Egypt and the Red Sea area. The possibility that the Axis would close the canal led the British to develop the port of Suez to supply their Egyptian army. At times during the war the canal was closed, once by mines dropped from German planes, and the resulting strain on British shipping was severe.

SUFFOLK, H.M.S. Royal Navy heavy cruiser of 10,000 tons, completed in 1927 at Portsmouth and armed with eight 8-inch and eight 4-inch guns, smaller weapons, eight 21-inch torpedo tubes (later removed) and four aircraft. *Suffolk* served in the Home Fleet until 1943, participating in the Norwegian campaign and various bombardment and strike operations in the far north, including cover for convoys to Russia. In May 1941 she particularly distinguished herself by tenacious shadowing and accurate reporting of the movements of the BISMARCK despite difficult conditions of snow, ice floes and rain. In 1943 *Suffolk* was moved to the Indian Ocean, where she served until 1945.

SUGAR LOAF HILL. A dominating point in the Japanese defenses ringed about SHURI, southeast of Amike on OKINAWA, first encountered by the U.S. 6th Marine Division on May 14, 1945. Its defenses were fully integrated with other positions on Half Moon and Horseshoe, and the taking of one was meaningless and just about impossible without capture of at least one of the other two. This complex did not fall to the Marines until a week later, after fierce fighting resulted in heavy casualties on both sides.

SUGIYAMA, Hajime (1880–1945). A Japanese Army field marshal who held virtually every important Army post during his career. Sugiyama was appointed Vice-Minister of War in 1930 and director of the Army's Aviation Headquarters in 1933. He became Inspector General of Military Education in 1936, Minister of War in 1937, Commander in Chief of the Japanese Army in northern China in 1938 and Chief of the Army General Staff in 1940. He was promoted to field marshal in 1943. As Chief of the General Staff, Sugiyama was responsible for overall Army strategy. Shortly after a devastating Allied raid on Japanese forces on the island of TRUK in mid-February 1944, Hideki TOJO, then both Prime Minister and War Minister, ousted Sugiyama from his position as Chief of Staff and took the post himself. When Tojo's cabinet was forced to resign in July 1944, Sugiyama became War Minister in the KOISO cabinet. Upon the resignation of this cabinet in April 1945, Sugiyama was appointed commander of the First Imperial Army and made responsible for Japan's home defenses. He and his wife committed suicide on September 12, 1945, in their home.

SUICIDE BOAT. Various small one-to-three-man craft, the Japanese Navy's counterparts of the KAMIKAZE, employed by surface raiding units. Many suicide boats were fast, 18½-foot plywood boats carrying several hundred pounds of explosive to make a crashing attack upon enemy ships at anchor in transport areas off landing beaches. Suicide boats appeared first at the LINGAYEN GULF landings in January 1945, and later that year were at OKINAWA.

SULFA DRUGS. Although the ability of sulfa drugs (medically known as sulfonamides) to kill bacteria in infected laboratory mice had not been reported until 1935, sulfa drugs were in general use during World War II. They were used in the treatment of diseases such as pneumonia, meningitis, dysentery, boils and other skin infections, blood poisoning and venereal diseases. Because some bacteria become increasingly resistant to sulfonamides, mass prophylaxis to control the spread of tonsillitis, scarlet fever and other diseases was not fully successful. Nevertheless, the use of sulfa drugs helped to keep the ratio of American fatalities per 100 wounded to less than one-half the ratio of World War I. *See also* MEDICINE.

SULLIVAN, William Aloysius (1894–). Captain Sullivan, USNR, rose to commodore as the Navy's number one salvage expert, plying his trade from the Mediterranean to Manila. He directed the clearing of the harbors at Casablanca, Palermo and NAPLES. Following the D-Day invasion, he cleared the harbor at CHERBOURG, where German mines presented more problems than did the actual efforts at demolition. MANILA was another story. Sullivan found the Japanese to be more efficient at demolition than the Germans. His method of dealing with sunken ships was to have divers seal the hulk, then pump it full of air. When the hulk surfaced, it was towed aside.

SULLIVAN BROTHERS. George T., 29, gunner's mate second class; Francis H., 26, coxswain; Joseph E., 23, seaman second class; Madison A., 22, seaman second class; and Albert L., 20, seaman second class. These five brothers, sons of Mr. and Mrs. Thomas F. Sullivan of Waterloo, Iowa, died when their ship, the cruiser JUNEAU, was sunk on November 14, 1942, during the battle for GUADALCANAL. The Navy's policy was to separate members of the same family in wartime service, but the brothers had enlisted (January 3, 1942), with the provision that they not be separated. Consequently, their loss was probably the greatest ever suffered by a single family in American naval history. A destroyer, *The Sullivans* (launched April 1943), was named after them, and 20th Century–Fox made a movie about their lives (1944).

SULTAN, Daniel Isom (1885–1947). A West Point graduate who saw prewar service in the U.S. Army Engineers, General Sultan arrived in India on January 2, 1944, where he first served as deputy to Lt. Gen. Joseph W. STILWELL, commander of the CHINA-BURMA-INDIA THEATER (CBI). Stilwell was recalled on October 18, 1944, and the CBI was split into the China Theater (CT) and the India-Burma Theater. Sultan was made commander of the latter with a primary mission of support to the CT in carrying out its responsibilities in China. Serving concurrently as a field commander, Sultan directed Allied combat forces in the reopening of overland communications to China and assisted the British in the defeat of the Japanese in BURMA. Subsequent to World War II, Sultan, a lieutenant general, was appointed Inspector General, U.S. Army.

SUMMERSBY, Kay (1908–1975). A native of County Cork, Ireland, Mrs. Summersby (née McCarthy-Morrogh) joined the British Transport Service in World War II and served as a chauffeur to Gen. Dwight D. EISENHOWER from July 1942 to October 1944, when she was given a direct commission in the U.S. WOMEN'S ARMY CORPS as a second lieutenant. Thereafter she served as a private secretary to General Eisenhower until the end of the war. She resigned her commission in 1946; in 1950 she was made a U.S. citizen. In 1952 she married Reginald H. Morgan; the couple were divorced in 1958.

SUNDA STRAITS. This narrow passage, which separates the islands of Sumatra and JAVA, was the scene of a savage action on the night of February 28, 1942, when the Australian cruiser PERTH and the U.S. cruiser HOUSTON encountered the Japanese invasion force which was attacking Java. The two cruisers had that morning reached Batavia after the disastrous Battle of the JAVA SEA, and were ordered by the Dutch Adm. Conrad HELFRICH to leave Batavia the same night and sail to TJILATJAP through the Sunda Straits. At 11 P.M. the two cruisers found the way barred by an overwhelming Japanese force; although they did much damage to the Japanese troop transports, both were eventually sunk after fighting until not a round was left in their magazines. Capt. H. M. L. Waller of the *Perth* and Capt. A. H. Rooks of the *Houston* were both lost with their ships.

SUNDERLAND. Descended from the Short Brothers Empire series of commercial flying boats, this British plane entered service in 1938 as a replacement for the biplane patrol craft being used by the RAF and remained with COASTAL COMMAND for 17 years. The Sunderland was a high-wing monoplane with fixed floats inboard of the wing tips. Because of its bristling armament—powered-operated turrets, each containing four .303-caliber machine guns, in both nose and tail and either manually operated beam guns or a two-gun dorsal turret—the Sunderland earned the nickname Flying Porcupine. Attacked by eight JUNKERS JU 88s over the Bay of Biscay, a lone Sunderland skimmed the waves to protect its vulnerable belly, shot down three of the German planes and drove off the rest. Early models were powered by four 1,065-horsepower Bristol Pegasus radials, replaced in the Sunderland V of August 1943 by Pratt and Whitney Wasps, each developing 1,200 horsepower. Although maximum speed was a mere 213 miles per hour, Sunderland V could fly 2,980 miles at 134 miles per hour and remain aloft for 13½ hours.

SUNFISH, U.S.S. Submarine, commanded by Lt. Comdr. E. E. Shelby, which sank two Japanese merchant ships off the Marianas in the early morning of February 23, 1944.

SUNFLOWER (Sonnenblume). Code name for the sending of German forces to the aid of the Italians in Tripolitania. The commander of these forces was Gen. Erwin ROMMEL, who arrived in Tripoli on February 12, 1941.

SUNRISE. Code name for the negotiations that led to the surrender of the German forces in ITALY in May 1945. Winston CHURCHILL, who closely followed the secret talks, independently gave them the name Crossword. *See also* DULLES, ALLEN.

SUOMUSSALMI. Site of a battle in the winter war, December 1940. The Russian 44th and 163d Divisions tried a pincers movement focusing on the East Karelian town of Suomussalmi. The 163d arrived at the town on December 7; the Finnish 9th Division attacked them on the 11th and virtually surrounded the force. The Russians twice were unable to break out. The Finnish Army killed or captured 30,000 Russian troops in the battle, took most of the divisional equipment and managed to hold their casualties to fewer than 3,000. *See also* SOVIET-FINNISH WAR.

SUPERCHARGE I. Code name for Gen. B. L. MONTGOMERY'S knockout blow, following LIGHTFOOT, during the second battle of ALAMEIN. Infantry was to attack at night with the armor following closely. The area of attack was a 4,000-yard front in the northern sector of the line. Supercharge began November 2, 1942, and had succeeded by November 4.

SUPERCHARGE II. Code name for Gen. B. L. MONTGOMERY'S shifted battle plan for the assault of the MARETH LINE, March 1943. When the main attack failed to penetrate, Supercharge II threw the main strength to Gen. Bernard FREYBERG'S flank attack. Plans included a daylight air assault and a rolling artillery barrage.

SUPERFORTRESS. *See* B-29.

SUPER-GYMNAST. Code name given at the ARCADIA CONFERENCE to a proposed Anglo-American landing in NORTHWEST AFRICA. The plan added a U.S. landing at Casablanca to an already planned British landing in Algeria (Gymnast). For various reasons, including setbacks to the British in the Libyan desert fighting, Super-Gymnast did not become operational. The Northwest African landing that ultimately was carried out (November 1942) was called Torch.

SUPREME COUNCIL FOR THE CONDUCT OF THE WAR. A Japanese body instituted in August 1944 soon after the KOISO cabinet was formed. It was made up of the Prime Minister, the Foreign Minister and the chiefs of the armed services.

SUPREME HEADQUARTERS, ALLIED EXPEDITIONARY FORCE (SHAEF). SHAEF succeeded the organization known as COSSAC (Chief of Staff to the Supreme Allied Commander), which conducted the early planning for the invasion of northwest Europe. SHAEF was generally functioning by the middle of January 1944, and U.S. Gen. Dwight D. EISENHOWER assumed formal command on February 13. SHAEF was at first quartered in the former COSSAC headquarters at Norfolk House, London, but moved in March 1944 to BUSHY PARK in the suburbs. There were also advance headquarters in England (SHARPENER) and France (SHELLBURST). On September 1, 1944, SHAEF moved to Jullouville in Normandy, and on September 15 to Versailles, being quartered in the Trianon Palace Hotel and other buildings. An advance headquarters was opened at Gueux, near Reims, on September 19, and on February 17, 1945, the forward echelon of SHAEF made the move to Reims. During these moves SHAEF continued to maintain rear offices in England.

It was at the Reims headquarters that the Allies accepted the German surrender on May 7, 1945. In December 1943 the COSSAC staff consisted of 215 U.S. officers, 204 U.S. enlisted men, 274 British officers and 410 other ranks. By July 12, 1944, SHAEF had 1,185 officers, 101 warrant officers and 3,628 enlisted personnel. The chart at right shows the organization of SHAEF on the day of the Normandy INVASION.

SUPREME WAR COUNCIL. The name given to meetings of British and French leaders from the beginning of the war to the fall of France in 1940. The last meeting was at Briare, near Orléans, on June 11-12.

SURABAYA. Port on the northeast coast of JAVA, the main naval headquarters of the Dutch Squadron in those waters when the Japanese entered the war in December 1941. It was the principal Allied base, with Dutch, American, British and Australian ships under Dutch overall command, until the whole of Java was overrun (March 1942). When the Allied forces were later able to turn to the offensive, Surabaya was heavily attacked by naval aircraft from the carriers of the British Eastern Fleet in May 1944 and considerable damage done to the oil refinery and dockyard.

SURCOUF. French submarine, the largest in the world at the time. She was armed with 10 torpedo tubes and

SUPREME HEADQUARTERS, ALLIED EXPEDITIONARY FORCE, JUNE 6, 1944

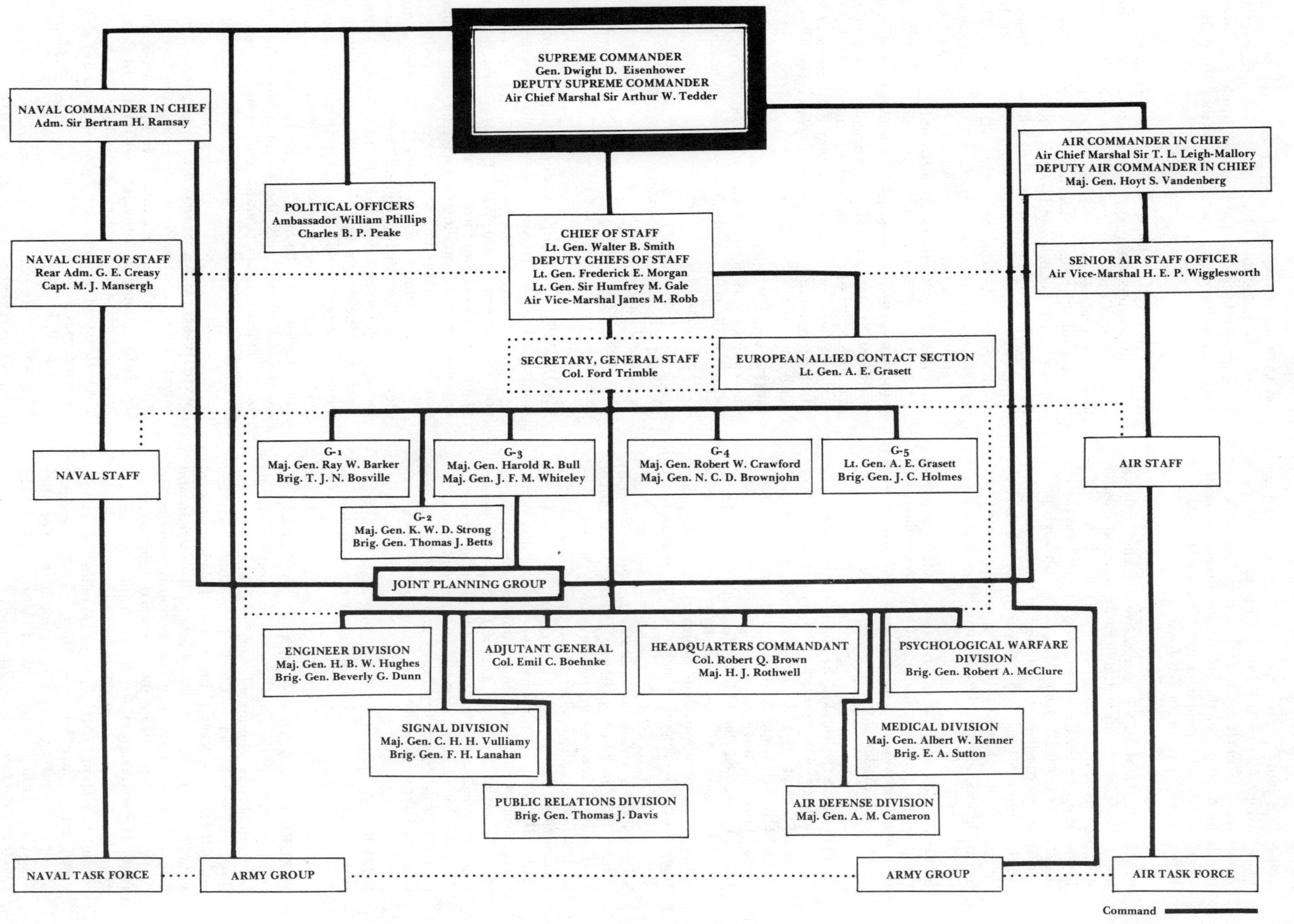

two 8-inch guns and equipped with a watertight seaplane hangar. After the fall of France, *Surcouf* came under Free French control. Declared lost with 207 hands in April 1942, the submarine presumably sank after collision with the merchant ship *Thompson Lykes* on February 18, 1942, in the Caribbean.

SURIBACHI, MOUNT. An active volcano 556 feet high, the most prominent and easily recognizable terrain feature of the island of Iwo Jima. It was a key defensive position for the Japanese, who could see the entire U.S. beachhead from its top. The photograph by Joe Rosenthal of the flag-raising on Suribachi by five marines and a Navy hospital corpsman on February 23, 1945, was one of the outstanding pictures of the war. Suribachi was called by the code name Hotrocks.

SUSDAL. Town northeast of Moscow, site of a prison camp where Axis prisoners were kept in conditions of extreme deprivation. Two hundred men a day were said to have died of starvation.

SUTHERLAND, Richard Kenneth (1893–1966). U.S. Army officer who served as Gen. Douglas MacArthur's chief of staff between 1939 and 1945. In 1944 Sutherland was promoted to lieutenant general. At the Japanese surrender ceremony on the U.S.S. Missouri, he learned that Col. L. Moore Cosgrave of Canada had signed on the wrong line. Sutherland lined through the names of four countries above misplaced signatures and wrote in the names of the countries.

SUWANNEE, U.S.S. Sangamon-class escort aircraft carrier, built in 1938–39 as the commercial oil tanker *Markay* and taken over by the Navy in 1941 as the fleet oiler *Suwannee*. She operated with the Atlantic Fleet in this capacity for six months. Early in 1942 she began conversion to an aircraft carrier and recommissioned in September of that year. In November she supported the invasion of North Africa. In December, *Suwannee* was reassigned to the Pacific. Off the Philippines during the battle for Leyte, *Suwannee* was damaged by a kamikaze that crashed her flight deck and ignited a gasoline fire. She later took part in the capture of Okinawa.

SUZUKAZE. Japanese Shiratsuyu-class destroyer, sunk by an American submarine off the Carolines on January 26, 1944.

SUZUKI, Kantaro (1867–1948). During his 40 years of active service in the Japanese Navy, Admiral Suzuki held numerous commands and positions, including those of Commander in Chief of the Combined Fleet and Chief of the Navy General Staff. Following his retirement in 1929, he became Grand Chamberlain and concurrently a privy councillor. Seriously wounded by Army extremists during the attempted coup d'état of 1936, Suzuki resigned as Grand Chamberlain but remained a member of the Privy Council, of which he became president in 1944. A political moderate who favored peace, Suzuki formed Japan's last war cabinet (April 7–August 15, 1945), resigning as Premier after Emperor Hirohito's broadcast of his acceptance of the Allied peace terms.

SWAMP. An Allied naval and air operation developed in 1943 to make life so hazardous for German submarines in the Mediterranean that they would have to stay under until forced up for air, when they would be attacked.

SWASTIKA. The symbol of the Nazi German regime (officially adopted in 1935). The swastika was in form an equal cross with arms bent at right angles in a clockwise direction. Because of the belief that it was an Aryan symbol, the swastika came to represent for the Nazis racial superiority and anti-Semitism. The official flag of the Third Reich consisted of a black swastika in a white circle on a red background. This banner had been adopted by the Nazi Party in 1920; in Mein Kampf, Adolf Hitler claimed it as his invention, though it actually appears to have been designed by a party member named Friedrich Krohn.

SWEENEY, Charles W. (1919–). Pilot of a U.S. B-29, *The Great Artiste*, that carried observers and scientific gear in support of the Hiroshima bombing. On August 9, 1945, Major Sweeney flew another B-29, Bock's Car, which dropped the atomic bomb on Nagasaki.

SWIFT, Innis Palmer (1882–1953). U.S. Army officer who commanded the 1st Cavalry Division in the Pacific theater in 1941–44 and subsequently commanded a corps.

SWORD BEACH. Code name of the British assault area (the Lion-sur-Mer beach) on the extreme left of the Allied line in the Normandy invasion, June 6, 1944.

SWORDFISH. An open-cockpit biplane torpedo bomber and reconnaissance plane, which entered service with Britain's Fleet Air Arm in 1936 and saw action throughout World War II. Fairey designed the plane as a private venture and naval authorities were impressed with its handling characteristics and its ability to carry a 1,610-pound, 18-inch aerial torpedo or a 1,500-pound mine or 1,500 pounds of bombs. Armament was one forward-firing machine gun and another mounted in the rear cockpit. The radial engine, either a 690-horsepower or 750-horsepower Bristol Pegasus, gave the fabric-covered plane a top speed of 139 miles per hour; range was 770 miles. Nicknamed the Stringbag, it took part in the attack on the Italian fleet at Taranto and helped sink the German battleship Bismarck. Fitted with floats and launched by catapult, the Swordfish served as a naval gunfire spotter.

SWORDFISH, U.S.S. Sargo-class submarine, commissioned in 1939. In the Philippines when the Pacific war began, she conducted her first three war patrols in that area before sailing to Australia after the fall of Corregidor. She carried out nine more Pacific war patrols. On her 13th patrol, in February 1945, she was lost to unknown causes.

SYMBOL. Code name of the American-British Casablanca Conference, January 14–23, 1943.

Swordfish

SYRACUSE. Gen. B. L. MONTGOMERY's British EIGHTH ARMY landed south of Syracuse (Siracusa) on July 10, 1943, and secured this Sicilian port the following day.

SYRIA. After the Franco-German armistice in 1940, Germans began to exert considerable influence in Syria, a French colony. Following successful operations in IRAQ, the British, together with FREE FRANCE forces, opened hostilities in Syria on June 8, 1941. They were opposed by VICHY French forces whose loyalties were divided, and native troops. The British sought to secure their Middle Eastern flank. After a little more than a month of fighting, an armistice was declared on July 12. The British won the right to occupy Syria for the duration of the war.

SZILARD, Leo (1898–1964). A Hungarian-born and -educated nuclear physicist who left Germany in 1933 and eventually made his way to the United States, where he became a key figure in the development of the ATOMIC BOMB. One of his most important contributions was a continuing attempt to get the U.S. Government to sponsor development of the bomb; at his and other scientists' urging, Albert EINSTEIN in 1939 signed a letter to President ROOSEVELT recommending immediate action in view of Germany's progress in nuclear research. Szilard, known as a most competent and energetic scientist, was deeply involved in every aspect of the MANHATTAN DISTRICT but later became a leading opponent of use of the bomb because of the nuclear proliferation that would inevitably follow.

T

T2. The U.S. Maritime Commission basic designation for a type of mass-produced fuel tanker built in large numbers and in a variety of individual configurations. Five hundred feet long or more and averaging 16,000 deadweight tons, T2 tankers served the U.S. Navy and merchant shipping lines. The basic T2 was turbine-powered, with an overall length of 501 feet. The later T2-SE-A1, -A2 and -A3 were 23 feet longer, with turboelectric propulsion.

T-34. *See* TANK.

TACLOBAN. Capital of LEYTE, near which troops of the U.S. SIXTH ARMY landed on October 20, 1944. It was taken the next day. On October 24 Gen. Douglas MACARTHUR presided at a ceremony in Tacloban at which the civil government of the Philippines was restored under President Sergio OSMEÑA.

TACOMA, U.S.S. Frigate and class, American-built version of the ASHEVILLE class. One hundred of these ships were contracted for by the U.S. Maritime Commission, since Navy shipbuilding facilities were strained at the time. Like the Asheville class, they had twin screws and reciprocating engines. Seventy-five Tacomas commissioned in the U.S. Navy during 1943–45 and were manned by Coast Guardsmen; 21 more went to Britain; four were canceled. They were armed with three 3-inch guns, light antiaircraft guns, depth-charge tracks and K-guns (depth-charge projectors).

TAGANROG. German forces bastion town in southern Russia, on the Sea of Azov. It was retaken by Soviet forces on August 30, 1943.

TAIHO. Japanese aircraft carrier, begun in 1941 but not completed until 1944. Eight hundred fifty-two feet long and displacing over 29,000 tons, *Taiho* had an armored flight deck and, unlike the case with most other Japanese carriers, her stack was incorporated into her island rather than being trunked outboard below the flight deck. In her first action, the Battle of the PHILIPPINE SEA, *Taiho* was torpedoed by an American submarine. The torpedoing itself should not have mortally injured her, but a massive blast of ignited fuel vapors set her ablaze and doomed her.

TAKAGI, Sokichi (1893–). Japanese career naval officer, primarily a research specialist. Takagi served as chief of the research section of the Navy Ministry from 1939, as chief of staff of the Maizuru Naval Station from 1942 and as chief of the education bureau of the Navy Ministry in 1944. In September 1943 he began a secret study of Japan's shipping and air losses. This research convinced him that Japan had to seek peace. He urged Koichi KIDO and Admirals YONAI and INOUYE to oust Premier TOJO and try to end the war. He became a key figure behind the peace movement undertaken by the naval officers. Author of a number of books about the war, Takagi was appointed a lecturer at the Naval Staff College and the National Defense College in 1956.

TAKAGI, Takeo (1892–1944). A career naval officer, Vice-Admiral Takagi was one of Japan's most active and successful naval commanders during the war. In command of support forces during the invasions of the PHILIPPINES, JAVA, PORT MORESBY and MIDWAY in 1942, he achieved significant victories over Allied commanders in the Battle of the JAVA SEA and the Battle of the CORAL SEA. He took command of Japan's Sixth (Submarine) Fleet in 1943, which was then stationed at Saipan. He was killed in action in the Central Pacific in July of the following year.

TAKAHASHI, Ibo (1888–1947). Japanese naval officer, a graduate of the Naval Academy (1908) and the Naval War College (1919), promoted to vice-admiral in 1939. Prior to the outbreak of the Pacific war, he was appointed commander in chief of the Third Fleet, which he commanded in the invasions of the PHILIPPINES and the Netherlands East Indies. After serving as commander in chief of the Southwest Area Fleet from April to November 1942 and subsequently as commanding officer of the Kure naval base, he retired from active duty in 1944.

TAKAO. Japanese heavy cruiser and class (often called in wartime publications the ATAGO class). Takaos were ships of 13,160 tons displacement and had a main battery of ten 8-inch guns, together with sixteen 24-inch torpedo tubes and eight 5-inch dual-purpose guns. Top speed was 34 knots. The four ships in the group were sometimes divided into two subclasses, depending on the position of the mainmast and on differences in the midship structure; *Takao* and *Atago* had the mainmast stepped farther aft than did CHOKAI and MAYA. *Takao* was put out of action at LEYTE GULF by the U.S. submarine *Darter* (Comdr. David McClintock).

TAKESHITA, Masahiko (1908–). A graduate of the Japanese Military Academy (1930) and the War College (1938), Lieutenant Colonel Takeshita became a member of the staff of the military affairs bureau of the War Department in April 1945. He was one of the most active members of the conspiracy against the Emperor, which had as its objective the continuation of the war.

TALISMAN. Code name originally given to Allied plans for governing Germany after the end of hostilities. Because a compromise of security was believed to have occurred, the code name was changed to Eclipse.

TALLINN (Revel). Capital of Estonia and after the Soviet occupation in 1940 the base of the Baltic Red Banner Fleet. In November 1941 it became the base of the German naval command Ostland. It was seized by the Soviets on September 22, 1944.

TAMAN PENINSULA. Following the disaster at STALINGRAD, elements of German Army Group A escaped into the Taman Peninsula, south of the Sea of Azov. They held the bridgehead until October 10, 1943, when the last resistance was eliminated.

TANAKA, Raizo (1892–1969). One of Japan's most brilliant naval commanders, Tanaka took part in many battles during the first year of the war. He commanded the naval escort vessels for the invasions of Jolo Island in the South PHILIPPINES, AMBON, TIMOR and JAVA. He also took part in the Battle of MIDWAY. Tanaka won fame, however, under Adm. Gunichi MIKAWA for his tenacity in trying to reinforce GUADALCANAL in the second half of 1942. He decisively defeated superior American forces at the Battle of TASSAFARONGA on the night of November 30, 1942, the last major naval battle in the Solomons. During the Guadalcanal campaign Tanaka strongly criticized the lack of coordination between air and surface operations, and he was an early advocate of the abandonment of Guadalcanal. Angered by such criticisms, the Japanese naval high command relieved Tanaka of his command and refused to give him another sea command for the duration of the war.

TANG, U.S.S. BALAO-class submarine, completed in 1943, which set the record for the most enemy ships sunk on one war patrol (10, on her third patrol, East China Sea and Yellow Sea, June 1944). Her commander was Richard H. O'KANE, the top U.S. submarine ace of the war. On her fifth and last patrol (October 1944) *Tang* sank seven Japanese ships, the third highest total of ships sunk on one patrol. But on October 24, immediately after sinking the two freighters that raised the bag to seven, *Tang*, in attempting to finish off still another freighter, was sunk by one of her own torpedoes that circled back and struck her. Eight men survived, including the skipper, O'Kane. They were taken prisoner by the Japanese.

TANK. Disarmed by the Allies after World War I, Germany did not have a stockpile of obsolete equipment to hinder developments in armor. After exhaustive study and field testing, the Germans concluded that the role of armor was to achieve a breakthrough of the enemy lines and then exploit it. Their new equipment reflected this theory, the Germans rearming with a series of light and medium tanks that were more heavily armed and faster than others of that time.

Although France began modernization in 1926, the real impetus came with Germany's rearming in 1934. The planned increases were delayed by nationalization of French war industries and Communist agitation. Despite these problems, France was able by 1939 to field about 3,100 tanks, of which 2,285 were modern types.

Stalin tanks (JS-III) rumble through Red Square

U.S.-built M3 medium tanks in the North African desert

French tanks combined thick curved armor with light suspension, keeping overall weights down, and controlled differential steering, permitting constant power to the track drive even when turning. In the Battle of FRANCE, in the early part of the war, the use of tanks was characterized by 1914–18 tactical concepts. The tank force, better equipped in many ways than that of the Germans, was never given a full chance to prove itself. The major French types were the R-35 (Renault Model 1935) and the H-35 (Hotchkiss Model 1935), both armed with short 37-mm. guns; the Char B-1*bis*, a 33-ton medium with a hull-mounted 75-mm. gun, a turret-mounted 47-mm. gun and two machine guns; and the excellent Somua S-35, a 20-ton vehicle with a cast-steel hull of 40 mm., carrying a 47-mm. gun and one machine gun and powered by a Somua V-8 gasoline engine which drove it at 29 miles per hour. Of the latter two there were approximately 800—somewhat more than the 627 modern types Germany ranged against France. The French tank force was hampered by poor operating ranges, lack of radio communications and limitation to an infantry role.

When Germany attacked Poland in 1939, she had four tank types in service: the Pz.Kw. (Panzerkampfwagen) I, a 5½-ton, two-man light tank armed with two machine guns; the Pz.Kw. II, a three-man, 11½-ton light with turret-mounted 20-mm. gun and one machine gun; the Pz.Kw. III, a five-man medium of 24½ tons carrying a 37-mm. gun in the turret and a machine gun in the hull; and the Pz.Kw. IV, a 26-ton, five-man medium with a short-barreled 75-mm. gun and a machine gun. In the attack on France the same models predominated, with a fifth being added, the Czech Pz.Kw. 35(t). Of the 2,687 German tanks employed in France only 627 were mediums; the rest were obsolescent light types.

The abandoned tanks of the French and British expeditionary corps formed the RED ARMY's armored force after the revolution; the Russians began building their own vehicles in 1928. The poor quality of their gasoline forced them to adopt diesel engines of the German type; German torsion suspension was also copied. Various designs were field-tested in the Spanish Civil War and the 1938–39 Soviet-Japanese clashes. The SOVIET-FINNISH WAR exposed serious design faults, but production of existing models continued because of bureaucratic inertia. When the German invasion came, the Russians had some small amphibious tanks; light T-6s, copies of the Vickers 6-ton model; BT mediums, weighing about 11 tons and mounting a 47-mm. gun; other assorted medium types; and a few heavies. Some of these tanks were ultramodern but, though the armored force as a whole was more numerous than the German, they were generally of poor quality and badly handled.

German heavy tank, the Panther (Pz.Kw. V)

Japanese medium tank, Type 97

Most small nations bought their tanks from Great Britain, France, Sweden or Czechoslovakia. The Czechs had a fine fast, light tank, the LTM-35. Built by Skoda, it was a 10½-ton tank armed with a 37-mm. gun and one machine gun. Another fine Czech tank was the TNHP-S of 1938, a modern medium/light of 9.7 tons also armed with a 37-mm. gun and a machine gun. It was taken into German service as the Pz.Kw. 35(t) and formed about a fourth of Germany's tank force in 1941–42, when German industry was unable to produce enough medium tanks to satisfy demand. The Japanese made use of foreign tanks until 1928, when they began building their own for the Army and Navy. Japanese vehicles were characterized by a great number of interchangeable parts and by the employment of diesel engines. The major types were the light 9-ton Type 98 Ke-ni, armed with a 37-mm. gun; the medium 30-ton Type 4 Chi-ito, armed with a 75-mm. gun, introduced in 1942; and another medium, the Type 97.

Poland, Austria, Belgium, Hungary, Canada and Italy built tanks of their own design and others under license. During World War II the Italians utilized a series of light tanks developed from the British Carden-Loyd carriers, most of which mounted two machine

British infantry tanks, Mark IV—the Churchill (A22)

German medium tank, (Pz.Kw. III)

German heavy tank, the Tiger (Pz.Kw. VI)

guns and an assortment of other types. The standard Italian medium was the M-13/40, a 14-ton, four-man vehicle armed with an excellent 47-mm. gun and three 8-mm. machine guns and with a maximum armor of 40 mm.

Differences in tactical concepts as the war wore on were reflected in the designs produced by different armies. The Germans built heavily armed and armored machines, since for them strategic surprise was gone by 1942 and the remainder of the war would be characterized by slugging matches between nearly equal armored forces. The tank design race became one of projectile and armor, a race the Germans always led. The most important German tank, numerically, was the Pz.Kw. IV, of which 7,071 were built in several models from 1937 to 1944. The G model weighed 24 tons, carried a crew of five and had a top speed of 25 miles per hour on roads and a range of 130 miles. It was armed with a long-barreled 75-mm. KwK 40 (L-43) gun and two Type 34 7.92-mm. machine guns. The maximum hull

Japanese medium tanks (Type 94) advancing on Manila, 1942

U.S. medium tank, T26

U.S. light tank, M24

frontal armor was 50 mm. thick and was increased by the addition of a 30-mm. spaced plate.

From 1939 to 1944 Germany built 42,932 armored vehicles. As they went on the defensive the Germans built more armored assault guns and tank destroyers than tanks, since these could be produced with less effort and material. Generally, German tanks mounted heavier guns than those of other nations, and the Germans constantly increased the weight of armor; their theory held that a tank's armor should be proof against its own weapon. Of the types built, the best was the Pz.Kw. V Panther, which was Germany's answer to Russia's T-34. More than a match for any Allied tank, the Panther was introduced in 1943. It could go 30 miles an hour on roads for 100 miles and carried a 75-mm. gun and two 7.92 Type 34 machine guns. It had thick (120-mm. maximum), well-sloped armor of welded construction and weighed 47 tons.

The first product of Germany's heavy tank program was the Pz.Kw. VI Tiger I, Ausf. (model) E, introduced in 1942. A total of 1,350 had been built when production halted in August 1944. The tank weighed 55 tons, carried an 88-mm. gun and two Type 34 7.92-mm machine guns, had 110-mm. frontal armor and went 25 miles per hour over 60 miles, carrying a crew of five.

Germany's final operational heavy tank entered production in January 1944 and service in May 1944. Only 485 units of the 68-ton Pz.Kw. VI Tiger II, called the Royal Tiger or King Tiger, were made. Two models were built—the Porsche (50) and the Henschel (435); they were differentiated only by their turrets. The Tiger II carried a crew of five; it had 185 mm. of frontal armor and was armed with a long-barreled 88-mm. gun and two Type 34 7.92-mm. machine guns. This was a hard-hitting tank, but it was underpowered and had limited mobility, in addition to being mechanically unreliable. Late in the war an even heavier tank, the Pz.Kw. E-100—of 100 tons and mounting a 150-mm. gun—was planned but never entered production.

Great Britain lost most of its tank force at DUNKIRK.

U.S. medium tank, M4 (Sherman), with "scorpion" mine destroyer attached

The rapid development and production of new types led to a group of tanks full of mechanical problems. The Cruiser Mark VI Crusader and the Infantry Mark II Matilda and Infantry Mark III Valentine all failed to live up to expectations. The American-built M3 (Stuart or Honey, in British service) and the modified medium M3 Lee (another version was called the Grant in British service) helped stave off defeat in the desert. Britain's best tanks were the Churchill Mark I—which had a five-man crew, weighed 40 tons, carried a turret-mounted 75-mm. gun and machine gun and a 3-inch howitzer or machine gun in the hull and traveled 100 miles at 17 miles an hour—and the Comet and Cromwell fast cruiser tanks with 75-mm. and 95-mm. guns, respectively. In addition, the British built a large number of tanks for specific tasks such as minesweeping, fortification assault and battlefield lighting. During the war Britain built about 24,000 armored vehicles and received an additional 3,600 from Canada and 25,600 from the United States.

Although a number of the Soviet tanks were obsolescent in 1941, the revolutionary vehicles planned in 1938–39 were in service and came as a rude shock to the Germans, who had underestimated the armored capabilities of the Russians. The T-34/76 was a 26-ton medium with well-sloped armor varying from 1.8 to 2.5 inches; it carried a 76.2-mm. gun (later the T-34/85 of 1943 carried an 85-mm. piece) and two machine guns, and had a crew of four. Its Christie suspension, wide (24-inch) tracks and double road wheels, coupled with a 500-horsepower liquid-cooled V-12 diesel engine, gave the tank superb cross-country performance with a top speed of 30 miles per hour on roads. Many observers consider this the best tank of the war. The KV-1, named for Kliment VOROSHILOV, was the Soviets' first new heavy tank. It weighed 52 tons, carried a 76.2-mm. gun and two machine guns and had a 210-mile range; its frontal armor was 75 mm. (maximum), and turret armor was 90 mm. front and rear. A five-man crew operated the vehicle. With these two the Soviets burst into the forefront of tank design. Before the end of the war a third tank series appeared, the JS (Joseph Stalin) I, II and III. Developed from the KV-I, the JS (or IS, as it is sometimes rendered) series was a logical step from the earlier tanks. The JS-III weighed 46 tons and carried a 122-mm. gun, a 7.6-mm. machine gun in the turret and a 12.7-mm. heavy machine gun atop the turret. It carried a crew of four, went at a top speed of 23 miles per hour and had 200-mm. armor at crucial points. The USSR built about 100,000 vehicles during the war; the United States sent about 13,000 assorted combat vehicles, Canada about 1,220 tanks and Britain about 4,260 tanks and, in addition, huge numbers of BREN GUN CARRIERS. Soviet tank losses are estimated at about 100,000. The Russian tank was turned out with the fewest possible man-hours of production, with simplic-

German Royal Tiger tank (Pz.Kw. VI-Tiger II) passes a line of U.S. soldiers captured in the Battle of the Bulge

ity highlighted and absolutely no emphasis on finish or crew comfort.

After Poland fell, the United States began a confused and feverish rearmament. After Pearl Harbor, almost impossible production goals were set and industry tried to meet them. The M6 heavy-tank program was dropped in favor of greater medium-tank production. Despite disputes between the Army Service Forces and the civilian WAR PRODUCTION BOARD, 289,425 combat vehicles of all types were built, along with enough spare parts to build half again as many. From 1940 to 1945 U.S. tank production totaled 88,410; in 1943, the peak year of production, 29,497 tanks were turned out.

The original medium tank, the M3 General Lee, had a sponson-mounted 75-mm. gun in the hull, a 37-mm. gun and machine gun in the offset turret and a .30-caliber machine gun in a cupola atop the turret. It weighed 32 tons and went a maximum of 22 miles per hour powered by a Wright R-975-EC aircraft engine. The hull armor was 1½ to 2 inches thick, with a 2-inch-thick cast turret. The M3 was used in almost every theater of the war and by Russia and Britain; one version, which received a British-designed turret, was called the General Grant. A total of 6,258 M3s were built by Chrysler, American Locomotive and Baldwin Locomotive from August 1941 to December 1942.

Another U.S. tank important to the war was the light M3 (General Stuart to the British) series tank, a development of the M2A4 light. Weighing about 15 tons fully loaded, it carried a 37-mm. gun and four machine guns, although the two side-mounted machine guns were usually removed for combat. It was powered by a 250-horsepower Continental W670-9A radial engine; later models had a comparable Guiberson diesel engine, which drove it to 37 miles an hour on roads. Owing to its short range, extra fuel tanks were introduced. The M3 Stuart's hull armor varied from 1 to 1½ inches in thickness, and the turret had 1½ inches maximum; it was heavier than any other nation's light tanks. A direct descendant was the M5 Stuart light, the main difference being a fully sloped glacis plate and a raised deck to accommodate the twin Cadillac V-8 engines; in addition, it could go 160 miles over roads or 100 miles under battlefield conditions. The M5A1 had a 37-mm. gun stabilized in elevation, permitting accurate fire while rolling.

The workhorse of the Western Allies' tank forces was the U.S. M4 series (christened by the British with the name of still another Civil War general, Sherman—the name by which it is commonly known), of which 49,234 were built; numbers and mechanical reliability gave the M4 an edge over the dwindling German armored force. Introduced in North Africa, these vehicles saw more service than any other Western Allied tanks, in almost every theater of operations and in a wide variety of roles. The final refinement was the M4A3E8 with power turret, high-velocity 76-mm. gun (some models had a 105-mm. howitzer) and two machine guns and 80-mm. maximum frontal hull armor; it weighed 35 tons, went 26 miles an hour, had a 100-mile range and carried a five-man crew. A compromise between this tank and the heavy M6, which did not perform satisfactorily in tests, was the 45-ton T25E1 Pershing, a few of which saw service in Germany and Okinawa before the war ended. **W.S.**

TANK DESTROYER. U.S. Army term for SELF-PROPELLED ARTILLERY designed to combat enemy tanks. Principal American tank destroyers included the Gun Motor Carriage M3, a French-designed 75-mm. gun mounted on an M3 half-track. This combination was developed in 1941 and used in the Pacific and European theaters. The Gun Motor Carriage M10 was a modified M4 Sherman tank chassis with a high-velocity 76-mm. gun in an open-top revolving turret. The later GMC M36, nicknamed the Jackson, had a similar turret mounting a 90-mm. gun. The British mounted their own 17-pounder high-velocity gun in the M10, designating it Achilles. The principal rationale behind tank destroyers of this type was that the sacrifice of some armor protection enabled a heavier gun to be mounted.

TAPOTCHAU, MOUNT. Tapotchau stands 1,554 feet high in the center of SAIPAN. The island's key terrain feature, it afforded the Japanese command an excellent observation of the U.S. Marine beachhead for 10 days after the initial landing. Its rugged foothills were also strongly defended by the enemy in well-organized positions.

TARANTO. A port and naval base on the Ionian Sea in southern Italy, the scene of a raid by British naval aircraft on the Italian battle fleet in November 1940. The attack on Taranto, code-named Operation Judgment, was intended to provide cover for several British Mediterranean convoys and at the same time to cripple the Italian battleship fleet, which was usually based at Taranto. On November 11 at 10:00 P.M., 21 SWORDFISH torpedo planes in two waves were launched from the carrier ILLUSTRIOUS about 170 miles from Taranto. Twelve of the Swordfish carried torpedoes, the remainder flares or bombs. Because of the slow speed and poor defensive capability of the Swordfish, the attack was to be made at night, when the more modern Italian fighter planes would not be a danger.

Anchored in the Mare Grande, the outer harbor of Taranto, were two new Italian battleships, LITTORIO and VITTORIO VENETO, and three older battleships—CONTE DI CAVOUR, GIULIO CESARE and *Caio Duilio*—along with three cruisers and seven destroyers. In the inner harbor, or Mare Piccolo, were the cruisers *Trieste, Trento, Bolzano* and *Pola* with four destroyers. The torpedo-net defenses of the base were incomplete, and many of the barrage balloons protecting the outer harbor had been swept away in a recent storm. Moreover, the Italian torpedo nets extended down only to the maximum draft of the battleships, not to the bottom of the harbor. The British had perfected a new type of torpedo which could pass under the nets and detonate under the keel of the target vessel.

Attacking at an altitude of under 35 feet on the clear, moonlit night, the six torpedo planes of the first wave attacked the battleships *Littorio* and *Conte di Cavour*, damaging the *Littorio* and sending the *Cavour* to the bottom. The second wave of aircraft continued to punish the *Littorio* and put a torpedo into the battleship *Caio Duilio*. By morning three of the five Italian ships had been crippled, the *Cavour*, though refloated, being lost for the remainder of the war. British losses were two aircraft lost and two damaged. The successful action ensured British naval superiority in the Mediterranean for the next half year. More important, it marked the debut of the aircraft carrier and its planes as the dominant weapon of naval warfare.

TARAWA. The keystone of the Japanese defenses in the GILBERT ISLANDS. The invasion of Tarawa in 1943 marked the opening of the American Central Pacific campaign. On November 20 the 2d Marine Division landed on BETIO, at the southwest tip of the atoll. It was strongly defended by 5,000 Japanese naval troops and Korean laborers, manning hundreds of guns which ranged in size from 7.7-mm. machine guns to four 8-inch rifles that the Japanese had captured at Singapore. Three runways had been built on the island, but the rest of Betio consisted of mutually supporting pillboxes and fortifications constructed from coconut logs, reinforced concrete and coral. Besides these man-made obstacles on the beach, a reef surrounding the island thwarted any crossing by landing craft, which meant that assault waves had to make the trip to the beach by amphibian tractors (*see* AMTRAC). Marines in subsequent waves were forced to go over the side of the landing craft or debark from their ramp bows and wade in to the beaches against withering fire. H-hour was originally set for 0830, but it was extended to 0900 when enemy shore batteries kept firing, indicating that the pre-invasion naval gunfire and air bombardment had not been very effective. Although some marines in the amtracs gained the beaches, those wading in through waist-deep water became easy targets of fire from shore or victims of mortar or shell fragments; others drowned when they stepped into potholes and were carried under by the weight of their packs. Those who did reach the beaches were exhausted, disorganized and often weaponless.

Meanwhile, those units in the initial assault waves which had established the beachhead were pinned down and unable to move. By nightfall Col. David M. SHOUP, senior officer ashore, held a shallow foothold near the base of a pier that jutted some 500 yards out into the water. No enemy attack was launched that night, and the next day the marines pushed out from the beachhead and began reducing the enemy fortifications. That afternoon 2d Battalion, 6th Marines, took Bairiki Island, blocking the Japanese avenue of escape, and emplaced artillery to support operations on Betio.

On the morning of the second day ashore the 1st Battalion, 8th Marines, which had spent the night afloat in landing craft, reached the beach, but with very heavy losses. But the tide of battle seemed to turn in favor of the Americans. On November 22 they attacked from positions in both the south and west of the island, pushing the Japanese into a pocket, from which the enemy counterattacked toward the eastern part of Betio. By 0500 the next morning, this attack was spent. After 76 hours of some of the heaviest fighting in the war to date, the Japanese were finished, unable to put up any sort of coordinated defense. At 1330 on the 23d, the island was declared secure. The cost for Tarawa was heavy—984 marines dead and 2,072 wounded. The only enemy left were 17 wounded prisoners and 129 Korean laborers. *See also* GALVANIC.

TARZAN. Code name for the India-based portion of the offensive to recapture BURMA, part of an overall plan called Champion. Adopted by SOUTHEAST ASIA COMMAND on November 7, 1943, Tarzan was favored by the British staff and criticized by the Americans. The Allied decision to give first priority to Europe in 1944 resulted in the Burma operations being decreased in scope from the original plans. Tarzan was finally modified into Gripfast, planned as an attack on north and central Burma coupled with an airborne landing at Indaw.

U.S. marines stalk and capture a Japanese pillbox on Tarawa

TASK FORCE. A temporary assignment of U.S. Navy ships and other units under a commander, set up to accomplish a single operation or constituted on a more or less permanent basis to carry out a continuing mission. Generally speaking, a task force (TF) could be subdivided into task groups (TG). These were, in turn, divided into task units (TU); a task unit could be further divided into task elements (TE). None of these organizations had any prescribed structure; they could be established and disestablished, rearranged and altered at will as the need arose. This principle provided a fleet commander with a highly flexible command structure which could be reshuffled in any manner that seemed desirable, taking into account the military situation and the forces available.

TASSAFARONGA, BATTLE OF. On the night of November 30–December 1, 1942, a U.S. cruiser and destroyer force took up positions at the entrance to Savo Sound to prevent Japanese landings in the Tassafaronga area, on the northwest coast of GUADALCANAL west of Kokumbona. Although the Americans opened fire first on the Japanese destroyer force, preventing the landings, superior enemy torpedo attacks severely damaged the cruisers PENSACOLA, NEW ORLEANS, *Minneapolis* and NORTHAMPTON, causing the latter to sink on December 1. The Japanese suffered the loss of only one destroyer, another being damaged.

TAUTOG, U.S.S. Tambor-class submarine, completed in 1940, credited with sinking the most ships (26) of any American submarine during the war. Her commanders were Joseph H. Willingham, William B. "Barney" Sieglaff and Thomas S. Baskett. Second in number of ships sunk was TANG, and third was *Silversides*.

TAYLOR, Maxwell Davenport (1901–). To Taylor's fellow cadets at West Point, from which he graduated in 1922, and his contemporaries during World War II, he was an "intellectual," a scholar who had an affinity for foreign languages. That may have been one reason he was called upon in 1943 for one of the war's more unusual missions, a daring trip by patrol boat to the Italian coast near Rome, thence by Red Cross ambulance into the capital for what turned out to be a futile attempt to gain Italian complicity in a landing of American airborne divisions to occupy Rome coincident with Italian surrender. He was one of the U.S. Army's early airborne enthusiasts and fought in SICILY and ITALY as artillery commander of the 82D AIRBORNE DIVISION. He commanded the 101ST AIRBORNE DIVISION in airborne assaults on D-Day in Normandy, in Operation MARKET in the Netherlands and in ground operations during the Battle of the BULGE and the drive through Germany. His post–World War II career involved major assignments: superintendent at West Point, commander of the Eighth Army in Korea, U.S. Army Chief of Staff, special military adviser to Presidents John F. KENNEDY and Lyndon B. Johnson, chairman of the Joint Chiefs of Staff and ambassador to the Republic of Vietnam. His final military rank was full general.

TAYLOR, Telford (1908–). American lawyer, U.S. chief prosecution counsel at the NUREMBERG (war crimes) TRIALS. Taylor was commissioned a major in the Army in 1942, and in April 1946 became a brigadier general. A professor of law at Columbia University, he wrote extensively about the war.

TBD. The Douglas TBD-1 Devastator, the U.S. Navy's first all-metal monoplane carrier aircraft, was introduced in late 1937 to replace earlier biplane torpedo bombers. By mid-1942 it was still standard, though slated for gradual replacement by the Grumman TBF Avenger (*see* TBF). It served in the Pacific raids of early 1942, and at the CORAL SEA TBDs shared in the sinking of the Japanese carrier SHOHO. During the Battle of MIDWAY on June 4, 1942, three American torpedo squadrons made courageous but fruitless attacks on the Japanese carrier striking force. Virtually every account of this action stresses the "antiquated" performance of the TBD and places much of the blame for the practically complete destruction of all three attacking torpedo squadrons on its "inadequate" performance. Of 41 Devastators launched in the Midway battle, only six returned. Granted, the Devastator's maximum speed (carrying its torpedo) of 207 miles per hour was low. Still, attacking under the same circumstances, faster TBF-1s and B-26s (*see* B-26) lost heavily and had no better success, though the TBD's relatively low speed—the original XTBD-1 had flown in 1935—did contribute to its vulnerability. Wartime experience showed that coordinated attacks by fighters, bombers and torpedo planes were essential to hold down losses among the slower and more vulnerable bomber types. By 1945 the U.S. Navy had decided to focus on single-seat attack planes with external weapon stowage to supplant such multiplace, internal-weapon-bay planes as the TBF. Experience gained with the TBD, TBF, SBD and SB2C (*see* SBD; SB2C), as well as in operations against comparable Japanese aircraft such as the D3A and B5N (*see* D3A; B5N), had convinced many airmen that the weight put into larger air crews and rearward-firing defensive armament was a poor investment.

TBF. The Grumman Avenger, U.S. Navy torpedo bomber that made its first test flights in 1941 and became operational in early 1942. A versatile and widely used midwing monoplane, the Avenger flew from both carriers and land bases; it was variously armed, depending on its mission. It had a belly power turret and

TBD Devastator

carried three or four other machine guns, a 21-inch torpedo (internally) or four 500-pound bombs or eight rockets. Maximum speed was about 270 miles per hour, range about 1,100 miles. The power plant was a 1,850-horsepower Wright radial.

After Grumman had built about 2,300 TBF-1s, the production model, it handed over production of the plane to the Eastern Aircraft Division of General Motors. The designation therefore changed to TBM (M being Eastern's identification letter), and two versions were produced, the TBM-1 and the TBM-3. Avengers of all three kinds were extensively used by the Royal Navy as well as by the American. In one version, the Avenger became a carrier-based night bomber operating with night fighters.

A large aircraft of its type, the Avenger was 41 feet long and had a wingspan of 54 feet 2 inches.

TÉBESSA. An Algerian city of ancient Roman, Byzantine, Christian, French and Arab culture, Tébessa was an important road center linking Algiers with the GAFSA–GABÈS area. General FREDENDALL and part of U.S. II Corps moved to Tébessa in January 1943 to establish a southern flank guard for the Allied forces in northern TUNISIA. After KASSERINE, the entire II Corps was stationed in the Tébessa area to provide a solid link between Generals MONTGOMERY and ANDERSON.

TÉBOURBA. Essential for either attack or defense of Tunis, Tébourba (12 miles west of Tunis) lay in the river plains backed by hills and had a bridge over the MEDJERDA RIVER. Allied forces seized it November 27, 1942, only to be thrown out by December 4. Tébourba was held by the Axis until May 6, 1943, then evacuated under pressure of the final Allied offensive.

TEDDER, Arthur William Tedder, 1st Baron (1890–1967). A graduate of Magdalene College, Cambridge, Tedder served in the British Army before transferring to the Royal Flying Corps in World War I and thence as a career officer to the RAF. He was appointed to a new post in the Air Ministry, director general of research and development, in 1938 and named deputy air member for development and production in the Ministry of Aircraft Production in 1940. He succeeded Air Marshal Sir Arthur LONGMORE as AOC-in-C Middle East in 1941. During the campaigns in the WESTERN DESERT he evolved techniques of cooperation between air and land forces and used pattern bombing effectively to clear the advance of Gen. B. L. MONTGOMERY'S EIGHTH ARMY. Tedder's partnership with Gen. Dwight EISENHOWER began in 1943, when he was appointed Air Commander in Chief Mediterranean. He became responsible to Eisenhower, the theater commander, for all the air operations in the vast MEDITERRANEAN THEATER. He soon learned to work as an Allied rather than a national commander. His policy for the central control and application of air power independently or in support of naval and ground forces was coherent and consistent. He became, in fact, one of the outstanding Allied commanders of the war.

The preparatory bombing of communications which preceded the Allied INVASION of Normandy (the TRANSPORTATION PLAN) owed much to Tedder's planning and resolution. An air chief marshal, he became Deputy Supreme Commander to General Eisenhower in December 1943, and in a remarkable spirit of understanding and regard they remained together until the Germans signed the instrument of surrender in May 1945.

After his retirement from the RAF in 1950 Tedder—now Lord Tedder—became chairman of the British Joint Services Mission in Washington, 1950–51. He was made chancellor of Cambridge University in 1951.

TEDDER PLAN. One of the various names given to the Allied bombing of railway facilities in the invasion area of France. *See also* TRANSPORTATION PLAN.

TEHERAN CONFERENCE. This first meeting of the Big Three—Winston S. CHURCHILL, Joseph STALIN and Franklin D. ROOSEVELT—took place in the Iranian capital, November 28–December 1, 1943.

Roosevelt had been anxious to meet Stalin personally for a long time, hoping to establish the intimate relationship he considered essential for Allied cooperation. Stalin had temporized, feeling that the tide of war in Russia must decidedly turn before he could discuss the future from a position of strength in a formal meeting with his Western allies. He asserted Soviet prestige by making Roosevelt come all the way to Teheran, by excluding CHIANG KAI-SHEK from the conference and by lodging Roosevelt in the Soviet embassy as his guest, thereby reducing his communication with Churchill.

At the first meeting of the conference, to Roosevelt's delight, Stalin declared that after Germany's defeat the Soviet Union would declare war on Japan. There were extensive discussions of the future operations against Germany. Churchill elaborated on the advantages of the Mediterranean strategy (in anticipation of a major invasion of France), proposing an attack through Yugoslavia. Stalin, suspecting the British of seeking to reach Vienna and Budapest before the Red Army, categorically opposed this plan. Roosevelt, whose military chiefs for the most part strongly favored an invasion of northwest Europe, supported Stalin. Although the Soviets were anxious to see the Allies strike directly at Germany, they had to accept May 1944 as the target date for the invasion.

Agreement was reached about the eastern frontier of Poland, which was to be compensated at the expense of Germany for the loss of territory to the Soviety Union. Stalin's claim to Königsberg was also accepted. Roosevelt proposed to partition Germany into five autonomous states. He was supported in this proposal by Churchill, who also advanced his idea of creating a Danubian confederation of Austria, Hungary and Bavaria. But Stalin's opposition, and probably the sweeping nature of these proposals, precluded specific agreement.

Other discussions included the outlines of the future UNITED NATIONS ORGANIZATION and the question of the veto power of the Big Four ("Four Policemen," in Roosevelt's terminology) in the Security Council, where the United States, Great Britain, the Soviet Union and the Republic of China were to be permanent members.

Agreements were reached on Iran, then under Allied occupation, which was promised full independence after the war, and on a shift of Allied support in Yugoslavia from the forces of Draža MIHAJLOVIĆ to Marshal TITO's partisans, considered by Churchill much more active in fighting the Axis. Churchill's other idea, that of pressing Turkey into joining the Allies in the war against Germany, was objected to by Stalin.

Discussions and decisions at the Teheran Conference were kept so secret that even U.S. Secretary of State Cordell HULL was not informed of them. The very fact of the conference was not announced until after it had adjourned. Teheran marked the high point of Allied wartime cooperation, and the cordiality of the discussions may have given Stalin a degree of hope that the Western Allies would approve most of the Soviet territorial and political objectives.

TELEGRAPH COTTAGE. Gen. Dwight D. EISENHOWER's weekend retreat near Richmond Park, outside London.

TELEKI, Paul (1879–1941). As Premier of Hungary, Count Teleki chose to commit suicide on April 3, 1941, rather than give in to Adolf HITLER's pressure on the Hungarian Government to attack Yugoslavia, a traditional friend. Teleki had tried unsuccessfully between 1939, when he became Premier, and 1941 to align Hungary with the Axis without falling under Nazi domination.

TELLER, Edward (1908–). The Hungarian-born Edward Teller contributed notably to the advancement of atomic physics. Ultimately to become known as the father of the hydrogen bomb, Teller studied and did his early work in Germany. Owing to Adolf HITLER's racial decrees, however, Teller left the country, finally emigrating, in 1935, to the United States. In August 1939, motivated by a report of rapid progress by the Third Reich in the realm of nuclear physics, a group of scientists, including Teller, prevailed upon Albert EINSTEIN to sign a letter to President ROOSEVELT informing him of the possibility of creating an artificial chain reaction that could lead ultimately to the development of an ATOMIC BOMB. Acquiring U.S. citizenship in 1941, Teller worked on theoretical studies with J. Robert OPPENHEIMER at the University of California at Berkeley, where the possibility of fusion came to light, and he was later among the scientists recruited to create the first fission bomb at Los ALAMOS. But, annoyed because priority during the years 1943 to 1945 was given to the uranium bomb, Teller was ultimately relieved of duties with the fission weapon and allowed to pursue his own ideas on the "Super," which he called "my baby." After the war Teller became the prime mover in the creation of the H-bomb, first detonated in 1952.

TELLERMINE. Any of a series of German antitank mines. Two models of the Tellermine 35 were followed by the war-designed Tellermine 42 and Tellermine 43; the latter was also referred to as the *Pilz* (mushroom), from its shape. All these mines were circular metal boxes, 12½ to 12¾ inches in diameter and 3 to 4 inches deep, with a 12-pound TNT charge.

TEMPEST. This British aircraft was Hawker's attempt to correct the problems encountered with the TYPHOON, some of whose aerodynamic difficulties stemmed from its extremely thick wing. As more data on compressibility became available, Hawker's chief designer, Sydney Camm, selected a thinner airfoil and an elliptical wing. All three subspecies of the single-seat Tempest used this new wing. Tempest I boasted a 2,240-horsepower Napier Sabre liquid-cooled engine. Instead of the distinctive chin radiator of the Typhoon, Tempest I, which did not enter production, had oil cooler and radiator built into the leading edge of the wing.

Tempest II, the most powerful single-engine, piston-powered fighter ever acquired by the RAF, appeared in October 1944. Intended for service against the Japanese, this version did not see combat. A 2,520-horsepower Bristol Centaurus air-cooled radial engine gave the plane a top speed of 422 miles per hour at 15,500 feet.

Tempest V featured a liquid-cooled Napier Sabre developing 2,260 horsepower and returned to the chin radiator characteristic of the Typhoon. Its top speed of 416 miles per hour at 4,600 feet and armament of four 20-mm. cannon made the plane especially effective against the German V-1 (*see* V-WEAPONS). Tempest V received credit for destroying more than 600 of the buzz bombs.

TEMPLER, Sir Gerald Walter Robert (1898–). British Army officer, a corps commander, commander of divisional and the 56th (London) Division, which he led at ANZIO, and the 6th Armored Division (1944–45). He was director of military government, 21ST ARMY GROUP, in 1945–46. Subsequently (1955–58) he was Chief of the Imperial General Staff.

TENARU RIVER, BATTLE OF THE. In the early maps provided to the U.S. 1st Marine Division for the GUADALCANAL operation, the names of the Ilu and Tenaru Rivers were transposed. The battle that took place in August at the Ilu was therefore incorrectly identified as the Battle of the Tenaru and remains so named to this day. At 0310 on August 21, 1942, about 200 soldiers of Col. Kiyono ICHIKI's force rushed the sand spit at the river's mouth, only to be met by point-blank fire, most of it coming from canister-firing 37-mm. antitank guns of the 2d Battalion, 1st Marines. A few enemy got into U.S. lines but were captured, while a counterattack drove the rest back across the river. Ichiki attempted another attack, preceded by an artillery and mortar barrage, but this attempt, too, was unsuccessful. Dawn revealed a gruesome scene—the sand spit was covered with the bodies of Japanese soldiers who had been cut down in their attacks. Meanwhile, the 1st Battalion, 1st Marines, had crossed the Ilu upriver in a successful attempt to encircle the fleeing enemy soldiers. By 1400 the Japanese were penned in completely by the river, the beaches and the Marine envelopment from the left and rear. At 1500 Gen. A. A. VANDEGRIFT ordered a tank attack across the spit to rid this portion of his perimeter of this threat. The battle was over by 1700. Nearly 800 Japanese were killed, 15 were captured and only a few escaped into the jungle. Colonel Ichiki committed suicide, disgraced by his utter defeat.

TEN GO. A Japanese plan for air operations over the East China Sea in defense of the home islands, issued February 2, 1945. Ten Go anticipated a decisive and successful air attack upon the advancing U.S. forces mainly in the island chain connecting the Japanese homeland and Taiwan. By July 1945 the concept of a decisive air battle had deteriorated into a series of small-scale hit-and-run raids.

10-in-1 RATION. Packed in a large box designed to provide one meal for 10 men (or 10 meals for one man), this late-war U.S. Army field ration contained a rather extensive variety of popular canned and packaged food items and was highly thought of by troops. It never replaced the C RATION or K RATION, particularly for infantry or marines, for whom the large box was often impractical.

TENNANT, Sir William (1890–1963). British admiral who organized the naval side of the withdrawal of the BRITISH EXPEDITIONARY FORCE at DUNKIRK in 1940. In 1944 he served in the Normandy INVASION, being in charge of the towage and assembly of the two prefabricated harbors, known as MULBERRIES. Later that year he was appointed Flag Officer Levant and Eastern Mediterranean, and his final naval service was as Commander in Chief America and West Indies Station, 1946–49.

TENNESSEE, U.S.S. Battleship and class (32,600 tons; twelve 14-inch guns). Commissioned in 1920–21, *Tennessee* and CALIFORNIA were never modified before World War II on the scale of earlier American battleship classes, although some minor changes were made. In appearance they were virtually identical to the three ships of the COLORADO class except that where the Tennessees had four triple 14-inch turrets, the Colorados had four 16-inch twins. The two classes were colloquially dubbed the "Big Five." *Tennessee* was damaged at PEARL HARBOR; she was later given a complete modernization. Her hull was considerably widened to provide additional underwater protection, and she received a new streamlined superstructure which gave her a superficial resemblance to the newer SOUTH DAKOTA class.

TENRYU. Class of Japanese light cruisers, built during World War I. *Tenryu* and *Tatsuta* displaced nearly 4,000 tons and had four 5.5-inch guns and six 21-inch torpedo tubes. They served in the early Pacific naval actions; *Tenryu* was sunk in the Bismarck Sea by an American submarine in December 1942, while *Tatsuta* was lost off Japan in March 1944.

TENTH AIR FORCE. This U.S. force was activated on February 12, 1942, at Patterson Field, Ohio, but it remained a paper organization until the 25th of that month, when Maj. Gen. Lewis H. BRERETON arrived in India. A veteran of the unsuccessful defense of the PHILIPPINES and the Netherlands East Indies. Brereton assumed command of the handful of bombers already based in the area; they were the nucleus of the Tenth. It flew its first mission against the Andaman Islands on April 3, with General Brereton in the lead. Reinforcements soon arrived in sufficient numbers to enable him to begin bombing targets in enemy-held BURMA. While it was making these first strikes, Tenth Air Force helped establish an aerial supply route across the Himalayas to support Brig. Gen. Claire CHENNAULT's China Air Task Force. For the remainder of the war Tenth Air Force fighters protected the AIR TRANSPORT COMMAND units flying over the HUMP.

Brereton left India for the Middle East in July 1942; He yielded command of the Tenth in June to Brig. Gen. Earl L. Naiden, who was replaced in August by Maj. Gen. Clayton L. BISSELL. Reinforcements and new equipment greatly enhanced the accomplishments of the Tenth in 1943 and 1944. Achievement of complete air supremacy over Burma multiplied enemy losses. The Tenth's mounting of raids that destroyed shipping, supply dumps, convoys and oil refineries and its cooperation with ground troops were important in stopping Japanese advances into India and China and in the success of the Allied campaign which resulted in the recapture of MYITKYINA, Burma, in August 1944.

TENTH ARMY (U.S.). The field army that invaded and captured the RYUKYU ISLANDS, the chief of which is OKINAWA. It was activated in June 1944, and Lt. Gen. Simon B. BUCKNER, Jr., assumed command in September. The principal components of Tenth Army were XXIV Army Corps and III Amphibious Corps (Marine). The former, consisting of the 7th and the 96th Infantry Divisions, was commanded by Maj. Gen. John R. HODGE. III Amphibious Corps, made up of the 1st and 6th Marine Divisions, was under the command of Maj. Gen. Roy S. GEIGER. Three more divisions—the 27th and the 77th Infantry Divisions and the 2d Marine Division—were under the direct control of Tenth Army for use in special operations and as reserves.

Although Tenth Army as such was a new formation, its elements had all seen action prior to the invasion of the Ryukyus, which began on April 1, 1945. On June 18, while at a forward observation post on Okinawa, General Buckner was killed by enemy gunfire. General Geiger, the senior officer on the island, assumed command of the Tenth Army. On June 23 he was succeeded by Gen. Joseph W. STILWELL. The campaign, the last American battle of World War II, was declared over on July 2.

TENTH FLEET. U.S. Navy designation for the organization established on May 20, 1943, to control antisubmarine operations in Atlantic areas under American command. It was responsible not only for warfare against enemy submarines but also for control and protection of shipping and for American antisubmarine training and development. The Tenth Fleet included a civilian scientific council, as well as operational research and analysis groups. It coordinated technical developments with the training going on in the fleets, providing up-to-date information on Allied and Axis developments and activities to fleet and force commanders responsible for operational planning. It developed new tactical methods based on combining experience with operations research. A shore activity with its headquarters in Washington, the Tenth Fleet was a fleet without a ship or an airplane under its command. Its effect on the antisubmarine war, however, was very real. On June 15, 1945, the Tenth Fleet was dissolved.

TERAUCHI, Count Hisaichi (1879–1946). Japanese field marshal, the son of Masatake Terauchi—also a field marshal—who served as Governor General of Korea and Prime Minister of Japan. After graduating from the Military Academy and the Military War College, the younger Terauchi briefly served as an instructor at the War College. He later held a number of important Army posts, including chief of staff of the Imperial Guards Division and commander of the Japanese Army in Taiwan. As War Minister in the Hirota cabinet, Terauchi crushed the *Kodoha* (Imperial Way faction) Army dissidents of 1936, who desired Japanese expansion north at the expense of the Soviet Union instead of south into China and Southeast Asia. After serving briefly as Inspector of Military Education, Terauchi became commander in chief of Japanese forces in northern China following the outbreak of war there in 1937. In 1941 he became commander in chief of all Japanese Army forces in Southeast Asia (the Southern Area Army), making his headquarters in Saigon. He was promoted to field marshal in 1943. Terauchi surrendered to the Allied command in late November 1945.

TERBOVEN, Josef (1898–1945). Terboven, a native-German Nazi gauleiter, was appointed Reich Commissioner for occupied NORWAY on April 24, 1940. His self-serving and repressive regime brought him into repeated conflict with the puppet government of Vidkun QUISLING and with German military and naval commanders in Norway.

TERMINAL. Code name of the Allied conference at POTSDAM, July 16–August 2, 1945.

TETRYL (trinitrophenylmethylnitramine). An explosive more sensitive than TNT and with a high shattering force. It was used by the U.S. services as a booster and for loading explosive shells for 20-mm. aircraft and antiaircraft guns, after being found too sensitive for heavier-caliber use.

TETRYTOL. A war-developed Allied explosive for use in mines and demolition charges. Tetrytol was a 7–3 composition of TETRYL and TNT.

TÊTU, Marcel (1888–). A World War I pilot and commander, General Têtu commanded all French aviation on the German front from early 1940 and was designated for eventual command of the French Air Force. Following the Franco-German armistice, he held an administrative post in French Africa.

TEXAS, U.S.S. Battleship, second ship of the NEW YORK class, a veteran of landings in NORTHWEST AFRICA, Normandy, SOUTHERN FRANCE, IWO JIMA and OKINAWA.

THAILAND. Japanese troops landed on the southeast coast of Thailand (Siam), on December 8, 1941, requesting permission—virtually an ultimatum—to use Thai soil in their advances on BURMA and Malaya (*see* SINGAPORE). The Thai Prime Minister, who was sympathetic to the Japanese, acceded to the demand, and the two countries entered into an uneasy alliance. Officially, therefore, Thailand came into the war on the side of the Axis, but its ambassador to the United States, Seni Promoj, refused to deliver the declaration of war to the U.S. Government. During the war a strong, well-led underground movement maintained close contact with the Allies. A general distaste for the Japanese presence by most of the Thai people, and cooperation with the Allies by many Thai government officials, fostered an American view that Thailand was not an enemy but a "country to be liberated from the enemy." Thailand was therefore not dealt with as an opponent after World War II.

THALA. Axis forces in TUNISIA struck north from KASSERINE toward Thala on February 22, 1943. They met a strong defense, including artillery, which halted the advance and made Field Marshal ROMMEL decide to abandon the Kasserine offensive.

THEOBALD, Robert Alfred (1884–1957). U.S. Navy officer, a graduate of the Naval Academy in 1907. Theobald became chief of staff to Adm. Claude C. BLOCH in 1939 and Commander of Destroyers Pacific Fleet in December 1941. A rear admiral, in 1942 he served as commander of Task Force 8 in the Aleutians, where he suffered some minor defeats at the hands of the Japanese. In January 1943 he was replaced by Rear Adm. Thomas KINKAID, and he retired in February 1945. "Fuzzy" Theobald attracted considerable attention some years after the war with the publication of his book *The Final Secret of Pearl Harbor: The Washington Background of the Pearl Harbor Attack* (1954), in which he claimed that President Franklin D. ROOSEVELT had "arranged" the Japanese attack on PEARL HARBOR in order that Japan might commit the first act of war in 1941.

THERMOPYLAE. The famous site of a heroic but unsuccessful attempt of 400 Spartans under Leonidas to halt the Persian invasion of Greece in 480 B.C., the pass, which was only a few yards wide in ancient times, has been widened to approximately three miles in modern times. During World War II, retreating British forces (mostly Australian and New Zealand troops) held back the onrushing Germans here during late April 1941. Their stand made it possible to evacuate large numbers of British troops that might otherwise have had to surrender. The British position was held during the day of April 24. That night the defenders were moved back.

THETIS. A German RADAR-deception buoy used extensively in the Bay of Biscay, a submarine transit area heavily patrolled by Allied land-based planes. It created a radar image similar to that of a submarine; U-boats passing through the bay dropped numbers of these decoys to create multiple radar images and confuse possible attackers.

THIRD ARMY (U.S.). Originally created in France just before the armistice in 1918, the Third Army performed occupation duty in Germany before being deactivated; it was reactivated in 1932 as one of four U.S. field armies. Third Army headquarters departed for duty in the European theater in January 1944; Lt. Gen. George S. PATTON, Jr., assumed command in England.

In July 1944, following the INVASION of Normandy, Third Army headquarters moved across the Channel to the COTENTIN PENINSULA. Already some Third Army divisions had been sent to the Continent for service with the First Army, and on August 1 the Third Army became operational. Its commander, General Patton, was one of the most colorful and controversial figures of the entire war; but in addition to being flamboyant, he was hard-driving and imaginative, and possessed a masterly knowledge of military history. Many of his personal traits and views had been adopted by the members of his command, whose part in the campaign was to overrun Brittany and exploit the breakout by the First Army. It was a part, observes the British historian Maj. Gen. H. Essame, for which "both he and his troops were, above all others, supremely well qualified." During the month of August, says the U.S. official historian, Martin Blumenson, "Patton and his army . . . were to find a situation perfectly suited to the expression of their principles of combat."

The result was the Third Army's spectacular dash across France, one of the greatest American accomplishments of the war. In the Battle of the Bulge, the Third Army came to the relief of Bastogne. Subsequently it moved into Germany, crossed the Rhine, crossed Germany, moved over the Danube and ended its fighting in Czechoslovakia. Six corps (III, V, VIII, XII, XV and XX) at various times made up the Third Army; 40 U.S. divisions and one foreign division were assigned to it for varying periods.

Following the end of hostilities, the Third Army was assigned to occupation duty in Germany, as it had been after World War I. *See also* Western Front.

THIRD FLEET (U.S.). Force established in April 1942 as the South Pacific Force under Vice-Adm. R. L. Ghormley, redesignated the Third Fleet on March 15, 1943; Adm. William F. Halsey had assumed command the previous October, and held the title throughout the Pacific war. During 1944 and 1945, however, the Third Fleet and the Fifth Fleet were actually the same force; their command element alternated between operations. When commanded by Admiral Halsey, the force was called the Third Fleet; when commanded by Adm. Raymond Spruance, it was the Fifth Fleet.

THIRTEENTH AIR FORCE. Formed in December 1942 from the U.S. Air Force units rushed to the South Pacific in order to check the Japanese advance toward Australia and launch a counterthrust into the Solomon Islands, and nicknamed the Jungle Air Force, the Thirteenth supported the advance from the Solomons, by way of the Admiralties, to the Philippines.

In April 1943, P-38s of the Thirteenth (*see* P-38) intercepted the plane carrying Adm. Isoroku Yamamoto and shot it down, thus killing Japan's most prominent naval leader. Besides pounding the Japanese base at Rabaul, New Britain, the Jungle Air Force launched B-24s (*see* B-24) from the northernmost Solomons to attack Truk, an overwater mission that involved more than 13 hours in the air. The bombing of Truk and other bases in the Caroline Islands continued as American amphibious forces, assisted by Thirteenth Air Force squadrons, seized bases in the Marianas.

Following the Marianas invasion, B-24 squadrons commenced operations from northeastern New Guinea against targets in the Philippines and the Netherlands East Indies. By the summer of 1945, when Japan at last surrendered, Thirteenth Air Force Liberators were flying 18-hour missions from Palawan in the southwestern Philippines against Batavia in Java and Balikpapan in Borneo.

THOMA, Wilhelm Ritter von (1891–1948). German Army officer who played a leading role in the development of Germany's armored forces after 1934. Between 1936 and 1939 Thoma commanded all the German ground forces in Spain, where he was called the Butcher of Guernica. He led a panzer brigade in Poland in 1939 and then became the director of mobile forces on the General Staff. In 1940 Adolf Hitler sent him to Cyrenaica to study ways to help the Italians, but Thoma reported that North Africa was an unpromising theater with difficult supply problems.

During 1941 and most of 1942 Thoma led a panzer division and then a corps in Russia, but in September 1942 Hitler sent him to North Africa to command the Afrika Korps. In the Battle of Alamein, Thoma briefly commanded all the Axis forces (Panzer Army Africa) after the death of General Stumme, until the return of Field Marshal Rommel from sick leave. Thoma was taken prisoner at the front during this battle and had dinner with Field Marshal Montgomery; he was held prisoner during the rest of the war. Liddell Hart assessed him as a "tough but likeable type," who loved fighting for the zest of it and would fight without ill-feeling, respecting any worthy opponent.

THOMAS, Georg (1890–1946). German Army officer (General der Infanterie), chief of the war economy and armaments office of the OKW in 1938–44 (*see* OKW). He opposed the launching of war in 1939, arguing that Germany lacked adequate raw materials, food supplies and financial resources.

THOMPSON, Charles Ralfe (1894–1966). Commander Thompson, Royal Navy, was personal assistant to Prime Minister Winston Churchill, 1940–45. The main responsibility of the "Flag Commander," as Churchill called him, was to organize Churchill's travels.

THOMSEN, Hans (1891–1968). German diplomat, chargé d'affaires in Washington after the recall of Ambassador Hans Dieckhoff in November 1938, following the Nazi wave of violence against Jews in Germany. Thomsen worked assiduously to promote the German cause in the news media and among politicians, and at the same time he attempted to present his government with a realistic picture of American opinion.

THOR. A German 61.5-mm. (24.2-inch) antifortress mortar, also known as Karl, Thor was the second heaviest artillery piece used by any combatant in World War II. Firing a 2¼-ton concrete-piercing projectile, the mortar contributed to the reduction of the Sevastopol stronghold in June 1941.

THOUSAND PLAN. Name for the first RAF 1,000-bomber raid, on Cologne on May 30, 1942. Following this attack, Sir Arthur Harris, chief of Bomber Command, launched a "thousand" attack on Essen on June 1. Once again, aircraft and crews from training units supplemented the operational crews from Bomber Command. Immediately after the Essen attack the thousand force was disbanded. Harris, however, conceived the idea of four "thousand" attacks per month. With the support of the Chief of Air Staff and the Prime Minister, plus cooperation from the First Sea Lord, a third "thousand" attack was launched, against Bremen on the night of June 25–26. However, increased casualties, particularly among the operational training aircraft, compelled Bomber Command to conserve its reserves, and the attack on Bremen was the last "thousand" attack on a single target in a single night until 1944.

THUNDERCLAP. Code name for the Allied bombing of DRESDEN, February 1945.

THUNDERSTORM (Gewitter). Name given to the roundup by the GESTAPO of thousands of suspects following the July 20, 1944, attempt to assassinate Adolf HITLER. *See also* OPPOSITION TO HITLER.

THURSDAY. Code name for the advance of the CHINDITS behind Japanese lines in BURMA in March 1944. Gen. Orde WINGATE, the Chindits' commander, died in a plane crash in this operation.

TIBBETS, Paul W., Jr. (1915–). After flying antisubmarine patrols along the Atlantic coast of the United States, Tibbets went to the European theater and flew 25 B-17 missions (*see* B-17), among them the raid on ROUEN–SOTTEVILLE, the first attack by EIGHTH AIR FORCE bomber command against Nazi-occupied Europe. He saw further combat in North Africa, then was ordered to the United States in 1943, where he flight-tested B-29s (*see* B-29). Then Gen. Henry H. ARNOLD personally selected him from a list of officers to command a special combat unit for training crews to deliver ATOMIC BOMBS. On August 6, 1945, Colonel Tibbets piloted the B-29 ENOLA GAY over HIROSHIMA to deliver history's first atomic attack.

TIDAL WAVE. Code name for the American operation to bomb PLOESTI, Rumania, August 1, 1943.

TIGER. Code name for a British operation to pass a convoy of five fast merchant ships loaded with tanks through the Mediterranean in May 1941. With German dive-bombers based in Sicily and Italy, this was certain to be a hazardous operation. The convoy was escorted by FORCE H and the Mediterranean Fleet. One merchant ship (*Empire Song*) was sunk by a mine, but the remaining four reached Alexandria safely, bringing welcome reinforcements for the Eighth Army of 238 tanks and 43 Hurricane aircraft.

TIGER MOTH. Royal Air Force de Havilland elementary biplane trainer, first delivered in 1932 as a development of the earlier Gipsy Moth trainer and utility plane of the 1920s. Production of Tiger Moths I and II continued into 1945 in Britain, Canada, New Zealand and Australia. More than 7,000 were produced, of which some were converted to radio-controlled Queen Bee gunnery-target drones. Tiger Moths served throughout the British Commonwealth until well after World War II as primary training planes, being suitable for instrument flying and aerobatics. During its long service career, the Tiger Moth was a universally known and deservedly popular aircraft. It had a 130-horsepower (120 horsepower in the Mark I) liquid-cooled engine, which gave it a top speed of 109 miles per hour, and a wingspan of 20 feet 4 inches.

TIGER TANK. German heavy TANK.

TIKHVIN. City southeast of Lake LADOGA, a key point on the Soviet supply route to LENINGRAD. It was taken by the Germans on November 8, 1941, and retaken by the Red Army on December 9.

TIMOR. Largest of the Lesser Sunda Islands, Netherlands East Indies (NEI), Timor was strategically located less than 400 miles from Australia's north coast. The Japanese landed in two places on February 20, 1942, in their overall conquest of the NEI. Three days later the island was under Japanese control, but Allied troops, who had avoided capture, continued to conduct effective guerrilla warfare operations until December, when they were withdrawn to Australia. The island was not reoccupied by the Allies until the surrender of Japan.

TIMOSHENKO, Semën K. (1895–1970). A young man at the time of the Russian Revolution, Timoshenko was a Red cavalry leader in the ensuing Civil War and became a friend of Joseph STALIN's—a fact that may have enabled him to survive the political purges of the 1930s. In 1940 he was the victorious commander in the SOVIET-FINNISH WAR, and in May he was made a marshal and appointed Defense Minister; in this post he worked on improving the RED ARMY's organization and training, which were still suffering from the effects of the purge of officers.

In June 1941, after the German onslaught came, Timoshenko temporarily became Commander in Chief of the Soviet armies, but on July 10 Stalin claimed the post for himself and Timoshenko was assigned to command of the West Theater, on the approaches to Moscow. In August he was in command at SMOLENSK, where his forces managed to slow down the German advance. In September he was put in command of the new Southwest Front, to retrieve what could be saved from the massive defeat suffered by Soviet forces under Marshal BUDËNNY.

In May 1942 Timoshenko, under pressure from Stalin, led a Soviet attack at KHARKOV; its disastrous outcome and other reverses appear to have lowered Timoshenko in Stalin's esteem, and he was called to Moscow in July. Subsequently he commanded in the northwest and served as a troubleshooter on various fronts, coordinating actions of armies for the SOVIET HIGH COMMAND (of which he had been an original member). But he never returned to the eminence he had attained in the early days of the war.

TINDALL. *See* COCKADE.

TINIAN. Separated by only three miles of water from SAIPAN, Tinian sits in the middle of the MARIANA ISLANDS. The Marianas were chosen as a U.S. strategic objective because of the need for bases from which B-29s could bomb Japan (*see* B-29). Saipan was thus selected as a target because it could serve as a base from which Tinian could be attacked. In mid-1944 Tinian, the least mountainous island of the Marianas, held three fine airfields and one more under construction, which the Japanese had developed for use in staging aircraft to and from the home islands. Scheduled to be invaded on July 24, 1944, Tinian received the most thorough pre-invasion bombardment of any island objective in the war.

The landing on Tinian was unique in that it was possible to take Marine unit commanders on reconnaissance flights over the objective. Another unusual aspect of this operation was that it was one of the few shore-to-shore (as opposed to ship-to-shore) landings of the war. And it was on Tinian that NAPALM bombs were first employed in the war. The landing went off as scheduled, with the 4th Marine Division landing on the 24th and expanding the beachhead the next day; on the 26th it was joined by the 2d Marine Division. On August 1 organized resistance ended. In this operation, 317 marines were killed, 1,550 wounded and 27 missing. Japanese losses were much higher, with nearly 5,000 killed.

TINY TIM. U.S. naval high-velocity aircraft rocket with a large (11.75-inch) head diameter. It carried 150 pounds of high explosive and had a range of one mile.

TIRPITZ. German battleship completed in 1941, sister ship of the more famous BISMARCK. One of the most powerful battleships in the world, with a displacement of 42,000 tons and a main armament of eight 15-inch guns, the *Tirpitz* spent her war career in Norwegian waters operating against the Allied convoys to Russia. Her presence obliged the Allies to maintain a large fleet in northern waters to guard against her, and repeated attempts were made to sink her. In September 1943 she was damaged by British MIDGET SUBMARINES, and in April 1944 she was attacked in the Altenfjord by torpedo bombers from British aircraft carriers. Partially crippled, she was transferred to Tromsö, where she was finally sunk by the famous DAM BUSTERS squadron of the RAF on November 12, 1944.

TISO, Josef (1887–1947). Roman Catholic priest who became active in Slovak nationalist politics after World War I and in 1938 became head of the Slovak People's Party. After the MUNICH AGREEMENT, Monsignor Tiso became Prime Minister of the new autonomous Slovakian Government. The Czech Government removed him from office in March 1939, but, with HITLER's help, Slovakia became independent and Tiso regained his office. In October he was elected President of the puppet Slovak republic.

TITO (1892–). Tito, whose real name was Josip Broz (or Brozovitch), was the general secretary of the Yugoslav Communist Party before World War II. After the German invasion and occupation of Yugoslavia in June 1941, Tito organized a resistance movement, calling his forces PARTISANS after the irregular units which had fought against Napoleon in Spain in 1808 and in Russia in 1812. The Partisans were Communists. Their slogan was "Death to Fascism, Liberty to the People."

Within weeks of their formation, the Partisans had liberated a substantial amount of territory in western Serbia. In the liberated area they established so-called people's councils (*odbors*) modeled on the soviets in revolutionary Russia, and they opened schools, published a newspaper, performed plays and even encouraged sports events.

In the fall of 1942 Tito set up the Anti-Fascist Council of National Liberation of Yugoslavia (AVNOJ) to function as a rudimentary future government. AVNOJ's program included a guarantee of equal rights for all minorities, respect for private property and postponement of any social change until national elections after the war. In 1943 AVNOJ created the National Liberation Committee as a temporary cabinet, with Tito as Premier. At the same time, at TEHERAN, President ROOSEVELT and Prime Minister CHURCHILL agreed to give large-scale military aid to the Partisans.

Throughout this entire period Tito's forces vied for the loyalties of the people with two other groups—the CHETNIKS, a Serbian nationalist movement organized by Draža MIHAJLOVIĆ, and the prewar Yugoslav Government under King PETER, who escaped to England in 1941. Mihajlović loathed Communism and resisted all efforts by Tito to combine forces under joint command. In November 1941 Mihajlović ordered the Chetniks to attack the Partisans, and for the rest of the war the two resistance movements fought each other. After the war Mihajlović was arrested and subsequently was executed on the charge of collaborating with the Germans.

The situation with the royal government-in-exile was more complicated. Initially Tito declined all suggestions to negotiate with King Peter, because of the King's support of Mihajlović in 1941. In 1943 the British began supporting Tito and supplying him with matériel; the Americans soon followed suit. In 1944, under pressure from the British, Peter appealed for unity. On June 11 Tito and Peter reached an accord in which the King recognized the achievements of AVNOJ along with the Partisans. In return Tito played down his Communism and sent two representatives to form a new regime. Several months later a second agreement was signed, which provided for a regency to act for the King until the long-awaited plebiscite on the nature of the government could be held. In early 1945 the new government took office with Tito as Premier and Ivan SUBASIĆ, representing the King, as Foreign Minister. Of the 28 cabinet posts, only five were not held by members of Tito's group. Following the conclusion of hostilities, AVNOJ, its membership temporarily swollen by members of the prewar Parliament as well as other non-Communists, became the National Provisional Parliament. Most of the other parties, convinced of their weakness, boycotted the elections that were then held, and Tito's Communist-dominated provisional government received a full vote of confidence. In November the constituent assembly declared Yugoslavia a republic and condemned King Peter as having supported collaborationists. Marshal Tito was in full control of Yugoslavia.

TIZARD, Sir Henry Thomas (1885–1959). As head of the Tizard Committee, 1935–36, Tizard was the scientist primarily responsible for the initial development of RADAR in Britain, and, as chairman of the Aeronautical Research Committee, 1933–43, he was personally responsible for the early development of airborne radar. Renowned as an administrator as well as a scientist, Tizard also served during the war as chairman of the

Committee for the Scientific Survey of Air Defence, 1939–40, an offshoot of which was a committee to investigate the feasibility of the ATOMIC BOMB. In 1940 Tizard was leader of a British scientific mission to Canada and the United States, which gave Canada her start in war research and enormously assisted American radar research and development. In 1941–42 he served on the Aircraft Supply Committee and represented the Ministry of Aircraft Production in the Air Council. His influence on British war science was severely curtailed by the antipathy existing between him and Professor Lindemann (Lord CHERWELL), scientific adviser to Winston CHURCHILL throughout the war.

TJILATJAP. Port on the south coast of JAVA, used as a base by the ABDA (Allied) fleet in early 1942. The ABDA COMMAND was dissolved on March 1, 1942, and the ships ordered to withdraw.

TOBRUK. At one time the main Italian fortress in Libya, Tobruk was important to the British as a port through which to supply their Desert Army. Italian fortifications, utilizing wire, an antitank ditch, booby traps and inner defensive posts, formed a 30-mile perimeter around the area, eight to nine miles from the harbor. Tobruk was captured by the British from the Italians in one day, January 21, 1941; besieged by Gen. Erwin ROMMEL from April to December 1941; and captured by Rommel in a one-day battle, June 21, 1942. Winston CHURCHILL, receiving the news of Tobruk's fall while in Washington conferring with President ROOSEVELT, called it "one of the heaviest blows I can recall during the war."

Tobruk changed hands for the last time on November 13, 1942, when it was taken by the British EIGHTH ARMY's 10th Corps. *See also* NORTH AFRICA.

TODT, Fritz (1891–1942). One of the outstanding organizers and engineers of the Third Reich, Dr. Todt had joined the Nazi Party in 1922. After the party came to power in 1933, he undertook the building of the famous autobahns. Under Hermann GÖRING's "Four-Year Plan," he was in charge of the entire German construction industry. His "Todt Organization" built the WEST WALL and, later, roads and other facilities in occupied countries. In 1940 he was appointed Minister of Armaments and Munitions. Many of these posts were held simultaneously; as Albert SPEER observed, he "held the positions of three ministers." On April 8, 1942, Dr. Todt was killed when his airplane crashed after taking off from Adolf HITLER's headquarters at Rastenburg, East Prussia. He was immediately succeeded by Speer.

TOGO, Shigenori (1882–1950). Several years after graduating from Tokyo Imperial University in 1908, Togo entered the Japanese foreign service. First posted to Mukden, Manchuria, he served in Switzerland, at the Versailles peace conference and in Germany before returning to Japan. He married a German woman shortly after coming home. Between 1921 and 1925 he was in charge of the Russian section of the European-American affairs bureau of the Foreign Office. Then he was again sent abroad, as first secretary to the embassy in Washington (1925–29) and then in Berlin (1929–33). Togo returned to Japan in 1933 to become director of the European bureau of the Foreign Office. Four years later he became ambassador to Germany (December 1937–October 1938); he then went to the Soviet Union as ambassador (October 1938–August 1940).

Appointed Foreign Minister in Hideki TOJO's cabinet in October 1941, Togo failed to achieve any breakthrough in the negotiations with the United States. He resigned in September 1942 in protest against Tojo's plan to create a Greater East Asian Ministry to handle Japan's relations with allied Asian nations apart from the Foreign Ministry. Togo again became Foreign Minister in Japan's last wartime cabinet under Kantaro SUZUKI. Sentenced to 20 years' imprisonment by the INTERNATIONAL MILITARY TRIBUNAL FOR THE FAR EAST in 1948 for "crimes of conspiracy against peace," Togo died in an American military hospital in July 1950, shortly after finishing the first draft of his book *The Cause of Japan.*

TOJO, Hideki (1884–1948). Premier of Japan from October 16, 1941, until July 18, 1944, General Tojo was the leader and spokesman of the militarists who felt war was a necessary route toward Japanese national goals.

The son of a self-made military man, Tojo as a child was spirited, competitive, self-confident and perhaps unusually quarrelsome. He attended Japan's Military Academy, was commissioned into the Army and graduated from the War College with honors in 1915.

During the early 1930s, when the Japanese Army was beginning to force government policy, Tojo became one of the leaders of the so-called Control Group within the Army—a group which favored increasing control of the state by the military and looked to China and Southeast Asia as a solution to Japan's economic and population problems. The belief was widespread in Japan that the West was hostile to Japan's best interests and thus Japan must be aggressive in defense of her national well-being. During the disorder and internal violence of the 1930s, Tojo's career progressed rapidly. In 1935 he was made commander of the military police of the Japanese KWANTUNG ARMY in Manchuria. There he had the opportunity to demonstrate a strong belief in "law and order," for he took the position that any action not sanctioned by the Emperor made one a rebel. In 1937, the year the government adopted the policy of making Japan the "stabilizing influence" in Asia, he was made chief of staff of the Kwantung Army. In 1937 he proved an effective leader in combat. In March 1938 he entered the government as Vice-Minister for War.

Tojo, a direct, simple man, had no personal misgivings about the legitimacy of the use of force to overcome obstacles or the reality of the threats to Japan's existence. The NEW ORDER he considered of "fundamental importance" to Japan: Japan needed China for trade and food; both countries would benefit, and the concept had a "moral basis."

In July 1940 Tojo was named War Minister in the KONOYE cabinet. He did not play a major role in forming the AXIS alliance, but he approved of it because it ended Japan's "isolation." During 1941 Japan gradually became committed to a state policy of aggression to achieve its long-range goals. Prince Konoye continued to seek a satisfactory settlement by negotiation with the

United States, but in October, when a decision had to be made about agreeing to American terms, Tojo insisted that Japan cease negotiations rather than give up any of the gains in China. The Army and Navy were not agreed on the issue of war, and the Konoye cabinet fell. On October 16 Tojo was instructed to form a government, and he was told the Army and Navy must come to some agreement. Tojo was also given a clean slate; the new government was to decide its policy free of earlier decisions to go to war if negotiations did not bring the desired gains. Tojo later said he might not have accepted the position without the "clean slate."

Although associated in the Western mind with Hitler and Mussolini, Tojo was not their equal in power and did not approach war leadership in the same way. Unlike the other two Axis leaders, he did not use invective or attempt to degrade the enemy. Rather than looking on Japan's enemies with contempt, Tojo sought to caution the Japanese people against the intoxication of victory and prepare them for a long, hard effort. In actual fact, Japan was a dictatorship, but the power was held by the supreme command, even though after February 1944 Tojo was Premier, War Minister and Army Chief of Staff. After the war Tojo said the power of the supreme command had been too great and he felt the imbalance in the government had been a prime cause of Japan's defeat.

Japan's losses mounted from 1942 onward, and after the fall of SAIPAN in 1944 pressure from within the cabinet and from influential elder statesmen forced him to resign. Almost overnight he became an object of abuse, blamed for Japan's failures. His wife, who had an unusual amount of education for a Japanese woman of her generation, also came under harsh criticism. They lived private lives until September 1945, when the Americans occupied Japan.

When American soldiers came to his residence to arrest him, Tojo shot himself through the chest. American doctors saved his life, and he spent the following months in prisons. During the long, tedious war crimes trial conducted by the INTERNATIONAL MILITARY TRIBUNAL FOR THE FAR EAST, he tried to take all blame upon himself and establish the Emperor's complete innocence. He lived out his last months calmly, and in his final statement he expressed contrition for atrocities committed by Japanese forces. He was hanged on December 22, 1948.

TOKYO EXPRESS. Journalists' term for the Japanese surface forces which brought reinforcements and supplies to GUADALCANAL during the battle for that island. They were called the CACTUS EXPRESS by American forces in the area.

TOKYO FIRE RAID. Disappointed by the results of high-altitude precision attacks against Japanese industry, Gen. Henry H. ARNOLD, commander of U.S. Army Air Forces, and his advisers decided to try area bombing, employing incendiary bombs to burn out the cities in which Japan's industry was concentrated. Selected to carry out this program of destruction was Maj. Gen. Curtis E. LEMAY, who in January 1945 assumed command of the MARIANAS-based XXI Bomber Command.

LeMay led off with tests, raids during which the B-29s (*see* B-29) dropped their incendiaries from high altitude, but high winds scattered the six-pound bombs and results were judged to be poor. He next proposed attacking at night from low altitude, where wind would not be a major factor, but his staff argued that this would be suicidal. LeMay insisted, however, that Japanese RADAR was too primitive to cope with hundreds of low-flying B-29s.

He put his theory to the test on the night of March 9, 1945, when more than 300 B-29s took off from the Marianas, roared over Tokyo in loose streams (guided by PATHFINDERS) rather than the usual compact formations, and from altitudes between 4,900 and 9,200 feet burned large portions of the city to ashes. The B-29s, which carried no guns or ammunition (except for the tail gun position) so that they could accommodate a greater weight of bombs, rained down incendiaries and napalm containers. The devastation was appalling. Japanese records showed 267,171 homes—nearly 25 percent of all buildings in the capital city of Japan—were consumed by fire, 1,008,005 persons left homeless, 83,793 killed and 40,918 injured. Twenty-five days passed before the last of the dead were dug from the ruins.

This raid established a new pattern for the air war. By June 15 a similar fate had been visited upon Nagoya, Kobe, Osaka, Yokohama and Kawasaki. The six cities thus destroyed had a combined urban area of 257.2 square miles, of which 105.6 miles were devoured by flame. Japanese industry was crippled, millions were driven from their homes and hundreds of thousands were killed or injured. The havoc was wrought by 41,592 tons of bombs dropped during some 6,000 B-29 sorties. Only 136 bombers were lost.

TOKYO ROSE (Iva Ikuko Toguri D'Aquino) (1916–). An American citizen of Japanese parentage whose broadcasts on Tokyo radio were designed to weaken the morale of American troops through supposedly upsetting references to life back home. The nickname came from the men in the South Pacific, who in fact enjoyed her programs, which featured nostalgia and good dance music. After the war Mrs. D'Aquino was convicted of treason and sentenced to 10 years' imprisonment and a fine of $10,000. She was released after serving six years. Some 30 years after the end of the war she sought a Presidential pardon, on the grounds that she had been trapped in Japan at the time of Pearl Harbor and had been forced to broadcast for the Japanese and that she was only one of various persons dubbed "Tokyo Rose." On his last full day in office—January 19, 1977—President Gerald Ford granted the pardon.

TOLBUKHIN, Fedor I. (1894–1949). Soviet general, commander of the Fifty-seventh Army, which played a principal role in the encirclement of the German SIXTH ARMY inside STALINGRAD in early 1943. In 1944 Tolbukhin was placed in command of the Fourth Ukrainian Front for the liberation of the CRIMEA. Subsequently he headed the attack on Bulgaria after the Soviet Government declared war on that country in September 1944. After the occupation of Bulgaria, he led his forces into Hungary, capturing BUDAPEST in February 1945. Tolbukhin rose to the rank of Marshal of the Soviet Union.

TOMIOKA, Sadatoshi (1900–1970). Japanese admiral, chiefly responsible for planning overall naval operations. From October 1940 to January 1943 he was operations section chief of the Naval General Staff, from September 1943 to November 1944 chief of staff of the Southeast Area Fleet and from November 1944 to the end of the war the operations bureau chief of the Naval General Staff. Tomioka unsuccessfully opposed both the PEARL HARBOR and MIDWAY operations, but strongly supported plans to invade Australia and to seize PORT MORESBY. Following the war Tomioka edited a Japanese naval history of the Pacific war, served as a member of the 12-man commission advising the Japanese Government on setting up a defense program in 1951 and lectured at the Japanese Defense Research Institute.

TONE. Japanese heavy cruiser and class, of more than 14,000 tons loaded displacement, with eight 8-inch guns (4×2). A development of the MOGAMI class, they reflected the stress placed on cruiser reconnaissance in Japanese fleet doctrine. Their 8-inch guns were concentrated forward in a unique arrangement of four twin turrets; the after deck was equipped with two catapults and tracks for handling five scout floatplanes. Both of these fast ships served extensively throughout the Pacific war. CHIKUMA was lost in the battle for LEYTE GULF. *Tone,* sunk in shallow water by carrier planes during raids on the Inland Sea late in July 1945, was later scrapped.

TORCH. Code name for the Allied invasion of NORTHWEST AFRICA, November 8, 1942, and the subsequent advance into TUNISIA.

TORGAU. German town on the Elbe River where on April 25, 1945, an American patrol under 2d Lt. William D. Robertson, 273d Infantry, 69th Division, met Russians of the 173d Rifle Regiment, 58th Guards Infantry Division. Although another patrol farther upstream met the Russians 45 minutes earlier, the patrol leader reported erroneous map coordinates of his position, so that Lieutenant Robertson's was officially designated as first contact. Division and corps commanders met on succeeding days, while on the 30th the U.S. First Army Commander, Lt. Gen. Courtney H. HODGES, ceremoniously greeted the commander of the First Ukrainian Front.

TORPECKER. U.S. Navy slang term for a torpedo bomber and also for TORPEDO.

TORPEDO. In addition to being carried by surface craft and submarines, as was the case in World War I, torpedoes were delivered during World War II by naval aircraft, as in the British attack on the Italian fleet at TARANTO and the Japanese assault on PEARL HARBOR. As the PACIFIC WAR developed, torpedo planes played a key part in a new kind of naval battle—carrier versus carrier—such as the CORAL SEA and MIDWAY. But, of course, submarines continued to use the torpedo with devastating effect: the Germans sank 14 million tons of Allied shipping (3 million more than in World War I), and the Americans destroyed the bulk of Japanese shipping, sending 5 million tons to the bottom. Various navies also had small surface torpedo boats—the American PT, the British MTB, the German E-boat, the Italian MAS-boat (see separate articles for these craft).

Torpedoes were of two general types, air-steam-propelled and electric (powered by batteries). Electric torpedoes tended to have shorter ranges and slower speeds, but they had the advantage of leaving no telltale wake.

The Japanese developed an electric torpedo (the Type 92, Mod-1) as early as 1934, but by the beginning of the war were giving first place to a very satisfactory air-steam torpedo (the Type 95, Mod-1). For surface-craft use they had the famous oxygen-fueled 24-inch LONG LANCE torpedo. The Germans likewise started the war with an electric torpedo, which they used to particular effect against American coastal shipping in the first months of 1942. The Americans salvaged several of these; this not only gave impetus to the Americans' own electric-torpedo project, already under way (the Mark II), but led to the establishment of another development project (the Mark XVIII), a combination of American and German features.

The most widely used German air-steam torpedo was the 21-inch G7a, called ultimately the T I. The Germans pioneered the acoustic torpedo, which was designed to home on the propeller noise of a convoy escort ship; the cargo ships themselves would be attacked by regular torpedoes. This acoustic torpedo was called the Wren (Zaunkönig—the T V). The Allied riposte was the Foxer, a noisemaking device—more alluring to a torpedo than a propeller—towed at a safe distance behind a ship.

American submarines were vexed by various torpedo problems. The standard Mark XIV air-steam torpedo sometimes worked well but often failed to function; it would not run at the set depth, would explode en route to the target or would fail to explode on hitting the target. The magnetic exploder was thought by some to be the chief problem (the Germans had tried and discarded magnetic exploders), but even when it was disconnected, problems remained; the deficiencies were various and interconnected. The problem was not solved until the autumn of 1943, after a great deal of engineering labor and bureaucratic hassling. Finally the Mark XVIII was ready; 30 percent of the torpedoes fired in 1944 were electric, and from July of that year submarines carried 75 percent electric torpedoes.

TORPEDO JUNCTION. American slang expression referring to the portion of the Coral Sea between the SOLOMONS and ESPIRITU SANTO, New Hebrides, patrolled by Japanese submarines. It was used as the title of a wartime book on the Solomons fighting.

TORPEX. A British war-developed explosive, intended primarily for use in underwater ordnance, originally a combination of 45 percent RDX (*see* RDX), 37 percent TNT and 18 percent powdered aluminum (the proportion of TNT was later increased to 40 percent). Adopted by the U.S. Navy in 1942, it was used in mines and depth charges as well as in warheads for torpedoes. Nearly half again as powerful as TNT, it produced a greater blast effect than any other production burster explosive.

TOTALIZE. Code name of the Canadian FIRST ARMY attack toward Falaise (France), August 8, 1944.

TOTAL WAR. Conflict that involves the complete national mobilization of all available material and manpower resources for the attaining of victory. Its tridimensional (land, sea and air) character tends to obliterate any distinction between combatants and noncombatants.

TOULON. The French naval base and port city of Toulon, with 175,000 inhabitants, suffered severely during World War II. From the summer of 1940 most of the French fleet moved to this VICHY-controlled port. On November 11, 1942, the Germans invaded Vichy France, but it seemed they might be persuaded to leave Toulon in Vichy hands. On November 27, however, German troops forced their way onto the base in a surprise attempt to seize the ships, only to find that Adm. Jean de LABORDE had ordered the three battleships, seven cruisers, 32 destroyers and sundry other units scuttled; only a few of the light units escaped, and none of the major vessels served the Axis. Following the occupation Toulon was the target of devastating Allied air attacks until its liberation in August 1944.

TOVEY, John Cronyn, 1st Baron Tovey of Langton Matravers (1885–1971). As a young Royal Navy officer, Tovey spent much of his time in destroyers and made a considerable name for himself when commanding H.M.S. *Onslow* at the Battle of Jutland on May 31, 1916. He was Rear Admiral, Destroyers, in the Mediterranean at the outbreak of the Second World War, and after promotion to vice-admiral became second-in-command of the Mediterranean Fleet. In 1940 he was brought home to relieve Adm. Sir Charles FORBES as commander in chief of the Home Fleet, an appointment he held until 1943, through the most difficult and anxious years of the war. His main responsibilities during this period were the protection of the big troop convoys from Britain to the Middle East, the organization and escorting of convoys to Russia, the guarding of the Atlantic trade routes against attack by German raiders and the neutralization of enemy warships along the Norwegian coast. He is probably best remembered for his chase and destruction of the German battleship BISMARCK when she broke out into the Atlantic in May 1941, but the real measure of his success lies more in his steady control of the Atlantic throughout his period of chief command, when the sea blockade of Germany was maintained without danger of a break.

On completion of his tenure of this high command in 1943 he was promoted to Admiral of the Fleet, and he completed the war as commander in chief the Nore (the naval command for eastern England), an appointment which brought him into close association with the planning and execution of Operation Overlord, the Allied INVASION of northwest Europe.

TOWNSEND, Peter (1914–). RAF fighter pilot who on February 3, 1940, led his HURRICANE section against a German HEINKEL HE 111 bomber, which became the first enemy plane shot down over England in the war. He was in the thick of the Battle of BRITAIN, his squadron being based at Croydon. A resourceful commander, he was credited with 11 kills overall. He has written about the Battle of Britain in *Duel of Eagles*.

TOYODA, Soemu (1885–1957). After graduating from the Japanese Naval Academy and the Naval War College, Toyoda held a variety of posts. He was captain of several warships and he participated in naval education. He was also involved in naval construction, eventually serving as director of the naval construction department, 1939–41. In September 1941 he was appointed commander in chief of the Kure Naval District. He replaced Adm. Mineichi KOGA as Commander in Chief of the COMBINED FLEET in 1944. The Japanese Navy under his command lost repeatedly to superior American naval forces in the seas off the Philippines and Formosa. Admiral Toyoda became Chief of the Naval General Staff in May 1945, and in that position strongly supported the Army hard-liners, Gen. Korechika ANAMI and Gen. Yoshijiro UMEZU, who hoped to continue the war. Acquitted of war crimes by the INTERNATIONAL MILITARY TRIBUNAL FOR THE FAR EAST, Toyoda went into retirement after the war.

TRACTABLE. Code name of a Canadian push toward Falaise (France), a follow-up to Operation TOTALIZE.

TRANSPORTATION PLAN. Known also as the railway bombing plan, the Tedder plan, the Zuckerman plan and the AEAF plan. Put forward and strongly supported by SHAEF, the Transportation Plan called for the bombing of railway yards and facilities in the area of the Normandy INVASION. It was based on an analysis by Prof. Solly ZUCKERMAN and was vigorously advocated by Air Chief Marshal Sir Arthur TEDDER, the Deputy Supreme Allied Commander. The purpose, Tedder wrote, was to "delay and disorganize enemy ground movement both during and after the . . . assault." The plan encountered some strong opposition from British and U.S. bomber commanders, who objected to the diversion of effort from "strategic" targets in Germany, and from members of the WAR CABINET, including the Prime Minister, because of the political and other implications of large-scale bombing of France. The Supreme Commander, Gen. Dwight D. EISENHOWER, pressed hard for a favorable decision, and the French Gen. Marie Pierre KOENIG gave his support. A railway bombing plan was carried out beginning in May 1944; by D-Day 76,200 tons of bombs had been dropped on rail centers, bridges and open tracks. All routes over the Seine north of Paris were closed and remained so for the next month. Railway traffic was cut almost in half between the middle of May and June 9.

TRAPANI. After the capture of Palermo, SICILY, Col. James M. GAVIN and the 505th Parachute Infantry were directed to take Trapani. Much of their advance was like a parade, as Sicilians welcomed them with fruit. A roadblock and several hours of artillery fire delayed them just outside Trapani, which was nevertheless captured quickly (July 23, 1943).

TREADWAY BRIDGE. U.S. Army engineers in 1941 designed this bridge (primarily for tracked vehicles) with interlocking parallel metal tracks supported by pontoon floats. The bridge was used in different theaters, primarily to span narrow rivers bordered by low banks.

TREBLINKA. Nazi EXTERMINATION CAMP in Poland. Along with AUSCHWITZ and Maidenek, Treblinka was designed as a death camp for the Jews of Poland and eastern Europe. Though the exact number of those murdered there is not known, several hundred thousand people perished in the camp's gas chambers. *See also* FINAL SOLUTION.

TRESCKOW, Henning von (1901–1944). As chief of staff in the German Army Group Center command in Russia, General von Tresckow established a center of anti-Nazi activity. The originator of Operation Flash, which placed a bomb in Adolf HITLER's personal aircraft in March 1943, only to have it fail to explode, he was also Count von STAUFFENBERG's collaborator in revising military plans to support the overthrow of the Nazi government. Rather than betray his friends to GESTAPO investigators after the plot failed on July 20, 1944, Tresckow walked into an open field near his headquarters the following day and killed himself with a hand grenade. *See also* OPPOSITION TO HITLER.

TRIBUTS, Vladimir F. (1900–). Soviet naval officer who commanded the Baltic Red Banner Fleet. In 1943 he was promoted to admiral.

TRIDENT. Code name of the American-British conference in Washington, May 12–25, 1943, with President Franklin D. ROOSEVELT, Prime Minister Winston CHURCHILL and the COMBINED CHIEFS OF STAFF. At this conference the target date for the cross-Channel INVASION was set for May 1, 1944; a pre-invasion air offensive against Germany was decided on, as was the bombing of the PLOESTI (Rumania) oil fields; and the American plan to drive on Japan through the Central Pacific was approved.

TRIPARTITE PACT. Agreement among Germany, Italy and Japan, signed in Berlin on September 27, 1940. Among its terms, Japan recognized "the leadership of Germany and Italy in the establishment of a new order in Europe" (Article 1), and Germany and Italy reciprocated with respect to Japan in "Greater East Asia" (Article 2). The parties agreed to come to each other's aid if one of them were attacked by a power "not involved in the European War or in the Sino-Japanese conflict" (Article 3). The Germans explained that this clause referred to the United States, and the pact explicitly affirmed the existing "political status" with the Soviet Union (Article 5). Nevertheless, after the signing of the agreement the Germans made efforts to mollify Russia and to draw her into the pact. Joseph STALIN displayed interest, sending V. M. MOLOTOV to Berlin in November, but his terms were too high to suit Adolf HITLER. Shortly thereafter Hitler issued his plan for Operation BARBAROSSA—the invasion of the Soviet Union.

TRIPOLI. Tripoli, Libya, was used as a port of entry and supply for the Axis desert forces. General MONTGOMERY's British EIGHTH ARMY occupied Tripoli on January 23, 1943. The retreating Axis tried to raze the city, including the harbor and airfield, but it was quickly repaired and put in use by the Allies.

TRITONAL. A war-developed American mixture of TNT and aluminum powder for use in GENERAL-PURPOSE BOMBS where a heavy blast effect was required.

TROBRIAND ISLANDS. Group of tropical islands, the largest being Kiriwina, about 115 miles north of MILNE BAY in southeastern NEW GUINEA. Within fighter and medium-bomber range of RABAUL, on New Britain, Kiriwina was taken on June 30, 1943, as the initial operation of the CARTWHEEL campaign. The islands were not occupied by the Japanese; the U.S. 158th RCT (Separate) encountered no opposition. Air operations began from the island on August 18. A companion piece was the unopposed seizure of Woodlark Island.

TROINA. A mountain fastness west of Mount Etna, in SICILY, grimly defended by the Axis. The U.S. 1st Division was delayed by a week of hard fighting before taking Troina on August 6, 1943.

TROIS PONTS. Belgian town at the confluence of the Salm and Amblève Rivers where on December 18, 1944, during the Battle of the BULGE, a company of the U.S. 51st Engineer Combat Battalion blew bridges and denied passage to the spearhead of the Sixth Panzer Army (Task Force PEIPER). The denial forced the Germans onto side roads and helped impose sufficient delay for American reinforcements to bottle up the column.

TROMSØ. Seaport on the northwest coast of NORWAY that became in late April 1940 the site of the Norwegian Government. In early June the King and government boarded a British cruiser and were evacuated to England.

TRONDHEIM. This Norwegian seaport, founded in A.D. 996, was the medieval capital of the country and continued to be the site of the crowning of kings. NORWAY's third largest city, it has a fine harbor. Though some opposition was made to German ships which sailed up the Trondheimsfjord, the city was taken easily on April 9, 1940. Trondheim was of strategic importance because it controlled central Norway and the entrance to northern Norway as well. From the city two routes led south to Oslo and a rail line extended to the north. Another railroad ran east to Sweden. The Allies hoped to recapture Trondheim, but efforts ceased when in late April the decision was made to evacuate central Norway.

TROOP CARRIER COMMAND. U.S. command created on June 20, 1942, as a result of an overhaul of the existing U.S. air transport organization. The new command assumed responsibility for providing transports to carry airborne infantry and parachute troops, to tow and fly gliders and to move men and cargo within the combat theater. Troop Carrier Command increased so rapidly in numbers and skill that it was able to provide C-47s (*see* C-47) and CG-4A GLIDERS for both the American and British airborne landings in SICILY in July

1943. The initial American contingent, some 3,400 men of the 82D AIRBORNE DIVISION, required 226 C-47s, and 144 planes of the same type later returned to drop reinforcements. In a notable disaster, however, 23 C-47s were shot down and 37 badly damaged by misdirected Allied fire during the Sicilian operation.

During the war, U.S. Army Air Forces acquired some 15,000 gliders for Troop Carrier Command and trained 5,000 glider pilots. In addition, about 4,500 four-man crews were trained to fly the organization's C-47s and C-46s (*see* C-46).

TROTT ZU SOLZ, Adam von (1909–1944). One of the younger conspirators against Adolf HITLER and a sometime intermediary between the KREISAU CIRCLE and the BECK-GOERDELER group. A proponent of traditional German values, even of the monarchy, an anti-Bolshevik, educated in international law in German and English universities and employed in the German Foreign Office as a counselor, Trott traveled widely in Europe and the United States in 1939, even after the war had begun, to contact Allied and then-neutral American leaders on behalf of the German resistance movement. His ideas on postwar Europe were grounded in the Kreisau conception of a federation similar to that of the United States. Having also maintained close liaison with Count von STAUFFENBERG until the evening before the bomb attempt on Hilter's life on July 20, 1944, Trott was arrested after the failure of the coup and was executed on August 26, 1944. *See also* OPPOSITION TO HITLER.

TRUK. An island group in the central CAROLINES, consisting of 11 larger islands and many small islets or atolls. The major islands are Moen, Tol, Udot, Fefan and Uman, all within a 38-mile-wide lagoon encircled by a reef, which is pierced by about 20 passages, of which only four are navigable. The chief town in this group is Truk, on Dublon Island; it served as the headquarters and base of the Japanese COMBINED FLEET. Truk's importance lay in its strategic location combined with the naval and air strength it held, which threatened Allied advances in the Central and South Pacific Areas. Of great concern was the fact that one of the two largest battleships in the world, the MUSASHI, was based at Truk, which for a long while had in the minds of

Japanese shipping at Truk is raided on February 16, 1944

American planners a degree of impregnability rivaled only by Gibraltar. There was a conflict among the Americans whether Truk should be captured on the road to Tokyo or whether it should be bypassed since its capture might prove to be a bloody endeavor. In the end the proponents of letting Truk wither on the vine won over, and from the first major naval strike on February 17, 1944, Truk became the target of continual air and naval bombardment, nullifying its value to the Japanese.

TRUMAN, Harry S. (1884–1972). The 33d President of the United States, serving between 1945 and 1953. Unable to attend West Point because of his poor eyesight, Truman could not otherwise go to college because of family finances, and he was thus the only President in the 20th century who did not graduate from college. He worked as a bank clerk, road overseer and local postmaster before he took over the family farm in 1906. As a member of the Missouri National Guard, he served in World War I as a junior officer, seeing combat in 1918 as commander of Battery D, 129th Field Artillery, 35th Division.

Returning from the war, he married his childhood sweetheart, Elizabeth (Bess) Wallace, in 1919. In the same year he went into a haberdashery partnership in Kansas City, but it went out of business in the hard times of 1921 (Truman made a point in the ensuing years of paying off all debts the business had incurred).

At this point, later than is generally the case, Truman got into politics. With the backing of boss Tom Pendergast, the leader of the Kansas City Democratic machine, he won election as a county court judge, serving between 1922 and 1924. In this nonjudicial position he quickly established a reputation for honesty and efficiency. In 1924 Truman was defeated by a non-Pendergast Democrat who was supported by the Ku Klux Klan, but he was again elected judge in 1926, holding the post until 1934. In that year he moved into national politics, winning the Democratic nomination for Senator in a close race and following that victory with an easy triumph in the general election. As a Senator he was a loyal New Deal Democrat, studious and modest.

When 1940 came, his career seemed to be over, with Tom Pendergast convicted of income tax evasion and President ROOSEVELT leaning to a rival candidate. But Truman himself was not corrupt, and he was a fighter. He won both the nomination and the election. In his second term his most notable accomplishment was his chairmanship of the Special Committee Investigating National Defense—the Truman Committee—established in February 1941. The committee served as a watchdog over the nation's huge and rapid military and industrial expansion. It uncovered conflicts of interest, under-the-table arrangements, military waste and rivalry, and labor abuses. The Truman Committee was notably successful in avoiding partisanship, in confining itself to facts rather than rumors and in resisting any temptation to dabble in the operational side of the war. As the chairman of the committee, Senator Truman was responsible for much of its record of integrity and effectiveness, and his public stature was greatly enhanced thereby. In 1944 Roosevelt chose him to replace the controversial Henry WALLACE as Democratic Party candidate for Vice-President, though Truman does not appear to have had any great desire for the post. Then, with Roosevelt's death on April 12, 1945, Truman found himself President.

He entered on his new task in many ways unprepared for the decisions he would be called upon to make. Roosevelt had established no pattern of conferring with his Vice-President, an omission that in normal times would not have been noteworthy. However, Harry HOPKINS was able to give Truman much of Roosevelt's thinking. As the war approached its climax, important international issues had to be faced—including the establishment of the UNITED NATIONS ORGANIZATION—and there was also the progress on the ATOMIC BOMB, about which the new President had not been previously informed.

The SAN FRANCISCO CONFERENCE opened on April 25, 1945, amid various conflicts between the West and the Soviet Union, some of which were subsequently eased by conversations in Moscow between Joseph STALIN and Hopkins, who had gone as Truman's personal emissary. Hopkins also reached agreement with Stalin about a Big Three conference to be held in Berlin, the capital of the now-defeated German foe, in July. This meeting—the POTSDAM CONFERENCE—convened on July 17 and, with an interlude for the British election (which resulted in the replacement at the council table of Winston CHURCHILL by Clement ATTLEE), continued until August 2. Although there was discussion of the war against Japan, the principal talks dealt with the transition to postwar Europe. It was President Truman's first appearance at a summit meeting, as such gatherings later came to be called, and his illustrious partner Churchill later spoke of his "gay, precise, sparkling manner and obvious power of decision."

On July 16, before the conference had formally opened, Truman received news of vital significance: the atomic bomb had been successfully tested in New Mexico. The President gave the news to Stalin in a casual way, telling him after the session of July 24 that the United States had a new weapon "of unusual destructive force." Stalin seemed unimpressed, remarking only that he hoped the Americans would "make good use of it against the Japanese." No one in the Allied group seems to have wondered whether he might already have had the news. After Truman had been told of the existence of the bomb, he had formed a committee of top political and scientific leaders, the Interim Committee, to advise him as to its use. Their report of June 1945 calling for quick use, without warning and against a joint civilian-military target (i.e., a city), was approved by Truman and led to the dropping of the two atomic bombs in August 1945. For the rest of his life, Truman maintained that he was correct in making this decision. Shortly after the two bombings, Japan surrendered and World War II was over.

Although Truman was President during the last phases of the war, he is chiefly remembered as the President who had to deal with the problems presented by the fact that the war left only the United States and the Soviet Union as great powers. But his decision to use the atomic bomb (or, it might more precisely be put, his decision not to overrule his scientific and military advisers and not use it) was historic. In 1948, in a fiery campaign against what seemed impossible odds, Truman won election to the Presidency in his own right. Although he was eligible to run again, he chose to retire from politics in 1953. At the time he was at a nadir of public esteem, but the public view of him has since changed markedly. He is remembered as straightforward, scrappy and plain-talking, with his characteristic sayings "The buck stops here" and "If you can't stand the heat, get out of the kitchen." **K.P.U.; T.P.**

TRUNCHEON. Code name for the raid on LEGHORN by British carrier-borne aircraft, February 9, 1941.

TRUSCOTT, Lucian King, Jr. (1895–1965). U.S. Army officer who was sent as a brigadier general to Britain to study COMMANDO units. He organized an American counterpart, the RANGERS, and led them at PORT-LYAUTEY in the 1942 NORTHWEST AFRICA invasion. In 1942–43 he served as field deputy to General Dwight D. EISENHOWER, and then became commanding general of the 3d Infantry Division. After fighting in Africa, SICILY and ITALY, he commanded the VI Corps in the 1944 invasion of SOUTHERN FRANCE. Truscott was promoted to lieutenant general and returned to Italy to command the FIFTH ARMY in 1944. As a cavalry colonel, Truscott had served on General Eisenhower's staff at Fort Lewis, Wash. Of ability demonstrated during this connection came his rise to high rank.

TSOUDEROS, Emmanuel (1882–1956). Prime Minister of Greece when the Germans invaded the country in April 1941. Tsouderos with his cabinet fled to Cairo, where for three years he headed the Greek government-in-exile. Following the liberation of Greece in 1944, he served as Deputy Premier.

T-STOFF. A German rocket fuel mixture of hydrogen peroxide and water.

TSUJI, Masanobu (1902–1968). One of the most important Japanese Army staff officers. He served in turn on the staffs of the Japanese Expeditionary Force in northern China (1937), of the KWANTUNG ARMY (1937) and of armies in Malaya, the Netherlands East Indies, GUADALCANAL, the PHILIPPINES and THAILAND. Colonel Tsuji is credited with doing much of the planning for the brilliant Japanese campaign that took Malaya and SINGAPORE in 1941. An ultranationalist, he has been charged with war crimes by numerous historians. At the end of the war he donned the garb of a Buddhist monk to avoid capture by the Allied forces, eventually reaching China, where he was given protection in return for serving as an adviser to CHIANG KAI-SHEK. After returning to Japan in 1949 he wrote several books about World War II and entered politics. In 1961 he tried to enter North Vietnam and has been missing since then. In 1968 he was officially declared dead.

TUAPSE. Port in the Caucasus, used (along with BATUM and Poti) by the Soviet Black Sea Fleet as a base after the loss of SEVASTOPOL and NOVOROSSISK to the Germans.

TUBE ALLOYS. British name for atomic research in the early part of the war, before British and American efforts were combined. *See* ATOMIC BOMB.

TUG ARGAN PASS. Outside Berbera, the capital of British Somaliland, this pass was the scene of a four-day battle between British and South African troops and the invading Italians in August 1940. The Italians, who greatly outnumbered the defenders, then pushed on to Berbera. *See also* EAST AFRICA.

TULA. Important city south of Moscow, on the line of advance of German mobile units in the autumn of 1941. Although Tula was outflanked for a time in November, it did not fall.

TULAGI. Island that had one of the few great fleet anchorages in the Pacific and was desirable as a base for that reason. South of Florida Island and 22 miles north of GUADALCANAL across Sealark Channel, Tulagi was taken by the Japanese on May 3, 1942. On August 7, 1942, the day of the main U.S. landing at Guadalcanal, it was assaulted by the 1st Raider Battalion (EDSON's Raiders) and the 2d Battalion, 5th Marines. Japanese resistance was only perfunctory, and at nightfall the marines were set in their lines, which were attacked four times by the Japanese without success. The island was declared secured the following day.

TUNIS. Tunis served as a major port of supply for the Axis forces in Africa after the Allied landings. Gen. Kenneth ANDERSON's British FIRST ARMY entered it on May 7, 1943, and on May 20 the Allies celebrated victory in North Africa with a parade through the streets of the city.

TUNISIA. The Tunisian theater of operations, from November 1942 until May 1943, was roughly the triangle enclosed by the coastal road from Constantine (Algeria) through Bizerte and Tunis to Gabès, then through Tébessa back to Constantine. *See also* NORTHWEST AFRICA.

TUPOLEV ANT-6. One of the oldest Soviet aircraft used in World War II. The ANT-6 became operational in 1930 as a heavy bomber; production ceased in 1936. It was used as a transport until 1944, when it was phased out. It had four 830-horsepower engines and flew at a maximum speed of 155 miles per hour; its range was 1,243 miles. Manned by an eight-man crew, it carried 30 passengers.

TUPOLEV SB-2. Twin-engine medium bomber introduced as the ANT-40 in 1936. It was first used in the Spanish Civil War. Though obsolete in 1941, it was successfully employed as a night bomber until late 1943.

TUPOLEV TU-2. A ground-support aircraft which entered limited service in 1943. Few were used in the war, since the PETLYAKOV PE-2 had priority over it. It was powered by two 1,850-horsepower engines, had a maximum speed of 345 miles per hour and carried a four-man crew. It was armed with two 23-mm. guns and five 12.7-mm. machine guns, and carried 5,000 pounds of bombs.

TURBULENT, H.M.S. British submarine built under the War Emergency Program as a medium patrol boat of 1,090 tons. She operated successfully in the Mediterranean, based on MALTA, in 1942 and 1943, being commanded by Lt. Comdr. J. W. LINTON.

TURNER, Richmond Kelly (1885–1961). U.S. Navy officer, a graduate of the Naval Academy in 1908, who became one of the leading experts in and practitioners of amphibious warfare. Turner served as a gunnery officer in the First World War, qualified as a naval aviator in 1927 and was a technical adviser to the American delegation to the Geneva Disarmament Conference of 1932. At the time of PEARL HARBOR in 1941, Turner was director of the War Plans Division of the Navy Department, and he was appointed assistant chief of staff for plans to Adm. Ernest J. KING when the latter took command of the Navy. In 1942 Turner was appointed commander of the Amphibious Force of the Pacific Fleet; his first operation was the invasion of GUADALCANAL in August 1942. Admiral Turner planned and personally directed the American attacks in the central SOLOMONS—where his flagship was sunk—in the GILBERTS and the MARSHALLS (where his command became the V Amphibious Force), in the MARIANAS, at IWO JIMA and at OKINAWA, where he commanded the Joint Expeditionary Force. He was promoted to admiral in 1945 and retired from active duty in 1947.

TUSCALOOSA, U.S.S. NEW ORLEANS–class heavy cruiser, completed in 1934, that saw considerable service in European waters in support of the landings at CASABLANCA, UTAH BEACH and SOUTHERN FRANCE. In 1943 *Tuscaloosa* was part of an American task force operating with the British Home Fleet from SCAPA FLOW. It was while cruising on *Tuscaloosa* in December 1940 that President ROOSEVELT conceived the idea of LEND-LEASE.

TUSKEGEE AIRMEN. Title given to the black officers who trained at Tuskegee Army Airfield and served in U.S. Army Air Forces during World War II. Although legislation adopted in April 1939 forced the Civil Aeronautics Authority to admit blacks to its training programs, which used equipment provided by the War Department, the Air Corps refused until 1940 to accept them in any capacity at all. Gen. Henry H. ARNOLD, who headed the Air Corps, invoked a traditional argument when he declared that "Negro pilots cannot be used in our present Air Force, since this would result in having Negro officers over white enlisted men."

Even as he was citing the conventional wisdom, Arnold realized that the influence of civil rights organizations would ultimately prevail, for he promptly authorized planning toward the establishment of black units, segregated, of course, as was the custom of the time. Finally, in December 1940, he announced an experimental program to recruit some 500 blacks, 47 of whom would receive commissions. Not all of these officers would be pilots, however.

Initially, this experiment included the creation near Chicago of a training base for black aviators and ground crews. The high cost of land caused the Air Corps to shift the training site to an airfield being operated by the Civil Aeronautics Authority at Tuskegee Institute in Alabama, the school founded by Booker T. Washington. This decision dismayed many influential blacks, who complained that the War Department not only was perpetuating racial segregation in the armed forces but in doing so was assigning the black airmen to an area where racial discrimination had the force of law. But these critics soon fell silent, apparently persuaded that a segregated aviation unit was better than no unit at all.

Life for the Tuskegee airmen was not easy, since Army Air Forces discouraged any sort of social contact between blacks and whites. Black officers from Tuskegee could not, for example, stay overnight at nearby Maxwell Field, where the visiting officers' quarters were closed to them. Also off limits was the Maxwell Field officers' club. For good reason, the Tuskegee airmen were called the Lonely Eagles.

Perhaps the most galling aspect of segregation was the absence of useful work for most of the black officers. The segregated combat and service units were too few to absorb the number of officers trained at Tuskegee. As a result, tables of organization listed such absurdities as assistant to the assistant supply officer and assistant area beautification officer.

Despite the injustice of segregation and the resulting waste of manpower, Tuskegee produced effective combat units, such as the 99th Pursuit Squadron, commanded by Lt. Col. Benjamin O. Davis, Jr. The first black aviation unit to see combat, the 99th became a first-rate outfit, although it required an extended shakedown overseas to compensate for hurried training prior to its deployment. Colonel Davis later assumed command of a larger black unit, the 332d Fighter Group, consisting at the end of the war of the 99th, 100th, 301st and 302d Squadrons. After the war he rose to the grade of lieutenant general, the first black to achieve three-star status in the services.

Of particular importance to the postwar air arm was the experience of Lt. Col. Noel F. Parrish, a white, who assumed command at Tuskegee in 1942. Influenced by his experiences there, he helped set the U.S. Air Force on the path toward racial integration.

TWADDLE, Harry L. (1888–). U.S. Army officer who took command of the 95th Infantry Division as a major general in 1942. The division arrived in Europe in September 1944 and fought in France, Holland and Germany.

TWELFTH AIR FORCE. Established on August 20, 1942, at Bolling Field, Washington, D.C., the U.S. Twelfth Air Force was entrusted in September to Maj. Gen. James H. DOOLITTLE, who served as its commanding general during the NORTHWEST AFRICA invasion of November 1942. When the organization commenced operation in Africa, it possessed some 500 planes. By mid-February 1943, when it joined Royal Air Force units to form the NORTHWEST AFRICAN AIR FORCES under Gen. Carl SPAATZ, its aerial strength had doubled.

As the Northwest African fighting approached its climax, Twelfth Air Force P-40s (*see* P-40) pounced on the German JUNKERS JU52/3MS and MESSERSCHMITT ME 323s delivering supplies to forces in Tunisia and claimed the destruction of 79 of the enemy transports. Twelfth Air Force combat squadrons also bombed the ports and roads upon which German troops in Tunisia depended.

The command participated in the reduction of PANTELLERIA, an Italian-held island that surrendered in June 1943 after a savage aerial bombardment. Next came the invasions of SICILY and ITALY.

For most of the Italian campaign, Twelfth Air Force was part of the Mediterranean Allied Air Forces. Under Maj. Gen. John K. CANNON, the Twelfth aided the advance on Rome by bombing Monte CASSINO, believed fortified by the enemy, and also took part in Operation STRANGLE, designed to isolate the German armies in Italy. The organization supported the landings in SOUTHERN FRANCE and the ensuing operations. Its planes also bombed and strafed the retreating enemy in northern Italy, maintaining unremitting pressure until April 29, 1945, when German forces in that country surrendered (effective May 2).

12th ARMY GROUP. Activated in London on October 19, 1943, as the First United States Army Group (FUSAG) under the command of Lt. Gen. Omar N. BRADLEY; the mission was operational planning for Overlord (the cross-Channel INVASION) and RANKIN (operations in case Germany collapsed before Overlord). All planning was carried out in close cooperation with the British 21ST ARMY GROUP. FUSAG was superseded by 12th Army Group on July 14, 1944, with no change in personnel or commander. Headquarters moved to the Continent on July 22, 1944. On August 1, 12th Army Group assumed operational control of U.S. FIRST ARMY (Lt. Gen. Courtney HODGES) and U.S. THIRD ARMY (Lt. Gen. George S. PATTON), while itself remaining under command of 21st Army Group (British) until September 1, when it came under command of SUPREME HEADQUARTERS, ALLIED EXPEDITIONARY FORCE (SHAEF). All offensive operations ceased on May 8, 1945, when the Germans surrendered. The 12th Army Group was inactivated on July 31, 1945, in Germany; all operational control over U.S. forces in Germany passed to United States Forces, European Theater (USFET). *See also* WESTERN FRONT.

TWENTIETH AIR FORCE. U.S. force created for the strategic bombardment of Japan using the new Boeing Superfortress (*see* B-29). Headquarters of the organization was located in Washington, with operational control vested in the Joint Chiefs of Staff, who designated Gen. Henry H. ARNOLD, commanding general of U.S. Army Air Forces, as their executive agent. Arnold, in turn, exercised command through a deputy, Brig. Gen. Lauris NORSTAD.

Training and combat operations were conducted by the XX and XXI Bomber Commands. First to see action was XX Bomber Command, which in June 1944 launched strikes against Japan from airfields in China. Maj. Gen. Kenneth B. WOLFE commanded these early efforts until his return to the United States in July to assist in the B-29 engineering program. Brig. Gen. LaVerne Saunders took over until September, when Maj. Gen. Curtis E. LEMAY arrived. The XXI Bomber Command, led by Brig. Gen. Haywood Hansell, went into action in November 1944, operating from bases in the MARIANA ISLANDS.

These first efforts proved disappointing. Because of difficulties in supplying and defending the Chinese airfields, a sustained B-29 offensive could be mounted only from the Marianas. Schooled in the doctrine of high-altitude precision bombing, which required larger formations than he could muster, Hansell could not achieve the results General Arnold desired. This key organization was then entrusted to LeMay, whose low-altitude incendiary attacks devastated Japan's cities. While XXI Bomber Command was razing the enemy's urban centers, XX Bomber Command was hitting targets from Thailand to Manchuria.

At the end of the war, General Arnold was in the process of reorganizing his command structure for the Pacific area, moving Twentieth Air Force headquarters, now under Lt. Gen. Nathan F. TWINING, to the Marianas and setting up U.S. Army Strategic Air Forces, Pacific, under Gen. Carl SPAATZ, with LeMay as his chief of staff.

21st ARMY GROUP. Allied (later British) ground force in the INVASION of Normandy and the ensuing campaign into Germany. It was activated in July 1943 under the command of Gen. Sir Bernard PAGET, who was responsible for its initial training. In December 1943 he was succeeded by Gen. Sir Bernard MONTGOMERY, who not only commanded British ground forces in the assault but was de facto commander of all Allied ground forces, the 21st Army Group including, until August 1, 1944, the American as well as the British forces. On that date U.S. 12TH ARMY GROUP became operational, but General Montgomery continued to exercise overall control until September 1. The 21st Army Group at that time included the Canadian FIRST ARMY (General CRERAR) and the British SECOND ARMY (General DEMPSEY). *See also* WESTERN FRONT.

TWINING, Nathan Farragut (1897–). U.S. Army air officer who served as chief of staff of Army Air Forces in the South Pacific in 1942–43. In January 1943 he was forced down at sea and was adrift for six days. Promoted to major general in 1943, Twining commanded the THIRTEENTH AIR FORCE and in July became Commander Air Forces, Southwest Pacific. In 1944–45 he was the commanding general of the FIFTEENTH AIR FORCE in Italy and of the Allied Strategic Air Forces in the Mediterranean. Twining ended the war as the commander of the TWENTIETH AIR FORCE. Between 1953 and 1957 he served as the Chief of Staff of the Air Force and between 1957 and 1960 as chairman of the Joint Chiefs of Staff.

TYPHOON (Taifun). Code name for a planned decisive attack by the German Army Group Center toward Moscow, September 1941.

TYPHOON. One of two aircraft begun by Sydney Camm and his Hawker design team to meet a 1938 British Air Ministry requirement for a 2,000-horsepower single-seat fighter and ground-attack aircraft. The other plane, the Tornado, presented aerodynamic problems that kept it from entering production. The Typhoon also had its share of problems.

First flown in February 1940, the Typhoon encountered buffeting at high speed and exhibited dangerous handling characteristics during takeoff. Although these failings were corrected, production was delayed so that

Hawker and Gloster could concentrate on the proven HURRICANE. In 1941 the first Typhoon rolled from the production line and promptly demonstrated that its 2,100-horsepower Sabre I engine was not dependable. The more powerful Sabre II proved satisfactory and encouraged FIGHTER COMMAND to use the plane against the FOCKE-WULF FW 190s that were making nuisance raids over the British Isles. A series of accidents ensued, owing to aileron reversal at speeds approaching 500 miles per hour and structural failure during dives. The installation of fishplates just forward of the tail surfaces cured the structural problem, and pilots learned to avoid the danger of compressibility. As a result, the Typhoon performed successfully as a fighter-bomber, especially against German armor, and was used to protect British convoys in the English Channel from German fighter-bombers based in France and the Low Countries.

Some 3,300 Typhoons were built. The plane bore some resemblance to the Hurricane, except for enlarged tail surfaces and a bulbous chin radiator for the liquid-cooled engine. It mounted four 20-mm. Hispano cannon. Late models carried eight rockets. Maximum speed was 405 miles per hour at 18,000 feet. Train "busting" was profitable for the Typhoon, because, with its four cannon, it could destroy a locomotive with ease.

TYULENEV, Ivan V. (1892–). Soviet Army officer who fought in the Russian Civil War and at the outbreak of World War II commanded the Moscow District. In 1942 Tyulenev was shifted to the Transcaucasus Front. He held the rank of general of army.

U

UDET, Ernst (1896–1941). A genial veteran of the German World War I Richthofen flying organization—where he flew with Hermann GÖRING—and winner of the POUR LE MÉRITE, General Udet became chief of LUFTWAFFE supply and procurement and head of the Luftwaffe technical office. It was not a job for which his talents equipped him. His death, on November 17, 1941, ostensibly in an aircraft crash, was in reality a suicide resulting from his despair over the course of the war and his own inability to carry out his official duties.

UGAKI, Matome (1890–1945). A Japanese career naval officer, Ugaki was an instructor at the Naval War College before World War II. He served as chief of staff of the COMBINED FLEET under Adm. Isoruku YAMAMOTO, until the death of his commander in April 1943. Later Ugaki served on Adm. Takeo KURITA's staff as commander of battleship squadrons. As commander of the 5th Air Fleet in 1945, Ugaki, a vice-admiral, controlled all naval air forces in Kyushu at the end of the war. On the day of the Emperor's broadcast of surrender, Ugaki stripped his uniform of its gold braid and insignia and climbed aboard a dive-bomber to lead a final 11-plane KAMIKAZE attack from Oita Air Base on Kyushu. The planes disappeared, never reaching a target.

U GO. Code name for the Japanese invasion of India, March 1944. *See also* IMPHAL; KOHIMA.

ULITHI. Located in the western Carolines, Ulithi is an atoll, whose chief islands are Falalop, Mog Mog and Asor. Its lagoon, 19 miles long by 5 to 10 miles wide, provides one of the finest deep-water fleet anchorages in the Pacific. On September 23, 1944, it was captured without opposition and became the hub of U.S. naval operations in the western Pacific from that date until the end of the war.

ULTRA. Special security classification given by the British to information gained from breaking the code of the standard German radio enciphering machine, the ENIGMA, and also the designation of the intelligence thus obtained. The Poles presented copies of the Enigma to both the British and the French just before the outbreak of war in 1939. Because of daily changes of the code and different codes used by each of the armed forces, the Germans considered it totally secure, and in the face of extraordinary security precautions practiced by the British and Americans (who were let in on the secret) never learned otherwise until near the end of the war. The British early solved the code and its changes through means of a special deciphering machine built by British scientists and mathematicians.

Although the existence of Ultra did not preclude the clash of men, machines, planes and ships, it was of invaluable assistance to Allied leaders and senior field commanders—the most extraordinary intelligence coup of the war. During the Battle of BRITAIN, for example, Ultra told the Royal Air Force in advance how many bombers the Germans were to employ, where and when. It afforded precise information on German intentions in North Africa, including when supply ships would sail. It enabled the British to defeat the Italian fleet at CAPE MATAPAN, and in 1943 to turn the tide in the Atlantic by revealing when and where German U-boats met their supply submarines. Ultra kept the British informed of German knowledge of plans for D-Day in Normandy, enabling them to plant information to maintain the fiction that the main INVASION would occur in the Pas de Calais. Ultra's big failure was the lack of advance warning of the Battle of the BULGE, attributable to such extraordinary German secrecy that no information was transmitted by wireless.

UMBERTO, Prince (1904–). Son of King VICTOR EMMANUEL III of Italy, Umberto commanded Italy's Army of the Alps, which attacked France in 1940. In 1944, as Lieutenant General of the Realm, he assumed the regency, and in May 1946, on his father's abdication, became King Umberto II. In June, however, the Italian people voted to abolish the monarchy, and Umberto went into exile after a reign of 35 days.

UMEZU, Yoshijiro (1882–1949). A graduate of the Japanese Military Academy and the Naval War College, Umezu held staff positions during most of his career. After serving as commander of the Japanese garrison in China (1934–35), he was appointed Vice-Minister of War in 1936. He was influential in furthering the interests of the *Toseiha* (Control Faction) of the Army and ridding the Army of dissident officers. Appointed commander of the KWANTUNG ARMY in Manchuria and ambassador plenipotentiary to MANCHUKUO in September 1939, Umezu was the most powerful Japanese in Manchuria and China until 1944. He replaced Hideki TOJO as Army Chief of Staff in July 1944, serving until the end of the war, and signed the document of surrender on the U.S.S. MISSOURI. Sentenced to life imprisonment for war crimes. Umezu died in prison of cancer.

UMIKAZE. Japanese SHIRATSUYU-class destroyer, sunk by an American submarine in the Caroline Islands area on February 1, 1944.

UMNAK. Island in the Aleutians, used as a U.S. air base from May 1942.

UNCLE TOM. British aircraft rocket, comparable in size and power to the U.S. TINY TIM.

UNCONDITIONAL SURRENDER. Phrase used to describe UNITED NATIONS policy toward the Axis. It was first publicly employed on January 24, 1943, at CASA-

BLANCA, when it was used by President ROOSEVELT at a press conference immediately following the Anglo-American meeting. Although the President made it appear to be an impromptu utterance, the idea had previously been discussed and agreed upon between the two governments, but it had not been included in the official communiqué of the conference. The policy was reaffirmed at the Moscow CONFERENCE of foreign ministers in October 1943. Its influence on the course of the war has occasioned continuing debate.

UNDERTONE. Code name of the U.S. SEVENTH ARMY operation to breach the WEST WALL and establish a bridgehead over the Rhine River in the vicinity of Worms, March–April 1945.

UNDERWATER DEMOLITION TEAM. Frogmen who prepared the way for an amphibious attack by destroying underwater obstacles shielding a landing beach.

UNEXPLODED BOMBS (UXB). In September 1940 the Germans began dropping delayed-action bombs on England. Special squads made up of civilian volunteers were formed to disarm or dispose of them. The composure and courage of these teams became legendary. One group, called the Holy Trinity, was made up of the Earl of Suffolk, his female private secretary and his elderly chauffeur.

UNITED NATIONS. The name, adopted on January 1, 1942, for the coalition of powers fighting against the AXIS. *See also* JOINT DECLARATION.

UNITED NATIONS ORGANIZATION. The international body established by the members of the victorious wartime coalition (*see* UNITED NATIONS above) at the United Nations Conference on International Organization, April 25–June 26, 1945, with the primary aim of preserving peace in the postwar world. The charter came into effect October 24, 1945. *See also* SAN FRANCISCO CONFERENCE.

UNITED NATIONS RELIEF AND REHABILITATION ADMINISTRATION. Agency established on November 9, 1943, by 44 nations to provide food, clothing, shelter, medical assistance and other aid to the people of countries liberated from Axis control. The funding of UNRRA came from the founding countries, each contributing an amount equal to 2 percent of its national income in 1943; more than half of the total came from the United States. Ultimately the number of participating countries reached 52. Among its services, UNRRA cared for millions of displaced persons, returning about 7 million to their home countries and housing another million who did not wish to return. The original director general was Herbert H. Lehman, former governor of New York; successors were former New York City mayor Fiorello H. LAGUARDIA and Maj. Gen. Lowell Rooks, a staff officer at Allied headquarters in Europe.

UNITED SERVICE ORGANIZATIONS. The USO was established to provide off-duty services and comforts to members of the U.S. armed forces and, in some instances, to workers in war plants in areas where social services were strained by the demands made on them. Created on February 4, 1941, it was the unified effort of a number of agencies—the YMCA and YWCA, the National Catholic Community Service, the National Jewish Welfare Board, the Salvation Army and the National Travelers Aid Association. At the end of the war there were about 2,500 USO clubs in the United States and overseas, offering "home away from home" facilities. A highly popular activity was USO Camp Shows, which sent more than 4,000 entertainers to posts and hospitals around the world. During the war USO is estimated to have served more than a billion persons (including audiences at Camp Shows).

UNITED STATES ARMY. At the outbreak of the war in Europe in 1939, the Regular Army numbered about 174,000 men; in mid-1941, with the inclusion of National Guard units and selectees, the Army's strength was about 1.4 million; by V-E Day it had reached about 8 million. The SELECTIVE SERVICE SYSTEM supplied males between ages 21 and 36 (later 18 to 38). Women could volunteer for the WOMEN'S ARMY CORPS, which had about 100,000 members in 1945. In 1942 the Army planned for a strength of 105 divisions and 8,248,000 troops, but in mid-1943 this figure was scaled down to 90 divisions and 7.7 million troops. The strength of the Army Air Forces was set at 2,340,000 men and 273 combat groups.

Among the Allied nations the United States was second to the Soviet Union in the total number of men and women mobilized (22 million to 15 million; of the U.S. figure, 10,420,000 served in the Army, including Army Air Forces). The Germans mobilized 17 million persons. The American figures demonstrated, as Gen. George C. MARSHALL observed, "how heavily the United States was concentrating on aerial warfare, on the production and movement of arms for its own troops and those of its Allies, and the meaning in terms of manpower of waging war from 3,000 to 7,000 miles from our shores"; thus "our ground strength was, for the size of our population, proportionately much smaller than that of the other belligerents."

Since every Army division was in an operational theater and all but two had seen combat action by V-E Day, the number of battle casualties suffered was substantial. Casualties in Atlantic area theaters (Africa and the Middle East, the Caribbean and South Atlantic, Europe, the Mediterranean) totaled 765,751 (177,100 dead). In the Pacific (including India-Burma and China) there were 169,635 battle casualties (57,137 dead). The overall totals, including casualties en route or not classifiable by theater, were 936,259 (234,874 dead). Total personnel captured and interned amounted to 124,079, and 30,314 were reported as missing (of whom some 24,000 returned to duty; the balance are included in the total of deaths). The Army Air Forces portion of the total casualty figures was 115,382 (52,173 dead).

Having fought in 34 specific campaigns and having awarded 1,400,409 decorations, exclusive of PURPLE HEARTS, the Army began to demobilize immediately after V-E Day. A point system based on length of service, overseas service, decorations, battle stars and dependent children was worked out to set up a priority ranking for discharges. Those with the highest number of points were the first discharged, usually in less than 48 hours after processing began.

The Order of Battle tables (below through page 648) show the deployment of U.S. Army forces at the cessation of hostilities in the various theaters. *See also* entries for numbered armies (e.g., FIRST ARMY [U.S.]).

UNITED STATES ARMY AIR FORCES. Organization established on June 20, 1941, as the result of efforts by Gen. George C. MARSHALL, the Chief of Staff, and by Secretary of War Henry L. STIMSON to bring the two elements of the air arm, GHQ Air Force and the Air Corps, under centralized control. Prior to this change the commanding general of the GHQ Air Force had concerned himself with combat effectiveness, while the Chief of the Air Corps had been responsible for individual and crew training and for procurement of equipment.

Arriving on the scene in 1940, Stimson installed Robert A. Lovett as Assistant Secretary of War for Air, and Lovett undertook to increase aircraft production and to push the reorganization of the air arm. This reorganization took the form of appointing Maj. Gen. Henry H. ARNOLD as Chief, Army Air Forces, making him directly responsible to the Army Chief of Staff and giving him authority over both the Air Corps and the Air Force Combat Command, which had succeeded GHQ Air Force. As Chief, Army Air Forces, Arnold had an air staff to assist him. He also retained his post as deputy for air to the Army Chief of Staff and remained the principal contact between Army Air Forces and the War Department. In March 1942 Army Air Forces became one of the coequal commands of the Army along with Army Ground Forces and the Services of Supply (later Army Service Forces).

During the war the peak strength of the Army Air Forces was 2,411,294, made up of 306,889 officers and 2,104,405 enlisted personnel. The AAF suffered 115,382 battle casualties. The number of airplanes employed was colossal: from July 1, 1940, to August 31, 1945, the Army accepted 229,554 aircraft. *See also* UNITED STATES ARMY and entries for numbered air forces (e.g., FIFTH AIR FORCE).

UNITED STATES COAST GUARD. During the war the Coast Guard came under the administration of the Navy rather than of the U.S. Treasury Department, its peacetime administrator. It increased greatly in both ships and personnel. In 1940, for example, it had 1,351 officers, 12,261 enlisted persons and 144 cadets, for a total of 13,756; in 1945 the total was 171,192 (12,683 officers; 158,290 enlisted persons and 219 cadets). At its peak in 1945 the Coast Guard manned 802 vessels greater than 65 feet in length as well as 351 Navy vessels and 288 Army craft. On June 30, 1945, the Coast Guard had 1,677 craft of its own, including 600 cutters and numerous small craft used in escort duties and harbor security.

Coast Guard personnel performed a great variety of wartime tasks. They served in captain-of-the-port activities involving the regulation of merchant shipping; supervision of loading explosives; and the protection of shipping, harbors and waterfront activities, including the guarding of 5 million linear feet of wharfage. The Coast Guard also manned some troop transports and landing craft as part of combat operations.

Other duties the Coast Guard performed during the war included the establishment of mounted and foot patrols on beaches, the manning of coastal lookout stations, and operating section bases and certain inshore patrol activities formerly handled by the Navy.

The Coast Guard grew in other respects besides personnel and vessels. By early 1944 its aviation activities had tripled in size. Under the operational control of Navy SEA FRONTIER commanders, Coast Guard aviators flew missions in convoy coverage, antisubmarine warfare, and search and rescue. In addition, certain units carried out aerial mapping and checking for the U.S. Coast and Geodetic Survey and ice observation on the Great Lakes. By 1945 the Coast Guard had nine air stations on U.S. coasts with a total of 165 planes for search and rescue. In fiscal year 1945 Guard aviators handled 5,357 emergency medical cases and saved 786 lives.

UNITED STATES MARINE CORPS. As of June 20, 1939, some two months before the outbreak of the war in Europe, Marine Corps strength stood at 19,432 officers and enlisted men, of whom 4,840 (including aviation components) were assigned to the Fleet Marine Force. FMF ground units were organized in two units, designated brigades, each actually an understrength infantry regiment reinforced by skeletonized supporting elements. The 1st Brigade was based on the East Coast at Quantico, Va.; the 2d Brigade was on the West Coast at San Diego, Calif. Each brigade had the support of a Marine aircraft group with a corresponding numerical designation. By November 30, 1941, just before PEARL HARBOR, Marine Corps strength had grown to 65,881, largely due to the mobilization in November 1940 of the entire Organized Marine Corps Reserve, both ground and air. At the end of the war, the corps numbered more than 450,000 officers and men.

On February 1, 1941, the brigades stationed on the East and West Coasts were redesignated as, respectively, the 1st Marine Division and 2d Marine Division. To effect the necessary expansion to divisional size (three infantry regiments, an artillery regiment, other units), cadres were drawn from existing units around which new units of the same type could be built and trained. This proved to be a slow and laborious process, and months passed before the two divisions could be built up to authorized strength. Growth of Marine Corps aviation kept pace with that of the ground forces; again, the pace appeared faster on paper than it was in reality. Simultaneously with the transformation of the two brigades into divisions, their supporting air groups were redesignated the 1st and 2d Marine Aircraft Wings.

During the course of the war, the organization of the Marine division underwent numerous changes reflecting combat experience and new developments in the conduct of amphibious assaults. Although the unit designation was the same, there was, for example, considerable difference between the strength and organization of the 1st Marine Division that landed on GUADALCANAL in 1942 and of the 1st Division that landed on OKINAWA three years later.

The Marine Corps chain of command in the Pacific was relatively simple and uncluttered. Until FLEET MA-

ORDER OF BATTLE, MEDITERRANEAN THEATER OF OPERATIONS (AS OF MAY 2, 1945)

Unit	Commander	Location
Fifteenth Army Group	Gen. Mark W. Clark	Florence, Italy
Fifth Army	Lt. Gen. Lucian K. Truscott	Verona, Italy
II Corps	Lt. Gen. Geoffrey Keyes	Italy
10th Mountain Division	Maj. Gen. George P. Hays	Italy
85th Infantry Division	Maj. Gen. John B. Coulter	Italy
88th Infantry Division	Maj. Gen. Paul W. Kendall	Italy
IV Corps	Maj. Gen. Willis D. Crittenberger	Italy
1st Armored Division	Maj. Gen. Vernon E. Prichard	Italy
34th Infantry Division	Maj. Gen. Charles L. Bolte	Italy
92d Infantry Division	Maj. Gen. Edward M. Almond	Italy
British Eighth Army	Lt. Gen. Sir R. L. McCreery	Italy
91st Infantry Division	Maj. Gen. William G. Livesay	Italy
U.S. Army Air Forces in MTO	Lt. Gen. J. K. Cannon	Caserta, Italy
Twelfth Air Force	Maj. Gen. B. W. Chidlaw	Florence, Italy
XXII Tactical Air Command	Brig. Gen. T. C. Darcy	Italy
Fifteenth Air Force	Maj. Gen. N. F. Twining	Bari, Italy
XV Fighter Command	Brig. Gen. D. C. Strother	Italy

ORDER OF BATTLE, EUROPEAN THEATER OF OPERATIONS (AS OF MAY 7, 1945)

Unit	Commander	Location
Supreme Headquarters, Allied Expeditionary Force	General of the Army Dwight D. Eisenhower	Main Hdqrs., Versailles, France Advance Hdqrs., Reims, France
Northern Group of Armies (21st Army Group)	FM Sir Bernard L. Montgomery	Suchteln, Germany
First Canadian Army	Gen. H. D. G. Crerar	Holland
Second British Army	Lt. Gen. Sir Miles C. Dempsey	Germany
XVIII Corps (Airborne)	Maj. Gen. M. B. Ridgway	Germany
5th Armored Div.	Maj. Gen. L. E. Oliver	Germany
7th Armored Div.	Maj. Gen. R. W. Hasbrouck	Germany
82d Airborne Div.	Maj. Gen. J. M. Gavin	Germany
8th Infantry Div.	Maj. Gen. B. E. Moore	Germany
Central Group of Armies (12th Army Group)	Gen. Omar N. Bradley	Wiesbaden, Germany
Ninth Army	Lt. Gen. William H. Simpson	Braunschweig, Germany
XIII Corps	Maj. Gen. A. C. Gillem, Jr.	Germany
35th Infantry Div.	Maj. Gen. Paul W. Baade	Germany
84th Infantry Div.	Maj. Gen. A. R. Bolling	Germany
102d Infantry Div.	Maj. Gen. F. A. Keating	Germany
XVI Corps	Maj. Gen. J. B. Anderson	Germany
29th Infantry Div.	Maj. Gen. C. H. Gerhardt	Germany
75th Infantry Div.	Maj. Gen. R. E. Porter	Germany
79th Infantry Div.	Maj. Gen. I. T. Wyche	Germany
95th Infantry Div.	Maj. Gen. H. L. Twaddle	Germany
XIX Corps	Maj. Gen. R. S. McLain	Germany
2d Armored Div.	Maj. Gen. I. D. White	Germany
8th Armored Div.	Maj. Gen. J. M. Devine	Germany
30th Infantry Div.	Maj. Gen. L. S. Hobbs	Germany
83d Infantry Div.	Maj. Gen. R. C. Macon	Germany
First Army	Gen. Courtney H. Hodges	Weimar, Germany
78th Infantry Div.	Maj. Gen. E. P. Parker, Jr.	Germany

ORDER OF BATTLE, EUROPEAN THEATER OF OPERATIONS (*continued*)

Unit	Commander	Location
VII Corps	Lt. Gen. J. L. Collins	Germany
3d Armored Div.	Brig. Gen. Doyle O. Hickey	Germany
9th Infantry Div.	Maj. Gen. L. A. Craig	Germany
69th Infantry Div.	Maj. Gen. Emil F. Reinhardt	Germany
104th Infantry Div.	Maj. Gen. Terry Allen	Germany
VIII Corps	Maj. Gen. Troy H. Middleton	Germany
6th Armored Div.	Brig. Gen. George W. Read, Jr.	Germany
76th Infantry Div.	Maj. Gen. William R. Schmidt	Germany
87th Infantry Div.	Maj. Gen. Frank L. Culin, Jr.	Germany
89th Infantry Div.	Maj. Gen. Thomas D. Finley	Germany
Third Army	Gen. George S. Patton, Jr.	Erlangen, Germany
4th Infantry Div.	Maj. Gen. Harold W. Blakeley	Germany
70th Infantry Div.	Maj. Gen. A. J. Barnett	Germany
III Corps	Maj. Gen. James A. Van Fleet	Germany
14th Armored Div.	Maj. Gen. Albert C. Smith	Germany
99th Infantry Div.	Maj. Gen. Walter E. Lauer	Germany
V Corps	Maj. Gen. Clarence R. Huebner	Germany
9th Armored Div.	Maj. Gen. John W. Leonard	Germany
16th Armored Div.	Brig. Gen. John L. Pierce	Czechoslovakia
1st Infantry Div.	Maj. Gen. Clift Andrus	Czechoslovakia
2d Infantry Div.	Maj. Gen. Walter M. Robertson	Czechoslovakia
97th Infantry Div.	Brig. Gen. Milton B. Halsey	Czechoslovakia
XII Corps	Maj. Gen. Stafford Leroy Irwin	Germany
4th Armored Div.	Maj. Gen. William M. Hoge	Czechoslovakia
11th Armored Div.	Maj. Gen. Holmes E. Dager	Austria
5th Infantry Div.	Maj. Gen. Albert E. Brown	Germany
26th Infantry Div.	Maj. Gen. Willard S. Paul	Austria
90th Infantry Div.	Maj. Gen. Herbert L. Earnest	Czechoslovakia
XX Corps	Lt. Gen. Walton H. Walker	Germany
13th Armored Div.	Maj. Gen. John Milliken	Germany
65th Infantry Div.	Maj. Gen. Stanley E. Reinhart	Austria
71st Infantry Div.	Maj. Gen. Willard G. Wyman	Austria
80th Infantry Div.	Maj. Gen. Horace L. McBride	Austria
Fifteenth Army	Lt. Gen. Leonard T. Gerow	Bad Neunahr, Germany
66th Infantry Div.	Maj. Gen. Herman F. Kramer	France
106th Infantry Div.	Maj. Gen. Donald A. Stroh	France
XXII Corps	Maj. Gen. Ernest N. Harmon	Germany
17th Airborne Div.	Maj. Gen. William M. Miley	Germany
94th Infantry Div.	Maj. Gen. Harry J. Malony	Germany
XXIII Corps	Maj. Gen. Hugh J. Gaffey	Germany
28th Infantry Div.	Maj. Gen. Norman D. Cota	Germany
Southern Group of Armies (6th Army Group)	Gen. Jacob L. Devers	Heidelberg, Germany
Seventh Army	Lt. Gen. Alexander M. Patch	Schwäbisch-Gmünd, Germany
12th Armored Div.	Maj. Gen. Roderick R. Allen	Germany
63d Infantry Div.	Maj. Gen. Louis Hibbs	Germany
45th Infantry Div.	Maj. Gen. Robert T. Frederick	Germany
100th Infantry Div.	Maj. Gen. W. A. Burress	Germany
XXI Corps	Maj. Gen. Frank W. Milburn	Germany
101st Airborne Div.	Maj. Gen. Maxwell D. Taylor	Germany
36th Infantry Div.	Maj. Gen. John E. Dahlquist	Austria
XV Corps	Lt. Gen. Wade H. Haislip	Germany
20th Armored Div.	Maj. Gen. Orlando Ward	Germany
3d Infantry Div.	Maj. Gen. John W. O'Daniel	Germany
42d Infantry Div.	Maj. Gen. Harry J. Collins	Germany
86th Infantry Div.	Maj. Gen. Harris M. Melasky	Austria
VI Corps	Maj. Gen. Edward H. Brooks	Germany
10th Armored Div.	Maj. Gen. William H. H. Morris, Jr.	Austria

ORDER OF BATTLE, EUROPEAN THEATER OF OPERATIONS (*continued*)

Unit	Commander	Location
44th Infantry Div.	Maj. Gen. William F. Dean	Austria
103d Infantry Div.	Maj. Gen. Anthony C. McAuliffe	Austria
First French Army	Gen. Jean J. de Lattre de Tassigny	Lindau, Germany
SHAEF Reserve		
First Allied Airborne Army	Lt. Gen. Louis H. Brereton	Maison LaFitte, France
13th Airborne Div.	Maj. Gen. Elbridge G. Chapman, Jr.	France
U.S. Strategic Air Forces in Europe*	Gen. Carl A. Spaatz	Reims, France
Eighth Air Force	Lt. Gen. James H. Doolittle	High Wycombe, Bucks, England
1st Air Div.	Maj. Gen. Howard McC. Turner	England
2d Air Div.	Maj. Gen. Wm. E. Kepner	England
3d Air Div.	Maj. Gen. Earle E. Partridge	England
Ninth Air Force	Lt. Gen. Hoyt S. Vandenberg	Wiesbaden, Germany
IX Bomb Div.	Maj. Gen. Samuel E. Anderson	Belgium
IX Tactical Air Command	Maj. Gen. Elwood R. Quesada	Germany
XIX Tactical Air Command	Maj. Gen. Otto P. Weyland	Germany
XXIX Tactical Air Command	Brig. Gen. Richard E. Nugent	Germany
First Tactical Air Force (Prov.)	Maj. Gen. Robt. M. Webster	Heidelberg, Germany
XII Tactical Air Command	Brig. Gen. Glenn O. Barcus	Darmstadt, Germany
1st French Air Command	Gen. de Brig. Paul Gerardot	Issenheim, France
IX Troop Carrier Command	Maj. Gen. Paul L. Williams	Louvecienne, France

*Exercised operational control over Fifteenth Air Force shown under Mediterranean Theater of Operations.

ORDER OF BATTLE, U.S. FORCES IN CHINA THEATER (AS OF AUGUST 14, 1945)

Unit	Commander	Location
Hdqrs., U.S. Forces, China Theater	Lt. Gen. A. C. Wedemeyer	Chungking
U.S. Army Air Forces, China Theater	Lt. Gen. G. E. Stratemeyer	Chungking
Tenth Air Force	Maj. Gen. H. C. Davidson	Liuchow
Fourteenth Air Force	Maj. Gen. C. B. Stone, 3d	Kunming

ORDER OF BATTLE, U.S. ARMY FORCES IN THE PACIFIC (AS OF AUGUST 14, 1945)

Unit	Commander	Location
General Headquarters, U.S. Army Forces in the Pacific	General of the Army Douglas MacArthur	Manila, Luzon, Philippine Islands
Sixth Army	Gen. Walter Krueger	Luzon, Philippine Islands
40th Infantry Div.	Brig. Gen. D. J. Myers	Panay, Philippine Islands
11th Airborne Div.	Maj. Gen. J. M. Swing	Luzon, Philippine Islands
I Corps	Maj. Gen. I. P. Swift	Luzon, Philippine Islands
25th Infantry Div.	Maj. Gen. C. L. Mullins	Luzon, Philippine Islands
33d Infantry Div.	Maj. Gen. P. W. Clarkson	Luzon, Philippine Islands
41st Infantry Div.	Maj. Gen. J. A. Doe	Mindanao, Philippine Islands
IX Corps	Maj. Gen. C. W. Ryder	Leyte, Philippine Islands
77th Infantry Div.	Maj. Gen. A. D. Bruce	Cebu, Philippine Islands
81st Infantry Div.	Maj. Gen. P. J. Mueller	Leyte, Philippine Islands
XI Corps	Lt. Gen. C. P. Hall	Luzon, Philippine Islands
43d Infantry Div.	Maj. Gen. L. F. Wing	Luzon, Philippine Islands
Americal Infantry Div.	Maj. Gen. W. H. Arnold	Cebu, Philippine Islands
1st Cavalry Div.	Maj. Gen. W. C. Chase	Luzon, Philippine Islands

ORDER OF BATTLE, U.S. ARMY FORCES IN THE PACIFIC (*continued*)

Unit	Commander	Location
Eighth Army	Lt. Gen. R. L. Eichelberger	Leyte, Philippine Islands
93d Infantry Div.	Maj. Gen. H. H. Johnson	Morotai Is., New Guinea, and Philippine Islands
96th Infantry Div.	Maj. Gen. James L. Bradley	Okinawa, Ryukyu Islands, and Mindanao, P.I.
X Corps	Maj. Gen. F. C. Sibert	Mindanao, Philippine Islands
24th Infantry Div.	Maj. Gen. R. B. Woodruff	Mindanao, Philippine Islands
31st Infantry Div.	Maj. Gen. C. A. Martin	Mindanao, Philippine Islands
XIV Corps	Lt. Gen. O. W. Griswold	Luzon, Philippine Islands
6th Infantry Div.	Maj. Gen. C. E. Hurdis	Luzon, Philippine Islands
32d Infantry Div.	Maj. Gen. W. H. Gill	Luzon, Philippine Islands
37th Infantry Div.	Maj. Gen. R. S. Beightler	Luzon, Philippine Islands
38th Infantry Div.	Maj. Gen. F. A. Irving	Luzon, Philippine Islands
Tenth Army	Gen. J. W. Stilwell	Okinawa, Ryukyu Islands
XXIV Corps	Lt. Gen. J. R. Hodge	Okinawa, Ryukyu Islands
7th Infantry Div.	Maj. Gen. A. V. Arnold	Okinawa, Ryukyu Islands
27th Infantry Div.	Maj. Gen. G. W. Griner, Jr.	Ie Shima and Okinawa, Ryukyu Islands
U.S. Army Forces, Middle Pacific	Lt. Gen. R. C. Richardson, Jr.	Oahu, Hawaiian Islands
98th Infantry Div.	Maj. Gen. A. M. Harper	Oahu, Hawaiian Islands
U.S. Army Forces, Western Pacific	Lt. Gen. W. D. Styer	Luzon, Philippine Islands
Far East Air Forces	Gen. G. C. Kenney	Okinawa, Ryukyu Islands
Fifth Air Force	Lt. Gen. E. C. Whitehead	Okinawa, Ryukyu Islands
Seventh Air Force	Brig. Gen. T. D. White	Saipan, Mariana Islands
Thirteenth Air Force	Maj. Gen. P. B. Wurtsmith	Leyte, Philippine Islands

ORDER OF BATTLE, U.S. ARMY STRATEGIC AIR FORCES (AS OF AUGUST 14, 1945)

Headquarters, U.S. Army Strategic Air Forces, Guam, Mariana Islands:
- Commanding General .... Gen. Carl Spaatz
- Deputy Commander .... Lt. Gen. B. McK. Giles
- Chief of Staff .... Maj. Gen. C. E. LeMay

Eighth Air Force, Okinawa, Ryukyu Islands:
- Commanding General .... Lt. Gen. James H. Doolittle

Twentieth Air Force, Guam, Mariana Islands:
- Commanding General .... Lt. Gen. Nathan F. Twining

Tables from *Biennial Report of the Chief of Staff of the U.S. Army 1943–45*.

RINE FORCE, PACIFIC, was established in 1944, the divisions came under corps control. Organized at Camp Elliott, San Diego, on October 1, 1942, the First (later I) Marine Amphibious Corps (IMAC) sailed for NOUMEA on the 15th and arrived there on the 28th, where it became the supra-echelon organization for coordination of all Fleet Marine Force units in the South Pacific. As such, it exercised no tactical control over the 1st Marine Division operation on Guadalcanal, being concerned only with administrative matters.

As the tempo of operations in the South Pacific speeded up, IMAC became the amphibious operations planning agency for Adm. William HALSEY's SoPac Command. The first IMAC commander, Maj. Gen. Clayton B. Vogel, who had taken the corps to the South Pacific, was relieved on July 1, 1943, by Lt. Gen. Alexander A. VANDEGRIFT, former commander of the 1st Marine Division. His task was to continue IMAC planning for the coming BOUGAINVILLE operation and to monitor the activities of Marine units then involved in the central SOLOMONS campaign. Vandegrift, who had been selected to become the 18th Commandant of the Marine Corps, was in turn relieved on September 15 by the former commander of the 3d Marine Division, Maj. Gen. Charles D. Barrett, one of the pioneers in developing amphibious warfare doctrine. However, Barrett suddenly died, and at Halsey's request Vandegrift remained in the South Pacific, resuming command of IMAC on October 18. Vandegrift completed the planning for Bougainville and witnessed the start of the operation before relinquishing command on November 9 to Maj. Gen. Roy S. GEIGER, a veteran Marine aviator and commander of Marine aviation on Guadalcanal during that campaign. On April 15, 1944, IMAC became III Amphibious Corps, still under Geiger with headquarters on Guadalcanal. On June 30 Maj. Gen. Keller E. Rockey relieved Geiger of the IIIAC command, Geiger then going on to Pearl Harbor, where he relieved Lt. Gen. Holland M. SMITH as Commanding General, Fleet Marine Force, Pacific.

V Amphibious Corps was organized on September 4, 1943, at Pearl Harbor with Smith (then a major general) as its commander. VAC was to train and control the troops required for future operations in the PACIFIC OCEAN AREAS. Under VAC, Marine divisions conducted operations in the GILBERTS and the MARSHALLS. Smith wore two hats, commanding both FMFPac and VAC, during the Central Pacific campaigns, only relinquishing the latter in mid-October 1944 to Maj. Gen. Harry SCHMIDT, former commander of the 4th Marine Division, who headed VAC until the end of the war.

The Marine divisions were commanded as follows:

1st (activated February 1, 1941, at Guantanamo Bay, Cuba)—Maj. Gen. Holland M. Smith, Maj. Gen. Philip Torrey (June 1941), Maj. Gen. Alexander A. Vandegrift (March 1942), Maj. Gen. William H. Rupertus (June 1943), Maj. Gen. Pedro A. del Valle (November 1944)

2d (activated February 1, 1941, at Camp Elliott, Calif.)—Maj. Gen. Clayton B. Vogel, Maj. Gen. Charles F. B. Price (December 1941), Maj. Gen. John Marston (April 1942), Maj. Gen. Julian C. Smith (April 1943), Maj. Gen. Thomas E. Watson (April 1944), Maj. Gen. LeRoy P. Hunt (April 1945)

3d (activated September 16, 1943, at Camp Elliott, Calif.)—Maj. Gen. Charles D. Barrett, Maj. Gen. Allen H. Turnage (September 1943), Brig. Gen. Alfred H. Noble (September 1944), Maj. Gen. Graves B. Erskine (October 1944)

4th (activated August 16, 1943, at Camp Pendleton, Calif.)—Maj. Gen. Harry Schmidt, Maj. Gen. Clifton B. Cates (July 1944)

5th (activated November 11, 1943, at Camp Pendleton, Calif.)—Maj. Gen. Keller E. Rockey, Maj. Gen. Thomas E. Bourke (June 1945)

6th (activated September 7, 1944, on Guadalcanal)—Maj. Gen. Lemuel C. Shepherd, Jr.

In Marine Corps aviation, only two groups and 10 squadrons existed at the beginning of the war, and overall pilot strength was 708 marines. Total aviation strength was only 10,412 men. At its peak, in January 1945, Marine Corps aviation consisted of 10,412 pilots and a total of 125,162 marines. At that time the Marine Corps had 5 aircraft wings, 29 groups and 132 squadrons of various types, as well as subordinate units and detachments with various functions. The senior Marine air command in the Pacific was Aircraft, Fleet Marine Force, Pacific. As parent organization of all Marine air in the Pacific, it administered, organized, deployed and supplied every unit committed in the war from Guadalcanal to the Japanese surrender. Its commanding generals were: Maj. Gen. Ross E. Rowell (August 1941), Maj. Gen. Francis P. Mulcahy (September 1944) and Maj. Gen. James T. Moore (February 1945 to the end of the war). Of the five Marine aircraft wings activated during the war, four of them—the 1st, 2d, 3d and 4th—actually fought, while the 9th Wing remained at Marine Corps Air Station, Cherry Point, N.C., in a strictly training and equipping capacity.

In the Marine Corps campaigns of the PACIFIC WAR, 80 marines won the MEDAL OF HONOR, 48 of them posthumously; 957 NAVY CROSSES were presented for valor in these same actions. Marine Corps casualties were as follows: killed in action, 15,161; died of wounds, 3,259; captured and died, 268; missing, presumed dead, 795; prisoner of war, presumed dead, 250; nonbattle casualties in combat zone, 4,778; wounded in action, 67,207—for a grand total of 91,718. **B.M.F.**

UNITED STATES NAVY. When the war began in 1939, the U.S. Navy was a battleship-oriented force organized around a battle line of 15 capital ships, ranging in age from ARKANSAS (27 years) to COLORADO and WEST VIRGINIA (16 years). Eight more battleships were under construction or projected. The battle line was supported by 5 aircraft carriers, with 2 more under construction; 18 heavy cruisers; and 19 light cruisers (9 new, 10 dating from the early 1920s), with 4 more on order. A considerable number of World War I–designed FLUSH-DECKER destroyers were still on hand; 49 newer destroyers were in commission, with another 24 commissioning during 1939 and early 1940; 23 more were projected or building. Sixty-one old submarines, of World War I or later design, were active or in reserve. These had been followed, by the end of 1939, by 35 newer boats. Patrol craft included some old gunboats and World War I–program "Eagle boats" and wooden submarine chasers, with two 1930s Erie-class seagoing gunboats armed with 6-inch guns.

The Navy began its real expansion after the passage of the "Two-Ocean Navy Act" of July 1940. An earlier act, in May 1938, had authorized an 11 percent expansion in total displacement tonnage, but this new legislation provided for a 70 percent increase. In mid-1940 the Navy, Marines and Coast Guard had a combined personnel strength of 203,127. By December 1941 this had more than doubled, to meet the early demands of the new expansion, to 486,226; by August 31, 1945, the total came to 4,064,455. The Navy alone numbered 3,383,196 by June 20, 1945. Of these, 1,574,614 were stationed afloat, while the rest were assigned to shore duty in the United States or overseas.

Construction of ships and small craft steadily increased, as the Two-Ocean Act was followed by a massive early-wartime maximum effort building program. Between July 1, 1940, and August 31, 1945, the Navy completed or acquired:

Battleships	10
Aircraft carriers (CV, CVL)	27
Escort carriers (CVE)	111
Cruisers (CB, CA, CL)	47
Destroyers	370
Destroyer escorts	504
Submarines	217
Minecraft	975
Patrol ships and craft	1,915
Auxiliary ships	1,612
Landing ships and craft	66,055
District craft (yard craft)	3,053
	74,896

Construction priorities constantly shifted as the tides of war changed in the Atlantic and Pacific theaters.

Early emphasis was placed on carriers and antisubmarine craft to meet the twin threats of the Japanese offensive and the U-boat war. Construction of fleet carriers (CV) proceeded fairly constantly into 1945; 1943 was the top year for carrier completions, with six CVs and nine CVLs being joined by 19 CVEs. Submarine construction rose to a peak of 79 in 1944, dropping back in 1945 as the end of the war approached. Ten modern battleships, of the NORTH CAROLINA, SOUTH DAKOTA and IOWA classes, were completed, but five larger ships of a projected Montana class were canceled. To help fill the needs of the growing FAST CARRIER TASK FORCE for offensive operations in the Pacific, nine light cruiser hulls were completed as light carriers (CVL). As the submarine threat in the Atlantic was brought under control, production of antisubmarine craft was curtailed so that building ways could be devoted to construction of the enormous numbers of landing ships and craft required for large-scale amphibious offensives on both sides of the globe.

Development and production of aircraft and weapons had to keep pace; quantity had to be modified by improvements in quality to cope with more powerful enemy weapons. Prewar electronics had consisted principally of radio sets and radio direction finders; some development and small production of RADAR had taken place, as well as of SONAR. The electronic suits of naval ships mushroomed during the war years, to the point where even auxiliary ships and such small combatant craft as PT boats were equipped with radar. Airplanes and airships were also provided with search and gunnery radars in many instances. By August 31, 1945, nearly $3 billion had been spent on electronics, the greater part of this for radar equipment.

Over 75,000 aircraft were delivered between July 1, 1940, and August 31, 1945, more than two-thirds of these combat types. One hundred and sixty-five patrol and training BLIMPS were delivered to join the 10 already on hand when the United States entered the war. Production of aircraft was reflected in the training of aviation personnel. Total sea-service aviation strength went from 10,923 (2,965 pilots) in mid-1940 to 437,524 (60,747 pilots) by the end of the war.

Antiaircraft and antisubmarine weapons were produced in massive quantities during the war years. Large-scale manufacture of the Bofors-designed 40-mm. and Oerlikon 20-mm. automatic antiaircraft guns was supplemented by production of the dual-purpose 5-INCH 38-caliber gun; around 8,500 of these useful weapons had been built by the end of the war. Fire-control systems, coupled with precise gunnery radars, were intensively worked on, as were improved dual-purpose rapid-fire 6-inch and 8-inch main-battery turrets for cruisers; these last were not completed by V-J Day, but saw extensive postwar use. The performance and capabilities of naval aircraft jumped greatly between Pearl Harbor and the end of the war. Speed, altitude, endurance and ordnance capacities of Navy airplanes were highly developed. New types of acoustic and magnetic mines were developed; laid from airplanes and submarines by the thousands, they contributed to the strangling of the Japanese merchant marine.

A usually ignored aspect of Navy development was the unprecedented use of two- and three-dimensional training aids on a service-wide scale. Prewar and wartime expansion meant that enormous numbers of inexperienced men and women had to be quickly and effectively trained in the complex ways of a highly technical service. This extended in many directions and to a variety of degrees, from basic indoctrination of recruits to the advanced operational training of carrier pilots. The best brains and resources available were devoted to the creation of a huge and varied system of teaching, using an amazing array of textbooks, charts, three-dimensional teaching devices and sophisticated simulators. Clarity and effectiveness were stressed; results were what counted. For instance, simulators were produced which permitted the entire crew of a new submarine to practice dry-run attacks on land, using simulated devices which operated just as the real ones did.

Operational research became big business. Operations and techniques were studied and analyzed in search of the most effective weapons for use, for example, against U-boats or KAMIKAZE planes. Operational testing provided both realistic training for fleet personnel and active tryouts for new weapons and tactics. Operational researchers worked closely with intelligence personnel, combining the best available information on the enemy with the new technical developments. Here, as in other areas, the interchange of information and ideas with opposite numbers in other Allied services, particularly the British, benefited all concerned.

By V-J Day the battleship Navy of prewar days had been replaced by a much larger and more complex—both technically and organizationally—service, oriented toward carrier striking forces and large-scale amphibious operations, along with offensive submarine warfare on an oceanic scale. An enormous body of operational experience had been accumulated and reported on; a great deal of this had been studied and analyzed, but many wartime lessons remained to be sifted from the staggering bulk of information that was now available. The advent of the ATOMIC BOMB was to have an increasing effect on the development and operation of the postwar Navy and Marine Corps, but this was only on the horizon when the Pacific war ended in Tokyo Bay.

J.C.R.

UNITED STATES NAVY AIRCRAFT NAMES. Descriptions of the planes can be found under their numerical designations.

Hellcat	F6F fighter
Wildcat	F4F
Corsair	F4U
Tigercat	F7F
Helldiver	SB2C scout bomber
Dauntless	SBD
Devastator	TBD torpedo bomber
Avenger	TBF/TBM
Sea Hawk	SC scout-observation floatplane
Seagull	SOC
Kingfisher	OS2U
Sentinel	OY-1 land-based liaison and observation plane (*see* L-2)
Privateer	PB4Y-2 land-based patrol bomber
Ventura	PV-1 land-based patrol bomber
Harpoon	PV-2
Nomad	PBN flying boat

Catalina	PBY flying boat
Coronado	PB2Y
Mariner	PBM flying boat

UNITED STATES STRATEGIC AIR FORCES IN EUROPE. During the latter months of 1943 the American daylight air offensive against Germany was in danger of defeat. EIGHTH AIR FORCE formations, operating from bases in the British Isles, suffered disabling losses in attempting to bomb targets deep within Germany, and the FIFTEENTH AIR FORCE in Italy was not yet ready to make much of a contribution to the air war. The creation of U.S. Strategic Air Forces in Europe in January 1944 marked an attempt to coordinate the efforts of the two air forces.

Lt. Gen. Carl SPAATZ, Deputy Commanding General, Mediterranean Allied Air Forces, returned to Britain to take charge of the new headquarters in London. With him came Maj. Gen. James H. DOOLITTLE, former commander of the Fifteenth Air Force, who turned over his post to Maj. Gen. Nathan F. TWINING and assumed command of the Eighth Air Force. Lt. Gen. Ira C. EAKER, whose U.S. Army Air Forces in the United Kingdom was abolished, went to the Mediterranean to become commanding general of Allied air forces there.

UNITED STATES STRATEGIC AIR FORCES, PACIFIC. As early as fall 1944, the Air Force chief Gen. Henry H. ARNOLD began urging the creation of a single headquarters whose commander would coordinate the strategic bombarbment of Japan and report directly to the Commanding General, U.S. Army Air Forces. He wanted this commander for air to be the equal of the senior land and sea commanders who would conduct the final phase of the war against Japan.

Such an arrangement, however, would require the appointment of a supreme commander, a step the JOINT CHIEFS OF STAFF were reluctant to take. As a result, General MACARTHUR and Admiral NIMITZ continued to share responsibility for the war against Japan, and Arnold's plan could not be carried out.

General Arnold finally had to settle for the establishment of U.S. Army Strategic Air Forces, Pacific, which basically was a redesignation of TWENTIETH AIR FORCE headquarters. The change of title took place in July 1945. Gen. Carl SPAATZ, former commander of U.S. Strategic Air Forces in Europe, went to Guam and began organizing his headquarters. He had scarcely begun the work of coordinating the B-29 offensive (*see* B-29) with the operations of Far East Air Forces when the ATOMIC BOMB signaled Japan's defeat.

UNITED STATES STRATEGIC BOMBING SURVEY. As early as the spring of 1944, officers serving with U.S. Strategic Air Forces in Europe, and others stationed at U.S. Army Air Forces headquarters at Washington, began examining the possibility of a comprehensive study of the contribution of the bomber offensive to the defeat of Germany, an analysis that would both aid in the conquest of Japan and assist in postwar planning. On April 5, Gen. Carl SPAATZ, then in the United Kingdom, forwarded such a suggestion to Gen. Henry H. ARNOLD, who approved the idea, along with Secretary of War Henry L. STIMSON. Planning started under the guidance of Maj. Gen. Orvil A. Anderson and Maj. Gen. Laurence Kuter. President ROOSEVELT gave his blessing to the project, and in the autumn of 1944 Franklin D'Olier, president of the Prudential Life Insurance Co., became chairman of the U.S. Strategic Bombing Survey with authority to recruit as many as 350 civilians, 350 military officers and 500 enlisted men to carry out the ambitious undertaking.

In April 1945 the first trained investigative teams entered conquered German territory to begin three months of intensive work that produced some 200 reports, which included information obtained from interviews with German officers and civil authorities. Since promised Russian cooperation failed to materialize, some targets in eastern Germany could not be examined.

The survey of strategic bombing in Europe pointed out certain errors in the conduct of operations, among them the unrewarding attacks on submarine pens, the erroneous belief in the vulnerability of the ball-bearing industry and the delay in attacking the synthetic-oil plants. The investigation reached the conclusion that although air power might have been more effectively employed at various times and places, "Allied air power was decisive in the war in western Europe. . . . It brought home to the German people the full impact of modern war with all its horror and suffering. Its imprint on the German nation will be lasting."

A similar bombing survey was conducted after Japan surrendered, but its scope was broadened to include Navy and Marine air operations and the contribution of Army tactical aviation. Unresolved differences among service viewpoints prevented unanimity. General Anderson, for example, insisted that air power, especially land-based aviation, had been the decisive factor in the war against Japan. Besides being unsupportable by available evidence, such an assertion was unacceptable to the Navy, which, understandably, argued for the importance of its submarines, aircraft carriers and amphibious forces.

UNIVERSITY OF CHICAGO. For many years prior to the explosion of the first ATOMIC BOMB, the University of Chicago sponsored an active program in nuclear physics. Two of the university's nuclear activities were of notable importance during the war years. The first was the series of experiments, directed by Enrico FERMI, which led to the operation of an atomic pile—the first sustained and controlled release of nuclear energy in history—in December 1942. Actually built in a modified squash court located under the west stands of Stagg Field, an athletic stadium, the atomic pile was of crucial importance to the advancement of nuclear physics. The second University of Chicago–centered activity was the Chicago Metallurgical Laboratory, originally established for developing a method of producing plutonium. Code-named the Metallurgical Project, it developed lines of research that eventually became quite varied and widespread. Beginning in 1945, the university's war-related scientific endeavors were scaled down as soon as they had been carried as far as the demands of national defense required.

UNRYU. Class of Japanese aircraft carriers, similar to the SORYU class but all having their islands on the starboard side. Three of them—*Unryu, Amagi* and *Katsu-*

ragi—were completed as 741-foot 6-inch ships displacing over 17,000 tons and having a capacity of 64 or 65 planes. Three more carriers—*Aso, Ikoma* and *Kasagi*—were never completed. Ten more were projected but never begun.

Unryu was sunk by an American submarine in December 1944; *Amagi* was sunk by carrier planes in the Inland Sea shortly before V-J Day. *Katsuragi,* the only survivor of her class, was later scrapped. Big, fast (32 to 34 knots) ships, the Unryus were not completed until long after Japanese carrier aviation had been crippled.

UNTERMENSCHEN. Nazi term, meaning subhuman beings, applied to people regarded as racially inferior, particularly Jews and Slavs. Untermenschen were either to be exterminated or to be used as slaves of the NEW ORDER.

UNYO. Japanese escort carrier of 16,500 gross tons, formerly the merchant ship *Yawata Maru.* She was taken into the Navy in 1939 and was sunk in November 1944.

UPHOLDER, H.M.S. One of the small U-class (540 tons) British submarines which were based on MALTA and operated against enemy sea communications between Italy and North Africa in 1941 and 1942. Under the command of Lt. Comdr. David WANKLYN, she carried out 24 patrols and was credited with having sunk 97,000 tons of enemy shipping and three U-boats and one destroyer, while an Italian cruiser and another destroyer were severely damaged by her torpedoes.

URANUS. Code name of the main Soviet counteroffensive at STALINGRAD, November 1942.

UREY, Harold Clayton (1893–). American chemist and Nobel laureate, an important figure in the development of the ATOMIC BOMB. Educated at the Universities of Montana and California and the Institute for Theoretical Physics at Copenhagen, he taught at Montana and Johns Hopkins and, from 1929 to 1942, at Columbia, becoming famous as the discoverer of heavy water. In 1942–45 he was in charge of the work conducted at Columbia on the development of the gaseous diffusion method for producing the isotope U-235, needed for the bomb. After the war (1945–58) Urey taught at the University of Chicago and, following retirement, at California.

URQUHART, Robert (1901–). A major general, a veteran of NORTH AFRICA (51st Highland Division) and a brigade commander in SICILY and ITALY, "Roy" Urquhart was commander of the British 1ST AIRBORNE DIVISION at ARNHEM (Operation MARKET-GARDEN), September 1944.

USHIJIMA, Mitsuru (1887–1945). A Japanese career Army officer, Ushijima was appointed commandant of the Japanese Military Academy in 1942. Two years later, in August 1944, he was given command of the 32d Army on OKINAWA; he was to take command of all Japanese forces on the island once fighting commenced. He committed suicide by hara-kiri in June 1945 with one of his chief subordinates.

UTAH. Originally commissioned as a battleship by the U.S. Navy in 1911, *Utah* was demilitarized under the terms of the London naval limitation treaty of 1930. Her armor and most of her 12-inch guns removed, she was reclassified as a naval auxiliary ship and used for gunnery training and also as a radio-controlled target ship. On the morning of December 7, 1941, *Utah* was moored at PEARL HARBOR. Mortally hit by Japanese planes, she capsized and sank. Some accounts say that the Japanese mistook her for an aircraft carrier; this is incorrect. In her training-target role she retained her battleship superstructure and cage foremast, and bore no resemblance to a carrier. Like that of ARIZONA, her hull still rests on the bottom at Pearl Harbor.

UTAH BEACH. Code name of the American assault area (south of les Dunes de Varreville) on the extreme right of the Allied line in the Normandy INVASION, June 6, 1944.

V

V-1, V-2. *See* V-WEAPONS.

V-3. Giant German cannon designed to fire on London from across the North Sea. The original design was 492 feet long and would fire a 165-pound shell 80 miles. Small tubes extending laterally from the main barrel held supplementary charges that boosted the main charge. These tubes caused the crew to nickname the weapon Tausendfüssler (Thousand Legs). The Germans employed a 197-foot V-3 in the BULGE.

V-5. The U.S. naval aviation cadet program that procured and trained officer pilots. At its peak in 1943–44 it included 30,000 men, who upon completion of a six-stage training course were commissioned ensigns in the Naval Reserve or Marine second lieutenants.

V-7. A U.S. Naval Reserve officer training program through which volunteers with sufficient postsecondary education (typically a bachelor's degree) were trained as line officers for surface vessels.

V-12. A U.S. Naval Reserve officer training program through which volunteers received military training while completing their bachelor's degrees.

VAAGSØ RAID. A British COMMANDO operation against Vaagsø and Maaloy Islands, central Norway, December 27, 1941. The primary aim was to reinforce the German view that the Allies might invade Norway, and thus keep German forces tied up; the raid was chiefly directed against the company-sized German garrison in the town of South Vaagsø. It has been described by Brig. Peter Young, who participated, as a "minor classic of amphibious warfare."

VAERST, Gustav von (1894–). General der Panzertruppen Vaerst succeeded General von ARNIM in command of the Fifth Panzer Army in TUNISIA in January 1943. On May 9 Vaerst accepted Gen. Omar BRADLEY's unconditional surrender demand, making the Fifth Panzer Army the second German army to capitulate to the Allies (the first was PAULUS's SIXTH ARMY at STALINGRAD).

VALIANT, H.M.S. Royal Navy battleship of 31,000 tons, completed in 1915 by Fairfield and rebuilt 1937–39. Her World War II armament comprised eight 15-inch and twenty 4.5-inch guns, smaller weapons and four aircraft. *Valiant* served in home waters, escorting convoys and participating in the Norwegian campaign, until June 1940 when she was moved to the Mediterranean, there taking part in the attack on the French Navy at MERS-EL-KÉBIR, the Battle of CAPE MATAPAN and the CRETE evacuation operations. In December 1941 she and the *Queen Elizabeth* were severely damaged in an audacious attack by Italian "human torpedoes" (small, mine-carrying craft) in ALEXANDRIA harbor. After repairs and a brief spell in the Eastern Fleet, *Valiant* returned to the Mediterranean in 1943 for the Sicilian and Italian landing operations, after which she returned to the Indian Ocean for operations against the Japanese in the East Indies.

VALKYRIE (Walküre). A German code name with a double significance. Originally, Operation Valkyrie was the name given to military measures to be taken in case of internal disruption or revolt (notably, rebellion by the slave laborers imported into Germany). Troops would come from the Replacement Army (Ersatzheer), commanded by Gen. Friedrich FROMM, and an important feature of the plan was that those forces would occupy key offices and points in Berlin. The conspirators against Adolf HITLER used this plan (which, ironically, had been approved by Hitler) as a cover for their own actions to be taken after Hitler's assassination. *See also* OPPOSITION TO HITLER.

VALMONTONE. Town northeast of ANZIO (Italy), where the Germans fought a rearguard action against units of the U.S. VI Corps on June 1–2, 1944. The Germans abandoned Valmontone on the latter day. The action provoked Allied controversy because the U.S. FIFTH ARMY commander, Gen. Mark CLARK, turned the bulk of his forces toward Rome rather than trying to cut off German forces by a rapid thrust to Valmontone, as the overall Allied commander, Field Marshal Sir Harold ALEXANDER, wished him to do.

VANDEGRIFT, Alexander Archer (1887–1973). As a young U.S. Marine officer, Vandegrift served in Nicaragua and the occupation of Veracruz before World War I. In 1914 he participated in the fighting against the Caco bandits in Haiti. In the 1930s he was one of the first officers assigned to the Fleet Marine Force. Then he served as military secretary to the Commandant of the Corps for three years before his appointment as assistant to the Commandant in 1940, when he was promoted to brigadier general. In November 1941 he was assigned to the 1st Marine Division as assistant division commander, and in March 1942, upon promotion to major general, he was named to head the division. As commanding general Vandegrift was responsible for its training and for getting it up to combat fitness before he took it to the South Pacific in May, the first Marine division ever to take the field against the enemy.

Vandegrift arrived in Wellington, N.Z., with the advance echelon of the division on June 14, and 12 days later he learned that he was slated to lead his marines in a landing on GUADALCANAL on August 7. Aside from the fact that there was no hard intelligence available about the target, Vandegrift was faced with the fact that his division was not complete—part of it was still en route to New Zealand, while one regiment was attached to Marine forces in Samoa. Further, supporting units were spread out from the South Pacific to the United States, and there was only about a month and a half in which to plan the operation and conduct rehearsals. Nonetheless, Vandegrift and his staff overcame all obstacles to conduct the Guadalcanal landing, which was the first large-scale offensive against the Japanese in the war.

For his outstanding service as commanding general of the 1st Marine Division in the attack on Guadalcanal, TULAGI and Gavutu, Vandegrift was awarded the NAVY CROSS, and for the subsequent occupation and defense of the island, against all odds, and his inspiring leadership "accomplished at the constant risk of his life," he was awarded the MEDAL OF HONOR.

In July 1943 he assumed command of I Marine Amphibious Corps and directed the planning for the landing on BOUGAINVILLE on November 1. After the beachhead was established, he was relieved by Maj. Gen. Roy S. GEIGER and returned to Washington as the Commandant-designate of the Marine Corps, assuming the post on January 1, 1944, as a lieutenant general. A little more than a year later, on April 4, 1945, he was appointed general, the first Marine officer on active duty to attain four-star rank.

VANDENBERG, Arthur Hendrick (1884–1951). U.S. Senator from Michigan, originally a leader of the isolationist bloc in the Senate. He co-authored the Nye-Vandenberg resolution, providing for a Senate investigation designed to promote peace by taking the profit out of war, and was one of the authors of a clause in the NEUTRALITY ACT of 1937 requiring the President to proclaim an embargo on the sale of arms to belligerents. He fought the repeal of this arms embargo requested by President ROOSEVELT in 1939. After PEARL HARBOR, however, Vandenberg took a strong stand for American leadership in world affairs. At the end of the war in 1945 he made a historic speech proposing that the United States, Great Britain, the Soviet Union, France and China enter into treaties to guarantee the permanent disarmament of Germany and Japan. After his return from YALTA, Roosevelt appointed Vandenberg a member of the U.S. delegation to the UNITED NATIONS conference in San Francisco. He played a leading role in the formulation of the U.N. Charter, particularly Article 14, which provided for the General Assembly to arbitrate situations which were "likely to impair the general welfare or friendly relations among nations," and after the San Francisco meeting was a leading advocate of the United Nations in the U.S. Senate and thus instrumental in its acceptance. Subsequently, he gave strong support to the Marshall Plan.

VANDENBERG, Hoyt S. (1899–1954). Considered one of the U.S. air arm's most capable staff officers, Vandenberg rose during the war from lieutenant colonel in the Air Staff's operations and training section to lieutenant general in command of the NINTH AIR FORCE. He took part in the preparations for Operation TORCH, and as a brigadier general helped organize the TWELFTH AIR FORCE in North Africa, served as that organization's chief of staff and flew missions over Tunisia, the Mediterranean islands and Italy. In August 1943 he returned to Washington as Deputy Chief of the Air Staff, but he soon departed for Russia as a member of a mission headed by Ambassador Averell HARRIMAN.

Vandenberg became Deputy Air Commander in Chief, Allied Expeditionary Force, as a major general, and participated in planning the INVASION of Europe. He took over Ninth Air Force in August 1944, received a promotion to lieutenant general in March 1945 and as the war was ending returned to Washington for staff duty. He later served as Chief of Staff of the U.S. Air Force.

VAN FLEET, James A. (1892–). U.S. Army officer who commanded the 8th Infantry Regiment on UTAH BEACH on D-Day, then served as assistant division commander of the 2d Division at SAINT-LÔ and BREST. Promoted to major general in the fall of 1944, Van Fleet assumed command of the 90th Division. He ended the war as the commander of the III Corps. In the Korean War he commanded the Eighth Army (1951–53), after Gen. Matthew B. RIDGWAY was moved up to the Supreme Command. He had earlier led the U.S. military effort to aid Greece in suppressing Communist revolution. Jim Van Fleet always looked the part of a soldier. A large, burly man, he was rated an ideal leader of combat troops.

VANSITTART, Robert Gilbert Vansittart, 1st Baron (1881–1957). As the Permanent Under-Secretary at the British Foreign Office, Vansittart was a vigorous prewar opponent of the British policy of APPEASEMENT. He was accused of fostering hostility to Germany despite the government's efforts to the contrary. In 1938, as a consequence, he was "demoted" to the specially created post of Chief Diplomatic Adviser to H.M. Government, being replaced by Sir Alexander CADOGAN.

VARGAS, Getulio (1883–1954). The dominant political figure in Brazil from 1930 until his death in 1954. During the war President Vargas's government strongly supported inter-American solidarity, and as North American support of the Allies increased, so did Brazil's. In July 1942 Brazil declared war against Germany and Italy. The Brazilian Navy joined the fight against Axis submarines, and the accessibility of Brazilian ports to Allied ships greatly facilitated this aspect of the war. In addition, Brazil was the only South American state to commit ground forces to the struggle. In October 1945 Vargas was overthrown in a bloodless coup. He returned to office in 1951. *See also* BRAZILIAN EXPEDITIONARY FORCE.

VARSITY. Code name for an Allied airborne assault on March 24, 1945, designed to assist the British 21ST ARMY GROUP to cross the Rhine River in the vicinity of WESEL. More aircraft (880 escorting fighters, 1,696 transport planes and 1,348 gliders) participated and more men (22,000) landed on the first day than in any other airborne operation, although more troops overall (36,000) arrived by air in an earlier assault, Operation MARKET.

The objectives of the airborne troops (the British 6th and American 17th Airborne Divisions) were wooded high ground affording observation of the river crossing sites, exits from Wesel and crossings of nearby streams to deny movement of German reserves. To enable ground troops to utilize darkness for the river crossing and to avoid interference with the airborne landings by artillery fire, the airborne attack began well after the amphibious assault, an unusual procedure. It involved the first use of a new C-46 transport aircraft designed with specific attention to the needs of paratroopers (*see* C-46).

Before the assault, Radio Berlin boasted that the Germans were lying in wait. In reality, they anticipated an attack farther behind the Rhine, but Allied losses nevertheless were heavy. Although contact was established quickly with British ground troops and all objectives were in hand by the end of the first day, controversy remained as to whether a costly airborne assault was necessary when German forces were so depleted. Two American infantry divisions crossing the river nearby, for example, lost but 41 men killed, while the two airborne divisions lost 506.

VASEY, George Alan (1895–1945). Australian Army officer (major general), a veteran of World War I in Europe, who commanded the Australian 7th Division in New Guinea.

VASILEVSKY, Alexander M. (1895–1977). Vasilevsky enlisted as a private and later served as an officer in the Imperial Russian Army during the First World War. After the Bolshevik Revolution he entered the Red Army and rose rapidly through the ranks. He was chief of the operations directorate of the General Staff when the German invasion came in 1941. In this capacity he had the task of informing Joseph Stalin of the many grave situations facing the nation during the early period of the war. It is likely that Vasilevsky gained Stalin's regard during those trying times, and the two remained close thereafter. In January 1942 he was appointed Chief of the General Staff and, although charged with supervising the staff, most often found himself in the field as the representative of the Soviet High Command. Vasilevsky, who achieved the rank of Marshal of the Soviet Union, remained as Chief of Staff until 1948 except for periods when he commanded the Third Belorussian Front and when he was named commander of Soviet forces in the Far East theater during the short period of hostilities against Japan.

VASILYEV. A code name used by Joseph Stalin in Soviet military transmissions.

VATUTIN, Nicholas F. (1901–1944). Soviet general who distinguished himself in 1941 during the Battle of Moscow and, a year later, at the Battle of Stalingrad,

Marshal Vasilevsky leads a group of Soviet staff officers

where he helped organize the great Soviet counteroffensive that resulted in the annihilation of the German SIXTH ARMY. According to Marshal ZHUKOV, on February 29, 1944, while Vatutin was commanding the First Ukrainian Front, his car was ambushed by PARTISANS believed to be Ukrainian nationalists opposed to the restoration of Soviet rule (Zhukov called them "BANDERA bandits"). Vatutin died of his wounds shortly thereafter.

V-E DAY. Victory-in-Europe Day, formally marking the end of the war in Europe, May 8, 1945. General JODL signed the instrument of unconditional surrender at the Allied headquarters at Reims at 2:41 A.M. on May 7; this was ratified at Berlin just before midnight on May 8, at Soviet headquarters.

VELIKYE LUKI. Russian railroad town some 250 miles west of Moscow. It was the scene of heavy fighting and strong Soviet resistance to the German advance on Moscow in the fall of 1941.

VELLA GULF, BATTLE OF. On the night of August 6–7, 1943, two U.S. destroyer divisions, under the command of Comdr. Frederick Moosbrugger, intercepted a Japanese troop and supply convoy in Vella Gulf in the central Solomons. The Japanese ships were carrying reinforcements to the garrison on KOLOMBANGARA Island. The Japanese had been spotted by a search plane, and Moosbrugger estimated that they would arrive in the gulf, between Kolombangara and VELLA LAVELLA, about midnight. With his ships formed into two parallel columns about a mile apart, Moosbrugger steered a dogleg course to bring his ships onto a parallel reciprocal course with the Japanese force. While still out of visible range of the Japanese, Moosbrugger's first division, using RADAR control, fired their torpedoes and quickly turned away to avoid possible Japanese torpedoes. Three Japanese destroyers of Capt. Kaju Sugiura's four-ship force were mortally hit. Moosbrugger's second division now opened up with 5-inch guns and torpedoes, and the first division joined in. The three damaged Japanese ships went down under this barrage. The remaining Japanese destroyer, the SHIGURE, retired, believing that the area was under American air attack. Moosbrugger's force turned southward, having suffered neither damage nor casualties. This short and successful encounter upheld the destroyermen's belief that they could get good results operating by themselves in night actions instead of being tied to cruiser forces, as they had been in earlier battles.

VELLA LAVELLA. One of the SOLOMON ISLANDS, some 12–15 miles northwest of KOLOMBANGARA. On August 15, 1943, the U.S. Army 35th Regimental Combat Team, reinforced by Army and Navy support forces and the Marine 4th Defense Battalion, landed on this hitherto-ignored island, after the landings on NEW GEORGIA. The U.S. forces were later augmented by the 14th New Zealand Brigade. On the night of August 17–18 the Japanese attempted a small-scale landing on the opposite end of the island; troops were embarked in small barges and torpedo boats. These were screened by four destroyers, commanded by Rear Adm. Matsuji Ijuin. The Japanese force was met north of Vella Lavella shortly after midnight by four American destroyers under Capt. Thomas Ryan. In a gun and torpedo action, Japanese destroyers *Hamakaze* and *Isokaze* were slightly damaged. During this action the troop-carrying barges and small craft scattered; some were sunk, but most succeeded in reaching their destination. The engagement was referred to in many contemporary sources as the Battle of Vella Lavella.

This name is also used to identify a later action, fought on the night of October 6–7, 1943. The Japanese evacuated Kolombangara during the first few nights of October. They then decided to withdraw the small garrison that had been landed on Vella Lavella in August. Rear Admiral Ijuin commanded a force of three destroyers and 12 smaller craft that were to load the garrison; six more destroyers formed a covering force. On the evening of October 6 two patrolling American groups of three destroyers each converged on the area from the north and south. In the hours before midnight Ijuin's screening force and the American northern force—three ships under Capt. Frank Walker—made RADAR and visual contact and deployed to engage.

Maneuvering at high speeds in the darkness, the two forces engaged with torpedoes and gunfire. Japanese destroyer YUGUMO was hit and left in flames, but one of her torpedoes blew the bow off *Chevalier*. Destroyer O'BANNON collided with *Chevalier* and was temporarily put out of action with a mutilated bow. Walker's third destroyer, *Selfridge*, continued the action but took a LONG LANCE torpedo, which shattered her bow and caused severe flooding. By now the three ships of the American southern destroyer group were nearing the area. A Japanese reconnaissance plane reported them to Ijuin, who ordered his ships and the three destroyer-transports to head for RABAUL. The Japanese smaller craft were not detected, and completed the evacuation of Vella Lavella in the dark early hours of October 7. The American southern force found no one to fight; it assisted the damaged *O'Bannon* and *Selfridge* and escorted them back down the SLOT for repairs. *Chevalier* was judged beyond help; her crew was taken off, and an American torpedo sent her to the bottom.

It is this action that is called the Battle of Vella Lavella in postwar histories. The earlier action, of August 17–18, is simply described as a destroyer action off Vella Lavella. Samuel Eliot MORISON refers to it as a destroyer action "off Horaniu," a small anchorage on Vella Lavella.

The October Vella Lavella battle was a tactical victory for the Japanese. One U.S. destroyer was sunk and two more crippled, at a cost of one Japanese ship. The scheduled evacuation of the island went off without interference. The strategic outcome was a minus for the Japanese; with their troops gone from Vella Lavella and Kolombangara, CHOISEUL remained the only Japanese foothold in the central Solomons. Another rung on the ladder toward Rabaul had been climbed.

VELVET. Code name for a proposal, made toward the end of 1942, for Allied air assistance to strengthen the Russian southern flank. An Anglo-American air force of 20 squadrons was to be established in Transcaucasia to assist the Soviet land and air forces in holding the line of the Caucasus Mountains and the Black Sea coast.

After protracted delay, the Russians declined the offer of aid.

VENERABLE. Code name of the operation by French forces to open the port of Bordeaux, April 14, 1945.

VENGEANCE. A two-place, low-wing dive-bomber built in the United States for service with the British and powered by a 1,700-horsepower Wright radial. Vultee developed the plane, and some 1,200 were acquired by the RAF. It rendered valuable service during the reconquest of BURMA, but lacked the speed and firepower to survive without fighter protection. The U.S. Army Air Forces designated its Vengeances either A-31 OR A-35.

VENTURA. Based on the American Lockheed Lodestar transport, this U.S.-built British aircraft closely resembled the older HUDSON. Major differences included more powerful engines—2,000-horsepower Pratt and Whitney radials—a ventral gun position, four rather than two forward-firing machine guns and capacity for 1,500 pounds of bombs. British Venturas entered service with BOMBER COMMAND in 1942 and participated in the pinpoint daylight destruction of a radio factory at Eindhoven, but were withdrawn from combat in 1943 in favor of faster aircraft. The plane continued to see action with COASTAL COMMAND, however, and with Canadian, South African, Australian and New Zealand squadrons. American designations were B-34 (Army) and PV-1 (Navy) (*see* PV).

VERITABLE. Code name for the Canadian FIRST ARMY's portion of Field Marshal MONTGOMERY's post-BULGE double envelopment designed to result in a linkup on the Rhine River with Operation GRENADE being conducted by the U.S. NINTH ARMY. Gen. Henry D. G. CRERAR launched his forces to the southeast from NIJMEGEN and the Reichswald Forest on February 8, 1945. Owing to high water in front of Ninth Army positions, the American attack originally scheduled for February 10 did not jump off until the 23d. Thus the enemy was able to mass his reserves against Crerar.

VERNON, H.M.S. The ROYAL NAVY's school at Portsmouth for TORPEDO, MINE and electrical instruction, and development and research in these branches of naval activity. An immediate problem at the beginning of the war was the use by Germany of magnetic mines laid by U-boats and aircraft. Although there was nothing new in magnetic mines, knowledge of their polarity had to be acquired before effective countermeasures could be taken. This came when a German magnetic mine was recovered from the mud flats off Shoeburyness on November 23, 1939, and successfully stripped by Lt. Comdr. J. G. D. Ouvry. With the knowledge obtained, *Vernon* was able to devise a system of protection to ships by DEGAUSSING (producing a counteracting magnetic field) and a method of exploding the mines by a sweep towed by minesweepers. Similar problems, having to do with more sophisticated influence mines and with acoustic and other target-seeking torpedoes developed by the Germans, were solved. At the same time, research and development in British torpedoes and mines were carried out, and a great deal of basic training in minesweeping and allied techniques was undertaken at *Vernon* and other temporary wartime establishments under its control.

VERSAILLES. Location of SHAEF (Allied SUPREME HEADQUARTERS) from September 20, 1944.

V FOR VICTORY. The V for Victory campaign, which was conducted by the BRITISH BROADCASTING CORPORATION, had the aim of encouraging and stiffening resistance to the Germans in the occupied countries of Europe. The idea is credited to Victor de Laveleye, a Belgian refugee who broadcast from London to his countrymen asking them to chalk the letter *V* in public places. In July 1941 the BBC's COLONEL BRITTON opened the campaign in seven languages, telling his listeners to tap out the Morse Code *V* sign—dot-dot-dot-dash—with car horns and train whistles, on doors and so on. He also suggested what became the famous hand sign—waving with the first two fingers making a *V*. The first four notes of Beethoven's Fifth Symphony became the aural symbol. Dr. GOEBBELS, the German Propaganda Minister, made an attempt to counter this highly successful campaign by declaring that *V* stood for *Viktoria*—German victory.

VIAN, Sir Philip (1894–1968). Then a captain in the Royal Navy, Vian first made his name in command of H.M.S. *Cossack* in February 1940 when he intercepted the German tanker *Altmark* in Jössing Fjord, Norway, and rescued 299 British merchant seamen, captured by the ADMIRAL GRAF SPEE, after a sharp fight (*see* ALTMARK INCIDENT). He was still commanding the *Cossack* during the chase of the German battleship BISMARCK in 1941, his flotilla shadowing the enemy through the night of May 26 and attacking her with torpedoes.

On promotion to rear admiral Vian commanded a cruiser squadron in the Mediterranean, and in the spring of 1942, during the passage of a convoy from ALEXANDRIA to MALTA, fought a spirited action with his cruisers and destroyers against heavy units of the Italian fleet, driving them off and succeeding in reaching Malta with much-needed food, ammunition and fuel. This action is known as the Battle of Sirte, a brilliant feat of arms which brought Vian a knighthood. He commanded the aircraft carrier force which supported the Allied landing at SALERNO in September 1943 (Operation Avalanche), and was brought home in 1944 to command the naval task force covering the British landings in the INVASION of Normandy (Operation Neptune). His success was outstanding, and it led to his appointment as commander of the British carrier force in the Pacific in 1945. After the war he commanded the Home Fleet and reached the rank of Admiral of the Fleet.

VICHY. Spa in south-central France that gave its name to the French Government formed after the defeat by the Germans. On July 1, 1940, the French Government, under the Premier, Marshal Philippe PÉTAIN, moved from the town of Clermont-Ferrand, its most recent stopping place in its flight from Paris, to Vichy, which as a resort had ample hotel accommodations. On July 10 the National Assembly voted, in effect, to give full power to the marshal, thus bringing to an end the Third Republic, the longest-lived French government since the Revolution. The resolution, which passed 569 to 80, empowered Pétain to draw up a new constitution, which was never completed; he did, however, set out to form a state based on "Work, Family and Fatherland," following many of the ideals of the French Right; this state was the government for the one-third of France not occupied by the Germans. The Vichy government was from the start divided into two factions—the traditionalist, Catholic conservatives and the fascist and semi-fascist elements, most of whose leaders had originally been leftists. In structure, the government tended to be decentralized.

Pétain functioned as head of state. Pierre LAVAL, who had much to do with bringing Vichy into being, was the first head of the government (he was styled Vice-President of the Council of Ministers). Laval was dismissed by Pétain in December 1940, being followed briefly by Pierre Etienne FLANDIN, who held the portfolio of Foreign Minister, and then in February 1941 by Adm. François DARLAN, who was given Laval's rank. At German dictation, Laval returned as Chief of the Government (the new title) in April 1942. At this time Pétain withdrew from active participation in the work of the administration. Laval continued as head of the government until the dissolution of the Vichy government in the summer of 1944, following Allied victories in northern France. In actuality the government had ceased to have real power after November 1942, when, following the Allied landings in North Africa, the Germans had taken over the unoccupied zone of France.

VICTOR EMMANUEL III (1869–1947). Italy's "Little King" reigned for 46 years—from 1900, when he ascended the throne following the assassination of his father, until 1946, when he abdicated in favor of his son. His reign is remembered for three bloody wars and the 21-year dominance of Benito MUSSOLINI and Fascism.

As a child Victor Emmanuel was small and sickly, but he was educated in a Spartan regimen and later won from Queen Victoria the tribute that he was one of the most talented and intelligent princes in Europe. As King, however, he had only limited constitutional powers, which he was careful to stay within. He has been criticized for being too concerned with the preservation of the House of Savoy, for having unrealistic imperial ambitions and for lacking forcefulness.

Victor Emmanuel spent the years of World War I at the front, living the simple life of a soldier and doing what he could to maintain morale among his army. The postwar years were hard ones for both Italy and the monarchy. When Mussolini and his Fascists agitated for power in 1922, the King yielded. Three days before the Fascist march on Rome, he wired his Prime Minister that "the only way of avoiding dangerous shocks [civil war] is in associating fascism with the Government by legal means." Critics assert that had the King followed the Prime Minister's advice and declared martial law, the Fascists would have been defeated without difficulty.

For whatever motives, Victor Emmanuel linked his monarchy with Fascism. Twice weekly Mussolini conferred with the King. There was considerable respect between them, although Count CIANO records that Mussolini often ridiculed the King in private. The King, on the other hand, consistently spoke well of Mussolini, even after the Duce's fall.

There is little doubt who wielded the power. The King often protested Mussolini's decisions, but usually acquiesced. Disliking the Germans and fearful that Italy did not have the economic or military resources to take part successfully in another war, Victor Emmanuel nevertheless took no drastic steps to prevent Mussolini from leading Italy into the Second World War. On June 1, 1940, Ciano described the King as "now resigned, no, more than resigned, to the idea of war."

As the war advanced steadily toward disaster for Italy, Victor Emmanuel was finally moved to action. On July 25, 1943, he told Mussolini he must step down. With Marshal Pietro BADOGLIO as his new Prime Minister, the King tried to avoid a unilateral breach of the AXIS alliance and prevent military action between Germany and Italy, but neither aim was achieved. An armistice was signed with the Allies on September 3, but on the 9th Victor Emmanuel and his government fled Rome, leaving the country to drift at this critical moment.

The Allies supported the King's government, reestablished at Brindisi, as an alternative to establishing an Allied military government for Italy; however, Victor Emmanuel was urged to abdicate. He was discredited with the Italian people. But not until June 5, 1944, after the Allies took Rome, did he relinquish power by naming his son, Crown Prince UMBERTO (Humbert II), Lieutenant General of the Realm. Two years later he abdicated in favor of Umberto. Victor Emmanuel and his wife, Elena of Montenegro, spent the following months in exile in Alexandria, Egypt, where he died on December 28, 1947.

VICTORIA CROSS. The highest British military award for bravery. The decoration was instituted in 1856 by a royal warrant for all "who had performed some signal act of valour." The medal could be granted without regard to rank or branch of service. It was first awarded by Queen Victoria in 1857 to Crimean War veterans. In 1902 King Edward VII decreed that the medal could be awarded posthumously. The medal is a Maltese cross of bronze, impressed with the imperial crown and crest, with the words "For Valour" on a scroll. Victoria Crosses were originally cast from cannon used in the Crimean War, and all are finished by hand.

VICTORIOUS, H.M.S. Royal Navy aircraft carrier of 23,000 tons, completed early in 1941 by Vickers-Armstrong, armed with sixteen 4.5-inch guns and smaller weapons. *Victorious* had an aircraft capacity of 40 to 50, depending on size, and an armored flight deck. On completion she joined the Home Fleet; her aircraft assisted in the pursuit of the BISMARCK, and she was used as cover for convoys to Russia and other operations. After participating in the August 1942 convoy (*see* PEDESTAL) to Malta and covering the Allied landings in NORTHWEST AFRICA in November 1942, she was lent to the U.S. Navy for use in the South Pacific in 1943. On her return to the Home Fleet, aircraft from *Victorious* scored several bomb hits on the TIRPITZ in the attack of April 3, 1944; after this and other operations she returned to the Far East.

VICTORY SHIP. A mass-producible cargo ship designed by the U.S. Maritime Commission as a replacement for the LIBERTY SHIP, faster and with better postwar commercial possibilities; this latter consideration had been ignored in producing the Liberty. Some Victory ships were diesel-powered and designated VC2-M-AP4, while others had turbines and the type designation VC2-S-AP2. The VC2-S-AP3 had a more powerful turbine plant than the -AP2, while the -AP5 type was a modification constructed for the Navy as the Haskell class of attack transports (*see* APA).

VIENNA. The former (and subsequent) Austrian capital was entered on April 7, 1945, by troops of the Soviet Third Ukrainian Front. Joined by troops of the Second Ukrainian Front, they completed the capture of the city on April 13, after considerable street fighting.

VIERLING. German name for a quadruple 20-mm. antiaircraft gun mount, referred to as a 2-cm. Flakvierling. It was widely used on land, in fixed positions or mounted on a tank or halftrack chassis or on a two-wheeled trailer, as well as in ships. It was effective against both surface and air targets.

VIETINGHOFF GENNANT SCHEEL, Heinrich Gottfried von (1887–1952). German Army officer, commander in chief in Italy in the last phases of the war. A veteran of World War I, Vietinghoff rose through the grades, becoming a Generalleutnant (equivalent to major general) in 1938. He commanded a panzer division in Poland, served in the Balkans and commanded a corps on the Eastern Front and an army in France. In August 1943, now a colonel general, he was appointed to command of the new Tenth Army in southern Italy, his first mission being to assure the withdrawal of German forces northward to Rome before Italy surrendered. In October 1944, when Field Marshal KESSELRING was injured in a car accident, Vietinghoff became temporary German commander in chief in Italy. Kesselring returned in January but in March was dispatched by Adolf HITLER to the Western Front, Vietinghoff then officially succeeding him. Vietinghoff and SS General Karl WOLFF participated in the secret negotiations with Allen DULLES, head of the OFFICE OF STRATEGIC SERVICES in Switzerland, that led to the surrender of German forces on May 2, 1945, six days before V-E Day.

VIET MINH. A revolutionary Indochinese organization formed in 1941 and ultimately led by Ho CHI MINH, the Viet Minh was in reality a Chinese-sponsored coalition of Vietnamese anti-French and anti-Japanese Communist and non-Communist nationalist groups. It was the only anti-Japanese movement of consequence during the war, producing some intelligence of use to the Allies and responsible for minor guerrilla forays against the Japanese.

VIGAN. The Japanese secured the Vigan area (northwestern Luzon) on December 10, 1941, opposed only by American air attacks and rough seas, and began fighter operations from there the next day. The last Japanese convoy to reach Luzon during the war put in near Vigan on December 30, 1944, suffering heavily at the hands of FIFTH AIR FORCE planes. The United States Army Forces in the PHILIPPINES (Northern Luzon), a guerrilla organization under Col. Russell W. Volckmann, cleared the Vigan area during April 1945, forcing the small Japanese garrison of some 750 troops to withdraw southward and inland.

VIGOROUS. Code name of an unsuccessful British attempt to convoy supplies to MALTA from Alexandria, June 1942.

VIIPURI (Vyborg). City on the western side of the KARELIAN ISTHMUS in northwestern Russia. Before the war it was the second largest city in Finland, with a population considerably greater than it has today. In 1940, at the conclusion of the SOVIET-FINNISH WAR, it was ceded to the Soviet Union. The annexation of Viipuri was a major factor in Finland's decision to go to war against the Soviet Union a second time in 1941 as Germany's ally.

VILLERS-BOCAGE. Twenty miles inland from the Normandy INVASION beaches, this important communications center was entered by troops of the British 7th Armored Division on June 13, 1944, but the division withdrew and the town was not retaken until August 4, when it fell to the British 50th Division.

VINCENNES. The command post of the Anglo-French Commander in Chief, Gen. Maurice GAMELIN. *See also* GRAND QUARTIER GÉNÉRALE.

VINCENNES, U.S.S. NEW ORLEANS–class heavy cruiser of 9,400 tons, completed in 1937. She was sunk by Japanese gunfire and torpedoes in the poorly handled and costly Battle of SAVO ISLAND, in the early morning hours of August 9, 1942.

VINSON, Frederick Moore (1890–1953). A strongly pro–New Deal member of the U.S. House of Representatives during the 1930s, Vinson was a federal judge when the United States entered the war. He resigned in 1943 to become director of the OFFICE OF ECONOMIC STABILIZATION, and in April 1945 became director of the OFFICE OF WAR MOBILIZATION. The latter position made him the country's top economic figure. He was greatly admired by President TRUMAN, who appointed him Secretary of the Treasury in July 1945 and, in the following year, Chief Justice of the United States.

VISTULA RIVER. From its bridgehead over the Vistula at Baranow, the Soviet First Ukrainian Front (Marshal KONEV) launched its great offensive toward and into Germany on January 12, 1945.

VITEBSK. Belorussian city captured by the Germans in the first weeks of the invasion of Russia, 1941. Vitebsk was retaken by the Soviets in 1944 in a campaign which resulted in the encirclement of a large German force and the capture of many prisoners.

VITTORIO VENETO. Italian battleship of 35,000 tons, completed at Trieste in 1940 and armed with nine 15-inch, twelve 6-inch and twelve 3.5-inch guns, smaller weapons and three aircraft. *Vittorio Veneto* participated in the Mediterranean fighting in 1941, being damaged at the Battle of CAPE MATAPAN; in December 1941 she was torpedoed by the Royal Navy submarine *Urge* and seriously damaged. In September 1943 she was one of the major units of the Italian fleet which surrendered at Malta.

V-J DAY. Victory-over-Japan Day, formally marking the end of the war in the Pacific, August 15, 1945. The Japanese accepted Allied surrender terms on August 14, soon after ATOMIC BOMBS were dropped on HIROSHIMA (August 6) and NAGASAKI (August 9). September 2, 1945, the day the Japanese signed the instrument of surrender, is also called V-J Day.

VLASOV, Andrei A. (1900–1946). General Vlasov was a rising star in the Red Army when the war came. In 1938–39 he had served in China as an adviser. In January 1941 he became commander of the IV Armored Corps in Lvov, and one month later he was awarded the Order of Lenin. During the Battle of Moscow, Joseph STALIN appointed Vlasov commander of the new Twentieth Army, which played a key part in repelling the German attack on the capital. In January 1942 he was made lieutenant general and awarded the ORDER OF THE RED BANNER. His new command—the Second Shock Army—took him to the Volkhov front. Encircled by the Germans with most of his troops, he was captured in July 1941.

Vlasov's anti-Stalinist, anti-Soviet feelings were doubtless deep-rooted and were possibly due to the horrors that accompanied the collectivization of farming and the bloody purges in the 1930s. Thus Vlasov allowed the Germans to exploit him as a rallying figure for a Russian Army of Liberation (*see* ROA), to be formed out of Russian POWs that would join the German war effort. Adolf HITLER opposed this OKW plan, and it never acquired the expected political dimensions. ROA units performed auxiliary functions; Vlasov and other former Soviet generals in the movement had no control over them.

Not until November 1944, when Germany's military situation had gravely deteriorated, was Vlasov permitted to launch the "Committee for the Liberation of the Peoples of Russia." One poorly equipped division, together with some oddments, was placed under his nominal command. They surrendered to the U.S. SEVENTH ARMY. In conformity with an agreement made at YALTA, Vlasov and six other generals were turned over to the Soviets. All of them were hanged in Moscow in August 1946. *See also* PRAGUE UPRISING.

VL FOKKER CX. A Dutch two-place, single-engine tactical reconnaissance and army liaison biplane designed by Fokker. About 35 were built for the Finnish Air Force. Bomb load was 880 pounds, and a defensive armament of two machine guns was normally carried.

VOGELKOP. On July 30, 1944, the reinforced 1st Infantry of the U.S. 6th Division began landing near Mar, at the northern tip of the Vogelkop—the "bird head" peninsula of western NEW GUINEA—and on offshore Amsterdam and Middleburg Islands to secure airfield sites for the support of further drives toward the PHILIPPINES. A PT base was established on Amsterdam Island, a fighter field was ready on Middleburg on August 17 and a medium-bomber base became operational near Mar on September 3. Ultimately, the entire 6th Infantry Division staged in the Mar area for the invasion of Luzon.

VOLGA RIVER. One of the German strategic aims in the 1942 campaign in Russia was the cutting off of Volga River traffic. However, this purpose, which could have been achieved elsewhere, became intermingled with (at least in HITLER's mind) and subsidiary to the capture of STALINGRAD.

VOLKSSTURM. The "People's Militia," a HITLER creation of the latter part of the war (order of September 25, 1944). Units of the Volkssturm appeared in the fighting on both the Eastern and Western Fronts and figured prominently in the final struggle in Berlin. The Volkssturm was made up chiefly of older men (up to 60) and boys of 16 or sometimes younger, with a number of other men physically unfit for service in the armed forces proper. In addition to these handicaps, Volkssturm units were inadequately armed and equipped. They were supposed to be fired with strong Nazi convictions, but essentially the Volkssturm was a last-gasp effort. A German joke of the time said that a person called up for the Volkssturm would be exempted if he could prove that he had a father already serving.

VOLOKOLAMSK. A defense point on the 1941 MOZHAISK Line, about 80 miles west of Moscow. In its winter counteroffensive the Red Army made a breakthrough near Volokolamsk on January 13, 1942.

VOLTURNO RIVER. The Germans held a defense line along this river north of Naples in October 1944. The U.S. FIFTH ARMY began its assault crossing on October 12, the start of a slow advance in the face of strong German delaying action and harsh terrain that finally ended at the fortified GUSTAV LINE.

VORONEZH. An important city on the east bank of the Don River north of STALINGRAD. It fell to the German Fourth Panzer Army on July 6, 1942. The German forces in Voronezh constituted a salient on the east bank of the river, and on January 22, 1943, this bulge was assaulted by troops of the Soviet Voronezh Front. These forces completed the capture of the city on January 25.

VORONOV, N. N. (1899–1968). Voronov entered Soviet military service in 1918 and served throughout his career in artillery. He took part in the Civil War, was a POW in Poland in 1920–21 and saw duty as Soviet military attaché in Italy (1932). After taking part in the SOVIET-FINNISH WAR, he served as first deputy chief of the Main Artillery Directorate. In June 1941 he was chief of artillery of the General Staff. At the same time he was appointed to the permanent board of advisers to the SOVIET HIGH COMMAND. He is noted by Marshal ZHUKOV as being instrumental in planning the STALINGRAD counteroffensive. He remained on the staff until the end of the war. His highest rank was colonel general of artillery.

VOROSHILOV, Kliment E. (1881–1969). A member of the Communist Party since 1903, Voroshilov became Red Army commander during the Civil War. Commis-

First Allied crossing of the Volturno River took place above and below the hairpin turn

sar of Defense and a staunch supporter of Joseph STALIN, he survived the purge of 1937–38. Following the initially disastrous, though ultimately successful war with Finland (November 1939–March 1940), Voroshilov was relieved in the reshuffle of positions (May 1940) and appointed Deputy Premier. On July 3, 1941, along with Stalin, MOLOTOV, BERIA and MALENKOV, he was named to the STATE DEFENSE COMMITTEE and at the same time was appointed to represent the SOVIET HIGH COMMAND at the LENINGRAD front. He was a member of the Soviet delegation at the TEHERAN CONFERENCE, and in 1944–45 was assigned to the headquarters of PARTISAN movements. From the end of the war until 1947, Marshal Voroshilov was the chief of the Soviet Control Commission in Hungary. He was Soviet President in 1953–60.

VT FUZE. The U.S. term for PROXIMITY FUZE. For security reasons, the abbreviation VT (with the meaningless literal signification, *variable time*) was used in references to this device. It continued in use even after the enemy had become aware of the existence of the proximity fuze.

VUILLEMIN, Joseph (1883–1963). A French bomber commander of legendary courage and leadership in World War I, named Chief of Staff of the FRENCH AIR FORCE early in 1938. His forces were too weak to face the LUFTWAFFE in 1938 and were thus a factor in the French capitulation at MUNICH. By the fall of 1939 Vuillemin had made progress, but his forces proved unequal to the Luftwaffe in the campaign of 1940. Following the armistice Vuillemin retired, but returned briefly in 1943 to command a bomber group for the forces of FREE FRANCE.

VULCAN. Code name of the final Allied offensive in TUNISIA, launched on May 6, 1943.

V-WEAPONS. In 1943 Adolf HITLER threatened to use secret weapons against the Allies, partly in reprisal for the bombing of Germany. The threat was backed up by two weapons, the V-1 and V-2 (Vergeltungswaffe 1 and 2; Reprisal Weapons 1 and 2). There was also a cannon called the V-3.

The V-1 was designated the FZG76 (Fernzielgerät—Long-Range Target Apparatus—76) by the Germans. It was also known as the doodlebug, the flying bomb and the buzz bomb. The V-1 was a pulse-jet-powered flying bomb, 25 feet long with a 16-foot wingspan, and carried a 1-ton warhead 152 miles at about 400 miles per hour. The range was later increased to 250 miles. It was first successfully flown on December 24, 1943. Usually launched from the ground from concrete ramps, it was also fired from modified HEINKEL HE 111 bombers manned by a special LUFTWAFFE unit. The latter method came into use after Allied forces overran the V-1's continental coastal launching sites. The weapon could be hit by antiaircraft fire or intercepted by RADAR-guided fighters. It was first used against targets in England several weeks after the Normandy INVASION. The only Allied planes capable of catching it by matching its speed were the Gloster METEOR I's of the RAF's 616th Squadron. The V-1 was plagued by an unreliable guidance system, and it is estimated that fewer than one-fifth of the 8,000 fired at England ever hit their intended targets. As a demoralizing agent, however, it was far superior to the V-2.

The second V-weapon was the V-2 rocket bomb, or A-4 (fourth model in the "A" series begun in 1933). It was first successfully fired on October 3, 1942, at PEENEMÜNDE. This weapon was a liquid-fuel rocket, 46 feet long and weighing 13 tons, with a 1-ton warhead. It reached Mach 1 in under 30 seconds, with a total burn time of 65–70 seconds. For long-range targets the V-2 attained a height of 50–60 miles. Greater altitudes could be reached if range was no object. The V-2 offensive began in September 1944 and ended on March 27, 1945. Because of a number of problems with the mechanism of the rockets, many did not reach their intended

V-1 dives toward the Piccadilly area of London

targets. The ones that did so caused a great deal of damage and a large number of casualties. Main targets were London, ANTWERP and Liège. There was no effective defense against this weapon once it was launched. Its great incoming speed caused it to impact at 3,500 feet per second five minutes after launching, which meant that the missile penetrated its target to some depth; thus it frequently expended much of its energy blowing a great hole in the ground.

The German missile offensive was aimed at both England and the Continent. About 2,500 people were killed in England by the V-2; France and Belgium were also hard hit, especially the city of Antwerp, the Allies' main port of entry, which suffered over 30,000 casualties. More than 13,000 V-1s and 5,000 V-2s had been fired by the end of the war, and there was a plan to tow containerized V-2s to America with U-boats and fire them at selected targets.

The weapons, especially the V-1, came at an auspicious time for Germany, supplying an aerial offensive capability when the Luftwaffe's conventional bomber force could no longer carry out such a program. However, Albert SPEER has recorded his view that the resources devoted to the V-weapons program could have been better used in the building of much-needed airplanes. *See also* BRAUN, WERNHER VON.

VYAZMA. Located east of Smolensk (USSR) on the road to Moscow, this town was taken by the Germans in October 1941 and held until the spring of 1943. During the occupation thousands of local inhabitants were deported to Germany as slave laborers. Just prior to their withdrawal from Vyazma, the Germans destroyed practically the entire city.

VYSHINSKY, Andrei Y. (1883–1954). A criminal lawyer by education, Vyshinsky became famous in the 1930s as a state prosecutor in the Moscow show trials of Old Bolsheviks. As Chief Prosecutor of the USSR in 1935–40, he was one of the principal organizers of Joseph STALIN's purges, including the purge of the RED ARMY. In 1940 he was appointed Deputy People's Commissar of Foreign Affairs and supervised the incorporation of LATVIA into the Soviet Union. During the war years, as Foreign Minister V. M. MOLOTOV's deputy, Vyshinsky took part in all Big Three conferences, and at Marshal ZHUKOV's Berlin headquarters he witnessed the signing of the terms of unconditional surrender. His hard-hitting, dogmatic demeanor made him Stalin's natural choice as Soviet spokesman in dealing with Western ambassadors in Moscow, in forcing King MICHAEL of Rumania to replace Prime Minister Radescu with Petru Groza and in outlining Soviet positions at the United Nations. His book, *The Law of the Soviet State*, interpreting the 1936 Constitution of the USSR, was a major text for a generation of Soviet lawyers in the Stalin era.

W2. Headquarters built for Adolf Hitler's use in directing operations against the Allies after the Normandy invasion. It was located between Laôn and Soissons, France, and was the site of a conference between Hitler and Field Marshal Rommel on June 17, 1944. After this meeting the Führer observed that the location of W2 in partisan-ridden France made it "unsafe."

WACHI, Tsunezo (1900–). In 1940 Commander Wachi became Japanese naval attaché in Mexico City, where he did double duty as chief of "L," Japan's largest overseas espionage ring. His principal mission was to intercept U.S. naval messages and report on all fleet movements in the Atlantic. From February to October 1944 Wachi commanded Japanese naval forces on Iwo Jima.

WADHAM. *See* Cockade.

WADIS (Akarit, Faregh, Matratir, Zebbeus, Zessar, Zeuss, Zigzaou, etc.). A wadi is a deep gorge or ravine, dry except during the rainy season. In North Africa wadis were often used as antitank obstacles or sites for gun emplacements. They are sometimes veritable canyons or fairly flat washes. Almost invariably they directly influence military operations.

WAFFEN SS. The permanent volunteer combat units of the German SS (Schutzstaffel—Protection Detachment) (*see* SS) dated from the establishment of Adolf Hitler's Headquarters Guard in March 1933. Similar units, political alert units of battalion size (called standards), were organized about the same time in some of the SS territorial headquarters. In 1936 these scattered battalions were organized into two regiments under the designation SS Verfügungstruppe. Hitler's Headquarters Guard, renamed the Body Guard Standard (Leibstandarte), was also considered a part of the SS Verfügungstruppe. Some of these units took part in the occupation of Austria and Czechoslovakia under Army command.

The mission of the SS Verfügungstruppe was defined when Hitler issued a decree in August 1938 which stated that the SS Verfügungstruppe was neither a part of the armed forces nor a part of the police but a permanent armed force at his personal disposal (Verfügung). The future mission of this force was outlined by Hitler in August 1940, when he stated that after the war Germany would encompass within its borders large groups of non-Germanic peoples who would not necessarily be friendly to the Reich. To keep these people in a proper state of order and discipline it would therefore be necessary to have a permanent state police force. This was to be the role of the SS Verfügungstruppe.

At the outbreak of war in 1939 the SS Verfügungstruppe, soon to be known as the Waffen SS, had been augmented until it reached a strength of approximately 18,000 men, with all the supporting troops necessary to constitute a motorized infantry division. These troops and other SS troops were not used as complete divisions in the Polish and French campaigns; instead, they were attached to regular Army divisions and committed at most in the strength of reinforced regiments. By the beginning of the Russian campaign in June 1941 the Waffen SS had reached a strength of over 150,000 men organized into and committed as separate SS divisions. The strength of the SS continued to grow throughout the war years until by December 1944 the Waffen SS had approximately 600,000 men under one Army headquarters, 12 corps headquarters and more than 30 divisions.

Units of the Waffen SS operating under the tactical control of the Army utilized the regular Army supply channels for rations, fuel, heavy equipment and ammunition. In addition, the SS maintained its own system of supply, which was not under armed forces control. For this purpose the SS had organized a network of depots and stores, mainly in Germany but extending into the occupied areas. With regard to administrative support, the SS maintained its own personnel, replacement, training and military justice systems. For constitution of new units and the rehabilitation of its divisions the SS enjoyed preferential treatment in comparison with the Army.

WAGNER, Eduard (1897–1944). German Army officer, Quartermaster General in 1941, when he participated in the planning of the invasion of Russia. His highest rank was general. As a man of action, he had previously advocated a policy of aggressive operations during the phony war period of 1939–40. When he saw the direction that military operations were taking, Wagner became increasingly disaffected with Adolf Hitler's leadership. Consequently he became involved in the plot to kill Hitler, and when the putsch of July 20, 1944, failed he committed suicide on July 26 rather than face trial. *See also* Opposition to Hitler.

WAHOO, U.S.S. Gato-class submarine, completed in 1942, which sank nine Japanese ships on her fourth war patrol (March 1943), the second-highest total for one patrol in the Pacific war. The *Wahoo*'s commander was Dudley W. "Mush" Morton. Overall, *Wahoo*, under the command of Morton and his predecessor, Marvin G. "Pinky" Kennedy, sank 20 ships, giving her seventh place among American submarines in the Pacific. *See also* Tang, U.S.S.

WAINWRIGHT, Jonathan Mayhew (1883–1953). U.S. Army officer who went to the Philippines in 1940 as a major general. When Gen. Douglas MacArthur was withdrawn from the Philippines in 1942, Wainwright was left in command of U.S. and Philippine forces. He was forced to surrender, and was a Japanese prisoner of war until 1945. Promoted to lieutenant general in 1942 and to general in 1945, Wainwright was present at the surrender ceremonies in Tokyo Bay in September 1945. To the Army, in which he became virtually a revered figure, he was always "Skinny" Wainwright.

WAKDE. Name applied during World War II to Insoemoar Island, the larger of the two Wakde Islands, off the northwest shore of NEW GUINEA. By June 1943 the Japanese had built an excellent airfield on Wakde, which the Allies needed to support Gen. Douglas MACARTHUR's drive toward the PHILIPPINES and Adm. Chester NIMITZ's drive across the Central Pacific. The 163d RCT of the U.S. 41st Division began landing on the New Guinea mainland opposite Wakde on May 17, 1944, and sent a reinforced battalion against Wakde the next day. By noon on the 20th Wakde was in American hands.

WAKE ISLAND. In 1941 Wake Island—actually an atoll consisting of three islands, Wilkes, Peale and Wake—was expected to become a forward base for U.S. Pacific Fleet submarines. Although civilian contractors were hired to build the naval base initially, at the time war broke out the work on the island's defenses had been done in the main by the men who were to man them, marines of the 1st Defense Battalion, commanded by Maj. James P. S. DEVEREUX. The Marine air element on Wake was Marine Fighter Squadron 211. At 11:58 A.M. on December 7, 1941, the island was subjected to its first Japanese air raid of the war. Raids continued daily until December 11, when a large enemy naval force appeared off the island and attempted an assault landing. Despite being outgunned by the Japanese ships, marine-manned coast artillery returned heavy fire and thwarted the attempt. On the 23d approximately 1,500 Japanese Special Naval Landing Force troops were put ashore. They were held off for about 12 hours before the overwhelmed marines were forced to capitulate. On January 12, 1942, the survivors of what President ROOSEVELT called "this great fight" were evacuated to spend the rest of the war in Japanese prison camps.

WALCHEREN ISLAND. With SOUTH BEVELAND ISLAND to the east, saucer-shaped Walcheren Island forms the north bank of the SCHELDT ESTUARY connecting Antwerp with the sea. On October 3–4, 1944, the RAF bombed dikes to flood the low-lying interior, but hard fighting was required to conquer German defenses on narrow strips of higher ground. Last resistance ended on November 8.

WALDAU, Otto Hoffmann von (1898–1943). When he died in a plane crash at the age of 45, Waldau was one of the youngest generals in the LUFTWAFFE. At the time he was on a mission in the eastern Mediterranean. Waldau had previously served on the Air Staff, as deputy to the Chief, and as air commander in Africa. He had recently become German air commander in the eastern Mediterranean.

WALKER, Frederick J. (1896–1944). One of the Royal Navy's most brilliant antisubmarine specialists. At the start of the war Walker was appointed to the staff of Adm. Sir Bertram RAMSAY, Flag Officer Dover, and was commended for his service there. He joined H.M.S. *Stork,* the ship with which his name will always be associated, in October 1941 as senior officer, 36th Escort Group. Two months later, escorting an ATLANTIC convoy, his group destroyed four U-boats in five days, and in April 1942, a fifth. He was promoted to captain in June 1942, and after commanding the escort base at Liverpool he became senior officer of the 2d Escort Group. In the next 12 months this group destroyed 16 U-boats around the convoys it was escorting. Captain Walker died in the naval hospital at Liverpool on July 9, 1944, following a stroke.

WALKER, Walton Harris (1889–1950). U.S. Army officer who commanded the 3d Armored Division and then the IV Armored Corps in 1942. In 1943 the IV Corps was redesignated the XX Corps; Walker led it for the rest of the war. In 1945 he was promoted to lieutenant general and was presented his three stars by Gen. George S. PATTON, the same three stars which Patton had gotten from Gen. Dwight EISENHOWER. Walker was killed in a jeep accident while commanding the Eighth Army in Korea during the 1950 Christmastide. A tough commander, not given to sentiment, reticent of manner and short of speech in any public appearance, Walker was not popular with soldiers. But he performed ably in Korea, and his defense of the Naktong Line is regarded as a military classic.

WALLACE, Henry Agard (1888–1965). A prominent American agricultural economist and editor, Wallace was appointed Secretary of Agriculture by President ROOSEVELT in 1933. In 1940 he resigned to campaign for the Vice-Presidency, the office he held in 1941–45. He had other duties as well. Before the United States entered the war, Wallace held two positions in the national defense program. He was appointed chairman of the Board of Economic Warfare and of the Supply Priorities and Allocations Board, which in 1942 was merged into the new WAR PRODUCTION BOARD. But friction developed between Wallace as chairman of the Board of Economic Warfare and Jesse JONES, head of the Reconstruction Finance Corporation, over administering the acquisition of war materials from foreign sources. Wallace lost the battle, and the Board of Economic Warfare was eliminated.

Continuously active in foreign affairs, Wallace visited China in 1944 to stimulate the government to continue its fight against the Japanese. In 1945 Roosevelt appointed him Secretary of Commerce in succession to his old adversary, Jesse Jones. The Senate confirmed him in the position but refused to approve his concomitant appointment as head of the RFC. A highly controversial political figure, Wallace was a hero to labor and a vague, irresponsible dreamer to conservatives. In 1948 he ran for the Presidency on the Progressive Party ticket.

WALLIS, Sir Barnes Neville (1887–). British aeronautical designer and engineer who designed some of the war's most notable bombs—the superheavy GRAND SLAM and Tall Boy and the skip bombs used by the famous DAM BUSTERS squadron in the Ruhr in May

1943. Details of Upkeep, as the dam-busting bomb was code-named, were not made public until the 1960s. It was shaped like a fat oil drum, being five feet long and almost five feet in diameter. When it was dropped, it had already been given a backspin of some 500 revolutions per minute by an auxiliary motor inside the bomber. When it hit the water it bounced like a stone until it came up against the target dam; then the backspin caused it to cling to the wall and crawl downward until it reached 30 feet below the surface, the depth for which its hydrostatic fuze was set.

In earlier years Wallis, who spent much of his career with Vickers Armstrong, had pioneered the geodetic system of aircraft construction. An airship man in the 1920s, he was the designer of the dirigible *R-100*.

WALRUS. Small single-engine biplane catapult flying boat built by Supermarine of England. Although obsolete in 1939, the plane served throughout the war in a variety of roles—as a spotter, in reconnaissance and, especially, in air–sea rescue in the North Sea and the Mediterranean and in the Far East. The lumbering Shagbat, as it was popularly known, had its biplane wings set above the hull. It carried a crew of four and had a normal range of 600 miles and a maximum speed of 135 miles per hour.

WALSH, Kenneth A. (1916–). U.S. Marine Corps major who scored 21 aerial victories in the Pacific. In May 1943 he became the war's first F4U Corsair ace (*see* F4U). He was awarded the MEDAL OF HONOR for two actions in August 1943; in the first he claimed three kills, and in the second he alone attacked 50 enemy aircraft and was credited with four victories.

WALTHER P-38. German semiautomatic pistol, 9 mm. in bore size, with an eight-cartridge capacity. *See also* SMALL ARMS.

WANG CHING-WEI (1884–1944). A one-time radical revolutionary associate of Dr. Sun Yat-sen, who overthrew the last Chinese dynasty to found the Chinese republic in 1911. With Chinese reverses in the Sino-Japanese War in 1938, Wang came to believe in an Axis victory, and he attempted to negotiate a peace between CHIANG KAI-SHEK and the Japanese. Wang became a Japanese puppet overlord based at Nanking.

WANKLYN, David (1911–1942). Captain of the British submarine *Upholder* in the Mediterranean, Wanklyn, a lieutenant commander, was awarded the VICTORIA CROSS for his gallantry in attacking a strongly escorted Italian troop convoy on May 24, 1941. He sank the 18,000-ton troopship *Conte Rosso* and was hunted by the destroyer escort, 37 depth charges being dropped near him. Wanklyn worked his way clear of the attack and returned safely to harbor. The *Upholder,* with Wanklyn still in command, was lost in April 1942, having failed to return from her 25th patrol.

WANNSEE CONFERENCE. Summoned by Adolf EICHMANN on behalf of Reinhard HEYDRICH, the secret Nazi interdepartmental conference held on January 20, 1942, at Wannsee, a suburb of Berlin, was convened to discuss organizational problems connected with the genocide operation against the Jews in the whole of German-occupied Europe, an operation to which Heydrich had been assigned by Hermann GÖRING. In addition to Heydrich and Eichmann, Heinrich MÜLLER of the Gestapo attended, and the key ministries sent high-level representatives. The minutes of the meeting survive; they reveal that the problems were discussed, territory by territory, largely in terms of evacuation of Jews to the east, though the ultimate FINAL SOLUTION demanded by Göring was referred to by Heydrich, as was the use of Jews as SLAVE LABOR.

WANZ. A German submarine-mounted RADAR search receiver. It incorporated automatic scanning but could not pick up higher-frequency Allied radar pulses; by 1944 it was considered ineffective against newer radars.

WAR CABINET. The British body charged with the formulation and direction of war policy. The War Cabinet was instituted on the declaration of war on September 3, 1939. It consisted of the following ministers: the Prime Minister, Neville CHAMBERLAIN; the Chancellor of the Exchequer, Sir John SIMON; the Foreign Secretary, Lord HALIFAX; the Minister for the Coordination of Defence, Admiral of the Fleet Lord Chatfield; the First Lord of the Admiralty, Winston S. CHURCHILL; the Secretary of State for War, Leslie HORE-BELISHA; the Secretary of State for Air, Sir Kingsley WOOD; the Lord Privy Seal, Sir Samuel HOARE; Minister Without Portfolio, Lord Hankey. In the National Coalition Government of Winston Churchill (May 11, 1940) the War Cabinet consisted of Churchill, Chamberlain, Halifax and two representatives of the Labour Party, Clement ATTLEE and Arthur GREENWOOD. At the end of the National Government (May 1945) the members of the War Cabinet were Churchill; the Chancellor of the Exchequer, Sir John ANDERSON; the Foreign Secretary, Anthony EDEN; the Home Secretary, Herbert MORRISON; the Minister of Labour and National Service, Ernest BEVIN; the Lord President of the Council, Attlee; the Minister of Production, Oliver LYTTELTON; and the Minister of Reconstruction, Lord WOOLTON.

WAR CRIMES COMMISSION. On October 7, 1942, the United States and Great Britain called on the members of the UNITED NATIONS to help establish a War Crimes Commission which would investigate alleged war crimes against nationals of the U.N. member states. A total of 16 nations sought representation on the commission, which began its work in London on October 20, 1943. Unlike the other U.N. members, the Soviets chose instead to establish their own commission on November 2, 1942. The U.N. commission gathered and evaluated evidence, affixed individual responsibility for war crimes, if possible, and took alleged war criminals into custody. It did not have, however, any judicial or prosecutorial functions similar to those of the INTERNATIONAL MILITARY TRIBUNAL at Nuremberg.

WARD, Orlando (1891–). U.S. Army officer who as a major general in 1942 assumed command of the 1st Armored Division, which he led in the fighting in TUNISIA. After a temporary setback to the division at the KASSERINE PASS he was relieved of command, and subsequently commanded the Tank Destroyer Center and

Field Artillery School in the United States before obtaining command of the 20th Armored Division in October 1944 and leading it through combat in Germany with a distinguished record.

WARD, U.S.S. FLUSH-DECKER destroyer, completed in 1918, that was on patrol duty off the entrance to PEARL HARBOR on the morning of December 7, 1941. About 0645 *Ward* shot at and depth-charged a Japanese MIDGET SUBMARINE, sinking her. The destroyer's commanding officer, Comdr. W. W. Outerbridge, promptly notified naval headquarters, but the news did not arouse the base.

WAR LABOR BOARD. *See* NATIONAL WAR LABOR BOARD.

WARLIMONT, Walter (1894–). An important German staff officer throughout the war, Warlimont had represented the Defense Ministry at General FRANCO's headquarters during the Spanish Civil War. In September 1938, then a colonel, he was appointed to the high command (*see* OKW). In 1939 he became Deputy Chief of the Armed Forces Operational Staff (Wehrmachtführungsstab) under Gen. Alfred JODL. He was promoted to major general in 1940, lieutenant general in 1942 and General der Artillerie in 1944. In the July 20, 1944, attempt on Adolf HITLER's life, Warlimont was injured, suffering a mild concussion.

WAR MANPOWER COMMISSION. U.S. agency established by President Franklin D. ROOSEVELT by executive order on April 18, 1942. Its primary task was to plan and supervise the recruitment, training and distribution of workers in the face of a critical domestic labor shortage. Directed by Paul V. MCNUTT, formerly governor of Indiana and head of the Federal Security Agency, the commission was unable to enforce its decisions and often was at odds with organized labor, and it had but limited success. In 1945 it was incorporated into the Department of Labor.

WAR PRODUCTION BOARD. U.S. agency created by President ROOSEVELT by an executive order of January 16, 1942. The board was to replace the OFFICE OF PRODUCTION MANAGEMENT and the Supply Priorities and Allocations Board. The first chairman was Donald M. NELSON, a Sears, Roebuck executive. The board was responsible for coordinating the production and distribution of both raw materials and manufactured goods. Nelson found himself in frequent conflict with some of his associates and with Army and Navy procurement officers; much of this had to do with Nelson's determination to maintain civilian control of production and his unwillingness to strengthen large firms at the expense of smaller ones. In September 1944 he was sent by President Roosevelt on a mission to China, being replaced at the WPB by Julius A. Krug. Yet the board was relatively successful. It was absorbed by the Civilian Production Administration after the end of the war.

WARSAW UPRISINGS. The Polish capital was the stage for two remarkable episodes of resistance to the German occupiers.

The first, generally called the Warsaw Ghetto Uprising, took place in early 1943. As a means of control of the city's Jewish population, the ghetto had been created in 1940 by the Nazis, and all the Jews of Warsaw, numbering about 400,000, had been forcibly moved into it. By 1943, however, the number had dwindled to about 60,000; in the summer of 1942 more than 300,000 of the people had been deported to the TREBLINKA death camp. In January 1943 Heinrich HIMMLER, the Reichsführer SS (see SS), ordered that this "resettlement," as it was euphemistically termed, be completed by February 15. But the Jews of the ghetto, led by the Jewish Combat Organization (ZOB—Zydowska Organizacja Bojowa) and the Jewish Coordinating Committee (ZKK—Zydowski Komitet Koordynacyjny), had determined to resist; very few could question any longer the meaning of "resettlement." On January 18 fighting broke out between ZOB units and the Germans, and after three days the latter abandoned their efforts to seize Jews for transportation to the death camps. The respite was purely temporary, but owing to German logistical problems it was prolonged until April.

On April 19, 1943, the morning of Passover, some 2,000 SS and Army troops, several hundred of them men from Eastern European satellites, moved into the ghetto, which by then had shrunk to a size of little more than half a mile in length by 300 yards in width. These forces, armed with at least one tank, armored cars, flamethrowers and other equipment, were met by a hail of MOLOTOV COCKTAILS, and after a number of hours of fighting were forced to withdraw. After four more similarly unsuccessful days of this guerrilla struggle, during which increasing numbers of ghetto buildings erupted in flames, the German commander, SS Brigadeführer Jürgen STROOP, decided "to destroy the entire Jewish area by setting every block on fire." Thus he would systematically destroy the Jews' primary defensive device—the maze of buildings itself. There would be little the 1,500 ZOB fighters, who were armed with a collection of pistols, rifles and machine guns in addition to their Molotov cocktails, could do with the battlefield itself destroyed. The results were gruesome. Stroop wrote in his report: "Despite the danger of being burned alive, the Jews and bandits often preferred to return into the flames rather than risk being caught by us."

No one had ever had any doubt about the outcome of the ghetto uprising. It was a moral action—a refusal to continue to die passively—rather than a military action for strategic purposes. The ZOB had no line of retreat, nor was there anywhere to turn for outside help. The fighting nevertheless went on for exactly 28 days, but on May 16 Stroop reported that "the former Jewish quarter of Warsaw is no longer in existence." The final action was the blowing up of the Tlomacki synagogue. The Germans, according to Stroop's figures, had captured or killed 56,065 Jews during the battle. The fighting example set by the ZOB was not lost on Jews elsewhere; other uprisings took place in Vilna, Cracow, Lodz and other Polish cities.

In the summer of 1944 came the second great uprising in Warsaw. August 1 of that year saw the beginning of one of the most controversial episodes of the entire war, the rising of the Polish underground forces (the Home Army—Armia Krajova) and the failure of the Red Army to extend a helping hand across the Vistula while the Germans crushed the revolt. On October 2 the last remnants of the Home Army surrendered.

The Home Army drew its guidance from the Polish government-in-exile in London, which viewed the Russians with deep suspicion, not only because of past animosities but also because they had clamped Communist control on the occupied areas to the east of Warsaw and had established the LUBLIN COMMITTEE as a supposedly indigenous political force and, along with it, a new Polish Army. Of course, as the future was to make clear, the Kremlin had no use whatever for the anti-Communist London Poles. In spite of these ideological differences, however, the Home Army had cooperated with the Russians as they advanced into Poland, for example in the liberation of Lublin itself.

This being the background, the Home Army—commanded by General BOR-KOMOROVSKI—appears to have decided, as a Soviet force moved into the Warsaw suburb of Praga across the Vistula, that it should demonstrate its power by beating the Russians to the capture of the capital. The decision was not made in isolation, since at the end of July the Soviets, by leaflets and by calls over Radio Moscow, were urging the Poles to rise against the Germans. The Russians later complained that they had not been notified of the rebellion, but the explanation seems patently self-serving. In any case, on August 1 the Poles attacked the Germans, who did not have strong forces in Warsaw. The Home Army numbered in the 35,000–50,000 range, and the people spontaneously fought along with it. Within three days, unaided, it had gained control of a large part of the city. Then SS detachments of even greater than customary depravity moved in and, to the accompaniment of massive atrocities, broke up the Home Army into small, beleaguered units, bombarded the areas in which they took refuge and savagely pursued them even through the sewers of the city. Lacking supplies and ammunition, the Poles fought on through all of August and September.

Across the Vistula the Russians sat as interested spectators. Soviet commentators have subsequently maintained that the Second Tank Army had been stopped at Praga by German resistance and that their forces as a whole had outdistanced their supplies. But these explanations do not account for the continuing Soviet advances across the Vistula south of Warsaw or for the Soviet refusal to allow British or American supply planes to land in Soviet territory. The Russians publicly washed their hands of the whole affair, STALIN even declaring to the Western leaders that "sooner or later the truth about the group of criminals who have embarked on the Warsaw adventure in order to seize power will become known to everybody."

In September, when the outcome was no longer in doubt, the Russians made token efforts to aid, or appear to aid, the Warsaw fighters. Some supplies and ammunition were dropped, the ammunition being useless because it fit Red Army weapons, which the Poles did not have. In October the Germans deported most of the population of Warsaw and razed most of the remaining buildings. By January 1945, when the Red Army finally took the city, 85 percent of it had been destroyed and half its prewar population (about 1.3 million) was dead. The most obvious political result of the Warsaw uprising was that the only organized Polish force that could oppose the Soviet occupiers had been destroyed.

WAR SHIPPING ADMINISTRATION. Established by President ROOSEVELT by an executive order of February 7, 1942, this U.S. agency was responsible for the supervision of wartime shipping. It had control of all vessels owned by the U.S. Maritime Commission and could allocate vessels to the armed services and other agencies. Under the direction of Rear Adm. Emory S. LAND, the agency successfully established transportation priorities (in cooperation with the WAR PRODUCTION BOARD), dealt with labor problems, supervised construction of ships totaling some 55 million tons and coordinated the use of the ships, as well as recruited for the merchant marine. By the end of the war, the United States had the world's greatest merchant fleet.

WARSPITE, H.M.S. Royal Navy battleship of 30,600 tons, completed at Devonport in 1915 and modernized in 1935–37. Her armament comprised eight 15-inch, twelve 6-inch and eight 4-inch guns, smaller weapons and four aircraft. *Warspite*'s war record was without equal in the Royal Navy. After convoy escort service in the early months of the war, *Warspite*'s first spectacular achievement was entry into the narrow waters of the NARVIK fjords at the head of a force of destroyers; this force shattered nine German destroyers and a submarine. She was then moved to the Mediterranean to become Adm. Sir Andrew CUNNINGHAM's flagship in the action off Calabria in 1940—where she scored the hit on the Italian flagship that led to the Italian withdrawal from the battle—and at the Battle of CAPE MATAPAN in 1941.

Damaged by German bombing during the CRETE evacuation, *Warspite* was repaired in the United States and served in the Indian Ocean in 1942 and early 1943. Moved to the Mediterranean once more, she participated in the Sicilian and Italian landings, led the Italian battle fleet into MALTA at the end of their surrender voyage and then suffered severe damage from a glider bomb while supporting the SALERNO landings. After further repairs *Warspite* was moved to home waters for use in support of the Normandy INVASION, during which she struck a mine, and she was again used for the bombardment of German positions at Brest, Le Havre and the island of Walcheren.

The stories about *Warspite* are innumerable. Perhaps the best to record here is the signal made to her by Admiral Cunningham after the ship had hurried to the support of the British Army in some difficulty in the Sicilian fighting: "Operation well carried out. There is no doubt that when the old lady lifts her skirt she can run."

WARWICK. British aircraft built by Vickers as a successor to the WELLINGTON. It retained the rugged geodetic construction of the older plane but mounted two of the unreliable Rolls-Royce Vulture engines, which prevented it from living up to expectations. As a result, this near-double for the successful Wellington served as a transport and as an air–sea rescue plane, carrying a lifeboat. Not until Bristol Centaurus radials became available did the plane emerge as a satisfactory antisubmarine patrol craft, but by then the end of the war was at hand.

WASHING MACHINE CHARLIE. A nickname given to Japanese patrol planes with distinctive humming motors that flew out of RABAUL and harassed American marines and sailors at Henderson Field on GUADALCANAL by circling them throughout the night and occasionally dropping bombs.

WASHINGTON, U.S.S. Battleship and class (which also included the NORTH CAROLINA). *Washington* was completed in 1942. She had a standard displacement of 35,000 tons and measured 704 feet in length by 108 feet in beam. She carried a main battery of nine 16-inch guns and a secondary of twenty 5-inch guns, with more than 100 smaller guns. Her complement was 2,500, and she could make better than 27 knots. *Washington* and *North Carolina* were the first new battleships added to the U.S. fleet in 18 years. At the naval battle of GUADALCANAL in November 1942, *Washington* was the flagship of Rear Adm. Willis A. LEE; expertly handled, she played the key part in the battleship victory of November 14–15. Earlier she had been part of an Allied task force protecting convoys on the northern Russia run. For the balance of the war she was one of the battleships in Admiral Lee's battle line.

WASP, U.S.S. Aircraft carrier of 14,700 tons, completed in 1940. Her complement, including flying personnel, was 1,800; she could carry up to 84 aircraft. She was 688 feet long and was armed with eight 5-INCH 38-caliber guns and many smaller ones. In April and May 1942, prior to joining the U.S. fleet in the Pacific, she ferried two loads of RAF Spitfires (47 each time) from Glasgow to MALTA, earning from Winston CHURCHILL the observation: "Who said a wasp couldn't sting twice?" *Wasp* then sailed for the Pacific, where she covered the GUADALCANAL landings in August. Because of refueling, she missed the fighting in the Battle of the EASTERN SOLOMONS later in the month. In September she was assigned as part of a covering force for a Marine troop convoy from ESPIRITU SANTO to Guadalcanal, and on the afternoon of September 15 she was fatally damaged by two torpedoes from the Japanese submarine *I-19*. Torpedoes from an American destroyer finished her off.

A second *Wasp*, an ESSEX-class fleet carrier, was completed in November 1943 and saw extensive service with the FAST CARRIER TASK FORCE before being damaged by KAMIKAZE attack.

WATCH ON THE RHINE (Wacht am Rhein). Code name for the German counteroffensive in the ARDENNES region of Belgium and Luxembourg in December 1944. The operation was originally called Christrose but was changed by Adolf HITLER to further the deception that the Germans were preparing merely to counter an expected Allied drive to the Rhine.

WATCHTOWER. Code name for the American invasion of TULAGI and GUADALCANAL, August 1942.

WATERFALL. Code name for the German C-2 rocket (*see* C-2).

WATSON, Edwin M. (1883–1945). U.S. Army officer who served as an aide to President Wilson in 1915–17 and in the same capacity for President ROOSEVELT. Watson became Roosevelt's secretary in 1939 and was promoted the next year to major general. He died on shipboard as the Presidential party was returning from the YALTA CONFERENCE. A man of benign appearance and manner, he was known in the White House as "Pa." Mainly out of his influence with the President had come the appointment of George C. MARSHALL as Army Chief of Staff.

WATSON-WATT, Sir Robert (1892–1973). This name is inseparably linked with the development of RADAR. Watson-Watt did early work for the British National Physical Laboratory at the Radio Research Station at Slough. This provided the theoretical basis for the development of detection of aircraft by radio methods, which led to the building of the chain of radar stations along the British coastline in the late 1930s. His vital contribution to research for the Air Ministry is recounted in his book *Three Steps to Victory;* the steps were Instantaneous Visual Radio Direction Finder (*see* HF/DF), radar and operational research.

WAVELL, Archibald Percival Wavell, 1st Earl (1883–1950). Field Marshal Wavell once wrote that he entered the British Army as "the line of least resistance," for his soldier father wanted him to become a soldier and he had "no particular bent" toward another profession. In school at Winchester he displayed an intellectual ability that suggested he could have succeeded in any number of fields. He graduated from Sandhurst in 1901 and was commissioned into the Black Watch. A tour of duty in South Africa was followed by five happy years in India, during which he grew as both soldier and man. In 1909 he got into the Staff College at Camberley by competitive examination, but peacetime promotions were few. He spent a year in Russia learning the language, held various staff positions and in World War I saw action in France as a brigade leader. He lost his left eye from a wound and found the war on the Western Front "very dull, unimaginative, heavy-footed business." In all he held 11 wartime appointments and considered his experiences "interesting and successful."

By 1935 Major General Wavell had a reputation as an outstanding officer, conscientious, contemplative and able to command and teach. In that year he was given the 2d Division, where his emphasis in training was to get men to think for themselves. In September 1937 he went to Palestine, in 1938 he became GOCinC Southern Command in England and in July 1939 he was appointed Commander in Chief MIDDLE EAST—a command that covered part of two continents. Much of his effort there involved setting up a sound administrative base for the vast theater.

Wavell quickly assessed the priorities in the coming war as oil, shipping, air power and sea power; though he felt confident Britain would win, access to British oil in the Middle East would be a vital factor. The administrative duties of his huge command were great, he had few troops with which to operate and he soon found himself in conflict with Prime Minister Winston CHURCHILL over plans and priorities. Despite his numerical inferiority, Wavell ordered small-scale offensive action against the Italians on the Egyptian-Libyan frontier at once. He also set in motion the LONG RANGE DESERT GROUP, for he was constantly seeking untried ways to fight effectively. On December 5, 1940, Wavell authorized Gen. Sir Richard O'CONNOR to begin action in Libya. O'Connor's 36,000 well-trained men began the drive that culminated with the victory at BEDA FOMM in February 1941. Wavell found it necessary to juggle forces, however, in an effort to reclaim EAST AFRICA from Italian conquest.

The times were hard for Britain, and Churchill pushed Wavell unmercifully. With limited resources and with operational problems that London did not always grasp, Wavell repeatedly had to weaken one effort to launch another. After Beda Fomm, O'Connor's successful DESERT ARMY was disbanded and an expeditionary force was sent to Greece. Events then followed swiftly. The German General ROMMEL came to Africa and launched an attack on March 31; on April 10 TOBRUK came under siege; on April 29 the British evacuated Greece with heavy losses; on May 5 revolution broke out in IRAQ; on May 20 the Germans invaded CRETE; on June 8 the British invaded SYRIA to forestall an Axis takeover. The East African campaign was successfully concluded, but elsewhere in the theater the pressures were intense. Churchill demanded victories, and Wavell's accomplishments failed to satisfy him. When the intervention in Iraq was being planned, Churchill was impressed by Gen. Sir Claude AUCHINLECK's willingness to send troops from India. He considered replacing Wavell with Auchinleck at that time, but the change was not made until July, after the failure of the BATTLEAXE offensive.

Wavell took his relief calmly and without protest, even though he had in many respects been badly used. His request for leave was not granted, and after turning command over to Auchinleck he proceeded to India. Belatedly Churchill realized the pressures Wavell had operated under, and a minister of state and an intendant-general were appointed to assist Auchinleck in political and administrative responsibilities.

When Wavell moved to India, he soon found himself presiding over inevitable disaster. Japan opened hostilities on December 7, 1941. At the ARCADIA CONFERENCE the Allies established the ABDA COMMAND, with Wavell as its head. The British were at first reluctant to have a British officer given command of the doomed area, but Wavell did not protest. He established headquarters in JAVA, but could do little. When Gen. Joseph STILWELL met him in February 1942, he found him a "tired, depressed man pretty well beaten down." At the end of February, ABDA was disbanded. Wavell questioned whether his prestige and influence remained sufficient for him to return to command in India, but Churchill praised his "admirable conduct" against "overwhelming odds."

As C-in-C India, Wavell worked with the Americans and the Chinese in planning Allied moves. The Americans, anxious to bolster China, favored a reconquest of BURMA, which Wavell did not wholeheartedly support. He sanctioned the formation of Wingate's CHINDITS to fight in Burma, but he had doubts about the effectiveness of the Chinese divisions and he questioned how much the Indian troops were willing to fight for the empire. The Americans complained of his defeatism, and Churchill decided, once again, to replace him with Auchinleck.

Wavell, who had been made a field marshal in January 1943, now became one of India's last viceroys. His first problem was relief for the Bengal famine, after which he became deeply involved in the delicate and volatile political situation as India moved toward self-government. He worked patiently, but he was often handicapped by having no clear statement of policy from London. The statement did not come until February 1947, when Wavell was replaced by Lord MOUNTBATTEN.

Wavell's career seems a succession of commands in crisis, from each of which he was removed once the crisis reached its peak. A lesser man might have complained, or sought to explain to the world. Wavell did neither. He spent his last years in retirement, traveling and writing. His memoirs were written only for his family and are not published, but his other books demonstrate the depth and variety of his ideas. **M.H.B.**

WAVES. Acronym for an organization of U.S. service women—Women Accepted for Volunteer Emergency Service—established on July 30, 1942, to provide for entry of women into the U.S. Naval Reserve. In 1944 the term WAVES was dropped and the women were simply called Women Reserves. During the war the Women Reserves performed shore duty in the United States, primarily in administrative positions. The peak strength during wartime was achieved in July 1945—approximately 90,000 women. In 1948 Congress provided for the continuance of women in the Navy by authorizing their integration into the Regular Navy. The director of the WAVES during the war was Capt. Mildred MCAFEE.

WEDEMEYER, Albert Coady (1897–). Educated at West Point, Wedemeyer spent most of his pre–World War II service as an infantry officer. During the early war years he served on the War Department staff, where he came to be regarded as an expert in war plans.

In September 1943 Wedemeyer was transferred to the SOUTHEAST ASIA COMMAND (SEAC), as deputy chief of staff under Adm. Lord Louis MOUNTBATTEN. For a year he was intimately acquainted with some of the more difficult of SEAC's many problems. For example, he was involved in Mountbatten's planning for the TARZAN offensive in BURMA, advocated the opening of a land or sea route to China as the fastest way to begin intensive air operations and served as one of several spokesmen for Mountbatten in Washington and London for SEAC's CULVERIN, a plan for assaulting Sumatra.

Duties with SEAC served him well for his next assignment. On October 18, 1944, as a major general, Wedemeyer was appointed Commander, U.S. Forces in the China Theater (CT), concurrently with President ROOSEVELT's recall of Lt. Gen. Joseph W. STILWELL and the split of the CHINA-BURMA-INDIA THEATER (CBI) into the CT and the India-Burma Theater (IBT). Additionally, he was made available to CHIANG KAI-SHEK as his chief of staff. Wedemeyer's missions were to advise and assist the Chinese in their conduct of military operations and, regarding U.S. forces, to carry out air operations from China. Wedemeyer established a pleasant working relationship with Chiang Kai-shek; his disarming personality helped make his advice palatable to the Chinese during a difficult time.

During his tenure in China, Wedemeyer brought about a number of improvements in the Chinese Army. Under his guidance the CT, among other things, prepared a superbly organized defense of KUNMING against feared Japanese intentions; reorganized itself to better accomplish the "advice and assistance" mission; made substantial progress in improving the lot of the Chinese soldier; planned and began the execution of a large-scale effort to open mainland China seaports (Operation Beta, ultimately Carborando); and by the end of the war had some 39 Chinese divisions undergoing training. That Wedemeyer's methods were effective was demonstrated in the Chinese Army's thwarting of the Japanese China Expeditionary Army's Chihchiang campaign, April 8–June 7, 1945. Chinese forces—not under General Wedemeyer's direct command—were advancing on Fort Bayard as a prelude to Carborando when the war ended.

Wedemeyer, aware of the difficulties China would face with the imposition of a "sudden peace," served in China until September 1946, when he returned to the United States to become commanding general of the Second Army.

WEHRMACHT. The German armed forces (literally, defense force). The term was sometimes used as though synonymous with "German Army," but it referred to the Navy and the Luftwaffe as well. *See also* OKW.

WEICHS, Maximilian, Baron von (1882–1954). German officer who joined the Army in 1900 and served on the General Staff in World War I. During the interwar period he commanded several cavalry divisions before receiving a promotion to lieutenant general in 1936. In October 1939 he commanded the Second Army on the Western Front. In July 1941 the Second Army was established in Belorussia and participated in the great drive into Russia. In June 1942 Weichs was given command of Group von Weichs, part of Army Group B under Field Marshal von BOCK, in the south; the next month he succeeded Bock as commander of Army Group B, which received STALINGRAD as its objective (General PAULUS's SIXTH ARMY was a component of Army Group B). However, most of Weichs's command, including the Sixth Army, was on Adolf HITLER's orders handed over to General von MANSTEIN in November.

Promoted to the rank of field marshal in February 1943, Weichs served as the supreme commander of German troops in southeast Europe from August 1943. When the Russians threatened eastern Germany in late 1944, Weichs was proposed as the commander of an army group to be called "Army Group Weichsel" to defend against the Soviets. Hitler subsequently rejected this plan. At the conclusion of the war U.S. forces arrested Weichs, but he was not put on trial at Nuremberg. He was released from prison in 1948.

WEIDLING, Helmuth (1897–1955). German Army officer, commander of the LVI Panzer Corps and last commander at BERLIN. It was he who ordered the surrender to the Soviet forces. General Weidling was taken prisoner and died in the USSR.

WEIZSÄCKER, Ernst, Baron von (1882–1951). Von Weizsäcker was among the career professionals in the German Foreign Office who entertained the mistaken belief that they could channel Adolf HITLER's foreign policy into traditional and acceptable directions without abandoning the basic policy of revision of the Treaty of Versailles. He became State Secretary, the senior executive officer, in the Foreign Office when the Nazis brought that agency under tighter party control by replacing Foreign Minister Baron Konstantin von NEURATH with Joachim von RIBBENTROP in February 1938. His distaste for Hitler's dilettantism and for Ribbentrop's complete lack of depth in international affairs led Weizsäcker to some involvement with the military and foreign-service opposition to the Nazi regime. He facilitated the earnest, clandestine and fruitless contacts between German resistance groups and figures within and outside the British Government during the Czech crisis in 1938.

After serving as ambassador to the Vatican from 1943 to the end of the war, Weizsäcker was tried by the Nuremberg tribunal for the Nazi Party membership that had become a precondition to official employment in Germany and for his honorary rank in the SS as much as for his presumed part in planning an aggressive and immoral foreign policy. His seven-year sentence was commuted in 1951.

WELKIN. Designed under the supervision of W. E. W. Petter, this airplane was Westland's response to a 1940 British Air Ministry requirement for a fighter capable of intercepting German bombers above 40,000 feet. The Welkin's 70-foot wing had an unusually high aspect ratio, and the plane featured de-icing gear, a pressurized cabin and two supercharged 1,250-horsepower Rolls-Royce Merlin liquid-cooled engines. Because the high-altitude threat failed to materialize, none of the 67 planes ever joined an operational unit. One plane, dubbed Welkin II, was modified to accept an airborne RADAR and its operator.

WELLES, Sumner (1892–1961). Welles, a native of New York, began his diplomatic career immediately after his graduation from Harvard. In 1937 he was appointed Under Secretary of State. During the PHONY WAR period in early 1940 he was sent to Europe by President ROOSEVELT to explore the possibility of a mediated settlement of the war. In 1941 he accompanied Roosevelt to his meeting at sea with Prime Minister CHURCHILL. In January 1942 he represented the United States at the RIO CONFERENCE of foreign ministers of the American republics, at which recommendations were adopted asking all states in Latin America to discontinue diplomatic, commercial and financial relations with the Axis powers.

Welles was an important and influential figure in that Roosevelt often chose to work with him rather than with Secretary of State Cordell HULL. He headed the U.S. body that carried out preparatory planning for the UNITED NATIONS ORGANIZATION. But in the summer of 1943 differences between the prestigious Hull and

Welles led to the Under Secretary's resignation. He was succeeded by Edward R. STETTINIUS, Jr.

WELLESLEY. British single-engine, two-place light bomber, which pioneered the use of geodetic construction, a technique devised by the British scientist Barnes WALLIS. The plane had a metal basket-weave skeleton covered with fabric, Wallis's answer to the problem of combining strength and lightness. A wing with an extremely high aspect ratio resulted in a service ceiling of 33,000 feet and a range of 1,100 miles. The crew had individual enclosed cockpits in the early Wellesleys, but later models had one elongated canopy for both men. A 925-horsepower Bristol Pegasus radial gave the plane a top speed of 228 miles per hour. Armament was a pair of machine guns, one firing forward and one aft. First flown in 1935, this Vickers product participated in the East African campaign but was retired from combat in 1941.

WELLINGTON. British twin-engine, midwing monoplane, which featured the basket-weave geodetic construction that Vickers Aircraft had first used in its WELLESLEY. Despite its fabric covering, the Wellington's latticework structure provided exceptional strength and enabled the plane to survive extensive flak damage. The Wellington IC, of which Vickers built more than 2,600, had powered turrets in the nose and tail, plus two manually operated beam guns, for a total of eight .303-caliber machine guns. Fitted with two 1,000-horsepower Bristol Pegasus radials, the plane had a top speed of 235 miles per hour, a bomb capacity totaling up to 6,000 pounds and a range of 2,550 miles with 1,000 pounds of bombs.

Prewar British plans called for employing the Wellington as a day bomber without fighter escort, but in December 1939 German fighters attacked a formation of some two dozen Wellington IAs, which had no beam guns, shot down 10 of the bombers and severely damaged three others. As a result, RAF BOMBER COMMAND shifted the plane to night operations. Later models, especially the more powerful Wellington III and Wellington X, remained first-line bombers throughout the war.

The plane also served with COASTAL COMMAND. One version mounted a hooplike device for detonating magnetic mines in shallow waters. Another carried a special searchlight, and one of these succeeded in locating a German submarine at night and destroying it. Still other Wellingtons were minelayers and torpedo planes, crew trainers, photo planes and transports.

Wellington

WELSH, Sir William (1891–1962). The RAF officer commanding Eastern Air Command in 1942, responsible for air support to Allied forces in the North African fighting in Algeria and TUNISIA. Air Marshal Welsh was head of the RAF delegation in Washington in 1943–44 before he retired from the RAF. *See also* NORTHWEST AFRICA.

WENCK, Walter (1901–). German Army tank officer who participated in the invasion of France in 1940. After serving on the Western Front, he was transferred to the Eastern Front as chief of staff of Army Group A, and in July 1944 he succeeded Gen. Adolf HEUSINGER as operations officer at the high command (*see* OKH). In the closing months of the war he took command of the Twelfth Army, which had the forlorn task of relieving BERLIN from Soviet encirclement in April 1945. When the job proved impossible, Wenck directed German soldiers and civilians across the Elbe River and thus into U.S. rather than Russian hands. His highest rank was General der Panzertruppen.

WERBOMONT. Belgian town on the Liège–Bastogne highway in the ARDENNES region that served as the focal point for the assembly of reserves to blunt the spearhead of the Sixth Panzer Army (Task Force PEIPER), which broke through American lines early in the Battle of the BULGE.

WEREWOLF (Werwolf). Adolf HITLER's field headquarters near Vinnitsa, in the Ukraine.

WEREWOLVES. A short-lived paramilitary guerrilla organization of fanatical young Germans formed by Heinrich HIMMLER (November 1944) to resist advancing Allied troops. The Werewolves were relatively ineffective, carrying out only one successful mission—the assassination of the chief burgomaster of Aachen in March 1945.

WESEL. Rail and road center north of the Ruhr at the confluence of the Rhine and Lippe Rivers. It was across the Wesel railroad and highway bridges that the last German units facing the 21ST ARMY GROUP west of the Rhine were withdrawn on March 9, 1945; the bridges were then blown. Wesel, situated on the east bank, was an important objective of the 21st Army Group's Rhine River crossing. It was assaulted on March 23 by the British 1st COMMANDO Brigade (SECOND ARMY), and its reduction by British and U.S. troops was completed on the 25th. Bridges were constructed at Wesel as soon as possible, and the city became an important Allied communications center.

WESER EXERCISE (Weserübung). Code name for the German occupation of Denmark and NORWAY. The operation commenced on April 9, 1940. The advantages were succinctly stated by Adolf HITLER in his directive: it "would anticipate English action against Scandinavia and the Baltic, would secure our supplies of ore from Sweden, and would provide the Navy and Air Force with expanded bases for operations against England." The Führer also observed, prophetically, that "weakness in numbers will be made good by skillful action and surprise in execution." Weserübung was divided into Weser Exercise South (Denmark) and Weser Exercise North (Norway).

WESTERN APPROACHES. The British naval command area from which the Allied war against U-boats in the Atlantic was commanded and administered. Originally the area comprised the waters south of Ireland, the southern half of the Irish Sea and the western Channel, with headquarters at Plymouth, but in February 1941 the headquarters was moved to Liverpool and the command area enlarged to absorb the western area of the Rosyth Command. The first commander in chief was Adm. Sir Martin DUNBAR-NASMITH, who was relieved on February 16, 1941, by Adm. Sir Percy NOBLE. Adm. Sir Max HORTON was appointed commander in chief on November 19, 1942, and remained in the post until the end of the war. *See also* ATLANTIC, BATTLE OF THE.

WESTERN DESERT. A fringe of the African Sahara, the Western Desert stretches across Egypt and extends into Libya to GAZALA. Bounded on the south by the oases of Jarabub and Siwa and the edges of the QATTARA DEPRESSION, the Western Desert measures roughly 240 by 150 miles. From December 1940 to December 1942 it was the battlefield for British and Axis forces, with control of the Suez Canal and the eastern Mediterranean at stake.

The Western Desert has two levels. A coastal strip of varying width edges the desert plateau 500 feet higher. The escarpment from plain to plateau is steep, and places where it could be negotiated by vehicles became strategic points, as did the harbors—SOLLUM and TOBRUK.

As a battleground, the desert—like the sea—offered free movement to forces. There was no civilian population to protect; only a few villages were scattered along the coast. Roads were few, but the desert's sandy surface, underlaid by hard limestone, could support vehicles and landing strips. Disadvantages, however, were numerous. The desert provided nothing for the support of an army. Water as well as all other supplies had to be provided from outside the battle area, thus limiting an army's performance to its supply capability.

Although essentially a healthful climate despite its discomforts, the desert placed the fighting men under bodily and mental strain. Heat, thirst, dust and clouds of flies were almost constant, and it was necessary to fight the desert as well as the enemy. The absence of landmarks, plus a haze caused by heat and dust, made it easy to lose perspective and necessitated navigating by compass and acquiring a "desert sense." Hot winds and dust storms are frequent, and vehicles had to be specially adapted to withstand the heat and dust.

The geography of the desert favored the mobile offense. There were no natural defensive positions, and the rocky undersurface made it difficult even to dig a foxhole. The crucial element, however, was supplies, and the area was popularly termed the "tactician's paradise, quartermaster's hell."

WESTERN FRONT—INVASION TO V-E DAY. Having landed approximately 150,000 American, British and Canadian troops in the Normandy INVASION on D-Day—June 6, 1944—the Allies, under the supreme command of Gen. Dwight D. EISENHOWER, faced an immediate task of putting enough additional men, tanks, artillery and supplies ashore to link the five beachheads and push far enough inland to be able to withstand the expected German counterattack. The best hope was that measures taken before the invasion would continue to delay movement of major German reserves. Allied planes, having virtually driven the LUFTWAFFE from the skies, could be counted upon to harass any German movement. An aerial campaign to cripple French railroads and demolish bridges and continuing sabotage by the FRENCH RESISTANCE would also help. Most important of all was maintaining an elaborate deception to mislead the Germans into believing the Normandy landings were but a preliminary to a forthcoming larger invasion farther north in the Pas de Calais. Through intelligence known as ULTRA, achieved by the British having broken the German military radio enciphering code, the Allies were able to monitor German traffic and reinforce the deception as needed.

In the event, all those measures helped delay a major German blow against the invasion beaches. Having reached the conclusion before the invasion through intuition that Normandy was to be the site of the main landings, Adolf HITLER now completely reversed himself, convinced that a larger second invasion was still to come. Refusing pleas of the Commander in Chief in the West, Field Marshal Gerd von RUNDSTEDT, and his

GI covers a surrendering German as the First Army moves out from the Remagen bridgehead

U.S. vehicles move through the ruins of Saint-Lô

principal subordinate, the commander of Army Group B, Field Marshal Erwin ROMMEL, to bring major reserves from the Pas de Calais for a decisive counterattack, he afforded them only seven PANZER divisions. That would nevertheless have been a formidable force had all been available at once, but one division had to come from southwestern France and was destined to be delayed 12 days by harassment from the French Resistance; three were already on hand, but to meet Allied advances had to be committed piecemeal to defensive roles; and two had to come from the Eastern Front and one from the Netherlands, which exposed them to incessant attack from Allied planes.

All Allied advances were nevertheless difficult, both because the German Seventh Army that had met the invasion was a powerful force and because of readily defensible terrain. Behind UTAH BEACH the U.S. FIRST ARMY under Lt. Gen. Omar N. BRADLEY faced vast stretches of flooded marshlands, and elsewhere there were HEDGEROWS, thick walls of earth reinforced by shrubs and trees, surrounding most fields.

While the British SECOND ARMY under Lt. Gen. Sir Miles C. DEMPSEY (composed at the time of British and Canadians) drove toward the city of CAEN, whence more open terrain beckoned in the direction of Paris, the Americans moved to cut the COTENTIN PENINSULA to ensure subsequent capture of the port of CHERBOURG and to gain the major road center of SAINT-LÔ, whence an attempt at breakout from the hedgerows might be launched. With most of the German armor deployed against the British and Canadians, Caen remained out of reach, but on June 18 the Americans cut the Cotentin Peninsula, although Saint-Lô, like Caen, remained in German hands.

Hitler meanwhile, on June 16, came to France to upbraid his field commanders, insisting that they do the job with the resources he had provided. They drew an assist for four days from June 19 through June 22 when a violent storm raged in the English Channel, halting all unloading of reinforcements and supplies. A churning sea wrecked scores of landing craft and smashed the two artificial harbors (*see* MULBERRY) that were helping the Allies to put reinforcements and equipment ashore. The American Mulberry was demolished beyond repair, and the British Mulberry was out of use for several days.

Yet that setback failed to provide the help the Germans needed. Cherboug fell on June 26, which within a few weeks would ease the job of putting Allied supplies ashore, and when the Germans at last counterattacked on June 29 against the British, it was far from a decisive blow. Only the two panzer divisions that finally had arrived from Russia could be employed, and their power was largely spent by the end of the first day.

By July 1 the Allies had matched the German buildup in Normandy and soon would exceed it. Almost a million men had arrived, along with 500,000 tons of supply and 177,000 vehicles. British and Canadians in the British Second Army totaled 4 corps, 3 armored and 10 infantry divisions, while the U.S. First Army had 4 corps, 2 armored and 11 infantry divisions. The beachhead was some 70 miles wide, yet in few places no deeper than 20 miles and in some less than 5.

The German commanders believed that if Hitler continued to deny additional forces from the Pas de Calais and persisted in a policy of no withdrawals the battle in France soon would be lost. When they so told Hitler, he relieved Rundstedt, replacing him with Field Marshal Günther von KLUGE. Rommel avoided such ignominy when on July 17 he was seriously wounded in a strafing by a British fighter plane. Kluge assumed command of Army Group B as well as serving as Commander in Chief.

Yet for all the German difficulties, the Allied advance was slow and costly. Particularly disappointing was the failure of the British to capture Caen and break into more open country; blame was heaped on the 21ST ARMY GROUP commander, Gen. Sir Bernard L. MONTGOMERY, who was also the overall ground commander. On the night of July 7 Montgomery attempted to still his critics by launching a main attack behind a heavy bombardment by 500 big bombers. The effort gained only that part of Caen lying west of the Orne River. At that time CHURCHILL visited Eisenhower and implied he was at liberty to relieve Montgomery.

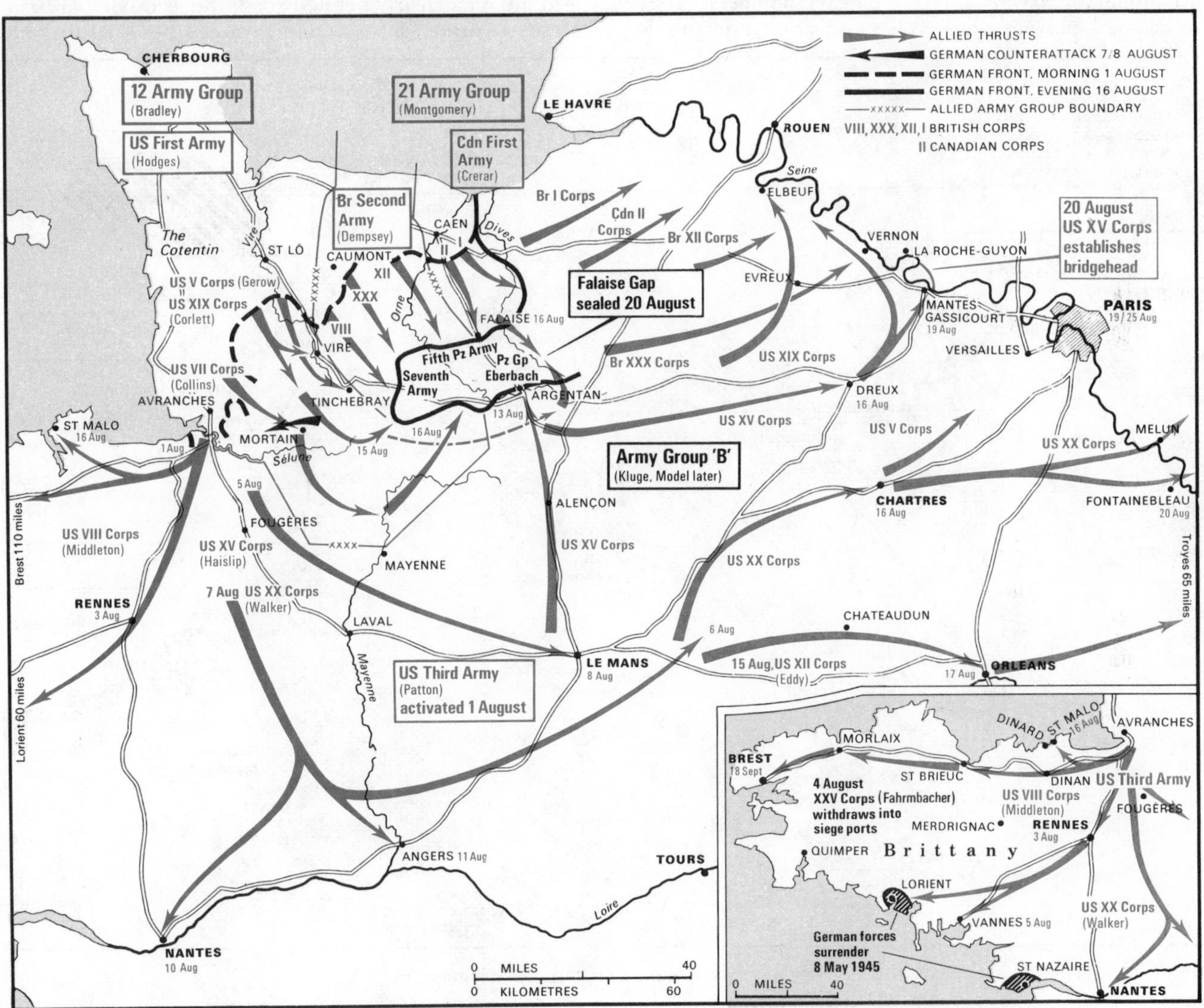

BREAKOUT: In August, Allied invasion forces poured out of the lodgment area and began sweeping across France

Ten days later, on July 18, even as men of the U.S. First Army at last captured Saint-Lô, Montgomery launched a similar attack, code-named Goodwood. A total of 2,100 planes dropped more than 8,000 tons of bombs in a preliminary bombardment, but again the advance was disappointingly short, carrying only six miles before bogging down. Shocked disappointment reverberated through the Allied command, but Montgomery insisted that the attack had accomplished what he expected of it. He was tying down the German panzer divisions near Caen, he explained, which would soon enable the U.S. First Army to launch a decisive attack to break out of the hedgerows near Saint-Lô.

Before that attack could take place, a cabal of officers in the German General Staff, convinced that Hitler was leading the nation to ruin, tried to assassinate the Führer, one of them exploding a bomb at his staff conference on July 20. Hitler survived and launched a terrible blood purge against the conspirators. Among those he thought implicated was Field Marshal Rommel. Recuperating from his wounds at his home, Rommel was forced to commit suicide. The attempted assassination convinced Hitler that virtually none of his generals were trustworthy and prompted him to take stronger control of operations (see OPPOSITION TO HITLER).

General Bradley gave the plan to break out of the hedgerows the code name Operation COBRA. Concentrating six divisions just west of Saint-Lô, he planned a preliminary strike by a mass of heavy bombers. After successive postponements because of unfavorable weather, the attack at last was set for July 24. Even then the weather was marginal, and at the last minute the attack had to be called off. Word of the postponement failed to reach the crews of some of the planes. When the bombardier in one plane inadvertently dropped his bombs short, bombardiers in 15 accompanying planes followed his lead. In the resulting holocaust on the ground, 131 American infantrymen were wounded and 27 killed.

Despite that tragedy, General Bradley decided to proceed with the attack the next day, July 25. That time 2,500 planes dropped more than 4,000 tons of bombs. Aiming on a clearly defined road, the lead bombardiers were accurate, but in later waves the bombardiers

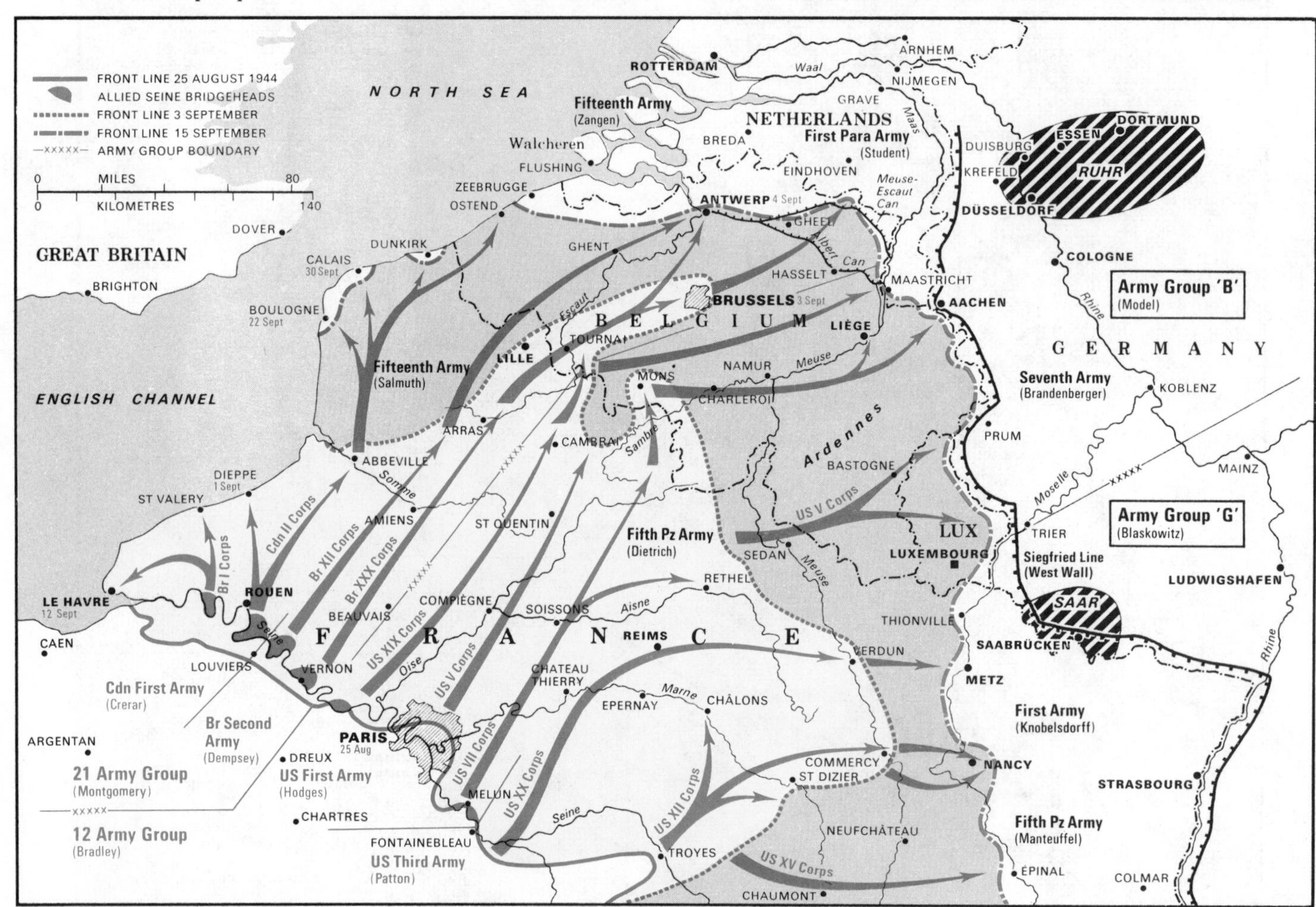

THE ALLIED ADVANCE: In September the Allies moved swiftly into Belgium and Luxembourg

found the road obscured by clouds of smoke and dust. They dropped their loads on the cloud line, unaware that it was drifting back over American infantrymen waiting to launch the ground attack. In the second holocaust in two days, 490 American soldiers were wounded and 111 killed. The bulk of the bombs had nevertheless rained devastation on German positions. That was insufficient to get the American attack moving swiftly on the first day, but commitment of two more divisions on the second day and a third on the next opened a tremendous breach in the German lines. The Americans poured through.

Bradley then ordered all four of his corps into action. American armored divisions were soon racing pell-mell through the countryside, the long weeks of plodding infantry fighting in the hedgerows at last at an end. Flying cover for the armor, fighter-bombers pounced on anything German that moved. Although Field Marshal von Kluge sent two panzer divisions to strike the flank of the penetrating forces, American planes so harried their movement that the riposte was ineffectual.

On July 31 the Americans seized the town of AVRANCHES at the base of the Cotentin Peninsula, which served as a gateway into the Brittany peninsula with its major ports. The next day Lt. Gen. George S. PATTON, Jr., took command of the corps that was turning into Brittany, plus another newly arrived corps, and a new American force entered the campaign: the THIRD

ARMY. At the same time Bradley turned over command of the First Army to Lt. Gen. Courtney H. HODGES, while he himself assumed command of the controlling headquarters, the 12TH ARMY GROUP. Montgomery's 21st Army Group had in the meantime, on July 23, been fleshed out with the arrival of the Canadian FIRST ARMY under Lt. Gen. Henry R. D. G. CRERAR. Thus four Allied armies were poised to exploit the penetration that the U.S. First Army had achieved.

Turning into Brittany, one of Patton's corps raced up the peninsula through countryside already largely cleared of Germans by the French Resistance. Taking the ports was another matter. There the Germans holed up and fought with grim determination. It took two weeks to reduce SAINT-MALO, and by the time the great port of BREST fell on September 18 the fighting had moved so far to the east that the planned development of Brittany as a major logistical base was no longer practical. While the entire Third Army joined the drive to the east, a new headquarters, the U.S. NINTH ARMY under Lt. Gen. William H. SIMPSON, took charge of the final fighting in Brittany.

Patton's other corps and the bulk of Hodges's First Army had in the meantime continued beyond Avranches to the southeast, the first step in a projected swinging movement to the Seine River and establishment of what was known as a "lodgment area." Before continuing the drive into Germany, the Allies intended to establish a vast lodgment area between the Seine and Loire Rivers in order to build a supply base for supporting the final drive. Yet despite the depth of the American penetration, it was less than 20 miles wide in the vicinity of Avranches, affording the Germans a tantalizing target for driving through to the sea and cutting off the American columns that had gone beyond Avranches. On Hitler's order, Kluge was to attack with eight of the nine panzer divisions then in Normandy. For the first time Hitler lifted restrictions on employing those divisions marking time in the Pas de Calais in anticipation of a second invasion.

The attack began around midnight on August 6. Forewarned by Ultra intelligence, General Bradley was already moving divisions to meet the thrust, and he was so confident they could defeat it that he made no move to call back any of the divisions that already had passed beyond Avranches. Although the Germans achieved early gains of from three to seven miles around the town of MORTAIN—hence the "Mortain counterattack"—it was apparent by the end of the first day that the effort was doomed. Kluge's concerns were increased the next day, August 8, when behind another heavy aerial bombardment, the Canadian First Army attacked southeastward toward the town of Falaise. An early three-mile gain by the Canadians posed the possibility of an enveloping maneuver. Instead of the Americans swinging in a broad arc to the Seine, General Bradley suggested to Montgomery, why not a shorter envelopment to link with the Canadians near Falaise and the nearby town of ARGENTAN, thereby trapping the eight German panzer divisions and all other Germans still defending in that part of Normandy?

When Montgomery agreed, Bradley sent two corps of the First Army and one of the Third racing toward Argentan. By August 13 Patton's corps was in sight of Argentan, but the Canadians meanwhile were having no such success. Because the American troops had reached the boundary separating the American and Canadian zones of operation and because Bradley feared a collision with a new Canadian attack to be launched with heavy aerial preparation the next day, he ordered the corps to halt in place. Two days later, on August 16, the Canadians reached Falaise, although a 25-mile gap between Argentan and Falaise remained.

As the German situation became more desperate, Hitler insisted that Kluge launch a new attack against the extended American corps near Argentan. In an effort to comply, Kluge on August 15 was visiting subordinate headquarters inside what was fast becoming a pocket when Allied planes forced him to take cover in a ditch. For 12 hours he was out of touch with his headquarters. When he finally returned, he received orders not only to attack but to stay out of the developing pocket. Hitler believed Kluge had spent those 12 hours in the pocket trying to contact Allied commanders in order to capitulate on the Western Front. Although the charge was never proved, Kluge had been somewhat involved in the OPPOSITION TO HITLER, and he was reluctant to order withdrawal from the pocket lest Hitler consider that evidence of his connivance in the conspiracy. Unknown to Kluge at the time, his days in command were numbered in any case, for Hitler had ordered Field Marshal Walther MODEL to France to take

Shouting "Americano! Americano!" a Russian soldier hugs a GI as troops of the two armies meet in Germany

DENMARK
BALTIC SEA
NORTH SEA
NETHERLANDS
BELGIUM
LUX
FRANCE
SWITZERLAND
GERMANY
CZECHOSLOVAKIA
AUSTRIA
ITALY
YUGOSLAVIA
Army Group 'H' (Blaskowitz)
Army Group 'B' (Model)
Army Group 'G' (Hausser)
21 Army Group (Montgomery)
12 Army Group (Bradley)
6 Army Group (Devers)
US Ninth Army
US First Army
US Third Army
US Seventh Army
Fr First Army
US Fifth Army
7 May
18 Apr
4 Apr
4 May
7May
OCCUPIED BY ALLIED FORCES, 28 MARCH 1945
BRITISH ATTACKS
US ATTACKS
FRENCH ATTACKS
GERMAN POCKETS
OCCUPIED BY RUSSIAN FORCES, 16 APRIL
CONCENTRATION CAMPS
MILES 0 120
KILOMETRES 0 200

his place. For all Kluge's reluctance to sanction withdrawal, when he learned around noon on August 16 that the Allies had staged an invasion of SOUTHERN FRANCE, he penned a message to Hitler saying that all was lost. He was, he said, withdrawing from what became known as the Argentan-Falaise pocket.

Field Marshal Montgomery, in the meantime, issued no orders to General Bradley to close the gap between Argentan and Falaise, deeming the Germans at that point too strong. Despairing of closing the gap, he ordered a second envelopment some 10 miles to the east. There the pincers were finally closed, but not before some 35,000 Germans escaped. The Argentan-Falaise pocket was nevertheless a scene of carnage, the graveyard for much of the German Seventh Army and the panzer divisions. Approximately 10,000 Germans were killed and 50,000 captured, and even those that escaped left behind most of their equipment, including 500 tanks and assault guns.

With Field Marshal Model's arrival in France to preside over the debacle, Field Marshal von Kluge left for Germany. On the way he committed suicide.

While waiting near Argentan for word to close the Argentan-Falaise gap, General Patton proposed to General Bradley that he turn part of his advance corps from Argentan to go on to the Seine River. Movement got under way on August 14, and five days later one division established a bridgehead over the river. A corps of the First Army soon came abreast.

The decision General Eisenhower faced at that point was whether to conform to the original plan of building a lodgment area between the Seine and the Loire before proceeding into Germany or to continue the pursuit. Because pursuit of a defeated enemy is axiomatic, he scarcely paused in making the decision to proceed. Troops of the Canadian First Army closest to the coast, then in order the British Second Army and the U.S. First and Third Armies were soon streaming to and across the Seine.

In the process the question of liberating PARIS came to the fore. In the hope of avoiding damage to the city and as long as possible avoiding the onus of having to feed the inhabitants, General Eisenhower had intended to bypass Paris. Hitler for his part ordered the capital turned into a fortress to be fought over until it was "a field of ruins." A spontaneous uprising by the French Resistance inside Paris on August 19 changed all plans. Lacking means to put down the uprising, the local German commander concluded a truce with Resistance leaders, while reports of grave food shortages and erroneous reports that the Germans were about to destroy the city prompted Eisenhower to change his mind. When he directed General Bradley to take the city, Bradley sent a Franco-American force. A French armored division was first into the city with a small contingent around midnight of August 24, but the liberation awaited the next day, when an American infantry division and more of the French armor arrived to a tumultuous welcome from the people.

Ten days earlier, on August 15, the Allies staged a second invasion in the south of France between Cannes and Toulon, the oft-postponed, on-again-off-again Operation ANVIL, known in the end as Operation Dragoon, designed to open additional ports and create a second line of communications. Behind heavy air and naval bombardment, three American divisions and an attached French armored combat command began landing early in the morning on either side of Saint-Tropez. An airborne task force of division size composed of American and British paratroopers landed behind the invasion beaches to cut roads and isolate the beach defenders. The overall commander was Lt. Gen. Alexander M. PATCH, commander of the U.S. SEVENTH ARMY.

The German force responsible for defending southern France, Army Group G under Generaloberst Johannes von BLASKOWITZ, had only 11 divisions for the task. Stretched thin, the Germans could muster only spotty resistance. In contrast to the vacillation Hitler had displayed in Normandy, he ordered Blaskowitz two days later to leave forces to hold the major ports and pull back into the Vosges Mountains of northeastern France.

On the first day of the invasion the Allies put ashore 86,000 men. In only a few days American divisions were fanning out from the beaches and heading north up the Route Napoléon toward Grenoble. Under Gen. Jean de LATTRE DE TASSIGNY, a follow-up French force swung against the ports of Toulon and MARSEILLES, where stubborn resistance ended on August 28. On the same day American troops seized MONTÉLIMAR, 75 miles up the Rhône River, but were too late to trap German columns withdrawing from southwestern France. In two weeks the Allies opened two major ports and took 57,000 prisoners at a cost of only 4,000 French and 2,700 American casualties. On September 11 patrols from the south met patrols of Eisenhower's northern force near Dijon. Four days later the troops in the south, organized as the 6th Army Group under Lt. Gen. Jacob L. DEVERS and composed of the U.S. Seventh and French First Armies, came under General Eisenhower's command.

For the drive into Germany, Eisenhower (who on September 1 had assumed direct command of the troops in France) had planned to advance on a broad front, the main effort to be in the north through Belgium, with Montgomery's 21st Army Group advancing north of the semimountainous ARDENNES region of Belgium and Luxembourg. That was the most direct route to the Ruhr industrial area, Germany's main source of industrial might. Bradley's 12th Army Group was to advance south of the Ardennes through a lesser industrial area, the Saar. Yet as the extent of the German defeat became apparent, Eisenhower yielded to persistent demands from Montgomery to strengthen the forces in the north. Leaving Patton's Third Army to advance south of the Ardennes, with support on the right from Devers's 6th Army Group, he sent Hodges's First Army northward alongside the British. That would at least help ensure early capture of the Channel ports, including the great port of ANTWERP, which was essential for any advance deep into Germany.

As General Crerar's Canadian First Army invested the minor Channel ports, the British on September 3 took Brussels and the next day seized Antwerp, its wharves and docks intact. Intent on driving on rapidly into Germany, Montgomery failed to send a force to clear the Germans from the banks of the SCHELDT ESTUARY, leading 60 miles to the sea. Without seaward access, Antwerp was useless as a port.

THE END IN EUROPE—the Allied advance into Germany

As patrols of the First Army crossed the German frontier on September 11, an early end to the war appeared likely. The ragged columns falling back into Germany seemed thoroughly beaten, and on the Eastern Front Soviet armies had begun to press into Poland. Day and night British and American heavy bombers continued to hammer German factories, railroads and cities. That the depleted German forces on the Western Front could hold at the German frontier seemed incredible, and even most of the German commanders saw the only hope to be quick withdrawal behind the historic moat of the Rhine River.

Hitler saw it differently. He still had more than 10 million men under arms, and German factories were still maintaining a high rate of production; indeed, they had yet to reach their wartime peak. He ordered the hurried formation of panzer brigades, to be rushed to the front until the shattered panzer divisions could be refitted. Although he could not hope to produce enough planes to redress the tremendous imbalance in the air, he put faith in the early appearance of new jet-propelled aircraft. He also put considerable faith in the frontier fortifications, known to the Germans as the WEST WALL, to the Allies as the Siegfried Line. To boost the morale of the troops, he recalled Field Marshal von Rundstedt on September 5 to become again Commander in Chief in the West. Field Marshal Model remained as commander of Army Group B. Hitler ordered Rundstedt to hold firm along the Dutch-Belgian border, in the West Wall and along the Moselle River in northeastern France. As soon as several panzer divisions could be regrouped, they were to counterattack into the south flank of the U.S. Third Army. Although he failed to communicate his long-range plan to Rundstedt, Hitler was already thinking of a major counteroffensive on the Western Front to impel the Western Allies to settle for a negotiated peace.

A strong factor in Hitler's confidence was his belief that the Allies had outrun their supply lines. In that he was correct, although General Eisenhower still hoped to get past the West Wall and establish bridgeheads over the Rhine before a pause became imperative. The problem was not a shortage of supplies on the Continent but the difficulty in getting them forward to troops that in some cases were more than 500 miles from the supply depots. The explosive nature of the advance out of the Normandy beachhead and the decision to forgo a pause at the Seine had denied the supply services time to build an orderly logistical apparatus. Despite such extraordinary measures as establishing a one-way truck route called the RED BALL EXPRESS, the supply troops simply could not keep pace. In view of the supply problems, Eisenhower's continued determination to proceed into Germany on a broad front seemed to Montgomery (promoted on September 1 to field marshal) to be a mistake. He insisted that all resources should be concentrated behind one part of the front, preferably his command in the north, for one sustained drive all the way to Berlin.

Although General Eisenhower rejected the argument (and also the insistence by General Patton that supplies be concentrated behind his Third Army for a quick thrust to the Rhine), he nevertheless sanctioned a plan proposed by Montgomery to use three airborne divisions to help the British Second Army across three major water obstacles in the Netherlands—the Maas (Meuse), Waal (Rhine) and Neder Rijn (Lower Rhine) Rivers. That accomplished, Montgomery might outflank the West Wall and be in a position to exploit on to the North German plain and encircle the Ruhr industrial area from the north. Concurrently, the 6th Army Group was to continue through the Vosges Mountains to the upper Rhine, the Third Army to drive into the Saar and the First Army to penetrate the West Wall near AACHEN and establish a bridgehead over the Rhine near Cologne.

As the FIRST ALLIED AIRBORNE ARMY under Lt. Gen. Lewis H. BRERETON prepared for the airborne assault, the Germans were reinforcing in the Netherlands. The German First Parachute Army gathered fleeing troops and several divisions that had escaped entrapment on the Channel coast by ferrying across the Scheldt Estuary and formed a line along the Dutch canals. Also present, but undetected by Allied intelligence until close to the target date, were two SS panzer divisions refitting near ARNHEM (see WAFFEN SS).

Labeled Operation MARKET, the airborne attack began on September 17 with one British and two American airborne divisions landing near Arnhem, NIJMEGEN and EINDHOVEN in history's largest airborne operation. The airborne troops were to establish a narrow corridor 65 miles deep, through which the British Second Army, in a companion ground attack known as Operation Garden, was to pass. Although the airborne drops were uniformly successful, the British ground column ran into staunch resistance and blown bridges that created critical delays. Before the ground troops could break through to the British airborne division at Arnhem, the German panzer divisions pinned the airborne troops to a minuscule bridgehead a few miles west of the city. On September 25 some 2,000 men of an original force of not quite 9,000 succeeded in withdrawing to the south bank of the river.

The outcome of Market-Garden in itself would have been enough to demonstrate that the pursuit was at an end, but in addition all Allied armies had run into trouble. In the forested foothills of the Vosges, the 6th Army Group could make only limited gains. Although the German counterattack against the Third Army's south flank was a case of too little and too late, a sharply contested Moselle River line and old forts around Metz stalled the Third Army. At Aachen and in the Ardennes the First Army pierced the West Wall but was too overextended to exploit the penetrations.

Although the logistical situation gradually improved, possession of Antwerp was still essential for any sustained offensive. When Montgomery finally turned full attention to clearing the banks of the Scheldt in mid-October, it was a slow process. Flooded lowlands and determined German defenders slowed the attacking Canadian First Army. The banks were at last secured on November 8, but the estuary still had to be cleared of mines; the first ship entered Antwerp only on November 28.

Still anxious at least to reach the Rhine before winter set in, Eisenhower ordered a new offensive even before Antwerp was functioning as a port. On November 16, following the heaviest aerial bombardment of the war in direct support of ground troops (Operation QUEEN—2,807 planes, 10,097 tons of bombs), the U.S.

First and Ninth Armies (the latter moved into the line between the U.S. First Army and the British) attacked east of Aachen. In an effort to avoid bombs falling short as in Normandy, Allied commanders allowed too great an interval between the attacking troops and the bomb line, so that the bombardment failed to do the job expected of it. It was well into December before the First and Ninth Armies could build up along the little Roer River, in places only seven miles beyond the line from which the offensive began. Even then the armies were powerless to cross the Roer, for a series of dams on the upper reaches of the river in the HÜRTGEN FOREST remained in German hands and might be blown to flood the river and trap any force that had crossed.

South of the Ardennes, the French First Army and the U.S. Third and Seventh Armies made greater gains despite flooded rivers and stubborn German defense. By early December the two armies of the 6th Army Group had compressed the Germans into a large bridgehead west of the Rhine known as the COLMAR POCKET, and the Third Army had drawn up before the West Wall along the face of the Saar. The British and Canadians meanwhile cleared all of the Netherlands west and south of the Meuse River.

That was the situation when on December 16 three German armies—the Fifth and Six Panzer and the Seventh—materialized out of the mists and snows of the Ardennes in a violent assault against the U.S. First Army's south wing. In that heavily forested, semimountainous region, General Eisenhower had sanctioned thinning the line to afford more troops for the offensives north and south of the Ardennes, and Hitler had seized upon that situation for his long-planned counteroffensive. He hoped to jump the Meuse River swiftly and drive on to Antwerp, thereby trapping the British and Canadians, the U.S. Ninth Army and that part of the U.S. First Army north of the Ardennes and precipitating a negotiated peace on the Western Front. From the bulge created in the American lines, the counteroffensive became known as the Battle of the Bulge. (For a detailed description of the battle, see the entry BULGE, BATTLE OF THE.)

The battle was all over by January 28. As Field Marshal von Rundstedt and other German field com-

Surrender at Reims: In the SHAEF war room, the Allies accept the unconditional surrender of the German high command. General Jodl (center foreground) prepares to sign the documents; he is accompanied by Admiral von Friedeburg, on his left, and Major Oxenius. Across the table are (from left) General Morgan, SHAEF deputy chief of staff; General Sevez, French representative; Admiral Burrough, Allied naval commander; General Smith, SHAEF chief of staff; General Susloparoff, Soviet representative; General Spaatz, U.S. strategic air commander; Air Marshal Robb, chief of the SHAEF air staff

manders had pointed out in advance, Hitler's plan was too ambitious for his resources; and the tenacity of American troops, even when they were broken into small, disorganized units, afforded ample time for highly mobile American forces to react. It was in the end the greatest pitched battle on the Western Front, involving 29 German and 33 Allied—mainly American—divisions, but the Germans achieved nothing more than possibly to delay a renewed Allied drive toward the Rhine and the Ruhr for about six weeks. The Americans incurred 81,000 casualties, of whom 19,000 were killed and 15,000 captured. Small British units that fought briefly in the tip of the bulge incurred 1,400 casualties. The Germans lost 100,000 men. Each side lost about 800 tanks. Yet the Americans could send in replacements swiftly, while the Germans could no longer make good their losses.

As an adjunct to the counteroffensive, Hitler directed a complementary strike in Alsace (Operation NORDWIND) to deter movement of American troops to the Ardennes. It was designed as an envelopment by the German First Army southward from the Saar and the Nineteenth Army northward from the Colmar pocket to trap part of the U.S. Seventh Army in northern Alsace. The attacks began just before midnight on December 31, but American intelligence was not again to be faulted. By January 25 the Germans were stopped with the loss only of a small portion of the northeastern corner of Alsace, and four days later the French First Army and the U.S. Seventh Army swung over to the offensive. They finished clearing the Colmar pocket on February 9, and by the end of the month had regained all of northeastern Alsace. However troublesome, Operation Nordwind failed to divert any American troops that might have been used in the Ardennes. The Americans incurred 16,000 casualties; the Germans, 25,000.

Despite pressure from General Bradley, who wanted to continue beyond the Ardennes to the Rhine, General Eisenhower returned to his concept of a main effort in the north and pulled divisions from the First and Third Armies to strengthen the Ninth Army near Aachen, under Montgomery's command. Montgomery was to launch the main drive to the Rhine with the Canadian First and U.S. Ninth Armies while the First Army in a subsidiary thrust captured the Roer River dams.

The Canadians attacked on February 8 in Operation VERITABLE but found the going slow because of mud, delay in the Ninth Army's attack when the Germans blew the Roer dams and flooded the river and the presence of the strongest force left to the Germans, Army Group H, organized in the fall under Generaloberst Kurt STUDENT with the First Parachute and Twenty-fifth Armies. Only when the Ninth Army was at last able to jump the Roer on February 23 did resistance weaken. On March 2 the Ninth Army reached the Rhine near Düsseldorf and turned to meet the Canadians.

Despite continued protests from Rundstedt, Hitler refused to sanction withdrawal behind the Rhine. As the bulk of the Allied armies swung to the offensive, the German forces thus were doomed to virtual annihilation. Troops of the U.S. First Army entered Cologne on March 5 while the Third Army was launching a devastating blow through the Eifel region opposite the Ardennes that by March 11 cleared the entire region north of the Moselle River. General Patton then turned southward to jump the Moselle and assist Patch's Seventh Army in sweeping the Saar. That was accomplished by March 25. In the entire battle for the Rhineland, the Germans lost more than 250,000 men.

Meanwhile, on March 7, one of the more electrifying events of the war had occurred. Reaching a bluff overlooking the Rhine at REMAGEN, men of a combat command of an American armored division were astonished to see that the Ludendorff railroad bridge across the Rhine was still standing. As a platoon rushed toward the bridge the Germans set off demolition charges, but they failed to do more than damage the bridge. In the face of small-arms and tank fire from the east bank, the American riflemen charged across. In a matter of minutes the Allies had a bridgehead over the Rhine, to which General Hodges rushed reinforcements.

Because terrain across the Rhine from Remagen was inhospitable for a major advance, Eisenhower planned no immediate breakout from the bridgehead. The crossing nevertheless attracted major German forces, thus weakening defense of the river elsewhere. Shortly before midnight on March 22 a division of the Third Army sneaked across at the town of Oppenheim against only scattered small-arms fire. It was a piece of calculated cunning on the part of General Patton to get across the river before Field Marshal Montgomery, making the Allied main effort, mounted a set-piece attack to jump the Rhine the next day.

Meanwhile, soon after the loss of the Ludendorff railroad bridge, Hitler on March 10 relieved Field Marshal von Rundstedt as Commander in Chief in the West and replaced him with Field Marshal Albert KESSELRING, who had been the German commander in Italy. Yet it would take more than a new commander to bring any order out of the chaos that at that point enveloped the German armies. Army Group G in the south was weakest of all; Army Group B in the center, preoccupied with the Remagen bridgehead, was in no position to repulse a major threat; and Army Group H, which had greater strength, was spread thin to protect the Ruhr. Through it all the mammoth Allied aerial campaign against German cities continued. In one day in March Allied planes flew 11,000 sorties. By the end of March, after dropping a record 245,000 tons of bombs during the month, Allied strategic bombers were almost out of targets. Although some German jet-propelled planes at last appeared, their arrival was too late to change the course of the war.

In contrast to American commanders, Field Marshal Montgomery left nothing to chance in his attack across the Rhine (Operation Plunder). Air attacks to isolate the battlefield began two weeks before the target date of March 23, a vast smoke screen hid preparations and two airborne divisions of the First Allied Airborne Army were assigned to help. Following heavy artillery fire, the British Second Army started crossing between Xanten and Rees soon after nightfall on March 23, with the U.S. Ninth Army following before daylight the next morning south of Wesel. The Ninth Army in particular met limited opposition, incurring for the entire first day losses of 41 killed and 450 wounded. The airborne divisions—one American, one British—began landing in midmorning of March 24 (Operation VARSITY) and by nightfall were in contact with British ground troops. By the end of the day the two Allied armies had established a firm bridgehead as deep as six miles in places.

The unqualified success in the north was the signal for all the Allied armies to begin the victory sweep through Germany. While approving a plan for the First and Ninth Armies to encircle the Ruhr with the Ninth remaining under Montgomery's command, General Eisenhower directed that as soon as the Ruhr was secured the Ninth Army was to revert to Bradley's 12th Army Group. Bradley's armies then were to make the Allied main effort through central Germany to link with the Russians.

The Seventh Army on March 26 made two crossings of the Rhine at Worms and Mannheim, while the French First Army sneaked across in the manner of Patton's Third Army before daylight on March 31 near Speyer. All the bridgeheads were soon joined except for that in the far north beyond the Ruhr.

Simpson's Ninth Army and Hodges's First, the latter attacking out of the Remagen bridgehead, swept rapidly to a juncture on the east face of the Ruhr industrial area on April 1 at Lippstadt, near Paderborn, in what Eisenhower subsequently called "the largest double envelopment in history." Caught in the Ruhr pocket was all of Army Group B with its Fifth Panzer and Fifteenth Armies and part of Army Group H's First Parachute Army. When the final mop-up was completed on April 18 the Army Group B commander, Field Marshal Model, was a suicide and the count of prisoners exceeded 325,000. A new U.S. Army headquarters, the FIFTEENTH under Lt. Gen. Leonard T. GEROW, came forward to supervise the final mop-up while the First and Ninth Armies continued to the east.

As seven Allied armies spread out over Germany, their advances exceeded even those of the great pursuit across France. Drives of 35 to 50 miles a day were not uncommon. Armored divisions usually led the way, followed by infantry mounted on tanks, tank destroyers and trucks. Many villages and towns lay undefended, improvised white flags decorating the houses. Nothing stood in the way of capturing others but roadblocks hastily constructed of heavy logs. Demolished bridges caused the longest delays, but with the Germans incapable of forming a solid line behind even sprawling streams such as the Weser River, infantrymen paddled across in assault boats to form bridgeheads while engineers quickly constructed pontoon bridges. In some cases a local German commander might fire his troops with some special bravado and bring on a fierce engagement in the midst of an otherwise rapid advance. That happened at Kassel and left the city in ruins. It happened also at Heilbronn on the Neckar River, where the U.S. Seventh Army required a week to reduce the city. It happened too in the Harz Mountains, where contingents of the U.S. First Army found themselves engaged for a full week in a real war again.

On the Reichsautobahnen, the superhighways with which Hitler had laced Germany to facilitate military movement, Allied columns raced up all four lanes while crowds of dejected German prisoners or ragged but exuberant slave laborers marched westward down the median strip. Some units discovered vast caches of money and works of art looted by the Nazis from all corners of Europe. Others came across grim evidence of human extermination factories and walking skeletons who somehow had survived Nazi concentration camps. Supplying the far-ranging motorized columns was a tremendous task. Trucks often had to make 700-mile round trips to railheads along the Rhine, and the most critical supplies—gasoline, rations and ammunition—had to be flown into captured airfields. On the return trips the planes often evacuated liberated prisoners of war.

In the north, the British Second Army reached the Elbe River on April 24, while a column on the British left advanced to Bremen on the 20th, there to fight a week-long battle against die-hard defenders. The columns on the right jumped the lower Elbe on the last two days of April and on May 2 took Lübeck without opposition, thereby cutting off the peninsula of Denmark. The great port of Hamburg surrendered the next day without a fight.

Driving to cut off the Germans in the Netherlands, the Canadian First Army faced the staunchest opposition still remaining. From a Rhine bridgehead near Emmerich, one column ran into one sharp fight after another en route to the naval bases at Emden and Wilhelmshaven. Farther west, another column quickly reached the North Sea, while still a third column jumped th Neder Rijn on April 12 and reached the IJsselmeer (Zuider Zee) on the 18th. Four days later, out of concern for a Dutch population already near starvation, Allied commanders suspended all attacks on the promise of the German high commissioner for the Netherlands, Arthur SEYSS-INQUART, that he would avoid large-scale flooding of the country. After a meeting between Seyss-Inquart and Eisenhower's chief of staff on April 30, the Allies began delivering food and supplies to the Dutch.

In the Allied center, armored spearheads of the Ninth Army reached the Elbe River near Magdeburg on April 11 and the next day established a bridgehead only 50 miles from BERLIN. The Germans reacted sharply, even calling in the almost defunct Luftwaffe in troublesome numbers, and forced abandonment of the bridgehead on the 14th; but a second bridgehead, established nearby on the preceding day, held fast. The bridgehead constituted no more than a threat, for by that time General Eisenhower had decided against proceeding to Berlin. Since mid-March Russian forces had stood only 28 miles east of the German capital with the apparent ability to take it whenever they chose. Eisenhower decided to concentrate instead on defeating the Germans in central Germany and driving into the south, where there were rumors of a last-ditch German stand in the Alps, the so-called NATIONAL REDOUBT. The Ninth Army, Eisenhower directed, was to halt at the Elbe, and the First Army at a tributary of the Elbe, the Mulde, and await contact with the Russians.

The First Army took LEIPZIG, Germany's fifth city, on April 18. An armored division already had bypassed the city to reach the Mulde River, and patrols ranging farther east made contact with Russian units on April 25. A formal meeting between American and Russian division commanders took place the following day at TORGAU.

As the First and Ninth Armies neared their final objectives, General Eisenhower directed the Third Army to sideslip southeastward for drives into Bavaria,

Czechoslovakia and Austria close alongside the Seventh Army. Breaking through hastily improvised defenses on the Isar and Inn Rivers, contingents of the Third Army on May 4 seized Linz. Others pushed into Pilsen, already in the hands of Czechoslovak partisans.

The two armies of General Devers's 6th Army Group meanwhile had swung southeast from their Rhine bridgeheads. After a hard fight at Heilbronn, troops of the Seventh Army had to battle three days for Nuremberg but took the city on April 20. The French swept through the Black Forest on the east bank of the Rhine and on April 22 took Stuttgart. Both armies crossed the Danube River on the 22d; Munich fell on the 30th; Salzburg on May 4; Berchtesgaden, site of Hitler's mountain retreat (Eagle's Nest), also on the 4th; and on the same day an American column pushed through Austria to the Brenner Pass to make contact with Allied forces in northern Italy. In the process the myth of a National Redoubt was exploded.

With Allied or Soviet armies sweeping to all parts of Germany, Adolf Hitler remained closeted in the Führerbunker in Berlin. Having composed a will on April 30 designating Grossadmiral Karl DÖNITZ as his successor, he committed suicide even as Russian troops were closing in on the bunker. Several of Hitler's top officials had been trying to arrange a capitulation to the Western Allies alone, but the heads of the Allied governments were adamant that unconditional surrender on all fronts was the only recourse. When the Allies on April 29 accepted the surrender of German forces in ITALY, to become effective on May 2, Admiral Dönitz nevertheless began to explore the possibility of other piecemeal surrenders to save German forces from the Russians. That led on May 4 to the surrender of all forces in the north, including those in Denmark and the Netherlands, to Field Marshal Montgomery. The next day a similar surrender occurred in the south, where Army Group G capitulated to General Devers.

A German representative authorized to open negotiations for all remaining forces in the west arrived at General Eisenhower's headquarters in Reims on May 5, but Eisenhower promptly made it known that simultaneous unconditional surrender in both east and west was mandatory. When Dönitz learned that, he sent Generaloberst Alfred JODL, head of the operations staff of the high command (*see* OKW) and a strong opponent of surrender in the east, to continue the negotiations. Eisenhower informed him that unless the Germans agreed quickly to unconditional surrender, he would break off negotiations and seal the Western Front to prevent further westward movement of German troops and civilians. With that, Jodl telegraphed Dönitz for permission to sign.

The Germans capitulated at 2:41 A.M., May 7. The next day, May 8, was officially designated as V-E (Victory-in-Europe) Day. A second surrender ceremony, with ranking Russians in attendance, took place in Berlin on May 9.

As hostilities came to an end, the German military forces and nation were crushed to a degree never before experienced in modern times, beaten by powerful Soviet armies and by an Allied force that at the end of the war totaled 4,581,000 men in a balanced air-ground military machine. Under Eisenhower's command on V-E Day were 9 armies, 23 corps and 93 divisions, plus air strength totaling 17,192 planes. Of the total force approximately two-thirds was American, including 65 divisions. Since D-Day in Normandy the Germans on the Western Front alone had lost 263,000 dead, 49,000 permanently disabled and 8,109,000 captured. Allied casualties were 186,900 dead, 545,700 wounded and 109,600 missing, most of whom were later declared dead. **C.B.M.**

WESTERN SEA FRONTIER. U.S. Navy designation for the SEA FRONTIER command responsible for the defense of the coastal waters off California and Mexico. When the NORTHWESTERN SEA FRONTIER was abolished in 1944, the Oregon, Washington and Alaskan areas were added.

WESTPHAL, Siegfried (1901–). German Army officer whose rise to prominence began with a short period of service with Gen. Erwin ROMMEL early in the war. In 1942 he received a promotion to major general, which made him one of the youngest officers of that rank in the German Army. In the spring of 1943 he became chief of staff to Field Marshal KESSELRING and thus directed much of the planning for the defense of SICILY and southern ITALY. Westphal earned fame for developing a ground defense without air support during this time. From Italy he moved to the WESTERN FRONT in September 1944, where he replaced Gen. Günther BLUMENTRITT as Field Marshal von RUNDSTEDT's chief of staff. In this capacity the "Paperwork Pedant," as Westphal was known, worked out the defense of the Western Front, especially the detailed planning of the ARDENNES offensive in late 1944. His highest rank was General der Kavallerie.

WEST VIRGINIA, U.S.S. COLORADO-class battleship, completed in 1923. On December 7, 1941, she was moored in BATTLESHIP ROW at PEARL HARBOR outboard of TENNESSEE. She took a number of torpedoes and two bombs, but prompt action by her crew allowed her to settle with little list onto the bottom. She was subsequently refloated and repaired and saw extensive service in the Pacific, notably as part of Adm. Jesse OLDENDORF's battle line at Surigao Strait (*see* LEYTE GULF) in October 1944.

WEST WALL. Known in Allied circles as the Siegfried Line, the West Wall (Germ. *Westwall*) was a series of fortifications along Germany's western frontier begun in 1938 under an able engineer, Dr. Fritz TODT, who built Germany's superhighways. Originally designed as a short belt in the Saar region opposite France's MAGINOT LINE, it was later extended to the Swiss and Dutch frontiers. Touted as impregnable, it contributed to German success in bluffing France and Britain at MUNICH. No thin line of major defensive works, as was the Maginot Line, the West Wall was a band approximately three miles deep of more than 3,000 mutually supporting concrete pillboxes, troop shelters and command posts. Where no natural antitank obstacles existed, a belt of pyramidal concrete projections called dragon's teeth barred the way. The intent was not to halt an attack, but to delay it until mobile reserves could counterattack to eliminate any penetration.

Neglected following the German victory over France in 1940, the line as Allied armies approached in Sep-

Dragon's-teeth tank obstacles in the West Wall

tember 1944 appeared to be little more than a Potemkin village. Few of the pillboxes could accommodate weapons developed in the interim between construction and confrontation, and mines, barbed wire and communications lines were missing. Yet Adolf HITLER decreed that it be held. Although German reserves in 1944 were feeble compared with what the line's designers intended, so were Allied troops, tired from a long race across France and lacking adequate logistical resources. The U.S. V Corps opposite the Belgian Ardennes and the VII Corps south of Aachen quickly pierced the sparsely manned line, but German reserves contained the penetrations. An attempt to outflank the line by a drive through the Netherlands assisted by an airborne attack (Operation MARKET-GARDEN) failed. A penetration in October by the U.S. XIX Corps north of Aachen led to no deep advance, so that not until the early spring of 1945, after German strength had been dissipated in a futile counteroffensive (the Battle of the BULGE), was the line pierced along its full length. Even then concrete helped empower the defense.

WEWAK. Town, port and airfield area on the north-central shore of northeastern NEW GUINEA. It was occupied by the Japanese in early spring 1942, but did not become important in Japanese strategy until the beginning of 1943, when they began to strengthen the base and expand air facilities to include four fields. Allied air power during late 1943 and early 1944 virtually destroyed the usefulness of Wewak as an air or logistical base, yet the area became an assembly point for Japanese ground forces withdrawing from eastern New Guinea. Late in March 1944 the Japanese 18th Army began sending troops northwest along the coast from Wewak, and in July these forces counterattacked American forces near AITAPE. Following the failure of this counterattack, the 18th Army fell back eastward upon Wewak, which Australian forces finally captured on May 10, 1945.

WEYGAND, Maxime (1867–1965). Graduating from Saint-Cyr, the French military academy, in 1887, Weygand became a devoted cavalryman. He served as chief of staff to Marshal Ferdinand Foch during World War I and headed the French military advisory mission to Poland in 1920. As head of the French General Staff in 1930 and overall Army commander between 1931 and 1935, he championed a limited modernization program and the restoration of the two-year service law. The world depression, coupled with his open right-wing sympathies, made it difficult for him to gain support for more comprehensive military reforms.

In 1939 the government recalled General Weygand from retirement to command the French Near East Theater of Operations from Beirut. On May 20, 1940, with the Allied armies reeling in northeastern France and Belgium, Weygand replaced Gen. Maurice GAMELIN as Allied ground Commander in Chief, and despite his advanced age (73), seemed an energetic figure. But his efforts were essentially futile. Too late to save the northern armies retreating to DUNKIRK, Weygand decided to make a final stand above Paris along the Somme and Aisne Rivers. When this failed he withdrew his forces south, but he refused to consider continuing the struggle from North Africa and instead pressed his superiors for an armistice.

At this point Weygand's political views began to overshadow his military activities. He, along with many conservative Frenchmen, feared that another long war of attrition with Germany would prove fatal to France as a nation and lead only to social disaster. To him, the threat of social revolution and Communism was greater than the more temporary one posed by German military strength. His dissatisfaction with internal French politics and Britain's wartime contributions to the Battle of FRANCE reinforced this attitude. As a result, Weygand refused the request of Prime Minister Paul REYNAUD for a separate capitulation of the metropolitan French armies and allied himself with Marshal Philippe PÉTAIN and others desiring an early armistice. Weygand was in full accord with Reynaud's resignation on June 16 and Pétain's request for terms shortly thereafter.

From June to September 1940 Weygand served as Defense Minister in the VICHY regime and presided over the establishment of the 100,000-man army allowed by the Germans. In this position he also tried to expand the tiny armistice army through further economic and political concessions to Germany and by emphasizing the British threat to the FRENCH NAVY and empire. Internal rivalry at Vichy ended his brief tenure of office, and he was sent to North Africa with the general mission of ensuring the French Army's strict neutrality. From September 1940 to November 1941 Weygand strove to minimize both Axis and Allied influence in France's African territories, so that the armistice might remain intact. One of his successes was the Murphy-Weygand agreement of February 26, 1941, which allowed the shipment of limited American supplies into French North Africa. Finally, after a long struggle with his chief rival, Adm. François DARLAN, Weygand was forced to resign.

Upon the German occupation of the Vichy zone in November 1942, Weygand was arrested and incarcerated in Germany until 1945. Following his liberation the French Fourth Republic tried the aging general for treason, but in 1948 he was exonerated of all charges.

WHALE. Roadway leading from shore to pierhead in a MULBERRY artificial harbor.

WHEELER, Raymond Albert (1885–1974). In 1941, when the U.S. War Department sought an "officer of broad engineering experience" to establish a military mission to Iran, the task was given to Colonel Wheeler, at the time an Acting Assistant Chief of Staff. A U.S. Military Academy graduate of 1911, he was a veteran construction engineer and a specialist in rail and highway matters, and had served as acting governor of the Canal Zone. It was the purpose of the new mission to develop supply facilities to support both the British and the Russians. After the United States entered the war, Wheeler (February 1942) was appointed commanding general of the Services of Supply for American forces in China, Burma and India, while retaining for the time his responsibilities in Iran. In autumn 1943 he was appointed to the SOUTHEAST ASIA COMMAND staff of Adm. Lord Louis MOUNTBATTEN, where he served as principal administrative officer and, from February 1944, as Deputy Supreme Commander.

Wheeler had been promoted to brigadier general in 1941 on receiving the Iranian command, and in 1944 attained the rank of lieutenant general, his highest. In June 1945 he became commanding general of the India-Burma Theater. Known as "Speck," General Wheeler was a highly competent officer whose capabilities were put to the test in extremely demanding circumstances—as, for example, the construction of the LEDO ROAD. After the war he served as Chief of Engineers of the U.S. Army.

WHEELER FIELD. The principal U.S. Army Air Corps pursuit base protecting PEARL HARBOR and one of the primary objects of Japanese bombing and strafing attacks, which destroyed 66 fighter planes. Several P-40s and P-36s took off from Wheeler the morning of December 7, 1941, to oppose the Japanese. One of the P-40 pilots, Lt. George S. Welch, claimed the destruction of four enemy planes.

WHIPCORD. Code name of an early British plan (1941) for the invasion of SICILY.

WHIRLWIND. The first twin-engine, single-seat fighter to serve with Britain's Royal Air Force. Designed by W. E. W. Petter of Westland, the plane was sleek—the nacelles housing the two Rolls-Royce Peregrine engines were slung beneath the wing, the cylindrical fuselage was atop the wing and the horizontal stabilizer was perched high on the tail. Mounted in the nose, which extended just forward of the wing and terminated aft of the propeller hubs, were four 20-mm. cannon. The plane was exceptionally maneuverable and easy to handle. Troubles with the supercharged engines, which were late in entering production, persuaded the RAF to cease production after acquiring about a hundred Whirlwinds. Despite the comparatively low-powered engines, each developing 850 horsepower, the plane was capable of 360 miles per hour at 15,000 feet.

WHITE, Isaac Davis (1901–). U.S. Army officer, an aggressive leader of armor. White saw action in NORTH AFRICA, SICILY and the Normandy INVASION. In 1945 he was promoted to major general and given command of the 2d Armored Division, which led the American advance to the Elbe River. In later years he was promoted to full general and commanded all U.S. Army forces in the Pacific. Known as "I.D." to the Army, he was equally popular with officers and ranks.

WHITE, William Allen (1868–1944). Editor of the Emporia (Kansas) *Gazette* and an influential Republican for almost 50 years. Known as the "sage of Emporia," White became famous in 1896 when his editorial "What's the Matter with Kansas?" became one of the most widely quoted arguments against the election of Democrat William Jennings Bryan as President. During the 1930s White strongly supported President ROOSEVELT's foreign policy, and when the war in Europe began he advocated supplying Britain and France with arms and war materials, although he was strongly opposed to American entry into the war. In 1940 he became chairman of the COMMITTEE TO DEFEND AMERICA BY AIDING THE ALLIES and was especially effective since he came from the traditionally isolationist Middle West.

WHITEHEAD, Ennis C. (1895–1964). In the summer of 1942, then a U.S. Air Force colonel, Whitehead went to the Southwest Pacific to become deputy commander of the FIFTH AIR FORCE under Maj. Gen. George C. KENNEY. He remained Kenney's close associate for the remainder of the war, receiving a promotion to brigadier general, then to major general in March 1943, and assuming command of the Fifth Air Force in June 1944. He became a lieutenant general in June 1945. His wartime career began with the repulse of the Japanese advance in NEW GUINEA and ended with the aerial offensive against the Japanese homeland.

WHITELEY, Sir John Francis Martin (1896–1970). British Army officer who as a major general served as deputy chief of staff at Gen. Dwight EISENHOWER's Allied Force Headquarters, moved to SHAEF as chief of intelligence and became deputy operations officer (*see* SHAEF) in May 1944, where he shared the operations responsibility with U.S. Maj. Gen. Harold R. BULL.

WHITE ROSE. An anti-Nazi student movement in Germany. It was fostered in Munich, the birthplace of the Nazi Party, and led by the youthful brother and sister Hans and Sophie Scholl. They were Catholic converts and took a strongly Christian line in the underground literature they began to publish on a hand-operated duplicator in 1939 and later, in 1942–43, in leaflet form bearing the emblem of a white rose (and so called the White Rose Letters). They worked in close association with a young academic, Prof. Kurt Huber. Their final demonstration consisted of openly distributing a broadsheet in the university, and this led to their arrest along with their associates. They were cruelly interrogated, "tried" by People's Court judge Roland FREISLER and beheaded. Hans was 25 and Sophie 22 at the time of their deaths. Arrests in connection with the White Rose movement amounted to some 100 persons and led to further executions of these outspoken idealists, including Huber. The White Rose movement, doomed from the start, nevertheless set a shining example to young Germans everywhere.

WHITLEY. Known as the Flying Barn Door because of its squarish lines and lack of speed, Britain's Armstrong Whitworth Whitley made its first flight in 1936. When hostilities broke out, six squadrons were ready for action, and on the first night of the war, September 3–4, 1939, 10 of the planes dropped 13 tons of propaganda leaflets on the Ruhr valley and the cities of Hamburg and Bremen. On March 19–20, 1940, 30 Whitleys and 20 HAMPDENS dropped the first bombs of the war on German soil, raiding the seaplane base at Hornum. The Whitley served with RAF BOMBER COMMAND until the spring of 1942, and RADAR-equipped models afterward flew antisubmarine patrols for COASTAL COMMAND. Whitleys also helped train parachutists and glider forces, dropped airborne COMMANDOS into enemy-held territory and flew occasional leaflet-dropping missions.

The most numerous subspecies of this slab-sided, midwing bomber was Whitley V. Powered by two 1,145-horsepower Rolls-Royce Merlins, the plane had a top speed of 222 miles per hour. Defensive armament was five .303-caliber machine guns, one in the nose and four in a power-operated tail turret.

WHITTLE, Sir Frank (1907–). British aeronautical engineer who developed the first British jet engine. For years Whittle had been a more or less isolated advocate of jet power for Great Britain and had received government subsidies to keep his small company, Power Jets, Ltd., in business. He finally achieved a successful trial flight in 1941, and was given support to proceed with the project. Although he had made plans for production of jets in 1942, technical problems developed, and no planes with Whittle-designed jet engines appeared in action during the war.

WHITWORTH, Sir William J. (1884–1973). Royal Navy officer serving as vice-admiral commanding the Battle Cruiser Squadron, Home Fleet, when the war broke out in 1939. He was in command at the second battle of NARVIK, flying his flag in H.M.S. WARSPITE, on April 13, 1940, in which eight German destroyers and one U-boat were sunk without loss or damage to the British force. In 1941 Admiral Whitworth came to the Admiralty as Second Sea Lord, and in 1944 he was appointed commander in chief ROSYTH. He retired in 1946.

WICKARD, Claude Raymond (1893–1967). A native of Indiana, Wickard was an agricultural specialist who in 1940 was appointed U.S. Secretary of Agriculture to succeed Henry A. WALLACE. LEND-LEASE in 1941 increased the demand for American food, and Wickard prepared a program of price supports for pork, poultry and dairy products as a means of stimulating production. Since the Department of Agriculture was designated as the purchasing agent for food supplies to be shipped to Britain, Wickard, in his efforts to meet this additional demand, established the first national production goals. They called for sharp increases in the production of dairy products, poultry, pork, beef, vegetables and oil-yielding crops. After the United States entered the war, Wickard set up agriculture defense boards at the state and local levels designed to assist farmers in meeting war-related needs, and introduced the rationing system for food.

WICKES, U.S.S. Destroyer and class (1,224 tons full load; antiaircraft: four 4-inch guns, one 3-inch gun; twelve 21-inch torpedo tubes; 35 knots). Destroyers Nos. 75–185, the first of two classes of FLUSH-DECKERS laid down during World War I, were referred to as "short-legged" in comparison with the later CLEMSON class, because of their relatively low (275-ton) fuel capacity. Unlike the Clemsons, most of the Wickes class fulfilled their contract speed and displacement requirements. Many alterations to the armament and appearance of these ships were made during the war years.

WIDEWING. Code name of SHAEF headquarters at Bushy Park, near London (*see* SHAEF).

WIGGLESWORTH, Sir (H. E.) Philip (1896–). An outstanding RAF staff officer in the Middle East and Mediterranean Commands. Wigglesworth rejoined Sir Arthur TEDDER, his old chief, as deputy chief of staff for air at SHAEF in 1944. He held the rank of air marshal. After the war he commanded the British air force in Germany.

WIGNER, Eugene Paul (1902–). A mathematical physicist from Hungary who had studied and taught in Germany, Wigner came to the United States in 1930 to teach at Princeton University. During the war he was a consultant to the Office of Scientific Research and Development, and he worked at the UNIVERSITY OF CHICAGO Metallurgical Laboratory from 1942 to 1945. He became the director of research and development at the OAK RIDGE Laboratories in 1946 and a consultant to the Atomic Energy Commission in 1947.

WILDFLOWER. U.S. code name for Great Britain.

WILFRED. Code name for the British operation of laying mines in Norwegian territorial waters to force merchant ships carrying iron ore to Germany out into the open sea, where they could be intercepted. Since this was early in the war, when NORWAY was still neutral, there were diplomatic objections to the plan, but agreement was finally reached to put it into operation at dawn on April 8, 1940. Three minelaying forces sailed, one as a subterfuge, the others to lay minefields off Bodö and Stadtlandet. As it happened, the date coincided with the sailing from Germany of considerable naval forces to attack and occupy Norway, of which no prior intelligence had been received in Britain. The minefield off Bodö was successfully laid, and that off Stadtlandet was canceled when the sighting of German warships in the area was confirmed. Wilfred received its name directly from Winston CHURCHILL, who said he used this designation because the operation "was so small and innocent."

WILHELMINA, Queen of the Netherlands (1880–1962). Wilhelmina had been sovereign of the Netherlands for a half-century when the German invasion came in 1940. She with members of her family and ministers of the government fled to London, which she proclaimed on May 13 to be the new seat of her government, and Dutch forces continued to take part in the war. Queen Wilhelmina returned to the liberated area of the Netherlands in March 1945 and took up residence again in April. She abdicated in favor of her daughter Juliana in 1948.

WILKES, John (1895–1957). Great-grandson of Adm. Charles Wilkes, the South Pole explorer, John Wilkes graduated from the U.S. Naval Academy in the class of 1916. He began World War II in the Pacific, escaping from CORREGIDOR aboard the submarine *Swordfish.* Having had submarine experience in World War I, Wilkes helped reorganize the Asian submarine fleet for the second war. He took part in the invasion of SICILY, and in 1944 assumed command of U.S. ports and bases in France. His most notable accomplishment, however, was the training of a 4,000-unit landing-craft force for the Normandy INVASION. Wilkes rose to rear admiral during the war. He served in the postwar occupation of Germany, and retired in 1951. *See also* NEPTUNE.

WILKINSON, Theodore Stark (1888–1946). Graduated first in the U.S. Naval Academy class of 1909, Wilkinson won the MEDAL OF HONOR for conduct in the occupation of Veracruz in 1914. In World War II he was prominent as an amphibious commander, his name being associated with victories at NEW GEORGIA, VELLA LAVELLA, Treasury Island, BOUGAINVILLE, PELELIU and ANGAUR in the Palaus, and LEYTE and LINGAYEN GULF in the Philippines. In 1941 Wilkinson served as chief of naval intelligence, where, according to Samuel Eliot MORISON, he "made the same underestimate of the enemy's capabilities and overestimate of their common sense as did everyone else." In 1942 he became commander of the III Amphibious Force under Adm. William F. HALSEY in the South Pacific. The III Amphibious Force played a decisive role under Wilkinson when it landed marines to occupy Peleliu, the gateway to Leyte Gulf and the Philippines. Wilkinson rose to vice-admiral during the war. He worked with the Joint Strategic Survey Committee of the JOINT CHIEFS OF STAFF until his death by drowning following an automobile crash.

WILLIS, Sir Algernon U. (1889–). British naval officer, chief of staff to Adm. Sir Andrew CUNNINGHAM in the Mediterranean at the outbreak of the war. In 1941 Admiral Willis was appointed Commander in Chief South Atlantic, a post he held until Japan entered the war and he was sent to the Eastern Fleet as second-in-command. In 1943 he was appointed Flag Officer Commanding FORCE H at Gibraltar, and was transferred later that year to the other end of the Mediterranean as Commander in Chief Levant. In 1944 he came to the Admiralty as Second Sea Lord, and finished his naval service as Commander in Chief Mediterranean, 1946–48, and Commander in Chief Portsmouth, 1948–50. He was promoted to Admiral of the Fleet in 1949.

WILLKIE, Wendell Lewis (1892–1944). A native of Indiana, Willkie moved to New York City in 1929 as legal counsel of a utilities holding company. He became president within four years and attracted national notice through his battle with the Tennessee Valley Authority, with which his firm was in competition. In 1940 he was the surprise winner of the Republican Presidential nomination, but he lost the election to Franklin ROOSEVELT, though winning more votes than any previous candidate except Roosevelt himself. An internationalist who strongly supported Roosevelt's war policies, Willkie was sent by Roosevelt to visit the United Kingdom in 1941, and in 1942 he left on a world trip as a Presidential envoy to the Middle East, Russia and China. He returned an apostle of what he called "one world" (and wrote a popular book of that title). These internationalist views did not endear him to a number of powerful forces in his own party. When he sought the 1944 nomination, his candidacy ran aground early, in the Wisconsin primary. He died before the November election. A large, tousled, vital person, Willkie had a candid manner that appealed to people of all kinds. Asked by a

Senate committee after the 1940 election to explain a certain attack on Roosevelt, he made the famous reply that it was just "campaign oratory."

WILLSON, Russell (1884–1948). During World War I Wilson, a 1906 graduate of the U.S. Naval Academy, worked with the Navy's signal and code section, winning a NAVY CROSS for his communications inventions. After PEARL HARBOR be became chief of staff to Adm. Ernest J. KING. He was promoted to vice-admiral in 1942, but in 1943 retired from active duty. The Navy immediately recalled him to work with the JOINT CHIEFS OF STAFF in communications. Again he was decorated for his work, this time with both Army and Navy DISTINGUISHED SERVICE MEDALS.

WILSON, Henry Maitland Wilson, 1st Baron (1881–1964). British Army officer who held high commands in the MIDDLE EAST and the Mediterranean. He was General Officer Commanding in Chief Egypt, 1939–41, and military governor and GOC-in-C CYRENAICA, 1941. He commanded British troops in the abortive operations in Greece in 1941, and later that year was commander in Palestine, Transjordan and Syria. In 1942 he became commander in chief of the Persia-Iraq Command, and in 1943 commander in chief in the Middle East. In 1944 he became Supreme Allied Commander, MEDITERRANEAN THEATER, and was promoted to field marshal. He was head of the British Joint Staff Mission in Washington in 1945–47, in succession to Sir John DILL. Known as "Jumbo," Wilson was a methodical, unspectacular soldier who exercised command with ability and caution.

WILSON, Sir Horace (1882–1972). British career civil servant who was chief industrial adviser to the government in 1930–39 and Permanent Secretary of the Treasury and head of the Civil Service in 1939–42. Much respected by Prime Minister Neville CHAMBERLAIN, Wilson, although not a specialist in foreign affairs, became the Prime Minister's close adviser on foreign policy. He played a leading part in the MUNICH negotiations in 1938 and in the immediately prewar diplomatic activity in 1939.

WILTZ. Town in Luxembourg on the Wiltz River that housed the command post of the U.S. 28th Infantry Division in the early stages of the Battle of the BULGE. On December 18, 1944, the division commander, Maj. Gen. Norman D. COTA, concentrated a hetereogeneous force of headquarters troops and stragglers to defend the town. Around midnight on the 19th the last American troops were forced to flee after heavy losses, but the stand afforded time for others to form to the west for defense of the crossroads town of BASTOGNE.

WINANT, John Gilbert (1889–1947). American politician, a liberal Republican who held elective and appointive U.S. offices and was director of the International Labor Organization in Geneva. In 1941 President ROOSEVELT appointed Winant ambassador to Britain, a post he held throughout the war. He was the American member of the EUROPEAN ADVISORY COMMISSION, which apportioned Germany and Berlin for the occupation. A man of quiet personal charm, he developed warm relationships with British leaders, including Winston CHURCHILL, and was considered an effective ambassador. He committed suicide in 1947.

WINCH. Code name of British plans to reinforce MALTA with aircraft, 1941.

WINDOW. Strips of metal foil dropped from airplanes to create a false image of an airplane on RADAR. The British developed Window for the purpose of deceiving German radar. The Americans gave Window the name "Chaff." *See also* ELECTRONIC COUNTERMEASURES.

WINGATE, Orde (1903–1944). British Army officer with a background in exploration, guerrilla fighting in Palestine (he was a convinced terrorist) and intelligence operations. Wingate was sent by General WAVELL (commanding in the Middle East) to the Sudan in 1940 to assist the Ethiopian nationalists and direct their revolt against the Italians. As the unrelenting leader of Gideon Force, Wingate made free use of bluff, maneuver and unorthodox tactics. Following the liberation of Ethiopia, Wingate was seriously ill and made an attempt at suicide, but after a convalescence he was called to India by Wavell, who appreciated his unconventional approaches. For BURMA, Wingate proposed LONG-RANGE PENETRATION GROUPS to conduct guerrilla operations behind the Japanese lines (*see* CHINDIT). A five-month test of this Chindit concept in 1943 earned Wingate the second bar to his DSO, though losses in men and equipment were high.

CHURCHILL, ever delighted by imaginative fighters, took General Wingate with him to the QUEBEC CONFERENCE in 1943. Although some opposed the idea, Wingate went back to India with authorization to conduct a long-range offensive under Adm. Lord Louis MOUNTBATTEN, Supreme Commander in SOUTHEAST ASIA, as part of the campaign to recapture Burma. In February 1944 Wingate's Chindits were dropped deep in Burma, but Wingate himself was killed in an air crash in India in March.

Wingate was a controversial figure, an intense, mercurial man who loved to innovate and lead but resented higher authority. He held a deep religious conviction that he was an instrument of a greater power, and he seemed infused with a mystical, almost fanatical quality. Gen. Sir William SLIM, who knew him both in Africa and in India, described him as a "strange, excitable, moody creature, but he had fire in him. He could ignite other men." Slim also said that his word was not reliable. Churchill considered Wingate "a man of genius."

WINKELMAN, Henri (1876–1952). Recalled from retirement in early 1940 to become Dutch Commander in Chief, General Winkelman planned to make a stand against a German invasion behind the great Dutch rivers. Despite his precautions, however, German airborne troops opening the way for panzers forced him to capitulate after five days of fighting.

WINTER STORM (Wintergewitter). Code name of General von MANSTEIN's operation to relieve German forces in STALINGRAD, December 1942.

WISCONSIN, U.S.S. Iowa-class battleship, completed in 1944. She was employed as part of a task force that bombarded the Japanese coast in 1945.

WITZLEBEN, Erwin von (1881–1944). An active conspirator to remove Adolf Hitler from power as early as 1938, Field Marshal von Witzleben was to have been commander in chief of all German armed forces had the bomb attempt against Hitler on July 20, 1944, succeeded. Tried for treason in the Nazi People's Court, Witzleben, as the principal Army officer among the accused, was treated with special ridicule. He was executed by hanging on August 8, 1944. *See also* Opposition to Hitler.

W. L. STEED. In the midst of a snowstorm off the Delaware capes, a German U-boat torpedoed the U.S. tanker *W. L. Steed* on February 2, 1942. Although the ship's crew was able to abandon their burning vessel in lifeboats, only six men survived the cold and exposure before being rescued. Of these six survivors, two died shortly thereafter.

WOLFE, Kenneth B. (1896–1971). U.S. Army Air Force officer whose greatest contribution to Allied victory was in supervising the development and testing of the Boeing B-29 Superfortress (*see* B-29). Wolfe was promoted to brigadier general in the spring of 1943 and in June of that year began organizing and training an operational B-29 wing. He prepared the XX Bomber Command for combat and commanded it when it began bombing Japan from bases in China. He returned to the United States to take part in aircraft development and production programs, then went to Okinawa in August 1945 as a major general to become chief of staff of the Fifth Air Force.

WOLFF, Karl Friedrich Otto (1900–). An officer of the Nazi SS (*see* SS), a member of the party from 1931 who was proud of his relatively low (indicating early) membership number. Wolff joined Heinrich Himmler's entourage in 1933, becoming the Reichsführer's adjutant and personal chief of staff, and soon his close friend. He rose quickly in the SS, reaching the ranks of Obergruppenführer and General der Waffen SS in 1942. In 1943 he was appointed military governor and head of the SS in northern Italy. When convinced that the war was lost, he arranged a secret meeting with Allen Dulles, the U.S. intelligence chief in Switzerland, in early March 1945 (*see* Office of Strategic Services). The ultimate result, after some delay, was the capitulation of the German forces in Italy on May 2, six days before V-E Day—which meant that a number of lives were saved. After the war Wolff was sentenced by a British tribunal to four years' imprisonment and was released in 1949. However, he was arrested again in 1962 and tried by a German court, which found him guilty of crimes relating to genocide. He was sentenced to 15 years.

WOLFPACK. An organized force of submarines coordinated against a specific target or on a specific mission. The Germans first employed wolfpack tactics during the Battle of the Atlantic, vectoring submarines in numbers against detected convoys. During the later months of the Pacific war, American submarines were sent out in task group–like wolfpacks, with nicknames based on the name of the wolfpack commander. German wolfpacks were coordinated from U-boat headquarters on shore, while the far smaller American wolfpacks (three to six boats) were controlled by the pack commander in one of the submarines on the scene.

WOLF'S LAIR (Wolfsschanze). Adolf Hitler's headquarters in the East Prussian forest near Rastenburg, described by visitors as a mixture of "monastery and concentration camp." It was surrounded by a minefield and a perimeter of barbed wire, which enclosed a group of small buildings. In the center, within a second perimeter, was a concrete bunker and a building containing a map room. The latter building was the scene of the attempt on Hitler's life on July 20, 1944.

WOLZEK. Nazi extermination camp in Poland.

WOMEN MARINES. The U.S. Marine Corps was the last of the line services to admit women to its ranks during World War II. In World War I, however, the Marine Corps had had the singular distinction of actually enlisting women—some 300 to perform clerical duties at its headquarters in Washington. The group was disbanded at the end of the war. On February 13, 1943, the Women's Reserve of the U.S. Marine Corps was established. The director of the corps was Ruth Cheney Streeter (February 1943 to December 1945). Initially a major, she was promoted eventually to the rank of colonel prior to leaving the service in December 1945. The peak strength of the Women's Reserve was 18,409, reached on June 31, 1945. The women served in 135 different jobs, primarily in the administrative field. In January 1945 Women Marines were assigned outside the continental United States for the first time, to Hawaii. On June 12, 1948, Congress authorized the enlistment of women in the regular Marine Corps.

WOMEN'S AIRFORCE SERVICE PILOTS (WASP). The wartime U.S. Army Air Forces organization in which licensed women aviators delivered aircraft and performed other flying duties within the United States. The idea originated with Jacqueline Cochran, a skilled racing pilot, who in 1939 had written Eleanor Roosevelt proposing the recruitment of women fliers. No action was taken on the Cochran plan, but after Pearl Harbor another woman aviator, Nancy Harkness Love, recommended that the Army's Ferrying Command employ skilled women volunteers to fly all types of planes from factory to air base. The coming of war lent urgency to Miss Cochran's idea, and during 1942 both Mrs. Love's Women's Auxiliary Ferrying Squadron and Miss Cochran's Women's Flying Training Detachment commenced operation.

Mrs. Love recruited 28 veteran pilots and put them immediately to work ferrying aircraft. Miss Cochran signed up a large number of less experienced fliers, arranged for additional training and made them available for a variety of noncombat jobs so as to release as many male pilots as possible for service overseas.

Rather than have two distinct organizations, Gen. Henry H. Arnold, the Air Force chief, in November

1942 ordered them merged under Miss Cochran's supervision, with Mrs. Love retaining responsibility for ferrying operations. The delivery of aircraft remained a principal activity of the newly merged unit, but the members also performed other duties, such as towing targets for aerial gunnery training and making weather flights. The Women's Airforce Service Pilots remained civilians, serving under Civil Service regulations.

Both General Arnold and Miss Cochran wanted the WASP converted into a military organization, similar to but distinct from the WOMEN'S ARMY CORPS. Congress objected to this apparent duplication, however. Predictions of an imminent surplus of male pilots in the U.S. Army Air Forces led to deactivation of the WASP in December 1944. A total of 916 women were on duty at that time.

WOMEN'S ARMY CORPS (WAC). First of the U.S. women's wartime services, the Women's Army Auxiliary Corps (WAAC) was established on May 14, 1942. In the following year the corps developed from a civilian auxiliary into an integral part of the Army of the United States (AUS—the expanded wartime Army) and the word Auxiliary was dropped from its title. The peak wartime strength—over 99,000 women—was reached in April 1945. Wartime director was Col. Oveta Culp HOBBY (May 1942–July 1945). Women served in almost all military occupational specialties during wartime, except those associated with combat duties. WACs were assigned in every overseas theater of war, beginning in January 1943. Regular Army status was awarded the WAC in 1948; by 1978 women were so integrated into the Army that the WAC was dissolved.

WOMEN'S AUXILIARY AIR FORCE (WAAF). Established on June 28, 1939, as a voluntary women's auxiliary to the Royal Air Force, the WAAF was awarded military status in 1941. Women in the WAAF performed varied duties—as balloon operators, airplane mechanics, instrument repairmen, control tower operators, meteorologists, parachute packers, air-ambulance nursing orderlies, radio operators, photographers, cooks, clerks and tailors. The WAAF attained its peak strength of 182,000 in June 1943; this total included volunteers and women drafted into national service. Unlike members of the other British women's services, WAAF personnel were (from 1941) authorized to use the titles of rank of the RAF and wore uniforms almost identical in style and color to the men's. Though WAAF members served primarily in Britain, some units were stationed in the Middle East, India and the Pacific. The wartime directors of the WAAF were K. Jane Trefusis Forbes (1939–43) and Air Commandant Lady Walsh. On February 1, 1949, the corps was integrated into the regular services as a component of the RAF and was retitled the Women's Royal Air Force (WRAF).

WOMEN'S AUXILIARY FERRYING SQUADRON (WAFS). Group of U.S. women pilots, with no military status, organized by Nancy Harkness Love in September 1942 at the New Castle Army Air Base in Delaware. These women were employed by the Ferrying Division of the AIR TRANSPORT COMMAND to transport light liaison and training planes within the United States and to Canada. When the WOMEN'S AIRFORCE SERVICE PILOTS was organized later in 1942, the Women's Auxiliary Ferrying Squadron was incorporated into it.

WOMEN'S LAND ARMY (WLA). British women's auxiliary that met a vital home-front necessity created by manpower shortages in agriculture and forestry. Women volunteered or were drafted, on a full- or part-time basis, to work on farms planting, cultivating and harvesting seasonal crops or in the timber industry to cut down trees and saw and haul timber for wartime use. The peak strength of 80,300 (full-time) was reached in December 1943. The group was disbanded in June 1945.

WOMEN'S ROYAL NAVAL SERVICE (WRNS). This British women's naval corps, first established in 1914, was demobilized after World War I and reactivated in 1939. During World War II its director was Vera Laughton MATHEWS, who held the title of superintendent (equivalent to colonel). Members of the WRNS, affectionately called "Wrens," served throughout the war both on ship and ashore. They operated motorboats (ferrying men and supplies to ships anchored in home ports), water ambulances and fleet mail boats. On land they worked in torpedo maintenance shops and gunnery repair shops, drove ambulances and other military vehicles and performed a number of administrative duties. Some women served aboard transports crossing the Atlantic as cooks, stewards and teletype operators. The peak wartime strength of this corps was 74,000, achieved in June 1944. The WRNS was established as a component of the regular naval service (for shore duty only) on February 1, 1949.

WOMEN'S VOLUNTARY SERVICE (WVS). British organization founded in 1938 to involve women in air raid precautions. Having only a small staff, headed by the Marchioness of Reading, it rose during the war to a voluntary membership in the hundreds of thousands, who performed a great variety of practical services such as supplying food and clothing to the homeless, helping with the evacuation of children and preparing meals for farm workers.

WOOD, Sir (Howard) Kingsley (1881–1943). As British Secretary of State for Air in 1938–40, Wood presided over the creation and early development of the British Commonwealth Air Training Plan. In May 1940 he became Chancellor of the Exchequer in the CHURCHILL cabinet.

WOOD, John Stephen (1888–1966). U.S. Army officer who served with the 5th Armored Division in 1941–42. Promoted to major general in 1942, he commanded the 4th Armored Division between 1942 and 1944, participating in the French campaign. He was an aggressive commander and a keen student of armored tactics, but was relieved for reasons of health in the fall of 1944.

WOOFUS. The U.S. Navy Rocket Launcher Mark 24, an installation of 120 rails designed to be quickly mounted in, or removed from, the well of an LCM (*see* LCM). Each rail carried a 7.2-inch bombardment rocket with a range of 840 or 1,260 feet, depending on the size of the rocket motor used. This close-support area-bombardment weapon was used in combat during 1944 and 1945.

WOOLTON, Frederick James Marquis, 1st Earl (1883–1964). A British department store executive, a one-time social worker, who in 1940 was appointed Minister of Food, a position he filled with outstanding success. In 1943 Woolton became Minister of Reconstruction, serving until 1945. He was Winston CHURCHILL's first minister to be given full authority to deal with all aspects of Britain's postwar reconstruction policy.

WORKSHOP. Code name for a proposed British seizure of PANTELLERIA, 1940–41.

WRIGHT, Carleton Herbert (1892–). A 1912 graduate of the U.S. Naval Academy, Rear Adm. "Bosco" Wright commanded Task Force 67 in the Battle of TASSAFARONGA, a U.S. defeat during the GUADALCANAL campaign. Wright was a poor choice to command the task force, since he took over with little relevant experience; nor was the task force itself a trained one. To his credit, Wright accepted responsibility for U.S. losses due to his inexperience. Following Tassafaronga, Wright returned to Washington.

WRIGHT, Jerauld (1898–). U.S. naval officer whose first wartime service was in the Pacific, though he soon transferred to the staff of Adm. Ernest J. KING. In this capacity he helped plan the invasion of NORTHWEST AFRICA. In November 1942 he assumed temporary command of the British submarine SERAPH to bring Gen. Henri GIRAUD from southern France to Africa. Wright worked in the planning of the invasion of SICILY and the SALERNO landing and later commanded cruisers in the Pacific. In November 1944 he became a rear admiral. Following the war Wright held high commands in NATO.

WÜRZBURG. Code name of the German RADAR apparatus used in the ground control of fighters and in the direction of antiaircraft batteries.

WYCHE, Ira T. (1887–). U.S. Army officer who was named to command of the 79th Infantry Division as a major general in 1942. He led the division throughout its participation in action in western Europe.

WYOMING, U.S.S. Gunnery training ship, originally built as a battleship. Sister ship to ARKANSAS, *Wyoming* was first commissioned in 1912. She was later demilitarized under the terms of the London naval arms limitation treaty; her armor belt and most of her 12-inch guns were removed. Armed with a changing assortment of dual-purpose and antiaircraft guns, she trained thousands of gunnery personnel during the war. Her "commuter-type" training cruises in Chesapeake Bay earned her such nicknames as "Back Every Friday" and "Chesapeake Raider."

X

X-CRAFT. British MIDGET SUBMARINES. An X-Craft was 45 feet long and carried a crew of four.

X GERÄT (X Apparatus). German radio-beam device for guidance of aircraft at night. A radio receiver in the bomber guided it along a main beam aimed over the target; when the bomber reached intersecting cross beams, the bombs were released. X Gerät was adopted after the initial failure of the Luftwaffe in the Battle of BRITAIN. It was employed by a PATHFINDER group, Kampfgruppe 100.

X REPORT. Document drawn up early in the war, on behalf of members of the German OPPOSITION TO HITLER, by Hans von DOHNANYI. It contained suggested peace terms.

Y

YAHAGI. Japanese light cruiser of 6,600 tons, completed at Sasebo in 1943 and armed with six 6.1-inch and four 3-inch guns, numerous smaller weapons, depth charges, eight 24-inch torpedo tubes and two aircraft. *Yahagi* participated in the MARIANAS fighting and the battle for LEYTE GULF. She was sunk during the "last sortie" of the Japanese Navy, the battle of OKINAWA, being destroyed off Kyushu by U.S. Navy carrier-borne aircraft on April 7, 1945.

YAKOVLEV YAK-1 and YAK-7. Soviet single-seat fighter and fighter-bomber designed by Alexander Yakovlev. The Yak-1 was first flown in March 1939 and proved to be eminently successful; it entered service in 1941. The Yak-7V, a two-seat version, came soon after. The development of the Yak-7V led to an improved single-seat fighter, the Yak-7A. The Yak-7A was followed by the Yak-7B, which had a canopy with all-around vision. The Yak-1 had an 1,100-horsepower V-12 engine and flew at 364 miles per hour maximum speed. It carried one 20-mm. cannon, two 7.62-mm. machine guns and six rockets. Dimensions: wingspan, 32 feet 9¾ inches; length, 27 feet 9¾ inches; height, 8 feet 8 inches.

YAKOVLEV YAK-3. The Yak-3 was developed parallel with the YAK-9, but designed specifically for low-altitude combat and ground support. Introduced in August 1943, it operated in the 8,000- to 11,000-foot altitude range, where it was greatly superior to the German MESSERSCHMITT ME 109G and the FOCKE-WULF FW 190A. Its flying characteristics, as was true with other Yak fighters, were superlative. It was powered by a 1,222-horsepower V-12 engine; its top speed was 403 miles per hour. It was armed with one 20-mm. cannon and two 12.7-mm. machine guns. Dimensions: wingspan, 30 feet 2¼ inches; length, 27 feet 10¾ inches; height, 7 feet 10 inches.

YAKOVLEV YAK-9. Essentially a long-range version of the YAK-1 and Yak-7 series, the Yak-9 began operations in the area around STALINGRAD in October 1942. Two variants appeared in 1943. They were the Yak-9D (D indicating *dalnii,* or long-range), a Yak-9 with even greater range, and the Yak-9T (*tyazholy,* or heavy), so named because of the 37-mm. antitank cannon it carried. A later model, the Yak-9K, which carried a 45-mm. cannon, was flown successfully in 1943. Another variant was the Yak-9M, which carried two 12.7-mm. machine guns and a hub-mounted 20-mm. cannon. Well over half of the 30,000 Yak fighters built were Yak-9s. It was popular with the pilots and was an extremely effective combat plane. The Yak-9T, a close-support aircraft, was powered by a 1,260-horsepower V-12 engine and flew at a top speed of 364 miles per hour. Dimensions: wingspan, 32 feet 9¾ inches; length, 28 feet ½ inch; height, 8 feet.

Yakovlev Yak-9

YAKOVLEV YAK-9U. One of the first Soviet planes to compare favorably with contemporary Western aircraft. Though a part of the Yak series, it was virtually a new aircraft. It was an all-metal, more powerful fighter, powered by a 1,620-horsepower V-12 engine. It was armed with a hub-firing 20-mm. cannon and two 12.7-mm. machine guns and could carry two bombs. It was put into operation in late 1944 and was used until the early 1950s.

YALTA CONFERENCE. On February 4, 1945, the second meeting of the Allied Big Three—President Franklin D. ROOSEVELT, Prime Minister Winston S. CHURCHILL and Premier Joseph STALIN—opened at Yalta, a resort city in the Crimea about 30 miles southeast of Sevastopol. In the 14 months since the TEHERAN CONFERENCE, when the three first came together, the war picture had changed greatly. Victory in Europe was at hand, and the principal questions to be answered were more political than military. The Yalta Conference, code-named Argonaut by the British and Americans, was preceded by U.S.–British staff discussions at Malta, January 30–February 2. (These discussions bore the code name Cricket; the Yalta talks proper were called Magneto, both phases being considered part of the overall Argonaut operation by the planners.)

Although Churchill and Roosevelt had for some time felt that a meeting of the Big Three was necessary, it had for various reasons been deferred, one factor being the opening of a new U.S. Congress and the fourth-term inauguration of the President. After considerable discussion, the rather remote meeting place was agreed upon; Stalin insisted that his doctors would not allow him to leave the Soviet Union. With some reluctance the Western leaders acceded, largely because urgent and controversial problems demanded attention on the highest levels.

These included questions relating to Poland; to Germany, whose defeat seemed imminent; to the smaller states of southeastern Europe, through which the Red Army had moved or was moving; to the Soviet Union's part in the war against Japan; and to the establishment of the UNITED NATIONS ORGANIZATION.

Poland received a great deal of attention, since to the Russians it was a matter of prime interest (this is not to say that the British, who had gone to war in 1939 as the result of a guarantee to Poland, took Polish problems lightly). The Western Allies recognized the Polish government-in-exile that had been set up in London early in the war; the Russians had recently recognized the provisional government created by the Committee of National Liberation, composed of Poles who were Communist leaders (*see* LUBLIN COMMITTEE). The Lublin Poles supported the Soviet claim to most of the territory assigned to the Soviet Union by the SOVIET-GERMAN BOUNDARY AND FRIENDSHIP TREATY in 1939. The Russians succeeded in winning Western agreement to their claim, Poland to be compensated at the expense of Germany by moving the German-Polish boundary westward to the Oder-Neisse line, though the precise western boundary was not drawn at the conference (*see* NEISSE RIVER). Since Poland was completely within the Soviet military sphere, the Western Allies had little leverage, whatever they might have wished to do, particularly with respect to the composition of the Polish Government—although the conference did agree that the Lublin government should be reorganized "on a broader democratic basis," including members of the London government. The exact composition of the Polish Government was left to a three-power committee, headed by Soviet Foreign Minister V. M. MOLOTOV, to decide. This step, said Stalin and Molotov, would be followed by free elections as soon as all of Poland was liberated; the Russians, to use the idiom of a later day, stonewalled all Anglo-American questions as to the supervision and conduct of these elections. In the months following the conference, no progress was made toward this "democratic" government, while the Russians took complete control of Poland.

With respect to Germany, the conference reaffirmed the policy of UNCONDITIONAL SURRENDER and reached agreement on controlling the country following the surrender. Each of the three victorious powers was to have its own zone of occupation; an ALLIED CONTROL COUNCIL was to deal with matters affecting Germany as a whole; Berlin was to be a jointly controlled special zone. After some discussion during the conference, Stalin agreed with the Anglo-American request that France too should have a zone, though none of it should come from the zone assigned to the Soviet Union. The questions of dismembering Germany, of extracting reparations from her and of the punishment of war criminals were left for decision at lower levels since there was little consensus in these areas.

The Big Three took some cognizance of the unsettled situations in various smaller countries from which the Germans had been or were being driven, but to little practical effect. The United States and Britain continued predominant in Italy, the Soviet Union in the Balkans, except for GREECE. The conference did adopt a rather hopeful American statement of principles, called the Declaration on Liberated Europe, designed to allay Western fears that representative democratic governments in the smaller countries were being aborted before they could emerge.

Of paramount importance to the United States was Soviet entry into the war against Japan, and to secure this the Americans were prepared to make some concessions. (The ATOMIC BOMB, then only a theory, appears to have played no part at all in the American thinking.) Stalin reaffirmed his promise, given at Teheran, to enter the war against Japan, stating that Russia would do so about three months after the defeat of Germany. As prizes of victory, the Russians were promised the return of territories they had lost in the Russo-Japanese War of 1904–5; further, they were to receive concessions (Port Arthur, Manchurian railways) that infringed on Chinese sovereignty. They were also given guarantees that the status quo in the pro-Soviet Mongolian People's Republic would be maintained.

These agreements were embodied in an accord on the Far East, which was signed along with the other accords that were arrived at during the conference but was not made public. There were obvious reasons for this secrecy, such as the need to protect Soviet preparations for the attack on Japan. The sievelike security conditions in Chungking may well have made it inadvisable to include the Chinese in the secret, but at the same time the Western Allies were bargaining away China's property without consulting her. Ever since, as the historian Herbert Feis has written, "the secrecy has caused the agreement to be regarded in a sinister light. Undoubtedly this is one of the reasons why . . . its importance has been so exaggerated in public controversy." This controversy was particularly strong in the early years of the Cold War, when opponents of the American Democratic administrations sought to give the word "Yalta" the emotive power of "Munich."

Secrecy also caused a problem in another area, that of the proposed new world organization, the United Nations. The statesmen at Yalta took up questions that had been left unresolved at the DUMBARTON OAKS CONFERENCE, particularly that of the veto and that of voting strength (membership) in the planned General Assembly. The United States proposed that a major power have the right to veto sanctions against itself, and the Russians agreed. (In the face of Anglo-American demands, Stalin agreed that the veto would not apply in procedural matters as opposed to substantive ones.) In SAN FRANCISCO, Molotov reneged on this agreement, but Harry HOPKINS in his last trip to Moscow in June persuaded Stalin to overrule his Foreign Minister and reaffirm the previous agreement.) Stalin demanded that the Ukraine and Byelorussia be admitted to the Assembly, thus giving the Soviet Union three votes instead of one. (This proposal, scaled down from the 16 votes Molotov had asked for at Dumbarton Oaks, was in some measure a Soviet countermove to American advocacy of membership for six Latin-American countries not at war with the Axis.) Roosevelt was dedicated to the creation of an effective international organization and finally, though with reluctance, acquiesced; his agreement was predicated on British and Soviet promises of support, if necessary, for an equivalent three votes for the United States in the Assembly. (For a time he had angrily talked to his advisers of demanding 48 votes for the United States.) However, the President asked that his decision be kept secret for the present, presumably until he could deal with it politically at home, but before the end of the month the story was out. Although the decision was not really of much substantive significance, the fact of the secrecy made a bad impression in some quarters. Critics demanded to know what other secret agreements had been made at Yalta.

During a banquet on February 8 at which he was host, Marshal Stalin offered a prophetic response to a toast. He observed that it was easy for allies to maintain unity during a war but that "the difficult task came after the war when diverse interests tended to divide the allies." He added that he was sure that the "present alliance would meet this test." But a dispassionate look backward at Yalta suggests that the "diverse interests" were already well advanced—as in Poland—and that sentiments and agreements could have little effect unless they were in accordance with the realities of power and the divergent aims of Russia and the Western world. **T.P.**

YAMAGUCHI, Tamon (1892–1942). A graduate of the Japanese Naval Academy in 1912 and the Naval War College in 1925, Yamaguchi was considered one of the most brilliant officers in the Japanese Navy. He was promoted to rear admiral in 1938 and in 1940 was made commanding officer of the Second Carrier Division, which he led in the PEARL HARBOR attack, the operations in the Indian Ocean and in the Battle of MIDWAY. When the two carriers under his command were destroyed at Midway, he refused to leave his flagship, the HIRYU, and went down with her. He was posthumously promoted to vice-admiral.

YAMAGUMO. Japanese ASASHIO-class destroyer that sank the American submarine SCULPIN in an unusual (and utterly one-sided) surface gunfire duel on the night of November 18–19, 1943. *Yamagumo* saved the survivors. She herself was sunk in the Surigao Strait fighting (*see* LEYTE GULF) on October 25,1944.

YAMAMOTO, Isoruku (1884–1943). The son of a schoolmaster, Yamamoto graduated from the Japanese Naval Academy in 1904, just in time to fight as an ensign aboard the cruiser *Nishin* in the Russo-Japanese War. He lost two fingers of his left hand in battle. At the end of World War I he went to the United States, studying at Harvard and also independently. After his return to Japan he was dean of the Kasumigaura Air Training School, 1924–25. He then returned briefly to the United States as naval attaché in Washington. Largely responsible for the development of Japan's naval air forces in the 1920s and '30s, Yamamoto won considerable international mention and prestige at home in 1935 when he successfully fought against the extension of limitations on the Japanese fleet at the London Naval Conference.

As Commander in Chief of the COMBINED FLEET from 1939 until his death in 1943, Admiral Yamamoto was the person most responsible for Japanese naval strategy. Noted as a master games player—including bridge and poker—he conceived the plan of the attack on PEARL HARBOR, though he was not in fact in favor of war with the United States. He seems to have approached the war with a kind of fatalism. He was convinced that Japan's only chance to win was to cripple the U.S. Pacific Fleet, seize as much of the Pacific as possible and then sue for an early peace. When this was not forthcoming, he went on with his duties as effectively as possible.

Admiral Yamamoto (official portrait), 1943

On April 18, 1943, while Yamamoto was on an inspection tour in the Solomons, his plane was ambushed by U.S. P-38s; either Capt. Thomas G. LANPHIER or Lt. Rex T. BARBER is considered to have shot down the BETTY bomber carrying the admiral. Thus, as a direct result of the Americans having broken the Japanese naval code some time before, the Japanese Navy lost its chief strategist. His loss was equivalent to the loss of a great battle.

YAMASHIRO. Japanese FUSO-class battleship. She differed somewhat in appearance from her sister ship *Fuso;* like her, she was sunk in the Surigao Strait phase of the battle for LEYTE GULF.

YAMASHITA, Tomoyuki (1885–1946). After graduating from the Japanese War College in 1916, Yamashita served in various influential posts in the Army, including staff, command and attaché duties (Switzerland, Germany and Austria), and he was commander of an infantry brigade in Korea in 1937.

Known as an able strategist, General Yamashita was made commanding general of the 25th Army in 1941. Landing on December 8, 1941, at two places in southern Thailand and one in northern Malaya, the 25th Army began a march south which lasted nine weeks and ended in the unconditional surrender of SINGAPORE on February 15, 1942. In July 1942 Yamashita was named Commanding General, 1st Area Army, a geographical entity situated in the northeastern quarter of

Manchuria. He remained in Manchuria until the fall of 1944. On October 5, owing to the critical situation which was beginning to face Japan, and in view of the importance attached to the PHILIPPINES, the highly regarded general was made responsible for their defense. For this effort he was named commander of the 14th Area Army, under the direction of the Southern Area Army.

In spite of a tenacious defense and great tactical flexibility, Yamashita was unable to retain control of the Philippines. LEYTE was invaded by U.S. forces on October 20, 1944; effective Japanese resistance ended there by December 25. Luzon was invaded on January 9, 1945. Japanese resistance was steadfast, but MANILA fell after a month, though only after being reduced to rubble in desperate house-to-house fighting. A fanatical defense also continued on CORREGIDOR until February 26. The formal end to Pacific hostilities occurred while fighting was still going on in the Philippines; in spite of the disarray of Yamashita's army, his troops had continued their efforts in the highlands of Luzon and elsewhere. On September 2 General Yamashita was taken to Baguio, where he signed the instrument of surrender.

Although he pleaded not guilty, denying that he knew of atrocities committed in his command, Yamashita was tried and convicted on charges of being a war criminal in a trial that has been controversial ever since. On February 23, 1946, he was hanged.

General Yamashita

YAMATO. Class of Japanese battleships, of more than 72,000 tons, with nine 18.1-inch guns. The most powerful battleships ever built, *Yamato* and MUSASHI had the heaviest guns ever mounted in a warship (the Royal Navy had used a few 18-inch guns during World War I), with protection to match and a speed of 27-plus knots. Their existence and characteristics were kept highly secret, and the true caliber of their main battery was apparently not known by the Allies until after the Pacific war had ended. Designed for ship-for-ship superiority over any enemy battleship they might encounter, the Yamato class had a highly distinctive appearance, with a massive tower foremast and a sharply raked stack and mainmast. As completed in 1941–42, they had a secondary battery consisting of four 6.1-inch triple turrets, removed early from MOGAMI-class cruisers when they were rearmed with 8-inch guns. As the war went on, two of these were removed and the antiaircraft batteries were greatly augmented.

Both ships were war losses; *Musashi* was sunk by prolonged air attack during the battle for LEYTE GULF, and *Yamato* was similarly lost during a suicide mission toward Okinawa in April 1945. A third ship, SHINANO, was completed as a carrier; a fourth was scrapped on the building ways early in the war.

YANK. Founded in April 1942, by Col. Hyman Munson of the Special Service Division, as a magazine for and by the U.S. enlisted soldier, *Yank* had 15 editions printed weekly in 12 plants scattered across the globe from Britain to Honolulu. The magazine's main office was in New York. There a U.S. edition was published; rotogravure, offset and letterpress pages prepared for overseas editions; and correspondents dispatched to every theater of war. The material in *Yank* came from two sources—the magazine's own soldier correspondents, photographers and artists, and enlisted contributors on every front who wrote and sketched without pay. A lead feature of *Yank* was its "Mail Call" department, which served as a sounding board for soldiers' complaints and suggestions, and which evolved into a reference service for answering questions on every subject of interest to a soldier from the new GI BILL OF RIGHTS to obtaining better allotments for dependents. The result of all this was an impressionistic, sometimes irreverent magazine purportedly written in the soldier's idiom but of some literary merit. It ceased publication in 1945, as soon as the war came to an end.

YAP. After TRUK became unusable, Yap was the major Japanese naval base in the Central Pacific. Lying between ULITHI and PELELIU, Yap was bypassed when, after Ulithi was secure, the U.S. 1st Marine Division landed at Peleliu on September 15, 1944.

YARNELL, Harry Erwin (1875–1959). An 1897 graduate of the U.S. Naval Academy, Yarnell spent much of his career in the Far East. Promoted to admiral in 1928, he commanded the U.S. Asiatic Fleet in 1936–39. In this position he protected U.S. rights against Japanese aggression in the Far East, but avoided open combat. Thanks greatly to his efforts, the United States received an indemnity for the Japanese sinking of the gunboat *Panay* on the Yangtze River in 1937. Yarnell participated in an organization called the Committee for Non-Participation in Japanese Aggression. Although retired before the outbreak of World War II, Yarnell was twice recalled to active duty. A notable contribution was his report on the command structure of the Navy.

Yamato sinks under heavy bomb and torpedo attack

Y DAY. In the planning of Operation Overlord (the INVASION of Normandy), the date on which preparations had to be complete. It was fixed for June 1, 1944.

YEFREMOV (Efremov), Mikhail G. (1897–1942). Yefremov entered Soviet military service in 1917 as a member of the Red Guards. After a number of command assignments including the Volga, Transcaucasian, Transbaikal and Orel Military Districts, he was assigned to the Office of the Infantry Inspectorate as first deputy inspector general. In 1941 he commanded the Twenty-first and then the Thirty-third Armies as a lieutenant general in the defense of Moscow. In April 1942 the Thirty-third Army along with other units was operating in the rear of the German Army Group Center. Yefremov, wounded, was surrounded in the vicinity of Vyazma, near SMOLENSK. To prevent being taken by the Germans, he committed suicide (April 9, 1942). *See also* SOVIET-GERMAN OPERATIONS.

YENAN. Headquarters of the Chinese Communist Party from 1935 to 1946. Until 1935 Yenan was a small provincial town in northern China. As the de facto capital of Chinese Communism, as well as the headquarters of the Eighth Route Army, the military arm of the party, it became a symbol of determined resistance for many Chinese. In this city of caves, a generation of military and political cadres was schooled in MAO TSE-TUNG's tactics of guerrilla warfare.

YEO-THOMAS, Forest Frederick (1902–1974). British secret agent, best known as the White Rabbit, who worked with FRENCH RESISTANCE groups. In 1944, on his third tour in France, he was betrayed, captured by the Germans and forced to undergo severe torture in unsuccessful attempts to extort information from him. Transferred to BUCHENWALD, he escaped in April 1945.

YEREMENKO (Eremenko), Andrei I. (1892–1970). Yeremenko, a cavalry officer, entered the Red Army in 1918 after service as a Czarist NCO in World War I. In 1939 he commanded the 6th Cossack Division, which took part in the occupation of Poland, and in 1940–41 he commanded the 1st Special Red Banner Division in the Far East. When the Germans invaded Russia he was transferred, first to the Western and then to the newly formed Bryansk Front (August 1941). By mid-October his forces were the focal point of the German drive on Moscow. Both Yeremenko and KONEV were subsequently criticized by ZHUKOV for allowing a breakthrough on the common boundary of their fronts, which threatened the capital. Yeremenko was assigned to command the Fourth Assault Army in late 1941 and held this post until he was given command of the newly formed Southeast Front (later expanded to include the Stalingrad Front). With Nikita KHRUSHCHEV as the political member of the military council, he remained in this position until December. Yeremenko subsequently commanded the Southern and Kalinin Fronts (1942–43) and took part in the liberation of the CRIMEA as the commander of the Special Baltic Front. From March 1945 he commanded the Fourth Ukrainian Front during the drive into Czechoslovakia. His highest wartime rank was general of army. *See also* SOVIET-GERMAN OPERATIONS.

Y GERÄT (Y Apparatus). German radio-beam device for guidance of aircraft at night—a later development than X GERÄT. Bombers carrying special repeater-transmitters had their courses plotted even at very long range by means of Y Gerät, which could then give instructions for alterations in course as needed and for bombing. Later in the war Y Gerät was also used for the guidance of home defense night fighters.

YOKOSUKA. Japanese naval base in Tokyo Bay.

YONAI, Mitsumasa (1880–1948). In 1936–37 Admiral Yonai was Commander in Chief of the Japanese COMBINED FLEET. After serving as Navy Minister in the Hayashi, KONOYE and HIRANUMA cabinets (1937–39), he was named to the Supreme War Council. He served as Prime Minister from January to July 1940. Opposed to an alliance with Germany and Italy and favorable to reaching a *modus vivendi* with the United States, Yonai was ousted as Prime Minister by TOJO and his supporters. Yonai was one of the leading government critics who forced Tojo out of the office in July 1944, and he held the post of Navy Minister in the subsequent KOISO, SUZUKI, HIGASHIKUNI and Shidehara cabinets (1944–45).

YONTAN AIRFIELD. One of the primary objectives in the April 1, 1945, American landing on OKINAWA, Yontan airfield lay just off the Hagushi beaches on the west coast of the island.

YORCK VON WARTENBURG, Peter, Count (1904–1944). Yorck, descendant of the Prussian General Yorck of the Napoleonic Wars, was, with Count Helmuth von MOLTKE, founder of the KREISAU CIRCLE of German opponents of Hitler. Arrested in the BENDLERSTRASSE on July 20, 1944, Yorck was hanged on August 8, 1944. *See also* OPPOSITION TO HITLER.

YORKTOWN, U.S.S. Aircraft carrier and class, of 19,000 tons, 809 feet 6 inches long, with a capacity of more than 80 planes. *Yorktown* and ENTERPRISE were involved in the Pacific war from the outset. *Yorktown* was at the CORAL SEA. Damaged, she was quickly patched up in time for MIDWAY. Here, with *Enterprise* and HORNET, a slightly modified near-sister, she helped win a decisive victory. Again damaged, she was finally sent to the bottom by Japanese submarine torpedoes.

A second *Yorktown,* one of the ESSEX class, commissioned in 1943 and served well through the end of the Pacific war. She continued on active duty for years afterward. Much modernized, and bearing little resemblance to her World War II self, she is on display at Charleston, S.C.

YOSHIKAWA, Takeo (1912–). Yoshikawa contributed significantly to the successful Japanese attack on PEARL HARBOR by providing valuable information on the harbor facilities, on the movement, number and kind of American ships and on American defense capabilities. Adopting the alias Tadashi Morimura, Yoshikawa studied at Nippon University, passed the foreign service examination and departed for Hawaii in late March 1941. Officially employed as a minor functionary by the Japanese consul general, Nagao KITA, Yoshikawa spent all his time gathering information on Pearl Harbor until his arrest on December 7, 1941.

YUBARI. Completed in 1923, this unusual Japanese ship displaced only about 3,100 tons but was armed with six cruiser-weight 5.5-inch guns and four 24-inch torpedo tubes, and was classed as a light cruiser. Experience gained in her design and construction was valuable in building later 8-inch-gun cruisers. *Yubari* was sunk by an American submarine in April 1944.

YUDACHI. A Japanese SHIRATSUYU-class destroyer, lost in the cruiser battle at GUADALCANAL on the night of November 13–14, 1942.

YUGUMO. Class of Japanese destroyers, a development of the KAGERO class with six 5-inch guns and eight 24-inch torpedo tubes. Like their predecessors, they proved useful and effective ships. Their 5-inch guns could elevate to 75 degrees, giving them a greater antiaircraft capability than the ASASHIOS or Kageros. Various combinations of increased light antiaircraft guns and antisubmarine weapons were installed during the Pacific war. Twenty-eight Yugumos were projected, but the last eight were canceled before being laid down; all of the completed ships of this class were war losses.

YUNAGI. Japanese KAMIKAZE-class destroyer that figured in the Battle of SAVO ISLAND, August 9, 1942. She was completed in 1925; she displaced 1,270 tons and carried four 4.7-inch guns. *Yunagi* was sunk by the U.S. submarine PICUDA in August 1944.

YUNNAN. A province in southwest China, important as a communications link between Chinese provinces to the northeast and BURMA. Considerations of strategy dictated Yunnan as a logical area for CHINA-BURMA-INDIA THEATER training facilities and supply depots: the airlift over the Himalayan HUMP terminated in Yunnan (Kunming), as did the BURMA ROAD and the Yunnan–Indochina railway. Japanese forces penetrated Yunnan as far north as the SALWEEN RIVER after their 1942 capture of Burma, but were evicted by the Chinese during May and June 1944.

Z

Z. Japanese code name for the attack on PEARL HARBOR, December 7 (8), 1941. "Z" was a code flag originally used by Admiral Togo at Tsushima in the Russo-Japanese War. It meant: "The fall and rise of the Empire depends upon the outcome of this sea battle. Everyone shall do his utmost." Prior to World War II, Admiral YAMAMOTO decided to use this famous code in the forthcoming war. In fact, it was used not only in the Pearl Harbor attack but in some other sea battles, such as the MARIANAS and LEYTE GULF.

ZAKHAROV, Georgi F. (1897–1957). Zakharov served as a Czarist junior infantry officer in World War I and entered the Red Army in 1918. From 1939 until 1941 he served as chief of staff of the Ural Military District; in mid-1941 he went as chief of staff to the Twenty-second Army in the northern sector of operations. He became General YEREMENKO's chief of staff in the Bryansk Front in the battle for Moscow, then served as deputy commander of the Western Front in December 1941. From April to July 1942 he served in the Caucasus, then again joined Yeremenko, this time as deputy commander of the Southeast Front. General Zakharov thereafter commanded the Fifty-first Army (February–July 1943) and the Second Guards Army from July 1943. After participating in the liberation of the CRIMEA, he was given command of the old Bryansk Front, now called the Second Belorussian Front, in mid-1944. In November 1944 ROKOSSOVSKY took Zakharov's command and Zakharov was moved to the Fourth Guards Army in Hungary. In January 1945 he was appointed deputy commander of the Fourth Ukrainian Front, where he remained until the end of the war. His highest rank was general of army.

ZAKHAROV, Matvey V. (1898–1972). After taking part in the Bolshevik Revolution, Zakharov entered the Red Army in April 1918 as an artillery officer. By June 1941 he had advanced to the rank of major general and was assigned duties with the Rear Services Directorate in Moscow. He subsequently served as chief of staff of a number of fronts, primarily working with Marshal KONEV. Zakharov, who reached the rank of general of army, was assigned to the Transbaikal Front after the defeat of Germany, and was named a HERO OF THE SOVIET UNION for his service against the Japanese.

ZAMBOANGA. Town at the southern tip of the Zamboanga Peninsula ("where the monkeys have no tails") of southwestern MINDANAO in the PHILIPPINES. Japanese naval troops occupied the area on March 2, 1942. It was reoccupied on March 10, 1945, by the U.S. 41st Division. By the beginning of April effective Japanese resistance in the mountains to the north had ended. Meanwhile, American engineers had opened an airfield near Zamboanga on March 15, a field vitally important to the support of subsequent operations along the Sulu Archipelago and in the Netherlands East Indies.

ZANUSSI, Giacomo (1894–1966). Italian Army officer who as chief of staff to Gen. Mario ROATTA participated in the negotiations with the Allies in August and September 1943. Zanussi, a brigadier general, tried unsuccessfully to ensure that the setting of the date of the proposed armistice would not be left in Allied hands and to get the Allies to agree to carry out a landing north of Rome that would protect the capital from the Germans.

ZEIDLITZ. Code name for German operations against Soviet PARTISANS.

ZEITZLER, Kurt (1895–1963). German Army officer who in the autumn of 1942 succeeded Gen. Franz HALDER as Chief of the General Staff. A much younger man, Zeitzler had been a regimental colonel just before the war. In 1940 he was chief of staff of General von KLEIST's panzer group, a post in which he distinguished himself by his logistical planning in connection with the panzer dash across northern France. In 1942 Zeitzler was chief of staff to Field Marshal von RUNDSTEDT, Commander in Chief West. When Adolf HITLER dismissed Halder with the observation that "we need National Socialist ardor now, not professional ability," he was expressing his distaste for Halder's repeated criticisms of the STALINGRAD campaign; the younger Zeitzler presumably would be more pliant, an expectation that proved true only briefly, since the weakness of the German position was apparent. Zeitzler soon was trying to persuade Hitler not to leave the SIXTH ARMY exposed in Stalingrad. Hitler ignored the Chief of Staff, and relations between the two became more and more distant. Several times Zeitzler tried to resign, his request finally being granted in June 1944 "without the right to wear the uniform." He was succeeded by Gen. Heinz GUDERIAN.

ZEMKE, Hubert A. (1914–   ). Commander of the 56th Fighter Group, U.S. Army Air Forces, which fought in the European theater and boasted 47 ACES, each of whom destroyed five or more enemy planes in aerial combat. Among these aces were Maj. Robert S. JOHNSON, Maj. Walker M. MAHURIN and Lt. Col. Francis S. GABRESKI, who together accounted for 94¾ victories. Colonel Zemke himself had received credit for downing 17¾ (revised) planes before his P-51 broke up in a storm on October 31, 1944, and he became a prisoner. During the European campaign the group's P-47s destroyed 1,006½ German aircraft, 671½ in the air and the rest on the ground.

ZERO. *See* A6M.

ZERSTÖRER (Destroyer). The Luftwaffe's term for a long-range strategic fighter. The MESSERSCHMITT ME 110 twin-engine fighter was designed for this role, at which it proved a conspicuous failure.

ZERVAS, Napoleon (1891–1957). As the leader of the Greek Republican Guard, Zervas was forced out of the Greek Army in 1926 and then in 1933 exiled to France for political activities. In 1938 he returned to Athens and four years later joined the guerrilla band EDES (Greek National Democratic Army), which cooperated closely with the British in fighting the Nazis. When not fighting the Germans, the EDES frequently fought the leftist partisans belonging to the ELAS (National Popular Liberation Army). Following the liberation of Greece, civil war between these two rival groups broke out. The ELAS eventually drove the EDES to a refuge on the island of Corfu. From there General Zervas's rightist force regrouped and returned to the mainland, gradually achieving political dominance over the ELAS. In early 1947 Zervas took over as Minister of Public Safety and proceeded to harass all leftist groups, including the Communists. *See also* GREECE—CIVIL WAR.

ZHDANOV, Andrei A. (1896–1948). One of the most powerful members of the Soviet Politburo, Zhdanov was Communist Party secretary in LENINGRAD during the first year of the siege (1941–42). He was responsible for a number of emergency measures, the most important of which was the mobilization of the city's population and the subsequent formation of militia units. Though he was not popular with the military, Zhdanov's Draconian policies did prepare the city to meet the prolonged battle. During the rest of the war, Zhdanov served in Moscow. His death in 1948 has been the subject of speculation. The announced cause was a heart attack, but rumors have persisted that he was poisoned. In 1953 the Soviet press attributed his death to what became known as the Kremlin "doctors' plot." Talk of the plot died away, however, after Joseph STALIN died.

ZHITOMIR. Important Ukrainian rail center east of KIEV, taken from the Germans by Soviet forces in the November 1943 offensive (November 12), lost again on November 19 under enemy pressure and finally retaken by Soviet forces on December 31.

ZHUKOV, Georgi K. (1896–1974). The son of peasants, Zhukov was conscripted into the Czarist army at the start of World War I and, four years later following the Bolshevik Revolution in 1917, he joined the Red Army in October 1918. Zhukov's entire military career, until he entered the Soviet high command in 1939, was in the cavalry and then in the armored mobile forces.

Zhukov's meteoric rise to fame dates from 1939, when he was sent to command the Soviet troops fighting the Japanese along the Mongolian border in the Far East (*see* SOVIET-JAPANESE BORDER CONFLICT). By January 1941, already Chief of the General Staff, he was involved in organizing Soviet military defenses along the western boundary. Soon after the war began, Stalin sent Zhukov to assist Marshal VOROSHILOV with the defense of LENINGRAD. His next assignment brought him back to Moscow, where he designed the great Soviet counterattack in late 1941. The attack succeeded in driving the Germans back from the gates of Moscow, and they never again threatened the Soviet capital.

Zhukov became the Deputy Supreme Commander of the Red Army in August 1942 and remained in that post until the end of the war. His name was synonymous with the historic Battles of Moscow and STALINGRAD, as well as with the final Soviet push across Poland into Germany, where he led the assault on BERLIN.

Marshal Zhukov

However, except for two periods of field command in early 1944 and the last six months of the war, Zhukov spent most of this time with Stalin at Supreme Headquarters in Moscow, helping the Generalissimo develop strategic plans for the war. From time to time Zhukov traveled to various battle sectors, issuing orders and coordinating local movements. He was generally regarded by both Soviet and Allied military observers as a decisive and innovative commander, one who did not hesitate to punish incompetence or to reward excellence on the part of his subordinates.

During the war Zhukov's popularity was second only to Stalin's, but soon afterward and throughout the last years of Stalin's reign Zhukov suffered political eclipse and his name was deleted from the annals of the war. Subsequently his prestige was restored.

ZIEGENBERG. An estate near Bad Neuheim, northeast of Frankfurt, site of elaborate headquarters built for Adolf HITLER in 1939. It was his intention to direct operations in the west from Ziegenberg, but, according to Albert SPEER, he "abruptly decided that the place was too luxurious for him." In 1944, from a headquarters near Ziegenberg, Hitler temporarily directed the ARDENNES offensive.

ZIEGLER, Heinz (1894–1964). German Army officer (General der Artillerie, 1944) who served as deputy commander to Gen. Jürgen von ARNIM in TUNISIA in 1942–43 and later commanded the Fourteenth Army in ITALY.

ZIP. Signal used by British commanders to denote the start of an operation.

Z-LIGHTER. A British 134-foot, engines-aft harbor landing craft with a bow ramp, somewhat resembling an LCT in appearance (*see* LCT). It was used in the Mediterranean for shuttling troops, vehicles and cargo from ships to beaches, and was primarily intended for use as a utility craft rather than for assault landings.

ZOSSEN. Site of German Army headquarters southeast of Berlin.

Z PLAN. Drawn up in 1938 and adopted in January 1939, this German plan called for the German Navy to approach the British Navy in strength by 1944–45. It was predicated on the maintenance of peace during the period.

ZUCKERMAN, Solly, 1st Baron (1904–). British scientist who was a consultant to various British and Allied headquarters, notably on the effects of bombing. He was particularly involved in the development of the TRANSPORTATION PLAN for disrupting German railway traffic in the INVASION area of France in 1944.

ZUIHO. Japanese SHOHO-class light aircraft carrier. Completed in late 1940, she had been begun as a submarine tender named *Takasaki* but was converted and renamed during construction. *Zuiho* served through nearly three years of the Pacific war before being lost in the battle for LEYTE GULF; her antiaircraft battery was considerably increased during the war. *Zuiho* was 712 feet long, displaced over 13,000 tons and had an operating capacity of 30 aircraft.

ZUIKAKU. Japanese SHOKAKU-class aircraft carrier. After taking part in most of the major campaigns in the Pacific war, *Zuikaku* was lost during the battle for LEYTE GULF.

Glossary of Terms and Abbreviations

World War II gave rise to an enormous number of positions, commands, area designations, devices and other new entities for which, of necessity, acronyms or other shortened names were created. The reader of the literature of the war will frequently encounter examples of these, as well as abbreviations of previously existing organizations and other entities (for example, RN for Royal Navy). Likewise, many unabbreviated terms that may be unfamiliar, particularly German words, occur in World War II texts. This glossary gives brief definitions of abbreviations and terms that do not appear as entries in the main body of this book. It is intended to serve as a convenient reference for general World War II reading.

AA	Antiaircraft
AAA	Antiaircraft artillery
AAF	Allied Air Forces
AAI	Allied Armies in Italy
AASC	Allied Air Support Command (Mediterranean)
A/B	Airborne
AB	U.S. Navy ship-type symbol for crane ship, the old battleship *Kearsarge* of 1900 converted to a hulk and fitted with a heavy rotating crane
ABS	British abbreviation for automatic bombsight
ACMF	Allied Central Mediterranean Force
AD	U.S. Navy ship-type symbol for destroyer tender
ADGB	Air Defence of Great Britain
Adler	German code name for a radio set designed for submarine-to-aircraft communication
AE	U.S. Navy ship-type symbol for ammunition ship
AEAF	Allied Expeditionary Air Force (Europe)
AEF	Allied Expeditionary Force
AF	U.S. Navy ship-type symbol for provision storeship, a refrigerated cargo ship
AFD	Mobile floating drydock
AFHQ	Allied Force Headquarters (Mediterranean)
AFPAC	U.S. Army Forces, Pacific
AFV	Armored fighting vehicles
AG	U.S. Navy ship-type symbol for miscellaneous auxiliary, a "catchall" designation
AGC	Amphibious force command ship
AGF	Army Ground Forces (U.S.)
AGP	U.S. Navy ship-type symbol for motor torpedo boat tender
AGS	U.S. Navy ship-type symbol for surveying ship
AIF	Australian Imperial Force
AK	U.S. Navy ship-type symbol for cargo ship
AKS	U.S. Navy ship-type symbol for general stores issue ship
AKV	U.S. Navy ship-type symbol for cargo ship and aircraft ferry
ALFSEA	Allied Land Forces Southeast Asia
AM	U.S. Navy ship-type symbol for minesweeper
AMET	Africa–Middle East Theater
AMLG	Allied Military Headquarters, Greece
AMMISCA	American Military Mission to China
AN	U.S. Navy ship-type symbol for net-laying ship
ANB	U.S. abbreviation for Army-Navy-British, applied to joint material standards
AND	British abbreviation for Admiralty net defence
Anlage	Appendix or annex (Ger.)
AO	U.S. Navy ship-type symbol for oiler
AOC	Air Officer Commanding (U.K.)
AOC-in-C	Air Officer Commanding in Chief (U.K.)
AOG	U.S. Navy ship-type symbol for gasoline tanker
AP	Armor-piercing; aiming point
AP	U.S. Navy ship-type symbol for transport
APB	U.S. Navy ship-type symbol for barrack ship, self-propelled
APD	U.S. Navy ship-type symbol for transport, high speed
ARP	Air raid precautions (U.K.)
ASC	Air Support Command

ASCOM	Army Service Command (U.S.)
A-Stoff	German dichloracetylene rocket fuel
ASV	Air-to-surface vessels, a British designation for an early airborne surface-search radar first tested in 1938
AT	U.S. Navy ship-type symbol for oceangoing tug
ATC	Air Transport Command
AUS	Army of the United States
BB	U.S. Navy ship-type symbol for battleship
BC	Bomber command
BCT	Battalion combat team
CA	U.S. Navy ship-type symbol for heavy cruiser
CACW	Chinese-American Composite Wing
CAD	Civil Affairs Division (SHAEF)
CAI	Chinese Army in India
CAM ship	Catapult-armed merchant ship (U.K.)
CAP	Combat air patrol
CAS	Chief of the Air Staff (U.K.)
CB	Naval construction battalion
CC	Combat command
CCA	Combat Command A
CCB	Combat Command B, etc.
CCS	Combined Chiefs of Staff
CenPac	Central Pacific
CG	Commanding general
CH	Chain Home, name given to early British radar stations
CIGS	Chief of the Imperial General Staff (U.K.)
C-in-C	Commander in Chief
Cinclant	Commander in Chief Atlantic Fleet
Cincmed	Commander in Chief Mediterranean
Cincpac, Cincpoa	Commander in Chief Pacific Fleet, Pacific Ocean Areas
Cincswpa	Commander in Chief Southwest Pacific Area
CL	U.S. Navy ship-type symbol for light cruiser
CM	U.S. Navy ship-type symbol for minelayer
CMF	Citizen Military Forces (New Guinea)
CNO	Chief of Naval Operations (U.S.)
CO	Commanding officer
Comairspac	Commander Air South Pacific
Comgenpoa	Commanding General Pacific Ocean Areas
Cominch	Commander in Chief United States Fleet
Comsopac	Commander in Chief South Pacific
COM Z	Communications zone
COS	Chiefs of Staff (U.K.)
CP	Command post
CV	U.S. Navy ship-type symbol for aircraft carrier
CVE	U.S. Navy ship-type symbol for aircraft carrier, escort
CVL	U.S. Navy ship-type symbol for aircraft carrier, small
DCS	Deputy Chief of Staff
DD	U.S. Navy ship-type symbol for destroyer
DE	U.S. Navy ship-type symbol for destroyer escort
DM	U.S. Navy ship-type symbol for light minelayer
DMS	U.S. Navy ship-type symbol for minesweeper, high speed
Dumbo	Patrol seaplane equipped for rescue
Düppel	German name for Window (radar-jamming metal foil), from the North German town where strips of this substance, dropped by Allied airplanes, were first discovered
EAC	Eastern Air Command (CBI)
Eierhandgranate	German egg grenade
ETO, ETOUSA	European Theater of Operations (U.S.)
FA	Field Artillery
FAAA	First Allied Airborne Army
Fall	Literally, case; the term used by the Germans for a military operation

Fallschirm	Parachute (Ger.)
FEAF	Far East Air Force
FEC	French Expeditionary Force
FF	Free French
FFI	Forces Françaises de l'Intérieur
FFO	Forces Françaises de l'Ouest
Flugabwehrkanone (flak)	Antiaircraft cannon (Ger.)
FMF	Fleet Marine Force
Führungsgruppe	Operations group (Ger.)
Führungsstab	Operations staff (Ger.)
FUSAG	First U.S. Army Group (paper organization designed to deceive the Germans before the 1944 invasion)
Gen.St.d.H.	Generalstab des Heeres (General Staff of the Army) (Ger.)
Geschwader	Wing (i.e., a group) of airplanes (Ger.)
G-5	Civil Affairs Division of SHAEF
GHQ	General headquarters
GOC	General Officer Commanding (U.K.)
GOC-in-C	General Officer Commanding in Chief (U.K.)
GP	U.S. abbreviation of general purpose, used with reference to bombs
GQG	Grand Quartier Générale (French HQ)
HE	High explosive
Heeresgruppe	Army group (Ger.)
HMAS	His Majesty's Australian Ship
HMCS	His Majesty's Canadian Ship
HMNZS	His Majesty's New Zealand Ship
HMS	His Majesty's Ship (Royal Navy)
HNMS	Her Netherlands Majesty's Ship
IBT	India-Burma Theater
IJN	Imperial Japanese Navy
JCS	Joint Chiefs of Staff
Jinking	Evasive swerving maneuver practiced by aircraft
JPS	Joint Staff Planners (U.S.)
JSM	Joint Staff Mission (British mission to Washington)
Kampfgruppe	Battle group (Ger.)
Kriegsmarine	German Navy
KTB	Kriegstagebuch (war diary) (Ger.)
LRP	Long-range penetration
MAAF	Mediterranean Allied Air Forces
MAC	Marine Amphibious Corps (U.S.)
MAC ship	Merchant aircraft carrier (U.K.)
MAD	Magnetic anomaly detection; airborne device capable of detecting the magnetic field present around the steel hull of a submarine
MAG	Marine Aviation Group (U.S.)
Marshmallow	"Torpedo track sighted" (U.S. Navy)
MATAF	Mediterranean Allied Tactical Air Force
ME	Middle East
MEDCOS	Chiefs of Staff, Mediterranean (U.K.)
MEF	Middle East Forces
MG	Machine gun; military government
MGB	British abbreviation for motor gunboat
MTOUSA	Mediterranean Theater of Operations, USA
NAAF	Northwest African Air Force
NATO	North African Theater of Operations
NATOUSA	North African Theater of Operations, USA
Naxos	German submarine-mounted radar search receiver
NCAC	Northern Combat Area Command (Burma)

Ob.d.H.	Oberbefehlshaber des Heeres (Commander in Chief of the Army) (Ger.)
O-Boat	U.S. Navy nickname for old submarines of the World War I o–1 class
Oberkommando	Headquarters of an army or higher military organization (Ger.)
OPD	Operations Division
Op.(H)	Operations Abteilung (*H*) (Operations Branch [Army]) (Ger.)
Opnl	Operational
Org.Abt.	Organisations Abteilung (staff section in charge of organization) (Ger.)
OTC	Officer in Tactical Command
Pak	Panzerabwehrkanone; German antitank gun
Panzertruppe	Tank corps (Ger.)
PC	U.S. Navy ship-type symbol for submarine chaser (173 feet)
PCE, PCE(R)	U.S. Navy ship-type symbol for the escort (180 feet) and the escort (rescue) (180 feet)
PCS	U.S. Navy ship-type symbol for submarine chaser (136 feet)
PE	U.S. Navy ship-type symbol for Eagle, the designation applied to subchasers of World War I vintage, familiarly referred to as Eagle Boats
PF	U.S. Navy ship-type symbol for frigate
PG	U.S. Navy ship-type symbol for patrol vessel, gunboat
PGC	Persian Gulf Command
PGM	U.S. Navy ship-type symbol for motor gunboat
PGSC	Persian Gulf Service Command
POA	Pacific Ocean Areas
Potato masher	Popular English-language name for the German Stielhandgranate
PR	U.S. Navy ship-type symbol for river gunboat
PWE	Political Warfare Executive (U.K.)
PY	U.S. Navy ship-type symbol for yacht, used for seagoing yachts taken over for naval patrol work
Pz	Panzer
RAAF	Royal Australian Air Force
RAF	Royal Air Force
RCAF	Royal Canadian Air Force
RCT	Regimental Combat Team
SAC	Supreme Allied Commander
SACMED	Supreme Allied Commander, Mediterranean Theater
Sadir	German name for a submarine detection finder designed to take bearings on the aircraft homing beacons of Allied aircraft carriers
SAP	U.S. and British abbreviation for "semi-armor-piercing," a type of bomb or projectile with a thinner wall than the armor-piercing type, but with heavier explosive weight. (Both the British and the Americans used SAP bombs, but the U.S. did not use SAP gun projectiles.)
SC	U.S. Navy ship-type symbol for submarine chaser
SCAEF	Supreme Commander, Allied Expeditionary Force
SCAP	Supreme Commander, Allied Powers—the title borne by General of the Army Douglas MacArthur as commander of the forces occupying Japan
Schiffsflak	Naval antiaircraft gun (Ger.)
Schnellfeuehkanone	Rapid-fire gun (Ger.)
SEAC	Southeast Asia Command
SFHQ	Special Force Headquarters
SO	Special Operations
SOE	Special Operations Executive (U.K.)
SOPA	Senior Officer Present Afloat
So Pac	South Pacific
SPM	Self-propelled mount
SS	U.S. Navy ship-type symbol for submarine
Staffel	Squadron (Ger.)
SWPA	Southwest Pacific Area
TAF	Tactical Air Force
TD	Tank destroyer
TDC	Torpedo data computer; U.S. Navy term for an electromechanical computer used in submarines to set up a firing solution when attacking with torpedoes
TF	Task force

TG	Task group
TIS	Theater intelligence section
U-Boat	Unterseeboot; German submarine
UDT	Underwater demolition team
UP	Unrotated projectiles (i.e., rockets)
USAAF	U.S. Army Air Forces
USAAFUK	U.S. Army Air Forces in the United Kingdom
USAFBI	U.S. Army Forces, British Isles
USAFFE	U.S. Army Forces, Far East
USAFIA	U.S. Army Forces in Australia
USAFICPA	U.S. Army Forces in Central Pacific Area
USAFIME	U.S. Army Forces in the Middle East
USAFISPA	U.S. Army Forces in the South Pacific Area
USASOS	U.S. Army Services of Supply
USAT	U.S. Army transport; prefix used before the names of Army troop transport ships. The U.S. Army owned and operated a large number of such ships; the Navy also operated them under the designation AP.
USFET	U.S. Forces in the European Theater
USFIA	U.S. Forces in Australia
USFIP	U.S. Forces in the Philippines
USMC	U.S. Marine Corps
USN	U.S. Navy
USSAFE	U.S. Strategic Air Forces in Europe
USSBS	U.S. Strategic Bombing Survey
USSTAF	U.S. Strategic Air Forces
WDAF	Western Desert Air Force (U.K.)
Wehrmachtbefehlshaber	Armed Forces Commander (Ger.)
WFSt	Wehrmachtführungsstab (Armed Forces Operations Staff) (Ger.)

TABLE OF EQUIVALENT RANKS

U.S. and British Armies	**German Army and Air Force**	**German Waffen SS**
None	Reichsmarschall	None
General of the Army (U.S.); Field Marshal (Brit.)	Generalfeldmarschall	Reichsführer SS
General	Generaloberst	Oberstgruppenführer
Lieutenant General	General der Infanterie Artillerie Gebirgstruppen Kavallerie Nachrichtentruppen Panzertruppen Pioniere Luftwaffe Flieger Fallschirmtruppen Flakartillerie Luftnachrichtentruppen	Obergruppenführer
Major General	Generalleutnant	Gruppenführer
Brigadier General (U.S.); Brigadier (Brit.)	Generalmajor	Brigadeführer
None	None	Oberführer
Colonel	Oberst	Standartenführer
Lieutenant Colonel	Oberstleutnant	Obersturmbannführer
Major	Major	Sturmbannführer
Captain	Hauptmann	Hauptsturmführer
Captain (Cavalry)	Rittmeister	
First Lieutenant	Oberleutnant	Obersturmführer
Second Lieutenant	Leutnant	Untersturmführer

Chronology: The War in Synopsis

PRELUDE 1931–1939

1931

September 18	Japanese Kwantung Army seizes Mukden, Manchuria

1933

January 30	Adolf Hitler appointed German Chancellor
October 14	Hitler announces withdrawal of Germany from the League of Nations

1934

June 30	"Night of the Long Knives" in Germany
July 25	Nazis murder Austrian Chancellor Dollfuss
September 19	USSR joins League of Nations

1935

January 13	Voters in Saar plebiscite choose to rejoin Germany
March 16	Hitler decrees universal military service for Germany
May 2	Franco-Soviet Mutual Assistance Pact signed (ratified by France February 26, 1936)
October 3	Italians invade Ethiopia

1936

March 7	Germans reoccupy Rhineland
May 9	End of war in Ethiopia as the country is annexed by Italy
July 17–18	Outbreak of Spanish Civil War
November 25	Anti-Comintern Pact

1937

July 7	Sino-Japanese War begins
December 12	Japanese attack U.S. and British gunboats in Yangtze River, sinking *Panay*
December 13	Japanese take Nanking

1938

March 12	German Anschluss of Austria
July 28	Soviet and Japanese forces fight in Far East
September 29	Munich Conference opens (to September 30)
November 3	Announcement of Japanese "New Order in East Asia"

1939

March 15	Germans enter Prague
23	Germany annexes Memel
28	Madrid falls to Franco forces—end of Spanish Civil War
31	British Government abandons appeasement policy, announces aid to Poland
May 22	Germany and Italy sign "Pact of Steel"
28	New Soviet-Japanese fighting erupts at Khalkhin Gol
August 23	Soviet-German Nonaggression Pact signed

THE WAR 1939–1945

September 1	Germany invades Poland—World War II begins
	Marshall becomes U.S. Army Chief of Staff
3	Britain, France, Australia and New Zealand declare war on Germany
15	Soviet-Japanese Border Conflict ends

17	Soviets move into Poland
29	Soviet-German Boundary and Friendship Treaty signed
November 3	U.S. Congress passes "cash and carry" amendment to Neutrality Laws
30	USSR invades Finland—beginning of Soviet-Finnish (Winter) War
December 17	*Graf Spee* scuttled in Rio de la Plata

1940

March 12	Finland capitulates, ending Soviet-Finnish War
30	Japanese establish puppet Chinese government (Wang Ching-wei) at Nanking
April 9	Germans seize Denmark, invade Norway
14	British forces make landings in Norway
May 2	Allies evacuate Namsos, Norway
10	Germany invades Low Countries
	Chamberlain resigns as British Prime Minister, Churchill forms coalition government
14	Netherlands surrenders
26	Allied evacuation at Dunkirk (to June 4)
28	Belgium capitulates to Germans
June 9	Norway surrenders
10	Italy enters the war
22	France signs armistice with Germany
July 3	British neutralize French fleet (Operation Catapult)
4	Italians invade British Somaliland
18	British close Burma Road
26	First U.S. embargo on war trade with Japan
August 15	Eagle Day—Battle of Britain
September 3	U.S.–British destroyers–bases deal
7	"Blitz" on London begins
13	Italian Army advances into Egypt
22	Japanese forces move into Indochina
27	Japan signs Tripartite Pact
October 18	Burma Road reopened
28	Italians invade Greece
29	British land in Crete
November 3	British land in Greece
5	Roosevelt elected to third term as U.S. President
11	British attack Italian fleet at Taranto
14	Greeks launch counterattack on Italians
December 9	British attack Italians in Western Desert
11	British capture Sidi Barrani

1941

January 19	British advance into Eritrea
22	British capture Tobruk
February 5	British victorious at Beda Fomm
12	Rommel arrives in Tripoli
22	Axis attacks at El Agheila
March 9	Italians attack Greece from Albania
11	U.S. Lend-Lease Act signed
24	Axis (Rommel) takes El Agheila
	British complete clearing of British Somaliland
27	Prince Paul overthrown in Yugoslavia
28	Battle of Cape Matapan
April 3	Rashid Ali coup in Iraq
6	Germans invade Balkans
9	Axis captures Bardia
10	Axis siege of Tobruk begins
13	USSR and Japan sign Neutrality Pact
17	Yugoslavia capitulates
18	British land at Basra
22	British begin withdrawal from Greece
23	Greek Army surrenders to Germans
27	Axis occupies Halfaya Pass
28	Axis takes Sollum

May 2 British complete evacuation from Greece
6 British defeat Iraqi forces at Habbaniya
15 British recapture Sollum
20 Germans invade Crete
22 British withdraw from Crete airfields
27 *Bismarck* sunk
30 Rashid Ali flees Iraq
June 1 British complete evacuation of Crete
8 British and Free French troops invade Syria
15 British launch Operation Battleaxe offensive in Western Desert
17 British withdraw in Western Desert
22 Germany invades USSR
July 1 Wavell appointed British C-in-C India, Auchinleck C-in-C Middle East
U.S. forces begin occupying Iceland
5 Germans complete roundup of 300,000 prisoners west of Minsk
9 Vichy French surrender in Syria
12 (see above)
August 5 Germans eliminate Russian resistance in Smolensk pocket
9 Roosevelt and Churchill meet in Atlantic Conference (to August 12); Atlantic Charter proclaimed
17 Germans take Kiev
25 British and Soviet troops occupy Iran
September 15 Germans complete investment of Leningrad
October 7 Germans take 650,000 prisoners at Vyazma
17 Tojo becomes Premier of Japan
19 Stalin announces state of siege in Moscow
31 U.S. destroyer *Reuben James* sunk by U-boat
November 15 Germans resume drive on Moscow
18 British open Crusader desert offensive
Brooke replaces Dill as British CIGS
30 British Eighth Army links up with Tobruk garrison
December 6 Soviets begin counteroffensive before Moscow
7 Pacific war begins with Japanese attacks on U.S. and British posts (Pearl Harbor, Malaya, etc.) (December 8 west of International Date Line)
8 United States declares war on Japan
10 Siege of Tobruk is lifted
Japanese sink H.M.S. *Prince of Wales* and *Repulse*
Japanese take Guam, make first landings on Luzon
11 Germany and Italy declare war on United States, which takes reciprocal action
16 Japanese invade Borneo
17 Nimitz replaces Kimmel as C-in-C of U.S. Pacific Fleet
19 Hitler assumes personal command of German Army, replacing Brauchitsch
20 King is appointed C-in-C of U.S. Fleet
23 Wake Island falls
24 Arcadia Conference begins in Washington (to January 14)
British reenter Benghazi
25 Hong Kong surrenders to Japanese
31 Allied ABDA Command established under Wavell

1942

January 1 United Nations Declaration signed
4 Japanese begin air attacks on Rabaul
7 Siege of Bataan begins
11 Japanese invade Netherlands East Indies
17 Halfaya garrison surrenders to British
19 Japanese capture Tavoy, Burma
22 In new Axis offensive, Rommel retakes Agedabia
24 U.S. destroyers sink Japanese shipping in Makassar Strait
27 British begin withdrawal from Malay Peninsula to Singapore
February 2 Stilwell designated chief of staff to Chiang Kai-Shek
11 German warships *Scharnhorst, Gneisenau, Prinz Eugen* make dash up English Channel (to February 13)
15 Singapore surrenders to Japanese
22 Roosevelt orders MacArthur to leave Philippines
25 ABDA Command dissolved
27 Fighting in Java Sea ends Allied naval resistance in Netherlands East Indies (to March 1)

March 7	Japanese land in New Guinea
	British Burma Army evacuates Rangoon
9	Japanese secure Java, completing conquest of East Indies
27	British raid Saint-Nazaire
30	MacArthur appointed Supreme Commander SWPA, Nimitz Cincpoa
April 3	Japanese open final Bataan offensive
9	Bataan surrenders
18	U.S. (Doolittle) B-25 raid on Japan
29	Japanese take Lashio, Burma Road terminus
May 4	Battle of the Coral Sea (to May 8)
6	Corregidor surrenders
8	Germans begin preliminary offensives in USSR
12	Russians open Kharkov offensive
17	Germans counterattack in Kharkov area, beginning Battle of Kharkov
20	Japanese complete conquest of Burma
27	Rommel attacks Gazala Line in large-scale Axis offensive
28	Battle of Kharkov ends in Soviet defeat
30	RAF stages 1,000-bomber raid on Cologne
June 3	Battle of Midway (to June 6)
7	Japanese invade western Aleutian Islands
9	Japanese conquest of Philippines completed
17	British withdrawal in Libya leaves Tobruk isolated
18	Churchill arrives in Washington for meetings
21	Tobruk falls to Rommel's forces
28	Axis takes Mersa Matrûh in Egypt
	Germans open summer offensive in USSR
July 1	First battle of El Alamein begins (to July 17)
	Sevastopol falls to German Army Group South
5	Soviet resistance in Crimea ends
8	Germans complete onslaught on Convoy PQ-17 to northern Russia
9	Germans open drives toward Rostov and Stalingrad
24	Rostov taken by German Army Group A
August 7	U.S. 1st Marine Division lands on Guadalcanal
8	Alexander appointed British C-in-C Middle East
	Battle of Savo Island (to August 9)
9	Civil disobedience campaign proclaimed in India
11	U-boats ravage Malta convoy
12	First Moscow Conference (Churchill-Stalin) (to August 15)
17	U.S. Eighth Air Force makes first attack on European target (Rouen-Sotteville)
19	Canadian and British force raids Dieppe
22	Brazil declares war on Germany and Italy
24	Battle of the Eastern Solomons (to August 25)
31	Battle of Alam Halfa (to September 7)
September 6	Germans capture Novorossisk
7	Japanese defeated in Milne Bay area, New Guinea
12	Eisenhower assumes post as C-in-C Allied Expeditionary Force (for Northwest Africa)
	Fighting on Bloody Ridge, Guadalcanal (to September 14)
16	German Army Group B enters suburbs of Stalingrad
25	Allied counteroffensive opens on Papua
October 11	Battle of Cape Esperance (to October 12)
23	Second battle of El Alamein begins (to November 4)
26	Battle of Santa Cruz Islands
November 3	Axis begins retreat at El Alamein
8	Allies land in Northwest Africa (Operation Torch)
9	Germans move into Tunisia
11	French cease resistance in Northwest Africa
	Germans occupy southern France
	British Eighth Army takes Bardia
12	Naval battle of Guadalcanal (to November 15)
13	British take Tobruk
19	Russians open counteroffensive at Stalingrad
22	Red Army units meet at Kalach, encircling German Sixth Army in Stalingrad
30	Battle of Tassafaronga
December 12	Manstein opens counterattack to relieve German Sixth Army
13	Axis begins retreat from Al Agheila

16 Germans abandon attempt to relieve Sixth Army
24 Darlan assassinated in Algiers

1943

January 14 Allied Casablanca Conference begins (to January 23)
15 British Eighth Army opens drive on Tripoli
22 Allies complete victorious Papuan campaign in Sanananda area
February 2 Final German resistance at Stalingrad ends
8 Chindits begin guerrilla warfare in Burma
9 U.S. forces complete Guadalcanal campaign
14 Red Army takes Rostov
19 Axis attacks at Kasserine Pass
March 1 Battle of the Bismarck Sea (to March 4)
9 Von Arnim replaces Rommel as Axis C-in-C in Africa
14 Germans retake Kharkov
16 Convoy battle is climax of Battle of the Atlantic (to March 20)
26 British Eighth Army breaks through Mareth Line
Battle of Komandorski Islands
April 18 U.S. planes shoot down Admiral Yamamoto
19 Rising in Warsaw ghetto
May 7 Allied 18th Army Group captures Tunis and Bizerte
9 Axis forces in northeast Tunisia surrender unconditionally
11 U.S. 7th Division lands on Attu
12 Trident Conference (Anglo-American) begins in Washington (to May 25)
All Axis resistance in North Africa ends
16 RAF Dam Busters attack Möhne and Eder dams
Destruction of Warsaw ghetto completed
26 Katyn massacre revealed
30 Japanese resistance on Attu ends
June 3 French announce creation of Committee of National Liberation
11 Pantelleria surrenders after bombing
30 Operation Cartwheel (Rabaul) launched in Southwest Pacific
July 5 Battle of Kursk (to July 12)
Battle of Kula Gulf (Kolombangara)
10 Allies invade Sicily
12 Red Army opens major attack on Orel salient
Battle of Kolombangara
22 Palermo falls to U.S. Seventh Army
24 Allied bombers incinerate Hamburg (to August 3)
25 Mussolini resigns; Badoglio becomes Italian Prime Minister
August 1 U.S. B-24s bomb Ploesti, Rumania (Operation Tidal Wave)
5 Red Army takes Orel and Belgorod
6 Battle of Vella Gulf (to August 7)
14 First Quebec Conference opens (to August 24)
15 U.S. force invades Kiska
17 U.S. B-17s raid Schweinfurt and Regensburg
Axis resistance ends in Sicily
23 Red Army retakes Kharkov
24 Mountbatten appointed Supreme Allied Commander in Southeast Asia
September 3 Allies land on Italian mainland; Italians surrender
8 Eisenhower announces Italian surrender
9 Allies land at Salerno
10 German forces occupy Rome
21 British midget submarines attack German battleship *Tirpitz*
October 6 Battle of Vella Lavella
12 U.S. Fifth Army attacks across Volturno River
13 Italy declares war on Germany
14 U.S. B-17s suffer heavy losses in raid on Schweinfurt
19 Allied foreign ministers meet in Moscow (to October 30)
31 U.S. 3d Marine Division lands on Bougainville; Battle of Empress Augusta Bay
November 6 Soviets retake Kiev
20 U.S. forces land on Makin and Tarawa
22 Allied Cairo Conference (to November 26)
25 Battle of Cape St. George

28 Allied Big Three begin Teheran Conference (to November 30)
30 Germans defeat Soviets at Korosten
December 1 Allies begin assaults on Winter Line in Italy
3 Allied meetings resume at Cairo (to December 7)
26 *Scharnhorst* sunk off North Cape
U.S. 1st Marine Division lands at Cape Gloucester, New Britain

1944

January 8 Red Army takes Kirovograd
11 Allied air forces begin Operation Pointblank against German aircraft industry and Luftwaffe
16 Eisenhower assumes duties as Supreme Commander, Allied Expeditionary Force
22 U.S. Fifth Army lands at Anzio
27 Leningrad–Moscow railroad is cleared
31 U.S. forces land on Kwajalein (secured February 7)
February 3 Soviet forces trap two German corps at Korsun
4 Japanese launch offensive operation in Arakan (Burma)
13 Combined Chiefs of Staff order intensive bomber offensive against Germany
15 Allies bomb abbey of Monte Cassino
17 U.S. forces land on Eniwetok (secured February 22)
20 "Big Week" of air attacks on Germany opens
29 U.S. Army force lands in Admiralty Islands
March 6 Japanese 15th Army opens offensive toward India
20 Germans occupy Hungary
30 RAF suffers heavy losses in raid on Nuremberg
April 3 British bombing again damages *Tirpitz*
5 U.S. Fifteenth Air Force bombers raid Ploesti, Rumania
9 Japanese invest Imphal, India
22 U.S. forces land in Hollandia area, New Guinea
May 9 Soviets retake Sevastopol
11 Allies open drive on Rome with attack on Gustav Line
18 U.S. forces land on Wakde, off New Guinea
21 Allies begin massive pre-invasion attacks on rail facilities on the Continent
23 U.S. Fifth Army breaks out at Anzio beachhead
27 U.S. Army forces land on Biak
June 4 U.S. Fifth Army enters Rome
6 Allies invade Normandy (Operation Overlord)
13 First V-1 bomb falls on England
15 U.S. marines invade Saipan
19 Battle of the Philippine Sea (Great Marianas Turkey Shoot) (to June 20)
22 Japanese offensive defeated at Imphal
23 Red Army opens summer offensive on central front
July 3 U.S. First Army opens "Battle of the Hedgerows" in Normandy
9 Fighting ends on Saipan
17 Rommel severely wounded in strafing attack, yields army group command in France
18 British Second Army opens offensive in Caen area (Operation Goodwood)
Tojo resigns as Japanese Premier, is subsequently replaced by Koiso
20 German Army officers attempt to assassinate Hitler
21 U.S. marines invade Guam
24 U.S. marines invade Tinian
25 U.S. Third Army breaks out at Saint-Lô (Operation Cobra)
28 Soviets take Brest Litovsk, cross the San River
August 1 U.S. 12th Army Group becomes operational in France
Warsaw Uprising begins
Organized resistance ends on Tinian
3 Myitkyina (Burma) falls to Allies
4 British Eighth Army takes Florence
7 Germans in Normandy begin counterattack toward Avranches
8 Japanese take Hengyang, China
9 Eisenhower establishes HQ in France
10 Organized resistance ends on Guam
12 German counterattack at Avranches ends in failure
15 Allies land in southern France (Operation Dragoon)
19 U.S. Third Army reaches Seine River
20 Canadian First Army forces seal Germans in Falaise-Argentan pocket

Date	Event
23	Rumania surrenders unconditionally to Soviet forces
	U.S. Seventh Army battles Germans at Montélimar (to August 28)
25	Paris liberated
	Aitape operation (New Guinea) ends in Allied victory
28	Germans surrender in Toulon and Marseilles
September 3	British Second Army force enters Brussels
	Southern France forces take Lyons
4	British Second Army takes Antwerp
	Fighting ends between USSR and Finland
8	First V-2 rocket falls on England
11	Allied Normandy and southern France invasion forces meet near Dijon
12	Second Allied Quebec Conference opens (to September 16)
15	U.S. Army units land on Morotai
	U.S. marines land on Peleliu
16	Red Army units enter Sofia
17	First Allied Airborne Army units dropped in Holland (Operation Market)
21	British Eighth Army takes Rimini
October 2	U.S. First Army assaults West Wall
10	Soviet forces reach Niemen River on border of Prussia
15	Allies open offensive in northern Burma
20	Belgrade taken by Soviet and Yugoslav forces
	U.S. Sixth Army lands on Leyte
21	U.S. First Army occupies Aachen
23	Battle for Leyte Gulf (to October 26)
November 7	Roosevelt elected to fourth term as U.S. President
12	*Tirpitz* sunk by air attack
16	U.S. First and Ninth Armies open offensive to clear Roer plain
23	French armored force enters Strasbourg
24	United States begins B-29 raids on Japan
27	Fighting ends on Peleliu
December 3	Civil war erupts in Athens
13	U.S. Third Army completes capture of Metz
15	U.S. force invades Mindoro
16	Germans attack in Ardennes (Battle of the Bulge)
26	U.S. Third Army armored relief column reaches Bastogne

1945

Date	Event
January 1	Germans launch offensive (Operation Nordwind) against U.S. Seventh Army
9	U.S. Sixth Army invades Luzon
12	Major Soviet winter offensive opens
	First convoy starts on Ledo Road
16	Allied counteroffensive reduces German bulge in Ardennes
17	Red Army takes Warsaw
20	Hungary signs armistice with Allies
30	Anglo-American talks prior to Yalta Conference begin at Malta
February 3	U.S. forces reach Manila
4	Yalta Conference begins (to February 12)
9	French First Army concludes Alsatian operations with victory at Colmar pocket
13	RAF bombers raid Dresden (followed by U.S. Eighth Air Force bombers next day)
	Budapest falls to Red Army
19	U.S. marines invade Iwo Jima
25	B-29 raid on Tokyo demonstrates effectiveness of incendiary bombs
March 3	Japanese resistance in Manila ends
5	U.S. First Army units enter Cologne (secured March 7)
7	Troops of U.S. 9th Armored Division cross Rhine on bridge at Remagen
9	U.S. B-29s begin incendiary campaign against Japanese cities
11	U.S. Eighth Army units land on Mindanao
22	In surprise action, troops of U.S. Third Army cross Rhine at Oppenheim
23	British Second Army begins crossing Rhine near Rees
26	Fighting ends on Iwo Jima
27	Last V-2 rocket lands in England
30	Soviets capture Danzig
	Meiktila (Burma) secured by British forces
April 1	U.S. forces land on Okinawa

5	Koiso resigns as Japanese Prime Minister; Suzuki succeeds
7	U.S. Navy planes sink Japanese battleship *Yamato* in East China Sea
9	Allies begin major attack on Gothic Line (Italy)
	Königsberg falls to Russians after 2½-month siege
11	Japanese begin two-day kamikaze onslaught against U.S. ships at Okinawa
12	Roosevelt dies; Truman succeeds as U.S. President
13	Soviets complete capture of Vienna
16	Soviets begin final offensive toward Berlin
18	U.S. forces complete Ruhr operations, taking more than 300,000 prisoners
	U.S. Third Army troops enter Czechoslovakia
20	U.S. Seventh Army takes Nuremberg
21	Allies take Bologna
23	Himmler makes surrender offer to Western Allies
	Russians break into Berlin
25	United Nations conference opens in San Francisco
	U.S. and Soviet forces meet near Torgau, splitting Germany in two
28	Mussolini is executed by partisans
30	Hitler dies in bunker; Dönitz is chosen as head of state
	U.S. Seventh Army takes Munich
May 2	Units of British Second Army reach Baltic
	Red Army completes capture of Berlin
	German forces surrender in Italy
3	Rangoon falls to British Indian force
5	German forces in Netherlands, northwestern Germany and Denmark surrender
	German Army Group G surrenders in Bavaria
	Uprising in Prague
7	All German forces surrender unconditionally (2:41 A.M. at Reims)
8	Proclaimed V-E Day
13	Last German resistance ceases in Czechoslovakia, thus ending fighting in Europe
20	Japanese begin pulling back from Chinese bases
June 22	U.S. Tenth Army completes capture of Okinawa
30	Luzon campaign concludes
July 1	Australian 7th Division lands at Balikpapan, Borneo
16	Big Three begin Potsdam Conference (to August 2)
	Atomic bomb successfully tested at Los Alamos
25	Organized resistance ends on Mindanao
26	Potsdam Declaration issued
	Churchill resigns following Conservative Party defeat; Attlee succeeds as British Prime Minister
August 6	Atomic bomb dropped on Hiroshima
8	USSR declares war on Japan
9	Atomic bomb dropped on Nagasaki
	Soviets invade Manchuria
14	Japan surrenders, ending World War II
September 2	Japan signs Instrument of Surrender

Selected Bibliography

The literature of World War II is vast, and its rate of growth appears undiminished by the passage of time. In fact, the opening during the 1970s of a number of previously sealed government archives acted as a stimulus to fresh writing and debate. Writing about the war, it seems, is very much with us and will continue to be. The overwhelming abundance of material available makes it evident that no overall book on World War II can present a bibliography that is more than partial and suggestive. What appears below is a list of full-length published books that were prominent among those consulted (although not necessarily endorsed) by the editors and writers who prepared this encyclopedia and that are generally available for those readers who wish to pursue particular areas of interest. The list does not include pamphlets, monographs, journal articles, documents or unpublished materials, although numerous sources of this kind were drawn upon in the creation of the encyclopedia, many of them in fact being written by contributors to it. Other sources used were interviews and personal recollections, a number of which have also gone into the official histories and other books written or edited by some of the contributors to this book.

The American and British official histories, being absolutely essential to serious study of the war, deserve special mention. The American historical series include the comprehensive *United States Army in World War II* (projected to be about 75 volumes), edited by various historians and published by the Office of the Chief of Military History (now the Center of Military History); *The Army Air Forces in World War II,* edited by W. F. Craven and J. L. Cate (7 vols.; Chicago: University of Chicago Press, 1948–58); *History of Marine Corps Operations in World War II,* published by the Historical Branch, Headquarters, U.S. Marine Corps; and the "semiofficial" and spirited *History of United States Naval Operations in World War II,* by Samuel Eliot Morison (15 vols.; Boston: Little, Brown, 1946–62). The Army and Marine Corps volumes are obtainable from the Superintendent of Documents, U.S. Government Printing Office, Washington, D.C. 20402. The British histories appear in the overall series *History of the Second World War: United Kingdom Military Series,* which includes subseries on military operations in the various theaters; *The War at Sea 1939–45,* by S. W. Roskill (4 vols.); air operations, strategy, etc. The series is published by H.M. Stationery Office, London. Readers in the United States may obtain a complete list from British Information Services, 845 Third Avenue, New York, New York 10022.

Those who wish to go deeper into bibliographic matters than is possible here may consult *World War II: Books in English 1945–65,* compiled by Janet Ziegler (Stanford, Calif.: Hoover Institution Press, 1971). This comprehensive listing is periodically brought up to date in the publications of the American Committee on the History of the Second World War; the present address of this committee is the Department of History, Southern Illinois University, Carbondale, Ill. 62901. Current coverage of publications in all languages appears in the quarterly *Revue d'histoire de la deuxième guerre mondiale,* published in Paris.

Accoce, Pierre, and Pierre Quet. *A Man Called Lucy.* New York: Coward-McCann, 1966.

Adams, Henry H. *1942: The Year That Doomed the Axis.* New York: David McKay, 1967.

———. *Years of Deadly Peril: The Coming of the War, 1939–1941.* New York: David McKay, 1969.

———. *Years of Expectation: Guadalcanal to Normandy.* New York: David McKay, 1973.

———. *Years to Victory.* New York: David McKay, 1973.

Ambrose, Stephen E. *The Supreme Commander: The War Years of General Dwight Eisenhower.* Garden City, N.Y.: Doubleday, 1970.

Arnold, Henry H. *Global Mission.* New York: Harper, 1949.

Asprey, Robert B. *War in the Shadows.* 2 vols. Garden City, N.Y.: Doubleday, 1975.

Ba Maw. *Breakthrough in Burma.* New Haven, Conn.: Yale University Press, 1968.

Baldwin, Hanson. *Battles Lost and Won: Great Campaigns of World War II.* New York: Harper & Row, 1966.

———. *The Crucial Years,* 1939–1941. New York: Harper & Row, 1976.

Barnett, Correlli. *Britain and Her Army, 1509–1970.* New York: Morrow, 1970.

———. *The Desert Generals.* New York: Viking Press, 1961.

Batchelor, John, and Ian Hogg. *Artillery.* New York: Ballantine, 1972.

Bergamini, David. *Japan's Imperial Conspiracy: How Emperor Hirohito Led Japan into War Against the West.* New York: Morrow, 1971.

Bethell, Nicholas. *The War Hitler Won: The Fall of Poland, September 1939.* New York: Holt, Rinehart and Winston, 1972.

Bialer, Seweryn. *Stalin and His Generals: Soviet Military Memoirs of World War II.* New York: Pegasus, 1969.

Blair, Clay, Jr. *Silent Victory: The U.S. Submarine War Against Japan.* 2 vols. New York: Lippincott, 1975.

Blumenson, Martin. *The Patton Papers, 1885–1945.* 2 vols. Boston: Houghton Mifflin, 1972, 1974.

Boelcke, Willi A. (ed.). *The Secret Conferences of Dr. Goebbels: The Nazi Propaganda War, 1939–1943.* Translated from the German by Ewald Osers. New York: Dutton, 1970.

Boldt, Gerhard. *Hitler: The Last Ten Days.* New York: Coward, McCann & Geoghegan, 1973.

Bradley, Omar N. *A Soldier's Story.* New York: Holt, Rinehart and Winston, 1951.

Bragadin, Marc' A. *The Italian Navy in World War II.* Edited by Giuseppe Finavanzo; translated by Gale Hoffman. Annapolis, Md.: Naval Institute Press, 1957.

Bramsted, Ernest K. *Goebbels and National Socialist Propaganda 1925–45.* East Lansing: Michigan State University Press, 1965.

Brown, Anthony Cave. *Bodyguard of Lies.* 2 vols. New York: Harper & Row, 1975.

Brownlow, Donald Grey. *Panzer Baron: The Military Exploits of General Hasso von Manteuffel.* Quincy, Mass.: Christopher Publishing House, 1975.

Bryant, Sir Arthur. *Triumph in the West, 1943–1946.* Garden City, N.Y.: Doubleday, 1959.

———. *The Turn of the Tide, 1939–1943.* Garden City, N.Y.: Doubleday, 1957.

Buchanan, A. Russell. *The United States and World War II.* 2 vols. New York: Harper & Row, 1964.

Buckley, Christopher. *Greece and Crete, 1941.* London: H.M. Stationery Office, 1952.

———. *Norway; the Commandos; Dieppe.* London: H.M. Stationery Office, 1952.

Bullock, Alan. *Hitler, A Study in Tyranny.* Rev. ed. New York: Harper & Row, 1964.

Burns, James M. *Roosevelt: The Lion and the Fox.* New York: Harcourt, Brace, 1956.

———. *Roosevelt: The Soldier of Freedom.* New York: Harcourt Brace Jovanovich, 1970.

Busch, Harold. *U-Boats at War.* Translated from the German by L. P. R. Wilson. New York: Ballantine, 1955.

Butcher, Harry C. *My Three Years with Eisenhower.* New York: Simon and Schuster, 1946.

Butow, Robert J. C. *Tojo and the Coming of the War.* Princeton, N.J.: Princeton University Press, 1961.

Calder, Angus. *The People's War: Britain, 1939–1945.* New York: Pantheon, 1969.

Calvocoressi, Peter, and Guy Wint. *Total War.* New York: Pantheon, 1972.

Campbell, Arthur. *The Siege: A Story from Kohima.* New York: Macmillan, 1956.

Carell, Paul. *The Foxes of the Desert.* Translated from the German by Mervyn Savill. New York: Dutton, 1960.

———. *Hitler Moves East, 1941–1943.* Translated from the German by Ewald Osers. Boston: Little, Brown, 1965.

Chamberlain, Peter, and Chris Ellis. *British and American Tanks of World War II.* New York: Arco, 1969.

Chapman, Guy. *Why France Fell.* New York: Holt, Rinehart and Winston, 1968.

Chennault, Claire L. *Way of a Fighter: The Memories of Claire Lee Chennault.* Edited by Robert Hotz. New York: Putnam, 1949.

Chuikov, Vasili I. *The Beginning of the Road: Battle for Stalingrad.* Translated from the Russian by Harold Salver. New York: Holt, Rinehart and Winston, 1964.

———. *The Fall of Berlin.* Translated from the Russian by Ruth Kisch. New York: Holt, Rinehart and Winston, 1968.

Churchill, Winston S. *The Second World War.* 6 vols. Boston: Houghton Mifflin, 1948–53.

Ciano, Count Galeazzo. *The Ciano Diaries, 1939–43.* Edited by Hugh Gibson. Garden City, N.Y.: Doubleday, 1946.

Clark, Alan. *Barbarossa: The Russian-German Conflict, 1941–45.* New York: Morrow, 1965.

———. *The Fall of Crete.* New York: Morrow, 1962.

Clark, Mark. *Calculated Risk.* New York: Harper, 1950.

Clark, Ronald W. *The Birth of the Bomb.* New York: Horizon Press, 1961.

Clark, Stanley. *The Man Who Is France: The Story of General Charles de Gaulle.* New York: Dodd, Mead, 1960.

Clubb, O. Edmund. *Twentieth Century China.* New York: Columbia University Press, 1966.

Cobban, Alfred. *A History of Modern France.* New York: George Braziller, 1965.

Cocchia, Aldo. *The Hunters and the Hunted: Adventures of Italian Naval Forces.* Translated from the Italian by Margaret Gwyer. Annapolis, Md.: Naval Institute Press, 1958.

Cole, Hubert. *Laval: A Biography.* New York: Putnam, 1963.

Collier, Basil. *The Battle of Britain.* New York: Macmillan, 1962.

———. *The War in the Far East, 1941–1945.* New York: Morrow, 1968.

Collins, Larry, and Dominique Lapierre. *Is Paris Burning?* New York: Simon and Schuster, 1965.

Commager, Henry Steele (ed.). *Documents of American History,* Vol. II, *Since 1898.* New York: Appleton-Century-Crofts, 1963.

Compton, Arthur H. *Atomic Quest.* New York: Oxford University Press, 1956.

Conquest, Robert. *The Great Terror: Stalin's Purge of the Thirties.* New York: Macmillan, 1973.

Craig, William. *Enemy at the Gates: The Battle for Stalingrad.* New York: Reader's Digest Press, 1973.

———. *The Fall of Japan.* New York: Dial Press, 1967.

Cross, Colin. *Adolf Hitler.* London: Hodder and Stoughton, 1973.

Cunningham, Andrew B. *A Sailor's Odyssey: The Autobiography of Admiral of the Fleet, Viscount Cunningham of Hyndhope.* New York: Dutton, 1951.

Davis, Burke. *Get Yamamoto.* New York: Random House, 1969.

Davis, Kenneth S. *Experience of War.* Garden City, N.Y.: Doubleday, 1965.

Dawidowicz, Lucy S. *The War Against the Jews 1933–1945.* New York: Holt, Rinehart and Winston, 1975.

Deakin, F. W. *The Brutal Friendship: Mussolini, Hitler and the Fall of Italian Fascism.* New York: Harper & Row, 1962.

———, and G. R. Storry. *The Case of Richard Sorge.* New York: Harper & Row, 1966.

Deutsch, Harold C. *The Conspiracy Against Hitler in the Twilight War.* Minneapolis: University of Minnesota Press, 1968.

Dietrich, Otto. *Hitler.* Translated from the German by Richard and Clara Winston. Chicago: Regnery, 1955.

Divine, Robert. *The Illusion of Neutrality.* Chicago: University of Chicago Press, 1962.

Dönitz, Karl. *Memoirs.* Cleveland: World, 1959.

Dorn, Frank. *Walkout with Stilwell in Burma.* New York: Crowell, 1971.

Dulles, Allen. *The Secret Surrender.* New York: Harper & Row, 1966.

Eisenhower, Dwight D. *Crusade in Europe.* Garden City, N.Y.: Doubleday, 1948.

Eisenhower, John S. D. *The Bitter Woods.* New York: Putnam, 1969.

Ellis, Chris, and Peter Chamberlain. *Fighting Vehicles.* New York: Hamlyn, 1972.

Ellsberg, Edward. *The Far Shore.* New York: Dodd, Mead, 1960.

Engle, Eloise, and Lauri Paananen. *The Winter War: The Russo-Finnish Conflict, 1939–40.* New York: Scribner, 1973.

Erickson, John. *The Soviet High Command: A Military-Political History, 1918–41.* New York: St. Martin's Press, 1962.

Essame, Hubert. *The Battle for Germany.* New York: Scribner, 1969.

———. *Patton: A Study in Command.* New York: Scribner, 1974.

Evans, Sir Geoffrey C., and Anthony Brett-James. *Imphal: A Flower on Lofty Heights.* New York: St. Martin's Press, 1962.

Fahey, James C. *The Ships and Aircraft of the U.S. Fleet.* 4 vols. [set combines 1939, 1941, 1942 and 1945 editions]. Annapolis, Md.: Naval Institute Press, 1976.

Farago, Ladislas. *The Broken Seal: The Story of Operation Magic and the Pearl Harbor Disaster.* New York: Random House, 1967.

———. *Patton: Ordeal and Triumph.* New York: Obolensky, 1964.

Feis, Herbert. *The China Tangle.* Princeton, N.J.: Princeton University Press, 1953.

———. *Churchill, Roosevelt and Stalin.* Princeton, N.J.: Princeton University Press, 1957.

———. *The Road to Pearl Harbor.* Princeton, N.J.: Princeton University Press, 1950.

Fest, Joachim C. *Hitler.* New York: Harcourt Brace Jovanovich, 1974.

Finer, Herman. *Mussolini's Italy.* New York: Holt, 1935.

FitzGibbon, Constantine. *20 July.* New York: Norton, 1956.

———. *The Winter of the Bombs.* New York: Norton, 1958.

Francillon, René J. *Japanese Aircraft of the Pacific War.* New York: Funk & Wagnalls, 1970.

Frank, Anne. *Diary of a Young Girl.* Garden City, N.Y.: Doubleday, 1952.

Frank, Wolfgang. *The Sea Wolves.* New York: Rinehart, 1955.

Freidin, Seymour, and William Richardson (eds.). *The Fatal Decisions.* New York: Sloane, 1956.

Friedlander, Saul. *Pius XII and the Third Reich.* New York: Knopf, 1968.

Friedman, Donald J. *The Road from Isolation.* Cambridge, Mass.: Harvard University Press, 1968.

Frischauer, Willi. *Himmler.* Boston: Beacon Press, 1953.

———, and Robert Jackson. *The Altmark Affair.* New York: Macmillan, 1955.

Fuller, J. F. C. *The Second World War: 1939–1945.* New York: Duell, Sloane & Pearce, 1962.

Gallagher, Richard. *The Malmédy Massacre.* New York: Paperback Library, 1964.

Galland, Adolf. *The First and the Last.* New York: Holt, 1954.

Gamelin, Maurice. *Servir.* 3 vols. Paris: Plon, 1946–47.

Gehlen, Reinhard. *The Service: The Memoirs of General Reinhard Gehlen.* New York: World, 1972.

Gilbert, Felix (ed.). *Hitler Directs His War.* New York: Oxford University Press, 1951.

Gilbert, Gustav M. *Nuremberg Diary.* New York: Farrar, Straus, 1947.

Gilbert, Martin, and Richard Gott. *The Appeasers.* Boston: Houghton Mifflin, 1963.

Gisevius, Hans Bernd. *To the Bitter End.* Boston: Houghton Mifflin, 1947.

Goebbels, Joseph. *The Goebbels Diaries, 1942–43.* Edited and translated by Louis P. Lochner. Garden City, N.Y.: Doubleday, 1948.

Görlitz, Walter. *The German General Staff, 1657–1945.* New York: Praeger, 1965.

———. *Paulus and Stalingrad.* New York: Citadel, 1963.

Goutard, Adolphe. *The Battle of France, 1940.* New York: Washburn, 1959.

Green, William. *Famous Bombers of the Second World War.* 2 vols. Garden City, N.Y.: Hanover House, 1960–61.

———. *War Planes of the Second World War.* 6 vols. Garden City, N.Y.: Doubleday, 1960–68.

Greenfield, Kent Roberts. *American Strategy in World War II: A Reconsideration.* Baltimore, Md.: Johns Hopkins Press, 1963.

Groueff, Stephane. *Manhattan Project: The Untold Story of the Making of the Atomic Bomb.* Boston: Little, Brown, 1967.

Groves, Leslie R. *Now It Can Be Told.* New York: Harper, 1962.

Grunberger, Richard. *The Twelve-Year Reich: A Social History of Germany 1933–45.* New York: Holt, Rinehart and Winston, 1971.

Guderian, Heinz. *Panzer Leader.* Translated from the German by Constantine FitzGibbon. New York: Dutton, 1952.

Halder, Franz. *Diary, 1939–42.* Nuremberg: Office of Military Government for Germany (U.S.), 1946.

———. *Hitler as War Lord.* Translated from the German by Paul Findlay. London: Putnam, 1950.

Halsey, William F., and J. Bryan. *Admiral Halsey's Story.* New York: McGraw-Hill, 1947.

Hassell, Ulrich von. *The von Hassell Diaries, 1938–1944.* Garden City, N.Y.: Doubleday, 1947.

Hechler, Ken. *The Bridge at Remagen.* New York: Ballantine, 1957.

Heiden, Konrad. *Der Führer: Hitler's Rise to Power.* Boston: Houghton Mifflin, 1944.

Henderson, Sir Nevile. *Failure of a Mission.* New York: Putnam, 1940.

Hersey, John. *Hiroshima.* New York: Knopf, 1946.

Hibbert, Christopher. *Il Duce: The Life of Benito Mussolini.* Boston: Little, Brown, 1962.

Hilberg, Raul. *The Destruction of the European Jews.* Chicago: Quadrangle, 1961.

Hitler, Adolf. *Hitler's Secret Conversations 1941–44.* Translated by Norman Cameron and R. H. Stevens. New York: Farrar, Straus & Young, 1953.

———. *Mein Kampf.* Boston: Houghton Mifflin, 1943. Unexpurgated English translation by James Murphy. (German original: Munich, 1925, 1927. The first volume, *Eine Abrechnung,* was published in 1925; the second, *Die Nationalsozialistische Bewegung,* in 1927. Subsequently the two were published in one volume.)

———. *The Testament of Adolf Hitler: The Hitler-Bormann Documents, February–April 1945.* London: Cassell, 1961.

Hoffschmidt, E. J., and W. H. Tantum IV (eds.). *Second World War Combat Weapons (German).* Greenwich, Conn.: WE, Inc., 1968.

Hogg, Ian V. *The Guns: 1939/45.* New York: Ballantine, 1970.

Hough, Richard. *Death of the Battleship.* New York: Macmillan, 1963.

Hoyle, Martha Byrd. *A World in Flames: A History of World War II.* New York: Atheneum, 1969.

Hoyt, Edwin P. *How They Won the War in the Pacific.* New York: Weybright and Talley, 1971.

Humble, Richard. *Hitler's High Seas Fleet.* New York: Ballantine, 1971.

International Military Tribunal. 42 vols. *Trial of the Major War Criminals Before the International Military Tribunal, Nuremberg, 14 November 1945–10 October 1946.* Nuremberg, 1947.

Irving, David. *Hitler's War.* 2 vols. New York: Viking, 1977.

———. *The Rise and Fall of the Luftwaffe: The Life of Field Marshal Erhard Milch.* Boston: Little, Brown, 1974.

Jablonski, Edward. *Airwar.* 4 vols. (Vol. I: *Terror from the Sky;* Vol. II: *Tragic Victories;* Vol. III: *Outraged Skies;* Vol. IV: *Wings of Fire*). Garden City, N.Y.: Doubleday, 1971–72.

Jackson, W. G. F. *The Battle for North Africa 1940–43.* New York: Mason/Charter, 1975.

Jacobsen, Hans-Adolf. *1934/1945. Der Zweite Weltkrieg in Chronik und Dokumenten.* Darmstadt: Wehr und Wissen, 1959.

James, Robert Rhodes. *Churchill: A Study in Failure.* New York: World, 1970

Jane's All the World's Aircraft. New York: McGraw-Hill, 1939–46.

Jane's Fighting Ships. New York: McGraw-Hill, 1939–46.

Jentschura, Hans-Georg, Dieter Jung, and Peter Mickel. *Warships of the Imperial Japanese Navy, 1869–1945.* Annapolis, Md.: Naval Institute Press, 1977.

Jetzinger, Franz. *Hitler's Youth.* Translated from the German by Lawrence Wilson. London: Hutchinson, 1958.

Johnson, M. M. *The Rifles and Machine Guns of the World's Armies.* Washington, D.C.: Combat Arms Press, 1944.

Jungk, Robert. *Brighter Than a Thousand Suns.* New York: Harcourt, Brace and World, 1958.

Karig, Walter, and others. *Battle Report.* New York: Rinehart, 1944–52.

Kase, Toshikazu. *Journey to the "Missouri."* New Haven, Conn.: Yale University Press, 1950.

Kelley, Douglas McG. *Twenty-two Cells in Nuremberg: A Psychiatrist Examines the Nazi Criminals.* New York: Greenberg, 1947.

Kemp, Peter K. *Key to Victory.* Boston: Little, Brown, 1957. (British title: *Victory at Sea, 1939–45.*)

Kennan, George. *Memoirs, 1925–1950.* Boston: Little, Brown, 1967.

Kennedy, Ludovic. *Pursuit: The Chase and Sinking of the Battleship "Bismarck."* New York: Viking, 1974.

King, Ernest J., and Walter M. Whitehill. *Fleet Admiral King.* New York: Norton, 1952.

Kirk, John, and Robert Young, Jr. *Great Weapons of World War II.* New York: Bonanza Books, 1961.

Kirkpatrick, Sir Ivone. *Mussolini: A Study in Power.* New York: Hawthorn, 1964.

Kogon, Eugen. *The Theory and Practice of Hell.* New York: Farrar and Straus, 1950.

Krancke, Theodor, and H. J. Brennecke. *Pocket Battleship: The Story of the "Admiral Scheer."* New York: Nórton, 1958.

Kubizek, August. *The Young Hitler I Knew.* Translated from the German by E. V. Anderson. Boston: Houghton Mifflin, 1955.

Lafore, Laurance D. *The End of Glory: An Interpretation of the Origins of World War II.* New York: Lippincott, 1970.

Lamont, Lansing. *Day of Trinity.* New York: Atheneum, 1965.

Langer, Walter C. *The Mind of Adolf Hitler.* New York: Basic Books, 1972.

Langer, William L. *Our Vichy Gamble.* New York: Knopf, 1947.

———. *The Undeclared War 1940–1941.* New York: Harper, 1953.

———, and S. Everett Gleason. *The Challenge to Isolation.* New York: Harper, 1952.

Lash, Joseph P. *Eleanor and Franklin.* New York: Norton, 1971.

Leahy, William D. *I Was There.* New York: Whittlesey House, 1950.

Leasor, James. *Singapore, the Battle That Changed the World.* Garden City, N.Y.: Doubleday, 1968.

Lenton, H. T. *American Battleships, Carriers, and Cruisers.* Warships of the Second World War Series. 2d ed. Garden City, N.Y.: Doubleday, 1970.

———. *British Battleships and Aircraft Carriers.* Warships of the Second World War Series. Garden City, N.Y.: Doubleday, 1972.

———. *German Surface Vessels.* 2 vols. Warships of the Second World War Series. Garden City, N.Y.: Doubleday, 1966.
———. *Japanese Battleships and Cruisers.* 3d ed. London: Macdonald, 1971.
Levine, Herbert S. *Hitler's Free City: A History of the Nazi Party in Danzig, 1925–39.* Chicago: University of Chicago Press, 1973.
Lewin, Ronald. *Montgomery as Military Commander.* New York: Stein and Day, 1971.
Liang, Chin-tung. *General Stilwell in China, 1942–1944: The Full Story.* Brooklyn: St. Johns University Press, 1972.
Liddell Hart, B. H. *The German Generals Talk.* New York: Morrow, 1948.
———. *History of the Second World War.* New York: Putnam, 1970.
———. *The Red Army.* New York: Harcourt, Brace, 1956.
——— (ed.). *The Rommel Papers.* New York: Harcourt, Brace, 1953.
Linebarger, Paul. *Psychological Warfare.* New York: Duell, Sloan and Pearce, 1954.
Lingeman, Richard R. *Don't You Know There's a War On? The American Home Front 1941–1945.* New York: Putnam, 1970.
Littlejohn, David. *The Patriotic Traitors.* Garden City, N.Y.: Doubleday, 1972.
Liu, F. F. *A Military History of Modern China.* Princeton, N.J.: Princeton University Press, 1956.
Loewenheim, Francis L., Harold D. Langley, and Manfred Jonas (eds.). *Roosevelt and Churchill, Their Secret Wartime Correspondence.* New York: Dutton, 1975.
Lord, Walter. *Day of Infamy.* New York: Holt, 1957.
———. *Incredible Victory.* New York: Harper & Row, 1967.
Lototskii, S. S. *The Soviet Army.* Moscow, 1969.
Lyall, Gavin (ed.). *The War in the Air: The Royal Air Force in World War II.* New York: Morrow, 1969.
Lyon, Peter. *Eisenhower: Portrait of the Hero.* New York: Little, Brown, 1974.
MacArthur, Douglas. *Reminiscences.* New York: McGraw-Hill, 1964.
MacDonald, Charles B. *Company Commander.* Washington, D.C.: Infantry Journal Press, 1947.
———. *The Mighty Endeavor: American Armed Forces in the European Theater in World War II.* New York: Oxford University Press, 1969.
Mackintosh, John Malcolm. *Juggernaut.* New York: Macmillan, 1967.
Maclean, Fitzroy. *Escape to Adventure.* Boston: Little, Brown, 1950.
McNeill, William H. *America, Britain and Russia: Their Co-operation and Conflict, 1941–1946.* New York: Oxford University Press, 1953.
Macksey, Kenneth, and John H. Batchelor. *Tank: A History of the Armoured Fighting Vehicle.* New York: Scribner, 1970.
Majdalany, Fred. *The Battle of El Alamein.* New York: Lippincott, 1965.
Malaparte, Curzio. *The Volga Rises in Europe.* London: Alvin Redman, 1957.
Manchester, William. *The Arms of Krupp, 1587–1968.* Boston: Little, Brown, 1968.
Mannerheim, Baron Carl. *The Memoirs of Marshal Mannerheim.* New York: Dutton, 1954.
Manstein, Erich von. *Lost Victories.* Chicago: Regnery, 1958.
Manvell, Roger. *The Conspirators: 20th July 1944.* New York: Ballantine, 1971.
———, and Heinrich Fraenkel. *The Canaris Conspiracy.* New York: David McKay, 1969.
———. *Doctor Goebbels.* New York: Simon and Schuster, 1960.
———. *Hermann Göring.* New York: Simon and Schuster, 1962.
———. *The Incomparable Crime: Mass Extermination in the Twentieth Century, the Legacy of Guilt.* New York: Putnam, 1967.
———. *The July Plot (The Men Who Tried to Kill Hitler).* New York: Coward-McCann, 1964.
Marshall, S. L. A. *Bastogne.* Washington, D.C.: Infantry Journal Press, 1946.
———. *Battle at Best.* New York: Pocket Books, 1964.
———. *Night Drop.* Boston: Atlantic–Little, Brown, 1962.
Martienssen, Anthony K. *Hitler and His Admirals.* New York: Dutton, 1949.
Maser, Werner. *Hitler.* New York: Harper & Row, 1973.
Mason, David. *Salerno: Foothold in Europe.* New York: Ballantine, 1972.
Mason, Herbert Molloy, Jr. *The Rise of the Luftwaffe 1918–1940.* New York: Dial Press, 1973.
Masson, Henri Le. *The French Navy.* 2 vols. Warships of the Second World War Series. Garden City, N.Y.: Doubleday, 1969.
Masson, Philippe. *De Gaulle.* New York: Ballantine, 1972.
Masterman, J. C. *The Double-Cross System in the War of 1939 to 1945.* New Haven, Conn.: Yale University Press, 1972.
Mee, Charles L., Jr. *Meeting at Potsdam.* New York: Evans, 1975.
Meinecke, Friedrich. *The German Catastrophe.* Cambridge, Mass.: Harvard University Press, 1950.
Mellenthin, F. W. von. *Panzer Battles.* Norman: University of Oklahoma Press, 1956.
Michel, Henri. *The Second World War.* 2 vols. New York: Praeger, 1975.
———. *The Shadow War.* New York: Harper & Row, 1972.
Millis, Walter (ed.). *The Forrestal Diaries.* New York: Viking, 1951.
Mitscherlich, Alexander, and Fred Mielke. *Doctors of Infamy: The Story of the Nazi Medical Crimes.* New York: McGraw-Hill, 1956.
Moltke, Count Helmuth von. *A German of the Resistance.* London: Geoffrey Cumberlege Oxford University Press, 1946.
Montagu, Ewen E. S. *The Man Who Never Was.* Philadelphia: Lippincott, 1954.
Montgomery, Bernard L. *Memoirs.* Cleveland: World, 1958.
———. *El Alamein to the River Sangro.* New York: Dutton, 1948.
———. *Normandy to the Baltic.* Boston: Houghton Mifflin, 1948.
Morison, Samuel Eliot. *The Two-Ocean War.* Boston: Little, Brown, 1963.
Mosley, Leonard. *Gideon Goes to War.* New York: Scribner, 1955.
———. *Hirohito, Emperor of Japan.* Englewood Cliffs, N.J.: Prentice-Hall, 1966.
———. *On Borrowed Time.* New York: Random House, 1969.
———. *The Reich Marshal.* Garden City, N.Y.: Doubleday, 1974.
Moulton, J. L. *The Norwegian Campaign of 1940.* London: Eyre & Spottiswoode, 1966.
Mrazek, James E. *The Fall of Eben Emael.* Washington, D.C.: Luce, 1971.
Munson, Kenneth. *Aircraft of World War II.* London: Ian Allen, 1962.
Murphy, Robert. *Diplomat Among Warriors.* New York: Doubleday, 1964.
Newcomb, Richard F. *Iwo Jima.* New York: Holt, Rinehart and Winston, 1965.
Nicolson, Nigel. *Alex.* New York: Atheneum, 1973.
Nyiszli, Miklos. *Auschwitz.* New York: Fell, 1960.
Papen, Franz von. *Memoirs.* New York: Dutton, 1953.
Patton, George S. *War As I Knew It.* Boston: Houghton Mifflin, 1947.
Paxton, Robert. *Parades and Politics at Vichy.* Princeton, N.J.: Princeton University Press, 1966.
Payne, Robert. *Chiang Kai-shek.* New York: Weybright and Talley, 1969.
———. *The Life and Death of Adolf Hitler.* New York: Praeger, 1973.
———. *The Rise and Fall of Stalin.* New York: Simon and Schuster, 1964.
Peillard, Leonce. *Sink the Tirpitz.* New York: Putnam, 1968.
Pendar, Kenneth W. *Adventure in Diplomacy: Our French Dilemma.* New York: Dodd, Mead, 1945.
Perrett, Geoffrey. *Days of Sadness, Years of Triumph: The American People, 1939–1945.* New York: Coward, McCann & Geoghegan, 1973.
Pertinax (André Geraud). *The Grave Diggers of France.* Garden City, N.Y.: Doubleday Doran, 1944.
Petrov, Vladimir (ed.). *June 22, 1941: Soviet Historians and the German Invasion.* Columbia: University of South Carolina Press, 1968.

Pogue, Forrest C. *George C. Marshall: Education of a General.* New York: Viking, 1964.

———. *George C. Marshall: Ordeal and Hope.* New York: Viking, 1966.

———. *George C. Marshall: Organizer of Victory.* New York: Viking, 1973.

Polenberg, Richard. *War and Society: The United States, 1941–1945.* Philadelphia: Lippincott, 1972.

Potter, E. B. *Nimitz.* Annapolis, Md.: Naval Institute Press, 1976.

Potter, John. *Yamamoto.* New York: Viking, 1965.

Prittie, Terence. *Germans Against Hitler.* New York: Little, Brown, 1964.

Rauch, Georg von. *History of Soviet Russia.* Translated from the German by Peter and Annette Jacobsohn. New York: Praeger, 1972.

Rauschning, Herman. *Hitler Speaks.* London: Butterworth, 1939.

Robertson, Terence. *Channel Dash.* New York: Dutton, 1958.

Robichon, Jacques. *The Second D-Day.* New York: Walker, 1962.

Rohwer, Jürgen, and Gerhard Hummelchen. *Chronology of the War at Sea.* 2 vols. New York: Arco, 1972.

Rokossovsky, Konstantin. *A Soldier's Duty.* Translated from the Russian by Vladimir Talmy. Moscow: Progress, 1970.

Roscoe, Theodore. *On the Seas and in the Skies.* New York: Hawthorn, 1970.

Roskill, S. W. *White Ensign: The British Navy at War, 1939–1945.* Annapolis, Md.: Naval Institute Press, 1960.

Ross, Davis R. B. *Preparing for Ulysses: Politics and Veterans During World War II.* New York: Columbia University Press, 1969.

Rothfels, Hans. *The German Opposition to Hitler.* Hinsdale, Ill.: Regnery, 1948.

Rowse, A. L. *Appeasement: A Study in Political Decline, 1933–39.* New York: Norton, 1961.

Rozek, Edward J. *Allied Wartime Diplomacy: A Pattern in Poland.* New York: Wiley, 1958.

Ruge, Friedrich. *Der Seekrieg: The German Navy's Story.* Annapolis, Md.: Naval Institute Press, 1957.

Ryan, Cornelius. *A Bridge Too Far.* New York: Simon and Schuster, 1974.

———. *The Last Battle.* New York: Simon and Schuster, 1966.

———. *The Longest Day.* New York: Simon and Schuster, 1959.

Sanderson, James D. *Behind Enemy Lines.* Princeton, N.J.: Van Nostrand, 1959.

Saraphis, Stephanos. *Greek Resistance Army: The Story of ELAS.* London: Birch Books, 1951.

Saundby, Sir Robert. *Air Bombardment: The Story of Its Development.* New York: Harper, 1961.

Schlabrendorff, Fabian von. *Revolt Against Hitler.* London: Eyre & Spottiswoode, 1948.

———. *The Secret War Against Hitler.* New York: Putnam, 1965.

Schmidt, Paul. *Hitler's Interpreter.* New York: Macmillan, 1951.

Schmitthenner, Walter (ed.). *The German Resistance to Hitler.* Berkeley: University of California Press, 1970.

Schoenbaum, David. *Hitler's Social Revolution: Class and Status in Nazi Germany 1933–1939.* Garden City, N.Y.: Doubleday, 1966.

Schofield, Brian B. *The Russian Convoys.* London: Batsford, 1964.

Schofield, William G. *Destroyers—60 Years.* Chicago: Rand McNally, 1962.

Schramm, Percy Ernst. *Hitler: The Man and the Military Leader.* Chicago: Quadrangle, 1970.

Seaton, Albert. *The Russo-German War, 1941–45.* New York: Praeger, 1971.

Semmler, Rudolf. *Goebbels—The Man Next to Hitler.* London: Westhouse, 1947.

Senger und Etterlin, F. M. von. *German Tanks of World War II.* New York: Galahad Books, 1969.

Sherwood, Robert E. *Roosevelt and Hopkins.* New York: Harper, 1948.

Shirer, William L. *The Collapse of the Third Republic.* New York: Simon and Schuster, 1969.

———. *The Rise and Fall of the Third Reich.* New York: Simon and Schuster, 1960.

Shtemenko, S. M. *The Soviet General Staff at War, 1941–1945.* Moscow: Progress, 1970.

Sixsmith, E. K. G. *Eisenhower As Military Commander.* New York: Stein and Day, 1972.

Slim, Sir William J. *Defeat into Victory.* New York: David McKay, 1961.

Smith, Bradley F. *Adolf Hitler: His Family, Childhood, and Youth.* Stanford, Calif.: Hoover Institution, 1967.

Smith, S. E. (ed.). *The United States Marine Corps in World War II.* New York: Random House, 1969.

Snell, John L. *Illusion and Necessity: The Diplomacy of Global War, 1939–1945.* Boston: Houghton Mifflin, 1963.

Snyder, Louis. *The War: A Concise History.* New York: Messner, 1960.

Spears, Sir Edward L. *Assignment to Catastrophe.* 2 vols. New York: Wyn, 1954–55.

Speer, Albert. *Inside the Third Reich.* New York: Macmillan, 1970.

Stamps, T. Dodson, and Vincent J. Esposito (eds.). *A Military History of World War II.* 2 vols. West Point, N.Y.: U.S. Military Academy, 1953.

Stein, George H. *The Waffen SS: Hitler's Elite Guard at War, 1939–1945.* Ithaca, N.Y.: Cornell University Press, 1966.

Steinert, Marles G. *23 Days: The Final Collapse of Nazi Germany.* New York: Walker, 1969.

Stevenson, William. *A Man Called Intrepid: The Secret War.* New York and London: Harcourt Brace Jovanovich, 1976.

Stewart, I. McD. G. *Struggle for Crete.* London: Oxford University Press, 1966.

Stimson, Henry L., and McGeorge Bundy. *On Active Service in Peace and War.* New York: Harper, 1947.

Strawson, John. *The Battle for North Africa.* New York: Scribner, 1970.

———. *Hitler's Battles for Europe.* New York: Scribner, 1971.

Suchenwirth, Richard. *Command and Leadership in the German Air Force.* New York: Arno, 1969.

Sykes, Christopher. *Orde Wingate.* Cleveland: World, 1959.

Taylor, Alan J. P. *Beaverbrook.* New York: Simon and Schuster, 1972.

———. *The Origins of the Second World War.* New York: Atheneum, 1962.

Taylor, John W. R. (ed.). *Combat Aircraft of the World.* New York: Putnam, 1969.

Taylor, Telford. *The March of Conquest: The German Victories in Western Europe, 1940.* New York: Simon and Schuster, 1958.

Tedder, Lord Arthur W. *With Prejudice.* Boston: Little, Brown, 1966.

Tissier, Pierre. *The Riom Trial.* London: Harrap, 1942.

Toland, John. *Adolf Hitler.* 2 vols. New York: Doubleday, 1976.

———. *Battle: The Story of the Bulge.* New York: Random House, 1959.

———. *But Not in Shame.* New York: Random House, 1961.

———. *The Last 100 Days.* Garden City, N.Y.: Doubleday, 1959.

———. *The Rising Sun.* 2 vols. New York: Random House, 1970.

Townsend, Peter. *Duel of Eagles.* New York: Simon and Schuster, 1970.

Trager, Frank N. *Burma—From Kingdom to Republic.* New York: Praeger, 1966.

Treadgold, Donald W. *Twentieth Century Russia.* Chicago: Rand McNally, 1971.

Trevor-Roper, H. R. (ed.). *Blitzkrieg to Defeat.* New York: Holt, Rinehart and Winston, 1965.

———. *The Last Days of Hitler.* New York: St. Martin's Press, 1947.

Truman, Harry S. *Year of Decisions, 1945.* Garden City, N.Y.: Doubleday, 1955.

Truman, Margaret. *Harry S. Truman.* New York: Morrow, 1973.

Tuchman, Barbara W. *Stilwell and the American Experience in China, 1911–1945.* New York: Macmillan, 1970.

Tunney, Christopher. *Biographical Dictionary of World War II.* London: J. M. Dent, 1972.

Ulam, Adam. *Expansion and Coexistence: Soviet Foreign Policy 1917–73.* New York: Praeger, 1974.

U.S. Chief of Counsel [Nuremberg]. *Nazi Conspiracy and Aggression.* 8 vols. Washington, D.C.: U.S. Government Printing Office, 1946–48.

Vanderveen, Bart H. *The Observer's Fighting Vehicles Directory, World War II.* London and New York: Frederick Warne, 1969.

Vasilevsky, Alexander M. *Delo vsei zhizni.* Moscow, 1974.

Von der Porten, Edward P. *The German Navy in World War Two.* New York: Crowell, 1969.

Wagner, Ray. *American Combat Planes.* New York: Hanover House, 1960.

Warburg, James P. *Unwritten Treaty.* New York: Harcourt, Brace, 1946.

Warlimont, Walter. *Inside Hitler's Headquarters, 1939–1945.* New York: Praeger, 1965.

War Reports of General of the Army George C. Marshall, General of the Army H. H. Arnold and Fleet Admiral Ernest J. King. Philadelphia: Lippincott, 1947.

Waters, John M., Jr. *Bloody Winter.* Princeton, N.J.: Van Nostrand, 1967.

Watts, Anthony J. *Japanese Warships of World War II.* Garden City, N.Y.: Doubleday, 1967.

———, and Brian Gordon. *The Imperial Japanese Navy.* Garden City, N.Y.: Doubleday, 1971.

Weizsäcker, Ernst von. *The Memoirs of Ernst von Weizsäcker.* Chicago: Regnery, 1951.

Werner, H. A. *Iron Coffins.* New York: Holt, Rinehart and Winston, 1969.

Werth, Alexander. *Russia at War, 1941–45.* New York: Dutton, 1964.

Westphal, Siegfried. *The German Army in the West.* London: Cassell, 1952.

Wheeler-Bennett, Sir John W. *Nemesis of Power.* New York: St. Martin's Press, 1964.

Whelan, R. *The Flying Tigers.* Garden City, N.Y.: Doubleday, 1944.

Whittle, Peter. *One Afternoon at Mezzegra.* Englewood Cliffs, N.J.: Prentice-Hall, 1969.

Wighton, Charles. *Heydrich.* Philadelphia: Chilton, 1962.

Wilmot, Chester. *The Struggle for Europe.* New York: Harper, 1952.

Wilson, Theodore A. *The First Summit.* Boston: Houghton Mifflin, 1969.

Winterbotham, F. W. *The Ultra Secret.* New York: Harper & Row, 1974.

Winton, John (pseud.) (ed.). *The War at Sea: 1939–45.* New York: Morrow, 1968.

Woodward, Sir Ernest L. *British Foreign Policy in the Second World War.* London: H.M. Stationery Office, 1962.

Woolf, S. J. (ed.). *European Fascism.* New York: Random House, 1969.

Wyke, Alan. *Heydrich.* New York: Ballantine, 1973.

Yeremenko, Andrei I. *Gody Vozmezdiia.* Moscow, 1967.

Young, Arthur N. *China and the Helping Hand 1937–1945.* Cambridge, Mass.: Harvard University Press, 1963.

Young, Kenneth. *Churchill and Beaverbrook.* London: Eyre & Spottiswoode, 1966.

Young, Peter (ed.). *Atlas of the Second World War.* New York: Putnam, 1973.

———. *Commando.* New York: Ballantine, 1969.

Zawodny, Janusz K. *Death in the Forest.* Notre Dame, Ind.: University of Notre Dame Press, 1962.

Zeman, Z. A. B. *Nazi Propaganda.* New York: Oxford University Press, 1964.

Zhukov, Georgi K. *Marshal Zhukov's Greatest Battles.* Edited by Harrison Salisbury. Translated from the Russian by Theodore Shabad. New York: Harper & Row, 1969.

———. *Memoirs.* New York: Delacorte Press, 1971.

Ziemke, Earl F. *Battle for Berlin: End of the Third Reich.* New York: Ballantine, 1969.

———. *The German Northern Theater of Operations, 1940–1945.* Washington, D.C.: U.S. Government Printing Office, 1960.

———. *Stalingrad to Berlin.* Washington, D.C.: U.S. Government Printing Office, 1968.

Zimmermann, Erich, and Hans-Adolf Jacobsen. *Germans Against Hitler.* Bonn: Press and Information Office of the Federal German Government, 1964.

Index

[Page references to entire articles are in **boldface.**]